AF814571

visualize

PHYSICAL CHEMISTRY

A COMPLETE BLUEPRINT FOR

JEE Main & Advanced

visualize PHYSICAL CHEMISTRY

A COMPLETE BLUEPRINT FOR

JEE Main & Advanced

Purushottam Singh
M.Sc. Chemistry (BHU IT)

arihant
SUCCESS AND NOTHING LESS

arihant
SUCCESS AND NOTHING LESS

Arihant Prakashan (Series), Meerut

卐 **Administrative & Production Offices**

Regd. Office

'Ramchhaya' 4577/15, Agarwal Road, Darya Ganj, New Delhi -110002
Tele: 011- 47630600, 43518550

Head Office

Kalindi, TP Nagar, Meerut (UP) - 250002
Tel: 0121-7156203, 7156204

卐 **Sales & Support Offices**

Agra, Ahmedabad, Bengaluru, Bareilly, Chennai, Delhi, Guwahati, Hyderabad, Jaipur, Jhansi, Kolkata, Lucknow, Nagpur & Pune.

卐 **PRICE** ₹675.00

卐 **PO No :** TXT-XX-XXXXXXX-X-XX

Published by Arihant Publications (India) Ltd.

For further information about the books published by Arihant, log on to www.arihantbooks.com or e-mail at info@arihantbooks.com

Follow us on

Preface

Physical Chemistry is one of the most dynamic and fascinating branches of chemistry, playing a pivotal role in the preparation for competitive exams like JEE Main and Advanced.

This book is meticulously crafted for students preparing for JEE Main and Advanced. With its clear explanations, systematic approach and extensive problem sets, it aims to provide a solid conceptual foundation while, also honing the problem-solving skills necessary for success in these high-stakes exams. The content is carefully curated to match the depth and difficulty required for both exams, with an emphasis on building a deep understanding of core principles that are critical to mastering Physical Chemistry.

Special Features of this First Edition are

- Modular theory and Practice as **Elements** and **Elemental Practice.**
- JEE Main & Advanced Analysis on the first page of every chapter as **Trend Insight** with **Insightful Advice.**
- Important JEE specific info as **JEE Spotlite** and **JEE Alert.**
- Theory and PYQs syncing through **JEE Mapper** and **JEE Quicker.**
- Figure Enhancement by merging text with figure as **Concept Visualizer** for better visualization and concept clarity.
- **Advanced Exclusive Different Strokes** as JEE Advanced targeted special tip/fact elaboration / important info.
- **Separate exercises for JEE Main and Advanced** with selected PYQs as **Check through PYQs**.

The book also incorporates the latest patterns of the JEE exams, ensuring that students are well-prepared for the types of questions they are likely to encounter. Furthermore, the inclusion of previous years' questions from both JEE Main and Advanced will help students understand the nature of the exam and gauge their progress.

As you embark on your journey to mastering **Physical Chemistry**, remember that success lies not only in memorizing formulas but in understanding the concepts and applying them in different contexts. With dedication, practice, and the right approach, you will not only excel in your exams but also develop an enduring interest in the world of chemistry.

We wish you all the best in your preparation and encourage you to make the most of this resource. Stay focused, stay curious, and keep pushing your limits!

Purushottam Singh

Key Features

Trend Insight

JEE Main & Advanced Analysis on the First Page of Every Chapter with Insightfull Advice

Trend Insights

JEE Main

Topics	2024 E	2024 M	2024 T	2024 O	2023 E	2023 M	2023 T	2023 O	2022 E	2022 M	2022 T	2022 O
Matter and Its Measurement	–	–	–	–	1	–	–	1	1	–	–	1
Chemical Formula, Mole Concept and Laws of Chemical Combination	–	2	5	7	–	2	1	3	1	–	–	1
Reaction Stoichiometry	–	1	2	3	–	1	1	2	2	3	1	6
Concentration Terms	1	2	–	3	2	2	–	4	1	2	1	4

JEE Advanced

Typology	Years				
	2024	2023	2022	2021	2020
1. Simple MCQ	–	–	–	–	–
2. One or More than one correct	–	–	1	–	–
3. Numerical Value	–	1	1	–	2
4. Matching Type	–	–	–	–	–
5. Paragraph	–	–	–	–	–

Element 1 Bohr's Model and Its Application

Imagine atoms as tiny, unseen building blocks that combine in various ways to create everything you see, touch and even taste. Despite their minuscule size, these particles possess a complex internal structure that defines their properties and behaviours. Understanding atomic structure is crucial for grasping the principles of chemistry and material science.

(vii) **Isoelectronic** Species having same number of electrons, e.g., N_2, CO, CN^-.

(viii) **Nuclear Isomers** Atoms with the same atomic number and same mass number but with different radioactive properties. Example of nuclear isomers is Uranium –*X* (half-life 1.4 min) and Uranium –*Z* (half life 6 7 hours)

Elements

Learning and Practice Modules of the Chapter as Elements and Practice Elements respectively.

JEE MAPPER

Example Similar to PYQ Asked in JEE Main 2023

The molality of a 20% (v/v) solution of iodine (I_2) in CCl_4 (carbon tetrachloride) is 'x'. $x =$ .... $\times 10^{-2}$ m (Nearest Integer)

[Given, Density of iodine $(I_2) = 3.4$ g cm^{-3}

Density of $CCl_4 = 1.6$ g cm^{-3}]

Sol. (209) 20 mL of solute (I_2) is present in 80 mL solvent (CCl_4).

Mass of solute = 20 mL × 3.4 g mL^{-1} = 68 g

Mass of solvent = 80 mL × 1.6 g mL^{-1} = 128 g

$$m = \frac{68 \times 1000}{254 \times 128} \approx 2.092 \text{ m}$$

$$= 209.2 \times 10^{-2} \approx 209$$

Competency Enhancer 4.1

The molality of a 10% (w/v) solution of ethyl alcohol in water is 'a'. The value of 'a' = ... $\times 10^{-2}$ mol/kg. (Nearest Integer)

JEE Mapper

Concept Enhancement tool, helpful in syncing PYQs with theory and provide additional practice with competency enhancer.

JEE Spotlite

- In case of extremely dilute solution, parts per billion (ppb) is used rather than ppm.

$$\text{ppb} = \frac{\text{Mass of solute}}{\text{Mass of solution}} \times 10^9$$

- Similar to percentage, ppm or ppb can also be expressed in terms of $\frac{W}{W'}, \frac{W}{V'}, \frac{V}{V'}$.

JEE Spotlite

Box Matter Having Pointers / Important info from JEE Perspective

Key Features

JEE Alert

The main advantage of using molality is that it is temperature independent because masses do not change when substances are heated or cooled (For those compounds which are thermally unstable).

JEE Alert

JEE Related Caution Points Helpful in Providing Usual Error Insights. Thus, helpful in Performance Enhancement.

JEE Quicker

Unique feature having PYQ facts and their elaborations as syncing of selected PYQs with theory.

JEE Quicker

If the Thomson model of the atom was correct, then the result of Rutherford's gold foil experiment would have been α-particles pass through the gold deflected by small angles and with reduced speed. ***JEE Main 2021***

- In Rutherford model, the particles were deflected at large angles but in thomson model, protons are diffused (charge is not centered). So, α-particles deviated by small angles and with reduced speed.

Concept Visualizer

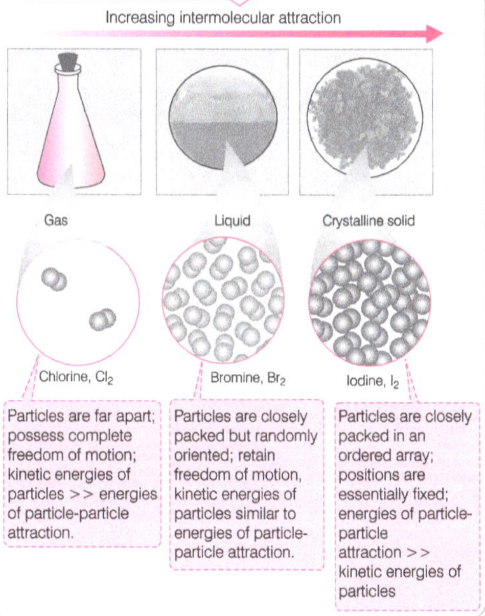

Concept Visualizer

Figure enhancement merged with text for better visualisation and concept clarity

Key Features

Advanced Exclusive Different strokes

JEE Advanced Targeted Content as Problem Solving Tips/Fact Elaborations/Important Info

Advanced Exclusive Different Strokes

Tips to solve problems related to Radial probability distribution curves.

For such problems it is very important to understand the interpretation of quantum waves.

Radial component of wave defines the probable radial distribution of electrons.

d

$$\psi_{nlm} = k\,[\text{Polynomial}]^{n-l-1}\left(\frac{Zr}{a_0}\right)^l e^{\frac{-Zr}{na_0}}$$

where,
n = Principal quantum number, a_0 = Bohr's radius
Z = Atomic number, l = Azimuthal quantum number

decreases because the area increases with larger extent with radius. For ψ^2_{nlm}: The graph will have positive solutions.

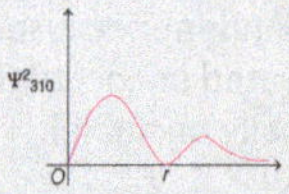

Graph of ψ_{nlm} and ψ^2_{nlm} vs radius for s-subshell will start from intercept where as for $p, d, f,...$ it will start from origin.

Elemental Practice 2.2

Type I 》 MCQs with Only One Correct Option

1. A particle of mass 1.0 mg has a velocity of 3600 km h^{-1}. Thus, wavelength associated with it is
   (a) 6.626×10^{-30} m (b) 6.626×10^{-31} m
   (c) 6.626×10^{-32} m (d) 6.626×10^{-33} m
2. The de-Broglie wavelength of the electron in the first excited state of He^+ is
   (a) 33.4 pm (b) 3.34 pm
   (c) 0.334 pm (d) 334 pm
3. The wavelength of electrons that have been accelerated from rest through a potential difference of 1.00 kV is
   (a) 1.23 pm (b) 38.8 pm
   (c) 123 pm (d) 0.123 pm

Elemental Practice

Scientifically designed first Practice Exercise to check Modular Learning.

Practice Element 1

JEE Main targeted practice with single choice correct MCQs and Integer/Numerical type questions.

PRACTICE ELEMENT 01 Target JEE Main

Objective Type Questions 》

1. If the radius of first Bohr orbit is x, then de-Broglie wavelength of the electron in 3rd orbit of H-atom is nearly
   (a) $2\pi x$ (b) $6\pi x$
   (c) $9x$ (d) $x/3$
2. If n and l are the principal and azimuthal quantum numbers respectively then the expression for calculating the total number of electrons in any energy level is
   (a) $\sum_{l=1}^{l=n} 2(2l+1)$ (b) $\sum_{l=1}^{l=(n-1)} 2(2l+1)$
   (c) $\sum_{l=0}^{l=(n+1)} 2(2l+1)$ (d) $\sum_{l=0}^{l=(n-1)} 2(2l+1)$

A. The negative sign in equation simply means that the energy of electron bound to the nucleus is lower than it would be if the electrons were at the infinite distance from the nucleus.
B. Larger the value of n, the larger is the orbit radius.
C. Equation can be used to calculate the change in energy when the electron changes orbit.
D. For $n = 1$, the electron has a more negative energy than it does for $n = 6$; which means that the electron is more loosely bound in the smallest allowed orbit.

Choose the correct answer from the options given below.
(a) B, C and D (b) C and D
(c) A and B (d) A, B and C

Key Features

PRACTICE ELEMENT 02 — Target JEE Advanced

Single Correct Choice MCQs

1. Select the incorrect statement about the following reaction when 0.80 mole of MnO_2 and 146 g of HCl are allowed to react

$$MnO_2 + 4HCl \longrightarrow MnCl_2 + Cl_2 + 2H_2O$$

(a) 0.80 mole of Cl_2 is formed
(b) 0.80 mole of HCl remains unreacted
(c) MnO_2 is the limiting reactant
(d) HCl is the limiting reactant

2. In the following reaction,

$$BaCl_2 + H_2SO_4 \longrightarrow BaSO_4 + 2HCl$$

If 100 mL of 20.8% $BaCl_2$ solution react with 50 mL of 9.8% H_2SO_4 solution $BaSO_4$ formed is,
(Ba = 137, S = 32 and Cl = 35.5)

(a) 23.3 g (b) 11.65 g
(c) 30.6 g (d) 15.30 g

3. A certain sample of phosphate rock contains 26.26% P_2O_5. A 0.5428 g sample is analysed by precipitating $MgNH_4PO_4 \cdot 6H_2O$ and igniting the precipitate to $Mg_2P_2O_7$. Thus, $Mg_2P_2O_7$ obtained is

(a) 0.8486 g (b) 1.1424 g
(c) 0.3648 g (d) 0.2220 g

4. Select the correct alternate about the following reaction.
(B = 11)

$$\underset{6.75\text{ g}}{B_2H_6} + \underset{8.55\text{ g}}{2NaH} \longrightarrow 2NaBH_4$$

	Limiting reactants	Excess reactants
(a)	B_2H_6	NaH = 1.80 g
(b)	NaH	B_2H_6 = 1.76 g
(c)	B_2H_6	NaH = 0.90 g
(d)	NaH	B_2H_6 = 1.8 g

5. In the reaction,

$$2Al(aq) + 6HCl(aq) \longrightarrow 2Al^{3+}(aq) + 6Cl^-(aq) + 3H_2(g)$$

(a) 6 mole HCl (aq) is consumed for every 3L $H_2(g)$ produced
(b) 33.6 L $H_2(g)$ is produced regardless of temperature and pressure of every mole Al that reacts
(c) 67.2 L $H_2(g)$ at STP is produced for every mole Al that reacts
(d) 11.2 L $H_2(g)$ at STP is produced for every mole HCl(aq) consumed

6. NH_3 is formed in the following step:

I. $Ca + 2C \longrightarrow CaC_2$ (50% yield)
II. $CaC_2 + N_2 \longrightarrow CaCN_2 + C$ (100% yield)
III. $CaCN_2 + 3H_2O \longrightarrow 2NH_3 + CaCO_3$ (50% yield)

2 moles of NH_3 are formed if we take

(a) 1 mol Ca (b) 2 mol Ca (c) 3 mol Ca (d) 4 mol Ca

Practice Element 2

JEE Advanced targeted practice with all formats covered as asked in Exam

Check Through PYQs

Element 2 Chemical Formula, Mole Concept & Laws of Chemical Combination

1. To check the principle of multiple proportions, a series of pure binary compounds (P_mQ_n) were analysed and their composition is tabulated below. The correct option(s) is (are) *2022 Adv.*

Compound	Weight % of P	Weight % of Q
1	50	50
2	44.4	55.6
3	40	60

(a) If empirical formula of compound 3 is P_3Q_4, then the empirical formula of compound 2 is P_3Q_5.
(b) If empirical formula of compound 3 is P_3Q_2 and atomic weight of element P is 20, then the atomic weight of Q is 45.
(c) If empirical formula of compound 2 is PQ, then the empirical formula of the compound 1 is P_5Q_4
(d) If atomic weight of P and Q are 70 and 35, respectively, then the empirical formula of compound 1 is P_2Q

(Atomic weights in g mol^{-1} : O = 16, S = 32, Pb = 207) *2018 Adv.*

6. The ammonia prepared by treating ammonium sulphate with calcium hydroxide is completely used by $NiCl_2 \cdot 6H_2O$ to form a stable coordination compound. Assume that both the reactions are 100% complete. If 1584 g of ammonium sulphate and 952 g of $NiCl_2 \cdot 6H_2O$ are used in the preparation, the combined weight (in grams) of gypsum and the nickel-ammonia coordination compound thus produced is____

(Atomic weights in g mol^{-1} : H = 1, N = 14, O = 16, S = 32, Cl = 35.5, Ca = 40, Ni = 59) *2018 Adv.*

7. To measure the quantity of $MnCl_2$ dissolved in an aqueous solution, it was completely converted to $KMnO_4$ using the reaction,

$$MnCl_2 + K_2S_2O_8 + H_2O \longrightarrow KMnO_4 + H_2SO_4 + HCl$$

(equation not balanced).

Few drops of concentrated HCl were added to this solution and gently warmed. Further, oxalic acid (225 g) was added in portions till the colour of the permanganate ion disappeared. The quantity of $MnCl_2$ (in mg) present in the initial solution is ....

(Atomic weights in g mol^{-1}: Mn = 55, Cl = 35.5) *2018 Adv.*

Check through PYQs

PYQ segment Present in Practice Elements 1 & 2 with selected Past year Questions of JEE Main and Advanced respectively.

Content

CHAPTER 1

Some Basic Concept of Chemistry

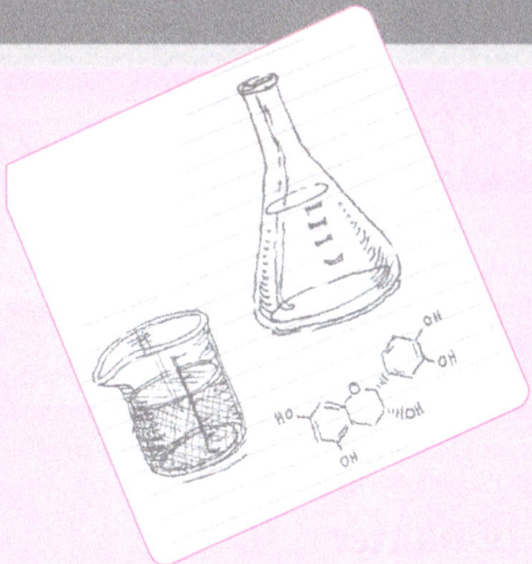

Learning Elements

Element 1 Matter and Its Measurement
States of matter, Classification of Matter, Properties of Matter, Measurement of Physical Quantities Uncertainity in Measurement, Significant Figures

Element 2 Chemical Formula, Mole Concept and Laws of Chemical Combination
Dalton's Atomic Theory, Atomic Mass and Average Atomic Mass, Molar Mass and Equivalent Mass, Chemical and Empirical Formula, Mole Concept, Law of Chemical Combination

Element 3 Reactions Stoichiometry
Stoichiometry, Concept of Limiting Reagents, Percentage Yield and Percentage Purity

Element 4 Concentration Terms
Reactions in Solutions and Concentration Terms, Relation between Different Concentration Terms

Practice Elements

Practice Element 1 Target JEE Main
Practice Element 2 Target JEE Advanced

Trend Insights

JEE Main

	2024				2023				2022			
Topics	**E**	**M**	**T**	**O**	**E**	**M**	**T**	**O**	**E**	**M**	**T**	**O**
Matter and Its Measurement	–	–	–	–	1	–	–	1	1	–	–	1
Chemical Formula, Mole Concept and Laws of Chemical Combination	–	2	5	7	–	2	1	3	1	–	–	1
Reaction Stoichiometry	–	1	2	3	–	1	1	2	2	3	1	6
Concentration Terms	1	2	–	3	2	2	–	4	1	2	1	4

E = Easy, **M** = Medium, **T** = tough, **O** = Overall

Current Dynamics

- Overall weightage of chapter has remained almost constant in recent years.
- More number of question on mole concept and law of chemical combination were asked in recent years.
- Questions based on mixed concepts of organic chemistry and stoichiometry were asked recent years.

JEE Advanced

Typology	Years				
	2024	**2023**	**2022**	**2021**	**2020**
1. Simple MCQs	–	–	–	–	–
2. One or More than one correct	–	–	1	–	–
3. Numerical Value/Integer	–	1	1	–	2
4. Matching Type	–	–	–	–	–
5. Paragraph Based	–	–	–	–	–

Current Dynamics

- Most of the questions from Mole concept, Atomic and molecular mass were asked in 2022.
- Numerical value type question asked in 2023 from stoichiometric application.
- Mostly numerical value type questions were asked from this chapter.
- No direct question were asked in recent years.

Insightful Advice

- This chapter is very crucial for grasping the basics of complete physical chemistry.
- The application of stoichiometry calculation is also used in other chapters of organic chemistry.
- Practice complex problems including limiting reagent and focus on formulas, calculations and conversion to build confidence over the concepts.

Element 1 Matter and Its Measurements

Matter constitutes the physical substance of the universe, encompassing anything that possesses mass and occupies space.

At the **microscopic level**, matter consists of atoms, which are the fundamental building blocks of all chemical elements.

On a **macroscopic scale**, matter encompasses vast structures such as planets, stars and galaxies.

States of Matter

Classification of matter is typically based on its composition and physical properties.

The three states of matter are discussed below:

(i) **Solids** In this state, the constituent particles of matter are held close to each other in an ordered arrangement. Its other characteristics are

- Solids have definite shape and volume, e.g. ice cube, iron bar, sugar crystals etc.
- In this state, the intermolecular forces between constituent particles are very strong.
- The constituent particles in a solid species, therefore, cannot leave their positions.

(ii) **Liquid** In this state, the constituent particles are not as much close as in the solid state. Its other characteristics are

- Liquid has definite volume but no definite shape; they take the shape of the vessel in which they are stored, e.g. water, oil, mercury etc.
- In this state, the intermolecular forces between constituent particles are very moderate.
- They have space around them so that they can leave their positions and move in a limited manner.

(iii) **Gases** In this state the constituent particles are far apart from each other as compared to solid state and liquid state. The other characteristics are

- In the gaseous state, the intermolecular force between constituent particles are very weak or negligible and molecules lie far apart from one another.
- These can leave their position and move everywhere in different directions colliding among themselves and against sides of the container, e.g. water vapour, air, oxygen, gas, nitrogen gas etc.

These states of matter are interconvertible by changing the conditions of the temperature and pressure, as shown in the figure.

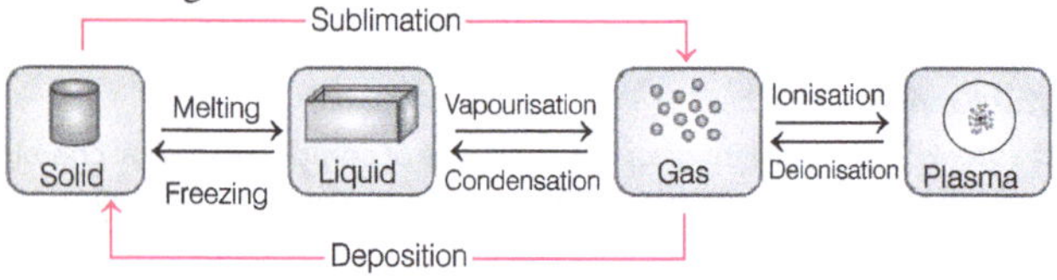

Interconversion of states of matter

JEE Spotlite

Alongwith solid, liquid and gases there are two more states of matter, plasma and Bose-Einstein condensate.

- **Plasma** Its a state containing gaseous ions and free electrons which is formed when gaseous state is heated to a very high temperature, e.g. electric arc, sun etc.
- **Bose-Einstein condensate** The concept and existence of this state is totally opposite to plasma. The state is achieved by a gas of extremely low density, at supercooled conditions, i.e. near absolute zero temperature.

Classification of Matter

Matter can be classified as pure substance and mixture on the basis of chemical properties.

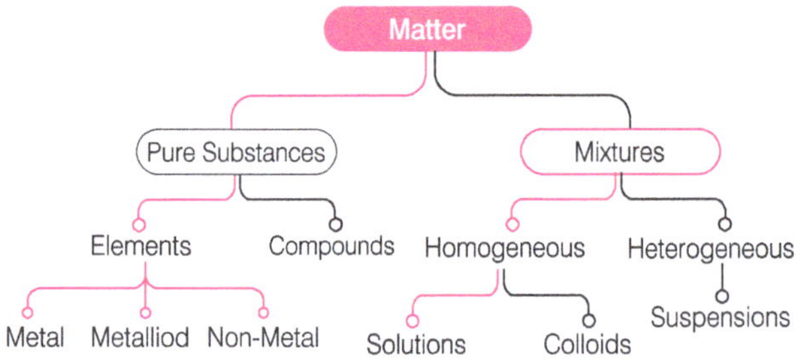

Pure Substances

These substances have fixed composition and their, constituents cannot be separated by physical methods, e.g. gold, silver, water etc.

They can be of two types

(i) **Element** An element consists of only one type of particles in the form of atoms or molecules.

- Sodium (Na), copper (Cu), hydrogen (H), oxygen (O), carbon (C) etc., are elements.
- Hydrogen, oxygen and nitrogen gases in which two atoms (of same type) combine to form molecule.

$$H + H \longrightarrow H_2,\ O + O \longrightarrow O_2$$

and $$N + N \longrightarrow N_2$$

(ii) **Compound** When two or more elements combine in a fixed ratio of mass then compound is formed.

e.g. $2H + O \longrightarrow H_2O$, $C + 2O \longrightarrow CO_2$

and $N + 3H \longrightarrow NH_3$

Properties of a compound are different from its constituent elements, e.g. H_2 and O_2 are gases but H_2O is a liquid.

Mixtures

Mixtures contain two or more components in any ratio. These can be classified as

(i) **Homogeneous Mixture** The mixture having components in a uniform composition and which are miscible into one each other is called homogeneous mixture. They are also called **solutions**.
e.g. Sugar solution (sugar in water)

(ii) **Heterogeneous Mixture** The mixture that has components in non-uniform variable composition and are not miscible into one other thus visible, is called heterogeneous mixture.
e.g. Mixture of sand and sugar

Properties of Matter

These are classified into following two properties

Physical Properties

These properties can be observed without changing the identity and composition of the substance. It include colour, mass, volume, temperature, density, melting point, boiling point, and hardness. Same major ones among then are explained below.

(i) **Mass and Weight** Mass represents the amount of matter present in a system, while weight represents the force that gravity exerts on that system.

$$\text{Weight } (W) = \text{mass } (m) \times \text{gravity } (g)$$

(ii) **Volume** It is the quantity of three-dimensional space enclosed by a matter. Volume of different bodies are calculated differently, e.g.
For a cuboidal body,

$$\text{Volume } (V) = \text{length } (l) \times \text{breadth } (b) \times \text{height } (h)$$

For a spherical body,

$$\text{Volume} = \frac{4}{3}\pi r^3$$

(iii) **Density** It is defined as mass per unit volume. It gives us an idea that how tightly or loosely a matter is packed.

$$\text{Density } (d) = \frac{\text{Mass } (m)}{\text{Volume } (V)}$$

(iv) **Temperature** Temperature is a measure of the average kinetic energy of the particles in a substance.

Chemical Properties

Chemical properties describe the way a substance may change, or react, to form other substances.

Measurement of Physical Quantities

Comparison of a physical quantity with a standard, is called **measurement**. Every measurement compares a physical quantity to be measured with some fixed standard known as the **unit of measurement**. For example, length of a room is 5.3 m, by this we can interpret that it is 5.3 times unit of measurement, which is one metre in this case.

To express the result of a measurement, two pieces of information are required, i.e.

- the **magnitude** or the numerical value which is 5.3 in the above example and
- the **unit**, which is metre in this case.

Unit

It is defined as "some fixed standard against which the comparison of a physical quantity can be done during measurement."

Various Systems of Measurement Units

Few important systems of measurement units are mentioned below

(i) **CGS System** It is based on centimetre (cm), gram (g) and second (s) as the units of length, mass and time respectively. It is also called as **Gaussian system**.

(ii) **FPS System** It is based on foot (ft); pound (lb) and second (s) an the fundamental units of length, mass and time respectively. It is also called as **British system**.

(iii) **MKS System** It is the system which uses metre (m), kilogram (kg) and second (s) respectively for length, mass and time. It is also called as **MKS system**.

(iv) **International System** In October 1960, the general conference of weights and measures adopted a particular choice now known as the international system of units (French : system international d'units) popularly known as **SI units**.

International system of units contains base units and supplementary units which are described below

Base or Fundamental SI Units

The SI unit has seven base units from where all other units are derived have been described in table (a) and (b).

(a) The seven base SI units

Physical quantity	Name of unit	Symbol for unit
Length	metre	m
Mass	kilogram	kg
Time	second	s
Temperature	kelvin	K
Amount of substance	mole	mol
Electric current	ampere	A
Luminous intensity	candela	cd

(b) Definitions of SI base units

Unit of length	**metre**	The metre is the length of the path travelled by light in vacuum during a time interval of 1/299 792 458 of a second, where the second is defined in terms of the caesium frequency $\Delta\nu_{Cs}$.
Unit of mass	**kilogram**	The kilogram, symbol kg, is the SI unit of mass. It is defined by taking the fixed numerical value of planck constant h to be $6.62607015 \times 10^{-34}$ when expressed in the unit of Js, where the metre and the second are defined in terms of c and $\Delta\nu_C$.
Unit of time	**second**	The second is the duration of 9 192 631 770 periods of the radiation corresponding to the transition between the two hyperfine levels of the ground state of the caesium-133 atom.
Unit of electric current	**ampere**	The ampere, symbol A, is the SI unit of electric current. It is defined by taking the fixed numerical value of the elementary charge e to be $1.602176634 \times 10^{-19}$ when expressed in the unit C, where the second is defined in terms of $\Delta\nu_{Cs}$.
Unit of thermodynamic temperature	**kelvin**	The kelvin symbol K, is the SI unit of thermodynamic temperature. It is defined by taking the fixed numerical value of the Boltzmann constant k to be 1.380649×10^{-23} when expressed in the unit JK^{-1}, where kilogram, metre and second are defined in terms of h, c and $\Delta\nu_{Cs}$.
Unit of amount of substance	**mole**	(i) The mole is the amount of substance of a system which contains exactly $6.02214076 \times 10^{23}$ elementary entities, its symbol is "mol." (ii) When the mole is used, the elementary entities must be specified and may be atoms, molecules, ions, electrons, other particles, or specified groups of such particles.
Unit of luminous intensity	**candela**	The candela is the luminous intensity, in a given direction, of a source that emits monochromatic radiation of frequency 540×10^{12} Hz and that has a radiant intensity in that direction of 1/683 watt per steradian.

The international system of units (SI) incorporates a system of prefixes that make it easier to express very large or very small quantities.

These prefixes are used to denote specific multiples or submultiples of bases units by powers of tens. The standard prefixes, which allow us to reduce or enlarge the base units are given in table.

SI prefixes

Multiple	Prefix	Symbol	Multiple	Prefix	Symbol
10^{24}	yotta	Y	10^{-1}	deci	d
10^{21}	zeta	Z	10^{-2}	centi	c
10^{18}	exa	E	10^{-3}	milli	m
10^{15}	peta	P	10^{-6}	micro	μ
10^{12}	tera	T	10^{-9}	nano	n
10^{9}	giga	G	10^{-12}	pico	p
10^{6}	mega	M	10^{-15}	femto	f
10^{3}	kilo	k	10^{-18}	atto	a
10^{2}	hecto	h	10^{-21}	zepto	z
10^{1}	deca	da	10^{-24}	yocto	y

Derived Units

The units of all other quantities, which are derived from the fundamental units are called **derived units**.

There are several smaller units of length, volume and energy which are not the SI units but commonly used in chemistry. Some of which are given in the table.

Non-SI units in common use

Quantity	Name of unit	Symbol of unit	SI equivalent
Length	angstrom	Å	10^{-10} m
Volume	litre	L	10^{-3} m^3
Mass	gram	g	10^{-3} kg
Energy	calorie	cal	$kg\, m^2/s^2$

Conversion Factor
(Dimensional Analysis)

The numerical value which must be multiplied or divided to the original unit to convert it into other unit is called **conversion factor**. A conversion factor must always have numerator and denominator representing equivalent quantities.

e.g. there are three common scales to measure temperature—°C (degree celsius), K (Kelvin) and °F (degree fahrenheit). Kelvin (K) scale represents the SI unit of temperature.

The relationship between various temperature units are as follows

Temperature in K = Temperature in °C + 273.15

Temperature in °C = Temperature in K − 273.15

and $$°F = \left(\frac{9}{5} \times °C\right) + 32 \Rightarrow °C = \frac{5}{9}(°F - 32)$$

Some important conversion factors (CF) listed in table.

Conversion factors

1 m	= 39.37 inch
1 inch	= 2.54 cm
1 L	$=1000\ mL = 1000\ cm^3 = 10^{-3} m^3 = 1\ dm^3$
1 cal	$= 4.184\ J = 2.611 \times 10^{19}$ eV
1 eV	$= 1.602189 \times 10^{-19}\ J = 3.827 \times 10^{-20}$ cal
1 eV/atom	$= 96.485\ kJ\ mol^{-1}$
1 amu	$= 1.6605653 \times 10^{-27}$ kg = 931.5016 MeV
1 J	$= 10^7$ erg
1 atm	$= 101325\ N\ m^{-2} = 101325$ Pa = 1.01325 bar
1 bar	$= 1 \times 10^5\ Nm^{-2} = 1 \times 10^5$ pascal
1 L atm	= 101.3 J = 24.21 cal
1 mol of a gas	= 22.4 L at STP
1 mol of a substance	$= N_0$ constituents
1 g atom	$= N_0$ atoms
$1\ g\ cm^{-3}$	$= 1000\ kg\ m^{-3}$

The SI system allows the use of prefix to indicate multiples or submultiples of a unit (to reduce a enlarge the base unit).

Graphical Analysis

In graphical analysis, values are derived based on graph. It requires less time to give more information and avoids lengthy and tedious calculations. For this one has to compare the results with a standard graph. Generally, we make a graph between Y- axis and X-axis. Nature and shape of graph varies from equation to equation.

Some examples of graph along with concerned equation are given below

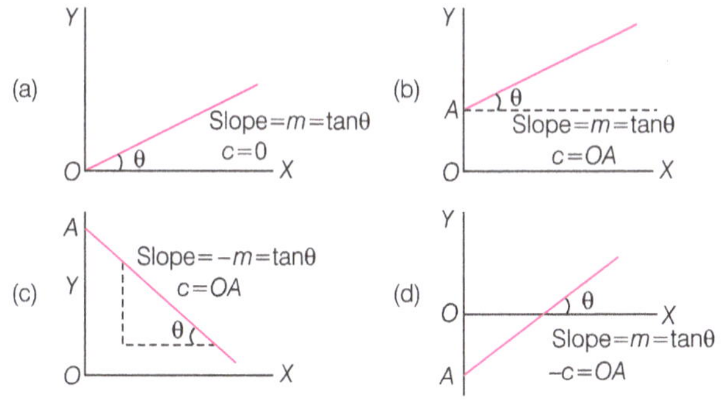

Graphical study

Graph	Equation	Slope	Intercept of on y-axis
1.2 (a)	$y = mx$	m	0
1.2 (b)	$y = mx + c$	m	$+c = OA$
1.2 (c)	$y = -mx + c$	$-m$	$+c = OA$
1.2 (d)	$y = mx - c$	m	$-c = OA$

Equation under study is required to converted in any form of (a), (b), (c) and (d) and graph is compared with a standard graph of linear equation as given in figure.

Uncertainty in Measurements

Experimental data as well as theoretical calculations in chemistry can be handled or processed in many ways. While dealing with calculations the meaningful way is to handle the number conveniently and present the data realistically with certainty to the possible extent.

These ideas are discussed below:

Scientific Notation

Exponential notation is used to express very large and very small numbers as a product of two numbers. The first number of the product, the digit term, is usually a number not less than 1 and not greater than 10. The second number of the product, the exponential term, is written as 10 with an exponent. For example

0.123 can be expressed as $1.23 \times 0.1 = 1.23 \times 10^{-1}$

Thus, they can be expressed as $N \times 10^n$

The power (exponent) of 10 is equal to the number of places the decimal is shifted to give the digit number.

4.13×10^3 interpreted as

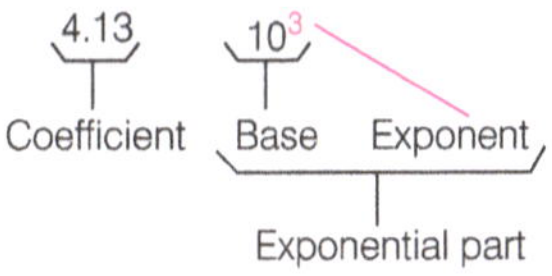

JEE Spotlite

- **Adding Exponentials** Add 5.00×10^{-5} and 3.00×10^{-3}
  $(5.00 \times 10^{-5}) + (300 \times 10^{-5}) = 305 \times 10^{-5} = 3.05 \times 10^{-3}$
- **Substracting Exponentials** Subtract 4.0×10^{-7} from 5.0×10^{-6}
  $(5.0 \times 10^{-6}) - (0.40 \times 10^{-6}) = 4.6 \times 10^{-6}$
- **Multiplying Exponentials** Multiply 4.2×10^{-8} by 2.0×10^3
  $(4.2 \times 10^{-8}) \times (2.0 \times 10^3) = (4.2 \times 2.0) \times 10^{(-8)+(+3)} = 8.4 \times 10^{-5}$
- **Dividing Exponentials** Divide 3.6×10^5 by 6.0×10^{-4}
  $\dfrac{3.6 \times 10^{-5}}{6.0 \times 10^{-4}} = \dfrac{3.6}{6.0} \times 10^{(-5)-(-4)} = 0.60 \times 10^{-1} = 6.0 \times 10^{-2}$
- **Squaring Exponentials** Square the number 4.0×10^{-6}
  $(4.0 \times 10^{-6})^2 = 4 \times 4 \times 10^{2 \times (-6)} = 16 \times 10^{-12} = 1.6 \times 10^{-11}$

Precision and Accuracy

For an experiment or observation, results should be precise and accurate.

- **Precision** refers to the closeness of various measurements for the same quantity.
- **Accuracy** is the agreement of a particular value (measured) to the correct values (true value) of the result.

Concept Visualizer

The concept of accuracy and precision can be visualised through target shooting.

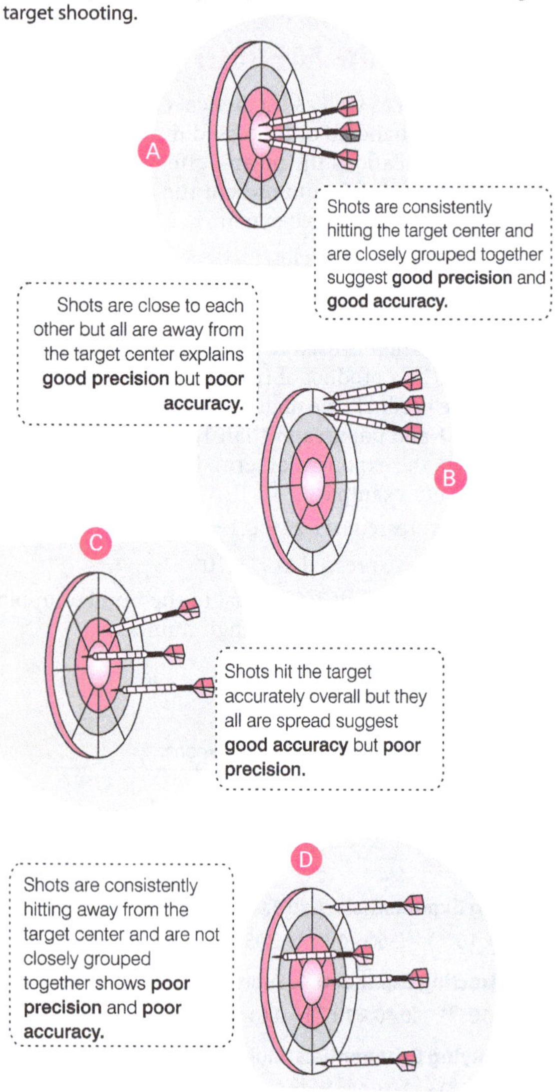

Solved Booster 1.1

The following measurements were made to determine the density of a material whose value was 1.15 g/mL.

Trial 1 – 0.95 g/mL Trial 2 – 1.16 g/mL

Trial 3 – 1.26 g/mL

These given measurements have:

(a) High accuracy and high precision

(b) High precision but low accuracy

(c) Low precision but high accuracy

(d) Low precision and low accuracy

Solution (d)

Low accuracy as there was spread of 0.31 between the first and third reading. Low precision as all results were different and not close in value.

Significant Figures

All digits of a measured quantity, including the uncertain one, are called **significant figures**.

Suppose you determine the mass of a dime on a balance capable of measuring to the nearest 0.0001 g. You could report the mass as 2.2405 ± 0.0001 g. The $\pm$ notation (read "plus or minus") expresses the magnitude of the uncertainty of your measurement.

- In much scientific work, we drop the $\pm$ notation with the understanding that there is always some uncertainty in the last digit reported for any measured quantity.
- Following rules are taken into consideration, while deciding the number of significant numbers.

Rule I All **non-zero digits** are significant.

Thus, 102 cm has three SF

0.92 g has two SF

Rule II Zeros preceding the **first non-zero digit** are not significant. Zeros of such types indicate the position of decimal point.

Thus, 0.003 has one SF

0.0052 has two SF

Rule III Zeros between **two non-zero digits** are significant.

Thus, 200.4 has four SF

105.01 has five SF

Rule IV Zeros at the end or right of a number are significant provided they are on the right side of the decimal point.

0.0 2 1 0 0 Has four SF

Non-significant Significant

Rule V When a number ends with zeros and has no decimal point, it is typically, assumed that the zeros are not significant.

Rule VI Exponential notation can be used to indicate whether end zeros are significant.

e.g., a mass of 10,300 g can be written to show three, four or five significant figures depending on how the measurement is obtained.

1.03×10^4 g (three siginificant figures)

1.030×10^4 g (four significant figures)

1.0300×10^4 g (five significant figures)

Solved Booster 1.2

Consider the following measurements.

(i) 0.036653 m (ii) 7.2100×10^{-3}g
(iii) 72.10 km (iv) ₹ 1400
(v) π

How many of them have four significant digits.

(a) 2 (b) 1 (c) 3 (d) 4

Solution (b)

(i) 0.036653 m - Five SF. (Zeros before a digit are not significant.)
(ii) 7.2100×10^{-3}g - Five SF. (7.2100: Significant; 10^{-3}: Non-significant)
(iii) 72.10 km - Four SF. (Significant)
(iv) Rs 1400 - Infinite SF. Exact number
(v) π = 3.14 ... (Infinite SF)

Significant Figures in Mathematical Operation

- **In addition and subtraction**

The sum or difference should contain as many digits to the right of the decimal as that in the least certain of the numbers used in the computation.

Add 4.383 g and 0.0023 g

4.383 g → 4 significant digits
0.0023 g → 2 significant digits
4.3853 g

Thus, result should be 4.385 → 4 significant digits

- **In multiplication and division** The product or quotient should contain no more digits than that in the factor containing the least number of significant figures.

Multiply 0.6238 by 6.6

$0.6238 \times 6.6 = 4.1.$

Solved Booster 1.3

Express the result of following calculations in required number of SF.

(i) $\frac{3.24 \times 0.08666}{5.0061}$ (ii) 0.58×324.65
(iii) $943 \times 0.00345 + 101$ (iv) $2.4 + 63.27 - 1.5678$

Solution

(i) $\frac{3.24 \times 0.08666}{5.0061}$ (3.24 → 3 (minimum); 0.08666 → 4; 5.0061 → 5)

= 0.05608725355

= 0.0561 (3 After three SF next number is 8>5 thus 0 rounded off to 1)

= 5.61×10^{-2}

(ii) $0.58 \times 324.65 = 188.297$ (0.58 → 2 (Minimum); 324.65 → 5)

$= 1.9 \times 10^{2}$ ← 2 SF

(iii) $(943 \times 0.00345) + 101$ (3, 3, 3)

= 3.25335 + 101

= 104.25335 (After 3 SF, next digit is 2 < 5. Thus, omitted.)

= 104 ← 3 SF

(iv) $2.4 + 63.27 - 1.5678$ (2, 4, 5) — One digit after decimal.

= 65.67 − 1.5678 — One digit is to be kept after decimal.

= 64.1022

= 64.1

Rounding Off

If the result of a calculation contains the non-significant figures then it is rounded off to nearest significant figures, e.g. we should express 15.433 as 15.5 and 14755 as 1.48×10^{4} if the results are reported to three significant figures.

Rule 1 Determine what your rounding digit is and look at the digit to the right of it. If the digit is 1, 2, 3, 4 simply drop all digits to the right of rounding digit.

e.g. 3.423 may be rounded off to 3.42 when rounded off to the nearest hundredths place.

3.4 when rounded off to the nearest tenths place.

3 when rounded off to the nearest units place.

Rule 2 Determine what your rounding digit is and look at the digit to the right of it. If the digit is 5, 6, 7, 8, 9 add one to the rounding digit and drop all digits to the right of rounding digit.

e.g. 2.786 may be rounded off to 2.79 when rounded off to the nearest hundredths place.

2.8 when rounded off to the nearest tenths place.

3 when rounded off to the nearest units place.

JEE Alert

If the right most digit to be rounded off is equal to 5, the preceeding number is not changed if it is even and increased by one if it is odd.

e.g. 3.25 is rounded off to 3.2.

2.35 is rounded off to 2.4.

Elemental Practice 1.1

Type I 》 MCQs with Only One Correct Option

1. An average adult has 5.2 L of blood. Volume of blood in m^3 is
(a) 5.2×10^3 m^3 (b) 5.2×10^{-3} m^3
(c) 5.2×10^{-6} m^3 (d) 5.2×10^{-2} m^3

2. 10.5 g cm^{-3} in SI unit will be
(a) 10.5×10^{-3} kg m^{-3} (b) 10.5×10^{-1} kg m^{-3}
(c) 10.5 kg m^{-3} (d) 10.5×10^3 kg m^{-3}

3. Solder is an alloy of tin and lead that is used in electronic circuits. It has melting point of 225°C. It is ....°F.
(a) 498 °F (b) – 437°F
(c) 437°F (d) 400 °F

4. x°C differ by 11° in Kelvin and Fahrenheit scale. Thus, x°C is
(a) 300 (b) 273
(c) 132 (d) None of these

5. 0.445 and 0.435 are round off to two SF as
(a) 0.44, 0.43 (b) 0.45, 0.44
(c) 0.44, 0.44 (d) 0.45, 0.45

6. For each of the following pairs, determine the quantity in which each value of pair have equal quantity.

	I	II
(a)	24.0 mg	24.0 cg
(b)	250 cm	0.25 m
(c)	0.8 nm	8 Å
(d)	10 L	10 m^3

7. At what temperature, will a Fahrenheit and Celsius thermometers will have same value but differ in sign?
(a) 12.3° (b) 16.6°
(c) 12.43° (d) 11.43°

8. Least count of an analytical balance is 0.0002 g. Which of the following is the correct recorded value?
(a) 9.3171 g (b) 9.3170 g
(c) 9.3175 g (d) 9.3173 g

9. Which choice best describes the degree of uncertainty in the measurement of 4.0032 g?
(a) The measurement is between 4.0031 and 4.0033
(b) The measurement is between 4.002 and 4.004
(c) The quantity is exact
(d) The uncertainty cannot be determined with given information

10. The largest volume of the following group is that of
(a) 445 g of water at 4°C (d = 1g cm^{-3})
(b) 600 g of chloroform at 20°C (d = 1.5 g cm^{-3})
(c) 155 cm^3 of steel
(d) 0.50 L of milk

11. Of the following substance, the greatest density is that of
(a) 1000 g of water at 4°C
(b) 100.0 cm^3 of chloroform weighing 198.9 g
(c) 10.0 cm^3 piece of wood weighing 7.72 g
(d) an ethyl alcohol-water mixture of density 0.83 g cm^{-3}

12. SI unit and metric unit of volume are
(a) m^3, L (b) m^3, m^3
(c) L, m^3 (d) dm^3, m^3

13. On the Reamur scale water freezes at 0°R and boils at 80°R. Hence,
(a) $\frac{°R}{80} = \frac{°C}{100}$
(b) $\frac{°R}{80} = \frac{°F - 32}{180}$
(c) $°R = 0.8°C = \frac{4}{9}(°F - 32)$
(d) All of these

14. Calculate the mean density of the three trials A, B and C

	Trial A	Trial B	Trial C
Mass (g)	2.5718	2.1532	3.3384
Volume (mL)	3.11	2.65	4.01
Density (kg/m^3)	......	......	......

(a) 789.6 (b) 913.5
(c) 675.1 (d) 824.0

15. The phenomenon of superconductivity was observed at 98 K. This temperature is nearly equal to
(a) – 289°F (b) – 146°C
(c) – 386°F (d) + 178°F

Type II 》 MCQs with One or More than One Correct Option

16. Select the correct statement(s) about two sets of readings of students X and Y, when correct value is 12.7 mL.

X		Y	
I	II	I	II
12.4	12.3	12.3	12.3

(a) Reading of both are precise but not accurate
(b) Reading of both are precise and accurate
(c) Reading of X are precise but not accurate
(d) Reading of Y are precise and accurate

17. Select the correct statement(s). The metre is the length of the path travelled by light.
(a) In air during a time interval of 1/299792458 of a second
(b) In vacuum during a time interval of 1/299792458 of a second
(c) In water during a time interval of 1/100 of a second
(d) Second is defined in terms of the cesium frequency, $\Delta\nu_{Cs}$.

18. Select the correct statement(s) among the following
    (a) Kilogram is equal to the mass of the international prototype of the kilogram.
    (b) Second is the duration of 9192631770 periods of the radiation corresponding to the transition between the two hyperline levels of the ground state of the Cs-133 atom.
    (c) National Metrology Institute (NMI) predicts climate conditions in each country.
    (d) The mole is the amount of substance containing $6.02214076 \times 10^{23}$ elementary entities.

19. Ratio of two units is 10^3 in the following.
    (a) pm/nm
    (b) nm/pm
    (c) Gm/Mm
    (d) hm/dm

20. Select derived SI units
    (a) molar volume $\rightarrow m^3 mol^{-1}$
    (b) pressure $\rightarrow kg\ m^{-1} s^{-2}$
    (c) force $\rightarrow g\ cm\ s^{-2}$
    (d) power $\rightarrow J\ s^{-1}$

Type III 》 Numerical Integer Answer Type Questions

21. Boiling point of helium is $-452°F$. The temperature expressed on a Kelvin scale is ……… .

22. Number of significant figures in the answer of the following will be x. The is value of x is ……… .

$$\frac{(29.2-20.2)(1.09 \times 105)}{1.69}$$

23. A thermometer reads the freezing point of water as 20°C and the boiling point as 150°C. The reading of the thermometer when the actual reading is 60°C is ……… .

24. The number of calories in 20.92 J is ……… .

25. Symbol G is for giga and symbol h for hecto. Ratio of G : h is 10^x. The value of x is ……… .

26. The value of 46.4°F in Celsius scale is ……… .

27. Final result of the following will be expressed in x SF. The value of x is ……… .
    $12.11 \div 18.0 + 1.012 - 1.02$

Elemental Practice 1.1 | Chapter 01

Connect with **Answers**

1. (b)	2. (d)	3. (c)	4. (d)	5. (c)	6. (c)
7. (d)	8. (b)	9. (a)	10. (d)	11. (b)	12. (a)
13. (d)	14. (d)	15. (a)	16. (a,c)	17. (b,d)	18. (b,d)
19. (b,c,d)	20. (a,b,d)	21. (4)	22. (2)	23. (98)	24. (5)
25. (7)	26. (8)	27. (2)			

Element 2 Chemical Formula, Mole Concept and Laws of Chemical Combination

This module explores the fundational concepts of atomic theory. It also covers mole concept which is essential for understanding of chemical reactions and stoichiometry.

Dalton's Atomic Theory (1808)

Main points of Dalton atomic theory are given below

(i) All elements are composed of minute particles called **atoms,** which do not undergo subdivision during chemical reactions and cannot be created or destroyed by any chemical process.

(ii) Atoms of the same element are similar to one another in all respects and are equal in mass.

(iii) Atoms of different elements have different masses (called atomic masses) and different properties.

(iv) Chemical combination between two or more elements takes place by interaction of their atoms in simple numerical proportions (as 1 : 1; 1 : 2; 1 : 3; etc.)

	Ratio
$H_2 + Cl_2 \longrightarrow 2HCl$	1 : 1
$N_2 + 3H_2 \longrightarrow 2NH_3$	1 : 3
$C + O_2 \longrightarrow CO_2$	1 : 1

(v) Combining masses of the elements represent the combining masses of the atoms. Dalton's atomic theory can explain various laws of chemical combination.

Limitations of Dalton's Atomic Theory

(i) It can explain the laws of chemical combination by mass, but it fails to explain Gay-Lussac's law of gaseous volume.

(ii) Distinction between the ultimate particles of an element and the smallest particle of a compound, both of which are made of atoms, could not be made.

(iii) It assumes that atoms of same element are like and have same mass. But this is not true for isotopes (two or more atoms with same atomic number but different atomic mass are called **isotopes**).

(iv) ${}^{12}_{6}C, {}^{13}_{6}C, {}^{14}_{6}C$, have atoms of same element but different masses. Similarly, ${}^{1}_{1}H, {}^{2}_{1}H, {}^{3}_{1}H$ have atoms of same element but different masses.

(v) It does not account for the existence of isobars. For examples, Calcium and Argon are two different element having same mass number.

JEE Quicker

As per Dalton's Atomic Theory statement 'Compounds are formed when atoms of different elements combine in any ratio' is incorrect. *JEE Main 2024*

➘ According to Dalton's Atomic Theory, compounds are formed when atoms of different elements combine in a fixed ratio.

Atomic Mass and Average Atomic Mass

- **Atomic mass** is the average relative mass of the element as compared to $\frac{1}{12}$ mass of an atom of carbon-12.

$$\text{Atomic mass} = \frac{\text{Mass of an atom}}{\frac{1}{12}\text{th mass of carbon-12 atom}}$$

- **Atomic mass unit (AMU)** The atomic mass unit is defined as the $\frac{1}{12}$th of the mass of single carbon atom of mass number 12.

$$\text{Thus, 1 amu} = \frac{1}{6.022 \times 10^{23}\ \text{g}} = 1.6605 \times 10^{-24}\ \text{g.}$$

- **Average atomic mass** is the weighed average mass of all the atoms in a naturally occuring isotopes.
- If $A_1, A_2, A_3, \ldots\ldots$ are the atomic masses of the different isotopes with percentages or ratios as $X_1, X_2, X_3, \ldots\ldots$ of their occurrence then, $\overline{A}$ average atomic mass or mass number of the element is

$$\overline{A} = \frac{\Sigma AX}{\Sigma X}$$

$$\overline{A} = \frac{A_1X_1 + A_2X_2 + A_3X_3 + \ldots.}{X_1 + X_2 + X_3 + \ldots.}$$

Solved Booster 2.1

If the average atomic mass number of two isotopes ${}^{10}_{5}B$ and ${}^{11}_{5}B$ is 10.2, then their percentage respectively are

(a) 20%, 80%
(b) 60%, 40%
(c) 80%, 20%
(d) 40%, 60%

Solution (c)

Let ${}^{10}_{5}B$ be = $X\%$

Then, ${}^{11}_{5}B = (100 - X) \Rightarrow 10.2 = \frac{10X + 11(100 - X)}{100}$

$\therefore \quad X = 80 \Rightarrow {}^{10}_{5}B = 80\% \Rightarrow {}^{11}_{5}B = 20\%$

Solved Booster 2.2

A divalent cation M^{2+} is isoelectronic of CO_2 and has $(Z+2)$ neutrons (Z is the atomic number of the divalent cation). What is the ionic mass of the divalent cation?

(a) 50 (b) 86 (c) 30 (d) 60

Solution *(a)*

M^{2+} is isoelectronic of CO_2

Electrons in $CO_2 = 6 + 16 = 22$

Electrons in $M^{2+} = 22$

Protons in $M^{2+} = 22 + 2 = 24$

Thus, atomic number of $M^{2+} = 24\ (Z)$

Neutrons in $M^{2+} = Z + 2 = 26$

Thus, ionic mass of $M^{2+} = P + N = 24 + 26 = 50$

Molar Mass

For any substance, molar mass is the mass in gram of 1 mole of the compound.

Molar mass is expressed in gm/mole.

Mass of 1 proton $= 1.672 \times 10^{-24}$ g

Mass of one mole proton = 1.007 g

Mass of 1 neutron $= 1.674 \times 10^{-24}$ g

Mass of one mole neutron = 1.008 g

Mass of 1 electron $= 9.12 \times 10^{-28}$ g

Mass of one mole electron = 0.0005 g

Mass of 1 mole of ${}_6C^{12}$ atoms contains

Mass of 6 moles $p = 6 \times 1.007$ g

Mass of 6 moles $n = 6 \times 1.008$ g

Mass of 6 moles $e = 6 \times 0.0005$ g

So, the molar mass of ${}_6C^{12} = 12.1008$ g/mol ≈ 12 g/mol

Molar Mass
- Atoms — Gram atomic mass
- Molecules — Gram molecular mass

Gram Atomic Mass

Gram atomic mass is synonymous with molar mass when referring to atomic elements. It is the mass of one mole or 6.022×10^{23} atoms expressed in gram.

1 mole O-atom $\equiv 6.022 \times 10^{23}$ O-atoms

$\equiv 15.99$ gm $\equiv 1$ gram-atom

2 mole O-atom $= 2 \times 6.022 \times 10^{23}$ O-atoms $= 2 \times 15.99$ g

$= 2$ gram-atom

Number of g-atom $\equiv$ number of moles

Example : 2 g-atom of Nitrogen

$\equiv 2$ mol of N-atoms

Gram Molecular Mass

Gram molecular mass is synonymous with molar mass when referring to molecules. It represents the mass of one mole of molecules in grams.

1 mole $H_2SO_4 \equiv 6.022 \times 10^{23}$ H_2SO_4 molecules $\equiv 98$ g

$\equiv 1$ g-molecule

2 mole $H_2SO_4 = 2 \times 6.022 \times 10^{23}$ H_2SO_4 molecules

$\equiv 196$ g $\equiv 2$ g-molecule

Number of g-molecule $\equiv$ number of moles of molecule

Equivalent Mass and Gram Equivalent Mass

Equivalent mass of a substance is the mass which can combine or displace 1 g hydrogen, or 8 g oxygen, or 35.5 g chlorine, or 80.0 g bromine, or 127.0 g iodine, or 12.0 g carbon, or 17.0 g OH^-.

Equivalent mass is a pure number, but when it is expressed in grams, it is called **gram equivalent mass.**

$$\text{Equivalent mass of an element} = \frac{\text{Atomic mass of element}}{\text{Valency of element}}$$

e.g. (i) $\underset{1\text{ mol}}{Zn + H_2SO_4} \longrightarrow ZnSO_4 + \underset{1\text{ mol}}{H_2}$

1 mole (= 2 g) H_2 is displaced by 1 mole H_2SO_4 (= 98 g)

$\therefore$ 1 g H_2 is displaced by = 49 g H_2SO_4

Thus, equivalent mass of $H_2SO_4 = 49$

(ii) $\underset{2\text{ mol}}{2Zn} + \underset{1\text{ mol}}{O_2} \longrightarrow 2ZnO$

1 mole O_2(32 g) combine with $= 2 \times 65.38$ g of Zn

Thus, 8 g O_2 combine with $= \frac{2}{32} \times 8 \times 65.38$ g

$= 32.62$ g of Zn

So, equivalent mass of Zn = atomic mass/valency

Here, 1 H is equivalent to $\left(\frac{\text{molar mass}}{2}\right)$ in H_2SO_4 and Zn.

It is written as $1\text{ H} \equiv \frac{\text{molar mass}}{2}$

(iii) $\underset{\substack{2\text{ mol}\\4\text{ g}}}{2H_2} + \underset{\substack{1\text{ mol}\\32\text{ g}}}{O_2} \longrightarrow \underset{\substack{2\text{ mol}\\36\text{ g}}}{2H_2O}$

For H_2O (with respect to H)

4 g $H_2 \equiv 36$ g H_2O,

1 g $H_2 \equiv 9$ g H_2O

For H_2O (with respect to O)

32 g $O_2 \equiv 36$ g H_2O,

8 g $O_2 \equiv 9$ g H_2O

Thus, equivalent mass of $H_2O = 9$

(iv) $N_2 + 3H_2 \longrightarrow 2NH_3$
1 mol 3 mol 2 mol
6 g 34 g

$$6\text{g H} \equiv 34 \text{ g NH}_3,$$

$$1\text{g H} \equiv \frac{34}{6}$$

$$= \frac{17}{3} \text{ g NH}_3$$

Thus, equivalent mass of $NH_3 = \frac{17}{3}$ g

$$\text{Number of equivalent} = \frac{\text{Mass (in gram)}}{\text{Equivalent mass (gram equivalent)}}$$

Equivalent Mass of an Acid or Base or Salt

Equivalent mass of a base or an acid or salt can be expressed in terms of n-factor

$$\text{Equivalent mass} = \frac{\text{Molar mass}}{n\text{-factor}}$$

***n*-factor for a base (i.e. acidity)** is the number of replaceable (ionisable) OH^- ions bonded to electropositive metal.

Acidity (or *n*-factor) of Some Common Bases

Base	Type	n-factor or number of OH^- ions per unit	Equivalent mass $= \frac{\text{Molar mass } (m)}{n \text{ - factor}}$
NaOH	monoacid	1	$= m$
KOH	monoacid	1	$= m$
NH_4OH	monoacid	1	$= m$
CH_3NH_2	monoacid*	1**	$= m$
$C_6H_5NH_2$	monoacid*	1**	$= m$
C_5H_5N	monoacid*	1**	$= m$
$Ca(OH)_2$	diacid	2	$= m/2$
$Ba(OH)_2$	diacid	2	$= m/2$
$Al(OH)_3$	triacid	3	$= m/3$

* Organic bases like CH_3NH_2, $C_6H_5NH_2$, C_5H_5N have the tendency to accept proton

** $$RNH_2 + H_2O \rightleftharpoons RNH_3^{\oplus} + OH^{\ominus}$$

$$\underset{\text{Methyl amine}}{CH_3NH_2} + H^{\oplus} \rightleftharpoons CH_3NH_3^{\oplus}$$

$$\underset{\text{Aniline}}{C_6H_5NH_2} + H^{\oplus} \rightleftharpoons C_6H_5NH_3^{\oplus}$$

$$\underset{\text{Pyridine}}{C_5H_5N} + H^{\oplus} \rightleftharpoons C_5H_5NH^{\oplus}$$

***n*-factor for an acid (i.e. basicity)** is the number of replaceable (ionisable) H^+ ions attached to O-atom/electronegative atoms as F, Cl, Br, and I

Basicity (or *n*-factor) Some Common Acids

Acid	Type	n-factor or number of H^+ per unit	Equivalent mass $= \frac{\text{Molar mass } (m)}{n\text{-Factor}}$
CH_3COOH	monobasic	1	$= m$
HCl	monobasic	1	$= m$
N_3H	monobasic	1	$= m$
HNO_3	monobasic	1	$= m$
HSO_4^-	monobasic	1	$= m$
H_3PO_2	monobasic	1	$= m$
H_2SO_4	dibasic	2	$= m/2$
$H_2C_2O_4$	dibasic	2	$= m/2$
H_3PO_3	dibasic	2	$= m/2$
H_3PO_4	tribasic	3	$= m/3$

JEE Spotlite

H_3PO_2, H_3PO_3 and H_3PO_4 all appear tribasic acids but respectively has one, two and three replaceable H^+ ions attached to O-atoms directly (encircled).

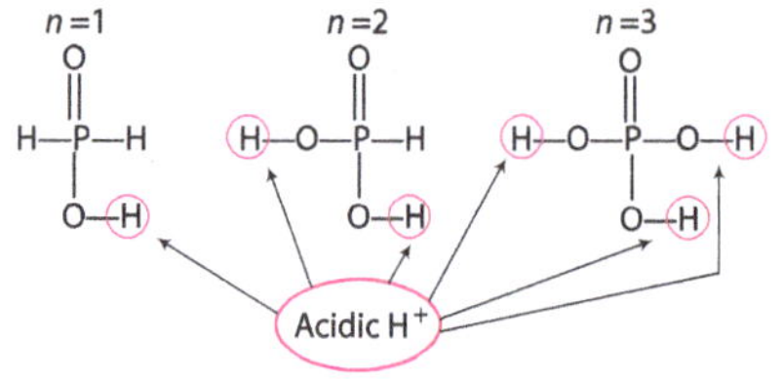

H attached to P directly exhibits reducing property and H attached to oxygen can get released as H^+ ions.

For a salt

n-factor is the total positive or negative charge on it.

$$KCl \rightleftharpoons K^+ + Cl^-; \quad n = 1, E = \frac{m}{1}$$

$$K_2SO_4 \rightleftharpoons 2K^+ + SO_4^{2-}; \; n = 2, E = \frac{m}{2}$$

$$AlPO_4 \rightleftharpoons Al^{3+} + PO_4^{3-}; \quad n = 3, E = \frac{m}{3}$$

$$Fe_2(SO_4)_3 \rightleftharpoons 2Fe^{3+} + 3SO_4^{2-}; n = 6, E = \frac{m}{6}$$

$$K_2SO_4 \cdot Al_2(SO_4)_3 \rightleftharpoons 2K^+ + 2Al^{3+} + 4SO_4^{2-}; n = 8, E = \frac{m}{8}$$

For Redox Change

***n*-factor** is the number of electrons gained (reduction) or lost (oxidation).

$$Fe^{3+} + e^- \longrightarrow Fe^{2+}; n = 1, E = \frac{m}{1}$$

$$Fe^{2+} + 2e^- \longrightarrow Fe; \quad n = 2, E = \frac{m}{2}$$

$$2H^+ + 2e^- \longrightarrow H_2; \qquad n=2, E=\frac{m}{2}$$

$$Cr_2O_7^{2-} + 6e^- \longrightarrow 2Cr^{3+}; \; n=6, E=\frac{m}{6}$$

$$MnO_4^- + 5e^- \longrightarrow Mn^{2+}; n=5, E=\frac{m}{5}$$

Solved Booster 2.3

Consider the following gases at STP.

(a) H_2 (b) O_2 (c) Cl_2 (d) HCl

How many of them have volume occupied by one equivalent equal to 11.2 L?

(a) 1 (b) 2 (c) 3 (d) 4

Solution (c)

(a) $H_2 \equiv 2H$

1 mole = 2 equivalents taking H as 1 g

$\therefore$ Volume of 1 equivalent H_2 at STP $= \frac{22.4}{2} = 11.2$ L

(b) $O_2 \equiv 2(O) = 32$ g

$\therefore \quad 8 \text{ g } O_2 \equiv \frac{32}{8} = 4$

Thus, 1 mole $O_2 \equiv 4$ equivalents O_2

Volume of 1 equivalent O_2 at STP = 5.6 L

(c) Volume of 1 equivalent Cl_2 = 11.2 L

(d) Volume of 1 equivalent HCl = 11.2 L

Chemical Formula

The chemical formula of a substance is a symbolic representation that provides information about the elements in a molecule and the number of atoms of each element. It signifies the chemical composition of the substance. Before going into detail first understand the term percentage composition.

Percentage Composition

Percentage composition of a chemical compound refers to the mass percentage of each element in the compound.

$$\text{Percentage of element} = \frac{\text{Mass of element}}{\text{Molecular mass}} \times 100$$

For example, for ethanol (C_2H_5OH)

1 mole of $C_2H_5OH = 46$ g/mol

mass of C = 2 mol × 12 g/mol = 24 g

mass of H = 6 mol × 1 g/mol = 6 g

mass of O = 1 mol × 16 g/mol = 16 g

$$\text{mass percent of C} = \frac{24}{46} \times 100 = 52.17\%$$

$$\text{mass percent of H} = \frac{6}{46} \times 100 = 13.04\%$$

$$\text{mass percent of O} = \frac{16}{46} \times 100 = 34.79\%$$

JEE MAPPER

Example Similar to PYQ Asked in JEE Main 2024

A sample of Li_2CO_3 and Na_2CO_3 weighed 3.51 g is ignited to constant weight of 1.9 g. The composition of mixture is [Given, molar mass in g mol^{-1} Li_2CO_3 : 74, Na_2CO_3 : 106]

(a) 3.15 g Li_2CO_3 + 0.36 g Na_2CO_3

(b) 2.658 g Li_2CO_3 + 0.852 g Na_2CO_3

(c) 0.36 g Li_2CO_3 + 3.15 g Na_2CO_3

(d) 0.852 g Li_2CO_3 + 2.658 g Na_2CO_3

Sol. (d) The reaction involved are

$$Li_2CO_3(s) \xrightarrow{\Delta} Li_2O(s) + CO_2(g)$$

$$Na_2CO_3(s) \xrightarrow{\Delta} Na_2O(s) + CO_2(g)$$

Let the weight of Li_2CO_3 be x g.

$\therefore$ Weight of $Na_2CO_3 = (3.51 - x)$ g

Moles of Li_2CO_3 decomposed = Moles of Li_2O formed

$$\frac{x}{74} = \text{Moles of } Li_2O \text{ formed}$$

$\therefore$ Weight of Li_2O formed $= \frac{x}{74} \times 30$

Moles of Na_2CO_3 decomposed = Moles of Na_2O formed

$$\frac{3.51 - x}{106} = \text{Moles of } Na_2O \text{ formed}$$

$$\therefore \quad \text{Weight of } Na_2O \text{ formed} = \frac{3.51 - x}{106} \times 62$$

$$\frac{(3.51 - x)}{106} \times 62 + \frac{x}{74} \times 30 = 1.9$$

$$\frac{217.62 - 62x}{106} + \frac{30x}{74} = 1.9$$

$$16103.88 - 4588x + 3180x = 1.9 \times 106 \times 74$$

$$16103.88 - 14903.6 = 1408x$$

$$x = 0.852 \text{ g}$$

$$= \text{Weight of } Li_2CO_3$$

$$\text{Weight of } Na_2CO_3 = 3.51 - 0.852$$

$$= 2.658 \text{ g}$$

Competency Enhancer 2.1

A sample of $CaCO_3$ and $MgCO_3$ weighted 4.41 g is ignited to constant weight of 2.232 g. The composition of mixture is [Given, molar mass in g mol^{-1} $CaCO_3$: 100, $MgCO_3$: 84]

(a) 3.03 g $CaCO_3$ + 1.38 g $MgCO_3$

(b) 1.58 g $CaCO_3$ + 2.83 g $MgCO_3$

(c) 1.38 g $CaCO_3$ + 5.03 g $MgCO_3$

(d) 2.84 g $CaCO_3$ + 1.57 g $MgCO_3$

Empirical Formula

Empirical formula represents the simplest ratio of atoms belonging to different elements in a molecule.

For Example

The molecular formula of hydrogen peroxide, H_2O_2. This formula indicates that each molecule of H_2O_2 consist of 2H-atoms and 2 O-atoms, i.e. the ratio of hydrogen to oxygen atoms in this molecule is 1 : 1. The empirical formula of hydrogen peroxide is HO.

Similarly, empirical formula of glucose (molecular formula $C_6H_{12}O_6$) is written CH_2O.

However, empirical formula of water is same to its molecular formula i.e., H_2O, because the ratio of H and O atoms in H_2O is already in their simplest ratio.

Empirical Formula Mass of a Compound

It is equal to the sum of atomic masses of all the atoms present in the empirical formula. e.g.

Empirical formula of hydrogen peroxide (H_2O_2) is HO.

So, empirical mass ≡17 g/mol

Steps to Find the Empirical Formula

What is the empirical formula of a compound which contains 52.96% carbon and 47.04% oxygen by mass?

Step 1 Take the mass percentage same as mass of atoms in gram.

Mass of carbon = 52.96 gm and oxygen = 47.04 gm

Step 2 Convert the mass in moles using atomic masses in grams.

$$\text{Moles of C} = \frac{52.96 \text{ g}}{12.01 \text{ g / mol}} = 4.410 \text{ mol}$$

$$\text{Moles of O} = \frac{47.04 \text{ g}}{16.00 \text{ g / mol}} = 2.940 \text{ mol}$$

Step 3 Divide all the numbers of moles by the smallest number to get an integral ratio.

$$C : \frac{4.410 \text{ mol}}{2.940 \text{ mol}} = 1.5$$

$$O : \frac{2.940 \text{ mol}}{2.940 \text{ mol}} = 1$$

Step 4 This ratio is still not integral. Multiplying these values by 2 yields integers.

$$C = 1.5 \times 2 = 3$$

$$O = 1 \times 2 = 2$$

The empirical formula = C_3O_2

JEE MAPPER

Example Similar to PYQ Asked in JEE Advanced 2022

A series of pure binary compounds (M_xN_y) were analysed and their composition is tabulated below.

Compound	Weight % of M	Weight % of N
1	70	30
2	40	60
3	25	75

The incorrect option's is(are)

(a) If empirical formula of compound '3' is M_3N_5, then the empirical formula of compound '2' is M_3N_4.

(b) If empirical formula of compound '3' is M_3N_2 and atomic weight of element M is 10, then the atomic weight of N is 45.

(c) If empirical formula of compounds 2 is MN then the empirical formula of the compound 1 is M_3N_2.

(d) If atomic weight of M and N are 75 and 25 respectively, then the empirical formula of compound 1 is M_6N_3.

Solution *(a, c, d)*

Among the given statements, a, c and d are incorrect while statement (b) is correct.

(a) If empirical formula of compound 3 is M_3N_5.

We know that, $\frac{3 \times M_M}{5 \times M_N} = \frac{\% \text{of } M}{\% \text{of } N}$

where, M_M = molar mass of M

M_N = molar mass of N

$$\frac{3M_M}{5M_N} = \frac{25}{75} = \frac{1}{3} \Rightarrow \frac{M_M}{M_N} = \frac{5}{9}$$

If empirical formula of compound 2 is M_3N_4

$$\frac{3M_M}{4M_N} = \frac{40}{60} \Rightarrow \frac{M_M}{M_N} = \frac{2}{3} \times \frac{4}{3} = \frac{8}{9}$$

Since, molecular weight ratio does not come out equal in two compounds, '2' and '3'. So, statement (a) cannot be correct.

(b) If empirical formula of '3' is M_3N_2

$$\frac{3M_M}{2M_N} = \frac{25}{75} = \frac{1}{3} \Rightarrow \frac{M_M}{M_N} = \frac{2}{9}$$

If atomic weight of M is 10 and that of N = 45

$$\frac{M_M}{M_N} = \frac{10}{45} = \frac{2}{9}$$

So, statement (b) is correct.

(c) If empirical formula of 2 is MN

$$\frac{M_M}{M_N} = \frac{40}{60} = \frac{2}{3}$$

and compound '1' is M_3N_2

$$\frac{3M_M}{2M_N} = \frac{70}{30} = \frac{7}{3}$$

Putting value of $\frac{M_M}{M_N} = \frac{2}{3}$

we get, $\frac{3}{2} \times \frac{2}{3} = 1$

So, statement (c) is incorrect.

(d) $M_M = 75, M_N = 25$

If empirical formula of compound '1' is M_6N_3.

$$\frac{6M_M}{3M_N} = \frac{70}{30} = \frac{7}{3}$$

$$\frac{M_M}{N_N} = \frac{7}{3} \times \frac{3}{6} \Rightarrow 6M_M = 7M_N$$

($6M_M$ is equal to $7M_N$)

But, M_M is shown as double to M_N

So, this statement is not correct.

So, only statement (b) is correct while all others are incorrect.

Competency Enhancer 2.2

A series of pure binary compounds (X_MY_N) were analysed and their composition is tabulated below.

Compound	Weight% of X	Weight% of Y
1	33.3	66.6
2	45	55
3	50	50

The correct option(s) is(are)

(a) If empirical formula of compound '1' is X_3Y_4, then the empirical formula of compound '2' is $X_{27}Y_{22}$.

(b) If empirical formula of compound '3' is X_3Y_2 and atomic weight of element X is 30, then the atomic weight of Y is 40.

(c) If empirical formula of compound '2' is XY, then the empirical formula of the compound '3' is X_3Y_5.

(d) If atomic weight of X and Y are 70 and 35 respectively, then the empirical formula of compound '3' is X_3Y_6.

Molecular Formula

The formula that represents exact number of atoms belonging to different elements in a molecule is called molecular formula.

For example, The molecular of hydrogen peroxide is H_2O_2 How to find the molecular formula using empirical formula mass and molecular formula mass.

Steps to Find the Molecular Formula

- **Step 1** Find the empirical formula mass
  e.g. $C_2H_3O : 12 \times 2 + 1 \times 3 + 16 = 43$ amu
  Molecular formula mass $= 86$ amu
- **Step 2** Divide the molecular mass by the empirical mass
  $$\frac{86 \text{ amu}}{43 \text{ amu}} = 2$$
- **Step 3** Multiply the number of atoms of each element in the empirical formula by the whole number found in Step 2
  $$(C_2H_3O) \times 2 = C_4H_6O_2$$

Mole

The term 'mole' in chemistry was introduced by the German Wilhelm Ostwald in the later 19th century. Mole is abbreviated as "mol". In chemistry, the mole is a fundamental unit of counting. One mole is the amount of a substance that contains as many particles or entities as there are atoms in exactly 12 g of ^{12}C isotope. Number of particles or entities in 1 mole of a substance is known as **Avogadro constant** or **Avagadro number** denoted by N_A or N_0.

One mole of a substance always contains the same number of particles, no matter what the substance may be.

Based on mass of one atom of ^{12}C determined by mass spectrometer value of N_A was derived.

Mass of one atom of $^{12}C = 1.992648 \times 10^{-23}$ g

Thus, 12 g of $^{12}C = \frac{12}{1.992648 \times 10^{-23}}$ atoms

$$= 6.0221367 \times 10^{23} \text{ atoms mol}^{-1}$$

Thus, 1 mole $= 6.022 \times 10^{23}$ electrons

1 mole of H-atom $= 6.022 \times 10^{23}$ atoms

1 mole of H_2O molecules $= 6.022 \times 10^{23}$ molecules

$$\text{Mole of a substance} = \frac{\text{Mass in grams}}{\text{Molar mass}}$$

$$\text{Mass of one molecule of a species} = \frac{\text{Molar mass}}{N_0}$$

Mass of one mole of a substance in grams is called its molar mass.

Each water molecules has two H-atoms and one O-atom, thus

1 mole of $H_2O = N_A$ water molecules

$= N_A$ oxygen atoms

$= 2N_A$ hydrogen atoms

Solved Booster 2.4

Gypsum is a hydrate of calcium sulphate. A 1.0 g sample contains 0.791 g $CaSO_4$. The sum of number moles of $CaSO_4$ and water in the sample is $x \times 10^{-3}$. The value of x is .... (nearest integer)

Solution (17)

Molar mass of $CaSO_4 = 40 + 32 + 64 = 136$ g mol^{-1}

$CaSO_4 = 0.791$ g

$H_2O = (1 - 0.791) = 0.209$ g

$$\text{Moles} = \frac{\text{Mass of the species (in g)}}{\text{Molar mass (in g mol}^{-1})}$$

$$\therefore \text{ Moles of } CaSO_4 = \frac{0.791}{136} = 5.816 \times 10^{-3}$$

$$\text{Moles of } H_2O = \frac{0.209}{18} = 11.611 \times 10^{-3}$$

$$\text{Sum of moles} = 5.816 \times 10^{-3} + 11.611 \times 10^{-3}$$

$$= 17.427 \times 10^{-3} \approx 17$$

Solved Booster 2.5

Analysis of chlorophyll shows that it contains 2.88% magnesium. The number of atoms of magnesium 1.20 g of chlorophyll contains is .... $\times 10^{20}$.
(round off upto 2 decimal place)

Solution *(8.67)*

$$1.20 \text{ g of chlorophyll has} = 1.20 \times \frac{2.88}{100} \text{ g Mg},$$

$$= 1.20 \times \frac{2.88}{100} \times \frac{1}{24} \frac{\text{g}}{\text{g mol}^{-1}} \text{ Mg}$$

$$= 1.44 \times 10^{-3} \text{ mol Mg}$$

$$= 1.44 \times 10^{-3} \times 6.02 \times 10^{23} \text{ Mg atoms}$$

$$= 8.6688 \times 10^{20} \text{ Mg atoms}$$

Solved Booster 2.6

Mass of one atom of X is 6.642×10^{-23}g. The number of moles of X are contained in 40 kg of it will be

(a) 1000 (b) 180
(c) 208 (d) 80

Solution *(a)*

$$\text{Atomic mass of } X = \text{Mass of one atom} \times N_0$$

$$= 6.642 \times 10^{-23} \text{g} \times 6.02 \times 10^{23} \text{mol}^{-1}$$

$$\approx 40.0 \text{g mol}^{-1}$$

$$\text{Moles of } X \text{ present in 40 kg} = \frac{40 \times 1000 \text{ g}}{40.0 \text{ g mol}^{-1}}$$

$$= 1000 \text{ mol}$$

Molar Volume Concept

Molar volume is the volume occupied by one mole of a gas at a defined temperature and pressure. It is typically denoted by the symbol "V_m".

At STP, the molar volume of an ideal gas is approximately 22.4 litres per mole.

STP : Standard Temperature → 273.15 K (0°C)

Standard Pressure → 1 atmosphere

Molar volume, if ideal gas is not at STP, is calculated using the ideal gas law : According to the ideal gas law, $pV = nRT$

where, p = pressure

V = volume

n = number of moles

T = temperature in Kelvin

'R' is the ideal gas constant which is approximately 0.0821 L atom-mol^{-1} K^{-1} or 8.314 Nm mol^{-1} K^{-1} or 8.314 J mol^{-1} K^{-1} or 2 cal mol^{-1} K^{-1}.

Mole Calculations

$$\text{Number of mole} = \frac{\text{Given number of chemical species}}{6.022 \times 10^{23}}$$

$$= \frac{\text{Given mass}}{\text{Molar mass}}$$

$$= \frac{\text{Given volume (L) at STP}}{22.4 \text{ L}} \text{ (for ideal gas only)}$$

$$= \frac{pV}{RT} \text{ (for ideal gas only)}$$

Solved Booster 2.7

16 g of an ideal gas SO_x occupies 5.6 L at STP. What is the molar mass of the gas? What is the value of x?

Solution (2)

1 mole of the gas = Molar mass of the gas = 22.4 L at STP

5.6 L of SO_x at STP of the gas = 16 g

$$22.4 \text{ L of the gas at STP} = \frac{16}{5.6} \times 22.4 = 64 \text{ g mol}^{-1}$$

$$\text{Molar mass of the gas} = 32 + 16x$$

$$\therefore \quad 32 + 16x = 64 \Rightarrow x = 2$$

Thus, gas is SO_2.

Laws of Chemical Combination

The combination of elements to form compounds is governed by a set of principles known as the laws of chemical combination.

Law of Conservation of Mass

According to this law "Mass is neither created nor destroyed in chemical reactions" i.e. total mass of reactants before chemical reaction is equal to the total mass of products after chemical reaction. For example, when hydrogen gas burns and combines with oxygen to yield water (H_2O), the mass of water formed is equal to the mass of hydrogen and oxygen consumed. This is in accordance with the law of mass conservation.

$$2H_2(g) + O_2(g) \longrightarrow 2H_2O(l)$$

Mass of reactants 4 g 32 g 36 g Mass of product

Law of Definite Proportions

This states "Different samples of a pure chemical substance always contain the same proportions of elements by mass".

e.g. Every samples of water (H_2O) contains 1 part hydrogen and 8 parts oxygen by mass.

$$\begin{array}{ccc} H_2 & & O \\ \downarrow & & \downarrow \\ 2 & : & 16 = 1:8 \end{array}$$

Every sample of carbon dioxide (CO_2) contains 1 part carbon and 2.67 parts oxygen by mass

$$\begin{matrix} C & O_2 \\ 12 : 32 = 1 : 2.67 \end{matrix}$$

Solved Booster 2.8

1.4 g of iron reacts with 0.8 g of sulphur directly to form iron (II) sulphide. 5.6 g of iron was dissolved in dilute HCl and excess of potassium sulphide was added. If the law of definite composition is followed, how much iron (II) sulphide is formed in the second case? (Fe=56 and S=32)

(a) 10 g
(b) 7.9 g
(c) 8.8 g
(d) 6.5 g

Solution *(c)*

$$\text{Based on law of definite proportions} = \frac{\text{Moles of Fe in case I}}{\text{Moles of Fe in case II}} = \frac{\text{Moles of S in case I}}{\text{Moles of S in case II}}$$

$$\left(\frac{1.4}{56}\right)\Big/\left(\frac{5.6}{56}\right) = \frac{0.8/32}{x/32}$$

$\therefore$ x (sulphur in case II) = 3.2 g

Total mass of iron and sulphur = 5.6 + 3.2

(Based on law of conservation of mass) = 8.8 g

Law of Multiple Proportions

According to this law "If two elements combine in different ways to form different substances, then the masses of one element that combine with a fixed mass of other element, are in the ratio of small whole numbers.

For example, 1g of hydrogen can combine with 8g of oxygen to yield H_2O or with 16g of oxygen to yield H_2O_2. Thus, hydrogen reacts in a multiple of 2.

$$\frac{\text{H : O mass ratio in } H_2O}{\text{H : O mass ratio in } H_2O_2} = \frac{(1g\ H/8g\ O)}{(1g\ H/16g\ O)} = 2$$

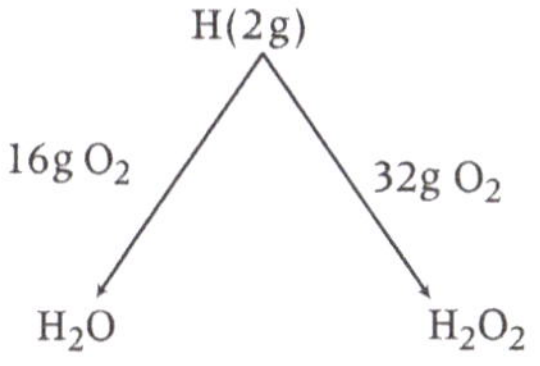

JEE Alert

Atoms of same elements will have same mass irrespective of the source. This is not valid in case of isotopes.

Solved Booster 2.9

Methane and ethane, both are constituents of natural gas. A sample of methane contains 11.4 g of carbon and 3.80 g of hydrogen, whereas a sample of ethane contains 4.47 g of carbon and 1.118 of hydrogen. This data illustrates the law of

(a) constant proportion (b) Gay-Lussac
(c) multiple proportion (d) reciprocal proportion

Solution *(c)*

S. No.	Carbon	Hydrogen	Ratio
Methane	11.4 g	3.80 g	$\frac{11.40}{3.80} = 3.00$
Ethane	4.47 g	1.118 g	$\frac{4.47}{1.118} = 4.00$

Thus, ratio of (C : H) in methane to ethane is = $\frac{3}{4}$

Thus, law of multiple proportion is followed.

Law of Reciprocal Proportions

If element A combines with element B and also with C, then if B and C combine together, the proportion by mass in which they do so will be either same or simple multiples of masses of B and C which separately combine with constant mass of A. e.g.,

(a) $C + 2H_2 \longrightarrow CH_4$ (b) $O_2 + 2H_2 \longrightarrow 2H_2O$
(c) $C + O_2 \longrightarrow CO_2$

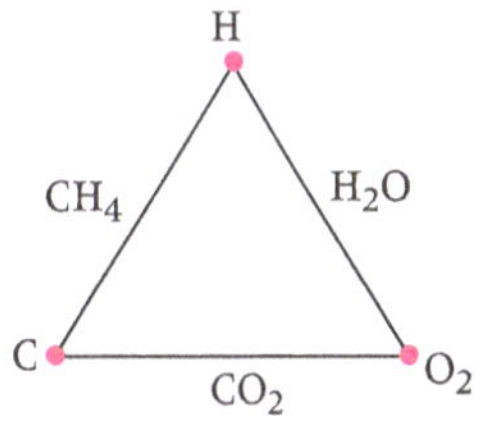

4 g H_2 combines with 12 g carbon in (a)
4 g H_2 combines with 32 g oxygen in (b)

Thus, ratio of carbon and oxygen in (a) and (b) by mass that combines with a definite mass of H_2 (in this case 4 g) =12:32 =3:8 in (c) or 12 g carbon combines with 32 g oxygen, and the ratio of carbon and oxygen (by mass) in CO_2 is 3 :8

This law is not applicable to isotopes.

Solved Booster 2.10

CuS contains 66.6% copper, CuO contains 79.9% of copper and SO_3 contains 40% of Sulphur. Show that the data illustrates the law of reciprocal proportions.

Solution

Consider CuS % of Cu = 66.6 and S = 33.4%

66.6 g Cu $\longrightarrow$ 33.4 g of S

1 g Cu $\longrightarrow \frac{33.4}{66.6}$ g of S = 0.5 g Sulphur

CuO Cu = 79.9% O = 20.1%

79.9 g Cu $\longrightarrow$ 20.1 g Oxygen

$1 \text{ g Cu} \longrightarrow \frac{20.1}{79.9} \text{ g of oxygen} = 0.25 \text{ g oxygen}$

* Ratio of masses of Sulphur and oxygen

$$1 \text{ g Cu} \left(\frac{S}{O}\right) = \frac{0.5}{0.25} = \frac{2}{1}$$

SO_3 $S = 40\%$ $O = 60\%$

The ratio of mass of sulphur and oxygen in SO_3

$$\left(\frac{S}{O}\right) = \frac{40}{60} = \frac{2}{3}$$

$$1 \text{ g Cu} \quad \frac{\left(\frac{S}{O}\right)}{\left(\frac{S}{O}\right)} = \frac{\frac{2}{1}}{\frac{2}{3}} = \frac{3}{1}$$

So, S and O combine together in a ratio of 1 : 3

Gay-Lussac's Law : The Law of Combining Volume of Gases

Based on experimental studies French chemist, Gay-Lussac concluded that the volumes of reactants and products in a large number of chemical reactions are related to each other by small integers, if volumes are measured at the same temperature and pressure. For example,

$$\underset{\substack{2\text{ V} \\ 100\text{ mL}}}{2H_2(g)} + \underset{\substack{1\text{ V} \\ 50\text{ mL}}}{O_2(g)} \longrightarrow \underset{\substack{2\text{ V} \\ 100\text{ mL}}}{2H_2O(g)}$$

If all the gases are measured at the same temperature and pressure (say 373 K and 1 bar pressure) then 100 mL of $H_2(g)$ combines with 50 mL of $O_2(g)$ to give exactly 100 mL of $H_2O(g)$.

Avogadro's Law

"The volume of a gas (at fixed temperature and pressure) is proportional to the number of moles (or molecules of gas present)".

Thus,

$$V \propto n \text{ (moles)} \propto nN_0 \text{ (molecules)}$$

Thus, in modified manner, **Avogadro's law can** be defined as **"Equal volumes of all gases under the same conditions of temperature and pressure contain equal number of molecules".**

Thus, both the Gay-Lussac and Avogadro laws can be summarised by the following equation.

$$\underset{1\text{ vol}}{N_2(g)} + \underset{3\text{ vol}}{3H_2(g)} \longrightarrow \underset{2\text{ vol}}{2NH_3(g)} \quad \text{By [Gay Lussac's Law]}$$

$$\underset{\substack{6.02\times10^{23} \\ \text{molecules}}}{1 \text{ mol } N_2} + \underset{\substack{3\times6.02\times10^{23} \\ \text{molecules}}}{3 \text{ mol } H_2} \longrightarrow \underset{\substack{2\times6.02\times10^{23} \\ \text{molecules}}}{2 \text{ mol } NH_3} \quad \text{[By Avogadro's law]}$$

Avogadro's hypothesis led to

(i) the word molecule and made the distinction between atoms and molecules.

(ii) conclude that molecules of hydrogen, chlorine, oxygen, nitrogen and fluorine are diatomic.

(iii) conclude that molecular weight $= 2 \times$ vapour density

(iv) conclude that one gram-molecular mass (molecular weight) has volume 22.4 L (22.4×10^{-3} m^3) at NTP (pressure = 1 atm and $T = 273.15$ K)

Number of molecules present in the amount equal to molecular weight (which we shall call one mole) are 6.02×10^{23} (called **Avogadro's number**)

Dalton's Theory as Modified by Avogadro's Hypothesis

(i) The smallest particle of an element, which take part in a chemical reactions are known as atoms; atoms may or may not have an independent existence.

(ii) The ultimate particles of a substance, element or compound which can exist in free state and possess all the physical and chemical properties of the substance are called molecules.

e.g. Hydrogen gas H_2; Oxygen gas O_2; Nitrogen gas N_2

- Monoatomic molecules : Na, Xe, He etc.
- Diatomic molecules : O_2, N_2, H_2 etc.
- Polyatomic molecules : CO_2, H_2O, BH_3 etc.

Polyatomic molecules can be further categorised to :

- Homoatomic molecules : Molecules that contain same type of atoms.

  e.g. O_2, H_2, O_3, S_8 etc.

- Heteroatomic molecules : Molecules that contain different types of atoms.

  e.g. CO_2, H_2O, SO_3, NO_2 etc.

  "They are also said to be compounds."

(iii) Chemical reactions are reconfiguration of atoms, i.e. breaking of old bonds and making new bonds.

$$NaOH + HCl \longrightarrow NaCl + H_2O$$

Solved Booster 2.11

Equal masses of N_2, O_2 and CO_2 have been taken in a container of volume V at temperature 25°C in identical conditions. The ratio of the volumes of the gases N_2, O_2 and CO_2 would be

(a) 14 : 32 : 44 (b) 88 : 77 : 176 : 56
(c) 176 : 77 : 56 (d) 64 : 56 : 32

Solution (b)

According to Avogadro's hypothesis under identical conditions equal masses of gases taken, ratio of the volume of gas will be equal to the ratio of their moles.

Let mass of each gas is 1 g.

Moles of $N_2 = \frac{1}{28}$, Moles of $O_2 = \frac{1}{32}$,

Moles of $CO_2 = \frac{1}{44}$

Ratio of volumes $= \frac{1}{28} : \frac{1}{32} : \frac{1}{44} = 88 : 77 : 56$

Elemental Practice 1.2

Type I MCQs with Only One Correct Option

1. One mole of oxygen gas at STP is equal to
   (a) 6.022×10^{23} molecules of oxygen
   (b) 12.044×10^{23} atoms of oxygen
   (c) 32 g of oxygen
   (d) All of the above

2. Which of the following pairs have the same number of atoms?
   I. 16 g of O_2 and 4 g of H_2
   II. 16 g of O_2 and 44 g of CO_2
   III. 28 g of N_2 and 32 g of O_2
   IV. 12 g of C and 23 g of Na
   (a) Both I and II (b) II, III and IV
   (c) Both III and IV (d) I, III and IV

3. 16 g of oxygen has same number of molecules as in
   (a) 16 g of CO (b) 28 g of N_2
   (c) 14 g of N_2 (d) 4 g of He

4. One requires 0.01 mole of Na_2CO_3. Mass of $Na_2CO_3 \cdot 10H_2O$ to be taken is
   (a) 1.06 g (b) 2.86 g (c) 1.80 g (d) 3.02 g

5. Number of atoms in 12g ($^{24}_{12}Mg$) is equal to
   (a) oxygen atoms in 11 g of CO_2
   (b) hydrogen atoms in 4 g of CH_4
   (c) nitrogen atoms in 46 g of N_2O_4
   (d) sulphur atoms in 79 g of $Na_2S_2O_3$

6. Select the correct statement.
   (a) At STP volume occupied by 1 mole liquid water is 22.4 L
   (b) 1 mole of every substance at STP has 22.4 L as volume
   (c) Volume occupied by 1 g of H_2 gas at STP is equal to volume occupied by 2g He at STP
   (d) CH_4 is a real gas if 1 g of it at STP has volume 1.4 L

7. A spherical ball of radius 7 cm contains 56% iron. If density of the metal (of the ball) is 1.4 g cm^{-3}, number of moles of Fe present is
   (a) 10 (b) 15 (c) 20 (d) 28

8. On heating $KClO_3$, 0.672 L of O_2 gas at STP is formed $KClO_3$ taken is
   (a) 0.02 mole (b) 0.02 molecules
   (c) 0.03 mole (d) 0.03 N_0 molecules

9. In the compounds X, Y and Z of aluminium, $X(Al_2O_3)$ contains 52.9% aluminium, $Y(CO_2)$ contains 27.27% carbon, Z(containing aluminium and carbon).
   If the law of reciprocal proportion is followed, percentage of aluminium in Z is
   (a) 24.99 (b) 56.0 (c) 45.00 (d) 75.00

10. Which of the following statements is correct about the reaction given below?
   $$4Fe(s) + 3O_2(g) \longrightarrow 2Fe_2O_3(g)$$
   (a) Total mass of iron and oxygen in reactants = total mass of iron and oxygen in product therefore it follows the law of conservation of mass
   (b) Total mass of reactants = total mass of product; therefore, law of multiple proportions is followed
   (c) Amount of Fe_2O_3 can be increased by taking any one of the reactants (iron or oxygen) in excess
   (d) Amount of Fe_2O_3 produced will decrease if the amount of any one of the reactants (iron or oxygen) is taken in excess

11. 1.0 g sample of NaCl and $CaCl_2$ is treated with Na_2CO_3, $CaCO_3$ thus precipitated gave 0.162 g CaO on heating. Thus % by mass of $CaCl_2$ in the mixture is
   (a) 15.2% (b) 21.8% (c) 32.1% (d) 11.7%

12. Which of the following postulates is incorrect about Dalton's atomic theory?
   (a) Chemical reactions involves reorganisation of atoms.
   (b) All the atoms of a given element have identical properties, including identical mass.
   (c) It could explain the laws of gaseous volumes.
   (d) Compounds are formed when atoms of different elements combine in a fixed ratio.

13. 1.947 g of iodine I_2 (I = 127) was allowed to react with 1.056 g of Sn(119) to form Sn_xI_y alongwith 0.601 g of unreacted Sn. Thus, Sn_xI_y is
   (a) SnI_2 (b) Sn_2I_3 (c) SnI_4 (d) SnI_3

14. Equivalent mass of a metal is 12 g mol^{-1}. Hence, equivalent mass of its oxide is
   (a) 24.0 g mol^{-1} (b) 28.0 g mol^{-1}
   (c) 20.0 g mol^{-1} (d) 34.0 g mol^{-1}

15. The equivalent mass of a metal is double that of oxygen. How many times is the equivalent mass of its oxide greater than the equivalent mass of the metal if the metal is alkaline earth metal?
   (a) 1.5 times (b) 2 times (c) 3 times (d) 4 times

16. A sample of ammonium phosphate, $(NH_4)_3PO_4$ contains 3.18 moles of hydrogen atoms. The number of moles of oxygen atoms in the sample is
   (a) 0.265 (b) 0.795 (c) 1.06 (d) 3.18

17. Copper forms two oxides. For the same amount of copper, twice as much oxygen was used to form the first oxide than to form second one. Ratio of the valencies of copper in the first and second oxides is
   (a) 1 : 2 (b) 2 : 1 (c) 1 : 1 (d) 1 : 3

18. In the combustion of 5.00 g of a metal, 9.44 g of metal oxide are formed. Hence, equivalent mass of metal is
   (a) 4.44 g (b) 9.00 g (c) 5.00 g (d) 2.22 g

19. The oxide of an element contains 67.67% of oxygen. Equivalent of the element is
   (a) 2.46 (b) 3.82 (c) 4.36 (d) 4.99

20. **Statement I** SO_2 and SO_3 follow "law of multiple proportion".

Statement II SO_2 has sulphur and oxygen in 1 : 1 mass ratio.

In the light of the below statements, choose the most appropriate answer from the options given below.
(a) Both Statement I and Statement II are false.
(b) Statement I is true and Statement II is false.
(c) Statement I is false but Statement II is true.
(d) Both Statement I and Statement II are true.

Type II 》 MCQs with One or More than One Correct Option

21. A bivalent metal ion (M^{2+}) has equivalent mass of 12. Then,
(a) equivalent mass of its oxide is 28
(b) molar mass of its oxide is 40
(c) equivalent mass of its hydride is 13
(d) atomic weight of the metal is 24

22. In diammonium hydrogen phosphate $(NH_4)_2HPO_4$, (a fertiliser), percentage of
(a) P_2O_5 is 53.78
(b) NH_3 is 25.81%
(c) N is maximum
(d) P is maximum

23. Which of the following statements are correct about the law of chemical combination?
(a) H_2O and H_2S contain 11.11% hydrogen and 5.88% hydrogen respectively, whereas SO_2 contains 50% sulphur. The above data prove the law of reciprocal proportions.
(b) Different proportions of oxygen in the various oxides of sulphur prove the law of multiple proportions.
(c) Potassium combines with two isotopes of chlorine (^{35}Cl and ^{37}Cl) to form two samples of KCl. Their formation follows the law of definite composition.
(d) 1.6 g of a hydrogen on combustion in excess of oxygen produces 1.2 g CO_2 and 0.4 of H_2O. The data illustrates the law of conservation of mass.

24. In which of the following pairs, 10 g of each have an equal number of molecules?
(a) N_2O and CO
(b) N_2 and C_3O_2
(c) N_2 and CO
(d) N_2O and CO_2

25. Consider the following percentage of elements of compound *A* and *B* given in table below.

Compound	% C	% H	% N
A (Molar mass = 162 g/mol)	74%	8.7%	17.3%
B (Molar mass = 108 g/mol)	66.7%	7.4%	25.9%

Select the correct option(s) is/are —
(a) The molecular formula of the compound *A* is $C_6H_8N_2$ and the molecular formula of the compound *B* is C_3H_4N.
(b) The value of *n*-factor for the both compound *A* and *B* is same.
(c) The empirical weight of compound *A* is double than the empirical weight of compound *B*.
(d) The molecular formula of the compound *A* is $C_{10}H_{14}N_2$ and the molecular formula of the compound *B* is $C_6H_8N_2$.

26. To check the principle of multiple proportions, a series of pure binary compounds (P_mQ_n) were analysed and their composition is tabulated below. The correct option(s) is/are —

Compound	Weight of %*P*	Weight of %*Q*
1	50	50
2	54.6	45.4
3	40	60

(a) If empirical formula of compound 3 is P_3Q_4, then the empirical formula of compound 2 is P_3Q_5. Both compounds has same molecular weight ratio.
(b) If empirical formula of compound 3 is P_3Q_2 and atomic weight of element *P* is 20, then the atomic weight of *Q* is 45.
(c) If empirical formula of compound 2 is *PQ*, then the empirical formula of the compound 1 is P_5Q_6.
(d) If atomic weight of *P* and *Q* are 50 and 25, respectively, then the empirical formula of compound 1 is

Type III 》 Numerical/Integer Type Questions

27. $Na_2SO_3 \cdot xH_2O$ has Na_2SO_3 and H_2O in equal mole ratio. Thus, *x* is .... in one molar unit.

28. Haemoglobin (molar mass = 67880 g mol^{-1}) contains 0.33% iron by weight. How many iron atoms are present in one molecule of haemoglobin (Fe = 56)?

29. Pure nitrogen is obtained by the decomposition of nitride of $M_x(N_3)_y$ of alkali metal *M*. What is the value of *x*?

30. A sample of ammonium phosphate contain 15 moles of hydrogen atoms.
How many moles of oxygen atoms are present in the given sample?

31. 10 mL of 0.2 N HCl and 30 mL of 0.1 N HCl together exactly neutralise 40 mL of solution of NaOH, which is also exactly neutralised by a solution in water of 0.61 g of an organic acid. The equivalent weight of the organic acid is ....

Elemental Practice 1.2 | Chapter 01

Connect with **Answers**

1. (d)	**2.** (c)	**3.** (c)	**4.** (b)	**5.** (a)	**6.** (c)
7. (c)	**8.** (a)	**9.** (d)	**10.** (a)	**11.** (c)	**12.** (c)
13. (c)	**14.** (c)	**15.** (a)	**16.** (c)	**17.** (b)	**18.** (b)
19. (b)	**20.** (d)	**21.** (b,d)	**22.** (a,b)	**23.** (a,b,d)	**24.** (c,d)
25. (b,d)	**26.** (b,c)	**27.** (7)	**28.** (4)	**29.** (1)	**30.** (5)
31. (122)					

Element 3 Reactions Stoichiometry

Chemical Equations

A chemical change involves a reorganisation of the atoms in one or more substances.

A chemical reaction is represented by a chemical equation with the reactants on the left side of an arrow and products are on the right side.

There must be the same number of each type of atom on the products side and on the reactants side to ensure atoms are neither created nor destroyed in a chemical reaction.

A Balanced Equation gives two important type of informations.

- Physical state of the reactants and products.
- The relative number of reatcants and products in terms of mole, mass number or volume.

Stoichiometry

Stoichiometry, is the branch of chemistry that deals with the quantitative relationships between the reactants and products in a chemical reaction.

In balanced equations, the numerical terms used to balance the number of atoms are called stoichiometric coefficients.

$$CH_4(g) + 2O_2(g) \longrightarrow CO_2(g) + 2H_2O(g)$$

Stoichiometric coefficients for the above reactants and products are $CH_4 = 1, O_2 = 2, CO_2 = 1, H_2O = 2$.

Significance of Stoichiometric Coefficients

(i) Stoichiometric coefficient for reactants and products can be changed by multiplying or dividing complete reactions by a number, still the balancing will not get disturbed.

$$CH_4(g) + 2O_2(g) \longrightarrow CO_2(g) + 2H_2O(g)$$

On multiplying by 2

$$2CH_4(g) + 4O_2(g) \longrightarrow 2CO_2(g) + 4H_2O(g)$$

(ii) Stoichiometric coefficients provide the mole ratio of reactants and products.

$$\underset{n_1}{3Fe(s)} + \underset{n_2}{4H_2O(l)} \longrightarrow \underset{n_3}{Fe_3O_4(s)} + \underset{n_4}{4H_2(g)}$$

$$\frac{n_1}{n_2} = \frac{3}{4}, \frac{n_1}{n_3} = \frac{3}{1}, \frac{n_1}{n_4} = \frac{3}{4}, \frac{n_1}{3} = \frac{n_2}{4}, \frac{n_1}{3} = \frac{n_3}{1}, \frac{n_1}{3} = \frac{n_4}{4}$$

So, $\frac{n_1}{3} = \frac{n_2}{4} = \frac{n_3}{1} = \frac{n_4}{4}$

In a balanced equation moles over their respective stoichiometric coefficients are same for all reactants and products.

(iii) Similarly, number of molecules can also be related as follows

$$\frac{n_1 N_A}{3} = \frac{n_2 N_A}{4} = \frac{n_3 N_A}{1} = \frac{n_4 N_A}{4}$$

N_A = Avogadro's number

If mole or number of molecules of any one compound is known, we can calculate same for any other compounds in the reaction.

Solved Booster 3.1

For a reaction,

$$C_6H_{12}O_6(s) + 6O_2(g) \longrightarrow 6CO_2(g) + 6H_2O(l)$$

If 4 moles of CO_2 formed in the reaction, find moles of $C_6H_{12}O_6(s)$ in the reaction.

(a) 4 (b) 2/3 (c) 4/3 (d) 1

Solution (b)

$$\frac{\text{Moles of } C_6H_{12}O_6}{1} = \frac{\text{Moles of } O_2}{6} = \frac{\text{Moles of } CO_2}{6} = \frac{\text{Moles of } H_2O}{6}$$

So, moles of $C_6H_{12}O_6 = \frac{4}{6}$ mol $= \frac{2}{3}$ mol

JEE Spotlite

It is better to convert mass to moles and use mole ratio.
Mass → Moles → Use coefficients from balanced equation → Find moles of other substances in the chemical reaction as in case (ii).
When all reactants and products are gaseous species, the volume ratio will be same as their mole ratio.

The Concept of Limiting Reagents (LR)

Limiting reagent is the reactant which is present in less amount as compared to the required amount in the balanced equation.

e.g. $$\underset{8\text{ moles}}{2H_2} + \underset{5\text{ moles}}{O_2} \longrightarrow 2H_2O$$

Moles of O_2 is less than the moles of H_2 but it does not mean O_2 is limiting reagent.

5 moles of O_2 required = 10 moles of H_2

5 moles of O_2 cannot react completely because the taken moles of H_2 are 8 moles which is less as per the requirement.

So, H_2 is LR.

The amount of LR is used to calculate the reacted amounts of reactants and produced amount of products.

HOW TO FIND LR

(i) Find the amount of any one of the product by the given amounts of the reactants, the one which forms least amount of the product will be the LR.

$$\underset{5\text{ moles}}{CH_4} + \underset{8\text{ moles}}{2O_2} \longrightarrow CO_2 + 2H_2O$$

5 moles of CH_4 = 5 moles of CO_2

8 moles of O_2 = 4 moles of CO_2

So, O_2 is LR.

(ii) Divide the given moles by their respective stoichiometric coefficient, the one with least value will be the LR

$$\underset{5\text{ moles}}{CH_4} + \underset{8\text{ moles}}{2O_2} \longrightarrow CO_2 + 2H_2O$$

$$\frac{5}{1} = 5, \frac{8}{2} = 4$$

O_2 is LR.

JEE Alert

Limiting Reagents get consumed completely in the reaction if reaction goes to completion.

Solved Booster 3.2

Consider the following reactions,

$$3Si + 2N_2 \longrightarrow Si_3N_4$$

When 21.44 moles of Si react with 17.62 moles of N_2, the number of moles of Si_3N_4 formed is ....

Solution (7.14)

$$3Si + 2N_2 \longrightarrow Si_3N_4$$

Moles : 21.44 17.62

$$\frac{21.44}{3} \quad \frac{17.62}{2}$$

7.14 8.81

Here, Si is limiting reagent.

Use moles of LR to find the moles of Si_3N_4 formed.

$$\frac{\text{Moles of Si}}{3} = \frac{\text{Moles of } Si_3N_4}{1}$$

$$7.14\text{ moles} = \frac{21.44}{3} = \text{moles of } Si_3N_4$$

Solved Booster 3.3

The amount of AgCl formed by adding 1 mol HCl to a solution containing 1.70 g of $AgNO_3$ will be (Ag = 108)

(a) 1.435 g (b) 2.865 g
(c) 3.752 g (d) 7.683 g

Solution (a)

$$1.70\text{ g } AgNO_3 = \frac{1.70}{170}\text{ mole} = 0.01\text{ mole } AgNO_3$$

1 mole $AgNO_3$ given = 1 mole AgCl

0.01 mole $AgNO_3$ given = 0.01 mole AgCl

1 mole HCl give = 1 mole AgCl

Thus, $AgNO_3$ is the limiting reactant.

AgCl formed = $0.01 \times 143.5 = 1.435$ g AgCl

Solved Booster 3.4

The combustion of propane gas produces CO_2 and H_2O vapour.

$$C_3H_8(g) + 5O_2(g) \longrightarrow 3CO_2(g) + 4H_2O(g)$$

The volume of oxygen is required to completely combust 0.65 L of propane is x and the volume of y is CO_2 is produced in the reaction? The sum of x and y is ....

Solution (5.20)

$$\frac{V_{C_3H_8}}{1} = \frac{V_{O_2}}{5} = \frac{V_{CO_2}}{3} = \frac{V_{H_2O}}{4}$$

Volume ratio and mole ratio are same if all gases are at same temperature and pressure.

$$\frac{V_{O_2}}{5} = \frac{0.65\text{ L}}{1} \Rightarrow V_{O_2} = 0.65 \times 5\text{ L} = 3.25\text{ L}$$

$$\frac{V_{CO_2}}{3} = \frac{0.65\text{ L}}{1}$$

$$\Rightarrow V_{CO_2} = 3 \times 0.65\text{ L} = 1.95\text{ L}$$

$$3.25 = x, \quad 1.95 = y$$

$$3.25 + 1.95 = 5.20$$

JEE MAPPER

Example Similar to PYQ Asked in JEE Main 2025, Adv. 2022

The '*A*' amount of benzylamine is subjected to diazotisation followed by hydrolysis to liberate dinitrogen gas and hydrochloric acid. The dinitrogen gas generated occupied 1.12 L volume at STP. The amount *A* is .... $\times 10^{-1}$ g.

Sol. (54) $C_6H_5CH_2NH_2 \xrightarrow{NaNO_2 + HCl} C_6H_5CH_2-\overset{\oplus}{N_2}\overset{\ominus}{Cl}$

$$\downarrow H_2O$$

$$C_6H_5CH_2OH + HCl + N_2 \; 28\text{ g/mol}$$

Given, that N_2 evolved in 1.12 L.

As we know, 1 mol of N_2 gas at STP occupy 22.4 liter.

0.05 mol of N_2 gas at STP occupy 1.12 liters

So, for 0.05 mole the benzylamine will be

$$107 \times 0.05 = 5.35\text{ g}$$

$$\approx 54 \times 10^{-1}\text{ g}$$

Competency Enhancer 3.1

The amount '*A*' of nitric acid required to produce 125.0 g of KNO_3 along with chlorine gas and water on reaction with 3 moles of potassium chloride give KNO_3.

The amount '*A*' of nitric acid is .... g. [Nearest integer]

[Given, Atomic mass of H, O, N and K are 1, 16, 14 and 39 respectively.]

Percentage Yield

If a reaction goes to completion, the yield of the reaction is taken 100%. But due to less purity of the reactants, some side reactions or because of lack of reaction conditions, the actual yield of the reaction is less then the theoretical yield of the reaction.

e.g.

For a given reaction $2H_2(g) + O_2(g) \longrightarrow 2H_2O(l)$

If 2 moles of H_2 and 1 mole O_2 form 30 g H_2O, then following conclusions can be drawn.

H_2 and O_2 are present in stoichiometry ratio, thus theoretical yield of H_2O is 2 moles (36 g) but experimentally actual yield was found to be 30 g.

Solved Booster 3.5

Silicon nitride (Si_3N_4) is made by direct combination of silicon and nitrogen at high temperature the yield of the reaction is 75%. The amount of silicon that react with excess nitrogen to prepare 140 g Si_3N_4 will be ($S_1 = 28$)?

(a) 78 g (b) 112 g (c) 80 g (d) 73 g

Solution (b)

$$\underset{\substack{3\text{ mol} \\ (3\times 28\text{ g}) = 84\text{ g}}}{3Si} + 2N_2 \longrightarrow \underset{\substack{1\text{ mol} \\ (3\times 28 + 4\times 14) = 140\text{ g}}}{Si_3N_4}$$

From the given amount of Si, amount actually needed by 75% yield can be calculated.

140 g Si_3N_4 is from = 84 g Si when yield is 100%

$$= 84 \times \frac{100}{75} \text{ g Si when yield is 75\%}$$

$$= 112.0 \text{ g.}$$

Percentage Purity

Percentage purity is a measure of how pure a substance is or the level of impurity in the substance.

Suppose you have a sample of a chemical with a mass of 10 grams and after analysis, it is determined that the pure substance within the sample is 9 grams.

$$\text{Percentage purity} = \frac{\text{Mass of pure substance}}{\text{Total mass of sample}} \times 100$$

$$= \frac{9\text{ g}}{10\text{ g}} \times 100 = 90\% \text{ purity}$$

Elemental Practice 1.3

Type I MCQs with Only One Correct Option

1. 2 moles of 50% pure $Ca(HCO_3)_2$ on heating form 1 mole of CO_2. Thus per cent yield of CO_2 is
(a) 50% (b) 75% (c) 80% (d) 100%

2. If 30 mL of H_2 at and 20 mL O_2 react to form water under standard condition, what is left at the end of reaction.
(a) 10 mL H_2 (b) 5 mL H_2
(c) 10 mL O_2 (d) 5 mL O_2

3. $CaCO_3$ on heating changes to CaO and CO_2. Percentages of Ca in reactant and product respectively are
(a) 100, 40 (b) 40, 56
(c) 56, 40 (d) 40, 71

4. A solution containing 145.0 g $AgNO_3$ is mixed with a $CaCl_2$ solution and 98.48 g of AgCl is recovered. Calculate the % yield of the reaction. (Ag = 108 and Ca = 40)
(a) 40.16% (b) 61.11%
(c) 61.99% (d) 80.39%

5. 17g of NH_3 is mixed with same amount of HCl. Thus, NH_4Cl formed is
(a) 17 g (b) 34 g
(c) 53.5 g (d) 24.9 g

6. The iron (III) oxide, Fe_2O_3, reacts with CO to give iron and CO_2.

$$Fe_2O_3 + 3CO \longrightarrow 2Fe + 3CO_2$$

The reaction of 480.0 g of Fe_2O_3 with excess of CO yields 252.0 g iron. Thus, per cent yield of iron is
(a) 100.0% (b) 91.2%
(c) 75.0% (d) 50.0%

7. In the Solvay process for producing sodium carbonate (Na_2CO_3), the following reactions occur in sequence :

$$NH_3 + CO_2 + H_2O \longrightarrow NH_4HCO_3$$
$$NH_4HCO_3 + NaCl \longrightarrow NaHCO_3 + NH_4Cl$$
$$2NaHCO_3 \longrightarrow Na_2CO_3 + H_2O + CO_2$$

How much of Na_2CO_3 would be produced per kg of NH_3 used if the processes were 100% efficient?
(a) 3.12 kg (b) 1.00 kg
(c) 2.00 kg (d) 0.56 kg

8. 10 g of magnesium and 10 g oxygen are allowed to react. Residual mixture contains (Mg = 24)
(a) 16.67 g MgO and 3.33 g O_2
(b) Only 10 g MgO
(c) Only 16.07 of MgO
(d) 25 g MgO and 4 g Mg

9. In the following reaction,

$$Zn(s) + 2HCl(aq) \longrightarrow ZnCl_2(aq) + H_2(g)$$

0.30 mole of Zn are added to 0.52 mole HCl containing aqueous solution when H_2 formed is (Zn = 65)
(a) 0.30 mol (b) 0.52 mol
(c) 0.15 mol (d) 0.26 mol

10. A sample of copper sulphate pentahydrate $CuSO_4 \cdot 5H_2O$ contains 1.595 g $CuSO_4$. Thus, it contains oxygen
(a) 1.44 g (b) 0.05 g
(c) 0.144 g (d) 14.40 g

11. Based on the following consecutive reactions
$$2KClO_3 \longrightarrow 2KCl + 3O_2$$
$$4Al + 3O_2 \longrightarrow 2Al_2O_3$$
2 moles of $KClO_3$ of 50% purity on strong heating and then with excess of Al, Al_2O_3 formed is
(a) 2 mol (b) 1 mol
(c) 3 mol (d) 1.5 mol

12. In the following set of reactions,
$$CaCO_3 \xrightarrow{\Delta} CaO + CO_2 \text{ (75\% yield)}$$
$$CO_2 + C \xrightarrow{\Delta} 2CO \quad \text{(50\% yield)}$$
CO formed at STP from 10 g of $CaCO_3$ is
(a) 2.24 L (b) 11.2 L
(c) 1.12 L (d) 1.68 L

13. How much $CaCO_3$ of 50% purity is required to yield 5.6 L of CO_2 at STP?
(a) 100 g (b) 50 g
(c) 25 g (d) 12.5 g

14. In the following reaction,
$$MnO_2 + 4HCl \longrightarrow MnCl_2 + 2H_2O + Cl_2$$
2 moles of MnO_2 react with 4 moles of HCl to form 11.2 L of Cl_2 at STP. Thus, per cent yield of Cl_2 is
(a) 25% (b) 50%
(c) 75% (d) 100%

15. Per cent yield of NH_3 in the following reactions is 80%
$$NH_2CONH_2 + 2NaOH \xrightarrow{\Delta} Na_2CO_3 + 2NH_3$$
NH_3 formed on heating 6 g NH_2CONH_2 and 8 g NaOH is
(a) 3.40 g (b) 11.20 g
(c) 4.25 g (d) 2.72 g

16. When a mixture consisting of 10 moles of SO_2 and 15 moles of O_2 was passed over a catalyst, 8 moles of SO_3 were formed. Thus, the percentage yield of SO_3 with respect to SO_2 is
(a) 50% (b) 95%
(c) 80% (d) 70%

17. 100 mL solution of NaOH (containing 4 g NaOH per litre) and 50 mL of HCl (containing 14.6 g HCl per litre) react as
$$NaOH(aq) + HCl(aq) \longrightarrow NaCl(aq) + H_2O(l)$$
0.42 g of NaCl is formed. Thus, the amount of unreacted NaOH is
(a) 0.586 g (b) 0.113 g
(c) 0.630 g (d) 1.361 g

18. 10 mL of 1 M $BaCl_2$ solution and 5 mL 0.5 M K_2SO_4 are mixed together to precipitate out $BaSO_4$. The amount of $BaSO_4$ precipitated will be
(a) 0.005 mol (b) 0.00025 mol
(c) 0.025 mol (d) 0.0025 mol

19. When 10 kg of N_2 reacts with 50 kg of H_2 to form NH_3. Then, what will be the limiting reagent and amount of NH_3 formed respectively?
(a) H_2, 10.312 kg (b) H_2, 15.631 kg
(c) N_2, 23.841 kg (d) N_2, 12.143 kg

20. For the reaction,
$$2Fe(NO_3)_3 + 3Na_2CO_3 \longrightarrow Fe_2(CO_3)_3 + 6NaNO_3$$
Initially 2.5 moles of $Fe(NO_3)_2$ and 3.6 moles of Na_2CO_3 are taken. If 6.5 moles of $NaNO_3$ is obtained then % yield of given reaction is
(a) 90.2 (b) 87.5
(c) 67.3 (d) 79.6

21. How many grams of phosphoric acid would be needed to neutralise 100 g of magnesium hydroxide?
(The molecular weights are : $H_3PO_4 = 98$ and $Mg(OH)_2 = 58.3$)
(a) 66.7 g (b) 252 g (c) 112 g (d) 168 g

Type II 》 MCQs with One or More than One Correct Option

22. 21.2 g sample of impure Na_2CO_3 is dissolved and reacted with a solution of $CaCl_2$, the weight of precipitate of $CaCO_3$ is 10.0 g. Which of the following statments is/are correct?
(a) The % purity of Na_2CO_3 is 50%
(b) The percentage purity of Na_2CO_3 is 60%
(c) The number of moles of Na_2CO_3 = $CaCO_3$ = 0.1mol
(d) The number of moles of NaCl formed is 0.1 mol

23. 100 g of sample of clay (containing 19% H_2O, 40% silica and inert impurities as rest) is partially dried so as to contain 10% H_2O.
Which of the following is/are correct statement(s)?
(a) The percentage of silica in partially dried clay is 44.4%
(b) The mass of partially dried clay is 90.0 g
(c) The percentage of inert impurity in partially dried clay is 45.6%
(d) The mass of water evaporated is 10.0 g

24. 1.0g mixture of $CaCO_3(s)$ and glass beads liberate 0.22 g of CO_2 upon treatment with excess of HCl. Glass does not react with HCl.
$$CaCO_3 + 2HCl \longrightarrow CO_2 + H_2O + CaCl_2$$
[M. wt. of $CaCO_3 = 100$, M. wt. of $CO_2 = 44$, Atomic weight of Ca = 40]
Which of the following statement(s) is/are correct?
(a) The weight of $CaCO_3$ in the original mixture is 0.5 g
(b) The weight of calcium in the original mixture is 0.2 g
(c) The weight percent of calcium in the original mixture is 40% Ca
(d) The weight percent of Ca in the original mixture is 20% Ca

25. Which of the following statements are correct?
A mixture containing 64.0 g H_2 and 64.0 g O_2 is ignited so that water is formed as follows :
$$2H_2 + O_2 \longrightarrow 2H_2O$$
(a) H_2 is the limiting reagent
(b) O_2 is the limiting reagent

(c) The reaction mixture contains 72.0 g of H_2O and 56.0 g of unreacted H_2

(d) The reaction mixture contains 56.0 g of H_2O and 72.0 g of unreacted H_2

26. Consider the following reactions,

(i) $P_4 + 5O_2 \longrightarrow P_4O_{10}$

(ii) $P_4 + 3O_2 \longrightarrow P_4O_6$

1.24 g of P_4 reacts with 8.0 g of O_2.

Which of the following statement(s) incorrect regarding the given data?

(a) P_4 is the limiting reagent in reaction (i)

(b) O_2 is the limiting reagent in reaction (i)

(c) Mass of P_4O_{10} obtained is 2.2 g

(d) Mass of P_4O_6 obtained is 2.84 g

Type III 》 Numerical/Integer Answer Type Questions

27. In a 2 L of 1.0 M impure H_2SO_4 sample, 1.0 M NaOH solution was added and a plot was obtained as follow :

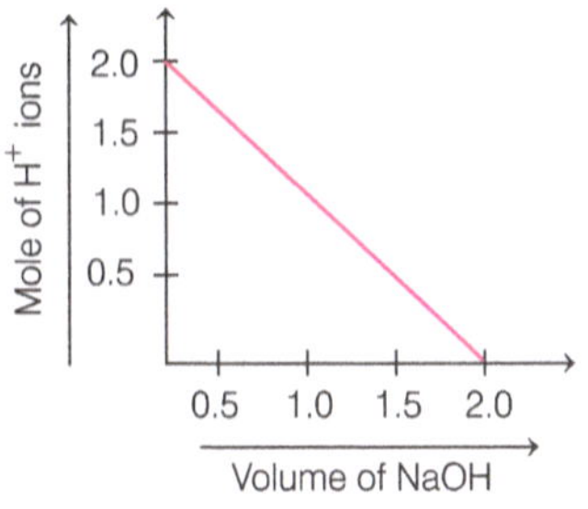

The percentage purity of H_2SO_4 is ....

28. Given the reaction,

$Pb(NO_3)_2(aq) + 2KI \longrightarrow PbI_2(s) + 2KNO_3(aq)$

The mass of PbI_2 that will precipitate if 10.2 g of $Pb(NO_3)_2$ is mixed with 5.63 g of KI in a sufficient quantity of H_2O is .... g. [Nearest integer]

[Given : Molar mass of Pb, I and K is 206, 127 and 39 respectively]

29. Antimony reacts with sulphur according to the given equation,

$$2Sb(s) + 3S(s) \longrightarrow Sb_2S_3(s)$$

The percentage yield for a reaction in which 1.40 g of Sb_2S_3 is obtained from 1.73 g of antimony and a slight excess of sulphur is .... [Nearest integer]

[Given : Molar mass of Sb_2S_3 is 340 g mol^{-1}]

30. SO_2Cl_2 on reaction with excess of water results into acidic mixture, $SO_2Cl_2 + 2H_2O \longrightarrow H_2SO_4 + 2HCl$

20 moles of NaOH is required for the complete neutralisation of the resultant acidic mixture.

The number of moles of SO_2Cl_2 used is ....

31. 5 g of activated charcoal was added to 55 mL of acetic acid solution (0.06 N) in a flask. After an hour it was filtered and the strength of the filtrate was found to be 0.042 N. The amount of acetic acid adsorbed (per gram of charcoal) is .... (mg). [Nearest integer]

1. (a)	**2.** (d)	**3.** (d)	**4.** (d)	**5.** (d)	**6.** (c)
7. (a)	**8.** (a)	**9.** (d)	**10.** (a)	**11.** (b)	**12.** (d)
13. (b)	**14.** (b)	**15.** (d)	**16.** (c)	**17.** (b)	**18.** (d)
19. (d)	**20.** (a)	**21.** (c)	**22.** (a, c)	**23.** (a,b,c,d)	**24.** (a,b,d)
25. (b,c)	**26.** (b,c,d)	**27.** (50)	**28.** (8)	**29.** (58)	**30.** (5)
31. (12)					

Elemental Practice 1.3 | **Chapter 01**

Connect with **Answers**

Element 4 Concentration Terms

A solution is a homogeneous mixture composed of two or more substances. The substance which is present in lesser amount is called solute while other present in greater amount is called solvent.

Reactions in Solutions and Concentration Terms

The reactions observed in laboratories are generally performed in solutions. Therefore, it is important to know about concentration terms. In chemistry, concentration terms describes the amount of a substance in a given quantity of solution. Concentration remains same if a part of solution is taken from the bulk.

The concentration of solution may be expressed by several ways as discussed ahead.

Percentage

It is defined as the amount of substance present in 100 parts of the solution.

It can be expressed in the following ways.

1. Mass Percentage (w/W)

It is defined as the mass of solute present in 100 g mass of the solution.

$$\text{Mass percentage} = \frac{\text{Mass of solute}}{\text{Mass of solution}} \times 100$$

Solved Booster 4.1

A solution is made by mixing 26 g methanol and 236 g ethanol at 298 K. The concentration of methanol in solution is

(a) 10% (b) 12.21% (c) 87% (d) 25%

Solution (a)

Mass of methanol (solute) = 26 g

Mass of ethanol (solvent) = 236 g

So, mass of solution = 26 + 236 = 262 g

Mass Percentage of methanol in solution

$$= \frac{\text{Mass of solute}}{\text{Mass of solution}} \times 100 = \frac{26}{262} \times 100 \approx 10\%$$

2. Volume Percentage (v/V)

It is defined as the volume of component present in 100 volume of the solution.

$$\% \text{ by volume} = \frac{\text{Volume of component}}{\text{Volume of solution}} \times 100$$

Solved Booster 4.2

1g methanol ($d = 0.75 \text{ g mL}^{-1}$) is mixed with 1g water ($d = 1 \text{ g mL}^{-1}$) at room temperature. The volume per cent of methanol will be

(a) 55% (b) 68% (c) 57% (d) 70%

Solution (c)

Given, mass of methanol and water is to be converted to volume.

Mass = Volume × Density

$$\therefore \quad \text{Volume} = \frac{\text{Mass}}{\text{Density}}$$

$$\therefore \quad \text{Volume of methanol} = \frac{1\text{g}}{0.75 \text{ g mL}^{-1}} = 1.33 \text{ mL}$$

$$\text{Volume of water} = \frac{1\text{ g}}{1.0 \text{ g mL}^{-1}} = 1.0 \text{ mL}$$

$$\text{Total volume} = 2.33 \text{ mL}$$

$$\text{Volume \%} = \frac{\text{Volume of methanol}}{\text{Total volume}} \times 100$$

$$\therefore \% \text{ methanol by volume} = \frac{1.33}{2.33} \times 100 = 57.08\%$$

3. Mass-Volume Percentage (w/V)

It is defined as the mass of component present in 100 mL of the solution.

$$\text{Mass Volume}\left(\frac{w}{V}\right)\% = \frac{\text{Mass of the component}}{\text{Volume of solution (mL)}} \times 100$$

Solved Booster 4.3

H_2SO_4 solution is 98% by mass of solution with density 1.8 g mL^{-1}. What is the mass by volume percentage of H_2SO_4?

(a) 100% (b) 176.4%

(c) 98.8% (d) 57.08%

Solution (b)

Let mass of solution = 100g

$$\text{Volume of solution} = \frac{\text{Mass}}{\text{Density}} = \frac{100 \text{ g}}{1.8 \text{ g mL}^{-1}} = \frac{1000}{18} \text{ mL}$$

Mass of H_2SO_4 (solute) = 98 g

$$\text{Thus, \% concentration} \left(\frac{w}{V}\right) = \left(\frac{98}{1000/18} \times 100\right) = 176.4\%$$

4. Percentage by Mole

It is defined as the number of moles of solute present in 100 mole in the solution.

$$\text{Percentage by mole} = \frac{\text{Moles of solute}}{\text{Moles of solution}} \times 100$$

5. Parts Per Million (ppm)

In very dilute solution, it is a convenient way to express concentration. It is the part of the component per million (10^6) of the solution.

$$\text{ppm} = \frac{\text{Mass of solute}}{\text{Mass of solvent}} \times 10^6$$

Solved Booster 4.4

A particular water sample is found to contain 96.0 ppm of SO_4^{2-} and 122.0 ppm of HCO_3^- with Ca^{2+} as the only cation. The concentration Ca^{2+} is X ppm. The value of X is ....

Solution

(80) $CaSO_4 \rightleftharpoons Ca^{2+} + SO_4^{2-}$

Thus, moles of Ca^{2+} = moles of SO_4^{2-}

$$96 \text{ ppm } SO_4^{2-} = 96 \text{ g } SO_4^{2-} \text{ in } 10^6 \text{ g } H_2O$$
$$= \frac{96}{96} \text{ mole } SO_4^{2-} \text{ in } 10^6 \text{ g } H_2O$$
$$= 1 \text{ mole } SO_4^{2-} \text{ in } 10^6 \text{ g } H_2O$$
$$= 1 \text{ mole } Ca^{2+} \text{ in } 10^6 \text{g } H_2O$$
$$= 40\text{g } Ca^{2+} \text{ in } 10^6 \text{ g } H_2O = 40 \text{ ppm } Ca^{2+}$$

$$Ca(HCO_3)_2 \rightleftharpoons Ca^{2+} + 2HCO_3^-$$

Thus, moles of $Ca^{2+} = \frac{1}{2}$ mol of HCO_3^-

As above

$$122 \text{ g } HCO_3^- = \frac{122}{61} \text{ moles } HCO_3^-$$
$$= 2 \text{ moles } HCO_3^-$$
$$= 1 \text{ moles } Ca^{2-}$$
$$= 40 \text{ ppm } Ca^{2+}$$

$\therefore$ Total $Ca^{2+} = 40 + 40 = 80$ ppm

JEE Spotlite

- In case of extremely dilute solution, parts per billion (ppb) is used rather than ppm.
$$\text{ppb} = \frac{\text{Mass of solute}}{\text{Mass of solution}} \times 10^9$$
- Similar to percentage, ppm or ppb can also be expressed in terms of $\frac{W}{W}, \frac{W}{V}, \frac{V}{V}$.

Strength (g/L)

It is defined as the amount of solute in grams present in 1000 mL or 1 L of the solution.

$$\text{Strength (g/L)} = \frac{\text{Mass of solute (g)}}{\text{Volume of solution (L)}}$$

Fraction

It is defined as the amount of solute/component present in unit amount of the solution.

The fraction can be expressed in following ways.

1. Mass Fraction

It defines mass of component in unit mass of the solution.

$$\text{Mass fraction} = \frac{\text{Mass of the component}}{\text{Mass of the solution}} = \frac{m_1}{m_1 + m_2 + m_3}$$

2. Volume Fraction

It defines volume of the component present in unit volume of the solution.

$$\text{Volume fraction} = \frac{\text{Volume of the component}}{\text{Volume of the solution}}$$
$$= \frac{V_1}{V_1 + V_2 + V_3}$$

3. Mole Fraction

It defines no. of moles of component present in one mole of the solution.

$$\text{Mole fraction} = \frac{\text{Mole of the component}}{\text{Moles of the solution}} = \frac{n_1}{n_1 + n_2}$$

where, n_1 = Number of moles of component (1) in solution.
n_2 = Number of moles of component (2) in solution.

JEE Alert

Mole fraction is unitless and temperature independent quantity.

Solved Booster 4.5

Aqueous glucose $(C_6H_{12}O_6)$ solution is 36% by mass of solution. What is the mole fraction of glucose in solution.

(a) 0.053 (b) 0.55 (c) 0.16 (d) 0.76

Solution *(a)*

Mass of glucose in 100 g aqueous solution = 36 g

Molar mass of glucose $(C_6H_{12}O_6) = 6 \times 12 + 12 \times 1 + 6 \times 16$
$$= 180 \text{ g mol}^{-1}$$

$$\text{Moles of glucose} = \frac{36}{180} = \frac{3.6}{18}$$

Mass of water in aqueous solution = 100 − 36 = 64 g

$$\text{Moles of water} = \frac{64}{18}$$

$$\text{Total moles} = \frac{3.6}{18} + \frac{64}{18} = \left(\frac{67.6}{18}\right)$$

$$\therefore \quad X_{\text{glucose}} = \frac{n(\text{Glucose})}{n(\text{Total})}$$
$$= \frac{3.6/18}{67.6/18} = \frac{3.6}{67.6} = 0.053$$

Solved Booster 4.6

Mole fraction of naphthalene ($C_{10}H_8$) in a solution of naphthalene and benzene (C_6H_6) is 0.2. The per cent concentration of naphthalene by mass of solution is

(a) 50% (b) 38.6%

(c) 20.2% (d) 29.1%

Solution *(d)*

Let the moles of naphthalene be $= n_1 = \frac{w_1}{m_1}$

and moles of benzene be $= n_2 = \frac{w_2}{m_2}$

Total moles of naphthalene and benzene (solution) $= (n_1 + n_2)$

$$X_1 \text{ (naphthalene)} = \frac{n_1}{(n_1+n_2)} = 0.2$$

$$X_2 \text{ (benzene)} = \frac{n_2}{(n_1+n_2)} = 0.8$$

$$\therefore \quad \frac{X_1}{X_2} = \frac{n_1}{n_2} = \frac{1}{4} = \frac{w_1}{m_1} \Big/ \frac{w_2}{m_2}$$

$$\Rightarrow \quad \frac{1}{4} = (w_1/128)/(w_2/78)$$

$$\frac{1}{4} = \frac{w_1}{w_2}\frac{78}{128} \qquad \Rightarrow \qquad \frac{w_1}{w_2} = \frac{128}{312}$$

Thus, if $w_1 = 128$ g naphthalene and $w_2 = 312$ g benzene and $(w_1 + w_2) = 440$ g solution

% concentration of naphthalene by mass of solution

$$= \frac{128}{440} \times 100 \approx 29.1\%$$

Molarity (M)

Number of moles of solute dissolved per litre of the solution is called molarity of the solution.

$$\text{Molarity } (M) = \frac{\text{Moles of solute}}{\text{Volume of solution in litres}}$$

Moles of solute = Molarity × Volume of solution in litres

$$\text{Molarity } (M) = \frac{\text{Number of moles of solute}}{\text{Volume of solution in ml}} \times 1000$$

$$\text{Or} \quad = \frac{\text{Mass of solute in grams}}{\text{Molecular weight} \times \text{Volume of solution in ml}} \times 1000$$

Molarity of a solution depends upon the temperature because volume of solution is temperature dependent.

Molarity Calculations

Molarity of solution can be discussed as per following different case.

Case I Molarity of solution after dilution

Dilution means number of moles of solute remains same on adding more amounts of the solvent i.e.,

Moles before dilution = Moles after dilution

$$M_1V_1 = M_2V_2$$

where M_1 and M_2 are the molarities before and after dilution. V_1 and V_2 are initial and final volume respectively.

Case II Molarity on mixing of two or more solutions

Sum of moles of solute on mixing different volume of the solutions = number of moles in the final solution

$$M_1V_1 + M_2V_2 + M_3V_3 \ldots = M_fV_f$$

$$M_f = \frac{M_1V_1 + M_2V_2 + M_3V_3 + \ldots}{V_f}$$

JEE Alert

Final volume is not always strictly additive when mixing solutions. This non-additivity occurs due to interactions between the solute and solvent molecules.

Case III Molarity in case of 100% ionisable solutes in the solvent

If 0.2 moles of $CaCl_2$ is present in 5 L of the solution,

(a) Molarity wrt $CaCl_2 = \frac{0.2 \text{ mol } CaCl_2}{5 \text{ L of solution}}$

$= 0.04$ M

(b) Assume 100% ionisation of $CaCl_2$ in water

Ca^{+2} ion = 0.2 mol

Cl^- ion = 0.4 mol

Total moles of solute (ions) = 0.6 mol

$$\text{Molarity of ions} = \frac{0.6 \text{ mol solute}}{5 \text{ L of the solution}} = 0.12 \text{ M}$$

$$\text{Molarity of } Cl^- \text{ ion} = \frac{0.4 \text{ mol } Cl^- \text{ ion}}{5 \text{ L of the solution}} = 0.08 \text{ M}$$

Solved Booster 4.7

Concentration of glucose ($C_6H_{12}O_6$) in normal blood is approximately 90 mg per 100 mL. The molarity of glucose solution in blood is $x \times 10^{-3}$. The value of x is ....

Solution *(5)*

$$\text{Moles of solute} = \frac{\text{Amount of solute in gram}}{\text{Molar mass in g mol}^{-1}}$$

$$\text{Molarity} = \frac{\text{Moles of solute}}{\text{Litres of solution}}$$

$$90 \text{ mg } C_6H_{12}O_6 = 90 \times 10^{-3} \text{g}$$

$$\text{Molar mass of } C_6H_{12}O_6 = 6 \times 12 + 12 \times 1 + 6 \times 16 = 180 \text{ g mol}^{-1}$$

100 mL solution = 0.1 L solution

$$\therefore \quad \text{Molarity} = \frac{90 \times 10^{-3}/180 \text{ mol}}{0.1 \text{ L}} = 0.005 \text{ M}$$

Molality (m)

The molality of a solution is defined as "**the number of moles of solute per kilogram of solvent**".

$$\text{Molality } (m) = \frac{\text{Moles of solute}}{\text{kg of solvent}}$$

It is expressed in mol kg^{-1}.

In the calculation of molality, mass of solvent (and not of solution) is taken in kg.

JEE Alert

The main advantage of using molality is that it is temperature independent because masses do not change when substances are heated or cooled (For those compounds which are thermally unstable).

Relation between Different Concentration Terms

(i) **Fraction is related to percentage by relation**

$$\text{Fraction} \times 100 = \text{Percentage}$$

(ii) **Molality (m) is related to molarity (M) by relation**

$$m = \frac{1000\,M}{1000\,d - Mm_1}$$

where, d = Density of solution in g mL^{-1}

m_1 = Molar mass of solute

(iii) **Molality (m) is also related to mole fraction of solute (χ_1) by relation**

$$m = \frac{1000\,\chi_1}{(1-\chi_1)m_2}$$

where, m_2 = Molar mass of solvent.

(iv) **Molality is related to mass fraction by relation**

$$m = \frac{x_m}{1-x_m} \times 1000$$

x_m = Mass fraction of solute

Mass of the solution is (g).

(v) **Relation between Molarity and Mole fraction**

When mole fraction and density of solution is given the molarity can be calculated

$$M = \frac{1000\,dx_1}{x_1M_1 + (1-x_1)M_2}$$

where, M_1 = Molar mass of solute and M_2 that of solvent.

(vi) **Relation between strength and molarity**

When strength and molar mass of solute is given, the molarity can be calculated as

$$\text{Molarity} = \frac{\text{Strength}}{\text{Molar mass of solute}}$$

Solved Booster 4.8

The molality of a 20% (v/v) solution of iodine (I_2) in CCl_4 (carbon tetrachloride) is 'x'. x = ... $\times 10^{-2}$ m (Nearest Integer)

[Given, Density of iodine (I_2) = 3.4 g cm^{-3}

Density of CCl_4 = 1.6 g cm^{-3}]

Solution *(209)*

20 mL of solute (I_2) is present in 80 mL solvent (CCl_4).

Mass of solute = 20 mL × 3.4 g mL^{-1} = 68 g

Mass of solvent = 80 mL × 1.6 g mL^{-1} = 128 g

$$m = \frac{68 \times 1000}{254 \times 128} \approx 2.092 \text{ m}$$

$$= 209.2 \times 10^{-2} \approx 209$$

Solved Booster 4.9

The density of 3 molal solution of NaOH is 1.110 g mL^{-1}. What is the molarity of the solution?

(a) 3 M (b) 2.8 M (c) 5.5 M (d) 1.2 M

Solution *(a)*

$$M(\text{molarity}) = \frac{m[1000\,d - Mm_1]}{1000} = m\left[d - \frac{Mm_1}{1000}\right]$$

$$M = 3\left[1.11 - \frac{M \times 40}{1000}\right]$$

$$M + 0.12\,M = 3.33$$

$$\therefore \quad M = \frac{3.33}{1.12} = 2.97\text{ M} \approx 3$$

JEE MAPPER

Example Similar to PYQ Asked in JEE Main 2023

If the density of 6 M solution of NaCl is 2.16 g mL^{-1}, then the molality of the solution will be

(a) 3 molal (b) 3.32 molal (c) 5.5 molal (d) 1.2 molal

Sol. (b) Molality (m) is related to molarity (M) and density (d), and molar mass (m_1) of solute by relation

$$m = \frac{1000\,M}{1000\,d - Mm_1}$$

$$\therefore \quad m = \frac{1000 \times 6}{(1000 \times 2.16 - 6 \times 58.5)} = \frac{6000}{2160 - 351} \approx 3.32 \text{ molal}$$

Competency Enhancer 4.1

The molality of a 10% (w/v) solution of ethyl alcohol in water is 'a'. The value of 'a' = ... $\times 10^{-2}$ mol/kg. (Nearest Integer)

Normality (*N*)

Concentration of the solution expressed in number of equivalents of solute dissolved per litre of solution is called normality.

$$\text{Normality } (N) = \frac{\text{Number of equivalent of solute}}{\text{Litre of solution}}$$

$$NV = \text{Milliequivalents and}$$

$$\frac{NV}{1000} = \text{Equivalents}$$

Normality $(N) \times$ **equivalent mass = concentration in g** $\mathbf{L^{-1}}$.

Normality is related to molarity as $N(\text{Normality}) = \text{Molarity} \times (n\text{-factor})$

$$\text{Equivalents} = \text{Moles} \times (n\text{-factor})$$

Normality Relation for Diluting a Solution

For diluting a solution from one concentration (1) to another concentration (2), following relations is found to be true

$$N_1V_1 = N_2V_2 \text{ [Normality equation]}$$

In **acid-base neutralisation reaction** or a **redox reaction**

Equivalent of an acid $\equiv$ Equivalent of base

Thus, $N_1V_1 \equiv N_2V_2$ is always true.

Thus, it is always desirable to convert moles into equivalents to simplify calculations.

(i) **For a mixture of strong acids, resultants normality** is

$$N \text{ (resultant)} = \frac{\Sigma NV}{\Sigma V} = \frac{N_1V_1 + N_2V_2 + \dots}{V_1 + V_2 + \dots}$$

(ii) **For a mixture of same type of basicity, resultant molarity** is

$$M \text{ (resultant)} = \frac{\Sigma MV}{\Sigma V} = \frac{M_1V_1 + M_2V_2 + \dots}{V_1 + V_2}$$

Solved Booster 4.10

100 mL of 0.1 M KOH is mixed with 200 mL of 0.1 M $Ca(OH)_2$ and 300 mL of 0.1 M H_2SO_4. The normality of the resultant mixture is .... $\times 10^{-3}$ N.

Solution (17)

First determine the normality of mixture of bases.

$$0.1 \text{ M KOH} \equiv 0.1 \text{ N, KOH} \equiv 0.1 \text{ N } [OH^-]$$

$$0.1 \text{ M } Ca(OH)_2 \equiv 0.2 \text{ N, } Ca(OH)_2 \equiv 0.2 \text{ N } [OH^-]$$

Resultant normality of base :

$$N(\text{base}) = \frac{\Sigma NV}{\Sigma V} = \frac{N_1V_1(\text{KOH}) + N_2V_2(Ca(OH)_2)}{V_1 + V_2}$$

$$= \frac{0.1 \times 100 + 0.2 \times 200}{100 + 200} = \frac{N}{6}$$

Thus, resultant basic mixture is = 300 mL of $\frac{N}{6}[OH^-]$

It is mixed with 300 mL of 0.1 M $H_2SO_4 \equiv$ 300 mL of 0.2 N H^+

Thus, $N_1V_1 \text{ (acid)} = 300 \times 0.2 = 60$

$$N_2V_2(\text{base}) = 300 \times \frac{1}{6} = 50$$

$$N_1V_1(\text{acid}) > N_2V_2 \text{ (base)}$$

Mixture is acidic., $N(H^+) = \frac{N_1V_1 - N_2V_2}{V_1 + V_2} = \frac{60-50}{600} = \frac{1}{60}$

$$\approx 0.017 \text{ N}$$

$$= 17 \times 10^{-3} \text{ N}$$

Percentage Labelling of Oleum

Oleum is forming sulphuric acid i.e., $H_2SO_4 \cdot xSO_3$.

Oleum is generally assessed according to the free SO_3 content by mass.

$$\underset{\text{1 mole}}{SO_3} + \underset{\text{1 mole}}{H_2O} = \underset{\text{1 mole}}{H_2SO_4}$$

Case I If percentage of oleum is labelled as 109.

It means 9 g of water would react with free SO_3 present in 100 g of oleum.

9 g H_2O = 0.5 mol $H_2O \equiv$ 0.5 mol $SO_3 \equiv$ 40 g SO_3

Therefore, 100 g of oleum contains 60 g H_2SO_4 and 40 g SO_3.

Case II If 100 g oleum contains 80 g H_2SO_4 and 20 g free SO_3.

% oleum labelling 20 g $SO_3 \equiv$ 0.25 mol of $SO_3 \equiv$ 0.25 mol $H_2O \equiv$ 4.5 g H_2O

To 100 gm oleum $\equiv$ 4.5 g H_2O can consume total free SO_3 present in 100 g oleum.

Therefore % oleum = 104.5

Volume Strength of H_2O_2

$$H_2O_2 \longrightarrow H_2O + \frac{1}{2}O_2$$

1 mole — 11.2 L of O_2 at STP

Concentration of H_2O_2 is measured by it's ability to release oxygen gas.

For example, H_2O_2 solution with a volume strength of 20 V, means 20 litres of O_2 at STP can be released by 1 litre solution of H_2O_2 upon decomposition.

$$H_2O_2 \longrightarrow H_2O + \frac{1}{2}O_2$$

1 mol — 11.2 L at STP

$\frac{1}{11.2} \times 20$ mol — 20 L at STP

1.785 mol of H_2O_2 is present in it's 1 litre solution.

Molarity of $H_2O_2 \times 11.2$ = Volume strength

Elemental Practice 1.4

Type I MCQs with Only One Correct Option

1. The molality of 9.2 g of ethanol in 18 mL of water ($d = 1 g/mL$) is
(a) 11.11 mol kg^{-1} (b) 11.92 mol kg^{-1}
(c) 11.11 M (d) 10.11 m

2. Which of the following represents 1.00 M KCl solution?
(a) 1.0 L of solution containing 100 g KCl
(b) 250.0 mL of solution containing 74.5 g KCl
(c) A solution containing 7.45 mg KCl / mL solution
(d) 5.00 L of solution containing 372.5 g KCl

3. What will be the molality of the solution containing 18.25 g of HCl in 500 g of water?
(a) 0.1 m (b) 10 m
(c) 0.5 m (d) 1.0 m

4. 100 mL of concentrated H_2SO_4 ($d = 1.8$ g mL^{-1}) is mixed with 100 mL of H_2O ($d = 1.0$ g mL^{-1}) thus percentage of H_2SO_4 by mass of solution in the mixture is
(a) 50.0 % (b) 60.0%
(c) 64.3% (d) 35.7 %

5. RH_2 is an ion exchange resin used to purify water in *RO* (water purifier). It can replace Ca^{2+} ions in hard water,
$RH_2 + Ca^{2+} \longrightarrow RCa + 2H^+$
Water coming out of ion exchange resin has $[H^+] = 0.01M$. Thus, hardness of water in ppm of Ca^{2+} ion is
(a) 100 (b) 200 (c) 50 (d) 125

6. 6.02×10^{20} molecules of urea are present in 10 mL solution. The concentration of urea solution is
(a) 0.001 M (b) 0.01 M
(c) 0.02 M (d) 0.10 M

7. 5.3 g of M_2CO_3 is dissolved in 150 mL of 1N HCl. Unused acid required 100 mL of 0.5 N NaOH. Thus, equivalent mass of *M* is
(a) 23 (b) 12 (c) 24 (d) 13

8. 1 mole of N_2 and 4 moles of H_2 are allowed to react in a vessel and after reaction, H_2O is added. Aqueous solution required 1 mole of HCl. Mole fraction of H_2 in the gaseous mixture after reaction is
(a) $\frac{1}{6}$ (b) $\frac{5}{6}$ (c) $\frac{1}{3}$ (d) $\frac{7}{3}$

9. The molality of 1 L solution with $x\%$ H_2SO_4 is equal to 10. The weight of the solvent present in the solution is 920 g. What will be the value of x?
(a) 80.23 (b) 90.16
(c) 76.13 (d) 79.12

10. Given below are two statements : one is labelled as Assertion (A) and the other is labelled as Reason (R).
Assertion (A) On changing volume of the solution by 20%, molarity of 1 M solution changes by 10%.
Reason (R) Molar concentration or molarity of solution decreases on 1 M dilution.
In the light of the above statements, choose the correct answer from the options given below.
(a) Both A and R are correct and R is the correct explanation of A.
(b) Both A and R are correct but R is not the correct explanation of A.
(c) A is true but R is false.
(d) A is false but R is true.

11. The normality of a mixture obtained by mixing 100 mL of 0.2 M H_2SO_4 with 100 mL of 0.2 M NaOH is
(a) 0.05 N (b) 0.10 N
(c) 0.15 N (d) 0.23 N

12. 350 mL of a barium carbonate solution contains 3.65 g of $BaCO_3$. If 10 mL of this solution is diluted to one litre, what is the concentration of the resultant solution?
[Molecular weight of $BaCO_3$ = 197 g/mol]
(a) 0.0005 M (b) 0.001 M
(c) 0.0312 M (d) 0.0413 M

13. 18 cc of a solution of H_2SO_4 neutralises 36 cc of $\frac{N}{10}$ NaOH solution. What is the strength in grams/litre of H_2SO_4 solution?
(a) 2.45 (b) 8.63 (c) 19.61 (d) 9.80

14. An oleum sample was labelled as 102.8 oleum. What is the percentage of free SO_3 in this sample?
(a) 13.80% (b) 17.60%
(c) 19.80% (d) 12.80%

15. The normality of a solution containing of 1.58 g of $KMnO_4$ in 50 mL acidic solution is
(a) 0.01 N (b) 0.1 N (c) 1 N (d) 0.5 N

Type II MCQs with One or More than One Correct Option

16. Mole fraction of ethanol in ethanol-water system is 0.25. Thus it has
(a) 25% ethanol by weight of solution
(b) 75% water by weight of solution
(c) 46% ethanol by weight of solution
(d) 54% water by weight of solution

17. Which of the following statements is/are correct?
20.0 mL of 6.0 M HCl is mixed with 50.0 mL of 2.0 M $Ba(OH)_2$ and 30 mL of water is added
(a) The concentration of $\overset{\ominus}{O}H$ remaining in solution is 0.5 M
(b) The concentration of $Cl^{\ominus}$ remaining in solution is 1.2 M
(c) The concentration of Ba^{2+} remaining in solution is 1.0 M
(d) 80 m moles of $\overset{\ominus}{O}H$ is in excess

18. 100 g sample of clay (containing 18% H_2O, 40% silica and inert impurities as rest) is partially dried so as to contain 10% H_2O.
Which of the following is/are correct statement(s)?
(a) The percentage of silica in it is 43.90%.
(b) The mass of partially dried clay is 60.
(c) The percentage of inert impurity in it is 46.1%.
(d) The mass of water evaporated is 10.0 g.

19. When 200 mL of 0.1 M KNO_3 and 400 mL of 0.2 M HCl and 400 mL of 0.3 M H_2SO_4 are mixed, then in the resulting solution
(a) The molarity of $K^{\oplus} = 0.02$ M
(b) The molarity of $SO_4^{2-} = 0.12$ M
(c) The molarity of $H^{\oplus} = 0.38$ M
(d) The molarity of $NO_3^{\ominus} = 0.08$ and $Cl^{\ominus} = 0.01$ M

20. If 100 mL of 1 M H_2SO_4 solution is mixed with 100 mL of 98% $\left(\frac{W}{W}\right)$ of H_2SO_4 solution ($d = 0.1$ g mL^{-1}), then
(a) Concentration of each component becomes double of the initial value.
(b) Volume of solution becomes 200 m.L
(c) Mass of H_2SO_4 in the solution is 98 g.
(d) Mass of H_2SO_4 in the solution is 19.6 g.

21. Which of the following solutions contains same molar concentration?
(a) 166 g KI in 1 L solution
(b) 33.0 g $(NH_4)_2SO_4$ in 200 mL solution
(c) 25.0 g $CuSO_4 \cdot 5H_2O$ in 100 mL solution
(d) 27.0 g Al^{3+} per 10^3 mL solution

Type III 》 Numerical/Integer Answer Type Questions

22. The volume of concentrated sulphuric acid which is 98% by mass required to prepare 6 dm^3 of 0.7 mol dm^{-3} solution of sulphuric acid is ....

23. The molality of a 10% $\left(\frac{V}{V}\right)$ solution of dibromine solution in toluene (C_7H_8) is 'x'.
The value of x is .... $\times 10^{-2}$ m.
[Nearest integer]
Given : Molar mass of $Br_2 = 160$ g mol^{-1}
Atomic mass of C and H is 12 and 1 g/mol respectively
Density of dibromine = 3.2 g cm^{-3}
Density of toluene = 0.86 g cm^{-3}
Molar mass of toluene = 92.14 g/mol

24. 5 mL of N-HCl, 20 mL of $\frac{N}{2}$ H_2SO_4 and 30 mL of $\frac{N}{3}$ HNO_3 are mixed together and the volume is made to 1 L. The normality of the resulting solution is $\frac{N}{x}$.
The value of x is ....

25. 100 g of propane is completely reacted with 1000 g of oxygen. The mole fraction of water in the resulting mixture is $x \times 10^{-4}$.
The value of x is .... [Nearest integer]
[Atomic weight : H = 1.008, C = 12.00, O = 16.00]

26. When 750 mL of 0.5 M nitrous acid is heated in a beaker, its volume is reduced to half and 11.5 g of nitrous acid is evaporated. The molarity of the remaining nitrous acid solution is $x \times 10^{-2}$ M. [Nearest integer]
[Molar mass of nitrous acid = 47 g/mol]
The value of x is ....

27. A sugar solution is obtained after mixing 150 g of its 20% solution and 350 g of its 40% solution (both by mass), the mass percentage of the resulting sugar solution is ....

Elemental Practice 1.4 | Chapter 01

Connect with **Answers**

1. (a)	**2.** (d)	**3.** (d)	**4.** (c)	**5.** (b)	**6.** (d)
7. (a)	**8.** (b)	**9.** (b)	**10.** (d)	**11.** (b)	**12.** (a)
13. (d)	**14.** (d)	**15.** (c)	**16.** (c,d)	**17.** (b,c,d)	**18.** (a,c)
19. (a,b)	**20.** (b,d)	**21.** (a,c,d)	**22.** (420)	**23.** (258)	**24.** (40)
25. (2537)	**26.** (35)	**27.** (34)			

Advanced Exclusive Different Strokes

Tips to Solve Problems Related to Equivalent Mass with the Help of Faraday

Chemical reactions involve electron sharing, exchange of electrons between cations and anions. In other words, electron transactions occurs in every chemical reaction. For one mole of electrons, charge transaction in coulombs is 96500 C or 1 Faraday.

The mass of chemical species deposited or released at the electrode upon the transaction of 1 Faraday electricity is called Equivalent mass. This is the generalised statement showing connectivity between Faraday and equivalent mass.

Suppose for a reaction,

$$M \longrightarrow M^{n+} + ne^-$$

If 1 mole of *M*, i.e. *m* grams releases *n* Faradays of charge as shown then equivalent mass of M will be m / n grams.

Let us understand this with the help of some examples

(a) $Fe \longrightarrow Fe^{3+} + 3e^-$

Above reaction can be interpreted as

1 mole of Fe i.e. 56 grams releases 3F Faraday of charge.

Equivalent mass of Fe is $\frac{56}{3}$

* One mole i.e. 56 g of Fe = 3 Faraday
= 3 equivalent mass

(b) $H_3PO_4 \longrightarrow HPO_4^{-2} + 2H^+$

1 mole of H_3PO_4 i.e., it's 98 grams releases 2 Faraday charges in terms of H^+.

Equivalent mass of H_3PO_4 is 98/2 g.

* One mole i.e. 98 grams of H_3PO_4
= 2 Faraday = 2 Equivalent mass

(c) $BaCl_2 + Na_3PO_4 \longrightarrow Ba_3(PO_4)_2 + NaCl$

One mole of $BaCl_2$ exchanges 2 Faraday of charges in terms of Ba^{+2} or $2Cl^-$

Equivalent mass of $BaCl_2 = M/2$

One mole of $BaCl_2$ represent 2 equivalent mass.

(d) $3Mn^{+2} \longrightarrow 2Mn^{+5} + 1Mn^{+7}$

Overall 3 moles of Mn^{+2} releases 11 mole of electrons or 11 Faraday of charges.

165 grams of Mn^{+2} releases 11 Faraday of charges.

Equivalent mass of Mn^{+2} is 165/11 g.

Conclusion

The number of Faradays lost always equal to the faradays gains meaning and the number of equivalents remains the same for species that directly react with each other. This concept can be used to determine equivalent masses without stating the complete reaction and using *n*-factor.

PRACTICE
ELEMENT 01

Target JEE Main

Objective Type Questions

1. The reaction between Al and dil. HCl produces $H_2(g)$ and Al^{3+} ions. The molar ratio of Al used to produced H_2 is
(a) 1 : 2 (b) 1 : 3
(c) 2 : 1 (d) 2 : 3

2. An ore contains 1.34% of mineral argentite, Ag_2S, by mass. How many grams of this ore would have to be processed in order to obtain 1.00 g of pure solid silver Ag? (Ag = 108 and S = 32)
(a) 74.60 g (b) 85.70 g
(c) 107.9 g (d) 154.0 g

3. Molality of 40% (by mass) urea solution is
(a) 0.40 (b) 0.60
(c) 11.11 (d) 0.17

4. An aqueous solution of a non-electrolyte solute has molality 11.11 mol kg^{-1}. Hence, mole fraction of solute in the solution is
(a) 0.17 (b) 0.83
(c) 0.40 (d) 0.60

5. Volume of 1.2 mole of ethanol in a sample of density 0.789 g mL^{-1} at 20°C is
(a) 55 mL (b) 58 mL
(c) 70 mL (d) 79 mL

6. Phosphorus forms two chlorides differing in composition. The equivalent mass of which element remains constant in these compounds
(a) chlorine (b) phosphorus
(c) Both (a) and (b) (d) None of these

7. The density of concentrated sulphuric acid is 1.85 g mL^{-1}. What volume of the acid (in mL) would contain 0.0755 mole?
(a) 4 mL (b) 8 mL
(c) 0.4 mL (d) 0.8 mL

8. $[Na^+]$, molar concentration of Na^+, in a solution prepared by mixing 30.0 mL of 0.12 M NaCl and 70.0 mL of 0.15 M Na_2SO_4 is
(a) 0.135 M (b) 0.141 M
(c) 0.210 M (d) 0.246 M

9. The same amount of a metal combines with 0.200 g of oxygen and 3.17 g of halogen. Hence, equivalent mass of halogen is
(a) 127 g (b) 80 g
(c) 35.5 g (d) 9 g

10. A boy drinks 400 mL of 9% glucose ($C_6H_{12}O_6$) solution per day. The number of glucose molecules consumed by him per hour is ($N_0 = 6.02 \times 10^{23} mol^{-1}$)
(a) 5.0×10^{21} (b) 1.20×10^{23}
(c) 2.17×10^{25} (d) 5.0×10^{23}

11. 5 g of CH_3COOH is dissolved in 1 L of ethanol. Assuming no reaction between reactants, molality of the solution is [d (ethanol) = 0.789g cm^{-3}]
(a) 0.0256 (b) 0.1056
(c) 0.1288 (d) 0.1476

12. Mole fraction of N_2 in air having O_2, 20% by volume in standard condition is
(a) 0.20 (b) 0.80 (c) 0.94 (d) 0.06

13. Solute and solvent have molar masses in 10 : 1 ratio. If a solution is 10% by mass of solvent, then mole fraction of solute in the solution is
(a) 9.9×10^{-3} (b) 1.0×10^{-4}
(c) 0.50 (d) 0.75

14. A solution of solute X contains 40% X by weight of solution. 800 g of this solution was cooled, when 100 g of solute is precipitated. Thus, percentage composition of solute in the remaining solution is
(a) 31.4% (b) 20.0% (c) 23.0% (d) 24.0%

15. A solution containing 40.0 g of $Fe_2(SO_4)_3$ has the same concentration as (molar mass = 400 g mol^{-1}) in
(a) 0.2 dm^3 solution is 1M Fe^{3+}
(b) 0.1 dm^3 solution is 2M Fe^{3+}
(c) 0.2 dm^3 solution is 3M SO_4^{2-}
(d) 0.1 kg solution is 3N Fe^{3+}

16. In the following reaction, $2A + B \longrightarrow C$ 8 moles of A and 5 moles of B will form
(a) 13 moles of C (b) 4 moles of C
(c) 5 moles of C (d) 8 moles of C

17. 1.575 g of a dibasic acid is neutralised completely by 100 mL of 0.25 N NaOH . Thus, molar mass of the acid is
(a) 15.75 g mol^{-1} (b) 157.50 g mol^{-1}
(c) 63.00 g mol^{-1} (d) 126.00 g mol^{-1}

18. In the following reaction,
$$2KClO_3 \longrightarrow 2KCl + 3O_2$$
5.0 g of $KClO_3$ gave 0.03 mole of O_2.
Hence, percent purity of $KClO_3$ is
(a) 49% (b) 50% (c) 95% (d) 98%

19. A sample of pure sodium carbonate 0.412 g is dissolved in water and titrated with HCl solution. A volume of 50 mL is required to reach the methyl orange end point. Calculate the molarity of the acid.
(a) 2.1 (b) 0.53
(c) 0.16 (d) 0.41

20. A sample of H_2SO_4 (density 1.8 g mL^{-1}) is 90% by weight. What is the volume of the acid that has to be used to make 1 L of 0.3 M H_2SO_4?
(a) 16.32 (b) 19.83
(c) 11.04 (d) 18.14

Numerical Type Questions

21. The aluminium sulphate hydrate $Al_2(SO_4)_3 \cdot xH_2O$ contains 8.20 per cent Al by mass. What is the value of $0.5x$ (Al = 27)?

22. On heating 2.495 g of $CuSO_4 \cdot xH_2O$, 0.05 mole of H_2O is lost forming $CuSO_4$. What is the value of x? (Cu = 63.5)

23. 5.0 g sample of 147% oleum ($H_2S_2O_7$) was diluted with water and the resulting solution required 25 mL solution of x M NaOH to neutralise the diluted oleum solution. Thus, value of x is ....

24. 1.25 g of gallium reacts with oxygen to give 1.68 g of Ga_xO_y. The value of $(x + y)$ is .... (Ga = 70)

25. Urea solution has molarity of 4.0 mol L^{-1} and molality 2.273 mol kg^{-1}. Thus, density (g mL^{-1}) of the given aqueous solution is........... .

26. 6.20 g of silane (Si_xH_y) is burnt in excess of oxygen forming 11.64 g SiO_2 and 6.980 g H_2O. The value of $(x + y)$ in silane is ....

27. $CaCO_3$ is decomposed by HCl (d = 1.825 g mL^{-1}). Calculate the volume of HCl required to decompose 10 g of $CaCO_3$ of 50% purity?

28. 2 moles of O_2 are formed in the following reaction with 66.67% yield.

$$2KClO_3 \longrightarrow 2KCl + 3O_2$$

How many moles of $KClO_3$ are taken?

29. What mass of CH_4 (in grams) produce 3.01×10^{23} H_2O molecules when burnt in excess of O_2?

30. 20.8 g of MCl_x (M = 137) on reaction with excess of K_2SO_4 yields 23.3 g of sulphate of metal M. The value of x is ....

Check Through PYQs

Element 1 Matter and Its Measurement

1. Which of the following have same number of significant figures? *2023, 8 April Shift-II*
(A) 0.00253 (B) 1.0003
(C) 15.0 (D) 163

Choose the correct answer from the options given below
(a) A, C and D
(b) A, B and C
(c) C and D
(d) B and C

2. Using the rules for significant figures, the correct answer for the expression $\frac{0.02858 \times 0.112}{0.5702}$ will be *2022, 29 June Shift-II*
(a) 0.005613
(b) 0.00561
(c) 0.0056
(d) 0.006

3. The number of significant figures in 0.00340 is .... *2021, 25 July Shift-II*

4. The number of significant figures in 50000.020×10^{-3} is .... *2021, 26 Feb Shift-I*

Element 2 Chemical Formula, Mole Concept & Laws of Chemical Combination

5. The compound contains 54.2% carbon, 9.2% hydrogen and the rest is oxygen. What is molecular formula of the compound, if molecular mass is 132 g/mol? *2025, 24 Jan Shift-II*
(a) $C_6H_{12}O_3$ (b) $C_4H_{12}O_3$
(c) $C_4H_{12}O_6$ (d) $C_6H_{13}O_6$

6. When 10^{21} molecules are removed from x mg of $CO_2(g)$, then 2.4×10^{-3} moles of CO_2 are left. Calculate the value of x. [Take $N_A = 6 \times 10^{23}$] *2025, 22 Jan Shift-II*

7. Choose the incorrect statement about Dalton's atomic theory. *2024, 4 April Shift-II*
(a) All the atoms of a given element have identical properties including identical mass.
(b) Matter consists of indivisible atoms.
(c) Chemical reactions involve reorganisation of atoms.
(d) Compounds are formed when atoms of different elements combine in any ratio.

8. A sample of $CaCO_3$ and $MgCO_3$ weighed 2.21 g is ignited to constant weight of 1.152 g. The composition of mixture is (Given, molar mass in g mol^{-1} $CaCO_3$: 100, $MgCO_3$: 84) *2024, 31 Jan Shift-II*

(a) 1.187 g $CaCO_3$ + 1.187 g $MgCO_3$
(b) 1.023 g $CaCO_3$ + 1.187 g $MgCO_3$
(c) 1.187 g $CaCO_3$ + 1.023 g $MgCO_3$
(d) 1.023 g $CaCO_3$ + 1.023 g $MgCO_3$

9. 0.05 cm thick coating of silver is deposited on a plate of 0.05 m^2 area. The number of silver atoms deposited on plate are .... $\times 10^{23}$.

(Atomic mass of Ag = 108, d = 7.9 g cm^{-3})
2024, 30 Jan Shift-I

10. A metal chloride contains 55.0% of chlorine by weight 100 mL vapours of the metal chloride at STP weigh 0.57 g. The molecular formula of the metal chloride is (Given, atomic mass of chlorine is 35.5 u) *2023, 12 April Shift-I*
(a) MCl_4 (b) MCl_2
(c) MCl (d) MCl_3

11. Match List-I with List-II.

List-I		List-II	
A.	16 g of $CH_4(g)$	I.	Weighs 28 g
B.	1 g of $H_2(g)$	II.	60.2×10^{23} electrons
C.	1 mole of $N_2(g)$	III.	Weighs 32 g
D.	0.5 mol of $SO_2(g)$	IV.	Occupies 11.4 L volume at STP

Choose the correct answer from the options given below
(a) A-I, B-III, C-II, D-IV *2023, 10 April Shift-II*
(b) A-II, B-IV, C-I, D-III
(c) A-II. B-III, C-IV, D-I
(d) A-II, B-IV, C-III, D-I

12. The number of molecules and moles in 2.8375 litres of O_2 at STP are respectively *2023, 10 April Shift-I*
(a) 7.527×10^{23} and 0.125 mol
(b) 1.505×10^{23} and 0.250 mol
(c) 7.527×10^{22} and 0.250 mol
(d) 7.527×10^{22} and 0.125 mol

13. The average molar mass of chlorine is 35.5 g mol^{-1}. The ratio of ^{35}C to ^{37}Cl in naturally occuring chlorine is close to
2020, 6 Sep Shift-II
(a) 4 : 1 (b) 3 : 1
(c) 2 : 1 (d) 1 : 1

Element 3 Reaction Stoichiometry

14. 2.32×10^3 kg of Fe_3O_4 reacts with 2.8×10^3 kg of CO according to the following reaction: *2025, 23 Jan Shift-I*

$$Fe_3O_4 + CO \longrightarrow CO_2 + Fe$$

If x kg of Fe is formed. Find the value of x?
(a) 2000 kg (b) 1680 kg
(c) 2780 kg (d) 1500 kg

15. If 2 g phenol is allowed to react with Br_2/H_2O. How much Br_2 (in g) will be required to produce 2, 4, 6 tribromophenol (Rounded off to nearest integer). *2025, 22 Jan Shift-II*

16. Consider the following reaction,

$$3PbCl_2 + 2(NH_4)_3PO_4 \longrightarrow Pb_3(PO_4)_2 + 6NH_4Cl$$

If 72 m mol of $PbCl_2$ is mixed with 50 m mol of $(NH_4)_3PO_4$, then the amount of $Pb_3(PO_4)_2$ formed is .... mmol (Nearest integer). *2024, 1 Feb Shift-I*

17. Zinc reacts with hydrochloric acid to give hydrogen and zinc chloride. The volume of hydrogen gas produced at STP from the reaction of 11.5 g of zinc with excess HCl is .... L. (Nearest integer)

(Given, molar mass of Zn is 65.4 g mol^{-1} and molar volume of H_2 at STP = 22.7 L) *2023, 31 Jan Shift-I*

18. 1 L, 0.02 M solution of $[Co(NH_3)_5SO_4]$ Br is mixed with 1 L, 0.02 M solution of $[Co(NH_3)_5Br]SO_4$.

The resulting solution is divided into two equal parts (X) and treated with excess of $AgNO_3$ solution and $BaCl_2$ solution respectively as shown below.
1 L solution (X) + $AgNO_3$ solution (excess) $\longrightarrow Y$
1 L solution (X) + $BaCl_2$ solution (excess) $\longrightarrow Z$
The number of moles of Y and Z respectively are
2023, 30 Jan Shift-II
(a) 0.02, 0.01 (b) 0.01, 0.02
(c) 0.02, 0.02 (d) 0.01, 0.01

19. Consider the reaction,

$$4HNO_3(l) + 3KCl(s) \longrightarrow Cl_2(g) + NOCl(g) + 2H_2O(g) + 3KNO_3(s)$$

The amount of HNO_3 required to produce 110.0 g of KNO_3 is

(Given, atomic masses of H, O, N and K are 1, 16, 14 and 39 respectively.) *[2022, 29 July Shift-II]*
(a) 32.2 g (b) 69.4 g
(c) 91.5 g (d) 162.5 g

20. A 1.84 mg sample of polyhydric alcoholic compound 'x' of molar mass 92.0 g/mol gave 1.344 mL of H_2 gas at STP. The number of alcoholic hydrogens present in compound 'x' is .... *2022, 29 July Shift-II*

21. $\underset{(20\text{ g})}{N_2(g)} + \underset{(5\text{ g})}{3H_2(g)} \longrightarrow 2NH_3(g)$

Consider the above reaction, the limiting reagent of the reaction and number of moles of NH_3 formed respectively are *2022, 29 July shift-I*
(a) H_2, 1.42 mol
(b) H_2, 0.71 mol
(c) N_2, 1.42 mol
(d) N_2, 0.71 mol

22. In the given reaction,

$$X + Y + 3Z \rightleftharpoons XYZ_3$$

if one mole of each of X and Y with 0.05 mole of Z gives compound XYZ_3. (Given : Atomic masses of X, Y and Z are 10, 20 and 30 amu, respectively.) the yield of XYZ_3 is ...... g. (Nearest integer) *2022, 28 July Shift-I*

23. Production of iron in blast furnace follows the following equation,

$$Fe_3O_4(s) + 4CO(g) \longrightarrow 3Fe(l) + 4CO_2(g)$$

when 4.640 kg of Fe_3O_4 and 2.520 kg of CO are allowed to react then the amount of iron (in g) produced is
[Given, molar atomic mass (g mol^{-1}) Fe = 56 molar atomic mass (g mol^{-1}) O = 16 and molar atomic mass (g mol^{-1}) C = 12.] *2022, 29 June Shift-I*
(a) 1400 (b) 2200
(c) 3360 (d) 4200

24. 1 L aqueous solution of H_2SO_4 contains 0.02 m mol H_2SO_4. 50% of this solution is diluted with deionised water to give 1 L solution (*A*). In solution (*A*), 0.01 m mol of H_2SO_4 are added. Total m mol of H_2SO_4 in the final solution is ... $\times 10^3$ m mol. *2022, 25 June Shift-I*

25. 0.4 g mixture of NaOH, Na_2CO_3 and some inert impurities was first titrated with $\frac{N}{10}$ HCl using phenolphthalein as an indicator, 17.5 mL of HCl was required at the end point. After this, methyl orange was added and titrated. 1.5 mL of same HCl was required for the next end point. The weight percentage of Na_2CO_3 in the mixture is .... (Rounded-off to the nearest integer) *2021, 25 Feb Shift-I*

26. $NaClO_3$ is used, even in spacecrafts, to produce O_2. The daily consumption of pure O_2 by a person is 492 L at 1 atm 300 K. How much amount of $NaClO_3$, in grams, is required to produce O_2 for the daily consumption of a person at 1 atm, 300 K .... ?
$NaClO_3(s) + Fe(s) \longrightarrow O_2(g) + NaCl(s) + FeO(s)$
$R = 0.082$ L atm mol^{-1} K^{-1} *2020, 8 Jan Shift-II*

27. A 20.0 mL solution containing 0.2 g impure H_2O_2 reacts completely with 0.316 g of $KMnO_4$ in acid solution. The purity of H_2O_2 (in %) is .... (mol. weight of $H_2O_2 = 34$; mol weight of $KMnO_4 = 158$) *2020, 04 Sep Shift-I*

Element 4 Concentration Terms

28. Density of 3 M NaOH is 1.25 g/mL. Molality of solution is *2025, 22 Jan Shift-II*
(a) 2.65 (b) 2.5
(c) 2.8 (d) 3

29. 200 mL of 0.2 M solution of NaOH is mixed with 400 mL of 0.5 M NaOH solution. Molarity of mixture is *2025, 22 Jan Shift-II*
(a) 0.4 (b) 0.6 (c) 4 M (d) 0.8 M

30. A solution is prepared by adding 1 mole ethyl alcohol in 9 mole water. The mass percent of solute in the solution is .... (integer answer) (Given : Molar mass in g mol^{-1}, ethyl alcohol : 46, water : 18) *2024, 8 April Shift-II*

31. Molality (*m*) of 3 M aqueous solution of NaCl is (Given : Density of solution = 1.25 g mL^{-1}, Molar mass in g mol^{-1}: Na-23, Cl-35.5) *2024, 6 April Shift-II*
(a) 2.90 m (b) 2.79 m
(c) 1.90 m (d) 3.85 m

32. The density of '*x*' M solution ('*x*' molar) of NaOH is 1.12 g mL^{-1}, while in molality, the concentration of the solution is 3m (3 molal). Then *x* is
(Given : Molar mass of NaOH is 40 g/mol) *2024, 6 April Shift-I*
(a) 3.5 (b) 3.0
(c) 3.8 (d) 2.8

33. The molality of a 10% (*V*/*V*) solution of dibromine solution in CCl_4 (carbon tetrachloride) is '*x*', *x* = ... $\times 10^{-2}$ m. (Nearest integer) *2023, 1 Feb Shift-II*
[Given, molar mass of Br_2 = 160 g mol^{-1}
atomic mass of C = 12 g mol^{-1}
atomic mass of Cl = 35.5 g mol^{-1}
density of dibromine = 3.2 g cm^{-3}
density of CCl_4 = 1.6 g cm^{-3}]

34. The density of 3 M solution of NaCl is 1.0 g mL^{-1}. Molality of the solution is .... $\times 10^{-2}$ m. (Nearest integer).
[Given, molar mass of Na and Cl is 23 and 35.5 g mol^{-1} respectively.] *2023, 1 Feb Shift-I*

35. Assume carbon burns according to following equation.
$$2C(s) + O_2(g) \longrightarrow 2CO(g)$$
When 12 g carbon is burnt in 48 g of oxygen, the volume of carbon monoxide produced is .... $\times 10^{-1}$ L at STP. [Nearest integer]
[Given, assume CO as ideal gas, mass of C is 12 g mol^{-1}, mass of O is 16 g mol^{-1} and molar volume of an ideal gas at STP is 22.7 L mol^{-1}] *2023, 31 Jan Shift-II*

36. 2 L of 0.2 M H_2SO_4 is reacted with 2 L of 0.1 M NaOH solution, the molarity of the resulting product Na_2SO_4 in the solution is .... millimolar. (Nearest integer) *2022, 28 July Shift-II*

37. The normality of H_2SO_4 in the solution obtained on mixing 100 mL of 0.1 M H_2SO_4 with 50 mL of 0.1 M NaOH is .... $\times 10^{-1}$ N. (Nearest integer) *2022, 27 July Shift-I*

38. 250 g solution of D-glucose in water contains 10.8% of carbon by weight. The molality of the solution is nearest to (Given: Atomic weights are H, 1u; C, 12u; O, 16u) *2022, 27 July Shift-I*
(a) 1.03 (b) 2.06
(c) 3.09 (d) 5.40

39. 56.0 L of nitrogen gas is mixed with excess of hydrogen gas and it is found that 20 L of ammonia gas is produced. The volume of unused nitrogen gas is found to be .... L. *2022, 25 July Shift-II*

40. A solution is prepared by adding 2 g of "*X*" to 1 mole of water. Mass per cent of "*X*" in the solution is *2022, 11 April Shift-II*
(a) 20% (b) 10%
(c) 5% (d) 2%

41. Sodium oxide reacts with water to produce sodium hydroxide. 20.0 g of sodium oxide is dissolved in 500 mL of water. Neglecting the change in volume, the concentration of the resulting NaOH solution is .... $\times 10^{-1}$ M. (Nearest integer)
[Atomic mass : Na = 23.0, O = 16.0, H = 1.0]
2021, 31 Aug Shift-II

42. The density of NaOH solution is 1.2 g cm^{-3}. The molality of this solution is .... m.
(Round off to the nearest Integer)
[Use : Atomic masses : Na : 23.0 u, O : 16.0 u, H : 1.0 u density of H_2O : 1.0 g cm^{-3}]
2021, 27 July Shift-I

43. 15 mL of aqueous solution of Fe^{2+} in acidic medium completely reacted with 20 mL of 0.03 M aqueous $Cr_2O_7^{2-}$. The molarity of the Fe^{2+} solution is ...... $\times 10^{-2}$ M (Round off to the nearest integer).
2021, 17 March Shift-I

44. The strengths of 5.6 volume hydrogen peroxide (of density 1 g/mL) in terms of mass percentage and molarity (*M*), respectively, are (Take molar mass of hydrogen peroxide as 34 g/mol)
2020, 3 Sep Shift-II
(a) 0.85 and 0.25
(b) 0.85 and 0.5
(c) 1.7 and 0.5
(d) 1.7 and 0.25

45. The mole fraction of glucose ($C_6H_{12}O_6$) in an aqueous binary solution is 0.1. The mass percentage of water in it, to the nearest integer, is ....
2020, 3 Sep Shift-I

46. The molarity of HNO_3 in a sample which has density 1.4 g/mL and mass percentage of 63% is ....
(Molecular weight of $HNO_3 = 63$)
2020, 9 Jan Shift-I

47. The volume (in mL) of 0.125 M $AgNO_3$ required to quantitatively precipitate chloride ions in 0.3 g of $[Co(NH_3)_6]Cl_3$ is ....
$M_{[Co(NH_3)_6]Cl_3} = 267.4$ g/mol
$M_{AgNO_3} = 169.87$ g/mol
2020, 8 Jan Shift-I

PRACTICE ELEMENT 02 Target JEE Advanced

Single Correct Choice MCQs

1. Select the incorrect statement about the following reaction when 0.80 mole of MnO_2 and 146 g of HCl are allowed to react

$$MnO_2 + 4HCl \longrightarrow MnCl_2 + Cl_2 + 2H_2O$$

(a) 0.80 mole of Cl_2 is formed
(b) 0.80 mole of HCl remains unreacted
(c) MnO_2 is the limiting reactant
(d) HCl is the limiting reactant

2. In the following reaction,

$$BaCl_2 + H_2SO_4 \longrightarrow BaSO_4 + 2HCl$$

If 100 mL of 20.8% $BaCl_2$ solution react with 50 mL of 9.8% H_2SO_4 solution $BaSO_4$ formed is,
(Ba = 137, S = 32 and Cl = 35.5)
(a) 23.3 g
(b) 11.65 g
(c) 30.6 g
(d) 15.30 g

3. A certain sample of phosphate rock contains 26.26% P_2O_5. A 0.5428 g sample is analysed by precipitating $MgNH_4PO_4 \cdot 6H_2O$ and igniting the precipitate to $Mg_2P_2O_7$. Thus, $Mg_2P_2O_7$ obtained is
(a) 0.8486 g
(b) 1.1424 g
(c) 0.3648 g
(d) 0.2220 g

4. Select the correct alternate about the following reaction. (B = 11)

$$\underset{6.75\text{ g}}{B_2H_6} + \underset{8.55\text{ g}}{2NaH} \longrightarrow 2NaBH_4$$

	Limiting reactants	Excess reactants
(a)	B_2H_6	NaH = 1.80 g
(b)	NaH	B_2H_6 = 1.76 g
(c)	B_2H_6	NaH = 0.90 g
(d)	NaH	B_2H_6 = 1.8 g

5. In the reaction,

$$2Al(aq) + 6HCl(aq) \longrightarrow 2Al^{3+}(aq) + 6Cl^-(aq) + 3H_2(g)$$

(a) 6 mole HCl (*aq*) is consumed for every 3L $H_2(g)$ produced
(b) 33.6 L $H_2(g)$ is produced regardless of temperature and pressure of every mole Al that reacts
(c) 67.2 L $H_2(g)$ at STP is produced for every mole Al that reacts
(d) 11.2 L $H_2(g)$ at STP is produced for every mole HCl(*aq*) consumed

6. NH_3 is formed in the following step:
I. $Ca + 2C \longrightarrow CaC_2$ (50% yield)
II. $CaC_2 + N_2 \longrightarrow CaCN_2 + C$ (100% yield)
III. $CaCN_2 + 3H_2O \longrightarrow 2NH_3 + CaCO_3$ (50% yield)
2 moles of NH_3 are formed if we take
(a) 1 mol Ca (b) 2 mol Ca (c) 3 mol Ca (d) 4 mol Ca

7. A mixture contains equal masses of urea (N_2OCH_4) tetrose ($C_4H_8O_4$) and glucose ($C_6H_{12}O_6$), mole fractions at points *A*, *B*, and *C* are that of

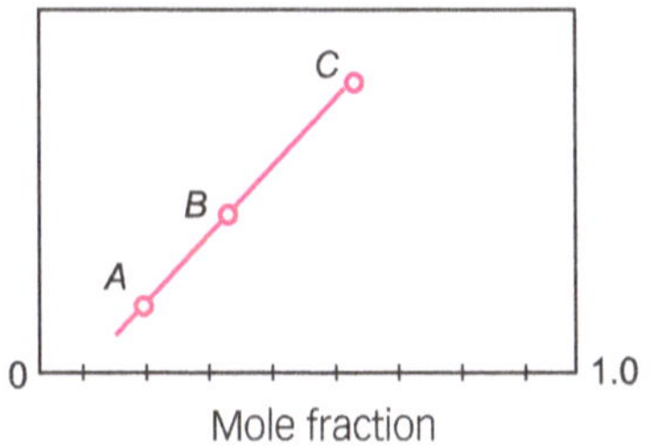

(a) glucose, tetrose, urea (b) glucose, urea, tetrose
(c) urea, tetrose, glucose (d) urea, glucose, tetrose

8. 0.7 g of iron reacts directly with 0.4 g of sulphur to form iron (II) sulphide. 2.8 g of iron was dissolved in dil. HCl and excess of potassium sulphide was added. If law of constant composition is followed, iron (II) sulphide formed in second case is
(a) 0.40 g (b) 0.44 g (c) 4.4 g (d) 1.1 g

9. In rhombic sulphur, sulphur atoms are catenated into S_8 molecules with density 2.07 g cm^{-3}. Number of S_8 molecules in a crystal of 0.568 mm^3 is
(a) 1.336×10^{21} (b) 2.212×10^{22}
(c) 2.765×10^{21} (d) 2.765×10^{18}

10. All the oxygen in 0.5434 g sample of a pure oxide of iron is removed by the reduction in a steam of H_2 gas. The loss in weight is 0.1210 g. Hence, formula of the iron oxide is (F = 56)
(a) Fe_2O_3 (b) FeO_2 (c) Fe_3O_4 (d) FeO

One or More than One Correct MCQs

11. An aqueous solution of glucose ($C_6H_{12}O_6$) contains 1 mole of glucose in 1.8 L solution, then,
(a) it is 10% aqueous solution
(b) its density is 0.1 g mL^{-1}
(c) solution contains 3.34×10^{20} glucose molecule per mL
(d) it is 0.56 molar solution

12. In the synthesis of urea (NH_2CONH_2) as given below:
$$2NH_3(g) + CO_2(g) \longrightarrow NH_2CONH_2(aq) + H_2O(l)$$
637.2 g of NH_3 are allowed to react with 1142 g of CO_2. In this
(a) NH_3 is the limiting reactant and CO_2 is in excess
(b) NH_3 is in excess and CO_2 is the limiting reactant
(c) 18.74 moles of urea is formed
(d) 5.00 moles of CO_2 is left unreacted

13. Consider 1.6g CH_4, 1.7g of NH_3 and 1.8 g H_2O, select the correct alternative(s).
(a) There are equal number of moles of each reactant
(b) Total number of atoms in $CH_4 > NH_3 > H_2O$
(c) Mole fraction of H_2O is maximum if equal moles of CH_4, NH_3 and H_2O are taken in the mixture
(d) Mixture contains 0.1 mole of (*aq*) NH_3 if taken in mixture

14. 800 g of 40% urea solution by weight of solution was cooled. 100 g of the solution is precipitated. Thus,
(a) percentage concentration of solution increases by 8.6
(b) percentage concentration of solution decreases by 8.6
(c) molality of solution increases by 7.65
(d) molality of solution decreases by 3.47

15. Select the correct statement(s) about I and II.
I. $P_4 + 5O_2 \longrightarrow P_4O_{10}$
II. $P_4 + 3O_2 \longrightarrow P_4O_6$
One takes 1.24 g P_4 and 8.00 g O_2 separately for each reaction.
(a) P_4 is the limiting reactant in I and O_2 is the limiting reactant in II
(b) P_4 is the limiting reactant in II and O_2 is the limiting reactant in I
(c) P_4 is the limiting reactant in both
(d) 2.20 g of P_4O_6 in II and 2.84 g of P_4O_{10} in I are formed

16. 2.4 g of magnesium is burnt in a closed vessel which contains 0.112 L oxygen at STP. Thus,
(a) equivalent of MgO formed is equal to equivalent of Mg taken
(b) equivalent of MgO formed is equal to oxygen taken
(c) reactant and product are in equal moles
(d) reactant and product are in equal equivalents

17. Which of the following statements is incorrect about molarity?
(a) 2.24 L of ammonia of STP neutralised 100 mL of a solution of H_2SO_4, the molarity of acid is 0.5 M.
(b) The density of a solution prepared by dissolving 120 g of urea in 1000 g of water is 1.15 g/mL, the molarity of this solution is 1.78 M.
(c) The molarity of H_3PO_4 (98% by mass of solution) has density 1.8 g/mL is 18 M.
(d) The molarity of a solution obtained by mixing 750 mL of 0.5 M HCl with 250 mL of 2 M HCl will be 1.75 M.

18. $KClO_4$ can be prepared by following reactions,
(i) $Cl_2 + 2KOH \longrightarrow KCl + KClO + H_2O$
(ii) $3KClO \longrightarrow 2KCl + KClO_3$
(iii) $4KClO_3 \longrightarrow 3KClO_4 + KCl$
Atomic weight of K, Cl and O are 39, 35.5 and 16 respectively.
The correct statements regarding the given data are —
(a) The amount of Cl_2 required to prepare 200 g of $KClO_4$ by above series of reaction is 294 g.
(b) The volume of KOH in litres used by Cl_2, if KOH is 1.5 M is 10.67 M.
(c) The amount of Cl_2 required to prepare 277 g of $KClO_4$ by above series of reaction is 568 g.
(d) The volume of KOH in litres used by Cl_2, if KOH us 1.5 M is 1.067 L.

19. Which of the following statements are incorrect?
(a) In the division of 6.85 by 112.04, the number of significant figures in the reported answer will be four.
(b) In the subtraction of 2.097 and 0.12 the number of significant figures in the reported answer will be three.

(c) Three different scientifc notations may be written for the result 10500 g.
(d) There are four significant figures in the answer of $\frac{(1.79 \times 10^5)(29.2 - 20.2)}{1.49}$.

20. If hardness of water sample is 200 ppm, then which of the following statements are correct?
(a) Mass ratio of $CaCO_3$ to H_2O is $\frac{0.02}{100}$
(b) 1m Eq. of $CaCO_3$ is present in 1 kg of hard water.
(c) Mole ratio of $CaCO_3$ to H_2O is 3.6×10^{-5}.
(d) Density of $CaCO_3$ present in hard water is 0.2 g/L.

Integer/Numerical Type Questions

21. The density of concentrated sulphuric acid is 1.85 g mL^{-1}. The volume of the acid (in mL) would contain 0.0755 mole is ....

22. A mineral consists of an equimolar mixture of carbonates of two bivalent metals. One metal is present to the extent 14.5% by mass. 3.0 g of the mineral an heating lost 1.40 g of CO_2. The % mass of the other metal is ....

23. A 1.10 g sample consisting of only CaC_2O_4 and MgC_2O_4 is heated at 500°C, converting the two salts of $CaCO_3$ and $MgCO_3$. The sample then weighs 0.835 g. If the sample had been heated to 900°C, where the products are CaO and MgO. The combined mixture of oxide weighs ....

24. The concentration of oxalic acid solution is 'x' mol. L^{-1}. 20 mL of this solution reacts with 16 mL of 0.02 M acidified $KMnO_4$. The pH of x M oxalic acid solution is ....

25. 2 moles of equimolar mixture of ferric oxalate and ferrous oxalate requires a mole of $KMnO_4$ in acidic medium for complete oxidation. a is ....

26. To a 20 mL, 0.5 M aqueous solution of Br_2, excess of NaOH is added so that all Br_2 is disproportionated to $Br^{\ominus}$ and $BrO_3^{\ominus}$. The resulting solution is free from $Br^{\ominus}$, by extraction and excess of $^{\ominus}OH$ neutralised by acidifying the solution. The resulting solution is sufficient to react with 4g of impure CaC_2O_4 ($M = 128$ g/mol) sample. The % purity of oxalate sample is ....

27. Chromium (III) ion forms many compounds with ammonia. In a titration of 1.580 g of $[Cr(NH_3)_xCl_3]$, 24.26 mL of 1.50 M HCl is used.

$$[Cr(NH_3)_xCl_3](aq) + xHCl(aq) \longrightarrow xNH_4^+(aq) + Cr^{3+}(aq) + (x+3)Cl^-(aq)$$

What is the value of x? (Cr = 52)

28. Automobile batteries are filled with an aqueous solution of H_2SO_4.
How many moles of H_2SO_4 in 500 mL of the battery solution are contained if the density of the solution is 1.303 g cm^{-3} of the 30.8% H_2SO_4 by mass?

Matching Type Questions

29. Match of compounds (1 mole each) in Column-I with corresponding properties in Column-II and select answer from the codes given below.

S. No.	Column-I		Column-II
(i)	H_2SO_4	(p)	60 g mol^{-1}
(ii)	H_3PO_4	(q)	98 g mol^{-1}
(iii)	H_3PO_3	(r)	N_0 ionisable H^+ ions per mol
(iv)	H_3PO_2	(s)	$2N_0$ ionisable H^+ ions per mol
(v)	CH_3COOH	(t)	$3N_0$ ionisable H^+ ions per mol
(vi)	NH_2CONH_2	(u)	$4N_0$ H atoms

Codes

	(i)	(ii)	(iii)	(iv)	(v)	(vi)
(a)	(q, r)	(q, t)	(t)	(r)	(r, u)	(p, u)
(b)	(q, r)	(q, t)	(t)	(t)	(p, r, u)	(p, u)
(c)	(q, s)	(q, t)	(s)	(r)	(p, r, u)	(p, u)
(d)	(q)	(q, t)	(t)	(t)	(r, u)	(p, u)

30. Match List-I with List-II.

	List-I (% of carbon)		List-II (Compound)
A.	52.2%	I.	Glucose
B.	40%	II.	Diaminomethanal
C.	20%	III.	Calcium carbonate
D.	12%	IV.	Ethanol

Choose the correct answer from the options given below.
(a) A-I, B-IV, C-II, D-III (b) A-III, B-I, C-IV, D-II
(c) A-IV, B-I, C-II, D-III (d) A-IV, B-III, C-I, D-II

31. Match List-I with List-II

	List-I		List-II
A.	3.74 g $Cu(NO_3)_2$	I.	60.2×10^{23} electrons
B.	2.8375 L of O_2 at STP	II.	6.023×10^{24} electrons
C.	16 g of $CH_4(g)$	III.	7.525×10^{22} molecules
D.	18 mL of H_2O	IV.	0.02 mol

Choose the correct answer from the options given below.
(a) A-II, B-IV, C-I, D-III (b) A-II, B-IV, C-III, D-I
(c) A-IV, B-I, C-II, D-III (d) A-IV, B-III, C-I, D-II

32. Match the species in Column-I with their concentration in Column-II and select the answers from the codes given below.

S. No.	Column-I		Column-II
(i)	98% H_2SO_4 (d = 1.8 g mL^{-1})	(p)	12 M
(ii)	98% H_3PO_4 (d = 1.2 g mL^{-1})	(q)	18 M
(iii)	63% HNO_3 (d = 1.2 g mL^{-1})	(r)	24 N
(iv)	82% H_3PO_3 (d = 1.2 g mL^{-1})	(s)	36 N
		(t)	12 N

Codes

	(i)	(ii)	(iii)	(iv)
(a)	(p, q)	(p, r)	(p, s)	(q, r)
(b)	(q, s)	(p, s)	(p, t)	(p, r)
(c)	(q, s)	(p, s)	(p, t)	(p, s)
(d)	(q, s)	(p, r)	(p, s)	(q, t)

33. Match the laws of chemical combination in Column-I with the examples followed in Column-II and select the answer for the codes given below.

S.No.	Column-I		Column-II
A.	Law of conservation of mass	p.	CH_4 has carbon and hydrogen in 3 : 1 mass ratio.
B.	Law of multiple proportion	q.	10 mL N_2 combines with 30 mL of H_2 to form 20 mL of NH_3.
C.	Law of definite proportion	r.	S and O_2 combine to form SO_2 and SO_3.
D.	Law of reciprocal proportion	s.	In H_2S and SO_2 mass ratio of H and O wrt sulphur is 1 : 16, hence in H_2O, mass ratio if H and O is 1 : 8.
E.	Gas Lussac's Law	t.	4.2 g $MgCO_3$ gives 2.0 g of residue on heating.

Codes

	A	B	C	D	E
(a)	(t)	(p)	(s)	(q)	(r)
(b)	(t)	(r)	(p)	(s)	(q)
(c)	(p)	(q)	(t)	(s)	(r)
(d)	(q)	(p, s)	(r)	(t)	(p)

34. Match List-I with List-II

	List-I (Reaction)		List-II (Mass)
A.	The mass of $(NH_4)_2CO_3$ which contains 0.5 mol NH_4^+	I.	12 g
B.	Mass of $(NH_4)_2CO_3$ which contains 6.02×10^{23} hydrogen atom	II.	2.98 g
C.	Mass of $(NH_4)_2CO_3$ which will produce 3 mol of CO_2 when treated with sufficient acid (HCl)	III.	24 g
D.	Mass of $(NH_4)_2CO_3$ is required to prepare 100 mL of 0.31 M $(NH_4)_2CO_3$ solution	IV.	288.0 g

Choose the correct answer from the options given below.

(a) A-IV, B-III, C-II, D-I
(b) A-II, B-I, C-IV, D-III
(c) A-I, B-II, C-III, D-IV
(d) A-III, B-I, C-IV, D-II

35. Match List-I with List-II

	List-I (Solution mixture)		List-II (Concentration)
A.	11.1 g $CaCl_2$ and 30.01g of NaCl are diluted with water to 100 mL.	I.	$[Ca^{2+}] = 0.8$ M $[Na^{\oplus}] = 1.5$ M $[Cl^{\ominus}] = 3.1$ M
B.	5.0 L of 3.0 M NaCl and 4.0 L of 2.0 M $CaCl_2$ are combined and diluted to 10.0 L	II.	$[Ca^{2+}] = 1$ M $[Na^{\oplus}] = 5.1$ M $[Cl^{\ominus}] = 7.1$ M
C.	300 mL of 3.0 M NaCl is added to 200 mL of 4.0 M $CaCl_2$	III.	$[Ca^{2+}] = 1.6$ M $[Na^{\oplus}] = 1.8$ M $[Cl^{\ominus}] = 5.0$ M
D.	100 mL of 2.0 M HCl + 200 mL of 1.0 M NaOH + 150 mL of 4.0 M $CaCl_2$ + 50 mL of H_2O	IV.	$[Ca^{2+}] = 1.2$ M $[Na^{\oplus}] = 0.4$ M $[Cl^{\ominus}] = 2.8$ M

Choose the correct answer from the options given below.

(a) A-II, B-III, C-IV, D-I
(b) A-II, B-I, C-III, D-IV
(c) A-III, B-IV, C-I, D-II
(d) A-III, B-IV, C-II, D-I

Paragraph Based Questions

Paragraph 1

An inorganic substance (*X*) has the composition as shown. On heating it forms oxide (*Y*) containing 63.63% N.

$\underline{X}$: N = 35%, H = 5%, O = 60%

36. Based on the given data, the molecular weight of '*X*' is .... g/mol.

37. Among the given compounds, HNO_2, HNO_3, $H_2N_2O_2$ and NH_4NO_3. The compound '*X*' which show maximum percentage of N. The percentage of N in compound '*X*' is ....

Paragraph 2

A mixture of FeO and Fe_3O_4 when heated in air to a constant weight to Fe_2O_3, gains 5.263% in its weight.

38. Fe_3O_4 and FeO are present in the molar ratio as $x : y$.
The value of $x + y$ is ....

39. Minimum amount of Fe_2O_3 formed is ....

Paragraph 3

When NaOH react with carbon dioxide it formed sodium carbonate with water. If 11.2 millimoles of CO_2 were passed into 1.0L of 0.15 N NaOH solution.

40. Resultant molarity of NaOH solution is ....

41. Molarity of sodium carbonate solution formed is ....

Species Selection (with 5 Species)

42. 116 g of a substance upon dissociation reaction, yield 7.5 g of hydrogen, 60 g of oxygen and 48.5 g of carbon. Given that, the atomic masses of H, O and C are 1, 16 and 12 respectively. The data agrees with how many formulae of the following compounds?
(i) CH_3OOCH_3 (ii) HCHO
(iii) CH_3COOH (iv) CH_3CHO
(v) CH_3COCH_3
(a) 4 (b) 1 (c) 3 (d) 2

43. Two samples of HCl of 1.0 M and 0.25 M are mixed. The volumes of these samples are taken in order to prepare 0.75 M HCl solution from the following is/are ....
[Assume no water is added]
(i) 20 mL, 10 mL (ii) 15 mL, 35 mL
(iii) 100 mL, 50 mL (iv) 40 mL, 20 mL
(v) 75 mL, 30 mL
(a) 4 (b) 1 (c) 3 (d) 2

44. Consider the following pairs.
(i) NaCl, NaBr (ii) H_2O, H_2Se
(iii) CuO, Cu_2O (iv) CaO, $CaCO_3$
(v) $SnCl_2$, $SnCl_4$
The number of pairs in which law of multiple proportion is followed
(a) 3 (b) 2 (c) 1 (d) 4

45. Which among the following combinations illustrates the law of reciprocal proportions?
(i) N_2O_3, N_2O_4, N_2O_5 (ii) NaCl, NaBr, NaI
(iii) H_2O, H_2S, SO_2 (iv) PH_3, P_2O_3, P_2O_5
(v) CS_2, CO_2, SO_2
(a) 2 (b) 1 (c) 3 (d) 4

46. In which of the following pairs, 10 g of each have an equal number of molecules
(i) N_2O and CO (ii) N_2 and CO
(iii) N_2O and CO_2 (iv) SO_3 and H_2O
(v) N_2 and C_3O_2
(a) 4 (b) 2 (c) 1 (d) 3

47. Among the following conversions,
(i) 1 zeta gram $= 10^{-18}$ g
(ii) 10 pounds = 3.54 kg
(iii) 360 miles per hour = 160.934 ms^{-1}
(iv) 100 million miles $= 1.6 \times 10^{11}$ m
(v) 200 lb = 90.7 kg
The correct unit conversion is/are
(a) 3 (b) 4 (c) 1 (d) 2

Species Selection (with 7 Species)

48. Consider the following solutions,
(i) 166 g KI per L
(ii) 33.0 g $(NH_4)_2SO_4$ in 200 mL
(iii) 25.0 g $CuSO_4 \cdot 5H_2O$ in 100 mL
(iv) 38.2 g NaCl in 50 mL
(v) 27.0 mg Al^{3+} per mL
(vi) 7.45 g KCl in 200 mL
(vii) 28.0 g CS_2 in 100 mL
The total number of solutions which contains same molar concentration is/are —
(a) 3 (b) 4 (c) 5 (d) 2

49. Consider the following reactions,
(i) $2Mg(s) + O_2(g) \longrightarrow 2MgO(s)$
(ii) $C_3H_8(g) + O_2(g) \longrightarrow CO_2(g) + H_2O(g)$
(iii) $P_4(s) + 5O_2(g) \longrightarrow P_4O_{10}(s)$
(iv) $CH_4(g) + 2O_2(g) \longrightarrow CO_2(g) + 2H_2O(g)$
(v) $2H_2(g) + O_2(g) \longrightarrow H_2O(l)$
(vi) $C_5H_{12}(l) + 7O_2(g) \longrightarrow 5CO_2(g) + 6H_2O(l)$
(vii) $2KI(aq) + Pb(NO_3)_2(aq) \longrightarrow PbI_2(s) + 2KNO_3(aq)$
The reactions which do not obey the law of conservation of mass —
(a) 2 (b) 4
(c) 3 (d) 5

50. Consider the following relation,
(i) $\dfrac{0.02858 \times 0.112}{0.5702}$
(ii) 5×5.364
(iii) 132.07×0.12
(iv) $0.0125 + 0.7864 + 0.0215$
(v) 1.0003
(vi) $\dfrac{(1.12 \times 10^{-3}) \times 0.2}{1.2}$
(vii) 18.38×23.54
How many of them have same number of significant figures?
(a) 5 (b) 4
(c) 2 (d) 3

51. Among the given solutions,
(i) 3.3 M solution of NaOH ($d = 1.25$ g ml^{-1})
(ii) 3.28 M HCl ($d = 1.25$ g ml^{-1})
(iii) 2.30 M H_2SO_4 ($d = 1.84$ g ml^{-1})
(iv) 2 M $BaCl_2$ ($d = 3.856$ g ml^{-1})
(v) 2.31 M KCl ($d = 1.69$ g ml^{-1})
(vi) 1.11 M NaCl ($d = 1.25$ g ml^{-1})
(vii) 3 M $CaCO_3$ ($d = 2.71$ g ml^{-1}, $Mw = 100$)
The total number of solutions which have the molality more than the 3 M aqueous solution of NaCl ($d = 1.25$ g ml^{-1}) is/are ....
(a) 5 (b) 3 (c) 4 (d) 2

52. Which of the following has equal mass of $Cl^{\ominus}$ ions in 1.0 L of each of the following solutions?
(i) 5% NaCl (density = 1.07 g mL^{-1})
(ii) 55.5 g $BaCl_2$
(iii) 5% KCl (density = 1.06 g mL^{-1})
(iv) 58.5 g NaCl
(v) 3% CCl_4 (density = 1.59 g mL^{-1})
(vi) 28.3 g S_2Cl_2
(vii) 95.2 g $MgCl_2$
(a) 5 (b) 3 (c) 4 (d) 2

Check Through PYQs

Element 2 Chemical Formula, Mole Concept & Laws of Chemical Combination

1. To check the principle of multiple proportions, a series of pure binary compounds (P_mQ_n) were analysed and their composition is tabulated below. The correct option(s) is (are) *2022 Adv.*

Compound	Weight % of *P*	Weight % of *Q*
1	50	50
2	44.4	55.6
3	40	60

(a) If empirical formula of compound 3 is P_3Q_4, then the empirical formula of compound 2 is P_3Q_5.
(b) If empirical formula of compound 3 is P_3Q_2 and atomic weight of element *P* is 20, then the atomic weight of *Q* is 45.
(c) If empirical formula of compound 2 is *PQ*, then the empirical formula of the compound 1 is P_5Q_4
(d) If atomic weight of *P* and *Q* are 70 and 35, respectively, then the empirical formula of compound 1 is P_2Q

Element 3 Reaction Stoichiometry

2. The stoichiometric reaction of 516 g of dimethyldichlorosilane with water results in a tertrameric cyclic product *X* in 75% yield. The weight (in g) of *X* obtained is ...... *2023 Adv.*

[Use, molar mass (g mol^{-1}) : H = 1, C = 12 , O = 16, Si = 28, Cl = 35.5]

3. Dissolving 1.24 g of white phosphorus in boiling NaOH solution in an inert atmosphere gives a gas Q. The amount of $CuSO_4$ (in g) required to completely consume the gas *Q* is ....

[Given, atomic mass of H = 1, O = 16, Na = 23, P = 31, S = 32, Cu = 63] *2022 Adv.*

4. Aluminium reacts with sulphuric acid to form aluminium sulphate and hydrogen. What is the volume of hydrogen gas in litre (L) produced at 300 K and 1.0 atm pressure, when 5.4 g of aluminium and 50.0 mL of 5.0 M sulphuric acid are combined for the reaction?

(Use molar mass of aluminium as 27.0 g mol^{-1}, $R = 0.082$ atm L mol^{-1} K^{-1}) *2020 Adv.*

5. Galena (an ore) is partially oxidised by passing air through it at high temperature. After some time, the passage of air is stopped, but the heating is continued in a closed furnace such that the content undergo self-reduction. The weight (in kg) of Pb produced per kg of O_2 consumed is ....

(Atomic weights in g mol^{-1} : O = 16, S = 32, Pb = 207) *2018 Adv.*

6. The ammonia prepared by treating ammonium sulphate with calcium hydroxide is completely used by $NiCl_2 \cdot 6H_2O$ to form a stable coordination compound. Assume that both the reactions are 100% complete. If 1584 g of ammonium sulphate and 952 g of $NiCl_2 \cdot 6H_2O$ are used in the preparation, the combined weight (in grams) of gypsum and the nickel-ammonia coordination compound thus produced is____

(Atomic weights in g mol^{-1} : H = 1, N = 14, O = 16, S = 32, Cl = 35.5, Ca = 40, Ni = 59) *2018 Adv.*

7. To measure the quantity of $MnCl_2$ dissolved in an aqueous solution, it was completely converted to $KMnO_4$ using the reaction,

$$MnCl_2 + K_2S_2O_8 + H_2O \longrightarrow KMnO_4 + H_2SO_4 + HCl$$

(equation not balanced).

Few drops of concentrated HCl were added to this solution and gently warmed. Further, oxalic acid (225 g) was added in portions till the colour of the permanganate ion disappeared. The quantity of $MnCl_2$ (in mg) present in the initial solution is ....

(Atomic weights in g mol^{-1}: Mn = 55, Cl = 35.5) *2018 Adv.*

Element 4 Concentration Terms

8. 5.00 mL of 0.10 M oxalic acid solution taken in a conical flask is titrated against NaOH from a burette using phenolphthalein indicator. The volume of NaOH required for the appearance of permanent faint pink color is tabulated below for five experiments. What is the concentration, in molarity, of the NaOH solution?

Exp. No.	Vol. of NaOH (mL)
1	12.5
2	10.5
3	9.0
4	9.0
5	9.0

2020 Adv.

9. The mole fraction of a solute in a solution is 0.1. At 298 K, molarity of this solution is the same as its molality. Density of this solution at 298 K is 2.0 g cm^{-3}. The ratio of the molecular weights of the solute and solvent, $\left(\frac{m_{solute}}{m_{solvent}}\right)$ is ... . *2016 Adv.*

HINTS & Solutions

Solutions : Competency Enhancer

2.1. ***(b)*** The reaction involved are

$$CaCO_3(s) \longrightarrow CaO(s) + CO_2$$

$$MgCO_3(s) \longrightarrow MgO(s) + CO_2$$

Let the weight of $CaCO_3$ be x g

$\therefore$ Weight of $MgCO_3 = (4.41 - x)$ g

Moles of $CaCO_3$ decomposed = Moles of CaO formed

$$\frac{x}{100} = \text{Moles of CaO formed}$$

$\therefore$ Weight of CaO formed $= \frac{x}{100} \times 56$

Moles of $MgCO_3$ decomposed = Moles of MgO formed

$$\frac{(4.41 - x)}{84} = \text{Moles of MgO formed}$$

$\therefore$ Weight of MgO formed $= \frac{(4.41 - x)}{84} \times 40$

$$\frac{(4.41 - x)}{84} \times 40 + \frac{x}{100} \times 56 = 2.232$$

$$100\,[176.4 - 40x] + 4704x = 2.232 \times 84 \times 100$$

$$17640 - 4000x + 4704x = 18748.8$$

$$704x = 1108.8$$

$$x = 1.58 \text{ g} = \text{Weight of } CaCO_3$$

Weight of $MgCO_3 = 4.41 - 1.58$

$= 2.83$ g

2.2. ***(a, d)*** Among the given statements, a and c are correct while b and d are incorrect.

(a) If empirical formula of compounds '1' is X_3Y_4.

We know that,

$$\frac{3 \times M_X}{4 \times M_Y} = \frac{\%\text{ of } X}{\%\text{ of } Y}$$

where, M_X = molar mass of X

M_Y = molar mass of Y

$$\frac{3M_X}{4M_Y} = \frac{33.3}{66.6}$$

$$\frac{M_X}{M_Y} = \frac{33.3 \times 4}{66.6 \times 3} = \frac{4}{6} = \frac{2}{3}$$

If empirical formula of compound '2' is $X_{27}Y_{22}$.

$$\frac{27M_X}{22M_Y} = \frac{45}{55}$$

$$\frac{M_X}{M_Y} = \frac{45}{55} \times \frac{22}{27} = \frac{2}{3}$$

Since, molecular weight ratio comes out equal in two compounds, '1' and '2'. So, statement (a) is correct.

(b) If empirical formula of '3' is X_3Y_2.

$$\frac{3M_X}{2M_Y} = \frac{50}{50} = 1$$

$$\frac{M_X}{M_Y} = \frac{2}{3}$$

If atomic weight of X = 30 and that of Y is 40

$$\frac{M_X}{M_Y} = \frac{30}{40} = \frac{3}{4}$$

So, statement (b) is incorrect, since the molecular weight ratio are not equal.

(c) If empirical formula of compound '2' is XY

$$\frac{M_X}{M_Y} = \frac{45}{55} = \frac{9}{11}$$

and compound '3' is X_3Y_5

$$\frac{3M_X}{5M_Y} = \frac{50}{50} = 1$$

$$\frac{M_X}{M_Y} = \frac{5}{3}$$

Molecular weight ratio are unequal in compounds '1' and '3'. So, statement (c) is incorrect.

(d) $M_X = 70$, $M_Y = 35$

$$\frac{M_X}{M_Y} = \frac{70}{35} = 2$$

If empirical formula of compound '3' is X_3Y_6

$$\frac{3M_X}{6M_Y} = \frac{50}{50} = 1$$

$$3M_X = 6M_Y$$

$$M_X = 2M_Y$$

M_X is double by M_Y

So, statement (d) is correct.

3.1. ***(104)*** The reaction proceeds as

$$4HNO_3(l) + 3KCl(s) \longrightarrow Cl_2(g)\uparrow + NOCl(g) + 2H_2O + 3KNO_3$$

Number of moles of $KNO_3 = \frac{125}{101} = 1.2376$

As, 3 moles of KNO_3 is produced from 4 moles of HNO_3.

$\therefore$ 1.2376 moles of KNO_3 is produced from

$$= \frac{4}{3} \times 1.2376$$

Mass of HNO_3 required is $= 1.650 \times 63$

$= 103.95 \approx 104$ g

4.1. ***(242)*** 10 g of ethyl alcohol is present in 90 mL of water

Density of water = 1 g/mL

Mass of solvent = 90 g

$$\text{Molality } (m) = \frac{10 \times 1000}{46 \times 90} \approx 2.415$$

$$= 242 \times 10^{-2}$$

Elemental Practice 1.1

1. ***(b)*** $5.2 \text{ L} = 5.2 \text{ dm}^3 = \frac{5.2 \text{ dm}^3}{1 \times 10^3 \text{ dm}^3/\text{m}^3} = 5.2 \times 10^{-3} \text{ m}^3$

2. ***(d)*** $1 \text{ g cm}^{-3} = 1000 \text{ kg m}^{-3}$

$\therefore \quad 10.5 \text{ g cm}^{-3} = 10.5 \times 10^3 \text{ kg m}^{-3}$

3. ***(c)*** $\frac{°F - 32}{180} = \frac{°C}{100}$ or $\left(\frac{9}{5}°C\right) + 32 = \frac{9}{5} \times 225 + 32$

$= 405 + 32 = 437 \text{ °F}$

4. ***(d)*** $x°C = (273 + x)\text{K}$

$$\frac{°F - 32}{180} = \frac{°C}{100}$$

$\therefore \quad °F = \frac{9}{5}(°C) + 32 = \left(\frac{9}{5}x + 32\right) °F$

$\therefore \quad (273 + x)\text{ K} - \left(\frac{9}{5}x + 32\right) °F = 11$

$\therefore \quad \left(x - \frac{9}{5}x\right) = 11 + 32 - 273$

$-\frac{4x}{5} = -230 \Rightarrow x = 287.5 \text{ °C}$

5. ***(c)***

Two SF → 0.445 — Even number before 5 thus, remains unchanged. Thus, 0.44

Two SF → 0.435 — Odd number before 5 thus, changes to 4. Thus, 0.44

6. ***(c)*** $0.8 \text{ nm} = 0.8 \times 10^{-9} \text{ m} = 8 \times 10^{-10} \text{ m} = 8 \text{ Å}$

Thus, both these pairs are equal.

7. ***(d)*** $x \text{ °C} = -x \text{ °F}$

$$\frac{x - 32}{180} = \frac{-x}{100}$$

$\therefore \quad x = 11.43°$

8. ***(b)*** The result should be recorded upto four decimal places and digit at the fourth decimal should be even (0, 2, 4, 6, 8), least count being 0.0002.

9. ***(a)*** The measurement 4.0032 is between 4.0031 and 4.0033

10. ***(d)*** (a) 445 g of water = 445 mL of water ($d = 1 \text{ g cm}^{-3}$)

(b) 600 g chloroform $= \frac{600 \text{ g}}{1.5 \text{ g cm}^{-3}} = 400 \text{ mL}$

(c) $155 \text{ cm}^3 = 155 \text{ mL}$

(d) 0.50 L = 500 mL

11. ***(b)***

(a) $d(H_2O \text{ at } 4° C) = 1 \text{ g cm}^{-3}$

(b) $d = \frac{\text{Mass}}{\text{Volume}} = \frac{198.9}{100} = 1.989 \text{ g cm}^{-3}$

(c) $d = \frac{7.72}{10} = 0.772 \text{ g cm}^{-3}$

(d) $d = 0.83 \text{ g cm}^3$

Thus, option (b) is correct

12. ***(a)*** SI unit of volume $= \text{m}^3$

Metric unit of volume $= \text{L} (\text{dm}^3)$

13. ***(d)*** On the Reamur scale, water freezes at 0° R and boils at 80° R.

Thus, $\frac{(°R)}{80} = \frac{(°C)}{100}$

Also $\frac{°C}{100} = \frac{°F - 32}{180}$

$\Rightarrow \quad \frac{°R}{80} = \frac{°C}{100} = \frac{°F - 32}{180}$

$\therefore \quad °R = 0.8 \text{ °C} = \frac{4}{9}(°F - 32)$

Thus, option (d) is correct.

14. ***(d)*** As we know, Density $= \frac{\text{Mass (kg)}}{\text{Volume } (\text{m}^3)}$

For trials *A*, density $= \frac{2.5718 \text{ g}}{3.11 \text{ mL}} = \frac{2.5718 \times 10^{-3} \text{ kg}}{3.11 \times 10^{-6} \text{ m}^3}$

$= 826.94 \text{ kg/m}^3$

For trials *B*, density $= \frac{2.1532 \text{ g}}{2.65 \text{ mL}} = \frac{2.1532 \times 10^{-3} \text{ kg}}{2.65 \times 10^{-6} \text{ m}^3}$

$= 812.53 \text{ kg/m}^3$

For trials *C*, density $= \frac{3.3384 \text{ g}}{4.01 \text{ mL}} = \frac{3.3384 \times 10^{-3} \text{ kg}}{4.01 \times 10^{-6} \text{ m}^3}$

$= 832.52 \text{ kg/m}^3$

The mean density of the three trials *A*, *B* and *C* is

$$= \frac{826.94 + 812.53 + 832.52}{3}$$

$$= 824.0 \text{ kg/m}^3$$

15. ***(a)*** $\frac{F - 32}{180} = \frac{K - 273.15}{100}$

$\Rightarrow \quad \frac{F - 32}{9} = \frac{95 - 273.15}{5}$

$\Rightarrow \quad \frac{F - 32}{9} = \frac{-178.15}{5}$

$\Rightarrow \quad F = -178.15 \times \frac{9}{5} + 32$

$= -320.67 + 32 \approx -289°\text{F}$

16. ***(a, c)*** In both case, readings are far away (± 0.4) from correct value. Thus, are not accurate. Readings of *X* as well as that of *Y* are precise being close to one another.

17. ***(b, d)*** Statement (b) and (d) are correct according to the 2019 redefinition of base unit accepted by IUPAC.

18. ***(b, d)*** Statements (b) and (d) are correct while statements (a) and (c) are incorrect. The correct form of statements (a) and (c) are:

Kilogram is defined by taking the fixed numerical value of Planck constant h to be $6.62607015 \times 10^{-34}$ when expressed in the unit of J.s, where the metre and the second are defined in terms of (c) and $\Delta\nu_C$.

National of Metrology Institute (NMT) maintains a country's national standard of measurement and ensures they are traceable to he international system of units.

19. ***(b, c, d)***

(a) $\frac{pm}{nm} = \frac{10^{-12}m}{10^{-9}m} = 1 \times 10^{-3}$

(b) $\frac{nm}{pm} = \frac{10^{-9}m}{10^{-12}} = 1 \times 10^{3}$

(c) $\frac{Gm}{Mm} = \frac{10^{9}m}{10^{6}m} = 1 \times 10^{3}$

(d) $\frac{hm}{dm} = \frac{10^{2}m}{10^{-1}m} = 1 \times 10^{3}$

20. ***(a, b, d)***
In (c) mass is in gram.
Others are derived SI units

21. ***(4)*** $\frac{°F - 32}{180} = \frac{°C}{100}$

$$\therefore \quad °C = \frac{5}{9}(°F - 32)$$
$$= \frac{5}{9}(-452 - 32)$$
$$\approx -269\,°C = -269\,°C + 273 = 4K$$

22. ***(2)*** $(29.2 - 20.2) = \overbrace{9.0}^{2}$ [Significant figures = 2]

$\overbrace{1.09}^{3}$ [Significant figures = 3]

$\overbrace{105}^{3}$ [Significant figures = 3]

$\overbrace{1.69}^{3}$ [Significant figures = 3]

$$\frac{9.0 \times 1.09 \times 105}{1.69} = 609.497 = \overbrace{6.1}^{2} \times 10^2$$

23. ***(98)*** Actual temperature = 60°C

Freezing point = 20°C

Boiling point = 150°C

Let the temperature on the thermometer at 60°C read x then,

$$\frac{x - 20}{150 - 20} = \frac{60}{100}$$
$$\Rightarrow \quad \frac{x - 20}{13} = 6$$
$$\Rightarrow \quad x - 20 = 78 \Rightarrow x = 98°C$$

24. ***(5)*** 1 cal = 4.18 J

$$\frac{20.92}{4.184} = x \text{ cal}$$
$$x = 5 \text{ cal}$$

25. ***(7)*** $\frac{G}{h} = \frac{10^9}{10^2} = 10^7 = 10^x$

$$\therefore \quad x = 7$$

26. ***(8)*** $\frac{°F - 32}{180} = \frac{°C}{100}$

$$\therefore \frac{46.4 - 32}{180} = \frac{C}{100}$$
$$\Rightarrow \quad C = 8°C$$

27. ***(2)*** $\overbrace{12.11}^{4} \div \overbrace{18.0}^{3} + \overbrace{1.012}^{4} - \overbrace{1.02}^{3}$

$$= \underline{0.672} + \underline{1.012} - \underline{1.02}$$
$$= \underline{1.684} - \underline{1.02}$$
$$= \underline{0.664} = \underline{0.66}$$

Elemental Practice 1.2

1. ***(d)*** One mol O_2 gas at STP

$$= N_0 \text{ molecules } (= 6.022 \times 10^{23} \text{mol}^{-1})$$

Thus, (a) is correct.

Each molecule of O_2 has two O-atoms

Thus, $2N_0 = 6.022 \times 10^{23} \times 2$
$= 12.044 \times 10^{23}$ O-atoms

Thus, (b) is correct

One mol = 1 × mol × 32 g mol^{-1}
= 32 g of O_2

Thus, (c) is correct.

2. ***(c)*** $16 \text{ g } O_2 = \frac{16}{32} \text{mol } O_2 = \left(\frac{1}{2} \times 2\right)$ mol O-atoms

$= N_0$ O-atoms

$4 \text{ g } H_2 = \frac{4}{2} \text{mol } H_2 = 2 \times 2$ mol H-atoms

$= 4N_0$ H - atoms

$44 \text{ g } CO_2 = \frac{44}{44}$ mol $= 1 \times 3$ mol C and O-atoms

$= 3N_0$ atoms

$28 \text{ g } N_2 = \frac{28}{28} \text{mol } N_2 = 1 \times 2$ mol N-atom

$= 2N_0$ N-atoms

$32 \text{ g } O_2 = \frac{32}{32}$ mol $O_2 = 1 \times 2$ mol O-atoms

$= 2N_0$ O - atoms

$12 \text{ g C} = \frac{12}{12} = 1$ mol C $= N_0$ C-atoms

$23 \text{ g Na} = \frac{23}{23} = 1$ mol Na $= N_0$ Na-atoms

So, both (III) and (IV) are correct.

3. ***(c)*** $16\text{ g } O_2 = \frac{16}{32}\text{ mol} = \frac{1}{2}\text{ mol}$

$14\text{ g } N_2 = \frac{1}{2}\text{ mol}$

4. ***(b)*** Molar mass of $Na_2CO_3 \cdot 10H_2O = 286\text{ g mol}$

$0.01\text{ mol } Na_2CO_3 = 0.01\text{ mol } Na_2CO_3 \cdot 10H_2O$

$= 2.86\text{ g } Na_2CO_3 \cdot 10H_2O$

5. ***(a)*** $12\text{ g } ({}^{24}_{12}Mg) = \frac{12}{24} = 0.5\text{ mol} = 0.5 N_0$ atoms

$11\text{ g } CO_2 = 0.25\text{ mol } CO_2 = 0.5 N_0$ O-atoms

$4\text{ g of } CH_4 = 0.25\text{ mol}$

$CH_4 = N_0$ H-atoms

$46\text{ of g } N_2O_4 = 0.50\text{ mol}$

$N_2O_4 = N_0$ O-atoms

$79\text{ g of } Na_2S_2O_3 = 0.5\text{ mol}$

$Na_2S_2O_3 = N_0$ S-atoms

6. ***(c)***

(a) Incorrect as volume of liquid H_2O at STP is not equal to 22.4 L.

(b) Only gases occupy 22.4 L mol^{-1} at STP.

(c) $1\text{ g of } H_2 = 2\text{ g He} = 0.5\text{ mol} = 11.2\text{ L}$ at STP

(d) If gas is real volume occupied by 1g of CH_4 at STP is different from 1.4 L

7. ***(c)*** Volume of spherical ball $= \frac{4}{3}\pi r^3 = \frac{4}{3}\pi (7)^3\text{ cm}^3$

Mass of ball = Volume × density

$= \frac{4}{3}\pi (7)^3 \times 1.4\text{ g}$

Mass of iron $= \frac{4}{3}\pi (7)^3 \times 1.4 \times \frac{56}{100}\text{ g}$

Mol of iron $= \frac{4}{3}\pi (7)^3 \times \frac{1.4}{56} \times \frac{56}{100}\text{ mol} = 20.11$

8. ***(a)*** $\underset{2\text{ mol}}{2KClO_3} \longrightarrow 2KCl + \underset{3\text{ mol} = 3\times 22.4\text{ L } O_2}{3O_2}$

$3\text{ mol} = 3 \times 22.4\text{ L } O_2$ is from $= 2\text{ mol } KClO_3$

$\therefore 0.672\text{ L } O_2$ is from $= \frac{2 \times 0.672}{3 \times 22.4} = 0.02\text{ mol } KClO_3$

9. ***(d)*** As, $4Al + 3O_2 \longrightarrow Al_2O_3$

$C + O_2 \longrightarrow CO_2$

Let the mass of oxygen = 1g

% of aluminium in aluminium oxide = 52.9%

% of oxygen in aluminium oxide = 100 − 52.9 = 47.1%

47.1 g of oxygen combine with aluminium = 52.9 g

1 g of oxygen combine with aluminium

$= \frac{52.9}{47.1} \times 1\text{ g} = 1.123\text{ g}$

% of carbon in $CO_2 = 27.27\%$

% of oxygen in $CO_2 = 100 - 27.27 = 72.73\%$

72.73 g of oxygen combine with carbon = 27.27 g

1 g of oxygen combine with carbon $= \frac{27.27}{72.73} \times 1\text{ g} = 0.375\text{ g}$

Hence, the ratio of aluminium : carbon will be 1.123 : 0.375 and it will be same in aluminium carbide i.e., '*Z*' compound as well.

% of aluminium in aluminium carbide $= \frac{1.123}{1.123 + 0.375} \times 100$

$= \frac{1.123}{1.498} \times 100 = 75\%$

10. ***(a)*** Among the given statements, statement (a) is correct regarding the given reaction.

Total mass of iron and oxygen in reactants is equal to the total mass of iron and oxygen in product therefore it follows the law of conservation of mass.

11. ***(c)*** $\underset{1\text{ mol}}{CaCl_2} \longrightarrow \underset{1\text{ mol}}{CaCO_3} \longrightarrow \underset{1\text{ mol}}{CaO}$

Let, the 1g mixture contain x g of $CaCl_2$.

Moles of $CaCl_2 = \frac{x}{111}$ while mole of CaO $= \frac{0.162}{56}$

1 mole of $CaCl_2$ produces 1 mole of CaO

$\therefore \frac{x}{111} = \frac{0.162}{56}$

$x = 0.321\text{ g}$

% of $CaCl_2 = \frac{0.321}{1} \times 100 = 32.1\%$

12. ***(c)*** Among the given statements, statement (c) is not correct because Dalton's theory explain the law's of chemical combination but it could not explain the laws of gaseous volumes.

13. ***(c)*** Sn taken as 1.056 g

Sn unreacted = 0.601 g

Sn used = 1.056 − 0.601 = 0.455 g

	Mole	Ratio
Sn	$\frac{0.455}{119} = 3.82 \times 10^{-3}$	1.0
Iodine	$\frac{1.947}{127} = 1.53 \times 10^{-2}$	4.0

Thus, compound is SnI_4.

14. ***(c)*** Equivalent mass of metal = 12 g/mol

Equivalent mass of oxygen = 8 g/mol

∴ Equivalent mass of metal oxide = 20 g/mol

15. ***(a)*** The equivalent mass of oxygen is 8.

The equivalent mass of metal is 16.

If it is a alkaline earth metal, then its molecular mass will be twice its equivalent mass. So, it will be 32.

The molecular mass of metal oxide will be = 32 + 16 = 48

The equivalent mass of metal oxide $= \frac{48}{2} = 24$

It is 1.5 times the equivalent mass of metal.

16. ***(c)*** In ammonium phosphate, 12 moles of H are present with 4 moles of oxygen atom.

$\therefore$ 3.18 moles of 'H' are present with $= \frac{4}{12} \times 3.18$

$= 1.06$ moles of oxygen atom

17. ***(b)*** For second oxide,

Let the 'X' g of Cu combines with 'y' g of oxygen.

For first oxide,

'X' g of Cu combines with '$2y$' g of oxygen

For a fixed amount of Cu,

$$\frac{(n_{Cu})_I}{(n_{Cu})_{II}} = \frac{\frac{Y}{M_O}}{\frac{2Y}{M_O}} = 2$$

$$\Rightarrow \quad (n_{Cu})_I = 2(n_{Cu})_{II}$$

So, ratio of the valencies of copper in the first and second oxides is 2 : 1.

18. ***(b)*** The mass of oxygen present in metal oxide

$= 9.44 - 5 = 4.44$ g

Equivalent weight of metal is equal to the mass of metal that combines with 8 g of oxygen.

Thus, equivalent weight of metal $= \frac{5}{4.44} \times 8 = 9.00$ g

19. ***(b)*** Given, oxygen = 67.67%

Metal = 100 − 67.67 = 32.33%

In 100 g metal oxide 67.67 g of oxygen and 32.33 g of metal is present.

Eq. wt. for oxygen = 8 g

$\because$ 67.67 g $O_2 \longrightarrow$ 32.33 g metal

8 g $O_2 \longrightarrow \frac{32.33}{67.67} \times 8 = 3.82$ g metal

Hence, equivalent weight of metal is 3.82 g.

20. ***(d)*** Both Statement I and Statement II are true.

21. ***(b, d)*** A bivalent metal ion (M^{2+}) has equivalent mass of 12, then molar mass of its oxide is 40.

Atomic weight = Equivalent weight × n-factor = 12 × 2 = 24

Molar mass of the oxide = Atomic weight of metal + Atomic weight of oxygen

= 24 + 16 = 40

22. ***(a, b)*** The molar mass of diammonium hydrogen phosphate is 132 g/mol and that of P_2O_5 is 142 g/mol.

1 mole of diammonium hydrogen phosphate contains 0.5 mol of P_2O_5.

132 g of diammonium hydrogen phosphate will contain 71 g of P_2O_5.

100 g of diammonium hydrogen phosphate will contain $\frac{71}{132} \times 100 = 53.78\%$.

% of $NH_3 = \frac{2 \times [14.01 + 3 \times 1.01]}{132.06} \times 100 = 25.81\%$

In $(NH_4)_2HPO_4$, the % compositions of elements are —

N = 21.21%

H = 6.870%

O = 48.46%

P = 23.45%

Hence, only statements (a, b) are correct.

23. ***(a, b, d)*** Among the statements, only statement (c) is incorrect while a, b and d are correct.

The correct form of statement 'c' is —

The reaction of potassium with isotopes of chlorine does not follow any of the mentioned laws and is a drawback of the law of constant proportions as no fixed ratio is obtained after a reaction with isotopes.

24. ***(c, d)*** Equal number of molecules are present when moles are same. For the same mass of the molecular weight has to be same for the same number of moles.

Hence, M. wt. of N_2 = M. wt. of CO = 28 g

and M. wt. of N_2O = M. wt. of CO_2 = 44 g

25. ***(b, d)*** Among the given statements, statement b and d are correct while other are incorrect.

The explanation of the statements are given as :

For Compound *A*			
Element	**%**	**Molar ratio**	**Integer ratio**
C	74%	$\frac{74}{12} = 6.16$	$\frac{6.16}{1.23} = 5$
N	17.3%	$\frac{17.3}{14} = 1.23$	$\frac{1.23}{1.23} = 1$
H	8.7%	$\frac{8.7}{1} = 8.7$	$\frac{8.7}{1.23} = 7$

Empirical formula = C_5NH_7

Empirical weight = (12 × 5) + (14 × 1) + (1 × 7) = 81 amu

$$n\text{-factor} = \frac{\text{Molecular weight}}{\text{Empirical weight}} = \frac{162}{81} = 2$$

Molecular formula = 2 × (Empirical formula) = $C_{10}N_2H_{14}$

Thus, the molecular formula is $C_{10}H_{14}N_2$.

For Compound *B*			
Element	**%**	**Molar ratio**	**Integer ratio**
C	66.7	$\frac{66.7}{12} = 5.56$	$\frac{5.56}{1.85} = 3$
H	7.4	$\frac{7.4}{1} = 7.4$	$\frac{7.4}{1.85} = 4$
N	25.9	$\frac{25.9}{14} = 1.85$	$\frac{1.85}{1.85} = 1$

Empirical formula = C_3H_4N

Empirical weight = (12 × 3) + (1 × 4) + (1 × 14)

= 36 + 4 + 14 = 54 amu

$$n\text{-factor} = \frac{\text{Molecular weight}}{\text{Empirical weight}} = \frac{108}{54} = 2$$

Molecular formula = 2 × (Empirical formula)

$$= 2 \times C_3H_4N = C_6H_8N_2$$

26. ***(b, c)*** Among the given statements, only (b) and (c) are correct while other are incorrect.

(a) If empirical formula of compound 3 is P_3Q_4.

We know that,

$$\frac{3 \times M_P}{4 \times M_Q} = \frac{\% \text{ of } P}{\% \text{ of } Q}$$

where M_P and M_Q are the molar masses of P and Q respectively.

$$\frac{3M_P}{4M_Q} = \frac{40}{60} = \frac{2}{3}$$

$$\frac{M_P}{M_Q} = \frac{8}{9}$$

If the empirical formula of compound 2 is P_3Q_5.

$$\frac{3M_P}{5M_Q} = \frac{54.6}{45.4} = \frac{6}{5}$$

$$\frac{M_P}{M_Q} = \frac{6}{5} \times \frac{5}{3} = \frac{2}{1}$$

Since, molecular weight ratio does not come out equal in two compounds. So, statement (a) is incorrect.

(b) If empirical formula of 3 is P_3Q_2.

$$\frac{3M_P}{2M_Q} = \frac{40}{60} = \frac{2}{3}$$

$$\frac{M_P}{M_Q} = \frac{4}{9}$$

If atomic weight of $P = 20$ and that of $Q = 45$

$$\frac{M_P}{M_Q} = \frac{20}{45} = \frac{4}{9}$$

So, statement (b) is correct.

(c) If empirical formula of 2 is PQ,

$$\frac{M_P}{M_Q} = \frac{54.6}{45.4} = \frac{6}{5}$$

and compound '1' is P_5Q_6

$$\frac{5M_P}{6M_Q} = \frac{50}{50} = \frac{1}{1}$$

Putting value of $\frac{M_P}{M_Q} = \frac{6}{5}$

we get $\frac{5}{6} \times \frac{6}{5} = 1$

So, statement (c) is correct.

(d) $M_X = 50$, $M_Y = 25$

If empirical formula of compound '1' is P_2Q.

$$\frac{2M_P}{M_Q} = \frac{50}{50} = 1 \Rightarrow M_P = \frac{M_Q}{2}$$

(M_P is half of M_Q)

But, M_P is shown as double to M_Q i.e., P_2Q.

So, this statement is incorrect.

So, only statement (b) and (c) are correct.

27. ***(7)*** Molecular mass of $Na_2SO_3 \times H_2O = 126 + 18X$

Hence, $\frac{18X}{126 + 18X} = 0.5$ (given)

$$X = 7$$

28. ***(4)*** Weight of Fe in haemoglobin

$$= \frac{0.33}{100} \times 67880 = 224.004 \text{ u}$$

Mass of one Fe atom = 56 M

$\therefore$ Total number of Fe atom $= \frac{224.004}{56} = 4$

29. ***(1)*** In the question, $M_x(N_3)_y$ compound is given where x and $3y$ are the valency of the element N and metal M respectively present in the given compound.

Decomposition reaction for the formation of pure nitrogen in the form of gas is written as below :

$$NaN_3(s) \longrightarrow Na(s) + N_2(g) \quad \ldots\text{(i)}$$

After balancing the equation (i), we get

$$2NaN_3(s) \longrightarrow 2Na(s) + 3N_2(g)$$

Here, sodium azide (NaN_3) decomposes to form pure nitrogen which means the compound that satisfies the molecular formula of $M_x(N_3)_y$ is sodium nitride i.e., NaN_3.

So, the value of x and y is 1 and 1 respectively.

30. ***(5)*** Ammonium phosphate = $(NH_4)_3PO_4$

Number of hydrogen atom in ammonium phosphate = 12

Number of oxygen atom in ammonium phosphate = 4

Number of hydrogen atoms = 3 × Number of oxygen atoms

Number of oxygen atoms $= \frac{15}{3} = 5$ moles of oxygen atoms

31. ***(122)*** 10 mL of 0.2 N HCl + 30 mL of 0.1 N HCl = 40 mL of NaOH (0.61 g of organic acid)

Molar equivalent of HCl = Molar equivalent of NaOH = Molar equivalent of organic acid

$$10 \times 0.2 + 30 \times 0.1 = \frac{0.61}{E} \times 1000$$

$$5 = \frac{0.61 \times 1000}{E} \Rightarrow E = \frac{610}{5} = 122$$

Elemental Practice 1.3

1. ***(a)*** $\underset{2\text{ mol}}{Ca(HCO_3)_2} \xrightarrow{\Delta} \underset{1\text{ mol}}{CaO} + \underset{2\text{ mol}}{2CO_2} + H_2O$

2 mol of 50% pure $Ca(HCO_3)_2$ = 1 mol pure $Ca(HCO_3)_2$

Theoretical yield = 2 mol

Experimental yield = 1 mol

Percentage yield $= \frac{1}{2} \times 100 = 50\%$

2. **(d)** $H_2(g)+\frac{1}{2}O_2(g) \longrightarrow H_2O(l)$

H_2	O_2	H_2O
1 mol	0.5 mol	1 mol
1 vol	0.5 vol	1 vol
30 mL	15 mL	30 mL

O_2 used = 15 mL for 30 mL H_2

O_2 taken = 20 mL

Thus, O_2 left ≡ 20 − 15 = 5 mL

3. **(d)** $CaCO_3 \longrightarrow CaO + CO_2$
100 g → 56 g

$$\% \text{ Ca in } CaCO_3 = \frac{40}{100} \times 100 = 40\%$$

$$\text{and in CaO} = \frac{40}{56} \times 100 = 71\%$$

4. **(d)** $2AgNO_3 + CaCl_2 \longrightarrow 2AgCl + Ca(NO_3)_2$

$2AgNO_3$	$2AgCl$
2 mol	2 mol
(2 × 170) g	(2 × 143.5) g
145 g	$\left(\frac{2 \times 143.5}{2 \times 170} \times 145\right)$ g

Theoretical yield = 122.4 g

Experimental yield = 98.4 g

$$\% \text{ yield} = \frac{98.4}{122.4} \times 100 = 80.39\%$$

5. **(d)** $NH_3 + HCl \longrightarrow NH_4Cl$

NH_3	HCl	NH_4Cl
17 g	36.5 g	53.5 g
17 g	17 g	?

HCl is the limiting reagent

NH_4Cl formed from 17 g

$$HCl = \frac{53.5}{36.5} \times 17 \text{ g} = 24.9 \text{ g}$$

6. **(c)** $Fe_2O_3 + 3CO \longrightarrow 2Fe + 3CO_2$
1 mol, 3 mol, 2 mol

160 g Fe_2O_3 give ⟶ 112 g Fe

480 g Fe_2O_3 give ⟶ 336 g Fe

Theoretical yield = 336 g

Experimental yield = 252 g

$$\% \text{ yield} = \frac{252}{336} \times 100 = 75\%$$

7. **(a)** $2NH_3 \longrightarrow 2NH_4HCO_3 \longrightarrow 2NaHCO_3 \longrightarrow Na_2CO_3$
2 mol, 34 g → 1 mol, 106 g

$$1000 \text{ g } NH_3 \text{ form} = \frac{106}{34} \times 1000 \text{ g } Na_2CO_3$$

$= 3117.659 = 3120$ g $= 3.120$ kg Na_2CO_3

8. **(a)** $2Mg + O_2 \longrightarrow 2MgO$

2Mg	O_2	2MgO
2 mol	1 mol	2 mol
48 g	32 g	80 g

$$10 \text{ g Mg form} = \frac{80}{48} \times 10 \text{ g MgO}$$
$$= 16.67 \text{ g MgO}$$
$$10 \text{ g } O_2 \text{ form} = \frac{80}{32} \times 10 \text{ g MgO}$$
$$= 25.00 \text{ g MgO}$$

Thus, Mg is the limiting reactant and some O_2 remains unreacted

$$10 \text{ g Mg react with} = \frac{32}{48} \times 10 \text{ g } O_2$$
$$= 6.67 \text{ g } O_2$$

O_2 unreacted = 10 − 6.67 = 3.33 g

MgO formed = 16.67 g

9. **(d)** $Zn(s) + 2HCl(aq) \longrightarrow ZnCl_2(aq) + H_2(g)$
1 mol, 2 mol, 1 mol, 1 mol

0.30 mol Zn forms = 0.30 mol H_2

0.52 mol HCl form = 0.26 mol H_2

Thus, HCl is the limiting reactant H_2 formed = 0.26 mol

10. **(a)** Mol of $CuSO_4 \cdot 5H_2O$ ≡ Mol of $CuSO_4$

$$1.595 \text{ g } CuSO_4 \equiv \frac{1.595}{159.5} = 0.01 \text{ mol}$$

1 mol $CuSO_4 \cdot 5H_2O$ ≡ 1 mol $CuSO_4$ ≡ 9 mol (O)

Thus, (O) atoms in 0.01 mol = 0.09

= (0.09 × 16) g

= 1.44 g

11. **(b)** $2KClO_3 \longrightarrow 2KCl + 3O_2$

$4Al + 3O_2 \longrightarrow 2Al_2O_3$

If $KClO_3$ is 100%, then 2 mol of $KClO_3$ form 2 mol of Al_2O_3.

But $KClO_3$ is 50% pure, thus 1 mol $KClO_3$ will form 1 mol Al_2O_3.

12. **(d)** $CaCO_3 \xrightarrow{\Delta} CaO + CO_2$

$CaCO_3$	CO_2
100 g	1 mol
10 g	0.1 mol with 100% yield
	0.075 mol with 75% yield

$CO_2 + C \longrightarrow 2CO$

CO_2	2CO
1 mol	2 mol
0.075	2 × 0.075 mol with 100% yield
	2 × 0.075 × 0.50 mol with 50% yield
	= 0.075 mol
	= 0.075 × 22.4 L at STP
	= 1.68 L at STP

13. **(b)** $CaCO_3 \longrightarrow CaO + CO_2$

$CaCO_3$	CO_2
1 mol	22.4 L at STP
0.25 mol $CaCO_3$	5.6 L at STP

0.25 mol $CaCO_3$ of 100% purity

0.50 mol $CaCO_3$ of 50% purity

0.50 mol $CaCO_3$ = 50 g $CaCO_3$

14. **(b)** $MnO_2 + 4HCl \longrightarrow MnCl_2 + Cl_2 + 2H_2O$
1 mol, 4 mol, 1 mol Cl_2 (22.4 L at STP)

2 mol of MnO_2 form = 44.8 L at STP

4 mol of HCl form = 22.4 L at STP

HCl is the limiting reactant

Cl_2 formed actually = 11.2 L

$$\text{Thus, per cent yield of } Cl_2 = \frac{11.2}{22.4} \times 100 = 50\%$$

15. **(d)** $NH_2CONH_2 + 2NaOH \xrightarrow{\Delta} Na_2CO_3 + 2NH_3$

NH_2CONH_2	$2NaOH$	$2NH_3$
1 mol	2 mol	2 mol
60 g	80 g	34 g
6 g	8 g	3.4 g

Both reactants are in exact quantity and thus NH_3 formed

$= 3.4$ g if 100% yield

$= 3.4 \times \frac{80}{100}$ if 80% yield $= 2.72$ g

16. **(c)** The reaction proceeds as follows

$2SO_2 + O_2 \longrightarrow 2SO_3$

	$2SO_2$	O_2	$2SO_3$
	2 mol	1 mol	2 mol
For SO_2,	10 mol	5 mol	10 mol
For O_2	30 mol	15 mol	30 mol

If 10 mol of SO_2 is taken, O_2 required is 5 mol, forming 10 mol of SO_3.

But, SO_3 actual formed = 8 mol

Thus, percentage yield of SO_3 w.r.t. $SO_2 = \frac{8}{10} \times 100 = 80\%$

17. **(b)** The given reaction is

$NaOH(aq) + HCl(aq) \longrightarrow NaCl + H_2O(l)$
(40 g, 36.5 g, 58.5 g)

NaOH in 100 mL = 0.4 g

HCl in 50 mL = 0.73 g

NaCl formed = 0.42 g

58.5 g NaCl is formed from = 40 g of NaOH

0.42 g NaCl is formed from $= \frac{40}{58.5} \times 0.42 = 0.287$ g NaOH

NaOH unreacted $= 0.4 - 0.287 = 0.113$ g

18. **(d)** The reaction proceeds as follow

$BaCl_2 + K_2SO_4 \longrightarrow BaSO_4 \downarrow + 2KCl$

$BaCl_2$	K_2SO_4
10 × 1	5 × 0.5
10 m mol	2.5 m mol

Here, K_2SO_4 is the limiting reagent.

1 m mol K_2SO_4 = 1 m mol $BaSO_4$

2.5 m mol K_2SO_4 = 2.5 m mol $BaSO_4$

$= \frac{2.5}{1000} = 0.0025$ mol $BaSO_4$

19. **(d)** The reaction takes place as

$N_2(g) + 3H_2(g) \longrightarrow 2NH_3(g)$

According to reaction,

$(14 \times 2 = 28\text{ g})$ of N_2 reacts with 6 g of H_2.

0.028 kg of N_2 reacts with 0.006 kg of H_2.

Thus, 10 kg of N_2 will reacts with

$= \frac{0.006}{0.028} \times 10 = 2.1428$ kg of H_2

But, we have 50 kg of H_2, so, N_2 is the limiting reagent and H_2 is present in excess.

As, 0.028 kg of N_2 forms = 0.034 kg of NH_3

10 kg of N_2 will form $= \frac{0.034}{0.028} \times 10$

$= 12.1428 \approx 12.143$ kg of NH_3

20. **(a)** The given reaction is

$2Fe(NO_3)_3 + 3Na_2CO_3 \longrightarrow Fe_2(CO_3)_3 + 6NaNO_3$
(2.5 mol, 3.6 mol)

(Mole Stoichiometric coefficient)

$\frac{2.5}{2} = 1.25 \qquad \frac{3.6}{3} = 1.2$

Limiting reagent is Na_2CO_3.

So, moles of $NaNO_3$ formed $= 3.6 \times 2 = 7.2$

$\%\text{ yield} = \frac{\text{Experimental yield} \times 100}{\text{Calculated yield}} = \frac{6.5}{7.2} \times 100 = 90.2\%$

21. **(c)** The reaction proceeds as follows

$3Mg(OH)_2 + 2H_3PO_4 \longrightarrow Mg_3(PO_4)_2 + 6H_2O$

$\frac{3 \times 58.3}{2 \times 98} = \frac{100}{W}$

$W = 112$ g

22. **(a, c)** Among the given statements, a and c are correct while statements b and d are incorrect.

Molar mass of $CaCO_3 = 100\text{ g mol}^{-1}$

Molar mass of $Na_2CO_3 = 106\text{ g mol}^{-1}$

$Na_2CO_3 + CaCl_2 \longrightarrow CaCO_3 + 2NaCl$

From stoichiometry,

Moles of $CaCO_3 = \frac{10}{100} = 0.1$ mol

Moles of Na_2CO_3 = moles of $CaCO_3 = \frac{1}{2} \times$ moles of NaCl

Mass of $Na_2CO_3 = 0.1 \times 106 = 10.6$ g

% purity $Na_2CO_3 = \frac{10.6}{21.2} = 100 = 50\%$

Moles of $CaCO_3 = \frac{10}{100} = 0.1$ mol = Moles of Na_2CO_3

Moles of NaCl $= 2 \times 0.1 = 0.2$ mol

23. **(a, b, c, d)** Among the given statements, all statements are correct.

Amount of partially dried sample of clay = 100 grams

Then, amount of silica = 40 grams

Amount of water = 10 grams

(in partially dried sample)

Rest of the component i.e., inert impurities

$= [100 - [40 + 10]] = 50$ g

Total non-water component = 90 g [100 – (40 + 50)]

Original clay sample : Amount of water = 19 grams

Total non-water component = 81 grams

Since, the proportion of non-water component remains same. Therefore, mass of silica $= \frac{40}{81} \times 90$

$= \frac{\text{Amount of silica}}{\text{Non-}H_2O\text{ component in original}} \times$ Non-water component in dried sample

$= 44.4\%$

Mass of inert impurity $= \frac{50}{90} \times 81 = 45.6\%$

24. ***(a, b, d)*** Among the given statements, (a), (b) and (d) are correct while statement (c) is incorrect.

Weight of $CaCO_3 = \frac{0.22 \times 100}{44} = 0.5\,g\ CaCO_3$

Moles of $CaCO_3$ = Moles of Ca $= \left(\frac{0.22}{44}\right) = 0.005$ mol

Weight of Ca $= 0.005 \times 40 = 0.2$ g Ca

Percentage of Ca $= \frac{0.2}{1.0} \times 100 = 20\%$ of Ca

25. ***(b, c)*** Among the given statements, (b) and (c) are correct while (a) and (d) are incorrect.

$$n_{H_2} = \frac{64}{2} = 32 \text{ mol}$$

$$n_{O_2} = \frac{64}{32} = 2 \text{ mol}$$

1 mol of O_2 requires = 2 mol of H_2

2 mol of O_2 requires = 4 mol g H_2

Since, H_2 is present in excess, therefore, O_2 is the limiting reagent,

2 mol of O_2 = 4 moles of $H_2O = 4 \times 18 = 72$ g H_2O

Moles of H_2 left $= 32 - 4 = 28$ mol $= 28 \times 2 = 56$ g H_2

Mixture contains = (72 g H_2O + 56 g H_2)

26. ***(b, c, d)*** Among the given statements (b), (c) and (d) are incorrect while statements (a) is correct. Their correct form are

$$n_{P_4} = \frac{1.24}{31 \times 4} = 0.01\text{ mol}, \ n_{O_2} = \frac{8}{32} = 0.25 \text{ mol}$$

In reaction (i), moles of O_2 required

$$= (0.01 \text{ mol } P_4)\left(\frac{5 \text{ mol } O_2}{\text{mol } P_4}\right)$$

$$= 0.01 \times 5 = 0.05 \text{ mol}$$

Since, there is more O_2 present than required

(a) Therefore, P_4 is the limiting reagent in reaction (i).

(c) [M_w. $P_4O_{10} = 284$]

0.01 mol of P_4 produces = 0.01 mol of P_4O_{10}

$$= (0.01 \text{ mol } P_4)\left(\frac{1 \text{ mol } P_4O_{10}}{\text{mol } P_4O_{10}}\right)\left(\frac{284 \text{ g } P_4O_{10}}{\text{mol } P_4O_{10}}\right)$$

$$= 0.01 \times 284 = 2.84 \text{ g}$$

(d) [*M.w.* of $P_4O_6 = 220$]

Weight of P_4O_6 produced

$$= (0.01 \text{ mol } P_4)\left(\frac{1 \text{ mol } P_4O_6}{\text{mol } P_4O_6}\right)\left(\frac{220 \text{ g } P_4O_6}{\text{mol } P_4O_6}\right)$$

$$= 0.01 \times 220 = 2.2 \text{ g}$$

27. ***(50)*** Moles of NaOH $= 1.0 \times 2.0$ L $= 2.0$ mol

Moles of $H_2SO_4 = 1.0 \times 2$ L $= 2.0$ mol

The reaction proceeds as follow

$$\underset{2 \text{ mol}}{2NaOH} + \underset{1 \text{ mol}}{H_2SO_4} \longrightarrow Na_2SO_4 + 2H_2O$$

2 moles of H_2SO_4 reacts with 1 mol NaOH.

Moles of H_2SO_4 required for neutralisation of 2 mol NaOH = 1 mol H_2SO_4

% purity of $H_2SO_4 = \frac{1 \times 100}{2} = 50\%$

28. ***(8)*** The given reaction is

$$\underset{330 \text{ g}}{Pb(NO_3)_2} + \underset{\substack{2 \times 166 \text{ g} \\ 332 \text{ g}}}{2KI} \longrightarrow \underset{460 \text{ g}}{PbI_2(s)} + 2KNO_3(aq)$$

330 g $Pb(NO_3)_2$ is mixed with 332 g of KI to produce 460 g of PbI_2.

The limiting reagent is KI.

The mass of PbI_2 that will precipitate is —

$$\frac{460}{332} \times 5.63 = 7.80 \approx 8 \text{ g}$$

29. ***(58)*** Theoretically, 244 g Sb gives 340 g Sb_2S_3.

1.73 g of Sb should give $= \frac{340}{244} \times 1.73 = 2.41$ g Sb_2S_3

% yield $= \frac{1.40 \times 100}{2.41} = 58.091 \approx 58\%$

30. ***(5)*** The given reaction is —

$$SO_2Cl_2 + 2H_2O \longrightarrow H_2SO_4 + 2HCl$$

Number of moles of NaOH required for complete neutralisation = 20

Now, as given chemical equation is balanced, so stoichiometric coefficients are equal to their moles respectively.

Number of moles of H^+ = 2 moles [from H_2SO_4] + 2 moles [from HCl] = 4 moles

So, moles of SO_2Cl_2 used

$$= \frac{\text{Moles of NaOH used in neutralisation}}{\text{Moles of acid } [H^+] \text{ formed from 1 mole of } SO_2Cl_2}$$

$$= \frac{20}{4} = 5$$

31. ***(12)*** Given, initial strength of acetic acid = 0.06 N

Final strength = 0.042 N

Volume given = 55 mL

∴ Initial number of moles of $CH_3COOH = 0.06 \times 55 = 3.3$

Final number of moles of $CH_3COOH = 0.042 \times 55 = 2.31$

∴ Number of moles of CH_3COOH adsorbed

$$= 3.3 - 2.31 = 0.99 \text{ m mol}$$

Hence, mass of CH_3COOH absorbed per gram of charcoal

$$= \frac{0.99 \times 60}{5} = \frac{59.4}{5} = 11.9 \approx 12 \text{ mg}$$

Elemental Practice 1.4

1. ***(a)*** Molality $= \frac{\text{Mol of ethanol}}{\text{kg of water}}$

$$= \frac{9.2/46}{18/1000} = 11.11 \text{ mol kg}^{-1}.$$

2. ***(d)*** $372.5 \text{ g KCl} = \frac{372.5}{74.5} \text{mol} = 5 \text{mol}$

$$\text{Molarity} = \frac{\text{Mol}}{\text{Litre}} = \frac{5}{5} = 1.0 \text{ M}$$

3. ***(d)*** $18.25 \text{ g HCl} = \frac{18.25}{36.5} \text{ mol HCl}$

500 g water = 0.500 kg water

$$\text{Molality} = \frac{\text{Mol}}{\text{kg}} = \frac{18.25}{36.5}/0.500 = 1.0 \text{ molal} = 1.0 \text{ m}$$

m(small letter) indicates molality and *M* (capital letter) indicates molarity.

4. ***(c)*** 100 mL of $H_2SO_4 = 100 \times 1.8 \text{ g } H_2SO_4 = 180 \text{ g } H_2SO_4$

100 mL of $H_2O = 100 \times 1.0 \text{ g } H_2O = 100 \text{ g } H_2O$

Total mass = 280 g

% H_2SO_4 by mass of solution, $\frac{180}{280} \times 100 = 64.3\%$

5. ***(b)*** Let $[Ca^{2+}] = x$ M

$\therefore \quad [H^+] = 2x \text{ m} = 0.01 \text{M}$

$\therefore \quad x = \frac{0.01}{2} = 0.005 \text{ M}$

$\therefore \quad [Ca^{2+}] = 0.005 \text{M} = 0.005 \times 40 \text{ g L}^{-1} = 0.2 \text{ g L}^{-1}$

1000 mL of water has $Ca^{2+} = 0.2$ g.

10^6 mL (ppm) of water has $Ca^{2+} = \frac{0.2}{1000} \times 10^6$

$= 200$ ppm

6. ***(d)*** 6.02×10^{23} urea molecules = 1 mol urea

6.02×10^{20} urea molecules = 0.001 mol urea

$$\text{Molarity} = \frac{\text{Mole}}{\text{Volume (in L)}} = \frac{0.001}{0.01} = 0.10 \text{ M.}$$

7. ***(a)*** $M_2CO_3 + 2HCl \longrightarrow MCl_2 + H_2O + CO_2$

Let, unused acid = V mL

V mL of 1N HCl ≡ 100 mL 0.5 N NaOH

$\therefore \quad V \times 1 = 100 \times 0.5$

$\therefore \quad V = 50$ mL

Used HCl = 150 − 50 = 100 mL

In neutralisation reaction,

Equivalent of acid ≡ Equivalent of base

Equivalent mass of $M_2CO_3 \equiv 2H^+ = \frac{\text{Molar mass}}{2}$

$$= \frac{2M + 60}{2} = (M + 30)$$

$m\, N \times V$ (mL) = milliequivalents

Equivalent of acid $= \frac{100 \times 1}{1000} = 0.1$

Equivalent base $= \frac{5.3}{M + 30}$

$\therefore \quad \frac{5.3}{M + 30} = 0.1$

$\therefore \quad M = 23$

8. ***(b)*** $\underset{1 \text{ mol}}{N_2} + \underset{4 \text{ mol}}{3H_2} \longrightarrow 2NH_3$

$\underset{1}{NH_3} + \underset{1}{HCl} \longrightarrow NH_4Cl$

$\therefore$ NH_3 formed = 1 mol

N_2 reacted = 0.5 mol

H_2 reacted = 1.5 mol

N_2 unreacted = 1 − 0.5 = 0.5 mol

H_2 unreacted = 4 − 1.5 = 2.5 mol

NH_3 formed = 1 mol

But, NH_3 gets dissolved in H_2O leaving N_2 and H_2.

$\therefore \quad x_{H_2} = \frac{2.5}{3.0} = \frac{5}{6}$

9. ***(b)*** As we know,

$$\text{Molality} = \frac{1000 \times \text{Weight of solute}}{M_w \times \text{Weight of solvent}}$$

$$10 = \frac{1000 \times W}{98 \times 920}$$

$$W = \frac{10 \times 98 \times 920}{1000}$$

$= 901.6 \text{ g L}^{-1} = 90.16$ g per 100 mL

10. ***(d)*** A is false but R is true.

The correct form of A is —

As, volume of solution changes by 20%, so it becomes

$$= 1 + \frac{20}{100} = 1.2 \text{ L}$$

∴ Molarity of resulting solution

$$= \frac{\text{Moles of solute}}{\text{Total volume of solution (L)}} \approx 0.8 \text{ M}$$

Change in molarity = 1 − 0.8 = 0.2 M

% Change in molarity $= \frac{0.2}{1} \times 100 = 20\%$

11. ***(b)*** Milli. equivalent of $H_2SO_4 = 100 \times 0.2 \times 2 = 40$

Milli. equivalent of NaOH = 100 × 0.2 × 1 = 20

Milli. equivalent of H_2SO_4 left = 40 − 20 = 20

Total volume = 100 + 100 = 200 mL

Normality of solution $= \frac{20 \text{ m Eq.}}{200 \text{ mL}} \approx 0.1 \text{ N}$

12. ***(a)*** Molarity of $BaCO_3$ solution $= \frac{3.65}{197} \times \frac{1000}{350} = 0.05$ M

As we know, $M_1V_1 = M_2V_2$

$0.05 \times 10 = M_2 \times 1000$

$$M_2 = \frac{0.05 \times 10}{1000} = 0.0005 \text{ M}$$

13. ***(d)*** As we know,

$N_1V_1 \; (H_2SO_4) = N_2V_2$ (NaOH)

$$N_1 = \frac{1}{10} \times \frac{36}{18} = 0.2$$

Strength = Normality × Equivalent weight

$= 0.2 \times 49 = 9.8$ g/L

14. ***(d)*** 102.8% oleum means that 100 g of this oleum when reacts with water, 102.8 g H_2SO_4 is formed by following reaction.

$$H_2SO_4 + SO_3 + H_2O \longrightarrow 2H_2SO_4$$

Mole of free SO_3 = Moles of H_2O added in the sample.

$\because$ Moles of H_2O added $= \dfrac{102.8 - 100}{18} \approx 0.16$

$\therefore$ Mass of SO_3 in 100 g oleum $= 0.16 \times 80 = 12.80$ g

$\therefore$ % of free $SO_3 = \dfrac{12.80}{100} \times 100\% = 12.80\%$

15. ***(c)*** Reaction of $KMnO_4$ in acidic solution

$$MnO_4^- + 8H^+ + 5e^- \longrightarrow Mn^{2+} + 4H_2O$$

Here, Mn(VII) is reduced to Mn(II) i.e. the reaction proceeds by transfer of $5e^-$. So, the valence factor is 5.

Molecular mass of $KMnO_4 = 158 \text{ g mol}^{-1}$

$$\text{Equivalent mass} = \frac{158}{5} = 31.6$$

$$\text{Normality } (N) = \frac{1.58 \times 1000}{31.5 \times 50} = 1\text{N}$$

16. ***(c, d)*** Mole fraction of ethanol $(C_2H_5OH) = 0.25 = \dfrac{n_1}{n_1 + n_2}$

Mole fraction of water $H_2O = 0.75 = \dfrac{n_2}{n_1 + n_2}$

$\therefore$ $$\frac{n_1}{n_2} = \frac{0.25}{0.75} = \frac{1}{3}$$

$C_2H_5OH = n_1 = 1 \text{ mole} = 46$ g

$H_2O = n_2 = 3 \text{ moles} = 54$ g

Total mass $= 46 + 54 = 100$ g

Thus, it is 46% ethanol by weight of solution and 54% water by weight of solution.

17. ***(b, c, d)*** Among the given statements, all are correct except statement (a).

m moles of HCl $\Rightarrow 20 \times 6 = 120$

$\Rightarrow$ 120 m mol $H^{\oplus}$ + 120 m mol $Cl^{\ominus}$

m moles of $Ba(OH)_2 \Rightarrow 50 \times 2 = 100 \Rightarrow$ 100 m mol

Ba^{2+} + 200 m mol $\overset{\ominus}{O}H$

$$H^{\oplus} + \overset{\ominus}{O}H \longrightarrow H_2O$$

Total volume $= 20 + 50 + 30 = 100$ mL

$\therefore$ $$[\overset{\ominus}{O}H] = \frac{(200 - 120) \text{ m mol}}{100 \text{ mL}} = 0.8 \text{M}$$

$$[Cl^{\ominus}] = \frac{120 \text{ m mol}}{100 \text{ mL}} = 1.2 \text{ M}$$

$$[Ba^{2+}] = \frac{100 \text{ m mol}}{100 \text{ mL}} = 1.0 \text{ M}$$

m moles of $\overset{\ominus}{O}H$ left $= 200 - 120 = 80$ m mol

18. ***(a, c)*** Among the given statements, only a and c are correct while b and d are incorrect.

	Silica	H_2O	Impurities
% in original clay ⇒	40	18	100 − (40 + 18) = 42
% after partial drying ⇒	*a*	10	100 − (*a* + 10) = 90 − *a*

On heating, only water evaporates from clay, whereas silica and impurities are left as it is. Therefore, % ratio of silica and impurities remains unchanged, i.e.,

$$\frac{40}{a} = \frac{42}{90 - a}$$

$\therefore$ $$a = 43.90\%$$

% of impurities after partial drying

$$= (90 - a) = (90 - 43.90) = 46.1\%$$

Mass of H_2O evaporated $= (18 - 10) = 8$ g

19. ***(a, b)*** Among the given statements, only a and b are correct while others are incorrect.

$$\underset{\begin{pmatrix}200 \times 0.1 \\ = 20 \text{ m mol}\end{pmatrix}}{KNO_3} + \underset{\begin{pmatrix}400 \times 0.2 \\ = 80 \text{ m mol}\end{pmatrix}}{HCl} + \underset{\begin{pmatrix}400 \times 0.3 \\ = 120 \text{ m mol}\end{pmatrix}}{H_2SO_4}$$

Total volume $= 200 + 400 + 400 = 1000$ mL

$$M_{K^{\oplus}} = \frac{20}{1000} = 0.02 \text{ M}$$

$$M_{SO_4^{2-}} = \frac{120}{1000} = 0.12 \text{ M}$$

$$M_{H^{\oplus}} = \frac{80 + 2 \times 120}{1000} = 0.32 \text{ M}$$

$$M_{NO_3^{\ominus}} = \frac{20}{1000} = 0.02 \text{ M}$$

$$M_{Cl^{\ominus}} = \frac{80}{1000} = 0.08 \text{ M}$$

20. ***(b, d)*** Among the given statements, only b and d are correct while a and c are incorrect.

100 mL of 1 M H_2SO_4 + 100 ml (98%, d = 0.1) H_2SO_4

$\Rightarrow 100 \times 1\text{M} + 100 \text{ mL} \times \left(\dfrac{98 \times 10 \times 0.1}{98}\right)$

$\Rightarrow 100 \times 1\text{M} + 100 \times 1\text{M}$

$\therefore$ $[H_2SO_4] = \dfrac{100 \times 1 + 100 \times 1}{200 \text{ mL}} = 1\text{M} = 98 \text{ g}/1000 \text{ mL}$

Mass of $H_2SO_4 = \dfrac{98 \text{ g} \times 200 \text{ mL}}{1000 \text{ mL}} = 19.6$ g

Concentration of each component becomes half of the initial value.

21. ***(a, c, d)*** Among the given solutions, a, c and d contains same molar concentration.

The molecular weight of KI, $(NH_4)_2SO_4$, $CuSO_4 \cdot 5H_2O$ and Al^{3+} are 166, 132, 250 and 27 g/mol respectively.

(a) $M = \dfrac{166 \times 1000}{166 \times 1000} = 1.0$ M

(b) $M = \dfrac{33 \times 1000}{132 \times 200} = 1.25$ M

(c) $M = \frac{25 \times 1000}{250 \times 100} = 1.0\text{ M}$

(d) $M = \frac{27 \times 10^{-3} \times 1000}{27 \times 1} = 1.0\text{ M}$

22. ***(420)*** Molarity of given sulphuric acid

$$= \frac{98}{98} \times \frac{1}{100} \times 1000 = 10 \text{ mol dm}^{-3}$$

As we know, $M_1V_1 = M_2V_2$

$$V_1 = \frac{0.7 \times 6}{10} = 0.42\text{ dm}^3$$

$$= 420\text{ mL}$$

23. ***(258)*** $10\%\left(\frac{V}{V}\right) = \frac{\text{Volume of solute}}{\text{Volume of solution}} \times 100$

$$10 = \frac{V_{Br_2}}{V_{Br_2} + V_{C_7H_8}} \times 100 \quad \ldots(i)$$

$\because$ $\text{Density} = \frac{\text{Mass}}{\text{Volume}}$

Mass of solute $= 3.2 \times V_{Br_2}$

Moles of solute $= 3.2 \times \frac{V_{Br_2}}{160}$

Mass of solvent $= 0.86 \times V_{C_7H_8} \times 10^{-3}$ kg

From equation (i), we get

$$\frac{V_{Br_2} + V_{C_7H_8}}{V_{Br_2}} = 10$$

$$\frac{V_{C_7H_8}}{V_{Br_2}} = 9$$

$$\text{Molality} = \frac{\frac{3.2 \times V_{Br_2}}{160}}{0.86 \times V_{C_7H_8} \times 10^{-3}}$$

$$= \frac{3.72 \times 10^3}{9 \times 160} = 2.58 = 258 \times 10^{-2}\text{ m}$$

24. ***(40)*** As we know,

$$N_1V_1 + N_2V_2 + N_3V_3 = N_4V_4$$

$$(V_4 = V_1 + V_2 + V_3 + V_4)$$

or $V_4 = \text{final volume} = 1\text{ L} = 1000\text{ mL}$

$$5 \times N + 20 \times \frac{N}{2} + 30 \times \frac{N}{3} = N_4 \times 1000$$

$\therefore$ $N_4 = \frac{N}{40}$

Thus, the value of x is 40.

25. ***(2537)*** $CH_3CH_2CH_3 + 5O_2 \longrightarrow 3CO_2 + 4H_2O$

	$CH_3CH_2CH_3$	O_2	CO_2	H_2O
	1	: 5	3	: 4
at $t = 0$	$\frac{100}{44} = 2.27$ mole	31.25 mol	0	0
at $t = t$	0	$31.25 - (5 \times 2.27)$ = 19.90 mol	3×2.27 = 6.81 mol	4×2.27 = 9.08 mol

When reaction is completed then 19.90 moles of O_2, 6.81 moles of CO_2 and 9.08 moles of steam are left in the flask.

$$\text{Mole fraction of } H_2O = \frac{\text{Moles of } H_2O}{\text{Total number of moles}}$$

$$= \frac{9.08}{19.90 + 6.81 + 9.08} = \frac{9.08}{35.79}$$

$$= 0.2537 = 2537 \times 10^{-4}$$

So, the value of x is 2537.

26. ***(35)*** Moles of nitrous acid = Volume (in L) × Molarity

$$= 750 \times 0.5 \times 10^{-3}$$

$$= 375 \times 10^{-3}$$

$$= 0.375 \text{ moles}$$

Weight of HNO_2 (nitrous acid)

= Number of moles × Molar mass

$= 0.375 \times 47$

$= 17.625$ g

Amount of HNO_2 remaining in the solution

$= 17.625 - 11.5$

$= 6.125$ g

$$\text{Molarity} = \frac{6.125}{47} \times \frac{1000}{375} = 0.3475$$

$$= 34.75 \times 10^{-2} \approx 35 \times 10^{-2}\text{ M}$$

Hence, the value of x is 35.

27. ***(34)*** Total mass of sugar in the given mixture is —

$0.20 \times 150 + 0.40 \times 350 = 170$

Hence, total mass of solution = 150 + 350

= 500 g

So, mass percentage of sugar $= \frac{170}{500} \times 100$

= 34%

Practice Element 01 : Target JEE Main

1. ***(d)*** $2Al + 6HCl \longrightarrow 2AlCl_3 + 3H_2$

$$1 \text{ mol Al} \equiv \frac{3}{2} \text{ mol } H_2$$

$\therefore$ Ratio = 2 : 3

2. ***(b)*** $2Ag \equiv Ag_2S$

(2×108) g $\equiv$ 248 g

216 g Ag is obtained from = 248 g Ag_2S (100% pure)

1g is obtained from

$= \frac{248}{216} \times 1$ g Ag_2S (100% pure)

$= \frac{248}{216} \times \frac{100}{1.34}$ g Ag_2S (1.34% pure) = 85.7 g

3. ***(c)*** 100 g solution has = 40 g urea

60 g H_2O has = 40 g urea

$$\therefore \text{ Molality} = \frac{\text{Moles of urea}}{\text{Weight of } H_2O \text{ (in kg)}} = \frac{40/60}{0.060} = 11.11$$

4. ***(a)*** Molality = 11.11 mol kg^{-1}
Thus, solute = 11.11 mol

Solvent (H_2O) = 1 kg = 1000 g = $\frac{1000}{18}$ mol

$$\therefore \quad \chi_{solute} = \frac{\text{Mol of solute}}{\text{Total mol}}$$

$$= \frac{11.11}{11.11 + \left(\frac{1000}{18}\right)} = \frac{11.11}{66.66} = \frac{1}{6} \approx 0.17$$

5. ***(c)*** 1.2 mol ethanol (C_2H_5OH) = 1.2 × 46 g

Since, $\frac{\text{Mass}}{\text{Volume}}$ = Density

$$\therefore \text{ Volume} = \frac{\text{Mass}}{\text{Density}} = \frac{1.2 \times 46 \text{ g}}{0.789 \text{ g mL}^{-1}} \approx 70.0 \text{ mL}$$

6. ***(a)*** Chlorides differ in composition due to different valencies of phosphorus; valency of chloride hence its equivalent mass remains constant.

7. ***(a)*** H_2SO_4 = 0 . 0755 mol = 0.0755 × 98 g = 7.4 g

$$\text{Density} = \frac{\text{Mass}}{\text{Volume}}$$

$$\therefore \text{ Volume} = \frac{\text{Mass}}{\text{Density}} = \frac{7.4}{1.85} = 4 \text{ mL}$$

8. ***(d)*** $Na_2SO_4 \equiv 2Na^+$

$NaCl \equiv Na^+$

$$\therefore \quad Na^+ \text{ (mixture)} = \frac{M_1V_1 + M_2V_2}{V_1 + V_2}$$

$$= \frac{0.12 \times 30 + 0.15 \times 2 \times 70}{100} = 0.246 \text{ M}$$

9. ***(a)*** 0.200 g of oxygen ≡ 3.17 g halogen

$$\therefore \quad 8 \text{ g of oxygen} \equiv \frac{3.170}{0.200} \times 8.00 = 126.8 \approx 127 \text{ g}$$

10. ***(a)*** Glucose present in 400 mL of 9% glucose solution

$$= \frac{400 \times 9}{100} \text{ g} = \frac{400 \times 9}{100 \times 180} \text{ mol per day}$$

$$= \frac{400 \times 9}{100 \times 180 \times 24} \text{ mol per hour}$$

$$= 5.0 \times 10^{21} \text{ molecules}$$

11. ***(b)*** 1 L ethanol = 1000 mL ethanol

= 1000 × 0.789 g ethanol = 0.789 kg

5 g CH_3COOH = $\frac{5}{60}$ mol CH_3COOH

$$\therefore \quad \text{Molality} = \frac{\text{Mol of } CH_3COOH}{\text{Weight of } CH_3CH_2OH} = \frac{5/60}{0.789} = 0.1056 \text{ molal}$$

12. ***(b)*** By Avogadro's law, equal mol occupy equal volumes.
O_2 = 20% by volume = 20% by mol
Thus, N_2 = 80% of volume = 80% by mol
∴ Total mol = 20 + 80 = 100

$$X_{N_2} = \frac{80}{100} = 0.80$$

13. ***(a)*** Solute = 10 g = $\frac{10}{10}$ mol

Solvent = 100 g = $\frac{100}{1}$ mol

Total mol = 101

$$X_{Solute} = \frac{1}{101} = 9.9 \times 10^{-3}$$

14. ***(a)*** Solute present in 800 g of 40%

X = 320 g

Solute remained after cooling = 320 − 100 = 220 g

Mass of solution = (800 − 100) = 700 g

Thus, % of X = $\frac{220}{700} \times 100$ = 31.4%

15. ***(b)*** $Fe_2(SO_4)_3$ = 40.0 g = $\frac{40.0}{400}$ = 0.1 mol

Fe^{3+} = 0.2 mol in 0.1 dm^3

$$= \frac{0.2}{0.1} = 2 \text{ M } Fe^{3+}$$

16. ***(b)*** $\underset{2\text{ mol}}{2A} + \underset{1\text{ mol}}{B} \longrightarrow \underset{1\text{ mol}}{C}$

8 mol of A will form = 4 mol of C
5 mol of B will form = 5 mol of C
Thus, A is the limiting reactant
C formed = 4 mol

17. ***(d)*** Equivalent of acid ≡ Equivalent of base

Equivalent of base = 100 mL of 0.25 N = $\frac{100 \times 0.25}{1000}$ = 0.025

Equivalent of an acid = 0.025 = $\frac{1.575}{E}$

$$\therefore \quad \frac{1.575}{E} = 0.025$$

$$\therefore \quad E = 63 \text{ g equiv}^{-1}$$

Molar mass = Basicity × E = 2 × 63 = 126 g mol^{-1}

18. ***(a)*** $\underset{\substack{2\text{ mol}\\0.02\text{ mol}}}{2KClO_3} \longrightarrow 2KCl + \underset{\substack{3\text{ mol}\\0.03\text{ mol}}}{3O_2}$

If $KClO_3$ is 100% pure = 0.02 mol

$KClO_3$ taken = 5.0 g = $\frac{5}{122.5}$ mol = 0.0408 mol

Thus, per cent purity of $KClO_3$ = $\frac{0.02 \times 100}{0.0408}$ = 49%

19. ***(c)*** The reaction proceeds as follow —

$Na_2CO_3 + 2HCl \longrightarrow 2NaCl + H_2O + CO_2$

At the equivalent point m mole of HCl
= 2 × m mol of Na_2CO_3

$$50 \times M = 2 \times \frac{0.412}{106} \times 1000$$

[Molecular weight of Na_2CO_3 = 106]

$$M = \frac{2 \times 0.412}{106 \times 50} \times 1000 \approx 0.16 \text{ M}$$

20. ***(d)*** As we know,

$M_1V_1 = M_2V_2$ $\left[M = \dfrac{\%\text{ by weight} \times 10 \times d}{MW_2}\right]$

$V_1 \times \dfrac{90 \times 10 \times 1.8}{98} = 0.3 \times 1\,L$

$V_1 = \dfrac{98 \times 0.3 \times 1}{90 \times 10 \times 1.8} = \dfrac{29.4}{1620} = 0.01814\,L = 18.14\,mL$

21. ***(9)*** Molar mass of $Al_2(SO_4)_3 \cdot xH_2O = (342 + 18x)$

$\%\,Al = 8.2 = \dfrac{54 \times 100}{(342 + 18x)}$

$\therefore\quad x \approx 18$

$\therefore\quad 0.5x = 9$

22. ***(5)*** $\underset{\substack{(159.5+18x)\\2.495\,g}}{CuSO_4 \cdot x\,H_2O} \longrightarrow \underset{\substack{18x\\0.05\,mol = (0.05 \times 18)\,g = 0.9\,g}}{xH_2O}$

$\therefore\quad \dfrac{159.5 + 18x}{2.495} = \dfrac{18x}{0.9}$

$\therefore\quad x = 5$

23. ***(6)*** '147 %' oleum contains 47 g H_2O in 100 g oleum. Thus, total mass is 147 g .

H_2SO_4 in 5 g oleum $= \dfrac{147 \times 5}{100} = 7.35\,g$

Equivalent of H_2SO_4 in 7.35 g $= \dfrac{7.35}{49} = 0.15$

Equivalent of NaOH used $= 25 \times \dfrac{x}{1000}$

$\therefore\quad \dfrac{25x}{1000} = 0.15$

$x = 6$

24. ***(5)*** Ga taken $= 1.25\,g = \dfrac{1.25}{70} \approx 0.018\,mol$

Ga_xO_y formed $= 1.68\,g$

Oxygen combined $= 0.43\,g$

$= \dfrac{0.43}{16} \approx 0.027\,mol$

Ratio of $\dfrac{\text{Gallium}}{\text{Oxygen}} = \dfrac{x}{y} = \dfrac{0.018}{0.027} = \dfrac{2}{3}$

$\therefore\quad x + y = 5$

25. ***(2)*** Urea solution $= 4.0\,mol\,L^{-1}$ (Molarity)

$= 240$ g in 1000 mL solution

Let density $= d\ g\,mL^{-1} = 240$ g in $1000\,d$ g solution

$\therefore$ Water present $= (1000\,d - 240)\,g$

Molality $= \dfrac{\text{Mol of solute}}{\text{kg of water}}$

$2.273 = \dfrac{4 \times 10^{-3}}{(1000\,d - 240)}$

$\therefore\quad d \approx 2.0\ g\,mL^{-1}$

26. ***(5)*** $Si_xH_y + \left(x + \dfrac{y}{4}\right)O_2 \longrightarrow x\,SiO_2 + \dfrac{y}{2}H_2O$

Si_xH_y taken $= 6.20\,g = \dfrac{6.20}{(30x + y)}$ mol

SiO_2 formed $= 11.64\,g = \left(\dfrac{11.64}{62}\right)$ mol

H_2O formed $= 6.98\,g = \dfrac{6.98}{18}$ mol

1 mol Si_xH_y forms $SiO_2 = x$ mol

$\therefore\quad \dfrac{6.20}{(30x + y)}(x) = \dfrac{11.64}{62}$

1 mol Si_xH_y forms $H_2O = \dfrac{y}{2}$ mol

$\therefore\quad \dfrac{6.20}{(30x + y)}\left(\dfrac{y}{2}\right) = \dfrac{6.98}{18}$

$\therefore\quad \dfrac{(x)}{\left(\dfrac{y}{2}\right)} = \dfrac{11.64}{62} / \dfrac{6.98}{18} \Rightarrow \dfrac{x}{y} \approx 0.25 = \dfrac{1}{4}$

$\therefore\quad x + y = 1 + 4 = 5$

27. ***(2)*** Volume of HCl $= V$ mL

Mass of HCl $= V \times d = 1.825V$

$CaCO_3 = 10$ g of 50% purity $= 5$ g of 100% purity

$\underset{\substack{100\,g\\5g}}{CaCO_3} + \underset{\substack{73\,g\\\left(\frac{73}{100} \times 5\right)g}}{2HCl} \longrightarrow CaCl_2 + H_2O + CO_2$

$\dfrac{73 \times 5}{100} = 1.825V \Rightarrow V = \dfrac{73 \times 5}{1.825 \times 100} = 2\,mL$

28. ***(2)*** $2KClO_3 \longrightarrow 2KCl + 3O_2$

O_2 formed $= 2$ mol with 66.67% yield

$= \dfrac{2 \times 100}{66.67}$ mol if 100% yield $= 3$ mol if 100% yield

As per reaction $KClO_3$ required $= 2$ mol

29. ***(4)*** $\underset{\substack{1\,mol\\16\,g}}{CH_4} + 2O_2 \longrightarrow CO_2 + \underset{\substack{2\,mol\\2N_0\text{ molecules}}}{2H_2O}$

$2 \times 6.02 \times 10^{23}$ water molecules are formed from $= 16\,g\,CH_4$

3.01×10^{23} water molecules are from $= 4\,g\,CH_4$

30. ***(2)*** $\underset{\substack{2\,mol\\2(M+35.5x)\,g}}{2MCl_x} + xK_2SO_4 \longrightarrow 2xKCl + \underset{\substack{1\,mol\\(2M+96x)\,g}}{M_2(SO_4)_x}$

Mol of $MCl_x = 2 \times$ mol of $M_2(SO_4)_3$

$\dfrac{20.8}{(M + 35.5x)} = 2\dfrac{(23.3)}{2M + 96x}$

$\dfrac{20.8}{(137 + 35.5x)} = \dfrac{23.3}{(137 + 48x)}$

$\therefore\quad \dfrac{(137 + 48x)}{(137 + 35.5x)} = \dfrac{23.3}{20.8}$

$\therefore\quad x = 2$

Check Through PYQs : JEE Main

1. ***(a)*** The number of significant figures of the given numbers are as follows.

0.00253	3
1.0003	5
15.0	3
163	3

Thus, (A), (C) and (D) have same number of significant figures.

2. ***(b)*** Answer should be reported with 3 significant figures.

$$\frac{0.02858 \times 0.112}{0.5702} = 0.00\underbrace{561}_{\text{3 significant figures}}$$

3. ***(3)*** Total number of significant figure = 3.

Here, $0.00\,34\,0$ — 0.00: Leading zero; 34: Non-zero digits; 0: Trailing zero

Non-zero digits and trailing zero are considered as significant figures.

4. ***(8)*** Zero's between 5 and 2 are all significant. Trailing zeroes after decimal are also significant.

50000.020×10^{-3}

↑

(Number of significant figures = 8)

5. ***(a)*** Let mass of compound be 100 g

	Mass (g)	Mole	Molar ratio
C	54.2	$\frac{54.2}{12} = 4.52$	2
H	9.2	$\frac{9.2}{1} = 9.2$	4
O	36.6	$\frac{36.6}{16} = 2.3$	4

Empirical formula = C_2H_4O

$\Rightarrow$ $MF = n(EF)$

$$n = \frac{\text{MF mass}}{\text{EF mass}}$$

$$MF = 3(C_2H_4O) = C_6H_{12}O_3$$

6. ***(179)*** Number of moles of CO_2 removed

$$= \frac{10^{21}}{6 \times 10^{23}} = 0.167 \times 10^{-2} \text{ mol}$$

Number of moles of CO_2 left = 2.4×10^{-3} mol

Total moles = $2.4 \times 10^{-3} + 1.67 \times 10^{-3} = 4.07 \times 10^{-3}$ mol

Mass of CO_2 present = $4.07 \times 44 \times 10^{-3}$

$= 179 \times 10^{-3}$ g = 179 mg

7. ***(d)*** Statement given in option (d) is incorrect. Its correct form is as follows: according to Dalton's atomic theory, compounds are formed when atoms of different elements combine in fixed ratio.

8. ***(c)*** The reaction involved are

$$CaCO_3(s) \xrightarrow{\Delta} CaO(s) + CO_2(g)$$

$$MgCO_3(s) \xrightarrow{\Delta} MgO(s) + CO_2(g)$$

Let the weight of $CaCO_3$ be x g.

$\therefore$ Weight of $MgCO_3$ = $(2.21 - x)$ g

Moles of $CaCO_3$ decomposed = Moles of CaO formed

$$\frac{x}{100} = \text{Moles of CaO formed}$$

$\therefore$ Weight of CaO formed = $\frac{x}{100} \times 56$

Moles of $MgCO_3$ decomposed = Moles of MgO formed

$$\frac{2.21 - x}{84} = \text{Mole of MgO formed}$$

$\therefore$ Weight of MgO formed = $\frac{2.21 - x}{84} \times 40$

$$\frac{2.21 - x}{84} \times 40 + \frac{x}{100} \times 56 = 1.152$$

$\therefore$ $x = 1.1886 \text{ g} \approx 1.187$ g

= Weight of $CaCO_3$

Weight of $MgCO_3$ = 1.0214 g ≈ 1.023 g

Hence, option (c) is correct.

9. ***(11)*** Given, thickness (d) = 0.05 cm

Area of plate (A) = 0.05 m^2

Volume of silver coating

$$V = A \times d = 0.05 \times 0.05 \times 10000 = 25 \text{ cm}^3$$

Mass of silver deposited = 25×7.9 g

Mole of Ag atoms = $\frac{25 \times 7.9}{108}$

Number of silver atoms = $\frac{25 \times 7.9}{108} \times N_A$

$$= \frac{25 \times 7.9}{108} \times 6.023 \times 10^{23}$$

$$= 11.01 \times 10^{23} \approx 11 \times 10^{23}$$

Hence, the number of Ag atoms are 11×10^{23}.

10. ***(b)*** Weight of metal chloride at STP is

$$= \frac{0.57}{100} \times 22400 = 127.68$$

Weight or mass of Cl in metal chloride = 127.68×0.55

= 70.224

Now, number of moles of Cl

$$= \frac{\text{Mass of Cl}}{\text{Molecular mass of Cl}}$$

$$= \frac{70.224}{35.5} \approx 2$$

Thus, the molecular formula is MCl_2.

11. ***(b)*** The correct match is A-II, B-IV, C-I, D-III.

(A) 16 g of CH_4 = 1 mole CH_4 contains $10 \times 6.02 \times 10^{23}$ electrons

$= 60.2 \times 10^{23}$

(B) 1 g H_2 = 0.5 mole H_2 gas occupy 1 mole contains = 22.7 L

$\therefore$ 0.5 mole contains 11.35 (approx) litre volume at STP.

(C) 1 mole of $N_2(g)$ = 28 g

(D) Mole of SO_2 = 64 g

0.5 mole of SO_2 = 32 g

12. ***(d)*** Number of moles $(n) = \frac{\text{Given volume}}{\text{Volume at STP}}$

$\therefore$ Number of moles of $O_2 = \frac{2.8375}{22.7} = 0.125$

Now, number of molecules = Moles × Avagadro's number

$= 0.125N_A = (0.125) \times (6.022 \times 10^{23})$

$= 7.527 \times 10^{22}$

13. ***(b)*** Suppose the mole ratio of ^{35}Cl be x and that of ^{37}Cl be y.

Average molar mass $= \frac{n_1m_1 + n_2m_2}{n_2 + n_2}$

$35.5 = \frac{35x + 37y}{x + y} \Rightarrow 1.5y = -0.5x$

$\Rightarrow \quad \frac{x}{y} = \frac{3}{1}$

14. ***(2)*** Balanced reaction

$$Fe_3O_4 + 4CO \longrightarrow 4CO + 3Fe$$

Given mass of $Fe_3O_4 = 2.32 \times 10^3$ kg

Mol. mass of $Fe_3O_4 = 232$ g $= 0.232$ kg

Moles of $Fe_3O_4 = \frac{2.32 \times 10^3}{0.232} = 10^4$ mol

Given mass of CO $= 2.8 \times 10^3$ kg

Mol. mass of CO = 28 g = 0.028 kg

Moles of CO $= 10^5$ mol

According to balanced reaction

1 mol Fe_3O_4 requires 4 mol CO

$\therefore$ 10^4 mol Fe_3O_4 requires 4×10^4 mol CO

$\therefore$ CO is in excess

1 mol Fe_3O_4 gives 3 mol Fe

10^4 mol Fe_3O_4 will gives 3×10^4 mol Fe

$\therefore$ Mass of Fe formed $= 3 \times 10^4 \times \frac{56}{1000} = 1680$ kg

15. ***(10)***

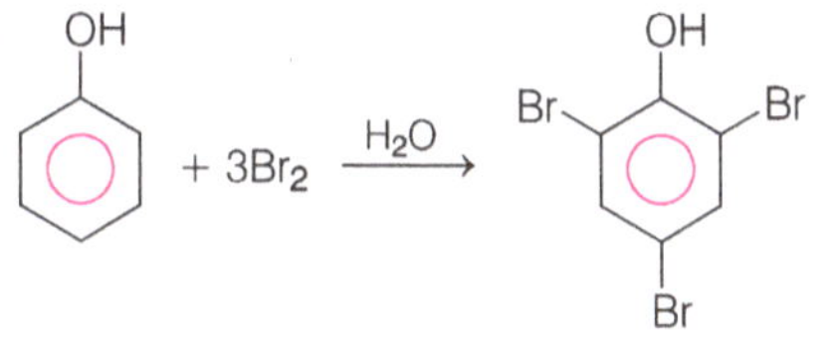

3 moles of Br_2 will be required to react with 1 mole phenol.

Br_2 requird for 2 g phenol $= \frac{2}{94} \times 160 \times 3$

$= 10.2$ g

16. ***(24)*** $3PbCl_2 + 2(NH_4)_3PO_4 \longrightarrow Pb_3(PO_4)_2 + 6NH_4Cl$

Limiting reagent is $PbCl_2$.

m mol of $Pb_3 \cdot (PO_4)_2$ formed $= \frac{\text{m mol of } PbCl_2 \text{ react}}{3}$

$= \frac{72 \text{ m mol}^{-1}}{3} = 24$ mmol

Hence, the amount of $Pb_3(PO_4)_2$ formed is 24 mmol.

17. ***(4)*** $Zn + 2HCl \longrightarrow ZnCl_2 + H_2\uparrow$

Amount of Zn = 11.5 g

Number of moles of Zn $= \frac{11.5}{65.4} = 0.176$

Number of moles of H_2 = Number of moles of Zn

Volume of H_2 liberated $= 0.176 \times 22.7$ L $= 3.99$ L ≈ 4 L

18. ***(d)*** Both complexes have equal volume and half concentration due to mixing.

$\underset{0.01\text{ M}}{[Co(NH_3)_5SO_4]Br}$

$\underset{0.01\text{ M}}{[Co(NH_3)_5Br]SO_4}$

(I) $\underset{\left(\frac{0.02}{2}\right)\text{mol}}{[Co(NH_3)_5SO_4]Br} + \underset{\text{(Excess)}}{AgNO_3} \longrightarrow \underset{\substack{0.01\text{ mol}\\(Y)}}{AgBr\downarrow}$

(II) $\underset{\left(\frac{0.02}{2}\right)\text{mol}}{[Co(NH_3)_5Br]SO_4} + \underset{\text{Excess}}{BaCl_2} \longrightarrow \underset{\substack{0.01\text{ mol}\\(Z)}}{BaSO_4\downarrow}$

Thus, option (d) is correct.

19. ***(c)*** The given reaction is

$$4HNO_3(l) + 3KCl(s) \longrightarrow Cl_2(g) + NOCl(g) + 2H_2O + 3KNO_3$$

Number of moles of $KNO_3 = \frac{110}{101} = 1.089$

As 3 moles of KNO_3 is produced from 4 moles or HNO_3

$\therefore$ 1.089 moles of KNO_3 is produced from $= \frac{4}{3} \times 1.089$

$= 1.452$ mol

Mass of HNO_3 required is $1.452 \times 63 \approx 91.5$ g

20. ***(3)*** $R(OH) \longrightarrow H_2$

$\therefore$ Number of moles of 'OH' present in x

$= \frac{1}{2}$ (Number of moles of H_2 formed)

$\Rightarrow \quad x\left(\frac{1.84 \times 10^{-3}\text{g}}{92\text{g mol}^{-1}}\right) = \frac{1}{2} \times \frac{1.344 \text{ mL}}{22.4 \times 10^3 \text{mL}} \times 2$

[Volume of 1 mole of gas at STP = 22.42]

$\Rightarrow \quad x = \frac{1.344 \times 2 \times 92 \times 1000}{2 \times 22.4 \times 1000 \times 1.84} \quad \Rightarrow x = 3$

So, number of alcoholic hydrogens present in compound 'x' is 3.

21. ***(c)*** $\underset{(20\text{ g})}{N_2(g)} + \underset{(5\text{ g})}{3H_2(g)} \longrightarrow 2NH_3(g)$

Number of moles of $N_2 = \frac{20}{28}$ mol

Number of moles of $H_2 = \frac{5}{2}$ mol

Limiting reagent can be calculated using a factor

$= \frac{\text{Number of moles}}{\text{Stoichiometric coefficient}}$

For $NH_3 = \frac{20}{28}$

For $H_2 = \frac{5}{2 \times 3} = \frac{5}{6}$

Clearly, $\frac{20}{28} < \frac{5}{6}$ so, N_2 is a limiting reagent and thus decides the formation of products.

1 mole of N_2 forms 2 mole of NH_3.

So, $\frac{20}{28}$ mole of N_2 forms $= 2 \times \frac{20}{28} = \frac{20}{14} = \frac{10}{7} = 1.42$ mol.

22. ***(2)*** 3 moles of Z are required to give 1 mole of XYZ_3.

So, 0.05 moles of Z are required to give

$$= \frac{1}{3} \times 0.05 \text{ mole of } XYZ_3$$

$$= 0.016 \text{ mole of } XYZ_3$$

Molecular weight of $XYZ_3 = 10 + 20 + (3 \times 30) = 120$ amu

$\therefore$ Number of moles of $XYZ_3 = \frac{\text{Weight of } XYZ_3}{\text{Molecular weight of } XYZ_3}$

$$0.016 = \frac{\text{Weight of } XYZ_3}{120}$$

$\therefore$ Weight of $XYZ_3 = 0.016 \times 120 = 1.92 \text{ g} \approx 2 \text{ g}$

23. ***(c)*** Molar mass of $Fe_3O_4 = 232$ g/mol

So, number of moles of Fe_3O_4 reacting $= \frac{4640}{232} = 20$ moles

Similarly,

Molar mass of $CO = (12 + 16)$ g/mol $= 28$ g/mol

$\therefore$ Number of moles of CO reacting $= \frac{2520}{28} = 90$ moles

As number of moles of Fe_3O_4 reacting is less than number of moles of CO, it is the limiting reagent and product formed will depend on number of moles of Fe_3O_4.

$\therefore$ Number of moles of iron formed

$$= 3 \times \text{moles of } Fe_3O_4$$

$$= 3 \times 20 = 60 \text{ moles}$$

Weight of iron produced $= 60 \times 56$ (in g) $= 3360$ g

24. ***(0)*** Moles of H_2SO_4 in solution $A = 50$ percent of original solution

$$= \frac{0.2}{2} = 0.1 \text{ m mol.}$$

Moles of H_2SO_4 in final solution $= 0.01 + 0.01$

$= 0.02$ m mol $= 0.00002 \times 10^3$ m mol

Solution of nearest integer = 0

25. ***(4)*** For first end point :

$$\underset{(a)}{NaOH} + \underset{(b)}{Na_2CO_3} + \underset{(c)}{2HCl} \longrightarrow \underset{(b)}{NaHCO_3} + 2NaCl + H_2O$$

Both NaOH and Na_2CO_3 are of basic character. Hence, they will not react with each other. However both of them will react with HCl.

According to law of equivalence

Equivalents of NaOH (a) + Equivalents of $Na_2CO_3 (b)$
= Equivalents of HCl (c)

and Equivalents of $Na_2CO_3 (b)$ = Equivalents of $NaHCO_3 (b)$

For second end point

$$\underset{(b)}{NaHCO_3} + \underset{(d)}{HCl} \longrightarrow H_2CO_3 + NaCl$$

According to law of equivalence

Equivalents of $NaHCO_3 (b)$ = Equivalents of HCl (d)

$\Rightarrow \qquad b = \frac{1}{10} \times 1.5 = 0.15$

From first end point, equivalents of $Na_2CO_3 = 0.15$

$\Rightarrow$ Mass of Na_2CO_3 = Number of eq. $\times$ Eq. mass

$$= 0.15 \times \frac{106}{1} \times 10^{-3} \text{ g} \approx 0.016 \text{ g}$$

Weight percentage of $Na_2CO_3 = \frac{0.016}{0.4} \times 100 = 4\%$.

26. ***(2130)*** To find the No. of moles of O_2 in the given question, use the formula $n = \frac{pV}{RT}$.

Then, use the value of n to find out the mass of $NaClO_3$.

Given, volume of $O_2 = 492$ L

$\therefore \qquad n = \frac{pV}{RT} = \frac{1 \text{ atm} \times 492 \text{ L}}{0.082 \text{ L atm K}^{-1} \text{ mol}^{-1} \times 300 \text{ K}}$

$$= \frac{492}{8.2 \times 3} \text{ mol}$$

From the reaction,

$$NaClO_3(s) + 5Fe(s) \longrightarrow O_2(g) + NaCl(s) + 5FeO(s)$$

$$n_{NaClO_3} = n_{O_2} = \frac{492}{82 \times 3} = 20 \text{ mol}$$

$$m_{NaClO_3} = n \times \text{molar mass of } NaClO_3$$

$$= 20 \times 106.5 = 2130 \text{ g}$$

The value in different situations may range from 2120 to 2140.

27. ***(85)*** $5H_2O_2 + 2\overset{(+7)}{Mn}O_4^- + 3H^+ \longrightarrow 2Mn^{2+} + 5O_2 + 8H_2O$

Moles of $KMnO_4 = \frac{0.316}{158} = 2 \times 10^{-3}$

(Molar mass of $KMnO_4 = 158$)

Equivalents of H_2O_2 = Equivalents of $KMnO_4$

Equivalents of $KMnO_4 = 2 \times 10^{-3} \times 5 = 0.01$

Moles of $H_2O_2 = \frac{\text{Equivalents of } H_2O_2}{n\text{-factor of } H_2O_2} = \frac{0.01}{2} = 0.005$

28. ***(1)*** $M = \frac{1000M}{1000d - M \times M_0} = \frac{3 \times 1000}{1250 - 3 \times 40} = \frac{3 \times 1000}{1130} = 2.65$

29. ***(1)*** $M_1 = 0.2$ M, $M_2 = 0.5$m,

$V_1 = 200$ mL, $V_2 = 400$ mL

Molarity of mixture $= \frac{M_1V_1 + M_2V_2}{V_1 + V_2} = \frac{0.2 \times 200 + 0.5 \times 400}{600}$ M

$$= \frac{40 + 200}{600} = \frac{240}{600} = 0.4 \text{ M}$$

30. ***(22)*** Mass percent of alcohol

$$= \frac{\text{Mass of ethyl alcohol}}{\text{Total mass of solution}} \times 100$$

$$= \frac{1 \times 46}{(1 \times 46) + (9 \times 18)} \times 100$$

$$= \frac{4600}{208} = 22.11$$

Nearest integer = 22

31. ***(b)*** Given,

density = 1.25 g mL^{-1}, $M = 3$ M

molar mass in g mol^{-1} :

Na = 23, Cl = 35.5

Molality = ?

$$\text{Molality } (m) = \frac{1000 \times M}{1000 \times d - (M \times W_{\text{Molecular weight of solute}})}$$

$$m = \frac{3 \times 1000}{1.25 \times 1000 - [3 \times 58.5]}$$

$m = 2.79$ m

32. ***(b)*** Given, molality = 3

Density of x M of NaOH = 1.12 g mL^{-1}

Using the formula for molality

$$\text{Molality} = \frac{1000 \times M}{1000 \times d - (M \times W_{\text{solute}})}$$

(Molecular weight = W)

$$3 = \frac{1000 \times x}{1000 \times 1.12 - (x \times 40)} \quad \ldots\text{(i)}$$

[40 = Molecular weight of NaOH]

By solving equation (i)

$$x = 3$$

33. ***(139)*** 10 mL solute in 90 mL solvent.

Mass of solute = 10 × 3.2 = 32 g

Mass of solvent = 90 × 1.6 g

$$m = \frac{32 \times 1000}{160 \times 90 \times 1.6} \approx 1.388$$

$$= 138.8 \times 10^{-2} = 139 \times 10^{-2} \text{ m}$$

34. ***(364)*** In this type of question, whenever the density and molarity is given, then use this formula of molality

i.e., $$m = \frac{1000 \times M}{1000d - M \times \text{molecular weight}}$$

$$m = \frac{1000 \times M}{1000d - M \times \text{molecular weight}}$$

$$= \frac{1000 \times 3}{1000 \times 1 - (3 \times 58.5)} = 3.6385 \text{ m}$$

$$\approx 3.64 \text{ m} = 364 \times 10^{-2} \text{ m}$$

35. ***(227)*** $2C(s) + O_2(g) \longrightarrow 2CO(g)$

$\underset{1\text{ mol}}{12\text{ g}}$ $\underset{1.5\text{ mol}}{48\text{ g}}$

Limiting reagent is carbon. One mole of carbon produces one mole of CO. Thus, volume at STP is 227×10^{-1} L.

36. ***(25)*** $H_2SO_4 + 2NaOH \longrightarrow Na_2SO_4 + 2H_2O$

	H_2SO_4	NaOH	Na_2SO_4	H_2O
Initial moles	0.4	0.2	0	0
Final moles	0.3	0	0.1	0.2

Limiting reagent ⟶ NaOH

$n_{Na_2SO_4} = 0.1$ mol

Total volume, $V = V_{H_2SO_4} + V_{NaOH} = 2 + 2 = 4$ L

$$\text{Molarity, } M_{Na_2SO_4} = \frac{0.1}{4} = 0.025 \text{ M}$$

$$= 25 \times 10^{-3} \text{ M} = 25 \text{ millimolar}$$

37. ***(1)*** Reaction involved

$$H_2SO_4 + 2NaOH \longrightarrow Na_2SO_4 + 2H_2O$$

Number of equivalents of H_2SO_4 = 100 × 0.1 × 2 = 20

Number of equivalent of NaOH = 50 × 0.1 = 5

$$\text{Normality} = \frac{\text{Number of gram equivalent}}{\text{Volume of the solution}}$$

Volume of the solution = 100 + 50 = 150 mL

$$\therefore \quad N = \frac{15}{150} = 0.1 = 1 \times 10^{-1} \text{ N}$$

38. ***(b)*** Percentage of carbon in glucose

$$10.8 = \frac{\text{Mass of C}}{250} \times 100 \Rightarrow \text{Mass of C} = \frac{10.8 \times 250}{100} = 27 \text{ g}$$

Molar mass of glucose = 180 g

72 g of carbon is present in 180 g of glucose.

$$\therefore 27 \text{ g of carbon present in} = \frac{180}{72} \times 27$$

$$= 67.5 \text{ g of glucose}$$

Mass of solvent = 250 g − 67.5 g = 182.5 g

$$\text{Molality} = \frac{\text{Moles of solute}}{\text{Mass of solvent}} \times 1000$$

$$= \frac{67.5 \times 1000}{180 \times 182.5} \approx 2.055 \text{ mol/kg}$$

39. ***(46)*** $N_2 + 3H_2 \longrightarrow 2NH_3$

Since the reactants and product are at same condition of temperature and pressure.

So, by Avogadro's law, $V \propto n$

56.0 L of N_2 gas = 56 moles of NH_3 gas

20.0 L of NH_3 gas = 20.0 moles of NH_3 gas

To produce 20 moles of NH_3, 10 mole of N_2 required.

So, to produce 20 L of NH_3, 10 L of N_2 required.

So, unused volume of N_2 will be = 56 − 10 = 46 L

46 L of N_2 will remain unused.

40. ***(b)*** Given,

Mass of solute (X) = 2g

Mass of solvent (H_2O) = 1 mole = 18 g

So, total mass of the solution = 18 + 2 = 20 g

$$\text{Mass \% of } X = \frac{\text{Mass of solute}}{\text{Total mass of the solution}} \times 100$$

$$= \frac{2}{20} \times 100 = 10\%$$

41. ***(13)*** For the reaction,

$$\underset{\frac{20}{62}\text{ mol}}{\underset{1\text{ mol}}{Na_2O}} + H_2O \longrightarrow \underset{x\text{ mol}}{\underset{2\text{ mol}}{2NaOH}}$$

1 mole of Na_2O forms 2 mol of NaOH

∴ Moles of NaOH formed

$$\Rightarrow x = \frac{20}{62} \times 2$$

$$\text{Concentration of NaOH} = \frac{\text{Moles of NaOH}}{\text{Volume of solution (in litre)}}$$

$$= \frac{\frac{20}{62} \times 2}{\frac{500}{1000}} = 1.29\text{ M} = 13 \times 10^{-1}\text{ M}$$

42. ***(5)*** Take 1 L solution

mass of solution = Vol. × density = 1.2 × 1000 g = 1200 g

Mass of 1 L solvent (water) = 1000 g (∵ density = 1 g cm^{-3})

⇒ Mass of NaOH = (1200 − 1000) g = 200 g

$$\Rightarrow \text{Moles of NaOH} = \frac{200\text{ g}}{40\text{ g/mol}} = 5\text{ mol}$$

$$\text{Molality} = \frac{\text{Number of moles of solute}}{\text{Mass of solvent (in kg)}}$$

$$\Rightarrow \text{Molality} = \frac{5\text{ mol}}{1\text{ kg}} = 5\text{ m}$$

43. ***(24)*** $\underset{+6}{Cr_2O_7^{2-}} + \underset{+2}{Fe^{2+}} \longrightarrow \underset{+3}{Cr^{3+}} + \underset{+3}{Fe^{3+}}$

Dichromate ($Cr_2O_7^{2-}$) oxidised Fe^{2+} to Fe^{3+} and itself get reduced to Cr^{3+}.

Valency factor of $Cr_2O_7^{2-}$ = 6 as Cr gets reduced from +6 to +3.

Valency factor of Fe^{2+} = 1 as it gets oxidised from +2 to +3.

From law of equivalence,

$$\underset{(Cr_2O_7^{2-})}{M_1V_1n_1} = \underset{(Fe^{2+})}{M_2V_2n_2}$$

$$(M_1 \times V_1) \times 6 = (M_2 \times V_2) \times 1$$

$$(0.03 \times 20) \times 6 = (M_2 \times 15) \times 1$$

$$\Rightarrow M_2 = 0.24\text{ molar} = 24 \times 10^{-2}\text{ molar}$$

44. ***(c)*** Volume of hydrogen = 5.6

Volume strength = 11.2 × molarity

$$\Rightarrow \text{Molarity} = \frac{\text{Volume strength}}{11.2} = \frac{5.6}{11.2} = 0.5$$

Suppose, that the solution taken is = 1L

Mass of solution = 1000 mL × 1 g/mL = 1000 g

Mass of solute = Moles × Molar mass = 0.5 × 34

[∵ molar mass of H_2O_2 = 34]

= 17 g

$$\Rightarrow \text{Mass \%} = \frac{17}{1000} \times 100 = 1.7\%$$

45. ***(47.00)*** Let, for glucose :

Mass = w_B g, mole = n_B

and mole fraction = χ_B

(Molar mass, M_B = 180 g mol^{-1})

For water : mass = w_A g,

mole = n_A and mole fraction = χ_A

(Molar mass, M_A = 18 g mol^{-1})

Where, $\chi_A + \chi_B = 1$

$$\Rightarrow \frac{\chi_B}{\chi_A} = \frac{\chi_B}{1-\chi_B} = \frac{0.1}{0.9} = \frac{1}{9}$$

$$\Rightarrow \frac{\frac{n_B}{n_A+n_B}}{\frac{n_A}{n_A+n_B}} = \frac{1}{9} \Rightarrow \frac{n_B}{n_A} = \frac{1}{9} \Rightarrow \frac{\frac{w_B}{180}}{\frac{w_A}{18}} = \frac{1}{9}$$

$$\Rightarrow \frac{w_B}{w_A} = \frac{10}{9} \Rightarrow \frac{w_B}{w_A} + 1 = \frac{10}{9} + 1$$

$$\Rightarrow \frac{w_A}{w_A + w_B} = \frac{9}{19}$$

$$\Rightarrow \frac{w_A}{w_A + w_B}\% = \frac{9}{19} \times 100 = 47.368 \approx 47.00\%$$

So, mass percentage of water (*A*) in the solution is 47.00.

46. ***(14)*** For 100 g sample of the solution,
mass of HNO_3 = 63 g,

$$\therefore n_{HNO_3} = \frac{63}{63} = 1\text{ mol}$$

$$\text{Volume of solution} = \frac{\text{Mass}}{\text{Density}} = \frac{100\text{ g}}{1.4\text{ g/mL}} = \frac{100}{1.4}\text{ mL} = \frac{1}{14}\text{ L}$$

$$\text{Molarity} = \frac{n}{V(L)} = \frac{1}{(1/14)} = 14\text{ M}$$

47. ***(26.92)*** Given, Mass of $[Co(NH_3)_6]Cl_3$ = 0.3 g

Molar mass = 267.46 g mol^{-1}

$$\therefore n = \frac{0.3}{267.46}\text{ mol}$$

From the formula, 1 mol complex will give 3 mol Cl^-.

$$\therefore n_{Cl^-} = \frac{0.3}{267.46} \times 3 = \frac{0.9}{267.46}$$

The precipitation reaction takes place as follows :

$$\underset{(0.3g)}{[Co(NH_3)_6]Cl_3} + \underset{(VmL, 0.125g)}{3AgNO_3} \longrightarrow 2AgCl$$

Let volume of $AgNO_3$ (in mL) be *V*.

Number of moles of Cl^- = number of moles of *N*

$$\therefore \frac{0.3 \times 3}{267.46} = 0.125 \times V \times 10^{-3}$$

$$= \frac{0.9 \times 1000}{0.125 \times 267.46} \approx 26.92\text{ mL}$$

Depending upon the accurancy of calculation this value may vary from 26.60 to 27.00.

Practice Element 02 : Target JEE Advanced

1. **(d)** $\underset{1\text{ mol}}{MnO_2} + \underset{4\text{ mol}}{4HCl} \longrightarrow MnCl_2 + Cl_2 + 2H_2O$

$MnO_2 = 0.80$ mol

$HCl = 146$ g $= 4.0$ mol

1 mol MnO_2 gives $= 1$ mol Cl_2

$\therefore$ 0.8 mol MnO_2 gives $= 0.80$ mol Cl_2, thus (a) is correct

MnO_2 is the limiting reactant, thus (c) is correct

HCl is in excess thus, (d) incorrect

HCl used by 0.8 mol $MnO_2 = 3.2$ mol

HCl remaining unreacted $= 0.8$ mol

So, (b) is correct.

2. **(b)** $BaCl_2 + H_2SO_4 \longrightarrow BaSO_4 + 2HCl$

$BaCl_2$	H_2SO_4	$BaSO_4$
1 mol	1 mol	1 mol
208 g	98 g	233 g
100 mL of 20.8%	50 mL of 9.8%	
20.8 g	4.9 g	?

$BaSO_4$ from 20.8 g of $BaCl_2 = 23.3$ g

$BaSO_4$ from 4.9 g of $H_2SO_4 = \frac{23.3}{2} = 11.65$ g

H_2SO_4 is the limiting reactant.

Thus, $BaSO_4$ formed is $= 11.65$ g

3. **(d)** $\underset{\substack{1\text{ mol}\\142\text{ g}}}{P_2O_5} \longrightarrow \underset{\substack{1\text{ mol}\\222\text{ g}}}{Mg_2P_2O_7}$

P_2O_5 in the mineral $= 0.5428 \times \frac{26.26}{100} = 0.1425$ g $= 0.001$ mol

Thus, $Mg_2P_2O_7$ formed $= 0.001$ mol ≈ 0.2220 g

4. **(b)** $\underset{\substack{1\text{mol}\\28\text{ g}}}{B_2H_6} + \underset{\substack{2\text{ mol}\\48\text{ g}}}{2NaH} \longrightarrow \underset{\substack{2\text{ mol}\\76\text{ g}}}{2NaBH_4}$

$NaBH_4$ formed from 6.75 g $B_2H_6 = \frac{76}{28} \times 6.75$ g ≈ 18.32 g

$NaBH_4$ formed from 8.55 g NaH $= \frac{76}{48} \times 8.55$ g ≈ 13.54 g

Thus, NaH is the limiting reactant.

B_2H_6 required by 8.55 g of NaH $= \frac{28}{48} \times 8.55 \approx 4.99$ g

B_2H_6 in excess $= 6.75 - 4.99 = 1.76$ g

5. **(d)** (a) 6 mol HCl is consumed for every 67.2 L $H_2(g)$ produced thus (a) incorrect

(b) Only at STP - thus (b) incorrect

(c) 1.5 mol = 33.6 L H_2 is formed at STP thus (c) incorrect.

(d) 6 HCl $\longrightarrow$ 3 mol H_2

1 HCl $\longrightarrow$ 0.5 mol $H_2 = 11.2$ L at STP

6. **(d)** In reaction I, CaC_2 formed $= 0.5$ mol (50% yield) from 1 mol Ca

$CaCN_2$ formed in reaction II from 0.5 mol $CaC_2 = 0.5$ mol (100% yield)

NH_3 formed in reaction III from

1 mol $CaCN_2 = 2.0$ mol NH_3 if (100% yield)

$= 1.0$ mol NH_3 (50% yield)

$\therefore$ NH_3 formed from 0.5 mol $CaCN_2 = 0.5$ mol NH_3 (50% yield)

Thus, in all 0.5 mol of NH_3 is formed from 1 mol Ca

$\therefore$ 2 mol of NH_3 is formed from 4 mol Ca

7. **(a)** Mass of each solute is equal $= w$ g

Compound	Moles	Mole fractions
Urea (60)	$w/60$	0.546 Max
Tetrose (120)	$w/120$	0.273
Glucose (180)	$w/180$	0.181 Min
Total	$11\,w/360$	

8. **(c)** **Case I**

$\underset{\substack{56\text{ g}\\0.7\text{ g}}}{Fe} + \underset{\substack{32\text{ g}\\0.4\text{ g}}}{S} \longrightarrow \underset{\substack{88\text{ g}\\1.1\text{ g (formed)}}}{FeS}$

Case II $\underset{2.8\text{ g}}{Fe} \xrightarrow{HCl} FeCl_2 \xrightarrow{K_2S} FeS$

If law of constant composition is true,

$$\frac{\text{FeS formed in Case II } (w)}{\text{FeS formed in Case I } (1.1)} = \frac{\text{Fe reacted in II}(2.8)}{\text{Fe reacted in I } (0.7)}$$

$\therefore \quad w = 4.4$ g

9. **(d)** 0.568 mm^3 cube $= 0.568 \times 10^{-3}$ cm^3

Mass of cube = Volume × Density

$= 0.568 \times 10^{-3} cm^3 \times 2.07$ gcm^{-3}

$= 1.17576 \times 10^{-3}$g

Moles $(S_8) = \frac{1.17576 \times 10^{-3}}{256}$

$\approx 4.593 \times 10^{-6}$

Molecules $= 4.593 \times 10^{-6} \times N_0$

$= 4.593 \times 10^{-6} \times 6.02 \times 10^{23}$

$\approx 2.765 \times 10^{18}$

10. **(d)** Oxygen is lost by reduction with H_2

$Fe_xO_y + yH_2 \longrightarrow xFe + yH_2O$

Oxygen lost $= 0.1210$ g

Fe present in oxide $= 0.5434 - 0.1210 = 0.4224$ g

	Amount	Mol	Ratio
Fe	0.4224 g	7.54×10^{-3}	1
O	0.1210 g	7.56×10^{-3}	1

Thus, oxide is FeO

11. **(a, b, c, d)**

1 mol glucose in 1.8 L solution

Thus, 180 g glucose in 1.8 L solution

Thus, percentage $= \frac{180\text{ g}}{1800} \times 100 = 10\%$

Density $= \frac{180\text{ g}}{1800\text{ mL}} = 0.1$ g mL^{-1}

1800 mL solution contains $= 1$ mol $= N_0$ molecules

$\therefore$ 1 mL contains $= \frac{N_0}{1800}$ molecules

$= \frac{6.02}{1800} \times 10^{23} = 3.34 \times 10^{20}$

Molarity $= \frac{1}{1.8} \approx 0.56 \text{ mol L}^{-1}$

12. **(a, c)** $\underset{\substack{2\text{ mol}\\34\text{ g}}}{2NH_3}(g) + \underset{\substack{1\text{ mol}\\44\text{ g}}}{CO_2}(g) \longrightarrow \underset{\substack{1\text{ mol}\\60\text{ g}}}{NH_2CO\,NH_2}(aq) + H_2O(l)$

34 g NH_3 react with 44 g CO_2

$\therefore$ 637.2 NH_3 react with $\frac{44}{34} \times 637.2 = 824.61 \text{ g } CO_2$

CO_2 taken = 1142 g

Thus, CO_2 is in excess.

CO_2 left unreacted $= 1142 - 824.61$

$= 317.4 \text{ g } CO_2 = \frac{317.4}{44} \approx 7 \text{ mol}$

NH_2CONH_2 formed

from 637.2 g $NH_3 = \frac{1}{34} \times 637.2$ g

$= \frac{637.2}{34}$ mol $= 18.74$ mol

13. **(a, b, d)**

Compound	Mass	Mol	Atom	Mole fraction
CH_4	1.6 g	0.1	5	0.33
NH_3	1.7 g	0.1	4	0.33
H_2O	1.8 g	0.1	3	0.33

$\underset{0.1\text{ mol}}{NH_3} + \underset{0.1\text{ mol}}{H_2O} \rightleftharpoons \underset{0.1\text{ mol}}{NH_4OH}$

Thus., mixture contains 0.1 mole of aqueous NH_3.

14. **(b, d)** Urea present in 800 g solution

$= \frac{800 \times 40}{100} = 320 \text{ g}$

Water present in 800 g solution

$= 800 - 320 = 480 \text{ g}$

$= 0.480 \text{ kg}$

After cooling urea separated = 100 g

Thus, urea left in solution = 320 – 100 = 220 g

Weight of solution after cooling = 800 – 100 = 700 g

Molality before cooling $= \frac{(320/60)\text{ mol}}{0.480\text{ kg}} \approx 11.11$

Molality after cooling $= \frac{(220/60)\text{ mol}}{0.480\text{ kg}} \approx 7.64$

Decrease in molality $= 11.11 - 7.64 = 3.47$

Percentage concentration after cooling (having 220 g urea in 700 g solution)

$= \frac{220}{700} \times 100 = 31.43\%$

Decreases in percentage concentration

$= 40.00 - 31.43 = 8.57 \approx 8.6$

15. **(c, d)** I. $\underset{\substack{1\text{ mol}\\1.24\text{ g}}}{P_4} + \underset{\substack{5\text{ mol}\\8.0\text{ g}}}{5O_2} \longrightarrow \underset{\substack{1\text{ mol}\\?}}{P_4O_{10}}$

1.24 g P_4(= 0.01 mol) gives 0.01 mol $P_4O_{10} = 2.84 \text{ g } P_4O_{10}$

8 g of O_2(= 0.25 mol) gives $= \frac{1}{5} \times 0.25$ mol P_4O_{10}

$= 0.05$ mol P_4O_{10}

Thus, P_4 is the limiting reactant and 2.84 g of P_4O_{10} is formed.

II. $\underset{\substack{1\text{ mol}\\1.24\text{ g}}}{P_4} + \underset{\substack{3\text{ mol}\\8\text{ g}}}{3O_2} \longrightarrow \underset{\substack{1\text{ mol}\\?}}{P_4O_6}$

P_4O_6 formed from 0.01 mol $P_4 = 0.01 = 2.20 \text{ g } P_4O_6$

P_4O_6 formed from 0.25 mol $O_2 = \frac{0.25}{3} = 0.083 \text{ mol } P_4O_6$

Thus, P_4 is the limiting reactant in II and 2.20 g of P_4O_6 is formed.

16. **(b)** Equivalent mass of $O_2 \equiv$ Mass equivalent to 8 g

$\equiv \frac{M}{4} = 8$

22.4 L O_2 gas or at STP = 1 mol

0.112 L O_2 gas at STP $= 5 \times 10^{-3}$ mol

Mg taken $= \frac{2.4}{24} = 0.1$ mol

$\underset{\substack{1\text{ mol}\\2\text{ equivalent}}}{Mg} + \underset{\substack{0.5\text{ mol}\\2\text{ equivalent}}}{\frac{1}{2}O_2} \longrightarrow \underset{\substack{1\text{ mol}\\2\text{ equivalent}}}{MgO}$

MgO formed from 0.1 mol Mg = 0.1 mol

= 0.2 equivalent

Mg taken = 0.2 equivalent

MgO formed from 5×10^{-3} mol $O_2 = 2 \times 5 \times 10^{-3}$ mol

= 0.01 mol = 0.02 equivalent

Thus, O_2 is the limiting reactant

O_2 taken $= 5 \times 10^{-3}$ mol

$= 5 \times 10^{-3} \times 4$ equivalent

$= 2 \times 10^{-2} = 0.02$ equivalent

Thus, equivalent of MgO formed = equivalent O_2 taken.

Reactants and products are neither in equal moles nor equivalent.

17. **(b, d)** Among the given statements, (b) and (d) are incorrect while statement (a) and (c) are correct.

The correct form of (b) and (d) are —

- Total mass of solution = 1000 g water + 120 g urea
  = 1120 g

Density of solution = 1.15 g /mL

Thus, volume of solution $= \frac{\text{Mass}}{\text{Density}} = \frac{1120 \text{ g}}{1.15 \text{ g/mL}}$

$= 973.91 \text{ mL} \approx 0.974 \text{ L}$

Mol of solute $= \frac{120}{60} = 2$ mol

$$\text{Molarity} = \frac{\text{Moles of solute}}{\text{Volume (L) of solution}} = \frac{2\text{ mol}}{0.9741\text{ L}} = 2.05\text{ mol L}^{-1}$$

- $\text{Molarity} = \frac{10 \times 1.8 \times 98}{98} = 18\text{ M}$
- The molarity of a resulting solution is given by

$$M = \frac{M_1V_1 + M_2V_2}{V_1 + V_2}$$

$$= \frac{750 \times 0.5 + 250 \times 2}{750 + 250}$$

$$= \frac{875}{1000} = 0.875\text{ M}$$

18. ***(b, c)*** Among the given statements, b and c are correct regarding the given data.

- According to given data,

$$1\text{ mol } Cl_2 = 2\text{ mol KOH} = 1\text{ mol KClO}$$

$$= \frac{1}{3}\text{ mol } KClO_3 = \frac{1}{4}\text{ mol } KClO_4$$

Moles of $KClO_4 = \frac{277}{138.5} = 2$

Moles of $Cl_2 = 2 \times 4 = 8$

Mass of $Cl_2 = 8 \times 71 = 568\text{ g}$

Hence, the amount of Cl_2 required to prepare 277 g of $KClO_4$ by above series of reaction is 568 g.

Moles of $KOH = 2 \times 8 = 16$

Volume of $KOH = \frac{16}{1.5} = 10.67\text{ L}$

So, the volume of KOH in litres used by Cl_2, if KOH is 1.5 M is 10.67 L.

19. ***(a, d)*** Among the given statements, a and d are incorrect while other statements b and c are correct.

Their correct form are —

(a) In the division of 6.85 by 112.04, the number of significant figures in the reported answer will be three. [$6.85 \div 112.04 = 0.061138878$, round off to 0.0611]

(d) There are three significant figures in the answer of

$$\frac{(1.79 \times 10^5)(29.2 - 20.2)}{1.49}$$

$$\Rightarrow \frac{(9.0)(1.79 \times 10^5)}{1.49} = \frac{16.1 \times 10^5}{1.49} = 10.8 \times 10^5$$

(b) $2.097 - 0.12 = 1.977$ round off to 1.98

So, the number of significant figures in the reported answer will be three.

(c) Three different scientific notations may be written for the result 10500 g i.e., 1.05×10^4, 1.050×10^4, 1.0500×10^4.

20. ***(a, c, d)*** Among the given statements, only (b) is incorrect while other statements a, c and d are correct.

Given : 200 g $CaCO_3$ in 10^6 g of water.

Mass of $CaCO_3 = 200\text{ g}$

Mass of $H_2O = 10^6\text{ g}$

(a) Mass ratio of $CaCO_3$ to $H_2O = \frac{200}{10^6} = \frac{0.02}{100}$

(c) Moles of $CaCO_3 = \frac{200}{100} = 2$ moles

Moles of $H_2O = \frac{10^6}{18} = \frac{10^6}{18}$ moles

Mole ratio of $CaCO_3$ to H_2O

$$= \frac{2}{10^6} \times 18 = \frac{36}{10^6} = 3.6 \times 10^{-5} = 0.36 \times 10^{-4}$$

(d) Density of water = 1 g/mL

$$\text{Volume} = \frac{\text{Mass}}{\text{Density}} = \frac{10^6\text{ g}}{1\text{ g/mL}} = 10^6\text{ mL} = 10^3\text{ L}$$

$\Rightarrow$ 200 g $CaCO_3$ is present in 10^3 L of water.

1 L of water contains $= \frac{200}{10^3}$ g $CaCO_3$

So, Mass of $CaCO_3$ present in hard water is 0.2 g/L

(b) 10^6 g hard water $\longrightarrow$ 200 g $CaCO_3$

10^3 kg $\longrightarrow$ 200 $CaCO_3$

1 kg of hardwater $= \frac{200}{10^3}$ g $CaCO_3 = 0.2$ g

$\Rightarrow$ 200 mg $CaCO_3$

Milimoles of $CaCO_3 = \frac{200}{100} = 2$

Miliequivalent of $CaCO_3 = 2 \times n$ factor of $CaCO_3$

$= 2 \times 2 = 4$

21. ***(4)*** $H_2SO_4 = 0.0755\text{ mol} = 0.0755 \times 98\text{ g} \approx 7.4\text{ g}$

$$\text{Density} = \frac{\text{Mass}}{\text{Volume}}$$

$$\therefore \text{ Volume} = \frac{\text{Mass}}{\text{Density}} = \frac{7.4}{1.85} = 4\text{ mL}$$

22. ***(21.83)*** Let the two equimolar carbonates be ACO_3 and BCO_3.

Mass of the metal $A = 3.0 \times 0.145 = 0.435$ g

$$ACO_3 + BCO_3 \longrightarrow AO + BO + 2CO_2$$

Two moles of carbonate (CO_3^{2-}) provide 2 moles of CO_2 or 60 g of CO_3^{2-} provide 44 g CO_2.

Total mass of CO_3^{2-} required to produce

$$1.40\text{ g of } CO_2 = \frac{60}{44} \times 1.40 \approx 1.91\text{ g}$$

Mass of metal $(A + B) = 3.0 - 1.91 = 1.90$ g

Mass of metal $B = (1.09 - 0.435)\text{ g} = 0.655$ g

$$\%\text{ of } B = \frac{0.655}{3.0} \times 100$$

$$\approx 21.83\%$$

23. ***(0.42)*** Let x g is the mass of CaC_2O_4 and $(1.8 - x)$ g is the mass of MgC_2O_4.

$$CaC_2O_4 \xrightarrow{\Delta} CaCO_3 + CO$$

$$MgC_2O_4 \xrightarrow{\Delta} MgCO_3 + CO$$

$$\text{Mass of } CaCO_3 \text{ produced} = \frac{x}{128} \times 100$$

$$\text{Mass of } MgCO_3 \text{ produced} = \frac{(1.10 - x)}{112} \times 84$$

$$\therefore \quad \frac{x}{128} \times 100 + \frac{(1.10 - x)}{112} \times 84 = 0.835 \Rightarrow x = 0.32 \text{ g}$$

Due to further heating

$$CaCO_3 \xrightarrow{\Delta} CaO + CO_2 \qquad \frac{x}{128}$$

$$MgCO_3 \xrightarrow{\Delta} MgO + CO_2 \qquad \frac{(1.10 - x)}{112}$$

Mass of CaO and MgO produced

$$= \left(\frac{0.32}{128} \times 56 + \frac{0.78}{112} \times 40\right) \text{ g}$$

$$\approx 0.42 \text{ g}$$

24. ***(1.097)*** $KMnO_4 + C_2O_4^{2-} \xrightarrow{H^+} Mn^{2+} + CO_2$

$n_f = 5$, 16 mL, 0.02 M; $n_f = 2$, 20 mL, x M

m.eq. of $C_2O_4^{2-}$ = m. eq. of $KMnO_4$

$$2 \times (20) \times x = 5 \times 16 \times 0.02$$

$$\Rightarrow \quad x = 0.04 \text{ M}$$

$$[H^+] = 2 \times 0.04 \text{ M} = 0.08 \text{ M}$$

$$pH = -\log [H^+] = -\log [0.08] \approx 1.097$$

25. ***(1.8)*** $Fe_2(C_2O_4)_3 + MnO_4^- + H^+ \longrightarrow 2Fe^{3+} + 6CO_2 + H_2O$ $(n = 6)$ $(n = 5)$

$FeC_2O_4 + MnO_4^- + H^+ \longrightarrow Fe^{3+} + 2CO_2 + H_2O$ $(n = 3)$ $(n = 5)$

Total equivalent of $(Fe_2(C_2O_4)_3 + FeC_2O_4)$ = equivalents of $KMnO_4$

$$\therefore \quad (1 \times 6 + 1 \times 3) = x \times 5$$

Moles of $KMnO_4 = x = 1.8$

26. ***(32)*** $3Br_2 + 6OH^{\ominus} \longrightarrow 5Br^{\ominus} + BrO_3^{\ominus} + 3H_2O$ ...(i)

$6H^+ + BrO_3^- + 3C_2O_4^{2-} \longrightarrow Br^- + 6CO_2 + 3H_2O$ ...(ii)

mmoles of $Br_2 = 20 \times 0.5 = 10$ mmol

10 mmol of Br_2 produces $\left(\frac{10}{3}\right)$ mmol of $BrO_3^{\ominus}$

mmoles of CaC_2O_4 required $= \frac{10}{3} \times 3 = 10$

$$\therefore \quad \text{Mass of } CaC_2O_4 = 10 \times 10^{-3} \times 128$$

$$\% \text{ purity} = \frac{10 \times 10^{-3} \times 128}{4} \times 100 = 32$$

27. ***(6)*** Molar mass of $[Cr(NH_3)_xCl_3] = (158.5 + 17x)$

x HCl ≡ x NH_3 ≡ mol of $[Cr(NH_3)_xCl_3]$

$$\therefore \quad \frac{24.26 \times 1.50}{1000x} = \frac{1.580}{(158.5 + 17x)} \Rightarrow x \approx 6$$

28. ***(2)*** H_2SO_4 is 30.8% by mass

100 g H_2SO_4 solution = 30.8 g H_2SO_4

$\left(\frac{100}{1.303}\right)$ mL H_2SO_4 solution = 30.8 g H_2SO_4

Thus, 500 mL H_2SO_4 solution

$$= \left(\frac{30.8 \times 1.303 \times 500}{100}\right) \text{g } H_2SO_4 = 200.66 \text{ g} \approx 2.00 \text{ mol}$$

29. ***(c)***

	Molar Mass	Ionisable (H^+)/mol	H-atoms* attached to O-atom
i. H_2SO_4	98 g	2 N_0	Two
ii. H_3PO_4	98 g	3 N_0	Three
iii. H_3PO_3	82 g	2 N_0	Two
iv. H_3PO_2	66 g	N_0	One
v. CH_3COOH	60 g	N_0	One
vi. NH_2CONH_2	60 g	–	Nil

Thus,

(i) → (q, s) (ii) → (q, t)

(iii) → (s) (iv) → (r)

(v) → (p, r, u) (vi) → (p, u)

30. ***(c)*** The correct match is A-IV, B-I, C-II, D-III

- C_2H_6O, $\%C = \frac{24 \times 100}{46} \approx 52.2\%$
- $\underset{180 \text{ g}}{C_6H_{12}O_6} = \underset{72 \text{ g}}{6C}$

$$\%C = \frac{72 \times 100}{180} = 40\%$$

- $\underset{60}{CN_2OH_4} = \underset{12 \text{g}}{1C}$

$$\%C = \frac{12 \times 100}{60} = 20\%$$

- $\underset{100 \text{ g}}{CaCO_3} = \underset{12 \text{ g}}{1C}$

$$\%C = \frac{12 \times 100}{100} = 12\%$$

31. ***(d)*** The correct match is — A-IV, B-III, C-I, D-II

- 3.74 g $Cu(NO_3)_2$; Moles $= \frac{3.74}{187} = 0.02$ mol

[Molar mass $Cu(NO_3)_2$ = 187 g/mol]

- 2.8375 L of O_2 at STP;

No. of moles of $O_2 = \frac{2.8375}{22.7} = 0.125$

Number of molecules = Moles × Avagadro's number

$= 0.125 \times 6.02 \times 10^{23} = 7.525 \times 10^{22}$

- 16 g of $CH_4(g)$ = 1 mole CH_4 contains

  $= 10 \times 6.02 \times 10^{23}$ electrons

  $= 60.2 \times 10^{23}$ electrons

- 18 mL of H_2O; considering density of water to be 1 g/mL, 18 mL of H_2O is 18 g of water and it contain Avogadro number of molecules.

  One molecule of H_2O contain = 10 electrons

  1 mole of H_2O contain $= 10 \times 6.023 \times 10^{23}$

  $= 6.023 \times 10^{24}$ electrons.

32. **(b)** $\text{Molarity} = \dfrac{\text{Percentage} \times \text{Density} \times 1000}{100 \times \text{Molar mass}}$

Normality = Basicity × Molarity

	Molar mass	%	Density (g mL^{-1})	Basicity	Molarity	Normality
i. H_2SO_4	98	98%	1.8	2	18 M	36 N
ii. H_3PO_4	98	98%	1.2	3	12 M	36 N
iii. HNO_3	63	63%	1.2	1	12 M	12 N
iv. H_3PO_3	82	82%	1.2	2	12 M	24 N

Thus,

(i) → (q, s) (ii) → (p, s)

(iii) → (p, t) (iv) → (p, r)

33. **(b)** The correct match is — A-t, B-r, C-p, D-s, E-q

34. **(d)** The correct match is — A-III, B-I, C-IV, D-II

- 2 mol $NH_4^{\oplus}$ = 1 mol of $(NH_4)_2CO_3$ = 96 g

  0.5 mol $NH_4^{\oplus} = \dfrac{96 \times 0.5}{2} = 24$ g

- 8 mol H atoms = 1 mol $(NH_4)_2CO_3$ = 96 g

  1 mol H atoms (6.02×10^{23} H atoms) $= \dfrac{96}{8} = 12.0$ g

- The reaction proceeds as follow

  $$(NH_4)_2CO_3 + 2HCl \longrightarrow 2NH_4Cl + CO_2 + H_2O$$

  1 mol CO_2 = 1 mol $(NH_4)_2CO_3$ = 96 g

  3 mol $CO_2 = 96 \times 3 = 288.0$ g

- 100 mL × 0.31 M = 31 m mol $(NH_4)_2CO_3$

  $= 31 \times 10^{-3} \times 96$

  ≈ 2.98 g

35. **(b)** The correct match is — A-II, B-I, C-III, D-IV

A. (i) Moles of $CaCl_2 = \dfrac{11.1}{111} = 0.1$ mol $CaCl_2$ = 0.1 mol Ca^{2+}

(ii) Moles of NaCl $= \dfrac{30.01}{58.5} = 0.51$ mol NaCl

$= 0.51$ mol $Na^{\oplus}$ + 0.51 mol $Cl^{\ominus}$

Adding (i) and (ii), we get

0.1 mol Ca^{2+} + 0.51 mol $Na^{\oplus}$ + 0.71 mol $Cl^{\ominus}$

∴ $[Ca^{2+}] = \dfrac{0.1}{0.1} = 1$ M

$[Na^{\oplus}] = \dfrac{0.51}{0.1} = 5.1$ M

$[Cl^{\ominus}] = \dfrac{0.71}{0.1} = 7.1$ M

B. (i) NaCl ⇒ $5 \times 3 = 15$

⇒ $Na^{\oplus}$ = 15 mol, $Cl^{\ominus}$ = 15 mol

(ii) $CaCl_2$ ⇒ $4 \times 2 = 8$

⇒ Ca^{2+} = 8 mol, $Cl^{\ominus}$ = 16 mol

Adding (i) and (ii), we get

15 mol $Na^{\oplus}$ + 8 mol Ca^{2+} + 31 mol $Cl^{\ominus}$

∴ $[Ca^{2+}] = \dfrac{8}{10} = 0.8$ M

$[Na^{\oplus}] = \dfrac{15}{10} = 1.5$ M

$[Cl^{\ominus}] = \dfrac{31}{10} = 3.1$ M

C. (i) NaCl = 300 × 3 = 900 mmol

⇒ 900 mmol $Na^{\oplus}$ + 900 mmol $Cl^{\ominus}$

(ii) $CaCl_2$ = 200 × 4 = 800 mmol

⇒ 800 mmol Ca^{2+} + 1600 mmol $Cl^{\ominus}$

Adding (i) and (ii), we get

800 mmol Ca^{2+} + 900 mmol $Na^{\oplus}$ + 2500 mmol $Cl^{\ominus}$

Total volume = 300 + 200 = 500 mL

∴ $[Ca^{2+}] = \dfrac{800 \text{ mmol}}{500 \text{ mL}} = 1.6$M

$[Na^{\oplus}] = \dfrac{900 \text{ mmol}}{500 \text{ mL}} = 1.8$M

$[Cl^{\ominus}] = \dfrac{2500 \text{ mmol}}{500 \text{ mL}} = 5$M

D. (i) HCl = 100 × 2 = 200 mmol

⇒ 200 mmol $H^{\oplus}$ + 200 mmol $Cl^{\ominus}$

(ii) NaOH = 200 × 1 = 200 mmol

⇒ 200 mmol $Na^{\oplus}$ + 200 mmol $\overset{\ominus}{O}H$

Since $H^{\oplus}$ and $\overset{\ominus}{O}H$ react to give H_2O.

$$\underset{200 \text{ mmol}}{H^{\oplus}} + \underset{200 \text{ mmol}}{\overset{\ominus}{O}H} \longrightarrow \underset{200 \text{ mmol}}{H_2O}$$

$Cl^{\ominus}$ = 200 mmol, $Na^{\oplus}$ ⇒ 200 mmol

(iii) $CaCl_2$ ⇒ 150 × 4 = 600 mmol

⇒ 600 mmol Ca^{2+} + 1200 mmol $Cl^{\ominus}$

(iv) Total volume = 200 + 100 + 150 + 50 = 500 mL

(v) Total Ca^{2+} = 600 mmol

$\therefore \quad [Ca^{2+}] = \frac{600}{500} = 1.2$ M

Total $\quad Na^{\oplus} = 200$ mmol

$\therefore \quad [Na^{\oplus}] = \frac{200}{500} = 0.4$ M

Total $Cl^{\ominus} = 200 + 1200 = 1400$ mmol

$\therefore \quad [Cl^{\ominus}] = \frac{1400}{500} = 2.8$ M

36. ***(80)***

Formula of *X*

	%	Mol	Ratio
N	35	2.5	1 = 2
H	5	5.0	2 = 4
O	60	3.75	1.5 = 3

X is $N_2H_4O_3$ (NH_4NO_3)

Formula of *Y*

	%	Mol	Ratio
N	63.63	4.54	2
O	36.47	2.27	1

Y is N_2O.

Hence, the compound '*X*' is NH_4NO_3 and its molecular weight is 80 g/mol.

37. ***(45.16)*** The percentage of *N* in the given compound is —

(a) N is $HNO_2 = \frac{14}{47} \times 100 = 29.78\%$

(b) N in $HNO_3 = \frac{14}{63} \times 100 = 22.22\%$

(c) N in $H_2N_2O_2 = \frac{28 \times 100}{62} = \frac{14 \times 100}{31} = 45.16\%$

(d) N in $NH_4NO_3 = \frac{28 \times 100}{80} = \frac{14 \times 100}{40} = 35\%$

Denominator of (c) is minimum hence it has maximum percentage of N.

Hence, the compound '*X*' i.e., ($H_2N_2O_2$) has maximum percentage of *N* i.e., 45.16% in the given compounds.

38. ***(2)*** Let FeO be $= x$ g $= \frac{x}{72}$ mol

and Fe_3O_4 be $= y$ g $= \frac{y}{232}$ mol

$$2\,FeO \xrightarrow{\Delta, O_2} Fe_2O_3$$
$$(2 \times 72)\text{ g} \qquad 160\text{ g}$$
$$x\text{ g} = \left(\frac{160\,x}{144}\right)\text{g} \quad Fe_2O_3$$

$$2\,Fe_3O_4 \xrightarrow{\Delta, O_2} 3\,Fe_2O_3$$
$$(2 \times 232)\text{ g} \qquad (3 \times 160)$$
$$y\text{ g} = \left(\frac{480\,y}{464}\right)\text{g } Fe_2O_3$$

Total mixture (FeO and Fe_3O_4) = $(x + y)Fe_2O_3$ formed

$= (x + y)\frac{105.263}{100}$, (given)

Actual formed $= \left(\frac{160\,x}{144}\right) + \frac{480y}{464}$

$\therefore \quad \frac{160x}{144} + \frac{480y}{464} = (x + y)\,1.05263$

$\frac{10x}{9} + \frac{30y}{29} = (x + y)\,1.05263$

$\frac{x}{9} + \frac{3y}{29} = (x + y)\,0.105263$

$\therefore \quad$ Mass ratio, $\frac{x}{y} = 0.3103$

$\therefore \quad$ Molar ratio $= \frac{x/72}{y/232} = \frac{0.3103 \times 232}{72} \approx 1:1$

Hence, the value of $x + y$ is 2.

39. ***(32)*** On solving $x = 7.2$ g and $y = 23.3$ g

Thus, Fe_2O_3 formed $= (7.2 + 23.2)\frac{105.263}{100} \approx 32.0$ g

40. ***(0.1276)*** 1.0 L of 0.15 N NaOH = 0.15 mol

	2NaOH	+	CO_2	$\longrightarrow$	Na_2CO_3	+	H_2O
	2 mol		1 mol		1 mol		
Given	0.15 mol		11.2×10^{-3} mol				
Reacted	11.2×10^{-3} mol		11.2×10^{-3} mol				
After	$(0.15 - 11.2 \times 10^{-3} \times 2)$		0		11.2×10^{-3} mol		

NaOH left = (0.15 − 0.0224) mol in 1L

$\therefore \quad M$ (NaOH) = 0.1276 M

41. ***(0.0112)*** Na_2CO_3 formed $= 0.0112$ mol $L^{-1} = 0.0112$ M

42. ***(d)*** Among the given compounds, only two i.e., (ii) and (iii) which agree with the given data.

Element	Percentage	Atomic mass	Relative number of atoms	Simplest atomic ratio	Simple whole number ratio
C	$\frac{48.5}{116} \times 100 = 41.8\%$	12	$\frac{41.8}{12} \approx 3.5$	$\frac{3.5}{3.23} \approx 1$	1
H	$\frac{7.5}{116} \times 100 \approx 6.5\%$	1	$\frac{6.5}{1} = 6.5$	$\frac{6.5}{3.23} \approx 2$	2
O	$\frac{60}{116} \times 100 = 51.7\%$	16	$\frac{51.7}{16} = 3.23$	$\frac{3.23}{3.23} = 1$	1

$\therefore$ Empirical formula is CH_2O.

Molecular formula = $n \times$ Empirical formula

If $n = 1$, molecular formula = CH_2O and HCHO.

If $n = 2$, molecular formula = $(CH_2O)_2$ or = CH_3COOH.

Hence, both (iii) CH_3COOH and (ii) CH_2O can relate to this formula.

43. ***(c)*** Among the given values of volumes of the given sample only three i.e., (i), (iii) and (iv) are taken in order to prepare 0.75 M solution.

Given, $M_1 = 1$ M

$M_2 = 0.25$ M

Let V_1 and V_2 are volumes required.

$$(1.0 \times V_1 + 0.25 \times V_2) = 0.75(V_1 + V_2)$$
$$0.25V_1 = 0.5V_2$$
$$V_1 : V_2 = 2:1$$

Hence, the value of volumes which are present in 2 : 1 ratio are taken in order to prepare 0.75 M HCl solution.

44. ***(b)*** Among the given pairs, only two i.e., (iii) and (v) in which law of multiple proportion is obeyed because these compounds are formed with same element.

45. ***(a)*** Among the given combinations, only two i.e., (iii) and (v) illustrates the law of reciprocal proportions.

This law states that if two different elements combine separately with a fixed mass of a 3rd element, the ratio of masses in which they do so are either the same as or multiple of the ratio of the masses in which they combine with each other.

Ex. In combination CS_2, CO_2, SO_2

$$CS_2, C:S = 12:32$$
$$CO_2, C:O = 12:16$$

$\therefore$ Applying the above ratio, we find

$$S:O = C:O \text{ or } C:S = \frac{12}{16} \times \frac{32}{12} = \frac{32}{16} = 2:1$$

Also, in SO_2, the ratio weight is

$$S:O = 32:16 = 2:1,$$

Similarly combination (iii) also obey law of reciprocal proportions.

46. ***(b)*** Among the given pairs, only two i.e., (ii) and (iii) have equal number of molecules.

- Equal number of molecules are present when moles are same. For the same mass the molecular weight has to be same.

Hence, Mw of N_2 = *Mw* of CO = 28 g

Mw of N_2O = Mw of CO_2 = 44 g

47. ***(a)*** Among the given conversions, only three i.e, (iii), (iv) and (v) are correct while other are incorrect.

Their correct form are —

- 1 zeta gram = 10^{21} g
- 10 pounds = 4.54 kg

$\because$ 1 pound = 454×10^{-3} kg

$\therefore$ 10 pound = $\frac{454 \times 10^{-3} \text{ kg}}{10}$ = 4.54 kg

48. ***(a)*** Among the given solutions, only three i.e., (i), (iii) and (v) solutions has same molar concentration.

As, *Mw* of KI, $(NH_4)_2SO_2$, $CuSO_4 \cdot 5H_2O$, NaCl, Al^{3+}, KCl and CS_2 are 166, 132, 249.5, 58.5, 27, 74.5 and 76 respectively.

(i) $M = \frac{166 \times 1000}{166 \times 1000} = 1.0$ M

(ii) $M = \frac{33 \times 1000}{132 \times 200} = 1.25$ M

(iii) $M = \frac{25 \times 1000}{249.5 \times 100} \approx 1.0$ M

(iv) $M = \frac{38.2 \times 1000}{58.5 \times 50} \approx 13.06$ M

(v) $M = \frac{27 \times 10^{-3} \times 1000}{27 \times 1} = 1.0$ M

(vi) $M = \frac{7.45 \times 1000}{74.5 \times 200} = 0.5$ M

(vii) $M = \frac{28 \times 1000}{76 \times 100} = 3.68$ M

49. ***(c)*** Among the given reactions, only three i.e., (ii), (v) and (vi) does not obey the law of conservation of mass because the total mass of the reactant is not equal to the total mass of the product.

50. ***(d)*** Among the given relations, only three i.e., (ii), (iv) and (vii) have same number of significant figures i.e., 4.

Relation	Significant figure
(i) $\frac{0.02858 \times 0.112}{0.5702}$ =	3
(iii) 132.07 × 0.12 =	2
(v) 1.0003 =	5
(vi) $\frac{(1.12 \times 10^{-3}) \times 0.2}{1.2}$ =	1

51. ***(d)*** Among the given solutions, only two i.e., (i) and (ii) have the molality more than the 3 M aq. solution of NaCl.

In case 3 M aqueous solution of NaCl

Given,

Density = 1.25 g mL^{-1}, $M = 3$ M

$$\text{Molality } (m) = \frac{1000 \times M}{1000 \times d - (M \times W_{solute})} \quad [Mw \text{ NaCl} = 58.5]$$

$$= \frac{1000 \times 3}{1000 \times 1.25 - [3 \times 58.5]} = 2.79 \text{ m}$$

(i) 3.3 M solution of NaOH

$d = 1.25$ g mL^{-1}, $M = 3.3$

Molecular mass of NaOH = 40

$$m = \frac{1000 \times 3.3}{1000 \times 1.25 - [3.3 \times 40]}$$

$$= \frac{3300}{1250 - 132} = 2.95 \text{ m}$$

(ii) $m = \frac{1000 \times 3.28}{1000 \times 1.2 - [3.28 \times 36.46]}$

$$= \frac{3280}{1080.41} = 3.03 \text{ m}$$

(iii) $m = \frac{1000 \times 2.30}{1000 \times 1.84 - [2.30 \times 98]} = \frac{2300}{1614.6} = 1.42$ m

(iv) $m = \dfrac{1000 \times 2}{1000 \times 3.856 - [2 \times 208.23]} = \dfrac{2000}{3439.54} = 0.58\,m$

(v) $m = \dfrac{1000 \times 2.31}{1000 \times 1.69 - [2.31 \times 75]} = \dfrac{2310}{1516.75} = 1.52\,m$

(vi) $m = \dfrac{1000 \times 1.11}{1000 \times 1.25 - [1.11 \times 58.5]} = \dfrac{1110}{1185} = 0.93\,m$

(vii) $m = \dfrac{1000 \times 3}{1000 \times 2.71 - [3 \times 100]} = \dfrac{3000}{2410} = 1.24\,m$

52. ***(d)*** Among the given solution, only two i.e., (ii) and (iv) has equal mass of $Cl^{\ominus}$ ions in 1.0 L.

Using the formula, $M = \dfrac{\%\text{ by weight} \times 10 \times d}{Mw_2}$;

$$M = \dfrac{w_2 \times 1000}{Mw_2 \times V_{sol}\text{ (in mL)}}$$

(i) $M = \dfrac{5 \times 10 \times 1.07}{58.5} = 0.91\,M$

($Cl^{\ominus} = 0.91,\ M = 0.91 \times 35.5 = 32.31\,g$)

(ii) $M = \dfrac{55.5 \times 1000}{111 \times 1000} = 0.5\,M$

($Cl^{\ominus} = 2 \times M = 2 \times 0.5 = 1\,M = 1 \times 35.5 = 35.5\,g$)

(iii) $M = \dfrac{5 \times 10 \times 1.06}{74.5} = 0.71\,M$

($Cl^{\ominus} = 0.71\ M = 0.71 \times 35.5 = 25.205\,g$)

(iv) $M = \dfrac{58.5 \times 1000}{58.5 \times 1000} = 1\,M$

($Cl^{\ominus} = 1\ M = 1 \times 35.5 = 35.5\,g$)

(v) $M = \dfrac{3 \times 10 \times 1.59}{154} = 0.3\,M$

($Cl^{\ominus} = 0.3\ M = 0.3 \times 4 \times 35.5 = 42.6\,g$)

(vi) $M = \dfrac{28.3 \times 1000}{135 \times 1000} = 0.2\,M$

($Cl^{\ominus} = 0.2 \times 2\ M = 0.2 \times 2 \times 35.5 = 14.2\,g$)

(vii) $M = \dfrac{952 \times 1000}{952 \times 1000} = 1\,M$

($Cl^{\ominus} = 2\ M = 2 \times 1 \times 35.5 = 71\,g$)

Check Through PYQs : JEE Advanced

1. ***(b,c)*** (a) If empirical formula of compound 3 is P_3Q_4.

We know that,

$$\frac{3 \times M_P}{4 \times M_Q} = \frac{\%\text{ of } P}{\%\text{ of } Q}$$

where, M_P = molar mass of P

M_Q = molar mass of Q

$$\frac{3M_P}{4M_Q} = \frac{40}{60} = \frac{2}{3}$$

$$\Rightarrow \quad \frac{M_P}{M_Q} = \frac{8}{9}$$

If empirical formula of compound 2 is P_3Q_5.

$$\frac{3M_P}{5M_Q} = \frac{44}{55}$$

$$\frac{M_P}{M_Q} = \frac{20}{15} = \frac{4}{3}$$

Since molecular weight ratio does not come out equal in two compounds, '2' and '3'. So, statement (a) cannot be correct.

(b) If empirical formula of '3' is P_3Q_2

$$\frac{3M_P}{2M_Q} = \frac{40}{60} = \frac{2}{3} \Rightarrow \frac{M_P}{M_Q} = \frac{4}{9}$$

If atomic weight of $P = 20$ and that of $Q = 45$

$$\frac{M_P}{M_Q} = \frac{20}{45} = \frac{4}{9}$$

So, statement (b) is correct.

(c) If empirical formula of 2 is PQ

$$\frac{M_P}{M_Q} = \frac{44}{55} = \frac{4}{5}$$

and compound '1' is P_5Q_4

$$\frac{5M_P}{4M_Q} = \frac{50}{50} = \frac{1}{1}$$

Putting value of $\dfrac{M_P}{M_Q} = \dfrac{4}{5}$,

we get $\dfrac{5}{4} \times \dfrac{4}{5} = 1$

So, statement (c) is correct.

(d) $M_P = 70$, $M_Q = 35$

If empirical formula of compound '1' is P_2Q.

$$\frac{2M_P}{M_Q} = \frac{50}{50} = 1$$

$\Rightarrow \quad 2M_P = M_Q$

$M_P = \dfrac{M_Q}{2}$ (M_P is half of M_Q)

But, M_P is shown as double to M_Q.

So, this statement is not correct.

So, only statements (b) and (c) are correct.

2. ***(222)***

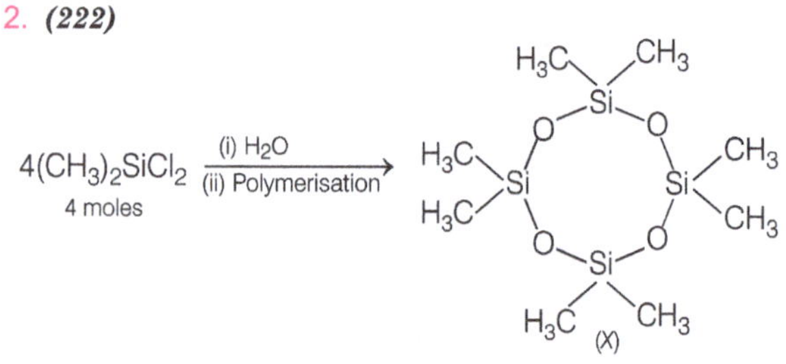

Molar mass of dimethyldichlorosilane = 129 g/mol

Moles of dimethyldichlorosilane initially taken $= \dfrac{516}{129} = 4$

Molar mass of product formed = 296

Moles of product formed = 1 × 0.75 moles = 0.75 moles

Mass of product formed = 0.75 × 296 = 222 g.

3. ***(2.38)*** Mass of white phosphorus, P_4 = 1.24 g

Molar mass of $P_4 = 4 \times 31 = 124 \text{ g mol}^{-1}$

$$\text{Moles of } P_4 = \frac{1.24}{124} = 0.01 \text{ mol}$$

Reaction involved,

$$P_4(s) + 3NaOH(aq) + 3H_2O(l) \longrightarrow PH_3(g) + 3NaH_2PO_2(aq)$$

NaOH is present in excess, so P_4 is limiting reagent. Thus, amount of PH_3 formed is 0.01 mole.

Reaction of PH_3 with $CuSO_4$, can written as

$$2PH_3 + 3CuSO_4 \longrightarrow Cu_3P_2 + 3H_2SO_4$$

2 moles PH_3 reacts with 3 moles $CuSO_4$ by double displacement reaction.

0.01 mole PH_3 reacts with $\frac{3 \times 0.01}{2} = 0.015$ mole $CuSO_4$.

$$\begin{aligned}\text{Molar mass of } CuSO_4 &= 63 + 32 + 4 \times 16\\ &= 63 + 32 + 64\\ &= 159 \text{ g mol}^{-1}\end{aligned}$$

Mass of $CuSO_4 = 0.015 \times 159 = 2.38$ g

4. ***(6.15)*** Aluminium reacts with sulphuric acid to form aluminium sulphate and hydrogen.

$$\underset{\left(\frac{5.4}{27} = 0.2 \text{ mol}\right)}{2Al} + \underset{\left(\frac{50 \times 5}{1000} = 0.25 \text{ mol}\right)}{3H_2SO_4} \longrightarrow Al_2(SO_4)_3 + 3H_2$$

H_2SO_4 is limiting reagent and moles of $H_2(g)$ produced = 0.25 mol

Using ideal gas equation,

$$pV = nRT$$

$$\Rightarrow \quad V = \frac{0.25 \times 0.082 \times 300}{1 \text{ atm}} \Rightarrow 6.15 \text{ L}$$

5. ***(6.47)*** The equations of chemical reactions occurring during the process are

In the presence of oxygen

$$2PbS + 3O_2 \longrightarrow 2PbO + 2SO_2 \quad \ldots\text{(i)}$$

By self reduction $2PbO + PbS \longrightarrow 3Pb + SO_2$

Thus, 3 moles of O_2 produces 3 moles of Pb

i.e. 32 × 3 = 96 g of O_2 produces 3 × 207 = 621 g of Pb

So, 1000 g (1kg) of oxygen will produce

$$\frac{621}{96} \times 1000 = 6468.75 \text{ g}$$

$$= 6.4687 \text{ kg} \approx 6.47 \text{ kg}$$

Alternate Method

From the direct equation, $\underset{32\text{ g}}{PbS + O_2} \longrightarrow \underset{207\text{ g}}{Pb} + SO_2$

So, 32 g of O_2 gives 207 g of Pb

1 g of O_2 will give $\frac{207}{32}$ g of Pb

$$\begin{aligned}1000\text{g of } O_2 \text{ will give } \frac{207}{32} \times 1000 &= 6468.75 \text{ g}\\ &= 6.46875 \text{ kg}\\ &\approx 6.47 \text{kg}\end{aligned}$$

6. ***(2992)*** Balanced equations of reactions used in the problem are as follows

(i) $\underset{\substack{1\text{ mol}\\132\text{ g}}}{(NH_4)_2SO_4} + Ca(OH)_2 \longrightarrow \underset{\substack{1\text{ mol}\\172\text{ g}}}{CaSO_4 \cdot 2H_2O} + \underset{\substack{2\text{ mol}\\(2\times17) = 34\text{ g}}}{2NH_3}$

(ii) $\underset{\substack{1\text{ mol}\\238\text{ g}}}{NiCl_2 \cdot 6H_2O} + \underset{\substack{6\text{ mol}\\102\text{ g}}}{6NH_3} \longrightarrow \underset{\substack{1\text{ mol}\\232\text{ g}}}{[Ni(NH_3)_6]Cl_2} + 6H_2O$

Now, in Eq. (i)

if, 1584 g of ammonium sulphate is used.

i.e., 1584 g $(NH_4)_2SO_4 = \frac{1584}{132} = 12$ mol

So, according to the Eq. (i) given above 12 moles of $(NH_4)_2SO_4$ produces

(a) 12 moles of gypsum $(CaSO_4 \cdot 2H_2O)$

(b) 24 moles of ammonia

Here, 12 moles of gypsum = 12 × 172 = 2064 g

and 24 moles of NH_3 = 24 × 17 = 408 g

Further, as given in question,

24 moles of NH_3 produced in reaction (i) is completly utilised by 952g or 4 moles of $NiCl_2 \cdot 6H_2O$ to produce 4 moles of $[Ni(NH_3)_6]Cl_2$.

So, 4 moles of $[Ni(NH_3)_6]Cl_2 = 4 \times 232 = 928$ g

Hence, total mass of gypsum and nickel ammonia coordination compound $[Ni(NH_3)_6]Cl_2$

$$= 2064 + 928 = 2992 \text{ g}$$

7. ***(126)*** The balanced equations are

(1) $2MnCl_2 + 5K_2S_2O_8 + 8H_2O \longrightarrow 2KMnO_4 + 4K_2SO_4 + 6H_2SO_4 + 4HCl$

(2) $2KMnO_4 + 5H_2C_2O_4 + 3H_2SO_4 \longrightarrow K_2SO_4 + 2MnSO_4 + 8H_2O + 10CO_2$

Given, mass of oxalic acid added = 225mg

So, millimoles of oxalic acid added $= \frac{225}{90} = 2.5$

Now from equation, 2, Millimoles of $KMnO_4$ used to react with oxalic acid = 1

and Millimoles of $MnCl_2$ required initially = 1

∴ Mass of $MnCl_2$ required initially = 1 × (55 + 71) = 126 mg

m moles of $MnCl_2$ = *m* moles of $KMnO_4 = x$ (let)

and M_{eq} of $KMnO_4 = M_{eq}$ of oxalic acid

So, $x \times 5 = \frac{225}{90} \times 2$

Hence, $x = 1$; $\therefore$ m moles of $MnCl_2 = 1$

Hence, mass of $MnCl_2 = (55 + 71) \times 1 = 126$mg.

8. ***(0.11)*** Oxalic acid solution titrated with NaOH solution using phenolphthalein as an indicator.

$$H_2C_2O_4 + 2NaOH \longrightarrow Na_2C_2O_4 + 2H_2O$$

Equivalent of $H_2C_2O_4$ reacted = Equivalent of NaOH reacted

$$= \frac{5 \times 2 \times 0.1}{1000}$$

$$= \frac{9 \times M_{(NaOH)} \times 1}{1000}$$

$$M_{(NaOH)} = \frac{1}{9} = 0.11$$

9. ***(9)*** Moles of solute, $n_1 = \frac{w_1}{m_1}$; Moles of solvent, $n_2 = \frac{w_2}{m_2}$

χ_1 (solute) = 0.1 and χ_2 (solvent) = 0.9

$$\therefore \quad \frac{\chi_1}{\chi_2} = \frac{n_1}{n_2} = \frac{w_1}{m_1} \cdot \frac{m_2}{w_2} = \frac{1}{9}$$

$$\text{Molarity} = \frac{\text{Solute (moles)}}{\text{Volume (L)}}$$

$$= \frac{w_1 \times 1000 \times 2}{m_1 (w_1 + w_2)}$$

Note Volume $= \frac{\text{Total mass of solution}}{\text{Density}}$

$$= \left(\frac{w_1 + w_2}{2}\right) \text{mL}$$

$$\text{Molality} = \frac{\text{Solute (moles)}}{\text{Solvent (kg)}}$$

$$= \frac{w_1 \times 1000}{m_1 \times w_2}$$

Given, molarity = molality

hence, $\frac{2000\, w_1}{m_1 (w_1 + w_2)} = \frac{1000\, w_1}{m_1\, w_2}$

$$\therefore \quad \frac{w_2}{w_1 + w_2} = \frac{1}{2}$$

$$\Rightarrow \quad w_1 = w_2 = 1$$

$$\therefore \quad \frac{w_1\, m_2}{m_1\, w_2} = \frac{1}{9}$$

$$\Rightarrow \quad \frac{m_1 \text{ (solute)}}{m_2 \text{ (solvent)}} = 9$$

CHAPTER 2

Atomic Structure

Learning Elements

Element 1 **Bohr's Model and its Application**

Subatomic Particles, Atomic Models, Electromagnetic Radiations, Black body Radiations, Electromagnetic Spectrum, Planck's Quantum Theory, Photoelectric Effect, Bohr's Model, Mathematical Application's of Bohr's Model

Element 2 **Dual Nature of Matter and Wave Mechanical Model**

Dual Behaviour of Matter, Wave Mechanical Model, Heisenberg's Uncertainity Principle, The Schrodinger's Equation, Radial Probability Distribution of Electrons, Shapes a Angular Distribution of Electrons, Quantum Numbers, Electronic Configuration of an Atom.

Practice Elements

Practice Element 1 Target JEE Main
Practice Element 2 Target JEE Advanced

Trend Insights

JEE Main

	2024				2023				2022				2021			
Topics	**E**	**M**	**T**	**O**	**E**	**M**	**T**	**O**	**E**	**M**	**T**	**O**	**E**	**M**	**T**	**O**
Bohr's Model and its Application	2	4	2	11	3	4	0	7	2	4	1	7	2	4	3	9
Dual Nature of Matter and Wave Mechanical Model	3	7	1	11	3	4	2	9	5	6	2	13	3	6	4	13

E = Easy, **M** = Medium, **T** = Tough, **O** = Overall

Current Dynamics

- Moderate level of questions on quantum mechanical model were asked in recent years.
- Weightage of preliminary models and dual nature of light has decreased in 2024.
- Similar questions were repeated multiple times in last 3 years.
- Direct formula based questions were asked from dual nature of matter and uncertainity principle.

JEE Advanced

Typology	Years				
	2024	2023	2022	2021	2020
1. Simple MCQs	1				
2. One or More than one correct	1				
3. Numerical Value/Integer		1		1	1
4. Matching Type					
5. Paragraph Based					

Current Dynamics

- In 2024, both questions were asked from application of Bohr's model.
- Mostly Numerical value type questions were asked in recent year.
- Overall Weightage of questions was increased in 2024.

Insightful Advice

- This chapter is important at JEE Main and advanced level. To master this chapter, understanding of key concept like Bohr's model, quantum number and visualisation of atomic structure is needed.
- Focus on mastering key formulas, practice PYQ's problems to reinforce the concepts and improve calculations and accuracy.
- At JEE advanced level, students should focus on Schrodinger wave equation and concept of probability density and wave function for different orbitals.

Element 1 Bohr's Model and Its Application

Imagine atoms as tiny, unseen building blocks that combine in various ways to create everything you see, touch and even taste. Despite their minuscule size, these particles possess a complex internal structure that defines their properties and behaviours. Understanding atomic structure is crucial for grasping the principles of chemistry and material science.

Subatomic Particles

Atoms can be further divided into sub-atomic particles, i.e., electrons, protons and neutrons called **fundamental particles.**

Nature of Fundamental Particles

Name	Electron	Proton	Neutron
Symbol	e^-	p	n
Approximate relative mass	1/1836	1	1
Mass in kg	9.109×10^{-31}	1.673×10^{-27}	1.675×10^{-27}
Mass in amu	5.485×10^{-4}	1.007	1.008
Charge (Coulomb)	-1.602×10^{-19}	1.602×10^{-19}	0
Actual charge (esu)	4.8×10^{-10}	4.8×10^{-8}	0
Discovered by	J.J. Thomson	Goldstein	Chadwick

In 1897, J.J. Thomson measured charge/mass ratio of the electron (-1.7588×10^8 C/g) and also its velocity by using cathode ray tube.

Atomic Species

Following species are common in relation to atoms.

(i) **Atomic Number** (Z) It represents the number of protons or electrons in a neutral atom.

(ii) **Mass Number** (A) It represents the total number of protons and neutrons in an atom.

(iii) **Nucleons** The sum of protons and neutrons which are present in a nucleus are collectively known as nucleons.

(iv) **Isotopes** Atoms of the element with same atomic number but different mass number. e.g., ${}_1H^1, {}_1H^2, {}_1H^3$.

(v) **Isobars** Atoms having the same mass number but different atomic numbers, e.g., ${}_{15}P^{32}$ and ${}_{16}S^{32}$.

(vi) **Isotones** Atoms having the same number of neutrons but different number of protons or mass number, e.g. ${}_6C^{14}, {}_8O^{16}, {}_7N^{15}$.

(vii) **Isoelectronic** Species having same number of electrons, e.g., N_2, CO, CN^-.

(viii) **Nuclear Isomers** Atoms with the same atomic number and same mass number but with different radioactive properties. Example of nuclear isomers is Uranium –X (half-life 1.4 min) and Uranium –Z (half life 6.7 hours).

(ix) **Isodiaphers** These species have same isotopic number, which is obtained by subtracting double of atomic number from atomic mass (or mass number). i.e. Isotopic number = mass number $- 2 \times$ atomic number.

e.g., ${}_{19}K^{39}$ and ${}_9F^{19}$ are isodiaphers.

Atomic Models

After the discovery of subatomic particles, their arrangement inside the atom became a new challenge for scientists. To solve this problem, various models were proposed. These models were called **atomic models.**

Thomson's Atomic Model

(Plum-pudding model)

Postulate Atom is a sphere of positive charge in which number of electrons are embedded.

Limitations Could not satisfactorily explain the results of scattering experiment carried out by Rutherford.

Rutherford's Model

Postulates

- Almost all the positive charge and mass of atom is present in its nucleus.
- Electrons revolve around the nucleus in circular orbits.
- There is strong electrostatic attraction between nucleus and electrons.

Limitations Could not explain stability and electronic structure of atom.

JEE Quicker

If the Thomson model of the atom was correct, then the result of Rutherford's gold foil experiment would have been α-particles pass through the gold deflected by small angles and with reduced speed. *JEE Main 2021*

In Rutherford model, the particles were deflected at large angles but in thomson model, protons are diffused (charge is not centered). So, α-particles deviated by small angles and with reduced speed.

Nature of Light and Electromagnetic Waves

To deepen the understanding of atomic structure, scientists aimed to visualise the arrangement of electrons around the nucleus. This comprehension based on the interactions between matter and various types of electromagnetic radiation. Danish physicist Niels Bohr enhanced Rutherford model by incorporating the dual nature of electromagnetic radiation.

Wave Nature of Electromagnetic Radiations

James Maxwell (1870) observed that when electrically charged particle moves under acceleration, alternating electrical and magnetic fields are produced and transmitted in the form of waves called **electromagnetic waves** or **electromagnetic radiations**.

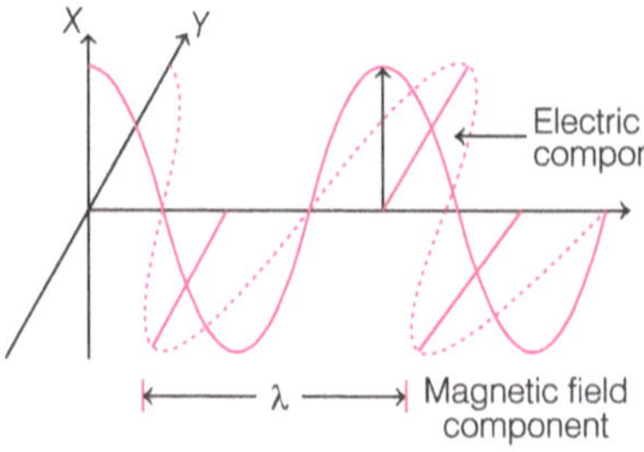

Simplified picture of electromagnetic waves

Wave theory considers light to be a form of wave motion of wavelength λ, related to frequency ν and velocity of light c by equation,

$$\nu = \frac{c}{\lambda}$$

Thus, velocity of light = frequency × wavelength

Characteristics of Wave

The electromagnetic radiations are characterised by different terms which are discussed below

(i) **Wavelength** It is defined as the distance between two consecutive crests or troughs of a wave. It is generally expressed in angstrom (Å) or nanometre (nm).

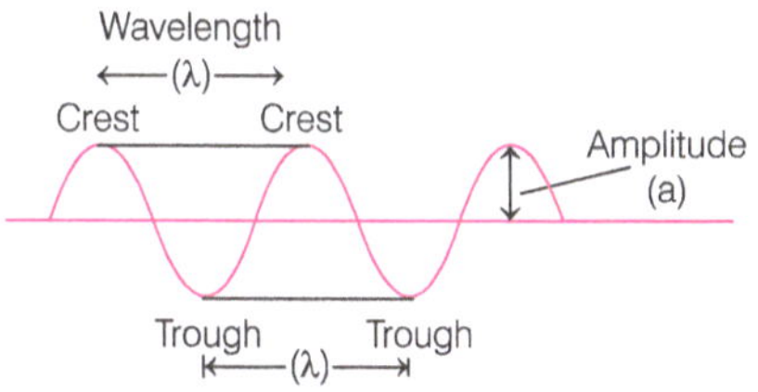

Propagation of Wave motion

(ii) **Frequency** (ν) of a wave is defined as the number of waves passing through a point in one second. It is expressed in Hertz (Hz) or cycles/sec or simply sec^{-1} or s^{-1}.

1 Hz = 1 cycle/sec

(iii) **Velocity** (v) of a wave is defined as the linear distance travelled by the wave in one second. It is expressed in cm/sec or m/sec (ms^{-1}).

(iv) **Amplitude** (a) of a wave is the height of the crest or the depth of the trough. It is expressed in the units of length.

(v) **Wave number** ($\bar{\nu}$) is defined as the number of waves present in 1 cm length. Evidently is equal to the reciprocal of the wavelength.

(vi) **Time period** (T) Time taken by the wave for one complete cycle or vibration is called time period. It is expressed in second per cycle.

Electromagnetic Spectrum

Various types of electromagnetic radiations having various wavelengths (or frequencies) are known and summarised in figure. They constitute the so called **electromagnetic spectrum.**

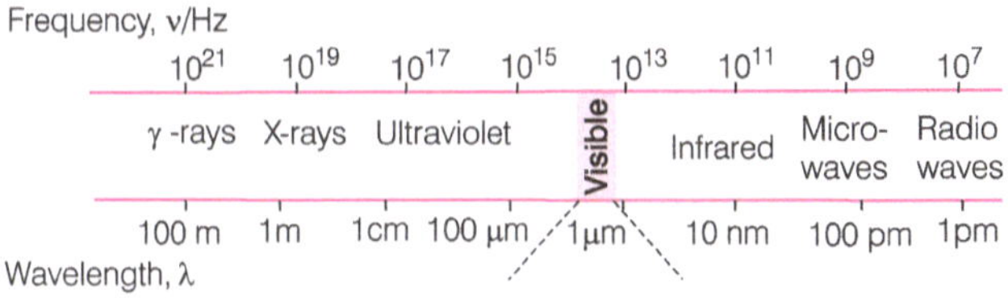

The spectrum of electromagnetic radiation

Visible light is just a small portion of electromagnetic radiation. The colours of visible light are given below

Colour	Wavelength range/nm
Red	740-625
Orange	625-590
Yellow	590-565
Green	565-490
Blue	490-440
Violet	440-390

JEE Alert

- In vacuum, all types of electromagnetic radiation regardless of their wavelength, travel at the same speed, i.e $3 \times 10^8\ ms^{-1}$.
- Unlike sound waves or water waves, electromagnetic waves do not require medium and can move in vacuum.

Moseley's Experiment

Moseley, working in Rutherford's team, in 1913, studied the wavelength of the characteristic X-rays that were produced by using different metals as anti-cathode that were placed in the path of cathode rays. He postulated that the frequency of the X-rays produced in this manner was related to the charge present on the nucleus of an atom of the element used as anti-cathode. By Moseley's equation,

$$\sqrt{\nu} = a(Z - b)$$

where, ν refers to the frequency, Z the nuclear charge (atomic number) and a and b are constants.

Particle Nature of Electromagnetic Radiations

Although wave theory successfully explained the phenomenon of interference and diffraction but it was unable to explain:

(i) The nature of emission of radiation from hot bodies i.e. black body radiation.
(ii) Ejection of electrons from metal surface i.e. photoelectric effect.
(iii) Line spectra of atoms.

Black Body Radiations

According to max Planck theory, an ideal body which emits and absorbs all frequencies of radiation uniformly is called a **black body** and the radiation emitted by this body is called **black body radiation.** The dependence is illustrated in figure which shows how the energy distribution varies with wavelength at several temperature.

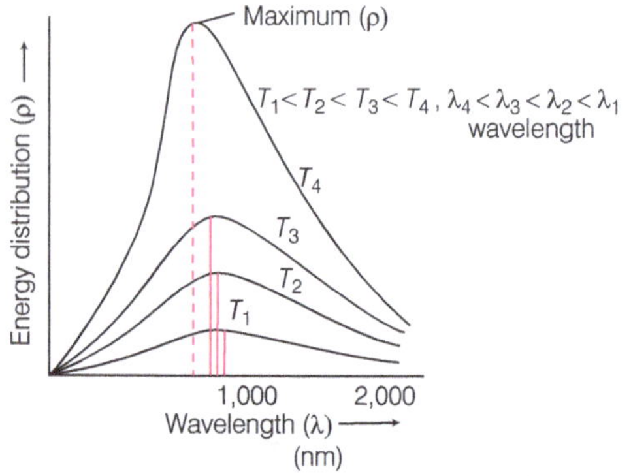

The energy distribution in a black body cavity at several temperatures, as the temperature is raised, the peak shifts to shorter wavelength

The exact frequency distribution of the emitted radiation from a black body depends on its temperature. At a given temperature, the intensity of radiation emitted increases with increase of wavelength, reaches a maximum value and then starts decreasing with further increase of wavelength.

Above figure shows that shorter wavelenghts contribute more to the energy density as the temperature is raised. Wien explained shift in terms of Wien's displacement law,

$$T\,\lambda_{max} = \text{constant}$$

where the value of constant is 2.9 mm K.

λ_{max} is the wavelength of the radiation that makes the greatest contribution to the energy density. Wien's law implies that as T increases, λ_{max} decreases enough to maintain the value of $T\,\lambda_{max}$ constant.

Planck's Quantum Theory : Quantisation of Light Energy

The black body radiation could not be explained on the basis of wave theory of light. Max Planck explained the behaviour of black body radiation.

The assumption of Planck's theory are given below

(i) The radiant energy is emitted or absorbed discontinuously in the form of small discrete packets of energy called a **quanta**. In case of light, the quantum of energy is known as **photon**.
(ii) The energy of quanta is proportional to its frequency and is expressed as $E = h\nu = \frac{hc}{\lambda}$ where, h is the proportionality constant called Planck's constant with the value 6.626×10^{-34} Js.

    The greater the frequency (i.e. the shorter the wavelength) the greater is the energy of the radiation.
(iii) The energy emitted or absorbed by a body is always an integral multiple of $h\nu$, i.e. $2h\nu$, $3h\nu$, ...

    Hence, $E = nh\nu$

    where, n is any integer

Solved Booster 1.1

The energy of one mole of photons having a wavelength of 5.42×10^{-6} m will be

(a) 25.078 (b) 60.280
(c) 22.078 (d) 56.280

Solution (c)

Energy is related to wavelength by Planck's equation

$$E = h\nu = \frac{hc}{\lambda}$$

$$E = \frac{6.626 \times 10^{-34}\ \text{Js} \times 3 \times 10^{8}\ \text{ms}^{-1}}{5.42 \times 10^{-6}\ \text{m}}$$

$= 3.6675 \times 10^{-20}$ J for one photon

$= 3.6675 \times 10^{-20} \times 6.02 \times 10^{23}$ J for one mol of photon

$= 22.078 \times 10^{3}\ \text{J mol}^{-1}$

$= 22.078\ \text{kJ mol}^{-1}$

Photoelectric Effect

In 1887, H. Hertz performed an experiment, in which electrons were ejected when light of a certain frequency strikes the surface of a cathode metal (like potassium, rubidium, caesium etc.,). This phenomenon of ejection of electrons from the structure of a metal when light of suitable frequency strikes it is called **photoelectric effect**. The electrons emitted are called **photoelectrons**. The apparatus used for this experiment is given below.

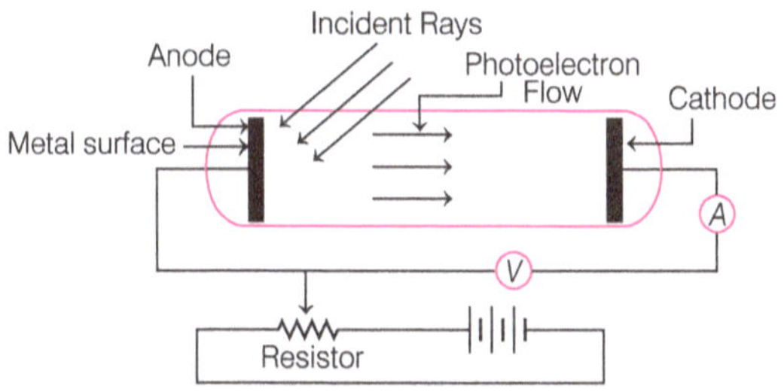

Some important **observations** made during the experiment of photoelectric effect are as follows

(i) There is **no time lag** between the striking of light beam and the ejection of electron from the metal surface.

(ii) For each metal, there is a characteristic minimum frequency, ν_0 (called **threshold frequency**) below which photoelectric effect is not observed. At a frequency $\nu > \nu_0$, the ejected electrons come out with certain kinetic energy, which increases with increase of frequency of light used.

JEE Alert

The kinetic energy of the electron ejected depends upon the frequencies of the incident radiation and is independent of its intensity.

(iii) The minimum energy above which electrons are ejected is called **work function**.

(iv) When potential is applied on collector, the KE of photoelectron is reduced and for a certain value of applied potential, the KE becomes zero. This minimum potential of anode to reduce the K.E of photoelectron to zero is known as stopping potential (V_0).

The kinetic energy of the emitted electrons is given by $KE = eV_0$

So by measuring V_0, maximum kinetic energy of the photoelectrons can be calculated.

Explanation

- Einstein explained the quantised nature of light while explaining the phenomenon of photoelectric effect.
- At a given frequency, increase in the intensity of light increases the number of photons, but not the energies of photons. Hence, when the intensity of light is increased, more electrons are ejected. But the energies of these electrons are not altered.
- If the energy of photon is more than the energy required to remove electron then

Energy of striking photon (ν) = threshold energy + maximum kinetic energy of ejected e^-

Minimum energy required to eject electron or threshold energy

$$= h\nu_0 = W_0 \text{ (work function also denoted by } \phi)$$

$$\therefore \quad h\nu = h\nu_0 + \frac{1}{2}mv^2 \quad \text{or } h\nu - h\nu_0 = \frac{1}{2}mv^2$$

where, m = mass of electron, v = velocity of ejected electron

Also, $$KE_{max} = h\nu - h\nu_0 = h(\nu - \nu_0) = hc\left[\frac{1}{\lambda} - \frac{1}{\lambda_0}\right]$$

Values of work function (W_0) of few metals are

Metal	Li	Na	K	Mg	Cu	Ag
W_0/eV	2.42	2.30	2.25	3.70	4.80	4.30

JEE MAPPER

Example Similar to PYQ Asked in JEE Advanced 2024

Values of work function (w_0) for a few metals are given below.

Metal	Li	Na	K	Mg	Cu
W_0/eV	2.42	2.3	2.25	3.7	4.8

The number of metals which will show photoelectric effect when light of wavelength 630 nm falls on it is ....

Given, $h = 6.6 \times 10^{-34}$ Js, $c = 3 \times 10^8$ ms^{-1}

$e = 1.6 \times 10^{-19}$ C

Sol. (0) Photoelectric effect will take place, only when the work function of given metals is lower than the energy incident light with wavelength 630 nm.

Energy of incident light $= h\nu = \dfrac{hc}{\lambda}$

$$E \text{ (eV)} = \frac{1240}{\lambda} = \frac{1240}{630} = 1.97 \text{ eV}$$

Thus, no metals will show photoelectric effect.

Competency Enhancer 1.1

Values of work function (w_0) for a few metals are given below.

Metal	K	Mg	Cu	Ag
W_0/eV	2.25	3.7	4.8	4.3

The number of metals which will show photoelectric effect when light of wavelength 350 nm falls on it is ....

Given, $h = 6.6 \times 10^{-34}$ Js, $c = 3 \times 10^8$ ms^{-1}

$e = 1.6 \times 10^{-19}$ C

Solved Booster 1.2

If P is the momentum of the fastest electron ejected from a metal surface after the irradiation of light having wavelength λ, then for 1.5 P momentum of the photoelectron, the wavelength of the light should be (Assume kinetic energy of ejected photoelectron to be very high in comparison to work function)

(a) $\frac{4}{9}\lambda$ (b) $\frac{3}{4}\lambda$ (c) $\frac{2}{3}\lambda$ (d) $\frac{1}{2}\lambda$

Solution *(a)*

The expression of kinetic energy of photo electrons,

$$KE = \frac{1}{2}mv^2 = E - E_0$$

When, $KE >> E_0$, the equation becomes, $KE = \frac{1}{2}mv^2 = E$

$$\frac{1}{2}mv^2 = \frac{1}{2} \times \frac{(mv)^2}{m} = \frac{1}{2}\frac{p^2}{m}$$

$$E = \frac{hc}{\lambda} = \text{energy of incident light}$$

So, $\frac{1}{2}mv^2 = \frac{hc}{\lambda} \Rightarrow \frac{P^2}{2m} = \frac{hc}{\lambda}$

$\Rightarrow \lambda = hc \times 2m \times \frac{1}{P^2} \Rightarrow \lambda \propto \frac{1}{P^2}$

As per the given condition, $\frac{\lambda_2}{\lambda_1} = \left(\frac{P_1}{P_2}\right)^2$

$\Rightarrow \frac{\lambda_2}{\lambda} = \left(\frac{P}{1.5 \times P}\right)^2 = \left(\frac{2}{3}\right)^2 = \frac{4}{9} \Rightarrow \lambda_2 = \frac{4}{9}\lambda$ $\left[\because \lambda_1 = \lambda,\ P_1 = P\right]$

Concept Visualizer

All the curves associated with photoelectric effect are given below.

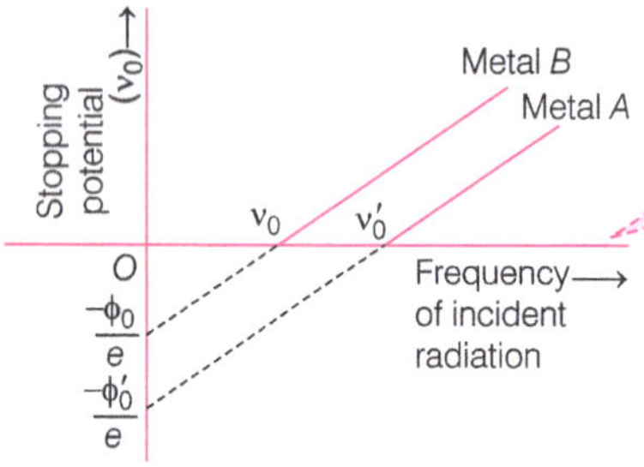

This graph shows as the work function of the metal increases, the threshold frequency (ν_0) increases (ν_0' (Metal A) > ν_0 (Metal B))

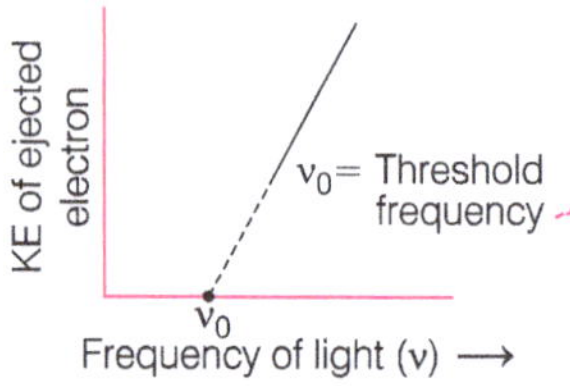

This graph shows that the kinetic energy of photoelectrons increases linearly with frequency of incident radiation.

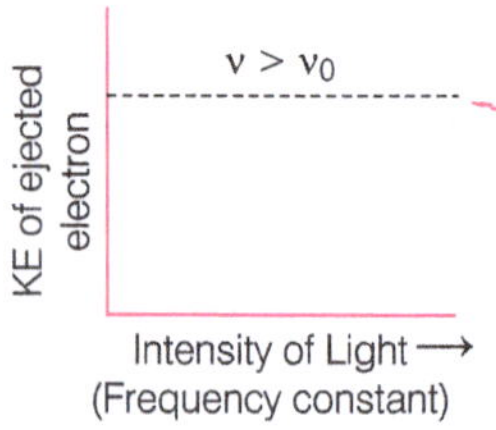

This graph shows that the kinetic energy does not depends on the intensity of light. Intensity affects the number of photoelectrons.

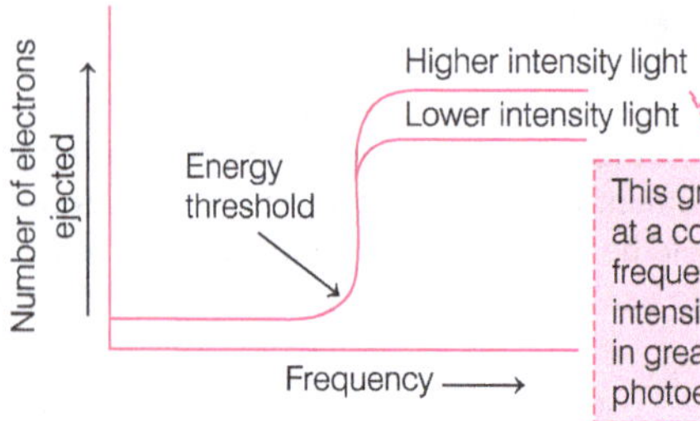

This graph shows that at a constant frequency, higher intensity of light results in greater number of photoelectrons.

Atomic Spectra

It is observed that when a ray of white light is passed through a prism, it undergo deviation. The angle of deviation is directly proportional to the frequency and inversely proportional to the wavelength of light. The wave with shorter wavelength bends more than the one with a longer wavelength.

Ordinary white light consist of waves with all the wavelengths in the visible light, hence a ray of white light is spread out into a series of coloured bands called spectrum.

In other words, "The pictorial representation of arrangement of radiations in increasing order of wavelength or decreasing order of frequency is called spectrum".

The spectrum of white light ranges from violet (at 7.50×10^{14}Hz) to red (at 4×10^{14} Hz). Such a spectrum is called **continuous spectrum**. It is continuous because violet merges into blue, blue into green and so on. The light of red colour with longest wavelength is deviated the least while the violet light with shortest wavelength is deviated the most.

When electromagnetic radiation interacts with matter, atoms and molecules may absorb energy and attain higher energy state called **excited state**. In excited state they are unstable, (lower the energy, more is the stability of the given state) hence emit radiation in various regions of electromagnetic spectrum and transit to lower energy state.

Depending upon the radiation absorbed or emitted, spectrum is classified into two categories given below.

Emission Spectrum

Atoms, molecules and ions which emit radiations after absorbing energy are said to be in excited state. The spectrum of such emitted radiation is called **emission spectra.**

- A substance may be excited either by passing electric discharge through a gas at low pressure or by heating the substance to high temperature.
- Each spectral line of emission spectra is characterised by one electronic transition from higher energy level to lower energy level (i.e. de excitation).

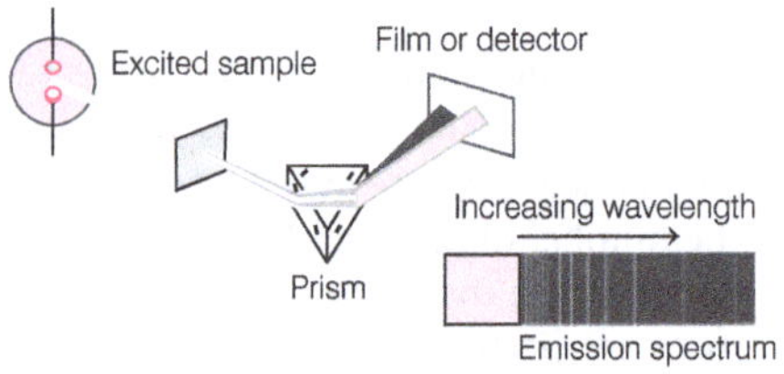

Representation of atomic emission specturm

Emission spectra is further classified into two types

(i) **Continuous Spectrum** When sunlight is passed through a prism, it gets dispersed into continuous bands of different colours. If the light of an incandescent object is resolved through prism or spectroscope, it gives continuous spectrum of colours. Thus, this spectrum appears like a continuous band of radiations.

(ii) **Line Spectrum** If the radiations: obtained by the excitation of a substance are analysed with the help of a spectroscope a series of thin bright lines of specific colours are obtained. There is dark space in between two consecutive lines. This type of spectrum is called line spectrum or atomic spectrum.

Absorption Spectrum

An **absorption spectra** is like the photographic negative of an emission spectra.

To obtain an absorption spectra a continum of radiation is passed through a sample which absorbs radiation of certain wavelength. The missing wavelength which corresponds to the radiation absorbed by the matter leave dark lines in the bright continuous spectrum. These lines constitute the **absorption spectrum.**

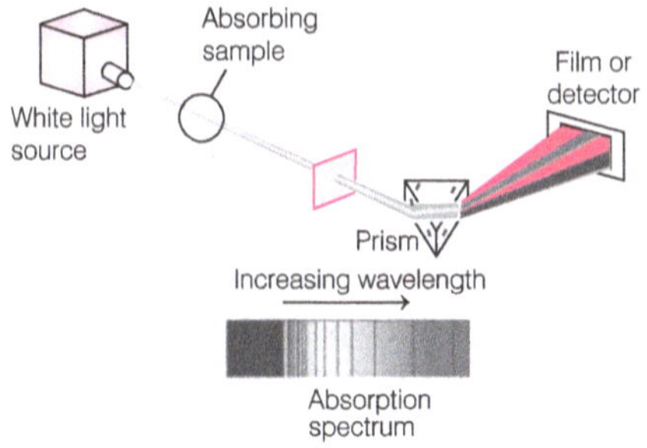

Representation of absorption spectrum

JEE Alert

Absorption and emission spectra are complementary to each other. A line missing in absorption spectrum will appear in emission spectrum.

Bohr's Model

In 1913, a Danish physicist named Niels Henrik David Bohr (1885-1962), developed a quantum model for the hydrogen atom. He combined the concept of the nuclear atom with the quantum theory of Max Planck and Albert Einstein.

Postulates of Bohr's Model

The main postulates of this model are as follows

(i) **Quantised Energy Levels** Electrons in an atom occupy specific, discrete energy levels or orbits around the nucleus. Electrons only exist in these quantised orbits and not in between them. The energy of these orbits is fixed and quantised.

(ii) **Electron Orbits** Electrons travel in circular orbits around the nucleus, and each orbit corresponds to a particular energy level. These orbits are also known as **"stationary states."** An electron in a particular orbit does not radiate energy and remains stable in that orbit. This explains the stability of an atom.

(iii) **Energy Absorption and Emission** Electrons can move between orbits by absorbing or emitting a photon with energy equal to the difference between the two orbits.

When an electron absorbs a photon, it moves to a higher energy orbit. When it emits a photon, it goes to a lower energy orbit. The frequency (or wavelength) of the emitted or absorbed photon correspond the energy difference between the orbits.

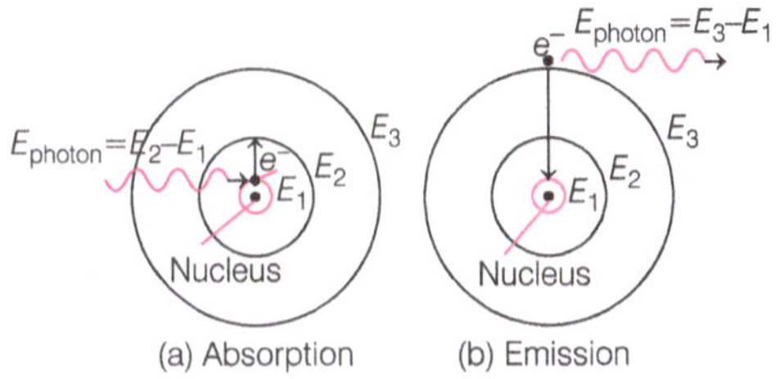

(a) Absorption (b) Emission

(iv) **Angular Momentum Quantisation** The angular momentum of an electron in orbit is quantised and is an integer multiple of $\left(\frac{h}{2\pi}\right)$

$$h = 6.63 \times 10^{-34} \text{ J-s} \qquad \left(\hbar = \frac{h}{2\pi}\right)$$

Mathematically, the angular momentum L (mvr) of an electron is given by $L = n\hbar$; where n is a positive integer (the principal quantum number).

This condition ensures stable orbits and explains the discrete nature of the energy levels. Angular momentum i.e. $mvr = \frac{nh}{2\pi}$

(v) **Hydrogen Atom Specifics** Bohr's model was particularly successful in explaining the spectral lines of hydrogen or Hydrogen like species (single electron atoms or ions e.g He^+, Li^{2+}, Be^{3+}). The model accurately predicts the wavelengths spectral lines of hydrogen by quantising the electron orbits and using them to calculate the energy differences responsible for the spectral lines.

Application of Bohr's Theory

Bohr's made following calculations through his postulates.

1. Bohr's Radius

The radii of the stationary states are expressed as

$$\boxed{r_n = \frac{n^2h^2}{4\pi^2mkZe^2}} \qquad \ldots\text{(i)}$$

For H-atom $Z = 1$ and in ground state $n = 1$

$$\therefore \quad r_1 = \frac{h^2}{4\pi^2 me^2 k} = a_0$$

Radius of the nth orbit $\boxed{r_n = \frac{n^2 a_0}{Z}}$

where, a_0 is called **Bohr's radius** of H-atom in its first orbit (i.e. ground state)

$$\boxed{a_0 = \frac{h^2}{4\pi^2 me^2 k} = 0.529\ \text{Å} = 52.9\ \text{pm}}$$

JEE MAPPER

Example Similar to PYQ Asked in JEE Main 2023

Assume that the radius of the first Bohr orbit of hydrogen atom is 2.1 Å. The radius of the second Bohr orbit of He^+ is .... pm. [Nearest integer]

Sol. (420) According to Bohr model, radius of hydrogen like species is,

$$r_n = a_0\left(\frac{n^2}{Z}\right)\text{Å}$$

where, n = number of orbit

Z = atomic number

for second Bohr orbit ($n = 2$)

For He^+ ($Z = 2$)

$$a_0 = 2.1\ \text{Å}$$

$$r_2 = 2.1\left[\frac{(2)^2}{2}\right]\text{Å} = 2.1 \times 2 = 4.2\ \text{Å}$$

$$= 4.2 \times 10^{-10}\ \text{m} = 4.2 \times 10^{-10} \times 10^{12}\ \text{pm}$$

$$= 4.2 \times 10^2\ \text{pm} = 420\ \text{pm}$$

Competency Enhancer 1.2

Assume that the radius of the first Bohr orbit of hydrogen atom is 3.17 Å. The radius of third Bohr orbit of beryllium ion with +3 oxidation state is .... picometer. [Nearest integer]

Solved Booster 1.3

Arrange the radii of the following in increasing order:

(i) He^+ in second orbit. (ii) Li^{2+} in third orbit.

(iii) Be^{3+} in fourth orbit. (iv) Be^{3+} in first orbit

(a) (i) < (ii) < (iv) < (iii) (b) (iv) < (iii) < (ii) < (i)

(c) (i) < (ii) < (iii) < (iv) (d) (iv) < (i) < (ii) < (iii)

Solution (d)

He^+, Li^{2+} and Be^{3+} are isoelectronic.

$$r_n = \frac{n^2 a_0}{Z}$$

where, n = number of shell (orbit), a_0 = Bohr's radius.

Z = atomic number.

(i) $r_2(He^+) = \frac{(2)^2 a_0}{2} = 2a_0$

(ii) $r_3(Li^{2+}) = \frac{(3)^2 a_0}{3} = 3a_0$

(iii) $r_4(Be^{3+}) = \frac{(4)^2 a_0}{4} = 4a_0$

(iv) $r_1(Be^{3+}) = \frac{(1)^2 a_0}{4} = 0.25a_0$

Thus, increasing order of ionic size is (iv) < (i) < (ii) < (iii).

2. Bohr Velocity or Velocity of Electron

The formula for the velocity of an electron within the orbit is

$$v = \frac{2\pi k Z e^2}{nh}$$

where, except n and Z all are constants. So, after putting the values of all the constants in the formula, we get

$$v = 2.18 \times 10^8 \left(\frac{Z}{n}\right)\ \text{cm/s}$$

Thus, the velocity of an electron in nth orbit of H-atom,

$$v_n = \frac{2\pi e^2}{nh} \quad (k = 1 \text{ in CGS})$$

$$= \frac{2.18 \times 10^8}{n}\ (\text{cm/s})$$

Solved Booster 1.4

The circumference of the first orbit of H-atom is 3.322×10^{-10} m. The velocity of the electron in this orbit as will be

(a) 2.192×10^6 (b) 3.98×10^7

(c) 3.79×10^7 (d) 1.59×10^6

Solution (a)

By Bohr's theory $mvr_n = \frac{nh}{2\pi} \Rightarrow v = \frac{nh}{2\pi r_n (m)_e}$

Here, $2\pi r_n = 2\pi r_1 = 3.322 \times 10^{-10}$m $(\because n = 1)$

$$\therefore \quad v = \frac{1 \times 6.626 \times 10^{-34}\ \text{J s}}{3.322 \times 10^{-10}\ \text{m} \times 9.1 \times 10^{-31}\ \text{kg}}$$

$$= 2.192 \times 10^6\ \text{ms}^{-1}$$

$[1\text{J} = 1\ \text{kg m}^2\text{s}^{-2}$

$2\pi r$ = Circumference of the circular path of radius (r)].

3. Energy of Electron

The total energy, E of the electron is the sum of its kinetic and potential energy.

$$E_n = \text{KE} + \text{PE} = \frac{-Zke^2}{2r_n}$$

Substituting for r_n, gives us

$$E = -\frac{2\pi^2 m Z^2 e^4 k^2}{n^2 h^2}$$

where n = 1,2,3,...

This expression shows that only certain energies are permissible for an electron.

After putting the values of constants in the formula we get following simplified expressions.

$$E = -21.8 \times 10^{-12} \times \frac{Z^2}{n^2} \text{ erg/atom}$$

$$= -21.8 \times 10^{-19} \times \frac{Z^2}{n^2} \text{ J/atom}$$

$$E_n = -13.6 \times \frac{Z^2}{n^2} \text{ eV / atom}$$

When only magnitude is compared $TE = KE = \frac{1}{2}PE$

Note The negative sign in all formulae of energy does not have any numerical implication. This sign only signifies that the energy of electron in an atom is lower than the energy of a free electron at infinity. The highest negative value is given for $n = 1$ corresponding to most stable orbit.

JEE MAPPER

Example Similar to PYQ Asked in JEE Advanced 2024

According to Bohr's model, the highest kinetic energy is associated with the electron in the

(a) second orbit of He^+ (b) first orbit of He^+

(c) first orbit of Li^{2+} (d) second orbit of Li^{2+}

Sol. (c) According to Bohr's model, the kinetic energy is given by,

$$K.E = +13.6 \times \frac{Z^2}{n^2}$$

For 2nd orbit of He^+

$$n = 2, Z = 2$$

$$K.E = +13.6 \text{ eV}$$

For 1st orbit of He^+

$$n = 1, Z = 2$$

$$K.E = +13.6 \times \frac{(2)^2}{(1)^2} = +54.4 \text{ eV}$$

For 1st orbit of Li^{2+}

$$n = 1, Z = 3$$

$$K.E = +13.6 \times \frac{(3)^2}{(1)^2} = +122.4 \text{ eV}$$

For 2nd orbit of Li^{2+}

$$n = 2, Z = 3$$

$$K.E = +13.6 \times \frac{(3)^2}{(2)^2} = +30.6 \text{ eV}$$

Thus, the highest energy is associated with orbit of Li^{2+}.

Competency Enhancer 1.3

According to Bohr's model, the lowest kinetic energy is associated with the electron in the

(a) first orbit of Be^{3+} (b) first orbit of H-atom

(c) first orbit of He^+ (d) first orbit of Li^{2+}

Hydrogen Spectrum

The atomic spectrum of hydrogen has been proved to be very helpful in the development of atomic structure.

It is an example of line emission spectrum or atomic emission spectrum. It is obtained when an electric discharge is passed through hydrogen gas at low pressure, a bluish light is emitted. This light shows discontinuous line spectrum of several isolated sharp lines when passed through prism.

- The lines in emission spectrum of hydrogen are classified into following six series which are named after the name of scientist who discovered them.
  1. Lyman series]—UV region
  2. Balmer series]—Visible region
  3. Paschen series
  4. Brackett series } — IR region
  5. Pfund series
  6. Humphery series — Far IR region
- To evaluate the wavelength of various H-lines Rydberg introduced the following expression.

$$\bar{\nu} = \frac{1}{\lambda} R_H \left[\frac{1}{n_1^2} - \frac{1}{n_2^2}\right]$$

Spectral lines of hydrogen atom

Series	n_1	$n_2 > n_1$	$\bar{\nu} = \frac{1}{\lambda} = R_H\left[\frac{1}{n_1^2} - \frac{1}{n_2^2}\right]$	Region of spectrum
Lyman	1	2, 3, ... ∞	$R_H\left[\frac{1}{1^2} - \frac{1}{n_2^2}\right]$	Ultraviolet
Balmer	2	3, 4, ... ∞	$R_H\left[\frac{1}{2^2} - \frac{1}{n_2^2}\right]$	Visible
Paschen	3	4, 5, ... ∞	$R_H\left[\frac{1}{3^2} - \frac{1}{n_2^2}\right]$	Infrared
Brackett	4	5, 6, ... ∞	$R_H\left[\frac{1}{4^2} - \frac{1}{n_2^2}\right]$	Infrared
Pfund	5	6, 7, ... ∞	$R_H\left[\frac{1}{5^2} - \frac{1}{n_2^2}\right]$	Infrared
Humphry	6	7, 8, ... ∞	$R_H\left[\frac{1}{6^2} - \frac{1}{n_2^2}\right]$	Infrared (Far)

The Balmer series of lines is the only series which appears in the visible region of EM spectrum.

- When an electron falls from nth, $(n-1)$th, $(n-2)$th level to ground level, then total number emission spectral lines $= \frac{n(n-1)}{2}$.
- When electron falls from n_2 shell to n_1 shell, total number of emission spectral lines $= \frac{(n_2 - n_1)(n_2 - n_1 + 1)}{2}$.

Explanation of Line Spectrum of Hydrogen

Bohr was successful in explaining the line spectrum of hydrogen.

When an electron drops from a higher enenrgy level (or orbit), say n_2, to lower energy level (or orbit) n_1, the electromagenetic radiation of discrete frequencies are emitted and appear in the form of sharp lines called spectrum.

Energy difference of n_2 and n_1 level is,

$$E_{n_1} = \frac{-2\pi^2 mZ^2 e^4 k^2}{n_1^2 h^2}$$

$$E_{n_2} = \frac{-2\pi^2 mZ^2 e^4 k^2}{n_2^2 h^2}$$

$$\therefore \quad \Delta E = E_{n_2} - E_{n_1}$$

$$\Delta E = \frac{2\pi^2 mZ^2 e^4 k^2}{h^2}\left[\frac{1}{n_1^2} - \frac{1}{n_2^2}\right]$$

Corresponding wave number and wavelength of the emitted radiation is

$$\bar{\nu} = \frac{1}{\lambda} = \frac{\Delta E}{hc} = \frac{2\pi^2 mZ^2 e^4 k^2}{h^3 c}\left[\frac{1}{n_1^2} - \frac{1}{n_2^2}\right] = R_H Z^2\left[\frac{1}{n_1^2} - \frac{1}{n_2^2}\right]$$

$$\Rightarrow \bar{\nu} = R_H Z^2\left[\frac{1}{n_1^2} - \frac{1}{n_2^2}\right]$$

where, $R_H = \frac{2\pi^2 me^4 k^2}{h^3 c} = 1.09677 \times 10^7 \ \text{m}^{-1}$ is called **Rydberg's constant**.

- Also in terms of (IE)

$$\bar{\nu} = \frac{(\text{IE})_Z n^2}{hc}\left[\frac{1}{n_1^2} - \frac{1}{n_2^2}\right] = \frac{(\text{IE})_H Z^2}{hc}\left[\frac{1}{n_1^2} - \frac{1}{n_2^2}\right]$$

where, $(\text{IE})_Z$ is the ionisation energy of the atom with atomic number Z and $(\text{IE})_H$ is the ionisation energy of H-atom.

$$(\text{IE})_Z = \frac{2\pi^2 mZ^2 e^4 k^2}{n^2 h^2} \text{ and } (\text{IE})_H = \frac{2\pi^2 me^4 k^2}{h^2}$$

Frequency ν of the emitted radiation can be calculated on multiplying related equations by c (velocity of light).

Thus, $$\nu = R_H Z^2 c\left[\frac{1}{n_1^2} - \frac{1}{n_2^2}\right]$$

The energy levels in the hydrogen atom and transitions of electrons between them can be visualised through the given figure.

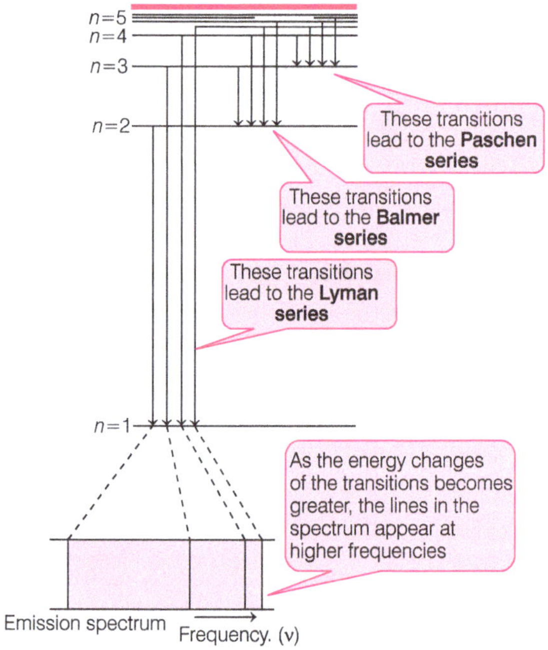

Spectral lines in the hydrogen atom

Merits and Demerits of the Bohr's Atomic Model Merits

Merits

Bohr's model of the atom successfully explained

(i) The stability of atoms

(ii) The origin of discontinuous line spectrum of H-atom

(iii) It also helped in understanding some related phenomenon like the production of characteristic X-ray by elements. The validity of the theory was also established quantitatively; satisfactory agreement with experimental results was observed for the Rydberg constant, excitation potential of atoms, characteristic X-rays etc.

Demerits

(i) Using instruments of high resolving power (like magnetic field a case of Zeeman's effect or electrical field—a case of Stark's effect) single line was found to consist of a number of closely spaced lines, i.e. resolution takes place. This fine structure of the spectral lines could not be explained with the help of the Bohr's theory.

(ii) It could not explain spectrum of multielectron atoms (as He, Le, ...).

(iii) Bohr's introduction of the concept of integers (n) in selecting the stable orbits for electrons was also arbitrary, merely to fit experimental results. There was no theoretical justification for it.

(iv) It could not explain the dual nature of matter and specially electrons.

JEE Quicker

The Statement "Bohr's theory accounts for the stability and line spectrum of Li^+ ion is false. *JEE Main 2021*

Bohr's theory accounts for the stability and spectrum of single electronic species or Hydrogen like species but Li^+ has two electron. Hence the given statement is false.

Bohr Sommerfeld Model

Bohr along with **Sommerfeld** (1915) suggested the existence of elliptical orbits alongwith circular orbits. This had the situation of nuclei at one of the foci of ellipse and was used to explain the fine structure in hydrogen spectrum.

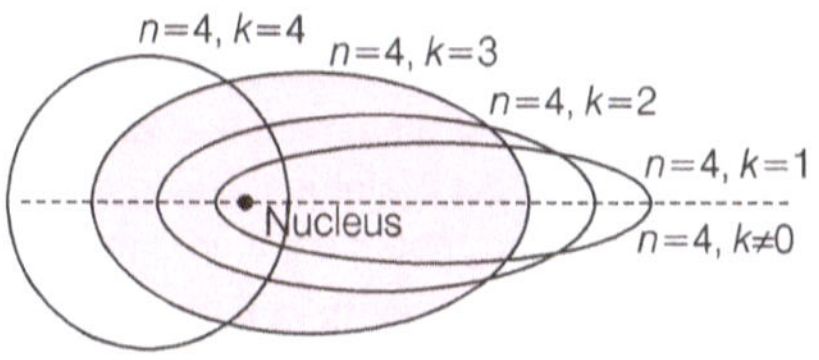

Due to the presence of such orbits, the tangential velocity of an electron at any instance can also be resolved into two components, i.e.

- the **radial velocity** means the one along the radius vector and
- the **transverse** or **angular velocity** means the one perpendicular to the radius vector.

These two velocities give rise to **radial** and **angular** or **azimuthal momentum** as,

$$\text{Radial momentum} = n_r \times \frac{h}{2\pi}$$

$$\text{Azimuthal momentum} = n_\phi \times \frac{h}{2\pi}$$

Here, n_r = radial quantum number

n_ϕ = azimuthal quantum number

These, n_r and n_ϕ are related to principal quantum number of Bohr (n) as

$$n = n_r + n_\phi$$

$$\frac{n}{n_\phi} = \frac{n_r + n_\phi}{n_\phi} = \frac{\text{length of major axis}}{\text{length of minor axis}}$$

Always remember that for a certain value of n,

(i) **The value of n_ϕ can never be zero,** because if $n_\phi = 0$, that means the minor axis of ellipse will also be zero.

So the electron is showing straight line motion which is impossible inside an atom.

(ii) **n_ϕ cannot be greater than n** because in such cases the path will not be elliptical as minor axis of ellipse exceeds its major axis.

(iii) **n_ϕ equal to n is possible** but in that case the orbit will be circular. Usually circular orbit is considered as the special case of ellipse, where major axis equals the minor axis.

(iv) **n_ϕ smaller than n is possible** and in all such cases the orbit will remain elliptical.

Elemental Practice 2.1

Type I MCQs with Only One Correct Option

1. An electron in H-atom in its ground state absorbs 1.5 times as much as energy as the minimum required for its escape (13.6 eV) from the atom. Thus, KE given to the emitted electron is
(a) 13.6 eV (b) 20.4 eV (c) 34.4 eV (d) 6.8 eV

2. Comparison of energy of H-atom in first orbit (E_1), He^+ in second orbit (E_2), Li^{2+} in third orbit (E_3) and Be^{3+} in fourth orbit (E_4) is
(a) $E_1(H) = \frac{E_2}{2}(He^+) = \frac{E_3}{3}(Li^{2+}) = \frac{E_4}{4}(Be^{3+})$
(b) $E_1(H) = 2E_2(He^+) = 3E_3(Li^{2+}) = 4E_4\ (Be^{3+})$
(c) $E_1(H) = E_2(He^+) = E_3(Li^{2+}) = E_4(Be^{3+})$
(d) $12E_1(H) = 6E_2(He^+) = 4E_3(Li^{2+}) = 3E_4(Be^{3+})$

3. **Assertion** In Lyman series of H-spectra, the maximum wavelength of lines is 125 nm.
Reason Wavelength is maximum if there is transition from the very next level.
(a) If both Assertion and Reason are true and Reason is the correct explanation of the Assertion.
(b) If both Assertion and Reason are true and Reason is not the correct explanation of the Assertion.
(c) Assertion is true but Reason is false.
(d) Assertion is false but Reason is true.

4. Which of the following triad of nuclei is isotonic?
(a) ${}^{18}_{8}O, {}^{19}_{9}F, {}^{15}_{7}N$
(b) ${}^{7}_{3}Li, {}^{14}_{6}C, {}^{17}_{9}F$
(c) ${}^{14}_{6}C, {}^{15}_{7}N, {}^{17}_{9}F$
(d) ${}^{12}_{6}C, {}^{14}_{7}N, {}^{15}_{7}N$

5. Velocity of the electron emitted by Li (ϕ (work function) $= 2.90$ eV) of light of frequency $4.77 \times 10^{15}\ s^{-1}$ is absorbed is ($1\ eV = 1.6 \times 10^{-19}$ J)
(a) $3.10 \times 10^6\ ms^{-1}$ (b) $6.20 \times 10^8\ ms^{-1}$
(c) $2.43 \times 10^6\ ms^{-1}$ (d) $4.86 \times 10^8\ ms^{-1}$

6. When an electron falls from a level of energy $4E/3$ to level of energy E, radiation of wavelength 3λ is observed. If electron falls from a level of energy $2E$ to a level of energy E, wavelength of the radiation is
(a) 3λ (b) $\frac{4\lambda}{3}$ (c) $\frac{3\lambda}{4}$ (d) λ

7. When electromagnetic radiation of wavelength 300 nm falls on the surface of sodium, electrons are emitted with a kinetic energy of $1.68 \times 10^5\ J\ mol^{-1}$. Minimum energy needed to remove an electron from sodium is
(a) 6.63×10^{-19} J (b) 3.99×10^5 J
(c) 2.31×10^5 J (d) 3.84×10^{-19} J

8. The radii of the any of the two of the first four Bohr orbits of H-atom are in the 1 : 4 ratio. Thus, energy difference between them is
(a) 10.2 eV or 2.55 eV (b) 13.6 eV or 3.4 eV
(c) 10.2 eV (d) 13.6 eV

9. Electron in H-atom is emitted from $n = 5$ state of $n = 2$ state. Wavelength associated with this transition is
(a) 434 nm (b) 217 nm
(c) 808 nm (d) 102 nm

10. Energy associated with the first orbit of He^+ is not equal to
(a) -8.70×10^{-18} J atom^{-1} (b) -5.24×10^6 J mol^{-1}
(c) -13.6 eV atom^{-1} (d) 1.6×10^{-19} J mol^{-1}

11. At what value of Z would the inner most orbit be expected to be pulled inside a nucleus of radius 1.0×10^{-13} cm, assuming simple Bohr theory and Bohr radius 0.5292 Å ?
(a) 5.292×10^4 (b) 5.292×10^2
(c) 0.5292 (d) 5.292

12. What is the work function of the metal; if the light of wavelength 3890 Å generates photoelectron of velocity $6 \times 10^5\ ms^{-1}$ from it?
[Given: Mass of electron $= 9.1 \times 10^{-31}$ kg
Velocity of light $= 3 \times 10^8$ m/s
Plank's constant $= 6.626 \times 10^{-34}$ Js
Charge of electron $= 1.6 \times 10^{-19}$ Je V^{-1}]
(a) 3.18 eV (b) 2.18 eV
(c) 1.38 eV (d) 3.56 eV

13. **Assertion** (A) The value of n for a line in Balmer series of hydrogen spectrum having the highest wavelength is 4 and 6.
Reason (R) For Balmer series of hydrogen spectrum, the value $n_1 = 2$ and $n_2 = 3, 4, 5$.
(a) If both Assertion and Reason are true and Reason is the correct explanation of the Assertion.
(b) If both Assertion and Reason are true and Reason is not the correct explanation of the Assertion.
(c) Assertion is true but Reason is false.
(d) Assertion is false but Reason is true.

14. The electron in the nth orbit of Li^{2+} is excited to $(n + 1)$ orbit using the radiation of energy 1.47×10^{-17} J (as show in the diagram). Find the value of n.
[Given: $R_H = 2.18 \times 10^{-18}$ J]
$4.4 \approx 4$

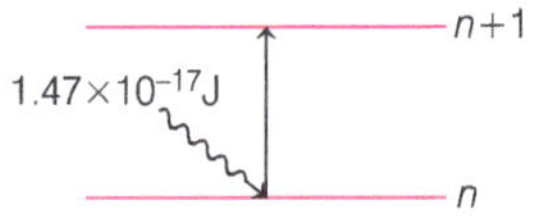

(a) 3 (b) 4 (c) 1 (d) 2

15. Given below are two statements.
Statement I In hydrogen spectrum, the series of lines appearing in ultra violet region of electromagnetic spectrum are called Lyman lines.
Statement II The limiting line in Balmer series will have a frequency of $3.65 \times 10^{14}\ s^{-1}$.
(a) Both Statement I and Statement II are false.
(b) Statement I is true and Statement II is false.
(c) Statement I is false but Statement II is true.
(d) Both Statement I and Statement II are true.

16. If the energy of electron in H-atom is given by expression, $-1312/n^2$ kJ mol^{-1}, then the energy required to excite the electron from ground state to second orbit is
(a) 678 kJ (b) 1312 kJ
(c) 328 kJ (d) 984 kJ

17. The wave number of the first line of Balmer series of hydrogen is 18700 cm^{-1}. The wave number of the first Balmer line of Li^{2+} ion is
(a) 136800 cm^{-1} (b) 168300 cm^{-1}
(c) 76000 cm^{-1} (d) 608000 cm^{-1}

Type II 》 MCQs with One or More than One Correct Option

18. Which of the following statements are correct?
(a) The ideal body, which emits and absorbs all frequencies uniformly, is called a black body.
(b) The exact frequency distribution of the emitted radiation from a black body depends upon its temperature.
(c) The radiation emitted goes from a lower frequency to a higher frequency as the temperature increases.
(d) At a given temperature, intensity of radiation emitted increases with the increase of wavelength continuously.

19. Select incorrect statement about nature of electromagnetic radiations.
(a) The oscillating electric and magnetic fields produced by oscillating charged particles are perpendicular to each other and both are perpendicular to the direction of propagation of the wave.

(b) Electromagnetic waves do not require medium and can move in vacuum.
(c) The velocity of X-rays is more than cosmic rays.
(d) The frequency of microwaves is more than that of UV rays.

20. Which of the following are not the characteristic of Planck's quantum theory of radiation?
(a) Magnitude of energy associated with a quantum is proportional to the frequency.
(b) The energy is not absorbed or emitted in whole number multiple of quantum.
(c) Radiation energy is not emitted or absorbed continuously but in the form of small packets called quanta.
(d) Radiations are not associated with energy.

21. Which of the following statements are correct about photoelectric effect?
(a) The number of electrons ejected is inversely proportional to the intensity or brightness of light.
(b) For each metal, below threshold frequency photoelectric effect is not observed.
(c) Kinetic energy of the ejected electrons does not depend upon the intensity of light.
(d) Photoelectric current depends on intensity of incident radiation and not on frequency.

22. Which of the following statements are incorrect about Bohr's model?
(a) It can explain that splitting of spectral lines in the presence of magnetic field or an electric field.
(b) It could not explain the ability of atoms to form molecules by chemical bonds.
(c) Qualitatively, the magnitude of velocity of electron increases with increase of positive charge on the nucleus and increase of principal quantum number.
(d) When the electron is free from the influence of nucleus, the energy is taken as zero.

Type IV 》 Numerical/Integer Answer Type Questions

23. The ionisation enthalpy of hydrogen atom is 1.312 $\times 10^6$ J/mol. The energy required to excite the electron in the atom from $n = 1$ to $n = 2$ is ...... $x \times 10^5$ J/mol. The value of x is .... (nearest integer)

24. Assume that the radius of the first Bohr orbit of hydrogen atom is 0.38 Å. The radius of the second Bohr orbit of helium with + 1 oxidation state is .... pm.
[Nearest integer]

25. One molecule of a substance absorbs one quantum of energy. The energy involved when 2.38 mole of the substance absorbs red light of frequency 6.35×10^{14} s^{-1} will be $x \times 10^5$ J. The value of x is .... (nearest integer)

26. Values of work function (W_0) for a few metals are given below.

Metal	Na	Mg	Cu	Ag
W_0 / eV	2.3	3.7	4.8	4.3

The number of metals which will show photoelectric effect when light of wavelength 410 nm falls on it is ....
[Given: $h = 6.6 \times 10^{-34}$ Js, $c = 3 \times 10^8$ ms^{-1}, $e = 1.6 \times 10^{-19}$ C]

27. Suppose, 10^{-17} J of energy is needed by the interior of human eye to see an object. The number of photons of green light ($\lambda = 550$ nm) are needed to generate this minimum amount of energy is .... (Nearest integer)

28. The wavelength of the spectral line when the electron in the hydrogen atom undergoes a transition from the energy level 4 to energy level 2 is $x \times 10^{-9}$ m.
The value of x is .... (nearest integer)

29. The ejection of the photoelectron from the silver metal in the photoelectric effect experiment can be stopped by applying the voltage of 0.45 V when the radiation 267.3 nm is used.
The work function for silver metal is .... (nearest integer)

30. The energy difference between two electronic states is 76.31 kcal/mol. The frequency of the light emitted when an electron drops from the higher to the lower energy state will be in $x \times 10^{14}$ cycles/sec.
[Given : Planck's constant $= 9.52 \times 10^{-14}$ kcal sec/mol]

Elemental Practice 2.1 | Chapter 02

Connect with **Answers**

1. (b)	2. (c)	3. (a)	4. (c)	5. (c)	6. (d)
7. (d)	8. (a)	9. (a)	10. (c)	11. (a)	12. (b)
13. (d)	14. (c)	15. (b)	16. (d)	17. (b)	18. (a,b,c)
19. (c,d)	20. (b,d)	21. (b,c,d)	22. (a,c)	23. (10)	24. (76)
25. (6)	26. (1)	27. (28)	28. (486)	29. (4.18)	30. (8)

Element 2 Dual Nature of Matter and Wave Mechanical Model

Since the Bohr's model had several drawbacks, scientists worked to develop a more suitable and generalised atomic model. The following two important developments led to the formulation of a model and explained demerits of earlier models.

Dual Nature of Matter

(de-Broglie Relationship)

de-Broglie based on Millikan's oil drop experiment (which showed particle nature) and diffraction study (which showed wave nature) suggested the dual nature of electron, both as a material particle and as a wave. This signifies that electron (or any microscopic particle) possesses both momentum as well as wavelength.

$$E_1 = mc^2 \quad \text{(by particle nature)}$$

$$E_2 = h\nu = \frac{hc}{\lambda} \quad \text{(by wave nature)}$$

Due to dual nature $E_1 = E_2$

$\therefore \quad mc^2 = \dfrac{hc}{\lambda}$

or $\quad \lambda = \dfrac{h}{mc}$

or $\quad \lambda = \dfrac{h}{p}$

Relationship between Wavelength and Kinetic Energy

According to de-Broglie's equation

$$\lambda = \frac{h}{p} = \frac{h}{mv} = \frac{h}{\sqrt{2m(\text{KE})}}$$

where, $p = mv = \sqrt{2m(\text{KE})}$ is called momentum of the particle of mass m moving with velocity v.

- If accelerating potential (V) is given, then $\lambda = \dfrac{h}{\sqrt{2m(\text{eV})}}$

  Also $\text{KE} = \dfrac{3}{2}RT = \dfrac{3}{2}kT$

  where, k is called Boltzmann's constant then $\lambda = \dfrac{h}{\sqrt{3mkT}}$

- Using above equation and assuming that one circular path of radius r can be divided into n waves of wavelength λ each, it can be shown that angular momentum is quantised in the multiple of $\dfrac{h}{2\pi}$,

  Also circumference of the nth orbit is equal to n times the wavelength of the electron.

$$2\pi r_n = n\lambda = n\frac{h}{mv} \Rightarrow mvr_n = \frac{nh}{2\pi}$$

where, n stands for principal quantum number. This shows that electron can move only in those orbits for which the **angular momentum is an integral multiple of $\dfrac{h}{2\pi}$.**

- If the wave is to remain continually in phase, the circumference of the circle is an integral multiple of wavelength λ and if the circumference is bigger or smaller than the value of $\dfrac{nh}{2\pi}$, the wave will no longer remain in phase.

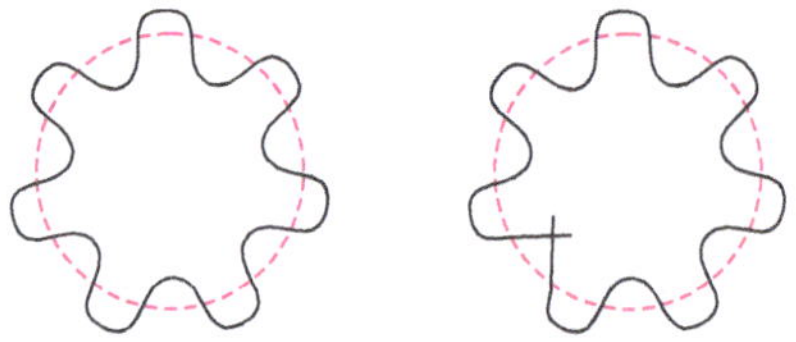

Wave continuity in phase   Wave not in phase

The expression for de-Broglie wavelength for subatomic particles are given as follows.

Particle	Electron	Proton	Neutron	α-particle	Gas molecule
de-Broglie wavelength	$\lambda = \frac{1.22}{\sqrt{V}}$ nm	$\lambda = \frac{0.0286}{\sqrt{V}}$ nm	$\lambda = \frac{0.0286}{\sqrt{V}}$ nm	$\lambda = \frac{0.0101}{\sqrt{V}}$ nm	$\lambda = \frac{h}{\sqrt{3mkT}}$

- The experimental confirmation of the de-Broglie relation was obtained when Davisson and Germer in 1927, observed that a beam of electrons is diffracted by a nickel crystal. Experimental values of λ and that determined using de-Broglie equation were in close agreement.

JEE Alert

de-Broglie equation is significant for microscopic objects only.
Reason The wavelengths associated with ordinary objects are so short (because of their large masses) that their wave properties can't be detected. The wavelengths associated with electrons and other subatomic particles (with very small masses) can be detected.

Solved Booster 2.1

An electron undergoes diffraction by crystals. Through what potential should a beam of electrons be accelerated so that its wavelength becomes equal to 154 pm.?

(a) 55.5 V (b) 63.6 V (c) 24 V (d) 36.8 V

Solution *(b)*

$$2 \times meV = \frac{h^2}{\lambda^2}$$

$$\Rightarrow eV = \frac{h^2}{2m\lambda^2} = \frac{(6.626 \times 10^{-34})^2 \text{ J}^2\text{s}^2}{2 \times 9.1 \times 10^{-31}\text{kg} \times (154 \times 10^{-12})^2 \text{m}^2}$$

$$eV = 1.0172 \times 10^{-17} \text{J} \, (1 \text{ eV} = 1.6 \times 10^{-19} \text{ J})$$

$$V = \frac{1.0172 \times 10^{-17}}{1.6 \times 10^{-19}} \text{ V} = 63.6 \text{ V}$$

JEE MAPPER

Example Similar to PYQ Asked in JEE Main 2023

If the radius of the first orbit of hydrogen atom is a_0, then de-Broglie's wavelength of electron in 1st excited state is

(a) $\frac{\pi a_0}{4}$ (b) $4\pi a_0$ (c) $\frac{\pi a_0}{2}$ (d) $2\pi a_0$

Sol. *(b)* Using the formula of de Broglie wavelength,

$$\lambda = h/mv$$

Also, angular momentum of an electron by Bohr is

$$mvr = \frac{nh}{2\pi} \text{ or } \frac{2\pi r}{n} = \frac{h}{mv}$$

$\therefore$ de-Broglie wavelength $\lambda = \frac{2\pi r}{n}$

de-Broglie wavelength of electron in 1st excited state $(n = 2)$

$$\lambda_2 = \frac{2\pi r_2}{n} \quad \text{...(i)}$$

$$r_2 = \text{radius of Ist orbit} \times n^2, r_2 = a_0 n^2, \frac{r_2}{n} = a_0 n \quad \text{...(ii)}$$

From (i) and (ii), equation, $\lambda_2 = 2\pi a_0 \times n$

$n = 2$ for (1st excited state) $\quad n = 2, \lambda_2 = 4\pi a_0$

Competency Enhancer 2.1

If the radius of the first orbit of hydrogen atom is a_0, then de-Broglie's wavelength of electron in 4th orbit is

(a) $8\pi a_0$ (b) $\frac{\pi a_0}{8}$ (c) $12\pi a_0$ (d) $\frac{\pi a_0}{12}$

Heisenberg's Uncertainty Principle

According to Heisenberg's uncertainity principle "It is not possible to determine precisely both the position and the momentum (or velocity) of a small moving particle (e.g. electron, proton, etc.)"

$$\Delta x \cdot \Delta p \geq \frac{h}{4\pi} = \frac{\hbar}{2} \left(\text{where, } \hbar = \frac{h}{2\pi}\right)$$

$$\Delta x \cdot \Delta v \geq \frac{h}{4\pi m}$$

where, Δx Δp and Δv are the uncertainties with regard to position, momentum and velocity, respectively. The sign $\geq$ means that the product of Δx and Δp (or of Δx and Δv) can be greater than, or equal to, but never smaller than $\frac{h}{4\pi}$. If Δx is made small, Δp increases and *vice-versa*.

For minimum uncertainties $\Delta x \cdot \Delta p \approx \frac{h}{4\pi}$

For large or macroscopic objects in motion, the exact position and velocity at any instant of time can be determined. But for microscopic objects like electron, involvement of the wave character undergoes considerable change in its path and velocity. Thus cannot determine simultaneously.

Solved Booster 2.2

The uncertainty for the calculation of ionic radius of Li^{2+} of the third orbit is 0.03%. The uncertainty in the measurement of velocity will be

(a) $1.217 \times 10^9 \text{ ms}^{-1}$ (b) $1.34 \times 10^{-9} \text{ ms}^{-1}$

(c) $0.235 \times 10^6 \text{ ms}^{-1}$ (d) $1.11 \times 10^{-21} \text{ ms}^{-1}$

Solution *(a)*

Ionic radius of H-like species (with one electron) is given by:

$$r_n = \frac{n^2 a_0}{Z}$$

$$r_3 (Li^{2+}) = \frac{(3)^2 (0.529 \times 10^{-10} \text{ m})}{3}$$

$$= 3 \times 0.529 \times 10^{-10} = 1.587 \times 10^{-10} \text{ m}$$

$$\Delta x = r_3 \times \frac{0.03}{100}$$

$$\therefore \quad \Delta x = 1.587 \times 10^{-10} \times \frac{0.03}{100} = 4.761 \times 10^{-14} \text{ m}$$

$$\therefore \text{ Since, } \Delta x \cdot \Delta p = \frac{h}{4\pi}$$

$$\Delta p = \frac{h}{4\pi \Delta x} = \frac{6.626 \times 10^{-34} \text{ Js}}{4\pi (4.761 \times 10^{-14} \text{ m})}$$

$$= 1.11 \times 10^{-21} \text{ kg ms}^{-1}$$

$$\Delta p = m\Delta v = 1.11 \times 10^{-21} \text{ kg ms}^{-1}$$

$$9.1 \times 10^{-31} \text{ kg } (\Delta v) = 1.11 \times 10^{-21}$$

$$\therefore \Delta v = \frac{1.11 \times 10^{-21}}{9.1 \times 10^{-31}} \text{ ms}^{-1} = 1.217 \times 10^9 \text{ ms}^{-1}$$

Significance of Heisenberg's Uncertainty Principle

In view of the uncertainty principle, Bohr's model in which electrons are considered as particles revolving in definite orbits with definite velocities become untenable. It is not possible to know exactly the position of an electron moving with a particular velocity as is implied in Bohr's model.

Instead, it is possible only to state or predict the **probability** of locating an electron moving with a particular velocity in a given region of space around the nucleus at a given time.

Uncertainty principle is also called **principle of indeterminacy**. One of the important implications of this principle is that it rules out existence of definite paths or trajectories of electrons.

JEE Spotlite

- **Heisenberg's uncertainity principle in terms of energy,** ΔE and uncertainty in time Δt, this principle is derived as

Since, $\Delta p = m\Delta v$

and $\frac{\Delta v}{\Delta t} = \Delta a$ (change in acceleration)

Put $m\Delta a = F$

and $F \cdot \Delta x = \Delta E$ (change in energy)

$$\Delta E \cdot \Delta t \geq \frac{h}{4\pi}$$

Similar conclusions are arrived from other considerations irrespective of the design of the experiment to measure these parameters. This shows that these uncertainties are inherent properties of the system itself resulting from wave particle dualism; it does not arise from the limitations of our instruments.

Quantum Mechanical Model of Atom

The Austrian physicist Erwin Schrodinger postulated that each of an atom's electrons can be visualised as occupying one of several volumes of space located around the nucleus. Each of these volume is called an **orbital** or an **atomic orbital**.

Quantum-mechanical model orbitals are very different from a **Bohr orbit**. A quantum-mechanical orbital is a three-dimensional region of space, somewhat like the space inside a very small balloon. While Bohr orbit is just a circular path on which electrons revolve.

Schrodinger Wave Equation

The allowable patterns for electron waves can be obtained through Schrodinger wave equation.

$$\frac{\partial^2\psi}{\partial x^2} + \frac{\partial^2\psi}{\partial y^2} + \frac{\partial^2\psi}{\partial z^2} + \frac{8\pi^2 m}{h^2}(E - V)\psi = 0$$

where, ψ (Greek letter psi) is called wave function.

$\frac{\partial^2\psi}{\partial x^2}, \frac{\partial^2\psi}{\partial y^2}$ and $\frac{\partial^2\psi}{\partial z^2}$ is the second derivative of ψ with respect to x only, y only and z only. m is the mass of the electron, E the permissible total energy of the electron, V the potential energy of the electron $\left(V = -\frac{Ze^2}{r}\right)$ and h the Planck's constant.

Wave functions contain three terms (called **quantum numbers** n, l and m). When specific values are assigned to these three quantum numbers, the result is called an **orbital**

Some important points related to quantum mechanical model are discussed below

- The probability of finding an electron at a certain radial distance is maximized at a particular value of x (like Bohr radius) and the electron density decreases as you move away from the nucleus.
- We can determine the probability of finding the electron at a given point located at a distance r from the nucleus if we calculate the value of ψ^2 at that point.

  The **radial probability density** indicates probability of finding the electron within the volume of a very thin spherical shell at a distance r from the nucleus.

Quantum Mechanical Model of the Hydrogen Atom

Schrodinger equation for the hydrogen atom can be written as

$$\hat{H}\psi = E\psi$$

where, $\hat{H}$ is called Hamiltonian operator and is the sum of kinetic energy operator ($\hat{T}$) and potential energy operator ($\hat{V}$).

$$\therefore \quad \hat{H} = \hat{T} + \hat{V}$$

Thus, $(\hat{T} + \hat{V})\psi = E\psi$

The wave function ψ is a mathematical function that varies with position. This variation means ψ is a function of **Cartesian coordinates** x, y and z and is written in shorthand as $\psi(x, y, z)$. Also atoms are spherical, it is more useful to represent the wave function as a function of distance, r, and two angle θ and ϕ. The parameters r, θ and ϕ are known as **spherical coordinates**. Cartesian and spherical coordinates are equally valid ways of specifying the position of a point wrt to an origin as shown in figure below.

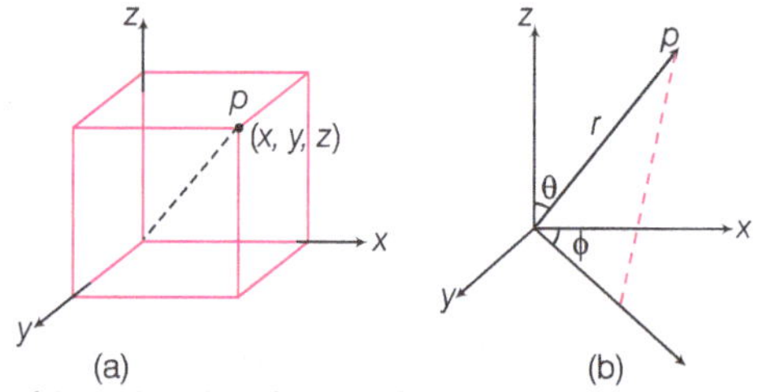

(a) (Position of the point p is defined in terms of x, y, z,)

(b) (Position of the point p is defined in terms of r, θ, and ϕ,)

Solution of the Schrodinger wave equation is based on coordinates x, y and z related to polar coordinates r, θ and ϕ

$$x = r\sin\theta\cos\phi$$

$$y = r\sin\theta\sin\phi$$

$$z = r\cos\theta$$

$$\therefore \quad x^2 + y^2 + z^2 = r^2$$

When wave equation in polar coordinates is solved for the hydrogen atom, it gives the possible energy states and the corresponding wave function [$\psi(r, \theta, \phi)$] which is called **hydrogenic orbital** or **atomic orbital**.

$$\psi(r, \theta, \phi) = \underbrace{R_{n,l}(r)}_{\text{Radial part}} \underbrace{\theta_{l,m}(\theta)\phi_m(\phi)}_{\text{Angular part}} = R(r) \times Y(\theta, \phi)$$

Radial wave function part is dependent on r and angular wave function is dependent on θ and ϕ. Radial wave function contains information about what happens to the wave function as the distance from the nucleus increases. Angular wave function contains information about shape of the orbital.

Radial Probability Function

- According to Max Born, probability of finding an electron in a small volume dV is $|\psi|^2\, dV$.
- Radial probability distribution function $= R^2 dV$. (where R = radial wave function)
- In order to find the value of dV, the entire space of the electron orbital around the nucleus is supposed to be divided into small imaginary concentric shells of very small thickness dr, each.
- Then, find out the volume of the space in between two such shells.

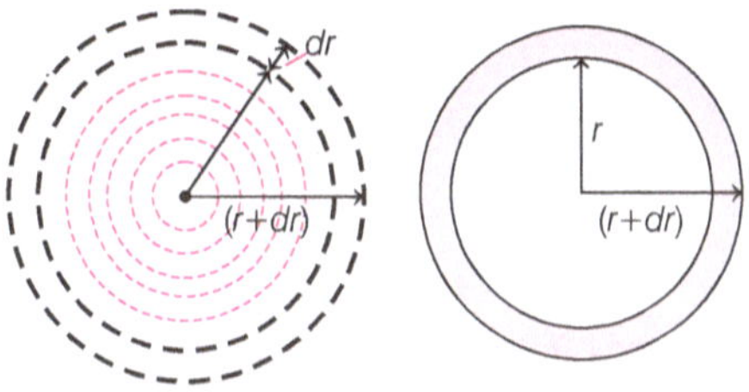

- The probability that the electron will be found between the inner and outer surfaces of this shell is $|\psi|^2 \times 4\pi r^2 dr$. This expression has the form $P(r)\, dr$, where

$$P(r) = 4\pi r^2 \psi^2$$

- A more general expression for orbitals which are not spherically symmetrical is $P(r) = r^2 R(r)$.

Variations of Radial Wave Function

1. Plots of Radial Wave Function R Against the Distance r

$R_{n,l}$ = Constant × Polynomial × Exponential

$R_{n,l}(r)$ v/s r plots

(i) 1s-orbital $R_{1,0} = 2\left(\dfrac{Z}{a_0}\right)^{3/2} \times 1 \times e^{\frac{-Zr}{a_0}}$

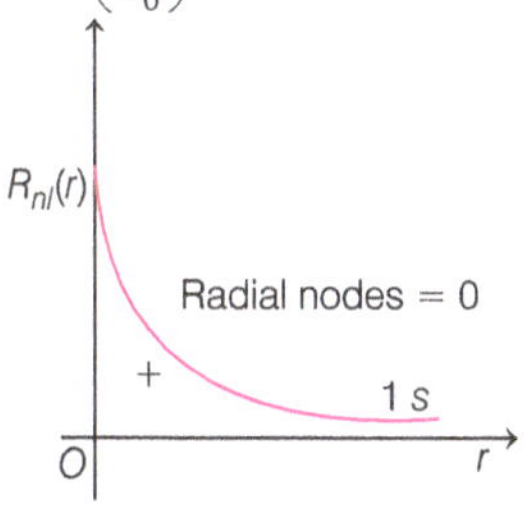

1s-orbital has a finite value of $R_{n,l}(r)$ at nucleus.

(ii) 2s-orbital $R_{2,0} = \left(\dfrac{Z}{a_0}\right)^{3/2} \dfrac{1}{2\sqrt{2}} \times \left(2 - \dfrac{Zr}{a_0}\right) \times e^{\frac{-Zr}{2a_0}}$

- If $2 > \dfrac{Zr}{a_0}$, then $R_{2,0}$ is + ve.
- If $\dfrac{Zr}{a_0} > 2$, then $R_{2,0}$ is – ve.
- If $\dfrac{Zr}{a_0} = 2$, then $R_{2,0}$ is 0.

At Radial node, $r = \dfrac{2a_0}{Z}$

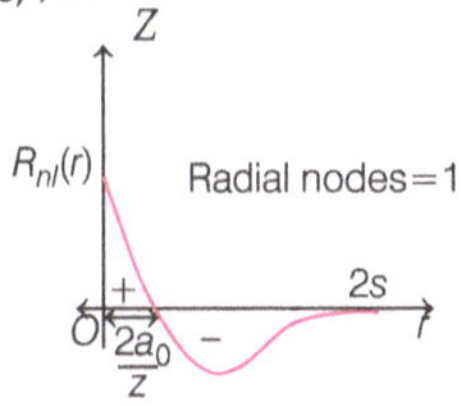

2s-orbital has a finite value of $R_{n,l}(r)$ at nucleus.

> **JEE Alert**
>
> The rate of exponential decay for 2s orbital (with respect to r) is slower than the rate of exponential decay for 1s orbital.

(iii) 2p-subshell

$$R_{2,1} = \left(\frac{Z}{a_0}\right)^{3/2} \frac{1}{2\sqrt{6}} \times \left(\frac{Zr}{a_0}\right) \times e^{\frac{-Ze}{2a_0}}$$

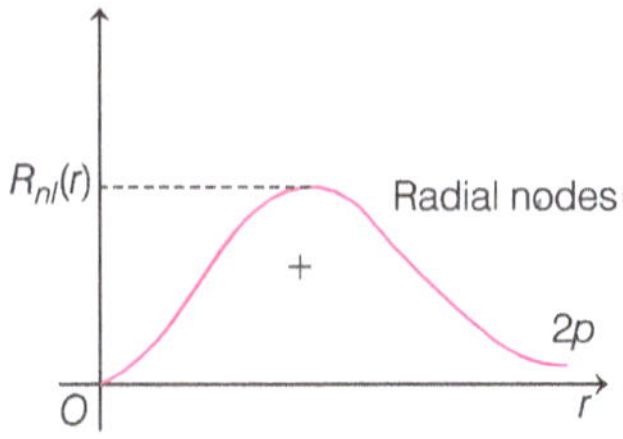

2p-orbital has zero value of $R_{n,l}(r)$ at nucleus.

2p-orbital has a maxima in the $R_{n,l}(r)$ v/s r plot.

(iv) 3s-orbital

$$R_{3,0} = \left(-\frac{Z}{a_0}\right)^{3/2} \frac{2}{81\sqrt{3}} \times \left(27 - 18\frac{Zr}{a_0} + \frac{2Z^2r^2}{a_0^2}\right) \times e^{\frac{-Zr}{3a_0}}$$

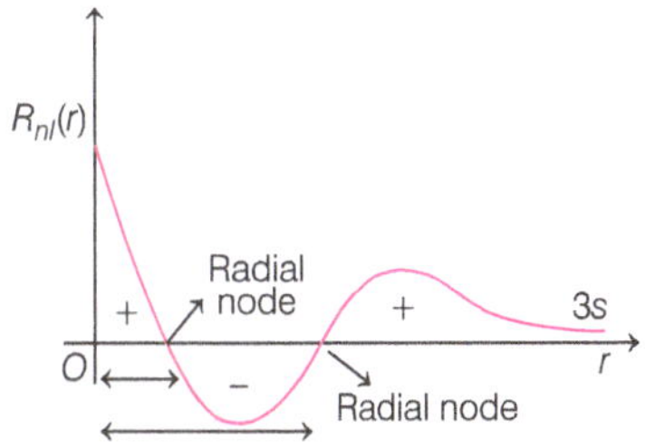

Radial nodes = 2

3*s*-orbital has a finite value of $R_{n,l}(r)$ at nucleus.

JEE Spotlite

- For all orbitals other than *s*-orbital, $R_{n,l}(r) = 0$ at the nucleus.
- For $R_{2,0}(r)$ has both +ve and –ve value.
- For the first orbital of other types (i.e. 2*p*, 3*d*, 4*f* etc), $R_{n,l}(r)$ may be + ve everwhere except at the origin
- For the second orbital of a given type (i.e. 2*s*, 3*p*, 4*d*, 5*f* etc.) $R_{n,l}(r)$ may be +ve or – ve but the radial wave function has only 1 sign change, i.e. they have 1 radial node.
- For the third orbital of a given type (i.e. 3*s*, 4*p*, 5*d*, 6*f* etc.), $R_{n,l}(r)$ may have 2 sign changes i.e. they have 2 radial nodes.

2. Plots of Radial Probability Density against the Distance *r*

$[R_{n,l}(r)]^2$ would always be + ve, irrespective of the sign of $R_{n,l}(r)$ for a given value of *r*. R^2 represents the probability density of finding electron at a particular point in space.

(i) 1*s*-orbital

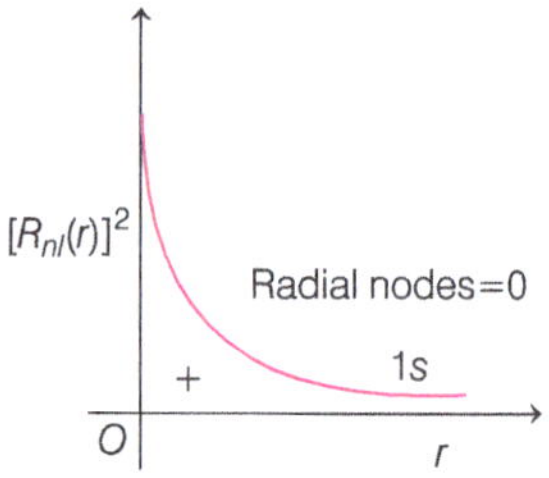

(ii) 2*s*-orbital

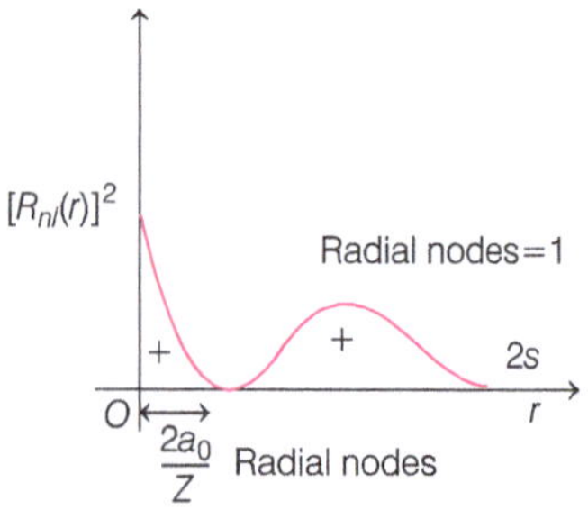

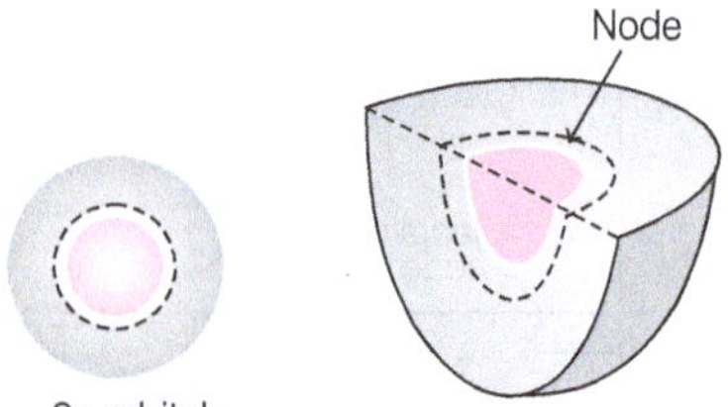

2s-orbital

(iii) 2*p*-subshell

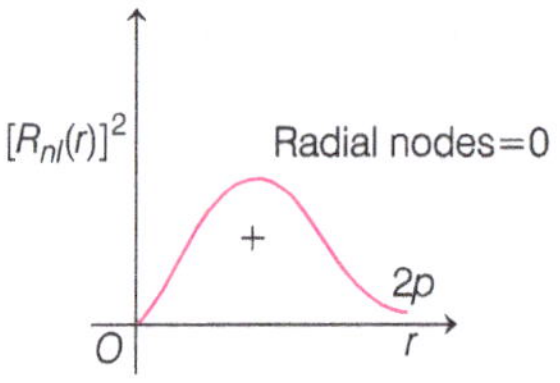

(iv) 3*s*-orbital

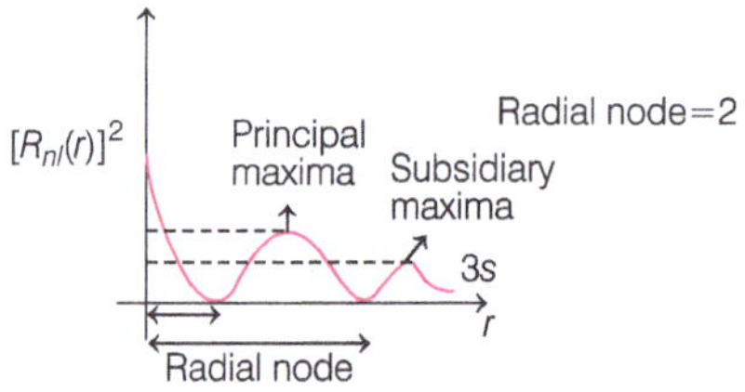

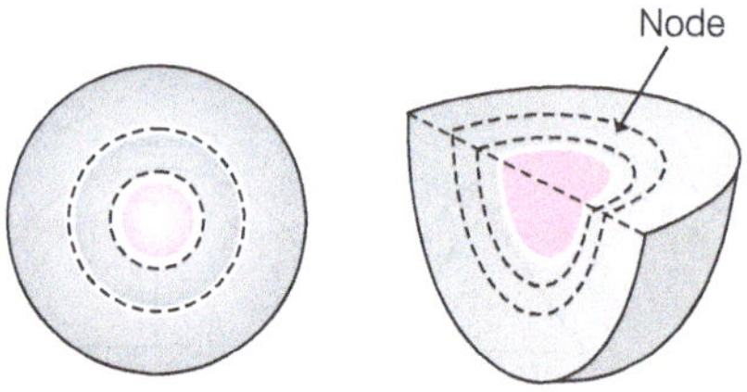

3s-orbital

3. Plot of $4\pi r^2[R_{n,1}(r)]^2$ *v/s r* Plots

Radial distribution function or radial probability distribution function (RPDF)

$$= p(r)dr = 4\pi r^2 [R_{n,1}(r)]^2 dr$$

$$p(r) = 4\pi^2 [R_{n,1}(r)]^2$$

The radial distribution is the probability function of choice to determine the most likely radius to find the electron for a given orbital (regardless of its direction).

Comparison between 3*s*, 3*p* and 3*d* orbitals.

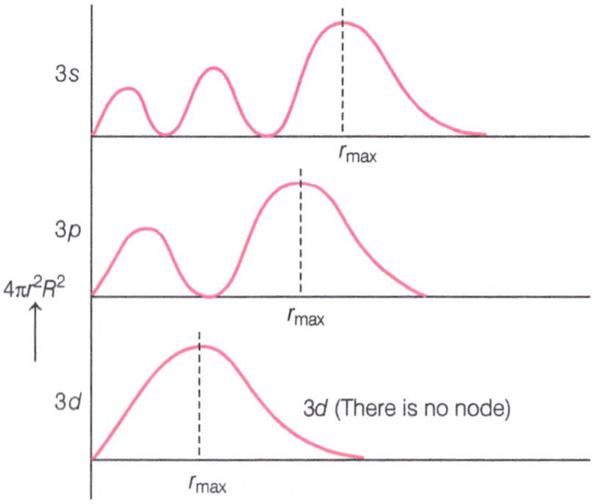

For the same value of *n*, the distance of max probability, r_{max} of various orbitals is inversely dependent upon the value of *l*.

$$(r_{max})_{3s} > (r_{max})_{3p} > (r_{max})_{3d}$$

Angular Wave Function θ, φ

Angular wave function θ, φ depends only on l and m_l and independent of n for a given type of orbital. Figure describes angular wave function.

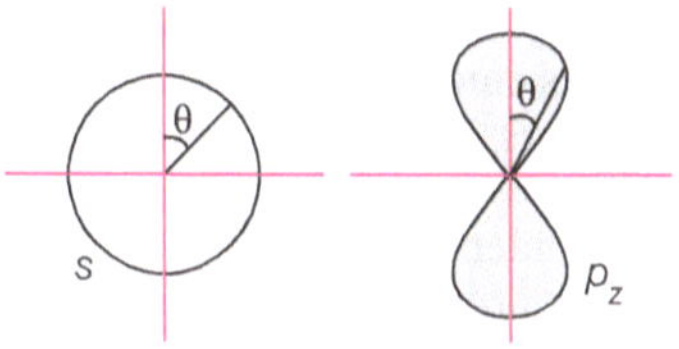

s-orbital and p_z-orbital
Angular part of the wave function for hydrogen like atom

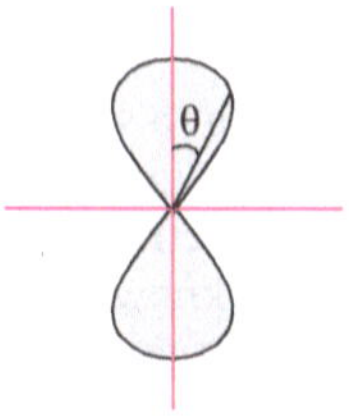

Angular part of probability density function $[\theta\phi]^2$ for p_z-orbital

The p-orbital (p_x, p_z and p_z) have same shape but differ in their orientations. Angular wave function depends on cos θ, boundary surface contains both positive and negative parts.

Interpretation of Wave Equation

- A principal tenet of quantum mechanics is that the wave function contains all the dynamical information about the system it describes.
- If the wave function of a particle has the value ψ at some point x, then probability of finding the particle between x and $(x + dx)$ is proportional to $|\psi|^2\, dx$.
- For a three dimensional wave function of a particle, if the wave function of a particle has the value at some point, then probability of finding a particle in a small volume (dV) around that point is $|\psi|^2\, dV$."

JEE Spotlite

- For a hydrogen atom, wave function of principal quantum number n, there are
  (i) $(n - l - 1)$ radial nodes
  (ii) l angular nodes
  (iii) $(n - 1)$ total nodes
  Thus, $1s(n = 1, l = 0)$ sub-shell is without any node.
  $2s(n = 2, l = 0)$ sub-shell will have only one radial node. While $2p(n = 2, l = 1)$ sub-shell will have only one angular node.
- If the node which occurs at $r = \infty$ is being included, then total number of nodes will be n and not $(n - 1)$.
- **Nodal plane** The plane in which the probability of finding an electron is zero is called a nodal plane.

- The wave function ψ is a probability amplitude in the sense that its square modulus ($|\psi|^2$) is a probability density.
- There is no physical significance of ψ but $|\psi|^2$ has a clear physical significance of being the probability density (probability per unit volume) of the location of particle.

Quantum Numbers

The position of an electron in an atom is determined by four quantum numbers

Principal Quantum Number

This is used to specify the position and energy of the electron in an orbit or shell. This is denoted by n.

$n = 1, 2, 3, \ldots, \infty$ (only positive integers)

It determines the average distance between nucleus and electron in an orbit and also their corresponding energy.

- The smaller the value of n the lower the energy.
- The size of an orbital and also depends on n. The larger the value of n is, the larger the orbital. Orbitals of the same quantum state 'n' are said to belong to the same shell. Shells are also denoted by letters :

Letter	K	L	M	N
n	1	2	3	4

Angular Quantum Number

This is also called subsidiary or azimuthal quantum number, denoted by l.

The value of l varies from $l = 0$ to $(n - 1)$

This is used to describe subshell. For $l = 0, 1, 2, 3, 4, 5, \ldots$, subshell $= s, p, d, f, g, \ldots$

where $s, p, d, f, g, \ldots$ are the symbols for sharp, principle, diffused, fundamental spectral lines.

Value of l	**Subshell** (notation)	**Number of orbitals** $(2l + 1)$
0	s (sharp)	1
1	p (principle)	3
2	d (diffused)	5
3	f (fundamental)	7
4	g*	9

*The letter g in atomic orbital does not have a historical association with specific spectral lines.

Any subshell is represented by 'nl' such that we write number for n and name for l.

Thus, $n = 1, l = 0$ will indicate ($1s$) subshell; $n = 2, l = 1$ will indicate ($2p$) subshell and so on.

- **Representation of a subshell**

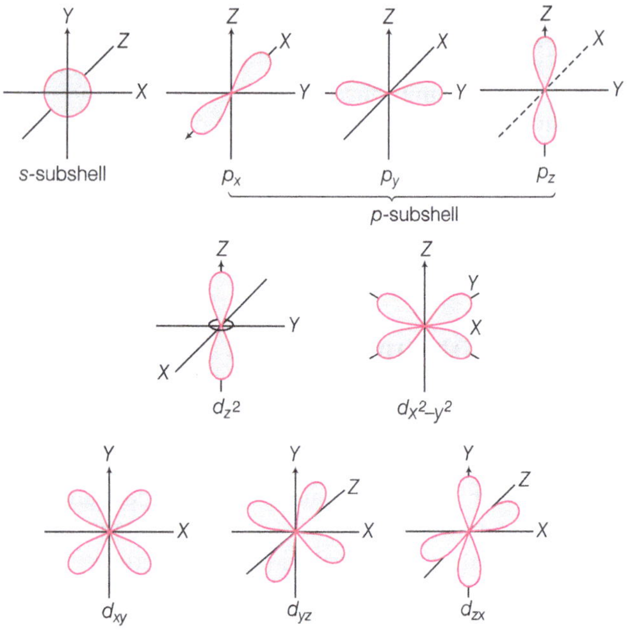

Shapes of orbitals

- Although the energy of an orbital is primarily determined by n, the energy also depends on l (except for H-atom) for a given n, the energy of an orbital increases with l.
- A subshell is only possible, if $l < n$.
- l also describes the shape of the orbital occupied by the electron.

  $l = 0$ (s) – spherical, $l = 1$ (p) – dumb-bell

  $l = 2$ (d) – double dumb-bell
- For the $d_{x^2-y^2}$ orbital both nodal planes bisect the X and Y-axes.
- For the d_{z^2} orbital there are two nodal cones instead of nodal planes.
- Orbital angular momentum, (L) is quantised and is given by

$$L = \sqrt{l(l+1)}\,\frac{h}{2\pi}, \left(\frac{h}{2\pi} = \hbar\right)$$

- The magnitude of magnetic moment (μ_L) is given by

$$\mu_L = \frac{eh}{4\pi mc}\sqrt{l(l+1)}$$

where, $\frac{eh}{4\pi mc} = 9.2732 \times 10^{-14}$ J

Magnetic Quantum Number

This quantum number denoted by m or m_l determines the preferred orientations of orbitals in space.

$$m \quad \text{or} \quad m_l = -l, \ldots, 0 \ldots, +l$$

Total values of $m = (2l + 1)$ = number of orbitals in a subshell (l)

Number of orbitals is equal to the number of ways in which they are oriented. Thus, s-subshell ($m = 0$) will have one orbital. p-subshell ($m = -1, -0, +1$) has three orbitals (p_x, p_y, p_z). They are identical in energy, (degenerate) shape and size which differ only in their directions in space.

d-subshell ($m = -2, -1, 0, +1, +2$) has five orbitals ($d_{xy}, d_{yz}, d_{zx}, d_{x^2-y^2}$ and d_{z^2}). These are also equal in energy. Degenerate orbitals have the same shape but different orientation in space.

Above three quantum numbers also help to designate the electron present in an orbital. Further since an orbital can contain a maximum of two electrons with opposite spins, an additional quantum number known as the magnetic spin quantum number (m_s) is also required to specify the spin of the electron.

Spin Quantum Number

An electron can be regarded as spinning on its axis, like a top, in a clockwise and anti-clockwise direction. This is called spin quantum number denoted s or m_s with value of $\left(\frac{1}{2}\right)$ for all electrons. Clockwise or anti-clockwise spins are distinguished by the spin magnetic quantum number m_s.

$$m_s = +\frac{1}{2} \quad \text{or} \quad \uparrow \text{(spin-up for clockwise)}$$

if $m_s = -\frac{1}{2}$ or $\downarrow$ (spin-down for anti-clockwise)

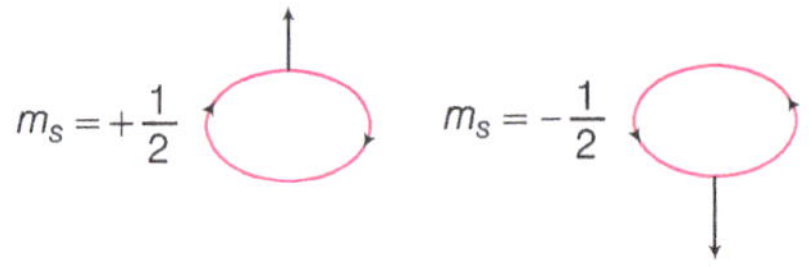

- In an orbital there are maximum of two electrons such that their spins are $+\frac{1}{2}$ and $-\frac{1}{2}$ and sum of spins is zero.

  $\uparrow\downarrow$

- There are maximum of 2 electrons in s-subshell, 6 electrons in p-subshell, 10 electrons in d-subshell, 14 electrons in f-subshell and 18 electrons in g-subshell.

  Spin angular momentum $= \sqrt{s(s+1)}\,\frac{h}{2\pi}$, where $s = \frac{1}{2}$
- The spin of electrons is responsible for most of the magnetic properties of atoms, molecules or ions. The spin magnetic moment (μ_s) is given by $\mu_s = \frac{eh}{2\pi mc}\sqrt{s(s+1)}$

Quantum numbers

The four quantum numbers				Max. number of electrons in each sublevel	Max. number of electrons in each principal level
Principal	**Subsidiary**	**Magnetic**	**Spin**		
$n=1$	$l=0$ (1s)	$m=0$	$\pm\frac{1}{2}$	2 s-electrons	2
$n=2$	$l=0$ (2s)	$m=0$	$\pm\frac{1}{2}$	2 s-electrons	8
	$l=1$ (2p)	$m=1$	$\pm\frac{1}{2}$	6 p-electrons	
		$m=0$	$\pm\frac{1}{2}$		
		$m=1$	$\pm\frac{1}{2}$		
$n=3$	$l=0$ (3s)	$m=0$	$\pm\frac{1}{2}$	2 s-electrons	18
	$l=1$ (3p)	$m=1$	$\pm\frac{1}{2}$	6 p-electrons	
		$m=0$	$\pm\frac{1}{2}$		
		$m=-1$	$\pm\frac{1}{2}$		
	$l=2$ (3d)	$m=2$	$\pm\frac{1}{2}$	10 d-electrons	
		$m=1$	$\pm\frac{1}{2}$		
		$m=0$	$\pm\frac{1}{2}$		
		$m=-1$	$\pm\frac{1}{2}$		
		$m=-2$	$\pm\frac{1}{2}$		

Solved Booster 2.3

Which of the following sets of quantum numbers are allowed? What atomic orbitals do the allowed combinations correspond to?

	n	l	m_l		n	l	m_l
(a)	2	2	2	(b)	5	3	−2
(c)	3	−1	1	(d)	2	1	1
(e)	4	0	1				

Solution **(b, d)**

A set of quantum number is allowed if for a given value of n,
$l = 0, 1, 2 \ldots (n-1)\,(l < n)$
$m_l = -l, 0, +l$

(a) $l = 2$ hence not allowed
(b) $n = 5, l = 3 < n, m_l = -2\ (-l, \ldots 0, \ldots +l)$. Thus, it is allowed
(c) l never takes −ve value, thus it is not allowed.
(d) $n = 2, l = 1 < n$, hence it is allowed.
(e) $m_l = 1$, it can take only 0 value for $l = 0$. Thus, it is not allowed.

(b) 5f (d) 2p

JEE Quicker

The statement "Atomic orbital is characterised by the quantum number n and l only is incorrect" *JEE Main 2022*

An atomic orbital is characterised by three quantum number n, l and m.

- n refers to principal quantum number which describes the orbit to which electron belongs.
- l refers to azimuthal quantum number which describes the shape and energy of subshells.
- m refers to magnetic quantum number which explains the number of possible orientation in a subshell.

Energies of Orbitals and Energy Level Diagram

A diagram representing relative energies of various orbitals in an atom is called **energy level diagram**.

Energy Level Diagram of Hydrogen Atom

In hydrogen atom, the energy of an electron is determined solely by the principal quantum number (n). Thus, the energy of an electron increases with an increase in n. The energy of the orbitals increases as follows:

$1s < 2s = 2p < 3s = 3p = 3d < 4s = 4p = 4d = 4f <\ldots$ so on and is depicted in figure.

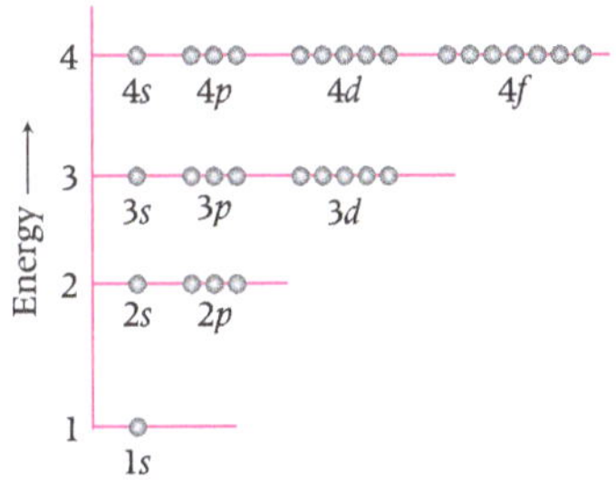

Energy level diagram for hydrogen atom

In the energy level diagram, it may be noted that orbitals for the same value of principal quantum number (n) have the same energies even for different azimuthal quantum numbers (l). e.g., the electron has the same energy when it is in 2s orbital as when it is present in 2p orbitals. The orbitals having the same energy are called **degenerates orbitals**.

Energy Level Diagram of Multi-electron Atoms

In case of multi-electron atoms, the energy of an electron, depends not only on its principal quantum number (shell), but also on its azimuthal quantum number (sub-shell).
As shown in figure for a particular energy level or shell, the various sub-shells such as *s, p, d*, ... have different energies.

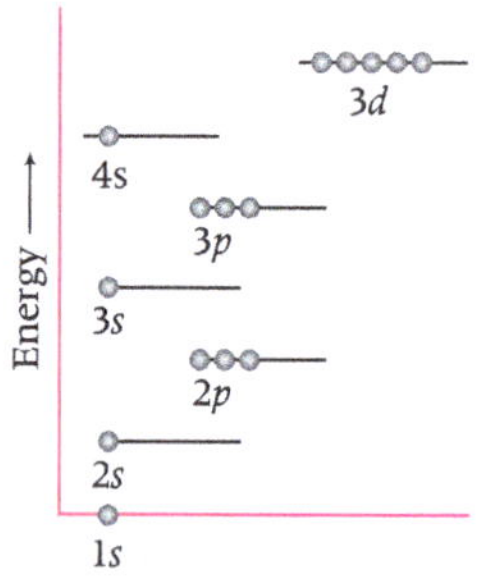

Energy level diagram for multielectron atoms

Thus, the order for the various sub-shells is

$1s < 2s < 2p < 3s < 3p < 4s < 3d < 4p < 5s < 4d < 5p < 4f$

The main reason for having different energies of the sub-shells is the mutual repulsion among the electrons in a multi-electron atom.

In hydrogen atom, there is only one electrical interaction present—the attraction between the negatively charged electron and the positively charged nucleus. But in a multi-electron atom, besides the attraction between the electron and the nucleus, there is repulsion between every electron and other electrons present in the atom.

Thus, the stability of an electron in a multi-electron atom is due to the reason that the total attractive interactions are greater than the total repulsive interactions.

Solved Booster 2.4

The quantum numbers of electrons are given below.

(a) $n = 4, l = 2, m_l = -2, m_s = -\frac{1}{2}$

(b) $n = 3, l = 2, m_l = 1, m_s = +\frac{1}{2}$

(c) $n = 4, l = 1, m_l = 0, m_s = +\frac{1}{2}$

(d) $n = 3, l = 2, m_l = -2, m_s = -\frac{1}{2}$

(e) $n = 3, l = 1, m_l = -1, m_s = +\frac{1}{2}$

(f) $n = 4, l = 1, m_l = +1, m_s = +\frac{1}{2}$

Choose the correct answer from the options given below.

(a) a < b < c < d < f < e (b) e < b = d < c = f < a
(c) b < d = c < e < f < a (d) f < e < d = c = b < a

Solution **(b)**

$e < b = d < c = f < a$

Rules for Filling Electrons in Orbitals

Aufbau Rule

('Building up') "Electrons in various sub-orbits of an orbit are filled in the increasing order of their energies". Smaller the value of $(n + 1)$, smaller the energy.

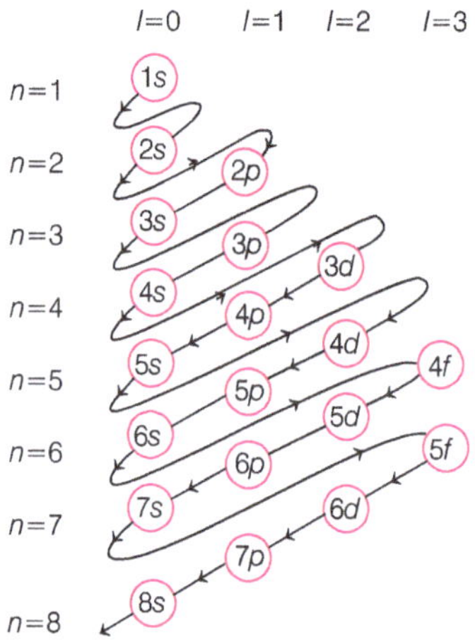

Increasing order of energy

If two or more sub-orbits have same values of $(n + l)$ sub-orbits with lower values of n has lower energy and thus will be filled first.

Energy order of $1s, 2s, 2p, 3s$, ... sub-orbits is given in Fig. (go in the direction of arrow to determine order).

Thus, the order in which the energies of the sub-orbits increase and hence the order in which the sub-orbits are filled is as follows:

$1s < 2s < 2p < 3s < 3p < 4s < 3d < 4p < 5s < 4d < 5p < 6s < 4f$

Based on $(n + l)$ rule, explanation of energy order is given in table .

Explanation of energy order

Sub-orbit	n	l	$(n + l)$	Comparison of energy
$1s$	1	0	1	$2s > 1s$
$2s$	2	0	2	$2p > 2s > 1s$
$2p$	2	1	3	$3s > 2p > 2s > 1s$ (lower n)
$3s$	3	0	3	
$3p$	3	1	4	$3p > 3s > 2p > 2s > 1s$
$3d$	3	2	5	$3d > 3p$
$4s$	4	0	4	$3d > 4s$ $(n+l)$ lower

This rule can be used to determine block of the element in a periodic table. Block is that in which last electron called **'differentiating electron'** is being filled. It is illustrated below.

Element	Z	Electronic configuration (EC)	Last electron goes into	Block
Na	11	$[Ne]\,3s^1$	$3s$	s
Al	13	$[Ne]\,3s^2 3p^1$	$3p$	p
Sc	21	$[Ar]\,4s^2 3d^1$	$3d$	d
Ce	58	$[Xe]\,6s^2 4f^2$	$4f$	f

JEE MAPPER

Example Similar to PYQ Asked in JEE Main 2024

Compare the energies of following sets of quantum numbers for multielectron system.

A. $n = 3, l = 2$ B. $n = 4, l = 0$ C. $n = 4, l = 3$ D. $n = 2, l = 1$
E. $n = 3, l = 0$

Choose the correct answer form the options given below.

(a) D > E > A > C > B (b) B > C > A > E > D
(c) D < E < B < A < C (d) E < D < A < B < C

Sol. (c) Energy level can be determined by comparing the value of $(n + l)$ rule, i.e. Bohr-Bury rule. i.e., lower is the value of $(n + l)$ lower is the energy. If the value of $(n + l)$ is equal then lower n corresponds to lower energy.

A. $n = 3, l = 2; n + l = 5$ B. $n = 4, l = 0; n + l = 4$
C. $n = 4, l = 3; n + l = 7$ D. $n = 2, l = 1; n + l = 3$
E. $n = 3, l = 0; n + l = 3$

So, the correct order is D < E < B < A < C.

Competency Enhancer 2.2

Compare the energies of following sets of quantum numbers for multielectron system

A. $n = 6, l = 0$ B. $n = 5, l = 3$
C. $n = 7, l = 1$ D. $n = 4, l = 1$
E. $n = 4, l = 2$

Choose the correct answer form the options given below.

(a) B > E > C > D > A (b) B > C > E > A > D
(c) D < A < E < C < B (d) D < E < A < B < C

Pauli Exclusion Principle

According to this principle, "No two electrons in an atom can have same set of all the four quantum numbers, i.e. n, l, m and s. In an atom any two electrons may have three quantum numbers identical but fourth quantum number must be different.

According to this principle, an orbital can accomodate maximum two electrons with their spins opposite to each other.

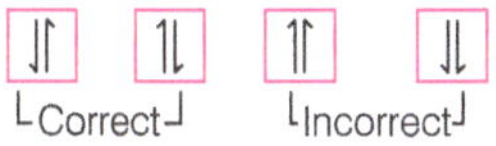

Hund's Rule of Maximum Multiplicity

This rule govern the fillings up of degenerate orbitals of the same subshell.

According to this rule, "Pairing of electrons in various orbitals (like p_x, p_y, p_z) of a sub-orbit (like np) takes place only after each orbital is half-filled/singly occupied."

The ground state electronic configuration of the atom of an element corresponds to the state of the lowest total electronic energy. The electronic configurations are written based on Aufbau rule and Hund's rule. But in cases (such as Cu and Cr) where the two subshells ($4s$ and $3d$) differ slightly in terms of energy,there can be a shift of an electron from a subshell of lower energy ($4s$) to a subshell of higher energy ($3d$) so as to give an electronic configuration of completely filled or half-filled orbitals of a subshell.

Elements with atomic number 24(Cr), 42(Mo) and 74(W) have $ns^1(n-1)d^5$ configuration and not $ns^2(n-1)d^4$ due to extra stability of these atoms. Elements with atomic number 29 (Cu), 47(Ag) and 79(Au) have $ns^1(n-1)d^{10}$ configuration instead of $ns^2(n-1)d^9$ due to extra stability of these atoms.

There is extra stability associated with these electronic configurations which can be due to :

(i) **Symmetrical Distribution of Electrons** The completely filled or half-filled subshells have symmetrical distribution of electrons in them and therefore are more stable. Electrons in the same subshell (with degenerate orbitals) have equal energy but different spatial distribution. As a result of it, their shielding of one-another is relatively small and the electrons are more strongly attracted by the nucleus.

(ii) **Exchange Energy** This stabilisation effect (of exchange energy) arises whenever two or more electrons with the same spin are present in the degenerate orbitals of a subshell. These electrons tend to exchange their positions, and the energy released due to this exchange is called exchange energy. When the subshell is half-filled or completely filled, the number of exchanges can be maximum and thus maximum exchange energy leads to the stabilisation of the atom. Possible exchanges for a d^5-configuration are show below.

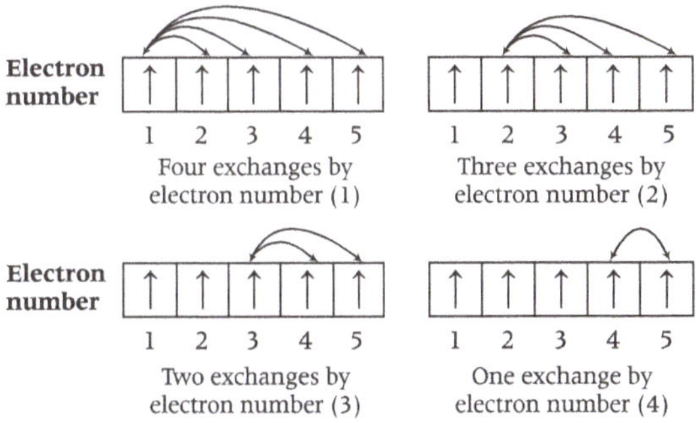

Electronic Configuration of Atoms

The distribution of electrons into orbitals of an atom is called its electronic configuration. Based on this, electronic configuration of various elements (upto $Z = 36$) are given in table.

Electronic configuration (EC) of elements $Z = 1$ to 36

Element	Atomic number	1s	2s	2p	3s	3p	3d	4s	4p	4d	4f
H	1	1									
He	2	2									
Li	3	2	1								
Be	4	2	2								
B	5	2	2	1							
C	6	2	2	2							
N	7	2	2	3							
O	8	2	2	4							
F	9	2	2	5							
Ne	10	2	2	6							
Na	11	2	2	6	1						
Mg	12	2	2	6	2						
Al	13	2	2	6	2	1					
Si	14	2	2	6	2	2					
P	15	2	2	6	2	3					
S	16	2	2	6	2	4					
Cl	17	2	2	6	2	5					
Ar	18	2	2	6	2	6					
K	19							1			
Ca	20			After 18 electrons				2			

Element	Atomic number	1s	2s	2p	3s	3p	3d	4s	4p	4d	4f
Sc	21						1	2			
Ti	22						2	2			
V	23						3	2			
Cr	24						5	1			
Mn	25						5	2			
Fe	26						6	2			
Co	27						7	2			
Ni	28						8	2			
Cu	29			After 18 electrons			10	1			
Zn	30						10	2			
Ga	31						10	2	1		
Ge	32						10	2	2		
As	33						10	2	3		
Se	34						10	2	4		
Br	35						10	2	5		
Kr	36	2	2	6	2	6	10	2	6		

JEE Spotlite

In the formation of ion, electrons of the outermost orbit are lost. Hence, whenever you are required to write electronic configuration of the ion, first write electronic configuration of its atom and take electron from outermost orbit. If we write electronic configuration of Fe^{2+} ($Z = 26$, 24 electrons), it will not be similar to Cr (with 24 e^-) but quite different

Fe $[Ar]\ 4s^2 3d^6$
Fe^{2+} $[Ar] 4s^0 3d^6$
} outermost orbit is 4th shell hence,

electrons from 4s have been removed to make Fe^{2+}.

Elemental Practice 2.2

Type I MCQs with Only One Correct Option

1. A particle of mass 1.0 mg has a velocity of 3600 km h^{-1}. Thus, wavelength associated with it is
(a) 6.626×10^{-30} m (b) 6.626×10^{-31} m
(c) 6.626×10^{-32} m (d) 6.626×10^{-33} m

2. The de-Broglie wavelength of the electron in the first excited state of He^+ is
(a) 33.4 pm (b) 3.34 pm
(c) 0.334 pm (d) 334 pm

3. The wavelength of electrons that have been accelerated from rest through a potential difference of 1.00 kV is
(a) 1.23 pm (b) 38.8 pm
(c) 123 pm (d) 0.123 pm

4. How fast would a particle of 1.0 g need to travel to have the same linear momentum as photon of radiation of wavelength 300 nm? (ms^{-1})
(a) 2.21×10^{-12} (b) 2.21×10^{-16}
(c) 2.21×10^{-24} (d) 2.21×10^{-18}

5. The speed of a certain proton is 350 km s^{-1}. If the uncertainty in its momentum is 0.01 per cent, what uncertainty in its location must be tolerated ?
(a) 9×10^{-10} m (b) 12×10^{-12} m
(c) 16×10^{-10} m (d) 18×10^{-12} m

6. If $2a_0$ be the radius of first Bohr's orbit of H-atom, the de-Broglie wavelength of an electron revolving in the 3rd Bohr's orbit will be
(a) $9\pi a_0$ (b) $\frac{\pi a_0}{6}$
(c) $6\pi a_0$ (d) $12\pi a_0$

7. In the formation of $Cu^+ \longrightarrow Cu^{2+} + e^-$ electron lost has

	n	l	m_l	m_s
(a)	4	0	0	$+\frac{1}{2}$
(b)	3	2	−2	$-\frac{1}{2}$
(c)	3	1	−1	$-\frac{1}{2}$
(d)	3	0	0	$+\frac{1}{2}$

8. The set of quantum numbers that represents the highest energy of an atom is
(a) $n = 4, l = 0, m_l = 0, m_s = +\frac{1}{2}$
(b) $n = 3, l = 2, m_l = 1, m_s = +\frac{1}{2}$
(c) $n = 3, l = 1, m_l = 1, m_s = +\frac{1}{2}$
(d) $n = 3, l = 0, m_l = 0, m_s = +\frac{1}{2}$

9. In a sub-orbit, there are three radial nodes. This sub-orbit can be
(a) 4*s* or 5*p* (b) 4*d* or 5*p*
(c) 4*s* or 4*p* (d) 3*s* or 3*p*

10. Electrons in various degenerate orbitals of a sub-shell can be filled (by changing spin etc.) by following arrangements, $\frac{x!}{(x-y)!y!}$ where, $x = 2 \times$ number of orbitals, y = number of electrons
A p^2-configuration can be written as many as
(a) 15 ways (b) 6 ways
(c) 45 ways (d) 10 ways

11. If azimuthal quantum number could have value of *n* also (in addition to normal value), then EC of V ($Z = 23$) would have been
(a) $1s^2, 2s^2, 2p^6, 3s^2, 3p^6, 4s^2, 3d^3$
(b) $1s^2, 1p^6, 2s^2, 2p^6, 2d^7$
(c) $1s^2, 1p^6, 2s^2, 2p^6, 3s^2, 2d^5$
(d) $1s^2, 1p^6, 2s^2, 2p^6, 3s^1, 2d^6$

12. Compare the energies of following sets of quantum numbers for multielectron system.
A. $n = 3, l = 0$ B. $n = 5, l = 1$
C. $n = 3, l = 1$ D. $n = 5, l = 0$
E. $n = 3, l = 4$
Choose the correct answer from the options given below:
(a) A < E < C < D < B (b) A < C < D < B < E
(c) D > B > A > C > E (d) D > A > B > E > C

13. A cricket ball of 0.25 kg is moving with a velocity of 250 ms^{-1}. The wavelength associated with its motion is
(a) 2.11×10^{-34} m (b) 1.81×10^{-33} m
(c) 1.06×10^{-35} m (d) 3.01×10^{-36} m

14. If the value of principal quantum number is 3, the total possible values for magnetic quantum number will be
(a) 9 (b) 4
(c) 12 (d) 16

15. The de-Broglie wavelength of a particle with mass 2g and velocity 200 m/s is
(a) 1.31×10^{-30} m (b) 1.65×10^{-33} m
(c) 1.45×10^{-35} m (d) 1.21×10^{-36} m

16. The correct set of four quantum numbers for the valence electron of caesium ($Z = 55$) is
(a) $6, 1, 1, +\frac{1}{2}$ (b) $6, 1, 0, +\frac{1}{2}$
(c) $6, 0, 0, +\frac{1}{2}$ (d) $6, 0, 1, +\frac{1}{2}$

17. An accelerated electron has a speed of 7×10^6 ms^{-1} with an uncertainty of 0.05%. The uncertainty in finding its location while in motion is $x \times 10^{-9}$ m. Find the value of x.

[Given : Mass of electron $= 9.1 \times 10^{-31}$ kg, $h = 6.63 \times 10^{-34}$, $\pi = 3.14$]

(a) 18.31 (b) 29.01 (c) 32.13 (d) 16.57

Type II 》 MCQs with One or More than One Correct Option

18. Which of the following statements are correct?

(a) The uncertainty principle is $\Delta E \times \Delta t \geq \frac{h}{4\pi}$.

(b) Half filled and fully filled orbitals have greater stability due to greater exchange energy, greater symmetry and more balanced arrangement.

(c) The energy of 2s-orbital is less than the energy of 2p-orbital in case of hydrogen like atoms.

(d) de-Broglie's wavelength is given by $\lambda = \frac{h}{mv}$, where m = mass of the particle, v = group velocity of the particle.

19. Which of the following statements are incorrect for an electron that has $n = 4$ and $m = -2$?

(a) The electron may or may not be present in a d-orbital.

(b) The electron is in the fourth principal electronic shell

(c) The electron may be in a p-orbital.

(d) The electron must have the spin quantum number $= +\frac{1}{2}$.

20. Which of the following statements are correct?

(a) The mass of a photon with wavelength 3.6 Å is 4.31×10^{-27} kg.

(b) The effect of Heisenberg uncertainty principle is significant only for motion of microscopic objects and is negligible for that of macroscopic objects.

(c) Heisenberg uncertainty principle is not valid for stationary particles and motor car.

(d) The qualitative order of de-Broglie wavelength for electron, proton and α particle is $\lambda_e > \lambda_p > \lambda_\alpha$ if kinetic energy is not same for all particles.

21. Which of the following statements are correct?

(a) The energy of an electron in an orbital of a hydrogen like species depends only on the principal quantum number n.

(b) The angular momentum of an electron in an orbital of a multielectron atom depends on the quantum numbers l and m.

(c) The expression of angular momentum of an electron in an orbitals is given as $\sqrt{l(l-1)}\left(\frac{h}{2\pi}\right)$.

(d) The z-component of angular momentum of an electron in an orbital is given as $m\left(\frac{h}{2\pi}\right)$.

22. Which of the following statements are incorrect?

(a) According to Pauli's exclusion principle, no two electrons in an atom can have the same values of quantum numbers n, l and m.

(b) The total energy of an electron in an orbital is half of its potential energy.

(c) The speed of an electron in an orbital increases with increase of quantum number n.

(d) The energy of an electron in an orbital decreases with increase of its quantum number n.

Type III 》 Numerical/Integer Answer Type Questions

23. An electron beam can undergo diffraction by crystals. Through, what potential should a beam of electrons be accelerated so that its wavelength becomes equal to 200 pm. The value of potential is .... [Nearest Integer]

24. The term degeneracy means the number of different quantum states of an atom or molecule having the same energy. The degeneracy of the $n = 5$ level is ....

25. The wavelength of helium atom with a velocity of 1×10^3 ms^{-1} is .... pm. [Nearest Integer]

26. If the uncertainties in the measurements of position and momentum are equal. Then, the uncertainty in the measurement of velocity (in ms^{-1}) of particle of mass 1.21×10^{-18} kg will be ....

27. Oxygen molecule (O_2) is travelling at the speed equal to root mean square velocity at 300 K. Then, its de-Broglie wavelength will be .... pm. [Nearest Integer]

Elemental Practice 2.2 | Chapter 02

Connect with **Answers**

1. (b)	**2.** (d)	**3.** (b)	**4.** (c)	**5.** (a)	**6.** (d)
7. (b)	**8.** (b)	**9.** (a)	**10.** (a)	**11.** (c)	**12.** (b)
13. (c)	**14.** (a)	**15.** (b)	**16.** (c)	**17.** (d)	**18.** (a,b,d)
19. (c,d)	**20.** (b,c)	**21.** (a,c,d)	**22.** (a,c)	**23.** (38)	**24.** (25)
25. (100)	**26.** (6)	**27.** (26)			

Advanced Exclusive Different Strokes

Tips to solve problems related to Radial probability distribution curves.

For such problems it is very important to understand the interpretation of quantum waves.

Radial component of wave defines the probable radial distribution of electrons.

$$\psi_{n,l,m} = k\,[\text{Polynomial}]^{n-l-1}\left(\frac{Zr}{a_0}\right)^{l} e^{\frac{-Zr}{na_0}}$$

where,

n = Principal quantum number, a_0 = Bohr's radius

Z = Atomic number, l = Azimuthal quantum number

Interpretations

r^l : The power term of r will show the type of subshell.

$e^{\frac{-Zr}{na_0}}$: n will show the shell number

$n-l-1$: will provide the number of radial nodes the degree of polynomial.

Let us understand this with the help of an example.

$$\psi = \frac{4\sqrt{2}}{3}\left(\frac{Z}{3a_0}\right)^{\frac{3}{2}}\left(\frac{Zr}{a_0}\right)\left(1-\frac{Zr}{6a_0}\right)e^{\frac{-Zr}{3a_0}}$$

Interpretations

(a) $n = 3$ third shell

(b) $\frac{Zr}{a_0}$: $l = 1$, p-subshell

(c) Degree of polynomial is 1, the graph will cut the 'r' axis at one point. Number of radial node is 1.

If $r \to 0$, $\psi \to 0$, the graph will start from the origin.

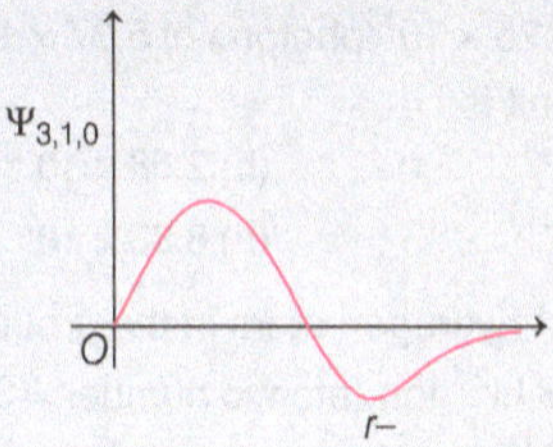

JEE Alert !

The graph of ψ vs r will have decreasing peaks with radius.

ψ^2_{nlm} : Radial probable density distribution.

The density of electron decreases with radius.

For instance, the probability getting of $3p$ electrons will increase with the radius till the distance of 3rd shell but the density decreases because the area increases with larger extent with radius. For ψ^2_{nlm}: The graph will have positive solutions.

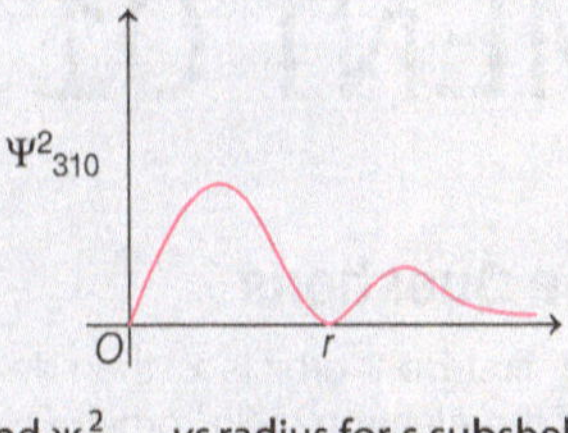

Graph of $\psi_{n,l,m}$ and $\psi^2_{n,l,m}$ vs radius for s-subshell will start from intercept whereas for p, d, f,... it will start from origin.

$\psi^2 4\pi r^2$: The probable radial distribution of electron.

The graph for $\psi^2 4\pi r^2$ vs r for all subshell will start from origin.

The peaks of graph will be increasing.

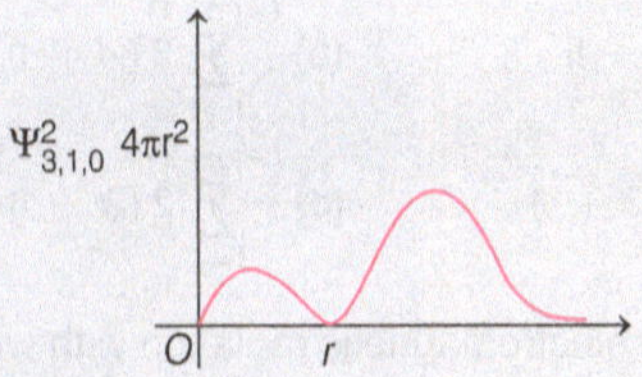

If the number of radial nodes is 'x', the number of maxima will be $(x+1)$.

Now, Interpret the wave function given below on the basis of above concept.

$$\psi_{300} = \frac{1}{81\sqrt{3\pi}}\left[\frac{1}{a_0}\right]^{\frac{3}{2}}\left[27 - \frac{18r}{a_0} + \frac{2r^2}{a_0^2}\right]e^{\frac{-r}{3a_0}}$$

Interpretations

(a) $n = 3$ represents third shell.

(b) 'r^l' missing : $l = 0$'s'-subshell

(c) degree of polynomial is '2' : number of radial node : 2 [The graph will cut the r axis at two points if $r \to 0$, $\psi \neq 0$, the graph will start from the intercept.

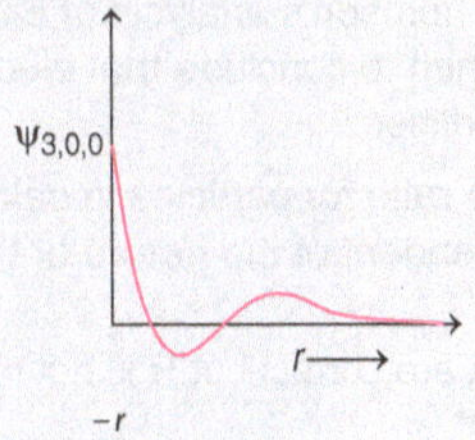

When the r is large, $e^{\frac{-r}{390}}$ plays major role $\to$ the graph will run parallel to 'r' axis till infinity.

PRACTICE
ELEMENT 01

Target JEE Main

Objective Type Questions

1. If the radius of first Bohr orbit is x, then de-Broglie wavelength of the electron in 3rd orbit of H-atom is nearly
(a) $2\pi x$ (b) $6\pi x$
(c) $9x$ (d) $x/3$

2. If n and l are the principal and azimuthal quantum numbers respectively then the expression for calculating the total number of electrons in any energy level is
(a) $\sum_{l=1}^{l=n} 2(2l+1)$ (b) $\sum_{l=1}^{l=(n-1)} 2(2l+1)$
(c) $\sum_{l=0}^{l=(n+1)} 2(2l+1)$ (d) $\sum_{l=0}^{l=(n-1)} 2(2l+1)$

3. A particular electromagnetic radiation with wavelength 200 nm
(a) has a higher frequency than radiation with wavelength 400 nm
(b) is in the visible region of the electromagnetic spectrum
(c) has a greater speed in vacuum than does radiation of wavelength 400 nm
(d) has a greater energy content per photon than does radiation with wavelength 100 nm

4. The ionisation energy of gaseous sodium atom is 495.80 kJ mol^{-1}. The lowest possible frequency of light that can ionise a sodium atom is
(a) $4.76 \times 10^{14} s^{-1}$ (b) $7.50 \times 10^{14} s^{-1}$
(c) $1.24 \times 10^{15} s^{-1}$ (d) $3.15 \times 10^{15} s^{-1}$

5. **Assertion** (A) Thomson's analysis of cathode ray experiment led him to conclude that electrons were fundamental particles.
Reason (R) e/m ratio for particles in cathode rays was found to be dependent of the nature of the gas taken in the tube.
(a) Both A and R are correct but R is not the correct explanation of A.
(b) Both A and R are correct and R is the correct explanation of A.
(c) A is correct but R is incorrect
(d) A is incorrect but R is correct

6. Based on equation, $E = -2.178 \times 10^{-18} \left(\frac{Z^2}{n^2}\right)$ J certain conclusions are written. Which of the following conclusions are correct?
A. The negative sign in equation simply means that the energy of electron bound to the nucleus is lower than it would be if the electrons were at the infinite distance from the nucleus.
B. Larger the value of n, the larger is the orbit radius.
C. Equation can be used to calculate the change in energy when the electron changes orbit.
D. For $n = 1$, the electron has a more negative energy than it does for $n = 6$; which means that the electron is more loosely bound in the smallest allowed orbit.

Choose the correct answer from the options given below.
(a) B, C and D (b) C and D
(c) A and B (d) A, B and C

7. The wave number of the spectral line in the emission spectrum of hydrogen will be equal to $\frac{8}{9}$ times the Rydberg's constant if the electron jumps from
(a) $n = 3$ to $n = 1$ (b) $n = 10$ to $n = 1$
(c) $n = 9$ to $n = 1$ (d) $n = 2$ to $n = 1$

8. If there were three possibilities of electron spin $\left(\text{as } +\frac{1}{2}, 0, -\frac{1}{2}\right)$, then K (19) would be placed in
(a) s-block (b) p-block
(c) d-block (d) f-block

9. Energy for 7.25×10^{15} photons of $5.37 \times 10^{14} s^{-1}$ frequency in Einstein unit is
(a) 1.20×10^{-8} (b) 2.58×10^{-3}
(c) 3.56×10^{-19} (d) 8.33×10^{7}

10. The radius of hydrogen atom in the ground state is 0.53 Å. The radius of Li^{2+} ion (atomic number = 3) in second excited state is
(a) 0.17 Å (b) 0.71 Å
(c) 0.53 Å (d) 1.59 Å

11. Uncertainty in position of an electron (mass $= 9.1 \times 10^{-31}$ kg) moving with a velocity of 3×10^{2} ms^{-1} accurate upto 0.001% will be
(a) 0.0193 m (b) 0.0384 m
(c) 0.0576 m (d) 0.0768 m

12. **Assertion** (A) If the potential difference applied to an electron is made 4 times, the de-Broglie wavelength associated is halved.
Reason (R) On making potential difference 4 times, velocity is doubled and hence λ is halved.

(a) Both A and R are correct and R is the correct explanation of A.
(b) Both A and R are correct but R is not the correct explanation of A.
(c) A is correct but R is not correct
(d) A is not correct but R is correct

13. Electrons with a kinetic energy of 6.02×10^4 J mol^{-1} are emitted from a surface of a metal, when it is exposed to radiation of wavelength =600 nm. The minimum amount of energy required to remove an electron from the metal atom is
(a) 2.313×10^{-19} J (b) 3×10^{-19} J
(c) 6.02×10^{-19} J (d) 6.62×10^{-34} J

14. Given below two statements.
Statement I The region in the electromagnetic spectrum where the Balmer series lines appear is ultraviolet region.
Statement II The spectral line obtained when an electron jumps from $n = 6$ to $n = 2$ level in hydrogen atom belongs to the Pfund series.
(a) Statement I is incorrect but Statement II is correct.
(b) Statement I is correct but Statement II is incorrect.
(c) Both Statement I and Statement II are incorrect.
(d) Both Statement I and Statement II are correct.

15. Which of the following pairs is not correctly matched?

(a)	Hund's rule	In orbitals of equivalent energy electron spins remain unpaired if possible
(b)	Pauli's exclusion principle	No two electrons can have all the four quantum numbers identical
(c)	Zeeman effect	The effect of magnetic field on the atomic spectra
(d)	Uncertainty principle	It is impossible to determine the position of an electron

16. Assume probability $= 4\pi r^2 \psi^2 \delta r$ and $\psi = \dfrac{e^{-r/a_0}}{(\pi a_0)^{3/2}}$ then probability that the electron will be found between a shell of radius a_0 and a shell of radius 1 pm greater is ($a_0 = 0.529$ Å and $e^{-2} = 0.14$)
(a) 0.01 (b) 10
(c) 100 (d) 0.10

17. Given below are two statements.
Statement I The maximum number of electrons in a subshell with $n = 4$ and $l = 3$ is 14.
Statement II The maximum numbers of electrons that can be associated with the ($n = 3, l = 1$ and $m = -1$) set of quantum numbers is six.
(a) Statement I is incorrect but Statement II is correct.
(b) Statement I is correct but Statement II is incorrect.
(c) Both Statement I and Statement II are incorrect.
(d) Both Statement I and Statement II are correct.

18. Which of the following statements are incorrect?
A. The first emission line on hydrogen spectrum in the Balmer series appears at $\frac{5}{36} R_H \text{ cm}^{-1}$.
B. In the Balmer series of H-spectrum, successive lines tend towards a limiting value of $\frac{R_H c}{2}$.
C. In Bohr's model of atom when an electron in Be^{3+} jumps from $n = 1$ to $n = 3$, the energy absorbed will be 12.09 eV.
D. The most intense line in the Brackett series of the spectrum of atomic hydrogen is given by the transition $n_2 = \infty$ to $n_1 = 4$.
Choose the correct answer from the options given below.
(a) A, B and D (b) B and C
(c) B, C and A (d) C and D

19. The shortest wavelength transition in the Paschen series in hydrogen occurs at 821 nm. At what wavelength does it occur in Li^{2+} (isoelectronic of hydrogen)?
(a) 91.2 nm (b) 273.6 nm (c) 821.0 nm (d) 7389.0 nm

20. If the de-Broglie wavelength of a particle of mass (m) is 100 times its velocity, then its value in terms of mass (m) and Planck's constant (h) is
(a) $\frac{1}{10}\sqrt{\frac{m}{h}}$ (b) $10\sqrt{\frac{h}{m}}$ (c) $\frac{1}{10}\sqrt{\frac{h}{m}}$ (d) $10\sqrt{\frac{m}{h}}$

Numerical Type Questions

21. The velocity of a particle A is 0.1 ms^{-1} and that of particle B is 0.05 ms^{-1}. If the mass of particle B is 5 times that of the particle A, the ratio of de-Broglie wavelengths associated with particles A and B is $x : y$.
The value of $x + y$ is ....

22. The value of Rydberg constant (R_H) is 2.18×10^{-18} J. The velocity of electron having mass 9.1×10^{-31} kg in Bohr's third orbit of lithium ion with + 2 oxidation state is $x \times 10^5$ ms^{-1}. The value of x is ....
[Nearest integer]

23. The wavelengths of the various lines in the hydrogen atomic emission spectrum can be related by a mathematical equation:
$$\frac{1}{\lambda} = R\left(\frac{1}{n^2} - \frac{1}{m^2}\right)$$
The value of n for the Pfund series of lines is ....

24. A hypothetical electromagnetic wave is shown below.

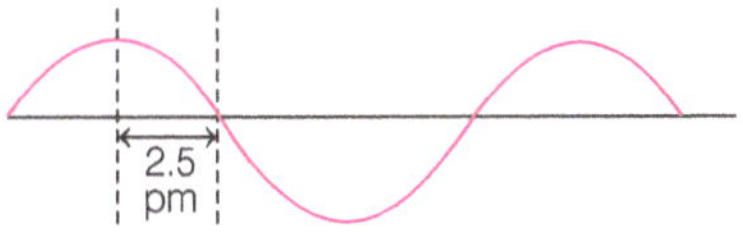

The frequency of the wave is 3×10^y kHz.
The value of y is ....

25. The energy of second Bohr orbit of the hydrogen atom is – 328 kJ mol^{-1}, hence the energy of fourth Bohr orbit will be (–) .... kJ/mol^{-1}.

26. The maximum number of orbitals associated with the principal quantum number 5 is ....

27. The number of radial nodes of 3*s* and 2*p* orbitals are *x* and *y* respectively. The sum of *x* and *y* is ....

28. Consider an imaginary ion $^{55}_{25}M^{3+}$. The nucleus contains '*a*' % more neutrons than the number of electrons in the ion. The value of '*a*' is .... [Nearest integer]

29. The radius of hydrogen atom in its ground state is 5.3×10^{-11} m. After collision with an electron it is found to have a radius of 21.2×10^{-11} m. The principal quantum number of the final state of the atom is '*n*'. The value of *n* is ....

30. The Azimuthal quantum number for the valence electrons of Ge^{+} ion is ....
[Atomic number of Ge = 32]

31. The wave function of an electron in the lowest energy state of H-atom is proportional to $e^{-\frac{r}{a_0}}$ ($a_0 = 52.9$ pm). Relative probability of finding the electron inside a small volume located in the nucleus to a distance a_0 from nucleus is ....[Nearest integer]

Check Through PYQs

Element 1 Bohr's Model and its Applications

1. An electron jumps from $A \rightarrow C$ emitting a wavelength of 2000 Å and also jumps from $B \rightarrow C$ by emitting a wavelength of 6000 Å, then wavelength of that electron; if it jumps from $A \rightarrow B$ *2025, 24 Jan Shift-I*
(a) 4000 Å (b) 3000 Å
(c) 8000 Å (d) 5000 Å

2. For a sample of hydrogen atom, the wavelength observed is 656 nm during a transition. The transition and corresponding series in hydrogen spectrum will be *2025, 24 Jan Shift-II*
(a) $3 \rightarrow 2$, Balmer (b) $4 \rightarrow 1$, Lyman
(c) $5 \rightarrow 2$, Balmer (d) $4 \rightarrow 3$, Paschen

3. For hydrogen atom, energy of an electron in first excited state is −3.4 eV, KE of the same electron of hydrogen atom is *x* eV. Value of *x* is ....$\times 10^{-1}$ eV. (Nearest integer) *2024, 6 April Shift-II*

4. The value of Rydberg constant (R_H) is 2.18×10^{-18} J. The velocity of electron having mass 9.1×10^{-31} kg in Bohr's first orbit of hydrogen atom = ... $\times 10^5 ms^{-1}$. (Nearest integer). *2024, 5 April Shift-I*

5. The ionisation energy of sodium in kJ mol^{-1}, if electromagnetic radiation of wavelength 242 nm is just sufficient to ionise sodium atom is .... *2024, 31 Jan Shift-I*

6. Match List-I with List-II. *2024, 29 Jan Shift-II*

	List-I (Spectral series for hydrogen)		**List-II** (Spectral region \ higher energy state)
A.	Lyman	I.	Infrared region
B.	Balmer	II.	UV region
C.	Paschen	III.	Infrared region
D.	Pfund	IV.	Visible region

Choose the correct answer from the options given below
(a) A-I, B-III, C-II, D-IV (b) A-II, B-IV, C-III, D-I
(c) A-I, B-II, C-III, D-IV (d) A-II, B-III, C-I, D-IV

7. Given below are two statements.
Statement I According to Bohr's model of hydrogen atom, the angular momentum of an electron in a given stationary state is quantised.
Statement II The concept of electron in Bohr's orbit, violates the Heisenberg uncertainty principle.
In the light of the above statements, choose the most appropriate answer from the options given below. *2023, 15 April Shift-I*
(a) Statement I is incorrect but Statement II is correct.
(b) Statement I is correct but Statement II is incorrect.
(c) Both Statement I and Statement II are incorrect.
(d) Both Statement I and Statement II are correct.

8. The energy of an electron in the first Bohr orbit of hydrogen atom is -2.18×10^{-18} J. Its energy in the third Bohr orbit is .... *2023, 13 April Shift-I*
(a) three times of this value (b) $\frac{1}{9}$th of this value
(c) one third of this value (d) $\frac{1}{27}$ of this value

9. Values of work function (W_0) for a few metals are given below *2023, 12 April Shift-I*

Metal	Li	Na	K	Mg	Cu	Ag
W_0 / eV	2.42	2.3	2.25	3.7	4.8	4.3

The number of metals which will show photoelectric effect when light of wavelength 400nm falls on it is ....
Given, $h = 6.6 \times 10^{-34}$ Js, $c = 3 \times 10^8$ ms^{-1}, $e = 1.6 \times 10^{-19}$C

10. Given below are two statements, one is labelled as Assertion (A) and the other is labelled as Reason (R).
Assertion (A) In the photoelectric effect, the electrons are ejected from the metal surface as soon as the beam of light of frequency greater than threshold frequency strikes the surface.
Reason (R) When the photon of any energy strikes an electron in the atom, transfer of energy from the photon to the electron takes place.

In the light of the above statements, choose the most appropriate answer from the options given below.
2023, 11 April Shift-I

(a) Both A and R are correct but R is not the correct explanation of A
(b) Both A and R are correct and R is the correct explanation of A
(c) A is correct but R is not correct
(d) A is not correct but R is correct

11. The number of incorrect statement/s about the black body from the following is .... *2023, 10 April Shift-I*
(a) Emit or absorb energy in the form of electromagnetic radiation.
(b) Frequency distribution of the emitted radiation depends on temperature.
(c) At a given temperature, intensity *vs* frequency curve passes through a maximum value.
(d) The maximum of the intensity *vs* frequency curve is at a higher frequency at higher temperature compared to that at lower temperature.

12. The number of following statement/s which is/are incorrect is *2023, 8 April Shift-I*
(a) line emission spectra are used to study the electronic structure.
(b) the emission spectra of atoms in the gas phase show a continuous spread of wavelength from red to violet.
(c) an absorption spectrum is like the photographic negative of an emission spectrum.
(d) the element helium was discovered in the sun by spectroscopic method.

13. Which transition in the hydrogen spectrum would have the same wavelength as the Balmer type transition from $n = 4$ to $n = 2$ of He^+ spectrum *2023, 31 Jan Shift-I*
(a) $n = 1$ to $n = 3$ (b) $n = 1$ to $n = 2$
(c) $n = 3$ to $n = 4$ (d) $n = 2$ to $n = 1$

14. The energy of one mole of photons of radiation of frequency 2×10^{12} Hz in J mol^{-1} is .... (Nearest integer)
[Given, $h = 6.626 \times 10^{-34}$ Js,
$N_A = 6.022 \times 10^{23}$ mol^{-1}] *2023, 30 Jan Shift-I*

15. Assume that the radius of the first Bohr orbit of hydrogen atom is 0.6 Å. The radius of the third Bohr orbit of He^+ is .... picometer. (Nearest integer) *2023, 29 Jan Shift-II*

16. The shortest wavelength of hydrogen atom in Lyman series is λ. The longest wavelength in Balmer series of He^+ is *2023, 29 Jan Shift-I*
(a) $\frac{5}{9\lambda}$ (b) $\frac{9\lambda}{5}$
(c) $\frac{5\lambda}{9}$ (d) $\frac{36\lambda}{5}$

17. If wavelength of the first line of the Paschen series of hydrogen atom is 720 nm, then the wavelength of the second line of this series is .... nm. (Nearest integer) *2023, 24 Jan Shift-I*

18. Consider an imaginary ion ${}^{48}_{22}X^{3-}$. The nucleus contains '*a*'% more neutrons than the number of electrons in the ion. The value of '*a*' is .... [nearest integer] *2022, 26 July Shift-II*

19. If the work function of a metal is 6.63×10^{-19} J, the maximum wavelength of the photon required to remove a photoelectron from the metal is ...... nm. [Nearest integer]
[Given, $h = 6.63 \times 10^{-34}$ Js, and $c = 3 \times 10^{8}$ m s^{-1}] *2022, 28 June Shift-I*

20 If the radius of the 3rd Bohr's orbit of hydrogen atom is r_3 and the radius of 4th Bohr's orbit is r_4. Then *2022, 26 June Shift-I*
(a) $r_4 = \frac{9}{16} r_3$ (b) $r_4 = \frac{16}{9} r_3$
(c) $r_4 = \frac{3}{4} r_3$ (d) $r_4 = \frac{4}{3} r_3$

21. The minimum energy that must be possessed by photons in order to produce the photoelectric effect with platinum metal is
[Given, the threshold frequency of platinum is $1.3 \times 10^{15} s^{-1}$ and $h = 6.6 \times 10^{-34}$ Js] *2022, 25 June Shift-II*
(a) 3.21×10^{-14} J (b) 6.24×10^{-16} J
(c) 8.58×10^{-19} J (d) 9.76×10^{-20} J

22. The energy of one mole of photons of radiation of wavelength 300 nm is
(Given, $h = 6.63 \times 10^{-34}$ Js, $N_A = 6.02 \times 10^{23}$, $c = 3 \times 10^{8} ms^{-1}$) *2022, 24 June Shift-II*
(a) 235 kJ mol^{-1} (b) 325 kJ mol^{-1}
(c) 399 kJ mol^{-1} (d) 435 kJ mol^{-1}

23. The kinetic energy of an electron in the second Bohr orbit of a hydrogen atom is equal to $\frac{h^2}{xma_0^2}$. The value of 10*x* is ....
(a_0 is radius of Bohr's orbit) (Nearest integer) [Given, $\pi = 3.14$] *2021, 27 Aug Shift-I*

24. Given below are two statements.
Statement I According to Bohr's model of an atom, qualitatively the magnitude of velocity of electron increases with decrease in positive charges on the nucleus as there is no strong hold on the electron by the nucleus.
Statement II According to Bohr's model of an atom, qualitatively the magnitude of velocity of electron increases with decrease in principal quantum number.
In the light of the above statements, choose the most appropriate answer from the options given below. *2021, 26 Aug Shift-I*
(a) Both Statement I and Statement II are false.
(b) Both Statement I and Statement II are true.
(c) Statement I is false but Statement II is true.
(d) Statement I is true but Statement II is false.

25. If the Thomson model of the atom was correct, then the result of Rutherford's gold foil experiment would have been *2021, 27 July Shift-II*

(a) all of the α-particles pass through the gold foil without decrease in speed.

(b) α-particles are deflected over a wide range of angles.

(c) all α-particles get bounced back by 180°.

(d) α-particles pass through the gold foil deflected by small angles and with reduced speed.

26. Given below are two statements.

Statement I Bohr's theory accounts for the stability and line spectrum of Li^+ ion.

Statement II Bohr's theory was unable to explain the splitting of spectral lines in the presence of a magnetic field.

In the light of the above statements, choose the most appropriate answer from the options given below : *2021, 18 March Shift-II*

(a) Both statements I and II are true.

(b) Statement I is false but statement II is true.

(c) Both statements I and II are false.

(d) Statement I is true but statement II is false.

27. According to Bohr's atomic theory,

I. Kinetic energy of electron is $\propto \frac{Z^2}{n^2}$

II. The product of velocity (v) of electron and principal quantum number (n), 'vn' $\propto Z^2$.

III. Frequency of revolution of electron in an orbit is $\propto \frac{Z^3}{n^3}$

IV. Coulombic force of attraction on the electron is $\propto \frac{Z^3}{n^4}$

Choose the most appropriate answer from the options given below. *2021, 24 Feb Shift-II*

(a) Only III

(b) Only I

(c) I, III and IV

(d) I and IV

28. The difference between the radii of 3rd and 4th orbits of Li^{2+} is ΔR_1. The difference between the radii of 3rd and 4th orbits of He^+ is ΔR_2. Ratio $\Delta R_1 : \Delta R_2$ is *2020, 5 Sep Shift-I*

(a) 3 : 2 (b) 8 : 3

(c) 2 : 3 (d) 3 : 8

29. Hydrogen has three isotopes (A), (B) and (C). If the number of neutron(s) in (A), (B) and (C) respectively, are (x), (y) and (z), the sum of (x), (y) and (z) is *2020, 8 Jan Shift-II*

(a) 4 (b) 3

(c) 2 (d) 1

30. For the Balmer series in the spectrum of H atom, $\bar{\nu} = R_H \left\{ \frac{1}{n_1^2} - \frac{1}{n_2^2} \right\}$, the correct statements among (I) to (IV) are :

I. As wavelength decreases, the lines in the series converge

II. The integer n_1 is equal to 2

III. The lines of longest wavelength corresponds to $n_2 = 3$

IV. The ionisation energy of hydrogen can be calculated from wave number of these lines *2020, 8 Jan Shift-I*

(a) I, II, IV (b) II, III, IV

(c) I, III, IV (d) I, II, III

Element 2 Dual Nature of Matter and Mechanical Model

31. An electron of He^+ is present in 3rd excited state. Find its de-Broglie wavelength. *2025, 22 Jan Shift-I*

(a) 6.64 Å (b) 1.66 Å

(c) 3.32 Å (d) 13.28 Å

32. Compare the energies of following sets of quantum numbers for multielectron system.

(A) $n = 4, l = 1$ (B) $n = 4, l = 2$

(C) $n = 3, l = 1$ (D) $n = 3, l = 2$

(E) $n = 4, l = 0$

Choose the correct answer from the options given below. *2024, 9 April Shift-I*

(a) (E) < (C) < (D) < (A) < (B)

(b) (C) < (E) < (D) < (A) < (B)

(c) (B) > (A) > (C) > (E) > (D)

(d) (E) > (C) > (A) > (D) > (B)

33. Frequency of the de-Broglie wave of electron in Bohr's first orbit of hydrogen atom is .... 10^{13} Hz (Nearest integer). [Given : R_H (Rydberg constant) = 2.18×10^{-18} J, h(Plank's constant) = 6.6×10^{-34} Js] *2024, 6 April Shift-I*

34. In an atom, total number of electrons having quantum numbers $n = 4$, $|m_l| = 1$ and $m_s = -\frac{1}{2}$ is .... *2024, 5 April Shift-I*

35. The maximum number of orbitals which can be identified with $n = 4$ and $m_l = 0$ is … . *2024, 4 April Shift-II*

36. The de-Broglie's wavelength of an electron in the 4th orbit is...... πa_0. (a_0 = Bohr's radius) *2024, 4 April Shift-I*

37. The number of radial nodes for $3p$-orbital is *2024, 1 Feb Shift-II*

(a) 1 (b) 2

(c) 4 (d) 3

38. According to the wave-particle duality of matter by de-Broglie, which of the following graph plot presents **most appropriate** relationship between wavelength of electron (λ) and momentum of electron (p)? *2024, 1 Feb Shift-I*

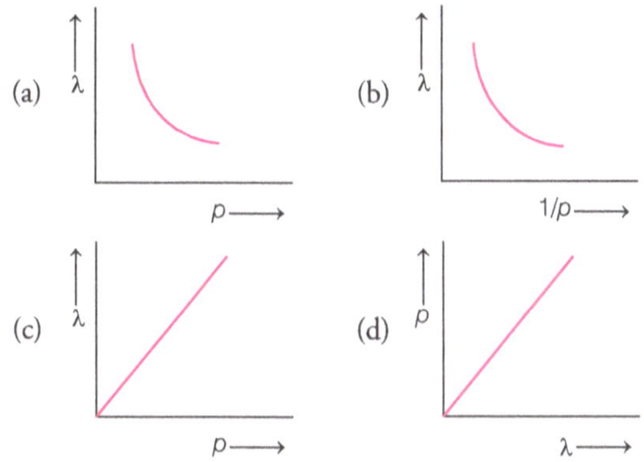

39. The four quantum numbers for the electron in the outermost orbital of potassium (atomic no. 19) are *2024, 31 Jan Shift-II*

(a) $n = 4, l = 2, m = -1, s = +\frac{1}{2}$

(b) $n = 2, l = 0, m = 0, s = +\frac{1}{2}$

(c) $n = 4, l = 0, m = 0, s = +\frac{1}{2}$

(d) $n = 3, l = 0, m = 1, s = +\frac{1}{2}$

40. Given below are two statements. *2024, 30 Jan Shift-I*

Statement I The orbitals having same energy are called as degenerate orbitals.

Statement II In hydrogen atom, 3*p* and 3*d* orbitals are not degenerate orbitals.

In the light of the above statements, choose the **most appropriate** answer from the options given below

(a) Statement I is false but Statement II is true.
(b) Both Statement I and Statement II are false.
(c) Statement I is true but Statement II is false.
(d) Both Statement I and Statement II are true.

41. The correct set of four quantum numbers for the valence electron of rubidium atom $(Z = 37)$ is *2024, 29 Jan Shift-I*

(a) $5, 1, 1, +\frac{1}{2}$ (b) $5, 1, 0, +\frac{1}{2}$

(c) $5, 0, 0, +\frac{1}{2}$ (d) $5, 0, 1, +\frac{1}{2}$

42. If the radius of the first orbit of hydrogen atom is a_0, then de-Broglie's wavelength of electron in 3rd orbit is *2023, 16 April Shift-II*

(a) $3\pi a_0$ (b) $\frac{\pi a_0}{3}$ (c) $6\pi a_0$ (d) $\frac{\pi a_0}{6}$

43. The number of correct statements from the following is *2023, 11 April Shift-II*

(a) For 1*s* orbital, the probability density is maximum at the nucleus.
(b) For 2*s* orbital, the probability density first increases to maximum and then decreases sharply to zero.
(c) Boundary surface diagrams of the orbitals encloses a region of 100% probability of finding the electron.
(d) *p* and *d*-orbitals have 1 and 2 angular nodes respectively.
(e) Probability density of *p*-orbital is zero at the nucleus.

44. The number of atomic orbitals from the following having 5 radial nodes is .... 7*s*, 7*p*, 6*s*, 8*p*, 8*d* *2023, 8 April Shift-II*

45. The wavelength of an electron of kinetic energy 4.50×10^{-29} J is .... $\times 10^{-5}$ m. (Nearest integer) *2023, 6 April Shift-I*

46. Electrons in a cathode ray tube have been emitted with a velocity of 1000 m s^{-1}. The number of following statements which is/are true about the emitted radiation is ....
[Given, $h = 6 \times 10^{-34}$ J s, $m_e = 9 \times 10^{-31}$ kg.] *2023, 1 Feb Shift-I*

(a) The de-Broglie wavelength of the electron emitted is 666.67 nm.
(b) The characteristic of electrons emitted depend upon the material of the electrodes of the cathode ray tube.
(c) The cathode rays start from cathode and move towards anode.
(d) The nature of the emitted electrons depends on the nature of the gas present in cathode ray tube.

47. The wave function (ψ) of 2*s* is given by

$$\psi_{2s} = \frac{1}{2\sqrt{2\pi}}\left(\frac{1}{a_0}\right)^{1/2}\left(2 - \frac{r}{a_0}\right)e^{-\frac{r}{2a_0}}$$

At $r = r_0$, radial node is formed. Thus, r_0 in terms of a_0 *2023, 30 Jan Shift-II*

(a) $r_0 = a_0$ (b) $r_0 = 2a_0$ (c) $r_0 = \frac{a_0}{2}$ (d) $r_0 = 4a_0$

48. The number of given orbitals which have electron density along the axis is .... $p_x, p_y, p_z, d_{xy}, d_{yz}, d_{z^2}, d_{x^2-y^2}$ *2023, 25 Jan Shift-II*

49. If the wavelength for an electron emitted from H-atom is 3.3×10^{-10} m, then energy absorbed by the electron in its ground state compared to minimum energy required for its escape from the atom, is .... times. (Nearest integer)
[Given, $h = 6.626 \times 10^{-34}$ Js] [Mass of electron = 9.1×10^{-31} kg] *2022, 28 July Shift-II*

50. Given below are two statements. One is labelled as Assertion (A) and the other is labelled as Reason (R).

Assertion (A) Energy of 2*s* orbital of hydrogen atom is greater than that of 2*s* orbital of lithium.

Reason (R) Energies of the orbitals in the same subshell decrease with increase in the atomic number.

In the light of the above statements, choose the correct answer from the options given below: *2022, 27 July, Shift-I*

(a) Both A and R are true and R is the correct explanation of A.
(b) Both A and R are true but R is not the correct explanation of A.
(c) A is true but R is false.
(d) A is false but R is true.

51. The wavelength of an electron and a neutron will become equal when the velocity of the electron is *x* times the velocity of neutron. The value of *x* is .... (Nearest integer) (Mass of electron is 9.1×10^{-31} kg and mass of neutron is 1.6×10^{-27} kg) *2022, 26 July Shift-I*

52. Which of the following is the correct plot for the probability density $\psi^2(r)$ as a function of distance 'r' of the electron from the nucleus for 2s orbital? *2022, 29 June Shift-II*

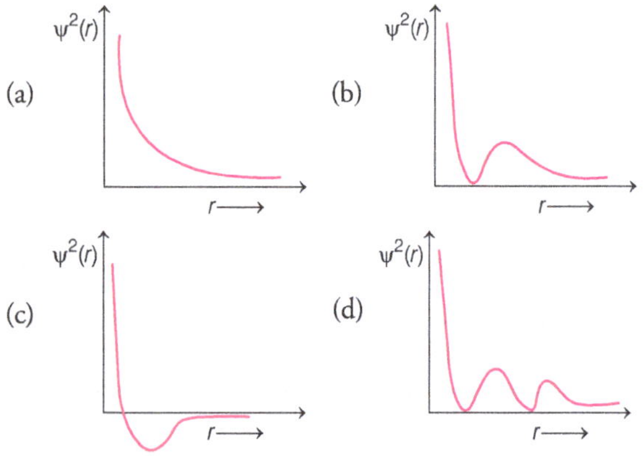

53. Which of the following statements are correct?
(A) The electronic configuration of Cr is $[Ar]3d^54s^1$.
(B) The magnetic quantum number may have a negative value.
(C) In the ground state of an atom, the orbitals are filled in order of their increasing energies.
(D) The total number of nodes are given by $n - 2$.
Choose the most appropriate answer from the options given below : *2022, 29 June Shift-I*
(a) (A), (C) and (D)
(b) (A) and (B)
(c) (A) and (C)
(d) (A), (B) and (C)

54. Consider the following statements.
(A) The principal quantum number 'n' is a positive integer with values of 'n' = 1, 2, 3, ...
(B) The azimuthal quantum number 'l' for a given 'n' (principal quantum number) can have values as 'l' = 0, 1, 2,... n.
(C) Magnetic orbital quantum number 'm_l' for a particular 'l' (azimuthal quantum number) has $(2l + 1)$ values.
(D) $\pm$ 1/2 are the two possible orientations of electron spin.
(E) For $l = 5$, there will be a total of 9 orbital.
Which of the above statements are correct?
(a) (A), (B) and (C) *2022, 28 June Shift-II*
(b) (A), (C), (D) and (E)
(c) (A), (C) and (D)
(d) (A), (B), (C) and (D)

55. Consider the following pairs of electrons : *2022, 24 June Shift-I*
(A) (a) $n = 3, l = 1, m_1 = -1, m_s = +1/2$
(b) $n = 3, l = 2, m_1 = 1, m_s = +1/2$
(B) (a) $n = 3, l = 2, m_1 = -2, m_s = -1/2$
(b) $n = 3, l = 2, m_1 = -1, m_s = -1/2$
(C) (a) $n = 4, l = 2, m_1 = 2, m_s = +1/2$
(b) $n = 3, l = 2, m_1 = 2, m_s = +1/2$
The pairs of electron present in degenerate orbitals is/are
(a) Only A (b) Only B
(c) Only C (d) Both (B) and (C)

56. Ge ($Z = 32$) in its ground state electronic configuration has x completely filled orbitals with $m_l = 0$. The value of x is *2021, 31 Aug Shift-I*

57. The Azimuthal quantum number for the valence electrons of Ga^+ ion is ....
(Atomic number of Ga = 31) *2021, 20 July, Shift-I*

58. When light of wavelength 248 nm falls on a metal of threshold energy 3.0 eV, the de- Broglie wavelength of emitted electrons is ...... Å.
[Round off to the nearest integer]
[Use : $\sqrt{3} = 1.73$, $h = 6.63 \times 10^{-34}$ Js, $m_e = 9.1 \times 10^{-31}$ kg, $c = 3.0 \times 10^8 \text{ms}^{-1}$, 1 eV = 1.6×10^{-19} J] *2021, 16 March Shift-I*

59. The plots of radial distribution functions for various orbitals of hydrogen atom against 'r' are given below. *2021, 25 Feb Shift-I*

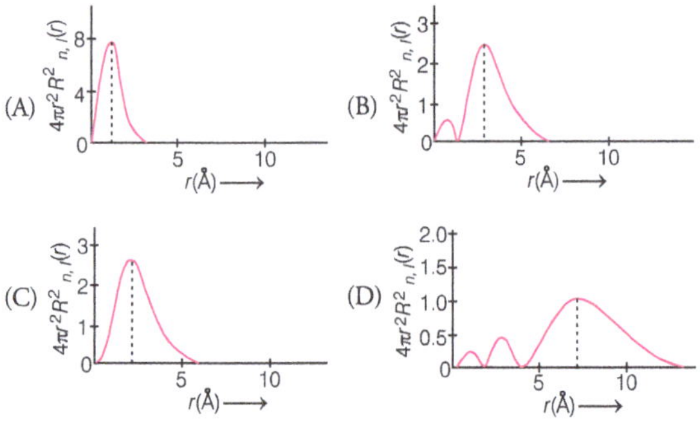

The correct plot for 3s-orbitals is
(a) A (b) B (c) (d) D

60. A proton and a Li^{3+} nucleus are accelerated by the same potential. If λ_{Li} and λ_P denote the de-Broglie wavelengths of Li^{3+} and proton respectively, then the value of $\frac{\lambda_{Li}}{\lambda_P}$ is $x \times 10^{-1}$. The value of x is ....
(Rounded off to the nearest integer)
(Mass of Li^{3+} = 8.3 mass of proton) *2021, 24 Feb Shift-I*

61. The correct statement about probability density (except at infinite distance from nucleus) is *2020, 5 Sep Shift-II*
(a) it can be zero for 1s orbital
(b) it can be negative for 2p orbital
(c) it can be zero for 3p orbital
(d) it can never be zero for 2s orbital

62. Consider the hypothetical situation where the azimuthal quantum number, l takes values 0, 1, 2, ... $n + 1$, where n is the principle quantum number. Then, the element with atomic number *2020, 3 Sep Shift-II*
(a) 8 is the first noble gas
(b) 13 has a half-filled valence subshell
(c) 9 is the first alkali metal
(d) 6 has a 2p-valence subshell

63. The de-Broglie wavelength of an electron in the 4th Bohr orbit is *2020, 9 Jan Shift-I*
(a) $6\pi a_0$ (b) $2\pi a_0$ (c) $8\pi a_0$ (d) $4\pi a_0$

PRACTICE
ELEMENT 02

Target JEE Advanced

Single Correct Choice MCQs

1. The wavelength of a neutron with a translatory kinetic energy equal to kT at 300 K is
(a) 178 pm (b) 200 pm (c) 17.8 pm (d) 20.0 pm

2. The normalised wave function of orbital is $\psi = \sqrt{N}e^{-Zr/a_0}$ and the radial distribution function $= 4\pi r^2\psi^2$ where,
$$N = \frac{1}{\pi}\left(\frac{Z}{a_0}\right)^3$$
Most probable distance at which the 1s electron of H-like atom with atomic number Z is to be found, is
(a) a_0 (b) $\frac{a_0}{Z}$ (c) $\frac{Z}{a_0}$ (d) $\frac{a_0^2}{Z}$

3. Consider the following figures A and B indicating distribution of charge density (electron probability ψ^2) with distance r. Select the correct statement(s).

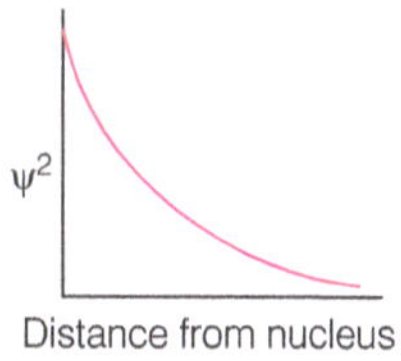

(A)

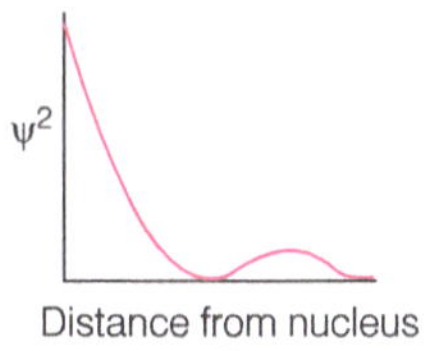

(B)

(a) A and B both are for 1s (b) A and B both are for 2s
(c) A is for 2s, B is for 1s (d) A is for 1s, B is for 2s

4. The correct set of quantum number for the unpaired electron of a chlorine atom is
(a) $2, 0, 0, +\frac{1}{2}$ (b) $2, 1, -1, +\frac{1}{2}$
(c) $3, 1, -1, +\frac{1}{2}$ (d) $3, 0, 0, +\frac{1}{2}$

5. According to Bohr's model, the highest kinetic energy is associated with the electron in the
(a) first orbit of H-atom (b) second orbit of Be^{3+}
(c) second orbit of Li^{2+} (d) second orbit of He^{+}

6. Two fast moving particles X and Y are associated with de-Broglie wavelength 1 nm and 4 nm respectively. If mass of X is nine times the mass of Y, the ratio of kinetic energies of X and Y would be
(a) 3 : 1 (b) 9 : 1
(c) 5 : 12 (d) 16 : 9

7. The energy (W) required to overcome the attractive forces on the electrons of some metals is listed below.

Metals	Li	Na	K	Mg	Cu	Ag	Fe	Pt	W
W (eV)	2.4	2.3	2.2	3.7	4.8	4.3	4.7	6.3	4.75

The number of metals showing photoelectric effect, when light of 300 nm falls on it is
(a) 6 (b) 8
(c) 5 (d) 4

8. Select the correct matching for $3d_{xy}$-orbital.

	n	l	Angular nodes	Radial nodes	Nodal plane
(a)	3	2	2	1	0
(b)	3	2	2	0	2
(c)	3	2	1	1	1
(d)	3	2	1	0	3

9. The position of both, an electron and a helium atom is known within 1.0 nm. Further the momentum of the electron is known within 5.0×10^{-26} kg ms^{-1}. The minimum uncertainty in the measurement of the momentum (in kg ms^{-1}) of the helium atom is
(a) 50 (b) 80
(c) 80×10^{-26} (d) 5.0×10^{-26}

10. The frequency of light emitted for the transition $n = 4$ to $n = 2$ of He^{+} is equal to the transition in H-atom corresponding to which of the following?
(a) $n = 3$ to $n = 1$
(b) $n = 2$ to $n = 1$
(c) $n = 3$ to $n = 2$
(d) $n = 4$ to $n = 3$

11. Which of the following is incorrectly matched?
(a) Energy equivalent to 100 m^{-1} $\longrightarrow 2 \times 10^{-23}$ J per atom
(b) Energy equivalent to 100 m^{-1} $\longrightarrow 1.204 \times 10^{-2}$ kJ mol^{-1} of photons
(c) Energy equivalent to 100 m^{-1} $\longrightarrow 2 \times 10^{-14}$ erg per photon
(d) Energy equivalent to 100 m^{-1} $\longrightarrow 2.9 \times 10^{-3}$ kcal mol^{-1} of photons

More than One Correct Choice MCQ

12. Electron in Li^{2+} ion falls from seventh level and subsequent lower levels to first level, then select the correct statements regarding the given data.
(a) total of six emission lines are obtained
(b) spectrum belongs to Lyman series
(c) minimum wave number obtained is 6.75 R_H
(d) maximum wave number obtained is 6.75 R_H

13. The probability density plots of 1s and 2s orbitals are given below, in which density of dots in a region represents the probability density of finding electrons in the region:

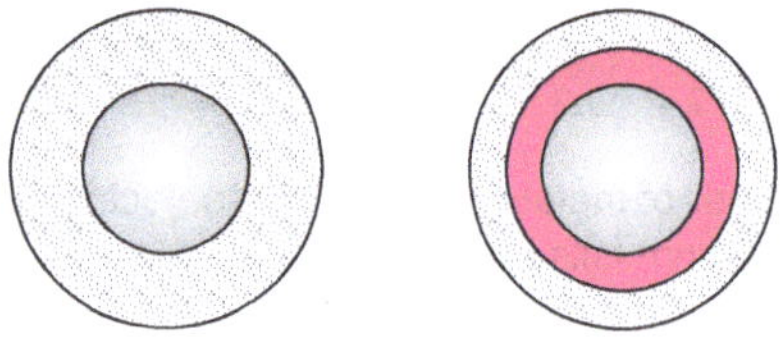

On the basis of above probability density plots,which of the following statements is/are correct?
(a) 1s and 2s are spherical in shape
(b) The probability of finding the electron is maximum near the nucleus
(c) The probability of finding the electron at a given distance is equal in all direction
(d) The probability density of electron for 2s orbitals decreases uniformly as distance from the nucleus increases

14. Which of the following statements are incorrect?
(a) The *d*-orbitals for which *n* equal to 3 have same shapes and size.
(b) The energy of 3*d* orbital may be greater than or lesser than, or equal to that of 4*s* orbital depending upon the atomic number of the atom.
(c) All *p* orbitals have the same type of angular dependence irrespective of the value of principal quantum number *n*.
(d) For a given shell, the Z_{eff} experienced by the electron increases with increase of azimuthal quantum number.

15. Which of the following statements are correct?
(a) The ideal body, which emits and absorbs radiations of all frequencies is called a black body
(b) The exact frequency distribution of the emitted radiation from a black body depends upon its temperature
(c) The radiation emitted goes from a lower frequency to higher frequency as temperature increases
(d) In vacuum, all types of electromagnetic radiations travel at the same speed

16. Which of the following statements are correct?
(a) For hydrogen like atom/ions, radius (r) of an orbit and energy (E) of an electron in an orbit respectively are: $r \propto \frac{1}{Z}$ and $E \propto Z^2$.
(b) Energy of the electron in 4th orbit of H-atom is more than of electron present in 4th orbit of $He^{\oplus}$ ion.
(c) If the radius of the second Bohr orbit of hydrogen atom is r_2, the radius of the fourth Bohr orbit will be $4r_2$.
(d) A hydrogen like atom has ground state binding energy 122.4 eV and a 80 eV photon can not excite it to a higher state.

17. Which of the following statements are incorrect?
(a) The de Broglie wavelength of a neutron at 2700 K is λ. The wavelength at 300 K is 6 λ.
(b) de-Broglie wavelength of an electron with velocity (v_e) is λ_e. The velocity of neutron (v_n) that has the same de-Broglie wavelength is 1840 v_e.
(c) The uncertainty in position of an electron is equal to its de-Broglie wavelength. The minimum percentage error in its measurement of velocity under this condition will be approximately 8%.
(d) An electron is continuously accelerated in vacuum tube by applying potential difference. If its de-Broglie wavelength is decreased by 2%, the change in the kinetic energy of the electron is increase by nearly 4%.

18. Which of the following statements are incorrect?
(a) Number of visible lines when an electron returns from 5th orbit to ground state in H-spectrum is four.
(b) Be^{3+} has the same orbit radius as that of the ground state of hydrogen atom when $n = 2$, for Be^{3+}.
(c) I.E of a single electron system is 11180 kJ mol^{-1}. The number of protons in the nucleus of the system will be three.
(d) The ratio of velocity of the electron in the third and fifth orbit of Li^{2+} will be 25 : 9.

19. Which of the following statements are correct about Hund's rule?
(a) It states that if more than one atomic orbital of the same energy is available, electrons will occupy different atomic orbitals with parallel spins, as far as possible, in the configuration of lowest energy
(b) Total energy of many electron atom with more than one electron occupying a set of degenerate orbitals is lowest, if as far as possible, electrons occupy different atomic orbitals and have parallel spins
(c) Hund's rule forbid any configuration that does not violate the Pauli's exclusion principle
(d) This rule simply tells us which of the possible configurations is lowest in energy and other configurations are those of excited states, higher in energy than the ground state.

Numerial Type Questions

20. For Be^{3+}, a transition takes place from the orbit of radius 138.2 pm to the orbit of radius 46.44 pm. The wavelength (in nm) of the emitted photon during the transition is .... nm.
[Use : Bohr radius, a = 52.9 pm
Rydberg constant, $R_H = 2.2 \times 10^{-18}$ J
Planck's constant, $h = 6.6 \times 10^{-34}$ Js
Speed of light, $c = 3 \times 10^8$ ms^{-1}]

21. Consider a boron (B) atom that absorbs a photon of wavelength 450 nm. The change in the velocity (in cm/s^{-1}) of B atom after the photon absorption is ....
(Assume, momentum is conserved, when photon is absorbed)
[Use : Planck's constant = 6.6×10^{-34} Js
Avogadro's number = 6×10^{23} mol^{-1}
Molar mass of B = 10 g/mol]

22. O_2 undergoes photochemical dissociation into two types of oxygen atoms, one normal (O) atom and the other more energetic (O^*). More energetic atom (O^*) has 1.967 eV more energy than normal (O) atom, then the maximum wavelength effective for the photochemical dissociation of O_2 will be x nm. (BDE of O_2 = 498 kJ mol^{-1})
The value of x is ....

23. The number of correct statements from the following is
A. In the energy levels of a certain atom when the system moves from $2E$ to E level, a photon of wavelength λ_1 is emitted. The wavelength (λ_2) of the photon produced during the transition from level $4E/3$ to level E is $2\lambda_1$

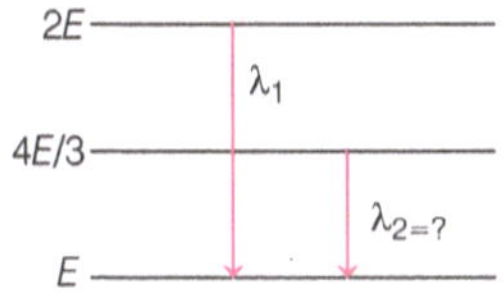

B. In the photoelectric effect, the slope of straight line graph between stopping potential(V_0) and frequency of incident light (v) gives ratio of h (planck's constant) and charge on electron (e).

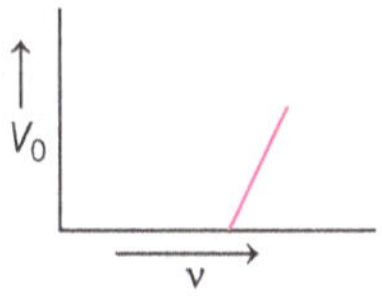

C. The graph for the stopping potential (V_0) vs ν (frequency) for two photoelectric surfaces A and B is shown as

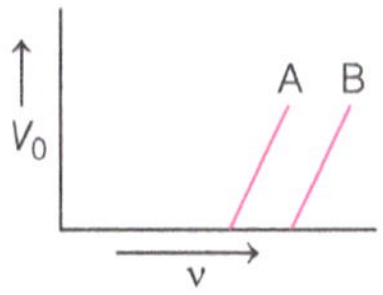

The graph shows that work function of B is greater than that of A.
D. In the emission of electrons from a metal surface when exposed to light radiation of appropriate wavelength (λ), the kinetic energy of photo electrons emitted does not depend on intensity but depends on frequency of the incident radiation.
E. The photoelectric work function depends upon the nature of the metal as a metal having higher ionisation energy has a greater value of photoelectric work function.

24. The energy required to excite 1 dm^3 of hydrogen gas (H_2) at 1 atm and 298 K to the first excited state of atomic hydrogen will be kJ.
Given: $H_2(g) \rightarrow 2H(g)$, $\Delta H° = 436$ kJ mol^{-1}

25. The difference in energy between 1st and 2nd Bohr's orbits for H-atom is 1.635×10^{-18} J. At what minimum atomic number, a transition from $n = 2 \rightarrow n = 1$ energy level would result in emission of X-ray with $\lambda = 3.0 \times 10^{-8}$ m.
[**Hint** Atomic number belongs to species like the H-atom]

26. The energy required for the ionisation of certain atom is 3.44 aJ (1a = 10^{-18}; a denotes 'atto'). The absorption of a photon of unknown wavelength ionises the atom and ejects an electron with a velocity of 1.03×10^6 ms^{-1}.
The wavelength of the incident radiation is .... Å.

27. The sum of degeneracy of s, p, d, f and g sub-orbits.

Matching Type Questions

28. Match List-I with List-II.

	List-I (Orbital)		List-II (Sum of nodes and radial nodes)
A.	$4f$	I.	10
B.	$6d$	II.	12
C.	$6s$	III.	3
D.	$7s$	IV.	8

Choose the correct answer from the options given below.
(a) A-II, B-I, C-IV, D-III
(b) A-III, B-I, C-II, D-IV
(c) A-III, B-IV, C-I, D-II
(d) A-II, B-IV, C-III, D-I

29. Neon gas is generally used is sign board, it emits radiations at 600 nm. Match the values derived given in Column-II with the corresponding parameter in Column-I and select answer from the codes given below:

S.No.	Column-I		Column-II
A.	Frequency of emission (in s^{-1})	I.	9×10^6
B.	Distance travelled by it (in km) in 30s	II.	3.31×10^{-22}
C.	Energy of quantum (in kJ)	III.	5×10^{14}
D.	Number of quanta present if it produce 2J of energy	IV.	6.04×10^{18}

Codes

	A	B	C	D
(a)	III	I	II	IV
(b)	I	III	IV	II
(c)	II	III	I	IV
(d)	III	II	I	IV

30. Wavelength of the spectral line of the H-like species (atomic number, Z) is given by $\frac{1}{\lambda} = R_H Z^2 \left(\frac{1}{n_1^2} - \frac{1}{n_2^2}\right)$.
Match the given parameter is Column I with their related values in Column II and select the answer from the codes given below:

S.No.	Column-I		Column-II
A.	Frequency of the α-line in Balmer series of He^+.	I.	$\frac{9}{16}R_H$
B.	Maximum wave number of spectral line in Brackett series of Li^{2+}.	II.	$\frac{16}{225}R_H$
C.	Minimum wave number of the spectral line in Lyman series of Be^{3+}.	III.	$\frac{5}{9}R_H$
D.	Wave number of β-line in Paschen series of H-atom.	IV.	$12R_H$

Codes

	A	B	C	D		A	B	C	D
(a)	I	III	IV	II	(b)	IV	II	I	III
(c)	II	III	I	IV	(d)	III	I	IV	II

31. λ_{max} and λ_{min} values of spectral lines of H-atom depends on the type of transition. Match the following, List-I contains series and List-II contain their λ_{max} and λ_{min} value respectively, $\left(x = \frac{1}{R_H}\right)$

List-I		List-II	
	Series		λ_{max} and λ_{min} value
A.	Lyman	I.	$\frac{9}{3}x, 2x$
B.	Balmer	II.	$\frac{400}{9}x, 16x$
C.	Paschen	III.	$\frac{36}{5}x, 4x$
D.	Brackett	IV.	$\frac{144}{7}x, 9x$
		V.	$\frac{4}{3}x, x$

Choose the correct answer from the options given below:

(a) A-III, B-IV, C-III, D-II (b) A-V, B-I, C-IV, D-III

(c) A-IV, B-V, C-II, D-I (d) A-V, B-III, C-IV, D-II

32. Match the isoelectronic species (atoms/ions) given in Column-I with the characteristics specified in Column-II and select the answer from the codes given below :

S.No.	Column-I		Column-II
A.	He^+	I.	Energy of 3rd orbit = − 13.6 eV
B.	Li^{2+}	II.	Radius of 2nd orbit = a_0
C.	Be^{3+}	III.	Ionisation energy = 54.4 eV
D.	B^{4+}	IV.	Ionisation energy = 340 eV
E.	H	V.	Radius in ground state = a_0

Codes

	A	B	C	D	E
(a)	I	II	III	IV	V
(b)	III	I	II	IV	V
(c)	III	II	I	V	IV
(d)	II	III	IV	V	I

33. Match the orbitals in Column-II with the properties (all of which have values = 0) given in Column-I and select the answer from codes gives.

S.No.	Column-I		Column-II
A.	Number of nodal planes	I.	4*f*
B.	Number of radial (spherical) nodes	II.	3*d*
C.	Total number of radial and angular nodes	III.	2*p*
D.	Azimuthal quantum number	IV.	2*s*
		V.	1*s*

Codes

	A	B	C	D
(a)	I	II	III	IV, V
(b)	II	III, IV	I	II, V
(c)	IV	I	II, III	V
(d)	IV, V	I, II,III, V	V	IV, V

Paragraph of Two Questions Each

Paragraph 1

In 1887, H. Hertz performed a very interesting experiment in which electrons (or electric current) were ejected when certain metals e.g. potassium, rubidium, caesium etc. were exposed to a beam of light known as photoelectric effect.

This effect can be expressed in terms of the following graph.

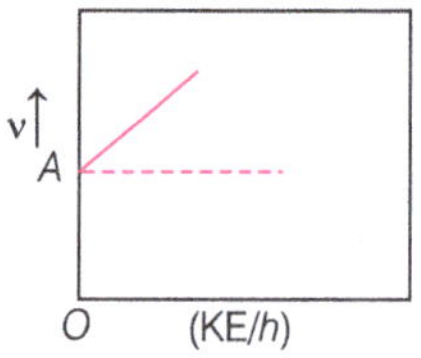

34. If work function of the given experiment is 199.262 kJ mol^{-1}. Then the value of *OA* will be ...... $\times 10^{13}$ s^{-1}.

35. Kinectic energy impacted to the moving electron at a wavelength of 250 nm is ...... kJ/mol. (nearest integer)

Paragraph 2

The emission of electrons from a metal surface when exposed to light radiation of appropriate wavelength is called photoelectric effect. The emitted electrons are called photo-electrons. Work function of threshold energy may be defined as the minimum amount of energy required to eject electrons from a metal surface.

36. If the threshold wavelength (λ_0) for ejection of electron from metal is 330 nm, then work function for the photoelectric emission will be .... $\times 10^{-19}$ J.

37. A certain metal when irradiated to light $(\nu = 3.2 \times 10^{16}$ Hz) emits photoelectrons with twice kinetic energy as did photoelectrons when the same metal is irradiated by light $(\nu = 2.0 \times 10^{16}$ Hz). The threshold frequency (ν_0) of metal is .... $\times 10^{14}$ Hz.

Paragraph 3

Besides the radial nodes (i.e., probability density function is zero), the probability density functions for the *np* and *nd* orbitals are zero at the plane, passing through the nucleus. The energy of an electron in a hydrogen atom is determined solely by the principal quantum number.

38. The number of nodal planes (planes of zero electron density) in the d_{xy} orbital is

39. The number of electrons in an atom with atomic number 105 can have $n + l = 8$ is ....

Paragraph 4

Neils Bohr (1913) was the first to explain quantitatively the general features of the structure of hydrogen atom and its spectrum. He used Planck's concept of quantisation of energy. Bohr's model for hydrogen atom is based on many facts i.e., the frequency of radiation absorbed or emitted when transition occurs between two stationary states that differ in energy by ΔE etc.

40. If each hydrogen atom in the ground state of 1.0 mol of H atoms is excited by absorbing photons of energy 8.4 eV, 12.09 eV and 15.0 eV of energy, then the number of spectral line emitted is equal to ....

41. The separation energy (in eV) for electron present in the first excited state of Be^{3+} is .... eV.

Species Selection (With 5 Species)

42. Among the orbitals $d_{z^2}, d_{x^2-y^2}, f_{5z^3-3zr^2}, d_{yz}$ and p_x, the number of orbitals, with exactly two modal planes are

(a) 2 (b) 3
(c) 4 (d) 5

43. Consider the following series,

(i) Lyman (ii) Paschen
(iii) Bracket (iv) Balmer
(v) Pfund

The total number of series in H-spectra which occurs in IR region is/are

(a) 2 (b) 5
(c) 4 (d) 3

44. Consider the following graphs.

If v = Velocity of electron in Bohr's orbit
r = Radius of electron in Bohr's orbit
P.E. = Potential energy of electron in Bohr's orbit
K.E. = Kinetic energy of electron in Bohr's orbit

(i) (ii)

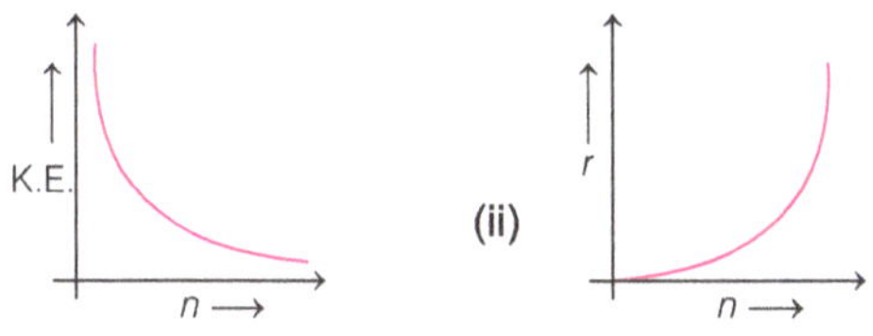

(iii) (iv)

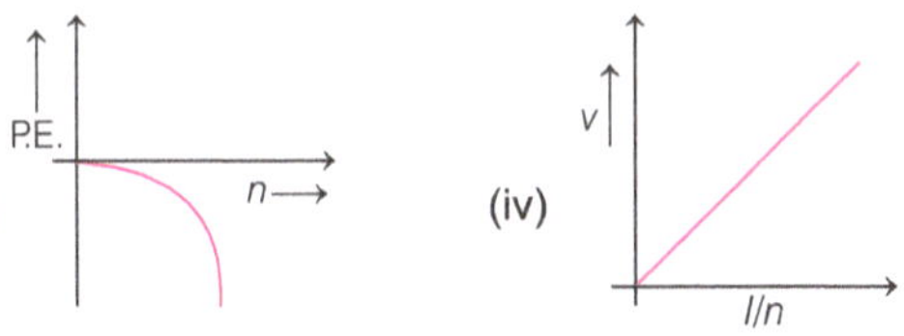

(v)

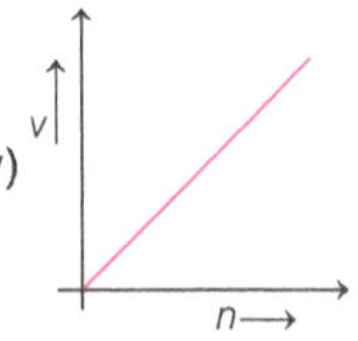

The total number of correct curves are

(a) 2 (b) 3 (c) 4 (d) 1

Species Selection (With 7 Species)

45. The radius of which of the following orbits is not same as that of the first Bohr's orbit of hydrogen atom is/are

(i) He^+ ($n = 2$) (ii) Li^{2+} ($n = 2$)
(iii) Li^{2+} ($n = 3$) (iv) Be^{3+} ($n = 2$)
(v) He^+ ($n = 1$) (vi) Be^{3+} ($n = 1$)
(vii) Li^{2+} ($n = 1$)

(a) 3 (b) 4
(c) 6 (d) 5

46. Consider the following set of quantum numbers,

	n	l	m_l	m_s
(i)	3	2	–2	$\frac{1}{2}$
(ii)	4	0	0	$\frac{1}{2}$
(iii)	3	2	–3	$\frac{1}{2}$
(iv)	5	3	0	$\frac{1}{2}$
(v)	6	1	–2	$\frac{1}{2}$
(vi)	2	1	–2	$\frac{1}{2}$
(vii)	4	3	–3	$\frac{1}{2}$

The set of quantum numbers which represents an impossible arrangement ......

(a) 3 (b) 4
(c) 5 (d) 2

47. Among the given set of quantum numbers,

(i) $n = 3, l = 2, m = 0, s = +\frac{1}{2}$

(ii) $n = 6, l = 2, m = 1, s = +\frac{1}{2}$

(iii) $n = 5, l = 1, m = 0, s = +\frac{1}{2}$

(iv) $n = 5, l = 3, m = 2, s = +\frac{1}{2}$

(v) $n = 7, l = 1, m = 0, s = +\frac{1}{2}$

(vi) $n = 4, l = 2, m = 2, s = +\frac{1}{2}$

(vii) $n = 2, l = 1, m = 0, s = +\frac{1}{2}$

The number of set of quantum numbers which have high energy than 5 *d* orbital is ....

(a) 6 (b) 3 (c) 5 (d) 4

48. Consider the following pairs of ions,

(i) ${}^{19}_{9}F$ and ${}^{13}_{6}C$ (ii) ${}^{40}_{18}Ar$ and ${}^{40}_{20}Ca$

(iii) ${}^{14}_{6}C$ and ${}^{23}_{11}Na$ (iv) ${}^{24}_{12}Mg$ and ${}^{23}_{11}Na$

(v) ${}^{4}_{2}He$ and ${}^{15}_{8}O$ (vi) ${}^{65}_{29}Cu$ and ${}^{52}_{24}Cr$

(vii) ${}^{39}_{19}K$ and ${}^{19}_{9}F$

The total pairs of ions which are isodiaphers ....

(a) 2 (b) 4 (c) 5 (d) 6

49. The frequency of light emitted for the transition $n = 4$ to $n = 2$ of He^+ is equal to the transition in H-atom corresponding to which of the following.

(i) $n = 3$ to $n = 1$ (ii) $n = 3$ to $n = 2$

(iii) $n = 2$ to $n = 1$ (iv) $n = 4$ to $n = 3$

(v) $n = 1$ to $n = 1$ (vi) $n = 3$ to $n = 4$

(vii) $n = 4$ to $n = 2$

(a) 3 (b) 4 (c) 1 (d) 5

Check Through PYQs

Element 1 Bohr's Model and Its Application

1. According to Bohr's model, the highest kinetic energy is associated with the electron in the *2024 Adv.*

(a) first orbit of H-atom (b) first orbit of He^+

(c) second orbit of He^+ (d) second orbit of Li^{2+}

2. For He^+, a transition takes place from the orbit of radius 105.8 pm to the orbit of radius 26.45 pm. The wavelength (in nm) of the emitted photon during the transition is ...... *2023 Adv.*

[**Use** Bohr radius, $a = 52.9$ pm

Rydberg constant, $R_H = 2.2 \times 10^{-18}$ J

Planck's constant, $h = 6.6 \times 10^{-34}$ Js

Speed of light, $c = 3 \times 10^8$ ms^{-1}]

3. The figure below is the plot of potential energy *versus* internuclear distance (d) of H_2 molecule in the electronic ground state. What is the value of the net potential energy E_0 (as indicated in the figure) in kJ mol^{-1}, for $d = d_0$ at which the electron-electron repulsion and the nucleus-nucleus repulsion energies are absent? As reference, the potential energy of H atom is taken as zero when its electron and the nucleus are infinitely far apart.

(**Use** Avogadro constant as 6.023×10^{23} mol^{-1}) *2020 Adv.*

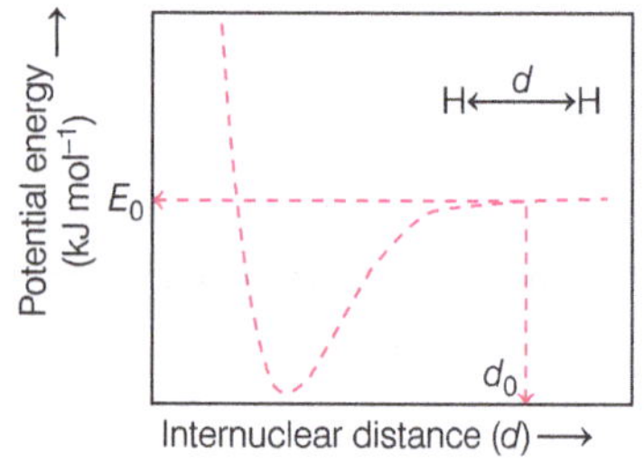

4. Consider the Bohr's model of a one-electron atom where the electron moves around the nucleus. In the following List-I contains some quantities for the *n*th orbit of the atom and List-II contains options showing how they depend on *n*.

	List-I		List-II
(I)	Radius of the *n* th orbit	(P)	$\propto n^{-2}$
(II)	Angular momentum of the electron in the *n*th orbit	(Q)	$\propto n^{-1}$
(III)	Kinetic energy of the electron in the *n*th orbit	(R)	$\propto n^0$
(IV)	Potential energy of the electron in the *n*th orbit	(S)	$\propto n^1$
		(T)	$\propto n^2$
		(U)	$\propto n^{1/2}$

Which of the following options has the correct combination considering List-I and List-II? *2019 Adv.*

(a) (III), (P) (b) (III), (S) (c) (IV), (U) (d) (IV), (Q)

Element 2 Dual Nature of Matter and Wave

5. Among the following the correct statement(s) for electrons in an atom is (are) *2024 Adv.*

(a) Uncertainty principle rules out the existence of definite paths for electrons.

(b) The energy of an electron in 2*s* orbital of an atom is lower than the energy of an electron that is infinitely far away from the nucleus.

(c) According to Bohr's model, the most negative energy value for an electron is given by $n = 1$, which corresponds to the most stable orbit.

(d) According to Bohr's model, the magnitude of velocity of electrons increases with increase in values of *n*.

6. Consider a helium (He) atom that absorbs a photon of wavelength 330 nm. The change in the velocity (in cm/s^{-1}) of He atom after the photon absorption is ....
(Assume, momentum is conserved, when photon is absorbed.

7. The ground state energy of hydrogen atom is -13.6 eV. Consider an electronic state Ψ of He^+ whose energy, azimuthal quantum number and magnetic quantum number are -3.4 eV, 2 and 0, respectively. Which of the following statement(s) is(are) true for the state Ψ? *2019 Adv.*

(a) It is a $4d$ state

(b) The nuclear charge experienced by the electron in this state is less than $2e$, where e is the magnitude of the electronic charge

(c) It has 2 angular nodes

(d) It has 3 radial nodes

Direction (Q.Nos. 8-10) by appropriately matching the information given in the three columns of the following table.

The wave function, ψ_{n,l,m_l} is a mathematical function whose value depends upon spherical polar coordinates (r, θ, ϕ) of the electron and characterised by the quantum number n, l and m_l. Here r is distance from nucleus, θ is colatitude and ϕ is azimuth. In the mathematical functions given in the Table, Z is atomic number and a_0 is Bohr radius. *2017 Adv.*

Column 1	Column 2	Column 3
I 1s-orbital	(i) $\psi_{n,l,m_l} \propto \left(\frac{Z}{a_0}\right)^{\frac{3}{2}} e^{-\left(\frac{Zr}{a_0}\right)}$	(P) Radial part of wave function (ψ) is plotted against 'r' wave function changes its sign at node.
II. 2s-orbital	(ii) One radial node	(Q) Probability density at nucleus $\propto \frac{1}{a_0^3}$
III. $2p_z$-orbital	(iii) $\psi_{n,l,m_l} \propto \left(\frac{Z}{a_0}\right)^{\frac{5}{2}} re^{-\left(\frac{Zr}{a_0}\right)} \cos\theta$	(R) Probability density is maximum at nucleus
IV. $3d_z^2$-orbital	(iv) xy-plane is a nodal plane	(S) Energy needed to excite electron from $n = 2$ state to $n = 4$ state is $\frac{27}{32}$ times the energy needed to excite electron from $n = 2$ state to $n = 6$ state

8. For He^+ ion, the only INCORRECT combination is

(a) (I) (i) (S)
(b) (II) (ii) (Q)
(c) (I) (iii) (R)
(d) (I) (i) (R)

9. For the given orbital in Column 1, the only CORRECT combination for any hydrogen-like species is

(a) (II) (ii) (P)
(b) (I) (ii) (S)
(c) (IV) (iv) (R)
(d) (III) (iii) (P)

10. For hydrogen atom, the only CORRECT combination is

(a) (I) (i) (P)
(b) (I) (iv) (R)
(c) (II) (i) (Q)
(d) (I) (i) (S)

11. P is the probability of finding the $1s$ electron of hydrogen atom in a spherical shell of infinitesimal thickness, dr, at a distance r from the nucleus. The volume of this shell is $4\pi r^2 dr$. The qualitative sketch of the dependence of P on r is *2016 Adv.*

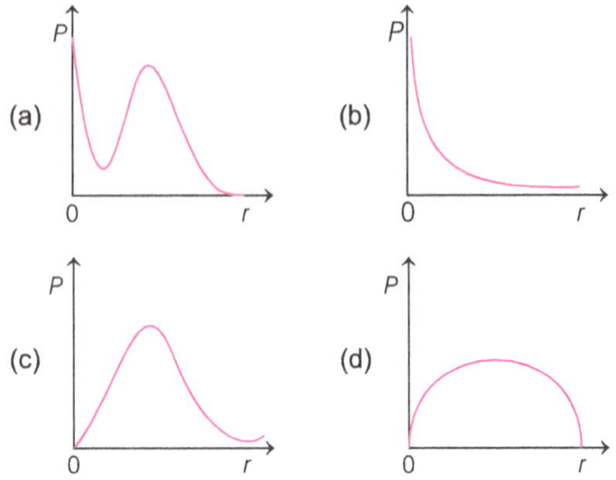

12. Not considering the electronic spin, the degeneracy of the second excited state ($n = 3$) of H-atom is 9, while the degeneracy of the second excited state of H^- is .... *2015 Adv.*

HINTS & Solutions

Solutions : Competency Enhancer

1.1 **(1)** Photoelectric effect will take place, only when the work function of given metals is lower than the energy of incident light with wavelength 350 nm.

Energy of incident light = $h\nu = \frac{hc}{\lambda}$

$$E\,(\text{eV}) = \frac{1240}{\lambda\,(\text{nm})} = \frac{1240}{350} = 3.54 \text{ eV}$$

Thus, only K will show photoelectric effect.

1.2 **(713)** According to Bohr model, radius of hydrogen like species is,

$$r_n = a_0\left(\frac{n^2}{Z}\right)\text{Å}$$

For third Bohr orbit ($n = 3$)

For Be^{+3} ($Z = 4$)

$$a_0 = 3.17\text{Å}$$

$$r_3 = 3.17\left[\frac{(3)^2}{4}\right]\text{Å}$$

$$= 7.13\text{Å} = 7.13 \times 10^{-10} \text{ m}$$

$$= 7.13 \times 10^{-10} \times 10^{12} \text{ pm}$$

$$= 7.132 \times 10^2 \text{ pm}$$

$$= 713.2 \text{ pm} \approx 713 \text{ pm}$$

1.3 **(b)** According to Bohr's model, the kinetic energy is given by,

$$\text{K.E} = +\,13.6 \times \frac{Z^2}{n^2}$$

For 1st orbit of Be^{3+}

$$n = 1, Z = 4$$

$$\text{K.E} = +\,13.6 \times \frac{(4)^2}{(1)^2} = +\,217.6 \text{ eV}$$

For 1st orbit of H-atom

$$n = 1, Z = 1$$

$$\text{K.E} = +\,13.6 \text{ eV}$$

For 1st orbit of He^{+}

$$n = 1, Z = 2$$

$$\text{K.E} = +\,13.6 \times \frac{(2)^2}{(1)^2} = +\,54.4 \text{ eV}$$

For 1st orbit of Li^{2+}

$$n = 1, Z = 3$$

$$\text{K.E} = +\,13.6 \times \frac{(3)^2}{(1)^2} = +\,122.4 \text{ eV}$$

Thus, the lowest energy is associated with first orbit of H atom.

2.1. **(a)** Using the formula of de-Broglie wavelength,

$$\lambda = \frac{h}{mv}$$

Also, angular momentum of an electron by Bohr's is :

$$mvr = \frac{nh}{2\pi}$$

$$2\pi r = \frac{nh}{mv}$$

$\therefore$ de-Broglie wavelenght $\lambda = \frac{2\pi r}{n}$

de-Broglie wavelength of electron in 4th orbit,

$$\lambda_4 = \frac{2\pi r_4}{n} \quad \text{...(i)}$$

Also radius of 4th orbit,

$$r_4 = \text{radius of 1st orbit} \times n^2$$

$$r_4 = a_0 \times n^2$$

$$\frac{r_4}{n} = a_0 \times n \quad \text{...(ii)}$$

From (1) and (2) equations,

$$\lambda_4 = 2\pi a_0 \times n$$

$$n = 4$$

$$\lambda_4 = 8\pi a_0$$

2.2. **(d)** Energy level can be determined by comparing he value of $(n + l)$ value i.e. Bohr-Bury rule.

A. $n = 6, l = 0; n + l = 6$

B. $n = 5, l = 3; n + l = 8$

C. $n = 7, l = 1; n + l = 8$

D. $n = 4, l = 1; n + l = 5$

E. $n = 4, l = 2; n + l = 6$

For same value of $n + l$, the orbital, having higher values of n, will have more energy.

So, the correct order is—

$$D < E < A < B < C$$

Elemental Practice 2.1

1. **(b)** Energy in the ground state = 13.6 eV

Energy absorbed = 13.6 × 1.5 = 20.4 eV

Energy in higher level = 20.4 + 13.6 = 34 eV

Thus, energy emitted (which is converted to KE)
= (34 – 13.6) = 20.4 eV

2. **(c)** $E_n = \frac{-\,13.6\,(Z^2)}{(n^2)}$ eV

$$E_1(\text{H}) = -\,13.6\left(\frac{1}{1}\right)^2 = -\,13.6 \text{ eV}$$

$$E_2(He^+) = -13.6\left(\frac{2}{2}\right)^2 = -13.6 \text{ eV}$$

$$E_3(Li^{2+}) = -13.6\left(\frac{3}{3}\right)^2 = -13.6 \text{ eV}$$

$$E_4(Be^{3+}) = -13.6\left(\frac{4}{4}\right)^2 = -13.6 \text{ eV}$$

Thus, $E_1(H) = E_2(He^+) = E_3(Li^{2+}) = E_4(Be^{3+})$

3. **(a)** $\frac{1}{\lambda} = R_H Z^2\left[\frac{1}{n_1^2} - \frac{1}{n_2^2}\right]$

For Lyman series, $n_1 = 1$, and $n_2 = 2$ for maximum λ (minimum wave number)

$$\therefore \quad \frac{1}{\lambda} = 1.0679 \times 10^7\left[\frac{1}{1^2} - \frac{1}{2^2}\right] \text{m}^{-1}$$

$$\therefore \quad \lambda = 1.25 \times 10^{-7} \text{m} = 125 \times 10^{-9} \text{m} = 125 \text{ nm}$$

Thus, Assertion (A) and Reason (R) are correct and Reason (R) is the correct explanation of Assertion (A).

4. **(c)** Among the given traid of nuclei, ${}^{14}_{6}C$, ${}^{15}_{7}N$ and ${}^{17}_{9}F$ are isotonic because all of these have same number of neutrons.

Number of neutrons in ${}^{14}_{6}C$, ${}^{15}_{7}N$, ${}^{17}_{9}F = 8$

5. **(c)** By Einstein's equation of photoelectric effect

$$h\nu = \phi \text{ (work function)} + \text{(KE)}$$

$$\therefore \quad \text{KE} = h\nu - \phi$$

$$\frac{1}{2}mv^2 = 6.626 \times 10^{-34} \text{Js} \times 4.77 \times 10^{15} \text{s}^{-1} - 2.90 \times 1.6 \times 10^{-19} \text{J}$$

$$= 31.61 \times 10^{-19} \text{ J} - 4.64 \times 10^{-19} \text{ J}$$

$$= 26.97 \times 10^{-19} \text{ J}$$

$$\therefore \quad v^2 = \frac{2 \times 26.97 \times 10^{-19} \text{ kg m}^2\text{s}^{-2}}{9.1 \times 10^{-31} \text{ kg}}$$

$$\therefore \quad v = 2.43 \times 10^6 \text{ ms}^{-1}$$

6. **(d)** In the transition,

$$\Delta E = E_2 - E_1 = \frac{4E}{3} - E = \frac{E}{3}$$

$$\Delta E = h\nu \Rightarrow \frac{E}{3} = \frac{hc}{3\lambda}$$

$$\therefore \quad E = \frac{3hc}{3\lambda} = \frac{hc}{\lambda}$$

In the transition, $\Delta E = E'_2 - E'_1 = 2E - E$

$$\Delta E = E \Rightarrow \frac{hc}{\lambda'} = \frac{hc}{\lambda}$$

$$\therefore \quad \lambda' = \lambda$$

7. **(d)** $E = h\nu = \frac{hc}{\lambda} = \frac{6.626 \times 10^{-34} \text{Js} \times 3 \times 10^8 \text{ ms}^{-1}}{300 \times 10^{-9} \text{m}}$

$$= 6.626 \times 10^{-19} \text{ J}$$

$$\text{KE} = 1.68 \times 10^5 \text{ J mol}^{-1}$$

$$= \frac{1.68 \times 10^5}{6.02 \times 10^{23}} \text{ J for one electron}$$

$$= 2.79 \times 10^{-19} \text{ J}$$

By photoelectric effect

$$E = h\nu_0 + \text{KE}$$

$$\therefore h\nu_0 = E - \text{KE} = (6.626 \times 10^{-19} - 2.79 \times 10^{-19}) \text{J} = 3.84 \times 10^{-19} \text{J}$$

Thus, minimum energy to emit one electron

$$= 3.84 \times 10^{-19} \text{ J}$$

8. **(a)** $r_n = \frac{n^2 a_0}{Z} \Rightarrow \frac{r_n}{r_{n'}} = \frac{1}{4} = \left(\frac{n}{n'}\right)^2 \quad \therefore \quad \frac{n}{n'} = \frac{1}{2}$

$\therefore \; n' = 2n$

Thus, if $n = 1$ or $n = 2$, $n' = 2$ or $n' = 4$

Thus, orbit can be first and second or second and fourth.

$$E_n = \frac{-13.6 Z^2}{n^2} \text{eV}$$

$$\therefore \; \Delta E = (E_2 - E_1) = 13.6\left[\frac{1}{1^2} - \frac{1}{2^2}\right] = 13.6 \times \frac{3}{4} \text{ eV} = 10.2 \text{ eV}$$

$$\Delta E = (E_4 - E_2) = 13.6\left(\frac{1}{2^2} - \frac{1}{4^2}\right) = 13.6 \times \frac{12}{16 \times 4} = 2.55 \text{ eV}$$

9. **(a)** $\Delta E = 2.18 \times 10^{-18}\left[\frac{1}{n_1^2} - \frac{1}{n_2^2}\right] \text{J}$

$$= 2.18 \times 10^{-18}\left[\frac{1}{2^2} - \frac{1}{5^2}\right] \text{J} = 4.578 \times 10^{-19} \text{J}$$

Also, $\Delta E = \frac{hc}{\lambda}$

$$\therefore \quad \lambda = \frac{hc}{\Delta E} = \frac{6.626 \times 10^{-34} \times 3 \times 10^8}{4.578 \times 10^{-19}} \text{ m}$$

$$= 4.34 \times 10^{-7} \text{ m} = 434 \text{ nm}$$

10. **(c)** By Bohr's theory

$$E_n = -\frac{13.6 Z^2}{n^2} \text{ eV}$$

For He^+ ion,

$Z = 2$ and $n = 1$ (given)

$$\therefore \quad E_1 = \frac{-13.6 \times 2^2}{1^2}$$

$= -54.4$ eV atom^{-1} (thus, (c) is incorrect)

$= -54.4 \times 1.6 \times 10^{-19}$ J atom^{-1}

$= -8.70 \times 10^{-18}$ J atom^{-1} (thus, (a) is correct)

$= -8.70 \times 10^{-18} \times 6.02 \times 10^{23}$ J mol^{-1}

$= -5.24 \times 10^6$ J mol^{-1} (thus, (b) is correct)

11. **(a)** $r_n = \frac{n^2 a_0}{Z}$

$$\therefore Z = \frac{n^2 a_0}{r_n} = \frac{(1)^2 \times 0.5292 \times 10^{-8}}{1.0 \times 10^{-13}} = 5.292 \times 10^4$$

12. ***(b)*** Work function of metal $(\phi) = h\nu_0$

where, ν_0 = threshold frequency

Also, $\frac{1}{2}m_e v^2 = h\nu - h\nu_0$ or $\frac{1}{2}m_e v^2 = h\nu - \phi$ ...(i)

$$\frac{1}{2}m_e v^2 = \frac{hc}{\lambda} - \phi \quad ...(ii)$$

Given: $\lambda = 3890 \text{ Å} = 3890 \times 10^{-10}$ m

$v = 6 \times 10^5 \text{ ms}^{-1}$

$m_e = 9 \times 10^{-31}$ kg, $c = 3 \times 10^8 \text{ ms}^{-1}$, $h = 6.626 \times 10^{-34}$ Js

Thus, on substituting all the given values in Eqs. (i), we get

$$\frac{1}{2} \times 9 \times 10^{-31} \text{ kg} \times (6 \times 10^5 \text{ ms}^{-1})^2$$

$$= \frac{6.626 \times 10^{-34} \text{ Js} \times 3 \times 10^8 \text{ ms}^{-1}}{3890 \times 10^{-10} \text{ m}} - \phi$$

$$\therefore \phi = 5.11 \times 10^{-19} \text{ J} - 1.62 \times 10^{-19} \text{ kg m}^2\text{s}^{-2}$$

$$[\because 1 \text{ kg m}^2\text{s}^{-2} = 1 \text{ J}, 1 \text{ eV} = 1.6 \times 10^{-19} \text{ J}]$$

$$= 3.49 \times 10^{-19} \text{ J} = 2.18 \text{ eV}$$

13. ***(d)*** A is false but R is true.

The correct form of A is.

As we know, that the line in Balmer series of hydrogen spectrum the highest wavelength or lowest energy is between $n_1 = 2$ and $n_2 = 3$ and for Balmer series of hydrogen spectrum, the value of $n_1 = 2$ and $n_2 = 3, 4, 5$.

14. ***(c)*** Given, radiation of energy $= 1.47 \times 10^{-17}$ J

$$R_H = 2.18 \times 10^{-18} \text{ J}$$

$$\Delta E = R_H Z^2 \left(\frac{1}{n_1^2} - \frac{1}{n_2^2}\right)$$

$$1.47 \times 10^{-17} = 2.18 \times 10^{-18} \times (3)^2 \left[\frac{1}{n^2} - \frac{1}{(n+1)^2}\right]$$

$$\frac{1.47}{1.962} = \frac{1}{n^2} - \frac{1}{(n+1)^2}$$

$$\frac{3}{4} = \frac{1}{n^2} - \frac{1}{(n+1)^2}$$

$$\therefore \quad n = 1$$

15. ***(b)*** Statement I is true but statement II is false.

The correct form of statement II is :

The limiting line of Balmer series refers to the transition from ∞ to 2nd orbit.

$$\nu = 3.29 \times 10^{15} \left(\frac{1}{n_1^2} - \frac{1}{n_2^2}\right) \text{s}^{-1} \; (n_1 = 2, n = \infty)$$

$$= 3.29 \times 10^{15} \left(\frac{1}{4}\right) = 8.22 \times 10^{14} \text{ s}^{-1}$$

16. ***(d)*** The energy of electron in H-atom is given by expression

$$= \frac{-1312}{n^2} \text{ kJ mol}^{-1}$$

For H-atom, $n = 1$

The energy required to excite the electron from ground state to second orbit is

$$n = 2, E = -\frac{1312}{(2)^2} \text{ kJ mol}^{-1}$$

$$E = \frac{-1312}{4}$$

$$\Delta E = \frac{-1312}{4} - \left(\frac{-1312}{1}\right) = -328 + 1312 = 984 \text{ kJ}$$

17. ***(b)*** As we know,

$$\bar{\nu}_H = R\left[\frac{1}{n_1^2} - \frac{1}{n_2^2}\right] = 18700 \text{ cm}^{-1}$$

$$\bar{\nu}_{Li^{2+}} = RZ^2\left[\frac{1}{n_1^2} - \frac{1}{n_2^2}\right] = (3)^2 \times 18700 \text{ cm}^{-1}$$

$$= 168300 \text{ cm}^{-1}$$

18. ***(a, b, c)*** Among the given statements, (a), (b) and (c) are correct while statement (d) is incorrect.

Its correct form is

- At a given temperature, intensity of radiation emitted increases with the increase of wavelength, reaches a maximum value at a given wavelength and then starts decreasing with further increase of wavelength.

19. ***(c, d)*** Among the given statements, (c) and (d) are incorrect while (a) and (b) are correct.

The correct form of (c) and (d) are

- The velocity of X-rays is more than microwaves.
- The frequency of microwaves is less than that of UV rays.

20. ***(b, d)*** Among the given statements, (b) and (d) are not the characteristic of Planck's quantum theory of radiation.

- The energy is absorbed or emitted in whole numbers or multiple of quantum.
- Radiations are associated with energy.

21. ***(b, c, d)*** Among the given statements, (b, c) and (d) are correct while statement (a) is incorrect about photoelectric effect.

Its correct form is

- The number of electrons ejected is proportional to the intensity or brightness of light.

22. ***(a, c)*** Among the given statements, (a) and (c) are incorrect about Bohr's model while statements b and d are correct.

The correct form of (a) and (c) is

- It could not explain the splitting of spectral lines in the presence of magnetic field (zeeman effect) or an electric field (stark effect).
- Qualitatively, the magnitude of velocity of electron increases with increase of positive charge on the nucleus and decreases with increase of principal quantum number.

23. ***(10)*** As we know,

$$\Delta E = E_2 - E_1$$

$$= \frac{-E_1}{2^2} + \frac{E_1}{1^2}$$

$$= \frac{-1.312 \times 10^6}{2^2} + 1.312 \times 10^6$$

$$= 9.84 \times 10^5 \text{ J/mol} \approx 10 \times 10^5 \text{ J/mole}$$

Hence, the value of x is 1.

24. ***(76)*** According to Bohr model, radius of hydrogen like species is,

$$r_n = r_0\left(\frac{n^2}{Z}\right) \text{Å}$$

For second Bohr orbit ($n = 2$)

For He^+ ($z = 2$)

$$r_2 = 0.38\left(\frac{(2)^2}{2}\right)$$

$$= 0.38 \times 2 \text{Å} = 0.76 \times 10^{-10} \text{ m}$$

$$= 0.76 \times 10^{-10} \times 10^{12} \text{ pm}$$

$$= 0.76 \times 10^2 \text{ pm} = 76 \text{ pm}$$

25. ***(6)*** For one molecule, $E = hv$

For 2.38 moles

$$E = 2.38 \times 6.023 \times 10^{23} \times hv$$

$$= 2.38 \times 6.023 \times 10^{23} \times 6.626 \times 10^{-34} \times 6.35 \times 10^{14}$$

$$= 603 \times 10^3 \approx 6.03 \times 10^5 \text{ J} \approx 6 \times 10^5 \text{ J}$$

26. ***(1)*** Photoelectric effect will take place, only when the work function of given metals is lower than the energy of incident light with wavelength 410 nm.

Energy of incident light $= hv = \frac{hc}{\lambda}$

$$E(\text{eV}) = \frac{1240}{\lambda} = \frac{1240}{410} = 3.02$$

Thus, only Na metal will show photoelectric effect.

27. ***(28)*** Let the number of photons required be n.

$$\frac{nhc}{\lambda} = 10^{-17}$$

$$n = \frac{10^{-17} \times \lambda}{hc} = \frac{10^{-17} \times 550 \times 10^{-9}}{6.626 \times 10^{-34} \times 3 \times 10^8}$$

$$= 27.6 \approx 28 \text{ photons}$$

28. ***(486)*** According to Rydberg equation, for H-atom ($Z = 1$)

$$\frac{1}{\lambda} = R\left(\frac{1}{n_1^2} - \frac{1}{n_2^2}\right)$$

$$R = 109678 \text{ cm}^{-1}; n_1 = 2; n_2 = 4$$

$$\frac{1}{\lambda} = 109678\left[\frac{1}{4} - \frac{1}{16}\right]$$

$$= 109678 \times \frac{3}{16}$$

$$\lambda = 486 \text{ nm} = 486 \times 10^{-9} \text{ m}$$

So, the value of x is 486.

29. ***(4.18)*** Energy of incident radiation $(E) = \frac{hc}{\lambda}$

$$= \frac{6.626 \times 10^{-34} \times 3 \times 10^8}{267.3 \times 10^{-9}}$$

$$= 0.0743 \times 10^{-17} = 7.43 \times 10^{-19} \text{ J}$$

$$= 4.63 \text{ eV } [1.602 \times 10^{-19} \text{ J} = 1 \text{ eV}]$$

The potential applied gives the kinetic energy to the electron KE of photoelectron $= eV_0$

$$= 1.6 \times 10^{-19} \times 0.45 = 7.2 \times 10^{-20} \text{ J}$$

$$= \frac{7.2 \times 10^{-20}}{1.602 \times 10^{-19}} = 0.449 \approx 0.45 \text{ eV}$$

$\therefore$ Work function $= (4.63 - 0.45)$ eV $= 4.18$ eV

30. ***(8)*** As we know,

$$\Delta E = h\nu$$

$$76.31 = 9.52 \times 10^{-14} \times \nu$$

$$\nu = \frac{76.31 \text{ kcal/mol}}{9.52 \times 10^{-14} \text{ kcal sec/mol}}$$

$$= 8.01 \times 10^{14} \text{ cycle/sec} = 8 \times 10^{14} \text{ cycle/sec}$$

Elemental Practice 2.2

1. ***(b)*** $\lambda = \frac{h}{mv}$, $m = 1.0$ mg $= 1 \times 10^{-6}$ kg

Velocity $(v) = 3600 \text{ km h}^{-1} = \frac{3600 \times 10^3 \text{ m}}{60 \times 60 \text{ s}} = 10^3 \text{ m s}^{-1}$

$$\therefore \quad \lambda = \frac{6.626 \times 10^{-34} \text{ Js}}{1 \times 10^{-6} \text{ kg} \times 10^3 \text{ ms}^{-1}} = 6.626 \times 10^{-31} \text{ m}$$

2. ***(d)*** Velocity of the electron of atomic number Z in nth orbit is $v_n = \frac{2.182 \times 10^6 Z}{n} \text{ ms}^{-1}$

$\therefore$ For He^+, $Z = 2$ and in first excited state $n = 2$

$\therefore$ $v_2(He^+) = 2.182 \times 10^6 \text{ ms}^{-1}$

$$\lambda = \frac{h}{mv}$$

$$\therefore \quad \lambda = \frac{6.626 \times 10^{-34} \text{ Js}}{9.1 \times 10^{-31} \text{ kg} \times 2.182 \times 10^6 \text{ ms}^{-1}}$$

$$= 3.34 \times 10^{-10} \text{ m}$$

$$= 334 \times 10^{-12} \text{ m} = 334 \text{ pm}$$

3. ***(b)*** 1 kV = 1000 V

$$eV = 1000 \times 1.6 \times 10^{-19} \text{ J}$$

By de-Broglie equation,

$$\lambda = \frac{h}{mv} = \frac{h}{\sqrt{2m_e eV}}$$

$$= \frac{6.626 \times 10^{-34} \text{ Js}}{\sqrt{2 \times 9.1 \times 10^{-31} \text{ kg} \times 1000 \times 1.6 \times 10^{-19} \text{J}}}$$

$$= 0.388 \times 10^{-11} \text{ m} = 38.8 \text{ pm}$$

$$1 \times 10^{-12} \text{m} = 1 \text{ pm}$$

4. *(c)* $\lambda = \dfrac{h}{mv}$

$\therefore\ mv = \dfrac{h}{\lambda} = \dfrac{6.626 \times 10^{-34}\ \text{Js}}{300 \times 10^{-9}\ \text{m}} = 2.21 \times 10^{-27}\ \text{kg ms}^{-1}$

For the particle of 1.0 g $(= 1 \times 10^{-3}\ \text{kg})$

$mv = 2.21 \times 10^{-27}\ \text{kg ms}^{-1}$

$\therefore\quad v = \dfrac{2.21 \times 10^{-27}\ \text{kg ms}^{-1}}{1 \times 10^{-3}\ \text{kg}} = 2.21 \times 10^{-24}\ \text{ms}^{-1}$

5. *(a)* $v = 350\ \text{km s}^{-1} = 350 \times 10^3\ \text{ms}^{-1}$

m (proton) $= 1.673 \times 10^{-27}$ kg

$mv = 350 \times 10^3 \times 1.673 \times 10^{-27}\ \text{kg ms}^{-1}$

$= 5.86 \times 10^{-22}\ \text{kg ms}^{-1}$

$\Delta p = m\Delta v = 5.86 \times 10^{-22} \times \dfrac{0.01}{100} = 5.86 \times 10^{-26}\ \text{kg ms}^{-1}$

As, $\Delta p \cdot \Delta x = \dfrac{h}{4\pi}$

$\therefore\quad \Delta x = \dfrac{h}{4\pi \times \Delta p}$

$= \dfrac{6.626 \times 10^{-34}\ \text{Js}}{4\pi \times 5.86 \times 10^{-26}\ \text{kg ms}^{-1}} = 9 \times 10^{-10}\ \text{m}$

6. *(d)* Using the formula of de-Broglie wavelength,

$$\lambda = \frac{h}{mv}$$

Also, angular momentum of an electron by Bohr is

$$mvr = \frac{nh}{2\pi}$$

$$\frac{2\pi r}{n} = \frac{h}{mv}$$

$$\therefore\quad \lambda = \frac{2\pi r}{n}$$

de-Broglie wavelength of electron in 3rd orbit,

$$\lambda_3 = \frac{2\pi r_3}{n} \quad \text{...(i)}$$

Also radius of 3rd orbit,

r_3 = radius of 3rd orbit $= 2a_0 \times n^2$

$$\frac{r_3}{n} = 2a_0 \times n \quad \text{...(ii)}$$

From (i) and (ii) equation,

$\lambda_3 = 2\pi \times 2a_0 \times n$

$n = 3$

So, $\lambda_3 = 2\pi \times 2a_0 \times 3$

$\lambda_3 = 12\pi a_0$

7. *(b)*

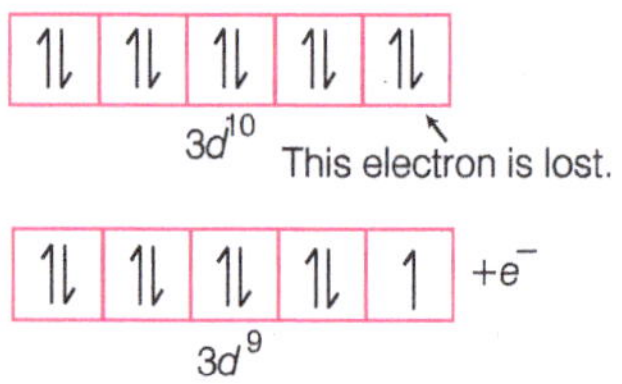

Thus, $n = 3, l = 2$

$m_l = -2, -1, 0, +1, +2$ (any one)

$m_s = +\dfrac{1}{2}$ or $-\dfrac{1}{2}$

8. *(b)*

		$n + l$
(a)	4s	4
(b)	3d	5
(c)	3p	4
(d)	3s	3

Energy order is $3s < 3p < 4s < 3d$

9. *(a)* Radial nodes $= (n - l - 1)$

		n	l	Radial nodes
(a)	4s	4	0	3 equal
	5p	5	1	3 equal
(b)	4d	4	2	1
	5p	5	1	3
(c)	4s	4	0	3
	4p	4	1	2
(d)	3s	3	0	2
	3p	3	1	1

10. *(a)* For a p-sub-orbit $l = 1$, total orbitals = 3

Possible arrangements $= \dfrac{x!}{(x-y)!\,y!}$

Here, $x = 6$ and $y = 2$

$\therefore$ Possible arrangements $= \dfrac{6!}{4!\,2!} = \dfrac{6 \cdot 5 \cdot 4!}{4!\,2!} = 15$ ways

11. *(c)* $l = 0, 1, 2, 3, \ldots n$

For a given value of n.

	l	Suborbit	Maximum capacity $[2(2l + 1)]$
$n = 1$	0	1s	2
	1	1p	6
$n = 2$	0	2s	2
	1	2p	6
	2	2d	10
$n = 3$	0	3s	2
	1	3p	6
	2	3d	10
	3	3f	14

Energy order is : $1s < 1p < 2s < 2p < 3s < 2d < 3p < 4s < 3d$

Thus, EC $(Z = 23)$ $1s^2 1p^6 2s^2 2p^6, 3s^2 2d^5$

12. ***(b)*** Energy level can be determined by comparing the value of $(n + l)$ value i.e., Bohr-Bury rule.

A. $n = 3, l = 0; n + l = 3$ B. $n = 5, l = 1; n + l = 6$

C. $n = 3, l = 1; n + l = 4$ D. $n = 5, l = 0; n + l = 5$

E. $n = 3, l = 4; n + l = 7$

For the same value of $n + l$, the orbital having higher values of n, will have more energy. So, the correct order is

A < C < D < B < E

13. ***(c)*** As we know,

$$\lambda = \frac{h}{mv} = \frac{6.626 \times 10^{-34}}{0.25 \times 250}$$

$$= 0.106016 \times 10^{-34} = 1.06 \times 10^{-35} \text{ m}$$

14. ***(a)*** Total possible values of magnetic quantum number $= n^2$

$$= 3^2 = 9$$

15. ***(b)*** As we know, $\lambda = \frac{h}{mv}$

$$m = 2g = 2 \times 10^{-3} \text{ kg}$$

$$v = 200 \text{ m/s}$$

$$h = 6.626 \times 10^{-34} \text{ Js}$$

$$\lambda = \frac{6.626 \times 10^{-34}}{2 \times 10^{-3} \times 200} = \frac{0.03313 \times 10^{-34} \times 10^3}{2}$$

$$= 0.0165 \times 10^{-31} = 1.65 \times 10^{-33} \text{ m}$$

16. ***(c)*** $Z = 55$ (Caesium)

$Cs = [Xe]\, 6s^1$

$n = 6$ (Principal quantum number)

$l = 0$ (Azimuthal quantum number)

$m = 0$ (Magnetic quantum number)

$s = +\frac{1}{2}$, or $-\frac{1}{2}$ (Spin quantum number)

Hence, option (c) is correct.

17. ***(d)*** Uncertainty in speed of electron $= \Delta v$

$$= \frac{0.05}{100} \times 7 \times 10^6 = 0.35 \times 10^6 \times 10^{-2}$$

$$= 35 \times 10^2$$

Uncertainty in position $= x \times 10^{-9}$ m

According to Heisenberg uncertainty principle,

$$\Delta x \cdot \Delta v = \frac{h}{4\pi m}$$

$$x \times 10^{-9} \text{ m} \times 10^2 \times 35 = \frac{6.63 \times 10^{-34}}{4 \times 3.14 \times 9.1 \times 10^{-31}}$$

$$35 \times x \times 10^{-7} = 0.058 \times 10^{-3}$$

$$x = \frac{0.058 \times 10^{-3}}{35 \times 10^{-7}} = 1.657 \times 10^{-3} \times 10^4$$

$$= 1.657 \times 10^1 = 16.57$$

18. ***(a,b,d)*** Among the given statements, (a), (b) and (d) are correct while statement (c) is incorrect. Its correct form is

- For a single electronic species like H-atom, energy depends on value of n and does not depend upon l. Hence, energy of $2s$ and $2p$ orbital is equal in case of H like atoms.

19. ***(c, d)*** Among the given statements are incorrect while statement (a), (c) and (b) is correct.

The correct form of statement (a), (c), and (d) are

- As given, $n = 4$ and $m = -2$

We know the value of m varies from $+l$ to $-l$ for d orbital, $l = 2$ and $m_l = +2$ to -2.

so, the electron may or may not be present in a d-orbital.

- For p-orbital, the value of $l = 1$ and the value of $m_l = +1$ to -1 so, the electron will not be present in a p-orbital.
- The electron may have the spin quantum number $= +\frac{1}{2}$. It will be either $+\frac{1}{2}$ or $-\frac{1}{2}$.

20. ***(b, c)*** Among the given statements, only (b) and (c) are correct while (a) and (d) are incorrect.

The correct form of (a) and (d) are

- The mass of a photon with wavelength 3.6 Å is 6.135×10^{-29} kg
- The qualitative order of de-Broglie wavelength for electron, proton and α-particle is $\lambda_e > \lambda_p > \lambda_\alpha$ if kinetic energy is same for all particles.

21. ***(a, c, d)*** Among the given statement, (a), (c) and (d) are correct while statement (b) is incorrect. Its correct form is

- The angular momentum depends only on the azimuthal quantum number.

22. ***(a, c)*** Among the given statements, (a) and (c) are incorrect while statement (b) and (d) are correct.

The correct form of (a), (c) and (d) are —

- No two electrons in an atom can have the same value of all four quantum numbers n, l, m and m_s.
- The expression of velocity is $v \propto \frac{1}{n}$; so the speed of an electron in an orbital decreases with increase of quantum number n.
- The expression of energy is $E \propto \frac{-13.6}{n^2}$

23. ***(38)*** By de-Broglie equation,

$$\lambda = \frac{h}{p} = \frac{h}{mv} = \frac{h}{\sqrt{2mKE}} = \frac{h}{\sqrt{2meV}}$$

$$\therefore \quad 2meV = \frac{h^2}{\lambda^2}$$

$$\therefore V = \frac{h^2}{\lambda^2 \times 2me} = \frac{(6.626 \times 10^{-34})^2}{(200 \times 10^{-12})^2 \times 2 \times 9.1 \times 10^{-31} \times 1.6 \times 10^{-19}}$$

$$= 37.69 \text{ V} \approx 38 \text{ V}$$

So, the value of x is 38.

24. ***(25)*** For

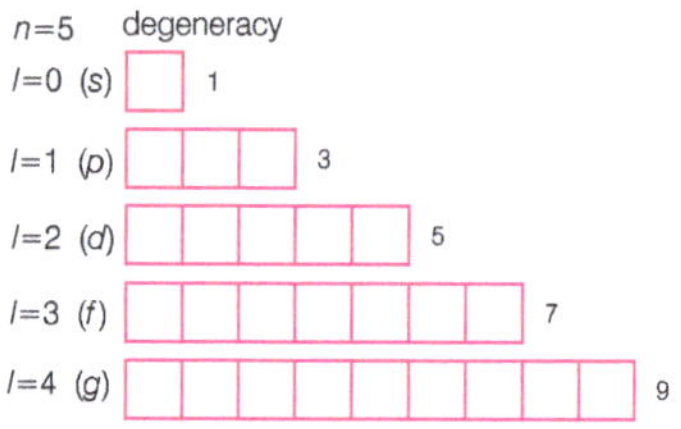

Total degeneracy of the nth level $= n^2 = 25$.

25. ***(100)*** Atomic mass of He = 4

Thus, mass of one atom $= \frac{4}{N_A}$ g

$$m = \frac{4 \times 10^{-3}}{6.02 \times 10^{23}} \text{ kg atom}^{-1}$$

$$\lambda = \frac{h}{mv} = \frac{6.626 \times 10^{-34} \text{ Js} \times 6.02 \times 10^{23}}{4 \times 10^{-3} \text{ kg} \times 1.0 \times 10^{3} \text{ ms}^{-1}}$$

$$= 9.97 \times 10^{-11} \text{ m} = 99.7 \times 10^{-12} \text{ m} = 99.7 \text{ pm} \approx 100 \text{ pm}$$

26. ***(6)*** By Heisenberg's uncertainty principle,

$$\Delta x \cdot \Delta p = \frac{h}{4\pi}$$

Given, Δx (in m) = Δp (in kg ms^{-1})

$$\therefore \quad \Delta p = \sqrt{\frac{h}{4\pi}}$$

$$\therefore \quad m\Delta v = \frac{1}{2}\sqrt{\frac{h}{\pi}}$$

$$\therefore \quad \Delta v = \frac{1}{2m}\sqrt{\frac{h}{\pi}}$$

$$= \frac{1}{2 \times 1.21 \times 10^{-18}}\sqrt{\frac{6.626 \times 10^{-34}}{\pi}} = 6.00 \text{ ms}^{-1}$$

27. ***(26)*** Velocity of O_2 molecule = root mean square velocity

$$= \sqrt{\frac{3RT}{M}} = \sqrt{\frac{3 \times 8.314 \times 300}{32 \times 10^{-3}}} = 484 \text{ms}^{-1}$$

By de-Broglie equation, $\lambda = \frac{h}{mv}$

$$m(O_2 \text{ molecule}) = \frac{32 \times 10^{-3}}{6.02 \times 10^{23}} \text{ kg} = 5.32 \times 10^{-26} \text{ kg}$$

$$\lambda = \frac{6.626 \times 10^{-34} \text{ Js}}{5.32 \times 10^{-26} \text{ kg} \times 484 \text{ ms}^{-1}}$$

$$= 2.575 \times 10^{-11} \text{ m} = 25.75 \times 10^{-12} \text{ m} = 25.75 \text{ pm} \approx 26 \text{ pm}$$

All values are in SI units.

$$M(O_2) = 32 \times 10^{-3} \text{ kg}$$

R(gas constant) $= 8.314 \text{ J mol}^{-1}\text{K}^{-1}$

$$1 \text{ J} = 1 \text{kg m}^2 \text{ s}^{-2}$$

Practice Element 01 : Target JEE Main

1. ***(b)*** Angular momentum is quantised.

$$mvr_n = \frac{nh}{2\pi}$$

Since, $r_n = \frac{n^2 a_0}{Z}$, $mv\left(\frac{n^2 a_0}{Z}\right) = \frac{nh}{2\pi}$

$$mvna_0 = \frac{h}{2\pi}$$

For H-atom, $Z = 1$ and in third orbit $n = 3$ and $a_0 = x$

$$\therefore \quad mv\,(3x) = \frac{h}{2\pi}$$

$$\therefore \quad mv = \frac{h}{6\pi x}$$

$$\lambda = \frac{h}{mv} = 6\pi x$$

2. ***(d)*** In a given shell (orbit) n, $l = 0, 1, \ldots, (n-1)$

Values of m_l are $-l \ldots 0, \ldots + l$

Total values of $m = (2l + 1)$ = total number of orbitals.

Each orbital can have maximum of = 2 electrons

Thus, total electrons $= 2(2l + 1)$

Thus, in a given energy level, n,

$$\text{Total electrons} = \sum_{l=0}^{l=(n-1)} 2\,(2l + 1)$$

3. ***(a)*** $\nu = \frac{c}{\lambda}$

$$\nu \propto \frac{1}{\lambda}$$

Thus, higher the wavelength, lower is the frequency.

4. ***(c)*** $E = h\nu$

$$\therefore \nu = \frac{E}{h}$$

$$E = 495.8 \text{ kJ mol}^{-1} = \frac{495.8 \times 10^3 \text{ J}}{6.02 \times 10^{23}} \text{atom}^{-1}$$

$$= 8.236 \times 10^{-19} \text{ J atom}^{-1}$$

$$\therefore \nu = \frac{E}{h} = \frac{8.236 \times 10^{-19} \text{ J}}{6.626 \times 10^{-34} \text{ Js}} = 1.24 \times 10^{15} \text{ s}^{-1}$$

5. ***(c)*** A is correct but R is incorrect.

The correct form of R is—

- e/m ratio for particles in cathode rays comes out to be same for all gases.

$$e/m = 1.76 \times 10^{11} \text{ C/kg}$$

This led to the conclusion that electrons were fundamental particles.

6. ***(d)*** Among the given statements, A, B and C are correct while the statement D is incorrect.

Its correct form is—

- As n increases, energy becomes less negative. Electron close to the nucleus is more tightly bound than the electron away from it.

7. ***(a)*** $\bar{\nu} = R_H Z^2 \left[\frac{1}{n_1^2} - \frac{1}{n_2^2}\right] = \frac{8}{9} R_H$

Thus, if $n_1 = 1$, $n_2 = 3$ then $\bar{\nu} = \frac{8}{9} R_H$

8. ***(b)*** If spins are $+\frac{1}{2}, 0, -\frac{1}{2}$ then each orbital can take three electrons, thus K(19) will have EC as $1s^3\ 2s^3, 2p^9, 3s^3, 3p^1$
Last electron goes into *p*-orbital thus *p*-block

9. ***(a)*** $E = Nh\nu$
$= 7.25 \times 10^{15} \times 6.626 \times 10^{-34}$ Js $\times 5.37 \times 10^{14}$ s^{-1}
1 Einstein unit = Energy of N_0 photons with same frequency
$E' = N_0\ h\nu$
$= 6.02 \times 10^{23} \times 6.626 \times 10^{-34}$ J s $\times 5.37 \times 10^{14}$ s^{-1}
Number of Einstein's $= \frac{E}{E'} = \frac{N}{N_0} = \frac{7.25 \times 10^{15}}{6.02 \times 10^{23}}$
$= 1.20 \times 10^{-8}$ Einstein

10. ***(d)*** $r_n = \frac{n^2 a_0}{Z}$
(a_0 = Bohr's radius = 0.53 Å)
For H-atom, $Z = 1$ and in ground state, $n = 1$
$\therefore\ r_1 = a_0 = 0.53$ Å
For second excited state $n = 3$
$\therefore\ r_3(\text{Li}^{2+}) = \frac{n^2 a_0}{Z} = \frac{9a_0}{3} = 3a_0 = 3 \times 0.53 = 1.59$ Å

11. ***(a)*** By Heisenberg's uncertainty principle,
$$\Delta x \cdot \Delta p \approx \frac{h}{4\pi}$$
$$\Delta x \cdot m\Delta v \approx \frac{h}{4\pi}$$
$$\therefore\ \Delta x \cdot \Delta v \approx \frac{h}{4\pi m}$$
$$\Delta x = \frac{h}{4\pi m\ \Delta v}$$
Given, $\Delta v = 3 \times 10^2 \times 0.001 / 100 = 3 \times 10^{-3}$
$$\Delta x = \frac{6.626 \times 10^{-34}\ \text{Js}}{4\pi \times 9.1 \times 10^{-31}\ \text{kg} \times 3 \times 10^{-3}} = 0.0193\ \text{m}$$

12. ***(a)*** Both A and R are true and R is the correct explanation of A.

13. ***(a)*** By photoelectric effect, $h\nu = h\nu_0 + (\text{KE})$
where $h\nu_0$ = Threshold frequency required to remove an electron from metal surface
$\therefore\ h\nu_0 = h\nu - (\text{KE})$
Given $h\nu = \frac{hc}{\lambda}$
$$= \frac{6.626 \times 10^{-34}\ \text{Js} \times 3 \times 10^8\ \text{ms}^{-1}}{600 \times 10^{-9}\text{m}}$$
$= 3.313 \times 10^{-19}$ J
KE $= 6.02 \times 10^4$ J mol^{-1}
$$= \frac{6.02 \times 10^4}{6.02 \times 10^{23}}\ \text{J atom}^{-1} = 1 \times 10^{-19}\ \text{J}$$
$\therefore\ h\nu_0 = 3.313 \times 10^{-19} - 1 \times 10^{-19} = 2.313 \times 10^{-19}$ J

14. ***(c)*** Both Statement I and Statement II are incorrect.
Their correct form are
- Balmer series lies in the visible region of the electromagnetic spectrum.
- The spectral line obtained when an electron jumps from $n = 6$ to $n = 2$ level in hydrogen atom belongs to the Balmer series.

15. ***(d)*** Among the given match, (d) is not correctly match. Its correct match is
Uncertainity principles states that it is impossible to determine the position and momentum of an electron simultaneously with same accuracy.

16. ***(a)*** Probability $= 4\pi r^2 \psi^2 \delta r$
$$= 4\pi r^2 \left(\frac{e^{-r/a_0}}{(\pi a_0)^{3/2}}\right)^2 \delta r = 4\pi r^2 \left(\frac{e^{-2r/a_0}}{(\pi a_0)^3}\right) \delta r$$
$$= 4r^2 \frac{e^{-2r/a_0}}{\pi^2 a_0^3} \delta r$$
Given, $\delta r = 1.0$ pm $= 1.0 \times 10^{-12}$ m and $r = a_0$
Then probability $= \frac{4a_0^2\ e^{-2}}{a_0^3} (\delta r) = \frac{4e^{-2}}{a_0}$
$$= \frac{4 \times 0.14 \times 1 \times 10^{-12}\ \text{m}}{0.529 \times 10^{-10}\ \text{m}} = 0.01$$

17. ***(b)*** Statement I is correct but Statement II is incorrect.
The correct form of statement II is—
- The maximum numbers of electrons that can be associated with the given set i.e., $n = 3, l = 1$ and $m = -1$ of quantum numbers is two.

$n = 3, l = 1$ represents $3p$

3p | ↿⇂ | ↿⇂ | ↿⇂ |

m can be $= -1, 0, +1$
Thus, orbital with $m = -1$ can accommodate maximum of two electron.

18. ***(b)*** Among the given statements, B and C are incorrect while A and D are correct. The correct form of B and C are—
(B) In the Balmer series of H-spectrum, successive lines tends towards a limiting value of $\frac{R_H c}{4}$.
For H-spectrum, wavelength is given by
$$\frac{1}{\lambda} = R_H \left[\frac{1}{n_1^2} - \frac{1}{n_2^2}\right]$$
For Balmer series, $n_1 = 2$ and when series converge, $n_2 = \infty$
$$\therefore\ \frac{1}{\lambda_{mix}} = \frac{R_H}{4}$$
But $\nu = \frac{c}{\lambda}$
$$\therefore\ \nu = \frac{c}{\lambda_{mix}} = \frac{R_H c}{4}$$

(C) In Bohr's model of atom when an electron in Be^{3+} jumps from $n = 1$ to $n = 3$, the energy absorbed will be 193.4 eV.

$$\Delta E = 13.6\,(Z^2)\left[\frac{1}{n_1^2} - \frac{1}{n_2^2}\right] \text{eV}$$

For Be^{3+}, $Z = 4$

$$\therefore \quad \Delta E = 13.6(4)^2\left[\frac{1}{1^2} - \frac{1}{3^2}\right] \text{eV} = 13.6 \times 16 \times \frac{8}{9}$$

$$= 193.4 \text{ eV}$$

19. ***(a)*** $\bar{\nu} = \frac{1}{\lambda} = R_H Z^2\left[\frac{1}{n_1^2} - \frac{1}{n_2^2}\right]$

For a given series

$$\lambda \propto \frac{1}{Z^2}$$

$$\therefore \frac{\lambda(\text{H})}{\lambda(\text{Li}^{2+})} = \left[\frac{Z(\text{Li}^{2+})}{Z(\text{H})}\right]^2 \Rightarrow \frac{821}{\lambda(\text{Li}^{2+})} = \left(\frac{3}{1}\right)^2 = 9$$

$$\therefore \lambda(\text{Li}^{2+}) = \frac{821}{9} = 91.2 \text{ nm}$$

20. ***(b)*** By de-Broglie equation, $\lambda = \frac{h}{mv}$

Given, $\lambda = 100v$

$$\therefore \quad v = \frac{\lambda}{100}$$

$$\therefore \quad \lambda = \frac{h \times 100}{m\lambda}$$

$$\therefore \quad \lambda^2 = \frac{100h}{m}$$

$$\therefore \quad \lambda = 10\sqrt{\frac{h}{m}}$$

21. ***(7)*** $\lambda = \frac{h}{mv}$

$$\frac{\lambda_A}{\lambda_B} = \frac{m_B v_B}{m_A v_A}$$

Given, $m_B = 5m_A$, $v_A = 0.1 \text{ ms}^{-1}$, $v_B = 0.05 \text{ ms}^{-1}$

$$\therefore \quad \frac{\lambda_A}{\lambda_B} = \frac{5m_A \times 0.05}{m_A \times 0.1} = \frac{0.25}{0.10} = \frac{5}{2}$$

The ratio of de-Broglie wavelengths associated with particles A and B is 5 : 2.

Hence, the sum of x and y is $5 + 2 = 7$.

22. ***(22)*** Velocity in Bohr' atomic model is given by—

$$v = 2.18 \times 10^6 \times \frac{Z}{n} = 2.18 \times 10^6 \times \frac{3}{3}$$

$$= 2.18 \times 10^6 = 21.8 \times 10^5$$

$$= 22 \times 10^5 \text{ ms}^{-1}$$

Hence, the value of x is 22.

23. ***(5)*** Pfund series mainly appears in the far infrared region. For, Pfund series the value of n will be 5.

24. ***(16)*** Wavelength of electromagnetic wave $= d \times 4$

$$\lambda = 2.5 \times 4 = 10.0 \text{ pm}$$

$$v = \frac{c}{\lambda} = \frac{3 \times 10^8}{10 \times 10^{-12}}$$

$$= 3 \times 10^{19} \text{ Hz} = 3 \times 10^{16} \text{ kHz}$$

Hence, the value of y is 16.

25. ***(82)*** As, $\frac{E_4}{E_2} = \frac{(2)^2}{(4)^2} = \frac{4}{16} = \frac{1}{4}$;

$$E_4 = \frac{E_2}{4} = \frac{-328}{4} = -82 \text{ kJ/mol}$$

26. ***(25)*** Number of orbitals can be calculated by using the formula $= n^2 = (5)^2 = 25$

27. ***(2)*** As, we know,

Number of radial nodes $= (n - l - 1)$

For $3s$; $n = 3, l = 0$

Radial nodes $= 3 - 0 - 1 = 2$

For $2p$; $n = 2, l = 1$

Radial nodes $= 2 - 1 - 1 = 0$

So, the radial nodes of $3s$ and $2p$ orbitals are 2 and 0 respectively.

Hence, the sum of x and y is $2 + 0 = 2$.

28. ***(36)*** The given symbol, ${}^{55}_{25}M^{3+}$ shows,

Atomic number = 25

Mass number = 55

Total electrons $= 25 - 3 = 22$

Total neutrons = Mass number – Atomic number

$$= 55 - 25 = 30$$

Neutron percentage which is more than number of

$$\text{electrons } (a) = \frac{\text{Number of neutrons} - \text{Number of electrons}}{\text{Number of electrons}} \times 100$$

$$= \frac{30 - 22}{22} \times 100 = 36.36 \approx 36$$

Hence, the value of 'a' is 36.

29. ***(2)*** Radius of H-atom in it ground state, $r_1 = 5.3 \times 10^{-11}$ m

Radius of Bohr atom in its nth orbit,

$$r_n = 5.3 \times 10^{-11} \frac{n^2}{Z} \text{ meters}$$

for H-atom, $Z = 1$ and $r_n = 21.2 \times 10^{-11}$ m

$$n = \left(\frac{21.2 \times 10^{-11}}{5.3 \times 10^{-11}}\right)^{1/2} = 2$$

Hence, the value of n is '2'.

30. ***(1)*** The electronic configuration of Ge $= 1s^2 2s^2 2p^6 3s^2 3p^6 3d^{10} 4s^2 4p^2$

$$\text{Ge}^+ = 1s^2 2s^2 2p^6 3s^2 3p^6 3d^{10} 4s^2 4p^1$$

Valence electron are present in p-orbital.

So, Azimuthal quantum number (l) for valence shell electrons is 1.

31. ***(7)*** As we know,

Probability $\propto e^2 \propto e^{-2r/a_0}$. At nucleus $r = 0$

$\therefore$ (Probability)$_{\text{nucleus}} \propto e^0 \propto 1$

At a distance $r = a_0$

$$(\text{Probability}) = e^{-2} = \frac{1}{e^2} = 0.14$$

$$\therefore \text{Relative probability} = \frac{1}{0.14} = 7.1 \approx 7$$

Check Through PYQs : JEE Main

1. ***(2)***

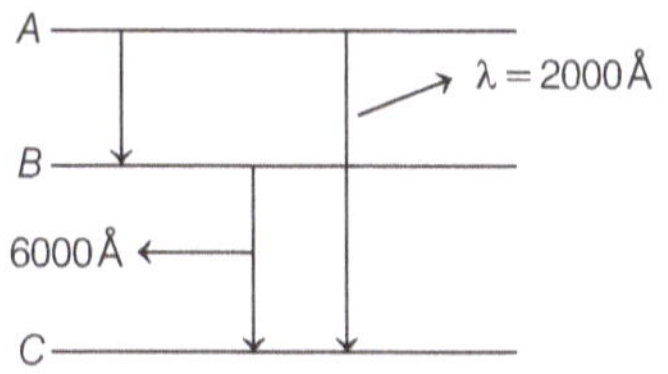

$$\left(\frac{hc}{\lambda}\right)_{AC} = \left(\frac{hc}{\lambda}\right)_{AB} + \left(\frac{hc}{\lambda}\right)_{BC}$$

$$\left(\frac{1}{\lambda}\right)_{AC} = \left(\frac{1}{\lambda}\right)_{AB} + \left(\frac{1}{\lambda}\right)_{BC}$$

$$\frac{1}{2000} = \frac{1}{\lambda_{AB}} + \frac{1}{6000}$$

$$\frac{1}{\lambda_{AB}} = \frac{1}{2000} - \frac{1}{6000}$$

$$\frac{1}{\lambda_{AB}} = \frac{6000 - 2000}{6000 \times 2000}$$

$$\frac{1}{\lambda_{AB}} = \frac{4000}{12 \times 10^6}$$

$$\frac{1}{\lambda_{AB}} = \frac{1}{3000}$$

$$\lambda_{AB} = 3000 \text{ Å}$$

2. ***(1)*** $\frac{1}{\lambda} = R_H Z^2 \left[\frac{1}{n_1^2} - \frac{1}{n_2^2}\right]$

$$\frac{1}{656 \times 10^{-7}} = 109677 \times (1)^2 \times \left[\frac{1}{2^2} - \frac{1}{n_2^2}\right] \text{cm}^{-1}$$

$$0.139 = 0.25 - \frac{1}{n_2^2} \Rightarrow \frac{1}{n_2^2} = 0.111$$

$$n_2 = 3$$

3. ***(34)*** First excited state is = − 3.4 eV

$$E_2 = -3.4 \text{ eV}$$

$$\text{KE} = -E_2$$

$$\text{KE} = 3.4 \text{ eV}$$

$$\text{KE} = 34 \times 10^{-1} \text{ eV}$$

compare it with given equation, value of x will be 34.

4. ***(22)*** Velocity in Bohr's atomic model is given by

$$v = 2.18 \times 10^6 \times \frac{Z}{n}$$

$$= 2.18 \times 10^6 \times \frac{1}{1} \approx 22 \times 10^5 \text{ m/s}$$

Hence, missing value is 22.

5. ***(493)*** To obtain ionisation energy of sodium in kJ/mol. First of all use the formula $E = \frac{1240 \text{ (eV)}}{\lambda \text{ (nm)}}$.

Then multiply the obtained value with 1.6×10^{19} to obtain energy in J/atom. After that multiply the calculated value in 2nd step with Avogadro number to get the final answer in kJ/mol.

Given, $\lambda = 242$ nm

using $E = \frac{1240 \text{ eV}}{\text{l (nm)}}$

$$E = \frac{1240}{242} \text{ eV} = 5.12 \text{ eV}$$

$$E = 5.12 \times 1.6 \times 10^{-19} \text{ J/atom}$$

$$E = 8.192 \times 10^{-19} \text{ J/atom}$$

or $E = 8.192 \times 10^{-19} \times 6.022 \times 10^{23}$ atom/mol

$= 493.32$ kJ/mol

≈ 494 kJ/mol

6. ***(b)*** The correct match is A-II, B-IV, C-III, D-I.

A. Lyman series lies in UV region.

B. Balmer series lies in visible region.

C. Paschen and Pfund series lies infrared region.

7. ***(d)*** Both Statement I and Statement II are correct.

According to Bohr's model, angular momentum is quantised for stationary orbits. In a given stationary state, it can be expressed as

$$mvr = n\frac{h}{2\pi}, \ n = 1, 2, 3, \ldots$$

It does not follow Heisenberg's uncertainty principle.

8. ***(b)*** Energy of hydrogen atom can be given as :

$$E_n = -2.18 \times 10^{-18} \left[\frac{Z^2}{n^2}\right] \text{J/atom}$$

$$E_1 = -2.18 \times 10^{-18} \text{ J / atom} \quad \ldots\text{(i)}$$

For 3rd orbit : $(n = 3)(Z = 1)$

$$E_3 = -2.18 \times 10^{-18} \left[\frac{(1)^2}{(3)^2}\right]$$

$$E_3 = -2.18 \times 10^{-18} \left[\frac{1}{9}\right] \text{J/atom} \quad \ldots\text{(ii)}$$

Hence, the energy in the 3rd Bohr orbit is (1/9th) of the energy of electron in the first Bohr orbit.

9. ***(3)*** Photoelectric effect will take place, only when the work function of given metals is lower than the energy of incident light with wavelength 400 nm.

Energy of incident light $= h\nu = \dfrac{hc}{\lambda}$

$$E(\text{eV}) = \frac{1240}{\lambda} = \frac{1240}{400} = 3.1 \text{ eV}$$

Thus, Li, Na, K will show photoelectric effect.

10\. ***(c)*** A is correct but R is not correct.

Emission of electron from metal surface take place only, when the photon with energy greater than work function strikes the metal surface. The ejected electrons leave with a specific amount of kinetic energy at a frequency $\nu > \nu_0$.

11\. ***(0)***

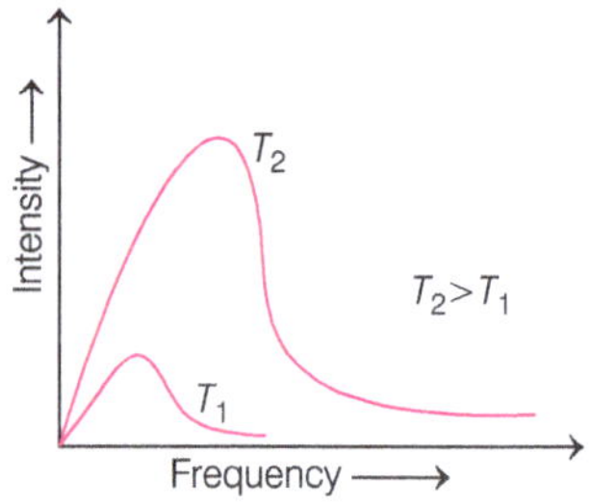

From the above graph we can see that, all statements (a), (b), (c) and (d) are also correct.

A black body can emit and absorb all the wavelength in electromagnetic spectrum. Hence, statement (a) is correct.

(b) The frequency distribution of the emitted radiation by a blackbody indeed depends on its temperature. This phenomenon is described by Planck's law. hence statement (b) is correct.

(c) The intensity *vs* frequency curve for a black body known as the planck's curve, pass through a maximum value for a given temperature. Statement (c) is correct.

(d) The frequency at which maximum intensity increase with increases in the temperature of the black body. Statement (d) is correct.

12\. ***(1)*** The emission spectra of atoms in gaseous phase do not show a continuous spread of wavelength from red to voilet, rather they emit light at specific wavelength with dark spaces between them. Hence, only statement i.e. (b) is incorrect.

13\. ***(d)*** Correct option is (d) i.e., $n = 2$ to $n = 1$.

For He^+ ion

$$\frac{1}{\lambda(\text{H})} = R(1)^2\left[\frac{1}{n_1^2} - \frac{1}{n_2^2}\right]$$

$$\frac{1}{\lambda(\text{He}^+)} = R(2)^2\left[\frac{1}{2^2} - \frac{1}{4^2}\right]$$

Given, Balmer series $\lambda(\text{H}) = \lambda(\text{He}^+)$.

$$\therefore \quad R(1)^2\left[\frac{1}{n_1^2} - \frac{1}{n_2^2}\right] = R(4)\left[\frac{1}{2^2} - \frac{1}{4^2}\right]$$

$$\frac{1}{n_1^2} - \frac{1}{n_2^2} = \frac{1}{1^2} - \frac{1}{2^2}$$

So, on comparing we will get, $n_1 = 1$ and $n_2 = 2$.

14\. ***(798)*** Given, $\nu = 2 \times 10^{12}$ Hz

$E = ?$

For one photon, $E = h\nu$

For one mole photon, $E = nh\nu$

where, h = Planck's constant

$n = 1$ mole

$$\therefore \quad E = 6.022 \times 10^{23} \times 6.626 \times 10^{-34} \times 2 \times 10^{12}$$

$$= 798.03 \text{ J} \approx 798 \text{ J}$$

15\. ***(270)*** According to Bohr model, radius of hydrogen like species is,

$$\left[r_n = r_0\left(\frac{n^2}{Z}\right) \text{Å}\right]$$

where, n = number of orbit

Z = atomic number

$\Rightarrow$ For 3rd Bohr orbit ($n = 3$)

For He^+ ($Z = 2$)

$r_0 = 0.6$ Å (Given)

$$\Rightarrow \quad r_3 = 0.6\left[\frac{(3)^2}{2}\right] \text{Å} = 2.7 \text{ Å}$$

$$= 2.7 \times 10^{-10} \text{ m} = 2.7 \times 10^{-10} \times 10^{12} \text{ pm}$$

$$= 2.7 \times 10^2 \text{ pm} = 270 \text{ pm}$$

$[\because 1 \text{ Å} = 10^{-10}\text{m}, 1 \text{ pm} = 10^{-12} \text{ m}]$

16\. ***(b)*** As we know that, $\lambda = \dfrac{hc}{\Delta E}$

For, λ = minimum, i.e. shortest,

ΔE = maximum

For Lyman series, $n = 1$ and for ΔE_{max} transition must be form $n = \infty$ to $n = 1$.

$$\text{So,} \quad \frac{1}{\lambda} = R_H Z^2\left(\frac{1}{n_1^2} - \frac{1}{n_2^2}\right) \qquad (\because n_1 = 1 \text{ and } n_2 = \infty)$$

$$\therefore \quad \frac{1}{\lambda} = R_H\left(\frac{1}{1^2} - \frac{1}{\infty^2}\right) \times (1)^2 \Rightarrow \lambda = \frac{1}{R_H}$$

For longest wavelength,

ΔE = minimum for Balmer series, $n = 3$ to $n = 2$ will have minimum ΔE.

For He^+, $Z = 2$

$$\text{So,} \quad \frac{1}{\lambda_2} = R_H \times 2^2\left(\frac{1}{n_1^2} - \frac{1}{n_2^2}\right)$$

$$\frac{1}{\lambda_2} = R_H \times 4\left(\frac{1}{4} - \frac{1}{9}\right)$$

$$\frac{1}{\lambda_2} = R_H \times \frac{5}{9} \Rightarrow \lambda_2 = \lambda \times \frac{9}{5}$$

17\. ***(492)*** We know that,

$$\frac{1}{\lambda} = R_H Z^2\left[\frac{1}{n_1^2} - \frac{1}{n_2^2}\right]$$

For first line of Paschen series,

$n_1 = 3, n_2 = 4$, on substituting the values, we will get

So, $\frac{1}{(\lambda_1)_P} = R_H Z^2\left[\frac{1}{(3)^2} - \frac{1}{(4)^2}\right]$

$$\frac{1}{(\lambda_1)_P} = R_H Z^2\left[\frac{1}{9} - \frac{1}{16}\right] \quad \text{...(i)}$$

Similarly, for second line of Paschen series

$n_1 = 3, n_2 = 5$

$$\frac{1}{(\lambda_2)_P} = R_H Z^2\left[\frac{1}{(3)^2} - \frac{1}{(5)^2}\right]$$

$$\frac{1}{(\lambda_2)_P} = R_H Z^2\left[\frac{1}{9} - \frac{1}{25}\right] \quad \text{...(ii)}$$

From Eqs. (i) and (ii), we get

$$\frac{(\lambda_2)_P}{(\lambda_1)_P} = \frac{\frac{7}{16\times 9}}{\frac{16}{25\times 9}} = \frac{25\times 7}{16\times 16} \Rightarrow (\lambda_2)_P = \frac{25\times 7}{16\times 16}\times 720$$

$(\lambda_2)_P = 492$ nm

18. ***(4)*** The symbol $^{48}_{22}X^{3-}$ shows,

Atomic number = 22; mass number = 48

Total electrons = 22 + 3 = 25

Total neutrons = Mass number − Atomic number

= 48 − 22 = 26

Neutron percentage which is more than number of electrons (*a*)

$$= \frac{\text{Number of neutrons} - \text{Number of electrons}}{\text{Number of electrons}}\times 100$$

$$= \frac{26-25}{25}\times 100 = 4$$

19. ***(300)*** Using equation, $E = w_0 + \text{KE}$

[E = energy given, w_0 = work function, KE = kinetic energy]

As electron is just ejected, so

$$\text{KE} = 0;\ E = W_0 = \frac{hc}{\lambda} = 6.63\times 10^{-19}$$

$$\Rightarrow \lambda = \frac{6.63\times 10^{-34}\times 3\times 10^8}{6.63\times 10^{-19}}$$

$\therefore \lambda = 3\times 10^{-7}$ m $= 300\times 10^{-9}$ m

Hence, $\lambda = 300$ nm

20. ***(b)*** Radius of *n*th Bohr's orbit of hydrogen atom is given as

$$r = 0.529\times\frac{n^2}{Z}\text{ Å} \quad (Z = 1 \text{ for hydrogen})$$

So, for 3rd Bohr's orbit

$$r_3 = 0.529\times\frac{(3)^2}{1} \Rightarrow r_3 = 0.529\times 9 \quad \text{...(i)}$$

For 4th Bohr's orbit ($n = 4$)

$$r_4 = 0.529\times\frac{(4)^2}{1} \Rightarrow r_4 = 0.529\times 16 \quad \text{...(ii)}$$

From Eqs. (i) and (ii),

$$\frac{r_4}{r_3} = \frac{0.529\times 16}{0.529\times 9} \Rightarrow \frac{r_4}{r_3} = \frac{16}{9} \Rightarrow r_4 = \frac{16}{9}r_3$$

21. ***(c)*** Minimum energy required to produce photoelectric effect is

$$E = E_0 = h\nu_0 = 6.6\times 10^{-34}\times 1.3\times 10^{15}$$
$$= 8.58\times 10^{-19}\text{ J}$$

22. ***(c)*** Energy of a photon is given by

$$E = \frac{hc}{\lambda} = \frac{6.63\times 10^{-34}\text{ Js}\times 3\times 10^8\text{ ms}^{-1}}{300\times 10^{-9}\text{m}}$$

$\Rightarrow E = 6.63\times 10^{-19}$ J

Energy of 1 mole of photon

$= 6.63\times 10^{-19}\times 10^{-3}\times 6.02\times 10^{23}$ kJ mol^{-1}

$= 6.63\times 6.02\times 10 = 39.9\times 10 = 399$ kJ mol^{-1}

23. ***(3155)*** Bohr's radius of *n*th orbit is given by $r_n = a_0 n^2$.

$$mvr = \frac{nh}{2\pi}$$

For second Bohr orbit $n = 2, r_2 = (2)^2 r_0 = 4a_0$

$$\therefore \text{Kinetic energy} = \frac{n^2h^2}{8\pi^2 mr^2}$$

$$= \frac{4h^2}{8\pi^2 m(4a_0)^2} = \left(\frac{4}{8\pi^2\times 16}\right)\frac{h^2}{ma_0^2}$$

$$= \frac{h^2}{xma_0^2} \quad \text{(Given)}$$

$$x = \frac{16\times 8\pi^2}{4} \Rightarrow x = 315.507$$

$10x = 3155.07 \approx 3155$

24. ***(c)*** According to Bohr's atom, velocity of electron is given by,

$$v \propto \frac{Z}{n} \quad \text{...(i)}$$

From Eq. (i), velocity of electron is directly proportional to atomic number of atom, corresponding to positive charge. So, as Z increases, velocity also increases. Hence, statement I is false, while statement II is true.

25. ***(d)*** According to J.J. Thomson model of our atom, positive charge and mass of an atom is uniformely distributed and electrons are embedded in it like seeds in water melon.

Hence, if the model was considered correct then on striking α-particles (consisting of 2 positive charge protons and 2 neutral neutrons i.e. of heavier mass than 1 proton) on a thin gold foil would result passage of α-particles through the gold foil with reduced speed and these will be deflected by some angle (due to charge repulsion)

26. ***(b)*** Statement I is false, because Bohr's theory accounts for the stability and spectrum of single electronic species (e.g. He^+, Li^{2+} etc.) but Li^+ has two electrons.

Bohr's theory fails to explain splitting of spectral lines in presence of magnetic field i.e. Zeeman effect.

∴ Statement II is true.

27. ***(d)*** According to Bohr's theory,

I. $\text{KE} \propto \frac{Z^2}{n^2}$ or $13.6\left(\frac{Z^2}{n^2}\right)\frac{\text{(eV)}}{\text{(atom)}}$, (∴ Correct)

II. Velocity of electron $\propto \frac{Z}{n}$

(Here, Z = atomic number, n = number of shells)

$\therefore \quad v \times n \propto Z$ ($\therefore$ Incorrect)

III. Frequency of revolution of electron $= \frac{v}{2\pi r}$

Frequency $\propto \frac{Z^2}{n^3}$ $\left(\because v \propto \frac{Z}{n}, r \propto \frac{n^2}{Z}\right)$

($\therefore$ Incorrect)

IV. Coulombic force of attraction on the electron is given by

$$F = \frac{kq_1q_2}{r^2} = \frac{kZe^2}{r^2}$$

$$F = \frac{Z}{\left(\frac{n^2}{Z}\right)^2}$$

$$F \propto \frac{Z^3}{n^4}$$ ($\therefore$ Correct)

Hence, only I, and IV are correct.

28. ***(c)*** Bohr's radius is given by,

$$r = 0.529 \frac{n^2}{Z} \text{ Å}$$

For Li^{2+} $(r_{Li^{2+}})_{n=4} - (r_{Li^{2+}})_{n=3}$

$$\Rightarrow \frac{0.529}{3}(16-9) = \Delta R_1 \quad \text{...(i)}$$

For He^+ $(r_{He^+})_{n=4} - (r_{He^+})_{n=3}$

$$\Rightarrow \frac{0.529}{2}(16-9) = \Delta R_2 \quad \text{...(ii)}$$

$$\frac{\Delta R_1}{\Delta R_2} = \frac{\frac{0.529}{3}(16-9)}{\frac{0.529}{2}(16-9)} = \frac{2}{3}$$

Hence, the ratio of $\Delta R_1 : \Delta R_2$ is 2 : 3.

29. ***(b)*** Number of neutrons in protium (^1_1H) is zero (x).
Number of neutrons in deuterium (^2_1H or ^2_1D) is 1 (y)
Number of neutrons in tritium (^3_1H or ^3_1T) is 2 (z)
So, the sum of x, y and z is $x + y + z = 3$

30. ***(d)*** Statements I, II and III are correct.
While the statement IV is incorrect.
It's corrected form is as follows: Ionisation energy of hydrogen can be calculated from Lyman series lines ($n = 1$) only by using the following formula,

$$\bar{v} = R_H \left[\frac{1}{(1)^2} - \frac{1}{\infty^2}\right]$$

31. ***(1)*** $n\lambda = 2\pi r$
For 3rd excited state, $n = 4$

$$4\lambda = 2 \times \pi \times a_0 \frac{n^2}{z}$$

$$4\lambda = 2 \times 0.529 \frac{16}{2} \text{ Å}$$

$$\lambda = 2 \times 3.14 \times 0.529 \times 2 \text{ Å} = 6.64 \text{ Å}$$

32. ***(b)*** Energy level can be determined by comparing the value of $(n + l)$ value i.e. Bohr-Bury rule.

(A) $n = 4, l = 1 \Rightarrow (n + l) = 5$
(B) $n = 4, l = 2 \Rightarrow (n + l) = 6$
(C) $n = 3, l = 1 \Rightarrow (n + l) = 4$
(D) $n = 3, l = 2 \Rightarrow (n + l) = 5$
(E) $n = 4, l = 0 \Rightarrow (n + l) = 4$

For the same value of $n + l$, the orbital having higher values of n, will have more energy
So, the correct order is

C < E < D < A < B

33. ***(661)*** According to de-Broglie hypothesis

$$\lambda = \frac{h}{mv} \Rightarrow \lambda = \frac{hv}{mv^2}$$

$$\Rightarrow \frac{mv^2}{h} = \frac{v}{\lambda} \quad \left(\frac{v}{\lambda} = \text{Frequency } (\nu)\right)$$

$$\nu = \frac{mv^2}{h} = \frac{2R_H}{h} = \frac{2 \times 2.18 \times 10^{-18}}{6.6 \times 10^{-34}} = 660.6 \times 10^{13} \text{ Hz}$$

Nearest integer = 661

34. ***(6)*** For principal quantum number n, $l = 0$ to $n - 1$ and for each l, m_l will be $-l$ to $+l$.

$n = 4$

l	m_l
0	0
1	−1, 0, +1
2	−2, −1, 0, +1, +2
3	−3, −2, −1, 0, +1, +2, +3

So, number of electrons associated with $n = 4$, $|m_l| = 1$, $m_s = -\frac{1}{2}$ are 6.

Hence, total number of electrons is 6.

35. ***(4)*** The possible combination of $n = 4$ and $m_l = 0$ is

$n = 4, l = 0, m_l = 0$
$n = 4, l = 1, m_l = 0$
$n = 4, l = 2, m_l = 0$
$n = 4, l = 3, m_l = 0$

So, total 4 orbitals can be identified with $n = 4$ and $m_l = 0$.

36. ***(8)*** The de-Broglie's wavelength of an electron is given by

$$2\pi r_n = n\lambda_d$$

or $$2\pi a_0 \frac{n^2}{Z} = n\lambda_d \quad \left(\because r_n = \frac{a_0 n^2}{Z}\right)$$

Here $n = 4$, $Z = 1$

Substitute the value of n and Z in above equation, we get

$$2\pi a_0 \frac{(4)^2}{1} = 4\lambda_d \Rightarrow \lambda_d = 8\pi a_0$$

37. ***(a)*** Number of radial nodes is given by

$$n - l - 1$$

For $3p$ orbital, the value of $n = 3$, $l = 1$

So, number of radial nodes $= 3 - 1 - 1 = 1$

38. ***(a)*** According to de-Broglie hypothesis,

$$\lambda \propto \frac{1}{p} \text{ (momentum)}$$

$$\lambda = \frac{h}{p}$$

$\Rightarrow$ $\lambda p = h$ (constant)

So, the plot between λ and p is rectangular hyperbola.

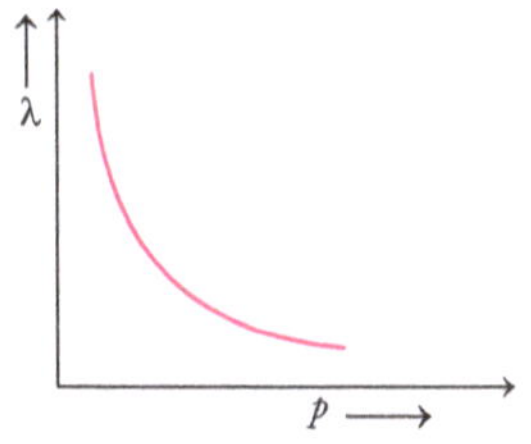

Hence, option (a) is correct.

39. ***(c)*** Electronic configuration of potassium is,

$$_{19}K = 1s^2 2s^2 2p^6 3s^2 3p^6 4s^1$$

Outermost orbital of K is 4s orbital.

For 4s,

n = Principal quantum number orbital = 4

l = Azimuthal quantum number = 0

m = Magnetic quantum number = 0

s = Spin quantum number = $\pm \frac{1}{2}$

Hence, option (c) is correct.

40. ***(c)*** Statement I is true but Statement II is false.

The correct form of Statement II is :

In hydrogen atom, $3p$ and $3d$ orbitals are degenerate orbitals as in single electron species, energy depends only on principal quantum number (n).

41. ***(c)*** $Z = 37$ (Rubidium)

Rb = [Kr] $5s^1$

$n = 5$ (Principal quantum number)

$l = 0$ (Azimuthal quantum number)

$m = 0$ (Magnetic quantum number)

$s = +\frac{1}{2}$, or $-\frac{1}{2}$ (spin-quantum number)

Hence, option (c) is correct.

42. ***(c)*** Using the formula of de-Broglie wavelength, $\lambda = \frac{h}{mv}$

also, angular momentum of an electron by Bohr is :

$$mvr = \frac{nh}{2\pi}$$

or

$$\frac{2\pi r}{n} = \frac{h}{mv}$$

$\therefore$ de-Broglie wavelength $\lambda = \frac{2\pi r}{n}$

de-Broglie wavelength of electron in 3rd orbit,

$$\lambda_3 = \frac{2\pi r_3}{n} \quad \ldots\text{(i)}$$

Also radius of 3rd orbit,

$$r_3 = \text{radius of 1st orbit} \times n^2$$

$$r_3 = a_0 \times n^2$$

$$\frac{r_3}{n} = a_0 \times n \quad \ldots\text{(ii)}$$

From Eqs. (i) and (ii) $\lambda_3 = 2\pi a_0 \times n$

for 3rd orbit, $n = 3$

$\therefore$ $\lambda_3 = 6\pi a_0$

43. ***(3)*** Statements given in (a), (d) and (e) are correct while, (b) and (c) are incorrect.

For $2s$ orbital, the probability density first decreases and then increases.

Boundary surface diagram of orbitals encloses a region of high probability (Not 100%) of finding an electron.

44. ***(3)*** Number of radial nodes in an orbital is given as $n - l - 1$

$7s : n = 7, l = 0;\ 7 - 0 - 1 = 6$

$7p : n = 7, l = 1;\ 7 - 1 - 1 = 5$

$6s : n = 6, l = 0;\ 6 - 0 - 1 = 5$

$8p : n = 8, l = 1;\ 8 - 1 - 1 = 6$

$8d : n = 8, l = 2;\ 8 - 2 - 1 = 5$

45. ***(7)*** Given, Kinetic energy = 4.5×10^{-29} J

Mass of electron = 9.1×10^{-31} kg

$$h = 6.626 \times 10^{-34} \text{ Js}$$

Wavelength of an electron = ?

We know that,

$$\text{wavelength } (\lambda) = \frac{h}{\sqrt{2KE\, m_e}} = \frac{6.626 \times 10^{-34} \text{ Js}}{\sqrt{2 \times 4.5 \times 10^{-29} \times 9.1 \times 10^{-31}}}$$

$$= 7.3 \times 10^{-5} \text{ m}$$

So, wavelength is $\lambda \approx 7 \times 10^{-5}$ m

46. ***(2)*** Statements (a) and (c) are correct while statements (b) and (d) are incorrect.

The characteristic of electrons emitted do not depend upon the material of the electrode of the cathode ray tube.

Nature of emitted electrons does not depend on nature of gas present in cathode ray tube.

47. ***(b)*** We know that, at node

$$\psi_{2s} = 0$$

So, $\left(2 - \frac{r}{a_0}\right) = 0$

$\Rightarrow$ If, $r = r_0 \Rightarrow 2 - \frac{r_0}{a_0} = 0$

$$2 = \frac{r_0}{a_0} \text{ or } r_0 = 2a_0$$

Thus, option (b) is correct.

48. ***(5)*** p_x, p_y, p_z, d_{z^2} and $d_{x^2-y^2}$ orbitals have electron density along the axis.

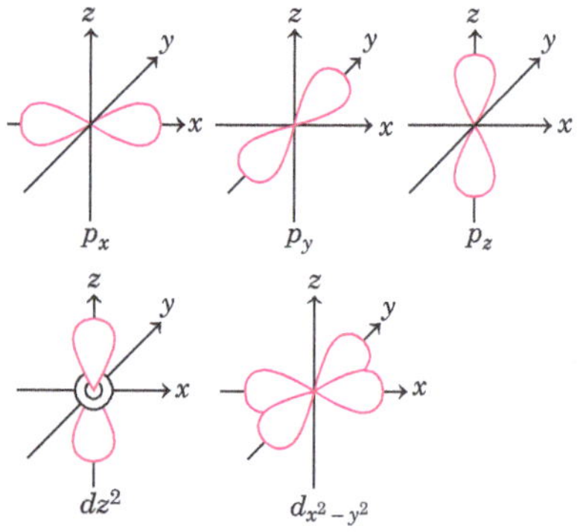

d_{xy} and d_{yz} have electron density between the axis.

49. ***(2)*** The de-Broglie wavelength of electron is given by

$$\lambda = \frac{h}{\sqrt{2mKE}} \Rightarrow KE = \frac{h^2}{2m\lambda^2}$$

$$= \frac{(6.626 \times 10^{-34})^2}{2 \times 9.1 \times 10^{-31} \times (3.3 \times 10^{-10})^2}$$

$KE = 2.215 \times 10^{-18}$

$E_{abs} = E_{req} + KE$

$$\frac{E_{abs}}{E_{req}} = 1 + \frac{KE}{E_{req}} = 1 + \frac{2.215 \times 10^{-18}}{13.6 \times 1.602 \times 10^{-19}} = 2.01 \simeq 2$$

50. ***(a)*** Energies of the orbitals in the same subshell decrease with increase in the atomic number (Z), e.g., energy of $2s$ orbital of hydrogen atom is greater than that of $2s$ orbital of lithium and that of lithium is greater than that of sodium and so on, i.e.,

So, $E_{2s}(H) > E_{2s}(Li) > E_{2s}(Na) > E_{2s}(K)$.

51. ***(1758)*** We know that wavelength,

$$\lambda = \frac{h}{mv}$$

$\therefore$ Wavelength of electron,

$$\lambda_e = \frac{h}{m_e \times v_e}$$

Wavelength of neutron,

$$\lambda_N = \frac{h}{m_N \times v_N} \Rightarrow \lambda_e = \lambda_N \quad \text{(given)}$$

when $v_e = xv_N$ ...(i)

$$\frac{h}{m_e \times v_e} = \frac{h}{m_N \times v_N} \quad \text{...(ii)}$$

By substituting Eq. (i) in Eq. (ii), we get

$$\frac{h}{m_e \times x \times v_N} = \frac{h}{m_N \times v_N} \Rightarrow x = \frac{m_N}{m_e}$$

m_N (mass of neutron) $= 1.6 \times 10^{-27}$

m_e (mass of electron) $= 9.1 \times 10^{-31}$

$$\Rightarrow \quad x = \frac{1.6 \times 10^{-27}}{9.1 \times 10^{-31}} = 1758$$

52. ***(b)*** The point at which the probability of finding an electron is zero is known as node or nodal surface. Number of nodes in any orbital $= n - l - 1$

In case of $2s$-orbital, number of nodes $= 2 - 0 - 1 = 1$

The correct plot for $\psi^2(r)$ as function of distance 'r'.

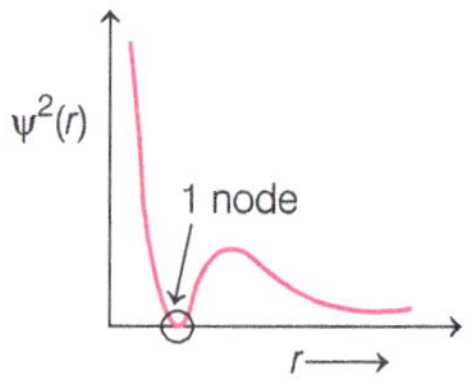

53. ***(d)*** Statement A, B and C are correct while statement D is incorrect. The correct explanation is given as

Total number of nodes present in atomic orbital is given by the formula $n - 1$, where n is principal quantum number.

So, the formula "$n - 2$" is incorrect.

54. ***(c)*** Statements A, C and D are correct while Statements B and E are incorrect.

The correct form of statements B and E are as follows

Azimuthal quantum number 'l' can have values from 0 to $(n-1)$ for a given 'n'. It describes the sub-shell and orbital angular momentum.

For any value of 'l', total number of orbitals are given by $(2l + 1)$ formula. So, for $l = 5$,

Total number of orbitals $= 2l + 1 = 2 \times 5 + 1 = 11$

55. ***(b)*** Electrons pair of the same shells and the same subshell have same energy and these electrons pairs are found in degenerated orbitals. So, only pairs of electron of (B) are present in degenerate orbitals as $n + l$ values in both are cases are same

(a) $n = 3, l = 2, \ n + l = 3 + 2 = 5$

(b) $n = 3, l = 2, n + l = 3 + 2 = 5$

56. ***(7)*** Ge ($Z = 32$) electronic configuration is

$$1s^2\, 2s^2\, 2p^6\, 3s^2 3p^6 3d^{10} 4s^2 4p^2$$

Thus, it has 7 fully filled orbital with $m_l = 0$

57. ***(0)*** The electronic configuration of Ga^+ is

$$1s^2 2s^2 2p^6 3s^2 3p^6 3d^{10} 4s^2$$

So, the valence electron is in s-orbital.

Hence, Azimuthal quantum No. (l) for valence shell electron is zero.

58. ***(9)*** Given, $(\lambda) = 248\ \text{nm} = 2480\ \text{Å}$

Threshold energy = 3.0 eV

de-Broglie wavelength is given by

$$\lambda = \frac{h}{mv} \Rightarrow \lambda = \frac{h}{\sqrt{2m\,(KE)}}$$

Putting mass of electron,

$m_e = 9.1 \times 10^{-31}$ kg

Charge of electron, $q = 1.6 \times 10^{-19}$ C

$$\lambda = \frac{0.491 \times 10^{-18}}{\sqrt{KE}} \quad \text{...(i)}$$

We know,

$$E_{\text{applied}} = \phi + \text{KE}_{\text{max}} \quad \ldots\text{(ii)}$$

$$E_{\text{applied}} = \frac{12400}{\text{l (Å)}} = \frac{12400}{2480} = 5\,\text{eV}$$

Putting value in Eq. (ii),

$$5 = 3 + \text{KE}_{\text{max}}$$

$$\Rightarrow \text{KE}_{\text{max}} = 2\text{ eV} = 2 \times 1.6 \times 10^{-19}\text{ J}$$

$$\lambda_e = \frac{0.49 \times 10^{-18}}{\sqrt{2 \times 1.6 \times 10^{-19}}} = 8.6$$

$$\lambda_e = 0.086 \times 10^{-8}\text{ m} \Rightarrow \lambda_e = 8.6\,\text{Å}$$

Nearest integer = 9

59. ***(d)*** The correct plot for 3*s*-orbital is

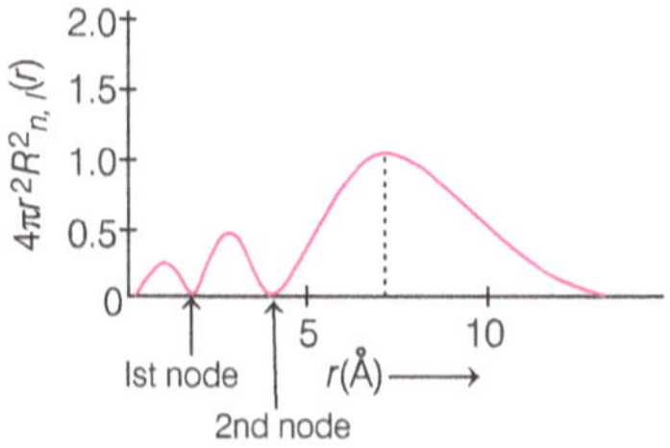

For 3*s*,

value of l = 0

value of n = 3

Number of radial nodes $= n - l - 1$

$= 3 - 0 - 1 = 2$

In graph *D*, two nodes are present, so this is the correct plot for 3*s*-orbital.

60. ***(2)*** Given, mass of Li^{3+} = 8.3 times of mass of proton formula,

De-Broglie wavelength,

$$\lambda = \frac{h}{\sqrt{2mqV}}$$

$$\lambda_{\text{Li}} = \frac{h}{\sqrt{2m_{\text{Li}}(3e)V}} \quad \ldots\text{(i)}$$

$$\lambda_{\text{P}} = \frac{h}{\sqrt{2m_{\text{P}}(e)V}} \quad \ldots\text{(ii)}$$

Divide Eq. (i) by Eq. (ii)

$$\frac{\lambda_{\text{Li}}}{\lambda_{\text{P}}} = \sqrt{\frac{m_{\text{P}}(e)V}{m_{\text{Li}}(3e)V}}$$

We know that $m_{\text{Li}} = 8.3\, m_p$

$$\frac{\lambda_{\text{Li}}}{\lambda_{\text{P}}} = \sqrt{\frac{m_{\text{P}} \times e \times V}{8.3\, m_{\text{P}} \times 3e \times V}}$$

$$= \sqrt{\frac{1}{8.3 \times 3}} = \frac{1}{5} = 0.2$$

$$= 2 \times 10^{-1}$$

Hence, $x \times 10^{-1}$, $x = 2$

61. ***(c)***

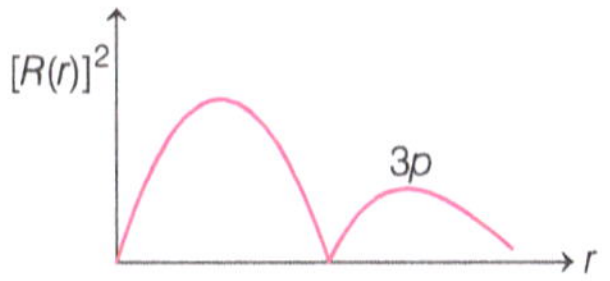

ψ^2 (Probability density) can be zero for 3*p* orbital other than infinite distance.

Since, $n = 3$, $l = 1$ for 3*p* orbital, the number of radial nodes $= 3 - 1 - 1 = 1$

62. ***(b)*** Hypothetical situation :

Azimuthal quantum number (l) = 0 – (n + 1)

n = Principal quantum number

For, $n = 1$, l = 0, 1, 2

↓ ↓ ↓

1s 1*p* 1*d*

$1s^2$ $1p^6$ $1d^{10}$

Number of electrons in *s*-orbital = 2

Number of electrons in *p*-orbital = 6

Number of electrons in *d*-orbital = 10

Z = 13 (Half-filled valence sub-shell)

For $n = 1$, $1s^2 1p^6 1d^5$ (Z = 13)

Number of electrons in 1*d*-orbital are 5. (It is half-filled).

Element with atomic number 9 is not first alkali metal but a *d*-block element with electronic configuration $1s^2 1p^6 1d^1$.

Atomic number 6 has $1s^2 1p^4$ electronic configuration, so it has 1*p* valence subshell, not 2*p*.

First noble gas has atomic number 2 not 8.

63. ***(c)*** The de-Broglie wavelength of an electron,

$$\lambda = \frac{h}{p}, \text{ or } \frac{h}{mv}$$

But, from the Bohr's postulate of quantisation of angular momentum of electrons, $l = mvr = \dfrac{nh}{2\pi}$,

$$\therefore \quad mv = \frac{nh}{2\pi r}$$

Upon substitution,

$$\lambda = \frac{h}{\left(\dfrac{nh}{2\pi r}\right)} = \frac{2\pi r}{n},$$

where, r is the radius of orbits in Bohr model $r = \dfrac{n^2 a_0}{Z}$

$$\therefore \lambda = \frac{2\pi \times n^2 \times a_0}{n \times Z} = \frac{2\pi n a_0}{Z} = 8\pi a_0 \quad \begin{Bmatrix} Z = 1 \text{ for hydrogen} \\ n = 4 \text{ (given)} \end{Bmatrix}$$

Practice Element 02 : Target JEE Advanced

1. ***(a)*** $\text{KE} = kT = \dfrac{R}{N_0}T$

where, $k = \dfrac{R}{N_0}$ (Boltzmann constant)

$$KE = \frac{8.314\ \text{J mol}^{-1}\ \text{K}^{-1} \times 300\ \text{K}}{6.02 \times 10^{23}\ \text{mol}^{-1}} = 4.1432 \times 10^{-21}\ \text{J}$$

m(neutron) $= 1.675 \times 10^{-27}$ kg

$$\therefore\ \lambda = \frac{h}{mv} = \frac{h}{\sqrt{2m\,KE}}$$

$$= \frac{6.626 \times 10^{-34}\ \text{Js}}{\sqrt{2 \times 1.675 \times 10^{-27} \times 4.143 \times 10^{-21}}}$$

$$= 1.778 \times 10^{-10}\ \text{m} = 177.8\ \times 10^{-12}\ \text{m} \approx 178\,\text{pm}$$

1×10^{-12} m $= 1$ pm

2. ***(b)*** Most probable distance is when

$$\frac{d}{dr}[4\pi r^2 \psi^2] = 0$$

$$\frac{d}{dr}[4\pi r^2\ Ne^{-2Zr/a_0}] = 0$$

$$\left[4\pi(2r)Ne^{-2Zr/a_0} + 4\pi r^2\left(-\frac{2Z}{a_0}\right)Ne^{-2Zr/a_0}\right] = 0$$

$$8\pi r Ne^{-2Zr/a_0}\left[1 - \frac{rZ}{a_0}\right] = 0 \quad \text{or} \quad 1 - \frac{rZ}{a_0} = 0,\ r = \left(\frac{a_0}{Z}\right)$$

3. ***(d)*** Highest electron density is at the nucleus thus A is 1s and B is 2s.

4. ***(c)*** Cl (17) $= 1s^2\ 2s^2, 2p^6, 3s^2, 3p^5$

↿⇂	↿⇂	↿

$3p^5$ ↑
Unpaired electron

$$n = 3, l = 1, m = -1 \text{ or } 0 \text{ or } +1, s = +\frac{1}{2} \text{ or } -\frac{1}{2}$$

5. ***(b)*** According to Bohr's model, the kinetic energy is given by,

$$K.E = +\ 13.6 \times \frac{Z^2}{n^2}$$

- First orbit of H-atom

$n = 1, Z = 1$

K.E $= +\ 13.6$ eV

- Second orbit of Be^{3+}

$n = 2, Z = 4$

$$KE = +13.6 \times \frac{(4)^2}{(2)^2} = +\ 54.4\,\text{eV}$$

Second orbit of Li^{2+}

$n = 2, Z = 3$

$$K.E = +\ 13.6 \times \frac{(3)^2}{(2)^2} = +\ 30.6\,\text{eV}$$

- Second orbit of He^{+}

$n = 2, Z = 2$

K.E $= +\ 13.6$ eV

Thus, the highest energy is associated with second orbit of Be^{3+}.

6. ***(d)*** Using de-Broglie equation,

$$\lambda = \frac{h}{\sqrt{2m\,KE}}$$

$$\therefore\quad \lambda^2 = \frac{h^2}{(2m)KE} \Rightarrow (KE) = \frac{h^2}{2m\lambda^2}$$

$$(KE) \propto \frac{1}{m\lambda^2} \Rightarrow \frac{(KE)_x}{(KE)_y} = \frac{m_y\lambda_y^2}{m_x\lambda_x^2}$$

Given, $\lambda_x = 1\,\text{nm}$

$\lambda_y = 4\,\text{nm}$

$m_x = 9m_y$

$$\therefore\quad \frac{(KE)_x}{(KE)_y} = \frac{m_y(4)^2}{9m_y(1)^2} = \frac{16}{9}$$

7. ***(d)*** $E = h\nu = \dfrac{hc}{\lambda}$

$$= \frac{6.626 \times 10^{-34}\ \text{Js} \times 3 \times 10^8\ \text{ms}^{-1}}{300 \times 10^{-9}\ \text{m}} = 6.626 \times 10^{-19}\ \text{J}$$

$$= \frac{6.626 \times 10^{-19}\,\text{J}}{1.6 \times 10^{-19}\ \text{J eV}^{-1}} = 4\ \text{eV}$$

Thus, any metal with threshold frequency less than 4.14 eV can emit electrons by this wavelength.

These metals are Li, Na, K and Mg

8. ***(b)*** Angular nodes $= l$, Radial nodes $= (n - l - 1)$

For $3d$, $n = 3, l = 2$

Thus, angular nodes $= 2$

radial nodes $= (3 - 2 - 1) = 0$

nodal planes $= 2$

9. ***(d)*** From Heisenberg uncertainity

$$\Delta x \cdot \Delta p \geq \frac{h}{4\pi}$$

$$\Delta x = 1.0\ \text{nm} = 10^{-9}\ \text{m}$$

$$\Delta p_e = 5.0 \times 10^{-26}\ \text{kg m/s}$$

$$\Delta p \geq \frac{h}{4\pi \cdot \Delta x}$$

$$= \frac{6.626 \times 10^{-34}\ \text{Js}}{4\pi\,(1.0 \times 10^{-9}\ \text{m})}$$

$$= 5.28 \times 10^{-26}\ \text{kg m/s}$$

$$\Delta p_{He} = 5.0 \times 10^{-26}\ \text{kg m/s}$$

10. ***(b)*** Frequency, $\nu = R_H Z^2 c\left[\dfrac{1}{n_1^2} - \dfrac{1}{n_2^2}\right]$

Case I For He^+, $n_1 = 2, n_2 = 4$

$$\therefore\ \nu_{(He^+)} = R_H(2)^2\,c\left[\frac{1}{(2)^2} - \frac{1}{(4)^2}\right] = 4R_H c\left[\frac{3}{16}\right] = \frac{3}{4}R_H c$$

Case II For H

$$\nu\,(H) = R_H\,c\left[\frac{1}{n_1^2} - \frac{1}{n_2^2}\right]$$

Given, $\nu(He^+) = \nu(H)$

$$\therefore \quad \left[\frac{1}{n_1^2} - \frac{1}{n_2^2}\right] = \frac{3}{4}$$

If $n_1 = 1$, $n_2 = 2$, then $\left[\frac{1}{1^2} - \frac{1}{2^2}\right] = \frac{3}{4}$

11. ***(c)*** Among the given match, (c) is incorrectly matched while other are correct.

$$E = h\nu = \frac{hc}{\lambda} = hc\bar{\nu}$$

where, $\frac{1}{\lambda} = \bar{\nu}$ (wave number)

$\bar{\nu} = 100\ m^{-1}$

$\therefore E = 6.626 \times 10^{-34}$ Js $\times 3 \times 10^8$ ms$^{-1} \times 100$ m^{-1}

$= 1.987 \times 10^{-23}$ J per atom

$\approx 2 \times 10^{-23}$ J per atom (correct)

$= 2 \times 10^{-23} \times 6.02 \times 10^{23}$ J mol^{-1} of photons

$= 12.04$ J mol^{-1} of photons.

$E = 1.2 \times 10^{-2}$ kJ mol^{-1} of photons (correct)

$E = 2 \times 10^{-23} \times 1 \times 10^7$ ergs per photon

$= 2 \times 10^{-16}$ ergs per photon (incorrect)

$$E = \frac{1.204 \times 10^{-2} \text{ kJ mol}^{-1}}{8.314 \times 10^{-3} \text{ kJ mol}^{-1}} \times 2 \times 10^{-3} \text{ kcal mol}^{-1}$$

$= 2.9 \times 10^{-3}$kcal mol^{-1} (correct)

Thus, (a), (b) and (d) are correct.

12. ***(a, b, c)*** Among the given statements, (a), (b) and (c) are correct while statement (d) is incorrect. Their explanation are give as

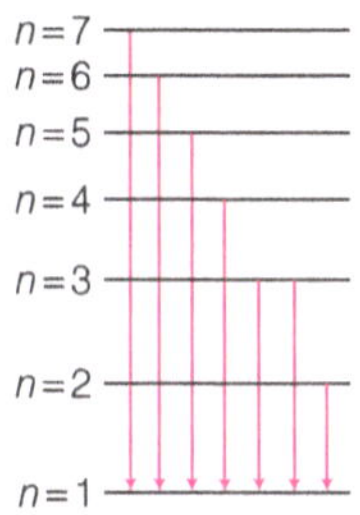

Electron falls from 7th, 6th, 5th, ... to 1st level.

Thus, total lines = 7

Thus (a) is correct.

Since, electron falls to first level, hence Lyman series.

Thus, (b) is correct

$$\bar{\nu} = R_H Z^2 \left[\frac{1}{n_1^2} - \frac{1}{n_2^2}\right]$$

For ,minimum $\bar{\nu}$, $n_1 = 1$ and $n_2 = (n_1 + 1)$

$$\therefore \quad \bar{\nu}_{min} = R_H (3)^2 \left(\frac{1}{1^2} - \frac{1}{2^2}\right) = 6.75\, R_H$$

Thus, (c) is correct.

13. ***(a, b, c)*** Among the given statements, (a), (b) and (c) are correct while the statement (d) is incorrect. Its correct form is—

- The probability density of electrons in 2*s*-orbital first increases then decreases and after that if increases again as distance increases from nucleus.

14. ***(a, d)*** Among the given statements, (a) and (d) are incorrect while (b) and (c) are correct.

The correct form of (a) and (d) are

- The *d*-orbitals for which *n* is greater than 3 have different shapes and size.
- For a given shell, the Z_{eff} experienced by the electron decreases with increase of azimuthal quantum number.

15. ***(a, b, c, d)*** Among the given statements, all the correct.

- As temperature increases, distribution of frequency ν (and energy *E*) increases. Thus, correct.
- As temperature *T* increases ($T_1 < T_2 < T_3$), radiation emitted is shifted to lower wavelength i.e. higher frequency. Thus, correct.
- All types of radiations have same speed. Thus, correct.

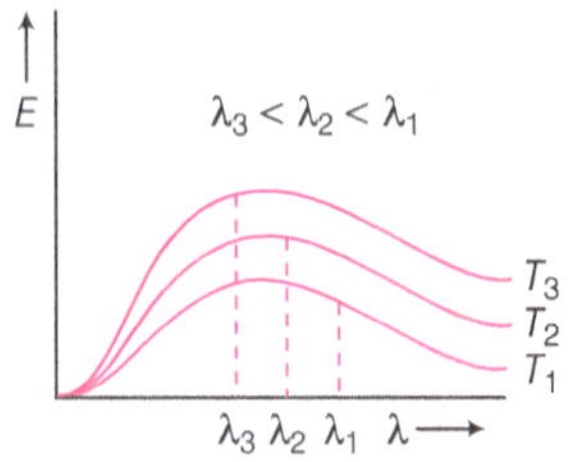

16. ***(a, b, c, d)*** Among the given statements, all statements are correct.

(a) $r = 0.529\,Å \times n^2 / Z$

Hence, $r \propto \frac{1}{Z}$ and $E \propto Z^2$

(– ve sign signifies the release of energy when the electron approaches nearer to the nucleus)

(b) E_H (for $n = 4$) $= -13.6 \times Z^2 / n^2$

$= (-13.6 \times 1/(4)^2 = -0.85$ eV

$E_{He^{\oplus}}$ (for $n = 4$) $= -13.6 \times (2)^2/(4)^2 = -3.4$ eV

$E_H(-0.85) > E_{He^{\oplus}}(-3.4)$

(c) As we know,

$$r = \frac{n^2h^2}{4\pi^2 m Ze^2}$$

$$\therefore \quad \frac{r_2}{r_4} = \frac{(2)^2}{(4)^2} = \frac{2 \times 2}{4 \times 4}$$

$$\frac{r_2}{r_4} = \frac{1}{4}$$

$r_4 = 4r_2$

(d) Ground state binding energy $= 13.6 \times Z^2 = 122.4$ eV

$\therefore \quad Z = 3$

First excitation energy $= 10.2 \times Z^2$

$= 10.2 \times (3)^2$

$= 91.8$ eV

Therefore, 80 eV photon can not excite it to a higher state.

17. ***(a, b)*** Among the given statements, (a) and (b) are incorrect while (c) and (d) statements are correct.

Their explanation are given as below

As we know,

(a) $\lambda = \frac{h}{\sqrt{2mkT}}$

$$\frac{\lambda_1}{\lambda_2} = \sqrt{\frac{T_2}{T_1}} = \sqrt{\frac{2700}{300}} = 3$$

$\lambda_1 = 3\lambda_2$

(b) $\lambda_e = \frac{h}{m_e v_e}$, $\lambda_n = \frac{h}{m_n v_n}$

$$\frac{h}{m_e v_e} = \frac{h}{m_n v_n}$$

$$v_n = \frac{m_e v_e}{m_n} = \frac{1}{1840} \times v_e \qquad \left[\because m_e = \frac{1}{1840} m_n\right]$$

(c) de Broglie wavelength $(\lambda) = \frac{h}{p}$

or Δx (uncertainty in position) $= \frac{h}{p}$

$\therefore \Delta x \cdot \Delta p = \frac{h}{4\pi}$ or $\frac{h}{p} \times \Delta p = \frac{h}{4\pi}$

$$\frac{\Delta p}{p} = \frac{1}{4\pi} \text{ or } \frac{m \times \Delta v}{m \times v} = \frac{1}{4\pi} \text{ or } \frac{\Delta v}{v} = \frac{1}{4\pi}$$

$\therefore$ % uncertainty in velocity $= \frac{\Delta v}{v} = \frac{1}{4\pi} \times 100$

$$= \frac{100}{4 \times 3.14} = 7.96 \approx 8\%$$

(d) $\lambda \propto \frac{1}{\sqrt{K.E}} = \sqrt{\frac{K.E_2}{K.E_1}} = \frac{\lambda_1}{\lambda_2} = \frac{\lambda_1}{(1 - 0.02)\lambda_1} = \frac{\lambda_1}{0.98\lambda_1}$

$\therefore$ $KE_1 = (0.98)^2 KE_2 = 0.96\, KE_2$

% change in KE $= \frac{K.E_2 - K.E_1}{K.E_1}$

$$= \frac{(K.E_2 - 0.96 K.E_2) \times 100}{K.E_1}$$

$$= \frac{(1 - 0.96)}{0.96} \times 100 \approx 4\%$$

18. ***(a, d)*** Among the given statements, (a) and (d) are incorrect while (b) and (c) are correct. Their explanation are given as

(a) No. of visible lines = 3

($5 \to 2$, $4 \to 2$, $3 \to 2$) visible region corresponds to $n = 2$.

(b) Radius of ground state of H-atom = 0.529 Å

$\therefore 0.529 = 0.529 \times n^2 / Z$ (Z for $Be^{+3} = 4$)

$0.529 = 0.529 n^2 / 4$

$\therefore \quad n = 2$

(c) IE (for H like atom) = IE (for H atom) $\times Z^2$

$$\therefore \quad Z^2 = \frac{11180}{1312} = 8.521$$

$Z = \sqrt{8.521} = 2.917 \approx 3$

(d) As we know $V \propto \frac{1}{n}$

So, $\frac{V_1}{V_2} = \frac{n_2}{n_1} = \frac{5}{3}$

So, the ratio of velocity of the electron in the third and fifth orbit will be 5 : 3.

19. ***(a, b, c, d)*** Among the given statements, all statements are correct about Hund's rule.

20. ***(40.5)*** The Bohr's radius of an orbit in atom is given by,

$$r_n = \frac{52.9 \times n^2}{Z} \text{ pm}$$

when $n = n_2$ [For Be; Z = 4]

$$138.2 = \frac{52.9 \times n_2^2}{4} \cdot n_2^2 = 10.44; n_2 = 3.23 \approx 3$$

When, $n = n_1$

$$46.44 = \frac{52.9 \times n_1^2}{4}$$

$n_1^2 = 3.51$; $n_1 = 1.87$, $n_1 \approx 2$

Now, the wavelength of the emitted photon can calculated from, $\frac{1}{\lambda} = RZ^2\left(\frac{1}{n_1^2} - \frac{1}{n_2^2}\right)$

$$\frac{1}{\lambda} = R \times 16 \times \left(\frac{1}{4} - \frac{1}{9}\right) \Rightarrow 16R \times \frac{5}{36} = 2.22\, R$$

$$\frac{hc}{\lambda} = 2.22R = 2.22 \times 2.2 \times 10^{-18} \text{ J}$$

$$\lambda = \frac{6.6 \times 10^{-34} \times 3 \times 10^8}{2.2 \times 10^{-18} \text{ J} \times 2.22} \text{ m} = 4.05 \times 10^{-8} \text{ m} = 40.5 \text{ nm}$$

So, the wavelength of the emitted photon during the transition is 40.5 nm.

21. ***(9.1)*** Wavelength of photon absorbed,

$\lambda = 450$ nm $= 450 \times 10^{-9}$ m

Planck's constant, $h = 6.6 \times 10^{-34}$ Js

Molar mass of B,

$M = 10$ g mol^{-1} $= 10 \times 10^{-3}$ kg mol^{-1}

Mass of one atom of B, $m = \frac{M}{N_A}$

$$= \frac{10 \times 10^{-3}}{6 \times 10^{23}} = \frac{10}{6} \times 10^{-26} \text{ kg}$$

Using, de-Broglie equation, $\lambda = \frac{h}{mv}$

$$v = \frac{h}{m\lambda} = \frac{6.6 \times 10^{-34}}{1.6 \times 10^{-26} \times 450 \times 10^{-9}}$$

$= 0.00916 \times 10^{-34} \times 10^{35}$

$= 0.0091 \times 10 = 0.091$ m/s $= 9.1$ cm/s

22. ***(174)*** $O_2 \rightarrow O + O^*$

Energy of O^* = Energy of O + 1.967 eV

Dissociation energy of O_2 = 498 kJ mol^{-1}

$$= \frac{498 \times 1000 \text{ J}}{6.02 \times 10^{23}} = 8.27 \times 10^{-19} \text{ J molecule}^{-1}$$

Energy required to convert O to O^* = 1.967 eV atom^{-1}

$$= 1.967 \times 1.6 \times 10^{-19} \text{ J atom}^{-1}$$

$$= 3.15 \times 10^{-19} \text{ J atom}^{-1}$$

Thus, total energy required to convert O_2 into O and O^*

$$= (8.27 \times 10^{-19} + 3.15 \times 10^{19}) \text{ J molecule}^{-1}$$

$$= 11.42 \times 10^{-19} \text{ J}$$

$$\lambda = \frac{hc}{E} = \frac{6.626 \times 10^{-34} \text{ Js} \times 3 \times 10^8 \text{ ms}^{-1}}{11.42 \times 10^{-19} \text{J}}$$

$$\approx 174 \times 10^{-9} \text{ m} = 174 \text{ nm}$$

23. ***(4)*** Among the given statements four statement i.e, B, C, D and E are correct while statement A is incorrect. Its correct form is

(A) (i) $\Delta E_{2E \rightarrow E} = E - 2E = \dfrac{hc}{\lambda_1}$

$$= -E = \frac{hc}{\lambda_1} \Rightarrow hc = -E\lambda_1 \quad \text{...(i)}$$

(ii) $\Delta E_{4E/3 \rightarrow E} = E - 4E/3 = \dfrac{hc}{\lambda_2}$

$$= \frac{-E}{3} = \frac{hc}{\lambda_2}$$

$$\Rightarrow \quad \lambda_2 = \frac{-3hc}{E} \quad \text{...(ii)}$$

Substituting the value of hc from equation (1) in equation (2)

$$\lambda_2 = \frac{-3}{E} \times -E\lambda_1 = 3\lambda_1$$

$$\therefore \quad \lambda_2 = 3\lambda_1$$

B. According of Einstein :

Maximum K.E of ejected electron

= Absorbed energy – Work function

$$\frac{1}{2} mv_{max}^2 = (h\nu - h\nu_0) = hc\left[\frac{1}{\lambda} - \frac{1}{\lambda_0}\right]$$

where ν_0 and λ_0 are threshold frequency and threshold wavelength respectively. Stopping potential is the minimum potential at which the photoelectric current becomes zero. If V_0 is the stopping potential then,

$$eV_0 = h(\nu - \nu_0)$$

$$\therefore \quad V_0 = \frac{h(\nu - \nu_0)}{e}$$

C. It is clear from the graph

D and E statements are also correct.

24. ***(98.126)*** By ideal gas equation,

$$pV = nRT = n(\text{moles}) = \frac{pV}{RT}$$

$$= \frac{1 \text{ atm} \times 1 \text{ dm}^3}{0.0821 \text{ dm}^3 \text{atm mol}^{-1} \text{ K}^{-1} \times 298 \text{ K}} = 0.04087 \text{ mol}$$

Bond dissociation energy = 436 kJ mol^{-1}

Thus, energy required to dissociate

0.04087 mol H_2 = 0.04087 × 436 = 17.81932 kJ

No. of H-atom = 0.04087 × 2 × 6.02 × 10^{23}

= 4.9207 × 10^{22} H-atom

Due to electronic transition of H-atom

$$\Delta E = 13.6\left[\frac{1}{n_1^2} - \frac{1}{n_2^2}\right] \text{eV} = 13.6 \times 1.6 \times 10^{-19}\left[\frac{1}{n_1^2} - \frac{1}{n_2^2}\right] \text{J}$$

First excited represents $n_2 = 2$

$$\text{Thus, } \Delta E = 13.6 \times 1.6 \times 10^{-19}\left[\frac{1}{1^2} - \frac{1}{2^2}\right] \text{J atom}^{-1}$$

$$= \frac{3}{4} \times 13.6 \times 1.6 \times 10^{-19} \text{ atom}^{-1}$$

Total transition energy of 4.9207 × 10^{22} H-atoms

$$= \frac{3}{4} \times 13.6 \times 1.6 \times 10^{-19} \times 4.9207 \times 10^{22} \text{ J}$$

$$= 80306 \text{ J} = 80.306 \text{ kJ}$$

Thus, total energy (conversion of H_2 to H and then excitation to $n_2 = 2$)

$$= 17.82 + 80.306 = 98.126 \text{ kJ}$$

25. ***(2)*** As we know,

$$\frac{1}{\lambda} = R_H Z^2\left(\frac{1}{n_1^2} - \frac{1}{n_2^2}\right)$$

$$\frac{1}{3 \times 10^{-8} \text{m}} = 1.097 \times 10^7 Z^2\left(\frac{1}{1} - \frac{1}{4}\right)$$

$$= \frac{3}{4} \times 1.097 \times 10^7 Z^2$$

$$Z^2 = \frac{4}{9 \times 1.097 \times 10^{-1}} = 4.05$$

$$Z = 2(\text{He}^+)$$

Hence, the atomic number will be 2.

26. ***(506)*** By Einstein's equation of photoelectric effect

$$h\nu = h\nu_0 + \frac{1}{2} mv^2$$

$$h\nu_0 = 3.44 \times 10^{-18} \text{ J} \quad \text{(given)}$$

$$\frac{1}{2} mv^2 = \frac{1}{2} \times 9.1 \times 10^{-31} \text{ kg } (1.03 \times 10^6)^2 \text{ m}^2\text{s}^{-2}$$

$$= 4.83 \times 10^{-19} \text{ J}$$

(**Note** 1 kg m^{2}s^{-2} = 1 J)

$$\therefore h\nu = 3.44 \times 10^{-18} \text{ J} + 4.83 \times 10^{-19} \text{ J} = 3.923 \times 10^{-18} \text{ J}$$

$$\frac{hc}{\lambda} = 3.923 \times 10^{-18} \text{ J}$$

$$\therefore \lambda = \frac{6.626 \times 10^{-34} \text{Js} \times 3 \times 10^8 \text{ms}^{-1}}{3.923 \times 10^{-18} \text{ J}} = 5.06 \times 10^{-8} \text{ m}$$

$$\approx 506 \text{ Å}$$

27. ***(25)*** In the presence of magnetic field, there is splitting of lines (Zeeman's effect)

Total lines = Total orbitals = $(2l + 1)$

Thus, total degeneracy = $(2l + 1)$

	l	Degeneracy
s	0	1
p	1	3
d	2	5
f	3	7
g	4	9

Hence, the sum of degeneracy of s, p, d, f and g sub-orbits is 25.

28. ***(c)*** The correct match is

A-III, B-IV, C-I, D-II

• $4f; n = 4, l = 3$

nodes $= (n-1) = 4-1 = 3$

Radial nodes $= (n-l-1) = 4-3-1 = 1-1 = 0$

$(n-1) + (n-l-1) = 3 + 0 = 3$

• $6d; n = 6, l = 2$

$(n-1) = 6-1 = 5$

$(n-l-1) = 6-2-1 = 3$

Sum of nodes $(n-1)$ and radial nodes $(n-l-1) = 5+3 = 8$

• $6s; n = 6, l = 0$

$(n-1) = 6-1 = 5$

$(n-l-1) = 6-0-1 = 5$

Sum of nodes $(n-1)$ and radial nodes $(n-l-1) = 5+5 = 10$

• $7s; n = 7, l = 0$

$(n-1) = 7-1 = 6$

$(n-l-1) = 7-0-1 = 6$

Sum of nodes $(n-1)$ and radial nodes $(n-l-1) = 6+6 = 12$

29. ***(a)*** The correct match is

A-III, B-I, C-II, D-IV

(A) $\nu = \frac{c}{\lambda} = \frac{3\times 10^8 \text{ ms}^{-1}}{600\times 10^{-9}\text{ m}}$

$= 5\times 10^{14}\text{ s}^{-1}$

Thus, (A)-(III)

(B) Velocity $= \frac{\text{Distance}}{\text{Time}}$

$\therefore$ Distance $= v\times t = 3\times 10^8 (\text{ms}^{-1})\times 30\text{ s}$

$= 9\times 10^9\text{ m} = 9\times 10^6\text{ km}$

Thus, (B) - (I)

(C) $E = h\nu = 6.62\times 10^{-34}\text{ Js}\times 5\times 10^{14}\text{s}^{-1}$

$= 3.31\times 10^{-19}\text{ J}$

$= 3.31\times 10^{-22}\text{ kJ}$

Thus (C)-(II)

(D) $E = nh\nu$, $2\text{J} = n(3.31\times 10^{-19}\text{J})$

$n = 6.04\times 10^{18}$

Thus, (D)- (IV)

30. ***(d)*** The correct match is

A-III, B-I, C-IV, D-II

$\frac{1}{\lambda} = \bar{\nu}$ (wave number) $= R_H Z^2\left[\frac{1}{n_1^2} - \frac{1}{n_2^2}\right]$

(A) Frequency $= \nu = \frac{c}{\lambda}$

$= R_H c Z^2\left[\frac{1}{n_1^2} - \frac{1}{n_2^2}\right]$

For α-line in Balmer series (first line), for He^+, $n_1 = 2, n_2 = 3$, $Z = 2$.

$\therefore\ \nu = R_H c(2)^2\left(\frac{1}{2^2} - \frac{1}{3^2}\right) \Rightarrow \nu = \frac{5}{9}R_H c$

Thus, (A) - (III)

(B) For maximum wave number, $n_2 = \infty$

In Brackett series, $n_1 = 4$, $Li^{2+}(Z = 3)$

$\therefore \bar{\nu}_{max} = R_H(3^2)\left(\frac{1}{4^2}\right) = \frac{9}{16}R_H$

$\therefore$ (B) - (I)

(C) For minimum wave number $n_2 = (n_1 + 1)$

For Lyman series, $n_1 = 1$

$n_2 = 2$

$Be^{3+}(Z = 4)$

$\therefore\ \bar{\nu}_{min} = R_H(4)^2\left[\frac{1}{1^2} - \frac{1}{2^2}\right] = 12R_H$

Thus, (C) - (IV)

(D) For Paschen series, $n_1 = 3$,

$n_2 = 5$ for β-line

$\therefore\ \bar{\nu} = R_H\left(\frac{1}{3^2} - \frac{1}{5^2}\right) = \frac{16}{225}R_H$

Thus, (D) - (II)

31. ***(d)*** The correct match is

A-V, B-III, C-IV, D-II

As we know, $\bar{\nu}$ (wave number) $= \frac{1}{\lambda} = R_H Z^2\left[\frac{1}{n_1^2} - \frac{1}{n_2^2}\right]$

For H-atom, $Z = 1$

$\therefore\ \bar{\nu} = \frac{1}{\lambda} = R_H\left[\frac{1}{n_1^2} - \frac{1}{n_2^2}\right]$

If $\bar{\nu}$ is maximum, then, λ is minimum.

If $\bar{\nu}$ is minimum, then, λ is maximum.

$\frac{1}{\lambda_{min}} = R_H\left[\frac{1}{n_1^2}\right]\left(\frac{1}{n_2^2} = 0 \text{ as } n_2 = \infty\right)$

$\frac{1}{\lambda_{max}} = R_H\left[\frac{1}{n_1^2} - \frac{1}{(n_1+1)^2}\right]$

	Series	n_1	n_2	
(A)	Lyman	1	∞	$\frac{1}{\lambda_{min}} = R_H \therefore \lambda_{min} = \frac{1}{R_H} = x$
		1	2	$\frac{1}{\lambda_{max}} = R_H\left[\frac{1}{1^2} - \frac{1}{2^2}\right] = R_H\left(\frac{3}{4}\right)$ $\therefore \lambda_{max} = \frac{4}{3R_H} = \frac{4}{3}x$
(B)	Balmer	2	∞	$\lambda_{min} = 4x$
		2	3	$\lambda_{max} = \frac{36}{5}x$
(C)	Paschen	3	∞	$\lambda_{min} = 9x$
		3	4	$\lambda_{max} = \frac{144}{7}x$
(D)	Brackett	4	∞	$\lambda_{min} = 16x$
		4	5	$\lambda_{max} = \frac{400}{9}x$

32. ***(b)*** The correct match is A-III, B-I, C-II, D-IV, E-V.

E_n(energy in nth orbit) $= -\frac{13.6Z^2}{n^2} = -13.6$ eV

if $\left(\frac{Z^2}{n^2}\right) = 1$

Thus, for Li^{2+}, $Z = 3$

$n = 3$

Thus, (B) - (I)

Radius of nth orbit $= \frac{n^2 a_0}{Z} = a_0$

if $\frac{n^2}{Z} = 1$

If $n = 2, Z = 4$,

Thus, (C)-(II)

Ionisation energy $= -E_n$

$= \frac{13.6Z^2}{n^2}$ eV $= 54.4$ eV

if $\frac{Z^2}{n^2} = 4$

Thus, for He^+, $Z = 2$ and $n = 1$ (ground state)

Thus, (A) -(III)

Ionisation energy $= 13.6\frac{Z^2}{n^2} = 340$

Species (with one electron) is in ground state, thus $n = 1$

$\therefore \quad 13.6\left(\frac{Z^2}{1^2}\right) = 340$

$Z = 5$

Thus, B^{4+}

Thus, (D) - (IV)

Radius $= a_0$ = Bohr's radius of H-atom

Thus, (E) - (V)

33. ***(d)*** The correct match is A-(IV, V); B-(I, II, III, V); C-V; D-(IV, V)

(A) Number of nodal planes $= l = 0$ (given)

$l = 0$ for s-orbital.

Thus, (A) - (IV, V)

(B) Radial nodes $= (n - l - 1) = 0$ (given)

For, $4f$, $n = 4$, $l = 3$

$\therefore \quad (n - l - 1) = 0$

$3d$, $n = 3$, $l = 2$

$\therefore \quad (n - l - 1) = (3 - 2 - 1) = 0$

$2p$, $n = 2$, $l = 1$

$(2 - 1 - 1) = 0$

$2s$, $n = 2$, $l = 0$

$\therefore \quad (n - l - 1) = (2 - 0 - 1) = 1$

$1s$, $n = 1$, $l = 0$

$(n - l - 1) = (1 - 0 - 1) = 0$

Thus, (B) - (I, II, III, V)

(C) Total number of radial and angular nodes

$= n - l - 1 + l = (n - 1)$

It is zero only for 1s

$(n - 1) = (1 - 1) = 0$

Thus, (C) - (V)

(D) Azimuthal quantum number $= l = 0$

For s-orbital

Thus, $1s$ and $2s$

Thus, (D)-(IV, V)

34. ***(50)*** Photoelectric effect is given by equation,

$h\nu = h\nu_0 + \frac{1}{2}mv^2 = h\nu_0 + \text{K.E}$

$h\nu = w_0$(work function) + K.E

$\nu = \frac{w_0}{h} + \left(\frac{\text{KE}}{h}\right)$

$\nu = \text{constant} + \left(\frac{\text{KE}}{h}\right)$

As ν increases, $\left(\frac{\text{KE}}{h}\right)$ also increases

This represents a straight line $(y = c + mx)$

$\therefore OA = \frac{w_0}{h}$

$OA = \frac{199.262 \text{ kJ mol}^{-1}}{6.62 \times 10^{-34} \text{ Js}}$

$= \frac{199.262 \times 10^3 \text{ J electron}^{-1}}{6.02 \times 10^{23} \text{ mol}^{-1} \times 6.62 \times 10^{-34} \text{ J s}} = 5 \times 10^{14} \text{ s}^{-1}$

Hence, the value of OA will be 50×10^{13} s^{-1}.

35. ***(279)*** $\text{KE} = h\nu - (OA)h = \frac{hc}{\lambda} - (OA)h$

$= \frac{6.62 \times 10^{-34} \text{ Js} \times 3 \times 10^8 \text{ ms}^{-1}}{250 \times 10^{-9} \text{ m}}$

$-5 \times 10^{14} s^{-1} \times 6.62 \times 10^{-34}$ Js

$= 33.02 \times 10^{-14}$ J electron^{-1}

$= 33.02 \times 10^{-14} J \times 6.02 \times 10^{23} mol^{-1}$

$= 198.78 \times 10^{4}$ J mol^{-1} = 1987 kJ mol^{-1}

36. ***(6)*** As we know,

Work function = Threshold energy

$$h\nu_0 = \frac{hc}{\lambda_0} = \frac{6.6 \times 10^{-34} \text{ Js} \times 3 \times 10^8 \text{ ms}^{-1}}{330 \times 10^{-9} \text{ m}}$$

$= 6 \times 10^{-19}$ J

37. ***(80)*** As we know,

K.E $= h\nu - h\nu_0$

$h\nu_1 - h\nu_0 = 2(h\nu_2 - h\nu_0)$

$\nu_0 = 2(\nu_2) - \nu_1$

$= 2\,(2.0 \times 10^{16}) - (3.2 \times 10^{16})$

$= 8 \times 10^{15}$ s^{-1}

$= 80 \times 10^{14}$ s$^{-1} \approx 80 \times 10^{14}$ Hz

38. ***(2)*** There are two nodal planes with zero electron density for d_{xy} orbital.

39. ***(17)*** Given, atomic number = 105

Value of $n + l = 8$

The element with atomic number 105 has [Rn] $5f^{14} 6d^3 7s^2$ electronic configuration.

For $5f$, the value of $n + l = 8$

For $6d$, the value of $n + l = 8$

For $7s$, the value of $n + l = 7$

Hence, the (17) electrons in an atom with atomic number 105 can have $n + l = 8$ value.

40. ***(3)*** Ground state electron in H atom can only be excited by energy greater than 10.2 eV Thus, 15 eV photon energy will ionise the atom and 8.4 eV photon will not be able to excite the electron at all. Only 12.09 eV excite to higher states. Now, this will be excited to $n = 3$. During de-excitation, correspondence to three transitions: wavelength will be emitted.

– 0.85 eV .... $n = 4$

– 1.51 eV .... $n = 3$

– 3.4 eV .... $n = 2$

– 13.6 eV .... $n = 1$

41. ***(54.4)*** For Be^{3+}, $Z = 4$; $n = 2$

As we know,

The separation energy $(E_\infty - E_2) = +13.6\left(\frac{Z^2}{n^2}\right)$

$$= 13.6 \times \frac{4^2}{2^2} = 54.4 \text{ eV}$$

42. ***(a)*** Only $d_{x^2-y^2}$ and d_{yz} orbital has two nodal planes. d_{z^2} has two modal comes, $f_{5z^2-3zr^2}$ has one nodal plane along xy-plane and p_x orbital also has only one nodal plane.

43. ***(d)*** Among the given series, only three i.e, (ii), (iii) and (v) series in H-spectra which occur in *IR* region while

- Lyman series → Ultraviolet
- Balmer → Visible

44. ***(b)*** Among the given curves, only three i.e. (i), (ii) and (iv) are correct while curve (iii) are (v) are incorrect.

As we know,

- Velocity of an electron in Bohr's orbit $v \propto \frac{Z}{n}$ hence graph (iv) is correct.
- Radius of electron in Bohr's orbit $r \propto \frac{n^2}{Z}$ hence graph (ii) is correct.
- Potential energy (P.E) $= -\frac{KZe^2}{r_n}$ i.e., (P.E) $\alpha \left(-\frac{Z^2}{n^2}\right)$ hence graph (iii) is incorrect
- Kinetic energy (K.E) $= \frac{1}{2}\frac{KZe^2}{r_n}$ i.e., (K.E) $\propto \frac{Z^2}{n^2}$ hence graph (i) is correct.

45. ***(c)*** Among the given orbits, only one i.e., Be^{3+} has same radius as that of the Ist Bohr's orbit of H-atom while others have not same radius as that of the first Bohr's orbit of H-atom.

As we know, $r_n = \frac{r_0 \times n^2}{Z}$, where r_0 is the radius of Ist Bohr orbit or ground state of H-atom.

As given, $\frac{r_0 \times n^2}{Z} = r_0$

i.e. $n^2 = Z$ which is possible only for Be^{3+}.

For Be^{3+}, $n = 2$, $Z = 4$

Hence, only Be^{3+} has same radius as that of the first Bohr's orbit of hydrogen atom.

46. ***(a)*** Among the given set of quantum numbers, only three i.e, (iii), (v) and (vi) represents an impossible arrangement.

In (iii) i.e, $n = 3$, $l = 2$ and m_l should be – 2 to + 2.

In (v) i.e., $n = 6$, $l = 1$ and m_l should be – 1 to + 1.

In (vi) i.e., $n = 2$, $l = 1$ and m_l should be – 1 to + 1.

47. ***(b)*** Among the given set of quantum numbers, only three i.e., (ii), (iv) and (v) have high energy than $5d$ orbital because $n + l$ value of $5d$ obital is seven.

Energy order can be estimate on the basis of $n + l$ value higher the value of $n + l$ higher will be the energy of the orbital. If $(n + l)$ same then higher value of n have higher energy.

(i) $n = 3, l = 2, m = 0, s = +\frac{1}{2}$

$n + l = 5 < (n + l)$ value of $5d$-orbital

(ii) $n = 6, l = 2, m = 1, s = +\frac{1}{2}$

$n + l = 8, n > 5$ so high energy

(iii) $n = 5, l = 1, m = 0, s = +\frac{1}{2}$

$n + l = 6 < (n + l)$ value of $5d$-orbital

(iv) $n = 5, l = 3, m = 2, s = +\frac{1}{2}$

$n + l = 8, 5f > 5d$ (energy)

(v) $n = 7, l = 1, m = 0, s = +\frac{1}{2}$

$n + l = 8,\ n > 5d, (n + l)$ value of $5d$-orbital.

(vi) $n = 4, l = 2, m = 2, s = +\frac{1}{2}$

$n + l = 6 < (n + l)$ value of $5d$-orbital

(vii) $n = 2, l = 1, m = 0, s = +\frac{1}{2}$

$n + l = 3 < (n + l)$ value of $5d$-orbital

48. ***(a)*** Isodiaphers are species with different atomic numbers and mass numbers, but have same difference between number of neutron and number of proton.

(i) $^{19}_{9}F$ and $^{13}_{6}C$

in F no. of $p = 9$ and $n = 10$

in C no. of $p = 6$ and $n = 7$

$(n - p)$ in F $= 1$ equal to $(n - p)$ in C i.e, 1

So, it is a pair of isodiaphers.

(ii) $^{40}_{18}Ar$ and $^{40}_{20}Ca$

In Ar, $p = 18$; In Ca, $p = 20$

$n = 22$ $\qquad n = 20$

$(n - p = 4)$ in Ar $\neq (n - p = 0)$ in Ca

(iii) $^{14}_{6}C$ and $^{23}_{11}Na$

In C, $p = 6$; In Na, $p = 11$

$n = 8$ $\qquad n = 12$

$n - p = 8 - 6 = 2$ $\qquad n - p = 12 - 11 = 1$

So, $(n - p)$ in C $\neq (n - p)$ in Na

(iv) $^{24}_{12}Mg$ and $^{23}_{11}Na$

In Mg, $p = 12$; In Na, $p = 11$

$n = 12$ $\qquad n = 12$

$n - p = 0$ $\qquad n - p = 1$

So, $(n - p)$ in Mg $\neq (n - p)$ in Na

(v) $^{4}_{2}He$ and $^{15}_{8}O$

In He, $p = 2$; In O, $p = 8$

$n = 2$ $\qquad n = 7$

$n - p = 0$ $\qquad n - p = -1$

$(n - p)$ in He $\neq (n - p)$ in O

(vi) $^{65}_{29}Cu$ and $^{52}_{24}Cr$

$p = 29$ $\qquad p = 24$

$n = 36$ $\qquad n = 28$

$(n\text{-}p)$ in Cu $= 36 - 29$ $\qquad (n\text{-}p)$ in Cr $= 28 - 24 = 4$

So, $(n\text{-}p)$ in Cu $\neq (n\text{-}p)$ in Cr.

(vii) $^{39}_{19}K$ and $^{19}_{9}F$

In K; In F

$p = 19$ $\qquad p = 9$

$n = 20$ $\qquad n = 10$

$n - p = 1$ $\qquad n - p = 1$

$(n - p)$ in K $= (n - p)$ in F

So, it is a pair of isodiaphers.

49. ***(c)*** Among the given transition in H-atom only one i.e, (iii) Which is equal to the frequency of light emitted for the transition $n = 4$ to $n = 2$ of He^+ ion.

As we know,

$$\Delta E = h\nu = \frac{2\pi^2 m Z^2 e^4 k^2}{h^2}\left[\frac{1}{n_1^2} - \frac{1}{n_2^2}\right]$$

If electron falls from n_2-level to n_1-level.

$\therefore$ In He^+, for $n_2 = 4$ to

$n_1 = 2$ transition

$$\nu_{He^+} = \text{Constant}(4)\left[\frac{1}{2^2} - \frac{1}{4^2}\right] \quad [\because Z_{He^+} = 2]$$

$$= \text{Constant} \times 4\left[\frac{3}{16}\right] = \frac{3}{4} \times \text{Constant}$$

$$\nu(H) = \text{Constant}(1)^2\left[\frac{1}{n_1^2} - \frac{1}{n_2^2}\right] = \text{Constant}\left[\frac{1}{n_1^2} - \frac{1}{n_2^2}\right]$$

- For $n_2 = 3$ and $n_1 = 1$.

$$\nu(H) = \text{Constant}\left[\frac{1}{1} - \frac{1}{9}\right] = \frac{8}{9} \times \text{Constant} \neq \nu(He^+)$$

- For $n_2 = 2$ and $n_1 = 1$,

$$\nu(H) = \text{Constant} \times \left[\frac{1}{1} - \frac{1}{4}\right] = \frac{3}{4} \times \text{Constant} = \nu[He^+]$$

- For $n_2 = 3$ and $n_1 = 2$

$$\nu(H) = \text{Constant} \times \left[\frac{1}{2^2} - \frac{1}{3^2}\right] = \frac{5}{36} \times \text{Constant} \neq \nu(He^+)$$

- For $n_2 = 4$ and $n_1 = 3$

$$\nu(H) = \text{Constant} \times \left[\frac{1}{3^2} - \frac{1}{4^2}\right] = \frac{7}{144} \times \text{Constant} \neq \nu[He^+]$$

- For $n_2 = 4$ and $n_1 = 1$

$$\nu(H) = \text{Constant} \times \left[-\frac{1}{16} + \frac{1}{1}\right] = \frac{15}{16} \times \text{Constant} \neq \nu[He^+]$$

- For $n_2 = 3$, $n_1 = 4$

$$\nu(H) = \text{Constant}\left[\frac{1}{16} - \frac{1}{9}\right] = -\frac{7}{144} \times \text{Constant} \neq \nu[He^+]$$

- For $n_2 = 4$ and $n_1 = 2$

$$\nu(H) = \text{Constant}\left[\frac{1}{4} - \frac{1}{16}\right]$$

$$= \frac{3}{16} \times \text{Constant} \neq \nu[He^+]$$

Check Through PYQs : JEE Advanced

1. ***(b)*** According to Bohr's model, the kinetic energy is given by

$$K.E = +13.6 \times \frac{Z^2}{n^2}$$

For 1st orbit of hydrogen atom

$$n = 1, Z = 1 \Rightarrow K.E = 13.6 \text{ eV}$$

For 1st orbit of He^+

$$n = 1, Z = 2 \Rightarrow K.E = +54.4 \text{ eV}$$

For second orbit of He^+

$$n = 2, Z = 2 \Rightarrow K.E = +13.6 \text{ eV}$$

For second orbit of Li^{2+}

$$n = 2, Z = 3 \Rightarrow K.E = 30.6 \text{ eV}$$

Thus, the highest energy is associated with first orbit of He^+.

2. ***(30)*** The Bohr's radius of an orbit in atom is given by

$$r_n = \frac{52.9 \times n^2}{Z} \text{ pm}$$

$$105.8 = \frac{52.9 \times n_2^2}{2} \quad \therefore \quad n_2^2 = 4, n_2 = 2$$

$$26.45 = \frac{52.9 \times n_1^2}{2} \quad \therefore \quad n_1 = 1$$

Now, the wavelength of the emitted photon can calculated from

$$\frac{hc}{\lambda} = R_H Z^2 \left(\frac{1}{n_1^2} - \frac{1}{n_2^2}\right)$$

$$\frac{hc}{\lambda} = R_H \times 4 \times \frac{3}{4} = 3R_H$$

$$\frac{hc}{\lambda} = 3R_H = 3 \times 2.2 \times 10^{-18} \text{ J}$$

$$\lambda = \frac{6.6 \times 10^{-34} \times 3 \times 10^8}{3 \times 2.2 \times 10^{-18}} \text{ m}$$

$$= 3 \times 10^{-8} \text{ m} = 30 \text{ nm}$$

So, the wavelength of the emitted photon during the transition is 30 nm.

3. ***(−5242.42)*** Given that, electrons and nucleus are at infinite distance, so potential energy of H-atom is taken as zero.

Therefore, according to Bohr's model, potential energy of a H-atom with electron in its ground state = − 27.2 eV

At $d = d_0$, nucleus-nucleus and electron-electron repulsions are absent.

Hence, potential energy will be calculated for 2H atoms

$$= -2 \times 27.2 \text{ eV} = -54.4 \text{ eV}$$

Potential energy of 1 mol H atoms in kJ

$$= -\frac{54.4 \times 6.023 \times 10^{23} \times 1.6 \times 10^{-19}}{1000}$$

$$= -5242.419 \text{ kJ/mol} \approx -5242.42 \text{ kJ / mol}$$

4. ***(a)*** (III) Kinetic energy of the electron in nth orbit is given as

$$K.E = +13.6 \times \frac{Z^2}{n^2} \quad \text{or} \quad K.E \propto \frac{1}{n^2} \quad \text{or} \quad K.E \propto n^{-2}$$

From list-II, correct match is (III, P).

(IV) Potential energy of the electron in the nth orbit,

$$PE = -2 \times 13.6 \times \frac{Z^2}{n^2} \text{ eV}$$

$$PE \propto \frac{1}{n^2} \Rightarrow PE \propto n^{-2}$$

From List II, correct match is (IV, P).

Hence, correct matching from List-I and List-II on the basis of given option is (III, P).

5. ***(a, b, c)*** Due to wave nature of electrons, uncertainty principle rules out the existence of definite paths for an electron. Thus, this statement is correct.

As the distance of electron from nucleus increases its energy also increases. Then this statement is also correct.

According to Bohr's model, energy of an electron is given by

$$E = \frac{-13.6 \times Z^2}{n^2}, \text{ if } n = 1$$

then, $E = (-13.6 \times Z^2)$ eV is most negative value and hence it is most stable. Thus, this statement is also correct.

Velocity $= 2.186 \times 10^6 \times \frac{Z}{n}$, so if value of n is increased then velocity decreases. Thus, this statement is incorrect.

Hence, statement given in (a), (b) and (c) are correct while (d) is incorrect.

6. ***(30)*** Wavelength of photon absorbed,

$$\lambda = 330 \text{ nm} = 330 \times 10^{-9} \text{m}$$

Planck's constant, $h = 6.6 \times 10^{-34}$ J s

Molar mass of He,

$$M = 4 \text{ g mol}^{-1} = 4 \times 10^{-3} \text{ kg mol}^{-1}$$

Avogadro number, $N_A = 6 \times 10^{23} \text{ mol}^{-1}$

Mass of one atom of He, $m = \frac{M}{N_A}$

$$= \frac{4 \times 10^{-3}}{6 \times 10^{23}} = \frac{2}{3} \times 10^{-26} \text{ kg}$$

Velocity, = v m/s.

Using de-Broglie equation, $\lambda = \frac{h}{mv}$

$$\Rightarrow \quad v = \frac{h}{m\lambda} = \frac{6.6 \times 10^{-34}}{2/3 \times 10^{-26} \times 330 \times 10^{-9}}$$

$$= \frac{6.6 \times 3 \times 10^{-34} \times 10^{35}}{2 \times 330}$$

$$= 0.03 \times 10 = 0.3 \text{ m/s} = 30 \text{ cm/s}$$

7. ***(a,c)*** Given, ground state energy of hydrogen atom = − 13.6 eV

Energy of He^+ = − 3.4 eV, $Z = 2$

Energy of He^+, $E = -\frac{13.6 \times Z^2}{n^2}$ eV

$$-3.4 \text{ eV} = \frac{-13.6 \times (2)^2}{n^2}$$

$\Rightarrow \qquad n = \sqrt{\frac{13.6 \times 4}{3.4}} \Rightarrow n = 4$

Given, azimuthal quantum number $(l) = 2$ (d – subshell

Magnetic quantum number $(m) = 0$

$\therefore$ Angular nodes $(l) = 2$

Radial node $= n - l - 1 = 4 - 2 - 1 = 1$

$nl = 4d$ state

8. ***(c)*** In the wave function (ψ) expression for 1s-orbital of He^+, there should be no angular part (θ). Hence (iii) can't be true for ψ_{1s} of He^+.

9. ***(a)*** Correct : 2s orbital has one radial node.

No. of radial node $= n - l - 1 = 2 - 0 - 1 = 1$

Also, when radial part of wave function (ψ) is plotted against 'r', wave function changes its sign at node.

10. ***(d)*** (i) is the correct expression of wave function for 1s-orbital of hydrogenic system.

$$\frac{\Delta E^{H}_{Z \to 4}}{\Delta E^{H}_{Z \to 6}} = \frac{2.18 \times 10^{-18}\left(\frac{1}{2^2} \times \frac{1}{4^2}\right) \times 1^2 \text{ J}}{2.18 \times 10^{-8}\left(\frac{1}{2^2} - \frac{1}{6^2}\right) \times 1^2 \text{ J}} = \frac{3}{16} \times \frac{36}{8} = \frac{27}{32}$$

11. ***(c)*** This graph shows the probability of finding the electron within shell at various distances from the nucleus (radial probability). The curve shows the maximum, which means that the radial probability is greatest for a given distance from the nucleus. This distance is equal to Bohr's radius $= a_0$

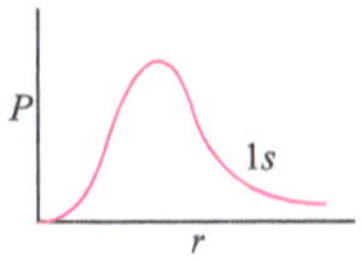

For other options,

(a) It is for 2s-orbital.

(b) It is radial wave function for 1s.

(c) Correct

(d) Probability cannot be zero at a certain distance from nucleus.

12. ***(3)*** In one electron (hydrogenic) system, all orbitals of a shell remains degenerate, hence in second excited state ($n = 3$) the degeneracy of H-atom is nine.

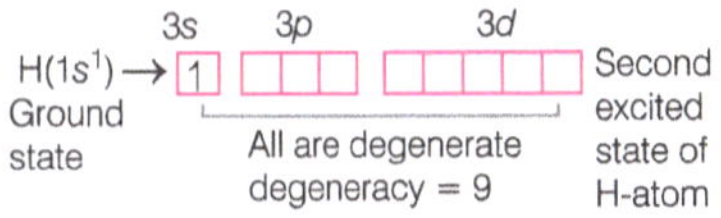

In case of many electrons system, different orbitals of a shell are non-degenerate. Hence,

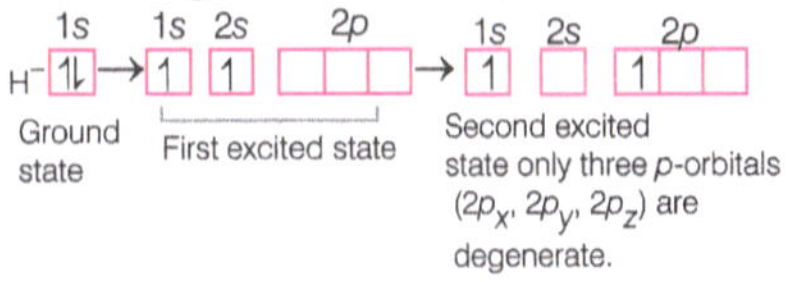

CHAPTER 3

States of Matter

Trend Insights

JEE Advanced

Typology	Years				
	2024	2023	2022	2021	2020
1. Simple MCQs	2	–	1	1	1
2. One or More than one correct	–	1	1	–	1
3. Numerical Value/Integer	–	1	–	–	–
4. Matching Type	–	–	–	–	–
5. Paragraph Based	–	–	–	–	–

E = Easy, **M** = Medium, **T** = tough, **O** = Overall

Current Dynamics

- Over recent years, the focus has been primarily on the solid state and gaseous state, with at least one question consistently appearing from each.
- The trend indicates questions from the liquid state, notably absent, suggesting its lower priority in JEE Advanced.

Insightful Advice

- Focus strongly on solid state topics, especially packing efficiency, radius ratio and fractions of ions in a unit cell.
- Priorities gaseous state especially master distribution of speeds (u_{av}, u_{rms}, u_{mp}) and compressibility factor.
- This chapter is important at JEE Advanced level as it has been removed from rationlised syllabus of JEE Mains.

Learning Elements

Element 1 The Gaseous State

Intermolecular Forces, Gases, Gas Laws, Ideal Gas Equation, Kinetic Molecular Theory of Gases, Different Type of Molecular Velocities, Graham's Law of Diffusion, The Real gas, Liquefaction of Gases

Element 2 The Liquid State

Properties of Liquid – Vapour Pressure, Surface tension, Viscosity, Boiling Point.

Element 3 The Solid State

Types of Solids, Coordination Number, Radius Ratio in Ionic Crystals, Packing Fraction, Density of Solids, Crystal Defects, Magnetic Properties of Solids.

Practice Element

Practice Element Target JEE Advanced

Element 1 The Gaseous State

The states of matter-solid, liquid and gas describe the physical forms of substances based on particle arrangement, intermolecular forces and energy.

Concept Visualizer

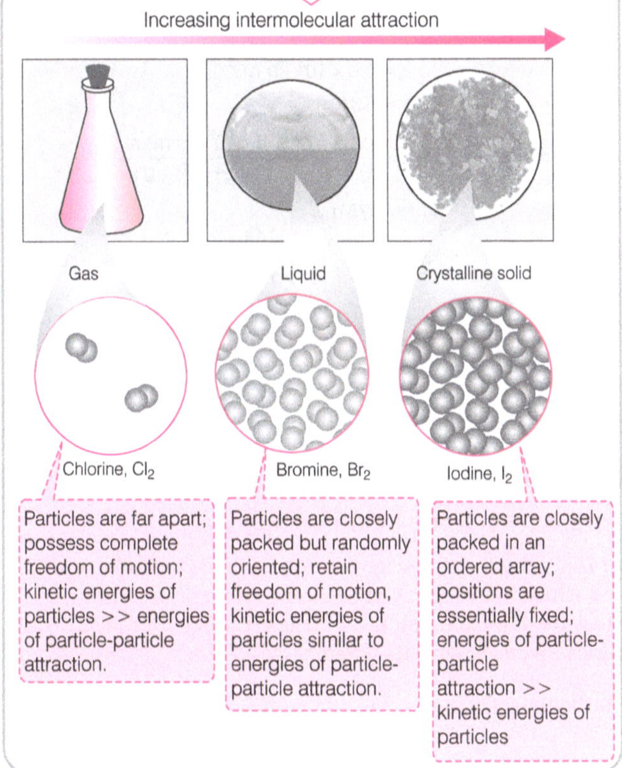

Forces Responsible for Physical States of Matter

The physical state of matter is determined by the balance between intermolecular forces and thermal energy.

Different types of intermolecular forces are given below.

van der Waals' Forces

This term broadly encompasses various types of weak intermolecular forces. It includes dispersion forces, dipole-dipole interactions, and other weak attractions.

1. Debye Forces (Permanent Dipole-Induced Dipole Forces)

When a dipole comes near the non-polar molecule, it can induce polarity in non-polar molecule resulting to **dipole-induced dipole interactions.**

e.g., Interaction between a water molecule and a helium atom.

2. Keesom Forces (Dipole-Dipole Forces)

These forces are interactions between molecules that have permanent dipoles. They occur when the positive end of one polar molecule is attracted to the negative end of another.

e.g., The interaction between molecules of HCl and CH_3COCH_3.

3. London Dispersion Forces

These are weak, temporary forces arising from the instantaneous and fluctuating distribution of electron density within an atom or molecule, leading to momentary dipoles.

Dispersion forces are present in all molecules, whether polar or non-polar. They become stronger with increasing molecular size and surface area.

e.g.,Intersection between neon (Ne) molecules.

Hydrogen Bond

Hydrogen bond is a attraction betwen a hydrogen atom attached to a highly electronegative atom (usually F, O, N) and a nearby small electronegative atom in another molecule or chemical group. It can be considered a special type of dipole-dipole attraction.

JEE Alert

Dipole-dipole interactions and hydrogen bonds are inversely proportional to 3rd power of the distance whereas dipole induced dipole interaction are inversely proportional to the sixth power of intermolecular distance.

Gases

It is the simplest state of matter and this allows a comparatively simple quantitative description. The important characteristics of gases can be described in terms of the following parameters.

1. Pressure (p)

Pressure of the gas is the force exerted by the gas molecules per unit area on the walls of the container. Instrument used for the measurement of the pressure of a gas is called manometer.

$$\text{Pressure} = \frac{\text{Force}}{\text{Area}}$$

2. Atmospheric Pressure

It is defined as the pressure exerted by the gases of the atmosphere. Instrument used for the measurement of atmospheric pressure is called a **barometer**. (Pressure at height h from sea level)

Atmospheric pressure $= \rho g h$

where, $h =$ height of mercury column (in barometer)

$g =$ acceleration due to gravity

$\rho =$ density of the mercury at room temperature

The SI unit of pressure, is pascal (Pa).

3. Volume (V)

The volume of a gas is defined as the space occupied by the gas due to its random motion. It is always equal to the volume of the container in which the gas is enclosed.

The SI unit of volume is m^3. Other units of volume are mL and dm^3 etc.

$$1\ L = 10^{-3}\ m^3 = 10^3 cm^3 = 1\ dm^3$$

$$1\ mL = 1\ cm^3 = 10^{-3} dm^3 = 10^{-6} m^3$$

$$1\ m^3 = 10^3 dm^3 = 10^6\ cm^3$$

4. Temperature (T)

It is the measure of hotness or coldness of the system and energy of the system. As the temperature of gas increases, the kinetic energy of gas molecules increases.

SI unit of temperature is kelvin (K). Other units of temperatures are celsius (°C) and fahrenheit (°F).

$$\boxed{K = {}^\circ C + 273} \quad \text{and} \quad F = \frac{9}{5} {}^\circ C + 32.$$

5. Mass (m)

The mass of a gas can be determined by weighing the container in which the gas is enclosed and again weighing the container after removing the gas. The difference between the two masses gives the mass of the gas. The amount of gas is related to number of moles of the gas.

$$\text{Moles of gas } (n) = \frac{\text{Mass in grams}}{\text{Molar mass}} = \frac{m}{M}$$

SI unit of mass is kg and unit of amount of substance is mol.

JEE Alert

Two sets of conditions are widely used as 'standard' values for reporting data.

Condition	T	p	V_m (molar volume)
STP/NTP	273.15 K	1 atm	22.414 L
SATP*	298.15 K	1 bar	24.800 L

SATP is Standard Ambient Temperature and Pressure.

Solved Booster 1.1

At 298 K, density of mercury is 13.6 g cm^{-3} and that of water is 1.0 g cm^{-3}. The height of a column of each liquid that would support a pressure of 1 atm will be

(a) 0.75 m, 10.2 m (b) 1.02 m, 0.75 m
(c) 0.75 m, 10.5 m (d) 7.5 m, 1.02 m

Solution (a)

$$p = 1\ atm \approx 1.0 \times 10^5\ Pa$$
$$= 1.0 \times 10^5\ kg\ m^{-1} s^{-2}$$
$$d = 1.0\ g\ cm^{-3}$$
$$= 1.0 \times 10^3\ kg\ m^{-3}$$
$$g = 9.81\ ms^{-2}$$

$$\therefore h\ (\text{mercury column}) = \frac{p}{dg} = \frac{1.0 \times 10^5\ kg\ m^{-1} s^{-2}}{13.6 \times 10^3\ kg\ m^{-3} \times 9.81\ ms^{-2}}$$
$$= 0.75\ m$$

$$h\ (\text{water column}) = \frac{1.0 \times 10^5\ kg\ m^{-1} s^{-2}}{1.0 \times 10^3\ kg\ m^{-3} \times 9.81\ ms^{-2}} = 10.2\ m$$

The Empirical Gas Law

The relationships among pressure, temperature and volume of a given mass of a gas are described by gas laws.

Boyle's law

(Pressure-Volume Relationship)

In 1662, Anglo-Irish scientist Robert Boyle formulated this law which states that "At constant temperature, the pressure of a fixed amount of a gas (number of moles, n) varies inversely with its volume".

Mathematically, $(p)_{n,T} \propto \frac{1}{V} \Rightarrow (p)_{n,T} = k\left(\frac{1}{V}\right)$

($k =$ constant of proportionality)

$(p)_{n,T}$ indicates that pressure is taken at constant temperature (T) for a fixed number of moles (amount of a gas).

or $\boxed{pV = k}$

The value of constant k depends upon the amount of gas, temperature of the gas and the units in which p and V are expressed.

On changing State I to State II at constant temperature (T). Then, by Boyle's law,

$$\boxed{p_1 V_1 = p_2 V_2 \Rightarrow \frac{p_1}{p_2} = \frac{V_2}{V_1}}$$

At constant temperature, Boyle' law can also be expressed in terms of density,

$$p = kd$$

$$\boxed{\frac{p_1}{p_2} = \frac{d_1}{d_2} = k}$$

Differential form of Boyle's Law

Since, $p = \frac{k}{V}$ at constant temperature

$$\therefore \qquad \left(\frac{\partial p}{\partial V}\right)_T = \left(\frac{-k}{V^2}\right)_T$$

Graphical Representation of Boyle's Law

Graph between p and V at constant temperature is called **isotherm.** Various isotherms are given below.

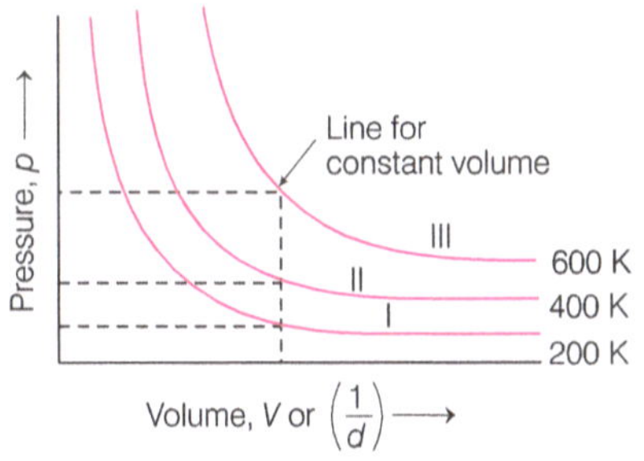

From the curve it is clear that same volume of gas exerts a larger pressure at a higher temperature.

Instead of V, density (d) can be taken and figure below gives isotherms of the variation of p with $\left(\frac{1}{V}\right)$ or density (d) at constant temperature. The straight line indicates that $\left(\frac{1}{V}\right)$ regularly increases with an increase in p.

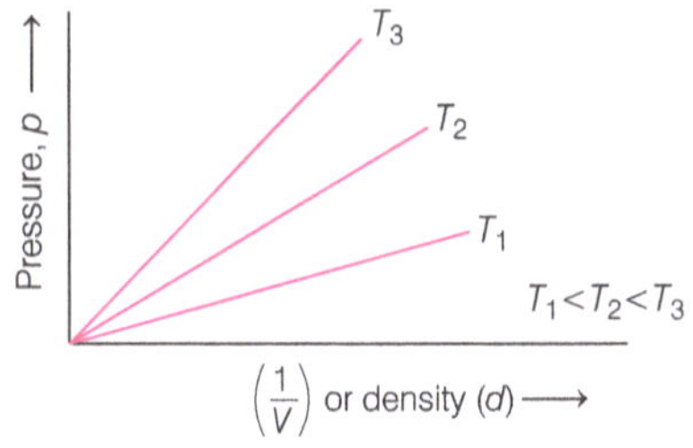

- Since, (pV = constant), hence isotherm shown in figure between (pV) and p is linear with zero slope

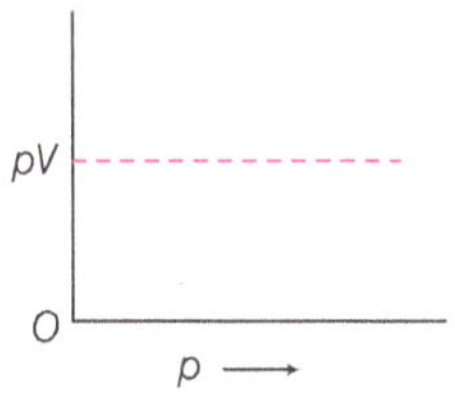

- Also equation $\left(p = \frac{k}{V}\right)$ in terms of logarithm can be expressed as

$$\boxed{\log p = \log\left(\frac{1}{V}\right) + \log k}$$

Graph between $\log p$ and $\log\left(\frac{1}{V}\right)$ under isothermal condition is of the type as shown in the figure with slope = 1 = tan 45° and intercept = $\log k$

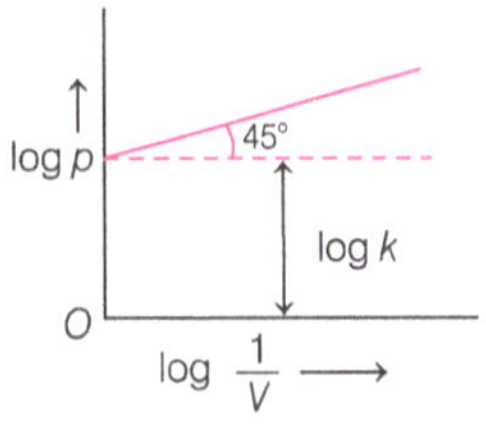

Solved Booster 1.2

Volume of CO_2 gas equal to 20.0 dm^3 was collected at 300 K and 1.00 bar pressure. What would be the volume of CO_2 collected at 300 K and at a pressure reduced by 25%?

(a) 26.67 (b) 42.37
(c) 32.47 (d) 53.70

Solution (a)

Given, $V_1 = 20.0\ dm^3$, $p_1 = 1.00$ bar

$$p_2 = 1.00 \times \frac{75}{100} = 0.75 \text{ bar}$$

(Pressure is reduced by 25%, thus new pressure is 75% of the initial value)

By Boyle's law, $(p_1V_1)_{T,n} = (p_2V_2)_{T,n}$

$$V_2 = \frac{p_1V_1}{p_2} = \frac{1.00 \times 20.0}{0.75} = 26.67\ dm^3$$

Solved Booster 1.3

Under isothermal condition, variation of $\log p$ with $\log\left(\frac{1}{V}\right)$ is given below for H_2 gas. When pressure is 0.2 bar, what will be its density?

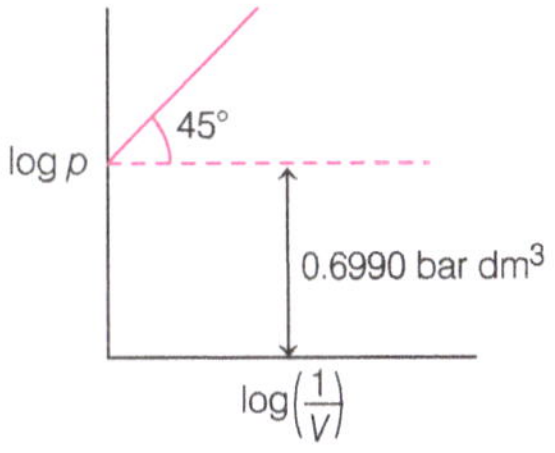

(a) 0.06 (b) 0.08
(c) 0.04 (d) 0.02

Solution (c)

$p = \frac{k}{V}$ for Boyle's law under isothermal condition.

Thus, $\log p = \log\frac{1}{V} + \log k$

Thus, $\log k = 0.6990$ bar dm^3 and slope = tan 45° = 1

$$\therefore \qquad k = \text{antilog of } 0.6990 = 5.0 \text{ bar } dm^3$$

$$\frac{1}{V} = \frac{p}{k} = \frac{0.2 \text{ bar}}{5 \text{ bar dm}^3} = 0.04 \text{ dm}^{-3}$$

$$\therefore \text{ Density} = \frac{\text{Mass}}{\text{Volume}} = 2 \times 0.04 = 0.08 \text{ g dm}^{-3}$$

Charles' Law

(Temperature-Volume Relationship)

According to Charles' law, 'for a fixed mass of a gas under isobaric condition (constant pressure), the gas expands as the temperature rises.'

$$V \propto T$$

$$(V)_{p,n} = kT$$

$(V)_{p,n}$ indicates volume is taken at constant pressure for a fixed number of moles (amount) of gas.

$$\boxed{\frac{V}{T} = k \text{ (constant)}}$$

$$V = kT = k\,(t + 273.15)$$

where, V is the volume and T is the temperature in absolute scale and t is the temperature in °C. If $t = 0$ °C, then $V = V_0$

Hence, $V_0 = k \times 273.15$

$$\therefore \quad k = \frac{V_0}{273.15}$$

$$\Rightarrow \quad V_t = \frac{V_0}{273.15}(t + 273.15)$$

$$\boxed{V_t = V_0\left(1 + \frac{t}{273.15}\right) = V_0(1 + \alpha t)}$$

where, α is the **volume coefficient**,

$$\alpha = \frac{1}{273.15} = 3.661 \times 10^{-3} \, {}^\circ\text{C}^{-1}$$

Thus, for every 1° change in temperature, the volume of gas changes by $\frac{1}{273.15}\left(\approx \frac{1}{273}\right)$ of the volume at 0°C.

Volume coefficient is the change in volume per degree change in temperature

$$\frac{V_t}{V_0} = 1 + \alpha t$$

$$\therefore \quad \alpha = \frac{V_t - V_0}{tV_0}$$

and $\alpha = \frac{1}{273}$ for all gases as shown above.

Differential form of Charles' Law

Under isobaric condition

$$V = kT \quad \therefore \quad \left(\frac{\partial V}{\partial T}\right)_p = k$$

Graphical Representation of Charles' Law

Graphs between V and T at constant pressure are called **isobars** [Fig. (a) and (b)]. If temperature is lowered, there is also decrease in volume at constant pressure.

- If temperature is taken in kelvin scale then the straight line obtained passes through the origin.

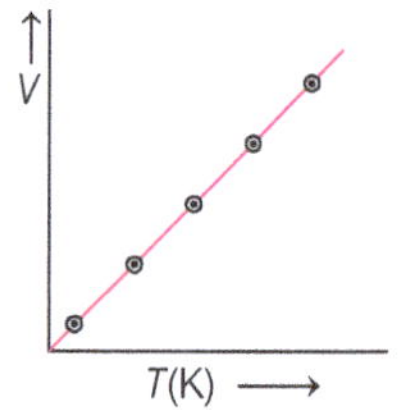

Fig. (a)

- If temperature is taken in Celsius then line intercepts the temperature axis at −273.15°C. The slopes of lines obtained at different pressures are different but at zero volume all lines meet the temperature axis at −273.15°C. The volume should, therefore, become zero at − 273.15° C.

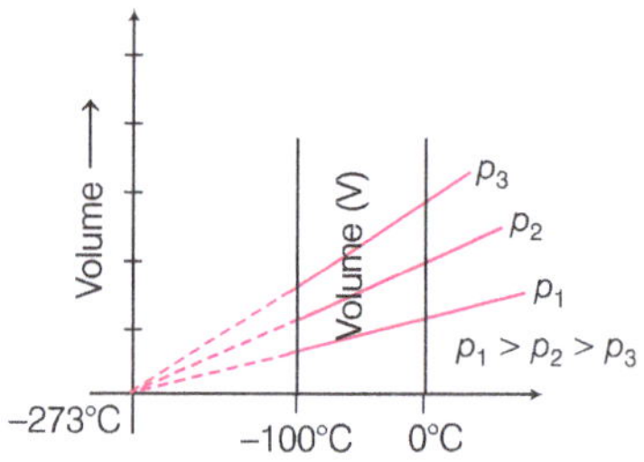

Fig. (b)

- Any further lowering is impossible, since it would imply negative volumes – a meaningless concept. – 273.15° C is the lowest possible temperature. It is called absolute zero of temperature and scale of temperature based on this choice of zero is known as the absolute scale of temperature.

The variation of log V with log T at constant pressure is a straight line.

$$\therefore \quad \log V = \log k + \log T.$$

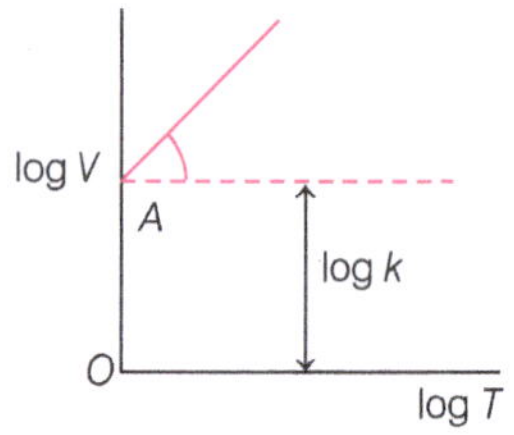

Plot of log V vs log T

Slope $= 1 = \tan 45°$ and intercept on log V axis $= \log k$

Gay-Lussac's Law

(Pressure-Temperature Relationship)

At constant volume, for a given mass of a gas the pressure is directly proportional to the temperature.

$$p \propto T$$

or $$p = kT$$

or $$\frac{p_1}{T_1} = \frac{p_2}{T_2}$$

Pressure coefficient is the change in pressure per degree change in temperature

$$p_t = p_0\left(1 + \frac{t}{273}\right) = p_0(1 + \alpha t)$$

α is called pressure coefficient, $\alpha = \frac{1}{t}\left(\frac{p_t}{p_0} - 1\right)$

$$\Rightarrow \quad \alpha = \frac{p_t - p_0}{p_0 t} \quad \Rightarrow \quad \alpha = \frac{1}{273} \text{ for all gases.}$$

Graphical Representation of Gay-Lussac's Law

A graph between p and T at constant V is called **isochore**. The shapes of various isochores at different volumes are different, but all lines meet temperature axis at 0 K.

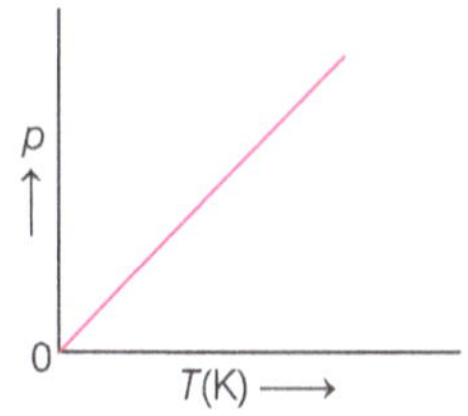

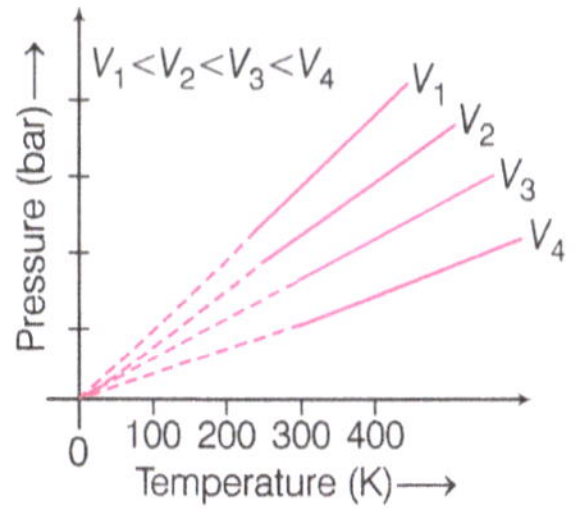

Pressure *versus* temperature (K) graph (isochores)

Logarithm Representation of Gay-Lussac's Law

By Gay-Lussac's law at constant volume, $p = kT$

$$\therefore \quad \log p = \log T + \log k$$

Thus, isochore between $\log p$ and $\log T$ is of the type as shown is figure.

Slope $= 1 = \tan 45°$ and intercept on $\log p$ axis $= \log k$. Thus, constant k is calculated.

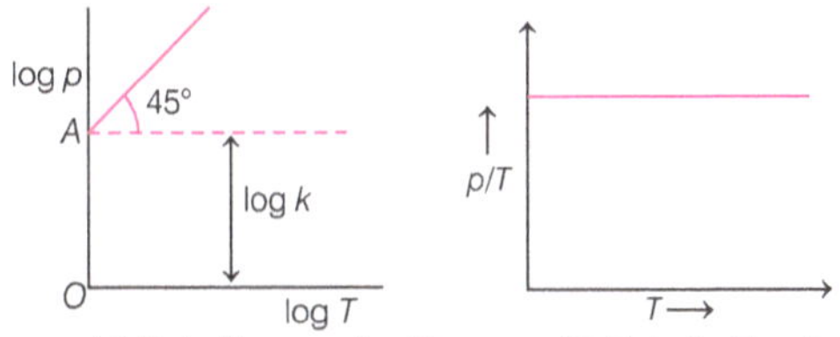

(a) Plot of log p *vs* log T (b) Plot of p/T *vs* T

Show different graphical representations of Gay-Lussac's law

Avogadro's Law

(Volume-amount Relationship)

Equal volumes of any two gases at the same temperature and pressure contain the same number of molecules.

One mole of any gas contains the same number of molecules (Avogadro's number $= 6.02 \times 10^{23}$) and by Avogadro's law must occupy the same volume at a given temperature and pressure. The volume of one mole of a gas is called **molar volume,** V_m which is 22.4 L mol^{-1} at STP (at 273.15 K and 1 atm).

$$V \propto n \; (p \text{ and } T \text{ constant})$$

or $$\frac{V_1}{n_1} = \frac{V_2}{n_2}$$

Solved Booster 1.4

Based on the following activity,

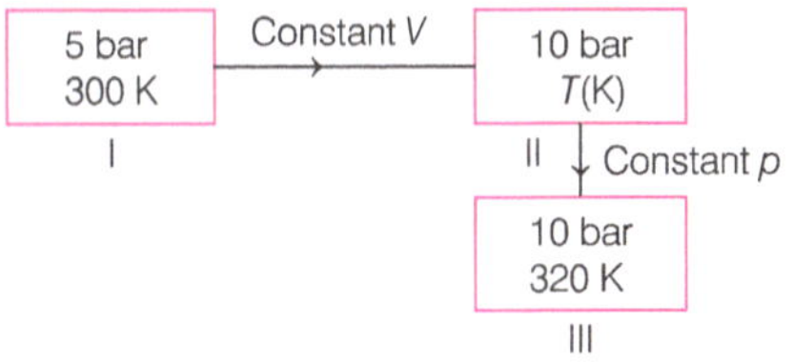

Volume of the given amount of ideal gas in stage II is 20 dm^3. The temperature (T) in stage II and volume (V) in stage III respectively are

(a) 600 K, 10.67 mL (b) 300 K, 20.3 mL

(c) 800 K, 100.2 mL (d) 600 K, 80 mL

Solution *(a)*

From stage I to stage II

$$\frac{5}{300} = \frac{10}{T} \Rightarrow T = \frac{10 \times 300}{5} = 600 \text{ K}$$

From stage II to stage III,

$$\frac{V_1}{T_1} = \frac{V_2}{T_2} \Rightarrow \frac{20}{600} = \frac{V_2}{320}$$

$$\Rightarrow \quad V_2 = \frac{20 \times 320}{600} = 10.67 \text{ dm}^3$$

The Ideal Gas Equation

The simple gas laws relating gas volume to pressure, temperature and amount of gas, respectively, are stated below

$$\frac{pV}{T} = \text{Constant}$$

For 1 mole, $\frac{pV}{T} = R$

This relation is known as ideal gas equation. For 'n' moles of gas, the equation is written as,

$\therefore$ $$pV = nRT$$

For two or more gases, $\frac{p_1V_1}{n_1T_1} = \frac{p_2V_2}{n_2T_2} = R$

$$\text{Units of } R = \frac{\text{(energy unit)}}{\text{(mol)(temperature unit)}}$$

$$\begin{aligned} R &= 8.314 \text{ J / mol-K} \\ &= 0.08205 \text{ L-atm/mol-K} \\ &= 1.99 \text{ cal / mol-K} \\ &= 5.189 \times 10^{19} \text{ eV mol}^{-1} \text{ K}^{-1}. \end{aligned}$$

Gas constant, R for a single molecule (6.023×10^{23}) is called **Boltzmann constant** $(k = R/N_A)$

$$\begin{aligned} &= 1.38 \times 10^{-16} \text{ erg mol}^{-1} \text{ degree}^{-1} \\ &= 1.38 \times 10^{-23} \text{ J mol}^{-1} \text{ degree}^{-1} \end{aligned}$$

- **Relationship between density (d) and molar mass**

From ideal gas equation (iii) density (d) can be written as,

$$d = \frac{pM}{RT} \qquad \left[\because \frac{m}{V} = d(\text{density})\right]$$

M and R are constant for a particular gas, so for two or more different temperatures and pressure,

$$\frac{d_1T_1}{p_1} = \frac{d_2T_2}{p_2} = \text{constant}$$

Solved Booster 1.5

Which one of the following graphs is not correct for ideal gas ?

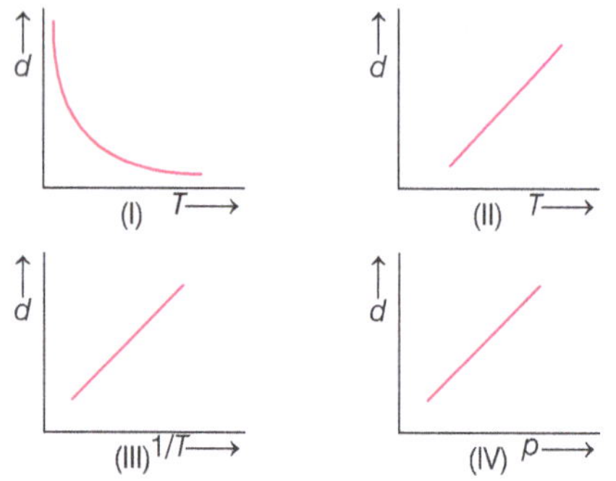

[**Key** : d = density, p = pressure, T = temperature]

(a) III (b) I (c) IV (d) II

Solution (d)

Graph (II) is not correct for ideal gas.

For n mole of an ideal gas,

$$pV = nRT = \frac{w}{M}RT$$

$$\Rightarrow \quad p = \frac{w}{V} \times \frac{RT}{M} = d \times \frac{RT}{M} \qquad \left[\because \frac{w}{M} = d\right]$$

$$\Rightarrow \quad d = \frac{p \cdot M}{RT}$$

where, p = pressure, V = volume,

T = temperature in K, R = molar gas constant,

w = mass of the gas in g, M = gram molar mass of the gas and

$d = \frac{w}{V}$ = density of the gas.

When, p = constant $\Rightarrow d \propto \frac{1}{T}$

So, nature of the plot, d vs T is rectangular hyperbolic (I) but not linear (II).

Again, nature of the plot, d vs $\frac{1}{T}$ will be linear as in (III).

When, T = constant $\Rightarrow d \propto p$

Here, nature of the plot, d vs p will be linear as in (IV).

JEE Spotlite

Gas densities differ from those of solids and liquids in some important ways:

Gas densities are generally stated in g/L instead of g cm^{-3}.

Gas densities are strongly dependent on pressure and temperature, T. It increases as the gas pressure increases and decreases as the temperature increases.

$$d \propto p, d \propto \frac{1}{T}$$

The density of a gas is directly proportional to its molar mass. No simple relationship exists between the density and molar mass of liquids and solids.

$$\text{Density of gas at STP} = \frac{\text{Molar mass (g mol}^{-1})}{22.4 \text{ L mol}^{-1}}$$

Also density of the atmosphere decreases rapidly with altitude and we also know that

$$\text{density} \propto \frac{1}{\text{temperature}}$$

hence, there is a limit to the height to which balloons with hot air can rise.

Dalton's Law of Partial Pressure

When two or more gases which do not react together chemically, are present in the same container, the total pressure exerted by the mixture is the sum of the partial pressure of each constituent gas

$$p_{\text{total}} = p_1 + p_2 + p_3 + \ldots \text{ (constant } V, T)$$

where, $p_1, p_2, p_3, \ldots$ are the partial pressure of gas number 1, 2, 3. In a mixture of gases, the pressure exerted by the individual gas when put alone under identical conditions of temperature and volume is called partial pressure.

If V is the total volume and $n_1, n_2, \ldots$ etc., are the number of moles of the gases 1, 2, ... etc., then

$$p_1 = \frac{n_1}{V} RT, p_2 = \frac{n_2}{V} RT, p_3 = \frac{n_3}{V} RT$$

$$\therefore \quad p_{total} = p_1 + p_2 + p_3 + \ldots$$

$$= \frac{n_1}{V} RT + \frac{n_2}{V} RT + \frac{n_3}{V} RT + \ldots$$

$$p_{total} = \frac{RT}{V}(n_1 + n_2 + n_3 + \ldots) = \frac{nRT}{V}$$

where, $n = n_1 + n_2 + n_3 + \ldots =$ total moles

Partial Pressure in Terms of Mole Fraction

For gas 1, $\frac{p_1}{p_{total}} = \frac{n_1 RT}{V} \frac{V}{n_{total} RT} = \frac{n_1}{n_{total}} = \chi_1$ (mole fraction)

Also, $p_1 = \frac{n_1}{n_{total}} p_{total} = \chi_1 p_{total}$ ($\chi_1 =$ mole fraction gas 1)

$$p_2 = \frac{n_2}{n_{total}} p_{total} = \chi_2 p_{total}$$

Gases are generally collected over water and are thus moist. Thus, to get the pressure of dry air

$$p_{(dry\ air)} = p_{(total)} - p_{(water\ vapours)}$$

Pressure of water vapour is called aqueous tension.

Relative humidity (RH) at a given temperature is given by,

$$RH = \frac{\text{Partial pressure of water in air}}{\text{Vapour pressure of water}}$$

Solved Booster 1.6

At a temperature of 20°C, vapour pressure of water is 17.5 torr. If relative humidity is 45%, calculate the moles of water present in 1 L of air at 20°C.

(a) 8.4×10^{-4} (b) 4.3×10^{-4}

(c) 2.7×10^{-3} (d) 3.8×10^{-3}

Solution (b)

$$\text{Relative humidity} = \frac{\text{Partial pressure of } H_2O \text{ in air}}{\text{Vapour pressure of } H_2O}$$

$$\Rightarrow \quad n = \frac{pV}{RT}$$

$$0.45 = \frac{p_{H_2O}}{17.5}$$

$$\therefore \quad p_{H_2O} = 0.45 \times 17.5 = 7.88 \text{ torr}$$

$$= 0.0104 \text{ atm}$$

Since, $pV = nRT$

$$\therefore \quad n = \frac{pV}{RT} = \frac{0.0104 \times 1}{0.0821 \times 293}$$

$$= 4.3 \times 10^{-4} \text{ mol}$$

Law of Partial Volumes

Partial volume of a gas in the mixture of chemically inert gases is the volume occupied by individual gas molecule under the identical conditions of same temperature and total pressure of the mixture.

It is useful in gas mixture e.g. air, to focus on one particular component like oxygen.

It can be calculated both from partial pressure and mole fraction.

$$V_x = V_{Total} \times \frac{p_x}{p_{Total}}$$

$$= V_{total} \frac{n_x}{n_{Total}}$$

V_x is the partial volume of a particular gas components

V_{Total} = total volume of gas mixture (air)

p_x is the partial pressure of gas X.

p_{Total} = total pressure of gas mixture.

n_x is moles of gas X.

n_{Total} is total amount of substance in the gas mixture.

The Kinetic Molecular Theory of Gases

It is based on the following assumptions. Since, all the assumptions are related to atoms and molecules which cannot be seen, the kinetic theory is said to provide a microscopic model of a gas. Properties studied earlier are part of macroscopic model.

(i) A gas consists of tiny particles, either atoms or molecules, moving randomly.

(ii) The volume of the particles themselves is negligible compared with total volume of the gas.

(iii) The gas particles act independently to one another; there are no attractive or repulsive forces between particles.

(iv) Collisions of the gas particles, either with other particles or with the walls of the container, are elastic, i.e. the total kinetic energy of the gas particles is constant at constant temperature.

(v) The average kinetic energy of the gas particles is proportional to the kelvin temperature of the sample.

(vi) The pressure exerted by a gas is the result of collisions of the particles with the walls of the container.

(vii) Gas molecule moves in straight line between two consecutive collision.

(viii) Identical gas molecule were considered in the container.

Kinetic Gas Equation

On the basis of postulates of kinetic theory of gases, the following gas equation was derived.

$$\therefore \quad pV = \frac{1}{3} mN_0u^2 = \frac{1}{3} Mu^2$$

where, $mN_0 = M$ (molar mass), $N_0 =$ Avogadro's number
$u =$ root mean square velocity (u_{rms})

Calculation of Kinetic Energy

Translatory kinetic energy of n moles $= \frac{1}{2} Mu^2$

But by kinetic gas theory $pV = \frac{1}{3} Mu^2$ or $pV = \frac{2}{3}\left(\frac{1}{2} Mu^2\right)$

$$\therefore \quad \frac{1}{2} Mu^2 = \frac{3}{2} pV$$

For ideal gas $\quad pV = nRT \Rightarrow \therefore \frac{1}{2} Mu^2 = \frac{3}{2} nRT$

Average Translational kinetic energy (per mole of gas) $= \frac{3}{2} RT$

Molecules in n moles $= nN_0$

Kinetic energy of n moles ($= nN_0$ molecules) $= \frac{3}{2} nRT$

hence average K.E $= \frac{3}{2}\frac{nRT}{nN_0} = \frac{3}{2} RT/N_0 = \frac{3}{2} kT$ (per molecule)

where, $\frac{R}{N_0}$ Boltzmann's constant $= k$

Average kinetic energy of gas molecules $= \frac{3}{2} kT$

- Average kinetic energy per mole or per molecule is independent of the type of the gas. It is dependent on temperature T (K).
- Average kinetic energy is proportional to absolute temperature. If $T = 0$ K (i.e. $-273.15°C$), then average of kinetic energy $= 0$
- Absolute zero (0 K) is the temperature at which molecular motion ceases. It is also the kinetic interpretation of temperature.
- Average kinetic energy is maintained because fraction of gas molecules with one speed range is fixed at the given temperature.

JEE Alert

The absolute speed of gas molecule is not constant. Because gas molecules are constantly colliding with each other and the walls of their container, causing their speeds to change randomly.

Collision Frequency and Mean Free Path

Collision frequency is the number of collisions that a molecule undergoes per second. It is denoted by Z. The number of collisions that a molecule will undergo in one second depends on the distance it moves and the number of gas molecules per unit volume (i.e. the pressure). In a given time period, a molecule will collide with any other molecule whose centre lies within a cylinder with cross-sectional area σ.

$\sigma = \pi d^2$, where, d is called **collision diameter**.

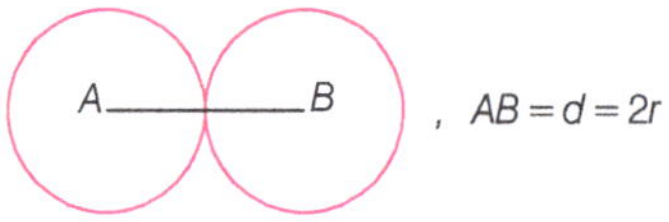

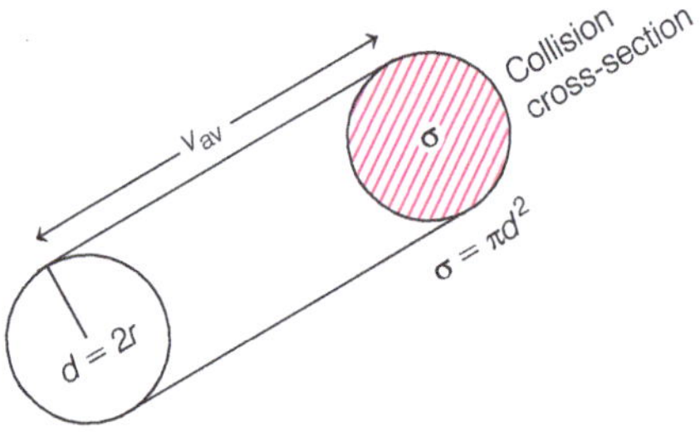

Since the radius of cylinder assumed is $2r$, so all gas molecules present in the assumed cylinder will collide with molecule moving gas molecule.

$$pV = nRT \Rightarrow \frac{n}{V} = \frac{p}{RT}$$

$\frac{N_A}{V} = N'$ number of gas molecule per unit volume.

So, number of gas molecules in the given cylinder is

$$Z = \sigma U_{av} N' \quad \text{where, } Z = \text{collision frequency}$$
$$= \pi d^2 U_{av} N'$$
$$Z = \sqrt{2} U_{av} \pi d^2 N'$$

$\sqrt{2} U_{av}$ is taken because it was assumed that two molecules collide while moving perpendicular to each other.

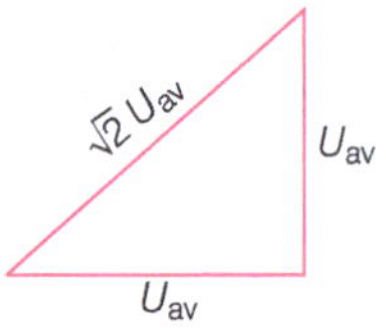

Effect of Collision Frequency on Mean Free Path

The average of the distance travelled by a molecule between successive collisions is called mean free path λ.

$$\lambda = \frac{\text{Distance travelled in 1 s}}{\text{Number of collisions in 1 s}} = \frac{U_{av}}{Z} = \frac{1}{\sqrt{2}\pi d^2 N'} = \frac{RT}{\sqrt{2}\pi d^2 N_A p}$$

JEE Spotlite

- Mean free path (λ) is dependent on temperature T ($\lambda \propto T$) and cross-sectional area σ, $\left(\lambda \propto \frac{1}{\sigma}\right)$
  Since, $\sigma = \pi(2r)^2 = 4\pi r^2$, hence smaller molecules have larger mean free path.
- Pressure p $\left(\lambda \propto \frac{1}{p}\right)$, if p increases λ decreases.
- If the volume of the gas is kept constant, there will be no effect of changing T or pressure on λ.

Solved Booster 1.7

At what pressure will the mean free path be equal to the collision diameter for He at 25°C. (Given, collision diameter of He = 0.218 nm)

(a) 820 bar (b) 893 bar (c) 362 bar (d) 598 bar

Solution (b)

$$\text{Mean free path } \lambda = \frac{RT}{\sqrt{2}\, N_A \sigma p} \qquad \text{...(i)}$$

where, σ = cross-sectional area $= \pi d^2 = \pi(2r)^2$

where, d is the collision diameter

Given, $\lambda = 2r$ (Collision diameter)

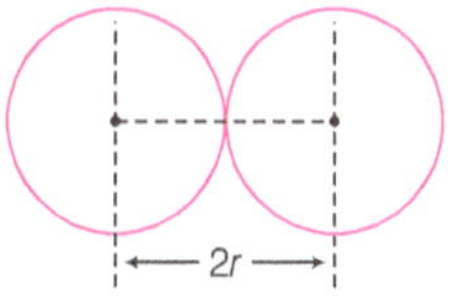

From (i), $\lambda\sigma = \frac{RT}{\sqrt{2}\, N_A\, p}$

$\Rightarrow$ $(2r)\pi(2r)^2 = \frac{RT}{\sqrt{2} N_A p}$

$\therefore$ $p = \frac{RT}{\sqrt{2}\, N_A\, (2r)^3 \pi}$

$$p = \frac{8.314 \text{ J mol}^{-1} \text{ K}^{-1} \times 298 \text{ K}}{\sqrt{2} \times 6.02 \times 10^{23} \text{ mol}^{-1}\ (0.218 \times 10^{-9})^3 \times \pi}$$

$= 8.93 \times 10^7$ Pa = 893 bar

Different Types of Molecular Velocities

Three types of molecular velocities are generally considered in the study of gases.

Most Probable Velocities

It is defined as the velocity possessed by maximum number of molecules of a gas at a given temperature.

$$\therefore \qquad U_{mp} = \sqrt{\frac{2RT}{M}}$$

Average Velocity

It is given by the arithmetic mean of different velocities possessed by the molecules of the gas at a given temperature

$$U_{av} = \frac{u_1 + u_2 + u_3 + \ldots u_n}{n}$$

where, $u_1, u_2, u_3 \ldots$ are the individual velocities of the total n gaseous molecules.

if u_1 is the velocity of n_1 molecules
u_2 is the velocity of n_2 molecules
$\vdots$

The $U_{av} = \frac{n_1 u_1 + n_2 u_2 + n_3 u_3 + \ldots}{n_1 + n_2 + n_3 \ldots}$

Based on distribution of molecular velocities,

$$U_{av} = \sqrt{\frac{8RT}{\pi M}}$$

Root Mean Square Velocity

It is the square root of the mean of the squares of different velocities possessed by molecules of a gas at a given temperature.

$$U_{rms} = \sqrt{\frac{u_1^2 + u_2^2 + u_3^2 + \ldots u_n^2}{n}} = \sqrt{\frac{3RT}{M}}$$

JEE Spotlite

Relation between different molecular velocities.

$$U_{rms} : U_{av} : U_{mp} = \sqrt{3} : \sqrt{\frac{8}{\pi}} : \sqrt{2}$$

$$U_{rms} = 1.2248 u_{mp}$$

$$U_{av} = 1.1284\, u_{mp}$$

$$U_{rms} = 1.0854 \mu_{av}$$

Solved Booster 1.8

The kinetic energy of 1 mole of CO gas at a temperature at which average speed is 100 ms^{-1} will be

(a) 1122 J mol^{-1} (b) 109.9 J mol^{-1}

(c) 339.2 J mol^{-1} (d) 230.1 J mol^{-1}

Solution (b)

$\text{KE} = \frac{1}{3} Mu^2$ Here, u represents rms speed

Also, $U_{av} = \sqrt{\frac{8RT}{\pi M}} \Rightarrow U_{rms} = \sqrt{\frac{3RT}{M}}$

$\Rightarrow$ $U_{rms} = \sqrt{\frac{3\pi}{8}} U_{av} = 1.0854\, U_{av} = 1.0854 \times 100 = 108.54 \text{ ms}^{-1}$

$\therefore$ $\text{KE} = \frac{1}{3} Mu^2 = \frac{1}{3} \times 28 \times 10^{-3} \text{kg} \times (108.54)^2 \text{ m}^2\text{s}^{-2}$

$= 109.96 \text{ J mol}^{-1}$

JEE MAPPER

Example Similar to PYQ Asked in JEE Advanced 2024

A closed vessel contains 10 g of an ideal gas X at 300 K which exerts 2 atm pressure. At the same temperature, 90 g of another ideal gas Y is added to it and the pressure become 6 atm. The ratio of root mean square velocities of X and Y at 300 K is

(a) $2\sqrt{3}:1$ (b) $1:\sqrt{3}$ (c) $\sqrt{3}:\sqrt{1}$ (d) $1:2\sqrt{3}$

Sol. (c) Given, For ideal gas X; For ideal gas Y

$m_1 = 10$ g $\quad m_2 = 90$ g

$T_1 = 300$ K $\quad T_2 = 300$ K

$p_1 = 2$ atm $\quad p_2 = 6$ atm

$$\frac{V_{rms}(X)}{V_{rms}(Y)} = ?$$

Substitute the given values in ideal gas equation,

$$pV = nRT$$

For gas X, $$2 \times V = \frac{10}{M_x} \times RT \quad \text{...(i)}$$

For gas Y, $$6 \times V = \frac{90}{M_y} \times RT \quad \text{...(ii)}$$

Divide Eqs. (ii) by Eq. (i)

$$\frac{6 \times V}{2 \times V} = \frac{\frac{90}{M_y} \times RT}{\frac{10}{M_x} \times RT}$$

$$3 = 9\frac{M_x}{M_y} \Rightarrow \frac{M_x}{M_y} = \frac{1}{3}$$

Now, we know that,

$$V_{rms} = \sqrt{\frac{3RT}{M}}$$

So, $$\frac{V_{rms}(X)}{V_{rms}(Y)} = \sqrt{\frac{M_Y}{M_X}} \Rightarrow \sqrt{\frac{3}{1}}$$

Thus, $$\frac{V_{rms}(X)}{V_{rms}(Y)} = \frac{\sqrt{3}}{\sqrt{1}}$$

Competency Enhancer 1.1

A closed vessel contains 20 g of an ideal gas X at 350 K, which exerts 4 atm pressure. At the same temperature, 60 g of another ideal gas Y is added to it and the pressure becomes 12 atm. The ratio of root mean square velocities of Y and X at 350 K is

(a) 1 : 1 (b) 1 : 3 (c) 2 : 1 (d) 1 : 2

Solved Booster 1.9

For gaseous state, if most probable speed is denoted by C^*, average speed by $\bar{C}$ and mean square speed by C, then for a large number of molecules, the ratios of these speeds are

(a) $C^*:\bar{C}:C = 1.225 : 1.128 : 1$ (b) $C^*:\bar{C}:C = 1.128 : 1.225 : 1$

(c) $C^*:\bar{C}:C = 1 : 1.128 : 1.225$ (d) $C^*:\bar{C}:C = 1 : 1.225 : 1.128$

Solution (c)

C^* = most probable speed = $\sqrt{2RT/M}$

$\bar{C}$ = average speed = $\sqrt{8RT/\pi M}$

C = Mean square speed, rms = $\sqrt{\frac{3RT}{M}}$

$$\therefore \quad C^*:\bar{C}:C = \sqrt{\frac{2RT}{M}}:\sqrt{\frac{8RT}{\pi M}}:\sqrt{\frac{3RT}{M}}$$

$$= \sqrt{2}:\sqrt{\frac{8}{\pi}}:\sqrt{3} = 1:\sqrt{\frac{4}{\pi}}:\sqrt{\frac{3}{2}}$$

Hence, $$C^*:\bar{C}:C = 1:\sqrt{\frac{4}{\pi}}:\sqrt{\frac{3}{2}} = 1 : 1.128 : 1.225$$

Graham's Law of Diffusion

If a tiny hole is made in the wall of a vessel containing a gas, then the rate at which gas molecules leak out of vessel will be proportional to the number of molecules that collide with unit area of the wall in unit time.

Diffusion is the tendency of any substance to spread throughout the space available to it.

Diffusion will take place in all direction and even against gravity. So gases diffuse through firm substances. The streaming of gas molecules through a small hole is called effusion.

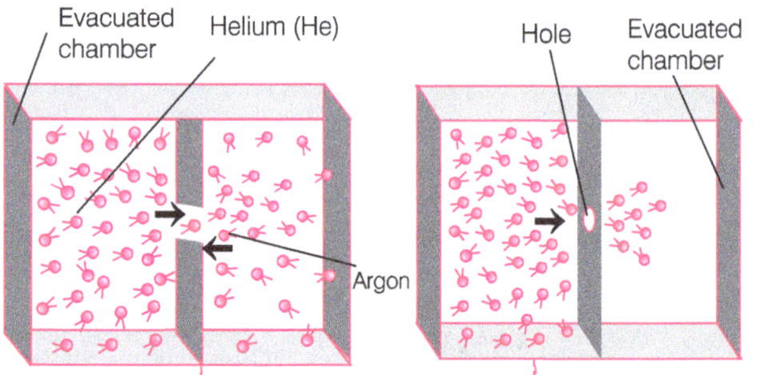

The movement of light gas (helium) into the Argon chamber through diffusion. This means that diffusion occurs from high concentration to low concentration

The escape of gaseous molecules through a small hole into evacuated space (vaccum). This suggest that, the movement of gases from high pressure to low pressure (vaccum) illustrates effusion.

According to Graham the rate of diffusion (effusion) of a gas at constant p and T is inversely proportional to square root of its molecular mass.

$$r \propto \sqrt{\frac{1}{M}} \text{ at constant } p \text{ and } T.$$

$$\therefore \quad \frac{r_1}{r_2} = \sqrt{\frac{M_2}{M_1}} \text{ at constant } p \text{ and } T.$$

The above equation is applicable only if two said gases are at same temperature and pressure, effusing through opening of identical geometry. The two gases may be in the combined system if they are non-reacting and at the same partial pressure.

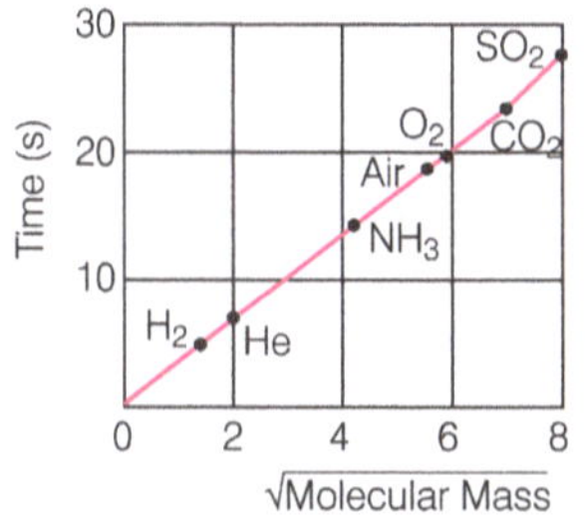

If a gaseous mixture consists of several components of different molar masses and at different partial pressure as well, initial rate of effusion of a component will depend on both molar mass and their partial pressure is outside pressure is zero or difference of pressure as

$$r_1 \propto p_i \quad \text{and} \quad r_i \propto \frac{1}{\sqrt{M_i}}$$

$\Rightarrow \quad r_i \propto \dfrac{p_i}{\sqrt{M_i}}$, if rate of effusion is linearly related to its partial pressure.

Under the above conditions, $\dfrac{r_1}{r_2} = \dfrac{p_1}{p_2} = \sqrt{\dfrac{M_2}{M_1}}$

Rate can be expressed in following terms

$$r = \frac{\text{Volume diffused } (V)}{\text{time taken}} = \frac{\text{moles diffused } (n)}{\text{time taken}}$$

$$r = \frac{\text{distance travelled in a narrow tube } (d)}{\text{time taken}}$$

Instantaneous Rate of Diffusion

Instantaneous rate of effusion will depend on the instantaneous partial pressure of that component, which decreases continuously with progress of effusion. Considering, instantaneous rate of decreases of partial pressure $\left(\dfrac{-dp}{dt}\right)$ to be directly proportional to instantaneous gas pressure and inversely proportional to square root of molar mass, instantaneous pressure at any time can be written as

$-\dfrac{dp}{dt} = \dfrac{K.p.}{\sqrt{M}}$ where K is constant of proportionality.

$$\Rightarrow \quad \int_{p_1}^{p_2} -\frac{dp}{p} = \frac{K}{\sqrt{M}} \int_0^t dt$$

$$\Rightarrow \quad \ln\left(\frac{p_1}{p_2}\right) = \frac{Kt}{\sqrt{M}}$$

$$\text{or} \quad p_2 = p_1 \exp\left(-\frac{Kt}{\sqrt{M}}\right)$$

Hence, partial pressure decreases exponentially with time as

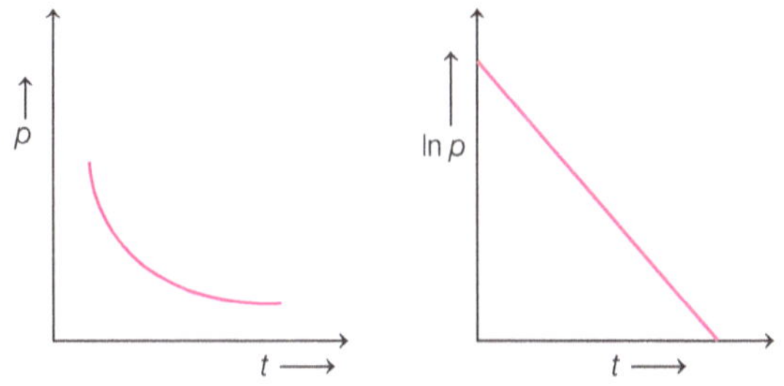

Separation of Gases Using Diffusion

When a gaseous mixture with lighter and heavier components is passed through a series of connected diffusion chambers, the lighter component progressively becomes more concentrated at each step. By performing diffusion through a set number of these chambers in succession, a desired level of enrichment of the lighter component can be achieved as described below.

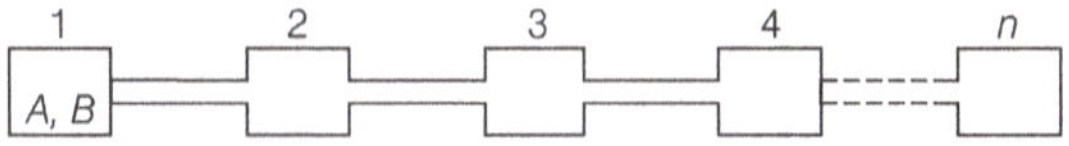

From the 1st chamber:

$$\left(\frac{r_A}{r_B}\right)_1 = \left(\frac{n_A}{n_B}\right)_1 \sqrt{\frac{M_B}{M_A}} = \left(\frac{n_A}{n_B}\right)_2$$

From the 2nd chamber

$$\left(\frac{r_A}{r_B}\right)_2 = \left(\frac{n_A}{n_B}\right)_2 \sqrt{\frac{M_B}{M_A}} = \left(\frac{n_A}{n_B}\right)_1 \left(\frac{M_B}{M_A}\right)^{2/2} = \left(\frac{n_A}{n_B}\right)_3$$

From the 3rd chamber

$$\left(\frac{r_A}{r_B}\right)_3 = \left(\frac{n_A}{n_B}\right)_3 \sqrt{\frac{M_B}{M_A}} = \left(\frac{n_A}{n_B}\right)_1 \left(\frac{M_B}{M_A}\right)^{3/2} = \left(\frac{n_A}{n_B}\right)_4$$

Similarly, from $(n-1)$th chamber

$$\left(\frac{r_A}{r_B}\right)_{n-1} = \left(\frac{n_A}{n_B}\right)_{n-1} \sqrt{\frac{M_B}{M_A}} = \left(\frac{n_A}{n_B}\right)_1 \left(\frac{M_B}{M_A}\right)^{\frac{n-1}{2}} = \left(\frac{n_A}{n_B}\right)_n$$

$$\Rightarrow \quad \left(\frac{r_A}{r_B}\right)_{n-1} = \left(\frac{n_A}{n_B}\right)_1 \left(\frac{M_B}{M_A}\right)^{\frac{n-1}{2}} = \left(\frac{n_A}{n_B}\right)_n$$

This equation indicates that after $(n-1)$ th step of diffusion a specific enrichment $\left(\dfrac{n_A}{n_B}\right)_n$ can be achieved in the nth chamber.

Solved Booster 1.10

A gas of unknown identity effuses at the rate of 83.3 mL s^{-1} in an effusion apparatus in which carbon dioxide effuses at the rate of 102 mL s^{-1}. Calculate the molar mass of the unknown gas.

(a) 50 (b) 66 (c) 26 (d) 44

Solution (b)

By Graham's law of effusion, $\frac{r_1}{r_2} = \sqrt{\frac{M_2}{M_1}}$

$r_1, r_2, M_1(CO_2)$ are given. Thus, M_2(Molar mass of the unknown gas can be derived).

$$r_1(CO_2) = 102 \text{ mL s}^{-1}$$
$$r_2(X) = 83.3 \text{ mL s}^{-1}$$
$$M_1(CO_2) = 44.0 \text{ g mol}^{-1}$$

$$\therefore \quad \frac{102}{83.3} = \sqrt{\frac{M_2}{44}} = 1.2245$$

$$\therefore \quad M_2 = 44(1.2245)^2$$
$$\approx 66.0 \text{ g mol}^{-1}$$

The Real Gas

The ideal gas law $pV = nRT$ holds fairly true for most gases but over a limited range of temperature and pressure. However, when the range and accuracy of measurements were extended and improved, real gases were found to deviate from expected behaviour of an ideal gas.

For instance pV_m (V_m = molar volume of a gas) does not have same value for all gases at a given temperature. Also plot of pV_m *vs* p are not same for all gases at a given temperature. The graph in figure describes the real pressure dependence of volume for one mole of different gases at same temperature.

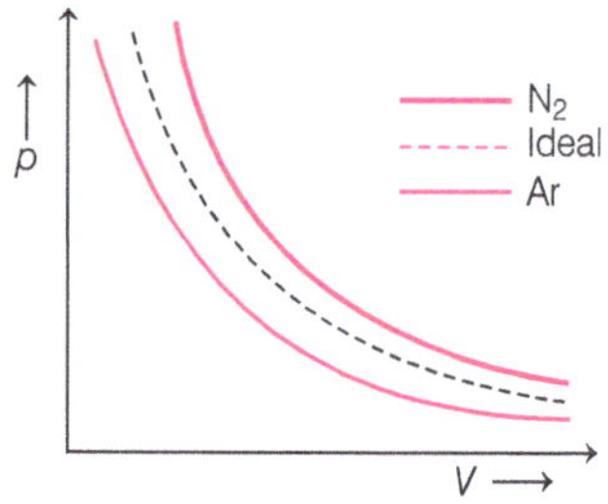

Plots of p *vs* V for real gas and comparison with ideal gas curve

Compression Factor (Z)

It is measure of deviation form ideal bahaviour and defined as

$$Z = \frac{V_m\,(\text{Red})}{V_m\,(\text{Ideal})}$$
$$= \frac{pV_m}{RT}$$

For an ideal gas $Z = 1$ and for a non-ideal gas $Z \neq 1$. Therefore, departure from unity indicates non-ideal behaviour, since each gas will have different interaction amongst their molecules, i.e., the behaviour of Z can be expected to be different for different gases. The following diagram showing plot of Z *vs* p for several gas depicts the variations typically observed.

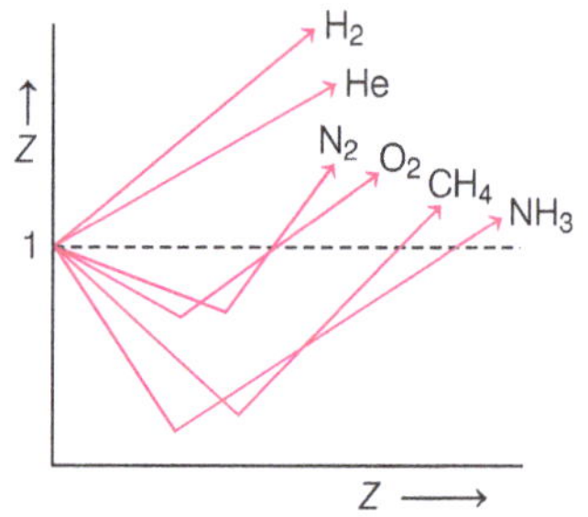

Plot of compression factor (Z) *versus* pressure for several gases at 273 K.

The shape of initial negative slope of some of these gases can be related to the attractive forces ($Z < 1$) prevalent among the molecules. It can be illustrated in the following manner.

- Z measure of deviation from ideal behaviour.

  Thus, if there exists attractive forces among the gas molecules, they will be attracted towards one another and will collide to the wall of container with less momentum. This results in lowering of observed pressure than expected.

  $$p_{\text{real}} < p_{\text{ideal}} \quad \text{and} \quad Z < 1$$

- Initial positive slope ($Z > 1$) indicates that repulsive forces among the gas molecules dominate. In case of repulsion, gas molecules will collide to the walls of container with greater effective momentum as compared to independent collision and a greater value of pressure will be observed.

  $$p_{\text{real}} > p_{\text{ideal}} \quad \text{and} \quad Z > 1$$

  All gases, at sufficiently high pressure will have $Z > 1$, since molecules come closer and repulsive forces start to dominate.

- As $p \to 0$, curves for all gases approaches $Z = 1$, with different slopes. Hence, as $p \to 0$ (low pressure and high temperature) gases approaches to ideality.

Reasons for Deviation from Ideality

Gases deviate form ideal behaviour because the assumptions made in deriving kinetic gas equation, do not hold true under all conditions of pressure and temperature. Two assumptions, which are mainly responsible for deviation form ideal behaviour, are

(i) **Molecular Volume** According to kinetic theory of gases, gas molecules have negligible volume due to their masses. In actual practice, gases can be liquefied and solidified, the volume occupied by gas molecules are finite and its contribution to the total volume becomes significant under specific conditions of temperature and pressure.

(ii) **Intermolecular Interactions** In kinetic theory of gases, gas molecules were assumed to be independent of attractive or repulsive forces by other molecules. In real situation, gases exert either attractive or repulsive force on one another depending upon conditions of temperaure and pressure.

Derivation of van der Waals' Equation

The equation proposed by van der Waals' can be derived from mathematical consideration in a number of ways. An easiest, but not so rigid method is as follows:

1. Correction for Pressure

If the molecules in a gas attract each other, then a molecule situated in the interior of a gas assembly is under the influence of attractive force from all sides of this. This serves to cancel the forces in the different directions mutually and to allow the molecule to freely move in any direction. On the other hand, when a molecule goes to strike the wall (which is responsible for the pressure exerted by the gas) it is attracted by the molecules situated on rear side as shown in figure.

In other words, the observed pressure (p) is smaller than the ideal pressure (p_i). Thus, in order to get the ideal pressure (p_i) a correction term has to be added to the observed pressure (p').

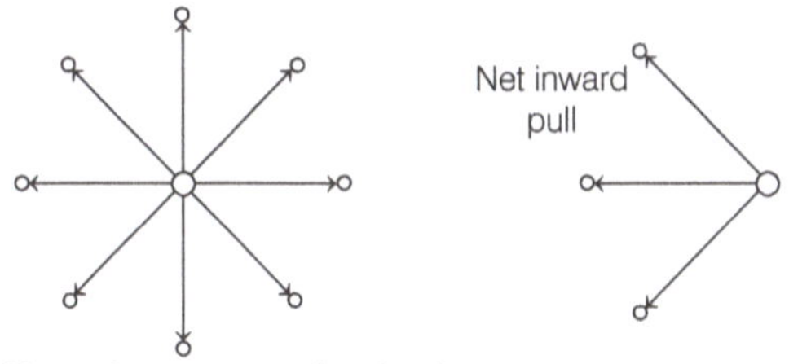

No net force on cental molecule

Net inward pull to the molecules near to the wall of container.

(i) Now this "p" known as pressure correction factor depends on the number of molecules attracting the molecules, which are about to strike the wall $p \propto n/V$. where, 'n' is the number of moles of gas and V is the volume of container. Inward pull depends on the density of gas.

(ii) Also 'p' depends on the number of molecules colliding per unit area of wall, and is, therefore, proportional to the total number of molecules per unit volume, i.e. n/V. Hence,

$$p \propto \frac{n^2}{V^2}$$

or $p = \dfrac{n^2 a}{V^2}$ where 'a' is the proportionality constant and is measure of the forces of attraction between the molecules.

The unit of the term $\dfrac{an^2}{V^2}$ is same as that of pressure.

2. Volume Correction

V in the ideal gas equation represents a volume where the molecules can move freely. In real gases, a part of the total volume is, however, occupied by the molecules of the gas due to their masses. If b represents the effective volume occupied by the molecules of 1 mole of a gas due to their masses, then for the amount n moles of the gas V_i is given by

$$V = V_{\text{container}} - nb$$

where b is called the excluded volume or co-volume. The numerical value of b is four times the actual volume occupied by the gas molecules due to their masses. This can be shown as follows. If we consider only bimolecular collisions, then the volume occupied by the sphere of radius $2r$ represents the excluded volume per pair of molecules as shown in figure.

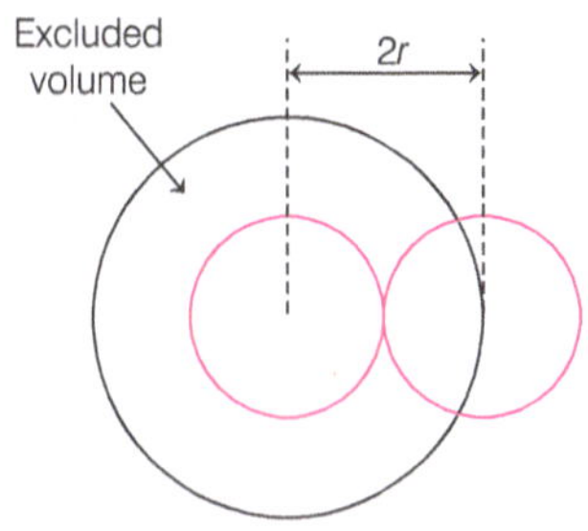

Thus excluded volume per pair of molecules

$$\frac{4}{3}\pi(2r)^3 = 8\left(\frac{4}{3}\pi r^3\right)$$

Excluded volume per molecule

$$= \frac{1}{2}\left[8\left(\frac{4}{3}\pi r^3\right)\right] = 4\left(\frac{4}{3}\pi r^3\right)$$

(volume occupied by a molecule)

Since b represents excluded volume per mole of the gas,

$$b = N_A\left[4\left(\frac{4}{3}\pi r^3\right)\right].$$

van der Waals' Equation

van der Waal's equation introduced corrections to the pressure and volume terms of the ideal gas law in order to account for intermolecular interactions and molecular size respectively. The equation is given below.

$$\left(p + \frac{a}{V_m^2}\right)(V_m - b) = RT$$

This equation is applicable to real gases and is known as van der Waal's equation.

JEE Spotlite

- **Volume correction factor**, depends on molecular size and larger molecule will have larger b. eg size of He, CH_4, CF_4, C_4H_{10} ..., are in order of He < CH_4 < CF_4 < C_4H_{10} and same will be the order of b.
- **Pressure correction factor** $\dfrac{n^2a}{V^2}$, depends on intermolecular force of attraction. Hence, larger the intermolecular force of attraction larger the value of 'a', for same n and V. e.g. intermolecular force of attraction among the molecules H_2, CO_2, NH_3,... are in order of $H_2 < CO_2 < NH_3$ (H-bonding) and same is the order of a.
- **Compressibility of gas (Z)** will depend on both 'a' and 'b'... "For greater compressibility, a gas should have small 'b' and large 'a'

Explanation of the Behaviour of Real Gases by van der Waal's Equation

(i) In low pressure region, volume will be large enough so that b can be ignored in comparison to V and van der Waals' equation takes the form

$$\left(p + \frac{n^2a}{V^2}\right)(V) = nRT$$

$$\Rightarrow \quad \left(p + \frac{a}{V_m^2}\right)V_m = RT$$

$$\Rightarrow \quad Z = \frac{pV_m}{RT} = 1 - \frac{a}{V_mRT} < 1 \quad \ldots(i)$$

Therefore, in low pressure region $Z < 1$, attractive forces dominate

(ii) In high pressure region,

$$p > \frac{a}{V_m^2} \text{ and } p + \frac{a}{V_m^2} = p$$

$$\Rightarrow \quad p(V_m - b) = RT \quad \Rightarrow Z = 1 + \frac{bp}{RT} > 1 \quad \ldots(ii)$$

Eq. (ii) indicates that in high pressure region, $Z > 1$, i.e. repulsive forces dominate.

(iii) At low pressure and high temperature conditions both attractive forces and finite size of gas molecules can be ignored due to high random motion and large volume of container.

$pV = RT$, Ideal gas approximations can be considered.

- The compressibility factor even for lighter gas can be less than 1, if they are at or less then their critical temperature.
- For lighter gas molecules e.g. H_2 or He, at room temperature attractive forces are not considered because of high random motion, $p(V - b) = RT$.
- There is one more point where $Z = 1$, when attractive forces balance the repulsive forces.
- $Z > 1$ permanent gas zone and $Z < 1$: liquification zone

van der Waals' constants

Gas	a kPa dm^{6}mol^{-2}	b dm^{3}mol^{-1}	Gas	a kPa dm^{6}mol^{-2}	b dm^{3}mol^{-1}
H_2	21.764	0.02661	CH_4	228.825	0.04278
He	3.457	0.02370	C_2H_6	556.173	0.06380
N_2	140.842	0.03913	C_3H_8	877.880	0.08445
O_2	137.802	0.03183	$C_4H_{10}(n)$	1466.173	0.1226
Cl_2	657.903	0.05622	$C_4H_{10}(iso)$	1304.053	0.1142
NO	135.776	0.02789	$C_5H_{12}(n)$	1926.188	0.1460
NO_2	535.401	0.04424	CO	150.468	0.03985
H_2O	553.639	0.03049	CO_2	363.959	0.04267

JEE MAPPER

Example Similar to PYQ Asked in JEE Advanced 2023

A gas has a compressibility factor of 0.3 and a molar volume of 0.2 dm^3 mol^{-1} at a temperature of 750 K and pressure x atm. If it shows ideal gas behaviour at the same temperature and pressure, the molar volume will be y dm^3 mol^{-1}. The value of $\left(\frac{x}{y}\right)$ is ....

[Use : Gas constant, $R = 8 \times 10^{-2}$ L atm K^{-1} mol^{-1}]

Sol. (136.4) Given, compressibility factor (Z) = 0.3

$V_m = 0.2$ dm^3 mol^{-1}, $T = 750$ K,

$p = x$ atm, $\quad R = 8 \times 10^{-2}$

We know that,

$$Z = \frac{pV_m}{RT}$$

$$0.3 = \frac{x \times 0.2}{8 \times 10^{-2} \times 750}$$

$$x = \frac{0.3 \times 8 \times 10^{-2} \times 750}{0.2} \Rightarrow 90$$

For ideal condition, $Z = 1$ and molar volume will be y dm^3 mol^{-1}.

Using, $Z = \frac{pV_m}{RT} \Rightarrow 1 = \frac{90 \times y}{0.08 \times 750}$

$$y = \frac{0.08 \times 750}{90} = 0.66$$

Now, $\frac{x}{y} = \frac{90}{0.66} = 136.36 \approx 136.4$

Competency Enhancer 1.2

A gas has a compressibility, factor of 0.7 and molar volume of 0.4 dm^3 mol^{-1} at a temperature of 850 K and pressure x atm. If it show ideal gas behaviour at the same temperature and pressure, the molar volume will be y dm^3 mol^{-1}.

The value of $\left(\frac{x}{y}\right)$ is ....

[**Use** Gas constant, $R = 8 \times 10^{-2}$ L atm K^{-1} mol^{-1}]

Liquefaction of Gases

A gas can be liquefied when its temperature is below critical temperature, i.e. by cooling or compressing it.

As a gas is compressed at a given temperature, the intermolecular distance decreases and intermolecular forces come into effect.

The kinetic energy of the molecules gradually decreases and the gas is said to be undergoing *liquefaction*.

During liquefaction, the pressure remains constant. The process of liquefaction spreads over a definite time interval.

(i) Gases which have high critical temperatures (such as CO_2, SO_2, NH_3, Cl_2 etc.) can be liquefied by applying a suitable pressure alone. Permanent gases (such as H_2, N_2, O_2 etc.) cannot be liquefied by the action of pressure and cooling.

(ii) A gas can be liquefied by "lowering the temperature" or "increasing the pressure".

(iii) **Andrews** in 1861 studied the effect of pressure on the volume of CO_2 at different constant temperatures.

Some of the effect are shown in the form of isotherm is in the following figure

- At 13.1°C (low temperature) and low pressure CO_2 exists as a gas as shown at the point X.
- The volume of the gas decreases along the curve XY, as the pressure is increased. At, Y liquefaction of gas starts and complete at point Z (volume is decrease along moving from Y to Z).

- After that increase in pressure has very little effect on volume due to which a steep curve (ZM) is obtained. Because liquids are very slightly compressible.
- As the temperature is increased, horizontal portion becomes smaller and smaller. At critical point, it reduced to a point P.
- 31.1°C is the critical temperature, pressure corresponding to their temperature is its critical pressure p_c (73.9 atm), and volume occupied by 1 mol of gas under these condition is its critical volume V_c (95.6 mL).

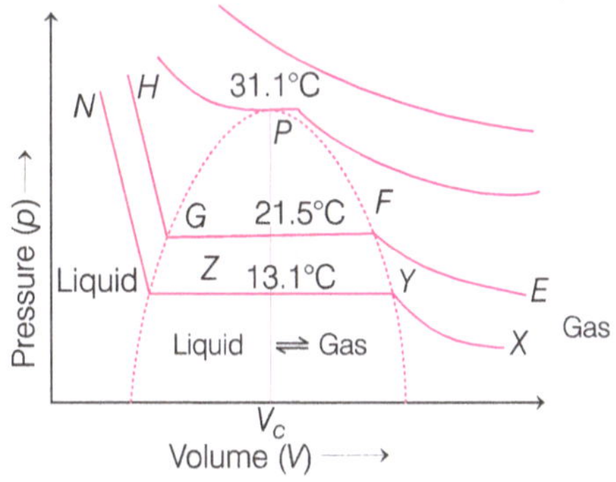

Isotherms of CO_2 at different temperatures

JEE Spotlite

Methods of Liquefaction of Gases

Two modern methods of cooling the gas to or below their T_c and hence, of liquefaction of gases are Linde's method and Claude's method.

(i) **Linde's Method** This process is based upon Joule-Thomson effect which states that "when a gas is allowed to expand adiabatically from a region of high pressure to a region of extremely low pressure, it is accompanied by cooling."

(ii) **Claude's Method** This process is based upon the principle that when a gas expands adiabatically against an external pressure (as a piston in an engine), it does some external work. Since work is done by the molecules at the cost of their kinetic energy, the temperature of the gas falls causing cooling.

Critical Constants

Different critical constant are as follows

(i) **Critical State** A state for every substance at which its vapour and liquid states are indistinguishable is known as critical state.

At this state, following conditions are achieved

(ii) **Critical Temperature** There is a temperature below which the gas can be liquefied but above it the gas defies liquefaction. This temperature is called critical temperature (T_c).

It is given by, $T_c = \dfrac{8a}{27Rb}$

(iii) **Critical Pressure** The critical pressure (p_c) is the minimum pressure required to liquefy the gas at its critical temperature. It is given by, $p_c = \dfrac{a}{27b^2}$

(iv) **Critical Volume** The critical volume (V_c) is the volume occupied by a mole of the gas at the critical temperature and critical pressure. It is given by $V_c = 3b$

From the above, the critical compressibility factor (Z_c) is given by,

$$Z_c = \frac{p_c V_c}{RT_c} = \frac{3}{8} = 0.375$$

All the gases behaves as a van der Waal's gas, its critical compressibiity factor (Z_c) is equal to 0.375.

Solved Booster 1.11

Consider the van der Waals' constants, a and b, for the following gases.

Gas	Ar	Ne	Kr	Xe
a/(atm dm^6 mol^{-2})	1.3	0.2	5.1	4.1
b/(10^{-2} dm^3 mol^{-1})	3.2	1.7	1.0	5.0

Which gas is expected to have the highest critical temperature?

(a) Kr (b) Xe (c) Ar (d) Ne

Solution *(a)*

Critical temperature is the temperature of a gas above which it cannot be liquefied what ever high the pressure may be. The kinetic energy of gas molecules above this temperature is sufficient enough to overcome the attractive forces. It is represented as T_c.

$$T_c = \frac{8a}{27Rb}$$

For Ar, $T_c = \dfrac{8 \times 1.3}{27 \times 8.314 \times 3.2} = 0.0145$

For Ne, $T_c = \dfrac{8 \times 0.2}{27 \times 8.314 \times 1.7} = 0.0042$

For Kr, $T_c = \dfrac{8 \times 5.1}{27 \times 8.314 \times 1.0} = 0.18$

For Xe, $T_c = \dfrac{8 \times 4.1}{27 \times 8.314 \times 5.0} = 0.03$

The value of T_c is highest for Kr (Krypton).

Elemental Practice 3.1

Type I MCQs with Only One Correct Option

1. Variation of log (p) with log $\left(\frac{1}{V}\right)$ is shown in the following isotherm at 300 K. If $OA = 0.3010$ bar dm^3. Then the volume at 2.0 bar is

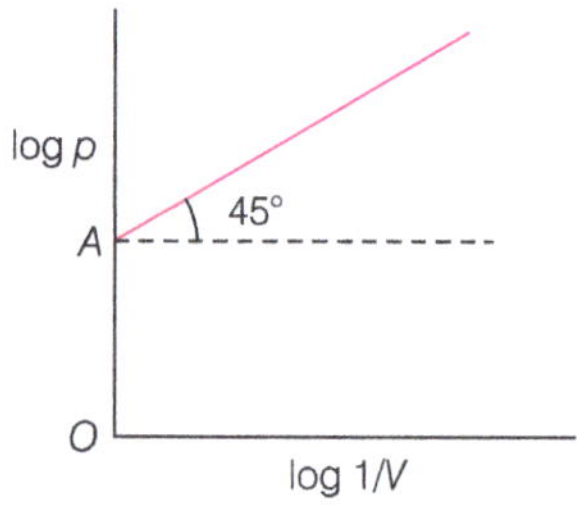

(a) 3.0 (b) 2.1
(c) 1.8 (d) 1.0

2. I, II and III are three isobars respectively at p_1, p_2 and p_3 as shown:

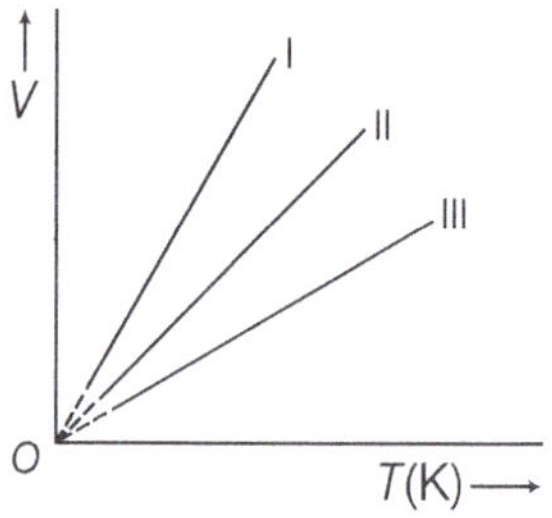

Arrange p_1, p_2 and p_3 in increasing order.
(a) $p_1 < p_2 < p_3$
(b) $p_3 < p_2 < p_1$
(c) $p_1 = p_2 = p_3$
(d) $p_3 < p_1 < p_2$

3. **Assertion (A)** In van der Waals' equation

$$\left(p + \frac{n^2a}{V^2}\right)(V - nb) = nRT$$

Pressure correction $\left(\frac{n^2a}{V^2}\right)$ is due to force of attraction between molecules.

Reason (R) Pressure of the gas is due to collisions of molecules against sides of the container.
(a) Both Assertion (A) and Reason (R) are correct and Reason (R) is a correct explanation of Assertion (A)
(b) Both Assertion (A) and Reason (R) are correct but Reason (R) is not the correct explanation of Assertion (A)
(c) Assertion (A) is correct, Reason (R) is incorrect
(d) Assertion (A) is incorrect, Reason (R) is correct.

4. The vapour pressure of liquid water is 23.8 torr at 25 °C. By what factor does the molar volume of water increases as it vaporises to form an ideal gas under these conditions? The density of liquid water is 0.997 g cm^{-3} at 298 K?
(a) 4.32×10^4 (b) 2.31×10^{-5}
(c) 4.32×10^6 (d) 2.31×10^{-7}

5. Which of the following temperature is correctly matched with their value?
(a) Critical temperature $\longrightarrow \frac{8b}{27Ra}$
(b) Boyle temperature $\longrightarrow \frac{2a}{Rb}$
(c) Inversion temperature $\longrightarrow \frac{a}{Rb}$
(d) Reduced temperature $\longrightarrow \frac{T}{T_c}$

6. 1.00 mole of O_2 and 3.00 moles of H_2 are mixed isothermally in a 125.0 L flask at 400 K. Gaseous mixture undergoes reaction to form H_2O vapours. Assume ideal behaviour. Total pressure after $H_2O(g)$ is formed is
(a) 0.80 bar (b) 1.056 bar
(c) 0.528 bar (d) 0.78 bar

7. A gaseous mixture containing He, CH_4 and SO_2 was allowed to effuse through a fine hole. If mixture contain He, CH_4 and SO_2 in 1 : 2 : 3 mole ratio, calculate the molar ratio of gases effusing out initially.
(a) 4 : 4 : 3 (b) $\sqrt{2} : \sqrt{2} : 3$
(c) 6 : 6 : 1 (d) 2 : 2 : 3

8. Pressure (p / bar) and temperature (T / K) needed to confine 1.0×10^{25} gas molecules, each with a mass of 1.0×10^{-25} kg and rms speed of 1.0×10^3 ms^{-1} in a 1.0 m^3 container are

	p (bar)	T (K)
(a)	3.33	2411
(b)	9.91	2411
(c)	3.33	1200
(d)	1.11	800

9. A and B are two ideal gases with the following parameters.

Gas	Molecules	Temperature	Kinetic energy
A	N_A	–123°C	E_A
B	N_B	27°C	E_B

If $(E_B/E_A) = 2$, then N_B/N_A is
(a) 1 (b) 2 (c) 3 (d) 4

10. **Assertion (A)** The collision frequency increases with decrease the pressure of the gas.

Reason (R) At constant temperature, molecules take less time to travel to its neighbour (before collision) in high pressure of the gas.

(a) Both Assertion (A) and Reason (R) are correct; Reason (R) is a correct explanation of Assertion (A)
(b) Both Assertion (A) and Reason (R) are correct; Reason (R) is not the correct explanation of Assertion (A)
(c) Assertion (A) is correct, Reason (R) is incorrect
(d) Assertion (A) is incorrect, Reason (R) is correct.

11. Given J-tube has 2.4 mL of air at a pressure of 1 atm. On adding mercury, volume of air is reduced to 1.9 mL as shown. Difference in the level of mercury in two columns is

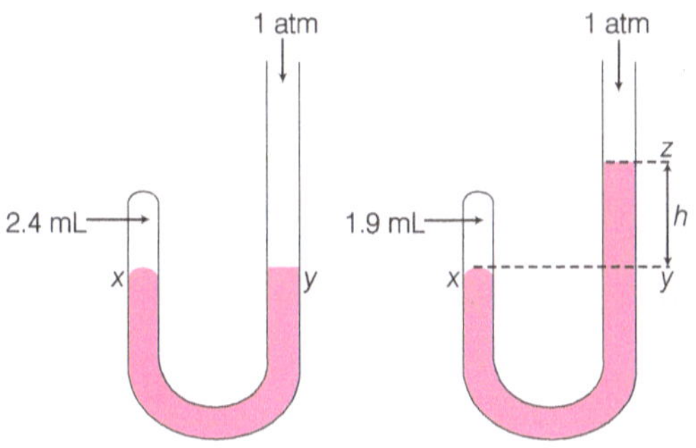

(a) 700 mm (b) 200 mm
(c) 960 mm (d) 760 mm

12. A closed vessel contains 30 g of an ideal gas *X* at 450 K, which exerts 4 atm pressure. At the same temperature 70 g, of another ideal gas *Y* is added to it having pressure 6 atm. The ratio of root mean square velocities of *X* and *Y* at 450 K is

(a) $2\sqrt{2} : 3$ (b) $\sqrt{14} : 3$
(c) $\sqrt{12} : \sqrt{17}$ (d) $3 : 2\sqrt{2}$

13. Which of the following gases follows non-ideal behaviour ?

(a) N_2 gas having density 1.25 g L^{-1} at STP
(b) 2.8 g CO gas in 0.1L flask exerting a pressure of 24.63 atm at 300 K
(c) 1.6 g CH_4 in 0.5 L flask at 273 K exerting a pressure of 4 atm
(d) 0.1 g H_2 gas at STP occupies volume of 1.12 L

14. Mean free path of krypton atom (radius = 1.85 Å) at 20°C and 1 bar pressure is

(a) 665 Å (b) 26.64 pm
(c) 333 nm (d) 472 pm

15. If densities of two gases are in the ratio 1 : 2 and their temperature are in the ratio 2 : 1, then the ratio of their respective molar mass at certain pressure is

(a) 4 : 1 (b) 2 : 1
(c) 1 : 2 (d) 1 : 1

Type II 》 MCQs with One or More than One Correct Option

16. Which of the following statements are incorrect? As critical point is approached

(a) the density of CO_2 (*l*) decreases and that of CO_2 (*g*) increases and at $T = T_C$ densities are equal.
(b) the density of CO_2 (*l*) increases and that of CO_2 (*g*) decreases and at $T = T_C$ densities are equal
(c) the density of CO_2 (*l*) and that of CO_2 (*g*) increases
(d) the density of CO_2 (*l*) and that of CO_2 (*g*) decreases

17. Which of the following statements are correct?

(a) Mass density of O_2 gas at 25° C and 1 atm is 1.31×10^{-3} kg m^{-3}
(b) Number density of O_2 gas at 25°C and 1 atm is 2.96×10^{25} molecules m^{-3}
(c) Mass density differs from gas to gas
(d) Number density at a given temperature and pressure is same for all gases

18. An ideal gas is at 300 K and 1 atm. The volume remains constant if

(a) temperature is doubled and pressure is halved
(b) temperature is halved and pressure is halved
(c) temperature is doubled and pressure is doubled
(d) Only temperature is doubled

19. Consider gases confined by a liquid, as shown in figure. Density of the liquid = *d* (all values in SI unit).

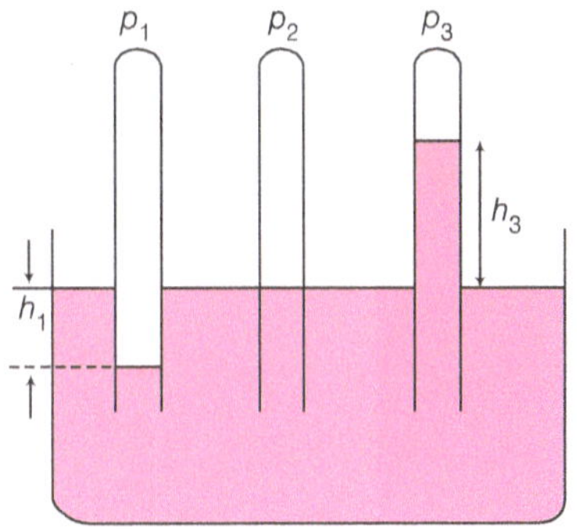

Then, identify the correct statement(s).

(a) in terms of barometric pressure (p_{atm}), p_1 is $p_{atm} + h_1dg$
(b) barometers pressure is $p_1 + p_2 + p_3$
(c) in terms of barometric pressure (p_{atm}), p_3 is $p_{atm} - h_3dg$
(d) barometric pressure is p_2

20. When two gaseous molecules of equal radii *r* collide,

(a) their centres are separated by 2*r* at the point of contact
(b) effective volume occupied by two molecules is eight times of the volume of each molecule
(c) excluded volume is four times of volume of each molecule
(d) greater the excluded volume, greater the deviation from ideal behaviour

Type IV 》 Numerical/Integer Answer Type Questions

21. A gas has a compressibility factor of 0.8 and molar volume of 0.7 $dm^3 \, mol^{-1}$ at a temperature of 950 K and pressure x atm. If it shows ideal gas behaviour at the same temperature and pressure, the molar volume will be $y \, dm^3 \, mol^{-1}$. The value of $\left(\frac{x}{y}\right)$ is ....

    [Use : Gas constant, $R = 8 \times 10^{-2}$ L atm $K^{-1} \, mol^{-1}$]

22. A mixture of N_2 and O_2 has a density of 1.00 g dm^{-3} at 300 K and 600 mm of Hg pressure. Mole fraction of N_2 in the mixture is $10x$. The value of 'x' is ....

23. At what temperature (in °C), root mean square speed of O_2 gas at 300 K is equal to most probable velocity of Ne gas (20 g mol^{-1})? [Nearest integer]

24. Consider the following data

Gas	Volume of container	Temperature	Pressure
N_2	5 L	300 K	3 bar
H_2	2 L	400 K	5 bar

Moles of N_2 occupied under given conditions are n-times that of H_2. What is value of n is ....

25. How many times the pressure of an ideal gas inside a cubic box of side l is affected, if side is reduced to $\frac{l}{2}$ and temperature is kept constant?

1. (d)	**2.** (a)	**3.** (b)	**4.** (a)	**5.** (d)	**6.** (d)
7. (a)	**8.** (a)	**9.** (a)	**10.** (d)	**11.** (b)	**12.** (b)
13. (c)	**14.** (a)	**15.** (d)	**16.** (b,c,d)	**17.** (b,c,d)	**18.** (b,c)
19. (a,c,d)	**20.** (a,b,c,d)	**21.** (99.25)	**22.** (0.02)	**23.** (8)	**24.** (2)
25. (8)					

Elemental Practice 3.1 | **Chapter 03**

Connect with **Answers**

Element 2 The Liquid State

In liquid state, the intermolecular force of attraction are stronger than in gaseous state but weaker than solid state. The molecules of liquids are held together by attractive intermolecular forces. They are strong enough to hold the constituting particles together but are not so strong to cease their translational motion.

Properties of Liquids

The key properties of liquids are:

Definite Volume

Liquids have a definite volume, which means they occupy a specific amount of space. Unlike gases, which can expand to fill their container, liquids maintain their volume regardless of the shape of the container.

No Definite Shape

Liquids do not have a definite shape. They adapt the shape of their container, taking on its form but maintaining their volume. This property is due to the relatively loose arrangement of particles compared to solids.

Density

Liquids have much higher density than gases. In liquids, molecules are quite closely packed. Therefore, their densities are much higher (about 1000 times) than the densities of gases under comparable conditions.

e.g.

- Density of water liquid at 373 K and 1 atm is 0.95 g/mL.
- Density of water vapour at the same temperature and pressure is 0.000588 g mL^{-1}.

JEE Alert

When density of liquid and vapour becomes the same; the clear boundary between liquid and vapours disappears. This temperature is called critical temperature.

Incompressibility

Liquids are much less compressible than gases. This may be accounted by the very small free space available in liquids.

Diffusion

Like gases, liquid also diffuse but they do so rather slowly. Since, diffusion involves movement of molecules from one position to another, in the liquid state molecules will undergo a number of collisions with the neighbouring molecules even as they move through a small distance.

Miscibility

It refers to a liquid's ability to mix with another liquid without forming separate layer. Miscible liquids, like alcohol and water, mix uniformly, while immiscible liquids, such as oil and water, do not.

Thermal Expansion

Unlike solids, liquids typically expand when heated and contract when cooled, leading to changes in density. This property affects various phenomena, including the operation of thermometers and the behaviour of fluids in different temperature conditions.

Vapour Pressure

The pressure exerted by the vapour molecules of a liquid in equilibrium with its liquid phase at a given temperature. It represents the tendency of the liquid to evaporate.

As temperature rises, the kinetic energy of the molecules increases, leading to more molecules escaping from the liquid phase into the vapour phase. Consequently, vapour pressure increases with temperature.

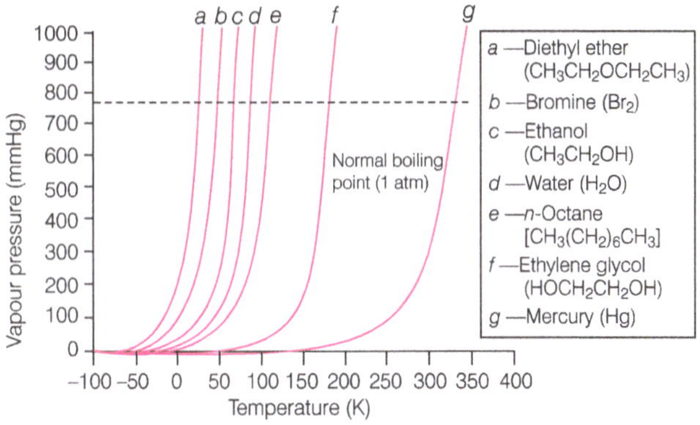

Clausius-Clapeyron Equation

This equation relates vapour pressure to temperature and is used to calculate the vapour pressure at different temperature.

$$\ln\left(\frac{p_2}{p_1}\right) = \frac{\Delta H_{vap}}{R}\left(\frac{1}{T_1} - \frac{1}{T_2}\right)$$

where p_1 and p_2 are the vapour pressure at temperature T_1 and T_2 respectively. ΔH_{vap} is the enthalpy of vaporisation, and R is the gas constant.

Solved Booster 2.1

Chloroform, $CHCl_3$, a volatile liquid was once used as an anaesthetic, but has been replaced by safer compounds. It boils at 61.7°C at 760 mmHg and has a heat of vaporisation of 31.4 kJ mol^{-1}. What is its vapour pressure at 25°C?

(a) 146.2 (b) 189.4 (c) 163.4 (d) 128.3

Solution *(b)*

Using Clausius-Clapeyron equation,

$$\Delta H = \frac{2.303\, RT_1T_2}{(T_2 - T_1)} \log \frac{p_2}{p_1}$$

$$T_1 = (273 + 61.7) = 334.7\ K,\ T_2 = 298\ K$$

$$p_1 = 760\ \text{mmHg},\ p_2 = ?$$

$$\Delta H = 31.4\ \text{kJ mol}^{-1} = 31.4 \times 10^3\ \text{J mol}^{-1}$$

$$= \frac{2.303 \times 8.314\ \text{J mol}^{-1}\ \text{K}^{-1} \times 334.7\ \text{K} \times 298\ \text{K}}{(298 - 334.7)\ \text{K}} \log \frac{p_2}{760}$$

$$\therefore \log\left(\frac{p_2}{760}\right) = -0.6034$$

$$\therefore \frac{p_2}{760} = 0.2492$$

$$p_2 \approx 189.4\ \text{mmHg}$$

Boiling Point

The temperature at which a liquid's vapour pressure equals the external pressure is known as the boiling point. At this temperature, bubbles of vapour form within the liquid and rise to the surface.

- At standard atmospheric pressure (1 atm or 101.3 kPa), the boiling point of water is 100°C (212°F). However, boiling points vary with changes in atmospheric pressure.
- **Effect of Temperature** Increasing the temperature increases the vapour pressure of the liquid until it reaches the external pressure, causing the liquid to boil. Conversely, lowering the temperature decreases the vapour pressure, which can prevent boiling if the external pressure is not reduced.

Surface Tension

It is the property of liquid due to which it has a tendency to have a shape that has minimum surface area. Surface Tension can be described as force per unit length at right angles to an imaginary lines drawn on the free surface of the liquid.

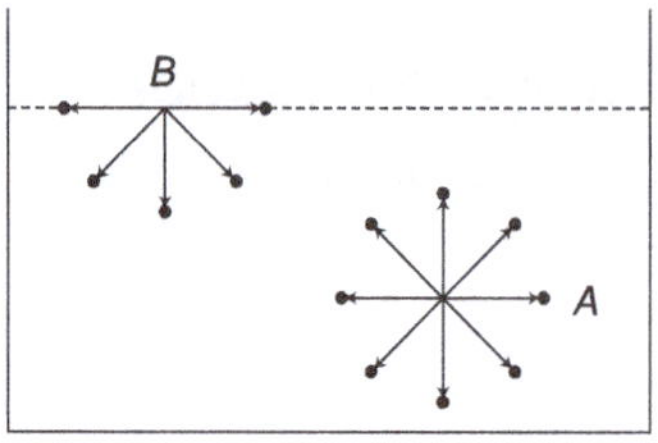

Surface tension

Molecules in liquid state attract each other. Consider **molecule *A*,** which lies entirely inside the liquid is attracted equally on all sides and the net pull on the molecule is zero. Now, consider the case of the **molecule *B*** at the surface is however different. It is only partially surrounded by other molecules and there being no molecules above it, it is subjected only to attractive forces of molecules below it.

Molecule *B*, therefore, experiences a net downward attractive force that is perpendicular to the plane of the surface. This attractive force pulls as many molecules as possible from the surface to the interior of the liquid and tends to make the surface area of the liquid as small as possible. The surface of the liquid, therefore, contracts and exhibits a state of tension.

$$\text{Surface tension } (\gamma) = \frac{\text{Force}}{\text{Length}}$$

The **work necessary to create or extend unit area of a surface is called the surface energy**. The surface tension is numerically the same as the surface energy per unit area of liquid.

$$\text{Surface energy} = \text{Surface tension} \times \text{Area}$$

Unit of surface tension and surface energy is Nm^{-1} and J/m^2 respectively.

JEE Spotlite

(i) Surface tension causes a drop of liquid to assume a spherical shape because a sphere has a minimum surface area for a given volume of liquid. The water drop in vacuum is perfectly spherical. The shape of water drop is distorted due to action of gravity.

(ii) **Meniscus Formation** Capillarity, or capillary action occurs when a liquid rises or falls in a column or porous material due to adhesive and cohesive forces.

The height of liquids in column rise in the capillary is given by $h = \frac{2\gamma \cos\theta}{r\rho g}$

where, r = radius of capillary, ρ = density of liquid, γ = the surface tension, θ = contact angle.

Effect of Temperature on Surface Tension

Since, the intermolecular attractive forces (which are responsible for surface tension) are comparatively smaller at higher temperature, surface tension decreases with rise in temperature and this decrease continues upto the critical temperature of the liquid at which there is no distinction between liquid and vapour state, i.e. surface disappears and thus surface tension is zero.

Variation of γ with temperature is given by **Eotvos equation,**

$$\gamma\left(\frac{M}{d}\right)^{2/3} = a - kt$$

where, M is molar mass, d the density, a and k constants and t the temperature (in °C), when $t = t_c$ (critical temperature), $\gamma = 0$. Therefore, $a = kt_c$ at critical temperature.

Effect of Soap and Detergent on Surface Tension

Surface tension is affected when substances are dissolved in a liquid, e.g. soaps and detergents lower the surface tension of water to a marked degree and thus improve the spreading property of these substances.

Solved Booster 2.2

The surface tension of liquid mercury is 0.490 N/m, and its density is 13.6×10^3 kg/m^3. When a glass capillary with 0.40 mm radius is placed in a dish of mercury the depression in mercury level is

(a) 24.8 (b) 18.4 (c) 19.3 (d) 25.5

Solution (b)

$$\gamma = \frac{rhdg}{2} \Rightarrow h = \frac{2\gamma}{rdg}$$

$\gamma = 0.49$ N/m or 0.49 kg/s^2, $r = 0.40$ mm $= 0.40 \times 10^{-3}$ m,

$d = 13.6 \times 10^3$ kg/m^3, $g = 9.8$ m/s^2

$$h = \frac{2(0.49\ \text{kg/s}^2)}{(0.40 \times 10^{-3}\ \text{m})(13.6 \times 10^3\ \text{kg/m}^3)(9.80\ \text{m/s}^2)}$$

$= 0.0184$ m $= 18.4$ mm

Viscosity

It refers to a liquid's resistance to flow. It determines how easily a liquid can move. For example, honey has high viscosity and flows slowly, whereas water has low viscosity and flows easily.

Viscosity depends on temperature and the nature of the liquid.

$$F \propto A\left(\frac{du}{dx}\right) \Rightarrow F = -\eta A\left(\frac{du}{dx}\right)$$

or

$$\frac{F}{A} = -\eta\left(\frac{du}{dx}\right)$$

where, η is called **coefficient of viscosity**, du the difference in velocity of two layers at a distance dx apart.

$\left(\frac{du}{dx}\right)$ is also called **velocity gradient**.

If $\left(\frac{du}{dx}\right) =$ velocity gradient $= 1$ then $\frac{F}{A} = -\eta$

Hence, **coefficient of viscosity is the tangential force per unit area required to maintain a unit velocity gradient** (velocity difference of unity between two layers at unit distant apart.)

Units of coefficient of viscosity

CGS dyne cm^{-2}s, g cm^{-1}s^{-1} (called poise)

MKS Nm^{-2}s (Pascal s), kg m^{-1}s^{-1}

$$1 \text{ poise} = 1 \text{ g cm}^{-1}\text{s}^{-1} = 10^{-1} \text{ kg m}^{-1}\text{s}^{-1}$$

The reciprocal of viscosity is called **fluidity** and is denoted by ϕ. Thus, $\phi = \frac{1}{\eta}$

Greater the viscosity, the more slowly the liquid flows.

Effect of Temperature on Viscosity

The viscosity of a liquid generally decreases with rise in temperature. The decrease is appreciable, being about 2 per cent per degree rise of temperature in many cases. This has been explained in terms of the **'hole theory'** of liquids.

- According to this theory, there are vacancies or holes in a liquid. The liquid molecules keep on moving continuously into these vacancies and it requires energy.
- A certain amount of energy called **activation energy** E_a, is required to move into a **hole**. As the activation energy becomes increasingly available at increasing temperature, a liquid can flow more easily at higher temperature hence, viscosity decreases.
- Variation of η with temperature T is given by

$$\eta = Ae^{E_a/RT}$$

(where, A is constant).

$$\log_e \eta = \log_e A + \frac{E_a}{RT}$$

or

$$\log_{10} \eta = \log_{10} A + \frac{E_a}{2.303\ RT}$$

If $\log \eta$ is plotted *vs* $\frac{1}{T}$, graph is linear as shown in figure.

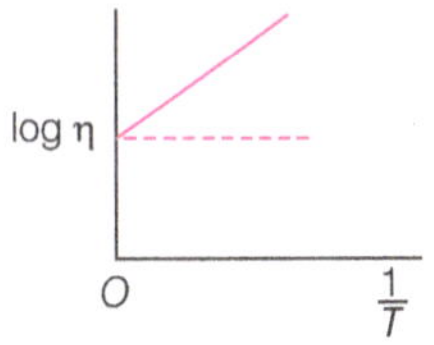

Effect of temperature on viscosity

This shows that as $\left(\frac{1}{T}\right)$ increases, $\log \eta$ decreases. Thus, on increasing temperature, η decreases.

Effect of Pressure on Viscosity

The viscosity of liquids, however, increases with increase in pressure. This is attributed to decrease in number of 'holes' as the pressure is increased. Consequently, it becomes more difficult for liquid molecules to move around and thus it becomes more difficult for them to flow. Also by Poiseuille's equation,

$$\eta = \frac{\pi r^4 tp}{8\ Vl}$$

Thus,

$$\eta \propto p$$

Elemental Practice 3.2

Type I MCQs with Only One Correct Option

1. Surface tension of water is 73 dyne cm^{-1} at 20°C. If surface area is increased by 0.10 m^2, work done is
   (a) 7.3 erg (b) 7.3×10^4 erg
   (c) 73 J (d) 0.73 J
2. Vapour pressure of a liquid is 380 mmHg at 300 K and 570 mmHg at 350 K. Thus, its normal boiling point is (log 2 = 0.3010, log1.5 = 0.1761)
   (a) 400 K (b) 397 K
   (c) 380 K (d) 300 K
3. Calculate mass of water per litre of air at given 27°C of % relative humidity is 50%.
   (a) 1.5 milligram (b) 1.25 milligram
   (c) 12.5 milligram (d) 0.125 milligram
4. Select the incorrect statement.
   (a) The properties of liquid crystals are intermediate between liquids and solids.
   (b) Surface tension of a liquid is maximum at critical temperature.
   (c) Viscosity decreases with increase in temperature.
   (d) CO_2 and H_2O show the unusual properties of supercritical fluids.
5. **Assertion (A)** As temperature is increased, less work is required to extend the surface of a liquid therefore surface tension decreases.
   Reason (R) As the temperature and hence the intensity of molecular motion increases, intermolecular forces becomes less effective.
   (a) Both Assertion (A) and Reason (R) are correct; Reason (R) is a correct explanation of Assertion (A)
   (b) Both Assertion (A) and Reason (R) are correct; Reason (R) is not the correct explanation of Assertion (A)
   (c) Assertion (A) is correct, Reason (R) is incorrect
   (d) Assertion (A) is incorrect, Reason (R) is correct.
6. The density of a vapour of substance at 1 atm pressure and 500 K is 0.36 kg/m^3. The vapours effuses through a small hole at a rate of 4/3 times faster than oxygen. Under some conditions, calculate its compression factor (Z) and which forces among the gas molecule are dominating the attraction or repulsion?
   (a) 1.22 repulsive force
   (b) 0.122 repulsive force
   (c) 0.22 repulsive force
   (d) 0.122 attractive force
7. If soap water has a surface tension of 24.3 dyne cm^{-1}, what is the pressure difference between the inside and outside of a bubble whose radius is 1.75 cm?
   (a) 22.77 bar (b) 55.54 bar
   (c) 55.54×10^{-3} bar (d) 5.554×10^{-5} bar
8. Heat of vaporisation of H_2O is 40.6 kJ mol^{-1}. At a 4000 m altitude, the atmospheric pressure is about 0.605 atm. What boiling point would you expect for water under these conditions?
   (a) 100°C (b) 90°C
   (c) 86.2°C (d) 56.2°C
9. A chemist decides to find the vapour pressure of water by the gas saturation method. 100 L of N_2 gas is passed through 65.44 g of water. After passage of the gas, 63.13 g water remained. The temperature of water is 298 K. Thus, vapour pressure of water is
   (a) 23.86 mmHg (b) 652.13 mmHg
   (c) 676 mmHg (d) 736.14 mmHg
10. Arrange the following in increasing order of surface tension.
    I. (Water) II. (Ethanol) III. (Hexane)
    (a) I < II < III (b) II < I < III
    (c) III < I < II (d) III < II < I
11. Across the surface of a droplet of water of radius r, change in pressure (Δp) in terms of change in area (dA), change in volume (dV) and surface tension (γ) is $\Delta p = \gamma\,(dA/dV)$. It is
    (a) $\Delta p = \frac{2\gamma}{r}$ (b) $\Delta p = \gamma / r$
    (c) $\Delta p = 4\gamma / r$ (d) $\Delta p = r/4$
12. The surface tension of liquid mercury is 435.5 dyne / cm. This value is equal to
    (a) 435.5×10^{-3} N / m (b) 435.5×10^{-7} N / m
    (c) 435.5×10^{-5} N / m (d) 435.5×10^{-4} N / m
13. Consider the following equation:
    $$p = Ae^{-\Delta H / RT}$$
    $$\text{If } \log_{10} p(\text{mmHg}) = 5 - \frac{400K}{T}$$
    Calculate the value of vapour pressure p in mmHg at 200 K, A and ΔH (kcal/mol) respectively
    (a) 1600, 10^5, 2.3421
    (b) 400, 10^5, 1.3410
    (c) 1000, 10^5, 1.8424
    (d) 980, 10^5, 2.1312
14. If following equation holds true (η in poise),
    $$\log_{10} \eta = -5 + \frac{200\,(K)}{T\,(K)}$$
    What is the value of viscosity at 200 K and E_a (energy of activation to move a hole) respectively?
    (a) 10^5, 2.1321 kJ mol^{-1}
    (b) 10^4, 2.1321 kJ mol^{-1}
    (c) 10^{-5}, 3.8294 kJ mol^{-1}
    (d) 10^{-4}, 3.8294 kJ mol^{-1}

Type II 》 MCQs with One or More than One Correct Option

15. Select the correct statement(s).
    (a) Cohesive forces are the intermolecular forces between like molecules and adhesive forces are between unlike molecules.
    (b) A drop maintains its shape if cohesive forces are stronger than adhesive forces.
    (c) If cohesive forces are weak compared to adhesive forces, drop collapses and spreads into film.
    (d) Cohesive forces in mercury, consist of metallic bonds between atoms, are strong; thus it does not wet glass.

16. Which of the following statements are correct? A 10 cm column of air is trapped by column of Hg of 8 cm long. The capillary tube is horizontally fixed at 1 atm pressure. Then, Select the correct statements.
    (a) The length of air column when the tube is fixed at same temperature is 84 cm.
    (b) The pressure of air measured when tube is held vertically with open end up is approximately 9.0 cm.
    (c) The pressure of air when tube is held vertically with open end down is 13.02 cm.
    (d) The pressure of air when the tube is held at 45° from horizontal with open end up is 9.3 cm.

17. Select the correct statement(s) when vaporisation takes place.
    (a) The molecules moving away from the surface and towards the vapour phase will escape if their kinetic energies are greater than the minimum value of potential energy.
    (b) Mercury column in the barometer moves downward.
    (c) Mercury column in the barometer moves upward.
    (d) As the number of molecules in the vapour phase increases, more and more gaseous molecules collide with the liquid water surface exerting pressure.

18. Which of the following statements are correct?
    (a) The water drop in vacuum is perfectly spherical.
    (b) The shape of water drop is distorted due to action of gravity.
    (c) Soaps and detergents drastically decrease the surface tension of water.
    (d) Due to increase in temperature, surface tension also increases and becomes maximum at critical temperature.

19. Which of the following statements regarding a liquid is/are correct?
    (a) The vapour pressure of a liquid increases with increase in temperature.
    (b) If a non-volatile solute is added to a liquid, vapour pressure increases.
    (c) In presence of non-volatile solute, boiling point is increased.
    (d) At the normal boiling point, vapour pressure is 1 atm.

Type IV 》 Numerical/Integer Answer Type Questions

20. Boiling point of water is 100°C at 760 mmHg. The value of its boiling point at 700 mmHg will be x.
    Given: Latent heat of vaporisation, $\Delta H_{vap} = 10$ kcal mol^{-1}
    The value of x is .... K.

21. Coefficient of viscosity (η) is 2.76×10^{-4} Pa-s at $-40°$C. If energy of activation for viscosity is 5.984 kJ mol^{-1}. The value of viscosity at $-50°$C is $x \times 10^{-5}$ Pa-s. The value of x is ....

22. A certain liquid has a viscosity of 1.00×10^4 poise and a density of 3.2 g mL^{-1}. How long will it take for a platinum ball with a 2.5 mm radius to fall 1.00 cm through the liquid?
    [Given : The density of platinum is 21.4 g cm^{-3}]

23. The boiling point of water at 38 torr pressure will be x K. If the average ΔH_{vap} over the temperature range is 10.12 kcal mol^{-1}. The value of x is ....

24. A tube of $x \times 10^{-4}$ m diameter was placed in a sample of water at 20° C. As a result of capillary action, the water rod inside the tube to a height of 10.00 cm.
    The value of x is ....
    (γ (H_2O) $= 73 \times 10^{-3}$ Nm^{-1}, $d(H_2O) = 1.0$ g cm^{-3})

Elemental Practice 3.2 | Chapter 03

Connect with **Answers**

1. (b)	**2.** (b)	**3.** (c)	**4.** (b)	**5.** (a)	**6.** (a)
7. (d)	**8.** (c)	**9.** (a)	**10.** (d)	**11.** (a)	**12.** (a)
13. (c)	**14.** (d)	**15.** (a,b,c,d)	**16.** (a,d)	**17.** (a,b,d)	**18.** (a,b,c)
19. (a,c,d)	**20.** (370.72)	**21.** (31.7)	**22.** (40.3)	**23.** (305.5)	**24.** (3)

Element 3 The Solid State

In this section, we will delve into the core concepts of solid-state chemistry, beginning with the structure and classification of solid materials.

The solid state of matter is mainly characterised by its rigidness, i.e. tendency to maintain a definite shape.

Types of Solids

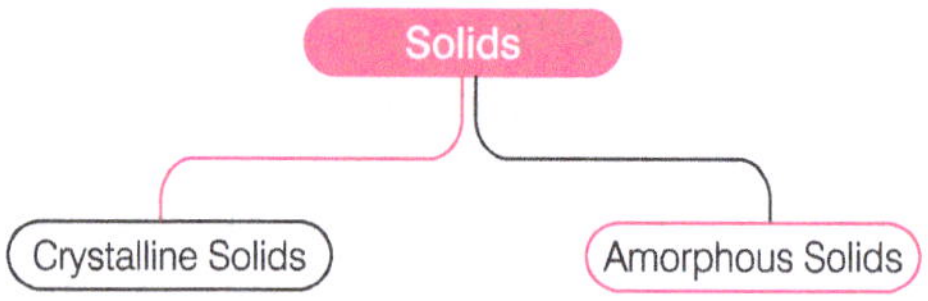

1. Crystalline Solids

These solids have long range order. The long range order means the atoms or ions or molecules are arranged in a regular fashion and this symmetrical arrangement extends throughout the crystal length.

2. Amorphous Solids

An amorphous solid differs from a crystalline substance in being without any shape of its own and has a completely random particle arrangements, i.e., no regular arrangement. e.g., Glass, Plastic

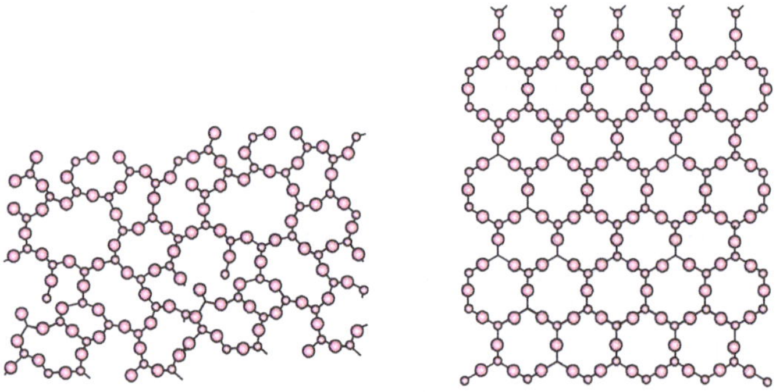

Amorphous solid   Crystalline solid

	Crystalline Solids	Amorphous Solids
1.	They have definite and regular geometry due to definite and orderly arrangement of atoms, ions or molecules in three-dimensional space.	They do not have any pattern of arrangement of atoms, ions or molecules and, thus do not have any definite geometrical shape.
2.	They have sharp melting points and change abruptly into liquids	Amorphous solids do not have sharp melting points and do not change abruptly into liquids.
3.	Crystalline solids are anisotropic.	Amorphous solids are isotropic.
4.	These are considered as true solids	These are considered pseudosolids or supercooled liquid.
5.	Crystalline solids are rigid and their shape is not distorted by mild distorting forces	Amorphous solids are not very rigid. These can be distorted by bending or compressing forces.
6.	e.g., NaCl, KCl, Sugar, Quartz, etc.	e.g., Plastic, Glass, Rubber etc.

Concept Visualizer

Let us understand the concept of isotropy and anisotropy with the help of visualisation of 2D arrangement of atoms.

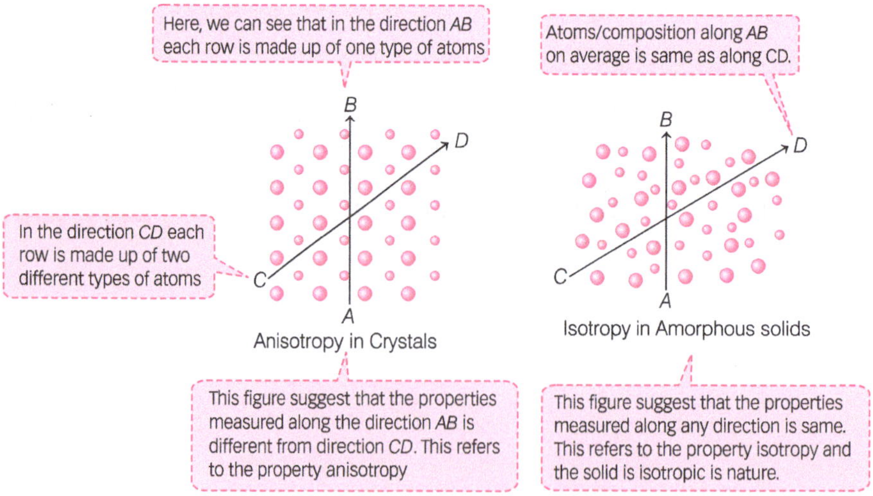

Classification of Crystalline Solids

Types of solid	Constituents	Bonding	Examples	Physical nature	Melting point	Boiling point	Electrical conductivity
1. Ionic	Ions	Electrostatic (coulombic) forces of attraction	NaCl, KCl CaO, MgO CaF_2, ZnS	Hard but brittle	High ≃1000K	High (≃2000K)	Conductor (in molten state and in aqueous solution) Insulator in solid state
2. Covalent	Atoms	Covalent bond due to sharing of e^-	SiO_2 (quartz), SiC, AlN C (diamond) C (graphite)	Hard except graphite	Very High (≃ 4000 K)	Very High (≃ 500K)	Insulator Conductor
3. Molecular solids	Simple covalent molecules	Dispersion or London forces, Dipole-dipole interactions H-bonding	I_2, S_8, CCl_4 HCl Starch	Soft or hard (in case of H-bonding)	Low (≃300K to 600 K)	Low (~450 to 800 K)	Insulator
4. Metallic	Positive ions in a sea of delocalised electrons	Metallic bond	Sodium, magnesium, metals and alloys.	Ductile malleable lustrous	High (≃800K to 1000 K)	High (≃1500K to 2000 K)	Conductors in solid as well as in molten state

Terms and Concepts

1. Space Lattice or Crystal Lattice

It may be defined as a regular three dimensional arrangement of identical points in space. The positions which are occupied by atoms, ions or molecules in the crystal lattice are called **lattice points** or **lattice sites.**

2. Unit Cell

A space lattice can be sub-divided into a number of small cells known as unit cells. It can be defined as the smallest block from which entire crystal can be built up by its translational repetition in three dimensions.

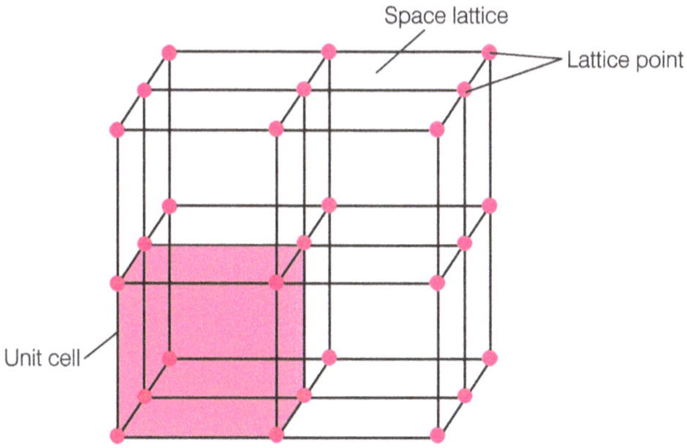

Space Lattice and Unit Cell

3. Crystal Parameters

The geometry of a crystal can be best described in terms of 3 non-coplanar coordinate axes, called the **crystallographic axes.** These axes namely x, y and z may be mutually at right angles to each other or may be inclined to each other at different angles.

As per convention, the angle between y and z-axes is called α, between z and x is called β and between x and y is called γ.

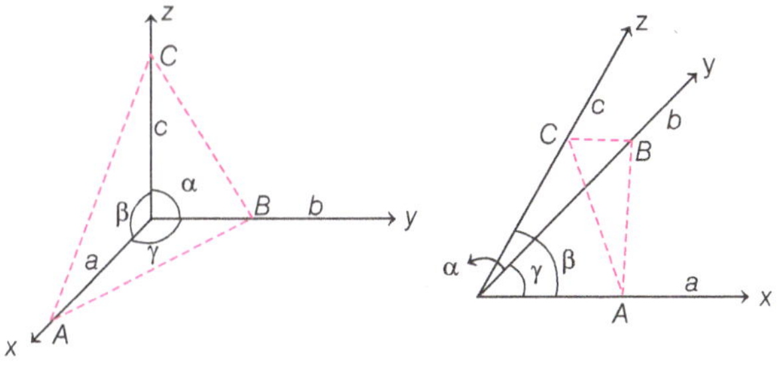

(a) α,β, and γ when perpendicular to each other, i.e. $\alpha = \beta = \gamma = 90°$

(b) α,β,γ, when inclined at different angle

Crystallographic axes showing angles

Any face of the crystal may cut into one or more crystallographic axes. The face which cuts all the three axes is called **standard** or **unit plane.** The distances of the points where the standard plane cuts the three axes from the origin are called **intercepts**. The intercepts a, b and c and axes x, y and z respectively are called **crystal parameters**.

In actual practice, the ratio $a : b : c$ is called the **axial ratio** and it depends upon the point where all the three axes meet.

Types of Lattices and Types of Unit Cell

1. Primitive or Simple Unit Cells

In a primitive unit cell, the same type of particles are present at all the corners of the unit cell. There are seven primitive crystal systems.

2. Non-primitive or Centred Unit Cells

There are three types of non-primitive unit cells as follows:

(i) **Face centred** When atoms are present in all 8-corners and six face centres in a cubic unit cell then this arrangement is known as FCC.

(ii) **End-centred** When in addition to particles at the corners, there are particles at the centres of the end faces.

(iii) **Body centred** When atoms are present at 8 corners as well as in the body centre in a cubic unit cell then this arrangement is known as BCC.

The unit cell relationships for the seven (primitive) crystal systems

S.No.	System	Unit cell			Example (common name)
		Possible variation	Lengths	Angles	
1.	Cubic	Primitive body-centred face-centred	$a = b = c$	$\alpha = \beta = \gamma = 90°$	NaCl, zinc blende, KCl, (ZnS), diamond, Cu
2.	Tetragonal	Primitive, body-centred	$a = b \neq c$	$\alpha = \beta = \gamma = 90°$	TiO_2, $CaSO_4$, white tin, SnO_2, NH_4Br
3.	Orthorhombic	Primitive, body-centred face-centred, end-centred	$a \neq b \neq c$	$\alpha = \beta = \gamma = 90°$	$MgSO_4 \cdot 7H_2O$, Rhombic sulphur, KNO_3, $BaSO_4$
4.	Monoclinic	Primitive, end-centred	$a \neq b \neq c$	$\alpha = \gamma = 90°; \beta \neq 90°$	$CaSO_4 \cdot 2H_2O$ ($Na_2SO_4 \cdot 10H_2O$ monoclinic sulphur)
5.	Triclinic	Primitive	$a \neq b \neq c$	$\alpha \neq \beta \neq \gamma \neq 90°$	$K_2Cr_2O_7$, ($CuSO_4 \cdot 5H_2O$, H_3BO_3)
6.	Hexagonal	Primitive	$a = b \neq c$	$\alpha = \beta = 90°; \gamma = 120°$	SiO_2 graphite, ZnO, CdS
7.	Rhombohedral or trigonal	Primitive	$a = b = c$	$\alpha = \beta = \gamma \neq 90°$	$CaCO_3$, HgS, $NaNO_3$, ICl

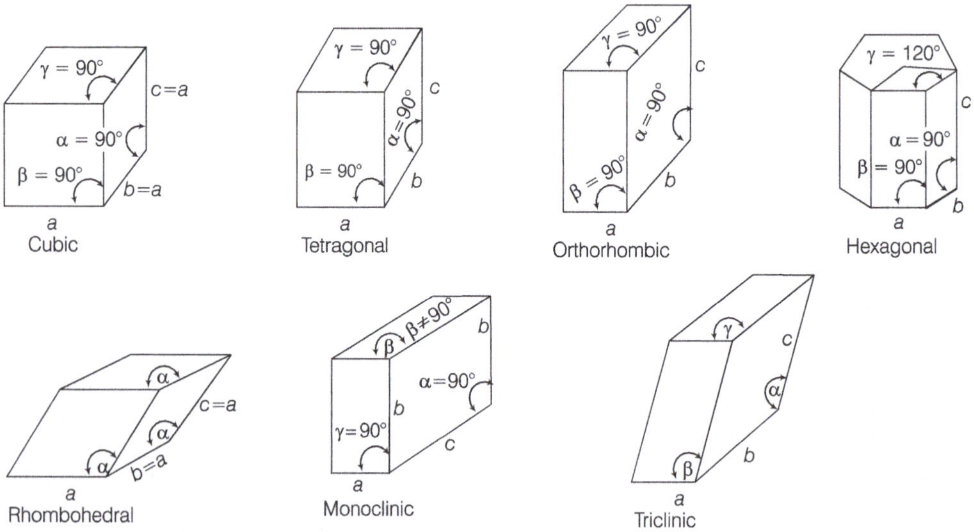

Seven primitive unit cells in crystals

Symmetry in Crystal

A crystal said to be symmetric, if it has plane of symmetry, axis of symmetry and centre of symmetry.

1. Centre of Symmetry

It is the point in the crystal such that any line passing through it divides it (crystal) into two symmetric portions

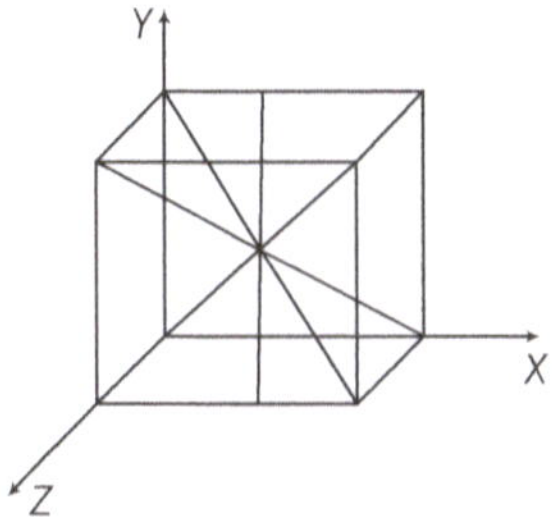

2. Axis of Symmetry

It is the line about which rotation of the crystal gives same appearance more than once in one complete rotation (from 0° to 360°). If same appearance is formed *n*-times than symmetry is *n*-fold.

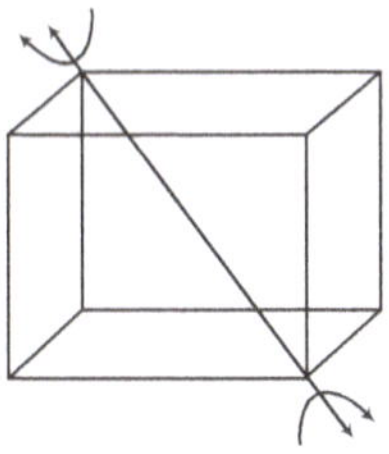

There are three types of axis of symmetry for a crystal lattice.

(i) **Axis of Four-fold Symmetry** A cubical box has four-fold symmetry, i.e. when a cube is rotated above the line as axis, the original appearance of cube occurs four times during the course of rotation through 0 ° to 360 °. There are three axis of four-fold symmetry.

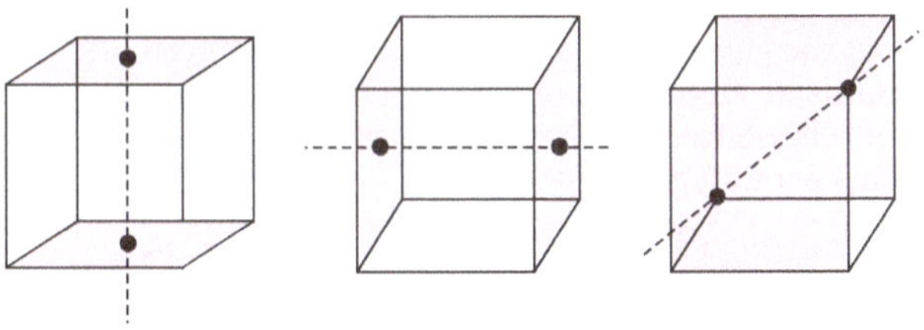

(ii) **Axis of Two-fold Symmetry** A cubical box has two-fold symmetry, if it is rotated about a line as axis passing through the centres of two diagonals opposite edges of a cube,

We get identical appearance two times during the rotation through each 180°.

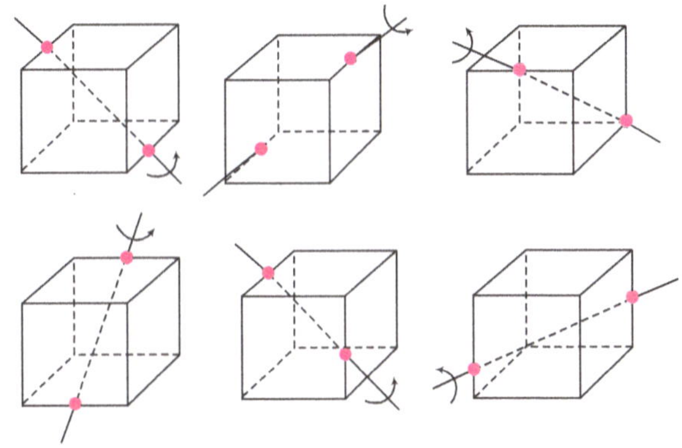

3. Plane of Symmetry

The plane passing through the centre of the crystal such that it divides the crystal in two equal parts which are mirror images of one each other.

ABCD is a plane of symmetry and each divided part is mirror image of the other. There are so many others.

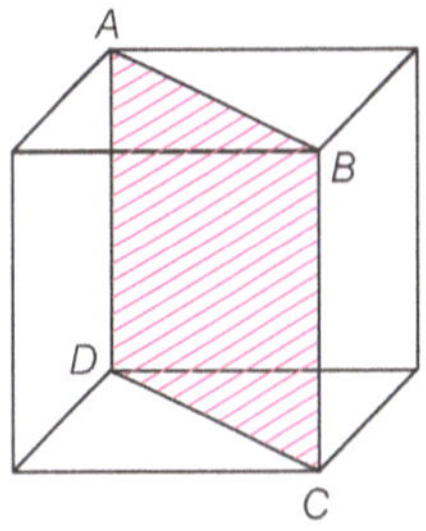

PQRS is also plane of symmetry.

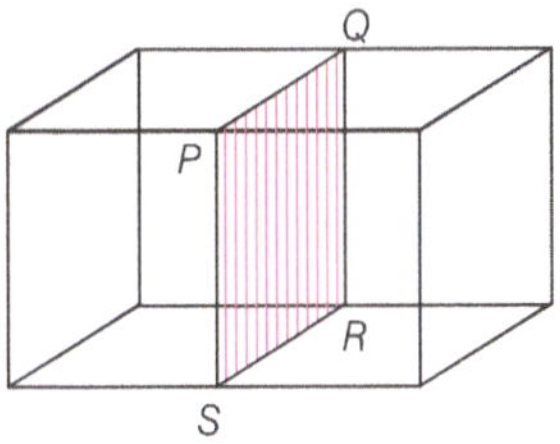

There are two types of plane of symmetry.

(i) **Rectangular Plane of Symmetry** The planes of symmetry which are located mid-way parallel to opposite faces, are called rectangular plane of symmetry. In a cube having 6 faces, there are three rectangular planes of symmetry as shown in figure.

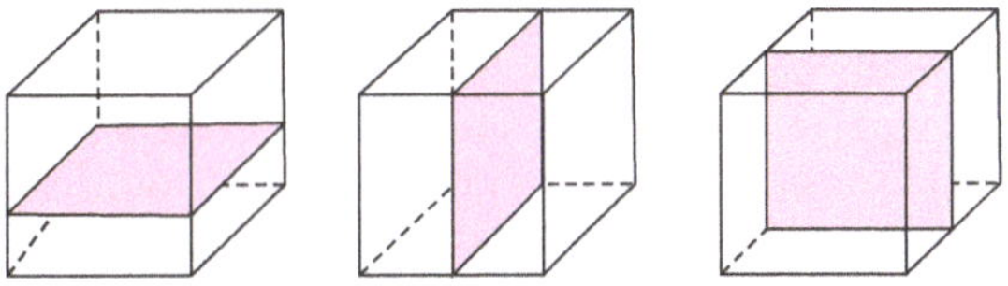

Rectangular planes of symmetry in a cube

(ii) **Diagonal Plane of Symmetry** The planes of symmetry that touch their opposite edges lie on the diagonal of opposite faces. In a cube there are six diagonal planes of symmetry.

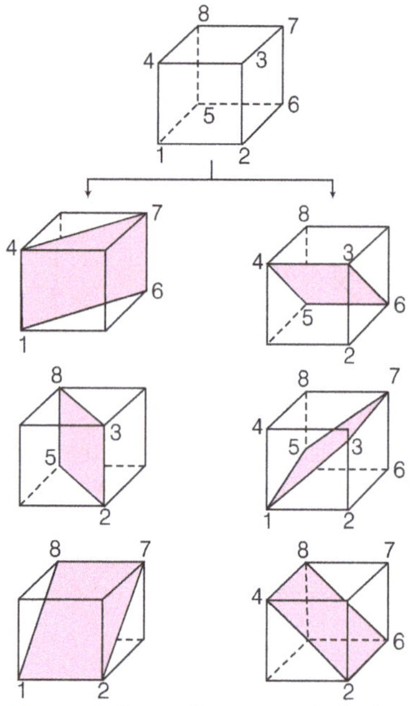

Diagonal planes of symmetry in a cube

The seven crystal systems have been given in table.

JEE Spotlite

The essential symmetries of the seven crystal systems are as follows

The system	Essential symmetries
Triclinic	None
Monoclinic	One two-fold axis
Orthorhombic	Three perpendicular two-fold axes
Rhombohedral	One three-fold axis
Tetragonal	One four-fold axis
Hexagonal	One six-fold axis
Cubic	Four three-fold axes in a tetrahedral arrangement

Coordination Number

The number of atoms in a crystal surrounding a particular atom as its nearest neighbour atoms in its neighbourhood is called its **coordination number**. In ionic compounds, coordination number is defined as the no of ions of opposite charges in the nearby surrounding of a given ion. In a simple language, coordination number of cations is the number of sorrounding ions or *vice-versa*, e.g. in NaCl, each Cl^- is surrounded by six Na^+ ions and *vice-versa*.
Hence, CN of Na^+ is six in NaCl (and also for Cl^-).

- **For simple cubic or primitive system**
  Coordination number = 6
- **For face-centred cubic** (fcc)
  Number of atoms surrounding the face-centre of any face = 12
  Hence, coordination number = 12
- **For body-centred cubic** (bcc)
  Number of atoms surrounding the body centre = 8
  Hence, coordination number = 8

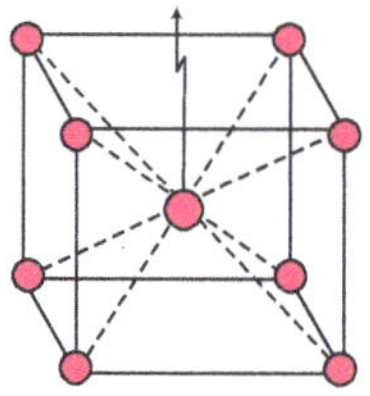

Calculation of Number of Particles in a Unit Cell (Z)

In different types of unit cell, the number of atoms per unit cell can be calculated as follows

1. Primitive or Simple Cubic Unit Cell

From the given figure, it is clear that here eight atoms which are present at 8 corners are shared by 8 unit cells. Hence,

contribution of each atom present at the corner $= \frac{1}{8}$,

Thus, total number of atoms present per unit cell

$$= 8 \times \frac{1}{8} = 1 \text{ atom}$$

Simple cubic unit cell

2. Body Centered Cubic Unit Cell

From the given figure, it is clear that this unit cell has 1 complete atom additional to that present in simple cubic unit cell. Hence, the total number of atoms present = 1 + 1 = 2 atoms per unit cell.

Body centred cubic unit cell

3. Face Centered Cubic Unit Cell

From the given figure it is clear that here

(i) 8 corner atoms $\times \frac{1}{8}$ atoms per unit cell $= 1$ atom

(ii) 6 face atoms (with representation of 1/2 atom per face) per unit cell, thus $6 \times \frac{1}{2} = 3$ atoms

Total atoms present per unit cell $= 1 + 3 = 4$ atoms

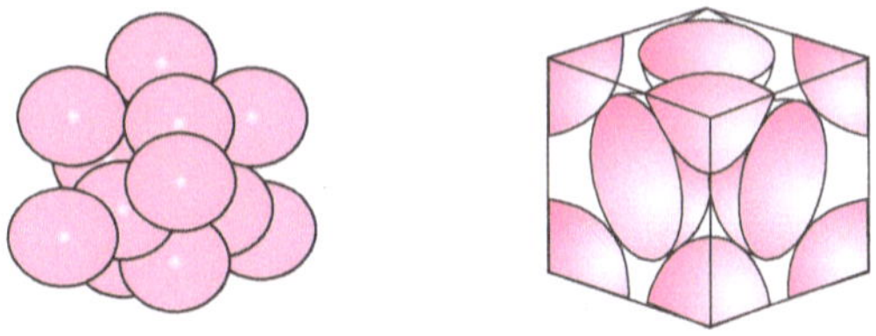

Face centered cubic unit cell

4. End Face Centered Cubic Unit Cell

Similarly, end face centered cubic unit cell have 1 instead of 3 face atoms present in face centered cubic unit cell. Rest distribution is same (because here only
2 parallel faces have one atom each at the centre of face shared by two unit cells).

Thus, the total number of atoms present per unit cell here is $1 + 1 = 2$ atoms per unit cell.

Number of Atoms in Different Unit Cells

Cubic unit cell	n_c	n_f	n_i	Total atoms in unit cell
Simple cubic	8	0	0	1
Body-centered cubic	8	0	1	2
Face-centered cubic	8	6	0	4

Solved Booster 3.1

A compound formed by elements X and Y has a cubic structure in which X atoms are at the corner of the cube and Y atoms are at the face centres. One atom X is missing from the corner. The formula of the compound is

(a) X_2Y_4 (b) X_7Y_{24}
(c) $X_{24}Y_7$ (d) X_7Y_3

Solution (b)

In a cube there are 8 atoms. Since, one atom X is missing from the corner. The number of X atoms at the corners = 7

Number of effective X atoms

$$= 7 \text{ corners} \times \frac{1}{8} \text{ per corner atom share} = \frac{7}{8} \text{ atom per unit cell}$$

$$\text{Number of effective } Y \text{ atoms} = 6 \text{ faces} \times \frac{1}{2} \text{ per face atom share}$$

$$= 3 \text{ atoms per unit cell}$$

Thus, formula of the compound is $X_{7/8}Y_3$.

Simplifying $= X_7Y_{24}$.

Close Packing in Crystals

In order to understand the packing of constituent particles. Let us study about their structures in different dimensions.

Close Packing in Two Dimensions

Two methods of crystal plane formation

- **Square Close Packing (SCP)** Spheres align horizontally and vertically, forming a square pattern. The coordiantion number in SCP is 4 as each sphere touches four other spheres.
- **Hexagonal Close Packing (HCP)** Spheres in the second row fit into depressions of the first row. The coordination number in HCP is 6 as each sphere touches six other spheres.

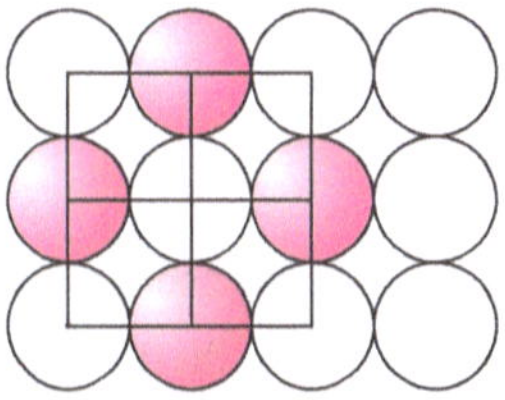

(a) square close packing (coordination number 4)

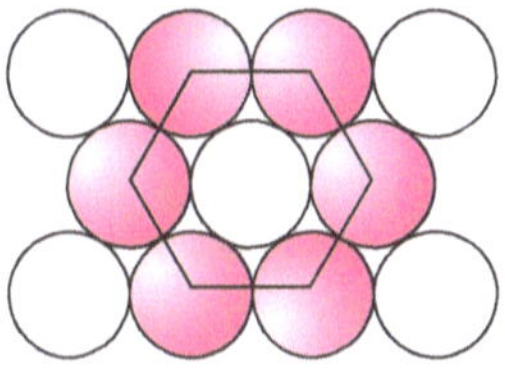

(b) Hexagonal close packing (coodination number 6)

Close Packing in Three Dimensions

- In 3*D* packing [figure (p)], the first layer has voids labeled (p) and (c).
- The second layer is represented with dotted circles. Spheres in the second layer can occupy either type of void but not both simultaneously.
- The third layer could be placed over second layer in such a way that it is
  - Over voids (c) from the second layer.
  - Over voids (d) from the second layer.

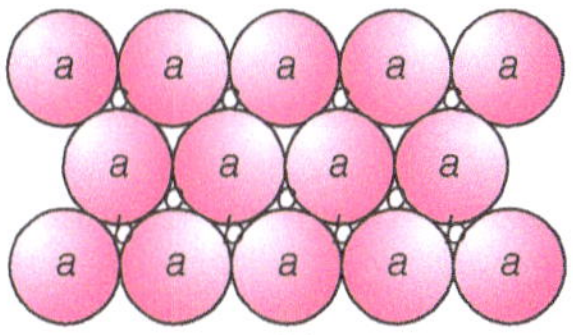

(p)

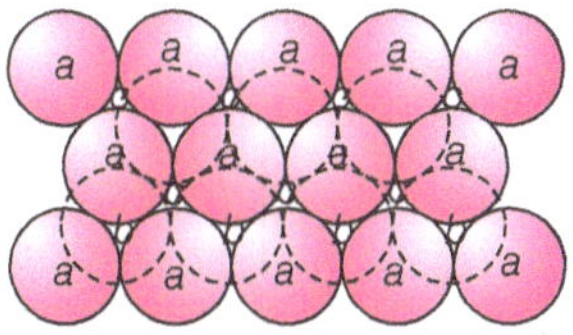

(q)

(i) When the third layer is placed over tetrahedral void (c) an arrangement known as ABAB... pattern (hexagonal close packing) is formed.

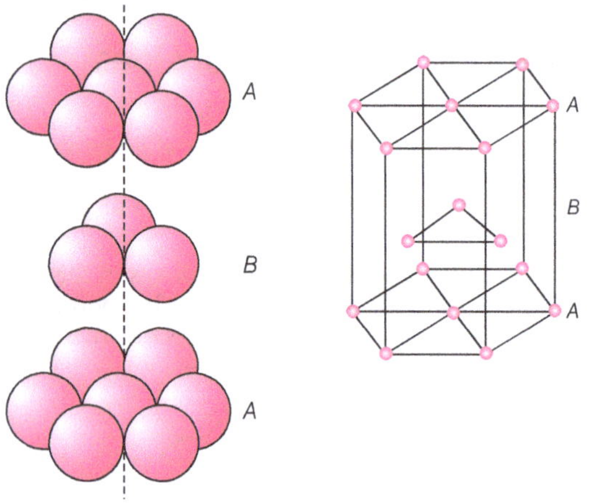

Hexagonal close packing (hcp)

- For HCP geometry coordination number = 12
- For HCP geometry number of atoms per unit cell

$$= 12 \text{ (corners)} \times \frac{1}{6} + 2 \text{ (face centres)} \times \frac{1}{2} + 3 \text{ (inside the body)}^* \times 1 = 6$$

*Three spheres are not totally inside the hexagonal unit but taken as 3 because part of spheres of other hexagonal unit from three sides enter the given hexagonal unit.

(ii) When the third layer is placed over the second layer such that the spheres cover the octahedral or 'd' voids, a layer *C* different from *A* and *B* is formed. This pattern is called *ABC ABC*...... pattern or cubic close packing (CCP).

The *ABC ABC* ...... packing has cubic symmetry and is known as cubic close packing (ccp). The cubic close packing has face centred cubic (fcc) unit cell.

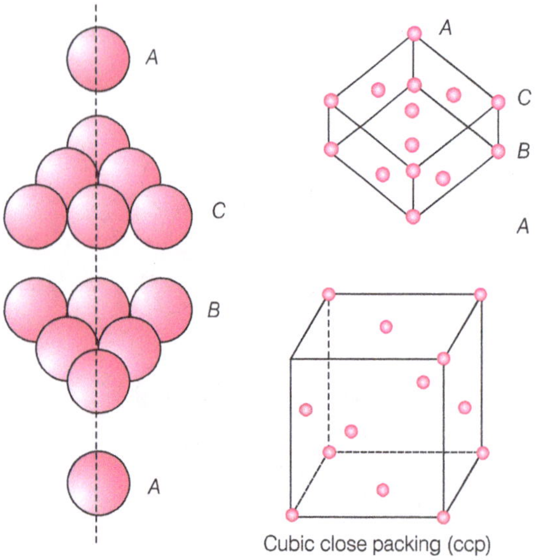

Cubic close packing (ccp)

Packing Fraction

(Density of Packing)

It is the ratio of the volume occupied by the total effective atoms in a cubic system to the volume of a cube (or unit cell)

Let, radius of the atom in the packing $= r$

Edge length of the cube $= a$

Volume of the cube $V = a^3$

Volume of the atom (spherical) $v = \frac{4}{3}\pi r^3$

then, packing density $= \frac{vz}{V} = \frac{\frac{4}{3}\pi r^3 z}{a^3}$

where '*z*' is the number of 'formulae units' (for effective atoms) in the unit cell.

1. In Simple Cubic Structure

Each corner atom is in contact with 8 corner atoms

$$2r = a$$

$$\Rightarrow \quad r = \frac{a}{2}$$

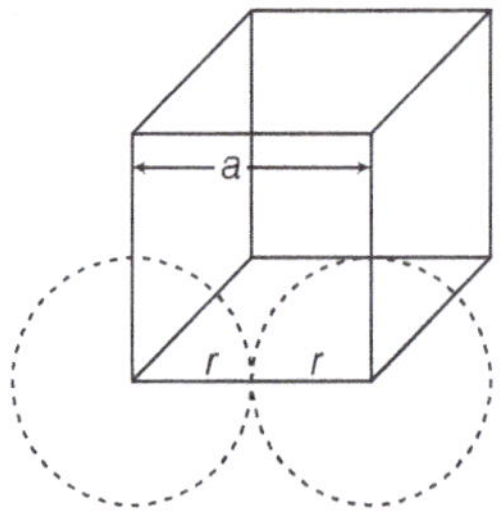

Simple cubic

$\therefore$ Volume of the atom (spherical)

$$v = \frac{4}{3}\pi r^3 = \frac{4}{3}\pi\left(\frac{a}{2}\right)^3 = \frac{\pi a^3}{6}$$

$\therefore$ Volume of the cube $= a^3$

$\therefore$ Packing density

$$= \frac{\text{Volume of the one spherical atom in unit cell}}{\text{Volume of the cube}}$$

$$= \frac{\pi a^3}{6a^3} = \frac{\pi}{6}$$

$$= 0.5236 \text{ (Thus } 52.36\%)$$

% empty space $= 100 - 52.36$

$$= 47.64\%$$

2. **In fcc Structure**

[Hexagonal Closest Packed (hcp) and Cubic Closest-Packed (ccp)]

Edge length $= a$ and $z = 4$

Face diagonal $= b = AC$

Also, $AC = 4r$

In ΔABC,

$$AC^2 = BC^2 + AB^2$$

$$b^2 = a^2 + a^2 = 2a^2$$

$$b = \sqrt{2}\,a$$

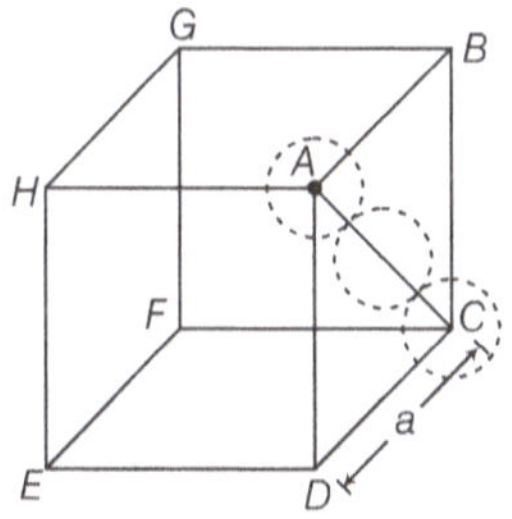

fcc structure

If radius of the spherical atom is r then

$$AC = b = \sqrt{2}\,a = 4r$$

$$\therefore \quad r = \frac{a}{2\sqrt{2}}$$

Volume of the four spherical atoms ($z = 4$) of radius r in the unit cell

$$= \frac{4}{3}\pi r^3 \times 4 = \frac{4}{3}\pi\left(\frac{a}{2\sqrt{2}}\right)^3 \times 4 = \frac{\pi a^3}{3\sqrt{2}}$$

Volume of the cube $= a^3$

$$\therefore \quad \text{Packing density} = \frac{\pi a^3}{3\sqrt{2} \times a^3} = \frac{\pi}{3\sqrt{2}} = 0.7405$$

(Thus, 74.05%)

% empty space $= 100 - 74.05 = 25.95\% \approx 26\%$

3. **In bcc** (body-centred cubic) **Structure**

Edge length $= a$ and $z = 2$

and radius of the spherical atom in the unit cell $= r$

face diagonal $= b$ and body diagonal $= c$

Atom at the centre touches other two atoms ($z = 2$) diagonally arranged

In ΔEFD, $FD^2 = EF^2 + ED^2$

$$b^2 = a^2 + a^2$$

$$\therefore \quad b = \sqrt{2}\,a$$

In ΔAFD, $AF^2 = AD^2 + FD^2$

$$c^2 = a^2 + b^2 = a^2 + 2a^2 = 3a^2$$

$$\therefore \quad c = \sqrt{3}\,a$$

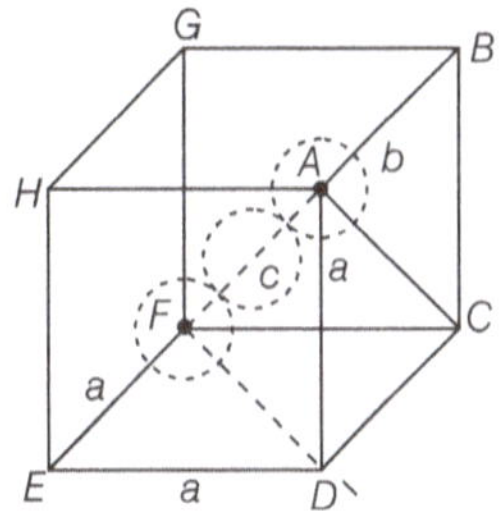

bcc structure

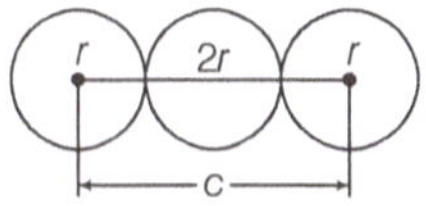

Also $\quad c = 4r \Rightarrow \sqrt{3}\,a = 4r$

$$\therefore \quad r = \frac{\sqrt{3}}{4}a$$

$\therefore$ Volume of two spherical atoms of radius r in a unit cell

$$= 2 \times \frac{4}{3}\pi r^3$$

$$= 2 \times \frac{4}{3}\pi\left(\frac{\sqrt{3}}{4}a\right)^3 = \frac{\pi\sqrt{3}\,a^3}{8}$$

and volume of the cube $= a^3$

$$\therefore \quad \text{Packing efficiency} = \frac{\pi\sqrt{3}\,a^3}{8\,a^3} = \frac{\sqrt{3}\,\pi}{8} = 0.6802 \text{ (Thus, 68.02\%)}$$

% empty space $= 100 - 68.02\% = 31.98 \approx 32\%$

An fcc unit cell occupies maximum space and hence, is referred as a close packed system.

4. **In HCP Structure**

Each corner atom would be common to 6 other unit cells, therefore their contribution to one unit cell would be 1/6. total number of atom in 1 hcp unit cell

$= \frac{12}{6}$ (from 12 corner) $+ \frac{2}{2}$ (from 2 face centred) $+ \frac{3}{1}$ (effective number of atoms from layer B)

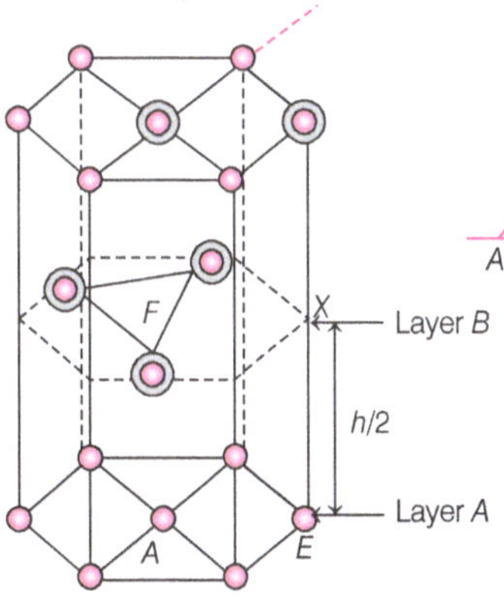

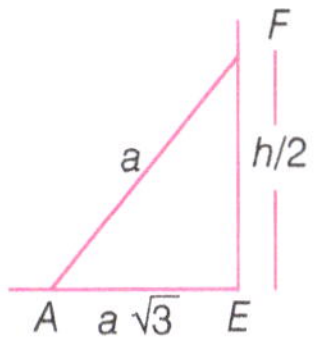

Atoms in the layer B are not totally inside the hexagonal structure. Some parts of sphere come out from three faces but some part of sphere also come inside it from adjacent hexagonal structures, Therefore effective 3 atoms can be considered from layer B.

$$XE = \frac{h}{2} = \sqrt{(2r)^2 - \left(\frac{2r}{\sqrt{3}}\right)^2}$$

$\therefore$ The height of unit cell $(h) = 4r\sqrt{\frac{2}{3}}$

The area of the base is equal to the area of six equilateral triangles, $= 6 \times \frac{\sqrt{3}}{2}(2r)^2$.

The volume of the unit cell $= 6 \times \frac{\sqrt{3}}{4}(2r)^2 \times 4r\sqrt{\frac{2}{3}}$.

Therefore, $PF = \dfrac{6 \times \frac{4}{3}\pi r^3}{6 \times \frac{\sqrt{3}}{4}(2r)^2 \times 4r\sqrt{\frac{2}{3}}} \approx \mathbf{0.74}$

$\therefore\ VF \approx 0.26$

JEE **MAPPER**

Example Similar to PYQ Asked in JEE Advanced 2022

Atom M occupies the body centred as well as half tetrahedral voids of the same lattice. The packing efficiency (in %) of the resultant solid is closest to

(a) 75% (b) 17%
(c) 63% (d) 34%

Sol. (*b*) For given lattice

$$\frac{\sqrt{3}a}{4} = 2r$$

$$\Rightarrow \quad a = \frac{8r}{\sqrt{3}}$$

There are 4 tetrahedral voids in bcc lattice but only 2 one occupied.

So, total number of atoms in bcc = 2 + 2 = 4 (as number of atoms on lattice site in BCC is 2)

$$\%\text{ packing efficiency} = \frac{\text{volume of 4 atoms}}{\text{volume of cell } (a^3)} \times 100$$

$$\%\text{ PE} = \frac{4 \times \frac{4}{3}\pi r^3}{\left(\frac{8r}{\sqrt{3}}\right)^3} \times 100$$

$$\%\text{ PE} = 17\%$$

Competency Enhancer 3.1

In diamond, carbon atom occupy fcc lattice point as well as alternate tetrahedral voids. The edge length of the unit all is 356.7 pm. The packing efficiency (in %) of total volume occupied by carbon atom is

(a) 42% (b) 55%
(c) 34% (d) 25%

Radius Ratio in Ionic Crystals

Ionic compounds occur in crystalline forms. Ionic crystals are made of cations and anions.

These ions are arranged in three-dimensional array to form an aggregate of the type $(A^+B^-)_n$. Since, the coulombic forces are non-directional, hence, the structures of such crystals are mainly governed by the ratio of the radius of cation (r_+) to that of anion (r_-). The ratio r_+ to $r_-(r_+ / r_-)$ is called as **radius ratio**.

$$\text{Radius ratio} = \frac{r_+}{r_-}$$

Structure of Some Common Ionic Compounds

Simple ionic compounds are typically of the form AB or AB_2, where A represents the positively charged ion and B represents the negatively charged ion.

In any solid of the type A_xB_y, the ratio of the coordination numbers of A to B would be $y : x$.

Structure of *AB* Type Crystals

Ionic compounds of the type AB means compounds having the positively and negatively charged ions in the ratio 1 : 1.

These compounds can have following three type of structures.

- Rock salt (NaCl) type
- Cesium chloride (CsCl) type
- Zinc blende (ZnS) type

1. Rock Salt Structure (NaCl)

(i) Cl^- forms a FCC unit cell in which Na^+ is in the octahedral voids. The co-ordination number of Na^+ is 6 and that of Cl^- would also be 6.

(ii) Ratio of ionic radii $= \left(\frac{r_{Na^+}}{r_{Cl^-}} = 0.525\right)$

(iii) Number of sodium ions $= 12$ (At edge centre) $\times \frac{1}{4} + 1$ (At body centre) $\times 1 = 4$

Number of chloride ions

$= 8$ (At corners) $\times \frac{1}{8} + 6$ (At face centres) $\times \frac{1}{2} = 4$

(Thus formula is Na_4Cl_4 i.e. NaCl)

(iv) Most of the halides of alkali metals and oxides of alkaline-earth metal have this type of structure. i.e. NaI, KCl, RbI and RbF.

FeO also has rock-salt structure in which oxide ions are arranged in ccp and Fe^{2+} ions occupy octahedral voids.

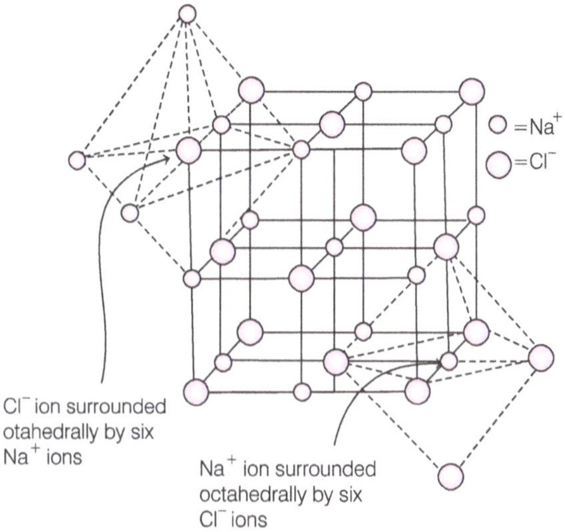

Sodium chloride structure

JEE Alert

If pressure is applied on NaCl type structure, it changes to CsCl type structure.

2. CsCl "Caesium Chloride"

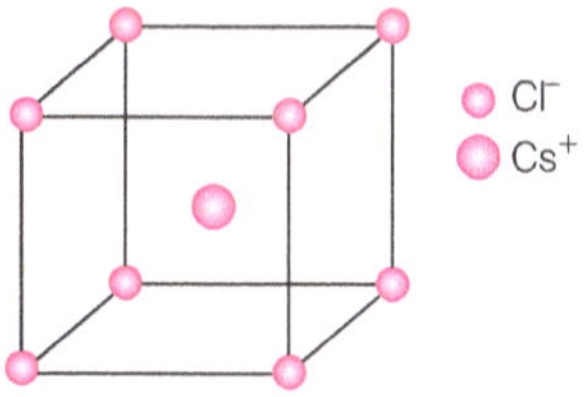

CsCl unit cell

In lattice each Cs^+ is surrounded by eight Cl^- and each Cl^- is surrounded by eight Cs^+. Coordination number of Cs^+ and Cl^- are 8 :8.

The radius ratio.

$$\Rightarrow \qquad \left(\frac{r_+}{r_-}\right) = 0.732$$

3. ZnS "Zinc Sulphide"

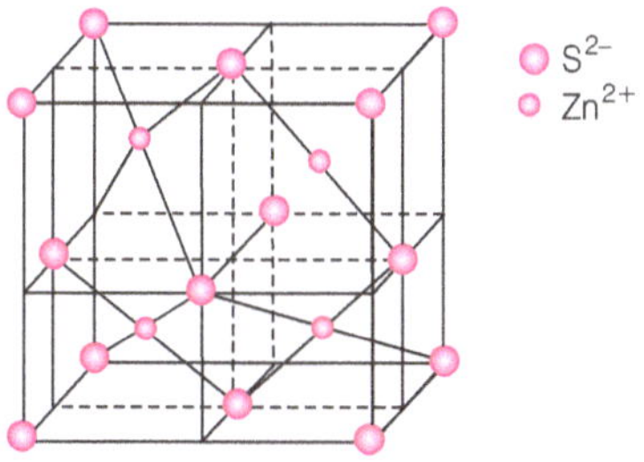

Zinc blend

In zinc blend structure, anions occupy the FCC positions and half of the tetrahedral holes are occupied by cations.

The radius ratio is

$$\Rightarrow \qquad \frac{r_+}{r_-} = 0.225$$

zinc blende type structure is observed in ZnO, CuCl, CuBr and CuI etc.

In lattice, each Zn^{2+} ions is tetrahedrally surrouded by S^{2-} ion each S^{2-} ion is tetrahedrally surrounded by Zn^{2+} ion. Thus, both the ions have equivalent positions and co-ordination number of Zn^{2+} and S^{2-} are 4 : 4.

Structure of AB_2 Type Crystals

Calcium fluoride (fluorite structure) is an example of AB_2 type crystal. Structure of fluorite unit cell is shown in the Figure in which Ca^{2+} ions form face-centred unit cell and F^- ions are present in the tetrahedral voids. Thus, each Ca^{2+} ion is surrounded by eight F^- ions and each F^- is sourrounded by four Ca^{2+} ions. Thus, the co-ordination number of Ca^{2+} and F^- ions are 8 : 4.

Fluorite structure to also observed in SrF_2, $BaCl_2$, HgF_2, CuF_2 etc.

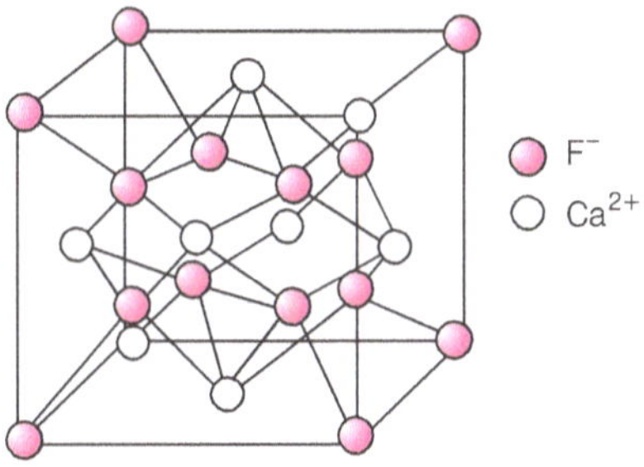

CaF_2 structure

Structure of A_2B Type Crystals

Na_2O is an example of A_2B type crystal and is having a related arrangement of ions as in fluorite structure, just their positions are changed, and is also known as antifluorite structure. In Na_2O, O^{2-} ions from face-centred unit cell in the lattice in which Na^+ ions are present in the tetrahedral voids. In antifluorite, co-ordination number of cation and anion are reversed as compared to fluoride.

Thus, the co-ordination number of Na^+ and O^{2-} are 4 :8.

Antifluorite structure is observed in Li_2O, K_2O, Rb_2O, Rb_2S etc.

Properties of Ionic Solids

Property	Rock-salt	CsCl (BCC)	Antifluorite	Zinc blende	Fluorite
Type	FCC-anions	BCC-cations	CCP-anions	CCP-anions	CCP-cations
Void	octahedral void-cation	BCC-cations	tetrahedral void-cations	1/2 tetrahedral void-cations	tetrahedral holes-anions
Ratio $A:B$	4 : 4	1 : 1	8 : 4	4 : 4	1/8 : 1/4
Formula	A_4B_4	AB	$A_8 : B_4, A_2B$	A_4B_4, AB	$A_{1/8}B_{1/4}, AB_2$
Example	NaCl, MgO	CsCl	Li_2O, Rb_2O	BeO, ZnS	UO_2, CaF_2
r^+/r^-	0.414–0.736	0.732 – 0.999	0.225 – 0.414	0.225 – 0.414	0.225 – 0.414
Neighbours	12	8	12		
co-ord-no.	6 each	8 each	4	cation-4 anion-8	cations-8 anions-4

JEE MAPPER

Example Similar to PYQ Asked in JEE Advanced 2024

In a metal deficient oxide sample, $M_xY_2O_4$ (M and Y are metals), M is present in both +2 and +3 oxidation states and Y is in +3 oxidation state. If the fraction of M^{2+} ions present in M is 1/4, the value of x is ....

(a) 0.67 (b) 0.72

(c) 0.81 (d) 0.35

Sol. (*b*) Average oxidation state of M will be given by

$$= \frac{1}{4} \times 2 + \frac{3}{4} \times 3 = + \frac{11}{4}$$

So, for the given sample $M_xY_2O_4$

$$\frac{11}{4} \times x + 3 \times 2 + 4(-2) = 0$$

$$\frac{11x}{4} = 2$$

$$\Rightarrow \quad x = \frac{8}{11} = 0.72$$

Competency Enhancer

In a metal deficient oxide sample, $M_xY_2O_3$ (M and Y are metals), M is present in both +2 and +3 oxidation states and Y is in +2 oxidation state. If the fraction of M^{2+} ions present in M is 2/3, the value of x is ....

(a) 0.65 (b) 0.34 (c) 0.71 (d) 0.85

Density of Solids

If there are n-units of particles is an unit cell (particle pertains to atom in case of atomic solid and formula unit in case of ionic solid), then, the mass of a unit cell

$$= \frac{nM}{6.023 \times 10^{23}}$$

This implies, density of the solid,

$$(\rho) = \frac{\text{Mass of unit cell}}{\text{Volume of unit cell}} = \frac{nM}{6.023 \times 10^{23}} \times \frac{1}{V}$$

In case of cubic unit cell "V" $= a^3$. In other geometries, V is determined from the given cell parameters.

Solved Booster 3.2

Titanium metal crystallises in a BCC arrangement and radius of an atom is 142 picometre. Determine atomic weight of titanium if density is 16.6 g/cm^3. Also determine the number of unit cells present in a 5 cm^3 block of titanium metals.

(a) $176, 1.42 \times 10^{23}$ (b) $192, 1.6 \times 10^{23}$

(c) $142, 2.4 \times 10^{23}$ (d) $128, 5.6 \times 10^{23}$

Solution (*a*)

(a) In BCC arrangement of atoms the relationship between edge length and radius of atom is

$$4r = \sqrt{3}a$$

$$\text{Density } (\rho) = \frac{NM}{N_A V}$$

Where, N = Number of atoms per unit cell,

M = Molar mass, N_A = Avogadro's number

V = Volume of unit cell

$$\Rightarrow \quad 16.6 = \frac{2M}{6.023 \times 10^{23} \left(\frac{4}{\sqrt{3}} \times 142 \times 10^{-10}\right)^3}$$

Here, radius is taken in cm unit since, density is in g/cm^3 unit.

Solving : $M = 176$. Also mass of 5 cm^3 block $= 5 \times 16.6 = 83$ g

$$\Rightarrow \text{Number of atoms in 5 cm}^3 \text{ block} = \frac{83}{176} \times 6.023 \times 10^{23}$$

$$\Rightarrow \text{Number of unit cells} = \frac{\text{No. of atoms}}{2}$$

$$= \frac{83 \times 6.23 \times 10^{23}}{2} = 1.42 \times 10^{23}$$

Crystal Defects

At absolute zero, crystals tend to have a perfectly ordered arrangement. As the temperature increases, the amount of thermal vibration of ions in their lattice sites increases, and if the vibration of a particular ion becomes large enough, it may jump out of its lattice site. This constitutes a point defect. The higher the temperature, the greater the chance that lattice sites may be unoccupied. Since, the number of defects depends on the temperature, they are sometimes called **thermodynamic defects**.

In a crystalline solid, the atoms, ions or molecules are arranged in a definite repeating pattern, but some defects may occur in the pattern. **Any departure from perfectly ordered arrangement of atoms/ions in a crystal is called crystal defect**. These defects have an important and sometimes dominating influence on the mechanical, electrical and optical properties of solids. Several types of **crystal defects** are known.

Classification of Lattice Defects (Imperfections)

Lattice imperfections are classified according to their geometric characteristics.

- **Point defects** involve only one or two lattice sites directly.
- **Line defects** have to do with alternations or displacements of a row of lattice sites.
- **Plane defects** arise when a whole plane of sites is imperfect.

Types of Point Defect

Point defects are of following types

Stoichiometric Defects

In stoichiometric compounds, the elements are present in specific, fixed proportions that adhere to the law of constant composition, meaning that a given chemical compound always contains the same elements in the same proportion by mass, regardless of its source or preparation method. However, when these compounds form crystals, defects can occur due to thermal vibrations or external influences. These defects can be broadly categorised into two types: Schottky defects and Frenkel defects.

Schottky Defects

A Schottky defect occurs when both cations and anions are missing from their respective lattice positions, creating vacancies. These vacancies are typically paired, meaning the number of cation vacancies equals the number of anion vacancies in the crystal. This is crucial because it ensures the crystal maintains its overall electrical neutrality.

For example, in the NaCl crystal structure, a Schottky defect would involve a Na^+ ion missing from its lattice position and a Cl^- ion missing from a neighboring site. Since the number of positive ions missing is equal to the number of negative ions missing, the crystal remains electrically neutral despite the vacancies.

Properties of Schottky Defects

(i) **Electrical Neutrality** The crystal remains neutral overall since both cation and anion vacancies are created in equal numbers.

(ii) **Decreased Density** The overall density of the crystal decreases because the lattice vacancies reduce the number of ions present in the crystal.

(iii) **Thermal Effect** Schottky defects are thermally activated, meaning they are more likely to occur at higher temperatures where ions in higher the lattice vibrate more vigorously and may escape their lattice positions.

(iv) **Impact on Crystal Properties** Schottky defects can influence various properties of the material, such as its density and ionic conductivity.

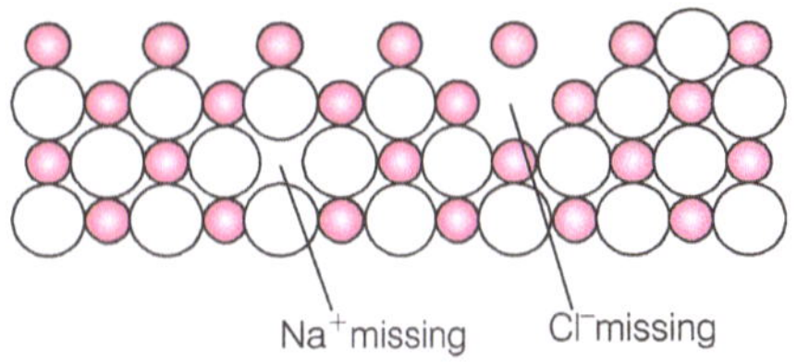

Frenkel Defects

A Frenkel defect, in contrast, involves the displacement of an ion (usually a cation) from its normal lattice position to an interstitial site, rather than creating a vacancy in both the cation and anion sites. In this case, the ion still remains in the crystal, but it is now located in an interstitial space (between the lattice points), rather than at its regular site. This defect results in the creation of a vacancy and an interstitial site. Unlike Schottky defects, Frenkel defects do not affect the electrical neutrality of the crystal but can affect its properties such as ionic conductivity and crystal stability.

Frenkel Defects in a Crystal

Ag^+	Br^-	Ag^+	Br^-	Ag^+	Br^-	Ag^+	Br^-	Ag^+
Br^-	Ag^+	Br^-	Ag^+	Br^-	Ag^+	Br^-	Ag^+	Br^-
Ag^+	Br^-	□ Ag^+	Br^-	Ag^+	Br^-	Ag^+	Br^-	Ag^+
Br^-	Ag^+	Br^-	Ag^+	Br^-	Ag^+	Br^-	Ag^+	Br^-

Frenkel defects appear in crystals in which the negative ions are much larger than the positive ions. Like Schottky defects, the Frenkel defects are also responsible for the conduction of electricity in crystals and also for the phenomenon of diffusion in solids.

JEE Alert

AgBr is a compound in which both Schottky and Frenkel defects are found because it is highly ionic and the large difference in sizes of Ag^+ and Br^-.

Non-Stoichiometric Defects

The defects discussed so far do not alter the stoichiometry of the crystalline substance. However, many non-stoichiometric inorganic solids exist, where the elements are present in non-stoichiometric ratios due to defects in their crystal structures. These compounds, known as non-stoichiometric or Berthollide compounds.

Some common properties of these compounds are:

- They do not follow the law of constant composition.
- Such compounds are common, especially among the oxides and sulphides of transition elements. For example, in compounds like FeO, FeS, or CuS, the ratios of Fe:O, Fe:S, or Cu:S deviate from the ideal 1:1 ratio.
- Electrical neutrality is maintained in such compounds by introducing extra electrons into the structure or by altering the charge on some of the metal ions. As a result, the structure becomes irregular and contains defects.
- These defects can be classified into two types: (i) metal excess defects and (ii) metal deficiency defects.

Metal Excess Defect

A metal excess defect can occur in two main ways:

F-Centres

This type of defect arises when a negative ion (anion) is absent from its lattice position, leaving a vacancy. This vacancy is then occupied by an electron, thus maintaining the electrical neutrality of the crystal.

These electron-filled anion vacancies are called F-centres, with "F" standing for Farbe, the German word for "colour". The presence of F-centres often imparts a colour to the crystal, which is a key characteristic of this type of defect.

This defect is typically found in crystals that would otherwise form Schottky defects. For example, when compounds like NaCl or KCl are heated in the presence of excess metal vapours or exposed to high-energy radiation, they become deficient in negative ions.

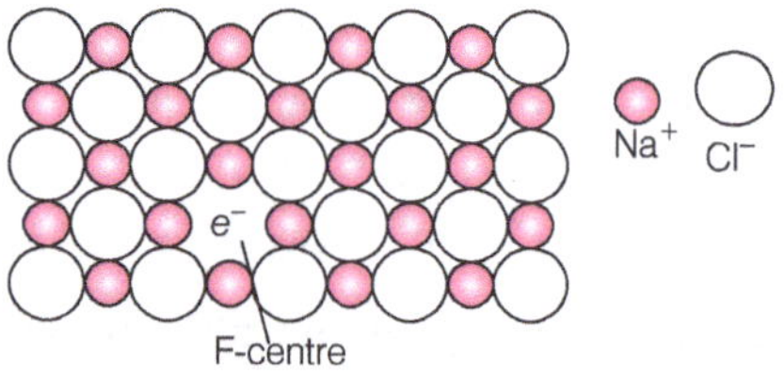

F-centres in a sodium chloride crystal

Interstitial Ions and Electrons

Metal excess defects also occur when an extra positive ion occupies an interstitial position in the lattice and electrical neutrality is maintained by the inclusion of an interstitial electron. Their composition may be represented by general formula $A_{1+\delta}X$. This kind of metal excess defect would be expected to form Frenkel defects. Examples include ZnO, CdO, Fe_2O_3.

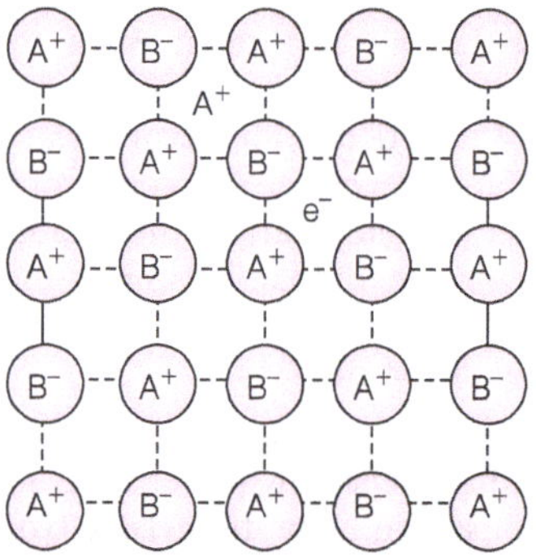

Metal excess defects caused by interstitial cations

Crystals with metal excess defect contain free electrons, and if these migrate they conduct an electric current. These free electrons may be excited to higher energy levels, giving absorption spectra and in consequence their compounds are often coloured e.g. non- stoichiometric NaCl is yellow, non-stoichiometric KCl is lilac.

Metal Deficiency Defects

In certain cases, one of the positive ions is missing from its lattice site and the extra negative charge is balanced by some nearby metal ion acquiring two charges instead of one. There is evidently, a deficiency of the metal ions although the crystal as a whole is neutral. This type of defect is generally found amongst the compounds of transition metals which can exhibit variable valency. Crystals of FeO, FeS and NiO show this type of defects. The existence of metal deficiency defects in the crystal of FeO is illustrated.

Metal deficiency defects

Fe^{2+}	O^{2-}	Fe^{2+}	O^{2-}	Fe^{2+}	O^{2-}	Fe^{2+}	O^{2-}	Fe^{2+}	O^{2-}
O^{2-}	Fe^{2+}	O^{2-}	Fe^{2+}	O^{2-}	Fe^{3+}	O^{2-}	Fe^{2+}	O^{2-}	Fe^{2+}
Fe^{2+}	O^{2-}	Fe^{2+}	O^{2-}	Fe^{2+}	O^{2-}	□	O^{2-}	Fe^{2+}	O^{2-}
O^{2-}	Fe^{2+}	O^{2-}	Fe^{2+}	O^{2-}	Fe^{2+}	O^{2-}	Fe^{3+}	O^{2-}	Fe^{2+}
Fe^{2+}	O^{2-}	Fe^{2+}	O^{2-}	Fe^{2+}	O^{2-}	Fe^{2+}	O^{2-}	Fe^{2+}	O^{2-}

It is evident from the above discussion that this defect results in the creation of vacancies or 'holes' in the lattice of the crystals. The presence of holes lowers the density as well as the lattice energy or the stability of the crystals. The presence of too many holes may cause a partial collapse of the lattice.

JEE Alert

When materials with *F*-centres are irradiated with light they become photoconductors. When electrons in the *F*-centres absorb sufficient light (or heat) energy, the electron is promoted into a conduction band, rather similar to the conduction bands present in metals. Since, conduction is by electrons it is *n*-type semiconduction.

Electrical Properties of Solids

Solids are classified into three groups on the basis of conduction power, namely

(i) **Conductors** It exhibit conductivity range of the order 10^4 to $10^7 (\Omega\ m)^{-1}$, e.g. metals.

(ii) **Semiconductors** It exhibit conductivity range $10^{-6} - 10^{+4}$ $(\Omega\ m)^{-1}$, e.g. semi-metals.

(iii) **Insulators** It show conductivity range $10^{-10} - 10^{-20}$ $(\Omega\ m)^{-1}$, e.g. non-metals.

In metals, conductivity strongly depends upon the number of valence electrons available per atom. The atomic orbitals form molecular orbitals which are so close to each other so as to form a **band.**

The conductivity of solids can be better explained on the basis of energy gap present between the conduction band (higher unoccupied band) and the valence band (lower occupied band).

Conductors

In conductors, the conduction band is almost overlapping with the valence band, i.e. there is no energy gap present between these two bands or valence band is not completely filled. Here, electrons can flow easily from valence band to conduction band.

Semiconductors

In the case of semiconductors, the gap between valence band and conduction band is small and therefore, some of the electrons may jump from valence band to conduction band and some conductivity is observed. The conductivity here increases with increase in temperature.

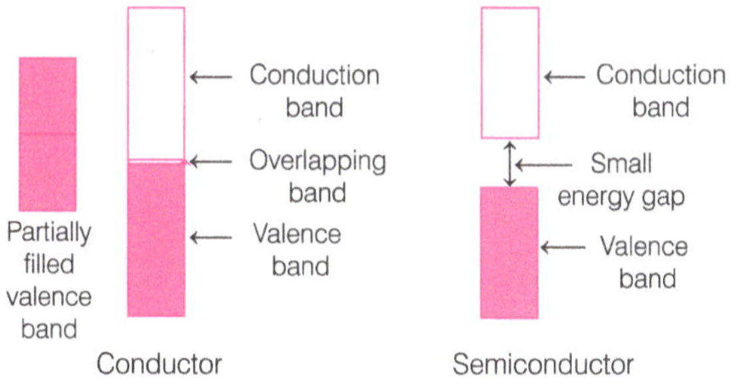

Semiconductors are of following two types, i.e. intrinsic and extrinsic.

(i) **Intrinsic semiconductors** Here, heat is responsible for ejection of electrons thus, leaving a (+)**ve charge** (positive hole). The crystal can now conduct electricity because on applying the electric field the electrons and holes migrate in opposite directions. Such type of conductance is called intrinsic **conductors** and these semiconductors showing such type of conductors are called undoped or intrinsic **semiconductors**, e.g. Si, Ge etc.

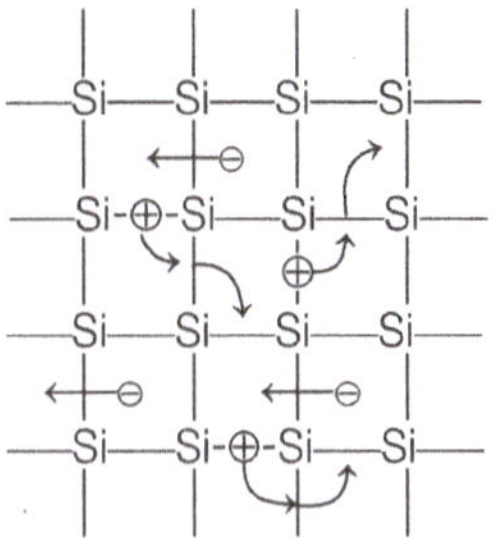

Electrical conduction in an intrinsic semiconductor

(ii) **Extrinsic semiconductor** For practical purposes the conductivity of pure Si and Ge is very low at room temperature.

In order to increase their conductance, the pure substances of group 14 are carefully doped (introduced with small amount of impurities in the form of elements of the 13 and 15 group of the periodic table).

Such semi conductor is called extrinsic semiconductor. Depending upon the nature of the elements used for doping, the extrinsic semiconductor can be of two types, *viz.*, *n*-types semiconductors and *p*-type semiconductors.

The group 15 elements have 1 electron excess to Si or Ge, after forming 4 covalent bonds with group 14 member (Si or Ge).

This excess free electron is responsible for electrical conductivity in them.

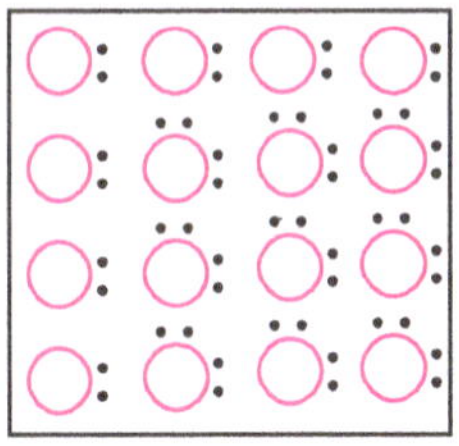

Normal silicon atom

Group 14 elements when doped with group 15 elements are called ***n*-type semiconductors**. Here, *n* specifies that negative charge flows in them.

The group 13 elements have 1 electron short to group 14 elements, thus giving rise to electron deficient band or a hole. Here, such holes are responsible for electrical conductivity.

Thus, group 14 elements when doped with elements of group 13 are called ***p*-type semiconductors**.

Here, *p* specifies that conduction is through positive holes in them.

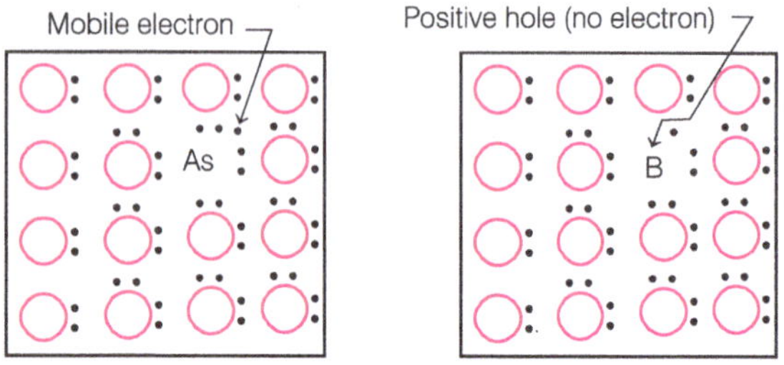

n and *p*-type semiconductors

Insulators

In case of **insulators,** the energy gap between valence band and conduction band is so large that it cannot even covered up even by supplying energy in the form of heat.

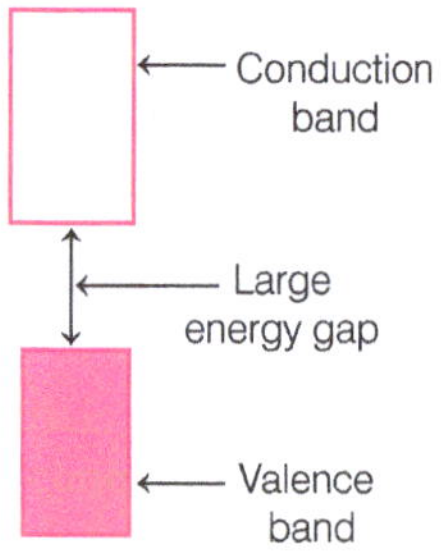

Insulators

Magnetic Properties of Solids

Solids can be divided into different classes. Depending on their response to magnetic fields.

(i) **Paramagnetic (weakly magnetic)** Such materials contain permanent magnetic dipoles due to the presence of atoms, ion or molecules with unpaired electrons e.g. O_2, Cu^{2+}, Fe^{3+} and they are attracted by the magnetic field. They however lose their magnetism in the absence of a magnetic field.

(ii) **Diamagnetic** They are weakly repelled by magnetic fields. Diamagnetism arises due to the absence of unpaired electrons e.g. H^-, Li^+, Be^{2+} (2 electron type), $O^{2-}, F^-, Na^+, Mg^{2+}$ (8 electron type), Ag^+, Zn^{2+}, Cd^{2+} (18 electron type).

(iii) **Ferromagnetic** It is caused by spontaneous alignment of magnetic moments in the same direction.

(iv) **Ferrimagnetism** It occurs when the moments are aligned in parallel and antiparalled direction in unequal number resulting in a net moment e.g. Fe_3O_4.

(v) **Antiferromagnetism** It occurs if the alignment of moments is in a compensatory way so as to give zero net moment e.g. MnO.

All magnetically ordered solids (ferromagnetic and antiferromagnetic solids) transform to the paramagnetic state at some elevated temperatures. This is most probably due to the randomisation of spins.

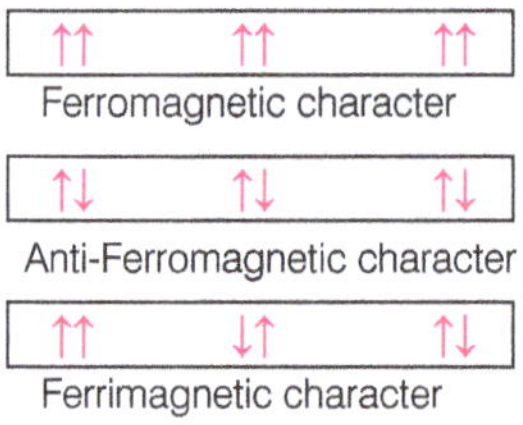

Elemental Practice 3.3

Type I MCQs with Only One Correct Option

1. In the following NaCl type structure.

Salt	Anion-anion distance	Cation-anion distance
MT	2.40 Å	1.70 Å
MQ	1.63 Å	1.15 Å
RT	2.66 Å	1.88 Å
RQ	2.09 Å	1.48 Å

MT is represented as

(a) 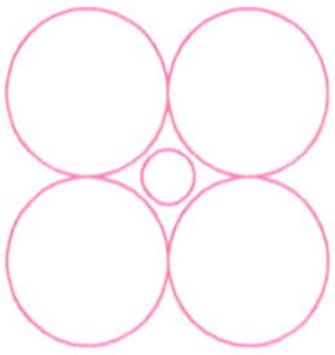
(b) 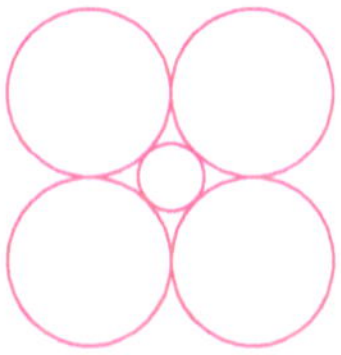

(c) 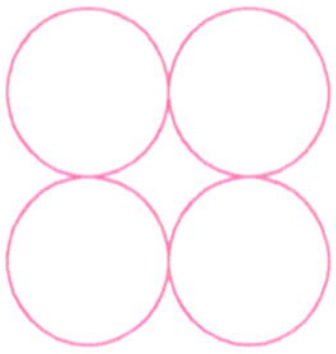
(d) 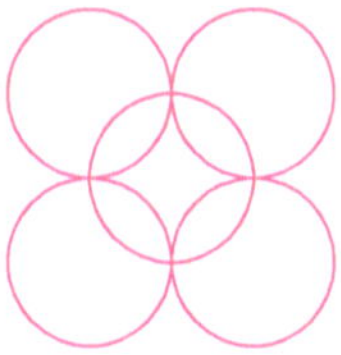

2. A solid has a structure in which *W*-atoms are located at the cube corners of the unit cell, O-atoms are located at the cube edges and the Na-atoms at the cube centres. Lattice is of the type with formula
(W is in +5 oxidation state)
(a) simple cubic, $NaWO_3$
(b) simple cubic, Na_2WO_3
(c) tetrahedral, $NaWO_3$
(d) body-centred, $NaWO_3$

3. In the structure of NaCl given below, ratio r_{Na^+}/r_{Cl^-} is

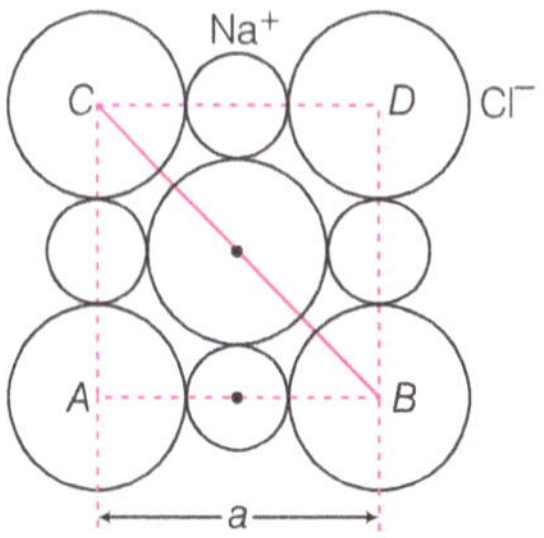

(a) 0.414
(b) 0.681
(c) 0.745
(d) 0.520

4. The length of the unit cell edge of a bcc lattice metal is 352 pm. Thus, volume of atoms in one mole of the metal is
(a) 8.91 cm^3
(b) 7.25 cm^3
(c) 1.21 cm^3
(d) 4.00 cm^3

5. In a face-centred cubic lattice, atom *A* occupies the corners of the cube and atom *B* occupies the face-centred positions. If one atom of *B* is missing from one of the face-centred points, the formula of the compound is
(a) A_2B
(b) AB_2
(c) A_2B_5
(d) AB

6. In which of the following oxides conducting or insulating property is dependent on temperature?
(a) TiO
(b) SiO_2
(c) Ti_2O_3
(d) MgO

7. Select the incorrect statement(*s*) about non-stoichiometric compounds.
(a) They are called Berthollide compounds.
(b) They do not obey the law of constant composition.
(c) Electrical neutrality is maintained either by having extra electrons in the structure or changing the charge on some of the metal ions.
(d) In compound FeO, FeS or CuS the ratio of Fe : O, Fe : S or Cu : S same from that indicated by the ideal chemical formula.

8. **Assertion (A)** The anionic sites occupied by unpaired electrons are called F-centres.
Reason (R) They impart yellow colour to the crystals of NaCl.
(a) Both A and R are correct and R is the correct explanation of A.
(b) Both A and R are correct and R is not the correct explanation of A.
(c) A is true but R is false.
(d) A is false but R is true.

9. The compound which is metallic compound as well as ferromagnetic at room temperature is
(a) MnO_2
(b) TiO_2
(c) CrO_2
(d) VO_2

10. Consider the following energy diagram.

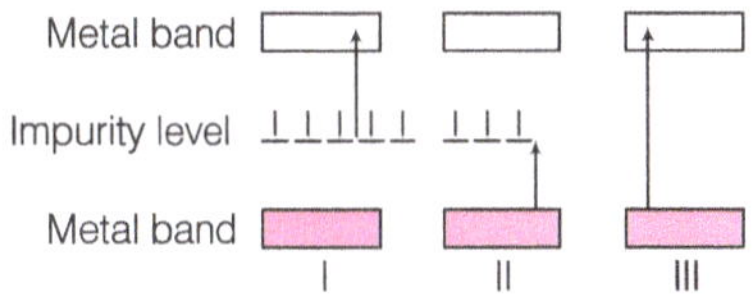

These energy diagrams are respectively, for semiconductors.

	I	II	III
(a)	*n*-type	*p*-type	Intrinsic
(b)	*n*-type	Intrinsic	*p*-type
(c)	*p*-type	Intrinsic	*n*-type
(d)	*p*-type	*n*-type	Intrinsic

11. In a closest packed structure of mixed oxides, it is found that lattice has O^{2-} (oxide ion) and one-half of octahedral voids are occupied by trivalent cations (A^{3+}) and one-eighth of tetrahedral voids are occupied by divalent cations (B^{2+}). Thus, mixed oxide is
(a) A_2BO_3 (b) A_2BO_4
(c) AB_2O_4 (d) ABO_3

12. Consider the following transition of iron at 1200 K.

$$\underset{\text{bcc lattice}}{Fe(\alpha\text{ - form})} \xrightarrow{1200\text{ K}} \underset{\text{fcc lattice}}{Fe(\gamma\text{ - form})}$$

Distance between the nearest neighbours is same in the two forms at the transition temperature 1200 K. Thus, ratio of the densities of the two forms at 1200 K is
(a) 1.09 (b) 1.00
(c) 0.92 (d) 2.18

13. Read the following question and answer as per the direction given below.

Assertion (A) Frenkel defect involving the migration of ions to interstitial sites is more likely for ionic compounds and for large (and highly polarisable) anions.

Reason (R) Large polarisable anions make it easier to accommodate the displaced cations and minimise repulsive effect.

(a) Both Assertion and Reason are correct and Reason is the correct explanation of Assertion.
(b) Both Assertion and Reason are correct but Reason is not the correct explanation of Assertion.
(c) Assertion is correct but Reason is incorrect.
(d) Reason is correct but Assertion is incorrect.

14. The cation/anion radius ratio for a triangular arrangement of anions in which the cation is in contact with the anions (but does not push them apart) as shown in the figure is

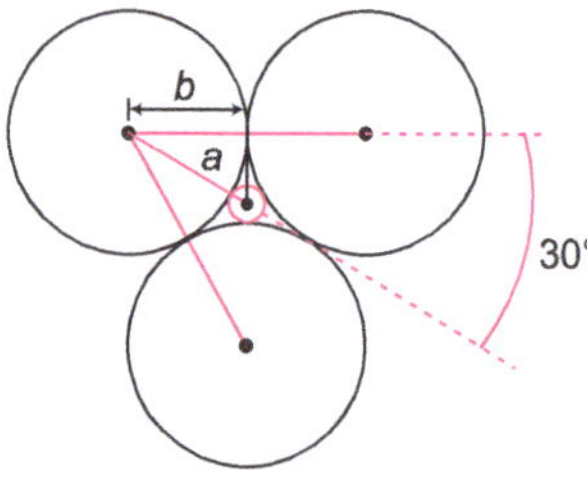

(a) 0.866 (b) 0.414
(c) 0.155 (d) 0.500

15. A crystal is formed by two elements *P* and *Q*. The element *Q* forms cubic close packing and atoms of *P* occupy one-third of tetrahedral voids. The compound is thus represented as
(a) PQ_3 (b) P_3Q
(c) P_2Q_3 (d) P_3Q_2

Type II 》 MCQs with One or More than One Correct Option

16. Select the correct statement(s).
(a) When silicon is doped with a group 15 elements (P or As), *n*-type semiconductor is formed
(b) When silicon is doped with a group 13 elements (B, Al, Ga), *p*-type semiconductor is formed
(c) In *n*-type semiconductor, increase in conductivity is due to the negatively charged electrons
(d) In *p*-type semiconductor, electrons move towards the positively charged plate through electronic holes under the influence of electric field

17. Silicon crystallises in a unit cell similar to that of diamond (a fcc unit cell containing a tetrahedron of atoms) with $a = 0.542$ nm. Thus,
(a) unit cell content for Si is 8.
(b) Si unit cell is predicated to be more efficiently packed than the fcc unit cell.
(c) Si unit cell is predicted to be less efficiently packed than the fcc unit cell.
(d) Si unit cell is packed as efficiently as fcc unit cell.

18. Which of the following statements are incorrect?
(a) The unit cell having crystal parameters. $a = b \neq c$, $\alpha = \beta = 90°, \gamma = 120°$ is hexagonal.
(b) The number of atoms per unit cell and the number of nearest neighbours in a simple cubic structures are 4 and 12 respectively.
(c) First three nearest neighbour distances for primitive cubic lattice are $\sqrt{3}a$, $\sqrt{2}a$ and a respectively. (a = edge length of unit cell)
(d) In sphalerite and antifluorite type structures, number of tetrahedral voids occupied are 2 and 4 respectively.

19. Which of the following statements are correct?
(a) Due to the pairing of electrons, magnetic moment is cancelled.
(b) Paramagnetic substances are weakly attracted by magnetic field.
(c) Ferromagnetic substances cannot be magnetised permanently.
(d) The domains in anti-ferromagnetic substances are oppositely oriented with respect to each other.

20. Which of the following statement(s) are incorrect?
(a) Vacancy defect results in the decrease in the density of the substance
(b) Interstitial defects result in the increase in the density of the substance
(c) Impurity defect has no effect on the density of the substance
(d) Frenkel defect results in an increase in the density of the substance

Type III 》 Integer/Numerical Answer Type Questions

21. A newly synthesised copper complex with molecular formula $C_{11}H_{29}N_2B_2Cu$ is found to crystallise in the orthorhombic system with $a = 14.749$ Å, $b = 17.604$ Å and $c = 13.907$ Å. The density is 1.17 g cm^{-3}. The number of molecules per unit cell will be .... (Nearest Integer)
[Given : Molar mass of B, Cu = 11 and 63.5 respectively]

22. M^+ forms $C_{60}M_3$ where C_{60}^{3-} fulleride (a superconductor). It forms octahedral holes. If radius of C_{60}^{3-} is 500 pm, then the radius of M^+ will be .... pm.

23. An element crystallises in fcc lattice having edge length 400 pm. Maximum radius of the atom which can be placed in the interstitial site without distorting the structure is $x \times 10^{-12}$ m. The value of x is ....

24. Experimentally it was found that a metal oxide has formula $A_{0.96}O$. The metal A, is present as A^{2+} and A^{3+} in its oxide. Fraction of the metal which exists as A^{3+} would be ....

25. The edge length of the unit cell of LiCl(NaCl-like structure, fcc) is 5.14 Å. Assuming that the lithium ion is small enough that the chloride ions are in contact.
The ionic radius for the chloride ions is ...x... Å.
The value of x is ....

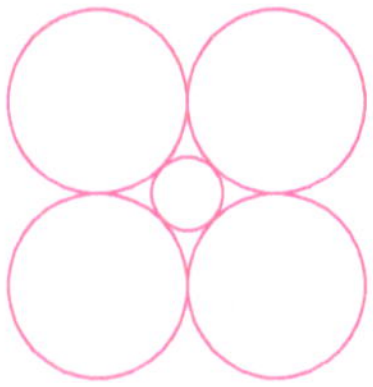

1. (a)	**2.** (d)	**3.** (a)	**4.** (a)	**5.** (c)	**6.** (c)
7. (d)	**8.** (b)	**9.** (c)	**10.** (a)	**11.** (b)	**12.** (c)
13. (a)	**14.** (c)	**15.** (c)	**16.** (a,b,c,d)	**17.** (a,c)	**18.** (b,c,d)
19. (a,b,d)	**20.** (c,d)	**21.** (9)	**22.** (207)	**23.** (58.55)	**24.** (8.16)
25. (1.8173)					

Elemental Practice 3.3 | **Chapter 03**

Connect with **Answers**

Advanced Exclusive Different Strokes

The Maxwell Boltzmann distribution of speeds provides a theoretical framework for the calculation of v_{av}, v_{rms}, v_{mp}. Questions based on these concepts have gained prominence in recent years.

The interpretation of Maxwell Boltzmann distribution have been discussed below.

Interpretation of Maxwell Boltzmann Distribution

The variation of molecular velocity with different parameters can be interpreted through Maxwell Boltzmann distribution.

At any particular time, different particles in a gas have different speeds hence different kinetic energy. This assumption is quite reasonable because a large number of particles imply a large number of collisions. As particles collide, we expect their speeds to change, but the distribution of speeds remains constant at a particular temperature. This distribution is referred to as the **Maxwell-Boltzmann distribution** and is shown in Figure at different temperatures. Maxwell proposed an equation for the distribution of molecular speeds as

$$\frac{1}{N}\left(\frac{dN}{du}\right) = 4\pi u^2 \left(\frac{B}{\pi}\right)^{3/2} e^{-Bu^2}$$

where, dN is the number of molecules distributed between velocities u and $(u + du)$

and $$B = \left(\frac{M}{2RT}\right)$$

The expression on the left hand side of the equation gives the fraction of molecules having velocity u to $u + du$.

Initial part of the graph is parabolic and later part of the graph is exponentially decreasing in the lower range of u, u^2 is decreasing faster whereas e^{-u^2} is decreasing in later part of the graph.

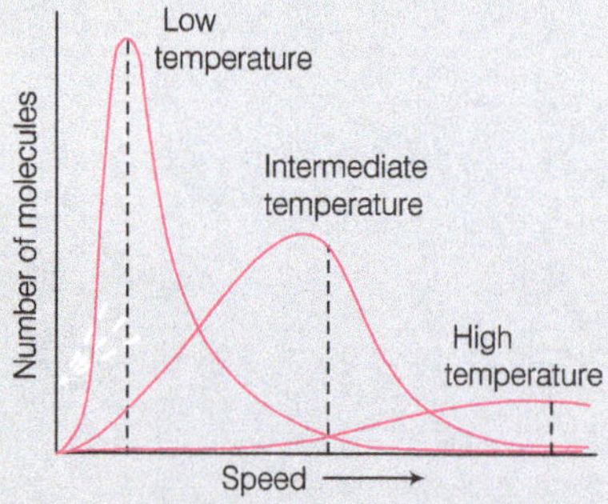

(a) The Maxwell distribution of speed with temperature

Effect of Temperature on Distribution of Molecular Velocities

- With increase in temperature, all velocity range increases since $u \propto \sqrt{T}$.
- With increase in temperature, fraction of molecules with most probable velocity decreases.
- With increase in temperature, fraction of molecules with average speed.
- With increase in temperature, fraction of molecules with rms speed increases.

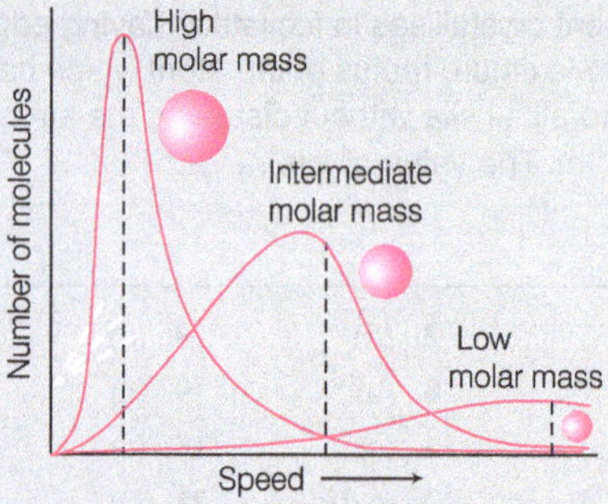

(b) The Maxwell distribution of speed based on molar mass

Effect of Molar Masses on Distribution of Molecular Velocities

The Maxwell distribution of speeds also depends on the molar mass of the molecules.

Molecules of low molar mass have a broad spread of speeds and a significant fraction may be found travelling much faster than the rms speed.

The distribution is much narrower for heavy molecules and most of them travel with speeds close to the *rms* value

Conclusion

(i) According to this figure, there are only a small number of molecules with very low velocities ($u \to 0$) or with high velocities ($u \to \infty$).

(ii) Most molecules have intermediate velocities. The largest number of molecules have a velocity corresponding to the maximum of the curve. This velocity is called **most probable velocity**.

PRACTICE ELEMENT

Target JEE Advanced

Objective Type Questions

1. Structure of unit cell is described in the given figure. Fraction of the unit cell is

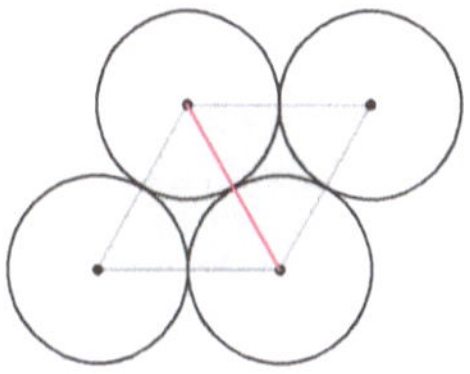

(a) 0.907 (b) 0.093
(c) 0.745 (d) 0.521

2. In a metal deficient oxide sample, $M_xY_2O_4$ (M and Y are metals), M is present in both +2 and +3 oxidation states and Y is in +2 oxidaion state. If the fraction of M^{2+} ions present in M is $\frac{3}{4}$, the value of x is

(a) 1.7 (b) 2.37
(c) 0.38 (d) 0.95

3. At 47°C and 16.0 atm, the molar volume of NH_3 gas is about 10% less than the molar volume of an ideal gas. This is due to

(a) NH_3 decomposes to N_2 and H_2 at 47°C
(b) the force of attraction between NH_3 molecules is significant at this temperature and pressure
(c) the volume occupied by NH_3 molecules themselves is a significant fraction of the volume of the container at this temperature and pressure
(d) at 16 atm, NH_3 molecules no longer move randomly

4. 60 mL mixture of nitrous oxide and nitric oxide undergoes explosive reaction with excess of hydrogen. If 38 mL of N_2 was formed, the volume of N_2O in the reaction mixture is

(a) 44 mL (b) 16 mL
(c) 32 mL (d) 48 mL

5. Germanium has been doped with impurity as shown in I, II, III and IV and followed by statements (A) to (D) based on it.

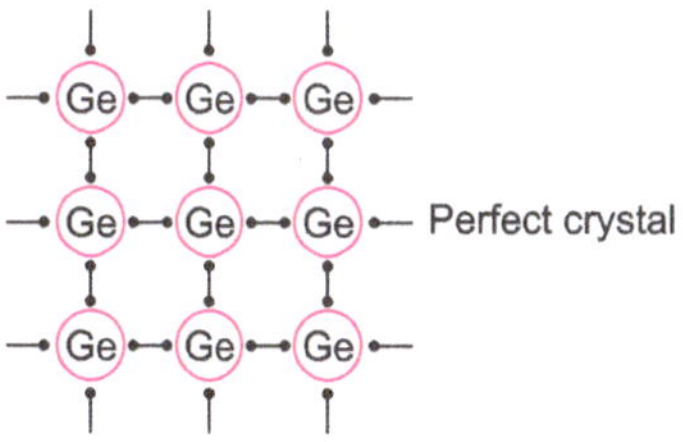

are given

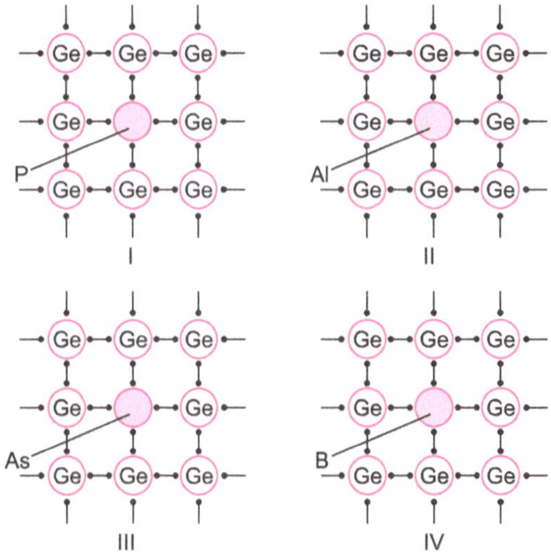

A. n-type semiconductor is formed in I and III
B. p-type semiconductor is formed in II and IV
C. n -type semiconductor is formed in II and IV
D. p-type semiconductor is formed in I and III
Select the correct statement(s).

(a) A, B (b) C, D (c) A, D (d) A, B, C

6. Select the incorrect match.

(a) Nearest neighbour distance in NaCl $\longrightarrow \frac{a}{2}$
(b) Nearest neighbour distance inCaF_2 $\longrightarrow \frac{a\sqrt{3}}{4}$
(c) Nearest neighbour distance in Na_2O $\longrightarrow \frac{a}{2\sqrt{2}}$
(d) Nearest neighbour distance is CsCl $\longrightarrow \frac{a\sqrt{3}}{2}$

7. Graphically variation of $\log_{10} p$ with $1/T$ is shown. If $\tan\theta$ (slope of the line) $= -2$K, latent heat of vaporisation of the given liquid is

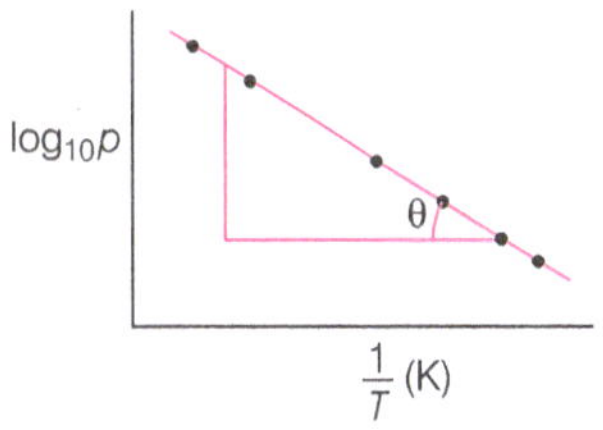

(a) 2.303 cal mol^{-1} (b) 4.606 cal mol^{-1}
(c) 9.212 cal mol^{-1} (d) 4.00 cal mol^{-1}

8. Consider the following isotherms (I-III) for gases.

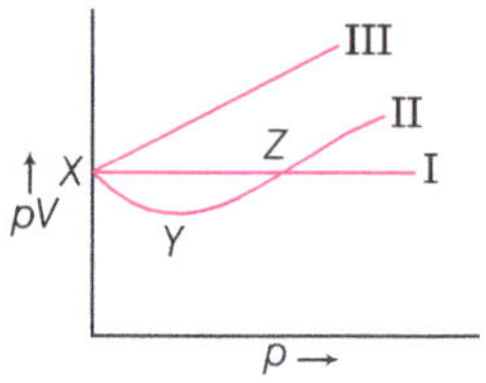

Select the correct statement(s) about these isotherms

(a) I is observed for ideal gases and for real gases under high temperature and low pressure

(b) *XY* nature of II is observed at low pressure and after *Y*, at high pressure

(c) III is observed for light gases

(d) All are correct statements

9. Under the condition, when $p \to 0$, isotherm showing variation of pV with p at 273 K has a slope of 0.1 dm^3. Assume ideal condition for approximation, van der Waals' constant a is (in unit of bar $\text{dm}^6 \text{mol}^{-2}$)

(a) 2.27 (b) 4.54

(c) 0.114 (d) 0.454

10. In an ionic crystal, anions occupy the corners of the cube while the cations along the face centres. The cations can be filled to octahedral holes. The packing fraction (in %) will be

(a) 75% (b) 36%

(c) 42% (d) 63%

More than One Correct Choice MCQs

11. Which of the following statements are incorrect?

(a) A mixture of non-reacting gases exert a pressure of 5 atm. If one of gases occupy 80% volume of the mixture, the partial pressure is 4 atm.

(b) Under identical condition of temperature and pressure helium will diffuse 2 times as compared to methane gas

(c) Dalton's law is not applicable to mixture of CO_2 and CO at room temperature

(d) A balloon filled with ethylene is picked with a needle and quickly dropped in a tank of H_2 gas under identical conditions. After a while, the balloon will shrink.

12. Which of following statements are incorrect for hexagonal close packing of sphere in three dimensions?

(a) In one unit cell there are 12 octahedral voids and all are completely inside the unit cell.

(b) In one unit cell there are six octahedral voids and all are completely inside the unit cell.

(c) In one unit cell there are six octahedral voids and of which four are completely inside the unit cell and other three are from contributions of octahedral voids which are partially inside the unit cell.

(d) In one unit cell there are 12 tetrahedral voids, all are completely inside the unit cell.

13. If the radius of $Cs^+ = 1.69$ Å and $Br^- = 1.95$ Å then which of the following is/are correct.

(a) The edge length of unit cell is 4.2 Å

(b) The coordination number of Cs^+ is 8.

(c) CsBr has bcc type structure

(d) Br^- ions touch each other along the edge

14. Which of the following statements are correct?

(a) The radius of the Na^+ is 95 pm and that of Cl^- ion is 181 pm. The coordination number of Na^+ is 8.

(b) The coordination number of Sr^{2+} ion in SrF_2, if ionic radii are $r(Sr^{2+}) = 113$ pm and $r(F^-) = 136$ pm is 6.

(c) The number of atoms in 100 g of an fcc crystal with density ($d = 5 \text{ g cm}^{-3}$) and all edge length (200 pm) is 10^{25}.

(d) An ionic compound *AB* has ZnS type of structure, if the radius of A^+ is 22.5 pm, then the ideal radius of B^- is 100 pm.

15. The temperature dependence of the surface tension of a liquid is given by the Sugden's equation, $\gamma = \gamma_0 \left(1 - \frac{T}{T_c}\right)^n$.

Select the correct statement(s).

(a) Surface tension approaches zero as critical temperature is attained, i.e. at $T = T_c$

(b) Plot of log γ against $\log\left(1 - \frac{T}{T_c}\right)$ is linear with a slope equal to n and an intercept equal to $\log \gamma_0$

(c) At reduced temperature equal to 1, surface disappears and $\gamma = 0$

(d) log γ decreases on increasing $\log\left(1 - \frac{T}{T_c}\right)$

16. Based on the following isotherms, select correct statements.

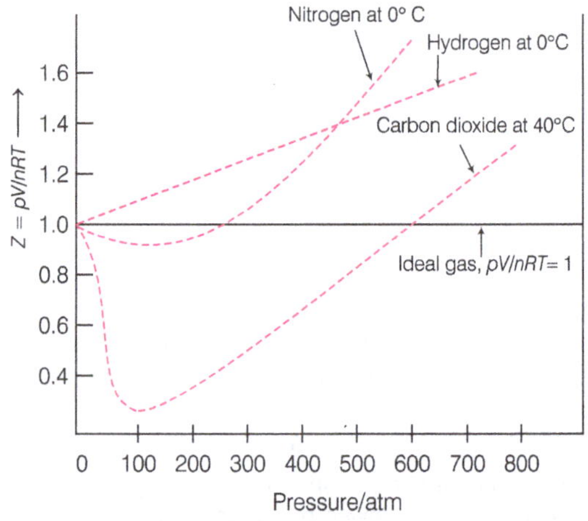

(a) For H_2 at 0° C, molecular attractive forces are weak and size effect dominates its behaviour resulting that $(Z > 1)$

(b) For N_2 at 0° C, attractive forces are large enough to cause negative deviation upto 150 atm and $Z < 1$ after which size effect dominates after which $(Z > 1)$

(c) For CO_2, intermolecular attraction is large even at 40°C resulting $(Z < 1)$ upto high pressures of 500 atm

(d) For CO_2 and N_2, two effects compensate each other at a particular pressure where, $Z = 1$

17. The given graph represents the variations of compressibility factor $(Z) = \frac{pV}{nRT}$, *versus* p, for three real gases A, B and C. Select the correct statements

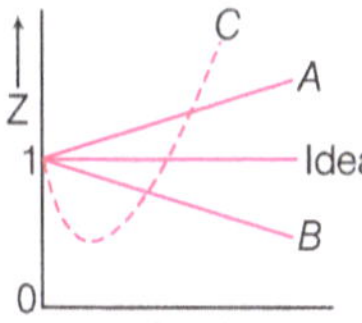

(a) For the gas A, $a = 0$ and its dependence on p is linear at all pressure
(b) For the gas B, $b = 0$ and its dependence on p is linear at all pressure
(c) For the gas C, which is typical real gas for which neither a nor $b = 0$. By knowing the minima and point of the intersection, with $Z = 1$ and the temperature a and b can be calculated
(d) At high pressure, the slope is positive for all real gases

18. Select the correct statement(s).
(a) Different types of velocities are related by equation, $u_{mp} < u_{av} < u_{rms}$
(b) Average kinetic energy of 1g H_2 gas and 8 g O_2 gas at 300 K are equal
(c) Kinetic energy of 1 mole of a gas in terms of u_{mp} is $\frac{3}{4}M(u_{mp})^2$
(d) Kinetic energy of 1 mole of a gas in terms of u_{rms} is $\frac{(u_{rms})^2 M}{2}$

19. Which of the following statements are correct?
(a) Dislocation of ion from lattice site to interstitial site is called Frenkel defect.
(b) In Frenkel defect, the dielectric constant of solid increases.
(c) In Schottky defect, the number of ion decreases, density of the solid also decreases.
(d) Non-stoichiometric NaCl has F-center due to anion vacancy defect.

Numerical/Integer Type Questions

20. KF has NaCl (fcc) structure with density 2.475 g/cm^3. The interionic distance in crystal of KF is .... pm.
[Given, Molar mass of K and F is 39 and 19 respectively].

21. A rigid vessel of volume 0.50 m^3 containing H_2 at 20.5°C and a pressure of 611×10^3 Pa is connected to a second rigid vessel of volume 0.75 m^3 containing Ar at 31.2°C and a pressure of 433×10^3 Pa. A valve separating the two vessels is opened and both are cooled to a temperature of 14.5°C. The final pressure in the vessel will be $x \times 10^5$ Pa. The value of x is ....

22. In zero-gravity environment, a sample of mercury has a spherical shape. And such sample has a radius of 1.00 cm. If 10 drops are formed $x \times 10^{-4}$ J work is performed. Surface tension of mercury is 414 erg/cm^2. Assume that only work done is related to change in surface energy. The value of x is ....

23. Calcium crystallises in a face-centred cubic unit cell with $a = 0.556$ nm. The fraction of Ca-atoms lie on the surface of a cubic crystal that is 1.00 cm in length will be $x \times 10^{-7}$. The value of x is ....

24. Metal M of radius of 50 nm is crystallised in fcc type and made cubical crystal such that face of unit cells aligned with face of cubical crystal. If the total number of metal atoms of M at all faces of cubical crystal is 24×10^{30}, then the area of one face of cubical crystal is $A \times 10^{16}$ m^2.
The value of A is ....

25. In the cubic crystal of CsCl ($d = 3.97$ g cm^{-3}) the eight corners are occupied by Cl^- ions with a Cs^+ at the centre and *vice-versa*. The radius ratio of two ions is 'y'. The value of y is ....

26. A liquid of density 850 kg m^{-3} having a surface tension of 0.058 Nm^{-1} will rise $x \times 10^{-2}$ m in a glass capillary of 1.4 mm inside a diameter. The is value of x is ....

27. A vessel of uniform cross-section of length 500 cm as shown in figure is divided in two parts by a weightless and frictionless piston one part contains 5 moles of He(g) and other part 2 moles of $H_2(g)$ and 4 moles of $O_2(g)$ added at the same temperature and pressure in which reaction takes place finally vessel cooled to 300 K and 1 atm.
The length of He compartment is .... cm.
(Assume volume of piston and vol. of $H_2O(l)$ formed are negligible)

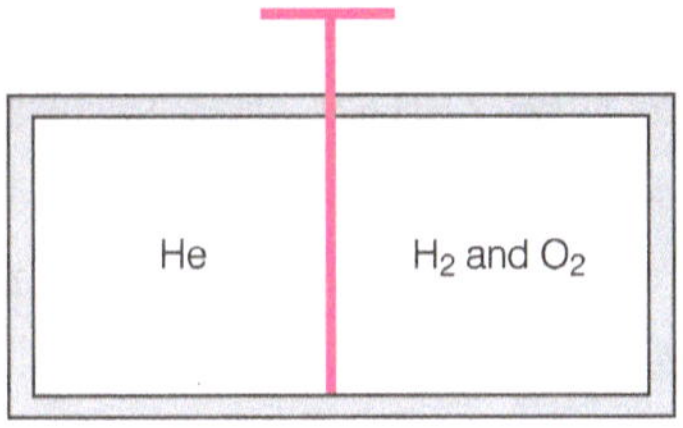

At initial stage

Matching Type Questions

28. Given below is the unit cell of NaCl.

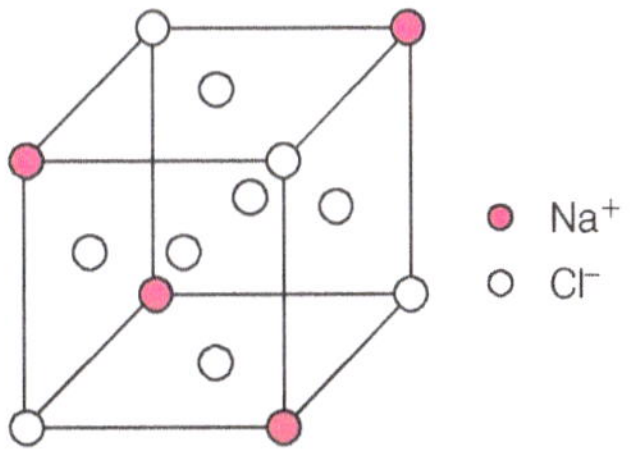

Match the questions in Column I with their answers in Column II and select answers from the codes given below.

S.No.	Column I		Column II
A.	The fraction of Cl^- at each corner of the cube within the unit cell	I.	$\frac{1}{4}$
B.	The fraction of a Cl^- appear in figure in each face	II.	$\frac{1}{2}$
C.	The fraction of each Na^+ along each face in the unit cell	III.	$\frac{1}{8}$
D.	In the simplest structure fraction of Cl^- ions out of total Na^+ and Cl^- ions in the unit cell	IV.	$\frac{7}{8}$

Choose the correct answer from the options given below

	A	B	C	D		A	B	C	D
(a)	I	II	III	IV	(b)	IV	I	II	III
(c)	III	II	I	IV	(d)	III	II	IV	I

29. Variation of vapour pressure with temperature is given by

$$\log_{10} p = \log_{10} A - \frac{\Delta H_V}{2.303\, RT}$$

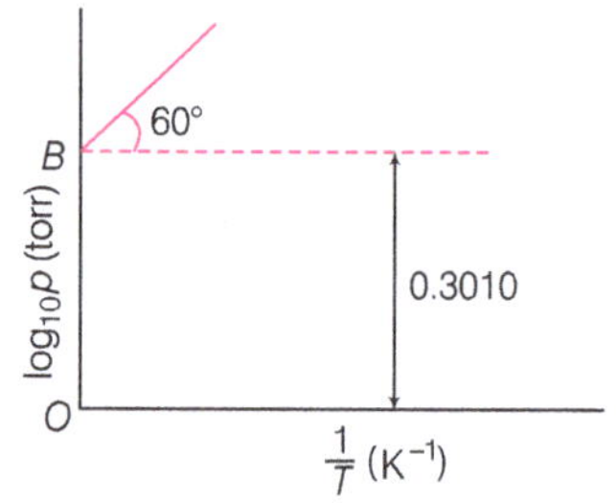

Match the parameters in Column I with their values in Column II and select the answer from the codes given.

	Column I		Column II
A.	ΔH_V in Cal	I.	2.0
B.	Vapour pressure when $T \to \infty$	II.	0.33
C.	ΔH_V in L atm mol^{-1} K^{-1}	III.	7.97
D.	Vapour pressure at 300 K (in torr)	IV.	1.97

Codes

	A	B	C	D
(a)	III	II	I	IV
(b)	III	I	II	IV
(c)	IV	I	III	II
(d)	II	IV	I	III

30. Interionic distances (bond length) of some compounds are given below

RbI = 3.67Å KCl = 3.14 Å

RbBr = 3.44Å NaCl = 2.79Å

KBr = 3.29Å NaF = 2 . 31Å

Ionic radius of iodide (I^-) ion = 2.19 Å.

Match the ion in Column I with ionic radius in Column II and select answer from codes given below.

S.No.	Column I		Column II
A.	Rb^+	I.	1.96 Å
B.	K^+	II.	1.81 Å
C.	Na^+	III.	1.33 Å
D.	Cl^-	IV.	0.98 Å
E.	Br^-	V.	1.48 Å

Codes

	A	B	C	D	E
(a)	V	III	II	IV	I
(b)	V	III	IV	II	I
(c)	II	III	IV	I	V
(d)	IV	V	I	II	III

31. 1.00 mole sample of O_2 and 3.00 moles sample of H_2 are mixed isothermally in a 100.0 L container at 400 K.

Match the partial pressures of different species in Column I with their values in Column II and select answer from codes given below.

	Column I		Column II
A.	Partial pressure of H_2 before reaction	I.	0.00 atm
B.	Partial pressure of O_2 after reaction	II.	1.3136 atm
C.	Total pressure before reaction	III.	0.6568 atm
D.	Partial pressure of H_2O reaction	IV.	0.9852 atm

Choose the correct answer from the options given below.

	A	B	C	D		A	B	C	D
(a)	I	II	III	IV	(b)	IV	III	II	I
(c)	IV	I	II	III	(d)	IV	II	III	I

32. Match the crystal given in Column I with the coordination number (of cation and anion) given in Column II and select the answer from the codes given below :

S.N.	Column I		Column II
A.	CsBr	I.	4-4
B.	NaCl	II.	6-6
C.	ZnS	III.	8-4
D.	CaF_2	IV.	8-8

Codes

	A	B	C	D		A	B	C	D
(a)	I	IV	III	II	(b)	IV	II	I	III
(c)	IV	II	III	I	(d)	IV	I	II	III

33. Assume that attractive forces are negligible and isobar (using Charles' law) giving variation of $V(dm^3)$ and $T(K)$ at constant p(atm) is of the type

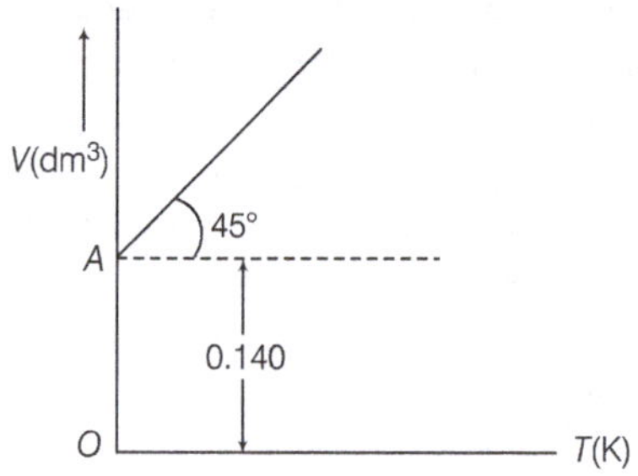

Match the parameters in Column I with their values in Column II and select the answer from the codes given below.

Column I		Column II	
A.	Pressure (atm)	I.	0.043
B.	van der Waals' constant (b)($dm^3 mol^{-1}$)	II.	0.140
C.	Volume at 300 K (dm^3)	III.	300.14
D.	van der Waals' constant (a) ($dm^6 atm\ mol^{-2}$) if pressure is the critical pressure	IV.	0.0821

Choose the correct answer from the options given below

	A	B	C	D		A	B	C	D
(a)	I	II	IV	III	(b)	III	IV	I	II
(c)	IV	II	III	I	(d)	II	III	IV	I

34. An isochore (at $0.1 dm^3$) showing Gay Lussac's law for one mole of a real gas is of the type

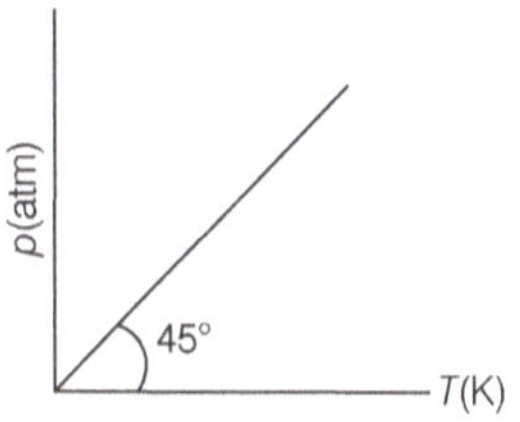

Match the parameters in Column I with their values in Column II and select the answer from codes given below.

Column I		Column II	
A.	van der Waals' constant 'b'	I.	0.0179
B.	Temperature at which p is 1 atm	II.	1.0
C.	$\left(\frac{\partial p}{\partial T}\right)_V$	III.	55.86
D.	Mean free path when $b = 4V$ at 1 atm	IV.	5.24

Choose the correct answer from the options given below.

	A	B	C	D		A	B	C	D
(a)	I	II	III	IV	(b)	I	II	II	IV
(c)	II	III	IV	I	(d)	III	IV	I	II

Paragraph of Two Questions Each

Paragraph 1

In the given sample of a gas all molecule do not posses same speed. Due to frequent molecular collisions, the molecules move with changing speeds and also with changing direction. There are three types of velocities:

(i) Root mean square velocity, (ii) average velocity and (iii) most probable velocity.

35. The density of a gas filled in electric lamp is $0.75 kg/m^3$. After the lamp has been switched on the pressure in it increases from 4×10^4 Pa to 9×10^4 Pa.

The increase in μ_{rms} is ....

36. A gaseous mixture contains 4 molecules with a velocity of 6 cm s^{-1}, 5 molecules with a velocity of 2 cm sec^{-1} and 10 molecules with a velocity of 3 cm sec^{-1}. The root mean square speed of the gas is .... cm sec^{-1}.

Paragraph 2

The quantity of heat required to evaporate a given liquid at constant temperature is defined as the heat of vaporisation. Variation of vapour-pressure with temperature is given by Clausius-Clapeyron equation.

A liquid is said to be at its boiling temperature. If its vapour pressure is equal to external pressure. Therefore, the boiling point of water in particular and of liquids in general decreases as altitude of a place increases where the external pressure is less than 1 atm.

37. For a given liquid at a given temperature vapour pressure is given by

$$\log_{10} p(\text{mm}) = -\frac{400\ (\text{K})}{T} + 10$$

Vapour pressure of the liquid at 400 K is .... mm.

38. The temperature at which the vapour pressure of liquid is 2 atm is .... °C.

Paragraph 3

A solid ball of radius 17.32 cm crystallises in a BCC pattern. During one such crystallisation, some oxygen gas is trapped inside the unit cell. The trapped oxygen at 640 K exerts a pressure of 5 atm. Assume

- The BCC arrangement is not disturbed due to the trapping of gas.
- The gas is uniformly distributed inside the unit cell. Given
- Universal gas constant $(R) = 0.08$ atm L $mol^{-1} K^{-1}$.
- Avogadro's number $(N_A) = 6 \times 10^{23}$
- Mass of the solid ball = 64 g.

39. The number of oxygen molecules present in a unit cell is $a \times 10^{24}$. The value of a is ....

40. The percentage increase in density of the solid ball due to the trapping of oxygen gas is ....

Species Selection (with 5 Species)

41. Consider the following mixture of gases

(i) Mixture of H_2 and N_2 (ii) Mixture of H_2 and CO_2
(iii) Mixture of H_2 and Cl_2 (iv) Mixture of He and Ar
(v) Mixture of N_2 and O_2

The total number of mixtures for which Dalton's law of partial pressure in not applicable is

(a) 1 (b) 2 (c) 3 (d) 4

42. In which case, compressibility factor of a given gas deviates from ideal behaviour?

(i) 1g H_2 gas occupies 11.2 dm^3 at STP
(ii) Mass of 5.6 dm^3 CO_2 gas is 11.0 g at STP
(iii) One mole of CO_2 occupies 0.4 dm^3 at 300 K and 40.0 bar
(iv) 6.9 g of a 1: 1 molar mixture of NO_2 and N_2O_4 exert a pressure of 24.9 bar at 300 K in 1 dm^3 flask.

(v) 1.6 g CH_4 occupies 13.1 dm^3 at STP.

(a) 2 (b) 3 (c) 1 (d) 4

43. Consider the given mixture of gases at room temperature,

(i) $SO_2(g)$ and $H_2O(g)$ (ii) $H_2(g)$ and $He(g)$
(iii) $NH_3(g)$ and $HCl(g)$ (iv) $CO_2(g)$ and $CO(g)$
(v) $H_2(g)$ and $Cl_2(g)$

Dalton's law of partial pressure is applicable to a mixture of

(a) 4 (b) 3 (c) 2 (d) 1

Species Selection (with 7 Species)

44. Consider the following pairs of gases *A* and *B*.

	A	*B*
(i)	CO_2	N_2O
(ii)	CO	N_2
(iii)	O_2	O_3
(iv)	H_2O	D_2O
(v)	$^{238}UF_6$	$^{235}UF_6$
(vi)	SO_2	CH_4
(vii)	N_2O_4	NO_2

The number of pairs which have same relative rates of effusion of gases *A* and *B* are

(a) 2 (b) 3 (c) 4 (d) 5

45. Which of the following variation of gaseous parameters (p, V, T) given in the form of graphs is/are correct for 1 mol of gas?

(i)
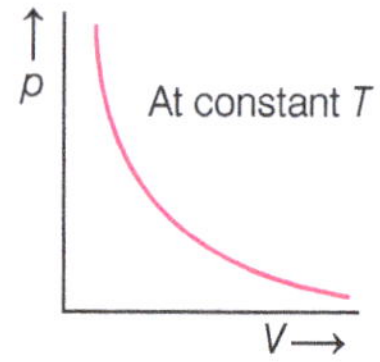

(ii)
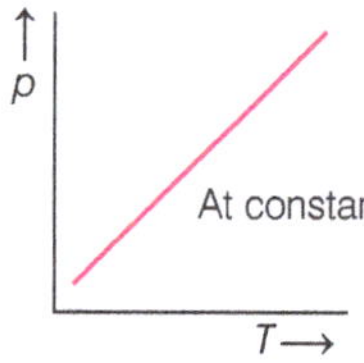

(iii)
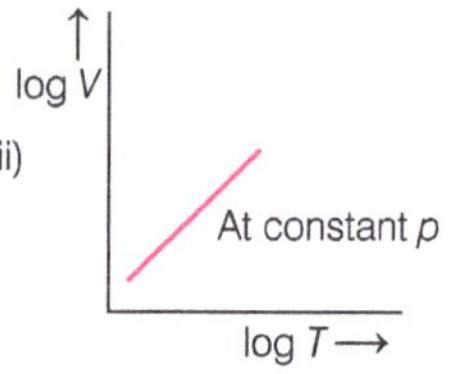

(iv)
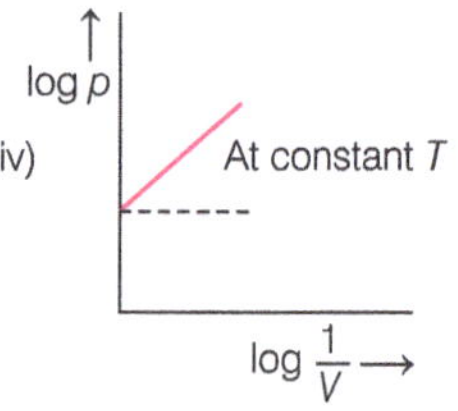

(v)
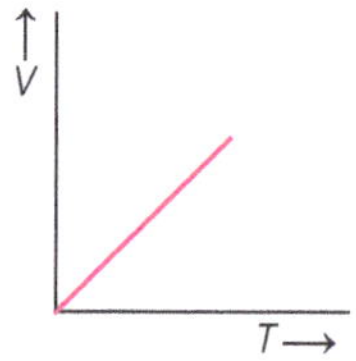

(vi)
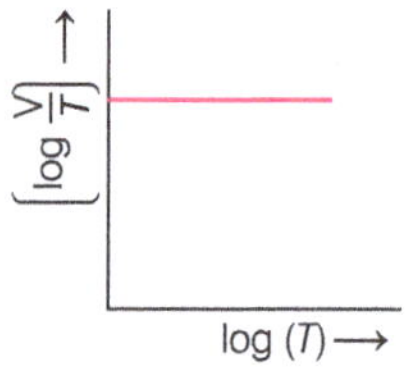

(vii)
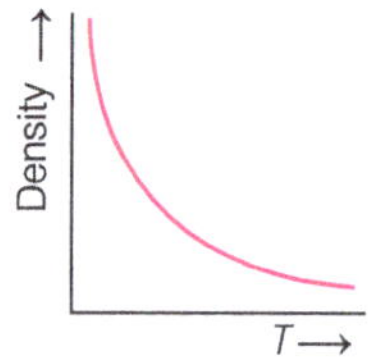

(a) 3 (b) 4
(c) 5 (d) 6

46. Consider the following crystal system,

(i) Cubic (ii) Tetragonal
(iii) Orthorhombic (iv) Monoclinic
(v) Triclinic (vi) Rhomobohedral
(vii) Hexagonal

The total number of crystal system, which have axial angle i.e., α and β value 90° is/are

(a) 1 (b) 2 (c) 4 (d) 3

47. Among the following elements,

The *p*-type semiconductor is obtained when Si is doped with Ga, Al, Ge, As, In, B, Sn

(a) 2 (b) 4 (c) 3 (d) 5

Check Through PYQs

Element 2 The Gaseous State

1. A closed vessel contains 10 g of an ideal gas *X* at 300 K, which exerts 2 atm pressure. At the same temperature, 80 g of another ideal gas *Y* is added to it and the pressure becomes 6 atm. The ratio of root mean square velocities of *X* and *Y* at 300 K is *2024 Adv.*

(a) $2\sqrt{2} : \sqrt{3}$ (b) $2\sqrt{2} : 1$
(c) 1 : 2 (d) 2 : 1

2. A gas has a compressibility factor of 0.5 and a molar volume of 0.4 $dm^3\ mol^{-1}$ at a temperature of 800 K and pressure *x* atm. If it shows ideal gas behaviour at the same temperature and pressure, the molar volume will be *y* $dm^3\ mol^{-1}$. The value of (x/y) is ......

[Use : Gas constant, $R = 8 \times 10^{-2}$ L atm $K^{-1}\ mol^{-1}$] *2023 Adv.*

3. If the distribution of molecular speeds of a gas is as per the figure shown below, then the ratio of the most probable, the average, and the root mean square speeds, respectively, is *2020 Adv.*

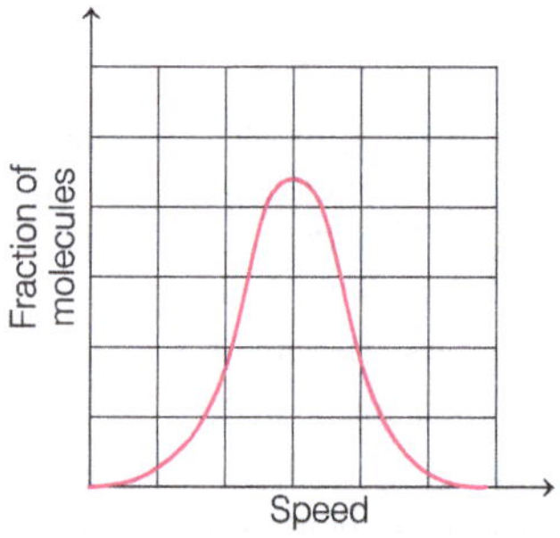

(a) 1 : 1 : 1 (b) 1 : 1 : 1.224
(c) 1 : 1.128 : 1.224 (d) 1 : 1.128 : 1

4. Which of the following statement(s) is(are) correct regarding the root mean square speed (U_{rms}) and average translational kinetic energy (E_{av}) of a molecule in a gas at equilibrium? *2019 Adv.*
(a) U_{rms} is inversely proportional to the square root of its molecular mass
(b) U_{rms} is doubled when its temperature is increased four times
(c) E_{av} is doubled when its temperature is increased four times
(d) E_{av} at a given temperature does not depend on its molecular mass

5. A closed tank has two compartments A and B, both filled with oxygen (assumed to be ideal gas). The partition separating the two compartments is fixed and is a perfect heat insulator (Fig. 1). If the old partition is replaced by a new partition which can slide and conduct heat but does not allow the gas to leak across (Fig. 2), the volume (in m^3) of the compartment A after the system attains equilibrium is ____. *2018 Adv.*

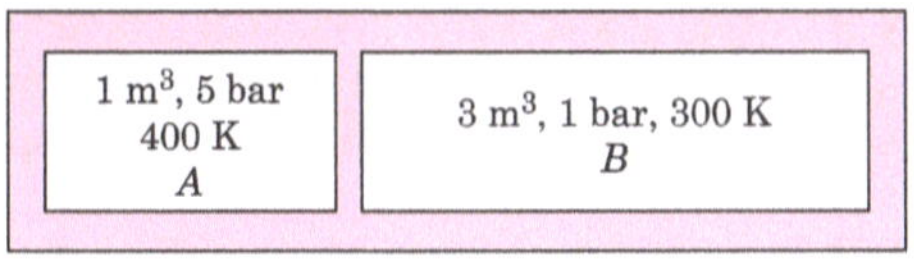

Fig. 1

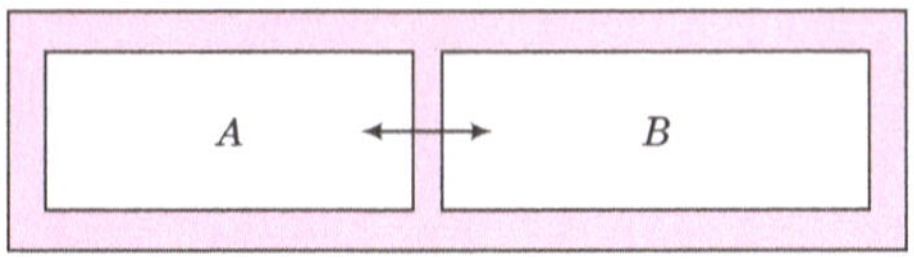

Fig. 2

6. The diffusion coefficient of an ideal gas is proportional to its mean free path and mean speed. The absolute temperature of an ideal gas is increased 4 times and its pressure is increased 2 times. As a result, the diffusion coefficient of this gas increases x times. The value of x is *2016 Adv.*

7. One mole of a monoatomic real gas satisfies the equation $p(V-b)=RT$ where, b is a constant. The relationship of interatomic potential $V(r)$ and interatomic distance r for gas is given by *2015 Adv.*

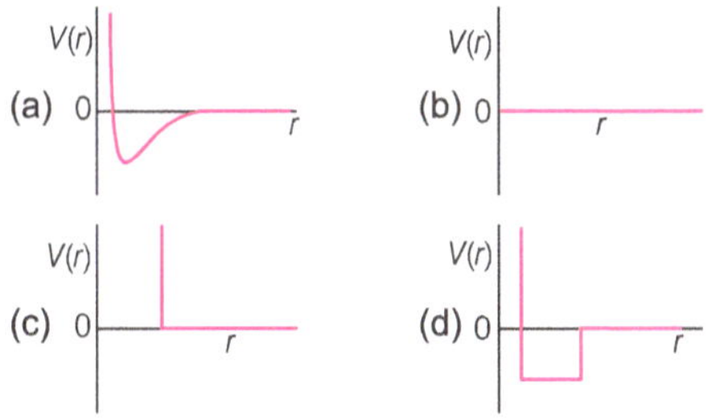

Element 3 The Solid State

8. In a metal deficient oxide sample, $M_xY_2O_4$ (M and Y are metals), M is present in both +2 and +3 oxidation states and Y is in +3 oxidation state. If the fraction of M^{2+} ions present in M is $\frac{1}{3}$, the value of x is .... *2024 Adv.*

(a) 0.25 (b) 0.33
(c) 0.67 (d) 0.75

9. Atoms of metals x, y and z form face-centred cubic (fcc) unit cell of edge length L_x, body-centred cubic (bcc) unit cell of edge length L_y and simple cubic unit cell of edge length L_z, respectively.

If $r_z = \frac{\sqrt{3}}{2} r_y; r_y = \frac{8}{\sqrt{3}} r_x; M_z = \frac{3}{2} M_y$

and $M_z = 3M_x$, then the correct statement(s) is(are)

[Given : M_x, M_y and M_z are molar masses of metals x, y and z, respectively.]

r_x, r_y and r_z are atomic radii of metals x, y and z respectively.] *2023 Adv.*

(a) Packing efficiency of unit cell of $x >$ packing efficiency of unit cell of $y >$ packing efficiency of unit cell of z
(b) $L_y > L_z$
(c) $L_x > L_y$
(d) Density of $x >$ Density of y

10. Atom X occupies the fcc lattice sites as well as alternate tetrahedral voids of the same lattice. The packing efficiency (in %) of the resultant solid is closest to *2022 Adv.*
(a) 25 (b) 35
(c) 55 (d) 75

11. For the given close packed structure of a salt made of cation X and anion Y shown below (ions of only one face are shown for clarity), the packing fraction is approximately.
(Packing fraction $= \frac{\text{Packing efficiency}}{100}$) *2021 Adv.*

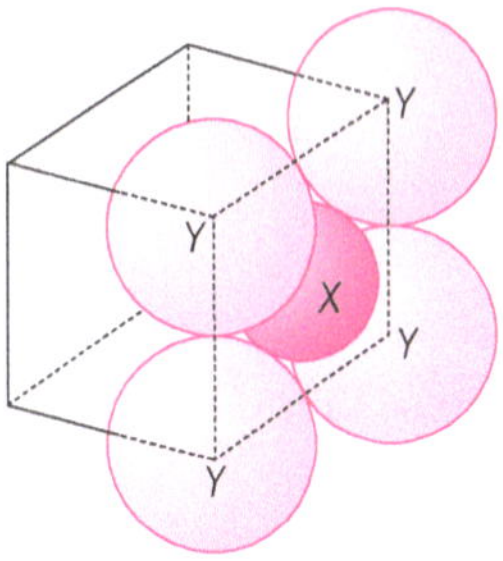

(a) 0.74 (b) 0.63
(c) 0.52 (d) 0.48

12. The cubic unit cell structure of a compound containing cation M and anion X is shown below. When compared to the anion, the cation has smaller ionic radius. Choose the correct statement(s). *2020 Adv.*

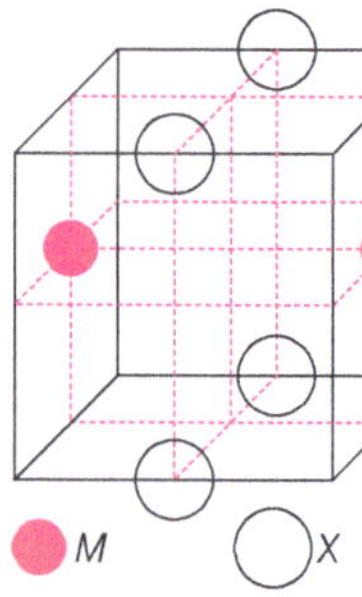

(a) The empirical formula of the compound is MX.
(b) The cation M and anion X have different coordination geometries.
(c) The ratio of $M—X$ bond length of the cubic unit cell edge length is 0.866.
(d) The ratio of the ionic radii of cation M to anion X is 0.414.

13. Consider an ionic solid MX with NaCl structure. Construct a new structure (Z) whose unit cell is constructed from the unit cell of MX following the sequential instruction given below. Neglect the charge balance. *2018 Adv.*

The value of $\left(\frac{\text{Number of anions}}{\text{Number of cations}}\right)$ in Z is ....

(i) remove all the anions (X) except the central one
(ii) replace all the face centered cations (M) by anions (X)
(iii) remove all the corner cations (M)
(iv) replace the central anion (X) with cation (M)

14. A crystalline solid of a pure substance has a face-centred cubic structure with a cell edge of 400 pm. If the density of the substance in the crystal is 8 g cm^{-3}, then the number of atoms present in 256 g of the crystal is $N \times 10^{24}$. The value of N is .... *2017 Adv.*

15. The correct statement(s) for cubic close packed (ccp) three dimensional structure is (are) *2016 Adv.*
(a) The number of the nearest neighbours of an atom. present in the top most layer is 12.
(b) The packing efficiency of atom is 74%.
(c) The number of octahedral and tetrahedral voids per atom are 1 and 2, respectively.
(d) The unit cell edge length is $2\sqrt{2}$ times the radius of the atom.

16. If the unit cell of a mineral has cubic close packed (ccp) array of oxygen atoms with m fraction of octahedral holes occupied by aluminium ions and n fraction of tetrahedral holes occupied by magnesium ions, m and n respectively, are *2015 Adv.*
(a) $\frac{1}{2}, \frac{1}{8}$ (b) $1, \frac{1}{4}$
(c) $\frac{1}{2}, \frac{1}{2}$ (d) $\frac{1}{4}, \frac{1}{8}$

HINTS & Solutions

Solutions : Competency Enhancer

1.1. ***(a)*** Given,

For ideal gas X;	For ideal gas Y
$m_1 = 20$ g	$m_2 = 60$ g
$T_1 = 350$ K	$T_2 = 350$ K
$p_1 = 4$ atm	$p_2 = 12$ atm

$$\frac{V_{rms}(X)}{V_{rms}(Y)} = ?$$

Substitute the given values in ideal gas equation,

$$pV = nRT$$

For gas X, $$4 \times V = \frac{20}{M_X} \times RT \quad \ldots\text{(i)}$$

For gas Y, $$12 \times V = \frac{60}{M_Y} \times RT \quad \ldots\text{(ii)}$$

Divide Eqs. (ii) by Eq. (i)

$$\frac{12V}{4V} = \frac{\frac{60}{M_y} \times RT}{\frac{20}{M_X} \times RT}$$

$$3 = \frac{60}{M_y} \times \frac{M_x}{20}$$

$$3 = 3\frac{M_x}{M_y} \Rightarrow \frac{M_x}{M_y} = 1$$

Now, we know that, $V_{rms} = \sqrt{\frac{3RT}{M}}$

So, $$\frac{V_{rms}(X)}{V_{rms}(Y)} = \sqrt{\frac{M_y}{M_x}} \Rightarrow \sqrt{\frac{1}{1}}$$

Thus, $$V_{rms}(X) : V_{rms}(Y) = 1:1$$

1.2. ***(208.7)*** Given, compressibility factor $(Z) = 0.7$

Molar volume $(V_m) = 0.4$ dm^3 mol^{-1}

$$T = 850 \text{ K}$$

$$p = x \text{ atm}$$

$$R = 8 \times 10^{-2}$$

We know that,

$$Z = \frac{pV_m}{RT}$$

$$0.7 = \frac{x \times 0.4}{8 \times 10^{-2} \times 850}$$

$$x = \frac{0.7 \times 8 \times 10^{-2} \times 850}{0.4} \Rightarrow 119$$

For ideal condition, $Z = 1$ and molar volume wil be y dm^3 mol^{-1}.

Using, $$Z = \frac{pV_m}{RT}$$

$$1 = \frac{119 \times y}{0.08 \times 850} \Rightarrow \frac{0.08 \times 850}{119}$$

Now, $$\frac{x}{y} = \frac{119}{0.57} = 208.7$$

3.1. ***(c)*** For given lattice,

$$\frac{\sqrt{3}a}{4} = 2r \Rightarrow 2r = \frac{\sqrt{3} \times 356.7}{4} = 154.45 \text{ pm}$$

$$r = 77.225 \text{ pm}$$

There are 8 tetrahedral voids in fcc but only 4 are occupied.

So, total number of atoms in fcc = 4 + 4 = 8

$$\% \text{ packing efficiency} = \frac{\text{Volume of 8 atoms}}{\text{Volume of all } (a^3)} \times 100$$

$$= \frac{8 \times \frac{4}{3}\pi r^3}{a^3} = \frac{8 \times \frac{4}{3} \times \frac{22}{7} \times (77.225 \times 10^{-12})^3}{(356.7 \times 10^{-12})^3} \times 100$$

$$= 0.34 \times 100 = 34\%$$

3.2. ***(d)*** Average oxidation state of M will be given by

$$= \frac{2}{3} \times 2 + \frac{1}{3} \times 3 = \frac{+7}{3}$$

So, far the given sample M_xY_2O

$$\frac{7}{3} \times x + 2 \times 2 + 3(-2) = 0$$

$$\frac{7}{4}x = 2$$

$$x = \frac{6}{7}$$

$$x = 0.85$$

Elemental Practice 3.1

1. ***(d)*** By Boyle's law, $p = \frac{k}{V}$

$\therefore$ $$\log p = \log\left(\frac{1}{V}\right) + \log k$$

It represents a straight line, $y = mx + C$

where, m = slope of line = tan 45° = 1

Intercept on $(\log p)$ axis $= OA = 0.3010$ bar dm^3

$\therefore$ $$\log k = 0.3010$$

$\therefore$ $$k = 2 \text{ bar dm}^3$$

Since, $pV = k = 2.0$ bar dm^3

$\therefore \quad V = \dfrac{2.0 \text{ bar dm}^3}{2.0 \text{ bar}}$

$= 1.0 \text{ dm}^3$

2. **(a)** This is a variation of V with T at constant p (Charles' law). Draw a line (ABC) at constant T.

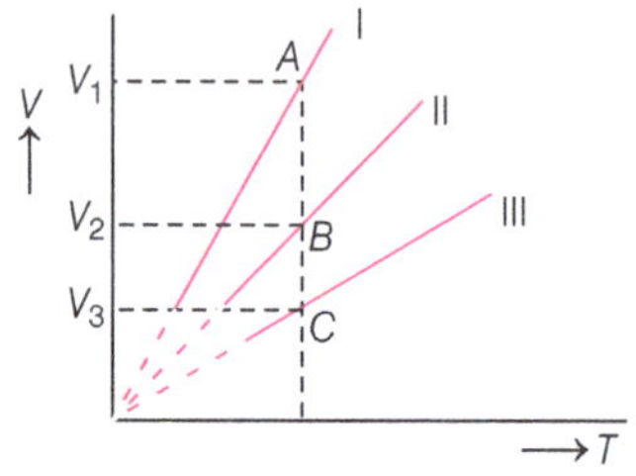

Volume at $A = V_1$ at $B = V_2$ at $C = V_3$

Since, $V_1 > V_2 > V_3$

Hence, $p_1 < p_2 < p_3$ (Boyle's law)

3. **(b)** A and R are true but R is not the correct explanation of A. The correct explanation of A is

Pressure arises due to collision of molecules against the side of the container. When there is force of attraction between molecules, number of collisions are less than expected. Hence, pressure of the gas is less than the ideal gas. Hence, $\left(\dfrac{n^2a}{V^2}\right)$ is the pressure correction.

4. **(a)** Volume of liquid water $(V_l) = \dfrac{\text{Mass}}{\text{Density}} = \dfrac{18 \text{ g mol}^{-1}}{0.997 \text{ g cm}^{-3}}$

$= \dfrac{18 \text{ g mol}^{-1}}{0.997 \times 10^3 \text{ g L}^{-1}}$

$= 0.01805 \text{ L mol}^{-1}$

Volume of water vapour $(V_g) = \dfrac{RT}{p}$

$= \dfrac{0.0821 \text{ L atm mol}^{-1}\text{K}^{-1} \times 298 \text{ K}}{\left(\dfrac{23.8}{760}\right) \text{atm}}$

$= 781.26 \text{ L mol}^{-1}$

Thus, $\dfrac{V_g}{V_l} = \dfrac{781.26}{0.01805} = 4.32 \times 10^4$ times

5. **(d)** Among the given match, (d) is correctly match while other are incorrect.

Their correct match are

- Critical temperature $\longrightarrow \dfrac{8a}{27Rb}$
- Boyle temperature $\longrightarrow \dfrac{a}{Rb}$
- Inversion temperature $\longrightarrow \dfrac{2a}{Rb}$

6. **(d)**

	$2H_2(g)$	+ $O_2(g)$	$\longrightarrow 2H_2O(g)$
Initial	3 mol	1 mol	–
After mixing	1 mol	0 mol	2 mol

All the O_2 is converted into water vapour and 1 mole of $H_2(g)$ remains unreacted. Thus, total moles of gaseous species

(1 mole of H_2 and 2 moles H_2O) = 3

$\therefore \quad p = \dfrac{n}{V}RT = \dfrac{3 \text{ mol} \times 0.081 \text{ bar L mol}^{-1}\text{K}^{-1} \times 400 \text{ K}}{125 \text{ L}}$

$= 0.78 \text{ bar}$

7. **(a)** As, $\dfrac{n'_{He}}{n'_{CH_4}} = \dfrac{1}{2}\sqrt{\dfrac{16}{4}} = \dfrac{1}{1}$

and $\quad \dfrac{n'_{He}}{n'_{SO_2}} = \dfrac{1}{3}\sqrt{\dfrac{64}{4}} = \dfrac{4}{3}$

$\therefore \quad n'_{He} : n'_{CH_4} : n'_{SO_2} = 4 : 4 : 3$

8. **(a)** By kinetic molecular theory,

$pV = \dfrac{1}{3} mNu^2 = \dfrac{1}{3} \times 1.0 \times 10^{-25} \times 1.0 \times 10^{25} \times (1 \times 10^3)^2$

$= 3.33 \times 10^5 \text{ Pa} = 3.33 \text{ bar}$

$pV = nRT$

$n = \dfrac{1 \times 10^{25}}{6.02 \times 10^{23} \text{mol}^{-1}} = 16.61$

$\therefore \quad T = \dfrac{pV}{nR} = \dfrac{3.33 \times 10^5 \text{ Pa} \times 1.0 \text{ m}^3}{16.61 \text{mol} \times 8.314 \text{ J mol}^{-1}\text{K}^{-1}}$

$T = 2411 \text{K}$

9. **(a)** $\text{KE} = \dfrac{3}{2} nRT$

Gas	N	n	T	(KE)
A	N_A	N_A / N_0	150 K	E_A
B	N_B	N_B / N_0	300 K	E_B

$E_A = \dfrac{3}{2} \dfrac{N_A}{N_0} R(150) \quad \Rightarrow \quad E_B = \dfrac{3N_B}{2N_0} R(300)$

$\dfrac{E_B}{E_A} = 2\left(\dfrac{N_B}{N_A}\right)$

Given, $\quad \dfrac{E_B}{E_A} = 2 \qquad \therefore \quad \dfrac{N_B}{N_A} = 1$

10. **(d)** A is incorrect but R is correct. The correct form of A is Collision frequency (Z) is the number of collisions per second.

$$(Z) = \frac{\sqrt{2} N_0 \sigma (U_{av}) p}{RT}$$

As $(Z) \propto p$, hence collision increases with increase of pressure. At constant temperature, molecules take less time to travel to its neighbour in a denser, high-pressure gas.

11. **(b)** Atmospheric pressure = 760 mm of Hg

$p_1V_1 = p_2V_2$

$p_2 = \dfrac{p_1V_1}{V_2} = \dfrac{760 \times 2.4}{1.9}$

$= 960 \text{ mm of Hg}$

Difference in column $= 960 - 760$

$= 200 \text{ mm of Hg}$

12. ***(b)*** Given,

For ideal gas X; $m_1 = 30$ g, $T_1 = 450$ K, $p_1 = 4$ atm

For ideal gas Y; $m_2 = 70$ g, $T_2 = 450$ K, $p_2 = 6$ atm

Substitute the given values in ideal gas equation,

$$pV = nRT$$

For gas X,

$$4 \times V = \frac{30}{M_x} RT \quad \ldots\text{(i)}$$

$$\left(\because n = \frac{\text{Mass}}{\text{Molar mass}}\right)$$

For gas Y,

$$6 \times V = \frac{70}{M_y} RT \quad \ldots\text{(ii)}$$

Divide Eqs. (ii) by Eq. (i)

$$\frac{6 \times V}{4 \times V} = \frac{70}{M_y} \times \frac{M_x}{30}$$

$$\frac{3}{2} = \frac{7}{3}\frac{M_x}{M_y} \Rightarrow \frac{M_x}{M_y} = \frac{9}{14}$$

Now, we know that,

$$V_{\text{rms}} = \sqrt{\frac{3RT}{M}}$$

So, $$\frac{V_{\text{rms}}(X)}{V_{\text{rms}}(Y)} = \sqrt{\frac{M_y}{M_x}} = \sqrt{\frac{14}{9}} \Rightarrow \frac{\sqrt{14}}{3}$$

Thus, $V_{\text{rms}}(X) : V_{\text{rms}}(Y) = \sqrt{14} : 3$

13. ***(c)*** If non- ideal behaviour is followed $pV \neq nRT$

(a) $pV = nRT$

$$pV = \frac{w}{M}RT \Rightarrow p = \frac{W}{V} \times \frac{RT}{M}$$

$$p = \frac{dRT}{M}$$

$$= \frac{1.25 \text{ g L}^{-1} \times 0.0821 \text{ L atm mol}^{-1}\text{K}^{-1} \times 273 \text{ K}}{28 \text{ g mol}^{-1}} = 1 \text{ atm}$$

thus correct (STP condition)

(b) $$p = \frac{w}{MV}RT = \frac{2.8 \text{ g} \times 0.0821 \text{ L atm mol}^{-1}\text{K}^{-1} \times 300 \text{ K}}{28 \text{ g mol}^{-1} \times 0.1\text{L}}$$

$= 24.63$ atm. Thus, correct

(c) $$p = \frac{w}{mV}RT = \frac{1.6 \text{ g} \times 0.0821 \times 273 \text{ K}}{16 \text{ g mol}^{-1} \times 0.5}$$

Thus, incorrect. It is non-ideal gas

(d) 0.1 g H_2 = 0.05 mol H_2 = 0.05 × 22.4 L = 1.12 L thus, correct

14. ***(a)*** λ (mean free path) $= \dfrac{kT}{\sqrt{2}\,\pi d^2 p}$

$$k(\text{Boltzmann constant}) = \frac{R}{N_0} = \frac{8.314 \text{ J mol}^{-1}\text{K}^{-1}}{6.02 \times 10^{23} \text{ mol}^{-1}}$$

$$= 1.38 \times 10^{-23} \text{ JK}^{-1}$$

$T = 293$ K

$d = 2r$ (collision diameter) $= 2 \times 1.85 \times 10^{-10}$ m

$p = 1.0$ bar $= 1 \times 10^5$ Pa

$$\therefore \quad \lambda = \frac{1.38 \times 10^{-23} \times 293}{\sqrt{2}\,\pi(3.7 \times 10^{-10})^2 \times 1 \times 10^5} = 6.65 \times 10^{-8} \text{ m}$$

$$= 665 \times 10^{-10} \text{ m} = 665 \text{ Å}$$

15. ***(d)*** As we know,

$$PM = dRT$$

$$PM \propto dT$$

$$\frac{M_1}{M_2} = \frac{d_1T_1}{d_2T_2} = \frac{1 \times 2}{2 \times 1}$$

$$\boxed{M_1 : M_2 = 1:1}$$

16. ***(b, c, d)*** Among the given statements, only (a) is correct while other (b), (c) and (d) are incorrect as critical point is approached.

When T_C is approached, density of liquid CO_2 decreases and that of gaseous CO_2 increases.

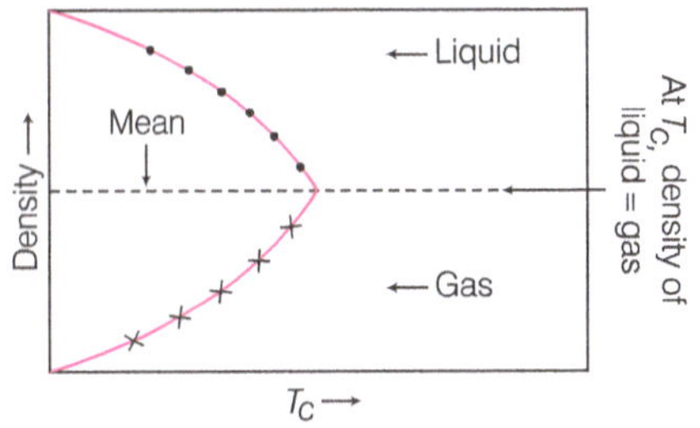

17. ***(b, c, d)*** Among the given statements (b), (c) and (d) are correct while (a) is incorrect.

As we know, $$pV = nRT = \frac{w}{M}RT$$

$$\therefore \quad p = \frac{w}{VM}RT \qquad \left(\frac{\text{Mass }(w)}{\text{Volume }(V)} = \text{Density}\right)$$

$$p = \frac{d}{M}RT$$

$$\therefore \quad d = pM/RT$$

$$d = \frac{1 \text{ atm} \times 32 \text{ g mol}^{-1}}{0.0821 \text{ L atm mol}^{-1}\text{ K}^{-1} \times 298 \text{ K}}$$

$$= 1.31 \text{ g L}^{-1} = 1.31 \times 10^{-3} \text{ kg L}^{-1}$$

$$= 1.31 \times 10^{-3} \times 10^3 \text{ kg m}^{-3} = 1.31 \text{ kg m}^{-3}$$

Thus (a) is incorrect.

(b) In terms of molecules, 32 g = 6.02×10^{23} molecules

$$d = \frac{1 \text{ atm} \times 6.02 \times 10^{23} \text{molecule mol}^{-1}}{0.0821 \text{ L atm mol}^{-1}\text{K}^{-1} \times 298 \text{ K}}$$

$$= 2.46 \times 10^{22} \text{ molecules L}^{-1}$$

$$= 2.46 \times 10^{22} \times 10^3 \text{ molecules m}^{-3}$$

$$= 2.40 \times 10^{25} \text{ molecules m}^{-3}$$

Thus correct.

(c) $d = \dfrac{m}{V}$ hence, differs as mass differs.

(d) Number density is independent of mass hence same for all gases.

18. **(b, c)**

(a) $pV = RT \Rightarrow V = \frac{RT}{p}$

$\therefore V_a = \frac{R(2T)}{p/2} = \frac{4RT}{p} = 4V$

Volume is made 4 time. Thus (a) is incorrect.

(b) $V_b = \frac{R(T/2)}{p/2} = \frac{RT}{p} = V$ (No change)

(c) $V_C = \frac{R(2T)}{2p} = \frac{RT}{p} = V$ (No change)

(d) $V_d = \frac{R(2T)}{p} = \frac{2RT}{p} = 2V$

Volume is doubled. Thus (d) is incorrect.

19. **(a, c, d)** The device shown is called eudiometer. It is used to compare the pressure of several gases.

(a) Pressure p_1 of the confined gas is equal to the barometric pressure plus the pressure needed to depress the column of the liquid.

Thus, p_1 = barometric pressure $+h_1dg = p_{atm} + h_1dg$

Thus (a) is correct.

(b) When $h = 0$ [as in (c)]

$p_2 = p_{atm}$ = barometric pressure.

Thus (b) is incorrect but (d) is correct.

(c) Pressure p_3 is equal to barometric pressure minus the pressure needed to support the column of liquid.

$p_3 = (p_{atm} - h_3dg)$

Thus (c) is correct.

20. **(a, b, c, d)**

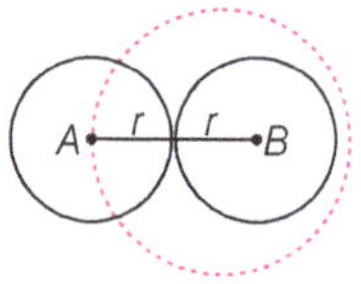

$AB = 2r$ (when in contact). Thus (a) is correct.

Volume of the molecule with radius $2r = \frac{4}{3}\pi(2r)^3 = 8\left(\frac{4}{3}\pi r^3\right)$

$= 8V$

$= 8 \times$ volume of the molecule of radius r. Thus, (b) is correct.

Volume of one molecule when in contact $= \frac{8V}{2} = 4V$.

This volume is called excluded volume. Thus, (c) is correct. Excluded volume is the volume correction in ideal gas volume.

Thus, $V_{ideal} = (V - b)$

Greater the value of b, greater the deviation. Thus, (d) is correct.

21. **(99.25)** Given, compressibility factor $(Z) = 0.8$

$$V_m = 0.7 \text{ dm}^3 \text{ mol}^{-1}$$
$$T = 950 \text{ K}$$
$$p = x \text{ atm}$$
$$R = 8 \times 10^{-2}$$

We know that,

$$Z = \frac{pV_m}{RT}$$

$$0.8 = \frac{x \times 0.7}{0.08 \times 950} \Rightarrow \frac{0.8 \times 0.08 \times 950}{0.7} = x$$

$$x = 86.85$$

For ideal condition, $Z = 1$ and molar volume will be y dm^3 mol^{-1}.

Using $Z = \frac{pV_m}{RT}$

$$1 = \frac{86.85 \times y}{0.08 \times 950}$$

$$y = \frac{0.08 \times 950}{86.85} \Rightarrow 0.875$$

Now, $\frac{x}{y} = \frac{86.85}{0.875} = 99.25$

22. **(0.02)** $pV = nRT = \frac{w}{M}RT \quad \therefore p = \frac{w}{VM}RT = \frac{d}{M}RT$

where, d (density) $= \frac{w}{V}$ (g dm^{-3})

$\therefore M$(molar mass) $= \frac{dRT}{p}$

$$= \frac{1.0 \text{ g dm}^{-3} \times 0.0821 \text{ L atm mol}^{-1}\text{K}^{-1} \times 300 \text{ K}}{\left(\frac{600}{760}\right) \text{atm}}$$

$$= 31.2 \text{ g mol}^{-1}$$

Average molar mass of mixture, $\bar{M} = \frac{M_{O_2}X_{O_2} + M_{N_2}X_{N_2}}{X_{O_2} + X_{N_2}}$

Since, $X_{O_2} + X_{N_2} = 1$

$\therefore X_{O_2} = (1 - X_{N_2})$

$\therefore 31.2 = \frac{32(1 - X_{N_2}) + 28X_{N_2}}{1}$

$0.8 = 4X_{N_2} \Rightarrow X_{N_2} = 0.2$

$\therefore 10x = 0.2 \Rightarrow x = 0.02$

23. **(8)** U_{rms} (O_2 at 300K) $= \sqrt{\frac{3R \times 300}{32}}$

U_{mp} (Ne at TK) $= \sqrt{\frac{2RT}{20}}$

Given, $\sqrt{\frac{3R \times 300}{32}} = \sqrt{\frac{2RT}{20}}$

$$\sqrt{\frac{900}{32}} = \sqrt{\frac{T}{10}} \Rightarrow \frac{900}{32} = \frac{T}{10}$$

$$T = 281.25\text{K} = 8.25°\text{C} \approx 8°\text{C}$$

24. **(2)** $pV = nRT$

$\therefore n(N_2) = \frac{pV}{RT} = \frac{3 \times 5}{300R} = \frac{1}{20R}$

$n(H_2) = \frac{pV}{RT} = \frac{5 \times 2}{400R} = \frac{1}{40R}$

$$\frac{n(N_2)}{n(H_2)} = \frac{40}{20} = 2$$

25. **(8)** $p = \frac{1}{3}\frac{mNu^2}{V} = \frac{2}{3V}\left(\frac{1}{2}mNu^2\right) = \frac{2}{3V}(KE)$

Temperature is constant, hence (KE) remains constant.

Volume initially of side $l = l^3$

Volume due to change to $\left(\frac{l}{2}\right) = \left(\frac{l^3}{8}\right)$

Thus, $p_1 = \frac{2}{3}\frac{(KE)}{l^3}$, $p_2 = \frac{2}{3}\left(\frac{KE}{l^3}\right)8$

$\therefore \frac{p_2}{p_1} = 8$

Pressure becomes 8 times.

Elemental Practice 3.2

1. **(b)** Work done = Surface tension × Increase in area

$$= 73 \text{ dyne cm}^{-1} \times 0.10 \text{ m}^2$$
$$= 73 \text{ g cm s}^{-2}\text{cm}^{-1} \times 0.10 \text{ m}^2$$
$$= \frac{73}{1000} \text{ kg s}^{-2} \times 0.10 \text{ m}^2$$
$$= 73 \times 10^{-4} \text{ kg m}^2\text{s}^{-2}$$
$$= 73 \times 10^{-4} \text{ J}$$
$$= 73 \times 10^{-4} \times 10^7 \text{ erg}$$
$$= 7.3 \times 10^4 \text{ erg}$$

2. **(b)** $\Delta H = \frac{2.303\, RT_1T_2}{(T_2 - T_1)} \log \frac{p_2}{p_1} = \frac{2.303\, RT_1T_3}{(T_3 - T_1)} \log \frac{p_3}{p_1}$

Given,

Temperature	VP
$T_1 = 300$ K	$p_1 = 380$ mmHg
$T_2 = 350$ K	$p_2 = 570$ mmHg
$T_3 = ?$	$p_3 = 760$ mmHg

$$\therefore \frac{T_2}{(T_2 - T_1)} \log \frac{p_2}{p_1} = \frac{T_3}{(T_3 - T_1)} \log \frac{p_3}{p_1}$$
$$\frac{350}{50} \log \frac{570}{380} = \frac{T_3}{(T_3 - 300)} \log \frac{760}{380}$$
$$7 \log 1.5 = \frac{T_3}{(T_3 - 300)} \log 2$$
$$\left(\frac{T_3 - 300}{T_3}\right) = \frac{0.3010}{0.1761 \times 7}$$
$$1 - \frac{300}{T_3} = 0.2442$$
$$T_3 = 397 \text{ K}$$

3. **(c)** $50 = \frac{P \times 100}{26}$

$$\frac{50 \times 26}{100} \text{ torr} = P$$
$$\Rightarrow P = 13 \text{ torr}$$
$$pV = \frac{WRT}{M}$$
$$\frac{13}{760} \times 1 = \frac{W}{18} \times 0.0821 \times 300$$
$$W = 12.5 \times 10^{-3} = 12.5 \text{ milligram}$$

4. **(b)** Among the given statements (b) is incorrect while others are correct statements.

The correct form of statement (b) is

- Surface tension of liquid is zero at critical temperature.

5. **(a)** Both A and R are true and R is the correct explanation of A.

6. **(a)** $d = 0.36 \text{ kg/m}^3 = 0.36$ g/L

$$r_V = \frac{4}{3} \times r_{O_2}$$
$$\Rightarrow \frac{r_V}{r_{O_2}} = \frac{4}{3} = \sqrt{\frac{32}{m_v}}$$
$$\Rightarrow m_v = 18 \text{ g}$$
$$d = \frac{M_v}{V_V}$$
$$\Rightarrow V_v = \frac{18}{0.36} = 50 \text{ L}$$
$$Z = \frac{pV_v}{RT} = \frac{1 \times 50}{0.0821 \times 500} = \frac{1}{0.821} = 1.22$$

Since, $Z > 1$ means repulsive force is dominating.

7. **(d)** Pressure difference between the inside and outside a bubble whose radius is r

$$= \frac{4\gamma}{r} = (4 \times 24.3 \text{ dyne cm}^{-1})\left(\frac{1}{1.75 \text{ cm}}\right)$$
$$= 55.54 \text{ dyne/cm}^2$$
$$= 55.54 \times 10^{-1} \text{ kg m}^{-1}\text{s}^{-2}$$
$$= 55.54 \times 10^{-1} \times 10^{-5} \text{ bar} = 5.554 \times 10^{-5} \text{ bar}$$

8. **(c)** $\Delta H = \frac{RT_1T_2}{(T_2 - T_1)} \log \frac{p_2}{p_1}$

$$\frac{\Delta H}{2.303\, R}\left[\frac{1}{T_1} - \frac{1}{T_2}\right] = \log \frac{p_2}{p_1}$$
$$\frac{40.6 \text{ kJ mol}^{-1}}{2.303 \times 8.314 \times 10^{-3} \text{kJmol}^{-1}\text{K}^{-1}}\left[\frac{1}{T_1(K)} - \frac{1}{373(K)}\right]$$
$$= \log \frac{1}{0.605}$$
$$\therefore \left(\frac{1}{T_1} - \frac{1}{373}\right) = 1.03 \times 10^{-4}$$
$$\therefore T_1 = 359.2 \text{ K}$$
$$T_1 = 359.2 - 273 = 86.2° \text{ C}$$

9. **(a)** Water converted into vapours

$$= 65.44 - 63.13 = 2.31 \text{ g}$$

$$= \frac{2.31}{18} \text{ mol}$$

$$p = \frac{n}{V} RT = \frac{2.31}{18} \times \frac{0.0821 \times 298}{100}$$

$$= 0.0314 \text{ atm} = 0.0314 \times 760 \text{ mmHg}$$

$$= 23.86 \text{ mmHg}$$

10. ***(d)*** As intermolecular force of attraction increases, surface tension also increases. Hexane with no H-bonding, has least force of attraction. There is excessive H-bonding in water as compared to ethanol, hence

$$\gamma_{hexane} < \gamma_{ethanol} < \gamma_{water}$$

11. ***(a)*** Surface area of droplet, $(A) = 4\pi r^2$

and volume of droplet, $(V) = \frac{4}{3}\pi r^3$

$$\therefore \quad \frac{dA}{dr} = 8\pi r$$

$$\frac{dV}{dr} = 4\pi r^2$$

$$\therefore \quad dp = \gamma\left(\frac{dA}{dV}\right) = \gamma \frac{(8\pi r)}{4\pi r^2} = \frac{2\gamma}{r}$$

12. ***(a)*** $1 \text{ dyne} = 1 \text{ g cm s}^{-2}$

$$1 \text{ dyne/cm} = \frac{1 \text{ g cm s}^{-2}}{\text{cm}} = 1 \text{ g s}^{-2}$$

$$= \frac{1}{1000} \text{ kg s}^{-2} = \frac{1}{1000} \text{ kg } \frac{\text{ms}^{-2}}{\text{m}}$$

$$= 10^{-3} \text{ Nm}^{-1} = 435.5 \times 10^{-3} \text{ N/m}$$

13. ***(c)*** $p = Ae^{-\Delta H/RT}$

It is called Clausius-Clapeyron equation

$$\log_e p = \log_e A + \log_e e^{-\Delta H/RT}$$

$$\log_e p = \log_e A - \frac{\Delta H}{RT}\log_e e = \log_e A - \frac{\Delta H}{RT}$$

$$\log_{10} p = \log_{10} A - \frac{\Delta H}{2.303 RT}$$

Given, $\log_{10} p = 5 - \frac{400 \text{ K}}{T}$

Thus, $\log_{10} A = 5$

$\therefore \quad A = 10^5 \text{ mmHg}$

At $\quad T = 200 \text{ K}$

$$\log_{10} p = 5 - \frac{400}{200} = 3$$

$\therefore \quad p = 1000 \text{ mm Hg}$

Also, $\frac{\Delta H}{2.303 R} = 400 \text{ K}$

$$\therefore \quad \Delta H = 2.303 R \times 400$$

$$= 2.303 \times 2.0 \times 10^{-3} \text{ kcal mol}^{-1}\text{K}^{-1} \times 400 \text{ K}$$

$$= 1.8424 \text{ kcal mol}^{-1}$$

14. ***(d)*** (i) $\log_{10} \eta = -5 + \frac{200}{200} = -4$

$$\eta = 10^{-4} \text{poise.}$$

(ii) $\eta = Ae^{-E_a/RT}$

$$\therefore \log_{10} \eta = \log_{10} A - \frac{E_a}{2.303RT}$$

On comparison

$$\frac{E_a}{2.303R} = 200 \text{ K}$$

$$\therefore \quad E_a = 200 \times 2.303 \times R$$

$$= 200 \times 2.303 \times 8.314 \text{ J mol}^{-1}\text{K}^{-1}\text{K}$$

$$= 3829.4 \text{ J mol}^{-1} = 3.8294 \text{ kJ mol}^{-1}$$

15. ***(a,b,c,d)*** Among the given statements, all are correct.

16. ***(a,d)*** Among the given statements, (a) and (d) are correct while (b) and (c) are incorrect statements.

The explanation of these statements are

(a) $p_1V_1 = p_2V_2$ or $p_1l_1a = p_2l_2a$

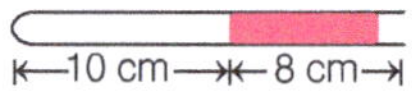

$\therefore p_2 = 76 + 8 = 84 \text{ cm}$

(b) $\therefore l_2 = \frac{p_1l_1}{p_2} = \frac{76 \times 10}{84} = 9.05 \text{ cm}$

$p_1l_1a = p_2l_2a$

(c) $\therefore p_2 = 76 - 8 = 68 \text{ cm}$

$\therefore l_2 = \frac{p_1l_1}{p_2} = \frac{76 \times 10}{68} = 11.18 \text{ cm}$

(d) When the tube is held at 45° with open up, the mass of Hg is borne partially by the gas and partially by the Hg. Vertical height of Hg is measure of additional pressure on gas, i.e.,

$$l = \frac{8}{\sqrt{2}}$$

Also $l_2 = \frac{p_1l_1}{p_2} = \frac{76 \times 10}{76 + \frac{8}{\sqrt{2}}} = 9.3 \text{ cm}$

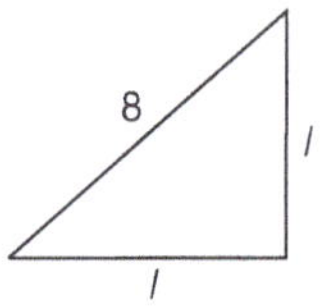

17. ***(a,b,d)*** Among the given statements, (a), (b) and (d) are correct while statement (c) is incorrect.

Its correct form is

As atmospheric pressure increases, the mercury is forced from the reservoir by the increasing air pressure and the column of mercury rises, when the atmospheric pressure decreases, the mercury flows back into the reservoir and the column of mercury is lowered.

18. ***(a,b,c)*** Among the given statements, (a), (b) and (c) are correct while the statement (d) is incorrect.

Its correct form is

Surface tension decreases with the increase of temperature and reaching a value of 0 K at the critical temperature.

19. ***(a,c,d)*** Among the given statements, (a), (c) and (d) are correct while statement (b) is incorrect.

(a) $H_2O(l) \longrightarrow H_2O(g)$, $\Delta H = +\text{ ve}$

Thus, increase in temperature favours the formation of more vapours, thus, increase in vapour pressure.

(b) On adding a non-volatile solute, vapour escape from surface decreases. Hence, VP decreases.

(c)

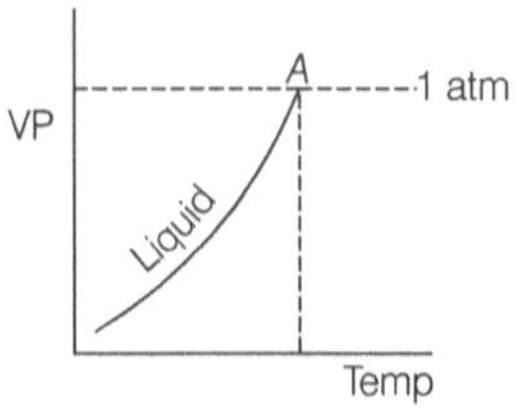

Temperature at which VP is equal to atmospheric pressure is the normal boiling point. On adding solute to liquid, VP falls hence boiling point of solution is increased.

20. ***(370.72)*** As we know,

$$\Delta H = \frac{2.303\,R\,T_1T_2}{(T_2 - T_1)} \log \frac{p_2}{p_1}$$

or $$\log \frac{p_2}{p_1} = \frac{\Delta H}{2.303R}\left[\frac{1}{T_1} - \frac{1}{T_2}\right]$$

Given $T_1 = ?$

$T_2 = 373\,K$

$p_1 = 700$ mmHg

$p_2 = 760$ mmHg

$\Delta H = 10$ kcal mol^{-1}

$$\therefore \quad \log \frac{760}{700} = \frac{10 \text{ kcal mol}^{-1}}{2.303 \times 0.002 \text{ kcal mol}^{-1}\text{K}^{-1}}\left[\frac{1}{T_1} - \frac{1}{373\,K}\right]$$

$$\left(\frac{1}{T_1} - \frac{1}{373}\right) = 1.645 \times 10^{-5}$$

$$\frac{1}{T_1} = 2.6974 \times 10^{-3}$$

$$\therefore \quad T_1 = 370.72\,K$$

21. ***(31.7)*** $\log_{10} \eta = \log_{10} A + \dfrac{E_a}{2.303\,RT}$

$$\therefore \quad \log \frac{\eta_2}{\eta_1} = \frac{E_a}{2.303R}\left(\frac{1}{T_2} - \frac{1}{T_1}\right)$$

$$\log \frac{\eta_2}{\eta_1} = \frac{5.984 \times 10^3 \text{ J mol}^{-1}}{2.303 \times 8.314 \text{ J mol}^{-1}\text{K}^{-1}}\left(\frac{1}{223} - \frac{1}{233}\right)$$

$$= 0.06015$$

$$\frac{\eta_2}{\eta_1} = 1.1485$$

$$\therefore \quad \eta_2 = 1.1485\,\eta_1 = 1.1485 \times 2.76 \times 10^{-4} \text{ Pa.s}$$

$$= 3.17 \times 10^{-4} \text{ Pa} \cdot \text{s}$$

$$= 31.7 \times 10^{-5} \text{ Pa} \cdot \text{s}$$

Hence, the value of x is 31.7.

22. ***(40.3)*** The mass of the platinum ball and of the liquid it displaces are determined from the respective densities and the volume of the ball.

Radius of the ball = 2.5 mm = 2.5×10^{-3} m

Volume of the ball $= \dfrac{4}{3}\pi r^3 = \dfrac{4}{3}\pi\,(2.5 \times 10^{-3})^3$ m^3

$= 6.545 \times 10^{-8}$ m^3

Mass (platinum) = Volume × Density

$= 6.545 \times 10^{-8}$ m$^3 \times 21.4 \times 10^3$ kg m^{-3}

$= 1.4 \times 10^{-3}$ kg

Mass (liquid) $= 6.545 \times 10^{-8}$ m$^3 \times 3.2 \times 10^3$ kg m^{-3}

$= 2.09 \times 10^{-4}$ kg

Thus, mass displaced $= (1.4 \times 10^{-3} - 2.09 \times 10^{-4})$ kg

$= 1.191 \times 10^{-3}$ kg

Also, $6\pi r\,\eta v = mg$

$$\therefore v \text{ (velocity)} = \frac{mg}{6\pi r\,\eta}$$

$$v = \frac{1.191 \times 10^{-3} \text{ kg} \times 9.8 \text{ ms}^{-2}}{6\pi \times 2.5 \times 10^{-3} \text{ m} \times 1.00 \times 10^4 \times 10^{-1} \text{ kg m}^{-1}\text{s}^{-1}}$$

$$= 2.48 \times 10^{-4} \text{ ms}^{-1}$$

$$\text{Time} = \frac{\text{Distance}}{\text{Velocity}} = \frac{1.00 \times 10^{-2} \text{ m}}{2.48 \times 10^{-4} \text{ ms}^{-1}} = 40.3 \text{ s}$$

23. ***(305.5)*** By Clausius-Clapeyron equation

$$\Delta H = \frac{2.303\,RT_1T_2}{(T_2 - T_1)} \log \frac{p_2}{p_1}$$

$$\frac{(T_2 - T_1)}{T_1T_2} = \frac{2.303\,R}{\Delta H} \log \frac{p_2}{p_1}$$

Given, p_2(1 atm = 760 torr),

T_2 (bp of water) = 373 K

p_1 (= 38 torr), $T_1 = ?$

$\Delta H = 10.12$ kcal mol^{-1},

$R = 0.002$ kcal mol^{-1}K^{-1}

$$\left(\frac{1}{T_1} - \frac{1}{373}\right) = \frac{2.303 \times 0.002}{10.12} \log \frac{760}{38}$$

$$\frac{1}{T_1} = \left(5.92 \times 10^{-4} + \frac{1}{373}\right)$$

$$\frac{1}{T_1} = 3.273 \times 10^{-3} \Rightarrow T_1 = 305.5\,K$$

24. ***(3)*** Force due to surface tension $= 2\pi r\gamma$

Force due to gravity $= mg = Vdg$

Volume of the liquid in the capillary at height, $h = \pi r^2 h$

$\therefore \quad mg = \pi r^2 hdg$

$\therefore \quad 2\pi r\,\gamma = \pi r^2 hdg$

$\therefore \quad \gamma = rhdg/2$

$$\therefore \quad r = \frac{2\gamma}{hdg}$$

$$= \frac{2 \times 73.0 \times 10^{-3} \text{ Nm}^{-1}}{10.0 \times 10^{-2} \text{ m} \times 1.0 \times 10^3 \text{ kg m}^{-3} \times 9.80 \text{ ms}^{-2}}$$

$= 1.5 \times 10^{-4}$ m

$\therefore$ Diameter $= 2r = 3.0 \times 10^{-4} = x \times 10^{-4}$ m

$\therefore \quad x = 3.0$

Elemental Practice 3.3

1. ***(a)*** In MT, anion-anion distance

$$T^-T^- = 2r_- = 2.40\text{Å}$$

$\therefore$ $r_- = 1.20\text{ Å}$

$\therefore$ $T^- = 1.20\text{ Å}$

From RT, $R^+ = 1.88 - 1.20 = 0.68\text{Å}$

From RQ, $Q^- = 1.48 - 0.68 = 0.80\text{Å}$

From MQ, $M^+ = 1.15 - 0.80 = 0.35\text{Å}$

$M^+ < T^-$ and cation-anion distance $= 1.20 + 0.35 = 1.55\text{Å}$
Actual $= 1.70\text{ Å}$

Thus, M^+ does not touch T^-.

2. ***(d)*** Total W-atoms at the corners

Thus, number of atoms

shared by 8 corners $= \frac{8}{8} = 1$

Thus, $W = 1$

O-atoms at the edges $= \frac{12}{4} = 3$

Thus, anion is (WO_3) and charge is (-1)

Na-atom at cube centre $= 1 \times 1 = 1$

Thus, lattice is $NaWO_3$.

Thus, body centred $NaWO_3$

3. ***(a)*** Along the edge,

$$AB = AC = 2(r_{Cl^-} + r_{Na^+}) = a$$

$\therefore$ $r_{Na^+} = \left(\frac{a}{2} - r_{Cl^-}\right)$

Also, $AC^2 + AB^2 = BC^2$

$\Rightarrow$ $a^2 + a^2 = (4r_{Cl^-})^2$

$\therefore$ $a = 2\sqrt{2}\, r_{Cl^-}$

$\therefore$ $r_{Na^+} = \left(\frac{2\sqrt{2}\, r_{Cl^-}}{2} - r_{Cl^-}\right)$

$$= r_{Cl^-}(\sqrt{2} - 1) = r_{Cl^-}(1.414 - 1)$$

$\therefore$ $\frac{r_{Na^+}}{r_{Cl^-}} = 0.414$

4. ***(a)*** In a bcc structure, the atoms touch each other along the body diagonal.

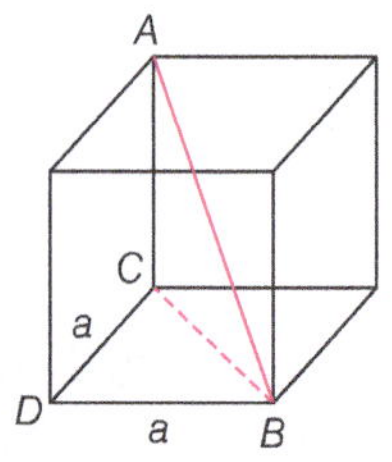

Radius of the atom $= r$

But $AB = 4r$

$\therefore$ $4r = \sqrt{3}a$

$r = \sqrt{3}a/4$

$r = \sqrt{3} \times \frac{352}{4}$ pm

$= \sqrt{3} \times \frac{352}{4} \times 10^{-12}$ m

$= \sqrt{3} \times \frac{352}{4} \times 10^{-10}$ cm

$= 152.42 \times 10^{-10}$ cm

Volume of one atom $= \frac{4}{3}\pi r^3 = \frac{4}{3}\pi(152.42 \times 10^{-10})^3 \text{ cm}^3$

$= 1.48 \times 10^{-23} \text{ cm}^3$

Volume of N_0 atoms in one mol of the metal

$= 6.02 \times 10^{23} \times 1.48 \times 10^{-23} \text{cm}^3 = 8.91 \text{cm}^3$

5. ***(c)***

Atom	Location	Number of atoms	Simple ratio
A	Corner	$\frac{8}{8} = 1$	2
B	Faces	$(6-1)\frac{1}{2} = \frac{5}{2} = 2.5$ (Since, one B is removed to make defect)	5
		The compound is A_2B_5	

6. ***(c)*** Ti_2O_3, conducting below 410 K and insulating at about 150 K.

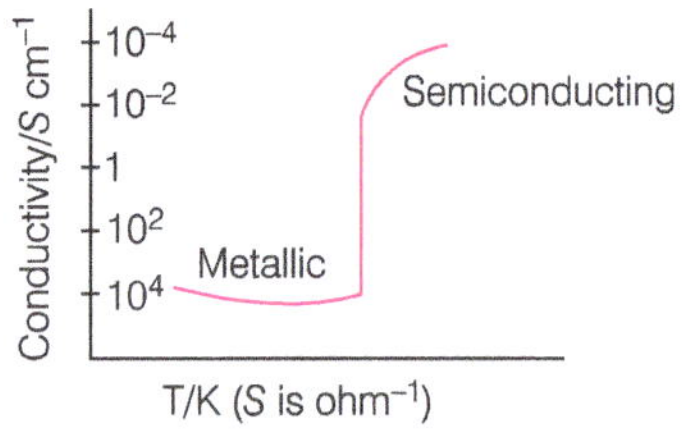

7. ***(d)*** Among the given statements, statement (d) is incorrect about non-stoichiometric compounds.

Its correct form is

In compound FeO, FeS or CuS the ratio of Fe : O, Fe : S or Cu : S differs from that indicated by the ideal chemical formula.

8. ***(b)*** Both A and R are true but R is not the correct explanation of A. The correct explanation of A is —

When crystal of NaCl is heated in the atmosphere of sodium vapour, Na-atoms are deposited on the surface of crystal and Cl^- ions diffuse on the surface and NaCl is formed.

$$Na(g) \longrightarrow Na^+(g) + e^-$$

Electrons released diffuse into the crystal and occupy interstitial sites. These anionic sites occupied by unpaired electrons are called F-centres (colour imparting) and appears yellow. Thus, both Statements I and II are correct. The colour results by excitation of these electrons when they absorb energy from the visible light falling on the crystals.

9. ***(c)*** Among the given compounds, CrO_2, it is metallic compound as well as ferromagnetic.

10. ***(a)***

I. An n-type semiconductor operates by thermally promoting an electron from an impurity level to an empty metal band so that conduction can occur.

II. A p-type semiconductor operates by thermally promoting an electron from a completely filled band to a partially empty impurity level so that conduction can occur in the originally filled band. The concept of hole is often used to describe conduction in this type of semiconductor.

III. If sufficient energy is available to promote an electron from the completely filled band to the completely empty band, conduction can occur. Thermal or light energy is the source of energy.

11. ***(b)*** In closest-packed structure lattice,

Number of octahedral voids = 1

Number of tetrahedral voids = 2

	Void	Ions	Simple ratio $(A_2B)^{x+}$
A^{3+}	1	1/2	2
B^{2+}	2	2/8	1

Charge on $(A_2B)^{x+} = (2\times3+2\times1)$

$= +8$

Thus, number of O-atoms $= \dfrac{8}{2} = 4$ (to balance charge)

Lattice is A_2BO_4.

12. ***(c)*** Z = number of atoms in unit cell

A = edge length, $M = 56$

Type	Z	a related to r	$d = \dfrac{Mz}{a^3N_0}$
bcc	2	$a = \dfrac{4}{\sqrt{3}}r$	$d(\alpha) = \dfrac{M\times2}{\left(\dfrac{4}{\sqrt{3}}r\right)^3 N_0}$
fcc	4	$a = 2\sqrt{2}r$	$d(\gamma) = \dfrac{M\times4}{(2\sqrt{2}r)^3N_0}$

$$\therefore \quad \frac{d(\alpha)}{d(\gamma)} = \frac{2(2\sqrt{2})^3}{4\left(\dfrac{4}{\sqrt{3}}\right)^3} = \frac{1}{2}\left(\frac{\sqrt{6}}{2}\right)^3 = 0.92$$

13. ***(a)*** Both (A) and (R) are true and (R) is the correct explanation of (A).

Larger the anion, smaller the cation, larger the polarisability. Frenkel defect is shown by ionic solids with smaller cation so that, it can migrate to interstitial site. Thus, repulsive effect is minimised.

14. ***(c)*** The lines joining the centres of the anions form an equilateral triangle with angle = 60°

Thus, $\dfrac{b}{a} = \sin 60° = \dfrac{r_X}{r_X + r_M} = 0.866$

$\therefore \quad r_X = 0.866r_X + 0.866r_M$

$0.134\,r_X = 0.866r_M$

$\therefore \quad \dfrac{r_M}{r_X} = \dfrac{0.134}{0.866} = 0.155$

15. ***(c)*** Let, the number of atoms in cubic close packing be x thus, number of tetrahedral voids $= 2x$

Number of atoms of $Q = x$

(due to cubic close packing)

P atoms occupy one-third of tetrahedral voids, thus number of P atoms $= \dfrac{2}{3}x$

Thus, $\dfrac{P\text{ atoms}}{Q\text{ atoms}} = \dfrac{2/3x}{x} = \dfrac{2}{3}$

Thus, compound is P_2Q_3.

16. ***(a,b,c,d)*** Among the given statements, all statements are correct.

Si (14) – [Ne] $3s^2\,3p^2$ (Group 14 element having four valence electrons). Thus, each atom of Si is covalently bonded to four neighbouring atoms.

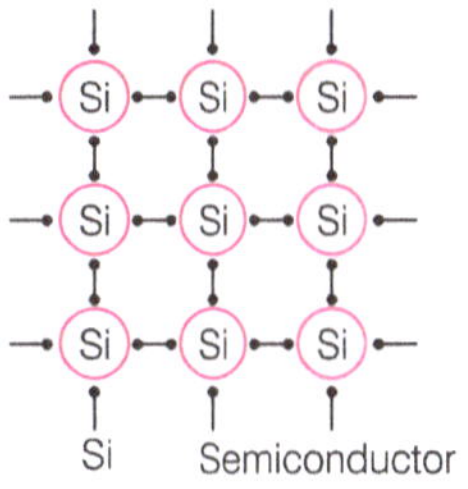

$\left.\begin{array}{l}\text{As (33)}\\ \text{P (15)}\end{array}\right\} ns^2np^3$ (five valence electrons)

Group 15 elements Four electrons are involved in bonding with four electrons of Si and one remaining electron becomes delocalised and increases the conductivity of Si. Thus, increase in the conductivity is due to doped negatively charged electron. This is called n-type semiconductor.

Group 13 elements

[B, Al, Ga] ns^2np^1

In this case, B, Al or Ga is short of one electron (as compared to Si). This is called electron hole or electron vacancy.

Under the influence of electric field, electron hole moves towards the positively charged plate and is called p-type semiconductor.

17. ***(a, c)*** Among the given statements, (a) and (c) are correct while (b) and (d) are incorrect.

Their explanation is given as

One-eighth of each corner atom, one-half of each face-centred, atom and the entire body-centred atom are contained within the unit cell, then

$$z = 8\left(\frac{1}{8}\right) + 6\left(\frac{1}{2}\right) + 4(1) = 1 + 3 + 4 = 8$$

For fcc type lattice

$$r = \frac{\sqrt{3}}{8} a \Rightarrow a = \left(\frac{8}{\sqrt{3}}\right) r$$

$$\therefore \text{Packing fraction} = \frac{8v}{a^3} = \frac{8\left(\frac{4}{3}\pi r^3\right)}{\left(\frac{8}{\sqrt{3}} r\right)^3} = 0.34$$

Thus, 34% packed which is much less than 74% packing.

18. ***(b, c, d)*** Among the given statements, (b), (c) and (d) are incorrect while statement (a) is correct.

The correct form of (b), (c) and (d) are

- The number of atoms per unit cell and the number of nearest neighbours in a simple cubic structures are 1 and 6 respectively.
- First three nearest neighbour distance for primitive cubic lattice are a, $\sqrt{2}a$ and $\sqrt{3}\,a$ respectively.
- In sphalerite (ZnS) and antifluorite (Na_2O) type structures, number of tetrahedral voids occupied are 4 and 8 respectively.

19. ***(a, b, d)*** Among the given statements, (a), (b) and (c) are correct while statement (d) is incorrect. Their correct explanation are given as

(a) 

Paramagnetic due to four unpaired electrons (n) and magnetic moment $= \sqrt{n\,(n+2)}$ BM

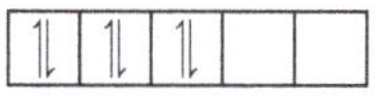 All paired thus,

$n = 0$, Magnetic moment $= 0$

Thus, (a) is correct.

(b) Paramagnetic substances are magnetised in a magnetic field in the same direction hence. weakly attracted thus, (b) is correct.

(c) Ferromagnetic substance can be magnetised permanently, thus, given statement is incorrect.

(d) Substances like MnO showing anti-ferromagnetism have domain structure similar to ferromagnetic substances, but their domains are oppositely oriented and cancel out each other magnetic moment.

↑ ↑ ↑ ↑ ↑ ↑ Ferromagnetic
↑ ↓ ↑ ↓ ↑ ↓ Anti-ferromagnetic
↑ ↑ ↓ ↓ ↑ ↑ Ferrimagnetic

20. ***(c, d)*** Among the given statements, (c) and (d) are incorrect while statements (a) and (b) are correct. Their correct form are given as

(a) When cation, anion or both are missing, molar mass is decreased. Since, density $= \frac{\text{Mass}}{\text{Volume}}$, hence density decreases, thus correct.

(b) When there is insertion of cation (A^+) in the interstitial site, it causes metal-excess defect. Thus, molar mass increases, hence density increases, thus correct.

(c) Presence of impurity increases molar mass (as doping of metal with P or Si), hence density changes, thus incorrect.

(d) In Frenkel defect, cation is dislocated without affecting molar mass thus, no change in density, thus incorrect.

21. ***(9)*** Density $= \frac{\text{Mass of unit cell}}{\text{Volume}}$

$$d = \frac{Mz}{VN_0} = \frac{Mz}{a \times b \times c \times N_0}$$

$$\therefore \quad z = \frac{a \times b \times c \times d \times N_0}{M}$$

$$= \frac{14.749 \times 10^{-8} \times 17.604 \times 10^{-8} \times 13.907 \times 10^{-8} \times 1{\cdot}17 \times 6.02 \times 10^{23}}{274.5}$$

$$= 9.26 \approx 9$$

22. ***(207)*** For octahedral hole

$$\frac{r_+}{r_-} = 0.414$$

$$\therefore \quad r_+(M^+) = 0.414 \times r_-(C^{3-}) = 0.414 \times 500 = 207 \text{ pm}$$

23. ***(58.55)*** For fcc structure

$$\frac{r_+}{r_-} = 0.414 \text{ for octahedral void}$$

$$= 0.225 \text{ for tetrahedral void}$$

Thus, maximum packing can be in octahedral void.

$$\therefore \quad r_{(+)} = 0.414 r_-$$

Also $\quad r_- = \frac{a}{2\sqrt{2}} = \frac{480}{2\sqrt{2}} = 141.42 \text{ pm}$

$$\therefore \quad r_+ = 0.414 \times 141.4 \text{ pm}$$

$$= 58.55 \text{ pm} = 58.55 \times 10^{-12} \text{ m}$$

Hence, the value of x is 58.55.

24. ***(8.16)*** Metal oxide $= A_{0.96}O$

If 'x' ions of A are in +3 state then

$$3x + (0.96 - x) \times 2 = 2 \Rightarrow x = 0.08$$

So, the percentage of metal in +3 state would be

$$\frac{0.08}{0.98} \times 100 \approx 8.16\%$$

25. ***(1.8173)*** Li^+ ion is so small that all the ions in the structure touch as shown :

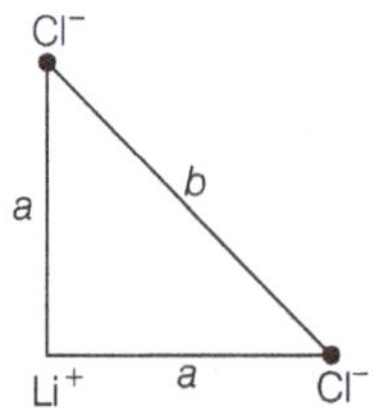

Let a = distance between the centres of Li^+ and Cl^- ions, then

$$a = \frac{5.14}{2} = 2.57 \text{ Å}$$

b = distance between the centres of two Cl^- ions then

$$b = \sqrt{a^2 + a^2} = \sqrt{2}\,a$$

$$= \sqrt{2} \times 2.57\ \text{Å} = 3.6345\ \text{Å}$$

$$r_{Cl^-} = \frac{b}{2} = 1.8173\ \text{Å}$$

Hence, the value of x is 1.8173.

Practice Element : Target JEE Advanced

1. ***(a)*** Packing fraction $= \dfrac{\text{Area occupied by circles}}{\text{Area of unit cell}}$

Let, edge length $= l$

Thus, radius $(r) = \dfrac{l}{2}$

From figure, it is clear that parallelogram has one complete circle.

Thus,

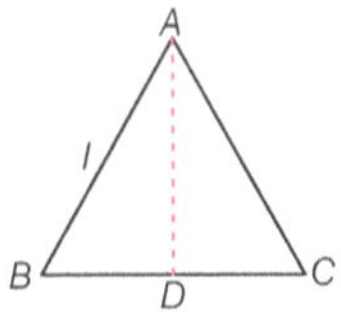

$$\text{Area of circle} = \pi r^2 = \pi\left(\frac{l}{2}\right)^2$$

Area of parallelogram = 2 (area of ΔABC)

$$\text{Area of } \Delta ABC = \frac{1}{2} BC \times AD$$

$$AD^2 = AB^2 - BD^2$$

$$= l^2 - \frac{l^2}{4} = \frac{3l^2}{4}$$

$$AD = \sqrt{3}\frac{l}{2}$$

$$\text{Area of } \Delta ABC = \frac{1}{2}\left(l \times \sqrt{3}\frac{l}{2}\right) = \sqrt{3}\frac{l^2}{4}$$

$\therefore$ Area of parallelogram

$$= 2 \times \text{Area of } \Delta ABC$$

$$= 2\sqrt{3}\frac{l^2}{4} = \sqrt{3}\frac{l^2}{2}$$

$$\therefore \text{Packing fraction} = \frac{\pi l^2/4}{\sqrt{3}l^2/2} = \frac{\pi}{2\sqrt{3}} = 0.907$$

2. ***(a)*** Average oxidation state of M will be given by

$$= \frac{3}{4} \times 2 + \frac{1}{4} \times 3 = \frac{+9}{4}$$

So, for the given sample $M_xY_2O_4$.

$$\frac{9}{4} \times x + 2 \times 2 + 4(-2) = 0$$

$$\frac{9}{4}x = 4$$

$$x = \frac{16}{9}$$

$$x = 1.7$$

3. ***(b)*** At 47°C and 16.0 atm, the molar volume of NH_3 gas is about 10% less than the molar volume of an ideal gas because the force of attraction between NH_3 molecules is significant at this temperature and pressure.

4. ***(a)*** Let the volume of NO in the mixture be x mL

	NO	+	N_2O	+	H_2	$\longrightarrow$	N_2	+	H_2O
	x mL		$(6 - x)$ mL				38 mL		
or	x moles		$(60 - x)$ moles				38 moles		

Since, N atoms are conserved, applying POAC for N atoms, we get

$1 \times$ moles of NO + 2 $\times$ moles of N_2O = 2 moles of N_2

$$x + 2(60 - x) = 2 \times 38$$

$$\Rightarrow \quad x = 44$$

So, the volume of N_2O formed = (60 − 44) = 16 mL

5. ***(a)*** I and III have been doped with pentavalent impurity (P and As) . There is one surplus electron that results in the formation of n-type semiconductor and thus conducting. In II and IV, doping has been done using trivalent B and Al. There is a hole formation which results in p-type semiconductor.

6. ***(c)*** Among the given match, (c) is incorrectly match while other are correct.

Its correct match is — Nearest neighbour distance in Na_2O is $\dfrac{a\sqrt{3}}{4}$

7. ***(c)*** By Clausius-Clapeyron equation

$$\log_{10} p = \log_{10} A - \frac{\Delta H}{2.303\,RT}$$

As $\left(\dfrac{1}{T}\right)$ increases, i.e. T decreases, vapour pressure decreases

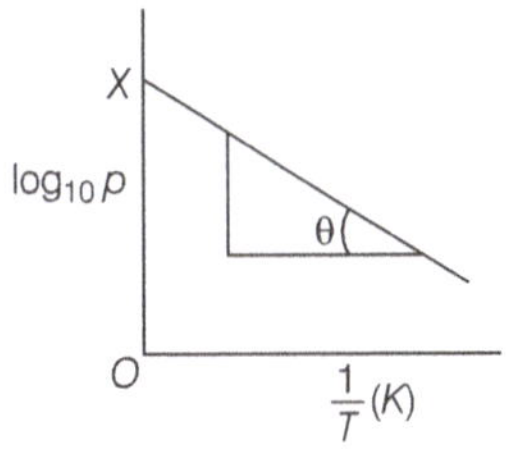

$OX = \log_{10} A$ = intercept on $(\log_{10} p)$ axis

$-\text{slope} = \tan\theta = -2K$

$$\therefore \quad -\frac{\Delta H}{2.303R} = -2\,K$$

$$\therefore \quad \Delta H = 2.303R \times 2\,K$$

$$= 2.303 \times 2\ \text{cal mol}^{-1}\,\text{K}^{-1} \times 2\,\text{K}$$

$$= 9.212\ \text{cal mol}^{-1}$$

8. ***(d)*** $pV = RT$

At constant temperature, pV = constant which is shown by the isotherm I.

Also if p is low, volume is high, then $(V - b) \approx V$

Also at high temperature, volume is high $(V \propto T)$. Thus, $(V - b) \approx V$ and molecules are far apart and the force of attraction between molecules is negligible. So, $\dfrac{a}{V^2}$(due to negligible attraction) = 0 and $\left(p + \dfrac{a}{V^2}\right) \approx p$

Hence, van der Waals' equation, $\left(p+\frac{a}{V^2}\right)(V-b)=RT$

is reduced to $pV = RT$ at low pressure and high temperature. So, (a) is correct.

At low pressure, V is high. Thus, $(V-b) \approx V$

Hence, $\left(p+\frac{a}{V^2}\right)V = RT$

$$pV = \left(RT - \frac{a}{V}\right) \approx (RT - a'p), V \propto \frac{1}{p}$$

Thus, on increasing pressure pV decreases in low pressure range. At high pressure, $\left(p+\frac{a}{V^2}\right) \approx p$

Hence, $p(V-b) = RT \Rightarrow pV = RT + pb$

Thus, pV increases as p increases, in high pressure range. So, (b) is correct.

If gases are light (H_2, He) ,force of attraction is negligible hence,

$$\left(p+\frac{a}{V^2}\right) \approx p$$

$\therefore$ $p(V-b) = RT$

$\therefore$ $pV = RT + pb$

Thus, pV increases as p increases as shown by isotherm III.

9. **(a)** $\left(p+\frac{a}{V^2}\right)(V-b)=RT$

When $p \rightarrow 0$, volume is very high thus,

$$\left(p+\frac{a}{V^2}\right)V = RT$$

$$pV + \frac{a}{V} = RT$$

$$pV = \left(RT - \frac{a}{V}\right)$$

If gas behaves ideally, $pV = RT$

$$\frac{1}{V} = \frac{p}{RT}$$

$$\therefore \quad pV = \left(RT - \frac{ap}{RT}\right)$$

Thus, isotherm of pV vs p is of the type

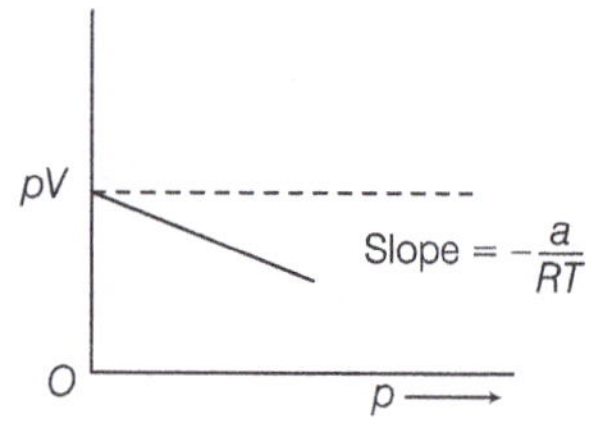

$$\therefore \quad -\frac{a}{RT} = -0.1\,dm^3$$

$\therefore$ $a = 0.1\,dm^3 \times RT$

$= 0.1\,dm^3 \times 0.0831\,dm^3$ bar $mol^{-1}K^{-1} \times 273$ K

$= (2.27\,dm^6$ bar $mol^{-1})$

10. **(d)** Total number of anions (present at corner) $= \frac{1}{8} \times 8 = 1$

Total number of cations (present at face centres) $= \frac{1}{2} \times 6 = 3$

r_a = radius of anions

r_c = radius of cations

$$\text{Packing fraction} = \frac{\left[1 \times \frac{4}{3}\pi r_a^3\right] + \left[3 \times \frac{4}{3}\pi r_c^3\right]}{(2r_a)^3}$$

$\because$ $2(r_c + r_a) = \sqrt{2} \times 2r_a$

Since the cations occupy octahedral holes. So,

$$\frac{r_c}{r_a} = 0.414$$

$$\text{Packing fraction} = \frac{\frac{4}{3}\pi\,[r_a^3 + 3(0.414)^3 r_a^3]}{(2r_a)^3} = \frac{\pi}{6}[1 + 3(0.414)^3]$$

PF. = 0.63

PF in% = 0.63 × 100 = 63%

11. **(c,d)** Among the given statements, (c) and (d) are incorrect while statement (a) and (b) are correct.

The correct form of statement (c) and (d) are —

(a) Partial pressure $= x \times p_{Total} = \frac{80}{100} \times 5 = 4$ atm

(b) $\frac{r_{He}}{r_{CH_4}} = \sqrt{\frac{Mw_{(CH_4)}}{Mw_{(He)}}} = \sqrt{\frac{16}{4}} = 2,$

$\therefore$ $r_{He} = 2r_{CH_4}$

(c) It is applicable since at room temperature CO_2 and CO does not react

(d) Rate of diffusion $(r) \propto \sqrt{\frac{1}{Mw}}$

Mw of H_2 < Mw of CH_4, hence H_2 will diffuse into the balloon and its size will increases

12. **(a,c,d)** Among the given statements, (a), (c) and (d) are incorrect while statement (b) is correct for hcp in 3D.

Their correct explanation given as below

- Total tetrahedral voids = 12 out of which 8 are completely inside but rest are shared by other unit cells.
- Total octahedral voids = 6 and all are completely inside the unit cell.

13. **(a, b, c)** $\frac{r_{Cs^+}}{r_{Br^-}} = \frac{1.69}{1.95} = 0.867$ (bcc structure)

Hence, Cs^+ ion lies at the body centre of cubic void where coordination number of $Cs^+ = 8$

CsBr has bcc structure with Br^- forming simple cubic lattice and Cs^+ ion in the void (at body centre)

For bcc,

$$2(r_{Cs^+} + r_{Br^-}) = \sqrt{3}a$$

$$2(1.69 + 1.95) = \sqrt{3}a \Rightarrow a = 4.2\,\text{Å}$$

14. ***(c, d)*** Among the given statements, (c) and (d) are correct while (a) and (b) are incorrect.

Their explanation are given below.

(a) The radius of the Na^+ is 95 pm and that of Cl^- ion is 181 pm then the coordination number of Na^+ is 6.

As, $\frac{r_+}{r_-}$ i.e., $\frac{r_{Na^+}}{r_{Cl^-}} = \frac{95}{181} = 0.525$

The radius ratio falls in the range 0.414 – 0.732 of octahedral arrangement which has coordination number 6.

(b) The coordination number of Sr^{2+} ion in SrF_2, if ionic radii are $r(Sr^{2+}) = 113$ pm and $r(F^-) = 136$ pm in 8.

As, $$\frac{r(Sr^{2+})}{r(F^-)} = \frac{113}{136} = 0.831$$

Radius ratio falls in the range of 0.732 – 1.0. Hence, coordination of Sr^{2+} is 8.

(c) As we know, $\rho = \frac{Z \times \text{weight}}{\text{Number of atoms} \times a^3}$

Number of atoms $= \frac{4 \times 100}{5 \times (200 \times 10^{-10})^3} = 10^{25}$ [For fcc, $Z = 4$]

(d) In ZnS, cation Zn^{2+} are present in tetrahedral voids created by S^{2-} ions.

Thus, in ZnS type structure,

r_+ i.e., size of tetrahedral site $= 0.225 r_-$

$$\therefore \quad r_{A^+} = 0.225 r_{B^-}$$

$$r_{B^-} = \frac{22.5}{0.225} = 100 \text{ pm}$$

15. ***(a,b,c)*** Among the given statements, (a), (b) and (c) are correct while statement (d) is incorrect.

Their explanation are given below:

As we know, $\gamma = \gamma_0 \left(1 - \frac{T}{T_C}\right)^n$

(a) at $T = T_C$, $\gamma = 0$

Thus, (a) is correct.

(b) $\log \gamma = \log \gamma_0 + n \log \left(1 - \frac{T}{T_C}\right)$

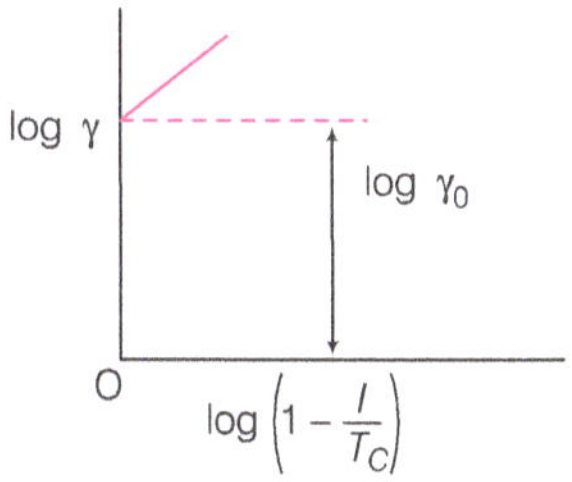

Plot between $\log \gamma$ and $\log \left(1 - \frac{T}{T_C}\right)$ is linear with slope $= n$ and intercept $= \log \gamma_0$

Thus, (b) is correct.

(c) $\frac{T}{T_C}$ is called reduced temperature, if

$$\frac{T}{T_C} = 1$$

$$\therefore \quad \gamma = 0$$

Thus (c) is correct.

(d) $\log \gamma$ increases on increasing, $\log \left(1 - \frac{T}{T_C}\right)$

Thus (d) is incorrect.

16. ***(a, b, c, d)***

(a) At 0°C, for H_2, attractive forces are weak due to its low molar mass.

Thus, $\frac{a}{V^2}$ (pressure correction) = 0

Thus, $\left(p + \frac{a}{V^2}\right)(V - b) = RT$

reduces to $pV - pb = RT$

$$pV = pb + RT$$

$$Z = \frac{pV}{RT} = \left(\frac{pb}{RT} + 1\right)$$

Thus $Z > 1$. Thus, (a) is correct.

(b) At lower pressure (at about below 150 atm), V is larger. Thus,

$(V - b) \approx V$

Thus, $\left(p + \frac{a}{V^2}\right) V = RT$

$$\Rightarrow \quad pV + \frac{a}{V} = RT$$

$$\therefore \quad Z = \frac{pV}{RT} = \left(1 - \frac{a}{RTV}\right)$$

Thus, $Z < 1$ for lower pressure range.

At higher pressure, as in (a),

$$Z = \frac{pV}{RT} = \left(\frac{pb}{RT} + 1\right) Z > 1$$

(c) As in (b)

(d) As is clear from graph, at a particular pressure (300 atm for N_2 and 500 atm for CO_2) $Z = 1$. Thus, ideal behaviour may be observed.

17. ***(a, c, d)*** The van der Waals equation of state for a real gas is

$$\left(p + \frac{an^2}{V}\right)(V - nb) = nRT \qquad \text{...(i).}$$

For a gas A, $a = 0$ the Eq. (i) reduces to

$$p(V - nb) = nRT$$

or $$\frac{pV}{nRT} - \frac{pb}{RT} = 1$$

or $$Z = 1 + \frac{bp}{RT}$$

i.e., the dependence of Z on p is linear at all pressure.

So, (a) is correct.

For a gas B, $b = 0$ the Eq. (i) reduces to

$$\left(p + \frac{an^2}{V}\right)V = nRT$$

or $$pV + an^2 = nRT$$

or $$Z = 1 - \frac{an}{RT}$$

i.e. the Z does not depends upon p when $b = 0$

So, (b) is incorrect.

For the gas C, if minima Z_{min} and $Z = 1$ (point of intersection is known for a given temperature a and b can be calculated.

When $Z = 1$

$$p_{int} = \frac{RT}{(V_{m,\,int} - b)} - \frac{a}{V^2_{m,\,int}}$$

$$\left[p_{int} \text{ in calculated from graph and } v_{m,\,int} = \frac{RT}{p_{int}}\right]$$

When $Z = 1$

$$Z_{min} = \frac{V_{m,\,min}}{(V_{m,\,min} - b)} - \frac{a}{RT\,V_{m,\,min}}$$

$$\left[\text{Again, } p_{m,\,int} \text{ is calculated from graph and } V_{m,\,min} = \frac{RT}{p_{min}}\right]$$

The two equation can be solved to calculate a and b. So, (c) is correct.

At high pressure, $Z > 1$ for real gases. So, (d) is correct.

18. ***(a, b, c, d)***

$$U_{mp} = \sqrt{\frac{2RT}{M}},\ U_{av} = \sqrt{\frac{8RT}{\pi M}},\ U_{rms} = \sqrt{\frac{3RT}{M}}$$

Thus, $U_{mp} < U_{av} < U_{rms}$

Thus, (a) is correct.

(b) $(KE)_{av} = \frac{3}{2}\frac{RT}{N_0}$. It is independent of amounts, thus (b) is correct.

(c) $KE = \frac{3}{2}RT$ per mol.

$$U_{mp} = \sqrt{\frac{2RT}{M}}$$

$$\therefore \quad \frac{(U^2_{mp})\,M}{2} = RT$$

$$\therefore \quad KE = \frac{3(U_{mp})^2\,M}{4}$$

Thus, (c) is correct.

(d) $U_{rms} = \sqrt{\frac{3RT}{M}} \Rightarrow \frac{(U_{rms})^2 M}{3} = RT$

$$KE = \frac{3}{2}RT = \frac{3}{2}\frac{(U_{rms})^2}{3}M = \frac{(U_{rms})^2 M}{2}$$

Thus, (d) is correct.

19. ***(a, b, c, d)*** Among the given statements, all statements are correct.

20. ***(380)*** Interionic distance in fcc $= 2(r_+ + r_-) = a\sqrt{2}$

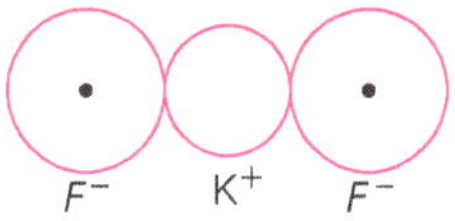

$$\therefore \quad (r_+ + r_-) = \frac{a}{\sqrt{2}}$$

$$d = \frac{Mz}{N_0 a^3}$$

$$\therefore \quad a^3 = \frac{Mz}{N_0\,d} = \frac{58\text{g mol}^{-1} \times 4}{6.02 \times 10^{23}\text{mol}^{-1} \times 2.475\text{g cm}^{-3}}$$

$$= 1.557 \times 10^{-22}\text{ cm}^3$$

$$\therefore \quad a \approx 5.38 \times 10^{-8}\text{ cm} = 5.38 \times 10^{-10}\text{ m}$$

$$= 538 \times 10^{-12}\text{ m} = 538\text{ pm}$$

$$\therefore \quad r_+ + r_- = \frac{a}{\sqrt{2}} = 380\text{ pm}$$

21. ***(4.84)*** Given,

A rigid vessel of containing H_2 at 20.5°C has

volume $= 0.50\text{ m}^3$

Pressure $= 611 \times 10^3$ Pa

A second rigid vessel containing Ar at 31.2°C has

volume $= 0.75\text{ m}^3$

pressure $= 433 \times 10^3$ Pa

As we know, $n_T = n_1 + n_2$ ...(i)

Substitute the value in Eq. (i) we get,

$$\frac{P \times 1.25}{R \times 287.5} = \frac{611 \times 10^3 \times 0.5}{293.5R} + \frac{433 \times 10^3 \times 0.75}{304.2R}$$

$$P = 4.84 \times 10^5\text{ Pa}$$

Hence, the value of x is 4.84.

22. ***(6)*** We need to calculate the ΔA(change in surface area) for going from 1.00 cm drop to 10 equal volume drops.

A(surface area of large drop) $= 4\pi r^2 = 4\pi(1)^2\text{ cm}^2 = 4\pi\text{ cm}^2$

V(volume of large drop) $= \frac{4}{3}\pi r^3 = \frac{4}{3}\pi(1)^3 = \frac{4}{3}\pi\text{ cm}^3$

V(volume of small drop of radius 'a') $= \frac{4}{3}\pi a^3$

$$\therefore \quad \frac{4}{3}\pi a^3 \times 10 = \frac{4}{3}\pi$$

$$\therefore \quad a^3 = 0.1$$

$$a = 0.4642\text{ cm}$$

A' (surface area of small drop) $= 4\pi a^2 = 4\pi(0.4642)^2$

$A'' =$ For 10 drops $= 10A'$

$A'' = 4\pi \times 10(0.4642)^2$

$$\therefore \quad \Delta A = (A'' - A)$$

$$= 4\pi\,[10\,(0.4642)^2 - 1] = 14.51\text{cm}^2$$

Work done $= \gamma \times \Delta A = 414 \times 14.51$

$= 6007.14$ dyne cm

$= 6007.14 \text{ erg} = \frac{6007.14}{10^7} \text{ J} \quad \left(\because \begin{array}{l} 1 \text{ dyne cm} = 1 \text{ erg} \\ 10^7 \text{ erg} = 1 \text{ J} \end{array}\right)$

$= 6.007 \times 10^{-4} \text{ J} = x \times 10^{-4}$ J

Thus, $x = 6$

23. ***(8.33)*** Volume of surface of cubic crystal $= 1 \text{cm}^3$

Volume of unit cell of Ca $= (0.556 \times 10^{-7})^3 \text{ cm}^3$

$\therefore$ Number of unit cells in $1\text{cm}^3 = \frac{1\text{cm}^3}{(0.556 \times 10^{-7})^3}$

$= 5.82 \times 10^{21}$

Number of atoms in one unit cell = 4

$\therefore$ Total atoms $= 4 \times 5.82 \times 10^{21}$

$= 2.328 \times 10^{22}$

There are total six faces in a cube.

Thus area of six surfaces $= 6 \times 1\text{cm}^2$

Area of one face in a unit cell $= (0.556 \times 10^{-7})^2 \text{ cm}^2$

$\therefore$ Number of surface cells $= \frac{6 \times 1\text{cm}^2}{(0.556 \times 10^{-7})^2 \text{ cm}^2}$

$= 1.94 \times 10^{15}$

Number of atoms on a surface of unit cell = 1

$\therefore$ Total atoms on given surfaces $= 1.94 \times 10^{15}$

Thus, fraction of the atoms on the surface

$$\frac{N \text{(Surface)}}{N \text{(Crystal)}} = \frac{1.94 \times 10^{15}}{2.328 \times 10^{22}} = 8.33 \times 10^{-8}$$

24. ***(8)*** Consider one face of unit all is shown below

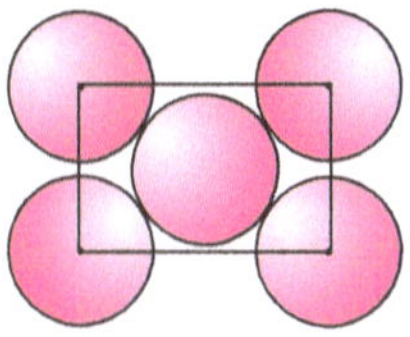

Number of atoms on one face = 4 (corners) $\times \frac{1}{8}$ (per corner share) + 1 (face centre) $\times \frac{1}{2}$ (face centre share)

$= \frac{1}{2} + \frac{1}{2} = 1$ per face

Given, number of atoms on all faces $= 24 \times 10^{30}$

Given, number of atoms on one face $= \frac{1}{6} \times 24 \times 10^{30}$

$= 4 \times 10^{30}$ atoms

Number of unit cells at one face of crystal $= \frac{24 \times 10^{30}}{6}$

$= 4 \times 10^{30}$

So, numbers of unit cells at the edge of crystal $= \sqrt{4 \times 10^{30}}$

$= 2 \times 10^{15}$

Now, edge length of unit cell $= \frac{4}{\sqrt{2}} \times 50$ nm

Edge length of cubical crystal $= \left(\frac{4}{\sqrt{2}} \times 50 \times 2 \times 10^{15} \text{ nm}\right)$

So, area of face of crystal $= \left(\frac{4}{\sqrt{2}} \times 50 \times 2 \times 10^{15}\right)^2 (\text{nm})^2$

$= \frac{16}{2} \times 25 \times 10^2 \times 4 \times 10^{30} (\text{nm})^2$

Hence, the value of A is $8 = 800 \times 10^{32} \times 10^{-18} \text{ m}^2$

$8 \times 10^{16} \text{ m}^2$

25. ***(0.73)*** CsCl has bcc structure with $z = 2, M = 168.5 \text{g mol}^{-1}$

$\therefore \quad d = \frac{Mz}{N_0 a^3}$

$\therefore \quad a^3 = \frac{Mz}{N_0 d}$

$\therefore \quad a^3 = \frac{168.5 \times 2}{6.02 \times 10^{23} \times 3.97}$

$\therefore \quad = 1.41 \times 10^{-22} \text{ cm}^3$

Side length (a) $= 5.2 \times 10^{-8}$ cm

Cs^+ and Cl^- are on diagonal

Thus, diagonal $= \sqrt{3} a$

$= \sqrt{3} \times 5.2 \times 10^{-8}$cm

$= 8.996 \times 10^{-8} \text{ cm} = 9$Å

Also diagonal $= 2r_+ + 2r_- = 9$Å

$r_+ + r_- = \frac{9\text{Å}}{2}$

Hence distance between Cs^+ and Cl^- = 4.5Å

we assume Cl^- ions touch each other.

Hence $r_- = \frac{5.2}{2}$ Å $= 2.6$ Å

$\therefore \quad r_+ = 4.5 - \frac{5.2}{2} = 1.9$Å

$\therefore \quad \frac{r_+}{r_-} = \frac{1.9}{2.6} = 0.73$

So, the value of x and y is 4.5 Å and 0.73 respectively.

Hence, the value of y is 0.73.

26. ***(2)*** Force due to surface tension $= 2\pi r\gamma$

Force which holds the liquid at height $h = mg$

Also mass $(m) = V \times d = \pi r^2 hd$

$\therefore \quad 2\pi r\gamma = (\pi r^2 hd) g$

$h = \frac{2\gamma}{rdg}$

$h = \frac{2 \times (0.058 \text{ kg s}^{-2})}{(0.70 \times 10^{-3} \text{ m}) (850 \text{ kg m}^{-3}) (9.80 \text{ ms}^{-2})}$

$\approx 2 \times 10^{-2}$ m

Thus, $x = 2$

[1 N = kg ms^{-2}

$\therefore$ 1N/m $= \frac{\text{kg ms}^{-2}}{\text{m}} = \text{kg s}^{-2}$]

27. ***(312.5)*** Moles of O_2 remaining after reaction = 4 − 1 = 3

$V \propto n$ is due to same T and p in each compartment after reaction.

$\therefore$ Length of He compartment,

$$\frac{5}{5+3} \times 500 = 312.5 \text{ cm}.$$

28. ***(c)*** The correct match is A-III, B-II, C-I, D-IV

A. An ion (Cl^-) at the corner contributes 1/8 of its volume to each of 8 adjacent cubes. Thus (A)-(III)

B. An ion (Cl^-) on the face of the unit cell contributes 1/2 of its volume of the cell.

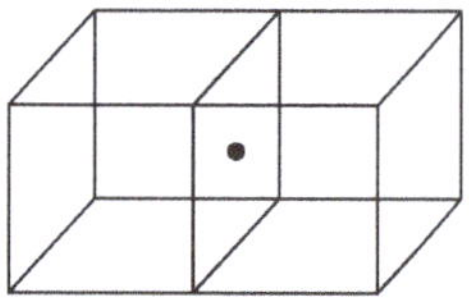

Thus (B)-(II)

C. Na^+ ion on the corner of the unit cell contribute 1/8 of their volume to the unit cell. Each face has two Na^+ ions. So, their overall contribution along a face $= \frac{1}{4}$.

Thus (C)-(I)

D. In the given structure, the contribution of Cl^- in each unit cell $= \left(\frac{1}{8} \times 4 + 6 \times \frac{1}{2}\right) = 3.5$

The contribution of Na^+ in the unit cell $= \left(\frac{1}{8} \times 4\right) = 0.5$

The fraction of Cl^- ions out of total Na^+ and Cl^- ion in a unit cell $= \frac{3.5}{4} = \frac{7}{8}$

Thus (D)-(IV)

29. ***(b)*** The correct match is A-III, B-I, C-II, D-IV.

$$\log_{10} p = \log_{10} A - \frac{\Delta H_v}{2.303\, RT}$$

where, $\frac{1}{T} = 0$, i.e $T = \infty$

$$\log_{10} p = \log_{10} A = OB = 0.3010$$

when $T \to \infty$, $\log_{10} p = 0.3010$

$\therefore \quad p = 2.0$ torr

Also, $\quad A = 2.0$ torr

Also slope of line $= \frac{\Delta H}{2.303\, R} = \tan 60$

$\therefore \quad \Delta H_v = 2.303 \times 2 \times \tan 60$

$\therefore \quad \Delta H_v = 7.97$ cal

$$\Delta H_V = 2.303 \times 0.0821 \times 1.732$$
$$= 0.327 \approx 0.33 \text{ L atm mol}^{-1} \text{K}^{-1}.$$

Vapour pressure at 300 K

$$\log_{10} p = 0.3010 - \frac{7.97}{2.303 \times 2 \times 300}$$

$$p \approx 1.97 \text{ torr}$$

30. ***(b)*** The correct match is — A-V, B-III, C-IV, D-II, E-I.

In all cases $r_+ + r_- =$ bond length

$$r_{Rb^+} + r_{I^-} = 3.67 \text{Å}$$

$$\therefore \quad r_{Rb^+} = 1.48 \text{Å}$$

Similarly, $r_{K^+} = 1.33$ Å, $r_{Na^+} = 0.98$Å, $r_{Cl^-} = 1.81$Å, $r_{Br^-} = 1.96$Å

31. ***(c)*** The correct match is — A-IV, B-I, C-II, D-III.

	$2H_2(g)$ +	$O_2(g)$ $\longrightarrow$	$2H_2O\,(g)$
Initial	3 mol	1 mol	0
After	(3 − 2)	(1 − 1)	2
	= 1mol	0	2 mol

$$\text{Initial } p_{H_2} = \frac{nRT}{V} = \frac{3 \times 0.0821 \times 400}{100} = 0.9852 \text{ atm}$$

Thus, A - IV

p_{O_2}(after) = 0.00 atm

Since, all O_2 is consumed.

Thus, B-I

Total moles before reaction = 1 + 3 = 4 mol

Thus, $p_{total} = \frac{4 \times 0.0821 \times 400}{100} = 1.3136$ atm

and C-II

After reaction there is 1 mol H_2 and 2 mol H_2O (g),

$p_{H_2O} = \frac{2 \times 0.0821 \times 400}{100} = 0.6568$ and D-III.

32. ***(b)*** The correct match is—A-IV, B-II, C-I, D-III

A. **Body-centred cubic** Every cation (Cs^+) is coordinated to eight anions. (Br^-) is coordinated to eight cations (Cs^+).

Thus, **A $\to$ (IV)**

B. **Face-centred cubic** Every cation (Na^+) is coordinated to six anions (Cl^-) and every anion (Cl^-) is coordinated to six cations (Na^+).

Thus, **B $\to$ (II)**

C. **Face-centred cubic** Every cation (Zn^{2+}) is coordinated to four anions (S^{2-}) and *vice-versa*.

Thus, **C $\to$ (I)**

D. **Face-centred cubic** (anti-fluorite) Every Ca^{2+} is coordinated to eight fluoride (F^-) and every F^- is coordinated to four Ca^{2+} (to balance charge).

$$4Ca^{2+} + 8F^-$$

Thus, **D $\to$ (III)**

33. ***(c)*** The correct match is—A-IV, B-II, C-III, D-I.

When attractive forces are negligible $\frac{a}{V^2} = 0$

Thus, for one mole $p(V - b) = RT$

$$\therefore \quad pV - pb = RT$$

$$\Rightarrow \qquad V = \left(\frac{RT}{p} + b\right)$$

Isobar at constant p, (between V and T) is of the type as given.

Thus, $OA = b =$ van der Waals' constant

$b = 0.140\ dm^3\ mol^{-1}$

Thus, B-II

Slope of the line $= \frac{R}{p} = \tan 45° = 1$

$\therefore \qquad p = R = 0.0821$ atm

Thus, A-IV

At 300 K, $V = \frac{0.0821 \times 300}{0.0821} + 0.14 = 300.14\ dm^3$

Thus C-III

When $\qquad p = p_C = \frac{a}{27b^2}$

$\therefore \qquad a = p_C \times 27b^2$

$= 0.0821\ atm \times 27 \times (0.140)^2\ (dm^3\ mol^{-1})^2$

$= 0.043\ atm\ dm^6\ mol^{-2}$

Thus, D-I

34. ***(a)*** The correct match is — A-I, B-II, C-III, D-IV.

$$\left(p + \frac{a}{V^2}\right)(V - b) = RT$$

Graph shows that attractive forces are negligible. Thus, $\frac{a}{V^2} = 0$

$$\therefore \qquad p = \frac{RT}{(V - b)}$$

Then, $p \propto T$

Isochore is formed between p and T at constant volume.

Thus, $\qquad$ slope $= \left(\frac{R}{V - b}\right) = \tan 45° = 1$

$\therefore \qquad R = (V - b)$

$\therefore \qquad b = V - R = (0.1 - 0.0821)$

$= 0.0179\ dm^3\ mol^{-1}$

Thus, A - I

$$p = \frac{RT}{(V - b)} = (1)T$$

When $p = 1$ atm, $T = 1$K

Thus, B - II

Also, $\left(\frac{\partial p}{\partial T}\right)_V = \frac{R}{V - b} = 1 \Rightarrow \frac{1}{b}\left(\frac{\partial p}{\partial T}\right)_V = \frac{1}{0.0179} \approx 55.86$

Thus, C - III

$$R = V - b$$

$$\lambda(\text{Mean free path}) = \frac{RT}{\sqrt{2}N_o \sigma p}$$

where, σ = cross-sectional area $= \pi d^2 = \pi(2r)^2$

r = radius of the molecule

Under given conditions (ii), $\frac{T}{p} = 1$

$$b = 0.0179\ dm^2\ mol^{-1}$$

Also, $\qquad b = 4V = 4N_0\left(\frac{4}{3}\pi r^3\right)$

where, V = volume of molecules in one mole of the gas

$$\therefore \quad r^3 = \frac{3}{16\pi N_0}(b) = \frac{3 \times (0.0179)\ dm^3}{16\pi \times 6.02 \times 10^{23}}$$

$$r^3 = 1.775 \times 10^{-27}\ dm^3$$

$$r = 1.21 \times 10^{-9}\ dm$$

$$\Rightarrow \quad \sigma = \pi d^2 = 4\pi r^2 = 4\pi(1.21 \times 10^{-9})^2\ dm^2$$

$$= 1.84 \times 10^{-17}\ dm^2$$

$$\therefore \quad \lambda = \frac{RT}{\sqrt{2}\ N_o\ \sigma\ p}$$

$$= \frac{0.0821 dm^3\ atm\ mol^{-1} K^{-1} \times 1K}{\sqrt{2} \times 6.02 \times 10^{23} mol^{-1} \times 1.84 \times 10^{-17} dm^2 \times 1 atm}$$

$$= 5.24 \times 10^{-9}\ dm$$

$$= 5.24 \times 10^{-10} m = 5.24 Å$$

Thus, D - IV.

35. ***(200)*** As we know,

$$\mu_1 = \sqrt{\frac{3p_1}{d}};\ \mu_2 = \sqrt{\frac{3p_2}{d}}$$

Given, density $= 0.75\ kg/m^3$

$p_1 = 4 \times 10^4$ Pa

$p_2 = 9 \times 10^4$ Pa

The increase in μ_{rms} is $= \sqrt{\frac{3p_1}{d}} - \sqrt{\frac{3p_2}{d}}$

$$= \sqrt{\frac{3}{0.75}}\,[\sqrt{9 \times 10^4} - \sqrt{4 \times 10^4}]$$

$$= \sqrt{\frac{3}{0.75}}\,[3 \times 10^2 - 2 \times 10^2]$$

$$= 2 \times 1 \times 10^2 = 200$$

36. ***(3.6)*** Given, 4 molecules $(v_1) = 6\ cm\ sec^{-1}$

5 molecules $(v_2) = 2\ cm\ sec^{-1}$

10 molecules $(v_3) = 3\ cm\ sec^{-1}$

$$\mu_{rms} = \sqrt{\frac{4 \times (6)^2 + 5(2)^2 + 10(3)^2}{19}}$$

$$\approx 3.6\ cm/sec.$$

37. ***(1)*** As the given equation,

$$\log_{10} p(mm) = \frac{-400\ K}{T} + 10 \qquad \ldots(i)$$

Given, $T = 400$ K

After putting the value in Eq. (i), we get

$$\log_{10} p(mm) = \frac{-400\ K}{400\ K} + 10 = 9$$

$$p = 1 \times 10^9\ mm$$

38. ***(-214.5)*** $p = 2\text{ atm} = 2 \times 760\text{ mm} = 1520\text{ mmHg}$

$$\log_{10} p\,(\text{mm}) = \frac{400\,(K)}{T} + 10$$

$$\log(1520) = -\frac{400(K)}{T} + 10$$

$$\frac{400(K)}{T} \approx 6.82 \Rightarrow T = 58.65\text{ K}$$

$$T(°\text{C}) = (58.65 - 273.15) = -214.5°\text{C}$$

39. ***(1.2)*** % of lattice which is vacant in BCC pattern = 32%

$$a = \frac{4}{\sqrt{3}} R \Rightarrow V = \left(\frac{4}{\sqrt{3}}\right)^3 \times R^3 = 64$$

$\Rightarrow 5(0.32 \times 64) = nRT \Rightarrow n = 2$ moles

Number of O_2 molecules $= 2 \times 6 \times 10^{23} \Rightarrow 1.2 \times 10^{24}$

$$a = 1.2$$

40. ***(50)*** % increase in density $= \dfrac{\Delta\text{ mass}}{\text{Initial mass}} \times 100$

$$\Rightarrow \frac{2 \times 32}{2 \times 64} \times 100 = 50\%$$

41. ***(a)*** The gases which react chemically do not follow Dalton's law of partial pressure. Among the given mixtures only (iii) react chemically (forming HCl) whereas (i), (ii), (iv) and (v) follow Dalton's law of partial pressure.

42. ***(b)*** In (iii), (iv) and (v) case, compressibility factor of a given gas deviates from ideal behaviour.

As we know,

If $Z \neq 1$, then there is deviation from ideal behaviour.

(i) $Z = \dfrac{pV}{nRT} = \dfrac{1\text{ atm} \times 11.2\text{ dm}^3}{0.5\text{ mol} \times 0.0821\text{ atm L mol}^{-1}\text{K}^{-1} \times 273\text{ K}}$

≈ 1 (ideal)

(ii) $Z = \dfrac{pV}{nRT} = \dfrac{1\text{ atm} \times 5.6\text{ dm}^3}{\left(\frac{11}{44}\right)\text{mol} \times 0.0821\text{ atm L mol}^{-1}\text{ K}^{-1} \times 273\text{ K}}$

≈ 1 (ideal)

(iii) $Z = \dfrac{pV}{nRT} = \dfrac{40.0\text{ bar} \times 0.4\text{ dm}^3}{1\text{ mol} \times 0.083\text{ bar dm}^3\text{ mol}^{-1}\text{K}^{-1} \times 300\text{ K}}$

$\approx 0.64 < 1$ (non-ideal)

(iv) N_2O_4 and NO_2 are in 1: 1 molar ratio

Thus, average molar mass $= \dfrac{M_1 X_1 + M_2 X_2}{X_1 + X_2}$

$$= \frac{92 \times 0.5 + 46 \times 0.5}{1} = 69\text{ g mol}^{-1}$$

Moles (mixture) $= \dfrac{6.9}{69} = 0.1$ mole

$\therefore\ Z = \dfrac{pV}{nRT} = \dfrac{24.9\text{ bar} \times 1\text{ dm}^3}{0.1\text{ mole} \times 0.083\text{ bar dm}^3\text{mol}^{-1}\text{K}^{-1} \times 300\text{ K}}$

$$= \frac{24.9}{2.49} = 10$$

$Z \neq 1$ (non-ideal)

(v) $Z = \dfrac{pV}{nRT} = \dfrac{1\text{ atm} \times 13.1\text{ dm}^3}{0.1\text{ mol} \times 0.0821\text{ atm L mol}^{-1}\text{ K}^{-1} \times 273\text{ K}}$

$$= \frac{13.1}{2.24} = 5.84$$

$Z \neq 1$ (non-ideal)

43. ***(c)*** Among the given mixture of gases, only two i.e., (ii) and (iv) for which Dalton's law of partial pressure is applicable because Dalton's law of partial pressure is applicable for non-interacting gases.

(i) SO_2 dissolves in H_2O.

(iii) NH_3 reacts with HCl.

(v) H_2 reacts with Cl_2.

44. ***(a)*** Among the given pairs, only two i.e., (i) and (ii) which have same relative rates of effusion of gases A and B.

As we know, $\dfrac{r_A}{r_B} = \sqrt{\dfrac{M_B}{M_A}}$

(i) $= \sqrt{\dfrac{44}{44}} = 1$ (ii) $= \sqrt{\dfrac{28}{28}} = 1$

(iii) $= \sqrt{\dfrac{48}{32}} = 1225$ (iv) $= \sqrt{\dfrac{20}{18}} = 1.054$

(v) $= \sqrt{\dfrac{352}{349}} = 1.004$ (vi) $= \sqrt{\dfrac{64}{16}} = 2$

(vii) $\sqrt{\dfrac{92}{46}} = 1.44$

45. ***(d)*** Among the given graphs, only one i.e., (iii) is incorrect while others are correct.

Their explanation are given as:

(i) $pV = k$ (constant) at constant temperature

Thus, $p \propto \dfrac{1}{V}$ (Boyle's law)

Thus, (i) is correct.

(ii) $pV = RT \Rightarrow p = \dfrac{RT}{V}$

At constant volume, $p \propto T$. Thus, (ii) is correct.

(iii) $V = kT$ (at constant p) –Charle's law

$$\log V = \log k + \log T$$

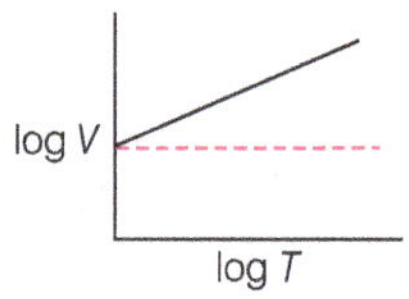

Thus (iii) is incorrect.

(iv) $p = \dfrac{k}{V}$ at constant T – Boyle's law

$$\therefore\ \log p = \log\frac{1}{V} + \log k$$

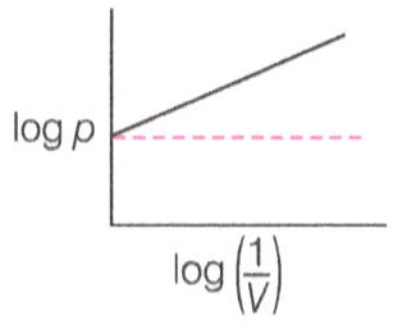

Thus (iv) is correct.

(v) $V = kT$ (at constant p) — Charle's law

Thus, (v) is correct.

(vi) $\frac{V}{T} = k$ (at constant p) — Charle's law

$$\Rightarrow \log\left(\frac{V}{T}\right) = \log k,$$

Thus, (vi) is correct.

(vii) Density $d = \frac{\text{Mass}}{\text{Volume}}$

$$\therefore \quad d \propto \frac{1}{V} \text{ or } V \propto \frac{1}{d}$$

$$\therefore \quad d \propto \frac{1}{T}$$

Thus, density increases with decrease in temperature.

Thus (vii) is correct.

46. ***(c)*** Among the given crystal system, only four i.e., (i), (ii), (iii) and (vii) has $\alpha = \beta = 90°$ while other have

(i) Cubic $\longrightarrow \alpha = \beta = \gamma = 90°$

(ii) Tetragonal $\longrightarrow \alpha = \beta = \gamma = 90°$

(iii) Orthorhombic $\longrightarrow \alpha = \beta = \gamma = 90°$

(iv) Monoclinic $\longrightarrow \alpha = \gamma = 90°, \beta \neq 90°$

(v) Triclinic $\longrightarrow \alpha \neq \beta \neq \gamma \neq 90°$

(vi) Rhomobohedral $\longrightarrow \alpha = \beta = \gamma \neq 90°$

(vii) Hexagonal $\longrightarrow \alpha = \beta = 90°, \gamma = 120°$

47. ***(b)*** A p-type semiconductor is a semiconductor created by doping an intrinsic semiconductor with an acceptor impurity. In a p-type semiconductor, a tetravalent semiconductor like Si or Ge is doped with a trivalent impurity like Al, Ga, In and B.

Check Through PYQs : JEE Advanced

1. ***(d)*** Given,

for ideal gas X for ideal gas Y

$m_1 = 10$ g $\quad m_2 = 80$ g

$T_1 = 300$ K $\quad T_2 = 300$ K

$p_1 = 2$ atm $\quad p_2 = 6$ atm

$$\frac{V_{rms}(X)}{V_{rms}(Y)} = ?$$

Substitute the given values in ideal gas equation,

$pV = nRT$

(where, symbols have their usual meaning)

for gas X,

$$2 \times V = \frac{10}{M_X} \times RT \quad \ldots\text{(i)}$$

$$\left(\because n = \frac{\text{mass}}{\text{molar mass}}\right)$$

For gas Y,

$$4 \times V = \frac{80}{M_Y} \times RT \quad \ldots\text{(ii)}$$

Divide Eq. (ii) by Eq. (i)

$$2 = \frac{80 \times M_X}{M_Y \times 10} \Rightarrow \frac{M_X}{M_Y} = \frac{1}{4}$$

Now, we know that, $V_{rms} = \sqrt{\frac{3RT}{M}}$

So, $\frac{V_{rms}(X)}{V_{rms}(Y)} = \sqrt{\frac{M_Y}{M_X}} \Rightarrow \sqrt{\frac{4}{1}} = \frac{2}{1}$

Thus, $\frac{V_{rms}(X)}{V_{rms}(Y)} = \frac{2}{1}$

2. ***(100)*** Given, compressibility factor $(Z) = 0.5$

Molar volume $(V_m) = 0.4 \text{ dm}^3\text{mol}^{-1}$

Temperature $(T) = 800$ K

Pressure $(p) = x$ atm

Gas constant $(R) = 8 \times 10^{-2}$

We know that,

$$Z = \frac{pV_m}{RT}$$

$$0.5 = \frac{x \times 0.4}{0.08 \times 800} \Rightarrow x = 80$$

For ideal condition, $Z = 1$ and molar volume will be $y \text{ dm}^3\text{mol}^{-1}$.

Using $Z = \frac{pV_m}{RT} \Rightarrow 1 = \frac{80 \times y}{0.08 \times 800}$

$$y = 0.8$$

Now, $\frac{x}{y} = \frac{80}{0.8} = 100$

3. ***(b)*** Fraction of molecules vs velocity graph is Maxwell distribution curve.

This curve is slightly unsymmetrical as shown below.

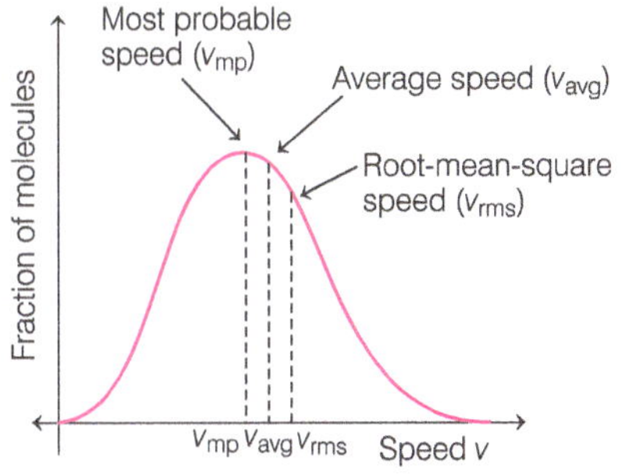

The ratio of most probable, the average and the root mean square speeds for this graph is 1 : 1.128 : 1.224

But the graph in question is completely symmetrical. Therefore, the most probable and the average speed will be same here but root mean square speed will be greater than average speed. So, the correct ratio is 1 : 1: 1224.

4. ***(a, b, d)*** The explanation of given statements are as follows:

(a) U_{rms} is inversely proportional to the square root of its molecular mass.

$$U_{rms} = \sqrt{\frac{3RT}{M}}$$

Hence, option (a) is correct.

(b) When temperature is increased four times then U_{rms} become doubled.

$$U_{rms} = \sqrt{\frac{3R}{M} \times 4T}$$

$$U_{rms} = 2 \times \sqrt{\frac{3RT}{M}}$$

Hence, option (b) is correct.

(c) and (d) E_{av} is directly proportional to temperature but does not depends on its molecular mass at a given temperature as $E_{av} = \frac{3}{2} K_B T$. If temperature raised four times than E_{av} becomes four time multiple.

Thus, option (c) is incorrect and option (d) is correct.

5. ***(2.22)*** Given

$p_1 = 5\,\text{bar}, V_1 = 1\,\text{m}^3, T_1 = 400\ \text{K}$

So, $n_1 = \frac{5}{400\,R}$ (from $pV = nRT$)

Similarly, $p_2 = 1\,\text{bar}, V_2 = 3\,\text{m}^3$, $T_2 = 300\ \text{K}, n_2 = \frac{3}{300\,R}$

Let at equilibrium the new volume of A will be $(1+x)\,\text{m}^3$

So, the new volume of B will be $(3-x)^3\ \text{m}^3$

Now, from the ideal gas equation.

$$\frac{p_1V_1}{n_1RT_1} = \frac{p_2V_2}{n_2RT_2}$$

and at equilibrium (due to conduction of heat)

$$\frac{p_1}{T_1} = \frac{p_2}{T_2}$$

So, $\frac{V_1}{n_1} = \frac{V_2}{n_2}$ or $V_1n_2 = V_2n_1$

After putting the values

$$(1+x) \times \frac{3}{300\,R} = (3-x) \times \frac{5}{400\,R}$$

or $(1+x) = \frac{(3-x)5}{4}$

or $4(1+x) = 15 - 5x$

or $4 + 4x = 15 - 5x$

or $x = \frac{11}{9}$

Hence, new volume of A i.e., $(1+x)$ will comes as $1 + \frac{11}{9} = \frac{20}{9}$ or $2.22\ \text{m}^3$

6. ***(4)*** Diffusion coefficient $[D] \propto \lambda C_{mean}$

Since, $\lambda \propto \frac{T}{p}$ and $C_{mean} \propto \sqrt{T}$

Therefore,

Diffusion coefficient $(D) \propto \frac{T\sqrt{T}}{p}$

Thus, $\frac{D_i}{D_f} = \frac{\frac{T\sqrt{T}}{p}}{\frac{4T\sqrt{4T}}{2p}} = \frac{1}{(4\times2)/2} = \frac{1}{4}$

or $\frac{D_f}{D_i} = \frac{4}{1}$

7. ***(c)*** Equation of state $p(V-b) = RT$ indicates absence of intermolecular attraction or repulsion. At larger interatomic distance (r), interatomic potential, $V(r)$ remains constant (as $a \to 0$). But when $r \to 0$, interatomic repulsion (electronic + nuclear) suddenly increases and $[V(r) > 0]$.

8. ***(d)*** Average oxidation state of M will be given by

$$= \frac{1}{3} \times 2 + \frac{2}{3} \times 3 = +\frac{8}{3}$$

So, for the given sample $M_xY_2O_4$

$$\frac{8}{3} \times x + 3(2) + 4(-2) = 0$$

$$\frac{8}{3}x = 2$$

$\Rightarrow$ $x = \frac{3}{4} = 0.75$

Thus, option (d) is the correct answer.

9. ***(a, b, d)*** Metal x forms fcc with edge length, $a_1 = L_x$,
Metal y forms bcc with edge length, $a_2 = L_y$,
Metal z forms simple cubic with edge length, $a_3 = L_z$.

Given, $r_z = \frac{3}{2} r_y, r_y = \frac{8}{\sqrt{3}} r_x, M_z = \frac{3}{2} M_y$ and $M_z = 3M_x$

(a) (i) For fcc $(Z = 4)$ metal 'x', $4r_x = \sqrt{2}L_x$

$$\text{PE} = \frac{Z \times \frac{4}{3}\pi (r_x)^3}{a_1^3} = \frac{4 \times \frac{4}{3}\pi (r_x)^3}{(L_x)^3} = \frac{4 \times \frac{4}{3}\pi (r_x)^3}{\left(\frac{4}{\sqrt{2}} r_x\right)^3} = 0.24\,\pi$$

(ii) For bcc $(Z = 2)$ metal 'y',

$4r_y = \sqrt{3}L_y$

$$\text{PE} = \frac{Z \times \frac{4}{3}\pi (r_y)^3}{a_2^3} = \frac{2 \times \frac{4}{3}\pi (r_y)^3}{(L_y)^3} = \frac{2 \times \frac{4}{3}\pi (r_y)^3}{\left(\frac{4}{\sqrt{3}} r_y\right)^3} = 0.22\,\pi$$

(iii) For simple cubic $(Z = 1)$ metal 'z',

$2r_z = L_z$

$$\text{PE} = \frac{Z \times \frac{4}{3}\pi (r_z)^3}{a_3^3} = \frac{1 \times \frac{4}{3}\pi (r_z)^3}{(L_z)^3}$$

$$= \frac{1 \times \frac{4}{3}\pi (r_z)^3}{(2r_z)^3} = \frac{\pi}{6} = 0.17\,\pi$$

$\therefore$ Packing efficiency of unit cell of x > Packing efficiency of unit cell of y > Packing efficiency of unit cell of z. Hence, option (a) is correct.

(b) $4r_y = \sqrt{3}L_y \qquad 2r_z = L_z$

$$L_y = \frac{4r_y}{\sqrt{3}}$$

$$\frac{L_y}{L_x} = \frac{4r_y}{\sqrt{3} \times 2r_z} = \frac{2r_y}{\sqrt{3}\,r_z} = \frac{2r_y}{\sqrt{3}\cdot\frac{\sqrt{3}}{2}r_y} = \frac{4}{3}$$

So, $L_y > L_z$ and hence, option (b) is correct.

(c) $4r_x = \sqrt{2}L_x,\ 4r_y = \sqrt{3}L_y$

$$L_x = \frac{4r_x}{\sqrt{2}},\ L_y = \frac{4r_y}{\sqrt{3}},\ \frac{L_x}{L_y} = \frac{3}{8\sqrt{2}}$$

So, $L_x < L_y$ and therefore, option (c) is incorrect.

(d) $$d_x = \frac{4 \times M_x}{\left(\frac{4r_x}{\sqrt{2}}\right)^3 \times N_A}$$

$$d_y = \frac{2 \times M_y}{\left(\frac{4r_y}{\sqrt{3}}\right)^3 \times N_A}$$

$$r_y = \frac{8}{\sqrt{3}}r_x,\ \frac{M_x}{M_y} = \frac{1}{2}$$

$$\frac{d_x}{d_y} = \frac{4Mx_x}{\left(\frac{4r_x}{\sqrt{2}}\right)^3 N_A} \times \frac{\left(\frac{4r_y}{\sqrt{3}}\right)^3}{2M_y} \times N_A$$

$$= 2\left(\frac{M_x}{M_y}\right) \times \left(\frac{4r_y}{\sqrt{3}} \times \frac{\sqrt{2}}{4r_x}\right)^3 = 2\left(\frac{M_x}{M_y}\right) \times \left(\frac{r_y}{r_x} \times \frac{\sqrt{2}}{\sqrt{3}}\right)^3$$

$$= 2\left(\frac{1}{2}\right) \times \left(\frac{8}{\sqrt{3}} \times \frac{\sqrt{2}}{\sqrt{3}}\right)^3 = 53.63$$

So, $d_x > d_y$ and hence, option (d) is correct.

10. ***(b)*** For given lattice

$$\frac{\sqrt{3}}{4}a = 2R$$

So, $$a = \frac{8R}{\sqrt{3}}$$

There are 8 tetrahedral voids in fcc but only 4 are occupied.

So, total number of atoms in fcc = 4 + 4 = 8 (as no. of atoms on lattice site in FCC is 4)

$$\%\text{ packing efficiency} = \frac{\text{Volume of 8 atoms}}{\text{Volume of cell}} \times 100$$

$$\%\text{ packing} = \frac{8 \times \frac{4}{3}\pi R^3}{a^3} \times 100$$

$$= \frac{8 \times \frac{4}{3}\pi R^3}{\left(\frac{8R}{\sqrt{3}}\right)^3} \times 100$$

$$\%\text{ packing} = 32.47\% \cong 35\%$$

So, option (b) is correct.

11. ***(b)***

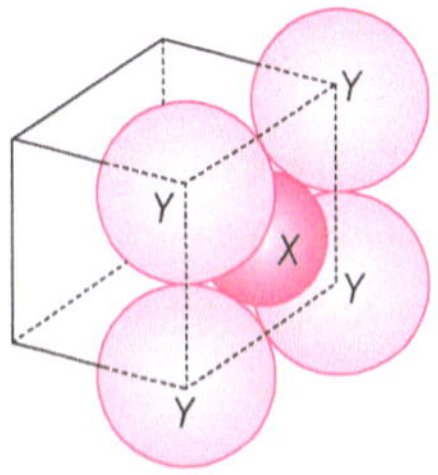

Radius of cation $X = r_+$

Number of cation X present $= 6 \times \frac{1}{2} = 3$

Radius of anion $Y = r_-$

Number of anion Y present $= \frac{1}{8} \times 8 = 1$

Side of unit cell $= a$

As two anions are touching each other, so side of unit cell, $a = 2r_-$

Volume of unit cell $= a^3 = (2r_-)^3 = 8r_-^3$

Radius ratio for cubic close packed structure,

$$\frac{r_+}{r_-} = 0.414$$

Packing efficiency

$$= \frac{(\text{Volume of cation} \times \text{Number of cations} + \text{Volume of anion} \times \text{Number of anions})}{\text{Volume of unit cell}} \times 100$$

$$\text{Packing fraction} = \frac{\text{Packing efficiency}}{100}$$

$$= \frac{1 \times \frac{4}{3}\pi r_-^3 + 3 \times \frac{4}{3}\pi r_+^3}{8r_-^3}$$

$$= \frac{4\pi}{3 \times 8}\left[\frac{r_-^3}{r_-^3} + \frac{3r_+^3}{r_-^3}\right] = \frac{\pi}{6}[1 + 3(0.414)^3]$$

$$= \frac{3.14}{6}(1 + 3 \times 0.0710)$$

$$= \frac{3.14}{6} \times 1.213 = 0.63$$

12. ***(a, c)*** The empirical formula of the compound:

Contribution of M and X : $M_{\left(2 \times \frac{1}{2}\right)} X_{\left(4 \times \frac{1}{4}\right)} \Rightarrow MX$

(b) Coordination number of both M and X is 8.

(c) Distance between M and $X = \sqrt{\frac{a^2}{4} + \frac{a^2}{2}} = \sqrt{\frac{3}{4}}a = \frac{\sqrt{3}}{2}a$

$\Rightarrow 0.866a$

(d) $r_M : r_X = (\sqrt{3} - 1) : 1 \Rightarrow 0.732 : 1,$

13. ***(3)*** In NaCl type of solids cations (Na^+) occupy the octahedral voids while anions (Cl^-) occupy the corners and face centre positions.

However, as per the demand of problem the position of cations and anions are swapped.

We also know that (for 1 unit cell)

(A) Total number of atoms at FCC = 4

(B) Total number of octahedral voids = 4

(as no. of atoms at FCC = No. of octahedral voids)

Now taking the conditions one by one

(i) If we remove all the anions except the central one then number of left anions. $= 4 - 3 = 1$

(ii) If we replace all the face centred cations by anions then effective number of cations will be $= 4 - 3 = 1$
Likewise effective number of anions will be $= 1 + 3 = 4$

(iii) If we remove all the corner cations then effective number of cations will be $1 - 1 = 0$

(iv) If we replace central anion with cation then effective number of cations will be $0 + 1 = 1$
Thus, as the final outcome, total number of cations present in Z after fulfilling all the four sequential instructions = 1
Likewise, total number of anions $= 4 - 1 = 3$
Hence, the value of $\frac{\text{Number of anions}}{\text{Number of cations}} = \frac{3}{1} = 3$

14. ***(2)*** Using the formula, $d = \frac{ZM}{N_A a^3}$

$$8 = \frac{4 \times M}{N_A (4 \times 10^{-8} \text{cm})^3}$$

$$\Rightarrow \quad M = 128 \times 10^{-24} N_A$$

$$\Rightarrow \quad \text{No. of atoms} = \frac{256}{M} \times N_A = \frac{256}{128 \times 10^{-24} N_A} \times N_A$$

$$= 2 \times 10^{24}$$

15. ***(b, c, d)***

(a) Nearest neighbour in the topmost layer of ccp structure is 9 thus, incorrect.

(b) Packing efficiency is 74% thus, correct.

(c) Tetrahedral voids = 2
Octahedral voids = 1 per atom thus, correct.

(d) For cubic close packed structure edge length,

$$a = \frac{4}{\sqrt{2}} r = 2\sqrt{2}r$$

Thus, correct.

16. ***(a)*** For ccp,

Z = number of oxygen atom

Number of octahedral voids = 4

$\therefore$ Number of tetrahedral voids $= 2 \times 4 = 8$

Number of Al^{3+} ion $= 4 \times m$

Number of Mg^{2+} ion $= 8 \times n$

Thus, the formula of the mineral is $Al_{4m}Mg_{8n}O_4$

$$4m(+3) + 8n(+2) + 4(-2) = 0$$

$$12m + 16n = 8$$

$$\Rightarrow \quad 3m + 4n = 2$$

So, the possible values of m and n are $\frac{1}{2}$ and $\frac{1}{8}$ respectively.

CHAPTER 4

Thermodynamics

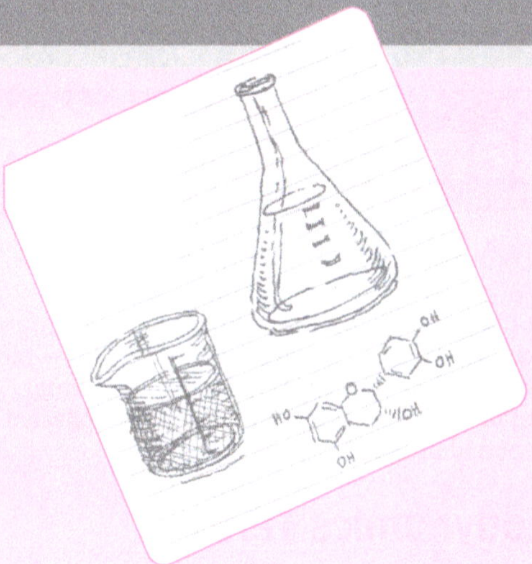

Learning Elements

Element 1 Fundamentals of Thermodynamics
Thermodynamics Terms, Thermodynamic Properties, The State of the System, Thermodynamic Equilibrium.

Element 2 First Law of Thermodynamics and Heat Capacity
Internal Energy, Enthalpy, Work, Heat, Heat Capacity, First Law of Thermodynamics, Carnot Cycle.

Element 3 Entropy and Second Law of Thermodynamics
Spontaneous Process or Spontaneity, Entropy, Entropy and Second Law of Thermodynamics, Entropy and Third Law of Thermodynamics, Gibb's Free Energy.

Element 4 Thermochemistry
Thermochemical Reactions and Equations, Enthalpy is a State Function, Enthalpies of Different Type of Reaction, Bond Energy or Bond Enthalpy, Hess's Law of Constant Heat Summation, Calorimetry.

Practice Elements

Practice Element 1 Target JEE Main
Practice Element 2 Target JEE Advanced

Trend Insights

JEE Main

	2024				2023				2022			
Topics	**E**	**M**	**T**	**O**	**E**	**M**	**T**	**O**	**E**	**M**	**T**	**O**
Fundamentals of Thermodynamics	–	–	–	–	–	2	–	2	1	–	–	1
First Law of Thermodynamics and Heat Capacity	–	1	6	7	–	–	3	3	–	1	3	4
Entropy and Second Law of Thermodynamics	–	1	4	5	1	–	3	4	1	1	1	3
Thermochemistry	–	1	8	9	–	–	12	12	–	–	13	13

E = Easy, **M** = Medium, **T** = Tough, **O** = Overall

Current Dynamics

- In recent years (2022 to 2024) overall weightage of this chapter has increased since 2022.
- Less number of questions involving fundamentals of thermodynamics were asked in previous years.
- Standard questions were asked from reaction related to enthalpies.
- The difficulty level of numerical value questions form reactions related to enthalpy and free energy change was increased in 2024 than the previous years.

JEE Advanced

Typology	Years				
	2024	**2023**	**2022**	**2021**	**2020**
1. Simple MCQs	–	–	–	–	–
2. One or More than one correct	–	–	–	1	1
3. Numerical Value/Integer	1	1	1	1, 1	1
4. Matching Type	–	–	–	–	–
5. Paragraph Based	–	1	–	–	–

Current Dynamics

- Mostly numerical value questions based on enthalpy calculation and heat absorbed were asked in recent year.
- Weightage of this chapter has remained constant in recent years.

Insightful Advice

- Focus on understanding how to use and manipulate Gibbs free energy, Helmholtz free energy and enthalpy for different chemical systems.
- Work on problems involving entropy changes during irreversible processes and heat transfer.
- Regularly solve previous year problems to reinforce these concepts and improve speed and accuracy.

Element 1 Fundamental of Thermodynamics

The subject of thermodynamics deals basically with the interaction of one body with another in terms of the quantities of heat and work. The entire formulation of thermodynamics is based on two fundamental laws which have been established on the basis of the experimental behaviour of macroscopic aggregates of matter, collected over a long period of time.

Thermodynamics Terms

In order to understand the transformation which are taking place with physical and chemical changes, we must understand some basic terms which are given below

System and Surroundings

The substance or mixture of substances under study in which a change occurs is called the **thermodynamic system** (or simply system). Everything else in the universe except system is called **surroundings**.

The region or interface separating the system from surrounding is called the **boundary**.

The system and the surroundings together constitute the universe.
System + Surrounding = Universe.

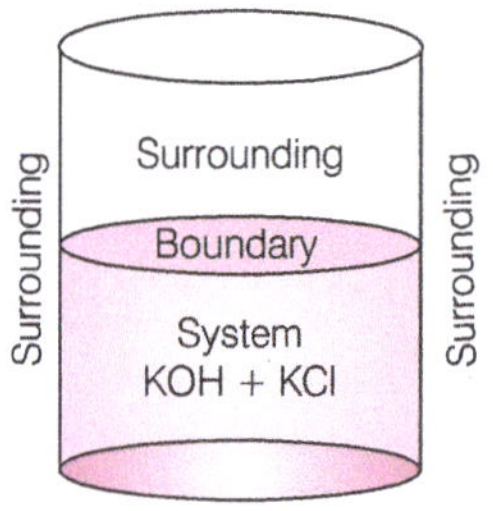

Types of System

On the basis of exchange of heat and matter between system and surroundings, they can be classified into three types

- **Open System** It can exchange both heat and matter with surroundings.
- **Closed System** It can exchange energy (as heat or work or both) but not the matter with surroundings.
- **Isolated System** It can neither exchange energy as heat and work nor matter with surroundings.

On the basis of composition, system can also be classified into following two types

(i) **Homogeneous System** A system composed a single phase, pure gas, pure liquid or pure solid.
Gaseous mixture is always one-phase system. For e.g.

$$2NH_3(g) \rightleftharpoons 3H_2(g) + N_2(g)$$

Since, all the components are in gaseous state. Hence, it is said to be one-state system.

(ii) **Heterogeneous System** A system composed of two or more phases. Mixture of matter in two or more than two different states as well as mixture having two or more solids is an example of heterogeneous system.

e.g $$CaCO_3(s) \rightleftharpoons CaO(s) + CO_2(g)$$

Thermodynamic Properties

Thermodynamics deals with macroscopic properties of matter.

The properties of the system which arise due to bulk behaviour of matter are called **macroscopic properties**.

These properties are always related by an equation of state e.g. $pV = nRT$ is an equation of state for gas. Macroscopic properties are; pressure, volume, mass, temperature, no. of moles, density etc. The macroscopic properties can be sub-divided into two types.

1. Intensive Properties

Those variables whose values on division remain the same in any part of the system are called **intensive variables**, These properties are independent of the quantity of matter in the system. e.g. temperature, pressure, concentration (molarity, normality), density, dipole, emf etc.

2. Extensive Properties

Those variables whose values in any part of the divided system are different from the entire system are called **extensive variables**. These properties depends on the quantity of matter present in the system. e.g. volume, energy, heat capacity.

JEE Spotlite

- An extensive property can be converted into intensive property when it is defined for unit amount of the substance.
  e.g. Mass per unit volume = density; $\left(d = \dfrac{m}{V}\right)$
- The ratio of two extensive properties indicates the intensive property.
  e.g. Density (Intensive) $= \dfrac{\text{Mass (extensive)}}{\text{Volume (extensive)}}$
- Intensive properties of a substance are non-additive in nature while extensive properties are additive in nature.

Thermodynamic Process

The operation by which a system changes from one state to another is called a **process**. A process is accompanied by change in energy (and matter also if system is open). Different types of process are defined below

(i) **Isothermal** If a process is taking place at constant temperature, it is said to be **isothermal** (iso-same, therm-heat, temperature) process. This is attained either by removing heat from the system or by supplying heat to the system, ($dT = 0$). The boundary will be diathermic.

(ii) **Isobaric** If a process is taking place at constant pressure, it is said to be **isobaric** process ($dp = 0$).

Mostly the closed boundary is flexible to maintain the pressure.

(iii) **Isochoric** If a process is taking place at constant volume, it is said to be **isochoric** process ($dV = 0$). i.e. boundary is rigid.

(iv) **Adiabatic** If no heat enters or leaves the system during any step of the process, it is said to be **adiabatic** process. The boundary is non-conducting i.e adiabatic boundary.

(v) **Cyclic Process** The process in which the system after undergone a number of different charges/process finally returns to its initial state, is called cyclic process.

(vi) **Reversible Process** A reversible process is a theoretical concept in thermodynamics where a system changes from one state to another in such a way that, if the process were reversed by the same path, the systems and 'its' surrounding would return to 'its' original state without any net changes.

The process occurs in infinite steps, allowing the system to return in thermodynamic equilibrium at all times (quasi-static system).

(vii) **Irreversible Process** An irreversible process is a thermodynamic process that cannot be reversed to restore the systems and surrounds to their original states without leaving a net change. e.g. If system is reversed in finite steps from same path, net work is not zero. During an irreversible process, the system move through finite steps.

The State of the System

The **thermodynamic state of a system** is defined by a set of conditions that completely specifies all the properties of the system. This set commonly includes the temperature, pressure, composition (identity and number of moles of each component), and physical state (gas, liquid, or solid) of each part of the system. Once the state has been specified, all other properties—both physical and chemical—are fixed.

State Function

A **state function** is a property of a system that depends only on its current state, not on the path taken to reach that state. State functions are essential in thermodynamics because they allow for the characterisation of systems without needing to know the history of how they arrived at their current condition.

Key Characteristics of State Functions

- The value of a state function is determined solely by the system's current state variables (like pressure, temperature and volume) and not by how the system got there.
- State functions provide information about the system's condition. Common example include

  Internal Energy (U), Enthalpy (H), Entropy (S), Gibbs Free Energy (G), Volume (V), Pressure (p)
- The cyclic integration involving a state function is zero.
- The state function has an exact differential, i.e. if $p = f(T, V)$ is a state function then

$$dp = \left(\frac{\partial p}{\partial t}\right)_V dT + \left(\frac{\partial p}{\partial V}\right)_T dV$$

with the condition that, $\frac{\partial}{\partial V}\left\{\left(\frac{\partial p}{\partial T}\right)_V\right\}_T = \frac{\partial}{\partial T}\left\{\left(\frac{\partial p}{\partial V}\right)_T\right\}_V$

JEE Quicker

Among internal energy (U), volume (V), heat (q) and enthalpy (H), the total number of state variables is 3 i.e. U, V and H.

JEE Main 2022

State variables are the variables that depend only on the initial or final state of the system. So, internal energy, volume and enthalpy are state variables. Heat is not a state variable, as it depends on the path taken during the process.

Path Function

The function that depend on the path followed are called path functions. e.g., work done, heat, etc. If q represents the heat, $q_1 \neq q_2$ (where, q_1 and q_2 are heat involved in two different paths).

Note Every path independent quantity is not necessary to be a state function but a state function is always path independent.

Thermodynamic Equilibrium

(Zeroth Law of Thermodynamics)

A system in which the macroscopic properties does not undergo any change with time is said to be in **thermodynamic equilibrium**. If there is net flow of heat from one portion of the system to another then system is said to be in **thermal equilibrium**. This is only possible if temperature remains constant throughout in all parts of the system. Two objects at different temperatures in thermal contact with each other tend to move towards the same temperature.

Zeroth law of thermodynamics states that if two objects in thermal equilibrium with the third one, they are in thermal equilibrium with each other. This law is also called law of thermal equilibrium.

Elemental Practice 4.1

Type I MCQs with Only One Correct Option

1. A system is said to be in thermodynamic equilibrium with the surroundings, if
   (a) it is only in thermal equilibrium with the surrounding.
   (b) it is in both thermal and chemical equilibrium with the surrounding.
   (c) it is in thermal, chemical as well as mechanical equilibrium with the surrounding.
   (d) it is in thermal and mechanical equilibrium, but not in chemical equilibrium with the surrounding.
2. Which of the following statement is true regarding pV, and T.
   (a) p and V are independent variables and T is dependent variable.
   (b) p and T are independent variable and V is dependent variable.
   (c) V and T are independent variables and p is dependent variable.
   (d) All are dependent as well as independent variables.
3. Out of the following which is not the set of intensive properties?
   (a) Boiling point, pH, molarity
   (b) Volume, area, length
   (c) Freezing point, elevation in boiling point, pressure
   (d) Refractive index, molality, density
4. Which of the following process is an example of reversible process?
   (a) Transfer of heat by radiation
   (b) Transfer of heat by conduction
   (c) Isothermal compression
   (d) Formation of curd from milk
5. Which of the following thermodynamic properties is not a macroscopic property?
   (a) Composition
   (b) Surface area enthalpy
   (c) Temperature
   (d) Collision frequency
6. The state of a gas can be described by quoting the relationship between
   (a) pressure, volume, temperature
   (b) temperature, amount, pressure
   (c) amount, volume, temperature
   (d) pressure, volume, temperature, amount
7. In thermodynamics, a process is called reversible when
   (a) surroundings and system change into each other
   (b) there is no boundary between system and surroundings
   (c) the surroundings are always in equilibrium with the system
   (d) the system changes into the surroundings spontaneously
8. Which of the following statement is correct?
   (a) The presence of reacting species in a covered beaker is an example of open system.
   (b) There is an exchange of energy as well as matter between the system and the surroundings in a closed system.
   (c) The presence of reactants in a closed vessel made up of copper is an example of a closed system.
   (d) The presence of reactants in a thermo flask or any other closed insulated vessel is an example of a open system.
9. Which of the following is incorrect statement?
   (a) Thermodynamics is concerned with mass change in a nuclear reactions.
   (b) At thermodynamic equilibrium, the macroscopic properties of a system do not change with time.
   (c) An isolated system is that system in which no exchange of energy and mass with surroundings.
   (d) Enthalpy is an extensive property.
10. Given below are two statements one is labelled as Assertion (A) and the other is labelled as Reason (R).
    Assertion (A) The heat absorbed during the isothermal expansion of an ideal gas against vacuum is zero.
    Reason (R) The volume occupied by the molecules of an ideal gas is negligible.
    In the light of the above statements, choose the most appropriate answer from the options given below.
    (a) Both (A) and (R) are correct and (R) is the correct explanation of (A).
    (b) Both (A) and (R) are correct but (R) is not the correct explanation of (A).
    (c) (A) is false but (R) is true.
    (d) (A) is true but (R) is false.
11. Which of the following is not an endothermic process?
    (a) Combustion of glucose
    (b) Decomposition of water
    (c) Dehydrogenation of ethane to ethene
    (d) Conversion of graphite to diamond
12. An ideal gas undergoes an adiabatic process. Which of the following statement is correct for the process?
    (a) The internal energy of the gas increases as it expands.
    (b) The temperature of the gas increases during expansion.
    (c) The work done by the gas is equal to the change in the enthalpy.
    (d) The relationship between pressure and volume is given by pV^{γ} = constant, where γ is the adiabatic index.
13. A gaseous system changes from state $A(p_1, V_1, T_1)$ to $B(p_2, V_2, T_2)$, B to $C(p_3, V_3, T_3)$ and finally from C to A. The whole process may be called—
    (a) reversible process (b) cyclic process
    (c) isobaric process (d) spontaneous process
14. p-V plots for two gases during adiabatic process are shown in fig. Plot 1 and 2 should correspond to respectively.

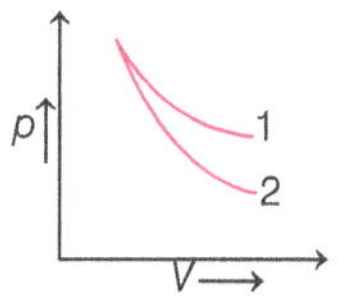

(a) He and O_2 (b) O_2 and He (c) He and Ar (d) O_2 and N_2

15. Which of the following is an example of open system?
(a) A well stoppered thermo flask containing some ice cubes.
(b) A calorimeter
(c) Some amount of hot water enclosed in a closed container which is not insulated.
(d) Warming ammonium chloride with sodium hydroxide in a test tube.

Type II 》 MCQs with One or More than One Correct Option

16. Select the incorrect statements from the following.
(a) A system may be a complex as a human body or as simple as a mixture consisting of a drop of water.
(b) A system is said to be macroscopic when it consists of large number of molecules, atoms or ions.
(c) Pressure, volume, temperature and surface area are some macroscopic properties.
(d) The internal energy of the system does not change when matter enters or leaves the system.
(e) The state of a thermodynamic system can not described by its measurable or macroscopic properties.

17. Which of the following statements are correct?
(a) Only a state function may be expressed as difference in its value at two states in any process.
(b) A process cannot be defined on the basis of initial and final states of the system.
(c) In a cyclic process, the internal energy of the system remains constant throughout.
(d) During irreversible process, the equation $pV = nRT$ is not applicable to ideal gas.

18. Which of the following statements are correct?
(a) When the system returns to its original condition, the overall change in a state function is zero.
(b) When a gas expands, work energy is released, hence work done is negative and is done by the system.
(c) In this Δn_g = zero, hence no work is done.

$$C(s) + CO_2(g) \longrightarrow 2CO(g)$$

(d) $2SO_2(g) + O_2(g) \longrightarrow 2SO_3(g)$; in this case work is done on the system.

19. Which of the following is/are state function?
(a) Internal energy (b) Temperature
(c) Volume (d) Enthalpy

20. Which of the following statement is correct?
(a) Work is a state function.
(b) Entropy is a state function.
(c) Change in the state is completely defined when the initial and final states are specified.
(d) Refractive index is an intensive property.

Type III 》 Numerical/Integer Answer Type Questions

21. The total number of non-additive properties from the following is ....
Boiling point, molarity, heat capacity, free energy, density, pressure, molar mass, mole

22. The number of examples for isobaric process is/are
(i) water heating in a pressure cooker.
(ii) thermal expansion of a gas in a balloon.
(iii) boiling of liquid at constant pressure.
(iv) heating of gas in a rigid container.
(v) combustion in a closed chamber.

23. Consider the following properties.

$$q, H, E, G, w$$

The total number of properties which are a path function is......

24. Among the following the total number of state function are
Gibbs free, irreversible expansion work, molar enthalpy, density, pressure.

25. Consider the following properties.
(a) Boiling point (b) Gibbs free energy
(c) Entropy (d) Surface tension
(e) pH (f) Pressure
(g) EMF of a cell (h) Density
The total number of extensive properties are ....

Elemental Practice 4.1 | Chapter 04
Connect with **Answers**

1. (c)	**2.** (b)	**3.** (b)	**4.** (c)	**5.** (d)	**6.** (d)
7. (c)	**8.** (c)	**9.** (a)	**10.** (b)	**11.** (a)	**12.** (d)
13. (b)	**14.** (b)	**15.** (d)	**16.** (d,e)	**17.** (a,c,d)	**18.** (a,b,d)
19. (a,b,c,d)	**20.** (b,c,d)	**21.** (5)	**22.** (3)	**23.** (2)	**24.** (4)
25. (2)					

Element 2

First Law of Thermodynamics and Heat Capacity

Internal Energy (U or E)

The total energy stored in a substance by virtue of its chemical nature and state is called it's internal energy. i.e. It is the sum of it's translation, vibrational, rotational, chemical bond, electronic energy, nuclear energy of constituent atoms and potential energy due to interaction with neighbouring molecules. It is also called intrinsic energy.

$$E = E_t + E_r + E_v + E_e + E_n + E_{PE}.$$

Internal energy is state function. It's absolute value can't be determined. However change in internal energy can be determined experimentally using bomb calorimetre under certain condition.

For a given substance internal energy depends on

- The quantity of substance.
- Chemical nature.
- Temperature, pressure and volume.

Energy for a closed system (where n is constant can be written as a function of temperature and volume i.e. $E = f(T, V)$

$$dE = \left(\frac{\partial E}{\partial T}\right)_V dT + \left(\frac{\partial E}{\partial V}\right)_T dV$$

(no attractive or repulsive forces are considered under ideal condition between gas molecules)

for ideal gas, $\left(\frac{\partial E}{\partial V}\right)_T = 0$

JEE Alert

- Change in internal energy for cyclic process is zero.
- It is an extensive property.

The internal energy of a system can change when

- heat passes into or out of the system.
- work is done on or by the system.
- matter enters or leaves the system.

Enthalpy

A new state function, enthalpy was introduced to relate the energy changes at constant pressure condition. Enthalpy is a thermodynamic function of the state variables i.e. 'H' is a state function, generally pressure and temperature.

Change in enthalpy for a given change of state is independent of the path and the change is zero for any cyclic process. It is an extensive property.

$$H = E + pV.$$

$$(dH) = q_p$$

Enthalpy change is equal to the heat exchanged by the system at constant pressure.

Relation between ΔH and ΔE

$$\Delta H = \Delta E + (p_2V_2 - p_1V_1)$$

(i) At constant pressure :

$$\Delta H = \Delta E + p(V_2 - V_1)$$

$$\Delta H = \Delta E + p\Delta V$$

(ii) When mole of gases is constant during expansion or compression :

$$\Delta H = \Delta E + (n_2RT_2 - n_1RT_1)$$

$$\Delta H = \Delta E + (nRT_2 - nRT_1)$$

$$\Delta H = \Delta E + nR\Delta T$$

(ii) In chemical reactions temperature is constant :

$$\Delta H = \Delta E + (\Delta n_g RT)$$

Δn_g = coefficient of gaseous product-coefficient of gaseous reaction.

$$\Delta H = nC_v\Delta T + (nR\Delta T) \Rightarrow \Delta H = nC_p\Delta T$$

$\therefore$ $\Delta H = q$ (at constant volume)

Under standard states when temperature is 298 K and pressure is 1 atm and all the species present are at unit activity.

$$\Delta H^\circ = \Delta E^\circ + \Delta n_g RT$$

Better way to specify standard states is to write temperature also

$$\Delta H^\circ_{298\text{ K}} = \Delta E^\circ_{298\text{ K}} + \Delta n_g R(298\text{ K})$$

and ΔH° etc., is to specify the temperature other than 298 K but at 1 atm and all the species at unit activity.

Work

By work, we mean work done by the system or on the system. It can be defined as the action/displacement of system against the force originating from surroundings and acting on the boundary of the system. Work is a mode of energy transfer to or from a system with reference to the surroundings or change the internal energy of the system.

- The SI unit of work is Joule (J).
- The SI convention is to take the work done on the system as the positive quantity whereas the work done by the system is taken as the negative quantity.

Expression for *p*-*V* Work

It is the work involve when the gas contracts or expands against the external pressure. To understand, this consider a cylinder containing gas fitted with a piston. The piston is assumed to be weightless and frictionless.

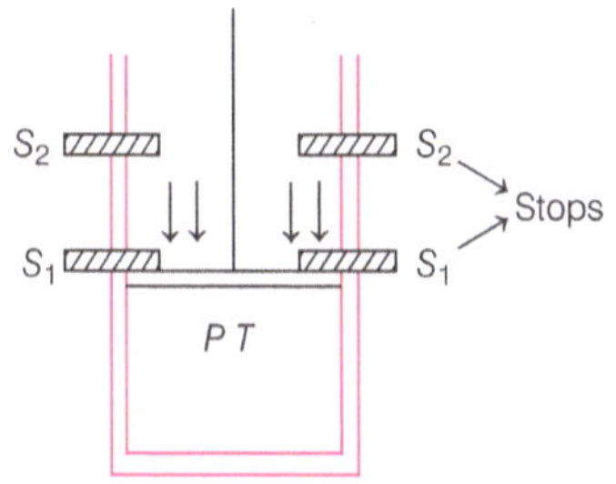

Process of expansion of a gas

If m is the mass that is put on the piston, then the force F acting downwards is $F = mg$ and the pressure acting downwards $p_{ext} = \frac{F}{A} = \frac{mg}{A}$ where A is the area of cross section of the piston.

- If the external pressure is greater than the internal pressure of the system, the piston moves downward. The volume of the system will decrease and it continues to decrease till the external pressure becomes equal to the internal pressure of the system.
- If the external pressure is smaller than the internal pressure, the piston moves upward resulting in expansion. Again, the volume will continue to increase till the external pressure becomes equal to the internal pressure. In the later, the external pressure may be different in each stage.

By definition, the work involved is given by:

$w = -$ (External force) (Distance through which piston moves)

(External pressure = force/Area)

or $w = -$ Pressure (Area of cross section) × (Distance through which piston moved)

or $w = p_{ext}(\Delta V)$ (ΔV = area × distance which piston moved)

where ΔV is the change in volume of the system. If the piston moves by an infinitesimal amount, the work involved is given by

$$dw = -p_{ext} dV$$

Work Done in Irreversible Process

If the volume of the system changes by a finite quantity from volume V_1 to V_2, then total work done w can be obtained as

$$= -p_{ex}(V_2 - V_1)$$
$$= -p_{ex}\Delta V \qquad \text{(In general, } \Delta V = V_f - V_i\text{)}$$

If the external pressure (p_{ex}) is slightly more than the pressure of the gas, the gas will contract. In that case, ΔV is negative and the work will be done by the surroundings on the system.

$$\therefore \qquad w = p\Delta V$$

Isothermal Reversible Process

The expression for the work involved in an isothermal expansion or compression from volume V_1 to V_2 can be worked out as follows:

Since, $dw = -p_{opp}dV$, therefore

$$w = -\int_{V_1}^{V_2} p_{opp} dV$$

In the reversible change of volume, the opposite pressure differs from the pressure of the gas by an infinitesimal amount, i.e., $p_{opp} = p_{int} \pm dp$

Where, + ve and – ve signs are meant for compression and expansion processes, respectively. Substituting this in the previous expression, we get

$$w = -\int_{V_1}^{V_2} (p_{int} \pm dp)\, dV = -\int_{V_1}^{V_2} p_{int} dV \pm \int_{V_1}^{V_2} dp\, dV$$

The second integration can be neglected, since it is the product of two infinitesimal small differentials. For gas, p_{int} is given by

$$p_{int} = \frac{nRT}{V}$$

With this the previous expression becomes

$$w = -\int_{V_1}^{V_2} \frac{nRT}{V} dV$$

Since temperature remains constant in an isothermal process, the work done is

$$w = -nRT \int_{V_1}^{V_2} \frac{dV}{V} = -nRT \ln \frac{V_2}{V_1}$$

In terms of pressure, we have

$$w = -nRT \ln \frac{p_1}{p_2}$$

Graphical Representation of Isothermal Process of a Gas

Isothermal Irreversible Process

The graph showing isothermal irreversible process are given below

Expansion

- **Expansion in One Stage** Let an isothermal expansion take place from V' to V'' against a constant external pressure p_{ext} and let p' and p'' be the respective pressures of the system at these two stages. The magnitude of the work involved is given by the shaded area in the p-V diagram.

  (For complete expansion or compression p_{ext} = final pressure of gas)

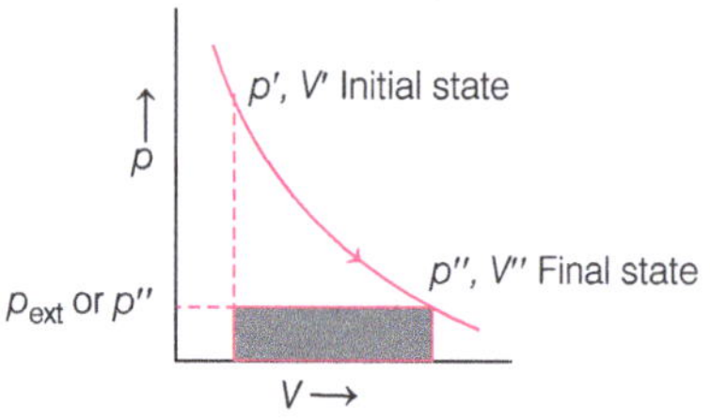

Expansion of a gas against a constant pressure

- **Expansion in Two Stages** If the above expansion is done in many stages, the magnitude of the work involved will be more than that involved in the one-stage expansion. This is evident from the graph in figure where the magnitude of the work involved in a two-stage expansion is shown by the shaded area.

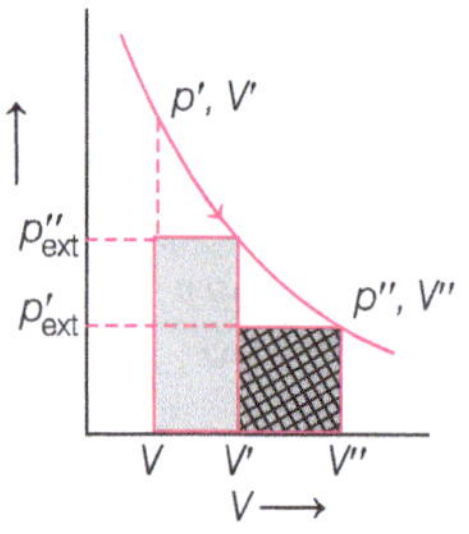

Expansion is two stages

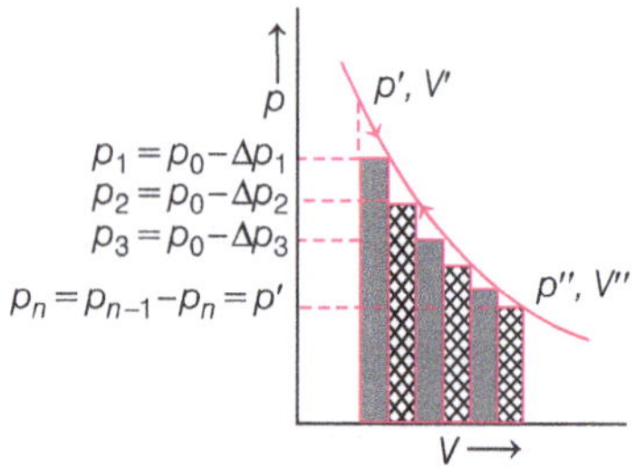

Expansion in many stages

Compression

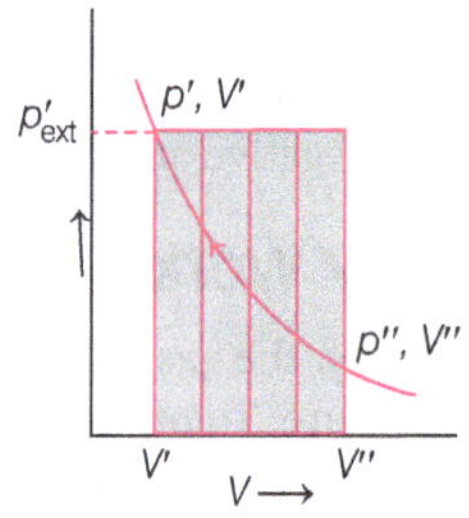

Compression in one stage

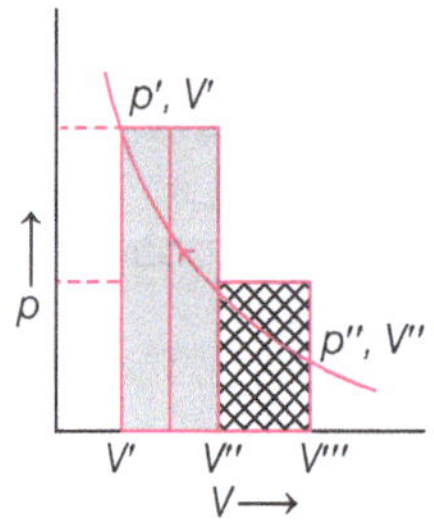

Compression two stage

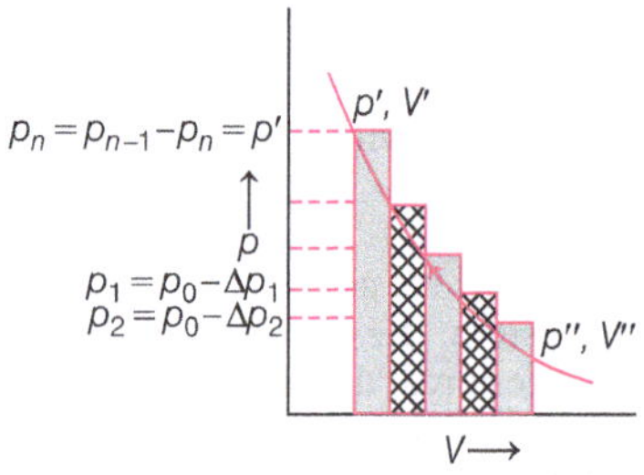

Compression in many stages

Isothermal Reversible Process

The graph showing isothermal reversible expansion and compression given below

Expansion

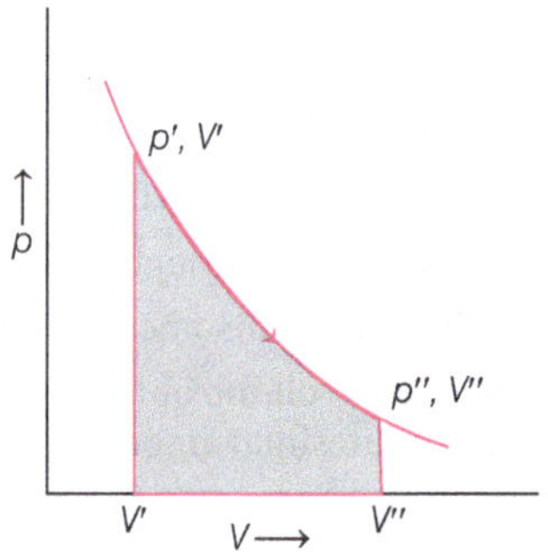

Expansion involving infinite number of stages

Compression

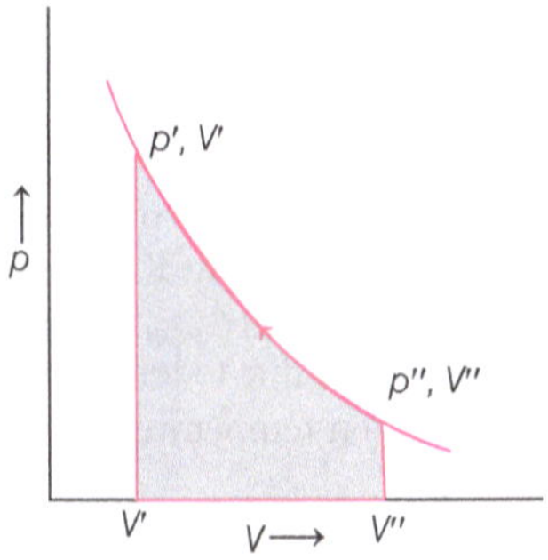

Compression involving infinite number of stages

Free Expansion

Expansion of a gas in vacuum ($p_{ex} = 0$) is called free expansion. No work is done during free expansion of an ideal gas whether the process is reversible or irreversible, $W = p_{ex}\Delta V = 0$.

JEE Spotlite

(i) Work involved in reversible expansion is greater than the work involved in irreversible expansion to same final volume.

(ii) Work involved in reversible compression is less than the work of compression in irreversible process to same extent.

(iii) In case of reversible cyclic process following same paths both for expansion and compression, net work is zero.

$$\oint w_{cycle} = 0$$

(iv) In case of irreversible cyclic process following same paths both for expansion and compression, net work is not equal to zero.

$$\oint w_{cycle} \neq 0$$

- Work expansion against vacuum is zero.
- Work compression against vacuum in not zero.

Polytropic Process

A polytropic process is a thermodynamic process that follows the relationship

$$pV^n = \text{constant}$$

where,

- p is the pressure,
- V is the volume.
- n is the polytropic index, which characterises the specific process.

The value of n determines the nature of the process:

- $n = 0$: Isobaric process (constant pressure)
- $n = 1$: Isothermal process (constant temperature)
- $n = \gamma$ (ratio of specific heats, C_p / C_v) Adiabatic reversible process (no heat transfer)
- $n = \infty$ Isochoric process (constant volume)

For a polytropic process, the relationship pV^n = constant can be expanded into various forms:

To derive the work done during a polytropic reversible process, we start from the relationship between pressure, volume, and the polytropic index n.

Work Done in a Polytropic Process

The work done W during a polytropic process from state 1 to state 2 can be expressed mathematically as:

$$W = -\int_{V_1}^{V_2} p\, dV$$

$$pV^n = \text{constant},$$

This integral becomes

$$W = -C\int_{V_1}^{V_2} V^{-n} dV$$

The integral of V^{-n} (for $n \neq 1$) is: $\int V^{-n} dV = \dfrac{V^{1-n}}{1-n} + \text{constant}$

Thus, we have

$$W = C\left[\frac{V^{1-n}}{1-n}\right]_{V_1}^{V_2}$$

Substituting the limits gives: $W = -C\left(\dfrac{V_2^{1-n}}{1-n} + \dfrac{V_1^{1-n}}{1-n}\right)$

This simplifies to

$$W = \frac{-C}{1-n}(V_2^{1-n} - V_1^{1-n})$$

Expressing in Terms of Pressure and Temperature

Now substituting back for C: $W = \dfrac{pV^n}{n-1}(V_2^{1-n} - V_1^{1-n})$

Alternatively, we can express this using pressures instead of volumes:

$$W = \frac{1}{n-1}(p_2V_2 - p_1V_1)\ (n \neq 1)$$

Heat

Heat is the energy that is transferred between a system and its surroundings because of the temperature difference between them. Heat flows from higher temperature to lower temperature. Its **SI unit is Joule (J).**

Heat and work are not state variables, they are two modes of energy transfer that could change the internal energy of the system.

According to SI convention, heat absorbed by the system is regarded as the positive quantity, whereas the heat released by the system is regarded as the negative quantity. To be more specific, the following alternate statements having the same meaning may be taken.

Heat involved = x kJ

heat absorbed by the system = x kJ

or heat released by the system = $-x$ kJ

Heat Capacity

It is the heat required to raise the temperature by unit degree Celsius or Kelvin for the given mass of the substance. It is an extensive property. It's unit is J/ ℃ or J/K

$$C = \frac{q}{\Delta T}$$

where, C represents the heat capacity.

Specific Heat Capacity

It is the heat required to raise the temperature by unit ℃ or Kelvin for unit mass of the substance. It is intensive property and unit is $JK^{-1}\ kg^{-1}$.

$$C = \frac{q}{m\Delta T},$$

where, q = heat required to raise the temperature by 1℃ or 1 K

C_s = specific heat capacity, m = mass

ΔT = temperature change (in ℃ or K)

Molar Heat Capacity

It is the heat required to raise the temperature by unit degree celsicus or Kelvin for one mole of the substance. It is an intensive property. Its SI unit is $JK^{-1}\ mol^{-1}$.

$$q = C_m \cdot n\Delta T \Rightarrow C_m = \frac{q}{n\Delta T}$$

where, n = number of moles and

C_m = molar heat capacity.

JEE Alert

Since q depends on the path, the molar heat capacity is also path dependent quantity.

Molar Heat Capacity at Constant Volume (Isochoric Process) The amount of heat required to raise the temperature of one mole of a gas by one degree at constant volume. It is measured when the system is at constant volume.

$$C_{v,m} = \left(\frac{q_V}{n\Delta T}\right) \text{or} \left(\frac{\Delta E}{n\Delta T}\right)_V$$

Heat Capacity at Constant Pressure (Isobaric Process) The amount of heat required to raise the temperature of one mole of a gas by one degree at constant pressure.

$$C_{p,m} = \frac{q_P}{n\Delta T} \text{ or } \left(\frac{\Delta H}{n\Delta T}\right)_p$$

Relation between $C_{p,m}$ and $C_{V,m}$

The difference between $C_{p,m}$ and $C_{V,m}$ will be the heat lost because of work of expansion for one mole of the gas when temperature is raised by unit degree Celsius.

$C_{p,m} - C_{V,m}$ = work of expansion for one mole of the gas when temperature is raised by unit Kelvin or degree celsius.

- For solids and liquids $C_{p,m}$ and $C_{V,m}$ are approximately same (expansion can be ignored due to temperature increase).
- Work of expansion when temperature is raised by 1°C for 1 mole of an ideal gas

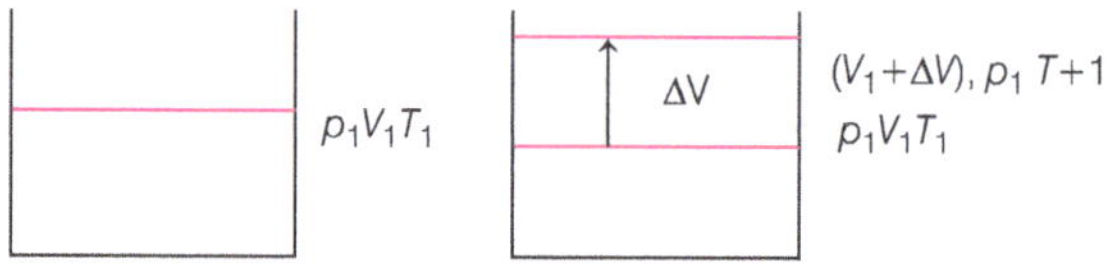

1 mole of the gas

$p_1V_1 = RT_1$

$p_1(V_1 + \Delta V) = R(T + 1)$

$p_1V_1 + p\Delta V = RT + R$

$p\Delta V = R$

$$C_p - C_V = R$$ for ideal gas.

C_p is Greater than C_V

Some of the heat supplied at constant pressure utilised in expansion and remaining heat utilised in increasing the temperature. Whereas heat supplied at constant volume is only utilised in increasing the temperature. That's why heat supplied at constant pressure must be higher to raise the temperature by same range as in constant volume condition.

Temperature Dependence of Heat Capacity

When the starting temp is low, the heat capacity is less and when the starting temperature is high, the heat capacity is higher because the material can absorb more heat due to more degree of freedom without significant change in temperature. It is convenient to define the heat capacity of the gas by the following empirical relation.

$$C_p = a + bT + cT^2 + dT^3 \ldots$$

a, b, c are constant and T is the absolute temperature.

$$dH = nC_p dT$$

$$\int dH = \int_{T_1}^{T_2} n(a + bT + cT^2 \ldots)\, dT$$

JEE Spotlite

- The degree of freedom of a system refers to a the number of independent ways in which the system can store energy. (Translational, rotational, vibrational)
- The ratio of C_p and C_V is equal to γ. The value of γ depends upon the atomicity of the gaseous molecule.

  For monoatomic gases $\gamma = 1.66$

  For diatomic gases $\gamma = 1.4$

  For triatomic gases $\gamma = 1.33$

JEE MAPPER

Example Similar to PYQ Asked in JEE Advanced 2024

Consider the following volume—temperature (V-T) diagram for the expansion of 6 moles of an ideal monoatomic gas.

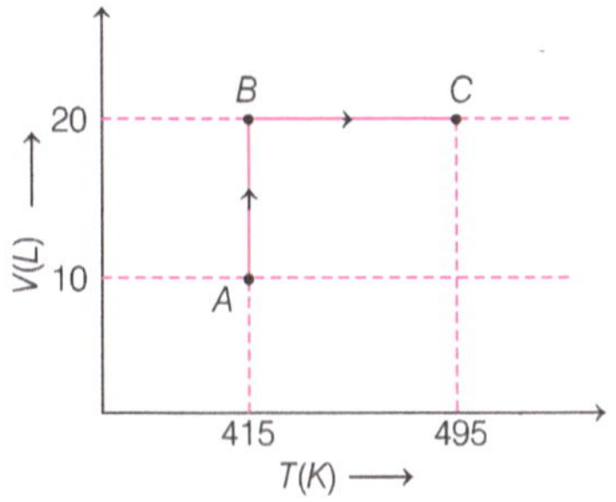

Considering only p-V work is involved, the total change in enthalpy (in Joule) for the transformation of state in the sequence A → B → C is ....

[Use the given data: Molar heat capacity of the gas for the given temperature range, $C_{v,m} = 14\,JK^{-1}\,mol^{-1}$ and $R = 8.3\,JK^{-1}\,mol^{-1}$]

Sol. (10704) Given, $n = 6$ mol

$C_{v,m} = 14\,JK^{-1}\,mol^{-1}$, $R = 8.3\,JK^{-1}\,mol^{-1}$, $T_2 = 495$ K

$T_1 = 415$ K, $V_2 = 20$ L, $V_1 = 10$ L

From the graph it is clear that $A \to B$ is an isothermal process ($dT = 0$)

So, $\Delta H_{A\to B} = nC_p dT = 0$

Also, $B \to C$ is an isochoric process.

$$\Delta U_{B\to C} = nC_V dT$$

$$\Delta U_{B\to C} = 6 \times 14 \times (495 - 415) \Rightarrow \Delta U_{B\to C} = 6720\,J$$

$$\Delta H_{B\to C} = \Delta U_{B\to C} + \Delta(PV)$$

$$\Delta H_{B\to C} = \Delta U_{B\to C} + nR\Delta T$$

$$= 6720 + (6 \times 8.3 \times 80) = 6720 + 3984$$

$$\Delta H_{B\to C} = 10704\,J$$

Competency Enhancer 2.1

One mole of an ideal monoatomic gas undergoes two reversible process ($X \to Y$ and $Y \to Z$) as shown in the given figure.

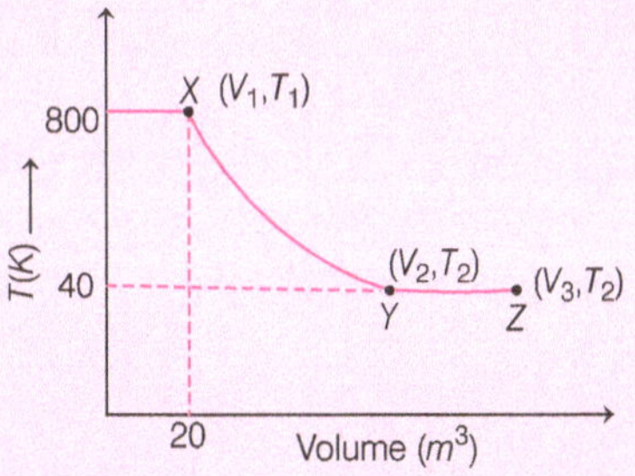

$X \to Y$ is an adiabatic process. If the total heat absorbed in the entire process ($X \to Y$ and $Y \to Z$) is $RT_2 \ln 20$, the value of $5\log V_3$ is .... (Nearest integer)

[Use, molar heat capacity of the gas at constant pressure, $C_{p,m} = 5/2R$]

First Law of Thermodynamics

"Energy may be converted from one form to another, but it is impossible to create or destroy it."

The principle of conservation of energy has been universely accepted as a basic law of nature and is retitled as the first law of thermodynamics.

Mathematical Formulation of The First Law

If a system is present in particular thermodynamic state say 'A' it has fixed amount of internal energy U_A. Suppose by a process the system is taken from state A to state B. In the process 'q' heat is involved with the system and w work involved with the system. Thus in the state 'B' total internal energy of system become

$$E_B = E_A + q + w \Rightarrow E_B - E_A = q + w$$

$$\Delta E = q + w \Rightarrow \Delta E = q - p\Delta V$$

Applications First Law of Thermodynamics

- **If Change is Cyclic** (reversible), $\Delta E = 0$, hence

$$q = -W = p\Delta V = pdV\ (W = -p\Delta V)$$

The net heat is lost to work,

- **If change is isothermal**

$$\Delta E = q + w \quad \text{since } \Delta E = 0$$

$$q = -w$$

(i) Isothermal expansion against constant external pressure.

$$w = -p_{ext}(V_2 - V_1) = -p_{ext}\left(\frac{nRT}{p_2} - \frac{nRT}{p_1}\right)$$

Since $\Delta T = 0$

$$\Delta E = nC_V(T_2 - T_1) = 0$$

$$\Delta H = nC_p(T_2 - T_1) = 0$$

(ii) Isothermal reversible expansion

$$dE = q + w,\quad dE = 0,\quad q = -w$$

(ii) Isothermal free expansion

Since $p_{ext} = 0$, $w = 0$, $\Delta E = 0$, $q = 0$, $\Delta H = 0$

$$\Delta H = nC_p dT = 0$$

$$\Delta E = nC_v dT = 0$$

- **If Change is Isochoric**, $V_i = V_f$

∴ $\Delta V = (V_f - V_i) = 0$

hence, $W = p\Delta V = 0$

by equation $\Delta E = q + W$

$\Delta E = q$

heat absorbed will only bring a change in internal energy.

- **If Change is Adiabatic,** $q = 0$, by equation $\Delta E = q + W$

$$\Delta E = W$$

(i) Reversible adiabatic expansion
In such cases work in done at the cost of internal energy.
If gas expands, W has negative sign, hence internal energy decreases causing decrease in temperature of the system.

$$W = -\Delta E = -C_V(T_2 - T_1) = C_V T_1\left(1 - \frac{T_2}{T_1}\right)$$

$$= C_V T_1\left[1 - \left(\frac{V_1}{V_2}\right)^{\gamma - 1}\right]$$

$$W = -\frac{(p_1V_1 - p_2V_2)}{(\gamma - 1)}$$

where, $\gamma = \dfrac{C_p}{C_V}$ and T_1 and T_2 are temperature $(T_2 < T_1)$.

Cooling takes place on adiabatic expansion of the gas. If gas compresses, W has positive sign, hence internal energy increases causing increase in temperature of the system. **System gets warmed on adiabatic compression of the gas.**

(ii) Adiabatic irreversible expansion

$$\Delta E = nC_v(T_2 - T_1) = W$$
$$\Delta H = nC_p(T_2 - T_1)$$

Since, $W_{rev} > W_{irr}$ in expansion, more cooling in reversible adiabatic expansion is observed.

(iii) Adiabatic free expansion $q = 0$, $w = 0$ $\Delta E = 0$, $\Delta n = 0$
No temperature change.

- **If Change is Isobaric** An isobaric process is a thermodynamic process in which the pressure remains constant.

$$\Delta E = nC_v(T_2 - T_1) \Rightarrow \Delta n = nC_p(T_2 - T_1) = q_p$$
$$w = -P_{ext}(V_2 - V_1)$$

Comparison between Reversible Work of Expansion (Isothermal and Adiabatic)

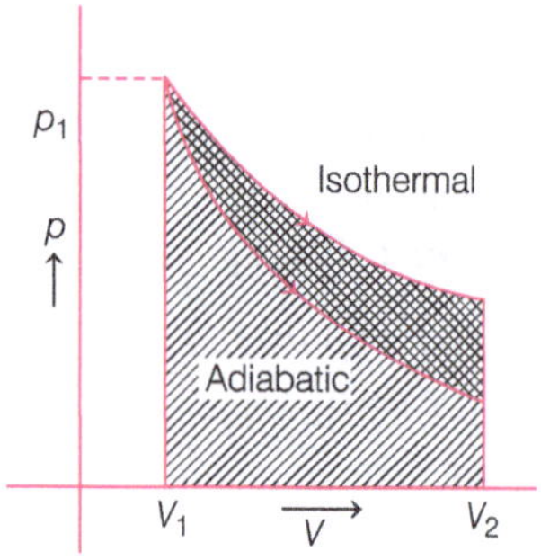

$|w|_{iso} > |w|_{Adia.}$

Expansion to same final volume.

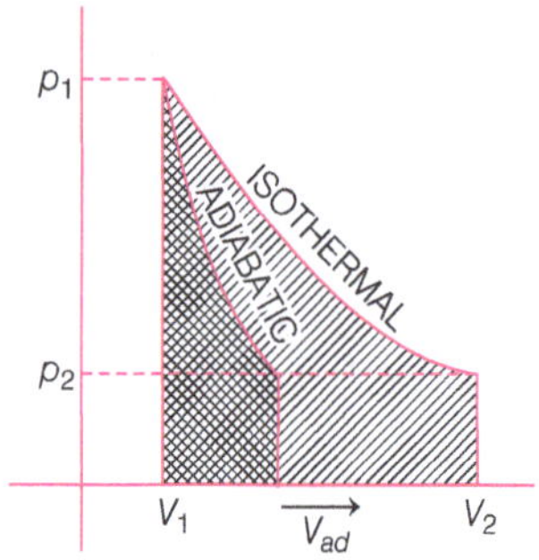

$|w|_{iso} > |w|_{Adia.}$

Work of expansion with the final pressure.

Equation of State in Adiabatic Process

If gas compresses, W has positive sign, hence internal energy increases causing increase in temperature of the system. System gets warmed on adiabatic compression of the gas.

Also, $\left(\dfrac{\Delta E}{\Delta T}\right)_V = C_V =$ molar heat capacity at constant volume

$\therefore \qquad \Delta E = C_V\Delta T = C_V dT$

$\Rightarrow \qquad W = -pdV$

and for adiabatic change

$$\Delta E = W$$

$\therefore \qquad C_V dT = -pdV \left(p = \dfrac{RT}{V}\right)$

$$C_V dT = -\frac{RT}{V}dV$$

$\therefore \qquad \dfrac{C_V}{R}\dfrac{dT}{T} = -\dfrac{dV}{V}$

In going from state I to state II as shown, above equation on integration gives.

$$\int_{T_1}^{T_2}\frac{dT}{T} = -\frac{R}{C_V}\int_{V_1}^{V_2}\frac{dV}{V}$$

$$\log\left(\frac{T_2}{T_1}\right) = -\frac{R}{C_V}\log\frac{V_2}{V_1} = \left(\frac{C_p - C_V}{C_V}\right)\log\left(\frac{V_1}{V_2}\right)$$

$$= \left(\frac{C_p}{C_V} - 1\right)\log\left(\frac{V_1}{V_2}\right) = (\gamma - 1)\log\left(\frac{V_1}{V_2}\right)$$

$$\log\left(\frac{T_2}{T_1}\right) = \log\left(\frac{V_1}{V_2}\right)^{\gamma - 1}$$

$\therefore \qquad \left(\dfrac{T_2}{T_1}\right) = \left(\dfrac{V_1}{V_2}\right)^{\gamma - 1}$

i.e, $\qquad T_2V_2^{\gamma-1} = T_1V_1^{\gamma-1}$

Also, $\qquad \dfrac{RT_2}{RT_1} = \dfrac{p_2V_2}{p_1V_1}$

$$\therefore \quad \frac{T_2}{T_1} = \frac{p_2V_2}{p_1V_1} \Rightarrow \frac{p_2V_2}{p_1V_1} = \left(\frac{V_1}{V_2}\right)^{\gamma - 1}$$

$$\therefore \quad p_1V_1^{\gamma} = p_2V_2^{\gamma}$$

or under adiabatic condition $p \propto \frac{1}{V^{\gamma}}$

Similarly, $p^{(1-x)}T^{\gamma}$ = constant

Thus, variation of p with V can be compared under adiabatic and isothermal conditions in figure.

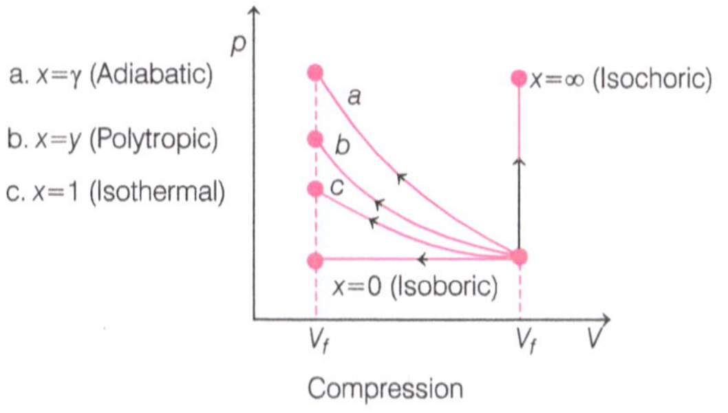

Comparison of p-V variation in isothermal, adiabatic and polytropic process.

JEE Spotlite

- For same extent of expansion from same initial state:
  (a) $p_{iso(final)} > p_{adi\ (final)}$
  (b) $\Delta p_{iso} < \Delta p_{adia}$
- For same extent of compression from same initial state.
  (a) $p_{adia\ final} > p_{iso\ final}$
  (b) $\Delta p_{adia} > \Delta p_{iso}$

Limitation

(i) First law of thermodynamics relates heat absorbed to work done ($\Delta U = q + W$) but it puts no restriction on the direction of flow of heat.

(ii) First law predicts that energy of an isolated system remains constant during a specified change of state; but it is unable to predict the type of specified change-physical or chemical can occur spontaneously or not.

(iii) First law predicts that energy of one form can be converted into equivalent amount of energy of another form. However, it is unable to predict that heat energy cannot be completely converted into an equivalent amount of work. Systems are not perfectly efficient.

(iv) Limitations of first law of thermodynamics led to second law of thermodynamics based on Carnot's cycle and entropy.

Carnot Cycle

It is a reversible engine comprises to four individual states two of expansion and two of compression, such that after these processes, engine returns to its original state.

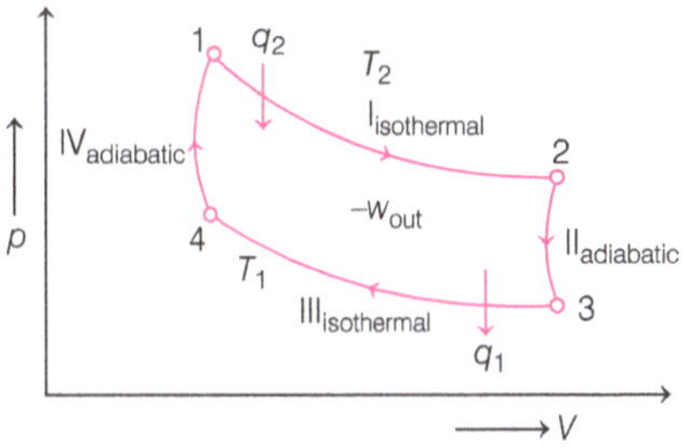

Let q_2 be the heat absorbed by the engine from the source of heat at T_2 and $-q_1$ be the heat lost to the sink (surroundings) at $T_1 (T_2 > T_1)$.

Hence, efficiency of the Carnot engine $= \frac{\text{work}}{\text{heat absorbed}}$

$$\eta = \frac{q_2 - q_1}{q_2}$$

It can also be proved that, $\eta = \frac{T_2 - T_1}{T_2} = \frac{q_2 - q_1}{q_2}$

$$\eta = 1 - \frac{T_1}{T_2} = 1 - \frac{q_2}{q_1} \Rightarrow \frac{q_1}{T_1} - \frac{q_2}{T_2} = 0$$

Since, $T_2 > T_1$, hence $\eta < 1$. Thus, it is impossible to convert heat into equivalent amount of work without compensation.

- If $T_1 = 0$ K (i.e. -273°C), then $\eta = 1$. Thus, engine is 100% efficient at -273°C (0 K). Since, temperature of 0 K (-273°C) cannot be attained practically, hence it is not possible to convert heat into equivalent amount of work.
- Greater the difference between T_2 and T_1 greater the value of η.

Elemental Practice 4.2

Type I MCQs with Only One Correct Option

1. A balloon containing air at 27°C and 1 bar initially is filled with air further, isothermally and reversibly till the pressure is 4 bar. If the initial diameter of the balloon is 1 m and the pressure at each stage is proportional to diameter of balloon, the magnitude of work done is
(a) -2.1×10^5 J (b) -1.17×10^6 J
(c) -3×10^4 J (d) -1×10^7 J

2. 5 moles of an ideal gas at 27° C are allowed to expand isothermally from an initial pressure of 10.0 atm to a final pressure of 4.0 atm against a constant external pressure of 1.0 atm. Thus, work done will be
(a) − 1870.6 J (b) + 1870.6 J
(c) − 18.47 J (d) + 18.47 J

3. 1.0 mole of a monoatomic ideal gas is expanded from state I to state II at 300 K.

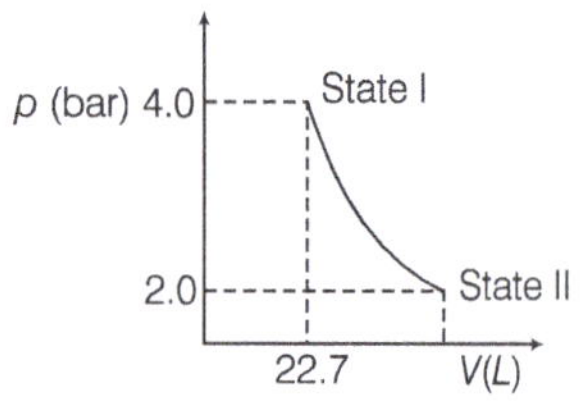

Thus, work done is
(a) − 1729 J (b) + 1729 J
(c) − 75.8 J (d) 17.07 J

4. During an adiabatic expansion, a gas obeys $VT^3 =$ constant. The gas must be
(a) monoatomic (b) diatomic
(c) polyatomic (d) never be polyatomic

5. One mole of an ideal mono-atomic gas at 27°C expands reversibly and adiabatically from a volume of 10 dm^3 to volume of 20 dm^3. The internal energy of the gas is

(Assume $C_v = \frac{3}{2}R$)
(a) −1384 J (b) 1384 J
(c) 1284 kJ (d) 12.84 J

6. Given below are two statements.

Statement I The enthalpy of solution of $CaCl_2 \cdot 6H_2O$ in a large volume of water is endothermic to the extent of 3.5 k cal/mol.

If $\Delta H = -23.2$ kcal for the reaction,

$$CaCl_2(s) + 6H_2O(l) \longrightarrow CaCl_2 \cdot 6H_2O(s)$$

Then heat of solution of $CaCl_2$(anh.) in a large volume of water is − 19.7 k cal/mol.

Statement II For the reaction,

$2Cl(g) \rightarrow Cl_2(g)$; the sign of ΔH and ΔS are negative.

In the light of the above statements, choose the most appropriate answer from the options given below:
(a) Both Statement I and Statement II are incorrect.
(b) Statement I is correct but Statement II is incorrect.
(c) Statement I is incorrect but Statement II is correct.
(d) Both Statement I and Statement II are correct.

7. 1 mole of $Al_4C_3(s)$ reacts with H_2O in a closed vessel and in an open vessel at 27°C against atmospheric pressure. Work done are respectively. (in cals)

	Closed	Open
(a)	−1800	− 1800
(b)	+1800	600
(c)	600	+ 1800
(d)	zero	− 1800

8. 3 moles of an ideal gas being initially at a temperature 273 K was isothermally expanded 5.0 times its initial volume and then isochorically heated so that the pressure in the final state became equal to that in the initial state. The total amount of heat transferred to the gas during the process equal 80 kJ. What will be the value of $C_{v,m}$ for this gas in cal/K-mol.
[Given ln 5 = 1.6]
(a) 5 cal/K-mol (b) 30 cal/K-mol
(c) 35 cal/K-mol (d) 15 cal/K-mol

9. A gas expands against a variable pressure given by $p = \frac{20}{V}$ (where p in atm and V in L). During expansion from volume of 1 L to 10 L, the gas undergoes a change in internal energy of 550 J. How much heat is absorbed by the gas during expansion?
(a) 5065.8 J (b) 5215.8 J
(c) 4660 J (d) 3831.6 J

10. In the following chemical changes taking place against external atmospheric pressure. The sign of work done is + ve

I. $N_2(g) + 3H_2(g) \longrightarrow 2NH_3(g)$
II. $NH_4HS(s) \longrightarrow NH_3(g) + H_2S(g)$
III. $C(s) + CO_2(g) \longrightarrow 2CO(g)$
IV. $C_2H_6(g) + 3.5O_2(g) \longrightarrow 2CO_2(g) + 3H_2O(l)$

Choose the correct answer from the option given below.
(a) I and IV (b) II and III
(c) I, II and IV (d) II, III and IV

11. 10 L of a non-linear triatomic ideal gas at 400 K and 2 atm pressure is suddenly released to 1 atm pressure and the gas expanded adiabatically against constant external pressure. The final temperature and volume of the gas respectively are
(a) 450 K, 13.6 L (b) 300 K, 12.5 L
(c) 350 K, 17.5 L (d) 27 K, 10.5 L

12. One mole of helium gas behaving ideally expands adiabatically at initial temperature T K against a constant external pressure of 1 atm such that volume is tripled. Thus, final temperature is

(a) 0.33 T (b) $\frac{T}{(3)^{5R/2}}$

(c) $T + \frac{2\text{ K}}{(0.0821 \times 1.5)}$ (d) $T - \frac{2\text{ K}}{(0.0821 \times 1.5)}$

13. Given below are two statements.

Statement I An ideal gas expands in volume from 10^{-3} m^3 to 10^{-2} m^3 at 300 K against a constant pressure of 10^5 Nm^{-2}, then the work done will be 900 J.

Statement II A process of expansion of an ideal gas which is isothermal as well as adiabatic must be a free-expansion work.

In the light of the above statements, choose the most appropriate answer from the options given below:

(a) Both Statement I and Statement II are incorrect.
(b) Statement I is correct but Statement II is incorrect.
(c) Statement I is incorrect but Statement II is correct.
(d) Both Statement I and Statement II are correct.

14. Which of the following equation is correctly matched with the given values?

(a) $NH_4HS(s) \longrightarrow NH_3(g) + H_2S(g) \longrightarrow \Delta H = \Delta U - 2RT$
(b) $PCl_5(g) \longrightarrow PCl_3(g) + Cl_2(g) \longrightarrow \Delta H = \Delta U + 2RT$
(c) $2SO_2(g) + O_2(g) \longrightarrow 2SO_3(g) \longrightarrow \Delta H = \Delta U - RT$
(d) $N_2(g) + 3H_2(g) \longrightarrow 2NH_3(g) \longrightarrow \Delta H = \Delta U + RT$

Type II 》 MCQs with One or More than One Correct Option

15. Heat is supplied to a certain water sample, at a uniform rate. Its temperature is plotted against time, as shown in the figure below.

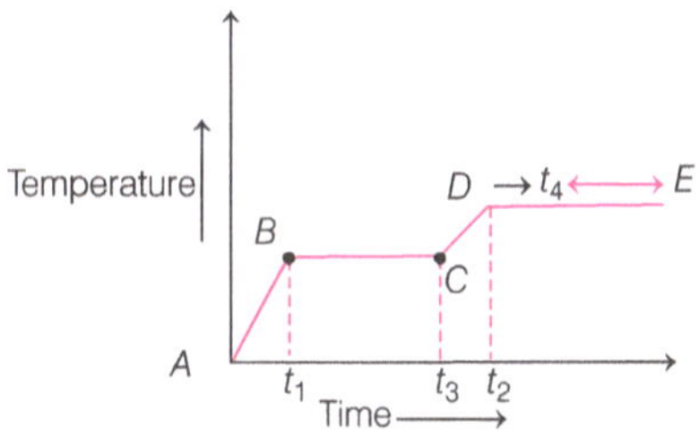

Which of the following conclusions can be drawn?

(a) Its specific heat capacity is greater in the solid state than in the liquid state.
(b) Its specific heat capacity is smaller in the solid state than in the liquid state.
(c) Its latent heat of vaporisation is greater than its latent heat of fusion.
(d) Its latent heat of vaporisation is smaller than its latent heat of fusion.

16. Which of the following statements are incorrect.

(a) If temperature of one mole of helium gas is increased by 1°C, then the increase in internal energy will be 3.5 cal.
(b) Among helium, oxygen and ozone, ozone gas has maximum internal energy.
(c) Internal energy is a state function and also an intensive property.
(d) If bond energy of N-H bond is x cal mol^{-1} then the change in internal energy in the process; $NH_3(g) \longrightarrow N_2(g) + 3H_2(g)$ will be $6x$ cal.

17. Which of the following statements are correct?

(a) The magnitude of work involved in an intermediate irreversible expansion is less than that involved in reversible expansion.
(b) Heat absorbed during intermediate irreversible expansion is more than that in intermediate reversible expansion.
(c) The magnitude of work involved in an intermediate reversible compression is more than that involved in intermediate irreversible compression.
(d) Heat released during intermediate irreversible compression is more than that in intermediate reversible compression.

18. A system consisting of 1 mole of water vapour $H_2O(g)$ at 100°C and 1 atm with a volume of 30.12 L condenses at a constant pressure of 1 atm to liquid water, $H_2O(l)$ at 100°C and 1 atm with a volume of 18.8 cm^3

$$H_2O(g) \longrightarrow H_2O(l), \quad \Delta H = -40.7 \text{ kJ}$$

On the basis of given data, select the correct statement from the following—

(a) The work done in kJ for the given transformation is – 3.05 kJ.
(b) The change in internal energy in kJ of the given process is – 37.65 kJ.
(c) The change in volume in the given process is – 30.1012 L.
(d) The change in internal energy in kJ of the given process is – 40.70 kJ.

19. Which of the following statements is correct for an ideal gas?

(a) the change in internal energy in a constant pressure process from temperature T_1 to T_2 is equal to $nC_V(T_2 - T_1)$ where C_V is the molar heat capacity at constant volume and n is no. of mole of gas.
(b) the change in internal energy of gas and the work done by the gas are equal in magnitude in an adiabatic process.
(c) the internal energy does not change is an isothermal process.
(d) no heat is added or removed in an adiabatic process.

20. Which of the following statements are correct?

(a) Work done when 3.4 g of H_2O_2 reacts against a pressure of 1.0 atm at 27°C.

$$2H_2O_2(l) \xrightarrow{\Delta} O_2(g) + 2H_2O(l) \text{ is } 134.5 \text{ J}$$

(b) An ideal gas expands against a constant P of 2.0 atm from 20 L to 40 L and absorbs 10 kJ of heat from surrounding ΔU of system is 5948 J.
(c) 2 mole of Zn is dissolved in HCl at 27°C. The work done in open vessel is – 5.0 kJ.
(d) For a system, $\Delta U = +400$ J, $q = 500$ J and work of expansion against 0.1 bar, then change in volume is 20 L.

Type III 》 Numerical/integer Type

21. A thermodynamic process is shown in the following figure. The pressure and volume corresponding to some points in the figure are $p_A = 3 \times 10^4$ Pa, $p_B = 8 \times 10^4$ Pa, $V_A = 2 \times 10^{-3}$ m^3, $V_D = 5 \times 10^{-3}$ m^3.

In the process AB, 600 J of heat is added to the system and in BC, 200 J of heat is added to the system.

The change in internal energy of the system in the process AC will be .... J.

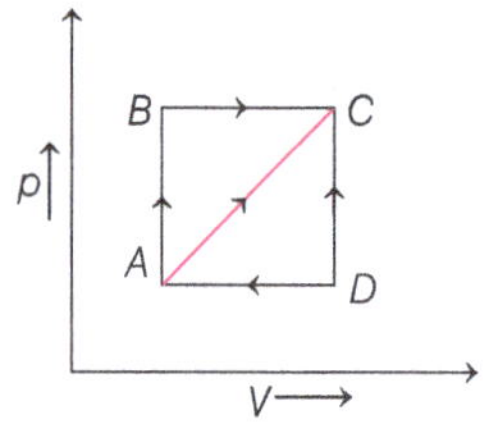

22. A 0.150 mole sample of an ideal gas is allowed expand at 294 K from 10.00 atm to 1.00 atm. If external pressure is kept constant at 1.00 atm work done is

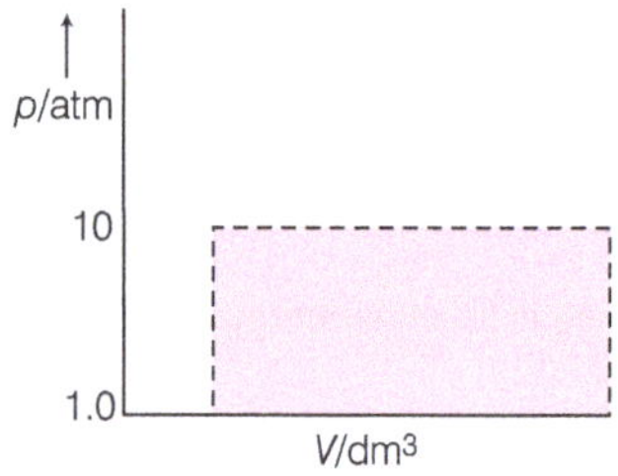

23. Two moles of a triatomic linear gas (neglect vibration degree of freedom) are taken through a reversible ideal process starting from A as shown in figure.

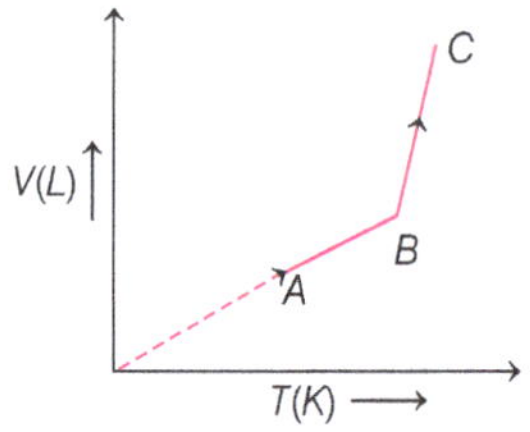

Given: The volume ratio $\frac{V_B}{V_A} = 4$; If the temperature at $A = 200$ K)

The work done by the gas in AB process approximately is (−).... kJ.

24. What is the value of change in internal energy at 1 atm in the given process?

$$H_2O(l, 323\text{ K}) \longrightarrow H_2O(g, 373\text{ K})$$

Given : $C_{V,m} = (H_2O, l) = 85.0$ JK^{-1} mol^{-1}

$C_{p,m}(H_2O, g) = 33.314$ JK^{-1} mol^{-1}

$\Delta H_{vap.}$ at 373 K = 40.7 kJ/mol

25. The internal energy change in the conversion of 1 mole of the calcite form of $CaCO_3$ to the 1 mol aragonite form is + 0.21 kJ. The enthalpy change (in J) in the conversion at 2.7 bar is .... J. (nearest integer)

[Given, the densities of the solids calcite and aragonite are 2.7 g cm^{-3} and 3.0 g cm^{-3} respectively.

Elemental Practice 4.2 | Chapter 04

Connect with **Answers**

1. (d)	2. (a)	3. (a)	4. (c)	5. (a)	6. (d)
7. (d)	8. (a)	9. (b)	10. (a)	11. (c)	12. (d)
13. (c)	14. (c)	15. (b,c)	16. (a,c,d)	17. (a,b,c,d)	18. (b,c)
19. (a,b,c,d)	20. (b,c)	21. (560)	22. (330)	23. (10)	24. (41.8)
25. (210)					

Element 3 Entropy and Second Law of Thermodynamics

Spontaneous Process or Spontaneity

A spontaneous process is an irreversible process. It can take place by itself under the given set of condition once it has been initiated, if necessary, is called spontaneous process.

- Combustion of coal into CO_2 is spontaneous as it burns to completely after it is ignited.
- Evaporation of $H_2O(l)$ into $H_2O(g)$ and fusion of $H_2O(s)$ into $H_2O(l)$ are spontaneous processes.
- Sugar dissolves in water spontaneously.

The interesting aspect of a spontaneous process is that the reverse process never happens under the same set of conditions.

Ice melts at 20°C and 1atm, but water at the same temperature and pressure will not spontaneously convert into ice.

Water boils at 100°C and 1 atm and is completely converted into vapour but reverse (liquefaction) does not take place under similar conditions. Thus, any process occurring spontaneously in one direction cannot take place spontaneously in the opposite direction.

JEE Alert

The direction of a spontaneous process for which the energy is constant is always the one that increases the molecular disorder or randomness.

Entropy

The thermodynamic property that measures the amount of molecular disorder is called **entropy**. It is denoted by S.

The entropy is a state function for a system. It is an extensive function. The change in the value of the entropy function in going from one state to another, is independent of the path, and the cyclic integral of dS for a cyclic change of state is always zero.

The unit of entropy function is energy unit divided by temperature unit, e.g. JK^{-1}, cal K^{-1}. A unit of 1 cal K^{-1} (non-SI) is known as an entropy unit.

$$\Delta S = S_2 - S_1$$

- Whenever there is an increase in randomness in a system, the entropy change is **positive** while if there is a decrease in the randomness in a system then the entropy change is **negative**.

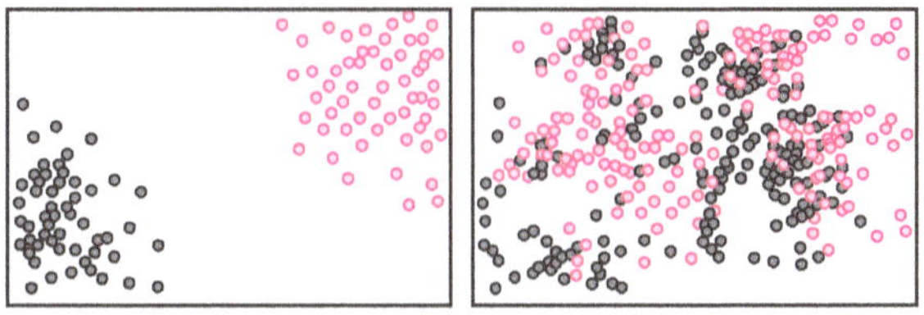

Entropy Changes in Reversible Process

If we assume that the surroundings transfer heat reversibly, then the entropy change in any process carried out reversibly will be the negative of the entropy change of the surroundings, i.e

$$\Delta S(\text{system}) = -\Delta S(\text{surroundings})$$

or $$\Delta S(\text{total}) = \Delta S(\text{system}) + \Delta S(\text{surroundings}) = 0$$

Entropy Changes in Irreversible Process

No matter what the interaction between system I and its surroundings in the irreversible process might be, the entropy of system + surrounding always increases.
We therefore, have

$$\Delta S(\text{total}) = \Delta S(\text{system}) + \Delta S(\text{surroundings}) > 0$$

Clausius assumed that the entire universe could be considered as an isolated system, in which all naturally occurring processes are irreversible.

The energy of the universe is constant, the entropy of the universe always tends toward a maximum.

Entropy changes adiabatic reversible/irreversible expansion or compression.

(i) Along path $(V_1T_1) \rightarrow (V_2, T_2)$

$$dS = \frac{dq_{\text{rev}}}{T} \qquad (dq)_p = dH$$

$$dS = \frac{dH}{T} = \frac{dE + pdV}{T} \Rightarrow dS = \frac{nC_V dT + pdV}{T}$$

$$dS = nC_V \frac{dT}{T} + nR\frac{dV}{V}$$

$$\int_{S_A}^{S_B} dS = nC_V \int_{T_1}^{T_2} \frac{dT}{T} + nR \int_{V_1}^{V_2} \frac{dV}{V}$$

$$\Delta S = nC_V \ln\frac{T_2}{T_1} + nR\ln\frac{V_2}{V_1} \quad \text{...(i)}$$

(ii) Along path $(p_1, T_1) \rightarrow (p_2, T_2)$ or $nC_V \ln\frac{T_2}{T_1} + nR\ln\left(\frac{p_1T_2}{p_2T_1}\right)$

$$= nC_p \ln\frac{T_2}{T_1} + nR\ln\frac{p_1}{p_2} \quad \text{...(ii)}$$

Equation (i) and (ii), can be applied for any thermodynamic process.

Note The condition of equilibrium in an isolated system is that the entropy has a maximum value.

Entropy Change in Mixing of Two Gases

If the two gases are separated by a partition, and allowed to mix together at constant temperature removing the partition as shown in the figure.

Mixing of two, non-reacting ideal gases from the different vessels at same temperature and pressure.

Final volume $= (V_1 + V_2)$

Change in entropy for the first gas, $\Delta S_1 = n_1 R \ln \frac{V_1 + V_2}{V_1}$

Change in entropy of the second gas, $\Delta S_2 = n_2 R \ln \frac{V_1 + V_2}{V_2}$

Also the mole fractions of two gases in the mixture are

$$x_1 = \frac{n_1}{n_1 + n_2} = \frac{V_1}{V_1 + V_2} \text{ and } x_2 = \frac{n_2}{n_1 + n_2} = \frac{V_2}{V_1 + V_2}$$

Total change in entropy,

$$\Delta S_{mix} = \Delta S_1 + \Delta S_2 = n_1 R \ln \frac{V_1 + V_2}{V_1} + n_2 R \ln \frac{V_1 + V_2}{V_2}$$

$$\Delta S_{mix} = -R(n_1 + n_2)[x_1 \ln x_1 + x_2 \ln x_2]$$

Entropy for Isothermal Phase Changes

The value of ΔS for any process measures the change in the molecular disorder or randomness when that process takes place. If a process is isothermal

$$\Delta S = q_{rev} / T$$

For a pure substance at a specified pressure, there is a unique temperature at which two phases are in equilibrium. Thus, phase changes are isothermal and using above equation we can calculate entropy change of that phase transition.

Entropy of Vaporisation

For a process, liquid $\rightleftharpoons$ vapour

$$\Delta S_{vap} = \frac{\Delta H_{vap}}{T_{bp}}$$

where, ΔH_{vap} is called heat of vaporisation which is the heat required to convert 1 mole of liquid into 1 mole of vapour at constant temperature (called boiling point T_{bp}) and constant pressure. As vaporisation is always endothermic, hence

$$\Delta H_{vap} > 0$$

Also, $\Delta S_{vap} = S_{vapour} - S_{liquid}$

thus, $S_{vap} > S_{liq}$. The entropy of 1 mol of a gas at its normal boiling point is always larger than the entropy of 1 mole of the liquid. This is a measure of the large increase in disorder or randomness that occurs on vaporisation.

Molecules in the vapour phase have more freedom of motion than molecules in the liquid.

JEE Alert

Trouton' rule states that entropy of vaporisation of most liquids is $88 \pm 5 \text{ J mol}^{-1} \text{K}^{-1}$ at the normal boiling point, hence, this law can be used to obtain a rough estimate of the heat of vaporisation.

Water and ethanol have unusually large entropies of vaporisation. That is because these liquids are more ordered than most other liquids, due to extensive hydrogen bonding which orients the molecules and increases the amount of molecular order. As a result, the increase in molecular disorder on converting 1 mole of liquid to vapour is greater for water and alcohols than for most other liquids and thus, ΔS_{vap} is larger.

Entropy of Fusion

For a process, Solid $\rightleftharpoons$ liquid $\Rightarrow \Delta S_{fusion} = \frac{\Delta H_{fusion}}{T_{mp}}$

where, ΔH_{fusion} is the heat required to convert 1 mole of solid at constant temperature (mp) and constant pressure into liquid, keeping the solid and liquid in equilibrium throughout the process.

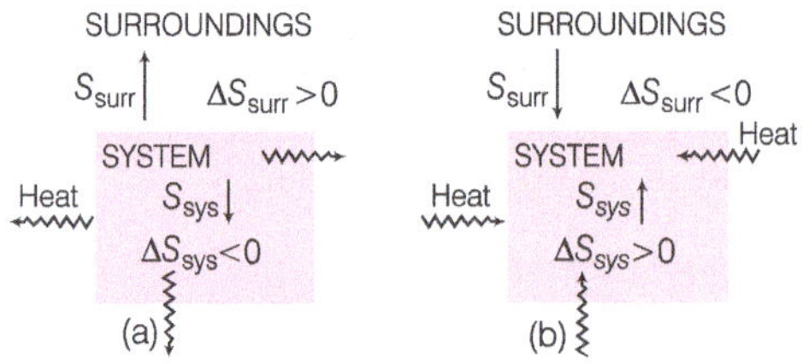

A schematic representation of heat flow and entropy changes for (a) freezing and (b) melting of a pure substance.

$$\Delta S_{fusion} = S_{liquid} - S_{solid}$$

Since, $\Delta H_{fusion} > 0$ (endothermic) and hence, $\Delta S_{fusion} > 0$,

thus, $S_{liquid} > S_{solid}$

- **Freezing below Melting Point** Below melting point, S_{surr} increases more than S_{sys} decreases, so $\Delta S_{univ} > 0$, and the process is spontaneous. Above melting point, S_{surr} is already high, so it cannot increase enough to compensate for the decrease in S_{sys}, and the process is not spontaneous.
- **Melting above Melting Point** Above melting point, S_{sys} increases more than S_{surr} decreases, so $\Delta S_{univ} > 0$ and the process is spontaneous. Below melting point, too little heat flows into the system, so S_{sys} cannot increase enough to make the process spontaneous.

Entropy of Transition

When one allotrope changes into the other, entropy changes.

Carbon (diamond) $\rightleftharpoons$ Carbon (graphite)

This takes place at a constant temperature

Thus, $\Delta S_{transition} = \frac{q_{transition}}{T}$

JEE MAPPER

Example Similar to PYQ Asked in JEE Advanced 2023

The entropy *versus* temperature plot for phases α and β at 1 bar pressure is given. S_T and S_0 are entropies of the phases at temperature T and 0 K, respectively.

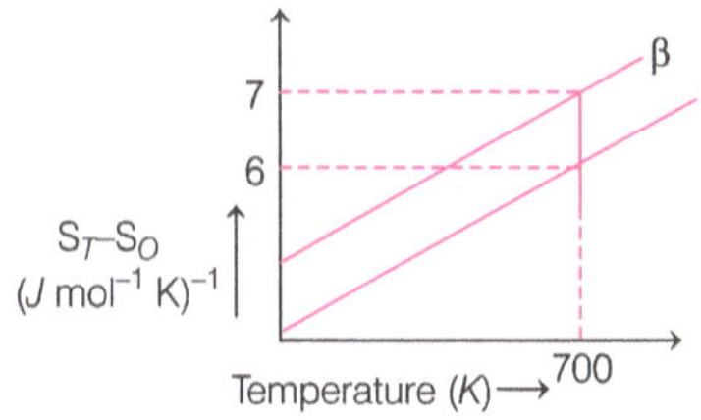

The transition temperature for α to β phase change is 700 K and $C_{p,\beta} - C_{p,\alpha} = 1$ J mol^{-1} K^{-1}. Assume $(C_{p,\beta} - C_{p,\alpha})$ is independent of temperature in the range of 200 to 800 K. $C_{p,\alpha}$ and $C_{p,\beta}$ are heat capacities of α and β phases, respectively.

1. The value of entropy change, S_β-S_α (in J mol^{-1} K^{-1}) at 300 K .... [Use : ln2 = 0.69, Given: $S_\beta - S_\alpha = 0$ at 0 K]
2. The value of enthalpy change, $H_\beta - H_\alpha$ (in J mol^{-1}), at 300 K is ....

Sol. 1. *(0.15)* S_T and S_0 are entropies of the phase at temperature T and 0 K, respectively.

$$S = S_0 + \int C_p \frac{dT}{T} \quad [S_0 = 0 \text{ at } 0 \text{ K}]$$

$$S_\alpha = S_0 + \int C_{p,\alpha} \frac{dT}{T} \Rightarrow S_\beta = S_0 + \int C_{p,\beta} \frac{dT}{T}$$

$$S_\beta - S_\alpha = [(C_{p,\beta} - (C_p)_\alpha] \int \frac{dT}{T}$$

Given, $C_{p,\beta} - C_{p,\alpha} = 1$

$S_\beta - S_\alpha = \ln T + C$ at any temperatures T.

$(S_\beta - S_\alpha)_{T_2} - (S_\beta - S_\alpha)_{T_1} = \ln T_2 - \ln T_1$

$T_2 = 700$ K, $T_1 = 300$ K from the graph, $S_\beta - S_\alpha$ at 700 K = 1

$(1) - (S_\beta - S_\alpha)_{300} = \ln 700 - \ln 300 \Rightarrow 1 - (S_\beta - S_\alpha)_{300} = 0.85$

$(S_\beta - S_\alpha)_{300} = 1 - 0.85 = 0.15$ J mol^{-1} K^{-1}

Sol. 2. *(300)* Change in Gibbs free energy transition from α to β phase = 0

Thus, $\Delta H = T\Delta S$

ΔH (at 700 K) = 700 × 1 = 700 J mol^{-1} $[\because \Delta S = 1]$

According to Kirchhoff's Law,

$$\Delta H_f - \Delta H_i = C_p(T_f - T_i) \quad \text{...(i)}$$

Using eq. (i), $\Delta H_{700} - \Delta H_{300} = 1 \times (C_{p,\beta} - C_{p,\alpha})(700 - 300)$

$700 - \Delta H_{300} = 1 \times 1 \times 400$

$\Delta H_{300} = 700 - 400 = 300$ J mol^{-1}

Competency Enhancer 3.1

5 mol of an ideal diatomic gas was heated and compressed from 298 K and 1 bar to 894 K and 3 bar. The change in entropy of the gas is ...... cal. K^{-1}

[Given : $C_{v,m}$ (gas) $= \frac{5}{2}R$; $R = 2$ cal, $^{-1}$. K^{-1}. mol^{-1}; ln3 = 1.098]

Physical Significance of Entropy

Entropy as a measure of the disorder of the system. A Spontaneous process is accompanied by increase in disorder of the system. eg.

- Melting of solid
- Evaporation of a liquid
- Expansion of a gas in vacuum
- Diffusion of two or more gases
- Diffusion of a solute from concentrated to a dilute solution

All these are spontaneous. In crystal lattice atoms or ions are arranged in a perfect order. The order is much less in liquid and gas. Increase in entropy means increase in disorder.

Entropy and Second Law of Thermodynamics

In terms of entropy second law of thermodynamics is defined as :

"Entropy of the system and surrounding remains constant in a reversible equilibrium process, while it increases in an irreversible process".

$$\Delta S_{\text{total}} = \Delta S_{\text{system}} + \Delta S_{\text{surroundings}}$$

In nature, all the process are irreversible (spontaneous) going to completion, hence entropy of the universe increases and tends to be maximum.

Table Entropy effects associated with melting and freezing

Change	Temp.	Sign of (a) ΔS_{sys}	Sign of (b) ΔS_{surr}	Comparison of (a) and (b)	ΔS_{univ}	Spontaneity
Melting	(i) > mp	+	−	>	>0	Spontaneous
(solid → liquid)	(ii) = mp	+	−	=	= 0	Equilibrium
	(iii) < mp	+	−	<	< 0	Non -spontaneous
Freezing	(i) > mp	−	+	>	< 0	Non -spontaneous
(liquid → solid)	(ii) = mp	−	+	=	= 0	Equilibrium
	(iii) < mp	−	+	<	>0	Spontaneous

Standard Molar Entropies

The standard molar entropy of a substance, denoted by $S°$, is the entropy of 1 mole of the pure substance at 1 atm pressure and at a specified temperature, usually at 25°C. Standard molar entropies are often called **absolute entropies** because they are measured with respect to an absolute reference point—the entropy of the perfectly ordered crystalline substance at 0 K ($S° = 0$ J K^{-1} mol^{-1} at $T = 0$ K).

Standard entropy of a reaction ΔS° is given by

$$\Delta S^\circ = S^\circ_{(\text{products})} - S^\circ_{(\text{reactants})}$$

Because S° values are quoted on a per mol basis, the S° value for each substance must be multiplied by the stoichiometric coefficients of that substance in a balanced chemical equation. Thus, for the general reaction

$$aA + bB \longrightarrow cC + dD$$

$$\Delta S^\circ = (cS^\circ_C + dS^\circ_D) - (aS^\circ_A + bS^\circ_B)$$

JEE Spotlite

- All reactions proceed spontaneously in the direction that increases the entropy of the system plus surroundings.
  Also $(\Delta S)_{\text{forward}} = -(\Delta S)_{\text{reverse}}$
  Thus, a reaction which is spontaneous in forward direction is non-spontaneous in reverse direction.
- Also for an **endothermic reaction**, system gains heat hence, entropy $\Delta S \left(= \frac{\Delta H}{T}\right)$ of the system increases
  $\Delta S_{\text{system}} > 0$ for endothermic reaction
- If this happens, surrounding loses heat, hence,
  $\Delta S_{\text{surroundings}} < 0$
  for endothermic reaction.
- For an **exothermic reaction**, system loses heat to the surroundings.
  $\therefore \left.\begin{matrix}\Delta S_{\text{system}} < 0 \\ \Delta S_{\text{surroundings}} > 0\end{matrix}\right\}$ for exothermic reaction

Solved Booster 3.1

The heat of vaporisation, $\Delta H^\circ_{\text{vap}}$ of CCl_4 at 25°C is 39.4 kJ mol^{-1}.

$$CCl_4(l) \rightleftharpoons CCl_4(g), \quad \Delta H^\circ_{\text{vap}} = 39.4 \text{ kJ mol}^{-1}$$

If 1 mole of liquid CCl_4 at 25°C has an entropy of 216 JK^{-1}. The entropy of 1 mole of the vapour in equilibrium with the liquid at this temperature is

(a) 360 J mol^{-1} K^{-1}
(b) 348.2 J mol^{-1} K^{-1}
(c) 480.7 J mol^{-1} K^{-1}
(d) 280.4 J mol^{-1} K^{-1}

Solution (b)

$$\Delta S^\circ_{\text{vap}} = \frac{\Delta H^\circ_{\text{vap}}}{T} = \frac{39.4 \times 10^3}{298} \text{ Jmol}^{-1}$$
$$= 132.2 \text{ J mol}^{-1}\text{K}^{-1}$$
$$\Delta S^\circ_{\text{liquid}} = 216.0 \text{ J mol}^{-1}\text{K}^{-1}$$
$$\therefore \Delta S^\circ_{\text{equilibrium}} = 132.2 + 216.0$$
$$= 348.2 \text{ J mol}^{-1}\text{K}^{-1}$$

Solved Booster 3.2

In which of the following pair former has the lower entropy per mole of substance than latter?

(a) H_2 at 25°C in a volume of 10 L or H_2 at 25°C in a volume of 50 L.
(b) O_2 at 25°C and 1 atm or O_2 at 25°C and 10 atm.
(c) H_2 at 25°C and 1 atm or H_2 at 100°C and 1 atm.
(d) CO_2 at STP or CO_2 at 100°C and 0.1 atm.

Solution (a)

(a) Larger the volume of the gas, greater the tendency of the molecules to set into motion, hence randomness increases. H_2 at 25°C in a volume of 50 L.
(b) O_2 at 25°C and 1 atm
(c) H_2 at 100°C and 1 atm
(d) CO_2 at 100°C and 0.1 atm

Temperature increases from 273 to 373 K but volume increases 10 times.

Entropy and Third Law of Thermodynamics

At absolute Zero (−273 °C), every substance is in solid state whose particles are rigidly fixed in a crystalline structure. If there is no residual orientational disorder, like that in CO, entropy of the substance at 0 K will be zero.

Third law of thermodynamics states **"At the absolute zero of temperature the entropy of every substance may become zero and does become zero in case of perfectly crystalline structure."**

$$\boxed{\lim_{T \to 0} S = 0}$$

In case of CO and NO molecules in solid state, there is randomness even at 0 K due to their dipole moment hence, entropy in such cases is not zero even at 0 K.

Gibb's Free Energy

The calculation of total entropy change require consideration of both the system and the surroundings. But in chemical thermodynamics, we prefer to focus ourselves on the system rather then the surroundings, so a new thermodynamics function called Gibbs free energy in thermodynamics was defined by J. Wiland Gibbs. Gibbs free energy G of a system at any moment of time is defined as the enthalpy of the system minus the product of the temperature times the entropy of the system.

$$\boxed{G = H - TS}$$

where, H is the enthalpy, T is the temperature in Kelvin scale, S is the entropy. TS is the part of system's energy that is already disordered (non-useful energy) and $H - TS (= G)$ is the part of system's energy that is still ordered, i.e., useful energy hence free (available) to cause spontaneous change by becoming disordered.

Gibbs energy is a state function because it is defined in terms of thermodynamic properties (enthalpy, entropy, and temperature) that are state functions.

Therefore,

$$\Delta G = G_{\text{final}} - G_{\text{inital}}$$

For any system, the change in Gibbs energy can be expressed as

$$\Delta G_{\text{system}} = \Delta H_{\text{system}} - T\Delta S_{\text{system}} - S_{\text{system}}\Delta T$$

For a process at constant temperature,

$$\mu_{\Delta T} = 0, \text{ therefore,}$$

$$\Delta G_{\text{system}} = \Delta H_{\text{system}} - T\Delta S_{\text{system}}$$

$$\Delta G = \Delta H - T\Delta S$$

In the expression for Gibbs energy, both ΔH and $T\Delta S$, are energy terms, therefore, change of Gibbs energy has units of energy.

The change in Gibbs energy is determined by change in both enthalpy and entropy of the system and should thus be a suitable parameter to predict spontaneity of a process.

Sign of ΔG can also be used to predict feasibility of a reaction at constant temperature and pressure.

For a reaction to be spontaneous if $\Delta S > 0$ then $\Delta G < 0$

Non-spontaneous if $\Delta S < 0$ then $\Delta G > 0$

At equilibrium if $\Delta S = 0$ then $\Delta G = 0$

Decrease in *G* Related to Work

We know that in all real processes, the enthalpy change is not completely converted into work as some amount of heat is lost to the surrounding and used in overcoming opposing forces. In the expression for Gibbs energy, if ΔH corresponds to the enthalpy change for the system, then $T\Delta S$ corresponds to the energy not available for doing work and ΔG corresponds to energy available for doing useful work.

$$\Delta G = \Delta H - T\Delta S = \Delta E + p\Delta V - T\Delta S \qquad \left(\because \Delta S = \frac{q}{T}\right)$$

$$= \Delta E - q + p\Delta V$$

($\Delta E = q - W$ by first law of Thermodynamics)

$$\Delta G = -W + p\Delta V$$

$$-\Delta G = W - p\Delta V = W_{\text{net}}$$

(W = total work and $p\Delta V$ = mechanical work)

$$-\Delta G = W_{\text{net}} = 2.303\, nRT \log \frac{V_2}{V_1}$$

Thus, decrease in G, $(-\Delta G)$, is equal to net work done (= total work − mechanical work).

Signs of enthalpy, entropy and free energy changes and reaction spontaneity at constant temperature and pressure

ΔH	ΔS	$\Delta G = \Delta H - T\Delta S$	**Reaction spontaneity**
−, − Exothermic	+	−	Spontaneous at all temperatures.
	−	−	Spontaneous at low temperatures.
		+	Non-spontaneous at high temperatures.
+, +, +, + Endothermic	+	+	Non-spontaneous at low temperatures.

(Assume both ΔH and ΔS are independent of temperature)

Solved Booster 3.3

Determine ΔG (reaction) at 298 K for the following chemical reaction

$$2H_2(g) + O_2(g) \longrightarrow 2H_2O(l)$$

Given			
ΔH_f kJ mol^{-1}	0	0	−285.83
S, J mol^{-1}K^{-1}	130.68	205.14	69.91

Solution (−474.31)

$$\Delta S = (S)_P - (S)_R,\ \Delta H_r = (\Delta H_f)_P - (\Delta G_f)_R,\ \Delta G = \Delta H - T\Delta S$$

$$\Delta S = 2S_{H_2O} - [2S_{H_2} + S_{O_2}]$$

$$= [2 \times 69.91] - [2 \times 130.68 + 205.14]$$

$$= -326.68\ \text{J K}^{-1} = -0.32668\ \text{kJ K}^{-1}$$

$$\Delta H_r = -285.83 \times 2$$

$$\therefore\ \Delta G = \Delta H - T\Delta S = -571.66 - 298 \times (-0.32668) = -474.31\ \text{kJ}$$

Free Energy Changes and Composition of the Reaction Mixture

ΔG (free-energy change) for a reaction under non standard-state conditions is related to $\Delta G°$ under standard-state condition by relation

$$\Delta G = \Delta G° + 2.303RT \log_{10} Q$$

where, Q is called reaction-quotient before equilibrium is attained.

$$aA + bB \longrightarrow cC + dD$$

$$Q = \frac{[C]^c[D]^d}{[A]^a[B]^b}$$

($[A]$, $[B]$, $[C]$ and $[D]$ are molar masses under non-equilibrium condition,

$Q = 0$ at the start of the reaction).

- When the reaction mixture is mostly reactants

$$Q << 1, RT \log_{10} Q << 0, \Delta G < 0$$

The total free energy decreases as the reaction proceeds spontaneously in the forward direction.

- When the reaction mixture is mostly products :

$$Q >> 1, RT \log_{10} Q >> 0, \Delta G > 0$$

- The total free energy decreases as the reaction proceeds spontaneously in the reverse direction.
- When $Q = 1$, $RT \log_{10} Q = 0$, $\Delta G = \Delta G°$
- When equilibrium is reached,

$$\Delta G = 0 \text{ then } Q = K (= K_p \text{ or } K_c).$$

$$\Delta G° = -2.303 RT \log K$$

Here, K is K_p for reactions involving gases and K_c for reaction involving solutes in solution. K is actually called thermodynamic equilibrium constant.

The relationship between $\Delta G°$ and thermodynamic equilibrium constant K has been given in Table.

- For a reaction in which a compound in its standard state is formed from its elements in their standard states, the free energy change is the standard free energy of formation, $\Delta G_f^°$

$$\Delta G_f^° = 0 \text{ for the elements,}$$

$$\Delta G_f^° = (\Delta G^°_{\text{products}} - \Delta G^°_{\text{reactants}})$$

$$= \Delta H° - T\Delta S°$$

- ΔG is an extensive property.
- ΔG changes sign when a process is reversed.

Relationship between the standard free-energy change and the equilibrium constant for a reaction :

$$\Delta G° = -2.303 RT \log K$$

$\Delta G°$	$\log K$	K	Comment
$\Delta G° = 0$	$\log K = 0$	1	The equilibrium mixture contains comparable amounts of reactants and products ($K = 1$ for 1 M concentrations and 1 atm partial pressures).
$\Delta G° < 0$	$\log K > 0$	$K > 1$	The equilibrium mixture is mainly products.
$\Delta G° > 0$	$\log K < 0$	$K < 1$	The equilibrium mixture is mainly reactants.

Solved Booster 3.4

For the equilibrium, $CO(g) + H_2O(g) \rightleftharpoons CO_2(g) + H_2(g)$ the standard enthalpy and entropy changes at 300 K and 1200 K for the forward reaction are as follows

$$\Delta H°_{300\,K} = -41.16 \text{ kJ mol}^{-1}$$

$$\Delta S°_{300\,K} = -0.0424 \text{ kJ mol}^{-1}$$

$$\Delta H°_{1200\,K} = -32.93 \text{ kJ mol}^{-1}$$

$$\Delta S°_{1200\,K} = -0.0296 \text{ kJ mol}^{-1}$$

In which direction will the reaction be spontaneous

(a) at 300 K and

(b) 1200 K, when $p_{CO} = p_{CO_2} = p_{H_2} = p_{H_2O} = 1$ atm?

Also calculate K_p for the reaction at each temperature

Solution

Using the relationship, $\Delta G° = \Delta H° - T\Delta S°$, we have

$$\Delta G°_{300\,K} = \Delta H°_{300\,K} - T\Delta S°_{300\,K}$$

$$= -41.16 - 300(-0.0424) = -28.44 \text{ kJ mol}^{-1}$$

and $\Delta G°_{1200\,K} = \Delta H°_{1200\,K} - T\Delta S°_{1200\,K}$

$$= -32.93 - 1200(-0.0296) = 2.59 \text{ kJ mol}^{-1}$$

we know that a process is spontaneous if $\Delta G° = -$ ve, therefore, the reaction

$$CO(g) + H_2O(g) \rightleftharpoons CO_2(g) + H_2(g)$$

is spontaneous at 300 K, whereas the reverse reaction is spontaneous at 1200 K. Also, $\Delta G° = -2.303\, RT \log K_p$

hence, at 300 K $-28.44 = -2.303 \times 8.314 \times 10^{-3} \times 300 \log K_p$

Thus, $K_p = 8.8 \times 10^4$

Similarly, K_p at 1200 K = 0.77

JEE Spotlite

Gibbs-Helmholtz equations

At constant pressure, it relates ΔG with ΔH

$$\Delta G = \Delta H + T\left[\frac{d(\Delta G)}{\Delta T}\right]_p \quad \text{or} \quad \frac{\Delta G - \Delta H}{T} = \left[\frac{d(\Delta G)}{\Delta T}\right]_p$$

Since, $\Delta G = \Delta H - T\Delta S$

$$\therefore \quad -\Delta S = \left[\frac{d(\Delta G)}{dT}\right]_p$$

using equation $\Delta G = -nFE_{cell}$, $\Delta S = nF\left(\frac{dE_{cell}}{dT}\right)_p$ thus,

temperature coefficient of the emf of a cell is $\left(\frac{dE_{cell}}{dT}\right)_p = \frac{\Delta S}{nF}$

Elemental Practice 4.3

Type I MCQs with Only One Correct Option

1. One mole of a substance is cooled at the rate of 0.4 kJ min^{-1} as shown in the graph. Curve AB, points B, C and curve CD represent respectively, the cooling of the liquid, start of freezing, completion of freezing and cooling of the solid based on this data. The entropy of fusion in J mol^{-1} K^{-1} is

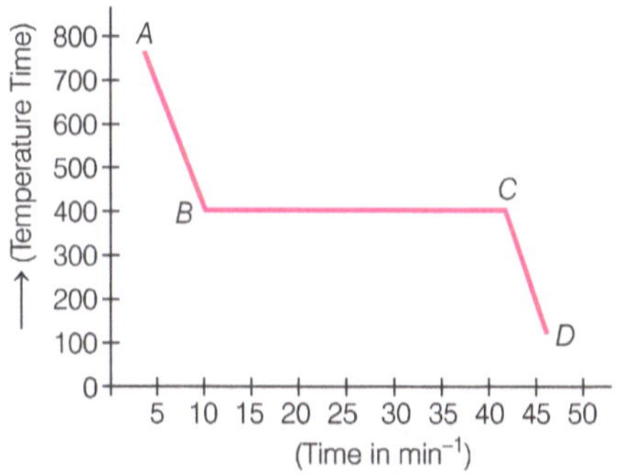

(a) 10 (b) 20 (c) 40 (d) 30

2. At 300 K, for a reaction, $\Delta G^\circ = -66.9$ kJ mol^{-1} and $\Delta H^\circ = -41.8$ kJ mol^{-1}
Thus, ΔG° for the same reaction at 330K is
(a) –25.1 kJ mol^{-1} (b) +25.1 kJ mol^{-1}
(c) 18.7 kJ mol^{-1} (d) –69.4 kJ mol^{-1}

3. Standard entropy change for the reaction,
$$Fe_2O_3(s) + 3H_2(g) \longrightarrow 2Fe(s) + 3H_2O(l) \text{ is}$$
Given : $S_m^\circ(Fe_2O_3, s) = 77.4$, $S_m^\circ(Fe, s) = 20.5$
$S_m^\circ(H_2, g) = 150.7$, $S_m^\circ(H_2O, l) = 70$ JK^{-1} mol^{-1}
(a) 90.5 kJ/mol (b) – 278.5 kJ/mol
(c) – 321.1 kJ/mol (d) 128 kJ/mol

4. 1 mole of benzene is mixed with 2 moles of toluene at 20°C and 1 atm. ΔG_{mix} due to mixing at the given temperature is (assume ideal solution)
(a) zero (b) – 4.54 kJ (c) 5.3 kJ (d) + 1.55 kJ

5. Given,
I. $C(diamond) + O_2(g) \longrightarrow CO_2(g); \Delta H^\circ = -91.0$ kcal mol^{-1}
II. $C(graphite) + O_2(g) \longrightarrow CO_2(g); \Delta H^\circ = -94.0$ kcal mol^{-1}
At 298 K, 2.4 kg of carbon (diamond) is converted into graphite form. Thus, entropy change is
(a) 10.07 cal K^{-1} (b) 2.013 kcal K^{-1}
(c) 305.4 cal K^{-1} (d) –2.013 kcal K^{-1}

6. For a perfectly crystalline solid $C_{p,m} = aT^3$, where a is constant. If $C_{p,m}$ is 0.42 J/K mol at 10 K, molar entropy at 20 K is
(a) 0.42 JK^{-1} mol^{-1} (b) 0.31 JK^{-1} mol^{-1}
(c) 1.38 JK^{-1} mol^{-1} (d) 1.12 JK^{-1} mol^{-1}

7. If for the cell, $Zn(s) + Cu^{2+}(aq) \rightleftharpoons Cu(s) + Zn^{2+}(aq)$ entropy change ΔS° is 96.5 JK^{-1} mol^{-1}, then temperature coefficient of the emf of a cell is
(a) 5×10^{-4} VK^{-1} (b) 1×10^{-3} VK^{-1}
(c) 2×10^{-3} VK^{-1} (d) 9.65×10^4 VK^{-1}

8. One mole of O_2 gas expands adiabatically against a constant pressure of 1 atm until the pressure balances. Initial temperature is 473 K and volume is 20 L. What will be the final temperature attained under adiabatic condition and entropy change respectively regarding the given data?
(a) 134.5 K, 1.17 JK^{-1} (b) 407.5 K, 1.175 JK^{-1}
(c) 200.0 K, 4.34 JK^{-1} (d) 400.0 K, 5.51 JK^{-1}

9. 10 dm^3 of an ideal monoatomic gas at 27°C and 1.01×10^5 N m^{-2} pressure are heated at constant pressure to 127 °C. Thus, entropy change is
(a) 2.422 JK^{-1} (b) 5.98 JK^{-1} (c) –2.422 JK^{-1} (d) –5.981 JK^{-1}

10. Using listed information, calculate $\Delta_f G^\circ$ (in kJ/mol^{-1}) at 300 K
$$Co_3O_4(s) + 4CO(g) \longrightarrow 3Co(s) + 4CO_2(g)$$
Given : at 300 K ΔH_f° (kJ/mol) for Co_3O_4, CO, Co and CO_2 are, – 900, – 100, 0.0, – 400 respectively.
S° (J/K-mol) for Co_3O_4, Co and CO_2 are 100, 190, 30, 200 respectively. [Ignore negative sign]
(a) 28.5 kJ/mol (b) 410 kJ/mol (c) 175 kJ/mol (d) 309 kJ/mol

11. For a particular reaction, $\Delta H^\circ = -38.3$ kJ and $\Delta S^\circ = -113$ J K^{-1}. This reaction is
(a) spontaneous at all temperatures
(b) non-spontaneous at all temperatures
(c) spontaneous at a temperature below 339 K
(d) spontaneous at a temperature above 339 K

12. For oxidation of iron at 298 K,
$$4Fe(s) + 3O_2(g) \longrightarrow 2Fe_2O_3(s)$$
$\Delta S^\circ = -549.4$ J K^{-1} mol^{-1} and $\Delta H^\circ = -1648.0$ kJ mol^{-1}
Calculate the free energy change for the given reaction and also determine the nature of the given reaction.
(a) + 1484.28 kJ mol^{-1}, Non-spontaneous
(b) – 3132.22 kJ mol^{-1}, Non-spontaneous
(c) + 3132.22 kJ mol^{-1}, Spontaneous
(d) – 1484.28 kJ mol^{-1}, Spontaneous

13. 1 mole of an ideal gas at 25°C is subjected to expand reversibly 20 times of its initial volume. The change in entropy of expansion is
(a) 19.15 JK^{-1} mol^{-1} (b) 24.91 JK^{-1} mol^{-1}
(c) 20.30 JK^{-1} mol^{-1} (d) 13.25 JK^{-1} mol^{-1}

14. Calculate ΔS for 2 mole of a diatomic ideal gas which is heated and compressed from 400 K and 3 bar to 800 K and 12 bar : [Given : $C_{V,m}$ (gas) $= \frac{5R}{2}$; ln(2) = 0.70; $R = 2$ cal K^{-1} mol^{-1}]
(a) 4.2 cal K^{-1} (b) – 4.2 cal K^{-1}
(c) 14 cal K^{-1} (d) – 14 cal K^{-1}

15. $A_2(g) + B_2(g) \rightleftharpoons 2AB(g)$

$\Delta_r G^\circ$ and $\Delta_r S^\circ$ for above reaction are 30 kJ/mol and – 30 JK^{-1} mol^{-1} respectively at 200 K.

If $\Delta_r C_p$ is 20 JK^{-1} mol^{-1} then $\Delta_r H^\circ$ at 400 K is

(a) 80 kJ/mol (b) 45 kJ/mol (c) 28 kJ/mol (d) 78 kJ/mol

Type II 》 MCQs with One or More than One Correct Option

16. Which of the following statements are correct?
(a) The net increase in entropy of the system is zero in any reversible cyclic process
(b) The isothermally available energy present in a system is called its free energy
(c) The change of free energy with pressure for one mole of a perfect gas at constant pressure is $\Delta G = RT \log_e p_2/p_1$
(d) For a spontaneous change $(\Delta G)_{T,p} > 0$

17. Consider a series of isotherms and adiabates as shown

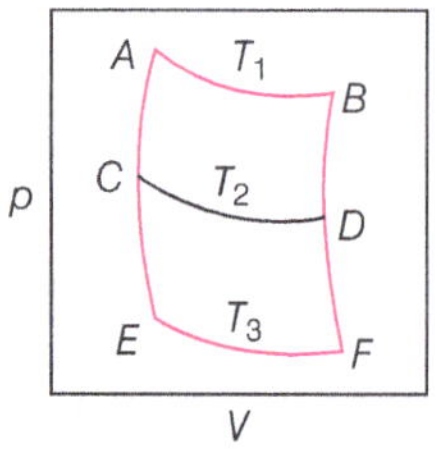

AB, CD and EF are isotherms.

AC, CE, BD and DF are adiabates.

Select the correct statement regarding the given data.

(a) $\Delta S_{(\text{system})}$ $A \to B$ is equal to $\Delta S_{(\text{system})}$ $A \to B \to D \to F$

(b) Among, $\frac{V_B}{V_A} = \frac{V_D}{V_C}$, $\frac{V_B}{V_A} = \frac{V_F}{V_E}$ and $\frac{V_B}{V_A} = \frac{V_C}{V_D}$ the relation $\frac{V_B}{V_A} = \frac{V_D}{V_C}$ is not true.

(c) $\Delta S_{(\text{system})}$ $A \to B$ and equal to $\Delta S_{(\text{system})}$ $A \to C \to E \to F$.

(d) $\Delta S_{(\text{system})}$ $A \to B$ is equal to $\Delta S_{(\text{system})}$ $A \to C \to D \to F$.

18. Select the correct reactions which has a negative sign for ΔS value
(a) $N_2(g) + 3H_2(g) \longrightarrow 2NH_3(g)$
(b) Desalination of water
(c) $3O_2(g) \longrightarrow 2O_3(g)$ (d) $C(s) + H_2O(l) \longrightarrow CO(g) + H_2(g)$

19. Which of the following statements are incorrect?
(a) For a reaction at 300 K, $X_2Y_4 \longrightarrow 2XY_2$ $\Delta H = 3$ kJ and $\Delta S = 30\ JK^{-1}$ at constant P and T, the reaction is spontaneous and entropy driven.
(b) Increases in temperature of an ideal at constant pressure is accompanied by increase in entropy of ideal gas.
(c) When $CaCO_3$ is heated to a high temperature it decomposes to CaO and CO_2, however it is quite stable at room temperature, because the term $\Delta_r H$ dominates $T\Delta S$ at high temperature.
(d) The normal boiling point of a liquid is 600 K. $\Delta H_{vap.}$ at normal boiling point is 60 kJ mol^{-1}. $\Delta G_{vap} > 0$ at 610 K and 1 atm.

20. Which of the following statements are correct?
(a) For an isolated system, the entropy either increases or remains constant but it never decreases.
(b) The normal boiling point of a liquid is 500 K ΔH_{vap} at normal boiling point is 50 kJ mol^{-1}. $\Delta S_{vap} < 100$ J mol^{-1} at 500 K and 2 atm.
(c) Molar Gibb's energy is an extensive property.
(d) Entropy of a closed system is maximum at equilibrium.

Type III 》 Numerical/Integer Type

21. In conversion of limestone to lime,

$$CaCO_3(s) \longrightarrow CaO(s) + CO_2(g)$$

The values of ΔH° and ΔS° are + 179.1 kJ mol^{-1} and 160.2 J/K mol respectively at 298 K and 1 bar. Assuming that ΔH° and ΔS° do not change with temperature, temperature above which conversion of limestone to lime will be spontaneous is .... K.

22. A sample of 20 g H_2O is slowly heated from 27°C to 87°C. Then change in entropy during heating is ....
(specific heat of water = 4200 J Kg^{-1} K^{-1}.

23. The reaction $N_2 + 3H_2 \longrightarrow 2NH_3$ is carried out at 300 K by mixing N_2 and H_2. The standard free energy of formation of NH_3 is – 16.4 kJ/mol. After a hour of mixing, the partial pressures of N_2, H_2 and NH_3 are 50 bar, 2 bar and 200 bar, respectively. The value of free energy at this stage of the reaction will be $(-x)$ kJ mol^{-1}.

24. On mole of an ideal gas at 400 K is in a 3.0 L vessel of thermally conducting walls, which are in contact with the surroundings. It undergoes isothermal reversible expansion from 3.0 L to 5.0 L against a constant pressure of 7 atm. The change in entropy of the surroundings (ΔS) is ...... $\times 10^{-3}$ JK^{-1}. [Nearest Integer]

Given, $R = 8.314$ JK^{-1} mol^{-1}

25. For a given chemical reaction, $X \to Y$ at 298 K, the free energy change is – 58.9 kJ mol^{-1} and the enthalpy of reaction is 67.8 kJ mol^{-1}. The entropy change of the reaction will be x JK^{-1} mol^{-1}. The value of x is ....

Elemental Practice 4.3 | Chapter 04

Connect with **Answers**

1. (d)	2. (d)	3. (b)	4. (b)	5. (b)	6. (d)
7. (a)	8. (b)	9. (a)	10. (d)	11. (c)	12. (d)
13. (b)	14. (a)	15. (c)	16. (a,b,c)	17. (a,c,d)	18. (a,b,c)
19. (c,d)	20. (a,b)	21. (1118)	22. (15.32)	23. (27.88)	24. (424)
25. (425)					

Element 4 Thermochemistry

Thermochemistry is the branch of chemistry that studies the energy changes, particularly, heat transfer, that occur during chemical reactions and phase changes. It focuses on understanding how heat is absorbed or released in various processes, which is essential for predicting the behavior of substances under different conditions.

Thermochemical Reactions and Equations

A balanced chemical equation which represents both, the chemical change as well as the heat change associated with it, is called thermochemical equation.

The physical state (along with allotropic states) of the substances can also be specified in these equations.

$$CH_4 + Cl_2 \longrightarrow CH_3Cl + HCl; \quad \Delta H = -115 \text{ kJ mol}^{-1}$$

$$C_2H_5OH(l) + 3O_2(g) \longrightarrow 2CO_2(g) + 3H_2O(l); \quad \Delta H = -1367 \text{ kJ mol}^{-1}$$

Depending upon the net release or absorption of heat, thermochemical reactions can be classified into two types; endothermic and exothermic reactions.

1. Endothermic Reaction

These are the reactions that involve transfer of heat to a chemical system from its surroundings. In other words, chemical reactions which proceed with the net absorption of heat are called **endothermic** reactions. For these reactions, the enthalpy of product is greater than reactant i.e. ΔH is + ve.

e.g. $N_2(g) + O_2(g) \longrightarrow 2NO\,(g);\ \Delta H^{\ominus} = +90.4$ kJ

The variation in the heat absorbed during endothermic reaction with time, i.e. as the reaction progress is shown in the graph given below.

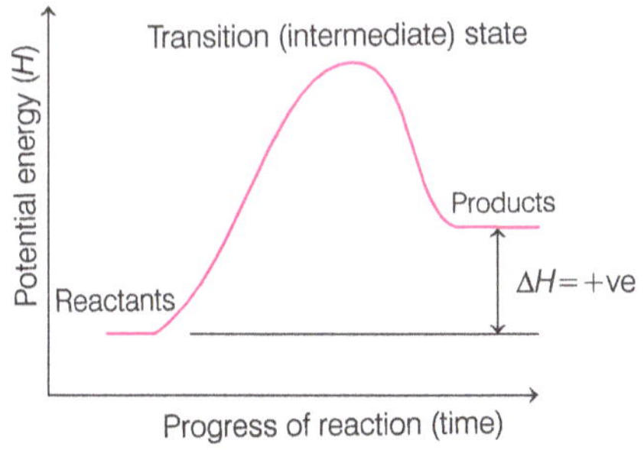

Net energy absorbed during an endothermic reaction

2. Exothermic Reaction

These are the reactions that involve transfer of heat from a chemical system to its surroundings. In other words, chemical reactions which proceed with the net release of heat are called **exothermic** reactions. For these reactions, the enthalpy of product is less than that of the reactant i.e ΔH is negative.

e.g. $4Al(s) + 3O_2(g) \longrightarrow 2Al_2O_3(s);\ \Delta H^{\ominus} = -1676$ kJ

The variation in the heat involved during exothermic reaction with time, i.e. as the reaction progress is shown in the graph given below.

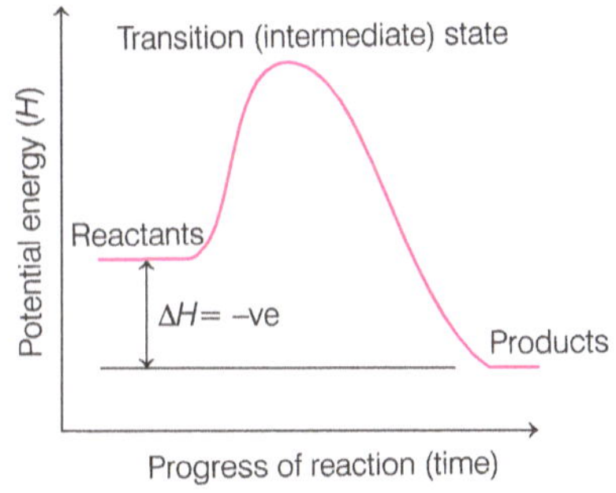

Net energy evolved during an exothermic reaction

Standard Enthalpy of Reaction

Standard enthalpy of a reaction is the enthalpy change for a reaction when all the reactants and products are in their standard states. It is represented by $\Delta_r H°$.

Factors Affecting Enthalpy of Reaction

There are a number of factors that affect the magnitude of the enthalpy of reactiod.

1. Reaction takes Place at Constant Pressure or Constant Volume

If chemical reaction occurs at constant volume, then heat change is called enthalpy of reaction at constant volume. Similarly, if reaction is taking place at constant pressure then heat change is called enthalpy of reaction at constant pressure. **These two values are almost same, if solids and liquids are involved in chemical reaction.**

In case of gases, there two values are considerably different

$$\Delta H° = \Delta E° + p\Delta V \Rightarrow \Delta H° = \Delta E° + \Delta n_g RT$$

where, $\Delta H°$ = enthalpy of reaction at constant p

$\Delta E°$ = enthalpy of reaction at constant V

Δn_g = difference of **coefficients** of gaseous products and reactants.

2. Effect of Temperature

Enthalpy of a substance increases when temperature increases. It happens due to variation in heat capacity of the system (reactants and products) with temperature.

The variation of enthalpy of reaction with temperature is given by **Kirchhoff's equation.**

Case I When ΔC_p is constant between two temperature T_1 and T_2

$$\Delta H_2 - \Delta H_1 = \Delta C_p (T_2 - T_1) \quad \ldots(\text{i})$$

$$\Delta E_2 - \Delta E_1 = \Delta C_V \cdot (T_2 - T_1) \quad \ldots(\text{ii})$$

Eqs. (i) and (ii) are known as **Kirchhoff's equations.**

Case II ΔC_p varies with temperature, $aA \longrightarrow rR$

$$\therefore \quad \Delta H = \Delta H_0 + \int \Delta C_p \, dT \quad \ldots(\text{iii})$$

where, ΔH_0 refers to the enthalpy change at absolute zero.

$$\because \quad (C_p = \alpha + \beta T + \gamma T^2)$$

or $$C_{pA} = \alpha_A + \beta_A T + \gamma_A T^2$$

$$C_{pR} = \alpha_R + \beta_R T + \gamma_R T^2$$

3. Physical States of the Reactants and Products

Since, an appreciable change is involved in changing a substance from one state of matter to another, that is the reason that physical state always affects the enthalpy of reaction. It is important that a state symbol is attached to all the formulae given in an equation, e.g.

(i) $H_2(g) + \frac{1}{2}O_2(g) \longrightarrow H_2O(l), \ \Delta H° = -285.9 \text{ kJmol}^{-1}$

(Formation of water in liquid state).

(ii) $H_2(g) + \frac{1}{2}O_2(g) \longrightarrow H_2O(g), \ \Delta H° = -241.8 \text{ kJ mol}^{-1}$

(Formation of water in gaseous state).

4. Strength of Intermolecular Attractions

The magnitude of enthalpy change depends on the strength of the intermolecular attractions in the substance undergoing the phase transformations.

(i) In water molecules, there is strong hydrogen bonding which holds the molecules together.

(ii) In acetone molecular, dipole-dipole interactions are weak compared to water.

Thus, molar enthalpy of vaporisations of acetone is less than that of water.

5. Quantities of Reactants

The enthalpy of reaction also depends on quantities of reactants. It increases with increase in number of moles of reactants. It is doubled when number of moles of reactants is doubled.

Enthalpy is a State Function

Enthalpy is a state function, a change in enthalpy is independent of the path between two states. Thus, same value of $\Delta H°$ will be obtained however the change is brought about (so long as the initial and final states are the same).

Consider the conversion of solid to vapour by two paths.

Path I $H_2O(s) \longrightarrow H_2O(g), \ \Delta H°_{sub}$

Path II $H_2O(l) \longrightarrow H_2O(g), \ \Delta H°_{vap}$

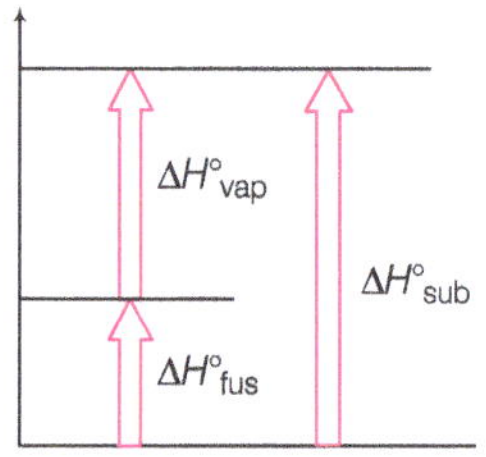

Step I $H_2O(s) \longrightarrow H_2O(l), \ \Delta H°_{fus}$

Step II $H_2O(l) \longrightarrow H_2O(g), \ \Delta H°_{vap}$

Overall $H_2O(s) \longrightarrow H_2O(g)$

$$\Delta H°_{sub} = \Delta H°_{fus} + \Delta H°_{vap}$$

Step I and Step II involve phase change from solid to liquid and then from liquid to vapour.

Enthalpy required to convert one mole of solid phase (ice) to liquid phase (water liquid) is called **molar enthalpy of fusion** ΔH_{fus} ($\Delta H°_{fus}$ in standard state) and molar enthalpy of vaporisation ΔH_{vap} or in general enthalpy of phase transition. Because the overall result of the indirect path II is the same as that of the direct path I, the overall enthalpy change is the same in each case.

Solved Booster 4.1

Given $H°_{C_2H_4} = +52.5 \text{ kJ mol}^{-1}$ or $H°_{C_2H_6} = -83.8 \text{ kJ mol}^{-1}$

What is $\Delta_r H°$ of a reaction at 298 K in which 1 mole of $C_2H_4(g)$ is hydrogenated to $C_2H_6(g)$.

(a) −160.3 (b) 180.6

(c) −133.8 (d) 196.7

Solution

$\Delta_r H° = H°_{C_2H_6} - [H°_{C_2H_4} + H°_{H_2}]$

$= -83.8 - [52.5 + 0] = -136.3$ kJ mol^{-1}

$\Delta H° = \Delta E° + \Delta n_g RT$

$\Delta n_g = 1 - 2 = -1$

$\Delta E° = \Delta H° - \Delta n_g RT$

$= -136.3 - (-1)\, 8.3143 \times 10^{-3} \times 298$

$= -133.8$ kJ mol^{-1}

Enthalpies of Different Types of Reaction

Based on type of reaction taking place, enthalpy change is defined in that term and different terms have been summarised in Table.

Enthalpy of Formation

The enthalpy change which occurs when one mole of a compound is formed from its constituent elements, is known as enthalpy of formation. If compound is formed under standard conditions, from its elements in their standard states, then it is known as the **standard enthalpy (or heat) of formation** of the substance. It is denoted by ΔH°_f.

e.g.

(i) $H_2(g) + \frac{1}{2}O_2(g) \longrightarrow H_2O\,(l)$, $\Delta H°_f = -286$ kJ mol^{-1}

(ii) $H_2(g) + Cl_2(g) \longrightarrow 2HCl(g)$, $\Delta H° = -92.3$ kJ

for two moles of HCl(g)

Hence, $\Delta H^\circ_f(HCl) = -\frac{92.3}{2}$ kJ mol^{-1}

(iii) $C(s) + 2H_2(g) \longrightarrow CH_4(g)$, $\Delta H°_f = -74.8$ kJ

The standard enthalpy of formation is defined as follows:

The standard enthalpy of formation of a compound is the change in the standard enthalpy when one mole of the compound is formed starting from the requisite amounts of elements in their stable states of aggregation.

JEE Alert

The standard enthalpy of formation of every element in its stable state of aggregation at one bar pressure and at specified temperature is assigned a zero value.

The specified temperature is usually taken as 25 °C.

A few example are

$\Delta_f H°(O_2, g) = 0$

$\Delta_f H°$ (C, graphite) $= 0$ $\Delta_f H°$ (C, diamond) $\neq 0$

$\Delta_f H°(Br_2, 1) = 0$

$\Delta_f H°$ (S, rhombic) $= 0$ $\Delta_f H°$ (S, monoclinic) $\neq 0$

$\Delta_f H°$ (P, white) $= 0$ $\Delta_f H°$ (P, black) $\neq 0$

All the calculations are based on the enthalpy changes, and not an actual enthalpy values.

This will make the **thermochemical calculations quite easier**.

Solved Booster 4.2

Calculate enthalpy of formation of benzene if enthalpy change of the given reaction is −3303 kJ

$$C_6H_6(l) + 7.5O_2 \longrightarrow 6\,CO_2(g) + 3H_2O(l)$$

Given, $\Delta H^\circ_f(CO_2) = -393.5$ kJ mol^{-1}

$\Delta H_f(H_2O) = -285.8$ kJ mol^{-1}

(a) 84.6 (b) 89.0 (c) −28.9 (d) −49.0

Solution (a)

We use simple concept that

ΔH°_f (of a substance) = Enthalpy of that Substance

H (element) = zero

$\therefore\ \Delta H° = [6\Delta H_f°(CO_2) + 3\Delta H_f°(H_2O)] - [\Delta H_f°(C_6H_6) + 7.5\Delta H_f°(O_2)]$

$-3303 = 6 \times (-393.5) + 3(-285.8) - \Delta H_f°(C_6H_6) - 0$

$\therefore\ \Delta H_f°(C_6H_6) = 84.6$ kJ mol^{-1}

JEE **MAPPER**

Example Similar to PYQ Asked in JEE Advanced 2022

2 moles of Mg(s) is combusted in a fixed volume bomb calorimeter with excess of O_2 at 298 K and 1 atm in MgO(*s*). During the reaction, temperature increases from 298.0 K to 316.5 K. If heat capacity of the bomb calorimeter and enthalpy of formation of Mg(*s*) is 22 kJ K^{-1} and 60.22 kJ mol^{-1} at 298 K, respectively, the calculated standard molar enthalpy of formation MgO(*s*) at 298 K is *X* kJ mol^{-1}. The value of $|X|$ is ......

[Given, gas constant $R = 8.3\ JK^{-1}\ mol^{-1}$]

Sol. *(144.5)* The combustion reaction is

$$2Mg(s) + O_2(g) \longrightarrow 2MgO(s)$$

Given, heat capacity of calorimeter,

$$C = 22\ kJ\ K^{-1},\ T_i = 298\ K,\ T_f = 316.5\ K$$

Change in temperature $(\Delta T) = 298 - 316.5 = -18.5\ K$

Heat evolved in reaction,

$$q = C\Delta T = 22 \times -18.5\ K = 407\ kJ$$

Since, the reaction is taking place under constant volume

$$\Delta U_r = -407\ kJ$$

Enthalpy of reaction,

$$\Delta H_r^\circ = \Delta U^\circ + \Delta n_g RT$$
$$= -407\ kJ - 1 \times 8.3 \times 10^{-3}\ kJ\ mol^{-1}\ K^{-1} \times 298\ K$$
$$= -407\ kJ - 2.47\ kJ = -409.47\ kJ$$

Also,

$$\Delta H_r^\circ = 2\Delta H_f^\circ[MgO(s)] - 2\Delta H^\circ f[Mg(s)] - \Delta H_f^\circ[O_2(g)]$$
$$= -409.47 = 2\Delta H_f^\circ[MgO(s)] - 2 \times 60.22 - 0$$
$$2\Delta H_f^\circ[MgO(s)] = -289.03$$
$$\Delta H_f^\circ[MgO(s)] = \frac{-289.03}{2} = -144.5\ kJ\ mol^{-1}$$
$$|X| = 144.5\ kJ\ mol^{-1}$$

Competency Enhancer 4.1

1 mole of propane is combusted in a fixed volume bomb calorimeter with excess of O_2 at 298 K and 1 atm in $CO_2(g)$ and $H_2O(l)$. During the reaction, temperature increases from 298 K to 325 K. If heat capacity of the bomb calorimeter and enthalpy of formation of propane is 30 kJ K^{-1} and 66.44 kJ mol^{-1} at 298 K, respectively, the calculated standard molar enthalpy of formation of $H_2O(l)$ at 298 K is *X* kJ mol^{-1}. The value of $|X|$ is ....

[Given, $\Delta H_f^\circ[(CO_2(g)] = 20\ kJ\ mol^{-1}$, $R = 8.3\ JK^{-1}\ mol^{-1}$]

Enthalpy of Combustion

The enthalpy decrease (ΔH = –ve, exothermic change) that takes place when one mole of the substance is completely burnt in oxygen is called enthalpy of combustion. If combustion takes place in standard conditions, i.e. all reactants and products are brought to 25°C and 1 bar pressure, then enthalpy change is called **standard enthalpy of combustion.**

e.g.

(i) $CH_4(g) + 2O_2(g) \longrightarrow CO_2(g) + 2H_2O(l)$,
$\Delta H^\circ = -890\ kJ\ mol^{-1}$

(ii) $C(graphite) + \frac{1}{2}O_2(g) \longrightarrow CO(g);\ \Delta H_1^\circ = -108.7\ kJ\ mol^{-1}$

This (b) does not represent heat of combustion of carbon since $CO(g)$ can be further oxidised to CO_2

$$CO(g) + \frac{1}{2}O_2(g) \longrightarrow CO_2(g);\ \Delta H_2^\circ = -284.4\ kJ\ mol^{-1}$$

Thus, $C(graphite) + O_2 \longrightarrow CO_2$;

$$\Delta H^\circ = \Delta H_1^\circ + \Delta H_2^\circ = -393\ kJ\ mol^{-1}$$

Heat of combustion of hydrocarbons, food materials fuels, etc can be converted into **calorific values** which are measured **per gram** of the substance. If heat of combustion of graphite is 393 kJ mol^{-1}, its **calorific value** is taken as 32.75 kJ g^{-1}. Calorific values of LPG is determined by this.

Enthalpy of Neutralisation

The enthalpy of neutralisation of an acid with an alkali is the enthalpy of reaction which takes place when an amount of acid or alkali is neutralised to form one mole of water in dilute aqueous solution.

$$HCl(aq) + NaOH(aq) \longrightarrow NaCl(aq) + H_2O(l);\quad \Delta H = -57.3\ kJ\ mol^{-1}$$

$$H^+(aq) + OH^-(aq) \longrightarrow H_2O(l);\ \Delta H = -57.3\ kJ\ mol^{-1}$$

Since, HCl, NaOH and NaCl are strong electrolytes.

- **Heat of neutralisation of strong acid with strong base is constant and is –57.3 kJ mol^{-1}.**

  It is explained on the basis of theory of ionisation. In all cases when a strong acid is neutralised by a strong base, it is actually a reaction between H^+ ion (from a strong acid) and OH^- ion (from a strong base).

  $$HCl(aq) + NaOH(aq) \rightleftharpoons NaCl(aq) + H_2O(l)$$
  $$H^+(aq) + Cl^-(aq) + Na^+(aq) + OH^-(aq) \rightleftharpoons Na^+(aq) + Cl^-(aq) + H_2O(l)$$

  On cancelling common ions

  $$H^+(aq) + OH^-(aq) \rightleftharpoons H_2O(l)$$

  Thus, enthalpy of neutralisation of a strong acid by a strong base is constant (= –57.3 kJ mol^{-1}).

- **Heat of neutralisation of strong acid and weak base or weak acid and strong base or weak acid and weak base is less than –57.3 kJ mol^{-1}** since, some heat is also absorbed in the ionisation of weak electrolyte.

  Enthalpy of neutralisation of acetic acid by strong base (NaOH) is –55.4 kJ mol^{-1}

Explanation

Neutralisation involves

Step I $CH_3COOH(aq) \rightleftharpoons CH_3COO^-(aq) + H^+(aq);\ \Delta H° = q$
Weak acid

Step II $NaOH(aq) \rightleftharpoons Na^+(aq) + OH^-(aq);\ \Delta H° = 0$
Strong base

Step III $H^+(aq) + OH^-(aq) \rightleftharpoons H_2O(l);\ \Delta H° = -57.3\ \text{kJ mol}^{-1}$

Net $CH_3COOH(aq) + OH^-(aq) \rightleftharpoons CH_3COO^-(aq) + H_2O(l);$

$$\Delta H° = q + 0 - 57.3$$

$$\therefore \quad q + 0 - 57.3 = -55.4$$

$$\therefore \quad q = 1.9\ \text{kJ mol}^{-1}$$

$1.9\ \text{kJ mol}^{-1}$ is absorbed in the ionisation of weak acid hence enthalpy of neutralisation of weak acid by a strong base is less than 57.3 kJ.

- For the case of neutralisation of weak acid by a weak base, enthalpy of neutralisation further decreases as heat is also absorbed in the ionisation of weak base.

JEE Alert

HF is a weak acid, but heat of neutralisation is much higher than that of strong acid and strong base i.e. 68.6 kJ mol^{-1}. It is due to the fact that it also involves hydration of F^- ion.

Solved Booster 4.3

What is heat of neutralisation on mixing 100 mL of 1 M $Ca(OH)_2$ and 100 mL of 1M H_2SO_4? (consider electrolytes as strong) in kJ.

(a) −550 (b) −26.5

(c) −11.46 (d) −279

Solution (c)

$$Ca(OH)_2 = \frac{100 \times 1}{1000} = 0.1\,\text{mol} = 02\ \text{mol}\ OH^-$$

$$H_2SO_4 = \frac{100 \times 1}{1000} = 0.1\,\text{mol} = 02\ \text{mol}\ H^+$$

$$\therefore\ 2H^+(aq) + 2OH^-(aq) \longrightarrow 2H_2O(l)$$

$$\therefore\ \Delta H° = 0.2 \times (-57.3)\ \text{kJ} = -11.46\ \text{kJ}$$

Enthalpy of Solution ($\Delta_{sol}H°$)

It is well known fact that dissolution of solute in a solvent is exothermic or endothermic depending on the nature of solute. The total energy released or absorbed when one mole of solute is dissolved in large excess of a solvent so that further addition of solvent does not produce further heat change, is called enthalpy of solution.

Endothermic $KCl(s) + H_2O(l) \rightleftharpoons KCl(aq);\ \Delta H° > 0$

Exothermic $CaO(s) + H_2O(l) \rightleftharpoons Ca(OH)_2;\ \Delta H° < 0$

Enthalpy of Dilution

It is defined as the enthalpy change when solution containing one mole of solute diluted from one concentration to other concentration.

$$HCl(g) + 5H_2O \longrightarrow HCl\cdot 5H_2O, \qquad \Delta H_1 = x_1$$

$$HCl(g) + 25H_2O \longrightarrow HCl\cdot 25H_2O, \qquad \Delta H_2 = x_2$$

$$HCl\cdot 5H_2O + 20H_2O \longrightarrow HCl\cdot 25H_2O, \qquad \Delta H = (x_2 - x_1)$$

The differential heat of solution depends on the concentration of the solution. It is impractical to measure the differential heat of solution directly, but it can be calculated from the integral heat of solution data.

When ΔH value is plotted against the moles of solute (mole per kg solvent, i.e. the molality) the slope of the tangent at a given concentration gives the differential heat of solution ΔH.

If ΔH is the enthalpy change when n_2 moles of a solute are mixed with n_1 moles of solvent, then

$$\left(\frac{\partial \Delta H}{\partial n_2}\right)_{T,\,P,\,n_1} = \Delta H = \text{Differential enthalpy of solution}$$

and $$\left(\frac{\partial \Delta H}{\partial n_1}\right)_{T,\,P,\,n_2} = \Delta H' = \text{Differential enthalpy of dilution}$$

Thus, total enthalpy change is $\Delta H_T = n_2 \Delta H + n_1 \Delta H'$

if 1 kJ of water is taken then $n_1 = \frac{1000}{18} = 55.55$ mol

$$\therefore \quad \Delta H_T = n_2 \Delta H + 55.55 \Delta H'$$

Enthalpy of Hydration

It is defined as the enthalpy change when one mole of solute is hydrated.

$$CuSO_4(s) + 5H_2O(l) \longrightarrow CuSO_4\cdot 5H_2O(s),$$

$$\Delta H_{\text{Hydration}} = -78.21\ \text{kJ mol}^{-1}$$

Hydration is generally **exothermic change**.

If integral heat of solution of the hydrated and anhydrous salt is known, then heat of hydration can be calculated.

e.g.

(a) $CuSO_4(\text{anhy.}) + 800H_2O(l) \longrightarrow CuSO_4(800H_2O);$

$$\Delta H = -66.50\ \text{kJ}$$

(b) $CuSO_4\cdot 5H_2O + 795H_2O(l) \longrightarrow CuSO_4(800H_2O);$

$$\Delta H = 11.71\ \text{kJ}$$

Thus, $(a - b)$ gives

$$CuSO_4(s) + 5H_2O(l) \longrightarrow CuSO_4\cdot 5H_2O(s),$$

$$\Delta H_{\text{hydration}} = -78.21\ \text{kJ}$$

- $\Delta H_{\text{solution}} = (\Delta H_{\text{hydration}} - \text{lattice energy})$
- If $\Delta H_{\text{hydration}} >$ lattice energy, solute dissolves in water.
- If $\Delta H_{\text{hydration}} <$ lattice energy, solute does not dissolve in water.
- If $\Delta H_{\text{hydration}} =$ lattice energy, solute remains in equilibrium with given solvent, i.e. H_2O.

Solved Booster 4.4

At 298 K, the heat of solution of $MgSO_4(s)$ is -91.21 kJ mol^{-1} and that of $MgSO_4 \cdot 7H_2O(s)$ is 13.81 kJ mol^{-1}. Calculate heat of hydration of $MgSO_4(s)$, i.e. ΔH for the reaction.

$$MgSO_4(s) + 7H_2O(l) \longrightarrow MgSO_4 \cdot 7H_2O(s)$$

(a) -105.02 kJ mol^{-1} (b) -279.5 kJ mol^{-1}

(c) -3900 kJ mol^{-1} (d) -469.7 kJ mol^{-1}

Solution (a)

(i) $MgSO_4(s) + (aq) \longrightarrow MgSO_4 \cdot 7H_2O(aq)$, $\Delta H_1 = 91.21$ kJ mol^{-1}

(ii) $MgSO_4 \cdot 7H_2O(s) + (aq) \longrightarrow MgSO_4 \cdot 7H_2O(aq)$, $\Delta H_2 = 13.81$ kJ mol^{-1}

Equation (i) involve two steps:

(iii) $MgSO_4(s) + 7H_2O \longrightarrow MgSO_4 \cdot 7H_2O(s)$, $\Delta H_3 = ?$

(iv) $MgSO_4 \cdot 7H_2O(s) + (aq) \longrightarrow MgSO_4 \cdot 7H_2O(aq)$, $\Delta H_2 = 13.81$ kJ mol^{-1}

We find (iii) + (iv) = ((i)

$\because$ $[xH_2O + (aq) \longrightarrow (aq)]$, $\Delta H_3 + \Delta H_2 = \Delta H_1$

Thus, for

$$MgSO_4(s) + 7H_2O \longrightarrow MgSO_4 \cdot 7H_2O(s)$$

$$\Delta H_3 = \Delta H_1 - \Delta H_2 = -91.21 - 13.81$$

$$= -105.02 \text{ kJ mol}^{-1}$$

Different types of standard enthalpy changes (based on IUPAC recommendations)

S. No.	Transition enthalpy	Examples	Definition	Symbol
1.	Enthalpy of formation	$Na(s) + \frac{1}{2}Cl(g) \longrightarrow NaCl(s)$	One mole of the compound formed from its elements.	$\Delta_f H^\circ$ or ΔH_f°
2.	Enthalpy of combustion	$CH_4(g) + 2O_2 \longrightarrow CO_2(g) + 2H_2O(l)$	One mole of the compound (fuel) is burnt completely in oxygen (oxidation).	$\Delta_c H^\circ$ or ΔH_c°
3.	Enthalpy of fusion	$H_2O(s) \longrightarrow H_2O(l)$	One mole of the liquid is formed from the solid without a change in temperature.	$\Delta_{fus} H^\circ$ or ΔH_{fus}°
4.	Enthalpy of vaporisation	$H_2O(l) \longrightarrow H_2O(g)$	One mole of the vapour formed from the liquid without a change in temperature.	$\Delta_{vap} H^\circ$ or ΔH_{vap}°
5.	Enthalpy of sublimation	$H_2O(s) \longrightarrow H_2O(g)$	One mole of the vapour formed from the solid.	$\Delta_{sub} H^\circ$ or ΔH_{sub}°
6.	Enthalpy of atomisation	$H_2(g) \longrightarrow 2H(g)$	One mole of the substance broken into isolated atoms in the gas phase.	$\Delta_{at} H^\circ$ or ΔH_{at}°
7.	Enthalpy of reaction	$A \longrightarrow B$	Enthalpy change taking place in a reaction.	$\Delta_r H^\circ$ or ΔH_r°
8.	Enthalpy of neutralisation	$HCl(aq) + NaOH(aq) \longrightarrow H_2O + NaCl(aq)$	One mole of water formed by the neutralisation of an acid by a base.	$\Delta_n H^\circ$ or ΔH_n°
9.	Enthalpy of ionisation	$Na(g) \longrightarrow Na^+(g) + e^-$	One mole atoms ionised - all species in gaseous phase.	$\Delta_{ion} H^\circ$ or ΔH_{ion}°
10.	Electron gain enthalpy	$X(g) + e^- \longrightarrow X^-(g)$	One mole of anions being formed all species in the gaseous phase.	$\Delta_{eg} H^\circ$ or ΔH_{eg}°
11.	Lattice enthalpy	$K^+Cl^-(s) \longrightarrow K^+(g) + Cl^-(g)$	One mole of a crystal completely separated into isolated particles in the gaseous phase. For reverse reaction in which lattice is formed.	$\Delta_L H^\circ$ or ΔH_L° $-\Delta_L H^\circ$ or $-\Delta H_L^\circ$
12.	Bond dissociation enthalpy (bond $A-B$)	$HX(g) \longrightarrow H(g) + X(g)$	One mole of bonds broken-all species in the gaseous phase.	ΔH_{A-B}°
13.	Enthalpy of solution	$A(s) + H_2O$ (excess) $\longrightarrow A(aq)$	One mole of the solute dissolved in excess of solvent so that further dilution produces no enthalpy change.	$\Delta_{sol} H^\circ$ or ΔH_{sol}°
14.	Enthalpy of hydration	$X^\pm(g) \longrightarrow X^\pm(aq)$	One mole of the ion in gaseous phase is hydrated.	$\Delta_{hyd} H^\circ$ or ΔH°_{hyd}
15.	Enthalpy of mixing	Pure substance $\longrightarrow$ mixture	One mole each of the two or more substances is mixed.	$\Delta_{mix} H^\circ$ or ΔH°_{mix}

Bond Energy or Bond Enthalpy

Chemical reactions involve breaking and making of chemical bonds. Energy is required to break a bond and energy is released when a bond is formed. The bond enthalpies are very important quantities as reaction enthalpy arises from the changes that accompany the breaking of old bond and formation of the new ones. We can predict enthalpy for a reaction in gas phase if bond enthalpies are known.

Average of the energy required to break all bonds of one type present in one mole of the gaseous covalent substance to form products in the gaseous state is called **bond energy**.

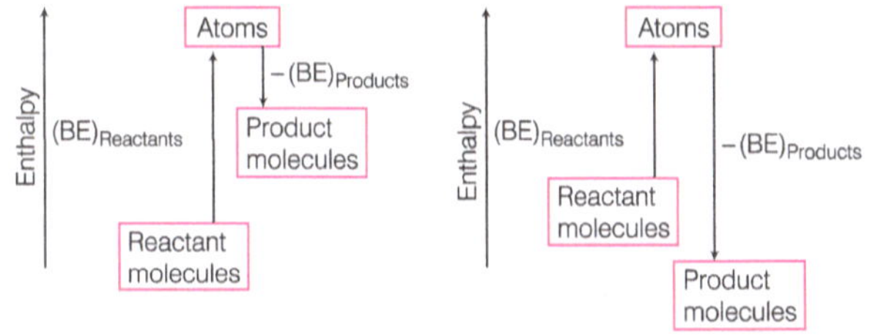

(a) (b)

(a) Bond enthalpy change in endothermic reaction.
(b) Bond enthalpy change in an exothermic reaction.

Consider a polyatomic molecule like $CH_4(g)$

Its four C—H bonds are cleaved in steps as given: $\Delta H°$

$CH_4(g) \longrightarrow CH_3(g) + H(g)$,	427 kJ mol^{-1}
$CH_3(g) \longrightarrow CH_2(g) + H(g)$,	439 kJ mol^{-1}
$CH_2(g) \longrightarrow CH(g) + H(g)$,	452 kJ mol^{-1}
$CH(g) \longrightarrow C(g) + H(g)$,	347 kJ mol^{-1}
Overall $CH_4(g) \longrightarrow C(g) + 4H(g)$	1665 kJ mol^{-1}

We now define the 'average' bond energy of C—H bond in CH_4 as :

$$= \frac{1}{4}\Delta H° = \frac{1665}{4} = 416.25 \text{ kJ mol}^{-1}$$

Bond Dissociation Enthalpy

The energy required to break a given bond in some specific compound is defined as the **bond dissociation energy**. It is a definite quantity and dependent on the presence of other groups in the molecule.

$$H—O—H(g) \longrightarrow H(g) + OH(g);\ \Delta H^\circ_{298} = 498 \text{ kJ mol}^{-1}$$

$$O—H(g) \longrightarrow H(g) + O(g);\quad \Delta H^\circ_{298} = 430 \text{ kJ mol}^{-1}$$

Thus, the bond dissociation energy of O—H bond in H_2O molecule is 498 kJ mol^{-1} and that of O—H bond in hydroxyl group is 430 kJ mol^{-1}.

Bond breaking is an endothermic process and is thus a compaired by absorption of energy, it resulting into a **positive value of bond dissociation enthalpy**.

On the other hand, bond formation is an exothermic process and is thus accompanied by release of energy resulting into a **negative value of bond dissociation enthalpy**.

JEE Quicker

At 298.2 K the relationship between enthalpy of bond dissociation (in kJ mol^{-1}) for hydrogen (E_H) and its isotope, deuterium (E_D), is best described by $E_H \approx E_D - 7.5$ kJ/mol.
JEE Main 2021

Deuterium is an isotope of hydrogen that contains an extra neutron in its nucleus, making it heavier than hydrogen. The lighter mass of hydrogen leads to a higher vibrational frequency and higher zero point energy, which means that less energy in required to break the bond in H_2 compared to D_2.

Atomisation Enthalpy ($\Delta_a H°$)

Enthalpy change on breaking one mole of bonds completely to obtain atoms in the gas phase is called **atomisation enthalpy.**

For all diatomic molecules, the bond dissociation enthalpy is same as enthalpy of atomisation. e.g. polyatomic molecules, the bond dissociation enthalpy for different bonds is different within the same molecule.

$$H_2(g) \longrightarrow 2H(g),\qquad \Delta_a H° = 435 \text{ kJ mol}^{-1}$$

In this case atomisation enthalpy is also the bond dissociation enthalpy.

In the following example,

$$CH_4(g) \longrightarrow C(g) + 4H(g);\quad \Delta H° = 1665 \text{ kJ mol}^{-1}$$

atomisation enthalpy of $CH_4(g)$ is 1665 kJ mol^{-1}, but bond energy of (C—H) bond is $= \frac{1665}{4} = 416.25$ kJ mol^{-1}

Application of Bond Energy

1. Determination of Enthalpy of Reaction

With the help of bond enthalpy, we can calculate enthalpies of reaction in gaseous phase involving elements or compounds having covalent bonds.

e.g. 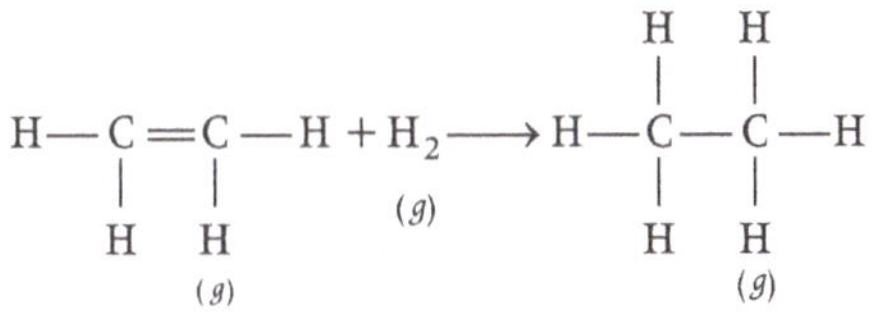

$$\Delta H = (BE)_{Reactants} - (BE)_{Products}$$
$$= [(BE)_{C=C} + 4(BE)_{C—H} + (BE)_{H—H}] - [6(BE)_{C—H} + (BE)_{C—C}]$$

$$H_2(g) + \frac{1}{2}O_2(g) \longrightarrow H_2O(l)$$

In this case, heat required to convert $H_2O(l)$ into $H_2O(g)$ is also added.

$$\Delta H = [(BE)_{H—H} + \frac{1}{2}(BE)_{O=O}] - [2(BE)_{O—H} + \text{Heat of vaporisation of } H_2O(l)]$$

2. Determination of Heat of Formation

The enthalpy of formation or a dissociation of a compound can be calculated from the bond energies of the constituent bonds.

In the above example, $H_2O(l)$ is formed from its element, hence heat of formation can also be evaluated using bond enthalpy values.

3. Determination of Resonance Energy

For a compound exhibiting resonance, there is a difference between heat of formation based on experimental and theoretical values.

This difference is due to stablisation by resonance, which is a measure of resonance energy. (using BE).

Resonance energy = (Experimental value of $\Delta H_f^\circ - \Delta H_f^\circ$ based on bond energies)

Solved Booster 4.5

Use values of mean bond enthalpies (given below) The standard enthalpy change for the gas phase isomerisation of methoxymethane to form ethanol is

$$CH_3—O—CH_3(g) \longrightarrow CH_3CH_2OH(g)$$

Bond	(BE)/kJ mol^{-1}
C—H	412
C—O	358
C—C	347
O—H	464

Solution

$\Delta_{isom}H^\circ$ = (BE of all bonds in reactants) – (BE of all bonds in products)

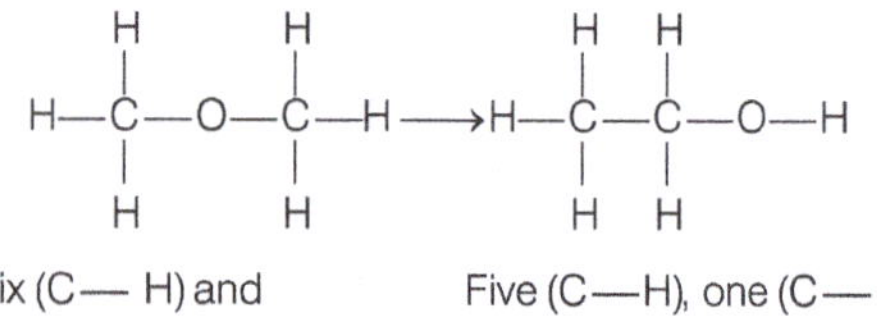

Six (C— H) and two (C—O) bonds

Five (C—H), one (C—O), one (C—C) and one (O—H) bonds

$$\Delta H^\circ = [6(BE)_{C—H} + 2(BE)_{C—O}] - [5(BE)_{C—H} + (BE)_{C—O} + (BE)_{O—H} + (BE)_{C—C}]$$

$$= (BE)_{C—H} + (BE)_{C—O} - (BE)_{O—H} - (BE)_{C—C}$$

$$= 412 + 358 - 464 - 347$$

$$= -41 \text{ kJ mol}^{-1}$$

Hess's Law of Constant Heat Summation

For a chemical equation that can be written as the sum of two or more steps, the enthalpy change for the overall equation is equal to the sum of the enthalpy changes for the individual steps.

Thus, Hess's law enables us to break down a reaction into so many intermediate steps and assign to each step an individual enthalpy change. The sum of the individual changes must, of course, equal the overall enthalpy change provided the initial and final states are the same in each case. **Thus it is a special case of first law of thermodynamics**.

Application of Hess's law

1. Born-Haber Cycle

This cycle is based on thermochemical changes taking place in the formation of a lattice. This cycle can be used to determine **lattice energy** which cannot be directly measured. It is defined as the energy released when one mole of the ionic compound (lattice) is formed from its isolated ions in the gaseous state under standard condition.

$$nA^{m+}(g) + mB^{n-}(g) \longrightarrow A_nB_m(s)$$

$\Delta H = -U$ (lattice energy)

Formation of NaCl (s) lattice involves

Direct method

$$Na(s) + \frac{1}{2}Cl_2(g) \longrightarrow NaCl(s);\ \Delta H_1 = q$$

Step-wise method

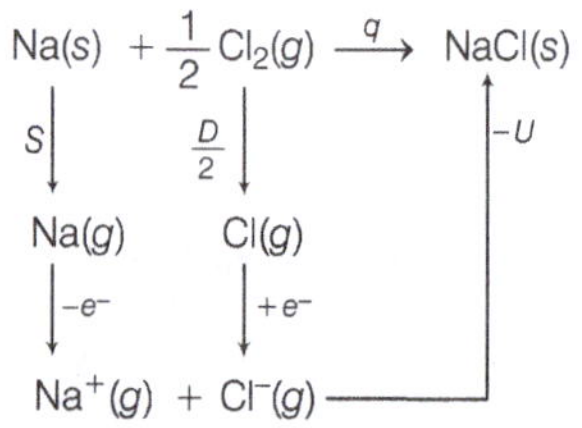

Assume

S = heat of sublimation of Na(s)

I = ionisation energy of Na(g)

D = dissociation energy of Cl_2

E = electron affinity of Cl(g)

U = lattice energy

q = heat of formation of NaCl(s)

$$Na(s) \longrightarrow Na(g); \quad \Delta H = S$$

$$Na(g) \longrightarrow Na^+(g) + e^-; \quad \Delta H = I$$

$$\frac{1}{2}Cl_2(g) \longrightarrow Cl(g); \quad \Delta H = \frac{D}{2}$$

$$Cl(g) + e^- \longrightarrow Cl^-(g); \qquad \Delta H = -E$$

$$Na^+(g) + Cl^-(g) \longrightarrow Na^+Cl^-(s); \qquad \Delta H = -U$$

$$\text{Net } Na(s) + \frac{1}{2}Cl_2(g) \longrightarrow NaCl(s);$$

$$\Delta H_2 = (S + I + \frac{D}{2} - E - U)$$

Both methods involve same chemical reaction, hence

$$\Delta H_1 = \Delta H_2$$

Thus, $S + I + \frac{D}{2} - E - U = q$

$$U = (S + I + \frac{D}{2} - E - q)$$

If lattice is $MgX_2(s)$, then

$$S + (I_1 + I_2) + D - 2E - U = q$$

where, $(I_1 + I_2)$ = total ionisation energy to form $Mg^{2+}(g)$.

2. Enthalpy of Intermediate Step

With the help of Hess's law, energy of intermediate step of a reaction can be determined.

CO_2 can be prepared by

I. **Direct method**

$$C(s) + O_2(g) \longrightarrow CO_2(g); \qquad \Delta H_1^\circ = x_1 \text{ (say)}$$

II. **Indirect method** (with steps)

(a) $C(s) + \frac{1}{2}O_2(g) \longrightarrow CO(g); \Delta H = x_2$

(b) $CO(g) + \frac{1}{2}O_2(g) \longrightarrow CO_2(g); \Delta H = x_3$

$$\text{Net } C(s) + O_2(g) \longrightarrow CO_2(g)$$

$$\Delta H_2 = x_2 + x_3$$

If enthalpy of step (a) is not known then it can be derived since, $\Delta H_1 = \Delta H_2$

$$x_1 = x_2 + x_3$$

$$\therefore \quad x_2 = (x_1 - x_3)$$

Solved Booster 4.6

From the reactions,

I. $2Na(s) + \frac{1}{2}O_2(g) \longrightarrow Na_2O, \Delta H = x$

II. $Na_2O + H_2O \longrightarrow 2NaOH, \Delta H = -56$ kcal

III. $2Na + 2H_2O \longrightarrow 2NaOH + H_2, \Delta H = -88$ kcal

IV. $H_2 + \frac{1}{2}O_2 \longrightarrow H_2O, \Delta H = -68$ kcal

For these value, the value of x is ......

Solution (−100)

By application of Hess's law, value of x, i.e. the enthalpy of formation of Na_2O can be evaluated. NaOH can be formed directly or by algebraic summation of above thermochemical reactions.

Adding I and II

$$2Na + H_2O + \frac{1}{2}O_2 \longrightarrow 2NaOH, \qquad \Delta H_1 = x - 56$$

Adding III and IV

$$2Na + H_2O + \frac{1}{2}O_2 \longrightarrow 2NaOH, \Delta H_2 = -156 \text{ kcal}$$

Both represent same chemical change, hence,

$$\Delta H_1 = \Delta H_2$$

$$\therefore \quad x - 56 = -156$$

$$x = -100 \text{ kcal}$$

Calorimetry

In the laboratory, heat changes in physical and chemical processes are measured with a calorimeter which is a insulated (closed) container and is used specifically for this purpose. Calorimetry, the measurement of heat changes, requires the concepts of

Specific heat (s) which is the amount of heat required to raise the temperature of one gram of the substance by one degree.

Heat capacity (C) which is the amount of heat required to raise the temperature of given quantity of the substance by one degree.

$$C = ms$$

where, m is the mass of the substance in grams.

Specific heat has the unit J/g °C and heat capacity has the unit J/°C. $\quad q = ms\Delta t = C\Delta t$

Δt (change in temperature) $= (t_{final} - t_{initial})$

For endothermic change, q is positive and for exothermic change, q is negative.

Constant Volume Calorimetry

Heat of combustion is usually measured by placing a known mass of a compound in a steel container called a **constant volume bomb calorimeter.**

Concept Visualizer

To understand the process of measurement of heat in a constant volume bomb calorimeter can be visualised as

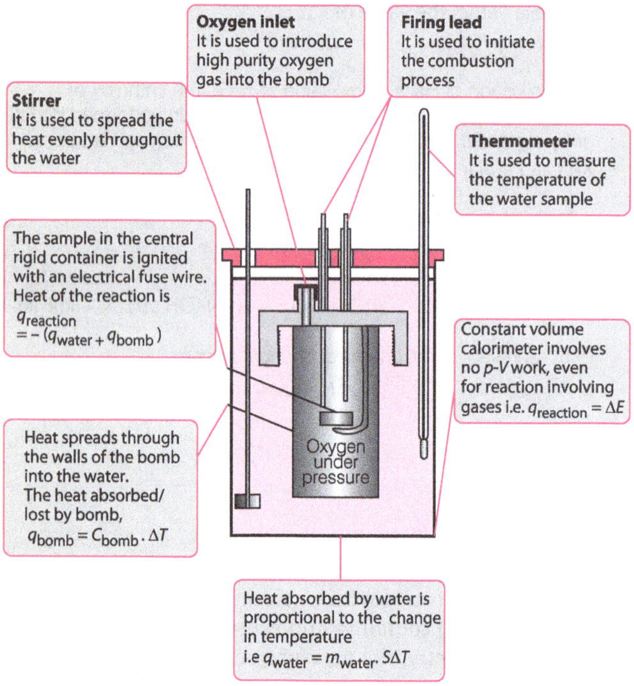

We assume that the system is perfectly insulated (isolated) so that no heat is lost to the surrounding during measurements. Thus,

Heat lost by the sample = Heat gained by water

$$q_{system} = q_{water} + q_{bomb} + q_{reaction} = 0$$

$$\therefore \quad q_{reaction} = -(q_{water} + q_{bomb})$$

Also, $q_{water} = m(\text{water})s(4.184\ \text{J/g}\,°\text{C})\Delta t$

$$q_{bomb} = C_{bomb}\ \Delta t$$

Thus, $q_{recation}$ (heat of reaction) is calculated.

Even for reaction involving gases, there is no work done as $\Delta V = 0$.

Thus, $$\boxed{q_{reaction} = \Delta E}$$

Constant Pressure Calorimetry

A simple device than the constant volume calorimeter is the constant-pressure calorimeter used to determine the heat change for non-combustion reactions (e.g. neutralisation, solution, hydration etc.). Because, the pressure is constant, the heat change for the process is equal to ΔH.

$$\boxed{q_p = \Delta H}$$

- $\Delta H = q_p =$ +ve, heat is absorbed by the system from surroundings.
- $\Delta H = q_p =$ –ve, heat is evolved and system loses heat to the surroundings.

Elemental Practice 4.4

Type I MCQs with Only One Correct Option

1. Determine C—C and C—H bond enthalpy (in kJ/mol)
Given: $\Delta_f H° = (C_2H_6(g)) = -85$ kJ/mol
$\Delta_f H°(C_3H_8, g) = -120$ kJ/mol
$\Delta_{sub} H°(C, s) = 700$ kJ/mol, B.E (H—H) = 550 kJ/mol
(a) 417.5 and 320
(b) 325 and 318.3
(c) 217 and 413
(d) 360 and 462.5

2. Given, $H_2S(g) \longrightarrow HS(g) + H(g)$; $\Delta H° = 376.6$ kJ mol^{-1}
$H_2(g) + S(g) \longrightarrow H_2S(g)$; $\Delta H° = -20.1$ kJ mol^{-1}
$H_2(g) \longrightarrow 2H(g)$; $\Delta H° = 436.0$ kJ mol^{-1}
$S(s) \longrightarrow S(g)$; $\Delta H° = 277.0$ kJ mol^{-1}
Thus, $\Delta_f H°$(HS) is
(a) 138.5 kJ mol^{-1} (b) –138.5 kJ mol^{-1}
(c) –277.0 kJ mol^{-1} (d) +277.0 kJ mol^{-1}

3. Hydration energies of Li^+ and Cl^- are –689 and –512 kJ mol^{-1}. If lattice energy of LiCl is –918 kJ mol^{-1}, heat of solution of LiCl is ....
(a) 741 kJ/mol (b) – 1621 kJ/mol
(c) + 1222 kJ/mol (d) – 283 kJ/mol

4. From the following detail, calculate the enthalpy change for the combustion of cyclopropane at 298 K. The enthalpy of formation of $CO_2(g)$, $H_2O(l)$ and propene (g) are –393.5, –285.8 and 20.42 kJ mol^{-1} respectively. The enthalpy of isomerisation of cyclopropane to propene is –33.0 kJ mol^{-1}.
(a) – 2058.32 kJ (b) – 2091.32 kJ
(c) – 1189.13 kJ (d) – 2501.38 kJ

5. Enthalpy of neutralisation of HF(aq)
$HF(aq) + OH^-(aq) \longrightarrow F^-(aq) + H_2O(l)$ is –68.60 kJ mol^{-1} and enthalpy change for the reaction
$H^+(aq) + OH^-(aq) \longrightarrow H_2O(l)$ is –55.83 kJ.mol^{-1}
Thus, enthalpy change (kJ mol^{-1}) for the dissociation is
$$HF(aq) \longrightarrow H^+(aq) + F^-(aq)$$
(a) – 12.77 (b) + 12.77
(c) – 124.43 (d) + 124.43

6. Given below are two statements: one is labelled as Assertion (A) and the other is labelled as Reason (R).
Assertion (A) The enthalpy change for the combustion of methane (CH_4) calculated using bond enthalpies differs slightly from the value obtained experimentally.
Reason (R) Bond enthalpy values are averages taken over different molecules, and they do not consider specific molecular environments.
In the light of the above statements, choose the correct answer from the options given below.
(a) Both A and R are true but R is not the correct explanation of A.
(b) A is true but R is false.
(c) A is false but R is true.
(d) Both A and R are true and R is the correct explanation of A.

7. At 25°C, when 1 mole of $MgSO_4$ was dissolved in water, the heat evolved was found to be 80 kJ/mol. One mole of $MgSO_4 \cdot 7H_2O$ on dissolution gives a solution of the same composition accompanied by an absorption of 12 kJ/mol. The enthalpy of hydration for the reaction is
$$MgSO_4(s) + 7H_2O(l) \longrightarrow MgSO_4 \cdot 7H_2O(s)$$
(a) – 76 kJ/mol (b) – 92 kJ/mol
(c) + 92 kJ/mol (d) + 76 kJ/mol

8. Given, $CH_3COOH(aq) \rightleftharpoons CH_3COO^-(aq) + H^+(aq)$;
$\Delta_r H° = 0.005$ kcal g^{-1}. Enthalpy change when 1 mole of $Ca(OH)_2$, a strong base, is completely neutralised by $CH_3COOH(aq)$ in dilute solution is
[$H°(H_2O) = -13.7$ kcal.mol^{-1}]
(a) – 27.4 kcal mol^{-1} (b) – 13.4 kcal mol^{-1}
(c) – 26.8 kcal mol^{-1} (d) – 27.1 kcal mol^{-1}

9. Given below are two statements
Statement I If $\Delta H_f°(NH_3) = -46.1$ kJ and $\Delta H°$ of the reaction, $N_2H_4(g) + H_2(g) \longrightarrow 2NH_3(g)$ is –187.6 kJ, then $\Delta H_f°(N_2H_4)$ will be –95.4 kJ.
Statement II The standard mole enthalpy of formation of molecular O_2 at 298 K is zero. Its value at 315 K will be 0.5 kJ mol^{-1} ($C_P(O_2)$ is 29.4 JK^{-1} mol^{-1}).
In the light of the above statements, choose the most appropriate answer from the options given below:
(a) Both Statement I and Statement II are incorrect.
(b) Statement I is correct but Statement II is incorrect.
(c) Statement I is incorrect but Statement II is correct.
(d) Both Statement I and Statement II are correct.

10. The standard enthalpy of formation of octane (C_8H_{18}) is –300 kJ/mol. Calculate the enthalpy of combustion of C_8H_{18}. The enthalpy of formation of $CO_2(g)$ and $H_2O(l)$ are –400 kJ/mol and –300 kJ/mol respectively.
(a) – 5500 kJ/mol (b) – 5600 kJ/mol
(c) + 5200 kJ/mol (d) – 5200 kJ/mol

11. Given, $CH_4(g) \longrightarrow C(g) + 4H(g)$; $\Delta H° = 360$ kcal mol^{-1}
$C_2H_6(g) \longrightarrow 2C(g) + 6H(g)$; $\Delta H° = 620$ kcal mol^{-1}
Thus, bond enthalpy of (C—C) bond is
(a) 260 kcal mol^{-1} (b) 180 kcal mol^{-1}
(c) 130 kcal mol^{-1} (d) 80 kcal mol^{-1}

12. The standard enthalpies of combustion of fumaric acid and maleic acid (to CO_2 and H_2O) are – 1436.0 kJ mol^{-1} and – 1459.2 kJ mol^{-1}, respectively.

Thus, enthalpy of the following isomerisation process is

$$\text{maleic acid} \rightleftharpoons \text{fumaric acid}$$

(a) – 2695.2 kJ/mol^{-1} (b) – 23.2 kJ/mol^{-1}
(c) + 23.2 kJ/mol^{-1} (d) 2695.2 kJ/mol^{-1}

13. Calculate resonance energy of N_2O from the following data

$\Delta_f H°(N_2O) = 82$ kJ mol^{-1}

Assume structure $\overset{\ominus}{N} = \overset{\oplus}{N} = O$

BE of $(N \equiv N)$ bond = 946 kJ mol^{-1}

$(N = N)$ bond = 418 kJ mol^{-1}

$(O = O)$ bond = 498 kJ mol^{-1}

$(N = O)$ bond = 607 kJ mol^{-1}

(a) – 358 kJ mol^{-1} (b) 170 kJ mol^{-1}
(c) – 88 kJ mol^{-1} (d) – 170 kJ mol^{-1}

14. Oxidising power of chlorine in aqueous solution can be determined by the parameters indicated below:

$$\frac{1}{2}Cl_2(g) \xrightarrow{\frac{1}{2}\Delta_{diss}H°} Cl(g) \xrightarrow{\Delta E_A H°} Cl^-(g) \xrightarrow{\Delta_{hyd.}H^\ominus} Cl^-(aq)$$

The energy involved in the conversion of $\frac{1}{2}Cl_2(g)$ to $Cl^-(aq)$ (using the data, $\Delta_{diss}H^\ominus_{Cl_2} = 240$ kJ mol^{-1}, $\Delta_{EA}H°_{Cl} = -249$ kJ/mol^{-1}, $\Delta_{hyd} \cdot H°_{Cl} = -481$ kJ mol^{-1})

(a) + 152 kJ mol^{-1} (b) – 610 kJ mol^{-1}
(c) – 850 kJ mol^{-1} (d) + 120 kJ mol^{-1}

15. A 0.05 L sample of 0.2 M aqueous HCl acid is added to 0.05 L of 0.2 M aqueous NH_3 in a calorimeter. Heat capacity of entire calorimeter system is 480 J/K. The temperature increase is 1.0 K. Calculate $\Delta_r H°$ in kJ/mol for the following reaction.

$$HCl(aq) + NH_3(aq) \longrightarrow NH_4Cl(aq)$$

(a) – 48 kJ/mol (b) – 60 kJ/mol
(c) – 55 kJ/mol (d) – 58 kJ/mol

Type II 》 MCQs with One or More than One Correct Option

16. A quantity of 100 mL of 0.5 M HCl is mixed with 100 mL of 0.5 M NaOH in a constant pressure calorimeter that has a heat capacity of 335 J/°C. There was increase in temperature of the reaction mixture by 2.4°C.

Density of solution = 1.00 g mL^{-1}

Specific heat of solution = 4.184 J/g°C.

Select the incorrect statement from the following on the basis of given data.

(a) Enthalpy of solution on mixing is 3.02 kJ
(b) Enthalpy of calorimeter (calorimeter constant) is 0.804 kJ
(c) Enthalpy of reaction is – 2.812 kJ
(d) Enthalpy of neutralisation is – 76.12 kJ mol^{-1}.

17. Dissociation energy of $A_2(g)$ is x kJ, that of $B_2(g)$ is $\frac{x}{2}$ kJ and that of $A-B(g)$ is $2x$ kJ.

If $\Delta H_f°(A-B)$ is – 200 kJ mol^{-1}, then

(a) dissociation energy of $A-B$ is + 200 kJ mol^{-1}
(b) dissociation energy of A_2 is 160 kJ mol^{-1}
(c) dissociation energy of $A-B$ is 320 kJ mol^{-1}
(d) $\Delta H_f°$ of A_2B $(A-B-A)$ is – 460 kJ mol^{-1}

18. Select the correct alternative(s).

(a) If $C_{p,m} = 3 + (2 \times 10^{-2})T$ cal mol^{-1} K^{-1} then $C_{V,m} = 1 + (2 \times 10^{-2})T$ cal mol^{-1} K^{-1}
(b) $\Delta H = C_{p,m}(T_2 - T_1)$
(c) $\Delta H = (C_{V,m} + R)(T_2 - T_1)$
(d) $\Delta E = (C_{p,m} - R)(T_2 - T_1)$

19. The diagram below shows the enthalpy change for the chemical reactions between N_2, O_2, NO and NO_2.

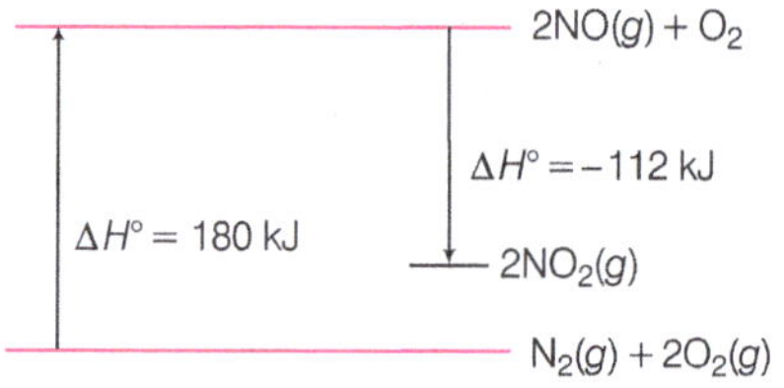

Select the correct statement(s).

(a) The standard heat of formation of NO_2 is 34 kJ mol^{-1}
(b) The oxidation reaction of N_2 to NO_2 is endothermic
(c) The standard heat of formation of NO is 90 kJ mol^{-1}
(d) The oxidation reaction of NO to NO_2 is endothermic

20. The standard enthalpies of combustion of fumaric acid and maleic acid are –1359.2 and –1336.0 kJ mol^{-1}

$$\Delta_f H°(CO_2) = -393.5 \text{ kJ mol}^{-1}$$

$$\Delta_f H°(H_2O) = -285.8 \text{ kJ mol}^{-1}$$

(a) heat is absorbed in the conversion of maleic acid to fumaric acid
(b) heat is evolved in the conversion of maleic acid to fumaric acid
(c) maleic acid is more stable than fumaric acid
(d) fumaric acid is more stable than maleic acid

21. Given,

$2C(\text{graphite}) + O_2(g) \longrightarrow 2CO(g)$; $\Delta_r H° = -52.0$ kcal

$CO(g) + \frac{1}{2}O_2(g) \longrightarrow CO_2(g)$; $\Delta_r H° = -68.0$ kcal

Thus, standard heat of formation of

(a) CO_2 is – 68.0 kcal mol^{-1}
(b) CO is – 26.0 kcal mol^{-1}
(c) CO_2 is – 94.0 kcal mol^{-1}
(d) CO is – 52.0 kcal mol^{-1}

22. A quantity of 200 mL of 0.862 M HCl is mixed with 200 mL of 0.431M $Ba(OH)_2$ in a constant pressure calorimeter that has a heat capacity of 435 JK^{-1}.

The initial temperature of the HCl and $Ba(OH)_2$ solution is the same at 20.48°C. For the process the heat of neutralisation for

$H^+(aq) + OH^-(aq) \rightleftharpoons H_2O(aq)$ is -56.2 kJ mol^{-1}

Select the correct statement(s).

(a) Enthalpy change of the process is – 9.69 kJ

(b) Final temperature is 25.11°C

(c) Some HCl is left unreacted

(d) Some $Ba(OH)_2$ is left unreacted

Type III 》 Single Integer Answer (0-9) Type Questions

23. Consider the following reactions,

I. $NH_4HS(s) \rightleftharpoons NH_3(g) + H_2S(g)$

II. $CaCO_3(s) \rightleftharpoons CaO(s) + CO_2(g)$

III. $PCl_5(g) \rightleftharpoons PCl_3(g) + Cl_2(g)$

IV. $C(s) + 2H_2O(g) \longrightarrow 2H_2(g) + CO_2(g)$

V. $C_3H_8(g) + 5O_2(g) \longrightarrow 3CO_2(g) + 4H_2O(g)$

The total number of reactions in which the value of $\Delta H - \Delta E = RT$ are .....

24. Given, enthalpy of combustion of carbon (s)

$= -94$ kcal mol^{-1}

$H_2(g) = -68$ kcal mol^{-1} and

$C_xH_4 = -318$ kcal mol^{-1} and

$\Delta_f H°(C_xH_4) = -100$ kcal mol^{-1}

The value of x is ....

25. Graphite is burnt in oxygen to given CO and CO_2. If the product mixture is 33% CO and 67% CO_2, by mass, The heat from the combustion of 1.00 g of mixture is (–)... kJ

[Given: ΔH_f° of CO $= -110.5$ kJ mol^{-1}

ΔH_f° of $CO_2 = -393.5$ kJ mol^{-1}]

26. $CO_2(g)$ can be prepared from diamond.

Method I (a) C(diamond) $\longrightarrow$ C(graphite); $\Delta H = 3$ kcal

(b) C (graphite) + $O_2(g) \longrightarrow CO_2(g)$; $\Delta H = -94$ kcal

Method II (a) C(diamond) $\longrightarrow$ C(graphite); $\Delta H = x_1$

(b) C(graphite) $+ \frac{1}{2} O_2(g) \longrightarrow CO(g)$; $\Delta H = x_2$

(c) $CO(g) + \frac{1}{2} O_2(g) \longrightarrow CO_2(g)$; $\Delta H = -68$ kcal

The sum of x_1 and x_2 is (–) ...... kcal.

27. The number of incorrect statements from the following is ....

I. The standard state of a substance is the pure substance at 1 bar

II. If dissociation energy of $H_2(g)$ is q then enthalpy of formation of H is q

III. If dissociation energy of H_2 is q, then enthalpy of formation of H_2 is $-q$

IV. $2H_2(g) + O_2(g) \longrightarrow 2H_2O(g)$

If $\Delta S^\circ_{298} = -1.92$ kJ K^{-1}

then $\Delta H_f^\circ(H_2O)$ is -572.16 kJ mol^{-1}

V. If ΔH_f° of SO_2 is -297.5 kJ mol^{-1} at 298 K then the energy required for the decomposition of 32 g of SO_2 is 148.75 kJ.

28. Based on the following thermochemical data of the given process, answer the questions.

$C(s) \longrightarrow C(g)$; $\Delta H° = 172$ kcal mol^{-1}

$H_2(g) \longrightarrow 2H(g)$; $\Delta H° = 104$ kcal mol^{-1}

$H_2(g) + \frac{1}{2} O_2(g) \longrightarrow H_2O(l)$; $\Delta H° = -68$ kcal mol^{-1}

$C(s) + O_2(g) \longrightarrow CO_2(g)$; $\Delta H° = -94$ kcal mol^{-1}

$\Delta_c H°(C_2H_6) = -372.0$ kcal mol^{-1}

$\Delta_c H°(C_3H_8) = -530.0$ kcal mol^{-1}

The bond energy of C—C bond is x k cal mol^{-1} and then bond energy of C—H bond is y k cal mol^{-1}.

The value of $x + y$ is .... k cal.

29. Given, $X_2(g) \longrightarrow 2X(g)$; $\Delta H = q$

$Y_2(g) \longrightarrow 2Y(g)$; $\Delta H = \frac{q}{2}$

$X-Y(g) \longrightarrow X(g) + Y(g)$; $\Delta H = q$

$X_2(g) + Y_2(g) \longrightarrow 2XY(g)$; $\Delta H = -400$ kJ

Bond enthalpy of $X_2(g)$ is $n \times 100$ kJ mol^{-1}

The value of n is ....

Elemental Practice 4.4 | Chapter 04

Connect with **Answers**

1. (d)	**2.** (a)	**3.** (d)	**4.** (b)	**5.** (a)	**6.** (d)
7. (b)	**8.** (c)	**9.** (c)	**10.** (b)	**11.** (d)	**12.** (b)
13. (c)	**14.** (b)	**15.** (a)	**16.** (a,d)	**17.** (b,c,d)	**18.** (a,b,c,d)
19. (a,b,c)	**20.** (b,d)	**21.** (b,c)	**22.** (a, b)	**23.** (3)	**24.** (3)
25. (6.871)	**26.** (23)	**27.** (3)	**28.** (181)	**29.** (8)	

Advanced Exclusive Different Strokes

Numericals based on entropy change for different thermodynamic processes have been asked in recent years.

Tips and formulas to solve problems related to entropy changes in thermodynamic process.

For such problem, it is important to understand the different thermodynamic process.

(i) Entropy change in isothermal expansion or compression of an ideal gas 1.

Isothermal reversible expansion from $T_1 = T_2$

$V_1 \rightarrow V_2$

$$\Delta S_{\text{system}} = R \ln \frac{V_2}{V_1} = \frac{q_{\text{rev}}}{T}$$

$$\Delta S_{\text{Surrounding}} = \frac{-q_{\text{rev}}}{T}$$

$$\Delta S_{\text{system}} + \Delta S_{\text{surrounding}} = 0$$

Isothermal irreversible expansion from $V_1 \rightarrow V_2$

Since for system 'S' is a state function

$$\Delta S_{\text{system}} = R \ln \frac{V_2}{V_1}$$

$$\Delta S_{\text{surroding}} = -\frac{q_{\text{irrev.}}}{T}$$

$$\Delta S_{\text{system}} + \Delta S_{\text{surrounding}} > 0$$

Isothermal free expansion from $V_1 \rightarrow V_2$

$$\Delta S_{\text{system}} = R \ln \frac{V_2}{V_1}$$

Since $\Delta T = 0$ and free expansion

$\Delta E = 0, w = 0$ $\Delta S_{\text{surrounding}} = 0$

$\Delta S_{\text{system}} + \Delta S_{\text{surrounding}} > 0$

(ii) Entropy changes in adiabatic expansion or compression of an ideal gas.

—Adiabatic reversible expansion from $(V_1, T_1) \rightarrow (V_2, T_2)$

$$\Delta S = C_V \ln \frac{T_2}{T_1} + R \ln \frac{V_2}{V_1}$$

Adiabatic expansion leads to cooling of gas. Therefore increase in entropy due to expansion gets compensated with decrease in entropy because of decrease in temperature.

So, $$C_V \ln \frac{T_2}{T_1} = -R \ln \frac{V_2}{V_1}$$

$$\Delta S_{\text{system}} = 0$$

and

$\Delta S_{\text{surrounding}} = 0$ (Since no heat flow between system and surrounding)

Adiabatic irreversible expansion from $(V_1, T_1) \rightarrow (V_2, T_2)$

$$\Delta S_{\text{system}} = C_V \ln \frac{T_2}{T_1} + R \ln \frac{V_2}{V_1}$$

$\Delta S_{\text{surrounding}} = 0$

$\Delta S_{\text{system}} + \Delta S_{\text{surrounding}} > 0$

Adiabatic free expansion from $V_1 \rightarrow V_2$

(Since $q_{\text{ex}} = 0, w = 0, \Delta E = 0, T_1 = T_2$)

$$\Delta S_{\text{system}} = R \ln \frac{V_2}{V_1}$$

$\Delta S_{\text{surrounding}} = 0$

$\Delta S_{\text{system}} + \Delta S_{\text{surrounding}} > 0$

Conclusion

- For isothermal expansion or compression, the enropy change is linked to heat exchange with the surroundings at a constant temperature.
- For an adiabatic expansion or compression, for reversible expansion $\Delta S_{\text{total}} = 0$ while that for irreversible expansion $\Delta S_{\text{total}} > 0$

PRACTICE
ELEMENT 01

Target JEE Main

Objective Type Questions

1. For the equilibrium at 300 K,

$$COCl_2(g) \rightleftharpoons CO(g) + Cl_2(g)$$

$\Delta H° = 12$ kJ mol^{-1} and $\Delta S° = 60$ JK^{-1} mol^{-1}

The value of equilibrium constant is

(a) 5.36 (b) 15.01 (c) 11.08 (d) 1.044

2. 2.56 g of sulphur is burnt in a constant volume calorimeter with excess of $O_2(g)$. Temperature increases from 21.25°C to 26.72°C. The bomb has a heat capacity of 923 J K^{-1}. Calorimeter contains 815 g of water. Thus, change in internal energy per mole of SO_2 formed for the reaction is

$$S_8(s) + 8O_2(g) \longrightarrow 8SO_2(g)$$

(Specific heat of water is 4.184 J K^{-1}g^{-1})

(a) – 296.27 kJ (b) + 296.27 kJ

(c) – 2370.13 kJ (d) + 2370.13 kJ

3. One mole of an ideal gas is put through a series of changes as shown in the figure in which 1, 2, 3 mark the three stages of the system.

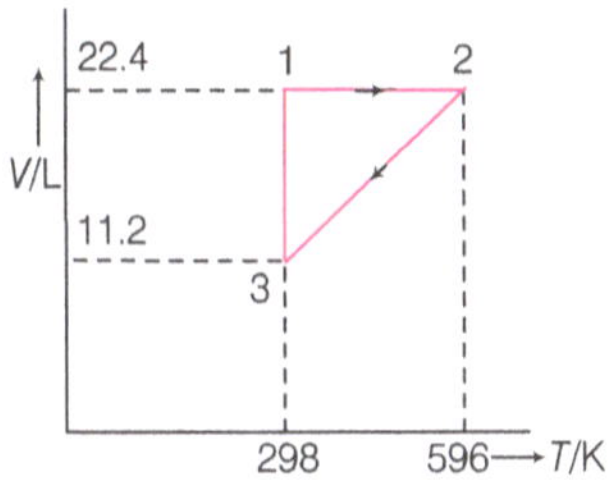

Pressure at the stages 1, 2 and 3 respectively will be (in bar)

	1	2	3
(a)	1.107	2.214	1.107
(b)	1.107	1.107	2.214
(c)	2.214	1.107	2.214
(d)	1.107	2.214	2.214

4. In the following case.

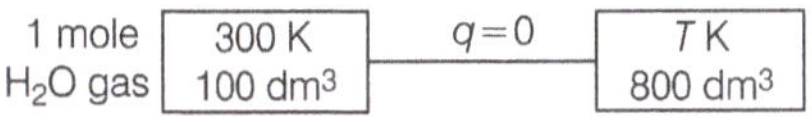

	Work done	Final temperature
(a)	900 cal	150 K
(b)	900 cal	300 K
(c)	1200 cal	150 K
(d)	1200 cal	300 K

5. The enthalpy changes for the following processes are listed below :

$Cl_2(g) = 2Cl(g)$,	242.3 kJ mol^{-1}
$I_2(g) = 2I(g)$,	151.0 kJ mol^{-1}
$ICl(g) = I(g) + Cl(g)$,	211.3 kJ mol^{-1}
$I_2(s) = I_2(g)$,	62.76 kJ mol^{-1}

Given that standard states for iodine and chlorine are $I_2(s)$ and $Cl_2(g)$, the standard enthalpy of formation of $ICl(g)$ is

(a) – 14.6 kJ mol^{-1} (b) – 16.8 kJ mol^{-1}

(c) + 16.8 kJ mol^{-1} (d) + 244.8 kJ mol^{-1}

6. Standard entropies of X_2, Y_2 and XY_3 are given below the reaction,

$$1/2\,X_2 + 3/2\,Y_2 \rightleftharpoons XY_3; \quad \Delta H = -30 \text{ kJ mol}^{-1}$$

S : 60 40 50 JK^{-1} mol^{-1}

At what temperature, reaction would be in equilibrium?

(a) 500 K (b) 750 K

(c) 1000 K (d) 1250 K

7.

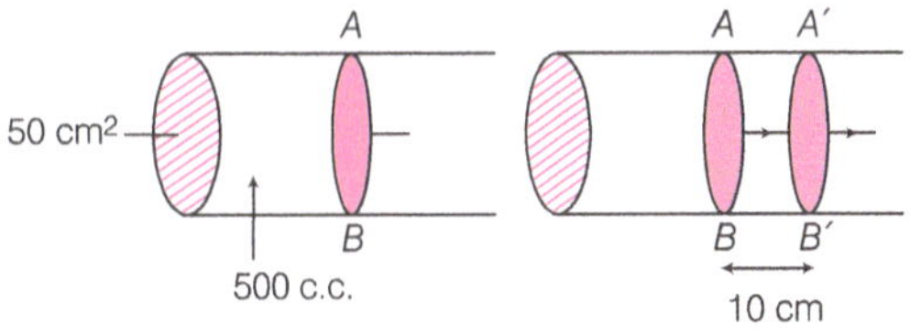

Piston AB moves to new position $A'B'$. Initially it occupies 500 cc at 298 K and 2 atm. What is change in entropy in going from AB to $A'B'$.

(a) 0.24 JK^{-1} (b) 4.2 JK^{-1}

(c) zero (d) – 0.24 JK^{-1}

8. One mole of an ideal gas at 27°C and 10 atm pressure is

I. allowed to expand to 1 atm isothermally and reversibly.

II. allowed to expand against a constant pressure of 1 atm isothermally.

III. allowed a free expansion.

Work obtained is in order

(a) I < II < III (b) III < II < I

(c) I = II < III (d) III < I < II

9. Given,

I. $NH_3(g) + 3Cl_2(g) \longrightarrow NCl_3(g) + 3HCl(g); \; -\Delta H_1$

II. $N_2(g) + 3H_2(g) \longrightarrow 2NH_3(g); \; -\Delta H_2$

III. $H_2(g) + Cl_2(g) \longrightarrow 2HCl(g); \; \Delta H_3$

$\Delta_f H^\circ(NCl_3)$ in terms of ΔH_1, ΔH_2 and ΔH_3 is

(a) $-\left(\Delta H_1 + \frac{\Delta H_2}{2} + \frac{3}{2}\Delta H_3\right)$

(b) $\left(\Delta H_1 + \frac{\Delta H_2}{2} - \frac{3}{2}\Delta H_3\right)$

(c) $\left(\Delta H_1 - \frac{\Delta H_2}{2} - \frac{3}{2}\Delta H_3\right)$

(d) $\left(\Delta H_1 + \frac{\Delta H_2}{2} + \frac{3}{2}\Delta H_3\right)$

10. $H_2O(g) \rightleftharpoons H_2O(l)$, $\Delta H = -10$ kcal mol^{-1}. For this transition, vapour pressure change with temperature as given

(a)
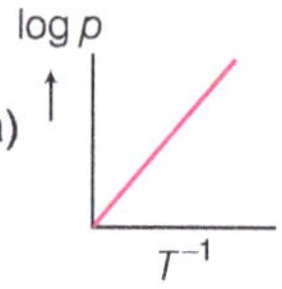

(b)
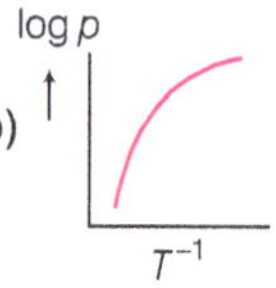

(c)

(d)
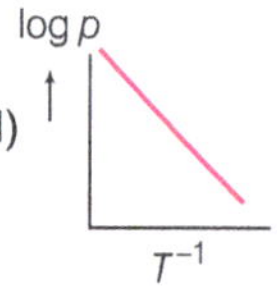

11. Choose the reaction from the following options, for which the standard enthalpy of reaction is not equal to the standard enthalpy of formation.

(a) $\frac{3}{2}O_2(g) \longrightarrow O_3(g)$

(b) $\frac{1}{8}S_8(s) + O_2(g) \longrightarrow SO_2(g)$

(c) $2H_2(g) + O_2(g) \longrightarrow 2H_2O(l)$

(d) $\frac{1}{2}N_2(g) + \frac{3}{2}H_2(g) \longrightarrow NH_3(g)$

12. When 6 moles of He gas expand isothermally and reversibly at 300 K from 10 L to 20 L, the magnitude of the maximum work obtained is

(Given, $R = 8.3$ JK^{-1}mol^{-1} and $\log 2 = 0.3010$)

(a) 3467.5 J (b) 10356.45 J

(c) 4426.8 J (d) 5327.4 J

13. One mole of an ideal gas at 300 K in thermal contact with surroundings expands isothermally from 4.0 L to 8.0 L against a constant pressure of 5 atm.

In this process, the change in entropy of surroundings (ΔS_{surr}) in JK^{-1} atm = 101.3 J)

(a) –6.89 (b) –6.75 (c) –8.26 (d) –3.45

14. In which of the following cases, entropy of I is larger than that of II?

	I	II
(a)	$NO_2(g)$	$N_2O_2(g)$
(b)	Dry ice (solid CO_2)	$CO_2(g)$ at 0°C
(c)	Pure alumina	Ruby
(d)	$N_2(g)$ at 1 bar	$N_2(g)$ at 5 bar

15. An engine takes up 80.0 kJ of heat to complete the cycle as shown. Thus, efficiency is

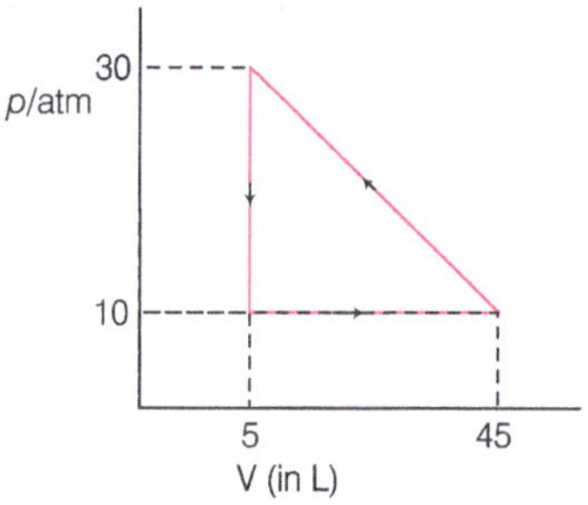

(a) 40.1% (b) 20.6%

(c) 70.2% (d) 50.6%

16. 1 mole each of CaC_2, Al_4C_3, Mg_2C_3 reacts with H_2O in separate open flask. Numerical value of work done by the system is in order

(a) $CaC_2 < Al_4C_3 = Mg_2C_3$ (b) $CaC_2 < Al_4C_3 < Mg_2C_3$

(c) $CaC_2 = Mg_2C_3 < Al_4C_3$ (d) $CaC_2 = Mg_2C_3 = Al_4C_3$

17. The density of ice at 0°C is 0.915 g cm^{-3} and that of liquid water at 0°C is 1.0 g cm^{-3}. Work done for melting 1 mole of ice at 1.00 bar is

(a) 0.167 J (b) – 0.167 J

(c) 0.00 J (d) – 1.67 J

18. For the reaction, at 298 K

$$CaCO_3(s) \longrightarrow CaO(s) + CO_2(g),$$
$$\Delta H^\circ = 178.3 \text{ kJ}, \Delta S^\circ = 160 \text{ J K}^{-1}$$

Select the correct statement(s).

(a) The reaction is spontaneous at this temperature (298 K)

(b) If temperature is decreased forward reaction is favoured

(c) The reaction is spontaneous in forward direction only at temperature above 1000 K

(d) The reaction is spontaneous in forward direction only at temperature above 1114 K

19. Given at 298 K, $\Delta_f H^\circ$(cyclohexane) = – 156.0 kJ mol^{-1}

$\Delta_f H^\circ$ (benzene) = + 49.0 kJ mol^{-1}

Cyclohexene + $H_2 \longrightarrow$ Cyclohexane, $\Delta_r H^\circ = -119$ kJ mol^{-1}.

The resonance energy of benzene is

(a) – 152.0 kJ mol^{-1} (b) + 152.0 kJ mol^{-1}

(c) – 107.0 kJ mol^{-1} (d) – 226.0 kJ mol^{-1}

20. For following reaction, 10 mL of 0.10 M NaOH(aq) + 10 mL of 0.10 M HCl(aq), enthalpy change is $\Delta_r H_1^\circ$. On further adding 20 mL of 0.10 M HCl(aq) and 20 mL of 0.1 M NaOH, enthalpy change is $\Delta_r H_2^\circ$. Thus, these values are

	$\Delta_r H_1^\circ$	$\Delta_r H_2^\circ$
(a)	– 13.7 cal	– 13.7 cal
(b)	– 13.7 cal	– 27.4 cal
(c)	– 13.7 kcal	– 13.7 kcal
(d)	– 13.7 kcal	– 27.4 kcal

Numerical Type Questions

21. A person consumes 200 g of sucrose providing 3200 kJ of energy. During a workout person uses 60% of this energy. To avoid storage in the body, calculate the mass of water the person would need to evaporate through perspiration. Assume that enthalpy of evaporation of water is 44 kJ/mol. (Nearest integer)
22. The standard Gibbs' free energy ($\Delta G°$) [in cal mol^{-1}] for a certain reaction is given by $\Delta G° = 300 + 2T \log_{10} T - 15T$ What is value of $\Delta S°$ at 100 K?
23. A quantity of 0.50 mole of an ideal gas at 300 K expands isothermally against a constant pressure of 2.0 atm form 1.0 L to 5.0 L. Thus, ΔS (universe) is ...... JK^{-1}.
24. The molar heat capacity of oxygen at constant pressure is given by 1.45 (25.7 T + 0.0130 T) 10^{-3}kJ mol^{-1}. The change in enthalpy upon temperature is increased from 25°C to 94°C is ...... kJ. (Nearest integer)
25. About 1 dm^3 gastric juice is produced per day in the human body from other body fluids such as blood, whose pH is 7.6021 at 53° C. Calculate the minimum work (in kJ) required to produce 1 dm^3 gastric juice whose pH may be taken as unity. (Nearest integer)
26. In a constant volume calorimeter, 3.5 g of a gas (molar mass = 28 g mol^{-1}) was burnt in excess of O_2 at 298 K. This increased the temperature of calorimeter by 0.45 K. Heat capacity of the calorimeter is 2.5 KJ K^{-1}. Thus, numerical value of the combustion of gas is ...... kJ mol^{-1}.
27. When 50 mL of 1 M HCl was mixed with 50 mL of 1 M NaOH in an insulated beaker at constant pressure, a temperature increase of 2.85°C was measured for the beaker and its content. In a second experiment 50 mL of 1M CH_3COOH and 50 mL of 1 M NaOH on mixing gave rise in temperature of 2.80°C. Thus, enthalpy of dissociation of CH_3COOH in kJ mol^{-1} is ....
28. Standard enthalpy of formation of $CH_3OH(l)$ can be evaluated using bond-enthalpy values.

$$C(s) + \frac{1}{2} O_2(g) + 2H_2(g) \longrightarrow CH_3OH(l)$$

The number of types of energy parameter (bond enthalpy, atomisation etc) required are

29. Given, $\Delta_f H°$ of the following in kJ mol^{-1}.

Compound	$\Delta_f H°$
$CO(g)$	– 110
$H_2O(g)$	– 242
$CO_2(g)$	– 394
$CH_4(g)$	– 75

The ratio taking derived values per unit volume of fuel $\frac{\Delta_c H°(CH_4)}{\Delta_c H° \{\text{water gas } (CO + H_2)\}}$ is .... (Nearest integer)

30. The heat of formation of liquid methyl alcohol in kJ per mol using following data is ....

$$\Delta H°_{vap}(CH_3OH, l) = 38 \text{ kJ mol}^{-1};$$
$$\Delta H°_f(H) = 218 \text{ kJ mol}^{-1}$$

$\Delta H°_f$ are of gaseous atoms

$$\Delta H°_f(C) = 715 \text{ kJ mol}^{-1}$$
$$\Delta H°_f(O) = 249 \text{ kJ mol}^{-1}$$
$$BE(C—H) = 415 \text{ kJ mol}^{-1}$$
$$BE(C—O) = 356 \text{ kJ mol}^{-1}$$
$$BE(O—H) = 463 \text{ kJ mol}^{-1}$$

Check Through PYQs

Element 1 Fundamental of Thermodynamics

1. What happens when methane undergoes combustion in systems *A* and *B* respectively? *2023, 13 April Shift-II*

	System A (Adiabatic system)	System B (Diathermic container)
(a)	Temperature remains same	Temperature rises
(b)	Temperature falls	Temperature remains same
(c)	Temperature falls	Temperature rises
(d)	Temperature rises	Temperature remains same

2. The total number of intensive properties from the following is .... Volume, molar heat capacity, molarity, $E°_{cell}$, Gibbs free energy change, molar mass, mole.

Element 2 First Law of Thermodynamics

3. An ideal gas undergoes following process from $A \to B \to C \to D \to E$. Find work done. *2025, 23 Jan Shift-II*

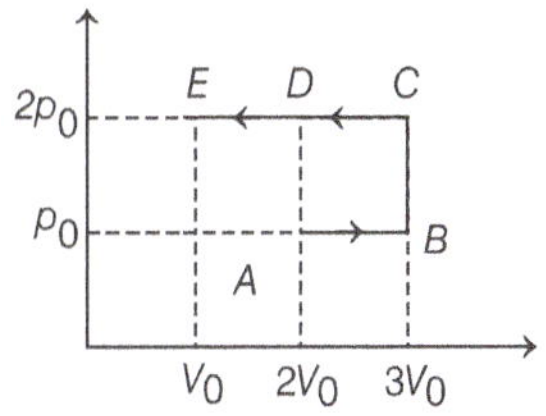

(a) $-3p_0V_0$ (b) $2p_0V_0$ (c) $3p_0V_0$ (d) $\frac{3p_0V_0}{2}$

4. 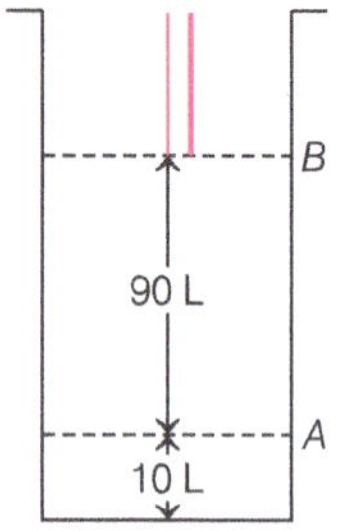

Consider the figure provided.

1 mol of an ideal gas is kept in a cylinder, fitted with a piston, at the position A, at 18°C. If the piston is moved to position B, keeping the temperature unchanged, then 'x' L atm work is done in this reversible process.

$x =$ ...... L atm (nearest integer)

[Given : Absolute temperature = °C + 273.15, $R = 0.08206$ L atm mol^{-1} K^{-1}]. **2024, 8 April Shift-I**

5. Choose the correct option for free expansion of an ideal gas under adiabatic condition from the following: **2024, 1 Feb Shift-I**

(a) $q = 0, \Delta T = 0, w = 0$ (b) $q \neq 0, \Delta T = 0, w = 0$
(c) $q = 0, \Delta T < 0, w \neq 0$ (d) $q = 0, \Delta T \neq 0, w = 0$

6. If 5 moles of an ideal gas expands from 10 L to a volume of 100 L at 300 K under isothermal and reversible condition then work, w, is $-x$ J. The value of x is ....
(Given, $R = 8.314$ JK^{-1} mol^{-1}) **2024, 31 Jan Shift-II**

7. 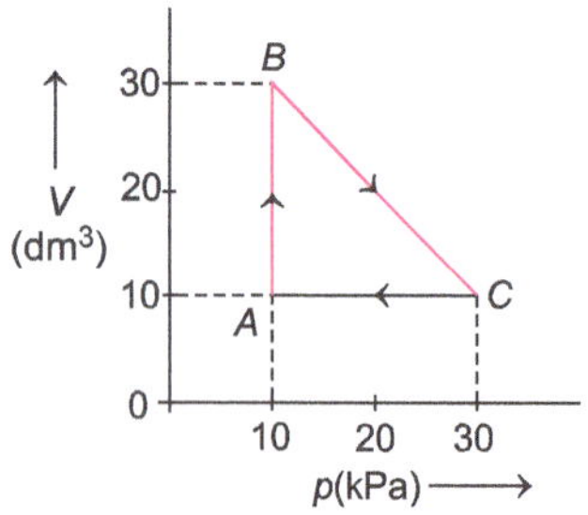

An ideal gas undergoes a cyclic transformation starting from the point A and coming back to the same point by tracing the path $A \to B \to C \to A$ as shown in the diagram above. The total work done in the process is .... J. **2024, 30 Jan Shift-I**

8. If three moles of an ideal gas at 300 K expand isothermally from 30 dm^3 to 45 dm^3 against a constant opposing pressure of 80 kPa, then the amount of heat transferred is .... J. **2024, 27 Jan Shift-I**

9. When a 60 W electric heater is immersed in a gas for 100s in a constant volume container with adiabatic walls, the temperature of the gas rises by 5°C. The heat capacity of the given gas is .... JK^{-1}. (Nearest integer) **2023, 8 April Shift-I**

10. 1 mole of ideal gas is allowed to expand reversibly and adiabatically from a temperature of 27°C. The work done by the system 3 kJ mol^{-1}. The final temperature of the gas is .... K. (Nearest integer).
[Given : $C_V = 20$ J mol^{-1} K^{-1}.] **2023, 30 Jan Shift-II**

11. 4.0 L of an ideal gas is allowed to expand isothermally into vacuum until the total volume is 20 L. The amount of heat absorbed in this expansion is ...... L atm. **2022, 28 June Shift-I**

12. At 25°C, 50 g of iron reacts with HCl to form $FeCl_2$.
The hydrogen gas evolved expands against a constant pressure of 1 bar. The work done by the gas during this expansion is ...... J. (Round off to the nearest integer)
[Given, $R = 8.314$ J mol^{-1} K^{-1}. Assume, hydrogen is an ideal gas]
[Atomic mass of Fe is 55.85 u] **2021, 16 March Shift-II**

13. Five moles of an ideal gas at 293 K is expanded isothermally from an initial pressure of 2.1 MPa to 1.3 MPa against at constant external pressure 4.3 MPa. The heat transferred in this process is .... kJ mol^{-1}. (Rounded off to the nearest integer)
[$R = 8.314$ J $mol^{-1}K^{-1}$] **2021, 25 Feb Shift-II**

14. The magnitude of work done by a gas that undergoes a reversible expansion along the path ABC shown in the figure is .... **2020, 8 Jan Shift-I**

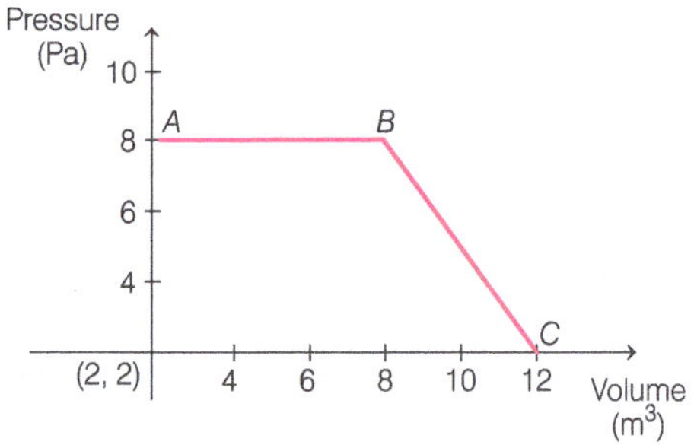

Element 3 》 Entropy and Second Law of Thermodynamics

15. Consider the given values:
$\Delta H = 55$ kJ mol^{-1}, $\Delta S = 175$ J mol^{-1} K^{-1}, $T = 25°C$
Calculate the value of Gibbs free energy change (ΔG) in J mol^{-1}. **2025, 22 Jan Shift-II**

16. For the reaction at 298 K, $2A + B \to C$. $\Delta H = 400$ kJ mol^{-1} and $\Delta S = 0.2$ kJ mol^{-1} K^{-1}. The reaction will become spontaneous above .... K. **2024, 6 April Shift-II**

17. For a certain reaction at 300 K, $K = 10$, then $\Delta G°$ for the same reaction is .... $\times 10^{-1}$ kJ mol^{-1}(Given, $R = 8.314$ JK^{-1} mol^{-1}) **2024, 1 Feb Shift-II**

18. Which of the following is not correct? **2024, 29 Jan Shift-I**
(a) ΔG is positive for a spontaneous reaction
(b) ΔG is positive for a non-spontaneous reaction
(c) ΔG is zero for a reversible reaction
(d) ΔG is negative for a spontaneous reaction

19. For a certain thermochemical reaction, $M \to N$ at $T = 400$ K, $\Delta H^{\ominus} = 77.2$ kJ mol^{-1}, $\Delta S = 122$ JK^{-1}, log equilibrium constant (log K) is $-$...... $\times 10^{-1}$. **2024, 27 Jan Shift-II**

20. One mole of an ideal gas at 350 K is in a 2.0 L vessel of thermally conducting walls, which are in contact with the surroundings. It undergoes isothermal reversible expansion from 2.0 L to 3.0 L against a constant pressure of 4 atm. The change in entropy of the surroundings (ΔS) is ………… JK^{-1}. (Nearest integer)

Given, $R = 8.314\ JK^{-1}\ mol^{-1}$ *2023, 12 April Shift-I*

21. Consider the graph of Gibbs free energy G vs extent of reaction. The number of statements from the following which are true with respect to points (a), (b) and (c) is ………. *2023, 6 April Shift-I*

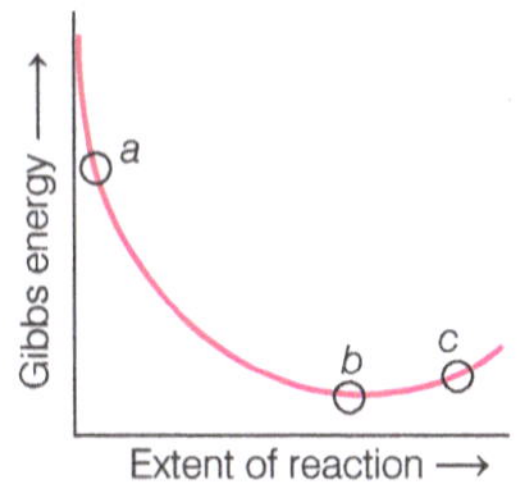

A. reaction is spontaneous at (a) and (b)
B. reaction is at equilibrium at point (b) and non-spontaneous at point (c)
C. Reaction is spontaneous at (a) and non-spontaneous at (c)
D. Reaction is non-spontaneous at (a) and (b)

22. Which of the following relations are correct?

A. $\Delta U = q + p\Delta V$
B. $\Delta G = \Delta H - T\Delta S$
C. $\Delta S = \frac{q_{rev}}{T}$
D. $\Delta H = \Delta U - \Delta nRT$ *2023, 29 Jan Shift-II*

(a) A and C (b) B only (c) B and C (d) A and D

23. The standard entropy change for the reaction,

$4Fe(s) + 3O_2(g) \longrightarrow 2Fe_2O_3(s)$ is $-550\ JK^{-1}$ at 298 K.

[Given, the standard enthalpy change for the reaction is $-165\ kJ\ mol^{-1}$]. The temperature in K at which the reaction attains equilibrium is … [Nearest integer] *2022, 25 June Shift-I*

24. The standard free energy change (ΔG°) for 50% dissociation of N_2O_4 into NO_2 at 27°C and 1 atm pressure is $-x$ J mol^{-1}. The value of x is ……… . (Nearest integer) [Given : $R = 8.31\ J K^{-1} mol^{-1}$, log 1.33 = 0.1239 ln 10 = 2.3] *2022, 25 June Shift-I*

25. The incorrect expression among the following is *2021, 31 Aug Shift-II*

(a) $\frac{\Delta G_{System}}{\Delta S_{Total}} = -T$ (at constant p)

(b) $\ln K = \frac{\Delta H^\circ - T\Delta S^\circ}{RT}$

(c) $K = e^{-\frac{\Delta G^\circ}{RT}}$

(d) For isothermal process, $W_{reversible} = -nRT \ln \frac{V_f}{V_i}$

26. Data given for the following reaction is as follows.

$$FeO(s) + C_{(graphite)} \longrightarrow Fe(s) + CO(g)$$

Substance	ΔH° (kJ mol^{-1})	ΔS° (J mol^{-1} K^{-1})
$FeO(s)$	– 266.3	57.49
$C_{(graphite)}$	0	5.74
$Fe(s)$	0	27.28
$CO(g)$	– 110.5	197.6

The minimum temperature in K at which the reaction becomes spontaneous is ……….. (Integer answer) *2021, 27 Aug Shift-II*

27. The true statement amongst the following is *2020, 9 Jan Shift-II*

(a) S is not a function of temperature but ΔS is a function of temperature.
(b) Both ΔS and S are functions of temperature.
(c) Both S and ΔS are not functions of temperature.
(d) S is a function of temperature but ΔS is not a function of temperature.

28. For the reaction; $A(l) \longrightarrow 2B(g)$

$\Delta U = 2.1$ kcal, $\Delta S = 20$ cal K^{-1} at 300 K.

Hence, ΔG in kcal is …… . *2020, 8 Jan Shift-I*

Element 4 》 Thermochemistry

29. The heat of solution of anhydrous $CuSO_4$ and $CuSO_4 \cdot 5H_2O$ are -70 kJ mol^{-1} and $+12$ kJ mol^{-1} respectively.

The heat of hydration of $CuSO_4$ to $CuSO_4 \cdot 5H_2O$ is $-x$ kJ. The value of x is …….. (Nearest integer). *2024, 9 April Shift-I*

30. An ideal gas, $C_V = \frac{5}{2}R$, is expanded adiabatically against a constant pressure of 1 atm until it doubles in volume. If the initial temperature and pressure is 298 K and 5 atm, respectively then the final temperature is ……. K (Nearest integer).

[C_V is the molar heat capacity at constant volume] *2024, 6 April Shift-I*

31. Given below are two statements : one is labelled as **Assertion (A)** and other is labelled as **Reason (R).** *2024, 5 April Shift-I*

Assertion (A) Enthalpy of neutralisation of strong monobasic acid with strong monoacidic base is always -57 kJ mol^{-1}.

Reason (R) Enthalpy of neutralisation is the amount of heat liberated when one mole of H^+ ions furnished by acid combine with one mole of OH ions furnished by base to form one mole of water.

In the light of the above statements, choose the **most appropriate** answer from the options given below.

(a) A is false, but R is true.
(b) Both A and R are true and R is the correct explanation of A.
(c) A is true, but R is false.
(d) Both A and R are true but R is not the correct explanation of A.

32. Given,

(A) $2CO(g) + O_2(g) \longrightarrow 2CO_2(g)$; $\Delta H_1^\circ = -x$ kJ mol^{-1}

(B) C (graphite) + $O_2(g) \longrightarrow CO_2(g)$; $\Delta H_2^\circ = -y$ kJ mol^{-1}

The ΔH° for the reaction

C (graphite) + $\frac{1}{2}O_2(g) \longrightarrow CO(g)$ is *2023, 10 April Shift-I*

(a) $\frac{x+2y}{2}$ (b) $\frac{x-2y}{2}$ (c) $\frac{2x-y}{2}$ (d) $2y - x$

33. Enthalpies of formation of $CCl_4(g)$, $H_2O(g)$, $CO_2(g)$ and $HCl(g)$ are -105, -242, -394 and -92 kJ mol^{-1} respectively. The magnitude of enthalpy of the reaction given below is – .... kJ mol^{-1}. (Nearest integer) *2023, 31 Jan Shift-II*

$$CCl_4(g) + 2H_2O(g) \longrightarrow CO_2(g) + 4HCl(g)$$

34. A gas (molar mass = 280 g mol^{-1}) was burnt in excess O_2 in a constant volume calorimeter and during combustion the temperature of calorimeter increased from 298.0 K to 298.45 K. If the heat capacity of calorimeter is 2.5 kJ K^{-1} and enthalpy of combustion of gas is 9 kJ mol^{-1} then amount of gas burnt is .... g. (nearest integer) *2022, 27 July Shift-II*

35. While performing a thermodynamics experiment, a student made the following observations.

$$HCl + NaOH \longrightarrow NaCl + H_2O; \Delta H = -57.3 \text{ kJ mol}^{-1}$$

$$CH_3COOH + NaOH \longrightarrow CH_3COONa + H_2O; \Delta H = -55.3 \text{ kJ mol}^{-1}$$

The enthalpy of ionisation of CH_3COOH as calculated by the student is .... kJ mol^{-1}. [nearest integer] *2022, 25 July Shift-II*

36. 2.2 g of nitrous oxide (N_2O) gas is cooled at a constant pressure of 1 atm from 310 K to 270 K causing the compression of the gas from 217.1 mL to 167.75 mL. The change in internal energy of the process, ΔU is '$-x$' J. The value of 'x' is [Nearest integer]

(Given, atomic mass of N = 14 g mol^{-1} and of O = 16 g mol^{-1}. Molar heat capacity of N_2O is 100 JK^{-1} mol^{-1}) *2022, 29 June Shift-II*

37. A fish swimming in water body when taken out from the water body is covered with a film of water of weight 36 g. When it is subjected to cooking at 100°C, then the internal energy for vaporisation in kJ mol^{-1} is ... . [Nearest integer] [Assume steam to be an ideal gas. Given, $\Delta_{vap}H^\ominus$ for water at 373 K and 1 bar is 41.1 kJ mol^{-1}; $R = 8.31$ JK^{-1} mol^{-1}] *2022, 26 June Shift-II*

38. At 25°C and 1 atm pressure, the enthalpies of combustion are as given below

Substance	H_2	C (graphite)	$C_2H_6(g)$
$\frac{\Delta_c H^\ominus}{\text{kJ mol}^{-1}}$	−286.0	−394.0	−1560.0

The enthalpy of formation of ethane is *2022, 24 June Shift-II*

(a) + 54.0 kJ mol^{-1} (b) − 68.0 kJ mol^{-1}

(c) − 86.0 kJ mol^{-1} (d) + 97.0 kJ mol^{-1}

39. 200 mL of 0.2 M HCl is mixed with 300 mL of 0.1 M NaOH. The molar heat of neutralisation of this reaction is −57.1 kJ. The increase in temperature in °C of the system on mixing is $x \times 10^{-2}$. The value of x is .... (Nearest integer)

[Given, specific heat of water = 4.18 J g^{-1} K^{-1}

Density of water = 1.00 g cm^{-3}]

(Assume no volume change on mixing) *2021, 27 Aug Shift-I*

40. At 298.2 K the relationship between enthalpy of bond dissociation (in kJ mol^{-1}) for hydrogen (E_H) and its isotope, deuterium (E_D), is best described by *2021, 25 July Shift-I*

(a) $E_H = \frac{1}{2}E_D$ (b) $E_H = E_D$

(c) $E_H \simeq E_D - 7.5$ (d) $E_H = 2E_D$

41. For one mole of an ideal gas, which of these statements must be true? *2020, 04 Sept Shift-I*

(1) U and H each depends only on temperature

(2) Compressibility factor Z is not equal to 1

(3) $C_{p,m} - C_{V,m} = R$

(4) $dU = C_V dT$ for any processes

(a) (1) and (3) (b) (2), (3) and (4)

(c) (3) and (4) (d) (1), (3) and (4)

42. The heat of combustion of ethanol into carbon dioxides and water is −327 kcal at constant pressure. The heat evolved (in cal) at constant volume and 27°C (if all gases behave ideally) is ($R = 2$ cal mol^{-1} K^{-1}) .... *2020, 2 Sep Shift-II*

PRACTICE ELEMENT 02

Target JEE Advanced

Single Correct Choice MCQs

1. 0.5 mole of an ideal monoatomic gas initially at 5 atm pressure and 273 K is allowed to expand against a constant external pressure of 0.5 atm such that the final volume is 10 times the initial volume. The value of ΔS and ΔG are respectively.
(a) $-6.37\ JK^{-1}$, -2613.6 J
(b) $8.34\ JK^{-1}$, $-9.57\ JK^{-1}$
(c) $9.57\ JK^{-1}$, -1382.3 J
(d) $9.57\ JK^{-1}$, -2613.6 J

2. In the following reactions,
I. 30 mL of 0.1 M $Ba(OH)_2(aq)$ + 30 mL of 0.1M $H_2SO_4(aq)$, rise in temperature = ΔT_1
II. 90 mL of 0.1 M $Ba(OH)_2(aq)$ + 90 mL of 0.1 M $H_2SO_4(aq)$, rise in temperature = ΔT_2.
Thus, $[\Delta H^\circ(H_2O) = -13.7\ \text{k cal. mol}^{-1}]$
(a) $\Delta T_2 = 3\Delta T_1$ (b) $\Delta T_1 = \Delta T_2$
(c) $\Delta T_1 = 3\Delta T_2$ (d) $\Delta T_1 = 2\Delta T_2$

3. The factor of ΔG values is important in metallurgy. The ΔG values for the following reactions at 800°C are given as
I. $S_2(s) + 2O_2(g) \longrightarrow 2SO_2(g)$; $\Delta G = -544$ kJ
II. $2Zn(s) + S_2(s) \longrightarrow 2ZnS(s)$; $\Delta G = -293$ kJ
III. $2Zn(s) + O_2(g) \longrightarrow 2ZnO(s)$; $\Delta G = -480$ kJ
The ΔG for the reaction,
$2ZnS(s) + 3O_2(g) \longrightarrow 2ZnO(s) + 2SO_2(g)$ will be
(a) -357 kJ (b) -731kJ (c) -773 kJ (d) -229 kJ

4. Given the following thermochemical data at 298 K and 1 bar
$$\Delta H^\circ_{vap}(CH_3OH) = 38.0\ \text{kJ mol}^{-1}$$
$$\Delta_f H^\circ : H(g) = 218\ \text{kJ mol}^{-1},\ O(g) = 249\ \text{kJ mol}^{-1}$$
$$C(g) = 715\ \text{kJ mol}^{-1}$$
Bond dissociation energy,
$(C—H) = 415\ \text{kJ mol}^{-1}$,
$(C—O) = 356\ \text{kJ mol}^{-1}$, $(O—H) = 463\ \text{kJ mol}^{-1}$
The $\Delta_f H^\circ$ of liquid methyl alcohol in kJ mol^{-1} is
(a) $-170\ \text{kJ mol}^{-1}$ (b) $+170\ \text{kJ mol}^{-1}$
(c) $-266\ \text{kJ mol}^{-1}$ (d) $+266\ \text{kJ mol}^{-1}$

5. A 150 W heater was placed in 1.00 kg of methanol (CH_3OH) and turned on for exactly 1 min. The temperature increased by 3.54 K. Assuming that all the heat is absorbed by methanol, then molar heat capacity of methanol is
(a) $81.4\ \text{J mol}^{-1}\text{K}^{-1}$ (b) $2.60\ \text{J mol}^{-1}\text{K}^{-1}$
(c) $9.0\ \text{J mol}^{-1}\text{K}^{-1}$ (d) $1.36\ \text{J mol}^{-1}\text{K}^{-1}$

6. What is the entropy change of the reaction,
$$2H_2(g) + O_2(g) \longrightarrow 2H_2O\ (l)$$
at 99°C and standard pressure?
$$C_p(H_2)(g) = 28.8\ \text{J mol}^{-1}\ \text{K}^{-1}$$
$$C_p(O_2)(g) = 29.4\ \text{J mol}^{-1}\ \text{K}^{-1},$$
$$C_p\ (H_2O)(l) = 75.3\ \text{J mol}^{-1}\ \text{K}^{-1}$$
Assume ideal gas behaviour and molar quantities based on chemical equation $H_2O(l)$ is at 25°C and $\Delta S\,(\text{reaction}) = -326.7\ \text{J K}^{-1}$
(a) $-312.6\ JK^{-1}$
(b) $-418.1\ JK^{-1}$
(c) $-287.3\ JK^{-1}$
(d) $-631.3\ JK^{-1}$

7. A 3 mole sample of a triatomic (non-linear) ideal gas at 300 K is allowed to expand under isobaric reversible adiabatic expansion from 5 L to 40 L.
The value of ΔE and ΔH are respectively.
(a) -11.224 kJ, -18.361 kJ
(b) -11.224 kJ, -14.965 kJ
(c) -14.312 kJ, -14.965 kJ
(d) -7.361 kJ, -316.311 kJ

8. A gas expands against a variable opposing pressure given by $p = \frac{5}{V}$ atm, where V is the volume of the gas at each stage of the expansion. The heat absorbed when gas expands from 5 L to 50 L is 1373.85 J. The internal energy of the gas during this expansion will be
(a) 207.85 J (b) 1801.02 J
(c) 972.33 J (d) 3501.21 J

9. The value of ΔS for the process of 1 mole $H_2O(l)$ to $H_2O(s)$
$H_2O(l)$ at -10°C $\longrightarrow$ $H_2O(s)$ at -10° C given specific heat of water = 1.0 cal $K^{-1}g^{-1}$ and specific heat of ice = 0.5 cal $K^{-1}g^{-1}$.
Given: $\Delta H_{fusion} = 80.0\ \text{cal g}^{-1}$.
(a) -6.01 cal k^{-1}
(b) -4.93 cal k^{-1}
(c) -2.38 cal k^{-1}
(d) -8.31 cal k^{-1}

10. Given below are two statements: one is labelled as Assertion (A) and the other is labelled as Reason (R).

Assertion (A) For oxidation of iron

$$4Fe(s) + 3O_2(g) \longrightarrow 2Fe_2O_3(s)$$

($\Delta S° = -549.4\ JK^{-1}\ mol^{-1}$ at 298 K, $\Delta H° = -1648\ kJ\ mol^{-1}$)

Inspite of negative change in entropy, the reaction is spontaneous at 298 K.

Reason (R) Every exothermic reaction is spontaneous.

In the light of the above statements, choose the correct answer from the options given below.

(a) Both A and R are true and R is not the correct explanation of A.

(b) A is true but R is false.

(c) A is false but R is true.

(d) Both A and R are true and R is the correct explanation of A.

One or More than One Correct MCQs

11. One mole of an ideal mono-atomic gas is taken round cyclic process *ABCA* as shown in figure below.

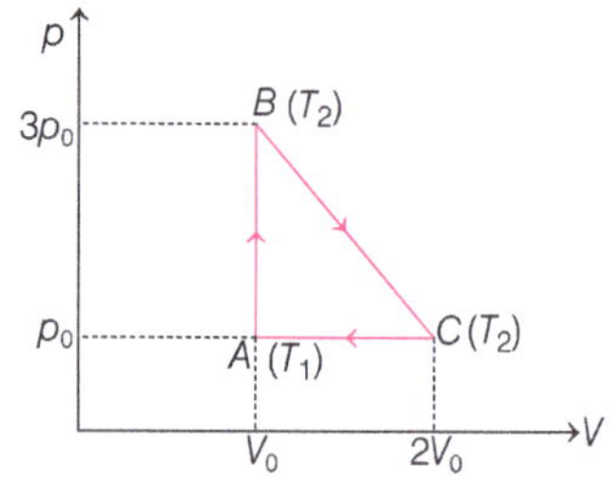

Choose the correct statement regarding the given data.

(a) The total work done by the gas is $-p_0V_0$.

(b) The heat rejected by the gas in the path *CA* is $+3p_0V_0$.

(c) The net heat absorbed by the gas in the path *BC* is p_0V_0.

(d) The maximum temperature attained by the gas during the cycle is $\frac{3p_0V_0}{R}$.

12. When $HCl(g)$ and $NH_3(g)$ come in contact, they react producing a white cloud of solid NH_4Cl

$$NH_3(g) + HCl(g) \rightleftharpoons NH_4Cl(s)$$

For this,

(a) $\Delta S°_{(universe)} > 0, \Delta G° < 0$

(b) $\Delta S°_{(system)} < 0, \Delta S°_{(surrounding)} > 0$

(c) $\Delta H° > 0, \Delta G° > 0$

(d) $\Delta S°_{(universe)} = 0, \Delta S°_{(system)} = -\Delta S°_{(surrounding)}$

13. Which of the following statements are true?

(a) The entropy of a substance increases on going from the liquid to the vapour state at any temperature

(b) An exothermic reaction will not be spontaneous at high temperature

(c) Reactions with a positive ($\Delta H°$ and $\Delta S°$) can never be product favoured

(d) If $\Delta G°$ for a reaction is negative, the reaction will have an equilibrium constant greater than one

14. Consider the following process.

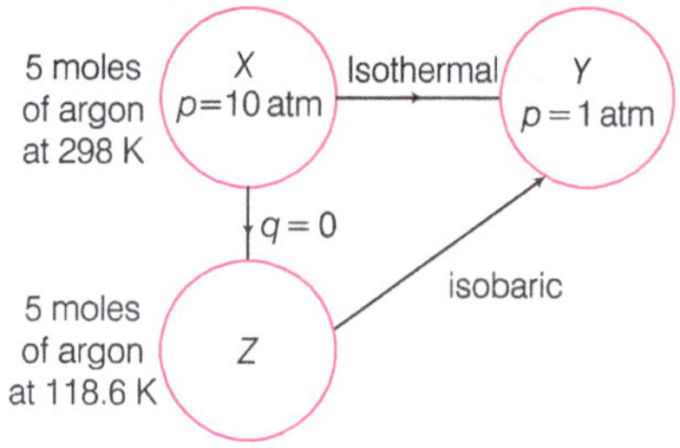

Select correct choices(s).

(a) $\Delta S_{X \to Y} = 95.7\ JK^{-1}$

(b) $\Delta S_{X \to Z} = 0$

(c) $\Delta S_{X \to Y} = \Delta S_{X \to Z} + \Delta S_{Z \to Y} = 95.75\ JK^{-1}$

(d) $\Delta S_{X \to Z \to Y} = 0$

15. Based on following figure.

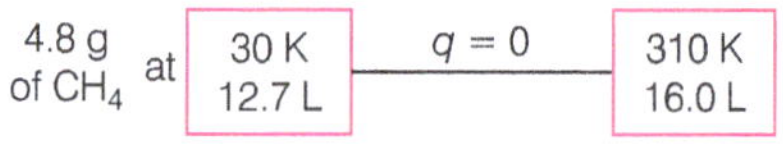

External pressure = 380 torr

(a) work done when gas expands isothermally against external pressure is -167.2 J

(b) work done when gas expands isothermally and reversibly is smaller than -167.2 J

(c) work done when gas expands under vacuum is zero

(d) work done when gas expands isothermally or isothermally reversibly is same

16. Select correct alternative based on the following experiment : A quantity of 0.850 mole of an ideal gas initially at a pressure 15.0 atm and 300 K is allowed to expand isothermally until its final pressure is 1.00 atm. Work done

(a) is zero if expansion is carried out against vacuum

(b) is -19.5 L atm if expansion is carried out against a constant external pressure of 1.0 atm

(c) is -5.74×10^3 J if expansion is carried our reversibly

(d) is zero if expansion is carried out adiabatically if gas is monoatomic.

17. A sample containing 1.0 mole of an ideal gas is expanded isothermally and reversibly to ten time of its original volume, in two separate experiments. The expansion is carried out 300 K and at 600 K, respectively. Choose the correct option.

(a) Work done at 600 K is 20 times the work done at 300 K

(b) Work done at 300 K is twice the work done at 600 K

(c) Work done at 600 K is twice the work done at 300 K

(d) $\Delta E = 0$ in both cases

18. One mole of methane gas at STP is expanded adiabatically against a pressure of 0.375 atm until its volume is doubled. Thus, [$C_V(CH_4) = 3R$]

(a) Work done is -8.4 L atm (b) $W = \Delta U$

(c) Temperature falls by 34 K (d) $W > \Delta U$

Integer/Numerical Type Questions

19. Two moles of an ideal gas at 300 K is held in a cylinder by a piston at a pressure of 150 atm. The pressure is released in four stages–first to 100 atm, then to 50 atm, then to 20 atm and finally to 1 atm, as shown

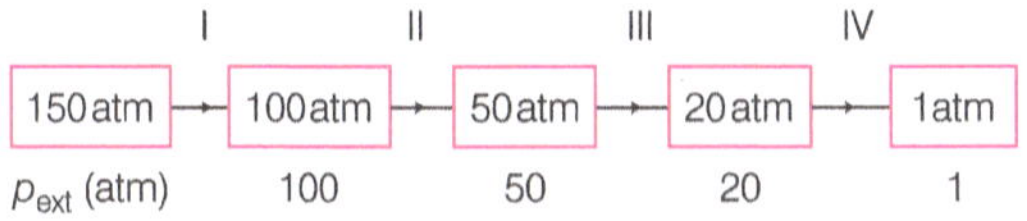

If temperature remains constant at 300 K total work done under irreversible condition is ..... kJ. (Nearest integer)

20. 2 moles of methanol (l) is combusted in a fixed volume bomb calorimeter with excess of O_2 at 298 K and 1 atm in CO_2 and water. During the reaction, temperature increases from 298 K to 330 K. If heat capacity of the bomb calorimeter and enthalpy of formation of methanol is 20.00 kJ K^{-1} and 60.32 kJ mol^{-1} at 298 K, respectively. The calculated standard molar enthalpy of formation of $H_2O(l)$ at 298 K is X kJ mol^{-1}. The value of $|X|$ is ....

[Given, $\Delta H_f^\circ[CO_2(g)] = 25$ kJ mol^{-1} and $R = 8.3$ JK^{-1} mol^{-1}]
(Nearest integer)

21. In the reaction,

I. $H_2(g) \longrightarrow 2H(g), \quad \Delta H^\circ = 236\,kJ$

II. $O_2 \longrightarrow 2O(g), \quad \Delta H^\circ = 498\,kJ$

III. $H_2(g) + \frac{1}{2}O_2(g) \longrightarrow H_2O(l), \Delta H^\circ = -241.8\,kJ$

IV. $2H(g) + \frac{1}{2}O_2(g) \longrightarrow H_2O(l), \Delta H^\circ = x$

V. $2H(g) + O(g) \longrightarrow H_2O(l), \Delta H^\circ = y$

Thus, $3x/y$ is ....

22. Consider the following volume-temperature (V-T) diagram for the expansion of 4 moles of an ideal monotomic gas.

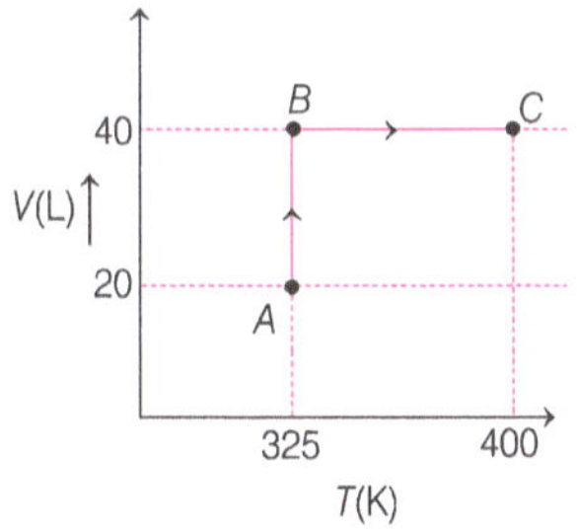

Considering only p-V work is involved, the total change in enthalpy (in J) for the transformation of state in the sequence $A \rightarrow B \rightarrow C$ is ....

[Use the given data, $C_{V,m} = 13$ JK^{-1} mol^{-1},
$R = 8.3$ JK^{-1} mol^{-1}]

23. 0.4 mole of monoatomic gas fills a 1 dm^3 container to a pressure of 1.0 kPa. It is expanded reversibly and adiabatically until a pressure of 0.1 kPa is reached. The final volume and temperature are 'X' dm^3 and 'Y' K respectively. The work done in expansion is 'Z' J.

The value of $X + Y + Z$ (excluding) units is ....

24.

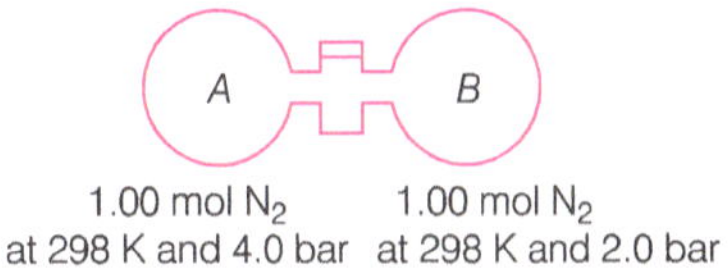

The stopcock connecting A and B is of negligible volume. Stopcock is opened and gases are allowed to mix isothermally.

The final pressure after mixing is X bar and the entropy change for the system is Y JK^{-1}.

The value of Y is ....

[Given: $R = 0.08314$ bar L mol^{-1} K^{-1}]

25. One mole of an ideal gas is taken from a to b along two paths denoted by the solid and the dashed lines as shown in the graph below. If the work done along the solid line path is W_s and that along the dotted line path is W_d, then the integer closest to the ratio W_d/W_s is

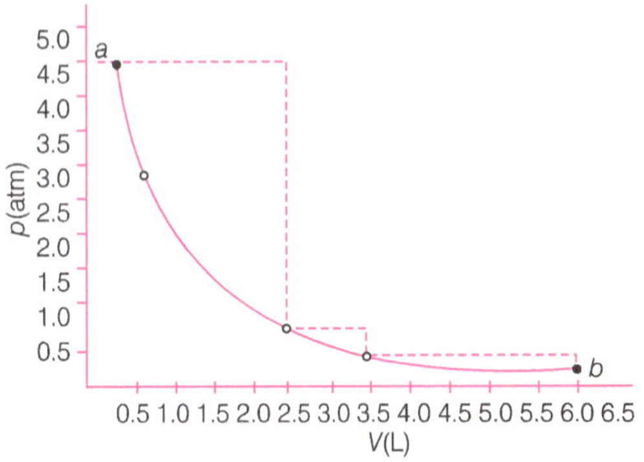

26. One mole of an ideal monoatomic gas undergoes two reversible process ($A \rightarrow B$ and $B \rightarrow C$) as shown in the given figure.

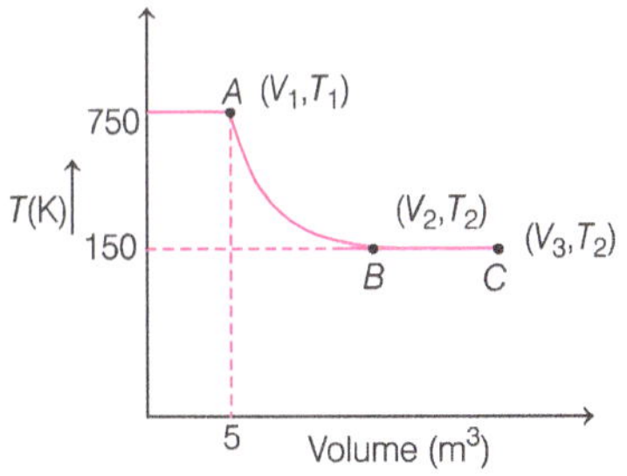

$A \rightarrow B$ is an adiabatic process. If the heat absorbed in the entire process ($A \rightarrow B$ and $B \rightarrow C$) is $RT_2 \ln 25$, the value of $6 \log V_3$ is .... (Nearest integer)

[Use, molar heat capacity of the gas at constant pressure, $C_{p,m} = \frac{5}{2}R$]

Matching Type Questions

27. Based on the following thermodynamic data,

Substance	S°/cal mol^{-1} K^{-1}	ΔH_f° /kcal mol^{-1}
CO	47.3	– 26.4
Cl_2	53.3	0
$COCl_2$	69.1	– 53.3

Match the thermodynamic functions for the following equilibrium at 298 K

$$CO(g) + Cl_2(g) \rightleftharpoons COCl_2(g)$$

in Column I and their values in Column II and select answers from the codes given

Colum I		Column II	
(i)	ΔS° (cal mol^{-1} K^{-1})	p.	– 26.9
(ii)	ΔH°(kcal mol^{-1})	q.	– 31.5
(iii)	ΔG° (kcal mol^{-1})	r.	12.7
(iv)	$\log K_{eq}$	s.	–17.5

Codes

	(i)	(ii)	(iii)	(iv)
(a)	(p)	(q)	(s)	(r)
(b)	(q)	(p)	(s)	(r)
(c)	(s)	(p)	(q)	(r)
(d)	(p)	(s)	(r)	(q)

28. Match the thermodynamic properties in Column I with the corresponding equations in Column II and select answers from the codes

Column I		Column II	
(i)	Free energy change of a reactions (ΔG)	p.	$-RT \log_e K$
(ii)	Enthalpy change of a reaction in a standard state (ΔH°)	q.	$RT^2\left(\frac{d \log K}{dT}\right)$
(iii)	Entropy change (ΔS°)	r.	$-nF\,\Delta G < 0$
(iv)	Free energy change of a reaction in equilibrium	s.	$-\left(\frac{d\Delta G^\circ}{dT}\right)_p$
		t.	$nR \log \frac{V_2}{V_1}$
		u.	$\Delta E^\circ + p\Delta V$

Codes

	(i)	(ii)	(iii)	(iv)
(a)	(s)	(t)	(p,q)	(s,u)
(b)	(p)	(q)	(r,s)	(t,u)
(c)	(r)	(q,u)	(s,t)	(p)
(d)	(r)	(q,u)	(s)	(p,t)

29. Bond energies (in kcal mol^{-1}) are given below

Bond	BE
H—H	104
H—Cl	103
H—C	87
H—O	111
C=O	193
Cl—Cl	58
C—Cl	79
O=O	118
C—C	83

Match the reactions in Column I with their $\Delta_r H^\circ$ (based on BE values) in Column II and select answer from the codes:

Column I		Column II (in kcal mol^{-1})	
i.	$2H_2(g) + O_2(g) \longrightarrow 2H_2O(g)$	p.	– 246
ii.	$CH_4(g) + 2O_2(g) \longrightarrow CO_2(g) + 2H_2O(g)$	q.	+ 46
iii.	$CH_4(g) + Cl_2(g) \longrightarrow CH_3Cl(g) + HCl(g)$	r.	– 118
iv.	$C_2H_6(g) + Cl_2(g) \longrightarrow C_2H_5Cl(g) + HCl(g)$	s.	– 37

Codes

	i	ii	iii	iv		i	ii	iii	iv
(a)	p	q	r	s	(b)	s	q	r	p
(c)	r	p	s	q	(d)	s	p	q	r

30. Variation of equilibrium constant with temperature is given by

$$\frac{d \log K}{dT} = \frac{\Delta H^\circ}{2.303\,RT^2}$$

Given,

Temperature (K)	K_{eq}
298 K	8.85
373 K	88.5

Match the parameters in Column I with their values in Column II and select answers from the codes
($\log 8.85 = 0.947$)

Column I		Column II	
(i)	ΔH°(kJ mol^{-1})	p.	– 5.40
(ii)	ΔG° (at 298 K, kJ mol^{-1})	q.	–13.9
(iii)	ΔG°(at 373 K, kJ mol^{-1})	r.	0.1
(iv)	K_1 / K_2	s.	+ 28.4

Codes

	(i)	(ii)	(iii)	(iv)		(i)	(ii)	(iii)	(iv)
(a)	(s)	(p)	(q)	(r)	(b)	(s)	(q)	(p)	(r)
(c)	(p)	(q)	(r)	(s)	(d)	(s)	(q)	(r)	(p)

31. Thermodynamic equilibrium constant K is related to temperature by equation $\log_{10} K = -\frac{2000}{T}(K) + 5$

Match the thermodynamic parameters given in Column I with respective values given in Column II and select answers from the codes given below the table.

	Column I		Column II
(i)	$\Delta H°$ (in kcal)	p.	10.0
(ii)	$\Delta S°$ (in kcal)	q.	9.212
(iii)	$\Delta G°$ (in kcal) at 1000 K	r.	0.023
(iv)	Equilibrium constant at 500 K	s.	−13.8

Codes

	(i)	(ii)	(iii)	(iv)		(i)	(ii)	(iii)	(iv)
(a)	(q)	(r)	(s)	(p)	(b)	(p)	(r)	(s)	(q)
(c)	(r)	(p)	(q)	(s)	(d)	(p)	(q)	(r)	(s)

32. I. A sample of an ideal gas underwent an expansion against a constant external pressure of 1.0 bar from 1.0 m^3, 10.0 bar, and 273 to10.0 m^3, 1.0 bar and 273 K. Work done by the system on the surroundings is W_1 (in J).

II. The external pressure was increased to 10.0 bar and the gas sample was isothermally compressed from 10.0 m^3 and 1.0 bar to 1.0 m^3 and 10.0 bar. Work done on the system by the surroundings is W_2 (in J).

III. Total work done is W_3 (in J) in the above processes.

IV. Least amount of work needed to restore the system to the original p-V conditions is W_4 (in J) by same path.

Match W_1, W_2, W_3 and W_4 in Column I with corresponding values in Column II.

	Column I		Column II
(i)	W_1	p.	8.1×10^6 J
(ii)	W_2	q.	9.0×10^6 J
(iii)	W_3	r.	2.3×10^6 J
(iv)	W_4	s.	-9.0×10^5 J

Codes

	(i)	(ii)	(iii)	(iv)		(i)	(ii)	(iii)	(iv)
(a)	(s)	(q)	(p)	(r)	(b)	(s)	(p)	(q)	(r)
(c)	(p)	(q)	(s)	(r)	(d)	(r)	(p)	(s)	(q)

Paragraph of Two Questions Each

33. Acetic acid, CH_3CO_2H can form dimer $(CH_3CO_2H)_2$ in the gas phase.

$2CH_3CO_2H(g) \rightleftharpoons (CH_3CO_2H)_2(g); K_p = 1.3 \times 10^3$ at 298 K

The dimer is held together by two hydrogen bonds with a total strength of 66.5 kJ mol^{-1} of dimer.

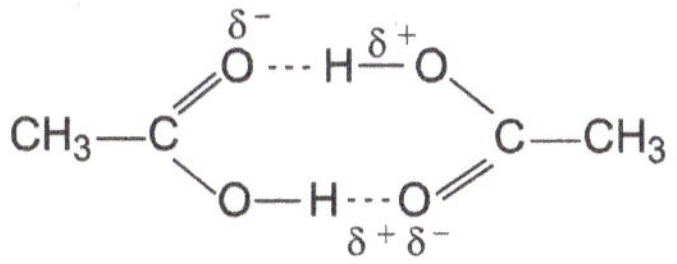

(i) The value of entropy change ($\Delta S°$) in kJ mol^{-1} at 298 K is (–) ....

(ii) The value of ΔG (in kJ mol^{-1}) when reaction quotient is 10^3 at 298 K is (–) ....

34. One mole of an ideal monoatomic gas (with $C_V = 3.0$ cal K^{-1} mol^{-1}) initially at STP is put through the following reversible cycle.

I. State I to State II, heated at constant volume to twice the initial temperature.

II. State II to state III expanded adiabatically until it is back to initial temperature.

III. State III to state I compressed isothermally back to state I.

(i) The volume due to adiabatic expansion in state II is .... L.

(ii) The total work done in this reversible cycle (I → II → III → I) is .... cal. [Nearest integer]

35. An ideal monoatomic gas undergoes a cyclic process consisting of 3 steps. In Ist step ($A \rightarrow B$) the gas is heated at constant volume, increasing its temperature from 300 K to 600 K. In the 2nd step, ($B \rightarrow C$), the gas expands reversing isothermally at 600 K, doubling its initial volume. Finally reversing in 3rd step ($C \rightarrow A$), the gas is compressed adiabatically back to its original state.

$p_A = 1$ atm, $V_A = 10$ L and $T_A = 300$ K respectively.

(i) Calculate the heat added to the gas during the isochoric process ($A \rightarrow B$).

(ii) Determine the workdone by the gas during the isothermal expansion ($B \rightarrow C$).

36. Consider the following reactions,

(i) $C_2H_4(g) + H_2(g) \longrightarrow C_2H_6(g)$
(ii) $C(s) + CO_2(g) \longrightarrow 2CO(g)$
(iii) $NH_4HS(s) \longrightarrow NH_3(g) + H_2S(g)$
(iv) $CH_4(g) + 2O_2(g) \longrightarrow CO_2(g) + 2H_2O(g)$
(v) $2H_2(g) + N_2(g) \longrightarrow 2NH_3(g)$

The total number of reactions which have equal values of change in enthalpy and change in internal energy at constant temperature.

(a) 1 (b) 3 (c) 4 (d) 2

37. Out of internal energy (i), temperature (ii), work (iii), enthalpy (iv) and pressure (v), the number of state functions are

(a) 1 (b) 3 (c) 2 (d) 4

38. Consider the following relation, regarding the given equation, $G = H - TS$

(i) $(dG) = -SdT + Vdp$ (ii) $(dG)_p = -SdT$

(iii) $(dG)_T = Vdp$ (iv) $(dG)_T = RT\frac{dp}{p}$

(v) $(dG)_p = nRT\frac{dV}{V}$

The total correct relation is

(a) 2 (b) 3 (c) 1 (d) 4

39. Among the following properties,

(i) Emf of a cell (ii) pH

(iii) Density (iv) Dielectric constant
(v) Refractive index (vi) Entropy
(vii) Viscosity

The total number extensive properties are

(a) 6 (b) 4 (c) 5 (d) 1

40. Consider the following reactions,

(i) $2H_2O(g) \longrightarrow 2H_2(g) + O_2(g)$
(ii) $CO(g) + 2H_2(g) \longrightarrow CH_3OH(g)$
(iii) $C_2H_5OH(g) + 3O_2(g) \longrightarrow 2CO_2(g) + 3H_2O(g)$
(iv) $2SO_2(g) + O_2(g) \longrightarrow 2SO_3(g)$
(v) $NH_4HS(s) \longrightarrow NH_3(g) + H_2S(g)$
(vi) $C_2H_6(g) + 3.5O_2(g) \longrightarrow 2CO_2(g) + 3H_2O(l)$
(vii) $CaCO_3(s) \longrightarrow CaO(s) + CO_2(g)$

The number of reactions for which the standard entropy change is positive.

(a) 5 (b) 3 (c) 4 (d) 6

41. Consider the following equation,

(i) $H_2(g) + \frac{1}{2}O_2(g) \longrightarrow H_2O(l)$
(ii) $CaO(s) + O_2(g) \longrightarrow CaCO_3(s)$
(iii) $2C(\text{Graphite}) + 3H_2(g) + \frac{1}{2}O_2(g) \longrightarrow C_2H_5OH(l)$
(iv) $CO(g) + 2H_2(g) \longrightarrow CH_3OH(l)$
(v) $C(\text{Graphite}) + 2H_2(g) \longrightarrow CH_4(g)$
(vi) $N_2(g) + 3H_2(g) \longrightarrow 2NH_3(g)$
(vii) $C(\text{Diamond}) + \frac{1}{2}O_2(g) + 2H_2(g) \longrightarrow CH_3OH(l)$

The number of equations which do not represent the standard enthalpy of formation (ΔH_f°) are ....

(a) 4 (b) 5
(c) 3 (d) 6

42. Consider the following chemical changes, taking place against external atmospheric pressure,

(i) $C(s) + O_2(g) \longrightarrow 2CO(g)$
(ii) $C_2H_6(g) + 3.5O_2(g) \longrightarrow 2CO_2(g) + 3H_2O(l)$
(iii) $3H_2(g) + N_2(g) \longrightarrow 2NH_3(g)$
(iv) $CH_4(g) + 2O_2(g) \longrightarrow CO_2(g) + 2H_2O(g)$
(v) $CaCO_3(s) \longrightarrow CaO(s) + CO_2(g)$
(vi) $NH_4HS(s) \longrightarrow NH_3(g) + H_2S(g)$
(vii) $PCl_5(g) \longrightarrow PCl_3(g) + Cl_2(g)$

The total number of chemical changes in which the sign of work done (based on SI convention) is negative

(a) 4 (b) 3
(c) 5 (d) 2

43. Consider the following reactions,

(i) $C_6H_6(l) + 4.5O_2(g) \longrightarrow 6CO(g) + 3H_2O(l)$, $\Delta H = -200$ k cal
(ii) $CH_4(g) + 2O_2(g) \longrightarrow CO_2(g) + 2H_2O(l)$, $\Delta H = -210$ k cal
(iii) $2C(g) + O_2(g) \longrightarrow 2CO(g)$, $\Delta H = -94$ k cal
(iv) $C_3H_8(g) + 5O_2(g) \longrightarrow 3CO_2(g) + 4H_2O(l)$, $\Delta H = -526$ k cal
(v) $C_2H_4(g) + H_2(g) \longrightarrow C_2H_6(g)$, $\Delta H = -34.11$ k cal
(vi) $C_2H_6(g) + 3.5O_2(g) \longrightarrow 2CO_2(g) + 3H_2O(l)$, $\Delta H = -368$ k cal
(vii) $2CH_3OH(l) + 3O_2(g) \longrightarrow 2CO_2(g) + 4H_2O(l)$, $\Delta H = -3003$ k cal

The total number of reactions which represents the enthalpy of combustion are

(a) 6 (b) 4
(c) 3 (d) 2

Check Through PYQs

Element 2 First Law of Thermodynamics

1. Consider the following volume-temperature (V-T) diagram for the expansion of 5 moles of an ideal monoatomic gas.

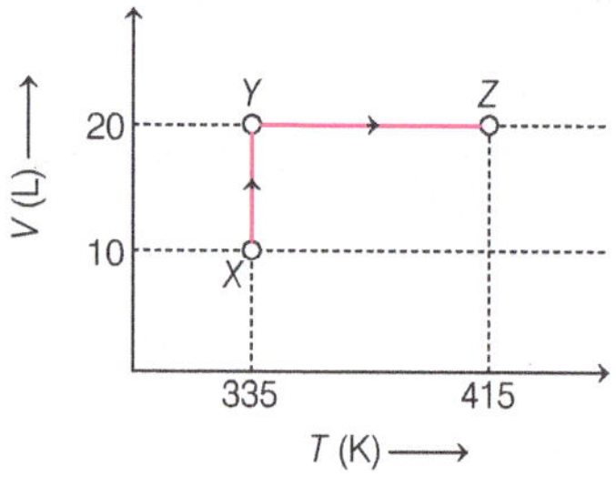

Considering only p-V work is involved, the total change in enthalpy (in Joule) for the transformation of state in the sequence $X \rightarrow Y \rightarrow Z$ is ....

[Use the given data : Molar heat capacity of the gas for the given temperature range, $C_{v,m} = 12\ \text{J K}^{-1}\ \text{mol}^{-1}$ and gas constant, $R = 8.3\ \text{J K}^{-1}\text{mol}^{-1}$]

(2024 Adv.)

2. One mole of an ideal monoatomic gas undergoes two reversible process ($A \rightarrow B$ and $B \rightarrow C$) as shown in the given figure.

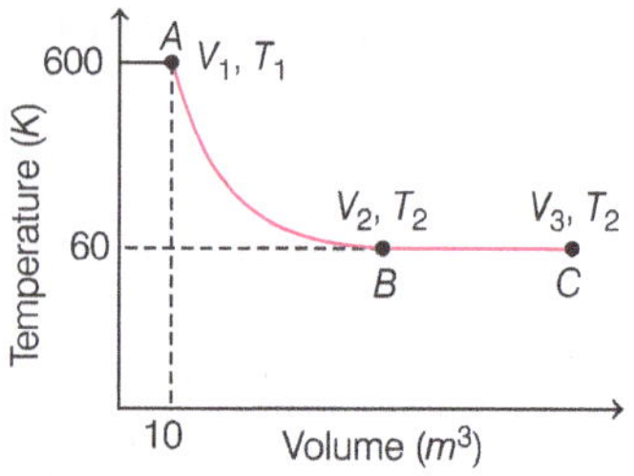

$A \rightarrow B$ is an adiabatic process. If the total heat absorbed in the entire process ($A \rightarrow B$ and $B \rightarrow C$) is RT_2 ln 10, the value of $2 \log V_3$ is ________ .

[Use, molar heat capacity of the gas at constant pressure, $C_{p,m} = \frac{5}{2}R$] **(2023 Adv.)**

3. A reversible cyclic process for an ideal gas is shown below. Here, p, V and T are pressure, volume and temperature, respectively. The thermodynamic parameters q, w, H and U are heat, work, enthalpy and internal energy, respectively. **(2018 Adv.)**

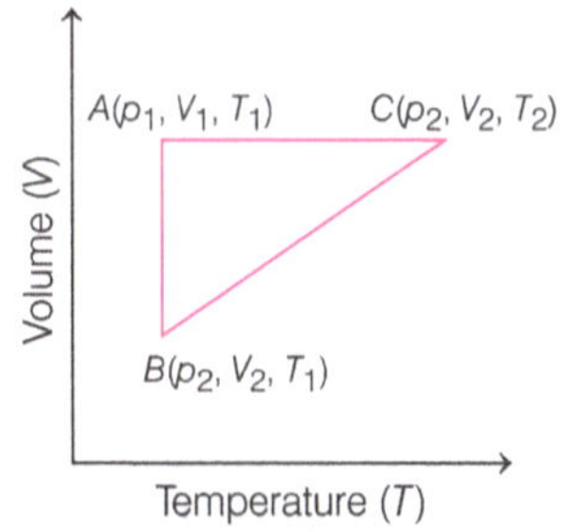

(a) $q_{AC} = \Delta U_{BC}$ and $w_{AB} = p_2(V_2 - V_1)$
(b) $w_{BC} = p_2(V_2 - V_1)$ and $q_{BC} = \Delta H_{AC}$
(c) $\Delta H_{CA} < \Delta U_{CA}$ and $q_{AC} = \Delta U_{BC}$
(d) $q_{BC} = \Delta H_{AC}$ and $\Delta H_{CA} > \Delta U_{CA}$

4. An ideal gas is expanded form (p_1, V_1, T_1) to (p_2, V_2, T_2) under different conditions. The correct statement(s) among the following is (are) **(2017 Adv.)**
(a) The work done on the gas is maximum when it is compressed irreversibly from (p_2, V_2) to (p_1, V_1) against constant pressure p_1
(b) The change in internal energy of the gas is (i) zero, if it is expanded reversibly with $T_1 = T_2$, and (ii) positive, if it is expanded reversibly under adiabatic conditions with $T_1 \neq T_2$
(c) If the expansion is carried out freely, it is simultaneously both isothermal as well as adiabatic
(d) The work done by the gas is less when it is expanded reversibly from V_1 to V_2 under adiabatic conditions as compared to that when expanded reversibly form V_1 to V_2 under isothermal conditions.

5. In thermodynamics, the p-V work done is given by

$$w = -\int dV\, p_{ext}$$

For a system undergoing a particular process, the work done is

$$w = -\int dV \left(\frac{RT}{V-b} - \frac{a}{V^2}\right)$$

This equation is applicable to a **(2020 Adv.)**
(a) system that satisfies the van der Waals' equation of state
(b) process that is reversible and isothermal
(c) process that is reversible and adiabatic
(d) process that is irreversible and at constant pressure

Element 3 Entropy and Second Law of Thermodynamics, Entropy

The entropy *versus* temperature plot for phases α and β at 1 bar pressure is given. S_T and S_0 are entropies of the phases at temperatures T and 0 K, respectively.

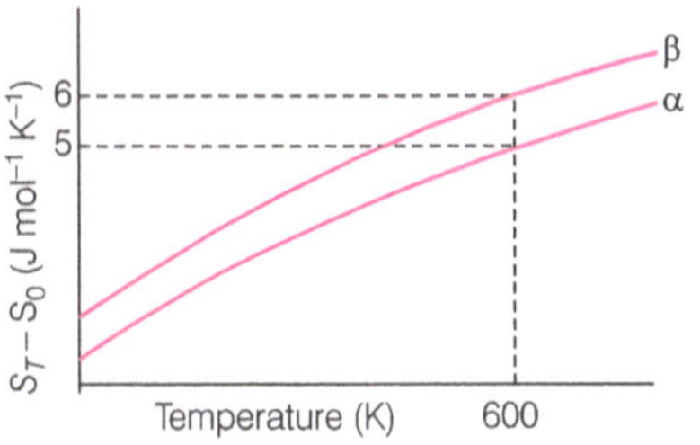

The transition temperature for α to β phase change is 600 K and $C_{p,\beta} - C_{p,\alpha} = 1$ J mol^{-1}K^{-1}. Assume $(C_{p,\beta} - C_{p,\alpha})$ is independent of temperature in the range of 200 to 700 K. $C_{p,\alpha}$ and $c_{p,\beta}$ are heat capacities of α and β phases, respectively. **(2023 Adv.)**

6. The value of entropy change, $S_\beta - S_\alpha$ (in J mol^{-1} K^{-1}) at 300 K is ....
[Use : ln 2 = 0.69; Given : $S_\beta - S_\alpha = 0$ at 0 K]

7. The value of enthalpy change, $H_\beta - H_\alpha$ (in J mol^{-1}), at 300 K is ....

8. For the reaction, $X(s) \rightleftharpoons Y(s) + Z(g)$, the plot of $\ln \frac{p_Z}{p^\circ}$ *versus* $\frac{10^4}{T}$ is, given below (in solid line), where p_Z is the pressure (in bar) of the gas Z at temperature T and $p^\circ = 1$ bar.

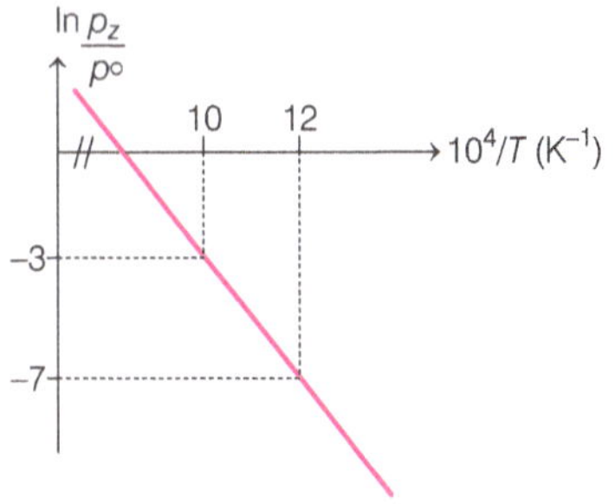

(Given, $\frac{d(\ln K)}{d\left(\frac{1}{T}\right)} = -\frac{\Delta H^\circ}{R}$, where the equilibrium constant, $K = \frac{p_Z}{p^\circ}$ and the gas constant, $R = 8.314$ JK^{-1}mol^{-1}) **(2021 Adv.)**

(i) The value of standard enthalpy, ΔH° (in kJ mol^{-1}) for the given reaction is ....
(ii) The value of, ΔS° (in JK^{-1} mol^{-1}) for the given reaction, at 1000 K is ....

9. One mole of an ideal gas at 900 K, undergoes two reversible processes, I followed by II, as shown below. If the work done by the gas in the two processes are same, the value of $\ln V_3/V_2$ is .... *(2021 Adv.)*

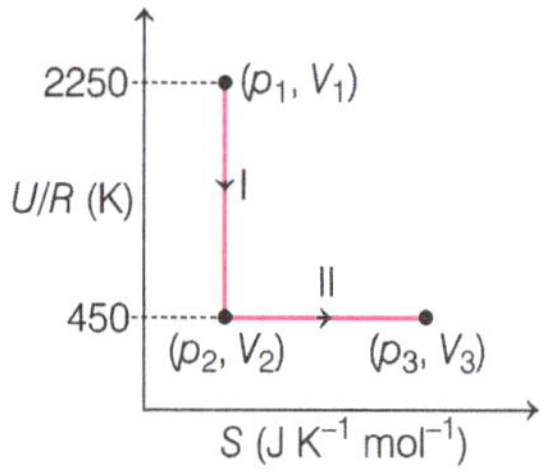

(U = internal energy, S = entropy, p = pressure, V = volume, R = gas constant)

(Given, molar heat capacity at constant volume, $C_{V,\,m}$ of the gas is $5/2\,R$)

10. An ideal gas undergoes a reversible isothermal expansion from state I to state II followed by a reversible adiabatic expansion from state II to state III. The correct plot(s) representing the changes from state I to state III is(are) (p = pressure, V = volume, T = temperature, H = enthalpy, S = entropy) *(2021 Adv.)*

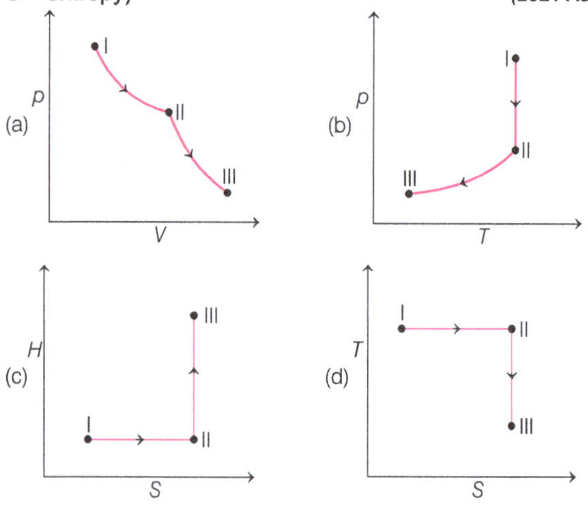

11. Consider the reaction,

$$A \rightleftharpoons B \text{ at } 1000\text{ K}.$$

At time t', the temperature of the system was increased to 2000 K and the system was allowed to reach equilibrium. Throughout this experiment the partial pressure of A was maintained at 1 bar. Given, below is the plot of the partial pressure of B with time.

What is the ratio of the standard Gibbs energy of the reaction at 1000 K to that at 2000 K?

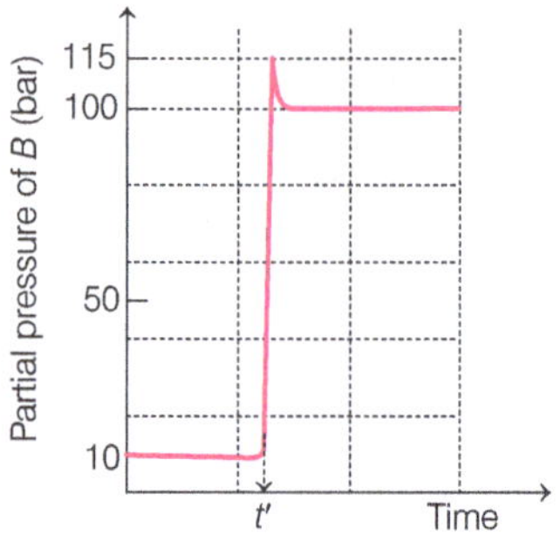

(2020 Adv.)

12. One mole of an ideal gas at 300 K in thermal contact with surroundings expands isothermally from 1.0 L to 2.0 L against a constant pressure of 3.0 atm.

In this process, the change in entropy of surroundings (ΔS_{surr}) in JK^{-1} is (1 L atm = 101.3 J) *(2016 Adv.)*

(a) 5.763 (b) 1.013 (c) – 1.013 (d) – 5.763

Element 4 Thermochemistry

13. 2 moles of Hg(g) is combusted in a fixed volume bomb calorimeter with excess of O_2 at 298 K and 1 atm into HgO(s). During the reaction, temperature increases from 298.0 K to 312.8 K. If heat capacity of the bomb calorimeter and enthalpy of formation of Hg(g) 20.00 kJ K^{-1} and 61.32 kJ mol^{-1} at 298 K, respectively, the calculated standard molar enthalpy of formation of HgO(s) at 298 K is X kJ mol^{-1}. The value of $|X|$ is ....

[Given, gas constant $R = 8.3\text{J K}^{-1}\text{ mol}^{-1}$] *(2022 Adv.)*

14. Choose the reaction(s) from the following options, for which the standard enthalpy of reaction is equal to the standard enthalpy of formation. *(2019 Adv.)*

(a) $2C(g) + 3\ H_2(g) \longrightarrow C_2H_6(g)$

(b) $2H_2(g) + O_2(g) \longrightarrow 2H_2O(l)$

(c) $\frac{3}{2}O_2(g) \longrightarrow O_3(g)$

(d) $\frac{1}{8}S_8(s) + O_2(g) \longrightarrow SO_2(g)$

HINTS & Solutions

Solutions : Competency Enhancer

2.1. ***(23)*** $X \rightarrow Y$ (reversible adiabatic)

$$\therefore \quad T_1V_1^{\gamma-1} = T_2V_2^{\gamma-1}$$

$$T_1 = 800, V_1 = 20, T_2 = 40$$

$$\gamma = \frac{5}{3} \qquad \left(\text{from } C_{p,m} = \frac{5}{2}R\right)$$

$$\therefore \quad (800)(20)^{\frac{2}{3}} = (40)(V_2)^{\frac{2}{3}} \Rightarrow (20)(20)^{\frac{2}{3}} = (V_2)^{\frac{2}{3}}$$

$$(V_2)^{\frac{2}{3}} = (20)^{\frac{5}{3}} \Rightarrow (V_2) = (20)^{\frac{5}{2}}$$

Also, $q_{XY} = 0$ and $q_{XZ} = RT_2 \ln 20$

$$\therefore \quad q_{YZ} = nRT_2 \ln\left(\frac{V_3}{V_2}\right) = RT_2 \ln\left(\frac{V_3}{V_2}\right) \quad (\because n = 1)$$

$$q_{XZ} = q_{YZ}$$

$\therefore$ Total heat absorbed $= RT_2 \ln\left(\frac{V_3}{V_2}\right) = RT_2 \ln 20$

$$\frac{V_3}{V_2} = 20$$

$$V_3 = 20 \times V_2 = 20 \times (20)^{\frac{5}{2}} = (20)^{\frac{7}{2}}$$

Now, the value of

$$5\log V_3 = 5\log (20)^{\frac{7}{2}}$$

$$= 5 \times \frac{7}{2} \times 1.30 = 22.75 \approx 23$$

3.1. ***(27.46)*** $\Delta S = nC_{p,m} \ln \frac{T_2}{T_1} + nR \ln \frac{p_1}{p_2}$

$$= 5 \times \frac{7}{2} R \ln\left[\frac{894}{298}\right] + 5R \ln\left[\frac{1}{3}\right]$$

$$= 5 \times \frac{7}{2} \times 2 \text{ cal. K}^{-1} \ln^3 - 5 \times 2 \text{ cal. K}^{-1} \ln (3)$$

$$= 27.46 \text{ cal.K}^{-1}$$

4.1. ***(202.75)*** The combustion reaction is

$$C_3H_8(g) + 5O_2(g) \longrightarrow 3CO_2(g) + 4H_2O(l)$$

Given, heat capacity of calorimeter,

$$C = 30 \text{ kJ K}^{-1}$$

$$T_i = 298 \text{ K}$$

$$T_f = 325 \text{ K}$$

Change in temperature $(\Delta T) = 298 - 325 = -27$ K

Heat evolved in reaction,

$$q = C\Delta T = 30 \times -27 = 810 \text{ kJ}$$

Since, the reaction is taking place under constant volume

$$\Delta U_r = -810 \text{ kJ}$$

Enthalpy of reaction,

$$\Delta H_r^\circ = \Delta U^\circ + \Delta n_g RT$$

$$= -810 \text{ kJ} + (-3) \times 8.3 \text{ JK}^{-1} \text{ mol}^{-1} \times 298 \text{ K} \times 10^{-3} \text{ kJ/J}$$

$$= -810 \text{ kJ} - 7.42 \text{ kJ} = -817.42 \text{ kJ}$$

Also, $\Delta H_r^\circ = 3\Delta H_f^\circ [CO_2(g)] + 4\Delta^\circ H_f[H_2O(l)] - \Delta^\circ H_f[(C_3H_8(g)] - 5\Delta H_f^\circ [O_2(g)]$

$$-817.42 = 3 \times 20 + 4\Delta^\circ H_f[H_2O(l)] - 66.44 - 0$$

$$-817.42 + 6.44 = 4\Delta^\circ H_f[H_2O(l)]$$

$$\Delta^\circ H_f[H_2O(l)] = -\frac{810.98}{4}$$

$$|X| = 202.75 \text{ kJ mol}^{-1}$$

Elemental Practice 4.1

1. ***(c)*** A system is said to be in thermodynamic equilibrium with the surroundings, if it is in thermal, chemical as well as mechanical equilibrium with the surrounding.
2. ***(b)*** Out of p, V and T, p and T are independent variable while V is dependent variable.
3. ***(b)*** Among the given sets, option (b) i.e., volume, area and length are not set of intensive properties as they all are extensive.
4. ***(c)*** Among the given process, isothermal compression is an example of reversible process.
5. ***(d)*** Among the given thermodynamic properties, collision frequency is not a macroscopic property.
6. ***(d)*** The state of a gas can be described by quoting the relationship between pressure, volume, temperature and amount. The ideal gas equation is $pV = nRT$.

   Thus p, V, T and n describe the state of the system.
7. ***(c)*** A process is called reversible when the surroundings are always in equilibrium with the system.
8. ***(c)*** In a closed vessel made of copper, no matter can exchange between the system and the surroundings but energy exchange can occur through its walls, copper being conducting.
9. ***(a)*** Thermodynamics is concerned with energy changes in a system.
10. ***(b)*** Both (A) and (R) are true but (R) is not the correct explanation of (A).

    The correct explanation of A is

    - The heat absorbed during the isothermal expansion of an ideal gas against vacuum is zero because $\Delta U = 0$ and $w = 0$ hence $q = 0$.
11. ***(a)*** Among the given processes, combustion of glucose is not an endothermic process while other are endothermic process.

12. ***(d)*** For an ideal gas, the relationship between pressure and volume in adiabatic process is given by

$$pV^{\gamma} = \text{constant} \left(\text{where } \gamma = \frac{C_p}{C_V} \right)$$

13. ***(b)*** The given process is called cyclic process.

14. ***(b)*** For an adiabatic process, $pV^{\gamma} = \text{constant}$.

$$\frac{dp}{dV} = \frac{-\gamma p}{V}$$

Thus, the slope of p-V curve is proportional to $-\gamma$.

For a diatomic gas, $\gamma = \frac{7}{5}$, is less than for a monoatomic gas for which $\gamma = \frac{5}{3}$

Therefore, the slope of the p-V curve is less for a diatomic gas than for a monoatomic gas.

Hence, curve 1 corresponds to diatomic gas and curve 2 for monoatomic gas.

15. ***(d)*** Among the given options, option (d) is an example of open system while others are—

(a) Example of an isolated system
(b) Example of a closed system
(c) Example of a closed system

16. ***(d, e)*** Among the given statements, only a, b and c are correct while the other d and e are incorrect. Their correct form are

- The internal energy (U) of the system may change when matter enters or leaves the system.
- The state of a thermodynamic system can be described by its measurable or macroscopic properties.

17. ***(a, c, d)*** Among the given statements, (a), (c) and (d) are correct while statement (b) is incorrect. Its correct form is

A process can be defined on the basis of initial and final states of the system.

18. ***(a, b, d)*** Among the given statements all are correct except (c).

In the reaction,

$$C(s) + O_2(g) \longrightarrow 2CO(g)$$

$\Delta n_g \neq 0$, and work is done by the system.

19. ***(a, b, c, d)*** A state function is a property of a system that depends only on the current state of system and not on the path or process used to react that state.

Among the given function internal energy, temperature volume and enthalpy all are state function.

20. ***(b,c,d)*** Among the given statements all are correct except a. The correct form of a is

- Work is a path function.

21. ***(5)*** As we know, extensive properties are additive in nature while intensive properties are non-additive in nature.

So, among the given properties only five i.e, boiling point, molarity, density, pressure and molar mass are non-additive in nature while heat capacity, free energy and mole are additive in nature.

22. ***(3)*** Heating of a gas in a rigid container, and combustion in a closed vessel are examples of isochoric process whereas others are examples of isobaric process.

23. ***(2)*** Among the given properties only three i.e. H, E and G are not a path function instead of they are state function, heat (q) and work (w) are path function.

24. ***(4)*** Among the given all are state functions except irreversible expansion work.

25. ***(2)*** An intensive property is a physical property of a system that does not depend on the amount or size of the material or substance in the system. Among the given properties only a, d, e, f, g and h are intensive property while b and c are extensive property.

Elemental Practice 4.2

1. ***(d)*** As, $p = k \cdot l$ (l = diameter)

For initial condition, 1 bar $= k \times 1$ m

$$\Rightarrow \quad k = 1\,\text{bar/m} \Rightarrow p = l \quad \text{and } V = \frac{4}{3}\pi r^3 = \frac{\pi}{6} l^3$$

Differentiation on both sides, we get;

$$dV = \frac{\pi}{2} l^2 dl$$

Now,

$$w = -\int_{V_1}^{V_2} p\,dV = -\int_{l_1}^{l_2} (k \cdot l)\left(\frac{\pi}{2} l^2 dl\right)$$

$$= \frac{-k\pi}{2} \cdot \frac{l_2^4 - l_1^4}{4}$$

$$= -10^5 \frac{\text{N/m}^2}{\text{m}} \times \frac{\pi}{2} \times \frac{(4^4 - 1^4)}{4} \text{m}^4$$

$$= -1 \times 10^7 \text{ J}$$

2. ***(a)*** Gas is being expanded against external pressure. Thus, work is done by the system, work is negative.

$$W = -p_{ext}[V_2 - V_1] = -p_{ext}\left[\frac{nRT}{p_2} - \frac{nRT}{p_1}\right]$$

$$= -nRTp_{ext}\left[\frac{1}{p_2} - \frac{1}{p_1}\right]$$

$$= -5 \times 0.0821 \text{L atm mol}^{-1}\text{ K}^{-1} \times 1\left[\frac{1}{4} - \frac{1}{10}\right] \times 300 \text{ K}$$

$$= -18.4725 \text{ L atm}$$

$$= -\frac{18.4725 \text{ L atm} \times 8.314 \text{ J}}{0.0821 \text{ L atm}} = -1870.6 \text{ J}$$

3. ***(a)*** It is clear from the figure that process is reversible expansion

$$W = -2.303 nRT \log\frac{V_2}{V_1} = 2.303\, nRT \log\frac{p_1}{p_2}$$

$$= -2.303 \times 1 \times 8.314 \times 300 \log\left(\frac{4}{2}\right)$$

$$= -2.303 \times 1 \times 8.314 \times 300 \times \log\left(\frac{2}{1}\right)$$

$$\therefore \quad W \approx -1729 \text{ J}$$

4. **(c)** Given, VT^3 = Constant

Also, $V^{\gamma-1}T$ = Constant for adiabatic expansion.

$$T^{\frac{1}{\gamma-1}}V = \text{constant} \quad \text{or} \quad \frac{1}{\gamma-1} = 3 \Rightarrow \gamma = \frac{4}{3}$$

So, the gas must be polyatomic gas.

5. **(a)** $$\frac{C_V}{R}\ln\frac{T_2}{T_1} = \ln\frac{V_1}{V_2}$$

$$\frac{3}{2}\ln\frac{T_2}{300} = \ln\left(\frac{10}{20}\right)$$

$$T_2 = 189\,\text{K} \Rightarrow dU = C_V dT$$

For a finite change involving n moles

$$\Delta U = nC_V\Delta T$$
$$= n \times \frac{3}{2}R(189 - 300)$$
$$= 1 \times \frac{3}{2} \times 8.314\,\text{J mol}^{-1}\text{K}^{-1} \times (-111\,\text{K})$$
$$\approx -1384\,\text{J}$$

6. **(d)** Both Statement I and II are correct.

7. **(d)** $$\underset{1\text{ mol}}{Al_4C_3(s)} + 12H_2O(l) \longrightarrow 4Al(OH)_3(s) + \underset{3\text{ mol}}{3CH_4(g)}$$

V_1 = Initial volume (solid) = 0, V_2 = Volume of 3 mol = $\frac{nRT}{p}$

In open vessel

$$\therefore\ W = -p(V_2 - V_1) = -p\left(\frac{nRT}{p} - 0\right) = -nRT$$
$$= -3\,\text{mol} \times 2\,\text{cal mol}^{-1}\,\text{K}^{-1} \times 300\,\text{K} = -1800\,\text{cal}$$

If vessel is closed, volume remains constant

$$\therefore \quad \Delta V = 0 \Rightarrow W = -p\Delta V = 0$$

In an open vessel $W = -1800$ cal.

8. **(a)** According to the given question,

State I $\xrightarrow{\text{Isothermal}}$ State II $\xrightarrow{\text{Isochoric}}$ Star-III

$T_1 = 273\,\text{K}$	$T_2 = 273\,\text{K}$	$T_3 = 5 \times 273\,\text{K}$
$V_1 = V$	$V_2 = 5V$	$V_3 = 5V$
$p_1 = p$	$p_2 = \frac{p}{5}$	$p_3 = p$

$$q_{\text{total}} = nRT\ln\frac{V_2}{V_1} + nC_{v,m}(T_3 - T_2)$$

$$80 \times 10^3 = 3 \times 8.314 \times 273 \times \ln 5 + 3 \times C_{v,m} \times 4 \times 273$$

$$\therefore \quad C_{v,m} \approx 21\,\text{J/K-mol} \approx 5\,\text{cal/K-mol}$$

9. **(b)** Work done at constant pressure is given by

$$\int dw = \int -pdV$$
$$w = -\int 20\frac{dV}{V}$$
$$= -20 \times 2.303\log\frac{V_2}{V_1} \quad [V_2 = 10\,\text{L and } V_1 = 1\,\text{L}]$$
$$= -46.06\,\text{L atm}$$
$$= -46.06 \times 101.3 = -4665.8\,\text{J}$$

According to first law of thermodynamics,

$$\Delta U = q + w$$
$$550 = q - 4665.8\,\text{J}$$
$$q = 5215.8\,\text{J}$$

10. **(a)** Δn_g = moles of gaseous products – Moles of gaseous reactants

Δn_g = + ve means expansion while – ve means compression.

I. $\Delta n_g = -2$ Compression take place

$$W = -p_{\text{ext}}(-\text{ve}) = +\text{ve}$$

II. $\Delta n_g = +2$ (only gaseous species)

$$W = -p_{\text{ext}}(+\text{ve}) = -\text{ve}$$

III. $\Delta n_g = +1$, $W = -$ ve

IV. $\Delta n_g = -2.5$, $W = +$ ve

11. **(c)** For adiabatic expansion, $q = 0$

So, According to first law of thermodynamics,

$$\Delta U = q + w$$
$$\Delta U = w \quad [\because q = 0]$$

$$\frac{nR}{\gamma - 1}[T_2 - T_1] = -p_{\text{ext.}}\left[\frac{nRT_2}{p_2} - \frac{nRT_1}{p_1}\right]$$

$$3(T_2 - T_1) = -1\left(\frac{T_2}{1} - \frac{T_1}{2}\right)$$

$$3T_2 - 3T_1 = -T_2 + \frac{1}{2}T_1 \Rightarrow 4T_2 = \frac{7}{2}T_1$$

$$T_2 = \frac{7}{8} \times 400 = 350\,\text{K}$$

By using, $$\frac{p_1V_1}{T_1} = \frac{p_2V_2}{T_2} = \frac{2 \times 10}{400} = \frac{1 \times V_2}{350}$$

$$V_2 = 17.5\,\text{L}$$

12. **(d)** For Helium, $\gamma = \frac{C_p}{C_V} = \frac{(5/2)R}{(3/2)R} = \frac{5}{3}$

$$(V_2 - V_1) = 3V - V = 2V \Rightarrow C_V = \frac{3}{2}R$$

$$\Delta E = q + w$$

If adiabatic, $q = 0$ $\quad \therefore\ \Delta E = W$

$\Rightarrow \frac{\Delta E}{n\Delta T} = C_V \quad \therefore\ \Delta E = nC_V\Delta T$

$\Rightarrow W = -p\Delta V$

Since internal energy decreases in adiabatic expansion,

$$\Delta E = -\text{ve}\ \Delta E = -w$$

$$\therefore \quad -nC_V\Delta T = p\Delta V$$

$$\therefore \quad \Delta T = -\frac{p\Delta V}{nC_V}$$

$$= \frac{-1\,\text{atm} \times 2\text{L}}{1\,\text{mol} \times \frac{3}{2} \times 0.0821\text{L atm mol}^{-1}\text{K}^{-1}}$$

$$= -\frac{2\,\text{K}}{1.5 \times 0.0821}$$

$$\Rightarrow \quad T_{final} - T = \frac{-2\text{ K}}{1.5 \times 0.0821}$$

$$\therefore \quad T_{final} = T - \frac{2\text{ K}}{(1.5 \times 0.0821)}$$

13. ***(c)*** Statement I is incorrect but statement II is correct.
The correct form of statement I is
- An ideal gas expands in volume from 10^{-3} m^3 to 10^{-2} m^3 at 300 K against a constant pressure of 10^5 Nm^{-2}, then the work done will be – 900 J.

14. ***(c)*** Among the given match, option (c) is correct while other are incorrect. Their correct match is

(a) $NH_4HS(s) \longrightarrow NH_3(g) + H_2S(g)$

$$\Delta n_g = 2 - 0 = 2$$
$$\Delta H = \Delta U + \Delta n_g RT = \Delta U + 2RT$$

(b) $PCl_5(g) \longrightarrow PCl_3(g) + Cl_2(g)$

$$\Delta n_g = 2 - 1 = 0$$
$$\Delta H = \Delta U + RT$$

(d) $N_2(g) + 3H_2(g) \longrightarrow 2NH_3(g)$

$$\Delta n_g = 2 - 4 = -2$$
$$\Delta H = \Delta U - 2RT$$

15. ***(b, c)*** On the basis of given graph, only b and c conclusions can be drawn.
From graph,
The time (t_1) taken for melting A; time (t_2) taken for vaporisation C; time t_3 is the total time of liquification process and time t_4 is the total time of vaporisation process.
As we know, $Q = mc\Delta t$
As, $t_1 < t_2$ so heat supplied in t_1 < heat supplied in t_2.

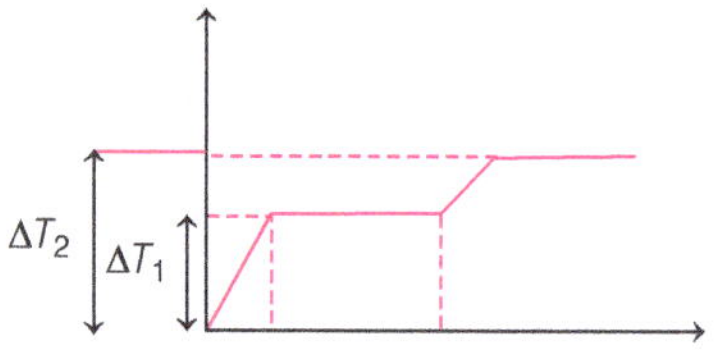

As, $\Delta T_2 > \Delta T_1$ so, specific heat capacity is smaller in the solid state than in the liquid state and the latent heat of vaporisation is greater than its latent heat of fusion for water.

16. ***(a, c, d)*** Among the given statements (a), (c) and (d) are incorrect while statement (b) is correct.
Their correct explanation are

(a) $\left(\frac{\Delta E}{\Delta T}\right)_V = C_V$

$\therefore \quad \Delta E = C_V \Delta T$

	C_V	C_p	C_p / C_V
Mono atomic	$\frac{3}{2}R$	$\frac{5}{2}R$	$\frac{5}{3}R$
Diatomic	$\frac{5}{2}R$	$\frac{7}{2}R$	$\frac{7}{5}R$
Triatomic/Polyatomic	$3R$	$4R$	$\frac{4}{3}R$

Helium is monoatomic gas,

$$C_V = \frac{3}{2}R, \Delta T = 1°$$

$$\therefore \quad \Delta E = \frac{3}{2} \times 2\text{cal} \times 1° = 3 \text{ cal}$$

- With maximum degrees of freedom ozone gas has maximum internal energy.
- Internal energy is a state function and also an extensive property.
- If bond energy of N—H bond is x cal mol^{-1} then the change in internal energy in the process; $NH_3(g) \longrightarrow N_2(g) + 3H_2(g)$ will be $3x$ cal.

17. ***(a, b, c, d)*** Among the given statements, all statements are correct.

18. ***(b, c)*** Among the given statements, (b) and (c) are correct while (a) and (d) are incorrect.
As given process is—

$$H_2O(g) \longrightarrow H_2O(l)$$
$$\Delta V = V\text{ (liquid)} - V\text{ (vapour)}$$
$$= 18.8 \times 10^{-3}\text{ L} - 30.12\text{ L} = -30.1012\text{L}$$
$$W = -p(\Delta V) = -1\,(-30.10212)$$
$$= +30.1012\text{ Latm}$$
$$= \frac{30.1012\text{ L atm} \times 8.314\text{ J mol}^{-1}\text{K}^{-1}}{0.0821\text{ L atm mol}^{-1}\text{ K}^{-1}}$$
$$= 3048\text{ J} = 3.048\text{ kJ}$$
$$\Delta E = W + q = (-40.7 + 3.048)\text{ kJ} = -37.65\text{ kJ}$$

19. ***(a, b, c, d)*** Among the given statements, for an ideal gas all are correct.

20. ***(b, c)*** Among the given statements, (b) and (c) are correct while statements (a) and (b) are incorrect. Their explanation given as below
Given reaction,

$$2H_2O_2(l) \xrightarrow{\Delta} O_2(g) + 2H_2O(l)$$
$$nH_2O_2 = \frac{3.4}{34} = 0.1;\ nO_2 = \frac{0.1}{2}$$
$$\Rightarrow \quad \Delta n_g = 0.05$$
$$w = -\Delta n_g RT = -(0.05) \times 8.314 \times 300 = -124.71\text{ J}$$
$$w = -\text{ve (work of expansion)};\ q = +\text{ve}$$
$$w = -p_{ext}\Delta V = -2 \times (40 - 20) = -40\text{ L atm}$$

As, $\Delta U = q + w$ [$\because$ 1 L-atm = 101.3 J]

$$= 10 \times 1000\text{ J} - 40 \times 101.3 = 5948\text{ J}$$
$$2Zn(s) + 4HCl(aq) \longrightarrow 2ZnCl_2(s) + 2H_2(g)$$
$$\Delta n_g = 2,\ w = -\text{ve (work done by the system)}$$
$$w = -p_{ext} \cdot \Delta V = -\Delta n_g RT$$
$$= -2 \times 8.314 \times 300 = -4988.4\text{ J}$$
$$= -4.98\text{ kJ} \approx -5\text{ kJ}.$$

21. ***(560)*** $q_{ABC} = 600 + 200 = 800$ J
From the given figure,
$w_{AB} = 0$ at constant volume and w_{BC} at constant pressure will be

$$w_{BC} = -\left(8 \times 10^4 \frac{N}{m^2}\right)[5 \times 10^{-3} - 2 \times 10^{-3}] m^3$$

$$= -240 \text{ J}$$

So, $w_{ABC} = -240$ J

$\therefore$ $\Delta U_{AC} = \Delta U_{ABC} = q_{ABC} + w_{ABC}$

$$= 800 - 240 = 560 \text{ J}$$

22. ***(330)*** $V_1(\text{initial}) = \frac{nRT}{p_1}$, $V_2(\text{final}) = \frac{nRT}{p_2}$

$\therefore$ $\Delta V = (V_2 - V_1) = nRT\left(\frac{1}{p_2} - \frac{1}{p_1}\right)$

$$\Delta V = 0.15 \times 0.0821 \times 294\left(\frac{1}{1} - \frac{1}{10}\right) = 3.26 \text{ dm}^3$$

External pressure $p = 1$ atm

$\therefore$ $W = -p\Delta V = -3.26 \text{ dm}^3\text{atm} \approx -330\text{J}$

$$1\text{L atm} = \frac{8.314\text{J}}{0.0821} = 101.267\text{J}$$

23. ***(10)*** As we know,

$$V \propto T$$

$$\frac{V_B}{V_A} = \frac{T_B}{T_A} = 4$$

$\therefore$ $T_B = 4T_A$ $[\because T_A = 200 \text{ K}$

$T_B = 4 \times 200 = 800 \text{ K}]$

The work done by the gas in AB process will be

$$w = -p_{ext} \cdot \Delta V$$
$$= -nR \times \Delta T$$
$$= -2 \times 8.314 [800 - 200]$$
$$= -9976.8 \text{ J} = -9.97 \text{ kJ} = -10 \text{ kJ}$$

24. ***(41.84)*** According to the given process,

$$H_2O(l, 323\text{K}) \xrightarrow{\Delta U_1} H_2O(l, 373\text{ K}) \xrightarrow{\Delta U_2} H_2O(g, 373\text{ K})$$

As we know,

$$C_{v,m}(H_2O, g) = (C_{p,m} - R)$$
$$= 33.314 - 8.314$$
$$= 25 \text{ JK}^{-1} \text{ mol}^{-1}$$
$$\Delta U_2 = \Delta H_2 - \Delta n_g RT$$
$$= (40.7 \times 10^3 \text{ J mol}^{-1} - 1 \times 8.314 \times 373 \text{ J mol}^{-1})$$
$$= 37598.8 \text{ J mol}^{-1}$$
$$= 37.59 \text{ kJ mol}^{-1}$$
$$\Delta U_{\text{Total}} = \Delta U_1 + \Delta U_2$$

$C_{v,m}(H_2O, l)\,\Delta T + 37.59$

$$= 85 \times 10^{-3} \times (373 - 323) + 37.59$$
$$= 85 \times 50 \times 10^{-3} + 37.59$$
$$= 4.25 + 37.59 = 41.84 \text{ kJ mol}^{-1}.$$

25. ***(210)*** Given,

$$\text{Calcite} \longrightarrow \text{Aragonite}$$

By using the formula,

$$\Delta H = \Delta U + \Delta n_g RT$$
$$= \Delta U + p \cdot \Delta V$$
$$= (0.21 \times 10^3 \text{J}) + \left(2.7 \times 10^5 \frac{N}{m^2}\right)\left(\frac{100}{3} - \frac{100}{2.7}\right) \times 10^{-6} m^3$$

$\because$ $\text{density} = \frac{\text{mass}}{\text{volume}}$

$$= 209.72 \text{ J mol}^{-1} = 210$$

Elemental Practice 4.3

1. ***(d)*** The cooling shows fusion process for 30 minute (40-10) at 400 K

$$\Delta S = \frac{q}{T} = \frac{0.4 \times 10^3 \times 30}{400} = 30 \text{ J/K.}$$

2. ***(d)*** $\Delta H°$ and $\Delta S°$ remain constant in the given temperature range.

$$\Delta G° = \Delta H° - T\Delta S°$$
$$\Delta S° = \frac{\Delta H° - \Delta G°}{T} = \frac{-41.8 - (-66.9)}{300 \text{ K}}$$
$$= \frac{25.1}{300} = 0.08367 \text{ kJ K}^{-1}\text{mol}^{-1}$$

$\therefore$ $\Delta G° = \Delta H° - T\Delta S° = (-41.8 - 330 \times 0.08367)$

$$= -69.4 \text{ kJ mol}^{-1}$$

3. ***(b)*** As we know,

The standard entropy change

$$\Delta_r S° = \Sigma n_p S°_{(P)} - \Sigma n_R S°_{(R)}$$
$$= [2 \times 20.5 + 3 \times 70] - [1 \times 77.4 + 3 \times 150.7]$$
$$= 41 + 210 - 77.4 - 452.1$$
$$= 251 - 529.5$$
$$= -278.5 \text{ kJ/mol}$$

4. ***(b)*** X_1 (benzene) $= \frac{1}{3}$, X_2(toluene) $= \frac{2}{3}$

Solution is ideal, $\Delta V_{mix} = 0 \Rightarrow \Delta H_{mix} = 0$

$\therefore$ $\Delta G = \Delta H - T\Delta S \Rightarrow \Delta G = -T\Delta S$

$$\Delta S_{mix} = -2.303 \times n \times R [X_1 \log X_1 + X_2 \log X_2] \quad (n = n_1 + n_2)$$
$$= -2.303 \times 3 \times 8.314 \text{ J mol}^{-1}\text{K}^{-1}\left[\frac{1}{3}\log\frac{1}{3} + \frac{2}{3}\log\frac{2}{3}\right]$$
$$= 5.29 \times 3 = 15.50 \text{ JK}^{-1}$$

$\therefore$ $\Delta G_{mix} = -293 \text{ K} \times 15.50 = -4544 \text{ J} = -4.54 \text{ kJ}$

5. ***(b)*** Eq. (i) Eq. (ii) gives

$$C(\text{diamond}) \longrightarrow C(\text{graphite})$$
$$\Delta H = -91 - (-94) = +3.0 \text{ kcal mol}^{-1}$$

$$\text{Moles of diamond} = \frac{2.4 \times 1000 \text{ g}}{12 \text{ g mol}^{-1}} = 200 \text{ mol}$$

$\Delta H°$ (to convert 200 mol diamond into graphite)

$$= 200 \times 3.0 \text{ kcal} = 600.0 \text{ kcal}$$

$\therefore$ $\Delta S = \frac{\Delta H°}{T} = \frac{600 \text{ kcal}}{298 \text{ K}} = 2.013 \text{ kcal K}^{-1}$

6. ***(d)*** Given, $C_{p,m} = aT^3$ $[C_{p,m} = 0.42]$

$$0.42 = a(10)^3$$

$$a = 0.42 \times 10^{-3}$$

$$S_m = \int_0^{20} \frac{C_{p,m}}{T} dT$$

$$= \int_0^{20} aT^2 dT = \frac{a}{3}[(20)^3 - 0]$$

$$= \frac{0.42 \times 10^{-3}}{3} \times (20)^3$$

$$= 1.12 \text{ JK}^{-1} \text{ mol}^{-1}$$

7. ***(a)*** By Gibbs-Helmholtz equation

$$\Delta G^\circ = \Delta H^\circ + T\left[\frac{d(\Delta G^\circ)}{dT}\right]_p$$

$$\frac{\Delta G^\circ - \Delta H^\circ}{T} = \left[\frac{d(\Delta G^\circ)}{dT}\right]_p$$

But $\Delta G^\circ = \Delta H^\circ - T\Delta S^\circ$

$\therefore$ $-\Delta S^\circ = \left[\frac{d\Delta G^\circ}{dT}\right]_p$

But $\Delta G^\circ = -nFE^\circ_{cell}$

$\therefore$ $\Delta S^\circ = nF\left(\frac{dE^\circ_{cell}}{dT}\right)_p$

$\left[\frac{dE^\circ_{cell}}{dT}\right]$ represents variation of emf of a cell with temperature. It is called temperature coefficient of emf of a cell.

$\therefore$ $\left(\frac{dE^\circ_{cell}}{dT}\right) = \frac{\Delta S^\circ}{nF} = \frac{96.5 \text{ J K}^{-1} \text{ mol}^{-1}}{2 \times 96500}$

$\therefore$ $\frac{dE^\circ_{cell}}{dT} = 5 \times 10^{-4} \text{ VK}^{-1}$

Note n = number of electrons exchanged = 2,
$F = 96500 \text{ C mol}^{-1}$

8. ***(b)*** In adiabatic irreversible expansion

Work, $W = +p_{ext}(V_2 - V_1)$

Also, $W = -C_V(T_2 - T_1)$

$\therefore p_{ext}(V_2 - V_1) = -C_V(T_2 - T_1)$

$$1 \text{ atm}\left(\frac{RT_2}{p_2} - \frac{RT_1}{p_1}\right) = -\frac{5}{2}R(T_2 - T_1)$$

$$p_2 = 1 \text{ atm},\ p_1 = \frac{RT_1}{V_1}$$

$$p_1 = \frac{0.0821 \text{ L atm mol}^{-1}\text{K}^{-1} \times 473 \text{ K}}{20 \text{ L}} = 1.94 \text{ atm mol}^{-1}$$

$$\therefore \left(T_2 - \frac{T_1}{1.94}\right) = -\frac{5}{2}(T_2 - T_1) = \frac{5}{2}(T_1 - T_2)$$

Taking $T_1 = 473\text{K}$

$\therefore$ $T_2 = 407.5 \text{ K}$

$$\Delta S = 2.303\left(C_p \log\frac{T_2}{T_1} + R\log\frac{p_1}{p_2}\right)$$

$$= 2.303\left[\frac{7}{2}R\log\frac{T_2}{T_1} + R\log\frac{p_1}{p_2}\right]$$

$$= 2.303 \times 8.314 \text{ J mol}^{-1}\text{K}^{-1} \times 1 \text{ mol}\left[3.5\log\frac{407.5}{473} + \log\frac{1.94}{1.0}\right]$$

$$= 1.172 \text{ J K}^{-1}$$

9. ***(a)*** Gas is being heated from T_1 and T_2 at constant pressure.

$$\Delta S = 2.303 n\, C_p \log\frac{T_2}{T_1}$$

$$n = \frac{pV}{RT} = \frac{1.01 \times 10^5 \text{Nm}^{-2} \times 10 \times 10^{-3} \text{ m}^3}{8.314 \text{ J mol}^{-1} \text{ K}^{-1} \times 300 \text{ K}}$$

$= 0.405 \text{ mol}$ $\quad$ ($\because$ 1 Nm = 1 J)

$C_p = \frac{5}{2}R = 2.5R$ (for monoatomic gas)

$T_1 = 300 \text{ K},\ T_2 = 400 \text{ K}$

$R = 8.314 \text{ J mol}^{-1} \text{ K}^{-1}$

$\therefore$ $\Delta S = 2.303 \times 0.405 \times 2.5 \times 8.314 \log\frac{400}{300}$

$\therefore$ $\Delta S = 2.422 \text{ JK}^{-1}$

$\Rightarrow$ Moles have not been given thus calculated indirectly.

10. ***(d)*** $\Delta_r H^\circ = 3\Delta_f H^\circ(\text{Co}, s) + 4\Delta_f H^\circ(\text{CO}_2, g) - \Delta_f H^\circ(\text{Co}_3\text{O}_4, s) - 4 \cdot \Delta_f H^\circ(\text{CO}, g)$

$\Delta_r H^\circ = 3 \times 0 + 4(-400) - (-900) - 4(-100)$

$\Delta_r H^\circ = -300 \text{ kJ/mol}$

$\Delta_r S^\circ = 3 \times 30 + 4 \times 200 - 100 - 4 \times 190$

$= 30 \text{ J/K mol}$

$\therefore$ $\Delta_r G^\circ = \Delta_r H^\circ - T \cdot \Delta_r S^\circ$

$$= -300 - \frac{300 \times 30}{1000} = -309 \text{ kJ/mol}$$

11. ***(c)*** $\Delta G^\circ = \Delta H^\circ - T\Delta S^\circ = -38.3 \text{ kJ} - T(-113 \times 10^{-3} \text{kJ K}^{-1})$

$= -38.3 + 113 \times 10^{-3} T$

If $\Delta G^\circ = -$ ve for spontaneous reaction

then $113 \times 10^{-3} T < +38.3$

$$T = \frac{+38.3 \times 1000}{113} = 339\text{K}$$

Thus, below 339K, $\Delta G = -$ ve, hence spontaneous

12. ***(d)*** $\Delta S^\circ_{(total)} = \Delta S^\circ_{(surrounding)} + \Delta S^\circ_{(system)}$

$\Delta H^\circ = -1648.0 \text{ kJ mol}^{-1}$

Thus, reaction is exothermic.

$\therefore$ $\Delta S^\circ_{(surrounding)} = \frac{-\Delta H^\circ}{T} = \frac{+1648 \times 10^3 \text{ J mol}^{-1}}{298}$

$= +5530.2 \text{ J mol}^{-1} \text{ K}^{-1}$

$\Delta S^\circ_{(system)} = -549.4 \text{ J mol}^{-1} \text{ K}^{-1}$

$\therefore$ $\Delta S^\circ_{(total)} = 5530.2 - 549.4$

$= +4980.80 > 0$

Thus, reaction is spontaneous – true.

$\Delta S^\circ_{(surr)} > 0$ true $\Rightarrow$ $\Delta S^\circ_{(total)} > 0$ true

$$\Delta G^\circ = \Delta H^\circ - T\Delta S^\circ$$

$= -1648.0 \text{ kJ mol}^{-1} - 298 \text{ K}\left(\frac{-549.4}{1000} \text{ kJ K}^{-1}\text{mol}^{-1}\right)$

$= -1648.0 + 163.72$

$\therefore \Delta G° = -1484.28 \text{ kJ mol}^{-1}$

13. **(b)** $\Delta S = \frac{q_1}{T} = \frac{2.303\, nRT \log_{10} \frac{V_2}{V_1}}{T}$

Given, $n = 1, R = 8.314 \text{ J}, T = 298 \text{ K}, V_1 = V, V_2 = 20 \text{ V}$

$\therefore \quad \Delta S = 2.303 \times 1 \times 8.314 \log_{10} \frac{20 \text{ V}}{V}$

$= 2.303 \times 8.314 \times \log_{10} 20$

$= 24.91 \text{ JK}^{-1} \text{ mol}^{-1}$

14. **(a)** By using the formula,

$$\Delta S = nC_{p,m} \ln \frac{T_2}{T_1} + nR \ln \frac{p_1}{p_2}$$

($C_{p,m}$ for diatomic ideal gas $= \frac{7R}{2}$)

$$\Delta S = 2 \times \frac{7}{2} \times R \ln \left(\frac{800}{400}\right) + 2 \times R \ln \left(\frac{3}{12}\right)$$

$= 7 \times 2 \text{ cal} \cdot \ln 2 + 2 \times 2 \text{ cal } \ln \frac{1}{4}$

$[14 \times 0.7 - 4 \ln (2)^2]$

$= 9.8 - 4 \times 2 \ln 2 = 9.8 - 8 \times 0.7$

$= 9.8 - 5.6 = 4.2 \text{ cal K}^{-1}$

15. **(c)** $\Delta G°_{200} = \Delta H°_{200} - T\Delta S°_{200}$

$\Delta H°_{200} = \Delta G°_{200} + T\Delta S°_{200}$

$= 30 \text{ kJ} + 200 \text{ K } (-30 \times 10^{-3}) \text{ kJ}$

$\Delta H°_{200} = 30 - 6 = 24 \text{ kJ/mol}$

$\Delta H°_{T_2} = \Delta H°_{T_1} + \Delta C_p (T_2 - T_1)$

$\Delta H°_{400} = \Delta H°_{200} + \frac{20 \times (400 - 200)}{1000} \text{ kJ mol}^{-1}$

$= 24 + 4 = 28 \text{ kJ/mol}$

16. **(a, b, c)** Among the given statements *a*, *b* and *c* are correct while the statement (d) is incorrect. For spontaneous change, $(\Delta G)_{T,p} < 0$.

17. **(a, c, d)** Among the given statements *a*, *c* and *d* are correct while statement (b) is incorrect.

Its correct from is—

Among, $\frac{V_B}{V_A} = \frac{V_D}{V_C}, \frac{V_B}{V_A} = \frac{V_F}{V_E}$ and $\frac{V_B}{V_A} = \frac{V_C}{V_D}$, the relation $\frac{V_B}{V_A} = \frac{V_C}{V_D}$ is not true.

Their explanation is given as:

Along the adiabatics (*AC, CE, BD* and *DF*), $q = 0$

Thus, $\Delta S_{(\text{system})} = \frac{q}{T} = 0$

For the isothermal change

$(A \longrightarrow B)$, $\Delta S_{(\text{system})\, A \longrightarrow B} = 2.303 nR \log \frac{V_B}{V_A}$

$(C \longrightarrow D)$, $\Delta S_{(\text{system})\, C \longrightarrow D} = 2.303 nR \log \frac{V_D}{V_C}$

$(E \longrightarrow F)$, $\Delta S_{(\text{system})\, E \longrightarrow F} = 2.303 nR \log \frac{V_F}{V_E}$

Temperature and volume along adiabates are related as

$(A \longrightarrow C)$, $\quad V_A T_1^{\gamma - 1} = V_C T_2^{\gamma - 1}$

$\therefore \quad \frac{V_A}{V_C} = \left(\frac{T_2}{T_1}\right)^{\gamma - 1}$

$(A \longrightarrow E)$, $\quad V_A T_1^{\gamma - 1} = V_E T_3^{\gamma - 1}$

$\therefore \quad \frac{V_A}{V_E} = \left(\frac{T_3}{T_1}\right)^{\gamma - 1}$

$(B \longrightarrow D)$, $\quad V_B T_1^{\gamma - 1} = V_D T_2^{\gamma - 1}$

$\therefore \quad \frac{V_B}{V_D} = \left(\frac{T_2}{T_1}\right)^{\gamma - 1}$

$(B \longrightarrow F)$, $\quad \frac{V_B}{V_F} = \left(\frac{T_1}{T_3}\right)^{\gamma - 1}$

Thus, $\frac{V_A}{V_C} = \frac{V_B}{V_D}$ or $\frac{V_A}{V_B} = \frac{V_C}{V_D}$ and $\frac{V_A}{V_E} = \frac{V_B}{V_F}, \frac{V_A}{V_B} = \frac{V_E}{V_F}$

Thus, $(\Delta S)_{\text{system}} = \Delta S_{(\text{system}) C \to D}$

$= \Delta S_{(\text{system}) E \to F} = 2.303 \log \frac{V_B}{V_A}$

(a) $\Delta S_{(\text{system}) A \longrightarrow B \longrightarrow D \longrightarrow F}$

$= \Delta S_{(\text{system}) A \longrightarrow B} + 0 + 0$

$= \Delta S_{(\text{system}) A \longrightarrow B}$

(c) $\Delta S_{(\text{system}) A \longrightarrow C \longrightarrow E \longrightarrow F} = 0 + \Delta S_{(\text{system}) E \longrightarrow F} + 0$

$= \Delta S_{(\text{system}) A \longrightarrow B}$

(d) $\Delta S_{(\text{system}) A \longrightarrow C \longrightarrow D \longrightarrow F} = 0 + \Delta S_{(\text{system}) C \longrightarrow D} + 0$

$= \Delta S_{(\text{system}) A \longrightarrow B}$

Thus (a), (c) and (d) are correct.

18. **(a, b, c)** Among the given reaction, *a*, *b* and *c* are the reactions in which randomness of gas molecules decrease hence the sign for ΔS will be negative.

(a) $N_2(g) + 3H_2(g) \longrightarrow 2NH_3(g)$; $\Delta S = -$ ve decrease the number of gaseous molecules.

(b) Desalination of water : $\Delta S = -$ ve desalination is the opposite of solution.

(c) $3O_2(g) \longrightarrow 2O_3(g)$; $\Delta S = -$ ve decrease the number of gases molecules.

(d) $C(s) + H_2O\,(l) \longrightarrow CO(g) + H_2(g)$; $\Delta S = +$ ve, increase the number of gaseous molecules.

19. **(c, d)** (a) By using,

$(\Delta G)_{p,T} = \Delta H - T\Delta S$

$= 3 \times 1000 \text{ J} - (30 \times 300) \text{ J} = -6000 \text{ J mol}^{-1}$

$\Delta G = -$ ve, and $\Delta S = +$ ve

spontaneous, and entropy driven

So, statement (a) is correct.

Statement (c) is incorrect.

Correct (c) $CaCO_3 \xrightarrow{\Delta} CaO + CO_2$, $\Delta H = -ve$

Reaction becomes spontaneous at high temperature because the term $T\Delta S$ dominates over the term $\Delta_r H$.

Statement (d) is incorrect.

Correct (d)

$$\Delta S_{vap} = \Delta H / \text{b.pt.} = 60 \times \frac{1000}{600} = 100 \text{ J mol}^{-1}$$

$$\Delta G = \Delta H - T\Delta S$$

$$= 60 \times 1000 \text{ J} - 610 \times 100 = -1000 \text{ J}$$

$$\Delta G = -ve$$

20. ***(a, b)*** Among the given statements a and b are correct while statement c and d are incorrect. Their explanation are given as

(b) $\Delta S_{vap.} = \frac{\Delta H}{\text{b.pt}} = \frac{50 \times 1000}{500} = 100 \text{ J mol}^{-1}$

When, $p = 2$ atm. b.pt > 500 K

pressure increases so b.pt increase.

Therefore, $\Delta S_{vap.} < 100 \text{ J mol}^{-1}$

(c) Molar Gibb's energy is an intensive property.

(d) Entropy of a closed system is not maximum at equilibrium.

21. ***(1118)*** The entropy change can be given as

$$\Delta S = \frac{\Delta H}{T} \quad \Rightarrow \quad \Delta S = 160.2 \text{ J/K}$$

$$\Rightarrow \quad \Delta H = 179.1 \times 10^3 \text{ J/mol}$$

$$\Rightarrow \quad T = \frac{179.1 \times 10^3 \text{ J/mol}}{160.2 \text{ J/K·mol}}$$

$$= 1117.97 \text{ K} \approx 1118 \text{ K}$$

22. ***(15.32)*** $\Delta S = 2.303 \times m \times C_p \times \log \frac{T_2}{T_1}$

$$= 2.303 \times \frac{20}{1000} \times 4200 \log \frac{360}{300} = 15.32 \text{ J}$$

23. ***(27.88)*** By using the formula,

$$\Delta G = \Delta G° + RT \ln \left[\frac{p(NH_3)^2}{(p_{N_2})(p_{H_2})^3} \right]$$

Partial pressure of N_2 = 50 bar

Partial pressure of H_2 = 2 bar

Partial pressure of NH_3 = 200 bar

Temperature = 300 K

Standard energy of formation of NH_3 = – 16.4 kJ/mol

$$-16.4 \text{ kJ mol}^{-1} = \Delta G° + 8.3145 \times 300 \ln \left[\frac{(200)^2}{(50)(2)^3} \right]$$

$$\Delta G° = -16.4 \text{ kJ mol}^{-1} - 2494.35 \times 4.606 \text{ J mol}^{-1}$$

$$= -16.4 \text{ kJ mol}^{-1} - 11.488 \text{ kJ mol}^{-1}$$

$$\Delta G° = -27.88 \text{ kJ mol}^{-1}$$

Thus, the value of x is 27.88.

24. ***(424)*** Given, $n_1 = 1$, $R = 8.314$

$$V_2 = 5 \text{ L}, V_1 = 3 \text{ L}$$

$$\Delta S_{system} = nR \ln \left(\frac{V_2}{V_1} \right)$$

$$\Delta S_{system} = 1 \times 8.314 \ln \left(\frac{5}{3} \right)$$

$$\Delta S_{system} = 1 \times 8.314 \times [1.60 - 1.09]$$

$$= 4.24 \text{ JK}^{-1} = 424 \times 10^{-3} \text{ JK}^{-1}$$

25. ***(425)*** By using the formula,

$$\Delta G° = \Delta H° - T\Delta S°$$

$$-58.9 = 67.8 - (298)\Delta S°$$

$$-\Delta S° = -\left[\frac{58.9 + 67.8}{298} \right]$$

$$-\Delta S° = \frac{-126.7}{298} = 0.425 \text{ kJ mol}^{-1} \text{ K}^{-1}$$

$$= 425 \text{ JK}^{-1} \text{ mol}^{-1}$$

Thus, the value of x is 425.

Elemental Practice 4.4

1. ***(d)*** The reaction proceeds as follow

$$2C(s) + 3H_2(g) \longrightarrow C_2H_6(g)$$

Let B.E of (C—C) and (C—H) are x and y respectively.

$$\Delta_f H° = [2 \times \Delta_{sub.}(C, s) + 3 \times \text{B.E (H—H)}] - [\text{B.E (C—C)} + 6 \times \text{B.E (C—H)}]$$

$$-85 = 2 \times 700 + 3 \times 550 - (x + 6y)$$

$$x + 6y = 3135 \qquad \text{...(i)}$$

Similarly, for $C_3H_8(g)$

$$3C + 4H_2(g) \longrightarrow C_3H_8(g)$$

$$\Delta_f H° = 3 \times 700 + 4 \times 550 - (2x + 8y)$$

$$2x + 8y = 4420 \qquad \text{...(ii)}$$

From Eq. (i) and (ii)

$$x = 360 \Rightarrow y = 462.5$$

2. ***(a)*** $\frac{1}{2} H_2(g) + S(s) \longrightarrow HS(g)$

This requires dissociation energy of (H—S) bond of HS (g). This can be derived from $\Delta_f H°(H_2S)$.

$\Delta_f H_2S\,(g)$ = [BE of H_2 + sublimation energy of S(s)]

– [BE of first HS bond + BE of second HS bond]

$$-20.1 = [436 + 277] - [376.6 + x]$$

$$\therefore \quad x = 436 + 277 - 376.6 + 20.1 = 356.5 \text{ kJ mol}^{-1}$$

For the formation of HS (g)

$$\frac{1}{2} H_2(g) + S(s) \longrightarrow HS(g)$$

$$\Delta_f H\,(HS) = \frac{1}{2} \text{BE}(H_2) + \text{sublimation energy of S(s)} - \text{BE (second H—S bond)}$$

$$= (218 + 277) - (356.5) = 138.5 \text{ kJ mol}^{-1}$$

3. ***(d)*** As we know,

$$\Delta_{sol} H^\circ = -\Delta_{lattice} H^\circ + \Delta_{hyd.} H^\circ$$
$$= -(-918) + [-689 + (-512)]$$
$$= 918 - 1201 = -283 \text{ kJ mol}^{-1}$$

4. ***(b)***  $\rightleftharpoons CH_3CH = CH_2; \Delta H = -33.0$ kJ

(b) $CH_3CH = CH_2 + 4.5O_2 \longrightarrow 3CO_2 + 3H_2O; \Delta H = x$ kJ

$$\Delta H = (a + b) = -33.0 + x$$

From (b), $x = 3\Delta H_f^\circ(CO_2) + 3\Delta H_f^\circ(H_2O) - \Delta H_f^\circ(C_3H_6)$

$$= -393.5 \times 3 - 285.8 \times 3 - 20.42$$
$$= -2058.32 \text{ kJ}$$

Net $\Delta H = -33 + x = -2091.32$ kJ

5. ***(a)*** $HF(aq) \longrightarrow H^+(aq) + F^-(aq); \Delta H^\circ = x$ kJ

$H^+(aq) + \overline{O}H(aq) \longrightarrow H_2O(l); \Delta H^\circ = -55.83$ kJ

$HF(aq) + \overline{O}H(aq) \longrightarrow H_2O(l) + F^-(aq); \Delta H^\circ = (x - 55.83)$ kJ

Given, $\Delta H^\circ = -68.60$ kJ

$\therefore$ $x - 55.83 = -68.60$

$\therefore$ $x = -12.77$ kJ

Ionisation is $HF(aq)$ is exothermic (and not endothermic), it is due to excessive H-bonding, enthalpy of which overcomes enthalpy of ionisation.

6. ***(d)*** Both A and R are true and R is the correct explanation of A.

7. ***(b)*** Given,

$MgSO_4(s) + nH_2O(l) \longrightarrow MgSO_4 \cdot (nH_2O)$ ...(i)

$\Delta_r H_1 = -80$ kJ/mol.

$MgSO_4 \cdot 7H_2O(s) + (n-7)H_2O \longrightarrow MgSO_4(nH_2O)$

$\Delta_r H_2 = 12$ kJ/mol ...(ii)

Eq. (i) – (ii), then we get

$$\Delta H_{hyd.} = \Delta_r H_1 - \Delta_r H_2 = -80 - 12$$
$$= -92 \text{ kJ/mol}$$

8. ***(c)*** $CH_3COOH(aq) \rightleftharpoons CH_3COO^-(aq) + H^+(aq);$

$$\Delta_r H^\circ = 0.005 \text{ kcal g}^{-1}$$
$$= 0.005 \times 60 \text{ kcal mol}^{-1}$$
$$= 0.3 \text{ kcal mol}^{-1}$$

$H^+(aq) + OH^-(aq) \rightleftharpoons H_2O(l);$

$\Delta_r H^\circ = -13.7$ kcal mol^{-1}

$Ca(OH)_2(aq) \longrightarrow Ca^{2+}(aq) + 2OH^-(aq)$

Thus, $2CH_3COOH(aq) + 2OH^-(aq)$

$\rightleftharpoons 2CH_3COO^-(aq) + 2H_2O(l);$

$\Delta H^\circ = (-13.7 + 0.3) \times 2 = -26.8$ kcal mol^{-1}

9. ***(c)*** Statement I is incorrect but statement II is correct. Its correct form is

If $H_f^\circ(NH_3) = -46.1$ kJ and ΔH° of the reaction,

$N_2H_4(g) + H_2(g) \longrightarrow 2NH_3(g)$ is -187.6 kJ, then $\Delta H_f^\circ(N_2H_4)$ will be $+95.4$ kJ.

$$\Delta_r H^\circ = -187.6 = 2\Delta H_f(NH_3) - \Delta H_f(N_2H_4)$$

$\therefore$ $\Delta H_f(N_2H_4) = -2 \times 46.1 + 187.6 = 95.4$ kJ

$$\Delta H_{315}^\circ = \Delta H_{298}^\circ + \Delta C_p(T_2 - T_1)$$
$$= 0 + 29.4(315 - 298) \text{ J mol}^{-1}$$
$$= 499.8 \text{ J mol}^{-1} = 0.5 \text{ kJ mol}^{-1}$$

10. ***(b)*** The complete combustion reaction of C_8H_{18} proceeds as follows

$$C_8H_{18}(g) + \frac{25}{2}O_2(g) \longrightarrow 8CO_2(g) + 9H_2O(l)$$

$$\Delta_r H^\circ = 8 \times (-400) + 9 \times (-300) - (-300)$$
$$= -3200 - 2700 + 300$$
$$= -5600 \text{ kJ/mol}$$

11. ***(d)*** $CH_4(g) \longrightarrow C(g) + 4H(g); \Delta H^\circ = 360$ kcal mol^{-1}

Thus, BE of (C—H) bond $= \frac{360}{4} = 90$ kcal

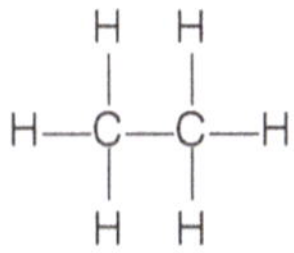 $\longrightarrow 2C(g) + 6H(g)$

Let, BE of (C—C) $= x$

Then, $x + 6 \times 90 = 620$

$\therefore$ $x = 80$ kcal mol^{-1}

12. ***(b)*** $\Delta H^\circ = -\Delta H_C^\circ$ (fumaric acid) $+ \Delta H_C^\circ$ (maleic acid)

$$= +1436.0 + (-1459.2) = -23.2 \text{ kJ/mol}^{-1}$$

13. ***(c)*** We calculate theoretical value of $\Delta_f H^\circ$ of N_2O. Difference of experimental and theoretical value gives resonance energy.

$$N_2(g) + \frac{1}{2}O_2(g) \longrightarrow \overset{\ominus}{N} = \overset{\oplus}{N} = O(g)$$

$$\Delta_f H^\circ(N_2O) = \left[(BE)_{(N\equiv N)} + \frac{1}{2}(BE)_{O=O}\right] - [(BE)_{N=N} + (BE)_{N=O}]$$

$$= \left[946 + \frac{498}{2}\right] - [418 + 607] = 170 \text{ kJ}$$

$\Delta_f H^\circ$(experimental) = 82 kJ

Thus, resonance energy of

$N_2O = 82 - 170 = -88$ kJmol^{-1}

14. ***(b)*** The given reaction is

$$\frac{1}{2}Cl_2(g) \longrightarrow Cl^-(aq)$$

$$\Delta H = \frac{1}{2}\Delta_{diss.}H^\circ(Cl_2) + \Delta_{EA}H^\circ(Cl) + \Delta_{hyd}H(Cl^-)$$

$$= \frac{240}{2} - 249 - 481 = 120 - 730$$

$$= -610 \text{ kJ/mol}^{-1}$$

15. ***(a)*** mole of acid $= 0.05 \times 0.2 = 0.01$

$$\Delta_r H^\circ = -\frac{480 \times 1.0}{0.01 \times 1000} = -48 \text{ kJ/mol}$$

16. ***(a, d)*** Among the given statements, a and d are incorrect while b and c are correct on the basis of given data. Their explanation is given as

$\therefore \quad \Delta H_{\text{reaction}} = -(\Delta H_{\text{solution}} + \Delta H_{\text{calorimeter}})$

$\Delta H_{\text{solution}} = ms\,\Delta T$

$= (200 \text{ mL} \times 1 \text{g mL}^{-1}) \times 4.184 \text{ J g}^{-1}{}^\circ\text{C}^{-1} \times 2.40\,^\circ\text{C}$

$= 2008.32 \text{ J} = 2.008 \text{ kJ}$

$\Delta H_{\text{calorimeter}} = C \times \Delta T = 335 \text{ J/}^\circ\text{C} \times 2.40\,^\circ\text{C}$

$= 804 \text{ J} = 0.804 \text{ kJ}$

$\Delta H_{\text{reaction}} = -(2.008 + 0.804) \text{ kJ} = -2.812 \text{ kJ}$

Millimoles of HCl (NaOH) $= 100 \times 0.5$

$$\text{Moles} = \frac{100 \times 0.5}{1000} = 0.05 \text{ mol}$$

$$\text{Thus, enthalpy of neutralisation} = \frac{-2.812 \text{ kJ}}{0.05 \text{ mol}}$$

$$= -56.24 \text{ kJ mol}^{-1}$$

17. ***(b, c, d)***

1. $A_2(g) + B_2(g) \longrightarrow 2AB(g)$

$\Delta H_f^\circ = (AB) = -200 \text{ kJ mol}^{-1}$

$\Delta_r H = (\text{BE})_{A-A} + (\text{BE})_{B-B} - 2(\text{BE})_{A-B}$

$-400 \text{ kJ} = x + \frac{x}{2} - 4x = -2.5x$

$\therefore \quad x = 160 \text{ kJ}, \frac{x}{2} = 80 \text{ kJ}$

Thus, BE $(A-B) = 2x = 320 \text{ kJ mol}^{-1}$

$A_2(g) + \frac{1}{2}B_2(g) \longrightarrow A_2B(g)$

$\Delta H_f^\circ (A_2B) = \text{BE}_{(A-A)} + \frac{1}{2}\text{BE}_{(B-B)} - 2\text{BE}_{(A-B)}$

$= 160 + \frac{80}{4} - 2(320) = 160 + 20 - 640 = -460 \text{ kJ}$

18. ***(a, b, c, d)***

(a) $C_{p,m} = 3 + (2 \times 10^{-2})T \text{ cal mol}^{-1}\text{ K}^{-1}$

$C_{p,m} - C_{V,m} = R = 2 \text{ cal mol}^{-1}\text{ K}^{-1}$

$\therefore \quad C_{V,m} = C_{p,m} - R = (3-2) + (2 \times 10^{-2})T \text{ cal mol}^{-1}\text{ K}^{-1}$

$= 1 + (2 \times 10^{-2})T \text{ cal mol}^{-1}\text{ K}^{-1}$

Thus, option (a) is correct.

(b) $\therefore \; \Delta H = nC_{p,m}(\Delta T) = C_{p,m}(T_2 - T_1)$

Thus, option (b) is correct.

(c) Since, $C_{p,m} - C_V = R$

$\therefore \quad C_p = (C_V + R)$

$\therefore \quad \Delta H = n(C_V + R)(T_2 - T_1)$

Thus, option (c) is correct.

(d) $\Delta E = nC_{V,m}\Delta T = (C_{p,m} - R)(T_2 - T_1)$

Thus, option (d) is correct.

19. ***(a, b, c)*** Among the given statements, (a) and (c) are correct while (b) and (d) are incorrect.

I. $N_2 + O_2 \longrightarrow 2NO; \; \Delta H^\circ = 180 \text{ kJ}$

II. $2NO + O_2 \longrightarrow 2NO_2; \; \Delta H^\circ = -112 \text{ kJ}$

III. $N_2 + 2O_2 \longrightarrow 2NO_2; \; \Delta H^\circ = 68 \text{ kJ}$

Thus, $\Delta H_f^\circ (NO_2) = \frac{68}{2} = +34 \text{ kJmol}^{-1}$ Thus (a) is correct.

ΔH° III > 0 endothermic thus (b) is correct

$\Delta H_f^\circ(NO)$ from I $= \frac{180}{2} = 90 \text{ kJ mol}^{-1}$. Thus, (c) is correct.

$\Delta H_{II} < 0$ thus exothermic hence (iv) is incorrect

20. ***(b, d)***

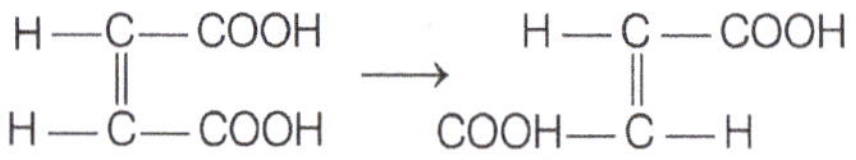

Maleic acid (*A*) Fumaric acid (*B*)

I. $A + 3O_2 \longrightarrow 4CO_2 + 2H_2O; \; \Delta_C H^\circ = -1359.2 \text{ kJ mol}^{-1}$

II. $B + 3O_2 \longrightarrow 4CO_2 + 2H_2O; \; \Delta_C H^\circ = -1336.0 \text{ kJ mol}^{-1}$

Thus, $A \longrightarrow B$, $\Delta_{\text{iso}}H^\circ = -23.2$ kJ (thus exothermic) and (b) is correct.

From I, $\Delta_C H^\circ = -1359.2$

$= (-4 \times 393.5) + 2(-285.8) - \Delta_f H^\circ(A)$

$\therefore \quad \Delta_f H^\circ(A) = -786.4 \text{ kJ mol}^{-1}$

Similarly, $\Delta_f H^\circ(B) = -809.6 \text{ kJ mol}^{-1}$

Thus, (*B*) is more stable than (A).

21. ***(b, c)*** $2\text{C (graphite)} + O_2(g) \longrightarrow 2CO\,(g); \; \Delta_r H^\circ = -52$ kcal

Two moles of CO are formed from its elements. Thus,

$\text{C(graphite)} + \frac{1}{2}O_2(g) \longrightarrow CO(g); \; \Delta_f H^\circ = -26.0 \text{ kcal mol}^{-1}$

Thus, option (b) is correct.

$CO(g) + \frac{1}{2}O_2(g) \longrightarrow CO_2(g); \; \Delta_r H^\circ = -68.0 \text{ kcal}$

Thus, $C\text{(graphite)} + O_2(g) \longrightarrow CO_2(g);$

$\Delta_f H^\circ(CO_2) = -94.0 \text{ kcal mol}^{-1}$

Thus, option (c) is correct.

22. ***(a, b)*** Moles of HCl $= \frac{200 \times 0.862}{1000} = 0.1724$ mol

$= 0.1724 \text{ mol H}^+$

Moles of $Ba(OH)_2 = \frac{200 \times 0.431}{1000} = 0.0862$ mol

Moles of $(OH^-) = 2 \times \frac{200 \times 0.431}{1000} = 0.1724 \text{ mol } (OH^-)$

Thus, moles of H^+ = moles of OH^-

There is complete reaction of HCl and $Ba(OH)_2$.

Hence, (c) and (d) are incorrect.

Hence, enthalpy change of reaction of HCl and $Ba(OH)_2$

$= -56.2 \times 0.1724 \approx -9.69 \text{ kJ}$

Thus, option ***(a)*** is correct

$\Delta H_{\text{calorimeter}} = C_p \Delta T$

$\Delta H_{\text{calorimeter}} = 435 \text{ JK}^{-1}$

Total volume of solution = 400 mL

Assume density $= 1 \text{ g L}^{-1}$

Hence, 400 mL = 400 g solution

$$\Delta H_{solution} = 400\text{ g} \times 4.184\text{ Jg}^{-1}\text{ K}^{-1}(T - 293.48)$$
$$= 0.400 \times 4.148\,(T - 293.48)\text{ kJ}$$
$$\Delta H_{reaction} = -(\Delta H_{solution} + \Delta H_{cal}) = -9.69$$
$$9.69 = [0.400 \times 4.148 + 0.435][T - 293.48]$$
$$T = 298.11\text{ K or } (298.11 - 273) = 25.11°\text{C}$$

Thus, option (b) is correct.

23. ***(3)*** Among the given reaction, only three i.e, (II), (III) and (V) in the value of $\Delta H - \Delta E = RT$ because Δn_g is equal to 1.

24. ***(3)*** $C(s) + O_2(g) \longrightarrow CO_2(g)$;

$$\Delta_f H°(CO_2) = -94\text{ kcal mol}^{-1}$$
$$H_2(g) + \frac{1}{2}O_2(g) \longrightarrow H_2O(l);\ \Delta_f H°(H_2O) = -68\text{kcal mol}^{-1}$$

Enthalpy of combustion of carbon is also the enthalpy of formation of CO_2 and enthalpy of combustion of $H_2(g)$ is also the enthalpy of formation of H_2O.

$$C_xH_4(g) + (x+1)\,O_2(g) \longrightarrow xCO_2 + 2H_2O\,(l)$$
$$\Delta_c H° = -318 = -94x - 2 \times 68 - (-100)$$
$$-318 = -94x - 36$$
$$\therefore \quad 94x = 282 \Rightarrow x = 3$$

(C_xH_4 is C_3H_4, $HC \equiv C—CH_3$, propyne)

25. ***(6.871)*** Let, amount of graphite changing to

$$CO = x\text{ g}$$

and that changing to $CO_2 = (1 - x)$ g

$$C + \frac{1}{2}O_2 \longrightarrow CO$$
$$12\text{ g} \qquad\qquad 28\text{ g}$$

12 g graphite gives = 28 g CO

x g graphite gives $= \left(\frac{28x}{12}\right)$ g CO

$$C + O_2 \longrightarrow CO_2$$
$$12\text{ g} \qquad 44\text{ g}$$

$(1-x)$ g graphite gives $= \frac{44(1-x)}{12}$ g CO_2

Total mass of CO and $CO_2 = \frac{28x}{12} + \frac{44(1-x)}{12}$

$$CO = \frac{\frac{28x}{12} \times 100}{\frac{28x}{12} + \frac{44(1-x)}{12}} = 0.33\text{ (given)}$$
$$\therefore \quad \frac{7x}{0.33} = 7x + 11(1-x)$$
$$21.21x = 7x + 11 - 11x$$
$$25.21x = 11 \Rightarrow x = 0.4364\text{ g}$$

Thus, C(graphite) forming CO = 0.4364 g ≈ 0.0165 mol

Thus, $\Delta H_f°$ due to CO = – (0.0166 × 110.5) = – 1.834 kJ

Thus, C(graphite) forming

$$CO_2 = 0.5636\text{ g} = 0.0128\text{ mol}$$

Thus, $\Delta H_f°$ due to CO_2 = – 0.0128 × 393.5 kJ = – 5.0368 kJ

Total heat = – 1.834 – 5.0368 ≈ – 6.871 kJ

26. ***(23)*** It is based on Hess's law of constant heat summation. Add I (a) and I (b)

$$C\text{ (diamond)} + O_2(g) \longrightarrow CO_2(g);\ \Delta H_1° = -91\text{ kcal}$$

Add II (a), II (b) and II (c)

$$C\text{ (diamond)} + O_2(g) \longrightarrow CO_2(g);\ \Delta H_2° = x_1 + x_2 - 68$$

Both represent same chemical change.

Also I ***(a)*** and II ***(a)*** represent same physical change hence, $x_1 = 3$ kcal

$$\Delta H_1 = \Delta H_2 \Rightarrow -91 = x_1 + x_2 - 68$$
$$-91 = 3 + x_2 - 68$$
$$\therefore \quad x_2 = -26\text{ kcal}$$

Hence the sum of x_1 and x_2 is 3 + (– 26) = –23 k cal

27. ***(3)*** Among the given statements, only three i.e, II, III and IV are incorrect while I and V are correct. Their explanation are—

I. Standard state of a pure substance is taken at 1bar. Thus I is correct.

II. $H_2(g) \longrightarrow 2H(g);\ \Delta H = q$

then $\Delta H_f(H) = \frac{q}{2}$. Thus, (II) is incorrect.

III. Enthalpy change of an element (H_2) which is in its most stable form is 0

Thus, option (III) is incorrect.

IV. $\Delta S°_{298} = -1.92\text{ kJ K}^{-1}$

$$\therefore \quad \Delta S°_{298} = \frac{\Delta H°}{T}$$
$$\therefore \quad \Delta H° = \Delta S°_{298} \times T = -1.92 \times 298 = -572.16\text{ kJ}$$
$$\therefore \quad \Delta H_f°(H_2O) = -\frac{572.16}{2} = -286.08\text{ kJ mol}^{-1}$$

Thus, option (IV) is incorrect

V. $S(s) + O_2(g) \longrightarrow SO_2(g)\ \Delta H_f° = -297.5\text{ kJ mol}^{-1}$

$$1\text{ mol} = 64\text{ g}$$
$$SO_2(g) \longrightarrow S(s) + O_2(g),\ \Delta H_f° = +297.5\text{ kJ mol}^{-1}$$

Thus, 32g $= \frac{1}{2}$ mol, $\Delta H° = \frac{297.5}{2}$

$$= 148.75\text{ kJ}$$

Thus, V is correct.

28. ***(181)*** From the values of $\Delta_c H°$ of C_2H_6 and C_3H_8, their $\Delta_f H°$ values are derived.

$$C_2H_6(g) + 3.5O_2 \longrightarrow 2CO_2(g) + 3H_2O(l)$$
$$\Delta_c H° = -372 = 2\Delta_f H°(CO_2) + 3\Delta_f H°(H_2O) - \Delta_f H°(C_2H_6)$$
$$\Delta_f H°(C_2H_6) = +372 - 2 \times 94 - 3 \times 68$$
$$= -20\text{ kcal}$$
$$C_3H_8(g) + 5O_2(g) \longrightarrow 3CO_2(g) + 4H_2O(l)$$
$$\Delta_f H°(C_3H_8) = +530 - 3 \times 94 - 4 \times 68 = -24\text{ kcal}$$

Based on BE values, BE(C— H) = x

BE(C—C) = y

For C_2H_6, $2C(s) + 3H_2(g) \longrightarrow C_2H_6(g)$

$$-20 = \Delta_f H°(C_2H_6) = (2 \times 172 + 3 \times 104) - [6x + y]$$

$\therefore \quad 6x + y = 344 + 312 + 20 = 676 \text{ kcal} \quad \ldots(i)$

For C_3H_8, $3C(s) + 4H_2(g) \longrightarrow C_3H_8$

$$-24 = \Delta_f H^\circ(C_3H_8) - [8x + 2y]$$
$$= 3\times172 + 4\times104 - [8x + 2y]$$
$$8x + 2y = 3\times172 + 4\times104 + 24$$
$$8x + 2y = 956 \quad \ldots(ii)$$

On solving Eqs. (i) and (ii) we get,

$$x = 99 \text{ kcal}, \quad y = 82 \text{ kcal}.$$

Hence, the value of $x + y$ is 181 k cal.

29. ***(8)*** $X_2(g) + Y_2(g) \longrightarrow 2XY(g)$

$$\Delta H_f = -400 = (BE)_{X-X} + (BE)_{Y-Y} - 2(BE)_{X-Y}$$
$$-400 = q + \frac{q}{2} - 2q = -\frac{q}{2}$$

$\therefore \quad q = 800 \text{ kJ mol}^{-1} = 8\times100 \text{ kJ mol}^{-1}$

$\therefore \quad n = 8$

Practice Element 01 : Target JEE Main

1. ***(c)*** $COCl_2(g) \rightleftharpoons CO(g) + Cl_2(g)$

$$\Delta H^\circ = 12 \text{ kJ mol}^{-1}$$

and $\quad \Delta S^\circ = 60 \text{ J mol}^{-1}\text{K}^{-1}$

$\therefore \quad \Delta G^\circ = \Delta H^\circ - T\Delta S^\circ$

$$\Delta G^\circ = 12 \text{ kJ mol}^{-1} - \frac{60}{1000}\text{kJ K}^{-1}\text{ mol}^{-1} \times 300 \text{ K}$$
$$= -6 \text{ kJ mol}^{-1}$$

Also, $\quad \Delta G^\circ = -2.303RT\log K$

$$-6 \text{ kJ mol}^{-1} = -2.303\times8.314 \times10^{-3}\text{ kJ mol}^{-1}\text{K}^{-1}\times300\text{ K}\times\log K$$

$\therefore \quad \log K = 1.044$

$\therefore \quad K = 11.08$

2. ***(a)*** Moles of $S_8 = \dfrac{2.56}{256} = 0.01$

Moles of SO_2 formed = 0.08

Rise in temperature = $(273 + 26.72)\text{K} - (273 + 21.25)\text{K}$
$= 5.47 \text{ K}$

Total change in internal energy (as system is at constant volume)

$$= -(923 \text{ J K}^{-1}\times5.47\text{ K} + 815\text{ g} \times4.184\text{ JK}^{-1}\text{g}^{-1}\times5.47\text{ K})$$
$$= -23701.29 \text{ J} = -23.70129 \text{ kJ}$$

Thus, change in internal energy per moles of SO_2 formed

$$= -\frac{23.70129}{0.08\text{ mole}} = -296.27 \text{ kJ mol}^{-1}$$

3. ***(d)*** At stage (1)

$$V = 22.4\text{ L} = 22.4\times10^{-3}\text{m}^3$$
$$T = 298\text{ K}, n = 1\text{ mol}$$
$$p = \frac{nRT}{V} = \frac{1\text{ mol}\times8.314\text{ Pa m}^3\text{mol}^{-1}\text{K}^{-1}\times298\text{ K}}{22.4\times10^{-3}\text{m}^3}$$
$$= 1.107\times10^5\text{ Pa} = 1.107\text{ bar}$$

At stage (2) temperature is doubled but volume is constant.

Thus, $p \propto T = 2.214$ bar

At stage (3), T is 298 K and V is 11.2 L and as in stage (1)

$$p = \frac{nRT}{V} = 2.214\text{ bar}$$

4. ***(a)*** Since, $q = 0$, hence, adiabatic change

For H_2O, $\dfrac{C_p}{C_V} = \gamma = 1.33$, $\dfrac{T_2}{T_1} = \left(\dfrac{V_1}{V_2}\right)^{\gamma-1}$

$$T_2 = T_1\left(\frac{V_1}{V_2}\right)^{\gamma-1} = 300\left(\frac{100}{800}\right)^{0.33}$$
$$= 300\left(\frac{1}{8}\right)^{\frac{1}{3}} = 300\times\frac{1}{2} = 150\text{ K}$$

By first law, $\Delta E = q + W \Rightarrow \Delta E = W(q = 0)$

$$\left(\frac{\Delta E}{\Delta T}\right)_V = C_V \qquad \therefore \quad \Delta E = C_V\Delta T$$
$$W = C_V\Delta T = 3R(T_2 - T_1)$$
$$= -3\times2\times150 = -900\text{ cal}$$

5. ***(c)*** $\frac{1}{2}I_2(s) + \frac{1}{2}Cl_2(g) \longrightarrow ICl(g)$

$$\Delta H = \left[\frac{1}{2}\Delta H_{s\to g}(I_2) + \frac{1}{2}\Delta H_{\text{diss}}(Cl_2) + \frac{1}{2}\Delta H_{\text{diss}}(I_2) - \Delta H(ICl)\right]$$
$$= \left(\frac{1}{2}\times62.76 + \frac{1}{2}\times242.3 + \frac{1}{2}\times151.0\right) - 211.3$$
$$= 228.03 - 211.3$$
$$\Delta H = 16.73\text{ kJ mol}^{-1} \approx 16.8\text{ kJ mol}^{-1}$$

6. ***(b)*** Reaction will be in equilibrium, when

$$\Delta G = 0$$

But $\quad \Delta G = \Delta H - T\Delta S$

Then, $\quad T = \dfrac{\Delta H}{\Delta S}$

$$\Delta H = -30\text{ kJ mol}^{-1}$$
$$\Delta S = S(XY_3) - \left[\frac{1}{2}S(X_2) + \frac{3}{2}S(Y_2)\right]$$
$$= 50 - \left[\frac{1}{2}\times60 + \frac{3}{2}\times40\right] = 50 - [30 + 60]$$
$$= -40\text{ J K}^{-1}\text{mol}^{-1}$$
$$T = \frac{-30\times1000\text{ J mol}^{-1}}{-40\text{ JK}^{-1}\text{mol}^{-1}} = 750\text{ K}$$

Hence, at 750 K, reaction would be in equilibrium.

7. ***(a)*** V_1 (initial volume) = 500 c.c.

Volume swept by piston = $50\text{ cm}^2\times10\text{ cm} = 500$ c.c.

Thus $V_2 = 500 + 500 = 1000$ c.c.

Initial moles $n = \frac{pV}{RT} = \frac{2\text{ atm} \times 0.5\text{ L}}{0.0821\text{ L atm mol}^{-1}\text{K}^{-1} \times 298\text{ K}}$

$= 0.041\text{ mol}$

$\therefore \quad \Delta S = 2.303\, nR \log \frac{V_2}{V_1}$

$= 2.303 \times 0.041\text{mol} \times 8.314\text{ J mol}^{-1}\text{ K}^{-1} \times \log \frac{1000}{500}$

$= 0.236\text{ J K}^{-1} \approx 0.24\text{ JK}^{-1}$

8. ***(b)*** I. $W_{rev} = -2.303\, nRT \log \frac{p_1}{p_2}$

$= -2.303 \times 1\text{mol} \times 8.314\text{ J mol}^{-1}\text{ K}^{-1} \times 300\text{ K} \log 10$

$= -5744.14\text{ J}$

II. $W = -p_{ext}(V_2 - V_1) = -p_{ext}\left(\frac{nRT}{p_2} - \frac{nRT}{p_1}\right)$

$= -p_{ext}\, nRT\left(\frac{1}{p_2} - \frac{1}{p_1}\right)$

$= -1\text{ atm} \times 1\text{ mole} \times 0.0821\text{ L atm mol}^{-1}\text{ K}^{-1} \times 300\text{ K}\left[\frac{1}{1\text{ atm}} - \frac{1}{10\text{ atm}}\right]$

$= -22.167\text{ L atm}$

$= -\frac{22.167\text{ L atm} \times 8.314\text{ J mol}^{-1}\text{K}^{-1}}{0.0821\text{ L atm mol}^{-1}\text{K}^{-1}} = -2244.78\text{ J}$

III. W(free expansion) = 0 (since $p = 0$). Thus, III < II < I

9. ***(a)*** $NCl_3(g)$ is formed from its elements by reaction,

$$\frac{1}{2}N_2(g) + \frac{3}{2}Cl_2(g) \longrightarrow NCl_3(g)$$

Thus, operate $\frac{1}{2} \times$ Eq. (ii) + Eq. (i) $- \frac{3}{2}$ Eq. (iii)

$$\frac{1}{2}N_2(g) + \frac{3}{2}H_2(g) + NH_3(g) + 3Cl_2(g) - \frac{3}{2}H_2(g) - \frac{3}{2}Cl_2(g) \longrightarrow NH_3(g) + NCl_3(g) + 3HCl(g) - 3HCl(g)$$

Final result is $\frac{1}{2}N_2(g) + \frac{3}{2}Cl_2(g) \longrightarrow NCl_3(g)$

$\Delta_f H° = -\Delta H_1 - \Delta H_2/2 - \frac{3}{2}\Delta H_3$

10. ***(c)*** By Clausius Clapeyron equation

$$\log_{10} p = -\frac{\Delta H}{2.303\, RT} + \text{Constant}$$

If $\Delta H = -ve$, $\log_{10} p = \frac{\Delta H}{2.303\, RT} + \text{Constant}$

$$y = mx + C$$

Thus, variation of $\log p$ with $\left(\frac{1}{T}\right)$ is shown in (c)

11. ***(c)*** The standard enthalpy of formation is defined as standard enthalpy change for formation of 1 mole of a substance from its elements, present in their most stable state of aggregation.

Among the given reaction only three i.e. a, b and d, standard enthalpy of reaction is equal to standard enthalpy of formation.

12. ***(b)*** Moles of He, $n = 6$ moles

Temperature at which expansion occur, $T = 300$ K

Volume before expansion, $V_1 = 10$ L

Volume after expansion, $V_2 = 20$ L

$\therefore$ Work done $= -nRT \ln \frac{V_2}{V_1}$

$= -6 \times 8.3 \times 300 \ln \frac{20}{10} = -10356.45\text{ J}$

The magnitude of maximum work obtained = 10356.45 J

13. ***(b)*** By first law, $\Delta E = Q + W$

For isothermal expansion,

$\Delta E = 0$

$Q = -W$

$Q_{irrev} = W_{irrev} = -p\Delta V$

$= -5(8-4) = -20\text{ L atm}$

Also, $\Delta S_{surr} = \frac{Q_{irrev}}{T} = \frac{(-20 \times 101.3)}{300}\text{ J} = -6.75\text{ JK}^{-1}$

14. ***(d)***

(a) Both NO_2 and N_2O_4 are gases. N_2O_4 is a larger molecule than NO_2 so is expected to have higher standard entropy.

(b) Randomness in gases is larger than in liquid/solid.

(c) When Cr^{3+} replaces Al^{3+} of Al_2O_3, ruby is formed. Size of $Cr^{3+} > Al^{3+}$

Thus, disorder increases, hence entropy increases.

(d) Due to increase in pressure, volume decreases, hence molecules are placed in order. Greater the volume, greater the randomness.

15. ***(d)*** Efficiency $= \frac{\text{Work} \times 100}{\text{Heat absorbed}}$

Work = area enclosed in the triangle

$= \frac{1}{2} \times \Delta p \cdot \Delta V$

$= \frac{1}{2}(20 \times 40) = 400\text{ L atm} = 40507\text{ J} = 40.507\text{ kJ}$

$0.0821\text{ L atm} = 8.314\text{ J}$

$\therefore$ Efficiency $= \frac{40.507}{80.0} \times 100 = 50.63\%$

16. ***(c)*** $\underset{1\text{ mol}}{CaC_2(s)} + 2H_2O(l) \longrightarrow Ca(OH)_2 + \underset{1\text{ mol}}{C_2H_2(g)}$

$\underset{1\text{ mol}}{Al_4C_3(s)} + 12H_2O(l) \longrightarrow 4Al(OH)_3 + \underset{3\text{ mol}}{3\,CH_4(g)}$

$\underset{1\text{ mol}}{Mg_2C_3(s)} + 4H_2O(l) \longrightarrow 2Mg(OH)_2 + \underset{1\text{ mol}}{C_3H_4(g)}$

Work is done due to formation of gases.

From 1 mole of each solid,

$$\underset{1}{C_2H_2} = \underset{1}{C_3H_4} < \underset{3}{CH_4}$$

$$CaC_2 = Mg_2C_3 < Al_4C_3$$

17. ***(a)*** For the isobaric and isothermal process

$$W = -\int_{V_1}^{V_2} p_{ext}dV = -p_{ext}(V_2 - V_1)$$

But density $(d) = \dfrac{\text{mass}}{V}$

Hence, $V = \dfrac{\text{mass}}{d}$

$\Rightarrow$ $W = -p_{ext}\left[\dfrac{\text{mass}}{d_2} - \dfrac{\text{mass}}{d_1}\right]$

$p_{ext} = 1.00 \text{ bar} = 1.0 \times 10^5 \text{ Pa}$

$m = 18 \text{ g} = 18 \times 10^{-3} \text{ kg}$

$d_1(\text{ice at } 0° \text{ C}) = 0.915 \text{ g cm}^{-3}$

$d_1 = \left(\dfrac{0.915}{10^3}\right) \text{kg } 10^6 \text{m}^{-3} = 915 \text{ kg m}^{-3}$

$d_2 = 1 \text{g cm}^{-3} = 1000 \text{ kg m}^{-3}$

$$W = -1.0 \times 10^5 \left[\frac{18 \times 10^{-3}}{1000} - \frac{18 \times 10^{-3}}{915}\right] \text{Pa m}^3$$

$$= -1.0 \times 10^2 \times 18 \left[\frac{1}{1000} - \frac{1}{915}\right]$$

$\therefore$ $W = +0.167 \text{ Pa m}^3 = 0.167 \text{ J}$

$1 \text{g cm}^{-3} = 1000 \text{ kg m}^{-3}$

18. ***(d)***

(a) incorrect $\Delta G° = \Delta H° - T\Delta S° = +\text{ve}$

(b) incorrect

(c) $\Delta G° = \Delta H° - T\Delta S°$. If spontaneous, $\Delta G° < 0$

$\therefore$ $T\Delta S° > \Delta H°$

$$T > \frac{\Delta H°}{\Delta S°} > \frac{178.3 \times 1000 \text{ J mol}^{-1}}{160 \text{ JK}^{-1}\text{mol}^{-1}}$$

$T > 1114 \text{ K}$

19. ***(a)***

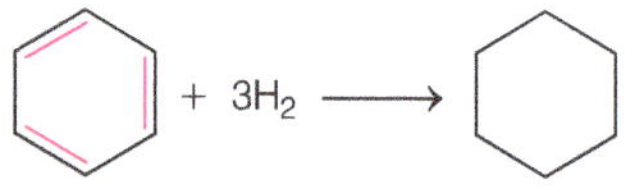

$\Delta_r H° = \Delta_f H°$ (cyclohexane) $- \Delta_f H°$ (benzene)

$= -156.0 - 49.0 = -205 \text{ kJ mol}^{-1}$

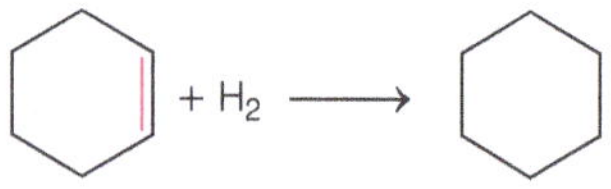

$\Delta_r H° = -119 \text{ kJ mol}^{-1}$

In cyclohexene $(C = C) =$ one

In benzene $(C = C) =$ three

Thus, theoretical value of heat of hydrogenation of benzene

$= -119 \times 3 = -357 \text{ kJ mol}^{-1}$

Thus, resonance energy $= -357 - (-205)$

$= -357 + 205$

$= -152 \text{ kJ mol}^{-1}$

20. ***(b)*** In first stage, 10 mL of 0.10 M HCl neutralise 10 mL of 0.10 M NaOH.

$H^+(aq) + OH^-(aq) \longrightarrow H_2O(l); \Delta H° = -13.7 \text{ kcal mol}^{-1}$

10 mL of 0.10 M HCl = 10 mL of 0.10 M NaOH

$= 1 \text{ millimol} = 1 \times 10^{-3} \text{ mol}$

Thus, $\Delta_r H_1°$ due to 1×10^{-3} mol of each reactant

$= -13.7 \text{ kcal mol}^{-1} \times 1 \times 10^{-3} \text{ mol}$

$= -13.7 \times 10^{-3} \text{ kcal} = -13.7 \text{ cal}$

In second stage, 20 mL of 0.10 M HCl neutralise remaining 20 mL of 0.1 M NaOH.

Millimol of HCl or NaOH reacted $= 20 \times 0.1 = 2 = 2 \times 10^{-3}$ mol

$H^+(aq) + OH^-(aq) \longrightarrow H_2O(l); \Delta H° = -13.7 \text{ kcal mol}^{-1}$

Thus, heat change in second state

$= -13.7 \times 2 \times 10^{-3}$

$= -27.4 \times 10^{-3} \text{ kcal}$

$= -27.4 \text{ cal}$

21. ***(524)*** Energy to dissipate = 40% of total energy

$= 0.40 \times 3200 = 1280 \text{ kJ}$

Moles of water needed = Energy/enthalpy of evaporation

$$= \frac{1280 \text{ kJ}}{44 \text{ kJ/mol}} = 29.09 \text{ moles}$$

Mass of water $= 29.09 \text{ moles} \times 18.015 \text{ g/mol}$

$= 524 \text{ g}$

22. ***(9)*** $\Delta G° = \Delta H° - T\,\Delta S°$

By Gibbs' Helmholtz equation,

$$\Delta G° = \Delta H° + T\left[\frac{d\,\Delta G°}{dT}\right]_p$$

Thus $\Delta S° = -\left[\dfrac{d\,\Delta G°}{dT}\right]_p$

$\therefore$ $\Delta G° = 300 + 2T \log_{10} T - 15T$

$\therefore$ $\left[\dfrac{d\,\Delta G°}{dT}\right] = 0 + 2\log T + \dfrac{2T}{T} - 15$

$= 2 \times \log 100 + 2 - 15$

$\therefore$ $\Delta S° = -\left[\dfrac{d\,\Delta G°}{dT}\right]_p = -2 \times 2 - 2 + 15$

$= 9 \text{ cal K}^{-1} \text{ mol}^{-1}$

23. ***(4)*** $\Delta S_{univ} = \Delta S_{surr} + \Delta S_{sys}$

$\Delta S_{sys} = 2.303\, nR \log \dfrac{V_2}{V_1}$

$= 2.303 \times 0.5 \times 8.314 \log \dfrac{5}{1} = 6.7 \text{ JK}^{-1}$

$\Delta S_{surr} = \dfrac{q_{surr}}{T}$

For irreversible change,

$\therefore$ $q_{surr} = -p\Delta V = -2(5-1) = -8.0 \text{ L atm}$

$$q_{surr} = \frac{-8.0 \text{ L - atm} \times 8.314 \text{ Jmol}^{-1}\text{K}^{-1}}{0.0821 \text{ L atm mol}^{-1}\text{K}^{-1}} = -810.1 \text{ J}$$

$\therefore \quad \Delta S_{surr} = \frac{-810.1}{300} = -2.7\ JK^{-1}$

$\therefore \quad \Delta S_{univ} = \Delta S_{sys} + \Delta S_{surr} = 6.7 - 2.7 = 4.0\ JK^{-1}$

24. **(3)** $C_p = \frac{\Delta H}{\Delta T}$

$\therefore \quad \Delta H = C_p \Delta T = \int_{T_1}^{T_2} C_p dT$

$= \int_{298\,K}^{367\,K} 1.45\,[25.7 + 0.013\,T] \times 10^{-3}\, dT\ kJ\ mol^{-1}$

$= 1.45 \left[25.7\,T + \frac{0.013T^2}{2} \right]_{298}^{367} \times 10^{-3}\ kJ$

$= 1.45 \left[[25.7\,(367 - 298)] + \frac{0.013}{2} [(367)^2 - (298)^2] \right] \times 10^{-3} kJ$

$\approx 3.00\ kJ$

25. **(4)** The production of gastric juice from body fluids is a slow process hence, the change may be considered as reversible one.

$$W = -2.303\, nRT \log \frac{V_2}{V_1}$$

Concentration $[H^+] \frac{mol}{L} \left(\propto \frac{1}{V} \right)$

Thus, $\frac{V_2}{V_1} = \frac{C_1}{C_2} \Rightarrow W = -2.303\, nRT \frac{C_1}{C_2}$

n = moles of H^+ ions present in 0.1 M

(pH = 1, $[H^+] = 10^{-1}$ M) of 1 dm^3 juice = 0.1

$C_1 = [H^+]_1 = 10^{-pH} = 10^{-7.6021} = 2.4 \times 10^{-8} M$

$C_2 = [H^+]_2 = 10^{-pH} = 10^{-1} = 0.1 M$

$R = 8.314 \times 10^{-3} kJ\ mol^{-1} K^{-1}$

$\Rightarrow \quad T = 326\,K$

$$W = -2.303 \times 0.1 \times 8.314 \times 10^{-3} \times 326 \log \frac{2.4 \times 10^{-8}}{0.1}$$

$= 4.125\ kJ = +\ 4.00\ kJ$

26. **(9)** Heat capacity $= C \times \Delta T$

$= 2.5\ kJ\ K^{-1} \times 0.45\ K = -1.125\ kJ$

$n = \frac{3.5\,g}{28\,g/mol} = 0.125\ mol$

$\therefore\ \Delta_C H^\circ$ of the gas $= \frac{-1.125}{0.125} kJ\ mol^{-1} = 9\ kJ\ mol^{-1}$

27. **(1)** $H^+(aq) + OH^-(aq) \longrightarrow H_2O(l)$;

$\Delta H^\circ = -57.0$ kJ (Standard value)

HCl (a strong acid) and NaOH (a strong base) are neutralised.

Moles of HCl $= \frac{50 \times 1}{1000} = 0.05$ mol

Moles of NaOH $= \frac{50 \times 1}{1000} = 0.05$ mol

$\therefore$ Enthalpy change for neutralisation of 0.05 mol

$= -57.0 \times 0.05 = -2.85$ kJ

Heat capacity $\times \Delta T = 2.85$ kJ

$\therefore \quad$ Heat capacity $= \frac{2.85\ kJ}{2.85°C} = 1.0 kJ/°C$

In second experiment, $\Delta T \times$ heat capacity = enthalpy

$2.8°C \times 1.0\ kJ/°C = 2.8\ kJ$

Moles of $CH_3COOH = \frac{50 \times 1}{1000} = 0.05$ mol

Moles of NaOH $= \frac{50 \times 1}{1000} = 0.05$ mol

$\therefore$ Enthalpy of neutralisation of CH_3COOH by NaOH

$= \frac{-2.8}{0.05} = -56.0\ kJ\ mol^{-1}$

Thus, enthalpy used in ionisation of

$CH_3COOH = 57.0 - 56.0 = 1.0\ kJ\ mol^{-1}$

28. **(7)** $C(s) \longrightarrow C(g)$, enthalpy of atomisation

$\frac{1}{2} O_2(g) \longrightarrow O(g)$ bond enthalpy of (O ═ O) bond

$H_2(g) \longrightarrow 2H(g)$ bond enthalpy of (H—H) bond

$C—H \longrightarrow C(g) + H(g)$ bond enthalpy of (C— H) bond

$O—H \longrightarrow O(g) + H(g)$ bond enthalpy of (O— H) bond

$C—O \longrightarrow C(g) + O(g)$ bond enthalpy of (C— O) bond

$CH_3OH(l) \longrightarrow CH_3OH(g)$ enthalpy of vaporisation of $CH_3OH(l)$.

29. **(3)** $CH_4(g) + 2O_2(g) \longrightarrow CO_2(g) + 2H_2O(g)$

$\Delta_c H^\circ(CH_4) = [\Delta_f H^\circ(CO_2) + 2\Delta_f H^\circ(H_2O)] - [\Delta_f H^\circ(CH_4) + \Delta_f H^\circ(O_2)]$

$= [-394 - 2 \times 242] - (-75 + 0) = -803\ kJ\ mol^{-1}$

$= -\frac{803}{1}$ kJ per unit volume of CH_4 (fuel)

$CO(g) + H_2(g) \longrightarrow CO_2(g) + H_2O$

$\Delta_c H^\circ$ (water gas) $= \Delta_f H^\circ(CO_2) + \Delta_f H^\circ(H_2O) - \Delta_f H^\circ(CO)$

$= -394 - 242 - (-110)$

$= -526$ kJ mol^{-1} of water gas

$= -\frac{526}{2}$ kJ per unit volume (one mole each of CO and H_2)

$= -263$ kJ per unit volume

Thus, $\frac{\Delta_c H^\circ(CH_4)}{\Delta_c H^\circ(\text{water gas})} = \frac{-803}{-263} = 3$

30. **(266)** The reaction for the formation of methyl alcohol proceeds as follow

$$C(s) + 2H_2(g) + \frac{1}{2} O_2(g) \longrightarrow CH_3OH\ (l)$$

ΔH = [Heat of atomisation of

$C(s) + 4\Delta H_f^\circ(H) + \Delta H_f^\circ(O)]$

$-[\Delta H_{vap}^\circ(CH_3OH) + 3(BE)_{C—H} + (BE)_{O—H} + (BE)_{C—O}]$

$= [715 + 4 \times 218 + 249] - [38 + 3 \times 415 + 463 + 356]$

$= -266\ kJ\ mol^{-1}$

If (BE) values are given, species should be in the gaseous state, thus additional enthalpy of vaporisation of liquid into vapour state is also involved.

Check Through PYQs : JEE Main

1. ***(d)*** Since in adiabatic system, no heat exchanges between system and surrounding, hence when methane undergo combustion, due to exothermic reaction, the temperature rises in container (*A*)

$$CH_4 + 2O_2 \longrightarrow CO_2 + 2H_2O + \text{heat}$$

In diathermic container, heat can change between system and surrounding, hence heat releases in to the surrounding and temperature of system (*B*) remains same.

2. ***(4)*** **Extensive properties** Mole, volume, Gibb's free energy

Intensive properties Molar mass, molar heat capacity, molarity, $E°_{cell}$

Thus, total number of intensive properties are 4.

3. ***(c)*** $|W|$ = Area under the curve

$$= 2p_0 \times [3V_0 - V_0] - p_0 \times [3V_0 - 2V_0]$$
$$= 3p_0V_0$$

Net work is done on the system.

4. ***(55)*** Given, $V_1 = 100$ L and $V_2 = 10$ L

Work done is given,

$$W = -nRT \ln \frac{V_2}{V_1}$$
$$= -1 \times 0.08206 \times 291.15 \times 2.303 \log \frac{10}{100}$$
$$= 55 \text{ L atm}$$

Hence, final answer is 55 L atm.

5. ***(a)*** For free expansion, $p_{external} = 0$

$\therefore$ Work done, $W = -p_{ext}\Delta V = 0$

$\because$ Adiabatic process, $q = 0$

Also from 1st law of thermodynamics.

$$\Delta U = q + W$$
$$\Rightarrow \quad \Delta U = 0$$

Internal energy is a function of temperature.

If internal energy is constant, $\Delta T = 0$

So, for free expansion, $q = 0$, $\Delta T = 0$, $W = 0$

Hence, option (a) is correct.

6. ***(28721)*** It is isothermal reversible expansion, so work done is negative.

Work done is given by

$$W = -2.303nRT \log\left(\frac{V_2}{V_1}\right)$$
$$= -2.303 \times 5 \times 8.314 \times 300 \log\left(\frac{100}{10}\right)$$
$$= -28720.713 \text{ J}$$
$$\approx -28721 \text{ J}$$

Hence, the value of x is 28721.

7. ***(200)*** Work done is given by area enclosed in the p vs V cyclic graph.

Sign is +ve for clockwise cyclic process for V vs p graph.

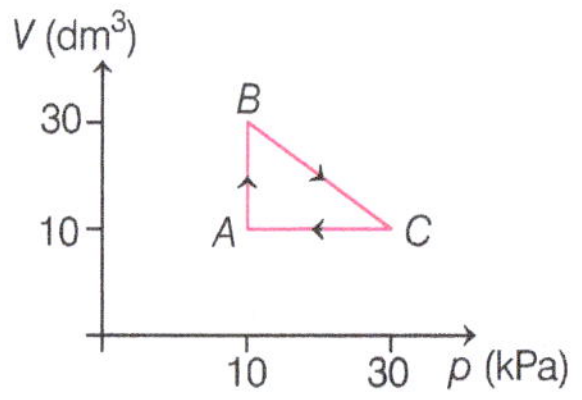

Work done = Area of triangle

$$= \frac{1}{2} \times \text{base} \times \text{height}$$
$$= \frac{1}{2} \times 20 \times 20 = 200 \text{ J}$$

Hence, work done is 200J.

8. ***(1200)*** For isothermal expansion at constant pressure, heat is given by

$$Q = -p_{ext}(V_2 - V_1)$$
$$= -80 \times 1000 \times (45 - 30) \times 10^{-3}$$
$$= -15 \times 80 = -1200 \text{ J}$$

Negative sign indicates heat is lost.

Hence, amount of heat transfer is 1200 J.

9. ***(1200)*** Power of heater = 60 W = 60 J/sec

Total energy emitted = $60 \times 100 = 6000$ J

heat capacity × temperature difference = total energy emitted

heat capacity × 5°C = 6000

$$\text{heat capacity} = \frac{6000}{5} = 1200 \text{ J/K}$$

10. ***(150)*** Given,

Number of moles = 1 mole

Temperature $(T_i) = 27°\text{C} = 300$ K

Since, the processes is adiabatic, hence, $q = 0$

$$\Rightarrow \quad W = \Delta U$$

On substituting values, we will get

$$W = nC_V\Delta T$$
$$-3 \times 10^3 = 1 \times 20\,[T_2 - 300]$$
$$T_2 - 300 = -150 \text{ or } T_2 - 150 \text{ K}$$

11. ***(0)*** Change in volume,

$$\Delta V = 20 - 4 = 16 \text{ L}$$

Work done, $W = -p_{ext}\Delta V$

but in vacuum, $p_{ext} = 0$

$$\therefore \quad W = -0 \times 16 = 0$$

For an isothermal expansion, $\Delta U = 0$

Using first law of thermodynamics,

$$\Delta U = q + W \Rightarrow 0 = q + 0 \Rightarrow q = 0$$

12. ***(2218)*** $Fe(s) + 2HCl(aq) \longrightarrow FeCl_2(aq) + H_2(g)$
50g

(Moles of Fe = Moles of H_2)

$$\text{moles} = \frac{50}{55.85} = 0.8952 \text{ mol} = 0.8952 \text{ mol}$$

Work done can be given by

$$W = -p_{ext}\Delta V = -\Delta n_g RT$$

Δ_{n_g} = (gaseous moles on product side) – (gaseous moles on reactant side)

$= 0.8952 - 0$

$W = -0.8952 \times 8.314 \times 298$

$= -2217.92$ J

Closest integer = 2218

13. ***(15)*** The gas performs isothermal irreversible work (W).

where, $\Delta U = 0$ (change in internal energy)

From, 1st law of thermodynamics,

$\Rightarrow \quad \Delta U = q + W \Rightarrow 0 = q + W$

$\Rightarrow \quad q = -W$

Now, $\quad W = -p_{ext}(V_2 - V_1)$

$$= -p_{ext}\left(\frac{nRT}{p_2} - \frac{nRT}{p_1}\right)$$

$$= -p_{ext} \times nRT\left(\frac{1}{p_2} - \frac{1}{p_1}\right)$$

Given, $p_{ext} = 4.3$ MPa, $p_1 = 2.1$ MPa,
$p_2 = 1.3$ MPa, $n = 5$ mol,
$T = 293$ K

and $\quad R = 8.314 \text{ J mol}^{-1} \text{K}^{-1}$

$$= -4.3 \times 5 \times 8.314 \times 293\left(\frac{1}{1.3} - \frac{1}{2.1}\right)$$

$= -15347.70 \text{ J mol}^{-1}$

$= -15.347 \text{ kJ mol}^{-1}$

$\simeq -15 \text{ kJ mol}^{-1}$

$\Rightarrow \quad q = 15 \text{kJ mol}^{-1}$

14. ***(48)*** Work done is equal to the area under pV-curve.

$\therefore$ Work done $(W) = \frac{1}{2}(6 + 10) \times 6$

$= 48.00 \text{ Pa. m}^3 = 48.00$ J.

15. ***(2850)*** $\Delta S = \Delta H - T\Delta S$

$\Delta S = 55000 - 298 \times 175 \text{ J mol}^{-1}$

$\Delta G = 55000 - 52150$

$\Delta G = 2850 \text{ J mol}^{-1}$

16. ***(2000)*** From Gibb's free energy equation,

$$\Delta G = \Delta H - T\Delta S$$

For reaction to be spontaneous $\Delta G = -$ ve

For limiting case $\Delta G = 0$

$$\Delta H = T\Delta S$$

$$T = \frac{\Delta H}{\Delta S} = \frac{400 \text{ kJ/mol}}{0.2 \text{ kJ/mol-K}}$$

$= 2000$ K

Hence, reaction will become spontaneous above 2000 K.

17. ***(57)*** $\Delta G° = -RT \ln K_{eq}$

$= -2.303RT \log K_{eq}$

$= -2.303 \times 8.314 \times 300 \times \log 10$

$= -5744.14 \text{ J/mol} = -5.744 \text{ kJ/mol}$

$= -57.44 \times 10^{-1} \text{ kJ/mol}$

Thus, the value is 57.

18. ***(a)*** Among the given options (a) is incorrect.

Its correct form is : (ΔG) is positive for non-spontaneous reaction.

19. ***(37)*** Given, $T = 400$ K

$\Delta H^{\ominus} = 77.2$ kJ / mol

$\Delta S = 122 \text{ JK}^{-1}$

Free energy is given by

$\Delta G° = \Delta H° - T\Delta S°$

$= 77.2 \times 10^3 - 400 \times 122 = 28400$ J

$\Delta G° = -2.303RT \log K$

$28400 = -2.303 \times 8.314 \times 400 \times \log K$

$\log K = -3.708$

or $\quad \log K = -37.08 \times 10^{-1}$

Hence, the missing value is 37.

20. ***(3)*** Given $n = 1, R = 8.314$

$V_2 = 3\text{ L}, V_1 = 2\text{ L}$

$$\Delta S_{\text{system}} = nR \ln\left(\frac{V_2}{V_1}\right)$$

$$\Delta S_{\text{system}} = 1 \times 8.314 \ln\left(\frac{3}{2}\right)$$

$\Delta S_{\text{system}} = 3.37 \text{ JK}^{-1}$

$\Delta S_{\text{surrounding}} = 3.37 \approx 3 \text{ JK}^{-1}$

21. ***(2)*** Graph between Gibbs free energy *vs* extent of energy.

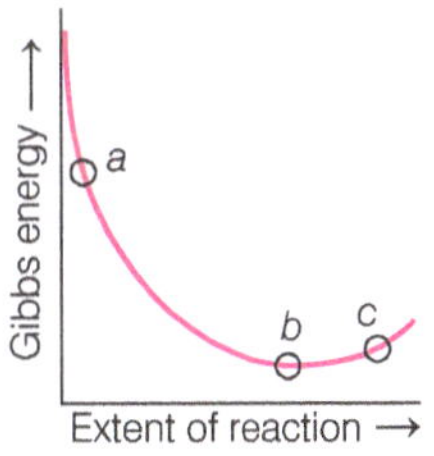

At *a* point we observe $\Delta_r G < 0$

So, reaction is spontaneous.

At *b* point $\Delta G = 0$ (equilibrium)

At *c* point gibbs free energy $\Delta_r G > 0$

So, reaction is non-spontaneous

Two statements, B and C are correct (2).

22. ***(c)*** The most appropriate relations are given in B and C only.

(B) Gibbs free energy is equal to the enthalpy of the system minus the product of the temperature and entropy.
$\Delta G = \Delta H - T\Delta S$ at constant temperature.

(C) Entropy is the measure of disorderness or randomness of the particular system. It can be expressed as

$$\left[\Delta S = \frac{q_{rev}}{T}\right]$$

23. ***(300)*** The relation between enthalpy, entropy and Gibb's free energy is given by equation

$$\Delta G = \Delta H - T\Delta S$$

At equilibrium, $\Delta G = 0$

$$0 = -165 \times 10^3 - T(-550)$$

$$\Rightarrow \quad T = \frac{165 \times 10^3}{550} = 300 \text{ K}$$

24. ***(711)*** From the given equilibrium equation:

$$N_2O_4 \rightleftharpoons 2NO_2$$

initially ($t = 0$) [1 mol]
after (time = t) $[1 - 0.5]$ mol $= 0.5$ mol; 0.5×2 mol $= 1$ mol

Total pressure = 1 atm

$$\therefore \quad K_p = \frac{[NO_2]^2}{[N_2O_4]} = \frac{\left[\frac{1}{1.5} \times 1\right]^2}{\left[\frac{0.5}{1.5} \times 1\right]} = \frac{100}{75} = [1.33]$$

$(\Delta G°)$ for the equilibrium reaction can be given by :

$$\Delta G° = -2.303\, RT \log K$$
$$= -2.303 \times 8.31 \times 300 \times \log(1.33)$$
$$= -2.303 \times 8.31 \times 300 \times 0.1239$$
$$\Delta G° = -711.35 \text{ J/mol} \simeq 711 \text{ J/mol}$$

25. ***(b)*** All the expression of thermodynamics are correct except

$$\ln k = \frac{\Delta H° - T\Delta S°}{RT}$$

As we know,

$$\Delta G = \Delta H - T\Delta S° \quad \text{...(i)}$$

Also $\quad \Delta G = -RT \ln K \quad$ ...(ii)

$\therefore$ From (i) and (ii),

$$-RT \ln K = \Delta H - T\Delta S°$$

$$\therefore \quad \ln K = \frac{-\Delta H}{RT} + \frac{\Delta S°}{R}$$

The correct expression is

$$\ln K = \frac{-\Delta H°}{RT} + \frac{\Delta S°}{R}$$

26. ***(964)***

$$\Delta H° = [\Delta H°_{f(Fe)} + \Delta H°_{f(CO)}] - [\Delta H°_{f(FeO)} + \Delta H°_{f(C)}]$$
$$= [0 + (-110.5)] - [-266.3 + 0]$$
$$= 155.8 \text{ kJ}^{-1} \text{ mol}^{-1}$$
$$\Delta S° = [\Delta S°_{(Fe)} + \Delta S°_{(CO)}] - [\Delta S°_{(FeO)} + \Delta S°_{(C)}]$$
$$= [27.28 + 197.6] - [57.49 + 5.74]$$
$$= 161.6 \text{ J K}^{-1} \text{ mol}^{-1}$$

The reaction becomes spontaneous when $\Delta G°$ is atleast zero or negative.

$$0 = \Delta H° - T\Delta S°$$
$$\Rightarrow \quad T\Delta S° = \Delta H°$$
$$\Rightarrow \quad T = \frac{\Delta H°}{\Delta S°} = \frac{155.8 \text{ kJ mol}^{-1}}{161.6 \text{ J K}^{-1} \text{ mol}^{-1}}$$
$$= \frac{155800 \text{ mol}^{-1}}{161.6 \text{ J K}^{-1} \text{ mol}^{-1}} = 964 \text{ K}$$

The temperature at which reaction becomes spontaneous is 964 K.

27. ***(b)*** Statement (b) is correct whereas all other statements are incorrect.

By definition,

$$dS = \frac{dQ}{T} \quad \text{and} \quad \Delta S = \frac{\int dQ}{T}$$

$\therefore$ ΔS is a function of temperature.

S is also a function of temperature.

28. ***(2.70)*** Given : $\Delta U = 2.1$ kcal

$$\Delta S = 20 \text{ cal K}^{-1} = \frac{20}{1000} \text{ kcal K}^{-1}$$

$$A(l) \rightleftharpoons 2B(g)$$

$$\therefore \quad \Delta n_g = 2 \text{ mol}$$
$$R = 2 \text{ cal K}^{-1} \text{ mol}^{-1}$$
$$= \frac{2}{1000} \text{ kcal K}^{-1} \text{ mol}^{-1}$$

As we know,

$$\Delta G = \Delta H - T\Delta S$$

and $\quad \Delta H = \Delta U + \Delta n_g RT$

$$\therefore \quad \Delta G = \Delta U + \Delta n_g RT - T\Delta S$$

$$\therefore \quad \Delta G = 2.1 + \frac{2 \times 2 \times 300}{1000} - \frac{300 \times 20}{1000}$$
$$= 2.1 + 1.2 - 6 = -2.70$$

29. ***(82)*** $CuSO_4(s) + H_2O(l) \longrightarrow CuSO_4(aq)$;

$$\Delta H = -70 \text{ kJ} \quad \text{...(i)}$$

$CuSO_4.5H_2O(s) + H_2O(l) \longrightarrow CuSO_4(aq) + 5H_2O$;

$$\Delta H = 12 \text{ kJ} \quad \text{...(ii)}$$

Subtracting Eq. (i) and (ii)

$$CuSO_4 + 5H_2O \longrightarrow CuSO_4 \cdot 5H_2O;$$
$$\Delta H = -70 - 12 = -82 \text{ kJ}$$

30. ***(274)*** In adiabatic condition, $q = 0$

Then, equation for change in internal energy will be given by

$$\Delta U = q + W \quad (q = 0)$$
$$nC_V\Delta T = -p_{ext}(V_2 - V_1) \text{...(i)}$$

as $\quad (W = p\Delta V)$

$$V_2 = 2V_1 \quad \text{(given)}$$

$$\frac{nRT_2}{p_2} = \frac{2nRT_1}{p_1} \quad \text{...(ii)}$$

$$p_1 = 5\,\text{atm},\ T_1 = 298\,\text{K}$$

p_2 from Eq. (ii) will be

$$p_2 = \frac{5T_2}{2 \times 298}$$

Now from Eq. (i)

(Put p_{ext} = 1 atm)

$$n\frac{5}{2}R(T_2 - T_1) = -1\left[\frac{nRT_2}{p_1} - \frac{nRT_1}{p_2}\right]$$

Put, $T_1 = 298$ and $p_2 = \dfrac{5T_2}{2 \times 298}$

$$\frac{5n}{2}R\,[T_2 - 298] = nR\left[\frac{T_2}{5} - \frac{298}{\left(\dfrac{5T_2}{2 \times 298}\right)}\right] \quad \text{...(iii)}$$

On solving Eq. (iii)

$$T_2 = 274.16\,\text{K}$$

Hence, nearest integer value of temperature is 274 K.

31. ***(b)*** The enthalpy of neutralisation of strong acid and strong base is always –57 kJ/mol. The reason for that is, strong monoacid gives one mole of H^+ and strong mono base gives on mole of OH^- which form one mole of water.

32. ***(b)*** Given equation

(A) $2CO(g) + O_2(g) \longrightarrow 2CO_2(g)$, $\quad \Delta H_1^\circ = -x$ kJ mol^{-1}

(B) $C(\text{graphite}) + O_2(g) \longrightarrow CO_2(g)$, $\quad \Delta H_2^\circ = -y$ kJ mol^{-1}

We have to find ΔH° for the reaction,

$$C(\text{graphite}) + \frac{1}{2}O_2(g) \longrightarrow CO(g) \quad \text{...(i)}$$

$$C(\text{graphite}) + O_2(g) \longrightarrow CO_2(g) \quad \text{...(ii)}$$

$$\Delta H_1 = -y\ \text{kJ/mol}^{-1}$$

$$CO_2(g) \longrightarrow CO(g) + \frac{1}{2}O_2(g) \quad \text{...(iii)}$$

$$\Delta H_2 = \frac{x}{2}\ \text{kJ/mole}$$

Eq. (i) = Eq. (ii) + Eq. (iii)

$$\therefore \quad \Delta H = -y + \frac{x}{2}$$

$$\Delta H = \frac{x}{2} - y \ \Rightarrow\ \Delta H = \frac{x - 2y}{2}$$

33. ***(173)*** $CCl_4(g) + 2H_2O(g) \longrightarrow CO_2(g) + 4HCl(g)$

$$\Delta H_r = (\Delta H_f CO_2 + 4\Delta H_f HCl) - (\Delta H_f CCl_4 + 2\Delta H_f H_2O)$$
$$= [-394 + 4 \times (-92)] - [-105 + 2 \times (-242)]$$
$$= -173\ \text{kJ/mol}$$

34. ***(35)*** Given, molar mass of gas = 280 g

Increase in temperature of calorimeter

$$= 298.45\ \text{K} - 298.0\ \text{K}$$

$$\Delta T = 0.45\,\text{K}$$

Enthalpy of calorimeter

$$\Delta H_{\text{Comb}} = 9\ \text{kJ mol}^{-1}$$

$$q = C\,\Delta T = 2.5 \times 0.45 = 1.125\,\text{kJ}$$

Considering $q = \Delta H$ (enthalpy change)

So, total enthalpy change $= q = 1.125$ kJ

Enthalpy change for 1 mole of gas, $\Delta H = 9$ kJ mol^{-1}

Thus, $\quad n_{gas} = \dfrac{q}{\Delta H} = \dfrac{1.125\ \text{kJ}}{9\ \text{kJ mol}^{-1}}$

and mass of gas taken $= n_{gas} \times$ molar mass

$$= \frac{1.125}{9} \times 280 \approx 35\,\text{g}$$

35. ***(2)*** $HCl + NaOH \longrightarrow NaCl + H_2O \quad \Delta H = -57.3$ kJ/mol

Since, HCl, NaOH and NaCl are strong acid, strong base and salt respectively. So, are completely ionised.

$$H^+ + Cl^- + Na^+ + OH^- \longrightarrow Na^+ + Cl^- + H_2O$$

$$\Delta H = -57.3\ \text{kJ/mol}$$

$$\Rightarrow \quad H^+ + OH^- \longrightarrow H_2O$$

$$\Delta H = -57.3\,\text{kJ/mol}$$

$$\Rightarrow \quad H_2O \longrightarrow H^+ + OH^- \quad \text{...(i)}$$

$$\Delta H = +57.3\ \text{kJ/mol}$$

$$\underset{\text{Weak acid}}{CH_3COOH} + \underset{\text{Strong base}}{NaOH} \longrightarrow CH_3CO\overset{-}{O}\overset{+}{Na} + H_2O$$

$$\Delta H = -55.3\,\text{kJ/mol}$$

We can also write above equation as

$$CH_3COOH + OH^- \longrightarrow CH_3COO^- + H_2O \quad \text{...(ii)}$$

$$\Delta H = -55.3\,\text{kJ/mol}$$

On adding Eq. (i) and Eq. (ii), we get,

$$CH_3COOH + OH^- + H_2O \longrightarrow CH_3COO^- + H_2O + H^+ + OH^-$$

$$CH_3COOH \rightleftharpoons CH_3COO^\ominus + H^\oplus$$

$$\Delta H = +57.3 - 55.3 = 2\ \text{kJ/mol}$$

So, ionisation of acid requires 2 kJ/mol of energy.

36. ***(195)*** $q = nC\Delta T$

$$= \frac{22}{44} \times 100 \times (270 - 310) = -200\ \text{J}$$

$$w = -p\Delta V$$

$$= -1 \times (101.3) \times (167.75 - 217.1) \times 10^{-3} = 4.999\ \text{J}$$

$$\Delta E = q + w = -200 + 4.999 \cong -195\,\text{J}$$

$$\therefore \quad x = 195$$

37. ***(38)*** $H_2O(l) \longrightarrow H_2O(g)$

Given, weight of water = 36 g

Moles of $H_2O = \dfrac{36\ \text{g}}{18\ \text{g}} = 2$ moles

Internal energy, $\Delta U = \Delta H - \Delta n_g RT \quad (\Delta n_g = 1 - 0 = 1)$

$$= 41.1 - \frac{1 \times 8.31 \times 373}{1000}\ \text{kJ/mol}$$

$$= 38\,\text{kJ/mol}$$

38. ***(c)*** The reaction between carbon and hydrogen can be written as

$$2C + 3H_2 \longrightarrow C_2H_6 \quad \ldots(R)$$

Combustion equation of ethane

$$C_2H_6\,(g) + \frac{7}{2}\,O_2(g) \longrightarrow 2CO_2 + 3H_2O \quad \ldots(i)$$

$$\Delta H^\circ_{comb} = -1560 \text{ kJ/mol (given)}$$

$$2 \times [C(s) + O_2(g) \longrightarrow CO_2(g)] \quad \ldots(ii)$$

$$\Delta H^\circ_{comb} = -394 \text{ kJ/mol}$$

$$3 \times \left(H_2(g) + \frac{1}{2}\,O_2 \longrightarrow H_2O\,(g)\right) \quad \ldots(iii)$$

$\Delta H^\circ_{comb} = -286$ kJ/mol

$2 \times$ Eq. (ii) + $3 \times$ Eq. (iii) – Eq (i) = Eq. (R)

$$= (-394 \times 2) + (-286 \times 3) - (-1560)$$

$$\Delta H_f^\circ = -86.0 \text{ kJ/mol}$$

39. ***(82)*** Millimoles of HCl $= 200 \times 0.2 = 40$

Millimoles of NaOH $= 300 \times 0.1 = 30$

Heat released (q) $= n \times$ molar heat

$$= \frac{30}{1000} \times 57.1 \times 1000 = 1713 \text{ J}$$

Mass of solution $= 500 \times 1 = 500$ g

We know that,

$$\Delta T = \frac{q}{mc} = \frac{1713 \text{ J}}{500 \text{ g} \times 4.18 \text{ J/g-K}}$$

$$= 0.8196 \text{ K} = 81.96 \times 10^{-2} \text{ K}$$

$$x \approx 82$$

40. ***(c)*** Enthalpy of bond dissociation (kJ/mol) at 298.2 K

For hydrogen = 435.88 kJ/mol

For deuterium = 443.35 kJ/ mol

Hence, difference in energy of deuterium and hydrogen is approx. 7.50 kJ/mol

Therefore, equation is [$E_H \simeq E_D - 7.5$]

41. ***(d)*** (1) From enthalpy, $H = U + pV$, and for ideal gas, $pV = nRT$

So, [$H = U + nRT$]

and (H) depends only on temperature.

(2) For an ideal gas, compressibility factor ($Z = 1$)

(3) $C_p - C_V = R$

(4) For all processes, [$\Delta U = C_V dT$]

42. ***(326400)*** The combustion equation of ethanol (C_2H_5OH or C_2H_6O) is

$$C_2H_6O(l) + 3O_2(g) \longrightarrow 2CO_2(g) + 3H_2O(l)$$

$$\Delta n_g = (2 + 0) - (0 + 3) = -1$$

$$\Rightarrow \quad \Delta q_p = \Delta u_v + \Delta n_g RT$$

$$\Rightarrow \quad \Delta U_v = \Delta q_p - \Delta n_g RT$$

$$= -327 - (-1) \times (2 \times 10^{-3}) \times 300$$

$$= -326.400 \text{ kcal} = -326400 \text{ cal}$$

Practice Element 02 : Target JEE Advanced

1. ***(d)*** V_1(initial volume) $= \dfrac{nRT_1}{p_1}$

$$= \frac{0.5 \text{ mole} \times 0.0821 \text{ L atm mol}^{-1}\text{K}^{-1} \times 273 \text{ K}}{5 \text{ atm}}$$

$$= 2.24 \text{ L}$$

V_2 (final volume) $= 10\,V_1 = 22.4$ L

p_2(final pressure) = 0.5 atm

Thus final temperature $= \dfrac{p_2V_2}{nR} = \dfrac{0.5 \times 22.4}{0.5 \times 0.0821} \approx 273$ K

Being isothermal, $\Delta U = 0$, $\Delta H = 0$

$$\Delta S = 2.303\, nR \log \frac{V_2}{V_1}$$

$$= 2.303 \times 0.5 \text{ mol} \times 8.314 \text{J mol}^{-1}\text{ K}^{-1} \log \frac{22.4}{2.24}$$

$$= 9.57 \text{ JK}^{-1}$$

$$\Delta G = -2.303\, nRT \log \frac{V_2}{V_1}$$

$$= -2.303 \times 0.5 \text{ mol} \times 8.314 \text{Jmol}^{-1}\text{ K}^{-1} \times 273 \text{K} \log \frac{22.4}{2.24}$$

$$= -2613.6 \text{ J}$$

2. ***(a)*** $H^+(aq) + OH^-(aq) \rightleftharpoons H_2O(l)$; $\Delta H^\circ = -13.7$ kcal mol^{-1}

$$0.1 \text{ M } Ba(OH)_2 \equiv 0.2 \text{ N } Ba(OH)_2$$

$$0.1 \text{ M } H_2SO_4 \equiv 0.2 \text{N } H_2SO_4$$

Equivalent of $Ba(OH)_2$ or H_2SO_4 neutralised in (I)

$$= \frac{30 \times 0.2}{1000} = 6 \times 10^{-3}$$

Thus, $\Delta H_1 = 6 \times 10^{-3} \times -13.7$ kcal $= -0.0822$ kcal

Thus, heat released will warm the reaction mixture and temperature increase is ΔT_1.

Equivalent of $Ba(OH)_2$ or H_2SO_4 neutralised in (II)

$$= \frac{90 \times 0.2}{1000} = 18 \times 10^{-3}$$

Thus, $\Delta H_2 = 18 \times 10^{-3} \times -13.7$ kcal $= -0.2466$ kcal

Thus, heat released will warm the reaction mixture and temperature increase is ΔT_2.

[Temperature increase $\propto$ heat released]

$$\frac{\Delta T_1}{\Delta T_2} = \frac{0.0822}{0.2466} = \frac{1}{3}$$

$$\Delta T_2 = 3\Delta T_1$$

3. ***(b)*** The ΔG values, for the following reactions at 800°C are given as

I. $S_2(s) + 2O_2(g) \longrightarrow 2SO_2(g)$; $\Delta G = -544$ kJ ...(i)

II. $2Zn(s) + S_2(s) \longrightarrow 2ZnS(s)$; $\Delta G = -293$ kJ ...(ii)

III. $2Zn(s) + O_2(g) \longrightarrow 2ZnO(s)$; $\Delta G = -480$ kJ ...(iii)

By adding (i) with (iii) then subtract from (ii)

$$\Delta G = -731 \text{ kJ}$$

4. ***(c)*** $C(g) + 4H(g) + O(g) \longrightarrow$ 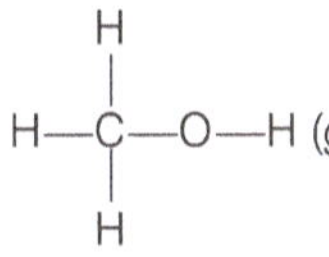 (g)

$$\Delta_r H^\circ = \Delta H_f^\circ(C, g) + 4\Delta_f H^\circ(H, g) + \Delta_f H(O, g)$$
$$- [3\,(BE)_{C-H} + (BE)_{C-O} + (BE)_{O-H}]$$
$$= [(715 + 4 \times 218 + 249) - (3 \times 415 + 356 + 463)]$$
$$= -228\text{ kJ}$$
$$CH_3OH\,(g) \longrightarrow CH_3OH\,(l); \quad \Delta H^\circ = -38\text{ kJ}$$

Thus, $\Delta_f H^\circ (CH_3OH, l) = -228 - 38 = -266\text{ kJ mol}^{-1}$

$\Delta_f H^\circ$, based on (BE) values requires all species in gaseous state, that –38 kJ of heat is released which converts $CH_3OH(g)$ into $CH_3OH(l)$.

5. ***(a)*** $150\text{ W} = 150\text{ J s}^{-1}$

Heat supplied in 1 min(60 s) = 150 × 60 = 9000 J

Methanol = 1 kg = 1000 g

$$\Delta T = 3.54\text{K}$$
$$\therefore \quad Q = mC\Delta T$$
$$n\text{ (specific heat)} = \frac{Q}{m\Delta T} = \frac{9000\text{ J}}{1000\text{ g} \times 3.54\text{ K}}$$
$$= 2.5424\text{ J g}^{-1}\text{K}^{-1}$$
$$Cm = 2.5424 \times 32\text{ J mol}^{-1}\text{K}^{-1}$$
$$= 81.4\text{ J mol}^{-1}\text{K}^{-1}$$

6. ***(a)*** **Step I** Change in entropy when temperature of H_2 and O_2 changes from 99°C to 25°C

$$\Delta S = nC_p \ln \frac{T_2}{T_1} = 2.303\, nC_p \log \frac{T_2}{T_1}$$
$$\therefore \quad \Delta S_1 = 2.303 \times 2 \times 28.8 \log \frac{298}{372} + 2.303 \times 1 \times 29.4 \log \frac{298}{372}$$
$$= -19.3\text{ JK}^{-1}$$

Step II $\Delta S_2\text{(reaction)} = -326.7\text{ JK}^{-1}$

Step III Change in entropy of converting $H_2O(l)$ to $H_2O(g)$

$$\Delta S_3 = 2.303\, nC_p \log \frac{T_2}{T_1}$$
$$= 2.303 \times 2 \times 75.3 \log \frac{372}{298} = 33.4\text{ JK}^{-1}$$
$$\because \quad \Delta S = \Delta S_1 + \Delta S_2 + \Delta S_3 = -312.6\text{ J K}^{-1}$$

7. ***(b)*** Gas is allowed to expand under adiabatic expansion hence, temperature falls

$$T_2 = T_1 \left(\frac{V_1}{V_2}\right)^{\gamma - 1}$$

Thus, T_2 is calculated.

$$\left(\frac{\Delta E}{\Delta T}\right)_V = C_V$$
$$\therefore \quad \Delta E = nC_V \int_{T_1}^{T_2} dT$$

Similarly, $\Delta H = nC_p \int_{T_1}^{T_2} dT$

Thus, ΔE and ΔH can also be calculated.

Gas is triatomic, hence,

$$\gamma = 1.33, C_V = 3R, C_p = 4R, T_1 = 300\text{K}$$
$$T_2 = 300\left(\frac{5}{40}\right)^{1.33-1} = 300\left(\frac{1}{8}\right)^{0.33}$$
$$= 300\left(\frac{1}{8}\right)^{1/3} = 300\left(\frac{1}{2}\right) = 150\text{ K}$$

(i) $\Delta E = nC_V \int_{T_1}^{T_2} dT = nC_V (T_2 - T_1)$

$$= 3 \times 3\,R(T_2 - T_1) = 3 \times 3 \times 8.314 \times (150 - 300)$$
$$= -11224\text{ J} = -11.224\text{ kJ}$$

(ii) $\Delta H = nC_p \int_{T_1}^{T_2} dT = 3 \times 4R\,(T_2 - T_1)$

$$= -3 \times 4 \times 8.314 \times 150$$
$$= -14965\text{ J} = -14.965\text{ kJ}$$

8. ***(a)*** $dW = -p_{ext}\, dV \Rightarrow dW = -\frac{5}{V} dV$

$$\therefore \quad \int dW = -5 \int_{V_1}^{V_2} \frac{dV}{V}$$
$$W = -2.303 \times 5 \log \frac{50}{5} = -2.303 \times 5\text{ L atm}$$
$$= -\frac{2.303 \times 5\text{ L atm} \times 8.314\text{ J mol}^{-1}\text{ K}^{-1}}{0.0821\text{ L atm mol}^{-1}\text{ K}^{-1}} = -1166\text{ J}$$
$$Q = ?$$
$$\Delta U = Q + W = 1373.85\text{ J} + (-1166\text{ J}) = 207.85\text{ J}$$

9. ***(b)*** Conversion involves following steps

Step I $H_2O\ (l)$ at –10°C $\longrightarrow$ $H_2O\ (l)$ at 0°C

Temperature changes: $\Delta S_1 = 2.303 \times nC_V \log \frac{T_2}{T_1}$

$$= 2.303 \times 1 \times 1.0\text{ cal} \times 18 \log \frac{273}{263}$$
$$= 0.67\text{ cal K}^{-1}$$

Step II $H_2O(l)$ at 0°C $\longrightarrow$ H_2O (s) at 0°C

$$\Delta S_2 = -\frac{18 \times 80}{273} = -5.27\text{ cal K}^{-1}$$

Entropy decreases due to increase in order. (it is a case of phase change)

Step III H_2O(s) at 0°C $\longrightarrow$ H_2O (s) at –10°C

Temperature changes

$$\therefore \quad \Delta S_3 = 2.303 \times 1 \times 0.5 \times 18 \log \frac{263}{273}$$
$$= -0.33\text{ cal K}^{-1}$$
$$\therefore \quad \Delta S_{Total} = \Delta S_1 + \Delta S_2 + \Delta S_3 = -4.93\text{ cal K}^{-1}$$

10. ***(b)*** A is true but R is false. The correct form of R is

$$\Delta S_{total} = (\Delta S_{system} + \Delta S_{surr})$$
$$\Delta S_{surr} = -\text{ (enthalpy change)}/T$$
$$= -\frac{(-1648 \times 10^3\text{ J mol}^{-1})}{298} = 5530.2\text{ J mol}^{-1}\text{ K}^{-1}$$

$\therefore \quad \Delta S_{total} = (-549.4 + 5530.2)\ J\ mol^{-1}\ K^{-1}$
$= 4980.8\ J\ mol^{-1} K^{-1}$

Since $\Delta S_{Total} > 0$, hence reaction is spontaneous.

As we know, $\Delta G° = \Delta H° - T\Delta S°$

If $\Delta H° = -$ ve and $\Delta S° < 0$

Then $\Delta G° = -\Delta H° + T\Delta S°$

If reaction is spontaneous, $\Delta G° < 0$

It is only when $(-\Delta H°) > T\Delta S°$

Thus, every exothermic reaction is not spontaneous.

11. ***(a, d)*** Among the given statement, only a and d are correct while b and c are incorrect regarding the given data.

(a) Their correct explanation is

$$W = \text{Area enclosed } ABC$$
$$W = \frac{1}{2}(V_0)(2p_0)$$
$$W = p_0V_0$$

Since it is overall expansion, so $w = -p_0V_0$

(b) For the path CA, i.e. isobaric

$$q_3 = n \times C_p \times (T_A - T_C) = 1 \times \frac{5}{2}R\left[\frac{p_AV_A - p_CV_C}{R}\right]$$
$$= \frac{5}{2}[p_0V_0 - 2p_0V_0]$$
$$q_3 = -\frac{5}{2}p_0V_0$$

(c) The path BC is isothermic for which $\Delta U = 0 \Rightarrow q = -w$

$$\Rightarrow q = \left(-\frac{1}{2} \times V_0 \times 3p_0\right) \Rightarrow q = \frac{3}{2}p_0V_0$$

(d) Also, $\frac{p_0V_0}{T_1} = \frac{3p_0V_0}{T_2}$

$$\Rightarrow T_2 = 3T_1 = \frac{3p_0V_0}{R}$$

12. ***(a, b)*** The reaction occurs spontaneously and is product favoured.

Thus, $\Delta S°(\text{universe}) > 0$

and $\Delta G° < 0$

Reaction occurs with loss of heat $\Delta H° < 0$.

$$\Delta S°_{(universe)} = \Delta S°_{(system)} + \Delta S°_{(surrounding)}$$

Thus, $\Delta S°_{(system)} = \frac{\Delta H°}{T} = -$ ve

$\Delta S°_{(surrounding)} = +$ ve

Thus, $\Delta S°_{(system)} < 0$

$\Delta S°_{(surrounding)} > 0$

13. ***(a, d)***

(a) $H_2O\,(l) \rightleftharpoons H_2O\,(g)$

Liquid molecules are more ordered than that of gaseous molecule. When a liquid changes to vapour state, randomness increases, hence entropy increases.

Thus, (a) is true.

(b) $\Delta G = \Delta H - T\Delta S$

$\Delta H = -$ ve for exothermic reaction if temperature is very low such that $\Delta S < 0$. and $(-T\Delta S) > \Delta H$.

Then, $\Delta G > 0$ thus non-spontaneous. Thus, exothermic reaction will be spontaneous only at high temperature.

Thus, (b) is not true.

(c) $\Delta G = \Delta H - T\Delta S$

If $T\Delta S > \Delta H$, then $\Delta G < 0$

and reaction will be product favoured.

Thus, (c) is not true.

(d) $\Delta G° = -2.303RT \log K$. If $K > 1$, say (2),

then $\Delta G° = -2.303\,RT \log 2 = -ve$

Thus (d) is true.

14. ***(a, b, c)***

(a) $\Delta S_{(X \longrightarrow Y)}$ taking place at constant temperature is

$$\Delta S = 2.303\,nR \log\frac{V_2}{V_1} = 2.303\,nR \log\frac{p_1}{p_2}$$
$$= 2.303 \times 5\ mol \times 8.314\ J\ mol^{-1}\ K^{-1} \log\left(\frac{10}{1}\right) = 95.7\ J\ K^{-1}$$

Thus, true.

(b) $q = 0,\ \Delta S_{(X \longrightarrow Z)} = \frac{q}{T} = 0$

(c) $X \longrightarrow Z$ takes place adiabatically hence, temperature falls to 118.6 K.

$$\Delta S_{X \longrightarrow Z} = 0,\ C_p = \frac{5}{2}R$$

For monoatomic gas

and $\Delta S_{Z \longrightarrow Y} = 2.303\,nC_p \log\frac{T_2}{T_1}$

$$= 2.303 \times 5 \times 2.5 \times 8.314 \log\frac{298}{118.6}$$
$$= 95.75\ JK^{-1}$$

Thus, $\Delta S_{X \to Y} = \Delta S_{X \to Z} + \Delta S_{Z \to Y} = 95.75\ JK^{-1}$

(d) $\Delta S_{X \longrightarrow Z \longrightarrow Y} \neq 0$

Thus, (d) is incorrect.

15. ***(a, b, c)***

(a) Process is isothermal expansion against a constant external pressure

$$p_{ext} = 380\ Torr = \frac{380}{760}\ atm = 0.5\ atm$$
$$W_1 = -p_{ext}(V_f - V_i)$$
$$= -0.5\,(16.0 - 12.7) = -0.5\ atm \times 3.3\ L$$
$$= -1.65\ L\ tm = -167.2\ J$$

$(R = 0.0821\ L\ atm\ mol^{-1}\ K^{-1} = 8.314\ J\ mol^{-1}\ K^{-1})$

(b) Under isothermal reversible condition

$$W_2 = -2.303\,nRT \log\frac{V_2}{V_1}$$
$$= -2.303 \times \left(\frac{4.8}{16}\right) \times 8.314 \times 310\ \log\left(\frac{16}{12.7}\right)$$

$W_2 = -178.64$ J

$\therefore \quad W_2 < W_1$

(c) Expansion in vacuum, $p = 0$

$\therefore \; W = -p(\Delta V) = 0$

(d) $W_1 \neq W_2$ (Hence, option (d) is incorrect)

16. ***(a, b, c)***

(a) $p_{ext} = 0, -p_{ext}\, \Delta V = 0,$
Thus, (a) is correct.

(b) $W = -p_{ext}[V_2 - V_1] = -p_{ext}\left[\frac{nRT}{p_2} - \frac{nRT}{p_1}\right]$

$= -nRTp_{ext}\left[\frac{1}{p_2} - \frac{1}{p_1}\right]$

$= -0.850 \text{ mol} \times 0.0821 \text{ L atm mol}^{-1}\text{K}^{-1} \times 300 \text{ K} \times 1.00 \text{ atm}\left[\frac{1}{1.0 \text{ atm}} - \frac{1}{15 \text{ atm}}\right]$

$= -19.54$ L atm

Thus, (b) is correct.

(c) For an isothermal reversible expansion

$W = -2.303 nRT \log \frac{p_1}{p_2}$

$= -2.303 \times 0.850 \text{ mol} \times 8.314 \text{ Jmol}^{-1}\text{K}^{-1} \times 300 \text{ K} \log \frac{15.0}{1}$

$= -5.74 \times 10^3$ J

Thus, (c), is correct.

(d) Work done $\neq 0$ if the expansion is carried out adiabatically. Thus (d) is incorrect

17. ***(c, d)***

At 300 K	At 600 K
$W_{300} = 2.303 nRT_1 \log \frac{V_2}{V_1}$	$W_{600} = 2.303 nRT_2 \log \frac{V_2}{V_1}$

$$\frac{W_{600}}{W_{300}} = \frac{600}{300} = 2$$

Process is isothermal reversible then $\Delta E = 0$

18. ***(a, b, c)***

1 mol at STP occupies volume = 22.4 L (initially)

Final Volume = 44.8 L

$\therefore \; W = -p_{ext}(V_2 - V_1) = -0.375 \text{ atm } (44.8 - 22.4) \text{ L}$
$= -8.4$ L atm

Since $\quad q = 0$

$\therefore \quad \Delta U = q + W = W$

For adiabatic expansion $(T_2 < T_1)$

$W = -nC_V(T_2 - T_1)$
$= -nC_V \Delta T$

For CH_4, $C_V = 3R$ (polyatomic gas mole)

$\therefore \; -8.4 \text{ L atm} = -1 \text{ mol} \times 3 \times 0.0821 \text{ L atm mol}^{-1}\text{ K}^{-1} \times \Delta T$

$\therefore \quad \Delta T = 34.1 \approx 34$ K

19. ***(11.90)*** Work done in irreversible process $= -p(V_2 - V_1)$

	p	V_2	V_1
Stage I	100	$\frac{nRT}{100}$	$\frac{nRT}{150}$
Stage II	50	$\frac{nRT}{50}$	$\frac{nRT}{100}$
Stage III	20	$\frac{nRT}{20}$	$\frac{nRT}{50}$
Stage IV	1	$\frac{nRT}{1}$	$\frac{nRT}{20}$

$n = 2, R = 8.314 \text{ J mol}^{-1}\text{ K}^{-1}, T = 300$ K

$\therefore \quad W_{Total} = W_1 + W_2 + W_3 + W_4$

$= nRT\left[100\left(\frac{1}{100} - \frac{1}{150}\right) + 50\left(\frac{1}{50} - \frac{1}{100}\right) + 20\left(\frac{1}{20} - \frac{1}{50}\right) + 1\left(\frac{1}{1} - \frac{1}{20}\right)\right]$

$= nRT\left[\left(1 - \frac{2}{3}\right) + \left(1 - \frac{1}{2}\right) + \left(1 - \frac{2}{5}\right) + \left(1 - \frac{1}{20}\right)\right]$

$= nRT\left(\frac{143}{60}\right)$

$= 2 \text{ mol} \times 8.314 \text{ Jmol}^{-1}\text{ K}^{-1} \times 300 \text{ K} \times \frac{143}{60}$

$= 11889 \text{ J} \approx 11.90$ kJ

20. ***(63)*** The combustion reaction is

$$2CH_3OH(l) + 3O_2(g) \longrightarrow 2CO_2(g) + 4H_2O(l)$$

Given, heat capacity of calorimeter,

$$C = 20 \text{ kJ K}^{-1}, T_i = 298 \text{ K}, T_f = 330 \text{ K}$$

Change in temperature $(\Delta T) = 330 - 298 = 32$ K

Heat evolved in reaction, $q = C\Delta T = 20 \times 32 = 640$ kJ

Since, the reaction is taking place under constant volume,

$$\Delta U_r = -\frac{640}{2} \text{ kJ} = -320 \text{ kJ mol}^{-1}$$

Enthalpy of reaction,

$\Delta H_r^\circ = \Delta U^\circ + \Delta n_g RT$

$= -320 \text{ kJ mol}^{-1} + (-1) \text{ mol} \times 8.3 \times 10^{-3} \text{ kJ mol}^{-1}\text{ K}^{-1} \times 298$ K

$= -322.4 \text{ kJ mol}^{-1}$

Also, $\Delta H_r^\circ = 2[\Delta H^\circ_f (CO_2)] + 4(\Delta H^\circ_f (H_2O)] - 2 \times \Delta H^\circ_f [CH_3OH] - 3 \times \Delta H^\circ_f [(O_2)]$

$-322.4 \text{ kJ mol}^{-1} = 2 \times 25 + 4[\Delta H^\circ_f (H_2O)] - 2 \times 60.32 - 0$

$X = 62.94 \text{ kJ mol}^{-1} \approx 63 \text{ kJ mol}^{-1}$

21. ***(2)*** (d) (I) $H_2(g) \longrightarrow 2H(g); \quad \Delta H^\circ = 236$ kJ

(IV) $2H(g) + \frac{1}{2}O_2(g) \longrightarrow H_2O(l); \; \Delta H^\circ = x$

(III) $H_2(g) + \frac{1}{2}O_2(g) \longrightarrow H_2O(l); \; \Delta H^\circ = -241.8$ kJ

$\therefore \quad 236 + x = -241.8$ kJ

$\therefore \quad x = -477.8$ kJ

I. $H_2(g) \longrightarrow 2H(g);\ \Delta H° = 236$ kJ

II. $\frac{1}{2}O_2(g) \longrightarrow O(g);\ \Delta H° = \frac{498}{2} = 249$ kJ

V. $2H(g) + O(g) \longrightarrow H_2O(l);\ \Delta H° = y$

III. $H_2(g) + \frac{1}{2}O_2(g) \longrightarrow H_2O(l);\ \Delta H° = -241.8$ kJ

$\therefore\ 236 + 249 + y = -241.8$ kJ $\Rightarrow\ y = -726.8$ kJ

Thus, $\frac{x}{y} = \frac{-477.8}{-726.8} \approx 0.66 = \frac{2}{3} \quad \Rightarrow \quad \frac{3x}{y} = 2$

22. ***(6390)*** Given, $n = 4$ mol

$$C_{v,m} = 13\ \text{JK}^{-1}\ \text{mol}^{-1}$$
$$R = 8.3\ \text{JK}^{-1}\ \text{mol}^{-1}$$
$$T_2 = 400\ \text{K}$$
$$T_1 = 325\ \text{K}$$
$$V_2 = 40\ \text{L}$$
$$V_1 = 20\ \text{L}$$

From the graph, it is clear that $A \rightarrow B$ is an isothermal process ($dT = 0$)

So, $\Delta H_{A \rightarrow B} = nC_p dT = 0$

Also, $B \rightarrow C$ is an isochoric process

$$\Delta U_{B \rightarrow C} = nC_{v,m} dT$$
$$\Delta U_{B \rightarrow C} = 4 \times 13 \times (400 - 325) = 3900\ \text{J}$$
$$\Delta H_{B \rightarrow C} = \Delta U_{B \rightarrow C} + \Delta(pV)$$
$$= \Delta U_{B \rightarrow C} + nR\Delta T$$
$$= 3900 + (4 \times 8.3 \times 75)$$
$$= 3900 + 2490 = 6390\ \text{J}$$

23. ***(5)*** For adiabatic expansion, $p_1V_1^\gamma = p_2V_2^\gamma$. Thus, V_2 is calculated.

Also $T_2 = T_1\left(\frac{V_1}{V_2}\right)^{\gamma-1}$. Thus, T_2 is calculated.

Also $W = -nC_V\Delta T = -nC_V(T_2 - T_1)$

Thus, W is calculated.

For monoatomic gas $\gamma = \frac{5}{3}$ and $C_V = \frac{3}{2}R$.

Given monoatomic gas is being expanded adiabatically, $p_1 = 1.0$ k Pa $= 1000$ Pa, $V_1 = 1\ \text{dm}^3 = 0.001\ \text{m}^3$

Initial temperature

$$T_1 = \frac{p_1V_1}{nR} = \frac{1000 \times 0.001}{0.4 \times 8.314} = 0.300\ \text{K}$$

Hence, $\quad p_1V_1^\gamma = p_2V_2^\gamma \left(\gamma = \frac{5}{3} \text{ for monoatomic gas}\right)$

$$(V_2)^{5/3} = \frac{p_1V_1^\gamma}{p_2} = \frac{1.0 \times (1)^{5/3}}{0.1} = 10$$

$\therefore \quad V_2 = 3.98\ \text{dm}^3$

$$T_2 = T_1\left(\frac{V_1}{V_2}\right)^{\gamma-1}$$

Also $\quad T_2 = 0.300\left(\frac{1}{3.98}\right)^{(5/3-1)} = 0.300\ (0.398) \approx 0.12\ \text{K}$

$$W = -nC_V(T_2 - T_1)$$
$$W = -0.4 \times \frac{3}{2} \times 8.314(0.12 - 0.300) \approx +0.900\ \text{J}$$

Hence, the value of $X + Y + Z = 3.98 + 0.12 + 0.900 = 5$

24. ***(0.96)*** Given, $R = 0.08314$ bar L mol^{-1} K^{-1}

First we calculate volume of each flask under given conditions

$$V_A = \frac{nRT}{p_A} = \frac{1 \times 0.08314 \times 298}{4.0} = 6.194\ \text{L}$$
$$V_B = \frac{1 \times 0.08314 \times 298}{2} = 12.388\ \text{L}$$

Total volume after mixing $= 18.582$ L

Total moles $= 2$ mol

Thus, final pressure after mixing $= \frac{nRT}{V}$

$$p = \frac{2 \times 0.08314 \times 298}{18.582} = 2.67\ \text{bar}$$

The entropy change for each gas is calculated assuming the gas to expand reversibly from its original pressure p_A to p_{total}, and p_B to p_{total}.

$$\Delta S(\text{system})_A = -2.303nR\log\frac{p_{total}}{p_A}$$
$$= -2.303 \times 1 \times 8.314 \log\frac{2.67}{4.00} = +3.36\ \text{JK}^{-1}$$
$$\Delta S(\text{system})_B = -2.303 \times 1 \times 8.314 \log\frac{2.67}{2.00} = -2.40\ \text{JK}^{-1}$$

$\therefore\ \Delta S(\text{system})_{A+B} = 3.36 - 2.40 = 0.96\ \text{JK}^{-1}$

25. ***(2)*** Work done along dashed line is Irreversible $-W_d = \Sigma p\Delta V$

$$W_d = 4.5(2.5 - 0.5) + 0.25(6.0 - 3.5) + 0.5(3.5 - 2.5)$$
$$= 4.5 \times 2 + 0.5 \times 1 + 0.25 \times 2.5 = 10.125\ \text{L atm}$$
$$W_d = -10.125\ \text{L atm}$$

Along solid line work is reversible

$$w_d = -10.125\ \text{L-atm}$$
$$p_1 = 4.5\ \text{atm},\quad V_1 = 0.5\ \text{L}$$
$$-W_s = 2.303RT\log\frac{V_2}{V_1} = 2.303p_1V_1\log\frac{V_2}{V_1}$$
$$= 2.303 \times 2.25\log\frac{6.0}{0.5} = 5.592\ \text{L atm}$$
$$W_s = -5.592$$
$$\frac{W_d}{W_s} = \frac{-10.125}{-5.592} \approx 1.81 \approx 2$$

26. ***(19)*** $A \rightarrow B$ (Reversible adiabatic)

$\therefore \quad T_1V_1^{\gamma-1} = T_2V_2^{\gamma-1}$

$$T_1 = 750,\ V_1 = 5,\ T_2 = 150$$

$$\gamma = \frac{5}{3} \qquad \left(\text{from } C_{p,m} = \frac{5}{2}R\right)$$

$$\therefore \quad (750)(5)^{2/3} = (150)(V_2)^{2/3}$$

$$(5)^{5/3} = (V_2)^{2/3}$$

$$V_2 = (5)^{5/2}$$

Also, $q_{AB} = 0$ and $q_{AC} = RT_2 \ln 25$

$$\therefore \quad q_{BC} = nRT_2 \ln\left(\frac{V_3}{V_2}\right)$$

$$= RT_2 \ln\left(\frac{V_3}{V_2}\right) \qquad (\because n = 1)$$

$$\Rightarrow \quad q_{AC} = q_{BC}$$

$\therefore$ Total heat absorbed $= RT_2 \ln\left(\frac{V_3}{V_2}\right) = RT_2 \ln 25$

$$\frac{V_3}{V_2} = 25$$

$$V_3 = (5)^2 \times V_2 = (5)^2 \times (5)^{5/2}$$

$$V_3 = (5)^{9/2}$$

Now, the value of, $6 \log V_3 = 6 \log (5)^{9/2}$

$$= 6 \times \frac{9}{2} \times \log 5$$

$$= 18.8 \approx 19$$

27. ***(b)*** $\Delta S° = S°(COCl_2) - [S°(CO) + S°(Cl_2)]$

$$= 69.1 - [47.3 + 53.3]$$

$$= -31.5 \text{ cal.mol}^{-1}\text{K}^{-1}$$

$$\Delta H° = -53.3 - [-26.4 + 0] = -26.9 \text{ kcal mol}^{-1}$$

$$\Delta G° = \Delta H° - T\Delta S° = -26.9 - 298\left(-\frac{31.5}{1000}\right)$$

$$= -17.51 \text{ kcal mol}^{-1}$$

$$\Delta G° = -2.303 RT \log K$$

$$\therefore \log K = \frac{-\Delta G°}{2.303 RT} = \frac{-(-17.51)}{2.303 \times 0.002 \times 298} = 12.76$$

Thus (i)—(q), (ii)—(p), (iii)—(s), (iv)—(r)

28. ***(c)*** (i) $\Delta G < 0$

(ii) $\Delta H° = \Delta E° + p\Delta V$

Also $\Delta H° = RT^2 \frac{d(\log K)}{dT}$ by van't Hoff equation

(iii) $\Delta S° = \frac{q_{rev}}{T} = \frac{nRT \log \frac{V_2}{V_1}}{T} = nR \log \frac{V_2}{V_1}$

$$\Delta G° = \Delta H° - T\Delta S° \Rightarrow \Delta G° = \Delta H° + T\left(\frac{d(\Delta G°)}{dT}\right)_p$$

By Gibb's Helmholtz equation, $\Delta S° = -\left(\frac{d(\Delta G°)}{dT}\right)_p$

(iv) $\Delta G° = -RT \log K$

(i) —(r) (ii)—(q, u)

(iii) —(s, t) (iv)—(p)

29. ***(c)*** The correct match is (i)-r, (ii)-p, (iii)-s, (iv)-q

(i) $2H_2(g) + O_2(g) \longrightarrow 2H_2O(g)$

$$\Delta_r H° = [2(BE)_{H-H} + (BE)_{O=O}] - 4(BE)_{O-H}$$

$$= (2 \times 104 + 118) - 4 \times 111 = -118 \text{ kcal mol}^{-1}$$

Thus, (i) $\rightarrow$ (r)

(ii) $CH_4(g) + 2O_2(g) \longrightarrow CO_2(g) + 2H_2O(g)$

$$\Delta_r H° = [4(BE)_{C-H} + 2(BE)_{O=O}] - [2(BE)_{C=O} + 4(BE)_{O-H}]$$

$$= (4 \times 87 + 2 \times 118) - (2 \times 193 + 4 \times 111)$$

$$= -246 \text{ kcal mol}^{-1}$$

Thus, (ii) $\rightarrow$ (p)

(iii) $CH_4(g) + Cl_2(g) \longrightarrow CH_3Cl(g) + HCl(g)$

$$\Delta_r H° = [4(BE)_{C-H} + (BE)_{Cl-Cl}] - [3(BE)_{C-H} + (BE)_{C-Cl} + (BE)_{H-Cl}]$$

$$= (4 \times 87 + 58) - [3 \times 87 + 79 + 103]$$

$$= -37 \text{ kcal mol}^{-1}$$

Thus (iii) $\rightarrow$ (s)

(iv) $C_2H_6(g) + Cl_2(g) \longrightarrow C_2H_5Cl(g) + HCl(g)$

$$\Delta_r H° = [6(BE)_{C-H} + (BE)_{C-C} + (BE)_{Cl-Cl}] - [5(BE)_{C-H} + (BE)_{C-Cl} + (BE)_{H-Cl}]$$

$$= [6 \times 87 + 83 + 58] - [5 \times 87 + 79 + 103]$$

$$= 46 \text{ kcal mol}^{-1}$$

Thus, (iv)–(q)

30. ***(a)*** If $\frac{d \log K}{dT} = \frac{\Delta H°}{2.303 RT^2}$

$$\int d \log K = \frac{\Delta H°}{2.303 R} \int \left(\frac{dT}{T^2}\right)$$

$$\therefore \quad \log K = \frac{-\Delta H°}{2.303 RT} + C \text{ (Constant)}$$

$$\therefore \quad \Delta H° = \frac{2.303 RT_1T_2}{(T_2 - T_1)} \log \frac{K_2}{K_1}$$

$$= \frac{2.303 \times 8.314 \times 10^{-3} \times 298 \times 373}{(373 - 298)} \times \log \frac{88.5}{8.85}$$

$$= 28.38 \text{ kJ}$$

Thus, (i)—(s)

$$\Delta G°_{298} = -2.303 \times 8.314 \times 10^{-3} \times 298 \times \log 8.85$$

$$= -5.40 \text{ kJ mol}^{-1}$$

Thus, (ii)—(p)

$$\Delta G°_{373} = -2.303 \times 8.314 \times 10^{-3} \times 373 \times \log 88.5$$

$$= -13.90 \text{ kJ mol}^{-1}$$

(iii)—(q)

$$K_1/K_2 = 0.1$$

Thus, (iv)—(r)

31. ***(a)*** $\log_{10} K = -\frac{2000}{T} + 5$

Also, $\Delta G° = \Delta H° - T\Delta S°$

$$\Delta G° = -2.303 RT \log K$$

Thus, $-2.303\,RT\log K = \Delta H° - T\Delta S°$

$\therefore \quad \log K = \dfrac{-\Delta H°}{2.303\,RT} + \dfrac{\Delta S°}{2.303\,R} \Rightarrow \dfrac{\Delta H°}{2.303\,R} = 2000$

$\therefore \quad \Delta H° = 2000 \times 2.303\,R = 2000 \times 2.303 \times 2 \times 10^{-3}$ kcal

$= 9.212$ kcal

Thus, (i) → (q)

$$\frac{\Delta S°}{2.303\,R} = 5$$

$\therefore \quad \Delta S° = 2.303 \times R \times 5 = 2.303 \times 2 \times 10^{-3} \times 5$ kcal

$= 0.023$ kcal

Thus, (ii) → (r)

$\Delta G° = \Delta H° - T\Delta S°$

$= 9.212 - 1000 \times 0.023 = -13.8$ kcal

Thus, (iii) → (s)

At 500 K

$$\log_{10} K = \frac{-2000}{500} + 5 = -4 + 5 = 1$$

$\therefore \quad K = 10$

Thus, (iv) → (p)

32. ***(a)*** (i) W_1 (for an isothermal expansion in which p_{ext} is constant.)

1 bar $= 1.0 \times 10^5$ Pa

$$W_1 = -\int_{V_1}^{V_2} p_{ext}\,dV = -p_{ext}[V_2 - V_1]$$

$= -1 \times 10^5$ Pa $[10.0\text{ m}^3 - 1.0\text{ m}^3]$

$W_1 = -9.0 \times 10^5\text{ m}^3\text{ Pa} = -9.0 \times 10^5$ J

Work done by the system $= -9 \times 10^5$ J

Thus, (i) → (s)

(ii) W_2 (for an isothermal compression at 10.0 bar external pressure)

$$W_2 = -\int_{V_1}^{V_2} p_{ext}\,dV = -p_{ext}[V_2 - V_1]$$

$= -10 \times 10^5$ Pa $[1.0\text{ m}^3 - 10.0\text{ m}^3]$

$= +9.0 \times 10^6\text{ m}^3\text{ Pa} = +9.0 \times 10^6$ J

Work done on the system $= +9.0 \times 10^6$ J

Thus, (ii) → (q)

(iii) $W_3 = W_{total} = W_1 + W_2 = -9.0 \times 10^5 + 9.0 \times 10^6 = 8.1 \times 10^6$

Thus, $W_3 = W_1 + W_2 = 8.1 \times 10^6$

Since, $W_{total} \neq 0$ hence, work is not a state function but work is a path function.

Thus, (iii) → (p)

(iv) Most efficient process will be one that is carried out reversibly.

$$W_4 = -\int_{V_1}^{V_2} p_{ext}\,dV = -nRT\int_{V_1}^{V_2}\frac{dV}{V} = -2.303\,nRT\log\frac{V_2}{V_1}$$

Here, $\quad n = \dfrac{pV}{RT}$

$V_2 = 1.0\text{ m}^3,\ V_1 = 10.0\text{ m}^3$

$\therefore \quad W_4 = -2.303\left(\dfrac{pV}{RT}\right)RT\log\dfrac{V_2}{V_1}$

$W_4 = -(10 \times 10^5\text{Pa})\,(1.0\text{m}^3) \times 2.303\log\dfrac{1}{10}$

$= 2.303 \times 10^6$ J

Thus, (iv) → (r)

33. ***(i) 0.1635, (ii) −0.65***

As we know,

$\Delta G° = -2.303\,RT\log K_p$

$= -2.303 \times 8.314 \times 10^{-3}$ kJ mol^{-1} K^{-1} $\times 298$ K $\log 1.3 \times 10^3$

$= -17.77$ kJ mol^{-1}

$\Delta G° = \Delta H° - T\Delta S°$

$\therefore \Delta S° = \dfrac{\Delta H° - \Delta G°}{T} = \dfrac{-66.5\text{kJ} - (-17.77)}{298} = -0.1635$ kJ mol^{-1}

As we know,

$\Delta G = \Delta G° + 2.303\,RT\log Q$

$\Delta G = -17.77 + 2.303 \times 8.314 \times 10^{-3}$ kJ mol^{-1} K^{-1} $\times 298$ K$(\log 10^3)$

$= -0.65$ kJ mol^{-1}

34. ***(i) 64.0, (ii) 1392***

Stage I.	I	⟶	II
Volume	V_1(22.4L)		V_1(22.4)
Temperature	T_1(273K)		T_2(546 K)
Stage II	II	⟶	III
Volume	V_1(22.4L)		V_2(64 L)
Temperature	T_2(546K)		T_1(273 K)
Stage III	III	⟶	I
Volume	V_2(64 L)		V_1(22.4 L)
Temperature	T_1(273K)		T_1(273 K)

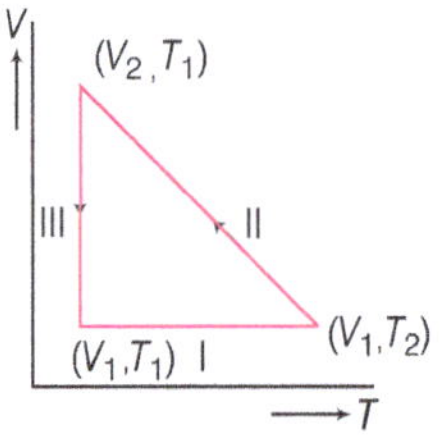

Stage I. $W = 0$ (since $\Delta V = 0$)

Stage II. $\left(\dfrac{V_2}{V_1}\right)^{\gamma-1} = \left(\dfrac{T_2}{T_1}\right)$ for

adiabatic expansion, $\gamma = \dfrac{C_p}{C_V} = \dfrac{3\text{ cal} + 2\text{ cal}}{3\text{ cal}} = 1.66$

$(C_p - C_V = R : C_p = R + C_V)$

$\therefore \quad \left(\dfrac{V_2}{22.4}\right)^{1.66-1} = \left(\dfrac{546}{273}\right) = 2$

$\therefore \quad 0.66\log\left(\dfrac{V_2}{22.4}\right) = \log(2) = 0.3010$

$\log\left(\dfrac{V_2}{22.4}\right) = \dfrac{0.3010}{0.66} \Rightarrow V_2 \approx 64.0$ L

Since, process is adiabatic

$$q = 0$$

$$\therefore \quad W = -\Delta E = -C_V \Delta T$$

$$= -3\,(273 - 546) = 819 \text{ cal}$$

Stage III. process is isothermal

$$W = -2.303\, nRT \log \frac{V_2}{V_1}$$

$$= -2.303 \times 1 \text{ mol} \times 2 \text{ cal mol}^{-1}\text{ K}^{-1} \times 273\text{K} \log \frac{22.4}{64.0}$$

$$= 573.3 \text{ cal}$$

Total work $= 819 + 573.3 = 1392.3 \approx 1392$ cal

35. ***(i) 1523, (ii) –1407***

(i) In an isochoric process

$$q_{\text{isochoric}} = nC_V \Delta T$$

for monoatomic gas

$$C_V = \frac{3}{2} R$$

$$\Delta T = T_B - T_A = 600 - 300 = 300 \text{ K}$$

$$n = \frac{p_A V_A}{RT_A} = \frac{1 \text{ atm} \times 10 \text{ L}}{0.0821 \text{ L atm mol}^{-1}\text{K}^{-1} \times 300 \text{ K}}$$

$$q_{\text{isochoric}} = 0.407 \times \frac{3}{2} \times R \times 300 \text{ K}$$

$$= 0.407 \times \frac{3}{2} \times 8.314 \times 300$$

$$= 1522.7 \text{ J} \simeq 1523 \text{ J}$$

(ii) Workdone during isothermal expansion ($B \rightarrow C$)

$$W = -nRT \ln \frac{V_2}{V_1} \left(\frac{V_2}{V_1} = 2 \right)$$

$$= -0.407 \text{ moles} \times 8.314 \text{ J mol}^{-1}\text{ K}^{-1} \times 600 \times \ln 2$$

$$= -1407.3 \text{ J} \simeq -1407 \text{ J}$$

36. ***(a)*** Among the given reactions, only one i.e. (iv) which have $\Delta H = \Delta U$ because the value of Δn_g is zero.

As we know,

$$\Delta H = \Delta U + \Delta n_g RT \quad \text{(at constant } T\text{)}$$

if $\Delta n_g = 0$ then $\Delta H = \Delta U$

37. ***(d)*** Among the given functions, four i.e, internal energy (i), temperature (ii), enthalpy (iv) and pressure (v) are state functions.

38. ***(d)*** Among the given relation, regarding the given equation, $G = H - TS$ only four i.e. (i), (ii), (iii) and (iv) are correct.

Given, $\quad G = H - TS$

Also $\quad H = U + pV$

$\therefore \quad G = (U + pV) - TS$

$\therefore \quad dG = (dU + pdV + Vdp) - TdS - SdT$

By First law, $dU = q - W = q - pdV$ and $TdS = q$

$\therefore \quad dU = TdS - pdV$

$$dG = TdS - pdV + pdV + Vdp - TdS - SdT$$

$$dG = -SdT + Vdp \quad \text{...(a)}$$

If p = constant

$dp = 0$

$$\therefore \quad (dG)_p = -SdT \quad \text{...(b)}$$

If $\quad T$ = constant, $\quad dT = 0$

$$\therefore \quad (dG)_T = Vdp \quad \text{...(c)}$$

Since, $V = \frac{RT}{p}$ for one mole

$$\therefore \quad (dG)_T = RT \frac{dp}{p} \quad \text{...(d)}$$

39. ***(d)*** Among the given properties, only one i.e, (vi) is an extensive properties while others i.e., (i), (ii), (iii), (iv), (v) and (vii) are intensive properties.

40. ***(c)*** For which, $\Delta n_g > 0$, the standard entropy change ($\Delta S°$) will be positive. So, only four i.e., (i), (iii), (v) and (vii) for which $\Delta S°$ will be positive.

(i) $\Delta n_g = 3 - 2 = 1$	(ii) $\Delta n_g = 1 - 3 = -2$
(iii) $\Delta n_g = 5 - 4 = 1$	(iv) $\Delta n_g = 2 - 3 = -1$
(v) $\Delta n_g = 2 - 0 = 2$	(vi) $\Delta n_g = 2 - 4.5 = -2.5$
(vii) $\Delta n_g = 1 - 0 = 1$	

41. ***(a)*** Among the given equations, only three i.e, (i), (iii), (v) represent the standard enthalpy of formation.

$\because$ The standard enthalpy of formation is the heat change when 1 mole of substance is formed from its element in their most stable states.

So, (ii), (iv), (vi) and (vii) do not represent the standard enthalpy of formation equation.

42. ***(a)*** Among the given chemical changes, only four i.e. (i), (v), (vi) and (vii) in which work done will be negative.

If the value of Δn_g is negative then the work will be done on the system i.e., $w = +$ ve, while the value of Δn_g is positive then the work will be done by the system i.e, $w = -$ ve.

Hence, Δn_g for

(i) $\Delta n_g = +1$	(ii) $\Delta n_g = -2.5$
(iii) $\Delta n_g = -2$	(iv) $\Delta n_g = 0$
(v) $\Delta n_g = 1$	(vi) $\Delta n_g = 2$
(vii) $\Delta n_g = 1$	

43. ***(c)*** Among the reactions, only three i.e, (ii), (iv) and (vi) represents the enthalpy of combustion while reaction (i) does not give complete oxidation of C_6H_6 since, CO can be further oxidised to CO_2 and in reaction (iii) C(g) is in gaseous state and incomplete oxidation.

(v) is a hydrogenation reaction and not combustion.

(vii) does not represents the enthalpy of combustion as 2 moles of methanol is taken.

Check Through PYQs : JEE Advanced

1. ***(8120)*** Given,

$$n = 5 \text{ mol} \Rightarrow C_{V,m} = 12 \text{ JK}^{-1}\text{mol}^{-1}$$

$$R = 8.3 \text{ JK}^{-1}\text{mol}^{-1} \Rightarrow T_2 = 415 \text{ K}$$

$$T_1 = 335 \text{ K} \Rightarrow V_2 = 20 \text{ L}$$

$$V_1 = 10 \text{ L}$$

Now, from the graph it is clear that

$X \to Y$ is an isothermal process ($dT = 0$)

So, $\Delta H_{X \to Y} = n\, C_p dT = 0$

Also, $Y \to Z$ is an isochoric process

$$\Delta U_{Y \to Z} = n\, C_V dT$$
$$\Delta U_{Y \to Z} = 5 \times 12 \times (415 - 335)$$
$$\Delta U_{Y \to Z} = 4800 \text{ J}$$
$$\Delta H_{Y \to Z} = \Delta U_{Y \to Z} + \Delta(pV)$$

or
$$\Delta H_{Y \to Z} = \Delta U_{Y \to Z} + nR\Delta T$$
$$\Delta H_{Y \to Z} = 4800 + (5 \times 8.3 \times 80)$$
$$\Delta H_{Y \to Z} = 8120 \text{ J}$$

2. ***(7)*** $A \longrightarrow B$ (Reversible adiabatic)

$\therefore$
$$T_1V_1^{\gamma-1} = T_2V_2^{\gamma-1}$$
$$T_1 = 600, V_1 = 10, T_2 = 60,$$
$$\gamma = \frac{5}{3} \qquad \left(\text{from } C_{p,m} = \frac{5}{2}R\right)$$

$\therefore$
$$(600)(10)^{2/3} = (60)(V_2)^{2/3}$$
$$(V_2)^{1/2} = (10)^{5/3} \Rightarrow V_2 = (10)^{5/2}$$

Also, $q_{AB} = 0$ and $q_{AC} = RT_2 \ln 10$

$\therefore \quad q_{BC} = nRT_2 \ln\left(\frac{V_3}{V_2}\right) = RT_2 \ln\left(\frac{V_3}{V_2}\right) \qquad (\because n = 1)$

$\Rightarrow \quad q_{AC} = q_{BC}$

$\therefore$ Total heat absorbed $= RT_2 \ln\left(\frac{V_3}{V_2}\right) = RT_2 \ln 10$

$\Rightarrow \quad \ln\left(\frac{V_3}{V_2}\right) = \ln 10 \Rightarrow V_3 = 10\,V_2$

$$V_3 = 10\,(10)^{5/2} = (10)^{7/2}$$

Now, the value of $2\log V_3 = 2\log(10)^{7/2} = 2 \times \frac{7}{2}\log 10 = 7$

3. ***(b, c)*** In the given curve, AC represents isochoric process as volume at both the points is same, i.e. V_1.

Similarly, AB represents **isothermal process** (as both the points are at T_1 temperature) and BC represents **isobaric process** as both the points are at p_2 pressure.

Now (i) for option (a)

$$q_{AC} = \Delta U_{BC} = nC_V(T_2 - T_1)$$

where, $n =$ number of moles

$C_v =$ specific heat capacity at constant volume

However, $W_{AB} \neq p_2(V_2 - V_1)$ instead

$$W_{AB} = nRT_1 \ln\left(\frac{V_2}{V_1}\right)$$

So, this option is incorrect.

(ii) For option (b)

$$q_{BC} = \Delta H_{AC} = nC_p(T_2 - T_1)$$

where, $C_p =$ specific heat capacity at constant pressure

Likewise, $\quad W_{BC} = -p_2(V_1 - V_2)$

Hence, this option is correct.

(iii) For option (c)

as $nC_p(T_2 - T_1) < nC_V(T_2 - T_1)$

so $\Delta H_{CA} < \Delta U_{CA}$ and $q_{AC} = \Delta U_{BC}$

Hence, this option is also correct.

(iv) For option (d)

Although $q_{BC} = \Delta H_{AC}$

but $\Delta H_{CA} \not> \Delta U_{CA}$

Hence, this option is incorrect.

4. ***(a,c,d)***

(a) The work done on the gas is maximum during irreversible compression.

(b) Internal energy change,

$$\Delta U = nC_V\Delta T$$

When gas is expanded reversibly with $T_1 = T_2, \Delta U = 0$

When gas is expanded reversibly under adiabatic condition, $T_1 = T_2$.

$\therefore \quad \Delta U = -\text{ve}$

(c) $W = -p_{ext}\Delta V$

In free expansion, external pressure = 0

$\therefore \quad W = 0$

From first law of thermodynamics,

$$\Delta U = q + W$$

$\therefore \quad \Delta U = q$

If the expansion is carried out isothermally,

$$q = 0$$

($\because \Delta U = 0$ for isothermal process)

$\therefore$ It is an adiabatic process.

If the expansion is carried out adiabatically,

$$\Delta U = 0$$

($\because q = 0$ for adiabatic process)

$\therefore$ It is an adiabatic process.

Therefore, it is an isothermal process.

(d)

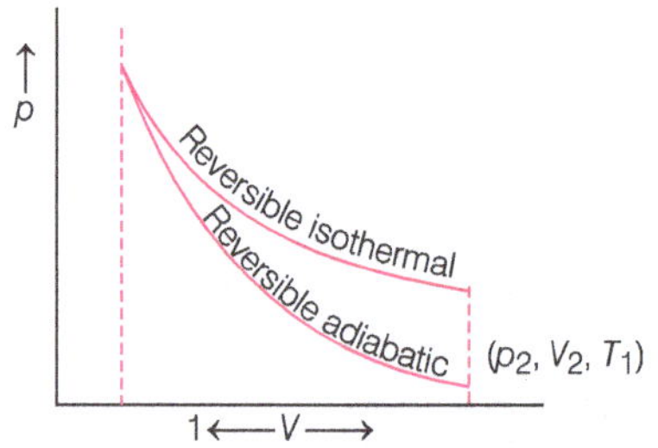

Thus, area under the curve in reversible adiabatic expansion is lesser than in reversible isothermal expansion.

5. ***(a,b,c)*** Given, $w = -\int p_{ext}dV$

For 1 mole van der Waals' gas

$$p = \left(\frac{RT}{V-b} - \frac{a}{V^2}\right)$$

For reversible process, $p_{ext} = p_{gas}$

$$w = -\int \left(\frac{RT}{V-b} - \frac{a}{V^2}\right) dV$$

But, it is not applicable for irreversible process which are carried out very fast. So, work done is calculated assuming final pressure remains constant throughout the process.

Thus, statement (a), (b) and (c) correct while statement (d) is incorrect.

6. ***(0.31)*** S_T and S_0 are entropies of the phases at temperatures T and 0 K, respectively.

$$S = S_\alpha + \int C_p \frac{dT}{T} \quad [S_0 = 0 \text{ at } 0\text{ K}]$$

$$\Rightarrow \quad S_\alpha = S_0 + \int (C_p)_\alpha \frac{dT}{T}$$

$$\Rightarrow \quad S_\beta = S_0 + \int (C_p)_\beta \frac{dT}{T}$$

$$\Rightarrow \quad S_\beta - S_\alpha = [(C_p)_\beta - (C_p)_\alpha] \int \frac{dT}{T}$$

Given, $C_{p_\beta} - C_{p_\alpha} = 1$

$S_\beta - S_\alpha = \ln T + C$ at any temperature T.

$\Rightarrow (S_\beta - S_\alpha)_{T_2} - (S_\beta - S_\alpha)_{T_1} = \ln T_2 - \ln T_1$

$T_2 = 600$ K, $T_1 = 300$ K, from the graph $S_\beta - S_\alpha$ at 600°C = 1

$$(1) - (S_\beta - S_\alpha)_{300} = \ln 600 - \ln 300$$

$$1 - (S_\beta - S_\alpha)_{300} = \ln 2 = 0.69$$

$$\Rightarrow \quad (S_\beta - S_\alpha)_{300} = 1 - 0.69$$

$$= 0.31 \text{ J mol}^{-1}\text{K}^{-1}$$

7. ***(300)*** Change in Gibbs free energy transition from α to β phase = 0

Thus, $\Delta H = T\Delta S$

$$\Delta H \text{ (at 600 K)} = 600 \times 1 \quad [\because \Delta S = 1]$$

$$= 600 \text{ J mol}^{-1}$$

According to Kirchhoff's law,

$$\Delta H_f - \Delta H_i = C_p(T_f - T_i) \quad \ldots\text{(i)}$$

Using the Eq. (i),

$$\Delta H_{600} - \Delta H_{300} = 1 \times (C_{p,\beta} - C_{p,\alpha})(600 - 300)$$

$$600 - \Delta H_{300} = 1 \times 1 \times 300$$

$$\Delta H_{300} = 600 - 300$$

$$= 300 \text{ J mol}^{-1}$$

8. ***(i) (166.28)*** $\Delta G° = -RT \ln K \quad \ldots$(i)

Also, $\Delta G° = \Delta H° - T\Delta S° \quad \ldots$(ii)

Comparing Eqs. (i) and (ii),

$$-RT \ln K = \Delta H° - T\Delta S°$$

Given, $K = \dfrac{p_Z}{p°}$ and $p° = 1$ bar

So, $-RT \ln\left(\dfrac{p_Z}{1}\right) = \Delta H° - T\Delta S°$

$$\ln\left(\frac{p_Z}{1}\right) = \frac{-\Delta H°}{RT} + \frac{\Delta S°}{R} \quad \ldots\text{(iii)}$$

In graph, slope $= \dfrac{-\Delta H°}{R}$

$$\text{Slope} = 10^4\left(\frac{Y_2 - Y_1}{X_2 - X_1}\right) = 10^4\left(\frac{-7+3}{12-10}\right)$$

$$= 10^4\left(-\frac{4}{2}\right) = -2 \times 10^4$$

Therefore, $-2 \times 10^4 = -\dfrac{\Delta H°}{R}$

$\Rightarrow \quad 2 \times 10^4 \times 8.314 = \Delta H°$

$$\Rightarrow \quad \Delta H° = 166280 \text{ J mol}^{-1}$$

$$= 166.28 \text{ kJ mol}^{-1}$$

(ii) (141.34) From graph, $\dfrac{10^4}{T} = 10$

Therefore, $T = 10^3$ K

Also, $\ln\left(\dfrac{p_2}{1}\right) = -3$

Substituting the value in Eq. (iii),

$$\ln\left(\frac{p}{1}\right) = -\frac{\Delta H°}{RT} + \frac{\Delta S°}{R}$$

$$-3 = -\frac{2 \times 10^4 \times R}{R \times 10^3} + \frac{\Delta S°}{R}$$

$$\Rightarrow \quad \frac{\Delta S°}{R} = 20 - 3 = 17$$

$$\Rightarrow \quad \Delta S° = +17 \times R$$

$$= +17 \times 8.314$$

$$= 141.34 \text{ JK}^{-1}\text{ mol}^{-1}$$

9. ***(10)*** For process 1, entropy is constant thus, q is constant

$$\therefore \quad W_{\text{I}} = \Delta U = nC_{V,m}\Delta T$$

$$= -(2250 - 450)R = -1800\,R \quad \ldots\text{(i)}$$

$$\Delta U = n\,C_{V,m}\,\Delta T$$

$$-1800R = 1 \times \frac{5R}{2} \times \Delta T \Rightarrow \Delta T = -720 \text{ K}$$

$$T_2 - T_1 = -720 \text{ K}$$

$$T_2 = -720 \text{ K} + 900 \text{ K} = 180 \text{ K}$$

For process II,

$$W_{\text{II}} = -nRT_2 \ln\left(\frac{V_3}{V_2}\right)$$

$$= -1 \times R \times 180 \ln\left(\frac{V_3}{V_2}\right) \quad \ldots\text{(ii)}$$

As, both work done for process I and II are equal.

Therefore, $W_{\text{I}} = W_{\text{II}}$

$$-1800\,R = -R \times 180 \times \ln\left(\frac{V_3}{V_2}\right)$$

$$\ln\left(\frac{V_3}{V_2}\right) = \frac{1800}{180} \Rightarrow \ln\left(\frac{V_3}{V_2}\right) = 10$$

10. ***(a,b,d)*** **From state I to II** Reversible isothermal expansion takes place. So, following changes take place,

- Pressure decreases.
- Volume increases.
- Temperature remains constant.
- Enthalpy, H remains constant.
- Entropy, S for expansion increases.

So, all options follows the above mentioned conditions, hence, all graphs are correct for state I and II.

From state II to III Reversible adiabatic expansion takes place. So, following changes take place.

- Pressure decreases.
- Volume increases.
- Temperature decreases.
- Enthalpy, H decreases.
- Entropy, S remains constant.

But in option (c) H increases instead of decreasing, so only option (c) is incorrect.

All other options, i.e. (a), (b) and (d) follows the above mentioned conditions.

Therefore, correct graphical representations are (a), (b) and (d).

11. ***(0.25)*** Given : $A \rightleftharpoons B \ (p_A = 1\,\text{bar})$

Using $\quad \Delta G = \Delta G^\circ + RT \ln K_p$

At equilibrium : $\quad \Delta G^\circ = -RT \ln K_p$

$$\Delta G_1^\circ = -RT_1 \ln K_{p_1} \quad \ldots \text{(i)}$$

$$\Delta G_2^\circ = -RT_2 \ln K_{p_2} \quad \ldots \text{(ii)}$$

From Eqs. (i) and (ii),

$$\frac{\Delta G_1^\circ}{\Delta G_2^\circ} = \frac{T_1}{T_2} \times \frac{\ln K_{p_1}}{\ln K_{p_2}}$$

$$= \frac{1000}{2000} \times \frac{\ln(10)}{\ln(100)}$$

$$= \frac{1}{4} = 0.25$$

12. ***(c)*** By first law, $\Delta E = Q + W$

For isothermal expansion,

$$\Delta E = 0$$

$$\therefore \quad Q = -W$$

$$-Q_{\text{irrev}} = W_{\text{irrev}} = p\Delta V$$

$$= 3(2-1) = 3\,\text{L atm}$$

Also, $\quad \Delta S_{\text{surr}} = \frac{Q_{\text{irrev}}}{T} = \frac{(-3 \times 101.3)\,\text{J}}{300\,\text{K}}$

$$= -\frac{303.9}{300} = -1.013\,\text{JK}^{-1}$$

13. ***(90.39)*** The combustion reaction is

$$2\text{Hg}(g) + \text{O}_2(g) \longrightarrow 2\text{HgO}(s)$$

Given, heat capacity of calorimeter,

$$C = 20\,\text{kJ K}^{-1}$$

Initial temperature, $T_i = 298\,\text{K}$

Final temperature, $T_f = 312.8\,\text{K}$

Change in temperature, $\Delta T_f = 312.8 - 298 = 14.8\,\text{K}$

Heat evolved in reaction, $q = C\Delta T = 20 \times 14.8 = 296\,\text{kJ}$

Since, the reaction is taking place under constant volume

$$\Delta U_r = -296\,\text{kJ}$$

Enthalpy of reaction,

$$\Delta H_r^\circ = \Delta U^\circ + \Delta n_g RT$$

$$\Delta H_r^\circ = -296\,\text{kJ} - 3\,\text{mol}^{-1} \times 8.3 \times 10^{-3}\,\text{kJ K}^{-1}\,\text{mol}^{-1} \times 298\,\text{K}$$

$$\Delta H_r^\circ = -296\,\text{kJ} - 7.42\,\text{kJ} = -303.42\,\text{kJ}$$

Also, $\quad \Delta H_r^\circ = 2\Delta H_f^\circ[\text{HgO}(s)] - 2\Delta H_f^\circ[\text{Hg}(g)] - \Delta H_f^\circ[\text{O}_2(g)]$

$$-303.42 = 2\Delta H_f^\circ[\text{HgO}(s)] - 2 \times 61.32\,\text{kJ mol}^{-1} - 0$$

$$\Delta H_f^\circ[\text{HgO}(s)] = -303.42 + 122.64 = -180.78\,\text{kJ}$$

$$\Delta H_f^\circ[\text{HgO}(s)] = \frac{-180.78}{2} = -90.39\,\text{kJ mol}^{-1}.$$

$$|X| = 90.39\,\text{kJ mol}^{-1}$$

14. ***(c, d)*** The standard enthalpy of formation is defined as standard enthalpy change for formation of 1 mole of a substance from its elements, present in their most stable state of aggregation.

$$\frac{3}{2}\text{O}_2(g) \longrightarrow \text{O}_3(g);$$

$$\frac{1}{8}\text{S}_8(s) + \text{O}_2(g) \longrightarrow \text{SO}_2(g)$$

In the above two reactions standard enthalpy of reaction is equal to standard enthalpy of formation.

CHAPTER 5

Chemical Equilibrium

Learning Elements

Element 1 **Chemical Equilibrium, Law of Mass Action and Equilibrium Constant**

State of Equilibrium, Equilibrium in Physical Process, Equilibrium in Chemical Process, Laws of Mass Action, and Equilibrium Constant, Relation between K_C and Kp, Types of Chemical Equilibria, Relationship between Vapour Density and Degree of Dissociation, Application of Equilibrium Constants, Thermodynamics of Chemical Equilibrium

Element 2 **Le-Chatelier's Principle and Factors Affecting Chemical Equilibrium**

Effect of Changes in Concentration, Effect of Pressure, Effect of Volume, Effect of Temperature, Effect of Catalyst, Effect of Inert Gas, Application of Le-Chatelier's principle

Practice Elements

Practice Element 1 Target JEE Main
Practice Element 2 Target JEE Advanced

Trend Insights

JEE Main

	2024				2023				2022			
Topics	**E**	**M**	**T**	**O**	**E**	**M**	**T**	**O**	**E**	**M**	**T**	**O**
Chemical Equilibrium, Law of Mass Action and Equilibrium Constant	4	3	1	8	–	–	3	3	–	–	2	2
Le-Chatelier's Principle and Factors Affecting Chemical Equilbrium	1	–	–	1	–	2	–	2	–	–	–	–

E = Easy, **M** = Medium, **T** = tough, **O** = Overall

Current Dynamics

- Moderate level of questions has been asked from calculation of equilibrium constants (K_c or K_p) based on the initial and equilibrium concentration in recent year.
- Most of the questions were asked from solubility product, common ion effect and application of Le-chatelier's in past years.
- Overall weightage of this chapter has increased in 2024 alongwith difficulty level.

JEE Advanced

Typology	Years				
	2024	**2023**	**2022**	**2021**	**2020**
1. Simple MCQs	–	–	–	–	–
2. One or More than one correct	–	–	–	–	–
3. Numerical Value/Integer	–	1	–	–	1
4. Matching Type	–	–	–	–	–
5. Paragraph Based	–	–	–	–	–

Current Dynamics

- Numerical value type question asked in 2023 from thermodynamics of chemical equilibrium.
- Mostly numerical value type questions were asked in this chapter. No direct question were asked in recent years.

Insightful Advice

- Students are advised to understand the concept of Le-chatelier's principle in the context of temperature changes and how it can be quantitatively related to thermodynamic properties.
- Study the condition for spontaneity ($\Delta G = 0$) and focus the relationship between Gibbs free energy and the equilibrium constant.
- Study the relationship between K_c and K_p and the equilibrium expression in terms of partial pressure.

Element 1 Chemical Equilibrium, Laws of Mass, Action and Equilibrium Constant

Chemical equilibrium is a fundamental concept in chemistry It describes the state of a reversible reaction when the rates of the forward and reverse processes are equal.

State of Equilibrium

In a closed system where the reactants or the products cannot escape, reactions rarely achieve completion. Instead, some reactants remain, and the concentration of products and reactants stabilise over time. At that point, when there is no further change in concentration of reactant and product, the reaction is said to have reached equilibrium.

Types of Equilibrium

The concept of equilibrium is applied to both physical and chemical processes.

(i) The equilibrium that exists in physical processes like evaporation of water, sublimation, dissolution of gases in liquids is called **physical equilibrium.**

(ii) The equilibrium that exits in chemical reactions like reaction of N_2 and H_2, decomposition of calcium carbonate, dissociation of PCl_5, is called **chemical equilibrium.**

Equilibrium in Physical Processes

This equilibrium is established between different physical states (or phases) of a substance at a particular temperature. As there are three physical states of matter, solid, liquid and gas, therefore three types of physical equilibrium exists as

- Solid $\rightleftharpoons$ Liquid : $[H_2O(s) \rightleftharpoons H_2O(l)]$
- Liquid $\rightleftharpoons$ Vapour : $[H_2O(l) \rightleftharpoons H_2O(g)]$
- Solid $\rightleftharpoons$ Vapour : $[H_2O(s) \rightleftharpoons H_2O(g)]$

1. Solid-Liquid Equilibrium

On heating a pure solid substance under atmospheric pressure, it gradually starts converting into liquid. Temperature at which solid and liquid are in equilibrium at atmospheric pressure is called the normal melting point of solid or normal freezing point of liquid.

e.g., $$H_2O(s) \rightleftharpoons H_2O(l)$$

The ice cubes melt to form water and some water in contact with ice may freeze to ice. Rates of transfer of molecules from ice to water and reverse transfer from water into ice are equal at 273 K and at atmospheric pressure because two opposing forces take place at the same time and at the same rate. Thus, in solid-liquid equilibrium,

- the system is in dynamic equilibrium.
- both the opposing processes occur simultaneously.
- both processes occur at the same rate and thus the amount of ice and water, remains constant.

2. Liquid-Vapour Equilibrium

Consider the evaporation of water in a closed vessel. On heating water, kinetic energy of molecules increases and more and more water molecules escape the surface of liquid. This process is called **vaporisation**. As the number of water molecules in vapour phase increases, some of them strike the liquid surface and convert back to liquid phase, this reverse process of vaporisation is called **condensation**.

After some time the rate of evaporation becomes equal to rate of condensation, thus a state of dynamic equilibrium is attained. Thus in liquid-vapour equilibrium,

$$H_2O(l) \rightleftharpoons H_2O(g)$$

$$\text{rate of evaporation} = \text{rate of condensation}$$

At equilibrium, the pressure exerted by the water molecules at a given temperature remains constant and is called vapour pressure of water. The water and water vapour remain in equilibrium position at atmospheric pressure and at 100°C in a closed vessel.

Temperature at which liquid is in equilibrium with its vapour at atmospheric pressure is called its normal boiling point. Boiling point of water = 100 °C at 1 atm (or at 1.013 bar) Boiling point alters as pressure varies.

JEE Spotlite

- At high altitude, the boiling point of water decreases due to decrease in atmospheric pressure.
- In a closed pressure cooker, the boiling point of water increases because the pressure inside the cooker in higher than atmospheric pressure.

3. Solid $\rightleftharpoons$ Vapour Equilibrium

Some solids directly form vapour without going into liquid state this phenomena is called **sublimation**.

We take the example of conversion of iodine to vapour for solid-vapour equilibrium. When iodine is heated in a closed vessel, after sometime the vessel gets filled up with violet vapours. The intensity of these violet coloured vapour increases with increase in time. After sometime, the intensity of colour becomes constant. At this stage, the rate of sublimation of solid becomes equal to the rate of condensation of vapours into solid. This stage is referred to as equilibrium state,

i.e. rate of sublimation $\rightleftharpoons$ rate of condensation

Or $I_2(\text{solid}) \rightleftharpoons I_2(\text{vapour})$

other e.g. are

$$\text{Camphor (solid)} \rightleftharpoons \text{Camphor (vapour)}$$
$$NH_4Cl\,(\text{solid}) \rightleftharpoons NH_4Cl\,(\text{vapour})$$

Equilibrium Involving Dissolution of Solids or Gases in Liquids

There are also physical equilibria which involve dissolution of solute (solid or gas) in a liquid solvent.

1. Solids in Liquids

When you dissolve a solute (solid) in a solvent (liquid), it dissolves upto a certain limit and after sometime no more solute can be dissolved in solvent. Such solution is called saturated solution. In a saturated solution, solute and solution remain in a state of dynamic equilibrium, like

$$\text{sugar} + H_2O \rightleftharpoons \text{sugar solution.}$$

This dynamic equilibrium can be studied by isotopic effect by using radioactive sugar. This radioactive sugar is added to a saturated solution of non-radioactive sugar. Initially there is no radioactivity in solution. But when dynamic equilibrium is attained, there is exchange between the radioactive and non-radioactive sugar molecules between the two phases.

Thus, the rate of formation of solution in which sugar goes into solution = Rate at which sugar in solution goes into solid state

Hence, radioactivity is transferred to both sides. Ratio of the radioactive to non-radioactive molecules in the solution increases and when dynamic equilibrium is attained, it becomes constant.

2. Gases in Liquids

When a gas is dissolved in water, an equilibrium is established between the gaseous molecule and dissolved molecules of the gas under pressure.

This equilibrium is attained under pressure, e.g. when CO_2 gas is dissolved in water under high pressure, there is a state of equilibrium between the CO_2 present in the solution and the vapours of the gas above the liquid surface at a given temperature.

$$CO_2(g) + H_2O(l) \rightleftharpoons CO_2(aq)$$

This equilibrium is explained by Henry's law. It states that the mole fraction of the gas in the solution is proportional to the partial pressure of the gas over the solution, $x = K_H p$.

where, K_H is the Henry's constant.

The amount of gas dissolved is determined by the pressure. for example When a soda water bottle is opened, the pressure decreases to the atmospheric pressure, so amount of gas dissolved in solution decreases and escapes rapidly.

Some features of physical equilibria are given below

Process	Property that becomes constant at equilibrium
Solid $\rightleftharpoons$ liquid	melting point or freezing point at constant pressure
Liquid $\rightleftharpoons$ vapour	vapour pressure [pressure of the vapours above the liquid] at constant temperature
Solute (s) + $H_2O\,(l) \rightleftharpoons$ solution (aq)	solubility (or concentration) of the solid solute at constant temperature
Gas (g) + $H_2O\,(l) \rightleftharpoons$ gas (aq)	solubility of the gas at constant pressure and temperature

Characteristics of Physical Equilibrium

Some of the important characteristics of equilibrium involving a physical process are as follows:

(i) Equilibrium is attained only in a closed system at a given temperature.

(ii) Equilibrium is dynamic in nature, i.e. the opposing processes do not stop but take place simultaneously and with the same rate.

(iii) At equilibrium, all the measurable properties of the system remain constant, like boiling point, melting point, vapour pressure.

(iv) The magnitude of parameters like pressure, concentration and temperature at any stage shows the extent of physical process upto which it has proceeded before reaching equilibrium.

Equilibrium in Chemical Processes

Like physical process, equilibrium in chemical process occurs when opposing process takes place in a chemical reaction. Such reactions are called **reversible reactions**.

Consider a reversible reaction,

$$P + Q \underset{\text{Backward Reaction}}{\overset{\text{Forward Reaction}}{\rightleftharpoons}} R + S$$

At the start of reaction, reactants undergo reaction to form product, i.e. initially only forward reaction takes place. After some time, when products are formed reverse reaction also takes place.

With time, rate of forward reaction decreases and rate of backward reaction increases and at a time rate of both reactions become equal.

$$\left(\frac{dx}{dt}\right)_f = \left(\frac{dx}{dt}\right)_b$$

Thus, the equilibrium is established in a system, when reactants combine to form products with the same rate at which products combine to form reactants. Such type of equilibrium established in chemical reactions is called **chemical equilibrium.**

At equilibrium state, concentrations of reactants and products do not change with time.

The variation of the reaction rates with time and attainment of chemical equilibrium may be represented as

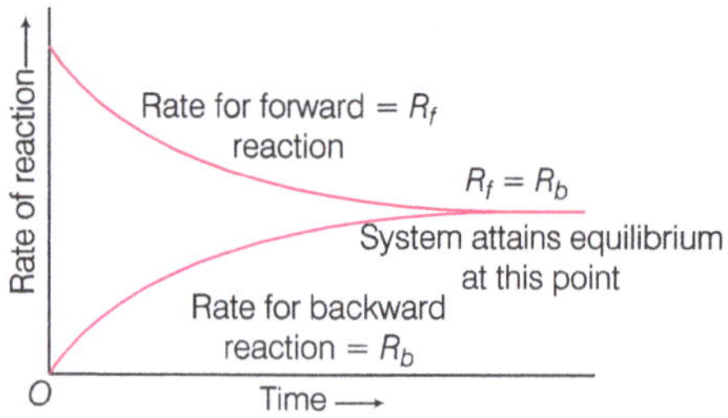

Variation in reaction rates for forward and backward reactions with time

We often use a double arrow ($\rightleftharpoons$) when writing an equation for a reversible reaction, i.e. both the forward and backward reaction occur simultaneously. e.g.

$$H_2(g) + I_2(g) \rightleftharpoons 2HI(g)$$

$$2Ag^+(aq) + Cu(s) \rightleftharpoons Cu^{2+}(aq) + 2Ag(s)$$

$$PCl_5(g) \rightleftharpoons PCl_3(g) + Cl_2(g)$$

Dynamic Nature of Chemical Equilibrium

At equilibrium, the reaction does not stop but the forward and backward reactions occur simultaneously at same rate. Thus, at equilibrium there is no change in concentration of reactants and products. Hence, the equilibrium state is a dynamic balance between the forward and backward reaction. This dynamic nature can be demonstrated by the following reaction.

$$N_2(g) + 3H_2(g) \rightleftharpoons 2NH_3$$

Forward reaction is

$$N_2 + 3H_2 \longrightarrow 2NH_3$$

When NH_3 starts forming, there is also the stage when NH_3 starts converting into N_2 and H_2.

$$\frac{1}{2}\frac{d[NH_3]}{dt} = k_f [N_2][H_2]^3$$

$$2NH_3 \longrightarrow N_2 + 3H_2$$

$$\frac{-1}{2}\frac{d[NH_3]}{dt} = k_b[NH_3]^2$$

A dynamic equilibrium is attained when rate of formation of NH_3 is equal to the rate of formation of N_2 and H_2. Graphically it is shown in below.

Concept Visualizer

The concept of chemical equilibrium can be visualised through given graphs.

This equilibrium ($k = 1$) shows that the concentration of reactant R is equal to the concentration of product (P)

This equilibrium ($k > 1$) shows that the concentration of reactant (R) is greater than product (P)

This equilibrium ($k < 1$) shows that the reactant concentration is less than the product (P)

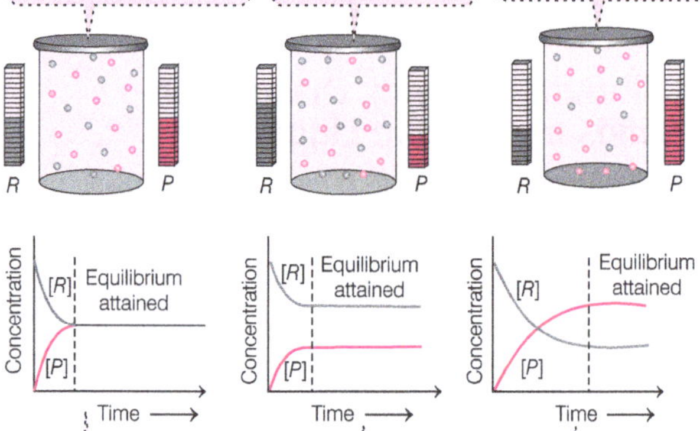

The concentration of reactant decreases while that of product increases till they arrive at the same constant equilibrium value

The concentration of reactant decreases while that of product increases till they arrive at a constant equilibrium value. The equilibrium concentration of reactant is more than the equilibrium concentration of product and the two curves do not intersect each other

The concentration of reactant decreases while that of product increases till they arrive at a constant equilibrium value. The equilibrium concentration of reactant is less than the equilibrium concentration of product and the two curves intersect.

Characteristics of Chemical Equilibrium

(i) Chemical equilibrium is attained only in reversible chemical reactions only.

(ii) Chemical equilibrium at a given temperature is characterised by constancy of certain observable properties such as pressure, concentration, density etc. i.e. these properties become constant at equilibrium

(iii) It can be attained from either side of the reaction i.e. from reactants as well as products side but only in a closed system

(iv) Chemical equilibrium is dynamic in nature.

(v) In the presence of a catalyst, equilibrium can be attained faster but does not alter the state of equilibrium.

(vi) At equilibrium, the free energy change (ΔG) during reaction is zero.

Law of Mass Action and Equilibrium Constant

"The law of mass action was put forward by **Guldberg** and **Waage** in 1864. This law states that the rate at which a substance reacts is proportional to its active mass and the rate of a chemical reaction is proportional to the product of the active masses of reacting substances at a given temperature". Here, the term active mass is the molar concentration in mol L^{-1}.

For a reaction,

$$A + B \longrightarrow C + D$$

According to law of mass action, rate of reaction $\propto [A]\ [B]$

or $\quad r = k[A][B]$

where k is the constant of proportionality.

This law of mass action can be applied to a reversible reaction to obtain a law of chemical equilibrium,

$$A + B \rightleftharpoons C + D$$

JEE Alert

Active masses of pure solids and liquids are taken as unity because their concentration remain same throughout the reaction. Since their activity coefficient approaches 1.

Thus, for the forward reaction

$$A + B \longrightarrow C + D$$

Rate of disappearance of A, $\dfrac{-d[A]}{dt} \propto [A]$

Rate of disappearance of B, $\dfrac{-d[B]}{dt} \propto [B]$

and rate of the forward reaction, $\left(\dfrac{dx}{dt}\right)_f \propto [A][B]$

$$\left(\frac{dx}{dt}\right)_f = K_f[A][B]$$

and similarly for the backward reaction

$$C + D \longrightarrow A + B$$

$$\left(\frac{dx}{dt}\right)_b = K_b[C][D]$$

where, K_f and K_b are rate constants of the forward and backward reactions respectively.

At dynamic equilibrium

$$\left(\frac{dx}{dt}\right)_f = \left(\frac{dx}{dt}\right)_b$$

$$K_f[A][B] = K_b\,[C][D]$$

$$\therefore \quad K_C = \frac{K_f}{K_b} = \frac{[C][D]}{[A][B]}$$

where K_c is called equilibrium constant. For a general reversible reaction,

For reaction $\quad aA + bB \rightleftharpoons cC + dD$

$$K_C = \frac{[C]^c[D]^d\ (\text{products})}{[A]^a[B]^b\ (\text{reactants})}$$

This represents equilibrium equation and is also known as the law of **chemical equilibrium.**

Thus, law of chemical equilibrium can be stated as :

At a given temperature, the product of concentrations of the reaction products raised to the respective stoichiometric coefficient in the balanced chemical equation divided by the product of concentrations of the reactants raised to their individual stoichiometric coefficients has a constant value.

As usual, square brackets $[A]$, $[B]$, $[C]$ and $[D]$ indicate the molar concentration of the substance (say A, B, C, and D) within brackets.

$$[A] = \frac{\text{mol}}{\text{litre}}\ (\text{mol}L^{-1})$$

Solved Booster 1.1

For the reaction, $A \rightleftharpoons B + C, \left(\dfrac{dx}{dt}\right)_f = k[A]$

If rate is 0.05 mol L^{-1} h^{-1} at $[A] = 0.170$ mol L^{-1} and $K_C = 0.5$ mol L^{-1}. The rate constant of backward reaction is

(a) 0.5882 L mol^{-1} h^{-1} (b) 0.9342 L mol^{-1} h^{-1}
(c) 0.3244 L mol^{-1} h^{-1} (d) 0.4732 L mol^{-1} h^{-1}

Solution *(a)*

$$\left(\frac{dx}{dt}\right)_f = K_f[A]$$

$$0.05\ \text{mol}\ L^{-1}\ h^{-1} = K_f[0.170]\ \text{mol}L^{-1}$$

$$K_f = 0.2941\ h^{-1}$$

Since, $K_f/K_b = 0.50$ mol $L^{-1} = K_C$

$$K_b = \frac{0.2941}{0.50} = 0.5882\ L\ mol^{-1}h^{-1}$$

Equilibrium Constant

The ratio of the concentrations of the products raised to the power of their stoichiometric coefficients to the concentrations of reactants raised to the power of their stoichiometric coefficients at equilibrium state is called the equilibrium constant (K).

For a reversible reaction at equilibrium,

$$aA + bB \rightleftharpoons cC + dD$$

The equilibrium constant (K) can be expressed in three ways:

(i) **Equilibrium constant is terms of molar concentration (K_C)** When the reactants and products are present is liquid, aqueous or gaseous state, the equilibrium constant is expressed in term of molar concentrations (molarity) as

$$K_C = \frac{[C]^c.[D]^d}{[A]^a.[B]^b}$$

(ii) **Equilibrium constant in terms of partial pressure (K_p).** When all the products and reactants of a reaction are in gaseous state, equilibrium constant can be expressed in terms of partial pressures as

$$K_p = \frac{p_C^c \cdot p_D^d}{p_A^a \cdot p_B^b}$$

(iii) **Equilibrium constant in terms of mole fraction (K_χ)** Using Dalton's law of partial pressure, equilibrium constant can also be expressed in terms of mole fraction (χ) as

$$K_\chi = \frac{\chi_C^c \cdot \chi_D^d}{\chi_A^a \cdot \chi_B^b}$$

Note According to Dalton's law of partial pressure,

$$p_i = \chi . p$$

where, p is the total pressure

JEE Spotlite

- Equilibrium constants are really defined in terms of activity, not concentration.
- Concentrations are related to activities by an activity coefficient (γ) to account ionic strength differences.
- The activity of a substance in a chemical reaction is a measure of its effective concentration relative to a standard state. It is defined as the ratio of the substance's concentration (or partial pressure for gases) to its standard concentration (or standard pressure).

The equilibrium constant is given by $K_C = \frac{(a_C)^c (a_B)^d}{(a_A)^a (a_B)^b}$

Solved Booster 1.2

In the following gaseous phase equilibrium in a 5 L flask at constant temperature, number of moles of SO_2 and SO_3 are equal. The number of moles of O_2 at equilibrium is

$$2SO_2 + O_2 \rightleftharpoons 2SO_3; K_C = 5$$

(a) 3 mol (b) 2 mol (c) 5 mol (d) 1 mol

Solution *(d)*

Let equilibrium moles of $SO_2 = SO_3 = x$ and that of $O_2 = y$

$$\therefore \quad [SO_2] = [SO_3] = \frac{x}{5} \text{ mol L}^{-1}$$

$$[O_2] = \frac{y}{5} \text{ mol L}^{-1}$$

$$K_C = \frac{[SO_3]^2}{[SO_2]^2[O_2]} = \frac{\left(\frac{x}{5}\right)^2}{\left(\frac{x}{5}\right)^2\left(\frac{y}{5}\right)} = 5 \text{ (given)}$$

$$y = 1$$

$\therefore$ Hence, O_2 at equilibrium = 1 mol

Characteristics of Equilibrium Constant

The magnitude of K_C is a measure of the extent to which reaction occurs. For any reaction the value of K_C

(i) is constant at a given temperature.

(ii) is independent of initial concentrations of the reactants.

Important Relationships Involving Equilibrium Constants

(i) If you reverse an equation, K_C or K_p is inverted i.e.

If $A + B \rightleftharpoons C + D$; $K_C = 10$

then $C + D \rightleftharpoons A + B$; $K_C' = 10^{-1}$

Thus, for **reverse chemical equation at equilibrium,** $K_C' = \frac{1}{K_C}$

(ii) If you multiply each of the coefficients in a balanced equation by a factor m, then equilibrium constant is raised to the same factor i.e. $K_C' = (K_C)^m$

If $\frac{1}{2}N_2 + \frac{1}{2}O_2 \rightleftharpoons NO; K_C = 5$

then for $N_2 + O_2 \rightleftharpoons 2NO; K_C' = K_C^2 = 5^2 = 25$

(iii) If you divide each of the coefficients in a balanced equation by the factor m, then new equilibrium constant is m^{th} root of the previous value., i.e. $K_c' = (K_c)^{1/m}$

If $2SO_2 + O_2 \rightleftharpoons 2SO_3$; $K_C = 25$

then for $SO_2 + \frac{1}{2}O_2 \rightleftharpoons SO_3$; $K_C' = (K_C)^{1/2} = \sqrt{25} = 5$

(iv) When you combine (i.e. add) individual equations, multiply their equilibrium constants to obtain the equilibrium constant for the net reaction.

If K_1, K_2, K_3 are stepwise equilibrium constants for

$$A \rightleftharpoons B \quad \ldots\text{(i)}$$

$$B \rightleftharpoons C \quad \ldots\text{(ii)}$$

$$C \rightleftharpoons D \quad \ldots\text{(iii)}$$

then for $A \rightleftharpoons D$ [obtained by adding Eqs. (i) (ii) and (iii)] net equilibrium constant is, $K = K_1 \cdot K_2 \cdot K_3$

JEE Alert

Equilibrium constant are never added nor substracted.

(v) Do not include concentration terms for pure solids and pure liquids in equilibrium constant expression.

Thus, for $C(s) + H_2O(g) \rightleftharpoons CO(g) + H_2(g)$

$$K_C = \frac{[CO]\,[H_2]}{[H_2O]}$$

and for $CaCO_3(s) \rightleftharpoons CaO(s) + CO_2(g)$

$$K_p = p_{CO_2} \quad \text{and} \quad K_C = [CO_2]$$

Solved Booster 1.3

For the equilibria given,

I. $C_6H_5COOH(aq) \rightleftharpoons C_6H_5COO^-(aq) + H^+(aq);$ $K_1 = 2 \times 10^{-5}$

II. $H_2O(l) \rightleftharpoons H^+(aq) + OH^-(aq); K_2 = 1 \times 10^{-14}$

The equilibrium constant of

III. $C_6H_5COO^-(aq) + H_2O(l) \rightleftharpoons C_6H_5COOH(aq) + OH^-(aq)$ is

(a) 5×10^{-10} (b) 3×10^{-10}

(c) 4×10^{-10} (d) 6×10^{-10}

Solution *(a)*

$$C_6H_5COOH(aq) \rightleftharpoons C_6H_5COO^-(aq) + H^+(aq);$$

$$K_1 = \frac{[C_6H_5COO^-][H^+]}{[C_6H_5COOH]} = 2 \times 10^{-5}$$

$$H_2O(l) \rightleftharpoons H^+(aq) + OH^-(aq)$$

$$K_2 = [H^+][OH^-]$$

$$K_3 = \frac{[C_6H_5COOH][OH^-]}{[C_6H_5COO^-]} = \frac{K_2}{K_1} = \frac{1 \times 10^{-14}}{2 \times 10^{-5}}$$

$$= 5 \times 10^{-10}$$

Note $H_2O(l)$ in K_2 and K_3 may be ignored.

JEE MAPPER

Example Similar to PYQ Asked in JEE Main 2024

For the given hypothetical reactions, the equilibrium constants are as follows:

$$X \rightleftharpoons Y; \quad K_1 = 1.0$$
$$Y \rightleftharpoons Z; \quad K_2 = 5.0$$
$$Z \rightleftharpoons W; \quad K_3 = 3.0$$

The equilibrium constant for the reaction $X \rightleftharpoons W$ is

(a) 16 (b) 18 (c) 15 (d) 32

Sol. *(c)*

$$X \rightleftharpoons Y; \quad K_1 = 1.0$$
$$Y \rightleftharpoons Z; \quad K_2 = 5.0$$
$$Z \rightleftharpoons W; \quad K_3 = 3.0$$

For the equilibrium constant value of

$$X \rightleftharpoons W; \quad K = K_1 \cdot K_2 \cdot K_3 = 1 \times 5 \times 3 = 15$$

Hence, option (c) is correct.

Competency Enhancer 1.1

The equilibrium constant for the reaction,

$NO_2(g) \rightleftharpoons NO(g) + \frac{1}{2}O_2(g)$ is $K_C = 4.89 \times 10^{-6}$. The value of K_C for the reaction given below is

$$2NO(g) + O_2(g) \rightleftharpoons 2NO_2(g) \text{ is}$$

(a) 4.182×10^{10} (b) 4.182×10^{11}

(c) 211.38×10^{8} (d) 0.231×10^{9}

Units of Equilibrium Constant

The units for K_C and K_p are determined on substituting concentration terms in mol L^{-1} and partial pressure in terms of bar (or atm or Pa). Thus, the units of equilibrium constant are based on molarity on pressure unless change in number of moles of gaseous products and reactant, $\Delta n_g = 0$

Equilibrium	Δn_g	K_p	K_C	K_x
$N_2(g) + O_2(g) \rightleftharpoons 2NO(g)$	0	—	—	Unitless
$PCl_5(g) \rightleftharpoons PCl_3(g) + Cl_2(g)$	1	bar	mol L^{-1}	Unitless
$2NO_2(g) \rightleftharpoons N_2O_4(g)$	−1	bar^{-1}	L mol^{-1}	Unitless

*Δn_g = (Stoichiometric coefficients of gaseous product) − (Stoichiometric coefficients of gaseous reactant) in a balanced chemical equation.

Relation between K_c and K_p

The relation between K_C and K_p can be established using ideal gas equation.

$$pV = nRT \Rightarrow p = \frac{n}{V}RT$$

Here $\frac{n}{V}$ i.e. moles per unit volume which is equal to concentration.

$$\therefore \quad p = [\text{active mass}]RT$$

Thus $p_A = [A](RT) \quad p_C = [C](RT)$

$p_B = [B](RT) \quad p_D = [D](RT)$

For a reaction $aA + bB \rightleftharpoons cC + dD$

$$K_C = \frac{[C]^c[D]^d}{[A]^a[B]^b} \quad \ldots(i)$$

$$\therefore \quad K_p = \frac{p_C^c \cdot p_D^d}{p_A^a \cdot p_B^b} \quad \ldots(ii)$$

Putting, $p = [\text{active mass}]\, RT$, in Eq. (ii)

$$K_p = \frac{[C]^c(RT)^c \cdot [D]^d(RT)^d}{[A]^a(RT)^a \cdot [B]^b(RT)^b}$$

$$= \frac{[C]^c \cdot [D]^d}{[A]^a \cdot [B]^b} \cdot (RT)^{(c+d)-(a+b)}.$$

$$K_p = K_C(RT)^{\Delta n_g}$$

where, Δn_g = (moles of gaseous products) − (moles of gaseous reactant)

JEE Alert

While computing value of Δn_g reactant and products in solid and liquid states are not considered. $K_p = K_C$, for all integral values of $\Delta n_g (= 0, < 0, > 0)$ such that $RT = 1$ or $T = \frac{1}{R} = \frac{1}{1.083} = 12.048$ K.

Relation between K_p and K_χ

According to Dalton's law, of partial pressure

$$p_i = \chi_i p$$

where p is total pressure.

Again for the reaction $aA + bB \rightleftharpoons cC + dD$

$$K_p = \frac{p_C^c \, p_D^d}{p_A^a \, p_B^b} \quad \ldots(i)$$

$$K_\chi = \frac{\chi_C^c \, \chi_D^d}{\chi_A^a \, \chi_B^b} \quad \ldots(ii)$$

K_χ is equilibrium constant when concentrations are in mole fraction.

Now $\quad p_C = \chi_C p \Rightarrow p_D = \chi_D p$

$\quad p_A = \chi_A p \Rightarrow p_B = \chi_B p$

$\therefore$ From Eq. (i) we get

$$K_p = K_\chi (p)^{\Delta n_g}$$

Relation between K_p, K_C and K_χ for different equilibrium reactions

Equilibrium	Δn_g	$K_p = K_c(RT)^{\Delta n_g}$	$K_p = K_\chi(p)^{\Delta n_g}$
$H_2(g) + I_2(g) \rightleftharpoons 2HI$	0	$K_p = K_C$	$K_p = K_\chi$
$N_2O_4(g) \rightleftharpoons 2NO_2(g)$	1	$K_p = K_C(RT)$	$K_p = pK_\chi$
$2SO_2(g) + O_2(g) \rightleftharpoons 2SO_3(g)$	−1	$K_C = K_p(RT)$	$K_x = pK_p$
$N_2(g) + 3H_2(g) \rightleftharpoons 2NH_3(g)$	−2	$K_C = K_p(RT)^2$	$K_x = p^2K_p$
$C(s) + O_2(g) \rightleftharpoons CO_2(g)$	0	$K_p = K_C$	$K_p = K_\chi$
$NH_4HS(s) \rightleftharpoons NH_3(g) + H_2S(g)$	2	$K_p = K_C(RT)^2$	$K_p = p^2K_\chi$
$NH_3(g) + H_2O(l) \rightleftharpoons NH_4OH(l)$	−1	$K_C = K_p(RT)$	$K_x = pK_p$

Solved Booster 1.4

Hydrogen is produced industrially by the steam-hydrocarbon re-forming process as given by

$$H_2O(g) + CH_4(g) \rightleftharpoons CO(g) + 3H_2(g)$$

If $K_C = 3.8 \times 10^{-3}$ at 1000 K,

The value of K_p at the same temperature is

Solution (25.61)

$\Delta n_g = (1 + 3) - (1 + 1) = 2$

$\therefore \quad K_p = K_C (RT)^{\Delta n_g}$

$= 3.8 \times 10^{-3} (0.0821 \times 1000)^2$

≈ 25.61 (units of K_p and K_C have been ignored)

Types of Chemical Equilibria

There are two types of chemical equilibria.

These are given below

Homogeneous Equilibrium

Equilibrium is said to be homogeneous if reactants and products are in same phase. For example, in the gaseous reaction, $N_2(g) + 3H_2(g) \rightleftharpoons 2NH_3(g)$, reactant and products are in the gaseous phase. Similarly, for the reaction,

$$CH_3COOH(l) + C_2H_5OH(l) \rightleftharpoons CH_3COOC_2H_5(l) + H_2O(l)$$

all the reactants and products are in the solution/liquid phase.

Solved Booster 1.5

If we start with 1 mole of A and 1 mole of B in 5 L flask, 0.5 mole of C is formed in the equilibrium of

$$A + B \rightleftharpoons C + D$$

The sum of molar concentration of each species if the reaction is carried with 2 moles of A and 1 mole of B in 5 L flask at the same temperature is

(a) 0.4 (b) 0.9

(c) 0.6 (d) 1.6

Solution (c)

		A +	B ⇌	C +	D	
Case I	Initial	1	1	0	0	
	change	$-x$	$-x$	$+x$	$+x$	$x = 0.5$
	At equilibrium	$(1-x)$	$(1-x)$	x	x	
Case II	Initial	2	1	0	0	
	change	$-y$	$-y$	$+y$	$+y$	
	At equilibrium	$(2-y)$	$(1-y)$	y	y	

$$\therefore \quad K_C = \frac{[C][D]}{[A][B]} = \frac{x^2/V^2}{\frac{(1-x)(1-x)}{V^2}}$$

$$= \frac{y^2/V^2}{\frac{(2-y)(1-y)}{V^2}}$$

Putting value of x, $K_C = \dfrac{\left(\frac{1}{2}\right)^2}{\left(\frac{1}{2}\right)\left(\frac{1}{2}\right)} = \dfrac{y^2}{(2-y)(1-y)}$

$$\frac{y^2}{(2-y)(1-y)} = 1$$

$$y^2 = [2 + y^2 - 3y]$$

$$\therefore \quad y = \frac{2}{3} \text{ mol}$$

$$[A]=\frac{\text{mol}}{\text{litre}}=\frac{2-\frac{2}{3}}{5}=\frac{4}{15}=0.267\text{ M}$$

$$[B]=\frac{1-\frac{2}{3}}{5}=\frac{1}{15}=0.067\text{ M}$$

$$[C]=\frac{2}{15}=0.133\text{ M}$$

$$[D]=\frac{2}{15}=0.133\text{ M}$$

Thus, the sum of each species $[A]+[B]+[C]+[D]$

$= 0.267 + 0.067 + 0.133 + 0.133 = 0.6$

Heterogeneous Equilibria

Equilibrium is said to be heterogeneous if reactants and products are in different phases.

e.g., $$CaCO_3(s) \overset{\Delta}{\rightleftharpoons} CaO(s) + CO_2(g)$$

All the constituent are not in same phase.

JEE MAPPER

Example Similar to PYQ Asked in JEE Main 2025

Consider the following reaction

$X_2Y(s) \rightleftharpoons X_2(g)+\frac{1}{2}Y_2(g)$. If α is the degree of dissociation. Calculate K_p in terms of P (total pressure)

(a) $K_p=\frac{2p^{3/2}}{3^{3/2}}$ (b) $K_p=\frac{2p^{3/2}}{3}$

(c) $K_p=\sqrt{\frac{2p}{3}}$ (d) $K_p=\frac{\sqrt{2}p}{3}$

Sol. (a) $X_2Y(s) \rightleftharpoons X_2(g)+\frac{1}{2}Y_2(g)$

t_{eq} $\quad p' \quad \frac{p'}{2}$

$$p_T=\frac{3p'}{2} \Rightarrow p'=\left(\frac{2p_T}{3}\right)$$

$$K_p=(p_{X_2})(p_{Y_2})^{1/2}$$

$$K_p=p'\left(\frac{p'}{2}\right)^{1/2}=\frac{(p')^{3/2}}{\sqrt{2}}$$

$$=\frac{\left(\frac{2p}{3}\right)^{3/2}}{\sqrt{2}}=\frac{2p^{3/2}}{3^{3/2}}$$

Compentency Enhancer 1.2

Some solid NH_4HS is placed in a flask containing 0.5 atm of NH_3. Upon heating following equilibrium is attained.

$$NH_4HS(s) \rightleftharpoons NH_3(g)+H_2S(g)$$

If K_p is 0.11, the pressure developed at equilibrium is

(a) 1.64 (b) 2.05 (c) 0.84 (d) 0.36

Applications of Equilibrium Constants

Some important applications of equilibrium are given below

Judging the Extent of Reactions

Knowing the value of the equilibrium constant for a chemical reaction is important in many ways. For example, it lets us judge the extent of the reaction, predict the direction of the reaction and calculate equilibrium concentration from any initial concentrations. We can make the following generalisations concerning the composition of equilibrium mixture.

- If $K_C > 10^3$, products predominate over reactants. If K_C is very large, the reaction proceeds almost all the way to completion.
- If $K_C < 10^{-3}$, reactants predominate over products. If K_C is very small, the reaction proceeds hardly at all.
- If K_C is in the range 10^{-3} to 10^3, appreciable concentration of both reactants and products are present.

This is illustrated in the following figure.

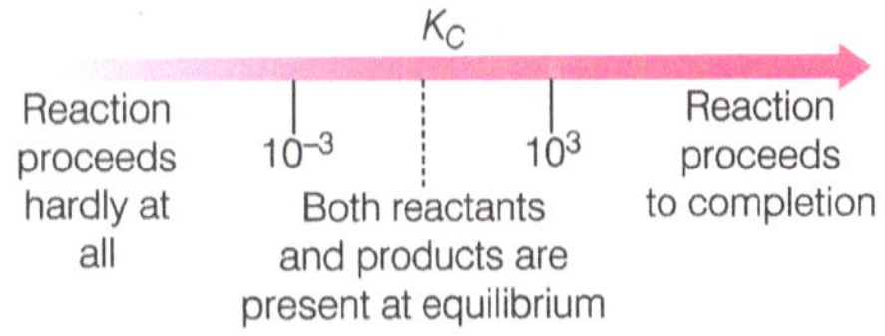

Judging the extent of a reaction. The larger the value of the equilibrium constant K_C, the farther the reaction proceeds to the right before reaching the equilibrium.

This can be explained clearly in the following examples :

(i) $2H_2+O_2 \rightleftharpoons 2H_2O, K_C=2.4\times 10^{47}$ at 500 K

Reaction proceeds almost to completion

(ii) $2H_2O \rightleftharpoons 2H_2+O_2$ at 500 K

Since, it is reverse of (a)

hence, $K'_C=\frac{1}{K_C}=4.17\times 10^{-48}$

This does not proceed at all.

(iii) $H_2+I_2 \rightleftharpoons 2HI, K_C=57$ at 700 K

This can proceed to attain equilibrium at which appreciable amount of both reactants and product are present.

(iv) $N_2O_4 \rightleftharpoons 2NO_2, K_C=4.69\times 10^{-3}$ at 298 K

This can also proceed to attain equilibrium at which appreciable amount of both reactants and product are present.

Predicting the Direction of a Reaction : The Reaction Quotient, Q

At each point in a reaction, we can formulate a ratio of concentration terms having the same form as the equilibrium constant expression. This ratio is called the **reaction quotient (Q)**. For a general reaction,

$$aA + bB \rightleftharpoons cC + dD$$

$$Q = \frac{[C]^c[D]^d}{[A]^a[B]^d}$$

where,

$[C]$, $[D]$ are the molar concentrations (or partial pressure) of the products at any points of time and $[A]$, $[B]$ are the molar concentrations (or partial pressures) of the reactants at any point of time. $a, b, c,$ and d are the stoichiometric coefficients from the balanced equation.

To predict the direction of any chemical reaction, we simply calculate the value of Q (reaction quotient) from the given values of molar concentration and compare the value of Q and K_C.

Condition	Direction
If $Q<K_C$	the reaction goes from left to right. i.e. the direction of products (forward reaction)
If $Q>K_C$	the reaction goes from right to left. i.e. in the direction of reactants (backward reaction)
If $Q=K_C$	the reaction mixture is already equilibrium, and no net reaction occurs.

This is illustrated in Figure

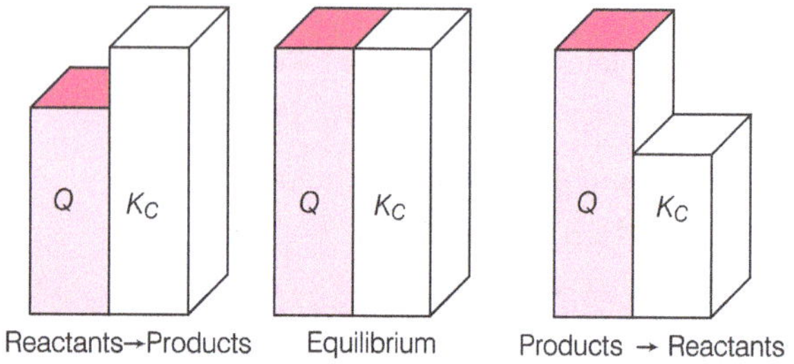

Predicting the direction of reaction, the direction of reaction depends on the relative values of Q and K_C

Solved Booster 1.7

For the following reaction, $PCl_5 \rightleftharpoons PCl_3 + Cl_2$; $K_C = 0.2$
0.4 mole of PCl_5, 0.2 mole of PCl_3 and 0.6 mole of Cl_2 are taken in 1L flask. The direction in which reaction proceeds:

(a) from right to left till, $K_C = Q$
(b) constant
(c) from right to left, $K_C > Q$
(d) from left to right, $K_C < Q$

Solution *(a)*

$$PCl_5(g) \rightleftharpoons PCl_3(g) + Cl_2(g)$$

$$\text{Reaction quotient, } Q = \frac{[PCl_3][Cl_2]}{[PCl_5]}$$

$$= \frac{\left(\frac{0.2}{1}\right)\text{mol L}^{-1}\left(\frac{0.6}{1}\right)\text{mol L}^{-1}}{\left(\frac{0.4}{1}\right)\text{mol L}^{-1}} = 0.3$$

But $K_C = 0.2 < Q$

Thus, reactions goes from right to left till

$K_C = Q$

Relations between Degree of Dissociation and Vapour Density

Degree of dissociation can be defined as the fraction that undergoes dissociation in a reaction.

$$\text{Degree of dissociation} = \frac{\text{Number of moles dissociated}}{\text{Initial number of moles}}$$

Vapour density of a substance is defined as the mass of certain volume of substance divided by the mass of same volume of hydrogen.

For gaseous reaction, we can relate vapour density with degree of dissociation.

In the following reversible chemical equation

	$A \rightleftharpoons$	yB
Initial :	1	0
At equilibrium	$(1-\alpha)$	$y\alpha$

where α = degree of dissociation

number moles of A and B at equilibrium

$$= 1-\alpha + y\alpha = 1 + \alpha(y-1)$$

If initial volume of 1 mole of A is V, then volume of equilibrium mixture of A and B is $=[1+\alpha(y-1)]V$

Vapour density before dissociation,

$$D = \frac{\text{molecular weight}}{\text{volume}} = \frac{m}{V}$$

Vapour density after dissociation, $d = \dfrac{m}{[1+\alpha(y-1)]V}$

$$\therefore \quad \frac{D}{d} = [1+\alpha(y-1)]$$

$$\therefore \quad \boxed{\alpha = \frac{D-d}{d(y-1)}}$$

y is the number of moles of products from one mole of reactant. $\frac{D}{d}$ is also called **van't Hoff factor.**

Thus, for the equilibria

I. $PCl_5(g) \rightleftharpoons PCl_3(g) + Cl_2(g)$, $y = 2$

II. $N_2O_4(g) \rightleftharpoons 2NO_2(g)$, $y = 2$

III. $2NO_2 \rightleftharpoons N_2O_4, y = \frac{1}{2}$

$$\therefore \quad \alpha = \frac{D-d}{d} \text{ for I and II}$$

$$\alpha = \frac{2(d-D)}{d} \text{ for III}$$

Also, $D \times 2$ = molecular weight (theoretical value)

$d \times 2$ = molecular weight (abnormal value) of the mixture.

Solved Booster 1.8

For the following equilibrium $PCl_5(g) \rightleftharpoons PCl_3(g) + Cl_2(g)$ Vapour density is found to be 100 when 1 mole of PCl_5 is taken in 10 L flask at 27°C. The sum of equilibrium pressure and percentage dissociation of PCl_5 will be

Solution (6.818)

$$PCl_5(g) \rightleftharpoons PCl_3(g) + Cl_2(g)$$

$y = 2$ (number of products from 1 mole reactant)

d (observed vapour density) = 100 (given)

$$D \text{ (theoretical vapour density)} = \frac{\text{molar mass}}{2} = \frac{208.5}{2} = 104.25$$

$$\alpha = \frac{D-d}{(y-1)d} = \frac{104.25-100}{(2-1)100} = 0.0425$$

$$\text{Thus, percentage dissociation of } PCl_5 = \frac{0.0425 \times 100}{1} = 4.25\%$$

	$PCl_5(g) \rightleftharpoons$	$PCl_3(g) +$	$Cl_2(g)$
Initial	1	0	0
At equilibrium	$(1-x)$	x	x

Total moles of gaseous

Species at equilibrium $= 1 - x + x + x = (1 + x)$

$= 1 + 0.0425 = 1.0425$

∴ Equilibrium pressure

$$p = \frac{n}{V}RT = \frac{1.0425 \text{ mol} \times 0.0821 \text{ L atm mol}^{-1}\text{K}^{-1} \times 300\text{K}}{10 \text{ L}}$$

$$\approx 2.568 \text{ atm}$$

Thus, the sum of equilibrium pressure and percentage dissociation of PCl_5 is $= 4.25 + 2.568 = 6.818$

Thermodynamics of Chemical Equilibrium

Spontaneity

A spontaneous or natural process is a process that occurs in a system left to right itself once started, no action from outside the system (external action) is necessary to make the process continue.

On the other hand, a non-spontaneous process will not occur unless some external action is continuously applied.

We say that the rusting of iron is spontaneous

$$2Fe(s) + 3O_2(g) \longrightarrow Fe_2O_3(s)$$

Reverse reaction is not impossible, but it is certainly non-spontaneous.

Gibbs Free Energy Change and Spontaneity

The Gibbs free energy 'G' for system is defined as

$$G = H - TS$$

and, for a change at constant T, $\Delta G = \Delta H - T\Delta S$

where, ΔG = change in Gibbs free energy G

ΔH = change in enthalpy H

ΔS = change in entropy S

Sign of ΔG is taken as the true criterion for spontaneity.

For a process occurring at constant T and p, if

(i) $\Delta G < 0$ (negative) the process is spontaneous.

(ii) $\Delta G > 0$ (positive) the process is non-spontaneous.

(iii) $\Delta G = 0$ (zero) the process is at equilibrium.

Sign of ΔG, based on equation ($\Delta G = \Delta H - T\Delta S$) can be decided depending on sign of ΔH and ΔS and magnitude of T, and is explained in table.

Criterion for spontaneous change, $\Delta G = \Delta H - T\Delta S$

Case	ΔH	ΔS	ΔG	Result	Example
1.	−	+	−	Spontaneous at all temperature.	$2N_2O(g) \longrightarrow 2N_2(g) + O_2(g)$
2.	−	−	−	Spontaneous at low temperature.	$H_2O(l) \longrightarrow H_2O(g)$
			+	Non-spontaneous at high temperature.	$2NH_3(g) \longrightarrow N_2(g) + 3H_2(g)$
3.	+	+	+	Non spontaneous at low temperature.	$N_2(g) + O_2(g) \longrightarrow 2NO(g)$
			−	Spontaneous at high temperature.	
4.	+	−	+	Non spontaneous at all temperature.	$3O_2(g) \longrightarrow 2O_3(g)$
5.	$T\Delta S = \Delta H$		0	Equilibrium	$A \rightleftharpoons B$

Relationship of $\Delta G°$ to the Equilibrium Constant (K) and Reaction Quotient (Q)

ΔG for a reaction under any set of conditions is related to its value for standard conditions, that is, $\Delta G°$ by equation

$$\Delta G = \Delta G° + 2.303\, RT \log Q$$

Under equilibrium condition

$$Q = K_p = K_C = K \text{ (where } \Delta n_g = 0)$$

and $\Delta G = 0$,

$$\Delta G° = -2.303\, RT \log K$$

$$\Delta G^\circ = -RT \log_e K$$

$$\therefore \quad K = e^{-\Delta G^\circ/RT}$$

$$R = 8.314 \text{ J K}^{-1} \text{ mol}^{-1}$$

As $K = e^{-\Delta G^\circ/RT}$, the spontaneity of reaction can be predicted in terms of ΔG° value.

If $\Delta G^\circ < 0, -\Delta G^\circ/RT$ is +ve and $e^{-\Delta G^\circ/RT} > 1$, making $K > 1$, which signifies that the reaction is spontaneous proceeding in forward direction.

If $\Delta G^\circ > 0, -\Delta G^\circ/RT$ is –ve and $e^{-\Delta G^\circ/RT}$ is -ve and $e^{-\Delta G^\circ/RT} < 1$, thus making $K < 1$, which signifies that the reaction is non-spontaneous.

JEE MAPPER

Example Similar to PYQ Asked in JEE Advanced 2023

In a one L flask, 12 moles of A undergoes the reaction, $A(g) \rightleftharpoons D(g)$. The progress of product formation at two temperature (in Kelvin), T_1 and T_2, is shown in the figure.

If $T_1 = 3T_2$ and $(\Delta G_2^\circ - \Delta G_1^\circ) = RT_2 \ln x$, then value of x is ....

[ΔG_1° and ΔG_2° are standard Gibbs' free energy change for the reaction at temperature T_1 and T_2 respectively]

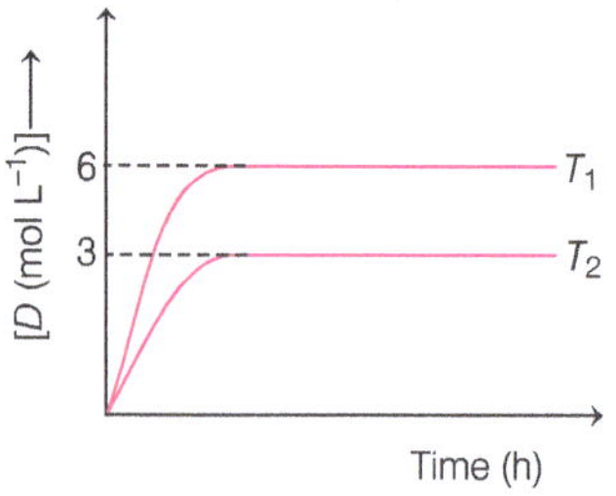

Sol. (16) Given reaction is:

	$A(g)$ $\rightleftharpoons$	$D(g)$
Initially	12	0
At equilibrium	$12-\alpha$	α

At T_1, $\alpha = 6$ (from graph)

$$(K_{eq})_1 = \frac{6}{6} = 1$$

At T_2, $\alpha = 3$ (from graph)

$$(K_{eq})_2 = \frac{3}{9} = \frac{1}{3}$$

Now, $\quad \Delta G_1^\circ = -RT_1 \ln (K_{eq})_1 \quad [\because T_1 = 3T_2]$

$$\Delta G_2^\circ = -3RT_2 \ln (K_{eq})_1$$

$$\Delta G_2^\circ = -RT_2 \ln (K_{eq})_2$$

$$\therefore \quad \Delta G_2^\circ - \Delta G_1^\circ = -RT_2 \ln (K_{eq})_2 + 3RT_2 \ln (K_{eq})_1$$

$$= RT_2 \ln \frac{(K_{eq})_1^3}{(K_{eq})_2}$$

$$= RT_2 \frac{\ln (1)^3}{(1/3)}$$

$$\Delta G_2^\circ - \Delta G_1^\circ = RT_2 \ln 3 \quad \text{...(i)}$$

By comparing Eq. (i) with

$$\Delta G_2^\circ - \Delta G_1^\circ = RT_2 \ln x$$

$$x = 3$$

Competency Enhancer 1.3

If densities of graphite and diamond are 22.5 and 3.51 g cm^{-3} respectively. The equilibrium pressure of conversion of graphite into diamond is 1.52×10^9 Pa. The standard Gibbs energy of the reaction is .... J/mol (Nearest integer)

Elemental Practice 5.1

Type I MCQs with Only One Correct Option

1. For the reactions,

$$NH_4^+ + 2\,H_2O \rightleftharpoons NH_4OH + H_3O^+; \quad K_1 = 5.56 \times 10^{-10}$$

$$H_2O + H_2O \rightleftharpoons H_3O^+ + OH^-; \quad K_2 = 1 \times 10^{-14}$$

K_3 of the reaction, $NH_4OH \rightleftharpoons NH_4^+ + OH^-$ is

(a) 1.8×10^5 (b) 1.8×10^{-5}

(c) 5.56×10^4 (d) 5.56×10^{-4}

2. The equilibrium constant for the reaction,

$$SO_3(g) \rightleftharpoons SO_2(g) + \frac{1}{2}O_2(g) \text{ is}$$

$K_C = 7.36 \times 10^{-3}\ L\ mol^{-1}$. The value of K_C for the reaction given below is

$$2SO_2(g) + O_2(g) \rightleftharpoons 2SO_3(g) \text{ is}$$

(a) 314×10^{-2} (b) 197.36×10^{-3}

(c) $211.01 \times 10^{+3}$ (d) 184.68×10^2

3. In the dissociation of N_2O_4 into NO_2, x varies with the vapour densities ratio $\left(\frac{D}{d}\right)$ as given by

(a)
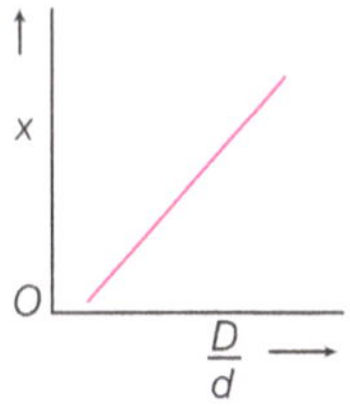

(b)
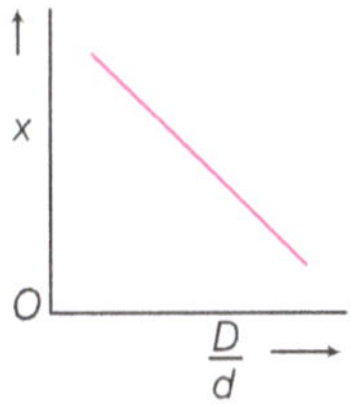

(c)
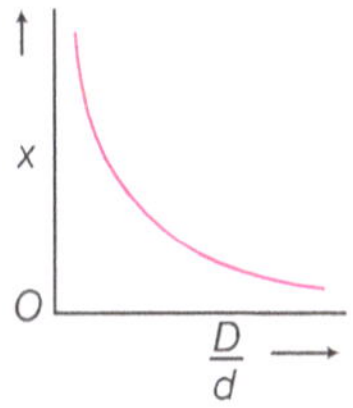

(d)
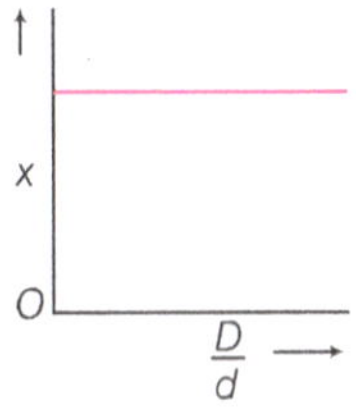

4. $CH_3OH(g)$ can be prepared using equation

$$CO(g) + 2H_2(g) \rightleftharpoons CH_3OH(g); K_C = 4 \times 10^2$$

At equilibrium, a 5 L flask contains equal moles of $CO(g)$ and $CH_3OH(g)$. Hence, number of moles of H_2 at equilibrium is

(a) 0.25 mol (b) 0.10 mol

(c) 0.50 mol (d) 0.125 mol

5. For the equilibrium

I. $C_6H_5COOH + H_2O \rightleftharpoons C_6H_5COO^- + H_3O^+; K_1 = 6.30 \times 10^{-5}$

II. $C_6H_5COOH + OH^- \rightleftharpoons C_6H_5COO^- + H_2O; K_2 = 6.30 \times 10^9$

III. $H_2O + H_2O \rightleftharpoons H_3O^+ + OH^-; K_3 = ?$

K_3 using the above equilibrium is

(a) $(6.30)^2 \times 10^4$ (b) 1.0×10^{-14}

(c) 1×10^{14} (d) $(6.30)^{-2} \times 10^{-4}$

6. In the following equilibria,

I. $A + 2B \rightleftharpoons C;\ K_{eq} = K_1$

II. $C + D \rightleftharpoons 3A;\ K_{eq} = K_2$

III. $6B + D \rightleftharpoons 2C;\ K_{eq} = K_3$

The correct option is

(a) $3K_1 \cdot K_2 = K_3$ (b) $K_1^3 \cdot K_2 = K_3$

(c) $3K_1 \cdot K_2^2 = K_3$ (d) $K_1^3 \cdot K_3 = K_2$

7. The rate of the elementary reaction $H_2(g) + I_2(g) \longrightarrow 2HI(g)$ at 25°C is given by

$$\text{Rate} = 1.7 \times 10^{-18}[H_2][I_2]$$

The rate of decomposition of gaseous HI to $H_2(g)$ and $I_2(g)$ at 25°C is rate $= 2.4 \times 10^{-21}[HI]^2$. Equilibrium constant for the formation of one mole of gaseous HI from $H_2(g)$ and $I_2(g)$ is

(a) 708 (b) 354

(c) 0.0014 (d) 26.61

8. At 800 K, $\Delta G°$ for the reaction

$$NiO(s) + H_2(g) \rightleftharpoons Ni(s) + H_2O\ (g) \text{ is } -9.0 \text{ kcal.}$$

Thus, ratio of pressures of water vapours and hydrogen in equilibrium with NiO and Ni at 800 K in terms of logarithm is

(a) 2.44 (b) 1.06

(c) 5.63 (d) − 2.44

9. For the reaction in equilibrium,

I. $CO(g) + \frac{1}{2}O_2(g) \rightleftharpoons CO_2(g)$

II. $2CO(g) + O_2(g) \rightleftharpoons 2CO_2(g)$

Equilibrium constant	Free energy change
K_1	ΔG_1
K_2	ΔG_2

Then,

(a) $K_1 = 2K_2, \Delta G_1 = 2\Delta G_2$ (b) $K_2 = 2K_1, \Delta G_2 = 2\Delta G_1$

(c) $K_2 = K_1^2, \Delta G_2 = 2\Delta G_1$ (d) $K_2 = K_1^2, \Delta G_2 = \Delta G_1^2$

10. Under standard state (at 1 bar and 298 K), K_p for the equilibrium

$$N_2O_4(g) \rightleftharpoons 2NO_2(g) \text{ is } 0.141.$$

What is ΔG under the given condition when $p_{N_2O_4} = 10$ bar and $p_{NO_2} = 1$ bar

(a) $0.37\ kJ\ mol^{-1}$ (b) $+ 0.85\ kJ\ mol^{-1}$

(c) $- 0.37\ kJ\ mol^{-1}$ (d) $- 0.85\ kJ\ mol^{-1}$

11. Given the equilibrium constant values,

I. $N_2(g) + \frac{1}{2}O_2(g) \rightleftharpoons N_2O(g); K_C = 2.7 \times 10^{-18}$

II. $N_2O_4\ (g) \rightleftharpoons 2NO_2\ (g); K_C = 4.6 \times 10^{-3}$

III. $\frac{1}{2}N_2(g) + O_2(g) \rightleftharpoons NO_2(g); K_C = 4.1 \times 10^{-9}$

Thus, for the reaction, $2N_2O(g) + 3O_2(g) \rightleftharpoons 2N_2O_4(g)$, K_C is

(a) 5.46×10^7 (b) 5.46×10^{-7}
(c) 1.832×10^6 (d) 1.832×10^{-6}

12. Given below are two statements.

Statement I Napthalene, a white solid used to make mothballs, has a vapour pressure of 0.10 mmHg at 27°C. The value of K_p and K_C for the equilibrium,

$C_{10}H_8(s) \rightleftharpoons C_{10}H_8(g)$ are 1.32×10^{-4} atm are 3.33×10^{-6} respectively.

Statement II For the given equilibrium,

$N_2O_4(g) \rightleftharpoons 2NO_2(g) K_p$ (in atm) is found to be equal to K_C (in mol L^{-1}) when temperature is 12.18 K.

In the light of the above statements, choose the most appropriate answer from the options given below

(a) Both Statement I and Statement II are incorrect
(b) Statement I is correct but Statement II is incorrect
(c) Statement I is incorrect but Statement II is correct
(d) Both Statement I and Statement II are correct

13. $H_2S(g)$ initially at a pressure of 10.0 atm and a temperature of 800 K, dissociates as

$$2H_2S(g) \rightleftharpoons 2H_2(g) + S_2(g)$$

At equilibrium, the partial pressure of S_2 vapour is 0.020 atm. Thus, K_p is

(a) 3.23×10^{-7} (b) 6.45×10^{-7}
(c) 1.55×10^6 (d) 6.20×10^7

14. A gaseous phase reaction taking place in 1L flask at 400 K is given, $N_2(g) + 3H_2(g) \rightleftharpoons 2NH_3(g)$.

Starting with 1 mole N_2 and 3 moles H_2, equilibrium mixture required 250 mL of 1M H_2SO_4. Thus, K_C is

(a) 0.006 (b) 0.08
(c) 0.029 (d) 2.05

15. Equilibrium constant for the following equilibrium,

$3ClO^-(aq) \rightleftharpoons 2Cl^-(aq) + ClO_3^-(aq)$

is 1.0×10^{28} at a temperature at which $RT = 2500$ J mol^{-1}. Gibbs free energy change ($\Delta G°$) is

(a) -70.0 kJ mol^{-1} (b) $+30.395$ kJ mol^{-1}
(c) -161.21 kJ mol^{-1} (d) $+371.24$ kJ mol^{-1}

16. Calculate the equilibrium constant for the reaction

$$CO + H_2O \rightleftharpoons CO_2 + H_2$$

if the equilibrium constants for

$$2CO + O_2 \rightleftharpoons 2CO_2; K = 40 \times 10^{-3}$$

$$2H_2 + O_2 \rightleftharpoons 2H_2O; K' = 36 \times 10^{-2}$$

(a) 1.02 (b) 2.113
(c) 0.056 (d) 0.333

Type II 》 MCQs with One or More than One Correct Option

17. Which of the following statements are correct?

(a) $N_2(g) + 3H_2(g) \rightleftharpoons 2NH_3(g)$ is a gaseous phase equilibrium reaction taking place in a 5 L flask at 400 K. For this $K_C = 5K_x$.
(b) The following reaction when heated in sealed tube, $2NaHCO_3(s) \rightleftharpoons Na_2CO_3(s) + CO_2(g) + H_2O(g)$, the equilibrium pressure is 1.0 atm at 300 K, then $K_p = 0.25$ atm.
(c) For the equilibria, $2NOCl(g) \rightleftharpoons 2NO(g) + Cl_2(g)$, the value of $K_p \neq K_c$.
(d) K_p or K_C are dimensionless, if pressure and concentration are expressed in standard state.

18. At 1700 K, and 1.10 atm, 1g of chlorine occupies 1.96 L in the following equilibrium

$$\frac{1}{2}Cl_2(g) \rightleftharpoons Cl(g)$$

If gas behaves ideally,

Then

(a) $K_p = K_C = K_\chi$
(b) $K_\chi = 0.187$
(c) $K_p = 0.196$ atm$^{1/2}$
(d) $K_C = 0.0166$ (mol $L^{-1})^{1/2}$

19. Pure nitrosyl chloride (NOCl) gas was heated to 240°C in a 1.00 L container. At equilibrium, the total pressure was 1.00 atm and the NOCl pressure was 0.64 atm.

$$2NOCl(g) \rightleftharpoons 2NO(g) + Cl_2(g)$$

Which of the following statements are correct about the given data?

(a) The equilibrium constant K_p for the given reaction is 0.27 atm.
(b) The partial pressure of NO in the system is 0.36 atm.
(c) The partial pressure of Cl_2 in the system is 0.12 atm.
(d) The equilibrium constant K_p for the given reaction is 0.017 atm.

20. The equilibrium constant for the gas-phase reaction,

$$H_2CO \rightleftharpoons H_2 + CO$$

has the numerical value of 0.50 at a given temperature. A mixture of H_2CO, H_2 and CO is introduced into a flask at this temperature. After a short time, analysis of a small sample of the reaction mixture shows the concentration to be $[H_2CO] = 0.50$M, $[H_2] = 1.50$ M and $[CO] = 0.25$ M. Which of the following statements about this reaction mixture is incorrect?

(a) The reaction mixture is at equilibrium.
(b) The reaction mixture is not at equilibrium, but no further reaction will occur.
(c) The reaction mixture is not at equilibrium but will more forward equilibrium by giving up more H_2CO.
(d) The forward rate is the same as the reverse rate for this reaction.

Type III 》 Numerical Value/Integer Answer Questions

21. For the equilibrium, $NH_3(g) \rightleftharpoons \frac{1}{2} N_2(g) + \frac{3}{2} H_2(g)$

degree of dissociation is...% at 1 bar.

if $K_p = 7.819 \times 10^{-3}$

22. For a certain reaction at 370 K, $K = 20$, then $\Delta G°$ for the same reaction is – .... $\times 10^{-1}$ kJ mol^{-1}.

[Given : $R = 8.314$ JK^{-1} mol^{-1}] (Nearest integer)

23. At 1000 K, pressure of CO_2 in equilibrium with $CaCO_3$ and CaO is equal to 2.105 atm. The equilibrium constant for the reaction,

$$C(s) + CO_2(g) \rightleftharpoons 2CO(g)$$

is 1.9 at the same temperature when pressure are in atm. Solid C, CaO, and $CaCO_3$ are mixed and allowed to come to equilibrium at 1000 K in a closed vessel. What is the pressure of CO (g) at equilibrium (in atm)?

24. One enzyme catalysed reaction in a biochemical cycle has an equilibrium constant that is 10 times the equilibrium constant of a second reaction. Standard Gibbs energy of the first reaction is – 300 kJ mol L^{-1} (at 300 K). Then, the standard Gibbs energy of the second reaction is – .... kJ mol^{-1}

25. The equilibrium constant K_{p_1} and K_{p_2} for the reactions $X \rightleftharpoons 2Y$ and $Z \rightleftharpoons P + Q$, respectively are in the ratio of 1:9. If the degree of dissociation of X and Z be equal, the sum of the ratio of that pressure at these equilibria is ....

Elemental Practice 5.1 | Chapter 05

Connect with **Answers**

1. (b)	**2.** (d)	**3.** (a)	**4.** (a)	**5.** (b)	**6.** (b)
7. (d)	**8.** (a)	**9.** (c)	**10.** (d)	**11.** (c)	**12.** (c)
13. (a)	**14.** (c)	**15.** (c)	**16.** (d)	**17.** (b,c,d)	**18.** (b,c,d)
19. (c,d)	**20.** (a,b,c,d)	**21.** (8)	**22.** (92)	**23.** (2)	**24.** (294.26)
25. (37)					

Element 2 Le-Chatelier's Principle and Factor Affecting Chemical Equilibrium

There are several factors that affect the equilibrium state of a system. The effect of such factors on equilibrium state is described by Le-Chatelier principle.

Le-Chatelier's Principle

The qualitative effect of the listed changes on the composition of an equilibrium mixture can be described by Le-Chatelier's principle given by Henry-Lousis Le-Chatelier:

"**If a stress is applied to a reaction mixture at equilibrium, reaction occurs in that direction that relieves the stress.**"

- Stress means a change in concentration, pressure, volume or temperature that disturbs the original equilibrium. The direction that the reaction takes (forward or backward) is the one that reduces the stress.
- If you increase concentration of the reactants, reaction goes in a direction that tends to decrease concentration.
- If you increase pressure (or decrease volume), reaction goes in a direction that tends to decrease pressure (or increase volume).
- If you increase temperature, reaction goes in a direction that tends to decrease the temperature.

Effect of Changes in Concentration

When an equilibrium is disturbed by the addition or removal of any reactant or product, Le-Chatelier's principle predicts that:

The stress of an added reactant or product is relieved by reaction in the direction that consumes the added substance.

The stress of a removed reactant or product is relieved by reaction in the direction that replenishes the removed substance.

For the equilibrium,

$$A + B \rightleftharpoons C$$

it can be stated that

(i) If you increase concentration of A and B (reactant) then equilibrium goes in the direction that consumes A or B i.e. forward direction.

(ii) If you increase concentration of C (product), then equilibrium goes in the direction that consumes C i.e. backward direction.

(iii) If you isolate C (product) then equilibrium goes in the direction in which its concentration increases (i.e. orward).

JEE Alert

If any of the species is in solid state, its addition does not alter the original equilibrium.

Effect of Changes in Pressure

The change in pressure affects the equilibrium in the case of gaseous reactions. If gases are not involved in a reaction at equilibrium, then there is a negligible effect of pressure change on the equilibrium.

In general, Le-Chatelier's principle predicts that

(i) An increase in pressure (by reducing the volume) will bring about net reaction in the direction that decreases the number of moles of gas.

(ii) A decrease in pressure (by enlarging the volume) will bring about net reaction in the direction that increases the number of moles of gas.

For an approximation, quantity of product (x) is dependent on pressure by equation $x \propto \left(\frac{1}{p}\right)^{\Delta n_g/2}$

where Δn_g = number of moles of gaseous product − number of moles of gaseous reactants. Increase in the value of x due to change in pressure implies a shift in the forward direction.

Δn_g	Variation	Direction
+ve	increase p	backward
−ve	increase p	forward
0	increase or decrease	no effect

JEE Spotlite

Effect of Pressure on Solid-Liquid Equilibria

- For most substances, increasing pressure tends to favour the solid phase because solids are generally denser than liquids. This means that, under increased pressure, the equilibrium may shift toward the solid phase (towards higher density).
- Water is a notable exception to this general rule. Ice (solid water) is less dense than liquid water, meaning that increasing pressure actually favours the melting of ice. In this case, raising the pressure can shift the equilibrium toward the liquid phase, promoting melting.

Effect of Change in Volume

The effect of change in volume is reverse to the effect of change in pressure.

According to ideal gas laws $V \propto \frac{1}{p}$, therefore

- On increasing volume, pressure decreases and the reaction will go in the direction where number of moles is more.
- On decreasing volume, pressure increases and the reaction will go in the direction where number of moles is less.

Solved Booster 2.1

In which of the following equilibria the number of moles of reaction products remains the same when each are subjected to a decrease in pressure (by increasing volume)?

(a) $2CO(g) \rightleftharpoons C(s) + CO_2(g)$

(b) $N_2O_4(g) \rightleftharpoons 2NO_2(g)$

(c) $CaO(s) + CO_2(g) \rightleftharpoons CaCO_3(s)$

(d) $3Fe\,(s) + 4H_2O(g) \rightleftharpoons Fe_3O_4(s) + 4H_2(g)$

Solution *(d)*

Species in the solid state are not to be considered.

Equilibria	Δn_g	Moles of reactant	Moles of product
(a)	−1	↑	↓
(b)	+1	↓	↑
(c)	−1	↑	↓
(d)	0	no effect	

In all of the above cases, you can also predict direction by using equation $x \propto \left(\frac{1}{p}\right)^{\Delta n_g/2}$

(a) $x \propto \sqrt{p}$, decrease in p, decreases x

(b) $x \propto \sqrt{\frac{1}{p}}$, decrease in p, increases x.

(c) $x \propto \sqrt{p}$, as in (a) (d) $x \propto p^0$, no effect

Effect of Change in Temperature

When an equilibrium is disturbed by a change in concentration, pressure or volume the composition of the equilibrium mixture changes, **but equilibrium constant remains unchanged**. But a change in temperature nearly always changes the value of equilibrium constant.

Dependence of K_p on temperature

According to Arrhenius equation of rate constant:

$$k_f = A_f e^{-E_{a_f}/RT} \quad \ldots(i)$$

where, k_f = Rate constant for forward reaction,

A_f = Arrhenius constant of forward reaction,

E_{a_f} = Energy of activation of forward reaction

$$k_r = A_r e^{E_{a_r}/RT} \quad \ldots(ii)$$

where, A_r = Arrhenius constant of reverse reaction,

E_{a_r} = Energy of activation of reverse reaction

Dividing Eqs. (i) by (ii), we get,

$$\frac{k_f}{k_r} = \frac{A_f}{A_r} e^{\frac{(E_{a_r} - E_{a_f})}{RT}}$$

We know that, $\frac{k_f}{k_r} = K$ (equilibrium constant)

$$\therefore \quad K = \frac{k_f}{k_r} \frac{A_f}{A_r} e^{\frac{(E_{a_r} - E_{a_f})}{RT}}$$

At temperature T_1 and T_2, the equilibrium constants are K_{T_1} and K_{T_2} respectively, then

$$\log \frac{K_{T_2}}{K_{T_1}} = \frac{E_{a_r} - E_{a_f}}{2.303R}\left(\frac{1}{T_2} - \frac{1}{T_1}\right) \quad \ldots(iii)$$

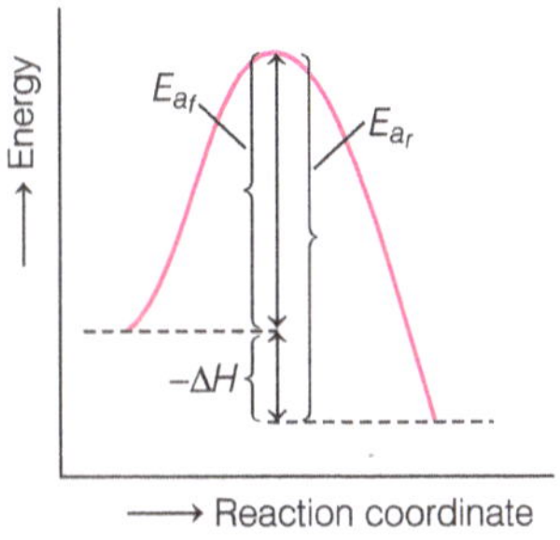

The enthalpy of a reaction is defined in terms of activation energies as $E_{a_f} - E_{a_r} = \Delta H$

$$\therefore \quad \log \frac{K_{T_2}}{K_{T_1}} = \frac{-\Delta H}{2.303R}\left(\frac{1}{T_2} - \frac{1}{T_1}\right) \quad \ldots(iv)$$

In general, the temperature dependence of the equilibrium constant depends on the sign of ΔH° (standard heat of reaction) for the given reaction.

$$K \propto T \text{ if } \Delta H^\circ = + \text{ ve}$$

$$K \propto \frac{1}{T} \text{ if } \Delta H^\circ = -\text{ve}$$

ΔH° = enthalpy of products − enthalpy of reactants

$= H^\circ$ (products) $- H^\circ$ (reactants)

For endothermic reactions, ΔH is positive and for exothermic reactions, ΔH is negative.

JEE Alert

- Exothermic reactions are favourable when temperature is lowered.
- Endothermic reaction are favourable when temperature is increased.

Effect of a Catalyst

A catalyst increases the rate of a chemical reaction by making available a new, lower energy pathway figure for conversion of reactants to products. Because the forward and backward reactions pass through the same transition state, a catalyst lowers the activation energy for the forward and reverse reactions by exactly the same amount. As a result, the rates of forward and backward reactions increase by the same factor.

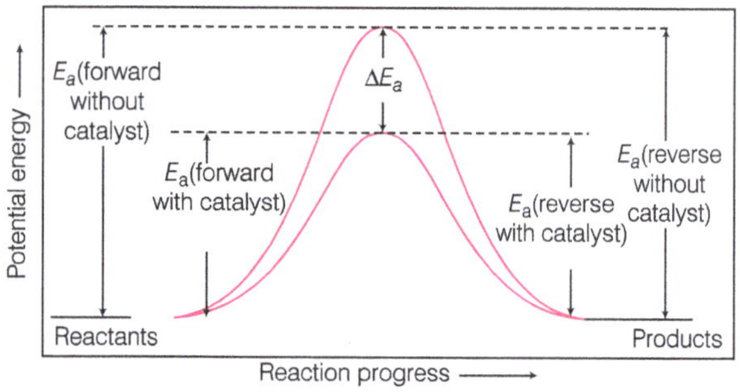

Potential energy profiles for a reaction whose activation energy is lowered by the presence of a catalyst

If a reaction mixture is at equilibrium in the absence of a catalyst, the forward and reverse rates are equal, it will still be at equilibrium after the addition of a catalyst because the forward and reverse rates, though faster, remain equal. **If a reaction mixture is not at equilibrium, a catalyst accelerates the rate at which equilibrium is reached, but it does not affect the composition of the equilibrium mixture.**

JEE Spotlite

The effect of varying conditions on the equilibrium

$aA + bB \rightleftharpoons cC + dD$, $\Delta n_g = (c+d) - (a+b)$

Changes imposed on the system at equilibrium	Equilibrium position moves	Equilibrium constant	Any other points
Conc of A and/or B increased	To right	No change	—
Conc. of C and/ or D increased	To left	No change	—
Pressure increased	To right if $(c+d) < (a+b)$, i.e. $\Delta n_g = -\text{ve}$	No change	Very little effect, if any, of in liquid solution.
	To left if $(c+d) > (a+b)$, i.e. $\Delta n_g = +\text{ ve}$	No change	
	No change if $(c+d) = (a+b)$, i.e. $\Delta n_g = 0$	No change	
Temperature increased	To left if $\Delta H = -\text{ve}$ (exothermic)	Value decreased	Equilibrium achieved faster.
	To right if $\Delta H = +\text{ve}$ (endothermic)	Value increased	
Addition of a catalyst	No change	No change	Equilibrium achieved faster.

Effect of Inert Gas

The addition of an inert gas to a system at equilibrium means the addition of an inert gas which neither reacts with reactants nor with products.

The influence of addition of inert gas to an equilibrium depends on the nature of equilibrium as well as condition of constant pressure or volume at which addition is made.

- For the equilibrium system where the $\Delta n_g > 0$, the addition of inert gas at constant pressure will increase the total volume of the system and decreases the molar concentration of reactant and the dissociation of reactant increases.
- For the equilibrium system where $\Delta n_g < 0$, the addition of inert gas at constant pressure will shifts the equilibrium to the backward direction.
- For the equilibrium system where $\Delta n_g = 0$, the addition of inert gas at constant pressure has no effect.
- At constant volume, addition of inert gas does not have any influence on the equilibrium system.

JEE Quicker

For the reaction,

$$PCl_5(g) \rightleftharpoons PCl_3(g) + Cl_2(g)$$

The effect of addition of helium gas in equilibrium state is that the equilibrium will shift in the forward direction and more of Cl_2 and PCl_3 gases will be produced. ***JEE Main 2023***

According to Le-Chatelier principle, effect of addition of inert gas at constant pressure will shift the reaction where number of moles of gaseous substances are more.

Applications of Le-Chatelier's Principle

This principle is applicable to physical as well as chemical equilibria and some of its applications are mentioned below.

1. Haber's Process of Synthesis of Ammonia

$$N_2(g) + 3H_2(g) \rightleftharpoons 2NH_3(g); \quad \Delta H = -22.4 \text{ kcal}$$

The favourable conditions are

(i) high concentration of N_2 or/and H_2
(ii) high pressure (as $\Delta n_g = -2$)
(iii) low temperature (as the reaction is exothermic)

Although, the low temperature favour the formation of NH_3. Yet, optimum temperature of **500°C** and pressure of **200 atm** is applied in practice.

To enhance the rate finally divided iron containing molybdenum (catalyst) is used.

2. Manufacture of Nitric Acid (Birkeland-Eyde Process)

$$N_2(g) + O_2(g) \rightleftharpoons 2NO(g);\ \Delta H = +43.2\ \text{kcal}$$

The factors favouring formation of NO are

(i) increase in concentration of N_2 and O_2

(ii) unaffected by pressure change (as $\Delta n_g = 0$)

(iii) increase in temperature (as the reaction is endothermic).

3. Melting of Ice

$$\underset{\substack{1\ \text{g} \\ 1.09\ \text{mL}}}{\text{Ice}} \rightleftharpoons \underset{\substack{1\ \text{g} \\ 1.01\ \text{mL}}}{\text{Water}} - x\ \text{kcal}$$

In the above case, forward change is accompanied with absorption of heat and a decrease in volume. Hence, on applying Le-Chatelier's principle, the favourable conditions for the melting of ice are high temperature (as forward reaction is endothermic) and high pressure (as forward reaction shows decrease in volume).

4. Boiling of Water

$$\underset{\text{(low volume)}}{\text{Water}} \rightleftharpoons \underset{\text{(higher volume)}}{\text{Steam}} - x\ \text{kcal}$$

The forward change is accompanied with absorption of heat and increase in volume. Hence, according to Le-Chatelier principle, the favourable conditions for vaporisation of water are

(i) high temperature

(ii) low pressure.

5. Solubility of Salts

If solubility of a salt is accompanied by absorption of heat.

e.g. Consider the solution of NaCl in water, following equilibrium exists

$$NaCl(s) + H_2O \rightleftharpoons NaCl(aq);\ \Delta H > 0$$

As the dissolution of NaCl proceeds with absorption of heat, it is favoured by high temperature.

If solubility of a salt is accompanied by evolution of heat, e.g. KOH dissolves in water with evolution of heat, the solubility of KOH, thus decreases with increase in temperature.

$$KOH(s) + H_2O \rightleftharpoons KOH(aq);\ \Delta H < 0$$

6. Manufacture of Sulphuric Acid by Contact Process

This process completes in several steps. The first step, which is rate determining step of the process is the conversion of SO_2 into SO_3.

$$2SO_2(g) + O_2(g) \rightleftharpoons 2SO_3(g);\quad K_C = 1.7 \times 10^{26} \quad \Delta H = -\text{ve}$$

This process is catalysed by using catalyst V_2O_5. Other conditions favouring this process are

- low temperature
- low concentration of SO_3
- high concentration of SO_2 and O_2.
- increase in pressure (as $\Delta n_g = -1$)

Elemental Practice 5.2

Type I MCQs with Only One Correct Option

1. Variation of $\log K_p$ with temperature (T) is given by the graph for the equilibrium:

$$NH_4HS(s) \rightleftharpoons NH_3(g) + H_2S(g)$$

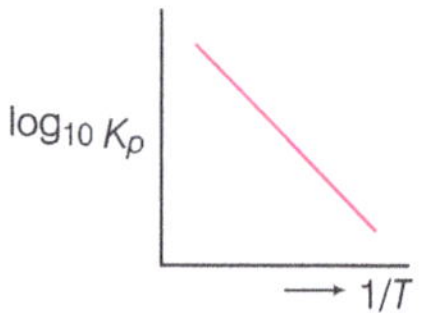

The equilibrium is displaced in forward direction on
(a) increasing temperature and decreasing pressure
(b) increasing temperature and pressure both
(c) decreasing temperature and pressure both
(d) decreasing temperature and increasing pressure.

2. The following pictures represent the composition equilibrium mixture of the reaction, $A + B \rightleftharpoons AB$ at 300 K and 400 K.

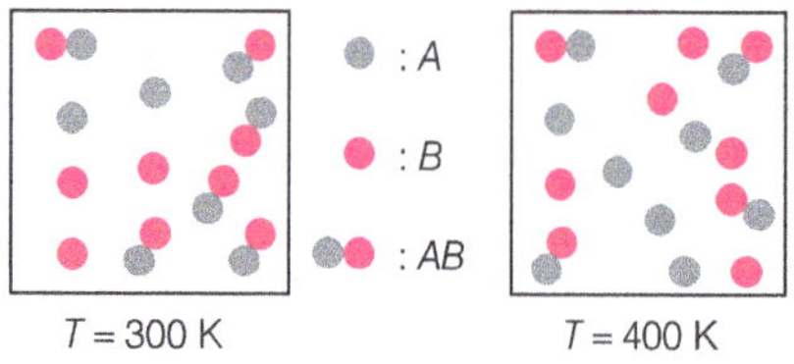

This represents that it is
(a) an exothermic reaction
(b) an endothermic reaction
(c) a non-thermodynamic reaction with $\Delta H° =$ zero
(d) nothing can be predicted

3. In the following equilibrium amount of $CO(g)$ can be decreased by

$$2CO(g) + O_2(g) \rightleftharpoons 2CO_2(g)$$

(a) decreasing volume at constant temperature
(b) adding argon gas
(c) adding O_2 gas
(d) All of the above

4. Given below are two statements.

Statement I Catalyst does not affect the equilibrium composition of a reaction mixture, it does not appear in the balanced chemical equation or in the equilibrium constant expression.

Statement II Catalyst lowers the activation energy for the forward and reverse reactions by different amount.

(a) Both Statement I and Statement II are incorrect
(b) Statement I is correct but Statement II is incorrect
(c) Statement I is incorrect but Statement II is correct
(d) Both Statement I and Statement II are correct

5. Pressure is doubled in each of the following equilibria. In which case yield is maximum?
(a) $C(s) + H_2O(g) \rightleftharpoons CO(g) + H_2(g)$
(b) $2H_2(g) + O_2(g) \rightleftharpoons 2H_2O(g)$
(c) $2Fe(s) + 3H_2O(g) \rightleftharpoons Fe_2O_3(s) + 3H_2(g)$
(d) $N_2O_4(g) \rightleftharpoons 2NO_2(g)$

6. Consider the following gas phase reaction.

$$2A(g) + B(g) \rightleftharpoons C(g) + D(g);\ \Delta H° = +\text{ve}$$

Which affects neither the composition nor the value of K_C?
(a) Addition of reactants
(b) Addition of helium
(c) Addition of catalyst
(d) Increase in temperature

7. When a sample of NO_2 is placed in a container, this equilibrium is rapidly established.

$$2NO_2(g) \rightleftharpoons N_2O_4(g)$$

Equilibrium mixture is darker in colour when temperature is increased and pressure is decreased. This indicates that
(a) ΔH is + ve and NO_2 is darker in colour than N_2O_4
(b) ΔH is + ve and N_2O_4 is darker in colour than NO_2
(c) ΔH is − ve and NO_2 is darker in colour than N_2O_4
(d) ΔH is − ve and N_2O_4 is darker in colour than NO_2

8. For the reaction, $PCl_5(g) \rightleftharpoons PCl_3(g) + Cl_2(g)$

The forward reaction at constant temperature is favoured by
I. introducing an inert gas at constant volume
II. introducing Cl_2 gas at constant volume
III. introducing an inert gas at constant pressure
IV. introducing PCl_5 at constant volume

(a) I, III
(b) II, III
(c) III, IV
(d) I, IV

9. Aerated water contains CO_2 dissolved in water

$$CO_2(g) + H_2O(l) \rightleftharpoons H_2CO_3(aq)$$

Variation of solubility (s) with pressure (p) is shown by

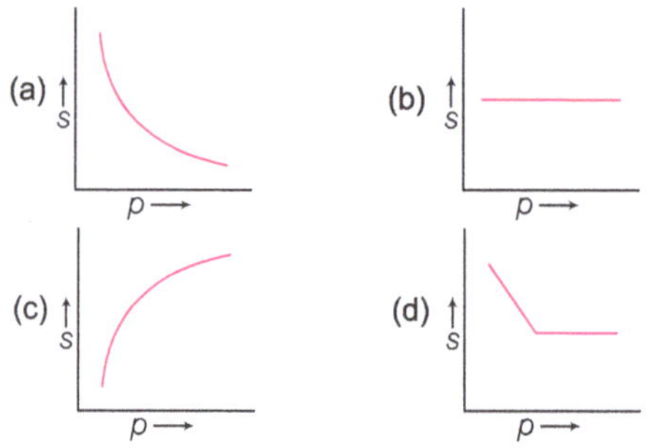

10. Given exothermic reaction,
$CoCl_4^{2-}(aq) + 6H_2O(l) \rightleftharpoons [Co(H_2O)_6]^{2+}(aq) + 4Cl^-(aq)$
Which one of the following will decrease the equilibrium concentration of $CoCl_4^{2-}$?
(a) Addition of HCl
(b) Addition of $CoCl_4^{2-}$
(c) The solution is diluted with water
(d) The temperature is increased

11. Consider the reaction when $K_p = 0.497$ bar at 500 K
$$PCl_5(g) \rightleftharpoons PCl_3(g) + Cl_2(g)$$
If the three gases are mixed in a closed vessel so that
$p_{PCl_5} = p_{Cl_2} = p_{PCl_3} = 1$ bar
Select the correct statement.
(a) More PCl_5 will be produced
(b) More PCl_3 will be produced
(c) Equilibrium will be established when 50% reaction is complete
(d) More Cl_2 will be produced

12. Under what conditions of temperature and pressure the formation of atomic hydrogen from molecular hydrogen will be favoured?
(a) High temperature and high pressure
(b) Low temperature and low pressure
(c) High temperature and low pressure
(d) Low temperature and high pressure

13. In the following endothermic equilibrium :
$$2NaNO_3(s) \rightleftharpoons 2NaNO_2(s) + O_2(g)$$
Select the incorrect statement.
(a) addition of $NaNO_2$ favours reverse reaction
(b) addition of $NaNO_3$ favours forward reaction
(c) increasing temperature favours forward reaction
(d) increasing pressure favours forward reaction

14. Consider the formation of SO_3 according to the reaction,
$$2SO_2(g) + O_2(g) \rightleftharpoons 2SO_3(g); \Delta H = -198 \text{ kJ}$$
Which of the following may change the value of equilibrium constant of the above reaction?
(a) Adding He gas to reaction vessel.
(b) Adding more of O_2 to the reaction vessel.
(c) Increasing the temperature
(d) Doubling the volume of reaction vessel.

Type II 》 MCQs with One or More than One Correct Option

15. For the gas phase reactions carried in a closed vessel,
$$C_2H_4(g) + H_2(g) \rightleftharpoons C_2H_6(g) \ (\Delta H = -136 \text{ kJ mol}^{-1})$$
equilibrium concentration of C_2H_4 can be increased by
(a) increasing the temperature
(b) decreasing the pressure
(c) removal of some H_2
(d) adding some C_2H_6

16. Variation of K_p with temperature T is given by the following equilibrium, $2NH_3(g) \rightleftharpoons N_2(g) + 3H_2(g)$

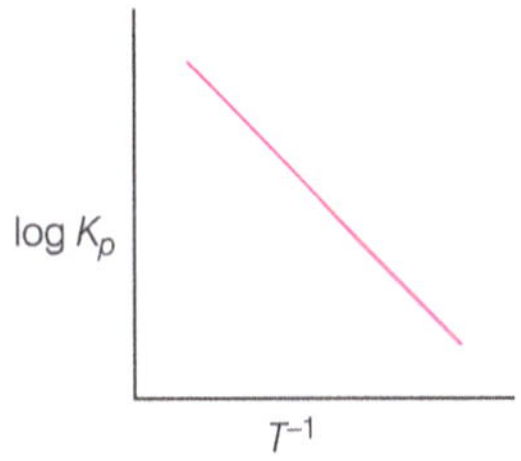

Thus, decomposition of $NH_3(g)$ can be prevented by
(a) lowering the temperature (b) increasing pressure
(c) isolation of $N_2(g)$ and $H_2(g)$ (d) adding $H_2(g)$

17. AgCl(s) is sparingly soluble salt,
$$AgCl(s) \rightleftharpoons Ag^+(aq) + Cl^-(aq)$$
There is
(a) increase in solubility if $NH_3(aq)$ is added
(b) increase in solubility if NaCl or $AgNO_3$ is added
(c) decrease in solubility if KCl is added
(d) decrease in solubility if H_2O is added

18. For the following equilibrium,
$$NH_4HS(s) + \text{Heat} \rightleftharpoons NH_3(g) + H_2S(g)$$
partial pressure of NH_3 will increase
(a) if pressure is decreased
(b) if H_2S is added after equilibrium is established
(c) temperature is increased
(d) volume of the flask is decreased

19. Combustion of $CO(g)$ can be increased in the following reaction by, $2CO(g) + O_2(g) \rightleftharpoons 2CO_2(g)$
(a) decreasing volume at constant temperature
(b) adding argon gas at constant pressure
(c) adding O_2 gas
(d) decreasing pressure at constant temperature

Type III 》 Numerical Value/Integer Answer Questions

20. Among the following statements, the number of incorrect statements are ....
A. In reaction, $C(s) + CO_2(g) \longrightarrow 2CO(g)$, when pressure is increased, the reaction goes in the reverse direction.
B. The equilibrium constant for an exothermic reaction increases as the temperature increases.
C. The addition of an inert gas at constant volume does not change the partial pressure or the molar concentrations of the substance involved in the reaction.
D. The equilibrium constant for an endothermic reaction decreases as the temperature increases.

21. The number of the following factors which do not affect the amount of H_2 present in an equilibrium mixture in the reaction is ....

$$3Fe(s) + 4H_2O(g) \rightleftharpoons Fe_3O_4(s) + 4H_2(g) \quad \Delta H^\circ = -150 \text{ kJ}$$

I. Raise the temperature of the mixture.
II. Introduce more $H_2O(g)$.
III. Double the volume of the container holding the mixture.
IV. Add an appropriate catalyst.

22. Increase in the pressure for the following equilibrium

$H_2O(l) \rightleftharpoons H_2O(g)$ result in the

I. Formation of more H_2O (*l*).
II. Formation of more H_2O (*g*).
III. Increase in boiling point of H_2O (*l*).
IV. Decrease in boiling point of H_2O (*l*).

The total number of results which are correct for the given reaction is ....

23. At a certain temperature, the equilibrium pressure of NO_2 and N_2O_4 are 1.6 bar and 0.58 bar respectively.

If the volume of the container is doubled at constant temperature, then the partial pressures of the gases when equilibrium is re-established will be *p* and *q* respectively.

$$N_2O_4(g) \rightleftharpoons 2NO_2(g).$$

The value of $p + q$ is ....

24. Among the following, the number of compounds, which on the addition will cause deep red colour to disappear are ......

$$\underset{\text{Pale yellow}}{Fe^{3+}(aq)} + \underset{\text{Colourless}}{SCN^-} \rightleftharpoons \underset{\text{Deep red}}{Fe(SCN)^{2+}(aq)}$$

I. $AgNO_3$
II. $HgCl_2$
III. $H_2C_2O_4$ (oxalic acid)

Elemental Practice 5.2 | Chapter 05

Connect with **Answers**

1. (a)	**2.** (a)	**3.** (d)	**4.** (b)	**5.** (b)	**6.** (c)
7. (c)	**8.** (c)	**9.** (c)	**10.** (c)	**11.** (a)	**12.** (c)
13. (d)	**14.** (c)	**15.** (a,b,c,d)	**16.** (a,b,d)	**17.** (a,c)	**18.** (a,c)
19. (a,b,d)	**20.** (2)	**21.** (2)	**22.** (2)	**23.** (1.17)	**24.** (3)

Advanced Exclusive Different Strokes

Equilibrium constant for exothermic and endothermic reactions are dependent on temperature. Questions based on graphs and their interpretation in terms of Δx°, ΔS° and ΔG° for both types of reactions have been asked in recent years.

The interpretation of temperature dependence of rate constant have been discussed below:

Intrepretation of temperature dependence of equilibrium constant for endothermic and exothermic reactions.

At equilibrium, $Q = K_C$ or K_p or $\Delta G = 0$

$$\Delta G^\circ = -2.303\, RT \log_{10} K$$

But $\Delta G^\circ = \Delta H^\circ - T\Delta S^\circ$

where, K is thermodynamic equilibrium constant and ΔH° is standard enthalpy change and ΔS° is the standard entropy change.

Quantitatively, variation of K with temperature T is given by van't Hoff equation.

$$\log_{10} K = -\frac{\Delta H^\circ}{2.303RT} + \frac{\Delta S^\circ}{2.303R}$$

ΔH° and ΔS° are temperature independent in the temperature range. If values of $\log_{10} K$ are plotted against $\frac{1}{T}$, a straight line of the type as shown in the figure below is obtained.

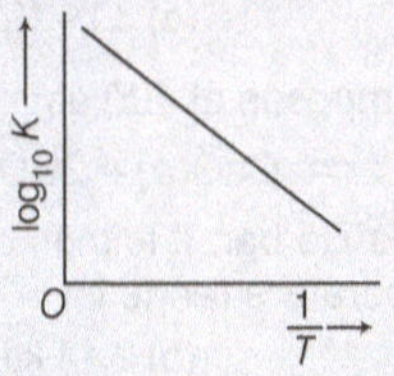

Figure Variation of $\log_{10}$ K and $1/T$ for an endothermic reaction.

$$\text{Slope} = -\frac{\Delta H^\circ}{2.\ 303R}$$

$$\therefore \quad \Delta H^\circ = -2.303R \times \text{slope}$$

Intercept on the coordinate $(\log_{10} K) = \frac{\Delta S^\circ}{2.303R}$

Thus, ΔH° can be evaluated for an endothermic reaction. From this graph, it is also clear that as $\frac{1}{T}$ increases, (T decreases), $\log_{10} K$ decreases.

Thus, **equilibrium constant K increases with increase in temperature for an endothermic reaction.**

$$K \propto T$$

For an exothermic reaction, $\Delta H^\circ = -$ve hence, van't Hoff equations is written as

$$\log_e K = \frac{\Delta H^\circ}{RT} + \frac{\Delta S^\circ}{R} \Rightarrow \log_{10} K = \frac{\Delta H^\circ}{2.303\, RT} + \frac{\Delta S^\circ}{2.303\, R}$$

For such case variation of $\log_{10} K$ with $\frac{1}{T}$ is given in figure below:

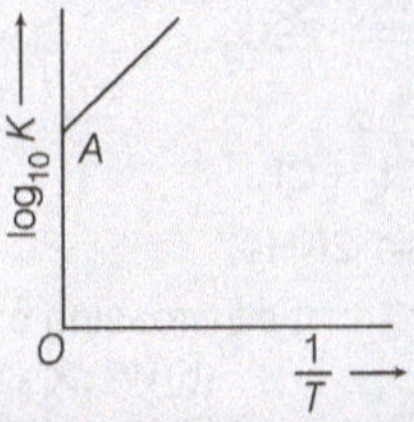

Figure Variation of $\log_{10} K$ with $1/T$ for an exothermic reaction.

$$\text{Slope} = \frac{\Delta H^\circ}{2.303\, R}$$

$$\Delta H^\circ = 2.303\, R \times \text{slope}$$

This graph shows that as $\frac{1}{T}$ increases (T decreases) $\log K$ increases.

Hence, equilibrium constant **K decreases with increase in temperature for an exothermic reaction.**

$$\boxed{K \propto \frac{1}{T}}$$

At, temperature T_1 and T_2, the two different relation is given by

$$\Delta H^\circ = \frac{2.303RT_1T_2}{(T_2 - T_1)} \log_{10} \frac{K_2}{K_1}$$

Conclusion

When $T_2 > T_1$ and $\Delta H^\circ > 0$ for endothermic reaction then $K_2 > K_1$. Thus, equilibrium constant increases with increase in temperature. For exothermic reaction, all the condition gets reversed.

PRACTICE ELEMENT 01

Target JEE Main

Objective Type Questions

1. For the following gaseous equilibria X, Y, Z and W at 300 K

   $X.\ 2SO_2 + O_2 \rightleftharpoons 2SO_3$

   $Y.\ 2HI \rightleftharpoons H_2 + I_2$

   $Z.\ PCl_5 \rightleftharpoons PCl_3 + Cl_2$

   $W.\ N_2 + 3H_2 \rightleftharpoons 2NH_3$

   Ratio of K_p and K_C in the increasing order is

   (a) $W < Y < Z < X$ (b) $W < X < Y < Z$
   (c) $X < W < Z < Y$ (d) $W < X < Y = Z$

2. 0.15 mole of CO taken in a 2.5 litre flask is maintained at 750 K alongwith a catalyst so that following reaction can take place, $CO(g) + 2H_2(g) \rightleftharpoons CH_3OH(g)$; hydrogen is introduced until the total pressure of the system is 8.5 atm at equilibrium and 0.08 mole of methanol are formed. The value of K_p and K_C are respectively.

   (a) 0.05, 187.85 (b) 0.08, 187.85
   (c) 0.08, 110.21 (d) 0.05, 130.21

3. $SO_3(g)$ is partially dissociated into $SO_2(g)$ and $O_2(g)$ at 900K and 1 atm as:

   $$SO_3(g) \rightleftharpoons SO_2(g) + \frac{1}{2}O_2(g)$$

   The density of the equilibrium mixture was found to be 0.866 g dm^{-3}. Thus, degree dissociation of $SO_3(g)$ is

   (a) 20% (b) 25% (c) 50% (d) 75%

4. Hot copper turnings can be used as an 'oxygen getter' far inert gas supplies by slowly passing the gas over the turnings, at 500 K.

   $$2Cu(s) + \frac{1}{2}O_2(g) \longrightarrow Cu_2O(s);\ \Delta G^\circ = -124.9 \text{ kJ}$$

   The number of molecules of O_2 that are left in 1.0 L of a gas supply after equilibrium has been reach are

   (a) 2.04×10^{-4} (b) 1.17×10^{-4}
   (c) 3.24×10^{-4} (d) 1.17×10^{-3}

5. Given below are two statements

   Statement I Two moles each of reactant A and B are taken in a reaction flask. They react as

   $$A(g) + B(g) \rightleftharpoons C(g) + D(g)$$

   When equilibrium is attained, the concentration of C becomes triple to that of B. The equilibrium constant K_C is than equal to 6.

   Statement II If $K_c = 4$ for the following equilibrium,

   $$N_2(g) + 3H_2(g) \rightleftharpoons 2NH_3(g)$$

   The mixture of 1 mol N_2, 3 moles H_2 and 2 moles NH_3 in 1 L flask is not in equilibrium.

   (a) Both Statement I and Statement II are incorrect.
   (b) Statement I is correct but Statement II is incorrect.
   (c) Statement I is incorrect but Statement II is correct.
   (b) Both Statement I and Statement II are correct.

6. At 700 K and 350 bar, a 1 : 3 mixture of $N_2(g)$ and $H_2(g)$ reacts to form an equilibrium mixture containing $x(NH_3) = 0.50$. Assuming ideal behaviour K_p for the equilibrium reaction, $N_2(g) + 3H_2(g) \rightleftharpoons 2NH_3(g)$ is

   (a) 2.03×10^{-4} (b) 3.55×10^{-3}
   (c) 1.02×10^{-4} (d) 3.1×10^{-4}

7. $Ca(HCO_3)_2$ decomposes at 400 as:

   $$Ca(HCO_3)_2(s) \rightleftharpoons CaO(s) + 2CO_2(g) + H_2O(g)$$

   pressure set-up is 7.5 bar. It is then cooled to 298K. ΔH° in the given temperature range is

   (a) -8.9 kJ mol^{-1} (b) 2.14 kJ mol^{-1}
   (c) -2.14 kJ mol^{-1} (d) 14.6 kJ mol^{-1}

8. Two systems $PCl_5(g) \rightleftharpoons PCl_3(g) + Cl_2(g)$ and $COCl_2(g) \rightleftharpoons CO(g) + Cl_2(g)$ are simultaneously in equilibrium in a vessel at constant volume. If some CO is added into the vessel then at the new equilibrium the concentration of

   (a) PCl_5 is greater (b) PCl_3 remains unchanged
   (c) PCl_5 is less (d) Cl_2 is greater

9. For the equilibrium at 298 K,

   $$A \rightleftharpoons B$$

   estimate the fraction 'f' for B in a solution where 'f' is defined by

   $$f = \frac{[B]}{[B] + [A]}$$

   Given, $\Delta G^\circ = 1.7$ kJ mol^{-1} at the given temperature

   (a) 0.33 (b) 1.21
   (c) 2.23 (d) 4.01

10. Given below are two statements:

    Statement I For a gaseous phase reaction $K_p > K_C$, the forward reaction is favoured at $(T > 15\text{ K})$ low pressure, if $\Delta n_g > 0$.

    Statement II At constant volume, addition of inert gas does not have any influence on the equilibrium system.

(a) Both Statement I and Statement II are correct.
(b) Statement I is correct but Statement II is incorrect.
(c) Statement I is incorrect but Statement II is correct.
(d) Both Statement I and Statement II are incorrect.

11. In the dissociation of Ag_2CO_3 at 1200 K in 1L closed vessel total pressure set-up is p atm.

$$Ag_2CO_3(s) \rightleftharpoons 2Ag(s) + CO_2(g) + \frac{1}{2}O_2(g)$$

Thus, equilibrium constant K_p is

(a) $2\left(\frac{p}{3}\right)^{3/2}$ (b) $\left(\frac{2p}{3}\right)^{3/2}$

(c) $\left(\frac{p}{3}\right)^{3/2}$ (d) $\left(\frac{2p}{3}\right)^{1/2}$

12. **Assertion (A)** The oxidation of SO_2 by O_2 to SO_3 is an exothermic reaction, the yield of SO_3 will be minimum if temperature is reduced and pressure is increased.

Reason (R) The given reaction associated with decrease in the number of moles.

(a) Both A and R are true and R is the correct explanation of A.
(b) A is false but R is true.
(c) A is true but R is false.
(d) Both A and R are true but R is not the correct explanation of A.

13. For the equilibrium $PCl_5(g) \rightleftharpoons PCl_3(g) + Cl_2(g)$

$K_{eq} = 100$ and $\Delta G° = -20.0$ kJ mol^{-1}

at a given temperature. For the equilibrium

$$\frac{1}{2}PCl_3(g) + \frac{1}{2}Cl_2 \longrightarrow \frac{1}{2}PCl_5(g)$$

K'_{eq} and $\Delta G'°$ respectively are

	K'_{eq}	$\Delta G'°$ (kJ mol^{-1})
(a)	0.01	− 10.0
(b)	0.10	− 10.0
(c)	0.10	+ 10.0
(d)	0.01	+ 10.0

14. Two solids X and Y dissociate into gaseous products as follows:

$$X(s) \rightleftharpoons A(g) + B(g); \quad K_{p_1} = 500$$
$$Y(s) \rightleftharpoons C(g) + B(g); \quad K_{p_2} = 900$$

At 298 K, the pressure over excess solid X is only 40 atm, and that over solid Y is only 80 atm.

The total pressure over solid mixture is
(a) 74.8 (b) 37.4 (c) 11.2 (d) 45.2

15. For the following reaction through stages I, II and III

$$A \xrightarrow{I} B \xrightarrow{II} C \xrightarrow{III} D$$

quantity of the product formed (X) varies with temperature (T) as given

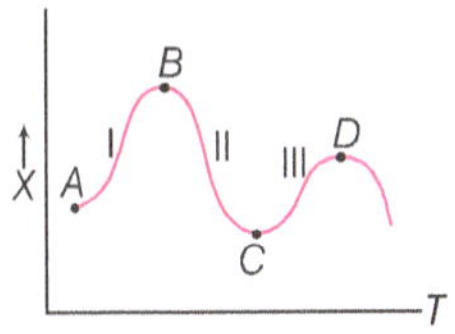

Select the correct statement.
(a) Stages I and III are endothermic but II is exothermic
(b) Stages I and III are exothermic but II is endothermic
(c) Stages II and III are exothermic but I is endothermic
(d) Stage I is exothermic but states II and III are endothermic

16. A sample of air consisting of N_2 and O_2 was heated to 2500 K until the equilibrium,

$$N_2(g) + O_2(g) \rightleftharpoons 2NO(g)$$

was established with an equilibrium constant, $K_C = 2.1 \times 10^{-3}$. At equilibrium, the mole % of NO was 1.8. What will be the mole fraction of N_2 in initial composition of air?
(a) 79.0 (b) 57.3
(c) 69.3 (d) 88.3

17. $N_2O_4 \rightleftharpoons 2NO_2$, $K_C = 4$. This reversible reaction is studied graphically as shown in the given figure. Select the correct statements out of I, II and III.

I. Reaction quotient has maximum value at point A.
II. Reaction proceeds left to right at a point when $[N_2O_4] = [NO_2] = 0.1$ M
III. $K_c = Q$ when point D or F is reached.

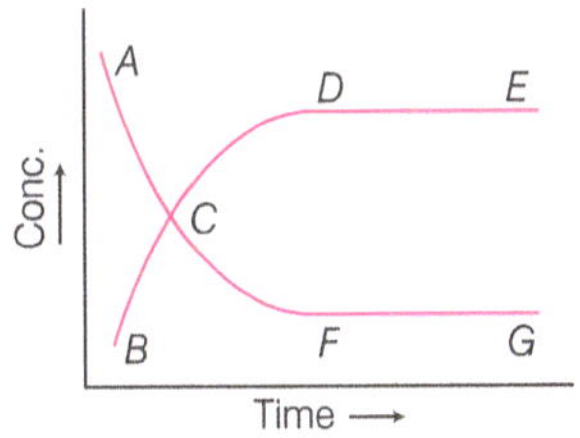

(a) I, II (b) II, III (c) I, III (d) I, II, III

18. The standard reaction enthalpy of

$$Zn(s) + H_2O(g) \longrightarrow ZnO(s) + H_2(g)$$

is approximately constant at + 224 kJ mol^{-1} from 920 K upto 1280 K. The standard reaction Gibbs function is + 33 kJ mol^{-1} at 1280 K. Assuming that both quantities remain constant, estimate the temperature at which the equilibrium constant becomes greater than 1.
(a) 1800 K (b) 1501.2 K
(c) 1000 K (d) 1302.3 K

19. For the reaction

$$[Ag(CN)_2]^- \rightleftharpoons Ag^+ + 2CN^-$$

the equilibrium constant, K_C at 25°C is 4.0×10^{-19}.

Calculate the silver ion concentration in a solution which is originally 0.10 M in KCN and 0.03 M in $AgNO_3$.
(a) 4.3×10^{-6} M (b) 3.2×10^{-10} M
(c) 1.12×10^{-12} M (d) 7.5×10^{-18} M

20. At 90°C, the following equilibrium is established

$$H_2(g) + S(s) \rightleftharpoons H_2S(g); \quad K_C = 6.8 \times 10^{-2}.$$

If 0.20 mole of hydrogen and 1.0 mole of sulphur are heated to 90°C in a 1.0 dm^3 flask, what will be the partial pressure of H_2S gas at equilibrium?

(a) 0.134 (b) 0.380 (c) 3.316 (d) 5.186

Numerical Type Questions

21. A mixture of SO_2 and O_2 at 1 atm in the mole ratio of 2 : 1 is passed through a catalyst at 1170°C at a rate sufficient for the attainment of equilibrium. The exit gas suddenly chilled and analysed is found to contain 87% of SO_3 by volume. The K_p for the reaction is (nearest integer)

$$2SO_2(g) + O_2(g) \rightleftharpoons 2SO_3(g)$$

22. In the following equilibrium, molar concentration were determined by $KMnO_4$ in acidic medium

$$2SO_2(g) + O_2(g) \rightleftharpoons 2SO_3(g)$$

Starting with 2 moles SO_2 and 1 mole O_2 in 1-L flask, mixture required 0.4 mole of $KMnO_4$ when equilibrium is reached. The value of equilibrium constant is ....

23. For the equilibrium in gaseous phase in 2-L flask,

$$2SO_2(g) + O_2(g) \rightleftharpoons 2SO_3(g)$$

2 moles of SO_2 and 1 mole O_2 at 3 atm are taken. Due to reactions, at equilibrium pressure changes to 2.5 atm. Thus, equilibrium constant K_c is

24. The number of correct statements involving equilibrium constant from the following is

A. The value of equilibrium constant is independent of initial concentrations of the reactants and products.

B. The numerical value of the equilibrium constant for a reaction indicates the extent of the reaction.

C. Equilibrium constant is temperature dependent having one unique value for a particular reaction at a given temperature.

D. When equilibrium is attained at a given temperature, the value of all its parameters become constant.

25. For the reaction, $A(g) \rightleftharpoons B(g)$ at 480 K, $\Delta_r G° = -7.38$ kJ mol^{-1}. If we start the reaction in a closed container at 480 K with 25 millimoles of A, the amount of B is the equilibrium mixture is .... millimoles. (Round off to the nearest integer)

$[R = 8.314\ JK^{-1}\ mol^{-1}, \ln 10 = 2.303]$

26. A mixture of 0.2 mol of N_2 and 0.6 mol of H_2 react to give NH_3 according to the equation,

$$N_2(g) + 3H_2(g) \rightleftharpoons 2NH_3(g)$$

at constant temperature and pressure. At equilibrium, 40% of N_2 was found to be present in the equilibrium mixture. Then, the ratio of the final volume to the initial volume of gases is $x : y$ respectively.

The sum of x and y is ....

27. For a contain thermochemical reaction, $X \longrightarrow Y$ at $T = 300$ K, $\Delta H° = 57.3$ kJ mol^{-1}, $\Delta S° = 136$ JK^{-1} mol^{-1}, log equilibrium constant (log K) is .... $\times 10^{-1}$ (Nearest integer)

28. In reaction $N_2(g) + 3H_2(g) \rightleftharpoons 2NH_3(g)$ starting with 1 mol of nitrogen and 3 mol of hydrogen, at equilibrium 50% of each had reacted. If the equilibrium pressure is p. The pressure of hydrogen at equilibrium would be $\frac{p}{x}$.

The value of x is ....

29. Bromine monochloride, BrCl decomposes into bromine and chlorine and reaches the equilibrium $2BrCl(g) \rightleftharpoons Br_2(g) + Cl_2(g)$ for which, $K = 32$ at 500 K. If initially pure BrCl is present at a concentration of 3.3×10^{-3} mol L^{-1}, then its molar concentration in the mixture at equilibrium will be $x \times 10^{-4}$. The value of x is ....

30. Solid ammonium carbamate dissociates as:

$NH_2COONH_4(s) \rightleftharpoons 2NH_3(g) + CO_3(g)$. In a closed vessel, solid ammonium carbamate is in equilibrium with its dissociation products. At equilibrium ammonia is added such that the partial pressure of NH_3 at new equilibrium now equals the original total pressure. The ratio of total pressure at new equilibrium to that of original total pressure is $x : y$.

The sum of x and y is ....

Check Through PYQs

Element 1 Chemical Equilibrium, Law of Mass Action and Equilibrium Constant

1. Given, $NH_2COONH_4(s) \rightleftharpoons 2NH_3(g) + CO_2(g)$

If the partial pressure of CO_2 gas at equilibrium is 0.4 atm and the total pressure is 1 atm, then the value of K_p at the same temperature is *2025, 22 Jan Shift-I*

(a) 0.027 atm^3

(b) 0.064 atm^3

(c) 0.144 atm^3

(d) 0.216 atm^3

2. Consider the given equilibrium reaction

$$CO_2(g) + C(g) \rightleftharpoons 2CO(g)$$

If initial pressure of CO_2 is 0.6 atm and after equilibrium is established, total pressure is 0.8 atm. Then, find K_p.

2025, 22 Jan Shift-I

(a) 0.4 (b) 0.2 (c) 0.6 (d) 0.8

3. For the given hypothetical reactions, the equilibrium constants are as follows: *2024, 8 April Shift-I*

$$X \rightleftharpoons Y; K_1 = 1.0$$

$$Y \rightleftharpoons Z; K_2 = 2.0$$

$$Z \rightleftharpoons W; K_3 = 4.0$$

The equilibrium constant for the reaction $X \rightleftharpoons W$ is

(a) 12.0 (b) 7.0
(c) 6.0 (d) 8.0

4. $A(g) \rightleftharpoons B(g) + \frac{C}{2}(g)$, the correct relationship between K_p, α and equilibrium pressure p is *2024, 31 Jan Shift-II*

(a) $K_p = \frac{\alpha^{3/2}p^{1/2}}{(2+\alpha)^{1/2}(1-\alpha)}$ (b) $K_p = \frac{\alpha^{1/2}p^{1/2}}{(2+\alpha)^{1/2}}$

(c) $K_p = \frac{\alpha^{1/2}p^{1/2}}{(2+\alpha)^{3/2}}$ (d) $K_p = \frac{\alpha^{1/2}p^{3/2}}{(2+\alpha)^{3/2}}$

5. For the given reaction, choose the correct expression of K_C from the following: *2024, 31 Jan Shift-I*

$$Fe^{3+}(aq) + SCN^{-}(aq) \rightleftharpoons (FeSCN)^{2+}(aq)$$

(a) $K_C = \frac{[FeSCN^{2+}]}{[Fe^{3+}][SCN^{-}]}$

(b) $K_C = \frac{[FeSCN^{2+}]^2}{[Fe^{3+}][SCN^{-}]}$

(c) $K_C = \frac{[FeSCN^{2+}]}{[Fe^{3+}]^2[SCN^{-}]^2}$

(d) $K_C = \frac{[Fe^{3+}][SCN^{-}]}{[FeSCN^{2+}]}$

6. Consider the following reaction at 298 K.
$\frac{3}{2}O_2(g) \rightleftharpoons O_3(g), K_p = 2.47 \times 10^{-29}$, $\Delta_r G^{-}$ for the reaction is .... kJ (Given, $R = 8.314\ JK^{-1}\ mol^{-1}$) *2024, 31 Jan Shift-I*

7. The following concentrations were observed at 500 K for the formation of NH_3 from N_2 and H_2. At equilibrium : $[N_2] = 2 \times 10^{-2}$ M, $[H_2] = 3 \times 10^{-2}$ M and $[NH_3] = 1.5 \times 10^{-2}$ M. Equilibrium constant for the reaction is .... *2024, 29 Jan Shift-II*

8. For a certain thermochemical reaction, $M \rightarrow N$ at $T = 400$ K, $\Delta H^{\ominus} = 77.2$ kJ mol^{-1}, $\Delta S = 122\ JK^{-1}$, log equilibrium constant (log K) is – ...... $\times 10^{-1}$. *2024, 27 Jan Shift-II*

9. A mixture of 1 mole of H_2O and 1 mole of CO is taken in a 10 litre container and heated to 725 K. At equilibrium 40% of water by mass reacts with carbon monoxide according to the equation $CO(g) + H_2O(g) \rightleftharpoons CO_2(g) + H_2(g)$. The equilibrium constant $K_C \times 10^2$ for the reaction is .... (Nearest integer) *2023, 11 April Shift-I*

10. (i) $X(g) \rightleftharpoons Y(g) + Z(g), K_{p_1} = 3$
(ii) $A(g) \rightleftharpoons 2B(g), K_{p_2} = 1$
If the degree of dissociation and initial concentration of both the reactants $X(g)$ and $A(g)$ are equal, then the ratio of the total pressure at equilibrium $\left(\frac{p_1}{p_2}\right)$ is equal to $x : 1$.
The value of x is .... (Nearest integer) *2023, 1 Feb Shift-I*

11. At 298 K
$N_2(g) + 3H_2(g) \rightleftharpoons 2NH_3(g); K_1 = 4 \times 10^5$
$N_2(g) + O_2(g) \rightleftharpoons 2NO(g); K_2 = 1.6 \times 10^{12}$
$H_2(g) + \frac{1}{2}O_2(g) \rightleftharpoons H_2O(g); K_3 = 1.0 \times 10^{-13}$
Based on above equilibria, the equilibrium constant of the reaction, $2NH_3(g) + \frac{5}{2}O_2(g) \rightleftharpoons 2NO(g) + 3H_2O(g)$ is .... $\times 10^{-33}$. (Nearest integer) *2023, 29 Jan Shift-II*

12. 4.0 moles of argon and 5.0 moles of PCl_5 are introduced into an evacuated flask of 100 litre capacity at 610 K. The system is allowed to equilibrate. At equilibrium, the total pressure of mixture was found to be 6.0 atm. The K_p for the reaction is [Given, $R = 0.082$ L atm K^{-1} mol^{-1}] *2022, 29 June Shift-II*

(a) 2.25 (b) 6.24
(c) 12.13 (d) 15.24

13. PCl_5 dissociates as
$$PCl_5(g) \rightleftharpoons PCl_3(g) + Cl_2(g)$$
5 moles of PCl_5 are placed in a 200 L vessel which contains 2 moles of N_2 and is maintained at 600 K. The equilibrium pressure is 2.46 atm. The equilibrium constant K_p for the dissociation of PCl_5 is ...... $\times 10^{-3}$. (Nearest integer)
(Given, $R = 0.082$ L atm K^{-1} mol^{-1}; assume ideal gas behaviour) *2022, 24 June Shift-II*

14. The reaction rate for the reaction
$$[PtCl_4]^{2-} + H_2O \rightleftharpoons [Pt(H_2O)Cl_3]^{-} + Cl^{-}$$
was measured as a function of concentrations of different species. It was observed that
$$\frac{-d[[PtCl_4]^{2-}]}{dt} = 4.8 \times 10^{-5}[[PtCl_4]^{2-}] - 2.4 \times 10^{-3}[[Pt(H_2O)Cl_3]^{-}][Cl^{-}].$$
where square brackets are used to denote molar concentrations. The equilibrium constant, $K =$ .... *2021, 26 Aug Shift-II*

15. For the reaction, $A(g) \longrightarrow B(g)$, the value of the equilibrium constant at 300 K and 1 atm is equal to 100.0. The value of $\Delta_r G$ for the reaction at 300 K and 1 atm in J mol^{-1} is – xR, where x is .... (Rounded off to the nearest integer)
($R = 8.31$ J mol^{-1} K^{-1} and ln10 = 2.3) *2021, 24 Feb Shift-I*

16. The value of K_C is 64 at 800 K for the reaction,
$$N_2(g) + 3H_2(g) \rightleftharpoons 2NH_3(g)$$
The value of K_C for the following reaction is
$$NH_3(g) \rightleftharpoons \frac{1}{2}N_2(g) + \frac{3}{2}H_2(g)$$ *2020, 6 Sep Shift-II*

(a) 1/64 (b) 8
(c) 1/4 (d) 1/8

17. The variation of equilibrium constant with temperature is given below *2020, 06 Sep Shift-I*

Temperature	Equilibrium constant
$T_1 = 25°C$	$K_1 = 10$
$T_2 = 100°C$	$K_2 = 100$

The values of $\Delta H°$, $\Delta G°$ at T_1 and $\Delta G°$ at T_2 (in kJ mol^{-1}) respectively, are close to

[use $R = 8.314$ J K^{-1} mol^{-1}]

(a) 28.4, –7.14 and –5.71 (b) 0.64, –7.14 and –5.71
(c) 28.4, –5.71 and –14.29 (d) 0.64, –5.71 and –14.29

18. For the equilibrium $A \rightleftharpoons B$, the variation of the rate of the forward (*a*) and reverse (*b*) reaction with time is given by *2020, 4 Sep Shift-I*

(a)
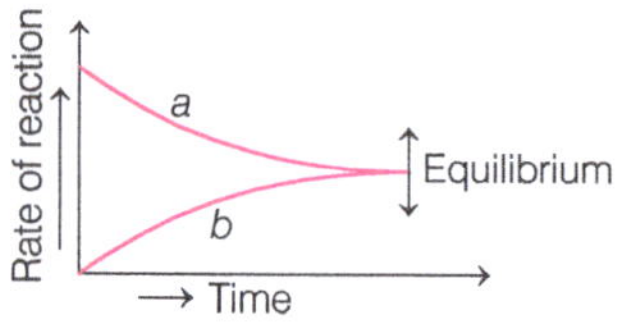

(b)
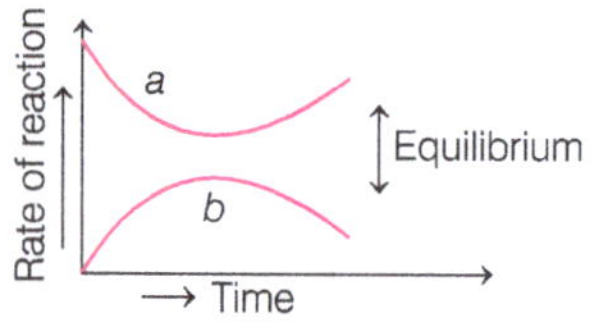

(c)
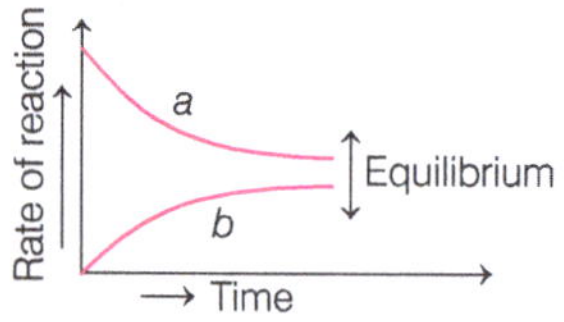

(d)
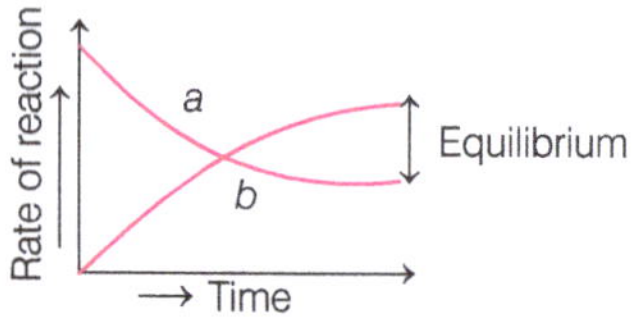

19. In the figure shown below, reactant *A* (represented by square) is in equilibrium with product *B* (represented by circle). The equilibrium constant is

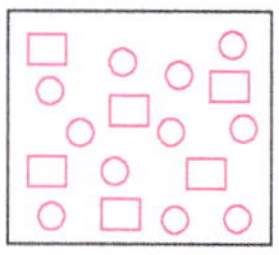

2020, 9 Jan Shift-II

(a) 4 (b) 2 (c) 8 (d) 1

Element 2 Le-Chatelier's Principle and Factor Affecting Chemical Equilibrium

20. The following reaction occurs in the blast furnace where iron ore is reduced to iron metal

$$Fe_2O_3(s) + 3CO(g) \rightleftharpoons Fe(l) + 3CO_2(g)$$

Using the Le-chatelier's principle, predict which one of the following will not disturb the equilibrium. *2024, 5th April Shift-I*

(a) Removal of CO
(b) Removal of CO_2
(c) Addition of CO_2
(d) Addition of Fe_2O_3

21. The number of correct statement/s involving equilibria in physical processes from the following is *2023, 10 April Shift-I*

(A) Equilibrium is possible only in a closed system at a given temperature.
(B) Both the opposing processes occur at the same rate.
(C) When equilibrium is attained at a given temperature, the value of all its parameters became equal.
(D) For dissolution of solids in liquids, the solubility is constant at a given temperature.

22. Consider the following equation:

$$2SO_2(g) + O_2(g) \rightleftharpoons 2SO_3(g), \Delta H = -190 \text{ kJ}$$

The number of factors which will increase the yield of SO_3 at equilibrium from the following is ....

A. increasing temperature
B. increasing pressure
C. adding more SO_2
D. adding more O_2
E. addition of catalyst *2023, 30 Jan Shift-II*

23. Consider the following reaction :

$$N_2O_4(g) \rightleftharpoons 2NO_2(g); \Delta H° = +58 \text{ kJ}$$

For each of the following cases (*A*, *B*), the direction in which the equilibrium shifts is

(*A*) temperature is decreased.
(*B*) pressure is increased by adding N_2 at constant *T*. *2020, 5 Sep Shift-I*

(a) (*A*) towards product, (*B*) towards reactant
(b) (*A*) towards reactant, (*B*) no change
(c) (*A*) towards reactant, (*B*) towards product
(d) (*A*) towards product, (*B*) no change

PRACTICE ELEMENT 02

Target JEE Advanced

Single Correct Choice MCQs

1. When 1-pentyne (A) is treated with 4N alcoholic KOH at 275°C, it is slowly converted into an equilibrium mixture of 1.3% 1-pentyne, (A) 95.2% of 2-pentyne (B) and 3.5% 1,2-pentadiene (C). The equilibrium was maintained at 275°C.

   The order of stability of A, B and C is

   (a) $A > B > C$ (b) $A > C > B$
   (c) $C > B > A$ (d) $B > C > A$

2. When NH_3 is heated in a 0.50 L flask at 700 K and 100 atm pressure, it decomposes into N_2 and H_2 and their equilibrium moles are given below

$$2NH_3(g) \rightleftharpoons N_2(g) + 3H_2(g)$$
$$0.30 \qquad 0.30 \qquad 0.90$$

   Which of the pairs given represents correct value?

	Initial moles of NH_3	K_c for NH_3 formation
(a)	0.80	9.72
(b)	0.90	9.72
(c)	0.80	0.103
(d)	0.90	0.103

3. Given below are two statements.

   Statement I An aqueous solution of hydrogen sulphide shows the equilibrium,

$$H_2S(aq) \rightleftharpoons H^+(aq) + HS^-(aq)$$

   If dilute hydrochloric acid is added to an aqueous solution of hydrogen sulphide without any change in temperature, then the concentration of HS^- will decrease.

   Statement II When $NaNO_3$ is heated in a closed vessel. Oxygen is liberated and $NaNO_2$ is left behind. At equilibrium addition of $NaNO_2$ favours forward reaction.

   (a) Statement I is correct but Statement II is incorrect
   (b) Statement I is incorrect but Statement II is correct
   (c) Both Statement I and Statement II are correct
   (d) Both Statement I and Statement II are incorrect

4. 20 g of sample of $CaCO_3(s)$ of 50% impurity is placed in a sealed vessel of 1L capacity at 400K were 50% dissociation takes place at equilibrium. If CO_2 gas at 0.5 atm is already present, per cent dissociation of $CaCO_3$ is

$$CaCO_3(s) \rightleftharpoons CaO(s) + CO_2(g)$$

   (a) 25.0% (b) 28.7%
   (c) 40.0% (d) 34.8%

5. Given, $COCl_2(g) \rightleftharpoons CO(g) + Cl_2(g)$

$$K_p = 8 \times 10^{-9} \text{ atm}; \ \Delta S° = 30 \text{ cal K}^{-1} \text{ at 373 K}.$$

   Temperature at which phosgene will be 0.1% dissociated at 2 atm ($R = 2$ cal mol^{-1} K^{-1}) is

   (a) 373 K (b) 413 K (c) 446 K (d) 512 K

6. A reaction system in equilibrium according to reaction;

$$2SO_2(g) + O_2 \rightleftharpoons 2SO_3(g)$$

   in 1 L vessel at a given temperature was found to be 0.12 mole each of SO_2 and SO_3 and 5 mole of O_2. In another vessel of 1 L contains 32 g of SO_2 at the same temperature. What mass of O_2 must be added to this vessel so that at equilibrium 20% of SO_2 is oxidised to SO_3?

   (a) 8.36 g (b) 20.1 g
   (c) 11.6 g (d) 15.3 g

7. Two moles of an equimolar mixture of two alcohols R_1—OH and R_2—OH undergoes esterification with one mole of acetic acid. If only 80% of the acid is consumed till equilibrium and the quantities of ester formed under equilibrium are in the ratio 3 : 2. What will be the value of equilibrium constant for the esterification of R_1—OH?

   (a) 4.62 (b) 2.31
   (c) 0.17 (d) 0.48

8. Assume that the decomposition of HNO_3 can be represented as

$$4HNO_3(g) \rightleftharpoons 4NO_2(g) + 2H_2O(g) + O_2(g)$$

   and that at a given temperature of 400 K and pressure of 30 atm, the reaction approaches equilibrium. At equilibrium, the partial pressure of $HNO_3(g)$ is 2 atm. The value of K_C (in m^3) for the reaction at 400 K is ($R = 0.082$ L-atm/K-mol)

   (a) 45 m^3 (b) 30 m^3
   (c) 48 m^3 (d) 26 m^3

9. Equimolar mixture of two gases A_2 and B_2 is taken in a rigid vessel at constant temperature 300 K. The gases achieve equilibrium as follows.

$$A_2(g) \rightleftharpoons 2A(g), \quad K_1 = x \text{ atm}$$
$$B_2(g) \rightleftharpoons 2B(g), \quad K_2 = y \text{ atm}$$
$$A_2(g) + B_2(g) \rightleftharpoons 2AB(g); \quad K_3 = 2$$

   If the initial pressure in the container was 2 atm and the final pressure at equilibrium is 2.75 atm in which the partial pressure of $AB(g)$ is 0.5 atm. What will be the value of $y : x$ if $(y > x)$?

   (a) 1 : 8 (b) 3 : 2
   (c) 2 : 3 (d) 8 : 1

One or More than One Correct MCQs

10. For the reaction, $2SO_3(g) \rightleftharpoons 2SO_2(g) + O_2(g)$.

When 2 moles of SO_3 are taken in a flask of 10.0 L at 350 K, at equilibrium ratio of SO_2 to SO_3 is 0.663. Thus,

(a) $K_{eq} = 0.0176 \text{ mol L}^{-1}$ (b) $\Delta G° = 11.76 \text{ kJ mol L}^{-1}$

(c) $[O_2] = 0.04 \text{ mol L}^{-1}$ (d) $[SO_3] = 0.12 \text{ mol L}^{-1}$

11. The equilibrium $SO_2Cl_2(g) \rightleftharpoons SO_2(g) + Cl_2(g)$

is attained at 298 K in a closed container and an inert gas helium is introduced. Which of the following statements is/are correct?

(a) Concentration of each species changes
(b) More Cl_2 is formed
(c) SO_2 decreases
(d) Both SO_2 and Cl_2 increases

12. One mole of $N_2O_4(g)$ at 300 K is kept in a closed container under one atmosphere. It is heated to 600 K when 20% by mass of $N_2O_4(g)$ decomposes to NO_2.

$$N_2O_4(g) \rightleftharpoons 2NO_2(g)$$

Thus,

(a) equilibrium pressure is 1.2 atm
(b) $K_p = 0.167$
(c) $K_C = 6.78 \times 10^{-3}$
(d) $K_p / K_C = 0.28$

13. For the equilibrium

$$Cl_2(g) \rightleftharpoons 2Cl(g)$$

degree of dissociation of Cl_2 is 0.071 at 1 atm and 1603 K. Thus

(a) $\chi_{Cl_2} > \chi_{Cl}$ (b) $K_\chi = 0.0204$

(c) $K_p = 0.0204$ atm (d) $K_C = 1.55 \times 10^{-4} \text{ mol L}^{-1}$

14. Which of the following factors will increase solubility of $NH_3(g)$ in H_2O?

$$NH_3(g) + H_2O\,(l) \rightleftharpoons NH_4OH(aq)$$

(a) Increase in pressure
(b) Addition of water
(c) Lowering of temperature
(d) Decreases in pressure

15. Select the correct relationships for the given equilibrium.

(a) $N_2(g) + O_2(g) \rightleftharpoons 2NO(g); K_{eq} = K_1$

$NO(g) \rightleftharpoons \frac{1}{2}N_2(g) + \frac{1}{2}O_2(g); K_{eq} = K_2$ thus, $K_1K_2^2 = 1$

(b) Free energy changes is ΔG_1° for

$2NO_2(g) \rightleftharpoons N_2O_4(g)$ and ΔG_2° for

$\frac{1}{2}N_2O_4(g) \rightleftharpoons NO_2(g)$, then, $2\Delta G_2^\circ + \Delta G_1^\circ = 0$

(c) van't Hoff equation is, $\Delta_r H^\circ\left(\frac{1}{T_2} - \frac{1}{T_1}\right) = \frac{\Delta_r G_2^\circ}{T_2} - \frac{\Delta_r G_1^\circ}{T_1}$

(d) For the equilibrium, $A(g) \rightleftharpoons 2B(g)$, $x = \sqrt{\frac{K_p}{K_p + 4p}}$

(x = Degree of dissociation)

16. For a reaction, $A(g) \rightleftharpoons B(g) + C(g). K_p$ at 400°C is 1.5×10^{-4} and K_p at 600°C is 6×10^{-3}. Which of the following statements are correct regarding the given data?

(a) The reaction is exothermic.
(b) Increase in temperature increases the formation of B.
(c) Increase in pressure increases the formation of A.
(d) Decrease in temperature and increase in pressure shift the equilibrium towards left.

17. Sulphuric acid is manufactured by the following reaction

$$2SO_2(g) + O_2(g) \rightleftharpoons 2SO_3(g) + Q$$

Reaction proceeds in the forward direction if

(a) some H_2O is added
(b) inert gas (helium) is passed into mixture
(c) temperature is lowered
(d) SO_3 is passed into mixture

Integer/Numerical Type Questions

18. A 4.72 g sample of methanol (CH_3OH) was placed in an otherwise empty 1.00 L flask and heated to 250°C to vapourise the methanol over time, the methanol vapour decomposed by the following reaction.

$$CH_3OH(g) \rightleftharpoons CO(g) + 2H_2(g)$$

After the system has reached equilibrium, a tiny hole is drilled in the side of the flask allowing gaseous compounds to effuse out of the flask. Measurements of the effusing gas show that it contains 33.0 times as much $H_2(g)$ as $CH_3OH(g)$. The value of equilibrium constant K for this reaction at 250°C is ....

19. The N_2O_4 and NO_2 equilibrium mixture in the flask on the left is allowed to expand into the evacuated flask on the right. The composition of gaseous mixture when equilibrium is established in the system consisting of the two flask is a and b respectively.

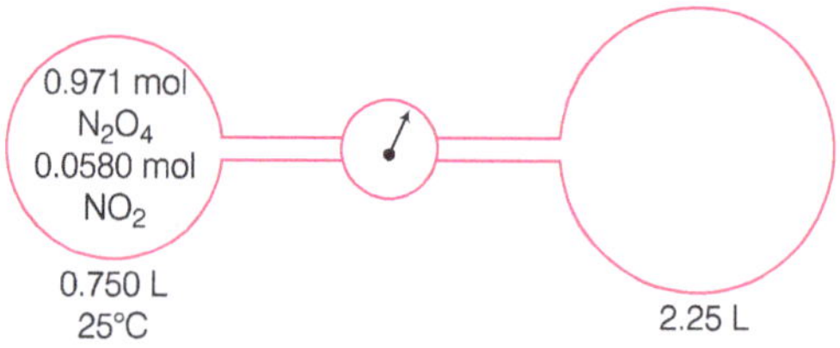

$K_C = 4.61 \times 10^{-3}$

The value of $a + b$ is .... mol.

20. An amount of 16 moles of H_2 and 4 moles of N_2 is confined in a vessel of volume one litre. The vessel is heated to a constant temperature until the equilibrium is established. At equilibrium, the pressure was found to be $\frac{9}{10}$th of the initial pressure. The value of K_C for the reaction,

$N_2(g) + 3H_2(g) \rightleftharpoons 2NH_3(g)$ is .... $\times 10^{-4}$ M^{-2}.

21. Consider the reaction $X \rightleftharpoons Y$ at 1800 K. At time *t*, the temperature of the system was increased to 3600 K and the system was allowed to reach equilibrium. Throughout this experiment the partial pressure of *X* was maintained at 1 bar. Given below is the plot of the partial pressure of *Y* with time. What is the ratio of the standard Gibbs energy of the reaction at 1800 K to that of 3600 K?

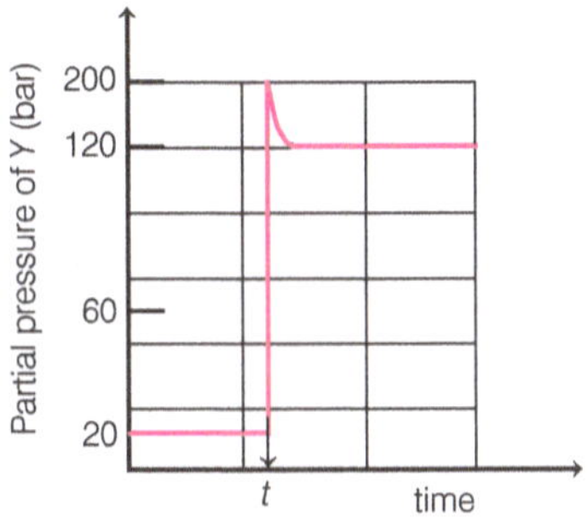

22. The equilibrium constant for the reaction:
$H_3BO_3 + \text{Glycerin} \rightleftharpoons (H_3BO_3 + \text{Glycerin complex})$ is 0.90.
How much glycerin should be added to 1 L of 0.10 M H_3BO_3 solution, so that 60% of the H_3BO_3 is converted to boric acid glycerin complex ....

23. For the equilibrium,
$$LiCl \cdot 3NH_3(s) \rightleftharpoons LiCl \cdot NH_3(s) + 2NH_3(g);$$
$K_p = 9\ \text{atm}^2$ at 37°C. A 5 litre vessel contains 0.1 mole of $LiCl \cdot NH_3$. How many moles of NH_3 should be added to the flask at this temperature to drive the backward reaction to completion?
[Given : $R = 0.082$ atm -L/mol K]

24. The value of *K* for the reaction,
$$A(g) + B(g) \rightleftharpoons C(g) + D(g)$$
Changed from 0.096 at 298 K to 1.4 at 373 K. The temperature above which the reaction becomes thermodynamically spontaneous in the forward direction assuming that $\Delta H°$ and $\Delta S°$ values for the reaction do not change with change in temperature is ....
[$\Delta S^{\circ}_{298\,K} = 102.96\ JK^{-1}$]

25. For the dissociation of phosgene gas, the value of K_p at 373 K is 6.7×10^{-9},
$$COCl_2(g) \rightleftharpoons CO(g) + Cl_2(g)$$
The fraction of phosgene dissociated at this temperature when 1 mole of phosgene is placed in a 100 L flask containing N_2 at a partial pressure of 1 bar is $x \times 10^{-4}$.
The value of *x* is ....

26. In a 1 L flask 16 moles of *A* undergoes the reaction, $X(g) \rightleftharpoons Z(g)$. The progress of product formation at two temperatures (in kelvin), T_1 and T_2 is shown in the figure.

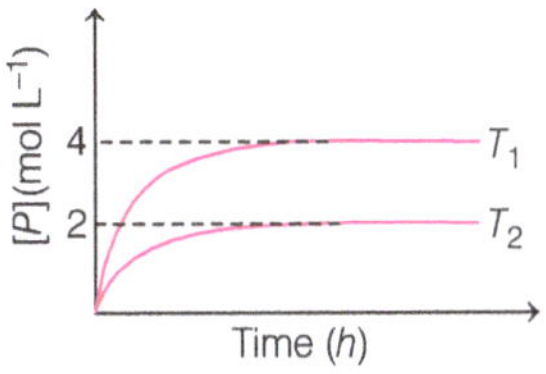

If $T_1 = 2T_2$ and $(\Delta G_2^{\circ} - \Delta G_1^{\circ}) = RT_2 \ln x$, then the value of *x* is ....
[ΔG_1° and ΔG_2° are standard Gibb's free energy change for the reaction at temperature T_1 and T_2 respectively]

Matching Type Questions

27. 4 moles of PCl_5 are placed in a 2-L flask when the following equilibrium is established :
$$PCl_5(g) \rightleftharpoons PCl_3(g) + Cl_2(g)$$
On analysis flask is found to contain Cl_2 of molar concentration 0.4 mol L^{-1}.
Match the parameters in Column I with their related values in Column II and select the correct answer from codes given below.

	Column I		Column II
i.	PCl_5 (mol)	p.	0.8
ii.	PCl_3 (mol)	q.	0.4
iii.	Cl_2 (mol L^{-1})	r.	3.2
iv.	K_{eq} (mol L^{-1})	s.	0.1

Codes

	i	ii	iii	iv		i	ii	iii	iv
(a)	p	r	q	s	(b)	s	q	p	r
(c)	r	p	q	s	(d)	p	q	s	r

28. In the following equilibrium, $H_2(g) + I_2(g) \rightleftharpoons 2HI(g)$ is set-up at 298 K in a 5 L flask. Experiment is carried by taking 0.1 mole each of $H_2(g)$ and $I_2(g)$.
After equilibrium is attained, $I_2(g)$ was dissolved in KI and required 100 mL of 0.1 M $Na_2S_2O_3$ solution.
Match the values given in Column II with the respective terms in Column I.

	Column I		Column II
i.	HI (mol) formed at equilibrium.	p.	0.005
ii.	H_2 (mol) at equilibrium.	q.	0.01
iii.	$Na_2S_2O_3$ (mole) reacted.	r.	1.00
iv.	K_C / K_p	s.	0.19

Codes

	i	ii	iii	iv		i	ii	iii	iv
(a)	s	p	r	q	(b)	s	q	p	r
(c)	s	p	q	r	(d)	p	s	q	r

29. Given at 298 K
I. $Fe_2O_3(s) + 3H_2(g) \rightleftharpoons 3Fe(s) + 3H_2O(l);\ K_p^{I} = 4.0 \times 10^{-6}$
II. $CO_2(g) + H_2(g) \rightleftharpoons CO(g) + H_2O(l);\ K_p^{II} = 3.2 \times 10^{-4}$
III. $Fe_2O_3(s) + 3CO\ (g) \rightleftharpoons 3CO_2(g) + 3Fe(s);\ K_p^{III} = ?$
Match the parameters given in List I with their respective value in List II.

	Column I		Column II
i.	K_p^{III}	p.	3.2×10^{-6}
ii.	p_{CO} / p_{CO_2} at equilibrium in III	q.	0.063×10^{3}
iii.	p_{H_2} at equilibrium in I	r.	2.0×10^{-2}
iv.	p_{CO} / p_{H_2} in II when $p_{CO_2} = 1 \times 10^{-2}$ bar	s.	1.2207×10^{5}

Codes

	i	ii	iii	iv
(a)	s	r	q	p
(b)	s	r	p	q
(c)	s	p	q	r
(d)	p	r	s	q

30. The hydrogenation of pyridine (C_5H_5N) to piperidine ($C_5H_{11}N$)

$$C_5H_5N(g) + 3H_2(g) \rightleftharpoons C_5H_{11}N(g)$$

is an equilibrium process whose equilibrium constant (K_p) is given by

$$\log_{10}K_p = -20.281 + \frac{10.560K}{T}$$

Match the thermodynamics parameters in column I with their respective values in column II.

	Column I		Column II
i.	$\log_{10} K_p$ at 500 K	p.	-388.32
ii.	$\Delta H°$ (in J)	q.	-20.26
iii.	$\Delta S°$ (in J)	r.	193.96×10^3
iv.	$\Delta G°$ at 500 K (in J)	s.	-202.19

Codes

	i	ii	iii	iv		i	ii	iii	iv
(a)	q	s	r	p	(b)	q	s	p	r
(c)	q	p	r	s	(d)	p	s	r	q

Paragraph of Two Questions Each

Paragraph 1

The variation of equilibrium constant K with temperature is given by van't Hoff equation

$$\ln K = \frac{\Delta_r S°}{R} - \frac{\Delta_r H°}{RT}$$

This equation can be used to evaluate $\Delta rH°$ if the equilibrium constants K_1 and K_2 at two temperatures T_1 and T_2 are known

$$\log\left\{\frac{K_2}{K_1}\right\} = \frac{\Delta_r H°}{2.303R}\left[\frac{1}{T_1} - \frac{1}{T_2}\right]$$

31. For an isomerisation reaction $A(g) \rightleftharpoons B(g)$, the temperature dependency of equilibrium constant is given by

$$\ln K = 5 - \frac{2000}{T}$$

The value of $\Delta_r S°$ at 400 K is .... JK^{-1}

32. The equilibrium constant K_p for the following reaction is 2 at 27°C and 8 at 47°C.

$$A(g) \rightleftharpoons B(g) + C(g)$$

The enthalpy change for the reaction below is (–) .... kcal.

$$B(g) + C(g) \rightleftharpoons A(g)$$

($R = 2$ cal /mol -K)

Paragraph 2

Case I Two moles of gaseous NH_3 are introduced in a 1.0 L flask and allowed to undergo partial decomposition at high temperature according to the reaction,

$$2NH_3(g) \rightleftharpoons N_2(g) + 3H_2(g)$$

At equilibrium 1.0 mole of $NH_3(g)$ remains.

Case II 1 mole $N_2(g)$ and 4 moles $H_2(g)$ are taken in 15 L flask at 27°C.

After the complete conversion of $N_2(g)$ into $NH_3(g)$, 5 L of H_2O is added.

33. The value of equilibrium constant K_C in case I will be ....

34. The sum of pressure set-up before and after adding H_2O in case II is .... atm.

Paragraph 3

N_2O_4 dissociates according to the equation

$$N_2O_4(g) \rightleftharpoons 2NO_2(g)$$

When 0.578 g of N_2O_4 was introduced into 1 dm^3 flask maintained at 308 K the equilibrium pressure was 24.12 kPa.

35. The degree of dissociation will be ....

36. The value of equilibrium constant (K_p) is $x \times 10^{-2}$ atm.

Species Selection (with 5 Species)

37. Consider the following reactions,
   (i) $H_2(g) + I_2(g) \rightleftharpoons 2HI(g)$
   (ii) $N_2(g) + 3H_2(g) \rightleftharpoons 2NH_3(g)$
   (iii) $Fe(s) + S(s) \rightleftharpoons FeS(s)$
   (iv) $N_2(g) + O_2(g) \rightleftharpoons 2NO(g)$
   (v) $C_{(diamond)} \rightleftharpoons C_{(graphite)}$

   The total reactions, for which Le Chatelier's principle is not applicable ....
   (a) 4 (b) 2 (c) 1 (d) 3

38. Consider the following matches:
   (i) $\Delta G° < 0, K > 1$
   (ii) $\Delta G° = 0, K = 1$
   (iii) $\Delta G° > 0, K < 1$
   (iv) $\Delta G° < 0, K < 1$
   (v) $\Delta G° > 1, K = 0$

   The total number of incorrect match is
   (a) 3 (b) 2 (c) 1 (d) 4

39. Consider the following equilibria,
   (i) $PCl_5(g) \rightleftharpoons PCl_3(g) + Cl_2(g)$
   (ii) $N_2(g) + 3H_2(g) \rightleftharpoons 2NH_3(g)$
   (iii) $N_2(g) + O_2(g) \rightleftharpoons 2NO(g)$
   (iv) $SO_2Cl_2(g) \rightleftharpoons SO_2(g) + Cl_2(g)$
   (v) $2N_2O_4(g) \rightleftharpoons 2NO_2(g)$

How many equilibria is not affected by change in volume of the flask?

(a) 4 (b) 3 (c) 2 (d) 1

40. For the equilibrium,

$$COCl_2(g) \rightleftharpoons CO(g) + Cl_2(g)$$

(i) $K_p = \frac{px^2}{(1-x^2)}$ (x = degree of dissociation)

(ii) $x = \sqrt{\frac{K_p}{p+K_p}}$

(iii) $K_C = \frac{x^2 V}{(1-x)}$

(iv) $K_C = \frac{x^2}{(1-x^2)V}$

(v) $K_p = \frac{px}{(1+x)^2}$

The correct expression is/are ....

(a) 4 (b) 3 (c) 1 (d) 2

Species Selection (with 7 species)

41. Consider the following reactions,

(i) $CaCO_3(s) \rightleftharpoons CaO(s) + CO_2(g)$
(ii) $H_2O(l) \rightleftharpoons H_2O(g)$
(iii) $3Fe(s) + 4H_2O(g) \rightleftharpoons Fe_3O_4(s) + 4H_2(g)$
(iv) $PCl_5(g) \rightleftharpoons PCl_3(g) + Cl_2(g)$
(v) $N_2(g) + O_2(g) \rightleftharpoons 2NO(g)$
(vi) $2NOCl(g) \rightleftharpoons 2NO(g) + Cl_2(g)$
(vii) $2SO_2(g) + O_2(g) \rightleftharpoons 2SO_3(g)$

The total number of reactions for which $K_p = K_C$ are ....

(a) 2 (b) 3 (c) 4 (d) 5

42. Consider the following reactions,

(i) $C_2H_5OH(g) + 3O_2(g) \rightleftharpoons 2CO_2(g) + 3H_2O(g)$
(ii) $2NOCl(g) \rightleftharpoons 2NO(g) + Cl_2(g)$
(iii) $NH_4Cl(s) \rightleftharpoons NH_3(g) + HCl(g)$
(iv) $4PH_3(g) \rightleftharpoons P_4(g) + 6H_2(g)$
(v) $CO(g) + H_2O(g) \rightleftharpoons CO_2(g) + H_2(g)$
(vi) $S(g) + 3F_2(g) \rightleftharpoons SF_6(g)$
(vii) $CH_4(g) + Cl_2(g) \rightleftharpoons CH_3Cl(g) + HCl(g)$

The total number of reactions in which backward reaction is favoured upon increasing the pressure are ....

(a) 3 (b) 6 (c) 5 (d) 4

43. Consider the following reactions,

(i) $PCl_5(g) \rightleftharpoons PCl_3(g) + Cl_2(g)$
(ii) $SO_2Cl_2(g) \rightleftharpoons SO_2(g) + Cl_2(g)$
(iii) $Cl_2(g) + 3F_2(g) \rightleftharpoons 2ClF_3(g)$
(iv) $N_2(g) + 3H_2(g) \rightleftharpoons 2NH_3(g)$
(v) $NO_2Cl_2(g) \rightleftharpoons NO_2(g) + Cl_2(g)$
(vi) $2SO_2(g) + O_2(g) \rightleftharpoons 2SO_3(g)$
(vii) $2NO_2(g) \rightleftharpoons 2NO(g) + O_2(g)$

The total number of reactions, which are favoured by introducing an inert gas at constant pressure to forward reaction at constant temperature are ....

(a) 7 (b) 5 (c) 3 (d) 4

44. Consider the following chemical reactions,

(i) $PCl_3(g) + Cl_2(g) \rightleftharpoons PCl_5(g)$
(ii) $N_2(g) + O_2(g) \rightleftharpoons 2NO(g)$
(iii) $N_2(g) + 3H_2(g) \rightleftharpoons 2NH_3(g)$
(iv) $2SO_2(g) + O_2(g) \rightleftharpoons 2SO_3(g)$
(v) $2HI(g) \rightleftharpoons H_2(g) + I_2(g)$
(vi) $2ICl(g) \rightleftharpoons I_2(g) + Cl_2(g)$
(vii) $2NOCl(g) \rightleftharpoons 2NO(g) + Cl_2(g)$

The chemical reaction in which the yield of the product cannot be increased or decreased by the application of high pressure is/are ....

(a) 2 (b) 3 (c) 4 (d) 6

45. Consider the following species:

A. SO_4^{2-} B. NO_3^-
C. Cl^- D. CN^-
E. SCN^- F. NCS^-

The total number of species in equilibrium

$2\overset{I}{Cu} \rightleftharpoons \overset{0}{Cu} + \overset{II}{Cu}$ in aqueous medium at 25°C that shifts towards the left is ....

(a) 5 (b) 4 (c) 3 (d) 2

Check Through PYQs

Element 1 Chemical Equilibrium, Law of Mass Action and Equilibrium Constant

1. In a one L flask, 6 moles of A undergoes the reaction $A(g) \rightleftharpoons P(g)$. The progress of product formation at two temperatures (in Kelvin), T_1 and T_2, is shown in the figure. *2023 Adv.*

If $T_1 = 2T_2$ and $(\Delta G_2^\ominus - \Delta G_1^\ominus) = RT_2 \ln x$, then the value of x is ______ .

[$\Delta G_1^\ominus$ and $\Delta G_2^\ominus$ are standard Gibb's free energy change for the reaction at temperatures T_1 and T_2, respectively.]

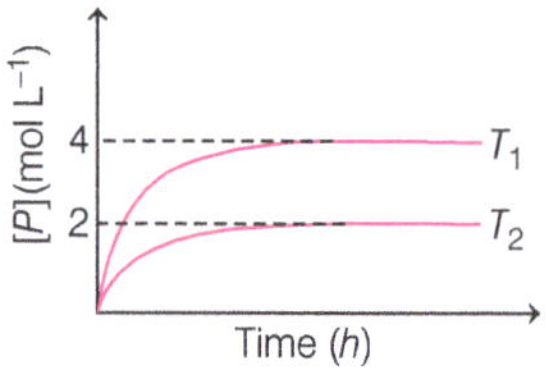

2. Consider the reaction $A \rightleftharpoons B$ at 1000 K. At time t, the temperature of the system was increased to 2000 K and the system was allowed to reach equilibrium. Throughout this experiment the partial pressure of A was maintained at 1 bar. Given below is the plot of the partial pressure of B with time. What is the ratio of the standard Gibbs energy of the reaction at 1000 K to that at 2000 K? *2020 Adv.*

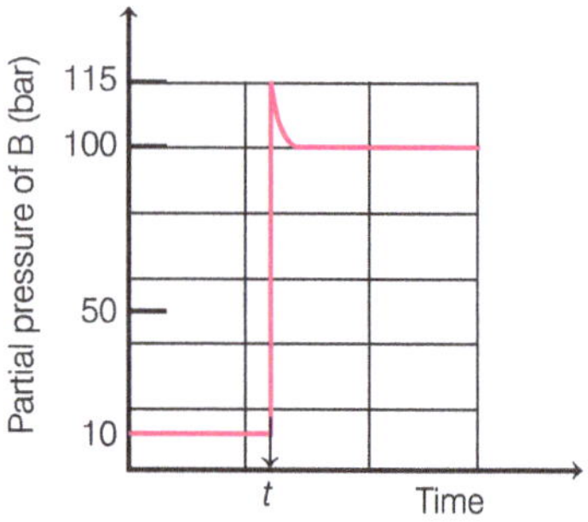

3. For a reaction, $A \rightleftharpoons P$, the plots of [A] and [P] with time at temperatures T_1 and T_2 are given below.

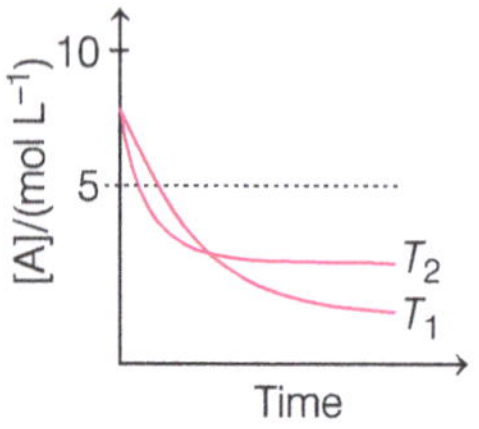

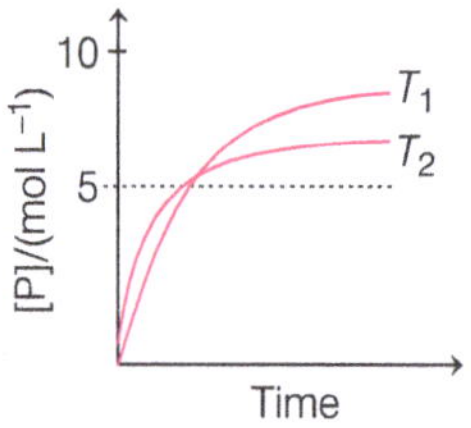

If $T_2 > T_1$, the correct statement(s) is are

(Assume $\Delta H^\ominus$ and $\Delta S^\ominus$ are independent of temperature and ratio of $\ln K$ at T_1 to $\ln K$ at T_2 is greater than T_2 / T_1. Here H, S, G and K are enthalpy, entropy, Gibbs energy and equilibrium constant, respectively.) *2018 Adv.*

(a) $\Delta H^\ominus < 0, \Delta S^\ominus < 0$

(b) $\Delta G^\ominus < 0, \Delta H^\ominus > 0$

(c) $\Delta G^\ominus < 0, \Delta S^\ominus < 0$

(d) $\Delta G^\ominus < 0, \Delta S^\ominus > 0$

4. The surface of copper gets tarnished by the formation of copper oxide. N_2 gas was passed to prevent the oxide formation during heating of copper at 1250 K. However, the N_2 gas contains 1 mole % of water vapour as impurity. The water vapour oxidises copper as per the reaction given below *2019 Adv.*

$$2Cu(g) + H_2O(g) \longrightarrow Cu_2O(s) + H_2(g)$$

p_{H_2} is the minimum partial pressure of H_2 (in bar) needed to prevent the oxidation at 1250 K. The value of $\ln(p_{H_2})$ is ....

(Given : total pressure = 1 bar, R (universal gas constant) $= 8\ J\ K^{-1}\ mol^{-1}$, $\ln(10) = 2.30$ Cu(s) and $Cu_2O(s)$ are mutually immiscible.)

At 1250 K : $2Cu(s) + 1/2\ O_2(g) \longrightarrow Cu_2O(s)$; $\Delta G^\ominus = -78{,}000\ J\ mol^{-1}$

$$H_2(g) + \frac{1}{2}O_2(g) \longrightarrow H_2O(g);$$

$\Delta G^\ominus = -1{,}78{,}000\ J\ mol^{-1}$; G is the Gibbs energy *2018 Adv.*

Passage (Q. Nos. 5-6)

Thermal decomposition of gaseous X_2 to gaseous X at 298 K takes place according to the following equation:

$$X_2(g) \rightleftharpoons 2X(g)$$

The standard reaction Gibbs energy, $\Delta_r G^\circ$, of this reaction is positive. At the start of the reaction, there is one mole of X_2 and no X. As the reaction proceeds, the number of moles of X formed is given by β. Thus, $\beta_{equilibrium}$ is the number of moles of X formed at equilibrium. The reaction is carried out at a constant total pressure of 2 bar. Consider the gases to behave ideally.

(Given, $R = 0.083\ L\ bar\ K^{-1}\ mol^{-1}$)

5. The equilibrium constant K_p for this reaction at 298 K, in terms of $\beta_{equilibrium}$ is *2016 Adv.*

(a) $\dfrac{8\beta^2_{equilibrium}}{2-\beta_{equilibrium}}$ (b) $\dfrac{8\beta^2_{equilibrium}}{4-\beta^2_{equilibrium}}$

(c) $\dfrac{4\beta^2_{equilibrium}}{2-\beta_{equilibrium}}$ (d) $\dfrac{4\beta^2_{equilibrium}}{4-\beta^2_{equilibrium}}$

6. The incorrect statement among the following for this reaction, is *2016 Adv.*

(a) decrease in the total pressure will result in the formation of more moles of gaseous X

(b) at the start of the reaction, dissociation of gaseous X_2 takes place spontaneously

(c) $\beta_{equilibrium} = 0.7$

(d) $K_C < 1$

Element 2 Le-Chatelier's Principle and Factor Affecting Chemical Equilibrium

7. The % yield of ammonia as a function of time in the reaction,

$N_2(g) + 3H_2(g) \rightleftharpoons 2NH_3(g); \Delta H < 0$ *2015 Adv.*

at (p, T_1) is given below.

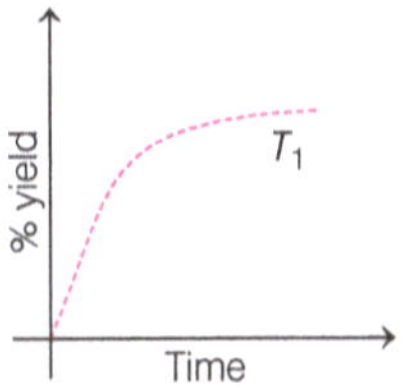

If this reaction is conducted at (p, T_1), with $T_2 > T_1$ the % yield by of ammonia as a function of time is represented by

(a)
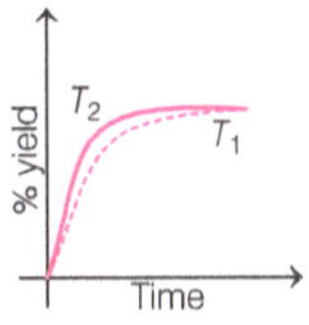

(b)
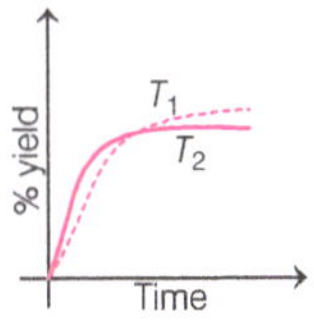

(c)
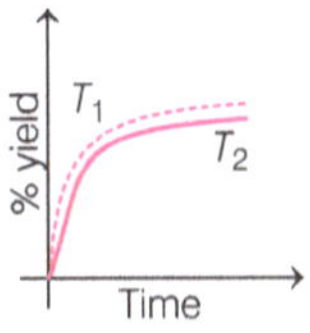

(d)
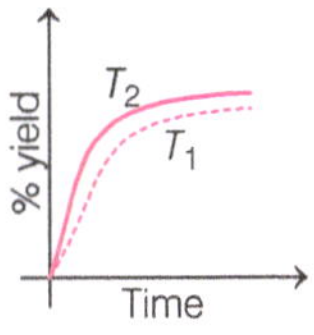

HINTS & Solutions

Solutions : Competency Enhancer

1.1. ***(a)*** The reaction, $2NO(g) + O_2(g) \rightleftharpoons 2NO_2(g)$ will be formed from the given reaction by multiplying it by 2 and the reversing it.

Thus, $$K_C' = \frac{1}{K_C^2} = \left(\frac{1}{4.89 \times 10^{-6}}\right)^2$$

$$= 0.04182 \times (10^6)^2$$

$$\approx 4.182 \times 10^{10}$$

1.2. ***(c)*** Initially there is $NH_3(g)$ at 0.5 atm.

$$NH_4HS(s) \rightleftharpoons NH_3(g) + H_2S(g)$$

Initially	– $(1-x)$	0.5 atm	0
At equilibrium		$(x+0.5)$	x

$\therefore \quad K_p = p_{NH_3} \cdot p_{H_2O} = (x+0.5)x = 0.11$

$x^2 + 0.5x - 0.11 = 0$

$\therefore \quad x \approx 0.17$

Hence, $p_{NH_3} = 0.17 + 0.50 = 0.67$ atm

$p_{H_2S} = 0.17$ atm

$p_{total} = p_{NH_3} + p_{H_2S} = 0.84$ atm

1.3. ***(–2903)*** Since, $\partial(\Delta G)_T = \Delta V \partial p$

$$\therefore \quad \int_g^d \partial(\Delta G) = \int_{p_1}^{p_2} \Delta V \, \partial p$$

$$\Rightarrow \quad (\Delta_f G_1^\ominus)_d - (\Delta_f G^\ominus)_g = \Delta V(p_2 - p_1)$$

$$\Delta V = (V_d - V_g)$$

$$= \left(\frac{12}{3.51} - \frac{12}{22.5}\right) \times 10^{-6} \text{ m}^3 \text{ mol}^{-1}$$

$$= -1.91 \times 10^{-6} \text{ m}^3 \text{ mol}^{-1}$$

$$\therefore \quad \Delta_r G = (\Delta_f G^\ominus)_d - (\Delta_f \Delta G^\ominus)_g$$

$$= -1.91 \times 10^{-6} \text{ m}^3 \text{ mol}^{-1} (1.52 \times 10^9 - 101325) \text{ Pa}$$

$$= -2903 \text{ J/mol}$$

Elemental Practice 5.1

1. ***(b)*** $K_1 = \dfrac{[NH_4OH]\,[H_3O^+]}{[NH_4^+]}$

$$K_2 = [H_3O^+]\,[OH^-] \Rightarrow K_3 = \frac{[NH_4^+]\,[OH^-]}{[NH_4OH]}$$

Thus, $$K_3 = \frac{K_2}{K_1} = \frac{1 \times 10^{-14}}{5.56 \times 10^{-10}} \approx 1.8 \times 10^{-5}$$

H_2O as reactant species is not a part of equilibrium constant.

2. ***(d)*** The reaction, $2SO_2(g) + O_2(g) \rightleftharpoons 2SO_3(g)$ will be formed from the given reaction by multiplying it by coefficient and then reversing it.

Thus, $$K_C' = \frac{1}{K_C^2} = \left(\frac{1}{7.36 \times 10^{-3}}\right)^2$$

$$\approx (0.1359 \times 10^3)^2$$

$$= 0.018468 \times 10^6 = 184.68 \times 10^2$$

3. ***(a)*** $$N_2O_4 \rightleftharpoons 2NO_2$$

At start	1	0
At equilibrium	$(1-x)$	$2x$

$y = 2$

(Total moles of products for 1 mole reactant)

$$\therefore \quad x = \frac{D-d}{d} = \frac{D}{d} - 1 \Rightarrow x + 1 = \frac{D}{d}$$

when $x = 0$

$D = d$

Thus, as x increases, $\dfrac{D}{d}$ also increases.

4. ***(a)*** $K_C = \dfrac{[CH_3OH]}{[CO]\,[H_2]^2}$

Given $n_{CO} = n_{CH_3OH}$ mol

Let $H_2 = x$ mol

$$\therefore \quad K_c = 4 \times 10^2 = \frac{\left(\frac{n}{5}\right)}{\left(\frac{n}{5}\right)\left(\frac{x}{5}\right)^2}$$

$$\therefore \quad 400 = \frac{25}{x^2} \Rightarrow x^2 = \frac{25}{400}$$

$$\Rightarrow \quad x = 0.25 \text{ mol}$$

5. ***(b)*** $K_3 = K_1 / K_2$

$$K_3 = \frac{K_1}{K_2} = \frac{6.30 \times 10^{-5}}{6.30 \times 10^9} = 1.0 \times 10^{-14}$$

6. ***(b)*** $K_1 = \dfrac{[C]}{[A]\,[B]^2};\ K_2 = \dfrac{[A]^3}{[C]\,[D]};\ K_3 = \dfrac{[C]^2}{[B]^6\,[D]}$

$$K_1^3 K_2 = \frac{[C]^3}{[A]^3\,[B]^6} \cdot \frac{[A]^3}{[C]\,[D]} = \frac{[C]^2}{[B]^6\,[D]} = K_3$$

7. ***(d)*** $H_2(g) + I_2(g) \rightleftharpoons 2HI(g)$

$$\left(\frac{dx}{dt}\right)_f = 1.7 \times 10^{-18}[H_2]\,[I_2]$$

$$2HI(g) \longrightarrow H_2(g) + I_2(g)$$

$$\left(\frac{dx}{dt}\right)_b = 2.4 \times 10^{-21}\,[HI]^2$$

For equilibrium $H_2(g) + I_2(g) \rightleftharpoons 2HI(g)$

$$K_C = \frac{K_f}{K_b} = \frac{1.7 \times 10^{-18}}{2.4 \times 10^{-21}}$$

$\therefore \quad \frac{1}{2}H_2(g) + \frac{1}{2}I_2(g) \rightleftharpoons HI(g)$

The equilibrium constant for the formation of one mole of gaseous HI, $K_C' = \sqrt{K_C}$

$$= \sqrt{\frac{1.7 \times 10^{-18}}{2.4 \times 10^{-21}}} \approx 26.61$$

8. **(a)** $NiO(s) + H_2(g) \rightleftharpoons Ni(s) + H_2O(g); \quad K_p = \frac{p_{H_2O}}{p_{H_2}}$

Thus, we require the value of $\log K_p$

$$\Delta G° = -2.303\,RT \log K_p$$

$$\therefore \quad \log K_p = \frac{-\Delta G°}{2.303\,RT}$$

$$= \frac{-(-9000)\text{ cal}}{2.303 \times 2\text{cal mol}^{-1}\text{ K}^{-1} \times 800\text{ K}} \approx 2.44$$

9. **(c)** $K_1 = \frac{[CO_2]}{[CO]\,[O_2]^{1/2}}$ and $K_2 = \frac{[CO_2]^2}{[CO]^2[O_2]} = K_1^2$

$$\Delta G_1 = -2.303\,RT \log K_1$$

$$\Delta G_2 = -2.303\,RT \log K_2 \equiv -2.303\,RT \log K_1^2$$

$$= +2 \times (-2.303\,RT \log K_1) = 2\Delta G_1.$$

10. **(d)** $\Delta G = \Delta G° + 2.303\,RT \log K_p$

$$= -2.303\,RT \log (K_p)_{\text{standard}} + 2.303\,RT \log \frac{p^2_{NO_2}}{p_{N_2O_4}}$$

$$= -2.303\,RT \left[\log 0.141 - \log \frac{1}{10}\right]$$

$$= (-2.303 \times 8.314 \times 10^{-3}\text{ kJ mol}^{-1}\text{K}^{-1} \times 298\text{ K})\,[\log 0.141 + 1]$$

$$\approx -0.85\text{ kJ mol}^{-1}$$

11. **(c)** Required final equation is obtained by

$4 \times$ Eq. III $-$ 2[Eq. I + Eq. II]

$$K = \frac{K_{III}^4}{K_I^2\,K_{II}^2} = \frac{(4.1 \times 10^{-9})^4}{(2.7 \times 10^{-18} \times 4.6 \times 10^{-3})^2} = 1.832 \times 10^6$$

12. **(c)** Statement I is incorrect but Statement II is correct. Its correct form is

- $C_{10}H_8(s) \rightleftharpoons C_{10}H_8(g)$

$$K_p = p_{C_{10}H_8} = 0.10\text{ mmHg} = \frac{0.10}{760}\text{ atm} \approx 1.32 \times 10^{-4}\text{ atm}$$

$$\Delta n_g = +1$$

$$K_p = K_C (RT)^{\Delta n_g}$$

$$\therefore \quad K_C = \frac{K_p}{(RT)^{\Delta n_g}} = \frac{K_p}{RT} = \frac{1.32 \times 10^{-4}}{0.0821 \times 300} \approx 5.36 \times 10^{-6}$$

From the given, equilibrium,

$$\Delta n_g = +1$$

$$K_p = K_C (RT)$$

$\therefore$ If $K_p = K_C$, then $T = \frac{1}{R}$

$$K_p = K_C (RT)$$

$$\text{atm} = \text{mol L}^{-1}\,(0.0821\text{ L atm mol}^{-1}\text{K}^{-1})T$$

$$\therefore \quad T = \frac{1}{0.0821}\text{ K} = 12.18\text{ K}.$$

13. **(a)** $2H_2S(g) \rightleftharpoons 2H_2(g) + S_2(g)$

	$2H_2S(g)$	$2H_2(g)$	$S_2(g)$
Initial	10 atm	0	0
At equil.	$(10 - 2x)$	$2x$	x

$$x = 0.020\text{ atm}$$

$\because \quad p_{H_2S} = 10 - 2x = 10 - 0.02 \times 2 = 9.96\text{ atm}$

$$p_{H_2} = 2x = 0.04\text{ atm}$$

$$p_{S_2} = x = 0.02$$

$$K_p = \frac{p_{S_2} \times p^2_{H_2}}{p^2_{H_2S}} = \frac{0.02 \times (0.04)^2}{(9.96)^2} \approx 3.23 \times 10^{-7}\text{ atm}$$

14. **(c)** $N_2(g) + 3H_2(g) \rightleftharpoons 2NH_3(g)$

	$N_2(g)$	$3H_2(g)$	$2NH_3(g)$
Initial	1	3	0
At equil.	$(1 - x)$	$3(1 - x)$	$2x$

$$2NH_3 + H_2SO_4 \rightleftharpoons (NH_4)_2SO_4$$

Moles of H_2SO_4 required $= \frac{MV}{1000} = \frac{250 \times 1}{1000} = 0.250$

Molarity $(\text{mol L}^{-1}) \times \text{mL} = $ millimoles

Since, $1\,H_2SO_4 \equiv 2NH_3$

Thus, $NH_3 = 0.500$ mol

$\therefore \quad 2x = 0.500 \Rightarrow x = 0.250$

$$K_C = \frac{[NH_3]^2}{[N_2]\,[H_2]^3} = \frac{\left(\frac{2x}{1}\right)^2}{\frac{(1-x)}{1}\left(\frac{1-x}{1}\right)^3 (3)^3}$$

$$= \frac{(0.50)^2}{(0.750)^4\,(27)} \approx 0.029$$

15. **(c)** $\Delta G° = -2.303\,RT \log K_p$

$$= -2.303 \times 2500\text{ J mol}^{-1} \log 1.0 \times 10^{28}$$

$$= -161.21 \times 10^3\text{ J mol}^{-1} = -161.21\text{ kJ mol}^{-1}$$

16. **(d)** $2CO + O_2 \rightleftharpoons 2CO_2,\ K = 40 \times 10^{-3}$

(i) $\therefore \quad CO + \frac{1}{2}O_2 \rightleftharpoons CO_2,$

$$K_1 = \sqrt{K} = \sqrt{40 \times 10^{-3}}$$

$$2H_2 + O_2 \rightleftharpoons 2H_2O, \quad K' = 36 \times 10^{-2}$$

$$\therefore \quad H_2 + \frac{1}{2}O_2 \rightleftharpoons H_2O,\ K_2 = \sqrt{K'} = \sqrt{36 \times 10^{-2}}$$

(ii) $\therefore \quad H_2O \rightleftharpoons H_2 + \frac{1}{2}O_2,\ K_3 = \frac{1}{K_2} = \frac{1}{\sqrt{36 \times 10^{-2}}}$

Adding (i) and (ii)

$\therefore \quad CO + H_2O \rightleftharpoons CO_2 + H_2,$

$$K_4 = K_1 K_3 = \sqrt{\frac{40 \times 10^{-3}}{36 \times 10^{-2}}} = 0.333$$

17. **(b, c, d)** Among the given statements, only three i.e., (b, c, d) are correct while statement (a) is incorrect.

Its correct form is

$\Delta n_g = -2$

$\therefore \quad K_C(RT)^{\Delta n_g} = (p)^{\Delta n_g} K_\chi \Rightarrow K_c = \left(\frac{p}{RT}\right)^{\Delta n_g} K_\chi$

But $pV = nRT = RT$ (for 1 mol)

$\therefore \quad \left(\frac{p}{RT}\right) = V^{-1}$

$$K_c = (V^{-1})^{\Delta n_g} K_\chi = (V^{-1})^{-2} K_\chi = V^2 K_\chi = (25) K_\chi$$

18. ***(b, c, d)*** $pV = nRT$

$\therefore \quad n\text{ (Total)} = \frac{pV}{RT} = \frac{1.1 \text{ atm} \times 1.96 \text{ L}}{0.0821 \text{ L atm mol}^{-1} \text{K}^{-1} \times 1700 \text{ K}}$

$= 0.0154 \text{ mol}$

If $Cl_2 = y \text{ g} = \frac{y}{71}$ mol

Then, $Cl = (1-y)\text{ g} = \frac{1-y}{35.5}$ mol

$\therefore \quad \frac{y}{71} + \frac{1-y}{35.5} = 0.0154 \Rightarrow y + 2 - 2y = 1.0934$

$\therefore \quad y = 0.9066 \text{ g}$

	Mass	Mole	Mole fraction
Cl_2	0.9066 g	0.0128 mol	0.8296
Cl	0.0934 g	2.63×10^{-3}	0.1704

$$K_\chi = \frac{\chi_{Cl}}{\sqrt{\chi_{Cl_2}}} = \frac{0.1704}{\sqrt{0.8296}} \approx 0.187$$

$$K_p = K_\chi p^{\Delta n_g} = 0.187\,(1.10)^{\frac{1}{2}} = 0.196 \text{atm}^{\frac{1}{2}}$$

$$K_C = K_p (RT)^{-\frac{1}{2}} = \frac{K_p}{\sqrt{RT}} = \frac{0.196}{\sqrt{0.0821 \times 1700}}$$

$$\approx 0.0166 (\text{mol L}^{-1})^{\frac{1}{2}}$$

19. ***(c, d)*** Among the given statements, (c) and (d) are correct while the statement (a) and (b) are incorrect.

Their explanation are given as

$$2NOCl(g) \rightleftharpoons 2NO(g) + Cl_2(g)$$

$p_{Total} = 1.0$ atm

$p_{NOCl} = 0.64$ atm

Since $2p_{Cl_2} = p_{NO}$

$\therefore p_{NO} + p_{Cl_2} = 0.36$ atm

$\therefore \quad 3p_{Cl_2} = 0.36$ atm

(c) $\therefore \quad p_{Cl_2} = 0.12$ atm

(b) and $\quad p_{NO} = 0.24$ atm

(d) $\therefore K_p = \frac{(p_{NO})^2 (p_{Cl_2})}{(p_{NOCl})^2} = \frac{(0.24)^2 (0.12)}{(0.64)^2} \approx 0.017$ atm

20. ***(a, b, c, d)*** Among the given statements all are incorrect about the given reaction mixture.

Their explanation are given as:

According to the given data,

$$Q = \frac{[H_2]\;[CO]}{[H_2CO]} = \frac{1.50 \times 0.25}{0.50} = 0.75$$

$K_C = 0.50$ (given)

(i) Since $Q > K_C$, hence system is not in equilibrium, thus (i) is false.

(ii) Since $Q > K_C$, reaction occurs in backward direction to attain equilibrium, thus (ii) is also false.

(iii) Thus, false based on (ii)

(iv) False since $Q \neq K_C$

21. ***(8)*** $\quad NH_3(g) \rightleftharpoons \frac{1}{2}N_2(g) + \frac{3}{2}H_2(g)$

	NH_3	N_2	H_2
Initial :	1	0	0
At equil.	$(1-x)$	$\frac{x}{2}$	$\frac{3}{2}x$

Total moles at equilibrium : $(1+x)$

$\therefore \quad p_{NH_3} = p\left(\frac{1-x}{1+x}\right) = \frac{1-x}{(1+x)}$

$$p_{N_2} = \frac{px}{2(1+x)} = \frac{x}{2(1+x)} \text{ and } p_{H_2} = \frac{3x}{2(1+x)}$$

$$K_p = p_{N_2}^{1/2}\, p_{H_2}^{3/2} / p_{NH_3}$$

$$= \left(\frac{x}{2(1+x)}\right)^{\frac{1}{2}} \left(\frac{3x}{2(1+x)}\right)^{\frac{3}{2}} \Big/ \left(\frac{1-x}{1+x}\right)$$

$$K_p = \frac{3^{3/2}\, x^2 (1+x)}{2^2 (1+x)^2 (1-x)} = \frac{1.3\, x^2}{(1-x^2)}$$

$$\therefore \quad x = \left(\frac{K_p}{1.3 + K_p}\right)^{\frac{1}{2}} = \left(\frac{0.00782}{1.3 + 0.00782}\right)^{\frac{1}{2}} \approx 0.08$$

$= 8\%$

22. ***(92)*** By using,

$$\Delta G^\circ = -RT \ln K_{eq}$$
$$= -2.303\, RT \log K_{eq}$$
$$= -2.303 \times 8.314 \times 370 \times \log 20$$
$$= -9217.07 \text{ J mol}^{-1}$$
$$= -9.217 \text{ kJ mol}^{-1}$$
$$= -92.17 \times 10^{-1} \text{ kJ mol}^{-1}$$

Thus, the value is 92.

23. ***(2)*** $\quad CaCO_3(s) \rightleftharpoons CaO(s) + CO_2(g)$

$$K_p = p_{CO_2} = 2.105 \text{ atm}$$

$$C(s) + CO_2(g) \rightleftharpoons 2CO(g);\; K_p = 1.9$$

$$K_p = \frac{p_{CO}^2}{p_{CO_2}} = 1.9$$

$$p_{CO}^2 = p_{CO_2} \times 1.9 = 2.105 \times 1.9 \approx 4.0$$

$\therefore \quad p_{CO} = 2.0$ atm

24. ***(294.26)*** Given, $K_1 = 10\, K_2$

$$\Delta G_1^\circ = -2.303\, RT \log K_1$$

$$-300 \text{ kJ mol}^{-1} = -2.303 \times 8.314 \times 10^{-3} \text{ kJ mol}^{-1}\text{K}^{-1} \times 300 \text{ K} \log K_1$$

$\therefore \quad \log K_1 = 52.227$

$\therefore \quad K_1 = 1.6866 \times 10^{52}$

$\therefore \quad K_2 = \frac{K_1}{10}$

$\log K_2 = \log 1.6866 \times 10^{51} = 51.227$

$\therefore \quad \Delta G_2^\circ = -2.303\, RT \log K_2 = -294.26 \text{ kJ mol}^{-1}$

25. ***(37)*** Given reaction,

	X	$\rightleftharpoons 2Y$
At initially.	1	0
Mole	$(1-\alpha)$	2α
Mole fraction	$\left(\frac{1-\alpha}{1+\alpha}\right)$,	$\left(\frac{2\alpha}{1+\alpha}\right)$
Partial pressure	$\frac{(1-\alpha)p}{(1+\alpha)}$	$\frac{2\alpha p_1}{(1+\alpha)}$

$$K_{p_1} = p_y^2 / p_x = \frac{4\alpha^2 p_1}{(1-\alpha^2)}$$

	Z	$\rightleftharpoons P$	$+ Q$
Initial	1	0	0
At equil.	$(1-\alpha)$	α	α
Mole fraction	$\left(\frac{1-\alpha}{1+\alpha}\right)$	$\frac{\alpha}{1+\alpha}$	$\frac{\alpha}{1+\alpha}$
Partial pressure	$\frac{(1-\alpha)p_2}{(1+\alpha)}$	$\frac{\alpha p_2}{(1+\alpha)}$	$\frac{\alpha p_2}{1+\alpha}$

$$K_{p_2} = \frac{p_P p_Q}{p_Z} = \frac{\alpha^2 p_2}{(1-\alpha^2)}$$

$$\Rightarrow \frac{K_{p_1}}{K_{p_2}} = \frac{4p_1}{p_2}$$

$$\frac{1}{9} = \frac{4p_1}{p_2} \quad \therefore \quad \frac{p_1}{p_2} = \frac{1}{36}$$

Hence, the sum of the ratio of total pressure at given equilbria is 37.

Elemental Practice 5.2

1. ***(a)*** $\log K_p$ decreases as $\frac{1}{T}$ increases or (T decreases).

Thus, $\Delta H > 0$ (endothermic)

Hence increase in temperature moves the equilibrium in forward direction

$\Delta n_g = +2$ (gaseous)

Thus $\quad x \propto \left(\frac{1}{p}\right)^{\Delta n_g/2} \Rightarrow x \propto \frac{1}{p}$

If p decreases x increases (forward direction).

2. ***(a)***

	A	$+ B$	$\rightleftharpoons AB$;	$K_C = [AB]/[A][B]$
At 300K	2	3	6	$K_1 = \frac{6}{6} = 1$
At 400K	5	5	4	$K_2 = \frac{4}{25}$

on increasing temperature, K_c decreases, thus it is an exothermic reaction.

3. ***(d)*** $\Delta n_g = -1$

$$x \propto \left(\frac{1}{p}\right)^{\Delta n_g/2} \Rightarrow \Rightarrow x \propto \sqrt{p}$$

(a) On decreasing volume, pressure is increased. Thus, formation of product is increased (and thus decreasing CO)

(b) Addition of argon (inert gas) increases pressure thus as in (a)

(c) O_2 (reactant) will react CO hence amount of CO decreases.

4. ***(b)*** Statement I is correct but Statement II is incorrect. Its correct form is

- Catalyst lowers the activation energy for the forward and reverse reactions by exactly the same amount.

5. ***(b)*** x (yield) $\propto \left(\frac{1}{p}\right)^{\Delta n_g/2}$

	Δn_g	x
(a)	1	$x \propto \sqrt{\frac{1}{p}}$
(b)	−1	$x \propto \sqrt{p}$
(c)	0	No effect
(d)	1	$x \propto \sqrt{\frac{1}{p}}$

Thus, on doubling pressure, amount of product is increased in (b).

6. ***(c)*** Among the given reactions, addition of catalyst does not affect the composition and the value of K_C.

7. ***(c)*** $\underset{\text{Dark brown}}{2NO_2(g)} \rightleftharpoons N_2O_4(g)$

On increasing temperature, equilibrium moves in the backward direction. Thus, reaction is **exothermic**.

Exothermic reactions are favoured at low temperature. $\Delta n_g = -1$, Thus, $x \propto \sqrt{p}$ here at low pressure, formation of N_2O_4 decreases.

Thus, at high temperature and low pressure, NO_2 is formed.

8. ***(c)*** By introducing an inert gas at constant pressure and PCl_5 at constant volume the given reaction will be favoured in forward direction at constant temperature.

9. ***(c)*** $\Delta n_g = -1$ (gaseous species)

$$x \propto \left(\frac{1}{p}\right)^{\Delta n_g/2}$$

$\therefore \quad x \propto \sqrt{p}$

Thus, on increasing pressure, solubility increases.

10. ***(c)*** H_2O will dilute $[CoCl_4]^{2-}$ thus, its concentration is decreased.

11. ***(a)*** $Q = \frac{p_{PCl_3} \cdot p_{Cl_2}}{p_{PCl_5}} = 1$ Then, $K_p < Q$

Hence, equilibrium shifts in backward direction producing more PCl_5.

12. ***(c)*** The reaction proceed as:

$$H_2(g) \longrightarrow 2H(g); \quad \Delta H = +\text{ve}$$

The above reaction is endothermic and accompanied with increase in number of moles. Therefore, favoured at high temperature and low pressure.

13. ***(d)*** In the given endothermic equilibrium, addition of $NaNO_2$ favours reverse reaction while addition of $NaNO_3$ favours forward reaction and increasing temperature also favours forward reaction.

$\Delta n_g = +1$, increasing pressure favours the reverse reaction. Thus, statement (d) is incorrect.

14. ***(c)*** According to the given reaction, K_{eq} is a function of temperature only, so increase the temperature may change the value of equilibrium constant.

15. ***(a,b,c,d)*** Increasing (C_2H_4) means backward reaction is favoured.

(a) Reaction is exothermic, thus on increasing temperature, backward reaction is favoured.

(b) Takes place with decrease in pressure ($\Delta n_g = -1$), thus on decreasing pressure, equilibrium is shifted in backward direction.

(c) If H_2 is removed, C_2H_4 is increased.

(d) If C_2H_6 is added, C_2H_4 is increased.

16. ***(a,b,d)*** K_p decreases as $\left(\frac{1}{T}\right)$ increases

(or T decreases)

Thus, reaction is endothermic

(a) If T is lowered, decomposition decreases

(b) $\Delta n_g = 2$

$$\therefore \quad x \propto \left(\frac{1}{p}\right)^{\Delta n_g/2} \Rightarrow x \propto \frac{1}{p}$$

17. ***(a,c)***

(a) NH_3 dissolves AgCl forming $[Ag(NH_3)_2]^+$

$$AgCl + 2NH_3 \longrightarrow [Ag(NH_3)_2]^+Cl^-$$

(b) Cl^-(from MCl) or Ag^+(from $AgNO_3$) decreases solubility by common ion effect

(c) As in (b)

(d) H_2O dissolves more AgCl (upto saturation point)

18. ***(a, c)*** For the given equilibrium,

$$NH_4HS(s) \rightleftharpoons NH_3(g) + H_2S(g)$$

$\Delta n_g = 2$. So, the forward reaction is favoured if the pressure is lowered and more NH_3 is formed. Also, the reaction is endothermic, so increase in temperature favours the forward reaction and the partial pressure of NH_3 increases.

19. ***(a,b,d)***

(a) $x \propto \left(\frac{1}{p}\right)^{\Delta n_g/2}$, $\Delta n_g = -1$, (x = product)

$$x \propto \left(\frac{1}{p}\right)^{-1/2} \Rightarrow x \propto \sqrt{(p)} \Rightarrow x \propto \sqrt{\frac{1}{V}}$$

Thus, if V decreases, x increases

(b) If Ar is added, p increases thus x increases

(c) Reactant (O_2) increases CO_2

(d) Decreasing pressure at constant temperature shifts the equilibrium in backward direction.

20. ***(2)*** Among the given statements, only two i.e., B and D are incorrect while A and C are correct. Their correct form is

- The equilibrium constant for an exothermic reaction decreases as the temperature increases.
- The equilibrium constant for an endothermic reaction increases as the temperature increases.

21. ***(2)***

I. $\Delta H° = -$ve, exothermic reaction, hence when equilibrium is set-up, temperature is increased the equilibrum shifts in the direction in which heat is absorbed, thus backward reaction is favoured.

II. H_2O (g) when added (as reactant) will form more $H_2(g)$.

III. $\Delta n_g = 0$, no effect.

IV. No effect, catalyst equally affects forward and backward reaction.

22. ***(2)*** Increase in the pressure for the following equilibrium

$$H_2O(l) \rightleftharpoons H_2O(g)$$

result in the formation of more $H_2O(l)$ and increase in boiling point of $H_2O(l)$.

$$\underset{\text{Low } p}{H_2O(l)} \rightleftharpoons \underset{\text{High } p}{H_2O(g)}$$

When pressure is applied, $H_2O(g)$ is liquefied, thus bp is elevated.

23. ***(1.17)*** $N_2O_4(g) \rightleftharpoons 2NO_2(g)$

If volume is doubled, pressure is halved

$\left(\text{as } p \propto \frac{1}{V} \text{ at constant temperature}\right)$

Initially

$$p_{N_2O_4} = 0.58 \text{ bar} \Rightarrow p_{NO_2} = 1.60 \text{ bar}$$

$$K_p = \frac{p^2_{NO_2}}{p_{N_2O_4}} = \frac{(1.60)^2}{0.58} = 4.41$$

Under new condition

$$p_{N_2O_4} = 0.29 \text{ bar}$$

$$\Rightarrow \quad p_{NO_2} = 0.80 \text{ bar}$$

Thus, partial pressure is affected to keep K_p constant.

	$N_2O_4(g)$ $\rightleftharpoons$	$2NO_2(g)$
Initially	0.29	0.80
at equil.	$(0.29 - x)$	$(0.80 + 2x)$

$$\therefore \quad K_p = 4.41 = \frac{(0.80 + 2x)^2}{(0.29 - x)}$$

$$\therefore \quad x \approx 0.0805$$

$\therefore$ New partial pressure of

$$p_{N_2O_4} = 0.29 - 0.0805 = 0.2095 \text{ bar} = p$$
$$p_{NO_2} = 0.80 + 0.161 = 0.961 \text{ bar} = q$$

Thus, the value of $x + y$ is 1.17.

24. **(3)** $Ag^+ + SCN^- \longrightarrow AgSCN$

$Hg^{2+} + 2SCN \longrightarrow Hg(SCN)_2$

$Fe^{3+} + 3C_2O_4^{2-} \longrightarrow [Fe(C_2O_4)_3]^{3-}$

Thus, SCN^- is removed by Ag^+ and Hg^{2+} and Fe^{3+} is removed by $C_2O_4^{2-}$.

So, all the given compounds which on addition will cause deep red colour to disappear in the given equilibrium.

Practice Element 01 : Target JEE Main

1. **(b)**

	Δn_g	$K_p = K_c(RT)^{\Delta n_g}$
X.	$2-3=-1$	$\frac{K_p}{K_C} = \frac{1}{RT} = \frac{1}{0.0821 \times 300} \approx 0.040$
Y.	$2-2=0$	$\frac{K_p}{K_C} = 1$
Z.	$2-1=1$	$\frac{K_p}{K_C} = RT = 0.0821 \times 300 = 24.63$
W.	$2-4=-2$	$\frac{K_p}{K_C} = \frac{1}{(RT)^2} = \frac{1}{(24.63)^2} = \frac{1}{606.64} \approx 1.64 \times 10^{-3}$

Hence, the correct increasing order is $W < X < Y < Z$.

2. **(a)** Given, $CO(g) + 2H_2(g) \rightleftharpoons CH_3OH(g)$

	$CO(g)$	$2H_2(g)$	$CH_3OH(g)$
Initial mole	0.15	a	0
Mole at equil.	$(0.15 - x)$	$(a - 2x)$	x

and mole of CH_3OH formed $= x = 0.08$

$\therefore$ Total mole at equilibrium $= 0.15 - x + a - 2x + x$

$$= 0.15 + a - 0.16 = a - 0.01$$

Also, total mole of equilibrium $(n) = \frac{pV}{RT} = \frac{8.5 \times 2.5}{0.0821 \times 750}$

$$= 0.345$$

$$a - 0.01 = 0.345 \Rightarrow a = 0.355$$

Or at equil. mole of $CO = 0.15 - 0.08 = 0.07$

Mole of $H_2 = 0.355 - 0.16 = 0.195$

Mole of $CH_3OH = 0.08$

So, $$K_C = \frac{[CH_3OH]}{[H_2]^2[CO]} = \frac{\frac{0.08}{2.5}}{\left(\frac{0.195}{2.5}\right)^2\left[\frac{0.07}{2.5}\right]}$$

$$\approx 187.85 \text{ mol}^{-2} \text{ litre}^2$$

By using,

$$K_p = K_C (RT)^{\Delta n}$$
$$= 187.85 \times (0.0821 \times 750)^{-2} \approx 0.05 \text{ atm}^2$$

So, the value of $K_p = 0.05$

$K_C = 187.85$

3. **(c)** $SO_3(g) \rightleftharpoons SO_2(g) + \frac{1}{2}O_2(g)$

y = number of moles of products from one mole reactant $= 1.5$

$$x = \frac{D-d}{d(y-1)} = \frac{D-d}{0.5d}$$

D = vapour density before dissociation $= \frac{M}{2} = \frac{80}{2} = 40$

d = vapour density after dissociation

$$pV = nRT = \frac{w}{m}RT$$

m (molar mass of mixture)

$$= \frac{wRT}{Vp} = \frac{\rho RT}{p} = \frac{0.866 \times 0.0821 \times 900}{1} \approx 64.0 \text{ g mol}^{-1}.$$

$\therefore$ $d = 32.0 \text{ g mol}^{-1}$

$\therefore$ $x = \frac{D-d}{0.5d} = \frac{40-32}{0.5 \times 32} = 0.5$

Thus, 50% dissociation.

4. **(b)** $\Delta G° = -2.303\, RT \log K_p$

$\therefore$ $$\log K_p = \frac{-124.9 \times 10^3}{-2.303 \times 8.31 \times 500} = 13.05$$

$$K_p = 1.12 \times 10^{13}$$

Now, for the equilibrium,

$$2Cu(s) + \frac{1}{2}O_2(g) \rightleftharpoons Cu_2O(s)$$

$$K_p = \frac{1}{(p_{O_2})^{1/2}}$$

$$p_{O_2} = \left\{\frac{1}{K_p}\right\}^2 = \left\{\frac{1}{1.12 \times 10^{13}}\right\}^2$$

$$= 7.97 \times 10^{-27} \text{ atm}$$

Again we have,

$$pV = nRT$$

$$n = \frac{pV}{RT} = \frac{7.97 \times 10^{-27} \times 1}{0.0821 \times 500}$$

$$= 1.94 \times 10^{-28} \text{ mol}$$

$\therefore$ Number of O_2 molecules

$$= (1.94 \times 10^{-28})(6.022 \times 10^{23})$$
$$= 1.17 \times 10^{-4} \text{ molecules per litre}$$

5. **(c)** Statement I is incorrect but Statement II is correct. The correct form of Statement I is

- The given equation is,

	$A(g)$ +	$B(g)$	$\rightleftharpoons C(g) + D(g)$
Initial	2	2	0
At equilibrium	$(2-x)$	$(2-x)$	x

Given, $[C] = 3[B]$

$x = 3(2-x)$ $\quad\therefore\; x = 1.5$

$\therefore$ $$K_c = \frac{[C][D]}{[A][B]} = \frac{1.5 \times 1.5}{0.5 \times 0.5} = 9.$$

6. **(d)** $N_2(g) + 3H_2(g) \rightleftharpoons 2NH_3(g)$

Mole fraction of $NH_3 = \chi(NH_3) = 0.50$

Also, $\chi(N_2) + \chi(H_2) + \chi(NH_3) = 1.0$

$$\chi(N_2) + \chi(H_2) = 0.50$$

Also, $\chi(H_2) = 3 \times (N_2)$

$$\therefore \quad 4\chi(N_2) = 0.50 \Rightarrow \chi(N_2) = \frac{0.50}{4} \Rightarrow \chi(H_2) = \frac{1.5}{4}$$

$p(\text{total}) = 350$ bar

$$\therefore \quad p_{NH_3} = 350 \times \frac{1}{2} = 175 \text{ bar}, \; p_{N_2} = 350 \times \frac{0.50}{4} \text{ bar}$$

$$p_{H_2} = 350 \times \frac{1.5}{4} \text{ bar}$$

$$K_p = \frac{p^2_{NH_3}}{p_{N_2} \cdot p^3_{H_2}} = \frac{(175)^2}{\left(350 \times \frac{0.5}{4}\right)\left(\frac{350 \times 1.50}{4}\right)^3}$$

$$= 3.1 \times 10^{-4}$$

7. **(d)** $Ca(HCO_3)_2(s) \rightleftharpoons CaO(s) + \underbrace{2CO_2(g) + H_2O(g)}$

Take only gaseous species

$$p_{total} = p_{CO_2} + p_{H_2O} \text{ at } 400 \text{ K} \Rightarrow 7.5 \text{ bar} = 2p + p = 3p$$

$$\therefore \quad p = 2.5 \text{ bar}$$

$$\therefore \quad p_{CO_2} = 5.0 \text{ bar} \Rightarrow p_{H_2O} = 2.5 \text{ bar}$$

$$\therefore \; K_p(400 \text{ K}) = p^2_{CO_2} p_{H_2O} = 25 \times 2.5 = 62.5 \text{ bar}$$

At 298 K, $H_2O(g)$ is condensed to $H_2O(l)$ and pressure set-up is due to CO_2 only.

$$\frac{p_{CO_2}(298 \text{ K})}{p_{CO_2}(400 \text{ K})} = \frac{298}{400}$$

$$p_{CO_2}(298 \text{ K}) = \frac{298}{400} \times 5.0 \text{ bar} = 3.725 \text{ bar}$$

$$\Delta H^\circ = \frac{2.303 RT_1T_2}{(T_2 - T_1)} \log \frac{K_p(400)}{K_p(398)}$$

$$= \frac{2.303 \times 8.314 \times 10^{-3} \text{ kJ mol}^{-1} \times 298 \text{ K} \times 400 \text{ K}}{(400 - 298) \text{ K}} \log \left(\frac{62.5}{13.88}\right)$$

$$= 14.6 \text{ kJ mol}^{-1}$$

8. **(c)** Given, two system,

$PCl_5(g) \rightleftharpoons PCl_3(g) + Cl_2(g)$

$COCl_2(g) \rightleftharpoons CO(g) + Cl_2(g)$; are simultaneously in equilibrium in a vessel at constant volume. If some CO is introduced into the vessel then at new equilibrium the concentration of PCl_5 will be less.

9. **(a)** Given, $f = \frac{[B]}{[A]+[B]} = \frac{[B]/[A]}{\frac{[A]}{[A]} + \frac{[B]}{[A]}} \Rightarrow f = \frac{K}{1+K}$

where, K (equilibrium constant) $= \frac{[B]}{[A]}$

By using the formula,

$$\Delta G^\circ = -2.303 RT \log K$$

$$1.7 \text{ kJ mol}^{-1} = -2.303 \times 8.314 \times 10^{-3} \text{kJ mol}^{-1} \text{ K}^{-1} \times 298 \text{ K} \log K$$

$$\therefore \quad \log K = -0.30$$

$$\therefore \quad K = 0.50$$

$$\therefore \quad f = \frac{0.5}{1 + 0.5} = \frac{1}{3} = 0.33$$

Thus, there is 33% B and 67% A at equilibrium.

10. **(a)** Both Statement I and Statement II are correct.

As given, $K_p > K_C$ means $\Delta n_g > 0$, i.e., $n_p > n_R$. So, the reaction accompanied with increase in number of moles are favoured at low pressure.

Addition of inert gas, at constant volume does not have any influence on the equilibrium system.

11. **(a)** $Ag_2CO_3(s) \rightleftharpoons 2Ag(s) + CO_2(g) + \frac{1}{2}O_2(g)$

	$Ag_2CO_3(s)$	$2Ag(s)$	$CO_2(g)$	$\frac{1}{2}O_2(g)$
Initial	1	0	0	0
At equil.			x	$\frac{x}{2}$
Mole fraction	–	–	$\frac{2}{3}$	$\frac{1}{3}$
Partial pressure			$\frac{2p}{3}$	$\frac{p}{3}$

$$\therefore \quad K_p = p_{CO_2} \cdot p^{\frac{1}{2}}_{O_2} = \left(\frac{2p}{3}\right)\left(\frac{p}{3}\right)^{\frac{1}{2}}$$

$$= 2\left(\frac{p}{3}\right)\left(\frac{p}{3}\right)^{1/2} = 2\left(\frac{p}{3}\right)^{3/2}$$

Only gaseous species considered.

12. **(b)** A is false but R is true.

The correct form of A is

The reaction proceed as :

$$2SO_2(g) + O_2(g) \rightleftharpoons 2SO_3(g), \; \Delta H = -ve$$

The given reaction is an exothermic reaction and associated with decrease in number of moles. Therefore, the yield of SO_3 will be maximum if temperature is reduced and pressure is increased.

13. **(c)** $PCl_5(g) \rightleftharpoons PCl_3(g) + Cl_2(g)$; $K_{eq} = 100$

$$\therefore \quad \Delta G^\circ_1 = -2.303 RT \log K_{eq}$$

$$= -20.0 \text{ kJ mol}^{-1} \text{ (given)}$$

For, $PCl_3(g) + Cl_2(g) \rightleftharpoons PCl_5(g)$; $K_{eq} = \frac{1}{100}$ and

for, $\frac{1}{2}PCl_3(g) + \frac{1}{2}Cl_2(g) \rightleftharpoons \frac{1}{2}PCl_5(g)$;

$$K_{eq} = \sqrt{\frac{1}{100}} = \frac{1}{10} = 0.1$$

$$\Delta G^\circ_2 = -2.303 RT \log (\sqrt{K_{eq}})^{-1}$$

$$= +\frac{2.303 RT \log K_{eq}}{2}$$

$$= -\frac{\Delta G^\circ_1}{2} = \frac{+20}{2} = +10 \text{ kJ mol}^{-1}$$

14. **(a)** When the two solids are taken together in a closed container, both decompose to give faces A, B and C. As B is the common gas, the dissociation of both the solids X

and Y shall be suppressed. Suppose that the partial pressures of A and B due to dissociation of only X are p_1 atm each, and the partial pressures of B and C due to dissociation of only Y are p_2 atm each.

$$X(s) \rightleftharpoons \underset{p_1}{A(g)} + \underset{p_1}{B(g)};\ K_{p_1} = 500$$

$$Y(s) \rightleftharpoons \underset{p_2}{C(g)} + \underset{p_2}{C(g)};\ K_{p_2} = 900$$

$\therefore$ $$K_{p_1} = p_A \cdot p_B = p_1(p_1 + p_2) = 500 \quad \ldots(i)$$

and $$K_{p_2} = p_C \cdot p_D = p_2(p_1 + p_2) = 900 \quad \ldots(ii)$$

Solving of Eqs. (i) and (ii),

$$p_1 = 13.36 \text{ atm},\ p_2 = 24.05 \text{ atm}$$

$\therefore$ Pressure over the solid mixture $= 2(p_1 + p_2)$

$$= 2(13.36 + 24.05)$$
$$= 74.8 \text{ atm}$$

15. ***(a)*** $A \xrightarrow{\text{I}} B$, x increases on increasing T thus, stage I is endothermic.

$B \xrightarrow{\text{II}} C$, x decreases on increasing T thus, stage II is exothermic.

$C \xrightarrow{\text{III}} D$ as in I

thus, stage III is endothermic.

16. ***(a)*** The given reaction is,

$$N_2(g) + O_2(g) \rightleftharpoons 2NO(g)$$

	N_2	O_2	NO
Initial	a	$100 - a$	0
Final	$a - x$	$100 - a - x$	$2x$

Mole % of NO at eq. $= \dfrac{2x}{100} = \dfrac{1.8}{100}$

$$x = 0.9$$

Here, $$K_C = \frac{[NO]^2}{[N_2][O_2]}$$

$$2.1 \times 10^{-3} = \frac{(2x)^2}{(a - x)(100 - a - x)}$$

$$2.1 \times 10^{-3} = \frac{(2 \times 0.9)^2}{(a - 0.9)(100 - a - 0.9)}$$

$$= \frac{(1.8)^2}{(a - 0.9)(99.1 - a)}$$

$$a = 79.46 \approx 79$$

$\therefore$ % N_2 in air = 79%

17. ***(b)*** I. $Q = \dfrac{[NO_2]^2}{[N_2O_4]}$

Since, $[NO_2]$ is maximum and $[N_2O_4]$ is minimum at point A, hence Q is minimum at this point. Thus, I is false.

II. $Q = \dfrac{(0.1)^2}{(0.1)} = 0.1 < K_C$

Thus, reaction proceeds left to right.
Thus, II is true

III. $K_C = Q$ when equilibrium is reached at point D or F

Thus, III is true.

18. ***(b)*** Equilibrium constant (K_1) can be calculated (using $\Delta G = -2.303\, RT \log K$) from the value of ΔG. ΔH in the temperature range has been given which is also related to equilibrium constants K_1 and K_2 by equation,

$$\Delta H = \frac{2.303\, RT_1T_2}{(T_2 - T_1)} \log \frac{K_2}{K_1}$$

Hence, T_2 is calculated at any temperature above which $K_2 > 1$

$$\Delta H = \frac{2.303\, RT_1\, T_2}{(T_2 - T_1)} \log \frac{K_2}{K_1} \quad \ldots(i)$$

Given, $\Delta H = +224$ kJ mol^{-1}, $T_1 = 1280$ K

$$\Delta G^\circ_{1280\,K} = +\ 33 \text{ kJ} = -2.303 \times 8.314 \times 10^{-3} \times 1280 \log K_1$$

$\therefore$ $K_1 = 4.5 \times 10^{-2}$, $K_2 = 1$

Using Eq. (i),

$$224 = 2.303 \times 8.314 \times 10^{-3} \left[\frac{1280\, T_2}{(T_2 - 1280)}\right] \times \log \frac{1}{4.5 \times 10^{-2}}$$

Hence, $T_2 \approx 1501.2$ K

At any temperature above 1501.2 K, equilibrium constant will be greater than 1.

19. ***(d)*** Ag^+ and CN^- react to form $[Ag(CN)_2]^-$ in a spontaneous reaction. $\left(K'_c = \dfrac{1}{K_c} = 0.25 \times 10^{19}\right)$. Thus, approximately all the Ag^+ ion has been complexed leaving x M Ag^+ for complexation equilibrium. Thus, x is calculated. Also $[Ag(CN)_2]^- = [Ag^+] = 0.03$ M.

$$Ag^+ + 2\,CN^- \rightleftharpoons [Ag(CN)_2]^-$$

	Ag^+	$2\,CN^-$	$[Ag(CN)_2]^-$
Initially	0.03 M	0.1M	0
At equil.	x M	$(0.1 - 0.03 \times 2)$ M	0.03 M

Putting these values in Eq, (i)

$$K'_C = 0.25 \times 10^{19} = \frac{(0.03)}{(x)(0.1 - 0.03 \times 2)^2}$$

$\therefore$ $x = [Ag^+] = 7.5 \times 10^{-18}$ M

20. ***(b)*** The given equilibrium as,

$$H_2(g) + S(s) \rightleftharpoons H_2S(g)$$

	$H_2(g)$	$S(s)$	$H_2S(g)$
At $t = 0$	0.20	1	0
At $t = t_{eq}$	$(0.20 - x)$	$1 - x$	x

$$K_C = \frac{[H_2S]}{[H_2]}$$

$$6.8 \times 10^{-2} = \frac{x}{0.20 - x}$$

$$1.068x = 1.36 \times 10^{-2}$$

$$x = 1.273 \times 10^{-2}$$

By using,

$$p_TV = n_TRT$$

$$p_T = \frac{n_TRT}{V}$$

n = total number of moles

$$= 0.20 - x + 1 - x + x$$

$$= 1.20 - 1.273 \times 10^{-2} \approx 1.1873$$

$$p_T = \frac{1.1873\,\text{mol} \times 0.0821\,\text{L atm K}^{-1}\text{mol}^{-} \times 363\,\text{K}}{1\,\text{L}}$$

$= 35.38$ atm

Thus, the partial pressure of H_2S at equilibrium

= Mole fraction of H_2S × Total pressure

$$= \frac{1.273 \times 10^{-2}}{1.1873} \times 35.38 = 0.379 \approx 0.38\,\text{atm}$$

21. ***(3322)*** As the given reaction,

	$2SO_2(g)$ +	$O_2(g) \rightleftharpoons$	$2SO_3(g)$
Initial	2	1	0
At equil.	$(2-2x)$	$(1-x)$	$2x$

Total moles $= 3-x$

Since, equal moles contain equal volumes (Avogadro's hypothesis)

∴ Total volumes $= (3-x)$

Given SO_3 by volume = 87%

$$\therefore \quad \frac{2x}{3-x} = \frac{87}{100} \Rightarrow x = 0.9094$$

∴ Total moles at equilibrium $= 3 - x = 2.0906$

Equilibrium pressure $= 2.0906 \times \frac{1}{3} \approx 0.7$ atm

(Initial pressure of 3 moles is 1 atm)

Mole fraction of $SO_2 = \frac{(2-2x)}{3-x} = \frac{0.1812}{2.0906} \approx 0.087$

Mole fraction of O_2

$$O_2 = \frac{(1-x)}{3-x} = \frac{0.0906}{2.0906} = 0.043$$

Mole fraction of $SO_3 = \frac{2x}{3-x} \approx 0.87$

Partial pressure of $SO_2 = 0.7 \times 0.087$ atm

Partial pressure of $O_2 = 0.7 \times 0.043$ atm

Partial pressure of $SO_3 = 0.7 \times 0.87$ atm

$$\therefore \quad K_p = \frac{p^2_{SO_3}}{p^2_{SO_2} p_{O_2}} = \frac{(0.7 \times 0.87)^2}{(0.7 \times 0.087)^2 (0.7 \times 0.043)} = 3322.3$$

≈ 3322

22. ***(2)***

	$2SO_2(g) +$	$O_2(g) \rightleftharpoons$	$2SO_3(g)$
Initial	2	1	0
At equili.	$(2-2x)$	$(1-x)$	$2x$

$$2MnO_4^- + 5SO_2 + 4H^+ \longrightarrow 5SO_4^{2-} + 2Mn^{2+} + 2H_2O$$

From above equation,

2 mol $MnO_4^- \equiv$ 5 mole SO_2

∴ 0.4 mol $MnO_4^- = \frac{5}{2} \times 0.4 = 1$ mol

∴ $(2-2x) = 1$

∴ $x = 0.5$ mol

$$\therefore \quad K_c = \frac{[SO_3]^2}{[SO_2]^2 [O_2]} = \frac{(2x/V)^2}{\left[\frac{2(1-x)}{V}\right]^2 \left(\frac{1-x}{V}\right)}$$

$$= \frac{\left(\frac{2 \times 0.5}{1}\right)^2}{\left(\frac{2\,(0.5)}{1}\right)^2 \left(\frac{0.5}{1}\right)} = 2$$

23. ***(4)***

	$2SO_2(g) + O_2(g) \rightleftharpoons 2SO_3$		
Initial mol	2	1	0
Moles at equil.	$(2-2x)$	$(1-x)$	$2x$

Initial moles $= 2 + 1 = 3$ at pressure 3 atm

Moles at equilibrium $= (3-x)$

At equilibrium pressure becomes 2.5 atm

Since, $pV = nRT$

Hence, $p \propto n$

Thus, $\frac{3-x}{3} = \frac{2.5}{3}$

∴ $x = 0.5$

$$[SO_2] = \frac{2-2x}{2} = 0.5\,\text{mol L}^{-1}$$

$$[O_2] = \frac{1-x}{2} = 0.25\,\text{mol L}^{-1}$$

$$[SO_3] = \frac{2x}{2} = 0.5\,\text{mol L}^{-1}$$

$$\therefore \quad K_c = \frac{[SO_3]^2}{[SO_2]^2[O_2]} = \frac{(0.5)^2}{(0.5)^2(0.25)} = 4$$

24. ***(4)*** Among the given statements, all the statements are correct.

25. ***(22)*** Given, $A(g) \rightleftharpoons B(g)$

By using,

$$\Delta G^\circ = -2.303\,RT \log K$$

$$\because \quad K = \frac{[B]}{[A]}$$

$$\log K = \frac{-\Delta G^\circ}{2.303RT}$$

$$= \frac{7.38\,\text{kJ mol}^{-1}}{2.303 \times 8.314\,\text{JK}^{-1}\,\text{mol}^{-1} \times 480\,\text{K}}$$

$\log K = 0.80 \Rightarrow K = 6.3$

Now,	$A(g) \rightleftharpoons$	$B(g)$
$t = 0$	25	0
$t = t$	$25 - x$	x

$$K = \frac{[B]}{[A]} = \frac{x}{25-x} = 6.3$$

$x = 157.5 - 6.3x$; $x = 21.5 \approx 22$

So, millimoles of $B = 22$

26. ***(9)*** The given equation is,

	$N_2(g) + $	$3H_2(g) \rightleftharpoons$	$2NH_3(g)$
At, $t = 0$	0.2	0.6	0
At, $t = t_{eq.}$	$0.2 - x$	$0.6 - 3x$	$2x$

$$x = \frac{40}{100} \times 0.2 = 0.08$$

Total number of initial moles $= 0.2 + 0.6 = 0.8$

Total number of final moles $= (0.2 - x) + (0.6 - 3x) + 2x$

$= 0.8 - 2x = 0.8 - 0.16 = 0.64$

Ratio of final volume of gases : Ratio of initial volume of gases

= Ratio of final moles : Ratio of initial moles

$= 0.64 : 0.8$ or $4 : 5$

Hence, the sum of x and y is $4 + 5 = 9$

27. **(29)** Given, $T = 300$ K

$$\Delta S = 136 \text{ JK}^{-1} \text{ mol}^{-1}$$
$$\Delta H° = 57.3 \text{ kJ mol}^{-1}$$

Free energy is given by,

$$\Delta G° = \Delta H° - T\Delta S°$$
$$= 57.3 \times 10^3 - 300 \text{ K} \times 136 \text{ JK}^{-1} \text{ mol}^{-1}$$
$$= 57300 \text{ J mol}^{-1} - 40800 \text{ J mol}^{-1}$$
$$= 16500 \text{ J mol}^{-1}$$

As we know,

$$\Delta G° = -2.303 RT \log K$$
$$16500 = -2.303 \times 8.314 \times 300 \times \log K$$
$$\log K = \frac{-16500}{2.303 \times 8.314 \times 300}$$
$$= -2.872 = -28.72 \times 10^{-1}$$

Hence, the mixing value is $28.72 \approx 29$.

28. **(2)** The given reaction is,

$$N_2(g) + 3H_2(g) \rightleftharpoons 2NH_3(g)$$

At, $t = 0$	1	3	0
At, $t = t_{eq}$	$1 - x$	$3 - 3x$	$2x$

Given, $x = 0.5$

Pressure of H_2 at equilibrium $= x_{H_2} \times p$

where, x_{H_2} is the mole fraction of H_2 at equilibrium.

$$\frac{1.5}{(0.5 + 1.5 + 1)} \times p = \frac{1.5}{3} \times p = \frac{p}{2}$$

Hence, the value of x is 2.

29. **(3)** The given reaction is

$$2BrCl(g) \rightleftharpoons Br_2(g) + Cl_2(g)$$

At, $t = 0$	3.3×10^{-3}	0	0
At, $t = t_{eq}$	$3.3 \times 10^{-3} - 2x$	x	x

$$k = \frac{x^2}{(3.3 \times 10^{-3} - 2x)^2} = 32$$
$$5.66 \approx \frac{x}{3.3 \times 10^{-2} - 2x}$$
$$12.32x = 5.66 \times 3.3 \times 10^{-3}$$
$$x \approx 1.5 \times 10^{-3}$$

Therefore, concentration of BrCl at equilibrium

$$= 3.3 \times 10^{-3} - 2 \times 1.5 \times 10^{-3}$$
$$= 0.3 \times 10^{-3} = 3 \times 10^{-4}$$

Hence, the value of x is 3.

30. **(58)** The given reaction is,

$$NH_2COONH_4(s) \rightleftharpoons 2NH_3(g) + CO_2(g)$$

Equ. partial	$2p_0$	p_0
New. equ. partial pressure	$3p_0$	p

Now, $k_p = (2p_0)^2 \cdot p_0 = (3p_0)^2 \cdot p$

$$p = \frac{4}{9} p_0$$

Now, $$\frac{3p_0 + p}{3p_0} = \frac{31}{27}$$

Hence, the sum of x and y is 58.

Check Through PYQs : JEE Main

1. **(3)** $NH_2COONH_4(s) \rightleftharpoons 2NH_3(g) + CO_2(g)$

Total pressure at equilibrium = 1.0 atm

Partial pressure of CO_2 at equilibrium = 0.4 atm

$\therefore$ Partial pressure of NH_3 at equilibrium = 0.6 atm

$$K_p = (p_{NH_3})^2(p_{CO_2})$$
$$= (0.6)^2(0.4) = 1.44 \text{ atm}^3$$

2. **(1)** $CO_2(g) + C(s) \rightleftharpoons 2CO(g)$

$t = 0$	0.6	0
$t = t_{eq}$	$0.6 - p$	$2p$

p_t at equilibrium $= 0.8 = 0.6 + p$

$$0.2 = p$$

$$k_p = \frac{(p_{CO})^2}{(p_{CO_2})} = \frac{(2p)^2}{0.6 - p} = \frac{4 \times 0.04}{0.6 - 0.2} = \frac{4 \times 0.04}{0.4} = 0.4$$

3. **(d)** $X \rightleftharpoons Y; K_1 = 1.0$

$Y \rightleftharpoons Z; K_2 = 2.0$

$Z \rightleftharpoons W; K_3 = 4.0$

For the equilibrium constant value of

$$X \rightleftharpoons W; K = K_1 \cdot K_2 \cdot K_3$$
$$K = 1 \times 2 \times 4$$
$$K = 8$$

Hence, option (d) is correct.

4. **(a)** $A(g) \rightleftharpoons B(g) + \frac{C}{2}(g)$

$t = t_{eq}$ $(1 - \alpha)$ $\quad \alpha \quad \frac{\alpha}{2}$

$$p_B = \frac{\alpha}{\left(1 + \frac{\alpha}{2}\right)} \cdot p, \; p_A = \frac{(1 - \alpha)}{\left(1 + \frac{\alpha}{2}\right)} \cdot p, \; p_C = \frac{a/2}{\left(1 + \frac{\alpha}{2}\right)} \cdot p$$

$$K_p = \frac{p_B \cdot p_C^{1/2}}{p_A} \quad \text{...(i)}$$

Substitute the value of p_A, p_B and p_C in Eq. (i)

$$\therefore \quad K_p = \frac{(\alpha)^{3/2} (p)^{1/2}}{(1 - \alpha)(2 + \alpha)^{1/2}}$$

5. **(a)** K_C is given by the equation

$$K_C = \frac{\text{Concentration of product ion}}{\text{Concentration of reactant ion}}$$

So, for the reaction

$$Fe^{3+}(aq) + SCN^-(aq) \rightleftharpoons (FeSCN)^{2+}(aq)$$

The value of K_C will be $= \frac{[FeSCN^{2+}]}{[Fe^{3+}][SCN^-]}$

6. ***(163)*** For the given reaction,

$$\frac{3}{2}O_2(g) \rightleftharpoons O_3(g)$$

$$K_p = 2.47 \times 10^{-29}$$

Using $\Delta_r G^\circ = -RT \ln K_p$

$$= -8.314 \times 10^{-3} \times 298 \times \ln(2.47 \times 10^{-29})$$

$$\Delta_r G^\circ = -8.314 \times 10^{-3} \times 298 \times (-65.87)$$

$$\Delta_r G^\circ = 163.19 \text{ kJ}$$

So, the value of x is 163.

7. ***(417)*** The formation of NH_3 is,

$$N_2 + 3H_2 \rightleftharpoons 2NH_3$$

Equilibrium constant is given by

$$K_C = \frac{[\text{Product}]}{[\text{Reactant}]} = \frac{[NH_3]^2}{[N_2][H_2]^3}$$

$$= \frac{(1.5 \times 10^{-2})^2}{(2 \times 10^{-2})(3 \times 10^{-2})^3} \approx 417$$

Hence, equilibrium constant is 417.

8. ***(37)*** Given, $T = 400$ K

$$\Delta H^\ominus = 77.2 \text{ kJ / mol}$$

$$\Delta S = 122 \text{ JK}^{-1}$$

Free energy is given by

$$\Delta G^\circ = \Delta H^\circ - T\Delta S^\circ$$

$$= 77.2 \times 10^3 - 400 \times 122$$

$$= 28400 \text{ J}$$

$$\Delta G^\circ = -2.303RT \log K$$

$$28400 = -2.303 \times 8.314 \times 400 \times \log K$$

$$\log K = -3.708$$

or $\log K = -37.08 \times 10^{-1}$

Hence, the missing value is 37.

9. ***(44)*** $CO(g) + H_2O(g) \rightleftharpoons CO_2(g) + H_2(g)$

	$CO(g)$	$H_2O(g)$	$CO_2(g)$	$H_2(g)$
at $t = 0$	1 mol	1 mol	0	0
at eq.	$1-x$	$1-x$	x	x

Given that 40% by mass, water reacts with CO at equilibrium.

$\Rightarrow$ $x = 0.4$ and $1 - x = 0.6$

So, $K_C = \frac{[CO_2][H_2]}{[CO][H_2O]} = \frac{0.4 \times 0.4}{0.6 \times 0.6} = 0.44$

or $K_C \times 10^2 = 44$

10. ***(12)*** For equilibrium equation.

(i) $X(g) \rightleftharpoons Y(g) + Z(g),\ K_{p_1} = 3$

	$X(g)$	$Y(g)$	$Z(g)$
at $t = 0$	1	0	0
at t_{eq}	$1-x$	x	x

Total number of moles $= 1 - x + x + x = 1 + x$

Partial pressure $\frac{(1-x)p_1}{1+x}$ $\frac{xp_1}{1+x}$ $\frac{xp_1}{1+x}$

$$\Rightarrow \quad Kp_1 = \frac{p_Y\, p_Z}{p_X}$$

$$= \frac{\left(\frac{xp_1}{1+x}\right)\left(\frac{xp_1}{1+x}\right)}{\left[\frac{(1-x)p_1}{1+x}\right]} = \frac{x^2}{1-x^2} \times p_1$$

(ii) $A(g) \rightleftharpoons 2B(g),\ K_{p_2} = 1$

	$A(g)$	$2B(g)$
at $t = 0$	1	0
at t_{eq}	$1-x$	$2x$
Partial pressure	$\frac{(1-x)p_2}{1+x}$	$\frac{(2x)p_2}{1+x}$

$$\Rightarrow \quad Kp_2 = \frac{(p_B)^2}{(p_A)} = \frac{\frac{(2x)^2 p_2^2}{(1+x)^2}}{\left(\frac{1-x}{1+x}\right)p_2}$$

$$= \frac{4x^2}{1-x^2} \times p_2$$

$$\Rightarrow \quad \frac{Kp_1}{Kp_2} = \frac{3}{1}$$

$$= \frac{x^2}{(1-x^2)} \times p_1 \times \frac{(1-x^2)}{4x^2} \times \frac{1}{p_2} = \frac{p_1}{4p_2}$$

$$\Rightarrow \quad \frac{p_1}{p_2} = \frac{12}{1} = \frac{x}{1} \quad \text{(Given)}$$

$$x = 12$$

11. ***(4)*** $N_2(g) + 3H_2(g) \rightleftharpoons 2NH_3(g);\ K_1 = 4 \times 10^5$ ...(i)

$N_2(g) + O_2(g) \rightleftharpoons 2NO(g);\ K_2 = 1.6 \times 10^{12}$ ...(ii)

$H_2(g) + \frac{1}{2}O_2(g) \rightleftharpoons H_2O(g);\ K_3 = 1 \times 10^{-13}$ ...(iii)

On solving above equation as

Eq. (ii) + 3 × Eq. (iii) – Eq. (i)

We have, $\left[2NH_3(g) + \frac{5}{2}O_2(g) \rightleftharpoons 2NO(g) + 3H_2O(g)\right]$

... required

Eq. (ii) + 3 × Eq. (iii) – Eq. (i)

$$K = \frac{K_2 \times (K_3)^3}{K_1}$$

or $K = \frac{1.6 \times 10^{12} \times (10^{-13})^3}{4 \times 10^5}$

or $K = 4 \times 10^{-33}$

12. ***(a)*** $p_{total} = \frac{nRT}{V} = \frac{9 \times 0.082 \times 610}{100} = 4.5$ atm

$$p_{PCl_5} = \frac{5 \times 4.5}{9} = 2.5 \quad [p_A = x_A p_T]$$

$$p_{Ar} = \frac{4 \times 4.5}{9} = 2$$

Now, $PCl_5 \rightleftharpoons PCl_3 + Cl_2$

PCl_5	PCl_3	Cl_2
$2.5 - p$	p	p

$$p_{total} = 2.5 - p + p + p + p_{Ar} = 6$$

$$p = 1.5$$

Now, $K_p = \frac{[PCl_3][Cl_2]}{[PCl_5]} = \frac{1.5 \times 1.5}{(2.5 - 1.5)} = 2.25$

13. ***(1107)*** $PCl_5 \rightleftharpoons PCl_3 + Cl_2$

	PCl_5	PCl_3	Cl_2
Initial mole	5	0	0
At equil.	$5(1-x)$	$5x$	$5x$

Total moles $= 5(1-x) + 5x + 5x$

$= 5(1+x) + 2$ (Nitrogen moles)

$$pV = nRT$$

$$n = \frac{2.46 \times 200}{0.082 \times 600} = 10$$

$$5(1+x) + 2 = 10$$

$$x = \frac{3}{5} = 0.6$$

Partial pressure of

$$p_{PCl_5} = \frac{5(1-x)}{7+5x} \times 2.46$$

Put value of $x = 0.6$

$$p_{PCl_5} = \frac{5 \times 0.4}{10} \times 2.46 = \frac{2.46}{5}$$

Partial pressure of p_{PCl_3} and p_{Cl_2}

$$p_{PCl_3} = p_{Cl_2} = \frac{5x}{5x+7} \times 2.46$$

Put $x = 0.6$

$$p_{PCl_3} = p_{Cl_2} = \frac{3}{10} \times 2.46$$

$$K_p = \frac{p_{PCl_3} \cdot p_{Cl_2}}{p_{PCl_5}} = \frac{\frac{3}{10} \times 2.46 \times \frac{3}{10} \times 2.46}{\frac{2}{10} \times 2.46}$$

$$= \frac{9}{10} \times \frac{2.46}{2} = 1.107 = 1107 \times 10^{-3}$$

14. ***(0.02)*** $[PtCl_4]^{2-} + H_2O \underset{K_b}{\overset{K_f}{\rightleftharpoons}} [Pt(H_2O)Cl_3]^- + Cl^-$

Rate of a reaction = Rate of forward reaction – rate of backward reaction

$$\frac{-d[[PtCl_4]^{2-}]}{dt} = k_f[[PtCl_4]^{2-}] - k_b[[Pt(H_2O)Cl_3]^-][Cl^-]$$

Comparing this equation with the given one :

$$\Rightarrow \quad K_{eq} = \frac{k_f}{k_b} = \frac{4.8 \times 10^{-5}}{2.4 \times 10^{-3}} = 0.02$$

15. ***(1380)*** For a reaction, $A(g) \longrightarrow B(g)$

Formula used

$$\Delta G° = -RT \ln K_p \quad \ldots (i)$$

Put given value in Eq (i), we get

$$\Delta G° = -R\,(300) \ln 100$$

$$\Delta G° = -R\,(300)\,(2) \ln (10)$$

$\because \quad \ln (10) = 2.3$

$$\Delta G° = -R(300)\,(2)\,(2.3)$$

$$\Delta G° = -1380\,R$$

Hence, $\Delta G° = -xR$

$$x = 1380$$

16. ***(d)*** Equilibrium constant for equation,

$$N_2(g) + 3H_2(g) \rightleftharpoons 2NH_3(g)$$

$$K_C = \frac{[NH_3]^2}{[N_2]\,[H_2]^3} = 64$$

and for $\quad 2NH_3(g) \rightleftharpoons N_2(g) + 3H_2(g)$,

$$K'_C = \frac{1}{K_C}$$

and for equation,

$$NH_3(g) \rightleftharpoons \frac{1}{2}N_2(g) + \frac{3}{2}H_2(g)$$

$$K'_C = \frac{1}{K_C^{1/2}} = \frac{1}{K_C^{1/2}} = \frac{1}{(64)^{1/2}} = \frac{1}{8}$$

17. ***(c)*** $\Delta G° = -RT \ln K$, $T_1 = 25°C$, $K_1 = 10$

$\Delta G°$ at $T_1 = 25°C$

$$T_1 = -8.314 \times 10^{-3} \times 298 \times 2.303 \times \log 10$$

$$\approx -5.71 \text{ kJ / mol}$$

$\Delta G°$ at $T_2(100°C) = -8.314 \times 10^{-3} \times 373 \times 2.303 \times \log (100)$

$$\approx -14.29 \text{ kJ/mol}$$

$$\Delta G° = \Delta H° - T\Delta S°$$

$\Rightarrow \quad -5.71 = \Delta H° - 298\,(\Delta S°)$

and $\quad -14.29 = \Delta H° - 373\,(\Delta S°)$

Hence,

At T_1

$$\Delta G° = -5.71 \text{ kJ/mol}$$

$$\Delta H° = 28.4 \text{ kJ/mol}$$

At T_2

$$\Delta G° = -14.29 \text{ kJ/mol}$$

$$\Delta H° = 28.4 \text{ kJ/mol}$$

18. ***(a)*** Equilibrium is the condition when a forward chemical reaction and its reverse reaction proceed at equal rates.

At equilibrium, $r_a = r_b$

For the equilibrium, $A \rightleftharpoons B$

The variation of the rate of the forward and reverse reaction can be illustrated by following graph.

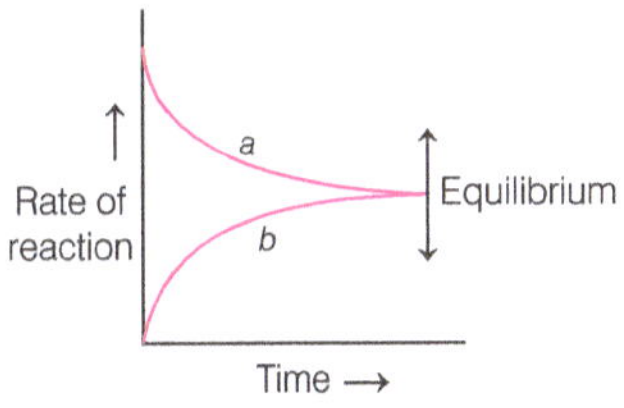

19. ***(b)*** Assuming the reaction to be

$$A \rightleftharpoons B,$$

Equilibrium constant, $K = \frac{[B]}{[A]}$

Number of circles in the figure = 11

Number of squares in the figure = 6

$$\therefore \quad K = \frac{11}{6} = 1.8 \approx 2$$

20. ***(d)*** According to Le-Chatelier's principle, if a solid is added, then there will be no effect on the equilibrium. Fe_2O_3 is a solid compound.
Hence, option (d) is correct.

21. ***(3)*** The number of correct statement involving equilibria in physical processes from the given statements are three i.e., A, B and D.
(A) Equilibrium is possible only in a closed system at a given temperature. All measurable properties of the system remain constant.
(B) The opposing processes occur at the same rate and there is dynamic but stable condition.
(C) At equilibrium the value of parameters become constant of a given temperature and not equal.
(D) For a given solid solute and a liquid solvent, solubility depends upon temperature only.

22. ***(3)*** $2SO_2(g) + O_2(g) \rightleftharpoons 2SO_3(g); \Delta H = -190$ kJ
The reaction is exothermic in nature.
On increasing pressure, equilibrium will shift in forward direction. Apart from that addition of more SO_2 and O_2 will also increase the yield of SO_3 at equilibrium while other factors decrease the yield of SO_3.

23. ***(b)*** $N_2O_4(g) \rightleftharpoons 2NO_2(g); \Delta H = +58$ kJ
In case of an endothermic reaction ($\Delta H = +$ ve), the equilibrium constant increases with rise in temperature and hence, the reaction moves in forward direction.On adding N_2, pressure is increased at constant T, and volume would also be constant, so no change is observed.

Practice Element 02 : Target JEE Advanced

1. ***(d)*** For the equilibrium, $B \rightleftharpoons A$

$$K = \frac{1.3}{95.2} \approx 0.0136$$

$$\Delta G_1^\circ = -2.303\, RT \log K$$

$$= -2.303 \times 8.314 \times 548 \times \log(0.0136)$$

$$= +19584\text{ J} = +19.58\text{ kJ}$$

For the equilibrium, $B \rightleftharpoons C$

$$K = \frac{3.5}{95.2} \approx 0.0368$$

$$\Delta G_2^\circ = -2.303\, RT \log K$$

$$= -2.303 \times 8.314 \times 548 \times \log(0.0368)$$

$$= +15048\text{ J} \approx +15.05\text{ kJ}$$

Further, negative value of $\Delta G°$ favours the forward reaction,

$\therefore$ For, $B \rightleftharpoons A$; $\Delta G_1^\circ = +19.58$ kJ; stability order is $B > A$.
and for, $B \rightleftharpoons C$; $\Delta G_2^\circ = +15.05$ kJ; stability order is $B > C$.
To determine the order of stability between A and C.

$A \rightleftharpoons B$; $\Delta G° = -19.58$ kJ
$B \rightleftharpoons C$; $\Delta G° = +15.05$ kJ
$A \rightleftharpoons C$; $\Delta G° = -4.53$ kJ; stability order is $C > A$

So, the decreasing order of stability is $B > C > A$.

2. ***(d)***

	$2NH_3(g) \rightleftharpoons$	$N_2(g)$ +	$3H_2(g)$
Initial	a	0	0
At equil.	$(a-2x)$	x	$3x$

$$x = 0.30$$

$\therefore \quad a - 2x = 0.30$

$\therefore \quad a = 0.90$

Thus, initial moles of $NH_3 = 0.90$ mol

$$K_C = \frac{[N_2][H_2]^3}{[NH_3]^2} = \frac{\left(\frac{0.30}{0.50}\right)\left(\frac{0.90}{0.50}\right)^3}{\left(\frac{0.30}{0.50}\right)^2} = 9.72$$

Thus, K_C for NH_3 formation

$$N_2(g) + 3H_2(g) \rightleftharpoons 2NH_3(g)$$

$$= \frac{1}{9.72} \approx 0.103.$$

3. ***(a)*** Statement I is correct but Statement II is incorrect.
Its correct form is
- The reaction proceed as

$$NaNO_3(s) \rightleftharpoons NaNO_2(s) + \frac{1}{2}O_2(g); \Delta H = +\text{ve}$$

Also, $K_p = (p_{O_2})^{1/2}$ and thus addition of $NaNO_3$ or $NaNO_2$ has no effect at equilibrium.
Instead at equilibrium, the increase in temperature will favour forward reaction.

4. ***(d)*** Pure $CaCO_3 = 20 \times \frac{50}{100} = 10\text{ g} = 0.1$ mol

Case I

	$CaCO_3(s) \rightleftharpoons$	$CaO(s)$ +	$CO_2(g)$
Initial	0.1	0	0
At equil.	–	–	x

$x = 0.05$ mol (50% of 0.1 mol)

$$p_{CO_2} = \frac{n}{V}RT = \frac{0.05}{1} \times 0.0821 \times 400 = 1.642\text{ atm}$$

Thus, $K_p = p_{CO_2} = 1.642$

Case II

	$CaCO_3(s) \rightleftharpoons$	$CaO(s)$ +	$CO_2(g)$
Initial	0.1 mol	0	0.5 atm
At equil.	–	–	$0.5 + y$

$$K_p = (0.5 + y) = 1.642$$

$\therefore \quad y = 1.142 \Rightarrow p = \frac{nRT}{V}$

$$1.142\text{ atm} = \frac{n \times 0.0821 \times 400}{1}$$

$$n \approx 0.0348\text{ (dissociated)}$$

Thus, percentage $= \frac{0.0348}{0.1} \times 100 = 34.8\%$

5. ***(c)*** **Step I** Calculation of $\Delta G°$

$$\Delta G° = -2.303\, RT \log K_p$$

$$= -2.303 \times 2 \times 373 \log 8 \times 10^{-9}$$

$$= +13910.8\text{ cal}$$

Step II Calculation of $\Delta H°$

$$\Delta G° = \Delta H° - T\Delta S°$$

$$\Delta H° = \Delta G° + T\Delta S° = 13910.8 + 373 \times 30$$

$$= 25100.8 \text{ cal}$$

Step III Calculation of K_2 (at temperature T_2 having 0.1% dissociation)

$$\alpha = \frac{0.1}{100} = 1 \times 10^{-3}$$

$$K_2 = \frac{p\alpha^2}{(1-\alpha^2)} = \frac{2(1\times10^{-3})^2}{[1-(1\times10^{-3})^2]} \approx 2\times10^{-6}$$

Step IV $\Delta H° = \frac{2.303\,RT_1T_2}{(T_2 - T_1)} \log \frac{K_2}{K_1}$

$$\frac{T_2 - T_1}{T_1T_2} = \frac{2.303R}{\Delta H°} \log \frac{K_2}{K_1}$$

$$\frac{1}{T_1} - \frac{1}{T_2} = \frac{2.303\times2}{25100.8} \log \frac{2\times10^{-6}}{8\times10^{-9}}$$

$$\frac{1}{373} - \frac{1}{T_2} = 4.4\times10^{-4} \Rightarrow \frac{1}{T_2} = \frac{1}{373} - 4.4\times10^{-4}$$

$$T_2 = 446 \text{ K}$$

6. ***(c)*** The given reaction is

$$2SO_2(g) + O_2(g) \rightleftharpoons 2SO_3(g)$$

$$K_C = \frac{(0.12)^2}{(0.12)^2 \times 5} = 0.2$$

Another vessel : $nSO_2 = \frac{32}{64} = 0.5$

	$2SO_2(g)$	$+ O_2(g)$	$\rightleftharpoons 2SO_3(g)$
At equilibrium	$0.5 - 2x$	$y - x$	$2x$

As per given : $2x = \frac{20}{100} \times 0.5 = 0.1$

$$x = 0.05$$

$$[SO_2] = 0.5 - 2x = 0.5 - 0.1 = 0.4$$

$$[O_2] = y - 0.05$$

$$[SO_3] = 2x = 2\times0.05 = 0.1$$

$$K_C = \frac{(0.1)^2}{(0.4)^2(y-0.05)} = 0.20$$

$$y = 0.3625 \text{ mole}$$

$\therefore$ Mass of O_2 added $= 0.3625 \times 32 = 11.6$ g

7. ***(a)*** The reaction proceeds as

	$R_1OH(aq)$	$+ CH_3COOH(aq)$	$\rightleftharpoons CH_3COOR_1(aq)$	$+ H_2O(l)$
Initial moles	1	1	0	0
Equ. moles	$1 - x$	$1 - (x + y)$	x	–

Similarly for R_2—OH;

	$R_2OH(aq)$	$+ CH_3COOH(aq)$	$\rightleftharpoons CH_3COOR_2(aq)$	$+ H_2O(l)$
Initial moles	1	1	0	0
Equil. moles	$1 - y$	$1 - (x + y)$	y	–

From question,

$$x + y = 0.8 \quad \text{and} \quad \frac{x}{y} = \frac{3}{2}$$

$\therefore$ $x = 0.48$ and $y = 0.32$

Now, $K_1 = \frac{x}{(1-x)[1-(x+y)]}$

$$= \frac{0.48}{0.52\times0.2} \approx 4.62$$

8. ***(b)*** The given reaction is,

	$4HNO_3(g)$	$\rightleftharpoons 4NO_2(g)$	$+ 2H_2O(g)$	$+ O_2(g)$
Initial pressure	p_0	0	0	0
Equil. partial pressure	$p_0 - 4x$	$4x$	$2x$	x

From question, $p_0 - 4x = 2$ atm

and $(p_0 - 4x) + 4x + 2x + x = 30$ atm

$\therefore$ $p_0 = 18$ atm and $x = 4$ atm

Now, $K_p = \frac{(4x)^4 \times (2x)^2 \times x}{(p_0 - 4x)^4} = \frac{(4\times4)^4 \times (2\times4)^2 \times 4}{(18 - 4\times4)^4}$

$$= 1048576 = 2^{20} \text{ atm}^3$$

and $K_C = \frac{K_p}{(RT)^{\Delta n_g}} = \frac{2^{20}}{(0.082\times400)^3} = 29.71 \text{ m}^3 \approx 30 \text{ m}^3$

9. ***(d)*** Given, $A_2(g) \rightleftharpoons 2A;\ K_1 = x$ atm

	$A_2(g)$	$2A$
Initial pressure	1 atm	0
Equ. partial pressure	$1 - (x + z)$	$2x$

$B_2(g) \rightleftharpoons 2B(g);\ K_2 = y$ atm

	$B_2(g)$	$2B(g)$
Initial partial pressure	1 atm	0
Equ. partial pressure	$1 - (y + z)$	$2y$

$A_2(g) + B_2(g) \rightleftharpoons 2AB(g);\ K_3 = 2$

	$A_2(g)$	$B_2(g)$	$2AB(g)$
Initial partial pressure	1	1	1
Equ. partial pressure	$1 - (x + z)$	$1 - (y + z)$	$2z = 0.5$

From question,

$$[1 - (x + z)] + 2x + [1 - (y + z)] + 2y + 2z = 2.75$$

$\therefore$ $x + y = 0.75$

Now, $K_3 = \frac{(0.5)^2}{(0.75 - x)(0.75 - y)} = 2$

$\Rightarrow$ $x = 0.25$ or 0.50

and $y = 0.50$ or 0.25

$$\frac{K_2}{K_1} = \frac{y}{x} = \frac{\frac{(2y)^2}{1-(y+z)}}{\frac{(2x)^2}{1-(x+z)}} = \frac{(2y)^2 \times (0.75 - x)}{(2x)^2 \times (0.75 - y)}$$

Given, $y > x$

So, the value of $y = 0.50$ and $x = 0.25$

then, $\frac{y}{x} = \frac{2\times0.50\times2\times0.50\times0.5}{2\times0.25\times2\times0.25\times0.25} = 8$

Hence, the value of $y : x$ is 8 : 1.

10. ***(a, b, c, d)***

	$2SO_3(g)$	$\rightleftharpoons 2SO_2(g)$	$+ O_2(g)$
Initial	2 mol	0	0
At equili.	$(2 - 2x)$	$2x$	x
Molar conc.	$\frac{2(1-x)}{10}$ mol L^{-1}	$\frac{2x}{10}$ mol L^{-1}	$\frac{x}{10}$ mol L^{-1}

Given, $\frac{[SO_2]}{[SO_3]} = 0.663$

$\therefore \quad \dfrac{2x}{2(1-x)} = 0.663$

$\therefore \quad x \approx 0.4$

$\therefore \quad K_{eq} = \dfrac{[SO_2]^2\,[O_2]}{[SO_3]^2} = (0.663)^2\left(\dfrac{0.4}{10}\right)$

$\approx 0.0176 \text{ mol L}^{-1}$

$\Delta G^\circ = -2.303\,RT \log K_{eq}$

$= -2.303 \times 8.314 \times 10^{-3} \text{ kJ mol}^{-1}\text{K}^{-1} \times 350 \text{ K} \log 0.0176$

$\approx 11.76 \text{ kJ mol}^{-1}$

$[O_2] = \dfrac{x}{10} = \dfrac{0.4}{10} = 0.04 \text{ mol L}^{-1}$

$[SO_3] = \dfrac{2(1-x)}{10} = 0.12 \text{ mol L}^{-1}$

11. ***(a, c)*** According to the given equilibrium,

$$SO_2Cl_2(g) \rightleftharpoons SO_2(g) + Cl_2(g)$$

which is attained at 298 K in a closed container, when an inert gas helium is introduced the concentration of each species changes and concentration of SO_2 decreases.

12. ***(a, b, c)***

	$N_2O_4(g) \rightleftharpoons$	$2NO_2(g)$
Initial	1	0
At equil	$(1-x)$	$2x$

1 mol N_2O_4 = 92 g

$20\%\ N_2O_4 = \dfrac{92 \times 20}{100} = 18.4\text{ g} = \dfrac{18.4}{92} = 0.2 \text{ mol}$

$\therefore \quad x = 0.2$

Total moles at equilibrium $= 1 + x = 1.2$

$$K_p = \frac{4x^2p}{(1-x^2)} = \frac{4 \times (0.2)^2 \times 1}{(1-0.04)} = 0.167$$

$$K_p = K_C(RT)^{\Delta n_g} = K_C RT$$

$$\therefore \quad K_C = \frac{K_p}{RT} = \frac{0.167}{0.0821 \times 300} = 6.78 \times 10^{-3}$$

13. ***(a, b, c, d)***

	$Cl_2 \rightleftharpoons$	$2Cl$
Initial	1	0
At equilibrium	$(1-x)$	$2x$

$x = 0.071$

$\therefore Cl_2 = (1-x) = 1 - 0.071 = 0.929 \text{ mol}$

$Cl = 0.142$ mol

$n_{total} = 0.929 + 0.142 = 1.071 \text{ mol}$

$\therefore \chi_{Cl_2} = \dfrac{0.929}{1.071},\ \chi_{Cl} = \dfrac{0.142}{1.071}$

Thus, $\chi_{Cl_2} > \chi_{Cl}$

As in (4)

$K_\chi = 0.0204$

$K_p = 0.0204$ atm

$K_c = 1.55 \times 10^{-4} \text{ mol L}^{-1}$

14. ***(a, c)*** Lowering of temperature and increased the pressure will increase solubility of $NH_3(g)$ in H_2O.

15. ***(a, b, c, d)*** (a) $N_2(g) + O_2(g) \rightleftharpoons 2NO(g)$

$$K_1 = \frac{[NO]^2}{[N_2]\,[O_2]}$$

$$NO(g) \rightleftharpoons \frac{1}{2}N_2(g) + \frac{1}{2}O_2(g)$$

$$K_2 = \frac{[N_2]^{\frac{1}{2}}\,[O_2]^{\frac{1}{2}}}{[NO]} \Rightarrow K_2^2 = \frac{[N_2]\,[O_2]}{[NO]^2}$$

Thus, $K_1K_2^2 = 1$

Thus, (a) is correct.

(b) Free energy can be obtained by algebraic summation.

$2NO_2(g) \rightleftharpoons N_2O_4(g);\ \Delta G_1^\circ$

$NO_2(g) \rightleftharpoons \dfrac{1}{2}N_2O_4(g);\ \dfrac{\Delta G_1^\circ}{2}$

$\dfrac{1}{2}N_2O_4(g) \rightleftharpoons NO_2(g);\ -\dfrac{\Delta G_1^\circ}{2}$

Thus, $\quad \Delta G_2^\circ = -\dfrac{\Delta G_1^\circ}{2} \Rightarrow 2\Delta G_2^\circ + \Delta G_1^\circ = 0$

Thus, (b) is correct.

(c) $\Delta_r H^\circ = \dfrac{2.303\,RT_1T_2}{(T_2 - T_1)} \log \dfrac{K_2}{K_1}$

or $\Delta_r H^\circ \dfrac{(T_2 - T_1)}{T_1T_2} = 2.303\,R \log K_2 - 2.303\,R \log K_1$

$$\Delta_r H^\circ \left[\frac{1}{T_1} - \frac{1}{T_2}\right] = \frac{2.303\,R\,T_2 \log K_2}{T_2} - \frac{2.303\,RT_1}{T_1} \log K_1$$

But $2.303\,RT \log K = -\Delta_r G^\circ$

$$\therefore \quad \Delta_r H^\circ \left[\frac{1}{T_1} - \frac{1}{T_2}\right] = -\frac{\Delta_r G_2^\circ}{T_2} - \left(-\frac{\Delta G_1^\circ}{T_1}\right)$$

$$\Delta_r H^\circ \left[\frac{1}{T_2} - \frac{1}{T_1}\right] = \frac{\Delta_r G_2^\circ}{T_2} - \frac{\Delta_r G_1^\circ}{T_1}$$

Thus, (c) is correct

(d)

	$A(g) \rightleftharpoons$	$2B(g)$
Initial	1	0
At equilibrium	$(1-x)$	$2x$

Total moles $= (1 + x)$

Partial pressure $p_A = \left(\dfrac{1-x}{1+x}\right)p,$

$$p_B = \frac{2xp}{(1+x)} \Rightarrow K_p = \frac{4x^2p}{(1-x^2)}$$

$$\Rightarrow \quad \frac{x^2}{(1-x^2)} = \frac{K_p}{4p}$$

On solving $x = \sqrt{\dfrac{K_p}{K_p + 4p}}$

Thus, (d) is correct.

16. ***(b, c, d)*** Among the given statements, (b), (c) and (d) are correct while statement (a) is incorrect regarding the given data. The given reaction is; $A(g) \rightleftharpoons B(g) + C(g)$
(a) With increase of temperature K_p increases, i.e., with increase of temperature, the reaction is favoured in forward direction and hence reaction is endothermic.
(b) Increase in temperature favours forward reaction and hence, the formation of B increases.
(c) $\Delta n = 1 + 1 - 1 = 1$
$\Delta n = +$ ve i.e., with the increase of pressure, reaction is favoured backward direction and hence the formation of $A(g)$ increases.
(d) As from the above statement in (i) and (iii), the reaction is favoured backward with decreased of temperature and increase of pressure.

17. ***(a, b, c)***
(a) H_2O removes SO_3 by dissolving it.
(b) Helium increases pressure thus forward reaction is favoured
(c) $\Delta H° < 0$, thus exothermic, low temperature favours forward reaction.

18. ***(1.26)*** The given reaction is

$$CH_3OH(g) \rightleftharpoons CO(g) + 2H_2(g)$$

At, $t = 0$ $\quad \frac{4.72}{32} = 0.1475 \quad 0 \quad 0$

At equilibrium $0.1475 - x \quad x \quad 2x$

Given that, $33(0.1475 - x) = 2x$

$$x = 0.139$$

From the reaction,

$$K = \frac{(2x)^2 x}{0.1475 - x} \text{ (as volume 1L)}$$

By putting the value of $x = 0.139$, $K = 1.26$

19. ***(1.05)*** $N_2O_4(g) \rightleftharpoons 2NO_2(g)$, $K_C = 4.61 \times 10^{-3}$

0.971 mol $\quad 0.058$ mol

Molar conc. $\frac{0.971}{0.750}$ mol L^{-1} $\quad \frac{0.058}{0.750}$ mol L^{-1}

$$\therefore \quad Q = \frac{[NO_2]^2}{[N_2O_4]} \text{ in LHS flask}$$

$$= \left(\frac{0.058}{0.750}\right)^2 \Big/ \left(\frac{0.971}{0.750}\right) = 4.61 \times 10^{-3} = K_C$$

In LHS flask, system is in equilibrium. In RHS flask $V = 2.25$ L

$\therefore \quad Q = 1.53 \times 10^{-3} << K_C$

Thus, equilibrium $N_2O_4 \rightleftharpoons 2NO_2$ is spontaneous in forward direction.

$$N_2O_4(g) \rightleftharpoons 2NO_2(g)$$

$0.971 \quad 0.058$

$(0.971 - x) \quad (0.058 + 2x)$

$$\therefore \quad [N_2O_4] = \left(\frac{0.971 - x}{2.25}\right) \text{ mol } L^{-1}$$

$$[NO_2] = \left(\frac{0.058 + 2x}{2.25}\right) \text{ mol } L^{-1}$$

$$\therefore \quad K_C = \frac{[NO_2]^2}{[N_2O_4]} = 4.61 \times 10^{-3}$$

$$\left(\frac{0.058 + 2x}{2.25}\right)^2 \Big/ \left(\frac{0.971 - x}{2.25}\right) = 4.61 \times 10^{-3}$$

$x = 0.021$

$[N_2O_4] = 0.971 - 0.021 = 0.950$ mol $= a$

$[NO_2] = 0.058 + 0.021 \times 2 = 0.100$ mol $= b$

Hence, the value of $a + b$ is 1.05 mol.

20. ***(6.07)*** Given equation

$$N_2(g) + 3H_2(g) \rightleftharpoons 2NH_3(g)$$

	$N_2(g)$	$3H_2(g)$	$2NH_3(g)$
Initial moles	4	16	0
Moles at equilibrium	$4 - x$	$16 - 3x$	$2x$

Total moles $= 4 - x + 16 - 3x + 2x = 20 - 2x$

From question, $20 \times \frac{9}{10} = 20 - 2x$

$x = 1$

Now,
$$K_C = \frac{(2x)^2}{(16 - 3x)^3 \times (4 - x)}$$
$$= \frac{4}{13 \times 13 \times 13 \times 3}$$
$$= 6.068 \times 10^{-4} \approx 6.07 \times 10^{-4} \text{ M}^{-2}$$

21. ***(3.19)*** Given, $\quad X \rightleftharpoons Y$

$$K_{eq} = \frac{p_Y}{p_X}$$

$$K_{1800\,K} = \frac{20}{1} = 20$$

$$K_{3600\,K} = \frac{120}{1} = 120$$

By using,

$$\Delta G° = -RT \ln K$$

$$\frac{\Delta G_2°}{\Delta G_1°} = \frac{-RT_2 \ln K_2}{-RT_1 \ln K_1}$$

$$= \frac{3600 \text{ K}}{1800 \text{ K}} \times \frac{\ln 120}{\ln 20} = \frac{2 \times 4.79}{3.00} \approx 3.19$$

22. ***(1.73)*** The given reaction is,

	H_3BO_3 +	Glycerin $\rightleftharpoons$	Complex
Initial concentration	0.1	a	0
Eq. concentration	$(0.1 - 0.06) = 0.04$	$(a - 0.06)$	(0.06)

Now,
$$K_{eq} = 0.9 = \frac{0.06}{0.04 \times (a - 0.06)}$$

$a = 1.73$ M

23. ***(0.79)*** The given equation is

$$LiCl \cdot 3NH_3(s) \rightleftharpoons LiCl \cdot NH_3(s) + 2NH_3(g); \; K_p = 9 \text{ atm}^2$$

Therefore, $\quad LiCl \cdot NH_3(s) + 2NH_3(g) \rightleftharpoons LiCl \cdot 3NH_3(s)$

	$LiCl \cdot NH_3(s)$	$2NH_3(g)$	$LiCl \cdot 3NH_3(s)$
Initial moles	0.1	a	0
Final moles at equ.	0	$a - 0.2$	0.1

$$\left[K_p' = \frac{1}{9} (\text{atm})^{-2}\right]$$

At equi. $K_p' = \frac{1}{(p_{NH_3}')^2}$ or $\frac{1}{9} = \frac{1}{(p_{NH_3}')^2}$

$\therefore \quad p_{NH_3}' = 3\,\text{atm}$

By using,

$$pV = nRT$$
$$3 \times 5 = n \times 0.082 \times 310$$
$$n = 0.59$$

$\therefore \quad a - 0.2 = 0.59$

$\therefore$ Initial moles of $NH_3 = 0.79$

24. ***(320.75)*** $\log \frac{K_2}{K_1} = \frac{\Delta H^\circ}{2.303R} \frac{(T_2 - T_1)}{T_1 T_2}$

$$\log \frac{1.4}{0.096} = \frac{\Delta H^\circ}{2.303 \times 8.314} \left(\frac{373 - 298}{373 \times 298}\right)$$
$$\Delta H^\circ = 33025\,\text{J}$$

Now, the temperature above which the forward reaction will be spontaneous is actually the temperature at which the reaction attains equilibrium, i.e., when $K = 1$ or $\log K = 0$

$\therefore \quad \Delta G^\circ = -2.303\,RT \log K = 0$

Also, $\quad \Delta G^\circ = \Delta H^\circ - T\Delta S^\circ$

$$0 = 33025 - T \times 102.96$$
$$T = 320.75\,\text{K}$$

25. ***(1.47)***

	$COCl_2(g)$ $\rightleftharpoons$	$CO(g)$ +	$Cl_2(g)$
Initial	1	0	0
At equili.	$(1-x)$	x	x
$\therefore$ Partial pressure	$\left(\frac{1-x}{1+x+n}\right) p$	$\frac{xp}{(1+x+n)}$	$\frac{xp}{(1+x+n)}$

where, n = moles of N_2

$$\therefore \quad K_p = \frac{p_{CO} \cdot p_{Cl_2}}{p_{COCl_2}} \Rightarrow 6.7 \times 10^{-9} = \frac{x^2 p}{(1-x)(1+x+n)}$$

Addition of N_2 at 1 bar increases number of moles. Hence in calculation of mole fraction of each species, moles of N_2 are added $n = \frac{pV}{RT}$

$$p = \frac{n_{total}}{V} RT$$

$$\therefore \quad \frac{p}{(1+x+n)} = \frac{RT}{V} = \frac{0.083\,\text{bar L mol}^{-1}\,\text{K}^{-1} \times 373}{100\,\text{L}}$$
$$\approx 0.31\,\text{bar mol}^{-1}$$

$$\therefore \quad 6.7 \times 10^{-9} = \frac{x^2}{(1-x)}(0.31) \approx x^2 \times 0.31$$
$$x = 1.47 \times 10^{-4}.$$

26. ***(7/9)*** Given reaction is

	$X(g)$ $\rightleftharpoons$	$Z(g)$
Initially	16	0
At equilibrium	$16 - \alpha$	α

at T_1, $\alpha = 4$ (from graph)

$$(K_{eq})_1 = \frac{4}{12} = \frac{1}{3}$$

at T_2, $\alpha = 2$ (from graph)

$$(K_{eq})_2 = \frac{2}{14} = \frac{1}{7}$$

Now, $\quad \Delta G_1^\circ = -RT_1 \ln (K_{eq})_1$

$$= -2RT_2 \ln (K_{eq})_1$$
$$\Delta G_2^\circ = -RT_2 \ln (K_{eq})_2$$

$$\therefore \quad \Delta G_2^\circ - \Delta G_1^\circ = -RT_2 \ln (K_{eq})_2 + 2RT_2 \ln (K_{eq})_1$$
$$= RT_2 \ln \frac{(K_{eq})_1^2}{(K_{eq})_2}$$
$$= RT_2 \ln \frac{\left(\frac{1}{3}\right)^2}{\frac{1}{7}} = RT_2 \ln \frac{7}{9} \qquad \ldots\text{(i)}$$

By comparing Eq. (i) with

$$\Delta G_2^\circ - \Delta G_1^\circ = RT_2 \ln x$$

Thus, x is $\frac{7}{9}$.

27. ***(c)***

	$PCl_5(g)$ $\rightleftharpoons$	$PCl_3(g)$ +	$Cl_2(g)$
Initial	4	0	0
At equilibrium	$(4 - x)$	x	x
Molar concentration	$\left(\frac{4-x}{2}\right)$	$\frac{x}{2}$	$\frac{x}{2}$

Given, $\frac{x}{2} = [Cl_2] = 0.4\,\text{mol L}^{-1}$

$\therefore \quad x = 0.8\,\text{mol}$

$$\therefore \quad [PCl_5] = \left(\frac{4 - 0.8}{2}\right) = 1.6\,\text{mol L}^{-1}$$
$$[PCl_3] = \frac{x}{2} = 0.4\,\text{mol L}^{-1}$$
$$[Cl_2] = \frac{x}{2} = 0.4\,\text{mol L}^{-1}$$
$$n(PCl_5) = 3.2\,\text{mol}$$
$$n(PCl_3) = n(Cl_2) = 0.8\,\text{mol}$$
$$K_C = \frac{[PCl_3][Cl_2]}{[PCl_5]} = \frac{(0.4)(0.4)}{(1.6)} = 0.1$$

Thus, (i)—(r); (ii)—(p); (iii)—(q); (iv)—(s)

28. ***(c)***

	$H_2(g) + $	$I_2(g)$ $\rightleftharpoons$	$2HI(g)$
Initial	0.1	0.1	0
At equil.	$(0.1 - x)$	$(0.1 - x)$	$2x$

Unreacted $I_2 = (0.1 - x) = 100\,\text{mL of}\ 0.1\ \text{M}\ Na_2S_2O_3$

$$I_2 + 2Na_2S_2O_3 \longrightarrow 2NaI + Na_2S_4O_6$$

$Na_2S_2O_3$ reacted $= \frac{100 \times 0.1}{1000}\,\text{mol} = 0.01\,\text{mol}$

$2\,\text{mol}\ Na_2S_2O_3 \equiv 1\,\text{mol}\ I_2$

$\therefore 0.01\,\text{mol}\ Na_2S_2O_3 = \frac{0.01}{2} = 0.005\,\text{mol}\ I_2$

Thus, H_2 at equilibrium $= 0.005\,\text{mol}$

Also $\quad 0.005 = (0.1 - x) \quad \therefore \quad x = 0.095$

$\therefore \quad HI = 2x = 0.095 \times 2 = 0.19\,\text{mol} \Rightarrow K_p = K_C(RT)^{\Delta n_g}$

But $\Delta n_g = 0$

$\therefore \quad \frac{K_C}{K_p} = 1$

Thus, (i) $\longrightarrow$ (s), (ii) $\longrightarrow$ (p),

(iii) $\longrightarrow$ (q), (iv) $\longrightarrow$ (r)

29. ***(a)*** Eq. (I) – Eq. (II) × 3 = Eq.III

Thus, $K_p^{III} = \frac{K_p^I}{(K_p^{II})^3} = \frac{4.0 \times 10^{-6}}{(3.2 \times 10^{-4})^3}$

$= 1.2207 \times 10^5$

From III, $\left(\frac{p_{CO_2}}{p_{CO}}\right)^3 = 1.2207 \times 10^5$

$\frac{p_{CO_2}}{p_{CO}} = (1.2207 \times 10^5)^{\frac{1}{3}} = 49.606$

$\Rightarrow \frac{p_{CO}}{p_{CO_2}} = 0.02$

From I, $K_p^I = \frac{1}{p_{H_2}^3} = 4.0 \times 10^{-6}$

$\Rightarrow \quad \frac{1}{p_{H_2}} = (4.0 \times 10^{-6})^{\frac{1}{3}} = 0.01587$

$p_{H_2} \approx 63.0$ bar

From II, $K_p^{II} = \frac{p_{CO}}{p_{CO_2} \cdot p_{H_2}} = 3.2 \times 10^{-4}$

$\frac{p_{CO}}{p_{H_2}} = 3.2 \times 10^{-4} \times p_{CO_2}$

$= 3.2 \times 10^{-4} \times 1 \times 10^{-2}$

$= 3.2 \times 10^{-6}$

Thus, (i) $\longrightarrow$ (s) (ii) $\longrightarrow$ (r)

(iii) $\longrightarrow$ (q) (iv) $\longrightarrow$ (p).

30. ***(b)*** $\log_{10} K_p = \frac{-\Delta H°}{2.303\, RT} + \frac{\Delta S°}{2.303 R}$

Given $\log_{10} K_p = + \frac{10.560\text{ K}}{T} - 20.281$

On comparison, $\frac{-\Delta H°}{2.303R} = 10.56$

$\therefore \quad \Delta H° = -10.56 \times 2.303 \times R$

$= -10.56 \times 2.303 \times 8.314 \text{ J}$

$= -202.19 \text{ J}$

Thus, (ii) $\rightarrow$ (s)

$\frac{\Delta S°}{2.303R} = -20.281$

$\therefore \quad \Delta S° = -20.281 \times 8.314 \text{ J mol}^{-1}\text{K}^{-1} \times 2.303$

$= -388.32 \text{ J mol}^{-1}\text{K}^{-1}$

Thus, (iii) $\rightarrow$ (p)

At 500 K, $\log_{10} K_p = -20.281 + \frac{10.560}{500}$

$= -20.26$

Thus, (i) $\rightarrow$ (q)

Also, $\Delta G° = \Delta H° - T\Delta S°$

$= -2.303 RT \log K_p$

$= -2.303 \times 8.314 \times 500 \times (-20.26)$

$= 193.96 \times 10^3$ J

Thus, (iv) $\rightarrow$ (r)

Solution for (Q. Nos. 31 and 32)

31. ***(41.57)*** Given,

$\ln K = \frac{\Delta_r S°}{R} - \frac{\Delta_r H°}{RT}$ ...(i)

$\ln K = 5 - \frac{2000}{T}$ ...(ii)

$\therefore \quad \Delta_r S° = 5R = 41.57 \text{ JK}^{-1}$

32. ***(13.31)*** $\log\left\{\frac{K_2}{K_1}\right\} = \frac{\Delta_r H°}{2.303R}\left[\frac{1}{T_1} - \frac{1}{T_2}\right]$

$\log\left\{\frac{8}{2}\right\} = \frac{\Delta_r H°}{2.303 \times 2}\left\{\frac{1}{300} - \frac{1}{320}\right\}$

$\Delta_r H° = 13311 \text{ cal}$

$= 13.31 \text{ kcal}$

$\therefore$ The enthalpy change for the reverse reaction,

$\Delta_r H° = -13.31 \text{ kcal}$

Solution for (Q. Nos. 33 and 34)

33. ***(1.6875)*** $2NH_3(g) \rightleftharpoons N_2(g) + 3H_2(g)$

	$2NH_3(g)$	$N_2(g)$	$3H_2(g)$
Initial	2	0	0
At equili.	$(2-2x)$	x	$3x$

Given, $(2 - 2x) = 1$

$\therefore \quad 2x = 1 \Rightarrow x = 0.5$

Then, $[NH_3]_{eq} = \frac{1}{1} = 1 \text{ mol L}^{-1}$

$[N_2] = \frac{x}{1} = 0.5 \text{ mol L}^{-1}$

$[H_2] = \frac{3x}{1} = 1.5 \text{ mol L}^{-1}$

$\therefore \quad K_C = \frac{[N_2]\,[H_2]^3}{[NH_3]^2}$

$= \frac{0.5 \times (1.5)^3}{(1)^2} = 1.6875$

34. ***(7.389)*** $N_2(g) + 3H_2(g) \rightleftharpoons 2NH_3(g)$

	$N_2(g)$	$3H_2(g)$	$2NH_3(g)$
Based on reaction	1 mol	3 mol	2 mol
Given	1 mol	4 mol	
After	(1 – 1)	(4 – 3)	2
Reaction	0	1	2

Thus, ammonia formed = 2 mol

H_2 unreacted = 1 mol

Pressure is developed due to NH_3 formed and unreacted H_2

$p = \frac{n_{H_2} + n_{NH_3}}{V} RT = \left(\frac{1+2}{15}\right) \times 0.0821 \times 300 = 4.926 \text{ atm}$

If H_2O is added, NH_3 is dissolved in it. Thus, pressure is due to H_2 only. Also volume of container is decreased by 5 L available effective volume = 15 − 5 = 10 L

$$p = \frac{n_{H_2}RT}{V}$$

$$= \frac{1 \times 0.0821 \times 300}{10}$$

$$= 2.463 \text{ atm}$$

Hence, the sum of pressure setup before and after adding H_2O is = 4.926 + 2.463 = 7.389 atm

Solution for (Q. Nos. 35 and 36)

35. ***(0.5)*** $N_2O_4(g) \rightleftharpoons 2NO_2(g)$

Normal molecular weight = 92 g mol^{-1}

∴ Vapour density (D) = 46

Equilibrium pressure = 24.12 k Pa = 24.12×10^3 Pa

If abnormal molecular weight = M

then moles of $N_2O_4 = \frac{0.578}{m}$

$$p = \frac{nRT}{V} = \frac{w}{m}\frac{RT}{V}$$

$R = 8.314 \text{ J mol}^{-1}\text{K}^{-1}, V = 1 \text{ dm}^3 = 1 \times 10^{-3} \text{ m}^3$

$$m = \frac{wRT}{pV} = \frac{0.578 \times 8.314 \times 308}{24.12 \times 10^3 \times 1 \times 10^{-3} \text{ m}^3}$$

$$= 61.36 \text{ g mol}^{-1}$$

$$\text{Abnormal VD} = (d) = \frac{61.36}{2} = 30.68$$

$$\therefore \text{Degree of dissociation} = \frac{D-d}{d} = \frac{46 - 30.68}{30.68} \approx 0.5$$

36. ***(31.74)*** $N_2O_4(g) \rightleftharpoons 2NO_2(g)$

	$N_2O_4(g)$	$2NO_2(g)$
Initial mol	1	0
At equilibrium	$(1 - x)$	$2x$

$$X_{NO_2} = \frac{2x}{1+x} = \frac{2}{3} \Rightarrow X_{N_2O_4} = \frac{1-x}{1+x} = \frac{1}{3}$$

$$\therefore p_{NO_2} = p_T \times \frac{2}{3} = 24.12 \times 10^3 \times \frac{2}{3} \text{ Pa}$$

$$p_{N_2O_4} = p_T \times \frac{1}{3} = 24.12 \times 10^3 \times \frac{1}{3} \text{ Pa}$$

$$\therefore K_p = \frac{p^2_{NO_2}}{p_{N_2O_4}} = \frac{\left(24.12 \times 10^3 \times \frac{2}{3}\right)^2}{24.12 \times 10^3 \times \frac{1}{3}}$$

$$= 32160 \text{ Pa}$$

$$= \frac{32160}{1.01325 \times 10^5} = 0.3174 \text{ atm}$$

$$\approx 31.74 \times 10^{-2} \text{ atm}$$

Hence, the value of x is 31.74.

37. ***(c)*** Le-Chatelier's principle is not applicable to (iii) only.

38. ***(b)*** For an ideal gas $\Delta G° = -RT \ln K$

$$\therefore \quad \ln K = \frac{-\Delta G°}{RT} \quad \text{and} \quad K = e^{-\Delta G°/RT}$$

Among the given only two matches are incorrect. i.e., (iv) and (v).

39. ***(c)*** Among the given equilibria, only two i.e., (iii) and (v) is not affected by change in volume of the flask because for these equilibria the value of $\Delta n_g = 0$.

40. ***(b)*** Among the given expression, for the given equilibrium reaction only three i.e., (i), (ii) and (iv) are correct.

$$K_C = \frac{px^2}{(1 - x^2)}$$

$$\therefore \quad K_C = \frac{x^2}{(1 - x^2)V}$$

$$K_p (1 - x^2) = px^2$$

$$K_p = K_p x^2 + px^2$$

$$= x^2 (K_p + p)$$

$$x = \sqrt{\frac{K_p}{K_p + p}}$$

41. ***(a)*** Among the given reactions only two i.e., (iii) and (v) have $K_p = K_C$.

The two constants K_p and K_C are equal only when, $\Delta n = 0$, meaning there is no change in the numbers of moles of gas between products and reactants in the balanced chemical equation.

42. ***(d)*** Among the given reactions four reactions i.e., (i), (ii), (iii) and (iv) will proceed in backward direction.

The system which has less number of gaseous reactants than products shall proceed in backward direction upon increasing pressure.

43. ***(d)*** Among the given reaction (i), (ii), (v) and (vii) are favoured by introducing an inert gas at constant pressure to forward reaction at constant temperature.

Addition of inert gas at constant volume has no effect on reactions having $\Delta n_g = 0$ or $\Delta n_g \neq 0$. But addition of inert gas at constant p has effect on reactions having $\Delta n_g \neq 0$, and no effect if $\Delta n_g = 0$. The given reaction which has $\Delta n_g \neq 0$ are favoured by introducing an inert gas at constant pressure to forward reaction at constant temperature.

44. ***(b)*** Among the given reactions, only (ii), (v) and (vi).

The yield of a product in a chemical reaction may not increase with the application of high pressure in reactions where there is no change in the number of moles of gas between the reactants and products.

45. ***(b)*** SO_4^{2-}, Cl^-, CN^- and CN^- forms precipitate with Cu(I), remove Cu(I) ion form equilibrium and reaction shifts in backward direction according to Le-Chatelier's principle.

Check Through PYQs : JEE Advanced

1. **(8)** Given reaction is :

$$A_{(g)} \rightleftharpoons P(g)$$

	$A_{(g)}$	$P(g)$
Initially	6	0
At equilibrium	$6-\alpha$	α

at T_1, $\alpha = 4$ (from graph)

$$(K_{eq})_1 = \frac{4}{2} = 2$$

at T_2, $\alpha = 2$

$$(K_{eq})_2 = \frac{2}{4} = \frac{1}{2}$$

Now, $\Delta G_1^\circ = -RT_1 \ln (K_{eq})_1$

$$\Delta G_1^\circ = -2RT_2 \ln (K_{eq})_1 \quad (\because T_1 = 2T_2)$$

$$\Delta G_2^\circ = -RT_2 \ln (K_{eq})_2$$

$$\therefore \Delta G_2^\circ - \Delta G_1^\circ = -RT_2 \ln (K_{eq})_2 + 2RT_2 \ln (K_{eq})_1$$

$$= RT_2 \ln \frac{(K_{eq})_1^2}{(K_{eq})_2} = RT_2 \ln \frac{(2)^2}{\left(\frac{1}{2}\right)}$$

$$\Rightarrow \Delta G_2^\circ - \Delta G_1^\circ = -RT_2 \ln 8 \quad \ldots(i)$$

By comparing Eq. (i) with

$$\Delta G_2^\circ - \Delta G_1^\circ = RT_2 \ln x \Rightarrow x = 8$$

2. **(0.25)** $A \rightleftharpoons B$

$$K_{eq} = \frac{p_B}{p_A}$$

$$K_{1000\,K} = \frac{10}{1} = 10$$

$$K_{2000\,K} = \frac{100}{1} = 100$$

Now, $\dfrac{\Delta G^\circ_{1000\,K}}{\Delta G^\circ_{2000\,K}} = \dfrac{(-RT \ln K_{eq})_{1000\,K}}{(-RT \ln K_{eq})_{2000\,K}}$

$$= \frac{1000 \times \ln 10}{2000 \times \ln 1000} = 0.25$$

Hence, $\Delta G^\circ_{1000\,K}$ is 0.25 times of $\Delta G^\circ_{2000\,K}$.

3. **(a, c)** For the reaction, $A \rightleftharpoons P$

Given, $T_1 < T_2$

$$\frac{\ln K_1}{\ln K_2} > \frac{T_2}{T_1} \quad \ldots(i)$$

It shows, that on increasing the temperature, K decreases so reaction is exothermic i.e., $\Delta H^\circ < 0$

Besides, graph shows $K > 1$

So $\Delta G^\circ < 0$

Now from equation (i)

$$T_1 \ln K_1 > T_2 \ln K_2$$

$$-\Delta G^\circ_1 > -\Delta G^\circ_2$$

Likewise $(-\Delta H^\circ + T_1 \Delta S^\circ) > (-\Delta H^\circ + T_2 \Delta S^\circ)$

or simply $T_1 \Delta S^\circ > T_2 \Delta S^\circ$

So, $(T_2 - T_1)\Delta S^\circ < 0$

$\therefore \Delta S^\circ < 0$

In other words, increase of ΔG with increase in temperature is possible only when $\Delta S^\circ < 0$. Hence, options (a) and (c) are correct.

4. **(14.6)** Given

(i) $2Cu(s) + \frac{1}{2}O_2(g) \longrightarrow Cu_2O(s)$;

$$\Delta G^\circ = -78000 \text{ J mol}^{-1} = -78 \text{ kJ mol}^{-1}$$

(ii) $H_2(g) + \frac{1}{2}O_2(g) \longrightarrow H_2O(g)$;

$$\Delta G^\circ = -178000 \text{ J mol}^{-1} = -178 \text{ kJ mol}^{-1}$$

So, net reaction is (By (i)-(ii))

$$2Cu(s) + H_2O(g) \longrightarrow Cu_2O(s) + H_2(g);$$

$$\Delta G = 100000 \text{ J/mol or } 10^5 \text{ J/mol}$$

$$= 100 \text{ kJ mol}^{-1}$$

Now , for the above reaction

$$\Delta G = \Delta G^\circ + RT \ln \left[\frac{p_{H_2}}{p_{H_2O}}\right]$$

and to prevent above reaction,

$$\Delta G \geq 0$$

So, $\Delta G^\circ + RT \ln \left[\dfrac{p_{H_2}}{p_{H_2O}}\right] \geq 0$

After putting the values,

$$10^5 + 8 \times 1250 \ln \left[\frac{p_{H_2}}{p_{H_2O}}\right] \geq 0$$

or $10^5 + 10^4 \ln \left[\dfrac{p_{H_2}}{p_{H_2O}}\right] \geq 0$

or $10^4(\ln p_{H_2} - \ln p_{H_2O}) \geq -10^5$

or $\ln p_{H_2} \geq -10 + \ln p_{H_2O}$

or $\ln p_{H_2} \geq -10 + 2.3 \log (0.01)$ (as $p_{H_2O} = 1\%$)

$\geq -10 - 4.6$

so $\ln p_{H_2} \geq -14.6$

5. **(b)** $X_2(g) \rightleftharpoons 2X(g)$

	$X_2(g)$	$2X(g)$
At $t = 0$	1	0
At equilibrium	$\left(1 - \frac{x}{2}\right)$	x (where, $x = \beta_{eq}$)

Total moles $= \left(1 + \dfrac{x}{2}\right)$

and Mole fraction, $X_2(g) = \dfrac{\left(1 - \frac{x}{2}\right)}{\left(1 + \frac{x}{2}\right)}$

$X(g) = \left(\dfrac{x}{1 + \frac{x}{2}}\right)$ and $p = 2$ bar

Partial pressure, $p_{X2} = \left(\dfrac{1-\dfrac{x}{2}}{1+\dfrac{x}{2}}\right).p$

and $$p_X = \frac{p\cdot x}{\left(1+\dfrac{x}{2}\right)}$$

$$\therefore K_p = p_X^2 / p_{X_2} = \frac{\left[px/\left(1+\dfrac{x}{2}\right)\right]^2}{p\dfrac{(1-x/2)}{\left(1+\dfrac{x}{2}\right)}}$$

$$= \frac{4px^2}{(4-x^2)} = \frac{8\beta_{eq}^2}{(4-\beta_{eq}^2)}$$

6. ***(c)*** $K_p = \dfrac{4px^2}{(4-x^2)} = px^2 \quad (\because 4 >>> x)$

$$\therefore \quad x \propto \sqrt{\frac{1}{p}}$$

If p decreases, x increases. Equilibrium is shifted in the forward side. Thus, statement (a) is correct.

(b) At the start of the reaction, $Q = 0$ where, Q is the reaction quotient $\Delta G = \Delta G° + 2.303RT \log Q$
Since, $\Delta G° > 0$, thus ΔG is –ve.
Hence, dissociation takes place spontaneously.
Thus, (b) is correct.

(c) If we use $x = 0.7$ and $p = 2$ bar then

$$K_p = \frac{4 \times 2(0.7)^2}{[4-(0.7)^2]} = 1.16 > 1$$

Thus, (c) is incorrect.

(d) At equilibrium, $\Delta G = 0$

$\therefore \quad \Delta G° = -2.303RT \log K_p$

Since, $\Delta G° = +\text{ve}$

Hence, $K_p < 1$

$$K_C = \frac{K_p}{(RT)}$$

Then $K_C < 1$. Thus, (d) is correct.

7. ***(b)*** Since, the reaction is exothermic, there will be less ammonia and higher temperature. However, rate of reaction increases with rise in temperature, NH_3 will be formed at faster rate in the initial stage when the temperature is high. Until it reaches the equilibrium (intersection point and its RHS of two curves)

CHAPTER 6

Ionic Equilibrium

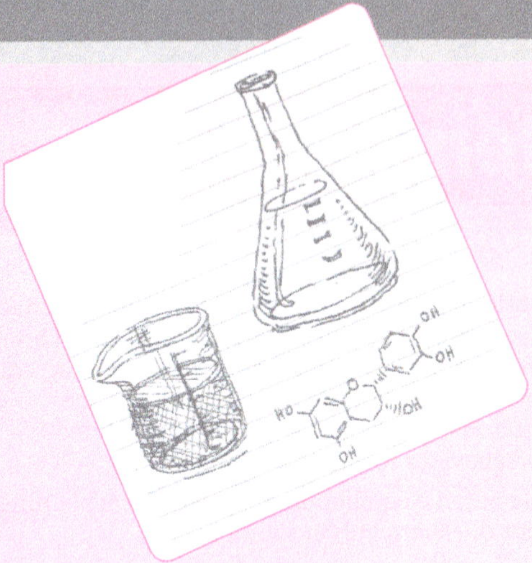

Learning Elements

Element 1 Ostwald's Dilution Law and Concept of Acids and Bases

Electrolytes, Ostwald Dilution Law, Acids and Bases, Acid Strength and Base Strength, Factors Affecting Acid, Strength, Lewis Acids and Bases, Ionisation Constants of Weak Acids and Bases, Ionisation of polyprotic Acid and Bases.

Element 2 pH, Buffer, Indicator and Salt Hydrolysis

pH Scale, pH Calculations, Hydrolysis, Detetction of the and point-Indicators, Theories of Indicators, Buffers, Acid-Base Titrations.

Element 3 Solubility Product and Common Ion Effect

Common Ion effect, Solubility and Solubility Product Constant, Applications of Common Ion Effect and Solubility Product.

Practice Elements

Practice Element 1 Target JEE Main

Practice Element 2 Target JEE Advanced

Trend Insights

JEE Main

	2024				2023				2022			
Topics	**E**	**M**	**T**	**O**	**E**	**M**	**T**	**O**	**E**	**M**	**T**	**O**
Ostwald's Dilution Law and Concepts of Acids and Bases	–	–	–	–	–	–	–	–	–	1	1	2
pH, Buffer, Indicator and Salt Hydrolysis	–	2	2	4	–	1	1	2	–	2	–	2
Solubility Product and Common Ion Effect	1	–	–	1	–	–	2	2	2	–	–	2

E = Easy, **M** = Medium, **T** = Tough, **O** = Overall

Current Dynamics

- Least number of questions were asked from dilution law and concept of acids and bases.
- Less number of questions involving the calculation of the degree of ionisation for weak acids and weak bases were asked in previous year.
- The difficulty level of numerical value questions from pH, buffer, solubility product and salt hydrolysis was increased in 2024 than in previous year.

JEE Advanced

Typology	Years				
	2024	**2023**	**2022**	**2021**	**2020**
1. Simple MCQs		1			
2. One or More than one correct					
3. Numerical Value/Integer			2		2
4. Matching Type					
5. Paragraph Based					

Current Dynamics

- Generally Numerical type question were asked in recent years.
- Questions Based on solubility product of sparingly soluble salt and buffer were frequently asked.

Insightful Advice

- Students are advised to understand the ionisation of water, especially for dilute solutions of strong acids or bases.
- Solve problems involving pH and hydrolysis constant.
- Understand the relationship between solubility product and ionisation constants for weak acids or salts.

Element 1 Ostwald's Dilution Law and Concept of Acids and Bases

Ionic equilibrium deals with the state of equilibrium that occurs in a solution when the rates of dissociation of an ionic compound and the recombination of its ions are equal. This equilibrium is important for understanding the behaviour of acids, bases, salts and sparingly soluble compounds behaviour in aqueous solutions.

The principle of ionic equilibrium is crucial for explaining the behaviour of electrolytes in solution.

Electrolytes

These are substances capable of conducting electricity when dissolved in water or in molten state. They possess the following characteristics:

- When an electrolyte is dissolved in a solvent (usually water) or is fused, it spontaneously dissociates into oppositively charged particles called ions, to a considerable extent.

$$H_2SO_4 \rightleftharpoons 2H^+ + SO_4^{2-}\ ;\ NaCl \rightleftharpoons Na^+ + Cl^-$$

  The positively charged ions are called cations and the negatively charged ions are called anions.
- Since the solution of an electrolyte, as a whole, is electrically neutral, the total charge on the cations is equal to the total charge on the anions.
- Electrolytic dissociation or ionisation produces equilibrium between unionised molecules and the ions in solution.
- The degree of dissociation of an electrolyte (α) is the fraction of one mole of the electrolyte that has dissociated under the given conditions.

Factor affecting degree of dissociation (α) are given below

(i) **Nature of the Electrolyte** Some electrolytes, e.g., mineral acids such as H_2SO_4, HCl and HNO_3, alkalis such as NaOH and KOH and all salts have a very high degree of ionisation (α nearly equal to 1) at all reasonable concentrations. They are known as **strong electrolytes.** The number of ions in solutions of strong electrolytes is large and thus such solutions have high conductance.

Some electrolytes, e.g. organic acids such as acetic acid, propionic acid etc., and bases like ammonium hydroxide have a low degree of ionisation in solution, They are called **weak electrolytes**. The number of ions in solutions of weak electrolytes is quite small and thus such solutions have low conductance.

(ii) **Nature of the Solvent** A solvent which has a high dielectric constant weakens the attractive force between the cations and anions. Hence a solvent of high dielectric constant favours the dissociation of the electrolyte.

Likewise a solvent which can solvate the ions readily, and can release energy by solvation, favours the dissociation of the electrolyte. Thus, the dissociation of acids in water is favoured by the hydration of the hydrogen ions to form hydronium ions. The enthalpy of hydration of the proton has a very high value.

(iii) **Temperature** Increase of temperature generally increases ionisation.

(iv) **Dilution** For some electrolytes, degree of dissociation increases with dilution as explained by Ostwald's dilution law.

Ostwald's Dilution Law

This states that "for a weak electrolyte degree of ionisation increases with dilution and is inversely proportional to the square root of molar concentration.

For a binary electrolyte *HA* dissociating in solution according to the following equation,

	HA	$+\ H_2O \rightleftharpoons$	H_3O^+	$+\ A^-$
Initially	C		0	0
At equilibrium	$C(1-\alpha)$		$C\alpha$	$C\alpha$

where α = degree of ionisation.

Dissociation constant, may be given as $K = \dfrac{C\alpha^2}{1-\alpha}$

For very weak electrolytes,

$$\alpha <<< 1 \Rightarrow (1-\alpha) \approx 1 \text{ (when } \alpha < 5\%)$$

$$K = C\alpha^2 \Rightarrow \alpha = \sqrt{K/C}$$

or $$\alpha \propto \frac{1}{\sqrt{C}} \propto \sqrt{V} \quad \left[C \propto \frac{1}{V}\right]$$

V = dilution of solution

where, C (mol/L) be the initial concentration of the electrolyte and α be the degree of dissociation.

Concentration of anion $= C\alpha = \sqrt{KC}$

Also $[H_3O^+] = C\alpha = \sqrt{KC}$.

Applications

This law is used

- to calculate the value of dissociation constant (K) of the weak acids and weak bases, by determining the degree of dissociation (α) from conductance measurement $\left(\dfrac{\lambda_V}{\lambda_\infty}\right)$ at any concentration C. [λ_V and λ_∞ are molar conductance at volume V and volume ∞].

- to calculate the degree of dissociation, α of weak acids and bases by knowing the value of K.

For weak acid, put $[A^-] = [H^+]$ and $K = K_a$

Similarly for weak bases, $[B^+] = [OH^-]$ and $K = K_b$

JEE Alert

The approximation $(1-\alpha) \approx 1$ can be applied only if $\alpha < 5\%$. If on solving a problem by applying the approximate formula; α comes out to be $> 5\%$, the problems may be solved by applying the exact formula and α may be calculated by applying the solution of the quadratic equation

$$\alpha = \frac{-b \pm \sqrt{b^2 - 4ac}}{2a} \text{ (for, } a\alpha^2 + b\alpha + c = 0)$$

Ostwald dilution law is applicable to weak electrolytes only.

Acids and Bases

Acids and base are the two terms of chemical compounds. According to experimentally observed properties of aqueous solutions, acids have sour taste and turns blue litmus to red, whereas bases have bitter taste turns red litmus blue and have a soapy feel. Some other concepts on which acids and bases can be explained are given below.

The Arrhenius Concept

Arrhenius classified a substance into an acid or a base in terms of the characteristic ions which it produces in aqueous solution. An acid is a substance which ionises in water to produce $H^+(aq)$ or the hydronium ion while a base is a substance which produces $OH^-(aq)$.

A generalised Arrhenius acid,

$$HA(aq) \rightleftharpoons H^+(aq) + A^-(aq)$$

H^+ ion is a proton and cannot exist in solutions as independent species. Thus, it combines with oxygen atom of a solvent water molecule to give hydronium ion H_3O^+.

$$H^+ + H_2O \longrightarrow H_3O^+$$

A generalised Arrhenius base,

$$MOH(aq) \rightleftharpoons M^+(aq) + OH^-(aq)$$

- The strength of an acid is defined in terms of concentration of $H^+(aq)$ that is present in the aqueous solution of a given concentration of the acid. Likewise, the strength of a base depends upon the relative concentration of $OH^-(aq)$ in an aqueous solution of the base.
- A neutralisation reaction involves the combination of H^+ and OH^- ions to form water,

$$H^+(aq) + OH^-(aq) \longrightarrow H_2O$$

Limitations

(i) The Arrhenius theory is restricted to aqueous solutions. Acid-base behaviour in non-aqueous solvents (like liquid NH_3, CO_2, alcohol) or in the gas phase was not covered by the Arrhenius theory.

(ii) This theory cannot be applied to the substances that show basic nature but do not contain OH^- ion, e.g. MgO, CaO, NH_3 etc. In the same way, it cannot applied to substances which show acidic nature but do not contain H^+ ion e.g. CO_2, SO_2, SO_3 etc.

Levelling Effect

In the context of the Arrhenius theory of acids and bases, the "levelling effect" refers to the tendency of strong acids and strong bases to exhibit similar behavior when dissolved in water, due to the limited extent of their dissociation in aqueous solutions.

However, the levelling effect occurs because, in water, any acid stronger than hydronium ion (H_3O^+) or any base stronger than the hydroxide ion (OH^-) will undergo complete dissociation to produce H_3O^+ or OH^- ions, respectively. This causes the observed behavior of acids and bases to "level out," meaning that any acid stronger than H_3O^+ or any base stronger than OH^- will essentially behave the same as H_3O^+ or OH^- in an aqueous solution.

Strong acids like HCl, H_2SO_4, and HNO_3 dissociate completely in water to produce H_3O^+ ions. The strength of these acids appears similar because they all result in the same hydronium ion concentration.

Strong bases like NaOH and KOH dissociate completely in water to produce OH^- ions. Again, their strength is equivalent in water because they both contribute to the same hydroxide ion concentration.

Bronsted-Lowry Protonic Concept

- According to this concept, a substance is known as an acid if it can donate a proton and as a base if it can accept a proton.
- The reaction of an acid with a base involves the transfer of a proton from the acid to the base.

  For a molecule or ion to accept a proton, it must have at least one unshared pair of electrons that it can use for bonding to proton.
- This theory is useful as it extends the scope of acid-base systems to cover the solvents such as liquid ammonia, glacial acetic acid, anhydrous sulphuric acid, on all hydrogen-containing solvents. All bases accept protons and there is no need for them to contain OH^- ions.

$$\underset{\substack{\text{Acid} \\ \text{(Proton donor)}}}{NH_4^+} + \underset{\substack{\text{Base} \\ \text{(Proton acceptor)}}}{NH_2^-} \longrightarrow \underset{\text{Solvent}}{2NH_3}$$

$$\underset{\text{Acid}}{H_3SO_4^+} + \underset{\text{Base}}{HSO_4^-} \longrightarrow \underset{\text{Solvent}}{2H_2SO_4}$$

Conjugate Acid-Base Pairs

Chemical species that differ in composition only by a single proton are called a 'conjugate pair'. Thus, every acid has a conjugate base, which is formed when the acid donates a proton. Similarly every base has a conjugate acid formed when the base accepts a proton.

$$\underset{\text{Acid}}{HA} \rightleftharpoons \underset{\text{Conjugate base}}{A^-} + H^+$$

$$\underset{\text{Base}}{B} + H^+ \rightleftharpoons \underset{\text{Conjugate acid}}{BH^+}$$

Thus, acid can be converted into a base by loss of H^+ ion and a base can be converted into an acid by gain of H^+.

The acid and base pair which differ by a proton are said to form **conjugate acid-base pair.**

In general, acid-base reactions are reversible,

$$\underset{\substack{H^+\text{donor}\\ \text{acid}}}{HA} + \underset{\substack{H^+\text{acceptor}\\ \text{base}}}{B} \rightleftharpoons \underset{\substack{H^+\text{donor}\\ \text{acid}}}{BH^+} + \underset{\substack{H^+\text{acceptor}\\ \text{base}}}{A^-}$$

Conjugate acid-base pairs

Consider the following reaction

$$\underset{\text{Base (2)}}{NH_3} + \underset{\text{Acid (1)}}{H_2O} \rightleftharpoons \underset{\text{Acid (2)}}{NH_4^+} + \underset{\text{Base (1)}}{OH^-}$$

In this reaction, H_2O acts as an acid. NH_3 and NH_4^+ is the conjugate base-acid pair and H_2O and OH^- is the conjugate acid-base pair.

JEE Spotlite

- The compound that can acts as acid as well as base are called amphoteric or amphiprotic e.g., H_2O, HCO_3^-, NH_3 etc.
- Any species that is an acid by the Arrhenius theory remains an acid in the Bronsted-Lowry theory. The same is true for bases.
  Certain species, because they do not contain the hydroxide group, would not be classified as bases by the Arrhenius theory. Yet they are so classified as bases by the Bronsted-Lowry theory, e.g. $OCl^-, H_2PO_4^-, HCO_3^-$.

Some conjugate acid-base pairs

Acid	Conjugate base
$HClO_4$ (Perchloric acid)	ClO_4^- (Percholorate ion)
H_2SO_4 (Sulphuric acid)	HSO_4^- (Hydrogen sulphate ion)
HCl (Hydrochloric acid)	Cl^- (Chloride ion)
HNO_3 (Nitric acid)	NO_3^- (Nitrate ion)
H_3O^+ (Hydronium ion)	H_2O (Water)
HSO_4^- (Hydrogen sulphate ion)	SO_4^{2-} (Sulphate ion)
H_3PO_4 (Ortho phosphoric acid)	$H_2PO_4^-$ (Dihydrogen phosphate ion)
CH_3COOH (Acetic acid)	CH_3COO^- (Acetate ion)
H_2S (Hydrogen sulphide)	HS^- (Hydrogen sulphide ion)
$\overset{+}{NH_4}$ (Ammonium ion)	NH_3 (Ammonia)
HCN (Hydrogen cyanide)	$\bar{CN}$ (Cyanide ion)
PhOH (Phenol)	PhO^- (Phenoxide ion)
H_2O (Water)	$\bar{O}H$ (Hydroxide ion)
C_2H_5OH (Ethanol)	$C_2H_5O^-$ (Ethoxide ion)
NH_3 (Ammonia)	$\overset{\ominus}{NH_2}$ (Amide ion)
CH_4 (Methane)	$^{\ominus}CH_3$ (Methinide ion)

Acid Strength and Base Strength

Strength of an acid or a base certains to the extent of ionisation when they are dissolved in water. Strength of an acid or base is expressed in terms of their acid dissociation constant or base dissociation constant as

For an acid $HA \rightleftharpoons H^+ + A^-$

and $$K_a = \left[\frac{[H^+][A^-]}{[HA]}\right]_{\text{At equilibrium}}$$

A strong acid is characterised by a greater extent of ionisation and hence higher K_a value and a weak acid is characterised by a smaller extent of ionisation and hence lower K_a value.

For a base $A^- + H_2O \rightleftharpoons HA + OH^-$

and $$K_b = \left[\frac{[HA][OH^-]}{[A^-]}\right]_{\text{At equilibrium}}$$

Also for a conjugate acid/base pair,

$$K_a \times K_b = [H^+][OH^-]$$

Therefore, as strength of a series of acids increases, the strength of their conjugate base decreases.

Consider the following acid-dissociation equilibrium,

$$\underset{\text{Acid}}{HA(aq)} + \underset{\text{Base}}{H_2O(l)} \rightleftharpoons \underset{\text{Acid}}{H_3O^+(aq)} + \underset{\text{Base}}{A^-(aq)}$$

H_2O and A^- both are competing for protons.

- If H_2O is a stronger base (a stronger proton acceptor than A^-), the H_2O molecules will get the protons and the solution will contain mainly H_3O^+ and A^-.
- If A^- is a stronger base than H_2O, the A^- ions will get the protons and the solution will contain mainly HA and H_2O.

JEE Alert

A Bronsted-Lowry acid-base reaction is always favoured in the direction from the stronger to the weaker acid/base combination.

Relative strengths of conjugate acids base pairs

	Acid, H*A*		Base, A^-		
Stronger acid	$HClO_4$	Strong acids, 100% dissociated in aqueous solution.	ClO_4^-	Very weak bases. Negligible tendency to be protonated in aqueous solution.	Weaker base
	HCl		Cl^-		
	H_2SO_4		HSO_4^-		
	HNO_3		NO_3^-		
	H_3O^+		H_2O		
	HSO_4^-	Weak acids. Exist in solution as a mixture of HA, A^-, and H_3O^+.	SO_4^{2-}	Weak bases. Moderate tendency to be protonated in aqueous solution.	
	H_3PO_4		$H_2PO_4^-$		
	HNO_2		NO_2^-		
	HF		F^-		
	CH_3COOH		$CH_3CO_2^-$		
	H_2CO_3		HCO_3^-		
	H_2S		HS^-		
	NH_4^+		NH_3		
	HCN		CN^-		
	HCO_3^-		CO_3^{2-}		
	H_2O	Very weak acid. Negligible tendency to dissociate.	OH^-	Strong bases 100% protonated in aqueous solution.	
	NH_3		NH_2^-		
	OH^-		O^{2-}		
Weaker acid	H_2		H^-		Stronger base

Factors Affecting Acid Strength

Various factors that affect acid strength are given below

1. Bond Strength and Electronegativity

- For binary acids of elements in the same group of the periodic table, the H—*A* bond strength decreases with increasing size of element *A* down the group, so acidity increases.
- That means when H—*A* bond strengths decrease, H*A* becomes stronger acid. Thus,

H—F H—Cl H—Br H—I
Max. ← Bond strength
Acid strength → Max.

$H_2O < H_2S < H_2Se < H_2Te$
Max. ← Bond strength
Acid strength → Max.

- As we move from left to right in a period, the increase in electronegativity causes the H–*A* bond to become more polar, making the partial positive charge (δ^+) on H greater. This makes it easier for hydrogen to separate as H^+, so the molecules becomes a better proton donor. So moving along left to right in a period, as the electronegativity of *A* increases, the strength of acid also increases.

Electronegativity of *A* (C, N, O, F) increases →

$CH_4 < NH_3 < H_2O < HF$

Acidic strength increase →

JEE Alert

1. For the elements of same group, H–*A* bond strength is the most important factor for determining acidity. While for the elements of same period, H—*A* bond polarity decides the acidic strength.
2. For the elements of different groups and different period, H—*A* bond strength decides the acid strength, weaker the H—*A* bond stronger the acid.

2. Strength of Oxoacids

The acids composed of hydrogen, oxygen and some other element are called oxoacids.

In the oxoacids of general formula, $(HO)_n YO_m$ (where, *Y* is non-metallic atom, such as C, N, S or Cl and *n* and *m* are integers) the atom *Y* is always bonded to one or more hydroxyl (—OH) groups and can be bonded, in addition, to one or more oxygen atoms.

There are two important factors that affect acidic strength are

(i) **Electronegativity of the central atom** If the central atom of oxoacids holds the same number of oxygen atoms, the acidic strength increases upward (from bottom to top) within a group and from left to right within a period.

(ii) **Number of oxygen atoms attached to the central atom** In an oxoacid, oxygen atom pulls electron density away from the central atom, which increases the central atom ability to draw electron density away from the O—H bond.

Therefore, the more oxygen atoms that are attached to a central atom, the more polar will be the O—H bonds of the acid and the stronger will be the acid. For e.g, the oxoacids of chlorine, $HClO < HClO_2 < HClO_3 < HClO_4$. Comparing their structures, we have

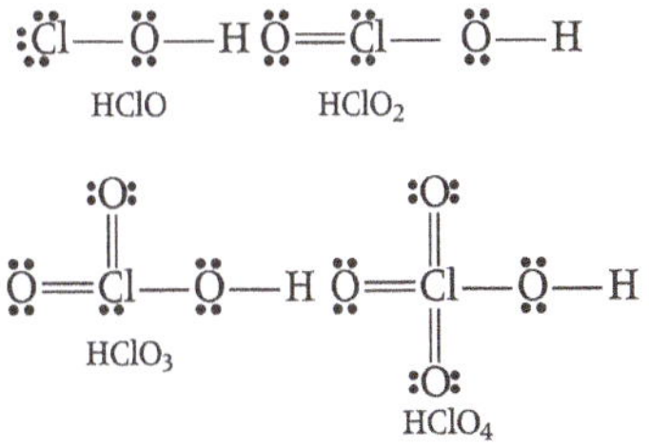

HClO HClO$_2$ HClO$_3$ HClO$_4$

Acid-strength and base-strength based on oxidation number been summarised.

Acid and base strength based on oxidation number (Acid is H_mYO_n)

	Acid	O.N. of Y	Acid strength	Base strength of conjugate base
Y = Halogen	I. HClO	+1	I < II < III < IV	IV < III < II < I
	II. $HClO_2$	+3		
	III. $HClO_3$	+5		
	IV. $HClO_4$	+7		
Y = Phosphorus	I. H_3PO_2	+1	I < II < III	III < II < I
	II. H_3PO_3	+3		
	III. H_3PO_4	+5		
Y = Sulphur	I. $H_2S_2O_3$	+2	I < II < III	III < II < I
	II. H_2SO_3	+4		
	III. H_2SO_4	+6		
Y = Nitrogen	I. $H_2N_2O_2$	+1	I < II < III	III < II < I
	II. HNO_2	+3		
	III. HNO_3	+5		

For oxoacids containing more than one hydrogen (poly basic), successive dissociation constants rapidly decreases, the acidic strength, i.e. the phosphate species formed on successive removal of H^+ becomes less acidic.

$$H_3PO_4 \rightleftharpoons H^+ + H_2PO_4^- ; \quad K_1 = 7.08 \times 10^{-3}$$

$$H_2PO_4^- \rightleftharpoons H^+ + HPO_4^{2-} ; \quad K_2 = 6.31 \times 10^{-8}$$

$$HPO_4^{2-} \rightleftharpoons H^+ + PO_4^{3-} ; \quad K_3 = 4.27 \times 10^{-13}$$

Thus, $K_1 > K_2 > K_3$

Limitations of Bronsted-Lowry Theory

The extent to which a dissolved substance can act as an acid or a base depends largely on the solvent. Thus, substances appearing as acids behave differently as bases. e.g. $HClO_4$ is an extremely strong proton donor. If liq. $HClO_4$ is used as solvent, then HF dissolved in this solvent is forced to accept protons, and thus acts as a base.

$$HClO_4 + HF \rightleftharpoons H_2F^+ + ClO_4^-$$

HNO_3 acts as proton acceptor in $HClO_4$ and HF both

$$HClO_4 + HNO_3 \rightleftharpoons H_2NO_3^+ + ClO_4^-$$

$$HF + HNO_3 \rightleftharpoons H_2NO_3^+ + F^-$$

The nature of solvent even makes some substances, as urea, which show no acidic properties in water, behave as weak acids.

$$NH_2CONH_2 + NH_3 \longrightarrow NH_4^+ + NH_2CONH^-$$

JEE Quicker

The Assertion-The amphoteric nature of water is explained by using Lewis acid/base concept is incorrect. *JEE Main 2022*

- Water can react with acids as well as base. This amphoteric nature is explained by Arrhenius acid/base concept.

Lewis Acids and Lewis Bases

Lewis defined acids and bases in the following manner

(i) **Lewis acid** is any ionic or molecular species that can accept a pair of electrons in the formation of a coordinate covalent bond. These substances have an incomplete valence shell, such as BF_3 or H^+.

(ii) **Lewis base** is any ionic or molecular species that can donate a pair of electrons in the formation of a coordinate covalent bond. These substances have completed valence shells and unshared pairs of electrons, such as NH_3, H_2O and O^{2-}.

Some Example of Lewis Acids

(i) Compounds where the central atom has incomplete octet are Lewis acids. This means all electron-deficient molecules can act as Lewis acids, like BF_3, BBr_3, $AlCl_3$, $FeCl_3$ and $GaCl_3$

(ii) Compounds in which the central atom has available vacant orbitals, like, SnF_4, $SnCl_2$, $SnCl_4$, PF_3, PF_4, SF_4 and TiCl.

(iii) Simple cations such as, Ag^+, Cu^{2+}, Al^{3+}, Co^{3+} and Mg^{2+}

e.g. $Cu^{2+} + 4NH_3 \rightleftharpoons [Cu(NH_3)_4]^{2+}$

(iv) Compounds which have multiple covalent bonds such as CO_2 (O=C=O), CS_2 (S=C=S), SO_2(O=S=O)

Under the influence of attacking Lewis base, one electron pair will be shifted towards more electronegative atom.

$$\underset{\text{Lewis acid}}{O{=}C{=}O} + \underset{\text{Lewis base}}{OH^-} \longrightarrow \underset{(HCO_3^-)}{O^-{-}\overset{\overset{O}{\|}}{C}{-}OH}$$

Some Example of Lewis Bases

(i) All simple anions are Lewis bases, like, NO_3^-, Cl^-, $\bar{O}H$.

(ii) Molecules containing one or more unshared pairs of electrons (lone pairs), like $H_2\ddot{O}:$, $\ddot{N}H_3$, $R\ddot{O}H$, $\ddot{N}X_3$ and $R_2\ddot{S}:$ are Lewis bases provided the octet of the central atom is complete

(iii) Multiple-bonded compounds which can donate the lone pair of electrons, like

$:C{=}O$, $\cdot\ddot{N}{=}O$, $CH_2{=}CH_2$, $CH{\equiv}CH$

Other examples of Lewis acid-base reactions are :

$$\underset{\text{Lewis acid}}{Cd^{2+}(aq)} + \underset{\text{Lewis base}}{4I^-} \rightleftharpoons [CdI_4^{2-}(aq)]$$

$$\underset{\text{Lewis Acid}}{Ni(s)} + \underset{\text{Lewis base}}{4(CO)(g)} \rightleftharpoons Ni(CO)_4(g)$$

$$\underset{\text{Lewis acid}}{Al^{3+}} + \underset{\text{Lewis base}}{6H_2O} \longrightarrow [Al(H_2O)_6^{3+}]$$

$$\underset{\text{Lewis acid}}{Cu^{2+}} + \underset{\text{Lewis base}}{4NH_3} \longrightarrow [Cu(NH_3)_4^{2+}]$$

$$\underset{\text{Lewis acid}}{SO_3} + \underset{\text{Lewis base}}{H_2O} \longrightarrow H_2SO_4$$

Factors Affecting Strength of Lewis Acids

(i) Greater the nuclear charge on central atom, larger is the Lewis acidic strength.

(ii) More the number of electronegative atoms attached more is the acidic strength, e.g. $HClO_3 > HClO_2$.

(iii) When charge is same on the cation, the decrease in the radii of cation increases the acidic strength, e.g.

$$\overset{+}{Li} \quad Na^+ \quad K^+$$

$\longrightarrow$ Size

$\longleftarrow$ Acidic strength

Limitations

(i) Protonic acid as HCl, H_2SO_4 etc., are not covered by this concept.

(ii) Acid-base strength of a species is dependent on the nature of reaction studied and not on the tendency of accepting or donating a pair of electrons.

Hard Soft Acid Base Concept

The Hard and Soft Acids and Bases (HSAB) theory, developed by Ralph Pearson in the 1960s.

Hard Acids and Hard Bases

Hard acids are species that are small, highly charged, and have high polarizing power or low polarisability. They tend to form stable complexes with hard bases, which have similar characteristics (small, highly charged, low polarisability). Hard acids and bases interact through ionic bonding.

Hard bases are species that are small, highly electronegative, and also have low polarisability. They tend to have localised electron pairs that are not easily distorted

e.g.

- Hard acids : $H^+, Li^+, Na^+, Mg^{2+}, Al^{3+}$
- Hard bases : OH^-, F^-, NH_3, H_2O

Soft Acid and Soft Base

Soft acids are larger, less charged, and more polarisable than hard acids. Soft acids prefer to form complexes with soft bases, which are also large, less charged, and more polarisable. Soft acids and soft bases interact through covalent bonding.

Soft bases are species that are more easily polarisable, and their electron pairs more diffuse and can be more readily shared.

e.g.

- Soft acids : $Cu^+, Ag^+, Hg^{2+}, Au^+$
- Soft bases : I^-, S^{2-}, PPh_3, RSH

JEE Alert

- All Bronsted bases are also Lewis bases but all Lewis acids are not Bronsted acids.
- NH_3 acts a Lewis base as well as Bronsted Lowry base as it can donate electron pair by accepting H^+ form NH_4^+ ion.

Acids and Bases in Proton Solvents and Ionic Product of Water

Water, as we know, is a unique solvent. One of its special properties is its ability to act either as an acid and as a base. Water functions as a base in reactions with acids such as HCl and CH_3COOH and as an acid in reactions with bases such as NH_3.

$$\underset{\text{Acid}}{HCl(aq)} + \underset{\text{Base}}{H_2O} \rightleftharpoons H_3O^+(aq) + Cl^-(aq)$$

$$\underset{\text{Base}}{NH_3(aq)} + \underset{\text{Acid}}{H_2O(l)} \rightleftharpoons NH_4^+(aq) + OH^-(aq)$$

Water is a very weak electrolyte and therefore, a poor conductor of electricity but it does undergo ionisation to a small extent.

$$H_2O(l) \rightleftharpoons H^+(aq) + OH^-(aq)$$

This reaction is called **autoionisation** of water.

In terms of Bronsted-Lowry protonic concept

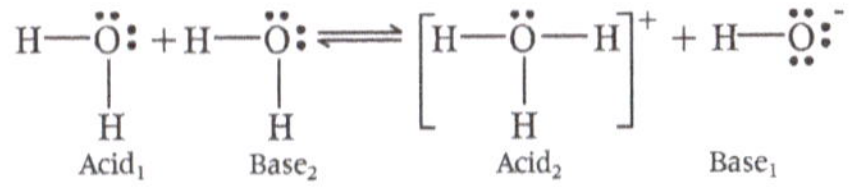

or $\quad 2H_2O(l) \rightleftharpoons H_3O^+(aq) + OH^-(aq)$

Equilibrium constant for this reaction is

$$K_c = \frac{[H_3O^+][OH^-]}{[H_2O]^2}$$

Water is weak acid, $H_2O(l) \rightleftharpoons H^+(aq) + OH^-(aq)$

It represents ionisation of H_2O and equilibrium constant is called **acid ionisation constant** K_a,

$$K_a(H_2O) \rightleftharpoons \frac{[H^+][OH^-]}{[H_2O]}$$

As the concentration of water remains almost constant, (being very large)

$$K_a[H_2O] = [H^+][OH^-]$$

At 298 K,

$$[H^+] = [OH^-] = 1 \times 10^{-7} M$$

(by experimental study)

$$K_w = [H^+][OH] = 1.0 \times 10^{-14}$$

Since, H^+ is associated with water as H_3O^+ we write

$$K_w = [H_3O^+][OH^-] = 1.0 \times 10^{-14}$$

The equilibrium constant for the self ionisation of water is **called ionic product of water or autoionisation constant or autoprotolysis constant and is represented as K_w.**

Whether we have pure water or solution or dissolved species, $K_w = [H_3O^+][OH^-] = 1 \times 10^{-14}$ is always true at 298K.

Ionisation Constant of Weak Acids and Weak Bases

Acids like CH_3COOH, HCN, H_2CO_3 ionise to smaller extent, thus $[H_3O^+]$ is not equal to the concentration of the acid.

$$CH_3COOH + H_2O \rightleftharpoons CH_3COO^- + H_3O^+$$

The equilibrium constant expression is

$$K_a = \frac{[CH_3COO^-][H_3O^+]}{[CH_3COOH]}$$

K_a is called **acid ionisation constant.**

For a weak base, K_b is called **base ionisation constant**.

$$NH_4OH \rightleftharpoons NH_4^+ + OH^-$$

$$K_b = \frac{[NH_4^+][OH^-]}{[NH_4OH]}$$

If K_a is the ionisation constant of a weak acid HA and K_b that of its conjugate base A^- such that

$$HA + H_2O \rightleftharpoons A^- + H_3O^+$$

$$K_a(HA) = \frac{[A^-][H_3O^+]}{[HA]}$$

and $$A^- + H_2O \rightleftharpoons HA + OH^-$$

$$K_b(A^-) = \frac{[HA][OH^-]}{[A^-]}$$

then $$K_a(HA) \cdot K_b(A^-) = [H_3O^+][OH^-] = K_w$$

For any conjugate acid-base pair, the product of the acid-dissociation constant for the acid and the base-dissociation constant for the conjugate base is always equal to ion-product constant for water.

JEE Spotlite

- In a solution of **weak acid** in water, unless the solution is unusually dilute or the value of K_a is very small assume that all the H_3O^+ in solution is produced by the weak acid. All the OH^- is produced by the self-ionisation of water.
- In a solution of a **weak base** in water, again unless the solution is unusually dilute or the value of K_b is very small, assume that all the OH^- ions are produced by the weak base. All the H_3O^+ ions are produced by the self-ionisation of water.

Ionisation of Polyprotic Acids or Bases

Acids that have more than one ionisable proton per molecule of acids are called **polyprotic acids**.

Let us take an example of H_2CO_3. Its ionisation in water may be represented as

Step I $H_2CO_3 \rightleftharpoons H^+ + HCO_3^-; K = K_{a_1}$

Step II $HCO_3^- \rightleftharpoons H^+ + CO_3^{2-}; K = K_{a_2}$

With each dissociation step, the acidic strength and hence, K_a values decreases,

$$K_{a_1} > K_{a_2}$$

The overall dissociation constant, $K_a = K_{a_1} \cdot K_{a_2}$

For tribasic acids like H_3PO_4, there are three ionisation constants.

JEE Alert

The concentration of any species present at equilibrium should be determined always from step by step dissociation, never by overall dissociation.

K_{a_1} of polyprotic acid is greater than K_{a_2} or K_{a_3} (i.e. $K_{a_1} > K_{a_2} > K_{a_3}$), because it is more difficult to remove a positively charged proton from a negative ion due to electrostatic forces. Similarly, it is more difficult to remove a proton from a doubly charged anion as compared to single charged anion.

Solved Booster 1.1

The overall ionisation constant of H_3PO_4 is
[Given $K_1 = 7.5 \times 10^{-3}; K_2 = 6.2 \times 10^{-8}; K_3 = 3.6 \times 10^{-13}$]

(a) 1.23×10^{-13} (b) 1.674×10^{-22}
(c) 3.271×10^{-21} (d) 3.384×10^{-13}

Solution

(b) For a polybasic acid (as H_3PO_4)

$$H_3PO_4 \rightleftharpoons H^+ + H_2PO_4^-, K_1 = \frac{[H^+][H_2PO_4^-]}{[H_3PO_4]}$$

$$H_2PO_4^- \rightleftharpoons H^+ + HPO_4^{2-}, K_2 = \frac{[H^+][HPO_4^{2-}]}{[H_2PO_4^-]}$$

$$HPO_4^{2-} \rightleftharpoons H^+ + PO_4^{3-}, K_3 = \frac{[H^+][PO_4^{3-}]}{[HPO_4^{2-}]}$$

Adding

$\therefore H_3PO_4 \rightleftharpoons 3H^+ + PO_4^{3-}$,

$$K = K_1 K_2 K_3$$
$$= 7.5 \times 10^{-3} \times 6.2 \times 10^{-8} \times 3.6 \times 10^{-13}$$
$$= 1.674 \times 10^{-22}$$

Elemental Practice 6.1

Type I MCQs with Only One Correct Option

1. $C_2H_5O^-$ is a X in C_2H_5OH solvent, NH_4NO_3 is a Y in NH_3 solvent. X and Y are

	X	Y
(a)	Strong acid	Strong acid
(b)	Strong base	Strong acid
(c)	Strong acid	Strong base
(d)	Weak acid	Weak base

2. In the following

$$\underset{A}{[Al(H_2O)_6]^{3+}} + \underset{B}{HCO_3^-} \rightleftharpoons \underset{C}{[Al(H_2O)_5OH]^{2+}} + \underset{D}{H_2CO_3}$$

Species behaving as Bronsted Lowry acids are
(a) A, D (b) B, C (c) B, D (d) A, C

3. Given below are two statements.

Statement I If 0.1 mol of HA is dissolved in 1 L of aqueous solution, then the % dissociated at equilibrium will be 1%. [K_a of HA at 25° is 10^{-5}]

Statement II HCOOH and CH_3COOH solutions have equal pH. If K_{a_1}/K_{a_2} is 4, then the ratio of their molar concentration will be 1 : 2.
(a) Both statement I and statement II are correct.
(b) Statement I is correct but statement II is incorrect.
(c) Statement I is incorrect but statement II is correct.
(d) Both statement I and statement II are incorrect.

4. The concentration of H_3O^+ ions in 0.005 M solution of $Ba(OH)_2$ at 298 K, assuming that $Ba(OH)_2$ is completely ionised under the given conditions.
(a) 10^{-1} (b) 10^{-11} (c) 10^{-12} (d) 10^{-13}

5. pH of 0.08 mol dm^{-3} HOCl solution is 2.85. Thus, its ionisation constant is
(a) 1.41×10^{-3} (b) 2.50×10^{-5}
(c) 2.00×10^{-6} (d) 1.60×10^{-7}

6. If following reactions proceed in forward side.

$HNO_2 + HF \rightleftharpoons H_2F^+ + NO_2^-$

$CH_3COOH + HF \rightleftharpoons F^- + CH_3COOH_2^+$

$H_2O + CH_3COOH \rightleftharpoons H_3O^+ + CH_3COO^-$

then increasing order of acid strength is
(a) $H_2O < CH_3COOH < HF < HNO_2$
(b) $HNO_2 < HF < CH_3COOH < H_2O$
(c) $HNO_2 < HF < H_2O < CH_3COOH$
(d) $HNO_2 < CH_3COOH < HF < H_2O$

7. The volume of water (in mL) that must be added to 300 mL of 0.2 M solution of CH_3COOH for its degree of dissociation to double is : [$K_a(CH_3COOH) = 1.8 \times 10^{-5}$]
(a) 450 mL (b) 700 mL
(c) 900 mL (d) 800 mL

8. At 298 K, K_w of water is 1×10^{-14}. Thus, ionisation constant of water is
(a) 1×10^{-14} (b) 5.55×10^{-15}
(c) 1.8×10^{-16} (d) 55.5×10^{-10}

9. Consider the following equilibrium,
$HONO\,(aq) + CN^- \rightleftharpoons HCN\,(aq) + ONO^-(aq)$;
$K_{eq} = 1.1 \times 10^6$.

The incorrect statement about this is
(a) CN^- is stronger base than ONO^-
(b) HCN is stronger acid than HONO
(c) The conjugate base of HONO is ONO^-
(d) $\Delta G = 0$

10. Consider the following statements:
Statement I HCO_3^- is an amphiprotic species.
Statement II H_2O is an amphoteric oxide.
(a) Both Statement I and Statement II are correct.
(b) Both Statement I and Statement II are incorrect.
(c) Statement I is correct but Statement II is incorrect.
(d) Statement I is incorrect but Statement II is correct.

11. Consider the K_a values of the given species

$K_a(HSO_4^-) = 1.2 \times 10^{-2}$; $K_a(H_2PO_4^-) = 6.3 \times 10^{-8}$

$K_a(HCO_3^-) = 4.7 \times 10^{-11}$

The species which is the strongest base is
(a) CO_3^{2-} (b) H_2SO_4 (c) SO_4^{2-} (d) HPO_4^{2-}

12. The dissociation constant of a 0.1 M weak acid, HA is 4.9×10^{-8}. The percentage ionisation of the acid is
(a) 7×10^{-2} (b) 16×10^{-2} (c) 1.2×10^{-2} (d) 4×10^{-3}

13. Three reactions involving $H_2PO_4^-$ are given below.
I. $H_3PO_4 + H_2O \longrightarrow H_3O^+ + H_2PO_4^-$
II. $H_2PO_4^- + H_2O \longrightarrow HPO_4^{2-} + H_3O^+$
III. $H_2PO_4^- + OH^- \longrightarrow H_3PO_4 + O^{2-}$
In which of the given reactions does $H_2PO_4^-$ act as an acid?
(a) Only II (b) Both I and II (c) Only III (d) Only I

14. Which of the following is amphiprotic species?
(a) $H_2PO_2^-$ (b) HPO_3^{2-} (c) HCO_3^- (d) $CH_3CO_2^-$

15. Which of the following is not Lewis acid?
(a) BCl_3 (b) $B(CH_3)_3$ (c) $AlCl_3$ (d) PH_3

Type II MCQs with One or More than One Correct Option

16. Which of the following statements are correct?
(a) CH_3COOH (a weak acid) behaves as a strong acid in NH_3.
(b) HNO_3 (a strong acid) behaves as a base in HF.
(c) H_2SO_4 dissociates to a very small extent in glacial CH_3COOH
(d) $B(CH_3)_3$ is a Lewis base and $N(CH_3)_3$ is a Lewis acid.

17. Consider the following reactions,

I. $[Al(OH)_3(H_2O)_3] + OH^- \rightleftharpoons [Al(OH)_4(H_2O)_2]^- + H_2O$

II. $[Al(OH)_3(H_2O)_3] + H_3O^+ \rightleftharpoons [Al(OH)_2(H_2O)_4]^+ + H_2O$

Select the correct statement(s).

(a) $[Al(OH)_3(H_2O)_3]$ is an amphoteric species
(b) $[Al(OH)_3(H_2O)_3]$ is a Lowry-Bronsted acid
(c) H_2O (product) is an acid in I and a base in II
(d) In both I and II, $[Al(OH)_3(H_2O_3)]$ is an acid

18. Which of the following statements are correct?

(a) In weak electrolytes, equilibrium is established between ions and the unionised molecules.
(b) The electrostatic forces between two charges are directly proportional to dielectric constant of the medium.
(c) The extent to which ionisation occurs depends upon the strength of the bond but not on the extent of solvation of ions produced.
(d) Hydrochloric acid and acetic acid both are polar covalent but the former is completely ionised into its constituent ions, while the latter is only partially ionised (< 5%) in water.

19. Select the correct statement(s).

(a) NH_4Cl is a strong acid in liquid NH_3
(b) $NaNH_2$ is a strong base in liquid NH_3
(c) CH_3COOH is a base in H_2SO_4
(d) H_3O^+ is the strongest acid that can exist in aqueous solution

20. Which of the following statements are correct?

(a) A Bronsted-Lowry acid-base reaction is always favoured in the direction from stronger to weaker acid/base combination.
(b) Ostwald dilution law is applicable to weak electrolytes only.
(c) All Bronsted bases are Lewis bases but all Bronsted acids are not Lewis acids.
(d) A solvent which has a high dielectric constant strengthens the attractive forces between the cation and anion.

Type III 》 Numerical/Integer Answer Type Questions

21. An aqueous solutions is prepared by dissolving 0.1 mole H_2CO_3 in sufficient water to get 100 ml solution at 25°C. For, H_2CO_3, $K_{a_1} = 4.0 \times 10^{-6}$ and $K_{a_2} = 5.0 \times 10^{-11}$. Then,

$[H^+] = a \times 10^{-3}$ M; $[HCO_3^-] = b \times 10^{-3}$ M

$[CO_3^{2-}] = c \times 10^{-11}$ M; $[OH^-] = d \times 10^{-12}$ M

The value of $a + b + c + d$ is ....

22. What is the ratio of $\dfrac{K_a(HCOOH)}{K_a(CH_3COOH)}$ if their aqueous solutions have equal pH when ratio of molar concentration is 0.25?

23. A 0.1 molar solution of weak base BOH is 1% dissociated. If 0.2 mol of BCl is added in 1 L solution of BOH. The degree of dissociation of BOH will become $x \times 10^{-5}$ M. The value of x is ......

24. Among $H_2PO_4^-$, SO_3^{2-}, ClO^-, Fe^{3+} and BCl_3 the total number of Bronsted-Lowry base will be ....

25. Consider the following species

HNO_2, HNO_3, NH_4^+, Cl^-, H^-, O^{2-}, H_2SO_4

The total number of species that behave as strong base in aqueous solution is ....

Elemental Practice 6.1 | Chapter 06

Connect with **Answers**

1. (b)	**2.** (a)	**3.** (b)	**4.** (c)	**5.** (b)	**6.** (a)
7. (c)	**8.** (c)	**9.** (b)	**10.** (a)	**11.** (a)	**12.** (a)
13. (a)	**14.** (c)	**15.** (d)	**16.** (a,b,c)	**17.** (a,b,c)	**18.** (a,d)
19. (a,b,c,d)	**20.** (a,b,c)	**21.** (14)	**22.** (4)	**23.** (5)	**24.** (3)
25. (2)					

Element 2 pH, Buffer, Indicators and Salt Hydrolysis

pH-scale

The pH of a solution is defined as "the negative logarithms to the base 10 of the concetration of H^+ions which it contains".

Thus, $$pH = -\log_{10}[H^+]$$
$$[H^+] = 10^{-pH}$$

pOH Value

Just as pH indicates H^+ ion concentration, pOH represents the OH^- ion concentration,

$$[OH^-] = 10^{-pOH}$$
$$pOH = -\log[OH^-]$$

Relation between pH and pOH

Since, $[H_3O^+][OH^-] = K_w = 1\times 10^{-14}$

or $\log[H_3O^+] + \log[OH^-] = \log K_w$

$$= \log 1\times 10^{-14}$$

or $-\log[H_3O^+] - \log[OH^-] = -\log K_w = 14$

$\therefore$ $pH + pOH = pK_w = 14$

Case I If solution is neutral (as in water)

$$[H_3O^+] = [OH^-] = \sqrt{K_w}$$

Thus, $pH = pOH = 7$

At 25°C, for pure water or for neutral solution, pH or pOH is 7.

Case II If solution is **acidic**,

$$[H^+] > [OH^-]$$

Thus $pH < 7$ and $pOH > 7$

As a solution becomes more acidic, its $[H_3O^+]$ increases and its pH decreases.

Case III If solution is **basic**,

$$[H^+] < [OH^-]$$

and $[OH^-] > 1\times 10^{-7}$ M

Thus, $pH > 7$

$pOH < 7$

As a solution becomes more basic, its $[OH^-]$ increases, its pOH decreases and its pH increases.

Limitations of pH Scale

The pH values of the solutions do not give the exact idea of their relative strengths. e.g.

(i) A solution of pH = 1, has $[H^+]$ 100 times than that of a solution of pH = 3, and not 3 times.

(ii) A 4×10^{-5} M HCl is twice concentrated as compared to 2×10^{-5} M HCl solution but the pH values of these solutions are 4.4 and 4.7, respectively and not double.

(iii) pH = 0 is obtained in 1N solution of a strong acid, but for concentrations 2N, 3N, 10N, etc., the value can be negative too. Similarly, for a concentrated solution of a strong base (> 1M), pH can be greater than 14.

(iv) A 10^{-7}M and 10^{-8}M solution of strong acid can not have pH = 7 and 8, respectively.

JEE Alert

When a strong acid is added to water, there are two potential sources of H^+ in the aqueous solution i.e. acid and water. So,

$$[H^+]_{Net} = [H_3O^+]_{Acid} + [H_3O^+]_{Water}$$

If $[H_3O^+]_{Acid} \geq 10^{-6}$, $[H_3O^+]_{Water}$ may be ignored in the calculation of pH.

If $[H_3O^+]_{Acid} < 10^{-6}$, then $[H_3O^+]_{Water}$ is added.

Solved Booster 2.1

The pH of 10^{-8} M HCl is

(a) 6.98 (b) 7.02 (c) 6.34 (d) 5.49

Solution *(a)*

If we do not consider $[H^+]$ from H_2O, then

$[HCl] = [H^+] = 10^{-8}$ M

pH = 8, which is not possible since, acidic solution should have pH < 7

	H_2O	$\rightleftharpoons H^+$	+ OH^-
Initial	C	0	0
After dissociation	$C-x$	x	x

$\therefore$ Total $[H^+] = [H^+]$ from H_2O + $[H^+]$ from HCl = $(x + 10^{-8})$

$[OH^-] = x$

$\therefore$ $[H^+][OH^-] = K_w = 1\times 10^{-14}$

$$(x + 10^{-8})x = 1\times 10^{-14}$$
$$x^2 + 10^{-8}x - 1\times 10^{-14} = 0$$
$$x = \frac{-10^{-8} + \sqrt{10^{-16} + 4\times 10^{-14}}}{2}$$

$x = 9.51 \times 10^{-8}$M

$\therefore [H^+]_{Total} = 10^{-8} + 9.51 \times 10^{-8}$ M

$= 10.51 \times 10^{-8}$M

$pH = -\log [H^+]$

$= -\log (10.51 \times 10^{-8})$

$= 8 - \log 10.51 \approx 6.98$

JEE Quicker

pH of water is 7 at 25°C, then the pH of water at 80°C will decreases. *JEE Main 2025*

Dissociation of water (H_2O) is an endothermic process. So, the dissociation constant (K_w) of water increaes, leading to higher concentrations of H^+ and OH^-. This lowers the pH of pure water even through it remains neutral (since $[H^+] = [OH^-]$).

At 25°C, pH of pure water is 7.

At 50°C, pH of pure water is 6.6

At ~100°C, pH of pure water is 6.1.

pH Calculations

- **pH of weak acids** pH of a weak monobasic acid

$$pH = -\log [H_3O^+] = -\log \sqrt{K_a C}$$

$$pH = -\frac{1}{2}\log K_a - \frac{1}{2}\log C$$

$$= \frac{1}{2}[pK_a - \log C]$$

- **pH calculation for strong acids and weak acids**

Case I Total $[H_3O^+]$ in a mixture of weak acid and a strong acid

$$[H_3O^+] = \frac{C_2 + \sqrt{C_2^2 + 4K_aC_1}}{2}$$

where, C_1 is the concentration (in mol L^{-1}) of the weak acid (K_a) and C_2 that of strong acid.

Case II Total $[H_3O^+]$ in a mixture of two weak acids,

$$[H_3O^+] = \sqrt{K_1C_1 + K_2C_2}$$

where K_1 is ionisation constant of first weak acid and K_2 that of second weak acid.

- **pOH of a weak bases** pOH of a weak monoacid base,

$$pOH = -\log [OH^-]$$

$$= -\log(K_b.C)^{1/2}$$

$$= -\frac{1}{2}[\log K_b + \log C]$$

$$= \frac{1}{2}[pK_b - \log C]$$

- **pOH calculation for mixtures of weak bases**

Total $[OH^-]$ in a mixture of two weak bases

$$[OH^-] = \sqrt{K_1C_1 + K_2C_2}$$

Degree of ionisation using Ostwald's dilution law

Solved Booster 6.3

The sum of the pH of 0.08 M solution of hypochlorous acid (HOCl) and the degree of dissociation of HOCl, if the ionisation constant of the acid is 2.5×10^{-5} ....

(a) 3.4212 (b) 2.8677

(c) 4.3061 (d) 8.3241

Solution

(b) $HOCl(aq) + H_2O(l) \rightleftharpoons H_3O^+(aq) + ClO^-(aq)$

By Ostwald's dilution law,

$[H_3O^+] = \sqrt{K_aC} = \sqrt{2.5 \times 10^{-5} \times 0.08} = 1.41 \times 10^{-3}$ M

$\therefore \quad pH = -\log [H_3O^+] = -\log [1.41 \times 10^{-3}]$

$pH = 2.85$

Also, (degree of dissociation) $= \sqrt{\frac{K_a}{C}}$

$$x = \sqrt{\frac{2.5 \times 10^{-5}}{0.08}} = 0.0177 = 1.77\%$$

Thus, $2.85 + 0.0177 = 2.8677$

Hydrolysis

Interaction of cation or anion or both of a salt with water to give acidic or basic or neutral solution is termed as hydrolysis.

$$\underset{\text{Cation}}{B^+} + H_2O \rightleftharpoons \underset{\text{Weak base}}{BOH} + \underset{\text{Acidic}}{H^+}$$

$$\underset{\text{Anion}}{A^-} + H_2O \rightleftharpoons \underset{\text{Weak acid}}{HA} + \underset{\text{Basic}}{OH^-}$$

$$\underset{\text{Cation}}{B^+} + \underset{\text{Anion}}{A^+} + H_2O \rightleftharpoons \underset{\text{Weak acid}}{HA} + \underset{\text{Weak base}}{BOH}$$

Hydrolysis will occur only if a chemical reaction can produce a **weak acid** or **weak base.**

JEE Alert

The interaction of cation or anion or both with H^+ or OH^- ions of H_2O is possible if the acid or base formed will have $\alpha < 1$, so that they will not give back the H^+/OH^- ion.

1. Hydrolysis of Salts of Strong Acid and Strong Base

$$\underset{\text{Salt}}{NaCl} + H_2O \rightleftharpoons \underset{\text{Strong base}}{NaOH} + \underset{\text{Strong acid}}{HCl}$$

or, $$H_2O \rightleftharpoons OH^- + H^+$$

- No hydrolysis takes place.
- Neutral solution, no effect on litmus paper.
- pH = 7

2. Hydrolysis of Salts of Strong Base and Weak Acid

$$\underset{}{CH_3COONa} + H_2O \rightleftharpoons \underset{\text{Weak acid}}{CH_3COOH} + \underset{\text{Strong base}}{NaOH}$$

$$CH_3COO^- + H_2O \rightleftharpoons CH_3COOH + OH^-$$

$$CO_3^{2-} + 2H_2O \rightleftharpoons H_2CO_3 + 2OH^-$$

Characteristics

- Anion of the salt (or conjugate base of weak acid) is hydrolysed.
- Free OH^- ions are formed. Number of OH^- ions formed due to hydrolysis is equal to the charge on the anion.
- Greater the charge, greater the number of OH^- ions hence, greater the pH.
- Solution is alkaline, pH > 7.

$$pH = \frac{pK_w + pK_a + \log C}{2}$$

or $$\text{pH at } 25°C = 7 + \frac{pK_a + \log C}{2}$$

Hydrolysis constant, K_h, of the Salt

	$CH_3COO^- + H_2O \rightleftharpoons$	$CH_3COOH +$	OH^-
Initial	C	0	0
After hydrolysis	$(C - Cx)$	Cx	Cx

$$K_h = \frac{[CH_3COOH][OH^-]}{[CH_3COO^-]}$$

$$= \frac{Cx^2}{(1-x)} \approx Cx^2 \text{ (if } x << 1)$$

where, x is degree of hydrolysis and C is the concentration (mol L^{-1})

Also $CH_3COOH \rightleftharpoons CH_3COO^- + H^+$

$$\therefore \quad K_a = \frac{[CH_3COO^-][H^+]}{[CH_3COOH]}$$

$$\therefore \quad K_h \cdot K_a = [H^+][OH^-] = K_w$$

$$\therefore \quad K_h = \frac{K_w}{K_a}$$

$$x = \sqrt{\frac{K_h}{C}} = \sqrt{\frac{K_w}{K_a C}}$$

$$[OH^-] = Cx = \sqrt{\frac{K_w C}{K_a}}$$

$$\Rightarrow \quad [H^+] = \frac{K_w}{[OH^-]} = \sqrt{\frac{K_w K_a}{C}}$$

3. Hydrolysis of Salts of Strong Acid and Weak Base

In aqueous solution such as salt BA exhibit following equation

$$B^+ + A^- + H_2O \rightleftharpoons BOH + HA$$

$$NH_4Cl + H_2O \rightleftharpoons \underset{\text{Weak base}}{NH_4OH} + \underset{\text{Strong acid}}{HCl}$$

$$NH_4^+ + H_2O \rightleftharpoons NH_4OH + H^+$$

Characteristics

- Cation of the salt (or conjugate acid of weak base) is hydrolysed.
- Free H^+ (H_3O^+) ions are formed. Number of H^+ ions, formed due to hydrolysis is equal to charge on the cation.
- Greater the charge, greater the number of H^+ ions, hence lower the pH.
- Solution is acidic, pH < 7.

$$pH = \frac{pK_w - (pK_b + \log C)}{2} = 7 - \left(\frac{pK_b + \log C}{2}\right)$$

Hydrolysis Constant; K_h, of the Salt

	$NH_4^+ + H_2O \rightleftharpoons$	$NH_4OH +$	H^+
Initial	C	0	0
After **hydrolysis**	$(C - Cx)$	Cx	Cx

$$K_h = \frac{[NH_4OH][H^+]}{[NH_4^+]} = \frac{K_w}{K_b} = \frac{Cx^2}{(1-x)} \approx Cx^2 \text{ (if } x << 1)$$

$$x = \sqrt{\frac{K_h}{C}} = \sqrt{\frac{K_w}{K_b C}}$$

$$[H^+] = Cx = \sqrt{\frac{K_w C}{K_b}}$$

4. Hydrolysis of Salt of Weak Acid and Weak Base

$$CH_3COONH_4 + H_2O \rightleftharpoons CH_3COOH + NH_4OH$$

$$CH_3COO^- + NH_4^+ + H_2O \rightleftharpoons CH_3COOH + NH_4OH$$

Characteristics

- Cation and anion both parts of the salt are hydrolysed.
- Solution can be acidic ($K_a > K_b$) or basic ($K_a < K_b$) or neutral ($K_a = K_b$) depending on relative values of ionisation constants.

$$pH = \frac{pK_w + pK_a - pK_b}{2} = 7 + \left(\frac{pK_a - pK_b}{2}\right)$$

—If $K_a > K_b (pK_b > pK_a)$, pH < 7 and solution is acidic.

—If $K_a < K_b (pK_a > pK_b)$, pH > 7 and solution is basic

—If $K_a = K_b (pK_a = pK_b)$, pH = 7 and solution is neutral.

Hydrolysis Constant, K_h, of the Salt

$$CH_3COO^- + NH_4^+ + H_2O \rightleftharpoons CH_3COOH + NH_4OH$$

	CH_3COO^-	NH_4^+	CH_3COOH	NH_4OH
Initial	C	C	0	0
After hydrolysis	$(C - Cx)$	$(C - Cx)$	Cx	Cx

$$K_h = \frac{[CH_3COOH][NH_4OH]}{[CH_3COO^-][NH_4^+]}$$

$$K_a(CH_3COOH) = [CH_3COO^-][H^+]/[CH_3COOH]$$

$$K_b[NH_4OH] = [NH_4^+][OH^-]/[NH_4OH]$$

$$\therefore \quad K_h \cdot K_a \cdot K_b = [H^+][OH^-] = K_w$$

$$\therefore \quad K_h = \frac{K_w}{K_a \cdot K_b}$$

Also, $$K_h = \frac{x^2}{(1-x)^2}$$

$$\sqrt{K_h} = \frac{x}{1-x} \text{ (if } x \text{ is not neglected compared to 1)}$$

$$\approx x \text{ if } x << 1$$

$$\boxed{x = \sqrt{K_h} = \sqrt{\frac{K_w}{K_a K_b}}}$$

JEE Alert

There is no effect of dilution on pH for such types of salt.

5. Hydrolysis of Amphiprotic Anion

If cation is not hydrolysed, salts such as $NaHCO_3$, NaHS, etc., can undergo ionisation to form H^+ ion and can undergo hydrolysis to form OH^- (Na^+ ion is not hydrolysed)

(i) $$HCO_3^- + H_2O \xrightleftharpoons{\text{Ionisation}} \underset{\text{Acid}}{CO_3^{2-} + H_3O^+}$$

$$HCO_3^- + H_2O \xrightleftharpoons{\text{Hydrolysis}} \underset{\text{Base}}{H_2CO_3 + OH^-}$$

Thus, HCO_3^- is amphiprotic anion.

$$H_2CO_3 \rightleftharpoons H^+ + HCO_3^-$$

K_{a_1} = first ionisation constant

$$HCO_3^- \rightleftharpoons H^+ + CO_3^{2-}$$

K_{a_2} = second ionisation constant

$$pH\ (HCO_3^-) = \left(\frac{pK_{a_1} + pK_{a_2}}{2}\right)$$

6. Hydrolysis of Amphiprotic Cation

(If Cation is also hydrolysed) $[H_3O^+]$ in salts like $NH_4^+HCO_3^-$, $NH_4^+HS^-$, (in which HCO_3^-, HS^- are amphiprotic and NH_4^+ ion is also hydrolysed) is

$$[H_3O^+] = \sqrt{K_{a_1}\left(\frac{K_w}{K_b} + K_{a_2}\right)}$$

Results of hydrolysis of different types of salts are summarised.

Hydrolysis constant (K_h), degree of hydrolysis (x) and pH of salts.

	Salt	Example	Hydrolysed ion	Nature of solution	K_h	x	pH (at 298 K)
I	Strong acid and strong base	NaCl, K_2SO_4	None	Neutral	—	—	7
II	Strong acid and weak base	NH_4Cl, $CuSO_4$, $AlCl_3$	Cation	Acidic	$\frac{K_w}{K_b}$	$\sqrt{\frac{K_w}{K_b C}}$	$\left(7 - \frac{pK_b}{2} - \frac{\log C}{2}\right)$
III	Weak acid and strong base	CH_3COONa, Na_2CO_3	Anion	Basic	$\frac{K_w}{K_a}$	$\sqrt{\frac{K_w}{K_a C}}$	$\left(7 + \frac{pK_a}{2} + \frac{\log C}{2}\right)$
IV	Weak acid and weak base	CH_3COONH_4, NH_4CN	Both	Depends on K_a and K_b	$\frac{K_w}{K_a K_b}$	$\sqrt{\frac{K_w}{K_a K_b}}$	$7 + \left(\frac{pK_a - pK_b}{2}\right)$
V	Amphiprotic anion	$NaHCO_3$	Anion	— do—	—	—	$\left(\frac{pK_{a_1} + pK_{a_2}}{2}\right)$

Detection of the End-Point : Indicators

When there is reaction of an acid with a base, the equivalence point is reached, where acid neutralises a base. The point at which the reaction is observed to be complete is called the end-point. A measurement is chosen such that the end-point coincides with or is very close to the equivalence point.

End-point can be detected by measuring the pH at different points of titration using a pH meter. Also, it can be detected by a change in colour. For this a number of indicators are preferred.

Characteristics

(i) It is usually more convenient to add an indicator to the solution and usually detect a colour change.

(ii) An indicator for an acid-base titration is a weak acid or weak base.

(iii) The colour of the ionised form is markedly different from that of unionised form. One form may be colourless, but the other form must be coloured.

Assume that the indicator is a weak acid, designated as HIn

$$\underset{\text{Colourless}}{HIn} \rightleftharpoons H^+ + \underset{\text{Coloured}}{In^-}$$

$$K_{In} = \frac{[H^+][In^-]}{[HIn]} \Rightarrow [H^+] = K_{In}\frac{[HIn]}{[In^-]}$$

$$\therefore \quad pH = pK_{In} + \log\frac{[In^-]}{[HIn]}$$

The indicator changes colour over a pH range. The transition range depends on the ability to detect small colour changes.

With indicators in which both forms are coloured, generally one colour is observed if the ratio of the concentration of the two forms is 10 : 1.

Case I When only colour of unionised form (HIn) is seen,

$$\frac{[In^-]}{[HIn]} = \frac{1}{10}$$

Thus, $pH = pK_a + \log\frac{1}{10} = pK_a - 1$

Case II When only the colour of the ionised form (In^-) is observed,

$$\frac{[In^-]}{[HIn]} = \frac{10}{1} \quad \therefore pH = pK_a + 1$$

pH in going from one colour to the other has changed from ($pK_a - 1$) to ($pK_a + 1$); this is a pH changes of 2, and most indicators require a transition of two pH units.

Case III Mid-way in the transition, the concentration of the two forms are equal

$$[HIn] = [In^-]$$

So, $pH = pK_a + \log 1 = pK_a$

Obviously, the pK_a of the indicator should be close to the pH of the equivalence point.

Similarly for weak base indicators, same transition range is observed and $pOH = pK_b$ at the mid-way or $pH = (14 - pK_b)$.

A weak base indicator should be selected such that $pH = 14 - pK_b$.

The transition is easier to see if one form is colourless. For this reason, phenolphthalein is usually used as an indicator for strong acid-base titrations.

Table gives colours and transition ranges of some commonly used indicators.

pH transition ranges and colours of some common indicators

Indicator	pH range	Colour in Acid solution	Colour in Alkaline solution
Thymol blue (acid)	1.2-2.8	Red	Yellow
Bromophenol blue	3.1- 4.6	Yellow	Purple
Methyl orange	3.1- 4.5	Red	Yellow
Methyl red	4.2-6.3	Red	Yellow
Bromothymol blue	6.0-7.5	Orange	Blue
Phenol red	6.4-8.2	Yellow	Red
Thymol blue (base)	8.1-9.6	Yellow	Blue
Phenolphthalein	8.0-9.8	Colourless	Pink
Thymophthalein	9.3-10.5	Colourless	Blue
Alizarin yellow *R*	10.1-12.1	Yellow	Lilac

Theories of Indicators

Ostwald's Theory

According to this theory

- Indicator is a weak electrolyte : a weak acid/a weak base.
- Unionised form is colourless and ionised form is coloured. If both forms are coloured then they have different colours (refer table above)
- In the presence of acid or base (pH changes) there is ionisation of the indicator, hence colour change appears.
- **Phenolphthalein behaves as a weak acid** (PhH)

$$\underset{\text{Colourless in acid}}{PhH} \rightleftharpoons \underset{\text{Pink in base}}{Ph^-} + H^+ \quad \ldots(i)$$

$$H^+ + OH^- \rightleftharpoons H_2O$$

Phenolphthalein is colourless in acid solution and pink in basic solution. In the presence of an acid (H^+) equilibrium (i) is displaced towards the left hand side (a case of Le-Chatelier's principle); when strong base like NaOH is added, this equilibrium is displaced towards right hand side and there is colour change from colourless to pink when pH changes.

- **Limitation of Phenolphthalein Indicator** This indicator is not suitable for titrating weak base (NH_4OH). Weak base can't furnish enough OH^- that can react with H^+ of the phenolphthtalein and impart pink colour which is obtained only after excess of NH_4OH is added.

$$\underset{\text{Colourless}}{PhH} + \underset{\text{Excess}}{NH_4OH} \rightleftharpoons \underset{\text{Pink}}{PhNH_4} + H_2O$$

This pink colour disappears instantly due to hydrolysis.

$$\underset{\text{Pink}}{Ph^-NH_4^+} + H_2O \rightleftharpoons \underset{\text{Colourless}}{PhH} + NH_4OH$$

- **Methyl Orange Behaves as a Weak Base**

Methyl orange is widely used pH indicator in titrations, but it is not universally applicable for all types of reactions. It is suited for strong acid-strong base titrations since its operational range lies between pH 3.1 to 4.4, where it shifts from red to orange/yellow.

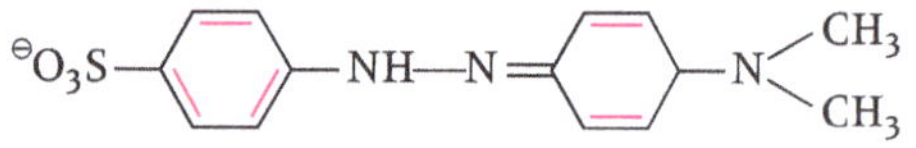

Quinonoid form - Acidic solution (red)

$^{-}OH \rightleftharpoons H^{+}$

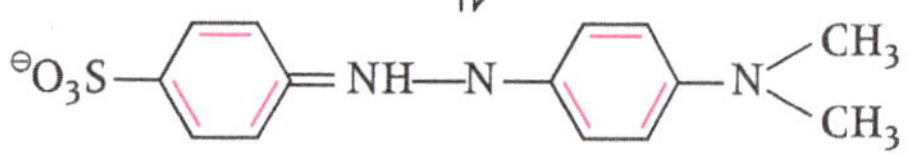

Azo form - Basic solution (yellow)

Buffers

A buffer is defined as a solution that resists change in pH when a small amount of an acid or base is added or when the solution is diluted.

This is very useful for maintaining the pH for a reaction at an optimum value. In order for a solution to act as a buffer it must have two components, one of which is able to neutralise acids and the other bases. Common buffer solutions are mixtures containing a

- weak acid and salt of its conjugate base : acidic buffer.
- weak base and salt of its conjugate acid : basic buffer.
- Salt of weak acid and weak base : salt buffer

Acidic Buffers

A solution of a weak acid and the salt of weak acid is called as acidic buffer. e.g. $CH_3COOH + CH_3COONa$

pH of Acidic Buffer

pH of an acidic buffer is given by

$$pH = pK_a + \log \frac{[Salt]}{[Acid]}$$

Hence, $$pH = pK_a + \log \frac{[Proton\ acceptor]}{[Proton\ donor]}$$

All these relations are called **Henderson-Hasselbalch equations**.

Buffer Action

When an aqueous solution of weak acid $[HA]$ and its salt (say, NaA) is taken, the solution mainly contains unionised acid molecules $[HA]$ and its conjugate base $[A^-]$ due to common ion effect of A^-.

$$HA \rightleftharpoons H^+ + A^-$$

(dissociation is suppressed by common ion effect of A^-)

$$NaA \rightleftharpoons Na^+ + A^-$$

(ionises almost completely in water)

Effect of Addition of Acid or Base on Acidic Buffer on pH

(i) **If OH^- ion is added to the acidic buffer**, equivalent amount of the acid is neutralised, thus decreasing the concentration of the acid and increasing the concentration of its conjugate base, thus increasing pH.

$$HA + OH^- \rightleftharpoons A^- + H_2O$$

	HA	OH^-	A^-	
Initially	C_1		C_2	mol L^{-1}
Added		x		mol L^{-1}
After	$(C_1 - x)$	0	$(C_2 + x)$	mol L^{-1}

$$pH = pK_a + \log \frac{[A^-]}{[HA]}$$

$$pH = pK_a + \log\left(\frac{C_2}{C_1}\right) \text{ (if no } OH^- \text{ is added)}$$

$$pH' = pK_a + \log \frac{(C_2 + x)}{(C_1 - x)} \text{ (if } OH^- \text{ is added)}$$

$pH' > pH$

if $pH' \approx pH$, then buffer action is appreciable.

(ii) **If H^+ is added to the acidic buffer**, equivalent amount of the conjugate base is converted to the acid thus, decreasing pH.

$$A^- + H^+ \rightleftharpoons HA$$

	A^-	H^+	HA	
Initially	C_2		C_1	mol L^{-1}
Added		x		mol L^{-1}
After	$(C_2 - x)$	0	$(C_1 + x)$	mol L^{-1}

$$pH'' = pK_a + \log \frac{(C_2 - x)}{(C_1 + x)'}$$

$(pH'' < pH)$

if $pH' \approx pH$, then buffer action is appreciable

(iii) At half neutralisation $[HA] = [A^-]$

$\therefore$ $pH = pK_a$

Thus no effect on pH.

(iv) Due to dilution, no effect on pH.

JEE MAPPER

Example Similar to PYQ Asked in JEE Main 2021

In order to prepare a buffer solution of pH 5.25, sodium acetate is added to acetic acid. If the concentration of acetic acid in the buffer is 0.5 M, the concentration of sodium acetate in the buffer is ...... M (Nearest integer)

$[pK_a(CH_3COOH) = 4.74]$

Sol. (2) $pH = pK_a + \log \frac{[Salt]}{[Acid]}$

$\Rightarrow$ $5.25 = 4.74 + \log \frac{[CH_3COONa]}{0.5}$

$\Rightarrow$ $0.51 = \log[CH_3COONa] - \log(0.5)$

$\Rightarrow$ $0.51 + \log(0.5) = \log[CH_3COONa]$

$\Rightarrow$ $[CH_3COONa] = 1.618\ M \approx 2$

Competency Enhancer 2.1

A buffer solution of benzoic acid and sodium benzoate has a pH 5.20. If the concentration of sodium benzoate in the buffer is 0.1 M, the concentration of benzoic acid in the buffer is ...... M (Nearest integer).

$[pK_a(C_6H_5COOH) = 4.20]$

Basic Buffer

A solution of a weak base and the salt of weak base is called as a basic buffer e.g. $NH_4OH + NH_4Cl$ etc.

pH of a Basic Buffer

pH of basic buffer is also given by **Henderson-Hasselbalch** equation.

$$pOH = pK_b + \log \frac{[Salt]}{[Base]}$$

$$pH = pK_a \text{ (Conjugate acid)} + \log \frac{[Base]}{[Conjugate\ acid]}$$

and $pH = 14 - pOH$

Buffer Action

When an aqueous solution of weak base (BOH) and its salt (say, BCl) is taken, the solution mainly contain unionised base molecules (BOH) and its (conjugate) acidic form (B^+), due to common ion effect of B^+

$$BOH \rightleftharpoons B^+ + OH^-$$

(dissociation is suppressed by common ion effect of B^+)

$BCl \longrightarrow B^+ + Cl$ (ionises almost completely in water)

Effect of Addition of Acid or Base on Basic Buffer on pH

(i) Addition of H^+ ion into the basic buffer will decrease pH due to increase in the concentration of conjugate acid B^+or BH^+.

$$BOH + H^+ \rightleftharpoons B^+ + H_2O$$

	BOH	B^+	
Initially	C_1	C_2	mol L^{-1}
Added	x		mol L^{-1}
After	$(C_1 - x)$	$(C_2 + x)$	mol L^{-1}

(ii) Addition of OH^- ion into the basic buffer will increase pH due to increase in the concentration of base BOH.

$$B^+ + OH^- \rightleftharpoons BOH$$

	B^+	BOH	
Initially	C_2	C_1	mol L^{-1}
Added		x	mol L^{-1}
After	$(C_2 - x)$	$(C_1 + x)$	mol L^{-1}

(iii) At half neutralisation of the base, where $[BOH] = [B^+]$, $pOH = pK_b$, $pH = 14 - pK_b$.

(iv) Due to dilution, there is no effect on pH

Salt Buffers

A salt buffer is a solution of a salt which itself can act as a buffer. Such salt is the salt of a weak acid and weak base.

For example in an aqueous solution of CH_3COONH_4

$$CH_3COONH_4 \longrightarrow CH_3COO^- + NH_4^+.$$

When acid is added to this solution, CH_3COO^- ion consumes it to give CH_3COOH (Weak Acid) and when a base is added, NH_4^+ ion consumes it to given NH_4OH (Weak Base). Hence it acts as a buffer.

For such solutions, $[H^+] = \sqrt{\frac{K_w K_a}{K_b}}$

and $$pH = \frac{1}{2} pK_w + \frac{1}{2} pK_a - \frac{1}{2} pK_b$$

Buffer Capacity

We measure the effectiveness of a buffer in terms of its **buffer capacity** (β), which is the amount of acid or base that must be added to the buffer to produce a unit change of pH. In other words, it is defined as **the number of moles of acid or base that causes the change in pH of a buffer solution by one unit.**

Buffer capacity

$$= \frac{\text{Number of moles of acid or base added to 1 L of buffer}}{\text{Change in pH}}$$

JEE Spotlite

Buffer capacity of an acidic buffer is maximum when $pH = pK_a$ or [Acid] = [Salt]

(i) Buffer capacity of a basic buffer is maximum when $pOH = pK_b$ or, [Base]= [Salt].

(ii) A solution of weak acid and its salt is regarded as a buffer only when $pH = pK_a \pm 1$ or, $\frac{1}{10} \le \frac{[Salt]}{[Acid]} \le 10$

(iii) A solution of weak base and its salt is regarded as a buffer only when $pOH = pK_b \pm 1$ or, $\frac{1}{10} \le \frac{[Salt]}{[Base]} \le 10$

Applications of Buffer Solution

- Normal blood has pH of 7.4 despite various acid and base producing reaction going on in our body. If blood would not have this buffer nature, we could not eat a veriety of foods and species. This pH is maintained by buffer action of following two buffers
  (i) buffer of carbonic acid (H_2CO_3 and $NaHCO_3$)
  (ii) buffer of phosphoric acid ($H_2PO_4^-$, HPO_4^{2-})
- Buffers are used for the removal of phosphate ion in the qualitative inorganic analysis after second group. For this purpose $CH_3COOH + CH_3COONa$ buffer is used.
- $CH_3COOH + CH_3COONa$ is used for the precipitation of lead chromate quantitatively in gravimetric analysis.
- $NH_4Cl + NH_4OH$ buffer is used for the precipitation of hydroxides of third group of qualitative analysis.
- Buffers find numerous applications in industrial processes, like manufacture of paper, drugs, dyes, inks, paints, electroplating, photographic material etc.
- These are used as preservatives of foods and fruits.

Solved Booster 6.5

1L of a buffer contains 0.17 g $NH_3(aq)$ and 1.32 g $(NH_4)_2SO_4$. The pH value is .... pH. $pK_b(NH_3) = 4.74$

(a) 3.47 (b) 8.96

(c) 8.81 (d) 3.42

Solution *(b)*

(b) It is a case of basic buffer

$$[NH_3] = 0.17 \text{ g L}^{-1} = \frac{0.17\text{g L}^{-1}}{17\text{g mol}^{-1}} = 0.01 \text{ mol L}^{-1}$$

$$[(NH_4)_2SO_4] = 1.32 \text{ g L}^{-1} = \frac{1.32 \text{ g L}^{-1}}{132 \text{ g mol}^{-1}} = 0.01 \text{ mol L}^{-1}$$

but $(NH_4)_2SO_4 \rightleftharpoons 2NH_4^+ + SO_4^{2-}$

0.01 M 0.02 M

$\therefore [NH_4^+]_{buffer} = 0.02$ M

By Henderson – Hasselbalch equation for basic buffer

$$pOH = pK_b + \log\frac{[NH_4^+]}{[NH_3]}$$

$$pOH = 4.74 + \log\frac{0.02}{0.01}$$

$$pOH = 5.04 \Rightarrow pH = 14 - 5.04 = 8.96$$

Acid-Base Titrations

An acid-base titration involves a neutralisation reaction in which an acid is reacted with an equivalent amount of a base. By constructing a titration curve, we can easily explain how the end points of these titrations can be detected. A titration curve is constructed by plotting the pH of the solution as a function of the volume of titrant added. **The titrant is always a strong acid or a strong base. The analyte may be either a strong base or acid or a weak base or acid.**

Titration of Strong Acid *versus* Strong Base

In the case of a strong acid *versus* a strong base, both the titrant and the analyte are completely ionised.

$$\begin{array}{ccccc} HCl & + & NaOH & \longrightarrow & NaCl + H_2O \\ \downarrow & & \downarrow & & \downarrow \end{array}$$

$$H^+ + Cl^- + Na^+ + OH^- \longrightarrow Na^+ + Cl^- + H_2O$$

or

$$H^+ + OH^- \rightleftharpoons H_2O$$

Thus, the neutralisation involves reaction of H^+ with OH^- to form H_2O. As OH^- is added to acid solution, $[H^+]$ decreases $[OH^-]$ increases, hence pH goes on increasing. As the **equivalence point** is approached (the point at which stoichiometric amount of base is added), the $[H^+]$ is rapidly reduced, a neutral solution of NaCl remains and the pH is 7.0. As we continue to add NaOH, the $[OH^-]$ rapidly increases from 10^{-7} M at the equivalence point and levels off between 10^{-2} and 10^{-1} M = $[OH^-]$ used for titration; thus the pH remains fairly constant on either side of the equivalence point figure and there is an inflexion in pH near the equivalence point.

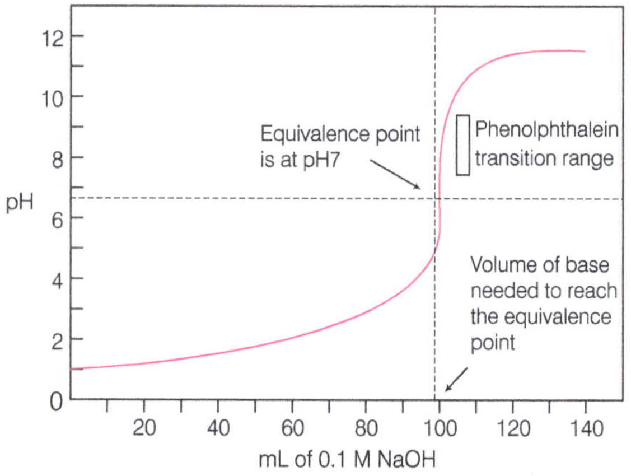

Titration curve for 10 mL 1 M HCl (Analyte) versus 0.1 M NaOH (Titrant)

Since, number of indicators change their colour over this large change in pH and therefore all of these can be used to note the end point.

Concept Visualizer

As the molar concentration of acid decreases, the steep part of the titration curve becomes smaller.

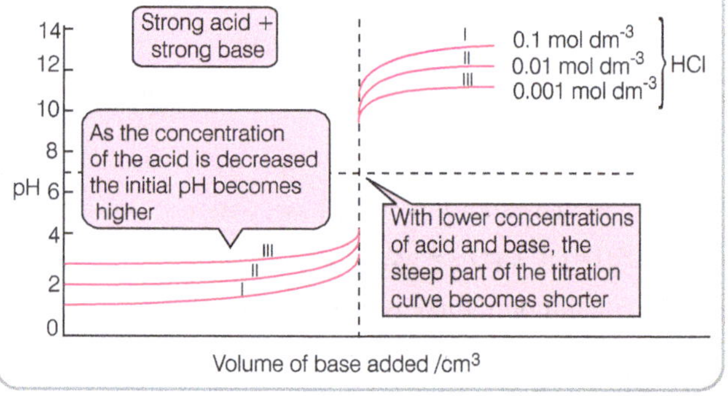

Titration of Weak Acid *versus* Strong Base

The titration curve for 100 mL of 0.1 M AcOH titrated with 0.1 M NaOH is shown in figure.

$$AcOH + NaOH \rightleftharpoons H_2O + AcONa$$

or $$AcOH + OH^- \rightleftharpoons H_2O + AcO^-$$

The acetic acid, which is only a few per cent ionised, depending on the concentration, is neutralised to H_2O and an equivalent amount of the salt, AcONa.

Initially we have 0.1M AcOH and pH is calculated using

$$pH = \frac{1}{2}[pK_a - \log C]$$

As soon as the titration is started, some of AcOH is **converted to AcONa and a buffer system is set up and pH** slowly increases. At the mid-point of the titration,

$$[AcOH] = [AcONa]$$

and, thus pH = $pK_a \cdot Ac\bar{O}Na^+$ is a Bronsted-Lowry base, hence at the equivalence point solution is alkaline.

$$AcO^- + H_2O \rightleftharpoons AcOH + OH^-$$

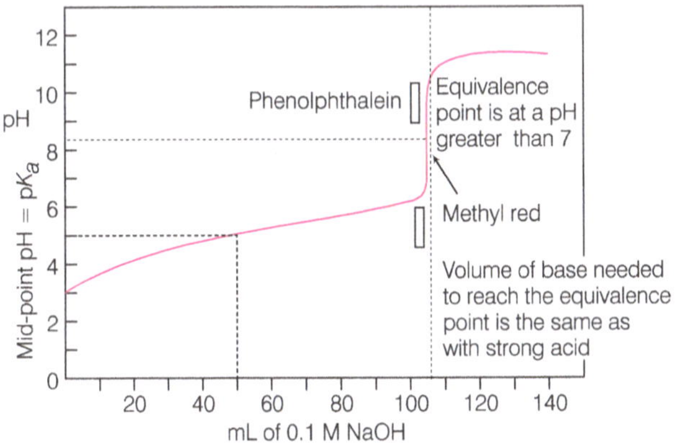

Titration curve for 100 mL 0.1 M AcOH versus 0.1 M NaOH

As excess of NaOH is added beyond the equivalence point, the ionisation of the base AcO^- is decreased to a negligible amount (common ion effect) and the pH is determined only by the excess $[OH^-]$ and titration curve beyond the equivalence point follows that for the titration of a strong acid.

Titration of Weak of Base *versus* Strong Acid

The titration curve of a weak base with a strong acid begins with a high pH, gradually decreases in buffer region, declines more steeply around the equivalence point and then stabilises at a lower pH beyond the equivalence point because of extra amount of strong acid.

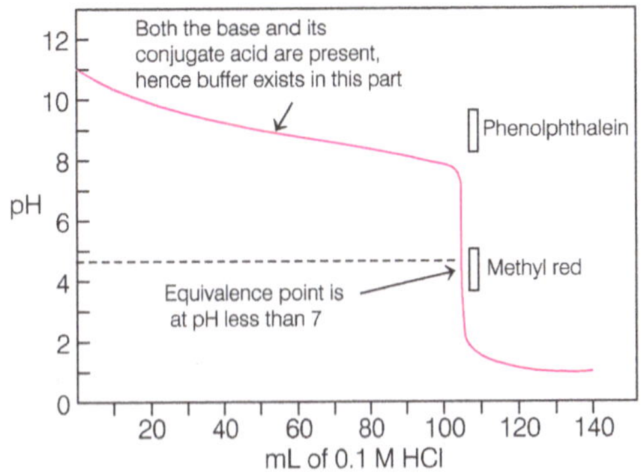

Titration curve for 100 mL NH_3 versus 0.1 M HCl

JEE Spotlite

- In general, weak acids ($K_a \approx 5\times10^{-6}$) should be titrated by using thymol blue, thymolphthalein or phenolphthalein indicators.
  (i) Phenolphthalein and thymolphthalein are not good indicators for titration of 0.1 MNH_3, (weak base).
  (ii) In the titrations using weak acid and strong base, thymolphthalein gives more accurate results than phenolphthalein.
- Weak bases, having $K_b \approx 5.0\times10^{-6}$ may be titrated with strong acids by using bromophenol blue or bromocresol green indicators.
- Very weak bases, having $K_b \approx 10^{-7}$ are titrated against strong acids by using bromophenol blue or methyl orange. In such titrations bromocresol green or methyl red do not give sharp end point.

Solved Booster 6.6

A given indicator when placed in a buffer solution of pH 4.63 was found to exhibit a colour which corresponds to 25% acid and 75% basic form. The pK_a of the indicator.

(a) 8.04×10^{-5} (b) 5.02×10^{-6}

(c) 7.02×10^{-5} (d) 2.07×10^{-7}

Solution *(c)*

Given, pH = 4.63

$\therefore$ $[H^+] = 10^{-4.63} = 2.34\times10^{-5}$ M

If $[In^-] = 75$, $[HIn] = 25$

$$K_{In} = 2.34\times10^{-5}\times\frac{75}{25} = 7.02\times10^{-5}\text{ M}$$

Elemental Practice 6.2

Type I MCQs with Only One Correct Option

1. The pH of 0.2 M $NaHCO_3$ solution at 25°C is 8.2. A 22 mL 2.0 M solution of H_2CO_3 when treated with 80 mL 0.5 M NaOH results into formation of $H_2CO_3 + NaHCO_3$ buffer with pH of 9.6. Hence, pK_{a_2} of H_2CO_3 is
(a) 10.8 (b) 7.8 (c) 9.2 (d) 8.6

2. The pH of 1×10^{-7} M aqueous solution of HCl at 25°C. ($k_w = 10^{-14}$ mol^2 dm^{-6})
(a) 6.79 (b) 5.34
(c) 2.39 (d) 7.34

3. A solution of weak acid *HA* was titrated with base NaOH. The equivalence point was reached when 40 mL of 0.1 M NaOH has been added. Now 20 mL of 0.1 M HCl were added to titrated solution, the pH was found to be 5.0. What will be the pH of the solution obtained by mixing 20 mL of 0.2 M NaOH and 20 mL of 0.2 M *HA*?
(a) 7 (b) 9
(c) 11 (d) None of these

4. When a 20 mL of 0.08 M weak base *BOH* is titrated with 0.08 M HCl, the pH of the solution at the end point is 5. What will be the pOH if 10 mL of 0.04 M NaOH is added to the resulting solution?
[Given: $\log 2 = 0.30$ and $\log 3 = 0.48$]
(a) 5.40 (b) 5.88 (c) 4.92 (d) 3.45

5. In the titration of a solution of a weak acid *HA* and NaOH, the pH is 5.0 after 10 mL of NaOH solution has been added and 5.60 after 20 mL NaOH has been added. The value of pK_a is
(a) 5.15 (b) 5.3 (c) 5.6 (d) 4.2

6. A buffer is 0.01 M each in ethanoic acid and 0.01 M calcium ethanoate. If $[H_3O^+]$ is 9.0×10^{-6}, ionisation constant of ethanoic acid is
(a) 5.55×10^{10} (b) 1.8×10^{-5} (c) 2.0×10^{-9} (d) 9.0×10^{-6}

7. Given below are two statements.
Statement I pH value of acidic buffer solution change, if buffer solution is diluted upto very larger extent.
Statement II If water is heated upto 50°C then pH will decrease and K_w increase with increase in temperature.
In the light of the above statements choose the most appropriate answer from the options given below.
(a) Both Statement I and Statement II are true.
(b) Statement I is true but Statement II is false.
(c) Statement I is false but Statement II is true.
(d) Both Statement I and Statement II are false.

8. 10 mL of H_2A (weak diprotic acid) solution is titrated against 0.1 *M* NaOH. pH of the solution is plotted against volume of strong base added and following observation is made.

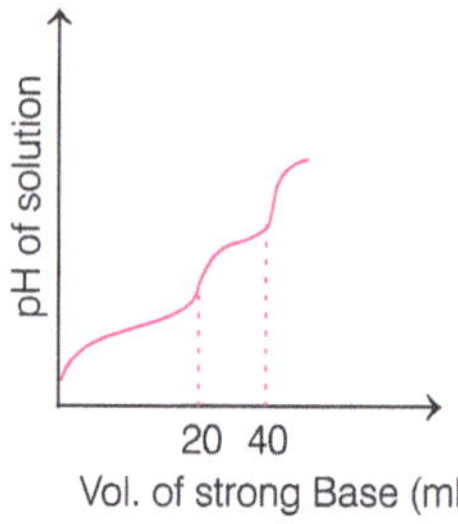

If pH of the solution at first equivalence point is pH_1 and at second equivalence point is pH_2. The value of $(pH_2 - pH_1)$ at 25°C is
Given: For H_2A, $pK_{a_1} = 4.6$ and $pK_{a_2} = 8$, $\log 25 = 1.4$
(a) 2 (b) 5 (c) 3 (d) 4

9. *HX* is a weak acid. It forms salt Na*X* on reacting with caustic soda. If K_a of *HX* is 1×10^{-5}, degree of hydrolysis of 0.1 M Na*X* solution is
(a) 0.01% (b) 0.001% (c) 0.1 % (d) 0.5 %

10. Which of the following is incorrect match?
(a) pK_b of *HX* (K_a of HX = 10^{-6}) → 8
(b) pH of 10^{-8} M HCl → 6.9
(c) pH of 10^{-2} M acetic acid solution (take K_a of acetic acid $= 1.6 \times 10^{-5}$) → 3.4
(d) pOH of a solution obtained by mixing equal volumes of solution with pH 3 and 5 → 10.0

11. The pH of a 0.04 M NH_4Cl solution will be [given, K_b $(NH_4OH) = 10^{-5}$] and $\log 2 = 0.3010$]
(a) 3.10 (b) 3.80
(c) 4.25 (d) 3.50

12. When 0.003 mol of acid is added to 200 ml of a buffer solution, pH decreases by 0.03 units. The buffer capacity of the system is
(a) 0.5 (b) 0.4
(c) 0.7 (d) 0.3

13. 0.1 mol of RNH_2 ($K_b = 5.2 \times 10^{-5}$) is mixed with 0.09 mol of HCl and diluted to 1l. The $[H^+]$ in the solution is
(a) 8×10^{-11} M (b) 1.7×10^{-9} M
(c) 3.4×10^{-12} M (d) 4.8×10^{-8} M

14. The pH of a solution made by mixing 0.1 M NH_3 and 0.1 M $(NH_4)_2SO_4$ is .... (pK_b of $NH_3 = 4.76, \log 2 = 0.3$)
(a) 6.24 (b) 7.32
(c) 8.94 (d) 5.32

15. The pH of a solution obtained by mixing 50 ml of 1 M HCl and 30 mL of 1 M NaOH is $x \times 10^{-3}$. The value of *x* is
(a) 602 (b) 724
(c) 214 (d) 832

Type II 》 MCQs with One of More than One Correct Option

16. Which of the following statement(s) is/are correct?
   (a) The pH of a mixture containing 400 mL of 0.1 M H_2SO_4 and 400 mL of 0.1 M NaOH will be approximately 1.3.
   (b) A monobasic acid with $K_a = 10^{-5}$ has a pH = 5. The degree of dissociation of this acid is 50%.
   (c) Phenolphthalein is pH dependent indicator, remains colourless in acidic solution and given pink colour in basic medium.
   (d) 200 mL of 0.01 M HCl is mixed with 400 ml of 0.01 M H_2SO_4. The pH of the mixture is 3.02.
17. Which of the following statements are correct?
   (a) The conjugate base of $H_2PO_4^-$ is HPO_4^{2-}.
   (b) The pair of solution H_2CO_3, HCO_3^- and CH_3COOH, CH_3COONa forms buffer solution.
   (c) The pH of a solution obtained by mixing 50 mL of 1 M HCl and 30 mL of 1 M NaOH is 0.60.
   (d) Acidic/basic nature of salt solution of a salt of weak acid and weak base depends on K_a and K_b value of acid and base forming it.
18. Which of the following statement(s) is/are correct?
   (a) The pH of 1.0×10^{-8} M solution of HCl is 8.
   (b) On dilution of a buffer solution, ratio of salt and acid remains constant.
   (c) pH will increase slightly on dilution of a buffer because the activity coefficient of salt has been increased by decreasing the ionic strength.
   (d) When a solution of a weak monoprotic acid is titrated against a strong base, at half neutralisation point $pH = \frac{1}{2}(pK_a)$
19. Which of the following statements is/are correct?
   (a) Silver chloride is less soluble in very concentrated sodium chloride solution than in pure water.
   (b) The pH of a buffer solution does not change on addition of small amount of an acid or a base.
   (c) Addition of NH_4Cl does not affect the pH of a solution of NH_4OH
   (d) Degree of hydrolysis of ammonium acetate does not depend upon the concentration of ammonium acetate solution.
20. Which of the following is true for alkaline aqueous solution?
   (a) $pH > \frac{pK_w}{2}$
   (b) pH > pOH
   (c) $pOH < \frac{pK_w}{2}$
   (d) pH = pOH

Type III Numerical/Integer Answer Type Questions

21. Bromothymol blue is an indicator with a K_a value of 6×10^{-5}. The % of indicator in its basic form of pH 5 is ....
22. Amongst the following, the total number of compounds whose aqueous solution turns red litmus paper to blue is NaCN, Na_2SO_4, $(NH_4)_2C_2O_4$, NaCl, $Zn(NO_3)_2$, $FeCl_3$, K_2CO_3, NH_4NO_3, LiCN.
23. A buffer solution contains 0.2 mole of acetic acid and 0.25 mole of potassium acetate per litre. Then, 0.5 ml of 1 M HCl is added to it. The dissociation constant of acetic acid at room temperature is 2.75×10^{-5}. (The volume change on the addition of HCl may be neglected). The change in pH of the solution is ....
24. If the pK_a of acetic acid is 4, then the pH of 0.004 M calcium acetate solution at 25°C is ..... $\times 10^{-1}$. (nearest integer)
25. A certain weak acid has $K_a = 10^{-5}$. If the equilibrium constant for its reaction with a strong base is represented as 1×10^y then the value of y is ....

Elemental Practice 6.2 | Chapter 06

Connect with **Answers**

1. (d)	2. (a)	3. (b)	4. (b)	5. (b)	6. (b)
7. (a)	8. (d)	9. (a)	10. (d)	11. (b)	12. (a)
13. (b)	14. (c)	15. (a)	16. (a,b,c)	17. (a,b,c,d)	18. (b,c)
19. (a,b,d)	20. (a,b,c)	21. (85.7)	22. (3)	23. (0.0019)	24. (79.5)
25. (–19)					

Element 3 Solubility Product and Common Ion Effect

Common Ion Effect

The decrease in the ionisation of a weak electrolyte by the presence of a common ion from a strong electrolyte, is called the common ion effect.

- Ionisation of CH_3COOH (weak acid) is decreased by the addition of CH_3COONa (CH_3COO^- being the common ion)

$$CH_3COOH \rightleftharpoons CH_3COO^- + H^+ \quad \ldots \text{(i)}$$

$$CH_3COONa \longrightarrow CH_3COO^- + Na^+$$

In the presence of CH_3COO^- equilibrium (*A*) shifts in backward direction.

- Solubility of a sparingly soluble salt is decreased by the addition of common ion. Presence of $AgNO_3$ or KCl decreases the solubility of AgCl.

$$AgCl(s) \rightleftharpoons Ag^+(aq) + Cl^-(aq)$$

$$AgNO_3(aq) \longrightarrow \underset{\text{Common ion}}{Ag^+(aq)} + NO_3^-(aq)$$

$$KCl(aq) \longrightarrow K^+(aq) + \underset{\text{Common ion}}{Cl^-(aq)}$$

The common ion effect is thus based on Le-Chatelier's principle in which the stress on the equilibrium that results from raising one of the products concentration is relieved by shifting the equilibrium to the left.

Solved Booster 6.7

A solution contains 0.1 M H_2S and 0.3 M HCl. The product of concentration of S^{2-} and HS^- ions in solution is ..... Given, K_{a_1} and K_{a_2} for H_2S are 10^{-7} and 1.3×10^{-13}, respectively.

(a) 3.4261×10^{-27}

(b) 13.243×10^{-28}

(c) 4.425×10^{-21}

(d) 4.7952×10^{-28}

Solution (*d*)

$$H_2S \rightleftharpoons H^+ + HS^-$$
$$HCl \longrightarrow H^+ + Cl^-$$

H^+ ion is common ion, thus

Total $[H^+] = 0.3$ M (due to HCl only)

$$K_{a_1} = \frac{[H^+][HS^-]}{[H_2S]}$$

$$1 \times 10^{-7} = \frac{(0.3)\,[HS^-]}{(0.1)}$$

$$\therefore \quad [HS^-] = \frac{1 \times 10^{-7}}{3} = 3.33 \times 10^{-8} M$$

$$HS^- \rightleftharpoons H^+ + S^{2-}$$

$$K_{a_2} = \frac{[H^+][S^{2-}]}{[HS^-]}$$

$$H_2S \rightleftharpoons 2H^+ + S^{2-}$$

$$K_a = K_{a_1} K_{a_2} = \frac{[H^+]^2 [S^{2-}]}{[H_2S]}$$

$$\therefore \quad 1 \times 10^{-7} \times 1.3 \times 10^{-13} = \frac{(0.3)^2 [S^{2-}]}{(0.1)}$$

$$\therefore \quad [S^{2-}] \approx 1.44 \times 10^{-20} M$$

Thus, $[HS^-] \times [S^{2-}] = 4.7952 \times 10^{-28}$

Solubility and Solubility Product Constant, (K_{sp})

A solution which remains in contact with excess of the solute is said to be saturated. The amount of a solute, dissolved in a given volume of a solvent (in 1000 mL or in 1 L) to form a saturated solution at a given temperature, is termed as the **solubility** of the solute in the solvent at that temperature.

Certain salts like AgCl, $BaSO_4$, PbS have very low solubility and thus are are called sparingly soluble salts.

For a sparingly soluble salt, ionisation is very small and concentration of the salt may be considered as constant.

Thus, for AgCl.

$$AgCl(s) \rightleftharpoons Ag^+(aq) + Cl^-(aq); \quad K_c = [Ag^+][Cl^-]$$

AgCl (*s*) is not included in K_c.

Instead of writing K_c, we write constant as K_{sp} called the solubility product constant, for the equilibrium between undissolved solute and its ions in a saturated solution.

Thus, $K_{sp} = [Ag^+][Cl^-]$

If S represents solubility of AgCl (in mol L^{-1}), then

$$[Ag^+] = [Cl^-] = S \text{ mol } L^{-1}$$

$$K_{sp} = [Ag^+][Cl^-] = S^2$$

$$S = \sqrt{K_{sp}}$$

"A **solubility product** constant expression is the product of the concentrations of the ions appearing in the chemical equation for a solubility equilibrium, with each term raised to the power given by the coefficient in the chemical equation".

For a solute A_xB_y, (giving $(x + y)$ ions)

$$A_xB_y(s) \rightleftharpoons \underset{xS}{xA^{y+}} + \underset{yS}{yB^{x-}}$$

$$K_{sp} = [A^{y+}]^x[B^{x-}]^y$$

$$= (xS)^x(yS)^y = x^x y^y (S)^{x+y}$$

(i) For $BaSO_4$ (binary solute giving two ions)

$$BaSO_4(s) \rightleftharpoons \underset{S}{Ba^{2+}(aq)} + \underset{S}{SO_4^{2-}(aq)}$$

$$K_{sp} = [Ba^{2+}][SO_4^{2-}] = S^2$$

(ii) For PbI_2 (ternary solute giving three ions)

$$PbI_2(s) \rightleftharpoons \underset{S}{Pb^{2+}(aq)} + \underset{2S}{2I^-(aq)}$$

$$K_{sp} = [Pb^{2+}][I^-]^2$$

$$= (S)(2S)^2 = 4S^3$$

(iii) For $Al(OH)_3$ (quaternary solute giving four ions)

$$Al(OH)_3(s) \rightleftharpoons \underset{S}{Al^{3+}(aq)} + \underset{3S}{3OH^-(aq)}$$

$$K_{sp} = [Al^{3+}][OH^-]^3$$

$$= (S)(3S)^3 = 27S^4$$

Solved Booster 3.2

K_{sp} of silver chromate is 1.1×10^{-12}. Its solubility in presence of 0.01 M K_2CrO_4 is

(a) 3.02×10^{-3} M (b) 2.62×10^{-6} M

(c) 2.04×10^{-7} M (d) 3.17×10^{-3} M

Solution (b)

$$Ag_2CrO_4(s) \rightleftharpoons 2Ag^+(aq) + CrO_4^{2-}(aq)$$

$$K_{sp} = [Ag^+]^2[CrO_4^{2-}]$$

$1.1 \times 10^{-12} = (2S)^2(0.01)$ in presence of 0.01 M K_2CrO_4

($\because S << 0.01$)

$$\therefore \quad S = \frac{\sqrt{1.1 \times 10^{-10}}}{4}$$

$$= 2.62 \times 10^{-6} \text{ M}$$

Applications of Common ion Effect and Solubility Product

1. Precipitation Reactions

For the sparingly soluble solute AB,

$$AB(s) \rightleftharpoons A^+(aq) + B^-(aq)$$

Q is the equilibrium constant with the given $[A^+]$ and $[B^-]$,

$$Q = [A^+][B^-]$$

When applied to solubility product, Q is generally called the ionic product.

- **Precipitation occurs if $Q > K_{sp}$** the solution is said to be supersaturated.
- **Precipitation cannot occur if $Q < K_{sp}$** (a case of unsaturated solution).
- A solution is just saturated if $Q = K_{sp}$.
- **Calculation of Remaining Concentration after Precipitation** Remaining concentration of an ion after precipitation may be calculated as

$$[A^+]_{left} = K_{sp}\frac{[AB]}{[B^-]}$$

JEE Alert

Fractional precipitation of two or more substances is possible only if there is significant difference in the solubilities of the substances being separated (usually this means a significant difference in their K_{sp} values).

2. Solubility of a Solute in a Buffer

Solubility of a solute in acidic and basic buffer can be determined if values of K_{sp} are known. e.g. solubility of $Mg(OH)_2$ in basic buffer of pH = 12 is x mol L^{-1}.

$$pH = 12$$

$$\Rightarrow \quad pOH = 2$$

$$\therefore \quad (OH^-) = 1 \times 10^{-2} \text{ M}$$

$$K_{sp} = [Mg^{2+}][OH^-]^2 = x(10^{-2})^2$$

$$x = 10^4 \times K_{sp}$$

3. Qualitative Analysis and K_{sp}

Qualitative analysis of cation is largely based on the principle of solubility product and common-ion effect. Cations are separated into six groups depending on the solubility of their salts.

Group I As insoluble chloride

Only Ag^+, Hg_2^{2+} and Pb^{2+} form insoluble chlorides since they have low values of K_{sp}.

Group II As insoluble sulphide in acidic medium

K_{sp} values of second group sulphides (PbS, CuS, CdS, SnS, HgS, As_2S_3, Bi_2S_3, Sb_2S_3) are very low.

In acidic buffer, $[S^{2-}]$ is decreased due to common ion effect and this results in the precipitation of Pb^{2+}, Cu^{2+} etc., of second group as their sulphides.

Third and fourth group sulphides have high value of K_{sp}, hence, they remain soluble.

Group III As insoluble hydroxide in basic buffer of NH_4OH and NH_4Cl

The concentration of OH^- in ammoniacal solution decreases when NH_4Cl is added to it, because of the common ion effect. Thus, only for least soluble hydroxides of Fe^{3+}, Al^{3+}, Cr^{3+}, ionic product exceeds the corresponding solubility products, hence only these ions are precipitated.

Hydroxides of successive groups remain soluble due to high K_{sp} values. Infact, cations such as Co^{3+}, Ni^{2+}, Mg^{2+} etc., form complexes with ammonia and thus the amount of free ions in the solution is decreased to a very large extent. Consequently, a larger concentration of OH^- is required to precipitate these ions from the solution as compared to those required for the group III cations.

Group IV Insoluble sulphides in neutral or slightly alkaline medium

It contains Mn^{2+}, Zn^{2+}, Ni^{2+}, Co^{2+} which are precipitated as sulphides. The K_{sp} of these sulphides are high. The required amount of S^{2-} ions are provided by passing H_2S in the presence of NH_4OH. Here, H_2S is dissociated to a larger extent due to alkaline nature of testing solution.

Group V Insoluble carbonates in ammonium carbonate

It contains Mg^{2+}, Ba^{2+}, Sr^{2+} and Ca^{2+} which are precipitated as carbonates by adding an excess of sodium carbonate solution.

Group VI Soluble group/Insoluble phosphates

It contains Mg^{2+}, Na^+ and K^+, Mg^{2+} is precipitated as its phosphate while the remaining ions, if present in the mixture, are identified through flame test.

JEE MAPPER

Example Similar to PYQ Asked in JEE Advanced 2024

The concentration of H_2CO_3 and Na_2CO_3 is a solution is 1 M and 7.6×10^{-4} M, respectively. Molar solubility of $PbCO_3$ in the same solution is $Z \times 10^{-Y}$ M (expressed in scientific notation). The value of Y is ......

[Given, solubility product of $PbCO_3$ (K_{sp}) = 1.6×10^{-5}, For H_2CO_3, K_{a_1}, is very large and $K_{a_2} = 5.6 \times 10^{-5}$]

Sol. (1)

H_2CO_3 ionised as,

	$H_2CO_3 \xrightarrow{K_{a_1}}$	H^+	+ HCO_3^-
$t = 0$	1 M	0	0
$t = t$	0	1 M	1 M

Na_2CO_3 is a salt of weak acid and strong base. It ionises into ions as,

	$Na_2CO_3 \longrightarrow$	$2Na^+$	+ CO_3^{2-}
$t = 0$	7.6×10^{-4}	0	0
$t = t$	0	$(2 \times 7.6 \times 10^{-4})$M	(7.6×10^{-4})M

HCO_3^- is a weak acid its $K_{a_2} = 5.6 \times 10^{-5}$

	$HCO_3^- \rightleftharpoons$	H^+	+ CO_3^{2-}
$t = 0$	1 M	1 M	7.6×10^{-4}
$t = t$	$1 + x = 1$	$1 - x = 1$	$7.6 \times 10^{-4} - x$

$[\because Q_c > K_{a_2}]$

$$K_{a_2} = \frac{[H^+][CO_3^{2-}]}{[HCO_3^-]}$$

$$5.6 \times 10^{-5} = \frac{7.6 \times 10^{-4} - x}{1} \Rightarrow x = 7.04 \times 10^{-4}$$

$$[CO_3^{2-}] = 7.6 \times 10^{-4} - x = 7.6 \times 10^{-4} - 7.04 \times 10^{-4} = 5.6 \times 10^{-5} \text{ M}$$

Let the molar solubility of $PbCO_3$ = S mol/L

$$\underset{}{PbCO_3} \rightleftharpoons \underset{S}{Pb^{2+}} + \underset{S + 5.6 \times 10^{-5}}{CO_3^{2-}} \quad ; \quad K_{sp} = [Pb^{2+}][CO_3^{2-}]$$

$$1.6 \times 10^{-5} = S \times (S + 5.6 \times 10^{-5})$$

Since, $S <<< 5.6 \times 10^{-5} \Rightarrow 1.6 \times 10^{-5} = S \times 5.6 \times 10^{-5}$

$$S = \frac{1.6 \times 10^{-5}}{5.6 \times 10^{-5}} = 0.29 = 2.9 \times 10^{-1}$$

Thus, $Z = 2.9$ and $Y = 1$

Competency Enhancer 3.1

Concentration H_2SO_4 and K_2SO_4 in a solution is 1 M and 2.8×10^{-4} M, respectively. Molar solubility of $PbSO_4$ in the same solution is $P \times 10^{-N}$ M (expressed in scientific notation). The value of N is ....

[Given, solubility product of $PbSO_4$(K_{sp}) = 1.6×10^{-8}, for H_2SO_4, K_{a_1} is very large and $K_{a_2} = 1.2 \times 10^{-4}$]

Elemental Practice 6.3

Type I MCQs with Only One Correct Option

1. For a sparingly soluble salt AB_2, the equilibrium concentrations of A^{2+} ions and B^- ions are 2.1×10^{-3} M and 0.31×10^{-2} M respectively. The solubility product of AB_2 is
(a) 0.31×10^{-10} (b) 4.31×10^{-6}
(c) 1.38×10^{-4} (d) 2.02×10^{-8}

2. A 0.150 M Na_2SO_4 solution also saturated with Ag_2SO_4 has $[Ag^+] = 9.7\times 10^{-3}$ M. What is the value of K_{sp} for Ag_2SO_4?
(a) 2×10^{-13} (b) 1.85×10^{-4} (c) 1.41×10^{-5} (d) 3.16×10^{-6}

3. Given below are two statements.
Statement I If solubility of $BaSO_4$ in aqueous solution is 1×10^{-5} M, then the solubility in 0.1 M $BaCl_2$ will more than 1×10^{-5} M.
Statement II If K_{sp} of $Ni(OH)_2$ is 2.0×10^{-15} then the molar solubility of $Ni(OH)_2$ in 0.1 M NaOH is 2×10^{-13} M.
(a) Both statement I and statement II are correct.
(b) Statement I is correct but statement II is incorrect.
(c) Both statement I and statement II are incorrect.
(d) Statement I in incorrect but statement II is correct.

4. If solubility of AgCl (*s*) in water, 0.05 $AgNO_3$, 0.05 NaCl and in 0.01 M $CaCl_2$ be represented as S_1, S_2, S_3 and S_4. ($K_{sp} = 1\times 10^{-10}$) then
(a) $S_1 = S_2 = S_3 = S_4$ (b) $S_2 < S_2 = S_3 < S_4$
(c) $S_4 < S_3 < S_2 < S_1$ (d) $S_2 = S_3 < S_4 < S_1$

5. In a saturated solution of the sparingly soluble $AgIO_3$ (283 g mol^{-1}), the equilibrium which sets in is
$$AgIO_3(s) \rightleftharpoons Ag^+(aq) + IO^-_3(aq)$$
Given, K_{sp} ($AgIO_3 = 1.0\times 10^{-8}$)
Mass of $AgIO_3$ present in 100 mL of saturated solution is
(a) 28.3×10^{-2} g (b) 2.83×10^{-3} g
(c) 1.0×10^{-7} g (d) 1.0×10^{-4} g

6. Given below are two statements one is labelled as Assertion (A) and the other one is labelled as Reason (R).
Assertion (A) The solubility in water of a sparingly soluble salt AB_2 is 1.0×10^{-5} mol L^{-1}. Its solubility in presence of 0.1 M A^{2+} ion is 2.0×10^{-7} M.
Reason (R) In the presence of 0.1 M A^{2+}, solubility is decreased due to common ion effect.
(a) A is true but R is false.
(b) Both A and R are true but R is not the correct explanation of A.
(c) Both A and R are true and R is the correct explanation of A.
(d) A is false but R is true.

7. The solubility product of the salt $Al(OH)_3$ in water at 298 K is 2.7×10^{-11}. The concentration of Al^{3+} in saturated aqueous solution of the salt is
(a) 5.7×10^{-6} M (b) 5.7×10^{-4} M
(c) 1.0×10^{-4} M (d) 1.0×10^{-3} M

8. Solubility of $Mg(OH)_2$ in 0.1 M CH_3COONa is
[K_{sp} of $Mg(OH)_2 = 1.8\times 10^{-11}$, K_a (CH_3COOH) $= 1.8\times 10^{-5}$, $pK_a = 4.74$]
(a) 0.33 M (b) 0.66 M (c) 1.0×10^{-2} M (d) 1.8×10^{-3} M

9. H_2S is passed into 1 dm^3 of a solution containing 0.1 mole of Zn^{2+} and 0.01 mole of the Cu^{2+} till the sulphide ion concentration reaches 8.1×10^{-19} mole. Which one of the following statements is true? [K_{sp} of ZnS and CuS are 3×10^{-22} and 8×10^{-36}, respectively].
(a) Only ZnS precipitates
(b) Both CuS and ZnS precipitate
(c) Only CuS precipitate
(d) No precipitation occurs

10. A solution is found to contain $[Cl^-] = 1.5\times 10^{-1}$ M; $[Br^-] = 5.0\times 10^{-4}$ M; $[CrO_4^{2-}] = 1.9\times 10^{-2}$ M.
A solution of $AgNO_3$ (100% dissociated) is added to the above solution drop by drop. Which silver salt will precipitate first?
Given :$K_{sp}(AgCl) = 1.5\times 10^{-10}$, $K_{sp}(AgBr) = 5.0\times 10^{-13}$, $K_{sp}(Ag_2CrO_4) = 1.9\times 10^{-12}$)
(a) AgCl (b) Ag_2CrO_4
(c) AgCl and AgBr together (d) AgBr

11. One litre of saturated CaC_2O_4 solution required 200 mL of 1×10^{-4} M $KMnO_4$ solution in acidic medium. What is the value of K_{sp} for CaC_2O_4?
(a) 4.0×10^{-10} (b) 5.0×10^{-5}
(c) 3.0×10^{-9} (d) 2.5×10^{-9}

12. K_{sp} of $BaSO_4$ is 1.1×10^{-10}. In which case is $BaSO_4$ precipitated?
(a) 100 mL of 4×10^{-3} M $BaCl_2$ + 300 mL of 6.0×10^{-4} M Na_2SO_4
(b) 100 mL of 4×10^{-4} M $BaCl_2$ + 300 mL of 6.0×10^{-8} M Na_2SO_4
(c) 300 mL of 4×10^{-4} M $BaCl_2$ + 100 mL of 6.0×10^{-8} M Na_2SO_4
(d) In all cases

13. The solubility of $Ca(OH)_2$ in water is [Given: The solubility product of $Ca(OH)_2$ in water $= 5.4\times 10^{-9}$]
(a) 1.10×10^{-3} (b) 1.25×10^{-9}
(c) 2.10×10^{-4} (d) 2.06×10^{-3}

14. For a sparingly soluble salt AB_2, the equilibrium concentration of A^{2+} ions and B^- ions are 1.6×10^{-4} M and 0.4×10^{-3} M, respectively. The solubility product of AB_2 is
(a) 6.91×10^{-12} (b) 2.34×10^{-10}
(c) 2.56×10^{-11} (d) 3.42×10^{-12}

15. The K_{sp} for arsenic sulphide (+ 3) is 2.08×10^{-78}. Then, the solubility of arsenic sulphide in mol L^{-1} at 298 K is ....
(a) 3.4×10^{-10} (b) 1.14×10^{-16} (c) 1.0×10^{-15} (d) 4.2×10^{-8}

Type II 》 MCQs with One or More than One Correct Option

16. Which of the following statements are incorrect?
(a) If pH of a saturated solution of $Ba(OH)_2$ is 12 then the value of its K_{sp} is 6×10^{-7} M^3.
(b) At 25°C the solubility product of Hg_2Cl_2 in water is 3.2×10^{-17} mol^3 dm^{-9} then the solubility of Hg_2Cl_2 in water at 25°C is 4×10^{-6} M.
(c) The K_{sp} value of zirconium phosphate is $6912S^7$.
(d) For a salt to be able to dissolve in a particular solvent its solvation enthalpy must be greater than its lattice enthalpy.

17. Which of the following statements are correct?
(a) Solubility of AgBr increase in presence of common anion.
(b) Solubility of $Zn(OH)_2$ in acidic solution is less than that in pure water and in strongly basic solution is more than that in pure water.
(c) Solubility of $Fe(OH)_3$ in acidic solution is more that in pure water solubility decreases in presence of common anion.
(d) Solubility of AgCN in water is more than expected and solubility in acidic solution is more than that in pure water.

18. A solution containing a mixture of 0.05 M NaCl and 0.05 M NaI is taken. (K_{sp} of AgCl = 10^{-10} and K_{sp} of AgI = 4×10^{-16}). When $AgNO_3$ is added to such a solution.
(a) The concentration of $Ag^{\oplus}$ required to precipitate $Cl^{\ominus}$ is 2×10^{-9} mol L^{-1}.
(b) The concentration of $Ag^{\oplus}$ required to precipitate $I^{\ominus}$ is 8×10^{-15} mol L^{-1}.
(c) AgCl and AgI will be precipitate together.
(d) First AgCl will be precipitated.

19. Which of the following statements are correct regarding the given data—a solution of 0.01 M Fe^{2+} in a saturated H_2S solution and (i) 0.2 M of $H^{\oplus}$ (ii) 0.001 M of $H^{\oplus}$. (K_1 and K_2 of $H_2S = 10^{-21}$, K_{sp} FeS $= 3.7 \times 10^{-19}$)?
(a) FeS will precipitate in solution (i)
(b) FeS will not precipitate in solution (i)
(c) FeS will precipitate in solution (ii)
(d) FeS will not precipitate in solution (ii)

20. Which is/are correct statement(s) about the solubility of AgCl(*s*)?
Given: $K_{sp(AgCl)} = 10^{-10}$; $K_f[Ag(NH_3)_2^{\oplus}] = 10^8$
(a) Solubility of AgCl in 2 M NH_3 is 0.166 M
(b) Solubility of AgCl in 2 M $AgNO_3$ is 5×10^{-11} M
(c) Solubility of AgCl in 2 M KBr is 10^{-5} mol/L
(d) Solubility of AgCl in pure water is 143.5×10^{-5} gL^{-1}

Type III 》 Numerical/Integer Answer Type Questions

21. The solubility products of NiC_2O_4 and Na_3AlF_6 are the same at 298 K ($K_{sp} = 4 \times 10^{-10}$). Then the solubility of Na_3AlF_6 is *x* times more soluble than NiC_2O_4. The value of *x* is ....

22. A particular water sample has 136 ppm $CaSO_4$ ($K_{sp} = 9.0 \times 10^{-6}$). If 1L of this water is boiled in a tea kettle, how much water must be evaporated before $CaSO_4(s)$ begins to precipitate? (Assume solubility is temperature independent in working stage)

23. A solution is a mixture of 0.05 M NaCl and 0.05 M NaI. The concentration of iodide ion in the solution when AgCl starts precipitating is equal to $x \times 10^{-7}$ M [Given : $K_{sp}(AgCl) = 1 \times 10^{-10}$, $K_{sp}(AgI) = 4 \times 10^{-16}$]

24. A 2.0 L kettle contains 14.92 g of boiler scale ($CaCO_3$). This can be removed by dissolving $CaCO_3$ in distilled water based on solubility of $CaCO_3$ in water. If this process of filling the kettle is repeated 100 *n* times, what is the value of *n* (Nearest integer)? ($K_{sp}(CaCO_3) = 8.7 \times 10^{-9}$)

25. For a sparingly soluble salt A_2B, $K_{sp} = 1 \times 10^{-16}$. What is the value of OP in the graph of pK_A *vs* pK_B at constant temperature?
($pK_A = -\log[A^+]$, $pK_B = -\log[B^{2-}]$)

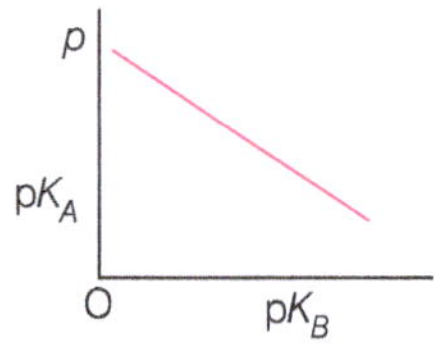

26. 25 mL of 0.060 M, $Ca(NO_3)_2$ is mixed with 25 mL of 0.030 M NaF. K_{sp} of CaF_2 is 0.6×10^{-4} at 298 K. The ratio of $[Ca^{2+}][F^-]^2$ and K_{sp} is .... $\times 10^{-4}$ (Nearest integer).

Elemental Practice 6.3 | Chapter 06

Connect with **Answers**

1. (d)	2. (c)	3. (d)	4. (c)	5. (b)	6. (c)
7. (d)	8. (a)	9. (b)	10. (c)	11. (d)	12. (a)
13. (a)	14. (c)	15. (b)	16. (a,b)	17. (c,d)	18. (a,b)
19. (b,c)	20. (a,b,c,d)	21. (100)	22. (667)	23. (2)	24. (8)
25. (8)	26. (1125)				

Advanced Exclusive Different Strokes

Tips to solve problems related to Solubility of Salts

(i) Solubilities of AgCl (salt of a strong acid and strong base) in water:

AgCl would dissolve in water as,

$$AgCl(s) \rightleftharpoons Ag^+(aq) + Cl^-(aq)$$

If the solubility of the salt is x moles/l

$\therefore [Ag^+] = x$ M, $[Cl^-] = x$ M

$\Rightarrow \quad x^2 = K_{sp}$

$x = \sqrt{K_{sp}}$

(ii) Solubility of AgCl in a solution that is having 0.1 M in $AgNO_3$:

AgCl would dissolve and finally reach saturation.

$$AgCl(s) \rightleftharpoons Ag^+(aq) + Cl^-(aq)$$

The K_{sp} of AgCl is approximately 10^{-10}. If AgCl were to be dissolved in water (pure), its solubility would have been 10^{-5} M (as explained in (i)). In the presence of 0.1 M $AgNO_3$, its solubility will decreases due to common ion effect. This means that $[Ag^+]$ from AgCl would be less than 10^{-5} M. Hence, we can ignore the contribution of Ag^+ from AgCl.

If the solubility of AgCl is x' moles / l in the presence of 0.1 M $AgNO_3$, then

$[Ag^+] = 0.1$ M, $[Cl^-] = x'M$

$\therefore \quad x' = \dfrac{K_{sp}}{0.1} = 10^{-9}$ moles / l

(iii) Solubility of CH_3COOAg (salt of weak acid and strong base) in water:

CH_3COOAg dissolves and reaches saturation. Since it is a salt of weak acid and strong base, it would hydrolyse. If the solubility of the salt is x moles/ l then

$$CH_3COOAg(s) \rightleftharpoons \underset{x-y}{CH_3COO^-(aq)} + \underset{x}{Ag^+(aq)}$$

At equ. $\quad x - y \quad x$

$$CH_3COO^-(aq) + H_2O \rightleftharpoons CH_3COOH(aq) + OH^-(aq)$$

At equ. $\quad x - y \qquad y \qquad y$

where y is the amount of CH_3COO^- ion that is hydrolysed.

$\therefore \qquad (x - y)x = K_{sp}$

$$\frac{y^2}{(x-y)} = \frac{K_w}{k_a}$$

Knowing the values of K_{sp} and K_a, solubility of the salt can be calculated.

(iv) Solubility of CH_3COOAg (salt of a weak acid and strong base) in an acid buffer of pH = 4 (assuming that the buffer does not have any common ion with CH_3COOAg):

CH_3COOAg would dissolve and reach equilibrium. It would then be hydrolysed. If the solubility of the salt is x' M in this solution, then

At equ. $CH_3COOAg(s) \rightleftharpoons \underset{x'-y'}{CH_3COO^-(aq)} + \underset{x'}{Ag^+(aq)}$

$$\underset{x'-y'}{CH_3COO^-(aq)} + \underset{10^{-4}}{H^+} \rightleftharpoons \underset{x'}{CH_3COOH(aq)}$$

Since the solution is a buffer, the pH will be maintained.

$(x' - y')x' = K_{sp}$

$$\frac{y'}{10^{-4} \times (x'-y')} = \frac{1}{K_a}$$

Since in presence of basic buffer, the degree of hydrolysis will be suppressed by already existing ^-OH ions, therefore the approximated formula which can be used is

$x'^2 = K''_{sp}$ ((CH_3COOAg) (neglecting y'')

Knowing K_{sp} and K_a, the solubility can be calculated.

(v) Solubility of CH_3COOAg in an buffer solution of pH = 9

Following the same logic as give in the earlier section,

$$CH_3COOAg(s) \rightleftharpoons CH_3COO^-(aq) + Ag^+(aq)$$

At. equ. $\quad x'' - y'' \quad x''$

$$CH_3COO^-(aq) + H_2O \rightleftharpoons CH_3COOH + OH^-$$

At eq: $\quad x'' - y'' \qquad y'' \qquad 10^{-5}$

where x'' M is the solubility of the salt and y'' the extent to which it is hydrolysed.

$\therefore \qquad (x'' - y'')x'' = K_{sp}$

$$\frac{y'' \times 10^{-5}}{(x''-y'')} = \frac{K_w}{K_a}$$

Knowing, K_{sp} and K_a, the solubility can be calculated.

Conclusion

- The solubility of salts depends on the nature of the salt and the solution it is dissolved in.
- Common ion effect can significantly reduce the solubility of a salt.
- Buffer solutions can affects the solubility of salts, especially those of weak acids or bases.
- Problems based on solubility of salts in buffer and common ion effect have frequently appeared in JEE advanced.

PRACTICE
ELEMENT 01

Target JEE Main

Objective Type Questions

1. 200 mL of an aqueous solution of HCl (pH = 2) is mixed with 300 mL of an aqueous solution of NaOH (pH = 12). Thus, pH of the resultant mixture is
(a) 14.0
(b) 10.2
(c) 7.9
(d) 11.3

2. A solution is 0.1 M with respect to Ag^+, Ca^{2+}, Mg^{2+} and Al^{3+} which will precipitate at lowest concentration of $[PO_4^{3-}]$ when solution of Na_3PO_4 is added?
(a) Ag_3PO_4 ($K_{sp} = 1 \times 10^{-6}$)
(b) $Ca_3(PO_4)_2$ ($K_{sp} = 1 \times 10^{-33}$)
(c) $Mg_3(PO_4)_2$ ($K_{sp} = 1 \times 10^{-24}$)
(d) $AlPO_4$ ($K_{sp} = 1 \times 10^{-20}$)

3. The silver ion in a solution is precipitated by the addition of chloride ion.
$Ag^+(aq) + Cl^-(aq) \rightleftharpoons AgCl(s)$, $K = 1 \times 10^{-10}$.
The final volume of the solution is 500 mL. At a point when not more than 0.10 mg of Ag^+ ion remains unprecipitated, $[Cl^-]$ ion is
(a) 5.4×10^{-5} M
(b) 1.9×10^{-6} M
(c) 5.4×10^{-4} M
(d) 1.9×10^{-7} M

4. K_{sp} of Ag_2CrO_4, AgCl, AgBr and AgI are respectively 1.1×10^{-12}, 1.8×10^{-10}, 5.0×10^{-13} and 8.3×10^{-17}. Which one of the following salts will precipitate last if $AgNO_3$ solution is added to the solution containing equal moles of NaCl, NaBr, NaI and Na_2CrO_4?
(a) AgCl
(b) AgBr
(c) Ag_2CrO_4
(d) AgI

5. Titration curve if a strong base is titrated with strong acid is

(a) 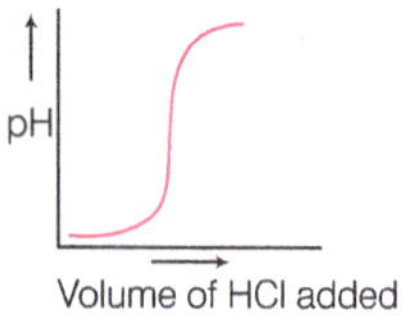

(b) 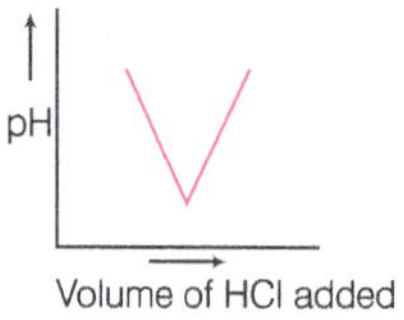

(c) 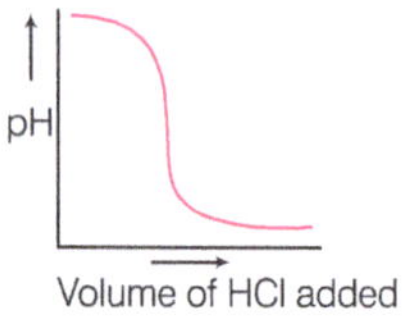

(d) 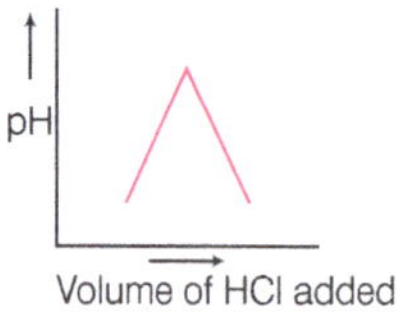

6. Given, $H_2S + H_2O \rightleftharpoons H_3O^+ + HS^-$, $K_{a_1} = 9.1 \times 10^{-8}$
$HS^- + H_2O \rightleftharpoons H_3O^+ + S^{2-}$, $K_{a_2} = 1.2 \times 10^{-13}$
Thus, $[S^{2-}]$ in the presence of 0.1 M HCl due to 0.1 M H_2S is
(a) 1.10×10^{-20} M
(b) 1.32×10^{-6} M
(c) 1.02×10^{-27} M
(d) 1.10×10^{-19} M

7. Given below are two statements.
Statement I pK_{a_1} and pK_{a_2} of H_2SO_3 are 1.82 and 7.20 respectively. pH after addition of 20 mL of 0.160 M NaOH is added to in 40 mL of 0.080 M H_2SO_3 is 4.51.
Statement II The acid ionisation (hydrolysis) constant of Zn^{2+} is 1.0×10^{-9} then, the pH of 0.001 M solution of $ZnCl_2$ is 3.
(a) Both Statement I and Statement II are correct.
(b) Statement I is correct but Statement II is incorrect.
(c) Both Statement I and Statement II are incorrect.
(d) Statement I is incorrect but Statement II is correct.

8. The solubility product of a salt having formula M_2X_3 is 2.2×10^{-20}. If the solubility of an another salt having formula M_2X is twice the molar solubility of M_2X_3, then solubility product of M_2X is
(a) 3×10^{-12}
(b) 9.16×10^{-5}
(c) 4.58×10^{-5}
(d) 2.76×10^{-18}

9. K_a of HCN and CH_3COOH are respectively 4.5×10^{-10} and 1.5×10^{-5} at 298K.
Thus, equilibrium constant for
$CN^- + CH_3COOH \rightleftharpoons CH_3COO^- + HCN$ would be
(a) 3.1×10^5
(b) 3.2×10^{-5}
(c) 3.3×10^{-4}
(d) 3.3×10^4

10. pH of the blood (which is 7.40) is controlled by $H_2PO_4^-$ and HPO_4^{2-}. pK_a of $H_2PO_4^-$ is 7.10. What is the ratio of $\dfrac{[H_2PO_4^-]}{[HPO_4^{2-}]}$ in the blood?
(a) 2 : 1
(b) 1 : 2
(c) 3 : 1
(d) 1 : 3

11. A 50.00 mL sample of acetic acid was titrated with 0.12 M KOH and 38.62 mL of base were required to reach the equivalence point. What was the pH of the titration mixture, when 19.31 mL of base has been added? [pK_a (acetic acid) = 4.74]
(a) 2.94
(b) 3.54
(c) 4.74
(d) 5.74

12. The atmospheric SO_2 concentration over a certain region is 0.12 ppm by volume. Assuming 100% ionisation as
$H_2O + SO_2 \rightleftharpoons H^+ + HSO_3^-$
pH of rain water (acid rain) due to this pollution is
(a) 5.73 (b) 3.92
(c) 8.27 (d) 10.08

13. 1 M NH_4OH and 1 M HCl are mixed to make total volume of 300 mL. If pH of the mixture is 9.26 and $pK_a(NH_4^+) = 9.26$ then volume ratio of NH_4OH and HCl will be
(a) 1:1 (b) 1:2 (c) 2:1 (d) 3:1

14. A buffer solution of pH 9.80 is to be prepared from 1M NH_4Cl and 1M NH_3 solution. pK_b of NH_3 is 4.74. In 1L of the buffer solution, volume of NH_4Cl is
$[\log(0.288) = -0.54]$
(a) 200 mL (b) 775 mL (c) 500 mL (d) 224 mL

15. The average concentration of SO_2 in the atmosphere over a city on a certain day is 10 ppm, when the average temperature is 298K. Given that the solubility of SO_2 in water at 298K is 1.3653 mol L^{-1} and pK_a of H_2SO_3 is 1.92, estimate the pH of rain on that day.
(a) 4.56 (b) 3.81 (c) 6.12 (d) 2.37

16. What concentration of free CN^- must be maintained in a solution that is 1.8 M $AgNO_3$ and 0.327 M NaCl to prevent AgCl(*s*) from precipitating?
Given, $K_{sp}[AgCl(s)] = 1.8 \times 10^{-10}$
$Ag^+(aq) + 2CN^-(aq) \rightleftharpoons Ag(CN)_2^-(aq); K_f = 5.6 \times 10^{18}$
(a) 3.61×10^{-3} M (b) 6.31×10^{-2} M
(c) 4.33×10^{-1} M (d) 2.42×10^{-5} M

17. Saturated $CaC_2O_4(aq)$ is prepared and 250.0 mL of the solution is withdrawn and titrated with 6.3 mL of 0.00102 M $KMnO_4(aq)$. What is the value of K_{sp} for CaC_2O_4? The titration reaction is
$5C_2O_4^{2-}(aq) + 2MnO_4^-(aq) + 16H^+(aq) \longrightarrow$
$2Mn^{2+}(aq) + 8H_2O(l) + 10CO_2(g)$
(a) 4.13×10^{-9} (b) 5.38×10^{-11}
(c) 12.36×10^{-10} (d) 6.31×10^{-6}

18. The partial pressure of CO_2 in air saturated with water vapour at 25°C and 1.00 atm is 3.04×10^{-4}atm. Henry's constant for CO_2 in water is 2.3×10^{-2} mol L^{-1}atm^{-1} and for carbonic acid pK_a is 6.37. Calculate pH of normal (CO_2 mixed) rain water.
(a) 3.41 (b) 6.31 (c) 5.76 (d) 2.31

19. Given the following thermodynamic quantities. Calculate the dissociation constant for
$$NH_4OH \rightleftharpoons NH_4^+ + OH^- \text{ at } 25°C.$$

Reaction	$\Delta H°$, kJ mol^{-1}	$\Delta S°$, JK^{-1} mol^{-1}
$NH_3 + H^+ \longrightarrow NH_4^+$	− 52.2	+ 1.67
$H_2O \longrightarrow H^+ + OH^-$	56.6	− 78.20

(a) 1.7×10^{-5} (b) 3.1×10^{-2}
(c) 4.31×10^{-1} (d) 2.31×10^{-5}

20. Given below are two statements one is labelled as Assertion (A) and the other is labelled as Reason (R).
Assertion (A) The higher order ionisation constants are smaller than the lower order ionisation constant of a polyprotic acid.
Reason (R) It is more difficult to remove a positively charged proton from a negative ion due to electrostatic forces.
(a) Both A and R are true and R is the correct explanation of A.
(b) A is true but R is false.
(c) A is false but R is true.
(d) Both A and R are true but R is not the correct explanation of A.

Numerical Type Questions

21. 0.3 moles of a weak acid $HA(K_a = 3.0 \times 10^{-6})$ is dissolved in 1.0 L of 0.1 M HCl solution. The degree of dissociation of *HA* is $x \times 10^{-5}$ (Round off to the nearest integer).
[Neglect volume change on adding *HA*. Assume degree of dissociation << 1]

22. The molar solubility of $Zn(OH)_2$ in 1 M ammonia solution at room temperature is $x \times 10^{-5}$ mol dm^{-3}. The value of *x* is ....
$[K_{sp}\ [Zn(OH)_2] = 1.8 \times 10^{-17}; K_{stab}$ of $[Zn(NH_3)_4]^{2+}$
$= 1.64 \times 10^{10}$.]

23. The pH of an aqueous solution obtained by mixing 25 ml of 0.2 M HCl with 50 ml of 0.25 M NaOH .....
[Take $k_w = 10^{-14}$ mol^2 dm^{-6} at 25°C]

24. Solubility product of silver bromide is 4.0×10^{-12}. The quantity of potassium bromide (molar mass taken as 120 g mol^{-1}) to be added to 1 L of 0.03 M solution of silver nitrate to start the precipitation of AgBr is $x \times 10^{-12}$ g. The value of *x* is .... [upto nearest integer]

25. The self ionisation equilibrium of pure formic acid $2HCOOH \rightleftharpoons HCOOH_2^+ + HCOO^-$ has ionisation product $K = 10^{-6}$ mol^2/lit^2 at 298 K. If percentage ionisation is 4×10^{-5}. The density of acid in g/mL is $Z \times 10^{-1}$. The value of *Z* is

26. The pH of 0.2 M solution of NH_4Cl is ...... Given K_b for NH_4OH is 1.8×10^{-5}. (nearest integer)

27. A solution is a mixture of 0.05 M NaCl and 0.05 M NaI. The concentration of iodide ion in the solution when AgCl just start precipitating is equal to $x \times 10^{-7}$. (K_{sp}AgCl $= 1 \times 10^{-10}$ M^2; K_{sp} AgI $= 4 \times 10^{-16}$ M^2). The value of *x* is ....

28. A weak monoatomic base is titrated against HCl of 0.3 M and end point has reached on adding 20 mL of the acid. To this solution, 120 mg of NaOH if added. The pH of the resulting solution is $x \times 10^{-1}$. The value of *x* is [pK_b of the base 4.2]

29. For a sparingly soluble salt AB_2, the equilibrium concentration of A^{2+} ions and B^- ions are 1.3×10^{-4} M and 0.3×10^{-2} M, respectively. The solubility product of AB_2 is ..... $\times 10^{-11}$.

30. The K_{sp} for bismuth sulphide (+3) is 1.08×10^{-73}. The solubility of bismuth sulphide in mol L^{-1} at 298 K is ...... $\times 10^{-15}$.

Check Through PYQs

Element 1 Ostwald's Dilution Law and Concept of Acids and Bases

1. K_{a_1}, K_{a_2} and K_{a_3} are the respective ionisation constants for the following reactions A, B, and C.

A. $H_2C_2O_4 \rightleftharpoons H^+ + HC_2O_4^-$

B. $HC_2O_4^- \rightleftharpoons H^+ + C_2O_4^{2-}$

C. $H_2C_2O_4 \rightleftharpoons 2H^+ + C_2O_4^{2-}$

The relationship between K_{a_1}, K_{a_2} and K_{a_3} is given as *2022, 25 July Shift-II*

(a) $K_{a_3} = K_{a_1} + K_{a_2}$ (b) $K_{a_3} = K_{a_1} - K_{a_2}$
(c) $K_{a_3} = K_{a_1} / K_{a_2}$ (d) $K_{a_3} = K_{a_1} \times K_{a_2}$

2. Given below are two statements one is labelled as Assertion (A) and the other is labelled as Reason (R).

Assertion (A) The amphoteric nature of water is explained by using Lewis acid/base concept.

Reason (R) Water acts as an acid with NH_3 and as a base with H_2S.

In the light of the above statements choose the correct answer from the options given below: *2022, 25 June Shift-II*

(a) Both A and R are true and R is the correct explanation of A.
(b) Both A and R are true but R is not the correct explanation of A.
(c) A is true but R is false.
(d) A is false but R is true.

3. Assuming that $Ba(OH)_2$ is completely ionised in aqueous solution under the given conditions the concentration of H_3O^+ ions in 0.005 M aqueous solution of $Ba(OH)_2$ at 298 K is ...... $\times 10^{-12}$ mol L^{-1}. (Nearest integer) *2021, 25 July Shift-II*

4. 0.01 moles of a weak acid HA ($K_a = 2.0 \times 10^{-6}$) is dissolved in 1.0 L of 0.1 M HCl solution. The degree of dissociation of HA is ...... $\times 10^{-5}$ (Round off to the nearest integer).

[Neglect volume change on adding HA. Assume degree of dissociation << 1] *2021, 17 March Shift-I*

Element 2 pH, Buffer and Indicators, Salt Hydrolysis

5. Given below are two statements: *2024, 8 April Shift-II*

Statement I A buffer solution is the mixture of a salt and an acid or a base mixed in any particular quantities.

Statement II Blood is naturally occurring buffer solution whose pH is maintained by $H_2CO_3/HCO_3^{\ominus}$ concentrations.

In the light of the above statements, choose the correct answer from the options given below:

(a) Statement I is false but Statement II is true.
(b) Both Statement I and Statement II are true.
(c) Both Statement I and Statement II are false.
(d) Statement I is true but Statement II is false.

6. K_a for CH_3COOH is 1.8×10^{-5} and K_b for NH_4OH is 1.8×10^{-5}. The pH of ammonium acetate solution will be .... *2024, 1st Feb Shift-I*

7. The pH of an aqueous solution containing 1 M benzoic acid ($pK_a = 4.20$) and 1 M sodium benzoate is 4.5. The volume of benzoic acid solution in 300 mL of this buffer solution is ...... mL. (Given, $\log 2 = 0.3$) *2024, 30 Jan Shift-II*

8. Given below are two statements: *2024, 27 Jan Shift-I*

Statement I Aqueous solution of ammonium carbonate is basic.

Statement II Acidic/basic nature of salt solution of a salt of weak acid and weak base depends on K_a and K_b value of acid and the base forming it.

In the light of the above statements, choose the most appropriate answer from the options given below.

(a) Statement I is correct but Statement II is incorrect.
(b) Statement I is incorrect but Statement II is correct.
(c) Both Statement I and Statement II are correct.
(d) Both Statement I and Statement II are incorrect.

9. 20 mL of 0.1 M NaOH is added to 50 mL of 0.1 M acetic acid solution. The pH of the resulting solution is .... $\times 10^{-2}$. (Nearest integer)

Given, pK_a (CH_3COOH) = 4.76

$\log 2 = 0.30$

$\log 3 = 0.48$ *2023, 13 April Shift-II*

10. If the pK_a of lactic acid is 5, then the pH of 0.005 M calcium lactate solution at 25°C is .... $\times 10^{-1}$. (Nearest integer)

Lactic acid 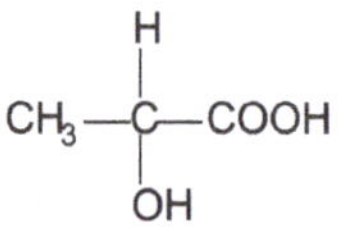

2023, 24 Jan Shift-II

11. Class XII students were asked to prepare one litre of buffer solution of pH 8.26 by their chemistry teacher. The amount of ammonium chloride to be dissolved by the student in 0.2 M ammonia solution to make one litre of the buffer is (Given, pK_b (NH_3) = 4.74, Molar mass of NH_3 = 17 gmol^{-1}, Molar mass of NH_4Cl = 53.5 g mol^{-1}) *2022, 26 July Shift-II*

(a) 53.5 g (b) 72.3 g (c) 107.0 g (d) 126.0 g

12. 50 mL of 0.1 M CH_3COOH is being titrated against 0.1 M NaOH. When 25 mL of NaOH has been added, the pH of the solution will be ...... $\times 10^{-2}$. (Nearest integer)

[Given, pK_a (CH_3COOH) = 4.76]
$\log 2 = 0.30$, $\log 3 = 0.48$, $\log 5 = 0.69$,
$\log 7 = 0.84$, $\log 11 = 1.04$ *2022, 26 June Shift-I*

13. The OH^- concentration in a mixture of 5.0 mL of 0.0504 M NH_4Cl and 2 mL of 0.0210 M NH_3 solution is $x \times 10^{-6}$ M. The value of x is .... (Nearest integer)

[Given $K_w = 1 \times 10^{-14}$ and $K_b = 1.8 \times 10^{-5}$]
2021, 26 Aug Shift-I

14. In order to prepare a buffer solution of pH 5.74, sodium acetate is added to acetic acid. If the concentration of acetic acid in the buffer is 1.0 M, the concentration of sodium acetate in the buffer is .... M. (Round off to the nearest integer).

[Given, pK_a (acetic acid = 4.74] *2021, 18 March Shift-I*

15. The solubility of AgCN in a buffer solution of pH = 3 is x. The value of x is

[Assume : No cyano complex is formed;
$K_{sp}(AgCN) = 2.2 \times 10^{-16}$ and $K_a(HCN) = 6.2 \times 10^{-10}$]
2021, 25 Feb Shift-I

(a) 1.9×10^{-5} (b) 1.6×10^{-6}
(c) 2.2×10^{-16} (d) 0.625×10^{-6}

16. Arrange the following solutions in the decreasing order of pOH.
(A) 0.01 M HCl
(B) 0.01 M NaOH
(C) 0.01 M CH_3COONa
(D) 0.01 M NaCl *2020, 6 Sep Shift-I*
(a) (A) > (C) > (D) > (B) (b) (A) > (D) > (C) > (B)
(c) (B) > (C) > (D) > (A) (d) (B) > (D) > (C) > (A)

17. 100 mL of 0.1M HCl is taken in a beaker and to it 100 mL of 0.1 M NaOH is added in steps of 2 mL and the pH continuously measured. Which of the following graphs correctly depicts the change in pH? *2020, 3 Sep Shift-II*

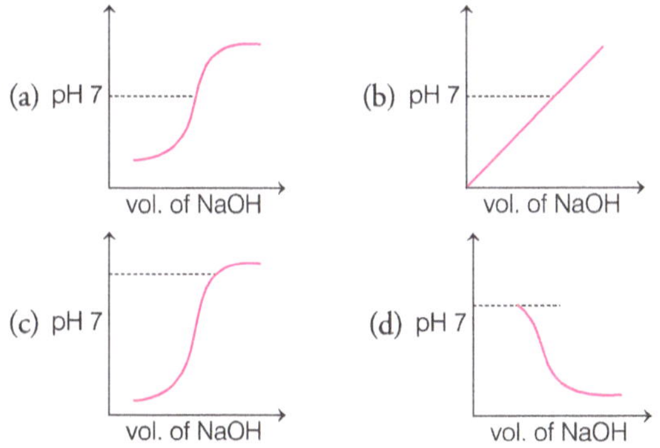

18. The strength of an aqueous NaOH solution is most accurately determined by titrating (Note; consider that an appropriate indicator is used) *2020, 8 Jan Shift-I*

(a) Aq. NaOH in a volumetric flask and concentrated H_2SO_4 in a conical flask
(b) Aq. NaOH in a pipette and aqueous oxalic acid in a burette
(c) Aq. NaOH in a burette and aqueous oxalic acid in a conical flask
(d) Aq. NaOH in a burette and concentrated H_2SO_4 in a conical flask

19. 3 g of acetic acid is added to 250 mL of 0.1 M HCl and the solution made up to 500 mL. To 20 mL of this solution 1/2 mL of 5 M NaOH is added. The pH of the solution is ....

[Given, pK_a of acetic acid = 4.75, molar mass of acetic acid = 60 g/mol, log 3 = 0.4771]

Neglect any changes in volume. *2020, 7 Jan Shift-II*

20. Two solutions, *A* and *B*, each of 100 L was made by dissolving 4 g of NaOH and 9.8 g of H_2SO_4 in water, respectively. The pH of the resultant solution obtained from mixing 40 L of solution *A* and 10 L of solution *B* is .... *2020, 7 Jan Shift-I*

Element 3 Solubility Product and Common Ion Effect

21. If the K_{sp} of $Cr(OH)_3$ is 1.6×10^{-30} M^4. The molar solubility of salt in water is 1.56×10^{-x}, then value of x is
2025, 24 Jan Shift-I
(a) 6 (b) 8 (c) 10 (d) 4

22. pH of water is 7 at 25°C, then the pH of water at 80°C will .... *2025, 23 Jan Shift-II*
(a) Increases
(b) Decreases
(c) H^+ increases, OH^- decreases
(d) Remains constant

23. For a sparingly soluble salt AB_2, the equilibrium concentrations of A^{2+} ions and B^- ions are 1.2×10^{-4} M and 0.24×10^{-3} M, respectively. The solubility product of AB_2 is *2024, 9 April Shift-II*
(a) 0.069×10^{-12} (b) 6.91×10^{-12}
(c) 0.276×10^{-12} (d) 27.65×10^{-12}

24. At 298 K, the solubility of silver chloride in water is 1.434 $\times 10^{-3}$ g L^{-1}. The value of $-\log K_{sp}$ for silver chloride is ....

(Given, mass of Ag is 107.9 g mol^{-1} and mass of Cl is 35.5 g mol^{-1}) *2023, 31 Jan Shift-II*

25. At 310 K, the solubility of CaF_2 in water is 2.34×10^{-3} g/100 mL. The solubility product of CaF_2 is ...... $\times 10^{-8} (mol/L)^3$.

(Given, molar mass of CaF_2 = 78 g mol^{-1}) *2022, 27 July Shift-I*

26. A_3B_2 is a sparingly soluble salt of molar mass M (g mol^{-1}) and solubility x g L^{-1}. The solubility product satisfies $K_{sp} = a\left(\frac{x}{M}\right)^5$. The value of a is .... (Integer answer)
2021, 31 Aug Shift-I

27. A solution is 0.1 M in Cl^- and 0.001 M in CrO_4^{2-}. Solid $AgNO_3$ is gradually added to it.
Assuming that the addition does not change in volume and $K_{sp}(AgCl) = 1.7 \times 10^{-10}\ M^2$ and $K_{sp}(Ag_2CrO_4) = 1.9 \times 10^{-12}\ M^3$
Select correct statement from the following *2021, 20 July Shift-II*
(a) AgCl precipitates first because its K_{sp} is high.
(b) Ag_2CrO_4 precipitates first as its K_{sp} is low.
(c) Ag_2CrO_4 precipitates first because the amount of Ag^+ needed is low.
(d) AgCl will precipitate first as the amount of Ag^+ needed to precipitate is low.

28. Two salts A_2X and MX have the same value of solubility product of 4.0×10^{-12}. The ratio of their molar solubilities i.e $\frac{S(A_2X)}{S(MX)} = \ldots\ldots$ (Round off to the nearest integer)
2021, 16 March Shift-I

29. For the following Assertion and Reason, the correct option is
Assertion (A) When Cu (II) and sulphide ions are mixed, they react together extremely quickly to give a solid.
Reason (R) The equilibrium constant of $Cu^{2+}(aq) + S^{2-}(aq) \rightleftharpoons CuS(s)$ is high because the solubility product is low. *2020, 2 Sep Shift-I*
(a) Both (A) and (R) are false.
(b) Both (A) and (R) are true and (R) is the explanation for (A).
(c) Both (A) and (R) are true but (R) is not the explanation for (A).
(d) (A) is false and (R) is true.

30. The solubility product of $Cr(OH)_3$ at 298 K is 6.0×10^{-31}. The concentration of hydroxide ions in a saturated solution of $Cr(OH)_3$ will be *2020, 9 Jan Shift-II*
(a) $(2.22 \times 10^{-31})^{1/4}$
(b) $(18 \times 10^{-31})^{1/4}$
(c) $(4.86 \times 10^{-29})^{1/4}$
(d) $(18 \times 10^{-31})^{1/2}$

31. The stoichiometry and solubility product of a salt with the solubility curve given below is, respectively : *2020, 8 Jan Shift-I*

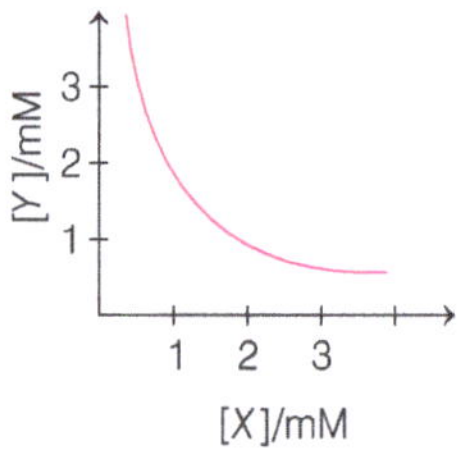

(a) X_2Y, $2 \times 10^{-9}\ M^3$
(b) XY, $2 \times 10^{-6}\ M^3$
(c) XY_2, $1 \times 10^{-9}\ M^3$
(d) XY_2, $4 \times 10^{-9}\ M^3$

PRACTICE ELEMENT 02
Target JEE Advanced

Single Correct Choice MCQs

1. In the following mixtures of acids and bases.
A : 100 mL of 1 M HCl + 100 mL of 0.5 M $Ca(OH)_2$
B : 100 mL of 1 M NaOH + 100 mL of 0.5 M H_2SO_4
C : 100 mL of 1 M NH_4OH + 100 mL of 1 M HCl
D : 100 mL of 1 M NaOH + 100 mL of 1 M CH_3COOH
neutral solutions are
(a) A and B
(b) C and D
(c) A and D
(d) A, B and C

2. Given below are two statements,
Statement I For the reaction,
$Hg^{2+} + 2Cl^- \rightleftharpoons HgCl_2, K = 1.65 \times 10^{13}$
Concentration of Hg^{2+} at the equivalence point in the titration of 2.0 m mol of Hg^{2+} with Cl^- when final volume is 100 mL is 2.87×10^6 M.
Statement II 0.1 mole of CH_3NH_2 ($K_b = 5 \times 10^{-4}$) is mixed with 0.08 mole of HCl and diluted to 1 L then, the $[H^+]$ concentration in the solution is 8×10^{-11} M.
(a) Statement I is correct but Statement II is incorrect.
(b) Both Statement I and Statement II are correct.
(c) Statement I is incorrect but Statement II is correct.
(d) Both Statement I and Statement II are incorrect.

3. The "fixing" of photographic film involves dissolving unexposed silver bromide in a thiosulphate (called hypo) solution.
$AgBr(s) + 2S_2O_3^{2-}(aq) \rightleftharpoons Ag(S_2O_3)_2^{3-}(aq) + Br^-(aq)$
Calculate equilibrium constant K for the dissolution reaction, and the molar solubility of AgBr(s) in 0.10 M $Na_2S_2O_3$ respectively.
[Given: $K_{sp}(AgBr) = 5.4 \times 10^{-13}$; $K_f[Ag(S_2O_3)_2^{3-}] = 2.9 \times 10^{13}$]
(a) 15.66, 0.044×10^{-2} M
(b) 13.31, 2.34×10^{-4} M
(c) 15.66, 4.44×10^{-2} M
(d) 13.31, 0.023×10^{-4} M

4. Calcium lactate is salt of a weak acid represented as $Ca(Lac)_2$. Its saturated solution contain 0.13 mole in 0.50 L solution and pH is 8.4. Assume complete dissociation of the salt, pK_a of the lactic acid is
(a) 6.16
(b) 3.084
(c) 10.92
(d) 5.80

5.

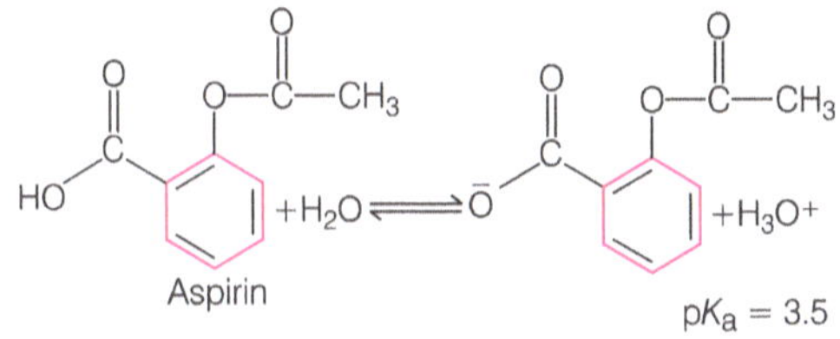

The pH of gastric juice in human stomach is about 2.3 and that in small intestine is about 8. Thus, aspirin will be

(a) unionised in the small intestine and in the stomach
(b) completely ionised in the small intestine and in the stomach
(c) ionised in the stomach and almost unionised in the small intestine
(d) ionised in the small intestine and almost unionised in the stomach

6. Given, $H_2CO_3 \rightleftharpoons H^+ + HCO_3^-, K_{a_1} = 4.3 \times 10^{-7}$

and $HCO_3^- \rightleftharpoons H^+ + CO_3^{2-}, K_{a_2} = 4.8 \times 10^{-11}$

Thus, fraction of carbonate present as H_2CO_3 in the solution of pH 10.00, is

(a) 3.2×10^{-4} (b) 4.6×10^{-4}
(c) 2.3×10^{-4} (d) 1.6×10^{-4}

7. A volume of 50.00 mL of a weak acid of unknown concentration is titrated with 0.10 M solution of NaOH. The equivalence point is reached after 39.30 mL of NaOH solution has been added. At the half-equivalence point (19.65 mL), the pH is 4.85. Thus, initial concentration of the acid and its pK_a values are

	$[HA]_{initial}$	pK_a
(a)	0.1 M	4.85
(b)	0.079 M	4.85
(c)	0.1 M	3.70
(d)	0.079 M	2.93

8. To precipitate as $Ag_2S(s)$, all the Ag^+ ions present in 338 mL of a saturated solution of $AgBrO_3$ requires 30.4 mL of $H_2S(g)$ measured at 23°C and 748 mm Hg. Thus, K_{sp} of $AgBrO_3$ is

$2Ag^+(aq) + H_2S(g) \longrightarrow Ag_2S(s) + 2H^+(aq)$

(a) 5.3×10^{-5} (b) 6.0×10^{-6}
(c) 7.3×10^{-3} (d) 2.5×10^{-3}

9. Given, $H_2S(aq) + H_2O(l) \rightleftharpoons H_3O^+(aq) + HS^-(aq)$;

$K = 9.1 \times 10^{-8}$ and for

$FeS(s) + H_2O(l) \rightleftharpoons Fe^{2+}(aq) + HS^-(aq) + OH^-(aq)$;

$K = 5 \times 10^{-19}$

Thus, molar solubility of FeS(s) in a buffer solution of pH = 3.0 in which $[H_2S]$ is fixed at 0.1 M, is

(a) 5.5×10^{-3} M
(b) 1.2×10^{-2} M
(c) 9.1×10^{-8} M
(d) 7.9×10^{-7} M

10. Following is the titration curve of CH_3COOH against NaOH added with phenolphthalein as the indicator.

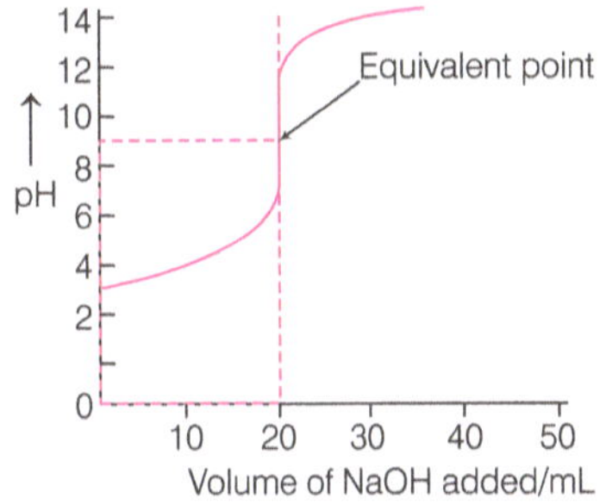

K_{In} value of phenolphthalein is 4.0×10^{-10}. Thus, incorrect statement is

(a) it begins to change colour from the pH 9.4
(b) it begins to change colour from acid colourless at pH 8.4 to the base form (reddish pink) at pH10.4
(c) phenolphthalein is suitable indicator for CH_3COOH — NaOH titration.
(d) phenolphthalein is a weak acid

More than One Correct Choice MCQs

11. Given, K_{sp} of AgCl = 1×10^{-10}. Select the correct statement(s).

(a) $p_{Ag} + p_{Cl} = 10$
(b) $p_{Cl} = 8$ in 0.01 M Ag^+
(c) $p_{Ag} + p_{Cl} < 10$ in the presence of Ag^+
(d) $p_{Ag} = p_{Cl} = 5$ in saturated AgCl solution

12. The concentration of sulphide ion in 0.1 M HCl solution saturated with H_2S is 1.0×10^{-19} M. If 10 mL of this solution is added to 5 mL of 0.04 M solution of the following.

$MnCl_2$	K_{sp} of MnS 2.5×10^{-13}
$ZnCl_2$	K_{sp} of ZnS 16×10^{-21}
$CdCl_2$	K_{sp} of CdS 8.0×10^{-27}
$CuSO_4$	K_{sp} of CuS 6.3×10^{-36}

in which of these solutions precipitation will take place?

(a) Mn^{2+} (b) Zn^{2+} (c) Cd^{2+} (d) Cu^{2+}

13. K_{sp} of $BaSO_4$ is 1.1×10^{-10}. In which case(s) $BaSO_4$ is/are precipitated?

(a) 100 mL of 4×10^{-3} M $BaCl_2$ + 300 mL of 6.0×10^{-4} M Na_2SO_4
(b) 100 mL of 4×10^{-4} M $BaCl_2$ + 300 mL of 6.0×10^{-8} M Na_2SO_4
(c) 300 mL of 4×10^{-4} M $BaCl_2$ + 100 mL of 6.0×10^{-8} M Na_2SO_4
(d) 300 mL of 4×10^{-4} M $BaCl_2$ + 300mL of 6.0×10^{-4} M Na_2SO_4

14. Select the correct statement(s).

Given, K_{sp} of LiOH = 1×10^{-6}; $Mg(OH)_2 = 1 \times 10^{-12}$

$Al(OH)_3 = 1 \times 10^{-27}$; $Si(OH)_4 = 1 \times 10^{-28}$

(a) $pH(LiOH) = p_{Li} + 8$ (b) $pH[Mg(OH)_2] = p_{Mg} + 8$
(c) $pH[Al(OH)_3] = \frac{p_{Al}}{3} + 5$ (d) $pH[Si(OH)_4] = \frac{p_{Si}}{4} + 7$

15. Select the correct fact(s) about H_3BO_3.
(a) It is weak monobasic acid
(b) It ionises as $H_3BO_3 \rightleftharpoons H^+ + H_2BO_3^-$
(c) It does not donate protons but accepts OH^-, thus it is a Lewis acid $B(OH)_3 + 2H_2O \rightleftharpoons [B(OH)_4]^- + H_3O^+$
(d) It is a tribasic acid

16. The buffer capacity (β) for a weak acid conjugate base buffer is defined as the number of moles of strong acid or strong base needed to change the pH of 1 L solution by 1 pH unit and is

$$\beta = \frac{2.303(C_A + C_B)K_a[H^+]}{([H^+] + K_a)^2}$$

where, C_A = molar concentration of weak acid
C_B = molar concentration of conjugate base
Which of the following statements are correct regarding the given data?
(a) The best buffering action will occur when pH = pK_a + 10.
(b) If $C_A = C_B$, then the value of β will be $\frac{2.303C_A}{2}$.
(c) The best buffering action will occur when $P_H = P_{K_a}$
(d) If $C_A = C_B$, then the value of β will be $\frac{2.303C_B}{2}$.

17. Which of the following statement(s) is/are correct?
(a) The value of K_w is temperature independent.
(b) The pH of a mixture containing 400 mL of 0.1 M H_2SO_4 and 400 mL of 0.1 M NaOH will be approximately 1.3.
(c) The pH of a 0.02 M NH_4Cl solution will be 5.35 if $K_b(NH_4OH) = 10^{-5}$ and log 2 = 0.301.
(d) pH value of 0.001 M NaOH solution is 9.

18. Which of the following expression for % dissociation of a monoacidic base (BOH) in aqueous solution at appreciable concentration is correct?
(a) $100 \times \sqrt{\frac{K_b}{c}}$
(b) $\frac{1}{1 + 10^{(pK_b - pOH)}}$
(c) $\frac{K_w[H^+]}{K_b + K_w}$
(d) $\frac{K_b}{K_b + [OH^-]}$

Numerical/Integer Type Questions

19. A 0.1 M solution of $[Cu(NH_3)_4]^+$ is stirred with an excess of potassium cyanide sufficient to convert all the ammonium complex to the corresponding cuprocyanide complex $[Cu(CN)_4]^{3-}$ and in addition to provide the solution with an excess of CN^- equal to 0.2 M. Calculate the maximum pH of the solution when the final solution is treated with hydrogen sulphide to maintain $[H_2S] = 0.1$ M and the precipitation of cuprous sulphide is prevented.
Given: The instability constant for $[Cu(CN)_4]^{3-}$ is 6.4×10^{-15}, K_a overall of $H_2S = 1.6 \times 10^{-21}$, K_{sp} of $Cu_2S = 2.56 \times 10^{-27}$.

20. A solution of weak acid was titrated with base NaOH. The equivalence point was reached when 36.12 ml of 0.1 M NaOH have been added. Now, 18.06 ml of 0.1 M HCl was added to the titrated solution, the pH was found to be 5.0. The pK_a of acid is ....

21. What is the sum of magic numbers of all solutions given below:
[Given: Magic number of a solution = pH of solution × weight factor]

	Solution	Weight Factor
A.	0.1 M HCN ($K_a = 10^{-10}$)	3
B.	0.1 M CH_3COOH + 0.1 M CH_3COONa ($K_a = 10^{-3}$)	2
C.	0.1 M HCl	3
D.	0.1 M NH_4OH ($K_b = 10^{-5}$)	2
E.	10 ml of 0.1 M CH_3COOH + 10 mL of 0.1 M NH_4OH	1

22. Fixed volume of 0.1 M benzoic acid ($pK_a = 4.2$) solution is added into 0.2 M sodium benzoate solution and formed a 300 mL, resulting acidic buffer solution. If pH of the resulting solution is 3.9, then added volume of benzoic acid is .... mL.

23. 3 g of acetic acid is added to 250 mL of 0.1 M HCl and the solution made up to 500 mL. To 20 mL of this solution 1/2 mL of 5 M NaOH is added. The pH of the solution is ....
[Given: pK_a of acetic acid = 4.75, molar mass of acetic acid = 60 g/mol, log 3 = 0.4771] Neglect any change in volume.]

24. In an attempted determination of the solubility product constant of Tl_2S, the solubility of this compound in pure CO_2 free water was determined as 2.0×10^{-6} M. Assume that the dissolved sulphide hydrolyses almost completely to HS^- and that the further hydrolysis to H_2S can be neglected, the value of computed K_{sp} is .... $\times 10^{-23}$.
[Given: for H_2S, $K_{a_1} = 1.4 \times 10^{-7}$, $K_{a_2} = 1.0 \times 10^{-14}$]

25. The K_{sp} of $K_2C_2O_4$ is 1.2×10^{-10} at 298 K. The solubility (in mol/L) of $K_2C_2O_4$ in a 0.1 M KNO_3 solution is $y \times 10^{-10}$.

26. The solubility of a salt of weak acid (AB) at pH 4 is mol L^{-1}. The value of Z is ....$\times 10^{-4}$ (Given that the value of solubility product of $AB(K_{sp}) = 3 \times 10^{-12}$ and the value of ionisation constant of $HB(K_a) = 2 \times 10^{-8}$.

Matching Type Questions

27 Compare the buffer in Column-I with their pH in Column-II and select the answer from the codes.
($pK_a(CH_3COOH) = 4.74$)

	Column-I		Column-II
i	0.05 M $(CH_3COO)_2Ca$ + 0.10 M CH_3COOH	p.	7.0
ii	50 mL of 0.10 M CH_3COOH + 25 mL of 0.10 M NaOH	q.	8.72
iii	50 mL of 0.10 M CH_3COOH + 50 mL of 0.10 M NaOH	r.	4.74
iv	50 mL of 0.1 M CH_3COOH + 100 mL of 0.1 M NaOH	s.	12.52

Codes

	i	ii	ii	iv		i	ii	ii	iv
(a)	r	r	q	s	(b)	q	r	p	s
(c)	r	p	q	s	(d)	s	p	q	r

28. 0.01 M phthalic acid, $C_6H_4(COOH)_2$ is being titrated with 0.01 M KOH. Compare the different stages as given in Column-I with the pH values of these stages in Column-II and select answer from the codes. ($pK_{a_1} = 2.89$, $pK_{a_2} = 5.41$)

	Column-I		Column-II
i	pH at the first half equivalence point	p.	8.47
ii	pH at the first equivalence point	q.	5.41
iii	pH at the second half equivalence point	r.	4.15
iv	pH at the second equivalence point	s.	2.89

Codes

	i	ii	ii	iv		i	ii	ii	iv
(a)	p	q	r	s	(b)	s	r	q	p
(c)	p	s	r	q	(d)	q	p	s	r

29. pK_a of different acids are given below.

Acid	pK_a
NH_4^+	9.26
CH_3COOH	4.74
C_6H_5COOH	4.20
HCN	9.21
$C_6H_5NH_3^+$	4.62

Match the species (salt) given in Column-I with their corresponding pH of 0.1 M solutions given in Column-II.

	Column-I		Column-II
i	$CH_3COONH_4^+$	p.	8.6
ii	C_6H_5COOK	q.	11.1
iii	$C_6H_5NH_3^+Cl^-$	r.	7.00
iv	NaCN	s.	2.81

Codes

	i	ii	ii	iv		i	ii	ii	iv
(a)	r	q	p	s	(b)	s	r	q	p
(c)	p	q	r	s	(d)	r	p	s	q

30. 100 mL of 0.01 M CH_3COOH is titrated with 0.01M KOH. Match the pH of the solution mixture in given Column-II with the stages of addition of KOH given in Column-I.
[$pK_a(CH_3COOH) = 4.74$]

	Column-I		Column -II
i	25 mL	p.	8.22
ii	50 mL	q.	4.26
iii	75 mL	r.	4.74
iv	100 mL	s.	5.22

Codes

	i	ii	ii	iv		i	ii	ii	iv
(a)	p	s	r	q	(b)	s	p	q	r
(c)	s	p	r	q	(d)	q	r	s	p

31. K_{sp} values of silver salts have been given

AgCl	1.8×10^{-10}
Ag_2CrO_4	1.1×10^{-12}
Ag_2S	6.0×10^{-51}
Ag_3AsO_4	1.0×10^{-22}

Match $[Ag^+]$ of the species in column-I with their values in Column-II.

	Column-I		Column-II
i	AgCl	p.	4.16×10^{-6} M
ii	Ag_2CrO_4	q.	2.28×10^{-17} M
iii	Ag_2S	r.	1.30×10^{-4} M
iv	Ag_3AsO_4	s.	1.34×10^{-5} M

Codes

	i	ii	ii	iv		i	ii	ii	iv
(a)	s	r	q	p	(b)	s	r	p	q
(c)	s	p	q	r	(d)	p	q	r	s

Paragraph 1

Acid-base indicators are either weak organic acids or weak organic bases. Indicator change colour in dilute solution when the hydronium ion concentration reaches a particular value. For example, phenolphthalein is a colourless substance in any aqueous solution with a pH less than 8.3. In between the pH range 8.3 to 10, transition of colour (colourless to pink) takes place and if pH of solution is greater than 10 solution is dark pink. Considering an acid indicator HIn, the equilibrium involving it and its conjugate base In can be represented as:

$$\underset{\text{acidic form}}{HIn} \rightleftharpoons H^+ + \underset{\text{basic form}}{In^-}$$

pH of solution can be computed as:

$$pH = pK_{In} + \log \frac{[In^-]}{[HIn]}$$

In general, transition of colour takes place in between the pH range $pK_{In} \pm 1$.

In titration curve of two weak acids HA and HB (5 milli-moles each) titrated agaisnt the strong base NaOH (0.1 M)

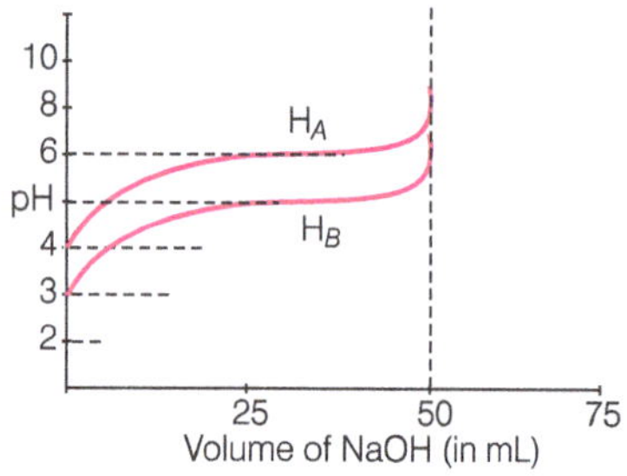

32. The pH at equivalent point when HB is titrated with NaOH.
33. The equilibrium constant for the reaction.
$HB(aq.) + NaA(aq.) \rightleftharpoons HA(aq.) + NaB(aq.)$ is

Paragraph 2

25 mL of a dilute aqueous solution of *p*-hydroxy benzoic acid is titrated with NaOH(*aq*). The solution has pH = 4.57 when 8.12 mL of 0.02 M NaOH had been added and pH = 7.02 when 16.24 mL of 0.02 M NaOH had been added (the equivalence point).

34. The value of pK_a of the following acid at first ionisation stage is

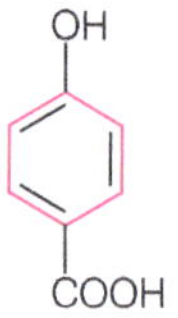

35. The value of pK_a at the second ionisation of the following acid?

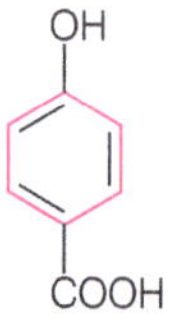

Paragraph 3

Read the following passage and answer the questions at the end of it:

Phosphoric acid is of great importance in fertilizer production. Besides, phosphoric acid its various salts have a number of applications in metal treatment, food, detergent and toothpaste industries.

$$pK_{a_1} = 2.12, pK_{a_2} = 7.21, pK_{a_3} = 12.32$$

Small quantities of phosphoric acid are extensively used to impart the sour or tart taste to many soft drinks such as colas and roots beers, in which a density of 1.00 g mL^{-1} contains 0.05% by weight of phosphoric acid.

Phosphoric acid is used as a fertilizer for agriculture, and an aqueous soil digesting 1.00×10^{-3} M phosphoric acid is found to have pH = 7. Zinc is an essential micro-nutrient for plant growth. Plants can absorb zinc in water soluble form only. In the given soil, zinc phosphate is only the source of zinc and phosphate ions. K_{sp} (Zinc phosphate) $= 9.1 \times 10^{-33}$.

36. Molar concentration of phosphates ion in the soil with pH = 7 is ......
37. Concentration of $[Zn^{2+}]$ in the soil is ....

Species selection (with 5 species)

38. Consider the following species,
(i) Glycine (ii) Salicyclic acid
(iii) Sulphanilic acid (iv) Anthranilic acid
(v) Acetic acid
The species which have Lowry-Bronsted acid as well as Lowry Bronsted base character
(a) 1 (b) 2
(c) 4 (d) 3
39. Among the given reactions,
(i) $AlCl_3 + Cl^- \longrightarrow AlCl_4^-$
(ii) $SO_2 + OH^- \longrightarrow HSO_3^-$
(iii) $NH_3 + B(CH_3)_3 \longrightarrow NH_3 \cdot B(CH_3)_3$
(iv) $2NH_3 + Ag^+ \longrightarrow Ag(NH_3)_2^+$
(v) $Cr^{3+} + 6H_2O \longrightarrow [Cr(H_2O)_6]^{3+}$
The total number of reactions which have the same lewis base are
(a) 3 (b) 1 (c) 2 (d) 4
40. Consider the following reactions,
(i) $H_2CO_3(aq) + HSO_4^-(aq) \rightleftharpoons H_2SO_4(aq) + HCO_3^-(aq)$
(ii) $HF(aq) + Cl^-(aq) \rightleftharpoons HCl(aq) + F^-(aq)$
(iii) $HF(aq) + NH_3(aq) \rightleftharpoons NH_4^+(aq) + F^-(aq)$
(iv) $HSO_4^-(aq) + CN^-(aq) \rightleftharpoons HCN(aq) + SO_4^{2-}(aq)$
(v) $NH_4^+(aq) + CN^-(aq) \rightleftharpoons NH_3(aq) + HCN(aq)$
The reactions which proceed towards the right are
(a) 1 (b) 3 (c) 2 (d) 4
41. Consider the following species:
$BCl_3, AlCl_3, SiCl_4, PH_3, B(OH)_3,$
The total number of species that will be Lewis acid is
(a) 2 (b) 3 (c) 4 (d) 1

Species selection (with 7 species)

42. Consider the following species,
(i) $H_2PO_2^-$ (ii) HPO_3^{2-}
(iii) HCO_3^- (iv) $H_2PO_3^-$
(v) $CH_3CO_2^-$ (vi) $H_2PO_4^-$
(vii) HPO_4^{2-}
The amphiprotic species are
(a) 4 (b) 5 (c) 3 (d) 2

43. Consider the following solutions,
(i) 100 mL of 0.1 M HCl + 100 mL of 0.1 M NaOH
(ii) 55 mL of 0.1 M HCl + 45 mL of 0.1 M NaOH
(iii) 10 mL of 0.1 M HCl + 90 mL of 0.1 M NaOH
(iv) 75 mL of 0.2 M HCl + 25 mL of 0.2 M NaOH
(v) 25 mL of 0.1 M HNO_3 + 25 mL of 0.1 M NH_3
(vi) 100 mL of 0.1 M CH_3COOH + 100 mL of 0.1 M KOH
(vii) 100 mL of 0.2 M H_2SO_4 + 100 mL of 0.3 M NaOH

The number of solutions when mixed will give a solution with pH greater than 7 are
(a) 3 (b) 4 (c) 2 (d) 5

44. Among the following, the total number of compounds whose aqueous solution turns red litmus paper blue is ....
(i) KCN (ii) K_2SO_4
(iii) $(NH_4)_2C_2O_4$ (iv) NaCl
(v) K_2CO_3 (vi) NH_4NO_3
(vii) $FeCl_3$
(a) 2 (b) 4 (c) 5 (d) 6

45. Consider the following expressions,
(i) $Cr(OH)_3(s)$; $K_{sp} = 27S^4$
(ii) $AlPO_4(s)$; $K_{sp} = S^3$
(iii) $Fe_2(SO_4)_3(s)$; $K_{sp} = 102\,S^5$
(iv) $NiC_2O_4(s)$; $K_{sp} = S^2$
(v) $Na_3AlF_6(s)$; $K_{sp} = 27\,S^4$
(vi) $CaSO_4(s)$; $K_{sp} = 2\,S^4$
(vii) $PbI_2(s)$; $K_{sp} = 2\,S^3$

The incorrect expressions are
(a) 6 (b) 5
(c) 3 (d) 4

46. A 1 litre solution containing NH_4Cl and NH_4OH has hydroxide ion concentration of 10^{-6} mol/litre. The total number of following hydroxides that could be precipitated when the solution is added to 1 litre solution of 0.1 M metal ions?
I. $Ba(OH)_2$ ($K_{sp} = 5 \times 10^{-3}$)
II. $Ni(OH)_2$ ($K_{sp} = 1.6 \times 10^{-16}$)
III. $Mn(OH)_2$ ($K_{sp} = 2 \times 10^{-13}$)
IV. $Fe(OH)_2$ ($K_{sp} = 8 \times 10^{-16}$)
V. $Ca(OH)_2$ ($K_{sp} = 4 \times 10^{-7}$)
(a) 1 (b) 2 (c) 3 (d) 5

Check Through PYQs

Element 1 Ostwald's Dilution Law and Concept of Acids and Bases

1. Dilution processes of different aqueous solutions, with water, are given in List-I. The effects of dilution of the solution on $[H^+]$ are given in List-II.

Note Degree of dissociation (α) of weak acid and weak base is << 1; degree of hydrolysis of salt << 1; $[H^+]$ represents the concentration of H^+ ions

List-I		List-II	
P.	(10 mL of 0.1 M NaOH + 20 mL of 0.1 M acetic acid) diluted to 60 mL	1.	the value of $[H^+]$ does not change on dilution
Q.	(20 mL of 0.1 M NaOH + 20 mL of 0.1 M acetic acid) diluted to 80 mL	2.	the value of $[H^+]$ changes to half of its initial value on dilution
R.	(20 mL of 0.1M HCl + 20 mL of 0.1 M ammonia solution) diluted to 80 mL	3.	the value of $[H^+]$ changes to two times of its initial value on dilution.
S.	10 mL saturated solution of $Ni(OH)_2$ in equilibrium with exces solid $Ni(OH)_2$ is diluted to 20 mL (solid $Ni(OH)_2$ is still present after dilution).	4.	the value of $[H^+]$ changes to $\frac{1}{\sqrt{2}}$ times of its initial value on dilution
		5.	the value of $[H^+]$ changes to $\sqrt{2}$ times of its initial value on dilution

Match each process given in List-I with one or more effect(s) in List-II. The correct option is *2018 Adv.*
(a) P → 4; Q → 2; R → 3; S → 1
(b) P → 4; Q → 3; R → 2; S → 3
(c) P → 1; Q → 4; R → 5; S → 3
(d) P → 1; Q → 5; R → 4; S → 1

Element 2 pH, Buffer, Indicators and Salt hydrolysis

2. On decreasing the pH from 7 to 2, the solubility of a sparingly soluble salt (*MX*) of a weak acid (*HX*) increased from 10^{-4} mol L^{-1} to 10^{-3} mol L^{-1}. The pK_a of HX is *2023 Adv.*
(a) 3 (b) 4
(c) 5 (d) 2

3. A solution is prepared by mixing 0.01 mole each of H_2CO_3, $NaHCO_3$, Na_2CO_3, and NaOH in 100 mL of water. pH of the resulting solution is ....
[Given, pK_{a_1} and pK_{a_2} of H_2CO_3 and 6.37 and 10.32, respectively; $\log 2 = 0.30$] *2022 Adv.*

4. A solution of 0.1 M weak base (*B*) is titrated with 0.1 M of a strong acid (*HA*). The variation of pH of the solution with the volume of *HA* added is shown in the figure below. What is the pK_b of the base? The neutralisation reaction is given by

$$B + HA \longrightarrow BH^+ + A^-.$$ *2020 Adv.*

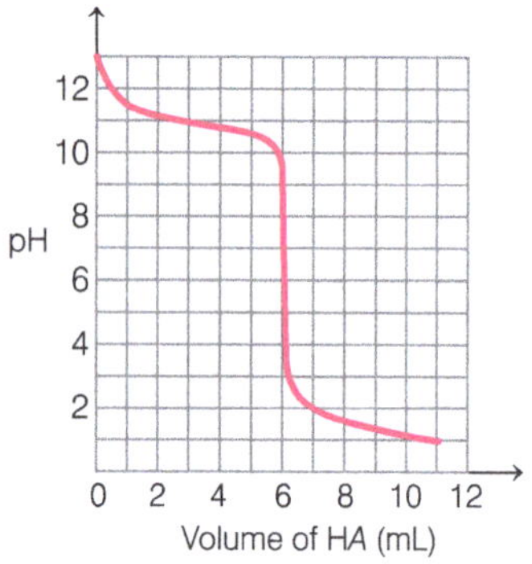

5. The molar conductivity of a solution of a weak acid H*X* (0.01 M) is 10 times smaller than the molar conductivity of a solution of a weak acid H*Y* (0.10 M). If $\lambda^\circ_{X^-} \approx \lambda^\circ_{Y^-}$ the difference in their pK_a values, pK_a (HX) – pK_a(HY), is (consider degree of ionisation of both acids to be <<1) *2015 Adv.*

Element 3 Solubility Product and Common Ion Effect

6. Concentration of H_2SO_4 and Na_2SO_4 in a solution is 1 M and 1.8×10^{-2}M, respectively. Molar solubility of $PbSO_4$ in the same solution is $X \times 10^{-Y}$ M (expressed in scientific notation). The value of *Y* is
[Given, solubility product of $PbSO_4 (K_{sp}) = 1.6 \times 10^{-8}$, for H_2SO_4, K_{a_1} is very large and $K_{a_2} = 1.2 \times 10^{-2}$]. *2022 Adv.*

7. An acidified solution of 0.05 M Zn^{2+} is saturated with 0.1 M H_2S. What is the minimum molar concentration (*M*) of H^+ required to prevent the precipitation of ZnS? Use $K_{sp}(ZnS) = 1.25 \times 10^{-22}$ and overall dissociation constant of H_2S, $K_{net} = K_1K_2 = 1 \times 10^{-21}$. *2020 Adv.*

8. The solubility of a salt of weak acid (*AB*) at pH 3 is $Y \times 10^{-3}$ mol L^{-1}. The value of *Y* is__ (Given that the value of solubility product of *AB* $(K_{sp}) = 2 \times 10^{-10}$ and the value of ionisation constant of H*B* $(K_a) = 1 \times 10^{-8}$ *2018 Adv..*

HINTS & Solutions

Solutions : Competency Enhancer

2.1 ***(0.01)*** $pH = pK_a + \log \frac{[Salt]}{[Acid]}$

$\Rightarrow \quad 520 = 420 + \log \frac{0.1}{[C_6H_5COOH]}$

$\Rightarrow \quad 1 = \log(0.1) - \log[C_6H_5COOH]$

$\Rightarrow \quad [C_6H_5COOH] = 0.01\,M$

3.1 ***(4)*** H_2SO_4 being a strong acid ionises completely into its ions.

$$H_2SO_4 \xrightarrow{K_{a_1}} H^+ + HSO_4^-$$

	H_2SO_4	H^+	HSO_4^-
$t = 0$	1 M	0	0
$t = t$	0	1 M	1 M

K_2SO_4 is a salt of strong acid and strong base, so it also ionises completely into its ions.

$$K_2SO_4 \longrightarrow 2K^+ + SO_4^{2-}$$

	K_2SO_4	$2K^+$	SO_4^{2-}
$t = 0$	2.8×10^{-4} M	0	0
$t = t$	0	$(2\times 2.8\times 10^{-4})$ M	2.8×10^{-4} M

HSO_4^- is a weak acid as its $K_{a_2} = 1.2\times 10^{-4}$

$$HSO_4^- \rightleftharpoons H^+ + SO_4^{2-}$$

	HSO_4^-	H^+	SO_4^{2-}
$t = 0$	1 M	1 M	2.8×10^{-4} M
$t = t$	$1 + x = 1$	$1 - x = 1$	$2.8\times 10^{-4} - x$

$[\because Q_c > K_{a_2}]$

$$K_{a_2} = \frac{[H^+]\,[SO_4^{2-}]}{[HSO_4^-]}$$

$$1.2\times 10^{-4} = \frac{2.8\times 10^{-4} - x}{1}$$

$$x = 1.6\times 10^{-4}$$

$$[SO_4^{2-}] = 2.8\times 10^{-4} - x$$

$$= 2.8\times 10^{-4} - 1.6\times 10^{-14} = 1.2\times 10^{-4}\,M$$

Let the molar solubility of $PbSO_4 = S$ mol/L

$$\underset{}{PbSO_4} \rightleftharpoons \underset{S}{Pb^{2+}} + \underset{S + 1.2\times 10^{-4}}{SO_4^{2-}} \quad K_{sp} = [Pb^{2+}]\,[SO_4^{2-}]$$

$$1.6\times 10^{-8} = S\times (S + 1.2\times 10^{-4})$$

Since, $S <<< 1.2\times 10^{-4}$

$$1.6\times 10^{-8} = S\times 1.2\times 10^{-4}$$

$$S = \frac{1.6\times 10^{-8}}{1.2\times 10^{-4}} = 1.3\times 10^{-4}\,M$$

$S = P\times 10^{-N}$

$S = 1.3\times 10^{-4}$ M

$P = 1.3$ and $N = 4$

Elemental Practice 6.1

1. ***(b)*** $\underset{\text{Solvent}}{2C_2H_5OH} \rightleftharpoons \underset{\text{Cation}}{C_2H_5OH_2^+} + \underset{\text{Anion}}{C_2H_5O^-}$

$$C_2H_5OH \longrightarrow \underset{\text{Anion}}{C_2H_5O^-} + H^+$$

$C_2H_5O^-$ is a strong base

$$2NH_3 \rightleftharpoons \underset{\text{Cation}}{NH_4^+} + \underset{\text{Anion}}{NH_2^-}$$

$$NH_4NO_3 \longrightarrow NH_4^+ + NO_3^-$$

NH_4^+ is a strong acid.

2. ***(a)*** H_2O in $[Al(H_2O)_6]^{3+}$ is a source of H^+, this proton is accepted by HCO_3^-.

Thus, $[Al(H_2O)_6^{3+}]$ is proton donor and HCO_3^- is proton-acceptor which is converted into H_2CO_3(acid).

Thus, Bronsted-Lowry acids are : $[Al(H_2O)_6^{3+}]$ and H_2CO_3.

3. ***(b)*** Statement I is correct but statement II is incorrect. Their explanation is given as:

(I) As we know, $\alpha = \sqrt{\frac{K_a}{C}} = \sqrt{\frac{10^{-5}}{0.1}} = 10^{-2}$

$$\%\alpha = 10^{-2}\times 100 = 1\%$$

(II) HCOOH and CH_3COOH solutions have equal pH. If $\frac{K_{a_1}}{K_{a_2}}$ is 4, then the ratio of their molar concentration will be 1 : 4.

Since, pH is same for two acids

$\therefore \quad [H^\oplus]_1 = [H^\oplus]_2$

Thus, $C_1\alpha_1 = C_2\alpha_2$

$$\frac{K_{a_1}}{K_{a_2}} = \frac{C_1\alpha_1^2}{C_2\alpha_2^2} = \frac{\alpha_1}{\alpha_2} \quad \text{...(i)}$$

$$\alpha_1 = \sqrt{\frac{K_{a_1}}{C_1}}, \quad \text{...(ii)}$$

$$\alpha_2 = \sqrt{\frac{K_{a_2}}{C_2}} \quad \text{...(iii)}$$

$$\therefore \quad \frac{\alpha_1}{\alpha_2} = \sqrt{\frac{K_{a_1}C_2}{K_{a_2}C_1}}$$

Substituting from equation (i), the value of $\frac{\alpha_1}{\alpha_2}$

$$\frac{K_{a_1}}{K_{a_2}} = \sqrt{\frac{K_{a_1}C_2}{K_{a_2}C_1}}$$

$$\therefore \quad \frac{K_{a_1}}{K_{a_2}} = \frac{C_2}{C_1} \Rightarrow \frac{C_2}{C_1} = 4$$

$C_1 : C_4 = 1 : 4$

4. **(c)** $Ba(OH)_2(aq) \longrightarrow Ba^{2+}(aq) + 2OH^-(aq)$

Since, $Ba(OH)_2$ is completely ionised and on ionisation its one molecule gives two OH^- ions.

$$\therefore \quad [OH^-] = 2[Ba(OH)_2] = 2 \times 0.005 = .01 \text{ mol L}^{-1} = 1 \times 10^{-2} \text{ mol L}^{-1}$$

$$H_3O^+ = \frac{K_w}{[OH^-]} = \frac{1 \times 10^{-14}}{1 \times 10^{-2}} = 1 \times 10^{-12} \text{ mol L}^{-1}$$

5. **(b)** pH = 2.85

$\therefore [H_3O^+] = 10^{-2.85} = 10^{-3} 10^{0.15} = 1.41 \times 10^{-3}$

Also in a weak acid, by Ostwald's dilution law,

$$[H_3O^+] = \sqrt{K_a C}$$

$$1.41 \times 10^{-3} = \sqrt{K_a \times 0.08}$$

$$\therefore \quad K_a = 2.48 \times 10^{-5} \approx 2.5 \times 10^{-5}$$

6. **(a)** HNO_2 is proton-donor thus it is stronger acid than HF. HF is proton-donor thus it is stronger acid than CH_3COOH. CH_3COOH is proton-donor and is thus stronger acid than H_2O.

7. **(c)** Let the degree of dissociation of CH_3COOH be x. Then,

	$CH_3COOH \rightleftharpoons$	CH_3COO^-	$+ H^+$
Initial Concentration	0.2	0	0
Concentration At equilib.	$0.2(1-x)$	$0.2x$	$0.2x$

$$K_a = \frac{0.2x \times 0.2x}{0.2(1-x)} = 1.8 \times 10^{-5}$$

$$\Rightarrow \quad x \approx 9.5 \times 10^{-3}$$

Now, let the solution be diluted to c mole per litre in order to double the degree of dissociation, x. So,

$$K_a = \frac{(c \times 2x) \times (c \times 2x)}{c(1-2x)} = \frac{c(2x)^2}{(1-2x)}$$

$$\Rightarrow 1.8 \times 10^{-5} = \frac{c \times (2 \times 9.5 \times 10^{-3})^2}{(1 - 2 \times 9.5 \times 10^{-3})}$$

$$\Rightarrow \quad c \approx 0.05 \text{ M}$$

Let V mL of water is to be added to dilute 300 mL of CH_3COOH solution to change its concentration from 0.2 M to 0.05 M. So, $0.2 \times 300 = 0.05 \times (300 + V)$

$$\Rightarrow \quad V = 900 \text{ mL}$$

8. **(c)** $H_2O + H_2O \rightleftharpoons H_3O^+ + OH^-$

$$K_w = [H_3O^+][OH^-] = 1 \times 10^{-14}$$

Since, $[H_3O^+] = [OH^-]$

Hence, $[H_3O^+]^2 = 1 \times 10^{-14}$

$$[H_3O^+] = 1 \times 10^{-7} \text{ M}$$

For H_2O, density = 1g mL^{-1} = 1000 g L^{-1}

Thus, molar concentration $= \frac{1000}{18}$ mol L^{-1}

By Ostwald's dilution law, $[H_3O^+] = \sqrt{K_a C}$

$$1 \times 10^{-7} = \sqrt{K_a \times \frac{1000}{18}} \Rightarrow 1 \times 10^{-14} = K_a \times \frac{1000}{18}$$

$$\therefore \quad K_a = \frac{18 \times 10^{-14}}{1000} \Rightarrow K_a = 1.8 \times 10^{-16}$$

9. **(b)** $K_{eq} = 1.1 \times 10^6$, thus equilibrium is predominantly in forward side. Equilibrium is shifted towards the formation of weak acid and weak base.

HCN is a weak acid, thus

CN^- is a stronger base

ONO^- is a weak base, hence

HONO is a stronger acid

There (a) is correct; (b) is incorrect; (c) is correct

(d) $\Delta G = 0$ at $K_{eq} = 1$ and $\Delta G° = -2.302\, RT \log K_{eq} \neq 0$. So, (d) is incorrect.

10. **(a)** $HCO_3^- \rightleftharpoons H^+ + CO_3^{2-}$

$HCO_3^- + H^+ \rightleftharpoons H_2CO_3$

HCO_3^- is H^+ ion donor as well as H^+ ion acceptor. Thus, HCO_3^- is amphiprotic

H_2O is also amphiprotic and amphoteric oxide.

It can react with both acids and bases.

Thus, both statements I and II are correct.

11. **(a)** $HCO_3^- \rightleftharpoons H^+ + CO_3^{2-}$

$$K_a = \frac{[H^+][CO_3^{2-}]}{[HCO_3^-]} = 4.7 \times 10^{-11}$$

Since, $K_a \cdot K_b = K_w$

$$\Rightarrow \quad K_b = \frac{K_w}{K_a} = \frac{(1 \times 10^{-14})}{(4.7 \times 10^{-11})} = 2.13 \times 10^{-4}$$

Among the given species K_b value is largest for CO_3^{2-}. So, it is the strongest base.

12. **(a)**

	$HA \rightleftharpoons$	H^+	$+ A^-$
Initial Concentration	0.1M	0	0
Concentration at equilib.	$0.1(1-x)$	$0.1x$	$0.1x$

$$K_a = \frac{0.1x \times 0.1x}{0.1(1-x)} = 4.9 \times 10^{-8}$$

$$x = 7 \times 10^{-4}$$

$\therefore$ % ionisation $= 7 \times 10^{-2}$ %

13. **(a)** $H_2PO_4^-$ is an acid if it donote H^+.

14. **(c)** HCO_3^- is proton donor as well as proton acceptor. Hence, HCO_3^- is amphiprotic species.

15. **(d)** PH_3 is a Lewis base, phosphorous has a lone pair of electrons on it, which can be donated to an electron deficient species.

16. **(a,b,c)** Among the given statements, a, b and c are correct while statement d is incorrect. Its correct form is

$B(CH_3)_3$is electrons deficient hence it is Lewis acid and $N(CH_3)_3$ is a Lewis base.

17. ***(a, b, c)***

I. $[Al(OH)_3(H_2O)_3] + OH^- \rightleftharpoons [Al(OH)_4(H_2O)_2]^- + H_2O$

H_2O (ligand) donates a proton thus, $[Al(OH)_3(H_2O)_3]$ is an acid.

OH^- accepts a proton thus, H_2O (product) is an acid.

II. $[Al(OH)_3(H_2O)_3] + H_3O^+ \rightleftharpoons [Al(OH)_2(H_2O)_4]^+ + H_2O$

OH^- (ligand) accepts a proton thus, $[Al(OH)_3(H_2O)_3]$ is a base. H_3O^+ donotes a proton. and changes to H_2O.

Thus, H_2O (product) is a base.

Thus, (a), (b) and (c) are correct.

18. ***(a, d)*** Among the given statements, a and d are correct while b and c are incorrect. Their correct form are—

- The electrostatic forces between two charges are inversely proportional to dielectric constant of the medium.
- The extent to which ionisation occurs depends upon the strength of the bond and the extent of solvation of ions produced.

19. ***(a,b,c,d)***

$$\underset{\substack{\uparrow \\ NH_4Cl}}{} NH_3 + NH_3 \longrightarrow \underset{\text{Cation}}{NH_4^+} + \underset{\text{Anion}}{NH_2^-}$$

NH_4Cl ⟶ ↑ (cation) ↑ ⟵ $NaNH_2$ (anion)

Species which gives cation of solvent is a strong acid.

Species which gives anion of solvent is a strong base.

CH_3COOH accepts a proton from a strong acid H_2SO_4 thereby acting as a base.

$$\underset{\text{Strong acid}}{H_2SO_4} + CH_3COOH \rightleftharpoons CH_3COOH_2^+ + HSO_4^-$$

H_2O is the weakest base in aqueous solution. Thus, H_3O^+ is the strongest acid.

20. ***(a, c)*** Among the given statements, (a), (b) and (c) are correct while incorrect from is as

A solvent which has a high dielectric constant weakens the attractive force between the cation and anions. Hence a solvent of high dielectric constant favours the dissociation of the electrolyte.

21. ***(14)***

	H_2CO_3	$\rightleftharpoons$	H^+	+	HCO_3^-
	$\frac{0.1}{100} \times 1000$ M		0		0
Equilibrium	$(1-x)M$		$(x+y)M$		$(x-y)M$
	HCO_3^-	$\rightleftharpoons$	H^+	+	CO_3^{2-}
Equilibrium	$(x-y)M$		$(x+y)M$		yM

Now, $K_{a_1} = \frac{[H^+][HCO_3^-]}{[H_2CO_3]}$

$\Rightarrow \quad 4 \times 10^{-6} = \frac{(x+y)\cdot(x-y)}{(1-x)} \approx \frac{x \cdot x}{1}$

$\therefore \quad x = 2 \times 10^{-3}$

and $\quad K_{a_2} = \frac{[H^+][CO_3^{2-}]}{[HCO_3^-]}$

$\Rightarrow \quad 5 \times 10^{-11} = \frac{(x+y)\cdot y}{(x-y)} \approx \frac{x \cdot y}{x}$

$\therefore \quad y = 5 \times 10^{-11}$

$\therefore \quad [H^+] = (x+y) \approx x = 2 \times 10^{-3}$ M

$[HCO_3^-] = (x-y) \approx x = 2 \times 10^{-3}$ M

$[CO_3^{2-}] = (y) = 5 \times 10^{-11}$ M

$[OH^-] = \frac{K_w}{[H^+]} = \frac{10^{-14}}{2 \times 10^{-3}} = 5 \times 10^{-12}$ M

Hence, the sum of x, y, z and w is $= 2 + 2 + 5 + 5 = 14$.

22. ***(4)*** If pH are equal, it mean

By Ostwald's dilution law,

$$[H^+] = \sqrt{K_a C}$$

$$[H^+](HCOOH) = [H^+](CH_3COOH)$$

$$\sqrt{K_a C}\,(HCOOH) = \sqrt{K_a C}(CH_3COOH)$$

$$\sqrt{\frac{K_a\,(HCOOH)}{K_a\,(CH_3COOH)}} = \sqrt{\frac{C\,(CH_3COOH)}{C\,(HCOOH)}}$$

$$\Rightarrow \frac{K_a\,(HCOOH)}{K_a\,(CH_3COOH)} = \frac{1}{0.25} = 4$$

23. ***(5)*** $\alpha = \frac{1}{100} = 10^{-2}$

$$BOH \rightleftharpoons B^{\oplus} + OH^{\ominus}$$

$$K_b = \frac{C\alpha^2}{1-\alpha} = C\alpha^2$$

$$= 0.1 \times (10^{-2})^2 = 10^{-5}$$

When 0.2 mol of BCl is added, due to common ion effect of $B^{\oplus}$($BCl \longrightarrow B^{\oplus} + Cl^{\ominus}$), suppression of ionisation of BOH occurs, and α becomes α'.

$\therefore \quad \alpha' = \frac{K_b}{M}$ (M = molarity of common ion added)

$$= \frac{10^{-5}}{0.2} = 5 \times 10^{-5} \text{ M}$$

Hence, the value of x is 5.

24. ***(3)*** Among the given species only SO_3^{2-}, $H_2PO_4^-$ and ClO^- are bronsted lowry base while Fe^{3+} and BCl_3 are Lewis acid.

25. ***(2)*** Among the given species only two i.e. H^- and O^{2-} are behave as strong base in aqueous solution.

Elemental Practice 6.2

1. ***(d)*** Moles of H_2CO_3, $n_{H_2CO_3} = 0.022\text{ L} \times 2\text{ M} = 0.04$ mol

Moles of NaOH, $n_{NaOH} = 0.080\text{ L} \times 0.5\text{ M} = 0.04$ mol

	H_2CO_3 +	NaOH ⟶	$NaHCO_3$ +	H_2O
Initial moles	0.044	0.04	—	—
Moles at eq.	0.004	0	0.040	—

Total volume of the solution = 22 mL + 80 mL

= 102 mL = 0.102 L

Concentration of H_2CO_3 left $= \frac{0.004}{0.102} = 0.0392$ M

Concentration of $NaHCO_3$ left $= \frac{0.040}{0.102} = 0.392$ M

$$pH = pK_{a_2} + \log \frac{(0.392)}{(0.0392)}$$

$$9.6 = pK_a + 1 \Rightarrow pK_a = 8.6$$

2. **(a)** The dissociation of water may be represented as

	H_2O	$\rightleftharpoons$ H^+	+ OH^-
Concs. if no dissociation	c	10^{-7} (from HCl)	0
Concs. after dissociation:	$c - x$	$(10^{-7} + x)$	x

where x is the molar amount of H_2O per litre of the solution which dissociates.

If we consider that there is no dissociation of water, then, $[H^+]$ contribution comes only from HCl. If we recognize that a small amount (x mole) of water does dissociate, then the $[H^+]$ contribution would be $(10^{-7} + x)$ mol dm^{-3}. Now, at 25°C,

$K_w = [H^+][OH^-] = 10^{-14}$ mol^2 dm^{-6} $= (10^{-7} + x)$ mol dm^{-3} $\times x$ mol dm^{-3}.

which reduces to the quadratic equation

$$x^2 + 10^{-7}x - 10^{-14} = 0$$

The roots of this equation are given by

$$x = \frac{-10^{-7} \pm \sqrt{(10^{-7})^2 + 4 \times 10^{-14}}}{2}$$

Neglecting the negative root which has no physical meaning,

$$x = \frac{-10^{-7} + \sqrt{10^{-14} + 4 \times 10^{-14}}}{2} = \frac{-10^{-7} + 2.24 \times 10^{-7}}{2}$$

$$= 0.62 \times 10^{-7} \text{ mol dm}^{-3}$$

$$\therefore [H^+] = 10^{-7} + x = 10^{-7} + 0.62 \times 10^{-7}$$

$$= 1.62 \times 10^{-7} \text{ mol dm}^{-3}$$

$$\therefore pH = -\log [H^+] = -\log(1.62 \times 10^{-7}) = 6.79$$

3. **(b)** $HA + NaOH \longrightarrow NaA + H_2O$

milli-moles of salt NaA or $A^- = 40 \times 0.1 = 4$

Now,

	A^-	+ H^+	$\longrightarrow$ HA
Initial milli-moles	4	2	
Final milli-moles	2	—	2

Acidic buffer solution is formed and $[A^-] = [HA]$

$$pH = pK_a + \log \frac{[A^-]}{[HA]} \Rightarrow pK_a = 5$$

Now, $HA + NaOH \longrightarrow NaA + H_2O$

Hydrolysis of A^- will takes place

$$[Na\,A] = \frac{\text{milli moles of acid}}{\text{Total volume}} = \frac{20 \times 0.2}{20 + 20} = 0.1$$

$$pH = \frac{1}{2}(pK_w + pK_a + \log C) = \frac{1}{2}[14 + 5 - 1] = 9$$

4. **(b)** $BOH + HCl \longrightarrow BCl + H_2O$

At equilibrium point $N_1V_1 = N_2V_2$; $V_2 = 20$ mL

$$[BCl] = \frac{20 \times 0.08}{20 + 20} = 0.04$$

$$pH = \frac{1}{2}[pK_w - pK_b - \log (C)] \Rightarrow pK_b = 5.4$$

	B^+	+ OH^- $\longrightarrow$	BOH; Basic Buffer is formed
Initial milli-moles	1.6		–
Final milli-moles	1.2		0.4

$$pOH = pK_b + \log \frac{[B^+]}{[BOH]} = 5.4 + \log\left(\frac{1.2}{0.4}\right) = 5.4 + 0.48$$

$$pOH = 5.88$$

5. **(b)** Let a is initial milli-moles of HA and molarity of NaOH solution is x

$$HA + NaOH \longrightarrow NaA + H_2O$$

In both case solution is acidic, so acidic buffer solution is formed.

$$5 = pK_a + \log \frac{10x}{a - 10x}$$

$$\Rightarrow \quad 5.60 = pK_a + \log \frac{20x}{a - 20x}$$

$$\Rightarrow \quad 0.60 = \log \frac{20x}{(a - 20x)} \times \frac{(a - 10x)}{10x}$$

$$\Rightarrow \quad 4 = \frac{2(a - 10x)}{(a - 20x)} \Rightarrow a = 30x$$

$$\therefore \quad 5 = pK_a + \log \frac{10x}{20x}$$

or $\quad pK_a = 5.3$

6. **(b)** $(CH_3COO)_2Ca \rightleftharpoons 2CH_3COO^- + Ca^{2+}$

0.01M $\quad$ 0.02 M

$CH_3COOH + H_2O \rightleftharpoons CH_3COO^- + H_3O^+$

$$K_a = \frac{[CH_3COO^-][H_3O^+]}{[CH_3COOH]} = \frac{0.02 \times 9.0 \times 10^{-6}}{0.01} = 1.8 \times 10^{-5}$$

7. **(a)** Both Statement I and Statement II are true.

8. **(d)** $H_2A + NaOH \longrightarrow NaHA + H_2O$

$$pH_1 = \frac{1}{2}(pK_{a_1} + pK_{a_2}) = \frac{1}{2}(4.6 + 8) = 6.3$$

$$N_1V_1 = N_2V_2$$

$$N_1 \times 10 = 0.1 \times 20$$

$$N_1 = 0.2$$

$NaHA + NaOH \longrightarrow Na_2A + H_2O$

$$c = \frac{2\text{m mole}}{50 \text{ mL}} = \frac{1}{25}M$$

$$pH_2 = 7 + \frac{1}{2}(pK_{a_2} + \log c)$$

$$pH_2 = 10.3$$

$$pH_2 - pH_1 = 10.3 - 6.3 = 4$$

9. ***(a)*** NaX is salt of weak acid and strong base.

$X^- + H_2O \rightleftharpoons HX + OH^-$

We can consider X^- as a base.

$$K_b(X^-) = \frac{K_w}{K_a} = \frac{1\times 10^{-14}}{1\times 10^{-5}} = 1\times 10^{-9} \text{ then}$$

$$x = \sqrt{\frac{K_b}{C}} = \sqrt{\frac{1\times10^{-9}}{0.1}} = 1\times10^{-4} \text{ M}$$

Thus, percentage $= 1\times 10^{-4} \times 100 = 0.01\%$

10. ***(d)*** pOH of a solution obtained by mixing equal volumes of solution with pH 3 and 5 is 10.7.

11. ***(b)*** For salt of weak base and strong acid,

$$pH = 7 - \frac{1}{2}pK_b - \frac{1}{2}\log C$$

$$pH = 7 - \frac{5}{2} - \frac{1}{2}\log(4\times 10^{-2})$$

$$= 7 - \frac{5}{2} - 0.7 = 3.8$$

12. ***(a)*** $$\text{Buffer capacity} = \frac{\left[\begin{array}{l}\text{Number of moles per}\\ \text{litre of acid or base added}\end{array}\right]}{\text{Change in pH or pOH}}$$

$$[\text{Acid}] = \frac{0.003\times 1000}{200} = 0.015 \text{ mol L}^{-1}$$

$$\text{Buffer capacity} = \frac{0.015}{0.03} = 0.5$$

13. ***(b)***

	RNH_2	+ HCl ⟶	$R\overset{\oplus}{N}H_3$	+ $\overset{\ominus}{Cl}$
Initial mole	0.1	0.09	0	0
Final mole	0.01	0	0.09	0.09

W_B is left behind so basic buffer is formed.

Use Hendreson's equation:

$$[\bar{O}H] = K_b\frac{[\text{Base}]}{[\text{Salt}]} = 5.2\times 10^{-5}\times\frac{0.01}{0.09}$$

$$= 0.57\times 10^{-5} = 5.7\times 10^{-6}$$

$$\therefore\ [H^+] = \frac{K_w}{[\bar{O}H]} = \frac{10^{-14}}{5.7\times 10^{-6}}$$

$$= 0.17\times 10^{-8} = 1.7\times 10^{-9}\text{ M}$$

14. ***(c)*** $[\text{Base}] = [NH_3] = 0.1\text{M}$

$[\text{Salt}] = [(NH_4)_2SO_4] = 0.2$ M

$[(NH_4)_2SO_4] \longrightarrow 2\overset{\oplus}{N}H_4 + SO_4^{2-}]$

$$pOH = pK_b + \log\frac{[\text{Salt}]}{[\text{Base}]}$$

$$= 4.76 + \log\frac{0.2\text{ M}}{0.1\text{M}}$$

$$= 4.76 + \log 2 = 4.76 + 0.3 = 5.06$$

$$pH = 14 - 5.06 = 8.94$$

15. ***(a)***

	$HCl(aq.)$ +	$NaOH(aq.)$ ⟶	$NaCl(aq.)$ +	$H_2O(l)$
Initial	50 mm	30 mm	—	—
Final	20 mm	—	30	30

The concentration of $[H^+]$ ions is

$$[H^+] = \frac{20}{80} = 0.25\text{ M}$$

$$pH = -\log(2.5\times 10^{-1})$$

$$= 0.602 = 602\times 10^{-3}$$

16. ***(a, b, c)*** Among the given statements all are correct expect statement (d).

The corrected form of statement (d) is :

When 200 mL of 0.01 M HCl is mixed with 400 mL of 0.01 M H_2SO_4, the pH of the mixture is 2.

17. ***(a,b,c,d)*** All the given statements are correct.

18. ***(b, c)*** Among the given statements only b and c are correct, while a and d are incorrect. The corrected form of incorrect statement is ....

- pH of 10^{-8} M solution will be between 6 and 7 but never 8.
- At the mid point of titration, pH = pK_a

19. ***(a, b, d)*** Among the given statements all statements are correct expect c. The corrected form of statement c is, Addition of NH_4Cl to NH_4OH decrease the dissociation of NH_4OH, which causes the pH to decrease:

20. ***(a,b,c)*** For an alkaline aqueous solution, pH is not equal to pOH.

21. ***(85.7)*** $HIn \rightleftharpoons H^+ + In^-$
Acid Base

$$K_a = \frac{[H^+][In^-]}{[HIn]}$$

Let x be the percentage of indicator in its basic form. So,

$$6\times 10^{-5} = \frac{10^{-5}(x)}{(100-x)}$$

$$\Rightarrow \qquad x = 85.7\%$$

22. ***(3)*** Basic salt solutions will have pH >7, will change colour of litmus paper red to blue, NaCN, K_2CO_3 and LiCN are the only basic salts among these.

23. ***(0.0019)*** $pH = pK_a + \log([\text{Salt}]/[\text{Acid}])$

$pK_a = -\log K_a = -\log 2.75\times 10^{-5} = 4.57$

pH of the solution before adding HCl will be given by

$$pH = pK_a + \log\frac{0.25}{0.20} = 4.57 + 0.0969 = 4.6669$$

Amount of HCl added = 0.5 ml of 1 M HCl = 0.5 millimole = 0.0005 mole

Assuming HCl to be completely dissociated, the amount H^+ ions added will be = 0.0005 mole

The addition of H^+ ion will result in the reaction

$$CH_3COO^- + H^+ \longrightarrow CH_3COOH$$

i.e., the amount of acetic acid will increase and that of the salt will correspondingly decrease by 0.0005 mole.

∴ After adding HCl,

$$[CH_3COOH] = 0.20 + 0.0005 = 0.2005 \text{ mol dm}^{-3}$$

and $[CH_3COOK] = 0.25 - 0.0005 = 0.2495 \text{ mol dm}^{-3}$

(The change of volume resulting from the addition of HCl is negligible)

$$pH = pK_a + \log([\text{Salt}]/[\text{Acid}]) = 4.57 + \log\frac{0.2495}{0.2005}$$

$$= 4.57 + 0.095 = 4.665$$

∴ Change of pH = Change in pH

$$= 4.665 - 4.6669 = -0.0019$$

$$pH = 5.8143 - 4.6669 = 1.147$$

24. ***(79.5)*** Concentration of acetate ion

$$= 2 \times 0.004 = 0.008 \text{ M}$$

As we know that calcium acetate is a salt of weak acid and strong base so salt hydrolysis will take place.

$$pH = 7 + \frac{1}{2}(pK_a + \log C) = 7 + \frac{1}{2}[4 + \log(2 \times 0.004)]$$

$$= 7 + \frac{1}{2}[4 + \log 0.008] = 7 + \frac{1}{2}[4 - 2.09]$$

$$= 7 + \frac{1}{2} \times 1.90 = 7 + 0.95 = 7.95 = 79.5 \times 10^{-1}$$

25. ***(– 19)***

$$HX(aq.) \rightleftharpoons H^+(aq.) + X^-(aq.);\ K_a = 10^{-5}$$

$$H^+(aq.) + OH^-(aq.) \rightleftharpoons H_2O(l);\ K_w = 10^{-14}$$

Addition

$$HX(aq.) + OH^-(aq.) \rightleftharpoons H_2O(l) + X^-(aq.)$$

$$K_{eq.} = K_a \times K_w$$

$$1 \times 10^y = 10^{-5} \times 10^{-14}$$

$$10^y = 10^{-19} \Rightarrow y = -19$$

Elemental Practice 6.3

1. ***(d)*** For $AB_2 \rightleftharpoons A^{2+} + 2B^-$

$$K_{sp} = [A^{2+}][B^-]^2$$

$$= (2.1 \times 10^{-3})(0.31 \times 10^{-2})^2$$

$$= 0.20181 \times 10^{-7} \approx 2.02 \times 10^{-8}$$

2. ***(c)*** $Ag_2SO_4(s) \rightleftharpoons 2Ag^+(aq) + SO_4^{2-}(aq)$

$$[Ag^+] = 9.7 \times 10^{-3} \text{M}$$

$$[SO_4^{2-}] = 0.150 \text{ M (from } Na_2SO_4)$$

$$K_{sp} = [Ag^+]^2 [SO_4^{2-}] = (9.7 \times 10^{-3})^2 (0.15)$$

$$= 1.41 \times 10^{-5} \text{M}^3$$

3. ***(d)*** Statement I is incorrect but statement II is correct. Its correct form is—

- If solubility of $BaSO_4$ in aqueous solution is 1×10^{-5} M, then the solubility in 0.1 M $BaCl_2$ will be less than 1×10^{-5} M.

$$BaSO_4(s) \rightleftharpoons Ba^{2+}(aq) + SO_4^{2-}(aq);$$

$$K_{sp} = [Ba^{2+}][SO_4^{2-}] = S^2 = (1 \times 10^{-5})^2 = 1 \times 10^{-10}$$

In the presence of $BaCl_2$, solubility is decreased due to common (Ba^{2+}) ion effect.

$$\underset{0.1\text{ M}}{BaCl_2(aq)} \rightleftharpoons \underset{0.1\text{ M}}{Ba^{2+}}(aq) + \underset{0.2\text{ M}}{2Cl^-}(aq)$$

∴ $1 \times 10^{-10} = [Ba^{2+}][SO_4^{2-}] = (0.1)(S')$

∴ $S' = 1 \times 10^{-9}$

$$S' = (1.0 \times 10^{-9}\text{M}) << 1 \times 10^{-5}\text{M}$$

$$Ni(OH)_2(s) \rightleftharpoons Ni^{2+}(aq) + 2OH^-(aq)$$

; $K_{sp} = [Ni^{2+}][OH^-]^2$

$$2 \cdot 0 \times 10^{-15} = [Ni^{2+}](0 \cdot 1)^2$$

∴ $(Ni^{2+}) = 2 \cdot 0 \times 10^{-13}\text{M}$

4. ***(d)***

$$AgCl(s) \longrightarrow Ag^+(aq) + Cl^-(aq)$$

$$AgNO_3(aq) \longrightarrow Ag^+(aq) + NO_3^-(aq)$$

$$NaCl(aq) \longrightarrow Na^+(aq) + Cl^-(aq)$$

$$CaCl_2(aq) \longrightarrow Ca^{2+}(aq) + 2Cl^-(aq)$$

In presence of common ion (Ag^+ or Cl^-) solubility is decreased.

Thus S_1 is maximum

In water, $S_1 = \sqrt{K_{sp}} = \sqrt{1 \times 10^{-10}} = 1 \times 10^{-5}$ M

In 0.05 M Ag^+, $S_2 = \frac{K_{sp}}{0.05} = \frac{1 \times 10^{-10}}{0.05} = 2.0 \times 10^{-9}$ M

In 0.05 M Cl^-,

$$S_3 = \frac{K_{sp}}{0.05} = 2.0 \times 10^{-9} \text{ M}$$

In 0.02 M Cl^- (from $CaCl_2$)

$$S_4 = \frac{K_{sp}}{0.02} = \frac{1 \times 10^{-10}}{0.02} = 5 \times 10^{-9}\text{M}$$

Thus, $S_2 = S_3 < S_4 < S_1$

5. ***(b)*** $K_{sp} = (Ag^+)[IO_3^-] = S^2$

$$\therefore S = \sqrt{K_{sp}} = 1.0 \times 10^{-4} \text{mol L}^{-1}$$

$$= 1.0 \times 10^{-4} \times 283 \text{ g mol}^{-1} \text{ mol L}^{-1}$$

$$= 283 \times 10^{-4} \text{ g L}^{-1}$$

$$= \frac{283 \times 10^{-4} \times 100}{1000} \text{ g in 100 mL}$$

$$= 2.83 \times 10^{-3} \text{ g}$$

6. ***(c)*** Both A and R are true and R is the correct explanation of A.

$$AB_2(s) \rightleftharpoons \underset{S}{A^{2+}}(aq) + \underset{2S}{2B^-}(aq)$$

$$K_{sp} = [A^{2+}][B^-]^2 = (S)(2S)^2 = 4S^3$$

$$= 4(1.0 \times 10^{-5})^3 = 4 \times 10^{-15}$$

In the presence of 0.1 M A^{2+}, solubility is decreased due to common ion effect.

$\therefore \quad [A^{2+}][B^-]^2 = 4\times10^{-15}$

$(0.1)[B^-]^2 = 4\times10^{-15}$

$[B^-]=2\times10^{-7}M$

7. **(d)** $Al(OH)_3(s) \rightleftharpoons Al^{3+}(aq) + 3OH^-(s)$

Solubility $= S$ mol L^{-1}

$\therefore \quad K_{sp} = [Al^{3+}][OH^-]^3 = (S)(3S)^3$

$2.7\times10^{-11} = 27S^4$

$\therefore \quad S^4 = 10^{-12}$

$S = 10^{-3}$mol L^{-1}

$[Al^{3+}] = 1\times10^{-3}$ mol L^{-1}

8. **(a)** Aqueous solution of CH_3COONa is basic due to hydrolysis of CH_3COO^-.

$CH_3COO^-(aq) + H_2O \rightleftharpoons CH_3COOH(aq) + OH^-(aq)$

$$pH = 7+\frac{pK_a}{2}+\frac{\log C}{2} = 7+\frac{4.74}{2}+\frac{\log 0.1}{2} = 8.87$$

$\therefore$ pOH $= 14 - 8.87 = 5.13$

$[OH^-] = 10^{-pOH} = 10^{-5.13} = 10^{-6}10^{0.87} \approx 7.4\times10^{-6}$ M

Let, solubility of $Mg(OH)_2 = x$ in 0.1M CH_3COONa

$Mg(OH)_2(s) \rightleftharpoons Mg^{2+}(aq) + 2OH^-(aq)$

$K_{sp} = [Mg^{2+}][OH^-]^2$

$1.8\times10^{-11} = (x)(7.4\times10^{-6})^2$

$x = 0.33$ M

9. **(b)** $[Zn^{2+}][S^{2-}] = 10^{-1}\times 8.1\times10^{-19}$

$= 8.1\times10^{-20} > K_{sp}$ of ZnS (3×10^{-22})

$[Cu^{2+}][S^{2-}] = 10^{-2}\times 8.1\times10^{-19}$

$= 8.1\times10^{-21} > K_{sp}$ of CuS (8×10^{-36})

Hence, both ions are precipitated as sulphides.

10. **(c)** For precipitation, $[Ag^{\oplus}]$ ion should be minimum in the solution.

$$\text{For AgCl: } [Ag^{\oplus}]_{min} = \frac{K_{sp}(AgCl)}{[Cl^{\ominus}]} = \frac{1.5\times10^{-10}}{1.5\times10^{-1}} = 10^{-9}\text{ M}$$

$$\text{For AgBr: } [Ag^{\oplus}]_{min} = \frac{K_{sp}(AgBr)}{[Br^{\ominus}]} = \frac{5.0\times10^{-13}}{5.0\times10^{-4}} = 10^{-9}\text{ M}$$

For Ag_2CrO_4 : $[Ag^{\oplus}]_{min}$

$$= \sqrt{\left(\frac{K_{sp}\ Ag_2CrO_4}{[CrO_4^{2-}]}\right)} = \sqrt{\left(\frac{1.9\times10^{-12}}{1.9\times10^{-2}}\right)} = 10^{-5}\text{ M}$$

Therefore, $[Ag^{\oplus}]$ min in solution is equal for AgCl and AgBr, so both will be precipitated together.

11. **(d)** Saturated CaC_2O_4 contains maximum amount of CaC_2O_4 and thus refers to its solubility

$2MnO_4^- + 5C_2O_4^{2-} + 16H^+ \longrightarrow 2Mn^{2+} + 10CO_2 + 8H_2O$

Equivalent in 1 mol $MnO_4^- = 5$

Equivalent in 1 mol $C_2O_4^{2-} = 2$

Thus, molarity $\times 5 =$ normality for MnO_4^-

Molarity $\times 2 =$ normality for CrO_4^{2-}

Let, molarity of $CrO_4^{2-} = x$

Normality $= 2x$

$n(MnO_4^-) = 5\times1\times10^{-4}$

then $N_1V_1 = N_2V_2$

$C_2O_4^{2-} \qquad MnO_4^-$

$(2x)\times1000 = (5\times1\times10^{-4})\times200$

$x = 5\times10^{-5}$

$\therefore \quad [C_2O_4^{2-}] = 5\times10^{-5}$M

$K_{sp}(CaC_2O_4) = (5\times10^{-5})^2 = 2.5\times10^{-9}M^2$

12. **(a)** Consider dilution factor due to mixing. $BaSO_4$ is precipitated if

$[Ba^{2+}][SO_4^{2-}] > K_{sp}$

$$[Ba^{2+}]_{mix} = \frac{4\times10^{-3}}{4} = 10^{-3}\text{M}$$

$$[SO_4^{2-}]_{mix} = \frac{3\times6\times10^{-4}}{4} = 4.5\times10^{-4}\text{M}$$

$[Ba^{2+}][SO_4^{2-}] = 4.5\times10^{-7} > K_{sp}$

13. **(a)** Let, solubility of $Ca(OH)_2$ in pure water $= S$ mol/L

$$Ca(OH)_2 \rightleftharpoons \underset{S\ mol/L}{Ca^{2+}} + \underset{2\times S\ mol/L}{2\bar{O}H}$$

$K_{SP} = [Ca^{2+}][\bar{O}H]^2\ S\times(2s)^2 = 4S^3$ (mol/L)

$$S = \left(\frac{K_{sp}}{4}\right)^{\frac{1}{3}} = \left(\frac{5.4\times10^{-9}}{4}\right)^{\frac{1}{3}}$$

$$= (1.35\times10^{-9})^{\frac{1}{3}} = 1.10\times10^{-3}$$

14. **(c)** For $AB_2 \rightleftharpoons A^{2+} + 2B^-$

$K_{sp} = [A^{2+}][B^-]^2 = [1.6\times10^{-4}][0.4\times10^{-3}]^2$

$= 0.64\times10^{-7}\times0.4\times10^{-3}$

$= 0.256\times10^{-10} = 2.56\times10^{-11}$

15. **(b)** Given, K_{sp} for

$As_2S_3 = 2.08\times10^{-78}$

$As_2S_3(s) \rightleftharpoons 2As^{3+}(aq) + 3S^{2-}(aq)$

$K_{sp} = [As^{3+}]^2[S^{2-}]^3$

So, $K_{sp} = [2s]^2[3s]^3 = 4s^2\times27s^3$

$K_{sp} = 108s^5$

$$\Rightarrow \quad S = \left(\frac{K_{sp}}{108}\right)^{1/5} = \left(\frac{2.08\times10^{-78}}{108}\right)^{1/5}$$

$= (1.92\times10^{-80})^{1/5} = 1.14\times10^{-16}$

Hence, solubility, $S = 1.14\times10^{-16}$

16. **(a, b)** Among the given statements, a and b are incorrect while c and d are correct. The correct form of a and b are

(a) pH = 12

$\therefore$ pOH = 2

$\therefore \quad [OH^-] = 10^{-2}$

$Ba(OH)_2 \rightleftharpoons Ba^{2+} + 2OH^-$

$$\therefore [Ba^{2+}] = \left(\frac{10^{-2}}{2}\right)\text{M}$$

$\therefore \quad K_{sp} = [Ba^{2+}][OH^-]^2 = \left(\frac{10^{-2}}{2}\right)(10^{-2})^2 = 5.0 \times 10^{-7}\ M^3$

(b) $Hg_2Cl_2(s) \rightleftharpoons \underset{(S)}{Hg_2^{2+}} + \underset{(2S)}{2Cl^-}$

$K_{sp} = 4S^3$

$S = \sqrt[3]{\frac{K_{sp}}{4}} = \sqrt[3]{\frac{3.2 \times 10^{-17}}{4}} = 2 \times 10^{-6}\ M$

(c) Zirconium phosphate $Zr_3(PO_4)_4$

$Zr_3(PO_4)_4 \rightleftharpoons \underset{(3S)}{3Zr^{4+}} + \underset{(4S)}{4PO_4^{3-}}$

$K_{sp} = (3S)^3 (4S)^4 = 6912\ S^7$

17. ***(c, d)*** Among the given statements, (c) and (d) are correct while statement a is incorrect.

(a) For AgBr, $K_{sp} = [Ag^\oplus][Br^\ominus]$

So on increase in $[Br^\ominus]$, solubility of AgBr decreases.

(b) For $Zn(OH)_2$, $K_{sp} = [Zn^{2+}][\overset{\ominus}{O}H]^2$

$Zn(OH)_2$ is amphoteric in nature, so it solubility increases in both acidic as well as in strongly basic solution.

(c) For $Fe(OH)_3$, $K_{sp} = [Fe^{3+}][\overset{\ominus}{O}H]^3$.

In acidic solution $[^\ominus OH]$ decreases, so solubility increases.

Solubility decreases in presence of $^\ominus OH$.

(d) For AgCN, $K_{sp} = [Ag^\oplus][CN^\ominus]$

$CN^\ominus$ undergoes hydrolysis, so solubility in water is more than expected.

In acidic solution, $CN^\ominus$ gets protonated. So, solubility of AgCN increases.

AgCN forms complex $Ag(CN)_2^\ominus$ with excess of $CN^\ominus$.

18. ***(a, b)*** Among the given statements, a and b are correct regarding the given data.

(a) $\underset{0.05\ M}{NaCl} + \underset{0.05\ M}{NaI}$

When $AgNO_3$ is added, then the minimum concentration of $Ag^\oplus$ required to start precipitation.

$[Ag^\oplus]_{AgCl} = \frac{K_{sp}(NaCl)}{[Cl^\ominus]} = \frac{10^{-10}}{0.05} = 2 \times 10^{-9} M$

$[Ag^\oplus]_{AgI} = \frac{K_{sp(AgI)}}{[I^\ominus]} = \frac{4 \times 10^{-16}}{0.05} = 8 \times 10^{-15}\ M$

(c) Since, there is a very high difference between the minimum concentrations of $Ag^\oplus$, precipitation is selective and AgI will precipitate first.

19. ***(b, c)*** Among the given statements, (b) and (c) are correct regarding the given data.

$$K_1K_2 = \frac{[H^\oplus]^2[S^{2-}]}{[H_2S]} = 10^{-21}$$

Note Saturated H_2S means 0.1 M H_2S.

$\frac{(0.2)^2[S^{2-}]}{0.1} = 10^{-21}$

$\therefore \quad [S^{2-}] = \frac{10^{-22}}{0.04} = 2.5 \times 10^{-21}$

$K_{sp} = [Fe^{2+}][S^{2-}] = 3.7 \times 10^{-19}$

Since $(0.01)(2.5 \times 10^{-21}) < 3.7 \times 10^{-19}$

FeS will not precipitate in solution (i).

$\frac{(0.001)^2/[S^{2-}]}{0.1} = 10^{-21}$, $[S^{-2}] = 10^{-16}$.

Since $(0.01)(10^{-16}) > 3.7 \times 10^{-19}$

FeS will precipitate in solution (ii).

20. ***(a, b, c, d)*** Among the given statement, (a), (b), (c) and (d) all are correct about the solubility of AgCl.

(a) $AgCl(s) \rightleftharpoons Ag^\oplus + Cl^\ominus$

$Ag^\oplus + 2NH_3 \rightleftharpoons [Ag(NH_3)_2]^\oplus$

$AgCl(s) + 2NH_3 \rightleftharpoons [Ag(NH_2)_2]^\oplus + Cl^\oplus$

$K = \frac{[Ag(NH_3)_2]^\oplus \times Cl^\ominus}{[NH_3]^2} = K_{sp} \times K_f$

$\frac{S^2}{(2-2S)^2} = 10^8 \times 10^{-10} = 10^{-2} S = 0.166 M$

(b) $AgCl(s) \rightleftharpoons Ag^\oplus + Cl^\ominus$ in 2M $AgNO_3$

$S + 2 \approx 2\ S$ (Since 2 M >> S)

$10^{-10} = 2\ S \Rightarrow S = 10^{-10}/2 = 5 \times 10^{-11}$

(c) $S = 10^{-5}$ mol L^{-1} (No common ion)

(d) $S = \sqrt{K_{sp}} = \sqrt{10^{-10}} = 10^{-5}$ mol L^{-1}

$= 10^{-5} \times 143.5\ g\ L^{-1}$

21. ***(100)*** $NiC_2O_4(s) \rightleftharpoons \underset{(S)}{Ni^{2+}(aq)} + \underset{(S)}{C_2O_4^{2-}(aq)}$

$K_{sp} = [Ni^{2+}][C_2O_4^{2-}] = S^2$

$\therefore \quad S\ (NiC_2O_4) = \sqrt{K_{sp}} = \sqrt{4 \times 10^{-10}} = 2.0 \times 10^{-5} M$

$Na_3AlF_6(S) \rightleftharpoons \underset{3S}{3Na^+(aq)} + \underset{S}{AlF_6^{3-}(aq)}$

$K_{sp} = (Na^+)^3[AlF_6^{3-}] = (3S)^3(S) = 27S^4$

$S' = \sqrt[4]{\frac{K_{sp}}{27}} = \left(\frac{4 \times 10^{-10}}{27}\right)^{1/4}$

$S'(Na_3AlF_6) = 1.96 \times 10^{-3} M$

$\therefore \quad \frac{S\ (NiC_2O_4)}{S'(Na_3AlF_6)} = \frac{2.0 \times 10^{-5}}{1.96 \times 10^{-3}} = 0.01$

Na_3AlF_6 is 100 times more soluble than NiC_2O_4.

22. ***(667)*** $CaSO_4$ = 136 ppm = 136 g in 10^6 mL solution

= 0.136 g in 1000 mL solution

$= \frac{0.136}{136} = 1 \times 10^{-3}$ mol L^{-1}

$K_{sp} = [Ca^{2+}][SO_4^{2-}] = 9 \times 10^{-6}$

Maximum solubility,

$(CaSO_4) = \sqrt{9 \times 10^{-6}} = 3 \times 10^{-3} M$

Thus, $CaSO_4$ will precipitate.

3×10^{-3} mol is present $=1000$ mL

1×10^{-3} mol is present $=\frac{1000}{3}$ mL

Thus, water evaporated $=1000-\frac{1000}{3}=667$ mL

23. **(2)** $K_{sp}(AgCl) > K_{sp}(AgI)$

Hence, precipitation of AgI starts first.

$[Ag^+][Cl^-]=1\times10^{-10}$

$[Ag^+]$ required to precipitate $[Cl^-]=\frac{1\times10^{-10}}{0.05}=2.0\times10^{-9}$

$[I^-]$ at this stage $=\frac{K_{sp\,(AgI)}}{[Ag^+]\text{ required for }(Cl^-)}$

$=\frac{4.0\times10^{-16}}{2.0\times10^{-9}}=2.0\times10^{-7}M$

24. **(8)** $CaCO_3(s) \rightleftharpoons Ca^{2+}(aq)+CO_3^{2-}(aq)$

$K_{sp}=(Ca^{2+})[CO_3^{2-}]=S^2$

$\therefore S=\sqrt{K_{sp}}=8.7\times10^{-9}=9.32\times10^{-5}$ mol L^{-1}

$=9.327\times10^{-5}\times100$ g $L^{-1}=9.327\times10^{-3}$ g L^{-1}

$=9.327\times10^{-3}$ g $L^{-1}=9.327\times10^{-3}\times2$g / 2 L

$=0.0187$ g

In one time $CaCO_3$ removed $=0.0187$ g

Number $=\frac{14.92\text{ g}}{0.0187\text{ g}}\approx800$

$=100\times8=100\,n$

25. **(8)** $A_2B \rightleftharpoons 2A^+ + B^{2-}$

$K_{sp}=[A^+]^2[B^-]=K_{sp}$

$\log[A^+]^2+\log[B^{2-}]=\log K_{sp}$

$2\log[A^+]+\log[B^{2-}]=\log1\times10^{-16}$

$-2\log[A^+]-\log[B^{2-}]=+16 \Rightarrow -\log[A^+]-\frac{1}{2}\log[B^{2-}]=8$

$pK_A+\frac{1}{2}pK_B=8 \Rightarrow pK_A=-\frac{pK_B}{2}+8$

$y=-mx+C$

Thus, intercept is $C=8$

(and Slope $=\frac{1}{2}=\tan\theta$)

26. **(0.125)** If equal volume are mixed, concentration become half

$Ca(NO_3)_2 \rightleftharpoons Ca^{2+}+2NO_3^-$

Before mixing $=[Ca^{2+}]=0.06$ M

After mixing $[Ca^{2+}]=\frac{0.06}{2}=0.03$ M ...(i)

$CaF_2 \rightleftharpoons Ca^{2+}+2F^{\ominus}$

Before mixing, $F^{\ominus}=0.03$ M

After mixing, $F^{\ominus}=\frac{0.03}{2}=0.015$ M ...(ii)

From Eqs. (i) and (ii),

$Q=[Ca^{2+}][F^-]^2=(0.03)\times(0.015)^2$

$=6.75\times10^{-6}$

Since, $Q<K_{sp}$

So, the ratio of $[Ca^{2+}][F^-]^2$ and K_{sp}.

$=\frac{[Ca^{2+}][F^-]^2}{K_{sp}}=\frac{6.75\times10^{-6}}{0.6\times10^{-4}}=0.1125$

Practice Element 01 : Target JEE Main

1. **(d)** pH [HCl] = 2.0

$\therefore$ $[H^+]=10^{-2}$ M

$[HCl]=10^{-2}$ M

Volume $=200$ mL

pH [NaOH] = 12.0

pOH = 2.0

$[OH^-]=10^{-2}$ M

$[NaOH]=10^{-2}$ M

Volume $=300$ mL

N_1V_1(acid) $=200\times10^{-2}=2$

N_2V_2 (base) $=300\times10^{-2}=3$

$N_2V_2>N_1V_1$

Thus, resultant mixture is basic.

$N(OH^-)=\frac{N_2V_2-N_1V_1}{V_1+V_2}=\frac{3-2}{500}=2\times10^{-3}$ M

$pOH=-\log(2\times10^{-3})=2.7$

$\therefore$ $pH=14-pOH=14-2.7=11.3$

2. **(d)**

(a) $Ag_3PO_4 \rightleftharpoons 3Ag^+ + PO_4^{3-}$; $K_{sp}=[Ag^+]^3[PO_4^{3-}]$

$[PO_4^{3-}]=\frac{K_{sp}}{(0.1)^3}=\frac{1\times10^{-6}}{10^{-3}}=10^{-3}$ M

(b) $Ca_3(PO_4)_2 \rightleftharpoons 3Ca^{2+}+2PO_4^{3-}$;

$K_{sp}=[Ca^{2+}]^3[PO_4^{3-}]^2$

$10^{-33}=(0.1)^3[PO_4^{3-}]^2$

$[PO_4^{3-}]^2=\frac{10^{-33}}{10^{-3}}$

$[PO_4^{3-}]^2=10^{-30}$M

$[PO_4^{3-}]=1\times10^{-15}$ M

(c) $Mg_3(PO_4)_2 \rightleftharpoons \underset{0.1}{3Mg^{2+}}+2PO_4^{3-}$

as in (b)

$[PO_4^{3-}]^2=\frac{10^{-24}}{10^{-3}}=10\times10^{-22}$

$[PO_4^{3-}]=3.16\times10^{-11}$ M

(d) $AlPO_4=\underset{0.1}{Al^{3+}}+\underset{x}{PO_4^{3-}}$

$PO_4^{3-}=\frac{K_{sp}}{0.1}=\frac{10^{-20}}{0.1}=10^{-19}$M

3. ***(a)*** $Ag^+(aq) + Cl^-(aq) \rightleftharpoons AgCl(s), K = 1 \times 10^{-10}$

Thus, K_{sp} of $AgCl = 1 \times 10^{-10}$

$[Ag^+] = 0.10$ mg in 0.5 L $= 0.10 \times 10^{-3}$g in 0.5L

$= \dfrac{0.10 \times 10^{-3}}{108}$ mol in 0.5L

Thus, $[Ag^+] = \dfrac{9.26 \times 10^{-7}}{0.5} = 1.85 \times 10^{-6}$M

Also, $[Ag^+][Cl^-] = 1 \times 10^{-10}$

Thus, $[Cl^-] = \dfrac{1 \times 10^{-10}}{[Ag^+]} = \dfrac{1 \times 10^{-10}}{1.85 \times 10^{-6}} = 5.4 \times 10^{-5}$ M

4. ***(c)*** Salt with maximum solubility (S) will be precipitated at last.

	K_{sp}	Related to S	S
Ag_2CrO_4	1.1×10^{-12}	$4S^3 = K_{sp}$	6.50×10^{-5}M
AgCl	1.8×10^{-10}	$S^2 = K_{sp}$	1.34×10^{-5}M
AgBr	5.0×10^{-13}	$S^2 = K_{sp}$	7.07×10^{-7}M
AgI	8.3×10^{-17}	$S^2 = K_{sp}$	9.1×10^{-9}M

Ag_2CrO_4 has maximum solubility and AgI has least solubility.

AgI < AgBr < AgCl < Ag_2CrO_4

First of all precipitated ... last precipitated

5. ***(c)***

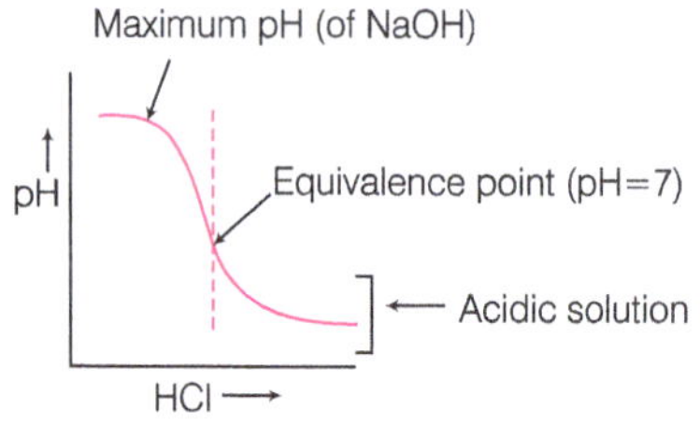

6. ***(d)*** S^{2-} is obtained from HS^-.

$[HS^-]$ in the presence of 0.1 M HCl is due to H_2S

$H_2S + H_2O \rightleftharpoons H_3O^+ + HS^-$

$$K_{a_1} = \frac{[H_3O^+][HS^-]}{[H_2S]}$$

$$\therefore [HS^-] = K_{a_1}\frac{[H_2S]}{[H_3O^+]} = \frac{9.1 \times 10^{-8} \times 0.1}{0.1} = 9.1 \times 10^{-8}\text{M}$$

$HS^- + H_2O \rightleftharpoons S^{2-} + H_3O^+$

$$K_{a_2} = \frac{[S^{2-}][H_3O^+]}{[HS^-]}$$

$$\Rightarrow 1.2 \times 10^{-13} = \frac{[S^{2-}][0.1]}{9.1 \times 10^{-8}}$$

$$\therefore \quad [S^{2-}] = \frac{1.2 \times 10^{-13} \times 9.1 \times 10^{-8}}{0.1} = 1.1 \times 10^{-19}\text{ M}$$

7. ***(b)*** Statement I is correct but statement II is in incorrect. It correct form is

If the acid ionisation (hydrolysis) constant of Zn^{2+} is 1.0×10^{-9}, then the pH of 0.001 M solution of $ZnCl_2$ is 6.

$Zn^{2+} + H_2O \rightleftharpoons Zn(OH)^+ + H^+$

$$K_h = 1 \times 10^{-9} \Rightarrow K_h = \frac{K_w}{K_b[Zn(OH)_2]}$$

$$\therefore \quad K_b = \frac{K_w}{K_h} = 1 \times 10^{-5}$$

$pK_b = 5$

$$\therefore \quad pH = 7 - \left(\frac{pK_b - \log C}{2}\right) = 7 - \frac{(5-3)}{2} = 6$$

I. $H_2SO_3 + NaOH \rightleftharpoons NaHSO_3 + H_2O$

20 mL of 0.160 M NaOH ≡ 3.2 millimol NaOH

40 mL of 0.080 M H_2SO_3 = 3.2 millimol H_2SO_3

Thus, H_2SO_3 is converted into $NaHSO_3$ and HSO_3^- is amphiprotic (H^+ ion donor as well as acceptor)

$\underset{\text{Acid}}{HSO_3^-} \rightleftharpoons H^+ + SO_3^{2-}$

$\underset{\text{Base}}{HSO_3^-} + H^+ \rightleftharpoons H_2SO_3$

$$pH = \frac{pK_{a_1} + pK_{a_2}}{2} = \frac{1.82 + 7.20}{2} = 4.51$$

8. ***(a)*** $M_2X_3 \rightleftharpoons \underset{2S}{2M^{3+}} + \underset{3S}{3X^{2-}}$ (where, S = solubility)

$$K_{sp} = (2S)^2 \cdot (3S)^3 = 108S^5$$

or $2.2 \times 10^{-20} = 108S^5$

$\therefore \quad S = 4.59 \times 10^{-5}$M

For M_2X, $M_2X \rightleftharpoons \underset{2s}{2M^+} + \underset{s}{X^{2-}}$

$K_{sp} = (2S)^2 \cdot (S) = 4S^3$M

$K_{sp} = 4(2 \times 4.59 \times 10^{-5})^3$

[∵ Solubility of $M_2X = 2 \times$ solubility of M_2X_3]

$= 3 \times 10^{-12}$

9. ***(d)*** $HCN \rightleftharpoons H^+ + CN^-, K_a = 4.5 \times 10^{-10}$

$CH_3COOH \rightleftharpoons H^+ + CH_3COO^-, K_{a'} = 1.5 \times 10^{-5}$

$CN^- + H^+ \rightleftharpoons HCN, K_a'' = \dfrac{1}{K_a}$

$CH_3COOH + CN^- \rightleftharpoons HCN + CH_3COO^-, K_{eq} = K_a' \cdot K_a''$

$$= 1.5 \times 10^{-5} \times \frac{1}{4.5 \times 10^{-10}} = 3.33 \times 10^4$$

10. ***(b)*** $pH = pK_a + \log\dfrac{[HPO_4^{2-}]}{[H_2PO_4^-]}$

$\because \; 7.40 = 7.10 + \log\dfrac{[HPO_4^{2-}]}{[H_2PO_4^-]}, \quad \log\dfrac{[HPO_4^{2-}]}{[H_2PO_4^-]} = 0.30$

$\dfrac{[HPO_4^{2-}]}{[H_2PO_4^-]} = \dfrac{2}{1}$ (Antilog of 0.3 = 2.0)

$\therefore \quad \dfrac{[H_2PO_4^-]}{[HPO_4^{2-}]} = \dfrac{1}{2}$

11. ***(c)*** When 19.31 mL of base added,
CH_3COOH is neutralised 50%
Thus $[CH_3COOH] = [CH_3COONa]$
$$\therefore \quad pH = pK_a + \log \frac{[CH_3COONa]}{[CH_3COOH]}$$
$$pH = pK_a$$

12. ***(a)*** SO_2 is pollutant of acid-rain. SO_2 dissolved in H_2O forming H_2SO_3 (sulphurous acid) which is ionised 100% as H^+ and HSO_3^-.

Thus, 0.12 ppm = 0.12 g per 10^6 mL $= \frac{0.12}{64}$ mol per 10^6 mL
$$= \left(\frac{0.12 \times 1000}{64 \times 10^6}\right) \text{mol L}^{-1} = 1.875 \times 10^{-6} \text{ M}$$
$$\therefore \quad [H^+] = 1.875 \times 10^{-6} \text{ M}$$
$$\therefore \quad pH = -\log[H^+] = -\log(1.875 \times 10^{-6}) = 5.73$$

13. ***(c)*** pH = 9.26 indicates $[NH_4OH] > [HCl]$ and thus mixture is a buffer since HCl will react with equivalent amount of NH_4OH forming NH_4Cl.
$$M \times V = \text{millimol}$$
Let, HCl $= x$ mL $= x$ mmol
$NH_4OH = (300 - x)$ mL $= (300 - x)$ mmol
NH_4Cl formed $= x$ millimol
NH_4OH unreacted $= 300 - x - x = (300 - 2x)$ mmol
$$pOH = 14 - 9.26 = 4.74$$
$$pK_b = 14 - 9.26 = 4.74$$
$$pOH = pK_b + \log \frac{[NH_4^+]}{[NH_4OH]}$$
$$4.74 = 4.74 + \log \frac{x}{(300 - 2x)} \Rightarrow \frac{x}{300 - 2x} = 1$$
$$x = 100 \text{ mL} = \text{volume of HCl}$$
$(300 - x) = 200$ mL = volume of NH_4OH, hence 2:1.

14. ***(d)*** Buffer is a mixture of V mL of 1 M NH_4Cl and $(1000 - V)$ mL of 1 M NH_4OH
$$pH = 9.80$$
$$\therefore \quad pOH = 4.2$$
$$\therefore \quad pOH = pK_b + \log \frac{[NH_4Cl]}{[NH_4OH]}$$
$$\because \quad MV = \text{millimol}$$
$$\therefore \quad [NH_4Cl] = V \text{ millimol}$$
and $[NH_4OH] = (1000 - V)$ millimol
$$\therefore \quad 4.20 = 4.74 + \log \frac{(V)}{(1000 - V)}$$
$$-0.54 = \log\left(\frac{V}{1000 - V}\right)$$
$$\log 0.288 = \log\left(\frac{V}{1000 - V}\right)$$
$$\therefore \quad \frac{V}{1000 - V} = 0.288$$
$$V = 288 - 0.288\,V$$
$$\therefore \quad V = 223.6 \approx 224 \text{ mL}$$

15. ***(b)*** SO_2 in atmosphere = 10 ppm = 10 g in 10^6 mL H_2O
$$= \frac{10}{64} \text{mol in } 10^6 \text{ mL } H_2O$$
$$= \frac{10 \times 10^3}{64 \times 10^6} \text{mol L}^{-1} = 1.5625 \times 10^{-4} \text{M}$$
Given, solubility of SO_2 is 1.3653 M. Thus, all the atmospheric SO_2 dissolves in H_2O giving H_2SO_3 of 1.5625×10^{-4} M.
$$H_2O + SO_2 \rightleftharpoons H_2SO_3$$
$$H_2SO_3 \rightleftharpoons H^+ + HSO_3^- \text{ (first ionisation considered)}$$

	H_2SO_3	H^+	HSO_3^-
Initial	C	0	0
After ionisation	$C - Cx$	Cx	Cx

$$K_a = \frac{[H^+]\,[HSO_3^-]}{[H_2SO_3]}, \; pK_a = 1.92$$
$$\therefore \quad K_a = 10^{-1.92} = 10^{0.08} \times 10^{-2} = 1.20 \times 10^{-2}$$
$$1.2 \times 10^{-2} = \frac{Cx^2}{(1 - x)} \Rightarrow 1.2 \times 10^{-2} = \frac{1.5625 \times 10^{-4} x^2}{(1 - x)}$$
$$x = 0.9873$$
$$\therefore \quad [H^+] = Cx = 1.5625 \times 10^{-4} \times 0.9873 \text{M}$$
$$= 1.5427 \times 10^{-4} \text{M} \Rightarrow pH = -\log [H^+] = 3.81$$

16. ***(d)*** Formation constant, K_f, of the complex $[Ag(CN)_2^-]$ is very high hence, it is assumed that all the Ag^+ has been complexed such that $[Ag(CN)_2^-] = 1.8$ M

Thus, $[CN^-]$ can be evaluated.

$Ag^+(aq)$ from AgCl (s) undergoes complex formation with CN^-
$$AgCl(s) \rightleftharpoons Ag^+(aq) + Cl^-(aq), K_1 = K_{sp}$$
$$Ag^+(aq) + 2CN^-(aq) \rightleftharpoons [Ag(CN)_2]^-, K_2 = K_f$$
$$AgCl(s) + 2CN^-(aq) \rightleftharpoons [Ag(CN)_2]^-(aq); + Cl^-(aq)$$
$$K = \frac{[Ag(CN)_2^-]\,[Cl^-]}{[CN^-]^2} = K_1K_2 = K_{sp} \cdot K_f$$
$$[Ag^+] = [Ag(CN)_2^-] = 1.8 \text{ M}$$
(Since value of K_f is very high, all Ag^+ is complexed)
$$[Cl^-] = 0.327 \text{ M}$$
$$\therefore \quad \frac{1.8 \times 0.327}{[CN^-]^2} = 1.8 \times 10^{-10} \times 5.6 \times 10^{18}$$
$$\therefore \quad [CN^-] = 2.42 \times 10^{-5} \text{M}$$

17. ***(a)*** $C_2O_4^{2-}$ from saturated CaC_2O_4 is oxidised to CO_2 by MnO_4^- in acidic medium. Moles of MnO_4^- and $C_2O_4^{2-}$ are determined.

Also 5 mol of $C_2O_4^{2-} \equiv 2$ mol of MnO_4^-

hence, $[C_2O_4^{2-}]$ and K_{sp} of CaC_2O_4 is calculated.

Let, molarity of $CaC_2O_4(aq) = M_1$

Moles of $CaC_2O_4 = \frac{250\ M_1}{1000} = 0.250\ M_1$ mol

Moles of $MnO_4^- = \frac{6.3 \times 0.00102}{1000} = 6.426 \times 10^{-6}$ mol

Since 2 mol MnO_4^- = 5 mol $C_2O_4^{2-}$

$\therefore 6.426 \times 10^{-6}$ mol $MnO_4^- = \frac{5}{2} \times 6.426 \times 10^{-6}$ mol $C_2O_4^{2-}$

$= 1.6065 \times 10^{-5}$ mol $C_2O_4^{2-}$

$\therefore\ 0.250 M_1 = 1.6065 \times 10^{-5}$ mol $C_2O_4^{2-}$

$[Ca^{2+}] = [C_2O_4^{2-}] = M_1 = 6.426 \times 10^{-5}$ M

$\therefore K_{sp}(CaC_2O_4) = [Ca^{2+}][C_2O_4^{2-}] = 4.13 \times 10^{-9}$

18. ***(c)*** Molar solubility S of a gas in aqueous solution is dependent on pressure given by Henry's law.

$$S = k\,p_{gas}$$

where, k is Henry's constant. Thus, S is known

$$H_2O + CO_2 \rightleftharpoons H_2CO_3$$

$$H_2CO_3 \rightleftharpoons H^+ + HCO_3^-$$

For weak acid, by Ostwald's dilution law,

$$[H^+] = \sqrt{K_aC} = \sqrt{K_aS}$$

hence, pH is calculated.

Molar solubility of CO_2 in H_2O

$S = k\,p_{CO_2}$

$S = 2.3 \times 10^{-2} \times 3.04 \times 10^{-4} = 6.992 \times 10^{-6}$ mol L^{-1}

$$H_2CO_3 \rightleftharpoons H^+ + HCO_3^-$$

$$[H^+] = \sqrt{K_aS} \Rightarrow \text{pH} = \frac{1}{2}[pK_a - \log S]$$

$$\therefore \text{pH} = \frac{1}{2}[6.37 - \log 6.992 \times 10^{-6}] = \frac{1}{2}[6.37 + 5.16]$$

pH = 5.76 s

19. ***(a)*** $\Delta G° = -2.303RT \log K$ and $\Delta G° = \Delta H° - T\Delta S°$.

Thus, from the values of $\Delta H°$ and $\Delta S°$, $\Delta G°$ is calculated.

Hence, $K = K_b$, dissociation constant of NH_4OH is calculated.

Given, $NH_3 + H^+ \longrightarrow NH_4^+$

$$H_2O \longrightarrow H^+ + OH^-$$

adding, (alongwith energy parameters)

$$NH_3 + H_2O \rightleftharpoons NH_4^+ + OH^-$$

or $$NH_4OH \rightleftharpoons NH_4^+ + OH^-,$$

$$K_b = \frac{[NH_4^+][OH^-]}{[NH_4OH]}$$

hence, $\Delta H° = -52.2 + 56.6$ kJ mol^{-1} = 4.4 kJ mol^{-1}

and similarly

$\Delta S° = -76.53$ JK^{-1}mol^{-1} = -76.53×10^{-3} kJK^{-1}mol^{-1}

using $\Delta G° = \Delta H° - T\Delta S°$

$\Delta G° = +4.4 - 298 \times (-76.53 \times 10^{-3}) = +27.21$ kJ mol^{-1}

also $\Delta G° = -2.303RT \log K_b$

$\therefore\ 27.21 = -2.303 \times 8.3143 \times 10^{-3} \times 298 \times \log K_b$

$\therefore\ K_b = 1.7 \times 10^{-5}$

20. ***(a)*** Both A and R are true and R is the correct explanation of A.

21. ***(3)*** Given, $[HA] = 0.3$

$[HCl] = 0.1$ M

When strong acid (HCl) is completely dissociated,

$$\underset{0.1}{HCl} \longrightarrow \underset{0.1}{H^+(aq)} + \underset{0.1}{Cl^-(aq)}$$

For weak acid, dissociation is very less,

	$HA \rightleftharpoons$	$H^+(aq) +$	$A^-(aq)$
At, $t = 0$	0.3	0.1	0
At, $t = t_{eq}$	$0.3 - 0.3\alpha$	$0.1 + 0.3\alpha$	0.3α

$$K_a = \frac{[H^+][A^-]}{[HA]} = 3.0 \times 10^{-6}$$

$$3 \times 10^{-6} = \frac{(0.1 + 0.3\alpha)(0.3\alpha)}{(0.3 - 0.3\alpha)} \quad \begin{bmatrix} 0.3\alpha << 0.1 \\ 0.3\alpha < 0.3 \end{bmatrix}$$

$$\therefore\ 3 \times 10^{-6} = \frac{0.1 \times 0.3\alpha}{0.3}$$

$$\alpha = \frac{3 \times 10^{-6} \times 0.3}{0.1 \times 0.3} = 30 \times 10^{-6} = 3.0 \times 10^{-5}$$

$\Rightarrow\ x = 3$

22. ***(419)*** The solubility equilibrium in this case is represented as

(i) $Zn(OH)_2(s) \rightleftharpoons Zn^{2+}(aq) + 2OH^-(aq)$

$$K_{sp} = [Zn^{2+}][OH^-]^2 = 1.18 \times 10^{-17}$$

(ii) $Zn^{2+} + 4NH_3(aq) \rightleftharpoons [Zn(NH_3)_4]^{2+}$

$$K_{stab} = \frac{[Zn(NH_3)_4]^{2+}}{[Zn^{2+}][NH_3]^4}$$

The overall reaction is obtained by adding reactions (i) and (ii):

$$Zn(OH)_2(s) + \underset{1-4x}{4NH_3(aq)} \rightleftharpoons \underset{x}{[Zn(NH_3)_4]^{2+}} + \underset{2x}{2OH^-(aq)}$$

$$K_{eq} = \frac{[Zn(NH_3)_4]^{2+}[OH^-]^2}{[NH_3]^4}$$

$$= \frac{[Zn^{2+}][OH^-]^2[Zn(NH_3)_4]^{2+}}{[Zn^{2+}][NH_3]^4}$$

$$= K_{sp}K_{stab}$$

If x is the molar solubility of $Zn(OH)_2$ in 1 M NH_3 solution, then, at equilibrium,

$[NH_3] = 1 - 4x$: $[OH^-] = 2x$ and $[Zn(NH_3)_4]^{2+} = x$

$$K_{eq} = \frac{x(2x)^2}{(1-4x)^4} = 4x^3 \text{ (since } 4x << 1)$$

$$4x^3 = K_{eq} = K_{sp}K_{stab} = (1.8 \times 10^{-17})(1.64 \times 10^{10})$$

$$x = 4.19 \times 10^{-3} \text{ mol dm}^{-3} = 419 \times 10^{-5}$$

$$x = 419$$

23. ***(13)*** Knowing that the product of volume in millilitres and molarity gives the number of millimoles of the acid or the base, we have

Number of millimoles of the acid in the solution

$= 25 \times 0.2 = 5$

Number of millimoles of the alkali in the solution

$= 50 \times 0.25 = 12.5$

Number of millimoles of the alkali left in the solution after the addition of the acid $= 12.5 - 5 = 7.5$

Total volume of the solution $= 50 + 25 = 75$ ml

Concentration of OH^- ions $= \dfrac{7.5 \times 1000}{75 \times 1000} = 0.10 \text{ mol dm}^{-3}$

$[H^+][OH^-] = 10^{-14} \text{ mol}^2 \text{ dm}^{-6}$ at 25°C

$[OH^-] = 0.10 \text{ mol dm}^{-3}$

$[H^+] = 10^{-14} \text{ mol}^2 \text{ dm}^{-6}/0.10 \text{ mol dm}^{-3} = 10^{-13} \text{ mol dm}^{-3}$

$pH = -\log [H^+] = -\log(10^{-13}) = 13$

24. ***(16000)*** $[AgBr] = [Ag^+] = 0.03$ M

$AgBr \rightleftharpoons Ag^+ + Br^-$

$K_{sp}[AgBr] = [Ag^+][Br^-]$

$$[Br^-] = \frac{K_{sp}[AgBr]}{[Ag^+]} = \frac{4.0 \times 10^{-12}}{0.03} = 133.33 \times 10^{-12}$$

Moles of KBr needed to precipitate AgBr

$= [Br^-] \times V = 133.33 \times 10^{-12} \text{ mol L}^{-1} \times 1 \text{ L}$

$= 133.33 \times 10^{-12}$ mol

Therefore, amount of KBr needed to precipitate AgBr

$= 133.33 \times 10^{-12} \text{ mol} \times 120 \text{ g mol}^{-1}$

$= 15999.6 \times 10^{-12} \text{ g} \approx 16000 \times 10^{-12}$ g

25. ***(23)*** $[HCOOH_2^+][HCOO^-] = 10^{-6}$

$\therefore [HCOO^-] = 10^{-3}$

$$\underset{C-2x}{2HCOOH} \rightleftharpoons \underset{x}{HCOOH_2^+} + \underset{x}{HCO_2^-}$$

$\therefore \quad \alpha = \dfrac{2x}{C}$

$4 \times 10^{-5} = \dfrac{2 \times 10^{-3}}{C}$

$\therefore \quad [HCOOH] = 50$ M

$d = 2.3 \text{ g/L} = 23 \times 10^{-1}$ g/L

Thus, the value of Z is 23.

26. ***(5)***

	$NH_4Cl + H_2O$	$\rightleftharpoons$	NH_2OH	$+ HCl$
Before hydrolysis	1		0	0
After hydrolysis	$1-h$		h	h

where, h is the degree of hydrolysis.

$\therefore \quad [H^{\oplus}] = C \cdot h = C\sqrt{(K_h/C)} = \sqrt{(K_h \cdot C)}$

$= \sqrt{(K_w \cdot C/K_b)}$

$= \sqrt{\dfrac{10^{-14} \times 0.2}{1.8 \times 10^{-5}}} = 1.054 \times 10^{-5}$

$\therefore \quad pH = -\log [H^{\oplus}] = -\log (1.054 \times 10^{-5})$

$= 4.9771 \approx 5$

27. ***(2)*** Concentration of Ag^+ when AgCl starts precipitating is 2×10^{-9}

So concentration of I^- when AgCl start precipitating

$= \dfrac{4 \times 10^{-16}}{2 \times 10^{-9}} = 2 \times 10^{-7}$ M

28. ***(98)*** $BOH + HCl \rightleftharpoons BCl + H_2O$

No. of mmoles of BCl in solution = 6

No. of mmoles of NaOH added = 3

	BOH	$+ HCl \rightleftharpoons$	$BCl + H_2O$
Intial mole	6	3	—
equil mole	3	—	3

$\therefore \quad pOH = pK_b = 4.2$

Then $pH = 9.8 = 98 \times 10^{-1}$

Thus, the value of x is 98.

29. ***(117)*** For $AB_2 \rightleftharpoons A^{2+} + 2B^-$

$K_{sp} = [A^{2+}] \times [B^-]^2$

$= (1.3 \times 10^{-4}) \times (0.3 \times 10^{-2})^2$

$= 0.117 \times 10^{-8} = 117 \times 10^{-11}$

30. ***(1)*** $Bi_2S_3 \rightleftharpoons 2Bi^{3+} + 3S^{2-}$

$K_{sp} = (2S)^2 (3S)^3 = 108S^5$

$S^5 = \dfrac{1.08 \times 10^{-73}}{108}$

$S^5 = 10^{-2} \times 10^{-73}$

$S^5 = 10^{-75}$

$S = 1 \times 10^{-15}$

Check Through PYQs : JEE Main

1. ***(d)*** $H_2C_2O_4 \overset{K_{a_3}}{\rightleftharpoons} 2H^+ + C_2O_4^{2-}$

$H_2C_2O_4 \overset{K_{a_1}}{\rightleftharpoons} H^+ + HC_2O_4^-$

$HC_2O_4^- \overset{K_{a_2}}{\rightleftharpoons} H^+ + C_2O_4^{2-}$

$$K_{a_3} = \frac{[H^+]^2[C_2O_4^{2-}]}{[H_2C_2O_4]} \quad \ldots(i)$$

$$K_{a_1} = \frac{[H^+][HC_2O_4^-]}{[H_2C_2O_4]} \quad \ldots(ii)$$

$$K_{a_2} = \frac{[H^+][C_2O_4^{2-}]}{[H_2C_2O_4]} \quad \ldots(iii)$$

In order to obtain Eq. (iii) we have to multiply Eq. (i) and (ii)

$$\therefore \quad K_{a_1} \times K_{a_2} = \frac{[H^+][HC_2O_4^-]}{[H_2C_2O_4]} \times \frac{[H^+][C_2O_4^{2-}]}{[HC_2O_4^-]}$$

$$= \frac{[H^+]^2[C_2O_4^{2-}]}{[H_2C_2O_4]} = Ka_3$$

$K_{a_1} \times K_{a_2} = K_{a_3}$

So, option (d) is correct.

2. ***(d)*** Assertion is false but Reason is true. The amphoteric nature of water can be explained by Bronsted-Lowry concept.

$$\underset{\text{Acid}}{H_2S} + \underset{\text{Base}}{H_2O} \rightleftharpoons H_3O^+ + HS^-$$

$$\underset{\text{Acid}}{H_2O} + \underset{\text{Base}}{NH_3} \rightleftharpoons NH_4^+ + \bar{O}H$$

3. ***(1)*** $Ba(OH)_2$ is completely ionised in aqueous solution.

$$Ba(OH)_2 \longrightarrow Ba^{2+} + 2OH^-$$

$$[Ba(OH)_2] = 0.005\,M$$

$$\Rightarrow \quad 2 \times 0.005 \Rightarrow 0.01$$

$$\Rightarrow \quad [OH^-] = 10^{-2}$$

At 298 K, in aqueous solution ;

$$[H_3O^+]\,[OH^-] = 10^{-14}$$

$$[H_3O^+] = \frac{10^{-14}}{10^{-2}} = 10^{-12}$$

$$[H_3O^+] = 1 \times 10^{-12}\,M$$

4. ***(2)*** Given, $HA = 0.01$ mole

$$[HCl] = 0.1\,M$$

When strong acid (HCl) is completely dissociated,

$$\underset{0.1}{HCl} \longrightarrow \underset{0.1}{H^+(aq)} + \underset{0.1}{Cl^-(aq)}$$

For weak acid, dissociation is very less,

	HA	$\rightleftharpoons$ $H^+(aq)$	$+ A^-(aq)$
$t = 0$	0.01	0.1	0
$t = t_{eq}$	$0.01 - 0.01\alpha$	$0.1 + 0.01\alpha$	0.01α

$$K_a = \frac{[H^+]\,[A^-]}{[HA]} = 2 \times 10^{-6}$$

$$\Rightarrow \quad \frac{(0.1 + 0.01\alpha)\,(0.01\alpha)}{(0.01 - 0.01\alpha)} = 2 \times 10^{-6}$$

As $0.01\alpha << 0.1$ $[H^+] = 0.1$

and $0.01\alpha << 0.01$ $[HA] = 0.01$

$$\therefore 2 \times 10^{-6} = \frac{(0.1)\,(0.01\alpha)}{0.01}$$

$$\Rightarrow \alpha = 2 \times 10^{-5} \quad \Rightarrow x = 2$$

5. ***(a)*** Statement I is false but statement II is true. The correct form of statement I is, Buffer solution is the mixture of weak acid or weak base with their conjugate ions.

Hence, option ***(a)*** is correct.

6. ***(7)*** Ammonium acetate is a salt of weak acid and weak base. So, to calculate the pH value of ammonium acetate, we have to first calculate pK_a and pK_b values of acetic acid and ammonium hydroxide. Further apply the formula

$$pH = 7 + \frac{1}{2}[pK_a - pK_b]$$

Given, K_a of $CH_3COOH = 1.8 \times 10^{-5}$

K_b of $NH_4OH = 1.8 \times 10^{-5}$

Using the formula,

$$pH = 7 + \frac{1}{2}[pK_a - pK_b] \quad \text{...(i)}$$

$$pK_a = -\log(K_a) = -\log(1.8 \times 10^{-5})$$

$$= +\,4.7447 \quad \text{...(ii)}$$

$$pK_b = -\log(K_b)$$

$$= -\log\,(1.8 \times 10^{-5})$$

$$= 4.7447 \quad \text{...(iii)}$$

Put value of Eq. (ii) and (iii) in Eq. (i)

$$pH = 7 + \frac{1}{2}[4.7447 - 4.7447] = 7$$

7. ***(100)*** Given,

Solution contains = 1 M benzoic acid (V_a mL)

+ 1 M sodium benzoate (V_s mL)

Total volume of buffer solution = 300 mL

$$pH = 4.5,\ pK_a = 4.20$$

$$pH = pK_a + \log\frac{[\text{salt}]}{[\text{acid}]} \quad \text{...(i)}$$

$$4.5 = 4.2 + \log\left[\frac{V_s}{V_a}\right]$$

$$\frac{V_s}{V_a} = 2 \quad \text{...(ii)}$$

$$V_s + V_a = 300 \quad \text{...(iii)}$$

From Eqs. (ii) and (iii)

$$V_a = 100\text{ mL}, V_s = 200\text{ mL}$$

Hence, volume of benzoic acid is 100 mL.

8. ***(c)*** Both the Statement I and Statement II are correct.

9. ***(458)*** 20 mL of 0.1 M NaOH = 2 m mole of NaOH (base)

50 mL of 0.1 M CH_3COOH = 5 m mole of CH_3COOH (acid)

Now, when acid reacts with base, gives salt and water. This reaction is called neutralisation reaction.

$$\underbrace{\underset{5\text{ m mol}}{CH_3COOH} + \underset{2\text{ m mol}}{NaOH}}_{\substack{3\text{ m mol of}\\(CH_3COOH\text{ will}\\\text{left})}} \longrightarrow \underset{\substack{(2\text{ m mol}\\\text{of salt}\\\text{will formed})}}{CH_3COONa} + H_2O$$

Now, with weak acid and the salt of weak acid, a buffer solution will be formed, pH can be calcualted from Henderson equation

$$pH = pK_a + \log\left[\frac{A^\ominus\text{ ion}}{HA\text{ acid}}\right]$$

$$pH = 4.76 + \log\left[\frac{2\text{ m mol}}{3\text{ m mol}}\right]$$

$$pH = 4.76 + \{\log(2) - \log(3)\}$$

$$pH = 4.76 + [0.30 - 0.48]$$

$$pH = 4.58 \text{ or } (458 \times 10^{-2})$$

10. ***(85)*** Concentration of lactate ion $= (2 \times 0.005)$ M.

As we know that, calcium lactate is a salt of weak acid and strong base so salt hydrolysis will take place.

$$pH = 7 + \frac{1}{2}(pK_a + \log c)$$

$$= 7 + \frac{1}{2}[5 + \log(2 \times 0.005)]$$

$$= 7 + \frac{3}{2} = \frac{17}{2} = 8.5 = 85 \times 10^{-1}.$$

Therefore, the pH of 0.005 M calcium lactate solution at 25°C is 85×10^{-1}.

11. ***(c)*** Given, [Base] = $[NH_3] = 0.2$ M

pH of buffer = 8.26

$pK_b (NH_3) = 4.74$

Molar mass of NH_3 = 17 g mol^{-1}

Molar mass of NH_4Cl = 53.5 g mol^{-1}

We know, $pOH = 14 - pH = 14 - 8.26 = 5.74$

Using the expression,

$$pOH = pK_b + \log \frac{[Salt]}{[Base]}$$

or, $$5.74 = 4.74 + \log \frac{[NH_4Cl]}{[0.2]}$$

or $[NH_4Cl] = 2$ moles

Moles of NH_3 = Moles of $NH_4Cl = 2$

So, the amount of NH_4Cl required

= Number of moles × Molecular mass

$= 2 \times 53.5 = 107$ g

12. ***(476)*** Moles of CH_3COOH

= Molarity of CH_3COOH × Volume of CH_3COOH(in L)

$= 0.1\ M \times \frac{50}{1000}\ L = 0.005$ moles

Similarly, moles of NaOH = 0.0025 moles

	NaOH +	$CH_3COOH \longrightarrow$	CH_3COONa +	H_2O
Initial conc.	0.0025 mol	0.005 mol	0	0
Final conc.	0	0.0025	0.0025 mol	0.0025 mol

So, buffer is formed, according to Henderson-Hasselbalch equation

$$pH = pK_a + \log\left(\frac{[Salt]}{[Acid]}\right) = pK_a + \log\left(\frac{\frac{0.0025}{75}}{\frac{0.0025}{75}}\right)$$

$= pH = 4.76 = 476 \times 10^{-2}$

13. ***(3)*** $NH_3 + H_2O \rightleftharpoons NH_4^+ + OH^-$

$[NH_3] = 2 \times 0.0210 = 0.042$ m mol

$NH_4Cl \longrightarrow NH_4^+ + Cl^-$

$[NH_4Cl] = 5 \times 0.0504 = 0.252$ m mol

By Henderson-Hasselbalch equation,

$$pOH = pK_b + \log \frac{[Salt]}{[Base]} = -\log (1.8 \times 10^{-5}) + \log \frac{0.252}{0.042}$$

$= 4.74 + 0.77 = 5.51$

$[OH^-] = 10^{-5.51} = 3.09 \times 10^{-6} \approx 3 \times 10^{-6}$

The value of x is 3.

14. ***(10)*** Concentration of acetic acid in buffer = 1.0 M

Acetic acid and its conjugate base sodium acetate makes acidic buffer.

$CH_3COOH + CH_3COONa \longrightarrow$ (Acidic buffer)

Using formula,

$$pH = pK_a + \log \frac{[CH_3COONa]}{[CH_3COOH]}$$

$$5.74 = 4.74 + \log \frac{[CH_3COONa]}{[CH_3COOH]}$$

$$\Rightarrow \frac{[CH_3COONa]}{[CH_3COOH]} = 10 \qquad \therefore [CH_3COOH] = 1$$

$[CH_3COONa] = [10 \times 1] = 10$

Thus, the concentration of sodium acetate in buffer is 10 M.

15. ***(a)*** $AgCN \rightleftharpoons Ag^+ + CN^-$

Solubility of AgCN is x.

$pH = 3 \Rightarrow [H^+] = 10^{-3}$

$HCN \rightleftharpoons H^+ + CN^-$

$$K_a = \frac{[H^+][CN^-]}{[HCN]}$$

$$\Rightarrow \frac{[10^{-3}][CN^-]}{[HCN]} = 6.2 \times 10^{-10} \Rightarrow \frac{[CN^-]}{[HCN]} = 6.2 \times 10^{-7}$$

Each CN upon hydrolysis to give one HCN as:

$CN^- + H_2O \rightleftharpoons HCN + OH^-$

HCN is a weak acid, thus,

$[HCN] >> [CN^-]$

$x = [Ag^+] = [CN^-] + [HCN]$

$\Rightarrow x = [Ag^+] \approx [HCN]$

$\Rightarrow [CN^-] = x \times 6.2 \times 10^{-7}$

$K_{sp}(AgCN) = [Ag^+][CN^-]$

$\Rightarrow 2.2 \times 10^{-16} = (x)(x \times 6.2 \times 10^{-7})$

$\Rightarrow x^2 = 3.55 \times 10^{-10}$

$\Rightarrow x = 1.88 \times 10^{-5} \approx 1.9 \times 10^{-5}$

16. ***(b)*** Given molar concentration are same. So strongest acid (HCl) will have max. pOH

Strongest base (NaOH) will have min. pOH

Neutral salt (NaCl) will have pOH equal to 7.

CH_3COONa is the salt of weak acid and strong base thus having pOH value less than 7.

Thus, order of pOH value :

(A) > (D) > (C) > (B)

Hence, the correct option is (b).

17. ***(a)*** Volume of HCl = 100 mL

Molarity of HCl = 0.1 M

Volume of NaOH = 100 mL

Molarity of NaOH = 0.1 M

Initially when only HCl is present in the beaker, then the pH is less than 7, so the graph looks like.

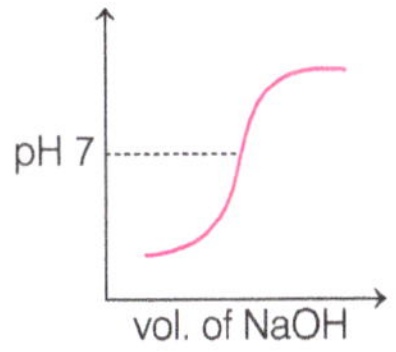

On adding 2 mL of NaOH continuously the pH value gradually increases and reach to equivalence point at pH = 7. On further addition of NaOH the pH value increases further beyond the equivalence point so, the final graph look like.

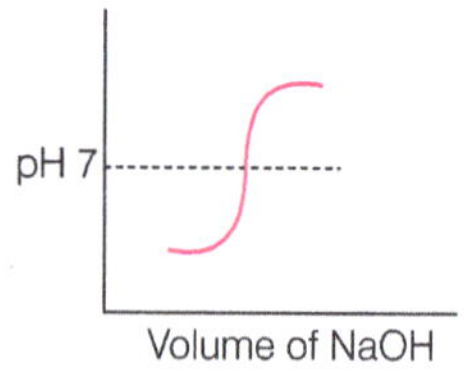

Hence, option (a) is correct.

18. ***(c)*** The strength of aqueous NaOH solution is most accurately determined by titrating aqueous NaOH in burette and aqueous oxalic acid in conical flask with phenolphthalein (used as an indicator). For weak acid-strong base titration, methyl orange cannot be used.

Thus, solution turns colourless to pink at the end point.

19. ***(5.23)*** 3g CH_3COOH $(M = 60) = \frac{3}{60} = \frac{1}{20}$ mol

250 mL of 0.1 M HCl $= M \times V = \frac{250}{1000} \times 0.1$

$= 25 \times 10^{-3}$ mol

After mixing solution is diluted to 500 mL.

Then from that solution, 20 mL is taken.

Number of moles of both CH_3COOH and HCl will be now only $\frac{20}{500} = \frac{1}{25}$ of original solution.

$$n_{CH_3COOH} = \frac{1}{20} \times \frac{1}{25} = \frac{1}{500} = 2 \times 10^{-3} \text{ mol}$$

$$n_{HCl} = 25 \times 10^{-3} \times \frac{1}{25}$$

$$= 10^{-3} \text{ mol}$$

$$n_{NaOH} \text{ added} = M \times V = \frac{1}{2} \times 5 \times 10^{-3}$$

$$= 2.5 \times 10^{-3}$$

After mixing, all HCl and NaOH will be neutralised. Remaining number of moles.

$n_{NaCl} = 10^{-3}$

$n_{CH_3COONa} = 1.5 \times 10^{-3}$

n_{CH_3COOH} (unreacted) $= 0.5 \times 10^{-3}$

∴ Now the solution is a buffer solution.

$$= pK_a + \log \frac{(n_{CH_3COONa})}{(n_{CH_3COOH})}$$

$$= 4.75 + \log 3 = 4.75 + 0.4771 = 5.2271 \approx 5.23$$

20. ***(10.60)*** (*A*) 4 g NaOH in 100 L

$$\Rightarrow M = \frac{4/40}{100} = 10^{-3} \text{ mol L}^{-1}.$$

(*B*) 9.8 g H_2SO_4 in 100 L

$$\Rightarrow M = \frac{9.8/98}{100} = 10^{-3} \text{ mol L}^{-1}$$

40 L of solution *A* contains

$= 40 \times 10^{-3}$ mol NaOH $\quad (\because n = M \times V)$

$= 40 \times 10^{-3}$ mol OH^-

10 L of solution *B* contains $= 10 \times 10^{-3}$ mol H_2SO_4

$= 20 \times 10^{-3}$ mol H^+

When they are mixed, total volume = 50 L

and all H^+ is neutralised by OH^-.

Number of moles (n_{OH^-}) of excess OH^-.

$= (40 - 20) \times 10^{-3} = 20 \times 10^{-3}$

$$[OH^-] = \frac{n_{OH^-}}{V_{solution}} \text{ (in litre)}$$

Or $$[OH^-] = \frac{n_{OH^-}}{\text{Total volume}}$$

$$= \frac{20 \times 10^{-3}}{50} = 4 \times 10^{-4} \text{ M}$$

As we know,

$pOH = -\log[OH^-]$

∴ $pOH = -\log 4 \times 10^{-4} = 4 - \log 4$

or $pH = 14 - pOH$

$= 14 - (4 - \log 4) = 10 + \log 4 = 10.602$

21. ***(b)*** $Cr(OH)_3(s) \rightleftharpoons Cr^{3+}(aq) + 3OH^-(aq)$

$\quad s \quad 2s$

$$K_{sp} = s^1(3s)^3$$

$$K_{sp} = 27s^4$$

$$s^4 = \frac{1.6}{27} \times 10^{-30} \text{ M}^4$$

$$s^4 = \frac{160}{27} \times 10^{-32}$$

$$= 5.92 \times 10^{-32}$$

$$s = 1.56 \times 10^{-8}$$

$$x = 8$$

22. ***(b)*** As water is heated degree of ionisation increases $[H^+]$ ion concentration increases pH decreases.

23. ***(b)*** For $AB_2 \rightleftharpoons A^{2+} + 2B^-$

$$K_{sp} = [A^{2+}][B^-]^2$$

$$= (1.2 \times 10^{-4})(0.24 \times 10^{-3})^2$$

$$= 0.0691 \times 10^{-10}$$

$$K_{sp} = 6.91 \times 10^{-12}$$

24. ***(10)*** To solve this question, the concept of solubility can be used. For this, write the equation involved in the reaction. Then use the formula of K_{sp} in terms of solubility *S*. Then solve the required value i.e., $-\log K_{sp}$.

$AgCl(s) \rightleftharpoons \underset{S}{Ag^+(aq)} + \underset{S}{Cl^-(aq)}$

$$K_{sp} = S^2 = \left(\frac{1.434}{143.4} \times 10^{-3}\right)^2 = 10^{-10}$$

$$-\log K_{sp} = -(-10)\log 10 = 10$$

25. ***(0)*** $CaF_2 \rightleftharpoons \underset{(S)}{Ca^{2+}} + \underset{(2S)}{2F^-}$

Solubility product constant,

$$K_{sp} = S \times (2S)^2 = 4S^3$$

$$\text{Solubility} = \frac{2.34 \times 10^{-3} \times 10}{78} = 3 \times 10^{-4} \text{ mol/L.}$$

$$K_{sp} = 4 \times (3 \times 10^{-4})^3 = 108 \times 10^{-12}$$
$$= 0.0108 \times 10^{-8} \text{ (mol/L)}^3$$
$$\simeq 0 \times 10^{-8} \text{ (mol / L)}^3$$

26. ***(108)*** $A_3B_2 \rightleftharpoons \underset{3S}{3A^{2+}(aq)} + \underset{2S}{2B^{3-}(aq)}$

$$K_{sp} = [A^{2+}]^3 [B^{3-}]^2$$
$$K_{sp} = (3S)^3 (2S)^2 = 108S^5$$

Also, $S = \frac{x}{M}$

$$K_{sp} = 108\left(\frac{x}{M}\right)^5$$

Given that, $K_{sp} = a\left(\frac{x}{M}\right)^5$

$\therefore \quad a = 108$

27. ***(d)*** $K_{sp}(AgCl) = 1.7 \times 10^{-10} \text{ M}^2$

$K_{sp}\ (Ag_2CrO_4) = 1.9 \times 10^{-12} \text{ M}^3$

(i) $[Ag^+]$ required to ppt. AgCl(s)

$$K_{sp} = [Ag^+]\ [Cl^-]$$
$$\Rightarrow 1.7 \times 10^{-10} = [Ag^+]\ [0.1]$$
$$[Ag^+] = 1.7 \times 10^{-9} \text{ M}$$

(ii) $[Ag^+]$ required to ppt. $Ag_2CrO_4(s)$

$$K_{sp} = [Ag^+]^2[CrO_4^{2-}]$$
$$\Rightarrow 1.9 \times 10^{-12} = [Ag^+]^2[0.001]$$
$$[Ag^+] = \sqrt{1.9 \times 10^{-9}}$$
$$= \sqrt{19} \times 10^{-5}$$
$$= 4.3 \times 10^{-5} \text{ M}$$

$\because$ $[Ag^+]$ required to precipitate AgCl is low, so AgCl will precipitate first.

28. ***(50)*** Let the solubility of A_2X be 'S'.

$$A_2X(s) \rightleftharpoons \underset{2S}{2A^+(aq)} + \underset{S}{X^{2-}(aq)};$$

$$K_{sp_1} = 4 \times 10^{-12}$$
$$K_{sp_1} = [A^+]^2[X^{2-}]$$
$$4 \times 10^{-12} = (2S)^2(S)$$
$$4 \times 10^{-12} = 4S^3$$
$$\Rightarrow \quad S = 10^{-3} \text{ M}$$

Let the solubility of MX be 'S_1'.

$$MX(s) \rightleftharpoons \underset{S_1}{M^+(aq)} + \underset{S_1}{X^-(aq)},$$

$$K_{sp_2} = 4 \times 10^{-12}$$
$$K_{sp_2} = [M^+][X^-]$$
$$K_{sp_2} = (S_1)^2$$
$$4 \times 10^{-12} = (S_1)^2$$
$$\Rightarrow \quad S_1 = 2 \times 10^{-6} \text{ M}$$
$$\frac{[A_2X]}{[MX]} = \frac{S}{S_1} = \frac{10^{-4}}{2 \times 10^{-6}} = 50$$

29. ***(c)*** Both (A) and (R) are true but (R) is not the correct explanation of (A).

Because of high stability CuS, the value of K_{eq} is high, i.e. the value of K_{sp} of CuS will be low.

30. ***(b)*** K_{sp} of $Cr(OH)_3$ at 298 K is 6.0×10^{-31}.

$$Cr(OH)_3 \rightleftharpoons \underset{S}{Cr^{3+}} + \underset{3S}{3OH^-}$$

In a saturated solution,

$$K_{sp} = [Cr^{3+}][OH^-]^3$$
$$= S(3S)^3 = 27S^4 = 6.0 \times 10^{-31}$$
$$\therefore \quad S^4 = \frac{6.0 \times 10^{-31}}{27}$$
$$\Rightarrow \quad S = \left(\frac{6.0 \times 10^{-31}}{27}\right)^{1/4}$$
$$[OH]^- = 3S = 3\left(\frac{6.0 \times 10^{-31}}{27}\right)^{1/4}$$
$$= (18 \times 10^{-31})^{1/4}$$

31. ***(d)*** Units given for all options is M^3, or $(mol\ L^{-1})^3$, which implies that, the equilibrium has three ions. Therefore,

$$XY_2 \rightleftharpoons X^{2+}(aq) + 2Y^-(aq),$$
$$K_{sp} = [X^{2+}][Y^-]^2$$

or $X_2Y \rightleftharpoons 2X^+(aq) + Y^{2-}(aq),$

$$K_{sp} = [X^+]^2[Y^{2-}]$$

(i) K_{sp} in case of XY_2,

$$K_{sp} = (1 \times 10^{-3})(2 \times 10^{-3})^2 = 4 \times 10^{-9} \text{ M}^3$$

(ii) K_{sp} in case of X_2Y,

$$K_{sp} = (1 \times 10^{-3})^2 (2 \times 10^{-3}) = 2 \times 10^{-9} \text{ M}$$

The only matching value of K_{sp} from options that satisfies the concentration values from graph is

$$[X^{2+}] = 1 \text{ mM} = 1 \times 10^{-3} \text{ M}$$

and $[Y^-] = 2\text{mM} = 2 \times 10^{-3}$ M

Thus, salt is XY_2 and

$$K_{sp} = (10^{-3})(2 \times 10^{-3})^2 = 4 \times 10^{-9} \text{ M}^3$$

Practice Element 02 : Target JEE Advanced

1. ***(a)*** Solution is neutral if

equivalent of an acid ≡ equivalent of a base

$$H_2SO_4 \equiv 2H^+$$

$$Ca(OH)_2 \equiv 2OH^-$$

In (C), NH_4^+ is formed but it acts as an acid

$$NH_4^+ + H_2O \rightleftharpoons NH_4OH + H^+$$

In (D), CH_3COO^- is formed but it acts as a base

$$CH_3COO^- + H_2O \rightleftharpoons CH_3COOH + OH^-$$

2. ***(c)*** Statement I is incorrect but statement II is correct. Their explanation is given as:

$[Hg^{2+}]$ = 2.0 millimol in 100 mL solution

$$= \frac{2 \times 10^{-3}\ \text{mol}}{0.1\,L} = 2 \times 10^{-2}\ \text{M}$$

$$= 0.02\ \text{M}$$

Since, stability constant of $HgCl_2$ is large (1.65×10^{13}) the value of $[Hg^{2+}]$ should be small.

At the end point

$$[Cl^-] = 2\,[Hg^{2+}]$$

$$[HgCl_2] = 0.020 - [Hg^{2+}] \approx 0.02\ \text{M}$$

$$\therefore \quad \frac{[HgCl]}{[Hg^{2+}]\,[Cl^-]^2} = 1.65 \times 10^{13}$$

$$\frac{0.02}{[Hg^{2+}]\,[2(Hg^{2+})]^2} = 1.65 \times 10^{13}$$

$$\therefore \quad 4[Hg^{2+}]^3 = \frac{0.02}{1.65 \times 10^{13}}$$

$$\therefore \quad [Hg^{2+}] = 6.72 \times 10^{-6}\ \text{M}$$

	CH_3NH_2 +	HCl ⇌	$CH_3NH_3^+$ + Cl^-
Initial	0.1	0.08	0
Final	0.02	—	0.08 M

$$CH_3NH_2 + H_2O \rightleftharpoons CH_3NH_3^+ + OH^-$$

$$K_b = \frac{[CH_3NH_3^+]\,[OH^-]}{[CH_3NH_2]} \Rightarrow 5 \times 10^{-4} = \frac{(0.08)\,[OH^-]}{(0.02)}$$

$$[OH^-] = 1.25 \times 10^{-4}\ \text{M}$$

$$[H^+] = \frac{K_w}{[OH^-]} = \frac{1 \times 10^{-14}}{1.25 \times 10^{-4}} = 8 \times 10^{-11}\ \text{M}$$

3. ***(c)*** Since, K_f of $Ag(S_2O_3)_2^{3-}$ is very high hence, it is assumed that all the Ag^+ from AgBr is complexed, hence molar solubility of AgBr in $S_2O_3^{2-}$ can be calculated.

$$AgBr(s) \rightleftharpoons Ag^+(aq) + Br^-(aq),\ K_1 = K_{sp}$$

$$Ag^+ + 2S_2O_3^{2-} \rightleftharpoons Ag(S_2O_3N)_2^{3-}(aq),\ K_2 = K_f$$

$$AgBr(s) + 2S_2O_3^{2-} \rightleftharpoons Ag(S_2O_3)_2^{3-} + Br^-,\ K = K_{sp} \cdot K_f$$

Initial conc.	0.1	0	0
Change	$-2x$	$+x$	$+x$
Equilibrium conc.	$(0.1-2x)$	x	x

$$\therefore \quad K = K_{sp} \cdot K_f = 5.4 \times 10^{-13} \times 2.9 \times 10^{13} = 15.66$$

Also, $K = \dfrac{[Ag(S_2O_3)_2^{3-}]\,[Br^-]}{[S_2O_3^{2-}]^2} \Rightarrow 15.66 = \dfrac{(x)(x)}{(0.1-2x)^2}$

$$\therefore \quad x^2 = (0.1-2x)^2\,15.66$$

$$\therefore \quad x = 0.0444 \times 10^{-2}\text{M} = 4.44 \times 10^{-2}\ \text{M}$$

Hence, solubility of AgBr(s) in 0.1 M $S_2O_3^{2-}$ is 4.44×10^{-2} M.

4. ***(b)*** $Ca(Lac)_2 \rightleftharpoons 2Lac^- + Ca^{2+}$

Lactic acid is a weak acid

$$[\text{Salt}] = \frac{0.13}{0.50} = 0.26\ \text{mol L}^{-1}$$

$\therefore$ [Lactate] = 0.26 × 2 = 0.52 M

Solution is alkaline due to hydrolysis of Lactate ion

$$Lac^- + H_2O \rightleftharpoons HLac + \overline{OH}$$

$$pH = 7 + \frac{pK_a}{2} + \frac{\log C}{2}$$

$$8 \cdot 4 = 7 + \frac{pK_a}{2} + \frac{\log 0.52}{2} = 7 + \frac{pK_a}{2} + \left(\frac{-0.284}{2}\right)$$

$$pK_a = 3.084$$

5. ***(d)***

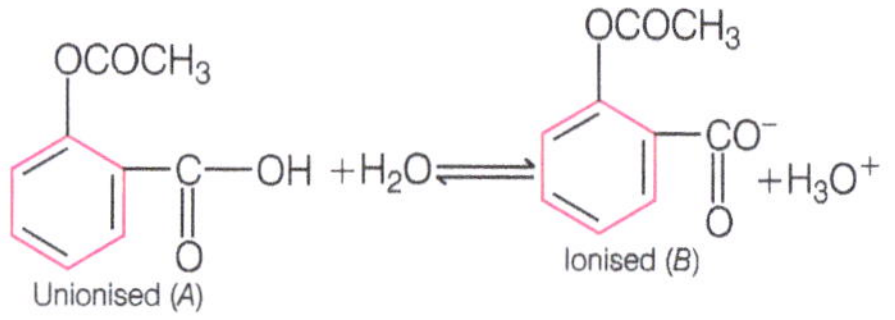

$$pH = pK_a + \log\frac{[B]}{[A]}$$

In stomach (pH = 2.3) < pK_a

Hence, [A] > [B].

Thus, in stomach it exists as unionised form.

In small intestine, (pH = 8) > pK_a

Hence, [B] > [A]

Thus, ionised form in small intestine.

6. ***(d)*** $H_2CO_3 \rightleftharpoons H^+ + HCO_3^-$

$$K_{a_1} = \frac{[H^+]\,[HCO_3^-]}{[H_2CO_3]}$$

$$\Rightarrow \quad pH = 10,\ [H^+] = 10^{-10}$$

$$\therefore \quad 4.3 \times 10^{-7} = 1 \times 10^{-10}\,\frac{[HCO_3^-]}{[H_2CO_3]}$$

$$\therefore \quad \frac{[HCO_3^-]}{[H_2CO_3]} = \frac{4.3 \times 10^{-7}}{1 \times 10^{-10}} = 4.3 \times 10^3$$

Also, $$HCO_3^- \rightleftharpoons H^+ + CO_3^{2-}$$

$$K_{a_2} = \frac{[H^+]\,[CO_3^{2-}]}{[HCO_3^-]}$$

$$4.8 \times 10^{-11} = \frac{1 \times 10^{-10}[CO_3^{2-}]}{[HCO_3^-]}$$

$$\therefore \quad \frac{[CO_3^{2-}]}{[HCO_3^-]} = \frac{4.8 \times 10^{-11}}{1 \times 10^{-10}} = 0.48$$

$$\text{Fraction of } [H_2CO_3] = \frac{[H_2CO_3]}{[H_2CO_3]+[HCO_3^-]+[CO_3^{2-}]}$$

$$= \frac{[H_2CO_3]/[HCO_3^-]}{\frac{[H_2CO_3]}{[HCO_3^-]}+1+\frac{[CO_3^{2-}]}{[HCO_3^-]}}$$

$$= \frac{\left(\frac{1}{4.3\times10^3}\right)}{\left(\frac{1}{4.3\times10^3}\right)+1+0.48} = 1.6\times10^{-4}$$

7. **(b)** $M_1V_1 = M_2V_2$ (Acid, Base)

$M_1 \times 50.0 = 0.10 \times 39.30$

$\therefore \quad M_1 = \frac{0.10\times39.30}{50} = 0.0786\text{ M}$

When half-equivalence point is reached

$[HA] = [A^-]$

$pH = pK_a + \log\frac{[A^-]}{[HA]}$

$\therefore \quad pH = pK_a = 4.85$

8. **(a)** $AgBrO_3(s) \rightleftharpoons Ag^+(aq) + BrO_3^-(aq)$

Ag^+ is precipitated by H_2S

$pV = nRT$

$\therefore \quad n(H_2S) = \frac{pV}{RT} = \frac{\left(\frac{748}{760}\right)\text{atm}\times\left(\frac{30.4}{1000}\right)\text{L}}{[0.0821\text{ L atm mol}^{-1}\text{K}^{-1}\times296\text{ K}]}$

$= 1.23\times10^{-3}\text{mol}$

$2Ag^+(aq) + S^{2-}(aq) \longrightarrow Ag_2S(s)$

Thus, $[Ag^+] = 2\times H_2S = 2.46\times10^{-3}\text{mol in } 338\text{ mL}$

$\therefore [Ag^+] = 7.28\times10^{-3}\text{mol in} 1000\text{ mL}$

$\therefore K_{sp} = [Ag^+][BrO_3^-] = [Ag^+]^2 = (7.28\times10^{-3})^2 = 5.3\times10^{-5}$

9. **(a)** pH = 3,

$pOH = 14-3 = 11 \Rightarrow [OH^-] = 1\times10^{-11}\text{ M}$

$H_2S(aq) + H_2O(l) \rightleftharpoons H_3O^+(aq) + HS^-(aq)$

$K_a = \frac{[H_3O^+][HS^-]}{[H_2S]}$

$9.1\times10^{-8} = \frac{(1\times10^{-3})[HS^-]}{0.1}$

$\therefore \quad [HS^-] = 9.1\times10^{-6}\text{ M}$

$FeS(s) + H_2O(l) \rightleftharpoons Fe^{2+}(aq) + HS^-(aq) + OH^-(aq);$

$K = [Fe^{2+}][HS^-][OH^-]$

$[Fe^{2+}][HS^-][OH^-] = 5\times10^{-19}$

$\therefore \quad [Fe^{2+}] = \frac{5\times10^{-19}}{9.1\times10^{-6}\times1\times10^{-11}} = 5.50\times10^{-3}\text{ M}$

10. **(a)** $pK_{In} = -\log K_{In} = \log(4\times10^{-10}) = 10-\log 4 = 9.4$

Thus, it is equivalent point. pH colour change starts from ($pK_{In}-1$) and completes at ($pK_{In}+1$).

Thus, (a) is incorrect

11. **(a,b,d)** Given,

$[Ag^+][Cl^-] = K_{sp} = 1\times10^{-10}$

$\log[Ag^+] + \log[Cl^-] = \log 1\times10^{-10}$

$-\log[Ag^+] - \log[Cl^-] = 10(\log 10)$

$\therefore p_{Ag^+} + p_{Cl^-} = 10, [p_x = -\log x]$

Thus, (a) is correct.

$[Ag^+][Cl^-] = 1\times10^{-10}$

When, $[Ag^+] = 0.01\text{ M}$

$[Cl^-] = 1\times10^{-8}$

$\therefore \quad p_{Cl^-} = 8$

Thus, (b) is correct.

In all cases, $p_{Ag^+} + p_{Cl^-} = 10$

Thus, (c) is incorrect.

Since, $[Ag^+] = [Cl^-]$

Thus, $[Ag^+]^2 = [Cl^-] = 1\times10^{-10}$

$[Ag^+] = [Cl^-] = 1\times10^{-5}$

$-\log[Ag^+] = -\log[Cl^-] = -\log 1\times10^{-5}$

$p_{Ag^+} = p_{Cl^-} = 5$

Thus, (d) is correct.

12. **(c,d)** $M^{2+} + S^{2-} \longrightarrow MS$

MS is precipitated if $[M^{2+}][S^{2-}] > K_{sp}$

On mixing, total volume = 15 mL

$[S^{2-}]_{mix} = 1\times10^{-19}\times\frac{10}{15} = \frac{1\times10^{-18}}{15}\text{M}$

$[M^{2+}]_{mix} = 0.04\times\frac{5}{15} = \frac{0.04}{3}\text{M}$

$[M^{2+}][S^{2-}] = \frac{1\times10^{-18}}{15}\times\frac{0.04}{3} = 8.89\times10^{-22}$

MS	K_{sp}	Precipitate
MnS	$2.5\times10^{-13} > [M^{2+}][S^{2-}]$	No
ZnS	$1.6\times10^{-21} > [M^{2+}][S^{2-}]$	No
CdS	$8.0\times10^{-27} < [M^{2+}][S^{2-}]$	Yes
CuS	$6.3\times10^{-36} < [M^{2+}][S^{2-}]$	Yes

13. **(a,d)** $BaSO_4(s) \rightleftharpoons Ba^{2+}(aq) + SO_4^{2-}(aq)$

$BaSO_4$ is precipitated if $[Ba^{2+}][SO_4^{2-}] > K_{sp}$

On mixing two solutions, total volume changes and due to this dilution, molarity is affected.

	Total volume	$[Ba^{2+}]_{mix}$	$[SO_4^{2-}]_{mix}$	$[Ba^{2+}][SO_4^{2-}]$	ppt. Yes/No
a	400 mL	1×10^{-3}M	4.5×10^{-4}M	$4.5\times10^{-7} > K_{sp}$	Yes
b	400 mL	1×10^{-4}M	4.5×10^{-8}M	$4.5\times10^{-12} < K_{sp}$	No
c	400 mL	3×10^{-4}M	1.5×10^{-8}M	$4.5\times10^{-12} < K_{sp}$	No
d	600 mL	3×10^{-4}M	4.5×10^{-4}M	$1.35\times10^{-7} > K_{sp}$	Yes

14. ***(a, c, d)***

(a) $LiOH \rightleftharpoons Li^+ + OH^-$

$[Li^+]\,[OH^-] = K_{sp} = 1\times10^{-6}$

$\therefore p_{Li} + pOH = pK_{sp} = 6$

$\therefore \quad pOH = 6 - p_{Li}$

Since, $pH + pOH = 14$

$\therefore\ pH = 14 - pOH = 14 - 6 + p_{Li} = 8 + p_{Li}$

Thus, (a) is correct.

(b) $Mg(OH)_2 \rightleftharpoons Mg^{2+} + 2OH^-$

$[Mg^{2+}]\,[OH^-]^2 = K_{sp} = 1\times10^{-12}$

$p_{Mg} + 2pOH = pK_{sp} = 12 \Rightarrow 2pOH = 12 - p_{Mg}$

$pOH = 6 - \frac{p_{Mg}}{2} \Rightarrow 14 - pH = 96 - \frac{p_{Mg}}{2}$

$\therefore \quad pH = 8 + \frac{p_{Mg}}{2}$

Thus, (b) is incorrect

(c) $Al(OH)_3 \rightleftharpoons Al^{3+}(aq) + 3OH^-(aq)$

$K_{sp} = [Al^{3+}]\,[OH^-]^3 = 1\times10^{-27}$

$\log[Al^{3+}] + 3\log[OH^-] = -27\log10 = 27$

$\therefore -\log[Al^{3+}] - 3\log(OH^-) = 27$

$p_{Al} + 3pOH = 27$

$\frac{p_{Al}}{3} + pOH = 9 \Rightarrow \frac{p_{Al}}{3} + 14 - pH = 9$

$\therefore\ pH = \frac{p_{Al}}{3} + 5$

This (c) is correct

(d) $K_{sp} = [Si^{4+}][OH^-]^4 = 1\times10^{-28}$

$\therefore\ \log[Si^{4+}] + 4\log[OH^-] = -28$

$p_{Si} + 4pOH = 28$

$\frac{p_{Si}}{4} + pOH = 7 \Rightarrow \frac{p_{Si}}{4} + 14 - pH = 7$

$\therefore \quad pH = \frac{p_{Si}}{4} + 7$

Thus (d) is correct

15. ***(a,c)*** Orthoboric acid H_3BO_3 is soluble in water. It does not release H^+ ion. Thus, it is not a Lowry-Bronsted acid nor Arrhenius acid.

In aqueous solution, it accepts OH^- ion from H_2O and H^+ is released.

$B(OH)_3 + 2H_2O \rightleftharpoons H_3O^+ + [B(OH)_4]^-$

$pK_a = 925$

Thus, it is a Lewis acid.

16. ***(b, c, d)*** Among the given statements, b, c and d are correct while statement (a) is incorrect. Their explanation are given as—

Best buffering action will occur when $\frac{\partial\beta}{\partial[H^+]} = 0$

$$\therefore\ 2.303(C_A + C_B)K_a \times \left[\frac{1}{([H^+]+K_a)^2} + \frac{-2[H^+]}{([H^+]+K_a)^3}\right] = 0$$

$$1 - \frac{2[H^+]}{[H^+]+K_a} = 0$$

$\therefore \quad [H^+] = K_a$

$\therefore \quad pH = pK_a$

If $C_A = C_B$ then $HA \rightleftharpoons H^+ + A^-$

$$K_a = \frac{[H^+][A^-]}{[HA]} = [H^+]\frac{C_B}{C_A} = [H^+]$$

At this stage $[H^+] = K_a$

$$\therefore\ \beta = \frac{2.303(2C_A)(K_a)^2}{(2K_a)^2} = \frac{2.303C_A}{2} \text{ or } = \frac{2.303C_B}{2}$$

17. ***(b, c)*** Among the given statements, (b) and (c) are correct while a and d are incorrect. Their correct form are—

The value of K_w is temperature dependent.

pH value of 0.001 M NaOH solution is 11.

0.001 M NaOH will contain 0.001 M OH^- ions.

$\therefore$ Concentration of OH^- ions.

$[OH^-] = 10^{-3}$ m

$pOH = -\log[OH^-] = 3$

$\because \quad pH = 14 - pOH = 11$

Hence, pH value of 0.001 M NaOH solution is 11.

Millimoles of $H^+ = 400 \times 0.1 \times 2 = 80$

Millimoles of $OH^- = 400 \times 0.1 = 40$

$\therefore$ Millimoles of H^+ left $= 80 - 40 = 40$

$$[H^+] = \frac{40}{400+400} = \frac{1}{20}\text{ M}$$

$$\because \quad pH = -\log[H^+] = -\log\left(\frac{1}{20}\right)$$

$= -0 + 0.301 + 1 = 1.30$

Given, $K_b(NH_4OH) = 10^{-5}$

$\therefore \quad pK_b = -\log K_b$

$= -\log(10^{-5}) = 5$

$C = 0.02$

$C = 2\times10^{-2}$ M

Now, $\quad pH = 7 - \frac{1}{2}(pK_b + \log C)$

On substituting the given values in above equation, we get

$= 7 - \frac{1}{2}[5 + \log(2\times10^{-2})]$

$= 7 - 1.65 = 5.35$

18. ***(a, b, d)***

$BOH(aq.) \rightleftharpoons B^+(aq.) + OH^-(aq.)$

At equilibrium $\quad c(1-\alpha) \quad c\alpha \quad c\alpha$

$$K_b = \frac{[B^+][OH^-]}{[BOH]}$$

neglect α w.r.t. 1 as concentration is appreciable,

$$\%\alpha = 100 \times \sqrt{\frac{K_b}{c}}$$

Total dissolved base present in solution as BOH and B^+.

So, $\alpha = \frac{[B^+]}{[B^+]+[BOH]} \Rightarrow \frac{1}{1+\frac{[BOH]}{[B^+]}} = \frac{1}{1+\frac{[OH^-]}{K_b}}$

$$\Rightarrow \frac{K_b}{K_b + [OH^-]} \Rightarrow \frac{K_b \cdot [H^+]}{K_b[H^+] + K_w}$$

Also $pOH = -\log [OH^-]$; $[OH^-] = 10^{-pOH}$;

$K_b = 10^{-pK_b}$

$$\alpha = \frac{1}{1+\frac{10^{-pOH}}{10^{-pK_b}}} \Rightarrow \frac{1}{1+10^{(pK_b - pOH)}}$$

19. ***(10)*** From the given data,

$[Cu(CN)_4]^{3-} = 0.1\,M$ and $[CN^-] = 0.2\,M$

$\therefore \quad [Cu^+] = \frac{K_{Instab.} \cdot [Cu(CN)_4]^{3-}}{[CN^-]^4} = \frac{6.4 \times 10^{-15} \times 0.1}{(0.2)^4}$

$= 4 \times 10^{-13}\,M$

Now, $[S^{2-}] = \frac{K_{sp}(Cu_2S)}{[Cu^+]^2} = \frac{2.56 \times 10^{-27}}{(4 \times 10^{-13})^2}$

$= 1.6 \times 10^{-2}\,M$

$\therefore \quad [H^+] = \sqrt{\frac{K_a + [H_2S]}{[S^{2-}]}} = \sqrt{\frac{1.6 \times 10^{-21} \times 0.1}{1.6 \times 10^{-2}}} = 10^{-10}\,M$

$\because \quad pH = -\log[H^+]$

Hence, pH = 10

20. ***(5)*** Let, HA is a weak acid.

According to the given data,

$$HA + OH^- \rightleftharpoons A^- + H_2O$$

	HA	OH^-	A^-
	36.12×0.1		0
Equ. point	0	0	3.612 millimole

$$A^- + H^+ \rightleftharpoons HA$$

	A^-	H^+	HA
	3.612 millimol	18.06×0.1 milli mole	0
Final	1.806	0	1.806 millimole

$\therefore \quad pH = pK_a + \log \frac{[A^-]}{[HA]} = pK_a + \log \frac{1.806}{1.806}$

$pH = 5 = pK_a$

21. ***(54.5)*** A. HCN is a weak acid;

$$pH_{WA} = \frac{1}{2}(pK_a - \log C)$$

$$= \frac{1}{2}(-\log 10^{-10} - \log 10^{-1}) = \frac{1}{2}[10 + 1] = 5.5$$

B. $0.1\,M CH_3COOH + 0.1\,M CH_3COONa$ is an acidic buffer;

$$pH_{\text{acidic buffer}} = pK_a + \log \frac{0.1}{0.1} = -\log 10^{-3} = 3$$

C. HCl is a strong acid;

$pH = -\log(0.1) = 1$

D. NH_4OH is a weak base;

$$pOH_{W_B} = \frac{1}{2}(pK_a - \log C)$$

$$= \frac{1}{2}(-\log 10^{-5} - \log 10^{-1}) = \frac{1}{2}(5+1) = 3$$

$pH = 14 - pOH = 14 - 3 = 11$

E. 10 ml of 0.1 M CH_3COOH + 10 ml of 0.1 M NH_4OH is a salt of weak acid and weak base;

pH = 7

Hence, the sum of magic numbers of all solutions is

$= 5.5 \times 3 + 3 \times 2 + 1 \times 3 + 11 \times 2 + 7 \times 1$

$= 16.5 + 6 + 3 + 22 + 7 = 54.5$

22. ***(240)*** Let V mL of acid solution is taken.

mmol of acid $= 0.1 \times V$

mmol of salt $= 0.2\,M \times (300 - V)\,mL$

$\because \quad pH = pK_a + \log \frac{[Salt]}{[Acid]}$

$3.9 = 4.2 + \log \frac{[Salt]}{[Acid]}$

$-0.3 = \log \frac{[Salt]}{[Acid]}$

$\frac{[Acid]}{[Salt]} = 2$

$\therefore \quad [Acid] = 2[Salt]$

$\frac{0.1 \times V}{300} = 2 \times \left[\frac{0.2 \times (300 - V)}{300}\right]$

$V = 240\,mL$

23. ***(5.227)*** Millimoles of $CH_3COOH = \frac{3 \times 1000}{60} = 50$

Millimoles of HCl $= 250 \times 0.1 = 25$

Millimoles of CH_3COOH in 20 mL $= \frac{50}{500} \times 20 = 2$

Millimoles of HCl in 20 mL $= \frac{25}{500} \times 20 = 1$

$$NaOH + HCl \longrightarrow NaCl + H_2O$$

	NaOH	HCl	NaCl	H_2O
Initial (millimoles)	2.5	1	—	—
After reaction: (millimoles)	1.5	0	1	—

$$CH_3COOH + NaOH \longrightarrow CH_3COONa + H_2O$$

	CH_3COOH	NaOH	CH_3COONa	H_2O
Initial (millimoles)	2	1.5	—	—
After reaction: (millimoles)	0.5	0	1.5	—

As we know,

$$pH = pK_a + \log \frac{[CH_3COONa]}{[CH_3COOH]}$$

$$pH = pK_a + \log\left(\frac{1.5}{0.5}\right) = 4.75 + \log 3$$

$= 4.75 + 0.4771 = 5.227$

24. ***(6.4)*** According to the given data,

$$Tl_2S(s) \rightleftharpoons \underset{2S\,M}{2Tl^+} + S^{2-}$$

$$\underset{xM}{S^{2-}} + H_2O \rightleftharpoons \underset{SM}{HS^-} + \underset{SM}{OH^-}$$

$$K_h = \frac{K_w}{K_{a_2}}$$

$$\frac{10^{-14}}{10^{-14}} = \frac{2\times10^{-6}\times2\times10^{-6}}{x}$$

$$x = 4\times10^{-12}$$

$$\therefore \quad K_{sp} = (2\times2\times10^{-6})^2\times4\times10^{-12} = 6.4\times10^{-23}$$

25. ***(120)*** In presence of common ion (in this case Ag^+ ion) solubility of sparingly soluble salt is decreased.

Let solubility of $K_2C_2O_4$ in presence of 0.1 M KNO_3 = x

$$K_2C_2O_4 \rightleftharpoons \underset{2x}{2K^+} + \underset{x}{C_2O_4^{2-}}$$

$$KNO_3 \rightleftharpoons \underset{0.1}{K^+} + \underset{0.1}{NO_3^-}$$

Total $[K^+] = (2x + 0.1)$ M ≈ 0.1 M as $x <<< 0.1$ M

$[C_2O_4^{2-}] = x$ M

Thus, $[K^+][C_2O_4^{2-}] = K_{sp}$

$$(0.1)^2x = 1.2\times10^{-10}$$

$$x = \frac{1.2\times10^{-10}}{(0.1)^2} = 120\times10^{-10}$$

Thus, the value of y is 120.

26. ***(1.2)*** Given, pH = 4, So $[H^+] = 10^{-4}$

$$K_a = 2\times10^{-8}$$

$$K_{sp} = 3\times10^{-12}$$

After putting the value in formula solubility

$$= \sqrt{3\times10^{-12}\left(\frac{10^{-4}}{10^{-8}\times2}+1\right)} = 1.224\times10^{-4}\text{ M}$$

$$\approx 1.2\times10^{-4}\text{ M}$$

Hence the value of Z is 1.2.

27. ***(a)***

(i) 0.05M $(CH_3COO)_2Ca$= 0.10 M CH_3COO^-

$$pH = pK_a + \log\frac{[CH_3COO^-]}{[CH_3COOH]}$$

$$= 4.74 + \log 1 = 4.74$$

(i) - (r)

(ii) CH_3COOH is 50% neutralised, thus at 50% neutralisation

$[CH_3COOH] = [CH_3COONa]$

$\therefore$pH = 4.74 + log1 = 4.74

$\therefore$ (ii) - (r)

(iii) CH_3COONa is formed when is hydrolysed to make solution alkaline.

$$CH_3COO^- + H_2O \rightleftharpoons CH_3COOH + OH^-$$

$$\therefore \quad pH = 7 + \frac{pK_a}{2} + \frac{\log C}{2} \Rightarrow [CH_3COONa] = \frac{0.10}{2} = 0.05\text{ M}$$

Since, total volume is 100 mL hence, molar concentration of CH_3COONa is halved $(M_1V_1 = M_2V_2)$

$$pH = 7 + \frac{4.74}{2} + \frac{\log 0.05}{2} = 9.37 - \frac{1.30}{2} = 9.37 - 0.65 = 8.72$$

Thus (iii) - (q)

(iv) NaOH is in excess,

$M_2V_2(NaOH) > M_1V_1(CH_3COOH)$

$$\therefore [NaOH]_{mix} = \frac{M_1V_1 - M_1V_1}{V_1 + V_2} = \frac{5}{150} = \frac{1}{30}$$

$$\therefore [OH^-] = \frac{1}{30}$$

$$\therefore pOH = -\log\frac{1}{30} = \log 30 = 1.48$$

$$\therefore pH = 14 - 1.48 = 12.52$$

Thus (iv) - (s)

28. ***(b)***

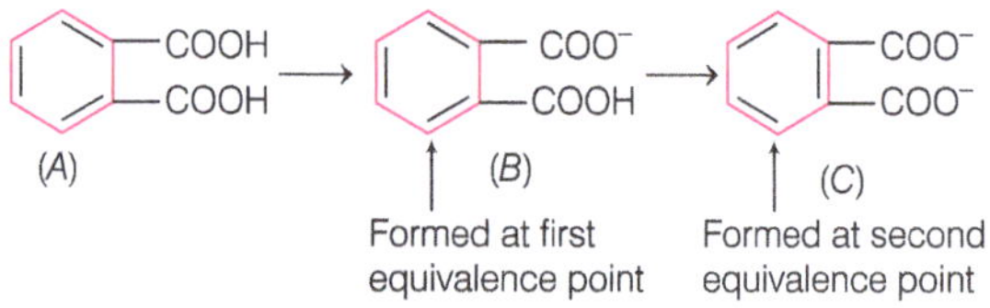

(i) When the first half-equivalence point is reached, mixture contains 50% A and 50% B. Thus, it is a buffer.

Thus, $pH = pK_{a_1} + \log\frac{[B]}{[A]} = pK_{a_1} = 2.89$

(i) - (s)

(ii) At the first equivalence point, B is formed.

B is proton donor as well as proton acceptor. Thus, it is amphiprotic.

$$pH = \frac{pK_{a_1} + pK_{a_2}}{2}$$

$$= \frac{2.89 + 5.41}{2} = 4.15$$

(ii) - (r)

(iii) When second half-equivalence point is reached, mixture contains 50% B and 50 % C.

Thus, it is a buffer.

$$\therefore \quad pH = pK_{a_2} + \log\frac{[C]}{[B]} = pK_{a_2} = 5.41$$

(iii) - (q)

(iv) At the second equivalence point, there is complete neutralisation of A changing to

$$A + 2NaOH \longrightarrow C + H_2O$$

V mL of 0.01 M A = $2V$ mL of 0.01 M NaOH

C formed = V mL of 0.01 M

But total volume = $3V$

$$\text{Thus, } [C]_{mix} = \left(\frac{0.01}{3}\right)\text{ M}$$

C is hydrolysed to *B* back forming basic solution

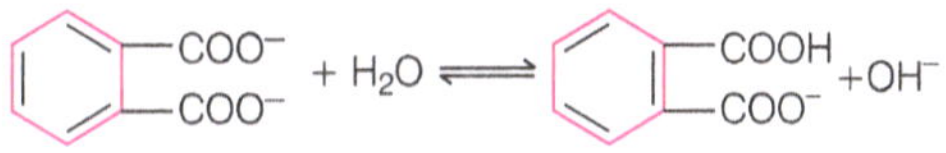

$$pH = 7 + \frac{pK_{a_2}}{2} + \frac{\log C}{2}$$

$$= 7 + \frac{5.41}{2} + \frac{\log(0.01/3)}{2} = 8.47$$

Then (iv) - (p)

29. ***(d)***

(i) $CH_3COONH_4^+$ it is salt of weak acid and weak base.

$$pH = 7 + \frac{pK_a - pK_b}{2}$$

$$pK_a(CH_3COOH) = 4.74,\ pK_a(NH_4^+) = 9.26$$

$\therefore$ $pK_b(NH_3) = 4.74$

$\therefore$ $pH = 7$

Thus, (i) $\rightarrow$ (r)

(ii) C_6H_5COOK

It is salt of weak acid and strong base. Solution is basic.

$$C_6H_5COO^- + H_2O \rightleftharpoons C_6H_5COOH + OH^-$$

$$pH = 7 + \frac{pK_a}{2} + \frac{\log C}{2} = 7 + \frac{4.20}{2} + \frac{\log 0.1}{2}$$

$$= 7 + 2.10 - 0.5 = 8.6$$

Thus, (ii) $\rightarrow$ (p)

(iii) $C_6H_5NH_3^+Cl$ It is salt of weak base and strong acid. Solution is acidic.

$$C_6H_5NH_3^+ + H_2O \rightleftharpoons C_6H_5NH_3OH + H^+$$

$$pK_a(C_6H_5NH_3^+) = 4.62,\ pK_b(C_6H_5NH_2) = 9.38$$

$$pH = 7 - \frac{pK_b}{2} - \frac{\log C}{2}$$

$$= 7 - \frac{9.38}{2} - \frac{\log 0.1}{2} = 2.81$$

Thus, (iii) $\rightarrow$ (s)

(iv) NaCN is a salt of weak acid and strong base. Solution is basic

$$CN^- + H_2O \rightleftharpoons HCN + OH^-$$

$$pH = 7 + \frac{pK_a}{2} + \frac{\log C}{2}$$

$$= 7 + \frac{9.21}{2} + \frac{\log 0.1}{2} = 11.1$$

Thus, (iv) $\rightarrow$ (q)

30. ***(d)*** $CH_3COOH + KOH \rightleftharpoons CH_3COOK + H_2O$

$$CH_3COOH = 100 \times 0.01 = 1 \text{ mmol}$$

I. 25 mL of KOH = 0.25 mmol
II. 50 mL of KOH = 0.50 mmol
III. 75 mL of KOH = 0.75 mmol
IV. 100 mL of KOH = 1.00 mmol

After KOH added

Stage	$[CH_3COOH]$ millimol	$[CH_3COOK]$ millimol	$pH = pK_a + \log\frac{[CH_3COOK]}{[CH_3COOH]}$
I.	0.75	0.25	$4.74 + \log\frac{1}{3} = 4.26$
II.	0.50	0.50	4.74
III.	0.25	0.75	$4.74 + \log 3 = 5.22$
IV.	0.00	1.00	8.22

In stages I, II and III, a buffer is formed thus, pH is derived from Henderson-Hasselbalch equation.

After CH_3COOH is completed neutralised, CH_3COOK is hydrolysed back forming a basic solution.

$$CH_3COO^- + H_2O \rightleftharpoons CH_3COOH + OH^-$$

$$pH = 7 = \frac{pK_a}{2} + \frac{\log C}{2}$$

Also total volume is = 200 mL containing 1 millimol of CH_3COOK

$$\therefore \quad [CH_3COOK] = \frac{1 \times 10^{-3}\text{mol}}{0.2\text{L}} = 0.005 \text{ M}$$

$$pH = 7 + \frac{4.74}{2} + \frac{\log 0.005}{2}$$

$$= 7 + 2.37 - 1.15 = 8.22$$

$\therefore$ (i) $\rightarrow$ (q); (ii) $\rightarrow$ (r); (iii) $\rightarrow$ (s); (iv) $\rightarrow$ (p)

31. ***(a)*** For a salt of A_xB_y, $K_{sp} = x^x y^y (S)^{x+y}$

	Salt	K_{sp}	S	$[Ag^+]$
i	AgCl	$[Ag^+][Cl^-] = S^2$	$S = \sqrt{K_{sp}}$ $= \sqrt{1.8 \times 10^{-10}}$ $= 1.34 \times 10^{-5}$M	1.34×10^{-5}M
ii	Ag_2CrO_4	$[Ag^+]^2[CrO_4^{2-}]$ $= 4S^3$	$S = \sqrt[3]{\frac{K_{sp}}{4}}$ $= \sqrt[3]{\frac{1.1 \times 10^{-12}}{4}}$ $= 6.5 \times 10^{-5}$M	$6.5 \times 10^{-5} \times 2$ $= 1.30 \times 10^{-4}$M
iii	Ag_2S	$[Ag^+]^2[S^{2-}]$ $= 4S^3$	$S = \sqrt[3]{\frac{K_{sp}}{4}}$ $= \sqrt[3]{\frac{6.0 \times 10^{-51}}{4}}$ $= 1.14 \times 10^{-17}$ M	$= 2.28 \times 10^{-17}$M
iv	Ag_3AsO_4	$[Ag^+]^3[AsO_4^{3-}]$ $= 27S^4$	$S = \left(\frac{K_{sp}}{27}\right)^{1/4}$ $= \left(\frac{1.0 \times 10^{-22}}{27}\right)^{1/4}$ $= 1.387 \times 10^{-6}$M	$= 4.16 \times 10^{-6}$M

$\therefore$ (i) $\rightarrow$ (s), (ii) $\rightarrow$ (r), (iii) $\rightarrow$ (q), (iv) $\rightarrow$ (p)

32. ***(8.85)*** When $V_{NaOH} = 0$ mL; pH = 3

or $[H^+] = 0.001$

$$K_{a(HB)} = \frac{C\alpha^2}{(1-\alpha)} = \frac{(0.001)\alpha}{1-\alpha} = 10^{-5}$$

$$\alpha = 0.01$$

$$C = \frac{0.001}{0.01} = 0.1 = \frac{n_{HB}}{V}$$

$$0.1 = \frac{5}{V}; V = 50 \text{ mL}$$

$$\therefore \quad [NaB] = \frac{\text{milli-moles of acid}}{\text{total volume}} = \frac{5}{50+50} = 0.05$$

$$pH = \frac{1}{2}[pK_w + pK_a + \log C]$$

$$= \frac{1}{2}[14 + 5 + \log(0.05)] = 8.85$$

33. ***(10)*** $K_{eq} = \dfrac{K_a(HB)}{K_a(HA)} = \dfrac{10^{-5}}{10^{-6}} = 10$

Solutions for Q. Nos. 34-35

It is given that equivalence point occurs when 16.24 mL has been added.

Thus, after 8.12 mL of NaOH has been added, there is 50% neutralisation of the acid.

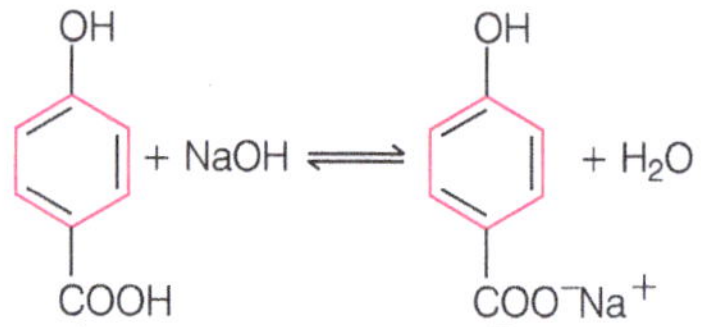

A B

At this point $[A] = [B]$, and mixture behaves as a buffer.

Thus, by Henderson-Hasselbalch equation,

$$pH = pK_{a_1} + \log\frac{[B]}{[A]} \Rightarrow 4.57 = pK_{a_1} + \log 1 = pK_{a_1}$$

Thus, pK_a of (A) at first ionisation stage is = 4.57

After (B) is formed, it behaves as amphiprotic species.

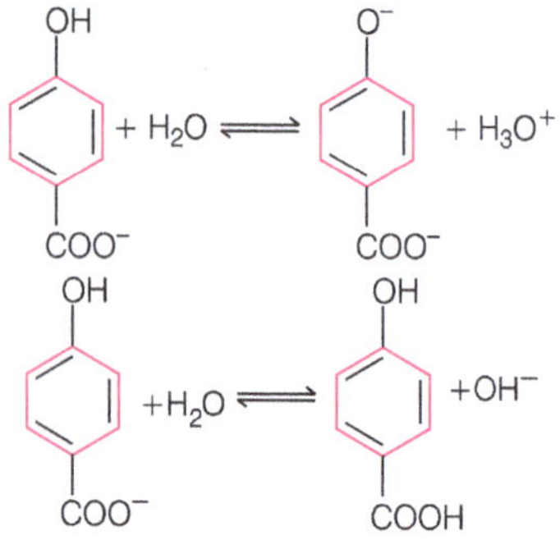

Thus, $\quad pH = \dfrac{pK_{a_1} + pK_{a_2}}{2}$

$$\therefore \quad 7.02 = \frac{4.57 + pK_{a_2}}{2}$$

$$\therefore \quad pK_{a_2} = 9.47$$

34. ***(4.57)***

35. ***(9.47)***

Solution for Q. No. 36-37

$$\text{Molarity of } H_3PO_4 = \frac{0.05}{98} \times \frac{1000}{100} = 5.1 \times 10^{-3}$$

$$pH = \frac{1}{2}[pK_a - \log 5.1 \times 10^{-3}] = 2.2$$

36. ***(2.2 × 10⁻⁴ m)*** $H_3PO_4 \rightleftharpoons 3H^+ + PO_4^{-3}$ $K = K_1K_2K_3$

$$K_1K_2K_3 = \frac{(10^{-7})^3 (PO_4^{-3})}{10^{-3}}$$

$$PO_4^{-3} = 2.2 \times 10^{-4} \text{ m}$$

37. ***(5.65 × 10⁻⁹)*** $K_{sp} = (Zn^{2+})^3 (PO_4^{-3})^2$

$$9.1 \times 10^{-33} = (Zn^{2+})^3 (2.2 \times 10^{-4})^2$$

$$Zn^{+2} = 5.65 \times 10^{-9} \text{ M}$$

38. ***(c)*** Among the given species, only four i.e., (i), (iii), (iv) and (v) have Lowry-Bronsted acid as well as Lowry Bronsted based character.

(i) (a)

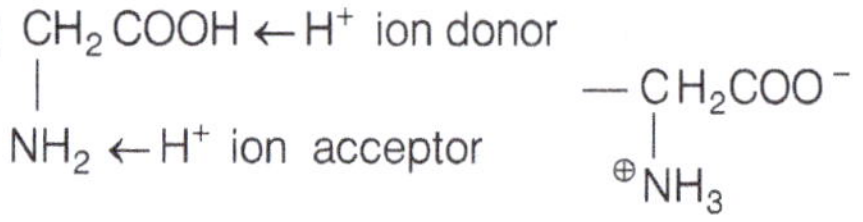

(ii)

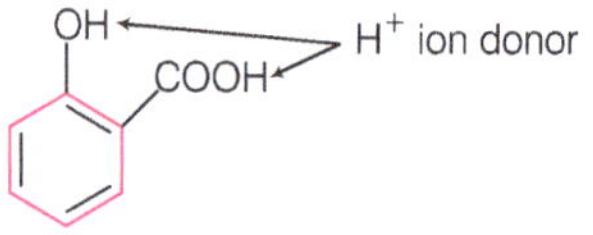

(iii)

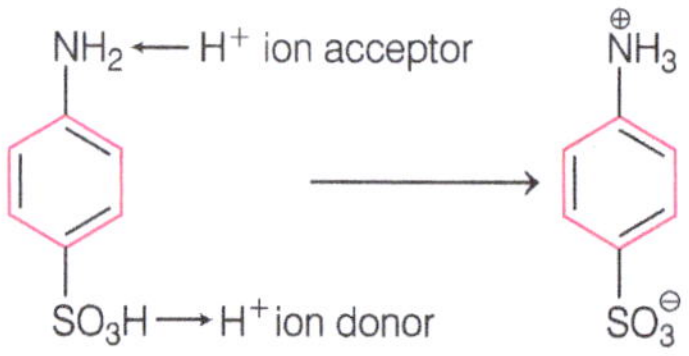

(iv)

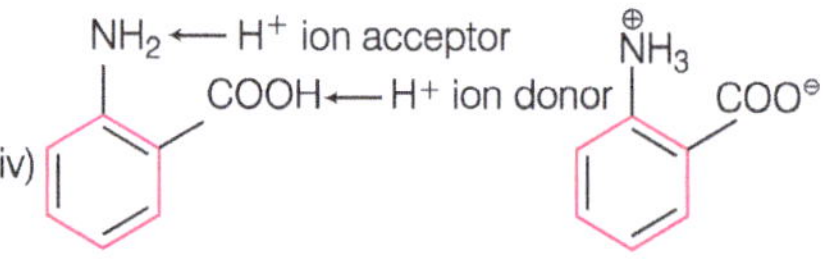

(v) Acetic acid CH_3COOH can behave as Lowry Bronsted acid as well as Lowry Bronsted base.

39. ***(c)*** Among the given reactions, only two i.e., (iii) and (iv) have same lewis base—

	Lewis acid	Lewis base
(i)	$AlCl_3$	Cl^-
(ii)	SO_2	OH^-
(iii)	$B(CH_3)_3$	NH_3
(iv)	Ag^+	NH_3
(v)	Cr^{3+}	H_2O

40. ***(c)*** Among the given reactions, only (iv) and (v) proceed towards right.
∵ Equilibrium is displaced in the direction of weak acid and weak base.

41. ***(c)*** Among the given species only four i.e. BCl_3, $AlCl_3$, $SiCl_4$ and $B(OH)_3$ are lewis acid.

42. ***(a)*** Among the given species, only four i.e., (iii), (iv), (vi) and (vii) are amphiprotic species (i.e, proton donor as well as proton acceptor).

43. ***(c)*** Among the given solutions, only two i.e, (iii) and (vi) when mixed will give a solution with pH greater than 7.
in (iii) $N_1V_1(\text{Base}) > N_2V_2(\text{Acid})$
In (vi) $CH_3COOH + KOH \rightleftharpoons CH_3COOK + H_2O$
Salt of weak acid and strong base is formed. CH_3COOK formed is hydrolysed to form alkaline solution. Thus pH > 7.

$$pH = 7 + \frac{pK_a}{2} + \frac{\log C}{2}$$

44. ***(a)*** Basic salts solution will have pH > 7, will change colour of litmus paper red to blue KCN and K_2CO_3 are the only basic salts among these.

45. ***(d)*** Among the given expression, only i.e., (ii), (iii), (vi) and (vii) are incorrect while others are correct.
(i) $Cr(OH)_3(s) \rightleftharpoons Cr^{3+} + 3OH^-$
$K_{sp} = [Cr^{3+}][OH^-]^3 = (S)(3S)^3 = 27S^4$
(ii) $AlPO_4(s) \rightleftharpoons Al^{3+} + PO_4^{3-}$
$K_{sp} = [Al^3]^+ [PO_4^{3-}] = S^2$
(iii) $Fe_2(SO_4)_3(s) \rightleftharpoons 2Fe^{3+} + 3SO_4^{2-}$
$K_{sp} = [Fe^{3+}]^2 [SO_4^{2-}]^3 = (2S)^2(3S)^3 = 108S^5$
(iv) $NiC_2O_4(s) \rightleftharpoons Ni^{2+} + C_2O_4^{2-}$
$K_{sp} = [Ni^{2+}][C_2O_4^{2-}] = S^2$
(v) $Na_3AlF_6(s) \rightleftharpoons 3Na^+ + AlF_6^{3-}$
$K_{sp} = [Na^+]^3[AlF_6^{3-}]^3 = (3S)^3 \cdot S$
(vi) $CaSO_4(s) \rightleftharpoons Ca^{2+} + SO_4^{2-}$
$K_{sp} = [Ca^{2+}][SO_4^{2-}] = S^2$
(vii) (a) $PbI_2(s) \rightleftharpoons Pb^{2+} + 2I^-$
$K_{sp} = [Pb^{2+}][I^-]^2 = 4S^3$

46. ***(b)*** When 1 litre each solution are mixed
$[OH^-] = 10^{-6} M$ (Buffer solution)
$M^{n+} = 0.05M$
for $Q = [0.5][10^{-6}]^2 = 5 \times 10^{-14}$
$Q > K_{sp}$ for Fe^{2+} and Ni^{2+}
So $Fe(OH)_2$ and $Ni(OH)_2$ are ppt.

Check Through PYQs : JEE Advanced

1. ***(d)*** P → 1, Q → 5, R → 4, S → 1

For *P*,
i.e. (10 mL of 0.1 M NaOH + 20 mL of 0.1 M acetic acid) is diluted to 60 mL
The correct match is 1, i.e. the value of $[H^+]$ does not change on dilution due to the formation of following buffer.

	$NaOH$	+ CH_3COOH ⇌	$CH_3COO^-Na^+ + H_2O$
Initial mmol	1	2	0
Final mmol	0	1	1

Final volume = 30 mL (20 + 10) in which millimoles of CH_3COOH and $CH_3COO^-Na^+$ are counted.

For *Q*, i.e. (20 mL of 0.1 M NaOH + 20 mL of 0.1 M CH_3COOH) is diluted to 80 mL
The correct match is 5, i.e. the value of $[H^+]$ changes to $\sqrt{2}$ times of its initial value on dilution.
As per the condition given in *Q*, the resultant solution before dilution contain 2 millimoles of $CH_3COO^-Na^+$ in 40 mL solution. Hence, it is the salt of weak acid and strong base.

So, $$[H^+]_{\text{initial}} = \sqrt{\frac{K_W K_C}{K_a}}$$

After dilution to 80 mL, the new '*C*' becomes $\frac{C}{2}$, So,

$$[OH^-]_{\text{new}} = \sqrt{\frac{K_W}{K_a} \times \frac{C}{2}}$$

or $$[H^+]_{\text{initial}} \times \sqrt{2}$$

For *R*, i.e. (20 mL of 0.1 M HCl + 20 mL of 0.1 M NH_3) is diluted to 80 mL
The correct match is 4, i.e. the value of $[H^+]$ changes to $\frac{1}{\sqrt{2}}$ times of its initial value of dilution.
As per the condition given in *R*, the resultant solution before dilution contains 2 millimoles of NH_4Cl in 40 mL of solution. Hence, a salt of strong acid and weak base is formed.
For this,

$$[H^+]_{\text{initial}} = \sqrt{\frac{K_W \times C}{K_b}}$$

Now, on dilution upto 80 mL new conc. becomes $C/2$.

So, $$[H^+]_{\text{new}} = \sqrt{\frac{K_W \times \frac{C}{2}}{K_b}}$$

or $$[H^+]_{\text{new}} = [H^+]_{\text{initial}} \times \frac{1}{\sqrt{2}}$$

For S, i.e. 10 mL saturated solution of $Ni(OH)_2$ in equilibrium with excess solid $Ni(OH)_2$ is diluted to 20 mL and solid $Ni(OH)_2$ is still present after dilution.

The correct match is 1.

$$Ni(OH)_2(s) \rightleftharpoons Ni^{2+} + 2OH^-$$

as per the condition given it is a sparingly soluble salt. Hence, on dilution the concentration of OH^- ions remains constant in saturated solution.

So for this solution, $[H^+]_{new} = [H^+]_{initial}$

2. ***(b)*** $MX \rightleftharpoons M^+ + X^-$

$X^- + H^+ \rightleftharpoons HX$

$$\text{Solubility, } S = \sqrt{K_{sp}\left[\frac{[H^+]+K_a}{K_a}\right]}$$

At pH = 7

$$10^{-4} = \sqrt{K_{sp}\left[\frac{10^{-7}+K_a}{K_a}\right]} \quad \text{...(i)}$$

At pH = 2

$$10^{-3} = \sqrt{K_{sp}\left[\frac{10^{-2}+K_a}{K_a}\right]} \quad \text{...(ii)}$$

On squaring and dividing both Eq.

$$10^{-2} = \frac{10^{-7}+K_a}{10^{-2}+K_a} \Rightarrow 10^{-4} + 10^{-2}K_a = 10^{-7} + K_a$$

$$0.999 \times 10^{-4} = 0.99\, K_a$$

$\therefore K_a = 10^{-4}$

$\therefore pK_a = 4$

3. ***(10.02)*** Moles of NaOH, $n_{NaOH} = 0.01$ mol

Moles of H_2CO_3, $n_{H_2CO_3} = 0.01$ mol

Moles of $NaHCO_3$, $n_{NaHCO_3} = 0.01$ mol

Moles of Na_2CO_3, $n_{Na_2CO_3} = 0.01$ mol

Acid-base reaction can be written as

	H_2CO_3	+ NaOH $\longrightarrow$	$NaHCO_3$ + H_2O
$t = 0$	0.01 mol	0.01 mol	0.02
After neutralisation	0	0.01 + 0.01	= 0.02 mol

This is a buffer solution,

By Henderson – Hasselbalch equation

$$pH = pK_{a_2} + \log\frac{[\text{Salt}]}{[\text{Acid}]}$$

$$pH = pK_{a_2} + \log\frac{[Na_2CO_3]}{[NaHCO_3]}$$

$$= 10.32 + \log\frac{0.01}{0.02}$$

$$= 10.32 - \log\left(\frac{1}{2}\right)$$

$$= 10.32 - 0.30 = 10.02$$

4. ***(3)*** From the given diagram, 6 mL volume of HA used till equivalene point. At half of equivalence point, solution will be basic buffer with B and BH^+.

$$\because \quad pOH = pK_b + \log\frac{[BH^+]}{[B]}$$

At half equivalence point :

$$[BH^+] = [B] \quad (\because pH = 11)$$

Therefore, $pOH = pK_b = 14 - 11 = 3$

$\because \quad pK_b = 3.00$

5. ***(3)*** Degree of ionisation $(\alpha) = \dfrac{\Lambda_m}{\Lambda^\infty}$

Let $\Lambda_m(HY) = x$

$$\Rightarrow \Lambda_m(HX) = \frac{X}{10}$$

$$\Rightarrow \frac{\Lambda_m(HX)}{\Lambda_m(XY)} = \frac{1}{10} = \frac{\alpha(HX)}{\alpha(HY)} \quad [\because \Lambda^\infty(HX) = \Lambda^\infty(HY)]$$

Also : $K_a(HX) = (0.01)[\alpha(HX)]^2$ ...(i)

$$K_a(HY) = (0.10)[\alpha(HY)]^2$$
$$= 0.10\,[10\,\alpha(HX)]^2$$
$$= 10\,[\alpha(HX)]^2 \quad \text{...(ii)}$$

$$\Rightarrow \frac{K_a(HX)}{K_a(HY)} = \frac{0.01}{10} = \frac{1}{1000}$$

$\Rightarrow \log K_a(HX) - \log K_a(HY) = -3$

$\Rightarrow -\log K_a(HX) - [-\log K_a(HY)] = 3$

$\Rightarrow pK_a(HX) - pK_a(HY) = 3$

6. ***(6)*** H_2SO_4 being a strong acid ionises completely into its ions.

	$H_2SO_4 \xrightarrow{K_{a_1}}$	H^+ +	HSO_4^-
$t = 0$	1M	0	0
$t = t$	0	1M	1M

Na_2SO_4 is a salt of strong acid and strong base, so it also ionises completely into its ions.

	$Na_2SO_4 \longrightarrow$	$2Na^+$ +	SO_4^-
$t = 0$	1.8×10^{-2}M	0	0
$t = t$	0	$2 \times (1.8 \times 10^{-2})$M	1.8×10^{-2}M

HSO_4^- is a weak acid as its $K_{a_2} = 1.2 \times 10^{-2}$

	$HSO_4^- \rightleftharpoons$	H^+ +	SO_4^-
$t = 0$	1M	1M	1.8×10^{-2}M
$t = t$	$1 + x \approx 1$	$1 - x \approx 1$	$1.8 \times 10^{-2} - x$

$[\because Q_C > K_{a_2}]$

$$K_{a_2} = \frac{[H^+][SO_4^-]}{[HSO_4^-]}$$

$$1.2 \times 10^{-2} = \frac{(1.8 \times 10^{-2} - x)}{1}$$

$$x = 0.6 \times 10^{-2}$$

$$[SO_4^{2-}] = (1.8 \times 10^{-2} + x)\text{M}$$
$$= (1.8 \times 10^{-2} - 0.6 \times 10^{-2})\text{M}$$
$$= 1.2 \times 10^{-2}\text{M}$$

Let the molar solubility of $PbSO_4 = S$ mol/L

$$PbSO_4 \rightleftharpoons \underset{S}{Pb^{2+}} + \underset{S + 1.2 \times 10^{-2}}{SO_4^{2-}}$$

$$K_{sp} = [Pb^{2+}][SO_4^{2-}]$$

$$1.6 \times 10^{-8} = (S)(S + 1.2 \times 10^{-2})$$

Since $K_{sp} <<< 1.2 \times 10^{-2}$

$$1.6 \times 10^{-8} = S \times 1.2 \times 10^{-2}$$

$$\Rightarrow \quad S = \frac{1.6 \times 10^{-8}}{1.2 \times 10^{-2}} = 1.3 \times 10^{-6}\ \text{M}$$

$$S = X \times 10^{-Y} = 1.3 \times 10^{-6}\ \text{M}$$

$$\Rightarrow \quad X = 1.3 \Rightarrow Y = 6$$

7. ***(0.20)*** $ZnS(s) \longrightarrow \underset{(0.05\ M)}{Zn^{2+}}(aq) + S^{2-}(aq)$

$$K_{sp}(ZnS) = [Zn^{2+}][S^{2-}] = 1.25 \times 10^{-22}$$

$$0.05 \times [S^{2-}] = 1.25 \times 10^{-22}$$

$$\Rightarrow [S^{2-}] = \frac{1.25 \times 10^{-22}}{0.05} = 25 \times 10^{-22}\ \text{M}$$

For H_2S, $\underset{(0.1\ M)}{H_2S} \rightleftharpoons 2H^+ + \underset{(25 \times 10^{-22}\ M)}{S^{-2}}$

$$K_{net} = 1 \times 10^{-21} = \frac{[H^+]^2\,[S^{2-}]}{[H_2S]}$$

$$1 \times 10^{-21} = \frac{[H^+]^2 \times 25 \times 10^{-22}}{[0.1]}$$

$$[H^+]^2 = \frac{1}{25}$$

$$[H^+] = \frac{1}{5} \Rightarrow 0.2\ \text{M}$$

8. ***(4.47)*** Solubility of salt of weak acid (AB) in presence of H^+ ions from buffer solution can be calculated with the help of following formula.

$$\text{Solubility} = \sqrt{K_{sp}\left[\frac{[H^+]}{k_a} + 1\right]}$$

Given, pH = 3, so $[H^+] = 10^{-3}$

$$K_a = 1 \times 10^{-8} \Rightarrow K_{sp} = 2 \times 10^{-10}$$

after putting the values in formula

$$\text{Solubility} = \sqrt{2 \times 10^{-10}\left(\frac{10^{-3}}{10^{-8}} + 1\right)} \approx \sqrt{2 \times 10^{-5}} = 4.47 \times 10^{-3}\text{M}$$

Hence, the value of $y = 4.47$

CHAPTER 7

Solution and Colligative Properties

Learning Elements

Element 1 Types and Concentration of Solution

Components of a Solution, Types of Solutions, Methods of Expressing Concentration of a Solution, Concentration terms, Expressing One Concentration Unit in Terms of Other Unit.

Element 2 Solubility, Vapour Pressure and Raoult's Law

Solubility, Henry's Law, Vapour Pressure, Raoult's law, Ideal Solution, Non-ideal Solution, Azeotropes.

Element 3 Colligative Properties, Abnormal Molecular Masses and Van't Hoff-Factor

Relative Lowering of Vapour Pressure, Elevation in Boiling Point, Depression in Freezing Point, Osmosis and Osmotic Pressure, Isotonic, Hypertonic and Hypotonic Solutions, Abnormal Molar Mass, Relationship between Van't, Hoff Factor (i) and Colligative Properties

Practice Elements

Practice Element 1 Target JEE Main
Practice Element 2 Target JEE Advanced

Trend Insights

JEE Main

	2024				2023				2022			
Topics	**E**	**M**	**T**	**O**	**E**	**M**	**T**	**O**	**E**	**M**	**T**	**O**
Types and Concentration of Solution	3	–	4	7	–	–	2	2	–	2	2	4
Solubility, Vapour Pressure and Raoult's law	–	–	3	3	–	2	–	2	–	2	2	4
Colligative Properties, Abnormal Molecular Masses and Van't Hoff Factor	–	3	9	12	–	3	15	18	–	1	12	13

E = Easy, **M** = Medium, **T** = tough, **O** = Overall

Current Dynamics

- Most of the questions from colligative properties, Raoult's law, vapour pressure, boiling point elevation and freezing point depression have been asked in previous years.
- Overall weightage of questions is nearly same in recent years.
- Moderate to tough question were asked in recent years.

JEE Advanced

Typology	Years				
	2024	**2023**	**2022**	**2021**	**2020**
1. Simple MCQs	–	–	–	–	–
2. One or More than one correct	–	–	–	–	–
3. Numerical Value/Integer	1	1	1	–	–
4. Matching Type	–	–	–	–	–
5. Paragraph Based	–	–	–	1	–

Current Dynamics

- Mostly numerical problems based on colligative properties and van't Hoff factor were asked from this chapter.
- The weightage of questions has remained constant in recent year.

Insightful Advice

- Focus on solving numerical problems, especially combining concepts of molality, mole fraction and colligative properties.
- Study the degree of dissociation (α) and association for solutes and its impact on colligative properties.
- Understand the concept of azeotropes, osmotic pressure and its applications.
- Review all PYQs and advanced level problems that combine multiple topics.

Element 1 Types and Concentration of Solution

A solution is a homogeneous mixture of two or more than two substances. It is a single-phase system, where the all components are evenly distributed at the molecular or ionic level. This uniformity is a defining characteristic of solutions, distinguishing them from heterogeneous mixtures where the components remain separate.

Components of a Solution

A solution has two essential components which are explained below

(i) **Solvent** The solvent is typically the component present in the largest quantity and is the medium in which the solute dissolves. Common solvents include water (often referred to as the "universal solvent" due to its ability to dissolve many substances). The solvent's physical and chemical properties significantly influence the behaviour of the solution.

(ii) **Solute** The solute is any substance that can be dissolved in the solvent, and it can exist in various forms : solids (e.g., salt, sugar), liquids (e.g., vinegar), or gases (e.g., carbon dioxide in carbonated beverages). The solute's identity and concentration determine the properties of solution.

Types of Solutions

Solutions are classified on the following three bases

On the Basis of Number of Components

Solution can be classified as

(i) **Binary Solution** If only two components are present.

(ii) **Ternary Solution** with three components, it is referred ternary.

(iii) **Quaternary Solution** with four components it is referred as quaternary.

In this chapter, we shall consider only binary solution.

On the Basis of Physical States of Solution

Solution can be classified as

1. Solid Solutions

These solutions are formed by mixing two solid components. It can be of two types

- **Substitutional solid solution** in which atoms, molecules or ions of one substance take the place of similar species of other substance in its crystal lattice. Brass, bronze, monel [nickel alloys with Cu, Zn, Mn] and steel are common examples.
- **Interstitial solid solution** in which atoms of one kind are placed into voids in the lattice of atoms of other substance. Tungsten carbide (WC) is this type of solution, being extremely hard, it is used in making of cutting and grinding tools.

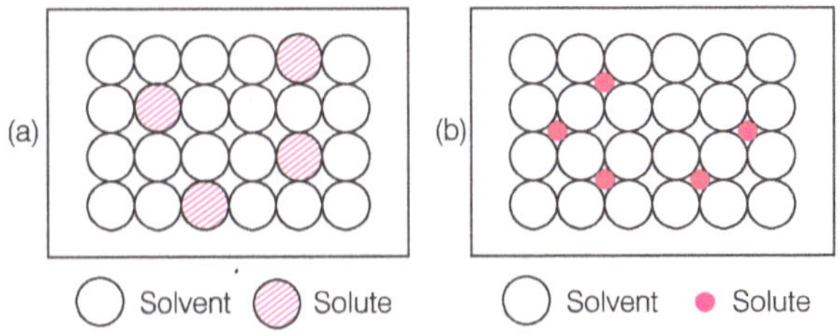

(a) Substitution solid solution
(b) Interstitial solid solution

2. Gaseous Solutions

All the gases form a homogeneous mixture known as gaseous solution, e.g. air is a gaseous solution.

3. Liquid Solutions

A liquid solution is a homogeneous mixture in which two or more substances are evenly distributed at the molecular level in a liquid medium.

Different Types of Binary Solution

Types of Solution	Solute	Solvent	Examples
Solid solutions	Gas	Solid	Solution of hydrogen in palladium.
	Liquid	Solid	Amalgam of mercury with sodium.
	Solid	Solid	Copper and gold alloy.
Gaseous solutions	Gas	Gas	Mixture of nitrogen and oxygen gas.
	Liquid	Gas	Chloroform mixed with nitrogen gas.
	Solid	Gas	Camphor in nitrogen gas, dust or smoke.
Liquid solutions	Gas	Liquid	Oxygen dissolved in water.
	Liquid	Liquid	Ethanol dissolved in water.
	Solid	Liquid	Glucose dissolved in water.

JEE Alert

Majorly, the solvent is decided by the final state of the solution i.e. it is the state of solution decides the state of solvent.

On the Basis of Concentration of Solute

On the above basis, solutions can be classified as follows.

1. Unsaturated Solution

A solution is unsaturated if it can still dissolve more solute at the same pressure and temperature. Thus, unsaturated solution contains lesser solute than the amount of solute it can dissolve.

2. Saturated Solution

A solution which can dissolve no more of the solute at the same pressure and temperature is said to be saturated. The saturated solution is in dynamic equilibrium with undissolved solute and contains the maximum amount of solute in a given amount of solvent thus its concentration is called its **solubility**.

3. Supersaturated Solution

A supersaturated solution is a solution that contains more solute than can normally be dissolved in a solvent at a given temperature and pressure. This state is achieved under specific conditions and is often unstable.

By dissolving more solute at a higher temperature, the solubility increases. As the solution cools slowly, it retains the excess solute and may avoid crystallisation if it is left undisturbed, resulting in a supersaturated state.

Methods of Expressing Concentration of a Solution

The amount of solute in a solution can be expressed in terms of two system of units.

(i) **Group *A*** Units specify the amount of solute in a given volume of solution because volume changes with temperature such as density, molarity, normality etc.

(ii) **Group *B*** Units specify the amount of solute for a given mass of solvent because mass will not change with temperature or solution, such as weight%, mole fraction, molality etc.

The advantage of group *A* units is the ease of solution preparation and **that of group *B* units is temperature independence**.

Expressing Concentration of Solutions Group *A*

The concentration of the solution in group *A* may be expressed in any of the following ways

(i) **Volume Per cent** (v/V) It is defined as volume of a solute present in 100 mL of solution.

Volume % of a component

$$= \frac{\text{Volume of the component}}{\text{Total volume of solution}} \times 100$$

(ii) **Mass by Volume Percentage** (w/V) It is the mass of solute dissolved in 100 mL of the solution.

$$\text{Mass\% of component} = \frac{\text{Mass of solute}}{\text{Volume of solution}} \times 100$$

(iii) **Molarity** (M) It is defined as the number of moles of solute dissolved in one litre (1 dm^3, 1000 cm^3) of solution.

$$\text{Molarity } (M) = \frac{\text{Number of moles of solute dissolved}}{\text{Volume of solution (in L)}}$$

$$\text{or } \frac{\text{Mass of solute (g)}}{\text{Molar mass of solute} \times \text{Volume of solution (in L)}}$$

$$M = \frac{w_B}{M_B \times V}$$

where, w_B is mass of solute.
M_B is molar mass of solute.
V is volume of solution (in L)

Solved Booster 1.1

The molarity of a solution containing 5 g NaOH in 450 mL solution is

(a) 0.278 (b) 0.323 (c) 0.523 (d) 0.628

Solution (a)

$$\text{Moles of NaOH} = \frac{5\text{ g}}{40\text{ g mol}^{-1}} = 0.125\text{ mol}$$

$$\text{Volume} = 450\text{ mL} = \frac{450\text{ mL}}{1000\text{ mL L}^{-1}} = 0.450\text{ L}$$

$$\therefore \quad \text{Molarity} = \frac{0.125\text{ mol}}{0.450\text{ L}} \approx 0.278\text{ M}$$

(iv) **Formality** (F) It is defined as the number of moles of formula units of solute per litre of solution, but focuses on the total amount of solute before any dissociation or reaction.

It can be expressed as

$$F = \frac{\text{Moles of solute}}{\text{Volume of solution in litres}}$$

JEE Spotlite

- **Differences between Formality and Molarity**
- **Molarity** is often used when discussing solutions of non-ionic compounds or when the solution's behavior is well-defined and does not change significantly with concentration.
- **Formality** is particularly useful for ionic compounds and solutions where the solute can dissociate into ions. It helps to find the concentration of the original solute before dissociation.

(v) **Strength** It is defined as gram of solute present in one litre of solution i.e. g/L.

(vi) **Normality** (N) It is defined as the number of gram equivalent of solute present in one litre of the solution.

$$N = \frac{\text{Number of gram equivalent of solute}}{\text{Volume of solution (in L)}}$$

$$= \frac{\text{Mass of solute (in g)} \times 1000}{\text{Equivalent weight (E)} \times \text{Volume of solution (in mL)}}$$

$$N = \frac{w_B \times 1000}{E_B \times V(\text{mL})}$$

Where, w_B is mass of solute

E_B = Equivalent weight of solute

V = Volume of solution.

Case I If a solution is diluted from V_1 to V_2, the normality of that solution changes accordingly, i.e.,

$$\underset{\text{Before dilution}}{N_1V_1} = \underset{\text{After dilution}}{N_2V_2}$$

Case II If a solution of normality N_1 and volume V_1 is mixed with normality N_2 and volume V_2 of the same solute then normality of the final solution is given by

$$N_1V_1 + N_2V_2 = N_3V_3 \qquad [V_3 = V_1 + V_2]$$

Expressing of the Concentration of Solution Group *B*

The concentration of group *B* solution are expressed as given below

(i) **Mass Percentage** (w / W) It is defined as mass of a solute present in 100 g of the solution.

Mass percentage solute

$$= \frac{\text{Mass of the solute in the solution}}{\text{Total mass of the solution}} \times 100$$

e.g. 20% w / W solution of KCl in water means that 20 g of KCl is dissolved in 80 g of water resulting in a 100 g solution.

(ii) **Mole Fraction** (χ) It is defined as number of moles of one component out of unit moles of all the components present in the solutions. It is expressed by χ. It is dimensionless quantity.

For example, in a binary solution containing the components *A* and *B*.

$$\text{Mole fraction of } A(\chi_A) = \frac{n_A}{n_A + n_B}$$

$$\text{Mole fraction of } B(\chi_B) = \frac{n_B}{n_A + n_B}$$

n_A = no. of moles of *A*, (Solute)

n_B = no of moles of *B*, (Solvent)

Sum of mole fraction of solute and solvent is always unity. So, $\chi_A + \chi_B = 1$

(iii) **Parts Per Million (ppm) and Parts Per Billion (ppb)** These are the concentration units which are closely related to mass per cent and particularly useful for dilute solutions.

Parts per million (ppm)

$$= \frac{\text{Mass of solute component}}{\text{Total mass of solution}} \times 10^6$$

Parts per billion (ppb)

$$= \frac{\text{Mass of solute component}}{\text{Total mass of solution}} \times 10^9$$

JEE MAPPER

Example Similar to PYQ Asked in JEE Advanced 2019

The mole fraction of urea in an aqueous urea solution containing 887g of water is 0.04. It the density of the solution is 1.32 g cm^{-3}, then molarity of urea solution is ....

[Given : Molar mass of urea and water are 60 g/mol and 18 g/mol, respectively.]

Sol. (2.72) $\text{Molarity} = \frac{\text{No. of moles of solute}}{\text{Volume of solution (in mL)}} \times 1000$

Given, mole fraction of urea $(\chi_{\text{urea}}) = 0.04$

Mass of water = 887 g

Density = 1.32 g/cm^3

$$\chi_{\text{urea}} = \frac{n_{\text{urea}}}{n_{\text{urea}} + 50}$$

$$\left[\therefore \text{ Moles of water } = \frac{887}{18} = 49.28 \approx 50\right]$$

$$0.04 = \frac{n_{\text{urea}}}{n_{\text{urea}} + 50}$$

$$0.04\, n_{\text{urea}} + 2 = n_{\text{urea}}$$

$$2 = 0.96\, n_{\text{urea}}$$

$$n_{\text{urea}} \approx 2.083 \text{ moles}$$

$$w_{\text{urea}} = n_{\text{urea}} \times (M.w)_{\text{urea}} = (2.083 \times 60) \text{ g}$$

$$V = \frac{(2.083 \times 60) + 887}{1.32}$$

$$= 766.65 \text{ mL}$$

Now,

$$\text{Molarity} = \frac{2.083 \times 1000}{766.65} \approx 2.72 \text{ M}$$

Competency Enhancer 1.1

The mole fraction of acetic acid in an aqueous acetic acid solution containing 927 g of water is 0.34. If the density of the solution is 1.86 gcm^{-3}, then molarity of acetic acid solution is ....

[Given : Molar masses of acetic acid and water are 60 g mol^{-1} and 18 g mol^{-1} respectively.]

(iv) **Molality** (m) It is defined as the number of moles of solute present in 1 kg of solvent. It is denoted by *m* and its unit is mol/kg.

$$m = \frac{\text{Number of moles of solute}}{\text{Mass of solvent (in kg)}}$$

Or $$m = \frac{\text{Mass of solute (in gram)}}{\text{Molar mass} \times \text{Mass of solvent (in kg)}}$$

$$m = \frac{w_B}{M_B \times W_A}$$

where, w_B is mass of solute in gram.
M_B is molar mass of solute in gram.
W_A is mass of solvent in kg.

Expression One Concentration Unit in Terms of Other Unit

One concentration unit can be easily converted into other. This helps in solving the numerical quickly without going through lengthy and tedious calculations.

1. Molarity Related to Molality

Molarity (M) is related to molality (m) by

$$m = \frac{1000\ M}{(1000d - Mm_2)} \quad \text{and} \quad M = \frac{1000\ d \times m}{(1000 + mm_2)}$$

where d is the density in g cm^{-3} of solution.
M = molarity, m = molality, m_2 = molar mass of solute

2. Relation between Molality (m) and Mole Fraction (χ)

These can be related as

$$m = \frac{\chi_2 \times 1000}{\chi_1 \times M_1}$$

where, m = molality, χ_1 = mole fraction of solvent,
χ_2 = mole fraction of solute, M_1 = molar mass of solvent.

3. Relation between Normality and Molarity

$$\text{Normality} = n\text{-factor} \times \text{molarity}$$
$$N = n\text{-factor} \times M$$

4. Relation between Molarity (M) and mole Fraction of the Solute (χ)

$$M = \frac{\chi_2 \times d \times 1000}{\chi_1 m_1 + \chi_2 m_2}$$

where, χ_1 = mole fraction of solvent
χ_2 = mole fraction of solute
m_1 = molar mass of solvent
m_2 = molar mass of solute
M = molarity, d = density of the solution (g mL^{-1})

Solved Booster 1.2

$Na_2S_2O_3$ solution is 5% by mass of solution. (Density = 1.04 g mL^{-1}). The concentration in terms of molarity, molality and mole fraction of solute respectively are .... M, ... mol kg^{-1} and ....

Solution *(0.329, 0.333, 6×10^{-3})*

Solution is 5% by weight of solution.

Thus, 100 g solution ($w_1 + w_2$) has = 5g (w_1) solute.

Thus, $w_1 = 5\text{ g} = \frac{5}{158}$ mole $Na_2S_2O_3$

$w_2 = 95\text{ g} = \frac{95}{18}$ moles H_2O

$= \frac{95}{1000}$ kg water

Volume of solution $= \frac{100}{1.04}\text{mL} = \frac{1}{10.4}\text{ L}$

Thus, (a) Molarity $= \frac{\text{Moles of solute}}{\text{Volume in L}} = \frac{\frac{5}{158\text{ mole}}}{\frac{1}{10.4\text{ L}}} = \frac{5 \times 10.4}{158}$

$= 0.329\text{ M}$

(b) Molality $= \frac{\text{Moles of solute}}{\text{kg of solvent}} = \frac{5/158\text{ mole}}{95/1000\text{ kg}} = 0.333\text{ mole kg}^{-1}$

(c) Total moles $= \left(\frac{5}{158} + \frac{95}{18}\right) = 5.31$

$\Rightarrow \chi_{\text{solute}} = \frac{5/158}{5.31} \approx 6 \times 10^{-3}$

JEE MAPPER

Example Similar to PYQ Asked in JEE Main 2024

Molarity (M) of an aqueous containing x g of anhyd. $ZnSO_4$ in 620 mL solution at 30° C is 3×10^{-1} M

Its molality will be .... $\times 10^{-3}$ m. (Nearest integer)
[Given density of the solution = 3.54 g/mL]

Sol. *(86)* $m_{\text{sol}} = V_{\text{sol}} \times d_{\text{sol}}$

$= 620 \times 3.54 = 2194.8$ g

Mass of solute (x) $= 0.3 \times 0.62 \times 161.47$

$= 30.03$ g

$n_{\text{solute}} = \frac{30.03\text{g}}{161.47\text{ g / mol}} = 0.186$

Mass of solvent = Mass of solution − Mass of solute

$= 2194.8\text{ g} - 30.03\text{ g}$

$= 2164.8$ g

Now, using the formula of molality,

Molality $= \frac{\text{No. of moles of solute}}{\text{Mass of solvent (in g)}} \times 1000$

$= \frac{0.186 \times 1000}{2164.8} = 0.08592$

$= 85.92 \times 10^{-3} \approx 86 \times 10^{-3}$ m

Compentency Enhancer 1.2

If the amount of anhydrous $CuSO_4$ present in 550 mL of 0.4 M solution is x g then the molality of solution will be .... $\times 10^{-2}$ m. (nearest integer)

[Given : density of the solution = 1.25 g/mL]

Elemental Practice 7.1

Type I MCQs with Only One Correct Option

1. If the density of 20% (mass/mass) aqueous KI solution is 1.202 g/mL, then its molality, molarity and mole fraction respectively are
(a) 1.403 m, 1.326 M, 0.213
(b) 1.506m, 1.448 M, 0.0264
(c) 1.306 m, 1.448 M, 0.0264
(d) 1.506 m, 1.481 M, 0.0264

2. Density of a 3.06 M solution of acetic acid in water is 1.02g/mL. The molality of the solution is
(a) 2.18 mol kg^{-1} (b) 3.66 mol kg^{-1}
(c) 0.381 mol kg^{-1} (d) 5.31 mol kg^{-1}

3. Given below are two statements.

Statement (I) The molarity of concentrated sulphuric acid (density = 1.834 g cm^{-3}) containing 90% of H_2SO_4 by mass is 14.32 M.

Statement (II) The volume of concentrated sulphuric acid which is 98% by mass (density = 1.84 g cm^{-3}) required to prepare 5 dm^3 of 0.5 mol dm^{-3} solution of sulphuric acid is 136 mL.

In the light of above statements, choose the correct answer from the options given below.
(a) Both Statement (I) and Statement (II) are correct.
(b) Both Statement (I) and Statement (II) are incorrect.
(c) Statement (I) is correct but Statement (II) is incorrect.
(d) Statement (I) is incorrect but Statement (II) is correct.

4. A sample of drinking water is contaminated with $CHCl_3$ to the level of 15 ppm by mass. Thus, mass percentage and molality of chloroform respectively are

	Mass %	Molality
(a)	15×10^{-3}	1.225×10^{-6}
(b)	15×10^{-6}	1.225×10^{-5}
(c)	15×10^{-2}	1.502×10^{-4}
(d)	15×10^{-4}	1.255×10^{-4}

5. If one assumes the volumes are additive, what is $[NO_3^-]$ in a solution obtained by mixing 275 mL of 0.200 M KNO_3, 325 mL of 0.40 M $Mg(NO_3)_2$ and 400 mL H_2O?
(a) 0.185 M (b) 0.600 M
(c) 0.315 M (d) 0.630 M

6. 250 mL of a sodium carbonate solution contains 2.65 g of Na_2CO_3. If 10 mL of this solution is diluted to one litre, what is the concentration of the resultant solution? [Molecular weight of Na_2CO_3 = 106]
(a) 10^{-4}M (b) 0.21 M
(c) 0.114 M (d) 0.001 M

7. The required amount (in mL) of glycerol ($C_3H_8O_3$) of density 1.26 g mL^{-1} must be added per kilogram of water to produce a solution with 4.85 mole per cent of $C_3H_8O_3$ is
(a) 207 mL (b) 115 mL
(c) 215 mL (d) 122 mL

8. If $H_2S(g)$ is bubbled through water at 298 K with a total pressure of 1 atm, what would be the molarity of H_2S in this solution ? Assume density of water is 1.0 g mL^{-1}. Henry's law constant of $H_2S = 4.12\times10^5$ torr at 298 K.
(a) 0.0234 mol L^{-1} (b) 0.1024 mol L^{-1}
(c) 1.368 mol L^{-1} (d) 0.0034 mol L^{-1}

9. Consider the following concentration terms at 298 K.
I. 0.1 m (molal) solution
II. 0.1 M (molar) solution
III. 0.05 mole fraction of urea
IV. 0.80 weight fraction of glucose solution

If temperature is increased to 315 K, concentration will not change in
(a) Both I and II (b) I, II and III
(c) I, III and IV (d) Both II and IV

10. Laboratory ammonia is 14.8 M $NH_3(aq)$ with a density of 0.8980 g / mL . Mole fraction of NH_3 in this solution is
(a) 0.292 (b) 0.708
(c) 0.148 (d) 0.852

11. We have
I. 25 mL of 1 M NaOH
II. 10 mL of 0.50 M HCl

On mixing the two solutions, molar concentrations of Na^+, OH^- and Cl^- respectively, are

	$[Na^+]$	$[OH^-]$	$[Cl^-]$
(a)	1.50 M	1.00 M	0.50 M
(b)	0.85 M	0.85 M	0.85 M
(c)	0.85 M	0.71 M	0.14 M
(d)	0.57 M	0.57 M	0.14 M

12. The molarity of each of the following solution is
(i) 30g $Co(NO_3)_2\cdot6H_2O$ in 4.3 L solution [Co = 59]
(ii) 30 mL of 0.5 M H_2SO_4 diluted to 500 mL
(a) 0.11 M, 0.21 M
(b) 0.32 M, 1.32 M
(c) 1.32 M, 0.32 M
(d) 0.02 M, 0.03 M

13. Molarity (M) of an aqueous solution containing *x* g of an aqueous solution of urea in 600 mL solution at 33°C is 5×10^{-1} M. Its molality will be
(a) 488×10^{-3} m (b) 388×10^{-3} m
(c) 432×10^{-3} m (d) 332×10^{-3} m

[Given : Density of the solution = 1.32 g/mL]

14. The mole fraction of sulphuric acid in an aqueous solution containing 738 g of water is 0.02. If the density of the solution is 1.84 g/cm^3, then molarity of urea solution is
(a) 18.22 (b) 18.39
(c) 1.87 (d) 1.70
[Given, Molar mass of sulphuric acid and water are 98 g/mol and 18g/mol, respectively]

15. 20 mL of 0.2 N HCl and 40 mL of 0.1 N HCl together exactly neutralise 40 mL solution of NaOH, which is also exactly neutralised by a solution in water of 0.61 g of an organic base. The equivalent weight of organic base is
(a) 152.5 (b) 38.125
(c) 60.25 (d) 76.25

Type II 》 MCQs with One or More than One Correct Option

16. Which of the following statements are correct?
(a) The density of solution of glucose if molarity and molality are equal to 1 is 1.18 g mL^{-1}.
(b) An aqueous solution is 6% methanol (CH_3OH) by mass with $d = 0.988$ g mL^{-1}. Thus the molarity of CH_3OH in this solution will be 1.8525 M.
(c) Mole fraction of a solute in an aqueous solution is 0.2. The molality of the solution will be ≈ 13.9.
(d) The density of 1 M solution of NaCl is 1.0585 g mL^{-1}, then the molality of the solution is 1 m.

17. 1 kg of aqueous solution has 0.40 kg NaOH. Thus, this solution is
(a) 66.67% by weight of water
(b) 40.00% by weight of aqueous solution
(c) 16.67 molal
(d) 16.67 molar

18. An ethanol-water solution is prepared by dissolving 10.00 mL of ethanol (C_2H_5OH, $d = 0.789$ g mL) in a sufficient volume of water to produce 100 mL of solution with a density, $d = 0.982$ g mL^{-1}.
Which of the following statements are correct?
(a) Molarity of the solution is 1.71 mol L^{-1}.
(b) Mole % of ethanol is 2.38%.
(c) Molality of the solution is 1.89 mol kg^{-1}.
(d) Mass % of ethanol is 5.03%.

19. 20 mL of 6.0 M HCl is mixed with 50.0 mL of 2.0 M $Ba(OH)_2$, and 30 mL of water is added.
The correct statement(s) is/are
(a) The concentration of $OH^{\ominus}$ remaining in the solution is 0.8 M.
(b) The concentration of $Cl^{\ominus}$ remaining in the solution is 1.2 M.
(c) The concentration of Ba^{2+} remaining in the solution is 1.0 M.
(d) The concentration of $OH^{\ominus}$ is in excess.

20. If 50 mL of 2 M H_2SO_4 solution is mixed with 100 mL of 98% (w/w) of H_2SO_4 ($d = 0.1$ g mL^{-1}), then
(a) concentration of solution becomes half
(b) volume of solution becomes 200 mL
(c) mass of H_2SO_4 in the solution is 98 g
(d) mass of H_2SO_4 in the solution is 19.6g

Type II 》 Numerical/Integer Answer Type Questions

21. An aqueous solution of 34% H_3PO_4 by mass and has density 1.209 gmL^{-1}. The value of molarity, molality and normality is xM, ym and zN.
The sum of x, y and z is ....

22. The sum of mole fraction of ethanol and water, if 3 moles of ethanol are dissolved in 1000 g of water ....

23. When 730 mL of 0.4 M sulphuric acid is heated in a beaker, its volume is reduced to half and 11.5 g of sulphuric acid is evaporated. The molarity of the remaining nitric acid solution is $x \times 10^{-2}$ M. (Nearest integer)

24. Molality of an aqueous solution of urea is 2.45 m. Mole fraction of urea in solution is $x \times 10^{-2}$. The value of x is .... (nearest integer)

25. 250 mL of Na_3PO_4 solution contains 3.65 g of sodium. The molarity of the solution is $x \times 10^{-2}$ mol L^{-1}. (nearest integer)
[Given ; Atomic mass Na : 23.0 u, O : 16.0 u, P : 31.0 u]

Elemental Practice 7.1 | Chapter 07

Connect with **Answers**

1. (b)	**2.** (b)	**3.** (d)	**4.** (d)	**5.** (c)	**6.** (d)
7. (a)	**8.** (b)	**9.** (c)	**10.** (a)	**11.** (d)	**12.** (d)
13. (b)	**14.** (c)	**15.** (d)	**16.** (a,b,c,d)	**17.** (a,b,c)	**18.** (a,c)
19. (a,b,c,d)	**20.** (b,d)	**21.** (22.02)	**22.** (1)	**23.** (48)	**24.** (4)
25. (20)					

Element 2 Solubility, Vapour Pressure and Raoult's Law

Solubility

The maximum amount of solute dissolved in a given amount of the solvent to form a saturated solution at a particular temperature is called **solubility**.

It depends upon the nature of solute and solvent as well as temperature and pressure.

Solubility of a Solid in a Liquid

Every solid does not dissolve in given liquid, e.g. NaCl and sugar dissolve readily in water while naphthalene and anthracenes do not.

The following factors affects the solubility of a solid in a liquid.

Nature of the Solute and the Solvent

When a solid or liquid dissolves, the structural units (ions, molecules) and the spaces between them is occupied by the solvent molecules. During dissolution, the energy required to break the bond arises from the new bond formed between the solute and the solvent particles (solvation).

In the case of ionic solutes, only water or other highly polar solvents are able to dissolve ionic compounds appreciably.

Non-polar or weakly polar compounds dissolve in non-polar or weakly polar solvents, highly polar solvents, highly polar compounds dissolve in highly polar solvents. It follows "Like dissolves like" rule.

Temperature

On the basis of the effect of temperature on solubility in water the various ionic substances are divided into three categories.

(i) Solutes whose solubility increases continuously with increase of temperature.

Most of the substances like $NaNO_3$, KNO_3, NaCl, KCl etc fall into this category. The reason for this behaviour is that for such substances, the process of dissolution is endothermic i.e.

$$\text{Solute} + \text{Solvent} + \text{Heat} \rightleftharpoons \text{Solution}$$

Applying Le Chatelier's principle as the temperature is increased, equilibrium will shift in a direction in which heat is being absorbed i.e. in the forward direction. Consequently more of the solute passes into the solution.

(ii) Solutes whose solubility decreases continuously with increase of temperature.

There are a few substances like cerium sulphate, lithium carbonate, sodium carbonate monohydrate ($Na_2CO_3 \cdot H_2O$) etc whose solubility decreases with increase of temperature.

This is due to the fact that the process of dissolution of these substances is exothermic and accompanied by evolution of heat.

(iii) Solutes substances whose solubility does not increase or decrease continuously.

There are some substances which on heating change at a particular temperature from one polymorphic form to another (like α to β-form as in the case of ammonium nitrate) to form one hydrated form to another (like $CaCl_2 \cdot 6H_2O \longrightarrow CaCl_2 \cdot 4H_2O \longrightarrow CaCl_2 \cdot 2H_2O$) or from hydrated to anhydrous form (e.g. $Na_2SO_4 \cdot 10H_2O \longrightarrow Na_2SO_4$.)

Such substances donot show a continuous increase or decrease of solubility.

> **JEE Alert**
> Pressure does not have any significant effect on solubility of a solid in liquids.

Solubility of a Gas in a Liquid

All gases are soluble in water as well as in other liquids to a greater or smaller extent.

The solubility of gases in liquids depends upon certain factors which are discussed below.

1. Nature of the Solute and the Solvent

Like solid solute, the gases too follow the thumb rule, "like dissolves like" For example, gases like, ammonia, sulphur dioxide and hydrogen chloride are highly soluble in water.

$$NH_3 + H_2O \rightleftharpoons NH_4OH \rightleftharpoons NH_4^+ + OH^-$$

$$SO_2 + H_2O \rightleftharpoons H_2SO_3 \rightleftharpoons HSO_3^- + H^+$$

$$HCl + H_2O \rightleftharpoons H_3O^+ + Cl^-$$

2. Effect of Pressure

The quantitative relation connecting the solubility with pressure was stated by *W*. Henry and is known as Henry's law.

The law states. "At a given temperature the mass of dissolved gas in a given volume of solvent is proportional to the pressure of the gas with which it is in equilibrium"

If 'm' is the mass of the gas dissolved by unit volume of solvent at equilibrium pressure 'p' then according to Henry's law we have

$$m \propto p \quad \text{or} \quad m = Kp \qquad \ldots\text{(i)}$$

where K is the constant of proportionality

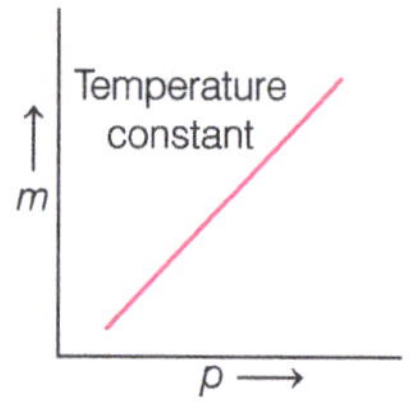

If solubility of the gas is known at one particular pressure, then it can be calculated at other pressures using the following relation,

$$\frac{m_1}{m_2} = \frac{p_1}{p_2} \quad \ldots \text{(ii)}$$

where 'm_1' is the solubility of the gas at pressure 'p_1'. and 'm_2' is the solubility of the gas at pressure 'p_2'.

When a mixture of two or more non-reacting gases is brought in contact with a solvent each constituent gas dissolves in proportion to its own partial pressure. Henry's law can be applied to each individual gas independent of the presence of other gas. If we use the mole fraction of the gas in the solution as a measure of its solubility, then the law can be stated as, "mole fraction of the gas in a solution is proportional to the partial pressure of the gas."

$$x \propto p$$

where, x = mole fraction of the gas in solution and

p = partial pressure of the gas

$$x = K'p$$

$$p = \frac{1}{K'}x = K_H x \left(K_H = \frac{1}{K'}\right) \quad \ldots \text{(iii)}$$

K_H is called Henry's law constant. Different gases have different values of K_H at a definite temperature for a given solvent.

Higher the K_H value, lesser will be the solubility of a gas in a solvent at a given pressure and temperature.

3. Effect of Temperature

In general, the solubility of a gas decreases with increase in temperature. This is expected because on heating the solution of a gas, some gas is usually expelled out of the solution.

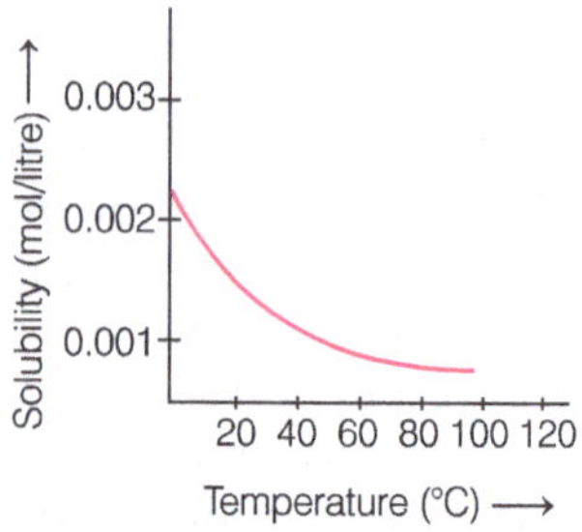

Temperature dependence of O_2 gas solubility in water

JEE Spotlite

K_H values for both N_2 and O_2 increases with increase of temperature and thus solubility of gases decreases with increase in temperature. When dissolved, the gas molecules are present in liquid phase and the process of dissolution can be considered similar to condensation in which heat is evolved. Hence, aquatic species are more comfortable in cold water rather than warm water.

Applications of Henry's Law

- To increase the solubility of CO_2 in soft drinks and soda water the bottle is sealed under high pressure.
- In lungs, when oxygen is present in air with high partial pressure, haemoglobin combines with oxygen to form oxyhaemoglobin. In tissues, when partial pressure of oxygen is low, oxyhaemoglobin releases O_2 for utilisation in cellular activities.

Limitations of Henry's Law

Henry's Law holds good if the following conditions are fulfilled

- The pressure is not too high,
- The temperature is not very low,
- The gas does not chemically combine with the solvent. The gas molecules do not either dissociate or associate in the solvent. In case the dissolved gas reacts with the solvent, higher solubilities can result. The solubility of ammonia in water is much higher than expected.

Solved Booster 2.1

Henry's law constant of CO_2 in water is 1.67×10^8 Pa at 298 K. The mass of CO_2 in 500 mL soda water under 2.5 atm CO_2 pressure at 298 K is ....

Solution *(1.852)*

$\therefore \quad p_{CO_2} = 2.5 \text{ atm} = 2.5 \times 1.01325 \times 10^5 \text{ Pa}$

By Henry's law

$$p_{CO_2} = K_H \chi_{CO_2}$$

$$\therefore \quad \chi_{CO_2} = \frac{p_{CO_2}}{K_H}$$

$$\chi_{CO_2} = \frac{2.5 \times 1.01325 \times 10^5 \text{Pa}}{1.67 \times 10^8 \text{Pa}} = 1.5168 \times 10^{-3}$$

If $\quad n_{CO_2} = n$

and $\quad n_{H_2O} = 500 \text{ mL } H_2O = 500 \text{ g } H_2O \; (d = 1 \text{ g mL}^{-1})$

$$= \frac{500}{18} \text{ mol} = 27.78 \text{ mol}$$

$\therefore$ Total moles $= n + 27.78$

$\therefore$ Mole fraction of $CO_2 = \dfrac{n}{n_{total}}$

$$1.5168 \times 10^{-3} = \frac{n}{n + 27.78} \approx \frac{n}{27.78}$$

$\therefore \quad n(CO_2) = 1.5168 \times 10^{-3} \times 27.78 = 0.0421 \text{ mol}$

$m(CO_2) = 0.0421 \times 44 \text{ g} = 1.852 \text{ g } CO_2$

Vapour Pressure

The pressure exerted by the vapour (the molecules in the vapour phase) above the liquid at equilibrium at a given temperature is known as the vapour pressure of the liquid. It is constant for a given liquid irrespective of amount of liquid and shape or volume of vessels. The vapour pressure is influenced by several factors which are explained below.

1. Effect of Temperature

As the temperature of a liquid increases, its molecules move more rapidly, leading to a rise in their average kinetic energy. At higher temperatures, a greater number of molecules gain sufficient energy to overcome the energy barrier, resulting in more molecules transitioning into the vapour phase. Consequently, the vapour pressure of the liquid increases.

2. Nature of the Liquid

The vapour pressure of a liquid is also affected by the strength of intermolecular forces between its molecules. Liquids with weaker intermolecular forces tend to evaporate more readily, resulting in higher vapour pressures and classifying them as volatile. Conversely, liquids with stronger intermolecular forces exhibit a lower tendency to escape as vapour, leading to lower vapour pressures and designating them as less volatile or non-volatile. For instance, ethyl alcohol has a higher vapour pressure due to its weaker intermolecular forces compared to water. Thus, a volatile liquid typically has a lower boiling point than a non-volatile liquid.

3. Surface Area

More number of volatile liquid molecules present per unit area on surface allows more molecules to escape into the gas phase, increasing vapour pressure.

Lowering of Vapour Pressure of a Liquid in Solution

- When a non-volatile solute (say glucose) is dissolved in solvent (say water) to form a solution the vapour pressure of the solution is due to the vapour pressure of the solvent alone (water) as non-volatile solute does not evaporate. It is found that the vapour pressure of the solution is less than that of the pure liquid (pure water).
- When a volatile solute (say C_2H_5OH) is dissolved in water to form a solution, the vapour phase consists of the vapours of both the components of the solution (both C_2H_5OH and H_2O). In such a case vapour pressure of the solution is the sum of the partial vapour pressures of each component. It is found that partial vapour pressure of each component depends upon the molar concentration (or mole fraction) respective component in solution

Explanation

In terms of thermodynamics, the higher the entropy of a substance the lower its free energy. If we compare the entropy of a solution to that of a pure solvent, the entropy of the solution will be higher. Therefore, the free energy of the solution will be lower than that of the pure solvent. Lower free energy is more stable. From a thermodynamic standpoint, the solution is more stable than a pure solvent. Because the solution is more stable, fewer molecules are leaving to the gas phase. This lower evaporation rate leads to a lower vapour pressure.

If $p°$ is the vapour pressure of the pure liquid and p that of liquid in solution., then

Lowering of vapour pressure = $p° - p$

Greater the no. of particles of the solute in solution greater is the lowering of vapour pressure of the solution.

$p° - p \propto$ Molar concentration of particles of solute in solution.

Concept Visualizer

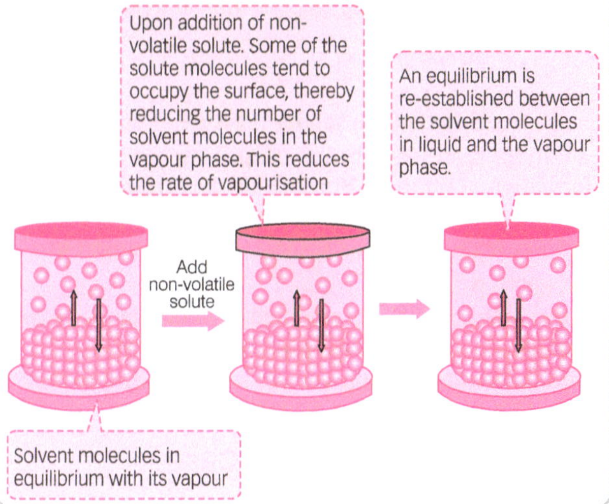

Raoult's Law

The French Chemist, Francois Marie Raoult's in 1886 studied the vapour pressure of volatile and non-volatile solution.

Raoult's Law for Volatile Solute

(For Ideal Solution)

This law states that "the partial pressure of any volatile constituent of a solution at a constant temperature is equal to the vapour pressure of pure constituent multiplied by the mole fraction of that constituent in the solution.

Mathematically, such a relationship is described as

$$p_{\text{solution}} = \chi_{\text{solvent}} \, p^{\circ}_{\text{solvent}}$$

Let us assume that a mixture is prepared containing n_A and n_B moles of liquid A and B, respectively.

Further, let p_A and p_B be the partial pressures of A and B, respectively and p_A° and p_B° be the vapour pressure in pure state.

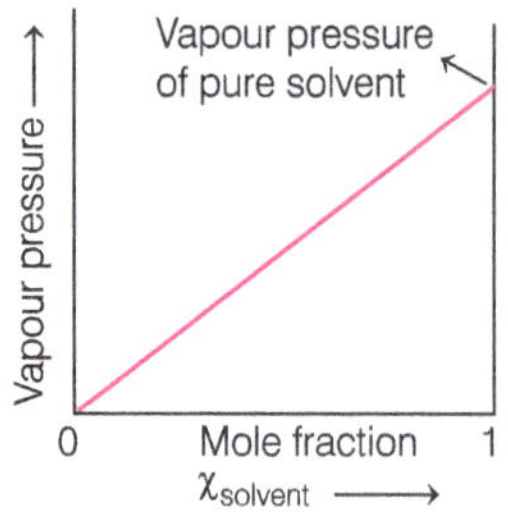

Then, according to Raoult's law,

$$p_A = p_A^\circ \chi_A \quad \text{and} \quad p_B = p_B^\circ \chi_B$$

Vapour pressure of the mixture $= p_A^\circ \chi_A + p_B^\circ \chi_B$

Raoult's Law for Non-Volatile Solute

At a given temperature, vapour pressure of a solution containing a non-volatile solute is equal to the partial vapour pressure of the solvent.

$$p_{\text{solution}} = p_{\text{pure solvent}} \times \text{Mole fraction of solvent}$$

$$p_S = p_A^\circ \chi_A \quad \text{or} \quad \frac{p_A^\circ - p_S}{p_A^\circ} = \chi_B$$

Here, $p_A^\circ - p_S$ (difference in vapour pressure of pure solvent and solution) represents the lowering in vapour pressure on the formation of solution. Now, by dividing the lowering in vapour pressure with the vapour pressure of the pure solvent, i.e., $(p_A^\circ - p_S)/p_A^\circ$ we get the relative lowering in vapour pressure.

Thus, the Raoult's law in its modified form may be stated as :

"The relative lowering in vapour pressure of an ideal solution containing the non-volatile solute is equal to the mole fraction of the solute at a given temperature."

Raoult's Law as a Special Case of Henry's Law

Raoult's law may be regarded as a special case of Henry's law. According to Raoult's law, the vapour pressure of a volatile component in given solution is given by the relation.

$$p_A = p_A^\circ \chi_A$$

In the case of solution of a gas in a liquid, the gaseous component is volatile component. Its solubility is governed by Henry law which gives the relation.

$$p = K_H \chi$$

From the comparison of equation of Raoult's law and Henry's law shows that the Raoult's law is a special case of Henry law in which K_H becomes equal to p_A°.

JEE MAPPER

Example Similar to PYQ Asked in JEE Advanced 2018

Liquids A and B form ideal solution over the entire range of composition. At temperature T, equimolar binary solution of liquids A and B has vapour pressure 65 torr. At the same temperature, a new solution of A and B having mole fractions χ_A and χ_B, respectively, has vapour pressure of 25.5 torr. The value of χ_A / χ_B in the new solution is ....

[Given : The vapour pressure of pure liquid A is 20 torr at temperature T]

Solution (15.66)

By using the formula,

$$P_{\text{total}} = p_A^\circ \times \chi_A + p_B^\circ \times \chi_B$$

and for equimolar solutions $\chi_A = \chi_B = \frac{1}{2}$

Given, $P_{\text{total}} = 65$ torr for equimolar solution

$p_A^\circ = 20$ torr

So, $$65 = p_A^\circ \times \frac{1}{2} + p_B^\circ \times \frac{1}{2} = \frac{1}{2}(p_A^\circ + p_B^\circ)$$

$$p_A^\circ + p_B^\circ = 130 \text{ torr}$$

But we know, $p_A^\circ = 20$ torr

So, $p_B^\circ = 110$ torr

Now, for the new solution

Given, $P_{\text{total}} = 25.5$ torr

So,
$$25.5 = 20\chi_A + (110)(1-\chi_A)$$
$$25.5 = 20\chi_A + 110 - 110\chi_A$$
$$25.5 = 110 - 90\chi_A$$
$$\chi_A = \frac{110 - 25.5}{90} = 0.939 \approx 0.94$$

Thus, $\chi_B = 1 - 0.94 = 0.06$

Hence, the ratio

$$\frac{\chi_A}{\chi_B} = \frac{0.94}{0.06} = 15.67$$

Competency Enhancer 2.1

The total pressure observed by mixing two liquids A and B is 360 mmHg when their mole fractions are 0.6 and 0.4 respectively.

The total pressure becomes 400 mmHg if the mole fractions are changed to 0.3 and 0.7 respectively for A and B.

The vapour pressure of pure A is .... mmHg. (Nearest integer)

Consider the liquids and solutions behave ideally.

Ideal Solution

A solution can be termed as ideal, if it falls into any one of the given below categories:

1. Molecular Interactions

An ideal solution is defined as the solution in which the intermolecular interactions between the components are of the same magnitude as the intermolecular attractions found in the pure components.

In general, substances forming similar structure and polarities form nearly ideal solution For example,

- Benzene and toluene
- Hexane and heptane
- Ethyl bromide and ethyl iodide
- Chlorobenzene and bromobenzene

2. Thermodynamics

An ideal solution is defined as the one in which no volume change and enthalpy change takes place on mixing the solute and the solvent in any proportion i.e.,

$$\Delta V_{\text{mixing}} = 0$$

and $$\Delta H_{\text{mixing}} = 0$$

> **JEE Alert**
> In actual practice, no solution is ideal. However, when concentration of solute is very low the solution behaves ideally. Therefore, very dilute solutions are ideal in behaviour.

3. Raoult's Law

An ideal solution is that solution in which each component obey's Raoult's law under all conditions of temperature and pressure.

Graphical Representation

- Generally a volatile solute is a liquid. Since the solvent is also a liquid, it is quite normal to treat either of them as a solute and the other as a solvent.
- Let us assume that liquid '*A*' is the solvent and liquid '*B*' is the solute and χ_A and χ_B are the mole fractions of two volatile miscible liquids *A* and *B* having vapour pressures p°_A and p°_B respectively at temperature *T* K.

Therefore, vapour pressure of solution is given by

$$\begin{aligned} p_{\text{total}} &= p_A + p_B \\ &= \chi_A p^\circ_A + \chi_B p^\circ_B \\ &= \chi_A p^\circ_A + (1 - \chi_A) p^\circ_B \\ &= \chi_A (p^\circ_A - p^\circ_B) + p^\circ_B \end{aligned}$$

- A plot between p_{Total} and χ_A is linear with slope equal to $(p^\circ_A - p^\circ_B)$ and intercept equal to p°_B. Thus, the total pressure increases with increase in χ_A as shown in graph

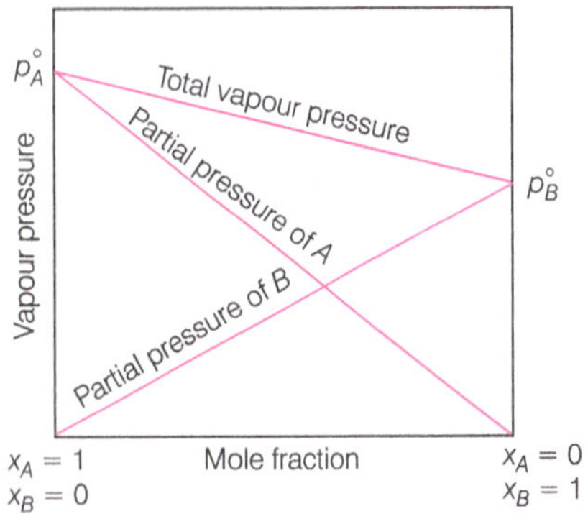

Relation between Mole Fraction in Liquid and Vapour Phase of a Volatile Solute

If χ'_A and χ'_B are the mole fractions of *A* and *B* in the vapour phase, then according to Dalton's law of partial pressure, we can write

$$p_A = \chi'_A \times p_{\text{total}}$$

$$\therefore \qquad \chi'_A = \frac{p_A}{p_{\text{Total}}} = \frac{\chi_A p^\circ_A}{\chi_A p^\circ_A + \chi_B p^\circ_B}$$

and $$\chi'_B = \frac{\chi_B p^\circ_B}{\chi_A p^\circ_A + \chi_B p^\circ_B} = 1 - \chi'_A.$$

Condensation of Vapours of Solution

Consider two containers given below

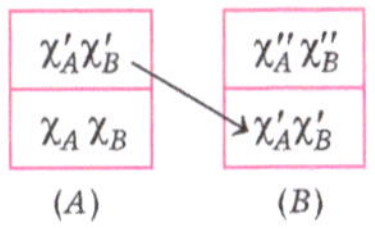

Vapour pressure in container *A*

According to Raoult's law, $p_A = \chi_A p^\circ_A = \chi_A' p_T$ ...(i)

$$p_B = \chi_B p^\circ_B = \chi_B' p_T \quad \text{...(ii)}$$

Divide Eqs. (i) and (ii) we get,

$$\frac{\chi_A p^\circ_A}{\chi_B p^\circ_B} = \frac{\chi_A'}{\chi_B'} \quad \text{...(iii)}$$

For container (*B*)

$$p'_A = \chi'_A p^\circ_A = \chi_A'' p'_T \quad \text{...(iv)}$$

$$p'_B = \chi'_B p^\circ_B = \chi''_B p'_T \quad \text{...(v)}$$

Divide Eqs. (iv) and (v), we get

$$\frac{\chi'_A p^\circ_A}{\chi'_B p^\circ_B} = \frac{\chi_A''}{\chi_B''} \quad \text{...(vi)}$$

Using Eqs. (iii) and (vi), we get

$$\frac{\chi_A}{\chi_B}\left(\frac{p^\circ_A}{p^\circ_B}\right)^2 = \frac{\chi''_A}{\chi''_B}$$

It shows, $$\frac{\chi_A}{\chi_B}\left(\frac{p_A^\circ}{p_B^\circ}\right)^n = \frac{Y_A}{Y_B}$$

where, χ_A and χ_B are mole fraction in liquid phase is 1st container and Y_A and Y_B are mole fraction in vapour phase after 'n' time condensation and evaporation.

Non-ideal Solutions

In terms of Raoult's law a non-ideal solution is defined as the one which does not obeys Raoult's law. These are divided into two types as explained below:

Non-Ideal Solutions Showing Positive Deviations

These can be defined on the basis of

1. Molecular Interactions

A non-ideal solution showing positive deviation is defined as the one in which the intermolecular forces of interactions between the molecules is weaker than the interactions found in any one of the pure components or both.

2. Thermodynamics

A non-ideal solution is showing positive deviation the one in which there is a slight increase in volume on mixing and absorption of heat takes place on mixing.

$$\Delta V_{\text{mixing}} = \text{positive}, \Delta H_{\text{mixing}} = \text{positive}.$$

Examples

- Acetone (dipole) + Ethyl alcohol (hydrogen bonding)
- Acetone (dipole) + Benzene (van der Waal's)
- Carbon tetrachloride (van der Waal's) + Chloroform (dipole)
- Methyl alcohol (hydrogen bonding) + Water

Graphical Representation

For one intermediate composition, the total vapour pressure of such a solution will be the highest and the boiling point will be the lowest.

- This solution acquires the property of boiling at a constant temperature and its composition remains unchanged.
- Liquid mixtures, which boil out without any change in the composition are called azeotropes or azeotropic mixtures.
- In case of positive deviations, we get minimum boiling azeotropes.

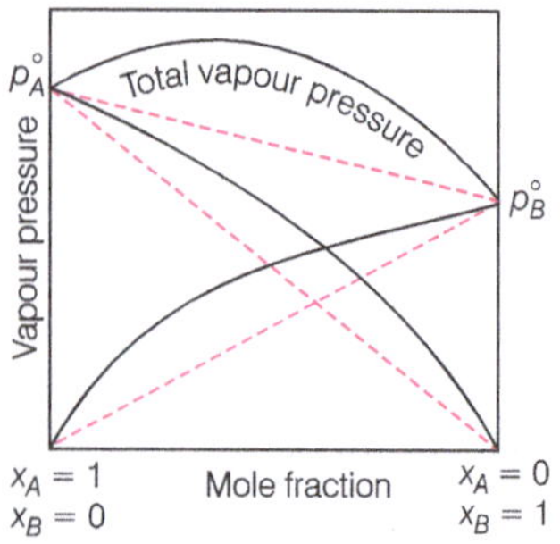

Positive deviations from Raoult's law

JEE Quicker

Among carbon tetrachloride + methanol, carbon disulphide + acetone, benzene + toluene, phenol + aniline, only carbon tetrachloride + methanol and carbon disulphide + acetone showing positive deviation from Raoult's law at 35°C.

JEE Adv. 2016

↘ When the intermolecular forces of attraction between the molecules is smaller than that between the pure components then mixture is more vapourised and showing positive deviation from Raoult's law.

Non-Ideal Solutions Showing Negative Deviations

These can be defined on the basis of

1. Molecular Interactions

Solutions in which forces of interactions between the components is more than that in between the pure components are the ones showing negative deviation from Raoult's law.

2. Thermodynamics

In case of such solutions, a slight decrease in volume and evolution of heat takes place on mixing i.e, ΔV_{mixing} = negative and ΔH_{mixing} = negative.

Examples

- Chloroform (dipole) + Acetone (dipole)
- Acetone(dipole) + Aniline (weak hydrogen bond)
- Acetic acid (hydrogen bonding) + Pyridine (van der Waal's)
- HCl + Water
- HNO_3 + Water

Graphical Representation

- For such solutions, at one intermediate composition, the total pressure exhibited by the components is the least and hence the boiling point of the liquid mixture at that composition would be highest.
- The solution will thus distil without a change in composition and provide an example of maximum boiling azeotrope.

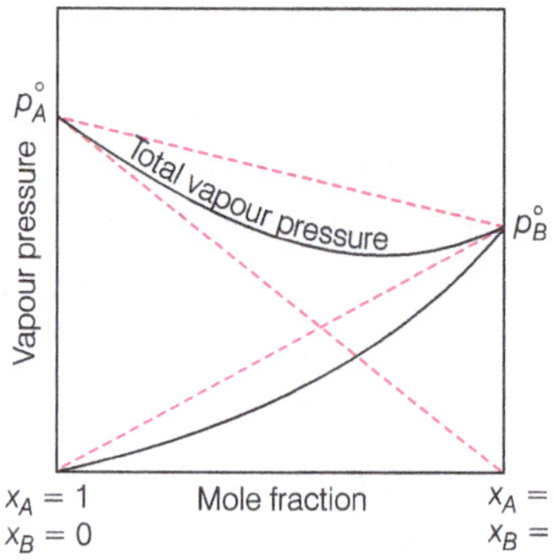

Negative deviations from Raoult's law

Vapour Pressure of Two Immiscible Liquid

- When a volatile liquid is added to another volatile liquid, which are completely immiscible with each other, each liquid will behave independent of the other and will exert its own vapour pressure.
- The total vapour pressure of the system will be the sum of vapour pressure of both the volatile liquids.

$$\therefore \quad p_{\text{Total}} = p_A + p_B$$
$$= p_A^\circ + p_B^\circ \qquad (\text{as } \chi_A \text{ and } \chi_B = 1)$$

- The total vapour pressure of the system remain constant as long as both the volatile liquids are present and will not depend on the relative amounts of the two liquids.

  The total vapour pressure of a mixture containing immiscible volatile liquids is greater than that of either of the pure constituents, thus the mixture will boil at a temperature, which is lower than the boiling point of either of the pure constituents.
- This composition of the vapour above the liquid mixture can be calculated using Dalton's law of partial pressures Thus,

$$p_A = p_A^\circ = P_{\text{total}}\chi'_A \qquad \ldots\text{(i)}$$
$$p_B = p_B^\circ = P_{\text{total}}\chi'_B \qquad \ldots\text{(ii)}$$

where χ'_A and χ'_Brepresents the mole fraction of A and B in the vapour phase Let n_A and n_B are the moles of A and B, respectively in the vapour phase

Then, $$\frac{w_B}{w_A} = \frac{p_B^\circ \times M_B}{p_A^\circ \times M_A}$$

- Thus, the masses of the constituents in the vapour (distillate) will be proportional to their respective molar mass and vapour pressure.

Solved Booster 2.3

At 300 K, vapour pressure of $CHCl_3$ and CH_2Cl_2 are 200 mmHg and 415 mmHg respectively. The solution prepared by mixing 42.5 g CH_2Cl_2 and 47.8 g $CHCl_3$ at 300 K.

The mole fraction of $CHCl_3$ and CH_2Cl_2 in the vapour phase above mixture respectively are ...... and ....

Solution *(0.28, 0.72)*

Molar mass of CH_2Cl_2 (say component 1) = 85 g mol^{-1}

Molar mass of $CHCl_3$ (say component 2) = 119.5 g mol^{-1}

$$\therefore \quad n_1 = \frac{42.5}{85} = 0.5 \Rightarrow n_2 = \frac{47.8}{119.5} = 0.4$$
$$\chi_1 = \frac{0.5}{0.9} = \frac{5}{9} \Rightarrow \chi_2 = \frac{0.4}{0.9} = \frac{4}{9}$$
$$\therefore \quad p_{\text{total}} = p_1^\circ\chi_1 + p_2^\circ\chi_2 = 415 \times \frac{5}{9} + 200 \times \frac{4}{9}$$
$$\approx 319.4 \text{ mmHg}$$

Mole fraction of CH_2Cl_2 in vapour phase

$$\chi_1' = \frac{p_1^\circ \chi_1}{p_{\text{total}}} = \frac{\frac{415 \times 5}{9}}{319.4} = 0.72$$

and that of $CHCl_3$ in vapour phase $\chi_2' = 1 - \chi_1' = 0.28$

Greater the vapour pressure of the given component, greater will be its mole fraction in vapour phase in the mixture of volatile liquids.

Azeotropes

In case of positive and negative deviations from Raoult's law the boiling point composition curves have minima or maxima. The separation of such solutions into their component can't be obtained by simple or fractional distillation and these are called azeotropic mixture.

A binary mixture having similar composition in liquid and vapour phase and which boils at a constant temperature and distils over without undergoing any change in its composition is called an **azeotrope.**

Types of Azeotropes

There are two types of azeotropes called as minimum boiling azeotrope and maximum boiling azeotrope, respectively.

(i) **Minimum Boiling Azeotropes** It comprises of non-ideal solution that shows positive deviation from Raoult's law. e.g. solution of ethanol and water shows such a large deviation from Raoult's law that there is a maximum in the vapour pressure curve and hence a minimum in the boiling point curve as shown in figure below.

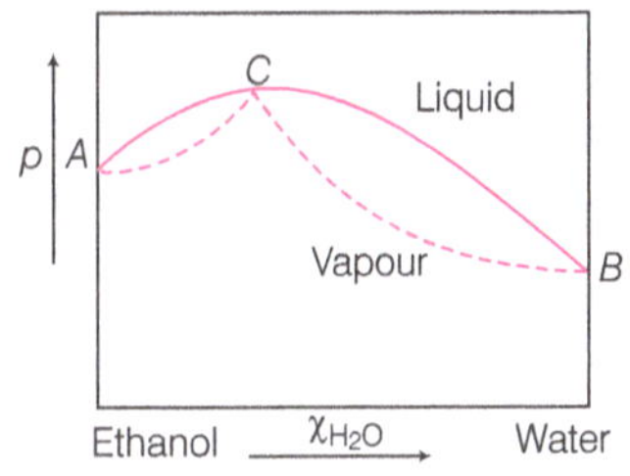

Vapour pressure curve for ethanol-water mixture (95% ethanol)

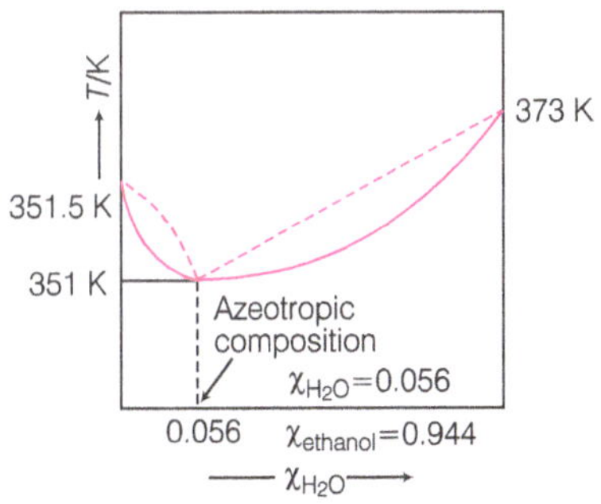

The boiling point curve for ethanol-water mixture (95% ethanol)

(ii) **Maximum Boiling Azeotropes** It comprises of non-ideal solutions that shows negative deviation from Raoult's law. e.g. HNO_3 and H_2O shows such a negative deviation from Raoult's law that there is a minimum in the vapour pressure curve and hence, a maximum in the boiling point as shown is below.

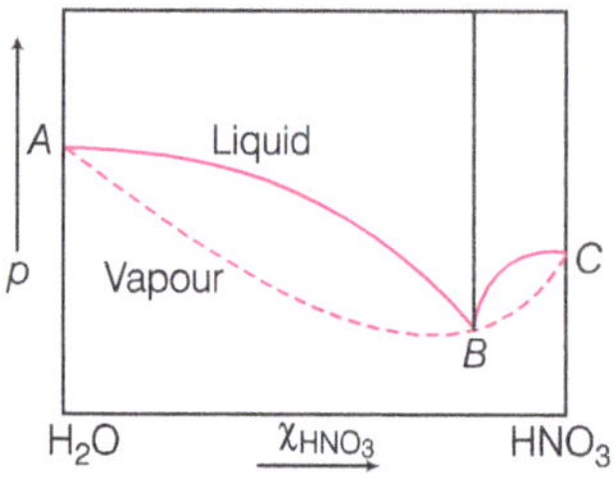

Vapour pressure curve for HNO_3 and H_2O

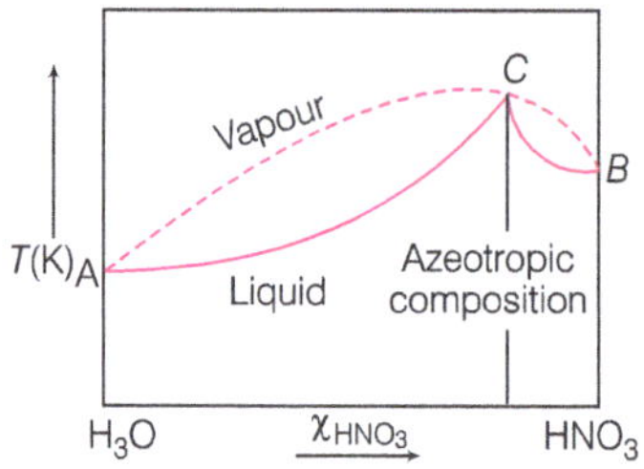

Boiling point curve from HNO_3 and H_2O

Elemental Practice 7.2

Type I MCQs with Only One Correct Option

1. At 400 K, the vapour pressure of C_6H_5Cl is 940 Torr and that of C_6H_5Br is 496 Torr. What will be the composition (mol %) of the vapour at 400 K temperature? [Assume ideal behaviour]
   (a) $C_6H_5Cl = 83.6\%$, $C_6H_5Br = 16.4\%$
   (b) $C_6H_5Cl = 73.6\%$, $C_6H_5Br = 26.4\%$
   (c) $C_6H_5Cl = 69\%$, $C_6H_5Br = 31\%$
   (d) $C_6H_5Cl = 26.4\%$, $C_6H_5Br = 73.6\%$

2. An organic compound (molar mass = 204 g mol^{-1}) is immiscible with water and also steam distilled under 1 atm. The vapour pressure of water at this temperature is 710 mm. What weight percentage of the organic liquid is present in the given amount of distillate?
   (a) 44.38% (b) 51.31% (c) 34.31% (d) 28.42%

3. Vapour pressure of pure water at 298 K is 23.8 mm. Thus, vapour pressure of 20% glucose (weight/volume) solution is (d = 0.9971 g mL^{-1})
   (a) 23.342 mm (b) 23.169 mm
   (c) 23.334 mm (d) 23.217 mm

4. Osmotic pressure of 3% aqueous solution of a non-volatile, non-electrolyte solute A at 298 K is 3.632 atm. Thus, its vapour pressure is ($p^\circ_{H_2O}$ = 23.7 mm at 298 K)
   (a) 23.64 mm (b) 22.15 mm (c) 23.42 mm (d) 22.76 mm

5. Given below are two statements.
   Statement I A solution of two liquids boils at a temperature more than the boiling point of either them, so the binary solution shows negative deviation from Raoult's law.
   Statement II Raoult's law becomes a special case of Henry's law in which K_H is equal to mole fraction of solvent.
   In the light of the above statements, choose the correct answer from the options given below.
   (a) Both Statement (I) and Statement (II) are correct.
   (b) Both Statement (I) and Statement (II) are incorrect.
   (c) Statement (I) is correct but Statement (II) is incorrect.
   (d) Statement (I) is incorrect but Statement (II) is correct.

6. The solubility of urea in methanol is 17g/100 mL methanol. Density of methanol is 0.792 g mL^{-1} at 293 K, at which vapour pressure of methanol is 96.0 mm Hg. Thus, vapour pressure of saturated solution of urea in methanol (in mmHg) is
   (a) 86.11 (b) 90.27 (c) 88.03 (d) 80.12

7. On addition of a solute, the vapour pressure of a liquid reduces to $\left(\frac{9}{10}\right)^{th}$ of original value. If 2g of solute (molar mass = 100) is added to 100 g of the liquid to attain this reduction then calculate the molar mass of the liquid.
   (a) 500 g mol^{-1} (b) 240 g mol^{-1}
   (c) 730 g mol^{-1} (d) 380 g mol^{-1}

8. Henry's law constant for N_2 at 293 K is 76.48 kbar. N_2 exerts a partial pressure of 0.987 bar. If N_2 gas is bubbled through water at 293 K, then number of millimoles of N_2 that will dissolve in 1L of water is
   (a) 0.716 (b) 129×10^{-5} (c) 1.29×10^{-2} (d) 5.55

9. Given below are two statements, one is labelled as Assertion (A) and the other one is labelled as reason (R).
   Assertion (A) Variation of K_H (Henry's law constant) with temperature T is shown by following graphs I-IV.

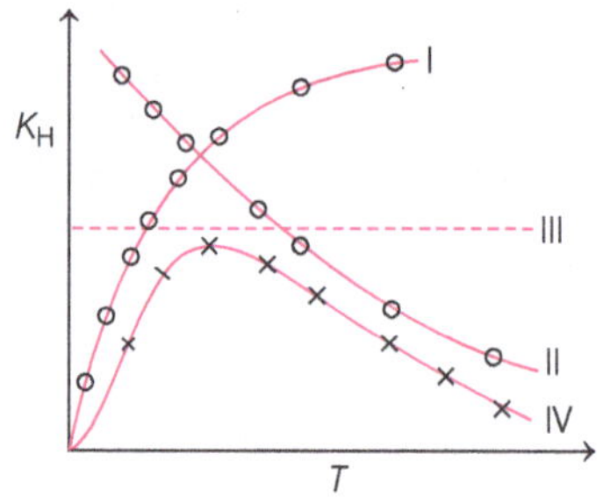

The correct representation is I.

Reason (R) K_H increases with increase in temperature.

In the light of above given statements, choose the correct answer from the options given below.

(a) Both (A) and (R) are true and (R) is the correct explanation of (A).
(b) Both (A) and (R) are true but (R) is not the correct explanation of (A).
(c) (A) is correct but (R) is incorrect.
(d) (A) is incorrect but (R) is correct.

10. H_2S gas is used in qualitative analysis of inorganic cations. Its solubility in water at STP is 0.195 mol kg^{-1}. Thus, Henry's law constant (in atm $molal^{-1}$) for H_2S is

(a) 0.195 (b) 5.128
(c) 3.897×10^3 (d) 2.565×10^{-4}

11. Following data has been given for CO_2 for the concentration in H_2O.

Temperature	Henry's constant	Pressure
273 K	728 atm	0.10 atm
333 K	3410 atm	p_2

If solution of CO_2 in H_2O is heated from 273 to 333 K, pressure (p_2) needed to keep CO_2 in the solution is

(a) 0.108 atm (b) 0.805 atm
(c) 0.212 atm (d) 0.468 atm

12. On the basis of information given below mark the correct option

Information On adding acetone to methanol some of the hydrogen bonds between methanol molecules break at specific composition methanol-acetone mixture will form

(a) Minimum boiling azeotrope and will show positive deviation from Raoult's law.
(b) Maximum boiling azeotrope and will show positive deviation from Raoult's law.
(c) Minimum boiling azeotrope and will show negative deviation from Raoult's law.
(d) Maximum boiling azeotrope and will show negative deviation from Raoult's law.

13. At 35°C, the vapour pressure of carbon disulphide (CS_2) is 512 mmHg and that of acetone (CH_3COCH_3) is 344 mmHg. A solution of CS_2 and CH_3COCH_3 in which mole fraction of CS_2 is 0.25 has a total vapour pressure of 600 mmHg. Which of the following statement(s) is/are correct?

(a) A mixture of 100 mL of CH_3COCH_3 and 100 mL of CS_2 has a volume of 200 mL.
(b) When CH_3COCH_3 and CS_2 are mixed at 35°C, heat must be absorbed in order to produce a solution at 35°C.
(c) Process of mixing is exothermic.
(d) Entropy of mixing is zero.

14. Given below are two statements one is labelled as Assertion (A) and the other one is labelled as Reason (R).

Assertion (A) Given diagram represents low boiling azeotrope

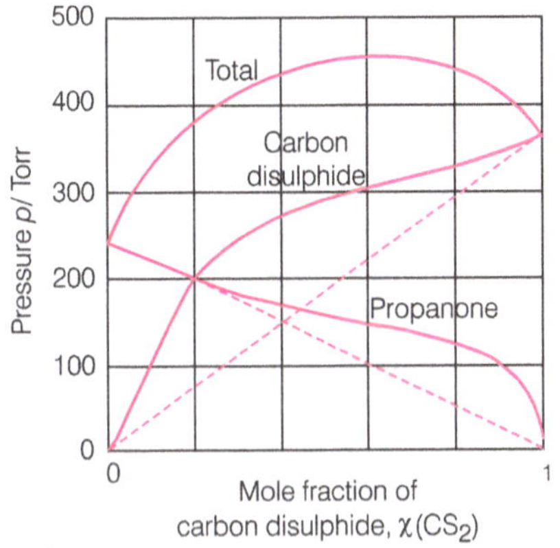

Reason (R) Mixture of carbon disulphide and propanone shows negative deviation from Raoult's law.

In the light of the above statements, choose the correct answer from the options given below.

(a) Both (A) and (R) are true and (R) is the correct explanation of (A).
(b) Both (A) and (R) are true but (R) is not the correct explanation of (A).
(c) (A) is correct but (R) is incorrect.
(d) (A) is incorrect but (R) is correct.

15. The vapour pressure of two pure liquids *A* and *B*, that form an ideal solution are 400 and 400 torr respectively at temperature *T*. This liquid solution of *A* and *B* is composed of 1 mole of *A* and 1 mole of *B*. What will be the pressure, when 1 mole of mixture has been vaporised?

(a) 500 torr
(b) 800 torr
(c) 400 torr
(d) 200 torr

Type II 》 MCQs with One or More than One Correct Option

16. Which of the following statements are correct?

(a) 1 mol benzene ($p^\circ_{benzene}$ = 42 mm) and 2 mol toluene ($p^\circ_{toluene}$ = 36 mm) will have total vapour pressure of 38 mm.
(b) Minimum boiling azeotropic mixture boils at temperature lower than either of the two pure components.
(c) Chlorobenzene and bromobenzene will not show any change in volume and heat.
(d) According to Henry's law, the solubility of a gas in given volume of liquid increases with increase in temperature only.

17. Select the correct statement(s).
(a) Gases which form ions in the solvent are soluble in that solvent.
(b) Gases which are liquefied easily are more soluble in water than the other gases which are not liquefied easily.
(c) Higher the value of K_H at a given pressure, lower is the solubility of the gas in the liquid.
(d) Higher the value of K_H at a given pressure, larger the solubility of the gas in the liquid.

18. Total vapour pressure of mixture of 1 mole of a volatile component $A\,(p^\circ_A = 100$ mmHg) and 3 moles of volatile component $B\,(p^\circ_B = 60$ mmHg) is 75 mmHg. For such case,
(a) there is positive deviation from Raoult's law.
(b) there is negative deviation from Raoult's law.
(c) boiling point is lowered.
(d) force of attraction between A and B is smaller than that between A and A, and A and B.

19. Which of the following statements are incorrect?
(a) The solution which is in dynamic equilibrium with undissolved solute is the saturated solution.
(b) In a nearly saturated solution, if the dissolution process is endothermic, the solubility should decrease with rise in temperature.
(c) Solids and liquids are highly incompressible and practically remain unaffected by changes in pressure.
(d) The solubility of gases decrease with increase of pressure.

20. Select the correct statement(s).
(a) K_H (Henry's law constant) is a function of nature of gases.
(b) Higher the value of K_H at a given pressure, the lower is the solubility of the gas in the liquid.
(c) K_H increases with increase in temperature.
(d) K_H increases with increase in partial pressure.

Type III 》 Numerical/Integer Answer Type Questions

21. The concentration of O_2 in water required to support aerobic aquatic life is about 3.856 mg dm^{-3}. Minimum partial pressure (in kPa) of oxygen in the atmosphere that can achieve this concentration is .... (nearest integer)
$K_H(O_2) = 74.68$ kPa m^3 mol^{-1}

22. A gaseous mixture of two substance A and B under a total pressure of 0.7 atm is in equilibrium with an ideal liquid solution. The mole fraction of substance A is 0.5 in the vapour phase and 0.3 in the liquid phase. The vapour pressure of pure liquid A is $x \times 10^{-1}$ atm then find $x \times 30$.

23. The vapour pressure of a solvent is decreased by 10 mmHg when a non-volatile solute having mole fraction as 0.2 is added to the solvent.

How many times the vapour pressure is changed when mole fraction of solvent is decreased by 25% ?

24. At 450 K, the vapour pressure of a solution containing 2 moles of *n*-heptane and 5 moles of nonane is 670 mm of Hg. At the same temperature, if one more mole of *n*-nonane is substracted from the solution, the vapour pressure of the solution increases by 10 mm of Hg. What is the vapour pressure in mmHg of *n*-nonane in its pure state is .... atm.

25. The total vapour pressure of a 4 mole % solution of NH_3 in water at 293 K is 60.0 torr. The vapour pressure of pure water is 18.5 torr at this temperature. Applying Henry's and Raoult's laws, calculate the total vapour pressure for a 5 mole % solution.

Elemental Practice 7.2 | Chapter 07

Connect with **Answers**

1. (b)	**2.** (a)	**3.** (d)	**4.** (a)	**5.** (c)	**6.** (a)
7. (a)	**8.** (a)	**9.** (a)	**10.** (b)	**11.** (d)	**12.** (a)
13. (b)	**14.** (c)	**15.** (c)	**16.** (a,b,c)	**17.** (a,b,c)	**18.** (a,c,d)
19. (b,d)	**20.** (a,b,c)	**21.** (9)	**22.** (35)	**23.** (2)	**24.** (610)
25. (70.38)					

Element 3 Colligative Properties, Abnormal Molecular Mass and Van't Hoff Factor

Colligative properties are properties of solutions that depend on the amount of species present (i.e., colligative properties are directly proportional to the number of moles of solute) in the solution. It does not depend on the nature and size of solute particles. Only those solutions which are ideal, show these properties. These properties are discussed below.

Relative Lowering of Vapour Pressure

- When a non-volatile solute is mixed with a volatile solvent, the vapour pressure of solution (p_s) becomes less than the vapour pressure of pure solvent ($p°$). It is called lowering of vapour pressure.
- According to Raoult's law, the lowering of vapour pressure of a solvent is given by

$$p_r = p_S^o \chi_{\text{solvent}}$$

$$p_r = p_S^o (1 - \chi_{\text{solute}})$$

Thus, $$\frac{p° - p_S}{p°} = \chi_{\text{solute}} \quad \ldots(3.1)$$

- The expression $(p° - p_S)/p°$ is known as the relative lowering of vapour pressure and according to Eq. (3.1), this is equal to the mole fraction of the solute in the solution.

$$\chi_{\text{solute}} = \frac{n_{\text{solute}}}{n_{\text{solute}} + n_{\text{solvent}}}$$

- It can be assumed $n_{\text{solute}} << n_{\text{solvent}}$ therefore in the denominator, n_{solute} can be ignored in comparison to n_{solvent}. Thus, $n_{\text{solute}} \approx \frac{n_{\text{solute}}}{n_{\text{solvent}}}$.
- Based on Eq. (3.1) it can also be derived that, $\frac{p° - p_S}{p_S} = \frac{n_{\text{solute}}}{n_{\text{solvent}}}$ which can be used for solving problems.

Elevation in Boiling Point

At boiling point, vapour pressure of the solution becomes equal to the atmospheric pressure. In the presence of a non-volatile solute the vapour pressure of the solution decreases. Correspondingly the boiling point (T) of the solution is higher than that of the solvent (T_0). It is called **elevation in boiling point**, ΔT_b.

Figure indicates the variation of vapour pressure with temperature, T_0 is the boiling point of the pure solvent corresponding to 1 atm at point A, and T is the boiling point of solution corresponding to 1 atm at point B.

The solution containing w_1 g of non-volatile solute (molar mass = m_1) in w_2 g solvent, corresponding to 1 atm at point B.

$T_0 < T$

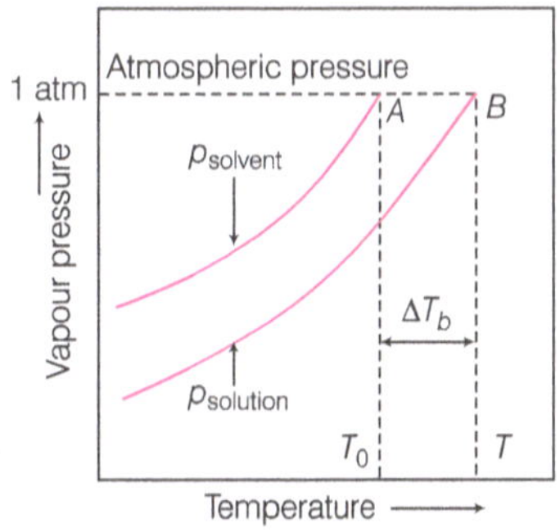

Variation of vapour pressure with temperature and showing elevation in boiling point

Based on this, $\Delta T_b = 1000 K_b \frac{w_1}{m_1 w_2} = K_b m$

where, $m(\text{molality}) = \frac{1000\, w_1}{m_1 w_2} \Rightarrow \Delta T_b = T - T_0$

$\therefore \quad T = (T_0 + \Delta T_b)$

K_b is the **molal boiling point elevation constant** (Ebullioscopic constant) and is equal to elevation in boiling point when one mole of solute is dissolved in 1000 g solvent or K_b is the elevation in boiling point of one molal solution. It is also related to boiling point of solvent (T_0) and enthalpy of vapourisation (ΔH_v) by equation

$$K_b = \frac{RT_0^2 m_2}{1000 \Delta H_v}$$

In this equation, ΔH_v is to be taken per mol of solvent

Molar mass (m_1) of the solute is $m_1 = \frac{1000 K_b w_1}{\Delta T_b w_2}$

JEE Alert

The elevation in boiling points for 1 molal solution in the given solvent of different types of non-dissociable or associables non-volatile solutes will be same.

Solved Booster 3.1

Water boils at 1 atmospheric pressure and 1 molal glucose solution boils at 100.52°C. Urea solution is 20% by weight of solution. The boiling point of were solution is ....

Solution *(102.17°C)*

Urea and glucose are non-electrolytes,

Water boils at 1 atmospheric pressure, it means boiling point of water is 100°C.

ΔT_b (glucose solution) = 100.52 − 100.00 = 0.52°

ΔT_b (glucose solution) = mK_b

$0.52 = 1 \times K_b$

$\therefore \quad K_b = 0.52° \text{ mol}^{-1} \text{ kg}$

(Urea solution is 20% by weight of solution, it means 100 g solution (solute + solvent) has 20 g solute and 80 g solvent)

$$\Delta T_b \text{ (urea solution)} = \frac{1000 K_b w_1}{m_1 w_2} = \frac{1000 \times 0.52 \times 20}{60 \times 80} \approx 2.17°$$

∴ Boiling point of urea solution = 100.00 + 2.17 ° = 102.17 °C

JEE MAPPER

Example Similar to PYQ Asked in JEE Main 2024

3.4 g of a non-volatile, non-electrolyte is dissolved in 150 g of water at 25°C. The solution showed a boiling point elevation by 3°C. Assuming the solute concentration is negligible with respect to the solvent concentration, the vapour pressure of the resulting aqueous solution is .... mmHg. (Nearest integer)

[Given: Molal boiling point elevation constant of water (K_b) = 0.52 K kg mol^{-1}, 1 atm pressure = 760 mm of Hg, molar mass of water = 18 g mol^{-1}]

Solution *(681)*

Given that, $\Delta T_b = 3$, $K_b = 0.52$, $p° = 760$ mmHg

$M_{\text{solvent}} = 18$

Now using,

$$\Delta T_b = K_b . m$$

$$3 = 0.52 \times m$$

$$m = \frac{3}{0.52}$$

Now, according to question, since the solution is very diluted.

Hence,

$$\frac{\Delta p}{p°} = \frac{n_{\text{solute}}}{n_{\text{solvent}}} \Rightarrow \frac{\Delta p}{p°} = \frac{m}{1000} \times M_{\text{solvent}}$$

$$\Delta p = 760 \times \frac{\left(\frac{3}{0.52}\right)}{1000} \times 18$$

$$\Delta p = 78.92$$

So, $\quad p_S = 760 - 78.92 = 681.08$

Hence, nearest integer is 681 mmHg.

Compentency Enhancer 3.1

1.32 g of a non-volatile, non-electrolyte is dissolved in 120 g of water at 25°C. The solution showed a boiling point elevation by 3.2°C. Assuming the solute concentration is negligible with respect to the solvent concentration, the vapour pressure of the resulting aqueous solution is .... mm of Hg. (Nearest integer)

[Given : Molal boiling point elevation constant of water (K_b) = 0.52 K kg mol^{-1}, 1 atm pressure = 760 mm of Hg, molar mass of water = 18 g mol^{-1}]

Depression in Freezing Point

Freezing point of a liquid is defined as that temperature at which it is in equilibrium with its solid state,

$$H_2O\,(l) \xrightleftharpoons{0°C} H_2O(s)$$

At freezing point of a solvent, liquid and solid states will have same vapour pressure. Therefore, a solution will freeze when its vapour pressure becomes equal to the vapour pressure of pure solvent.

If a non-volatile solute is added to the solvent, there is decrease in vapour pressure of the solution and thus the freezing point of the solution (T) is less than that of pure solvent (T_0). It is called depression in freezing point, ΔT_f.

The given figure, indicates variation of vapour pressure with temperature, T_0 is the freezing point of the pure solvent corresponding to 1 atm at point A and T is the freezing point of the solution containing w_1 g of non-volatile solute in w_2 g of solvent corresponding to 1 atm point B.

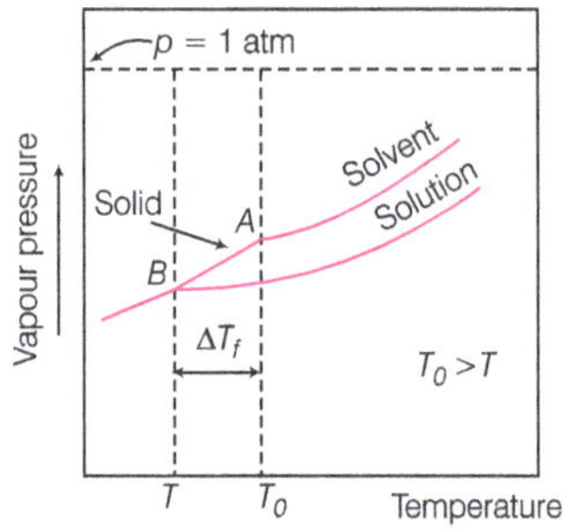

Phase diagram for a pure solvent and solution for depression in freezing point

It is clear that, $T < T_0$

i.e. Freezing point is depressed, $\Delta T_f = (T_0 - T)$

T (Freezing point of solution) = $(T_0 - \Delta T_f)$

For this case $\quad \boxed{\Delta T_f = \dfrac{1000\, K_f w_1}{m_1 w_2} = K_f m}$

where, $m \left(= \dfrac{1000\, w_1}{m_1 w_2} \right)$ is the molality (mol kg^{-1} solvent) of the solution, and K_f is the molal freezing point depression constant.

Molal freezing point depression constant is equal to depression in freezing point of 1 molal solution (having 1 mole solute in 1 kg solvent). K_f is related to freezing point (T_0) and enthalpy of fusion (ΔH_f) of the solvent by equation

$$K_f = \frac{RT_0^2 m_2}{1000\, \Delta H_f}$$

Solved Booster 3.2

45 g of ethylene glycol ($C_2H_6O_2$) is mixed with 600 g of water. The freezing point of the solution is ....
($K_f(H_2O) = 1.86$ kg mol^{-1})

Solution (270.75)

$$\Delta T_f = \frac{1000\, K_f\, w_1}{m_1\, w_2} = \frac{1000 \times 1.86 \text{ kg mol}^{-1} \times 45 \text{ g}}{62 \text{ g mol}^{-1} \times 600 \text{ g}} = 2.25° \text{ K}$$

Freezing point = 273 − 2.25 = 270.75 K

JEE Alert

An aqueous solution of an ethylene glycol, has much lower freezing point than that of pure water. Thus, it works as an antifreeze and is used in car radiators in hill stations.

Osmosis and Osmotic Pressure

Spontaneous flow of solvent molecules from dilute solution (it may be pure solvent, i.e. region of low concentration) into the concentrated solution (i.e. region of high concentration) through a semi-permeable membrane is called **osmosis**. This process continues till the concentration on both sides of the membrane becomes equal.

As a result of osmosis, the level of solution in the tube rises, whereas that of the pure solvent falls. After sometime an equilibrium is reached where the level of the solution in the tube does not rise further. At this stage, the excessive hydrostatic pressure created on the solution side that exactly balances the tendency of the solvent to pass through the membrane and prevents the passage of solvent molecules as shown in a figure below.

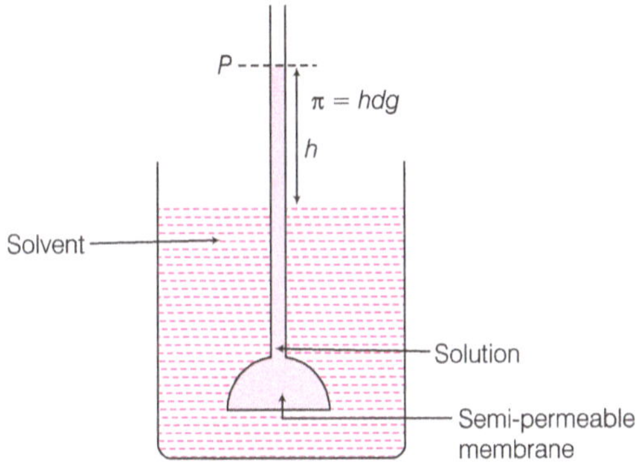

Osmosis and osmotic pressure

The excessive hydrostatic pressure which is applied to solution to prevent osmosis is known as the osmotic pressure of the solution and is represented by symbol π. It prevents the passage of solvent molecules through semi-permeable membrane into the solution.

The osmotic pressure of a dilute solution is equal to the pressure which the dissolved substance would exert if it existed as a gas under the same condition of temperature and volume.

Also $$\pi = \frac{n}{V}RT = \left(\frac{w}{m}\right)\frac{RT}{V} = \frac{dRT}{m} = CRT$$

where $n = \frac{w}{m}$ = moles and $d = \frac{w}{V}$ = density (in g L^{-1})

Osmotic Pressure of Mixture of two or More Solution

If n_1 moles of solute (1) are in V_1 litres and n_2 moles of solute (2) are in V_2 litres then

$$\pi = \pi_1 + \pi_2$$

In mixture total volume = $(V_1 + V_2)$ litres

then $\pi_1 = \left(\frac{n_1}{V_1 + V_2}\right)RT$ and $\pi_2 = \left(\frac{n_2}{V_1 + V_2}\right)RT$

$$\therefore \quad \pi = \frac{(n_1 + n_2)RT}{(V_1 + V_2)}$$

Importance of Osmosis

- Plasma membrane in animal cells is a semi-permeable membrane. If an egg which had the outer shell removed by treatment with dil. HCl is placed in water, it will float and expand as water passes through the external membrane.
- In a concentrated solution of salt, however it sinks and shrinks as water passes out of the egg into the surrounding solution. Animal cells preserve their shapes when they exist in isotonic environment having osmotic pressure equal to that of their cells.
- Osmosis is a process of prime importance in living organisms. The salt concentration in blood plasma of different species is equivalent to 0.9% aqueous NaCl solution by mass. If blood cells are placed in pure water, water molecules rapidly move into the cell.
- As a result of osmosis of water molecules into the cells, salt concentration decreases and blood cells swell and burst. Hence, one must be careful to ensure that solutions that flow into the blood stream are of the same osmotic pressure as that of the blood.
- Na^+ and K^+ ions are responsible for maintaining proper osmotic pressure balance inside and outside the cells of organism. Osmosis is also critically involved in the functioning of kidneys.

JEE MAPPER

Example Similar to PYQ Asked in JEE Advanced 2023

45 mL of 0.3 molal urea solution (density = 1.361 g mL^{-1} at 300 K) is mixed with 240 mL of a solution containing 0.03 g of urea. Both the solutions were prepared in the same solvent. The osmotic pressure (in torr) of the resulting solution at 300 K is ....

[Use : Molar mass of urea = 60 g mol^{-1}, gas constant $(R) = 62$ L torr K^{-1} mol^{-1}; Assume, $\Delta_{mix}H = 0$, $\Delta_{mix}V = 0$]

Sol. *(1207.37)* 0.3 molal means 0.3 moles in 1000 g of solvent.

$\therefore$ Number of moles of urea = 0.3 mol

Weight of urea = 0.3 × 60 = 18 g

Weight of solvent = 1000 g

Weight of solution = 1000 + 18 = 1018 g

So, volume $= \frac{\text{Mass}}{\text{Density}} = \frac{1018}{1.361} = 747.98$ mL

7.98 mL solution contains 0.3 moles

$\therefore$ 45 mL solution contains $= \frac{0.3}{7.98} \times 45 = 0.018$ mol

$$n_1 = 0.018 \text{ mol}$$

So, number of moles of urea in another solution (n_2)

$$= \frac{0.03}{60} = 0.0005$$

$$\text{Final molarity } (M) = \frac{n_1 + n_2}{V_1 + V_2} = \frac{0.018 + 0.0005}{\frac{45 + 240}{1000}} = \frac{0.0185}{0.285} \text{ M}$$

Now, osmotic pressure $(\pi) = CRT$

$$= \left(\frac{0.0185}{0.285}\right) \times 62 \times 300 = 1207.37 \text{ torr.}$$

Competency Enhancer 3.2

70 mL of 0.2 molal urea solution (density = 3.102 g mL^{-1} at 450 K^{-1}) is mixed with 330 mL of a solution containing 0.04 g of urea. Both the solutions were prepared in the same solvent. The osmotic pressure (in torr) of the resulting solution at 450 K is ....

[Use : Molar mass of urea = 60g mol^{-1}; gas constant, $R = 71.3$ L torr K^{-1} mol^{-1}; Assume, $\Delta_{mix}H = 0$, $\Delta_{mix}V = 0$]

Isotonic, Hypertonic and Hypotonic Solutions

Isotonic Solutions

Two or more solutions having equal osmotic pressure under given conditions are called **isotonic solutions**. When such solutions are separated by a semi-permeable membrane, no osmosis occurs, thus, no transference of solvent from one solution to the other.

For isotonic solutions: $\pi_1 = \pi_2$

$$\frac{n_1RT_1}{V_1} = \frac{n_2RT_2}{V_2} \Rightarrow \frac{w_1}{m_1}\frac{RT_1}{V_1} = \frac{w_2}{m_2}\frac{RT_2}{V_2} \quad \text{...(i)}$$

Hypertonic and Hypotonic Solutions

Osmotic pressure associated with the fluid inside the blood cell is equivalent to that of 0.9% (*w/V*) sodium chloride, called normal saline solution and it is safe to inject intravenously.

If we place the cells in a solution containing NaCl of concentration more than 0.9% (*w/V*), water will flow out of cells and thus shrinking occurs. Such solution is said to be **hypertonic**. Thus, hypertonic solution is more concentrated with respect other solution.

If NaCl < 0.9% (*w/V*) the reverse will take place and solution is said to be **hypotonic**. Thus, hypotonic solution is less concentrated with respect other solution.

Osmosis like all other colligative properties, results from an increase in entropy as pure solvent passes through the membrane and mixes with the solution.

Reverse Osmosis

Generally, osmosis takes from pure solvent to solution, but the direction of osmosis can be reversed by applying pressure on solution side. Due to which the solvent starts flowing from solution side to the pure solvent through the semi-permeable membrane. This process is called reverse osmosis. Reverse osmosis is used for water purification and desalination of sea water. A schematic set up for the reverse osmosis is represented below.

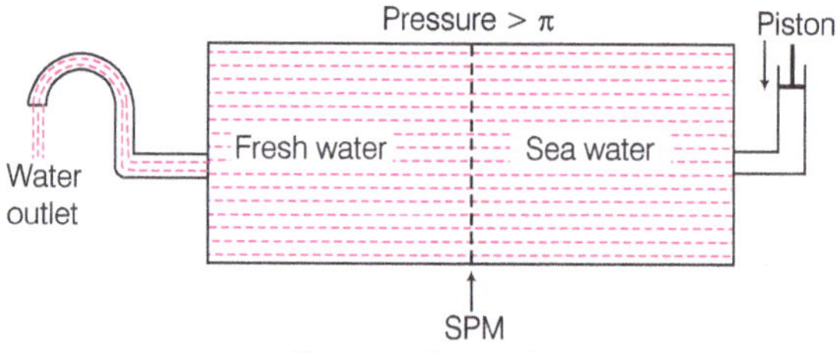

Reverse Osmosis

Solved Booster 3.3

A solution containing 8.6 gdm^{-3} of urea (molar mass 60g mol^{-1}) was found to be isotonic with a 5% solution of an organic non-volatile solute (*A*). The molar mass of the solute (*A*), assuming isothermal condition is

(a) 350 g mol^{-1} (b) 450 g mol^{-1}

(c) 500 g mol^{-1} (d) 550 g mol^{-1}

Solution *(a)*

$$\pi(\text{urea}) = MRT$$

$$M \text{ (molar concentration)} = \frac{8.6 \text{ g dm}^{-3}}{60 \text{ g mol}^{-1}} \approx 0.143 \text{ mol dm}^{-3}$$

$\therefore$ $\pi(\text{urea}) = 0.143\, RT$, $\pi(A) = MRT$

$$M = 5 \text{ g in 100 mL solution}$$

$$= \left(\frac{5}{m_1}\right) \text{mol in 100 mL}$$

$$\text{solution} = \left(\frac{50}{m_1}\right) \text{mol dm}^{-3}$$

$$\therefore \quad \pi(A) = \left(\frac{50}{m_1}\right) RT$$

Since, solutions are isotonic hence

$$\pi(\text{urea}) = \pi(A)$$

$$\therefore \quad 0.143RT = \frac{50}{m_1} RT$$

$$\Rightarrow \quad m_1(A) = \frac{50}{0.143} \approx 350 \text{ g mol}^{-1}$$

Abnormal Molar Mass

It is commonly observed that the difference between the observed and calculated molecular masses of a solute arises due to the association and dissociation of solute molecules in solution. This variation molar mass is referred to as abnormal molar mass.

The van't Hoff factor (i) is a correction factor that happen due to dissociation or association of solute in solvent in measuring colligative properties.

There may be change in number of moles of solute due to ionisation or association hence, colligative properties may be affected.

Number of moles of the product is related to degree of ionisation or association by van't Hoff factor i, given by

$$i = [1 + (y - 1)\,x]$$

where, 'x' is degree of association/dissociation y is the number of products (ions or molecules) obtained per mole of the reactant.

The factor 'i' is also related to molar mass of the solute, m_1, and colligative properties by equation

$$i = \frac{\text{Normal molar mass } (m_1)}{\text{Abnormal molar mass}(m_1') \text{ (due to dissociation or association)}}$$

$$\text{or } i = \frac{\text{Observed value of colligative property due to dissociation or association}}{\text{Theoretical value of colligative property without dissociation or association}}$$

$$\text{or } i = \frac{\text{No. of solute particles after association or dissociation}}{\text{No. of solute particles before association or dissociation}}$$

Case I For **association,** observed molar mass is more than the normal so value of van't Hoff factor (i) is less than 1.

Case II For **dissociation,** observed molar mass is less than the normal so value of van't Hoff factor is more than 2.

Case III For the solute which does not undergo any association or dissociation in solvent, value of van't Hoff factor is 1.

van't Hoff Factor for Different Cases of Solutes Undergoing Ionisation and Association

Solute	Example	Ionisation/ Association (x = degree)	y*	van't Hoff factor $i = [1 + (y-1)\,x]$	Abnormal molecular weight (m_1')
Non-electrolyte	Urea-glucose, sucrose, etc.	None	1	1	Normal molecular weight (m_1)
Electrolyte of type A^+B^-	NaCl, KCl, HCl, CH_3COOH, $FeSO_4$, etc.	$\underset{1-x}{AB} \rightleftharpoons \underset{x}{B^+} + \underset{x}{B^-}$	2	$(1 + x)$	$\frac{m_1}{(1 + x)}$
Electrolyte of type A_2B, AB_2	K_2SO_4, $BaCl_2$, $K_2[PtCl_6]$, etc.	$\underset{1-x}{A_2B} \rightleftharpoons \underset{2x}{2A^+} + \underset{x}{B^{2-}}$ $\underset{1-x}{AB_2} \rightleftharpoons \underset{x}{A^{2+}} + \underset{2x}{2B^-}$	3	$(1 + 2x)$	$\frac{m_1}{(1 + 2x)}$
Electrolyte of type A_3B, AB_3	Na_3PO_4, $AlCl_3$, $K_3[Fe(CN)_6]$, $FeCl_3$, etc.	$\underset{1-x}{A_3B} \rightleftharpoons \underset{3x}{3A^+} + \underset{x}{B^{3-}}$ $\underset{1-x}{AB_3} \rightleftharpoons \underset{x}{A^{3+}} + \underset{3x}{3B^-}$	4	$(1 + 3x)$	$\frac{m_1}{(1 + 3x)}$
Associated solute	Benzoic acid in benzene forming dimer	$2A \rightleftharpoons A_2$ $\underset{(1-x)}{A} \rightleftharpoons \underset{x/2}{\frac{1}{2}A_2}$	$\frac{1}{2}$	$\left(1 - \frac{x}{2}\right) = \left(\frac{2-x}{2}\right)$	$\frac{2m_1}{(2-x)}$
	Any solute forming polymer A_n	$nA \rightleftharpoons A_n$ $\underset{(1-x)}{A} \rightleftharpoons \underset{(x/n)}{\frac{1}{n}A_n}$	$\frac{1}{n}$	$\left[1 + \left(\frac{1}{n} - 1\right)x\right]$	$\left[\frac{m_1}{1 + \left(\frac{1}{n} - 1\right)x}\right]$
General	One mole of solute giving y mol of products	$A \rightleftharpoons yB$	y	$[1 + (y-1)x]$	$\frac{m_1}{[1 + (y-1)x]}$

**Number of products from one mole solute.*

Solved Booster 3.4

van't Hoff factor for aqueous 0.01 M monobasic acid HA is 1.08. The per cent ionisation of HA and ionisation constant are ....% and .... $\times 10^{-5}$

Solution *(8,6.96)*

HA is a monobasic acid

$$HA + H_2O \rightleftharpoons H_3O^+ + A^-$$

$$y = 2$$

$$i = [1 + (y-1)x]$$

$$1.08 = (1 + x)$$

$$x = 1.08 - 1 = 0.08$$

$\therefore$ Per cent ionisation of $HA = 8\%$

$$K_a \text{ (ionisation constant)} = \frac{Cx^2}{(1-x)} = \frac{0.01 \times (0.08)^2}{(1-0.08)}$$

$$= 6.96 \times 10^{-5}$$

Relationship between van't Hoff Factor(i) and Colligative Properties

We know that Colligative properties depend on number of solute particles. So in case of solute that associates or dissociates in solution, the number of particles of solute changes as compared to the number of particles added in solid state, so, the equation of colligative properties need to be modified to include van't Hoff factor. The modified equation for colligative properties are given below:

- **Relative lowering of vapour pressure** $= \dfrac{p_A^\circ - p_A^\circ}{p_A^\circ} = i\dfrac{n_B}{n_A}$
- **Elevation of boiling point** $= \Delta T_b = iK_b m$
- **Depression in freezing point** $= \Delta T_f = iK_f m$
- **Osmotic pressure** $= \pi = i\dfrac{n_B}{V}RT$

Solved Booster 3.6

12.2 g of benzoic acid (C_6H_5COOH) in 100 g of benzene shows a depression in freezing point equal to 2.45 K. Molal depression constant for benzene is 4.9 K kg mol^{-1}. The percentage of dimer formation of benzoic acid is ....

Solution *(100)*

$$\text{Abnormal mass} = \frac{1000 \times 4.90 \times 12.2}{2.45 \times 100} = 244 \text{ g mol}^{-1}$$

$$\text{Normal molar mass} = 122 \text{ g mol}^{-1}$$

$$\therefore \quad i = \frac{122}{244} = \frac{1}{2}$$

$$\Rightarrow \quad \left(1 - \frac{x}{2}\right) = \frac{1}{2}$$

$\therefore x = 1$ (100% dimer formation)

JEE MAPPER

Example Similar to PYQ Asked in JEE Advanced 2024

Vessel-1 contains w_2 g of a non-volatile solute X dissolved in w_1 g of water. Vessel-2 contains w_2 g of another non-volatile solute Y dissolved in w_1 g of water. Both the vessels are at the same temperature and pressure. The molar mass of X is 75% of that of Y. The van't Hoff factor for X is 2.1 times of that of Y for their respective concentrations.

The elevation of boiling point for solution in vessel-1 is .... % of the solution in Vessel-2.

Sol. *(280)* In Vessel 1

$$(\Delta T_b)_1 = i_1 K_b \times \frac{\left(\frac{w_2}{M_x}\right)}{\left(\frac{w_1}{1000}\right)}$$

In Vessel 2

$$(\Delta T_b)_2 = i_2 K_b \times \frac{\left(\frac{w_2}{M_y}\right)}{\left(\frac{w_1}{1000}\right)}$$

$$\Rightarrow \quad \frac{(\Delta T_b)_1}{(\Delta T_b)_2} = \frac{i_1 \times M_y}{i_2 \times M_x} = 2.1 \times \frac{1}{0.75} = 2.8$$

$$\Rightarrow \quad (\Delta T_b)_1 = 2.8\,(\Delta T_b)_2$$

$$\Rightarrow \quad \frac{(\Delta T_b)_1}{(\Delta T_b)_2} \times 100 = 280\%$$

Competency Enhancer 3.3

Container-1 contains w_2 g of a non-volatile solute X dissolved in w_1 g of water. Container-2 contains w_2 g of another non-volatile solute Y dissolved in w_1 g of water. Both the containers are at the same temperature and pressure. The molar mass of X is 55.7% of that of Y. The van't Hoff factor for X is 1.6 times of that of Y for their respective concentrations.

The elevation of boiling point for solution in container-1 is .... % of the solution in container-2.

Solved Booster 3.7

Considering acetic acid dissociates in water, its dissociation constant is 7.38×10^{-5}. If 4 mL of acetic acid is dissolved in 1L water, the solution will freeze at $x \times 10^{-4}$°C, provided pure water freezes at 0°C. x = ... (nearest integer)

Given : (K_f) water = 1.86 KKg mol^{-1}

Density of acetic acid is 1.2 g mol^{-1}

Molar mass of water = 18 g mol^{-1}

Molar mass of acetic acid = 60 g mol^{-1}

Density of water = 1 g cm^{-3}

Acetic acid dissociates as

$$CH_3COOH \rightleftharpoons CH_3COO^{\ominus} + H^{\oplus}$$

Solution **(1533)**

Mass of $CH_3COOH = V \times d$

$$V = 4\text{ mL}, d = 12\text{ g/mL} = 4 \times 1.2 = 4.8\text{ g}$$

$$n_{CH_3COOH} = \frac{\text{Mass}}{\text{Molar mass}} = \frac{4.8}{60} = 0.08$$

$$m_{CH_3COOH} \simeq M_{CH_3COOH}$$
$$= \frac{0.08}{1} = 0.08\text{ M}$$

$$\begin{array}{lcc} CH_3COOH \rightleftharpoons & CH_3COO^{\ominus} + & H^{\oplus} \\ C & 0 & 0 \\ C - C\alpha & C\alpha & C\alpha \end{array}$$

$$K_\alpha = \frac{C\alpha^2}{1-\alpha}$$

$$1 - \alpha \approx 1 \Rightarrow K_\alpha = C\alpha^2$$

$$\alpha = \sqrt{\frac{K_\alpha}{C}} = \sqrt{\frac{7.38 \times 10^{-5}}{0.08}}$$
$$= \sqrt{92.25 \times 10^{-5}}$$
$$= 0.03037 = 30.4 \times 10^{-3}$$

By using,

$$i = 1 + \alpha(n-1)$$
$$= 1 + \alpha(2-1) = 1 + \alpha$$
$$= 1 + 30 \times 10^{-3} = 1.0304$$

As we know,

$$\Delta T_f = iK_f.m = (1.0304) \times (1.86)(0.08)$$
$$= 0.15332 \approx 1533 \times 10^{-4}$$

Hence, the value of x is 1533.

Concept Visualizer

Ostwald Walker Experiment-Designed to calculate the relative lowering of vapour pressure of a solution The principle behind this experiment is that when a gas is passed through another gas, the later diffuses into the former which is visualised below.

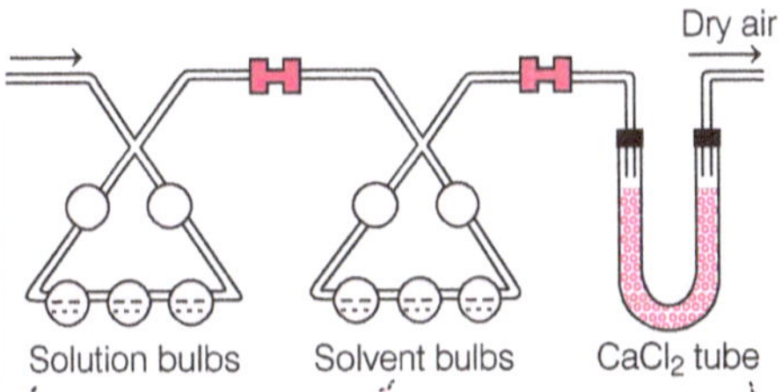

Dry air is bubbled successively through the solution, pure solvent and reagent.

These three bulb contain a weighed amount of the solution under examination. When dry air is bubbled through a solution, the vapour present in it diffuse into air. The diffusion takes place till the pressure of the vapours in air becomes equal to that of the vapours in the container. Therefore, there will be a loss of weight in this container. $\Delta m_1 \propto p_S$

These three bulb contain a weighted amount of pure solvent. When the air carrying the vapours from the solution container moves to this container, vapours from the solvent container diffuse into the partially saturated air. The pressure exerted by vapours in the air is p_S while the pressure exerted by the vapours in the solvent container is $p°$. So the vapours that diffuse into the air now have a pressure of $p° - p_S$. Therefore, the solvent container also loses weight. $\Delta m_2 \propto p° - p_S$

As the air, passes through this container i.e. $CaCl_2$ tube, all the vapours get absorbed by the absorbing agent, which makes the third container gain weight equal to the loss of the first two. Thus, $(\Delta m_1 + \Delta m_2) \propto p°$

Elemental Practice 7.3

Type I MCQs with Only One Correct Option

1. The total sum of van't Hoff factor in each of the following cases is
   (i) *aq.* $K_4[Fe(CN)_6]$ which is 20% ionised.
   (ii) PCl_5 which is 50% dissociated
   (iii) Solution of K_2HgI_4 which is 40% ionised.

   (a) 3.2 (b) 8.1 (c) 5.1 (d) 4.37

2. Arrange the following solutions in order of decreasing freezing point, ionisation being 100% in each case, assume molarity = molality.
   A. 0.05 M $NaNO_3$ B. 0.08 M $CuSO_4$
   C. 0.14 M Glucose D. 0.037 M $BaCl_2$
   E. 0.06 M $(NH_4)_2SO_4$

   (a) B > D > E > C > A (b) A > D > C > B > E
   (c) B > C > E > A > D (d) A > B > C > E > D

3. A 0.0140 g of sample of an ionic compound with the formula $[Cr(NH_3)_5Cl_3]$ was dissolved in water to give 25.0 mL of solution at 25°C. The osmotic pressure was determined to be 119 mmHg. How many ions are obtained from each formula unit when the compound is dissolved in water? (Molar mass of the compound is 243.5 g mol^{-1}). Assume 100% ionisation.

   (a) 5 (b) 7 (c) 3 (d) 2

4. When phenol (C_6H_5OH) is dissolved in a particular solvent, it is partially dimerised. If 1.88 g of phenol is dissolved in 100 g of the solvent, freezing point is depressed by 1.41. Calculate the % of phenol dimerised.
   Use : K_f (solvent) = 14.1° mol^{-1} kg

   (a) 50% (b) 100%
   (c) 120% (d) 75%

5. In benzene, ethanoic acid forms dimer as

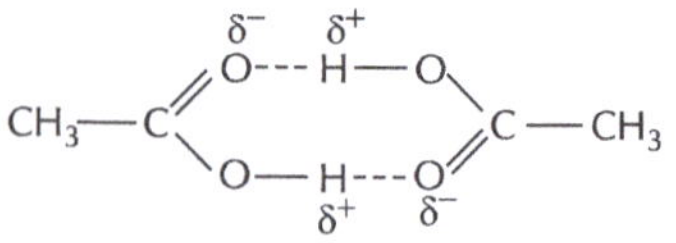

   Its van't Hoff factor is 0.75. The abnormal mass of ethanoic acid in benzene and the % dimer formation respectively is

   (a) 120 gmol^{-1} 40% (b) 120 g mol^{-1} 60%
   (c) 80 g mol^{-1}, 50% (d) 80 g mol^{-1}, 75%

6. An aqueous solution containing 0.25 g of a solute dissolved in 20 g of water freeze at −0.42°C. What will be the molar mass of the solute?
   [Given: Molar heat of fusion of ice at 0°C is 6.025 kJ mol^{-1}]

   (a) 71.31 g mol^{-1} (b) 55.06 g mol^{-1}
   (c) 62.08 g mol^{-1} (d) 40.31 g mol^{-1}

7. It is found that elevation in boiling point of a given *aq.* KCl solution is equal to depression in freezing point of 0.35 molal aq. Na_2CO_3 solution. If $K_f = 1.86°\ mol^{-1}$ kg and $K_b = 0.52°$ kg/mol. Calculate molality of KCl solution, assume complete ionisation of KCl and Na_2CO_3 in aqueous solution.

   (a) 1.87 (b) 1.34
   (c) 1.56 (d) 1.74

8. Three solutions are given alongwith their ΔT_b.

	Solutions	Concentration	Elevation in BP (ΔT_b)
I	Urea	6% by mass of solvent	x_1
II	glucose	18 % by mass of solvent	x_2
III	(mixture of I and II)		x_3

   Then
   (a) $x_1 + x_2 = x_3$ (b) $3x_1 + x_2 = x_3$
   (c) $x_1 = x_2 = x_3$ (d) $x_1 < x_2 < x_3$

9. A dilute solution contains *n* mole of solute '*A*' in 1 kg of a solvent with molal elevation constant K_b. The solute *A* undergoes dimerisation as $2A \rightleftharpoons A_2$. If ΔT_b is the elevation in boiling point of a given solution and molality = molarity, the equilibrium constant K_C for dimer formation is

   (a) $\dfrac{K_b(n \cdot K_b - \Delta T_b)}{(2 \cdot \Delta T_b - n \cdot K_b)}$ (b) $\dfrac{K_b(n \cdot K_b - \Delta T_b)}{(2 \cdot \Delta T_b - n \cdot K_b)^2}$

   (c) $\dfrac{K_b n \cdot \Delta T_b}{(2 \cdot \Delta T_b - n \cdot K_b)^2}$ (d) $\dfrac{n \cdot K_b - \Delta T_b}{(2 \cdot \Delta T_b - 2 \cdot K_b)^2}$

10. The relative decrease in vapour pressure of an aqueous glucose dilute solution is found to be 0.019. Hence, the elevation in boiling point is (it is given 1 molal aqueous glucose solution boils at 100.54°C at atm pressure) $K_b = 0.54°$ C kg mol^{-1}.

    (a) 0.064°C (b) 0.019°C
    (c) 0.58°C (d) 0.762° C

11. Latent heat of fusion and latent heat of vaporisation of a solvent are in the ratio of 1:6 and freezing point and boiling point (in Kelvin scale) are in the ratio of 2:3. Thus, ratio of elevation in boiling point to depression in freezing point of 1 molal solution is

    (a) 1/2 (b) 1/4
    (c) 3/4 (d) 3/8

12. Given below are two statements.
    Statement (I) An aqueous solution of a solute *AB* has boiling point of 101.08°C (*AB* is 100% ionised in bp of the solution) and freezes at −1.80° C ($K_b / K_f = 0.3$) hence, *AB* behaves as non-electrolyte at the freezing point of the solution.

Statement (II) The vapour pressure of water is lowered from 760 mmHg to 741 mmHg when 0.04 mole of $Ca(NO_3)_2$ is added to 4 moles of H_2O, thus the value of van't Hoff factors is 1.56.

In the light of above statements, choose the correct answer from the options given below.

(a) Both statement (I) and Statement (II) are correct.

(b) Both Statement (I) and Statement (II) are incorrect.

(c) Statement (I) is correct but Statement (II) is incorrect.

(d) Statement (I) is incorrect but statement (II) is correct.

13. 1 kg of 1 molal aqueous solution of sucrose is cooled and maintained at – 3.53 °C. $K_f(H_2O) = 1.86$ K mol^{-1} kg, calculate relative lowering of vapour pressure and how much ice will separate under the given conditions respectively?

(a) 0.018,353.0 g (b) 0.020, 745 g

(c) 55.56, 392.0 g (d) 78.31, 658.0 g

14. The osmotic pressure of 40% (weight/ volume) urea solution is 1.64 atm and that of 3.42 % (weight / volume) canesugar is 2.46 atm. When equal volumes of the above two solutions are mixed, the osmotic pressure of the resulting solution is

(a) 4.10 atm (b) 2.05 atm (c) 1.64 atm (d) 3.21 atm

15. A solution was prepared by dissolving 8.0 g an organic compound in 100 g of water. Calculate the osmotic pressure of this solution at 298 K, when the boiling point of the solution is 110.3°C. (Density = 1g mL^{-1}).

(K_b for water = 0.52 Km^{-1} and R = 0.082 L atm K^{-1}mol^{-1})

(a) 9.398 atm (b) 447.99 atm

(c) 936.5 atm (d) 438.2 atm

16. 1 mole each of the following solutes are taken in 5 moles of water.

(A) NaCl (B) K_2SO_4 (C) Na_3PO_4 (D) Glucose

Assume 100% ionisation of the electrolytes. Relative decrease in vapour pressure will be in order

(a) $A < B < C < D$ (b) $D < C < B < A$

(c) $D < A < B < C$ (d) $C < B < D < A$

17. Which of the following is correctly match with the given value of van't Hoff factor?

(a) *aq.* Na_2SO_4 solution which is 50% ionised $\rightarrow$ 0.5

(b) NO_2 which forms dimer to the extent of 40% $\rightarrow$ 3.5

(c) KCl which is 100% ionised in aqueous solution $\rightarrow$ 1

(d) *aq.* $K_4[Fe(CN)_6]$ which is 20% ionised $\rightarrow$ 1.8

18. 0.01 molal solution of $[Pt(NH_3)_4Cl_4]$ in water has a freezing point depression of 0.0056°C. $K_f(H_2O) = 1.86°$ C kg mol^{-1}. [Assume 100% ionisation of the complex]. What will be the value of van't Hoff factor of the given solution?

(a) 2 (b) 3 (c) 4 (d) 5

19. AB and CD are two non-volatile solutes dissolved in same solvent, showing following behaviour.

$$AB \rightleftharpoons A^+ + B^-$$

AB is ionised in the given solvent, α being degree of ionisation.

$$CD \rightleftharpoons \frac{1}{2}(CD)_2$$

CD is dimerised to the extent of β in the same solvent. If $\alpha = 0.8$ and $\Delta T_b(AB) = 2\Delta T_b(CD)$, then β is

(a) 0.50 (b) 0.40 (c) 0.80 (d) 0.20

20. 17.4% K_2SO_4 solution at 27°C is isotonic to 4% NaOH solution at 27°C. What is the ratio of their degree of ionisation? Given $[K_b(H_2O) = 0.52°\text{ mol}^{-1}\text{ kg}]$

(a) $\frac{1}{4}$ (b) $\frac{2}{3}$ (c) $\frac{3}{4}$ (d) $\frac{1}{2}$

Type II 》 MCQs with One or More than One Correct Option

21. One molal aqueous glucose solution has density 1.180 g mL^{-1}. Also, $K_f / K_b = 3$.

Thus,

(a) $\Delta T_b / \Delta T_f = 3$

(b) osmotic pressure at 300 K is 24.63 atm

(c) osmotic pressure at 300 K is 29.06 atm

(d) $\Delta T_b / \Delta T_f = 0.33$

22. Following solutions have been provided at temperature T K.

I. 1M aqueous glucose solution.

II. 1M aqueous sodium chloride solution.

III. 1M aqueous ammonium phosphate solution.

IV. 1M benzoic acid in benzene.

Select the correct statements for the above solutions.

(a) All are isotonic solutions

(b) III is hypertonic of I, II and IV

(c) IV is hypotonic of I, II and III

(d) II is hypotonic of III but hypertonic of I and IV

23. In which case(s), there will be change in the value of van't Hoff factor. (Assume 100% ionisation before and after additional solute shown by underlined is mixed)

(a) $HgI_2(s)$ + KI $\longrightarrow$ (b) $Fe(CN)_2$ + KCN $\longrightarrow$

(c) AgCl(s) + NH_3 $\longrightarrow$ (d) AgCN + KCN $\longrightarrow$

24. 10% aqueous solution of a non-electrolyte solute of molar mass (m) has elevation in boiling point x, then

(a) graphically

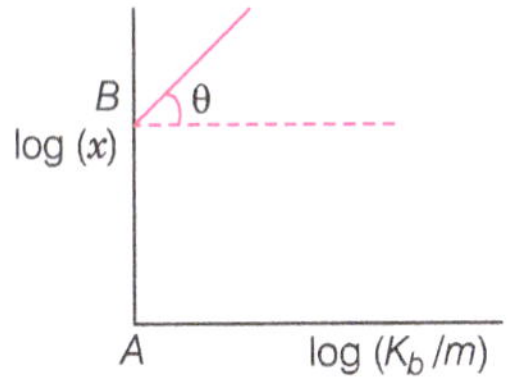

(b) $AB = 2$ and $\tan\theta = 1$

(c) x is dependent on (K_b/m)

(d) $\log\left(\frac{K_b}{m}\right) \rightarrow 0$, when boiling point of the solution is twice the boiling point of water (in °C)

25. Which of the following statements are correct?
(a) If all the molecules of ethanoic acid associate in benzene, then ΔT_b or ΔT_f for ethanoic acid will be half of the normal value.
(b) The value of i for aqueous KCl is less than unity while for ethanoic acid in benzene is more than unity.
(c) For 0.01 M $CH_3COOH(aq)$ solution, van't Hoff factor is 1.04, it means CH_3COOH is 4% ionised in the solution.
(d) 1 molal aqueous solution of $FeSO_4 \cdot (NH_4)_2SO_4$ (40% ionised) has $\Delta T_b = 2.6 K_b$. [$K_b(H_2O) = 0.52°$ kg mol^{-1}]

26. Consider following observations,

	Solution	Freezing point
A.	Water	0°C
B.	0.10 m $HgCl_2$	−0.186° C
C.	0.10 m $Hg(NO_3)_2$	−0.558°C
D.	1.0 m Urea	−1.86° C

Based on above observations, select the correct statements.
(a) $HgCl_2$ does not ionise in aqueous solution.
(b) Molal elevation constant of water is 1.86° molal^{-1}.
(c) $Hg(NO_3)_2$ is ionised to 100% in aqueous solution.
(d) The van't Hoff factor value of urea and $HgCl_2$ is same.

27. The freezing point depression of 0.001 m aqueous HCl solution is 3.608×10^{-3} K. ($K_f = 1.86°$ C kg mol^{-1} for H_2O). Select the incorrect statement from the following on the basis of given data.
(a) Its elevation in boiling point is 13×10^{-3} if $\frac{K_b}{K_f} = 3.6$.
(b) Its osmotic pressure is 0.025 bar at 300 K, if 0.001 M = 0.001m.
(c) HCl is 90% ionised under given condition
(d) pH of HCl solution is 1.2.

Type II 》 Numerical/Integer Answer type Questions

28. A motor vehicle radiator was filled with 8 L of water to which 2 L of methyl alcohol (density 0.8 g/mL) was added. What is lowest temperature at which the vehicle can be parked outdoors without a danger that water in the radiator will freeze?
[Given, K_f of water = 1.86° C kg mol^{-1}] (Excluding negative sign)

29. 2.01 g of a monobasic acid when dissolved in 100 g of water lowers the freezing point by 0.316. 20 mL of 0.1 M KOH was required to neutralise a solution containing 0.246 g of the acid upto phenolphthalein end point. If K_f for water is 1.86°C molal^{-1}, then the degree of ionisation of monobasic acid is ....

30. What osmotic pressure would the 1.35 molal sucrose aqueous solution exhibit at 298 K? [Given, the density of the solution is 1.34 g mL^{-1}] [upto nearest integer]

31. The freezing point of an aqueous solution of 0.200 molal KCN solution was − 0.781° C. On adding 0.100 mole $Hg(CN)_2$, the freezing point increased by 0.417°C. Assume $Hg(CN)_2$ and KCN form complex and KCN is 100% ionised then the value of van't Hoff factor when complex formation takes place is .... [Nearest integer]

32. Consider following observations for a solute X which is non-electrolyte and non volatile.

Solute	Solvent	K_f	ΔT_f	State
w_2gX	w_1 g of A	1.86°C molal^{-1}	α	$2X \rightleftharpoons X_2$ (100%)
w_2 gX	w_1 g of B	1.46°C molal^{-1}	β	$3X \rightleftharpoons X_3$ (100%)

The ratio of $\left(\frac{\alpha}{\beta}\right)$ is .... $\times 10^{-2}$. (Nearest integer).

33. Variation of log ΔT_f with log(m_i) is given, (where, (m) is the molal concentration and (i) is the van't Hoff factor for 0.5 molal $K_4[Fe(CN)_6]$. Degree of ionisation of the solute is .... when log $\Delta T_f = 0.56$.

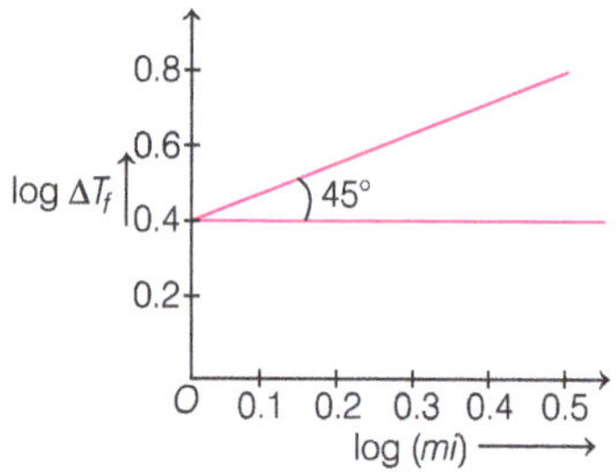

34. A and B are two non- volatile solutes. A in a given solvent ionise as

$$A \rightleftharpoons X + Y$$

and B in the same solvent and with same molar concentration dimerises as

$$2B \rightleftharpoons B_2$$

Degree of ionisation of $A = \alpha = 0.8$ and degree of dimerisation of $B = \beta$

If the elevation in boiling point of the solution A is twice that of solution B. Then, the value of β is ....

1. (c)	**2.** (b)	**3.** (c)	**4.** (b)	**5.** (c)	**6.** (b)
7. (a)	**8.** (c)	**9.** (b)	**10.** (c)	**11.** (d)	**12.** (c)
13. (a)	**14.** (b)	**15.** (b)	**16.** (c)	**17.** (d)	**18.** (b)
19. (d)	**20.** (d)	**21.** (b,d)	**22.** (b,c,d)	**23.** (a,b,c,d)	**24.** (a,b,c,d)
25. (a,c,d)	**26.** (a,b,c,d)	**27.** (b,c,d)	**28.** (11.625)	**29.** (0.04)	**30.** (30)
31. (2)	**32.** (191)	**33.** (0.5)	**34.** (0.2)		

Elemental Practice 7.3 | **Chapter 07**

Connect with **Answers**

Advanced Exclusive Different Strokes

Problems based on positive and negative deviation from Raoult's law especially classification of a given mixture into minimum boiling or maximum boiling azeotropes are important for the purpose of JEE Advanced.

Interpretation of Azeotropes

An azeotrope is a special type of mixture that has a contant boiling point and composition. This means that when you try to separate the components of an azeotropes by boiling it, the vapour that forms has the same composition as the liquid state.

There are two main azeotropic mixtures types.

1. Minimum Boiling Azeotrope (Positive Deviation)

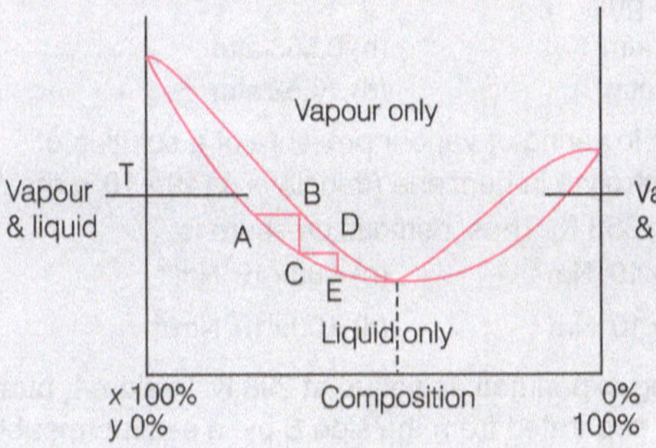

$A \rightarrow B$ 1st container.

A : composition in liquid phase and B : composition in vapour phase (container 1)

$B \rightarrow C$ container 2

Vapours of 1st container condensed in the 2nd container (C : composition in liquid phase in container 2 and D : composition in vapour phase in 2nd container.

The process is repeated till we arrive at a point where the composition in the liquid and vapour phase becomes constant. Such a solution is called azeotropes.

Solutions that show a large positive deviation from Raoult's law typically form minimum boiling azeotropes. This means that the mixture has a boiling point higher that what would be expected based on Raoult's law, which assumes ideal behaviour.

Example : Ethanol-water mixture, obtained by fermentation of sugars on fractional distillation yields a solution containing approximately 95.57% v/v ethanol. This specific composition represents the minimum boiling azeotrope, and during distillation, the vapour phase and the liquid phase maintain the same composition.

2. Maximum Boiling Azeotrope (Negative Deviation)

Solutions that show a large negative deviation from Raoult's law typically form maximum boiling azeotropes. in this case, the mixture has a boiling point lower than what Raoult's law predicts.

Example : Nitric acid-water mixture is an azeotrope formed by nitric acid and water. This azeotrope has an approximate composition of 68% nitric acid and 32% water by mass, with a boiling point of 393.5 K. During distillation, the vapour phase and the liquid phase maintain this composition, and separation becomes challenging due to the constant boiling point.

Conclusion

- Minimum boiling azeotropes show a large positive deviation from Raoult's law.
- Maximum boiling point azeotropes show a large negative deviation from Raoult's law.

PRACTICE

ELEMENT 01

Target JEE Main

Objective Type Questions 》

1. The ozone layer in the earth's stratosphere has an average total pressure of 10 mm with partial pressure of ozone layer, 1.2×10^{-6}mm. What is the concentration of ozone (in ppm) assuming that the average molar mass of air is 29 g mol^{-1} ?
(a) 0.56 ppm (b) 1.31 ppm
(c) 0.20 ppm (d) 2.06 ppm

2. The average human with a body weight of 70 kg has a blood volume of 5.00 L. Henry's law constant K_H for N_2 is 9.04×10^4 bar at 298 K. Density of blood and water is 1.00 kg L^{-1}. Calculate the number of moles of N_2 absorbed by this amount of blood when exposed to air with a composition of 80% N_2 at sea level when the pressure of 1 bar and 50 bar respectively.
(a) 0.134,1.31 (b) 2.31, 3.26
(c) 1.24×10^{-2}, 0.312 (d) 2.46×10^{-3}, 0.123

3. 122 g of benzoic acid is dissolved in 1000 g of benzene at 10°C at which vapour pressure of benzene is 66.6 cm of Hg. Vapour pressure of this solution, when benzoic acid is completely dimerised in benzene is
(a) 66.20 cm of Hg (b) 66.00 cm of Hg
(c) 64.10 cm of Hg (d) 65.92 cm of Hg

4. Given below are two statements.
Statement (I) If the molality and molarity of sucrose solution are equal to 0.1 then the density of solution will be 1.0342 g mL^{-1}.
Statement (II) If the mole fraction of solute and molality of solution are equal to 0.1 then the molar mass of solvent will be 1011 g mol^{-1}.
In the light of the above statements, choose the correct option.
(a) Both Statement I and Statement II are correct.
(b) Both Statement I and Statement II are incorrect.
(c) Statement I is correct but Statement II is incorrect.
(d) Statement I is incorrect but Statement II is correct.

5. For a dilute solution containing 2.5 g of a non-electrolyte and non-volatile solute in 100 g water, the elevation in boiling point is 2° at 1 atm. Assume a dilute solution. Thus, vapour pressure of solution (in mm Hg) is,
($K_b = 0.52$ K kg mol^{-1})
(a) 724.0 (b) 740
(c) 707 (d) 718

6. A 0.86 percent by mass solution of NaCl is called "physiological saline" because its osmotic pressure is equal to that of the solution in blood cells. Calculate the osmotic pressure of this solution at normal body temperature (37°C). [Given, density of the saline solution is 1.005 gmL^{-1}]
(a) 2.38 atm (b) 0.568 atm
(c) 7.52 atm (d) 10.52 atm

7. Relative lowering of vapour pressure of a solution of non-electrolyte in benzene (density = $8.149 \times 10^2 g\ dm^{-3}$) is 0.013 at 353 K. Thus, osmotic pressure is
(a) $3.94 \times 10^5 Nm^{-2}$ (b) $4.00 \times 10^5 Nm^{-2}$
(c) $3.94 \times 10^6 Nm^{-2}$ (d) $4.00 \times 10^6 Nm^{-2}$

8. Following experiment is set up at 298 K. In side *A*, pure water is separated from the side *B* by a semipermeable membrane (SPM), side *B* contains 20 g of haemoglobin in 1 L of solution. When equilibrium is attained, difference in height of the water in column in side *A* is and that in side *B* is 77.8mm.

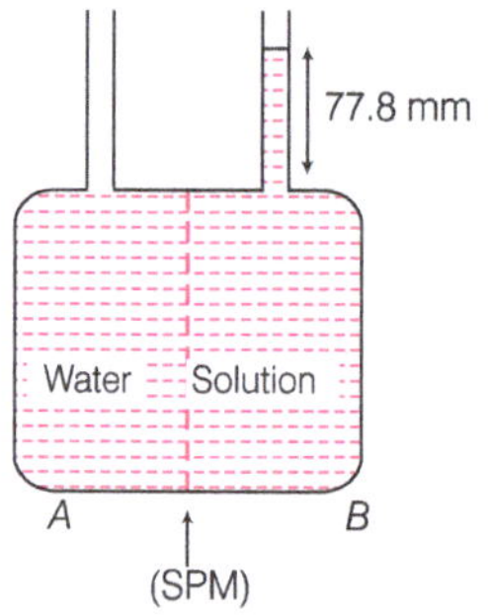

Calculate the osmotic pressure of the solution and molar mass of haemoglobin respectively.
(a) 76.3 Nm^{-2}, 6.49 kg mol^{-1}
(b) 763 Nm^{-2} , 64.90 kg mol^{-1}
(c) 86.3 Nm^{-2}, 0.649 kg mol^{-1}
(d) 0.763 Nm^{-2}, 0.0649 kg mol^{-1}

9. Consider following aqueous solutions at isothermal conditions exerting osmotic pressure as specified.

	Solutions	Osmotic pressure
1	10 g glucose in 200 mL solution	p_1
2	10 g urea in 100 mL solution	p_2
3	10 g sucrose in 50 mL solution	p_3

Thus,

(a) $p_1 > p_2 > p_3$ (b) $p_1 < p_2 < p_3$

(c) $p_2 > p_1 > p_3$ (d) $p_1 < p_3 < p_2$

10. Based on the given graph, molar mass of solute X (non-electrolyte) is

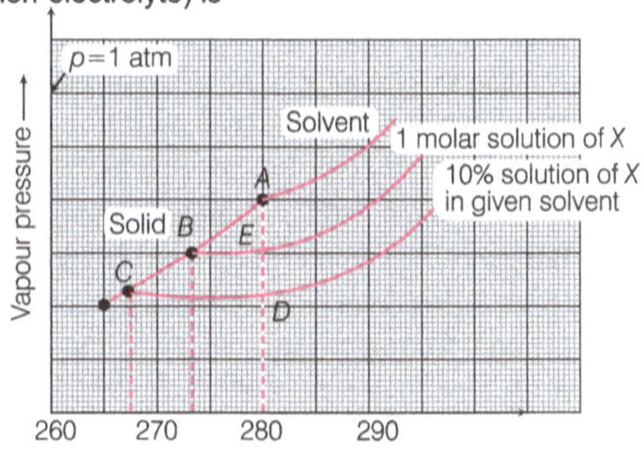

(a) 54.5g mol^{-1} (b) 109.0g mol^{-1}

(c) 120.0g mol^{-1} (d) 77.2g mol^{-1}

11. Pure benzene freezes at 5.3°C. A solution of 0.223 g of phenyl acetic acid, A ($C_6H_5CH_2COOH$ = 136 g mol^{-1}) in 4.4 g benzene freezes at 4.47°C. From this it is concluded that K_f(benzene) = 5.12° kg mol^{-1})

(a) A exists as such in solution.

(b) A undergoes partial ionisation in benzene.

(c) A undergoes complete ionisation in benzene.

(d) A undergoes dimerisation.

12. A mixture of ethyl alcohol and propyl alcohol has a vapour pressure of 280 mm at 300 K. The vapour pressure of propyl alcohol is 240 mm. If the mole fraction of ethyl alcohol is 0.4, its vapour pressure (in mm) at the same temperature will be

(a) 640 (b) 700

(c) 480 (d) 340

13. Benzene and toluene form nearly ideal solutions. At 20°C, the vapour pressure of benzene is 78 torr and that of toluene is 25 torr. The partial vapour pressure of benzene at 20°C for a solution containing 78g of benzene and 46 g of toluene in torr is

(a) 37.5 (b) 68

(c) 52 (d) 75.5

14. 3.4 mL of acetic acid is dissolved in water to make 3.0 L of solution. The depression in freezing point observed for this strength of acid is 0.1382°C. Calculate the percentage of dissociation of the acid.

[Given, density of acetic acid is 1.02 g mL^{-1} and molar mass of acetic acid is 60 g mol^{-1}, $K_f(H_2O)$ = 1.85 K kg mol^{-1}]

(a) 28.7 (b) 287

(c) 320 (d) 32.01

15. The freezing point of benzene decreases by 0.48°C when 0.3 g of acetic acid is added to 20 g of benzene. If acetic acid associates to form a dimer in benzene, percentage association of acetic acid in benzene will be (K_f for benzene = 5.32 K kg mol^{-1})

(a) 94.6% (b) 111.1%

(c) 88.7% (d) 128%

16. 1.36 g of a biopolymer dissolved in a 100 mL water at 300 K exerted an osmotic pressure of 2.34×10^{-3} bar.

Calculate the molar mass of the biopolymer.

[Use : $R = 0.083$ L bar mol^{-1} K^{-1}]

(a) 147.23×10^{-3} g/mol (b) 120×10^{-2} g/mol

(c) 15.02×10^4 g/mol (d) 137.74×10^2 g/mol

17. Elevation in boiling point of a solution of non-electrolyte in non-polar solvent (toluene) is 0.3°. Mole fraction elevation in boiling point constant of non-polar solvent is 36.1 K. Thus molality (in mole kg^{-1}) of the solution is

(a) 1.012 mol kg^{-1} (b) 0.321 mol kg^{-1}

(c) 0.023 mol kg^{-1} (d) 0.091 mol kg^{-1}

18. 25 mL of an aqueous solution of KCl was found to require 20 mL of 1.0 M $AgNO_3$ solution when titrated using K_2CrO_4 as an indicator. Thus, depression in freezing point of KCl solution with 100% ionisation will be

[$K_f(H_2O)$ = 2.0° mol^{-1} kg] (Assume molarity = molality)

(a) 5.0° (b) 3.2°

(c) 1.6° (d) 0.8°

19. At 0°C and pressure of 1.00 atm, the aqueous solubility of $O_2(g)$ is 48.9 g O_2 per litre. Thus, molarity of O_2 in a saturated water solution when the O_2 is under the normal partial pressure of 0.2095 atm, is

(a) 4.57×10^{-4} M (b) 2.18×10^{-3} M

(c) 4.57×10^{-2} M (d) 2.18×10^{-5} M

20. A handbook lists the solubility of carbon monoxide in water at 0°C and 1 atm pressure as 0.0354 mL CO per mL of H_2O. What should be the pressure of CO (g) above the solution to obtain 0.010 M CO solution?

(a) 0.633 atm (b) 6.33 atm

(c) 1 atm (d) 0.01 atm

Numerical Type Questions

21. 1 g mixture of Na_2CO_3 and $NaHCO_3$ each having 1 : 1 molar ratio required X mL of 0.05 M H_2SO_4 solution for complete reaction. The value of X is .... mL.

22. A certain mass of a substance dissolved in 100 g of benzene lowers the freezing point by 1.28°C. The same mass of solute dissolved in 100 g of water lowers the freezing point by 1.40°C. If the substance has a normal molecular weight in benzene and is completely dissociated in water, what is van't Hoff factor of substance? [Given, K_f (benzene/kg (water) = 2.75]

23. Solute X (non-electrolyte and non-volatile) exists as dimer in solvent (A)(K_f (A) = 1.86° mol^{-1} kg) and as trimer in solvent (B)($K_f(B)$ = 1.36° mol^{-1} kg). Depression in freezing point in solvent (A) is α and that of in solvent (B) is β. What

is ratio of α and β? (in both cases, solutions have same amount of solute and there is 100% polymerisation.

24. Variation of π/c vs c (c is concentration of solute in g dm^{-3}) is given. At 300 K, for a solute of molar mass 308 g mol^{-1}, $OA = x \times 10^{-y}$ in scientific notation with x as single digit integer. What is value of x ? ($R = 0.0821$ L atm mol^{-1} K^{-1})

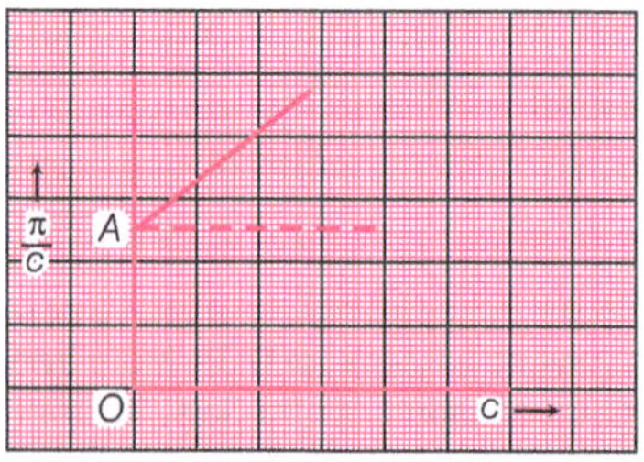

25. For an aqueous solution of a non-volatile solute X, relative lowering of vapour pressure is 0.05. When ΔT_f is the depression in freezing point assuming a dilute solution and $\Delta T'_f$ is the depression in freezing point of a moderate concentrated solution. Calculate the difference in $(\Delta T_f - \Delta T'_f)$ $x \times 10^{-2}$°C. The value of x is ....
[Given : $K_f(H_2O) = 1.86°$ mol^{-1} kg]

26. The freezing point of an aqueous solution of KCN containing 0.2 mole/ kg water was −0.80°C. On adding 0.1 mole of $Hg(CN)_2$ in the solution containing 1 kg of water, the freezing point of the solution was −0.6°C. Assuming that the complex is formed according to the following equation.

$$Hg(CN)_2 + mCN^- \longrightarrow Hg(CN)_{m+2}^{m-}$$

and $Hg(CN)_2$ is the limiting reactant, the value of m is ....
[Assume molality = molarity]

27. The freezing point of benzene decrease by 0.38°C when 0.3 g of acetic acid is added to 35 g of benzene. If acetic acid association to form a dimer in benzene, percentage association of acetic acid in benzene will be .... (nearest integer) [K_f for benzene = 5.12 K kg mol^{-1}]

28. A solution containing 0.2563 g of naphthalene (molecular mass = 128 g mol^{-1}) in 56 g of carbon tetrachloride yields a boiling point elevation of 0.211°C while a solution of 0.6216 g of an unknown solute in the same mass of the solvent gives a boiling point elevation of 0.647°C. The molecular mass of unknown solute will be ....

29. Ethylene glycol is used as an antifreeze in a cold climate. Mass of ethylene glycol which should be added to 4 kg of water to prevent it from freezing at -6°C will be (K_f for water = 1.86 K kg mol^{-1} and molar mass of ethylene glycol = 62 g mol^{-1})

30. The osmotic pressure of a dilute solution of an ionic compound XY in water is four times that of a solution of 0.02 M $BaCl_2$ in water. Assume complete dissociation of the given ionic compounds in water, the concentration of XY (in mol L^{-1}) in solution is $x \times 10^{-2}$ mol L^{-1}.
The value of x is ....

Check Through PYQs

Element 1 Types and Concentrations of Solution

1. Molarity (M) of an aqueous solution containing x g of anhyd. $CuSO_4$ in 500 mL solution at 32°C is 2×10^{-1} M. Its molality will be .... $\times 10^{-3}$ m. (Nearest integer).
[Given density of the solution = 1.25 g/mL.]
2024, 9 April Shift-I

2. The molarity (M) of an aqueous solution containing 5.85 g of NaCl in 500 mL water is
(Given: Molar mass Na: 23 and Cl: 35.5 $gmol^{-1}$)
2024, 4 April Shift-I
(a) 4 (b) 0.2 (c) 2 (d) 20

3. If a substance 'A' dissolves in solution of a mixture of 'B' and 'C' with their respective number of moles as n_A, n_B and n_C. Mole fraction of C in the solution is
2024, 30 Jan Shift-I
(a) $\dfrac{n_C}{n_A \times n_B \times n_C}$ (b) $\dfrac{n_C}{n_A - n_B - n_C}$
(c) $\dfrac{n_C}{n_A + n_B + n_C}$ (d) $\dfrac{n_B}{n_A + n_B}$

4. A solution of H_2SO_4 is 31.4% H_2SO_4 by mass and has a density of 1.25 g/mL. The molarity of the H_2SO_4 solution is .... M (Nearest integer).
[Given, molar mass of H_2SO_4 = 98 g mol^{-1}]
2024, 29 Jan Shift-I

5. Some amount of dichloromethane (CH_2Cl_2) is added to 671.141 mL of chloroform ($CHCl_3$) to prepare 2.6×10^{-3} M solution of CH_2Cl_2 (DCM). The concentration of DCM is .... ppm (by mass).
Given, atomic mass C = 12, H = 1, Cl = 35.5,
density of $CHCl_3$ = 1.49 g cm^{-3}
2023, 30 Jan Shift-I

6. 250 g of solution of D-glucose in water contains 10.8% of carbon by weight. The molality of the solution is nearest to (Given : Atomic weights are H : 1u, C : 12 u, O : 16 u)
2022, 27 July Shift-I
(a) 1.03 (b) 2.06 (c) 3.09 (d) 5.40

7. When 800 mL of 0.5 M nitric acid is heated in a beaker, its volume is reduced to half and 11.5 g of nitric acid is evaporated. The molarity of the remaining nitric acid solution is $x \times 10^{-2}$ M. (Nearest integer) *2022, 26 July Shift-I*

8. Given below are two statements. One is labelled as Assertion (A) and the other is labelled as Reason (R).

Assertion (A) At 10°C, the density of a 5M solution of KCl [atomic masses of K and Cl are 39 and 35.5 g mol^{-1} respectively], is 'x' g mL^{-1}. The solution is cooled to –21°C. The molality of the solution will remain unchanged.

Reason (R) The molality of a solution does not change with temperature as mass remains unaffected with temperature.

In the light of the above statements, choose the correct answer from the options given below. *2022, 27 June Shift-I*

(a) Both (A) and (R) are true and (R) is the correct explanation of (A)
(b) Both (A) and (R) are true but (R) is not the correct explanation of (A)
(c) (A) is true but (R) is false
(d) (A) is false but (R) is true

9. A commercially sold conc. HCl is 35% HCl by mass. If the density of this commercial acid is 1.46 g/mL, the molarity of this solution is
(Atomic mass : Cl = 35.5 amu, H = 1 amu) *2022, 26 June, Shift-I*

(a) 10.2 M (b) 12.5 M
(c) 14.0 M (d) 18.2 M

10. If 80 g of copper sulphate $CuSO_4 \cdot 5H_2O$ is dissolved in deionised water to make 5 L of solution. The concentration of the copper sulphate solution is $x \times 10^{-3}$ mol L^{-1}. The value of x is ....
[Atomic masses Cu = 63.54 u, S = 32 u, O = 16 u, H = 1 u] *2021, 1 Sep Shift-II*

11. The molarity of the solution prepared by dissolving 6.3 g of oxalic acid ($H_2C_2O_4 \cdot 2H_2O$) in 250 mL of water in mol L^{-1} is $x \times 10^{-2}$. The value of x is .... (Nearest integer)
[Atomic mass H = 1.0, C = 12.0, O = 16.0] *2021, 31 Aug Shift-I*

12. A 6.50 molal solution of KOH (aq) has a density of 1.89 g cm^{-3}. The molarity of the solution is ...... mol dm^{-3} (Round off to the nearest integer).
[Atomic masses: K : 39.0 u, O : 16.0 u, H : 1.0 u] *2021, 16 March Shift-I*

13. 4.5 g of compound A (MW = 90) was used to make 250 mL of its aqueous solution. The molarity of the solution in M is $x \times 10^{-1}$. The value of x is .... (Rounded off to the nearest integer). *2021, 24 Feb Shift-I*

14. The hardness of a water sample containing 10^{-3} M $MgSO_4$ expressed as $CaCO_3$ equivalents (in ppm) is...... (molar mass of $MgSO_4$ is 120.37 g/mol) *2020, 9 Jan Shift-II*

15. 10.30 mg of O_2 is dissolved into a litre of sea water of density 1.03 g/mL. The concentration of O_2 in ppm is *2020, 9 Jan Shift-II*

Element 2 Solubility, Vapour Pressure and Raoult's Law

16. The vapour pressure of pure benzene and methyl benzene at 27°C is given as 80 torr and 24 torr, respectively. The mole fraction of methyl benzene in vapour phase, in equilibrium with an equimolar mixture of those two liquids (ideal solution) at the same temperature is .... $\times 10^{-2}$. (Nearest integer) *2024, 9 April Shift-II*

17. Identify the mixture that shows positive deviations from Raoult's law. *2024, 31 Jan Shift-I*

(a) $(CH_3)_2CO + CS_2$ (b) $CHCl_3 + C_6H_6$
(c) $(CH_3)_2CO + C_6H_5NH_2$ (d) $CHCl_3 + (CH_3)_2CO$

18. The vapour pressure vs temperature curve for a solution solvent system is shown below.

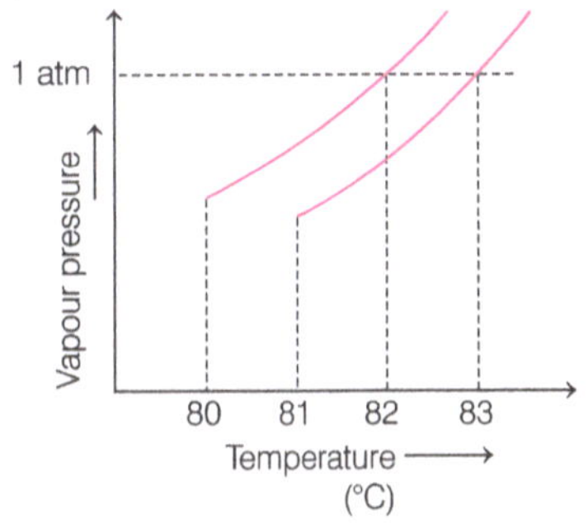

The boiling point of the solvent is .... °C. *2023, 8 April Shift-I*

19. The total pressure observed by mixing two liquids A and B is 350 mm Hg when their mole fractions are 0.7 and 0.3 respectively.
The total pressure becomes 410 mm Hg if the mole fractions are changed to 0.2 and 0.8 respectively for A and B. The vapour pressure of pure A is .... mm Hg. (Nearest integer)
Consider the liquids and solutions behave ideally. *2023, 24 Jan Shift-II*

20. 'x' g of molecular oxygen (O_2) is mixed with 200 g of neon (Ne). The total pressure of the non-reactive mixture of O_2 and Ne in the cylinder is 25 bar. The partial pressure of Ne is 20 bar at the same temperature and volume. The value of 'x' is ....
[Given : Molar mass of O_2 = 32 g mol^{-1}.
Molar mass of Ne = 20 g mol^{-1}] *2022, 29 July Shift-II*

21. If O_2 gas is bubbled through water at 303 K, the number of millimoles of O_2 gas that dissolve in 1 litre of water is .... (Nearest integer).
(Given, Henry's law constant for O_2 at 303 K is 46.82 k bar and partial pressure of O_2 = 0.920 bar)
(Assume, solubility of O_2 in water is too small, nearly negligible.) *2022, 29 July Shift-I*

22. The vapour pressures of two volatile liquids A and B at 25°C are 50 torr and 100 torr, respectively. If the liquid mixture contains 0.3 mole fraction of A, then the mole fraction of liquid B in the vapour phase is $\frac{x}{17}$. The value of x is .... *2022, 28 June Shift-I*

23. CO_2 gas is bubbled through water during a soft drink manufacturing process at 298 K. If CO_2 exerts a partial pressure of 0.835 bar then .... x m mol of CO_2 would dissolve in 0.9 L of water. The value of x is .... (Nearest integer)
(Henry's law constant for CO_2 at 298 K is 1.67×10^3 bar) *2021, 25 July Shift-I*

24. The vapour pressures of A and B at 25°C are 90 mm Hg and 15 mm Hg respectively. If A and B are mixed such that the mole-fraction of A in the mixture is 0.6, then the mole fraction of B in the vapour phase is $x \times 10^{-1}$. The value of x is .... (Nearest integer) *2021, 20 July Shift-II*

25. The oxygen dissolved in water exerts a partial pressure of 20 kPa in the vapour above water. The molar solubility of oxygen in water is .... $\times 10^{-5}$ mol dm^{-3}. (Round off to the Nearest integer)
[Given : Henry's law constant = $K_H = 8.0 \times 10^4$ kPa for O_2. Density of water with dissolved oxygen = 1.0 kg dm^{-3}] *2021, 17 March Shift-I*

26. At 300 K, the vapour pressure of a solution containing 1 mole of n-hexane and 3 moles of n-heptane is 550 mm of Hg. At the same temperature, if one more mole of n-heptane is added to this solution, the vapour pressure of the solution increases by 10 mm of Hg. What is the vapour pressure in mm Hg of n-heptane in its pure state .... ? *2020, 4 Sep Shift-I*

27. A graph of vapour pressure and temperature for three different liquids X, Y, and Z is shown below : *2020, 8 Jan Shift-I*

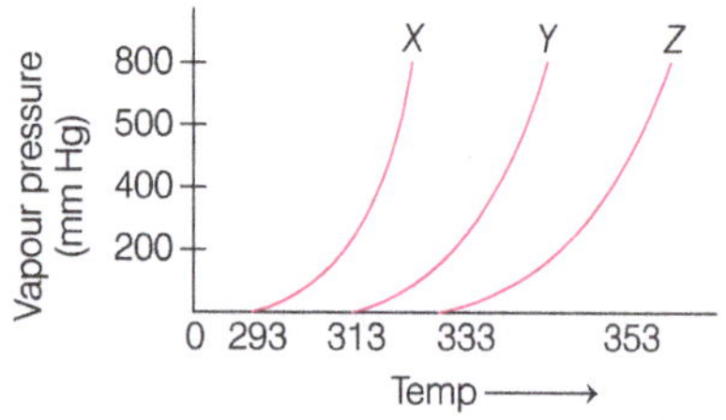

The following inference are made :
A. X has higher intermolecular interactions compared to Y.
B. X has lower intermolecular interactions compared to Y.
C. Z has lower intermolecular interactions compared to Y.

The correct inference(s) is/are :
(a) (C) (b) (B)
(c) (A) (d) (A) and (C)

28. At 35°C, the vapour pressure of CS_2 is 512 mm Hg and that of acetone is 344 mm Hg. A solution of CS_2 in acetone has a total vapour pressure of 600 mm Hg. The false statement amongst the following is *2020, 7 Jan Shift-I*
(a) Raoult's law is not obeyed by this system
(b) CS_2 and acetone are less attracted to each other than to themselves
(c) a mixture of 100 mL CS_2 and 100 mL acetone has a volume < 200 mL
(d) heat must be absorbed in order to produce the solution at 35°C

Element 3 Colligative Properties, Abnormal Molecular Mass and van't Hoff Factor

29. When a non-volatile solute (A) is added to a volatile solvent, the vapour pressure of solvent decreases by 10 mmHg. Mole fraction of solute is 0.2. If second solute (B) is added to the same solution and vapour pressure of solution decreases by 20 mmHg, calculate mole fraction of second solute in the final solution. *2025, 23 Jan Shift-II*
(a) 0.3 (b) 0.4
(c) 0.5 (d) 0.6

30. Compare boiling point of given solutions *2025, 22 Jan Shift-I*
I. 10^{-4} M NaCl II. 10^{-3} M NaCl
II. 10^{-2} M NaCl IV. 10^{-4} M urea
(a) I > II > III > IV
(b) III > II > I > IV
(c) II > I > III > IV
(d) III > I > II > IV

31. 0.05 M $CuSO_4$ when treated with 0.01 M $K_2Cr_2O_7$ gives colour solution of $Cu_2Cr_2O_7$. The two solutions are separated as shown below.
[SPM : Semi-permeable membrane] *2024, 9 April Shift-I*

$K_2Cr_2O_7$	$CuSO_4$
Side X	Side Y

SPM

Due to osmosis
(a) molarity of $K_2Cr_2O_7$ solution is lowered.
(b) green colour formation observed on side X.
(c) molarity of $CuSO_4$ solution is lowered.
(d) green colour formation observed on side Y.

32. When $x \times 10^{-2}$ mL methanol (molar mass = 32 g : density = 0.792 g/cm^2) is added to 100 mL water (density = 1 g/cm^3), the following diagram is obtained. *2024, 6 April Shift-II*

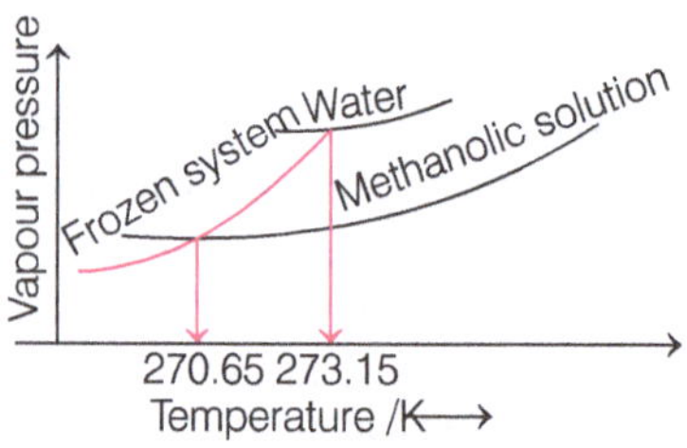

x = ... (nearest integer)
[Given : Molal freezing point depression constant of water at 273.15 K is 1.86 K kg mol^{-1}]

33. Considering acetic acid dissociates in water, its dissociation constant is 6.25×10^{-5}. If 5 mL of acetic acid is dissolved in 1 L water, the solution will freeze at $-x \times 10^{-2}$ °C, provided pure water freezes at 0 °C.

$x =$ .... (Nearest integer)

Given: $(K_f)_{water} = 1.86$ K kg mol^{-1}.

density of acetic acid is 1.2 g mol^{-1}

molar mass of water = 18 g mol^{-1}.

molar mass of acetic acid = 60 g mol^{-1}

density of water = 1g cm^{-3}

Acetic acid dissociates as

$CH_3COOH \rightleftharpoons CH_3COO^{\ominus} + H^{\oplus}$ *2024, 5 April Shift-II*

34. 2.7 kg of each of water and acetic acid are mixed. The freezing point of the solution will be $-x$°C. Consider the acetic acid does not dimerise in water, nor dissociates in water, $x =$......... (Nearest integer)

[given: Molar mass of water = 18 g mol^{-1},
acetic acid = 60 g mol^{-1}

$K_{f_{H_2O}}$: 1.86 K kg mol^{-1}

$K_{f_{acetic\ acid}}$: 3.90 K kg mol^{-1}

Freezing point: H_2O = 273 K, acetic acid = 290 K]

2024, 4 April Shift-II

35. The solution from the following with highest depression in freezing point/lowest freezing point is *2024, 30 Jan Shift-II*
(a) 180 g of acetic acid dissolved in water
(b) 180 g of glucose dissolved in water
(c) 180 g of acetic acid dissolved in benzene
(d) 180 g of benzoic acid dissolved in benzene

36. The vapour pressure of 30% (w/v) aqueous solution of glucose is .... mm Hg at 25°C.

[Given, the density of 30% (w/v), aqueous solution of glucose is 1.2 g cm^{-3} and vapour pressure of pure water is 24 mm Hg.] (Molar mass of glucose is 180 g mol^{-1})

2023, 15 April Shift-I

37. What weight of glucose must be dissolved in 100 g of water to lower the vapour pressure by 0.20 mm Hg ? (Assume, dilute solution is being formed)

Given, vapour pressure of pure water is 54.2 mm Hg at room temperature. Molar mass of glucose is 180 g mol^{-1}

2023, 11 April Shift-II

(a) 3.69 g (b) 3.59 g
(c) 2.59 g (d) 4.69 g

38. Sea water contains 29.25% NaCl and 19% $MgCl_2$ by weight of solution. The normal boiling point of the sea water is .... °C (Nearest integer)

Assume 100% ionisation for both NaCl and $MgCl_2$. (Given, $K_b(H_2O)$ = 0.52 K kg mol^{-1} Molar mass of NaCl and $MgCl_2$ is 58.5 and 95 g mol^{-1} respectively.) *2023, 10 April Shift-II*

39. If the boiling points of two solvents X and Y (having same molecular weights) are in the ratio 2:1 and their enthalpy of vaporisations are in the ratio 1:2, then the boiling point elevation constant of X is m times the boiling point elevation constant of Y. The value of m is .... (Nearest integer). *2023, 8 April Shift-II*

40. 20% of acetic acid is dissociated when its 5 g is added to 500 mL of water. The depression in freezing point of such water is .... $\times 10^{-3}$°C. Atomic mass of C, H and O are 12, 1 and 16 amu, respectively.
[Given, molal depression constant and density of water are 1.86 K kg mol^{-1} and 1 g cm^{-3} respectively].

2023, 1 Feb Shift-II

41. 25 mL of an aqueous solution of KCl was found to require 20 mL of 1 M $AgNO_3$ solution when titrated using K_2CrO_4 as an indicator. What is the depression in freezing point of KCl solution of the given concentration? .... (Nearest integer) (Given, K_f = 2.0 K kg mol^{-1})

Assume

1. 100% ionisation and
2. density of the aqueous solution as 1 g mL^{-1}

2023, 1 Feb Shift-I

42. At 27°C, a solution containing 2.5 g of solute in 250.0 mL of solution exerts an osmotic pressure of 400 Pa. The molar mass of the solute is .... g mol^{-1}. (Nearest integer)
(Given : R = 0.083 L bar K^{-1} mol^{-1}) *2023, 31 Jan Shift-I*

43. Evaluate the following statements for their correctness.
A. The elevation in boiling point temperature of water will be same for 0.1 M NaCl and 0.1 M urea.
B. Azeotropic mixtures boil without change in their composition.
C. Osmosis always takes place from hypertonic to hypotonic solution.
D. The density of 32% H_2SO_4 solution having molarity 4.09 M is approximately 1.26 g mL^{-1}.
E. A negatively charged sol is obtained when KI solution is added to silver nitrate solution.

Choose the correct answer from the options given below.

2023, 31 Jan Shift-II

(a) B and D (b) A and C
(c) A, B and D (d) B, D and E

44. The osmotic pressure of solutions of PVC in cyclohexanone at 300K are plotted on the graph. The molar mass of PVC is .... g mol^{-1}. (Nearest integer)

2023, 25 Jan Shift-I

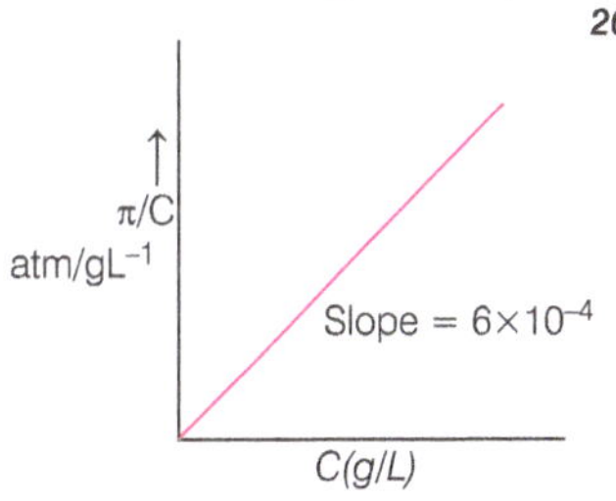

(Given : R = 0.083 L atm K^{-1} mol^{-1}).

45. 1.2 mL of acetic acid is dissolved in water to make 2.0 L of solution. The depression in freezing point observed for this strength of acid is 0.0198°C. The percentage of dissociation of the acid is .... (Nearest integer)

[Given, density of acetic acid is 1.02 g mL^{-1}, molar mass of acetic acid is 60 g mol^{-1} $K_f(H_2O) = 1.85$ K kg mol^{-1}] *2022, 29 June Shift-I*

46. 150 g of acetic acid was contaminated with 10.2 g ascorbic acid ($C_6H_8O_6$) to lower down its freezing point by $(x \times 10^{-1})$°C. The value of x is .... (Nearest integer)

[Given $K_f = 3.9$ K kg mol^{-1}; molar mass of ascorbic acid = 176 g mol^{-1}] *2022, 28 July Shift-I*

47. A 0.5 per cent solution of potassium chloride was found to freeze at – 0.24°C. The percentage dissociation of potassium chloride is .... (Nearest integer)

(Molal depression constant for water is 1.80 K kg mol^{-1} and molar mass of KCl is 74.6 g mol^{-1}) *2022, 26 June Shift-I*

48. A 1 molal $K_4Fe(CN)_6$ solution has a degree of dissociation of 0.4. Its boiling point is equal to that of another solution which contains 18.1 weight per cent of a non- electrolytic solute A. The molar mass of A is .... u. (Round off to the nearest integer).

[Density of water $= 1.0$ g cm^{-3}] *2021, 17 March Shift-II*

49. 1.22 g of an organic acid is separately dissolved in 100 g of benzene (K_b = 2.6 K kg mol^{-1}) and 100 g of acetone (K_b = 1.7 K kg mol^{-1}). The acid is known to dimerise in benzene but remain as a monomer in acetone. The boiling point of the solution in acetone increases by 0.17°C. The increase in boiling point of solution in benzene in °C is $x \times 10^{-2}$. The value of x is .... (Nearest integer)

[Atomic mass : C = 12.0, H = 1.0, O = 16.0] *2021, 31 Aug Shift-II*

50. The elevation of boiling point of 0.10 m aqueous $CrCl_3 \cdot x\,NH_3$ solution is two times that of 0.05 m aqueous $CaCl_2$ solution. The value of x is ....

[Assume 100% ionisation of the complex and $CaCl_2$, coordination number of Cr as 6, and that all NH_3 molecules are present inside the coordination sphere] *2020, 6 Sep Shift-I*

51. When 12.2 g of benzoic acid is dissolved in 100 g of water, the freezing point of solution was found to be – 0.93°C ($K_f(H_2O)$ = 1.86 K kg mol^{-1}). The number (n) of benzoic acid molecules associated (assuming 100% association) is .... *2021, 26 Feb Shift-II*

52. A cylinder containing an ideal gas (0.1 mol of 1.0 dm^3) is in thermal equilibrium with a large volume of 0.5 molal aqueous solution of ethylene glycol at its freezing point. If the stoppers S_1 and S_2 (as shown in the figure) are suddenly withdrawn, the volume of the gas in litres after equilibrium is achieved will be ....

(Given, K_f (water) = 2.0 K kg mol^{-1}, $R = 0.08$ dm^3 atm $K^{-1}mol^{-1}$) *2020, 9 Jan Shift-II*

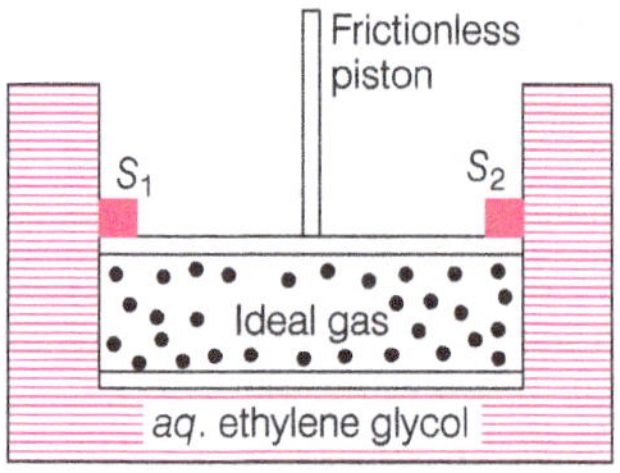

53. How much amount of NaCl should be added to 600 g of water ($\rho = 1.00$ g/mL) to decrease the freezing point of water to – 0.2° C? ...... (The freezing point depression constant for water = 2 K kg mol^{-1}) *2020, 9 Jan Shift-I*

PRACTICE ELEMENT 02

Target JEE Advanced

Single Correct Choice MCQs

1. The vapour pressure of a substance of low volatility can be measured by passing an unreactive gas over a sample of the substance and analysing the composition of the resulting gas mixture. When nitrogen was passed over mercury at 23°C, the mixture was analysed to 0.6 mg of Hg, 55.4g of nitrogen at a total pressure of 760 torr. The vapour pressure of mercury at this temperature is
(a) 1.15×10^{-3} torr (b) 1.6×10^{-2} torr
(c) 2.11×10^{-2} torr (d) 1.58×10^{-4} torr

2. Ideal mixture of two miscible liquids A and B is placed in a cylinder containing piston. The piston is pulled out isothermally so that volume of liquid decreases but that of vapours increases. When negligibly small amount of liquid was left, the mole fraction of A in vapour phase is 0.4. If $p_A^\circ = 0.4$ atm and $p_B^\circ = 1.2$ atm at the experimental temperature, the total pressure at which the liquid is almost evaporated will be
(a) 0.667 atm (b) 5.012 atm
(c) 3.33 atm (d) 0.316 atm

3. A very small amount of non-volatile solute (that does not dissociate) is dissolved in 56.8 cm^3 of benzene (density 0.623 g cm^{-3}). At room temperature, vapour pressure of this solution is 200 mmHg while that of benzene is 204 mmHg. If the freezing temperature of this solution is 1.53 degree lower than that of benzene, then what is the value of molal freezing point depression constant of benzene?
(a) 4.37 degree/molal (b) 6.81 degree/molal
(c) 2.31 degree/molal (d) 6.07 degree/molal

4. A non-volatile solute 'X' completely dimerises in water if the temperature is below $-3.72°$ C and the solute completely dissociates as $X \longrightarrow Y + Z$ if the temperature is above 100.26°C. In between these two temperatures (including both temperatures), the solute is neither dissociated nor associated. One mole of 'X' is dissolved in 1.0 kg water ($K_b = 0.52$ K. Kg/mol, $K_f = 1.86$ K-Kg/mol). Identify the incorrect information related with the solution.
(a) The freezing point of solution is $-1.86°$ C.
(b) The boiling point of solution is 101.04°C
(c) When the solution is cooled to -7.44°C, 75% of water present initially will separate as ice.
(d) When the solution is heated to 103.08°C, 99% of water present initially will escape out as vapour.

5. The osmotic pressure of a solution of a synthetic polyisobutylene in benzene was determined at 25°C. A sample containing 0.20 g of a solute per 100 cm^3 of solution developed a rise of 2.4 mm at osmotic equilibrium. The density of the solution was 0.88 g/cm^3. What is the molecular weight of the polyisobutylene?
(a) 58.3016×10^2 g mol^{-1} (b) 23.9406×10^4 g mol^{-1}
(c) 37.9041×10^5 g mol^{-1} (d) 46.2019×10^3 g mol^{-1}

6. Relative lowering of vapour pressure of a non-volatile solute X in water is 0.05 and $K_b(H_2O) = 0.52°$ C mol^{-1} kg
Assume ΔT_b = elevation in boiling point assuming a dilute solution.
$\Delta T_b'$ = elevation in boiling point assuming a moderate concentrated solution.
Then $(\Delta T_b - \Delta T_b')$ is
(a) 0.21° (b) 0.08°
(c) $-0.08°$ (d) 0.16°

7. A solution containing 0.1 mol of a non-volatile solute and 0.4 mol of benzene is cooled out, until some benzene is frozen out. The solution is then decanted off from the solid and warmed upto 353 K where its vapour pressure was found to be 680 torrs. The normal freezing point and normal boiling point of benzene are 278.5 K and 353 K respectively and molal depression constant of benzene is equal to 5 K Kg mol^{-1}. The temperature to which the solution was cooled originally is [Assume ideal behaviour]
(a) 275 K (b) 278.28 K
(c) 239.48 K (d) 262.48 K

8. The molar volume of liquid benzene (density = 0.877 g mL^{-1}) increase by a factor of 2750 as it vapourises at 20°C and that of liquid toluene (density 0.867 g mL^{-1}) increases by a factor of 7720 at 20°C. A solution of benzene and toluene at 20°C has a vapour pressure of 46.0 torr. The mole fraction of benzene in the vapour above the solution is ....
(a) 0.34 (b) 0.21 (c) 0.46 (d) 0.73

More than One Correct Choice MCQs

9. The freezing point of 0.02 mole fraction solution of acetic acid in benzene is 298.95 K. Acetic acid exists partly as a dimer. Freezing point of benzene is 300 K and its heat of fusion is 36 cal/g and $R = 2$ cal/deg/mol. Which of the following statements are incorrect regarding the given data?

(a) The molality of the solution is 0.195 m.
(b) The value of molal cryoscopy constant for the given solution is 10 K kg mol^{-1}.
(c) The percentage dimerisation of acid is 39.2%.
(d) The value of molal cryoscopy constant for the given solution is 17.5 K Kg mol^{-1}.

10. A certain vessel *X* has water and nitrogen gas at a total pressure of 2 atm and 300 K. All the contents of vessel are transferred to another vessel *Y* having half the capacity of the vessel *X*. The pressure of N_2 in this vessel was 3.8 atm at 300 K. The vessel *Y* is heated to 320 K and the total pressure observed was 4.32 atm. Assume that the volume occupied by the gases in vessel is equal to the volume of the vessel. Select the correct statements regarding the given data.
(a) Pressure of $H_2O(g)$ in *X* at 320 K is 0.1 atm.
(b) Enthalpy of vapourisation is 39.65 kJ mol^{-1}
(c) Pressure of N_2 at 320 K is 4.05 atm.
(d) Pressure of water vapour at 320 K is 0.32 atm.

11. 2 L of molar solution of a complex salt $CrCl_3 \cdot 6H_2O$ (Mw = 266.5) shows an osmotic pressure of 98.52 atm at 300 K. The solution is now treated with 1 L of 6 M $AgNO_3$, which of the following are correct?
(a) Weight of AgCl precipitated is 761 g.
(b) The clear solution will show an osmotic pressure of 65.68 atm.
(c) 2 mol of $[Cr(H_2O)_6](NO_3)_3$ will be present in the solution.
(d) Weight of AgCl precipitated is 861 g.

12. For a mixture of binary components *A* and *B* with vapour pressures p_A° and p_B° in pure state, total vapour pressure is

$p_{total} = p_A^\circ + (p_B^\circ - p_A^\circ)\chi_B$

Where, χ_B is mole fraction of component *B* in the mixture. From this equation, it is concluded that
(a) total vapour pressure over the solution can be related to the mole fraction of any component
(b) total vapour pressure over the solution varies linearly with the mole fraction of the component *B*
(c) total vapour pressure over the solution may decrease or increase with increase of mole fraction of component *A* depending on vapour pressures of individual components.
(d) $p_{total} = p_B^\circ + (p_A^\circ - p_B^\circ)\chi_A$

13. A mixture of liquids '*A*' and '*B*' in the molar ratio 1 : 2 forms a maximum boiling azeotrope. Identify the correct statement, if '*A*' is more volatile. (Molar masses : *A* = 100, *B* = 50 respectively)
(a) A liquid solution of '*A*' and '*B*' having mass% of *A* = 50 will have vapour having mass % of *A* = 50.
(b) A liquid solution of '*A*' and '*B*' having mass% of *A* > 50 will have vapours having mass% of *A* > 50.
(c) A mixture of '*A*' and '*B*' in the molar ratio 1 : 3 can be separated into azeotropic mixture and pure '*A*'.
(d) A mixture of '*A*' and '*B*' in the molar ratio 2 : 3 can be separated into azeotropic mixture and pure '*A*'.

14. Compartments *A* and *B* have the following combinations of solutions.

	A	B
1.	0.1 M KCl	0.2 M KCl
2.	0.1% (*m/v*) NaCl	10% (*m/v*) NaCl
3.	18 g L^{-1} Glucose	34.2 g L^{-1} Sucrose
4.	20% (*m/v*) Glucose	10% (*m/v*) Glucose

Which of the following statements are correct?
(a) The concentration of 18 g L^{-1} glucose is same to 34.2 g L^{-1} sucrose.
(b) For solution 1 and 2 the concentration in compartment *B* is higher than in *A*.
(c) For solution 3 there will be no change in the level of the solution in the compartments *A* and *B*.
(d) In solution 1, 2 compartment *B* will show an increase in volume.

15. You have been provided with 10.00% by mass solution of ethanol in water.

At 15°C, density = 0.9831 g mL^{-1}

At 25°C, density = 0.9804 g mL^{-1}

Select the correct statement(s).
(a) Molarity at 15°C is larger than that at 25°C.
(b) Molarity at 25°C is larger than that at 15°C.
(c) Molality at both temperature are equal.
(d) Molality at 25°C is larger than that at 15°C.

16. Based on the given diagram, which of the following statements regarding the solutions of two miscible volatile liquids I and II are correct?

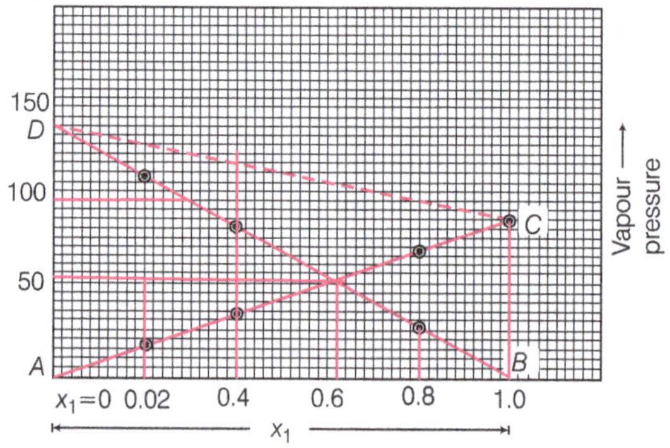

(a) Plots *AC* and *BD* show that Raoult's law is obeyed for the solution in which I is solute and II is solvent and as well as for that in which II is solute and I is solvent.
(b) Plots *CD* shows that Dalton's law of partial pressure is observed for the binary solution of components I and II.
(c) In pure state, vapour pressures of volatile liquid differ by 50 units.
(d) Vapour pressure of a mixture containing 40 mole % of II is about 105 units.

17. Which of the following statement(s) is/are correct?
   (a) Two different solutions of sucrose of same molality prepared in different solvents will have the same depression in freezing point.
   (b) Osmotic pressure of a solution is given by $\pi = CRT$ where C is the molar concentration of the solution.
   (c) Osmotic pressure of 0.01 M aqueous solution of different solutes will be in order $BaCl_2 > KCl > CH_3COOH >$ Sucrose.
   (d) By Raoult's law, the vapour pressure exerted by a volatile component of a solution is directly proportional to its mole fraction.

18. A solution containing 3.5 g of solute X in 50.0 g of water has a volume of 52.5 mL and a freezing point of $-0.86°C$. Thus, (K_f of H_2O = 1.86° C mol^{-1} kg)
   (a) molality of the solution is 0.46 mol kg^{-1}
   (b) molarity of the solution is 0.44 mol L^{-1}
   (c) molar mass of solute X is 152 g mol^{-1}
   (d) mole fraction of solute X is 0.0082

Integer/Numerical Type Questions

19. Total volume of a mixture of 46 g ethanol (C_2H_5OH) and 72 g water (H_2O) based on the given figure is .... cm^3

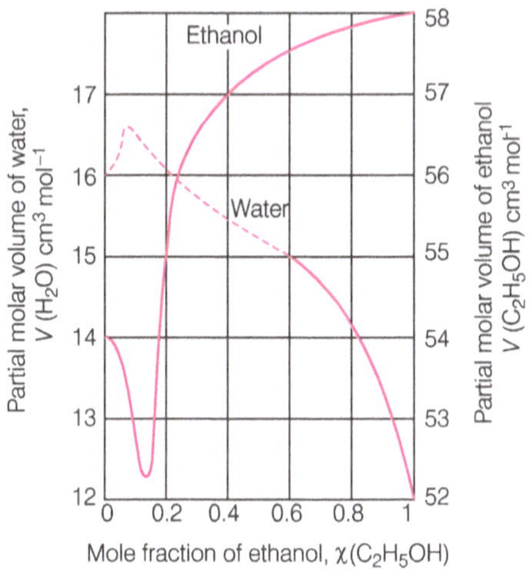

20. When cells of the skeletal vacuole of a frog were placed in a series of NaCl solution of different concentrations at 10°C, it was observd microscopically that they remained unchanged in x% NaCl solution, it shrink in more concentrated solutions and swells in more dilute solutions. Water freezes from the x% salt solution at $-0.40°$ C. If the osmotic pressure of the cell cytoplasm at 10°C is $Z \times 0.0821$ atm.

    The value of Z is ....

    [Given : The value of K_f = 1.86 K Kg mol^{-1}]

21. Two liquids X and Y form are ideal solution. At 300 K, vapour pressure of the solution containing 1 mole of X and 3 mole of Y is 570 mmHg. At the same temperature if 1 mole of Y is further added to this solution, vapour pressure of the solution increases by 10 mmHg. The ratio of vapour pressure (in mmHg) of X and Y in their pure states will be .... $\times 10^{-2}$.

22. 0.0700 g sample of an ionic compound with the formula $Cr(NH_3)_5Cl_3$ was dissolved in water to give 125.0 mL of solution at 25°C. The osmotic pressure was 119 mmHg. How many ions are obtained from each formula unit when the compound is dissolved in water?

    Molar mass of $Cr(NH_3)_5Cl_3$ = 243 .5 g mol^{-1}

23. Mole fraction of a non-electrolyte (A) in aqueous solution is 0.07. One molal sucrose solution freezes at $-1.86°$ C. Thus, depression in freezing point of solution of solute (A) is

24. Vessel-1 contains w_2 g of a non-volatile solute X dissolved in w_1 g of water. Vessel-2 contains w_2 g of another non-volatile solute Y dissolved in w_1 g of water. Both the vessels are at the same temperature and pressure. The molar mass of X is 60% of that of Y. The van't Hoff factor for X is 3 times of that of Y for their respective concentrations.

    The elevation of boiling point for solution in Vessel-1 is .... % of the solution in Vessel-2.

25. To 500 cm^3 of water 3.0×10^{-3}kg of acetic acid is added. If 23% of acetic acid is dissociated then the depression in freezing point will be ...... K_f and density of water are 1.86 K kg mol^{-1} and 0.997 g cm^{-3} respectively.

26. For a dilute solution containing 3.7 g of a non-volatile, non-electrolyte solute in 210 g of water, the elevation in boiling point at 1 atm pressure is 4°C. Assume concentration of solute is much lower than the concentration of solvent. The vapour pressure (mm of Hg) of the solution is ...... taken K_b = 0.76 K kg mol^{-1}.

Matching Type Questions

27. The major components of air are O_2 and N_2 with approximate proportion of 21% and 79% by volume at 298 K. The water is in equilibrium with air at a pressure of 10 atm. At 298 K, $K_H(N_2) = 6.51 \times 10^7$mm, $K_H(O_2) = 3.30 \times 10^7$mm.

    Match the parameters in Column I with their values in Column II and select the answer from the codes given below.

Column I		Column II	
(i)	Mole fraction of N_2	(p)	4.84×10^{-5}
(ii)	Mole fraction of O_2	(q)	2.69×10^{-3}
(iii)	Moles of N_2 in 1 kg H_2O	(r)	9.22×10^{-5}
(iv)	Moles of O_2 in 1 kg H_2O	(s)	5.12×10^{-3}

Codes

	(i)	(ii)	(iii)	(iv)
(a)	p	q	s	r
(b)	p	r	s	q
(c)	r	p	q	s
(d)	r	p	s	q

28.

Volatile component	Vapour pressure at 350 K	Molar mass
A	24 kPa	60 g mol^{-1}
B	12 kPa	40 g mol^{-1}

100 g of binary mixture of A and B contains 60% of A. Mixture is subjected to the following operation.

Original mixture I $\xrightarrow{\text{Distil}}$ II containing vapours of A and B

$\xrightarrow{\text{Condense}}$ III (liquid) $\xrightarrow{\text{Distil}}$ IV containing vapours of A and B

Match the content of Column I with their values in Column II and select the answer from the codes given below.

Column I (Mole fraction of A)	Column II
(i) Mixture I	(p) 0.25
(ii) Mixture II	(q) 0.50
(iii) Mixture III	(r) 0.67
(iv) Mixture IV	(s) 0.80

Codes

	(i)	(ii)	(iii)	(iv)
(a)	p	q	q	s
(b)	p	r	s	q
(c)	q	r	r	s
(d)	s	q	p	p

29. Match the different solutions in Column I with their ΔT_b (in terms of K_b) in Column II and select the answer from the codes given below.

Column I	Column II
(i) 1 molal urea solution	(p) K_b
(ii) 1 molal KCl solution with 100% ionisation	(q) 15 K_b
(iii) 1 molal K_2SO_4 solution with 75% ionisation	(r) 2.0 K_b
(iv) 1 molal $K_4[Fe(CN)_6]$ solution with 50% ionisation	(s) 2.5 K_b
(v) 1 molal iron (III) sulphate (VI) solution with 25% ionisation	(t) 3.0 K_b

Codes

	(i)	(ii)	(iii)	(iv)	(v)
(a)	p	r	s	t	r
(b)	p	q	s	t	r
(c)	p	r	t	s	q
(d)	r	s	t	p	q

30. Given, K_f of $H_2O = 1.86°$ C mol^{-1} kg.

Match the solution given in Column I with their depression in freezing points given in Column II and select the answer from the codes given below.

Column I	Column II
(i) 6.0% urea solution	(p) 3.72°C
(ii) 9.6% methanol solution	(q) 1.86°C
(iii) 17.1% sucrose solution	(r) 5.58°C
(iv) 36.0% glucose solution	(s) 0.93°C

Codes

	(i)	(ii)	(iii)	(iv)
(a)	p	q	s	r
(b)	p	r	s	q
(c)	q	r	p	s
(d)	q	r	s	p

31. 17.1 g sucrose ($C_{12}H_{22}O_{11}$) is dissolved in 1000 g of water.

$p°(H_2O) = 26.50$ mm

$K_f(H_2O) = 1.86$ mol^{-1} kg

$K_b(H_2O) = 0.52°C$ mol^{-1} kg.

Match the colligative properties in Column I with their values in Column II and select the answer from the codes given below.

Column I	Column II
(i) Δp (in mm)	(p) 1.2315
(ii) ΔT_f (in K)	(q) 0.026
(iii) ΔT_b (in K)	(r) 0.093
(iv) π (in atm) at 300 K	(s) 0.024

Codes

	(i)	(ii)	(iii)	(iv)
(a)	p	q	r	s
(b)	r	s	p	q
(c)	p	r	s	q
(d)	s	r	q	p

Paragraph of Two Questions Each

Paragraph 1

Depression in freezing point in a given solvent is dependent on nature of solute.

$$\Delta T_f = i\,K_f m$$

where i = van't Hoff factor

K_f = molal depression constant

m = molality

For 1 molal solution of different solutes of the type *AB*, it is represented graphically.

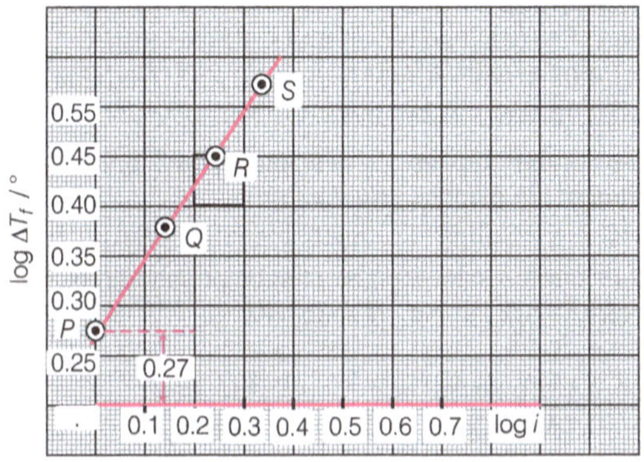

32. The value of K_f for the given solvent is .... K mol^{-1} kg.

33. The degree of ionisation at the point *R* is ....

Paragraph 2

Vapour pressure of C_6H_6 and C_7H_8 mixture at 50°C are given by $p = 180\ X_B + 90$ in mm, where X_B is mole fraction of C_6H_6. 936 gm of benzene and 736 gm of toluene are mixed. The vapours are formed. The vapours are removed and condensed into liquid and again brought to the temperature of 50°C.

34. The mole fraction of benzene in vapour phase of first liquid ....

35. Mole fraction of benzene in vapour phase of condensed liquid is ....

Paragraph 3

Properties such as boiling point, freezing point and vapour pressure of a pure solvent change when solute molecules are added to get homogeneous solution. These are called colligative properties. Applications of colligative properties are very useful in day-to-day life.

One of its examples is the use of ethylene glycol and water mixture as anti-freezing liquid in the radiator of automobiles.

A solution *M* is prepared by mixing ethanol and water. The mole fraction of ethanol in the mixture is 0.9.

Given, freezing point depression constant of water

$$(K_{f,\ water}) = 1.86\ K\ kg\ mol^{-1}$$

Freezing point depression constant of ethanol

$$(K_{f,\ ethanol}) = 2.0\ K\ kg\ mol^{-1}$$

Boiling point elevation constant of water

$$(K_{b,\ water}) = 0.52\ K\ kg\ mol^{-1}$$

Boiling point elevation constant of ethanol

$$(K_{b,\ ethanol}) = 1.2\ K\ kg\ mol^{-1}$$

Standard freezing point of water = 273 K

Standard freezing point of ethanol = 155.7 K

Standard boiling point of water = 373 K

Standard boiling point of ethanol = 351.5 K

Vapour pressure of pure water = 32.8 mm Hg

Vapour pressure of pure ethanol = 40 mm Hg

Molecular mass of water = 18 g mol^{-1}

Molecular mass of ethanol = 46 g mol^{-1}

In answering the following questions, consider the solutions to be ideal dilute solutions and solutes to be non-volatile and non-dissociative.

36. The freezing point of the solution '*M*' is .... K.

37. Water is added to the solution *M* such that the mole fraction of water in the solution becomes 0.9. The boiling point of this solution is .... K.

Species Selection (with 5 Species)

38. Among the following terms,
    (i) Molality (ii) Mole fraction
    (iii) Mass percentage (iv) Molarity
    (v) Parts per million
    the terms which do not change with temperature is/are
    (a) 2 (b) 3
    (c) 1 (d) 4

39. Consider the following pairs of solution which will be isotonic at the same temperature.
    (i) 1.4 M *aq.* H_2SO_4 and 0.5 M *aq.* C_2H_5OH
    (ii) 1 M *aq.* NaCl and 2 M *aq.* Urea
    (iii) 1 M *aq.* $CaCl_2$ and 1.5 M *aq.* KCl
    (iv) 1.5 M *aq.* $AlCl_3$ and 2 M *aq.* Na_2SO_4
    (v) 2.5 M *aq.* KCl and 1 M *aq.* $Al_2(SO_4)_3$
    The number of pairs of solution is/are ....
    (a) 4 (b) 3
    (c) 2 (d) 1

40. Among the following units,
    (i) Mole (ii) Mole-fraction
    (iii) Molarity (iv) PPM
    (v) Mass percent
    Which are used to express concentration of solutions?
    (a) 1 (b) 2
    (c) 4 (d) 3

Species Selection (with 7 Species)

41. Consider the following mixtures,
    (i) water + hydrochloric acid
    (ii) benzene + methanol
    (iii) water + nitric acid
    (iv) acetone + chloroform
    (v) Carbon disulphide + propanone
    (vi) Chloroform + benzene
    (vii) acetone + aniline
    The total number of mixtures that show positive deviation from Raoult's law are
    (a) 2 (b) 5
    (c) 4 (d) 3

42. Of the following aqueous solutions, total number of these solutions whose freezing point is lower than that of 0.10 M aqueous solution of C_2H_5OH is/are ....

(Assume, Molarity = molality)

(i) 0.10 M $Ba_3(PO_4)_2$
(ii) 0.10 M K_2HgI_4
(iii) 0.10 M Li_3PO_4
(iv) 0.10 M $NaAlO_2$
(v) 0.10 M Na_2SO_4
(vi) 0.10 M $FeSO_4(NH_4)_2SO_4$
(vii) 0.10 M KCl

(a) 4 (b) 7 (c) 5 (d) 6

43. Out of the following pairs of volatile solvents how many form azeotropic mixture?

(i) $CCl_4 + CHCl_3$ (ii) $C_6H_{14} + C_7H_{16}$
(iii) *o*-nitrophenol + $C_6H_5CH_3$ (iv) $C_6H_5Cl + C_6H_5Br$
(v) $HNO_3 + CHCl_3$ (vi) $CH_3Br + CH_3Cl$
(vii) $CH_3CH_2OH + C_6H_{12}$

(a) 5 (b) 4 (c) 6 (d) 3

44. Consider the following pairs of solution,

(i) 0.02 M $KCl \cdot MgCl_2 \cdot 6H_2O$ (*aq*) and 0.05 M KCl (aq)
(ii) 0.500 M C_2H_5OH (*aq*) and 0.25 M KBr (*aq*)
(iii) 0.250 M KBr(*aq*) and 0.125 M Na_3PO_4(*aq*)
(iv) 0.100 M $K_4[Fe(CN)_6]$ (*aq*) and 0.100 M $FeSO_4(NH_4)_2SO_4$(*aq*)
(v) 0.500 M C_2H_5OH (*aq*) and 0.100 M $Mg_3(PO_4)_2$(*aq*)
(vi) 0.05 M $K_4[Fe(CN)_6]$ (*aq*) and 0.25 M NaCl (*aq*)
(vii) 0.15 M NaCl (*aq*) and 0.1 M $BaCl_2$(*aq*)

The number of pairs of the solutions having the same value of the osmotic pressure are

(a) 3 (b) 4 (c) 5 (d) 6

45. Consider the following pair of substances with osmotic pressure of π_1 and π_2 respectively.

	π_1	π_2
(i)	0.1 M glucose	0.1 M urea
(ii)	0.1 M NaCl	0.1 M Na_2SO_4
(iii)	0.1 M NaCl	0.1 M KCl
(iv)	0.1 M $CuSO_4$	0.1 M Sucrose
(v)	0.1 M glucose	0.1 M NaCl
(vi)	0.1 M glucose	0.1 M Sucrose
(vii)	0.1 M $Al_2(SO_4)_3$	0.1 M $MgCl_2$

The number of pairs in which π_2 is hypertonic to π_1 are

(a) 2 (b) 3
(c) 4 (d) 5

Check Through PYQs

Element 1 Types and Concentrations of Solution

1. The mole fraction of urea in an aqueous urea solution containing 900 g of water is 0.05. If the density of the solution is 1.2 g cm^{-3}, then molarity of urea solution is ...... (Given data : Molar masses of urea and water are 60 g mol^{-1} and 18 g mol^{-1}, respectively) *2019 Adv.*

Element 2 Solubility, Vapour Pressure and Raoult's Law

2. Liquids *A* and *B* form ideal solution for all compositions of *A* and *B* at 25°C. Two such solutions with 0.25 and 0.50 mole fractions of *A* have the total vapour pressure of 0.3 and 0.4 bar, respectively. What is the vapour pressure of pure liquid *B* in bar? *2020 Adv.*

3. Liquids *A* and *B* form ideal solution over the entire range of composition. At temperature *T*, equimolar binary solution of liquids *A* and *B* has vapour pressure 45 torr. At the same temperature, a new solution of *A* and *B* having mole fractions x_A and x_B, respectively, has vapour pressure of 22.5 torr. The value of x_A / x_B in the new solution is ____.
(Given that the vapour pressure of pure liquid *A* is 20 torr at temperature *T*) *2018 Adv.*

4. For a solution formed by mixing liquids *L* and *M*, the vapour pressure of *L* plotted against the mole fraction of *M* in solution is shown in the following figure. Here x_L and x_M represent mole fractions of *L* and *M*, respectively, in the solution. The correct statement(s) applicable to this system is (are) *2017 Adv.*

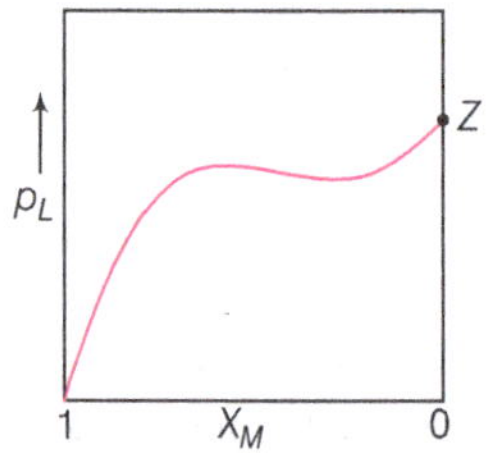

(a) The point *Z* represents vapour pressure of pure liquid *M* and Raoult's law is obeyed from $x_L = 0$ to $x_L = 1$
(b) Attractive intermolecular interactions between *L* - *L* in pure liquid *L* and *M* - *M* in pure liquid *M* are stronger than those between *L* - *M* when mixed in solution
(c) The point *Z* represents vapour pressure of pure liquid *M* and Raoult's law is obeyed when $x_L \to 0$
(d) The point *Z* represents vapour pressure of pure liquid *L* and Raoult's law is obeyed when $x_L \to 1$

5. Mixture(s) showing positive deviation from Raoult's law at 35°C is (are) *2016 Adv.*

(a) carbon tetrachloride + methanol
(b) carbon disulphide + acetone
(c) benzene + toluene
(d) phenol + aniline

Element 3 Colligative Properties, Abnormal Molecular Mass and van't Hoff Factor

6. Vessel-1 contains w_2 g of a non-volatile solute X dissolved in w_1 g of water. Vessel-2 contains w_2 g of another non-volatile solute Y dissolved in w_1 g of water. Both the vessels are at the same temperature and pressure. The molar mass of X is 80% of that of Y. The van't Hoff factor for X is 1.2 times of that of Y for their respective concentrations.

   The elevation of boiling point for solution in Vessel-1 is .... % of the solution in Vessel-2. *2024 Adv.*

7. 50 mL of 0.2 molal urea solution (density = 1.012 g mL^{-1} at 300 K) is mixed with 250 mL of a solution containing 0.06 g of urea. Both the solutions were prepared in the same solvent. The osmotic pressure (in torr) of the resulting solution at 300 K is ....

   [Use : Molar mass of urea = 60 g mol^{-1}; gas constant, $R = 62$ L torr K^{-1} mol^{-1}; Assume, $\Delta_{mix}H = 0, \Delta_{mix}V = 0$]

   2023 Adv.

8. An aqueous solution is prepared by dissolving 0.1 mol of an ionic salt in 1.8 kg of water at 35°C. The salt remains 90% dissociated in the solution. The vapour pressure of the solution is 59.724 mm of Hg. Vapour pressure of water at 35°C is 60.000 mm of Hg. The number of ions present per formula unit of the ionic salt is .... *2022 Adv.*

Passage Based Questions (Q. Nos. 9 & 10)

The boiling point of water in a 0.1 molal silver nitrate solution (solution A) is x°C. To this solution A, an equal volume of 0.1 molal aqueous barium chloride solution is added to make a new solution B. The difference in the boiling points of water in the two solutions A and B is $y \times 10^{-2}$ °C.

(Assume: Densities of the solutions A and B are the same as that of water and the soluble salts dissociate completely).

Use : Molal elevation constant (Ebullioscopic constant), $K_b = 0.5$ K kg mol^{-1}; (Boiling point of pure water as 100°C.)

2021 Adv.

9. The value of x is ....

10. The value of y is ....

11. On dissolving 0.5 g of a non-volatile non-ionic solute to 39 g of benzene, its vapour pressure decreases from 650 mmHg to 640 mmHg. The depression of freezing point of benzene (in K) upon addition of the solute is ....

    (Given data : Molar mass and the molal freezing point depression constant of benzene are 78 g mol^{-1} and 5.12 K kg mol^{-1}, respectively). *2019 Adv.*

12. Pure water freezes at 273 K and 1 bar. The addition of 34.5 g of ethanol to 500 g of water changes the freezing point of the solution. Use the freezing point depression constant of water as 2 K kg mol^{-1}. The figures shown below represent plots of vapour pressure (V.P.) *versus* temperature (T). [Molecular weight of ethanol is 46 g mol^{-1}] *2017 Adv.*

    Among the following, the option representing change in the freezing point is

(a)
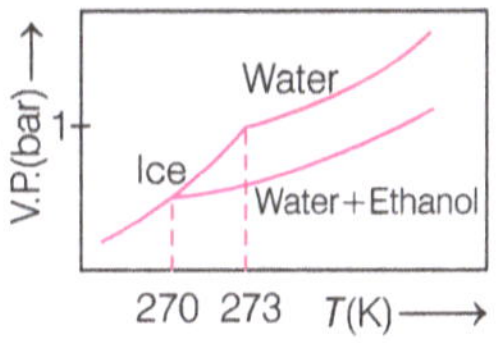

(b)
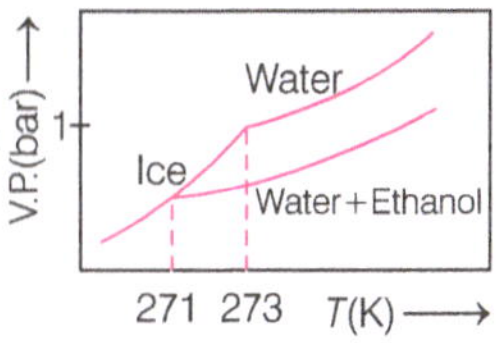

(c)
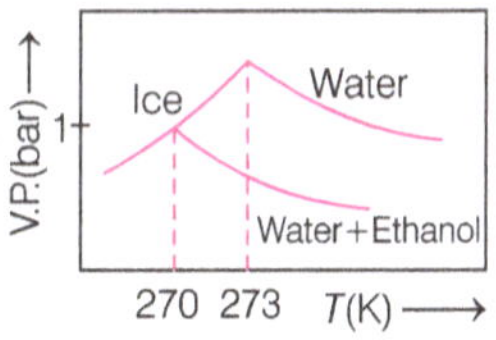

(d)
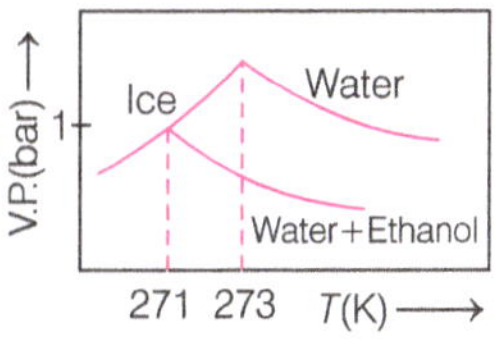

13. If the freezing point of a 0.01 molal aqueous solution of a cobalt (III) chloride-ammonia complex (which behaves as a strong electrolyte) is – 0.0558°C, the number of chloride(s) in the coordination sphere of the complex is [K_f of water = 1.86 K kg mol^{-1}] *2015 Adv.*

HINTS & Solutions

Solutions : Competency Enhancer

1.1. ***(19.66)*** Given, mole fraction of acetic acid $(\chi_{A.A}) = 0.34$

Mass of water = 927 g

Density = 1.86 g/cm^3

$$\chi_{\text{acetic acid}} = \frac{n_{\text{acetic acid}}}{n_{\text{acetic acid}} + 52}$$

$$\left[\text{Moles of water } = \frac{927\text{g}}{18 \text{ g/mol}} = 51.5 \approx 52 \text{ mol}\right]$$

$$0.34 = \frac{n_{\text{acetic acid}}}{n_{\text{acetic acid}} + 52}$$

$$n_{\text{acetic acid}} \approx 26.79$$

$$w_{\text{acetic acid}} = n_{\text{acetic acid}} \times (\text{M.w})_{\text{acetic acid}}$$

$$= (26.79 \times 60) \text{ g}$$

$$V = \frac{(26.79 \times 60) + 927}{1.86} = 1362.58 \text{ mL}$$

Now, $\quad \text{molarity} = \frac{\text{No. of moles of solute}}{\text{Volume of solution (mL)}} \times 1000$

$$= \frac{26.79 \times 1000}{1362.58} = 19.66$$

1.2. ***(32)*** $m_{\text{soln}} = V_{\text{soln}} \times d_{\text{soln}}$

$$= 550 \times 1.25 = 687.4 \text{ g}$$

Mass of solute $(x) = 0.4 \times 0.55 \times 159.5 = 35.09$

$$n_{\text{solute}} = \frac{35.09}{159.5 \text{ g/mol}} = 0.22$$

Mass of solvent = Mass of solution − Mass of solute

$$= 687.5 - 0.22 = 687.28 \text{ g}$$

By using the formula of molality,

$$\text{Molality} = \frac{\text{No. of moles of solute} \times 1000}{\text{Mass of solvent (in g)}}$$

$$= \frac{0.22 \times 1000}{687.28} = 0.320 \text{ m}$$

$$= 32 \times 10^{-2} \text{ m}$$

2.1. ***(333.3)*** Given,

Mole fraction of $A_1 = 0.6$

Mole fraction of $B_1 = 0.4$

Total pressure, $p_1 = 360$ mmHg

Let vapour pressure of pure A be p_A° and B be p_B°

When mole fraction of $A_1 = \chi_{A_1} = 0.6$ and

mole fraction of $B_1 = \chi_{B_1} = 0.4$ and total pressure $p_1 = 360$

$$\Rightarrow \quad 360 = p_A^\circ \times 0.6 + p_B^\circ \times 0.4 \quad \text{...(i)}$$

Similarly for $A_2 = \chi_{A_2} = 0.3$, $B_2 = \chi_{B_2} = 0.7$ and $p_2 = 400$

$$\Rightarrow \quad 400 = p_A^\circ \times 0.3 + p_B^\circ \times 0.7 \quad \text{...(ii)}$$

Multiply Eq. (i) by 0.3 and Eq. (ii) by 0.6, we get,

$$108 = 0.18 p_A^\circ + 0.12 p_B^\circ \quad \text{...(iii)}$$

$$240 = 0.18 p_A^\circ + 0.42 p_B^\circ \quad \text{...(iv)}$$

$$- \quad - \quad -$$

$$-132 = -0.30 \, p_B^\circ$$

$$p_B^\circ = 440 \text{ mmHg}$$

Now, put the value of p_B° in Eq. (i)

$$0.6 \, p_A^\circ + 0.4 \times 400 = 360$$

$$0.6 \, p_A^\circ = 360 - 160$$

$$p_A^\circ = 333.3 \text{ mmHg}$$

Therefore, the vapour pressure of pure A is 333.3 mmHg.

3.1. ***(676)*** Given that,

$\Delta T_b = 3.2$, $K_b = 0.52$, $p^\circ = 760$ mmHg, $M_{\text{solvent}} = 18$

Now using, $\quad \Delta T_b = K_b . m$

$$3.2 = 0.52 \times m,$$

$$m = \frac{3.2}{0.52}$$

Now, according to question, since the solution is very diluted.

Hence,

$$\frac{\Delta p}{p^\circ} = \frac{n_{\text{solute}}}{n_{\text{solvent}}} \Rightarrow \frac{\Delta p}{p^\circ} = \frac{m}{1000} \times M_{\text{solvent}}$$

$$\Delta p = 760 \times \frac{\left(\frac{3.2}{0.52}\right)}{1000} \times 18 = 84.19$$

So, $\quad p_S = 760 - 84.19 = 675.81$ mmHg

Hence, nearest integer is 676 mmHg.

3.2. ***(3288.7)*** 0.2 molal means 0.2 moles in 1000 g of solvent.

∴ Number of moles of urea = 0.2 mol

Weight of urea = 0.2 × 60 = 12 g

Weight of solvent = 1000 g

Weight of solution = 1000 + 12 = 1012 g

So, Volume = Mass / density $= \frac{1012}{3.102} = 326.24$ mL

326.24 mL solution contains 0.2 moles

∴ 70 mL solution contains $= \frac{0.2}{326.24} \times 70$ moles ≈ 0.04 mol

$$\therefore \quad n_1 = 0.04 \text{ mol}$$

So, number of moles of urea in another solution

$$(n_2) = \frac{0.06}{60} = 0.001$$

$$\text{Final molarity } (M) = \frac{n_1 + n_2}{V_1 + V_2} = \frac{0.04 + 0.001}{\frac{70 + 330}{1000}}$$

$$M = \frac{0.041}{0.4}$$

$$\text{Now, osmotic pressure } (\pi) = CRT = \frac{0.041}{0.4} \times 71.3 \times 450$$

$$= 3288.7 \text{ torr}$$

3.3. ***(287.2)*** In Container 1

$$(\Delta T_b)_1 = i_1 K_b \times \frac{\left(\frac{w_2}{M_x}\right)}{\left(\frac{W_1}{1000}\right)}$$

In Container 2

$$(\Delta T_b)_2 = i_2 K_b \times \frac{\left(\frac{w_2}{M_y}\right)}{\left(\frac{W_1}{1000}\right)}$$

$$\frac{(\Delta T_b)_1}{(\Delta T_b)_2} = \frac{i_1 \times M_y}{i_2 \times M_x} = 1.6 \times \frac{1}{0.557} = 2.872$$

$$\Rightarrow \quad (\Delta T_b)_1 = 2.872\, (\Delta T_b)_2$$

$$\frac{(\Delta T_b)_1}{(\Delta T_b)_2} \times 100 = 287.2\%$$

Elemental Practice 7.1

1. ***(b)*** KI solution is 20% mass by mass.

Thus, 100 g KI solution has KI = 20 g

solvent = 80 g = 0.080 kg

$$\text{Thus, volume of solution} = \frac{\text{Mass}}{\text{Density}}$$

$$= \frac{100 \text{ g}}{1.202 \text{ g mL}^{-1}} = \frac{100}{1.202} \text{ mL}$$

$$= \frac{1}{12.020} \text{ L}$$

$$\text{KI (solute)} = \frac{20 \text{ g}}{166 \text{ g mol}^{-1}} = \frac{20}{166} \text{ mol}$$

$$\text{(a) Molality} = \frac{\text{Moles of solute}}{\text{Mass of solvent(kg)}}$$

$$= \frac{20/166 \text{ mol}}{0.080 \text{ kg}} = 1.506 \text{ molal}$$

$$\text{(b) Molarity} = \frac{\text{Moles (solute)}}{\text{Volume (solution in L)}}$$

$$= \frac{20/166}{1/12.020} = 1.448 \text{ M}$$

$$\text{(c) Moles of solute} = \frac{20}{166} \text{ moles KI}$$

$$\text{Moles of water} = \frac{80}{18} \text{ moles } H_2O$$

$$\text{Total moles} = \left(\frac{20}{166} + \frac{80}{18}\right)$$

$$X_{KI} = \frac{20/166}{\left(\frac{20}{166} + \frac{80}{18}\right)} = 0.0264$$

2. ***(b)*** 3.06 M means 3.06 mol of acetic acid in one litre.

weight of solute = 3.06 × 60 = 183.6 g

Molecular weight of acetic acid = 60 g mol^{-1}

Weight of solution = 1.02 × 1000 = 1020 g

∴ Weight of solvent = 1020 − 183.6 = 836.4 g

$$\text{Molality} = \frac{3.06 \times 1000}{836.4} = 3.658 \approx 3.66 \text{ mol kg}^{-1}$$

3. ***(d)*** Statement I is incorrect but Statement II is correct. Their correct explanation is given as:

(I) 90% by mass means 100 g of acid contains 90g H_2SO_4.

$$\text{Volume of acid} = \frac{100}{1.834} \text{ mL}$$

$$\text{Molarity} = \frac{90}{98} \times \frac{1.834}{100} \times 1000 = 16.84 \text{ M}$$

$$\text{(II) Molarity of given sulphuric acid} = \frac{98}{98} \times \frac{1.84}{100} \times 1000$$

$$= 18.4 \text{ mol dm}^{-3}$$

By using, $M_1V_1 = M_2V_2$

$$V_1 = \frac{0.5 \times 5}{18.4} = 0.136 \text{ dm}^3 \approx 136 \text{ mL}$$

4. ***(d)*** The level of $CHCl_3$ is 15 ppm,

Thus 10^6g of H_2O has $CHCl_3$ = 15 g

$$\text{and 100 g of } H_2O \text{ has } CHCl_3 = \frac{15}{10^6} \times 100 = 15 \times 10^{-4}\ \%$$

Thus mass% = 15×10^{-4} %

$$\text{Moles of } CHCl_3 = \frac{15}{119.5} = 0.1255$$

Water = 10^6g = 10^3kg

$$\therefore \quad \text{Molality} = \frac{0.1255 \text{ mole}}{10^3 \text{ kg}} = 1.255 \times 10^{-4} \text{ mole kg}^{-1}$$

5. ***(c)*** $[NO_3^-]$ without adding $H_2O = \left(\frac{M_1V_1 + M_2V_2}{V_1 + V_2}\right)$

$$= \frac{0.2 \times 275 + 0.8 \times 325}{600} = 0.525 \text{ M}$$

600 mL of 0.525 M is further diluted to 1000 mL by adding 400 mL H_2O. i.e.,

$$600 \times 0.525 \text{ M} = 1000 \times M'$$

$$\therefore \quad M' = 0.315 \text{ M.}$$

6. ***(d)*** Molarity of Na_2CO_3 solution $= \frac{2.65}{106} \times \frac{1000}{250} = 0.1$ M

By using,

$$M_1V_1 = M_2V_2$$

$$0.1 \times 10 = M_2 \times 1000$$

$$M_2 = 0.001 \text{ M}$$

7. ***(a)*** Mole % of $C_3H_8O_3 = 4.85$

$\therefore \quad X_{C_3H_8O_3} = 0.0485$

$X_{H_2O} = 0.9515$

$\therefore \quad \frac{n_{C_3H_8O_3}}{n_{total}} = 0.0485$

$\frac{n_{H_2O}}{n_{total}} = 0.9515$

$\therefore \quad \frac{n_{C_3H_8O_3}}{n_{H_2O}} = \frac{0.0485}{0.9515}$

$\frac{w\,(C_3H_8O_3)}{92} / \frac{1000}{18} = \frac{0.0485}{0.9515}$

$\because \quad w\,(C_3H_8O_3) = 260.52\ g$

$\therefore \quad \text{Volume} = \frac{w}{d} = \frac{260.52\ g}{1.26\ g\ mL^{-1}} \approx 207\ mL$

8. ***(b)*** By Henry's law, $p_{H_2S} = X_{H_2S}\,K_H(H_2S)$

$\therefore \quad X_{H_2S} = \frac{p_{H_2S}}{K_H} = \frac{760\ torr}{4.12 \times 10^5 torr} = 1.845 \times 10^{-3}$

$n_{H_2O} = \frac{1000}{18} = 55.55$

$n_{total} = n_{H_2S} + n_{H_2O} \approx n_{H_2O}$

$\therefore \quad = 55.55$

$X_{H_2S} = \frac{n_{H_2S}}{n_{total}}$

$n_{H_2S} = X_{H_2S} \cdot n_{total}$

$= 1.845 \times 10^{-3} \times 55.55$

$= 0.1024$ mol in 1L H_2O

$\therefore \quad [H_2S] = 0.1024\ mol\ L^{-1}$

9. ***(c)*** Among the following only molarity is dependent on temperature because it involves volume, which can expand or contract with temperature change. Molality, mole fraction and weight fraction are independent of temperature because they rely on mass or ratios of moles, which are not affected by temperature changes.

10. ***(a)*** NH_3 solution is = 14.8 M

Thus, $\quad 1L = 1000mL = 898$ g NH_3 solution

NH_3 present = 14.8 mol

$= 14.8 \times 17\ g = 251.6\ g$

H_2O present $= 898 - 251.6 = 646.4\ g$

$= \frac{646.4}{18} = 35.91$ mol

Total moles of H_2O and $NH_3 = 35.91 + 14.8 = 50.71$

$\therefore \quad X_{NH_3} = \frac{n(NH_3)}{n(\text{total})} = \frac{14.80}{50.71} = 0.292.$

11. ***(d)*** NaOH = $25 \times 1 = 25$ millimol

HCl $= 10 \times 0.5 = 5$ millimol

Thus, $\quad$ NaOH > HCl

$\therefore \quad [NaOH]_{mix} = \frac{M_1V_1\,(NaOH) - M_2\,V_2\,(HCl)}{V_1 + V_2}$

$= \frac{25-5}{25+10} = \frac{4}{7} = 0.57\ M$

Thus, H^+ is completely neutralised

$\therefore \quad [H^+] = 0.0\ M$

$[Cl^-] = 0.14$

$[OH^-] = 0.57\ M$

$[Na^+] = 0.14 + 0.57 = 0.714\ M$

12. ***(d)*** (i) 30g $Co(NO_3)_2 \cdot 6H_2O$ in 4.3 L solution,

Atomic number of Co = 27

Given, atomic mass of Co = 59

Molar mass of $Co(NO_3)_2 \cdot 6H_2O = 291\ g\ mol^{-1}$

$\therefore$ Molarity $= \frac{30}{291 \times 4.3L} = 0.0239 \approx 0.02\ M$

(ii) 30 mL of 0.5 M H_2SO_4 diluted to 500 mL for the case of dilution,

$M_1V_1 = M_2V_2$

$0.5 \times 30 = M_2 \times 500$

$M_2 = \frac{0.5 \times 30}{500} = 0.03\ M$

13. ***(b)*** $m_{sol} = V_{sol} \times d_{sol} = 600 \times 1.32 = 792\ g$

Mass of solute $(x) = 0.5 \times 0.6 \times 60.06 = 18\ g$

$n_{solute} = \frac{18g}{60\ g/mol} = 0.3$

Mass of solvent = Mass of solution − Mass of solute

$= 792g - 18g = 774\ g$

Now, by using the formula of molality,

$\text{Molality} = \frac{\text{No. of moles of solute}}{\text{Mass of solvent (in kg)}} \times 1000$

$= \frac{0.3 \times 1000}{774} = 0.3876\ m$

$= 387.6 \times 10^{-3} m \approx 388 \times 10^{-3} m$

14. ***(c)*** Given, mole fraction of sulphuric acid $(\chi_{S.A.}) = 0.02$

Mass of water = 738 g

Density = $1.84\ g/cm^3$

$\chi_{\text{Sulphuric acid}} = \frac{n_{\text{Sulphuric acid}}}{n_{\text{Sulphuric acid}} + 41}$

$\left[\text{Moles of water} = \frac{738}{18} = 41\ mol\right]$

$0.02 = \frac{(n_{S.A.})}{n_{S.A.} + 41}$

$n_{S.A.} = 83.67 \times 10^{-2}$ mol

$w_{S.A.} = n_{S.A.} \times (m.wt)_{S.A.}$

$= 83.67 \times 10^{-2}\ mol \times 98\ g/mol$

$V = \frac{(83.67 \times 10^{-2}\ mol \times 98) + 738}{1.84}$

$= 445.64\ mL$

Now,

$$\text{Molarity} = \frac{\text{No. of moles of solute}}{\text{Volume of solution (mL)}} \times 1000$$

$$= \frac{83.67 \times 10^{-2} \times 1000}{445.67} = 1.87$$

15. ***(d)*** 20 mL of 0.2 N HCl + 40 mL of 0.1 N HCl

$\equiv$ 40 mL of NaOH $\equiv$ 0.61 g of organic base

Or m Eq. of HCl $\equiv$ m Eq. of NaOH $\equiv$ *m* Eq. of organic base

$$20 \times 0.2 + 40 \times 0.1 = \frac{0.61}{E} \times 1000$$

$$E = \frac{0.61 \times 1000}{8} = 76.25$$

16. ***(a, b, c, d)*** Among the given statements, all are correct. Their explanation are given as:

(a) $d = \dfrac{M(1000 + m \cdot M_w)}{1000\,m}$

$$= \frac{1(1000 + 1 \times 180)}{1 \times 1000} = 1.180 \text{ g . mL}^{-1}$$

where M is molarity, m is molality and M_w is the molar mass of solute.

(b) 100 g of aqueous solution has 6 g CH_3OH

Aqueous 6% methanol solution by mass means

$$\because \quad V = \frac{m}{d} = \frac{100}{0.988} = 101.2 \text{ mL}$$

$$\text{Molarity} = \frac{\text{Moles of } CH_3OH}{\text{Volume (in L)}}$$

$$= \frac{6/32}{(101.2 \text{ mL})/1000} = 1.8525 \text{ M}$$

(c) $\chi_B = 0.2$, $\chi_A = 0.8$

$$m = \frac{\chi_B \times 1000}{\chi_A \times Mw_A} = \frac{0.2 \times 1000}{0.8 \times 18} \approx 13.9$$

(d) $d = M\left\{\dfrac{Mw}{1000} + \dfrac{1}{m}\right\}$

$$\Rightarrow 1.0585 = 1\left\{\frac{58.5}{1000} + \frac{1}{m}\right\} \quad \Rightarrow m = 1$$

17. ***(a, b, c)*** 1000 g aqueous solution has

NaOH = 0.40 kg = 400 g

water = 1000 − 400 = 600 g

Thus % of NaOH by weight of water $= \dfrac{400}{600} \times 100 = 66.67\%$

% of NaOH by weight of aqueous solution $= \dfrac{400}{1000} \times 100$

$= 40.00\%$

$$\text{Molality} = \frac{\left(\frac{400}{40}\right)\text{mol}}{(0.600)\text{ kg}} = 16.67 \text{ molal}$$

If $d = 1$ gm L^{-1}

$$\text{Molarity} = \left(\frac{\frac{400}{40}}{1\text{ L}}\right) = 10 \text{ mol L}^{-1} \text{ (incorrect)}$$

18. ***(a, c)*** Among the given statements, only a and c are correct while b and d are incorrect.

Their explanation are given as

(a) $\text{Molarity} = \dfrac{\text{Moles of solute (ethanol)}}{\text{Volume of solution (in L)}}$

$$= \frac{0.171}{0.100} = 1.71 \text{ mol L}^{-1}$$

(b) Mass of ethanol solution (ethanol + water) = 98.20 g

Ethanol = 7.89 g

Thus, water = 98.20 − 7.89 = 90.31 g

$$n(\text{ethanol}) = \frac{7.89}{46} = 0.171$$

$$n(H_2O) = \frac{90.31}{18} = 5.017$$

Total moles = 5.188

$$\chi_{\text{ethanol}} = \frac{0.171}{5.188} = 0.0329$$

Mole % = 3.29%

(c) $\text{Molality} = \dfrac{\text{Mole of solute (ethanol)}}{\text{kg of } H_2O}$

$$= \frac{0.171 \text{ mol}}{0.09031 \text{ kg}} = 1.89 \text{ mol kg}^{-1}$$

(d) Since, $\text{Density} = \dfrac{\text{Mass}}{\text{Volume}}$

m (ethanol) $= V \times d = 10 \times 0.789 = 7.89$ g

100 mL solution = 100 × 0.982 = 98.2 g

$$\text{Mass \% of ethanol} = \frac{7.89}{98.2} \times 100 = 8.03\%$$

19. ***(a,b,c,d)*** m moles of HCl = 20 × 6

$= 120$ m mol $H^{\oplus}$ + 120 m mol $Cl^{\ominus}$

m moles of $Ba(OH)_2$ = 50 × 2 = 100 m mol

m moles of OH^- = 200 m mol

Total volume = 20 + 50 + 30 = 100 mL

$$[OH^{\ominus}] = \frac{(200 - 120)}{100 \text{ mL}} \text{ m mol} = 0.8 \text{ M}$$

$$[Cl^-] = \frac{120 \text{ m mol}}{100 \text{ mL}} = 1.2 \text{ M}$$

$$[Ba^{2+}] = \frac{100 \text{ m mol}}{100 \text{ mL}} = 1 \text{ M}$$

m moles of $OH^{\ominus}$ left = 200 − 120 = 80 mmol

20. ***(b, d)*** 50 mL of 2 M H_2SO_4 + 100 mL (98%, d = 0.1) H_2SO_4

$= 100$ m mol H_2SO_4 + 100 mL $\times \dfrac{(98 \times 10 \times 0.1)}{98}$ M H_2SO_4

$= 100$ m mol H_2SO_4 + 100 m mol H_2SO_4

$\therefore [H_2SO_4] = \dfrac{(100 \times 1 + 100 \times 1)}{200 \text{ mL}}$ m mol

$= 1\text{ M} = 98\text{ g}/1000\text{ mL}$

Mass of $H_2SO_4 = \dfrac{98\text{ g} \times 200\text{ mL}}{1000\text{ mL}} = 19.6\text{ g}$

21. ***(22.02)*** $H_3PO_4 \rightleftharpoons 3H^+ + PO_4^{3-}$

Thus, normality = 3 × molarity

H_3PO_4 is 34% by mass thus,

100 g H_3PO_4 solution = 34 g H_3PO_4

water = 66 g

or $\left(\dfrac{100}{1.209}\right)$ mL H_3PO_4 solution = 34 g H_3PO_4

$\therefore \quad H_3PO_4 = \left(\dfrac{34}{98}\right)$ mol

$H_2O = \dfrac{66}{1000} = 0.066\text{ kg}$

$\text{Solution} = \dfrac{100}{1.209} \times \dfrac{1}{1000} = \dfrac{1}{12.09}\text{L}$

$\therefore \quad \text{Molarity} = \dfrac{\text{Mol}}{\text{L}} = \left(\dfrac{34/98}{1/12.09}\right) = 4.19\text{ M}$

$\therefore \quad \text{Normality} = 4.19 \times 3 = 12.57$

$\therefore \quad \text{Molality} = \dfrac{\text{Moles}}{\text{kg}(H_2O)} = \dfrac{34/98}{0.066} = 5.26\text{ molal}$

Hence, the sum of x, y and z is $4.19 + 5.26 + 12.57 = 22.02$

22. ***(1)*** The molecular weight of $H_2O = \dfrac{\text{Given weight}}{\text{Molecular weight}}$

$= 55.5$ moles

Mole fraction of ethanol $= \dfrac{\text{Number of moles of ethanol}}{\text{Total moles}}$

$= \dfrac{3}{58.5}$

Mole fraction of ethanol = 0.05128

Mole fraction of $H_2O = \dfrac{55.5}{58.5} = 0.95$

The sum of mole fraction of ethanol and H_2O is

$= 0.05128 + 0.95 = 1.001$

23. ***(48)*** Moles of sulphuric acid $= 730 \times 10^{-3} \times 0.4 = 0.292$

Moles of sulphuric acid evaporated $= \dfrac{11.5}{98} = 0.117$

Moles left $= 0.292 - 0.117 = 0.175$

$\text{Molarity} = \dfrac{0.175 \times 10^3}{365} = 0.4794$

$= 47.94 \times 10^{-2} \approx 48 \times 10^{-2}$ M

Hence, the value of x is 48.

24. ***(4)*** As we know,

$$\frac{\chi_B}{\chi_A} = \frac{m \cdot M_A}{1000}$$

where, χ_B and χ_A = Mole fraction, m = molality

M_A = molar mass of solvent

$A \rightarrow$ Solvent, $B \rightarrow$ Solute

$\dfrac{\chi_B}{1-\chi_B} = \dfrac{2.45 \times 18}{1000}$ $[\chi_A + \chi_B = 1]$

$\dfrac{\chi_B}{1-\chi_B} = 0.04$

$\chi_B = 0.04 - 0.04\,\chi_B$

$1.04\,\chi_B = 0.04$

$\chi_B = 0.03846 \approx 3.9 \times 10^{-3} \approx 4 \times 10^{-2}$

Hence, the value of x is 4.

25. ***(20)*** Mole of $Na^+ = \dfrac{3.65}{23} = 0.15$

3 mole of Na^+ is present in $\dfrac{0.15}{3}$ mole of Na_3PO_4

$\text{Molarity} = \dfrac{0.15}{3 \times 250} \times 1000 = 0.2\text{ mol/L}$

$= 20 \times 10^{-2}$ mol / L

Thus, the value of x is 20.

Elemental Practice 7.2

1. ***(b)*** C_6H_5Cl and C_6H_5Br form ideal solution.

Let $C_6H_5Cl = X_1$ (mole fraction)

$C_6H_5Br = X_2 = (1 - X_1)$

$p_{total} = 760$ torr

$\therefore \quad p_{total} = p^\circ_{C_6H_5Cl} X_1 + p^\circ_{C_6H_5Br} X_2$

$760 = 940X_1 + 496(1 - X_1)$

$444X_1 = 264$

$\therefore \quad X_1 = 0.595$

Hence, C_6H_5Cl = 59.5 mol%

C_6H_5Br = 40.5 mol%

In vapour phase

$X'_{C_6H_5Cl} = \dfrac{p^\circ_{C_6H_5Cl} X_1}{p_{total}} = \dfrac{940 \times 0.595}{760} = 0.736$

Thus, in vapour phase

C_6H_5Cl = 73.6 mol%

and C_6H_5Br = 26.4 mol%

2. ***(a)*** As we know,

$p_{total} = p^\circ_{solute} + p^\circ_{H_2O} = 1$ atm

$760 = p^\circ_{solute} + 710$

$p^\circ_{solute} = 50$mm

Also vapour pressure is proportional to moles

$$\frac{p^\circ_{solute}}{p^\circ_{H_2O}} = \frac{n_{solute}}{n_{H_2O}} = \frac{w_{solute}}{w_{H_2O}} \times \frac{m_{H_2O}}{m_{solute}}$$

$$\frac{50}{710} = \frac{w_{solute}}{w_{H_2O}} \times \frac{18}{204}$$

$$\frac{w_{solute}}{w_{H_2O}} = \frac{50 \times 204}{710 \times 18} = 0.798$$

percentageand by weight of solution

$= \dfrac{0.798}{1.798} \times 100 = 44.38\%$

3. ***(d)*** 100 mL solution has glucose = 20g glucose

Given, $d = 0.9971 \text{ g mL}^{-1}$

$\therefore$ 99.71g solution has glucose = 20g glucose

Thus, solvent (water) = 99.71 – 20.0 = 79.71 g

$$n_2 = \frac{79.71}{18} \text{ mol } H_2O$$

$$\text{Solute } n_1 = \frac{20}{180} \text{ mol}$$

By Raoult's law,

$$\frac{\Delta p}{p^\circ} = X_{\text{solute}}$$

$$\frac{23.8 - p}{23.8} = \frac{20/180}{\frac{20}{180} + \frac{79.71}{18}} = 0.0245$$

$$\therefore \quad p = 23.8 - 23.8 \times 0.0245$$

$$= 23.217 \text{ mm}$$

4. ***(a)*** $\pi = \frac{n_1}{V} RT = \frac{w_1}{m_1 V} RT$

$\therefore m_1(\text{molar mass of solute}) = \frac{w_1 RT}{\pi V}$

$$m_1 = \frac{3 \text{ g} \times 0.0821 \text{ L atm mol}^{-1} \text{ K}^{-1} \times 298 \text{ K}}{3.632 \text{ atm} \times 0.1 \text{ L}}$$

$$= 202.085 \text{ g mol}^{-1}$$

By Raoult's law,

$$p_{\text{solution}} = p^\circ_{H_2O} X_{H_2O} = 23.7 \times \frac{n_{H_2O}}{n_{\text{total}}}$$

$$= 23.7 \times \frac{100/18}{\left(\frac{100}{18} + \frac{3}{202.085}\right)} = 23.64 \text{ mm}$$

5. ***(c)*** Statement I is correct but Statement II is incorrect. Its correct form is

Raoult's law becomes a special case of Henry's law in which K_H is equal to vapour pressure of solvent.

By Raoult's law, vapour pressure of solution is

$$p_s = p^\circ \chi_{\text{solvent}}$$

and by Henry's law

$$p = K_H \cdot \chi$$

Thus, on comparison

$$K_H = p^\circ$$

6. ***(a)*** Density of methanol = 0.792 g mL^{-1}

Thus 100 mL of methanol = 100 × 0.792 = 79.2 g

$$p_{\text{solution}} = p^\circ_{CH_3OH} X_{CH_3OH}$$

$$n_1(\text{urea}) = \frac{17}{60} \text{ mol}$$

$$n_2(CH_3OH) = \frac{79.2}{32} \text{ mol}$$

$$\therefore \quad X_{CH_3OH} = \frac{79.2/32}{\frac{79.2}{32} + \frac{17}{60}} = 0.897$$

$$\therefore \quad p_{\text{solution}} = 96 \times 0.897 = 86.11 \text{ mm Hg}$$

7. ***(a)*** If $p_{\text{solvent}} = p_0$

$$p_{\text{solution}} = \frac{9}{10} p_0$$

$$\therefore \quad \Delta p = \frac{p_0}{10}$$

$\therefore$ By using Raoult's law,

$$\frac{\Delta p}{p_0} = \frac{n_1}{n_1 + n_2} = \frac{n_1}{n_2}$$

$$\frac{p_0/10}{p_0} = \frac{w_1}{m_1} \times \frac{m_2}{w_2} = \frac{2}{100} \times \frac{m_2}{100}$$

$$m_2 = \frac{100 \times 100}{2 \times 10} = 500 \text{ g mol}^{-1}$$

8. ***(a)*** By Henry's law, $p_{N_2} = K_H X_{N_2}$

$0.987 \text{ bar} = 76.48 \times 10^3 \text{ bar } X_{N_2}$

$$\therefore \quad X_{N_2} = \frac{0.987}{76.48 \times 10^3} = 1.29 \times 10^{-5}$$

$$\therefore \quad X_{N_2} = \frac{n(N_2)}{n(N_2) + n(H_2O)}$$

$$1.29 \times 10^{-5} \approx \frac{n(N_2)}{n(H_2O)}$$

Since $n_{N_2} << n_{H_2O}$

$$\therefore n(N_2) = (1.29 \times 10^{-5}) \times n_{H_2O} \text{ mol} = 1.29 \times 10^{-5} \times \frac{1000}{18} \text{ mol}$$

$$= 0.716 \times 10^{-3} \text{ mol} = 0.716 \text{ millimol.}$$

9. ***(a)*** Both A and R are true and R is the correct explanation of A.

10. ***(b)*** Given, solubility = $0.195 \text{ mol kg}^{-1}$ = 0.195 molal

$$p_{H_2S} = K_H \times \text{solubility}$$

$$\therefore \quad K_H = \frac{p_{H_2S}}{\text{Solubility}} = \frac{1 \text{ atm}}{0.195 \text{ molal}}$$

$$= 5.128 \text{ atm molal}^{-1}.$$

Instead of mole fraction, solubility factor has been multiplied by K_H to obtain partial pressure of H_2S gas.

11. ***(d)*** By Henry's law,

$$p_{CO_2} = K_H X_{CO_2}$$

$$X_{CO_2} = \frac{p}{K_H} = \frac{0.10}{728}$$

At 273 K, $0.1 = 728 X_{CO_2}$

At 333 K, $p_2 = 3410 X_{CO_2}$

X_{CO_2} remains unchanged

Henry's law constant at 333 K

$$X_{CO_2} = \frac{p}{K_H} = \frac{p_2}{3410}$$

$$\frac{p_2}{3410} = \frac{0.10}{728}$$

$$\therefore \quad p_2 = 0.468 \text{ atm}$$

12. ***(a)*** Due to breakage of H-bonds, mixture is more vaporised, BP is lowered.

Thus it forms with a positive deviation from Raoult's law —a minimum boiling azeotrope

13. ***(b)*** (*A* for acetone, *C* for carbon disulphide)

$$p_A^\circ = 344\,\text{mmHg},\ \chi_A = 0.75$$
$$p_C^\circ = 512\,\text{mmHg},\ \chi_C = 0.25$$
$$p_{\text{total}} = p_A^\circ\chi_A + p_C^\circ\chi_C = 344\times 0.75 + 512\times 0.25$$
$$= 385\,\text{mm Hg}$$

but actual $p_{\text{total}} = 600\,\text{mmHg}$

Thus, there is positive deviation. Boiling point is lowered. $\Delta H > 0$ (endothermic) i.e. heat is absorbed.

14. ***(c)*** A is correct but R is incorrect. The correct form of *R* is

Mixture of CS_2 and CH_3COCH_3 shows positive deviation as force of attraction between CS_2 and CH_3COCH_3 is less than between CS_2 / CS_2 or CH_3COCH_3 / CH_3COCH_3. There is more vaporisation and BP is lowered - a low boiling azeotrope.

15. ***(c)*** Let n_B mole of *B* present in 1 mole of mixture that has been vaporised.

Thus, $$y_B = \frac{n_B}{1}$$

Mole fraction of *B* in the remaining liquid phase will be

$$\chi_B = \frac{1-n_B}{1}$$

$$\chi_B = \frac{p - p_T^\circ}{p_B^\circ - p_T^\circ} \quad \ldots\text{(i)}$$

$$[\because p = p_T^\circ + (p_B^\circ - p_T^\circ)\chi_B]$$

and $$y_B = \frac{p_B}{p} \Rightarrow \frac{p_B^\circ\chi_B}{p} \quad \ldots\text{(ii)}$$

After substitution of values of χ_B and y_B in (i) and (ii), we get

$$1-n_B = \frac{p - p_T^\circ}{p_B^\circ - p_T^\circ} \quad \ldots\text{(iii)}$$

and $$n_B = \frac{(1-n_B)\,p_B^\circ}{p} \quad \ldots\text{(iv)}$$

or $$n_B = \frac{p_B^\circ}{p + p_B}$$

So, $$\frac{p_B^\circ}{p + p_B} = \frac{p - p_T^\circ}{p_B^\circ - p_T^\circ}$$

$$p = \sqrt{p_B^\circ \cdot p_T^\circ} = \sqrt{400\times 400}$$
$$= 400\text{ torr.}$$

16. ***(a, b, c)*** Among the given statements a, b and c are correct while statement d is incorrect.

Its correct form is —

According to Henry's law, the solubility of a gas in given volume of liquid increases with increase in temperature and pressure.

17. ***(a, b, c)*** (a) $NH_3 + H_2O \rightleftharpoons NH_4OH \rightleftharpoons NH_4^+ + OH^-$

$CO_2 + H_2O \rightleftharpoons H_2CO_3 \rightleftharpoons 2H^+ + CO_3^{2-}$

$SO_2 + H_2O \rightleftharpoons H_2SO_3 \rightleftharpoons 2H^+ + SO_3^{2-}$

NH_3, CO_2, SO_3 ... gases form ions in water, hence these gases are soluble in water. O_2, N_2 ... do not form ions in water hence, insoluble thus correct.

(b) NH_3 and CO_2 are liquefied easily hence, soluble in water thus, correct.

(c) $p = K_H\chi,\ \chi \propto \dfrac{1}{K_H}$

Higher the value of K_H, smaller the solubility (χ) of the gas at a given pressure thus, correct.

18. ***(a, c, d)*** $p_A^\circ = 100\,\text{mmHg},\ n_A = 1\,\text{mol},\ \chi_A = 0.25$

$p_B^\circ = 60\,\text{mmHg},\ n_B = 3\,\text{mol},\ \chi_B = 0.75$

$$\therefore\quad p_{\text{total}} = p_A^\circ\chi_A + p_B^\circ\chi_B$$
$$= \frac{100\times 1}{4} + \frac{60\times 3}{4} = 70\,\text{mmHg}$$

But, actual vapour pressure = 75 mmHg. Vapour pressure is increased. Force of attraction between *A* and *B* is smaller than between *A* and *A* and between *B* and *B*. Thus, more vaporisation due to decrease in boiling point, a case of positive deviation.

19. ***(b, d)*** Among the given statements, b and d are incorrect while a and c are correct.

Their correct form are

In a nearly saturated solution, if the dissolution process is endothermic then the solubility will increase with rise in temperature.

The solubility of gases increase with increase of pressure.

20. ***(a, b, c)*** (a) At constant temperature, different gases have different K_H values. Thus, K_H is a function of nature of gases. Thus, correct.

(b) *p* (partial pressure) = $K_H\chi$

If *p* is constant and K_H value increases then χ (solubility) decreases. Thus, correct.

(c) K_H increases with increase in temperature thus, correct.

(d) K_H is independent of pressure thus, incorrect.

21. ***(9)*** $K_H(O_2) = 74.68\,\text{kPa m}^3\,\text{mol}^{-1}$

We use relation

$$p_{O_2} = K_H C_{O_2}$$

(Take this value in mol m^{-3})

$$C_{O_2} = 3.856\,\text{mg dm}^{-3}$$
$$= \left(\frac{3.856\times 10^{-3}}{32}\,\text{g}\right)\text{mol dm}^{-3}$$
$$= \frac{3.856\times 10^{-3}}{32}\times 10^3\,\text{mol m}^{-3}$$
$$= 0.1205\,\text{mol m}^{-3}$$

$$\therefore\quad p_{O_2} = 74.68\,\text{kPa m}^3\,\text{mol}^{-1}\times 0.1205\,\text{mol m}^{-3}$$
$$= 8.998\,\text{kPa} \approx 9.0\,\text{k Pa}$$

22. ***(35)*** Given, total pressure, $p_T = 0.7$ atm

Mole fraction of A in vapour phase, $y_A = 0.5$

Mole fraction of A in liquid phase, $\chi_A = 0.3$

Using equation,

$$p_A = y_A \times 0.5 = 0.5 \times 0.7$$
$$= 0.35 \text{ atm}$$

we know that,

$$p_A = \chi_A \cdot p_A^\circ$$

[p_A° = vapour pressure of pure A]

$$p_A^\circ = \frac{p_A}{\chi_A} = \frac{0.35}{0.3}$$

$$\frac{35}{30} = x$$

$$x \times 30 \approx 35.$$

23. ***(2)*** By Raoult's law,

$$\frac{\Delta p}{p^\circ} = x_{\text{solute}}$$

Case I $\left(\frac{\Delta p}{p^\circ}\right)_{\text{I}} = 0.2$, as $x_{\text{solute}} = 0.2$

Case II $x_{\text{solvent}} = 0.8 - \frac{0.8 \times 25}{100} = 0.6$

Hence, $x_{\text{solute}} = 0.4$

$$\left(\frac{\Delta p}{p^\circ}\right)_{\text{II}} = 0.4$$

$$\therefore \quad \frac{(\Delta p)_{\text{II}}}{(\Delta p)_{\text{I}}} = 2$$

24. ***(610)*** $p_{\text{total}} = \chi_{\text{heptane}} \times p^\circ_{\text{heptane}} + \chi_{\text{nonane}} \times p^\circ_{\text{nonane}}$

Given, $p_{\text{total}} = 670$ mm of Hg

$$\chi_{\text{heptane}} = \frac{2}{2+5} = \frac{2}{7};\ \chi_{\text{nonane}} = \frac{5}{7}$$

Substituting the values in above formula.

$$670 = \frac{2}{7} \times p^\circ_{\text{heptane}} + \frac{5}{7} \times p^\circ_{\text{nonane}} \quad \ldots\text{(i)}$$

After substracting the 1 mole of n-nonane then,

$$680 = \frac{2}{6} \times p^\circ_{\text{heptane}} + \frac{4}{6} \times p^\circ_{\text{nonane}} \quad \ldots\text{(ii)}$$

From Eq. (i) and (ii)

$$p^\circ_{\text{nonane}} = 610 \text{ atm}$$

25. ***(70.38)*** Given,

$$p_{\text{water}} = 18.5 \text{ torr}$$

$$P_{\text{total}} \text{ (4 mole \% solution)} = p_{NH_3} + p_{\text{water}} = 60.0 \text{ torr}$$

$$x_{NH_3} = 0.04 \text{ and } x_{\text{water}} = 0.96$$

Now, according to Raoult's law;

$$p_{\text{water}} = x_{\text{water}} \times p^\circ_{\text{water}}$$
$$= 0.96 \times 18.5 \text{ torr} = 17.76 \text{ torr}$$

Now, Henry's law constant for ammonia is

$$K_H(NH_3) = \frac{p_{NH_3}}{x_{NH_3}} = \frac{42.24 \text{torr}}{0.04} = 1056 \text{ torr}$$

Hence, for 5 mole % solution, we have

$$p_{NH_3} = K_H(NH_3) \times x_{NH_3}$$
$$= (1056) \times (0.05) = 52.8 \text{ torr}$$

$$p_{\text{water}} = p^\circ_{\text{water}} \times x_{\text{water}}$$
$$= (18.5)(0.95) = 17.575 \text{ torr}$$

Thus, P_{total} (5 mole % solution)

$$= p_{NH_3} + p_{\text{water}}$$
$$= 52.8 + 17.575 = 70.375 \text{ torr} \approx 70.38 \text{ torr}$$

Elemental Practice 7.3

1. ***(c)*** By using the formula,

$$i = [1 + (y-1)x]$$

(i) $K_4[Fe(CN)_6] \rightleftharpoons 4K^+ + [Fe(CN)_6]^{4-}$

$$\begin{array}{ccc} 1 & 0 & 0 \\ (1-x) & 4x & x \end{array}$$

$y = 5$

i (van't Hoff factor) $= 1 + (y-1)x$

$$= 1 + 4x = 1 + 4 \times 0.2 = 1.8$$

(ii) $PCl_5(g) \rightleftharpoons PCl_3(g) + Cl_2(g)$

$$\begin{array}{ccc} 1 & 0 & 0 \\ (1-x) & x & x \end{array}$$

$y = 2$

$$i = 1 + (y-1)x = 1 + x = 1 + 0.5 = 1.5$$

(iii) $K_2HgI_4 \rightleftharpoons 2K^+ + HgI_4^{2-}$

$$\begin{array}{ccc} 1 & 0 & 0 \\ (1-x) & 2x & x \end{array}$$

$$i = 1 + (y-1)x = 1 + 2x$$
$$= 1 + 2 \times 0.40 = 1.8$$

Hence, the total sum of i is $1.8 + 1.5 + 1.8 = 5.1$

2. ***(b)***

S.No.	Solution	i	$i \times m$
A	0.05 M $NaNO_3$	2	$2 \times 0.05 = 0.10$
B	0.08 M $CuSO_4$	2	$2 \times 0.08 = 0.16$
C	0.14 M Glucose	1	$1 \times 0.14 = 0.14$
D	0.037 M $BaCl_2$	3	$3 \times 0.037 = 0.111$
E	0.06 M $(NH_4)_2SO_4$	3	$3 \times 0.06 = 0.18$

$$\Delta T_f = K_f \times i \times m$$
$$\Delta T_f \propto mi$$

Freezing point $= T_0 - \Delta T_f$

Thus, lower the value of ΔT_f, higher will be the freezing point.

$$\Delta T_f = E > B > C > D > A$$

Freezing point $= A > D > C > B > E$

3. ***(c)*** Let number of ions from 1 unit of compound = y

Then, $i = [1 + (y - 1)x]$

$x = 1$

$\pi = MRTi$

$$\text{Molarity of the compound} = \frac{\left(\frac{0.0140}{243.5}\right)\text{mol}}{0.0250\text{ L}}$$

$$= 2.3 \times 10^{-3}\text{ M}$$

$$\pi = MRTi$$

$$\left(\frac{119}{760}\right)\text{atm} = 2.3 \times 10^{-3} \times 0.0821 \times 298 \times y$$

$$y = 2.78 \approx 3.0$$

$\therefore$ Number of ions = 3

4. ***(b)***

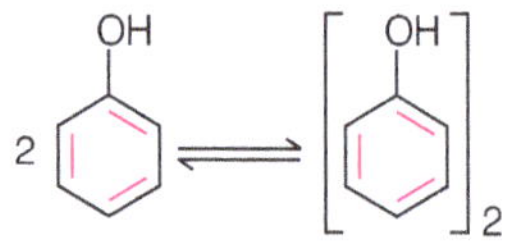

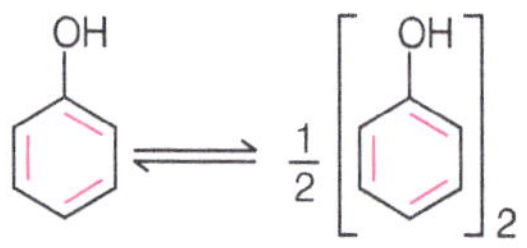

$$y = \frac{1}{2} = \text{species formed from 1 mole reactant}$$

$\therefore$ i = van't Hoff factor

$$= 1 + (y - 1)\,x = \left(1 - \frac{x}{2}\right)$$

x = degree of dimerisation

$$\Delta T_f = \frac{1000\,K_f\,w_1(i)}{m_1 w_2}$$

$$1.41 = \frac{1000 \times 14.1 \times 1.88}{94 \times 100}\left(1 - \frac{x}{2}\right)$$

$$\therefore \quad \left(1 - \frac{x}{2}\right) = 0.5$$

$$\therefore \quad x = 1.0$$

Thus, 100% dimer formation.

5. ***(c)*** Dimer formation is due to intermolecular H-bonding.

$$CH_3COOH \rightleftharpoons \frac{1}{2}(CH_3COOH)_2$$

$$y = \frac{1}{2}$$

$$i = 1 + (y - 1)x = 1 + \left(\frac{1}{2} - 1\right)x$$

$$0.75 = \left(1 - \frac{x}{2}\right)$$

$$\therefore \quad x = 0.50$$

Thus, 50% dimer formation.

$$\frac{\text{Normal molar mass}}{\text{Abnormal molar mass}} = i$$

$$\therefore \text{Abnormal molar mass} = \frac{\text{Normal molar mass}}{i}$$

$$= \frac{60}{0.75}\text{g mol}^{-1} = 80\text{ g mol}^{-1}$$

6. ***(b)*** By using the formula

$$\Delta T_f = \frac{1000\,K_f w_1}{m_1 w_2}$$

$$\Delta T_f = 0° - (-0.42°) = 0.42°$$

$$\therefore \quad m_1 = \frac{1000\,K_f w_1}{\Delta T_f w_2}$$

$$K_f = \frac{RT_0^2}{1000\Delta H_f}$$

$$\Delta H_f = 6.025\text{kJ mol}^{-1} = \frac{6.025}{18}\text{kJ g}^{-1}$$

$$\therefore \quad K_f = \frac{8.314 \times 10^{-3} \times (273)^2}{1000 \times \left(\frac{6.025}{18}\right)}$$

$$= 1.85°\text{ mol}^{-1}\text{ kg}$$

$$m_1 = \frac{1000 \times 1.85 \times 0.25}{0.42 \times 20} = 55.06\text{ g mol}^{-1}$$

7. ***(a)*** $\Delta T_b(KCl) = \Delta T_f(Na_2CO_3)$

$K_b = 0.52°\text{ mol}^{-1}\text{kg}$, $K_f = 1.86°\text{ mol}^{-1}\text{ kg}$

$m = ?$

$$KCl \rightleftharpoons K^+ + Cl^-$$

$$i = [1 + (y - 1)x]$$

$$Na_2CO_3 \rightleftharpoons 2Na^+ + CO_3^{2-}$$

$$i = 1 + 2x = 3$$

For KCl, $i = 1 + 2x = 2$ ($x = 1$ since complete ionisation)

$$\Delta T_b = K_b \times mi = 0.52 \times m \times 2$$

$$\Delta T_f = K_f \times mi = 1.86 \times 0.35 \times 3$$

Since, $\Delta T_b = \Delta T_f$

$$0.52 \times m \times 2 = 1.86 \times 0.35 \times 3$$

$$m = \frac{1.86 \times 0.35 \times 3}{0.52 \times 2} = 1.87\text{ molal}$$

8. ***(c)***

	w_1	m_1	Moles	w_2	$\Delta T_b = \frac{1000\,w_1 K_b}{m_1 w_2}$
I.	6g	60g	0.1	100 g	$x_1 = K_b$
II.	18g	180g	0.1	100 g	$x_2 = K_b$
III.			(0.1+ 0.1)	200 g	$x_3 = K_b$

$$\therefore \quad x_1 = x_2 = x_3$$

9. ***(b)***

	$2A \rightleftharpoons$	A_2
Initial conc.	nM	0
Equilibrium conc.	$(n - x)M$	$\frac{x}{2}M$

Now, $\Delta T_b = K_b.m = K_b.\left[n - x + \frac{x}{2}\right]$

$$\therefore \quad x = 2n - \frac{2\Delta T_b}{K_b}$$

Now,
$$K_C = \frac{[A_2]}{[A]^2} = \frac{\left(\frac{x}{2}\right)}{(n-x)^2} = \frac{n - \frac{\Delta T_b}{K_b}}{\left(\frac{2\Delta T_b}{K_b} - n\right)^2}$$
$$= \frac{K_b(n.K_b - \Delta T_b)}{(2\Delta T_b - n.K_b)^2}$$

10. **(c)** By using

$$\chi_B = \frac{\Delta p}{p_A^\circ} = 0.019$$
$$\Delta T_b = K_b . m = 0.54 \times 1$$
$$m = \frac{\chi_B}{1-\chi_B} \times \frac{1000}{MW_A}$$
$$m = \frac{0.019}{0.981} \times \frac{1000}{18} = 1.07$$
$$\Delta T_b = K_b \times m$$
$$= 0.54 \times 1.07 = 0.5°C$$

11. **(d)** $K_f = \frac{R(T_{f.p})^2}{1000\Delta H_f}$, $K_b = \frac{R(T_{b.p})^2}{1000\,\Delta H_V}$

$$\frac{K_b}{K_f} = \left(\frac{T_{b.p}}{T_{f.p}}\right)^2 \frac{\Delta H_f}{\Delta H_V} = \left(\frac{3}{2}\right)^2\left(\frac{1}{6}\right) = \frac{3}{8}$$
$$\Delta T_b = m K_b$$
$$\Delta T_f = m K_f$$
$$\therefore \quad \frac{\Delta T_b}{\Delta T_f} = \frac{K_b}{K_f} = \frac{3}{8}$$

12. **(c)** Statement I is correct but statement II is incorrect. Their explanation are given as :

(I) $\Delta T_b = m\,K_b\,i$

At boiling point

$$AB \rightleftharpoons A^+ + B^-, i = 2$$

$\therefore$ $1.08° = m \times K_b \times 2$

At freezing point

$$1.80° = m \times K_f \times i$$
$$\frac{1.08}{1.80} = \frac{2K_b}{i\,K_f} = \frac{2 \times 0.3}{i}$$
$$i = 1$$

Thus, no change in the state of AB when frozen.

(II) By Raoult's law,

$$\frac{\Delta p}{p^\circ} = iX_{solute}$$
$$Ca(NO_3)_2 \rightleftharpoons Ca^{2+} + 2NO_3^-$$
$$\therefore \quad i = [1 + (y-1)x] = (1 + 2x)$$
$$X_{solute} = \frac{0.04i}{0.04i + 4} = \left(\frac{0.01i}{0.01i + 1}\right)$$
$$\frac{760 - 741}{760} = \frac{0.01i}{0.01i + 1}$$
$$\frac{1}{40} = \frac{0.01i}{0.01i + 1}$$
$$0.01i + 1 = 0.4i$$
$$i = 2.56$$

Van't Hoff factor of solute is to be included in total moles as well as in individual solute.

13. **(a)** Given,

Molality = 1 mol kg^{-1},

Solute (sucrose) = 1 mol

Solvent (H_2O) = 1 kg = 1000 g = 55.55 mol

$$\chi_{solute} = \frac{1}{56.55}$$

By Raoult's law for binary mixture of non-volatile solute in volatile solvent, relative lowering of vapour pressure

$$= \chi_{solute}$$
$$\frac{\Delta p}{p^\circ} = \frac{1}{56.55} = 0.018$$

Sucrose solution is maintained at – 3.53°C.

Thus, $\Delta T_f = 3.534°$

Total mass of 1 molal solution

= 1000 g (solvent) + 342 g (solute) = 1342 g

1342 g solution contains sucrose =342 g

1000 g solution contains sucrose $= \frac{342 \times 1000}{1342} = 255$ g

H_2O present in 1000 g solution = 1000 – 255 = 745 g

Solvent actually required to keep 255 g sucrose in solution at – 3.534°C = w_2

$$\Delta T_f = \frac{1000 w_1 K_f}{w_2 m_1}$$
$$w_2 = \frac{1000\,w_1 K_f}{\Delta T_f m_1} = \frac{1000 \times 255 \times 1.86}{3.534 \times 342}$$
$$= 392.0 \text{ g (in liquid state)}$$

Thus, ice formed = 745 – 392 = 353 g (in solid state)

14. **(b)** $\pi = \frac{\pi_1 + \pi_2}{2}$, if equal volumes are mixed,

Then volume of solution becomes double.

Given,
$$\pi_1 = 1.64$$
$$\pi_2 = 2.46$$
$$\pi = \frac{1.64 + 2.46}{2}$$
$$= 2.05 \text{ atm}$$

15. **(b)** The given values are

$$w_{solute} = 8.0 \text{ g}, w_{solvent} = 100 \text{ g}, K_b = 0.52 \text{ Km}^{-1}$$
$$\Delta T_b = 110.3 - 100 = 10.3$$

By using the formula,

$$Mw_{solute} = \frac{K_b \times w_{solute} \times 1000}{\Delta T_b \times w_{solvent}(g)}$$

$$= \frac{0.52 \times 8.0 \times 1000}{10.3 \times 100} = 4.03 \text{ g mol}^{-1}$$

$$\begin{bmatrix} \text{Mass of solution} = 100 + 8 = 108 \text{ g} \\ d \text{ (soln)} = 1 \text{ g mol}^{-1} \\ V \text{ (soln)} = 108 \text{ mL} \end{bmatrix}$$

Now, $\pi = \frac{nRT}{V}; n = \frac{w_{solute}}{Mw_{solute}}$

$\therefore$ $n = \frac{8}{4.03} = 1.98$

$$\pi = \frac{1.98 \times 0.082 \times 298}{0.108} = 447.99 \text{ atm}$$

16. ***(c)*** n_1 = solute = 1

n_2 = solvent = 5

$$\frac{\Delta p}{p^\circ} = \frac{n_1 i}{n_1 i + n_2}$$

Solute	i	$\Delta p / p^\circ$
(A) NaCl	2	2 / 7 = 0.29
(B) K_2SO_4	3	3 / 8 = 0.38
(C) Na_3PO_4	4	4 / 9 = 0.44
(D) Glucose	1	1 / 6 = 0.17

Thus, $D < A < B < C$

17. ***(d)*** Among the given cases, option (d) is correct. Their explanation are given as :

(a) $Na_2SO_4 \rightleftharpoons \underbrace{2Na^+ + SO_4^{2-}}_{y=3}$

$$i = [1 + (y-1)x] = 1 + (3-1)\,0.5 = 2$$

(b) $2NO_2 \rightleftharpoons N_2O_4$

$NO_2 \rightleftharpoons \frac{1}{2}N_2O_4 \quad \left(y = \frac{1}{2}\right)$

$$i = 1 + \left(\frac{1}{2} - 1\right) 0.4 = 0.8$$

y = number of moles of products from 1 mole reactant

(c) $KCl = \underbrace{K^+ + Cl^-}_{y=2}$ $\quad i = 1 + (y-1)x = 1 + 1 = 2$

(d) $K_4[Fe(CN)_6] \rightleftharpoons \underbrace{4K^+ + [Fe(CN)_6]^{4-}}_{y=5}$

$\therefore$ $i = 1 + (y-1)x$

$= 1 + (5-1)\,0.2 = 1.8$

18. ***(b)*** Cl^- can be a part of inside coordinate sphere as well as that of outside

Let Cl^- is inside sphere = n

then outside sphere = $(4-n)$

and complex is $[Pt(NH_3)_4Cl_n]\,Cl_{4-n}$

$[Pt(NH_3)_4Cl_n]\,Cl_{4-n} \rightleftharpoons [Pt(NH_3)_4Cl_n]^{(4-n)} + (4-n)\,Cl^-$

Total ions from

1 mol complex $= 1 + (4-n) = (5-n) = y$

$x = 1$ (100% ionisation)

van't Hoff factor $i = [1 + (y-1)x]$

$i = 1 + (5 - n - 1)1$

$i = (5-n)$

$\Delta T_f = K_f m i$

$0.0056 = 1.86 \times 0.001 \times (5-n)$

$(5-n) = 3.01$

$\therefore$ van't Hoff factor $= 3.01 \approx 3$

19. ***(d)*** $AB \rightleftharpoons \underbrace{A^+ + B^-}_{y=2}$

$\therefore$ $i = 1 + (y-1)\,\alpha = 1 + \alpha = 1.8$

$\therefore$ $\Delta T_b\,(AB) = K_b m i = K_b \times m \times 1.8$

$CD \rightleftharpoons \underbrace{\frac{1}{2}(CD)_2}_{y=\frac{1}{2}}$

$\therefore$ $i = 1 + (y-1)\,\beta = \left(1 - \frac{\beta}{2}\right)$

$\therefore$ $\Delta T_b(CD) = K_b m i = K_b \times m \times \left(1 - \frac{\beta}{2}\right)$

Also, $\Delta T_b\,(AB) = 2\Delta T_b(CD)$

$\therefore$ $1.8\,K_b m = 2\left(1 - \frac{\beta}{2}\right) K_b m$

$1.8 = 2\left(1 - \frac{\beta}{2}\right) \Rightarrow \beta = 0.2$

20. ***(d)*** $[K_2SO_4 \rightleftharpoons 2K^+ + SO_4^{2-}]\; y = 3$

$i = 1 + (y-1)\,x_1 = (1 + 2x_1)$

$[NaOH \rightleftharpoons Na^+ + OH^-]\; y = 2$

$i = 1 + (y-1)\,x_2 = (1 + x_2)$

y = Number of ions formed

Solute	Molar mass	Conc.	Molarity	Reactants $\pi = MRTi$
K_2SO_4	174	17.4%	1 M	$\pi_1 = 300(1+2x_1)R$
NaOH	40	4.0%	1 M	$\pi_2 = 300(1+x_2)R$

Solutions are isotonic

$\pi_1 = \pi_2$

$\therefore$ $300\,(1 + 2x_1)R = 300\,(1 + x_2)R$

$1 + 2x_1 = 1 + x_2$

$\therefore$ $2x_1 = x_2$

$\therefore$ $\frac{x_1}{x_2} = \frac{1}{2}$

21. ***(b, d)*** Glucose solution is = 1 mol kg^{-1} water

Solute (glucose) = 180 g

Solvent (water) = 1000 g

Total mass of solution $= 1180 \text{ g} = \frac{1180}{1.180} \text{ mL} = 1000 \text{ mL}$

Thus, molarity $= 1 \text{ mol L}^{-1}$,

$$\frac{\Delta T_b}{\Delta T_f} = \frac{K_b}{K_f} = \frac{1}{3} = 0.33$$

Osmotic pressure,

$$\pi = MRT = 1 \times 0.0821 \times 300 = 24.63 \text{ atm}$$

22. ***(b, c, d)*** $\pi = MRTi$

I. Glucose (non-electrolyte), $i = 1 \; \pi = RT$

II. $NaCl \rightleftharpoons Na^+ + Cl^-, i = 2 \; \pi = 2RT$

III. $(NH_4)_3PO_4 \rightleftharpoons 3NH_4^+ + PO_4^{3-} \; i = 4, \; \pi = 4RT$

IV. $C_6H_5COOH \rightleftharpoons \frac{1}{2}(C_6H_5COOH) i = \frac{1}{2}, \; \pi = \frac{RT}{2}$

Thus, π is in order

$$IV < I < II < III$$

Thus, III is hypertonic of I, II and IV— correct

IV is hypotonic of I, II and III– correct II is hypotonic of III but hypertonic of I and IV— correct

23. ***(a, b, c, d)*** $i = [1 + (y - 1)x]$

where, y is the number of ions due to ionisation. $x = 1$ (given)

(a) Hg_2I_2(s) insoluble, $i = 1$

$$HgI_2 + 2KI \rightleftharpoons K_2HgI_4 \longrightarrow \underbrace{2K^+ + HgI_4^{2-}}_{y = 3}$$

$i = 3$

Thus, 'i' changes

(b) $Fe(CN)_2$, (insoluble), $i = 1$

$$Fe(CN)_2 + 4KCN \rightleftharpoons K_4Fe(CN)_6 \longrightarrow \underbrace{4K^+ + [Fe(CN)_6]^{4-}}_{y = 5}$$

$i = 5$

Thus, 'i' changes

(c) AgCl (insoluble), $i = 1$

$$AgCl + 2NH_3 \longrightarrow [Ag(NH_3)_2]Cl \rightleftharpoons \underbrace{[Ag(NH_3)_2]^+ + Cl^-}_{y = 2}$$

$i = 2$

Thus, 'i' changes

(d) AgCN (insoluble), $i = 1$

$$AgCN + KCN \rightleftharpoons K[Ag(CN)_2] \rightleftharpoons \underbrace{K^+ + [Ag(CN)_2]^-}_{y = 2}$$

$i = 2$

Thus, 'i' changes

24. ***(a, b, c, d)*** $\Delta T_b = \frac{1000 K_b w_1}{m_1 w_2}$

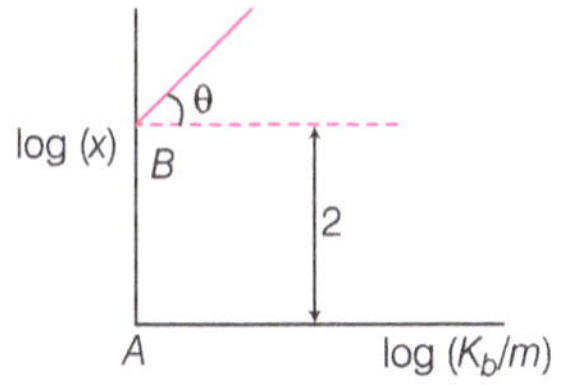

Given, $\Delta T_b = x$

$w_1 = 10 \text{ g}, m_1 = m, w_2 = 100 \text{ g}$

$$\therefore x = \frac{1000 \times K_b \times 10}{100 m} = 10^2 \left(\frac{K_b}{m}\right)$$

$$\log x = \log 10^2 + \log \left(\frac{K_b}{m}\right)$$

$$\log x = 2 + \log \left(\frac{K_b}{m}\right)$$

This represents linear equation.

With slope $= 1 = \tan \theta \; (\theta = 45^\circ)$

Intercept, $AB = 2$

(d) $T_b = 2T_b^\circ \Rightarrow \log (2T_b^\circ - T_b) = 2 + \log \left(\frac{k_b}{m}\right)$

$$\Rightarrow \quad \log T_b^\circ = 2 + \log \left(\frac{k_b}{m}\right) \cdot T_b = 100^\circ C$$

$$2 = 2 + \log \left(\frac{k_b}{m}\right) = \log \left(\frac{k_b}{m}\right) = 0$$

25. ***(a,c,d)*** Among the given statements a, c and d are correct while statement b is incorrect.

Their explanation are given as :

(b) The value of i for aqueous KCl is more than unity while for ethanoic acid in benzene it is less than unity.

(c) $CH_3COOH \rightleftharpoons CH_3COO^\ominus + H^\oplus$

	CH_3COOH	$CH_3COO^\ominus$	$H^\oplus$
Initial	C	0	0
After ionisation	(C – Cx)	Cx	Cx

$y = 2$

$$K_a = \frac{C\alpha^2}{1 - x}$$

$$i = 1 + (y - 1)x = 1 + x$$

$$1.04 = 1 + x$$

$$x = 0.04$$

Thus, it is 4% ionised. So, (c) is correct.

$$FeSO_4 \cdot (NH_4)_2SO_4 \rightleftharpoons Fe^{2+} + 2SO_4^{2-} + 2NH_4^+$$

$x = 0.4$

$y = 5$

$\therefore \quad i = 1 + (y - 1)x = 1 + 4x$

$i = 2.6$

By using,

$$\Delta T_b = m \,.\, K_b \,.\, i = 2.6 \times 1 \times K_b = 2.6 K_b$$

Thus (d) is also correct.

26. ***(a, b, c, d)*** Among the given statements, all the statements are correct. Their explanation are given as :

From (D) ΔT_f (urea) $= 1.86^\circ C$

$i = 1$ for urea (non-electrolyte)

$\therefore \quad \Delta T_f = m \times K_f \times i$

$1.86 = 1 \text{ molal} \times K_f \times 1$

$K_f = 1.86^\circ C \text{ molal}^{-1}$ for H_2O

So, (b) is correct.

From (B), $\Delta T_f(HgCl_2) = 0.186^\circ C$

$m = 0.10$ molal

$0.186 = 0.1 \times 1.86 \times i$

$i = 1$

Thus, $HgCl_2$ does not ionise in aqueous solution.

Thus, (a) is correct.

From (C), $\Delta T_f\ [Hg(NO_3)_2] = 0.558°C$

$$0.558°C = 0.10 \times 1.86 \times i$$

$$i = 3 = 1 + (y-1)x = 1 + 2x$$

$$Hg(NO_3)_2 = Hg^{2+} + 2NO_3^-$$

$$(1 + 2x) = 3$$

$$x = 1$$

Thus $Hg(NO_3)_2$ is 100% ionised in aqueous solution.

So, (c) is correct.

Thus van't Hoff factor value of urea and $HgCl_2$ is same i.e., 1.

27. ***(b, c, d)*** Among the given statements, b, c and d are incorrect while statement a is correct. Their explanation are given as :

(c) As we know, $\Delta T_f = K_f \times m \times i$

$$\therefore \quad i(HCl) = \frac{\Delta T_f}{K_f \times m} = \frac{3.608 \times 10^{-3}}{1.86 \times 0.001} = 1.9398$$

$$(1 + x) = 1.9398$$

$$x = 0.9398 \approx 0.94$$

Thus, HCl is 94% ionised.

(d) $[H^+]_{HCl} = 0.001 \times 0.94 = 9.4 \times 10^{-4}$ M

$$pH = -\log [H^+] = 3.03$$

So, (d) is incorrect.

(b) π(osmotic pressure) $= MRTi = 0.001 \times 0.083 \times 300 \times 1.94$

$$= 0.048 \text{ bar}$$

Thus, (b) is incorrect.

(a) As we know.

$$\frac{\Delta T_b}{\Delta T_f} = \frac{K_b}{K_f} = 3.6 \times 3.608 \times 10^{-3} \text{ K} = 13 \times 10^{-3} \text{ K}$$

Thus, (a) is correct.

28. ***(11.625)*** Mass of 8 L water, $w_A = 8000 \times 1.0 = 8000$ g

Mass of alcohol added,

$$w_B = 2000 \times 0.8 = 1600 \text{ g}$$

$$M_B = 32$$

By using the formula,

$$\Delta T_f = \frac{K_f \times 1000 \times w_B}{w_A \times m_B}$$

$$= \frac{1.86 \times 1000 \times 1600}{8000 \times 32}$$

$$= 11.625$$

Freezing point $= 0 - 11.625 = -11.625°$ C.

Vehicle may be parked outdoor not below than $-11.625°$ C temperature.

29. ***(0.04)*** By using,

$$\Delta T_f = 1000 \times K_f \times \frac{w_2}{m_2 w_1}$$

$\therefore$ m_2 (molar mass of acid) based on colligative property

$$= \frac{1000 \times K_f \times w_2}{w_1 \times \Delta T_f}$$

$$= \frac{1000 \times 1.86 \times 2.01}{100 \times 0.316}$$

$$m_2(\text{observed}) = 118.31 \text{ g mol}^{-1}$$

m_2 based on titration

$$20 \text{ mL of } 0.1 \text{ M KOH} = \frac{20 \times 0.1}{1000} \text{ mol}$$

$$= 2 \times 10^{-3} \text{ mol}$$

Moles of acid = Moles of KOH

$$\frac{0.246}{m_2} = 2 \times 10^{-3}$$

$$m_2 = 123 \text{ g mol}^{-1}$$

$$m_2 \text{ (theoretical)} = 123 \text{ g mol}^{-1}$$

$$i = \frac{m_2(\text{theoretical})}{m_2(\text{observed})} = \frac{123}{118.31} = 1.039 \approx 1.04$$

Also, $\quad i = 1 + (y-1)x$

Since, $\quad y = 2$

$$i = (1 + x)$$

$$\therefore \quad x = 1.04 - 1$$

$$x = 0.04$$

30. ***(30)*** Given, Molality $= 1.35$ mol kg^{-1}

$$\text{Molarity} = \left(\frac{1000 \text{ dm}}{1000 + mm_2}\right)$$

$$= \frac{1000 \times 1.34 \times 1.35}{1000 + 1.35 \times 342} = 1.23 \text{ M}$$

$$\pi = MRT$$

$$= 1.23 \times 0.0821 \times 298 = 30.27 \text{ atm}$$

$$\approx 30 \text{ atm}$$

31. ***(2)*** $KCN \rightleftharpoons K^+ + CN^-$

$$i = 1 + (y-1)x$$

$$= 1 + (2-1)1 = 2$$

$$\Delta T_f(KCN) = K_f \times mi$$

$$0.781 = K_f \times 0.2 \times 2$$

$$K_f = 1.95°C \text{ molal}^{-1}$$

On adding $Hg(CN)_2$

	$2KCN$ +	$Hg(CN)_2$ $\rightleftharpoons$	$K_2[Hg(CN)]$
Initial	0.2 mol	0.1 mol	0.1 mol
Final	—	—	0.1 mol

Thus $K_2[Hg(CN)_4]$ is 0.1 molal

$$T_f \text{ (complex)} = (-0.781 + 0.417)° \text{ C}$$

Freezing point of water = 0° C

$$\therefore \quad \Delta T_f \text{ (complex)} = (+0.781 - 0.417)° = 0.364°$$

$$\Delta T_f(\text{complex}) = K_f(0.1) \times i$$

$$i = \frac{0.364}{1.95 \times 0.1} = 1.86 \approx 2$$

32. ***(191)*** Solute X in A,

$$2X \rightleftharpoons X_2$$

$$X \rightleftharpoons \frac{1}{2} X_2$$

$$\because \quad i = 1 + (y-1)x$$

$$= 1 + \left(\frac{1}{2} - 1\right) 1 = \frac{1}{2}$$

By using, $\Delta T_f(A) = \dfrac{1000 \times K_f \times w_2 \times i}{w_1 \times m_2}$

$$\alpha = \frac{1000 \times w_2 \times 1.86}{w_1 \times m_2} \times \frac{1}{2}$$

Solute X in B

$$3X \rightleftharpoons X_3$$

$$X \rightleftharpoons \frac{1}{3} X_3$$

$$i = 1 + \left(\frac{1}{3} - 1\right) 1 = \frac{1}{3}$$

$$\Delta T_f \text{ (in } B)\beta = \frac{1000 \times K_f \times w_2 \times i}{w_1 \times m_2} = \frac{1000 \times w_2 \times 1.46}{w_1 \times m_2} \times \frac{1}{3}$$

Thus, $\dfrac{\alpha}{\beta} = \dfrac{1.86}{2} \times \dfrac{3}{1.46} = 1.910 = 191 \times 10^{-2}$

33. ***(0.5)*** By using,

$$\Delta T_f = K_f \times m \times i$$

Taking log on both side then we get,

$$\log \Delta T_f = \log K_f + \log (mi) \quad \ldots \text{(i)}$$

By comparing the Eq. (i) with $y = mx + c$

when $\quad \log \Delta T_f = 0.56, \log k_f = 0.4$

$$\log (mi) = 0.16$$

$$mi = 1.5$$

But $\quad m = 0.5$ molal

$$\therefore \quad i = 3$$

But, $\quad 1 + 4x = 3$

$$4x = 2$$

$$x = 0.5$$

34. ***(0.2)*** For solute $A \rightleftharpoons X + Y, y = 2$

$$x = \alpha = 0.8$$

$$\therefore \quad i(A) = 1 + (2-1)\, 0.8 = 1.8$$

For solute $B \quad B \rightleftharpoons \dfrac{B}{2}$

$$y = \frac{1}{2}$$

$$\therefore \quad i(B) = \left[1 + \left(\frac{1}{2} - 1\right)\beta\right] = \left(1 - \frac{\beta}{2}\right)$$

$$\Delta T_b(A) = K_b \times \text{molality} \times i = K_b \times m \times 1.8$$

$$\Delta T_b(B) = K_b \times m \times \left(1 - \frac{\beta}{2}\right)$$

$$\Delta T_b(A) = 2\Delta T_b(B) \text{ given}$$

$$1.8 = 2\left(1 - \frac{\beta}{2}\right) = 2 - \beta$$

$$\beta = 0.2$$

Practice Element 01 : Target JEE Main

1. ***(c)*** $p_{O_3} = p_{\text{total}} X_{O_3}$

$$12 \times 10^{-6} \text{ mm} = 10 \text{ mm } X_{O_3}$$

$$\therefore \quad X_{O_3} = 1.2 \times 10^{-7}$$

$$X_{\text{air}} = 1 - X_{O_3} \approx 1.0$$

$$\therefore \quad X_{O_3} = n_{\text{total}}\ (1.2 \times 10^{-7})$$

$$= (n_{O_3} + n_{\text{air}})(1.2 \times 10^{-7})$$

Since $n_{O_3} \lll n_{\text{air}}$

$$\therefore \quad n_{O_3} = n_{\text{air}}\ (1.2 \times 10^{-7})$$

$$\therefore \quad \frac{n_{O_3}}{n_{\text{air}}} = 1.2 \times 10^{-7}$$

$$\therefore \quad \frac{w\,(O_3)\, m\,(\text{air})}{w\,(\text{air})\, m\,(O_3)} = 12 \times 10^{-7}$$

$$\frac{w\,(O_3)}{w\,(\text{air})} = \frac{12 \times 10^{-7} \times 48}{29}$$

Thus, O_3 (in ppm) $= \dfrac{1.2 \times 10^{-7} \times 48}{29} \times 1.0 \times 10^{6}$

$$= 0.20 \text{ ppm}$$

2. ***(d)*** By Henry's law,

$$p_{\text{gas}} = K_H X_{\text{gas}} = K_H X_{N_2}$$

$$X_{N_2} = \frac{n_{N_2}}{n_{N_2} + n_{\text{blood}}} \approx \frac{n_{N_2}}{n_{\text{blood}}}$$

Since, $n_{N_2} \lll n_{\text{blood}}$

$$\therefore \quad p_{N_2} = K_H \frac{n_{N_2}}{n_{\text{blood}}}$$

$$\Rightarrow \quad n_{N_2} = p_{N_2} \frac{n_{\text{blood}}}{K_H}$$

$$n_{\text{blood}} = 5 \text{ L} = 5000 \text{ g} = \frac{5000}{18}$$

$$p_{N_2} = 0.80\ p_{\text{total}}$$

(i) When, $p_{\text{gas}} = 1.0$ bar

$$\therefore \quad p_{N_2} = 0.80 \text{ bar}$$

$$\therefore \quad n_{N_2} = 0.80 \frac{\left(\frac{5000}{18}\right) \text{bar}}{9.04 \times 10^{4} \text{ bar}}$$

$$= 2.46 \times 10^{-3} \text{ mol}$$

(ii) When $p_{\text{gas}} = 50.0$ bar

$$p_{N_2} = 50 \times 0.8 = 40 \text{ bar}$$

$$n_{N_2} = \frac{40 \times \frac{5000}{18}}{9.04 \times 10^{4}}$$

$$\therefore \quad n_{N_2} = 2.46 \times 10^{-3} \times 50$$

$$= 0.123 \text{ mol}$$

3. **(c)** $2C_6H_5COOH \rightleftharpoons (C_6H_5COOH)_2$

or $C_6H_5COOH \rightleftharpoons \frac{1}{2}(C_6H_5COOH)_2$

x, y = stoichiometric coefficient of C_6H_5COOH and $(C_6H_5COOH)_2$ viz.

$$y = \frac{1}{2}, x = 1 \text{ (100\% dimer formation)}$$

$\therefore$ i = van't Hoff factor $= 1 + (y-1)x = 1/2$

By Raoult's law,

$$\frac{\Delta p}{p^\circ} = X_{solute} = \frac{n_1 i}{n_1 i + n_2}$$

where $n_1 = \frac{122 \text{ g}}{122 \text{ g mol}^{-1}} = 1 \text{ mol}$

benzoic acid

$$n_2 = \frac{1000 \text{ g}}{78 \text{ g mol}^{-1}} = 12.8205 \text{ mol}$$

$$\therefore \quad \frac{\Delta p}{p^\circ} = \frac{i}{i + 12.8205} = \frac{0.5}{0.5 + 12.8205}$$

$$\Delta p = 66.6 \times 0.0375 = 2.5$$

$$\therefore \quad p^\circ - p = 2.5$$

$$\therefore \quad p = p^\circ - 2.5 = 66.6 - 2.5 = 64.10 \text{ cm of Hg}$$

4. **(c)** Statement I is correct but statement II is incorrect. Its correct form is : If the mole fraction of solute and molality of solution are equal to 0.1 then the molar mass of solvent will be 1111 g mol^{-1}. Their explanation are given as ;

(I) Molality (m) is related to molarity (M) density (d) and molar mass (m_1) of solute by equation :

$$m = \frac{1000\,M}{(1000d - Mm_1)}$$

$$0.1 = \frac{1000 \times 0.1}{(1000d - 0.1 \times 342)}$$

$$1000d = 1034.2$$

$$\therefore \quad d = \frac{1034.2}{1000} = 1.0342 \text{ g mL}^{-1}$$

(II) Molality (m) of solution and mole fraction χ_1 of solute and molar mass of solvent (m_2) are related to each other

$$m = \frac{1000\,\chi_1}{(1-\chi_1)m_2}$$

Given, $m = \chi_1 = 0.1$

$$0.1 = \frac{1000 \times 0.1}{0.9 \times m_2}$$

$$\therefore \quad m_2 = \frac{1000}{0.9} = 1111 \text{ g mol}^{-1}$$

5. **(c)** $\Delta T_b = \frac{1000\, w_1 K_b}{m_1 w_2}$

$$\therefore m_1 \text{(molar mass of solute)} = \frac{1000\, w_1 K_b}{\Delta T_b w_2}$$

$$= \frac{1000 \times 2.5 \times 0.52}{2 \times 100} = 6.5 \text{ g mol}^{-1}$$

$$\frac{\Delta p}{p^\circ} = \frac{w_1}{m_1}\frac{m_2}{w_2} \text{ for dilute solution}$$

$$= \frac{2.5 \times 18}{6.5 \times 100} = 0.07$$

$$\therefore \quad \Delta p = 0.07 \times 760 = 53.2 \text{ mm Hg}$$

$$\therefore \quad p^\circ - p_s = 53.2$$

$$p_s = 760 - 53.2 = 706.8 \approx 707 \text{ mm Hg}$$

6. **(c)** $\left(\frac{100}{1.005}\right)$ mL of NaCl solution has $\left(\frac{0.86}{58.5}\right)$ mol of NaCl.

$$\therefore \quad \text{M (NaCl)} = \frac{(0.86/58.5) \text{ mol} \times 1000}{\left(\frac{100}{1.005}\right) \text{L}} = 0.1477 \text{ M}$$

By using,

$$\pi = iMRT$$

$$= 2 \times 0.1477 \times 0.0821 \times 310 = 7.52 \text{ atm}$$

7. **(b)** By Raoult's law,

$$\frac{\Delta p}{p^\circ} = X_1 \text{(mole fraction of solute)}$$

$$= \frac{n_1}{n_1 + n_2} \approx \frac{n_1}{n_2} = \frac{w_1}{m_1}\frac{m_2}{w_2}$$

$$\therefore \quad \frac{w_1}{m_1 w_2} = \frac{\Delta p}{p^\circ\, m_2} = \frac{0.013}{78} \quad \ldots \text{(i)}$$

Osmotic pressure $\pi = \frac{n_1}{V}RT = \frac{w_1}{m_1 V}RT$

But $\frac{w_2}{V} = d$

$$V = \frac{w_2}{d} = \frac{w_2 \text{ g}}{8.149 \times 10^2 \text{ g}} \text{ dm}^3$$

$$= \frac{w_2}{8.149 \times 10^2 \times 10^3} \text{ m}^3 = \frac{w_2}{8.149 \times 10^5} \text{ m}^3$$

$$\therefore \quad \pi = \frac{w_1 \times 8.149 \times 10^5}{(m_1 \times w_2)} RT \quad \ldots \text{(ii)}$$

From Eqs. (i) and (ii)

$$\pi = \frac{0.013 \text{ mol} \times 8.149 \times 10^5 \times 8.3143 \text{ Nm mol}^{-1}\text{K}^{-1} \times 353 \text{ K}}{78 \text{ m}^3}$$

$$= 3.98 \times 10^5 \text{Nm}^{-2} \approx 4.0 \times 10^5 \text{ Nm}^{-2}$$

8. **(b)** Pressure = hdg

$$h = 77.8 \text{ mm} = 0.0778 \text{ m}$$

$$d = 1 \times 10^3 \text{ kg m}^{-3}$$

$$g = 9.81 \text{ms}^{-2}$$

π (osmotic pressure) = hdg

$$= 0.0778 \text{ m} \times 1 \times 10^3 \text{ kg m}^{-3} \times 9.81 \text{ms}^{-2}$$

$$= 763.2 \text{ kg m}^{-1}\text{s}^{-2} = 7632 \text{ Nm}^{-2}$$

Also, $\pi = \frac{nRT}{V} = \frac{w}{m}\frac{RT}{V}$

$$\therefore \quad m = \frac{wRT}{\pi V} = \frac{20 \times 10^{-3} \text{ kg} \times 8.314 \text{ Jmol}^{-1}\text{K}^{-1} \times 298 \text{ K}}{763.2 \text{ Nm}^{-2} \times 1 \times 10^{-3} \text{ m}^3}$$

$$= 64.92 \text{ kg mol}^{-1}$$

$1\ Nm^{-2} = 1\ kg\ ms^{-2}\ m^{-2} = 1\ kg\ m^{-1}\ s^{-2}$

$1\ J = 1\ Nm = 1\ kg\ ms^{-2} m = 1\ kg\ m^2\ s^{-2}$

$1\ N = 1\ kg\ ms^{-2}$

9. ***(d)***

Solutions	Osmotic Pressure
10 g glucose in 200 mL solution	$p_1 = \dfrac{\left(\frac{10}{180}\right)\text{mol}}{0.2\ L} RT = 0.28RT$
10 g urea in 100 mL solution	$p_2 = \dfrac{\left(\frac{10}{60}\right)\text{mol}}{0.1\ L} RT = 1.67\,RT$
10 g sucrose in 50 mL solution	$p_3 = \dfrac{\left(\frac{10}{342}\right)\text{mol}}{0.05\ L} RT = 0.585RT$

Thus, $p_1 < p_3 < p_2$.

10. ***(a)*** Solute X is non- electrolyte

For 1 molal solution of X,

$$\Delta T_f = BE = 279 - 273 = 6°$$

$$\therefore \quad \Delta T_f = K_f m = K_f \times 1$$

$$\therefore \quad K_f = \frac{\Delta T_f}{1} = 6°\ \text{mol}^{-1}\ \text{kg}$$

For 10% solution of X

$$\Delta T_f = CD = 279 - 268 = 11\,K$$

$$\therefore \quad \Delta T_f = \frac{1000\ w_1}{m_1 w_2} K_f$$

$$m_1 = \frac{1000 \times 10 \times 6}{11 \times 100} = 54.54\ \text{g mol}^{-1}.$$

11. ***(d)*** $\Delta T_f = \dfrac{1000\ K_f w_1\ (i)}{m_1 w_2}$

$$(5.3 - 4.47) = \frac{1000 \times 5.12 \times 0.223 \times i}{136 \times 4.4}$$

$$\therefore \quad i = 0.435$$

We observe $i < 1$, hence there is dimer formation of A in benzene

$$A \rightleftharpoons \frac{1}{2} A_2$$

$y = \dfrac{1}{2}$ = number of products formed from 1 mole reactants.

If $i = 1$, no change

$i > 1$, ionisation

$i < 1$, polymer formation.

12. ***(d)*** According to Raoult's law

$$p = p_A^\circ X_A + p_B^\circ X_B$$

$$280 = 240 \times 0.6 + p_B^\circ \times 0.4$$

$$136 = 0.4 p_B^\circ$$

$$p_B^\circ = 340\ \text{mm}$$

13. ***(c)*** Mixture contains 78 g benzene = 1 mol benzene and 46 g toluene = 0.5 mol toluene

Total moles of benzene and toluene = 1.5 mol

Mole fraction of benzene in mixture $= \dfrac{1}{1.5} = \dfrac{2}{3}$

Vapour pressure of benzene $p_B^\circ = 78$ torr

$\therefore$ Partial vapour pressure of benzene

$$= p_B^\circ \times X_B$$

$$= 78 \times \frac{2}{3}$$

$$= 52\ \text{torr}$$

14. ***(b)*** Number of moles of acetic acid $= \dfrac{V \times \rho}{\text{Molar mass}}$

Molar mass of acetic acid = 60 g mol^{-1}

$$= \frac{(3.4)\ \text{mL} \times (1.02)\text{gmL}^{-1}}{(60)\ \text{g mol}^{-1}}$$

$$= 0.0578\ \text{mol}$$

$$\text{Molality} = \frac{0.0578}{3000} \times 1000$$

[As 3 L solution in water is prepared so mass of solvent becomes 3000 g]

$$= 0.0193$$

By using,

$$\Delta T_f = i \times K_f \times m$$

$$i = \frac{\Delta T_f}{K_f \times m} = \frac{0.1382}{1.85 \times 0.0193}$$

Dissociation of acetic acid;

$$i = 3.870$$

$$CH_3COOH \rightleftharpoons CH_3COO^{\ominus} + H^{\oplus}$$

Initial	n	0	0
final	$n(1-x)$	nx	nx

Total moles $= n - nx + 2nx$

$$= n - nx$$

$$i = \frac{n(1-x) + nx + nx}{n}$$

$$i = 1 + x$$

$$3.87 = 1 + x$$

x (degree of dissociation) $= 3.87 - 1 = 2.870$

% degree of dissociation $= 2.870 \times 100 = 287\%$

15. ***(d)*** Let the degree of association of acetic acid in benzene is α, then,

$$2CH_3COOH \rightleftharpoons (CH_3COOH)_2$$

Initial moles	1	0
Moles at Eq.	$1-\alpha$	$\dfrac{\alpha}{2}$

$\therefore$ Total moles $= 1 - \alpha + \dfrac{\alpha}{2} = 1 - \dfrac{\alpha}{2}$

Now, $\quad \Delta T_f = i.\,K_f.m \quad$ ...(i)

$$m = \frac{0.3}{60} \times \frac{1000}{20}$$

By putting the value of Eq. (i), we get

$$0.48 = \left[1 - \frac{\alpha}{2}\right] \times (5.32) \left[\frac{0.3}{60} \times \frac{1000}{20}\right]$$

$$1 - \frac{\alpha}{2} = \frac{0.48 \times 60 \times 20}{5.32 \times 0.3 \times 1000}$$

$$1 - \frac{\alpha}{2} = 0.36 \Rightarrow \frac{\alpha}{2} = 1 - 0.36$$

$$\alpha = 0.64 \times 2 = 1.28$$

% of association = 128%

16. ***(a)*** By using, $\pi = CRT$

$$\text{Molarity} = \frac{1.36 \times 1000}{M \times 100 \text{ (mL)}} = \frac{1360}{100 \times M}$$

$$\pi = \frac{1360}{100 \times M} \times 0.083 \times 300$$

Given, $\pi = 2.34 \times 10^{-3}$ bar

$$\text{Therefore, } M = \frac{1360}{100 \times 2.3 \times 10^{-3}} \times 0.083 \times 300$$

$$= 147.23 \times 10^{-3} \text{g/ mol}$$

17. ***(d)*** When mole fraction elevation in boiling point is given, then

$$\Delta T_b = K_b \chi_{\text{solute}}$$

$$0.3 = 36.1\, \chi_{\text{solute}}$$

$$\therefore \quad \chi_{\text{solute}} = \frac{0.3}{36.1} = \frac{3}{361}$$

$$\chi_{\text{solvent}} = 1 - \frac{3}{361} = \frac{358}{361}$$

$$\therefore \quad \frac{\chi_{\text{solute}}}{\chi_{\text{solvent}}} = \frac{3}{358} \quad \text{or} \quad \frac{n_1(\text{solute})}{n_2(\text{solvent})} = 3/358$$

$$\frac{n_1}{w_2 / m_2} = \frac{3}{358}$$

$$\therefore \quad \frac{n_1(\text{solute})}{w_2(\text{solvent})} = \frac{3}{358 \times 92}$$

Thus solute = 3 mol

Solvent = (358 × 92) g = (0.358 × 92) kg

$$\therefore \quad \text{Molality} = \frac{\text{Moles of solute}}{\text{kg of solvent}} = \frac{3}{0.358 \times 92}$$

$$= 0.091 \text{ mol kg}^{-1}$$

18. ***(b)*** Dissociation of KCl is given as :

$$KCl \rightleftharpoons K^+ + Cl^-$$

$$Cl^- + Ag^+ \longrightarrow AgCl \downarrow$$

(White ppt.)

When Cl^- is completely precipitated, additional drop of $AgNO_3$ gives chocolate coloured precipitate with K_2CrO_4.

$$2Ag^+ + CrO_4^{2-} \longrightarrow Ag_2CrO_4 \downarrow$$

(Chocolate coloured ppt.)

At the end point,

$$M_1V_1 = M_2V_2$$

$$KCl = AgNO_3$$

$$M_1 \times 25 = 1.0 \times 20$$

$$M_1 = 0.8\,\text{M}$$

i(van't Hoff factor for KCl) $= 1 + x = 1 + 1 = 2$

By using, $\Delta T_f = i.K_f.m$

$$= 2 \times 2 \times 0.8 = 3.2^\circ$$

19. ***(a)*** Given conditions are that of STP when volume of $O_2 =$ 22400 mL mol^{-1}

$$\therefore 48.9 \text{ mL } O_2 \text{ at STP} = \frac{48.9}{22400} \text{ mol } O_2$$

$$= 2.183 \times 10^{-3} \text{mol L}^{-1}$$

Solubility ∝ pressure

$$\therefore \quad \frac{S_2}{S_1} = \frac{p_2}{p_1}$$

$$S_2 = S_1 \frac{p_2}{p_1}$$

$$= 2.183 \times 10^{-3} \text{ mol L}^{-1} \times \frac{0.2095 \text{ atm}}{1.0 \text{ atm}}$$

$$= 4.57 \times 10^{-4} \text{ mol L}^{-1}.$$

20. ***(b)*** Moles of CO$(n) = \dfrac{pV}{RT}$

$$= \frac{1 \text{ atm} \times \frac{0.0354}{1000} \text{L}}{0.0821 \text{ L atm mol}^{-1}\text{K}^{-1} \times 273 \text{ K}}$$

$$= 1.58 \times 10^{-6} \text{ mol mL}^{-1} \text{ water}$$

$$= 1.58 \times 10^{-3} \text{ mol L}^{-1} \text{ water}$$

Thus, solubility at 1 atm $= 1.58 \times 10^{-3}$ M

By Henry's law,

Solubility ∝ pressure

$$\therefore \quad \frac{S_2}{S_1} = \frac{p_2}{p_1}$$

$$\therefore \quad p_2 = p_1 \frac{S_2}{S_1} = \frac{1 \times 0.01}{1.58 \times 10^{-3}} = 6.33 \text{ atm}$$

21. ***(158)*** Let Na_2CO_3 be $= w$ g $= \dfrac{w}{106}$ mol

Thus, $NaHCO_3 = (1 - w)$ g $= \dfrac{(1-w)}{84}$ mol

$$\text{Given,} \quad \frac{w}{106} = \frac{1-w}{84}$$

$$\therefore \quad w = 0.5579 \text{ g } Na_2CO_3 = \frac{0.5579}{106} \text{ mol}$$

$$= 5.2632 \times 10^{-3} \text{ mol}$$

and $NaHCO_3 = 5.2632 \times 10^{-3}$ mol

$$Na_2CO_3 + H_2SO_4 \longrightarrow Na_2SO_4 + H_2O + CO_2$$

1 mol 1 mol

H_2SO_4 required by 5.2632×10^{-3} mol Na_2CO_3

$$= 5.2632 \times 10^{-3} \text{mole}$$

$$2NaHCO_3 + H_2SO_4 \longrightarrow Na_2SO_4 + 2H_2O + CO_2$$

2 mol 1 mol

H_2SO_4 required by 5.263×10^{-3} mol

$$NaHCO_3 = \frac{5.2632 \times 10^{-3}}{2} \text{ mol}$$

Thus, H_2SO_4 required

$$= \left(5.2632 + \frac{5.2632}{2}\right) \times 10^{-3} \text{ mol}$$

$$= 7.895 \times 10^{-3} \text{ mol}$$

But actual H_2SO_4 required $= x$ mL of 0.05 M

$$\frac{\text{Molarity} \times \text{Volume (in mL)}}{1000} = \text{moles of solute}$$

$$\therefore \quad \frac{x \times 0.05}{1000} = 7.895 \times 10^{-3}$$

$$\therefore \quad x = 157.9 \text{ mL} \approx 158.0 \text{ mL}$$

22. ***(3)*** In both case solvents are different but solute is same.

$$\Delta T_f(\text{in water}) = K_f(\text{water})\ mi$$

$$\Delta T_f(\text{in benzene}) = K_f(\text{benzene})\ m$$

$$\therefore \frac{\Delta T_f\ (\text{in water})}{\Delta T_f\ (\text{in benzene})} = \frac{K_f\ (\text{water})\ i}{K_f\ (\text{benzene})}$$

$$\therefore \quad i = \frac{1.40}{1.28} \times 2.75 = 3.0$$

23. ***(2)*** $\Delta T_f = K_f mi$

In solvent A,

$$2X \rightleftharpoons X_2$$

$$X \rightleftharpoons \frac{1}{2} X_2$$

$$y = \frac{1}{2}$$

$$\therefore \quad i = 1 + (y-1)\alpha = 1 + \left(\frac{1}{2} - 1\right) 1 = \frac{1}{2}$$

In solvent B, $\quad X \rightleftharpoons \frac{1}{3} X_3$

$$\therefore \quad y = \frac{1}{3}$$

$$\therefore \quad i = 1 + \left(\frac{1}{3} - 1\right) 1 = \frac{1}{3}$$

$$\therefore \Delta T_f\ (\text{in solvent } A) = \alpha = \frac{(K_f)_A\ m}{2} = \frac{1.86m}{2}$$

$$\Delta T_f\ (\text{in solvent } B) = \beta = \frac{(K_f)_B m}{3} = \frac{1.86m}{3}$$

$$\therefore \quad \frac{\alpha}{\beta} = \frac{1.86 \times 3}{1.36 \times 2} = 2.0$$

24. ***(8)*** Osmotic pressure, $\pi = \frac{n}{V} RT = \frac{w}{mV} RT$

$$\pi = \frac{CRT}{m}$$

$$\therefore \quad \frac{\pi}{C} = \frac{RT}{m}$$

Thus, $\frac{RT}{m} = OA$ when $C \to 0$

$$\therefore \quad OA = \frac{RT}{m} = \frac{0.0821 \times 300}{308} = 0.079$$

$$= 8.0 \times 10^{-2} = x \times 10^{-y}$$

Thus, $x = 8$

25. ***(27)*** By Raoult's law,

$$\frac{\Delta p}{p^\circ} = X_{\text{solute}} = \frac{n_{\text{solute}}}{n_{\text{solute}} + n_{H_2O}} = 0.05$$

Case I. If solution is dilute,

$n_{H_2O} >> n_{\text{solute}}$, then

$$\therefore \quad \frac{n_{\text{solute}}}{n_{H_2O}} = 0.05$$

Thus, if $n_{\text{solute}} = 0.05$ mol

water = 1 mol = 18 g = 0.018 kg

$$\therefore \text{Molality} = \frac{0.05}{0.018} \text{ mol kg}^{-1}$$

$$\therefore \quad \Delta T_f = K_f \cdot m$$

$$= 1.86 \times \frac{0.05}{0.018} = 5.17^\circ$$

Case II. Solution is of moderate concentration,

then $\frac{n_{\text{solute}}}{n_{H_2O} + n_{\text{solute}}} = 0.05$

$$\therefore \quad \frac{n_{\text{solute}}}{n_{H_2O}} = \frac{1}{19}$$

$\therefore$ If solute is 1 mol, then water is = 19 mol

$$= 19 \times 18 \text{ g} = 342 \text{ g}$$

$$= 0.342 \text{ kg}$$

$$\therefore \text{Molality} = \frac{1 \text{ mol}}{0.342 \text{ kg}} = 2.924 \text{ mol kg}^{-1}$$

$$\therefore \quad \Delta T_f' = 1.86 \times 2.924 = 5.44^\circ$$

$$\therefore \quad \Delta T_f - \Delta T_f' = 5.17 - 5.44^\circ$$

$$= -0.27^\circ = -(27 \times 10^{-2})^\circ$$

$$\therefore \quad x = 27$$

26. ***(2)*** By using,

$$\Delta T_f = K_f . m$$

For KCN solution

$$0.80 = K_f \times 0.2 \times 2$$

$$K_f = \frac{0.80}{0.4} \quad \ldots \text{(i)}$$

According to given equation,

$$Hg(CN)_2 + mCN \longrightarrow Hg(CN)_{m+2}^{m}$$

	$Hg(CN)_2$	mCN	$Hg(CN)_{m+2}^{m}$
Initial	0.1	0.2	0
final	0	(0.2 – 0.1 m)	(0.1)

Now, Molarity of $K^+ = 0.2$ M

Molarity of $CN^- = (0.2 - 0.1m)$ M

Final effective molality

$$= (0.2 - 0.1m) + 0.1 + 0.2 = 0.5 - 0.1m$$

Now, $0.60 = K_f \times (0.5 - 0.1\,m)$ ...(ii)

From Eqs. (i) and (ii)

$$0.60 = \frac{0.80}{0.4} \times (0.5 - 0.1\,m)$$

$$m = \frac{0.4}{0.2} = 2$$

27. ***(96)*** Let $A : CH_3COOH$

Then $2A \rightleftharpoons A_2$

i (van't Hoff factor) $= [1 + (y-1)x]$

$y = \frac{1}{2}$ = number of product from 1 mole of A.

$$i = \left(1 - \frac{x}{2}\right)$$

By using,

$$\Delta T_f = \frac{1000\, w_1 K_f}{m_1 w_2} \quad \text{...(i)}$$

$$0.38 = \frac{1000 \times 0.3 \times 5.12}{60 \times 35}\left(1 - \frac{x}{2}\right)$$

$$\left(1 - \frac{x}{2}\right) = \frac{0.38 \times 60 \times 35}{1000 \times 0.3 \times 5.12} = \frac{798}{1536} = 0.519$$

$$2 - x = 1.039$$

$$x = 0.961$$

Thus, 96%

28. ***(101)*** By using,

$$K_b = \frac{\Delta T_b \times w_1 \times Mw_2}{1000 \times w_2}$$

For CCl_4; $K_b = \frac{0.211 \times 56 \times 128}{1000 \times 0.2563} = 5.901$

$$Mw_2 = \frac{1000 \times K_b \times w_2}{\Delta T_b \times w_1}$$

$$= \frac{1000 \times 5.901 \times 0.6216}{0.647 \times 56} = 101.23 = 101$$

29. ***(800)*** As we know,

ΔT_f = freezing point of H_2O – freezing point of ethylene glycol solution.

$= 0 - (-6°) = 6°$

$K_f = 1.86°$ K kg mol^{-1}

w_1 = mass of ethylene glycol in grams

w_2 = mass of solvent (H_2O) in grams = 4000 g

m_1 = molar mass of ethylene glycol

= 62 g mol^{-1}

By using, $\Delta T_f = \frac{1000 \times K_f \times w_1}{m_1 \times w_2}$

$$6 = \frac{1000 \times 1.86 \times w_1}{62 \times 4000}$$

$$w_1 = 800 \text{ g}$$

30. ***(12)*** Given, concentration of $BaCl_2 = 0.01$ M

$$\pi_{xy} = 4\pi_{BaCl_2}$$

$$i \times CRT = 4 \times i \times CRT \quad \text{...(i)}$$

For the calculation of i,

$$XY \longrightarrow X^+ + Y^- \text{ (Here, } i = 2)$$

$$BaCl_2 \longrightarrow Ba^{2+} + 2Cl^- \text{ (Here, } i = 3)$$

Putting the value of i in Equ. (i)

$$2[XY] = 4 \times 3 \times [BaCl_2]$$

$$2[XY] = 12 \times 0.02$$

$$[XY] = 6 \times 0.02$$

So, the concentration of $[XY] = 0.12$

$= 12 \times 10^{-2}$ mol L^{-1}

So, the value of x is 12.

Check Through PYQs : JEE Main

1. ***(164)*** $M_{soln} = V_{soln} \times d_{soln}$

$= 500 \times 1.25 = 625$ g

Mass of solute $(x) = 0.2 \times 0.5 \times 159.5 = 15.95$ g

$$n_{solute} = \frac{15.95 \text{ g}}{159.5 \text{ g/mol}} = 0.1$$

Mass of solvent = Mass of solution – Mass of solute

$= 625 - 15.95 = 609.05$ g

Now using formula of molality

$$\text{Molality} = \frac{\text{Number of moles of solute} \times 1000}{\text{Mass of solvent (in kg)}}$$

$$m = \frac{0.1 \times 1000}{609.05}$$

$$m = 0.164 \text{ m}$$

$$m = 164 \times 10^{-3} \text{ m}$$

2. ***(b)*** Given,

Mass of NaCl = 5.85 g

Volume of water = 500 mL = 0.5 L

Using, $\text{Molarity} = \frac{\text{Number of moles of NaCl}}{\text{Volume of solution (in L)}}$

$$M = \frac{\frac{5.85}{58.5}}{0.5}$$

$\Rightarrow$ $M = 0.2$ M

3. ***(c)*** Mole fraction

$$= \frac{\text{Number of moles of component}}{\text{Total number of moles of all the component}}$$

From above definition of mole fraction, mole fraction of C will be $= \frac{n_C}{n_A + n_B + n_C}$

where n_A, n_B, n_C are number of moles of substance A, B and C.

Hence, option (c) is correct.

4. ***(4)*** Given, let mass of solution = 100 g

Mass of H_2SO_4 in solution = 31.4%

density = 1.25 g/mL

Molar mass of H_2SO_4 = 98 g/mol

$$\text{Molarity, } M = \frac{n_{\text{solute}}}{V} \times 1000$$

$$= \frac{(31.4/98)}{(100/125)} \times 1000 = 4.005 \approx 4\text{ M}$$

Hence, nearest integer is 4.

5. ***(148)*** $\text{Molarity} = \dfrac{\text{Number of moles of solute}}{\text{Volume of solution (L)}}$

$$2.6 \times 10^{-3} = \frac{x/85}{0.67141}$$

$$x = 0.148\text{ g}$$

$$\text{Conc. of dichloromethane in ppm} = \frac{0.148}{1.49 \times 671.141} \times 10^6$$

$$= 148\text{ ppm}$$

6. ***(b)*** The molecular mass of glucose is 180 g/mol

$$\text{Mass of carbon in 250 gram solution is} = \frac{250 \times 10.8}{100} = 27\text{ g}$$

We know that, 72 g of C is present in 180 g glucose

so, 27 g of carbon is present in $\dfrac{180}{72} \times 27$ g glucose

$$\Rightarrow \text{Weight of glucose} = \frac{180}{72} \times 27 = 67.5\text{ g}$$

So, mass of solvent = 250 − 67.5 = 182.5g

$$\Rightarrow \text{Molality} = \frac{67.5 \times 1000}{180 \times 182.5} = 2.055 \approx 2.06\text{ m}$$

7. ***(54)*** Moles of nitric acid = $800 \times 10^{-3} \times 0.5 = 0.4$

$$\text{Moles of niric acid evaporated} = \frac{11.5}{63} = 0.182$$

Moles left = 0.4 − 0.182 = 0.218

$$\text{Molarity} = \frac{0.218 \times 10^3}{400} = 0.545\text{ M} = 54.5 \times 10^{-2}\text{ M}$$

8. ***(a)*** Since, mass of a substance does not depend on temperature, the molality of KCl solution will remain same when the solution is cooled.

Therefore, both (A) and (R) are true and (R) is the correct explanation of (A).

9. ***(c)*** Given, density of commercial acid = 1.46 g/mL

So, mass of commercial acid = Density × Volume

= 1.46 × 1000 = 1460 g

Total mass of solution = 460 g

$$\text{Mass of HCl} = \frac{35}{100} \times 1460 = 511\text{g}$$

$$\text{Mole of HCl} = \frac{511}{36.5} = 14\text{ moles}$$

$$\text{Molarity} = \frac{n_{\text{HCl}}}{\text{Vol (L)}} = \frac{14}{1} = 14\text{ M}$$

10. ***(64)*** Given, mass of $CuSO_4 \cdot 5H_2O$ = 80 g

The concentration of copper sulphate solution is $x \times 10^{-3}$ mol/L.

Molar mass of $CuSO_4 \cdot 5H_2O$ = 63.54 + 32 + 16 × 4 + 5 × 18

= 249.54 g / mol

$$\text{Number of moles of solute} = \frac{\text{Weight of solute}}{\text{Molecular mass of solute}}$$

$$= \frac{80\text{ g}}{249.54\text{ g / mol}} = 0.32\text{ mol}$$

Volume of solution = 5 L

$$\text{Molarity} = \frac{\text{Number of moles of solute}}{\text{Volume of solution (in L)}}$$

$$\therefore \quad \text{Molarity} = \frac{0.32}{5}$$

$$= 64.11 \times 10^{-3}\text{ mol / L}$$

$$\therefore \quad x = 64.11$$

or $\quad x \approx 64$

Hence, answer is 64.

11. ***(20)*** $\text{Molarity} = \dfrac{\text{Weight of solute}}{\text{M.M. of solute} \times \text{Vol. of solution (in L)}}$

Molecular mass of solute of $[H_2C_2O_4 \cdot 2H_2O]$ = 126 g

$$x \times 10^{-2} = \frac{6.3\text{ g} / 126\text{ g}}{250\text{ mL}} \times 1000$$

$$x \times 10^{-2} = 0.2$$

$$x \times 10^{-2} = 20 \times 10^{-2}$$

$$\therefore \quad x = 20$$

12. ***(9)*** Molarity

$$(m) = \frac{M \times 1000}{\{(1000d) - M \times M_{\text{solute}}\}}$$

M_{solute} = molar mass of solute

Putting the values,

$$6.50 = \frac{M \times 1000}{(1000 \times 1.89) - (M \times 56)}$$

$$\text{On solving, } \quad M = \frac{12285}{1364}$$

$$M = 9\text{ molar}$$

13. ***(2)*** Given, weight of compound A = 4.5 g

Molecular weight of compound A = 90 g/mol

Volume of solution (in mL) = 250 mL

$$= \frac{\frac{4.5}{90}}{\frac{250}{1000}} = 0.2 \text{ or } = 2 \times 10^{-1}\text{ M}$$

Hence, $x \times 10^{-1} = 2 \times 10^{-1} \Rightarrow x = 2$

14. ***(100)*** Hardness in ppm

$$= \frac{\text{Mass of hardness causing substances} \times 10^6}{\text{Mass of water sample}}$$

Here, $[Mg^{2+}] = 10^{-3}$ M

$n_{Mg^{2+}} = 10^{-3}$ per 1 L water ≅ 1000 g

Mass of 10^{-3} moles of $CaCO_3$

$$= 10^{-3} \times 100\text{ g} = 0.1\text{g}$$

$$\therefore \quad \text{ppm} = \frac{0.1 \times 10^6}{1000} = 100\text{ ppm}$$

15. ***(10)*** Mass of O_2 = 10.30 mg (Given)

Mass of sea water solution

$$= \text{volume} \times \text{density} = 1\text{L} \times 1.03\text{ g/mL}$$

$$= 1000\text{ mL} \times 1.03\text{ g mL}^{-1} = 1030\text{ g}$$

$$\text{ppm} = \frac{\text{Mass of } O_2}{\text{Mass of solution}} \times 10^6$$

$$= \frac{10.30 \times 10^{-3}\text{ g} \times 10^6}{1030\text{ g}} = 10\text{ ppm}$$

16. ***(23)*** $y_A = \frac{p_{\text{methyl benzene}}}{p_{\text{total}}}$

$$y_A = \frac{24}{80 + 24} = 0.2307$$

$$y_A = 23.07 \times 10^{-2}$$

$$\Rightarrow \quad y_A \approx 23 \times 10^{-2}$$

17. ***(a)*** Among the given options $(CH_3)_2CO + CS_2$ shows positive deviation from Raoult's law. Since acetone-CS_2 attractions are and weaker than acetone-acetone attractions and $CS_2 - CS_2$ attractions.

18. ***(82)***

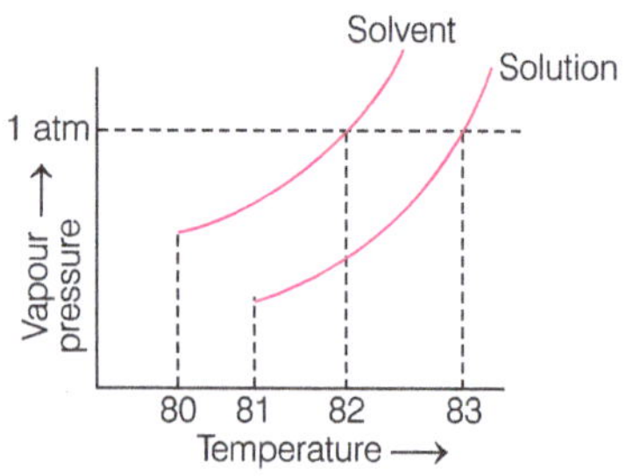

From the graph at 1 atm pressure, boiling point of solvent = 82° C

19. ***(314)*** Given;

Mole fraction of A_1 = 0.7

Mole fraction of B_1 = 0.3

Total pressure, p_1 = 350 mm Hg

Mole fraction of A_2 = 0.2

Mole fraction of B_2 = 0.8

Total pressure, p_2 = 410 mm Hg

Let vapour pressure of pure A be p_A° and B be p_B°.

When, mole fraction of $A_1 = \chi_{A_1} = 0.7$

and mole fraction of B_1,

$$= \chi_{B_1} = 0.3$$

and total pressure p_1 = 350.

$$\Rightarrow \quad (p_A^\circ \times 0.7) + (p_B^\circ \times 0.3) = 350 \quad \ldots\text{(i)}$$

When, mole fraction of A_2,

$$= \chi_{A_2} = 02$$

mole fraction of B_2, $= \chi_{B_2} = 0.8$

and, total pressure $p_2 = 410$

$$(p_A^\circ \times 0.2) + (p_B^\circ \times 0.8) = 410 \quad \ldots\text{(ii)}$$

Now, solving Eq. (i) and (ii), we get

$$0.7p_A^\circ + 0.3p_B^\circ = 350 \quad \ldots\text{(i)}$$

$$0.2p_A^\circ + 0.8p_B^\circ = 410 \quad \ldots\text{(ii)}$$

Multiply Eq. (i) by 0.2 and Eq. (ii) by 0.7, we get

$$0.14p_A^\circ + 0.06p_B^\circ = 70 \quad \ldots\text{(iii)}$$

$$0.14p_A^\circ + 0.56p_B^\circ = 287 \quad \ldots\text{(iv)}$$

$$- \quad - \quad -$$

$$0 - 0.5p_B^\circ = -217$$

$$\Rightarrow \quad -0.5p_B^\circ = -217$$

$$\Rightarrow \quad p_B^\circ = \frac{217}{0.5} = 434\text{ mm Hg}$$

Now put the value of p_B° in Eq. (i),

$$0.7p_A^\circ + 0.3(434) = 350$$

$$0.7p_A^\circ = 350 - 130.2$$

$$0.7p_A^\circ = 219.8$$

$$p_A^\circ = \frac{219.8}{0.7} = 314$$

Therefore, the vapour pressure of pure 'A' is 314 mm Hg.

20. ***(80)*** Total pressure of cylinder ,

$$p_{\text{total}} = 25\text{ bar}$$

Partial pressure of Ne, p_{Ne} = 20 bar

∴ Partial pressure of O_2

$$p_{O_2} = p_{\text{total}} - p_{\text{Ne}} = 25 - 20 = 5\text{ bar}$$

Moles of O $= \frac{x}{32}$ mol

Mass of Ne = 200 g

Moles of Ne $= \frac{200}{20}$ mol

Now, putting value of p_{O_2}

$$\Rightarrow \quad 5 = \frac{\frac{x}{32}}{\frac{x}{32} + \frac{200}{20}} \times 25$$

$$\Rightarrow \quad \frac{1}{5} = \frac{\frac{x}{32}}{\frac{x}{32} + 10}$$

$$\Rightarrow \quad 5x = x + 320 \quad \Rightarrow \quad 4x = 320$$

$$\Rightarrow \quad x = 80\text{ g}$$

So, the value of 'x' is 80.

21. ***(1)*** Given, Henry's constant,

$$K_H = 46.82 \text{ k bar} = 46.82 \times 10^3 \text{ bar}$$

Partial pressure of O_2, $p_{O_2} = 0.92$ bar

Using the Henry's equation,

$$p_{O_2} = K_H \cdot \chi_{O_2} \quad [\chi = \text{mole fraction}]$$

So, $$\chi_{O_2} = \frac{p_{O_2}}{K_H}$$

$$\chi_{O_2} = \frac{0.92 \times 10^{-3}}{46.82} = 0.02 \times 10^{-3}$$

Mole fraction of water,

$$\chi_{H_2O} = 1 - \chi_{O_2} = 1 - 0.02 \times 10^{-3} = 0.99$$

$$1 \text{ L water} = 1000 \text{ gm } (\rho_{H_2O} - 1 \text{ gmL}^{-1})$$

Moles of water $= \frac{1000}{18} = 55.55$ mol

So, moles of

$$O_2, n_{O_2} = \frac{55.55 \times 0.02 \times 10^{-3}}{0.99}$$

$$= 1.13 \times 10^{-3} \text{mol}$$

$$= 1.13 \text{m mol} \approx 1 \text{ m mol}$$

22. ***(14)*** Given, vapour pressure of liquid A, $p_A^\circ = 50$ torr

Vapour pressure of liquid B, $p_B^\circ = 100$ torr

Mole fraction of A, $\chi_A = 0.3$

Mole fraction of B, $\chi_B = 1 - \chi_A = 1 - 0.3 = 0.7$

According to Dalton's law of partial pressures,

$$p_{\text{Total}} = p_A^\circ \chi_A + p_B^\circ \chi_B$$

$$= 50 \times 0.3 + 100 \times 0.7$$

$$= 15 + 70 = 85 \text{ torr}$$

Using relation to calculate mole fraction in vapour phase

$p_B = p_{\text{Total}} Y_B$; Y_B = mole fraction of B in vapour phase

$$Y_B = \frac{p_B}{p_{\text{Total}}} = \frac{p_B^\circ \chi_B}{p_{\text{Total}}}$$

$$= \frac{0.7 \times 100}{85} = \frac{70}{85} = \frac{14}{17} = \frac{x}{17}$$

Hence, value of $x = 14$

23. ***(25)*** According to Henry's law,

$$p_{CO_2} = K_H X_{CO_2}$$

p_{CO_2}, K_H and X_{CO_2} are pressure of CO_2 gas, Henry's constant and mole fraction of CO_2 respectively.

$$\Rightarrow \quad X_{CO_2} = \frac{p_{CO_2}}{K_H} \quad \ldots(i)$$

Given, $K_H = 0.835 \times 2 \times 10^3 \text{ bar} = 1.67 \times 10^3$ bar

$$p_{CO_2} = 0.835 \text{ bar}$$

Put all values in equation (i), we get

$$X_{CO_2} = \frac{0.835}{0.835 \times 10^3 \times 2}$$

$$= 0.5 \times 10^{-3}$$

Volume of water = 0.9 L = 900 mL

Density of water = 1 g/mL

Mass of water = density × volume = 900 g

So, number of mole of water $= \frac{900}{18} = 50$ moles

So, $$\frac{n_{CO_2}}{n_{CO_2} + n_{H_2O}} = 0.5 \times 10^{-3}$$

$n_{CO_2} << H_2O = 50$ moles

So, $n_{CO_2} + n_{H_2O} = n_{H_2O}$

$$n_{CO_2} = 0.5 \times 10^{-3} \times 50$$

$$= 25 \times 10^{-3} \text{ mol}$$

Millimoles of $CO_2 = 0.025 \times 1000 = 25$

24. ***(1)*** Partial pressure of A,

$$p_A^\circ = 90 \text{ mm of Hg}$$

Partial pressure of B,

$$p_B^\circ = 15 \text{ mm of Hg}$$

Mole fraction of A, $\chi_A = 0.6$

Mole fraction of B,

$$\chi_B = 0.4$$

$$P_T = (0.6 \times 90) + (0.4 \times 15)$$

$$= 54 + 6 = 60 \text{ mm}$$

Now, mole fraction of B in vapour phase,

i.e. $$Y_B = \frac{p_B}{p_T} = \frac{\chi_B p_B^\circ}{60} = 0.1 = 1 \times 10^{-1}$$

$$x = 1$$

25. ***(25)*** $$S = \frac{P}{K_H} = \frac{20 \times 10^3}{8 \times 10^7} = 25 \times 10^{-5} \text{ mol/dm}^{-3}$$

26. ***(600)*** $p_{\text{Total}} = x_{\text{hexane}} p^\circ_{\text{hexane}} + x_{\text{heptane}} p^\circ_{\text{heptan}}$

Given that, $p_{\text{total}} = 550$ mm

$$x_{\text{hexane}} = \frac{1}{1+3} = \frac{1}{4},$$

$$x_{\text{heptane}} = \frac{3}{3+1} = \frac{3}{4}$$

Substituting the values in above formula

$$550 = \frac{1}{4} \times p^\circ_{\text{hexane}} + \frac{3}{4} \times p^\circ_{\text{heptane}} \quad \ldots(i)$$

After mixing 1 more mole of n-heptane

$$560 = \frac{1}{5} \times p^\circ_{\text{hexane}} + \frac{4}{5} \times p^\circ_{\text{heptane}} \quad \ldots(ii)$$

From Eq. (i) and (ii)

$$p^\circ_{\text{heptane}} = 600 \text{ mm Hg.}$$

27. ***(b)*** From given graph it can be seen that, X has higher vapour pressure as compared to Y at lower temperature (or to attain same vapour pressure, Y need higher temperature than X). It means that intermolecular interactions must be weaker in X as compared to Y.

28. ***(c)*** According to Raoult's law, vapour pressure of the solution p_{ideal} (ideal vapour pressure) $= p_A^\circ + (p_B^\circ - p_A^\circ)x_B$

(A = solvent : acetone, B = solute : CS_2)

Given; $p_A^\circ = 344$ mm Hg.

$p_B^\circ = 512$ mm Hg.

$\therefore \quad p_{\text{ideal}} = 344 + (512 - 344)x_B$

or $\quad p_{\text{ideal}} = 344 + 168x_B$

So, $\quad 0 < x_B < 1$.

Also, total vapour pressure $(p) = 600$ mmHg

$\therefore$ For any value of x_B, $p > p_{\text{ideal}}$.

Option (c) is incorrect. It is because, mixture of pure CS_2 and CH_3COCH_3 shows positive deviation from Raoult's law. For such solution $\Delta V_{\text{min}} > 0$ and $\Delta H_{\text{mix}} > 0$.

29. ***(c)*** For solute (A),

$$X_A = 0.2$$
$$\Delta p = 10 \text{ mm Hg}$$

Let p°_{solvent} be vapour pressure of pure solvent

$$\frac{\Delta p}{p^\circ_{\text{solvent}}} = X_A$$

$$p^\circ_{\text{solvent}} = \frac{10}{0.2} = 50 \text{ mm Hg}$$

For solute (B),

Let number of moles of solvent be 0.8 and n_B be the number of moles of (B) added, then

$$X_B = \frac{n_B}{0.2 + 0.8 + n_B} = \frac{n_B}{1 + n_B}$$

$$\Delta p' = 10 + 20 = 30 \text{ mm Hg}$$

$$\frac{\Delta p'}{p^\circ_{\text{solvent}}} = \frac{0.2 + n_B}{1 + n_B}$$

$$\frac{30}{50} = \frac{0.2 + n_B}{1 + n_B} \Rightarrow n_B = 1$$

$$X_B = \frac{1}{1+1} = 0.5$$

30. ***(b)*** Higher the elevation in boiling point, higher will be the boiling point.

$$\Delta T_b \propto i \times m$$

For urea $i = 1$

for NaCl $i = 2$

Boiling point order III > II > I > IV.

31. ***(c)*** Due to osmosis, net movement of water molecules takes place from low osmotic pressure to high osmotic pressure. Since the value of concentration of 0.05 M $CuSO_4$ solution is higher hence, it has higher osmotic pressure. So, movement of water molecule will take towards $CuSO_4$ solution. Due to which molarity of $CuSO_4$ is lowered.

32. ***(543)*** Given,

$$\Delta T_f = 2.5^\circ \text{C (from diagram)}$$
$$K_f = 1.86 \text{ K kg mol}^{-1}$$
$$\Delta T_f = K_f \times m$$

$$2.5 = 1 \times 1.86 \times \frac{n_B}{0.1}$$

$$n_B = 0.1344 \text{ mole}$$

Mass of methanol $= 0.1344 \times 32 = 4.3$ g

$$d = \frac{m}{V} \Rightarrow V = \frac{m}{d}$$

$$V = \frac{4.3}{0.792} = 5.43 \text{ mL} = 543 \times 10^{-2} \text{ mL}$$

Thus, the value of x is 543.

33. ***(19)*** Mass of $CH_3COOH = V \times d$

$V = 5$ mL, $d = 1.2$ g/mL (given)

$= 6$ g

$$n_{CH_3COOH} = \frac{\text{Mass}}{\text{Molar mass}} = \frac{6}{60} = 0.1 \text{ mol}$$

$$m_{CH_3COOH} \simeq M_{CH_3COOH} = \frac{0.1}{1} = 0.1 \text{ M}$$

$$\begin{array}{lccc} & CH_3COOH & \rightleftharpoons CH_3COO^- & + \ H^+ \\ & C & 0 & 0 \\ & C - C\alpha & C\alpha & C\alpha \end{array}$$

$$K_\alpha = \frac{C\alpha^2}{1-\alpha}$$

$$1 - \alpha \cong 1 \Rightarrow K_\alpha = C\alpha^2$$

$$\alpha = \sqrt{\frac{K_\alpha}{C}} = \sqrt{\frac{6.25 \times 10^{-5}}{0.1}} = 25 \times 10^{-3}$$

Using,

$$i = 1 + \alpha(n-1)$$
$$= 1 + \alpha(2-1) = 1 + \alpha$$
$$= 1 + 25 \times 10^{-3} = 1.025$$

$$\Delta T_f = iK_f m = (1.025)(1.86)(0.1)$$
$$= 0.19 = 19 \times 10^{-2}$$

34. ***(31)*** As the number of moles of water is greater than the moles of acetic acid. Thus, water acts as a solvent.

Now, calculating the molality of acetic acid

$$= \frac{2700}{60} \times \frac{1}{2.7} \text{ mol/kg}$$
$$= 16.667 \text{ mol/kg}$$

Now, using $\Delta T_f = K_f m = 1.86 \times 16.667 = 31$ K

35. ***(a)*** Highest depression in freezing point (colligative properties) is inversely proportional to experimental molar mass of non-volatile solute.

- On dissociation, experimental molar mass decreases.
- On association, experimental molar mass increases.

36. ***(23)*** Given,

weight of solute = 30 g
volume of solution = 100 mL
weight of solution = $1.2 \times 100 = 120$ g
weight of solvent = 120 − 30 = 90 g

$$m = \frac{30 \times 1000}{180 \times 90} = 1.85$$

$$\frac{24 - p_S}{p_S} = \frac{1.85 \times 18}{1000} \Rightarrow 24 - p_S = 0.0333 p_S$$

$$p_S\,(1.033) = 24 \Rightarrow p_S = 23.22$$

37. ***(a)*** According to Raoult's law, for dilute solution

$$\frac{p^\circ - p}{p^\circ} = \frac{n}{N}$$

[where n = number of moles of glucose, N = number of moles of H_2O]

On substituting the values

$$\frac{0.2}{54.2} = \frac{n \times 18}{100} \Rightarrow n = \frac{100}{271 \times 18}$$

Now weight of glucose = number of moles × molar mass

$$w = \frac{100}{271 \times 18} \times 180 \Rightarrow w = 3.69\text{ g}$$

38. ***(116)*** Elevation in boiling point = [$\Delta T_b = i \times K_b \times$ molality]

Since two solute are present which dissociates completely, hence for NaCl ($i = 2$),

$MgCl_2$, ($i = 3$)

⇒ Mass of NaCl = 29.25% (by weight) = 29.25 g

⇒ Mass of $MgCl_2$ = 19 g

So, total mass of solute = 29.25 + 19 = 48.25 g ...(i)

So, mass of solvent = 100 − 48.25 = 51.75 g ...(ii)

$$\Delta T_b = K_b \left[\frac{i \times n_1 + i \times n_2}{\text{Mass of solvent (kg)}}\right] = 0.52 \left[\frac{2 \times \frac{29.25}{58.5} + 3 \times \frac{19}{95}}{\frac{51.75}{1000}}\right]$$

$$\Rightarrow \quad \frac{0.52\,(1 + 0.6)}{0.05175} \Rightarrow [16.07]$$

So, boiling point of solution = 100 + 16.07 = 116° C

39. ***(8)*** The boiling point elevation constant (K_b) of a volatile liquid is given by the following expression

$$K_b = \frac{RT_b^2 M}{\Delta Hv}$$

where, T_b = boiling point of the liquid

M = molar mass of the liquid

ΔHv = enthalpy of vaporisation

Given, $M_x = M_y$

$$(Tb)_x = 2(Tb)_y \Rightarrow 2(\Delta Hv)_x = (\Delta Hv)_y$$

$$\therefore \quad \frac{(K_b)_x}{(K_b)_y} = \left(\frac{2}{1}\right)^2 \times \frac{2}{1} = \frac{8}{1} = m$$

$$\therefore \quad m = 8$$

40. ***(372)*** $i = 1 + (n - 1)\alpha$

$[i = 1 + 0.2(2 - 1) = 1.2]$

$$\Delta T_f = iK_b m = 1.2 \times 1.86 \times \frac{5 \times 1000}{60 \times 500}$$

$$= 0.372 = 372 \times 10^{-3}$$

Thus, the depression in freezing point of water is 372×10^{-3}°C.

41. ***(3)*** Reaction equation of titration is

$$\underset{\substack{V = 25\text{ mL} \\ M}}{KCl} + \underset{\substack{20\text{ mL} \\ 1\text{ M}}}{AgNO_3} \longrightarrow AgCl + KNO_3$$

At equivalent point

Millimole of KCl = Millimole of $AgNO_3$ = 20 millimole

(i) Volume of KCl solution = 25 mL

(ii) Mass of KCl solution = 25(g) (assuming, d = 1 g/mL)

(iii) Mass of KCl (solute) = $(20 \times 10^{-3} \times 74.5)$

[∵ Molar Mass of KCl = 39 + 35.5 = 74.5 g/mol]

(iv) Mass of solvent = Mass of solution − Mass of solute

$= 25 - [20 \times 10^{-3} \times 74.5]$

$= 23.51$ g

$= 23.51 \times 10^{-3}$ kg

$$m_{KCl} = \frac{20 \times 10^{-3}}{23.51 \times 10^{-3}} = 0.85\text{ m}$$

Depression of freezing point of the KCl solution,

$$\Delta T_f = i \times K_f \times m$$

[∵ i for KCl = 2 assuming it gets 100% dissociated in water]

$$= 2 \times 2 \times 0.85 = 3.4 \approx 3$$

42. ***(62250)*** Osmotic pressure (π) = CRT

Given : solute mass = 2.5 g

Volume of solution = 250 mL

osmotic pressure = 400 pa

$$\text{So, } \frac{400\text{Pa}}{10^5} = \frac{2.5\text{g}/M}{250/1000} \times 0.083 \frac{\text{L-bar}}{\text{K mol}} \times 300\text{K}$$

$\therefore M = 62250$ g mol^{-1}

43. ***(a)*** $\Delta T_b \propto i \times C$.

$$NaCl \rightleftharpoons Na^+ + Cl^- \quad (i = 2)$$

$NH_2CONH_2 \longrightarrow$ Non-ionic solution

Statement (B) and (D) are correct.

44. ***(41500)***

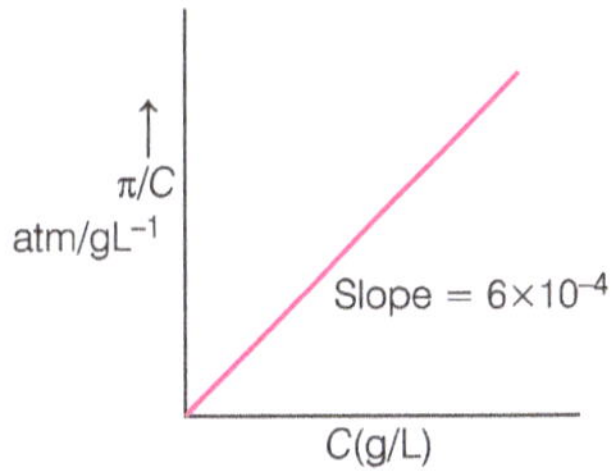

$R = 0.0831$ L atm/K/mol

Osmotic pressure, π = Molar concentration × RT

$$\pi = \frac{C}{M} RT \Rightarrow \frac{\pi}{C} = \frac{RT}{M}$$

Assuming π/C vs C graph

$$\frac{RT}{\text{Slope}} = \frac{RT}{M} = \frac{0.083 \times 300}{6 \times 10^{-4}}$$

M = 41500 g/mol

45. ***(5)*** Number of moles of acetic acid $= \dfrac{V \times \rho}{\text{Molar mass}}$

Molar mass of acetic acid $= 60 \text{ g mol}^{-1}$

$$= \frac{(1.2)\text{mL} \times (1.02)\text{g/mL}}{(60)\text{g/mol}}$$

$$= 0.0204 \text{ mol}$$

Molality $(m) = \dfrac{\text{Moles of solute}}{\text{Mass of solvent } (g)} \times 1000$

$$= \frac{0.0204}{2000} \times 1000$$

(As 2 L solution in water is prepared so mass of solvent becomes 2000 g).

$$= 0.0102$$

$$\Delta T_f = i \times K_f \times m$$

$\Delta T_f =$ Depression in freezing point

$$= 0.0198^\circ \text{C}$$

$$i = \frac{\Delta T_f}{K_f \times m}$$

$$= \frac{0.0198}{1.85 \times 0.0102} = 1.049$$

$$CH_3COOH \rightleftharpoons CH_3COO^- + H^+$$

	CH_3COOH	CH_3COO^-	H^+
Initial	n	0	0
Final	$n(1-x)$	nx	nx

[n = number of moles, x = degree of dissociation]

Total moles $= n - nx + 2nx$

$$= n - nx$$

$$i = \frac{n(1-x) + nx + nx}{n} = \frac{n[1 - x + x + x]}{n}$$

$\Rightarrow \quad i = 1 + x$

$\therefore \quad 1.049 = 1 + x$

x (degree of dissociation) $= 1.049 - 1$

$$= 0.049$$

$$\approx 0.05$$

% degree of dissociation $= 0.05 \times 100 = 5\%$

46. ***(15)*** We know that,

$$\Delta T_f = K_f \times m$$

$$= 3.9 \times \frac{10.2 \times 1000}{176 \times 150} = 1.5^\circ \text{C}$$

or 15×10^{-1} °C

47. ***(98)*** We are given with 0.5% of KCl solution.

$\therefore$ Molality of KCl solution,

$$m = \frac{0.5}{74.6} \times \frac{100}{99.5}$$

$$0.24 = i \times 1.80 \times \frac{0.5}{74.6} \times \frac{1000}{99.5}$$

$$\Rightarrow \quad i = \frac{0.24 \times 74.6 \times 0.1}{0.5 \times 1.80}$$

$$= 1.979$$

$$KCl \rightleftharpoons K^+ + Cl^-$$

	KCl	K^+	Cl^-
Initial	1	0	0
At equilibrium	$1 - x$	x	x

{x is the amount of KCl dissociated}

$$i = x + x + (1 - x)$$

$$1.979 = 1 + x$$

$$x = 0.979 \Rightarrow \%x = 97.9\% \approx 98\%$$

$\therefore$ Percentage of dissociation of KCl is 98%

48. ***(85)*** $K_4Fe(CN)_6 \rightleftharpoons 4K^+ + [Fe(CN)_6]^{4-}$

	$K_4Fe(CN)_6$	$4K^+$	$[Fe(CN)_6]^{4-}$
Initial conc.	1 m	0	0
Final conc.	$(1-0.4)$ m $= 0.6$ m	$4 \times 0.4 = 1.6$ m	0.4 m

Effective molality $= 0.6 + 1.6 + 0.4 = 2.6$ m

Molality of non-electrolyte solution

$$= \text{molality of } K_4[Fe(CN)_6] = 2.6 \text{ m}$$

Now, 18.1 weight per cent solution means 18.1 g solute is present in 100 g solution and hence, (100 − 18.1 =) 81.9 g water.

Molality

Now, $2.6 = \dfrac{18.1/M}{81.9/1000}$

Molar mass of solute, $M = 85$

49. ***(13)*** With benzene as solvent, RCOOH dimerises.

$$2RCOOH \rightleftharpoons (RCOOH)_2$$

$\therefore \quad i = \dfrac{1}{2}$

$$\Delta T_b = i \times K_b \times m$$

On substituting the values, we get

$$\Delta T_b = \frac{1}{2} \times 2.6 \times \frac{1.22/M_w}{100/1000} \quad \ldots(i)$$

With acetone as solvent, no dimerisation.

$\therefore \quad i = 1$

$$\Delta T_b = i \times K_b \times m$$

$$0.17 = 1 \times 1.7 \times \frac{1.22/M_w}{100/1000} \quad \ldots(ii)$$

Eq. (i) divide by Eq. (ii),

$$\frac{\Delta T_b}{0.17} = \frac{\frac{1}{2} \times 2.6 \times \frac{1.22/M_w}{100/1000}}{1 \times 1.7 \times \frac{1.22/M_w}{100/1000}}$$

$\Rightarrow \quad \Delta T_b = \dfrac{0.26}{2} = 13 \times 10^{-2}$

$$x = 13$$

50. ***(5.00)*** $\Delta T_b = i \times m \times K_b$

For $CaCl_2$, $i = 3$, $m_{(CaCl_2)} = 0.05$ m

$\therefore \quad \Delta T_b = 3 \times 0.05 \times K_b = 0.15 K_b$

Molality of $CrCl_3 \cdot xNH_3 = 0.1$ m

$\therefore \quad \Delta T_b' = i \times m \times K_b = 0.1 i K_b$

Given that : $0.1 i K_b = 2 \times 0.15 \times K_b$

$\therefore$ $i = 3$ and coordination number is 6.

Thus, complex will be $[Cr(NH_3)_5Cl]Cl_2$

$\therefore$ $x = 5$

Hence, the correct answer is 5.

51. **(2)** $n\,\underset{\text{Benzoic acid}}{PhCOOH} \xrightarrow{\text{Association}} (PhCOOH)_n$

Assuming 100% association ($\alpha = 1$),

$$\Rightarrow \quad i = 1 - \alpha\left(1 - \frac{1}{n}\right) = \frac{1}{n} \qquad [\because \alpha + 1]$$

Now, $\Delta T_f = K_f \times m \times i$

$$0 - (0.93) = 1.86 \times \frac{w_B \times 1000}{w_A \times M_B} \times \frac{1}{n}$$

[$\because w_B$ = mass of PhCOOH = 12.2 g

w_A = mass of H_2O = 100 g

M_B = molar mass of PhCOOH

= 122g mol^{-1}]

$$= 1.86 \times \frac{12.2 \times 1000}{100 \times 122} \times \frac{1}{n}$$

$$\Rightarrow \quad n = \frac{1.86 \times 12.2 \times 1000}{0.93 \times 100 \times 122} = 2$$

$\therefore$ Number of benzoic acid molecules associated, $n = 2$

52. **(2.18)** $K_f = 2.0$ (Given) $m = 0.5$ m (Given)

$\Delta T_f = K_f \times m = 2 \times 0.5 = 1$

$\therefore$ T_f = Actual freezing point of water $- \Delta T_f$.

$= 273 - 1 = 272$ K.

Pressure of gas after the stoppers are withdrawn = 1 atm (atmospheric pressure)

$$\therefore \quad V = \frac{nRT}{p}$$

$$= \frac{0.1 \times 0.08 \times 272}{1 \text{ atm}}$$

$= 2.176\text{ L} \approx 2.18\text{ L}$

53. **(1.76)**

$$\Delta T_f = \frac{i \times K_f \times w_{NaCl} \times 1000}{\underset{(=58.5)}{M_{NaCl}} \times w_{H_2O}}$$

$$(m = \text{molality}) = \frac{w_B \times 1000}{M_B \times w_A}$$

$\Delta T_f = 0.2$ because

freezing point $= -0.2°$ C

K_f of water 2 K kg mol^{-1} (Given)

i = van't Hoff factor, for NaCl = 2

$$\therefore \quad w_{NaCl} = \frac{\Delta T_f \times M_{NaCl} \times w_{H_2O}}{i \times K_f \times 1000}$$

$$= \frac{0.2 \times 58.5 \times 600}{2 \times 2 \times 1000}$$

$= 1.755$ g

≈ 1.76 g

Practice Element 02 : Target JEE Advanced

1. **(a)** According to Henry's law,

$$p_{Hg} = \chi_{Hg} \cdot p_{total} \qquad \ldots(i)$$

$$\text{Mole fraction of mercury (Hg)} = \frac{\dfrac{0.6 \times 10^{-3}}{200}}{\dfrac{0.6 \times 10^{-3}}{200} + \dfrac{55.4}{28}}$$

$= 0.00000151$

Put the value of χ_{Hg} in Eq. (i) we get

$$p_{Hg} = 0.00000151 \times 760 = 1.15 \times 10^{-3} \text{ torr}$$

2. **(a)** Let χ_A and χ_B mole fraction of A and B be present in solution of A and B and p_M is vapour pressure of mixture, then

By Raoult's law,

$$p_M = p_A^\circ \chi_A + p_B^\circ \chi_B$$

$$p_M = (0.4)\chi_A + (1.2)\chi_B \qquad \ldots(i)$$

$$\chi_A' = \frac{p_A^\circ \cdot \chi_A}{p_M} \quad \text{and} \quad \chi_B' = \frac{p_B^\circ \chi_B}{p_M}$$

where χ'_A and χ'_B are mole fraction of A and B in gaseous phase. So,

$$(0.4)\chi_A = P_M \cdot (0.4)$$

$$p_M = \chi_A \qquad \ldots(ii)$$

and $(1.2)\chi_B = p_M(0.6) \Rightarrow p_M = 2\chi_B \qquad \ldots(iii)$

Solving Eq. (ii) and (iii),

$$\chi_A = 2\chi_B$$

$\because$ $\chi_A + \chi_B = 1$

$$\chi_A = \frac{2}{3} \text{ and } \chi_B = \frac{1}{3}$$

From Eq. (i)

$$p_M = 0.4 \times \frac{2}{3} + 1.2 \times \frac{1}{3} = 0.667 \text{ atm}$$

3. **(d)** Given, $p^\circ = 204$

$p = 200$

$\Delta T_f = 1.53°$C

$K_f = ?$

If the molality of solution is m, then,

$$\frac{p^\circ - p}{p^\circ} = \frac{n_1}{n_2}$$

$$\frac{204 - 200}{204} = \frac{m}{1000/78}$$

$$\frac{4}{204} = \frac{78.m}{1000} \Rightarrow m = \frac{4 \times 1000}{204 \times 78} = 0.252$$

By using,

$$\Delta T_f = K_f.m$$

$$\frac{1.53}{0.252} = K_f$$

$K_f = 6.07$ degree/molal

4. ***(c)*** Among the given statements, statement (c) is incorrect.

(a) $\Delta T_f = K_f . m = 1.86 \times 1 = 1.86°C$

$\therefore$ F. P of solution $= -1.86°$ C

(b) $\Delta T_b = K_b . m = 0.52 \times 1 = 0.52°C$

$\therefore$ B.P of solution should be 100.52°C. As the solute dissociates completely above 100.26°C, its actual $\Delta T_b = 0.52 \times 2 = 1.04°$ C and hence B.P = 101.04° C.

(c) $\Delta T_f = iK_f . m$

$$\Rightarrow 7.44 = 1.86 \times \frac{1/2}{m_{solvent}}$$

$$4 = \frac{1}{m_{solvent} \times 2} \Rightarrow m_{solvent} = 0.125 \text{ kg}$$

$\therefore$ Percentage of water separated as ice $= (1 - 0.125) \times 100$
$= 87.5\%$

(d) $\Delta T_b = iK_b . m$

$$\Rightarrow 103.08 = 0.52 \times \frac{2}{m_{solvent}}$$

$$198.23 \times m_{solvent} = 2$$

$$m_{solvent} = \frac{2}{198.23} = 0.010$$

$\therefore$ $m_{solvent}$ left = 0.01 kg

Percentage of water evaporated $= (1 - 0.01) \times 100 = 99\%$

5. ***(b)*** Osmotic pressure $\pi = hdg$

$h = 2.4 \text{ mm} = 2.4 \times 10^{-3} \text{m}$

$d = 0.88 \text{ g cm}^{-3} = 0.88 \times 10^3 \text{ kg m}^{-3}$

$g = 9.8 \text{ m s}^{-2}$

$\therefore$ $\pi = 2.4 \times 10^{-3} \text{ m} \times 0.88 \times 10^3 \text{kg m}^{-3} \times 9.8 \text{ m s}^{-2}$
$= 20.6976 \text{ kg m}^{-1}\text{s}^{-2} = 20.6976 \text{Nm}^{-2}$

Also $\pi = MRT$

where M = molarity

$20.6976 \text{ Nm}^{-2} = M \times 8.314 \text{ J mol}^{-1}\text{K}^{-1} \times 298 \text{ K}$

$\therefore$ $M = 8.354 \times 10^{-3} \text{mol m}^{-3}$

$$\frac{(0.20 \text{ g}/m_1)\text{mole}}{100 \times 10^{-6} \text{ m}^3} = 8.354 \times 10^{-3} \text{mol m}^{-3}$$

$\therefore$ $m_1 = 23.9406 \times 10^4 \text{ g mol}^{-1}$.

6. ***(c)*** $\frac{\Delta p}{p°} = X_1$

$\therefore$ $X_1 = 0.05$

Case I If solution is dilute $n_1 << n_2$

then, $X_1 = \frac{n_1}{n_1 + n_2} \approx \frac{n_1}{n_2} = \frac{w_1 m_2}{m_1 w_2}$

$\therefore$ $\frac{w_1}{m_1 w_2} = \frac{0.05}{18}$

$$\Delta T_b = \frac{1000 \, K_b w_1}{m_1 w_2} = \frac{1000 \times 0.52° \times 0.05}{18} = 1.44° \text{ C}$$

Case II If solution is not dilute

$X_1 = 0.05$

$X_2 = (1 - X_1) = 0.95$

$\therefore$ $\frac{X_1}{X_2} = \frac{n_1}{n_2} = \frac{w_1 m_2}{m_1 w_2} = \frac{1}{19}$

$\therefore$ $\frac{w_1}{m_1 w_2} = \frac{1}{19 \times 18}$

$\therefore$ $\Delta T'_b = \frac{1000 \times 0.52 \times 1}{19 \times 18} = 1.52$

$\therefore$ $\Delta T_b - \Delta T'_b = 1.44 - 1.52 = -0.08°$

7. ***(d)*** As we know,

$$\Delta T_f = K_f \frac{w_2}{M} \times \frac{1000}{w_1}$$

$$278.5 - T_f = 5\left(\frac{0.1 \times 1000}{31.2}\right)$$

$$T_f = 262.481 \text{ K}$$

8. ***(d)*** At 20°C, volume of 1 mole or 78 g benzene vapours $= \frac{78 \times 1}{0.877} \times 2750 \text{ mL}$

At 20°C, volume of 1 mole (or 92g) toluene

$$= \frac{92 \times 1}{0.867} \times 7720 \text{ mL}$$

Using ideal gas equation, $pV = nRT$

$$\frac{p_B^°}{760} \times \frac{78 \times 2750}{0.877 \times 1000} = 1 \times 0.0821 \times 293$$

$$p_B^° = 74.75 \text{ mm}$$

Similarly, $\frac{p_T^°}{760} \times \frac{92 \times 7720}{0.867 \times 1000} = 1 \times 0.0821 \times 293$

$$p_T^° = 22.32 \text{ mm}$$

Using Raoult's law,

$$p_M = p_B^° . X_B + p_T^° X_T$$

$$p_M = p_B^° . X_B + p_T^°(1 - X_B)$$

$$46 = 74.75 X_B + 22.32(1 - X_B)$$

$$X_B = 0.45$$

$\because$ $X_B + X_T = 1 \Rightarrow X_T = 0.55$

Also, $p_B = p_B^° . X_B = p_M . X_B'$

$74.74 \times 0.45 = 46 \, X_B'$

$\Rightarrow X'_B$(in gas phase) = 0.73.

9. ***(a, b, d)*** Among the given statements a, b and d are incorrect while c is correct. Their explanation are given as :

$$X_2 = \frac{n_2}{n_1 + n_2} = 0.02$$

$$\frac{n_2}{n_1} = \frac{1}{49}$$

$$\frac{n_2}{w_1} \times MW_1 \times \frac{1000}{1000} = \frac{1}{49}$$

$$m = \frac{1000}{49 \times 78} = 0.261 \text{ m}$$

$$K_f = \frac{RT^2M}{1000\,\Delta H} = \frac{2(300)^2}{1000 \times 36} = 5\text{ K kg mol}^{-1}$$

$$\Delta T_f = K_f i\, m$$

$$300 - 298.95 = 5i\,(0.261)$$

$$i = 0.804$$

$$CH_3COOH \longrightarrow (CH_3COOH)_2$$

$$1-\alpha \qquad \frac{\alpha}{2}$$

$$i = 1 - \frac{\alpha}{2}$$

$$0.804 = 1 - \frac{\alpha}{2}$$

$$\alpha = 39.2\%$$

10. ***(a, b, c)*** Among the given statements, a, b and c are correct while statement d is incorrect. Their explanation are given as :

Pressure of N_2 in $X = 1.9$ atm

Total pressure of vessel 'X' = 2 atm

$\therefore$ Pressure of $H_2O(g)$ in X at 320 K = 2 − 1.9 = 0.1 atm

Pressure of N_2 in $Y = 3.8$ atm

Pressure of N_2 at 320 K $= \frac{3.8}{300} \times 320 = 4.05$ atm.

Total pressure at 320 K = 4.32 atm

$\therefore$ Pressure of water vapour at 320 K = 4.32 − 4.05 = 0.27 atm

Enthalpy of vapourisation ($\Delta_{vap}H$)

$$\Rightarrow \quad \log\frac{p_1}{p_2} = \frac{\Delta H}{2.303R}\left[\frac{1}{300} - \frac{1}{320}\right]$$

$$\log\frac{0.27}{0.10} = \frac{\Delta H}{2.303R}\left[\frac{1}{300} - \frac{1}{320}\right]$$

$$\Delta_{vap}H = 39.65\text{ kJ mol}^{-1}$$

11. ***(b,c,d)*** Among the given statements, b, c and d are correct while statement (a) is incorrect.

Their explanation are given as :

Given complex salt, $CrCl_3 \cdot 6H_2O$

$$\pi = CRT\,(1 - \alpha + x\alpha + y\alpha)$$

$$98.52 = 1 \times 0.0821 \times 300 \times (x + y)\ (\alpha = 1)$$

$\therefore \quad (x + y) = 4$

$\therefore CrCl_3 \cdot 6H_2O$ can be written as :

$$[Cr(H_2O)_6]Cl_3 \rightleftharpoons [Cr(H_2O)_6]^{3+} + 3Cl^{\ominus}$$

1	0	0
$1-\alpha$	α	3α

3 mol of $AgNO_3$ will react with 1 mol of $Cr(H_2O)_6Cl_3$

$$Cr(H_2O)_6Cl_3 + 3AgNO_3 \longrightarrow [Cr(H_2O)_6](NO_3)_3 + 3AgCl$$

	$Cr(H_2O)_6Cl_3$	$3AgNO_3$	$[Cr(H_2O)_6](NO_3)_3$	$3AgCl$
moles	2 × 1 = 2	1 × 6 = 6	0	0
	0	0	2	6

$\therefore$ Moles of AgCl formed = 6

Weight of AgCl formed = 6 × 143.5 = 861 g

$$[Cr(H_2O)_6](NO_3)_3 = \frac{2}{3}$$

$$\Rightarrow \quad \pi = CRT \times (1 + 3\alpha)$$

$$= \frac{2}{3} \times 0.0821 \times 300 \times 4$$

$$= 65.68\text{ atm}$$

12. ***(a, b, c, d)*** Let χ_A = mole fraction of component A

χ_B = mole fraction of component B

p_A° = vapour pressure of pure A

p_B° = vapour pressure of pure B

p_A = vapour pressure of A in binary mixture

$= p_A^{\circ}\chi_A$ by Raoult's law

Similarly, $p_B = p_B^{\circ}\chi_B$

$$p_{total} = p_A + p_B = p_A^{\circ}\chi_A + p_B^{\circ}\chi_B$$

$$= p_A^{\circ}\chi_A + p_B^{\circ}(1 - \chi_A)$$

$$= p_A^{\circ}\chi_A + p_B^{\circ} - p_B^{\circ}\chi_A$$

$$= p_B^{\circ} + (p_A^{\circ} - p_B^{\circ})\chi_A$$

(in terms of mole fraction of A)

Thus, (a) and (d) are correct.

Variation of p_A with χ_A, p_B with χ_B and p_{total} with χ_A and χ_B both can be represented as

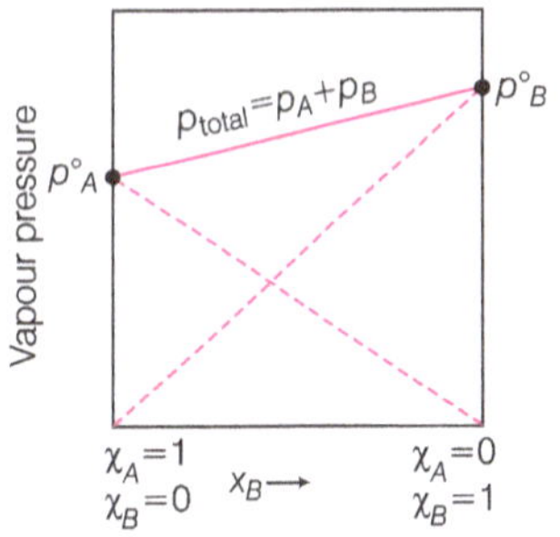

At start $\chi_A = 1$ thus, p_A° is the vapour pressure of pure A. As B is added into it, χ_B increases. Hence, p_A decreases and that of p_B increases. When $\chi_B = 1$, vapour pressure of $B = p_B^{\circ}$ (pure).

Thus, vapour pressure of B increase as χ_B increases and decreases as χ_A decreases.

Line joining p_A° and p_B° represent total vapour pressure.

Thus, (b) and (c) are also correct.

13. ***(a, b, d)*** Among the given statements a, b and d are correct while statement (c) is incorrect. Their correct explanation is gives as

(a) Mass percent of $A = 50 \Rightarrow n_A : n_B = 1:2 \Rightarrow$ Azeotrope
Hence, vapour will have the same composition of liquid.

(b) Mass percent of $A > 50 \Rightarrow n_A : n_B = 1:2$
In this case, the vapour must be more rich in A than liquid.

(c) $X_B = \frac{3}{4} = 0.75 > \frac{2}{3} \Rightarrow$ pure A cannot be obtained.

(d) $X_B = \frac{3}{5} = 0.60 < \frac{2}{3} \Rightarrow$ pure A can be obtained.

Mixtures richer in one component can be separated into the azeotrope and excess component.

14. ***(a,b,c,d)*** All the given statements are correct.

15. ***(a, c)*** 10% ethanol by mass means

100 g (ethanol + water) solution has = 10 g ethanol

90 g H_2O has ethanol = 10 g ethanol

$$\text{Molality} = \frac{10/46}{0.09\,\text{kg}} = 2.415\,\text{mol kg}^{-1}$$

Molality does not involve density, hence same at 15°C and 25°C.

Thus, (c) is correct.

$$\frac{\text{Mass}}{\text{Volume}} = \text{Density}$$

$$\therefore \quad \text{Volume} = \frac{\text{Mass}}{\text{Density}}$$

$$V_{15} = \text{Volume at 15°C} = \frac{100}{0.9831}\,\text{mL} = 0.1017\,\text{L}$$

$$V_{25} = \text{Volume at 25°C} = \frac{100}{0.9804}\,\text{mL} = 0.1020\,\text{L}$$

$$\text{Molarity} = \frac{\text{mol}}{\text{L}},\ \text{thus molarity} \propto \frac{1}{V},\ V_{15} < V_{25}$$

Hence, molarity at 15°C > molarity at 25°C

Thus, (a) is also correct.

16. ***(a, b, c, d)*** Among the given statements all statements are correct regarding the solutions of two miscible volatile liquids I and II.

Their explanation are given as :

Raoult's law is followed by I and II, liquids being miscible.

Plot *CD* holds for Dalton's law of partial pressure for the components I and II

From graph

$AD = p^{\circ}_{\text{II}}$ (vapour pressure of pure II) $= 135$

when $X_{\text{I}} = 0$

$X_{\text{II}} = 1.0$

$BC = p^{\circ}_{\text{I}}$ (when $X_{\text{I}} = 1$) $= 85$

Thus, $p^{\circ}_{\text{II}} - p^{\circ}_{\text{I}} = 50$ units

Thus, (c) is correct

When $X_{\text{II}} = 0.40$

$X_{\text{I}} = 0.60$

$$\therefore \quad p_{\text{total}} = p^{\circ}_{\text{I}} X_{\text{I}} + p^{\circ}_{\text{II}} X_2$$

$$= 85 \times 0.60 + 135 \times 0.4$$

$$= 51 + 54 = 105\,\text{units}$$

Then, *d* is also correct.

17. ***(b, c, d)*** Among the given statements b, c, and d are correct while statement a is incorrect. Their explanation are given as :

(a) $\Delta T_f = K_f m$

Molality is same, but K_f is different for different solvents. Thus, ΔT_f will be different. Thus, (a) is incorrect.

(b) (b) is Correct

(c) $\pi = iCRT(i)$

i for $BaCl_2 > KCl > CH_3COOH >$ Sucrose

Thus, (c) is correct

(d) $p = p^{\circ} \chi_i$ thus (d) is correct

18. ***(a, b, c, d)*** Solute, $w_1 = 3.5\,\text{g}$

Solvent, $w_2 = 50.0\,\text{g}$

Volume of solution $= 52.5\,\text{mL}$

$$\Delta T_f = 0.86°\,\text{C}$$

$$K_f = 1.86°\,\text{C mol}^{-1}\text{kg}$$

$$\Delta T_f = \text{molality} \times K_f$$

(a) $$\text{Molality} = \frac{\Delta T_f}{K_f} = \frac{0.86°\,\text{C}}{1.86°\,\text{C mol}^{-1}\,\text{kg}} = 0.46\,\text{mol kg}^{-1}$$

Thus, (a) is correct.

(b) $$\frac{\Delta T_f}{K_f} = \frac{1000\,w_1}{m_1 w_2}$$

$$\therefore \frac{w_1}{m_1}(\text{mole}) = \frac{\Delta T_f}{1000\,K_f} w_2 = \frac{0.46 \times 50}{1000} = 0.023$$

$$\therefore \text{Molarity} = \frac{\text{Mole}}{\text{litre(v)}} = \frac{0.023\ \text{mol}}{0.0525\ \text{L}} = 0.44\,\text{mol L}^{-1}$$

Thus, (b) is correct.

(c) $$\frac{w_1}{m_1} = 0.023$$

$$\therefore \quad m_1 = \frac{w_1}{0.023} = \frac{3.5}{0.023} = 152\,\text{g mol}^{-1}$$

Thus, (c) is correct.

(d) $$X_{\text{solute}} = \frac{\frac{w_1}{m_1}}{\frac{w_1}{m_1} + \frac{w_2}{m_2}} = \frac{0.023}{0.023 + \frac{50}{18}} = 0.0082$$

Thus, (d) is correct

19. ***(115)*** $$46\text{ g ethanol} = \frac{46}{46} = 1\,\text{mol}$$

$$72\text{ g water} = \frac{72}{18} = 4\,\text{mol}$$

$$\text{Total moles} = 1 + 4 = 5$$

$$X_{\text{ethanol}} = \frac{1}{5} = 0.2$$

$$X_{\text{water}} = \frac{4}{5} = 0.8$$

From graph molar volume of water when ($X_{\text{water}} = 0.8$) is

$= 15\ \text{cm}^3\text{mol}^{-1}$

and molar volume of ethanol when ($X_{\text{ethanol}} = 0.2$) is

$= 55\ \text{cm}^3\text{mol}^{-1}$

$$V_{\text{mixture}} = (V_1 n_1)_{\text{water}} + (V_2 n_2)_{\text{ethanol}}$$

$$= 15 \times 4 + 55 \times 1 = 60 + 55 = 115\ \text{cm}^3.$$

20. ***(60.86)*** By using the formula,

$$\Delta T_f = K_f \times m \times i \qquad \ldots\text{(i)}$$

Given, $\Delta T_f = 0.40 \Rightarrow K_f = 1.86$

Put the values in Eq. (i) we get,

$$0.40 = 1.86 \times m \times 2$$

$\therefore$ Effective molality of NaCl solution $= \dfrac{20}{93 \times 2}$ m

Now, $\pi = iCRT = \dfrac{20 \times 0.0821 \times (273 + 10) \times 2}{93 \times 2}$

$$= 60.86 \times 0.0821 \text{ atm}$$

Hence, the value of z is 60.86.

21. ***(67.74)*** As we know,

$$p_M = p^\circ_X . X_X + p^\circ_Y . X_Y$$

$$570 = p^\circ_X\left(\frac{1}{1+3}\right) + p^\circ_Y\left(\frac{3}{1+3}\right)$$

$$p^\circ_X + 3p^\circ_Y = 2280 \quad \ldots\text{(i)}$$

When 1 mole of Y is further added to it

$$p_M = p^\circ_X . X_X + p^\circ_Y . X_Y$$

$$580 = p^\circ_X\left(\frac{1}{1+4}\right) + p^\circ_Y\left(\frac{4}{1+4}\right)$$

$$\therefore \quad p^\circ_X + 4p^\circ_Y = 2900 \quad \ldots\text{(ii)}$$

From Eq. (i) and (ii), we get

$$-p^\circ_Y = -620$$

$$p^\circ_Y = 620$$

and from Eq. (i)

$$p^\circ_X = 2280 - 1860$$

$$p^\circ_X = 420$$

The ratio of vapour pressure of X and Y is

$$\frac{p^\circ_X}{p^\circ_Y} = \frac{420}{620} = 0.6774 = 67.74 \times 10^{-2}$$

22. ***(3)*** $\pi = iMRT$

where, i = number of ions

= van't Hoff factor

M = mol/litre

$$M = \left(\frac{0.070 \text{ g}}{243.5 \text{ g mol}^{-1}}\right) / 0.125 \text{ L}$$

$$= 2.3 \times 10^{-3} \text{ M (mol L}^{-1})$$

$$R = 0.0821 \text{ atm L mol}^{-1}\text{K}^{-1}$$

$$T = 298 \text{ K}$$

$$\pi = 119 \text{ mm Hg} = \frac{119}{760} \text{ atm}$$

$$\frac{119}{760} \text{ atm} = 2.3 \times 10^{-3} \text{ mol L}^{-1} \times 0.0821 \text{ atm L mol}^{-1}\text{K}^{-1} \times 298 \text{ K} \times i$$

$$i = 2.78 \approx 3.0$$

Coordination number of Cr = 6

Thus, complex is $[Cr(NH_3)_5Cl]Cl_2$ ionising as

$$[Cr(NH_3)_5Cl]Cl_2 \rightleftharpoons [Cr(NH_3)_5Cl]^{2+} + 2Cl^-$$

23. ***(7.78)*** Molality (m) is related to mole fraction X_1 (solute) and molar mass (m_2) of solvent by equation

$$m = \frac{1000X_1}{(1 - X_1)m_2} = \frac{1000 \times 0.07}{0.93 \times 18} = 4.18$$

Also $\Delta T_f = mK_f$

For sucrose solution,

$$\Delta T_f = 1.86^\circ$$

$$1.86 = 1 \times K_f$$

$$\therefore \quad K_f = 1.86^\circ \text{ mol}^{-1} \text{ kg}$$

For soluton of solute (A)

$$\Delta T_f = 1.86 \times 4.18 = 7.78^\circ$$

24. ***(500)*** In Vessel 1

$$(\Delta T_b)_1 = i_1 K_b \times \frac{\left(\dfrac{w_2}{M_x}\right)}{\left(\dfrac{W_1}{1000}\right)}$$

In Vessel 2

$$(\Delta T_b)_2 = i_2 K_b \times \frac{\left(\dfrac{w_2}{M_y}\right)}{\left(\dfrac{W_1}{1000}\right)}$$

$$\frac{(\Delta T_b)_1}{(\Delta T_b)_2} = \frac{i_1 \times M_y}{i_2 \times M_x} = 3 \times \frac{1}{0.6} = 5 \Rightarrow (\Delta T_b)_1 = 5\,(\Delta T_b)_2$$

$$\frac{(\Delta T_b)_1}{(\Delta T_b)_2} \times 100 = 500\%$$

25. ***(0.229)*** Mass of solute $= 3.0 \times 10^{-3}$ kg = 3.0 g

Molecular mass of solute = 60

Mass of solvent $= 500 \times 0.997 = 498.5$ g

We know that degree of dissociation $(X) = \dfrac{i-1}{n-1}$

$$0.23 = \frac{i-1}{2-1}$$

$$i = 1.23$$

$$\Delta T_f = i \times K_f \times \text{molality}$$

$$= 1.23 \times 1.86 \times \frac{3 \times 1000}{60 \times 498.5} = 0.229$$

26. ***(688)*** As we know,

$$\Delta T_b = \frac{1000\, K_b w_1}{m_1 w_2}$$

Also, $$\frac{\Delta p}{p^\circ} = \frac{w_1 m_2}{m_1 w_2}$$

$$\frac{\Delta p}{p^\circ} = \frac{\Delta T_b m_2}{1000\, K_b}$$

$$\frac{\Delta p}{p^\circ} = \frac{4 \times 18}{1000 \times 0.76}$$

$$\frac{\Delta p}{p^\circ} = 0.09473$$

$$p^\circ = 1\,\text{atm} = 760\,\text{mmHg}$$
$$\Delta p = 0.09473 \times 760 = 72\,\text{mmHg}$$
$$\therefore \quad p_{\text{solution}} = 760 - 72 = 688\,\text{mm Hg}$$

27. ***(d)*** K_H is in pressure unit.

$$p = K_H\chi$$
$$\chi_{N_2} = \frac{p_{N_2}}{K_H} = \frac{10 \times 0.79 \times 760\,\text{mm}}{6.51 \times 10^7\,\text{mm}}$$
$$= 9.22 \times 10^{-5}$$

Also, $n(H_2O) = \frac{1000}{18} = 55.55$

$$\chi_{N_2} = \frac{n_{N_2}}{n_{O_2} + n_{N_2} + n_{H_2O}} \approx \frac{n_{N_2}}{n_{H_2O}}$$

(n_{N_2} and n_{O_2} being very small)

$$\therefore \quad n_{N_2} = \chi_{N_2} \times n_{H_2O}$$
$$= 9.22 \times 10^{-5} \times 55.55$$
$$= 5.117 \times 10^{-3}$$

Similarly,

$$\chi_{O_2} = \frac{p_{O_2}}{K_H} = \frac{10 \times 0.21 \times 760\,\text{mm}}{3.30 \times 10^7\,\text{mm}}.$$
$$= 4.84 \times 10^{-5}$$
$$\therefore \quad n_{O_2} = 4.84 \times 10^{-5} \times n_{H_2O}$$
$$= 4.84 \times 10^{-5} \times 55.5 = 2.686 \times 10^{-3}$$

(i) $\chi_{N_2} = 9.22 \times 10^{-5}$ (r) ...(r)

(ii) $\chi_{O_2} = 4.84 \times 10^{-5}$(p) ...(p)

(iii) Moles of $N_2 = 5.12 \times 10^{-3}$(s) ...(s)

(iv) Moles of $O_2 = 2.69 \times 10^{-3}$(q) ...(q)

28. ***(c)*** Initially, 60 g $A = \frac{60}{60} = 1\,\text{mol}$

$$40\text{ g } B = \frac{40}{40} = 1\,\text{mol}$$

Then, $\chi_A(\text{in I}) = \frac{1}{2} = 0.5$

Total vapour pressure of mixture in I

$$p_I = p_A^\circ\chi_A + p_B^\circ\chi_B$$
$$= \frac{24}{2} + \frac{12}{2} = 18\,\text{kPa}$$
$$\therefore \quad \chi_A(\text{in II}) = \frac{p_A^\circ\chi_A}{p_{\text{total}}} = \frac{12}{18} = 0.67$$

III is liquefied form of II, thus,

$$\chi_A(\text{in III}) = \chi_A(\text{in II}) = 0.67$$

Vapour pressure of III = $p_A^\circ\chi_A$ (III) + $p_B^\circ\chi_B$ (III)

$$= 24 \times \frac{2}{3} + 12 \times \frac{1}{3} = 20\,\text{kPa}$$

Mole fraction of A above liquid in IV

$$\chi_A(\text{in IV}) = \frac{p_A^\circ\chi_A(\text{III})}{p_{\text{total}}} = \frac{16}{20} = 0.8$$

Thus, (i) → (q), (ii) → (r), (iii) → r, (iv) → (s)

29. ***(a)*** $\Delta T_b = K_b m(i) = K_b\, i$, for molality, $m = 1$

$$\therefore \quad i = [1 + (y - 1)x]$$

		y	i	ΔT_b
(i)	Urea	1	1	K_b
(ii)	$KCl \rightleftharpoons K^+ + Cl^-$	2	$(1 + x) = 2$	$2K_b$
(iii)	$K_2SO_4 \rightleftharpoons 2K^+ + SO_4^{2-}$	3	$(1+2x) = 1 + 2 \times 0.75 = 2.5$	$2.5K_b$
(iv)	$K_4[Fe(CN)_6] \rightleftharpoons 4K^+ + [Fe(CN)_6]^{4-}$	5	$(1 + 4x) = (1 + 4 \times 0.5) = 3$	$3.0K_b$
(v)	$Fe_2(SO_4)_3 \rightleftharpoons 2Fe^{3+} + 3SO_4^{2-}$	5	$1 + 4x = 1 + 4 \times 0.25 = 2$	$2K_b$

Thus, (i) → (p), (ii) → (r), (iii) → (s), (iv) → (t), (v) → (r)

30. ***(d)*** $\Delta T_f = \frac{1000\,K_f w_1}{m_1 w_2}$

$$\Delta T_f(\text{i}) = \frac{1000 \times 1.86 \times 6}{60 \times 100} = 1.86^\circ\text{C}$$

Thus, (i) → (q)

$$\Delta T_f(\text{ii}) = \frac{1000 \times 1.86 \times 9.6}{32 \times 100} = 5.58^\circ\text{C}$$

Thus, (ii) → (r)

$$\Delta T_f(\text{iii}) = \frac{1000 \times 1.86 \times 17.1}{342 \times 100} = 0.93^\circ\text{C}$$

Thus, (iii) → (s)

$$\Delta T_f(\text{iv}) = \frac{1000 \times 1.86 \times 36.0}{180 \times 100} = 3.72^\circ\text{C}$$

Thus, (iv) → (p)

31. ***(d)*** $w_1(\text{solute}) = 17.1\,\text{g} = \frac{17.1}{342} = 0.05\,\text{mol}\ (n_1)$

$w_2(\text{solvent}) = 1000\,\text{g} = \frac{1000}{18} = 55.55\,\text{mol}\ (n_2)$

(i) $\frac{\Delta p}{p^\circ} = \chi_{\text{solute}} = \frac{n_1}{n_1 + n_2} \approx \frac{n_1}{n_2}$

$$\therefore \Delta p = p^\circ\frac{n_1}{n_2} = 26.50 \times \frac{0.05}{55.55} = 0.024\,\text{mm}$$

(ii) $\Delta T_f = \frac{1000K_f w_1}{m_1 w_2} = \frac{1000 \times 1.86 \times 17.1}{342 \times 1000} = 0.093^\circ\text{C}$

(iii) $\Delta T_b = \frac{1000K_b w_1}{m_1 w_2} = \frac{1000 \times 0.52 \times 17.1}{342 \times 1000} = 0.026^\circ\text{C}$

(iv) $\pi = MRT = \frac{w_1}{m_1 V}RT = \frac{0.05 \times 0.0821 \times 300}{1} = 1.2315$

Hence, (i) → (s), (ii) → (r), (iii) → (q), (iv) → (p)

32. ***(1.86°)*** As we know,

$$\Delta T_f = iK_f m$$

when, $m = 1\,\text{molal}\ (1\,\text{mol kg}^{-1})$

$$\Delta T_f = iK_f$$

$\therefore \quad \log \Delta T_f = \log i + \log K_f$

$AB \rightleftharpoons A^+ + B^-$

$i = (1 + x)$

when, $x = 0$ (no ionisation),

$\log i = \log 1 = 0$

$\log \Delta T_f = \log K_f = 0.27$ (from graph)

$\therefore \quad K_f = 1.86 \text{ K kg mol}^{-1}$

33. ***(0.78)*** At point R

$\log i = 0.25$

$\therefore \quad i = 1.78$

$\therefore \quad 1 + x = 1.78 \Rightarrow x = 0.78$

34. ***(0.818)*** Given,

$p = 180X_B + 90$

If $X_B = 1$, then $p = \overset{\circ}{p}_B$

$\overset{\circ}{p}_B = 270,\ \overset{\circ}{p}_T = 90$

Number of moles of benzene $(n_B) = \dfrac{936}{78} = 12$

Number of moles of toluene $(n_T) = \dfrac{736}{92} = 8$

Vapour pressure of Ist liquid is

$$p_M = \overset{\circ}{p}_B X_B + \overset{\circ}{p}_T X_T$$

$$= 270\left(\frac{12}{20}\right) + 90\left(\frac{8}{20}\right) = 198 \text{ mm}$$

By using,

$$\frac{X'_B}{X'_T} = \frac{\overset{\circ}{p}_B X_B}{\overset{\circ}{p}_T X_T} = \frac{270 \times \frac{3}{5}}{90 \times \frac{2}{5}} = \frac{9}{2}$$

$$\frac{X'_B}{1 - X'_B} = \frac{9}{2} \Rightarrow 2X'_B = 9 - 9X'_B$$

$$X'_B = \frac{9}{11} = 0.818$$

35. ***(0.931)*** Vapour pressure of condensed liquid

$$= \overset{\circ}{p}_B X'_B + \overset{\circ}{p}_T X'_T = 270\,(0.818) + 90(0.181)$$

$$p_M = 237.2 \text{ mm}$$

By using,

$$\frac{X''_B}{X''_T} = \frac{\overset{\circ}{p}_B X'_B}{\overset{\circ}{p}_T X'_T} = \frac{(270)\,(0.818)}{90(0.181)} = 13.55$$

$$\frac{X''_B}{1 - X''_B} = 13.55$$

$$X''_B = 13.55 - 13.55\, X''_B$$

$$X''_B = 0.931$$

36. ***(150.9)*** By using,

$$\Delta T_f = K_f \times m = 2 \times \frac{0.1}{0.9 \times 46} \times 1000 = 4.83 \text{ K}$$

Freezing point of solution (M),

$$T'_f = T^\circ_f - \Delta T_f = 155.7 - 4.83 \approx 150.9 \text{ K}$$

37. ***(376.2)*** By using,

$$\Delta T_b = K_b \times m$$

$$= 0.52 \times \frac{0.1}{0.9 \times 18} \times 1000$$

$$= \frac{520}{9 \times 18} = 3.20$$

The boiling point of the solution,

$$T'_b = T_b^\circ + \Delta T_b = 373 + 3.20$$

$= 376.2$ K [Standard b.pt of water $= 373$ K]

38. ***(d)*** Among the given terms, only four i.e., molality, mole fraction, mass percentage and ppm do not change with temperature while molarity is a function of temperature.

39. ***(c)*** Among the given pairs of solutions, only two i.e, (ii) and (v) are isotonic at same temperature.

To determine the number of pairs of solutions that are isotonic at the same temperature, we need to analyze the osmotic pressure of each solution by using the formula, $\pi = i.CRT$

(i) For 1.4 M *aq*. H_2SO_4; For 0.5 M *aq*. C_2H_5OH

$(i = 3)$ $(i = 1)$

$\therefore \quad \pi = 4.2RT \quad \therefore \quad \pi = 0.5RT$

(ii) For 1 M *aq* NaCl ; For 2 M *aq*. Urea

$(i = 2)$ $(i = 1)$

$\therefore \quad \pi = 2RT \quad \therefore \pi = 2RT$

(iii) For 1 M *aq*. $CaCl_2$; For 1.5 M *aq*. KCl

$(i = 2)$ $(i = 2)$

$\therefore \quad \pi = 2RT \quad \therefore \quad \pi = 3RT$

(iv) For 1 M *aq*. $AlCl_3$; For 2 M *aq*. Na_2SO_4

$(i = 4)$ $(i = 3)$

$\therefore \quad \pi = 4RT \quad \therefore \quad \pi = 6RT$

(v) For 2.5 M *aq*. KCl ; For 1 M *aq*. $Al_2(SO_4)_3$

$(i = 2)$ $(i = 5)$

$\therefore \quad \pi = 5RT \quad \therefore \quad \pi = 5RT$

Hence, (ii) and (v) solutions are isotonic at the same temperature.

40. ***(c)*** Among the given units, only four i.e, (ii), (iii), (iv) and (v) are used to express concentration of solutions.

41. ***(a)*** Among the given mixtures only two i.e., (ii) and (v) will show positive deviation from Raoult's law while others does not.

42. ***(b)*** By using, $\Delta T_f = i \times K_f \times m$; $\Delta T_f = T^\circ_f - T_f$ $\quad [\because T^\circ_f = 0]$

For C_2H_5OH the value of $i = 1$

$\therefore \quad T_f = -\,0.1K_f$

Similarly,

For, (i) $Ba_3(PO_4)_2$; $i = 5$; $\Delta T_f = 0.5K_f$ So, $T_f = -0.5K_f$

(ii) K_2HgI_4; $i = 3$; $\Delta T_f = 0.3\,K_f$ So, $T_f = -0.3\,K_f$

(iii) Li_3PO_4; $i = 4$; $\Delta T_f = 0.4K_f$ So, $T_f = -0.4K_f$

(iv) $NaAlO_2$; $i = 2$; $\Delta T_f = 0.2\,K_f$ So, $T_f = -0.2\,K_f$

(v) Na_2SO_4 ; $i = 3$; $\Delta T_f = 0.3K_f$ So, $T_f = -0.3K_f$

(vi) $FeSO_4(NH_4)_2SO_4$; $i = 5$; $\Delta T_f = 0.5K_f$ So, $T_f = -0.5K_f$

(vi) KCl ; $i = 2$; $\Delta T_f = 0.2\ K_f$ So, $T_f = -0.2\ K_f$

Hence, all the solutions have lower freezing point than 0.10 M C_2H_5OH.

43. ***(b)*** Among the given pairs of volatile solvents only four i.e., (i), (iii), (v) and (vii) form azeotropic mixture because they show deviations from Raoult's law in which (i), (iii) and (vii) show positive deviation (minimum boiling azeotrope while (v) show negative deviation (maximum boiling azeotrope).

44. ***(d)*** By using $\pi = i \times CRT$

$$\pi \propto iC$$

So, (i) 0.02 M $KCl.MgCl_2.6H_2O(aq)$; 0.05 M KCl (aq)

$i = 5$; $i = 2$

$\pi = 0.02 \times 5 = 0.1$; $\pi = 0.05 \times 2 = 0.1$

(ii) 0.5 M C_2H_5OH (aq); 0.25 M KBr (aq)

$i = 1$; $i = 2$

$\pi = 0.5 \times 1 = 0.5$; $\pi = 0.25 \times 2 = 0.5$

(iii) 0.250 M KBr (aq) ; 0.125 M $Na_3PO_4(aq)$

$i = 2$; $i = 4$

$\pi = 0.250 \times 2 = 0.5$; $\pi = 0.125 \times 4 = 0.5$

(iv) 0.1 M $K_4[Fe(CN)_6]$ (aq) ; 0.1 M $FeSO_4(NH_4)_2SO_4$ (aq)

$i = 5$; $i = 5$

$\pi = 0.1 \times 5$; $\pi = 0.1 \times 5$

$\pi = 0.5$; $\pi = 0.5$

(v) 0.5 M C_2H_5OH (aq); 0.1 M $Mg_3(PO_4)_2(aq)$

$i = 1$; $i = 5$

$\pi = 0.5$; $\pi = 0.5$

(vi) 0.05 M $K_4[Fe(CN)_6]$; 0.25 M NaCl (aq)

$i = 5$; $i = 2$

$\pi = 0.05 \times 5 = 0.25$; $\pi = 0.25 \times 2 = 0.5$

(vi) 0.15 M NaCl (aq) ; 0.4 M $BaCl_2$ (aq)

$i = 2$; $i = 3$

$\pi = 0.15 \times 2 = 0.3$; $\pi = 0.1 \times 3 = 0.3$

So, solution (i), (ii), (iii), (iv), (v) and (vii) have same value of osmotic pressure.

45. ***(a)*** The osmotic pressure, $\pi = iCRT$. Since the concentration and temperature in each of the pair are same, osmotic pressure is proportional to i. The number of pairs in which π_2 is hypertonic to π_1 are (ii) and (v).

(i), (iii) and (vi) are isotonic ($\pi_1 = \pi_2$)

(iv) and (vii) are hypotonic ($\pi_1 > \pi_2$)

Check Through PYQs : JEE Advanced

1. ***(2.98)*** Molarity

$$(M) = \frac{\text{Number of moles of solute} \times 1000}{\text{Volume of solution (in mL)}}$$

Also, volume $= \dfrac{\text{Mass}}{\text{Density}}$

Given, mole fraction of urea $(\chi_{urea}) = 0.05$

Mass of water = 900 g

Density = 1.2 g/cm^3

$$\chi_{urea} = \frac{n_{urea}}{n_{urea} + 50} \quad \left[\because \text{Moles of water} = \frac{900}{18} = 50\right]$$

$$0.05 = \frac{n_{urea}}{n_{urea} + 50}$$

$\Rightarrow$ $19n_{urea} = 50$

$n_{urea} = 2.6315$ moles

$w_{urea} = n_{urea} \times (M \cdot wt)_{urea} = (2.6315 \times 60)$ g

$$V = \frac{2.6315 \times 60 + 900}{1.2}$$

$$\left[\because \text{Density} = \frac{\text{Mass of solution}}{\text{Volume of solution}}\right]$$

= 881.57 mL

Now, molarity

$$= \frac{\text{Number of moles of solute} \times 1000}{\text{Volume of solution (mL)}}$$

$$= \frac{2.6315 \times 1000}{881.57}$$

= 2.98 M

2. ***(0.2)*** Using Raoult's law equation for a mixture of volatile liquids.

$$p_T = p_A^\circ \chi_A + p_B^\circ \chi_B$$

$$0.3 = 0.25 \times p_A^\circ + 0.75 \times p_B^\circ \quad \ldots (i)$$

$$0.4 = 0.5 \times p_A^\circ + 0.5 \times p_B^\circ \quad \ldots (ii)$$

By solving Eqs. (i) and (ii)

$p_A^\circ = 0.6$ bar and $p_B^\circ = 0.2$ bar

Thus, the vapour pressure of pure liquid B in bar is 0.2.

3. ***(19)*** Use the formula

$$p_{Total} = p_A^\circ \times \chi_A + p_B^\circ \times \chi_B$$

and for equimolar solutions $\chi_A = \chi_B = \dfrac{1}{2}$

Given, $p_{Total} = 45$ torr for equimolar solution

$p_A^\circ = 20$ torr

So, $45 = p_A^\circ \times \dfrac{1}{2} + p_B^\circ \times \dfrac{1}{2}$

$= \dfrac{1}{2}(p_A^\circ + p_B^\circ)$

or $p_A^\circ + p_B^\circ = 90$ torr ...(i)

But we know $p_A^\circ = 20$ torr

so, $p_B^\circ = 90 - 20 = 70$ torr (From Eq. (i))

Now, for the new solution from the same formula

Given, $p_{Total} = 22.5$ torr

So, $22.5 = 20\chi_A + 70(1-\chi_A)$

(As $\chi_A + \chi_B = 1$)

or $22.5 = 70 - 50\chi_A$

So, $\chi_A = \dfrac{70-22.5}{50} = 0.95$

Thus $\chi_B = 1 - 0.95 = 0.05$ (as $\chi_A + \chi_B = 1$)

Hence, the ratio

$$\frac{\chi_A}{\chi_B} = \frac{0.95}{0.05} = 19$$

4. ***(b,d)*** The graph shown indicates that there is positive deviation because the observed vapour pressure of L is greater than the ideal pressure

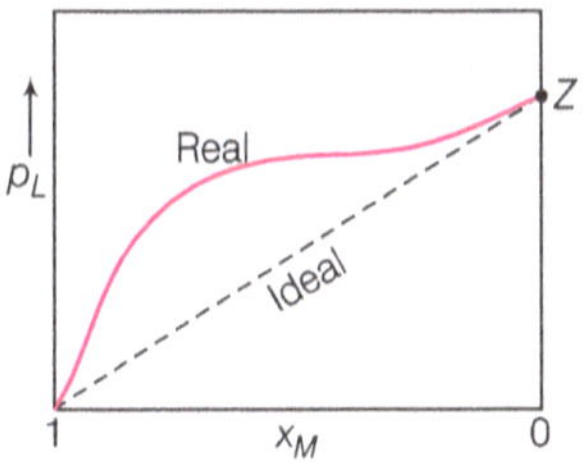

Since, deviation is positive, the intermolecular force between L and M is smaller than the same in pure L and pure M.

Also, as $x_L \to 1$, $x_M \to 0$ (for pure L), the real curve approaching ideal curve where Raoult's law will be obeyed.

5. ***(a,b)*** When intermolecular attraction between A and B in a mixture is smaller than that between A and A or B and B, then mixture is more vaporised, boiling point is lowered. It is a case of positive deviation from Raoult's law.

Methanol molecules (CH_3OH) are hydrogen bonded. In a mixture of CCl_4 and CH_3OH, extent of H-bonding is decreased. Mixture is more vapourised thus, positive deviation from Raoult's law.

Acetone molecules have higher intermolecular attraction due to dipole-dipole interaction. With CS_2, this interaction is decreased thus, shows positive deviation.

6. ***(150)*** In Vessel 1

$$(\Delta T_b)_1 = i_1 K_b \times \frac{\left(\frac{w_2}{M_x}\right)}{\left(\frac{W_1}{1000}\right)}$$

In Vessel 2

$$(\Delta T_b)_2 = i_2 K_b \times \frac{\left(\frac{w_2}{M_y}\right)}{\left(\frac{W_1}{1000}\right)}$$

$$\frac{(\Delta T_b)_1}{(\Delta T_b)_2} = \frac{i_1 \times M_y}{i_2 \times M_x} = 1.2 \times \frac{1}{0.8} = 1.5$$

$$\Rightarrow \quad (\Delta T_b)_1 = 1.5(\Delta T_b)_2$$

$$\frac{(\Delta T_b)_1}{(\Delta T_b)_2} \times 100 = 150\%$$

7. ***(682)*** 0.2 molal means 0.2 moles in 1000 g of solvent.

$\therefore$ Number of moles of urea = 0.2 mol

Weight of urea = $0.2 \times 60 = 12$ g

Weight of solvent = 1000 g

Weight of solution = $1000 + 12 = 1012$ g

So, Volume = Mass/density = $\dfrac{1012}{1.012}$

= 1000 mL

1000 mL solution contains 0.2 moles

$\therefore$ 50 mL solution contains

$$= \frac{0.2}{1000} \times 50 \text{ moles} = 0.01 \text{ mol}$$

$\therefore \quad n_1 = 0.01$ mol

So, number of moles of urea in another solution

$$(n_2) = \frac{0.06}{60} = 0.001$$

Final molarity

$$(M) = \frac{n_1 + n_2}{V_1 + V_2} = \frac{0.01 + 0.001}{\frac{(50+250)}{1000}} = 11/300 \text{ M}$$

Now, osmotic pressure $(\pi) = CRT$

$$= \frac{11}{300} \times 62 \times 300$$

= 682 torr

8. ***(5)*** Vapour pressure of water,

$p^\circ = 60$ mmHg

Vapour pressure of solution,

$p_s = 59.724$ mmHg

Let the number of ions present per formula unit of the ionic salt be n.

$$\begin{array}{ccc} S_n & \longrightarrow & nS \\ 0.1 & & 0 \\ 0.1(1-0.9) & & 0.1 \times 0.9 \times n \end{array}$$

$$i = \frac{0.1 \times 0.9 \times n + 0.1\,(1-0.9)}{0.1}$$

$$i = 0.1 + 0.9n$$

As we know,

$$\frac{p^\circ - p_s}{p^\circ} = i \times \text{mole fraction of solute}$$

$$\Rightarrow \frac{60 - 59.724}{60} = i \times \frac{0.1}{\frac{1800}{18} + 0.1}$$

$$\Rightarrow \quad i = 4.6$$

$$\Rightarrow \quad 0.1 + 0.9n = 4.6$$

$$\Rightarrow \quad n = 5.$$

9. ***(100.1)*** Complete reaction is as follows:

$$AgNO_3(aq) \longrightarrow Ag^+(aq) + NO_3^-(aq)$$

Concentration, $m = 0.1$ m

van't Hoff factor, $i = 2$

$$\Delta T_b = iK_b m$$

where, ΔT_b is change in boiling point of H_2O.
K_b is ebullioscopic constant = 0.5 K kg mol^{-1}

m is concentration of solution

$$\Delta T_b = 2 \times 0.5 \times 0.1 = 0.1°C$$

$T_b°$ = boiling point of pure water

T_b = boiling point of solution

$$T_b - T_b° = 0.1$$

$\Rightarrow \quad T_b = 100 + 0.1 = 100.1°C$

Boiling of solution, $x°\,C = 100.1°C$

10. ***(2.5)*** By adding equal volume of 0.1 m $BaCl_2$, the volume of solution doubles and concentration becomes half.

$$\underset{}{AgNO_3(aq)} \longrightarrow \underset{0.05\text{ m}}{Ag^+(aq)} + \underset{0.05\text{ m}}{NO_3^-(aq)}$$

$$BaCl_2(aq) \longrightarrow \underset{0.05\text{ m}}{Ba^{2+}(aq)} + \underset{0.1\text{ m}}{2Cl^-(aq)}$$

Ag^+ reacts with Cl^- to form ppt. of AgCl.

	$Ag^+(aq)$ +	$Cl^-(aq)$ ⟶	$AgCl(s)$
$t = 0$	0.05	0.1 m	–
$t = \infty$	0	0.05 m	0.05 m

Total species in solution are NO_3^-, Cl^- and Ba^{2+}. So, van't Hoff factor, $i = 3$.

Concentration of each species, $m = 0.05$ m

Elevation of boiling point

$$\Delta T_b = iK_b m$$

$$\Delta T_b = 3 \times 0.5 \times 0.05$$

$$= 0.075°C$$

$$T_b' - 100 = 0.075$$

$$T_b' = 100.075°C$$

Difference in boiling point, $T_b - T_b'$

$$= 100.1 - 100.075$$

$$= 0.025$$

$$= 2.5 \times 10^{-2}\,°C$$

So, $\quad y = 2.5$

11. ***(1.02)*** Weight of non-volatile solute = 0.5 g

Weight of solvent (benzene) = 39 g

From relative lowering of vapour pressure,

$$\frac{p° - p_s}{p°} = x_{\text{Solute}} = \frac{n_{\text{solute}}}{n_{\text{solute}} + n_{\text{solvent}}}$$

$$\frac{650 - 640}{650} = \frac{\frac{0.5}{\text{molar mass}}}{\frac{0.5}{\text{molar mass}} + \frac{39}{78}}$$

$$\frac{10}{650} = \frac{\frac{0.5}{\text{molar mass}}}{\frac{0.5}{\text{molar mass}} + 0.5}$$

$$0.5 + 0.5 \times \text{molar mass} = 65 \times 0.5$$

$\therefore$ Molar mass of solute = 64 g

From molal depression of freezing point,

$$\Delta T_f = K_f \times \text{molality} = \frac{K_f \times w_{\text{solute}}}{(MW)_{\text{solute}} \times w_{\text{solvent}}}$$

$$\Delta T_f = 5.12 \times \frac{0.5 \times 1000}{64 \times 39}$$

$\Rightarrow \quad \Delta T_f = 1.02$ K

12. ***(a)*** As we know, $\Delta T_f = iK_f m_2$

$$273 - T_f = 1 \times 2 \times \frac{34.5}{46 \times 500} \times 1000 = 3$$

$\therefore \quad T_f = 270$ K

We know, as the temperature increases, vapour pressure increases.

Vapour pressure curves shown in (a) is in agreement with the calculated value of ΔT_f.

13. ***(1)*** $\Delta T_f = iK_f m$

$$\Delta T_f = 0 - (-0.0558°C) = 0.0558°C$$

$$\Rightarrow i \text{ (van't Hoff's factor)} = \frac{0.0558}{1.86 \times 0.01} = 3$$

This indicates that complex upon ionisation produces three ions as:

$$[Co(NH_3)_5Cl]Cl_2 \longrightarrow [Co(NH_3)_5Cl]^{2+}(aq) + 2Cl^-(aq)$$

Thus, only one Cl is inside the coordination sphere.

CHAPTER 8

Redox Reactions & Electrochemistry

Learning Elements

Element 1 **Redox Reactions**

Oxidation-Reduction, Oxidation State of an Element, Types of Redox Reactions, Balancing of Redox Reactions.

Element 2 **Conductors, Conductance of Electrolytic Solution, Kohlrausch Law, Electrolysis**

Conductor, Conductance of Electrolytic Solutions, Kohlrausch's Law, Application of Kohlrausch's Law, Quantitative Aspects of Electrolysis, Qualitative Aspects of Electrolysis, Conductometric Titration.

Element 3 **Electrochemical Cells, Nernst Equation and Electrode Potential**

Cells, Electrode Potential and Standard Electrode Potential, Various Types of Half Cell Electrochemical Series, Thermodynamics in Cells EMF Measurement : Applications, Concentration Cells.

Element 4 **Batteries, Fuel Cell and Corrosion**

Batteries, Primary Batteries (Dry Cell), Secondary Batteries, Fuel Cells, Corrosion.

Practice Elements

Practice Element 1 Target JEE Main
Practice Element 2 Target JEE Advanced

Trend Insights

JEE Main

	2024				2023				2022			
Topics	**E**	**M**	**T**	**O**	**E**	**M**	**T**	**O**	**E**	**M**	**T**	**O**
Redox Reactions	–	2	3	5	1	2	1	4	2	2	–	4
Coductors, Conductors of Electrolytic Solutions, Kohlrausch Law, Electrolysis	3	7	6	16	–	2	5	7	–	2	7	9
Electrochemical Cells, Nernst Equation and Electrode Potential	–	3	6	9	2	–	13	15	–	1	8	9
Battery, Fuel Cell and Corrosion	–	–	3	3	–	–	1	1	–	–	1	1

E = Easy, **M** = Medium, **T** = tough, **O** = Overall

Correct Dyamics

- Frequent questions have been about calculating cell potential using the Nernst equation under non-standard conditions.
- Most of the questions have been asked from variation of conductivity with dilution and the use of Kohlrausch's law to determine limiting molar conductance.
- Questions are often asked from electrochemical series and Faraday's law.

JEE Advanced

Typology	Years				
	2024	2023	2022	2021	2020
1. Simple MCQs	–	1	–	–	–
2. One or More than one correct	1	–	1	–	–
3. Numerical Value/Integer	–	–	2	–	–
4. Matching Type	1	–	–	–	–
5. Paragraph Based	–	–	–	1	–

Current Dynamics

- Frequent questions have been asked from Nernst equation and thermodynamics of a cell.
- Most of the questions were asked from more than one correct and matching typology in recent years.

Insightful Advice

- Understand the concept of standard reduction potential, electrolysis, Kohlrausch's law and conductance.
- Practice problems based on Nernst equation and its applications.
- Solve numerical involving ΔG, E_{cell}, K and conductance.

Element 1 Redox Reactions

Oxidation-Reduction

Redox reactions are chemical reactions that involve the transfer of electrons between two substances. In these reactions, one substance loses electrons (Oxidation) and another substance gains electrons (reduction).

Oxidation and reduction are complementary processes that always occur together. A substance, which undergoes oxidation, acts as a **reducing agent** while a substance, which undergoes reduction, acts as an **oxidising agent**.

Oxidation State of an Element

The Oxidation state (or oxidation number) of an atom is a measure of the degree of oxidation (loss of electrons) or reduction (gain of electrons) of an element in a compound.

In case of covalent compound, it is the hypothetical charge an atom would have if all bonds to atom of different elements were considered to be completely ionic, with the more electronegative atom taking both electrons from the bond.

The oxidation state can be positive, negative, or zero, depending on whether the atom has lost or gained electrons.

Some Rules for Finding Oxidation State are as follows

(i) The oxidation number of an atom in free elements is zero, hydrogen in H_2, sulphur in S_8, phosphorus in P_4, oxygen in O_2 or O_3, all have zero oxidation number.

(ii) The most electronegative element, fluorine, oxidation number is – 1 in all of its compounds.

(iii) In most of compounds, oxidation number of oxygen is –2 except in peroxides, superoxides and oxygen fluorides.

In peroxides (O_2^{-2}), it's –1; superoxides (O_2^{-1}), it's –1/2; and in OF_2, the oxygen has an oxidation number of +2.

(iv) The oxidation number of hydrogen is +1 in all of its compounds except in metallic hydrides like NaH, BaH_2 etc. where it is –1.

(v) The oxidation number of a monoatomic ion is equal to the electrical charge present on it.

(vii) For polyatomic ions, the algebraic sum of oxidation numbers of all the atoms is equal to the net charge on the ion.

(viii) For neutral molecules, the algebraic sum of the oxidation numbers of all the atoms present in the molecule is zero.

The Paradox of Fractional Oxidation Number

Sometimes, we come across with certain compounds in which the oxidation number of a particular element in the compound is in fraction. This fractional oxidation state is the average oxidation state of the element. Examples are ;

- C_3O_2 [where oxidation number of carbon is (4/3)],
- Br_3O_8 [where oxidation number of bromine is (16/3)],
- $Na_2S_4O_6$ (where oxidation number of sulphur is 2.5).

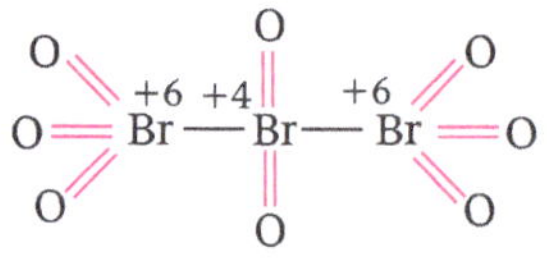

Tribromooctaoxide

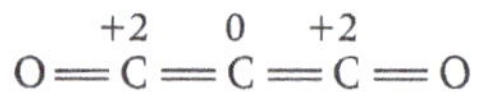

Structure of C_3O_2 carbon suboxide

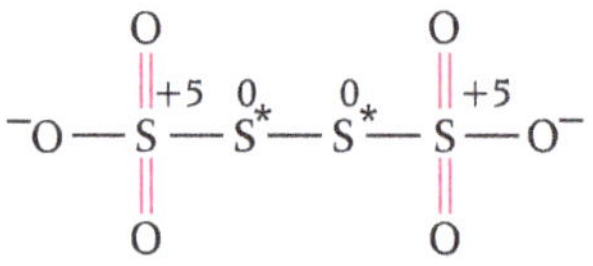

Structure of $S_4O_6^{2-}$ tetrathionate ion

In reality (revealed by structures only), the element in that particular species is present in more than one whole number oxidation states. $\overset{+8/3}{Fe_3O_4}$ ($\overset{+3}{Fe_2O_3}$ and $\overset{+2}{FeO}$), $\overset{+8/3}{Mn_3O_4}$ ($\overset{+2}{MnO}\cdot\overset{+3}{Mn_2O_3}$), $\overset{+8/3}{Pb_3O_4}$ ($\overset{+4}{PbO_2}\cdot 2\overset{+2}{PbO}$) are some of the other examples of the compounds, which are mixed oxides, where we come across with fractional oxidation states of the metal atom.

JEE Alert

In non-stoichiometric compound like $Fe_{0.94}O$, the oxidation state of iron is $\frac{2}{0.94}$.

Types of Redox Reactions

Various types of redox reactions are given below.

1. Combination Reactions

The reactions in which two atoms or molecules combines together to form a new molecule are called combination reactions. For e.g.

$$C + O_2 \xrightarrow{\Delta} CO_2,\ 3Mg + N_2 \xrightarrow{\Delta} Mg_3N_2,$$

$$CH_4 + 2O_2 \xrightarrow{\Delta} CO_2 + 2H_2O$$

2. Decomposition Reactions

The reactions in which a molecule break down to form two or more components, at least one of them must be in the elemental state. For e.g.

$$2H_2O \xrightarrow{\Delta} 2H_2 + O_2,\ 2NaH \xrightarrow{\Delta} 2Na + H_2,$$

$$2KClO_3 \xrightarrow{\Delta} 2KCl + 3O_2$$

3. Displacement Reactions

Reaction in which an atom or ion of a compound is replaced by an atom or ion of another element are called displacement reactions.

(i) **Metal Displacement** A more reactive metal displaces less reactive metal from the solution.

- **Metal-metal displacement**

$$Zn(s) + CuSO_4(aq) \longrightarrow ZnSO_4(aq) + Cu(s)$$

$$V_2O_5(s) + 5Ca(s) \xrightarrow{\Delta} 2V(s) + 5CaO(s)$$

$$TiCl_4(l) + 2Mg(s) \xrightarrow{\Delta} Ti(s) + 2MgCl_2(s)$$

(ii) **Non-metal displacement** A Non-metal can be displaced by a metal or another non-metal from the solution.

- **Metal-non metal displacement**

$$2Na(s) + 2H_2O(l) \longrightarrow 2NaOH(aq) + H_2(g)$$

$$Ca(s) + 2H_2O(l) \longrightarrow Ca(OH)_2(aq) + H_2(g)$$

$$2Fe(s) + 3H_2O(l) \longrightarrow Fe_2O_3(s) + 3H_2(g)$$

$$Zn(s) + 2HCl(aq) \longrightarrow ZnCl_2(aq) + H_2(g)$$

- **Non metal - non metal displacement**

$$Cl_2(g) + 2Br^-(aq) \longrightarrow 2Cl^-(aq) + Br_2(l)$$

$$Cl_2(g) + 2I^-(aq) \longrightarrow 2Cl^-(aq) + I_2(s)$$

A more electronegative halogen displaces less electronegative halogen from solution.

4. Disproportionation Reactions

In a disproportionation reaction, an element from the same oxidation state gets oxidised as well as reduced. One of the element in a disproportionation reaction should occur in at least three oxidation states.

The element in the reacting substance should be in the intermediate oxidation state and higher and lower oxidation state of the element are formed in the reaction.

$$2H_2O_2(aq) \longrightarrow 2H_2O(l) + O_2(g)$$

$$P_4(s) + 3OH^-(aq) + 3H_2O(l) \longrightarrow PH_3(g) + 3H_2PO_2^-(aq)$$

5. Comproportionation Reaction

These reactions are the reverse of disproportionation reaction. For example, Br^- and BrO_3^- in acidic medium undergoes oxidation and reduction to give Br_2.

$$5Br^- + BrO_3^- + 6H^+ \longrightarrow 3Br_2 + 3H_2O$$

JEE MAPPER

Example Similar to PYQ Asked in JEE Advance 2021

Which of the following reactions are disproportionation reactions?

A. $MnO_4^{2-} + 2H_2O \longrightarrow MnO_4^- + MnO_2 + 4OH^-$

B. $5NH_2OH + 3H^+ \longrightarrow 3NH_4^+ + 2NO + 3H_2O$

C. $3Sn^{2+} + 2H^+ \longrightarrow 3Sn^{4+} + H_2$

D. $Cl_2 + NaOH \longrightarrow NaCl + NaClO_3 + H_2O$

Choose the correct answer from the options given below.

(a) A, B and C (b) A, B, C and D
(c) A, B and D (d) B, C and D

Sol. (c) Disproportionation reactions are those in which same species is oxidised and reduced simultaneously.

A. $\overset{+6}{Mn}O_4^{2-} + 2H_2O \longrightarrow \overset{+7}{Mn}O_4^- + \overset{+4}{Mn}O_2 + 4OH^-$

B. $5\overset{-1}{N}H_2OH + 3H^+ \longrightarrow 3\overset{-3}{N}H_4^+ + 2\overset{+2}{N}O + 3H_2O$

C. $3Sn^{2+} + 2H^+ \longrightarrow 3Sn^{4+} + H_2$ is not a disproportionation reaction

D. $Cl_2 + NaOH \longrightarrow Na\overset{-1}{Cl} + Na\overset{+5}{Cl}O_3 + H_2O$

In A, B and D, same species is oxidised as well as reduced

So, these are disproportionation reaction.

Competency Enhancer 1.1

Which of the following reactions are disproportionation reactions?

A. $3H_3PO_2 \longrightarrow PH_3 + 2H_3PO_3$

B. $P_4 + 3NaOH + 3H_2O \longrightarrow PH_3 + 3NaH_2PO_2$

C. $Cl_2 + H_2O \longrightarrow HCl + HClO$

D. $3Cu + 8HNO_3 \longrightarrow 3Cu(NO_3)_2 + 4H_2O + NO$

Choose the correct answer from the options given below.

(a) A, C and D (b) B, C and D
(c) A, B, C and D (d) A, B and C

Balancing of Redox Reactions

The redox reactions can be balanced through

- Oxidation State Method
- Ion Electron Method

1. Oxidation State Method

This method is based upon the fact that the total increase in oxidation number must be equal to the total decrease in oxidation number. Let us understand the oxidation state method through an example

$$H_2\overset{+3}{C_2}O_4 + K\overset{+7}{Mn}O_4 \longrightarrow \overset{+4}{C}O_2 + K_2O + \overset{2+}{Mn}O + H_2O$$

(i) Find oxidation states of elements in the reaction.

(ii) Write separate equations for reduction and oxidation half taking the elements undergoing oxidation and reduction.

$$C_2^{+3} \longrightarrow 2C^{+4} \rightarrow \text{oxidation}$$
$$Mn^{+7} \longrightarrow Mn^{+2} \rightarrow \text{Reduction}$$

(iii) Add required number of e^- to balance charges

$$C_2^{+3} \longrightarrow 2C^{+4} + 2e^-$$
$$5e^- + Mn^{+7} \longrightarrow Mn^{+2}$$

(iv) Balance e^- lost and gained by cross multiplication, if lost and gained and not same

$$(C_2^{+3} \longrightarrow 2C^{+4} + 2e^-) \times 5$$
$$(5e^- + Mn^{+7} \longrightarrow Mn^{+2}) \times 2$$

(v) Write the complete reaction with same stoichiometric coefficients

$$5H_2C_2O_4 + 2KMnO_4 \longrightarrow 10CO_2 + K_2O + 2MnO + H_2O$$

(vi) Atoms other than 'O' and 'H' atoms are balanced

(vii) Balance 'O' atom (Acidic medium) by adding required number of H_2O on deficient side.

$$5H_2C_2O_4 + 2KMnO_4 \longrightarrow 10CO_2 + K_2O + 2MnO + 5H_2O$$

'H' atoms are balanced.

Solved Booster 1.1

Balance the following Oxidation - Reduction equation

$KMnO_4 + KCl + H_2SO_4 \longrightarrow MnSO_4 + K_2SO_4 + H_2O + Cl_2$

by oxidation number methods.

Solution

(a) Identify the oxidation & reduction half equations.

Reduction half : $KMnO_4 \longrightarrow MnSO_4$, Oxidation half : $KCl \longrightarrow Cl_2$

(b) Balance the atoms that undergo change in oxidation state

Reduction half : $KMnO_4 \longrightarrow MnSO_4$,

Oxidation half : $2KCl \longrightarrow Cl_2$

(c) Balance atoms other than O & H.

Reduction half : $2KMnO_4 + 3H_2SO_4 \longrightarrow 2MnSO_4 + K_2SO_4$

Oxidation half : $2KCl + H_2SO_4 \longrightarrow Cl_2 + K_2SO_4$

(d) Balance O & H's

Reduction half :

$2KMnO_4 + 3H_2SO_4 + 10H^+ \longrightarrow 2MnSO_4 + K_2SO_4 + 8H_2O$

Oxidation half : $2KCl + H_2SO_4 \longrightarrow Cl_2 + K_2SO_4 + 2H^+$

(e) Add the electrons lost or gained to each half equation.

Reduction half :

$2KMnO_4 + 3H_2SO_4 + 10H^+ + 10e^- \longrightarrow 2MnSO_4 + K_2SO_4 + 8H_2O$

Oxidation half : $2KCl + H_2SO_4 \longrightarrow Cl_2 + K_2SO_4 + 2H^+ + 2e^-$

(f) Multiply oxidation half with 5 and then add the two half reactions.

Reduction half :

$2KMnO_4 + 3H_2SO_4 + 10H^+ + 10e^- \longrightarrow 2MnSO_4 + K_2SO_4 + 8H_2O$

Oxidation half :

$10KCl + 5H_2SO_4 \longrightarrow 5Cl_2 + 5K_2SO_4 + 10H^+ + 10e^-$

Overall balanced reaction :

$2KMnO_4 + 10KCl + 8H_2SO_4 \longrightarrow 2MnSO_4 + 6K_2SO_4 + 8H_2O + 5Cl_2$

2. Ion-Electron Method

Let us take an example to balance the reaction by ion-electron method step wise.

$$H_2\overset{+3}{C_2}O_4 + K\overset{+7}{Mn}O_4 \longrightarrow \overset{+4}{C}O_2 + K_2O + \overset{+2}{Mn}O$$

(i) Write oxidation state of elements to find oxidation and Reduction.

(ii) Write separate equation for oxidation and reduction half

$$H_2C_2O_4 \longrightarrow CO_2 \text{ Oxidation}$$
$$KMnO_4 \longrightarrow MnO + K_2O \text{ Reduction}$$

(iii) Balance atoms other than 'O' and 'H' atoms

$$H_2C_2O_4 \longrightarrow 2CO_2$$
$$2KMnO_4 \longrightarrow 2MnO + K_2O$$

(iv) Balance 'O' and 'H' atoms (Acidic medium)

$$H_2C_2O_4 \longrightarrow 2CO_2 + 2H^+$$
$$10H^+ + 2KMnO_4 \longrightarrow 2MnO + K_2O + 5H_2O$$

(v) Balance charge for both halves by adding required number of electrons.

$$H_2C_2O_4 \longrightarrow 2CO_2 + 2H^+ + 2e$$
$$10e^- + 10H^+ + 2KMnO_4 \longrightarrow 2MnO + K_2O + 5H_2O$$

(vi) Balance lost and gained electrons

$$(H_2C_2O_4 \longrightarrow 2CO_2 + 2H^+ + 2e) \times 5$$
$$10e^- + 10H^+ + 2KMnO_4 \longrightarrow 2MnO + K_2O + 5H_2O$$
$$5H_2C_2O_4 + 2KMnO_4 \longrightarrow 10CO_2 + 2MnO + K_2O + 5H_2O$$

JEE Alert

Mostly, the medium in which a redox reaction is to be balanced is given in the problem. If the problem does not state the medium explicitly, then the medium is decided by looking at the reactants or products

Solved Booster 1.2

Balance the following redox equation,

$$AsO_3^{3-} + MnO_4^- \longrightarrow AsO_4^{3-} + MnO_2$$

using ion-electron method (alkaline medium).

Solution

(a) Identify the oxidation & reduction halves.

Reduction half : $MnO_4^- \longrightarrow MnO_2$,

Oxidation half; $AsO_3^{3-} \longrightarrow AsO_4^{3-}$

(b) Atoms of the element undergoing oxidation and reduction are already balanced.

(c) Balancing O atoms

Reduction half : $2H_2O + MnO_4^- \longrightarrow MnO_2 + 4OH^-$

Oxidation half : $2OH^- + AsO_3^{3-} \longrightarrow AsO_4^{3-} + H_2O$

(d) Balancing H atoms,

H atoms are already balanced in both the half-reactions.

(e) Balancing charge,

Reduction half : $3e^- + 2H_2O + MnO_4^- \longrightarrow MnO_2 + 4OH^-$ ...(B)

Oxidation half : $2OH^- + AsO_3^{3-} \longrightarrow AsO_4^{3-} + H_2O + 2e^-$ ...(A)

(f) Multiply equation (A) by 3 and equation (B) by 2 and then add (A) and (B).

$$[3e^- + 2H_2O + MnO_4^- \longrightarrow MnO_2 + 4OH^-] \times 2$$
$$[2OH^- + AsO_3^{3-} \longrightarrow AsO_4^{3-} + H_2O + 2e^-] \times 3$$
$$\overline{3AsO_3^{3-} + 2MnO_4^- + H_2O \longrightarrow 3AsO_4^{3-} + 2MnO_2 + 2OH^-}$$

Elemental Practice 8.1

Type I MCQs with Only One Correct Option

1. Which of the following coordination compounds has the metal in a zero oxidation state?

(a) $[Ni(CO)_4]$ (b) $[FeCl_4]^{2-}$

(c) $[Cu(NH_3)_4]^{2+}$ (d) $[MnO_4]^-$

2. An acidic medium contains 1 mole of $Cr_2O_7^{2-}$ reacts with 1.2 moles of a metal ion M^{y+} to form MO_4^- and Cr^{3+}. If the oxidation state of a metal M in MO_4^- is 7, the value of y is

(a) 2 (b) 3

(c) 4 (d) 1

3. In which of the following reactions is nitrogen (N) oxidised?

(a) $NH_4^+ \longrightarrow N_2$ (b) $N_2H_4 \longrightarrow NH_4^+$

(c) $NH_3 \longrightarrow NH_4^+$ (d) $NO_3^- \longrightarrow NO$

4. Given below are two statements.

Statement I In the reaction of $Cr_2O_7^{2-}$ with SO_3^{2-} in an acidic medium, chromium undergoes both oxidation and reduction, showing disproportionation.

Statement II In this case, $Cr_2O_7^{2-}$ undergoes disproportionation forming Cr^{3+} and CrO_4^{2-}.

In the light of the above statements choose the correct answer from the options given below.

(a) Both statement I and statement II are correct.

(b) Both statement I and statement II are incorrect.

(c) Statement I is correct but statement II is incorrect.

(d) Statement I is incorrect but statement II is correct.

5. In the unbalanced reaction

$$Cr_2O_7^{2-} + NO_2^- \longrightarrow Cr^{3+} + NO_3^-$$

If the stoichiometric coefficients of $Cr_2O_7^{2-}$, NO_2^-, Cr^{3+} and H_2O are a, b, c and d respectively in acidic medium. Then the numerical value of $\frac{a}{c} + \frac{b}{d}$ is

(a) 5/4 (b) 6/4 (c) 7/4 (d) 3/4

6. In a redox titration, potassium permanaganate ($KMnO_4$) is used to titrate sodium oxalate ($Na_2C_2O_4$) in an acidic medium. If 1 mole of $KMnO_4$ oxidises 5 moles of $Na_2C_2O_4$, what is the equivalent weight of $KMnO_4$?

(a) $\frac{M}{3}$ (b) $\frac{M}{4}$

(c) $\frac{M}{5}$ (d) $\frac{M}{1}$

7. Match list-I with list-II

List-I (Type of Reaction)		List-II (Example of Reaction)
A.	Decomposition	1. $3Cl_2 + 6OH^- \longrightarrow 5Cl^- + ClO_3^- + 3H_2O$
B.	Displacement	2. $2H_2O_2 \longrightarrow 2H_2O + O_2$
C.	Disproportionation	3. $2N_2 + 4H_2 \longrightarrow 2N_2H_4$
D.	Combination	4. $Mg + Cu(NO_3)_2 \longrightarrow Mg(NO_3)_2 + Cu$

Choose the correct answer from the options given below.

(a) A → 2, B → 4, C → 3, D → 1

(b) A → 4, B → 2, C → 1, D → 3

(c) A → 2, B → 4, C → 1, D → 3

(d) A → 4, B → 2, C → 3, D → 1

8. The oxidation number of Fe in brown ring complex is

(a) +2 (b) +1

(c) 0 (d) +3

9. Given below are two statements.

Assertion (A) In the reaction $2Ag_2O \longrightarrow 4Ag + O_2$, silver undergoes reduction and its oxidation state changes from +1 to 0.

Reason (R) In any decomposition reaction, the substance undergoing decomposition always experience a change in oxidation state.

In the light of the above statements, choose the correct answer from the options given below.
(a) Both (A) and (R) are correct and (R) is the correct explanation of (A).
(b) Both (A) and (R) are correct but (R) is not the correct explanation of (A).
(c) (A) is correct but (R) is incorrect.
(d) (A) is incorrect but (R) is correct.

10. Given below are some statement related to the reaction between H_2O_2 and $KMnO_4$ in acidic medium.
I. H_2O_2 reduces Mn^{7+} to Mn^{2+} and itself gets oxidised to oxygen gas (O_2).
II. H_2O_2 oxidises MnO_4^- to MnO_4^{2-}.
III. $KMnO_4$ acts as a reducing agent and H_2O_2 acts as an oxidising agent.
IV. Both H_2O_2 and $KMnO_4$ acts as reducing agent.
V. H_2O_2 acts as an oxidising as well as reducing agent.

Choose the correct answer from the options given below.
(a) I, II and III are correct. (b) I and V are correct.
(c) I, II IV and V are correct. (d) I, III and V are correct.

11. When sulphur is boiled with sodium hydroxide, two sulphur compounds are formed. What type of reaction it is and the oxidation state of S in the main products are?
(a) Redox, (+ 1) and (− 2)
(b) Redox, (+ 2) and (+ 2)
(c) Disproportionation, (+ 2) and (+ 2)
(d) Disproportionation, (+ 2), (− 2)

12. Which of the following reactions demonstrates the oxidising behavior of concentrated nitric acid (HNO_3)?
(a) $2Al + 6HNO_3(conc.) \longrightarrow 2Al(NO_3)_3 + 3H_2O$
(b) $3Cu + 8HNO_3(conc.) \longrightarrow 3Cu(NO_3)_2 + 2NO_2 + 4H_2O$
(c) $2Na + 2HNO_3 \longrightarrow 2NaNO_3 + H_2$
(d) $2Fe + 6HNO_3(conc) \longrightarrow 2Fe(NO_3)_3 + 3H_2O$

13. The decreasing order of oxidation state of sulphur anions is

Persulphate anion, Tetrathionate anion, Thiosulphate anion
(a) Persulphate anion > Thiosulphate anion > Tetrathionate anion
(b) Persulphate anion > Tetrathionate anion > Thiosulphate anion
(c) Tetrathionate anion >Persulphate anion > Thiosulphate anion
(d) Tetrathionate anion > Thiosulphate anion > Persulphate anion

14. In a redox reaction involving potassium permanganate, which of the following reactions is most likely to occur?
(a) Oxidation of primary alcohol to a carboxylic acid.
(b) Reduction of a ketone to an alcohol.
(c) Oxidation of a methyl group to a carboxyl group.
(d) Reduction of an aldehyde to a primary alcohol.

15. Consider the following reaction.

$$Cr_2O_7^{2-} + xH^+ + yFe^{2+} \longrightarrow zCr^{3+} + nFe^{3+} + pH_2O$$

The values of x, y, z, n and p in a balanced redox reaction are respectively
(a) 14, 3, 2, 1 and 10
(b) 12, 2, 4, 3 and 12
(c) 3, 5 6, 12 and 5
(d) 14, 6, 2, 7 and 6

Type II 》 MCQs with One or More than One Correct Option

16. Choose the correct statements related to the given redox reaction.

$$MnO_4^- + C_2O_4^{2-} + H^+ \longrightarrow Mn^{2+} + CO_2 + H_2O$$

(a) The oxidation state of C changes from + 4 to + 3
(b) The oxidation state of Mn changes from + 7 to + 2
(c) The reaction involves 5 electrons transferred per molecule of MnO_4^-.
(d) The reaction rate is catalysed by the presence of Mn^{2+}.

17. Select the reactions in which redox process is involved.
(a) $CaCO_3 \longrightarrow CaO + CO_2$
(b) $MnO_2 + 4HCl \longrightarrow MnCl_2 + 2H_2O + Cl_2$
(c) $ClO_2 + O_2^{2-} \longrightarrow ClO_2^- + O_2$
(d) $2Fe^{3+} + 2I^- \longrightarrow 2Fe^{2+} + I_2$

18. Which of the following are examples of disproportionation reaction?
(a) $2H_2O_2 \longrightarrow 2H_2O + O_2$
(b) $P_4 + 3OH^- + 3H_2O \longrightarrow PH_3 + 3H_2PO_2^{\ominus}$
(c) $3Br_2 + 6OH^- \longrightarrow 5Br^- + BrO_3^- + 3H_2O$
(d) $Cu + 2AgNO_3 \longrightarrow Cu(NO_3)_2 + 2Ag$

19. Consider the reaction:

$$Cr_2O_7^{2-} + 14H^+ + 6Br^- \longrightarrow 2Cr^{3+} + 7H_2O + 3Br_2$$

Which of the following are correct?
(a) The oxidation state of Cr changes from + 6 to + 3.
(b) Br^- acts as a reducing agent.
(c) The equivalent weight of $Cr_2O_7^{2-}$ in this reaction is $M/2$.
(d) The number of electrons transferred in the balanced equation is 6.

20. Select the incorrect statements.
(a) The oxidation number of an element is the same as its valency in all compounds.
(b) In CCl_4, carbon has valency of 4 and an oxidation number of + 4.
(c) The oxidation number is used to determine electrons lost or gained during a redox reaction.
(d) Valency can be fractional in some compounds, but oxidation numbers are always whole numbers.

21. For the element chlorine in the compounds NaCl, Cl_2, HClO, ClO_4^-, which of the following statements are true?
(a) The oxidation number of chlorine in NaCl is – 1.
(b) The valency of chlorine in HClO is 1.
(c) The oxidation number of chlorine in ClO_4^- is + 7.
(d) The valency of chlorine in Cl_2 is zero.

Type III 》 Numerical/Integer Answer Type Questions

22. In an acidic solution, 5 moles of potassium dichromate quantitatively oxidise iodide anions to produces *y* moles of a product containing iodine. The number of moles of electrons involved in the reaction are

23. In the compound potassium tetrathionate there are four sulphur atoms with two different oxidation states. The sum of the both the oxidation states is.....

24. Equal volumes of a reducing agent are titrated separately with 0.2 M $KMnO_4$ in acidic, basic and neutral solutions. The volume of $KMnO_4$ required are 15 mL in acidic, 75 mL in basic and 25 mL in neutral medium. The sum of oxidation state of Mn in each reduction product is

25. A 2g sample of copper (II) oxide (CuO) has 80% purity. It is dissolved in acid and reduced by heating with hydrogen gas. The resultant solution is cooled and made up to 250 mL. An aliquot of 50 mL of this solution is titrated. The number of electrons taken by the oxidant in the reaction of the above titration is .... $\times 10^{21}$ [Nearest Integer]

26. The oxidation states of the transition metal atoms in the following comopunds are denoted by *x*, *y* and *z* respectively. The product of *x*, *y* and *z* are ...
Chromium Oxide, Copper Sulphate, Ferric Chloride

Elemental Practice 8.1 | Chapter 8

Connect with **Answers**

1. (a)	**2.** (a)	**3.** (a)	**4.** (b)	**5.** (a)	**6.** (c)
7. (c)	**8.** (b)	**9.** (c)	**10.** (b)	**11.** (d)	**12.** (b)
13. (b)	**14.** (a)	**15.** (d)	**16.** (b,c,d)	**17.** (b,c,d)	**18.** (a,b,c)
19. (a,b,d)	**20.** (a,d)	**21.** (a,b,c)	**22.** (30)	**23.** (5)	**24.** (12)
25. (5)	**26.** (18)				

Element 2

Conductors, Conductance of Electrolytic Solution, Kohlrausch Law, Electrolysis

Electrochemistry is the branch of chemistry that deals with the relationship between electrical energy and chemical reactions. It focuses on how chemical changes can produce electricity and how electrical energy can drive chemical reactions.

Conductor

In electrochemistry, the term conductor refers to the materials that facilitate the flow of current. The conductors can be classified in two major ways.

1. Metallic Conductors

These are the materials which allow electricity primarily through the movement of electrons. Free electrons and holes (positive charges) are responsible for the conduction of such conductors. It is generally occurs in solid material.

Cs, Hg and Ga are metallic conductors but are liquids at or near room temperature.

2. Electrolytic Conductors

These are the materials that conduct electricity through the movement of ions rather than electrons. This category primarily includes solutions of electrolytes (substances that dissociate into ions in solution) and molten ionic compounds. The extent of conduction of different electrolytes in solutions is different. Electrolytes can be broadly categorised into two types, i.e. strong and weak electrolytes.

(i) **Strong Electrolytes** These substances are largely dissociated and form a highly conducting liquid in water. e.g. NaCl, HCl, KCl, NaOH, HNO_3, H_2SO_4 etc.

(ii) **Weak Electrolytes** These substances have less ability to dissociate in aqueous solution. e.g. H_2CO_3, CH_3COOH, $ZnCl_2$, $HgCl_2$ etc.

JEE Spotlite

- As temperature increases, metallic conductivity generally decreases because increased thermal vibrations of the lattice atoms hinder electron movement.
- In electrolytic conductors, increased temperature usually leads to higher conductivity due to increased ion mobility.
- All salts except ($CdBr_2$, $HgCl_2$), mineral acids like HCl, H_2SO_4, HNO_3, etc and bases like NaOH, KOH etc are strong electrolytes.
- All organic acids like HCN, H_2CO_3 etc., and bases like NH_3, amines etc are weak electrolytes.
- Electrical conductance of a solution increases as the viscosity of the solvent decreases.

Conductance in Electrolytic Solutions

Conductance is the power of an electrolyte to conduct electric current. Just like metallic conductors, electrolytic solutions also obey Ohm's law which states that "The current (I), flowing through a conductor is directly proportional to the potential difference (V) across it". i.e

$$V \propto I \text{ or } V = IR$$

1. Resistance (R)

It is the hindrance to the flow of cation and anion to the respective electrodes in the flow of current

From Ohm's law, $R = \frac{V}{I}$

Its unit is Ohm (Ω).

2. Electrical Conductance

The reciprocal of resistance R is called **electrical conductance.** It is the ease with which the electricity flows through a solution. It is represented by G.

$$G = 1/R$$

Its SI unit is mho or Siemen(S).

3. Resistivity

If a solution is placed between two parallel electrodes having cross-sectional area a and distance l apart, the resistance R is directly proportional to its length and inversly proportional to its area,

$$R \propto \frac{l}{a} \quad \text{or} \quad R = \rho\frac{l}{a}$$

where, ρ is called **specific resistance or resistivity**, It's SI unit is Ω–m. In electrolytic cell, it can be considered as resistance to flow of ions present in unit cube of a solution.

4. Specific Conductance

The reciprocal of resistivity (specific resistance) is called **conductivity** (specific conductance) and is represented by κ(kappa).

$$\therefore \quad \frac{1}{\rho} = \frac{l}{Ra} \Rightarrow \kappa = \frac{l}{Ra}$$

Specific conductance (κ) $= G \times \frac{l}{a}$

If $l = 1$ cm and $a = 1\text{ cm}^2$, then

then κ = Conductance.

In other words **specific conductance** is the conductance of ions present in one centimeter cube of a electrolytic solution. The SI unit of conductance is Ω^{-1}, i.e. siemens(S) Thus specific conductance is expressed is $S\,cm^{-1}$ or $ohm^{-1}cm^{-1}$.

5. Cell Constant

The ratio of length to the cross sectional area is called **cell constant**. It is a characteristic parameter of conductivity of cell used for experiment.

Cell constant, $G^* = \frac{l}{a}$

It is also represented as

$$G^* = R \times \kappa$$

The unit of cell constant is m^{-1} or cm^{-1}.

JEE Quicker

The statement "The nature of the electrode used does not affect electrolytic conductance of a solution" is correct.

JEE Main 2024

The conductivity of an electrolytic solution is primarily determined by the concentration and mobility of the ions present in the solution. The electrode serves as a surface for the ions to transfer charge to and from, rather than acting as an active participant in the conduction.

Measurement of Conductance and Cell Constant

The cell constant is usually determined by measuring the resistance of a cell containing a solution, whose conductivity is a standard (known) value. KCl solution conductivity in water is generally taken for this standarisation. Its conductivity values at different concentration are known.

Thus, $$G^* = \frac{l}{a} = R\kappa$$

Measurement of R is done using **Wheatstone Bridge** principle as shown in the circuit. R_1 and R_2 are known **resistances**,

R_3 is a variable resistance and R_4 is the unknown resistance (under study) of a conductivity cell.

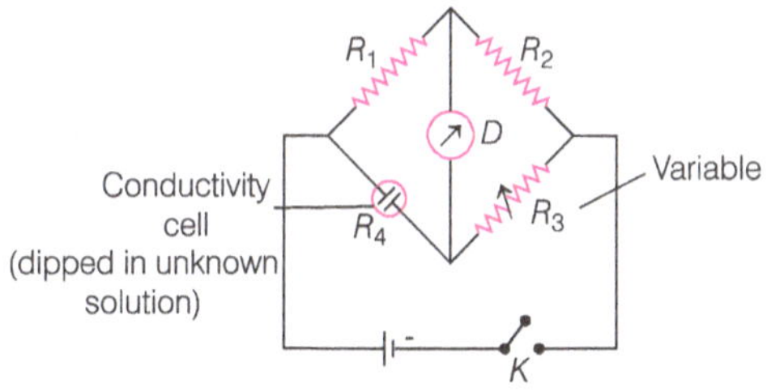

Arrangement for measuring the resistance of the solution of an electrolyte

R_3 is adjusted in such a way that when key (K) is pressed, detector (D) shows no deflection. At balanced point, when no current passes the detector $\frac{R_4}{R_3} = \frac{R_1}{R_2}$, thus R_4 is measured.

Generally, all measurements are made using conductivity water. If conductivity water is not available then true conductance

= (experimental value − conductance of water)

Conductance of conductivity water or deionized water is taken as zero.

Solved Booster 2.1

The resistance of a conductivity cell containing 0.001 M KCl solution at 298 K is 1500 Ω. The cell constant if conductivity of 0.001 M KCl solution at 298 K is $0.146 \times 10^{-3} S\ cm^{-1}$.

(a) 21.9 (b) 2.19 (c) 25.1 (d) 20.01

Solution *(a)*

$$G^* = \frac{l}{a} = R\kappa = 1500\ ohm \times 0.146 \times 10^{-3} ohm^{-1}cm^{-1}$$
$$= 0.219\ cm^{-1} = 21.9\ m^{-1}$$

Equivalent Conductance

- It is defined as the conducting power of all the ions produced by one gram- equivalent of an electrolyte in a given solution. It is denoted by Λ_{eq}.

  Equivalent conductance $\Lambda = \kappa V$

  where, κ is specific conductivity of solution and V is the volume of the solution containing 1gm-equivalent of the substance.
- If 1cc of a solution containing 1g-equivalent of the electrolyte is diluted to 100cc, then

  Equivalent conductance

  $$\Lambda_{eq} = 100 \times \text{specific conductance}$$

  On successive dilution to 1000 cc,

  $$\Lambda_{eq} = 1000 \times \text{specific conductance}$$

  In general, $\Lambda_{eq} = \kappa \times \phi$

  where, ϕ is the volume of the solution in cm^3 containing 1g-equivalent of the electrolyte.
- If concentration of the solution is C_{eq} gram-equivalent per litre (= normality) then the volume containing 1g-equivalent of the electrolyte will be $\frac{1}{C_{eq}}$ litres or $\frac{1000}{C_{eq}}\ cm^3$.

  $$\Lambda_{eq} = \kappa\phi$$

  $$\therefore \quad \Lambda_{eq} = \frac{1000\,\kappa(S\ cm^{-1})}{C_{eq}\ (\text{equivalent } L^{-1} \text{ or normality})}$$

  κ(specific conductance) is in $S\,cm^{-1}$ and ϕ in $equivalent^{-1}cm^3$, hence Λ_{eq} is practically written in the unit of $S\,cm^2\,equivalent^{-1}$.

Molar Conductivity

If the concentration (C_m) is expressed in mol L^{-1} then the volume (in cm^3) containing 1 mole of the electrolyte is $\frac{1000}{C_m} cm^3$, then the term molar conductance is used which is defined as the conducting power of all the ions produced by one mole of the electrolyte dissolved in a given solution.

$$\Lambda_m = \frac{1000\kappa \text{ (S cm}^{-1})}{C_m \text{ (mol L}^{-1})}$$

Λ_m is expressed (practically) in the unit of S $cm^2 mol^{-1}$.

JEE Spotlite

Relationship between Equivalent and Molar Conductance

If (v_+z_+) or (v_-z_-) is the total charge of cations (or anions) of a single electrolyte, it follows that

1 mol $= (v_+z_+)$ (1 equivalent)

$$N = n \text{ factor} \times M$$

$$N = (v_+z_+) \times M = \text{Total charge (cation or anion)} \times M$$

$$\Lambda_{eq} = \frac{\kappa}{(v_+z_+) \times M} = \frac{\Lambda_m}{(v_+z_+)}$$

$$\therefore \quad \Lambda_{eq} = \frac{\Lambda_m}{\text{Total charge of cations (or anions)}}$$

Or $\quad \Lambda_m = \Lambda_{eq} \times$ Total charge of cations (or anions)

Solved Booster 2.2

When a certain conductivity cell was filled with 0.020 M KCl which has a specific conductivity of 0.2768 $ohm^{-1}m^{-1}$, it had a resistance of 82.40 Ω at 25°C. With 0.0025 M K_2SO_4, it has a resistance of 326.0 Ω. The molar conductance of K_2SO_4 solution is

(a) 140×10^{-4} S m^2 eqv^{-1} (b) 280×10^{-4} S m^2 eqv^{-1}

(c) 70×10^{-4} S m^2 eqv^{-1} (d) 280×10^{-4} S m^2 eqv^{-1}

Solution *(a)*

$$\text{Specific conductance} = \frac{\text{Cell constant}}{\text{Resistance } (R)}$$

$\therefore$ Cell constant = Specific conductance × resistance

$$= 0.2768 \times 82.4 \approx 22.81 \text{ m}^{-1}$$

Thus, specific conductance of K_2SO_4 solution

$$= 22.81 / 326 \approx 0.07 \text{ ohm}^{-1}\text{m}^{-1} (\text{or S m}^{-1})$$

Equivalent conductance

$$\Lambda_{eq} = \frac{1000 \times \text{specific conductance}}{\text{normality}}$$

Specific conductance = 0.07 $ohm^{-1}m^{-1}$ = 0.0007 $ohm^{-1}cm^{-1}$

Normality = 0.0025 × 2 = 0.005 N

$$\Lambda_{eq} = \frac{1000 \times 0.0007}{0.005}$$

$$= 140 \text{ ohm}^{-1}\text{cm}^{-2}\text{equiv}^{-1}$$

$$= 140 \times 10^{-4} \text{ohm}^{-1}\text{m}^2\text{equiv}^{-1}$$

Variation of Conductivity and Molar Conductivity with Concentration

Equivalent and molar conductivity increase on dilution. On dilution the total volume V of a solution containing 1g equivalent or 1 mole of electrolyte increases which leads to more free movement of ions and increase in degree of dissociation of weak electrolyte.

For both strong and weak electrolytes, equivalent conductivity and molar conductivity increase with dilution.

Case I For Strong Electrolytes

In the lower concentration range, the molar conductivity of strong electrolytes is found to obey the following equation called **Debye-Huckel-Onsager equation**,

$$\Lambda_m = \Lambda_m^\infty - [A + B\Lambda_m^\infty]\sqrt{C}$$

where, Λ_m^∞ is limiting molar conductivity (A and B are called **Debye-Huckel constants**).

Λ_m^∞ is the limiting value of the molar conductivity at infinite dilution, i.e. when $C \to 0$

Thus, $$\lim_{C \to 0} \Lambda_m = \Lambda_m^\infty$$

The limiting molar conductivity varies for strong and weak electrolytes.

Graphical Interpretation of Limiting Molar Conductivity

If we plot molar conductivity against $\sqrt{C}$, the graph is linear in lower concentration range for strong electrolytes like KCl and there is slight deviation from linearity in higher concentration range. However, we can obtain Λ_m^∞ by extrapolating the graph to $\sqrt{C} = 0$.

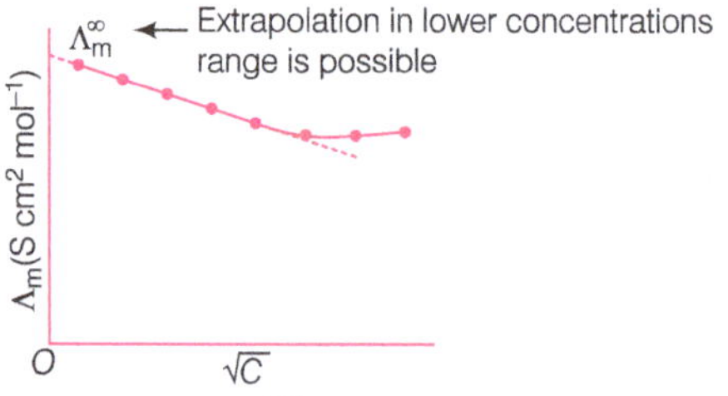

Variation of Λ_m *versus* $\sqrt{C}$ for KCl (strong electrolyte)

- This decrease is not due to a change in the number of ions with concentration, but due to change in the interionic attractions. At high concentrations, there are greater number of ions per unit volume which increases attraction between cation (K^+) and anion (Cl^-).

  Attraction between ions reduces the conducting ability of the ions, hence, Λ_m falls with increasing concentration.
- On dilution (concentration is decreased), due to decrease in ionic attractions, molar conductivity increases and it approaches a maximum **limiting value** at **infinite dilution**.

Case II For Weak Electrolytes

- In case of weak electrolytes (as CH_3COOH, NH_4OH, AgCl etc.), ionisation is very small compared to strong electrolytes, hence, Λ_m (or Λ_{eq}) of a weak electrolyte is low. In the very low concentration range, the degree of ionisation rises sharply, hence, Λ_m increases sharply, when solution is diluted in lower concentration range. The graph is not linear in lower concentration range and thus Λ_m^{∞} cannot be obtained by extrapolation.

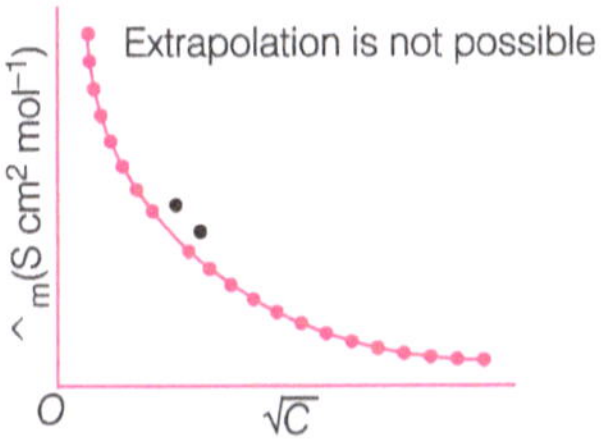

Variation of Λ_m with $\sqrt{C}$

- For weak electrolyte (CH_3COOH), Λ_m^{∞} cannot be obtained by extrapolation to $\sqrt{C} \to 0$. (Percentage dissociation for weak electrolytes is never 100%)

JEE MAPPER

Example Similar to PYQ Asked in JEE Main 2024

The molar ionic conductivities of a monovalent cation and anion are 50 S cm^2 mol^{-1} and 750 S cm^2 mol^{-1} respectively. The molar conductivity of a solution of an electrolyte containing these ions will be

(a) 120 S cm^2 mol^{-1} (b) 240 S cm^2 mol^{-1}

(c) 800 S cm^2 mol^{-1} (d) 30 S cm^2 mol^{-1}

Sol. (c) The molar conductivity of a solution is the sum of the molar ionic conductivities of the cation and the anion.

Therefore, the molar conductivity of the solution is

$750 + 50 = 800$ S cm^2 mol^{-1}

Competency Enhancer 2.1

The equivalent ionic conductivities of a trivalent cation and divalent anion are 65 S cm^2 mol^{-1} and 40 S cm^2 mol^{-1} respectively. The equivalent conductivity of a solution of an electrolyte containing these ions will be

(a) 260 S cm^2 eq^{-1} (b) 105 S cm^2 eq^{-1}

(c) 250 S cm^2 eq^{-1} (d) 520 S cm^2 eq^{-1}

Kohlrausch's Law

This law states that, "At infinite dilution, when ionisation is complete, each ion makes its contribution towards equivalent conductance (or molar conductance) of the electrolyte and at infinite dilution equivalent conductance (or molar conductance) is given by the sum of the equivalent conductances (molar conductances) of the contributing ions".

If λ_+^{∞} is the molar conductivity of the cations and λ_-^{∞} is the molar conductivity of the anions then by Kohlrausch's law of independent migration of ions is

$$\Lambda_m^{\infty} = x\lambda_+^{\infty} + y\lambda_-^{\infty}$$

Equivalent conductance at infinite dilution

$$\Lambda_{eq}^{\infty} = \lambda_+^{\infty} + \lambda_-^{\infty}$$

where, x and y are the number of ions per formula unit of the electrolyte.

Electrolyte	x	y
HCl	1	1
K_2SO_4	2	1
$BaCl_2$	1	2
$AlCl_3$	1	3
Na_3PO_4	3	1
$Fe_2(SO_4)_3$	2	3

The sharp increase in molar or equivalent conductivity (λ_m or λ_{eq}) at maximum dilution happens when electrolytes are dissociated to maximum, allowing ions to move freely in the solvent without any interactions between ion pairs.

Solved Booster 2.3

The Λ_m° and Λ_{eq}° for $CaCl_2$ is x Scm^2mol^{-1}, y Scm^2eq^{-1} and $MgSO_4$ is z Scm^2mol^{-1} and w Scm^2 eq^{-1} respectively. Given molar conductances at infinite dilution as

$\Lambda^{\circ}_{Ca^{2+}} = 119.0$ S cm^2 mol^{-1}; $\Lambda^{\circ}_{Cl^-} = 76.3$ S cm^2 mol^{-1}

$\Lambda^{\circ}_{Mg^{2+}} = 106.0$ S cm^2 mol^{-1}; $\Lambda^{\circ}_{SO_4^{2-}} = 160.0$ S cm^2 mol^{-1}

The sum of x, y, z and w is ......

Solution (806.4)

$$\Lambda^{\circ}_{m\,(CaCl_2)} = \Lambda^{\circ}_{Ca^{2+}} + 2\Lambda^{\circ}_{Cl^-} = 119.0 + 2 \times 76.3$$
$$= 271.6 \text{ S cm}^2 \text{ mol}^{-1}$$

$$\Lambda^{\circ}_m(MgSO_4) = \Lambda^{\circ}_{Mg^{2+}} + \Lambda^{\circ}_{SO_4^{2-}} = 106.0 + 160.0$$
$$= 266 \text{ S cm}^2 \text{ mol}^{-1}$$

$$\Lambda^{\circ}_{eq}(CaCl_2) = \frac{271.6}{2}$$
$$= 135.8 \text{ Scm}^2 \text{ equiv}^{-1}$$

$CaCl_2$ having one divalent Ca^{2+} and two monovalent Cl^-

$$\Lambda^{\circ}_{eq}(MgSO_4) = \frac{266}{2} = 133 \text{ S cm}^2 \text{ equiv}^{-1}$$

$$(x + y + z + w) = (273.6 + 266 + 135.8 + 133)$$
$$= 806.4$$

Solved Booster 2.4

For strong electrolytes the values of molar conductivity at infinite dilution are given below:

Electrolyte	Λ_m^∞ (S m^2 mol^{-1})
$BaCl_2$	280×10^{-4}
NaCl	126.5×10^{-4}
NaOH	248×10^{-4}

The value of $\Lambda^\infty_{[Ba(OH)_2]}$ will be

(a) 520×10^{-4} (b) 523×10^{-4} (c) 560×10^{-4} (d) 558×10^{-4}

Solution (b)

$$BaCl_2 + 2NaOH \longrightarrow Ba(OH)_2 + 2NaCl$$

Thus, $\Lambda^\infty_{[Ba(OH)_2]} = \Lambda^\infty_{(BaCl_2)} + 2\Lambda^\infty_{(NaOH)} - 2\Lambda^\infty_{(NaCl)}$

$= 280\times10^{-4} + 2\times248\times10^{-4} - 2\times126.5\times10^{-4}$

$= 523.0\times10^{-4}$ S m^2 mol^{-1}

Application of Kohlrausch's Law

Some other important application of kohlrausch law are as follows

1. Calculation of Degree of Dissociation (α)

For weak electrolytes, the degree of dissociation can be calculated by the formula, $\alpha = \Lambda_m / \Lambda_m^\circ$

where α = degree of dissociation

Λ_m = molar conductivity at any concentration

Λ_m° = molar conductivity at infinite dilution.

2. Calculation of Dissociation Constant of Weak Electrolysis (K_c)

For the determination of the ionisation constant of a weak electrolyte we can use this formula,

$K_c = \dfrac{C\alpha^2}{1-\alpha} = \dfrac{C\,\Lambda_m^2}{\Lambda_m^\circ(\Lambda_m^\circ - \Lambda_m)}$ where C is concentration of electrolyte.

3. Determination of the Solubility of a Sparingly

If a salt is less soluble in the given solvent then its conductivity can be calculated at some concentration as its conductivity at infinite dilution.

$$\lim_{c\to0} \lambda_q^c = \lambda_m^\circ = \frac{\kappa\times1000}{M} \text{ or } \frac{\kappa\times1000}{S}$$

(S = solubility in mol L^{-1})

Thus, K_{sp} can be calculated for any electrolyte A_xB_y

$K_{sp} = x^x y^y S^{x+y}$.

JEE MAPPER

Example Similar to PYQ Asked in JEE Advanced 2017

The conductance of 3×10^{-3} M aqueous solution of monobasic acid was determined by using a conductivity cell containing Pt electrode. The distance between the electrodes is 150 cm with an area of cross section of 1 cm^2. The resistance of this solution was found to be $2\times10^6\ \Omega$. If the pH of this solution is 3, the value of limiting molar conductivity (Λ_m°) of this weak monobasic acid in aqueous solution is .... $\times10^2$ S cm^2 mol^{-1}.

Sol. (75) $pH = C\alpha = 10^{-3} \Rightarrow \alpha = \dfrac{10^{-3}\text{ M}}{3\times10^{-3}\text{ M}} = \dfrac{1}{3}$

Also, resistance, $R = \rho\dfrac{l}{A} \Rightarrow R = \dfrac{1}{k}\dfrac{l}{A}$

$\Rightarrow \quad k = \dfrac{1}{R}\dfrac{l}{A} = \dfrac{1}{2\times10^6\ \Omega}\times\dfrac{150}{1} = 7.5\times10^{-5}$ S cm^{-1}

$\Rightarrow \quad \Lambda^c = \dfrac{k\times1000}{C} = \dfrac{7.5\times10^{-5}\times1000}{3\times10^{-3}}$

$\Lambda^\circ = \dfrac{\Lambda^c}{\alpha} = \dfrac{7.5\times10^{-5}\times1000}{3\times10^{-3}}\times\dfrac{3}{1} = 75$ S cm^2 mol^{-1}

Competency Enhancer 2.2

At 298 K, the limiting molar conductivity of a weak monobasic acid is 800 S cm^2 mol^{-1}. At 298 K, for an aqueous solution of the acid, the degree of dissociation is α and the molar conductivity is $a\times10^2$ S cm^2 mol^{-1}. At 298 K, upon 30 times dilution with water, the molar conductivity of the solution becomes $4a\times10^2$ S cm^2 mol^{-1}. The degree of dissociation α of the acid is ....

Quantitative Aspects of Electrolysis

Michael Faraday developed a quantitative relationship between the quantity of electricity passed and the amount of substance getting discharged.

1. Faraday's First Law

The mass of an ion discharged during electrolysis is proportional to the quantity of electricity passed. Mathematically,

$$W \propto Q$$

where,

W = Mass of ions librated in gram,

Q = Quantity of electricity passed in coulombs.

Q = current in amperes (I) × Time in sec (t)

$\therefore \quad W \propto I\times t$ or $W = Z\times I\times t$

where Z is a constant, known as electrochemical equivalent (ECE) of the ion deposited. When a current of 1 ampere is passed for 1 second (i.e. $Q = 1$), then

In case current efficiency (η) is given 100%, then $W = Z$.

Thus, electrochemical equivalent may be defined as the mass of the ion deposited by passing a current of one ampere for one second. Its unit is gram per coulomb.

1 F of charge = Charge on one mole of electron ≈ 96500 C

Equivalent mass is the mass that get discharged by 1 Faraday of charge i.e. 96500 C.

96500 C discharge E gm, (E is equivalent mass)

$$1\text{C discharges} = \frac{E}{96500}\text{g of ion} = Z$$

Now substituting the value of Z in the reaction

$$W = Z\,\text{It} = \frac{\text{EIt}}{96500}$$

or

$$\frac{W}{E} = \frac{\text{It}}{96500} = \frac{Q}{96500}$$

1 Faraday
- → Charge on one mole of e^{-1} s = 96500 C/mol
- → Charge that can deposit/discharge 1 gram-equivalent of the substance

JEE Alert

The amount of electric charge required to discharge one mole of substance at an electrode is equal to the number of elementary charges on that ion,

$Al^{3+} + 3e^- \longrightarrow Al$	Quantity of charge required = 3F
$MnO_4^- + 5e^- \longrightarrow Mn^{2+}$	Quantity of charge required = 5F
$Cr_2O_7^{2-} + 6e^- \longrightarrow 2Cr^{3+}$	Quantity of charge required = 6F

2. Faraday's Second Law

When the same quantity of electricity is passed through different electrolytes, the masses of different ions librated at the electrodes are directly proportional to their chemical equivalents weights. Suppose W_1 and W_2 are the weights of the elements deposited by passing a certain quantity of electricity through their salt solutions and E_1 and E_2 are their respective equivalent weights, then

$$\frac{W_1}{W_2} = \frac{E_1}{E_2} \text{ or } \frac{W_1}{E_1} = \frac{W_2}{E_2} = \text{Number of equivalents}$$

Solved Booster 2.5

A constant current of 30 A is passed through an aqueous solution of NaCl for a time of 1.00 h. What is volume of Cl_2 gas at STP produced?

(a) 1.12 L (b) 12.535 L

(c) 0.56 L (d) 25.36 L

Solution (b)

Due to electrolysis,

$$2H_2O(l) + 2e^- \longrightarrow H_2(g) + 2OH^-(aq)$$
$$2Cl^-(aq) \longrightarrow Cl_2(g) + 2e^-$$

Net : $2H_2O(l) + 2Cl^-(aq) \longrightarrow H_2(g) + Cl_2(g) + 2OH^-(aq)$

$Q = It = 30A \times 3600s = 108000\,C$

Number of moles of electrons

$$n_e = \frac{Q}{F} = \frac{108{,}000}{96500} \approx 1.12 \text{ mol}$$

Cl_2 formed $= \frac{1}{2}$ mol of NaOH (as in reaction given)

$= \frac{1.12}{2} = 0.56$ mol

$= 0.56 \times 22.4$ L at STP

$= 12.535$ L

JEE MAPPER

Example Similar to PYQ Asked in JEE Main 2022

The quantity of electricity in Faraday needed to reduce 1 mol of MnO_4^- to Mn^{2+} is

Sol. (5) The oxidation state of Mn changes from +7 to +2.

$$\underset{1\text{ mol}}{\overset{+7}{Mn}O_4^-} + \underset{5\text{ mol}}{5e^-} \longrightarrow Mn^{2+}$$

1 mol MnO_4^- requires ⟶ 5 mol of electrons

∴ Number of Faraday's of electricity required is 5.

Competency Enhancer 2.3

The quantity of electricity required to reduced 1 mol of Fe_3O_4 to Fe^{2+}.

Qualitative Aspects of Electrolysis

The qualitive aspects of electrolysis provide a deeper understanding of electrolysis and different factors that contribute to the discharge of products at either electrodes.

Electrolysis of Water using Pt Electrodes

Water is not a good conductor of electricity because of very low concentration of ions in it. So, we add a small quantity of strong electrolyte generally H_2SO_4 or NaOH to make it more conducting. HCl is not added because it may raise complications by the possibility of oxidation of Cl^- ion.

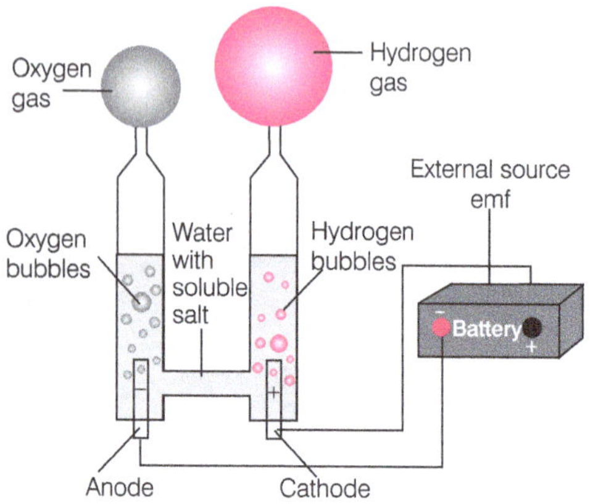

Reaction at anode $2OH^-(aq) \longrightarrow 1/2O_2(g) + H_2O(l) + 2e^-$

Reaction at cathode $2H_2O(l) + 2e^- \longrightarrow H_2(g) + 2OH^-(aq)$

Net reaction $H_2O(l) \longrightarrow 1/2O_2(g) + H_2(g)$

- In the net reaction, hydrogen and oxygen gases are always liberated in the molar ratio of 2:1 as long as the electrolysis of only water is taking place or only the above reactions of reduction and oxidation of water are taking place at cathode and anode respectively.
- In case of some solution, when water is oxidised along with some other species, then hydrogen and oxygen gases are not liberated in the molar ratio of 2:1.

Electrolysis of Molten NaCl using Pt Electrodes

- **Reaction at Cathode:** $Na^+ + e^- \longrightarrow Na$
- **Reaction at anode:** $Cl^- \longrightarrow 1/2Cl_2 + e^-$

Na is liberated at cathode while chlorine is released at anode.

Electrolysis of Aqueous NaCl using Pt Electrodes

- Possible Reactions **at cathode:**

$Na^+ + e^- \longrightarrow Na;\ E^\circ_{Na^+/Na} = -2.71$ V

$H^+ + e^- \longrightarrow 1/2H_2;\ E^\circ_{H^+/H_2} = 0.00$ V

- Possible Reactions **at anode:**

$Cl^- \longrightarrow 1/2Cl_2 + e^-;\ E^\circ_{Cl^-/Cl_2} = 1.36$ V

$2OH^- \longrightarrow 1/2O_2 + H_2O + 2e^-$

$E^\circ_{OH^-/O_2} = 0.41$ V

- H_2 is liberated at cathode while chlorine is released at anode.
- At anode, the oxidation of OH^- should take place but there is also the possibility of oxidation of Cl^-. If we look at the oxidation potential values, it suggests that the value is higher for OH^-, so it's oxidation should occur in preference to that of Cl^- ion. But in real scenario, it was found that Cl_2 gas is liberated at anode rather than O_2 gas. This is because of the difference in the observed potential and theoretical potential for the oxidation of OH^- to form O_2 gas. This difference in observed and theoretical potential is called overpotential or overvoltage.

Electrolysis of Very Dilute NaCl Solution using Pt Electrodes

- Possible reactions at cathode:

$Na^+ + e^- \longrightarrow Na,\ E^\circ_{Na^+/Na} = -2.71$ V

$H^+ + e^- \longrightarrow 1/2H_2,\ E^\circ_{H^+/H_2} = 0.00$ V

- Possible reactions at anode:

$Cl^- \longrightarrow 1/2Cl_2 + e^-,\ E^\circ_{Cl^-/Cl_2} = 1.36$ V

$2OH^- \longrightarrow 1/2O_2 + H_2O + 2e^-,\ E^\circ_{OH^-/O_2} = 0.41$ V,

$$E_{Cl^-/Cl_2} = E^\circ_{Cl^-/Cl_2} - \frac{RT}{2F}\ln\frac{p_{Cl_2}}{[Cl^-]^2};\ \text{As } [Cl^-]\downarrow,\ E_{Cl^-/Cl_2}\downarrow$$

- H_2 is liberated at cathode while oxygen is released at anode. The electrolysis of a very dilute NaCl solution is just like the electrolysis of water.

Electrolysis of Aqueous NaCl Solution using Hg Electrodes

- Possible reactions at cathode:

$Na^+ + e^- \longrightarrow Na,\ E^\circ_{Na^+/Na} = -2.71$ V

$Na + Hg \longrightarrow Na-Hg;\ H^+ + e^- \longrightarrow 1/2H_2,\ E^\circ_{H^+/H_2} = 0.00$ V

- Possible reactions at anode:

$Cl^- \longrightarrow 1/2Cl_2 + e^-,\ E^\circ_{Cl^-/Cl_2} = 1.36$ V

$2OH^- \longrightarrow 1/2O_2 + H_2O + 2e^-,\ E^\circ_{OH^-/O_2} = 0.41$ V

- Na is reduced preferentially at cathode forming sodium-amalgam as the overvoltage associated with liberation of H_2 gas at Hg electrode is high while chlorine is released at anode.

Electrolysis of Aqueous Na_2SO_4 Solution using Pt Electrodes

- Possible Reactions at cathode:

$Na^+ + e^- \longrightarrow Na,\ E^\circ_{Na^+/Na} = -2.71$ V

$H^+ + e^- \longrightarrow 1/2H_2,\ E^\circ_{H^+/H_2} = 0.00$ V

- Possible reactions at anode:

$$SO_4^{2-} \longrightarrow S_2O_8^{2-} + 2e^-, E^\circ_{SO_4^{2-}/S_2O_8^{2-}} = -2.01\text{ V}$$

$$2OH^- \longrightarrow 1/2O_2 + H_2O + 2e^-, E^\circ_{OH^-/O_2} = 0.41\text{ V}$$

- H_2 is liberated at cathode while oxygen is released at anode. The electrolysis of aqueous Na_2SO_4 solution is just like the electrolysis of water. Electrolysis of aqueous solutions of K_2SO_4 or $CaSO_4$ or $MgSO_4$ or Li_2SO_4 etc using Pt electrodes will undergo electrolysis just like aqueous Na_2SO_4.

Electrolysis of Aqueous $CuSO_4$ Solution using Pt Electrodes

- Possible reactions at cathode:

$$Cu^{2+} + 2e^- \longrightarrow Cu, E^\circ_{Cu^{2+}/Cu} = 0.34\text{ V}$$

$$H^+ + e^- \longrightarrow 1/2H_2, E^\circ_{(H^+/H_2)} = 0.00\text{ V}$$

- Possible reactions at anode:

$$SO_4^{2-} \longrightarrow S_2O_8^{2-} + 2e^-, E^\circ_{SO_4^{2-}/S_2O_8^{2-}} = -2.01\text{ V}$$

$$2OH^- \longrightarrow 1/2O_2 + H_2O + 2e^-, E^\circ_{OH^-/O_2} = 0.41\text{ V}$$

- Cu is deposited at cathode while oxygen is released at anode. The solution will become more acidic and will turn blue litmus paper red. The intensity of blue colour of solution decreases with time.

Electrolysis of Aqueous $CuSO_4$ Solution using Cu Electrodes

- Possible reactions at cathode:

$$Cu^{2+} + 2e^- \longrightarrow Cu, E^\circ_{Cu^{2+}/Cu} = 0.34\text{ V}$$

$$H^+ + e^- \longrightarrow 1/2H_2, E^\circ_{(H^+/H_2)} = 0.00\text{ V}$$

- Possible reactions at anode:

$$Cu \longrightarrow Cu^{2+} + 2e^-, E^\circ_{Cu/Cu^{2+}} = -0.34\text{ V}$$

$$SO_4^{2-} \longrightarrow S_2O_8^{2-} + 2e^-, E^\circ_{SO_4^{2-}/S_2O_8^{2-}} = -2.01\text{ V}$$

$$2OH^- \longrightarrow 1/2O_2 + H_2O + 2e^-, E^\circ_{OH^-/O_2} = 0.41\text{ V}$$

- Cu is deposited at cathode and copper is dissolved at anode. Thus concentration of Cu^{2+} in the solution remain same.

Electrolysis of Aqueous $CuCl_2$ Solution using Pt Electrodes

- Possible reactions at cathode:

$$Cu^{2+} + 2e^- \longrightarrow Cu, E^\circ_{Cu^{2+}/Cu} = 0.34\text{ V}$$

$$H^+ + e^- \longrightarrow 1/2H_2, E^\circ_{(H^+/H_2)} = 0.00\text{ V}$$

- Possible reactions at anode:

$$Cl^- \longrightarrow 1/2Cl_2 + e^-, E^\circ_{Cl^-/Cl_2} = 1.36\text{ V}$$

$$2OH^- \longrightarrow 1/2O_2 + H_2O + 2e^-, E^\circ_{OH^-/O_2} = 0.41\text{ V}$$

- Cu is deposited at cathode while chlorine gas is released at anode. The solution's acidity will decrease a little because of decrease in conc. of Cu^{2+}.

$$Cu^{2+}(aq) + 2H_2O(l) \longrightarrow Cu(OH)^+(aq) + H_3O^+(aq)$$

Electrolysis of Aqueous $CuCl_2$ Solution using Cu Electrodes

- Possible reactions at cathode:

$$Cu^{2+} + 2e^- \longrightarrow Cu, E^\circ_{Cu^{2+}/Cu} = 0.34\text{ V}$$

$$H^+ + e^- \longrightarrow 1/2H_2, E^\circ_{(H^+/H_2)} = 0.00\text{ V}$$

- Possible reactions at anode:

$$Cu \longrightarrow Cu^{2+} + 2e^-, E^\circ_{Cu/Cu^{2+}} = -0.34\text{ V}$$

$$Cl^- \longrightarrow 1/2Cl_2 + e^-, E^\circ_{Cl/Cl_2} = 1.36\text{ V}$$

$$2OH^- \longrightarrow 1/2O_2 + H_2O + 2e^-, E^\circ_{OH^-/O_2} = 0.41\text{ V}$$

- Cu is deposited at cathode and copper is dissolved at anode. Thus concentration of Cu^{2+} in the solution remain same.

Electrolysis of Molten $SnCl_2$ using Pt Electrodes

- Possible reactions at cathode:

$$Sn^{2+} + 2e^- \longrightarrow Sn, E^\circ_{Sn^{2+}/Sn} = -0.14\text{ V}$$

- Possible reactions at anode:

$$Cl^- \longrightarrow 1/2Cl_2 + e^-, \quad E^\circ_{Cl^-/Cl_2} = -1.36\text{ V}$$

$$Sn^{2+} \longrightarrow Sn^{4+} + 2e^-, \quad E^\circ_{Sn^{2+}/Sn^{4+}} = -0.13\text{ V}$$

Net reaction: $2Sn^{2+} \longrightarrow Sn^{4+} + Sn$

- During electrolysis of molten $SnCl_2$, Sn^{2+} is oxidised at anode and Sn^{2+} is reduced at cathode.

Electrolysis of Aqueous $AgNO_3$ Solution using Pt Electrodes

- Possible reactions at cathode:

$$Ag^+ + e^- \longrightarrow Ag, \quad E^\circ_{Ag^+/Ag} = 0.80\text{ V}$$

$$H^+ + e^- \longrightarrow 1/2H_2, \quad E^\circ_{H^+/H_2} = 0.00\text{ V}$$

- Possible reactions at anode :

$$2OH^- \longrightarrow 1/2O_2 + H_2O + 2e^-, E^\circ_{OH^-/O_2} = 0.41\text{ V}$$

- Ag is deposited at cathode while O_2 gas is released at anode.

Electrolysis of Aqueous $AgNO_3$ Solution using Ag Electrodes

- Possible reactions at cathode:

$$Ag^+ + e^- \longrightarrow Ag, \quad E^\circ_{Ag^+/Ag} = 0.80\text{ V}$$

$$H^+ + e^- \longrightarrow 1/2H_2, \quad E^\circ_{H^+/H_2} = 0.00\text{ V}$$

- Possible reactions at anode :

$Ag \longrightarrow Ag^+ + e^-, \quad E^\circ_{Ag/Ag^+} = -0.80\,V$

$2OH^- \longrightarrow 1/2O_2 + H_2O + 2e^-, \quad E^\circ_{OH^-/O_2} = 0.41\,V$

- Ag is deposited at cathode and silver is dissolved at anode to form Ag^+ ions. Thus concentration of Ag^+ in the solution remain same.

Electrolysis of Dilute H_2SO_4 Solution using Pt Electrodes

- Possible reactions at cathode:

$H^+ + e^- \longrightarrow 1/2H_2, E^\circ_{H^+/H_2} = 0.00\,V$

- Possible reactions at anode:

$2OH^- \longrightarrow 1/2O_2 + H_2O + 2e^-, E^\circ_{OH^-/O_2} = 0.41\,V,$

$SO_4^{2-} \longrightarrow S_2O_8^{2-} + 2e^-, E^\circ_{SO_4^{2-}/S_2O_8^{2-}} = -2.01\,V$

- H_2 gas is released at cathode and O_2 gas is liberated at anode.

JEE Quicker

The product obtained from the electrolytic acidified sulphate solution is HO_3SOOSO_3H. *JEE Main 2021*

Reaction at cathode

$H^+ + e^- \longrightarrow 1/2H_2, E^\circ_{H^+/H_2} = 0.00\,V, E_{H^+/H_2} = -0.41\,V$

Reactions at anode

$2OH^- \longrightarrow 1/2O_2 + H_2O + 2e^-, E^\circ_{OH^-/O_2} = 0.41\,V$

$SO_4^{2-} \longrightarrow S_2O_8^{2-} + 2e^-, E^\circ_{SO_4^{2-}/S_2O_8^{2-}} = -2.01\,V$

H_2 gas is liberated at cathode while at anode, perdisulphuric acid is formed as sulphate ion gets preferentially oxidized.

Electrolysis of Aqueous $NiSO_4$ Solution using Pt Electrodes

- Possible reactions at cathode:

$Ni^{2+} + 2e \longrightarrow Ni, E^\circ_{Ni^{2+}/Ni} = -0.26\,V$

$H^+ + e^- \longrightarrow 1/2H_2, E^\circ_{H^+/H_2} = 0.00\,V$

- Possible reactions at anode:

$2OH^- \longrightarrow 1/2O_2 + H_2O + 2e^-, E^\circ_{OH^-/O_2} = -0.41\,V,$

$E_{OH^-/O_2} = -0.82\,V$

$SO_4^{2-} \longrightarrow S_2O_8^{2-} + 2e^-, E^\circ_{SO_4^{2-}/S_2O_8^{2-}} = -2.01\,V$

- Ni is deposited at cathode and O_2 gas is liberated at anode.

Electrolysis of Aqueous $NiSO_4$ Solution using Ni Electrodes

- Possible reactions at cathode:

$Ni^{2+} + 2e \longrightarrow Ni, E^\circ_{Ni^{2+}/Ni} = -0.26\,V$

$H^+ + e^- \longrightarrow 1/2H_2, E^\circ_{H^+/H_2} = 0.00\,V$

- Possible reactions at anode:

$2OH^- \longrightarrow 1/2O_2 + H_2O + 2e^-, E^\circ_{OH^-/O_2} = -0.41\,V,$

$E_{OH^-/O_2} = -0.82\,V$

$SO_4^{2-} \longrightarrow S_2O_8^{2-} + 2e^-, E^\circ_{SO_4^{2-}/S_2O_8^{2-}} = -2.01\,V$

$Ni \longrightarrow Ni^{2+} + 2e^-, E^\circ_{Ni/Ni^{2+}} = 0.26\,V$

- Ni is deposited at cathode while at anode Ni is dissolving to form Ni^{2+} ions in the solution.

Conductometric Titration

Titration in which end point can be determined by measuring conductance at each addition of the titre solution (from burette) is called conductometric titration. We take the fact that conductance of non-electrolyte or insoluble solute is lower than that of electrolyte or its ion.

Type I Titration of HCl(*aq*) with NaOH(*aq*)

(Strong acid *vs* strong base).

$$HCl(aq) + NaOH(aq) \rightleftharpoons NaCl(aq) + H_2O(l)$$

$$H^+(aq) + OH^-(aq) \rightleftharpoons H_2O(l)$$

Initially, there is maximum conductance due to HCl (free H^+). As $NaOH(OH^-)$ is added from burette, equivalent H^+ ion is neutralised forming weak electrolyte H_2O. Thus, conductance falls. This decrease appears till all the HCl is neutralised. After complete neutralisation, further addition of NaOH will result in the increase in conductance.

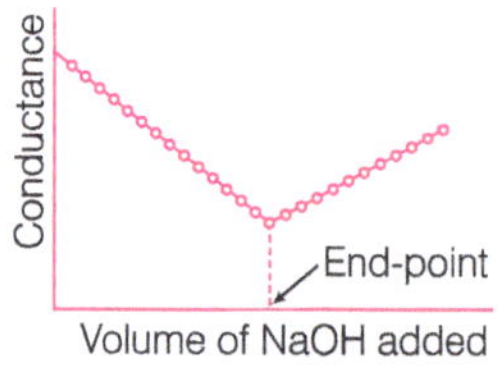

Titration of strong acid against a strong base

End point of the titration is where two linear curves intersect.

Type II Titration of $CH_3COOH(aq)$ with NaOH (aq)

(weak acid vs a strong base)

Before the addition of OH^- (or NaOH), the solution shows poor conductance due to feeble ionisation of CH_3COOH.

$$CH_3COOH(aq) + OH^-(aq) \rightleftharpoons CH_3COO^-(aq) + H_2O\ (l)$$

Every addition of OH^- ion from burette into CH_3COOH solution will form more conducting CH_3COO^- ion, thus conductance starts increasing slightly.

After complete neutralisation of CH_3COOH, further addition of OH^- ion will make rapid increase in conductance. End-point is that where two linear curves intersect.

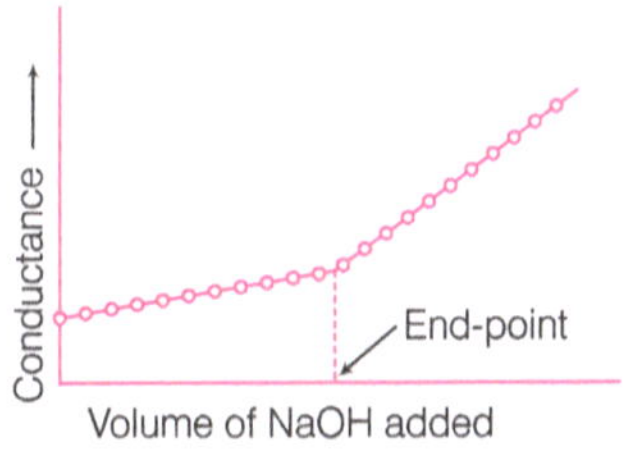

Titration of a weak acid against a strong base

Type III Titration of a Strong Acid against a Weak Base

$$\underset{\text{Strong acid}}{HCl(aq)} + \underset{\text{Weak base}}{NH_4OH(aq)} \longrightarrow NH_4Cl(aq) + H_2O(l)$$

or $H^+(aq) + NH_4OH(aq) \longrightarrow NH_4^+(aq) + H_2O(l)$

The conductance falls at first due to replacement of fast moving H^+ ions by slow moving NH_4^+ ions. After neutralisation of the acid, further addition of weakly ionised NH_4OH will not cause any appreciable change in the conductance as given in fig.

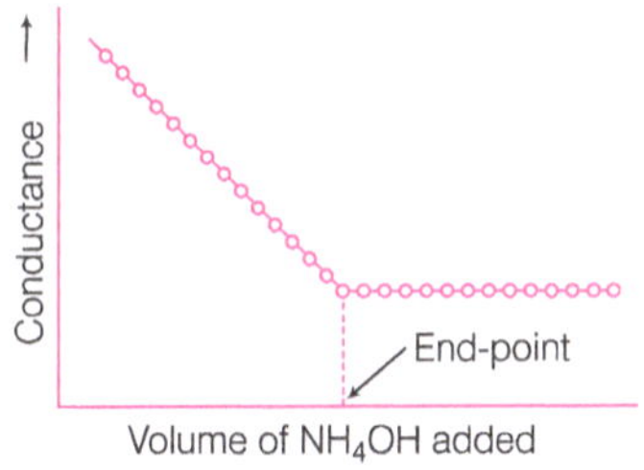

Titration of strong acid against a weak base

Type IV Titration of a Weak Acid Against a Weak Base

$$CH_3COOH(aq) + NH_4OH(aq) \longrightarrow CH_3COONH_4(aq) + H_2O$$

When weak base (say NH_4OH) is added to a weak acid (say CH_3COOH), salt (CH_3COONH_4) is formed. It is hydrolysed at the same time forming weak acid and weak base.

If K_a(acid) > K_b(base) or K_a(acid) < K_b(base)

then conductance may increase due to free H^+ ion (if $K_a > K_b$) or OH^- ion (if $K_b > K_a$).

After complete neutralisation, conductance remains constant (due to weak electrolyte) as shown in fig.

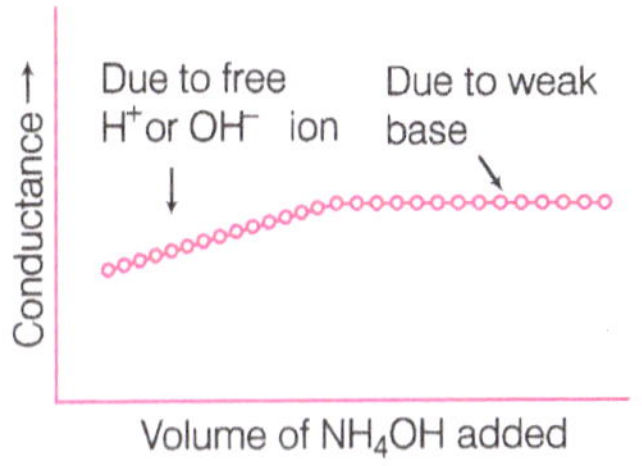

Titration of weak acid against a weak base

JEE Alert

If K_a(acid) = K_b(base), then conductometric titration is not possible since, there will be no change in conductance.

Type V Precipitation titration

If in any titration insoluble salt is formed, then it is a precipitation titration. In the titration of $AgNO_3$ against KCl, insoluble AgCl(*s*) is formed. Thus, conductance remains constant.

$$AgNO_3(aq) + KCl(aq) \longrightarrow AgCl(s) + KNO_3(aq)$$

By ionisation $Ag^+(aq) + Cl^-(aq) \longrightarrow AgCl(s)$

After complete precipitation of Ag^+ as AgCl, further addition of KCl(*aq*) causes increase in conductance.

Thus, end point is determined from conductometric titration curve.

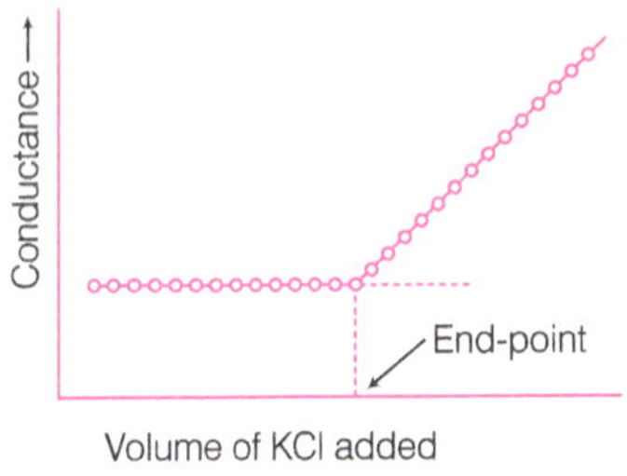

Titration of $AgNO_3$ against KCl

Elemental Practice 8.2

Type I MCQs with Only One Correct Option

1. A conductivity cell was filled with a 0.04 M NaCl solution which has a specific conductance of 4.768×10^{-3} $ohm^{-1} cm^{-1}$. If its resistance is 82.4 ohm at 25°C, the cell constant is
(a) 0.394 cm^{-1} (b) 0.393 cm^{-1}
(c) 0.398 cm^{-1} (d) 0.309 cm^{-1}

2. Specific conductance of 0.1 M HCl is 8.3×10^{-2} $ohm^{-1} cm^{-1}$. The molar conductance of solution is
(a) 100 $ohm^{-1} cm^2 mole^{-1}$
(b) 8300 $ohm^{-1} cm^2 mole^{-1}$
(c) 830 $ohm^{-1} cm^2 mole^{-1}$
(d) 315 $ohm^{-1} cm^2 mole^{-1}$

3. At infinite dilution, the molar conductance of Mg^{2+} and Cl^- are 254 and 128 $ohm^{-1} cm^2 mol^{-1}$. The equivalent conductivity (in $ohm^{-1} cm^2 eq^{-1}$) of $MgCl_2$ at infinite dilution is
(a) 250 (b) 252 (c) 294 (d) 255

4. Both metallic and electrolytic conduction differs in electrolytic conduction,
(a) with increase of temperature resistance increases
(b) with increase of temperature resistance decreases
(c) with current flow heat does not generate
(d) Resistance is independent of length of conductor

5. How many electrons flow when a current of 4 ampere is passed through a conductor for 300 seconds?
(a) 7.38×10^{21} (b) 7.50×10^{21}
(c) 7.50×10^{22} (d) 7.38×10^{20}

6. For 1000 s current of 8.45 ampere is passed through the aqueous solution of KCl using suitable electrode. The amount of KOH formed during electrolysis is
(a) 4.71 g (b) 4.85 g (c) 4.90 g (d) 4.10 g

7. The molarity of the solution at the end of electrolysis on passing current of 2.0 ampere for 5 hour through 1 L of 2 M solution of lead nitrate using lead electrodes will be
(a) 1.814 M (b) 1.914 M
(c) 1.514 M (d) 1.414 M

8. Iron rod is electro-plated with zinc using zinc chloride in HCl. The current was passed for 30 min and the increase in the weight of the rod was found to be 3g. [Zn = 65]. The current passed was
(a) 5.02 amp (b) 3.4 amp
(c) 4.948 amp (d) 3.45 amp

9. The specific conductance of a saturated solution of NaCl is 4.40×10^{-6} $ohm^{-1} cm^{-1}$ at 25°C.
If $\lambda_{Na^+} = 62.3$ $ohm^{-1} cm^2 mol^{-1}$ and $\lambda_{Cl^-} = 67.7$ $ohm^{-1} cm^2 mol^{-1}$, the solubility of NaCl at 25° C is
(a) 3.46×10^{-5} M (b) 3.38×10^{-5} M
(c) 3.8×10^{-5} M (d) 3.5×10^{-5} M

10. Given below are two statements.
Statement I For strong electrolyte, molar conductivity increases steeply with dilution.
Statement II For carbonic acid, molar conductivity increases slowly with dilution.
Choose the correct answer from the options given below.
(a) Both Statement I and Statement II are true.
(b) Both Statement I and Statement II are false.
(c) Statement I is true but Statement II are false.
(d) Statement I is false but Statement II are true.

11. In the given reactions.
$$Fe^{3+} + 2e^- \longrightarrow Fe^+, E^\circ = x_1 V$$
$$Fe^+ \longrightarrow Fe^{2+} + e^-, E^\circ = -x_2 V$$
$$Fe^{2+} \longrightarrow Fe^{3+} + e^-, E^\circ = ?$$
The value of E° in third reaction will be
(a) $(2x_1 + x_2)V$ (b) $+(2x_1 - x_2)V$
(c) $-(x_1 + x_2)V$ (d) $(x_1 + x_2)V$

12. Given,
$$Ge^{2+} + 2e^- \longrightarrow Ge; E^\circ = +0.23 \text{ V}$$
$$Pb^{4+} + 2e^- \longrightarrow Pb^{2+}; E^\circ = +1.67 \text{ V}$$
$$Ce^{4+} + e^- \longrightarrow Ce^{3+}; E^\circ = +1.61 \text{V}$$
$$Co^{3+} + e^- \longrightarrow Co^{2+}; E^\circ = +1.81 \text{V}$$
Oxidising power of the species will increase in the order.
(a) $Ge^{2+} < Ce^{4+} < Pb^{4+} < Co^{3+}$
(b) $Ce^{4+} < Pb^{4+} < Co^{3+} < Ge^{2+}$
(c) $Pb^{4+} < Ce^{4+} < Co^{3+} < Ge^{2+}$
(d) $Co^{3+} < Ce^{4+} < Ge^{2+} < Co^{3+}$

13. Match the Column I with Column II.

	Column-I		Column-II
A.	Kohlrausch law	p.	$\Lambda_m / \Lambda_m^\circ$
B.	Λ_m	q.	$\frac{1}{R} \times \frac{l}{A}$
C.	κ (kappa)	r.	$\Lambda_{m Na_2SO_4} = 2\lambda^\circ_{Na} + \lambda^\circ_{SO_4^{2-}}$
D.	α	s.	$k \times \frac{1000}{M}$

(a) (A-r); (B-s); (C-q); (D-p)
(b) (A-s); (B-r); (C-p); (D-q)
(c) (A-p); (B-q); (C-s); (D-r)
(d) (A-q); (B-p); (C-r); (D-s)

14. If the solution is diluted to 100 times at 298 K, then by how much will the potential of Zn^{2+} / Zn change.
(a) Increases by 59 mV (b) Decreases by 59 mV
(c) Increases by 29.5 mV (d) Decreases by 29.5 mV

15. Arrange the following compounds in order of increasing molar conductivity in aqueous solution.
$Pt(NH_3)_6Cl_4$, $Cr(NH_3)_6Cl_3$, $Co(NH_3)_4Cl_3$, K_2PtCl_6
(a) $Co(NH_3)_4Cl_3 < K_2PtCl_6 < Cr(NH_3)_6Cl_3 < Pt(NH_3)_6Cl_4$
(b) $K_2PtCl_6 < Co(NH_3)_4Cl_3 < Cr(NH_3)_6Cl_3 < Pt(NH_3)_6Cl_4$
(c) $Co(NH_3)_4Cl_3 < K_2PtCl_6 < Pt(NH_3)_6Cl_4 < Cr(NH_3)_6Cl_3$
(d) $Cr(NH_3)_6Cl_3 < K_2PtCl_6 < Co(NH_3)_4Cl_3 < Pt(NH_3)_6Cl_4$

Type II 》 MCQs with One or More than One Correct Option

16. Which of the following statement is/are correct?
(a) van't Hoff factor for 10^{-3} M CH_3COOH is 39/35 ($\Lambda^\circ_m = 350$ S cm^2 mol^{-1} and $k = 4 \times 10^{-5}$ S cm^{-1}).
(b) If Λ°_m of KCl, LiCl and KNO_3 are 150, 115 and 145 S cm^2 mol^{-1}, then that of $LiNO_3$ will be 110 S cm^2 mol^{-1}.
(c) In general, with increase in concentration, the specific conductance increases.
(d) The increase in molar conductivity of HCl with dilution is due to hydrolysis of HCl.

17. Which of the following statements are incorrect?
(a) For a dilute solution of a strong electrolyte, the variation of molar conductivity with concentration is given by $\Lambda_m = \Lambda^\circ_m - A\sqrt{C}$.
(b) A cell constant is generally found by measuring the conductivity of aqueous solution of KCl.
(c) Specific conductance of a solution increase with dilution, whereas molar conductance decreases with dilution.
(d) The increase in the value of molar conductivity of acetic acid with dilution is due to increase in self ionisation of water.

18. Which of the following statements are correct?
(a) Conductivity always decreases with decrease in concentration for both strong and weak electrolytes.
(b) The number of ions per unit volume that carry in a solution increases on dilution.
(c) The variation in molar conductivity is different for strong and weak electrolytes.
(d) For weak electrolytes, the change in molar conductivity with dilution decrease due to decrease in degree of dissociation.

19. Which of the following statement are correct?
(a) V and Hg ($E^\circ = +$ 1.19 V and 0.86 V) respectively have ability to reduce NO_3^- ($E^\circ = 0.96$ V).
(b) Limiting molar conductivity of KI is not greater than CH_3COOH.
(c) The decreasing order of deposition is $Fe^{2+} > Cu^{2+} > Au^{3+} > Mg^{2+}$.
(d) The cell potential for $Ni(s) \mid Ni^{2+}(aq\ 0.1M) \parallel Ag^+ (aq\ 0.1\ M) \mid Ag(s)$ is 0.4 V.

20. Which of the following statements are incorrect?
(a) The amount of electricity in coulomb required for the oxidation of 1 mol of H_2O to O_2 is 1.93×10^5 C.
(b) One Faraday of electricity liberates 5×10^{-1} gram atom of copper from copper sulphate.
(c) Nature of electrode affect the electrolytic conductance of a solution.
(d) The quantity of electricity in Faraday needed to reduce 1 mole of $Cr_2O_7^{2-}$ to Cr^{3+} is 4.

Type III 》 Numerical/Integer Answer Type Questions

21. If '*y*' litre of 0.4 M $ZnSO_4$ is reduced to Zn by a current of 0.965 A in 1 hour. Then value of '*y*' is

22. If ionic conductivity of Mg^{2+} and Cl^- at infinite dilution are 147 and 80 ohm^{-1} cm^2 mol^{-1} respectively. The equivalent conductivity of $MgCl_2$ at infinite dilution is

23. The anodic half-cell of lead-acid battery is recharged using electricity 0.06 Faraday. The amount of $PbSO_4$ electrolysed in *g* during the process is (Molar mass of $PbSO_4 = 303$ g mol^{-1}) [Nearest Integer]

24. The Gibbs energy for the decomposition of ZnO at 500°C is as follows

$$ZnO \longrightarrow Zn + O_2;\ \Delta G = +866 \text{ kJ mol}^{-1}$$

The potential difference needed for the electrolytic reduction of ZnO at 500°C is atleast.

25. The quinhydrone electrode (Q, H^+/H_2Q) is used in conjunction with a saturated calomel electrode as represented below:

$$Hg(l), Hg_2Cl_2(s) \mid KCl_{(saturated\ solution)} \parallel H^{\oplus}_{(unknown)} \mid Q, H_2Q, Pt$$

$EMF_{cell} = 0.364$ at 30°C. Calculate pH of unknown solution at this temperature.

Given, $E_{calomel} = 0.24$ V,
$E^\circ_{2H^+, Q|H_2Q} = 0.7$ V
$2.303 \frac{RT}{F}$ at 30° C = 0.06
$E_{SCE} = 0.24$ V

Elemental Practice 8.2 | Chapter 8

Connect with **Answers**

1. (b)	2. (c)	3. (d)	4. (b)	5. (b)	6. (c)
7. (a)	8. (c)	9. (b)	10. (b)	11. (b)	12. (a)
13. (a)	14. (b)	15. (a)	16. (a,b,c)	17. (c,d)	18. (a,c)
19. (b)	20. (c,d)	21. (0.045)	22. (153.5)	23. (9)	24. (– 4.17)
25. (1.6)					

Element 3 Electrochemical Cells, Nernst Equation and Electrode Potential

Cells

The device which converts chemical energy into electric energy and vice-versa is called **electrochemical cells** or **cell**. There are two types of cells in which chemical reactions are carried out.

Electrochemical or voltaic (galvanic) cells are of a type that produce electricity as a result of chemical reactions.

$$Cu(s) + 2Ag^{+}(aq) \longrightarrow Cu^{2+}(aq) + 2Ag(s)$$

Galvanic cells are further divided into chemical cells and concentration cells.

Daniel Cell

It is an electrochemical cell in which Zn/Zn^{2+} electrode is used as anode while Cu^{2+}/Cu electrode act as cathode. The electronic conductor and its electrolyte constitute an electrode. The physical structure containing them is called an electrode compartment.

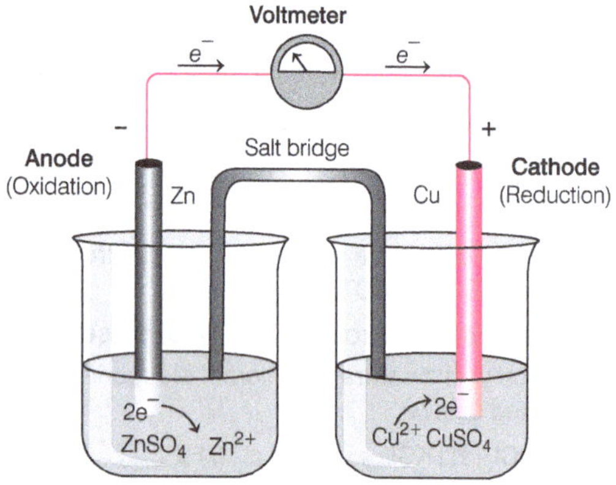

$$Zn(s) \mid ZnSO_4(aq) \parallel CuSO_4(sq) \mid Cu(s)$$

At anode, oxidation takes place

$$Zn(s) \longrightarrow Zn^{2+}(aq) + 2e^-$$

At cathode, reduction takes place

$$Cu^{2+}(aq) + 2e^- \longrightarrow Cu(s)$$

As the reaction proceeds in Daniel cell, the electrons released at the anode travel through the external circuit and electrons re-enter the cell at the cathode, where they bring about reduction. In order for Daniel Cell to function continuously, the charge in both the half cells needs to be balanced. To do so, we use Salt Bridge, which is a saturated paste of an ionic electrolyte in agar-agar or some jelly-like substance.

KCl is the preferred electrolyte because the ionic mobilities of cation and anion i.e. K^+ and Cl^- ions are comparable.

In fact K^+, NH_4^+, Cl^- and NO_3^- ions have not much difference in their ionic mobilities, that's why in place of KCl, we can also use KNO_3 or NH_4NO_3 or NH_4Cl.

JEE Alert

Care must be taken to choose the electrolyte in the salt bridge. For example, NO_3^- should not be used if the solution contains some oxidisable species or Cl^- should not be used if the solution contains Ag^+ or Hg_2^{2+} ions.

The significance of salt bridge includes

- It connects the solution of two half-cells, thus completes the cell circuit.
- It prevents transference or diffusion of the solutions from one half-cell to other.
- It helps in keeping the solution in two half-cells electrically neutral, i.e. it provides negative ions to anodic half-cell. Thus, preventing the accumulation of extra positive charge in the solution and around anode which normally hinders the flow of electrons from anode. Similarly, in cathodic half-cell, it provides positive ions to prevent the accumulation of extra negative ions in this half.
- It prevents **liquid-liquid junction potential**, i.e. the potential difference which arises between two solutions when these are in contact with each other due to different movement of ions.
- **Electrolytic Cell** are of a type in which we use electricity to produce non spontaneous chemical changes.

The two cells are of the reverse of each other.

The difference between electrolytic cell and Galvanic cell is given below in table.

Electrolytic Cell	Galvanic/Voltaic Cell
(a) Chemical change occur due to flow of electricity i.e. these cells consume an electric current.	Electricity flows due to chemical change or these cells produce an electric current.
(b) Use electrical energy to bring about non-spontaneous chemical transformation.	Produce electricity from energy released during spontaneous chemical reactions.
(c) Electrical Energy → Chemical Energy	Chemical Energy → Electrical Energy
(d) Cathode: negatively charged electrode Anode: positively charged electrode	Cathode: positively charged electrode Anode: negatively charged electrode
(e) If inert electrodes are used, the concentration of electrolytic solution go on decreasing because ions are continuously discharged.	Concentration of electrolyte increases in the anodic chamber while it decreases in cathodic chamber or may remains same.

JEE Quicker

An electrochemical cell can be converted into an electrolytic cell by applying an external potential greater than E°_{cell}.

JEE Main 2024

- If an external opposite potential is applied on the galvanic cell and increased reaction continues to take place till the opposing voltage reaches the value of 1.1 V. At this stage, no current flows and any further increase in the external potential then reaction starts functioning as electrolytic cell.

Electrode Potential and Standard Electrode Potential

If we connect two different electrodes, electrons will flow from the electrode of higher negative electric charge density to the electrode with a lower negative electric charge density and hence a potential difference is developed. The potential difference between the metal and the metal ion in which electrode is dipped, is called **electrode potential** denoted as E.

In the standard state, when pressure is 1 atm, (latest IUPAC convention uses 1 bar) and concentration is 1 M, electrode potential is called **standard electrode potential** denoted as $E°$. Temperature is generally taken as 298 K (i.e. 25°C).

The electrode potential can be of two types

- **Oxidation potential** It is the tendency of an electrode to get oxidised, i.e. to lose electrons.

  Half cell: $Zn \mid Zn^{+2}(aq)$

  Reaction: $Zn \longrightarrow Zn^{+2}(aq) + 2e^-$

  Oxidation potential: $E_{Zn \mid Zn^{+2}}$ or E_{ox}

- **Reduction potential** It is the tendency of an electrode to get reduced, i.e. to accept electrons.

  Half Cell: $Cu^{+2}(aq) \mid Cu$

  Reaction: $Cu^{+2}(aq) + 2e^- \longrightarrow Cu$

  Reduction potential: $E_{Cu^{+2} \mid Cu}$ or E_{red}

  General representation of oxidation and reduction potential

  Oxidation potential $E_{M \mid M^{+n}}$

  Reduction potential $E_{M^{+n} \mid M}$

  According to international convention, standard reduction potentials are now called standard electrode potentials.

Potential of a Cell or EMF

The flow of current from one electrode to other indicates that these electrodes are at different potential. The potential difference between the two electrodes is known as the cell potential. It is the maximum potential that a cell can generate and represented by E_{cell}. Since, the potential difference is the driving force for electrons, it is also called the **electromotive force** (emf) of the cell or the cell potential or the cell voltage. This driving force pushes the negatively charged electrons away from the anode (−ve electrode) and pulls them towards the cathode (+ ve electrode). EMF of cell is equal to cell potential when no current is being drawn from the cell potential depends on composition of electrodes, concentration of the ions in the half cells and the temperature. In standard conditions cell potential is called standard cell potential, denoted by E°_{cell}.

E°_{cell} or E_{cell} is the potential difference between two half-cells.

$$E^\circ_{cell} = E^\circ_{ox} + E^\circ_{red}$$

$$\Rightarrow \quad E_{cell} = E_{ox} + E_{red}$$

(If oxidation potential is taken for anode and reduction potential is taken for cathode.)

$$E_{Anode} - E_{Cathode} = E_{Cell}$$

if oxidation potential is taken for both electrode.

$E_{Cathode} - E_{Anode} = E_{Cell}$ (if reduction potential is taken for both electrodes.)

Solved Booster 3.1

For the cell reaction, $2Ce^{4+} + Co \longrightarrow 2Ce^{3+} + Co^{2+}$

E°_{cell} is 1.89 V. If $E_{Co^{2+}/Co}$ is −0.28 V, what is the value of $E^\circ_{Ce^{4+}/Ce^{3+}}$?

(a) 1.61 (b) − 1.61

(c) 2.17 (d) − 2.17

Solution (a)

$$E^\circ_{cell} = E^\circ_{ox} + E^\circ_{red} = E^\circ_{Co/Co^{2+}} + E^\circ_{Ce^{4+}/Ce^{3+}}$$

$$E^\circ_{cell} = -E^\circ_{Co^{2+}/Co} + E^\circ_{Ce^{4+}/Ce^{3+}}$$

$$1.89 = -(-0.28) + E^\circ_{Ce^{4+}/Ce^{3+}}$$

$$= 0.28 + E^\circ_{Ce^{4+}/Ce^{3+}}$$

$$\therefore E^\circ_{Ce^{4+}/Ce^{3+}} = 1.89 - 0.28 = 1.61 \text{ V}$$

Solved Booster 3.2

The following half-cell reactions are given:

I. $Cu^{2+}(aq) + e^- \longrightarrow Cu^+(aq)$; $E^\circ = 0.15$ V

II. $2H^+(aq) + 2e^- \longrightarrow H_2(g)$; $E^\circ = 0.00$ V

III. $CuI(s) + e^- \longrightarrow Cu(s) + I^-(aq)$; $E^\circ = -0.17$ V

IV. $Zn^{2+}(aq) + 2e^- \longrightarrow Zn(s)$; $E^\circ = -0.76$ V

The voltage of the cell is

$\underset{\ominus}{Zn} | Zn^{2+}(1\ M) || I^-(1\ M) | CuI | \underset{\oplus}{Cu}$

(a) – 0.59 (b) 0.59 (c) 0.93 (d) – 0.93

Solution (b)

Oxidation at LHS

$$Zn \longrightarrow Zn^{2+} + 2e^-;\ E^\circ_{ox} = 0.76\ \text{V (from IV)}$$

Reduction at RHS

$$\left.\begin{aligned} CuI + e^- &\longrightarrow Cu + I^- \\ \text{or}\quad 2CuI + 2e^- &\longrightarrow 2Cu + 2I^- \end{aligned}\right] E^\circ_{red} = -0.17\ \text{V (from III)}$$

Overall reaction $Zn + 2CuI \longrightarrow Zn^{2+} + 2Cu + 2I^-$

$$E^\circ = E^\circ_{ox} + E^\circ_{red} = 0.59\ \text{V}$$

Note Values given in I and II are not required.

Various Types of Half-Cell

Various type of half-cells have been used some as reference half-cells, to make complete cell with spontaneous reaction in forward direction. These half-cells alongwith half cells reactions are given below.

1. Metal-Metal Ion Half-Cell

- In this type of half-cell, the metal rod is dipped in a solution of the corresponding metal ion having concentration c-M.

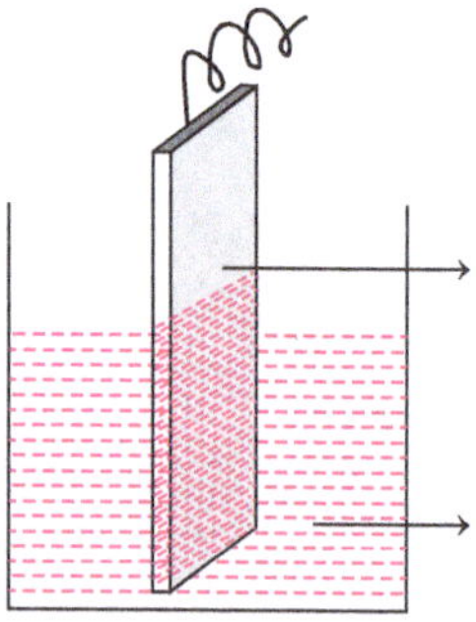

Metal-metal ion half-cell

- The given half-cell when functions as anode can be represented as: $M(s) | M^{n+}(c\text{-}M)$.
- The anodic half-cell reaction: $M(s) \longrightarrow M^{n+}(aq) + ne^-$
- The representation of the half-cell when it functions as cathode: $M^{n+}(c\text{-}M) + M(s)$.
- The cathodic half-cell reaction: $M^{n+}(aq) + ne^- \longrightarrow M(s)$.

- Examples of this type of half-cell when used as cathode are $Cu^{2+} | Cu$, $Zn^{2+} | Zn$, $Ag^+ | Ag$, $Sn^{2+} | Sn$, etc. The half cells or electrodes used in Daniel cell are of the metal-metal ion type.
- For such type of half-cells, very active metals cannot be used, because they react with water. For such highly reactive metals, an amalgam of the metal in mercury is used instead of pure metal.

2. Gas-Gas Ion Half-Cell

- In a gas-gas ion half-cell, a gas is bubbled into a solution of the gas ion, with a platinum rod having a sheet coated with platinum black being dipped in the gas ion solution. Platinum is used for making electrical contact because the gases are non-conducting and the platinum do not react with gas ions as it is an unreactive metal.
- Platinum black is used over the platinum sheet, which gives it a large surface area for the adsorption of gases.
- The half-cell assembly is shown in figure:

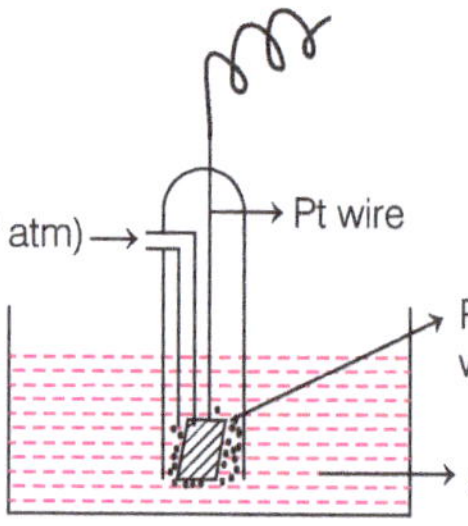

Gas-gas ion half-cell

The given half-cell when functions as anode can be represented as:

Pt | Gas (P atm) | Gas ion (c M).

- Let us consider a hydrogen gas half-cell, functioning as anode. It is represented as:

$$Pt | H_2(P\ atm) | H^+\ (c\ M)$$

and the anodic half-cell reaction:

$$H_2(Pt) \longrightarrow 2H^+(aq) + 2e^-(Pt)$$

- Let us consider a hydrogen half-cell, functioning as cathode. It is represented as:

$$H^+\ (c\ M) | H_2\ (P\ atm) | Pt$$

and the cathodic half-cell reaction:

$$2H^+(aq) + 2e^-(Pt) \longrightarrow H_2(Pt).$$

- The hydrogen electrode is called standard hydrogen electrode when the concentration of H^+ ion is 1 M and the pressure of H_2 gas is 1 atm.
- The standard hydrogen electrode (SHE) functions as reference electrode and is used for the measurement of standard reduction potentials of other half-cells or couples. The SRP values obtained in this manner are arranged in the decreasing order to give electrochemical series (ECS).

3. Redox Half-Cell

- In redox half-cell, a platinum rod is dipped in a solution containing two different oxidation states of a metal ion (M^{n_1+} and M^{n_2+}, where n_2 is greater than n_1).

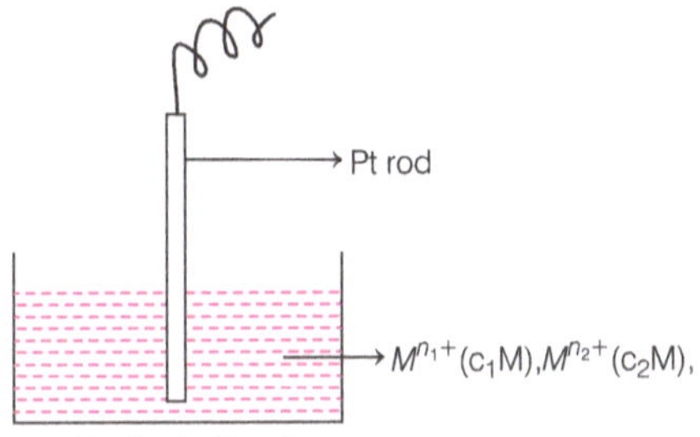

Redox half -cell

- The given half-cell when functions as anode can be represented as

$$\text{Pt} \mid M^{n_1+}(c_1\ \text{M}), M^{n_2+}(c_2\ \text{M})$$

and the anodic half-cell reaction is:

$$M^{n_1+} \longrightarrow M^{n_2+} + (n_2 - n_1)e^-$$

- The redox half-cell when functions as cathode can be represented as

$$M^{n_2+}(c_2\ \text{M}), M^{n_1+}(c_1\ \text{M}) \mid \text{Pt}$$

and the cathodic half-cell reaction is:

$$M^{n_2+} + (n_2 - n_1)e^- \longrightarrow M^{n_1+}$$

- Examples of this type of half-cell when used as anode are $\text{Pt}|Cr^{2+}(c_1\ \text{M}), Cr^{3+}(c_2\ \text{M})$; $\text{Pt}|Fe^{2+}(c_1\ \text{M}), Fe^{3+}(c_2\ \text{M})$; $\text{Pt}|Sn^{2+}(c_1\ \text{M}), SN^{4+}(c_2\ \text{M})$ etc. In such half cells, the oxidising and reducing agents are both metal ions.

JEE Spotlite

Redox half-cell can also be made with organic molecules that can exist in two different oxidation states.

- A couple of hydroquinone (QH_2) and quinone (Q) forms a redox half-cell. Its representation, when it functions as anode is

$$\text{Pt} \mid QH_2\ (1\ \text{M}), Q\ (1\ \text{M}), H^+(c\ \text{M})$$

and the anodic half-cell reaction is:

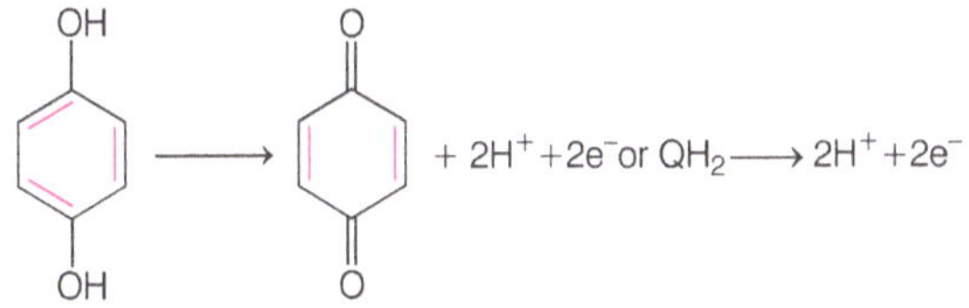

- This redox electrode having organic molecules is called quinhydrone electrode because of the charged complex formed between quinone and hydroquinone.

4. Metal-Metal Insoluble Salt-Anion Half-Cell

- In this type of half-cell, a metal strip is coated with an insoluble metal salt of the same metal and it is dipped in a solution containing the same anion (as that of the insoluble salt) but it's coming from a highly soluble salt.
- The essential condition is that the corresponding cation of the highly soluble salt should have the standard reduction potential less than the standard reduction potential of the cation in insoluble salt.

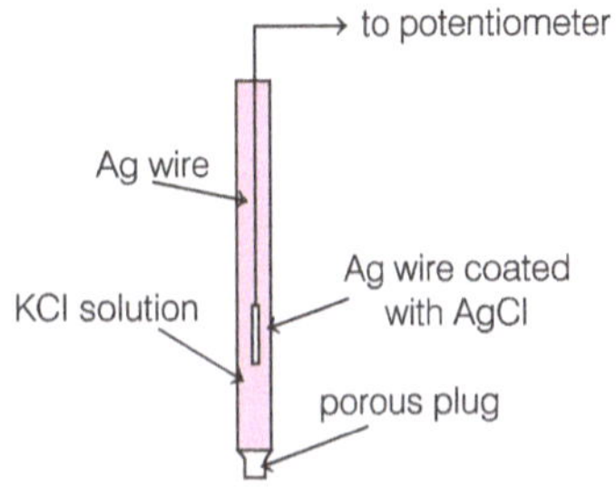

- The metal used is silver and metal insoluble salt is AgCl.

Few more examples of a metal-metal insoluble salt-anion half-cell acting as anode is

(i) $Hg(l) \mid Hg_2Cl_2(s) \mid KCl\ (c\ M)$

This is called calomel electrode as Hg_2Cl_2 commonly called as calomel

$$2Hg(l) + 2Cl^-(aq) \longrightarrow Hg_2Cl_2(s) + 2e^-$$

$$E_{Cl^-/Hg_2Cl_2/Hg} = E^\circ_{Cl^-/Hg_2Cl_2/Hg} + \frac{RT}{2F}\ln[Cl^-]^2$$

Hg and Hg_2Cl_2 won't appear in the Nernst equation as they are pure liquid and pure solid respectively and their activities are 1.

Calomel electrode
- → [KCl] = 1 M = 1 N : Standard/Normal/Molar calomel electrode
- → [KCl] = 0.1 M = 0.1 N : Decinormal/Decimolar calomel electrode
- → [KCl] = Saturated: Saturated calomel electrode (SCE)

(ii) $SO_4^{2-}(c\ M) \mid PbSO_4(s) \mid Pb(s)$

$$PbSO_4(s) + 2e^- \longrightarrow Pb(s) + SO_4^{2-}(aq)$$

$$E_{SO_4^{2-}/PbSO_4/Pb} = E^\circ_{SO_4^{2-}/PbSO_4/Pb} - \frac{RT}{2F}\ln[SO_4^{2-}]$$

Types of Half-Cells

S.N	Type	Example	Half-cell reaction	Q =	Reversible to	Electrode potential (oxidation), E =
1.	Gas-ion half-cell	$Pt(H_2)\|H^+(aq)$ $Pt(Cl_2)\|Cl^-(aq)$	$\frac{1}{2}H_2(g) \longrightarrow H^+(aq) + e^-$ $Cl^-(aq) \longrightarrow \frac{1}{2}Cl_2(g) + e^-$	$[H^+]$ $\frac{1}{[Cl^-]}$	H^+ ion Cl^- ion	$E° - 0.0591 \log [H^+]$ $E° + 0.0591 \log [Cl^-]$
2.	Metal-metal ion half-cell	$Ag\|Ag^+(aq)$	$Ag(s) \longrightarrow Ag^+(aq) + e^-$	$[Ag^+]$	Ag^+ ion	$E° - 0.0591 \log [Ag^+]$
3.	Metal-insoluble salt anion half-cell	$Ag, AgCl\|Cl^-(aq)$	$Ag(s) + Cl^-(aq) \longrightarrow AgCl(s) + e^-$	$\frac{1}{[Cl^-]}$	Cl^- ion	$E° + 0.0591 \log [Cl^-]$
4.	Calomel electrode	$Hg, Hg_2Cl_2\|Cl^-(aq)$	$2Hg(l) + 2Cl^-(aq) \longrightarrow Hg_2Cl_2(s) + 2e^-$	$\frac{1}{[Cl^-]^2}$	Cl^- ion	$E° + 0.0591 \log [Cl^-]$
5.	Metal-metal oxide hydroxide half-cell	$Hg, HgO\|OH^-(aq)$	$Hg(l) + 2OH^-(aq) \longrightarrow HgO(s) + H_2O(l) + 2e^-$	$\frac{1}{[OH^-]^2}$	OH^- ion	$E° + 0.0591 \log [OH^-]$
6.	Oxidation-reduction half-cell	$Pt\|Fe^{2+}_{(aq)}, Fe^{3+}_{(aq)}$	$Fe^{2+}(aq) \longrightarrow Fe^{3+}(aq) + e^-$	$\frac{[Fe^{3+}]}{[Fe^{2+}]}$	Fe^{2+}, Fe^{3+} ions	$E° - 0.0591 \log \frac{[Fe^{3+}]}{[Fe^{2+}]}$
7.	Mercury-mercury sulphate half-cell	$Hg, HgSO_4\|SO_4^{2-}(aq)$	$SO_4^{2-}(aq) + Hg(l) \longrightarrow HgSO_4(s) + 2e^-$	$\frac{1}{[SO_4^{2-}]}$	SO_4^{2-} ion	$E° + \frac{0.0591}{2} \log [SO_4^{2-}]$
8.	Quinhydrone half-cell	$Pt\|$ quinhydrone $\|H^+(aq)$	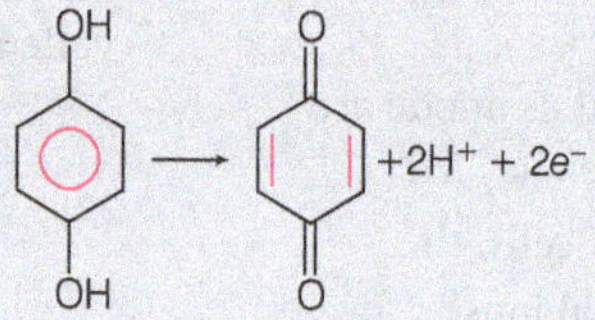	$[H^+]^2$	H^+ ion	$E° - 0.0591 \log [H^+]$

Solved Booster 3.6

The following oxidising agents in order of increasing strength under standard-state conditions:

$$Br_2(l), Fe^{3+}(aq), Cr_2O_7^{2-}(aq)$$

[Given, $Cr_2O_7^{2-} + 14H^+ + 6e^- \longrightarrow 2Cr^{3+} + 7H_2O$, $E_1^\circ = 1.33$ V

$Br_2(l) + 2e^- \longrightarrow 2Br^-(aq)$, $E_2^\circ = 1.06$ V

$Fe^{3+}(aq) + e^- \longrightarrow Fe^{2+}(aq)$, $E_3^\circ = 0.77$ V]

is

(a) $Fe^{3+} < Br_2 < Cr_2O_7^{2-}$

(b) $CrO_7^{2-} < Br_2 < Fe^{3+}$

(c) $Fe^{3+} < Cr_2O_7^{2-} < Br_2$

(d) $Br_2 < Fe^{3+} < Cr_2O_7^{2-}$

Solution *(a)*

$E°$ values given are standard reduction potentials. We find that $E_1^\circ > E_2^\circ > E_3^\circ$.

Thus, $Cr_2O_7^{2-}$ has the maximum tendency to be reduced, hence it is the best oxidising agent, order being $Fe^{3+} < Br_2 < Cr_2O_7^{2-}$.

> **JEE Alert**
> More positive value of the E°_{red} implies its greater tendency to be reduced hence, better oxidising agent.

Electrochemical Series

The arrangement of various electrodes in the order of their increasing values of standard reduction potentials is called **electrochemical** series.

Stronger reducing agent ↑ (left) — Weaker oxidising agent ↓ (right)

Electrode reaction	$E°/V$	Half-cell representation
$Li^+ + e^- \longrightarrow Li$	– 3.045	$Li^+ \mid Li$
$K^+ + e^- \longrightarrow K$	– 2.925	$K^+ \mid K$
$Na^+ + e^- \longrightarrow Na$	– 2.714	$Na^+ \mid Na$
$Mg^{2+} + 2e^- \longrightarrow Mg$	– 2.37	$Mg^{2+} \mid Mg$
$H_2 + 2e^- \longrightarrow 2H^-$	– 2.25	$H^- \mid H_2 \mid Pt$
$Al^{3+} + 3e^- \longrightarrow Al$	–1.66	$Al^{3+} \mid Al$
$2H_2O + 2e^- \longrightarrow H_2 + 2OH^-$	– 0.828	$OH^- \mid H_2 \mid Pt$
$Zn^{2+} + 2e^- \longrightarrow Zn$	– 0.763	$Zn^{2+} \mid Zn$
$Cr^{3+} + 3e^- \longrightarrow Cr$	–0.74	$Cr^{3+} \mid Cr$
$Fe^{2+} + 2e^- \longrightarrow Fe$	– 0.44	$Fe^{2+} \mid Fe$
$Cr^{3+} + e^- \longrightarrow Cr^{2+}$	– 0.41	$Cr^{3+}, Cr^{2+} \mid Pt$
$Cd^{2+} + 2e^- \longrightarrow Cd$	– 0.40	$Cd^{2+} \mid Cd$
$Co^{2+} + 2e^- \longrightarrow Co$	– 0.277	$Co^{2+} \mid Co$
$Ni^{2+} + 2e^- \longrightarrow Ni$	–0.26	$Ni^{2+} \mid Ni$
$AgI + e^- \longrightarrow Ag + I^-$	– 0.151	$I^- \mid AgI \mid Ag$
$Sn^{2+} + 2e^- \longrightarrow Sn$	– 0.136	$Sn^{2+} \mid Sn$
$Pb^{2+} + 2e^- \longrightarrow Pb$	– 0.126	$Pb^{2+} \mid Pb$
$Fe^{3+} + 3e^- \longrightarrow Fe$	– 0.036	$Fe^{3+} \mid Fe$
$2H^+ + 2e^- \longrightarrow H_2$	0.000	$H^+ \mid H_2 \mid Pt$
$AgBr + e^- \longrightarrow Ag + Br^-$	0.095	$Br^- \mid AgBr \mid Ag$
$Cu^{2+} + e^- \longrightarrow Cu^+$	0.153	$Cu^{2+}, Cu^+ \mid Pt$
$Sn^{4+} + 2e^- \longrightarrow Sn^{2+}$	0.15	$Sn^{4+}, Sn^{2+} \mid Pt$
$AgCl + e^- \longrightarrow Ag + Cl^-$	0.222	$Cl^- \mid AgCl \mid Ag$
$Hg_2Cl_2 + 2e^- \longrightarrow 2Hg + 2Cl^-$	0.2676	$Cl^- \mid Hg_2Cl_2 \mid Hg$ (Pt)
$Cu^{2+} + 2e^- \longrightarrow Cu$	0.337	$Cu^{2+} \mid Cu$
$O_2(g) + 2H_2O + 4e^- \longrightarrow 4OH^-$	0.401	$OH^- \mid O_2 \mid Pt$
$Cu^+ + e^- \longrightarrow Cu$	0.521	$Cu^+ \mid Cu$
$I_2 + 2e^- \longrightarrow 2I^-$	0.5355	$I_2, I^- \mid Pt$
$Fe^{3+} + e^- \longrightarrow Fe^{2+}$	0.771	$Fe^{3+}, Fe^{2+} \mid Pt$
$Hg_2^{2+} + 2e^- \longrightarrow 2Hg$	0.789	$Hg_2^{2+} \mid Hg$ (Pt)
$Ag^+ + e^- \longrightarrow Ag$	0.7991	$Ag^+ \mid Ag$
$O_2 + 4H^+ + 4e^- \longrightarrow 2H_2O$	1.229	$H^+ \mid O_2 \mid Pt$
$Br_2(l) + 2e^- \longrightarrow 2Br^-$	1.0562	$Br_2, Br^- \mid Pt$
$Cr_2O_7^{2-} + 14H^+ + 6e^- \longrightarrow 2Cr^{3+} + 7H_2O$	1.33	$Cr_2O_7^{2-}, Cr^{3+}, H^+ \mid Pt$
$Cl_2(g) + 2e^- \longrightarrow 2Cl^-$	1.3595	$Cl^- \mid Pt(Cl_2)$
$Ce^{4+} + e^- \longrightarrow Ce^{3+}$ (1 mol dm^{-3} H_2SO_4)	1.44	$Ce^{4+}, Ce^{3+} \mid Pt$
$Au^{3+} + 3e^- \longrightarrow Au$	1.455	$Au^{3+} \mid Au$
$MnO_4^- + 8H^+ + 5e^- \longrightarrow Mn^{2+} + 4H_2O$	1.51	$MnO_4^-, Mn^{2+}, H^+ \mid Pt$
$Co^{3+} + e^- \longrightarrow Co^{2+}$	1.82	$Co^{3+}, Co^{2+} \mid Pt$
$F_2(g) + 2e^- \longrightarrow 2F^-$	2.87	$F^- \mid Pt (F_2)$

Weaker reducing agent (left) — Stronger oxidising agent (right)

Applications of Electrochemical Series

The applications of electrochemical series are as follows

(i) Higher the reduction potential, greater is the tendency of the element to get reduced. Hence, the relative oxidising and reducing abilities of the elements can be compared easily.

(ii) A metal placed higher in the series is anodic to other metals which lie below it. An element can displace all elements that lie below it in the series, from their salt solutions.

(iii) Knowledge of electrochemical series helps in selection of electrode assemblies, to construct the galvanic cells of the desired EMF.

(iv) The polarity of the electrode system and the electrode reaction can be easily predicted.

(v) Spontaneity and feasibility of the cell under construction can be easily predicted.

Thermodynamics in Cells

$$\Delta_r G = \Delta_r G^\circ + RT \ln Q \qquad \ldots\text{(i)}$$

The reaction in galvanic cell is spontaneous, so it occurs with decrease in Gibbs energy. This decrease in Gibbs energy at any instant bring in an equivalent amount of non-pV work i.e electrical work the work done in forcing the electrons into the electrical circuit.

The maximum amount of non pV work W_{max}, available from a process carried out at constant temperature and pressure is equal to the free energy change ΔG for the process.

$$W_{max} = -\Delta G$$

We can write an equation that relates the potential of a cell and the free energy of the cell reaction, because the maximum amount of work available can be related both to the cell potential and to the free energy change of the cell reaction $W_{max} = nFE_{cell} = -\Delta G$

$$\Delta G = -nFE_{cell}$$

$$\Delta G^\circ_{298} = -nFE^\circ_{cell} \text{ for standard state conditions}$$

These equations relate the free energy change for a cell reaction, where the initial state is that of the reactants in the cell and the final state is that of the products in the cell.

The equation shows that a galvanic cell spontaneously produces current when it has a positive potential. A positive potential corresponds to a negative value of ΔG, which is the criterion for spontaneity of a reaction.

where, E_{cell} is EMF of cell n is moles of electrons involved in redox reaction.

F is Faraday = 96500 C

Putting Eq. (ii) and (iii) in Eq. (i)

$$-FE_{cell} = -nFE^\circ_{cell} + RT \ln Q$$

Dividing by $-nF$ throughout gives, $E_{cell} = E^\circ_{cell} - \frac{RT}{nE} \ln Q$

This is called **Nernst equation**.

Relation between Electrochemical Cell Potential and Gibbs Free Energy Change

If two reactions are added, E° cannot be just added. but ΔG° for the reactions can be added. However the potentials are additive for the process in which half- reactions are added to yield an overall reaction but they are not additive when added to yield to third half-reaction.

$$\Delta G_3 = \Delta G_1 + \Delta G_2$$

or $$-n_3FE_3 = -n_1FE_1 - n_2FE_2 = -F(n_1E_1 + n_2E_2)$$

or $$E_3 = \frac{n_1E_1 + n_2E_2}{n_3}$$

When the two half-reactions are added to yield an overall reaction, the number of moles of electrons involved in each half-reaction and the overall reaction are necessary the same, i.e. $n_1 = n_2 = n_3 = n$

$$\therefore \quad E_3 = \frac{nE_1 + nE_2}{n} = E_1 + E_2$$

However, when two half-reactions are added to yield a third half- reaction, the number of moles of electrons in all the three half- reactions cannot be the same.

JEE MAPPER

Example Similar to PYQ Asked in JEE Main 2025

For the half-cell reactions,

$Cu^{2+} + e^- \longrightarrow Cu^+$; $\quad E^\circ = 0.15$ V

$Cu^{2+} + 2e^- \longrightarrow Cu$; $\quad E^\circ = 0.34$ V

The E° of the half-cell reaction is

$$Cu^+ + e^- \longrightarrow Cu$$

(a) 0.80 (b) − 0.53 (c) 0.19 (d) 0.53

Sol. (d)

$Cu^{2+} + e^- \longrightarrow Cu^+$; $E^\circ = 0.15$ V

I. $Cu^+ \longrightarrow Cu^{2+} + e^-$; $\quad E_1^\circ = -0.15$ V, $n_1 = 1$

II. $Cu^{2+} + 2e^- \longrightarrow Cu$; $\quad E_2^\circ = 0.34$ V, $n_2 = 2$

(I + II) gives $Cu^+ + e^- \longrightarrow Cu$, $\quad E_3^\circ = ?$, $n_3 = 1$

$$\therefore \quad \Delta G_3^\circ = \Delta G_1^\circ + \Delta G_2^\circ \Rightarrow -n_3E_3^\circ = -n_1E_1^\circ - n_2E_2^\circ$$

$$E_3^\circ = \frac{n_1E_1^\circ + n_2E_2^\circ}{n_3} = \frac{1 \times (-0.15) + 2 \times (0.34)}{1}$$

$$= -0.15 + 0.68 = +0.53 \text{ V}$$

Competency Enhancer 3.1

The standard reduction potentials of Fe^{3+} / Fe^{2+} and Fe^{2+} / Fe are 0.77 V and − 0.44 V respectively. The standard electrode potential of Fe^{3+} / Fe half-cell is

(a) 0.14 (b) − 0.11 (c) − 0.037 (d) + 0.037

Interpretation of Nernst Equation

Electrode potential is given by $E = E^\circ - \dfrac{2.303\,RT}{nF}\log Q$

Case I

Electrode potential of oxidation half-cell $M/M^{n+}(aq)$ with reaction, $M(s) \longrightarrow M^{n+}(aq) + ne^-$ is

$$E_{ox} = E^\circ_{ox} - \frac{2.303\,RT}{nF}\log[M^{n+}]$$

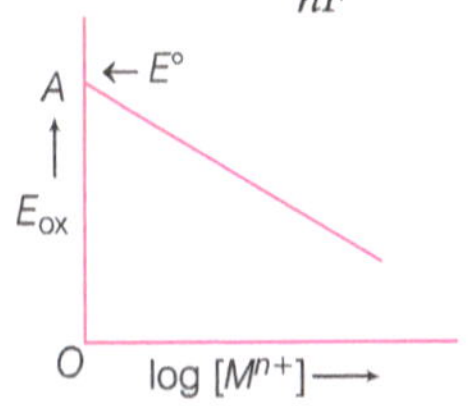

Variation of E_{ox} with $\log[M^{n+}]$

E_{ox} depends on

(i) **$[M^{n+}]$, concentration of ionic species**

If $[M^{n+}]$ increases, $\log[M^{n+}]$ increases, hence E_{ox} decreases (as shown in fig.

We can say electrode is reversible with respect to M^{n+}.

Slope $= \dfrac{2.303\,RT}{nF}$

and when $[M^{n+}] = 1\text{ M} \Rightarrow \log[M^{n+}] = 0$

then $OA = E^\circ_{ox}$

(ii) **Temperature (T)**

At constant $[M^{n+}]$, on increasing temperature, $\dfrac{2.303\,RT}{nF}$ increases

Hence, $E_{ox}\left(= E^\circ_{ox} - \dfrac{2.303\,RT}{nF}\log[M^{n+}]\right)$ decreases.

Variation of E_{ox} with $\log[M^{n+}]$ at temperature T_1, T_2 and T_3 is shown Fig.

$(T_1 < T_2 < T_3)$

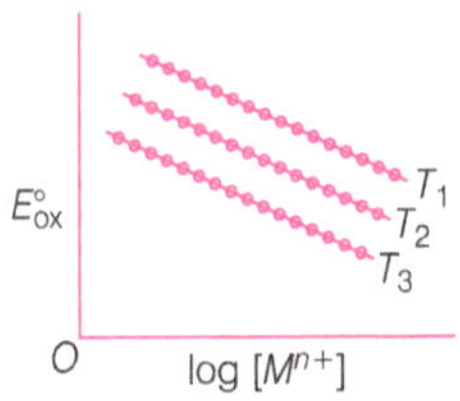

Variation of E_{ox} with $\log[M^{n+}]$ at different temperatures.

Case II

Electrode potential of reduction half-cell $M^{n+}(aq)/M$ with reaction, $M^{n+}(aq) + ne^- \longrightarrow M(s)$ is

$$E_{red} = E^\circ_{red} - \frac{2.303\,RT}{nF}\log\frac{1}{[M^{n+}]} = E^\circ_{red} + \frac{2.303\,RT}{nF}\log[M^{n+}]$$

E_{red} depends on

(i) **$[M^{n+}]$ concentration of ionic species**

If $[M^{n+}]$ increases, E_{red} increases, electrode is reversible to M^{n+} Fig.

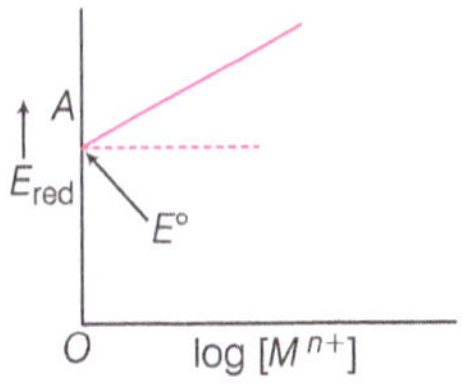

Variation of E_{red} with $\log[M^{n+}]$

Slope $= \dfrac{2.303\,RT}{nF}$ and when $[M^{n+}] = 1\,M$, $E^\circ_{red} = OA$

(ii) **Temperature, (T)**

If T increases at constant $[M^{n+}]$, E_{red} increases.

Variation of E_{red} with $\log[M^{n+}]$ at different temperatures is shown in Fig.

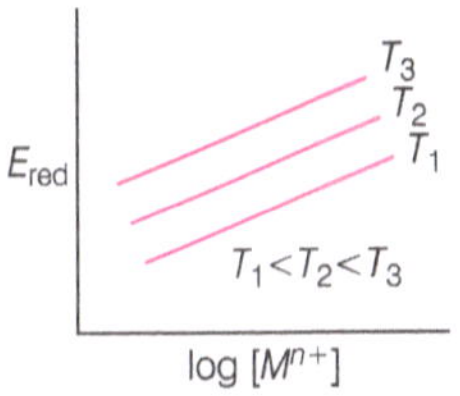

Variation of E_{red} with $\log[M^{n+}]$ at different temperatures

JEE Spotlite

Some Important Points Regarding Gibbs Energy Change and Cell Potential:

(i) Gibbs energy is an extensive variable whereas EMF is intensive variable. Intensive variables are non-additive in nature while extensive variables are additive in nature.

(ii) If two half-cells involving either oxidation or reduction reaction both are added to get the third reaction, then EMF is non-additive in nature.

$$M(s) \longrightarrow M^{n_1+}(aq) + n_1e^-; \quad \Delta G^\circ_1 = -n_1FE^\circ_{M/M^{n_1+}}$$

$$M^{n_1+}(aq) \longrightarrow M^{n_2+}(aq) + (n_2 - n_1)e^-;$$
$$\Delta G^\circ_2 = -(n_2 - n_1)FE^\circ_{M^{n_1+}/M^{n_2+}}$$

$$M(s) \longrightarrow M^{n_2+}(aq) + n_2e^-; \quad \Delta G^\circ_3 = -n_2FE^\circ_{M/M^{n_2+}}$$

n_1 may or may not be equal to $(n_2 - n_1)$ but will never be equal to n_2.

(iii) If two half-cell one involving oxidation and other involving reduction reaction...are added to get the third reaction, then EMF is additive in nature.

$$M(s) \longrightarrow M^{n_1+}(aq) + n_1e^-] \times n_2; \Delta G^\circ_1 = -n_1n_2\,FE^\circ_{M/M^{n_1+}}$$

$$N^{n_2^+}(aq) + n_2e^- \longrightarrow N(s);] \times n_1; \; \Delta G^\circ_2 = -n_1n_2\,FE^\circ_{N^{n_2+}/N}$$

$$n_2M(s) + n_1N^{n_2+}(aq) \longrightarrow n_2M^{n_1+}(aq) + n_1N(s);$$
$$\Delta G^\circ_3 = -n_1n_2\,FE^\circ_{cell}$$

EMF Measurements : Applications

EMF measurements have wide applications such as in the determination of pH, K_{sp}, ΔH, ΔS etc.

1. Determination of Thermodynamic Data

- ΔG can be determined as $\Delta G = -nFE_{cell}$
- Using Gibbs-Helmholtz equation, temperature coefficient of emf of the cell can be determined.

$$\Delta G = \Delta H + T\left(\frac{d(\Delta G)}{dT}\right)_p \quad \ldots(i)$$

Since, $\Delta G = -nFE_{cell}$

$$\therefore \quad -nFE_{cell} = \Delta H - nFT\left(\frac{dE_{cell}}{dT}\right)_p$$

$$\left(\frac{dE_{cell}}{dT}\right)_p = \frac{\Delta H + nFE_{cell}}{nFT}$$

$$\Rightarrow \left(\frac{dE_{cell}}{dT}\right)_p = \frac{\Delta H}{nFT} + \frac{E_{cell}}{T}$$

$\left(\frac{dE_{cell}}{dT}\right)$ is called temperature coefficient of EMF of the cell.

Enthalpy change can be determined.

$$\Delta H = -nFE_{cell} + nFT\left(\frac{dE_{cell}}{dT}\right)$$

$$= -nF\left[E_{cell} - T\left(\frac{dE_{cell}}{dT}\right)_p\right]$$

Entropy change can be determined,

$$\Delta G = \Delta H - T\Delta S$$

Compare it with Eq. (i)

$$\Delta S = -\left(\frac{d(\Delta G)}{dT}\right)_p$$

$$= -\left(\frac{d}{dT}(-nFE_{cell})\right)_p = nF\left(\frac{dE_{cell}}{dT}\right)_p$$

2. Determination of Solubility and Solubility Product

If half-cell contains electrolyte in saturated solution, as given

$$\underset{\ominus}{Ag \mid} Ag^+ \parallel Ag^+ \text{ (saturated } AgX(aq)) \underset{\oplus}{\mid Ag}$$

then

At anode: $Ag(s) \longrightarrow Ag^+(aq) + e^-$

At cathode: $AgX(s) + e^- \longrightarrow Ag(s) + X^-(aq)$

$$AgX(s) \longrightarrow Ag^+(aq) + X^-(aq)$$

$$K_{eq} = [Ag^+][X^-] = K_{sp}$$

Hence, K_{sp} (solubility product) can be evaluated.

$$E^\circ_{cell} = E^\circ_{Ag/Ag^+} + E^\circ_{X^-/AgX,\,Ag} \Rightarrow E^\circ_{cell} = \frac{0.0591}{n}\log K_{sp}$$

$$\log K_{sp} = \frac{nE^\circ_{cell}}{0.0591}$$

Thus, for AgCl type salt solubility $= \sqrt{K_{sp}}$

JEE MAPPER

Example Similar to PYQ Asked in JEE Advance 2018

Consider an electrochemical cell:

$$X(s)\,|\,X^{n+}(aq,\ 4M)\,||\,Y^{2n+}(aq, 2M)\,|\,Y(s)$$

The value of $\Delta H^\ominus$ for the cell reaction is 4 times the $\Delta G^\ominus$ at 300 K. If the EMF of the cell is zero, the $\Delta S^\ominus$ (in J.K^{-1}. mol^{-1}) of the cell reaction per mol of Y formed at 300 K is ....

(Given ln(2) = 0.7, R (universal gas constant) = 8.3 J.K^{-1} mol^{-1} H, S and G are enthalpy, entropy and Gibbs energy, respectively)

Sol. (52.29) The given cell representation is:

$$X(s) \mid X^{n+}(aq.\ 4M) \parallel Y^{2n+}(aq.\ 2M) \mid Y(s).$$

The reactions at respective electrodes will be:

Anode $\quad X(s) \longrightarrow X^{n+}(aq.) + ne^- \times 2$

Cathode $\quad Y^{2n+}_{(aq.)} + 2ne^- \longrightarrow Y(s)$

Overall reaction, $2X(s) + Y^{2n+}(aq.) \longrightarrow 2X^{n+}(aq.) + Y(s)$

Also, $\Delta H^\ominus = 4\Delta G^\ominus$ and $E_{cell} = 0$

So, using the Nernst equation

$$E_{cell} = E^\ominus_{cell} - \frac{RT}{nF}\ln\frac{[\text{Product}]}{[\text{Reactant}]} \Rightarrow 0 = E^\ominus_{cell} - \frac{RT}{nF}\ln\frac{[X^{n+}]^2}{[Y^{2n+}]}$$

$$\Rightarrow E^\circ_{cell} = \frac{RT}{2nF}\ln\frac{(4)^2}{(2)} = \frac{RT}{2nF}\ln 8$$

Since, $\Delta G^\ominus = -nFE^\ominus = -2nFE^\ominus_{cell} = -2nF \times \frac{RT}{2nF}\ln 8 = -RT\ln 8$

Finally, using the formula,

$$\Delta G^\ominus = \Delta H^\ominus - T\Delta S^\ominus \Rightarrow \Delta G^\ominus = 4\Delta G^\ominus - T\Delta S^\ominus$$

$$\Rightarrow \quad 3\Delta G^\ominus = T\Delta S^\ominus \Rightarrow \Delta S^\ominus = \frac{3\Delta G^\ominus}{T} = \frac{-3RT\ln 8}{T}$$

$$= -3R\ln 8 = -3 \times 8.3 \times 3 \times 0.7 = -52.29\ \text{J/K-mol}$$

Competency Enhancer 3.2

Consider an electrochemical cell:

$M(s)\,|\,M^{n+}(aq,\ 3M)\,||\,N^{3n+}(aq, 1.5M)\,|\,N(s)$

The value of $\Delta H^\ominus$ for the cell reaction is thrice the $\Delta G^\ominus$ at 300 K. If the EMF of the cell is zero, the $\Delta S^\ominus$ (in J.K^{-1}. mol^{-1}) of the cell reaction per mol of N formed at 300 K is ....

(Given ln(2) = 0.7 and ln 3 = 1.1, R (universal gas constant) = 8.3 J.K^{-1} mol^{-1} H, S and G are enthalpy, entropy and Gibbs energy, respectively)

3. Determination of Equilibrium Constant

$$\Delta G = \Delta G^\circ + 2.303\,RT \log Q$$

At equilibrium, $\Delta G = 0$ and $Q = K_{eq}$

$\therefore$ $$\Delta G^\circ = -2.303\,RT \log K_{eq}$$

$$-nFE^\circ_{cell} = -2.303\,RT \log K_{eq}$$

at 298 K, $\dfrac{2.303\,RT}{F} = 0.0591\,V$

$\therefore$ $$E^\circ_{cell} = \frac{0.0591}{n} \log K_{eq}$$

Solved Booster 3.7

The value of the equilibrium constant K, for the reaction between copper (II) and tin (II) ions in aqueous solution at 25° C is _____ $\times 10^6$

$$Cu^{2+}(aq) + Sn^{2+}(aq) \longrightarrow Sn^{4+}(aq) + Cu(s)$$

Given, $E^\circ_{Cu^{2+}/Cu} = 0.34$ V

$E^\circ_{Sn^{4+}, Sn^{2+}/Pt} = 0.154$ V

Solution (1.97)

First we determine E°_{cell} for the reaction,

Oxidation : $Sn^{2+}(aq) \longrightarrow Sn^{4+}(aq) + 2e^-$,

Reduction : $Cu^{2+}(aq) + 2e^- \longrightarrow Cu$

Net, $Sn^{2+}(aq) + Cu^{2+}(aq) \longrightarrow Sn^{4+}(aq) + Cu$

$$E^\circ_{ox} = E^\circ_{Pt/Sn^{2+}, Sn^{4+}} = -E^\circ_{Sn^{4+}, Sn^{2+}/Pt} = -0.154 \text{ V}$$

$$E^\circ_{red} = E^\circ_{Cu^{2+}/Cu} = 0.34 \text{ V}$$

$$E^\circ_{cell} = E^\circ_{ox} + E^\circ_{red} = -0.154 + 0.34 = +0.186 \text{ V}$$

The number of moles of electrons per mole of cell reaction is 2

$\therefore$ $$E^\circ_{cell} = \frac{0.0591}{2} \log K_{eq}$$

$$\log K_{eq} = \frac{2 \times 0.186}{0.0591} = 6.2944$$

$\Rightarrow$ $$K_{eq} = 1.97 \times 10^6$$

Solved Booster 3.8

$E^\circ_{Cu^{2+}/Cu} = 0.34$ V. The reduction potential at pH = 14 for the Cu^{2+}/Cu couples is K_{sp} of $Cu(OH)_2 = 1.0 \times 10^{-19}$.

Solution (– 0.22)

pH = 14

$\therefore$ pOH = 0, $[OH^-] = 1M$

$\therefore$ $[Cu^{2+}][OH^-]^2 = K_{sp} = 1.0 \times 10^{-19}$

$\therefore$ $[Cu^{2+}] = 1 \times 10^{-19}$ M; $Cu^{2+} + 2e^- \longrightarrow Cu$

$\therefore$ $$E_{Cu^{2+}/Cu} = E^\circ_{Cu^{2+}/Cu} - \frac{0.0591}{2} \log \frac{1}{[Cu^{2+}]}$$

$$= 0.34 - \frac{0.0591 \times 19}{2}$$

$$= -0.22 \text{ V}$$

4. Determination of a pH of a solution

Using a suitable reference half-cell, pH of the unknown solution can be determined.

(i) $Pt(H_2) \mid H^+(pH = x) \| Cl^-(1\ M) \mid \underset{\text{Calomel}}{Hg_2Cl_2, Hg}$

LHS half- cell, $H_2(g) \longrightarrow 2H^+ + 2e^-$; $E^\circ_{ox} = 0.00$ V

RHS half-cell, $Hg_2Cl_2(s) + 2e^- \longrightarrow 2Hg(l) + 2Cl^-$; $E^\circ_{red} = 0.2676$ V

Net, $H_2(g) + Hg_2Cl_2(s) \longrightarrow 2H^+(aq) + 2Hg(l) + 2Cl^-(aq)$; $E^\circ_{cell} = 0.2676$ V

$Q = [Cl^-]^2 [H^+]^2 = [H^+]^2$ (since, $[Cl^-] = 1$ M)

$$E_{cell} = E^\circ_{cell} - \frac{0.0591}{2} \log [H^+]^2$$

$$= E^\circ_{cell} + 0.0591 \text{ pH}$$

$\therefore$ $$\text{pH} = \frac{E_{cell} - E^\circ_{cell}}{0.0591}$$

In general, $$\text{pH} = \frac{E_{cell} - [E^\circ_{reference} + E^\circ_{SHE}]}{0.0591}$$

$\Rightarrow$ $$\text{pH} = \frac{E_{cell} - E^\circ_{reference}}{0.0591}$$

In this case reference half-cell is **calomel electrode**.

(ii) Instead of SHE, quinhydrone electrode can be used for quinhydrone electrode. $Q = [H^+]^2$,

$$E_{quinhydrone}(\text{oxidation}) = E^\circ_{quinhydrone}(\text{oxidation}) - \frac{0.0591}{2} \log [H^+]^2$$

$$E_{quinhydrone} = E^\circ_{quinhydrone} + 0.0591 \text{ pH}$$

Thus, pH can be evaluated.

$[E^\circ_{quinhydrone}(\text{oxidation}) = -0.6996 \text{ V}]$

JEE Alert

The quinhydrone electrode cannot be used for solutions of pH more than 8. It ionises appreciably and gets oxidised.

Solved Booster 3.9

The reversible reduction potential of pure water is − 0.413 V under 1.00 atm H_2 pressure. If the reduction is considered to be $2H^+ + 2e^- \longrightarrow H_2$. The pH of pure water is _____ (Nearest integer)

Solution (7)

$$2H^+ + 2e^- \longrightarrow H_2; \quad Q = \frac{1}{[H^+]^2}$$

$$E = E^\circ_{SHE} - \frac{0.0591}{2}\log\frac{1}{[H^+]^2}$$

$$\Rightarrow -0.413 = 0 + \frac{0.0591}{2}\log[H^+]^2$$

$$0.413 = -0.0591\log[H^+],$$

[since $-\log[H^+] = pH$] = 0.0591 pH

$$\therefore \quad pH = \frac{0.413}{0.0591} \approx 7$$

Concentration Cells

A concentration cell is a type of electrochemical cell in which both electrodes are made of the same material but are immersed in solutions of different concentrations of the same electrolyte. The electrochemical reaction in a concentration cell is driven by the difference in concentration of ions in the two half-cells, causing a flow of electrons from the electrode in the more concentrated solution to the electrode in the more dilute solution.

Characteristics of a Concentration Cell

- Both electrodes are identical in material.
- The electrolyte solution in each half-cell is of the same type but at different concentrations.
- A potential difference (voltage) arises due to the concentration gradient, and the cell generates an electric current.
- The side with the higher concentration of ions acts as the anode (where oxidation occurs).
- The side with the lower concentration of ions acts as the cathode (where reduction occurs).
- E° is the standard electrode potential (which is 0 for concentration cells).

Types of Concentration Cells

(i) **Concentration cell in which electrode is reversible with respect to cation**

(a) $Zn | Zn^{2+}(C_1) || Zn^{2+}(C_2) | Zn$

Half-cell

At LHS $Zn \longrightarrow Zn^{2+}(C_1) + 2e^-$; $E^\circ_L = 0.76$ V

At RHS $Zn^{2+}(C_2) + 2e^- \longrightarrow Zn$; $E^\circ_R = -0.76$ V

Net $Zn^{2+}(C_2) \longrightarrow Zn^{2+}(C_1)$ $E^\circ_{cell} = 0.00$ V

$$Q = \frac{[Zn^{2+}]_L}{[Zn^{2+}]_R} = \frac{C_1}{C_2}$$

$$E_{cell} = E^\circ_{cell} - \frac{0.0591}{2}\log\frac{C_1}{C_2}$$

$$\Rightarrow E_{cell} = \frac{0.0591}{2}\log\frac{C_2}{C_1}$$

Cell-reaction is spontaneous in forward direction if

$[Zn^{2+}]_{RHS}, (C_2) > [Zn^{2+}]_{LHS}, (C_1)$

(b) $Pt(H_2) | HCl\,(C_1) || HCl\,(C_2) | Pt\,(H_2)$
 1 atm 1 atm

at LHS : $\frac{1}{2}H_2(g) \longrightarrow H^+(C_1) + e^-$; $E^\circ_L = 0.00$ V

at RHS : $H^+(C_2) + e^- \longrightarrow \frac{1}{2}H_2$; $E^\circ_R = 0.00$ V

$H^+(C_2) \longrightarrow H^+(C_1)$ $E^\circ_{cell} = 0.00$ V

$$E_{cell} = E^\circ_{cell} - \frac{0.0591}{1}\log\frac{C_1}{C_2}$$

$$= 0.0591\log\frac{C_2}{C_1}$$

cell reaction is spontaneous in forward reaction if $C_2 > C_1$

(ii) **Concentration cell in which electrode is reversible with respect to anion**

$Pt\,(Cl_2) | Cl^-(C_1) || Cl^-(C_2) | Pt\,(Cl_2)$
1 atm 1 atm

at LHS : $Cl^-(C_1) \longrightarrow \frac{1}{2}Cl_2(g) + e^-$

at RHS : $\frac{1}{2}Cl_2(g) + e^- \longrightarrow Cl^-(C_2)$

$Cl^-(C_1) \longrightarrow Cl^-(C_2)$; $E^\circ_{cell} = 0.00$V

$$E_{cell} = \frac{0.0591}{1}\log\frac{C_1}{C_2}$$

For such cases, cell reaction is spontaneous in forward reaction if $C_1 > C_2$.

(iii) **Concentration cell having electrodes at different concentration dipped into same electrolyte**

$Pt(H_2) | HCl | Pt(H_2)$
at p_1 1 M at p_2

Two half-cells are joined by two salt-bridges, since they have common electrolyte.

LHS half-cell $H_2(p_1) \longrightarrow \underset{1\,M}{2H^+} + 2e^-$

RHS half-cell $\underset{1\,M}{2H^+} + 2e^- \longrightarrow H_2(p_2)$

Net $H_2(p_1) \longrightarrow H_2(p_2)$; $E^\circ_{cell} = 0.00$

$$E_{cell} = E^{\circ}_{cell} - \frac{0.0591}{2} \log \frac{p_2}{p_1}$$

Cell reaction is spontaneous in forward direction if $p_1(\text{LHS}) > p_2(\text{RHS})$.

The value of E_{cell} for concentration cells is quite small. When current is drawn from the cell, the cell potential decreases as the reaction proceeds. When the concentrations are the same in both half-cells, then the reaction comes to equilibrium. At this stage

$$\Delta G = 0 \quad \text{and} \quad E_{cell} = 0$$

The principle underlying concentration cells is important in cases where solutions of different electrolytes with different concentration are separated by a porous membrane. If one of the ions-say the positive ion can pass through the membrane but others cannot, the passage of ions will occur to equalise the concentrations. This leads to an excess of these ions on one side of the membrane. Thus, a potential difference is developed across the membrane which slows down and stops the movement of ions. This is called **Nernst potential** (also the **membrane potential**).

This type of potential is found in biological cells where the concentration of K^+, Na^+, Cl^- and other ions are different inside the cell compared with outside.

$$E = \frac{2.303\,RT}{nF} \log \frac{[M^+]_{outside}}{[M^+]_{inside}}$$

Solved Booster 3.10

A certain electrode has a reduction potential of 0.140 V, when measured against a standard calomel electrode. Its potential versus a SHE is ($E^{\circ}_{calomel}$(oxidation) = – 0.244 V)

(a) –0.384 V

(b) 0.244 V

(c) 0.140 V

(d) 0.384 V

Solution *(d)*

$$M^{n+} + ne^- \longrightarrow M, \qquad E^{\circ} = x$$

$$2Hg + 2Cl^- \longrightarrow Hg_2Cl_2 + 2e^-, \qquad E^{\circ} = -0.244\ V$$

$$E^{\circ}_{M^{n+}/M} + E^{\circ}_{cal} = 0.140\ V$$

$$E^{\circ}_{M^{n+}/M} - 0.244\ V = 0.140\ V$$

$$\therefore \quad E^{\circ}_{M^{n+}/M} = 0.140 + 0.244$$

$$= 0.384\ V$$

Since, $E^{\circ}_{SHE} = 0.00\ V$

$$\therefore \quad E^{\circ}_{cell}\ (\text{with respect to SHE}) = E^{\circ}_{SHE} + E^{\circ}_{M^{n+}/M}$$

$$= 0.00 + 0.384$$

$$= 0.384\ V$$

Elemental Practice 8.3

Type I MCQs with Only One Correct Option

1. At pH = 10, the reduction potential of a hydrogen electrode will be
(a) – 0.50 V (b) – 0.59 V (c) 0.059 V (d) – 0.059 V

2. Given below are two statements.
Statement I According to the Nernst equation EMF of a daniel cell = $E^\circ_{cell} + \frac{0.059}{2} \log \frac{[Cu^{2+}]}{[Zn^{2+}]}$.
Statement II EMF of cell will increase on increasing Cu^{2+} ion concentration.
(a) Both Statement I and Statement II are correct.
(b) Both Statement I and Statement II are incorrect.
(c) Statement I is correct and Statement II is incorrect.
(d) Statement I is incorrect and Statement II is correct.

3. Given below are two statements.
Statement I Electrode potential of any electrode will change of changing any of its intensive properties.
Statement II The cell potential becomes half if the a daniel cell reaction is divided by 2 throughout.
(a) Both Statement I and Statement II are correct.
(b) Both Statement I and Statement II are incorrect.
(c) Statement I is correct and Statement II is incorrect.
(d) Statement I is incorrect and Statement II is correct.

4. Given below are two statements, one is labelled Assertion and other is labelled as Reason.
Assertion In half reaction, if coefficients change, the number of electrons, get change to cancel effect of change in coefficient.
Reason E° values do not depend on the coefficient in the chemical equation.
(a) Assertion and Reason both are correct and Reason is correct explanation of Assertion.
(b) Assertion and Reason both are correct but Reason is not correct explanation of Assertion.
(c) Assertion is correct but Reason is incorrect.
(d) Assertion is incorrect but reason is correct.

5. For given latimer diagram.
Acid Medium
$$Fe \xrightarrow{E^\circ_{Fe|Fe^{2+}} = 0.44\ V} Fe^{2+} \xrightarrow{E^\circ_{Fe^{2+}|Fe^{3+}} = -0.77\ V} Fe^{3+}$$
Alkaline Medium
$$Fe \xrightarrow{E^\circ_{Fe|Fe^{2+}} = +0.88\ V} Fe^{2+} \xrightarrow{E^\circ_{Fe^{2+}|Fe^{3+}} = 0.56\ V} Fe^{3+}$$
A. In acid medium, positive value of $E^\circ_{Fe|Fe^{2+}}$ indicate iron do not dissolve in acid medium.
B. In acid medium positive value of $E^\circ_{Fe|Fe^{2+}}$ indicate iron dissolve to form Fe^{2+} ion.
C. $E^\circ_{Fe^{2+}|Fe^{3+}}$ negative, hence + 2 state is less stable than + 3 in acid medium.
D. Negative $E^\circ_{Fe^{2+}|Fe^{3+}}$ indicates + 2 state is more stable + 3 in acid medium.
Choose pair of correct statements.
(a) Both B and D are correct.
(b) Both A and C are correct.
(c) A and D are correct.
(d) C and B are correct.

6. By how much would the oxidising power of $Cr_2O_7^{2-}/Cr^{3+}$ couple change if the H^+ ions concentration is decreased 100 times at 25° C?
(a) increase by 275 mV (b) decreases by 275 mV
(c) increase by 27 mV (d) decrease by 27 mV

7. Given below are two statements.
Statement I Negative E°_{value} signifies that cell will not function in the manner it is represented.
Statement II Solution of $CuSO_4$ can be stored in a zinc container.
(a) Both Statements I and Statement II are true.
(b) Both Statements I and Statement II are false.
(c) Statement I is true; Statement II is false.
(d) Statement I is false; Statement II is true.

8. Given below are two reactions one is labelled as Assertion (A) and the other is labelled as Reason (R).
Assertion (A) In the given electrochemical cell $Pt(l)|Hg^{2+}/Hg_2^{2+}(a=1)||Ce^{4+}/Ce^{3+}(a=1)|Pt(2)$ current in the circuit will flow from Pt(2) cathode to Pt(1) anode.
Reason (R) Current in electrochemical cell flows from cathode to anode.
(a) Both Assertion and Reason are true and Reason is correct explanation.
(b) Both Assertion and Reason are true but Reason is not correct explanation.
(c) Assertion is true but Reason is false.
(d) Assertion is false but Reason is true.

9. Match the List-I and List-II.

List-I (Type of half-cell)		List-II (Half-cell reaction)
A. Hg—$HgSO_4$ electrode	p.	$Hg_2Cl_2 + 2e^- \rightleftharpoons 2Hg(l) + 2Cl^-(aq)$
B. Calomel electrode	q.	$AgCl_{(s)} + e^- \rightleftharpoons Ag + Cl^-(aq)$
C. Metal insoluble salt anion electrode	r.	$Ag^+(aq) + e^- \rightleftharpoons Ag(s)$
D. Metal-metal ion electrode	s.	$HgSO_4(s) + 2e^- \rightleftharpoons Hg(l) + SO_4^{2-}(aq)$

(a) A - s, B - p, C - q, D - r (b) A - p, B - q, C - s, D - r

10. Which of the following statements is incorrect about standard hydrogen electrode?
(a) It contains a metallic conductor which does not absorb hydrogen
(b) The hydrogen ion concentration is 1 M
(c) Temperature is 25°C
(d) Pressure of hydrogen is 1 atmosphere

11. Given below are two statements.

Statement I The reduction potential of an electrode is exactly equal in magnitude but opposite in sign to its oxidation potential.

Statement II In redox electrode, electrode reaction in standard condition is

Reduction : $MnO_4^- + 8H^+ + 5e^- \longrightarrow Mn^{2+} + 4H_2O$

(a) Both statement I and II are true.
(b) Both statement I and II are false.
(c) Statement I is false and II is true.
(d) Statement I is true and II is false.

12. For the following standard reduction potentials.

$E^\circ_{K^+/K} = -2.93$ V, $E^\circ_{Ag^+/Ag} = +0.80$ V, $E^\circ_{Hg^{2+}/Hg} = 0.79$ V,

$E^\circ_{Mg^{2+}/Mg} = -2.37$ V, $E^\circ_{Cr^{3+}/Cr} = -0.74$ V

The correct decreasing order of reducing power is
(a) K > Mg > Cr > Hg > Ag (b) Ag > Hg > Cr > Mg > K
(c) Mg > K > Cr > Hg > Ag (d) Cr > Hg > K > Mg > Ag

13. Among the following couples which will have highest value of emf?
(a) $Zn|Zn^{2+}||Ag^+|Ag$ (b) $Cu|Cu^{2+}||Ag^+|Ag$
(c) $Zn|Zn^{2+}||Cu^{2+}|Cu$ (d) $Mg|Mg^{2+}||Ag^+|Ag$

14. Calculate the emf of the cell $Zn|Zn^{2+}_{(2M)}||Ag^+_{(2M)}|Ag$.

Given emf E°

$Ag|Ag^+(2M)||Cu^{2+}(2M)|Cu$; $E^\circ = -0.46$ V

$Zn|Zn^{2+}(2M)||Cu^{2+}(2M)|Cu$; $E^\circ = +1.10$ V

(a) + 1.56 V (b) – 1.56 V (c) – 1.46 V (d) + 1.46 V

15. Arrange the following anions in increasing order of discharge at anode.
(a) $SO_4^{2-}, Cl^-, Br^-, NO_3^-$ (b) $F^-, Cl^-, OH^-, SO_4^{2-}$
(c) $SO_4^{2-}, NO_3^-, OH^-, Cl^-$ (d) I^-, Br^-, OH^-, NO_3^-

Type II 》 MCQs with One or More than One Correct Option

16. The Nernst, equation is given by:

$$E_{cell} = E^\circ_{cell} - \frac{RT}{nF}\ln Q$$

Where Q is the reaction quotient, R is gas constant and T is the temperature.

Which of the following statements are correct regarding Nernst equation?
(a) A cell potential decreases with an increase in temperature if the reaction is exothermic.
(b) The Nernst equation gives a positive value for the EMF at non-standard conditions.
(c) If $Q = 1$, the cell potential equals to the standard cell potential at any temperature.
(d) The Nernst equation shows that the cell potential decreases as the concentration of product increases and reactant decreases.

17. For a galvanic cell represented as:

$Fe(s)|Fe^{2+}(0.001\ M)||Ag^+(0.01\ M)|Ag(s)$.

The standard reduction potentials are:

$$E^\circ_{Fe^{2+}/Fe} = -0.44\ V;\ E^\circ_{Ag^+/Ag} = +0.80\ V$$

Select the correct statements.
(a) The standard cell potential, $E^\circ_{cell} = 1.24$ V
(b) The cell potential will increase if concentration of Fe^{2+} ions increases.
(c) The cell potential will increase if concentration of Ag^+ ions increases.
(d) The cell will stop working, when $Q = K_{eq}$.

18. For a redox reaction with a standard cell potential $E^\circ = 1.10$ V at 298 K. Which of the following is true about the equilibrium constant K?
(a) ΔG° is negative.
(b) The equilibrium constant $K > 1$
(c) K is temperature dependent
(d) At equilibrium, cell potential is zero
(e) The reaction is non spontaneous

19. Select the correct statements that are true for an electrolyte concentration cell.
(a) The electrolyte diffuses from lower concentration to higher concentration solutions.
(b) The electrode material and the solution in both half cells are composed of the different substances.
(c) The cell potential decreases as the concentration gradient decreases.
(d) Only the concentration of solution of the same substances is different in these cells.

20. Consider the equilibrium between a metal (M), its ions M^{n+} and the sparingly soluble salt MX (metal with anions). Choose the correct statements.
(a) The solubility product K_{sp} of the salt MX can be used to calculate $E^\circ_{MX|M}$.
(b) The standard electrode potential of the metal-salt electrode is more negative if the solubility of the salt MX is very low.
(c) The metal ion concentration is lower in the metal-metal ion electrode compared to the sparingly soluble salt electrode at standard conditions.
(d) Both $E^\circ_{MX|M}$ are influenced by temperature.

21. Identify the incorrect statement for the electrochemical cell?
(a) If for an electrode, the standard reduction potential is negative then it is a stronger oxidising agent.
(b) Negative electrode is the one where reduction occurs.
(c) In voltaic cell electron flow from cathode to anode.
(d) Anode is negative electrode and cathode is positive electrode in electrolytic cell.

Type III 》 Numerical/Integer Answer Type Questions

22. If the equilibrium $A^{2+}(aq) + A(s) \longrightarrow 2A^{+}(aq)$ established at 25°C corresponds to $\frac{[A^{2+}]}{[A^{+}]^2} = 4.040 \times 10^8$. Then the value of E°_{A/A^+} will be

    (Given $E^\circ_{A^{2+}/A} = 0.33$)

23. The equilibrium constant for the reaction $Zn(s) + Cu^{2+}(aq) \rightleftharpoons Zn^{2+}(aq) + Cu(s)$ is 1×10^{20} at 298 K. The magnitude of standard electrode potential of Cu/Cu^{2+} if $E^\circ_{Zn^{2+}/Zn} = -0.76$ V is .... $\times 10^{-2}$ V (nearest integer)

    Given: $\frac{2.303\,RT}{F} = 0.059$ V

24. For the given reactions,

    $$Fe^{2+} + 2e^- \longrightarrow Fe$$
    $$Fe^{3+} + 3e^- \longrightarrow Fe$$

    The electrode potentials are; $E^\circ_{Fe^{2+}/Fe} = -0.440$ V and $E^\circ_{Fe^{3+}/Fe} = -0.036$ V. The magnitude of standard electrode potential for Fe^{3+}/Fe^{2+} i.e. $E^\circ_{Fe^{3+}/Fe^{2+}}$ is .... $\times 10^{-2}$ V (nearest integer)

25. EMF of the following cell at 298 K in volt is $x \times 10^{-2}$.
    $Cd\,|\,Cd^{2+}(0.2\text{ M})\,||\,Ag^{+}(0.02\text{ M})\,|\,Ag$. The value of x is ....

    Given $E^\circ_{Cd^{2+}|Cd} = -0.403$; $E^\circ_{Ag^{+}/Ag} = +0.80$ V;

    $\frac{2.303\,RT}{F} = 0.059$

26. Calculate the electrode potential for zinc electrode immersed in a 0.1 M solution of zinc sulphate at 25° C. The standard electrode potential of Zn^{2+}/Zn system is 0.76 V at 298 K.

27. Calculate standard potential of $Zn^{2+}\,|\,Zn$ electrode, for following cell

    $Pt\,|\,Zn\,|\,Zn^{2+}\,(0.0018\text{ mol}^{-1}\text{L})\,||\,Ag^{+}(0.01\text{ mol}^{-1}\text{L})\,|\,Ag$

    The emf of this cell is found to be 0.54 volt. Calculate the standard potential of the half reaction

    $Zn^{2+} + 2e^- \longrightarrow Zn$, $E^\circ_{Ag^{+}/Ag} = 0.80$ volt.

28. Among following how many cations will not deposit at cathode before H^+ ion

    $K^+, Ca^{2+}, Na^+, Mg^{2+}, Cu^{2+}, Ag^+, Al^{3+}, Au^+, Fe^{2+}$

Elemental Practice 8.3 | Chapter 8

Connect with Answers

1. (b)	2. (a)	3. (c)	4. (a)	5. (a)	6. (b)
7. (c)	8. (a)	9. (a)	10. (a)	11. (a)	12. (a)
13. (d)	14. (a)	15. (c)	16. (a,d)	17. (a,c,d)	18. (a,b,c,d)
19. (c,d)	20. (a,b,d)	21. (a,b,c,d)	22. (–0.575)	23. (17)	24. (77)
25. (112)	26. (0.730)	27. (0.223)	28. (6)		

Element 4 Batteries, Fuel Cell and Corrosion

Batteries

By far the most important application of galvanic cells is their use as **batteries**. In multicell batteries, such as those in automobiles, the individual galvanic cells are linked in series, with the anode of each cell connected to the cathode of the adjacent cell and the voltage provided by the battery is the sum of the individual cell voltages.

Primary Batteries (Dry cell)

In such type of batteries, the reaction occurs only once and after use over a period, they become dead and cannot be reused again.

1. Leclanche Cell

It is a commercial dry cell containing a graphite (carbon) cathode in a zinc container (anode).

Anode Zinc metal acts as anode

Cathode Inert graphite rod surrounded by a paste of MnO_2 and carbon black.

Electrolyte moist paste of NH_4Cl and $ZnCl_2$.

Reactions

At anode, $Zn(s) \longrightarrow Zn^{2+}(aq) + 2e^-$

At cathode, $MnO_2(s) + NH_4^+(aq) + e^- \longrightarrow MnO(OH) + NH_3(g)$

2. Alkaline Dry Cell

This cell is a modified version of the Leclanche cell in which the acidic electrolyte (NH_4Cl) is replaced by an alkaline (basic) electrolyte (NaOH or KOH). It involves reactions:-

At anode, $Zn(s) + 2OH^-(aq) \longrightarrow ZnO(s) + H_2O(l) + 2e^-$

At cathode, $2MnO_2(s) + H_2O(l) + 2e^- \longrightarrow Mn_2O_3(s) + 2OH^-(aq)$

Net $Zn(s) + 2MnO_2(s) \longrightarrow ZnO(s) + Mn_2O_3(s)$

Advantages

- Cell potential is independent of OH^- concentration.
- Corrosion in alkaline medium takes place slowly as compared to in acidic medium hence, alkaline batteries have longer life.
- Alkaline cell also produces higher power and more stable current and voltage because of more efficient ion transport in the alkaline electrolyte.

3. Mercury Battery

It has anode made of zinc-mercury amalgam and cathode is a paste of HgO and carbon. The electrolyte is a paste of KOH and ZnO. Reactions are as follows

Anode $Zn(s) + 2OH^-(aq) \longrightarrow ZnO(s) + H_2O(l) + 2e^-$

Cathode $HgO(s) + H_2O(l) + 2e^- \longrightarrow Hg(l) + 2OH^-(aq)$

Net $Zn(s) + HgO(s) \longrightarrow ZnO(s) + Hg(l)$

Net reaction does not involve any ion hence, cell potential is independent of ion (OH^-) concentration.

Secondary Batteries

These are the cells which can be recharged and so can be reused.

1. Lead Storage Batteries

A typical 12 V battery consists of six cells connected in series, each cell providing a potential of about 2 V. The anode, a series of lead grids packed with spongy lead, and the cathode, a second series of lead grids packed with lead dioxide, dip into the electrolyte (which is an aqueous solution of H_2SO_4, 38% by weight).

When the cell is discharging (providing current) the reactions are :

Anode, $Pb(s) + H_2SO_4(aq) \longrightarrow PbSO_4(s) + 2e^- + 2H^+$, $E° = 0.296$ V

Cathode, $PbO_2(s) + 4H^+(aq) + SO_4^{2-}(aq) + 2e^- \longrightarrow PbSO_4(s) + 2H_2O(l)$, $E° = 1.628$ V

Overall $Pb(s) + PbO_2(s) + 2H_2SO_4(aq) \longrightarrow 2PbSO_4(s) + 2H_2O(l)$, $E° = 1.924$ V

- There is no need for the cell to have separate anode and cathode compartments because the oxidising and reducing agents are both solids (PbO_2 and Pb) that are kept from coming in contact by the presence of insulating spaces between the grids.

2. Nickel-cadmium Batteries

Nickel-cadmium or "ni-cad" batteries are rechargeable storage batteries. It has

Anode Cadmium metal.

Cathode Nickel (III) compound like NiO(OH) supported on nickel.

Reactions during discharging

At anode, $Cd(s) + 2OH^-(aq) \longrightarrow CdO(s) + H_2O(l) + 2e^-$

At cathode, $Ni(OH)_3(s) + e^- \longrightarrow Ni(OH)_2(s) + OH^-(aq)$

$$Cd(s) + 2Ni(OH)_3(s) \longrightarrow CdO(s) + H_2O_2(l) + 2Ni(OH)_2(s)$$

When charging takes place, reactions are reversed.

3. Lithium Batteries

Rechargeable lithium batteries are replacing other common batteries because of their light weight and high voltage (about 3.0 V). It has

Anode, Lithium metal

Cathode, Metal oxide or metal sulphide that can incorporate Li^+ ions (MnO_2 or MnS).

Electrolyte $LiClO_4$ in organic solvent (solid-state polymer electrolytes that can transport Li^+ ions, can also be used)

Reactions

At anode, $Li(s) \longrightarrow Li^+ + e^-$

At cathode $MnO_2(s) + Li^+ + e^- \longrightarrow LiMnO_2(s)$

Concept Visualizer

Nickel-Cadmium Batteries can be visualised through the given diagram.

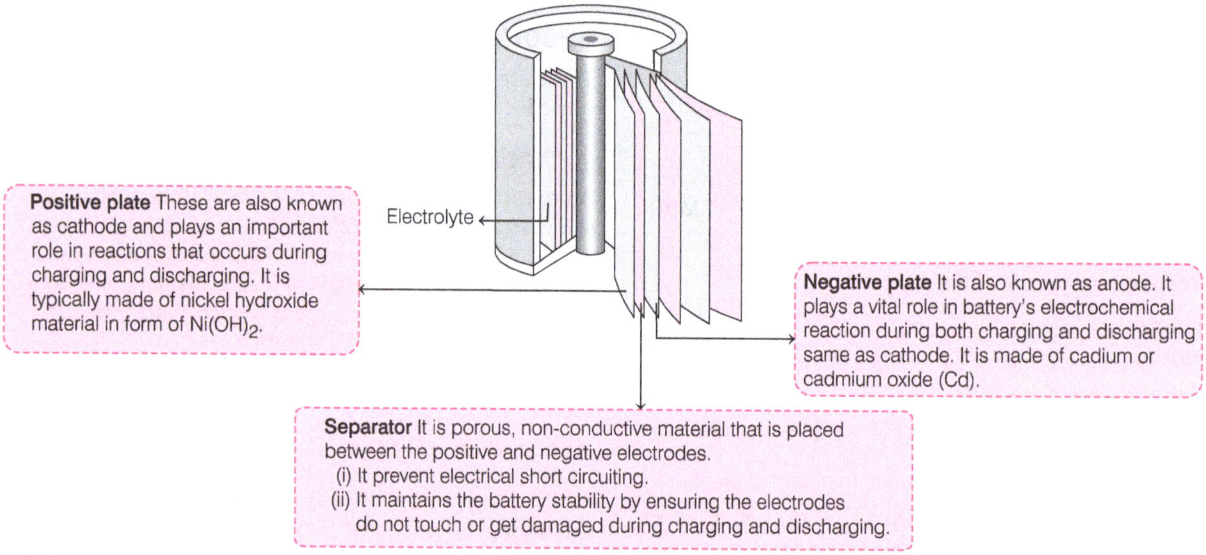

Fuel Cells

A fuel cell is a **galvanic cell** in which one of the reactants is a traditional fuel such as CH_4 or H_2 or CO.

Reactants are not contained within the cell but instead, are continuously supplied from an external reservoir.

Conventional conversion of chemical energy of fuels into electrical energy is carried out by burning the fuel, using the heat energy to raise steam which is then used for spinning the turbines connected with electric generators. The efficiency of this process, varies from 20 to 40 per cent. Fuel cells convert about 75 per cent of the available chemical energy into electrical energy.

- Electrodes are made of porous carbon impregnated with metallic catalysts (Pt, Ag or metal oxide), electrolyte is hot aqueous KOH.
- The fuel (gaseous H_2) and the oxidising agent (gaseous O_2) do not react directly but instead of flow into separate cell compartments where H_2 is oxidised at the anode and O_2 is reduced at the cathode.

Anode, $2H_2 \longrightarrow 4H^+ + 4e^-$

$$4H^+ + 4OH^- \rightleftharpoons 4H_2O$$

$$2H_2(g) + 4OH^-(aq) \longrightarrow 4H_2O(l) + 4e^-$$

Cathode $O_2(g) + 2H_2O(l) + 4e^- \longrightarrow 4OH^-(aq)$

Overall $2H_2(g) + O_2(g) \longrightarrow 2H_2O(l)$

Hydrogen-oxygen fuel cell is used as a source of electric power in space vehicles. Such fuel cells are also being investigated for automobiles. These electrochemical engine have greater efficiency and eliminate hazardous air pollutants such as CO, NO_x, SO_2, etc. The emf of the cell is found to be 1.0 V.

Corrosion

It is the oxidative deterioration of a metal, such as conversion of iron to rust $[Fe_2O_3 \cdot xH_2O]$, the tarnishing of silver (due to formation of Ag_2O), development of a green coating on copper and bronze.

Corrosion is basically an electrochemical phenomenon. A metal is oxidised by loss of electrons to oxygen, and forms metal oxide. Corrosion of iron (rusting) occurs in presence of water and oxygen (air).

Mechanism

The theory of corrosion can be explained by taking an example of rusting of iron.

At one spot of an iron object, oxidation occurs and this is thus the anode.

Anode $Fe(s) \longrightarrow Fe^{2+}(aq) + 2e^-, \quad E^\circ = 0.44\ V$

Electrons from the anode move through the metal and go another spot on the metal and reduce O_2 in presence of H^+ ions. (CO_2 gets dissolved in water forming H_2CO_3 and which releases H^+ ions, $CO_2 + H_2O \longrightarrow H_2CO_3, (H^+ + HCO_3^-)$). This spot where reduction takes place is the cathode.

Cathode: $O_2(g) + 4H^+(aq) + 4e^- \longrightarrow 2H_2O(l),$

$$E^\circ = 1.23\ V$$

Net: $2Fe(s) + O_2(g) + 4H^+(aq) \longrightarrow 2Fe^{2+}(aq) + 2H_2O(l),$

$$E^\circ_{cell} = 1.67\ V$$

Fe^{2+} ions move through water on the surface of the iron object. If water present is saline, it will help more in carrying the current in the electrochemical cell formed.

$$O_2(g) + 2H_2O(l) + 4e^- \longrightarrow 4OH^-; E^\circ = 0.40\ V$$

Fe^{2+} ions are further oxidised by atmospheric O_2 to Fe^{3+} (as Fe_2O_3) and comes out as rust in the form of a hydrated iron (III) oxide represented as $Fe_2O_3 \cdot xH_2O$.

$$4Fe^{2+}(aq) + O_2(g) + 4H_2O(l) \longrightarrow 2Fe_2O_3(s) + 8H^+$$

H^+ ions produced in this reaction help further in rusting .

$$Fe + 2H^+ \longrightarrow Fe^{2+} + H_2$$

Impurities present in iron also enhance rusting by setting a number of miniature cells.

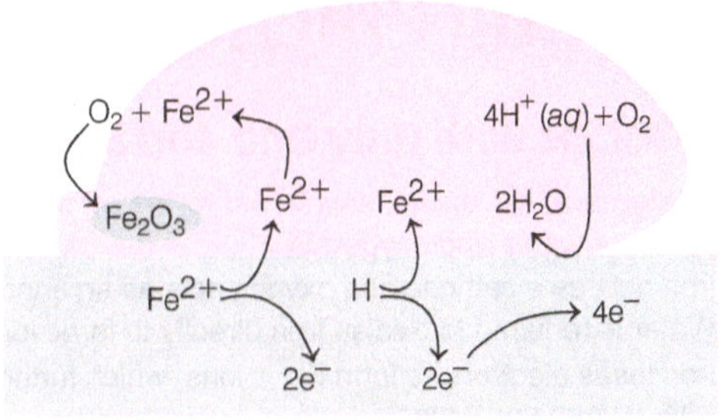

Figure Mechanism of rusting

- $Fe(s) \longrightarrow Fe^{2+}(aq) + 2e^-$ (Oxidation)
- $O_2(g) + 4H^+(aq) + 4e^- \longrightarrow 2H_2O(aq)$ (Reduction)
- $2Fe^{2+}(aq) + 2H_2O(l) + \frac{1}{2}O_2(g) \longrightarrow Fe_2O_3(s) + 4H^+(aq)$ (Atmospheric oxidation)

Prevention of Corrosion

(i) Corrosion of iron can be prevented or at least minimised by shielding the metal surface from oxygen and moisture.

(ii) A coat of point is effective for a while, but rust begins to form as soon as the paint is scratched.

(iii) Metals such as Cr, Sn, or Zn afford a more durable surface coating for Fe. The steel used in making automobiles is coated by dipping into a bath of molten zinc, a process known as galvanising. Since,

$$E^\circ_{Fe^{2+}/Fe} = -0.44\ V, \quad E^\circ_{Zn^{2+}/Zn} = -0.76\ V$$

zinc is oxidised more readily than iron, and it, in turn, reduces Fe^{2+} (formed during oxidation rusting) to Fe.

$$Fe^{2+} + Zn \longrightarrow Zn^{2+} + Fe, \quad E^\circ_{cell} = 1.20\ V$$

This reaction is spontaneous in forward side hence, Zn can reduce Fe^{2+} to Fe. As long as the zinc and iron are in contact, the zinc protects the iron from oxidation even if the zinc layer becomes scratched.

JEE Quicker

Statement "Coating of iron, surface by tin prevents rusting even if the tin coating is peeling off" is incorrect. *JEE Main 2024*

Tin is less reactive than iron so it prevents rusting when the tin coating is intact. However when the coating is scratched iron is exposed to the environment and undergo oxidation as it is more reactive than iron.

Elemental Practice 8.4

Type I MCQs with Only One Correct Option

1. The statement that explains why rust forms on iron in the presence of water and oxygen is
   (a) Iron acts as a cathode and oxygen acts as an anode.
   (b) Water is required to oxidise iron directly to ferric ions.
   (c) Iron loses electrons to form Fe^{2+} ions, which further react with oxygen and water.
   (d) Oxygen reacts directly with iron to form FeO.

2. Which of the following is the primary advantage of lithium ion batteries over nickel-cadmium batteries?
   (a) Lower cost
   (b) Higher weight
   (c) Higher energy density and less memory effect
   (d) Greater environmental impact

3. Match the following reactions in Column A with the type of batteries in Column B

	Column A		Column B
I.	$MnO_2 + NH_4^+ + e^- \longrightarrow MnO(OH) + NH_3$	A.	Anodic reaction in mercury cell
II.	$Zn(Hg) + 2OH^- \longrightarrow ZnO(s) + H_2O + 2e$	B.	Cathodic reaction in lead storage battery
III.	$PbO_2(s) + SO_4^{2-}(aq) + 4H^+(aq) + 2e^- \longrightarrow 2PbSO_4(s) + 2H_2O(l)$	C.	Cathodic reaction in leclanche cell
IV.	$Pb(s) + SO_4^{2-}(aq) \longrightarrow PbSO_4(s) + 2e^-$	D.	Anodic reaction in lead storage battery

   Choose the correct answer from the options given below :
   (a) I-C, II-A, III-B, IV-D (b) I-A, II-B, III-D, IV-C
   (c) I-C, II-A, III-D, IV-B (d) I-B, II-D, III-A, IV-C

4. Out of the following, that does not contribute to the prevention of corrosion in metals is
   (a) painting the metal surface
   (b) using sacrificial anodes
   (c) applying a strong acid to the metal surface
   (d) galvanising the metal surface

5. Given below are two statements one is labelled as Assertion (A) and the other is labelled as Reason (R).
   Assertion (A) Electrolytic refining is used to purify metals like copper and zinc.
   Reason (R) In electrolytic refining, the pure metal is used as the anode and the impure metal as the cathode.
   In the light of the above statements, choose the correct answer from the options given below.
   (a) Both (A) and (R) are true and (R) is the correct explanation of (A).
   (b) Both (A) and (R) are true but (R) is not the correct explanation of (A).
   (c) (A) is true but (R) is false.
   (d) (A) is false but (R) is true.

6. Select the electrolyte that is used in the Mercury cell.
   (a) MnO_2 + C
   (b) 38% H_2SO_4
   (c) KOH solution
   (d) ZnO + KOH(moist)

7. Consider the following statements.
   Statement I The rate of corrosion of metals can be increased by increasing the temperature of the environment.
   Statement II Corrosion is primarily an electrochemical process that involves the transfer of electrons.
   In the light of above statements, choose the correct answer from the options given below.
   (a) Both Statement I and Statement II are false.
   (b) Statement I is true but Statement II is false.
   (c) Statement I is false but Statement II is true.
   (d) Both Statement I and Statement II are true.

8. What is the purpose of adding a descaling agent to an electrolytic cell?
   (a) To remove calcium and magnesium impurities from the electrodes.
   (b) To minimize the resistance of the solution.
   (c) To increase the efficiency of the cell.
   (d) To prevent the formation of gas bubbles.

9. During the electrolytic refining of copper, which metal is commonly recovered as anode sludge?
   (a) Nickel (b) Lead
   (c) Gold (d) Manganese

10. Which of the statements regarding the electrolysis of water are true?
    I. Electrolysis of water produces hydrogen gas at the anode.
    II. Hydrogen is produced at the cathode.
    III. This process requires a minimum voltage to overcome the electrolysis barrier.
    IV. Acidic conditions enhance the conductivity of water during electrolysis.
    V. The overall reaction is $2H_2O \longrightarrow 2H_2 + O_2$.
    Choose the appropriate answer from the given options.
    (a) I, II and III (b) I, II, III and V
    (c) II, III, IV and V (d) II, IV and V

11. Commonly used species as a sacrificial anode to prevent the corrosion of iron is
    (a) Al (b) Zn
    (c) Cu (d) Pb

12. Consider the following species involved.
    I. Sodium ions (Na^+) II. Chlorine gas (Cl_2)
    III. Hydrogen gas (H_2) IV. Sodium hydroxide (NaOH)
    V. Chloride ions (Cl^-)
    Choose the species that are obtained after electrolysis of NaCl(brine) solution.
    (a) I, II, III and V (b) II, III and IV
    (c) I, II, III and IV (d) II, III and V

13. The reaction that takes place at anode in Nickel-Metal Hydride (Ni*M*H) battery is
(a) $MH + OH^- \longrightarrow M + \frac{1}{2}H_2 + H_2O + e^-$
(b) $Ni(OH)_2 + 2e^- + 2H_2O \longrightarrow Ni + 2OH^-$
(c) $MH + Ni(OH)_2 \longrightarrow M + Ni(OH)_2 + H_2 + e^-$
(d) $M + Ni(OH)_2 + H_2 + e^- \longrightarrow MH + Ni(OH)_2$

14. Which of the following involves the reduction of copper?
(a) $Cu + \frac{1}{2}O_2 \longrightarrow CuO$ (b) $Cu^{2+} + 4I^- \longrightarrow 2CuI + I_2$
(c) $CuCl_2 + 2F^- \longrightarrow CuF_2 + Cl_2$ (d) $Cu + I_2 \longrightarrow CuI_2$

15. The solution that turn blue when placed in copper vessel is....
(a) $AgNO_3$ (b) KNO_3 (c) $ZnSO_4$ (d) NaCl

Type II 》 MCQs with One or More than One Correct Option

16. Which of the following statements are true regarding primary batteries?
(a) Designed to be used once and discarded.
(b) Recharged multiple times.
(c) Alkaline and zinc-carbon batteries are common examples.
(d) Operate based on reversible chemical reactions.

17. Choose the statements true regarding the electrochemical series and its relation to corrosion.
(a) Metals lower in the series are more reactive and prone to corrosion.
(b) Metals higher in the series can protect metals lower in the series when used as coatings.
(c) Metals in the same group can exhibit similar corrosion behavior.
(d) More noble metals such as Pt and Au are less resistant to corrosion.

18. Select the correct statements that are related to rust formation on an iron.
(a) Rust is primarily composed of $Fe_2O_3 \cdot nH_2O$
(b) This process requires both oxygen and water.
(c) Rusting can occur in the absence of moisture if oxygen is present.
(d) It is an exothermic reaction.

19. Which of the following reactions are involved in a hydrogen fuel cell?
(a) $2H_2 + O_2 \longrightarrow 2H_2O$
(b) $2H_2 + 4OH^- \longrightarrow 4H_2O + 4e^-$
(c) $O_2 + 2H_2O + 4e^- \longrightarrow 4OH^-$
(d) $H_2O \longrightarrow H_2 + \frac{1}{2}O_2$

20. Choose the applications of electrolysis used in industries.
(a) Electroplating of metals for corrosion resistance.
(b) Production of chlorine and NaOH from brine.
(c) Electrorefining of metals to obtain pure metals.
(d) Synthesis of hydrocarbons from CO_2.

21. In commercial electrolysis, the purpose of using an electrolyte with high conductivity is/are
(a) enhances ion mobility
(b) increases power consumption
(c) enhances the flow of current
(d) improves yield and purity

Type III 》 Numerical/Integer Answer Type Questions

22. The number of factors that accelerate the rate of corrosion are ......
(a) presence of electrolytes
(b) high temperature
(c) low humidity
(d) increased surface area of metal
(e) electrical conductivity.

23. The number of examples that represents the secondary batteries......
(a) Lead-acid battery (b) Nickel-cadmium (NiCd) battery
(c) Lithium-ion battery (d) Zinc-carbon battery
(e) Alkaline battery

24. The number of correct statements regarding the following reaction are......
$$2NiO(OH)(s) + 2H_2O(l) + Cd(s) \longrightarrow Ni(OH)_2(s) + Cd(OH)_2(s)$$
I. Nickel oxyhydroxide is reduced to nickel hydroxide.
II. Cadmium is oxidised to cadmium hydroxide.
III. Reaction is reversible.
IV. Reaction produces energy that can be used to power devices.
V. The discharge voltage of NiCd battery is approximately 1.2 V per cell.

25. The number of species that are not observed during the electrolysis of dilute H_2SO_4 are......
I. H_2 gas at cathode II. O_2 gas at anode
III. SO_4^{2-} at anode IV. H_2O at cathode
V. H_2O acts as a source

26. The number of primary methods to prevent corrosion of metal structures are ....
I. galvanisation II. cathodic protection
III. adding Cl^- ions IV. painting/coating
V. anodisation

Elemental Practice 8.4 | Chapter 8

Connect with **Answers**

1. (c)	**2.** (c)	**3.** (a)	**4.** (c)	**5.** (c)	**6.** (d)
7. (d)	**8.** (a)	**9.** (c)	**10.** (c)	**11.** (b)	**12.** (b)
13. (a)	**14.** (b)	**15.** (a)	**16.** (a,c)	**17.** (b,c)	**18.** (a,b,d)
19. (a,b,c)	**20.** (a,b,c)	**21.** (a,c,d)	**22.** (4)	**23.** (3)	**24.** (5)
25. (2)	**26.** (4)				

Advanced Exclusive Different Strokes

Problem based on species evolved at an electrode was asked in 2024. Such problems become complicated when overvoltage occurs in a cell. This conept is of crucial importance for upcoming JEE Advance.

In order to decide which species will be produced at an electrode we must understand the crucial difference between electrode potential and overvoltage.

The standard electrode potential is the standard EMF of the cell with respect to the standard hydrogen electrodes.

Overvoltage is the difference between the potential of an electrode at which gas evolution occurs and the theoretical reversible potential for the same solution. Overvoltage depends on

(a) Nature of electrode: Metals with low MP has high overvoltage.

(b) Surface area of electrode: greater the surface area, lesser is the overvoltage.

(c) Temperature: Increase in temperature will decrease the overvoltage.

Hydrogen overvoltage at a smooth Pt electrode = 0.09 V. Oxygen overvoltage at a smooth Pt electrode = 0.45 V

Total excess potential = 0.54 V

Reversible EMF of the H_2—O_2 cell = 1.2 V (Theoretical potential)

Observed decomposition potential of the H_2—O_2 cell = 1.7 V

Let us understand this with an example

- When the electrolyte contains only one cation and one anion like in molten NaCl, then Na^+ will get reduced at cathode while Cl^- will get oxidised at anode.
- Complications will crop up only when the electrolyte contains more than 1 cation and more than 1 anion in the solution like in aqueous NaCl (in aqueous solutions, there would always be a dilemma to decide which species will get reduced and which species will get oxidised) but luckily for us, this dilemma is resolvable.
- During production of NaOH and Cl_2 by electrolysis of aqueous NaCl solution, oxidation of OH^- should be preferred over Cl^- based on $E°$ values at Pt electrode. But in actual practice liberation of Cl_2 is preferred over evolution of O_2 because of high overvoltage associated with liberation of O_2 gas.

$E^\circ_{OH^-/O_2} = -0.413\text{ V}$ $E_{OH^-/O_2} = -0.826\text{ V}$ (Theoretically)

$$E_{OH^-/O_2} = (-0.826 - 0.6)\text{ V} = -1.426\text{ V (Observed)}$$

$$E^\circ_{Cl^-/Cl_2} = -1.36\text{ V}$$

- When observed oxidation potential of OH^- ions is compared against the oxidation potential of Cl^- ions, it is found that OP of Cl^- ions is greater than the OP of OH^- ions. Thus, oxidation of Cl^- occurs in preference to oxidation of OH^- ions liberating Cl_2. This is attributed to the overvoltage associated with the release of O_2 gas by the oxidation of OH^-ions.
- In practice, in case of *aq* NaCl, H_2O or H^+ gets reduced at cathode but it's Cl^- that gets oxidised at anode.

PRACTICE ELEMENT 01

Target JEE Main

Objective Type Questions

1. The standard reduction potential of $Fe^{2+} + 2e^- \longrightarrow Fe$ is -0.44 V and $Zn^{2+} + 2e^- \longrightarrow Zn$ is -0.76 V, which of the following statement is correct for the cell reaction?
   (a) The cell potential is 0.32 V and Fe is oxidised.
   (b) The cell potential is 1.20 V and Zn is oxidised.
   (c) The cell potential is 0.32 V and Zn is oxidised.
   (d) The cell potential is 1.20 V and Fe is oxidised.

2. If the standard electrode potential (E°) for the reaction $A + B^+ \longrightarrow A^+ + B$ is negative. What does this indicate about the feasibility of the reaction under standard conditions?
   (a) Reaction is spontaneous.
   (b) Reaction is non-spontaneous.
   (c) Reaction is at equilibrium.
   (d) Reaction proceeds in the presence of catalyst only.

3. Which of the following solutions is expressed as the highest equivalent conductance?
   (a) 0.1 M HCl (b) 0.01 M HCl
   (c) 0.001 M HCl (d) 0.0001 M HCl

4. Given below are two statements.
   Statement I Molar conductivity of strong electrolytes increases slowly with dilution and approaches a limiting value at infinite dilution.
   Statement II Strong electrolytes are completely dissociated in solution, even at higher concentration.
   In the light of the above statements choose the correct answer from the options given below.
   (a) Both Statement I and Statement II are correct.
   (b) Both Statement I and Statement II are incorrect.
   (c) Statement I is correct but Statement II is incorrect.
   (d) Statement I is incorrect but Statement II is correct.

5. A current of I amp was passed for t seconds through cells A, B and C connected in series. These contain respectively silver nitrate, mercuric nitrate and mercurous nitrate. At the cathode of the cell A, 0.378 g of Ag was deposited. The weight of mercury deposited in the cathode of B and C are
   (a) 0.361 g and 0.802 g (b) 0.421 g and 0.521 g
   (c) 0.351 g and 0.702 g (d) 0.371 g and 0.712 g

6. Match List-I with List-II

	List-I		List-II
A.	Resistivity	I.	S/m
B.	Molar conductivity	II.	S cm²/mol
C.	Specific conductivity	III.	S
D.	Conductance	IV.	Ωm

   Choose the correct answer from the options given below.
   (a) A-IV, B-II, C-I, D-III (b) A-IV, B-I, C-II, D-III
   (c) A-II, B-IV, C-I, D-III (d) A-II, B-III, C-IV, D-I

7. Calculate the cell potential E at 298 K for a redox reaction where $E^\circ = 0.76$ V, $n = 2$ and the concentration are given as follows :
$$[Ox] = 0.10 \text{ M}$$
$$[Red] = 0.20 \text{ M}$$
   (a) 0.70 V (b) 0.72 V (c) 0.73 V (d) 0.75 V

8. Suppose you have a solution of $MgCl_2$ with a conductivity of 0.01 S/cm at a concentration of 0.05 mol/L. Using Kohlrausch's law, if the molar conductivities of Mg^{2+} and Cl^- are 106 S cm^2/mol and 76 S cm^2/mol, respectively. Then the expected conductivity of $MgCl_2$ will be
   (a) 0.0129 S/m (b) 0.129 S/cm
   (c) 0.0129 S/cm (d) 0.129 S/m

9. Given below are two statements, one is labelled as Assertion (A) and the other is labelled as Reason (R).
   Assertion (A) In a lead-acid battery, the electrolyte concentration decreases during discharge even though H_2SO_4 is produced at the cathode.
   Reason (R) The sulphate ions are consumed to form insoluble $PbSO_4$ at both electrodes, outweighing H_2SO_4 production.
   In the light of the above statements, choose the correct answer from the options given below.
   (a) Both (A) and (R) are true and (R) is the correct explanation of (A).
   (b) Both (A) and (R) are true but (R) is not the correct explanation of (A).
   (c) (A) is true but (R) is false.
   (d) (A) is false but (R) is true.

10. Arrange the following species in increasing order of their reduction power.
$$Cu^{2+}, Ag^+, Fe^{3+}, Pb^{2+}$$
   (a) $Pb^{2+} < Cu^{2+} < Fe^{3+} < Ag^+$
   (b) $Pb^{2+} < Fe^{3+} < Cu^{2+} < Ag^+$
   (c) $Fe^{3+} < Pb^{2+} < Cu^{2+} < Ag^+$
   (d) $Fe^{3+} < Pb^{2+} < Ag^+ < Cu^{2+}$

11. Select the correct statement.
   (a) In an electrolytic cell, the free energy of the system decreases while in an electrochemical cell it increases.
   (b) In an electrochemical cell, the free energy of the system decreases while in an electrolytic cell it increases.
   (c) Free energy remains same in both cells.
   (d) Free energy increases in both cells.

12. The curve given in graph indicates the electrolyte is :

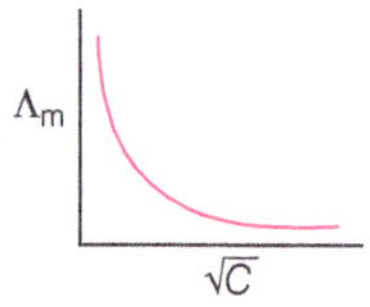

(a) HCl (b) HNO_3 (c) H_2SO_4 (d) H_2CO_3

13. How many grams of copper will be deposited when 2 Faradays of electricity passed through a copper sulphate solution?
(a) $\frac{2}{63.5}$ g (b) Zero
(c) 63.5 g (d) $\frac{1}{63.5}$ g

14. Given below are two statements.
Statement I Secondary batteries, such as lead-acid and lithium-ion batteries, can be recharged by reversing the chemical reaction that occurs during their discharge.
Statement II During the recharging process of a lead acid battery, the sulphuric acid concentration decreases as the battery approaches full charge.
In the light of the above statements choose the correct answer from the options given below.
(a) Both Statement I and Statement II are correct.
(b) Both Statement I and Statement II are incorrect.
(c) Statement I is correct but Statement II is incorrect.
(d) Statement I is incorrect but Statement II is correct.

15. The molar conductivity of acetic acid at infinite dilution is 390 S cm^2/mol. Calculate the degree of dissociation of 0.1 M acetic acid solution with a molar conductivity of 40 S cm^2/mol.
(a) 0.102 (b) 0.112
(c) 0.131 (d) 0.100

16. The EMF of a galvanic cell at 298 K is given as $E = 0.80$ V. The cell representation is
$Zn/Zn^{2+}(0.01\text{ M}) \,||\, Ag^+(0.01\text{M})/Ag$ $E^\circ_{Zn^{2+}/Zn} = -0.76$ V, $E^\circ_{Ag^+/Ag} = 0.80$ V
Calculate the EMF of the cell if the concentration of Zn^{2+} is changed to 1.0 M and that of Ag^+ is changed to 0.01 M.
(a) 1.36 V (b) 1.44 V
(c) 1.56 V (d) 1.46 V

17. The values of Λ^∞_m for KNO_3 and KCl_3 are 196.74 and 145.25 Ω^{-1} cm^2 mol^{-1}. Also $\Lambda^\infty_{Cl^-}$ is 81.44 Ω^{-1}cm^2 mol^{-1}. The value of $\Lambda^\infty_{NO_3^-}$ is
(a) 132.93 Ω^{-1} cm^2 mol^{-1} (b) 122.93 Ω^{-1} cm^2 mol^{-1}
(c) 145.93 Ω^{-1} cm^2 mol^{-1} (d) 131.93 Ω^{-1} cm^2 mol^{-1}

18. If the concentration of H*A* is increased to 0.5 M while keeping H*B* at 0.1 M, what will happen to the EMF?
(a) The EMF will remain the same.
(b) The EMF will increase.
(c) The EMF will decrease.
(d) The EMF will become zero.

19. Match List-I with List-II

	List-I		List-II
A.	Galvanic cell	I.	Uses the same metal for both electrodes
B.	Electrolytic cell	II.	Lead acid battery
C.	Fuel cell	III.	Zinc-copper cell
D.	Concentration cell	IV.	Converts hydrogen and oxygen electricity

Choose the correct answer from the options given below.
(a) A-III, B-II, C-IV, D-I
(b) A-III, B-II, C-I, D-IV
(c) A-IV, B-I, C-II, D-III
(d) A-IV, B-II, C-I, D-III

20. Which of the following statement(s) is/are true about electrochemical cells and resistance
1. The resistance of an electrochemical cell decreases with increasing concentration of the electrolyte solution.
2. A higher internal resistance in a galvanic cell results in a lower cell potential when measured under load conditions.
3. Increasing the surface area of the electrodes will increases the resistance of an electrochemical cell.
4. A lower concentration of ions in the solution leads to decreased mobility and higher resistance.

Choose the correct answer from the options given below.
(a) 1, 2, 3, 4 (b) 1, 2, 3
(c) 1, 2 (d) 1, 2, 4

21. A current of 2 A is passed through an electrolytic cell contaning $CuSO_4$ solution for 30 minutes. Calculate the mass of copper deposited at the cathode.
(a) 1.81 g (b) 1.72 g
(c) 1.23 g (d) 1.18 g

Numerical Type Questions

22. A 0.01 M solution of an electrolyte has a resistance of 250 ohm. The distance between electrodes is 1.5 cm and the area of the cross-section of electrodes is 4 cm^2. The molar conductivity of the solution in terms at .... $\times 10^{-3}$ S m^2/mol.

23. The cell potential when the following reaction $Cu^{2+} + 2e^- \longrightarrow Cu$ occurs at 25°C with concentration of Cu^{2+} 0.01 M and pH of the solution 3 is .... mV (nearest integer).

24. For the cell reaction,
$$Cu(s) + 2Ag^+(aq) \longrightarrow Cu^{2+}(aq) + 2Ag(s)$$
the standard reduction potential of Ag^+/Ag is 0.80 V and for Cu^{2+}/Cu is 0.34 V. The concentration of Cu^{2+} is 0.01 M and for Ag^+ is 1.0 M. The cell potential for the given reaction at 25°C will be .... mV.

25. A solution of $AgNO_3$ is electrolysed using a current of 3 A for a total time of 30 minutes. the mass of Ag deposited on the cathode (in g) .... (nearest integer).

26. A voltaic cell is constructed with zinc electrode in a 1.0 M $ZnSO_4$ solution and a silver electrode in a 1.0 M $AgNO_3$ solution. The equilibrium constant at 298 K will be .... $\times 10^{52}$ (nearest integer).

27. The molar conductance at infinite dilution (Λ_m) for NaCl, HCl and CH_3COONa are 126.4, 425.9, 91.0 S cm^2/mol, respectively. The molar conductance at infinite dilution for acetic acid using Kohlrausch's law of independent migration of ions is .... (nearest integer).

28. A solution of KCl has a conductivity of 0.012 S/m. If the molar conductivity at infinite dilution is 150.0 S cm^2/mol. The equivalent conductance of solution is .... S cm^2/mol.

29. The standard reduction potentials for the following half-reactions are :

$$Sn^{4+} + 2e^- \longrightarrow Sn^{2+}, E^\circ = +0.51 \text{ V}$$
$$Cu^{3+} + e^- \longrightarrow Cu^{2+}, E^\circ = -0.41 \text{ V}$$

A cell is constructed with these half cells. The cell reaction $Sn^{4+} + Cr^{2+} \longrightarrow Sn^{2+} + Cr^{3+}$ be spontaneous. The EMF of the cell is ....

30. The Daniel cell is represented as :

$$Zn(s)/Zn^{2+}(1 \text{ M}) \,||\, Cu^{2+}(1 \text{ M})/Cu(s)$$
$$E^\circ_{Zn^{2+}/Zn} = -0.76 \text{ V}, E^\circ_{Cu^{2+}/Cu} = +0.34 \text{ V}$$

The number of correct statements from the following is
(A) The EMF of the Daniel cell under standard conditions is 1.10 V.
(B) The copper electrode acts as cathode.
(C) Oxidation occurs at zinc electrode.
(D) Electrons flow copper to zinc in the external circuit.
(E) The reaction will be non-spontaneous.

31. The number of correct statements about the electrochemical series are :
(A) A more negative electrode potential indicates a stronger oxidising agent.
(B) The electrochemical series can be used to predict the spontaneity of redox reactions.
(C) The electrochemical series can predict the direction of electron flow in a galvanic cell.
(D) The reduction potential of an element can indicate its tendency to gain electrons.
(E) Strongly electropositive metals cannot displace weakly electropositive metals from their salt solutions.

32. In a galvanic cell constructed using the following half reactions

$$Ag^+ + e^- \longrightarrow Ag, (E^\circ = +0.80 \text{ V})$$
$$Pb^{2+} + 2e^- \longrightarrow Pb, (E^\circ = -0.13 \text{ V})$$

If the concentration of Ag^+ is 0.1 M and the concentration of Pb^{2+} is 0.01 M, the standard cell potential E°_{cell} ...... MV.

33. The number of correct statements corresponds to standard electrode potential are ....
(A) The standard electrode potential of hydrogen is defined as 0 V.
(B) Standard electrode potentials can be influenced by temperature and concentration.
(C) A half cell with a standard electrode potential of −0.80 V is weaker oxidising agent than one with +0.40 V.
(D) The potential of individual half cell can be measured.
(E) Negative standard electrode potential means hydrogen gas is less stable than the reduced form of species.

Check Through PYQs

Element 1 Redox Reactions

1. From the given list, the number of compounds with + 4 oxidation state of sulphur is ....

SO_3, H_2SO_3, $SOCl_2$, SF_4, $BaSO_4$, $H_2S_2O_7$ ***2024, 27 April, Shift-I***

2. The standard reduction potentials at 298 K for the following half cells are given below: ***2024, 9 April, Shift-I***

$$Cr_2O_7^{2-} + 14H^+ + 6e^- \longrightarrow 2Cr^{3+} + 7H_2O, \quad E^\circ = 1.33 \text{ V}$$
$$Fe^{3+}(aq) + 3e^- \longrightarrow Fe, \quad E^\circ = -0.04\text{V}$$
$$Ni^{2+}(aq) + 2e^- \longrightarrow Ni, \quad E^\circ = -0.25 \text{ V}$$
$$Ag^+(aq) + e^- \longrightarrow Ag, \quad E^\circ = 0.80 \text{ V}$$
$$Au^{3+}(aq) + 3e^- \longrightarrow Au, \quad E^\circ = 1.40 \text{ V}$$

Consider the given electrochemical reactions,

The number of metal(s) which will be oxidised by $Cr_2O_7^{2-}$, in aqueous solution is ....

3. Thiosulphate reacts differently with iodine and bromine in the reactions given below :

$$2S_2O_3^{2-} + I_2 \longrightarrow S_4O_6^{2-} + 2I^-$$
$$S_2O_3^{2-} + 5Br_2 + 5H_2O + 2SO_4^{2-} + 4Br^- + 10H^+$$

Which of the following statements justifies the above dual behaviour of thiosulphate? ***2024, 8 April Shift-I***
(a) Thiosulphate undergoes oxidation by bromine and reduction by iodine in these reactions
(b) Bromine is a weaker oxidant than iodine
(c) Bromine is a stronger oxidant than iodine
(d) Bromine undergoes oxidation and iodine undergoes reduction in these reaction.

4. The number of ions from the following that have the ability to liberate hydrogen from a dilute acid is Ti^{2+}, Cr^{2+} and V^{2+}. *2024, 5 April Shift-II*
(a) 1 (b) 0 (c) 2 (d) 3

5. In acidic medium, $K_2Cr_2O_7$ shows oxidising action as represented in the half reaction:

$$Cr_2O_7^{2-} + XH^+ + Ye^{\ominus} \longrightarrow 2A + ZH_2O$$

X, Y, Z and A are respectively are *2024, 1 Feb Shift-I*
(a) 8, 4, 6 and Cr_2O_3 (b) 8, 6, 4 and Cr_2O_3
(c) 14, 7, 6 and Cr^{3+} (d) 14, 6, 7 and Cr^{3+}

6. Given below are two statements. *2024, 31 Jan Shift-II*

Statement I S_8 solid undergoes disproportionation reaction under alkaline conditions to form S^{2-} and $S_2O_3^{2-}$.

Statement II ClO_4^- can undergo disproportionation reaction under acidic condition.

In the light of the above statements, choose the most appropriate answer from the options given below
(a) Both Statement I and Statement II are incorrect.
(b) Statement I is correct but Statement II is incorrect.
(c) Both Statement I and Statement II are correct.
(d) Statement I is incorrect but Statement II is correct.

7. $2MnO_4^- + bI^- + cH_2O \longrightarrow xI_2 + yMnO_2 + z\bar{O}H$

If the above equation is balanced with integer coefficients, the value of z is .... *2024, 30 Jan Shift-I*

8. Chlorine undergoes disproportionation in alkaline medium as shown below

$aCl_2(g) + bOH^-(aq) \longrightarrow cClO^-(aq) + dCl^-(aq) + eH_2O(l)$

The values of a, b, c and d in a balanced redox reaction are respectively *2024, 29 Jan Shift-I*
(a) 1, 2, 1 and 1 (b) 2, 4, 1 and 3
(c) 3, 4, 4 and 2 (d) 2, 2, 1 and 3

9. Which of the following cannot function as an oxidising agent? *2024, 27 Jan Shift-II*
(a) SO_4^{2-} (b) MnO_4^- (c) N^{3-} (d) BrO_3^-

10. See the following chemical reaction

$Cr_2O_7^{2-} + XH^+ + 6Fe^{2+} \longrightarrow YCr^{3+} + 6Fe^{3+} + ZH_2O$

The sum of X, Y and Z is .... *2023, 13 April Shift-II*

11. In alkaline medium, the reduction of permanganate anion involves a gain of .... electrons. *2023, 10 April, Shift-II*

12. $2IO_3^- + xI^- + 12H^+ \longrightarrow 6I_2 + 6H_2O$

What is the value of x? *2023, 8 April Shift-I*
(a) 6 (b) 2 (c) 10 (d) 12

13. Which of the following options are correct for the reaction.

$2[Au(CN)_2]^-(aq) + Zn(s) \longrightarrow 2Au(s) + [Zn(CN)_4]^{2-}(aq)$

A. Redox reaction
B. Displacement reaction
C. Decomposition reaction
D. Combination reaction

Choose the correct answer from the options given below *2023, 6 April Shift-I*
(a) C and D (b) A and B
(c) A and D (d) A only

14. Which one of the following is an example of disproportionation reaction? *2022, 26 June Shift-II*
(a) $3MnO_4^{2-} + 4H^+ \longrightarrow 2MnO_4^- + MnO_2 + 2H_2O$
(b) $MnO_4^- + 4H^+ + 4e^- \longrightarrow MnO_2 + 2H_2O$
(c) $10I^- + 2MnO_4^- + 16H^+ \longrightarrow 2Mn^{2+} + 8H_2O + 5I_2$
(d) $8MnO_4^- + 3S_2O_3^{2-} + H_2O \longrightarrow 8MnO_2 + 6SO_4^{2-} + 2OH^-$

15. Identify the process in which change in the oxidation state is five *2021, 25 July Shift-II*
(a) $Cr_2O_7^{2-} \longrightarrow 2Cr^{3+}$ (b) $MnO_4^- \longrightarrow Mn^{2+}$
(c) $CrO_4^{2-} \longrightarrow Cr^{3+}$ (d) $C_2O_4^{2-} \longrightarrow 2CO_2$

16. The species given below that does not show disproportionation reaction is *2021, 20 July Shift-I*
(a) BrO_4^- (b) BrO^-
(c) BrO_2^- (d) BrO_3^-

17. The oxidation states of iron atoms in compounds (A), (B) and (C), respectively, are x, y and z. The sum of x, y and z is

$$\underset{(A)}{Na_4[Fe(CN)_5(NOS)]}, \underset{(B)}{Na_4[FeO_4]}, \underset{(C)}{[Fe_2(CO)_9]}$$

2020, 9 Sep Shift-I

18. Consider the following equations :

$2Fe^{2+} + H_2O_2 \longrightarrow xA + yB$ (in basic medium)

$2MnO_4^- + 6H^+ + 5H_2O_2 \longrightarrow x'C + y'D + z'E$ (in acidic medium)

The sum of the stoichiometric coefficients x, y, x', y' and z' for products A, B, C, D and E, respectively, is .... *2020, 4 Sep Shift-II*

19. The redox reaction among the following is *2020, 7 Jan Shift-II*
(a) reaction of H_2SO_4 with NaOH
(b) reaction of $[Co(H_2O)_6]Cl_3$ with $AgNO_3$
(c) combination of dinitrogen with dioxygen at 2000 K
(d) formation of ozone from atmospheric oxygen in the presence of sunlight

Element 2 Conductors, Conductance of Electrolytic Solution, Kohlrausch Law, Electrolysis

20. Two ampere current is allowed to pass through molten $AlCl_3$ for 30 min. Find the mass (in mg) of aluminium deposited at cathode. (Nearest integer) *2025, 22 Jan Shift-II*

21. Which out of the following is a correct equation to show change in molar conductivity with respect to concentration for a weak electrolyte, if the symbols carry their usual meaning : *2024, 9 April Shift-II*
(a) $\Lambda_m - \Lambda_m^\circ - AC^{1/2} = 0$
(b) $\Lambda_m^2 C - K_a \Lambda_m^{\circ 2} + K_a \Lambda_m \Lambda_m^\circ = 0$
(c) $\Lambda_m - \Lambda_m^\circ + AC^{1/2} = 0$
(d) $\Lambda_m^2 C + K_a \Lambda_m^{\circ 2} - K_a \Lambda_m \Lambda_m^\circ = 0$

22. The molar conductivity for electrolytes A and B are plotted against $C^{1/2}$ as shown below. Electrolytes A and B respectively are *2024, 9 April Shift-I*

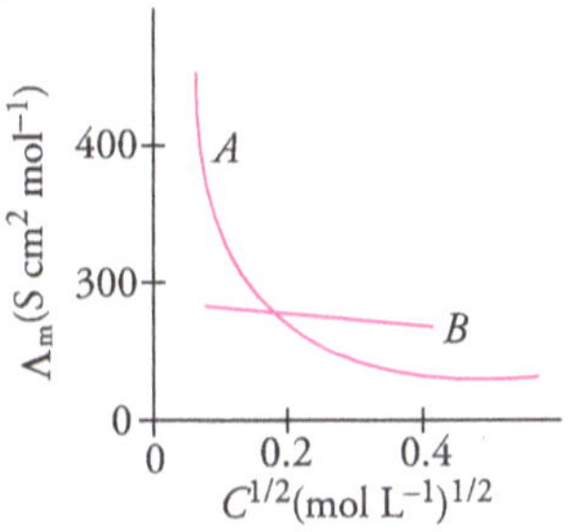

	A	*B*
(a)	Weak electrolyte	Strong electrolyte
(b)	Weak electrolyte	Weak electrolyte
(c)	Strong electrolyte	Weak electrolyte
(d)	Strong electrolyte	Strong electrolyte

23. A conductivity cell with two electrodes (dark side) are half-filled with infinitely dilute aqueous solution of a weak electrolyte. If volume is doubled by adding more water at constant temperature, the molar conductivity of the cell will *2024, 6 April Shift-I*

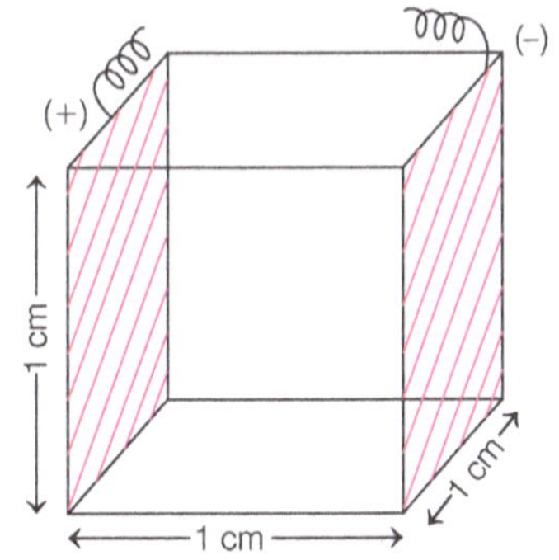

(a) depend upon type of electrolyte
(b) decrease sharply
(c) increase sharply
(d) remain same or can not be measured accurately

24. One of the commonly used electrode is calomel electrode. Under which of the following categories, calomel electrode comes? *2024, 4 April Shift-I*
(a) Gas- ion electrodes
(b) Oxidation-reduction electrodes
(c) Metal- insoluble salt-anion electrodes
(d) Metal ion-metal electrodes

25. The value of conductivity of some materials at 298.15 K in Sm^{-1} are 2.1×10^3, 1.0×10^{-16}, 1.2×10, 3.91, 1.5×10^{-2}, 1×10^{-7}, 1.0×10^3. The number of conductors among the materials is ... . *2024, 31 Jan, Shift-II*

26. The number of correct statement from the following is .... *2023, 15 April, Shift-I*
A. Conductivity always decreases with decrease in concentration for both strong and weak electrolytes.
B. The number of ions per unit volume that carry in a solution increases on dilution.
C. Molar conductivity increases with decrease in concentration.
D. The variation in molar conductivity is different for strong and weak electrolytes.
E. For weak electrolytes, the change in molar conductivity with dilution is due to decrease in degree of dissociation.

27. 1×10^{-5} M $AgNO_3$ is added to 1 L of saturated solution of AgBr. The conductivity of this solution at 298 K is .... $\times10^{-8}$ S m^{-1}.
[Given, K_{sp}(AgBr) = 4.9×10^{-13} at 298 K

$$\lambda^\circ_{Ag^+} = 6\times10^{-3}\,S\,m^2\,mol^{-1}$$
$$\lambda^\circ_{Br^-} = 8\times10^{-3}\,S\,m^2\,mol^{-1}$$
$$\lambda^\circ_{NO_3^-} = 7\times10^{-3}\,Sm^2\,mol^{-1}$$
2023, 1 Feb Shift-II

28. Resistance of a conductivity cell (cell constant 129 m^{-1}) filled with 74.5 ppm solution of KCl is 100 Ω (labelled as solution 1). When the same cell is filled with KCl solution of 149 ppm, the resistance is 50 Ω (labelled as solution 2). The ratio of molar conductivity of solution 1 and solution 2 is i.e. $\lambda_1/\lambda_2 = x\times10^{-3}$. The value of x is .... (Nearest integer) *2022, 29 July Shift-I*

29. Given below are two statements.
Statement I For KI, molar conductivity increases steeply with dilution.
Statement II For carbonic acid, molar conductivity increases slowly with dilution.
In the light of the above statements, choose the correct answer from the options given below. *2022, 27 July Shift-II*
(a) Both Statement I and Statement II are true.
(b) Both Statement I and Statement II are false.
(c) Statement I is true but Statement II is false.
(d) Statement I is false but Statement II is true.

30. A dilute solution of sulphuric acid is electrolysed using a current of 0.10 A for 2 hours to produce hydrogen and oxygen gas. The total volume of gases produced at STP is ...... cm^3. (Nearest integer) [Given, Faraday constant, $F = 96500$ C mol^{-1} at STP, molar volume of an ideal gas is 22.7 L mo1^{-1}] *2022, 29 June Shift-I*

31. The limiting molar conductivities of NaI, $NaNO_3$ and $AgNO_3$ are 12.7, 12.0 and 13.3 mS m^2 mol^{-1}, respectively (all at 25°C). The limiting molar conductivity of AgI at this temperature is ...... m S m^2 mol^{-1}. *2022, 27 June Shift-I*

32. The resistance of a conductivity cell containing 0.01 M KCl solution at 298 K is 1750 Ω. If the conductivity of 0.01 M KCl solution at 298 K is 0.152×10^{-3} S cm^{-1}, then the cell constant of the conductivity cell is ...... $\times 10^{-3}$ cm^{-1}.
2022, 24 June Shift-II

33. Given below are two statements.

Statement I The limiting molar conductivity of KCl (strong electrolyte) is higher compared to that of CH_3COOH (weak electrolyte).

Statement II Molar conductivity decreases with decrease in concentration of electrolyte.

In the light of the above statements, choose the most appropriate answer from the options given below
2021, 26 Aug Shift-I

(a) Statement I is true but Statement II is false.
(b) Statement I is false but Statement II is true.
(c) Both Statement I and Statement II are true.
(d) Both Statement I and Statement II are false.

34. Potassium chlorate is prepared by the electrolysis of KCl in basic solution $6OH^- + Cl^- \longrightarrow ClO_3^- + 3H_2O + 6e^-$. If only 60% of the current is utilised in the reaction, the time (rounded to the nearest hour) required to produce 10 g of $KClO_3$ using a current of 2 A is ....

(Given : F = 96,500 C mol^{-1}; molar mass of $KClO_3$ = 122 g mol^{-1})
2020, 6 Sep Shift-I

35. The variation of molar conductivity with concentration of an electrolyte (X) in aqueous solution is shown in the given figure.

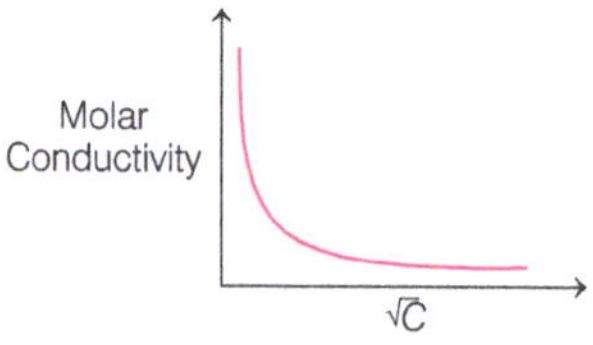

The electrolyte X is
2020, 5 Sep Shift-II

(a) HCl
(b) NaCl
(c) KNO_3
(d) CH_3COOH

36. 250 mL of a waste solution obtained from the workshop of a goldsmith contains 0.1 M $AgNO_3$ and 0.1 M AuCl. The solution was electrolysed at 2 V by passing a current of 1 A for 15 minutes. The metal /metals electrodeposited will be ($E^\circ_{Ag^+/Ag}$ = 0.80 V, $E^\circ_{Au^+/Au}$ = 1.69 V)
2020, 4 Sep Shift-II

(a) only silver
(b) silver and gold in equal mass proportion
(c) only gold
(d) silver and gold in proportion to their atomic weights

Element 3 Electrochemical Cells, Nernst Equation and Electrode Potential

37. $Ag^+ + e^- \longrightarrow Ag \quad E^\circ = x$ V

$Fe^{2+} + 2e^- \longrightarrow Fe \quad E^\circ = y$ V

$Fe^{3+} + 3e^- \longrightarrow Fe \quad E^\circ = z$ V

Then find the E°_{cell} for $Fe^{2+} + Ag \longrightarrow Fe^{3+} + Ag^+$
2025, 24 Jan Shift-I

(a) $x - 2y$
(b) $x + 2y - 3z$
(c) $x + y - z$
(d) $x + y + z$

38. The reaction,

$$\frac{1}{2}H_2(g) + AgCl(s) \longrightarrow H^+(aq) + Cl^-(aq) + Ag(s)$$

occurs in which of the following Galvanic cell :
2024, 8 April Shift-II

(a) Pt | $H_2(g)$ | HCl(soln.) | $AgNO_3(aq)$ | Ag
(b) Ag | AgCl(s) | KCl(soln.) | $AgNO_3(aq)$ | Ag
(c) Pt | $H_2(g)$ | HCl(soln.) | AgCl(s) | Ag
(d) Pt | $H_2(g)$ | KCl(soln.) | AgCl(s) | Ag

39. For the electrochemical cell $M | M^{2+} || X | X^{2-}$

If, $E^\circ_{(M^{2+}/M)} = 0.46$ V

and $E^\circ_{(X/X^{2-})} = 0.34$ V.

Which of the following is correct?
2024, 5 April Shift-II

(a) E_{cell} = 0.80 V
(b) E_{cell} = − 0.80 V
(c) $M + X \rightarrow M^{2+} + X^{2-}$ is a spontaneous reaction
(d) $M^{2+} + X^{2-} \longrightarrow M + X$ is a spontaneous reaction

40. Consider the following redox reaction,

$$MnO_4^- + H^+ + H_2C_2O_4 \longrightarrow Mn^{2+} + H_2O + CO_2$$

The standard reduction potentials are given as below (E°_{red}).

$$E^\circ_{MnO_4^-/Mn^{2+}} = +1.51 \text{ V}$$

$$E^\circ_{CO_2/H_2C_2O_4} = -0.49 \text{ V}$$

If the equilibrium constant of the above reaction is given as $K_{eq} = 10^x$, then the value of x = ... (Nearest integer)
2024, 1 Feb Shift-II

41. At 298 K, the standard reduction potential for Cu^{2+}/Cu electrode is 0.34 V.

Given : $K_{sp}Cu(OH)_2 = 1 \times 10^{-20}$

Take $\frac{2.303\,RT}{F} = 0.0591$V

The reduction potential at pH = 14 for the above couple is (−)$x \times 10^{-2}$ V.

The value of x is ....
2023, 13 April Shift-II

42. The number of correct statements from the following is ......

A. E_{cell} is an intensive parameter.

B. A negative $E^{\ominus}$ means that the redox couple is a stronger reducing agent than the H^+/H_2 couple.

C. The amount of electricity required for oxidation or reduction depends on the stoichiometry of the electrode reaction.

D. The amount of chemical reaction which occurs at any electrode during electrolysis by a current is proportional to the quantity of electricity passed through the electrolyte. *2023, 11 April Shift-II*

43. The standard reduction potentials at 298 K for the following half-cells are given below

$NO_3^- + 4H^+ + 3e^- \longrightarrow NO(g) + 2H_2O \quad E^\circ = 0.97\ V$

$V^{2+}(aq) + 2e^- \longrightarrow V \quad E^\circ = -1.19\ V$

$Fe^{3+}(aq) + 3e^- \longrightarrow Fe \quad E^\circ = -0.04\ V$

$Ag^+(aq) + e^- \longrightarrow Ag(s) \quad E^\circ = 0.80\ V$

$Au^{3+}(aq) + 3e^- \longrightarrow Au(s) \quad E^\circ = 1.40\ V$

The number of metal(s) which will be oxidised by NO_3^- in aqueous solution is .... *2023, 6 April Shift-II*

44. The electrode potential of the following half cell at 298 K $X | X^{2+}$ (0.001 M) $||$ Y^{2+} (0.01 M) $| Y$ is .... $\times 10^{-2}$ V. (Nearest integer).

[Given : $E^\circ_{X^{2+}/X} = -2.36$ V; $E^\circ_{Y^{2+}/Y} = +0.36$ V $\frac{2.303RT}{F} = 0.06$ V] *2023, 30 Jan Shift-II*

45. The equilibrium constant for the reaction

$Zn(s) + Sn^{2+}(aq) \rightleftharpoons Zn^{2+}(aq) + Sn(s)$ is 1×10^{20} at 298 K. The magnitude of standard electrode potential of Sn/Sn^{2+} if $E^\circ_{Zn^{2+}/Zn} = -0.76$ V is .... $\times 10^{-2}$ V.

(Nearest integer). Given, $\frac{2.303RT}{F} = -0.059$ V *2023, 29 Jan Shift-II*

46. $Pt(s) | H_2(g)(1\ bar) | H^+(aq)(1\ M) | M^{3+}(aq) \cdot | M^+(aq) | Pt(s)$

The E_{cell} for the given cell is 0.1115 V at 298 K when $\frac{[M^+(aq)]}{[M^{3+}(aq)]} = 10^a$

The value of a is ....

[Given, $E^\circ_{M^{3+}/M^+} = 0.2$ V, $\frac{2.303RT}{F} = 0.059$ V] *2023, 25 Jan Shift-II*

47. For the given reactions, $Sn^{2+} + 2e^- \longrightarrow Sn$

$Sn^{4+} + 4e^- \longrightarrow Sn$

The electrode potentials are $E^\circ_{Sn^{2+}/Sn} = -0.140$ V and $E^\circ_{Sn^{4+}/Sn} = 0.010$ V. The magnitude of standard electrode potential for Sn^{4+}/Sn^{2+} i.e., $E^\circ_{Sn^{4+}/Sn^{2+}}$ is .... $\times 10^{-2}$ V. (Nearest integer) *2022, 28 June shift-II*

48. $Cu(s) + Sn^{2+}(0.001M) \longrightarrow Cu^{2+}(0.01\ M) + Sn(s)$

The Gibb's free energy change for the above reaction at 298 K is $x \times 10^{-1}$ kJ mol^{-1}.

The value of x is .... [Nearest integer]

[Given, $E^\ominus_{Cu^{2+}/Cu} = 0.34$ V; $E^\ominus_{Sn^{2+}/Sn} = -0.14$ V; F $= 96500$ C mol^{-1}]. *2022, 26 June Shift-II*

49. Consider the following cell reaction,

$$Cd(s) + Hg_2SO_4(s) + \frac{9}{5} H_2O(l) \rightleftharpoons CdSO_4 \cdot \frac{9}{5} H_2O(s) + 2Hg(l)$$

The value of E°_{cell} is 4.315 V at 25°C.

If $\Delta H^\circ = -825.2$ kJ mol^{-1}, the standard entropy change ΔS° in J K^{-1} is .... (Nearest integer)

[Given, Faraday constant = 96487 C mol^{-1}] *2021, 31 Aug Shift-I*

50. For the cell

$Cu(s) | Cu^{2+}(aq)(0.1\ M) || Ag^+(aq)(0.01M) | Ag(s)$

the cell potential, $E_1 = 0.3095$ V

For the cell, $Cu(s) | Cu^{2+}(aq)(0.01\ M) || Ag^+(aq)(0.001M) | Ag(s)$

the cell potential = ... $\times 10^{-2}$ V.

(Round off the nearest integer). $\left[\text{Use} : \frac{2.303\,RT}{F} = 0.059\right]$ *2021, 27 July Shift-II*

51. Emf of the following cell at 298 K in V is $x \times 10^{-2}$,

$Zn | Zn^{2+}$ (0.1 M) $||$ Ag^+ (0.01 M) $| Ag$

The value of x is ....

(Rounded off to the nearest integer).

[Given, $E^\circ_{Zn^{2+}/Zn} = -0.76$ V, $E^\circ_{Ag^+/Ag} = +0.80$ V, $\frac{2.303RT}{F} = 0.059$] *2021, 26 Feb Shift-II*

52.

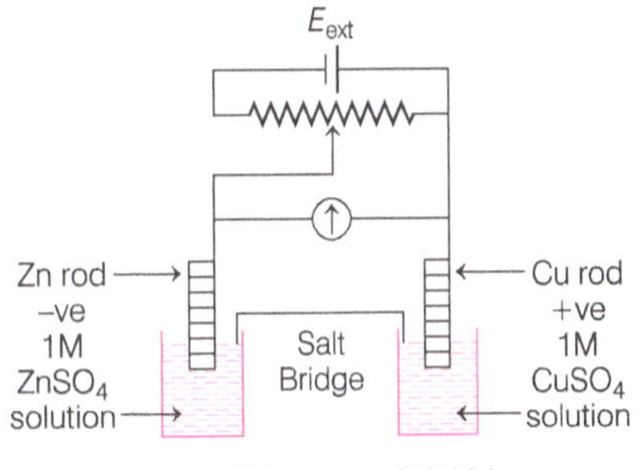

$E^\circ_{Cu^{2+}|Cu} = +0.34$ V

$E^\circ_{Zn^{2+}|Zn} = -0.76$ V

Identify the incorrect statement from the options below for the above cell. *2020, 4 Sep Shift-I*

(a) If $E_{ext} > 1.1$V, Zn dissolves at Zn electrode and Cu deposits at Cu electrode.

(b) If $E_{ext} = 1.1$V, no flow of electrons or current occurs.

(c) If $E_{ext} > 1.1$V, electrons flows from Cu to Zn.

(d) If $E_{ext} < 1.1$V, Zn dissolves at anode and Cu deposits at cathode.

53. For the disproportionation reaction $2Cu^+(aq) \rightleftharpoons Cu(s) + Cu^{2+}(aq)$ at 298 K, ln K (where K is the equilibrium constant) is ...... $\times 10^{-1}$.

Given : ($E^\circ_{Cu^{2+}/Cu^+} = 0.16$ V, $E^\circ_{Cu^+/Cu} = 0.52$ V and $\frac{RT}{F} = 0.025$)

2020, 2 Sep Shift-II

54. The Gibbs energy change (inJ) for the given reaction at $[Cu^{2+}] = [Sn^{2+}] = 1$ M and 298 K is

$$Cu(s) + Sn^{2+}(aq) \longrightarrow Cu^{2+}(aq) + Sn(s);$$

($E^\circ_{Sn^{2+}/Sn} = -0.16$ V, $E^\circ_{Cu^{2+}/Cu} = 0.34$ V,

Take, $F = 96500$ C mol^{-1}) *2020, 2 Sep Shift-I*

Element 4 Batteries, Fuel Cells and Corrosion

55. Match List-I with List-II.

List-I (Cell)		List-II (Use/Property/Reaction)	
A.	Leclanche cell	I.	Converts energy of combustion into electrical energy
B.	Ni – Cd cell	II.	Does not involve any ion in solution and is used in hearing aids
C.	Fuel cell	III.	Rechargeable
D.	Mercury cell	IV.	Reaction at anode $Zn \longrightarrow Zn^{2+} + 2e^-$

Choose the correct answer from the options given below *2024, 9 April Shift-II*

(a) A-III, B-I, C-IV, D-II (b) A-I, B-II, C-III, D-IV
(c) A-II, B-III, C-IV, D-I (d) A-IV, B-III, C-I, D-II

56. Fuel cell, using hydrogen and oxygen as fuels,
A. has been used in spaceship
B. has as efficiency of 40% to produce electricity
C. uses aluminum as catalysts
D. is eco-friendly
E. is actually a type of Galvanic cell only.

Choose the correct answer from the options given below: *2024, 4 April Shift-II*

(a) A, B and C
(b) A, B and D
(c) A, B, D and E
(d) A, D and E

57. Which of the following statements is not correct about rusting of iron? *2024, 27 Jan Shift-II*

(a) Dissolved acidic oxides SO_2, NO_2 in water act as catalyst in the process of rusting.
(b) Rusting of iron is envisaged as setting up of electrochemical cell on the surface of iron object.
(c) When pH lies above 9 or 10, rusting of iron does not take place.
(d) Coating of iron surface by tin prevents rusting, even if the tin coating is peeling off.

58. For lead storage battery pick the correct statements.
A. During charging of battery, $PbSO_4$ on anode is converted into PbO_2.
B. During charging of battery, $PbSO_4$ on cathode is converted into PbO_2.
C. Lead storage battery consists of grid of lead packed with PbO_2 as anode.
D. Lead storage battery ~ 38% solution of sulphuric acid as an electrolyte. *2023, 12 April Shift-I*

Choose the correct answer from the options given below.
(a) B and D
(b) B and C
(c) B, C and D
(d) A, B and D

59. Match List-I with List-II.

	List-I		List-II
(A)	$Cd(s) + 2Ni(OH)_3(s) \longrightarrow CdO(s) + 2Ni(OH)_2(s) + H_2O(l)$	(I)	Primary battery
(B)	$Zn(Hg) + HgO(s) \longrightarrow ZnO(s) + Hg(l)$	(II)	Discharging of secondary battery
(C)	$2PbSO_4(s) + 2H_2O(l) \longrightarrow Pb(s) + PbO_2(s) + 2H_2SO_4(aq)$	(III)	Fuel cell
(D)	$2H_2(g) + O_2(g) \longrightarrow 2H_2O(l)$	(IV)	Charging of secondary battery

Choose the correct answer from the options given below. *2022, 28 July Shift-I*

(a) (A) → (I), (B) → (II), (C) → (III), (D) → (IV)
(b) (A) → (IV), (B) → (I), (C) → (II), (D) → (III)
(c) (A) → (II), (B) → (I), (C) → (IV), (D) → (III)
(d) (A) → (II), (B) → (I), (C) → (III), (D) → (IV)

60. Compound A used as a strong oxidising agent is amphoteric in nature. It is the part of lead storage batteries. Compound A is *2021, 26 Feb Shift-I*

(a) PbO_2 (b) PbO
(c) $PbSO_4$ (d) Pb_3O_4

PRACTICE
ELEMENT 02

Target JEE Advanced

Single Correct Choice MCQs

1. The overall formation constant for the reaction of 6 mole of CN^- with cobalt (II) is 1×10^{19}. What is the formation constant for the reaction of 6 moles of CN^- with cobalt (III)
[Given: $[Co(CN)_6]^{3-} + e^- \longrightarrow [Co(CN)_6]^{4-}$; $E° = -0.83$ V, $Co^{3+} + e^- \longrightarrow Co^{2+}$; $E° = +1.81$ V and $2.303 \frac{RT}{F} = 0.06$]
(a) 1.0×10^{63} (b) 1.02×10^{60}
(c) 1.38×10^{-68} (d) 1.00×10^{-38}

2. If it is desired to construct the following galvanic cell :
$Ag(s)/Ag^+$ (saturated AgI) || Ag^+ (saturated AgCl, $x \times 10^{-4}$ M Cl^-)/$Ag(s)$ to have, $E_{cell} = 0.102$ V, what should be the value of x to get $[Cl^-]$, which must be present in the cathodic half-cell to achieve the desired EMF. Given, K_{sp} of AgCl and AgI are 1.8×10^{-10} and 8.1×10^{-17}, respectively, ($2.303\, RT/F = 0.06$, $\log 2 = 0.3$)
(a) 8 (b) 10 (c) 4 (d) 16

3. Quinhydrone electrode is used in indicator electrode in contact with platinum metal and can be used in acid-base potentiometric titration,

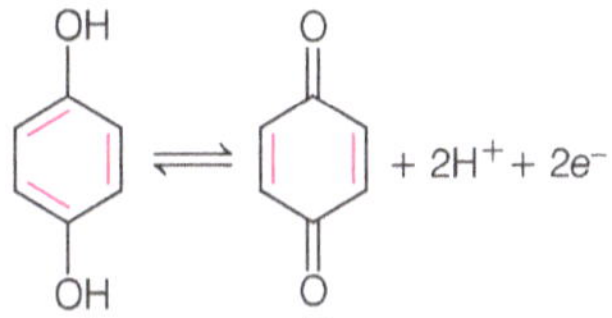

A B

At the equivalence point, $[A] = [B]$ and thus, EMF of the cell is dependent of pH. When NaOH is added to electrode in potentiometric titration, potentiogram is

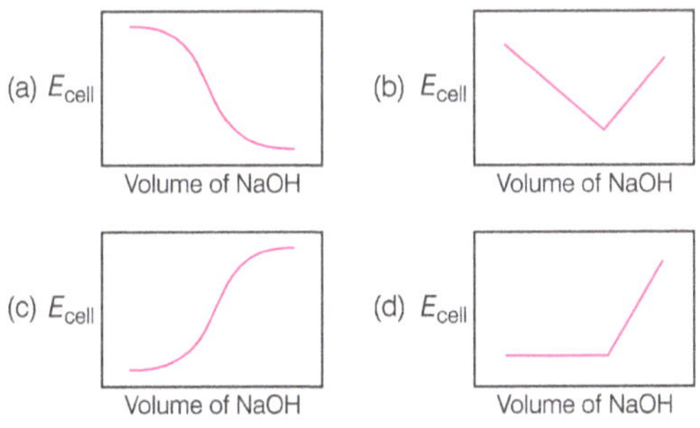

4. For the cell, Zn | Zn^{2+}(1M) || H^+(1M) |$Pt(H_2)$ (1 bar), $E°_{cell} = 0.76$ V and for the cell $Pt(H_2)$ | H^+(1M) || Ag^+(1M) | Ag, $E°_{cell} = 0.80$ V
Thus, E_{cell} for the Ag | Ag^+(0.1 M) || Zn^{2+}(0.1M)| Zn is .... and cell reaction is ....
(a) 1.44 V, spontaneous (b) 0.4 V, spontaneous
(c) – 1.44 V, non-spontaneous (d) – 1.53 V, non-spontaneous

5. For the calomel half-cell, Hg, Hg_2Cl_2 | $Cl^-(aq)$ values of electrode potentials are plotted at different log $[Cl^-]$. Variation is represented by

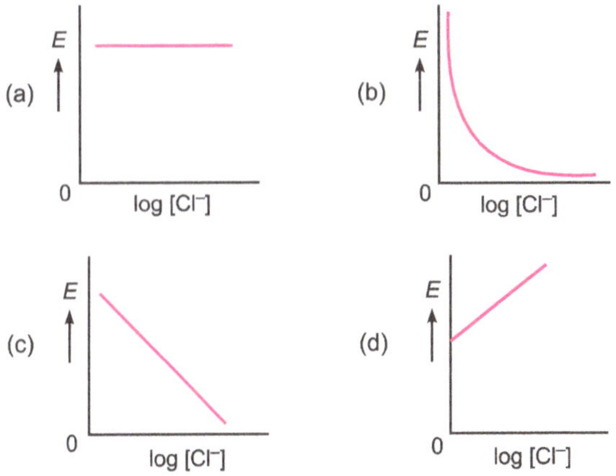

6. An excess of liquid mercury is added to an acidified solution of 10^{-3} M Fe^{3+}. It is found that 10% of Fe^{3+} remains at equilibrium at 25°C. The value of $E°_{Hg_2^{2+}/Hg}$ (in mV), assuming that the only reaction that occurs is :
$2Hg + 2Fe^{3+} \rightleftharpoons Hg_2^{2+} + 2Fe^{2+}$ (Given : $E°_{Fe^{3+}/Fe^{2+}} = 0.7724$ V, $\log 2 = 0.3$, $\log 3 = 0.48$, $2.303\, RT/F = 0.06$)
(a) 0.571 (b) 0.231 (c) 0.21 (d) 0.815 V

7. An acidic solution of Cu^{2+} salt containing 0.4 g of Cu^{2+} is electrolysed until all the copper is deposited. The electrolysis is carried for seven more minutes with the volume of solution kept at 100 mL and the current at 1.2 A. The volume of the gases evolved at STP during the entire electrolysis is
(a) 160 mL (b) 100 mL (c) 90 mL (d) 195 mL

8. Which of the following ($E_{cell} - E°_{cell}$) value is correctly match regarding the given cell?
(a) Zn/Zn^{2+} (0.01 M) || Cu^{2+} (1.00 M)/Cu $\longrightarrow$ 0.04 V
(b) Cu/Cu^{2+} (0.01 M) || Ag^+ (0.10 M)/Ag $\longrightarrow$ 0.0591 V
(c) Al/Al^{3+} (0.25 M) || Co^{2+} (0.05 M)/Co $\longrightarrow$ 0.021 V
(d) Pt(Br_2, l)/Br^- (0.5 M) || Cl^- (0.05 M)/Pt(Cl_2, 0.9 atm) $\longrightarrow$ 0.06 V

One or More than One Correct MCQs

9. Which of the following statements are correct?
   (a) The mass of Zn deposited at the cathode in 815 s, when 1.77 A of electric current is passed through a solution of Zn^{2+} (aq) is 0.486 g.
   (b) The time required to produce 1.96 g I_2 at the anode if a current of 3.14 A is passed through KI (aq) is 360 s.
   (c) 0.207 M $[Cu^{2+}]$ remaining in 335 mL of a solution that was originally 0.215 M $CuSO_4$, after the passage of 2.17 A for 235 s and the deposition of Cu at the cathode.
   (d) The time required to reduce $[Ag^+]$ in 255 mL of $AgNO_3\,(aq)$ from 0.185 M to 0.175 M by electrolysing the solution with Pt electrodes and a current of 1.92A is 130.26 s.

10. Select the correct statement(s) from the following.

    Given : $E^{\ominus}_{Li^{\oplus}|Li} = -3.05$ V

    $E^{\ominus}_{Na^{\oplus}|Na} = -2.71$ V

    $E^{\ominus}_{K^{\oplus}|K} = -2.93$ V

    Alkali metals react with water according to the following reaction (M = Alkali metals) :

    $$2M + H_2O \longrightarrow 2MOH + H_2$$

    It is found that Li reacts gently with water, whereas K reacts violently with water.

    (a) ΔG values have nothing to do with kinetics of the reaction.
    (b) The metal having large standard oxidation potential will have lesser reactivity.
    (c) Potassium (K) has low melting point and heat of reaction which is sufficient to make it melt or even vapourize. This leads to exponential increase in its surface area.
    (d) The ionisation potential of K is smaller than that of Li.

11. Consider the following half-reactions.

    I. $H^+(aq) + e^- \longrightarrow \frac{1}{2}H_2(g);\quad E^{\circ}_{cell} = 0.0$ V

    II. $2H_2O(l) \longrightarrow O_2(g) + 4H^+ + 4e^-;\quad E^{\circ}_{cell} = 1.23$ V

    III. $2SO_4^{2-}(aq) \longrightarrow S_2O_8^{2-}(aq) + 2e^-;\quad E^{\circ}_{cell} = 1.96$ V

    Select the correct statement(s) on the basis of the above data.
    (a) In dilute sulphuric acid, hydrogen ion will be reduced at cathode
    (b) In concentrated sulphuric acid, water will be oxidised at anode
    (c) In dilute sulphuric acid, water will be oxidised at anode
    (d) In dilute sulphuric acid, sulphate ion is oxidised to $S_2O_8^{2-}$

12. Select the correct statements(s) based on the following half-reaction

    $Cu^{2+} + 2e^- \longrightarrow Cu;\quad E^{\circ} = 0.34$ V

    $Zn^{2+} + 2e^- \longrightarrow Zn;\quad E^{\circ} = 0.76$ V

    $SO_4^{2-} + 4H^+ + 2e^- \longrightarrow SO_2 + 2H_2O;\quad E^{\circ} = 1.17$ V

    (a) Copper reacts with dil. H_2SO_4 forming H_2 and SO_2
    (b) Copper reacts with conc. H_2SO_4 forming SO_2
    (c) Zinc reacts with conc. H_2SO_4 forming SO_2
    (d) Zinc reacts with dill. H_2SO_4 forming H_2

13. Select the correct statement(s).
    (a) If salt-bridge is removed, potential falls to zero
    (b) Quinhydrone electrode is reversible to H^+ ion
    (c) Liquid-junction potential developed across the boundary of the two solutions of different concentration is minimised if concentration cells are used
    (d) Calomel electrode contains calcium chloride solution in contact with Pt electrode

14. For the reduction of CO_3^{2-} ion in an aqueous solution E° is +0.96 V. Values of E° for some metal ions are given below.

    $V^{2+}(aq) + 2e^- \longrightarrow V;\ E^{\circ} = -1.19$ V

    $Fe^{3+}(aq) + 3e^- \longrightarrow Fe;\ E^{\circ} = -0.04$ V

    $Au^{3+}(aq) + 3e^- \longrightarrow Au;\ E^{\circ} = +1.40$ V

    $Hg^{2+}(aq) + 2e^- \longrightarrow Hg;\ E^{\circ} = +0.86$ V

    The pair(s) of metals that is/are oxidised by CO_3^{2-} in aqueous solution is(are)
    (a) V and Hg
    (b) Hg and Fe
    (c) Fe and Au
    (d) Fe and V

15. Select the correct statement(s).
    (a) Λ_m^{∞} (molar conductance at infinite dilution) of weak electrolytes can be obtained by Kohlrausch's law.
    $\Lambda_m^{\infty} = x_+\lambda_+^{\infty} + y_-\lambda_-^{\infty}$
    (b) Λ_m^{∞} of strong as well as weak electrolytes can be obtained by extrapolation of graph between Λ_m and $\sqrt{C}$ to $\sqrt{C} \longrightarrow 0$
    (c) Λ^{∞}_{AgCl} can be obtained by known value of $\Lambda^{\infty}_{AgNO_3}$, Λ^{∞}_{HCl} and $\Lambda^{\infty}_{HNO_3}$
    (d) $\Lambda^{\infty}_{BaSO_4\,(molar)} = \Lambda^{\infty}_{BaCl_2} + \Lambda^{\infty}_{H_2SO_4} - 2\Lambda^{\infty}_{HCl}$

16. In the electrolysis of aqueous sodium chloride solution, two types of reactions can take place at anode.
    I. $2Cl^-(aq) \longrightarrow Cl_2(g) + 2e^-$
    II. $2H_2O(l) \longrightarrow O_2(g) + 4H^+(aq) + 4e^-$

    Select the correct statement(s) about these.
    (a) Electrode potentials of I and II are quite similar
    (b) I is favoured in higher concentration of NaCl and II is favoured in higher pH
    (c) Because of overvoltage, Cl_2 and not O_2 is formed
    (d) Electrode potentials of I and II are different

Integer/Numerical Type Questions

17. Consider an electrochemical cell :

    $A(s)|A^{n+}(aq,\ 3\ M)\ ||\ B^{2n+}(aq,\ 2\ M)|B(s)$. The value of $\Delta H^{\ominus}$ for the cell reaction is twice of ΔG° at 300 K. If the emf of the cell is zero, the $\Delta S^{\ominus}$ in $JK^{-1}\ mol^{-1}$ of the cell reaction per mole of B formed at 300 K is (–) ....

    [Given, ln (2) = 0.7, ln (3) = 1.0, $R = 8.3\ JK^{-1}\ mol^{-1}$, H, S and G are enthalpy, entropy and Gibbs energy respectively.]

18. In the following two half-cells
    I. $\underset{1\ bar}{Pt(H_2)}\ |\ HX(1\ M),\ K_a(HX) = 10^{-2}$
    II. $\underset{1\ bar}{Pt(H_2)}\ |\ HY(1\ M),\ K_a(HY) = 10^{-6}$ then E_{II}/E_I will be...

19. When silver chloride is dissolved in a large excess of ammonia, practically all silver ion can be assumed to exist in form of a single ionic species $[Ag_x(NH_3)_y]^{x+}$. Compute the values of x and y using the two following cells :

Cell I : $Ag|4.0 \times 10^{-4}$ M –AgCl, 1 M

$-NH_3||4 \times 10^{-2}$ M –AgCl, 1 M

$-NH_3|Ag$; $E_{cell} = 0.118$ V at 298 K.

Cell II : $Ag|3 \times 10^{-3}$ M –AgCl, 1 M

$-NH_3||3 \times 10^{-3}$ M –AgCl, 0.1 M

$-NH_3|Ag$; $E_{cell} = 0.118$ V at 298 K

The value of $x + y$ is ....

20. A conductivity cell has electrodes 0.656 cm apart and each of area 0.8 cm^2. Given, equivalent conductance of saturated solution of AgCl = 130 S cm^2 $equiv^{-1}$, solubility product of AgCl $= 1.6 \times 10^{-10}$. If (AgCl) offers resistance of $n \times 10^5$ ohm. What is value of n?

21. The reduction potential ($E°$, in V) of $FeO_4^{2-}|Fe$ is ....

[Given, $E^{\circ}_{FeO_4^{2-}(aq)/Fe^{3+}} = 1.74$ V ;

$E^{\circ}_{Fe^{3+}/Fe^{2+}} = 1.31$ V ; $E^{\circ}_{Fe^{2+}/Fe} = 1.05$ V]

22. In the following cell at 298 K,

$Ag|Ag^+$ (1 M) $||Cu^{2+}$(1M) $|Cu$

a current of 9.65 A is passed for 1 h.

What is the change in EMF (in centivolts)?

23. The reduction potential of $AsO_4^{3-}|AsO_2^-$ in a solution when 18 mL of 0.1 N solution of NaI is added to 20 mL of 0.1 N Na_3AsO_4 solution at pH = 5 is ______ .

[Given: The standard reduction potential of $AsO_4^{3-}|AsO_2^- = -0.70$ V]

24. H_2O_2 can be prepared by the successive reactions,

$$2NH_4HSO_4 \longrightarrow H_2 + (NH_4)_2S_2O_8$$

$$(NH_4)_2S_2O_8 + 2H_2O \longrightarrow 2NH_4HSO_4 + H_2O_2$$

The first reaction is an electrolytic reaction and the second a steam distillation. The current that will be used in first reaction to produce enough intermediate to yield 100 g pure H_2O_2 per hour is .... A. [Assume 50% current efficiency.]

Matching Type Questions

25. Half-cell reactions and $E°$ values are given.

	$E°$
A. $O_3(g) + 2H^+ + 2e^- \longrightarrow O_2(g) + H_2O$,	+2.075 V
B. $O_2(g) + 2H_2O + 4e^- \longrightarrow 4OH^-$,	+0.401 V
C. $O_2(g) + 4H^+ + 4e^- \longrightarrow 2H_2O$,	+1.229 V
D. $H_2O_2(aq) + 2H^+ + 2e^- \longrightarrow 2H_2O$,	+1.763 V
E. $Cr^{3+} + 3e^- \longrightarrow Cr$,	−0.74 V
F. $Cr^{2+} + 2e^- \longrightarrow Cr$,	−0.91 V
G. $2H^+(aq) + 2e^- \longrightarrow H_2(g)$,	0.00 V
H. $4H_2O + 4e^- \longrightarrow 2H_2 + 4OH^-$,	−0.83 V

Match the half-cell reaction in Column I with their values in Column II and select the answer from answer codes at the end.

	Column I		Column II
i.	$O_2(g) + 2H^+ + 2e^- \longrightarrow H_2O_2$	p.	0.695 V
ii.	$2H_2O + 2e^- \longrightarrow H_2 + 2OH^-$	q.	− 0.40 V
iii.	$O_3 + H_2O + 2e^- \longrightarrow O_2 + 2OH^-$	r.	1.245 V
iv.	$Cr^{3+} + e^- \longrightarrow Cr^{2+}$	s.	− 0.83 V

Codes

	i	ii	iii	iv		i	ii	iii	iv
(a)	p	s	r	q	(b)	r	q	p	s
(c)	s	q	p	r	(d)	q	p	s	r

26. The standard potential of the following cell is 0.23 V at 288 K and 0.21 V at 308 K,

$E^{\circ}_{Ag^+/Ag} = 0.80$ at 298 K

$Pt(H_2)\,|\,HCl(aq)\,||\,AgCl(s)\,|\,Ag(s)$

Match the parameters in Column I with their values in Column II and select the answer from the codes given below the list.

	Column I		Column II
i.	Temperature coefficient of EMF of the cell (in mV) K^{-1}	p.	− 9.81
ii.	Entropy change (in JK^{-1}) in the temperature range 288 K and 308 K	q.	− 96.5
iii.	Enthalpy change (in kJ mol^{-1}) at the temperature 288 K and 308 K	r.	− 50.0
iv.	Solubility product of AgCl in water and 298 K in terms of (log)	s.	− 1.0

Codes

	i	ii	iii	iv		i	ii	iii	iv
(a)	p	q	s	r	(b)	q	s	p	r
(c)	s	q	r	p	(d)	s	p	r	q

27. Four electrolytic cells containing solution of $ZnSO_4$, $AgNO_3$, $CuSO_4$ and dil. H_2SO_4 are connected in series. A steady current of 1.5 A was passed through them until 77 mL of O_2 gas at STP is formed in anode compartment of H_2SO_4 solution. Match the different elements/gas formed in Column I with their values in Column II and select the answer from the codes given below.

(Cu = 63.5, Zn = 65, Ag = 108, S = 32, H = 1 and O = 16)

	Column I		Column II
i.	Zn	p.	0.45 g
ii.	Ag	q.	1.485 g
iii.	Cu	r.	0.014 g
iv.	H_2	s.	0.44 g

Codes

	i	ii	iii	iv		i	ii	iii	iv
(a)	p	q	s	r	(b)	q	r	p	s
(c)	s	q	p	r	(d)	p	r	q	s

28. For H_2O at 298 K, $\lambda^\circ(H^+) = 3.5\times10^{-2}\,Sm^2mol^{-1}$,
$\lambda^\circ(OH^-) = 2.0\times10^{-2}\,S\,m^2\,mol^{-1}$
Specific conductance $(\kappa) = 5.7\times10^{-6}\,S\,m^{-1}$,
Density of water = 1.0 g cm^{-3}
Match the parameters in Column I (in terms of $-\log$ (value) i.e. p_{value}) with their values in Column II.

	Column I		Column II
i.	$p_x = -\log x$ (x = degree of dissociation)	p.	10.0
ii.	p_{Λ_c} (Λ_c = molar conductance)	q.	8.73
iii.	pH	r.	14.0
iv.	pK_w (K_w = ionic product)	s.	7.00

Codes

	i	ii	iii	iv
(a)	p	q	r	s
(b)	s	q	r	p
(c)	q	p	s	r
(d)	q	s	p	r

29. $\Lambda^\circ_m(CH_3COOH)$ = 390.5 S cm^2mol^{-1},
$K_a(CH_3COOH) = 1.8\times10^{-5}$, $[CH_3COOH] = 0.040$ M
Cell constant of the cell used = 0.206 cm^{-1}. Match the parameter given in Column I with the value in Column II and select answer from the codes given at the end.

	Column I		Column II
i.	Λ_m (S m^2 mol^{-1})	p.	8.28×10^{-4}
ii.	κ (S m^{-1})	q.	1.61×10^{-3}
iii.	Ω (kilo ohm)	r.	3.312×10^{-2}
iv.	S (ohm^{-1})	s.	0.622

Codes

	i	ii	iii	iv
(a)	p	r	s	q
(b)	p	q	s	r
(c)	q	s	p	r
(d)	p	q	r	s

30. Match the List-I with List-II

	List-I Name of cell/battery		List-II Electrolyte
A.	Lead storage battery	I.	KOH solution
B.	Dry cell	II.	38% H_2SO_4
C.	Fuel cell ($H_2 - O_2$)	III.	MnO_2 + C (touching cathode) and paste of NH_4Cl + $ZnCl_2$ (touching anode)
D.	Ni-Cd storage cell	IV.	Concentrated aqueous KOH solution

Choose the correct answer from the options given below.
(a) A-II, B-IV, C-I, D-III
(b) A-IV, B-III, C-II, D-I
(c) A-II, B-III, C-IV, D-I
(d) A-III, B-I, C-II, D-IV

Paragraph of Two Questions Each

Paragraph 1

The electrochemical cell shown below is a concentration cell. $M|M^{2+}$ (saturated solution of a sparingly soluble salt, MX_2)|| M^{2+} (0.001 mol dm^{-3})|M. The emf of cell depends on the difference in concentration of M^{2+} ions at the two electrodes. The emf of the cell at 300 K is 0.068 V.

31. The solubility product (K_{sp} : $mol^3\,dm^{-9}$) of MX_2 at 300 K based on the information available the given concentration cell is .... $\times10^{-15.9}$.
(Use : $2.303\times R\times300/F = 0.06$ V)

32. The value of ΔG (kJ mol^{-1}) for the given cell is (–) .... kJ. [Use : 1 F = 96500 C mol^{-1}]

Paragraph 2

A conductivity cell shows a conductance of 1.5×10^{-4} S, when filled with 0.001 M KCl. The same cell records a conductance of 4.25×10^{-4}S, when filled with 0.001 M HCl at 298 K. Assume K^+ and Cl^- ions have same mobility and specific conductance of 0.001 M KCl is 1.5×10^{-4} S cm^{-1}.

33. The equivalent conductance of 0.001 M HCl solution is .... $\times10^2$ S cm^2 $equiv^{-1}$.

34. Ionic conductance of H^+ ion is .... S cm^2 $equiv^{-1}$.

Paragraph 3

The electrochemical cell shown below is a concentration cell. $M(s)|M^{2+}$ (saturated solution of a sparingly soluble salt, MX_2)|| M^{2+} (0.001 mol dm^{-3})|$M(s)$.
The emf of the cell depends on the difference in concentrations of M^{2+} ions at the two electrodes. The EMF of the cell at 298 K is 0.059 V.

35. The value of ΔG (kJ mol^{-1}) for the given cell is – .... : (Use : 1 F = 96500 C mol^{-1}).

36. The solubility product (K_{sp} : $mol^3\,dm^{-3}$) of MX_2 at 298 K based on the information available for the given concentration cell is (take $2.303\times R\times298/F = 0.059$) is ...$x$...$10^{-15}$. The value of x is ....

Species Selection (with 5 Species)

37. Consider the following electrochemical changes,
(i) 0.8 mol of I_2 is converted to I^-
(ii) 118.7 g of Sn^{2+} is converted to Sn (Sn = 118.7)
(iii) 0.174 g of MnO_4^- is converted to Mn^{2+} in acidic medium
(iv) MnO_4^- in 15.80 mL of 0.1145 M MnO_4^- is converted to Mn^{2+}
(v) 1 L of O_2 at STP is converted to H_2O in acid solution; $O_2(g) + 4H^+(aq) + 4e^- \longrightarrow 2H_2O(l)$
In which changes, the mole of electrons are involved are less than one is/are —
(a) 3 (b) 1 (c) 2 (d) 4

38. Among the following batteries,

dry-cell battery, lead-storage (acid) battery, nickel-cadmium battery, lithium battery and fuel cell

The total number of rechargeable batteries are —

(a) 3 (b) 4
(c) 1 (d) 2

39. Given :

For $I_2 + 2e^- \longrightarrow 2I^{\ominus}$, standard reduction potential $= +0.54$ V. For $2Br^{\ominus} \longrightarrow Br_2 + 2e^-$, standard oxidation potential $= -1.09$ V. For $Fe \longrightarrow Fe^{2+} + 2e^-$, standard oxidation potential $= +0.44$ V. For $Cd^{2+} + 2e^- \longrightarrow Cd$, standard reduction potential $= -0.403$ V.

(i) $Br_2 + 2I^{\ominus} \longrightarrow 2Br^{\ominus} + I_2$

(ii) $Fe + Br_2 \longrightarrow Fe^{2+} + 2Br^{\ominus}$

(iii) $Fe + I_2 \longrightarrow Fe^{2+} + 2I^{\ominus}$

(iv) $I_2 + 2Br^{\ominus} \longrightarrow 2I^{\ominus} + Br_2$

(v) $Cd^{2+} + Fe \longrightarrow Cd + Fe^{2+}$

The total number of reactions which are spontaneous is(are) —

(a) 3 (b) 2
(c) 4 (d) 1

Species Selection (with 7 Species)

40. The standard reduction potentials at 298 K are given against each of the following half cell reactions :

(i) $E^{\circ}_{Zn^{2+}/Zn} = -0.76$ V (ii) $E^{\circ}_{Cr^{3+}/Cr} = -0.74$ V

(iii) $E^{\circ}_{H^{\oplus}/H_2} = 0.00$ V (iv) $E^{\circ}_{Fe^{3+}/Fe^{2+}} = +0.77$ V

(v) $E^{\circ}_{Al^{3+}/Al} = -1.66$ V (vi) $E^{\circ}_{Na^{+}/Na} = -2.71$ V

(vii) $E^{\circ}_{Cl_2/2Cl^-} = 1.36$ V

Based on the above data, which of the following is the stronger reducing agent than $E^{\circ}_{Pb^{2+}/Pb}$.

[$E^{\circ}_{Pb^{2+}/Pb} = -0.13$ V]

(a) 4 (b) 5
(c) 6 (d) 3

41. Consider the following relations,

(i) $E^{\circ}_{cell} = \dfrac{2.303\,RT}{nF} \log K_c$ at 298 K

(ii) $\Delta G^{\circ} = -RT \ln K$

(iii) $G = \dfrac{\rho A}{l}$

(iv) $G^{*} = \kappa R$

(v) $\Lambda_m = \Lambda^{\circ}_m + A\sqrt{C}$

(vi) $K_a = \dfrac{C\Lambda^2_m}{\Lambda^{\circ}_m(\Lambda^{\circ}_m - \Lambda_m)}$ (for strong electrolyte)

(vii) $\alpha = \dfrac{\Lambda_m}{\Lambda^{\circ}_m}$

The correct relations are

(a) 5 (b) 4 (c) 3 (d) 6

42. Consider the following electrode reactions,

(i) $MnO_2 + NH_4^+ + e^- \longrightarrow MnO(OH) + NH_3$ (at cathode)

(ii) $Zn(Hg) + 2OH^- \longrightarrow ZnO(s) + H_2O + 2e^-$ (at anode)

(iii) $PbO_2 + SO_4^{2-} + 4H^+ + 2e^- \longrightarrow PbSO_4 + 2H_2O$ (at cathode)

(iv) $Cd(s) + 2Ni(OH)_3 \longrightarrow CdO + 2Ni(OH)_2 + H_2O$

(v) $Pb(s) + SO_4^{2-} \longrightarrow PbSO_4(s) + 2e^-$ (at anode)

(vi) $Zn(s) \rightarrow Zn^{2+} + 2e^-$ (at anode)

(vii) $HgO + H_2O + 2e^- \longrightarrow Hg(l) + 2OH^-$ (at cathode)

The total number of electrode reactions which are related to secondary batteries are —

(a) 3 (b) 4
(c) 2 (d) 5

43. Consider the following electrolytes,

(i) Acetic acid (ii) Phosphoric acid
(iii) Sulphuric acid (iv) Potassium hydroxide
(v) Carbonic acid (vi) Hydrochloric acid
(vii) Nitric acid

The electrolytes which give straight line when a graph is plotted between Λ_m *vs* $\sqrt{C}$ are–

(a) 3 (b) 4
(c) 5 (d) 2

44. Consider the following solutions,

(i) $ZnSO_4$ (ii) $AgNO_3$
(iii) $AuCl_3$ (iv) $FeCl_3$
(v) $CuCl_2$ (vi) $CeCl_4$
(vii) $Cu(NO_3)_2$

The total number of solutions, which can be safely stored in a copper vessel are —

(a) 2 (b) 4 (c) 3 (d) 1

Check Through PYQs

Element 2 Conductors, Conductance of Electrolytic Solution, Kohlrausch Law, Electrolysis

1. An aqueous solution of hydrazine (N_2H_4) is electrochemically oxidised by O_2, thereby releasing chemical energy in the form of electrical energy. One of the products generated from the electrochemical reaction is $N_2(g)$.

   Choose the correct statement(s) about the above process. *2024 Adv.*

   (a) OH^- ions react with N_2H_4 at the anode to form $N_2(g)$ and water, releasing 4 electrons to the anode.
   (b) At the cathode, N_2H_4 breaks to $N_2(g)$ and nascent hydrogen released at the electrode reacts with oxygen to form water.
   (c) At the cathode, molecular oxygen gets converted to OH^-.
   (d) Oxides of nitrogen are major by-products of the electrochemical process.

2. In a conductometric titration, small volume of titrant of higher concentration is added stepwise to a larger volume of titrate of much lower concentration, and the conductance is measured after each addition.

   The limiting ionic conductivity (Λ_0) values (in mS m^2 mol^{-1}) for different ions in aqueous solutions are given below. *2024, Adv.*

Ions	Ag^+	K^+	Na^+	H^+	NO_3^-	Cl^-	SO_4^{2-}	OH^-	CH_3COO^-
Λ_0	6.2	7.4	5.0	35.0	7.2	7.6	16.0	19.9	4.1

   For different combinations of titrates and titrants given in List-I, the graph of 'conductance' *versus* 'volume of titrant' are given in List-II.

   March each entry in List-I with the appropriate entry in List-II and choose the correct option.

List-I		List-II	
(P)	Titrate : KCl Titrant : $AgNO_3$	(1)	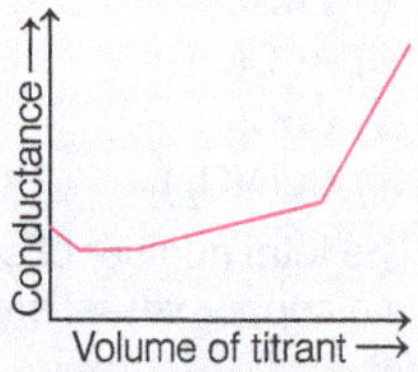
(Q)	Titrate : $AgNO_3$ Titrant : KCl	(2)	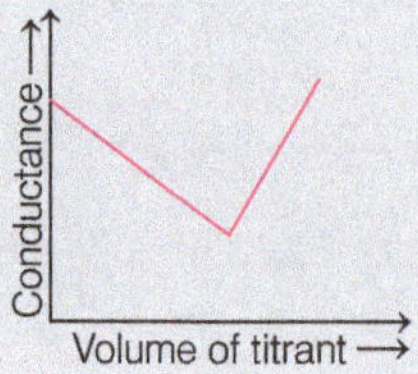
(R)	Titrate: NaOH Titrant : HCl	(3)	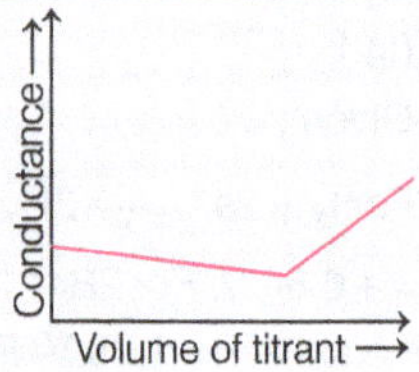
(S)	Titrate : NaOH Titrant : CH_3COOH	(4)	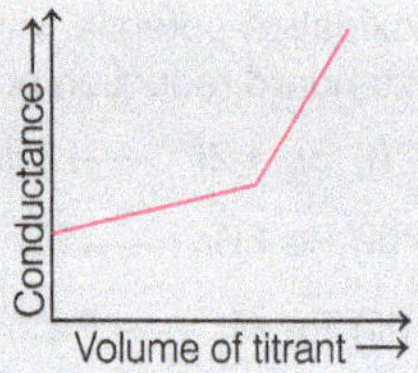
		(5)	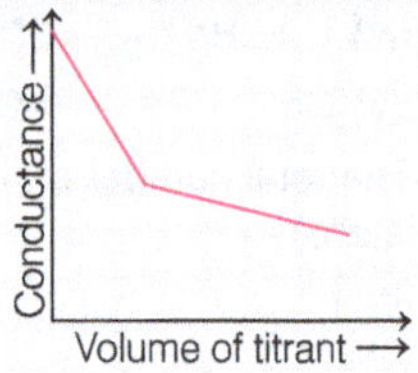

   (a) P - 4, Q - 3, R - 2, S - 5
   (b) P - 2, Q - 4, R - 3, S - 1
   (c) P - 3, Q - 4, R - 2, S - 5
   (d) P - 4, Q - 3, R - 2, S - 1

3. Plotting $1/\Lambda_m$ against $C\Lambda_m$ for aqueous solutions of a monobasic weak acid (HX) resulted in a straight line with *y*-axis intercept of *P* and slope of *S*. The ratio *P*/*S* is
   [Λ_m = molar conductivity
   Λ_m° = limiting molar conductivity
   C = molar concentration
   K_a = dissociation constant of HX] *2023 Adv.*

   (a) $K_a\Lambda_m^\circ$ (b) $K_a\Lambda_m^\circ/2$
   (c) $2K_a\Lambda_m^\circ$ (d) $1/(K_a\Lambda_m^\circ)$

4. Consider the strong electrolytes Z_mX_n, U_mY_p and V_mX_n. Limiting molar conductivity (Λ°) of U_mY_p and V_mX_n are 250 and 440 S cm^2 mol^{-1}, respectively. The value of $(m + n + p)$ is .... *2022 Adv.*

Ion	Z^{n+}	U^{p+}	V^{n+}	X^{m-}	Y^{m-}
λ° (S cm^2 mol^{-1})	50.0	25.0	100.0	80.0	100.0

   λ° is the limiting molar conductivity of ions.

The plot of molar conductivity (Λ) of Z_mX_n *vs* $C^{1/2}$ is given below.

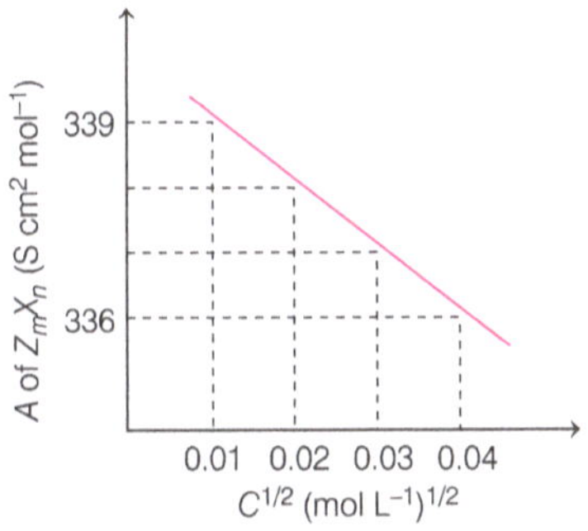

Paragraph

At 298 K, the limiting molar conductivity of a weak monobasic acid is $4 \times 10^2 \text{ S cm}^2 \text{ mol}^{-1}$. At 298 K, for an aqueous solution of the acid the degree of dissociation is α and the molar conductivity is $y \times 10^2 \text{ S cm}^2 \text{ mol}^{-1}$. At 298 K, upon 20 times dilution with water, the molar conductivity of the solution becomes $3y \times 10^2 \text{ S cm}^2 \text{ mol}^{-1}$. **2021 Adv.**

5. The value of α is ....
6. The value of y is ....
7. The conductance of a 0.0015 M aqueous solution of a weak monobasic acid was determined by using a conductivity cell consisting of platinised Pt electrodes. The distance between the electrodes is 120 cm with an area of cross section of 1 cm². The conductance of this solution was found to be 5×10^{-7} S.

   The pH of the solution is 4. The value of limiting molar conductivity (Λ_m°) of this weak monobasic acid in aqueous solution is
   $Z \times 10^2 \text{ S cm}^{-2} \text{ mol}^{-1}$. The value of Z is .... **2017 Adv.**

Element 3 Electrochemical Cells, Nernst Equation and Electrode Potential

8. The reduction potential (E°, in V) of $MnO_4^-(aq)/Mn(s)$ is

   [Given, $E^\circ_{MnO_4^-(aq)/MnO_2(s)} = 1.68$ V ; $E^\circ_{MnO_2(s)/Mn^{2+}(aq)} = 1.21$ V ;

   $E^\circ_{Mn^{2+}(aq)/Mn(s)} = -1.03$ V] **2022 Adv.**

9. Some standard electrode potentials at 298 K are given below :

Pb^{2+}/Pb;	-0.13 V,	Ni^{2+}/Ni;	-0.24 V
Cd^{2+}/Cd;	-0.40 V,	Fe^{2+}/Fe;	-0.44 V

   To a solution containing 0.001 M of X^{2+} and 0.1 M of Y^{2+}, the metal rods X and Y are inserted (at 298 K) and connected by a conducting wire. This resulted in dissolution of X. The correct combination(s) of X and Y, respectively, is(are)
   (Given : Gas constant, $R = 8.314 \text{ J K}^{-1} \text{ mol}^{-1}$, Faraday constant, $F = 96500 \text{ C mol}^{-1}$) **2021 Adv.**
   (a) Cd and Ni
   (b) Cd and Fe
   (c) Ni and Pb
   (d) Ni and Fe

10. For the electrochemical cell,
    $Mg(s)|Mg^{2+}(aq, 1\text{ M}) || Cu^{2+}(aq, 1\text{ M}) | Cu(s)$
    The standard emf of the cell is 2.70 V at 300 K. When the concentration of Mg^{2+} is changed to x M, the cell potential changes to 2.67 V at 300 K. The value of x is ....
    (Given, $\frac{F}{R} = 11500 \text{ K V}^{-1}$, where F is the Faraday constant and R is the gas contant, $\ln(10) = 2.30$) **2018 Adv.**

11. Consider an electrochemical cell :
    $A(s)|A^{n+}(aq, 2\text{M})||B^{2n+}(aq, 1\text{M})|B(s)$. The value of $\Delta H^\ominus$ for the cell reaction is twice of $\Delta G^\ominus$ at 300 K. If the emf of the cell is zero, the $\Delta S^\ominus$ (in J K⁻¹ mol⁻¹) of the cell reaction per mole of B formed at 300 K is ....
    (Given : $\ln(2) = 0.7$, R (universal gas constant) = $8.3 \text{ J K}^{-1} \text{ mol}^{-1}$. H, S and G are enthalpy, entropy and Gibbs energy, respectively.) **2018 Adv.**

12. For the following cell,
    $Zn(s)|ZnSO_4(aq)||CuSO_4(aq)|Cu(s)$
    when the concentration of Zn^{2+} is 10 times the concentration of Cu^{2+}, the expression for ΔG (in J mol⁻¹) is [F is Faraday constant; R is gas constant; T is temperature; E° (cell) = 1.1 V] **2017 Adv.**
    (a) $2.303\,RT + 1.1F$
    (b) 1.1 F
    (c) $2.303\,RT - 2.2F$
    (d) -2.2 F

13. For the following electrochemical cell at 298 K,
    $Pt(s)|H_2(g, 1\text{bar})|H^+(aq, 1\text{M})||M^{4+}(aq), M^{2+}(aq)|Pt(s)$
    $E_{cell} = 0.092$ V when $\frac{[M^{2+}(aq)]}{[M^{4+}(aq)]} = 10^x$

    Given : $E^\circ_{M^{4+}/M^{2+}} = 0.151$ V;

    $$2.303\frac{RT}{F} = 0.059 \text{ V}$$

    The value of x is **2016 Adv.**
    (a) -2 (b) -1
    (c) 1 (d) 2

HINTS & Solutions

Solutions : Competency Enhancer

1.1 ***(d)*** Disproportionation reactions are those in which same species is oxidised as well as reduced simultaneously.

A. $3H_3\overset{+1}{P}O_2 \longrightarrow \overset{-3}{P}H_3 + 2H_3\overset{+3}{P}O_3$

B. $\overset{0}{P_4} + 3NaOH + 3H_2O \longrightarrow \overset{-3}{P}H_3 + 3NaH_2\overset{+1}{P}O_2$

C. $\overset{0}{Cl_2} + H_2O \longrightarrow H\overset{-1}{Cl} + H\overset{+1}{Cl}O$

D. $3Cu + 8H\overset{+5}{N}O_3 \longrightarrow 3Cu(\overset{+5}{N}O_3)_2 + 4H_2O + \overset{+2}{N}O$

not is an disproportionation reaction.

In A, B and C same species is oxidised as well as reduced. So, these are disproportionation reactions.

2.1 ***(c)*** $\lambda_{\text{solution}} = 2 \times \lambda_c^{+3} + 3 \times \lambda_a^{2-}$

$= 2 \times 65 + 3 \times 40 = 130 + 120$

$= 250 \text{ S cm}^2 \text{ eq}^{-1}$

2.2 ***(0.135)*** Limiting molar conductivity,

$$\overset{\circ}{\Lambda}_m = 8 \times 10^2 \text{ S cm}^2 \text{ mol}^{-1}$$

Molar conductivity,

$$\Lambda_m = a \times 10^2 \text{ S cm}^2 \text{ mol}^{-1}$$

Molar conductivity on dilution,

$$\overset{\circ}{\Lambda}_m = 4a \times 10^2 \text{ S cm}^2 \text{ mol}^{-1}$$

Let the concentration before dilution be C

Concentration after dilution $= \frac{C}{30}$

Since, $\alpha = \frac{\Lambda_m}{\overset{\circ}{\Lambda}_m}$ ...(i)

$\Rightarrow$ Dissociation constant, $K_a = \frac{C\alpha^2}{(1-\alpha)}$

Using (i) in the above equation,

$$K_a = \frac{C\Lambda_m^2}{\overset{\circ}{\Lambda}_m^2 \left\{1 - \frac{\Lambda_m}{\overset{\circ}{\Lambda}_m}\right\}} = \frac{C\Lambda_m^2}{\overset{\circ}{\Lambda}_m (\overset{\circ}{\Lambda}_m - \Lambda_m)}$$

Dissociation constant before dilution,

$$K_a = \frac{C(a \times 10^2)^2}{(8 \times 10^2)(8 \times 10^2 - a \times 10^2)} \quad \text{...(ii)}$$

Dissociation constant after dilution,

$$K_a = \frac{\frac{C}{30}(4a \times 10^2)^2}{(8 \times 10^2)(8 \times 10^2 - 4a \times 10^2)} \quad \text{...(iii)}$$

Comparing equation (ii) and (iii),

$$\frac{C \times (a \times 10^2)^2}{(8 \times 10^2)(8 \times 10^2 - a \times 10^2)} = \frac{C(4a \times 10^2)^2}{30(8 \times 10^2)(8 \times 10^2 - 4a \times 10^2)}$$

$$\Rightarrow \frac{a^2 \times 10^4}{10^2(8-a)} = \frac{16a^2 \times 10^4}{30 \times 10^2 \times 4(2-a)}$$

$$\Rightarrow 30(2-a) = 4(8-a) \Rightarrow 60 - 30a = 32 - 4a$$

$$\Rightarrow 26a = 28 \Rightarrow a = \frac{28}{26}$$

$$\alpha = \frac{\Lambda_m}{\overset{\circ}{\Lambda}_m} = \frac{a \times 10^2}{8 \times 10^2} = \frac{28 \times 10^2}{26 \times 8 \times 10^2}$$

$$\approx 0.135$$

2.3 ***(8)*** Fe in Fe_3O_4 exists in oxidation states of + 2 and + 3 $(\overset{III}{Fe_2}O_3 \cdot \overset{II}{Fe}O)$.

The average oxidation state of Fe in

$$Fe_3O_4 = \frac{8}{3}$$

$$Fe_3O_4 + 8e^- \longrightarrow 3Fe^{2+} + 4O^{2-}$$

1 molecule of Fe_3O_4 contains 3 Fe atoms with + 8 / 3 oxidation state per Fe atom.

So, 1 mol of Fe_3O_4 requires 8 Faradays of electricity.

3.1 ***(c)*** $Fe^{3+} + e^- \longrightarrow Fe^{2+}, \Delta G_1^\circ = +0.77 \text{ V} (n = 1)$ ...(I)

$Fe^{2+} + 2e^- \longrightarrow Fe, \quad \Delta G_2^\circ = -2 \times 0.44 \text{ V} (n = 2)$ ...(II)

Adding I and II

$$Fe^{3+} + 3e^- \longrightarrow Fe, \Delta G_3^\circ = -3FE^\circ \text{ V}$$

$$\Delta G_3 = \frac{+0.77 - 2 \times 0.44}{3}$$

$$= \frac{0.77 - 0.88}{3} \approx -0.037 \text{ V}$$

3.2 ***(−48.14)*** The given cell representation is:

$$M(s) | M^{n+} (aq.\ 3M) || N^{3n+} (aq.\ 1.5M) | N(s)$$

The reactions at respective electrodes will be:

Anode $M(s) \longrightarrow M^{n+}(aq.) + ne^- \times 3$

Cathode $N^{3n+}_{(aq.)} + 3ne^- \longrightarrow N(s)$

Overall reaction

$$3M(s) + N^{3n+}(aq.) \longrightarrow 3M^{n+}(aq.) + N(s)$$

Also, $\Delta H^\ominus = 3\Delta G^\ominus$ and $E_{\text{cell}} = 0$

So, using the Nernst equation

$$E_{\text{cell}} = E^\ominus_{\text{cell}} - \frac{RT}{nF} \ln \frac{[\text{Product}]}{[\text{Reactant}]}$$

$$\Rightarrow 0 = E^\ominus_{\text{cell}} - \frac{RT}{nF} \ln \frac{[M^{n+}]^3}{[N^{3n+}]}$$

$$\Rightarrow E^\circ_{\text{cell}} = \frac{RT}{3nF} \ln \frac{(3)^3}{(1.5)} = \frac{RT}{3nF} \ln 18$$

Since, $\Delta G^\ominus = -nFE^\ominus = -3n\,FE^\ominus_{cell}$

$$= -3nF \times \frac{RT}{3nF} \ln 18 = -RT \ln 18$$

Finally, using the formula,

$$\Delta G^\ominus = \Delta H^\ominus - T\Delta S^\ominus$$

$$\Delta G^\ominus = 3\Delta G^\ominus - T\Delta S^\ominus$$

$$\Rightarrow \quad \Delta S^\ominus = \frac{2\Delta G^\ominus}{T} = \frac{-2RT \ln 18}{T}$$

$$= -2R \ln 18 = -2 \times 8.3 \times \ln(9.2)$$

$$= -2 \times 8.3 \times (\ln (3)^2 + \ln 2)$$

$$= -2 \times 8.3 \times (2 \ln 3 + \ln 2)$$

$$= -2 \times 8.3 \times (2 \times 1.1 + 0.7)$$

$$= -48.14 \text{ J.K}^{-1} \text{ mol}^{-1}$$

Elemental Practice 8.1

1. ***(a)***
   (a) In $[Ni(CO)_4]$, Ni is in zero oxidation state, as CO is a neutral ligand does not contribute to the oxidation state of the metal.
   (b) In $[FeCl_4]^{2-}$, Fe is in + 2 oxidation state as the Cl^- ions are anionic and contribute a charge of – 1 each.
   (c) In $[Cu(NH_3)_4]^{2+}$, Cu is in + 2 oxidation state, as the ammonia molecules (NH_3) are neutral ligand, and the complex has an overall charge of + 2.
   (d) In $[MnO_4]^-$, Mn is in + 7 oxidation state.

2. ***(a)*** In acidic medium

   Reduction half reaction (for $Cr_2O_7^{2-}$)

$$Cr_2O_7^{2-} + 14H^+ + 6e^- \longrightarrow 2Cr^{3+} + 7H_2O$$

   Oxidation half reaction (for M^{y+})

$$M^{y+} \longrightarrow MO_4^- + (7-y)e^-$$

   1 mole of $Cr_2O_7^{2-}$ reacts with 1.2 moles of M^{y+}

   1 mole of $Cr_2O_7^{2-}$ gains 6 electrons.

   For the redox reaction to be balanced:

$$1.2 \times (7-y) = 6$$

$$7 - y = \frac{6}{1.2} = 5$$

$$7 - y = 5$$

$$y = 2$$

3. ***(a)*** Oxidation occurs when there is an increase in an oxidation state of central atom.
   (a) $NH_4^+ \longrightarrow N_2$ (Oxidation state of N changes from – 3 to 0)
   (b) $N_2H_4 \longrightarrow NH_4^+$ (Oxidation state of N changes from – 2 to – 3)
   (c) $NH_3 \longrightarrow NH_4^+$ (Oxidation state of N changes from – 3 to – 3)
   (d) $NO_3^- \longrightarrow NO$ (Oxidation state of N changes from + 5 to + 2)

4. ***(b)*** Both statement I and statement II are incorrect.

   The reaction between $Cr_2O_7^{2-}$ and SO_3^{2-} in acidic medium is

$$Cr_2O_7^{2-} + 3SO_3^{2-} + 8H^+ \longrightarrow 2Cr^{3+} + 3SO_4^{2-} + 4H_2O$$

   The correct form of statement I and statement II are:

   Statement I In the reaction of $Cr_2O_7^{2-}$ with SO_3^{2-} in an acidic medium, Cr is reduced and S is oxidised.

   Statement II In this case $Cr_2O_7^{2-}$ is reduced to Cr^{3+}.

5. ***(a)*** The two half reactions are:

$$Cr_2O_7^{2-} \longrightarrow 2Cr^{3+} + 7H_2O$$

$$NO_2^- + H_2O \longrightarrow NO_3^-$$

   Balance H and O atoms:

$$Cr_2O_7^{2-} + 14H^+ \longrightarrow 2Cr^{3+} + 7H_2O$$

$$NO_2^- + H_2O \longrightarrow NO_3^- + 2H^+$$

   Balance the charges

$$Cr_2O_7^{2-} + 14H^+ + 6e^- \longrightarrow 2Cr^{3+} + 7H_2O$$

$$3NO_2^- + 3H_2O \longrightarrow 3NO_3^- + 6H^+ + 6e^-$$

   The total equation is

$$Cr_2O_7^{2-} + 8H^+ + 3NO_2^- \longrightarrow 2Cr^{3+} + 3NO_3^- + 4H_2O$$

$$\frac{a}{c} + \frac{b}{d} = \frac{1}{2} + \frac{3}{4} = \frac{2+3}{4} = \frac{5}{4}$$

6. ***(c)*** The reaction is

$$MnO_4^- + 8H^+ + 5e^- \longrightarrow Mn^{2+} + 4H_2O \times 2$$

   and

$$C_2O_4^{2-} \longrightarrow 2CO_2 + 2e^- \times 5$$

$$2MnO_4^- + 5C_2O_4^{2-} + 16H^+ \longrightarrow 2Mn^{2+} + 10CO_2 + 8H_2O$$

   Each MnO_4^- accepts 5 electrons

   ∴ Number of electrons transferred per mole of $KMnO_4 = 5e^-$

$$\text{Equivalent weight} = \frac{\text{Molar mass}}{n\text{-factor}} = \frac{M}{5}$$

7. ***(c)*** The correct match is: A-2, B-4, C-1, D-3

8. ***(b)*** The brown ring complex compound is formulated as $[Fe(H_2O)_5NO]SO_4$

$$[\overset{+1}{Fe}(H_2\overset{0}{O})_5\overset{+1}{N}O]^{2+}\,SO_4^{2-}$$

   Oxidation state of Fe is + 1.

9. ***(c)*** (A) is correct but (R) is incorrect.

$$2\overset{+1}{Ag_2}\overset{-2}{O} \longrightarrow 4\overset{(0)}{Ag} + O_2^0$$

   Not all the decomposition reactions involve oxidation changes.

   Example $\quad CaCO_3 \longrightarrow CaO + CO_2$

10. ***(b)*** Statement I and V are correct whereas II, III and IV are incorrect.

   The reaction between H_2O_2 and $KMnO_4$ is

$$5\overset{-1}{H_2O_2} + 2K\overset{+7}{Mn}O_4 + 3H_2SO_4 \longrightarrow 5O_2 + 8H_2O + 2\overset{+2}{Mn}SO_4 + K_2SO_4$$

   In this reaction H_2O_2 acts as a reducing as well as an oxidising agent and it will reduce MnO_4^- to Mn^{2+}.

11. ***(d)*** $\overset{(0)}{S_8} + 12NaOH \longrightarrow 2Na_2\overset{+2}{S_2}O_3 + 4Na_2\overset{-2}{S} + 6H_2O$
Sodium Thiosulphate, Sodium Sulphide

This is an example of disproportionation reaction because *S* is reduced as well as oxidised.

12. ***(b)***
(a) $2Al + 6HNO_3(conc.) \longrightarrow 2Al(NO_3)_3 + 3H_2O$
Al : 0 ⟶ + 3 (oxidised)
N stays (+ 5) (No reduction)
(b) $3Cu + 8HNO_3(conc.) \longrightarrow 3Cu(NO_3)_2 + 2NO_2 + 4H_2O$
Cu : 0 → + 2 (oxidised)
N : + 5 → + 4 (Reduced)
(c) $2Na + 2HNO_3 \longrightarrow 2NaNO_3 + H_2$
Na : 0 → + 1 (oxidised)
N : + 5 (No reduction)
(d) $2Fe + 6HNO_3(conc.) \longrightarrow 2Fe(NO_3)_3 + 3H_2O$
Fe : 0 to + 3 (Oxidised)
N : (+ 5) (No reduction)

13. ***(b)*** Persulphate anion ($S_2O_8^{2-}$),

$$2x + (-2)\times 6 + (-1)\times 2 = -2$$
$$2x - 14 = -2 \Rightarrow 2x = 12$$
$$\boxed{x = +6}$$

Tetrathionate anion ($S_4O_6^{2-}$)

$$4x + (-2)\times 6 = -2 \Rightarrow 4x - 12 = -2$$
$$4x = 10 \Rightarrow x = 2.5$$

Thiosulphate anion ($S_2O_3^{2-}$)

$$2x + (-2)\times 3 = -2 \Rightarrow 2x - 6 = -2$$
$$2x = 4 \Rightarrow x = +2$$

The correct order is

Per sulphate anion ($S_2O_8^{2-}$) > Tetrathionate anion ($S_4O_6^{2-}$) > Thiosulphate anion ($S_2O_3^{2-}$)

14. ***(a)*** Potassium permanganate ($KMnO_4$) is a strong oxidising agent that can oxidise primary alcohol to carboxylic acid.

15. ***(d)*** Reduction half reaction can be balanced as

$Cr_2O_7^{2-} + 14H^+ + 6e^- \longrightarrow 2Cr^{3+} + 7H_2O$

Oxidation half reaction is

$$Fe^{2+} \longrightarrow Fe^{3+} + 1e^-$$

On combining both equation and eliminating number of electrons, the overall equation we get,

$$Cr_2O_7^{2-} + 14H^+ + 6Fe^+ \longrightarrow 2Cr^{3+} + 7H_2O + 6Fe^{3+}$$

Hence, *x*, *y*, *z*, *n* and *p* respectively are 14, 6, 2, 7 and 6.

16. ***(b,c,d)*** Statements (b), (c), (d) are correct whereas (a) is incorrect. The correct form of (a) and (e) is
(a) The reaction is:

$$MnO_4^- + C_2O_4^{2-} + H^+ \longrightarrow Mn^{2+} + CO_2 + H_2O$$

The oxidation state of C in $C_2O_4^{2-}$ is

$$2x + (-2)\times 4 = -2 \Rightarrow x = +3$$

The oxidation state of C in CO_2 is

$$x - 4 = 0$$
$$x = +4$$

Thus, the oxidation state of C changes from + 3 to + 4.

17. ***(b,c,d)***
(a) $CaCO_3 \longrightarrow CaO + CO_2$ is a thermal decomposition reaction with no change in oxidation states.
(b) $MnO_2 + 4HCl \longrightarrow MnCl_2 + 2H_2O + Cl_2$ is a redox reaction in which Mn in MnO_2 is reduced and Cl^- is oxidised to Cl_2.
(c) $ClO_2 + O_2^{2-} \longrightarrow ClO_2^- + O_2$ is a redox reaction in which Cl in ClO_2 is reduced and O_2^{2-} is oxidised to O_2.
(d) $2Fe^{3+} + 2I^- \longrightarrow 2Fe^{2+} + I_2$ is a redox reaction in which Fe^{3+} is reduced to Fe^{2+} and I^- is oxidised to I_2.

18. ***(a,b,c)*** Disproportionation reactions are those in which same species is oxidised and reduced simultaneously.

19. ***(a,b,d)*** Statement (a), (b), (d) are correct whereas (c) is incorrect.
(a) In $Cr_2O_7^{2-}$, oxidation state of Cr is

$$2x - 14 = -2$$
$$2x = 12 \Rightarrow x = +6$$

Chromium is reduced from + 6 to + 3.
(b) Br^- is oxidised to Br_2. So, it will act as a reducing agent.
(c) The equivalent weight of $Cr_2O_7^{2-}$ is *M* / 6 because it undergoes 6 electron change.
(d) The balanced equation shows a transfer of 6 electrons.

20. ***(a, d)*** Statements (b, c) are correct whereas (a, d) are incorrect. The correct form of (a, d) is
(a) Valency and oxidation number can differ. For example, In NH_3, nitrogen has valency of 3 but an oxidation number is – 3.
(d) Valency is always a whole number whereas oxidation number may be fractional.

21. ***(a,b,c)*** Statements (a), (b), (c) are correct whereas (d) is incorrect. The correct form of (d) is:

The oxidation number of chlorine in Cl_2 is zero.

22. ***(30)*** Reduction of dichromate ($Cr_2O_7^{2-}$) in acidic solution.

$Cr_2O_7^{2-} + 14H^+ + 6e^- \longrightarrow 2Cr^{3+} + 7H_2O$

Oxidation of iodide (I^-)

$$2I^- \longrightarrow I_2 + 2e^-$$

The oxidation half reaction releases 2 electrons per $2I^-$, so 6 electrons requires 3 moles of I_2. The reduction half-reaction involves 6 electrons per 1 mole of $Cr_2O_7^{2-}$.

The balanced redox reaction is

$$Cr_2O_7^{2-} + 14H^+ + 6I^- \longrightarrow 2Cr^{3+} + 3I_2 + 7H_2O$$

The reduction of 1 mole of $Cr_2O_7^{2-}$ requires 6 moles of electrons

5 moles of $Cr_2O_7^{2-}$ will require = 5 × 6

= 30 moles of electrons

23. ***(5)*** The chemical formula for potassium tetrathionate is $K_2S_4O_6$ and its structure is

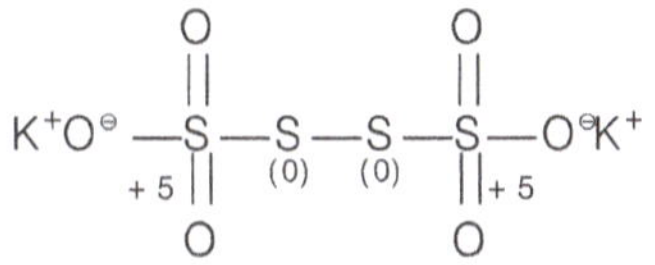

Let oxidation state of S is x.

$$x - 1 - 2 - 2 = 0 \Rightarrow x = +5$$

Oxidation state of central sulphur atom is 0.

Thus, the sum of the both oxidation states are $5 + 0 = 5$.

24. ***(12)*** In Acidic solution:
Potassium permanaganate ($KMnO_4$) reduces from Mn^{7+} to Mn^{2+}.

$$MnO_4^- \longrightarrow Mn^{2+}$$

In Neutral solution:
$KMnO_4$ reduces from Mn^{7+} to MnO_2

$$MnO_4^- \longrightarrow Mn^{4+}$$

In basic solution:
$KMnO_4$ reduces from Mn^{7+} to MnO_4^{2-}

$$MnO_4^- \longrightarrow Mn^{6+}$$

Sum of oxidation of Mn in each reduction product is $2 + 4 + 6 = 12$.

25. ***(5)*** Mass of CuO $= 2 \times \dfrac{80}{100}$

$$= 1.6 \text{ g of CuO}$$

Molar mass of CuO = 79.5 g/mol

Moles of CuO $= \dfrac{1.6\text{g}}{79.5 \text{ g / mol}} = 0.0201$ moles

Reaction with H_2.

$$CuO + H_2 \longrightarrow Cu + H_2O$$

$$Cu^{2+} + 2e^- \longrightarrow Cu$$

1 mole of CuO produces 1 mole of Cu

The solution is diluted to 250 ml, and 50 ml of this solution is titrated.

The fraction of the solution taken is:

$$= \frac{50}{250} = \frac{1}{5} \text{ of total solution}$$

Moles of Cu^{2+} in aliquot $= 0.0201 \times \dfrac{1}{5}$

$$= 0.00402 \text{ moles of } Cu^{2+}$$

Electron involved are, each Cu^{2+} takes 2 electrons

Total electrons $= 0.00402 \times 2 = 0.00804$ moles of electrons

$$= 0.00804 \times 6.022 \times 10^{23}$$

$$= 4.84 \times 10^{21} \approx 5 \times 10^{21} \text{ electrons}$$

26. ***(18)*** In Cr_2O_3, let oxidation state of Cr is x

$$2x + (-2) \times 3 = 0 \Rightarrow 2x - 6 = 0$$

$$2x = 6 \Rightarrow x = +3$$

In $CuSO_4$, let oxidation state of Cu is y

$$y + 6 + (-2) \times 4 = 0 \Rightarrow y + 6 - 8 = 0$$

$$y = +2$$

In $FeCl_3$, let oxidation state of Fe is z

$$z + (-1) \times 3 = 0 \Rightarrow z - 3 = 0$$

$$z = +3$$

The product of x, y and z is

$$3 \times 2 \times 3 = 18$$

Elemental Practice 8.2

1. ***(b)*** $R = \rho \dfrac{l}{A}$

$$\frac{l}{A} = \frac{R}{\rho} \Rightarrow \left(\frac{1}{\rho} = G\right)$$

$$\therefore \quad \frac{l}{A} = G \times R = 4.768 \times 10^{-3} \times 82.4 = 0.393$$

2. ***(c)*** $\lambda_m = \dfrac{\kappa \times 1000}{M}$

$$\lambda_m = \frac{8.3 \times 10^{-2} \times 1000}{0.1} = 830$$

3. ***(d)*** $MgCl_2 \longrightarrow Mg^{2+} + 2Cl^-$

$$\lambda^\infty_{MgCl_2} = \lambda^\infty_{Mg^{2+}} + 2\lambda^\infty_{Cl^-} = 254 + 2 \times 128 = 510$$

Equivalent conductivity $= \dfrac{510}{2} = 255$

4. ***(b)*** In electrolytic conductance on increasing temperature the kinetic energy of ions increases, led to the increase in mobility of ions, hence conductance increases and resistance decreases.

5. ***(b)*** $Q = It$

$$= 4 \times 300 = 1200 \text{ C}$$

Charge on 1 electron $= 1.6 \times 10^{-19}$ C

Number of electrons for 1200 C $= \dfrac{1200}{1.6 \times 10^{-19}}$

$$= 7.50 \times 10^{21}$$

6. ***(c)*** $KOH \longrightarrow K^+ + OH^-$

Equivalent mass $= \dfrac{56}{1}$

$$Q = 8.45 \times 1000$$

$$w = \frac{\left(\frac{56}{1}\right)}{96500} \times 8.45 \times 1000 = 4.90 \text{ g}$$

7. ***(a)*** Moles of $Pb(NO_3)_2$ in 1 L of $2M = 2 \times 1 = 2$ mol

Charge it $= 2 \times 5 \times 3600$ C $= 36000$ C

$$Pb^{2+} + 2e^- \longrightarrow Pb$$

2×96500 C deposits 1 mol of Pb

$$= 36000 \text{ C deposits } \frac{36000}{2 \times 96500} \text{ moles}$$

$$= \frac{180}{965} = 0.186$$

Moles of $Pb(NO_3)$ left $= 2 - 0.186 = 1.814$ moles

$$M = 1.814 \text{ M}$$

8. **(c)** $w = Zit$

$$3 = \frac{65}{2} \times \frac{i \times 30 \times 60}{96500} \Rightarrow i = 4.948\,A$$

9. **(b)** $\lambda_{Na^+} = 62.3\,\Omega^{-1}\,cm^2\,mol^{-1}$

$\lambda_{Cl^-} = 67.7\,\Omega^{-1}\,cm^2\,mol^{-1}$

$k_{NaCl} = 4.40 \times 10^{-6}\,\Omega^{-1}\,cm^{-1}$

$\lambda^{\infty}_{NaCl} = 62.3 + 67.7 = 130$

$$S = \frac{k \times 1000}{\lambda^{\infty}_{NaCl}} = \frac{4.40 \times 10^{-6} \times 1000}{130} = 3.38 \times 10^{-5}$$

10. **(b)** As dilution increases, dissociation of the electrolyte increases hence total number of ions increases ∴ molar conductivity increases. Carbonic acid is weak electrolyte, does not fully dissociate, as dilution increases, molar conductivity increase.

11. **(b)**

$Fe^{3+} + 2e^- \longrightarrow Fe^+, \quad \Delta G_1^\circ = -2x_1V \times F$ ...(i)

$Fe^+ + e^- \longrightarrow Fe^{2+} + e^-, \Delta G_2^\circ = +x_2V \times F$ ...(ii)

$Fe^{3+} + e^- \rightarrow Fe^{2+}, \quad \Delta G_3^\circ = -1 \times F \times E^\circ$

$$\Delta G_3^\circ = \Delta G_1^\circ - \Delta G_2^\circ$$
$$-F \times E^\circ = -2x_1VF + x_2VF$$
$$-E^\circ = -2x_1V + x_2V$$
$$E^\circ = (2x_1 - x_2)V$$

12. **(a)** Lower the reduction potential, lower is the tendency of species to get reduced and hence lesser oxidising power. Standard reduction potential increases in the order

$$Ge^{2+} < Ce^{4+} < Pb^{4+} < Co^{3+}$$

Hence, oxidising power of the species will increase in the order.

$$Ge^{2+} < Ce^{4+} < Pb^{4+} < Co^{3+}$$

13. **(a)** (A-r); (B-s); (C-q); (D-p)

14. **(b)** For $Zn^{2+} + 2e^- \longrightarrow Zn(s)$

$$E_{Zn^{2+}/Zn} = E^\circ - \frac{0.059}{2} \log \frac{1}{[Zn^{2+}]}$$

when Zn^{2+} solution diluted to 100 times, $[Zn^{2+}]$ decreases to 1/100.

Let new potential after dilution

$$E'_{Zn^{2+}/Zn} = E^\circ - \frac{0.059}{2} \log \frac{100}{[Zn^{2+}]}$$

$$E'_{Zn^{2+}/Zn} = E^\circ - \frac{0.059}{2} (\log 100 - \log [Zn^{2+}])$$

$$E'_{Zn^{2+}/Zn} = E^\circ - \frac{0.059}{2} \times 2 - \frac{0.059}{2} \log \frac{1}{[Zn^{2+}]}$$

$$E'_{Zn^{2+}/Zn} = E_{Zn^{2+}/Zn} - 0.059$$

Hence potential is decreased by 59 mV.

15. **(a)** CN for $Pt^{4+}, Cr^{3+}, Co^{3+} = 6$

$$Pt(NH_3)_6Cl_4 + aq \rightleftharpoons \overset{+4}{[Pt}(\overset{0}{NH_3})_6]^{4+} + 4Cl^-$$

[5 ions per molecule]

$$Cr(NH_3)_6Cl_3 + aq \rightleftharpoons \overset{+3}{[Cr}(NH_3)_6]^{3+} + 3Cl^-$$

[4 ions per molecule]

$$Co(NH_3)_4Cl_3 = [Co(NH_3)_4Cl_2]Cl \rightleftharpoons [\overset{+3}{Co}(NH_3)_4\overset{-1}{Cl_2}]^+ + Cl^-$$

[2 ions per molecule]

$$K_2PtCl_6 + aq \rightleftharpoons 2K^+ + [\overset{+4}{Pt}\ \overset{-6}{Cl_6}]^{-2}$$

[3 ions per molecule]

The more ions produced, the higher the molar conductivity.

16. **(a,b,c)** The increase in molar conductivity of HCl with dilution is due to a decrease in interionic forces.

17. **(c,d)** Specific conductance of a solution decreases with dilution, whereas molar conductance increase with dilution.

- The increase in the value of molar conductivity of acetic acid with dilution is due to decrease in interionic forces and increase in α.

18. **(a,c)** Only two statements (a, c) are correct whereas all other statements are incorrect.

- Change in molar conductivity is different for both strong and weak electrolyte with increase in dilution.
- The number of ions per unit volume decreases on dilution.

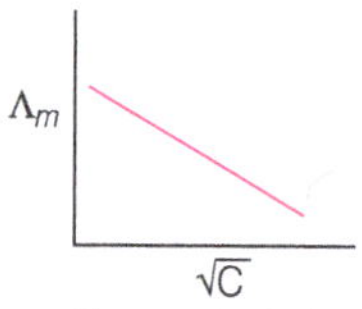

Strong electrolyte

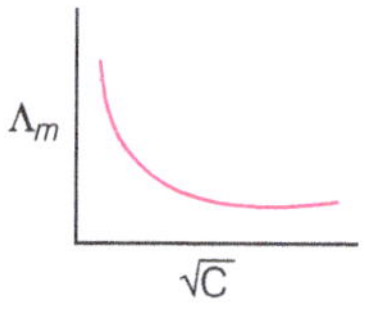

Weak electrolyte

19. **(b)** Statement given in (b) is correct. The corrected from of incorrect statement is

- Cation having higher standard reduction potential value will discharge first at cathode. Thus, the correct decreasing order of deposition is $Au^{3+} > Cu^{2+} > Fe^{2+} > Mg^{2+}$.
- The cell potential for $Ni(s)\,|\,Ni^{2+}(aq\ 0.1\ M)\ ||\ Ag^+(aq\ 0.1\ M)\,|\,Ag(s)$ is 1.02 V

$$E_{cell} = E^\circ_{cell} - \frac{0.0591}{2} \log \frac{[Ni^{2+}]}{[Ag^+]^2}$$

$$= (1.05 - 0.0295)\,V = 1.02\,V$$

20. **(c,d)** Nature of electrolyte does not affect the electrolytic conductance of a solution.

The oxidation state of Cr changes from + 6 to + 3

$$\overset{+6}{Cr_2}O_7^{2-} + 6e^- \longrightarrow 2Cr^{3+}$$
1 mol 6 mol

$1\,Cr^{3+}$ require ⟶ 3 mole of electron

$2\,Cr^{3+}$ require ⟶ 6 mole of electron

21. **(0.045)** $\underset{(0.4y)}{Zn^{2+}} + 2e^- \longrightarrow Zn(s)$

$$w = Zit$$

$$Z = \frac{M}{n\text{-factor} \times F} = \frac{65.4}{2 \times 96500}$$

$$w = \frac{65.4}{2 \times 96500} \times 0.965 \times 3600 \Rightarrow w = 1.1772 \text{ g}$$

$$\text{Moles} = \frac{w}{MM}$$

$$0.4 \times y = \frac{1.1772}{65.4} \Rightarrow y = 0.045$$

22. ***(153.5)*** Molar ionic conductivity of Mg^{2+}

$$\lambda^{\infty}_{[Mg^{2+}]} = 147\ \Omega^{-1}\ cm^2\ mol^{-1}$$

Molar ionic conductivity of Cl^-

$$\lambda^{\infty}_{[Cl^-]} = 80\ \Omega^{-1}\ cm^2\ mol^{-1}$$

Therefore, $\Lambda^{\infty}_{[MgCl_2]} = \lambda^{\infty}_{[Mg^{2+}]} + 2 \times \lambda^{\infty}_{[Cl^-]}$

$$= (147 + 2 \times 80)\ \Omega^{-1}\ cm^2\ mol^{-1}$$

$$= 307\ \Omega^{-1}\ cm^2\ mol^{-1}$$

Equivalent conductance

$$= \frac{\text{molar conductance}}{n-\text{factor}} = \frac{307}{2}$$

$$= 153.5\ \Omega^{-1}\ cm^2\ eq^{-1}$$

23. ***(9)*** $PbSO_4 \longrightarrow Pb^{2+} + SO_4^{2-}$

2 Faraday $\rightarrow$ 303 g mol^{-1} ($PbSO_4$ produced 2 moles of $e^{\ominus}$)

1 Faraday $\rightarrow \frac{303}{2} = 151.5$ g

1 Faraday liberate 151.5 g of $PbSO_4$.

$\therefore$ 0.06 Faraday $\rightarrow 151.5 \times 0.06 = 9.09 \approx 9$ g

24. ***(– 4.17)*** $ZnO \longrightarrow Zn + O_2$ $(n = 2)$

$$\Delta G = -nFE$$

$$E = -\frac{\Delta G}{nF}$$

$$= \frac{-866 \times 1000}{2 \times 96500} = -4.17\ V$$

25. ***(1.6)*** Equinhydrone $= E^{\circ}_{\text{quinhydrone}} - 0.06\text{pH}$ (at 30°C)

$$E^{\circ}_{\text{cell}} = E^{\circ}_{\text{RHS}} - E^{\circ}_{\text{LHS}} = E^{\circ}_{\text{quinhydrone}} - E^{\circ}_{\text{SCE}}$$

$$0.364 = 0.7 - 0.06\,\text{pH} - 0.24 \text{ (at 30°C)}$$

$$\text{pH} = \frac{0.7 - 0.24 - 0.364}{0.06}$$

$$\Rightarrow \quad \text{pH} = \frac{0.096}{0.06} = 1.6$$

Elemental Practice 8.3

1. ***(b)*** $E_{\text{cell}} = E^{\circ}_{\text{cell}} - \frac{0.0591}{1} \log \frac{\text{Product}}{\text{Reactant}}$

$$H^+ + e^- \longrightarrow \frac{1}{2}H_2$$

$$[H^+] = 10^{-10}$$

$$E = E^{\circ} - \frac{0.059}{1} \log \frac{1}{10^{-10}}$$

$$E = 0 - 0.059 \times 10$$

$$= -0.59\ V$$

2. ***(a)*** Both statement I and statement II are correct.

$$E_{\text{cell}} = E^{\circ}_{\text{cell}} + \frac{0.0591}{2} \log \frac{[Cu^{2+}]}{[Zn^{2+}]}$$

$$E_{\text{cell}} \propto [Cu^{2+}] \Rightarrow \propto \frac{1}{[Zn^{2+}]}$$

3. ***(c)*** Electrode potential is the potential difference between the charged metallic rods and salt solution. The electrode potential changes with the change in concentration of ions in solution in contact with metal.

   Cell potential is intensive property and always calculated for complete reaction.

4. ***(a)*** Both Assertion and reason are correct and reason is correct explanation.

   Standard electrode potential do not depend on the stoichiometric coefficient in a chemical equation because its an intensive property. i.e independent of the amount of substance involved or the extent of the reaction.

5. ***(a)*** Both (B) and (D) are correct. In acid medium positive value of $E^{\circ}_{Fe/Fe^{2+}}$ indicates that iron will dissolve in acid medium to form Fe^{2+} ion. Since $E^{\circ}_{Fe^{2+}/Fe^{3+}}$ is negative, hence + 2 state of iron is more stable than + 3 state in acid medium.

6. ***(b)*** decreases by 275 mV

$$Cr_2O_7^{2-} + 14H^+ + 6e^- \longrightarrow 2Cr^{3+} + 7H_2O$$

According to Nernst equation at 25°C.

$$E_{\text{red}} = E^{\circ}_{\text{red}} - \frac{0.059}{6} \log \frac{[Cr^{3+}]^2}{[Cr_2O_7^{2-}][H^+]^{14}}$$

Let $[H^+]_{\text{initial}} = X$

$$E_{\text{red(initial)}} = E^{\circ}_{\text{red}} - \frac{0.059}{6} \log \frac{[Cr^{3+}]^2}{[Cr_2O_7^{2-}][X]^{14}}$$

$$[H^+]_{\text{final}} = \frac{X}{100} = \frac{X}{10^2}$$

$$E_{\text{red(final)}} = E^{\circ}_{\text{red}} - \frac{0.059}{6} \log \frac{[Cr^{3+}]^2}{[Cr_2O_7^{2-}]\left[\frac{X}{10^2}\right]^{14}}$$

$$\Delta E = \frac{0.059}{6} \times 14 \times \log 100$$

$$= 2.75\ \text{mV}$$

7. ***(c)*** correct form of statement II is solution of $CuSO_4$ can not be stored in a zinc container as zinc is more reactive than Cu.

8. ***(a)*** Both Assertion and Reason are true and reason is correct explanation.

9. ***(a)*** A - s, B - p, C - q, D - r

10. ***(a)*** Statement (b), (c) and (d) are correct while statement (a) is incorrect. Its correct form is. It contains a metallic conductor (platinum) electrode which absorbs hydrogen.

11. ***(a)*** Both statement I and II are true.

12. ***(a)*** The lower the electrode potential, the stronger is the reducing agent. Therefore, the decreasing order of reducing power is K > Mg > Cr > Hg > Ag.

13. ***(d)*** EMF = $(SRP)_C - (SRP)_A$

(a) Zn, Ag EMF = 1.561 V (b) Cu, Ag EMF = 1.136 V

(c) Zn, Cu EMF = 1.099 V (d) Mg, Ag EMF = 3.17 V

14. ***(a)*** $E_{cell} = E_{Zn|Zn^{2+}} + E_{Ag^+|Ag}$

$Ag|Ag^+(2M)||Cu^{2+}(2M)|Cu, E° = -0.46V$

or $Cu|Cu^{2+}(2M)||Ag^+(2M)|Ag, E° = +0.46V$

$$+0.46 = E_{(Cu|Cu^{2+})} + E_{(Ag^+|Ag)} \quad ...(1)$$

$Zn|Zn^{2+}(2M)||Cu^{2+}|Cu, E° = 1.10V$

$$+1.10 = E_{(Zn|Zn^{2+})} + E_{Cu^{2+}|Cu} \quad ...(2)$$

Adding Eqs. (1) and (2)

$$+1.56 = E_{(Cu|Cu^{2+})} + E_{(Ag^+|Ag)} + E_{(Zn+Zn^{2+})} + E_{(Cu^{2+}+Cu)}$$

Since $E_{(Cu|Cu^{2+})} = -E_{(Cu^{2+}|Cu)}$

$$\therefore \quad +1.56 = E_{(Zn|Zn^{2+})} + E_{Ag^+|Ag}$$

15. ***(c)*** The anion which is stronger reducing agent (low value of standard reduction potential) is liberated first at anode. The increasing order of discharge of anion is SO_4^{2-}, NO_3^-, OH^-, Cl^-.

16. ***(a, d)***

(a) The cell potential is inversely related to the temperature. In exothermic reaction increase in temperature decreases the cell potential.

(b) The Nernst equation gives a negative value for the EMF at non-standard conditions.

(c) The cell potential is equal to the standard potential if $Q = 1$ only at standard conditions 298 K, 1 M concentration, 1 atm pressure).

(d) As the concentration of product increases, Q increases makes log Q larger. This results in a decrease in a cell potential.

17. ***(a, c, d)***

(a) The standard cell potential $E°_{cell} = E°_{cathode} - E°_{anode}$

$$= 0.80 - (-0.44) = 1.24V$$

(b) The cell potential will decrease, if concentration of Fe^{2+} ions increases.

(c) The cell potential will increase, if concentration of Ag^+ ions increases.

(d) The cell will stop operating when reaction reaches equilibrium and $Q = K_{eq}$, makes cell potential zero.

18. ***(a,b,c,d)***

(a) $\Delta G° = -nFE°$; $E°$ is positive, so $\Delta G°$ is negative.

(b) $E° = \frac{0.0592}{2} \log K$

Positive $E°$ implies that log K is positive

(c) Nernst equation is: $E_{cell} = E°_{cell} - \frac{RT}{nF} \ln K$

(d) At equilibrium, the cell has no driving force, so cell potential becomes zero.

(e) ΔG is –ve, reaction is spontaneous.

19. ***(c, d)***

(a) The electrolyte diffuses from higher concentration to lower concentration solutions.

(b) The electrode material and the solution in both half cells are composed of same substances.

(c) The cell potential is dependent on concentration. So, as the concentration decreases, cell potential also decreases.

(d) In electrolyte concentration cell, the concentrations of solutions of the same substances is different.

20. ***(a, b, d)***

(a) The Nernst equation can be used to express the potential in terms of concentration of the metal ions, indicated by K_{sp}.

$$E_{cell} = E°_{cell} - \frac{0.0591}{n} \log K_{sp}$$

(b) A lower concentration of metal ions typically results in a more negative standard electrode potential $E°_{MX|M}$.

(c) In a typical metal-metal ion electrode $(M|M^{n+})$, the concentration of M^{n+} is higher than in a sparingly soluble salt electrode.

(d) Temperature affects reaction kinetics and equilibrium positions, which can alter the values of $E°$.

21. ***(a,b,c,d)*** All (a), (b), (c) and (d) are incorrect and their correct form are

(a) If the standard reduction potential is negative then it is a stronger reducing agent.

(b) Negative electrode is the one where reduction occurs in electrolytic cell.

(c) In voltaic cell electron flow from anode to cathode

(d) Anode is positive electrode and cathode is negative electrode in electrolytic cell.

22. ***(–0.575)*** $E°_{cell} = +\frac{0.0591}{1} \log_{10} \frac{[A^+]^2}{[A^{2+}]} = \frac{0.0591}{1} \log\left(\frac{10^{-8}}{4.04}\right)$

$$E°_{cell} = -0.491 = E°_{A^{2+}/A^+} - E°_{A^+/A} \quad ...(i)$$

$$A^{2+} + 2e^- \longrightarrow A \;...(a) \Rightarrow \Delta G_a$$

$$A^+ + e^- \longrightarrow A \;...(b) \Rightarrow \Delta G_b$$

$$A^{2+} + e^{\ominus} \longrightarrow A^+ \;...(c) \Rightarrow \Delta G_c$$

We know, $\Delta G = -nFE$

$$\Delta G_c = \Delta G_a - \Delta G_b$$

$$-n_cFE_c = -n_aFE_a - (-n_bFE_b)$$

$$-n_cE_c = -2E_a + E_b$$

$$E_{A^{2+}/A^+} = 2E_{A^{2+}/A} - E_{A^+/A}$$

$$E_{A^{2+}/A^+} = 2 \times 0.33 - E_{A^+/A}$$

From equation (1) put value of E_{A^{2+}/A^+}

$$-0.491\text{ V} + E°_{A^+/A} = 0.66 - E_{A^+/A}$$

$$2E°_{A^+/A} = 0.66 + 0.491$$

$$E°_{A^+/A} = \frac{1.151\text{ V}}{2} = 0.575V$$

$$\therefore \quad E°_{A/A^+} = -0.575V$$

23. ***(17)*** $Zn(s) + Cu^{2+}(aq) \rightleftharpoons Zn^{2+}(aq) + Cu(s)$

$$\Delta G^\circ = -2.303\,RT \log_{10} K_{eq}$$
$$-nFE^\circ_{cell} = -2.303\,RT \log_{10} K_{eq}$$
$$E^\circ_{Zn/Zn^{2+}} + E^\circ_{Cu^{2+}/Cu} = \frac{0.059}{2}\log_{10} K_{eq}$$
$$0.76 + E^\circ_{Cu^{2+}/Cu} = \frac{0.059}{2}\log_{10} 10^{20}$$
$$0.76 + E^\circ_{Cu^{2+}/Cu} = \frac{0.059\times 20}{2}$$
$$E^\circ_{Cu^{2+}/Cu} = 0.59 - 0.76 = -0.17$$
$$E^\circ_{Cu/Cu^{2+}} = 17\times 10^{-2}\text{ V}$$

24. ***(77)*** $Fe^{3+} + 3e^- \longrightarrow Fe,\ E^\circ_1 = -0.036\text{ V}$

$$Fe^{2+} + 2e^- \longrightarrow Fe,\ E^\circ_2 = -0.440\text{ V}$$
$$Fe^{3+} + e^- \longrightarrow Fe^{2+},\ E^\circ_3 = ?$$
$$\Delta G^\circ_3 = \Delta G^\circ_1 - \Delta G^\circ_2$$
$$-n_3FE^\circ_3 = (-n_1FE^\circ_1) - (-n_2FE^\circ_2)$$
$$E^\circ_3 = 3E^\circ_1 - 2E^\circ_2 = 3\times(-0.036) - 2\times(-0.440)$$
$$= -0.108 + 0.88$$
$$= 0.772\text{ V} = 77.2\times 10^{-2} = 77\times 10^{-2}$$

25. ***(112)*** $E^\circ_{cell} = E^\circ_{cathode} - E^\circ_{anode}$

$$= 0.80 - (-0.403) = 1.203\text{ V}$$
$$E_{cell} = E^\circ_{cell} - \frac{0.059}{2}\log\frac{0.2}{(0.02)^2}$$
$$= 1.203 - \frac{0.059}{2}\times 2.70 = 1.203 - 0.080 = 1.123$$
$$= 112.3\times 10^{-2} \approx 112\times 10^{-2}$$

Therefore, the value of x is 112.

26. ***(0.730)*** $E_{red} = E^\circ_{red} + \dfrac{0.0591}{n}\log_{10}[\text{ion}]$

$$E_{red} = 0.76 + \frac{0.0591}{2}\log_{10}[0.1]$$
$$= 0.76 + 0.02955\times(-1) = 0.730\text{ volt}$$

27. ***(0.223)*** Cell reaction

$$Zn + 2Ag^+ \longrightarrow 2Ag + Zn^{2+}$$
$$E_{cell} = E^\circ_{cell} - \frac{0.0591}{2}\log\frac{[Zn^{2+}]}{[Ag^+]^2}$$
$$0.54 = E^\circ_{cell} - \frac{0.0591}{2}\log\frac{(0.0018)}{(0.01)^2}$$
$$E^\circ_{cell} = 0.54 + 0.037 = 0.577\text{ V}$$
$$E^\circ_{cell} = E^\circ_{cathode} - E^\circ_{anode}$$
$$E^\circ_{anode} = 0.80 - 0.577 = 0.223\text{ volt}$$

28. ***(6)*** When two or more positive and negative ions are present in solution, during electrolysis, certain ions are discharged in preference to others.

The ion which is stronger oxidising agent (high value of standard reduction potential) is discharged first at cathode.

Therefore $K^+, Ca^{2+}, Na^+, Mg^{2+} Al^{3+}$ and Fe^{2+} will not deposit at cathode before H^+.

Elemental Practice 8.4

1. ***(c)*** Iron loses electron to form Fe^{2+} ions, which further react with oxygen and water.

   Oxidation of Iron

$$Fe \longrightarrow Fe^{2+} + 2e^-$$

   Formation of Iron oxide

$$4Fe^{2+} + 3O_2 + xH_2O \longrightarrow 2Fe_2O_3\cdot xH_2O$$

2. ***(c)*** Lithium ion batteries store more energy in a smaller, lighter package and have minimal memory effect, allowing for more flexible charging patterns without affecting performance.

   Nickel-cadmium batteries suffer from the memory effect, where they lose capacity if not fully discharged before recharging.

3. ***(a)*** The correct match is

   I-C, II-A, III-B, IV-D

4. ***(c)*** Applying a strong acid to the metal surface would accelerate corrosion by lowering pH and increasing oxidation.

5. ***(c)*** In electrolytic refining, the impure metal is used as the anode and the pure metal is deposited at the cathode.

6. ***(d)*** $MnO_2 + C \rightarrow$ Used in Dry cell

   38% $H_2SO_4 \rightarrow$ Used in lead storage battery

   KOH solution $\rightarrow$ Used in Ni-Cd cell

7. ***(d)*** Both statement I and Statement II are true.

8. ***(a)*** A descaling agent helps to remove calcium and magnesium impurities from the electrodes, which can improve the efficiency of the electrolysis process.

9. ***(c)*** Anode sludge is a valuable by product in this process that often carries metals such as gold, silver. These metals are less reactive than copper and do not readily dissolve in the electrolytic solution. As a result, they settle at the bottom of the electrolytic cell as anode sludge.

10. ***(c)*** Only statement I is incorrect. The correct form of statement I is :

    Electrolysis of water produces hydrogen gas at the cathode.

11. ***(b)*** Zinc is often used as a sacrifical anode because it is more reactive than iron.

12. ***(b)*** Electrolysis of NaCl (brine) solution

$$NaCl + H_2O \xrightarrow{\text{Electrolysis}} NaOH + H_2 + Cl_2$$

13. ***(a)*** In nickel-metal hydride (NiMH) :

    Reaction occurs at anode (oxidation)

$$MH + OH^- \longrightarrow M + \frac{1}{2}H_2 + H_2O + e^-$$

    Reaction occurs at cathode (Reduction)

$$Ni(OH)_2 + 2e^- + 2H_2O \longrightarrow Ni + 2OH^-$$

14. ***(b)*** $Cu^{2+} + 4I^- \longrightarrow 2CuI + I_2$

Oxidation of copper decreases from +2 to +1.

15. ***(a)*** $2AgNO_3 + Cu \longrightarrow Cu(NO_3)_2 + 2Ag$

Due to presence of Cu^{2+} ions in solution, it will turn blue.

16. ***(a, c)*** Primary batteries are not rechargeable and their chemical reactions are irreversible.

17. ***(b, c)*** Metals lower in the series are less reactive. Noble metals such as Pt and Au are less reactive and more resistant to corrosion.

18. ***(a, b, d)*** Rust cannot occur in the absence of moisture, even if oxygen is present.

19. ***(a, b, c)*** In H_2 -O_2 fuel cell

Reaction occurs at cathode

$$O_2 + 2H_2O + 4e^- \longrightarrow 4OH^-$$

Reaction occurs at anode

$$2H_2 + 4OH^- \longrightarrow 4H_2O + 4e^-$$

Overall reaction

$$2H_2(g) + O_2(g) \longrightarrow 2H_2O(l)$$

20. ***(a, b, c)*** Direct synthesis of hydrocarbons from CO_2 is not a common industrial application of electrolysis.

21. ***(a, c, d)*** Electrolyte with high conductivity lowers the energy consumption.

22. ***(4)*** Presence of electrolytes, high temperature, increased surface area and electrical conductivity accelerate the rate of corrosion whereas low humidity generally decreases the rate of reaction.

23. ***(3)*** Lead acid, NiCd, Lithium ion are secondary batteries. Zinc-carbon, alkaline are primary batteries.

24. ***(5)*** Reaction occurs at anode

$$Cd(s) + 2OH^-(aq) \longrightarrow Cd(OH)_2(s) + 2e^-$$

Reaction occurs at cathode

$$2NiO(OH)(s) + 2H_2O(l) + 2e^- \longrightarrow 2Ni(OH)_2(s) + 2OH^-(aq)$$

Overall reaction

$$Cd(s) + 2NiO(OH)(s) + 2H_2O(l) \longrightarrow Cd(OH)_2(s) + 2Ni(OH)_2(s)$$

NiCd is a reversible secondary battery with discharge voltage of approximately 1.2 V per cell.

25. ***(2)*** SO_4^{2-} ions are not oxidised instead, water is oxidised at anode, releasing O_2 gas.

H_2O acts as a source of H^+ ions, which are reduced to produce H_2 gas, not H_2O itself.

26. ***(4)*** Adding Cl^- ions enhances the rate of corrosion.

Practice Element 01 : Target JEE Main

1. ***(c)*** The cell reaction is :

$$Fe^{2+}(aq) + Zn(s) \longrightarrow Fe(s) + Zn^{2+}(aq)$$

$$E^\circ_{cell} = E^\circ_{cathode} - E^\circ_{anode}$$

$$= E^\circ_{Fe^{2+}/Fe} - E^\circ_{Zn^{2+}/Zn}$$

$$= -0.44V - (-0.76V) = 0.32V$$

Zn is oxidised as it has more negative reduction potential value.

2. ***(b)*** A negative E° means the reaction is not spontaneous under standard conditions. The reverse reaction is more likely to be spontaneous.

3. ***(d)*** Equivalent conductance increases with dilution and HCl has highly mobile H^+ and Cl^- ions.

4. ***(a)*** Both Statement I and Statement II are correct.

5. ***(c)*** In B cell : g eq. of Hg^{2+} = g eq. of Ag^+

$$\frac{w}{\frac{200.6}{2}} = \frac{0.378}{108} \Rightarrow w = 0.351\,g$$

In C cell : g eq. of Hg^+ = g eq. of Ag^+

$$\frac{w}{\frac{200.6}{1}} = \frac{0.378}{108} \Rightarrow w = 0.702\,g$$

6. ***(a)*** The correct match is

A-IV, B-II, C-I, D-III.

7. ***(d)*** The reaction is represented as :

$$Q = \frac{[Red]}{[Ox]} = \frac{0.20}{0.10} = 2$$

Using the Nernst equation :

$$E = E^\circ - \frac{RT}{nF}\ln Q$$

$$E = 0.76 - \frac{8.314 \times 298}{2 \times 96500}\ln 2$$

$$E = 0.76 - 0.01284 \times 0.693$$

$$E = 0.751V$$

8. ***(c)*** $\Lambda_m, MgCl_2 = \lambda_{Mg^{2+}} + 2 \times \lambda_{Cl^-}$

$$= 106 + 2 \times 76$$

$$= 258\,S\,cm^2/mol$$

Expected conductivity $(\kappa) = C \cdot \Lambda_m$

$$= 0.05\,mol/L \times 258\,S\,cm^2/mol$$

$$= \frac{0.05\,mol}{1000\,cm^3} \times 258\,S\,cm^2/mol$$

$$= 0.0129\,S/cm$$

9. ***(a)*** Both (A) and (R) are true and (R) is the correct explanation of (A).

10. ***(a)*** Standard Reduction Potential values are :

$$Cu^{2+} + 2e^- \longrightarrow Cu, E^\circ = +0.34\,V$$

$$Ag^+ + e^- \longrightarrow Ag, E^\circ = +0.80\,V$$

$$Fe^{3+} + 3e^- \longrightarrow Fe, E^\circ = +0.77\,V$$

$$Pb^{2+} + 2e^- \longrightarrow Pb, E^\circ = -0.13\,V$$

Higher the standard reduction potential values, more is the reducing power of a substance.

$$Pb^{2+} < Cu^{2+} < Fe^{3+} < Ag^+$$

11. ***(b)*** In an electrochemical cell, the cell reaction is spontaneous and as such free energy of the system decreases. On the other hand, in electrolytic cell, the cell reaction is non-spontaneous and as such free energy of the system increases.

12. ***(d)*** Molar conductivity of a weak electrolyte is found to increase with dilution as dissociation increases with dilution. The magnitude of increase of molar conductance for a weak electrolyte is much larger than that for a strong electrolyte.

13. ***(c)*** Mass $= \frac{Q}{F} \times \frac{M}{n}$

Molar mass of copper = 63.5 g/mol

$$Cu^{2+} + 2e^- \longrightarrow Cu \quad (n = 2)$$

Mass of copper deposited $= \frac{2F}{F} \times \frac{63.5}{2} = 63.5$ g

14. ***(c)*** During the recharging process of a lead-acid battery, the sulphuric acid concentration actually increases as the battery reaches full charge.

15. ***(a)*** $\alpha = \frac{\Lambda_m}{\Lambda_m^\circ}$

$$= \frac{40 \text{ S cm}^2/\text{mol}}{390 \text{ S cm}^2/\text{mol}}$$

$$\alpha = 0.1025$$

16. ***(b)*** The cell reaction is

$$Zn(s) + 2Ag^+(aq) \longrightarrow Zn^{2+}(aq) + 2Ag(s)$$

$$E^\circ_{Zn^{2+}/Zn} = -0.76 \text{ V}, E^\circ_{Ag^+/Ag} = 0.80 \text{ V}$$

$$E^\circ_{cell} = E^\circ_{cathode} - E^\circ_{anode}$$

$$= 0.80 \text{ V} - (-0.76 \text{ V}) = 1.56 \text{ V}$$

Using the Nernst Equation

$$E_{cell} = E^\circ_{cell} - \frac{0.0591}{n} \log \frac{[Zn^{2+}]}{[Ag^+]^2}$$

$$= 1.56 - \frac{0.0591}{2} \log \frac{1.0}{(0.01)^2}$$

$$= 1.56 - 0.0296 \times 4$$

$$= 1.44 \text{ V}$$

17. ***(a)*** $\Lambda^\infty_{eq}(NO_3^-) = \Lambda^\infty(KNO_3) - \Lambda^\infty(KCl) + \Lambda^\infty_m(Cl^-)$

$$= (196.74 - 145.25 + 81.44)\ \Omega^{-1}\text{cm}^2\text{mol}^{-1}$$

$$= 132.93\ \Omega^{-1}\text{cm}^2\text{mol}^{-1}$$

18. ***(b)*** $E = E^\circ - \frac{RT}{nF} \ln Q$

Initial concentrations :

$$[HA] = 0.1 \text{ M}$$

$$[HB] = 0.1 \text{ M}$$

$$Q_{initial} = \frac{[HA]}{[HB]} = \frac{0.1}{0.1} = 1$$

New concentrations :

$$Q_{new} = \frac{[HA]}{[HB]} = \frac{0.5}{0.1} = 5$$

If Q increases, the term $\ln Q$ also increases.

The expression $-\frac{RT}{nF} \ln Q$ becomes more negative.

$$E = E^\circ - \frac{RT}{nF} \ln Q$$

$$E^\circ = 0$$

$$E = -\frac{RT}{nF} \ln Q$$

An increase in Q results in a more negative value for E, leading to an increase in the EMF.

19. ***(a)*** A-III, B-II, C-IV, D-I

20. ***(d)*** Increasing the surface area of the electrodes will decreases the resistance of an electrochemical cell.

21. ***(d)*** $Cu^{2+} + 2e^- \longrightarrow Cu$

$$Q = I \times t$$

$$= 2A \times 30 \times 60 \text{ s}$$

$$= 3600 \text{ C}$$

$$n = \frac{Q}{F} = \frac{3600 \text{ C}}{96500 \text{ C/mol}}$$

$$= 0.037 \text{ moles}$$

Moles of Cu $= \frac{0.037}{2} = 0.0186$ moles

Mass of Cu = 0.0186 moles × 63.5 g/mol

$$= 1.18 \text{ g}$$

22. ***(15)*** Distance between electrodes

$$(d) = 1.5 \text{ cm} = 0.015 \text{ m}$$

Area of the cross-section of electrodes

$$(A) = 4 \text{ cm}^2$$

$$= 4 \times 10^{-4} \text{ m}^2$$

Specific conductivity, $k = \frac{1}{R} \times \frac{d}{A}$

$$= \frac{1}{250} \times \frac{0.015}{4 \times 10^{-4}}$$

$$= 0.15 \text{ S/m} = 15 \times 10^{-2} \text{ S/m}$$

Molar conductivity $(\Lambda_m) = k \times \frac{1000}{C}$

$$C = 0.01 \text{ mol/L}$$

$$= 0.01 \text{ mol/L} \times 1000 \text{ L/m}^3$$

$$= 10 \text{ mol/m}^3$$

$$\Lambda_m = \frac{0.15 \text{ S/m}}{10 \text{ mol m}^{-3}}$$

$$= 0.015 \text{ S m}^2/\text{mol}$$

$$= 15 \times 10^{-3} \text{ S m}^2/\text{mol}$$

23. ***(458)*** $Cu^{2+} + 2e^- \longrightarrow Cu$

$$[H^+] = 10^{-pH} = 10^{-3}\ M = 0.001\ M$$

$$Cu^{2+} + 2e^- \longrightarrow Cu,\ E^\circ = +0.34\ V$$

$$2H^+ + 2e^- \longrightarrow H_2,\ E^\circ = 0\ V$$

$$E = E^\circ - \frac{RT}{nF}\ln Q$$

$$Q = \frac{[H^+]^2}{[Cu^{2+}]} = \frac{(0.001)^2}{0.01} = 0.0001$$

$$E = E^\circ - \frac{RT}{nF}\ln Q = 0.34 - \frac{0.059}{2}\log\frac{(0.001)^2}{0.01}$$

$$= 458 \times 10^{-3}$$

24. ***(519)*** $E^\circ_{cell} = E^\circ_{cathode} - E^\circ_{anode}$

$$= 0.80\ V - 0.34\ V = 0.46\ V$$

$$E_{cell} = E^\circ_{cell} - \frac{0.0591}{n}\log\frac{[Cu^{2+}]}{[Ag^+]^2}$$

$$= 0.46 - \frac{0.0591}{2}\log\frac{0.01}{(1.0)^2}$$

$$= 0.46 - 0.02955\log(0.01)$$

$$= 0.46 - 0.02955 \times (-2) = 0.5191\ V = 519\ mV$$

25. ***(6)***

$$Q = I \times t$$

$$= 3\ A \times (30 \times 60)\ s = 5400\ C$$

The reaction at the cathode is :

$$Ag^+ + e^- \longrightarrow Ag$$

Moles of Ag deposited $= \dfrac{Q}{nF}$

$$= \frac{5400\ C}{1 \times 96500} = 0.056\ \text{moles}$$

Mass of Ag deposited

$$= 0.056\ \text{moles} \times 108\ g/mol$$

$$= 6.048\ g \simeq 6\ g$$

26. ***(6)*** The cell reaction is :

$$Ag^+ + Zn \longrightarrow Zn^{2+} + Ag$$

$$E^\circ_{cell} = E^\circ_{cathode} - E^\circ_{anode}$$

$$= 0.80\ V - (-0.76\ V) = 1.56\ V$$

$$\Delta G^\circ = -nFE^\circ_{cell}$$

$$= -2 \times 96500\ C/mol \times (1.56\ V)$$

$$= -301080\ J/mol$$

$$= -301.08\ kJ/mol$$

$$\Delta G^\circ = -RT\ln K$$

$$\ln K = -\frac{(-301080)}{8.314 \times 298}$$

$$\Rightarrow \quad \ln K = 121.5$$

$$K = e^{121.5} = 5.8 \times 10^{52}$$

$$\simeq 6 \times 10^{52}$$

27. ***(391)***

$$\Lambda^\circ_m(CH_3COOH) = \Lambda^\circ_m(HCl) + \Lambda^\circ_m(CH_3COONa) - \Lambda^\circ_m(NaCl)$$

$$\Lambda^\circ_m(CH_3COOH) = 425.9 + 91.0 - 126.4$$

$$\Lambda^\circ_m(CH_3COOH) = \ = 390.5\ S\ cm^2/mol$$

$$\simeq 391\ S\ cm^2/mol$$

28. ***(150)***

Conductivity $(k) = 0.012$ S/m

$$= 1.2\ S/cm$$

$$k = C\Lambda_m$$

$$C = \frac{k}{\Lambda_m} = \frac{1.2\ S/cm}{150.0\ S\ cm^2/mol}$$

$$= 0.008\ mol/cm^3$$

$$= 8 \times 10^{-3}\ mol/cm^3$$

$$\Lambda_{eq} = \frac{K}{C} = \frac{1.2\ S/cm}{0.008\ mol/cm^3}$$

$$= 150\ S\ cm^2/mol$$

For KCl, $\Lambda_{eq} = \Lambda_m$ as each mole dissociates into one mole of K^+ and one mole of Cl^- ions.

29. ***(1)*** $E^\circ_{Sn^{4+}/Sn^{2+}} = +0.51\ V$

$$E^\circ_{Cu^{3+}/Cu^{2+}} = -0.41\ V$$

Since, tin has a higher reduction potential, it will undergo reduction at the cathode and chromium will undergo oxidation at the anode.

$$E^\circ_{cell} = E^\circ_{cathode} - E^\circ_{anode}$$

$$= 0.51 + 0.41 = 0.92 \approx 1\ V$$

EMF is positive, the reaction will be spontaneous. The EMF of the cell is 1 V.

30. ***(3)***

(A) $E^\circ_{cell} = E^\circ_{cathode} - E^\circ_{anode}$

$$= 0.34\ V - (-0.76\ V) = +1.10\ V$$

(B) The copper electrode is the cathode, where reduction occurs.

(C) The oxidation state of Zn changes from 0 to +2. So, zinc will oxidised to Zn^{2+}.

(D) Electrons will flow from anode to cathode.

(E) EMF is positive, reaction is spontaneous.

31. ***(3)*** A more negative electrode potential value indicates a stronger reducing agent.

Strongly electropositive metals can displace weakly electropositive metals from their salt solutions.

32. ***(9)*** The standard cell potential (E°_{cell}) is unaffected by the concentration changes.

$$E^\circ_{cell} = E^\circ_{Ag^+/Ag} - E^\circ_{Pb^{2+}/Pb}$$

$$= 0.80\ V - (-0.13\ V) = 0.93\ V$$

$$= 9.3 \times 10^{-7}\ MV \approx 9$$

33. ***(3)*** Only difference between two half cells potentials can be measured.

Negative standard potential means hydrogen gas is more stable than the reduced form of species.

Check Through PYQs : JEE Main

1. ***(3)*** Oxidation state of sulphur in given compound is calculated as,

$SO_3 \Rightarrow 0 = x - 6, x = 6$

$H_2SO_3 \Rightarrow 0 = 2 \times 1 + x - (2 \times 3), x = +4$

$SOCl_2 \Rightarrow 0 = x - 2 - (2 \times 1), x = +4$

$SF_4 \Rightarrow 0 = x - 4, x = +4$

$BaSO_4 \Rightarrow 0 = 2 + x - 8, x = +6$

$H_2S_2O_7 \Rightarrow 0 = 2 + 2x - 2 \times 7, x = +6$

Hence, in total 3 compounds sulphur have +4 oxidation state.

2. ***(3)*** Among the given metals, Fe, Ni and Ag will be oxidised by $Cr_2O_7^{2-}$ due to lower standard reduction potential values.

3. ***(c)*** In the reaction of $S_2O_3^{2-}$ with I_2, oxidation state of sulphur change from +2 to +2.5.

In the reaction of $S_2O_3^{2-}$ with Br_2, oxidation state of sulphur changes from +2 to +6.

$\therefore$ Both I_2 and Br_2 are oxidant (oxidising agent) and Br_2 is stronger oxidant than I_2.

4. ***(d)*** Strong reducing agents will liberate hydrogen from the dilute acid.

In given question, Ti^{2+}, V^{2+}, Cr^{2+} are strong reducing agents.

e.g. $2Cr^{2+}(aq) + 2H^+(aq) \longrightarrow 2Cr^{3+}(aq) + H_2(g)$

So, total number is 3.

Hence, option (d) is correct.

5. ***(d)*** The overall reaction is

$$Cr_2O_7^{2-} + 14H^+ + 6e^- \longrightarrow 2Cr^{3+} + 7H_2O$$

So, $X = 14$, $Y = 6$, $Z = 7$ and $A = Cr^{3+}$.

6. ***(b)*** Disproportionation reaction occurs in element who exhibits at least 3 oxidation states and must be less stable is one oxidation state.

Statement I is correct but Statement II is incorrect.

The correct form of Statement II is as follow,

ClO_4^- cannot undergo disproportionation reaction as chlorine is present in its highest oxidation state.

7. ***(c)*** $2MnO_4^- + I^- + H_2O \longrightarrow 2MnO_2 + IO_3^- + 2OH^-$

$Cr_2O_7^{2-} \downarrow + 14H^+ + 6e^- \longrightarrow 2Cr^{3+} + 7H_2O$

8. ***(a)*** $Cl_2 + 2OH^- \longrightarrow Cl^- + ClO^- + H_2O$

9. ***(c)*** N^{3-} cannot function as an oxidising agent. In N^{3-} ion 'N' is already present in its lowest possible oxidation state, hence it cannot be reduced further because of which it cannot act as an oxidising agent.
Hence, option (c) is correct.

10. ***(23)*** Reduction half reaction can be balanced as

$$Cr_2O_7^{2-} + 14H^{\oplus} + 6e^{\ominus} \longrightarrow 2Cr^{3+} + 7H_2O$$

Oxidation half reaction is

$$Fe^{2+} \longrightarrow Fe^{3+} + 1e^{\ominus}$$

On combining both equation and eliminate number of electrons, the overall equation we get

$$Cr_2O_7^{2-} + 14H^{\oplus} + 6Fe^{\ominus} \longrightarrow 2Cr^{3+} + 7H_2O + 6Fe^{3+}$$

Hence, $x = 14$, $y = 2$, $z = 7$

Thus, the sum of $x + y + z = 14 + 2 + 7 = 23$

11. ***(3)*** In alkaline medium,

$$MnO_4^- + 3e^- + 2H_2O \longrightarrow MnO_2 + 4OH^-$$

Number of electrons gained = 3
It has a tendency to release 4 electrons to attain + 4 oxidation state.
Hence, option (a) is correct.

12. ***(c)*** Number of iodine on reactant side = Number of iodine on product side

$$2 + x = 6 \times 2 \Rightarrow x = 12 - 2$$
$$x = 10$$

Thus, the equation will be

$$2IO_3^- + 10I^- + 12H^+ \longrightarrow 6I_2 + 6H_2O$$

13. ***(b)*** Consider the following reactions

$$\overset{(+1)}{2[Au(CN)_2]^-}(aq) + \overset{(0)}{Zn(s)} \longrightarrow \overset{(0)}{2Au(s)} + \overset{(+2)}{[Zn(CN)_4]^{2-}}(aq)$$

Reduction: Au (+1) → Au (0); Oxidation: Zn (0) → Zn (+2)

Above reaction is redox reaction as well as displacement reaction.
Hence, option (b) is correct.

14. ***(a)*** A chemical reaction in which the same species undergoes both reduction and oxidation is called disproportionation reaction.

Reduction (gain of electrons)

$$3\overset{+6}{Mn}O_4^{2-} + 4H^+ \longrightarrow 2\overset{+7}{Mn}O_4^- + \overset{+4}{Mn}O_2 + 2H_2O$$

Oxidation (loss of electrons)

15. ***(b)*** $MnO_4^- \longrightarrow Mn^{2+}$ $\quad$ ($\therefore$ $5e^-$ change)

$x - 8 + 1 = 0$ $\quad$ $x = +2$

$x = +7$

Hence, in the process of MnO_4^- to Mn^{2+} the change in oxidation state is five.

16. ***(a)*** BrO_4^- will not undergo disproportionation reaction because in it bromine is in its maximum oxidation state, i.e. + 7.

In option (a), we have the oxidation state of Br = + 7

In option (b), we have oxidation state of Br = + 1

In option (c), we have oxidation state of Br = + 3

In option (d), we have oxidation state of Br = + 5

The maximum and minimum possible oxidation state value for Br are + 7 and + 1 respectively. So, BrO_4^- cannot oxidise further. Hence, it cannot show disproportionation reaction.

17. ***(6)*** $Na_4[\overset{x}{Fe}(CN)_5NOS]$

$\Rightarrow \quad 4\times(+1)+x+5\times(-1)+(+1)+(-2)=0$

$\Rightarrow \quad x=+2$

$Na_4[\overset{y}{Fe}O_4] \Rightarrow 4(+1)+y+4\times(-2)=0$

$\Rightarrow \quad y=+4$

$[\overset{z}{Fe_2}(CO)_9] \Rightarrow 2\times z+9\times 0=0$

$\Rightarrow \quad z=0$

So, $x+y+z=(+2)+(+4)+(0)=6$

18. ***(19)*** In basic medium, the balanced equation is given by

$$2Fe^{2+}+H_2O_2 \longrightarrow 2Fe^{3+}+2OH^-$$

In acidic medium, the balanced equation is given by

$$2MnO_4^-+6H^++5H_2O_2 \longrightarrow 2Mn^{2+}+8H_2O+5O_2$$

$\therefore \quad x=2, y=2, x'=2, y'=8, z'=5$

$\therefore \quad x+y+x'+y'+z'=19$

19. ***(c)***

(a) The reactions in the given options are as follows:

$$\underset{(+6)}{H_2SO_4}+\underset{(+1)}{2NaOH} \longrightarrow \underset{(+1)\ (+6)}{Na_2SO_4}+2H_2O$$

(No change in oxidation state, so not a redox reaction).

(b) $\underset{(+3)}{[Co(H_2O)_6]Cl_3}+\underset{(+1)}{3AgNO_3} \longrightarrow \underset{(+3)}{[Co(H_2O)_6](NO_3)_3}+\underset{(+1)}{3AgCl\downarrow}$

(No change in oxidation state, so not a redox reduction).

(c) $\underset{(0)}{N_2}+\underset{(0)}{O_2} \xrightarrow{200\ K} \underset{(+2)\ (-2)}{2NO}$

(N_2 oxidised from 0 to +2 oxidation state and O_2 reduced from 0 to −2 oxidation state).

$\therefore$ This is redox reaction.

(d) $\underset{(0)}{3O_2} \overset{hv}{\rightleftharpoons} \underset{(0)}{2O_3}$

(No change in oxidation states, so not a redox reaction).

20. ***(336)*** Total charge passed $=2\times 30\times 60$ C

Number of Faraday passed $=\dfrac{2\times 30\times 60}{96500}$ F

Equivalents of Al deposited $=\dfrac{36}{965}$

Mass of al deposited $=\dfrac{36\times 9}{965}$ g

$=\dfrac{36\times 9\times 1000}{965}$ mg

$=335.75\ \text{mg}=336\ \text{mg}$

21. ***(b)*** For a weak electrolyte

$$HA(aq) \rightleftharpoons H^+(aq)+A^-(aq)$$

$$K_a=\frac{\alpha^2C}{1-\alpha}$$

$$\alpha^2C=K_a-K_a\alpha$$

$$\alpha^2C-K_a\alpha-K_a=0$$

$$\left(\frac{\Lambda_m}{\Lambda_m^\circ}\right)^2C+K_a\left(\frac{\Lambda_m}{\Lambda_m^\circ}\right)-K_a=0$$

$$\Lambda_m^2C+K_a\Lambda_m\Lambda_m^\circ-K_a\Lambda_m^\circ=0$$

22. ***(a)*** The electrolytes *A* and *B* are weak electrolyte and strong electrolyte respectively.

23. ***(d)*** As the given solution is already infinitely dilute hence no change in molar conductivity is observed upon addition of water.

24. ***(c)*** Calomel electrodes comes in the category of metal-insoluble salt-anion electrodes.

25. ***(4)*** Conductivity (Sm^{-1})

2.1×10^3
12×10
3.91
1×10^3
} Conductor at 298.15 K

1×10^{-16} Insulator at 298.15 K

26. ***(3)*** Only three statements A, C and D are correct whereas all other statements B, E are incorrect.

The correct form of B and E respectively are :

(B) The number of ions per unit volume in a solution on dilution, because the total number of ions in solution remains the same, but the volume increases.

(E) For weak electrolyte, the change in molar conductivity with dilution is due to an increase in the degree of dissociation.

27. ***(13)*** $\underset{10^{-5}}{AgNO_3} \longrightarrow \underset{10^{-5}}{Ag^+}+\underset{10^{-5}}{NO_3^-}$

$$AgBr \rightleftharpoons \underset{S}{Ag^+}+\underset{S}{Br^-}$$

$$K_{sp}=[Ag^+][Br^-]=4.9\times 10^{-13}$$

$\Rightarrow \quad S^2=4.9\times 10^{-13}$

$\Rightarrow \quad S=7\times 10^{-7}$ M

$\therefore \quad [Ag^+]=7\times 10^{-7}+100\times 10^{-7}$

$=107\times 10^{-7}$ M

$\therefore \quad [Br^-]=\dfrac{K_{sp}}{[Ag^+]}=\dfrac{4.9\times 10^{-13}}{107\times 10^{-7}}$

$=4.58\times 10^{-8}$

Conductivity $=u_{Ag^+}\lambda^\circ_{Ag^+}+u_{Br^-}\lambda^\circ_{Br^-}+u_{NO_3^-}\lambda^\circ_{NO_3^-}$

$=(107\times 10^{-7}\times 6\times 10^{-3})$

$+(4.58\times 10^{-8}\times 8\times 10^{-3})+(10^{-5}\times 7\times 10^{-3})$

$=(642\times 10^{-10})+(36.64\times 10^{-11})+(7\times 10^{-8})$

$=(642+3.664+700)\times 10^{-10}$

$=1346\times 10^{-10}\ Sm^{-1}$

or $13.46\times 10^{-8}\ Sm^{-1}\approx 13\times 10^{-8}\ Sm^{-1}$

28. ***(1000)*** In case of solution 1, cell constant

$$\frac{l}{A}=129\ m^{-1}$$

Resistance, $R = 100\ \Omega$

Specific conductivity,

$$\kappa = \frac{1}{R}\cdot\frac{l}{A} = \frac{1}{100}\times 129$$

$$= 129\Omega^{-1}m^{-1}$$

Concentration, $C = 74.5$ ppm

$$\text{Molarity, } M_1 = \frac{74.5}{\text{molar mass}\times 1000}$$

$$= \frac{74.5}{74.5\times 1000} = 10^{-3}\ \text{M}$$

$$\text{Molar conductivity } \Lambda_1 = \frac{\kappa}{M}$$

$$\Lambda_1 = \frac{129}{10^{-3}} = 1290\ \Omega^{-1}\ \text{m}^{-1}\ \text{M}^{-1}$$

or $\frac{129\times 10^3}{100}$

In case of solution 2,

Resistance, $R = 50\ \Omega$

$$\kappa = \frac{1}{50}\times 129 = \frac{129}{50}\ \Omega^{-1}\text{m}^{-1}$$

$$M = \frac{149}{74.5\times 1000} = 2\times 10^{-3}\ \text{M}$$

$$\lambda_2 = \frac{\kappa}{M} = \frac{129\times 10^3}{50\times 2}\ \Omega^{-1}\text{m}^{-1}\text{M}^{-1}$$

$$\frac{\lambda_1}{\lambda_2} = \frac{129\times 10^3\times 50\times 2}{100\times 129\times 10^3} = 1$$

$$\frac{\lambda_1}{\lambda_2} = 1 = 1000\times 10^{-3}.$$

Thus, the value of x is 1000.

29. ***(b)*** Molar conductivity of strong electrolyte (i.e. KI) increases slowly on dilution, while molar conductivity of weak electrolyte (i.e., H_2CO_3) increases steeply with dilution.

30. ***(127)*** **At anode**

$$2H_2O \longrightarrow O_2(g) + 4\ H^+ + 4e^-$$

At cathode

$$2H_2O + 2e^- \longrightarrow H_2(g) + 2OH^-$$

$$\text{Number of gram equivalent} = \frac{i\times t}{F}$$

$$= \frac{0.10\times 2\times 60\times 60}{96500}$$

$$= 0.00746$$

Now, volume of O_2 = number of moles of $O_2 \times 22.7$

$$= \frac{0.00746}{4}\times 22.7 = 0.0423\ \text{L}$$

Volume of H_2 = number of moles of

$$H_2\times 22.7\ \text{L} = \frac{0.00746}{2}\times 22.7 = 0.0846\ \text{L}$$

Total volume = (0.0423 + 0.0846) L

$= 0.1269$ L $\approx$ 127 mL or 127cm^3

31. ***(14)*** Given,

$$\Lambda^{\infty}_{AgI} = \Lambda^{\infty}_{AgNO_3} + \Lambda^{\infty}_{NaI} - \Lambda^{\infty}_{NaNO_3}$$

$$= 13.3 + 12.7 - 12.0$$

$$= 14\ \text{mS m}^2\ \text{mol}^{-1}.$$

32. ***(266)*** Given, $R = 1750\ \Omega$

$$\kappa = 0.152\times 10^{-3}\Omega^{-1}\ \text{cm}^{-1}$$

Conductivity = Cell constant × conductance

$$0.152\times 10^{-3} = \text{Cell constant}\times\frac{1}{1750}$$

Cell constant $= 0.152\times 10^{-3}\times 1750$

$= 266\times 10^{-3}\ \text{cm}^{-1}$

33. ***(d)*** Limiting molar conductivity of CH_3COOH is more than KCl. Hence, statement I is false.

With decrease in concentration of electrolyte, molar conductivity increases.

Hence, statement II is also false.

34. ***(11)*** For 1 mole of ClO_3^-, 6 F charge required but current efficiency is only 60%. So, to obtain 1 mol ClO_3^-, charge required is 10 F.

$$\text{Now, moles of } KClO_3 = \frac{10\ \text{g}}{122}$$

$$\therefore\ \text{Charge required} = \frac{10}{122}\times 10\ \text{F}$$

$\therefore$ Current = 2 A

Apply, $Q = I\cdot t$

$$\therefore\ 100\times\frac{96500}{122} = 2t$$

$$\Rightarrow\ t = 39549.18\ \text{sec}$$

$$= 10.98\ \text{h} \approx 11\ \text{h}$$

Hence, the correct answer is (11).

35. ***(d)*** The given graph of molar conductivity *vs* $\sqrt{C}$ is for weak electrolyte. Hence among the given options CH_3COOH is the correct answer, as it is a weak electrolyte(x).

36. ***(c)*** Species with higher value of standard reduction potential will get deposited at cathode. So, only Au ($E^{\circ}_{Au^+/Au} = 1.69$ V) will get electro deposited at cathode.

37. ***(4)*** $Fe^{2+} + 2e \longrightarrow Fe \quad E^{\circ} = y$

$$Fe \longrightarrow Fe^{3+} + 3e^- \quad E^{\circ} = -z$$

$$Fe^{2+} \longrightarrow Fe^{3+} + e^- \quad E^{\circ} = w\ \text{(say)}$$

$$1\times w = 2\times y - 3z$$

$$w = 2y - 3z$$

$$Fe^{2+} + Ag^+ \longrightarrow Fe^{3+} + Ag$$

$$E^{\circ}_{cell} = E^{\circ}_{Fe^{2+}/Fe^{3+}} + E^{\circ}_{Ag^+/Ag} = 2y - 3z + x$$

38. ***(c)*** The given reaction has the following half cell reaction;

$$\text{At anode}: \frac{1}{2}H_2 \longrightarrow H^+ + e^-$$

$$\text{At cathode}: AgCl + e^- \longrightarrow Ag + Cl^-$$

Overall redox reaction

$$\frac{1}{2}H_2(g) + AgCl(s) \longrightarrow H^+(aq) + Cl^+(aq) + Ag(s)$$

Hence, the overall cell representation is,

$$Pt|H_2(g)|HCl(aq)|AgCl(a)|Ag(s)$$

Hence, option (c) is correct.

39. ***(d)*** $M | M^{+2} || X | X^{2-}$

The cell potential is given by

$$E^\circ_{cell} = E^\circ_{M/M^{+2}} + E^\circ_{X/X^{-2}}$$
$$= -0.46 + 0.34 = -0.12\text{ V}$$

As E°_{cell} is negative, so anode becomes cathode and cathode becomes anode.

Spontaneous reaction will be

$$M^{+2} + X^{2-} \rightarrow M + X$$

Hence, option (d) is correct.

40. ***(338)*** $[Mn^{+7} + 5e^- \rightarrow Mn^{+2}] \times 2$

$$[C_2O_4^{-2} \rightarrow 2CO_2 + 2e^-] \times 5$$
$$2Mn^{+7} + 5C_2O_4^{-2} \rightarrow 2Mn^{+2} + 10CO_2$$
$$E^\circ_{cell} = 0.49 + 1.51 = 2.00\text{ V}$$

At equilibrium, $E_{cell} = 0$

So, $E^\circ_{cell} = \frac{0.0591}{n}\log K_{eq}$

$$\log K_{eq} = \frac{2 \times 10}{0.0591} \Rightarrow \log K_{eq} = 338.40$$
$$\log K_{eq} \approx 338 \Rightarrow K_{eq} = 10^{338}$$

Thus, $x = 338$

41. ***(25)*** For the reaction,

$$Cu^{2+} + 2e^- \longrightarrow Cu$$
$$pH = 14$$

means, $p_{OH} = 0$ or $[OH^-] = 1$ M

Also, $K_{sp} = [Cu^{2+}] \times [OH^-]^2$

Hence, $1 \times 10^{-20} = [Cu^{2+}]\,[1]^2$

or, $[Cu^{2+}] = 1 \times 10^{-20}$ ...(1)

The reduction potential of copper can be written as

$$E_{cell} = E^\circ_{cell} - \frac{0.0591}{2} \times \log[1/Cu^{2+}]$$
$$E_{cell} = E^\circ_{cell} + \frac{0.0591}{2} \times \log[Cu^{2+}]$$
$$E_{cell} = 0.34 + 0.0295 \times \log[10^{-20}]$$
$$E_{cell} + 0.34 + [0.0295 \times (-20)] = 0.34 + [-0.59] = -0.25$$

or -25×10^{-2}V

Thus, the value of $x = 25$

42. ***(4)*** All the given statements i.e. A, B, C and D are correct.

43. ***(3)*** For the redox reaction to be feasible, E°_{cell} must be positive. Therefore, E°_{cell} will be positive in case of 3 metals i.e., V, Fe and Au.

(i) $E^\circ_{cell} = E^\circ_{reduction} - E^\circ_{oxidation}$

$$E^\circ_{cell} = E^\circ_{NO_3^-/NO} - E^\circ_{V/V^{2+}} = 0.97 - (-1.19) = 2.16\text{V}$$

(ii) $E^\circ_{cell} = E^\circ_{NO_3^-/NO} - E^\circ_{Fe/Fe^{3+}}$

$$= 0.97 - (-0.04) = 1.01\text{V}$$

(iii) $E^\circ_{cell} = E^\circ_{NO_3^-/NO} - E^\circ_{Ag/Ag^+}$

$$= 0.97 - (0.80) = 0.17\text{ V}$$

44. ***(275)*** $E^\circ_{cell} = E^\circ_{Y^{2+}/Y} - E^\circ_{X^{2+}/X} = 0.36 - (-2.36) = 2.72$

From the Nernst equation,

$$E_{cell} = E^\circ_{cell} - \frac{0.06}{2}\log\frac{[X^{2+}]}{[Y^{2+}]}$$
$$= 2.72 - 0.03\log\left(\frac{0.001}{0.01}\right)$$
$$= 2.72 - 0.03\log(10^{-1}) = 2.72 - 0.03 \times (-1)$$
$$= 2.72 + 0.03 = 2.75 = 275 \times 10^{-2}\text{ V}$$

45. ***(17)*** $Zn(s) + Sn^{2+}(aq) \rightleftharpoons Zn^{2+}(aq) + Sn(s)$

$$\Rightarrow \quad \Delta G^\circ = -2.303RT\log_{10}K_{eq}$$
$$-nE^\circ_{cell} = -\frac{2.303RT}{F}\log_{10}K_{eq}$$
$$\Rightarrow \quad E^\circ_{cell} = E^\circ_{Zn/Zn^{2+}} + E^\circ_{Sn^{2+}/Sn}$$
$$= \frac{0.059}{2}\log_{10}K_{eq} \qquad [\because n = 2]$$
$$0.76 + E^\circ_{Sn^{2+}/Sn} = \frac{0.059}{2}\log_{10}10^{20} \qquad [\because E^\circ_{Zn^{2+}/Zn} = -0.76\text{V}]$$
$$0.76 + E^\circ_{Sn^{2+}/Sn} = \frac{0.059 \times 20}{2}$$
$$\Rightarrow \quad E^\circ_{Sn^{2+}/Sn} = 0.59 - 0.76$$
$$E^\circ_{Sn^{2+}/Sn} = -0.17$$
$$\Rightarrow \quad E^\circ_{Sn/Sn^{2+}} = 17 \times 10^{-2}\text{ V}$$

46. ***(3)*** To calculate the value of *a*, Nernst equation is used. First determine the value of E°_{cell} from given $E^\circ_{X^{2+}/X}$ and $E^\circ_{Y^{2+}/Y}$ value. Then use this value in Nernst Equation.

Given, $E^\circ_{M^{3+}/M^+} = 0.2$ V

$$\frac{2.303RT}{F} = 0.059\text{V}$$
$$\frac{[M^+(aq)]}{[M^{3+}(aq)]} = 10^a$$
$$E_{cell} = 0.1115\text{ V at 298 K}$$

Overall reaction of the cell is given by

$$H_2(g) + M^{3+}(aq) \longrightarrow M^+(aq) + 2H^+(aq)$$

According to Nernst equation,

$$E_{cell} = E^\circ_{(M^{3+}/M)} - \frac{0.059}{2}\log\frac{[M^+] \times 1^2}{[M^{+3}] \times 1}$$
$$0.1115 = 0.2 - \frac{0.059}{2}\log 10^a \qquad \left(\therefore \frac{[M^+]}{[M^{+3}]} = 10^a\right)$$
$$\Rightarrow \quad \frac{0.059}{2}\log 10^a = 0.2 - 0.115$$

$\Rightarrow \quad \frac{0.059}{2} \log 10^a = 0.0885$

$\Rightarrow \quad \log 10^a = \frac{0.0885 \times 2}{0.059}$

$\Rightarrow \quad \log 10^a = 3$

$\Rightarrow \quad a = 3$

So, the value of 'a' is 3.

47. ***(16)*** Given, $Sn^{2+}(aq) + 2e^- \longrightarrow Sn(s)$;

$E^\circ_{Sn^{2+}/Sn} = -0.140$ V

$\Delta G_1^\circ = -nFE^\circ_{Sn^{2+}/Sn}$

$= -2 \times (-0.14)\ F = 0.28\ F \quad \ldots(i)$

$Sn^{4+}(aq) + 4e^- \longrightarrow Sn(s)$;

$E^\circ_{Sn^{4+}/Sn} = 0.010$ V

$\Delta G_2^\circ = -nFE^\circ_{Sn^{4+}/Sn}$

$= -4 \times 0.01\ F = 0.04\ F \quad \ldots(ii)$

$Sn^{4+}(aq) + 2e^- \longrightarrow Sn^{2+}(aq);\ \Delta G_3^\circ \quad \ldots(iii)$

To get Eqs. (iii), subtract Eqs (i) from (ii)

So, we get

$Sn^{4+} + 4e^- \longrightarrow Sn\ ; \Delta G_2^\circ = -0.04F$

$\underline{Sn \rightarrow Sn^{2+} + 2e^-; -\Delta G_1^\circ = -0.28\ F}$

$Sn^{4+} + 2e^- \longrightarrow Sn^{2+}\ ;\ \Delta G_3^\circ = \Delta G_2^\circ - \Delta G_1^\circ$

$-nFE^\circ_{Sn^{4+}/Sn^{2+}} = -0.04F - 0.28\ F$

$-2FE^\circ_{Sn^{4+}/Sn^{2+}} = -0.32\ F$

$E^\circ_{Sn^{4+}/Sn^{2+}} = \frac{0.32\ F}{2\ F} = 0.16$ V

$E^\circ_{Sn^{4+}/Sn^{2+}} = 16 \times 10^{-2}$ V

48. ***(983)*** The given reaction is as follows

$Cu(s) + Sn^{2+}(0.001\ M) \longrightarrow Cu^{2+}(0.01\ M) + Sn(s)$

$E^\circ_{cell} = E^\circ_{cathode} - E^\circ_{anode}$

$= (-0.14) - (0.34) = -0.48$ V

$E_{cell} = E^\circ_{cell} - \frac{0.059}{2} \log \frac{[Cu^{2+}]}{[Sn^{2+}]}$

$= -0.48 - 0.0295 \log \frac{0.01}{0.001}$

$= -0.5095$ V

$\Delta G = -nFE_{cell}$

$= -2 \times 96500 \times (-0.5095)$

$= 98333.5$ J / mol

$= 98.3335$ kJ / mol

or $\quad 983.335 \times 10^{-1}$ kJ/mol

$\Delta G \approx 983 \times 10^{-1}$ kJ mol^{-1}

49. ***(25)*** $\Delta G^\circ = \Delta H^\circ - T\Delta S^\circ$

Also, $\Delta G^\circ = -nFE^\circ$

$\therefore \quad -nFE^\circ = \Delta H^\circ - T\Delta S^\circ$

$\Rightarrow \quad \Delta S^\circ = \frac{nFE^\circ + \Delta H^\circ}{T}$

$= \frac{(2 \times 96487\ C\ mol^{-1} \times 4.315\ V) + (-825.2\ kJ/mol)}{298\ K}$

$= \frac{832.682 \times 10^3 J\ mol\ or\ -825.2 \times 10^3\ J/mol}{298\ K}$

$\Delta S^\circ = 25.11$ J / K mol

50. ***(28)*** Cell reaction,

$Cu(s) + 2Ag^+(aq) \longrightarrow Cu^{2+}(aq) + 2Ag(s)$

$E_{cell} = E^\circ_{cell} - \frac{0.0591}{2} \log \frac{[Cu^{2+}]}{[Ag^+]^2} \qquad E_1 = 0.3095$

$= E^\circ_{cell} - \frac{0.0591}{2} \log \frac{(0.1)}{(0.01)^2}$

$E^\circ_{cell} = 0.3095 + \frac{0.0591}{2} \log(1000)$

$= 0.3095 + \frac{0.0591}{2} \log 10^3$

$E^\circ_{cell} = 0.3095 + \frac{0.0591}{2} \times 3 \quad \ldots(i)$

$E_2 = E^\circ_{cell} - \frac{0.0591}{2} \log \frac{(0.01)}{(0.001)^2} = E^\circ_{cell} - \frac{0.0591}{2} \log 10^4$

$E_2 = E^\circ_{cell} - \frac{0.0591}{2} \times 4$

From Eq. (i), we substitute E°_{cell}

$E_2 = 0.3095 + \frac{0.0591}{2} \times 3 - \frac{0.0591}{2} \times 4$

$= 0.3095 - 0.0295 = 0.28 = 28 \times 10^{-2}$ V

51. ***(147)***

$Zn | Zn^{2+}(0.1M) \,||\, Ag^+(0.01M) | Ag$

Cell reaction

$Zn(s) + \underset{0.01M}{2Ag^+} \longrightarrow \underset{0.1M}{Zn^{2+}} + 2Ag\ (s)$

$\Rightarrow \quad \frac{[P]}{[R]} = \frac{[Zn^{2+}]\ [Ag]^2}{[Zn]\ [Ag^+]^2} \qquad ([Ag] = [Zn] = 1)$

$= \frac{0.1 \times 1^2}{1 \times (0.01)^2} = 10^3$

$n = 2$

and $E^\circ_{cell} = E^\circ_{Ag^+/Ag} - E^\circ_{Zn^{2+}/Zn} = 0.8 - (-0.76) = 1.56$ V

$\Rightarrow \quad E_{cell} = E^\circ_{cell} - \frac{0.059}{n} \log \frac{[Zn^{2+}]}{[Ag^+]}$

$= 1.56 - \frac{0.059}{2} \log 10^3 = 1.4715$ V

$= 147.15 \times 10^{-2}$ V $= 147 \times 10^{-2}$ V

$x = 147$

52. ***(a)*** $E^\circ_{cell} = E^\circ_{Cu^{2+}/Cu} - E^\circ_{Zn^{2+}/Zn}$

$= 0.34 - (-0.76) = 1.10$ volt

If $E_{ext} < E^\circ_{cell}$, then e^-s flow from Zn to Cu and Zn dissolves at anode and Cu deposites at cathode.

Then, statement (a) is incorrect whereas all other statements are correct.

53. ***(144)*** $2Cu^+(aq) \rightleftharpoons Cu(s) + Cu^{2+}(aq)$

For the cell reaction, $E^\circ_{cell} = E^\circ_{Cu^+/Cu} - E^\circ_{Cu^{2+}/Cu^+}$

$= (0.52 - 0.16)\,V = 0.36\,V$

$\Rightarrow \quad \Delta G^\circ = -nFE^\circ_{cell}$

$\Delta G = -RT \ln K$

$\Rightarrow \quad -RT \ln K = -nFE^\circ_{cell}$

$\Rightarrow \quad \ln K = n \times \dfrac{E}{RT} \times E^\circ_{cell} = 1 \times \dfrac{1}{0.025} \times 0.36$

$\ln K = 14.4 = 144 \times 10^{-1}$

54. ***(96500)***

$$E^\circ_{cell} = (E^\circ_{Sn^{2+}/Sn} - E^\circ_{Cu^{2+}/Cu}) - \frac{0.0591}{2} \log \frac{[Cu^{2+}]}{[Sn^{2+}]}$$

$$= (-0.16 - 0.34) - \frac{0.0591}{2} \log \frac{1}{1} = -0.50\,V$$

$\Delta G = -nFE^\circ_{cell}$

$= -2 \times 96500 \times (-0.50)\,J = 96500.00\,J$

55. ***(d)*** The correct match is

A-IV, B-III, C-I, D-II

56. ***(d)*** Statements given in A, D and E are correct regarding fuel cells while B and C are incorrect.

It is because fuel cells produces electricity with an efficiency of about 70% and aluminium is not used a catalyst in it.

57. ***(d)*** Option (d) is incorrect among the given options while remaining all other options are correct.

The correct form of option (d) is as follows.

As tin coating is peeled off, then iron is exposed in atmosphere.

58. ***(a)*** Statements given in B, D only are correct.

On charging the lead storage battery, the reaction is reversed and $PbSO_4(s)$ on anode is converted into Pb instead of PbO_2.

Lead storage battery consists of lead anode and a grid of lead packed with lead oxide as cathode, a 38% solution of H_2SO_4 is used as an electrolyte.

59. The correct match is

A-II, B-I, C-IV, D-III.

60. ***(a)*** PbO_2 or Pb_3O_4 can be the compound *A*. But out of these two compounds only PbO_2 is used in lead storage batteries where a grid of lead packed with PbO_2 acts as cathode and also it is amphoteric in nature. It reacts with both acids and alkali.

Practice Element 02 : Target JEE Advanced

1. ***(a)*** Given, $Co^{3+} + e^- \longrightarrow Co^{2+}$; $\quad E^\circ = 1.81\,V$

$\Delta G^\circ_1 = -1 \times F \times 1.81$

$[Co(CN)_6]^{3-} + e^- \longrightarrow [Co(CN)_6]^{4-}$; $\quad E^\circ = -0.83\,V$

$\Delta G^\circ_2 = -1 \times F \times (-0.83)$

$Co^{2+} + 6CN^- \longrightarrow [Co(CN)_6]^{4-}$; $\quad K_f = 10^{19}$

$\Delta G^\circ_3 = -RT \times \ln 10^{19}$

Required, $Co^{3+} + 6CN^- \longrightarrow [Co(CN)_6]^{3-}$, $K_f = ?$

$\Delta G^\circ = -RT \times \ln K_f$

Now, $\Delta G^\circ = \Delta G^\circ_1 - \Delta G^\circ_2 + \Delta G^\circ_3$

or, $-RT \ln K_f = (-1.81\,F) - 0.83\,F + (-RT \ln 10^{19})$

or $RT \ln \dfrac{10^{19}}{K_f} = -2.64\,F$

$\Rightarrow \quad \log \dfrac{10^{19}}{K_f} = \dfrac{-2.64F}{2.303\,RT} = \dfrac{-2.64}{0.06}$

$\therefore \quad K_f = 10^{63} \approx 1.0 \times 10^{63}$

2. ***(c)*** Assuming the cell as concentration cell, net cell reaction is,

$$Ag^+\left(C_1 = \frac{K_{sp}\,(AgCl)}{[Cl^-]}\right) \longrightarrow Ag^+(C_2 = \sqrt{K_{sp}\,(AgI)})$$

and $E_{cell} = 0 - \dfrac{0.06}{1} \log \dfrac{C_2}{C_1}$

$$\text{or, } 0.102 = -0.06 \cdot \log \frac{\sqrt{8.1 \times 10^{-17}}}{\left(\dfrac{1.8 \times 10^{-10}}{[Cl^-]}\right)}$$

$\Rightarrow [Cl^-] = 4 \times 10^{-4}\,M$

The value of x is 4.

3. ***(c)***

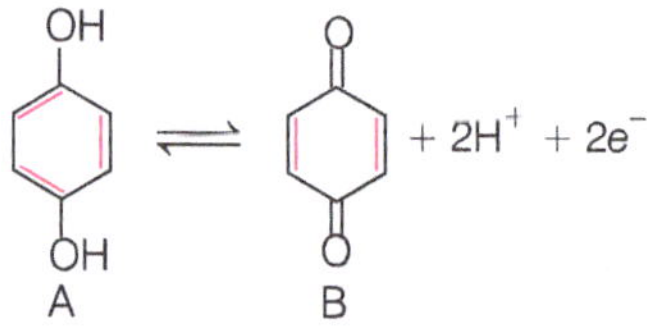

Reaction quotient,

$$(Q) = \frac{[B]\,[H^+]^2}{[A]} = [H^+]^2$$

$$\therefore \quad E = E^\circ - \frac{0.0591}{2} \log [H^+]^2$$

$$= E^\circ - 0.0591 \log [H^+] = E^\circ + 0.0591\,pH$$

Thus, E_{cell} is dependent on pH.

As (NaOH) is added to the electrode.

$$H^+ + \underset{\text{Being added}}{OH^-} = H_2O$$

Initially in acid (H^+) pH < 7, at neutral point pH = 7 and after H^+ is neutralised, pH increases due to further addition of NaOH.

Hence, E_{cell} also increases.

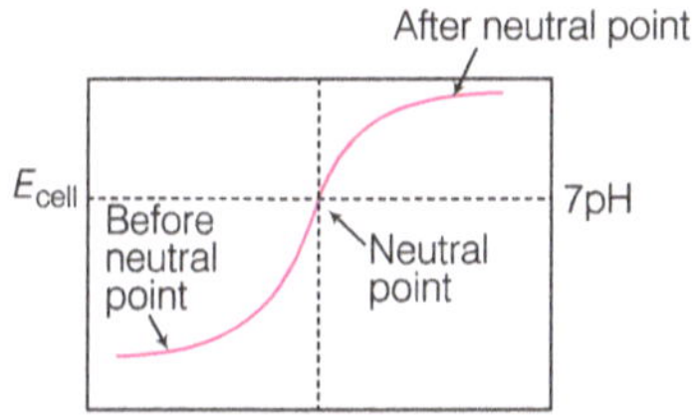

Volume of NaOH added to quinhydrone electrode

4. ***(d)*** For the cell,

$$Zn|Zn^{2+}(1M)||H^+(1M)|Pt(H_2)_{1bar}$$

$$E^\circ_{cell} = E^\circ_{Zn/Zn^{2+}} + E^\circ_{SHE}$$

$$0.76 = E^\circ_{Zn/Zn^{2+}} + 0.00$$

$\therefore \quad E^\circ_{Zn/Zn^{2+}} = 0.76$ V

For the cell, $E^\circ_{Zn^{2+}/Zn} = -0.76$ V

$$Pt(H_2) \mid H^+ (1M) \mid\mid Ag^+ (1\ M) \mid Ag$$

$$E^\circ_{cell} = E^\circ_{SHE} + E^\circ_{Ag^+/Ag} \Rightarrow 0.80 = 0.00 + E^\circ_{Ag^+/Ag}$$

$\therefore \quad E^\circ_{Ag^+/Ag} = 0.80$ V

$\therefore \quad E^\circ_{Ag/Ag^+} = -0.80$ V

For the cell,

$$Ag|Ag^+(0.1M)||Zn^{2+}(0.1M)|Zn$$

Oxidation at anode

$$2Ag \longrightarrow \underset{0.1\ M}{2Ag^+} + 2e^- ; \quad E^\circ_{Ag/Ag^+} = -0.80\ V$$

Reduction at cathode

$$\underset{0.1\ M}{Zn^{2+}} + 2e^- \longrightarrow Zn, \qquad E^\circ_{Zn^{2+}/Zn} = -0.76\ V$$

$$\underset{0.1M}{Zn^{2+}} + 2Ag \longrightarrow \underset{0.1M}{2Ag^+} + Zn \quad E^\circ_{cell} = -1.56\ V$$

Reaction quotient $(Q) = \dfrac{[Ag^+]^2}{[Zn^{2+}]} = \dfrac{(0.1)^2}{(0.1)} = \dfrac{1}{10}$

$\because \quad E_{cell} = E^\circ_{cell} - \dfrac{2.303RT}{nF}\log Q$

At 298 K, $\dfrac{2.303\,RT}{F} = 0.0591$ V

$\therefore \quad E_{cell} = -1.56 - \dfrac{0.0591}{2}\log\left(\dfrac{1}{10}\right)$

$= -1.56 + \dfrac{0.0591}{2}\log 10$

$= -1.56 + 0.0295$

$= -1.53$ V

$E_{cell} < 0$, hence reaction is non-spontaneous.

5. ***(d)*** This represents oxidation half-cell

$$2Hg + 2Cl^- \longrightarrow Hg_2Cl_2 + 2e^-$$

$\therefore \quad Q = \dfrac{1}{[Cl^-]^2}$

$\Rightarrow \quad E = E^\circ - \dfrac{0.0591}{2}\log Q$

$= E^\circ - \dfrac{0.0591}{2}\log\dfrac{1}{[Cl^-]^2}$

$= E^\circ + 0.0591\log[Cl^-]$

when $[Cl^-] = 1M$, $E = E^\circ$

and E increases on increasing log $[Cl^-]$

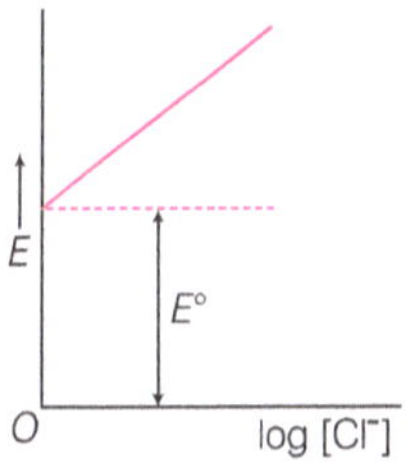

6. ***(d)*** $2Hg + 2Fe^{3+} \rightleftharpoons Hg_2^{2+} + 2Fe^{2+}$

excess $\quad 10^{-3}$ M

Equ. $\quad 10^{-3} - x \quad \dfrac{x}{2} \quad x$

$$[Fe^{3+}] = \frac{10}{100} \times 10^{-3}M = 10^{-4}$$

$\therefore \quad x = 9 \times 10^{-4}$

Now, $\quad K_{eq} = \dfrac{\dfrac{x}{2} \times x^2}{(10^{-3} - x)^2}$

$= \dfrac{\dfrac{9 \times 10^{-4}}{2} \times (9 \times 10^{-4})^2}{(1 \times 10^{-4})^2}$

$= \dfrac{9^3 \times 10^{-4}}{2}$

Now, $E^\circ_{cell} = E^\circ_{Fe^{3+}/Fe^{2+}} - E^\circ_{Hg_2^{2+}/Hg}$

Or $\quad E^\circ_{cell} = \dfrac{0.06}{2}\log K_{eq}$

or $0.7724 - E^\circ_{Hg_2^{2+}/Hg} = \dfrac{0.06}{2}\log\dfrac{9^3 \times 10^{-4}}{2}$

$\therefore \quad E^\circ_{Hg_2^{2+}/Hg} = 0.815$ V

7. ***(b)*** Anodic reaction is $\quad 2H_2O \longrightarrow O_2(g) + 4H^+ + 4e^-$

Cathodic reaction is $\quad 2Cu^{2+}(aq) + 4e^- \longrightarrow 2Cu(s)$

Net electrolysis reaction is $2Cu^{2+}(aq) + 2H_2O \longrightarrow 2Cu(s) + 4H^+ + O_2(g)$

Thus, in first part of electrolysis, O_2 gas is liberated. By Faraday's second law

$$\frac{\text{Weight of } O_2}{\text{Weight of Cu}} = \frac{\text{Equivalent weight of } O_2}{\text{Equivalent weight of Cu}}$$

$$\text{Weight of } O_2 = \text{Weight of Cu} \times \frac{\text{Equivalent weight of } O_2}{\text{Equivalent weight of Cu}}$$

$$= 0.4 \times \frac{8}{31.75} = 0.1008\ g = 0.00315\ mol\ O_2$$

$= 70.55$ mL of O_2 at STP

O_2 formed in further electrolysis :

$$2O^{2-} \longrightarrow O_2 + 4e^-$$

$$W = \frac{8 \times 1.2 \times 420}{96500} = 0.04178 \text{ g}$$

$$= 1.306 \times 10^{-3} \text{mol} = 29.25 \text{mL}$$

Total O_2 at STP $= 70.55 + 29.25$

≈ 100mL

8. ***(d)*** Among the given match only (d) is correctly match while others are incorrect. Their explanation are given as :

(a) $\frac{[Zn^{2+}]}{[Cu^{2+}]} = \frac{0.01}{1.00} = \frac{1}{100}$

$\therefore \; E - E° = -\frac{0.0591}{2} \log \frac{1}{100} = 0.0591 \text{V}$

(b) $\frac{[Cu^{2+}]}{[Ag^+]^2} = \frac{0.01}{(0.1)^2} = 1$

$\therefore \quad E - E° = 0$

(c) $\frac{[Al^{3+}]^2}{[Co^{2+}]^3} = \frac{(0.25)^2}{(0.05)^3} = 500$

$\therefore \quad E - E° = -\frac{0.0591}{6} \log 500$

$= -0.0266$ V

(d) $Br^- \longrightarrow \frac{1}{2} Br_2 + e^-$

$\frac{1}{2} Cl_2 + e^- \longrightarrow Cl^-$

$Br^- + \frac{1}{2} Cl_2 \longrightarrow \frac{1}{2} Br_2 + Cl^-$

$$K = \frac{[Cl^-]}{[Br^-]\sqrt{p_{Cl_2}}} = \frac{0.05}{0.5\sqrt{0.9}} = 0.105$$

$\therefore \; E - E° = -\frac{0.0591}{1} \log K$

$= -0.0591 \log 0.105 \approx 0.06$ V

9. ***(a, c)*** Among the given statements, only a and c are correct while b and d are incorrect. Their correct explanation is given as :

(a) By Faraday's first law :,

$$w = Zit$$

where, Z is electrochemical equivalent

$$= \frac{\text{Atomic weight}}{\text{Electron} \times 96500}$$

$$= \frac{65}{2 \times 96500}$$

i(current) $= 1.77$ A, and t (time) $= 815$ s

$Zn^{2+}(aq) + 2e^- \longrightarrow Zn$

$\therefore \quad w = \frac{65}{2 \times 96500} \times 1.77 \times 815 = 0.486$ g

(b) $2I^-(aq) \longrightarrow I_2 + 2e^-$

I_2 is formed at anode.

Using equation as in (a),

$$Z = \frac{\text{Molar mass of } I_2 \; (= 254)}{2 \times 96500}$$

$\therefore \quad w = iZt$

$$t = \frac{w}{iZ} = \frac{1.96 \times 2 \times 96500}{3.14 \times 254} \text{ s} = 474.3 \text{ s}$$

(c) $Cu^{2+}(aq) + 2e^- \longrightarrow Cu$, $Z = \frac{63.5}{2 \times 96500}$

Cu deposited at the cathode due to passage of 2.17 A current (i) for 235 s (t).

$$w = Zit = \frac{63.5}{2 \times 96500} \times 2.17 \times 235 \text{ g} = 0.1678\text{g}$$

$= 2.64 \times 10^{-3}$ mol Cu in 0.335 L

$\therefore \quad [Cu^{2+}]_{final} = 7.88 \times 10^{-3} \text{mol L}^{-1}$ (M)

$[Cu^{2+}]_{initial} = 0.215$ M

$\therefore \; [Cu^{2+}]_{remaining} = 0.215 - 7.88 \times 10^{-3} = 0.207$ M

(d) $Ag^+ + e^- \longrightarrow Ag$

$$Z = \frac{108}{1 \times 96500}$$

$[Ag^+]_{initial} = 0.185$ M

$[Ag^+]_{final} = 0.175$ M

$[Ag^+]_{changed} = 0.01$ M

$\therefore \; Ag^+$ in 255 mL ($= 0.255$ L) solution $= 0.01 \times 0.255$ mol

$= 0.01 \times 0.255 \times 108$ g

Using Faraday's first law,

$$w = Zit$$

$$t = \frac{w}{Zi} = \frac{0.01 \times 0.255 \times 108}{\frac{108}{1 \times 96500} \times 1.92} = 128.16 \text{ s}$$

10. ***(a, c)*** Statements (a) and (c) are correct.

(a) ΔG is a thermodynamic property so it is not related to rate of the reaction, i.e., kinetics of the reactions. So, (a) is correct.

(b) Large $E^{\ominus}_{oxidation}$ means more tendency of metal to undergo oxidation ($M \longrightarrow M^{\oplus} + e^-$), so more reactive metal. So, statement (b) is wrong.

(c) Factual statement and is correct.

(d) $E^{\ominus}_{\text{oxid Li}|\text{Li}^{\oplus}} > E^{\ominus}_{\text{oxid K}|\text{K}^{\oplus}}$.

It means higher the oxidation potential more easily the metal is oxidised, i.e., IE_1 of Li is smaller than K.

Although Li is smaller in size than K, so its IE_1 should be more. But due to high –ve hydration energy of $Li^{\oplus}$, it compensates the high IE_1 of Li.

$$Li(s) \xrightarrow{\Delta H_{Sub}} Li(g) \xrightarrow{IE_1} Li^{\oplus}(g) + e^-$$

$$Li^{\oplus}(g) \xrightarrow[\text{aq.}]{\Delta H_{Hydration}} Li^{\oplus}(aq)$$

$E^{\ominus}_{oxid} = \Delta H^{\ominus}_{Sub} + IE_1 + \Delta H^{\ominus}_{Hydration}$

So, IP (ionisation potential) is determined by all the three factors, i.e., sublimation, IE_1 and hydration energy.

So, statement (d) is wrong.

11. ***(a, c)*** $H_2SO_4(aq) \rightleftharpoons 2H^+ + SO_4^{2-}$
Dilute

$SO_4^{2-} + H_2O \rightleftharpoons H_2SO_4 + O^{2-}$

At cathode

$2H^+ + 2e^- \longrightarrow H_2$

Thus, (a) is correct.

At anode $2O^{2-} \longrightarrow O_2 + 4e^-$

Thus, (c) is correct.

Concentrated H_2SO_4 ionises as H^+ and HSO_4^- and then water is not oxidised in concentrated H_2SO_4. Thus, (b) is incorrect.

SO_4^{2-} is not oxidised to $S_2O_8^{2-}$ in dilute H_2SO_4.

Thus, (d) is incorrect.

12. ***(b, c, d)***

If dil. H_2SO_4 is used, then H^+ is the reacting species.

If conc. H_2SO_4 is used, then SO_4^{2-} is the reacting species.

(a) $2H^+ + 2e^- \longrightarrow H_2$, $E^\circ_{SHE} = 0.00$ V

$Cu \longrightarrow Cu^{2+} + 2e^-$, $E^\circ_{Cu/Cu^{2+}} = -0.34$

$Cu + 2H^+ \longrightarrow Cu^{2+} + H_2$; $E^\circ_{cell} = -0.34$ V; $E^\circ_{cell} < 0$.

Thus, copper does not react with H^+ (dil. H_2SO_4) forming H_2.

(b) $SO_4^{2-} + 4H^+ + 2e^- \longrightarrow SO_2 + 2H_2O, E^\circ = 1.17$ V

$Cu \longrightarrow Cu^{2+} + 2e^-$,
$E^\circ = -0.34$ V

$Cu + SO_4^{2-} + 4H^+ \longrightarrow Cu^{2+} + SO_2 + 2H_2O$;
$E^\circ_{cell} = 0.83$ V

Since, $E^\circ_{cell} > 0$, Thus, copper reacts with conc. H_2SO_4 forming SO_2.

(c) $Zn + SO_4^{2-} + 4H^+ \longrightarrow Zn^{2+} + SO_2 + 2H_2O$;
$E^\circ_{cell} = 0.41$ V,

$E^\circ_{cell} > 0$, thus zinc also reacts with conc. H_2SO_4 forming SO_2.

(d) $Zn + 2H^+ \longrightarrow Zn^{2+} + H_2, E^\circ_{cell} = 0.76$ V

$E^\circ_{cell} > 0$, thus zinc reacts with dil. H_2SO_4 forming H_2.

13. ***(a, b, c)***

(a) If salt-bridge is removed, the ions can no longer flow between the half-cells, and the circuit is incomplete. So, potential difference falls to zero i.e. (a) is correct.

(b) 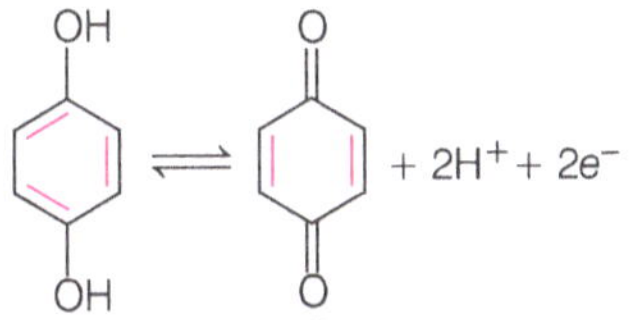

(A) (B)

Quinhydrone is a mixture of *A* and *B* in (1 : 1) molar ratio joined by H-bonding. Above equilibrium is set up in aqueous solution

$$K = [H^+]^2 \frac{[B]}{[A]} = [H^+]^2$$

$$E_{QH} = E^\circ_{QH} - \frac{0.0591}{n} \log K$$

$$E_{QH} = E^\circ_{QH} - \frac{0.0591}{2} \log [H^+]^2$$

$$E_{QH} = E^\circ_{QH} - 0.0591 \log [H^+]$$

If $[H^+]$ changes, E_{QH} also changes. Thus, quinhydrone electrode is reversible to H^+ ion i.e (b) is correct.

(c) Liquid junction potential is minimised by use of concentration cell i.e (c) is correct.

(d) Calomel electrode is $Hg(l)$, $Hg_2Cl_2(s) | Cl^-$.

Thus, (d) is incorrect

14. ***(a, b, d)*** Metals with E° value less than 0.96 V will be able to reduce CO_3^{2-} in aqueous solution. Therefore, metals V ($E^\circ = -1.19$ V), Fe ($E^\circ = -0.04$ V), Hg ($E^\circ = 0.86$ V) will all reduce. CO_3^{2-} but Au ($E^\circ = 1.40$ V) cannot reduce CO_3^{2-} in aqueous solution.

15. ***(a, c, d)***

(a) Yes, Λ^∞_m (molar conductance at infinite dilution) of weak electrolyte can be obtained by Kohlrausch law.

$\Lambda^\infty_m = x_+\Lambda^\infty_+ + \lambda_-\Lambda^\infty_-$

Thus, (a) is true

(b) 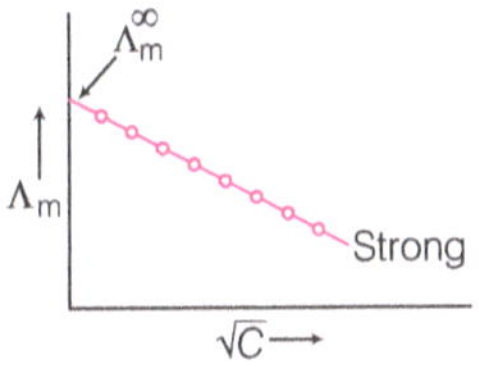

For strong electrolyte, variation in graph is uniform, hence Λ_m can be extrapolated to $\sqrt{C} \longrightarrow 0$, to obtain Λ^∞_m.

In case of weak electrolyte, variation of Λ_m with $\sqrt{C}$ is rapid in lower concentration range (higher dilution), hence graph is not uniform and Λ^∞_m cannot be obtained by extrapolation to $\sqrt{C} \longrightarrow 0$.

Thus, (b) is incorrect.

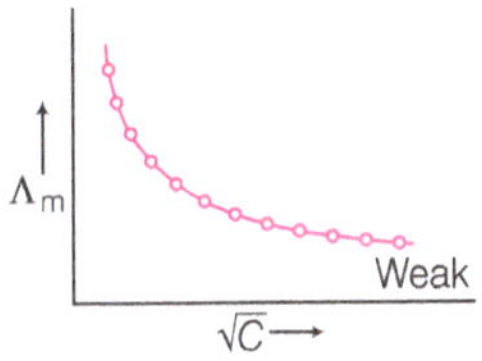

(c) $\Lambda^\infty_{AgCl} = \Lambda^\infty_{AgNO_3} + \Lambda^\infty_{HCl} - \Lambda^\infty_{HNO_3} = \Lambda^\infty_{Ag^+} + \Lambda^\infty_{Cl^-}$

Thus, correct based on Kohlrausch's law.

(d) Also, $\Lambda^\infty_{BaSO_4} = \Lambda^\infty_{BaCl_2} + \Lambda^\infty_{H_2SO_4} - 2\Lambda^\infty_{HCl}$

Thus, it is also correct based on Kohlrausch's law.

16. ***(a, b, c)***

(a) I : $2Cl^-(aq) \longrightarrow Cl_2 + 2e^-$; $E^\circ = -1.36$ V

II : $2H_2O(l) \longrightarrow O_2(g) + 4H^+ + 4e^-$; $E^\circ = -1.23$ V

Thus, E° values of I and II are quite closer – correct.

(b) $E_I = E^\circ_I - \frac{0.0591}{2} \log \frac{1}{[Cl^-]^2} = E^\circ_I + 0.0591 \log [Cl^-]$

If $[Cl^-]$ is high, $E_1 > E_1^\circ$ thus, I favoured.

$$E_{II} = E_{II}^\circ - \frac{0.0591}{4}\log [H^+]^4 = E_{II}^\circ + 0.0591\,pH$$

since, ($-\log [H^+] = pH$)

Thus, if pH is high

$E_{II} > E_{II}^\circ$ thus II favoured

Thus, (b) is correct.

(c) Experiment indicates that the applied voltage required is always greater than the voltage calculated from the standard E_{ox}° or E_{red}°. The additional voltage required is called overvoltage. Due to this, Cl_2 and not O_2 is formed.

Thus, (c) is correct,

17. ***(10.79)*** Given,

$A(s)\,|\,A^{n+}(aq, 3\text{ M})\,||\,B^{2n+}(aq, 2\text{ M})\,|\,B(s)$

So, reaction at respective electrode will be

Anode : $A(s) \to A^{n+} + ne^- \times 2$

Cathode : $B^{2n+} + 2ne^- \to B(s)$

Overall reaction

$$2A(s) + B^{2n+}(aq) \longrightarrow 2A^{n+}(aq) + B(s)$$

Further,

$\Delta H^\circ = 2\Delta G^\circ$ and $E_{cell} = 0$ is also given

Now, by using the Nernst equation,

$$E_{cell} = E_{cell}^\circ - \frac{RT}{nF}\times \ln\frac{[P]}{[R]}$$

After putting the values,

$$0 = E_{cell}^\circ - \frac{RT}{2nF}\ln\frac{[A^{n+}]^2}{[B^{2n+}]}$$

$$E_{cell}^\circ = \frac{RT}{2nF}\ln\frac{(3)^2}{(2)}$$

$$= \frac{RT}{2nF}\times[2\ln 3 - \ln 2] = \frac{RT}{2nF}[2 - 0.7]$$

$$= \frac{RT}{nF}\times 0.65 \qquad \text{...(i)}$$

Further from the formula,

$$\Delta G^\circ = -FE_{cell}^\circ$$

$$\Rightarrow \quad \Delta G^\circ = -2nFE_{cell}^\circ$$

Now, putting the value of E° from eq. (i)

$$\Delta G^\circ = -2nF\times\frac{RT}{nF}\times 0.65 = -1.3\,RT$$

Finally, using the formula,

$$\Delta G^\circ = \Delta H^\circ - T\Delta S^\circ$$

$$= 2\Delta G^\circ - T\Delta S^\circ$$

$$\Delta G^\circ = T\Delta S^\circ$$

$$\Delta S^\circ = \frac{\Delta G^\circ}{T} = \frac{-1.3\,RT}{T}$$

$$= -1.3\times 8.3$$

$$= -10.79$$

18. ***(3)*** HX and HY and weak acids

$[H^+] = \sqrt{K_aC}$ by Ostwald's dilution law

Also both are oxidation half-cell,

$$\frac{1}{2}H_2(g) \longrightarrow H^+ + e^-$$

$$\therefore \text{Reaction quotient } Q = \frac{[H^+]}{\sqrt{p_{H_2}}} = \frac{\sqrt{K_aC}}{1} = \sqrt{K_aC}$$

For half-cell I

$$E_I = E^\circ - \frac{0.0591}{1}\log [H^+]_{HX}$$

$$= 0 - \frac{0.0591}{1}\log\sqrt{K_a(HX)C_{HX}}$$

$$= -\frac{0.0591}{1}\log\sqrt{10^{-2}\times 1}$$

$$= 0.0591\log 10 = 0.0591$$

For half-cell II

$$E_{II} = E^\circ - \frac{0.0591}{1}\log\sqrt{K_a(HY)\,C_{HY}}$$

$$= 0 - \frac{0.0591}{1}\log\sqrt{10^{-6}}$$

$$= -\frac{0.0591}{1}\log 10^{-3}$$

$$= 3\times 0.0591\log 10 = 3\times 0.0591$$

$$\frac{E_{II}}{E_I} = 3$$

19. ***(3)*** $x\text{Ag}^+ + y\text{NH}_3 \rightleftharpoons [\text{Ag}_x(\text{NH}_3)_y]^{x+}$

	aM	bM	0	b >> a
At eq^m	—	bM	$\frac{a}{x}$ M	

$$K_f = \frac{\frac{a}{x}}{[Ag^+]^x\cdot b^y} \Rightarrow [Ag^+] = \left(\frac{a}{K_f\cdot x\cdot b^y}\right)^{1/x}$$

Cell reaction : $Ag^+(\text{Right}) \longrightarrow Ag^+(\text{Left})$

$$\therefore \quad E_{cell} = 0 - \frac{0.059}{1}\log\frac{[Ag^+]_{Left}}{[Ag^+]_{Right}}$$

$$\text{Case-I} : 0.118 = -0.059\cdot\log\left(\frac{4\times10^{-4}}{4\times10^{-2}}\right)^{\frac{1}{x}} \Rightarrow x = 1$$

$$\text{Case-II} : 0.118 = -0.059\log\left(\frac{0.1}{1}\right)^y$$

$$\Rightarrow \quad y = 2$$

$$x + y = 1 + 2 = 3$$

20. ***(5)*** Cell constant $= \frac{\text{Length}}{\text{Area}} = \frac{0.656\text{ cm}}{0.80\text{ cm}^2} = 0.82\text{ cm}^{-1}$

If solution is saturated, for a sparingly soluble salt, solubility can be taken as its concentration.

$$AgCl(s) \rightleftharpoons Ag^+(aq) + Cl^-(aq)$$

$$K_{sp} = [Ag^+]\,[Cl^-] = s^2$$

$$\therefore \quad s = \sqrt{K_{sp}}$$

$$= \sqrt{1.6 \times 10^{-10}} = 1.265 \times 10^{-5} \text{ mol L}^{-1}$$

$$= 1.265 \times 10^{-5} \text{ equiv L}^{-1}$$

$$\therefore \quad \Lambda_c = \Lambda_0 = \frac{1000 \times \text{specific conductance}}{\text{Concentration}} \quad (\text{Lim } C \to 0)$$

$$\therefore 130 \text{ ohm}^{-1} \text{cm}^2 \text{ equiv}^{-1} = \frac{1000 \times \text{specific conductance}}{1.265 \times 10^{-5} \text{equiv L}^{-1}}$$

$\therefore$ Specific conductance $= 1.6445 \times 10^{-6}$ ohm^{-1}cm^{-1}

Specific conductance = Cell constant × Conductance

$$\therefore \text{ Conductance} = \frac{1.6445 \times 10^{-6}}{0.82} = 2.0 \times 10^{-6} \text{ ohm}^{-1}$$

$$\text{Resistance} = \frac{1}{\text{Conductance}} = \frac{1}{2.0 \times 10^{-6}}$$

$$= 5.0 \times 10^5 = n \times 10^5 \text{ ohm}$$

$$\therefore \quad n = 5$$

21. ***(1.44)*** Latimer diagram,

$$\overset{+6}{FeO_4^{2-}} \xrightarrow[n_1 = 3]{E_1^\circ = 1.74\text{ V}} Fe^{3+} \xrightarrow[n_2 = 1]{E_2^\circ = 1.31\text{ V}}$$

$$Fe^{2+} \xrightarrow[n_3 = 2]{E_3^\circ = 1.05\text{ V}} \overset{0}{Fe}$$

$E_4^\circ = ?, n_4 = +6$

so, $n_4 E_4^\circ = n_1 E_1^\circ + n_2 E_2^\circ + n_3 E_3^\circ$

$$6E_4^\circ = 3 \times 1.74 + 1 \times 1.31 + 2 \times 1.05$$

$$E_4^\circ = \frac{5.22 + 1.31 + 2.1}{6} = 1.44$$

So, $E^\circ_{FeO_4^{2-}/Fe} = +1.44$ V

22. ***(1)*** At Ag | Ag^+ (anode)

Oxidation takes place $Ag \longrightarrow Ag^+ + e^-$

At Cu^{2+}| Cu (cathode)

Reduction takes place

$$Cu^2 + 2e^- \longrightarrow Cu$$

Net $Cu^{2+} + 2Ag \longrightarrow 2Ag^+ + Cu$

Reaction quotient

$$Q = \frac{[Ag^+]^2}{[Cu^{2+}]} = \frac{(1)^2}{(1)} = 1.0$$

$$\therefore \quad E_{cell} = E^\circ_{cell} - \frac{0.0591}{2} \log 1$$

$$= E^\circ_{cell} - 0 = E^\circ_{cell}$$

Current = 9.65 A

Time = 3600 s (= 1h)

Quantity of current passed = It

$$= 9.65 \times 3600 \text{ C}$$

$$= \frac{9.65 \times 3600}{96500} \text{ F} = 0.36 \text{ F}$$

Thus, $[Ag^+]$ formed = 0.36 equivalent = 0.36 mol

$\therefore [Ag^+]$ after current is passed = 1.36 M

$[Cu^{2+}]$ reduced = 0.36 equivalent $= \frac{0.36}{2} = 0.18$ mol

$\therefore [Cu^{2+}]$ after current is passed = 1.0 − 0.18 = 0.82 M

$\therefore$ Reaction quotient, is thus

$$Q = \frac{[Ag^+]^2}{[Cu^{2+}]} = \frac{(1.36)^2}{0.82} = 2.26$$

$$\therefore \quad E'_{cell} = E^\circ_{cell} - \frac{0.0591}{2} \log Q$$

$$= E^\circ_{cell} - \frac{0.0591}{2} \log 2.26 = E^\circ_{cell} - 0.01$$

Also, $\quad E_{cell} = E^\circ_{cell}$

$$\therefore \quad E_{cell} - E'_{cell} = 0.01 \text{ V} = 0.01 \times 100 = 1 \text{ centivolt}$$

23. ***(−1.329)*** The half-cell reaction is:

$$4H^+ + AsO_4^{3-} + 2e^- \longrightarrow AsO_2^- + 2H_2O$$

$$E_{(AsO_4^{3-}/AsO_2^-)} = E^\circ_{(AsO_4^{3-}/AsO_2^-)} - \frac{0.059}{2} \log \frac{[AsO_2^-]}{[AsO_4^{3-}][H^+]^4} \quad \text{...(i)}$$

$m_{eq.}$ of $AsO_4^{3-} = 20 \times 0.1 = 2$

$m_{eq.}$ of $I^- = 18 \times 0.1 = 1.8$

Therefore, 1.8 $m_{eq.}$ of I^- reacts with 1.8 $m_{eq.}$ of AsO_4^{3-} to give 1.8 $m_{eq.}$ of AsO_2^-

So, $m_{eq.}$ of $AsO_4^{3-} = 2 - 1.8 = 0.2\, m_{eq.}$

total volume of solution = (18 + 20) mL = 38 mL

Hence, $[AsO_4^{3-}] = \frac{0.2\, m_{eq.}}{38 \text{ mL}}, [AsO_2^-] = \frac{1.8\, m_{eq.}}{38 \text{ mL}}$

$$pH = 5 \Rightarrow [H^+] = 10^{-5}$$

substituting the value in Eq. (i).

$$E_{(AsO_4^{3-}/AsO_2^-)} = E^\circ_{(AsO_4^{3-}/AsO_2^-)} - \frac{0.059}{2} \log \frac{[AsO_2^-]}{[AsO_4^{3-}][H^+]^4}$$

$$= -0.70 \text{ V} - \frac{0.059}{2} \log \frac{(1.8/38)}{\left(\frac{0.2}{38}\right)(10^{-5})^4}$$

$$= -0.70 - \frac{0.059}{2} [\log 9 + \log 10^{20}]$$

$$= -0.70 - \frac{0.059}{2} [2 \times 0.48 + 20]$$

$$= -0.70 - 0.03 \times 20.96 \qquad [\log 3 = 0.48 \text{ and } 0.059 \approx 0.06]$$

$$= -0.7 - 0.629 \approx -1.329 \text{ V}$$

24. ***(315.56)*** Intermediate is $(NH_4)_2S_2O_8$

Mole of $(NH_4)_2S_2O_8$ = Mole of H_2O_2

$$\frac{w}{m} = \text{mole of } H_2O_2 = \frac{100}{34} = \frac{50}{17}$$

$$w = Zit$$

$$w = \frac{mit}{n \times 96500}$$

$$\text{or} \quad \frac{w}{m} = \frac{it}{n \times 96500}$$

By Faraday's first law $\frac{w}{m} = \frac{it}{n \times 96500}$

where, i = current in ampere = ?

t = time in second = $1 \times 60 \times 60$ s,

n = number of electrons = 2

$$\frac{50}{17} = \frac{i \times 3600}{2 \times 96500}$$

$i = 157.68$ A when 100% efficient

$= 315.36$ A when 50% efficient

25. ***(a)*** (i)

(C) $O_2 + 4H^+ + 4e^- \longrightarrow 2H_2O$,

$n_1 = 4, E_1^\circ = 1.229$ V

(D) $H_2O_2(aq) + 2H^+ + 2e^- \longrightarrow 2H_2O$,

$n_2 = 2, E_2^\circ = 1.763$ V

(C) – (D) gives (i)

$O_2 + 2H^+ + 2e^- \longrightarrow H_2O_2\,(aq),\ n_3 = 2, E_3^\circ = ?$

$\Delta G_3 = \Delta G_1 - \Delta G_2$

$-n_3FE_3^\circ = -n_1FE_1^\circ + n_2FE_2^\circ$

$$E_3^\circ = \frac{n_1E_1^\circ - n_2E_2^\circ}{n_3}$$

$$= \frac{4 \times 1.229 - 2 \times 1.763}{2}$$

$= 0.695$ V

Thus, (i) $\rightarrow$ (p)

(ii) (B) $O_2(g) + 2H_2O + 4e^- \longrightarrow 4OH^-$ $n_1 = 4, E_1 = 0.401$ V

(C) $O_2(g) + 4H^+ + 4e^- \longrightarrow 2H_2O,\ n_2 = 4, E_2 = 1.229$ V

(G) $4H^+ + 4e^- \longrightarrow 2H_2,\ n_3 = 4,\ E_3 = 0.00$ V

equal number of electrons are involved,

(B) + (G) – (C) gives (ii)

$4H_2O + 4e^- \longrightarrow 2H_2 + 4OH^-$

$2H_2O + 2e^- \longrightarrow H_2 + 2OH^-$

$\therefore$ $E_4 = 0.401 + 0.00 - 1.229 = -0.83$ V

Thus, (ii) $\rightarrow$ (s)

(iii) (A) $O_3 + 2H^+ + 2e^- \longrightarrow O_2(g) + H_2O$

or $2O_3 + 4H^+ + 4e^- \longrightarrow 2O_2 + 2H_2O,\ E_1^\circ = 2.075$ V

(G) $2H_2 \longrightarrow 4H^+ + 4e^-,\ E_2^\circ = 0.00$

(H) $4H_2O + 4e^- \longrightarrow 2H_2 + 4OH^-,\ E_3^\circ = -0.83$ V

(A) + (G) + (H) gives (iii)

$2O_3 + 2H_2O + 4e^- \longrightarrow 2O_2 + 4OH^-$

$O_3 + H_2O + 2e^- \longrightarrow O_2 + 2OH^-,\ E_{cell}^\circ = 1.245$ V

Thus, (iii)$\rightarrow$ (r)

(iv) (E) $Cr^{3+} + 3e^- \longrightarrow Cr,\ n_1 = 3, E_1^\circ = -0.74$ V

(F) $Cr^{2+} + 2e^- \longrightarrow Cr,\ n_2 = 2, E_2^\circ = 0.91$ V

$Cr^{3+} + e^- \longrightarrow Cr^{2+},\ n_3 = 1, E_3^\circ = ?$

(E) – (F) = (iv)

$\therefore$ $\Delta G_3 = \Delta G_1^\circ - \Delta G_2^\circ$

$-n_3FE_3^\circ = -n_1FE_1^\circ + n_2FE_2^\circ$

$\therefore$ $$E_3^\circ = \frac{n_1E_1^\circ - n_2E_2^\circ}{n_3}$$

$$= \frac{3(-0.74) + 2 \times 0.91}{1}$$

$= -2.22 + 1.82 = -0.40$ V

Thus, (iv) $\rightarrow$ (q)

26. ***(c)*** (i) Temperature coefficient of EMF

$$= \left(\frac{dE_{cell}}{dT}\right) = \frac{\text{Change in EMF}}{\text{Change in temperature}}$$

$$= \frac{E_{T_2}^\circ - E_{T_1}^\circ}{(T_2 - T_1)} = \frac{(0.21 - 0.23)\text{ volt}}{(308 - 288)\text{ K}}$$

$$= \frac{-0.02\text{ volt}}{20\text{ K}}$$

$= -1 \times 10^{-3}$ VK^{-1}

$= -1.0$ mV K^{-1}

Thus, (i) $\rightarrow$ (s)

(ii) $\Delta G^\circ = \Delta H^\circ - T\Delta S^\circ$

By Gibb's Helmholtz equation,

$$\Delta G^\circ = \Delta H^\circ + T \cdot \left[\frac{d\,\Delta G^\circ}{dT}\right]_p$$

$\therefore$ $$\Delta S^\circ = -\left(\frac{d\,(\Delta G^\circ)}{dT}\right)_p = -\left(\frac{-nF\,(dE_{cell}^\circ)}{dT}\right)_p$$

$$= +\frac{nF\,(dE_{cell}^\circ)}{dT} = nF\left(\frac{dE_{cell}^\circ}{dT}\right)$$

$= -1 \times 96500 \times 1.0 \times 10^{-3} = -96.5$ JK^{-1}

Thus, (ii) $\rightarrow$ (q)

(iii) $\Delta G^\circ = \Delta H^\circ - T\Delta S^\circ$

$-nFE_{cell}^\circ = \Delta H^\circ - T\Delta S^\circ$

At 288 K, $E_{cell}^\circ = 0.23$ V

$-1 \times 96500 \times (0.23) = \Delta H^\circ - 288\,(-96.5)$

$\therefore$ $\Delta H^\circ = [-96500 \times 0.23 - 288 \times 96.5]$ J

≈ -50000 J or -50 kJ

At 308 K, $E_{cell}^\circ = 0.21$ V

$-1 \times 96500 \times 0.21 = \Delta H^\circ - 308(-96.5)$

$\Delta H^\circ \approx -50000$ J ≈ -50 kJ

Thus. (iii) $\rightarrow$ (r)

At 298 K,

$-1 \times 96500\ E_{cell}^\circ = -50{,}000 - 298 \times (-96.5)$

$$E_{cell}^\circ = \frac{50000 - 298 \times 96.5}{96500}$$

$= 0.22$ V

$AgCl(s) + e^- \longrightarrow Ag + Cl^-;\ E^\circ = 0.22$ V

$Ag \longrightarrow Ag^+ + e^-;\ E^\circ = -0.80$ V

$AgCl(s) \longrightarrow Ag^+ + Cl^-\ E^\circ = -0.58$ V

$K = K_{sp} = [Ag^+]\,[Cl^-]$

$\therefore$ $$E^\circ = \frac{0.0591}{1}\log K_{sp}$$

$\therefore$ $$\log K_{sp} = -\frac{0.58}{0.0591} = -9.81$$

Thus (iv) $\rightarrow$ (p)

27. ***(a)*** By Faraday's second law,

$$\frac{\text{Amount of } X}{\text{Amount of } Y} = \frac{\text{Equivalent mass of } X}{\text{Equivalent mass of } Y}$$

$$Zn^{2+} + 2e^- \longrightarrow Zn, E\,(Zn) = \frac{65}{2}$$

$$Cu^2 + 2e^- \longrightarrow Cu, E\,(Cu) = \frac{63.5}{2}$$

$$Ag^+ + e^- \longrightarrow Ag, E\,(Ag) = \frac{108}{1}$$

$$2H^+ + 2e^- \longrightarrow H_2, E\,(H_2) = \frac{2}{2}$$

$$2O^{2-} \longrightarrow O_2 + 4e^-, E\,(O_2) = \frac{32}{4}$$

By electrolysis, amount formed are in equivalent ratio.
Thus, equivalent of Zn formed = equivalent of O_2 formed
O_2 formed = 77 mL O_2 at STP

$$= 0.077 \text{ L } O_2 \text{ at STP}$$

$$= \frac{0.077}{22.4} \text{ mol} = \frac{0.077}{22.4} \times 4 \text{ equivalents}$$

(i) (Zn formed) $= \frac{0.077 \times 4}{22.4}$ equiv

$$= \frac{0.077 \times 4}{22.4} \times \frac{65}{2} \text{ g}$$

$$= 0.45 \text{ g}$$

Thus (i)—(p)

(ii) (Ag) $= \frac{0.077 \times 4}{22.4}$ equiv

$$= \frac{0.077 \times 4}{22.4} \text{ g} \times 108(\text{g}) = 1.485 \text{ g}$$

Thus (ii) — (q)

(iii) (Cu) = equivalent of O_2

$$= \frac{0.077 \times 4}{22.4}$$

$$= \frac{0.077 \times 4}{22.4} \times \frac{63.5}{2} \text{ g} \approx 0.44 \text{ g}$$

Thus (iii) — (s)

(iv) (H_2) = equivalent of O_2

$$= \frac{0.077 \times 4}{22.4} = \frac{0.077 \times 4}{22.4} \times 1 \text{g } H_2$$

$$\approx 0.014 \text{ g}$$

Thus (iv) — (r)

28. ***(c)*** $\Lambda^\circ\,(H_2O) = \lambda^\circ\,(H^+) + \lambda^\circ\,(OH^-)$

$$= (3.5 \times 10^{-2} + 2.0 \times 10^{-2}) \text{ S m}^2\text{mol}^{-1}$$

$$= 5.5 \times 10^{-2} \text{ S m}^2\text{mol}^{-1}$$

Density of water = $1.0 \text{ g cm}^{-3} = 1000 \text{ g dm}^{-3}$

$\therefore$ Molarity (H_2O) $= \frac{1000}{18} = 55.55 \text{ mol dm}^{-3}$

$$= 55.55 \times 10^3 \text{ mol m}^{-3}$$

Λ_c (molal conductance)

$$= \frac{\kappa}{\text{Molarity (mol m}^{-3})}$$

$$= \frac{5.7 \times 10^{-6} \text{ S m}^{-1}}{55.5 \times 10^3 \text{ mol m}^{-3}}$$

$$= 1.027 \times 10^{-10} \text{ S m}^2\text{mol}^{-1}$$

$\therefore \quad p_{\Lambda_c} = 9.988 \approx 10.0$

Thus, (ii) $\rightarrow$ (p)

x (degree of ionisation)

$$= \frac{\Lambda_c}{\Lambda^\circ} = \frac{1.027 \times 10^{-10}}{5.55 \times 10^{-2}}$$

$$= 1.85 \times 10^{-9}$$

$$p_x = 8.73$$

Thus, (i) $\rightarrow$ (q)

In H_2O at 298 K

$[H^+] = [OH^-] = Cx = 55.55 \text{ M} \times 1.85 \times 10^{-9}$

$$= 1.03 \times 10^{-7} \text{ M}$$

$\therefore$ pH = $-\log [H^+] = 6.98 \approx 7.0$

Thus, (iii) $\rightarrow$ (s)

$K_w = [H^+]\,[OH^-]$

$$= (1.03 \times 10^{-7})^2 = 1.061 \times 10^{-14}$$

$\therefore pK_w = 13.97 \approx 14.0$

Thus, (iv) $\rightarrow$ (r)

29. ***(a)*** $x = \frac{\Lambda_m}{\Lambda_m^\circ}$

$\therefore \Lambda_m = x\Lambda_m^\circ$

By Ostwald's dilution law $x = \sqrt{\frac{K_a}{C}}$

(i) $\Lambda_m = \sqrt{\frac{K_a}{C}}\,\Lambda_m^\circ = \sqrt{\frac{1.8 \times 10^{-5}}{0.04}}\,390.5$

$$= 8.28 S \text{ cm}^2 \text{ mol}^{-1}$$

$$= 8.28 \times 10^{-4} \text{ S m}^2\text{mol}^{-1}$$

Thus, (i) $\rightarrow$ (p)

(ii) $\frac{\kappa\,(\text{conductivity}) \times 1000}{\text{Molarity}} = \Lambda_m$

$\therefore \quad \kappa\,(\text{conductivity}) = \frac{\Lambda_m \times \text{molarity}}{1000}$

$$= \frac{8.28 \times 0.04}{1000}$$

$$= 3.312 \times 10^{-4} \text{ S cm}^{-1}$$

$$= 3.312 \times 10^{-4} \times 100 \text{ S m}^{-1}$$

$$= 3.312 \times 10^{-2} \text{ S m}^{-1}$$

Thus, (ii) $\rightarrow$ (r)

(iii) Also κ (conductivity) $= \frac{\text{Cell constant}}{\text{Resistance}}$

$\therefore \quad \text{Resistance} = \frac{\text{Cell constant (cm}^{-1})}{\kappa\,(\text{conductivity}) \text{ S cm}^{-1}}$

$$= \frac{0.206 \text{ cm}^{-1}}{3.312 \times 10^{-4} \text{ S cm}^{-1}}$$

$= 622\ \Omega = 0.622$ kilo ohm

Thus, (iii) $\rightarrow$ (s)

(iv) Conductance $= \frac{1}{\text{Resistance}} = \frac{1}{622} = 1.61 \times 10^{-3} \text{ohm}^{-1}$

Thus, (iv) $\rightarrow$ (q)

30. ***(c)*** The correct match is —

A-II, B-III, C-IV, D-I

31. ***(4)*** For the given concentration cell, the cell reaction are,

$M \longrightarrow M^{2+}$ at left hand electrode

$M^{2+} \longrightarrow M$ at right hand electrode

$\Rightarrow M^{2+}$ (RHS electrode) $\longrightarrow M^{2+}$ (LHS electrode)

$E^\circ = 0$

Applying Nernst Equation,

$$E_{cell} = 0.068 = 0 - \frac{0.06}{2} \log \frac{[M^{2+}]}{0.001}$$

$$\log \frac{[M^{2+}]}{0.001} = -\frac{0.068 \times 2}{0.06} = -2.3$$

$\Rightarrow [M^{2+}]$ at LHS electrode $= 10^{-2.3} \times 0.001$

$= 10^{-5.3}$ M

The solubility equilibrium for MX_2 is

$$MX_2(s) \rightleftharpoons M^{2+}(aq) + 2X^-(aq)$$

Solubility product, $K_{sp} = [M^{2+}][X^-]^2$

$= 10^{-5.3} \times (2 \times 10^{-5.3})^2$

$= 4 \times 10^{-15.9}$

32. ***(13.124)*** By using,

$$\Delta G = -nEF$$

$$= \frac{-2 \times 0.068 \times 96500}{1000} \text{ kJ}$$

$= -13.124$ kJ

33. ***(4.25)*** Specific conductance = Cell constant × conductance.

1.5×10^{-4} S cm^{-1} = Cell constant $\times 1.5 \times 10^{-4}$ S

$$\therefore \quad \text{Cell constant} = \frac{1.5 \times 10^{-4} \text{ S cm}^{-1}}{1.5 \times 10^{-4} \text{ S}} = 1 \text{cm}^{-1}$$

$$\Lambda_{HCl} = \frac{1000 \times \text{conductance} \times \text{cell constant}}{\text{Concentration}}$$

$$= \frac{1000 \times 4.25 \times 10^{-4} \text{S} \times 1 \text{ cm}^{-1}}{0.001 \text{ N}}$$

$= 4.25 \times 10^2$ S cm^2 equiv^{-1}

34. ***(350)*** Also $\lambda_{K^+} = \lambda_{Cl^-}$

$$\therefore \quad \Lambda_{KCl} = \frac{1000 \times \text{ specific conductance}}{\text{Concentration}}$$

$$= \frac{1000 \times 1.50 \times 10^{-4}}{0.001}$$

$\Lambda_{KCl} = 150$ S cm^2 equiv^{-1}

$\Rightarrow \Lambda_{KCl} = \lambda_{K^+} + \lambda_{Cl^-} = 2\lambda_{Cl^-}$

$\therefore\ 2\lambda_{Cl^-} = 150 \Rightarrow \lambda_{Cl^-} = 75$ S cm^2 equiv^{-1}

$\Lambda_{HCl} = 425 = \lambda_{H+} + \lambda_{Cl^-}$

$\therefore\ \lambda_{H^+} = \Lambda_{HCl} - \lambda_{Cl^-} = 425 - 75 = 350$ S cm^2 equiv^{-1}

35. ***(11387)*** As we know,

$$\Delta G_{cell} = -nFE_{cell}$$

$= -2 \times 96500 \times 0.059 = -11387$ J

36. ***(4)*** By using,

$$E_{cell} = E^\circ_{cell} - \frac{0.059}{2} \log \frac{[M^{2+}]_{Left}}{[M^{2+}]_{Right}}$$

$$0.059 = 0 - \frac{0.059}{2} \log \frac{\left(\frac{K_{sp}}{4}\right)^{\frac{1}{3}}}{0.001}$$

$\Rightarrow \quad K_{sp} = 4 \times 10^{-15}$

Hence, the value of x is 4.

37. ***(a)*** In (iii), (iv) and (v) electrochemical changes the mole of electrons are involved are less than 1.

(i) $\frac{1}{2} I_2 \xrightarrow{+e^-} I^-$

0.5 mol $I_2 \equiv 1$ mol of electrons

0.8 mol $I_2 = 1.6$ mol of electrons

(ii) $\underset{1 \text{ mol}}{Sn^{2+}} + \underset{2 \text{ mol}}{2e^-} \longrightarrow Sn$

$\frac{118.7}{118.7} = 1$ mol

Thus 2 mol of electrons

(iii) $MnO_4^- + 5e^- \longrightarrow Mn^{2+} + 4H_2O + 8H^+$

1 mol of $MnO_4^- \equiv 5$ mol of electron

$\frac{0.174}{158} = 1.101 \times 10^{-3}$ mol MnO_4^-

$\equiv 5 \times 1.101 \times 10^{-3} = 5.505 \times 10^{-3}$ mol electrons

(iv) 15.80 mL of 0.1145 M $MnO_4^- = \frac{15.80 \times 0.1145}{1000}$ mol

$= 1.81 \times 10^{-3}$ mol MnO_4^-

$= 1.81 \times 10^{-3} \times 5$ mol of electron

$= 9.05 \times 10^{-3}$ mol of electron

(v) 22.4 L at STP = 1 mol O_2

1L at STP $= \frac{1}{22.4}$ mol O_2

$= \frac{4}{22.4}$ mol electrons

$= 0.1786$ mol electrons

38. ***(b)*** Among the given batteries, only four i.e., lead-storage (acid) battery, nickel-cadmium battery and lithium battery are rechargeable batteries.

39. ***(c)*** Among the given reactions, only four i.e., (i), (ii), (iii) and (v) are spontaneous.

(i) $E^\circ_{cell} = 1.09 - 0.54\ V > 0$

(ii) $E^\circ_{cell} = 1.09 - (-0.44)\ V > 0$

(iii) $E^\circ_{cell} = 0.54 - (-0.44)\ V > 0$

(iv) $E^\circ_{cell} = 0.54 - 1.09\ V < 0$

(v) $E^\circ_{cell} = -0.403 - (-0.44)$

$= 0.037\ V > 0$

40. ***(a)*** Among the given reduction potentials at 298 K only four i.e., (i), (ii), (v) and (vi) are strong reducing agent than $E^\circ_{Pb^{2+}/Pb}$. $(\because E^\circ_{Pb^{2+}/Pb = -0.13\ V})$

41. ***(b)*** Among the given relations only four i.e., (ii), (iv) (vi) and (vii) are correct while others are incorrect.

42. ***(a)*** Among the given electrode reactions, only three i.e., (iii), (iv) and (v) are related to secondary batteries while others related to primary batteries.

43. ***(b)*** Among the given electrolytes, only four i.e., (iii), (iv), (vi) and (vii) gives straight line when a graph is plotted between Λ_m vs $\sqrt{C}$ because they are the example of strong electrolyte.

44. ***(d)*** Among the given solutions, only one i.e., (i) can be safely stored in a copper vessel because it does not react with copper while other compounds reacts with copper and can not be stored in a copper vessel.

Check Through PYQs : JEE Advanced

1. ***(a, c)*** The correct statements are given in option (a) and (c).
   - **At anode,**

     $N_2H_4(aq.) + 4OH^-(aq.) \longrightarrow N_2(g) + 4H_2O(l) + 4e^-$
   - **At cathode,** $2H_2O(l) + O_2(g) + 4e^- \longrightarrow 4OH^-(aq)$

   Overall reaction

   $$N_2H_4 + O_2 \longrightarrow N_2 + 2H_2O$$

   The major by product is H_2O.

2. ***(c)*** The correct match is P—3, Q—4, R—2, S—5.

(P) Titrate — KCl

Titrant — $AgNO_3$

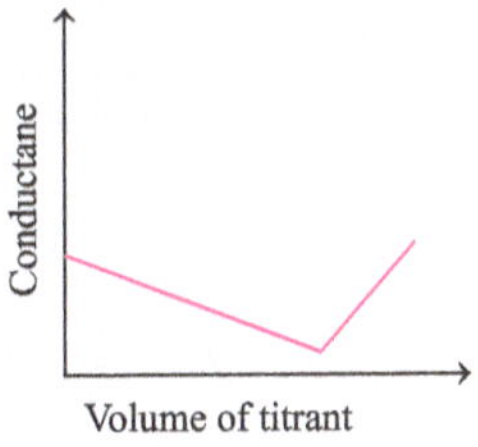

(Q) Titrate — $AgNO_3$

Titrant — KCl

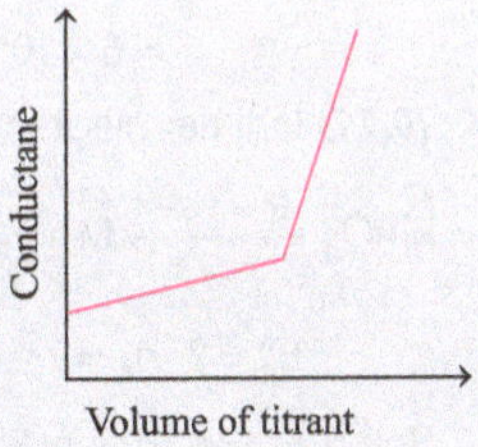

(R) Titrate — NaOH

Titrant — HCl

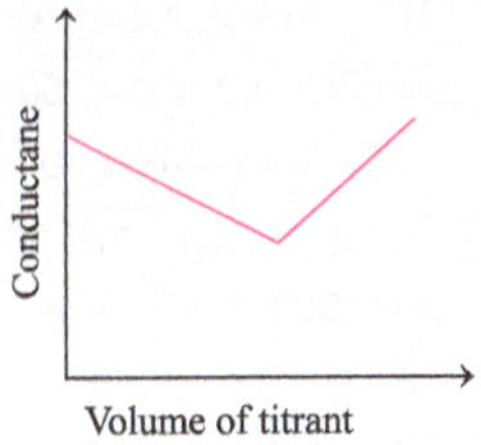

(S) Titrate — NaOH

Titrant — CH_3COOH

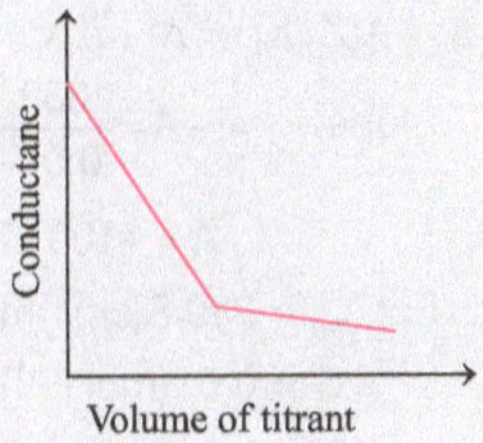

3. ***(a)*** Degree of dissociation, α for a given aqueous solution

$$= \frac{\Lambda_m}{\Lambda^\circ_m} \quad \ldots(i)$$

Dissociation constant (K_a) for a given aqueous solution

$$(K_a) = \frac{C\alpha^2}{1-\alpha} \quad \ldots(ii)$$

Put the value of α in Eq. (ii)

$$\therefore \quad K_a = \frac{C\left(\frac{\Lambda_m}{\Lambda^\circ_m}\right)^2}{1-\left(\frac{\Lambda_m}{\Lambda^\circ_m}\right)}$$

$$K_a = \frac{C\Lambda_m^2}{\Lambda^\circ_m(\Lambda^\circ_m - \Lambda_m)}$$

$$K_a\Lambda^{\circ 2}_m - K_a\Lambda^\circ_m\Lambda_m = C\Lambda_m^2$$

$$\frac{K_a\Lambda^{\circ 2}_m}{\Lambda_m} - K_a\Lambda^\circ_m = C\Lambda_m$$

$$\frac{K_a\Lambda^{\circ 2}_m}{\Lambda_m} = C\Lambda_m + K_a\Lambda^\circ_m$$

$$\frac{1}{\Lambda_m} = \frac{C\Lambda_m}{K_a\Lambda^{\circ 2}_m} + \frac{1}{\Lambda^\circ_m} \quad \ldots(iii)$$

By comparing Eq. (iii) with $y = mx + C'$, we will get,

Slope, $m = \frac{1}{K_a\Lambda^{\circ 2}_m} = S$

Intercept, $C' = \frac{1}{\Lambda^\circ_m} = P$

$$\therefore \quad \text{Ratio } \left(\frac{P}{S}\right) = \left(\frac{\frac{1}{\Lambda^\circ_m}}{\frac{1}{K_a\Lambda^{\circ 2}_m}}\right) = K_a\Lambda^\circ_m$$

4. ***(7)*** $\Lambda^\circ (U_mY_p) = m\lambda^\circ (U^{p+}) + p\lambda^\circ (Y^{m-})$

$\Rightarrow 25m + 100p = 250$

$\Rightarrow m + 4p = 10$ ...(i)

$\Lambda^\circ (V_mX_n) = m\lambda^\circ (V^{n+}) + n\lambda^\circ (X^{m-})$

$\Rightarrow 100m + 80n = 440$

$\Rightarrow 5m + 4n = 22$ ...(ii)

For electrolyte Z_mX_n from the given curve,

$\Lambda(Z_mX_n) = \Lambda^\circ (Z_mX_n) - A\sqrt{C}$

Slope, $= -A = \dfrac{339-336}{0.01-0.04}$

$A = +100$

For $\lambda_m = 339$ S cm^2 mol^{-1},

$\sqrt{C} = 0.01 \, (\text{mol L}^{-1})^{1/2}$

$339 = \Lambda^\circ (Z_mX_n) - 100 \times 0.01$

$\Rightarrow \Lambda^\circ (Z_mX_n) = 340$ S cm^2 mol^{-1}

$\Rightarrow m\lambda^\circ (Z^{n+}) + n\lambda^\circ (X^{m-}) = 340$

$\Rightarrow 50m + 80n = 340$

$\Rightarrow 5m + 8n = 34$ ...(iii)

By solving Eqs. (ii) and (iii)

$n = 3$ and $m = 2$

Putting value of m in Eq. (i),

$p = 2$

Therefore, $m + n + p = 2 + 3 + 2$

$= 7.$

5. ***(0.22)*** Degree of dissociation $= \alpha$

Limiting molar conductivity, $\Lambda^\circ_m = 4 \times 10^2$ S cm^2 mol^{-1}

Molar conductivity, $\Lambda_m = y \times 10^2$ S cm^2 mol^{-1}

Molar conductivity of dilution,

$\Lambda^\circ_m = 3y \times 10^2$ S cm^2 mol^{-1}

Concentration before dilution $= C$

Concentration after dilution $= \dfrac{C}{20}$

Using relation,

$$\alpha = \frac{\Lambda_m}{\Lambda^\circ_m} \quad \text{...(i)}$$

$\Rightarrow$ Dissociation constant, $K_a = \dfrac{C\alpha^2}{(1-\alpha)}$

Putting Eq. (i),

$$K_a = \frac{C\Lambda_m^2}{\Lambda^{\circ 2}_m \left(1 - \dfrac{\Lambda_m}{\Lambda^\circ_m}\right)} = \frac{C\Lambda_m^2}{\Lambda^\circ_m (\Lambda^\circ_m - \Lambda_m)}$$

$\Rightarrow$ Dissociation constant before dilution,

$$K_a = \frac{C(y \times 10^2)^2}{(4\times10^2)(4\times10^2 - y\times10^2)} \quad \text{...(ii)}$$

$\Rightarrow$ Dissociation constant after dilution,

$$K_a = \frac{\frac{C}{20}(3y \times 10^2)^2}{(4 \times 10^2)(4 \times 10^2 - 3y \times 10^2)} \quad \text{...(iii)}$$

Comparing Eqs. (ii) and (iii),

$$\frac{C(y \times 10^2)^2}{(4\times10^2)(4\times10^2 - y\times10^2)} = \frac{C(3y \times 10^2)^2}{20(4\times10^2)(4\times10^2 - 3y\times10^2)}$$

$\Rightarrow \dfrac{y^2 \times 10^4}{10^2(4-y)} = \dfrac{9y^2 \times 10^4}{10^2 \times 20(4-3y)}$

$\Rightarrow \dfrac{1}{(4-y)} = \dfrac{9}{20(4-3y)}$

$\Rightarrow 80 - 60y = 36 - 9y$

$\Rightarrow 80 - 36 = 60y - 9y$

$44 = 51y$

$\Rightarrow y = \dfrac{44}{51}$ ...(iv)

Putting in Eq. (i),

$\alpha = \dfrac{\Lambda_m}{\Lambda^\circ_m} = \dfrac{y \times 10^2}{4 \times 10^2}$

$\alpha = \dfrac{44}{51 \times 4} = \dfrac{11}{51}$

$\alpha = 0.22$

The value of α is 0.22.

6. ***(0.86)*** From equation (iv),

$y = \dfrac{44}{51}$

$\Rightarrow y = 0.86$

The value of y is 0.86.

7. ***(6)*** $\text{pH} = C\alpha = 10^{-4}$

$\Rightarrow \alpha = \dfrac{10^{-4}}{0.0015}$

Also, conductance $(G) = \kappa\left(\dfrac{A}{l}\right)$

$\Rightarrow \kappa = G\left(\dfrac{l}{A}\right) = 5 \times 10^{-7} \times \dfrac{120}{1} = 6 \times 10^{-5}$

$\Rightarrow \Lambda^c = \dfrac{\kappa \times 1000}{C} = \dfrac{6 \times 10^{-5} \times 1000}{0.0015}$

$\Rightarrow \Lambda^\circ = \dfrac{\Lambda^c}{\alpha} = \dfrac{6 \times 10^{-5} \times 1000}{0.0015} \times \dfrac{0.0015}{10^{-4}}$

$= 600$

$= 6 \times 10^2$ S cm^{2}mol^{-1}

8. ***(0.77)*** Latimer diagram

$$\overset{+7}{MnO_4^-} \xrightarrow[n_1 = 3]{E_1^\circ = 1.68\text{ V}} \overset{+4}{MnO_2} \xrightarrow[n_2 = 2]{E_2^\circ = 1.21\text{ V}} \overset{+2}{Mn^{2+}} \xrightarrow[n_3 = 2]{E_3^\circ = -1.03\text{ V}} \overset{0}{Mn}$$

$E_4^\circ = ?\ n_4 = 7$

So, $n_4E_4^\circ = n_1E_1^\circ + n_2E_2^\circ + n_3E_3^\circ$

$$7E_4^\circ = 3\times 1.68 + 2\times 1.21 + 2\times(-1.03)$$

$$\Rightarrow \quad E_4^\circ = \frac{5.04 + 2.42 - 2.06}{7} = \frac{5.4}{7} = 0.77\text{ V}$$

$$E^\circ_{MnO_4^-(aq)/Mn(s)} = +\,0.77\text{ V}$$

9. ***(a,b,c)*** Given,

At anode $X(s) \longrightarrow \underset{(0.001\text{ M})}{X^{2+}(aq)} + 2e^-$

At cathode $\underset{(0.1\text{ M})}{Y^{2+}(aq)} + 2e^- \longrightarrow Y(s)$

Overall reaction $X(s) + Y^{2+}(aq) \longrightarrow X^{2+}(aq) + Y(s)$

Nernst equation ,

$$E_{cell} = E^\circ_{cell} - \frac{0.06}{2}\log\frac{[X^{2+}]}{[Y^{2+}]}$$

$$E_{cell} = E^\circ_{cell} - 0.03\log\frac{0.001}{0.1}$$

$$E_{cell} = E^\circ_{cell} + 0.06$$

E_{cell} should be positive for a reaction to be spontaneous.

(a) $E^\circ_{Cd^{2+}/Cd} = -\,0.40\text{ V}, \quad E^\circ_{Ni^{2+}/Ni} = -\,0.24\text{ V}$

$$E^\circ_{cell} = E^\circ_{cathode} - E^\circ_{anode} = -\,0.24 - (-0.40)$$

$$E^\circ_{cell} = 0.16$$

$$E_{cell} = E^\circ_{cell} + 0.06 = 0.16 + 0.06 = 0.22\text{ V}$$

Reaction is spontaneous.

(b) $E^\circ_{Cd^{2+}/Cd} = -\,0.40\text{ V}$

$E^\circ_{Fe^{2+}/Fe} = -\,0.44\text{ V}$

$$E^\circ_{cell} = -\,0.44 + 0.40 = -\,0.04\text{ V}$$

$$E_{cell} = -0.04 + 0.06 = 0.02\text{ V}$$

Reaction is spontaneous.

(c) $E^\circ_{Ni^{2+}/Ni} = -\,0.24\text{ V}$

$E^\circ_{Pb^{2+}/Pb} = -\,0.13\text{ V}$

$$E^\circ_{cell} = -\,0.13 + 0.24 = 0.11\text{ V}$$

$$E_{cell} = 0.11 + 0.06 = 0.17\text{ V}$$

Reaction is spontaneous.

(d) $E^\circ_{Ni^{2+}/Ni} = -\,0.24\text{ V}$

$E^\circ_{Fe^{2+}/Fe} = -\,0.44\text{ V}$

$$E^\circ_{cell} = -0.44 + 0.24 = -\,0.20\text{ V}$$

$$E^\circ_{cell} = -\,0.20 + 0.06 = -\,0.14\text{ V}$$

Reaction is non-spontaneous.

Therefore, the correct combinations of X and Y are (a), (b) and (c).

10. ***(10)*** Equation of cell reaction according to the cell notation given, is

Reduction

$$Mg(s) + Cu^{2+}(aq) \longrightarrow Mg^{2+}(aq) + Cu(s)$$

Oxidation

Given, $E^\circ_{cell} = 2.70\text{ V}, T = 300\text{ K}$

with $[Mg^{2+}(aq)] = 1\text{ M}$ and $[Cu^{2+}(aq)] = 1\text{ M}$ and $n = 2$

Further, $E_{cell} = 2.67\text{ V}$

with $[Cu^{2+}(aq)] = 1\text{M}$ and $[Mg^{2+}(aq)] = x\text{M}$

and $\dfrac{F}{R} = 11500\text{ KV}^{-1}$

where, F = Faraday constant, R = gas constant

From the formula,

$$E_{cell} = E^\circ_{cell} - \frac{RT}{nF}\ln\frac{[Mg^{2+}(aq)]}{[Cu^{2+}(aq)]}$$

After putting the given values

$$2.67 = 2.70 - \frac{RT}{2F}\ln\frac{x}{1}$$

or $$2.67 = 2.70 - \frac{R\times 300}{2F}\times \ln x$$

or $$\ln x = \frac{0.03\times 2}{300}\times\frac{F}{R} = \frac{0.03\times 2\times 11500}{300} = 2.30$$

So, $\ln x = 2.30$

or $x = 10$ (as given $\ln(10) = 2.30$)

11. ***(-11.62)*** Given,

$A(s)\,|\,A^{n+}(aq, 2\text{M})\,||\,B^{2n+}(aq, 1\text{M})\,|\,B(s)$So, reactions at respective electrode will be

Anode $A(s) \longrightarrow A^{n+} + ne^- \times 2$

Cathode $B^{2n+} + 2ne^- \longrightarrow B(s)$

Overall reaction

$2A(s) + B^{2n+}(aq) \longrightarrow 2A^{n+}(aq) + B(s)$ Further,

$\Delta H^\circ = 2\Delta G^\circ$ and $E_{cell} = 0$ is also given

Now by using the Nernst equation

$$E_{cell} = E^\circ_{cell} - \frac{RT}{nF}\ln\frac{[\text{Product}]}{[\text{Reactant}]}$$

$\Rightarrow$ After putting the values

$$0 = E^\circ_{cell} - \frac{RT}{2nF}\ln\frac{[A^{n+}]^2}{[B^{2n+}]}$$

or $$E^\circ = \frac{RT}{2nF}\ln\frac{[2]^2}{[1]} = \frac{RT}{2nF}\ln 4 \qquad \ldots(i)$$

$\Rightarrow$ Further from the formula,

$$\Delta G^\circ = -nFE^\circ$$

$$\Rightarrow \quad \Delta G^\circ = -2nFE^\circ$$

Now putting the value of E° from eq. (i)

$$\Delta G^\circ = -2nF\times\frac{RT}{2nF}\ln 4 \qquad \ldots(ii)$$

$$\Delta G^\circ = -RT \ln 4$$

Finally, using the formula

$$\Delta G^\circ = \Delta H^\circ - T\Delta S^\circ$$

$$\Delta G^\circ = 2\Delta G^\circ - T\Delta S^\circ \quad \text{(as } \Delta H^\circ = 2\Delta G^\circ\text{, given)}$$

$$\Delta G^\circ = T\Delta S^\circ \quad \text{(from eq. (ii), } \Delta G^\circ = -RT \ln 4\text{)}$$

or $\Delta S^\circ = \dfrac{\Delta G^\circ}{T} = \dfrac{-RT \ln 4}{T}$

$$= -R \ln 4 = -8.3 \times 2 \times 0.7 \quad \text{(as all values given)}$$

$$= -11.62 \text{ J/K-mol}$$

12. ***(c)*** The redox reaction is :

$$Zn(s) + Cu^{2+} \longrightarrow Zn^{2+} + Cu$$

The Nernst equation is

$$E = E^\circ - \frac{2.303RT}{2F} \log 10$$

$$= 1.1 - \frac{2.303RT}{2F}$$

Also, $\Delta G = -nEF$

$$= -2F\left(1.1 - \frac{2.303RT}{2F}\right)$$

$$= -2.2F + 2.303RT$$

$$= 2.303RT - 2.2F$$

13. ***(d)*** Oxidation at anode

$$H_2(g) \longrightarrow 2H^+(aq) + 2e^-; \ E^\circ_{SHE} = 0.00 \text{ V}$$

Reduction at cathode

$$M^{4+}(aq) + 2e^- \longrightarrow M^{2+}(aq); \ E^\circ_{M^{4+}/M^{2+}} = 0.151 \text{ V}$$

Net: $M^{4+}(aq) + H_2(g) \longrightarrow M^{2+}(aq) + 2H^+(aq);$

$$\Rightarrow \quad K = \frac{[M^{2+}][H^+]^2}{[M^{4+}]\,p_{H_2}} = \frac{[M^{2+}]}{[M^{4+}]}$$

$$\Rightarrow \quad E_{cell} = E^\circ_{cell} - \frac{0.059}{2} \log K$$

$$0.092 = 0.151 - \frac{0.059}{2} \log \frac{[M^{2+}]}{[M^{4+}]}$$

$$0.059 = \frac{0.059}{2} \log 10^x$$

$\therefore \quad \log 10^x = 2$

$\therefore \quad x = 2$

CHAPTER 9

Chemical Kinetics

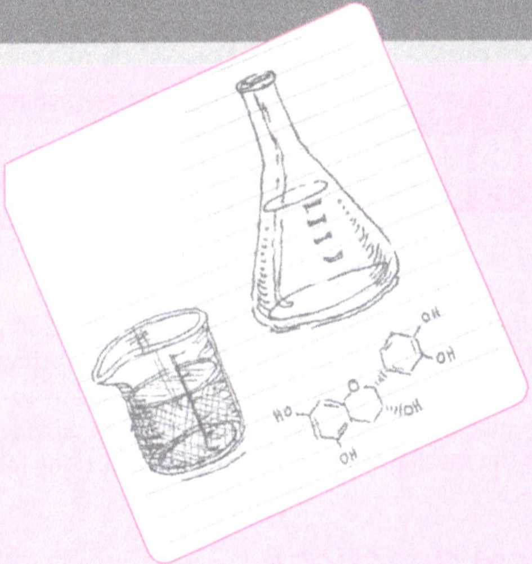

Learning Elements

Element 1 **Rate of a Reaction and Factor Affecting Rate of Reaction**

Chemical Reactions, Rate of a Chemical Reaction, Average and Instantaneous Rate, Factors affecting Rate of a Reaction, Law of Mass Action.

Element 2 **Rate Law, Order, Molecularity and Half-Life Period**

Rate Law, Rate Constant, Order of Reaction, Molecularity of a Reaction, Integrated Rate Equation, Half life period, Consecutive Reaction, Parallel Reaction, Reversible or Opposing Reaction

Element 3 **Arrhenius Theory, Activation Energy, Collision and Related Theories**

Temperature Coefficient, Arrhenius Equation, Activation Energy, Effect of Catalyst on E_a Collision Theory, Transition State Theory

Practice Elements

Practice Element 1 Target JEE Main

Practice Element 2 Target JEE Advanced

Trend Insights

JEE Main

	2024				2023				2022			
Topics	**E**	**M**	**T**	**O**	**E**	**M**	**T**	**O**	**E**	**M**	**T**	**O**
Rate of a Reaction and Factor Affecting, Rate of Reaction	–	–	4	4	–	–	–	–	–	–	1	1
Rate Law, Order, Molecularity and Half-Life Period	–	2	12	14	–	1	15	16	–	1	13	14
Arrhenius Theory, Activation Energy, Collision and Related Theories	–	–	2	2	1	1	5	7	–	–	4	4

E = Easy, **M** = Medium, **T** = tough, **O** = Overall

Current Dynamics

- During past three years problems based on rate law, order molecularity and half-life period were frequently from this chapter.
- Most of the questions has been asked from first order kinetics and rate constants and Arrhenius equations in recent years.
- Problems based on first order and zero order reactions and their half-life has been asked in previous years.

JEE Advanced

Typology	Years				
	2024	**2023**	**2022**	**2021**	**2020**
1. Simple MCQs	–	–	–	–	1
2. One or More than one correct	–	–	–	1	–
3. Numerical Value/Integer	1	–	–	–	–
4. Matching Type	–	–	–	–	–
5. Paragraph Based	–	–	–	–	–

Current Dynamics

- Numerical value type question was asked in 2024 from rate law, order and activation energy.
- Most of the questions from rate law, rate of a reversible reaction were asked in previous years.

Insightful Advice

- Practice plotting graph for different order of reaction and their interpretation.
- Focus on Arrhenius equation and reaction mechanisms to score well in exams.
- Memorise integrated rate equations for zero, first and second order reactions.

Element 1 Rate of a Reaction and Factor Affecting Rate of Reaction

Chemical kinetics is the branch of chemistry that examines the rates of chemical reactions and the factors that influence them. Understanding reaction rates not only helps us to predict how quickly a reaction will occur but also provides insight into the mechanisms by which these reactions take place.

Chemical Reactions

A chemical reaction occurs when one or more substances undergo a transformation, resulting in the formation of new substances with distinct compositions and properties. It involves breaking and forming chemical bonds. This process requires different amount of energy for different types of bonds, leading to variation in the rates or speed of different reactions.

Classification of Chemical Reactions

I. Depending on their rates or speeds chemical reactions can be classified as

1. Instantaneous or Fast Reactions

These are infact very fast reactions and it is practically impossible to measure the speed of such reactions. Typical examples of such reactions include ionic reactions, organic substitution reactions etc.

2. Extremely Slow Reactions

Such reactions proceed at very slow speed and here the speed is so slow that again it is not possible to measure the speed of such reactions, e.g. rusting of iron.

3. Moderately Slow Reactions

Reactions belonging to third category, i.e. **with moderate speed** are utilised for the study of chemical kinetics as in inversion of cane sugar and hydrolysis of starch.

II. Depending upon number of steps, chemical reactions are classified in the following ways

1. Elementary Reactions

An elementary reaction refers to a single step in a chemical reaction, where reactants directly interact and transform into products without any intermediate stages. In other words, it represents a reaction that occurs in a single, indivisible molecular collision or interaction between reactants.

2. Complex Reactions

These reactions involves multiple elementary steps (reactions), which together describe the overall reaction mechanism. Unlike elementary reactions, which occur in a single molecular collision or event, complex reactions occur through a series of individual elementary steps, each with its own molecularity and rate law.

Rate of a Chemical Reaction

The rate of a reaction is defined as the amount of change in concentration of products or reactants divided by the corresponding time intervals or rate is the concentration change per unit time.

$$\frac{\Delta x}{\Delta t} \quad \text{or} \quad \frac{dx}{dt} = \frac{(x_2 - x_1)}{t_2 - t_1}$$

where, Δx or dx is the concentration change, i.e. $(x_2 - x_1)$ in the time interval Δt or dt, i.e. $(t_2 - t_1)$.

Note Concentration is generally expressed as active mass, i.e. in units of molarity, mol L^{-1} or mol dm^{-3}.

As a reaction proceeds, the concentration of reactants decreases and that of products increases. Thus, the rate of a reaction, can also be expressed as;

$$\text{Rate of reaction} = \frac{\text{Decrease in concentration of reactants}}{\text{Time taken}}$$

$$= \frac{\text{Increase in concentration of products}}{\text{Time taken}}$$

For a reaction, $R \longrightarrow P$

$$\text{Rate of reaction} = \frac{-\Delta[R]}{\Delta t} = +\frac{\Delta[P]}{\Delta t}$$

$$\Delta t \longrightarrow 0$$

Here, –ve sign signifies the decrease in concentration of reactants with time and +ve sign signifies increase in concentration of products with time.

To express the rate, two terms are often used:

(i) Average rate (ii) Instantaneous rate

Average Rate of Reaction

The average rate of reaction can be defined as the ratio of the change in concentration (of products or reactants) to the time interval in which change in concentration takes place.

For a reaction, $R \longrightarrow P$

$$\text{Average Rate} = -\frac{\Delta[R]}{\Delta t} = \frac{\Delta[P]}{\Delta T}$$

Instantaneous Rate of Reaction

A reaction rate does not remain same throughout the reaction but changes as the reactants are used up because the rate depends upon the concentration of reactants which changes as the reaction goes. Thus, to measure the rate at any particular moment the term instantaneous rate is used.

The rate of the reaction at a particular instant in terms of the concentration of the reactants at that instant is called **instantaneous rate**.

For a simplest reaction,

$$\text{Reactant } (R) \longrightarrow \text{Product } (P)$$

$$\text{Instantaneous rate} = -\frac{d[R]}{dt} = \frac{d[P]}{dt} \text{ if } \Delta t \to 0$$

Concept Visualizer

The concept of Rate of reaction can be visualised from the graph given below

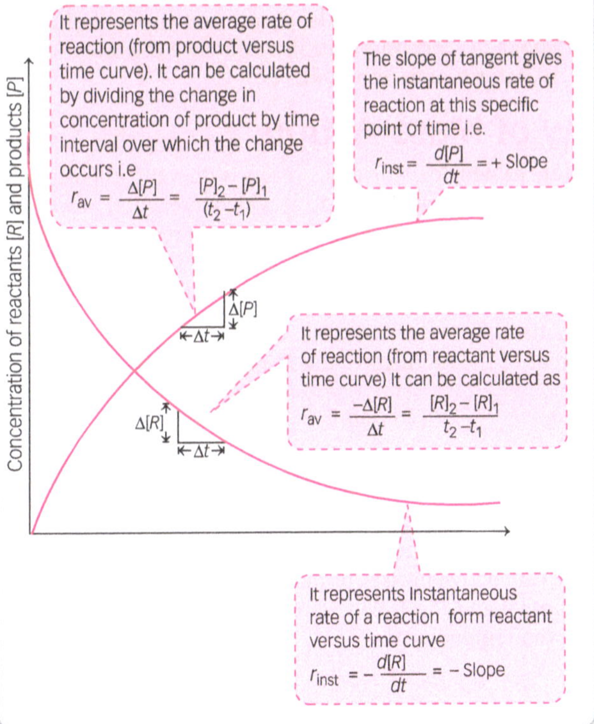

Instantaneous Rate based on Stoichiometry

For the reaction, $aA + bB \longrightarrow cC + dD$

Rate of disappearance of a reactant is negative.

$$\therefore \quad \text{Rate of disappearance of } A = -\frac{d[A]}{dt}$$

$$\text{Rate of disappearance of } B = -\frac{d[B]}{dt}$$

Rate of formation of a product is positive.

$$\text{Rate of formation of } C = \frac{d[C]}{dt}$$

$$\text{Rate of formation of } D = \frac{d[D]}{dt}$$

$$\text{Thus,} \quad \text{Rate of Reaction, } \frac{dx}{dt} = -\frac{1}{a}\frac{d[A]}{dt} = -\frac{1}{b}\frac{d[B]}{dt} = \frac{1}{c}\frac{d[C]}{dt} = \frac{1}{d}\frac{d[D]}{dt}$$

where, a, b, c and d are the **stoichiometric coefficients** of the substances A, B (reactants), C and D (products), respectively.

Negative sign before rate indicates that concentration of reactants decreases with time.

JEE Alert

Symbol 'Δ' is used for a large change. i.e., for average rate whereas symbol d is used for a small change, i.e. for instantaneous rate.

Solved Booster 1.1

In the following reaction, ammonia and oxygen react at high temperature as $4NH_3(g) + 5O_2(g) \longrightarrow 4NO(g) + 6H_2O(g)$

The rate of formation of NO is $1.2 \times 10^{-3}\ Ms^{-1}$.

The rate of disappearance of ammonia and the rate of formation of water (in $mol \cdot L^{-1}$) respectively are

(a) $1.2 \times 10^{-3}, 1.8 \times 10^{-3}$ (b) $1.5 \times 10^{-3}, 1.8 \times 10^{-3}$

(c) $1.5 \times 10^{-3}, 1.4 \times 10^{-3}$ (d) $1.2 \times 10^{-3}, 1.5 \times 10^{-3}$

Solution *(a)*

For the reaction,

$$4NH_3(g) + 5O_2(g) \longrightarrow 4NO(g) + 6H_2O(g)$$

$$\text{Rate} = \frac{1}{4}\frac{-d[NH_3]}{dt} = \frac{1}{5}\frac{-d[O_2]}{dt} = \frac{1}{4}\frac{d[NO]}{dt} = \frac{1}{6}\frac{d[H_2O]}{dt}$$

(a) Rate of disappearance of ammonia

$$= \text{Rate of appearance of NO} = 1.2 \times 10^{-3}\ mol\ L^{-1}s^{-1}$$

(b) Rate of formation of water $= \frac{d[H_2O]}{dt}$

From the rate equation, $\frac{1}{6}\frac{d[H_2O]}{dt} = \frac{1}{4}\frac{d[NO]}{dt}$

$$\therefore \quad \frac{d[H_2O]}{dt} = \frac{6}{4} \times 1.2 \times 10^{-3} = 1.8 \times 10^{-3}\ mol\ L^{-1}\ s^{-1}$$

JEE MAPPER

Example Similar to PYQ Asked in JEE Advanced 2015

In dilute aqueous HCl, the complex tetraaquadichloroferrate (II) is oxidised by $Cr_2O_7^{2-}$. For this reaction, the ratio of the rate of change of $[H^+]$ to the rate of change of $Cr_2O_7^{2-}$ is

Sol. *(14)* The reaction is

$$6[Fe(H_2O)_4Cl] + Cr_2O_7^{2-} + 14H^+ \longrightarrow 6[Fe(H_2O)_4Cl_2]^+ + 2Cr^{3+} + 7H_2O$$

$$\text{Rate} = -\frac{1}{14}\frac{d[H^+]}{dt} = \frac{-d[Cr_2O_7^{2-}]}{dt} = \frac{1}{2}\frac{d[Cr^{3+}]}{dt}$$

From the above rate equation, for every 1 mole of $Cr_2O_7^{2-}$ consumed 14 moles of H^+ ions are consumed. So, the ratio of the rate of change of $[H^+]$ to the rate of changes of $[Cr_2O_7^{2-}]$ is 14 : 1.

Compentancy Enhancer 1.1

In an acidic solution, the complex hexaquacobaltate (II) is oxidised by MnO_4^-. For this reaction, the ratio of the rate of change of $[H^+]$ to the rate of change of MnO_4^- is ....

Unit of Rate of Reaction

The unit of rate is concentration time^{-1}. If the concentration is in mol L^{-1} and the time is in seconds then the unit will be mol $L^{-1}s^{-1}$.

Rate of reaction may also be expressed in terms of pressure change per unit time, if amount of reactants and products are given in terms of their partial pressure.

Factors Affecting the Rate of Reaction

The rate of a chemical reaction may be affected by a number of factors, such as :

(i) **Concentration of the Reactants** Rate of a reaction is directly related to the concentration of reactants, greater the reactants concentration, faster the reaction.

(ii) **Temperature of the Reaction** The reaction rate increases with increase in temperature. Generally, the reaction rate doubles nearly with every 10 K rise of temperature.

(iii) **Presence of Light** Most of the reactions take place at a faster rate in the presence of light (or radiations). Like the reaction between H_2 and Cl_2 occurs at a lower rate in the absence of light. But in the presence of light, the reaction occurs rapidly at faster rate.

(iv) **Particle Size of a Solid** Related to the surface area of the solid particles, larger the surface area of the reactants, faster is the rate of reaction. Hence, finely divided reactants react more rapidly because smaller the particle size, greater the surface area and faster the reaction.

(v) **Presence of a Catalyst** A catalyst generally increases the speed of a reaction without itself being consumed in the reaction. In case of reversible reactions, a catalyst helps to attain the equilibrium quickly without disturbing the state of equilibrium.

(vi) **Nature of Reactants** In a chemical reaction, bonds present in the reactants are broken and new bonds in products are formed. The nature and strength of the bonds in reactant molecules influence the rate of its transformation into products.

Law of Mass Action

The rate at which a substance reacts is directly proportional to its active mass and the rate at which a reaction proceeds is proportional to the active masses of the reacting substances.

$$A + B \longrightarrow C + D$$

Concentration of the reactants A and B decreases with time and that of the products C and D increases with time.

Hence, $-\frac{d[A]}{dt} \propto [A]$ and $-\frac{d[B]}{dt} \propto [B]$

so that rate of the reaction $\left(\frac{dx}{dt}\right) \propto [A][B]$ or $\left(\frac{dx}{dt}\right) = k[A][B]$

where, k is called rate constant or velocity constant and $[A]$ and $[B]$ are active masses or molar concentration of the reactants A and B. k is constant for a particular reaction at the given temperature.

Elemental Practice 9.1

Type I MCQs with Only One Correct Option

1. Which of the following factors does not affect the rate of a chemical reaction?
(a) Concentration of reactants
(b) Temperature
(c) Nature of reactants
(d) Colour of reactants

2. For the reaction,
$$A + 2B \longrightarrow C + D$$
If the initial concentrations of A and B are halved, how will the rate of reaction change if the rate law is given by
$$\text{Rate} = k[A]^1[B]^2$$
(a) Rate remains the same
(b) Rate is halved
(c) Rate is reduced to $\frac{1}{4}$th
(d) Rate is reduced to $\frac{1}{8}$th

3. For the reaction,
$$2A + B \longrightarrow 2C$$
If the instantaneous rate of formation of C is 0.05 M/s, then the instantaneous rate of consumption of A is
(a) 0.05 M/s (b) 0.10 M/s
(c) 0.025 M/s (d) 0.15 M/s

4. Given below are two statements, one is labelled as Assertion (A) and the other is labelled as Reason (R).
Assertion (A) The rate constant of a reaction is dependent on the concentration of reactants.
Reason (R) The rate constant changes with temperature but remains constant at a given temperature.
In the light of the above statements, choose the correct answer from the options given below.
(a) Both (A) and (R) are true and (R) is the correct explanation of (A).
(b) Both (A) and (R) true but (R) is the incorrect explanation of (A).
(c) (A) is true but (R) is false.
(d) (A) is false but (R) is true.

5. Consider the following sequential reactions
$$X \xrightarrow{k_1} Y$$
$$Y \xrightarrow{k_2} Z$$
k_1 and k_2 be the rate constants for these reactions. If the rate of appearance of Z is given as 0.04 M/s. Then the rate of appearance of Y, assuming no accumulation of Y is
(a) 0.04 m/s (b) 0.08 m/s
(c) 0.02 m/s (d) 0.10 m/s

6. Match List I with List II

	List I		List II
(A)	The rate at which reactants are consumed or products are formed.	(1)	Rate constant
(B)	The reaction that involve more than one elementary reaction	(2)	Average rate
(C)	The change in concentration of a species over a small time interval.	(3)	Instantaneous rate
(D)	The proportionality constant specific to a given reaction and temperature	(4)	Complex reaction

Choose the correct answer from the options given below.
(a) A-2, B-4, C-1, D-3 (b) A-2, B-4, C-3, D-1
(c) A-3, B-1, C-4, D-2 (d) A-1, B-3, C-2, D-4

7. Which the following statement(s) regarding factor(s) affecting the rate of reaction is correct
(a) Increasing the surface area of a solid reactant increases the rate of reaction.
(b) Dilution of a reactant in a solution always decreases the rate of reaction
(c) The presence of inert gases does not affect the rate of reaction.
(d) The rate of a reaction cannot be affected by the nature of the solvent used.

8. For the reaction, $A \xrightarrow{k_1} B$, the initial concentration of A is $[A]_0$ and no B is present initially. If the reaction reaches to completion, what is the concentration of B at that point?
(a) $[A]_0$ (b) 0
(c) $[A]_0 - [A]$ (d) $[A]_0 + [B]_0$

9. Given below are two statements.
Statement I The rate of chemical reaction increases with an increase in temperature.
Statement II The rate constant of a reaction is temperature independent.
In the light of the above statements, choose the correct answer from the options given below.
(a) Both Statement I and Statement II are true.
(b) Both Statement I and Statement II are false.
(c) Statement I is true and Statement II is false.
(d) Statement I is false and Statement II is true.

10. The concentration of gases are expressed in their partial pressures, then the units of rate equation is
(a) atm s^{-1} (b) atm s
(c) No units (d) atm $mol^{-1}s^{-1}$

11. In a reaction, $A \longrightarrow$ Products, the concentration of A decreases from 0.6 mol L^{-1} to 0.2 mol L^{-1} in 10 minutes, then the rate during this interval will be
(a) 6.7×10^{-5} M/s
(b) 6.7×10^{-4} M/s
(c) 6.7×10^{-2} M/s
(d) 6.7×10^{-3} M/s

12. Consider the reaction $A \rightarrow B$. Generally the concentration of both the reactants and products varies with time. Which of the following figure correctly describes the change in concentration of reactant with time.

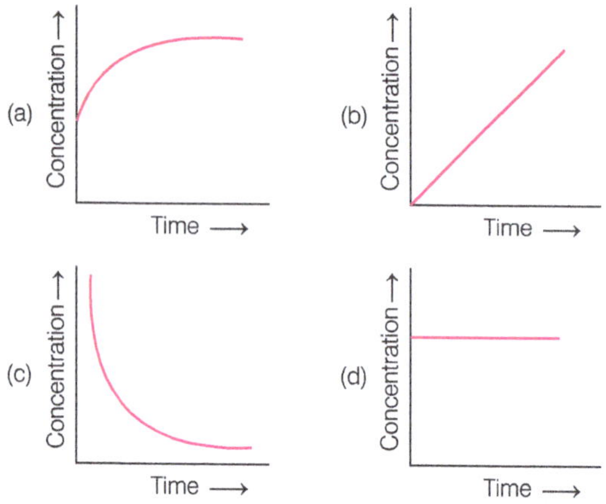

13. Given below are two statements, one is labelled as Assertion (A) and the other is labelled as Reason (R).

Assertion (A) The instantaneous rate of the reaction can be calculated using the tangent to the concentration *vs* time curve.

Reason (R) The instantaneous rate is the slope of the tangent to the concentration *vs* time curve at a specific point.

In the light of the above statements, choose the correct answer from the options given below.
(a) Both (A) and (R) are true and (R) is the correct explanation of (A).
(b) Both (A) and (R) true but (R) is not the correct explanation of (A).
(c) (A) is true but (R) is false.
(d) (A) is false but (R) is true.

14. If the average rate of hydrolysis of butyl chloride increases with increasing temperature, which of the following statement is true?
(a) The reaction is exothermic
(b) The reaction is endothermic
(c) The reaction does not depend on temperature
(d) The activation energy is zero.

15. Which of the following methods is commonly used to determine the instantaneous rate of a reaction at time t?
(a) Measuring the volume of gas produced at regular intervals.
(b) Taking the derivative of the concentration with respect to time at a specific moment.
(c) Using a spectrophotometer to measure absorbance at the beginning and end of the reaction.
(d) Recording the temperature change throughout the reaction.

16. If the reaction rate at a given temperature decreases then
(a) free energy of activation is lower
(b) free energy of activation is higher
(c) the concentration of reactant decreases
(d) initial concentration of reactants remain constant

17. In a catalytic reaction involving the formation of ammonia by Haber's process
$N_2 + 3H_2 \longrightarrow 2NH_3$, the rate of appearance of NH_3 was measured as 3.5×10^{-4} mol L^{-1} s^{-1}. The rate of disappearance of H_2 will be
(a) 5.25×10^{-5}
(b) 5.25×10^{-2}
(c) 5.25×10^{-4}
(d) 5.25×10^{-3}

18. In a reaction $A \rightarrow B$, the following data is observed

Time (min)	[A] (M)	[B] (M)
0	0.5	0
5	0.3	0.2
10	0.1	0.4

The average rate of formation of B at $t = 10$ min is
(a) 0.04 M/min
(b) 0.03 M/min
(c) 0.02 M/min
(d) 0.01 M/min

Type II 》 MCQs with One or More than One Correct Option

19. Which of the following statements about average and instantaneous rates of reaction are correct?
(a) The average rate over a time interval is always greater than the instantaneous rate at the end of the interval.
(b) The average rate of a reaction decreases over time for a reaction when the concentration of reactant decreases.
(c) The instantaneous rate at any given time can be determined from the slope of the concentration time graph.
(d) For a zero-order reaction, the instantaneous rate remains constant throughout the reaction.

20. For the reaction, $2A + B \rightarrow C$, if the rate of disappearance of A is 0.2 mol L^{-1} s^{-1}, what is/are the correct rate expressions?
(a) Rate of disappearance of $B = 0.1$ mol $L^{-1} s^{-1}$.
(b) Rate of formation of $C = 0.1$ mol L^{-1} s^{-1}.
(c) Rate of disappearance of $B = 2 \times$ Rate of formation of C.
(d) Rate of disappearance of $A = 2 \times$ Rate of disappearance of B

21. Which of the following statements about the rate of a chemical reaction are not true?
(a) The rate of a reaction is always positive.
(b) The average rate of reaction can be negative.
(c) The rate of reaction can depend on the temperature and concentration of reactants.
(d) The rate of reaction is independent of the presence of a catalyst.

22. For the reaction, $A + 2B \rightarrow C$. Which of the following statements are correct?
(a) The rate of disappearance of A is equal to the rate of appearance of C.
(b) The rate of appearance of C is twice the rate of disappearance of B.
(c) Catalyst increases the rate of a reaction.
(d) The reaction will not proceed if the concentration of B is zero.

23. Select the factors that affect the rate of a chemical reaction.
(a) Concentration of products
(b) Temperature
(c) Nature of reactants
(d) Presence of catalyst

Type III 》 Numerical/Integer Answer Type Questions

24. For a chemical reaction $A \rightarrow B$, it was found that concentration of B is increased by 0.4 mol L^{-1} in 20 min. The average rate of the reaction is .... $\times 10^{-2}$ mol L^{-1} h^{-1} (nearest integer)

25. The number of elementary reactions are ....
A. $N_2O_5 \longrightarrow NO_2 + NO_3$
B. $Cl + O_3 \longrightarrow ClO + O_2$
C. $H + C_2H_5 \longrightarrow C_2H_6$
D. $CH_4 + Cl_2 \xrightarrow{h\nu} CH_3Cl + HCl$
E. $NO + NO_3 \longrightarrow 2NO_2$

26. The number of correct statements related to the given reaction is/are ....

$$2A + B \longrightarrow C + D$$

I. The rate of reaction can be expressed as $-\frac{1}{2}\frac{d[A]}{dt} = \frac{d[C]}{dt}$
II. The rate of a reaction depends on concentration of reactants.
III. The instantaneous rate of reaction can change as the reaction progresses.
IV. The rate of formation of product C is equal to the rate of disappearance of reactant A.

27. For the reaction, $C_2H_4 + H_2 \longrightarrow C_2H_6$
under certain conditions the temperature and partial pressures of reactants, the rate of formation of C_2H_6 is 0.002 kg/h. The rate of conversion of H_2 under same condition is .... $\times 10^{-5}$ (nearest integer)

28. During the decomposition of H_2O_2 to give oxygen, 68g O_2 is formed per minute at a certain point of time. The rate of formation of water at this point is .... (nearest integer)

Elemental Practice 9.1 | Chapter 09

Connect with **Answers**

1. (d)	**2.** (d)	**3.** (a)	**4.** (d)	**5.** (a)	**6.** (b)
7. (a)	**8.** (a)	**9.** (c)	**10.** (a)	**11.** (b)	**12.** (c)
13. (a)	**14.** (b)	**15.** (b)	**16.** (c)	**17.** (c)	**18.** (a)
19. (b,c,d)	**20.** (a,b,d)	**21.** (b,d)	**22.** (a,c,d)	**23.** (b,c,d)	**24.** (120)
25. (4)	**26.** (3)	**27.** (13)	**28.** (4)		

Element 2 Rate Law, Order, Molecularity and Half-Life Period

Rate Law

Consider a reaction, $aA + bB \longrightarrow$ Product

where, a and b are the stoichiometric coefficients of reactants and products. The, rate of the above reaction be

$$\frac{dx}{dt} \propto [A]^x\,[B]^x \quad \ldots\text{(i)}$$

$$\left(\frac{dx}{dt}\right) = k\,[A]^x\,[B]^y \quad \ldots\text{(ii)}$$

Above equation is called **rate law**, since it describes the functional dependence of the reaction rate upon concentration of the various reactants.

Here, the exponents x and y may or may not be equal to the stoichiometric coefficients (a and b of the reactants).

Equation (ii) is known as differential rate equation and k is constant of proportionality.

Equation (i) which relates the rate of reaction to the concentration of reactants is called rate law or rate expression.

Thus, **rate law is the expression which relates the rate of reaction to the concentration of reactants with each term raised to some power which may or may not be equal to the stoichiometric coefficients of the reacting species in a balanced chemical equation.**

JEE Spotlite

- It must be noted that the rate law cannot be deduced from the equation for a given reaction. It is found by experiment only. Thus, the rate law may not bear a simple relationship as the stoichiometric equation.
- The rate law may not depend on the concentration of every reactant or product of the reaction.
- The rate law may depend on the concentration of species (e.g. catalyst) which do not appear in the equation for the overall reaction.

Rate Constant

From (ii) At a time when $[A] = [B] = 1\text{ mol L}^{-1}$, $\frac{dx}{dt} = k$

Thus, rate constant k is also called **specific reaction rate**. It is defined as the rate of the reaction, when the molar concentration of each of the reactants is unity.

Different Characteristics of rate constant are given below

(i) Larger the value of k, faster is the reaction and *vice-versa*. Therefore, rate constant is a measure of the rate of reaction for unit active mass.

(ii) The value of k remains constant for a reaction at the given temperature.

(iii) For a given reaction, the value of k is independent of concentration.

Order of Reaction

Consider the following reaction,

$$aA + bB + cC \longrightarrow dD + eE$$

Experimentally, rate law obtained is

$$\text{Rate} = k[A]^x[B]^y[C]^z$$

Here, x, y and z indicate how rate varies with the concentration of A, B and C. The sum of these exponents, gives the overall order of the reaction. Thus, $n = x + y + z$

where, x, y and z represent order with respect to reactants, A, B and C respectively. **Hence, the order of a reaction is given by the sum of powers of the concentration of the reactants in the rate law expression.**

Order of reaction is purely an experimental quantity not necessarily an integer.

Solved Booster 2.1

$$X + Y + Z \longrightarrow P$$

The rate of reaction is doubled when the concentration of Y was doubled, and when the concentration of both X and Y were doubled the rate becomes doubled and when the concentration of both Y and Z were doubled the rate becomes quadrupled. Total sum of order is

(a) 0 (b) 3 (c) 2 (d) 1

Solution (c)

$$r_1 = k[X]^a[Y]^b[Z]^c \quad \ldots\text{(i)}$$

$$r_2 = 2r_1 = k[X]^a[2Y]^b[Z]^c \quad \ldots\text{(ii)}$$

$$r_3 = 2r_1 = k[2X]^a[2Y]^b[Z]^c \quad \ldots\text{(iii)}$$

$$r_4 = 4r_1 = k[X]^a[2Y]^b[2Z]^c \quad \ldots\text{(iv)}$$

Solve for (a), (b) and (c), $a = 0, b = 1, c = 1$

Order w.r.t. $[X] = 0, [Y] = 1, [Z] = 1$

Total order $= 0 + 1 + 1 = 2$

Units of Rate Constants of Different Order Reactions

For a reaction, $aA + bB \longrightarrow$ Rate, $\left(\frac{dx}{dt}\right) = k\,[A]^x\,[B]^y$

when, $(x + y) =$ total order of reaction $= n$

$$k = \frac{\left(\frac{dx}{dt}\right)}{[A]^x\,[B]^y} = \frac{\text{conc.}}{\text{time (conc.)}^n}$$

$$k = \text{conc}^{(1-n)}\,\text{time}^{-1}$$

Taking the units of concentration as mol L^{-1} and time in seconds, then

n (Order)	Unit
0	mol $L^{-1}s^{-1}$
1	s^{-1}
2	$(\text{mol } L^{-1})^{-1}s^{-1}$ or L mol^{-1} s^{-1}

JEE MAPPER

Example Similar to PYQ Asked in JEE Advanced 2019

Consider the kinetic data given in the following table for the reaction.

$$X + Y + Z \longrightarrow \text{Product}$$

Exp. No.	[X] (mol dm^{-3})	[Y] (mol dm^{-3})	[Z] (mol dm^{-3})	Rate of reaction/mol dm^{-3} s^{-1}
1.	4	2	2	3.4×10^{-5}
2.	4	4	2	3.4×10^{-5}
3.	4	2	4	6.2×10^{-5}
4.	6	2	2	8.2×10^{-5}

The rate of the reaction for $[X] = 1.4$ mol dm^{-3}, $[Y] = 2.5$ mol dm^{-3} and $[Z] = 2.8$ mol dm^{-3} is found to be $P \times 10^{-8}$ mol dm^{-3} s^{-1}. The value of P is ....

Sol. *(549)* Rate $= k[X]^a[Y]^b[Z]^c$

$$\frac{(\text{Rate})_1}{(\text{Rate})_2} = \frac{(4)^a(2)^b(2)^c}{(4)^a(4)^b(2)^c} \Rightarrow \frac{3.4 \times 10^{-5}}{3.4 \times 10^{-5}} = \left(\frac{2}{4}\right)^b$$

$$b = 0$$

$$\frac{(\text{Rate})_1}{(\text{Rate})_3} = \frac{(4)^a(2)^b(2)^c}{(4)^a(2)^b(4)^c}$$

$$\frac{3.4 \times 10^{-5}}{6.2 \times 10^{-5}} = \left(\frac{1}{2}\right)^c \Rightarrow 0.5 = \left(\frac{1}{2}\right)^c$$

$$C \approx 1$$

$$\frac{(\text{Rate})_1}{(\text{Rate})_4} = \frac{(4)^a(2)^b(2)^c}{(6)^a(2)^b(2)^c} \Rightarrow \frac{3.4 \times 10^{-5}}{8.2 \times 10^{-5}} = \left(\frac{4}{6}\right)^a$$

$$a \approx 2$$

So, rate $= k[X]^2[Z]^1$

From exp. Ist, Rate $= 3.4 \times 10^{-5}$ mol dm^{-3} s^{-1}

$$3.4 \times 10^{-5} = k[4]^2[2]^1$$

$$3.4 \times 10^{-5} = k \times 32 \Rightarrow k \approx 0.1 \times 10^{-5}$$

Given, $[X] = 1.4$ mol dm^{-3}; $[Y] = 2.5$ mol dm^{-3}

$[Z] = 2.8$ mol dm^{-3}

$\therefore$ Rate $= 0.1 \times 10^{-5} \times [1.4]^2[2.5]^0[2.8]^1 = 54.88 \times 10^{-7}$

Rate $= 548.8 \times 10^{-8}$ mol dm^{-3} s^{-1}

Thus, $P \approx 549$

Competency Enhancer 2.1

Consider the kinetic data given in the following table for the reaction $M + N + O \longrightarrow$ Product

Exp. No.	[M] (mol dm^{-3})	[N] (mol dm^{-3})	[O] (mol dm^{-3})	Rate of reaction/mol dm^{-3} s^{-1}
1.	2.4	2.2	2.2	4×10^{-6}
2.	2.4	2.4	2.2	4×10^{-6}
3.	2.4	2.2	4.4	8×10^{-6}
4.	3.5	2.2	2.2	6×10^{-6}

The rate of the reaction for $[M] = 2.3$ mol dm^{-3}.

$[N] = 1.2$ mol dm^{-3} and $[O] = 2.4$ mol dm^{-3} is found to be $Z \times 10^{-8}$ mol dm^{-3} s^{-1}. The value of Z is ....

Molecularity of Reaction

The total number of reacting species (molecules, free radicals atoms or ions) taking part in an elementary reaction, is called **molecularity of reaction**.

It represents the number of reactant molecules undergoing collision to bring about the chemical reaction.

Consider a reaction,

$$aA + bB \longrightarrow \text{Products}$$

Here, molecularity of reaction $= a + b$. Value of molecularity can be 1, 2, 3 etc., depending upon the participation of one, two, three reactants in the reaction.

Depending upon the value of molecularity, reactions are classified as follows:

(i) **Unimolecular Reactions** The reactions which have molecularity one are called unimolecular reactions.

e.g. $$F_2O_2 \longrightarrow F_2 + O_2$$

(ii) **Bimolecular Reactions** The reactions which have molecularity two are called bimolecular reactions. These reactions involve simultaneous collision between two species as in dissociation of HI.

$$2HI \longrightarrow H_2 + I_2$$

(iii) **Trimolecular Reactions** The reactions which have molecularity three are called trimolecular reactions. These reactions involve simultaneous collisions between three reacting species.

$$2NO + O_2 \longrightarrow 2NO_2$$

Distinction between Order and Molecularity

The main difference between order and molecularity of a reaction are tabulated below.

Distinction between order and molecularity of a reaction

S. No.	Molecularity	Order
1.	Molecularity is always an integral value and never zero.	Order may be zero, fraction and even negative.
2.	Molecularity is based on the number of reactants in an elementary step. (of one-step reaction or a complex reaction)	Order is based on the rate law and is decided by rate-determining step (which is the slowest step). Order of an elementary step is always equal to its molecularity.
3.	Molecularity of the slowest step is same as order in a complex reactions.	Order is given by slowest step of the complex reactions.

Integrated Rate Equation

Integrated rate equation gives relation between directly measured experimental quantities, i.e. concentrations at different times. For different order reactions, integrated rate equations are different.

Zero Order Reaction

In zero order reactions, rate is independent of the concentration of the reactants, i.e. rate is proportional to zeroth power of the concentration of reactants.

Consider a reaction,

$$A \longrightarrow \text{Products}$$

Let, $[A]_0$ is the initial concentration of reactants and $[A]$ be the concentration at time t.

$$\text{Rate} = -\frac{d[A]}{dt}$$

$$= k_0[A]^0 = k_0$$

$$-d[A] = -k_0\,dt \quad \ldots\text{(i)}$$

Integrating both sides, we get

$$[A] = -k_0 t + I \quad \ldots\text{(ii)}$$

where, I = Constant of integration

At $t = 0$, $[A] = [A]_0$

$$\therefore \quad I = [A]_0$$

From eq.(ii) $$[A] = -k_0 t + [A]_0 \quad \ldots\text{(iii)}$$

or $$k_0 = \frac{[A]_0 - [A]}{t} \quad \ldots\text{(iv)}$$

This is the expression for the rate constant of zero order reactions. Thus, rate constant for zero order reactions is equal to the rate of reaction at all concentrations.

Graphical Representation

Eq. (iii) represents a straight line (plot of concentration A *vs* time) with a slope equal to $-k_0$ and intercept equal to $[A]_0$, as shown below

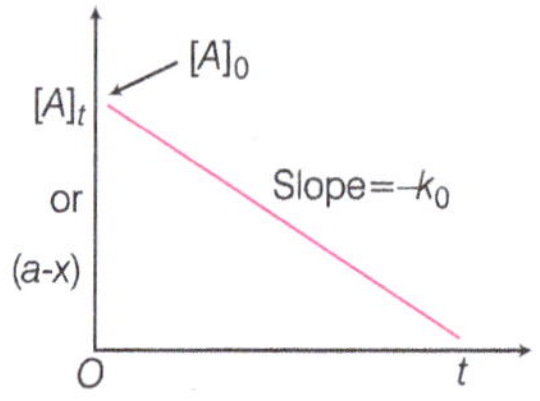

Plot of concentration A *versus* time

When reaction is completed 100%, then $[A]_0 = [A]$

i.e. $$[A]_0 - [A] = 0$$

$$\therefore \quad k_0 = \frac{[A]_0}{t} \quad \text{or} \quad t = \frac{[A]_0}{k_0} \quad \ldots\text{(v)}$$

$\therefore$ At time $t = [A]_0/k_0$, reaction is completed 100%.

Characteristics of Zeroth Order Reaction

(i) **Unit of Rate Constant** k_0 is expressed in the units of concentration. time^{-1} e.g. mol L^{-1} s^{-1}.

(ii) If concentration of the product is x_1 at time t_1, and x_2 at time t_2, then

$$k_0 t_1 = x_1 \quad \text{and} \quad k_0 t_2 = x_2 \quad \Rightarrow \quad k_0 = \frac{x_1 - x_2}{t_1 - t_2}$$

k_0 has unit conc. time^{-1}

(iii) **Half-life Period** The time required to reduce the initial concentration of the reactant to half of its initial value is called **half-life time** or **half-life period** and is denoted by $t_{1/2}$. When $[x] = [a]/2, t = t_{1/2}$, substituting these values in Eq. (v), we get

$$t_{1/2} = \frac{[A]_0}{2k_0}$$

Thus, the half-life period of zero order reaction is directly proportional to initial concentration, i.e., $t_{1/2} \propto [A]_0$

Hence, a graph of $t_{1/2}$ *vs* $[A]_0$ will be a straight line passing through origin and slope $= \frac{1}{2k_0}$

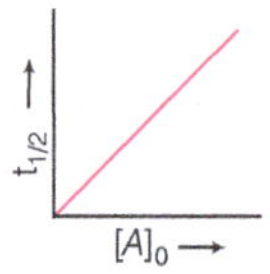

Graph of $t_{1/2}$ *versus* [a]

(iv) At $t = T_{75}$ (which is the time required by the reactant to decompose 75%), $x = \frac{3}{4}[A]_0$

$$\therefore \quad T_{75} = \frac{3a}{4k_0} = 1.5T_{50}$$

Thus, T_{75} or $T_{50} \propto [A]_0$

JEE Spotlite

- Change in concentration of the reactant has no effect on the rate in a zero order reaction.
- Zero order reaction for 100% completion take place in two half-lifes.

$$t_{100\%} = 2t_{50\%}$$

- The unit of rate and rate constant for zero order is same.
- For nth order reaction, the ratio of $\frac{T_{75}}{T_{50}} = 2^{n-1} + 1$

Solved Booster 2.2

A chemical reaction is known to be of zeroth order with $k = 5 \times 10^{-8}$ mol L^{-1}s^{-1}. How long does it take to change concentration from 4×10^{-2}mol L^{-1} to 2×10^{-2} mol L^{-1}.

(a) 1.98 h (b) 13.60 h (c) 102 h (d) 111.11 h

Solution *(d)*

$[A]_0$ = Initial concentration = 4×10^{-2} mol L^{-1}

$[A]_t$ = Concentration at time t = 2×10^{-2} mol L^{-1}

$$\therefore \quad t = \frac{(4 \times 10^{-2} - 2 \times 10^{-2}) \text{ mol L}^{-1}}{5 \times 10^{-8} \text{ mol L}^{-1}\text{s}^{-1}}$$

$$= 4.00 \times 10^5 \text{s} = 111.11 \text{h}$$

First Order Reaction

A reaction is said to be first order if rate of a reaction is determined by the variation of one concentration term.

Consider the reaction,

	A	$\longrightarrow$ Product
At $t = 0$	$a = [A_0]$	0
At time t	$(a - x)$	x

Rate law is $\left(\frac{dx}{dt}\right) = k_1 [A]^n = k_1 [A] = k_1 (a - x)$

$$\Rightarrow \quad \frac{dx}{a - x} = k_1 dt$$

Integration of this equation gives

$$\int \frac{dx}{(a - x)} = k_1 \int dt$$

$$\therefore \quad -\ln (a - x) = k_1 t + I \text{(integration constant)}$$

At $t = 0$, $x = 0$, above equation gives

$$\therefore \quad -\log_e a = I$$

$$\therefore \quad k_1 t = \ln a - \ln(a - x)$$

$$\therefore \quad k_1 = \frac{1}{t} \ln\left(\frac{a}{a - x}\right) = \frac{2.303}{t} \log_{10}\left(\frac{a}{a - x}\right) \quad \text{...(i)}$$

Fraction of reactant can be calculated using formula

$$\frac{x}{[A]_0} = (1 - e^{-kt})$$

Graphical Representation Rewriting equation of first-order into the form

$$\log_{10} (a - x) = -\frac{k_1 t}{2.303} + \log_{10} a$$

A graph between $\log_{10}(a - x)$ and time t is a straight line.

slope of the line $= \frac{-k_1}{2.303}$ and intercept OA on y-axis $= \log_{10} a$.

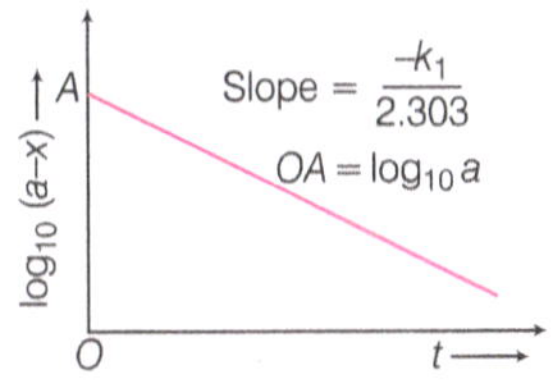

A plot between log $\frac{[a]}{[a - x]}$ and t, a staight line graph will be obtained with slope $= \frac{k_1}{2.303}$ as shown below,

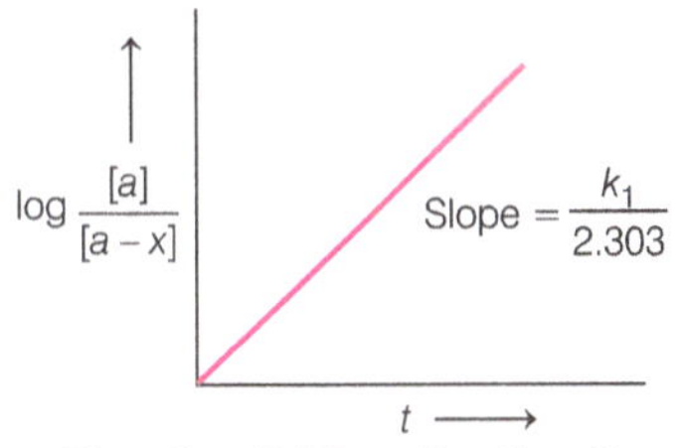

Plot of log ([a]/[a – x]) vs time (t)

Characteristics of First Order Reaction

(i) **Unit of Rate Constant** The unit of rate constant is expressed is time^{-1}. i.e. s^{-1} or min^{-1} or h^{-1}

(ii) **Half-life Period** It is the time taken to reduce the initial concentration of reactant to half of its initial value. For a first order reaction,

$$x = 0.5a \quad \text{and} \quad t = t_{1/2}$$

so,
$$k = \frac{2.303}{t_{1/2}} \log \frac{a}{0.5a}$$

$$= \frac{2.303}{t_{1/2}} \log 2 = \frac{0.693}{t_{1/2}}$$

or $t_{1/2}=\dfrac{0.693}{k}$

Thus, $t_{1/2}$ is independent of initial concentration a. First order reaction never goes to completion as after each half-time 50% reactant is left.

Half-life does not depends upon initial concentration of reactant.

(iii) Average life for first order reaction is inverse of rate constant or is equal to $1.443t_{1/2}$.

(iv) For a typical 1st order gas phase reaction $A(g) \rightarrow B(g) + C(g)$. The rate constant can be calculated by $k=\dfrac{2.303}{t}\log\dfrac{p_i}{2p_i-p_t}$

where, p_i be initial pressure and p_t the total pressure at time t.

(v) **Examples of First Order Reaction**

- Cyclopropane $\longrightarrow$ propene
- $2N_2O_5(g) \xrightarrow{\Delta} 4NO_2(g) + O_2(g)$
- $(CH_3)_3CCl + OH^-(aq) \longrightarrow (CH_3)_3COH + Cl^-(aq)$
- $SO_2Cl_2(g) \xrightarrow{\Delta} SO_2(g) + Cl_2(g)$

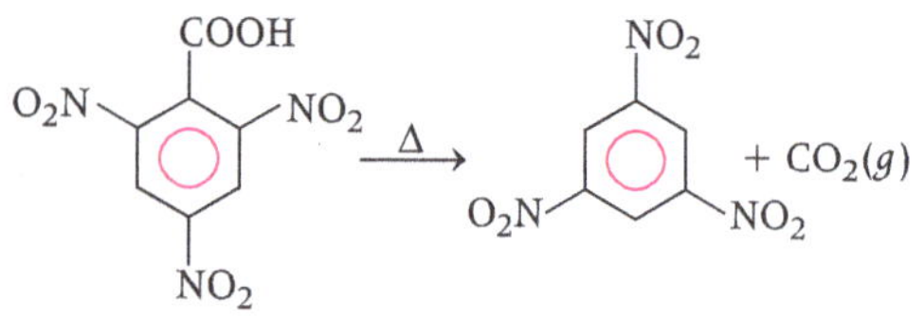

Solved Booster 2.3

Decomposition of H_2O_2 is studied by volumetric measurement of concentration of H_2O_2 by standard $KMnO_4$ solution at different intervals of time.

$$H_2O_2 \longrightarrow H_2O + \frac{1}{2}O_2$$

At any time t $H_2O_2 \equiv KMnO_4$

If 5 mL of H_2O_2 required 10 mL of 0.1 N $KMnO_4$ at the start of the reaction and after 10 min 5 mL of H_2O_2 required 5 mL of 0.1 N $KMnO_4$. The rate constant of

$$\frac{-d[H_2O_2]}{dt}=k[H_2O_2] \text{ in } (\text{min}^{-1}) \text{ is}$$

(a) 0.125 (b) 0.295

(c) 0.045 (d) 0.0693

Solution *(d)*

Since, $\dfrac{-d[H_2O_2]}{dt}=k[H_2O_2]$

Hence, it is first-order reaction

Also $H_2O_2 \equiv KMnO_4$

Initial concentration of H_2O_2 = $10 \times 0.1 = 1$ milliequivalent = a

$[H_2O_2]$ at 10 min = $5 \times 0.1 = 0.5$ milliequivalent = $(a-x)$

$$\therefore \quad k=\frac{2.303}{t}\log\left(\frac{a}{a-x}\right)$$

$$=\frac{2.303}{t}\log\frac{V_0}{V_t}$$

$$=\frac{2.303}{10}\log\frac{1}{0.5}$$

$$=\frac{2.303}{10}\log 2 = 0.0693\ \text{min}^{-1}$$

JEE MAPPER

Example Similar to PYQ Asked in JEE Main 2025

Consider the following first order reaction that takes place at 410 K:

$$2CO(g) \longrightarrow CO_2(g) + C(s)$$

The total pressure at the end of 410 s after starting with pure $CO(g)$ is found to be 0.313 atm. At the time when the reaction is 100% complete, the total pressure is found to be 0.1645 atm. Then, the rate constant of the reaction is .... $\times 10^{-5}$ s^{-1}.

Sol. *(25)*

	$2CO(g) \longrightarrow$	$CO_2(g)$ +	$C(s)$
or	$CO(g) \longrightarrow$	$\frac{1}{2}CO_2(g)$ +	$\frac{1}{2}C(s)$
Initial	p_0	0	0
At time t	$p_0 - p_i$	$\frac{p_i}{2}$	–
[100%] decomposition	0	$\frac{p_0}{2}$	–

$$\frac{p_0}{2}=0.1645 \Rightarrow p_0 = 0.329$$

Total pressure at time t

$$p_0 - p_i + \frac{p_i}{2} = 0.313$$

$$\therefore \quad p_i = 0.032 \Rightarrow k=\frac{2.303}{t}\log\frac{p_0}{p_0-p_i}$$

$$=\frac{2.303}{410}\log\frac{0.329}{(0.329-0.032)}$$

$$=\frac{2.303}{410}\log\frac{0.329}{0.297}=\frac{2.303}{410}\times 0.0444$$

$$\approx 2.5\times10^{-4}\ \text{s}^{-1} \Rightarrow k = 25\times10^{-5}\ \text{s}^{-1}$$

Competency Enhancer 2.2

Some PH_3 is introduced into a flask at 600°C containing inert gas. PH_3 decomposes to give $P_4(g)$ and $H_2(g)$. The total pressure as a function of time is given below.

Time (s)	0	60	120	∞
Pressure (mm) (total)	262.4	272.9	275.53	276.4

Then, the rate constant of the given reaction is .... 10^{-4} s^{-1}.

Second Order Reaction

It is a type of chemical reaction in which the rate of reaction is proportional to the square of the concentration of one reactant, sum of power terms of two or more reactants is 2.

Consider the reaction,

	A	+	A	$\rightarrow$	Product
or	A	+	B	$\rightarrow$	Product
At $t=0$	a		a		0
At time t	$(a-x)$		$(a-x)$		x
At time t_1	$(a-x_1)$		$(a-x_1)$		x_1
At time t_2	$(a-x_2)$		$(a-x_2)$		x_2

Rate law is $\left(\frac{dx}{dt}\right)=k_2[A]^n=k_2[A]^2=k_2[A][B]$ or

$$\left(\frac{dx}{dt}\right)=k_2(a-x)^2$$

Rate constant, k_2 of second-order reaction is

$$k_2=\frac{1}{t}\left[\frac{1}{(a-x)}-\frac{1}{a}\right]=\frac{1}{t}\frac{x}{a(a-x)} \quad \ldots\text{(i)}$$

Also $$k_2=\frac{1}{(t_2-t_1)}\left[\frac{(x_2-x_1)}{(a-x_1)(a-x_2)}\right]$$

where $(a-x_1)$ and $(a-x_2)$ are the concentration of the reactant A at time t_1 and t_2, respectively. Eq. (i) is integrated rate law for second order reaction.

Characteristics of Second Order Reaction

(i) **Unit of Rate Constant** k_2 is expressed in the unit of conc^{-1} time^{-1} (L mol$^{-1}\cdot$s^{-1})

(ii) **Half-life Period** If $t=t_{1/2}$

$$x=\frac{a}{2}$$

$$\therefore \quad k_2=\frac{1}{t_{1/2}}\left[\frac{a/2}{a(a/2)}\right]$$

$$\Rightarrow \quad t_{1/2}=\frac{1}{k_2a}$$

$$\Rightarrow \quad T_{1/2}\propto\frac{1}{a}$$

Thus, half-life period is inversely proportional to initial concentration.

(iii) **Graphical Representation** Equation of second-order can be rewritten as $\frac{1}{(a-x)}=k_2t+\frac{1}{a}$

A graph between $(a-x)^{-1}$ and time t is a straight line of slope $=k_2$ and intercept on y-axis $=\frac{1}{a}$

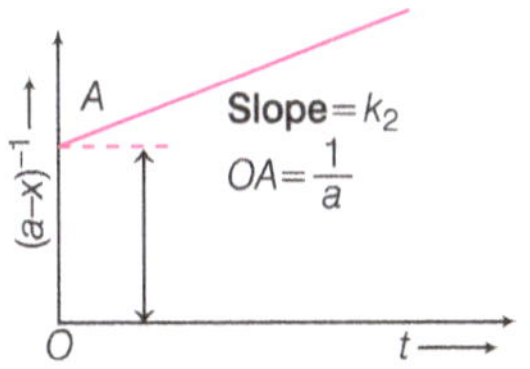

Graphical study of second order reaction

(iv) **Pseudo Unimolecular Reactions** If reactants A and B have different concentration, a and b respectively, then

$$k_2=\frac{2.303}{t(a-b)}\log_{10}\frac{b(a-x)}{a(b-x)}$$

If reactant A is in excess, i.e. $a>>b$, then, $(a-b)\approx a$, $(a-x)\approx a$, so that above equation reduces to

$$k_2=\frac{2.303}{ta}\log_{10}\left(\frac{b}{b-x}\right)$$

$$k_2'=k_2a=\frac{2.303}{t}\log_{10}\left(\frac{b}{b-x}\right)$$

(Since a being very large, may be treated as constant after the change).

Thus, the reaction follows first order kinetict with respect to the reactant taken relatively in small amount.

(v) **Example of Second Order Reaction** Following are some examples of the second-order reaction:

(i) $CH_3COOC_2H_5 + OH^- \longrightarrow CH_3COO^- + C_2H_5OH$

(ii) $S_2O_8^{2-} + 2I^- \longrightarrow 2SO_4^{2-} + I_2$

(iii) $CH_3I + OH^- \longrightarrow CH_3OH + I^-$

(iv) $2NOCl(g) \longrightarrow 2NO(g) + Cl_2(g)$

(v) $H_2O_2 + 2H^+ + 2I^- \longrightarrow 2H_2O + I_2$

JEE Spotlite

Rate constant and other parameters of different order reactions

Order	Rate constant**	*Unit of rate constant	Effect on rate by changing concentration to m times	(Half-life period $t_{1/2}$ =)
0	$k_0 = \frac{x}{t} = \frac{[A]_0 - [A]_t}{t}$	conc time^{-1} mol L^{-1} s^{-1}	no change	$\frac{a}{2k_0}$
1	$k_1 = \frac{2.303}{t}\log_{10}\left(\frac{a}{a-x}\right) = \frac{2.303}{t}\log_{10}\frac{[A]_0}{[A]_t}$ $C = C_0e^{-k_1t}$, $N = N_0e^{-k_1t}$, $k_1 = \frac{2.303}{(t_1-t_2)}\log_{10}\frac{(a-x_1)}{(a-x_2)}$ (when initial concentration 'a' is not given)	time^{-1}(s^{-1})	m times	$\frac{0.693}{k_1}$
2	$k_2 = \frac{1}{t}\left[\frac{1}{(a-x)} - \frac{1}{a}\right] = \frac{1}{t}\left[\frac{1}{[A]_t} - \frac{1}{[A]_0}\right] = \frac{x}{ta(a-x)}$ (for the case when each reactant has equal concentration) $k_2 = \frac{2.303}{t(a-b)}\log_{10}\left[\frac{b(a-x)}{a(b-x)}\right]$ (for the case when both reactants have different concentration)	conc^{-1} time^{-1} (mol L^{-1})$^{-1}$ s^{-1}, L mol^{-1} s^{-1}	m^2 times	$\frac{1}{k_2a}$
3	$k_3 = \frac{1}{2t}\left[\frac{1}{(a-x)^2} - \frac{1}{a^2}\right]$	conc^{-2} time^{-1} (mol L^{-1})$^{-2}$ s^{-1} L^2 mol^{-2} s^{-1}	m^3 times	$\frac{3}{2k_3a^2}$
n	$k_n = \frac{1}{(n-1)t}\left[\frac{1}{(a-x)^{n-1}} - \frac{1}{(a)^{n-1}}\right] n \neq 1$ (except for 1st order reaction)	conc$^{(1-n)}$time^{-1} (mol L^{-1})$^{(1-n)}$s^{-1} L$^{(n-1)}$ mol$^{(1-n)}$ s^{-1}	m^n times	$\frac{2^{n-1}-1}{(n-1)k_n(a)^{n-1}}$

** *In each case, coefficient of the reactant is one. If y is the number of reactants involved, then rate constant should be multiplied by y*

Experimental Determination of Rate Constant

Sometimes for chemical calculations we require the measurement of the concentration of the reactants or products or both at different intervals of time.

Various methods are adopted and the proper selection is based on experimental condition and nature of the reactants and products (e.g. their states, neutral or acidic or basic etc).

Volumetric Method

In this method a known volume of the reaction mixture is removed at various times and rapidly added to a larger volume of ice-cold water, which effectively stops the reaction or atleast slows it down considerably.

This is widely used in cases where reactants or products are acid or base or species undergoing a redox reaction.

(i) **Decomposition of H_2O_2**

$$H_2O_2 \longrightarrow H_2O + \frac{1}{2}O_2$$

At	$t = 0$	a
At time	$t = 0$	$(a - x)$

Concentration of H_2O_2 at different interval of time can be determined by titration of the reactant using $KMnO_4$ in acidic medium. At any time volume of $KMnO_4 \equiv [H_2O_2]$

If V_0 = volume of $KMnO_4$ at start = a

V_t = volume of $KMnO_4$ at time $t = (a - x)$

then for the first-order reaction,

$$k_1 = \frac{2.303}{t}\log\frac{V_0}{V_t}$$

(ii) **Acid Hydrolysis of Ethyl Acetate**

$$CH_3COOC_2H_5 + H_2O \xrightarrow{H^+} CH_3COOH + C_2H_5OH$$

	$CH_3COOC_2H_5$	CH_3COOH	C_2H_5OH
At $t = 0$	a	0	0
At time t	$(a - x)$	x	x
At time ∞	$(a - a)$	a	a

In this case reactants are neutral species and products formed have acid. Since, it is acid catalysed reaction, hence, concentration of the catalyst remains constant throughout but requires definite volume of the titrating substance (titre). Concentration of CH_3COOH formed can be measured by titration of the reaction mixture with suitable base (e.g. NaOH).

V_0 = volume of NaOH at start = Catalyst H^+

V_t = volume of NaOH at time t

= CH_3COOH formed at time t + catalyst $H^+ \equiv x + V_0$

V_∞ = volume of NaOH at infinite time

= total CH_3COOH + catalyst $H^+ = a + V_0$

This gives $a = (V_\infty - V_0)$, $(a - x) = (V_\infty - V_t)$

$$k_1 = \frac{2.303}{t} \log \frac{(V_\infty - V_0)}{(V_\infty - V_t)}$$

Volume Measurement Method

This method is to be used where we can measure the volume of one of the gaseous substances evolved.

$$N_2O_5(g) \longrightarrow 2NO_2(g) + \frac{1}{2}O_2(g)$$

	$N_2O_5(g)$	$2NO_2(g)$	$\frac{1}{2}O_2(g)$
At $t = 0$	a	0	0
At time t	$(a - x)$	2	$\frac{x}{2}$
At time ∞	$(a - a)$	2	$\frac{a}{2}$

$N_2O_5(g)$ and $NO_2(g)$ both are soluble in CCl_4, hence volume of $O_2(g)$ can be measured.

Let, V_t = volume of $O_2(g)$ at time $t \equiv \frac{x}{2}$

V_∞ = volume of $O_2(g)$ at ∞ time $\equiv \frac{a}{2}$

$$\therefore \quad a = 2V_\infty$$

$$(a - x) = 2(V_\infty - V_t)$$

$$k_1 = \frac{2.303}{t} \log \frac{2V_\infty}{2(V_\infty - V_t)}$$

Optical Rotation Method Inversion of Cane Sugar (Sucrose)

$$\underset{\substack{((+); 60.5^\circ) \\ \text{Dextro-rotatory}}}{C_{12}H_{22}O_{11}} + H_2O \xrightarrow{H^+} \underbrace{\underset{\substack{\text{Glucose} \\ ((+); 52.5^\circ)}}{C_6H_{12}O_6} + \underset{\substack{\text{Fructose} \\ ((-); -92^\circ)}}{C_6H_{12}O_6}}_{\textit{Laevo}\text{-rotatory}}$$

In this reaction by the hydrolysis of *dextro*-rotatory sucrose produces a mixture of glucose (*dextro*-rotatory) and fructose (laevo rotatory). As *laevo* rotation of fructose is more therefore the resulting mixture is *laevo* rotatory.

The kinetics of above reaction is studied by noting the angle of rotation at different intervals of time using polarimeter.

Say angle of rotation at the start of experiment = r_0

Angle of rotation at any time $t = r_t$

Angle of rotation at ∞ time = r_∞

Now, angle of rotation at any instant of time = $(r_0 - r_t) \propto$ amount of sucrose hydrolysed

or $\quad x \propto (r_0 - r_t)$

Similarly, angle of rotation at ∞ time = $(r_0 - r_\infty) \propto$ initial conc. of sucrose (a)

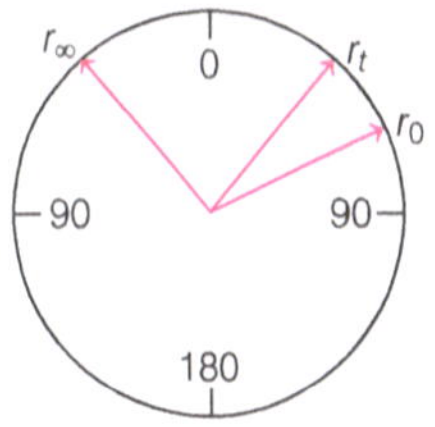

$$a \propto (r_0 - r_\infty)$$

Thus, $(a - x) \propto (r_0 - r_\infty) - (r_0 - r_t) \propto (r_t - r_\infty)$

Hence, $k = 2.303 \log \dfrac{r_0 - r_t}{r_t - r_\infty}$

Kinetics of Some Complex Reactions

Complex reactions can be decomposed into a series of well-defined kinetic steps. These reactions are classified based on their unique features and mechanisms.

Consecutive Reactions

Consecutive reactions may be represented as

$$A \xrightarrow{k_A} B \xrightarrow{k_B} C$$

Thus, reaction proceeds from reactants (A) to products (C) through one or more intermediate stages. The overall reaction is a result of several consecutive steps. Thus, each step

$$A \longrightarrow B \quad \text{or} \quad B \longrightarrow C$$

has its own reaction rate and also rate constant. Above reaction is a two-step reaction with velocity constants k_A and k_B of first-order reactions. The concentration of B will first increase and then it will decrease showing a maximum as shown in below.

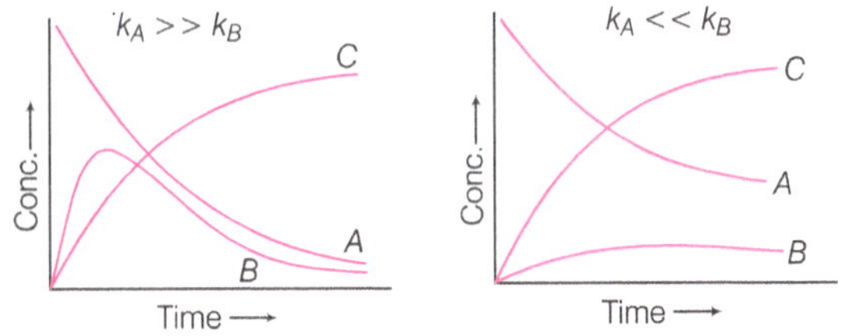

Consecutive reactions

For the concecutive reaction

$$[A] = [A]_0 e^{-k_A t}$$

$$[B] = \frac{k_A}{k_B - k_A}(e^{-k_A t} - e^{-k_B t})[A]_0$$

$$[C] = \left(\frac{k_A e^{-k_B t} - k_B e^{-k_A t}}{k_B - k_A} + 1\right)[A]_0$$

It can be shown that concentration of B is maximum when

$$\therefore \quad k_A e^{-k_A t} = k_B e^{-k_B t}$$

$$\Rightarrow \quad \frac{k_A}{k_B} = e^{(k_A - k_B)t}$$

$$\frac{dB}{dt} = 0, \log_e\left(\frac{k_A}{k_B}\right) = (k_A - k_B)t$$

$$\therefore \quad t_{max} = \frac{\log_e (k_A/k_B)}{(k_A - k_B)}$$

$$\Rightarrow \quad t_{max} = \frac{\log_e k_A - \log_e k_B}{(k_A - k_B)}$$

Parallel Reactions

Sometimes a reactant can undergo changes in more than one way. These are termed **parallel or side reactions**.

In these reactions, some side reactions take place leading to the formation of some byproducts alongwith the main product. There reactions can be represented as

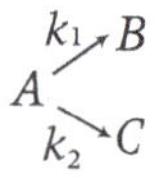

Let initial concentration of $A = a$ and amount disappeared in time $t = x$, partly as B and partly as C, K_1, and K_2 are rate constant.

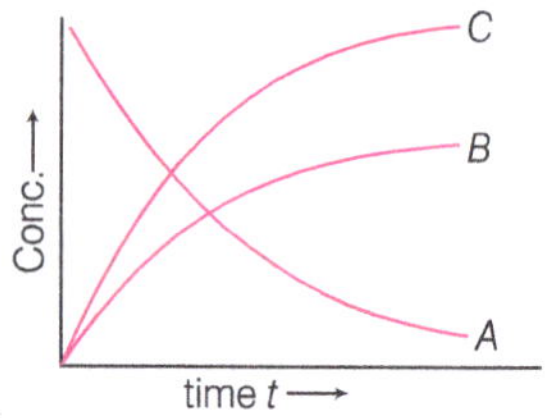

Parallel reactions

It can be shown

$$\frac{dA}{dt} = K_1 A_0 + K_2 A_0$$

$$(k_1 + k_2) = \frac{2.303}{t}\log_{10}\left(\frac{a}{a-x}\right) \qquad [K_{eff} = K_1 + K_2]$$

Also, $\dfrac{\text{rate of formation of } B}{\text{rate of formation of } C} = \dfrac{k_1(a-x)}{k_2(a-x)} = \dfrac{k_1}{k_2}$

and $\dfrac{\text{amount of } B \text{ at time } t}{\text{amount of } C \text{ at time } t} = \dfrac{k_1}{k_2}$

If after a time interval t, x M of B and y M of C are formed such that a $t = 0, [B] = [C] = 0$ then

% yield of $B = \dfrac{k_1}{k_1 + k_2}$ and % yield of $C = \dfrac{k_2}{k_1 + k_2}$

If E_1 and E_2 are activation energy of parallel reactions.

The effective energy $E_{eff} = \dfrac{k_1 E_1 + k_2 E_2}{k_1 + k_2}$ where $k_{eff} = k_1 + k_2$

JEE MAPPER

Example Similar to PYQ Asked in JEE Advanced 2021

For the reaction,

$$[Cu(NH_3)_4]^{2+} + H_2O \underset{k_b}{\overset{k_f}{\rightleftharpoons}} [Cu(NH_3)_3(H_2O)]^{2+} + NH_3$$

New rate is,

$$\left(\frac{dx}{dt}\right)_{net} = 4.0 \times 10^{-4}\ s^{-1}[Cu(NH_3)_4]^{2+} - 8.0 \times 10^{5}\ L\ mol^{-1}\ s^{-1}\ [Cu(NH_3)_3(H_2O)]^{2+}[NH_3]$$

The correct statement about the reaction is (are) ....

(a) The rate constant for the forward reaction is $8 \times 10^5\ L\ mol^{-1}\ s^{-1}$.

(b) Order is 2 in case of backward reaction with rate constant $8 \times 10^5\ L\ mol^{-1}\ s^{-1}$.

(c) Backward reaction is faster than forward reaction.

(d) The rate constant for the backward reaction is $4 \times 10^{-4}\ L\ mol^{-1}\ s^{-1}$.

Sol. *(b, c)* $\left(\dfrac{dx}{dt}\right)_f = k_f[Cu(NH_3)_4]^{2+}$

and $\left(\dfrac{dx}{dt}\right)_b = k_b[Cu(NH_3)_3(H_2O)]^{2+}[NH_3]$

by comparison, $k_f = 4.0 \times 10^{-4}\ s^{-1}$

$k_b = 8.0 \times 10^5\ L\ mol^{-1}\ s^{-1}$.

Backward reaction with rate constant in ($L\ mol^{-1}s^{-1}$) is second order as $(mol\ L^{-1})^{1-n}s^{-1} = (mol\ L^{-1})^1 s^{-1}$

$$1 - n = 1$$

$$n = 2$$

$\because k_b > k_f$, thus backward reaction is faster.

Compentency Enhancer 2.3

For the following reversible reaction,

$$N_2(g) + 3H_2(g) \rightleftharpoons 2NH_3(g)$$

$$\left(\frac{dx}{dt}\right)_{net} = 2.5 \times 10^{-2}[N_2][H_2]^3 - 8.0 \times 10^{-3}[NH_3]^2$$

The incorrect statement(s) is/are ....

(a) For a reversible reaction, net rate is the vector summation of the rates of the forward and backward reactions.

(b) Rate constant of forward reaction is 3.0×10^{-3}.

(c) Rate constant of backward reaction is 1.5×10^{-2}.

(d) Forward reaction is faster than backward reaction.

Reversible or Opposing Reactions

When the reaction rates are appreciable for both the forward and the reverse processes, then kinetics of both are considered.

$$\underset{(a-x)}{A} \underset{k_2}{\overset{k_1}{\rightleftharpoons}} \underset{x}{B}$$

For the above reaction k_1 and k_2 are the rate constants of the forward and backward reactions. If first order kinetics is considered then

$$\left(\frac{dx}{dt}\right)_{\text{forward}} = k_1[A] = k_1(a-x) \text{ and } \left(\frac{dx}{dt}\right)_{\text{backward}} = k_2[B] = k_2 x$$

Let, equilibrium concentration be x_e then

$$\frac{dx}{dt} = k_1(a - x_e) - k_2 x_e = 0$$

$$\therefore \quad k_2 = \frac{k_1(a - x_e)}{x_e}$$

$$\Rightarrow \quad k_1 = \frac{2.303 x_e}{at} \log_{10} \frac{x_e}{x_e - x}$$

Mechanism of a reaction is based on the slow step, which is also the rate-determining step. This step can also involve intermediate.

Pseudomolecular Reactions

There are several reactions which are considered as unimolecular, although in reality they are bi-or tri-molecular, e.g. consider the hydrolysis of methyl acetate in the presence of acid

$$CH_3COOCH_3 + H_2O \xrightarrow{\text{Acid}} CH_3COOH + CH_3OH$$

According to the law of mass action, this reaction seems to follow bimolecular process with the rate dependent on concentration of both ester and water. However, it is found that the rate is independent of concentration of water, it depends only on concentration of ester.

This can be explained on the basis of the fact that here water is present in such excess that its concentration remains practically constant during the course of reaction. Hence, reactions showing such a behaviour are called **pseudounimolecular reactions** or **pseudo first order reactions.**

Methods of Determination of Order of the Reaction

Determination of the order of the reaction is the most important part of the kinetics to study rate law. Order is generally deduced from the rate determining step which is generally the slowest step.

Following are some of the methods adopted to determine order of the given reaction.

Half-life Method

This method is employed only when the rate law involves only one concentration term.

The expression for half-life of a chemical reaction $t_{1/2} \propto a^{1-n}$ where n is the order of the reaction.

At two different concentration of the reactants, this time $t_{1/2}$ is determined.

$(t_{1/2})_1$ = time of completing 50% of the reaction of concentration a_1

$(t_{1/2})_2$ = time of completing 50% of the reaction of concentration a_2

then $$\frac{(t_{1/2})_1}{(t_{1/2})_2} = \left(\frac{a_2}{a_1}\right)^{n-1} \Rightarrow \log\left(\frac{t_{1/2}}{t_{1/2}}\right) = (n-1)\log\left(\frac{a_2}{a_1}\right)$$

$$n = \left[1 + \log\left(\frac{t_{1/2}}{t_{1/2}}\right)\right] / \log\left(\frac{a_2}{a_1}\right)$$

Thus, n can be determined using the above equation.

Plots of log $t_{1/2}$ VS log a

$$t_{1/2} \propto (a)^{1-n}$$

or $$t_{1/2} = k'(a)^{1-n}$$

where, k' is constant (but not rate constant)

or $\log(t_{1/2}) = (1-n)\log a + \log k'$

If $\log T_{50}$ is plotted against $\log a$, a straight line with a slope $(l-n)$ and intercept $\log k'$ as given is obtained.

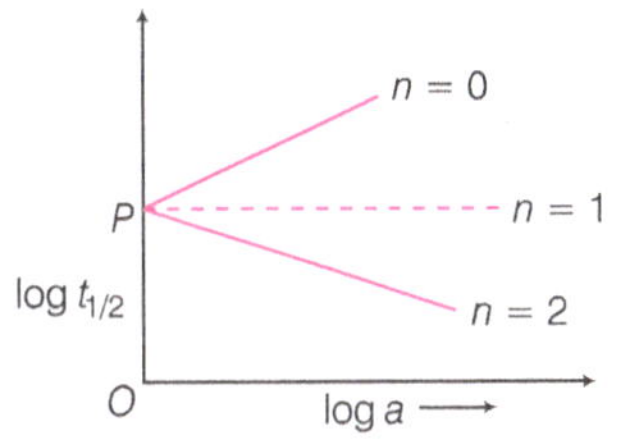

Graph between $\log t_{1/2}$ and $\log a$ for different order reaction. As the order increases, slope decreases

Integration Method

(Hit and Trial Method)

In this method, the data is substituted into the integrated rate equation for different order reactions. The equation which gives almost a constant value of k decides the order of the reaction.

In general for the reactions of order n, the rate equation of the form below is used

$$k_n = \frac{1}{t(n-1)}\left[\frac{1}{(a-x)^{n-1}} - \frac{1}{a^{n-1}}\right]$$

The above equation is applicable for all order except first order.

Graphical Method

This method requires less time and avoids tedious calculation. The rate constant of the reaction can be calculated from the slope of the resultant straight line plot. We may start plotting data in order given in Table

Graphical determination of order of the reaction

Order	Equation	Straight line Plot		Slope	Intercept on Y-axis
		Y-axis	X-axis		
Zero	$x = k_0 t$	x	t	k_0	0
One	$\log_{10}(a-x) = \frac{-k_1 t}{2.303} + \log_{10} a$	$\log_{10}(a-x)$	t	$\frac{-k_1}{2.303}$	$\log_{10} a$
Two	$(a-x)^{-1} = k_2 t + a^{-1}$	$(a-x)^{-1}$	t	k_2	a^{-1}
$n(>1)$	$(a-x)^{1-n} = (n-1)k_n t + a^{1-n}$	$(a-x)^{(1-n)}$	t	$(n-1)k_n$	a^{1-n}

It is clear from the above relations that the straight lines are obtained form a plot of $[x]$ *versus* t for a zero order reaction, of $\log(a-x)$ *versus* t for a first order reaction, and of $\frac{1}{(a-x)}$ *versus* t for second order reaction as shown below:

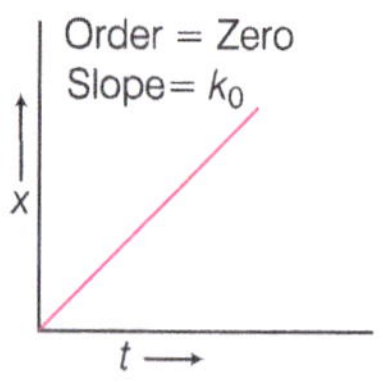

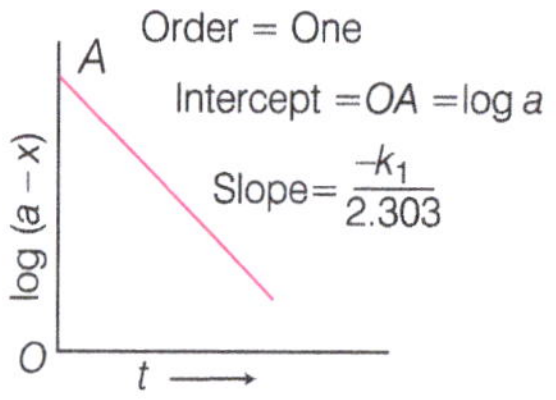

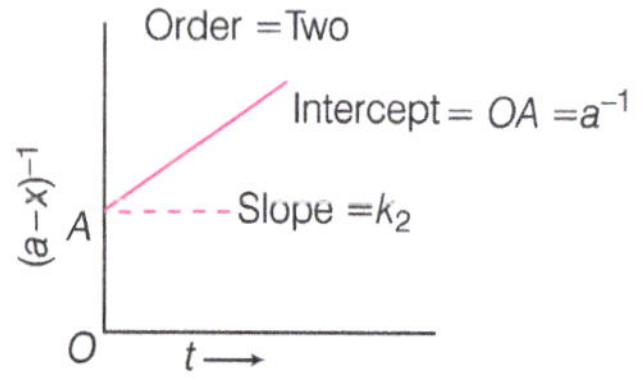

These curves also help to calculate the value of k from the slope of the straight line.

van't Hoff 's Differential Order Method (Initial Rate Method)

In this method, the order of the given reaction with respect to each of its reactants can be determined. For the reaction,

$$A + B \longrightarrow \text{Product}$$

Rate law can be $\left(\frac{dx}{dt}\right) = k[A]^a[B]^b$

If concentration of B is kept constant and new rate constant, $k' = k[B]^b$, then

$$R = \left(\frac{dx}{dt}\right) = k'[A]^a$$

Rate of the reaction at two different initial concentration of A is given by

or $$\log_{10}\left(\frac{R_1}{R_2}\right) = a\log_{10}\left(\frac{[A_1]}{[A_2]}\right)$$

$$a = \log_{10}\left(\frac{R_1}{R_2}\right) / \log_{10}\left(\frac{[A_1]}{[A_2]}\right)$$

Thus, a can be determined using above equations. Also

$$\boxed{\log_{10} R = a\log_{10}[A] + \log_{10} k'}$$

Ostwald's Isolation Method

It is similar to method described above. Concentration of the reactants is changed one by one and rates are compared.

If $$R = k[A]^a[B]^b[C]^c$$

we take four sets of rate R to determine order a, b and c.

If concentration is made m times of the nth order reaction, new rate is m^n times.

Let reaction be $aA + bB + cC \longrightarrow \text{Product}$

Its rate law is $\frac{dx}{dt} = k[A]^a[B]^b[C]^c$

Step I $[B]$ and $[C]$ are kept constant and $[A]$ is changed. Rates are compared.

$$\left(\frac{dx}{dt}\right)_1 = k[A_1]^a[B]^b[C]^c$$

$$\left(\frac{dx}{dt}\right)_2 = k[A_2]^a[B]^b[C]^c$$

$$\left(\frac{dx}{dt}\right)_1 \Big/ \left(\frac{dx}{dt}\right)_2 = \left(\frac{[A_1]}{[A_2]}\right)^a$$

Thus, a order wrt A is derived.

Step II $[A]$ and $[C]$ are kept constant and $[B]$ is changed.

Rates are compared as in step I.

This gives b order wrt B.

Step III $[A]$ and $[B]$ are kept constant and $[C]$ is changed.

Rates are compared.

This gives c order wrt C.

Elemental Practice 9.2

Type I MCQs with Only One Correct Option

1. For a reaction, $2A + B \rightarrow$ products, doubling the concentration of a results in a four fold increase in the rate, while doubling the concentration of B results in a two fold increase in the rate, then the rate law for this reaction is
(a) Rate $= k\,[A]\,[B]$
(b) Rate $= k\,[A]^2\,[B]$
(c) Rate $= k\,[A]^2\,[B]^2$
(d) Rate $= k\,[A]^4\,[B]^2$

2. For a reaction, $X \rightarrow Y$, the plot of $\ln[X]$ versus time is a straight line with a negative slope. What can be order of the reaction?
(a) Zero (b) second
(c) first (d) third

3. Given below are two statements, one is labelled as Assertion (A) and the other is labelled as Reason (R).
Assertion (A) A reaction with an overall order of 2 has a half-life that depends on the initial concentration of the reactants.
Reason (R) For a second-order, the half-life $t_{1/2}$ is given by $t_{1/2} = \dfrac{1}{k\,[A]_0}$.
In the light of the above statements, choose the correct answer from the options given below.
(a) Both (A) and (R) are true and (R) is the correct explanation of (A).
(b) Both (A) and (R) are true but (R) is not the correct explanation of (A).
(c) (A) is true but (R) is false.
(d) (A) is false but (R) is true.

4. For the reaction, $3X \rightarrow 2Y$, the following graph is obtained experimentally. The rate of reaction when $[X] = 0.3$ M, is

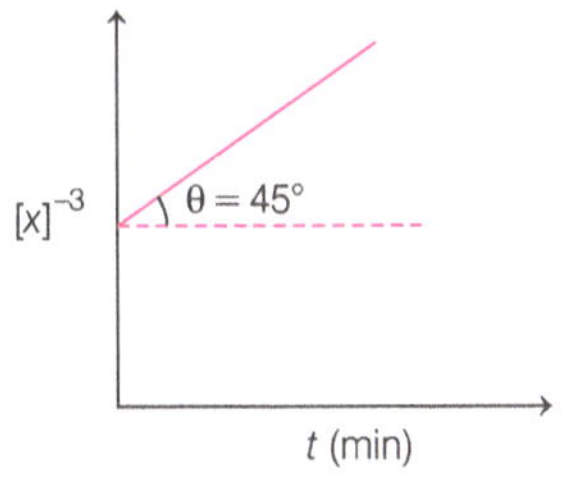

(a) 9×10^{-4} M min^{-1} (b) 3×10^{-4} M min^{-1}
(c) 9×10^{-4} M s^{-1} (d) 18×10^{-4} M min^{-1}

5. A sample of a radioactive isotope decays with a half-life of 20 days. The time taken by the isotope for 87.5% of the sample to decay is
(a) 50 days (b) 60 days
(c) 40 days (d) 80 days

6. The following graph shows the variation of $t_{1/2}$ of a reactant A changes with initial reactant concentration a_0. The order of a reaction will be

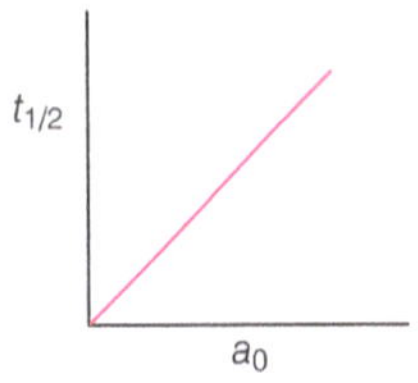

(a) zero (b) 1
(c) 2 (d) 3

7. Given below are two statements.
Statement I The molecularity of a reaction refers to the number of reactant molecules involved in the elementary step of the reaction.
Statement II The order of a reaction can be determined only from the stoichiometry of the balanced chemical equation.
In the light of the above statements, choose the correct answer from the options given below.
(a) Both Statement I and Statement II are correct.
(b) Both Statement I and Statement II are incorrect.
(c) Statement I is correct but Statement II is incorrect.
(d) Statement I is incorrect but Statement II is correct.

8. The rate law of the following reaction based on the data given below is :

$$A + B \rightarrow \text{Products}$$

Experiment	$[A]$ (M)	$[B]$ (M)	Rate (M/s)
1	0.1	0.1	0.01
2	0.1	0.2	0.04
3	0.2	0.1	0.04
4	0.2	0.2	0.16

(a) Rate $= k\,[A]^2\,[B]^2$
(b) Rate $= k\,[A]^2\,[B]$
(c) Rate $= k\,[A]\,[B]^2$
(d) Rate $= k\,[A]\,[B]$

9. Consider the reaction between reactants A and B, which follows the rate law :

$$\text{Rate} = k\,[A]\,[B]$$

If the concentration of B is much greater than that of A (*i.e.*, $[B] >> [A]$), the reaction can be Pseudo first order reaction. The initial concentration of A is $[A]_0 = 0.1$ M and the initial concentration of B is $[B]_0 = 1.0$ M, the rate constant k is 0.5 M^{-1} s^{-1}. What will be the pseudo first-order rate constant k' for the reaction?
(a) 0.2 s^{-1} (b) 0.4 s^{-1}
(c) 0.1 s^{-1} (d) 0.5 s^{-1}

10. The given reaction is :

$$A + 2B \rightarrow C + D$$

The overall reaction mechanism involves two elementary steps :

$$A + B \rightarrow E \text{ (unimolecular)}$$

$$E + B \rightarrow C + D \text{ (bimolecular)}$$

The molecularity of the overall reaction is

(a) 1 (b) 2

(c) can not be defined (d) 4

11. $C_{12}H_{22}O_{11} + \underset{\text{(excess)}}{H_2O} \xrightarrow{H^+} C_6H_{12}O_6 + C_6H_{12}O_6$ is an example of

(a) 1st order (b) Pseudo 1st order

(c) 2nd order (d) Zero order

12. For the following elementary steps of a reaction mechanism :

$$A \rightarrow B \text{ (Unimolecular)}$$

$$B + C \rightarrow D \text{ (Bimolecular)}$$

$$D \rightarrow E + F \text{ (Unimolecular)}$$

Which of the following are true regarding the overall reaction order?

A. The overall reaction is 3rd order.

B. Overall order depends on slowest step of the mechanism.

C. Overall order can be zero if rate law indicates it.

D. The overall molecularity of a reaction is the sum of the molecularities of all individual steps, regardless of their order.

(a) B, C, D (b) B, C (c) A, D (d) A, B, C, D

13. Reaction, $P + Q \rightarrow R + S$ follows the rate law, $r = k\,[P]^{1/2}[Q]^{1/2}$ starting with 1 M of P and Q each, what is the time taken for concentration of P to become 0.01 M ? (Given, $k = 2.303 \times 10^{-3}\ s^{-1}$)

(a) 1000 s (b) 2000 s (c) 4000 s (d) 1500 s

14. Given below are two statements, one is labelled as Assertion (A) and the other is labelled as Reason (R).

Assertion (A) In a parallel reaction, if one path has a much higher rate constant than the other, most of the reactant will not follow the path with higher rate constant.

Reason (R) The rate of a reaction path in parallel reactions is directly proportional to the rate constant of that path.

In the light of the above statements, choose the correct answer from the options given below.

(a) Both (A) and (R) are true and (R) is the correct explanation of (A).

(b) Both (A) and (R) are true but (R) is not the correct explanation of (A).

(c) (A) is true but (R) is false.

(d) (A) is false but (R) is true.

15. The decomposition of dinitrogen pentoxide, N_2O_5 in the gas phase is a first order reaction with rate constant $k = 5.1 \times 10^{-3}\ min^{-1}$ at a certain temperature.

The percentage of N_2O_5 decomposed after 200 minutes is ($e^{-1.02} = 0.360$)

(a) 64% (b) 36% (c) 54% (d) 34%

16. For an elementary reaction $H_2 + I_2 \rightarrow 2HI$, the volume of a container is doubled. The rate becomes

(a) $\frac{1}{2}$ (b) $\frac{1}{4}$ (c) $\frac{1}{6}$ (d) $\frac{1}{16}$

17. In a consecutive reaction where A converts to E_1 and E_1 further converts to B and C.

$$A \xrightarrow{k_1} E_1 \xrightarrow{k_2} B$$

$$E_1 \xrightarrow{k_3} C$$

Which of the following statement is true if the rate constant k_2 for the conversion of E_1 to B is greater than the rate constant k_3 for the conversion of E_1 to C?

(a) Concentration of C will increase faster than concentration of B.

(b) Concentration of B will increase steadily over time while concentration of C remains constant.

(c) Concentration of B will increase more rapidly than concentration of C.

(d) Both B and C will increase at the same rate.

18. The decomposition of acetaldehyde (CH_3CHO) follows the reaction :

$$2CH_3CHO \longrightarrow CH_4 + CO_2 + C_2H_4$$

The reaction is 2nd order w.r.t acetaldehyde and rate constant is 0.1 L mol s^{-1} at certain temperature.

If the initial concentration of CH_3CHO is 0.5 mol/L. The time required for the concentration to decrease to 0.25 mol/L is

(a) 10 s (b) 20 s (c) 30 s (d) 40 s

Type II 》 MCQs with One or More than One Correct Option

19. Select the correct statements regarding pseudo-first order reaction.

(a) Pseudo first order reaction is observed in enzyme catalysed reaction when substrate concentration is lower than enzyme concentration.

(b) Acidic hydrolysis of an ester is an example.

(c) Reaction that is 2nd order can become 1st order if one reactant is in excess.

(d) The half-life of pseudo-first order reaction does not depends on the concentration of excess reactant.

20. Choose the true statements about rate law.

(a) The units of rate constant depend on the overall order of the reaction.

(b) Rate constants are temperature dependent and can vary with changes in temperature.

(c) Rate laws can be determined experimentally by change in concentration of reactants or products over time.

(d) There is one rate determining step in any reaction mechanism.

21. Which of the following statements regarding the graphical representation of reaction orders are correct?
(a) For a zero-order reaction, a plot of concentration *vs* time yields a straight line with a slope of k.
(b) For a 2nd order reaction, a plot of the inverse of the concentration *vs* time yields as straight line with slope equal to k
(c) A plot of concentration *vs* time yields a straight line for a 1st order reaction.
(d) A half-life of a zero order reaction depends on the initial concentration of reactant.

22. Select the true statements about parallel reactions.
(a) The rate of formation of each product in a parallel reaction is independent of the formation rates of the other products.
(b) The rate constant for a parallel reaction is the sum of the rate constant for each pathway.
(c) Parallel reactions cannot occur in reversible manner.
(d) In parallel reactions, a single reactant can yield multiple products simultaneously.

23. The dimerisation reaction of a species A to form A_2 can be represented as

$$2A \rightarrow A_2$$

Rate of reaction, $r = k\,[A]^2$. Which of the following is/are correct?
(a) The reaction is 2nd order w.r.t. A.
(b) The overall order of the reaction is 1.
(c) The half-life of A is directly proportional to its initial concentration.
(d) The reaction is an example of second order reaction in terms of dimer A_2.

Type III 》 Numerical/Integer Answer Type Questions

24. A second-order reaction occurs as follows :

$$A \rightarrow \text{Products}$$

The rate constant k for a reaction is 0.04 $M^{-1}\,s^{-1}$ and initial concentration of reactant A is 0.5 M. Then concentration of A after 25 sec is ……$\times 10^{-3}$ M.

25. Consider the gas-phase decomposition of carbonic acid (H_2CO_3) which can decompose *via* two parallel reactions at 1123 K.
1. $H_2CO_3 \longrightarrow H_2O + CO_2 \quad (k_1 = 0.03\ s^{-1})$
2. $H_2CO_3 \longrightarrow H_2 + CO + O_2 \quad (k_2 = 0.05\ s^{-1})$

The percentage yield of CO at this temperature is

26. For a second order reaction, the activation energy E_a is 50 kJ/mol and the pre-exponential factor A is 1.2×10^7 L $mol^{-1}\,s^{-1}$. If the half life is observed to be 30 minutes at room temperature, then the value of the temperature at which the half life is 10 minutes will be ………
($\ln 3 = 1.098$) (nearest integer)

27. For the reaction,

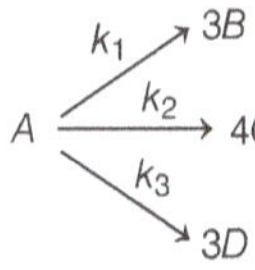

$4C$; At time $t = 0$, initial mole of A is 1.

The overall half-life of the reaction is 30 days. The number of moles of C after 90 days, if the ratio of $k_1 : k_2 : k_3$ is $4:2:1$, is ………

28. The radioactive decay of elements such as thorium and radon emitting alpha particles follows first-order kinetics. The number of alpha particles emitted per second by 1 g of pure ThO_2 if $t_{1/2}$ of Th^{232} is 1.39×10^{10} years ……

29. The decomposition of a compound 'P' at temperaure T, according to the following equation?

$$2A(g) \longrightarrow 4B(g) + C(g) + D(l)$$

is a first-order reaction. After 30 minutes, from the start of decomposition in a closed vessel, the total pressure developed is found to be 445 mm and after a long time, the total pressure is 625 mm. The vapour pressure of $D(l)$ at this temperature is 25 mm. The total pressure after 60 minutes is ……… .

Elemental Practice 9.2 | Chapter 09
Connect with **Answers**

1. (b)	**2.** (c)	**3.** (a)	**4.** (a)	**5.** (b)	**6.** (a)
7. (c)	**8.** (a)	**9.** (d)	**10.** (c)	**11.** (b)	**12.** (b)
13. (b)	**14.** (d)	**15.** (a)	**16.** (b)	**17.** (c)	**18.** (b)
19. (b,c,d)	**20.** (a,b,c,d)	**21.** (b,d)	**22.** (a,b,d)	**23.** (a,c)	**24.** (333)
25. (62.5)	**26.** (316)	**27.** (1)	**28.** (3602)	**29.** (535)	

Element 3 Arrhenius Theory, Activation Energy, Collision and Related Theories

Theories of Reaction Rate

The rate of chemical reaction is the speed at which reactants are converted into products. Several theories and models have been proposed to explain and predict the factors influencing the rate of reactions. The temperature dependence of the rate constants for elementary reactions has helped a great in the development of reaction rates.

Temperature Dependence of the Rate of a Reaction

The rate of chemical reaction generally increases on increasing the temperature. Generally the rate of reaction becomes double or triple for each 10°C rise in temperature, however actual amount of increase differs for reaction to reaction.

This increase in rate with temperature is expressed in the form of temperature coefficient.

Temperature coefficient of a reaction is defined as the ratio of rate constants at two temperatures differing by 10 K (generally 25° and 35°C). Observed value usually lies between 2 and 3 for most of the reactions.

Temperature coefficient

$$= \frac{\text{Rate constant at temperature } t^\circ}{\text{Rate constant at temperature } (t+10)^\circ} = \frac{k_t}{k_{t+10}}$$

Rate constant k is characteristic of the reaction and is constant for a particular temperature. Graph give below shows variation of the concentration of reactant against time for different temperatures and thus for different values of k.

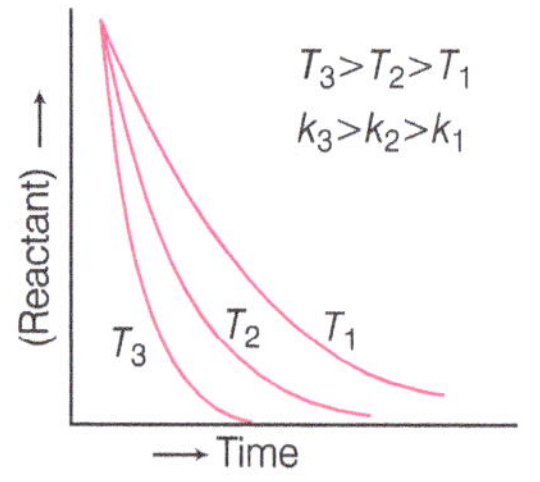

Plots of concentration of reactant against time at three different temperatures

Arrhenius Equation

Variation of rate constant k with temperature T (K) is given by Arrhenius equation

$$k = Ae^{-E_a/RT}$$

$$\log_e k = \log_e A - E_a/RT$$

$$\log_{10} k = \log_{10} A - \frac{E_a}{2.303\ RT}$$

where, A is called the frequency factor or the pre-exponential factor. Collectively A and E_a are called the Arrhenius parameters of the reaction.

JEE Quicker

The statement 'at lower temperature increase in temperature causes more change in the value of k than at higher temperature is incorrect. *JEE Main 2022*

According to Arrhenius equation,

$$k = Ae^{-E_a/RT}$$

$$\frac{dk}{dT} = \frac{E_a A e^{-E_a/RT}}{RT^2} = \frac{E_a k}{RT^2}$$

The value of the rate constant (k) increases with increasing temperature.

At lower temperature increase in temperature causes less change in the value of k than at higher temperature.

Graphical Variation of Rate Constant k with Temperature T

If the Arrhenius equation is obeyed, a plot of $\log_{10} k$ *versus* T^{-1} is a straight line with slope $-E_a/2.303\ R$ and intercept $\log_{10} A$. This enables one to determine E_a and A as shown below.

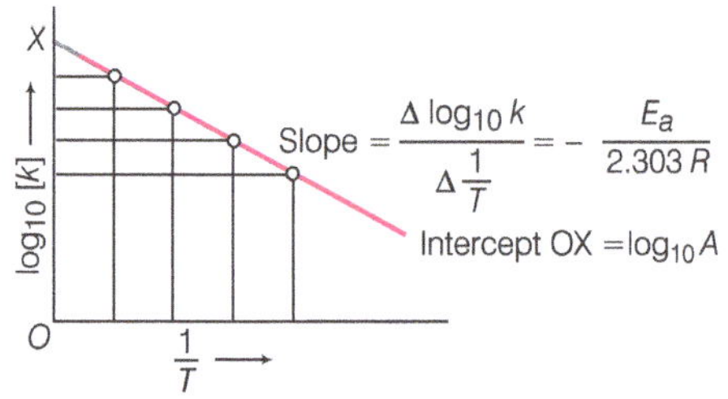

Plot showing variation of log k *versus* T^{-1}

This graph shows that as $\frac{1}{T}$ increases (i.e. T decreases) $\log k$ decreases. Hence, rate constant k increases with increase in temperature.

Activation Energy (E_a)

According to Arrhenius theory, for a reaction to take place the collision between reactant molecules must occur with a certain minimum energy before it is effective in yielding product molecules. This minimum energy is called activation energy (E_a).

This energy barrier determines the magnitude of threshold energy which reactant molecules must acquire before they can yield products.

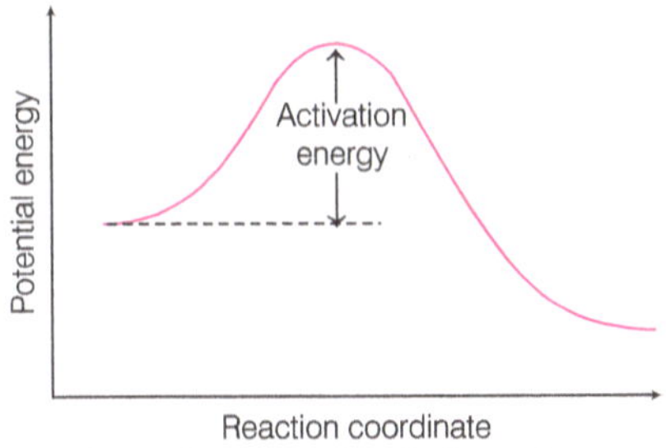

Energy barrier in chemical reactions

Different reactions have different amount of activation energy. A reaction which has higher activation energy is slow at ordinary temperatures while the reaction, having lower activation energy will proceed at a faster rate at a given temperature.

Thus, the difference in activation energy mainly responsible for observed difference in rates of reactions.

Determination of Energy of Activation

Energy of activation E_a has been determined based on graphical study. E_a can be determined experimentally by measuring rate constants at different temperatures.

Let k_1 = Velocity constant at temperature $T_1 K$

and k_2 = Velocity constant at temperature $T_2 K$

then $$\log_{10} k_2 = \log_{10} A - \frac{E_a}{2.303RT_2}$$

$$\log_{10} k_1 = \log_{10} A - \frac{E_a}{2.303RT_1}$$

$\therefore$ $$\log_{10}\frac{k_2}{k_1} = \frac{E_a}{2.303R}\left[\frac{1}{T_1} - \frac{1}{T_2}\right]$$

or $$E_a = \frac{2.303\, RT_1T_2}{(T_2 - T_1)}\log_{10}\left(\frac{k_2}{k_1}\right)$$

Since, rate constant, k is inversely proportional to $t_{1/2}$ at a given concentration, hence

$$E_a = \frac{2.303RT_1T_2}{(T_2 - T_1)} \cdot \log\frac{(t_{1/2})_{T_1}}{(t_{1/2})_{T_2}}$$

JEE MAPPER

Example Similar to PYQ Asked in JEE Main 2023

$$P \longrightarrow Q$$

The rate constants of the above reaction at 50°C and 100°C are $1.5 \times 10^7\ s^{-1}$ and $4.5 \times 10^7\ s^{-1}$ respectively. The activation energy for the reaction is .... kJ mol^{-1} (nearest integer)

Sol. (22) The Arrhenius equation is $k = A\exp(-E_a/RT)$

For the two temperatures, we get

$$\log\frac{k_2}{k_1} = \frac{E_a}{2.303R}\left(\frac{1}{T_1} - \frac{1}{T_2}\right)$$

Substituting the given data, we get

$$\log\frac{4.5 \times 10^7}{1.5 \times 10^7} = \frac{E_a}{(2.303)(8.314\ JK^{-1}\ mol^{-1})}\left(\frac{1}{323\ K} - \frac{1}{373\ K}\right)$$

or $$E_a = \frac{(2.303)(8.314)(373)(323)}{50}\log(3.0)$$

$$= 22012.7\ J\ mol^{-1} = 22.013\ kJ\ mol^{-1}$$

$$\approx 22$$

Competency Enhancer 3.1

For a first order reaction $X \to Y$, the temperature (T) dependent rate constant (k) was found to follow the equation $\log k = -(4000)\frac{1}{T} + 8.0$. The pre-exponential factor A and activation energy E_a, respecively are

(a) $1.0 \times 10^8\ s^{-1}$ and 9.2 kJ mol^{-1}

(b) 8.0 s^{-1} and 16.6 kJ mol^{-1}

(c) $1.0 \times 10^8\ s^{-1}$ and 16.6 kJ mol^{-1}

(d) $1.0 \times 10^8\ s^{-1}$ and 76.6 kJ mol^{-1}

Effect of Catalyst on E_a

In presence of catalyst (additional reactant) number of collisions increases, E_a is lowered and thus rate of the reaction increases.

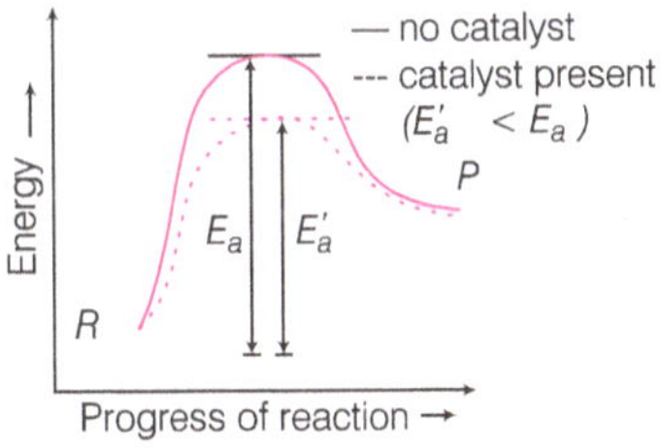

Effect of catalyst E_a

Significance of Activation Energy

According to Arrhenius, the molecules must acquire a certain energy before they would undergo chemical transformation. This means that before the chemical reaction can occur the molecule or molecules involved must be raised to a higher energy level, i.e. the molecules must be in an energy-rich or activated state before they can react.

Consider the following reaction

$$A \longrightarrow B; \Delta H < 0$$

Let average energy of the reaction A be E_A and that of the product B be E_B. A is not transformed into the product B directly even in the case if $E_A > E_B$.

There is minimum energy level for the reaction denoted by E_X to which the reactant molecules must be raised in order a reaction can take place.

The excess or additional energy $(E_x - E_A)$ which the reactant must acquire in order to undergo a chemical change is the activation energy. Molecules having energy E_X or above are said to be in activated state and only such molecules are able to undergo chemical change.

$(E_X + E_A)$ is called threshold energy.

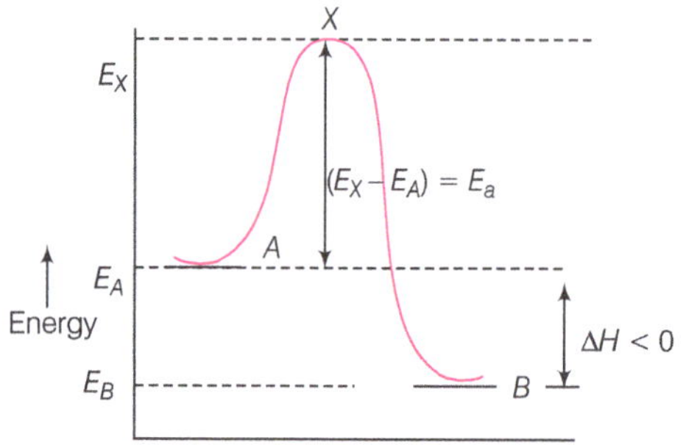

(a) Energy of the system *vs* reaction coordinate

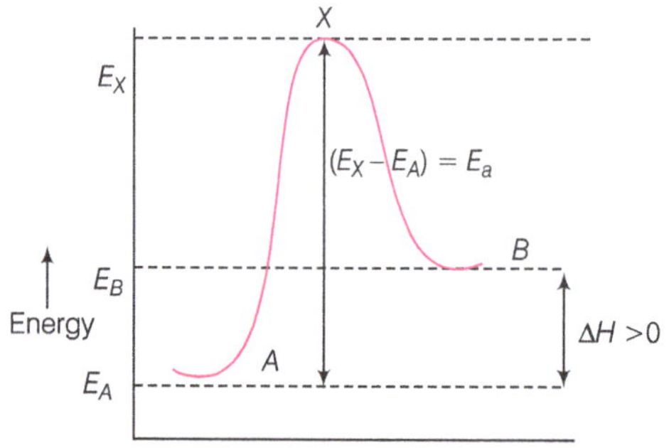

(b) Energy of the system *vs* reaction coordinate

The idea of the activated state has been qualitatively presented in Fig. (a) for exothermic reactions $(\Delta H < 0)$ and in Fig.(b) for endothermic reactions $(\Delta H > 0)$.

After the chemical change, the product have energy E_B.

If $E_B < E_A$, $\quad \Delta H = (E_B - E_A) = -\text{ve}$

a case of an endothermic reaction.

If $E_B > E_A$, $\quad \Delta H = (E_B - E_A) = +\text{ve}$

a case of an endothermic reaction.

JEE Spotlite

- When $T \to \infty$, then $k = A (\because e^{-E_a/RT} = 1)$ and the rate constant becomes equal to Arrhenius factor.
- Two reaction having same value of E_a do not necessarely have same rate because frequency factor (A) also affect the rate.
- $K = Ae^{-E_a/RT}$, because E_a is always positive so rate of elementary reactions will always increase with increase in temperature, irrespective of nature of reaction whether endothermic or exothermic. This hold good for majority of reactions but some complex reactions are also known for which rate of reaction decreases with increase in temperature e.g. $NO + \frac{1}{2}O_2 \longrightarrow NO_2 + \text{heat}$
- Activation energy can never be zero except radioactive reactions. If $E_a = 0$, then according to Arrhenius equation the value of k will become equal to A. This can never be true for ordinary reaction.

Solved Booster 3.1

The rate constants of a reaction at 500 K and 700 K are 0.1 s^{-1} and 0.35 s^{-1}, respectively. The value of frequency factor at 500 K will be

(a) 7.9 (b) 6.4 (c) 5.8 (d) 5.2

Solution *(a)*

$$\log \frac{k_2}{k_1} = \frac{E_a}{2.303R}\left[\frac{T_2 - T_1}{T_1 T_2}\right]$$

$$\log \frac{0.35}{0.1} = \left(\frac{E_a}{2.303 \times 8.314\ \text{JK}^{-1}\ \text{mol}^{-1}}\right)\left[\frac{700 - 500}{700 \times 500}\right]$$

$$0.544 = E_a \times 5.222 \times \frac{10^{-4}}{17.50}$$

$$E_a = \frac{0.544 \times 17.50}{5.222 \times 10^{-4}} = 18230.6\ \text{J}$$

Since,

$$k = Ae^{-E_a/RT}$$

$$\log k = \log A - \frac{E_a}{2.303RT}$$

$$\log A = \log k + \frac{E_a}{2.303RT}$$

$$\log A = \log(0.1) + \frac{18230.6\ \text{J mol}^{-1}}{2.303 \times 8.314\ \text{JK}^{-1}\ \text{mol}^{-1} \times 500\ \text{K}}$$

$$= -1 + 1.90 = 0.904 \approx 0.9$$

$$A = \text{Antilog}(0.9) \approx 7.943 \approx 7.9$$

Collision Theory of Bimolecular Gaseous Reactions

According to this theory, for a reaction to occur two molecules must collide with a certain minimum kinetic energy along their line of approach. The energy profiles used in the collision theory represent the potential energy of the two molecules as they approach and then collide and react to form the products.

Assume a bimolecular reaction between gaseous molecules A and B. Number of collisions per second between A and B is given by Z_{AB}.

$$Z_{AB} = \sigma\sqrt{\frac{8RN_0T}{\pi\mu}}$$

where Z is also called collision frequency (and is also the number of collisions per second per unit volume) σ is called collision cross-section, R gas constant, N_0 Avogadro's number, T temperature and

μ the reduced mass of the molecules A and B

$$\frac{1}{\mu} = \frac{1}{m_A} + \frac{1}{m_B}$$

The fraction of collisions with an energy equal to or greater than the activation energy E_a is represented as f

$$f = n/n_0 = e^{-E_a/RT}$$

Rate constant is related to collision frequency and fraction of collisions by

$$k = Z_{AB}\frac{n}{n_0}$$

$$= Z_{AB}e^{-E_a/RT}$$

Actually all the molecules do not undergo collisions to give products. Hence, above result is multiplied by probability p, **where the value of p is less than one**

$$k = pZ_{AB}e^{-E_a/RT}$$

On comparison with Arrhenius equations

$$k = Ae^{-E_a/RT}$$

thus, Arrhenius constant A

$$A = pZ_{AB} = p\sigma\sqrt{\frac{8RTN_0}{\pi\mu}}$$

The collisions in which molecules collide with sufficient kinetic energy (called threshold energy) and proper orientation resulting in breaking of bonds between reacting species and formation of new bonds (at the same time) to form products are called effective collisions. Hence, probability factor p was introduced.

p is sometimes called **steric factor**—the reactant needs to collide in a specific orientation to react.

JEE Spotlite

- Only a certain fraction of the total number of collisions are effective in forming the products.
- Activation energy and proper orientation of the molecules together determine the criteria for effective collisions and hence the rate of a chemical reaction.

JEE Alert

If steric factor > 1, the experimentally determined value of frequency factor is higher than the value predicted by Arrhenius equation.

Drawbacks of Collision Theory

(i) It considers atoms/molecules to be hard spheres.

(ii) It ignores structural aspects of molecules.

Activated Complex Theory

During a chemical reaction certain bonds are broken and certain new bonds are formed. The breaking of bonds requires energy whereas the formation of bonds results in the release of energy. In the beginning breaking of bonds predominates, so the energy of the system starts increasing and reaches a maximum called threshold energy.

Then the energy starts decreasing because after this, the bond formation predominates and finally leads to the product. The arrangement of atoms corresponding to energy maxima (threshold energy) is called activated complex. In this state, the system has partial reactant character and partial product character.

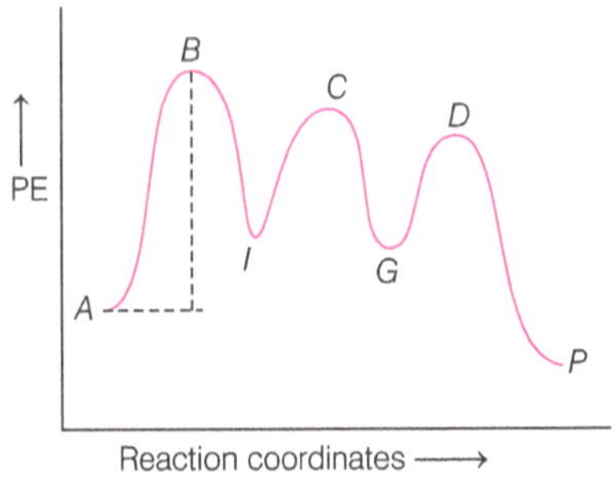

In the above graph, A is reactant, P is product B, C, D are activated complex or transition state while I and G are unstable intermediates.

Distinction between Unstable Intermediate and Transition State or Activated Complex

An unstable intermediate is an actual chemical species (which perhaps can be stabilised under different reaction conditions). It has normal bond orders for its atoms. It represents a minimum on the PE curve, albeit a small minimum.

The activated complex or transition state (TS) is the postulated species which has maximum energy during the conversion from reactants to products. No matter which way the bond lengths and strength vary, stabilisation results. The bond order of the atoms of the activation complex are sometimes unusual.

Elemental Practice 9.3

Type I MCQs with Only One Correct Option

1. Two different reactions have the same collision frequency but different activation energies, then their reaction rates will be
(a) same
(b) Reaction with lower E_a will be faster.
(c) Reaction with higher E_a will be faster.
(d) Reaction rates will be independent of E_a.

2. The temperature coefficient of a reaction is 3.2. If at 400 K, the rate constant is k, then at 410 K, the rate constant will be
(a) k (b) $3k$
(c) $3.2k$ (d) $3k^2$

3. The activation energy plot for an exothermic reaction is

(a) 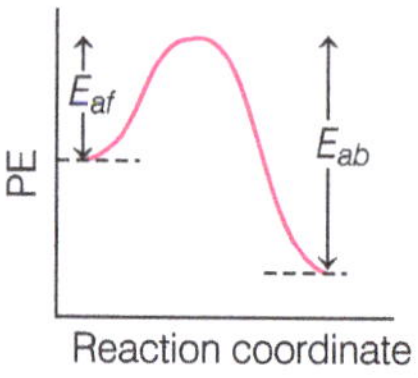

(b) 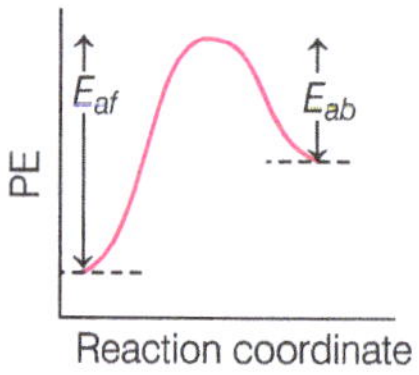

(c) 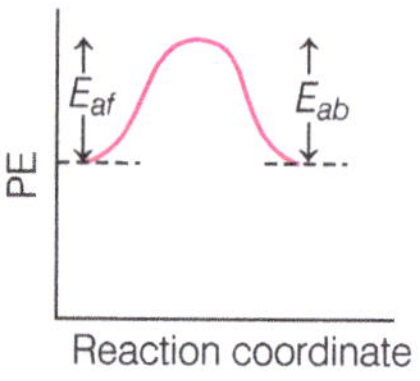

(d) 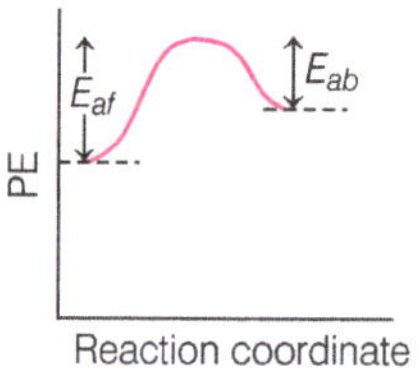

4. Match List-I with List-II.

	List-I		List-II
A.	Pre-exponential factor	1.	Describes the dependence of rate constant on temperature
B.	Transition state Theory	2.	Represents the collision frequency and orientation effects in the Arrhenius equation
C.	Arrhenius equation	3.	Minimum energy barrier required for reactants to form products.
D.	Activation energy	4.	Involves formation of an activated complex at the peak of the potential energy curve.

Choose the correct answer from the options given below.
(a) A-2, B-4, C-3, D-1
(b) A-2, B-4, C-1, D-3
(c) A-4, B-2, C-3, D-1
(d) A-4, B-2, C-1, D-3

5. Given below are two statements.

Statement I A catalyst participates in the reaction and is consumed in the reaction, thereby increasing the amount of reactant molecules that can successfully collide.

Statement II A catalyst provides an alternative path for the conversion of reactants to products and enhance the reaction rate.

In the light of the above statements, choose the correct answer from the options given below.
(a) Both Statement I and Statement II are correct.
(b) Both Statement I and Statement II are incorrect.
(c) Statement I is correct but Statement II is incorrect.
(d) Statement I is incorrect but Statement II is correct.

6. The rate constant k of a reaction increases with temperature. If the activation energy E_a is 50 kJ/mol, the temperature is increased from 300 K to 310 K. According to the Arrhenius equation, the rate constant will increases by
(a) About 91% (b) About 81%
(c) About 71% (d) About 75%

7. Given below are two statements, one is labelled as Assertion (A) and the other is labelled as Reason (R).

Assertion (A) According to Transition State Theory, the rate of reaction is determined by the concentration of the activated complex formed during the reaction.

Reason (R) The transition state is a high-energy, unstable intermediate that exists at the peak of the potential energy barrier between reactants and products.

In the light of the above statements, choose the correct answer from the options given below.
(a) Both (A) and (R) are true and (R) is the correct explanation of (A).
(b) Both (A) and (R) are true but (R) is not the correct explanation of (A).
(c) (A) is true but (R) is false.
(d) (A) is false but (R) is true.

8. A hydrogenation reaction is carried out at 500 K. If the same reaction is carried out in the presence of a catalyst at the same rate, the temperature required is 400 K. The activation energy of the reaction when the catalyst lowers the activation energy barrier by 20 kJ mol^{-1} is
(a) 40 kJ mol^{-1} (b) 60 kJ mol^{-1}
(c) 80 kJ mol^{-1} (d) 100 kJ mol^{-1}

9. The activation energies of a reaction at two different temperature are E_1 and E_2, where $E_1 < E_2$. Which of the following statement is true regarding the change in their rate constants k_1 and k_2?
(a) The rate constant k_1 with activation energy E_1 will be more than k_2 activation energy E_2.
(b) The rate constant k_1 with activation energy E_1 will be less than k_2 with activation energy E_2.
(c) The rate constants k_1 and k_2 will increase by same factor.
(d) The rate constant k_1 for the reaction with activation energy E_1 will not change with temperature, but k_2 will increase significantly.

10. The formation of product is

$$A + B \rightarrow C \rightarrow D$$

$\Delta H = x$ kJ mol^{-1}, $E_a = y$ kJ mol^{-1}

E_a for the backward reaction is

(a) $y - 2x$ (b) $y + 2x$ (c) $y + x$ (d) $y - x$

11. For a certain reaction, the rate constant at 298 K is 5.0×10^{-3} s^{-1}. The activation energy is 75 kJ/mol. The rate constant at 350 K is

(a) 0.643 (b) 0.449 (c) 0.573 (d) 0.723

12. The combustion of methane (CH_4) is represented by the following reaction :

$$CH_4(g) + 2O_2(g) \longrightarrow CO_2(g) + 2H_2O(g)$$

$\Delta H = -$ve, $\Delta S = +$ve and activation energy is high. Which of the following statement is true about the combustion of methane?

(a) The reaction is always be spontaneous regardless of temperature because activation energy is low.

(b) The combustion is exothermic, but the high activation energy makes ignition difficult.

(c) The reaction rate will be high at low temperatures due to the high activation energy.

(d) Reaction is non-spontaneous at high temperatures because negative ΔH cannot overcome positive ΔS..

13. Given below are some statements related to pre-exponential factor (A).

A. The pre-exponential factor A reflects the fraction of collisions that result in a reaction, given the total number of collisions.

B. The value of A is determined by the activation energy of the reaction.

C. This factor affects the rate constant at any temperature.

D. A is related to the probability of successful collisions between reactant molecules.

E. The larger value of A, the fewer the number of molecules available for the reaction.

Choose the correct answer from the options given below.

(a) A, B, C and D (b) C and D
(c) A, C and E (d) A, B, C, D and E

14. Which of the following is an example of auto catalysis?

(a) Decomposition of H_2O_2 in the presence of MnO_2.

(b) Formation of complex between NH_3 and BF_3.

(c) Formation of water using hydrogen and oxygen.

(d) Reaction between $KMnO_4$ and $(COOH)_2$ in acidic solution.

15. The region in the graph which shows fraction of additional molecules which react at ($t + 10$) is :

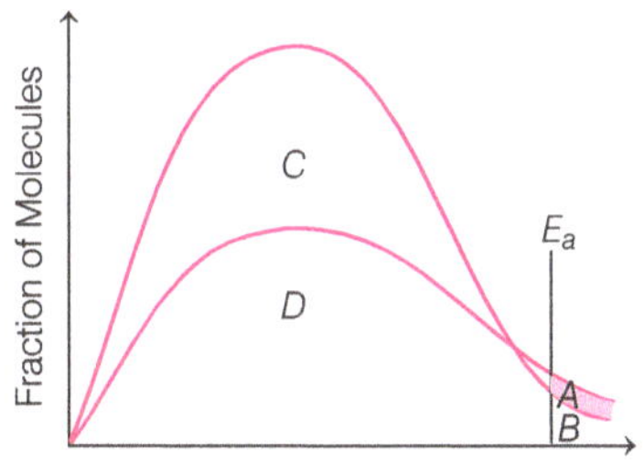

(a) B (b) A (c) D (d) C

16. The steric factor for a reaction is 0.01. This means that

(a) all collisions are effective.

(b) only 1% of collisions with proper orientation and energy leads to product.

(c) the reaction has no activation energy.

(d) 99% of the collision with proper orientation and energy leads to product.

17. Which of the following is best describes about an effective collision?

(a) A collision that results in the formation of products.

(b) A collision with sufficient energy but incorrect orientation.

(c) A collision that increases the entropy of system.

(d) A collision that lowers activation energy.

Type II 》 MCQs with One or More than One Correct Option

18. Select the correct statements related to collision theory.

(a) Rate of reaction increases with an increase in collision frequency.

(b) A reaction can occur even if the molecule do not have the proper orientation during a collision.

(c) Collision theory considers atoms/molecules to be hard sphere and ignore their structural aspect.

(d) The collisions in which molecule collide with insufficient kinetic energy is called threshold energy.

19. Which of the following statements are incorrect about Arrhenius equation?

(a) As temperature increases, the rate constant (k) increases exponentially.

(b) At very high temperatures, the value of the rate constant becomes very large, making the reaction approach completion immediately.

(c) The value of E_a cannot be determined from the slope of plot of ln k versus $\frac{1}{T}$.

(d) The Arrhenius equation can be used to estimate the rate of reaction at same temperature. If A and E_a are not known.

20. Choose the correct statement related to catalysts.

(a) A positive catalyst increases the rate of reaction by lowering the activation energy.

(b) Both positive and negative catalysts are consumed during the reaction.

(c) A positive catalyst can be used to speed up a reaction without changing the equilibrium of the reaction.

(d) The presence of positive catalysts changes the equilibrium constant of a reaction.

21. Select the true statements about Transition State Theory (TST).

(a) TST assumes that the transition state complex can be isolated and studied.

(b) According to this theory, the reaction rate depends on the concentration of activated complex.

(c) This theory provides an expression for the rate constant that includes Boltzmann and Planck constants.

(d) The energy required to reach the transition state is same as the activation energy of a reaction.

22. For a reversible reaction $C \rightleftharpoons D$, the $\Delta H = +3$ kcal, the pre-exponential factor (A) for forward and reverse are different.

Choose the correct statements for the given reversible reaction.

(a) The activation energy of the forward reaction is greater than that of reverse reaction.

(b) The rate constant of the forward reaction decreases as temperature decreases.

(c) If both reactions have same activation energy, the forward and reverse reactions would proceed at the same rate.

(d) At equilibrium, the ratio of the rate constants for the forward and reverse reactions is given by equilibrium constant.

Type III 》 Numerical/Integer Answer Type Questions

23. For the reaction $A \rightarrow B$, the rate constant (k) at 300 K is $2.0 \times 10^{-3}\ s^{-1}$. The activation energy for the reaction is 75 kJ/mol and the pre-exponential factor (A) is $1.5 \times 10^{21}\ s^{-1}$. Then the rate constant (k) at 350 K is $x$and time required for the concentration of A to decrease by half at 300 K is y. The value of xy is ....

24. Consider the following reaction taking place in three steps :

$$A \rightarrow B, E_{a_1} = 50 \text{ kJ/mol}$$
$$B \rightarrow C, E_{a_2} = 60 \text{ kJ/mol}$$
$$C \rightarrow D, E_{a_3} = 40 \text{ kJ/mol}$$

If the rate constant $k_1 = 10^{-3}\ s^{-1}$ and k_2 is $10^{-2}\ s^{-1}$ at 300 K, then the overall activation energy .... (nearest integer)

$$k_{overall} = \frac{k_1 k_2}{k_3}$$

25. For a reversible reaction, $X \rightleftharpoons Y$, the forward and reverse rate constants k_f and k_r follows the Arrhenius equation.

If $A_f = 2 \times 10^{13}\ s^{-1}$, $A_r = 4 \times 10^{12}\ s^{-1}$ and $\Delta H = +20$ kJ/mol

The value of equilibrium constant K_{eq} at 300 K is $x \times 10^{-3}$ and the temperature at which the forward and reverse rate constants k_f and k_r are equal is y. The value jof $x + y$ is ....

26. Consider a reaction with rate constant (k_1) at 300 K is $1.8 \times 10^{-4}\ s^{-1}$ and activation energy (E_a) is 75 kJ/mol. Also the collision frequency is 1.5×10^{12} collisions/mol/s. Then the steric factor for this reaction is ...... $\times 10^{-3}$ (nearest integer)

27. The number of correct statements regarding the effect of temperature on reaction rate is

A. The rate constant k increases by a factor of α.

B. The rate constant doubles, if $\alpha = 2$ when the temperature is increased by 10°C.

C. The activation energy increases with an increase in temperature.

D. The rate of reaction generally increases when the tempertature is increased because of the increase in the rate constant.

Elemental Practice 9.3 | Chapter 09

Connect with **Answers**

1. (b)	2. (c)	3. (a)	4. (b)	5. (d)	6. (a)
7. (b)	8. (c)	9. (a)	10. (d)	11. (b)	12. (b)
13. (b)	14. (d)	15. (b)	16. (b)	17. (a)	18. (a,c)
19. (c,d)	20. (a,c)	21. (b,c,d)	22. (a,b,d)	23. (0.912)	24. (70)
25. (1496)	26. (1)	27. (3)			

Advanced Exclusive Different Strokes

Radioactive disintegration follows first order kinetics. numerical problems on radioactive disintegration was asked in JEE Advance 2024. Similarly, determination of order from mechanism of reaction has been frequently asked in JEE Advance. So, these concepts are important for the purpose of JEE Advance.

Tips to solve problems related to radioactivity and half-life which follows first order kinetics.

The term radioactivity may be defined as a process in which nucleus of certain elements spontaneously disintegrate (transformation into another element by the ejection of α- or β-particle) at a rate characteristic for each particular active isotope. All the heavy elements from bismuth (atomic number 83) through uranium and also a few of the lighter elements possess radioactive properties. However, the radioactive property of the different radioactive elements differs widely, e.g. radium atoms have about three million times the activity of uranium atoms.

Radioactive disintegration

The atomic nuclei of radioactive elements can disintegrate any moment. During disintegration, atoms of new elements having different physical and chemical properties are formed, called daughter elements.

Disintegration occurs by the following processes:

(i) α-**particle emission** When an α-particle ($_2^4He$) is emitted from the nucleus of parent element, the new element formed called daughter element, possess atomic mass less by 4 unit and atomic number less by 2 units.

$$\text{Parent element} \xrightarrow{-\alpha} \text{Daughter element}$$

	Parent element	Daughter element
Atomic mass	A	$A-4$
Atomic number	Z	$Z-2$

For e.g., $_{92}^{238}U \longrightarrow {}_{90}^{234}Th + {}_2^4He$

(ii) β-**particle emission** When β-particle is emitted from parent element thus formed daughter elements possesses same atomic mass but atomic number is increased by 1 unit.

$$\text{Parent element} \xrightarrow{-\beta} \text{Daughter element}$$

	Parent element	Daughter element
Atomic mass	A	A
Atomic number	Z	$Z+1$

1. Rate of decay (acitivity, A) is the number of atoms undergoing decay to unit time; it is represented by $-\frac{dN_1}{dt}$.
2. Rate of decay of a nuclide is directly proportional to the number of atoms of that nuclide present at that moment, hence,

$$-\frac{dN_t}{dt} \propto N_t$$

or
$$-\frac{dN_t}{dt} = \lambda N_t$$

(the negative sign shows that the number of radioactive atoms, N_t decreases as time t increases)

3. Rate of decay of nuclide is independent of temperature, so its energy of activation is zero.
4. Since the rate of decay is directly proportional to the amount of the radioactive nuclide present and as the number of undecomposed atoms decreases with increase in time, the rate of decay also decreases with the increase in time. Various forms of equation for radioactive decay are

$$N_t = N_0 e^{-\lambda t}$$

$$\log N_0 - \log N_t = \frac{\lambda t}{2.303}$$

$$\log \frac{N_0}{N_t} = \frac{\lambda t}{2.303}$$

$$\lambda = \frac{2.303}{t} \log \frac{N_0}{N} \quad \text{...(i)}$$

where, N_0 = Initial number of atoms of the given nuclide, i.e. at time 0

N_t = No. of atoms of the nuclide present after t

λ = Decay constant

Note that the Eq. (i) is similar to that of first order reaction, hence we can say that radioactive disintegration are examples of first order reactions.

However, unlike first order rate constant (K), the decay constant (λ) is independent of temperature.

Tips to solve problems related to finding order from Reaction mechanism.

Following example illustrate this concept

- Mechanism of the reaction, $2NO + Cl_2 \rightarrow 2NOCl$ may be written as

$$2NO \underset{}{\overset{K'}{\rightleftharpoons}} (NO)_2 \text{...(fast)}$$

$$(NO)_2 + Cl_2 \xrightarrow{k} 2NOCl \text{...(slow)}$$

- Rate equation would be

$$r = k[(NO)_2][Cl_2]$$

Rate determining step is slowest step of complex reactions. The rate law is written according to rds and finally the rate law must appear in terms of reactants

$$K' = \frac{[(NO)_2]}{[NO]^2}$$

$$r = kK'[NO]^2[Cl_2]$$

Conclusion

- Radioactive decay follows first order kinetics.
- The rate law is determined by the slowest step of reaction and its final expression must not include intermediates.

PRACTICE ELEMENT 01

Target JEE Main

Objective Type Questions

1. For the reaction :

$$A + 2B \rightarrow C + D, \text{ rate} = k[A]^2[B]$$

Which of the following is the correct expression for the rate of disappearance of the reactants?

(a) $\frac{-\Delta[A]}{\Delta t} = k[A]^2[B]$

(b) $\frac{-\Delta[B]}{\Delta t} = k[A]^2[B]$

(c) $\frac{-\Delta[A]}{\Delta t} = 2k[A]^2[B]$

(d) $\frac{-\Delta[C]}{\Delta t} = k[A]^2[B]$

2. The decomposition of hydrogen peroxide (H_2O_2) follows the reaction :

$$2H_2O_2(g) \longrightarrow 2H_2O(l) + O_2(g)$$

The reaction follows first order kinetics with respect to H_2O_2 and the rate constant $k = 3.5 \times 10^{-4}$ s. If the initial concentration of H_2O_2 is 0.5 M, the time required for the concentration of H_2O_2 to decrease to 0.125 M is ($\log 2 = 0.3010$)

(a) 500 s (b) 1000 s (c) 2961 s (d) 3961 s

3. In a reaction to occur, according to collision theory, which of the following conditions must be satisfied?

(a) Molecules must collide with sufficient kinetic energy to overcome the activation energy barrier.

(b) The frequency of collisions between molecules does not affect the reaction rate.

(c) Every collision between reactant molecules leads to the formation of products.

(d) The reactant molecules not to be aligned in a specific orientation during the collision.

4. Consider the following elementary reaction :

$$A + B \underset{k_{-1}}{\overset{k_1}{\rightleftharpoons}} C$$

The correct expression that represents the net rate of formation of C at any point of time is

(a) $\frac{d[C]}{dt} = k_1[A][B] - k_{-1}[C]$

(b) $\frac{d[C]}{dt} = k_1[A][B] + k_1[C]$

(c) $\frac{d[C]}{dt} = k_1[A][B]$

(d) $\frac{d[C]}{dt} = k_1[C] - k_1[A][B]$

5. Match List I with List II.

List I (Reaction order)	List II (Reaction example)
A. Zero order	(i) $CH_3COOC_2H_5(aq) + H_2O(l) \longrightarrow CH_3COOH(aq) + C_2H_5OH(aq)$
B. First order	(ii) $2NO_2(g) + F_2(g) \longrightarrow 2NO_2F(g)$
C. Second order	(iii) $NH_3(g) \xrightarrow{\text{Mo or } h\nu} N_2(g) + 3H_2(g)$
D. Pseudo-first order	(iv) $NH_4NO_2(aq) \longrightarrow N_2(g) + 2H_2O(l)$

Choose the correct answer from the options given below.

(a) A-(iii), B-(iv), C-(i), D-(ii)
(b) A-(iii), B-(iv), C-(ii), D-(i)
(c) A-(iv), B-(iii), C-(i), D-(ii)
(d) A-(iv), B-(iii), C-(ii), D-(i)

6. For a zero-order reaction, $A \rightarrow$ Products, with a rate constant $k = 0.1 \text{ M s}^{-1}$, the initial concentration of A is 1.0 M. Then the percentage of A that remains after 5 seconds is

(a) 75% (b) 60%
(c) 50% (d) 65%

7. Given below are two statements, one is labelled as Assertion (A) and the other is labelled as Reason (R).

Assertion (A) According to transition state theory, the rate of a reaction depends on the height of the potential energy barrier.

Reason (R) The potential energy barrier corresponds to the activation energy required to form transition state.

In the light of the above statements, choose the correct answer from the options given below.

(a) Both (A) and (R) are true and (R) is the correct explanation of (A).
(b) Both (A) and (R) are true but (R) is not the correct explanation of (A).
(c) (A) is true but (R) is false.
(d) (A) is false but (R) is true.

8. The correct statement about the molecularity of the reaction is

(a) molecularity equal to the order of the reaction for an elementary reaction.
(b) molecularity is always less than or equal to the order of reaction.
(c) molecularity is always equal to the order of the reaction.
(d) molecularity and order are completely interdependent.

9. For a reaction, if the rate constant k_1 at temperature $T_1 = 300$ K is 0.02 s^{-1} and the rate constant k_2 at $T_2 = 350$ K

is $0.05\,s^{-1}$. The approximate activation energy for a reaction is ....

(Given, $R = 8.314\ J\ mol^{-1}\ K^{-1}$)

($\ln 2.5 = 0.916$)

(a) 15.45 J/mol (b) 15.45 kJ/mol
(c) 15.80 J/mol (d) 15.80 kJ/mol

10. For a reaction $A \rightarrow B$, the rate of reaction at an initial concentration of $[A] = 0.1$ M is measured to be $1.0 \times 10^{-3}\ mol^{-1}\ L\ s^{-1}$. When the concentration of A is increased to 0.2 M, the rate increases to $4.0 \times 10^{-3}\ mol^{-1}\ L\ s^{-1}$. What is the order of reaction w.r.t. A?

(a) 0 (b) 2 (c) 1 (d) 3

11. In a reaction where AB absorbs light and forms an excited complex AB^*, the rate of formation of AB^* is directly proportional to the intensity of absorbed light I and the concentration of AB (denoted by C). Which of the following statements correctly represents the rate law for the formation of AB^*?

(a) The rate of formation of AB^* is directly proportional to I and C^2.
(b) The rate of formation of AB^* is directly proportional to I and C.
(c) The rate of formation of AB^* is directly proportional to I^2 and C.
(d) The rate of formation of AB^* is inversely proportional to I and C.

12. Given below are two statements.

Statement I According to collision theory, increasing the temperature of a reaction mixture will always increase the rate of the reaction.

Statement II Decreasing the concentration of a reactant will always decrease the rate of the reaction for a zero order reaction.

In the light of the above statements, choose the correct answer from the options given below.

(a) Statement I is correct but Statement II is incorrect.
(b) Statement I is incorrect but Statement II is correct.
(c) Both Statement I and Statement II are correct.
(d) Both Statement I and Statement II are incorrect.

13. The number of graphs representing the zero order reaction is

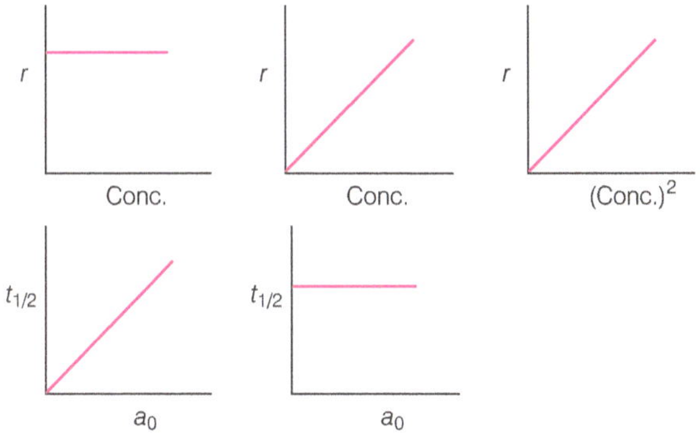

(a) 2 (b) 4 (c) 3 (d) 1

14. The pre-exponential factor A depends on the steric factor P and the collision frequency. Which of the following factor can influence the value of the steric factor P?

(a) Temperature
(b) The concentration of reactants
(c) The orientation and geometry of reacting molecules
(d) The activation energy of the reaction.

15. The following data is given for the reaction :

$$A \xrightarrow{k} \text{Products}$$

The concentration of A at different times is given as :

Time (s)	[A] (M)
0	0.80
10	0.60
20	0.50

Which of the following statements is correct?

(A) The average rate of the reaction between $t = 0$ and $t = 10$ seconds is $0.02\ s^{-1}$.
(B) The instantaneous rate at $t = 10$ seconds is $0.06\ s^{-1}$.
(C) The average rate between $t = 0$ and $t = 10$ s can be calculated as $\frac{0.80 - 0.60}{10}$.
(D) The instantaneous rate at $t = 10$ seconds can be calculated using the rate law for a first order reaction, Rate $= k\,[A]$.
(E) The instantaneous rate can be obtained by taking the slope of the concentration *vs* time curve at that point.

Choose the correct answer from the options given below.

(a) A, B, C and D (b) A, B, C, D and E
(c) B, C and D (d) A, C, D and E

16. The Arrhenius equation is given as :

$$k = Ae^{\frac{-E_a}{RT}}$$

$$\ln k = \ln A - \frac{E_a}{R} \cdot \frac{1}{T}$$

Which of the following graphs represents the relationship between $\ln k$ and $\frac{1}{T}$ for a reaction, where activation energy E_a is positive?

(a) A straight line with a positive slope.
(b) A straight line with a negative slope.
(c) A hyperbolic curve.
(d) A straight line with zero slope.

17. The decomposition of compound X follows pseudo first order kinetics with respect to X when compound Y is present in excess. The half-life of the reaction is 20 minutes when concentration of X is 0.2 M and the concentration of Y is 2.0 M. Then, the rate constant (k') for pseudo 1st order reaction is

(a) $5.8 \times 10^{-4}\ s^{-1}$ (b) $5.8 \times 10^{-3}\ s^{-1}$
(c) $5.8 \times 10^{-5}\ s^{-1}$ (d) $5.8 \times 10^{-6}\ s^{-1}$

18. The ester hydrolysis of ethyl acetate $(CH_3COOC_2H_5)$ is carried out separately in 0.1 M HCl and 0.1 M H_2SO_4. If the reaction is first order with respect to the ester and follows

pseudo first order kinetics in both acids, which of the following is true?

(a) The reaction will be slower in 0.1 M H_2SO_4 because it is weaker than HCl.

(b) The reaction rate will be same in both 0.1 M HCl and 0.1 M H_2SO_4, as both are strong acids.

(c) The reaction rate will be faster in 0.1 M H_2SO_4 than in 0.1 M HCl because H_2SO_4 is diprotic acid and releases more protons.

(d) The reaction rate will be faster in 0.1 M HCl due to the higher concentration of H^+ ions from HCl.

19. Which of the following statements about a catalyst is not true?

(a) A catalyst lowers the activation energy of a reaction.

(b) A catalyst increases the rate of both the forward and reverse reactions.

(c) A catalyst changes the equilibrium position of the reaction.

(d) A catalyst is not consumed in the reaction.

20. The given graph is a representation of kinetics of a reaction :

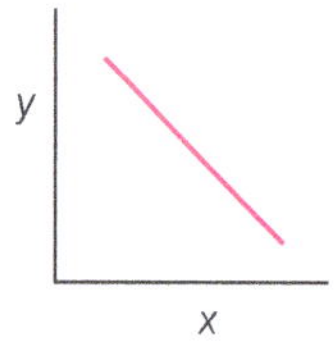

The x and y for zero and first order reaction is

(a) $x = t$, $y = [A]$ (for zero order), $x = t$, $y = \log [A]$ (for 1st order)

(b) $x = t$, $y = \log [A]$ (for zero order), $x = t$, $y = \log [A]$ (for 1st order)

(c) $x = t$, $y = \frac{1}{[A]}$ (for zero order), $x = t$, $y = \log [A]$ (for 1st order)

(d) $x = t$, $y = [A]$ (for zero order), $x = t$, $y = \log \frac{1}{[A]}$ (for 1st order)

Numerical Type Questions

21. The thermal decomposition of nitrous oxide (N_2O) follows first-order kinetics. The reaction is carried out in a constant volume container at 700°C. The half-life of decomposition reaction is 3.2 minutes and the initial pressure of nitrous oxide is 0.50 atm. Then the total pressure in the container after 9.6 minutes is .... $\times 10^{-1}$ atm. (nearest integer)

22. The rate constant equation is given by equation :

$$k = 2.5 \times 10^{10}\ s^{-1}\ e^{-25000\ J/mol/RT}$$

The decomposition reaction of C at 350 K follows 1st order kinetics. The time required for the concentration of C to decrease to 20% of its initial value is .... (nanoseconds) ($\ln 5 = 1.609$)

23. The decomposition reaction mechanism of ozone is given below

$$O_3 \rightleftharpoons O_2 + O \text{ (fast)}$$

$$O + O_3 \rightarrow O_2 + O_2 \text{ (slow)}$$

The overall order of the reaction will be ....

24. An organic compound undergoes first-order decomposition and it takes 200 seconds for 50% of the compound to decompose. The time required for 75% of the compound to decompose is ....

($\ln 2 = 0.693$, $\ln 4 = 1.386$)

25. For the reversible reaction

$$A \rightleftharpoons B$$

The activation energy for the forward reaction is 75 kJ/mol and for the backward reaction is 100 kJ/mol. The pre exponential factors for forward and backward reactions are given as :

$$A_{forward} = 1.2 \times 10^{13}\ mol^{-1}\ L\ s^{-1}$$

$$A_{backward} = 4.0 \times 10^{12}\ mol^{-1}\ L\ s^{-1}$$

At 298 K, the equilibrium constant will be .... $\times 10^4$. (Nearest integer)

26. Consider the following reaction

$$A + B \rightarrow C$$

$$\text{rate} = k\,[A][B]$$

Initial concentration of A and B is 0.6 M and 0.4 M and rate constant, k is 0.1 $M^{-1}\ min^{-1}$ respectively. Then, change in reaction rate when concentration of A is doubled ...... $\times 10^{-4}$ M/s (Nearest integer).

27. Consider two different first order reactions. The half life of reaction 1 is 3 times that of reaction 2. t_1 and t_2 are the time taken for 80% and 90% completion of reaction 1 and reaction 2 respectively. Then, value of ratio of $\frac{t_1}{t_2}$ is ....

($\ln 5 = 1.609$, $\ln 10 = 2.302$)

28. Consider the following reaction :

$$A + B \rightarrow C$$

The reaction follows second-order kinetics with respect to A and first order with respect to B i.e., rate law is

$$\text{Rate} = k\,[A]^2[B]$$

The number of correct statements regarding the instantaneous rate of reaction at any given time is

(A) The rate of the reaction increases with an increase in concentration of A in a quadratic manner.

(B) The rate of the reaction depends on the concentrations of both A and B linearly.

(C) If the concentration of A is doubled, the instantaneous rate will increase by a factor of 4.

(D) The rate of reaction is directly proportional to the concentration of B.

(E) The reaction will proceed faster if the concentration of B is increased, assuming $[A]$ remains constant.

29. For the decomposition of gaseous compound A at 298 K, the initial pressure is 100 kPa and half life is 200 sec. Then the pressure is changed to 50 kPa and half life becomes 100 s. Then, the order of the reaction is

30. In a reaction $B \rightarrow$ Products, the rate of the reaction is tripled when concentration of B increases by factor 27. If the 50% of reaction occurs in $3\sqrt{3}$ hours, then time taken for the completion of the reaction is ....

Check Through PYQs

Element 1 Rate of Reaction and Factor Affecting Rate of Reaction

1. Given below are two statements: *2024, 9 April Shift-I*

Statement I The rate law for the reaction $A + B \longrightarrow C$ is rate $(r) = k\,[A]^2\,[B]$. When the concentration of both A and B is doubled, the reaction rate is increased "x" times.

Statement II

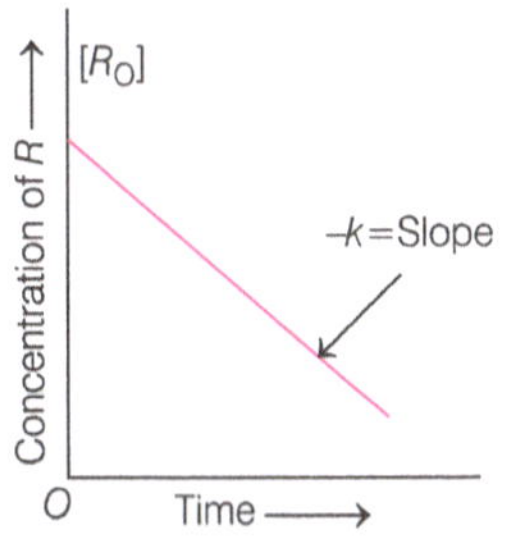

The figure is showing "the variation in concentration against time plot" for a "y" order reaction.

The value of $x + y$ is ....

2. For a reaction $A \xrightarrow{k_1} B \xrightarrow{k_2} C$

If the rate of formation of B is set to be zero then the concentration of B is given by : *2024, 8 April Shift-II*

(a) $\left(\frac{k_1}{k_2}\right)[A]$ (b) $(k_1 + k_2)[A]$
(c) $(k_1 - k_2)[A]$ (d) $k_1k_2\,[A]$

3. NO_2 required for a reaction is produced by decomposition of N_2O_5 in CCl_4 as by equation

$$2N_2O_5(g) \longrightarrow 4NO_2(g) + O_2(g)$$

The initial concentration of N_2O_5 is 3 mol L^{-1} and it is 2.75 mol L^{-1} after 30 minutes.

The rate of formation of NO_2 is $x \times 10^{-3}$ mol $L^{-1}min^{-1}$, value of x is ....

(nearest integer) *2024, 30 Jan Shift-II*

4. For a given chemical reaction,

$$\gamma_1 A + \gamma_2 B \longrightarrow \gamma_3 C + \gamma_4 D$$

concentration of C changes from 10 m mol dm^{-3} to 20 mmol dm^{-3} in 10 seconds. Rate of appearance of D is 1.5 times the rate of disappearance of B which is twice the rate of disappearance A. The rate of appearance of D has been experimentally determined to be 9 m mol dm^{-3} s^{-1}. Therefore, the rate of reaction is ... m mol dm^{-3} s^{-1}. [Nearest integer] *2022, 25 June Shift-I*

5. The reaction that occurs in a breath analyser, a device used to determine the alcohol level in a person's blood stream is

$$2K_2Cr_2O_7 + 8H_2SO_4 + 3C_2H_6O \longrightarrow 2Cr_2(SO_4)_3 + 3C_2H_4O_2 + 2K_2SO_4 + 11H_2O$$

If the rate of appearance of $Cr_2(SO_4)_3$ is 2.67 mol min^{-1} at a particular time, the rate of disappearance of C_2H_6O at the same time is .... mol min^{-1}. (Nearest integer) *2021, 27 Aug Shift-I*

6. For the reaction $2A + 3B + \frac{3}{2}C \rightarrow 3P$, which statement is correct? *2020, 3 Sep Shift-II*

(a) $\frac{dn_A}{dt} = \frac{2}{3}\frac{dn_B}{dt} = \frac{3}{4}\frac{dn_C}{dt}$ (b) $\frac{dn_A}{dt} = \frac{3}{2}\frac{dn_B}{dt} = \frac{3}{4}\frac{dn_C}{dt}$
(c) $\frac{dn_A}{dt} = \frac{dn_B}{dt} = \frac{dn_C}{dt}$ (d) $\frac{dn_A}{dt} = \frac{2}{3}\frac{dn_B}{dt} = \frac{4}{3}\frac{dn_C}{dt}$

Element 2 Rate Law, Order, Molecularity and Half-Life Period

7. $A(g) \longrightarrow 2B(g)$

For the given reaction, initial pressure was 0.6 atm and rate constant is 4.606×10^{-2} sec^{-1}. Find the pressure at 100 sec. *2025, 22 Jan Shift-II*

(a) 0.6 atm (b) 1.194 atm
(c) 0.594 atm (d) 0.006 atm

8. Consider the following reaction *2024, 8 Jan Shift-I*

$$A + B \longrightarrow C$$

The time taken for A to become $1/4^{th}$ of its initial concentration is twice the time taken to become 1/2 of the same. Also, when the change of concentration of B is plotted against time, the resulting graph gives a straight line with a negative slope and a positive intercept on the concentration axis.

The overall order of the reaction is ....

9. Consider the two different first order reactions given below. *2024, 6 April Shift-II*

$$A + B \longrightarrow C \text{ (Reaction 1)}$$
$$P \longrightarrow Q \text{ (Reaction 2)}$$

The ratio of the half-life of reaction 1 : reaction 2 is 5 : 2. If t_1 and t_2 represent the time taken to complete $\frac{2}{3}$rd and $\frac{4}{5}$th of reaction 1 and reaction 2, respectively, then the value of the ratio $t_1 : t_2$ is .... $\times 10^{-1}$ (Nearest integer).

[Given, $\log_{10}(3) = 0.477$ and $\log_{10}(5) = 0.699$]

10. During kinetic study of reaction, $2A + B \longrightarrow C + D$, the following results were obtained. *2024, 5 April Shift-I*

	A[M]	B[M]	Initial rate of formation of D
I.	0.1	0.1	6.0×10^{-3}
II.	0.3	0.2	7.2×10^{-2}
III.	0.3	0.4	2.88×10^{-1}
IV.	0.4	0.1	2.40×10^{-2}

Based on above data, overall order of the reaction is ....

11. Consider the following reaction, the rate expression of which is given below *2024, 4 April Shift-II*

$$A + B \rightarrow C$$

Rate $= k [A]^{1/2}[B]^{1/2}$

The reaction is initiated by taking 1 M concentration of A and B each. If the rate constant (k) is $4.6 \times 10^{-2} s^{-1}$, then the time taken for A to become 0.1 M is ...... sec. (Nearest integer)

12. A student has studied the decomposition of a gas AB_3 at 25°C. He obtained the following data.

p (mm Hg)	50	100	200	400
Relative $t_{1/2}$ (s)	4	2	1	0.5

The order of the reaction is *2023, 24 Jan Shift-II*

(a) 1 (b) 0 (zero)
(c) 0.5 (d) 2

13. For a chemical reaction, $A + B \longrightarrow$ Product, the order is 1 with respect to A and B.

Rate mol L^{-1} s^{-1}	**[A] mol L^{-1}**	**[B] mol L^{-1}**
0.10	20	0.5
0.40	x	0.5
0.80	40	y

What is the value of x and y? *2023, 11 April Shift-II*

(a) 80 and 4
(b) 80 and 2
(c) 40 and 4
(d) 160 and 4

14. The reaction $2NO + Br_2 \longrightarrow 2NOBr$ takes places through the mechanism given below

$$NO + Br_2 \rightleftharpoons NOBr_2 \text{ (fast)}$$
$$NOBr_2 + NO \longrightarrow 2NOBr \text{ (Slow)}$$

The overall order of the reaction is .... *2023, 12 April Shift-I*

15. The number of incorrect statements from the following is *2023, 10 April Shift-II*

A. The successive half lives of zero order reactions decreases with time.
B. A substance appearing as reactant in the chemical equation may not affect the rate of reaction
C. Order and molecularity of a chemical reaction can be a fractional number
D. The rate constant units of zero and second order reaction are mol $L^{-1}s^{-1}$ and mol L^{-1} s^{-1} respectively

16. A molecule undergoes two independent first order reactions whose respective half lives are 12 min and 3 min. If both the reactions are occurring then the time taken for the 50% consumption of the reactant is .... min. (Nearest integer) *2023, 10 April Shift-I*

17. $A \rightarrow B$

The above reaction is of zero order. Half-life of this reaction is 50 min. The time taken for the concentration of A to reduce to one-fourth of its initial value is .... min. (Nearest integer) *2023, 1 Feb Shift-II*

18. For certain chemical reaction $X \rightarrow Y$, the rate of formation of product is plotted against the time as shown in the figure. The number of correct statements from the following is .... *2023, 29 Jan Shift-I*

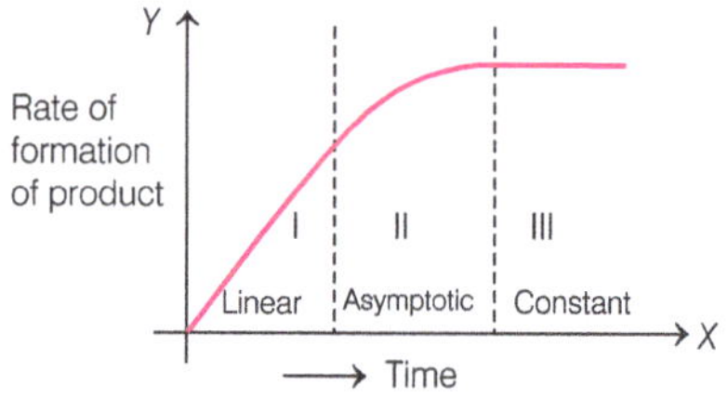

(A) overall order of this reaction is one
(B) order of this reaction can't be determined
(C) in region I and III, the reaction is of first and zero order respectively
(D) in region-II, the reaction is of first order
(E) in region-II, the order of reaction is in the range of 0.1 to 0.9.

19. A first order reaction has the rate constant, $k = 4.6 \times 10^{-3}$ s^{-1}. The number of correct statements from the following is/are ....

[Given, log 3 = 0.48] *2023, 25 Jan Shift-II*

A. reaction completes in 1000 s.
B. the reaction has a half-life of 500 s.
C. the time required for 10% completion is 25 times the time required for 90% completion.
D. the degree of dissociation is equal to $(1 - e^{-kt})$
E. the rate and the rate constant have the same unit.

20. The reaction between X and Y is first order with respect to X and zero order with respect to Y.

Experiment	**[X] (mol L^{-1})**	**[Y] (mol L^{-1})**	**Initial rate (mol L^{-1} min^{-1})**
I.	0.1	0.1	2×10^{-3}
II.	L	0.2	4×10^{-3}
III.	0.4	0.4	$M \times 10^{-3}$
IV.	0.1	0.2	2×10^{-3}

Examine the data of table and calculate ratio of numerical values of M and L. (Nearest integer) *2022, 29 July Shift-I*

21. For the given first order reaction $A \rightarrow B$, the half-life of the reaction is 0.3010 min. The ratio of the initial concentration of reactant to the concentration of reactant at time 2.0 min will be equal to .... (Nearest integer) *2022, 28 July Shift-I*

22. $[A] \longrightarrow [B]$
Reactant Product

If formation of compound $[B]$ follows the first order of kinetics and after 70 minutes the concentration of $[A]$ was found to be half of its initial concentration. Then the rate constant of the reaction is $x \times 10^{-6} s^{-1}$. The value of x is .... (nearest integer) *2022, 27 July Shift-II*

23. $2NO + 2H_2 \longrightarrow N_2 + 2H_2O$

The above reaction has been studied at 800°C. The related data are given in the table below.

Reaction serial number	Initial pressure of H_2/kPa	Initial pressure of NO/kPa	Initial rate $\left(\frac{-dp}{dt}\right)$/ (kPa/s)
1	65.6	40.0	0.135
2	65.6	20.1	0.033
3	38.6	65.6	0.214
4	19.2	65.6	0.106

The order of the reaction with respect to NO is...... . *2022, 27 July Shift-I*

24. For a first order reaction, the ratio of the time for 75% completion of a reaction to the time for 50% completion is ...... (Integer answer) *2021, 31 Aug Shift-I*

25. The following data was obtained for chemical reaction given below at 975 K.

$$2NO(g) + 2H_2(g) \longrightarrow N_2(g) + 2H_2O(g)$$

	[NO] mol L^{-1}	[H_2] mol L^{-1}	[Rate] mol L^{-1}
A.	8×10^{-5}	8×10^{-5}	7×10^{-9}
B.	24×10^{-5}	8×10^{-5}	2.1×10^{-8}
C.	24×10^{-5}	32×10^{-5}	8.4×10^{-8}

The order of the reaction with respect to NO is .... [Integer answer] *2021, 26 Aug Shift-I*

26. For a reaction of order n, the unit of the rate constant is *2021, 27 July Shift-I*

(a) $mol^{1-n} L^{1-n} s$ (b) $mol^{1-n} L^{2n} s^{-1}$
(c) $mol^{1-n} L^{n-1} s^{-1}$ (d) $mol^{1-n} L^{1-n} s^{-1}$

27. Sucrose hydrolyses in acid solution into glucose and fructose following first order rate law with a half-life of 3.33 h at 25°C. After 9 h, the fraction of sucrose remaining is f. The value of $\log_{10}\left(\frac{1}{f}\right)$ is ... $\times 10^{-2}$

(Rounded off to the nearest integer).
[Assume, $\ln 10 = 2.303$, $\ln 2 = 0.693$] *2021, 24 Feb Shift-II*

28. Gaseous cyclobutene isomerises to butadiene in a first order process which has a 'k' value of $3.3 \times 10^{-4} s^{-1}$ at 153°C. The time in minutes it takes for the isomerisation to proceed 40 % to completion at this temperature is ....
(Rounded off to the nearest integer) *2021, 24 Feb Shift-I*

29. If 75% of a first order reaction was completed in 90 minutes, 60% of the same reaction would be completed in approximately (in minutes) ....
(Take : $\log 2 = 0.30$; $\log 2.5 = 0.40$) *2020, 4 Sep Shift-I*

30. During the nuclear explosion, one of the products is ^{90}Sr with half-life of 6.93 years. If 1 μg of ^{90}Sr was absorbed in the bones of a newly born baby in place of Ca, how much time, in years, is required to reduce it by 90% if it is not lost metabolically .... *2020, 7 Jan Shift-I*

Element 3 Arrhenius Theory, Activation Energy, Collision and Related Theories

31. Let k_1, k_2 and k_3 be the rate constant of reaction and $k = \sqrt{\frac{k_1 k_3}{k_2}}$. Then find activation energy of overall reaction.
(Given : $E_{a_1} = 10$ kJ/mol, $E_{a_2} = 30$ kJ/mol, $E_{a_3} = 60$ kJ/mol) *2025, 24 Jan Shift-II*

32. Consider the following transformation involving first order elementary reaction in each step at constant temperature as shown below. *2024, 4 April Shift-I*

$$A + B \underset{\text{Step 3}}{\overset{\text{Step 1}}{\rightleftharpoons}} C \xrightarrow{\text{Step 2}} P$$

Some details of the above reactions are listed below.

Step	Rate constant (sec^{-1})	Activation energy (kJ mol^{-1})
1	k_1	300
2	k_2	200
3	k_3	Ea_3

If the overall rate constant of the above transformation (k) is given as $k = \frac{k_1 k_2}{k_3}$ and the overall activation energy (E_a) is 400 kJ mol^{-1}, then the value of Ea_3 is...... kJ mol^{-1}. (Nearest integer)

33. For a reversible reaction $A \rightleftharpoons B$, the $\Delta H_{\text{forward reaction}} = 20$ kJ mol^{-1}. The activation energy of the uncatalysed forward reaction is 300 kJ mol^{-1}. When the reaction is catalysed keeping the reactant concentration same, the rate of the catalysed forward reaction at 27°C is found to be same as that of the uncatalysed reaction at 327°C. The activation energy of the catalysed backward reaction is .... kJ mol^{-1}. *2023, 15 April Shift-I*

34. The number of given statement/s which is/are correct is *2023, 8 April Shift-I*

(A) The stronger the temperature dependence of the rate constant, the higher is the activation energy.
(B) If a reaction has zero activation energy, its rate is independent of temperature.
(C) The stronger the temperature dependence of the rate constant, the smaller is the activation energy.
(D) If there is no correlation between the temperature and the rate constant then it means that the reaction has negative activation energy.

35. The correct reaction profile diagram for a positive catalyst reaction is *2023, 8 April Shjift-II*

(a) 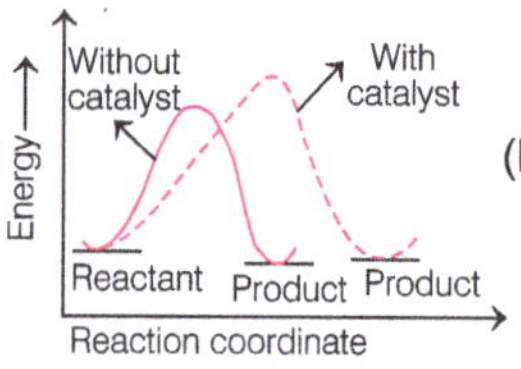

(b) 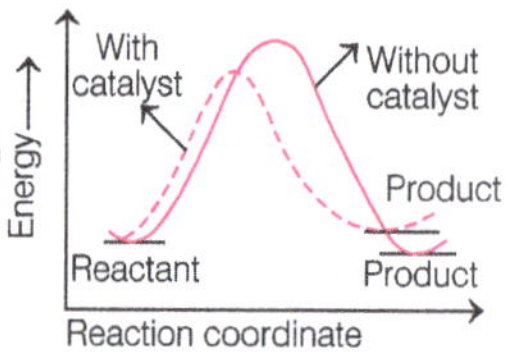

(c) 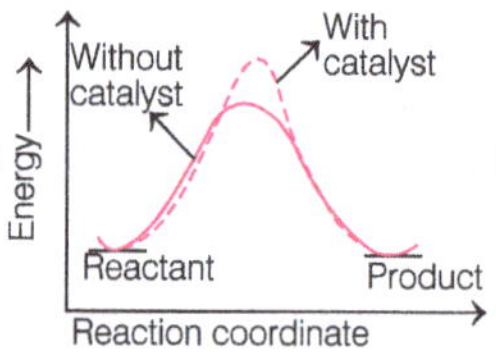

(d) 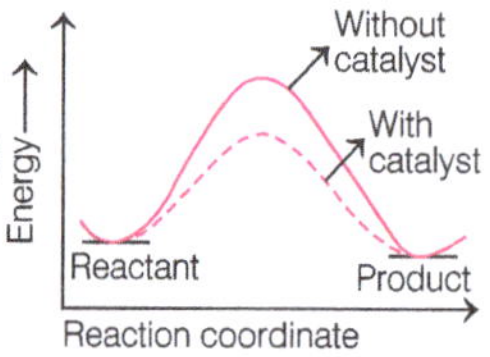

36. $A \rightarrow B$

The rate constants of the above reaction at 200 K and 300 K are 0.03 min^{-1} and 0.05 min^{-1} respectively. The activation energy for the reaction is .... J. (Nearest integer) [Given : $\ln 10 = 2.3$, $R = 8.3$ J K^{-1} mol^{-1}, $\log 5 = 0.70$, $\log 3 = 0.48$, $\log 2 = 0.30$] *2023, 31 Jan Shift-I*

37. Consider the following reaction that goes from A to B in three steps as shown below

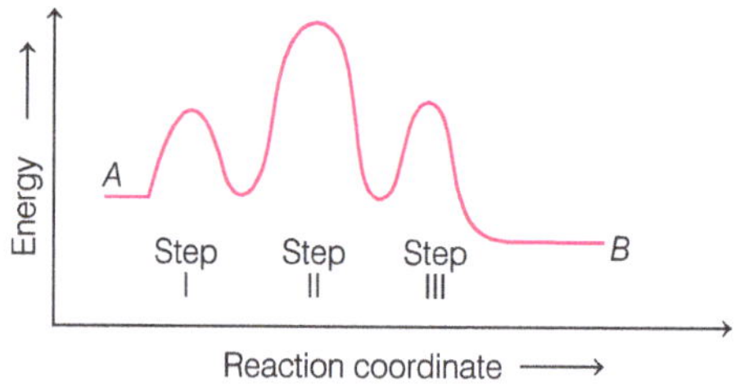

Choose the correct option *2023, 6 April Shift-II*

	Number of intermediates	Number of Activated complexes	Rate determining step
(a)	2	3	III
(b)	3	2	II
(c)	2	3	II
(d)	2	3	I

38. The number of correct statements from the following is .... *2023, 24 Jan Shift-I*

(A) larger the activation energy, smaller is the value of the rate constant.

(B) the higher is the activation energy, higher is the value of the temperature coefficient.

(C) at lower temperature, increase in temperature causes more change in the value of k than at higher temperature.

(D) a plot of $\ln k$ vs $\frac{1}{T}$ is a straight line with slope equal to $-\frac{E_a}{R}$

39. For the reaction $P \rightarrow B$, the values of frequency factor A and activation energy E_a are $4 \times 10^{13} s^{-1}$ and 8.3 kJ mol^{-1} respectively. If the reaction is of first order, the temperature at which the rate constant is $2 \times 10^{-6} s^{-1}$ is .... $\times 10^{-1}$ K. (Given, $\ln 10 = 2.3$, $R = 8.3$ J K^{-1} mol^{-1}, $\log 2 = 0.30$) *2022, 30 June Shift-I*

40. The equation, $k = (6.5 \times 10^{12} s^{-1}) e^{-26000\,K/T}$ is followed for the decomposition of compound *(a)*. The activation energy for the reaction is ... kJ mol^{-1}. [Nearest integer] (Given, $R = 8.314$ J K^{-1} mol^{-1}) *2022, 29 June Shift-II*

41. The activation energy of one of the reactions in a biochemical process is 532611 J mol^{-1}. When the temperature falls from 310 K to 300 K, the change in rate constant observed is $k_{300} = x \times 10^{-3} k_{310}$. The value of x is .... [Given, $\ln 10 = 2.3$, $R = 8.3$ J K^{-1} mol^{-1}] *2022, 29 June Shift-I*

42. It has been found that for a chemical reaction with rise in temperature by 9K the rate constant gets doubled. Assuming a reaction to be occurring at 300 K, the value of activation energy is found to be .... kJ mol^{-1}. [Nearest integer]
(Given, $\ln 10 = 2.3$, $R = 8.3$ $JK^{-1} mol^{-1}$, $\log 2 = 0.30$) *2022, 27 June Shift-II*

43. The rate constant for a first order reaction is given by the following equation

$$\ln k = 33.24 - \frac{2.0 \times 10^4 \text{ K}}{T}$$

The activation energy for the reaction is given by ...... kJ mol^{-1}. [In nearest integer]
(Given, $R = 8.3$ J K^{-1} mol^{-1}) *2022, 27 June Shift-I*

44. Which one of the following given graphs represents the variation of rate constant (k) with temperature (T) for an endothermic reaction? *2021, 1 Sep Shift-II*

(a) 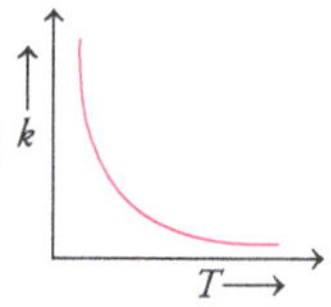

(b) 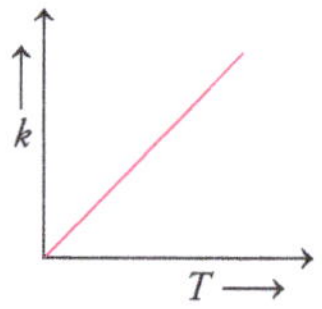

(c) 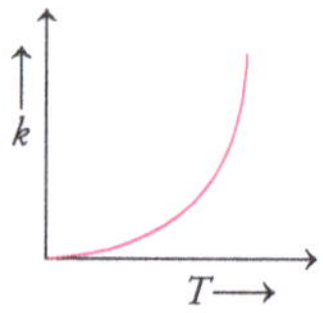

(d) 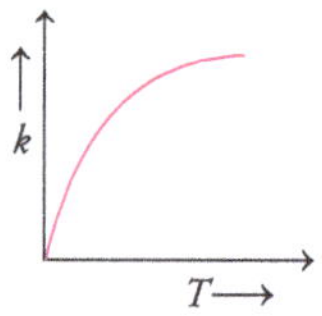

45. The rate constant (k) of a reaction is measured at different temperature (T), and the data are plotted in the given figure. The activation energy of the reaction in kJ mol^{-1} is (R is gas constant)

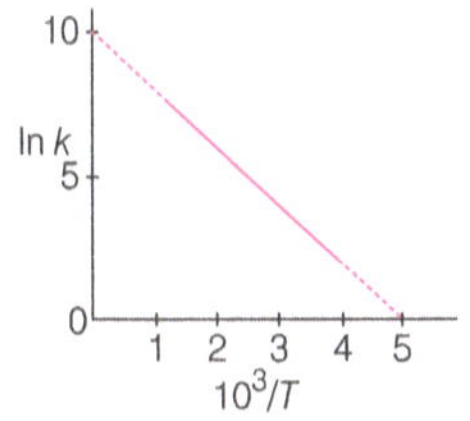

[2020, 5 Sep Shift-II]

(a) $\frac{2}{R}$ (b) $\frac{1}{R}$
(c) R (d) $2R$

46. Consider the following plots of rate constant *versus* $1/T$ for four different reactions. Which of the following orders is correct for the activation energies of these reactions?

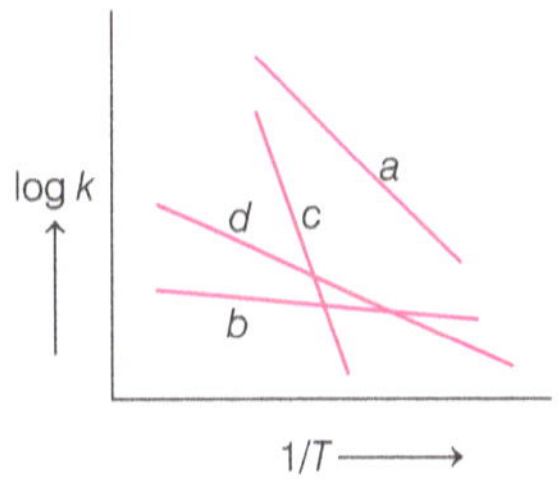

(a) $E_b > E_a > E_d > E_c$
(b) $E_a > E_c > E_d > E_b$
(c) $E_b > E_d > E_c > E_a$
(d) $E_c > E_a > E_d > E_b$

PRACTICE ELEMENT 02 Target JEE Advanced

Single Correct Choice MCQs

1. Consider the reversible reaction :

$$2SO_2(g) + O_2(g) \underset{k_2}{\overset{k_1}{\rightleftharpoons}} 2SO_3(g)$$

The rate of disappearance of SO_2 is equal to :
(a) $k_1[SO_2]^2[O_2] - k_2[SO_3]^2$
(b) $2(k_1[SO_2]^2[O_2] - k_2[SO_3]^2)$
(c) $k_1[SO_2]^2[O_2] + k_2[SO_3]^2$
(d) $2(k_1[SO_2]^2[O_2] + k_2[SO_3]^2)$

2. For a reaction $A \xrightarrow{k_1} B$ and $A \xrightarrow{k_2} C$, both occuring simultaneously (parallel reactions), the initial concentration of A is 0.5 M. If $k_1 = 0.1 s^{-1}$ and $k_2 = 0.2 s^{-1}$, then the concentration of A after 10 seconds is $(e^{-3} = 0.0498)$
(a) 0.0123 M (b) 0.0234 M
(c) 0.0143 M (d) 0.0249 M

3. The hydrolysis of an ester in acidic medium follows first-order kinetics with respect to the ester and first-order with respect to H^+ ions. The reaction is given by

$$\text{Ester} + H_2O \xrightarrow{H^+} \text{Carboxylic acid} + \text{Alcohol}$$

The half-life of the reaction is 40 minutes when the pH of the solution is 4. What will be the half-life of the reaction if the pH is changed to 3?
(a) 4 minutes (b) 5 minutes
(c) 6 minutes (d) 7 minutes

4. In a solution of 70% water and 30% ethanol at 25°C, methyl bromide (CH_3Br) reacts with sodium hydroxide (NaOH) via an S_N2 mechanism. The initial concentration of methyl bromide is 0.2 M and the concentration of OH^- is 0.1 M. Then the percentage of methyl bromide that reacts at $t = 3000$ seconds and the rate constant is 0.05 $M^{-1} s^{-1}$.
(a) 75% (b) 85%
(c) 65% (d) 55%

5. Given below are two statements.

Assertion (A) For a single step endothermic reaction, the increase in rate with temperature is more pronounced than for an exothermic reaction occuring in a single step.

Reason (R) The Arrhenius equation shows that the rate constant k increases exponentially with temperature and this increase is more significant when the activation energy is low.

In the light of the above statements, choose the correct answer from the options given below.
(a) Both (A) and (R) are correct and (R) is the correct explanation of (A).
(b) Both (A) and (R) are correct but (R) is not the correct explanation of (A).
(c) (A) is correct but (R) is incorrect.
(d) (A) is incorrect but (R) is correct.

6. Half-life for the zero order reaction $P(g) \longrightarrow Q(g) + R(g)$ and half-life for the first order reaction $A(g) \longrightarrow B(g) + C(g)$ are equal. If completion time for the zero order reaction is 14.56 min, then the rate

constant (in hr^{-1}) for the reaction $A(g) \longrightarrow B(g) + C(g)$ is ....

(a) 5 hr^{-1} (b) 6 hr^{-1} (c) 8 hr^{-1} (d) 12 hr^{-1}

7. Given below are two statements.

Statement I In heterogeneous catalysis, the rate of reaction is proportional to the surface area of the catalyst.

Statement II More number of molecules can pass the barrier in a given amount of time when the catalyst and reactants produce an activated complex with a lower potential energy.

In the light of the above statements, choose the correct answer from the options given below.

(a) Both Statement I and Statement II are correct.
(b) Both Statement I and Statement II are incorrect.
(c) Statement I is correct but Statement II is incorrect.
(d) Statement I is incorrect but Statement II is correct.

8. For a certain first-order reaction, the activation energy and pre-exponential factor values are 80 kJ mol^{-1} and 2.0×10^{10} s^{-1}. The temperature (in °C) at which the half-life of this reaction becomes 20 minutes will be

(a) 20.52°C (b) 30.52°C
(c) 35.51°C (d) 50.52°C

9. If the rate of reaction increases by factor 4 when the temperature changes from 20°C to 30°C, by what factor will the rate increase when temperature changes from 30°C to 40°C.

(a) 4.66 (b) 1.66 (c) 2.66 (d) 3.66

10. According to the transition state theory, the activation energy is related to the energy of the transition state. In the collision theory, the rate of reaction depends on the successful collisions betwen reactant molecules, which is influenced by factors such as temperature and activation energy.

Which of the following statements are incorrect regarding the transition state and collision theory?

(a) According to collision theory, a higher frequency of collisions increases rate of reaction.
(b) Higher temperature results in an increase in the fraction of molecules having energy greater than or equal to the activation energy.
(c) Transition state theory explains that the reaction rate depends on the activation energy and temperature independent of the molecular orientation during collisions.
(d) Transition state is a high-energy, unstable configuration of reactant molecules occurs at the peak of the energy barrier.

One or More than One Correct MCQs

11. Consider the reaction of ethyl bromide (CH_3CH_2Br) with hydroxide ion (OH^-).

$$CH_3CH_2Br + OH^- \longrightarrow CH_3CH_2OH + Br^-$$

Select the correct statements about the reaction rate.

(a) If the reaction proceeds *via* S_N2 mechanism, doubling the concentration of OH^- will double the reaction rate.
(b) Increasing the solvent polarity in a polar aprotic solvent will increase the rate of S_N2 reaction.
(c) The rate of reaction increases when nucleophile is weaker in S_N2 reaction.
(d) Increasing the concentration of CH_3CH_2Br will increase the reaction rate regardless of whether the reaction follows the S_N1 and S_N2 mechanism.

12. Consider a first order reaction where a reactant A dissociates as follows :

$$A \longrightarrow \text{Products}$$

Let the initial concentration of A be $[A]_0$ and the concentration at time t be $[A]$. Let α represent degree of dissociation of A at time t.

Choose the correct statements related to first order kinetics.

(a) The degree of dissociation α at time t is given by $\alpha = \dfrac{[A]_0 - [A]}{[A]_0}$.
(b) The plot of ln $[A]$ versus t is a straight line with a slope equal to $-k$.
(c) A plot of ln $[A]_0(1-\alpha)$ versus time t gives a straight line with a slope of $-k$.
(d) The half-life is independent of the initial concentration $[A]_0$.

13. The rate law is given as :

$$\text{Rate} = k\,[A]^n$$

where n is the order of the reaction and $n \neq 1$. Which of the following statements are correct?

(a) For $n > 1$, a plot of $\dfrac{1}{[A]^{n-1}}$ versus time t is non-linear
(b) For $n < 1$, the half-life of the reaction increases as the concentration $[A]_0$ increases.
(c) For $n > 1$, the half-life of the reaction increases with an increase in the initial concentraton $[A]_0$.
(d) For $n < 1$, the integrated rate law can be written as $[A]^{1-n} = [A]_0^{1-n} - (n-1)kt$.
(e) For any order $n > 0$, increasing the initial concentration $[A]_0$ always increases the initial rate of the reaction.

14. Select the correct statements about pseudo first order reactions.

(a) Reaction between an ester and water in dilute acid is pseudo first order.
(b) The concentration of one reactant is kept very high to ensure its effective concentration remains constant throughout the reaction.
(c) The rate law appears to be first-order with respect to both reactants, even if the reaction is second-order overall.
(d) Hydrolysis of sucrose in presence of excess of water can be treated as pseudo first order.

15. Consider a complex multistep reaction involving a single reactant A, leading to the final product. The reaction mechanism involves two elementary steps

$$A \xrightarrow{k_1} \text{Intermediate } X \text{ (fast)}$$

$$X \xrightarrow{k_2} \text{Product (slow)}$$

The rate constant for each step is k_1 and k_2 respectively. Select the correct statements about the overall reaction rate.

(a) The rate law of the overall reaction is determined by the slow step, $X \xrightarrow{k_2} \text{Product}$.

(b) The intermediate X does not appear in the overall rate law expression.

(c) If the first step is fast and reversible, the equilibrium concentration of X can be expressed as $[X] = K[A]$, where $K = \frac{k_1}{k_{-1}}$.

(d) If $k_2 << k_1$, the reaction rate can be approximated as Rate $= k_2[X] \simeq \frac{k_1k_2}{k_{-1}}[A]$.

(e) For a multistep reaction, the overall order of the reaction can be fractional or zero depending on the mechanism.

16. Which of the following statements is/are correct?

(a) The specific rate constant of a first order reaction depends on the time and temperature.

(b) For a reaction of order n, the unit of the rate constant is $mol^{1-n}\ L^{n-1}s^{-1}$.

(c) Higher order (> 3) reactions are rare due to low probability of simultaneous collision of all the reactions.

(d) Integrated rate law equation for a typical first order gas phase reaction is given by $k = \frac{2.303}{t}\log\left(\frac{p_i}{2p_i - p_t}\right)$.

where p_i is initial pressure and p_t is total pressure at time t.

17. Which of the following statement(s) is/are incorrect?

(a) The higher is the activation energy, higher is the value of the temperature coefficient.

(b) Overall rate constant 'K' for a reaction taking place in three steps at same temperature is $\frac{k_1k_2}{k_3}$. The value of E_{a_1}, E_{a_2} and E_{a_3} are 40, 50 and 60 kJ/mol respectively. Then, overall E_a is 30 kJ/mol.

(c) If there is no correlation between the temperature and the rate constant then it means that the reaction has negative activation energy.

(d) The equation, $k = (8.0 \times 10^{12}\ s^{-1})\, e^{-24000K/T}$ is followed for the decomposition of compound (P). Then, activation energy for the reaction is 280.53 kJ mol^{-1}.

18. For a parallel reaction, the concentraton of A as a function of time is given by :

$$[A](t) = [A]_0\, e^{-(k_1 + k_2)t}$$

The concentration of B and C will be

$$[B](t) = [A]_0\,(1 - e^{-k_1t})$$

$$[C](t) = [A]_0\,(1 - e^{-k_2t})$$

For the first order parallel reactions starting with 1 M of A, select the correct statements.

(a) The concentration of A increases exponentially with time according to the sum of the rate constants $k_1 + k_2$.

(b) The concentration of B increases according to the rate constant k_1 and follows 1st order kinetics.

(c) The concentration of C increases according to the rate constant k_2 and follows 1st order kinetics.

(d) The sum of the rates of formation of B and C is equal to the rate of disappearance of A.

(e) The concentration of A will never zero, but will approaches to zero as time increases.

Matching Type Questions

19. Match the List I with List II.

	List I (Reactions)		List II (Unit of Rate Constant)
A.	Decomposition of ammonia on a Pt surface at a high pressure.	1.	s^{-1}
B.	Radioactive decay of isotopes (e.g. carbon-14 decay)	2.	$mol^1\ L^{-1}s^{-1}$
C.	Decomposition of Hydrogen Iodide	3.	$L^2\ mol^{-2}\ s^{-1}$
D.	Oxidation of ferrous sulphate in water.	4.	$mol^{-1}\ L\ s^{-1}$

Choose the correct answer from the options given below.

(a) A-2, B-1, C-4, D-3
(b) A-2, B-1, C-3, D-4
(c) A-1, B-2, C-4, D-3
(d) A-1, B-2, C-3, D-4

20. Match the Column I with Column II.

	Column I (Graphs for reactions)		Column II (Coordinates, x axis *vs* y axis)
A.	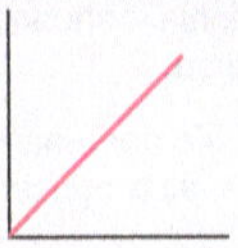	1.	time vs [conc.]
B.	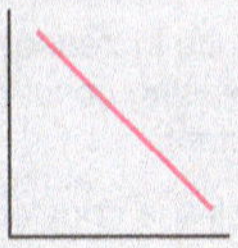	2.	$(conc)^2$ *vs* r
C.	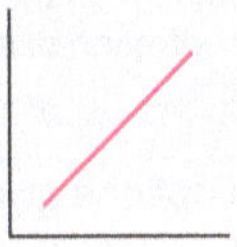	3.	conc. *vs* $t_{1/2}$
D.	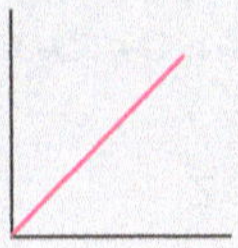	4.	$\frac{1}{conc}$ *vs* $t_{1/2}$

Choose the correct answer from the options given below.

(a) A-3, B-1, C-4, D-2
(b) A-2, B-1, C-4, D-3
(c) A-2, B-4, C-1, D-3
(d) A-3, B-2, C-3, D-1

21. Match the reaction type in List I with Rate expression or Integrated form in List II.

	List I		List II
A.	First-order	1.	Rate $= k'[A]$ (B is in excess)
B.	Second-order	2.	$\ln[A] = \ln[A]_0 - kt$
C.	Zero-order	3.	$[A] = [A]_0 - kt$
D.	Pseudo-first order	4.	$\frac{1}{[A]} = \frac{1}{[A]_0} + kt$

Choose the correct answer from the options given below.

(a) A-4, B-3, C-2, D-1
(b) A-2, B-4, C-1, D-3
(c) A-4, B-3, C-1, D-2
(d) A-2, B-4, C-3, D-1

22. Match the List I with List II.

List I (Rate Law Expression)	List II (Fraction of Reactant Converted)
A. Rate $= k$	1. $[A]_0 - \frac{[A]_t}{[A]_0}$
B. Rate $= k\,[A]$	2. $1-\frac{[A]_t}{[A]_0}$
C. Rate $= k\,[A]^2$	3. $1-e^{-kt}$
D. Rate $= k\,[A]\,[B]$ (when B is in excess)	4. $\frac{1}{[A]_0} - \frac{1}{[A]_t}$

Choose the correct answer from the options given below.

(a) A-2, B-3, C-4, D-1 (b) A-3, B-2, C-1, D-4
(c) A-2, B-3, C-1, D-4 (d) A-3, B-2, C-4, D-1

23. Match the Column I with Column II.

Column I (Half-life expression)	Column II (Characteristics of Half-life)
A. $t_{1/2} = \frac{0.693}{k}$	1. Half life is independent of the initial concentration of reactant.
B. $t_{1/2} = \frac{1}{k\,[A_0]}$	2. Half life decreases with increasing concentration of reactant.
C. $t_{1/2} = \frac{[A_0]}{2k}$	3. Half life increases with increasing concentration of reactant.
D. $t_{1/2} = \frac{0.693}{k'}$	4. Half life is constant and dependent on the concentration of excess reactant.

Choose the correct answer from the options given below.

(a) A-1, B-2, C-4, D-3 (b) A-2, B-1, C-3, D-4
(c) A-1, B-2, C-3, D-4 (d) A-2, B-1, C-4, D-3

24. The given reaction is

$$X \xrightarrow{k_1} Y \xrightarrow{k_2} Z$$

Initial concentration of X is $[X]_0$ and the reaction starts only with only X present at $t = 0$.

Match the expression of Column I with the formula of Column II.

Column I (Expression)	Column II (Formula)
A. $[X]\,(t)$	1. $\frac{k_1[X]_0}{k_2 - k_1}(e^{-k_1t} - e^{-k_2t})$
B. $[Y]\,(t)$	2. $[X]_0 e^{-k_1t}$
C. $[Z]\,(t)$	3. $k_1[X] - k_2[Y]$
D. Expression for rate of change of $[Y]$	4. $[X]_0 \frac{1-k_2e^{-k_1t} - k_1e^{-k_2t}}{k_2 - k_1}$

Choose the correct answer from the options given below.

(a) A-2, B-1, C-3, D-4 (b) A-2, B-1, C-4, D-3
(c) A-1, B-2, C-3, D-4 (d) A-1, B-2, C-4, D-3

Integer/Numerical Type Questions

25. A reaction follows the first-order kinetics and is represented by the decomposition of dinitrogen tetraoxide (N_2O_4) into nitrogen dioxide (NO_2):

$$N_2O_4 \longrightarrow 2NO_2$$

The rate constant for the reaction is $k = 5.0 \times 10^{-3}\ s^{-1}$. If at $t = 0$, the initial concentration of N_2O_4 is 0.6 M, then the time at which the molar ratio of NO_2 to N_2O_4 in the reaction mixture becomes 2.0 in hours is ....

26. In a reaction between hydrogen and iodine to form hydrogen iodide :

$$H_2(g) + I_2(g) \longrightarrow 2HI(g)$$

The rate law for the reaction is given as :

$$-\frac{\Delta[H_2]}{\Delta t} = k\,[H_2][I_2]$$

where the rate constant k is $4.5 \times 10^3\ M^{-1}\ s^{-1}$. A vessel contains hydrogen and iodine at 350 K, with the initial pressure of H_2 and I_2 as 100 mm Hg and 120 mm Hg, respectively.

The initial rate of decrease of the partial pressure of H_2 in mm Hg per second is

27. A mixture of two substances X and Y undergoes parallel first order reactions :

$X \to P$ with rate constant k_X

$Y \to P$ with rate constant k_Y

The initial concentration of X and Y are $[X_0] = 2.0$ M and $[Y_0] = 1.5$ M. The half lifes for the reactions are $t_{1/2}(X) = 5$ min and $t_{1/2}, Y = 10$ min. The concentration of P after 20 minutes. ($e^{-2.772} = 0.062$, $e^{-1.386} = 0.250$)

28. A chemical reaction is completed in 6 hours at 30°C. The temperature coefficient (Q_{10}) of the reaction is 3. If the reaction is carried out in 1 hour, approximately at what temperature must the reaction be carried out.

($\ln 6 = 1.791$, $\ln 3 = 1.099$)

29. In a certain polluted atmosphere, the steady state concentration of NO_2 is 3×10^{-8} M. The hourly production rate of NO_2 is estimated to be 6×10^{-15} M/h. If the mechanism for the destruction of NO_2 follows a second-order rate law, then the rate constant for the destruction of NO_2 is .... $10^{-6}\ m^3$/mol. s.

30. For two reactions :

$$A \to B \text{ (Reaction 1)}$$
$$B \to C \text{ (Reaction 2)}$$

Both follows first order kinetics. The rate constant of the reaction 1 doubles when temperature is raised from 290 K to 300 K. The half-life of reaction 2 at 300 K is 45 minutes. At 300 K, reaction 2 proceeds twice as fast as reaction 1. The activation energy for reaction 2 is 20 kJ/mol less than that for reaction 1. What is the ratio of rate constant $\frac{k_2(290)}{k_2(300)}$ for reaction 2 .

31. A 0.1 mL drop of a solution contains 5×10^{-8} moles of H^+. The rate constant for the disappearance of H^+ is 2×10^{-7} mol L^{-1} s^{-1}. The time taken by the H^+ concentration in the drop to decrease to $\frac{1}{10}$th of its initial value is .... (in hours)

32. For a substance undergoing decomposition, 0.005% of the substance is consumed in 2 milliseconds when the concentration is 0.01 M. In 4 milliseconds, 0.01% of the substance is consumed when the concentration is 0.02 M. The order of the reaction will be ....

33. For the reaction $A + B \rightarrow C + D$, the number of correct statements are
(a) The collision frequency of reactant molecules increases when temperature is increased.
(b) The rate constant (k) of a reaction increases with an increase in collision frequency and the steric factor.
(c) In an elementary reaction, the rate law is determined by the collision frequency and the rate constant depends on both steric factor and activation energy.
(d) The reaction rate is directly proportional to the number of collisions, but the steric factor has no effect on the rate constant.

34. Consider the following reaction,

$$NH_4Cl + NaNO_2 \xrightarrow{\text{Acidic medium}} N_2 + 2H_2O + NaCl$$

which follows the mechanism given below

$$NaNO_2 + HCl \underset{-k_1}{\overset{k_1}{\rightleftharpoons}} HNO_2 + NaCl \quad \text{(fast equilibrium)}$$

$$NH_4^+ + HNO_2 \xrightarrow{k_2} [NH_3 \cdot HNO_2]$$

$$\longrightarrow N_2 + H_2O \text{ (slow reaction)}$$

$$NH_4Cl + NaNO_2 + HCl \xrightarrow{k_3} N_2 + 2H_2O + NaCl$$

(fast reaction)

The order of reaction is ....

Paragraph of Two Questions Each

Paragraph 1

Consider the following parallel reaction

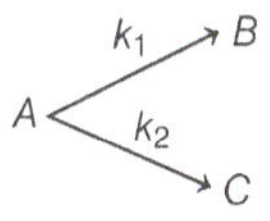

60% decomposition of A takes place in 20 min, at that time amount of B and C was 75% and 25%.

35. k_1 is related to k_2 as
(a) $k_1 = k_2$
(b) $k_2 = 3k_1$
(c) $k_1 = 3k_2$
(d) $k_1 = 2k_2$

36. Rate constant k_1 is
(a) 0.03435 min^{-1}
(b) 0.01145 min^{-1}
(c) 0.01717 min^{-1}
(d) 0.103 min^{-1}

Paragraph 2

For the displacement reaction,

$$[Co(NH_3)_5Cl]^{2+}(aq.) + H_2O(l) \longrightarrow [Co(NH_3)_5H_2O]^{3+} + Cl^-(aq.)$$

The rate constant is given by

$$\log_{10} k\,(min^{-1}) = \frac{-11067K}{T} + 31.330$$

37. Rate constant at 25°C is ....

38. Energy of activation of this reaction is ....

Paragraph 3

A reaction between substances A and B are represented as :

$$A + B \longrightarrow C$$

Observations on the rate of this reaction are obtained as :

Initial concentration $[A]_0$ M	$[B]_0$ M	Duration of experiment Δt / (h)	Final concentration $[A]_f$ M
0.1	1.0	0.50	0.0975
0.1	2.0	0.50	0.0900
0.05	1.0	2.00	0.0450

39. The sum of order of the reaction wrt A and B is ....

40. Rate constant of the overall reaction is .... M^2 h^{-1}.

Paragraph 4

The reaction, $I^-(aq.) + OCl^-(aq.) \rightarrow IO^-(aq.) + Cl^-(aq.)$ is believed to proceed through the following three-step mechanism:

Step I $OCl^- + H_2O \underset{k_{-1}}{\overset{k_1}{\rightleftharpoons}} HOCl + OH^-$; (Fast equilibrium)

Step II $I^- + HOCl \overset{k_2}{\rightleftharpoons} HOI + Cl^-$; (Slow equilibrum)

Step III $HOI + OH^- \overset{k_3}{\rightleftharpoons} H_2O + IO^-$; (Fast equilibrium)

41. Identify the false statement,
(a) The molecularity of each step is 2.
(b) The limiting step is II.
(c) HOCl is only the reaction intermediate.
(d) The reaction is a complex reaction.

42. What is the rate equation of the reaction?
(a) $r = \left(\frac{k_1 k_2}{k_{-1}}\right) \frac{[I^-][OCl^-]}{[OH^-]}$
(b) $r = k_2[I^-][HOCl]$
(c) $r = \left(\frac{k_{-1} k_1}{k_2}\right) \frac{[I^-][OCl^-]}{[OH^-]}$
(d) $r = k_2[HOI][Cl^-]$

Species Selection (With 5 Species)

43. The number of graphs showing the second order reaction is/are

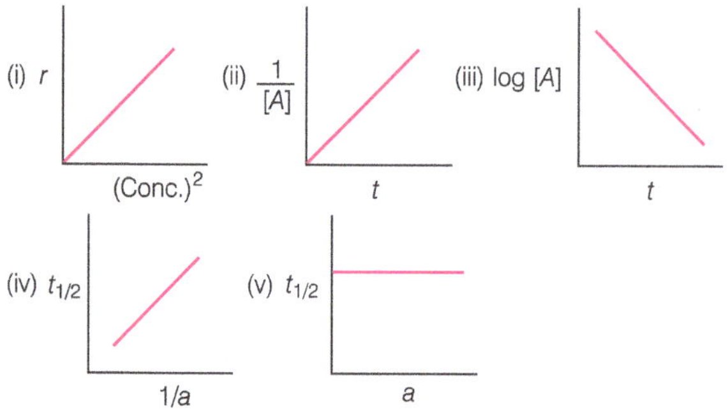

(a) 2 (b) 4 (c) 3 (d) 5

44. The number of reaction that corresponds to zero order reaction is/are ....

(i) H_2C—CH_2 (cyclopropane, ring CH_2) $\longrightarrow CH_3—CH{=}CH_2$

(ii) $2N_2O(g) \xrightarrow[\text{High pressure}]{\text{Hot Pt}} 2N_2(g) + O_2(g)$

(iii) $H_2(g) + Cl_2(g) \xrightarrow{h\nu} 2HCl(g)$

(iv) $CH_3COOC_2H_5(l) + OH^{\ominus}(aq) \longrightarrow CH_3COO^-(aq) + C_2H_5OH(l)$

(v) $2HI(g) \longrightarrow H_2(g) + I_2(g)$

(a) 1 (b) 2 (c) 3 (d) 4

45. The number of equations that represents the Arrhenius equation is/are

(i) $\log \frac{k_2}{k_1} = \frac{E_a}{2.303R}\left[\frac{T_2 - T_1}{T_1T_2}\right]$

(ii) $\frac{d \ln K}{dT} = \frac{E_a}{RT^2}$

(iii) $\log K - \log A - \frac{E_a}{RT}$

(iv) $k = Ae^{-E_a/RT}$

(v) $k = pZe^{-E_a/RT}$

(a) 5 (b) 4 (c) 3 (d) 2

Species Selection (with 7 Species)

46. The number of reactions that can be studied by the Isolation method are

(i) $C_{12}H_{12}O_{11} + H_2O \xrightarrow{H^+} C_6H_{12}O_6 + C_6H_{12}O_6$

(ii) $CH_3COCH_3 + I_2 \longrightarrow CH_3COCH_2I + HI$

(iii) $CH_3COOC_2H_5 + H_2O \longrightarrow CH_3COOH + C_2H_5OH$

(iv) $CH_3COOCH_3 + NaOH \longrightarrow CH_3COONa + CH_3OH$

(v) $HCl + NaOH \longrightarrow NaCl + H_2O$

(vi) $2H_2O_2 \longrightarrow 2H_2O + O_2$

(vii) $Br_2 + CH_3COCH_3 \longrightarrow CH_3COCH_2Br + HBr$

(a) 5 (b) 4 (c) 3 (d) 2

47. The number of equations which shows temperatures range from 190 K to 300 K in the given Arrhenius equation are

(i) $0.489 = 1 - \frac{800}{8.314 \times T}$

(ii) $0.508 = 2 - \frac{1000}{8.314 \times T}$

(iii) $0.549 = 1 - \frac{1100}{8.314 \times T}$

(iv) $0.508 = 2 - \frac{1100}{8.314 \times T}$

(v) $0.457 = 1 - \frac{1000}{8.314 \times T}$

(vi) $0.477 = 1 - \frac{1000}{8.314 \times T}$

(vii) $0.477 = 1 - \frac{1150}{8.314 \times T}$

(a) 7 (b) 4 (c) 5 (d) 6

48. The number of expressions that represents the first order reactions are

(i) $\log [A] = \log [A]_0 - \frac{k \cdot t}{2.303}$ (ii) $t_{1/2} = \frac{0.693}{k}$

(iii) $[A] = [A]_0 e^{-kt}$ (iv) $t_{1/2} = \frac{1}{k[A]_0}$

(v) $k = \frac{1}{t}\left[\frac{1}{[A]} - \frac{1}{[A]_0}\right]$ (vi) $t_{1/2} = \frac{[A]_0}{2k}$

(vii) $k = \frac{[A]_0 - [A]}{t}$

(a) 3 (b) 4 (c) 5 (d) 7

49. Consider the graph for the reaction $A \longrightarrow P$, where the mechanism involves several kinetic steps:

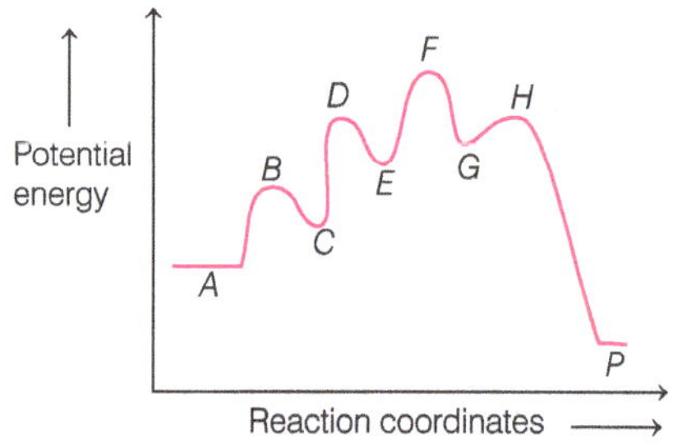

Among the species B, C, D, E, F, G, H, the number of species which are intermediates are

(a) 2 (b) 3 (c) 4 (d) 5

50. The number of equations related to first order are ....

(i) $T_{50} = t_{1/2} = 0.693 \times T_{av}$

(ii) $T_{av} = 1.44T_{50}$

(iii) $T_{75} = 1.5 \times T_{50}$

(iv) $T_{75} > T_{av} < T_{50}$

(v) $T_{av} = 2.44T_{50}$

(vi) $T_{50} = 1.5 \times T_{75}$

(vii) $T_{75} > T_{av} > T_{50}$

(a) 3 (b) 4 (c) 5 (d) 6

Check Through PYQs

Element 1 Rate of Reaction and Factor Affecting Rate of Reaction

1. In dilute aqueous H_2SO_4, the complex diaquadioxalatoferrate (II) is oxidised by MnO_4^-. For this reaction, the ratio of the rate of change of $[H^+]$ to the rate of change of $[MnO_4^-]$ is .... *2015 Adv.*

Element 2 Rate Law, Order, Molecularity and Half-Life Period

2. Consider the following reaction,

$$2H_2(g) + 2NO(g) \longrightarrow N_2(g) + 2H_2O(g)$$

which follows the mechanism given below

$$2NO(g) \underset{k_{-1}}{\overset{k_1}{\rightleftharpoons}} N_2O_2(g) \text{ (Fast equilibrium)}$$

$$N_2O_2(g) + H_2(g) \xrightarrow{k_2} N_2O(g) + H_2O(g) \text{ (Slow reaction)}$$

$$N_2O(g) + H_2(g) \xrightarrow{k_3} N_2(g) + H_2O(g) \text{ (Fast reaction)}$$

The order of the reaction is .... *JEE Adv. 2024*

3. A sample initially contains only U-238 isotope of uranium. With time, some of the U-238 radioactively decays into Pb-206 while the rest of it remains undisintegrated.
When the age of the sample is $P \times 10^8$ years, the ratio of mass of Pb-206 to that of U-238 in the sample is found to be 7. The value of P is ....
[Given: Half-life of U-238 is 4.5×10^9 years; $\log_e 2 = 0.693$] *2024, Adv.*

4. The plot of $\log k_f$ *versus* $1/T$ for a reversible reaction $A(g) \rightleftharpoons P(g)$ is shown.

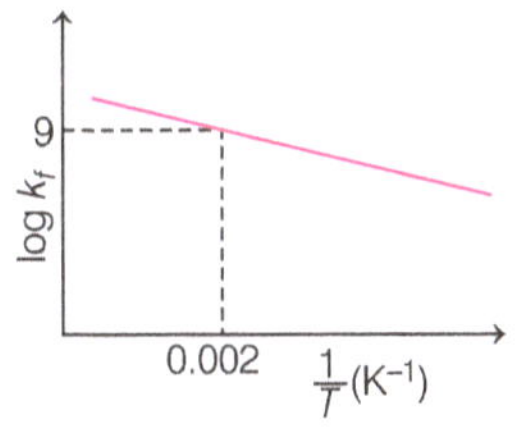

Pre-exponential factors for the forward and backward reactions are $10^{15}s^{-1}$ and $10^{11}s^{-1}$, respectively. If the value of $\log K$ for the reaction at 500 K is 6, the value of $|\log k_b|$ at 250 K is ....
[K = equilibrium constant of the reaction
k_f = rate constant of forward reaction
k_b = rate constant of backward reaction] *2023 Adv.*

5. Match the rate expressions in List-I for the decomposition of X with the corresponding profiles provided in List-II. X_s and k are constants having appropriate units. *2022 Adv.*

	List-I		List-II
(I)	rate $= \frac{k[X]}{X_s + [X]}$ Under all possible initial concentrations of X.	(P)	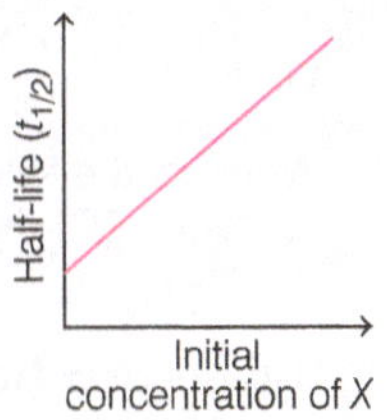
(II)	rate $= \frac{k[X]}{X_s + [X]}$, where initial concentrations of X are much less than X_s.	(Q)	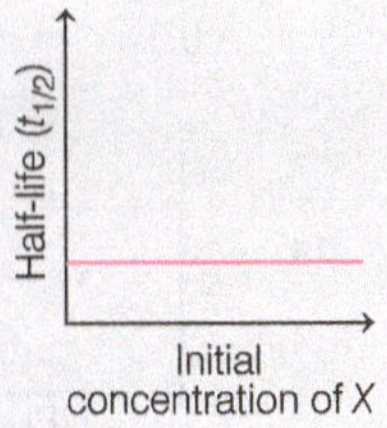
(III)	rate $= \frac{k[X]}{X_s + [X]}$, where initial concentrations of X are much higher than X_s.	(R)	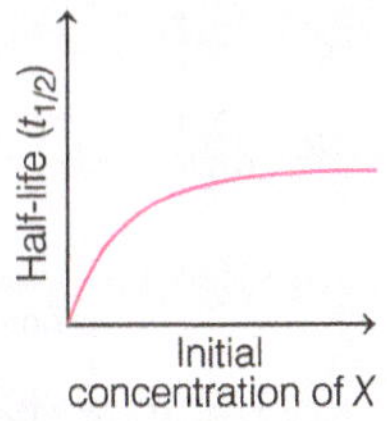
(IV)	rate $= \frac{k[X]^2}{X_s + [X]}$, where initial concentration of X is much higher than X_s.	(S)	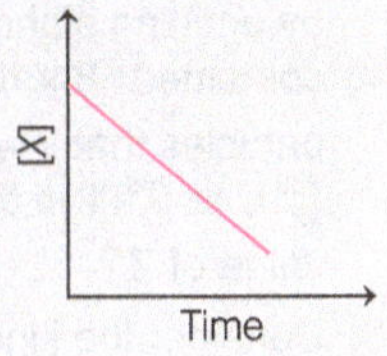
		(T)	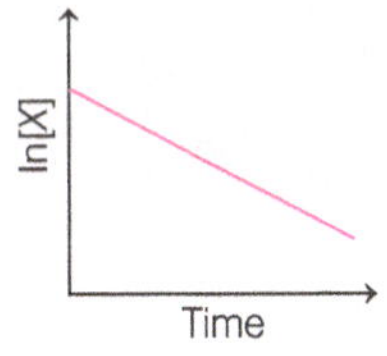

(a) I → P; II → Q; III → S; IV → T
(b) I → R; II → S; III → S; IV → T
(c) I → P; II → Q; III → Q; IV → R
(d) I → R; II → S; III → Q; IV → R

6. For the following reaction, $2X + Y \xrightarrow{k} P$
the rate of reaction is $\frac{d[P]}{dt} = k[X]$. Two moles of X are mixed with one mole of Y to make 1.0 L of solution. At 50 s, 0.5 mole of Y is left in the reaction mixture. The correct statement(s) about the reaction is(are) (Use $\ln 2 = 0.693$) *2021 Adv.*
(a) the rate constant k, of the reaction is $13.86 \times 10^{-4} s^{-1}$.
(b) half-life of X is 50 s.
(c) at 50 s, $-\frac{d[X]}{dt} = 13.86 \times 10^{-3} \text{mol L}^{-1}\text{s}^{-1}$.
(d) at 100 s, $-\frac{d[Y]}{dt} = 3.46 \times 10^{-3} \text{mol L}^{-1}\text{s}^{-1}$.

7. Which of the following plots is(are) correct for the given reaction? ($[P]_0$ is the initial concentration of P) *2020 Adv.*

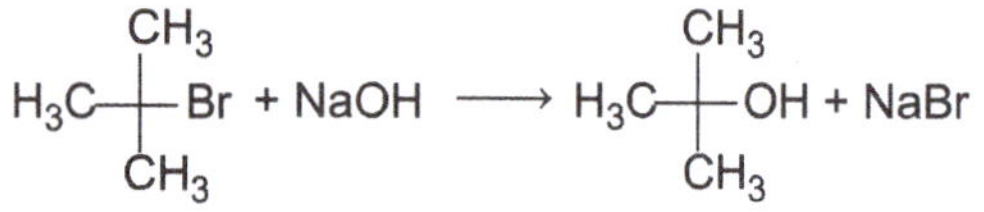

(P) (Q)

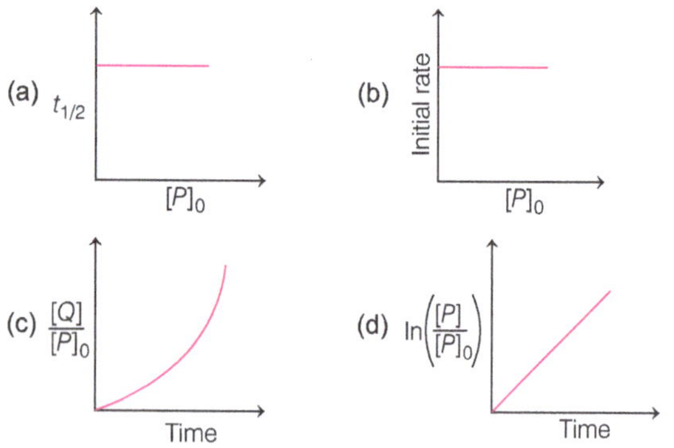

8. $^{238}_{92}U$ is known to undergo radioactive decay to form $^{206}_{82}Pb$ by emitting alpha and beta particles. A rock initially contained 68×10^{-6} g of $^{238}_{92}U$. If the number of alpha particles that it would emit during its radioactive decay of $^{238}_{92}U$ to $^{206}_{82}Pb$ in three half-lives is $Z \times 10^{18}$, then what is the value of Z? *2020 Adv.*

9. Consider the kinetic data given in the following table for the reaction $A + B + C \longrightarrow$ Product

Exp. No.	[A] (mol dm^{-3})	[B] (mol dm^{-3})	[C] (mol dm^{-3})	Rate of reaction (mol dm^{-3}s^{-1})
1	0.2	0.1	0.1	6.0×10^{-5}
2	0.2	0.2	0.1	6.0×10^{-5}
3	0.2	0.1	0.2	12×10^{-4}
4	0.3	0.1	0.1	9.0×10^{-5}

The rate of the reaction for $[A] = 0.15 \text{ mol dm}^{-3}$, $[B] = 0.25 \text{ mol dm}^{-3}$ and $[C] = 0.15 \text{ mol dm}^{-3}$ is found to be $Y \times 10^{-5} \text{ mol dm}^{-3}\text{s}^{-1}$. The value of Y is .... *2019 Adv.*

10. For a first order reaction, $A(g) \longrightarrow 2B(g) + C(g)$ at constant volume and 300 K, the total pressure at the beginning ($t = 0$) and at time t are p_0 and p_t, respectively. Initially, only A is present with concentration $[A]_0$, and $t_{1/3}$ is the time required for the partial pressure of A to reach 1/3rd of its initial value. The correct option(s) is (are) (Assume that all these gases behave as ideal gases) *2018 Adv.*

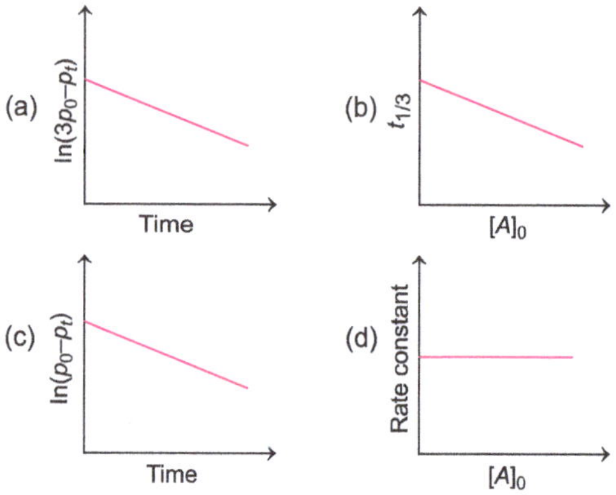

Element 3 Arrhenius Theory, Activation Energy, Collision and Related Theories

11. Consider the following reversible reaction,
$$A(g) + B(g) \rightleftharpoons AB(g)$$
The activation energy of the backward reaction exceeds that of the forward reaction by $2RT$ (in J mol^{-1}). If the pre-exponential factor of the forward reaction is 4 times that of the reverse reaction, the absolute value of $\Delta G°$ (in J mol^{-1}) for the reaction at 300 K is ....
(Given; $\ln(2) = 0.7$ $RT = 2500$ J mol^{-1} at 300 K and G is the Gibbs energy) *2018 Adv.*

12. In a bimolecular reaction, the steric factor P was experimentally determined to be 4.5. the correct option(s) among the following is(are) *2017 Adv.*
(a) the activation energy of the reaction is unaffected by the value of the steric factor
(b) experimentally determined value of frequency factor is higher than that predicted by Arrhenius equation
(c) the value of frequency factor predicted by Arrhenius equation is higher than that determined experimentally
(d) since $P = 4.5$, the reaction will not proceed unless an effective catalyst is used

13. According to the Arrhenius equation, *2016 Adv.*
(a) a high activation energy usually implies a fast reaction
(b) rate constant increases with increase in temperature. This is due to a greater number of collisions whose energy exceeds the activation energy
(c) higher the magnitude of activation energy, stronger is the temperature dependence of the rate constant
(d) the pre-exponential factor is a measure of the rate at which collisions occur, irrespective of their energy

HINTS & Solutions

Solutions : Competency Enhancer

1.1 ***(8)*** The equation is

$$5[Co(H_2O)_6]^{2+} + MnO_4^- + 8H^+ \longrightarrow 5[Co(H_2O)_6]^{3+} + Mn^{2+} + 4H_2O$$

$$\frac{-d\,[MnO_4^-]}{dt} = \frac{1}{8}\frac{d[H^+]}{dt} = \frac{1}{5}\cdot\frac{d[Co^{3+}]}{dt}$$

For every 1 mole of MnO_4^- consumed 8 moles of H^+ are also consumed. Therefore, the rate of change of $[H^+]$ is 8 times the rate of change of $[MnO_4^-]$.

2.1 ***(419)*** Rate $= k[M]^a[N]^b[O]^c$

$$\frac{(\text{Rate})_1}{(\text{Rate})_2} = \frac{[2.4]^a[2.2]^b[2.2]^c}{[2.4]^a[2.4]^b[2.2]^c}$$

$$\frac{4\times10^{-6}}{4\times10^{-6}} = (0.91)^b$$

$$1^0 \approx (1)^b$$

$$b = 0$$

$$\frac{(\text{Rate})_1}{(\text{Rate})_3} = \frac{(2.4)^a(2.2)^b(2.2)^c}{(2.4)^a(2.2)^b(4.4)^c}$$

$$\frac{4\times10^{-6}}{8\times10^{-6}} = (0.5)^c$$

$$0.5 = (0.5)^c$$

$$c = 1$$

$$\frac{(\text{Rate})_1}{(\text{Rate}_4} = \frac{(2.4)^a(2.2)^b(2.2)^c}{(3.5)^a(2.2)^b(2.2)^c}$$

$$\frac{(4\times10^{-6})}{(6\times10^{-6})} = \frac{(2.4)^a}{(3.5)^a}$$

$$0.66 \approx (0.68)^a$$

$$(0.6)^1 = (0.6)^a$$

$$a = 1$$

So, rate $= k[M]^1[O]^1$

From exp. Ist,

$$\text{Rate} = 4\times10^{-6}\ \text{mol dm}^{-3}\ \text{s}^{-1}$$

$$4\times10^{-6} = k[2.4][2.2]$$

$$k = 0.76\times10^{-6}$$

$$k = 7.6\times10^{-7}$$

Given, $[M] = 2.3\ \text{mol dm}^{-3}$

$[N] = 1.2\ \text{mol dm}^{-3}$

$[O] = 2.4\ \text{mol dm}^{-3}$

$\therefore$ Rate $= 7.6\times10^{-7}\times[2.3]^1[1.2]^0[2.4]^1$

$= 41.9\times10^{-7}$

Rate $= 419\times10^{-8}\ \text{mol dm}^{-3}\ \text{s}^{-1}$

Thus, $Z = 419$

2.2 ***(9)*** $4PH_3(g) \longrightarrow P_4(g) + 6H_2(g)$

$$PH_3(g) \longrightarrow \frac{1}{4}P_4(g) + \frac{3}{2}H_2(g)$$

Initial	p_0	0	0
Final	$p_0 - p_i$	$\frac{p_i}{4}$	$\frac{3}{2}p_i$

$$p_t = (p_0 - p_i) + \frac{p_i}{4} + \frac{3}{2}p_i$$

$$p_t = p_0 + \frac{3}{4}p_i$$

a. When $t = 0$, $p_0 = 262.4$

$t = 60$, $p_{60} = 272.9$

$$p_{60} = p_0 + \frac{3}{4}p_i = 272.9$$

$$\frac{3}{4}p_i = 272.9 - 262.4$$

$$p_i = \frac{4}{3}\times10.5 = 14$$

$$k = \frac{2.303}{60}\log\frac{262.4}{262.4-14}$$

$$= \frac{2.303}{60}\times\log(1.056) = 0.0009 = 9\times10^{-4}$$

2.3 ***(b, c)*** $N_2 + 3H_2 \rightleftharpoons 2NH_3$

$$\left(\frac{dx}{dt}\right)_f = k_f[N_2][H_2]^3$$

and

$$\left(\frac{dx}{dt}\right)_b = k_b[NH_3]^2$$

$$\left(\frac{dx}{dt}\right)_{net} = k_f[N_2][H_2]^3 - k_b[NH_3]^2$$

Given, net value,

$$\left(\frac{dx}{dt}\right)_{net} = 2.5\times10^{-2}\,[N_2][H_2]^3 - 8.0\times10^{-3}\,[NH_3]^2$$

Thus, $k_f = 2.5\times10^{-2}$

$k_b = 8.0\times10^{-3}$

$\because$ $k_f > k_b$, thus, forward reaction is faster than backward reaction.

3.1 ***(d)*** $\log k = 8 - \dfrac{4000}{T}$ ...(i)

According to Arrhenius equation,

$$\log k = \log A - \frac{E_a}{2.303RT} \quad \text{...(ii)}$$

Comparing Eqs. (i) and (ii) and solving, we get

$$\log A = 8 \Rightarrow A = 10^8\ \text{s}^{-1}$$

$$\frac{E_a}{2.303R} = 4000 \Rightarrow E_a \approx 76.59\ \text{kJ/mol}$$

Elemental Practice 9.1

1. ***(d)*** The colour of a reactant is related to its electronic structure and the wavelength of light it absorbs or reflects. It does not directly impact the rate of a reaction.

2. ***(d)*** Rate $= k[A]^1[B]^2$

   When concentrations are halved

   New concentration of $A = \frac{1}{2}[A]$

   New concentration of $B = \frac{1}{2}[B]$

   $$\text{New rate} = k\left(\frac{1}{2}[A]\right)^1\left(\frac{1}{4}[B]^2\right)$$
   $$= k\left(\frac{1}{2}[A]\right)^1\left(\frac{1}{4}[B]^2\right)$$
   $$= \frac{1}{2}\times\frac{1}{4} = \frac{1}{8}k[A][B]^2$$

3. ***(a)*** $$\text{Rate} = -\frac{1}{2}\frac{d[A]}{dt} = \frac{-d[B]}{dt} = \frac{1}{2}\frac{d[C]}{dt}$$
   $$\frac{-1}{2}\frac{d[A]}{dt} = \frac{1}{2}\frac{d[C]}{dt}$$
   $$\frac{-d[A]}{dt} = \frac{d[C]}{dt} = 0.05\text{ M/s}$$

4. ***(d)*** The rate constant does not depend on the concentration of reactants, it is specific to a given reaction at a certain temperature.

5. ***(a)*** In a sequential reaction, Y is an intermediate there is no accumulation.

   The rate of disappearance of Y = Rate of appearance of Z

   Thus, the rate of appearance of $Y = 0.04$ M/s

6. ***(b)*** A-2, B-4, C-3, D-1

7. ***(a)*** Statement (a) is correct, while Statement (b), (c) and (d) are incorrect.
   - **Dilution may have varying effects** Zero-order reactions remain unaffected by dilution. In reactions limited by diffusion, dilution might increase the rate by reducing the effects of crowding and improving the diffusion of reactants.
   - If the inert gas is added at constant pressure, the total volume of the system increases, which is turn causes the reactants to decrease reducing the reaction rate. In reactions involving gases at very high pressure the presence of inert gas might affect molecular collision or diffusion rates.
   - Polar solvents stabilise charged intermediates and can influence the rate of a reaction.

8. ***(a)*** Initial conditions

   $$[A] = [A]_0$$
   $$[B] = 0 \text{ (no } B \text{ initially)}$$

   when reaction reaches completion.

   All of A gets converted to B and no A remains.

   According to conservation of mass,

   total number of molecules remain constant

   $$\therefore \quad [B]_{\text{final}} = [A]_0$$

9. ***(c)*** Rate constant of a reaction usually depends on temperature. Most of the chemical reactions dependent on molecular collisions, which increases as temperature increases.

10. ***(a)*** In terms of partial pressure, the units of rate equation is given by atm s^{-1}.

11. ***(b)*** $$|\Delta A| = |A|_{\text{initial}} - |A|_{\text{final}}$$
    $$= 0.6\text{ M} - 0.2\text{ M} = 0.4\text{ M}$$
    $$A_t = 10\text{ min} = 10\times 60 = 600\text{ sec}$$
    $$\text{Rate} = \frac{-0.4\text{ M}}{600\text{ s}} = 6.7\times10^{-4}\text{ M/s}$$

12. ***(c)*** Concentration of reactant decreases exponentially w.r.t. time.

13. ***(a)*** Both (A) and (R) are true and (R) is the correct explanation of (A).

14. ***(b)*** The reaction is endothermic. In general reactions that exhibit increased rates with temperature are endothermic because they require heat to proceed.

15. ***(b)*** Taking the derivative of concentration wtih respect to time

    $$\text{Rate} = \frac{d[C]}{dt} \text{ at time } t$$

16. ***(c)*** As the concentration of reactant decreases, the rate of reaction decreases at a given temperature.

17. ***(c)*** $$\frac{-d[N_2]}{dt} = -\frac{1}{3}\frac{d[H_2]}{dt} = \frac{1}{2}\frac{d[NH_3]}{dt}$$
    $$-\frac{1}{3}\frac{d[H_2]}{dt} = \frac{1}{2}\frac{d[NH_3]}{dt}$$
    $$-\frac{d[H_2]}{dt} = \frac{3}{2}\times 3.5\times10^{-4}$$
    $$= 5.25\times10^{-4}\text{ mol L}^{-1}\text{ s}^{-1}$$

18. ***(a)*** Average rate of formation of B : from $t = 0$ to $t = 10$ min

    $$\Delta B = [B]_{10} - [B]_0 = 0.4 - 0 = 0.4\text{ M}$$

    Average rate of formation of $B = \frac{\Delta[B]}{\Delta t} = \frac{0.4}{10} = 0.04$ M/min

19. ***(b, c, d)*** The average rate can sometimes be lower than the instantaneous rate, depending on the time interval chosen.

20. ***(a,b,d)*** $$\frac{-d[A]}{2\,dt} = \frac{-d[B]}{dt} = \frac{d[C]}{dt}$$

    Rate of disappearance of B, $\frac{-d[B]}{dt} = 0.1\text{ mol}\cdot\text{L}^{-1}\text{s}^{-1}$

    Rate of formation of C, $\frac{d[C]}{dt} = 0.1\text{ mol L}^{-1}\text{s}^{-1}$

    Rate of formation of C is half of rate of disappearance of A.

21. ***(b, d)*** The average rate of reaction cannot be negative because it is defined as the change in concentration of a reactant or product over a time interval which is always positive.

The rate of a reaction can be significantly affected by the presence of catalyst, which lower the activation energy and increases the reaction rate.

22. ***(a, c, d)*** Rate, $r = \frac{-d[A]}{dt} = -\frac{1}{2}\frac{d[B]}{dt} = \frac{d[C]}{dt}$

So, (b) is incorrect as the rate of appearance of C is half the rate of disappearance of B.

23. ***(b, c, d)*** Rate of a chemical reaction depends on the concentration of reactant not products.

24. ***(120)*** Average rate $= \frac{\Delta[B]}{\Delta t} = \frac{0.4\,\text{mol L}^{-1}}{20\,\text{min}} = \frac{0.4\,\text{mol L}^{-1}}{\frac{20\,\text{h}}{60}}$

$$= 1.20\,\text{mol L}^{-1}\,\text{h}^{-1}$$
$$= 120 \times 10^{-2}\,\text{mol L}^{-1}\,\text{h}^{-1}$$

25. ***(4)*** $CH_4(g) + Cl_2(g) \xrightarrow{h\nu} CH_3Cl(g) + HCl(g)$

This is not an elementary reaction. It is an example of chain reaction involving radical mechanisms, thus occuring through multiple steps.

26. ***(3)*** The rate of formation of product C is half to the rate of disappearance of reactant A

$$\frac{-d[A]}{2\,dt} = \frac{d[C]}{dt}$$

So, IV is incorrect.

27. ***(13)*** Rate of formation of $C_2H_6 = 0.002$ kg/h

Molar mass of $C_2H_6 = 30.07$ g/mol

Moles of $C_2H_6 = \frac{\text{Rate of formation of } C_2H_6}{\text{Molar mass of } C_2H_6}$

$$= \frac{0.002\,\text{kg/h}}{30.07\,\text{g/mol}} \times 1000\,\text{g/kg}$$
$$\approx 0.0665\,\text{mol/h}$$

1 mole of C_2H_6 is produced from 1 mole of H_2

Moles of H_2 consumed = moles of C_2H_6 formed

$$= 0.0665\,\text{mol/h}$$

Mass of $H_2 = 0.0665\,\text{mol/h} \times 2.02\,\text{g/mol}$

$$= 0.1343\,\text{g/h}$$
$$= 0.0001343\,\text{kg/h}$$
$$= 13.43 \times 10^{-5}\,\text{kg/h}$$
$$\approx 13 \times 10^{-5}\,\text{kg/h}$$

28. ***(4)*** $2H_2O_2 \longrightarrow 2H_2O + O_2$

Rate of formation of $O_2 = \left(\frac{68}{32\,\text{g mol}^{-1}}\right)\text{min}^{-1}$

$$= 2.125\,\text{mol min}^{-1}$$

Rate of formation of H_2O

$$= 2 \times \text{Rate of formation of } O_2$$
$$= 2 \times 2.125\,\text{mol min}^{-1}$$
$$= 4.25\,\text{mol min}^{-1} \approx 4\,\text{mol min}^{-1}$$

Elemental Practice 9.2

1. ***(b)*** Doubling the concentration of $[A]$ causes the rate to increase by factor 4, this suggests that the reaction is 2nd order with respect to A.

Doubling the concentration of $[B]$ increase the rate by factor 2, this means reaction is 1st order with respect to B.

So, $\text{Rate} = k[A]^2[B]$

2. ***(c)*** For a 1st order reaction, the integrated rate law:

$$\ln[X] = -kt + \ln[X_0]$$

This equation is in the form of a straight line

$$y = mx + c$$
$$m\,(\text{slope}) = -k$$

3. ***(a)*** Both (A) and (R) are true and (R) is the correct explanation of (A).

4. ***(a)*** For $-\frac{d[A]}{dt} = k[A]^n$ and $n \neq 1$

$$[A]^{1-n} = [A]_0^{1-n} - k(1-n)\cdot t$$

For the given graph, $1 - n = -3 \Rightarrow n = 4$

and $-k(1-n) = \tan 45° \Rightarrow k(4-1) = 1$

$\therefore$ $k = \frac{1}{3}\,M^{-3}\,\text{min}^{-1}$

The rate of the reaction,

$$r_{\text{reaction}} = -\frac{1}{3}\frac{d[A]}{dt} = \frac{1}{3}k\cdot[A]^4$$
$$= \frac{1}{3} \times \frac{1}{3} \times (0.3)^4 = 9 \times 10^{-4}\,\text{M min}^{-1}$$

5. ***(b)*** For 1st order:

$$k = \frac{0.693}{t_{1/2}} = \frac{0.693}{20} = 0.03465\,\text{day}^{-1}$$

If 87.5% decays, then 12.5% remains

$$[A]_t = 0.125\,[A]_0$$
$$\ln\frac{[A]_0}{[A]_t} = kt$$
$$\ln\frac{[A]_0}{0.125\,[A]_0} = 0.03465 \times t$$
$$2.079 = 0.03465 \times t$$
$$t \approx 60\text{ days}$$

6. ***(a)*** $t_{1/2} \propto \frac{1}{a^{n-1}}$, For $n = 0$

$$t_{1/2} \propto \frac{1}{a^{-1}}$$

$\Rightarrow$ $t_{1/2} \propto a$

7. ***(c)*** Statement I is correct but Statement II is incorrect.

The correct form of Statement II is:

The order of a reaction is determined experimentally and can be different from stoichiometric coefficients in balanaced equation, especially in complex reactions.

8. ***(a)*** Compare experiment 1 and 2, to determine order w.r.t. *B*.

$$\frac{\text{Rate}_2}{\text{Rate}_1} = \frac{k[A_2]^m[B_2]^n}{k[A_1]^m[B_1]^n} = \frac{0.04}{0.01} = 4$$

$$\Rightarrow \quad 4 = \left(\frac{0.2}{0.1}\right)^n \Rightarrow n = 2$$

Compare experiment 1 and 3, to determine order w.r.t. *A*.

$$\frac{\text{Rate}_3}{\text{Rate}_1} = \frac{k[A_3]^m[B_3]^n}{k[A_1]^m[B_1]^n} = \frac{0.04}{0.01} = 4$$

$$4 = \left(\frac{0.2}{0.1}\right)^m \Rightarrow m = 2$$

The rate law can be expressed as:

$$\text{Rate} = k[A]^2[B]^2$$

9. ***(d)*** Rate constant $(k) = 0.5\,M^{-1}s^{-1}$ (second order reaction) To convert second order rate law into a pseudo first order, the concentration of reactant *B* will be effectively constant (concentration of *B* is much greater than *A*)

$$k' = k[B]_0$$
$$= (0.5\,M^{-1}s^{-1}) \times (1.0\,M)$$
$$= 0.5\,s^{-1}$$

10. ***(c)*** Molecularity is defined only for elementary reaction. The given reaction is a two step reaction with molecularity 1 and 2 respectively.

11. ***(b)*** The concentration of one reactant (water) is much larger than other. It's concentration of water remains constant. Rate of reaction is $r \propto [C_{12}H_{22}O_{11}]$. It is an example of pseudo first order reaction.

12. ***(b)*** Statement B and C are correct while A and B are incorrect. Its correct form are as follows:

The order of a reaction is not simply the sum of the orders from individual steps. It depends on the rate determining step and rate law. Overall molecularity is not defined for multistep reactions. Instead, it is ony applicable to individual elementary steps.

13. ***(b)***

	P	+	Q	$\longrightarrow$	R	+	S
$t = 0$	1 M		1 M		0		0
t	$(1 - x)$ M		$(1 - x)$ M		x M		x M

$$r = k[P]^{1/2}[Q]^{1/2}$$

$$\frac{dx}{dt} = k(1-x)^{1/2}(1-x)^{1/2}$$

$$= k(1-x)$$

$$\Rightarrow \quad t = \frac{1}{k}\ln\left(\frac{1}{1-x}\right)$$

$$= \frac{2.303}{2.303 \times 10^{-3}}\log\left(\frac{1}{0.01}\right) = 2000\text{ s}$$

14. ***(d)*** (A) is false but (R) is true.

In a parallel reaction, if one path has a much higher rate constant than the other, most of the reactant will follow the path with higher rate constant.

15. ***(a)*** The formula for the percentage decomposed, x is

$$x = 100\,(1 - e^{-kt})$$
$$x = 100\,(1 - e^{-(5.1 \times 10^{-3} \times 200)})$$
$$x = 100\,(1 - 0.360)$$
$$x = 64\%$$

16. ***(b)*** $\text{Rate} = k[H_2][I_2]$

When volume is doubled, the new concentration become

$$[H_2] = \frac{[H_2]_0}{2}$$

$$[I_2] = \frac{[I_2]_0}{2}$$

$$\text{New rate} = \frac{k\,[H_2]_0[I_2]_0}{4}$$

$$= \frac{1}{4}k[H_2]_0[I_2]_0 = \frac{1}{4}\text{ Initial rate}$$

17. ***(c)*** Since k_2 is greater than k_3, more of E_1 will be converted to *B* than *C*, leading to a more rapid increase in the concentration of *B* compared to *C*.

18. ***(b)*** For 2nd order reaction,

$$\frac{1}{[A]_t} - \frac{1}{[A]_0} = kt$$

$$\frac{1}{0.25} - \frac{1}{0.5} = (0.1) \times t$$

$$4 - 2 = 0.1 \times t$$

$$t = \frac{2}{0.1} = 20\text{ s}$$

19. ***(b, c, d)*** Statement (b), (c), (d) are correct. The correct form of statement (a) is

Pseudo 1st order reaction is observed in enzyme catalysed reaction when substrate concentration is higher than enzyme concentration.

20. ***(a, b, c, d)*** Statements (a), (b), (c) and (d) are true.

21. ***(b, d)*** Statements (b) and (d) are correct.

The correct form of (a) and (c) are

Zero order reaction, the plot of concentration *vs* time is a straight line but slope is $-k$.

$$[A] = [A]_0 - kt$$

A plot of concentration *vs* time for a 1st order reaction is not linear, it shows an exponential decay.

22. ***(a, b, d)*** Statements (a), (b) and (d) are correct.

The correct form of (c) is

Parallel reactions can occur both in reversible and irreversible manners.

23. ***(a, c)*** Statement (a), (c) is correct while (b), (d) is incorrect. The correct form of (b), (d) is

Reactions rate depends on $[A]^2$, making the overall reaction order 2.

$r = k[A]^2$ and does not depend on the concentration of A_2.

24. ***(333)*** Integrated rate-law for 2nd order reaction is

$$\frac{1}{[A]} - \frac{1}{[A]_0} = kt$$

$$\frac{1}{[A]} - \frac{1}{0.5} = 0.04 \times 25$$

$$\frac{1}{[A]} - 2 = 1$$

$$\frac{1}{[A]} = 3$$

$$[A] = \frac{1}{3} \approx 0.333\,\text{M}$$

$$= 333 \times 10^{-3}\,\text{M}$$

25. ***(62.5)*** Percentage yield $= \frac{k_2}{k_1 + k_2} \times 100$

$$= \frac{0.05}{0.03 + 0.05} \times 100 = 62.5\%$$

26. ***(316)*** For 2nd order reaction,

$$t_{1/2} = \frac{1}{k[A]_0}$$

Relationship two half-life and two temperature is

$$\frac{(t_{1/2})_2}{(t_{1/2})_1} = \frac{k_1}{k_2} \Rightarrow \frac{10 \times 60\,\text{s}}{30 \times 60\,\text{s}} = \frac{k_1}{k_2}$$

$$\frac{k_1}{k_2} = \frac{600}{1800} = \frac{1}{3} \Rightarrow \frac{k_2}{k_1} = 3$$

According to Arrhenius equation,

$$\ln \frac{k_2}{k_1} = \frac{E_a}{R}\left(\frac{1}{T_1} - \frac{1}{T_2}\right)$$

$$\ln 3 = \frac{50{,}000}{8.314}\left(\frac{1}{298} - \frac{1}{T_2}\right)$$

$$1.098 = 6013.9\left(\frac{1}{298} - \frac{1}{T_2}\right)$$

$$0.00018 = \frac{1}{298} - \frac{1}{T_2}$$

$$0.00018 = 0.00335 - \frac{1}{T_2}$$

$$T_2 = 315.5\,\text{K} \approx 316\,\text{K}$$

27. ***(1)***

$$A \begin{cases} \xrightarrow{k_1} 3B \\ \xrightarrow{k_2} 4C; \quad k_1 : k_2 : k_3 = 4 : 2 : 1 \\ \xrightarrow{k_3} 3D \end{cases}$$

Moles of A remaining after 90 days

$$= \frac{N_0}{2^n} = \frac{N_0}{2^{T/t_{1/2}}}$$

$$= \frac{1}{2^{90/30}} = \frac{1}{2^3} = \frac{1}{8}$$

Moles of A converted into product $= \frac{7}{8}$ mol

$$\text{Moles of } C = \frac{k_2}{k_1 + k_2 + k_3} \times \frac{7}{8} \times 4 = \frac{2}{7} \times \frac{7}{8} \times 4 = 1$$

28. ***(3602)*** $t_{1/2} = \frac{0.693}{\lambda}$

$$k_1 \equiv \lambda = \frac{0.693}{t_{1/2}} = \frac{0.693}{1.39 \times 10^{10}\,\text{yr}}$$

$$= \frac{0.693}{(1.39 \times 10^{10} \times 365 \times 24 \times 3600)\,\text{s}}$$

$$= 1.58 \times 10^{-18}\,\text{s}^{-1}$$

$$N = 6.022 \times 10^{23}\,\text{mol}^{-1} \times \frac{1\text{g}}{264\,\text{g/mol}}$$

$$= 2.28 \times 10^{21}$$

$$\frac{-dN}{dt} = \lambda N$$

$$= (1.58 \times 10^{-18}\,\text{s}^{-1})(2.28 \times 10^{21})$$

$$\approx 3.602 \times 10^3\,\text{s}^{-1} = 3602\,\text{s}^{-1}$$

29. ***(535)***

	$2A(g)$	$\longrightarrow$ $4B(g)$	$+ C(g)$	$+ D(l)$
At, $t = 0$	p_0	0	0	
At, $t = 30$ min	$(p_0 - x)$	$2x$	$\frac{x}{2}$	V.P. = 25
At, $t = 60$ min	$(p_0 - y)$	$2y$	$\frac{y}{2}$	V.P. = 25
At, $t = \infty$	0	$2p_0$	$\frac{p_0}{2}$	V.P. = 25

$$2p_0 + \frac{p_0}{2} + 25 = 625 \Rightarrow p_0 = 240$$

Also, $(p_0 - x) + 2x + \frac{x}{2} + 25 = 445 \Rightarrow x = 120$

$$\frac{1}{30} \cdot \ln \frac{p_0}{(p_0 - x)} = \frac{1}{60} \cdot \ln \frac{p_0}{(p_0 - y)}$$

$$\Rightarrow \quad 2 \ln \frac{240}{120} = \ln \frac{240}{(240 - y)}$$

$$\Rightarrow \quad \ln 2^2 = \ln \frac{240}{(240 - y)}$$

$$\Rightarrow \quad 4(240 - y) = 240$$

$$\Rightarrow \quad 4y = 720 \Rightarrow y = 180$$

$\therefore$ Pressure after 60 min $= (p_0 - y) + 2y + \frac{y}{2} + 25 = 535\,\text{mm}$

Elemental Practice 9.3

1. ***(b)*** Lower E_a means more molecules will have enough energy to surpass the activation barrier, leading to a higher reaction rate.

2. ***(c)*** Temperature coefficient $\frac{k_{410}}{k_{400}} = 3.2$

or $\quad k_{410} = 3.2 \times k_{400}$

$$k_{410} = 3.2 \times k$$

3. ***(a)*** In the plot of activation energy for an exothermic reaction activation energy of backward reaction is more than that of forward reaction i.e., $E_{ab} > E_{af}$

4. ***(b)*** The correct match is : A-2, B-4, C-1, D-3

5. ***(d)*** Statement I is incorrect but Statement II is correct.

   The correct form of Statement I is:

   A catalyst does indeed participate in the reaction, but it is not consumed in the reaction. It remains unchanged after the reaction and can be used again.

6. ***(a)*** According to Arrhenius equation,

$$k = Ae^{-Ea/RT}$$

For reaction at two different temperature:

$$\log\left(\frac{k_2}{k_1}\right) = \frac{E_a}{2.303R}\left(\frac{1}{T_1} - \frac{1}{T_2}\right)$$

$$= \frac{50 \times 10^3}{2.303 \times 8.314}\left(\frac{1}{300} - \frac{1}{310}\right)$$

$$= 0.28$$

$$\frac{k_2}{k_1} = 10^{0.28} \approx 1.91$$

$$k_2 = 1.91k_1$$

Increase in the value of rate constant $= (k_2 - k_1) = 0.91k_1$

$$\% \text{ increase} = \frac{0.91k_1}{k_1} \times 100 \approx 91\%$$

7. ***(b)*** Both (A) and (R) are true but (R) is not the correct explanation of (A).

8. ***(c)*** According to Arrhenius equation,

$$\log k = \log A - \frac{E_a}{2.303RT}$$

$$\log k_{500} = \log A - \frac{E_{a_1}}{2.303RT_1}$$

and
$$\log k_{400} = \log A - \frac{E_{a_2}}{2.303RT_2}$$

Given, $k_{500} = k_{400} \Rightarrow \log k_{500} = \log k_{400}$

or
$$\frac{E_{a_1}}{T_1} = \frac{E_{a_2}}{T_2} \Rightarrow \frac{E_{a_1}}{500} = \frac{E_{a_2}}{400}$$

$$\Rightarrow \quad \frac{E_{a_1}}{E_{a_2}} = \frac{5}{4} \qquad \ldots\text{(i)}$$

According to the given data,

$$E_{a_1} - E_{a_2} = 20 \qquad \ldots\text{(ii)}$$

∴ Substituting Eqs. (ii) in (i), we get

$$\frac{E_{a_1}}{E_{a_1} - 20} = \frac{5}{4}$$

$$\Rightarrow \quad 4E_{a_1} = 5E_{a_1} - 100$$

$$\Rightarrow \quad E_{a_1} = 100 \text{ kJ mol}^{-1}$$

and
$$E_{a_2} = 80 \text{ kJ mol}^{-1}$$

9. ***(a)*** The Arrhenius equation,

$$k = Ae^{-Ea/RT}$$

When temperature increases, the rate constant k increases because the factor $e^{-Ea/RT}$ becomes large. $E_1 < E_2$, the reaction with E_1 will experience a large relative increase in its rate constant compared to the reaction with E_2 when the temperature is raised from T_1 to T_2.

10. ***(d)***

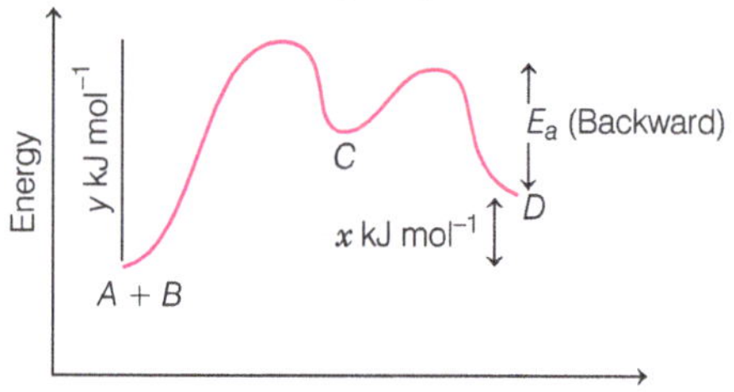

$$E_a\text{ (backward)} = E_a - \Delta H$$

$$= y - x \text{ kJ mol}^{-1}$$

11. ***(b)*** The Arrhenius equation is

$$\ln\left(\frac{k_2}{k_1}\right) = \frac{E_a}{R}\left(\frac{1}{T_1} - \frac{1}{T_2}\right)$$

$$k_2 = k_1 e^{\frac{E_a}{R}\left(\frac{1}{T_1} - \frac{1}{T_2}\right)}$$

$$k_2 = 5.0 \times 10^{-3} e^{\frac{75000}{8.314}\left(\frac{1}{298} - \frac{1}{350}\right)}$$

$$k_2 = 5.0 \times 10^{-3} e^{(4.497)}$$

$$k_2 = 0.449 \text{ s}^{-1}$$

12. ***(b)*** Despite being exothermic and having a positive entropy change, methane combustion has a high activation energy, which makes it difficult to ignite initially.

13. ***(b)*** Statement C and D are correct while A, B, E are incorrect. The correct form of A, B, E is:

    (A) The fraction of successful collisions is given by $e^{-E_a/RT}$ not A.

    (B) A is independent of E_a. A is not determined by the activation energy.

    (E) Larger A means more frequent collisions. So, the larger value of A, the large number of molecules available for the reaction.

14. ***(d)*** Autocatalysis is a phenomenon in which product formed is itself a catalyst.

$$2MnO_4^-(aq) + 6H^+(aq) + 5(COOH)_2(aq) \rightleftharpoons 2Mn^{2+}(aq) + 10CO_2(g) + 8H_2O(l)$$

15. ***(b)*** When the temperature is raised the maximum curve moves to the higher energy value and curve broadens out. The curve spreads to the right such that there is a greater proportion of molecules with higher energies.

16. ***(b)*** The steric factor (p) is a number that reflects the probability that a collision between reactant molecules will result in a successful reaction, given the proper orientation.

17. ***(a)*** Effective collision is one where the collision results in the formation of products, meaning the colliding molecules sucessfully overcome the activation energy and form new chemical bonds to generate products.

18. ***(a, c)*** Statement (a) and (c) are correct where as (b) and (d) are incorrect. The correct form of (b) and (d) is :

A reaction cannot occur if the molecules do not have the proper orientation during a collision.

The collisions in which molecule collide with sufficient kinetic energy is called threshold energy.

19. ***(c, d)*** The correct form of (c) and (d) is:

The value of E_a can be determined from the slope of plot of $\ln k$ versus $\frac{1}{T}$.

The Arrhenius equation can be used to estimate the rate of reaction at different temperatures.

20. ***(a, c)*** Statement (a) and (c) are correct while (b) and (d) are incorrect. The correct form of (b) and (d) is

(b) Both positive and negative catalysts are not consumed in the reaction.

(d) A positive catalyst does not affect the equilibrium constant. It only helps the system to reach equilibrium faster without, altering equilibrium concentrations.

21. ***(b, c, d)*** Statement (b), (c) and (d) are correct while (a) is incorrect. The correct form of (a) is:

The transition state is highly unstable and cannot be studied or isolated directly.

22. ***(a, b, d)*** Statments (a), (b) and (d) are correct while (c) is incorrect. The correct form of (c) is:

Pre-exponential factors (A) are different in this case. Even with same activaion energy different pre-exponential values (A) means different rate constants (k) values.

23. ***(0.912)*** The Arrhenius equation is given by

$$k = Ae^{-E_a/RT}$$

$$\frac{k_2}{k_1} = \frac{Ae^{-E_a/RT_2}}{Ae^{-E_a/RT_1}} = e^{\frac{-E_a}{R}\left(\frac{1}{T_2}-\frac{1}{T_1}\right)}$$

$$\frac{k_2}{k_1} = e^{-9021(-0.00048)} \Rightarrow \frac{k_2}{k_1} = e^{4.33} = 75.94$$

$$k_2 = k_1 \times 75.94 = 2.0 \times 10^{-3} \times 75.94$$

$$k_2 \approx 0.152\ s^{-1}$$

$$k_2 = 1.52 \times 10^{-1}\ s^{-1}$$

$$= 1.52 \times 10^{-1}\ s^{-1} = x$$

The reaction is a 1st order, half-life ($t_{1/2}$) is

$$t_{1/2} = \frac{\ln 2}{k}$$

$$= \frac{0.693}{2.0 \times 10^{-3}} = 346.5 \text{ second}$$

$$= 5.78 \text{ minutes}$$

$$\approx 6 \text{ min} = y$$

The value of $x \times y = 1.52 \times 10^{-1} \times 6 \approx 0.912$

24. ***(70)*** According to Arrhenius equation,

$$k = Ae^{E_{a_1}/RT}$$

$$k_{overall} = \frac{A_1e^{\frac{-E_{a_1}}{RT}}\ A_2e^{\frac{-E_{a_2}}{RT}}}{A_3e^{-E_{a_3}/RT}}$$

$$k_{overall} = \frac{A_1A_2}{A_3} e^{\frac{-(E_{a_1}+E_{a_2}-E_{a_3})}{RT}}$$

This gives overall activation energy,

$$E_{a_{overall}} = E_{a_1} + E_{a_2} - E_{a_3}$$

$$= 50 + 60 - 40 = 70 \text{ kJ/mol}$$

25. ***(1496)*** $K_{eq} = \frac{k_f}{k_r}$

Using Arrhenius equation,

$$K_{eq} = \frac{A_f\, e^{\frac{-E_f}{RT}}}{A_r\, e^{\frac{E_r}{RT}}}$$

$$K_{eq} = \frac{2 \times 10^{13}}{4 \times 10^{12}} e^{\frac{-20000}{8.314 \times 300}} \quad [\because E_f - E_r = \Delta H]$$

$$K_{eq} = \frac{2 \times 10^{13}}{4 \times 10^{12}} \times 3.29 \times 10^{-4}$$

$$= 1.64 \times 10^{-3} \approx 2 \times 10^{-3} = x \times 10^{-3}$$

Temperature at which $k_f = k_r$

$$A_fe^{\frac{-E_f}{RT}} = A_re^{-\frac{E_r}{RT}}$$

Taking natural logarithm,

$$\ln A_f - \frac{E_f}{RT} = \ln A_r - \frac{E_r}{RT}$$

$$T = \frac{E_f - E_r}{R(\ln A_f - \ln A_r)}$$

$$T = \frac{20000}{8.314 \times (30.63 - 29.02)}$$

$$T = 1494.1\text{K} \approx 1494\text{K} = y$$

The value of $x + y = 1496$.

26. ***(1)*** $k = pZ_{AB}e^{-E_a/RT}$

$$p = \frac{k}{Z_{AB}e^{-E_a/RT}}$$

$$p = \frac{1.8 \times 10^{-4}\ s^{-1}}{1.5 \times 10^{12} \times e^{-\frac{75000}{8.314 \times 300}}}$$

$$= \frac{1.8 \times 10^{-4}}{1.5 \times 10^{12} \times e^{-30.07}} = \frac{1.8 \times 10^{-4}}{1.5 \times 10^{12} \times 8.8 \times 10^{-14}}$$

$$= 0.00137 = 1.37 \times 10^{-3} \approx 1 \times 10^{-3}$$

27. ***(3)*** Statement (A), (B) and (D) are correct while (C) is incorrect.

The correct form of (C) is :

The activation energy E_a is a characteristic property of the reaction and is independent of the temperature. It does not change with a change in temperature.

Practice Element 01 : Target JEE Main

1. **(a)** $-\frac{\Delta[A]}{\Delta t} = -\frac{1}{2}\frac{[\Delta B]}{\Delta t} = \frac{\Delta[C]}{\Delta t} = \frac{\Delta[D]}{\Delta t} = k[A]^2[B]$

$$-\frac{\Delta[A]}{\Delta t} = k[A]^2[B]$$

$$-\frac{\Delta[B]}{\Delta t} = 2k[A]^2[B]$$

2. **(d)** For 1st order reaction,

$$t = \frac{2.303}{k}\log\frac{[A]_0}{[A]}$$

$$= \frac{2.303}{3.5\times10^{-4}}\log\left(\frac{0.5}{0.125}\right)$$

$$\approx 3961.16\,\text{s}$$

3. **(a)** According to collision theory, molecules must collide with sufficient kinetic energy and the reactant molecules must be aligned orientation during the collision.

4. **(a)** For elementary reaction

$$A + B \underset{k_{-1}}{\overset{k_1}{\rightleftharpoons}} C$$

Forward reaction rate $= k_1[A][B]$, represents the formation of C from A and B.

Reverse reaction rate k_{-1} [C], represents the decomposition of C back into A and B

Net rate of formation of C is given by:

$$\frac{d[C]}{dt} = k_1[A][B] - k_{-1}[C]$$

5. **(b)** The correct match is : A-(iii), B-(iv), C-(ii), D-(i)

6. **(c)** For zero order reaction:

$$[A] = [A]_0 - kt$$

$$[A] = 1.0 - (0.1)(5\,\text{s})$$

$$[A] = 1.0 - 0.5 = 0.5\,\text{M}$$

Percentage of $[A]$ remaining $= \frac{[A]}{[A]_0}\times 100$

$$= \frac{0.5\text{M}}{1.0\text{M}}\times 100 = 50\%$$

7. **(a)** Both (A) and (R) are true and (R) is the correct explanation of (A).

8. **(a)** Molecularity is the number of molecules or atoms colliding in an elementary reaction step and is always a whole number (0, 1, 2) while order of reaction is the sum of the power of the concentrations terms in rate law of a reaction.

In elementary reaction, order is equal to the molecularity but in complex or multi-step, order may be lower than molecularity.

9. **(d)** According to Arrhenius equation

$$\ln\frac{k_2}{k_1} = \frac{E_a}{R}\left(\frac{1}{T_1} - \frac{1}{T_2}\right)$$

$$\ln\frac{0.05}{0.02} = \frac{E_a}{8.314}\left(\frac{1}{300} - \frac{1}{350}\right)$$

$$\ln 2.5 = \frac{E_a}{8.314}\times 0.00048$$

$$0.916 = E_a \times 0.000058$$

$$E_a = 15793\ \text{J/mol}$$

$$\approx 15.80\ \text{kJ/mol}$$

10. **(b)** Rate $= k[A]^n$

$[A]_1 = 0.1\,\text{M}, [A]_2 = 0.2\,\text{M}$

$\text{Rate}_1 = 1.0\times10^{-3}\ \text{mol}^{-1}\,\text{L}\,\text{s}^{-1}$

$\text{Rate}_2 = 4.0\times10^{-3}\ \text{mol}^{-1}\,\text{L}\,\text{s}^{-1}$

$$\frac{\text{Rate}_2}{\text{Rate}_1} = \frac{k[A_2]^n}{k[A_1]^n}$$

$$\frac{4.0\times10^{-3}}{1.0\times10^{-3}} = \left(\frac{0.2}{0.1}\right)^n$$

$$\Rightarrow \quad 4 = 2^n \Rightarrow n = 2$$

11. **(b)** The rate of formation of the excited complex AB^* depends on both the intensity of light I and the concentration of the reactant AB

$$\text{Rate} = \text{K.I.C}$$

12. **(a)** Statement I is correct but Statement II is incorrect.

The correct form of Statement II is:

Zero order reactions rate does not depend on the concentration.

13. **(a)**

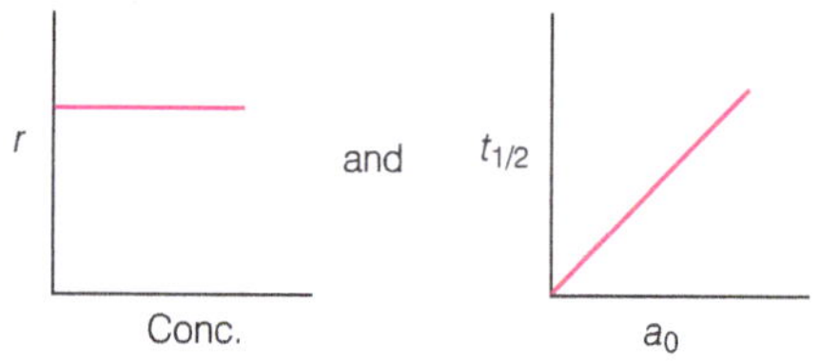

These graphs are of zero order reaction.

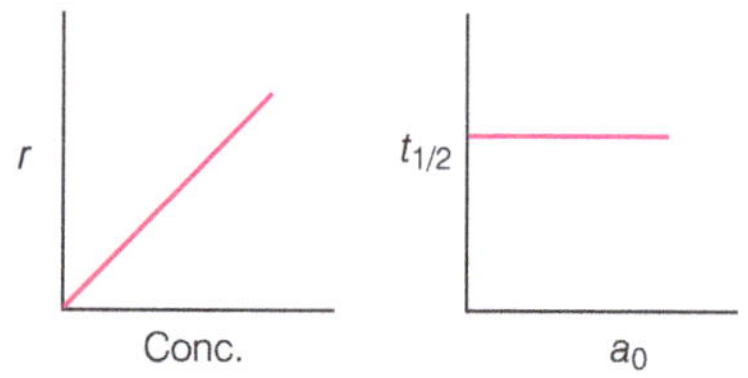

These are of 1st order reaction.

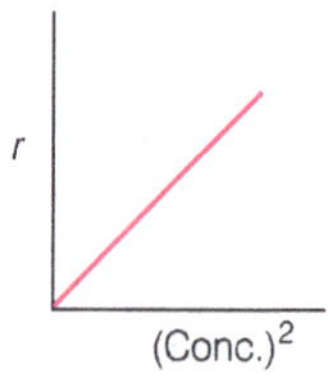

This follows 2nd order reaction.

14. **(c)** The steric factor is influenced by the orientation and geometry of reacting molecules.

15. ***(d)*** Statement (A), (C), (D) and (E) is correct and (B) is incorrect.

(A) Average rate $= \dfrac{\text{Change in concentration of } A}{\text{Change in time}}$

$$= \frac{0.80 - 0.60}{10}$$

$$= \frac{0.20}{10} = 0.02\ \text{s}^{-1}$$

(B) Instantaneous rate

$$\ln \frac{[A]_0}{[A]_t} = kt$$

$$\ln \frac{0.80}{0.60} = k \times 10$$

$$\ln (1.33) = k \times 10$$

$$0.285 = k \times 10$$

$$k = 0.0285\ \text{s}^{-1}$$

16. ***(b)*** $\ln k = \ln A - \dfrac{E_a}{R} \cdot \dfrac{1}{T}$

$$y = mx + c$$

$$m = -\frac{E_a}{R} \text{ (Slope of the line)}$$

$$c = \ln (A) \text{ (intercept)}$$

Since E_a is positive, the slope of the line is negative. This means as $\dfrac{1}{T}$ increases, $\ln (k)$ decreases indicating negative slope.

17. ***(a)*** The half-life for pseudo first order is

$$t_{1/2} = \frac{\ln 2}{k'}$$

$$k' = \frac{0.693}{20} = 0.03465\ \text{min}^{-1}$$

$$\approx 5.8 \times 10^{-4}\ \text{s}^{-1}$$

18. ***(c)*** HCl is a monoprotic acid, meaning it releases one proton per molecule.

H_2SO_4 is diprotic, releasing two protons per molecule, so it has a higher concentration of H^+ as compared to HCl of the same molarity.

19. ***(c)*** A catalyst does not change the equilibrium position of a reaction. It only helps the system to reach equilibrium faster by speeding up both the forward and reverse reactions.

20. ***(a)*** Plot of concentration $[A]$ vs time.

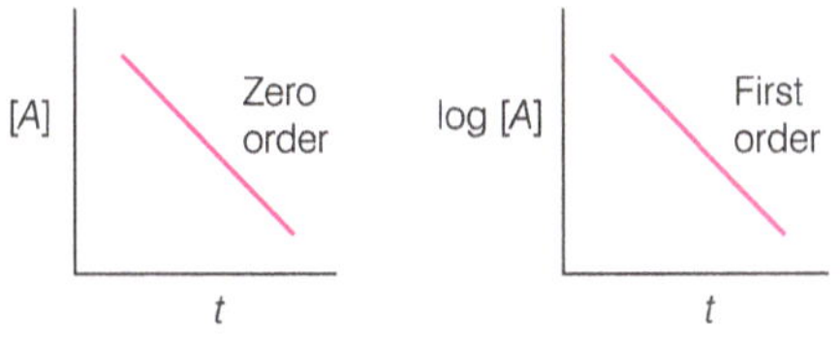

21. ***(7)*** The reaction can be represented as:

$$N_2O(g) \longrightarrow N_2(g) + \frac{1}{2}O_2(g)$$

Half-life for 1st order reaction is

$$t_{1/2} = \frac{0.693}{k}$$

$$\Rightarrow \quad k = \frac{0.693}{3.2\ \text{min}} \approx 0.2166\ \text{min}^{-1}$$

	$N_2O\ (g) \longrightarrow$	$N_2(g)\ +$	$\frac{1}{2}O_2(g)$
Initial pressure	0.50	0	0
Change in pressure	$-x$	$+x$	$+\frac{x}{2}$
Total pressure after 9.6 min	$0.50 - x$	$+x$	$+\frac{x}{2}$

$$p_{\text{remaining}} = p_{\text{initial}} \times e^{-kt}$$

$$= 0.50 \times e^{-0.2166 \times 9.6} \approx 6.25 \times 10^{-2}$$

$$x = p_{\text{initial}} - p_{\text{remaining}}$$

$$= 0.50 - 6.25 \times 10^{-2} = 0.4375\ \text{atm}$$

$$p_{\text{Total}} = (0.50 - x) + x + \frac{x}{2} = 0.50 + \frac{x}{2}$$

$$= 0.50 + \frac{0.4375}{2} \approx 7.188\ \text{atm}$$

$$= 7.188 \times 10^{-1}\ \text{atm} \approx 7 \times 10^{-1}\ \text{atm}$$

22. ***(350)*** $k = 2.5 \times 10^{10}\ e^{\frac{-25000}{8.314 \times 350}}$

$$= 2.5 \times 10^{10}\ e^{-8.59}$$

$$= 4.6 \times 10^{6} \approx 4 \times 10^{6}\ \text{s}^{-1}$$

For 1st order kinetics

$$t = \ln \frac{\text{(initial)}}{\text{(final)}} \Big/ k = \frac{\ln\left(\frac{1}{0.20}\right)}{4.6 \times 10^{6}}$$

$$= \frac{\ln 5}{4.6 \times 10^{6}} = \frac{1.609}{4.6 \times 10^{6}}$$

$$= 3.50 \times 10^{-7}\ \text{s}$$

$$= 3.50 \times 10^{-7} \times 10^{9}\ \text{nanoseconds}$$

$$= 350\ \text{nanoseconds}$$

23. ***(2)*** The overall order is determined by the slow step i.e, the rate determining step of the reaction.

So, rate of the reaction depends on the 2nd step of the reaction.

$$\text{rate} = k[\text{O}][\text{O}_3]$$

The reaction is 1st order w.r.t to O and O_3.

The overall order is 2. (second order)

24. ***(400)*** For the first-order reaction, the rate constant k can be calculated using the formula

$$k = \frac{\ln 2}{t_{50\%}}$$

$$k = \frac{\ln 2}{200} = \frac{0.693}{200}$$

$$= 0.003465\ \text{s}^{-1}$$

For 75% decomposition, 25% of the original compound remains.

$$\frac{[A]}{[A]_0} = 0.25 \Rightarrow \ln\left(\frac{[A]_0}{[A]}\right) = kt$$

$$\frac{[A]_0}{[A]} = \frac{1}{0.25} = 4 \Rightarrow \ln(4) = k \times t$$

$$1.386 = 0.003465 \times t \Rightarrow t = 400 \text{ s}$$

25. ***(7)*** According to Arrhenius equation,

$$k = Ae^{-E_a/RT}$$

Equilibrium constant $(k) = \frac{k_{\text{forward}}}{k_{\text{backward}}}$

$$k_{\text{forward}} = A_{\text{forward}}\, e^{\frac{-E_a^{\text{forward}}}{RT}}$$

$$= (1.2 \times 10^{13}) e^{\frac{-75 \times 10^3}{8.314 \times 298}}$$

$$= 1.2 \times 10^{13} \times 7.13 \times 10^{-14}$$

$$= 0.856 \text{ mol}^{-1} \text{ L s}^{-1}$$

$$= 8.56 \times 10^{-1} \text{ mol}^{-1} \text{ L s}^{-1}$$

$$k_{\text{backward}} = A_{\text{backward}}\, e^{-\frac{E_a^{\text{backward}}}{RT}}$$

$$= 4.0 \times 10^{12}\, e^{\frac{-100 \times 10^3}{8.314 \times 298}}$$

$$= 4.0 \times 10^{12} \times 2.96 \times 10^{-18}$$

$$= 1.18 \times 10^{-5} \text{ mol}^{-1} \text{ L s}^{-1}$$

$$k = \frac{8.56 \times 10^{-1}}{1.18 \times 10^{-5}} = 7.25 \times 10^4 \approx 7 \times 10^4$$

26. ***(8)*** Rate $= k[A][B]$

$$= 0.1 \text{M}^{-1} \text{min}^{-1} [0.6][0.4]$$

$$= 0.024 \text{ M/min} = 0.0004 \text{ M/sec} \approx 4 \times 10^{-4} \text{ M/sec}$$

The reaction is first order with respect to both A and B. If concentration of A is doubled, then rate will change according to the relationship

$$\text{Rate} \propto [A]$$

$$\text{Rate}_{\text{New}} = 2 \times 0.0004$$

$$= 0.0008 \text{ M/s} = 8 \times 10^{-4} \text{ M/s}$$

27. ***(2)*** Half-life for 1st order reaction

$$t_{1/2} = \frac{0.693}{k}$$

$$(t_{1/2})_1 = 3 \times (t_{1/2})_2 \Rightarrow \frac{0.693}{k_1} = 3 \times \frac{0.693}{k_2}$$

$$\frac{1}{k_1} = 3 \times \frac{1}{k_2} \Rightarrow \frac{k_1}{k_2} = \frac{1}{3}$$

For 80% completion of reaction 1, 20% of reactant remains

$$\frac{[A]}{[A]_0} = 0.20 \Rightarrow \ln\frac{[A]_0}{[A]} = kt$$

For reaction 1, $\ln\left(\frac{1}{0.20}\right) = k_1 t_1 \Rightarrow \ln 5 = k_1 t_1$

$$t_1 = \frac{1.609}{k_1}$$

For 90% completion of reaction 2, 10% of reactant remains

$$\frac{[A]}{[A]_0} = 0.10$$

$$\ln\left(\frac{1}{0.10}\right) = k_2 t_2 \Rightarrow t_2 = \frac{2.302}{k_2}$$

$$k_1 = \frac{k_2}{3} \Rightarrow t_1 = \frac{1.609}{\frac{k_2}{3}} = \frac{4.827}{k_2}$$

$$\frac{t_1}{t_2} = \frac{4.827/k_2}{2.302/k_2} \approx 2$$

28. ***(4)*** Statement (A), (C), (D) and (E) are true whereas (B) is incorrect. The correct form of (B) is

The rate law depends on $[A]^2$ and $[B]$, so rate is not linear with respect to $[A]$. The relation is quadratic with A and linear with B.

29. ***(0)*** The relationship between half-life $(t_{1/2})$ and initial concentration $[A_0]$ for a n order reaction is

$$t_{1/2} \propto [A_0]^{1-n}$$

For a gas phase reactions, pressure is proportional to concentration

$$[A] \propto p$$

$$\frac{(t_{1/2})_1}{(t_{1/2})_2} = \left(\frac{p_1}{p_2}\right)^{1-n} \Rightarrow \frac{200}{100} = \left(\frac{100}{50}\right)^{1-n}$$

$$2 = 2^{1-n}$$

$$1 = 1 - n \Rightarrow n = 0$$

Order of reaction is 0.

30. ***(14)*** $r = k[B]^n$

$3r = k(3^3)^n \cdot [B]^n \Rightarrow n = 1/3$

For a reaction of order 1/3.

$$t = \frac{3}{2k}([A]_0^{2/3} - [A]^{2/3})$$

So, $$t_{1/2} = \frac{3}{2k}\left([A]_0^{2/3} - \left(\frac{[A]_0}{2}\right)^{2/3}\right)$$

$$= \frac{3}{2k}[A]_0^{2/3}\left(\frac{2^{2/3} - 1}{2^{2/3}}\right)$$

The rate constant, $k = \frac{3}{2.3\sqrt{3}}[A]_0^{2/3}\left(\frac{2^{2/3} - 1}{2^{2/3}}\right)$

$$= \frac{1}{2\sqrt{3}}[A]_0^{2/3}\left(\frac{2^{2/3} - 1}{2^{2/3}}\right)$$

The time required for the completion of the reaction,

$$t = \frac{3}{2k}[A]_0^{2/3}$$

$$t = \frac{3[A]_0^{2/3}}{2 \cdot \left(\frac{1}{2\sqrt{3}}[A]_0^{2/3}\left(\frac{2^{2/3} - 1}{2^{2/3}}\right)\right)}$$

$$= \frac{3\sqrt{3} \cdot 2^{2/3}}{(2^{2/3} - 1)} \approx 14 \text{ h}$$

Check Through PYQs : JEE Main

1. **(8)** Given $r = k\,[A]^2\,[B]$

   If concentration is doubled

$$r' = k\,[2A]^2\,[2B]^1$$

$$r' = 8r \Rightarrow x = 8$$

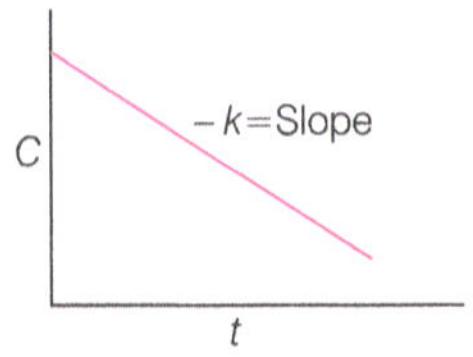

   Zero order $y = 0$

   So $x + y = 8$

2. **(a)** Given reaction,

$$A \xrightarrow{k_1} B \xrightarrow{k_2} C$$

   Rate of formation of B is,

$$\frac{d[B]}{dt} = k_1[A] - k_2[B] \Rightarrow 0 = k_1[A] - k_2[B]$$

$$\left[\frac{k_1}{k_2}\right][A] = [B]$$

3. **(17)** For reaction,

$$2N_2O_5(g) \longrightarrow 4NO_2(g) + O_2(g)$$

   Rate of reaction (ROR) $= -\frac{1}{2}\frac{\Delta[N_2O_5]}{\Delta t}$

$$= \frac{1}{4}\frac{\Delta[NO_2]}{\Delta t} = \frac{\Delta[O_2]}{\Delta t}$$

$$ROR = -\frac{1}{2}\frac{\Delta[N_2O_5]}{\Delta t} = -\frac{1}{2}\frac{(2.75-3)}{30}\ \text{mol L}^{-1}\text{min}^{-1}$$

$$ROR = -\frac{1}{2}\frac{(-0.25)}{30} = \frac{1}{240}\ \text{mol L}^{-1}\ \text{min}^{-1}$$

   Rate of formation of NO_2

$$= \frac{\Delta[NO_2]}{\Delta t} = 4 \times ROR = \frac{4}{240}$$

$$= 16.66 \times 10^{-3}\ \text{mol L}^{-1}\text{min}^{-1}$$

$$\approx 17 \times 10^{-3}\ \text{mol L}^{-1}\ \text{min}^{-1}$$

4. **(1)** Rate of reaction $= -\frac{1dA}{\gamma_1 dt} = -\frac{1dB}{\gamma_2 dt} = \frac{1dC}{Y_3\,dt} = \frac{1dD}{\gamma_4 dt}$

$$= -\frac{1}{\gamma_1} \times 3 = -\frac{1}{\gamma_2} \times 6 = \frac{1}{\gamma_3} \times 1 = \frac{1}{\gamma_4} \times 9$$

   Let us assume $\gamma_1 = 1$ then

$$\gamma_2 = 2;\ \gamma_3 = \frac{1}{3};\ \gamma_4 = 3$$

   Substituting in the reaction,

$$1A + 2B \longrightarrow \frac{1}{3}C + 3D$$

   Multiplying the coefficients by 3 to remove fraction 1/3 gives values of $\gamma_1 = 3;\ \gamma_2 = 6;\ \gamma_3 = 1$ and $\gamma_4 = 9$

$$3A + 6B \longrightarrow C + 9D$$

   Rate of reaction $= \frac{1dD}{\gamma_4 dt} = \frac{1}{9} \times 9\ \text{m mol dm}^{-3}\ \text{s}^{-1}$

$$= 1\ \text{m mol dm}^{-3}\ \text{s}^{-1}$$

5. **(4)** For the given reaction,

   rate of reaction $= -\frac{1}{2}\frac{d[K_2Cr_2O_7]}{dt}$

$$= \frac{-1}{8}\frac{d[H_2SO_4]}{dt} = \frac{-1}{3}\frac{d[C_2H_6O]}{dt}$$

$$= \frac{1}{2}\frac{d[Cr_2(SO_4)_3]}{dt} = \frac{1}{3}\frac{d[C_2H_4O_2]}{dt}$$

$$= \frac{1}{2}\frac{d[K_2SO_4]}{dt} = \frac{1}{11}\frac{d[H_2O]}{dt}$$

   Rate of appearence of 2 moles of $Cr_2(SO_4)_3$ is given as

$$\frac{d}{dt}[Cr_2(SO_4)_3] = 2.67\ \text{mol/min}$$

   Rate of disappearence of C_2H_6O can be calculated as

$$-\frac{1}{3}\frac{d[C_2H_6O]}{dt} = \frac{+1}{2}\frac{d[Cr_2(SO_4)_3]}{dt}$$

$$\frac{-d[C_2H_6O]}{dt} = \frac{2.67}{2} \times 3 = 4.005 = 4\ \text{mol/min}$$

6. **(d)** Rate of reaction

$$\frac{-1}{2}\frac{d\,[A]}{dt} = \frac{-1}{3}\frac{d\,[B]}{dt} = \frac{-2}{3}\frac{d\,[C]}{dt} = \frac{1}{3}\frac{d\,[P]}{dt}$$

$$\frac{d\,[A]}{dt} = \frac{2}{3}\frac{d\,[B]}{dt} = \frac{4}{3}\frac{d\,[C]}{dt} = -\frac{2}{3}\frac{d\,[P]}{dt}$$

7. **(2)**

	$A(g)$	$\longrightarrow$	$2B(g)$
$t = 0$	0.6		
$t = 100$ sec	$0.6 - p$		$2p$

$$kt = 2.303 \log \frac{0.6}{0.6 - p}$$

$$4.606 \times 10^{-2} \times 100 = 2.303 \log \frac{0.6}{0.6 - p}$$

$$(0.6 - p)\,100 = 0.6$$

$$60 - 100p = 0.6$$

$$p = 0.594\ \text{atm}$$

   Total pressure $= 0.6 + p = 0.6 + 0.594 = 1.194$ atm

8. **(1)** Given reaction,

$$A + B \longrightarrow C$$

$$A \xrightarrow{t = x} \frac{A}{2} \xrightarrow{t = 2x} \frac{A}{4}$$

   Order w.r.t. $A = 1$

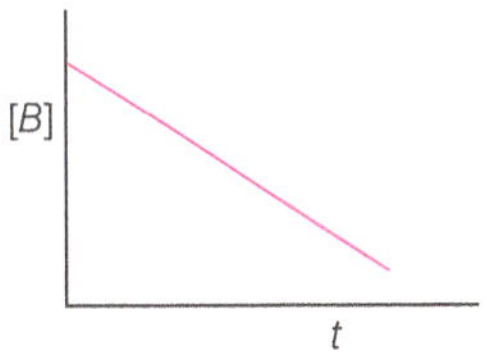

$$[B] = -kt + [B]_0$$

   Order w.r.t. B = zero order

   Overall order $= 1 + 0 = 1$

   Hence, the overall order is 1.

9. ***(17)***

$$A + B \rightarrow C \quad \text{...(i)}$$
$$P \rightarrow Q \quad \text{...(ii)}$$
$$t_{1/2} \propto \frac{1}{k}$$

We know that

$$\frac{(t_{1/2})_1}{(t_{1/2})_2} = \frac{k_2}{k_1} = \frac{5}{2}$$

$$\frac{t_{2/3}}{t_{4/5}} = \frac{k_2 \log 3}{k_1 \log 5} = \left(\frac{5}{2}\right)\frac{0.477}{0.699} = 1.7 = 17 \times 10^{-1}$$

Comparing it with given equation the value is 17.

10. ***(3)*** Reaction rate, $r = k\,[A]^x\,[B]^y$

for I, $r = 6 \times 10^{-3}$, $A = 0.1$, $B = 0.1$

$6 \times 10^{-3} = k\,[0.1]^x\,[0.1]^y$

Similarly for IV,

$$2.4 \times 10^{-2} = [0.4]^x\,[0.1]^y$$

Now divide IV by I

$$4 = 4^x \Rightarrow x = 1$$

For III,

$$2.88 \times 10^{-1} = k\,[0.3]^x\,[0.4]^y$$

For II,

$$7.2 \times 10^{-2} = k\,[0.3]^x\,[0.2]^y$$

III/II, $4 = 2^y \Rightarrow y = 2$

Overall order $= x + y = 1 + 2 = 3$

11. ***(50)*** Given $[A]_0 = 1$

$$[A] = 0.1$$
$$k = 4.6 \times 10^{-2}\,s^{-1}$$

Since the given reaction is of first order.
Hence, using

$$t = \frac{2.303}{k}\log\frac{[A]_0}{[A]}$$

On substituting the values

$$t = \frac{2.303}{4.6 \times 10^{-2}}\log\frac{1}{0.1}$$
$$t = 50 \text{ sec}$$

12. ***(d)*** $AB_3(g) \longrightarrow A(g) + 3B(g)$

As decomposition reaction of $AB_3(g)$ is not given, we assume that p (mm Hg) is for $AB_3(g)$ only.

So, half-life $t_{1/2} \propto (p_0)^{1-n}$

$$\frac{(t_{1/2})_1}{(t_{1/2})_2} = \frac{(p_0)_1^{1-n}}{(p_0)_2^{1-n}}$$

$$\Rightarrow \left(\frac{4}{2}\right) = \left(\frac{50}{100}\right)^{1-n} \Rightarrow 2 = \left(\frac{1}{2}\right)^{1-n}$$

$$\Rightarrow \quad n = 1 + 1 \Rightarrow n = 2$$

Therefore, the order of reaction is 2.

13. ***(b)*** We know that

$$r = k[A]^1[B]^1$$

From the given data

$$0.1 = k[20]^1[0.5]^1 \quad \text{...(i)}$$
$$0.40 = k[x]^1[0.5]^1 \quad \text{...(ii)}$$
$$0.80 = k[40]^1[y]^1 \quad \text{...(iii)}$$

Dividing Eqs. (i) and (ii)

$$\frac{0.1}{0.40} = \frac{k[20]^1\,[0.5]^1}{k[x]^1\,[0.5]^1}$$
$$\frac{10}{40} = \frac{[20]}{[x]}$$

$\therefore \quad x = 80$

Putting the value of x in Eq. (ii), we get

$$0.40 = k\,[80]^1\,[0.5]^1$$

Dividing the above Eq. by Eq. (iii) we get

$$\frac{0.40 = k\,[80]^1\,[0.5]^1}{0.80 = k\,[40]^1\,[y]^1}$$
$$\frac{1}{2} = \frac{2\,[0.5]^1}{[y]^1}$$

$\Rightarrow \quad y = 2$

14. ***(3)*** Slowest step is the rate determining step.

$$NOBr_2 + NO \longrightarrow 2NOBr$$
$$r = k\,[NOBr_2]\,[NO] \quad \text{...(i)}$$
$$NO + Br_2 \rightleftharpoons NOBr_2$$
$$K_{eq} = \frac{[NOBr_2]}{[NO]\,[Br_2]}$$
$$[NOBr_2] = k_{eq}[NO][Br_2] \quad \text{...(ii)}$$

Subtituting Eqs. (ii) in (i)

$$r = k \cdot k_{eq}\,[NO]\,[Br_2]\,[NO]$$
$$r = k'[NO]^2[Br_2]$$

Thus, the overall order = 3

15. ***(1)***

(A) For zero order, $t_{1/2} = \frac{[A]_0}{2k}$ as concentration decreases, life decreases. So, statement 'A' is correct.

(B) If order w.r.t that reactant is zero then it will not affect rate of reaction. So statement 'B' is correct.

(C) Order can be fractional but molecularity cannot be fractional. So statement 'C' is incorrect.

(D) For zero order reaction unit is mol $L^{-1}s^{-1}$ and for second order reaction unit is $mol^{-1}Ls^{-1}$. So statement 'D' is correct.

16. ***(2)*** Given, $(t_{1/2})_A = 12$ minute, $(t_{1/2})_B = 3$ minute

$$\frac{1}{(t_{1/2})_C} = \frac{1}{(t_{1/2})_A} + \frac{1}{(t_{1/2})_B}$$
$$= \frac{1}{12} + \frac{1}{3} = \frac{1+4}{12} = \frac{5}{12}$$

$$\Rightarrow \quad (t_{1/2})_C = \frac{12}{5} \text{ minutes} = 2.4 \text{ minutes} \approx 2$$

17. ***(75)*** Let initial conc. of $A = 1$ mol

For zero order reaction half-life period,

$$t_{1/2} = \frac{a}{2k}$$

$$\Rightarrow \quad k = \frac{a}{2t_{1/2}} = \frac{a}{2 \times 50} = \frac{1}{2 \times 50}$$

For 75% completion

$$\left(a - \frac{a}{4}\right) = kt \Rightarrow \frac{4a - a}{4} = kt \Rightarrow \frac{3a}{4} = kt$$

$$t = \frac{3}{4}\frac{a}{k} = \frac{3}{4} \times \frac{100}{1} = 75 \text{ min}$$

18. ***(2)*** Region (I) is the straight line for first order reaction and Region (III) is the constant line for zero order reaction, since for zero order, rate do not depend on the time but on the condition. (catalyst, $h\nu$) etc.

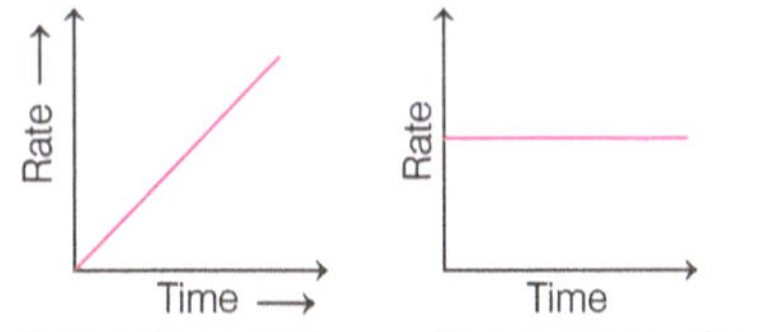

First order reaction   Zero order reaction

Hence, statement (C) is correct.

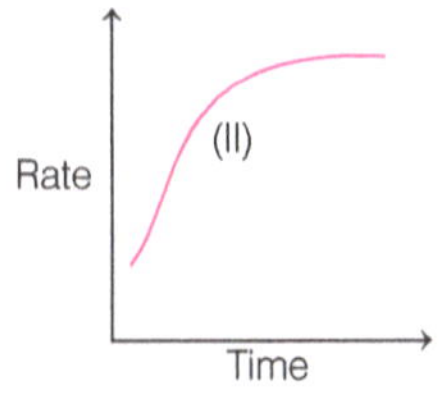

Since region (II) is asymptotic region it shows the running time, hence order cannot be determined.

Thus, statement *A* and *C* are correct.

19. ***(2)*** It takes infinite time for the completion of the reaction. So statement A is incorrect.

$$t_{1/2} = \frac{\ln 2}{k} = \frac{0.693}{(4.6 \times 10^{-3} s^{-1})} = 150.65 \text{ s}$$

So, statement B is incorrect.

Time required for 10% completion,

$$t_{10\%} = \frac{1}{\text{Rate constant }(k)} \ln\left(\frac{a}{a-x}\right)$$

$$\Rightarrow \quad t_{10\%} = \frac{1}{k}\ln\left(\frac{100}{100-10}\right) \Rightarrow t_{10\%} = \frac{2.303}{k}\ln\left(\frac{100}{90}\right)$$

$$t_{10\%} = \frac{2.303}{k} \times (0.04)$$

Similarly, $t_{90\%} = \frac{1}{k}\ln\left(\frac{a}{a-x}\right)$

$$t_{90\%} = \frac{1}{k}\ln\left(\frac{100}{100-90}\right) = \frac{1}{k}\ln\left(\frac{100}{10}\right) \Rightarrow t_{90\%} = \frac{2.303}{k}$$

Now, $\frac{t_{90\%}}{t_{10\%}} = \frac{\frac{2.303}{k}}{\frac{2.303 \times 0.04}{k}} = \frac{1}{0.04} = 25$

So, statement C is correct.

$$e^{kt} = \frac{a}{a-x}$$

By reversing the above equation

$$\frac{a-x}{a} = e^{-kt} \text{ or } 1 - \frac{x}{a} = e^{-kt} \Rightarrow x = a(1 - e^{-kt})$$

$$\Rightarrow \quad d = \frac{x}{a} = (1 - e^{-kt})$$

where, d is degree of dissociation.

So, statement D is also correct.

The rate has the unit of Ms^{-1} or atm s^{-1} while the rate constant for a first order reaction has unit s^{-1}. So, statement E is incorrect.

20. ***(40)*** Rate $= k[X][Y]^0 = k[X]$

Using data of experiment I and II,

$$\frac{\text{Rate}_I}{\text{Rate}_{II}} = \frac{k\,[X_I]}{k\,[X_{II}]}$$

$$\frac{2 \times 10^{-3}}{4 \times 10^{-3}} = \frac{0.1}{L}$$

$$\Rightarrow \quad L = 0.1 \times 2 = 0.2$$

Using experiment III and IV,

$$\frac{\text{Rate}_{III}}{\text{Rate}_{IV}} = \frac{k\,[X_{III}]}{k\,[X_{IV}]} \Rightarrow \frac{M \times 10^{-3}}{2 \times 10^{-3}} = \frac{0.4}{0.1}$$

$$M = 4 \times 2 = 8$$

So, $M : L = \frac{8}{0.2} = \frac{80}{2} = 40.$

21. ***(100)*** For a first order reaction,

$$\text{(half-life) } t_{1/2} = \frac{0.693}{k}$$

$$= \frac{0.693}{0.3010} \quad [\text{Given, } t_{1/2} = 0.3010]$$

$$= 2.303$$

The rate law for 1st order reaction is given as

$$k = \frac{2.303}{t}\log\frac{[A]_0}{[A]_t}$$

$$\therefore \quad 2.303 = \frac{2.303}{2}\log\frac{[A]_0}{[A]_t} \Rightarrow 2 = \log\frac{[A]_0}{[A]_t}$$

$$\Rightarrow \quad \frac{[A]_0}{[A]_t} = \text{antilog (2)} \Rightarrow \frac{[A]_0}{[A]_t} = 100$$

22. ***(165)*** Since after 70 minutes, the concentration of reactant [*A*] is halved.

So, $t_{1/2} = 70$ min

Half-life of first order reaction is given as

$$t_{1/2} = \frac{0.6932}{k}$$

[k = rate constant for 1st order reaction]

$$k = \frac{0.6932}{t_{1/2}} = \frac{0.6932}{70} = 0.0099 \text{ min}^{-1}$$

$$= \frac{0.0099}{60} s^{-1} = 165 \times 10^{-6} s^{-1}$$

The value of x is 165.

23. **(2)** Rate of reaction $(r) = k[NO]^x[H_2]^y$

From I data,

$$0.135 = k[40]^x[65.6]^y \quad \dots(i)$$

From II data,

$$0.033 = k[20.1]^x[65.6]^y \quad \dots(ii)$$

On dividing Eq. (i) by Eq. (ii),

$$\frac{0.135}{0.033} = \left[\frac{40}{20.1}\right]^x$$

$$4 = (2)^x \Rightarrow x = 2$$

∴ Order of reaction with respect to NO is 2.

24. **(2)** For 50% completion,

$$k = \frac{2.303}{t_{50\%}} \log \frac{100}{100-50} \quad \dots(i)$$

For 75% completion,

$$k = \frac{2.303}{t_{75\%}} \log \frac{100}{100-75} \quad \dots(ii)$$

From Eqs. (i) and (ii),

$$\frac{2.303}{t_{50\%}} \log \frac{100}{50} = \frac{2.303}{t_{75\%}} \log \frac{100}{25}$$

$$\frac{0.3010}{t_{50\%}} = \frac{0.6020}{t_{75\%}}$$

$$t_{75\%} = 2t_{50\%}$$

$$\therefore \quad \frac{t_{75\%}}{t_{50\%}} = \frac{2}{1}$$

25. **(1)** Rate of the reaction $= k[NO]^x [H_2]^y$

where k is rate constant and x, y are order of reaction w.r.t. NO and H_2 respectively.

From observations A and B

$$7 \times 10^{-9} = k\,(8 \times 10^{-5})^x (8 \times 10^{-5})^y \quad \dots(i)$$

and

$$2.1 \times 10^{-8} = k\,(24 \times 10^{-5})^x\,(8 \times 10^{-5})^y \quad \dots(ii)$$

Dividing Eqs. (i) by (ii)

$$\frac{7 \times 10^{-9}}{2.1 \times 10^{-8}} = \frac{k\,(8 \times 10^{-5})^x\,(8 \times 10^{-5})^y}{k(24 \times 10^{-5})^x\,(8 \times 10^{-5})^y}$$

$$\frac{1}{3} = \left(\frac{1}{3}\right)^x \Rightarrow x = 1$$

∴ Order of reaction w.r.t. NO is 1.

26. **(c)** $k = \dfrac{\text{Rate of reaction}}{[\text{Reactant}]^n} = \dfrac{\text{mol}^1\,\text{L}^{-1}\text{s}^{-1}}{[\text{mol}^n / \text{L}^n]}$

$$= \text{mol}^{1-n}\text{L}^{n-1}\text{s}^{-1}$$

Therefore, option (c) is correct.

27. **(81)** Given,

$$\underset{\text{Sucrose}}{C_{12}H_{22}O_{11}} + H_2O \xrightarrow{\text{1st order}} \underset{\text{Glucose}}{C_6H_{12}O_6} + \underset{\text{Fructose}}{C_6H_{12}O_6}$$

$$t_{1/2} = \frac{10}{3}\text{ h}$$

At $t = 0$, $a = [A]_0$ (initial conc.)

$t = 9\text{ h}$ $a - x = [A]_t$ [conc. at time t]

On using 1st order equation,

$$k = \frac{2.303}{t} \log \frac{[A]_0}{[A]_t}$$

$$\Rightarrow \quad \frac{k \times t}{2.303} = \log \frac{[A]_0}{[A]_t}$$

$$\frac{\ln 2 \times 9}{10/3 \times 2.303} = \log\left(\frac{1}{f}\right) \quad \left(\because k = \frac{\ln 2}{t_{1/2}}\right)$$

$$\Rightarrow \quad \log\left(\frac{1}{f}\right) = 0.8127$$

$$\log\left(\frac{1}{f}\right) = 81.27 \times 10^{-2}$$

$$x = 81.27$$

or $\quad x \approx 81$

28. **(26)** Integrated rate law for 1st order reaction is

$$kt = \ln \frac{[A]_0}{[A]_t} \quad \dots(i)$$

Given, $k = 3.3 \times 10^{-4}\text{ s}^{-1}$

$[A]_0 = 100$

$\Rightarrow \quad [A]_t = 100 - 40 = 60$

Put values in Eq. (i), we get

$$3.3 \times 10^{-4}\text{s}^{-1} \times t = \ln \frac{100}{60}$$

$$t = 1547.95\text{ s} = 25.79\text{ min}$$

$$\left(1\text{ min} = 60\text{ s or } 1\text{ s} = \frac{1}{60}\text{ min}\right)$$

$$= 26\text{ minutes}$$

29. **(60)** For first order reaction,

$$t = \frac{2.303}{k} \log\left(\frac{a_0}{a}\right)$$

For 75%,

$$t_{75\%} = \frac{2.303}{k} \log\left(\frac{100}{25}\right) \quad \dots(i)$$

For 60%,

$$t_{60\%} = \frac{2.303}{k} \log\left(\frac{100}{40}\right) \quad \dots(ii)$$

On dividing Eqs. (ii) by (i),

$$\frac{t_{60\%}}{t_{75\%}} = \frac{\frac{2.303}{k}\log\left(\frac{100}{40}\right)}{\frac{2.303}{k}\log\left(\frac{100}{25}\right)}$$

$$t_{60\%} = t_{75\%} \times \left(\frac{0.3979}{0.602}\right)$$

$$\Rightarrow \quad t_{60\%} = 90 \times \frac{0.3979}{0.602}$$

$$t_{60\%} = 59.49\text{ minute}$$

$$\approx 60\text{ min}$$

30. ***(23.03)*** All the radioactive reactions follows. Ist order kinetics.

Time taken for decay from N_0 to N_t is (N = number of nuclei)

$$t = \frac{1}{\lambda} \ln \frac{N_0}{N_t}$$

$$t = \frac{1}{\lambda} \times 2.303 \log \frac{N_0}{N_t} \quad \ldots \text{(i)}$$

Also, we know λ = (decay constant)

$$= \frac{0.693}{t_{1/2}}$$

where, $t_{1/2} = 6.93$ yr (given)

Also, we know 90% nuclei are decayed

$$\therefore \quad \frac{N_0}{N_t} = \frac{100}{10} = 10$$

Put the values of λ and $\frac{N_0}{N_t}$ in Eq. (i), we get

$$\therefore \quad t = \frac{6.93}{0.693} \times 2.303 \times \log 10$$

$$= 23.03 \text{ (yr)}$$

31. ***(20)*** $(E_a)_{\text{overall}} = \frac{1}{2}[E_{a_1} + E_{a_3} - E_{a_2}]$

$$= \frac{1}{2}[10 + 60 - 30]$$

$$= 20 \text{ kJ/mole}$$

32. ***(100)*** Given that, $K = \frac{K_1 K_2}{K_3}$

or $$Ae^{-E_a/RT} = \frac{A_1 e^{-\frac{E_{a_1}}{RT}} A_2 e^{-\frac{E_{a_2}}{RT}}}{A_3 e^{-E_{a_3}/RT}}$$

$$Ae^{-E_a/RT} = \frac{A_1 A_2}{A_3} e^{-\frac{(E_{a_1} + E_{a_2} - E_{a_3})}{RT}}$$

$$E_a = E_{a_1} + E_{a_2} - E_{a_3}$$

$$400 = 300 + 200 - E_{a_3}$$

$$E_{a_3} = 100 \text{ kJ/mole}$$

33. ***(130)*** Given, $E_a = 300$ kJ/mol

$$\frac{E_a}{T} = \frac{E_a'}{T'}$$ ($\because$ Rate of catalysed and uncatalysed reaction is same)

$$\frac{300}{600} = \frac{E_{a\,\text{Forward}}}{300}$$

$\Rightarrow \quad E_{a\,\text{Forward}} = 150$

Now, $\quad 20 = 150 - E_{a\,\text{Backward}}$

$\Rightarrow \quad E_{a\,\text{Backward}} = 130$

34. ***(2)*** Among the given statements A and B are correct.

We know that

$$k = Ae^{-E_a/RT}$$

or $$\log k = \log A - \frac{E_a}{2.303R} \times \frac{1}{T}$$

Thus, higher is the E_a values, stronger will be the temperature dependence of K.

Also, if activation energy (E_a) of a reaction is zero, then the rate is independent of temperature.

35. ***(d)*** A catalyst provides an alternate pathway or reaction mechanism by reducing the activation energy between reactants and products and therefore, lowering the potential energy barrier. Hence, the correct reaction profile diagram is as follows.

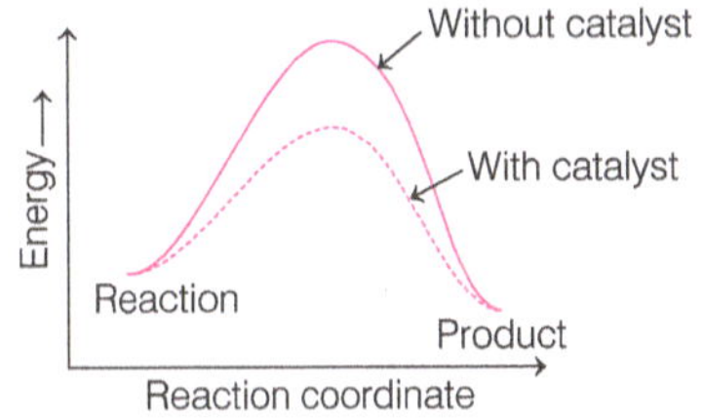

36. ***(c)***

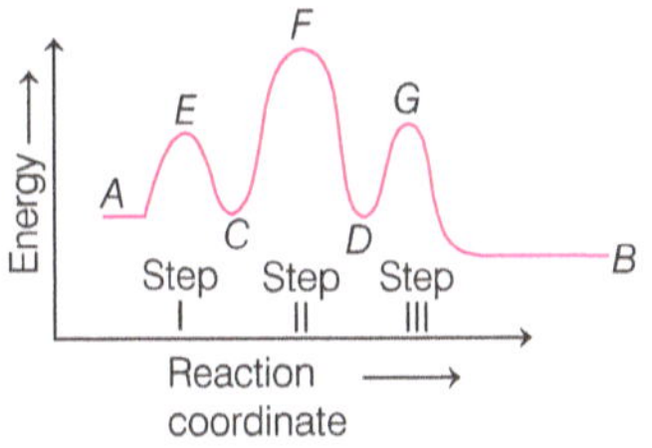

This is a 3-step reaction. Total number of intermediates are 2 (C and D) and transition states are 3 (E, F and G). The rate determining step is step II. Since it has highest activation energy and higher energy correspond to slowest step.

37. ***(2520)*** From Arrhenius equation of kinetics

$$\ln\left(\frac{k_2}{k_1}\right) = \frac{E_a}{R}\left(\frac{1}{T_1} - \frac{1}{T_2}\right)$$

$$\log\left(\frac{0.05}{0.03}\right) = \frac{E_a}{2.3 \times 8.3}\left[\frac{1}{200} - \frac{1}{300}\right]$$

$$[0.70 - 0.48] = \frac{E_a}{2.3 \times 8.3}\left[\frac{300 - 200}{300 \times 200}\right]$$

$$\Rightarrow \quad 0.22 = \frac{E_a}{2.3 \times 8.3}\left(\frac{1}{600}\right)$$

$$E_a = 0.22 \times 2.3 \times 8.3 \times 600$$

$$= 2519.88 \text{ J/mol}$$

$$\approx 2520 \text{ J/mol}$$

38. ***(3)*** Among the given statements A, B and D are correct. However, statement C is incorrect.

The correct statement for Statement (C) is that the value of k may be greater or lesser depending upon the temperature.

39. ***(225)*** Using Arrhenius equation,

$$k = Ae^{-E_a/RT}$$

Taking natural log on both sides,

$$\ln k = \ln A - \frac{E_a}{RT}$$

$$\Rightarrow \quad \log(2 \times 10^{-6}) = \log(4 \times 10^{13}) - \frac{8.3 \times 10^3}{8.3 \times T \times 2.3}$$

$$\Rightarrow \quad \log 2 - 6 = 2\log 2 + 13 - \frac{8.3 \times 10^3}{8.3 \times T \times 2.3}$$

$$\Rightarrow \quad -19.3 = -\frac{10^3}{T \times 2.3}$$

$$\Rightarrow \quad T = 225 \times 10^{-1}\ \text{K}$$

40. ***(216)*** $k = (6.5 \times 10^{12}\ \text{s}^{-1})e^{-26000\ \text{K}/T}$ ...(i)

From Arrhenius equation,

We know that, $k = Ae^{-E_a/RT}$ ... (ii)

∴ From (i) and (ii),

$$\frac{-E_a}{RT} = \frac{-26000\ \text{K}}{T}$$

$$E_a = 26000\ \text{K} \times R$$

$$= 26000\ \text{K} \times 8.314\ \text{J/K mol}^{-1}$$

$$= 216164\ \text{J/mol} = 216.164\ \text{kJ/mol}$$

i.e. 216 kJ/mol

41. ***(1)*** $k_{300} = x \times 10^{-3}\ k_{310}$ (Given)

$$\therefore \quad x = \frac{k_{300}}{k_{310} \times 10^{-3}}$$

From Arrhenius equation,

$$\log\left(\frac{k_2}{k_1}\right) = \frac{E_a}{2.303\,R} \times \left[\frac{1}{T_1} - \frac{1}{T_2}\right]$$

$$= \frac{532611}{2.303 \times 8.3} \times \left[\frac{1}{310} - \frac{1}{300}\right]$$

$$\log\frac{k_2}{k_1} = -2.9960$$

taking antilog,

$$\frac{k_2}{k_1} = \text{antilog}(-2.9960) = 1.009 \times 10^{-3}$$

$$x = \frac{k_2}{k_1} \times \frac{1}{10^{-3}} = \frac{1.009 \times 10^{-3}}{10^{-3}}$$

$$\therefore \quad = 1.009 \approx 1$$

42. ***(59)*** According to Arrhenius equation,

$$k = Ae^{-E_a/RT}$$

Taking ln both sides

$$\ln k = \ln A - \frac{E_a}{RT}$$

Rate constant when reaction occur at 300 K :

$$\ln k_1 = \ln A - \frac{E_a}{R \times 300} \quad \text{... (i)}$$

Rate constant when reaction occur at temperature 309 K

$$\ln k_2 = \ln A - \frac{E_a}{R \times 309} \quad \text{...(ii)}$$

$$\because \quad k_2 = 2k_1 \text{ (given)}$$

$$\ln(2k_1) = \ln A - \frac{E_a}{309R} \quad \text{...(iii)}$$

Subtract Eqs. (i) from (iii),

$$\ln(2k_1) - \ln k_1 = \frac{-E_a}{309R} + \frac{E_a}{300R}$$

$$\log(2) = \frac{E_a}{2.303\,R}\left[\frac{9}{300 \times 309}\right]$$

$$0.3 = \frac{E_a}{2.303 \times 8.3} \times \frac{9}{300 \times 309}$$

$$\Rightarrow \quad E_a = 59065.04\ \text{J/mol} = 59.06\ \text{kJ/mol}$$

43. ***(166)*** Given, $\ln k = 33.24 - \dfrac{2.0 \times 10^4}{T}$

Also, $\quad \ln k = \ln A - \dfrac{E_a}{RT}$

On comparing both above equations,

$$\frac{E_a}{R} = 2.0 \times 10^4$$

$$\therefore \quad E_a = 2.0 \times 10^4 \times R = 2.0 \times 10^4 \times 8.3\ \text{J/mol}$$

$$= 16.6 \times 10^4\ \text{J/mol} = 166\ \text{kJ/mol}$$

44. ***(c)*** According to Arrhenius equation,

$$k = Ae^{-E_a/RT}$$

As the temperature increases, rate constant k also increases which will generally speed up the process (increase the rate). So, graph will exponentially increases as in option (c).

45. ***(d)*** $k = Ae^{-E_a/RT}$

Taking natural logarithm on both sides, the Arrhenius equation becomes.

$$\Rightarrow \quad \ln k = \ln A - \left(\frac{E_a}{R}\right)\frac{1}{T} \Rightarrow \ln k = \ln A - \left(\frac{E_a}{R \times 10^3}\right) \times \frac{10^3}{T}$$

$$\text{Slope of a graph} = \frac{-E_a}{R \times 10^3} = \frac{-10}{5}$$

$$E_a = 2R \times 10^3\ \text{J mol}^{-1} \Rightarrow E_a = 2R\ \text{kJ/mol}$$

46. ***(d)*** According to Arrhenius equation

$$k = Ae^{-E_a/RT}$$

$$\Rightarrow \quad \log k = \log A - \frac{E_a}{2.303RT}$$

Slope of the graph of 'log k' vs $\dfrac{1}{T}$ is $\dfrac{-E_a}{2.303R}$

Greater the value of E_a, more will be the negative slope.

From the graph,

most –ve slope = c, followed by a, d and b.

∴ Order of activation energies must be

$$E_c > E_a > E_d > E_b$$

Practice Element 02 : Target JEE Advanced

1. **(b)** Rate of forward reaction (r_f) is given by

$$r_f = k_1 [SO_2]^2[O_2]$$

Rate of backward reaction (r_b) is given by

$$r_b = k_2[SO_3]^2$$

Rate of disappearance of SO_2 is

$$\frac{-d[SO_2]}{dt} = 2(r_f - r_b)$$

$$= 2(k_1[SO_2]^2[O_2] - k_2[SO_3]^2)$$

2. **(d)** Rate of consumption of $A = k_1[A] + k_2[A]$

$$k_{Total} = k_1 + k_2 = 0.1 + 0.2 = 0.3\,s^{-1}$$

Integrated 1st order reaction is

$$[A]_t = [A]_0 e^{-k_{Total}\,t}$$

$$[A]_{10} = 0.5 \times e^{-0.3 \times 10}$$

$$= 0.5 \times e^{-3}$$

$$\approx 0.5 \times 0.0498$$

$$= 0.0249\,M$$

3. **(a)** Rate Law for this reaction is

$$\text{Rate} = k[\text{Ester}][H^+]$$

Half life ($t_{1/2}$) for first order reaction is

$$t_{1/2} = \frac{\ln 2}{k[H^+]}$$

At pH = 4

$$[H^+] = 10^{-4}\,M$$

$$t_{1/2} = \frac{\ln 2}{k \times 10^{-4}}$$

$$k = \frac{\ln 2}{40 \times 10^{-4}}$$

At pH = 3 $\quad [H^+] = 10^{-3}\,M$

$$t'_{1/2} = \frac{\ln 2}{k \times 10^{-3}}$$

$$= \frac{\ln 2}{\dfrac{\ln 2}{40 \times 10^{-4}} \times 10^{-3}}$$

$$t'_{1/2} = 4 \text{ minutes}$$

4. **(a)** For a second order reaction rate law is

$$\text{Rate} = k[CH_3Br][OH^-]$$

The integrated form is

$$\frac{1}{[CH_3Br]_t} - \frac{1}{[CH_3Br]_0} = k[OH^-]t$$

$$\frac{1}{[CH_3Br]_t} - \frac{1}{0.2} = 0.05 \times 0.1 \times 3000$$

$$\frac{1}{[CH_3Br]_t} - 5 = 15$$

$$\frac{1}{[CH_3Br]_t} = 20$$

$$[CH_3Br]_t = 0.05\,M$$

$$\% \text{ Reacted} = \left(1 - \frac{0.05}{0.2}\right) \times 100$$

$$= (1 - 0.25) \times 100$$

$$= 0.75 \times 100 = 75\%$$

5. **(c)** (A) is correct but (R) is incorrect.

The correct form of (R) is

The Arrhenius equation shows that the rate constant k increases exponentially with temperature, and this increase is more significant when the activation energy is higher.

6. **(b)** For zero order,

$$2(t_{1/2}) = t_{complete}$$

$$(t_{1/2}) = \frac{14.56}{2} \quad \ldots(i)$$

For first order reaction,

$$(t_{1/2}) = \frac{0.693}{k_1}$$

Given,

$$(t_{1/2})_0 = (t_{1/2})_1$$

$$\frac{14.56}{2} = \frac{0.693}{k_1}$$

$$k_1 = 0.0951\,\text{min}^{-1}$$

$$= 0.1 \times 60\,\text{hr}^{-1}$$

$$k_1 = 6\,\text{hr}^{-1}$$

7. **(a)** Both Statement I and Statement II are correct.

8. **(c)** For a first order reaction, the half-life is given by

$$t_{1/2} = \frac{\ln 2}{k} \Rightarrow k = \frac{0.693}{20 \times 60\,s} = \frac{0.693}{1200\,s}$$

$$k = 5.78 \times 10^{-4}\,s^{-1}$$

The Arrhenius equation is

$$k = Ae^{-Ea/RT}$$

$$5.78 \times 10^{-4} = 2.0 \times 10^{10} e^{\frac{-80000}{8.314 \times T}}$$

Take natural logarithm on both sides

$$\ln(5.78 \times 10^{-4}) = \ln(2.0 \times 10^{10}) - \frac{80000}{8.314 \times T}$$

$$-7.456 = 23.719 - \frac{80000}{8.314 \times T}$$

$$-31.175 = \frac{-80000}{8.314 \times T}$$

$$\frac{31.175 \times 8.314}{80000} = \frac{1}{T}$$

$$T = 308.66\,K$$

$$T = 308.66 - 273.15 = 35.51°C$$

9. **(d)** Arrhenius equation, when temperature increases from 20°C to 30°C

$$\log 4 = \frac{E_a}{2.303R}\left(\frac{1}{293\,K} - \frac{1}{303\,K}\right) \quad \ldots(1)$$

Arrhenius equation, when temperature increases from 30° to 40°C

$$\log y = \frac{Ea}{2.303R}\left(\frac{1}{303\,K} - \frac{1}{313\,K}\right) \quad \ldots(2)$$

Divide Eqs. (2) by (1)

$$\frac{\log y}{\log 4} = \frac{293\,K}{313\,K} \Rightarrow \frac{\log y}{0.602} = 0.936$$

$$\Rightarrow \quad \log y = 0.563 \Rightarrow y = 3.66$$

10. ***(c)*** Transition state theory also consider the orientation of molecules during collision, as the correct orientation is necessary for effective collisions to form transition state.

11. ***(a, b, d)*** Statements (a, b, d) are correct while (c) is incorrect. The correct form of (c) is:

    The rate of reaction increases when nucleophile is stronger in S_N2 reaction.

12. ***(a, b, c, d)*** All the given statements are correct.

13. ***(c, d, e)*** Statements (c), (d), (e) are correct whereas (a), (b) are incorrect.

    The correct form of (a), (b) are:

    For $n > 1$, a plot of $\frac{1}{[A]^{n-1}}$ versus time t is linear.

    For $n < 1$, the half-life of the reaction decreases as the concentration $[A]_0$ increases.

14. ***(a, b, d)*** Statements (a), (b), (d) are correct whereas (c) is incorrect. The correct form (c) is

    The rate law appears to be first order with respect to only one reactant, not both. The reaction is orginally second-order, but due to the excess concentration of one reactant, it behaves as 1st order overall.

15. ***(a, b, c, d, e)*** All statements are correct.

16. ***(b, c, d)*** Among the given statement (b), (c) and (d) are correct except (a). Its corrected form is as

    Specific rate constant of the reaction depends on temperature.

17. ***(c, d)*** If there is no correlation between temperature and the rate constant, it does not necessarily imply that the activation energy is negative. In fact, negative activation energy is a rare phenomenon and usually indicates an unusual reaction mechanism.

$$k = Ae^{-E_a/RT}$$
$$= (8.0 \times 10^{12}\ s^{-1})e^{-24000\,K/T}$$
$$\frac{E_a}{8.314} = 24000 \Rightarrow E_a = 199.536\,kJ/mol.$$

18. ***(b, c, d, e)*** Statements (b), (c), (d), (e) are correct whereas statements (a) is incorrect.

    The correct form of (a) is

    The concentration of A decreases exponentially with time according to the sum of rate constants ($k_1 + k_2$).

19. ***(a)*** The correct match is: A-2, B-1, C-4, D-3

20. ***(b)*** The correct match is : A-2, B-1, C-4, D-3

21. ***(d)*** The correct match is : A-2, B-4, C-3, D-1

22. ***(a)*** The correct match is: A-2, B-3, C-4, D-1

23. ***(c)*** The correct match is : A-1, B-2, C-3, D-4

24. ***(b)*** The correct match is: A-2, B-1, C-4, D-3

25. ***(0.0385)*** The concentration of N_2O_4 at time t will be

$$[N_2O_4]_t = [N_2O_4]_0 - x = 0.6 - x$$
$$[NO_2]_t = 2x$$
$$\frac{[NO_2]_t}{[N_2O_4]_t} = 2.0 \Rightarrow \frac{2x}{0.6 - x} = 2.0$$
$$2x = 2 \times (0.6 - x)$$
$$2x = 1.2 - 2x$$
$$4x = 1.2$$
$$x = 0.3$$

The decomposition of N_2O_4 follows first order kinetics

$$\ln\left(\frac{[N_2O_4]_0}{[N_2O_4]_t}\right) = kt$$
$$[N_2O_4]_t = 0.6 - x = 0.6 - 0.3 = 0.3\,M$$
$$\ln\left(\frac{0.6}{0.3}\right) = 5.0 \times 10^{-3} \times t$$
$$\ln 2 = 5.0 \times 10^{-3} \times t$$
$$0.693 = 5.0 \times 10^{-3} \times t$$
$$t = \frac{0.693}{5.0 \times 10^{-3}} = 138.6\,sec$$
$$= 0.0385\,hours$$

26. ***(5.4× 10⁷)*** For ideal gases, the partial pressure are proportional to molar concentrations at constant temperature. Since the rate constant k is given in $M^{-1}s^{-1}$, then pressure can be directly treated as concentration in molarity.

$$[H_2] = 100\,M \Rightarrow [I_2] = 120\,M$$
$$\frac{-\Delta[H_2]}{\Delta t} = k[H_2][I_2] = (4.5 \times 10^3)(100 \times 120)$$
$$= 5.4 \times 10^7\,M/s$$

The initial rate of decrease of the partial pressure of H_2 is 5.4×10^7 mmHg/s

27. ***(3)*** The half-life ($t_{1/2}$) for a first-order reaction is

$$t_{1/2} = \frac{\ln 2}{k}$$
$$k_X = \frac{\ln 2}{t_{1/2,}(X)} = \frac{0.693}{5} = 0.1386\,min^{-1}$$
$$k_Y = \frac{\ln 2}{t_{1/2},(Y)} = \frac{0.693}{10} = 0.0693\,min^{-1}$$

For first order reaction, the concentration at time t is given by

$$[A]_t = [A]_0 e^{-kt}$$

For X after 20 minutes

$$[X]_{20} = 2.0 \times e^{-0.1386 \times 20}$$
$$[X]_{20} = 2.0 \times 0.062 = 0.124\,\text{M}$$

For Y after 20 minutes

$$[Y]_{20} = 1.5 \times e^{-0.0693 \times 20}$$
$$= 1.5 \times 0.250 = 0.375\,\text{M}$$

The amount of product P formed from each reactant is

From $X : P_X = [X]_0 - [X]_{20} = 2.0 - 0.124 = 1.876\,\text{M}$

From $Y : P_Y = [Y]_0 - [Y]_{20} = 1.5 - 0.375 = 1.125\,\text{M}$

Total concentration of P after 20 minutes

$$P_{\text{Total}} = P_X + P_Y = 1.874 + 1.125\,\text{M}$$
$$= 2.999\,\text{M} \approx 3\,\text{M}$$

28. ***(46.29°C)*** The time taken for a reaction is inversely proportional to the rate constant k

$$\frac{k_2}{k_1} = \frac{t_1}{t_2} \Rightarrow \frac{k_2}{k_1} = \frac{6}{1} = 6$$

The relationship between the rate constant at two temperatures is given by

$$\frac{k_2}{k_1} = Q_{10}^{\frac{T_2 - T_1}{10}}$$
$$6 = 3^{\frac{T_2 - 30}{10}}$$

Taking natural log on both sides:

$$\ln(6) = \ln 3^{(T_2 - 30)/10}$$
$$\ln 6 = \frac{T_2 - 30}{10} \ln 3$$
$$1.791 = \frac{T_2 - 30}{10} \times 1.099$$
$$\frac{1.791}{1.099} = \frac{T_2 - 30}{10}$$
$$1.629 = \frac{T_2 - 30}{10}$$
$$16.29 = T_2 - 30$$
$$T_2 = 46.29°\text{C}$$

29. ***(1.86)*** At steady state, the rate of production of NO_2 is equal to the rate of its destruction.

For second order kinetics

Rate of destruction $= k\,[NO_2]^2$

At state

$$\text{Rate of production} = \text{Rate of destruction}$$
$$6 \times 10^{-15}\,\text{M/h} = k(3 \times 10^{-8}\,\text{M})^2$$
$$\frac{6 \times 10^{-15}}{3600} = k(3 \times 10^{-8}\,\text{M})^2$$
$$1.67 \times 10^{-18} = k \times 9 \times 10^{-16}$$
$$k = 0.00186\,\text{M}^{-1}\text{s}^{-1}$$
$$= 0.00186\,\text{L mol}^{-1}\text{s}^{-1}$$
$$= 1.86 \times 10^{-6}\,\text{m}^3\,\text{mol}^{-1}\,\text{s}^{-1}$$

30. ***(1.514)*** For reaction 1

$$k_1(300) = 2 \times k_1(290)$$
$$\frac{k_1(300)}{k_1(290)} = e^{\frac{E_{a_1}}{R}\left(\frac{1}{290} - \frac{1}{300}\right)}$$
$$2 = e^{\frac{E_{a_1}}{R} \times 0.000115}$$
$$\ln 2 = \frac{E_{a_1}}{R} \times 0.000115$$
$$E_{a_1} = \frac{0.693 \times 8.314}{0.000115}$$
$$E_{a_1} = 50101\,\text{J/mol}$$
$$\approx 50\,\text{kJ/mol}$$
$$E_{a_2} = E_{a_1} - 20 = 50 - 20 = 30\,\text{kJ/mol}$$

For reaction 2

$$\frac{k_2(290)}{k_2(300)} = e^{\frac{Ea_2}{R}\left(\frac{1}{290} - \frac{1}{300}\right)}$$
$$\frac{k_2(290)}{k_2(300)} = e^{\frac{30 \times 10^3}{8.314} \times 0.000115}$$
$$\frac{k_2(290)}{k_2(300)} = e^{0.4150}$$
$$\frac{k_2(290)}{k_2(300)} = 1.514$$

31. ***(3197.22)*** Volume of drop

$$= 0.1\,\text{mL} = 0.1 \times 10^{-3}\,\text{L} = 1 \times 10^{-4}\,\text{L}$$

Initial concentration of H^+

$$[H^+]_0 = \frac{\text{moles of } [H^+]}{\text{Volume of solution}}$$
$$= \frac{5 \times 10^{-8}\,\text{moles}}{1 \times 10^{-4}\,\text{L}}$$
$$= 5 \times 10^{-4}\,\text{moles/L}$$

For the first order reaction, the concentration of H^+ at any time is given by

$$\ln\left(\frac{[H^+]_0}{[H^+]_t}\right) = kt$$

Concentration of H^+ is reduced to $\frac{1}{10}$th of its initial value

$$[H^+]_t = \frac{1}{10} \times [H^+]_0 = \frac{1}{10} \times 5 \times 10^{-4}$$
$$= 5 \times 10^{-5}\,\text{moles/L}$$
$$\ln\frac{(5 \times 10^{-4})}{(5 \times 10^{-5})} = (2 \times 10^{-7}) \times t$$
$$\ln 10 = 2 \times 10^{-7} \times t$$
$$2.302 = 2 \times 10^{-7} \times t$$
$$t = 1.151 \times 10^7\,\text{s}$$
$$\approx 3197.22\,\text{hours}$$

32. ***(1)*** $t_1 = 2\text{ ms}, \Delta x_1 = 0.005\% = 5\times10^{-5}, [A]_1 = 0.01\text{ M}$
$t_2 = 4\text{ ms}, \Delta_2 = 0.01\% = 1\times10^{-4}, [A]_2 = 0.02\text{ M}$

$$\text{Rate} = \frac{-d[A]}{dt} = k[A]^n$$
$$\Delta[A]_1 = 0.01\times5\times10^{-5} = 5\times10^{-7}\text{ M}$$
$$\text{Rate}_1 = \frac{(5\times10^{-7})\text{ M}}{(2\times10^{-3})\text{ s}}$$
$$= 2.5\times10^{-4}\text{ m/s}$$
$$\text{Rate}_1 = k(0.01)^n$$
$$\Delta[A]_2 = 0.02\times1\times10^{-4} = 2\times10^{-6}\text{ M}$$
$$\text{Rate}_2 = \frac{(2\times10^{-6})}{(4\times10^{-3})} = 5\times10^{-4}\text{ m/s}$$
$$\text{Rate}_2 = k(0.02)^n$$
$$\frac{\text{Rate}_2}{\text{Rate}_1} = \frac{(0.02)^n}{(0.01)^n}$$
$$\frac{5\times10^{-4}}{2.5\times10^{-4}} = \frac{(0.02)^n}{(0.01)^n}$$
$$\frac{50}{25} = 2^n$$
$$2 = 2^n$$
$$n = 1$$

33. ***(3)*** Statement (a), (b), (c) are correct but (d) is incorrect. The correct form of (d) is

Reaction rate is proportional to collisions, and the steric factor that affects the rate constant.

34. ***(3)*** Since, slowest step of any reaction is the rate determining step. Hence,

$$\text{Rate law} = k_2[NH_4^+][HNO_2]$$
$$k_1 = \frac{[HNO_2]}{[NaNO_2][HCl]}$$
$$[HNO_2] = k_1[NaNO_2][HCl]$$
$$\text{Rate law} = k_1k_2[NH_4^+][NaNO_2][HCl]$$

Order of the reaction:

order with respect to $[NH_4]^+ = 1$

and $[NaNO_2] = 1, [HCl] = 2$

overall order of the reaction $= 1 + 2 = 3$

Solution for (Q. Nos. 35 and 36)

This is a case of parallel reaction

$$k_1 + k_2 = \frac{2.303}{t}\log\left(\frac{a}{a-x}\right)$$
$$t = 20\text{ min}, x = 0.60\,a$$
$$\therefore \quad k_1 + k_2 = \frac{2.303}{20\text{ min}}\log\frac{a}{0.40a} = 0.0458\text{ min}^{-1}$$

After 20 min $[B] = 75\%$ and $[C] = 25\%$

$$\Rightarrow \frac{d[B]}{dt} = k_1[A] = k_1\times25$$
$$\Rightarrow \frac{d[C]}{dt} = k_2[A] = k_2\times75$$
$$k_1\times25 = k_2\times75$$
$$\frac{k_1}{k_2} = 3 \Rightarrow k_1 = 3k_2$$
$$k_1 + k_2 = 4k_2 = 0.0458\text{ min}^{-1}$$
$$k_2 = 0.01145\text{ min}^{-1}$$
$$k_1 = 0.03435\text{ min}^{-1}$$

35. ***(c)***

36. ***(a)***

Solution for (Q. Nos. 37 and 38)

$$\log k\ (\text{min}^{-1}) = -\frac{11067\text{ K}}{T} + 31.330$$

At 298 K, $\log k\ (\text{min}^{-1}) = -\dfrac{11067}{298} + 31.330$

$$= -5.8076\text{ min}^{-1}$$
$$k = 1.5574\times10^{-6}\text{ min}^{-1}$$
$$k = 2.596\times10^{-8}\text{ s}^{-1}$$
$$\log k = \log A - \frac{Ea}{2.303RT}$$

On comparing with given equation

$$\frac{Ea}{2.303R} = 11067\text{ K}$$
$$Ea = 2.303R\times11067\text{ K}$$
$$= 2.303\times8.314\times10^{-3}\text{ kJ mol}^{-1}\times11067\text{ K}$$
$$= 211.90\text{ kJ/mol}$$

37. ***(2.6 × 10^{-8})***

38. ***(211.90)***

Solution for (Q. 39 and 40)

Rate law, $-\dfrac{\Delta[A]}{\Delta t} = k[A]^a[B]^b$

where, a = order wrt A, b = order w.r.t B

Set	$[A]_0$	$[A]_t$	$[B]_0$	$\Delta[A]$	Δt (h)	$\frac{-\Delta[A]}{\Delta t}$ (hr^{-1})
1	0.10	0.0975	1.0	0.0025	0.50	5.0×10^{-3}
2	0.10	0.0900	2.0	0.0100	0.50	2.0×10^{-2}
3	0.05	0.04500	1.0	0.0050	2.00	2.5×10^{-3}

(i) $5\times10^{-3} = k[0.1]^a[1.0]^b$
(ii) $2\times10^{-2} = k[0.1]^a[2.0]^b$
(iii) $2.5\times10^{-3} = k[0.05]^a[1.0]^b$

From Eqs. (i) and (ii)

$$\frac{2.0\times10^{-2}}{5.0\times10^{-3}} = (2)^b \Rightarrow (4) = 2^b$$
$$(2)^2 = (2)^b \Rightarrow b = 2$$

Order wrt $B = 2$

From Eqs. (i) and (iii)

$$\frac{5.0\times10^{-3}}{2.5\times10^{-3}}=\left(\frac{0.10}{0.05}\right)^a$$

$$(2)=(2)^a \Rightarrow a=1 \Rightarrow \text{order w.r.t } A=1$$

From Eqs. (i), $5.0\times10^{-3}=k(0.1)(1.0)^2$

$$\Rightarrow \quad k=5.0\times10^{-2}\ M^{-2}h^{-1}$$

39. ***(3)***

40. ***(5×10^{-2})***

Solution for (Q. Nos. 41 and 42)

Molecularity of each step is 2. Thus, (a) is correct.

The limiting step of a complex reaction is always the slowest. Thus (b) is correct.

It involves more than one elementary step, thus it is a complex reaction. Thus, (d) is correct.

HOI appears in step II and disappears in III.

Thus, (c) is incorrect.

Slow step II is the rate-determining step

Thus, $\left(\frac{dx}{dt}\right)=k_2[I^-][HOCl]$

By Step I, $k_1[OCl^-]=k_{-1},[HOCl][OH^-]$

$$[HOCl]=k_1[OCl^-]/k_{-1}[OH^-]$$

$$\therefore \quad \left(\frac{dx}{dt}\right)=\frac{k_2[I^-]k_1[OCl^-]}{k_{-1}[OH^-]}$$

$$=\frac{k_1k_2[I^-][OCl^-]}{k_{-1}[OH^-]}$$

41. ***(c)***

42. ***(a)***

43. ***(c)*** Graphs follows 2nd order reaction

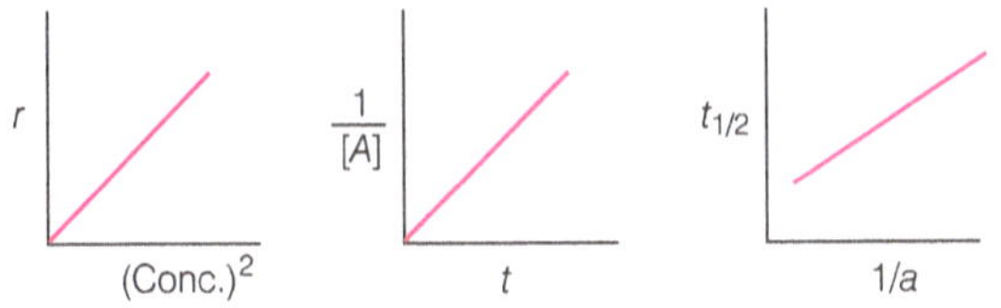

Graphs follows first order reaction.

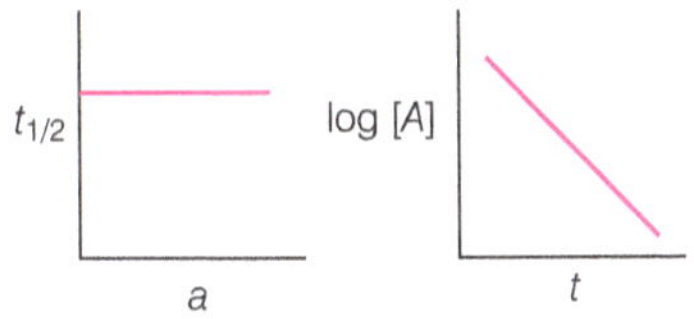

44. ***(b)***

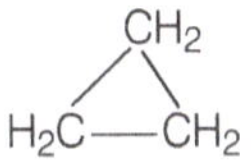

H_2C—CH_2 (cyclic, with CH_2) $\longrightarrow CH_3—CH=CH_2 \longrightarrow$ First order reaction

$$2N_2O(g)\xrightarrow[\text{High pressure}]{\text{Hot Pt}}2N_2(g)+O_2(g) \text{ zero order reaction}$$

$$H_2+Cl_2\xrightarrow{h\nu}2HCl \text{ — zero order reaction}$$

$$CH_3COOC_2H_5+OH^{\ominus}\longrightarrow CH_3COO^{\ominus}+C_2H_5OH \text{ and}$$

$$2HI\longrightarrow H_2+I_2 \text{ — Second order reaction.}$$

45. ***(a)*** All the expression are of Arrhenius Equation

46. ***(d)*** Reactions studied by Isolation method are:

$$C_{12}H_{22}O_{11}+H_2O\xrightarrow{H^+}C_6H_{12}O_6+C_6H_{12}O_6$$

$$CH_3COCH_3+I_2\longrightarrow CH_3COCH_2I+HI$$

Reactions studied by Titrimetric method

$$CH_3COOCH_3+NaOH\longrightarrow CH_3COONa+CH_3OH$$

Half-life method

$$CH_3COOC_2H_5+H_2O\longrightarrow CH_3COOH+C_2H_5OH$$

Conductometric method

$$HCl+NaOH\longrightarrow NaCl+H_2O$$

Initial rate method

$$2H_2O_2\longrightarrow 2H_2O+O_2$$

$$Br_2+CH_3COCH_3\longrightarrow CH_3COCH_2Br+HBr$$

47. ***(b)*** $0.549=1-\frac{1100}{8.314\times T}$ $\quad$ $0.477=1-\frac{1000}{8.314\times T}$

$\Rightarrow \quad T\approx293.36\,K$ $\quad$ $\Rightarrow \quad T\approx229.98\,K$

$0.477=1-\frac{1150}{8.314\times T}$ $\quad$ $0.457=1-\frac{1000}{8.314\times T}$

$\Rightarrow \quad T\approx264.48\,K$ $\quad$ $\Rightarrow \quad T\approx221.51\,K$

48. ***(a)*** The expressions for 1st order reaction is

$$\log[A]=\log[A]_0-\frac{kt}{2.303}$$

$$t_{1/2}=\frac{0.693}{k}$$

$$[A]=[A]_0e^{-kt}$$

The expressions for zero order reaction is

$$k=\frac{[A]_0-[A]}{t}$$

$$t_{1/2}=\frac{[A]_0}{2k}$$

The expression for second order reaction is

$$t_{1/2}=\frac{1}{k[A]_0}$$

$$k=\frac{1}{t}\left[\frac{1}{[A]}-\frac{1}{[A]_0}\right]$$

49. ***(b)*** Among the species only *C*, *E* and *G* are reaction intermediates while *B*, *D*, *F* and *H* are transition states or activated complex.

50. ***(b)*** Equations related to first order are:

$$T_{50}=t_{1/2}=0.693\times T_{av}$$

$$T_{av}=1.44T_{50}$$

$$T_{75}=1.5\times T_{50}$$

$$T_{75}>T_{av}>T_{50}$$

Check Through PYQs : JEE Advanced

1. **(8)** The reaction is

$$8H^+ + 5[Fe(H_2O)_2(Ox)_2]^{2-} + MnO_4^- \longrightarrow Mn^{2+} + 5[Fe(H_2O)_2(Ox)_2]^- + 4H_2O$$

$$\text{Rate} = -\frac{1}{8}\frac{d[H^+]}{dt} = -\frac{d[MnO_4^-]}{dt}$$

Hence, $\dfrac{\text{Rate of change } [H^+]}{\text{Rate of change of } [MnO_4^-]} = 8$

2. **(3)** Since, slowest step of any reaction is the rate determining step. Hence,

$$\text{Rate law} = k_2[N_2O_2]\,[H_2]$$

$\because \quad \dfrac{k_1}{k_{-1}} = \dfrac{[N_2O_2]}{[NO]^2}$

$\therefore \quad [N_2O_2] = \dfrac{k_1}{k_{-1}}[NO]^2$

$\therefore \quad \text{Rate} = k_2 \times \dfrac{k_1}{k_{-1}}[NO]^2[H_2]$

So, the order of the reaction is 3.

3. **(143)** The reaction involved is as follows

$$_{92}U^{238} \longrightarrow {}_{82}Pb^{206} + 8_2He^4 + 6_{-1}\beta^0$$

$$t = 0,\ N_0 = \left(\frac{1}{238} + \frac{7}{206}\right)\text{mol}$$

$$t = t\ N_t = \frac{1}{238}\text{mol}$$

$$x = \frac{7}{206}\text{mol}$$

For 1st order kinetics

$$\lambda_t = \ln\frac{N_0}{N_t}$$

$$\frac{\ln 2}{4.5\times10^9} = \frac{1}{t}\ln\cdot\frac{\left(\frac{1}{238} + \frac{7}{206}\right)}{\frac{1}{238}}$$

$\Rightarrow \quad t = \dfrac{4.5\times10^9}{\ln 2}\ln\dfrac{1872}{206}$

$$= 143\times10^8 \text{ years}$$

Thus, the value of P is 143.

4. **(5)** Given, A_f (Pre-exponential factor for forward reaction) $= 10^{15}$

A_b (Pre-exponential factor for backward reaction) $= 10^{11}$

$\log K$ at 500 K = 6

From graph, $\log k_f$ at 500 K = 9

$\log k_b$ at 500 K = ?

As $\quad \log K = \log\dfrac{k_f}{k_b} \qquad \left(\because K = \dfrac{k_f}{k_b}\right)$

$\therefore$ At 500 K,

$$6 = \log k_f - \log k_b$$

$$6 = 9 - \log k_b$$

$\therefore \quad \log k_b = 3$

According to Arrhenius equation,

$$\log k_b = \log A_b - \frac{E_{a(b)}}{2.3RT}$$

From graph, $\dfrac{1}{T} = 0.002$

$\therefore \quad 3 = 11 - \dfrac{E_{a(b)}}{2.3R}(0.002) \qquad [\because A_b = 10^{11}]$

$\therefore \quad \dfrac{E_{a(b)}}{2.3R} = \dfrac{8}{0.002} = 4\times10^3$

At 250 K,

$$\log k_b = 11 - \frac{E_{a(b)}}{2.3R}\left(\frac{1}{250}\right)$$

$$\log k_b = 11 - 4\times10^3\,(0.004)$$

$$\log k_b = 11 - 16$$

$\Rightarrow \quad \log k_b = -5$

$\therefore \quad |\log k_b| = 5$

5. **(a)** $\text{Rate} = \dfrac{k[X]}{X_s + [X]} = \dfrac{k}{\dfrac{X_s}{[X]} + 1} = k\,\dfrac{1}{\dfrac{X_s}{[X]} + 1}$

(I) When, $[X] \rightarrow \infty$

Rate = k

$\Rightarrow$ Rate is independent of concentration

$\Rightarrow$ Order of reaction = 0 (w.r.t. X)

$\therefore$ (I) $\rightarrow$ (P), (S)

(II) When $[X] << X_s$;

$\therefore \text{Rate} = k\,\dfrac{[X]}{[X]_s}$

$\Rightarrow$ Order of reaction = 1 (w.r.t. X)

$\therefore$ (II) $\rightarrow$ (Q), (T)

(III) $[X] >> X_s$;

$$\text{rate} = \frac{k[X]}{[X]} = k$$

$\Rightarrow$ Order of reaction = 0 (w.r.t. X)

$\therefore$ (III) $\rightarrow$ (P), (S)

(IV) $\text{Rate} = \dfrac{k[X]^2}{X_s + [X]}$

$[X] >> X_s$; Rate = $k[X]$

$\Rightarrow$ Order of reaction = 1 (w.r.t. X)

(IV) $\rightarrow$ (Q), (T)

6. **(b, c, d)**

	$2X$	$+\ Y \xrightarrow{k}$	P
$t = 0$	2 mol	1 mol	–
$t = 50\,s$	(2 – 1) mol = 1 mol	(1 – 0.5) mol = 0.5 mol	0.5 mol

$\Rightarrow$ As the concentration of reactant (X) becomes half at $t = 50$ s.

At $t_{1/2}$, $X = \dfrac{X_0}{2}$,

$$\ln\frac{2X_0}{X_0}=2kt_{1/2}$$

$$\Rightarrow \quad k=\frac{\ln 2}{2t_{1/2}}=\frac{0.693}{100}$$

$$=6.93\times10^{-3}\ s^{-1}$$

At, $t=50$ s, $-\frac{dX}{dt}=2k\ [X]^1;[X]=1\,\text{mol}$

So, $\frac{-d[X]}{dt}=2\times6.93\times10^{-3}\times1$

$$=13.86\times10^{-3}\ \text{mol L}^{-1}\ s^{-1}$$

At $t=100$ s, $-\frac{1}{2}\frac{d[X]}{dt}=\frac{-d[Y]}{dt}$

$$\Rightarrow \quad \frac{-d[Y]}{dt}=k[Y]^1;[Y]=\frac{1}{2}$$

$$-\frac{d[Y]}{dt}=6.93\times10^{-3}\times\frac{1}{2}$$

$$=3.46\times10^{-3}\ \text{mol L}^{-1}\ s^{-1}$$

7. ***(a)*** $(CH_3)_3CBr + NaOH \xrightarrow[\text{(First order reaction)}]{S_N1} (CH_3)_3C{-}OH + NaBr$

This is first order reaction and for first order reaction

$$t_{1/2}=\frac{0.693}{k}$$

So, half-life is independent of initial concentration.

Therefore, the plot (a) correct.

For first order reaction,

$$R=k\,[(CH_3)_3C{-}Br]$$

$$\ln\left(\frac{P_0}{P}\right)=kt \text{ or } \ln\left(\frac{P}{P_0}\right)=-kt$$

Hence, plot (b) and (d) are incorrect.

For first order reaction,

$$Q=[P_0](1-e^{-kt})$$

or $$\frac{[Q]}{[P_0]}=(1-e^{-kt})$$

Hence, plot (c) is incorrect.

8. ***(1.20)*** ${}^{238}_{92}U \longrightarrow {}^{206}_{82}Pb$

Initial moles of $U^{238}=\frac{68\times10^{-6}}{238}=x$

Number of α-particles emitted per nuclei of

$${}^{238}_{92}U=\frac{238-206}{4}=8$$

Moles of U^{238} decayed in three half-lives $=\frac{7}{8}x$

No. of α-particle emitted $=\left(\frac{7}{8}x\right)\times8\times N_A$

$$=7\times\frac{68\times10^{-6}}{238}\times6.022\times10^{23}$$

$$=1.204\times10^{18}$$

$\therefore \quad Z=1.20$

9. ***(6.75)*** Rate $=k[A]^x[B]^y[C]^z$

$$\frac{(\text{Rate})_1}{(\text{Rate})_2}=\frac{[0.2]^x\,[0.1]^y\,[0.1]^z}{[0.2]^x\,[0.2]^y\,[0.1]^z}$$

$$\Rightarrow \quad \frac{6\times10^{-5}}{6\times10^{-5}}=\left(\frac{1}{2}\right)^y$$

$\Rightarrow y=0$

$$\frac{(\text{Rate})_1}{(\text{Rate})_2}=\frac{[0.2]^x\,[0.1]^y\,[0.1]^z}{[0.2]^x\,[0.1]^y\,[0.2]^z}$$

$$\Rightarrow \quad \frac{6\times10^{-5}}{12\times10^{-4}}=\left(\frac{1}{2}\right)^z$$

$\Rightarrow Z=1$

$$\frac{(\text{Rate})_1}{(\text{Rate})_2}=\frac{[0.2]^x\,[0.1]^y\,[0.1]^z}{[0.3]^x\,[0.1]^y\,[0.1]^z}=\frac{6\times10^{-5}}{9\times10^{-5}}=\left(\frac{2}{3}\right)^x$$

$\Rightarrow x=1$

So, rate $=k[A]^1[C]^1$

From exp-Ist,

$$\text{Rate}=6.0\times10^{-5}\ \text{mol dm}^{-3}\ s^{-1}$$

$$6.0\times10^{-5}=k[0.2]^1[0.1]^1$$

$$k=3\times10^{-3}$$

Given, $[A]=0.15$ mol dm^{-3}

$[B]=0.25$ mol dm^{-3}

$[C]=0.15$ mol dm^{-3}

$\therefore$ Rate $=(3\times10^{-3})\times[0.15]^1[0.25]^0[0.15]^1$

$$=3\times10^{-3}\times0.15\times0.15$$

Rate $=6.75\times10^{-5}$ mol dm^{-3} s^{-1}

Thus, $Y=6.75$

10. ***(a, d)*** Given for the reaction

(at $T=300$ K and constant volume $=V$)

	$A(g)$	$\longrightarrow$	$2B(g)$	+	$C(g)$
at $t=0$	p_0		–		–
at $t=t$	p_0-x		$2x$		x
at $t=t_{1/3}$	$\left[p_0-\frac{2p_0}{3}\right]=\frac{p_0}{3}$		$\frac{4p_0}{3}$		$\frac{2p_0}{3}$

We can calculate,

$$p_t=p_0-x+2x+x=p_0+2x$$

or $$2x=p_t-p_0 \text{ or } x=\frac{p_t-p_0}{2}$$

Now, for first order reaction,

$$t=\frac{1}{k}\ln\frac{p_0}{(p_0-x)}$$

Putting the value of x in the equation,

$$t=\frac{1}{k}\ln\frac{p_0}{p_0-\left(\frac{p_t-p_0}{2}\right)}$$

$$=\frac{1}{k}\ln\frac{2p_0}{2p_0-p_t+p_0}$$

or $$kt=\ln\frac{2p_0}{(3p_0-p_t)}$$

or $$kt = \ln 2p_0 - \ln(3p_0 - p_t)$$

or $$\ln(3p_0 - p_t) = -kt + \ln 2p_0$$

It indicates graph between $\ln(3p_0 - p_t)$ vs 't' will be a straight line with negative slope , so option (a) is correct

$$t_{1/3} = \frac{1}{k}\ln\frac{p_0}{p_0/3} = \frac{1}{k}\ln 3$$

It indicates $t_{1/3}$ is independent of initial concentration so, option (b) is incorrect.

Likewise, rate constant also does not show its dependence over initial concentration. Thus, graph between rate constant and $[A]_0$ will be a straight line parallel to X-axis.

11. ***(8500)*** For the reaction,

$$A(g) + B(g) \rightleftharpoons AB(g)$$

Given $$E_{a_b} = E_{a_f} + 2RT$$

or $$E_{a_b} - E_{a_f} = 2RT$$

Further

$$A_f = 4A_b \quad \text{or} \quad \frac{A_f}{A_b} = 4$$

Now, rate constant for forward reaction,

$$k_f = A_f e^{-E_{af}/RT}$$

Likewise, rate constant for backward reaction,

$$k_b = A_b e^{-E_{ab}/RT}$$

At equilibrium,

Rate of forward reaction = Rate of backward reaction

i.e., $$k_f = k_b \quad \text{or} \quad \frac{k_f}{k_b} = K_{eq}$$

so $$K_{eq} = \frac{A_f e^{-E_{af}/RT}}{A_b e^{-E_{ab}/RT}}$$

$$= \frac{A_f}{A_b} e^{-(E_{af} - E_{ab})/RT}$$

After putting the given values

$$k_{eq} = 4e^2 \text{ (as } E_{a_b} - E_{a_f} = 2RT \text{ and } \frac{A_f}{A_b} = 4)$$

Now, $$\Delta G° = -RT \ln K_{eq}$$

$$= -2500 \ln(4e^2)$$

$$= -2500 (\ln 4 + \ln e^2)$$

$$= -2500 (1.4 + 2)$$

$$= -2500 \times 3.4 = -8500 \text{ J/mol}$$

Absolute value = 8500 J/mol

12. ***(a, c)*** Activation energy is not related to steric factor. If steric factor p is considered, the corrected Arrhenius equation will be

$k = pZe^{\frac{-E_a}{RT}}$ where A = frequency factor by Arrhenius = $p \times Z$

Hence, (a) and (c) is correct.

13. ***(b, c, d)*** Rate constant,

$$k = Ae^{-E_a/RT}$$

where, E_a = activation energy and

A = pre-exponential factor

(a) If E_a is high, it means lower value of k hence, slow reaction. Thus, (a) is incorrect.

(b) On increasing temperature, molecules are raised to higher energy (greater than E_a), hence number of collisions increases. Thus, (b) is correct.

(c) $\log k = \log A - \frac{E_a}{RT}$

$$\Rightarrow \frac{d(\log k)}{dT} = \frac{E_a}{RT^2}$$

Thus, when E_a is high, stronger is the temperature dependence of the rate constant. Thus, (c) is correct.

(d) Pre-exponential factor (A) is a measure of rate at which collisions occur. Thus, (d) is correct.

CHAPTER 10

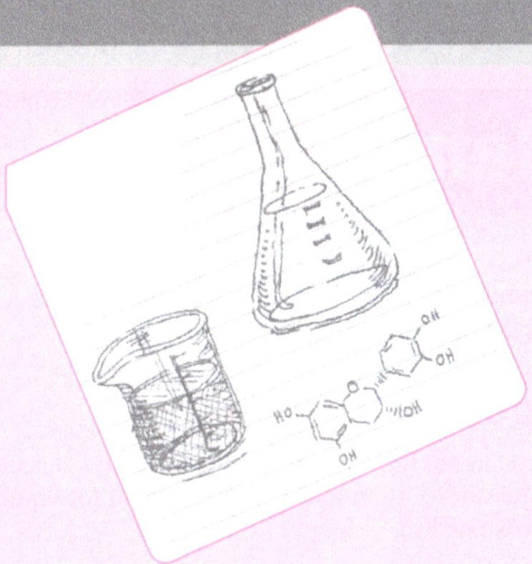

Surface Chemistry

Learning Elements

Element 1 Adsorption

Distinction between Adsorption and Absorption, Mechanism of Adsorption, Types of Adsorption, Freundlich Adsorption Isothern, Langmuir Adsorption Isotherm,

Element 2 Catalysis

Types of Catalysis-Homogeneous and Heterogeneous Catalysis, Based on the Mechanism, Activity and Selectivity of Catalyst, Theories of Catalysis, Enzyme Catalysis.

Element 3 Particle Size and Colloidal State

Classification of Solution, Critical Micelle Concentration (CMC), Preparation of Colloidal Solutions, Purification of Colloidal Solutions, Properties of Colloids, Coagulation and Hardy-Schulze Rule, Protective Collidal Sols and Gold Number Emulsions, Emulsifiers, Gels

Practice Elements

Practice Element Target JEE Advanced

Trend Insights

JEE Advanced

Typology		Years			
	2024	2023	2022	2021	2020
1. Simple MCQs	–	1	–	–	–
2. One or More than one correct	–	–	1	1	–
3. Numerical Value/Integer	1	–	–	–	–
4. Matching Type	–	–	–	–	–
5. Paragraph Based	–	–	–	–	–

E = Easy, **M** = Medium, **T** = tough, **O** = Overall

Current Dynamics

- A fair number of numerical problems, especially those involving adsorption isotherms, and catalysis have been asked in recent years.
- In recent years, questions basically focus on conceptual clarity, especially around the fundamentals of adsorption, colloids and surface active agents.
- The least few years have seen a marked increase in questions related to Langmuir and Freundlich adsorption isotherms with an emphasis on calculations of adsorption and surface area.

Insightful Advice

- Focus on understanding the types of catalysis, activation energy and the mechanism behind catalytic reactions.
- Master the concept of CMC and its significance in detergent and emulsification.
- Students are advised to understand the key theories like Langmiur adsorption isotherm and the conditions under which these theory applies.

Element 1 Adsorption

Surface chemistry deals with the phenomenon or changes that takes place at the surfaces or interfaces.

Adsorption

The phenomenon of higher concentration of any molecular species at the surface than in the bulk of a solid (or liquid) is known as **adsorption**.

The phenomena of adsorption is basically due to presence of residual forces at the surface of liquid or solid. In case of liquids, residual forces arise from the non-uniform distribution of molecules at the surface.

In case of solids, residual forces arise due to presence of unbalanced valence forces of atom or ions at surface. Due to residual forces, the surface of a solid (or a liquid) has a tendency to attract and retain molecules of other species with which it is brought into contact. Concentration of these species is more at the surface than in the bulk of the solid or liquid.

Solids, particularly when finely divided, have a large surface area, hence, this behaviour is predominantly on solid surfaces.

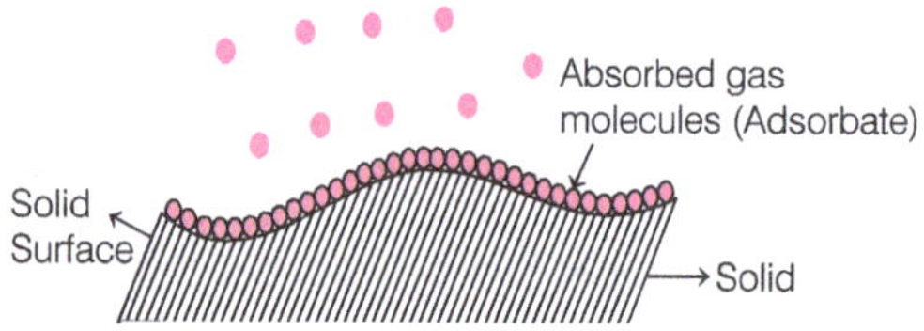

Adsorption of gas molecules over solid surface

For adsorption process, two components are required.

The solid that takes up a gas or vapour or a solute from solution, i.e. the solid at the surface of which adsorption takes place is called the **adsorbent** while the gas or the solute, which accumulates at the surface of the solid is called the **adsorbate**.

	Adsorption	Adsorbate	Adsorbent
(a)	Ink on chalk	Ink	Chalk
(b)	Acetic acid on charcoal	Acetic acid	Charcoal
(c)	H_2 on metal	H_2	Metal surface

The adsorption of gases on metal surfaces is called occlusion. Colloids, on account of their extremely small dimensions, have larger surface area per unit mass and these are good adsorbents.

Distinction between Adsorption and Absorption

Some point of difference between absorption and adsorption are given below in table.

	Absorption	Adsorption
1.	It is phenomenon as a result of which the species of one substance get distributed uniformly throughout the body of the other substance.	It is the phenomenon as a result of which the species of one substance get concentrated mainly at the surface of the other substance which adsorbs these.
2.	The concentration is the same throughout the material.	The concentration on the surface of the adsorbent is different from that in the bulk.
3.	It is a bulk phenomenon since it occurs throughout the bulk of the material.	It is only a surface phenomenon since it occurs only at the surface.
4.	Absorption proceeds at uniform rate.	Adsorption is rapid in the beginning and its rate slowly decreases with the non-availability of the surface.

- In some cases, adsorption and absorption take place simultaneously and it is difficult to determine the relative extent of adsorption and absorption. The term **sorption** is widely used in such cases.
- The removal of the adsorbed substance from a surface is called **desorption** when equilibrium is reached.
  At equilibrium,

$$\text{Rate of adsorption} = \text{Rate of desorption}$$

JEE Spotlite

There are some liquid solutions in which concentration of the adsorbate is less on the surface than in the bulk of the solution. This type of adsorption is referred to as **negative adsorption**.

Mechanism of Adsorption

Only the surface atoms in an adsorbent play an active role in adsorption. These atoms possess unbalanced forces of various types such as, van der Waals' forces and chemical bond forces.

These force arises because the molecules present at the surface are attracted by other molecules only from below unlike the molecules inside the bulk phase which are attracted uniformly from all sides.

Thus, molecules on surface have a tendency to move inside the bulk phase where force of attraction is uniform or the surface is under strain due to unbalanced residual forces.

To satisfy the residual force the surface has a tendency to attract and retain molecules of the adsorbate when brought in contact with them.

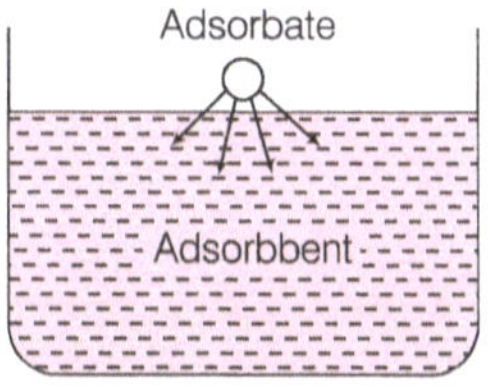

Mechanism for adsorption

When adsorption takes place residual forces of the surface decreases. This decrease in surface energy appears as heat. Thus, adsorption is an exothermic process.

i.e. $\Delta H < 0$

Also due to adsorption, gaseous molecules (adsorbate) are set into ordered state (i.e their randomness decreases). Hence, entropy which is the measure of disorder of the system decreases.),

i.e. $\Delta S < 0$

By thermodynamic relation $\Delta G = \Delta H - T\Delta S$

ΔH and ΔS both decrease, and adsorption process being spontaneous $\Delta G < 0$ at constant temperature and pressure.

Thus, ΔH is very high (as $T\Delta S$ is positive and to make ΔG negative, $\Delta H > T\Delta S$).

As adsorption proceeds, ΔH becomes less and less negative and when equilibrium is attained

$$\Delta G = 0, \text{ and } \Delta H = T\Delta S.$$

Types of Adsorption

Depending on the nature of attractive forces involved between adsorbent and adsorbate, adsorption can be :

(i) **Physical adsorption** (physisorption) in which adsorbate is held to the adsorbent by weak forces such as van der Waals' forces of attraction.

(ii) **Chemical adsorption** (chemisorption) in which adsorbate is held to the adsorbent by forces nearly as strong as a chemical bond.

Distinction between the two types of adsorption is summarised below.

Difference between physical and chemical adsorptions

S.No.	Physical adsorption	Chemical adsorption
1.	Reversible	Irreversible
2.	Formation of multimolecular layers	Formation of unimolecular layer
3.	The amount of gas adsorbed is related to the ease of liquefaction of the gas	No coorelation exists
4.	Forces of attraction between adsorbate and adsorbent are weak (van der Waals' forces)	Strong (as a chemical bond)
5.	Non-specific in nature, i.e. all gases adsorbed on all sides to some extent	Highly specific and occurs only if there is a possibility of compound formation between the gas being adsorbed and the solid adsorbent
6.	Low enthalpy of adsorption, 20-40 kJ mol^{-1}	High enthalpy of adsorption, 80-240 kJ mol^{-1}
7.	Occurs at low temperature and decreases with increasing temperature 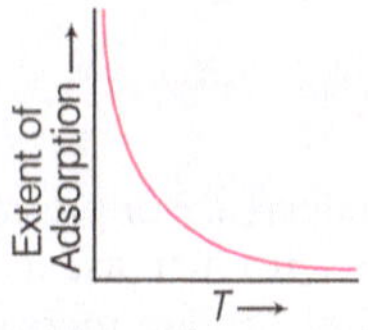	Occurs at higher temperature, extent of adsorption first increases and then decreases with increase in temperature 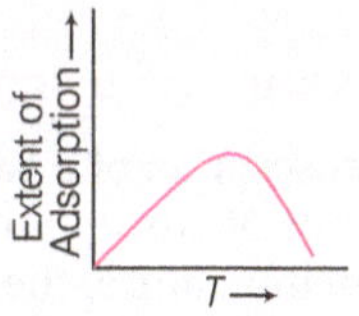
8.	Depends on the nature of the gas, more easily liquefiable gases are readily adsorbed	Depends on the nature of the gases. Those which can react with the adsorbent exhibit chemisorption
9.	No appreciable activation energy is required	High activation energy is required
10.	Increases with increase in surface area	Also increases with increase in surface area
11.	The rate of adsorption increases with increase in pressure of adsorbate	The rate of adsorption decreases with increase in pressure

Adsorption of Gases on Solids

Whenever a clean surface is exposed to a gas, the gas molecules get adsorbed on to the free surface. If the surface already having a weakly held adsorbate on it, the same is displaced by the substance which has a tendency to get adsorbed more strongly.

The activated charcoal used in gas masks is already exposed to atmosphere from where gases and water vapours are adsorbed. On exposing this adsorbate-rich charcoal to chlorine atmosphere, desorption of water vapours and other gases take place.

Factors Affecting Adsorption of Gases on Solids

1. Nature of Adsorbate (Gas)

It has been found that the more readily soluble and easily liquefiable gases such as NH_3, HCl, Cl_2, SO_2, etc., are adsorbed more than the so called permanent gases such as H_2, N_2 and O_2. Physical adsorption is non-specific in nature and therefore every gas gets adsorbed on the surface of any solid to a lesser or greater extent. The ease with which a gas can be liquefied is dependent on T_c, (critical temperature). **Higher the value of T_c of a gas, the more easily it will be liquefied and therefore, more readily it will be adsorbed on the solid.**

2. Nature and Surface Area of the Solid Adsorbent

Larger the surface area of the adsorbent, greater is the extent of adsorption. **The surface area per gram of the adsorbent is called specific surface area of the adsorbent**.

Finely divided solids having a large surface area show a much larger extent of adsorption.

3. Pressure of Adsorbate Gas

Since, adsorption of a gas leads to decrease of pressure, the magnitude of adsorption increases with increase in pressure. At low temperature, the extent of adsorption increases very rapidly with pressure. Over a small range of pressure, the extent of adsorption is found to be directly proportional to the pressure.

However, at higher pressure (closer to the saturation point of the vapour pressure of the gas), the adsorption tends to achieve a limiting value. At this point, formation of multilayers starts and a stage of **desorption** may be observed.

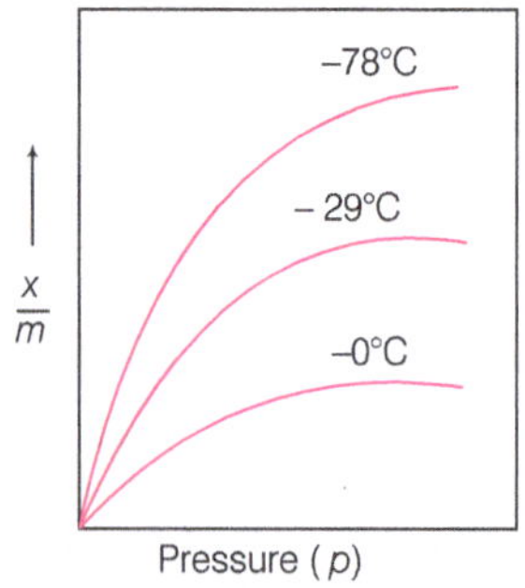

Adsorption isotherm

Above isotherms are obtained only when the adsorbate form a layer of one molecule thickness, the adsorption is monolayered.

4. Temperature

Adsorption is an exothermic process (taking place with evolution of heat), therefore in accordance with Le-Chatelier's principle, the magnitude of adsorption should increase with fall in temperature.

When temperature is lowered then due to lower thermal energy, more number of molecules are held to the surface by residual forces, i.e. higher adsorption. This actually happens except in chemisorption, where extent of adsorption first increases and then decreases with increase in temperature. In case of chemisorption, chemical reactions come into play for which to occur some activation energy is required.

The curve showing the effect of temperature on the extent of adsorption at a given pressure is called an **adsorption isobar**.

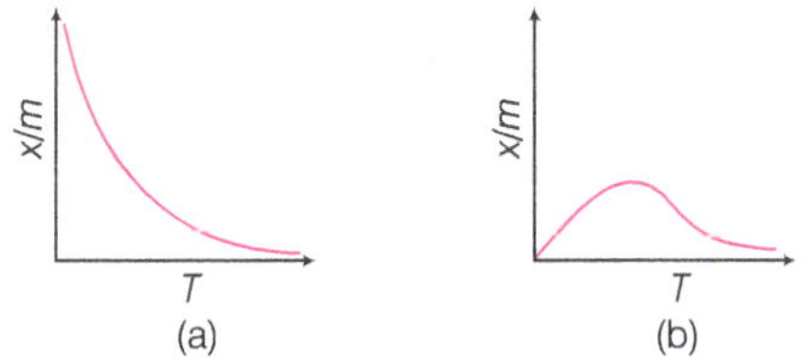

Effect of temperature on adsorption at constant pressure: (a) Physisorption and (b) Chemisorption

- Usually adsorption process is exothermic but some endothermic cases of chemisorption have also been observed.

(i) Adsorption of H_2 on glass surface is spontaneous and **endothermic.**

(ii) Adsorption of highly hydrated solutes on solid surfaces is also **endothermic**.

- **Adsorption isotere** The graphs plotted T *vs.* p for given amount of adosption are known as **"adsorption isotere"**.

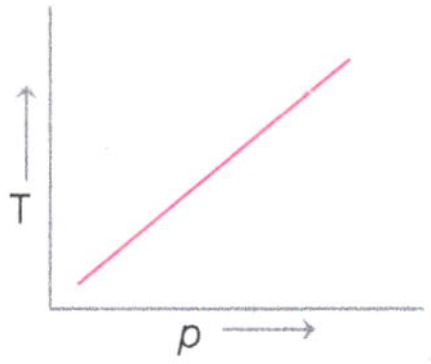

JEE Quicker

The statement "lowering the temperature favours physisorption process" is correct. *JEE Adv. 2022*

➘ Physisorption involves weak van der Waals' forces between the adsorbate and the adsorbent. These interaction are exothermic. Therefore, according to Le-Chatelier's principle, lowering the temperature shifts the equilibrium towards the adsorption process.

Freundlich Adsorption Isotherm

It gives a relationship between the quantity of gas adsorbed by unit mass of solid adsorbent and pressure at a particular temperature. The relationship can be expressed by

$$\frac{x}{m} = kp^{1/n}$$

where, $\left(\frac{x}{m}\right)$ is the amount of the gas adsorbed per unit mass of the adsorbent at pressure p. k and n are constants, $n \geq 1$.

For different value of n, the two cases are discussed below

Case I

When, $n=1$, $\frac{x}{m}=kp$ and $\frac{x}{m} \propto p$

This is observed in lower pressure range.

Case II

When n is large, $\frac{x}{m}=k$ (independent of pressure). This is observed at high pressure when saturation point is reached.

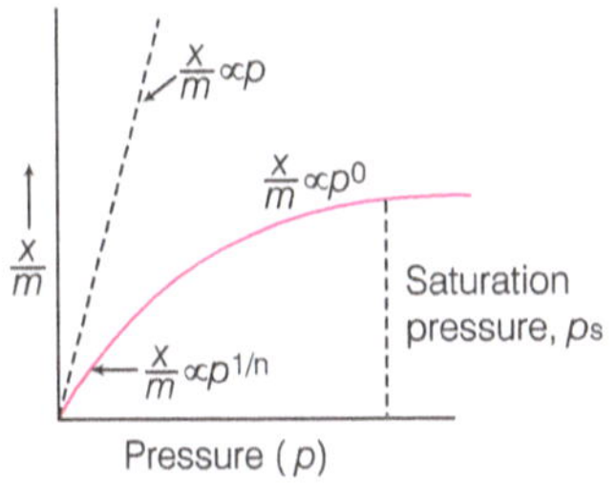

Variation x/m with increase in pressure at constant temperature.

Taking logarithm of the equation, $\frac{x}{m}=kp^{1/n}$

$$\log\frac{x}{m}=\log k+\frac{1}{n}\log p$$

Graph between $\log\left(\frac{x}{m}\right)$ and $\log p$ is a straight line with slope $\frac{1}{n}$ and intercept on the y-axis gives the value of $\log k$.

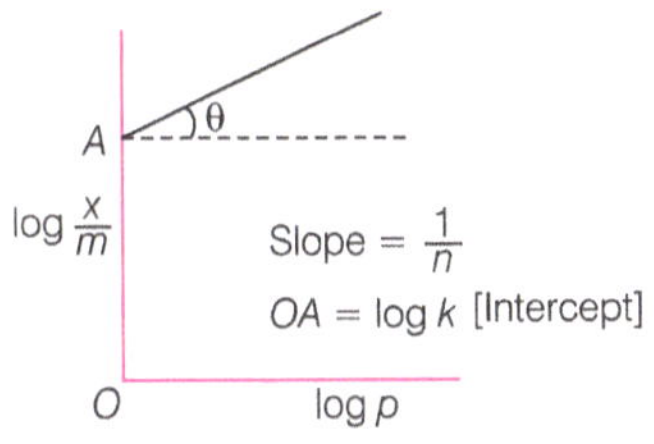

Freundlich adsorption isotherm

JEE Spotlite

Like adsorption of gases on solid surfaces, Freundlich isotherm can also be applied for **adsorption of solutes from solutions**, yet the precise mechanism of adsorption from solutions is not known.

In this case,

$$\frac{x}{m} \propto C^{1/n}$$

or

$$\frac{x}{m} = k \cdot C^{1/n}$$

where, C is the equilibrium concentration of the solute in solution.

In terms of logarithm $\log\left(\frac{x}{m}\right) = \frac{1}{n}\log(C) + \log k$

Validity of this equation can be checked by adsorption of CH_3COOH on charcoal.

Langmuir Adsorption Isotherm

Freundlich adsorption isotherm fails at high pressure and hence Langmuir adsorption isotherm is of importance which is based on kinetic consideration. He assumed that adsorption consists of following two opposing processes;

- adsorption of the gas molecules on the surface of the solid and
- desorption of the adsorbed molecules from the surface of the solid.

Langmuir believed that finally a dynamic equilibrium is established between rate of adsorption and rate of desorption. He assumed that each site can adsorb only one gas molecule i.e. adsorption is monolayered. Such type of adsorption is obtained for **chemisorption**.

Rate of (condensation) adsorption = Rate of (evaporation) desorption.

Based on above facts, Langmuir adsorption isotherm is represented as:

$$\frac{x}{m} = \frac{Kp}{1+Kp} = \theta$$

where,

θ = Ratio of number of adsorption sites occupied to adsorption of sites available.

K = Langmuir parameters constant

The variation of amount of gas adsorbed for different values of pressure are discussed below.

Case I If pressure p is very high

then $Kp >>> 1$, hence $1+Kp \approx Kp$

$$\frac{x}{m}=\frac{Kp}{Kp}=1 \text{ (constant)}$$

This indicates saturation point as shown along BC in the figure.

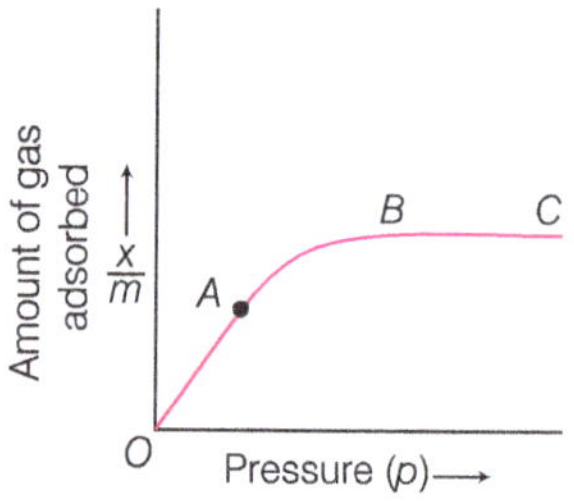

Langmuir adsorption isotherm

Case II At very low pressure,

$$Kp << 1 \qquad \therefore 1 + Kp \approx 1$$

$$\frac{x}{m} = Kp \qquad \therefore \frac{x}{m} \propto p$$

This is shown along OA in above Fig.

Solved Booster 1.1

In a laboratory experiment, 60 cc of a solution originally 0.21M CH_3COOH was permitted to come to equilibrium with a 10 g of sample of charcoal. At equilibrium 20 cc of CH_3COOH required 30 cc of 0.11 M NaOH for neutralisation.

Thus equilibrium concentration of the acid and the weight of CH_3COOH adsorbed per gram of charcoal is

(a) 0.024 (b) 0.016
(c) 0.362 (d) 0.054

Solution (b)

20 cc of CH_3COOH (at equilibrium) ≡ 30 cc of 0.11 M NaOH

$\therefore$ Equilibrium concentration of $(CH_3COOH)_f = \frac{30 \times 0.11}{20} = 0.165$ M

Initially $(CH_3COOH) = 0.21$ M

Thus, CH_3COOH adsorbed $= 0.210 - 0.165$ M $= 0.045$M

$= 60 \times 0.045$ millimoles CH_3COOH

$= \frac{60 \times 0.045}{1000} \times 60$g CH_3COOH

$= 0.16$ g CH_3COOH

Thus, amount of CH_3COOH adsorbed per gram of charcoal

$= \frac{0.16}{10} = 0.016$ g/g

JEE MAPPER

Example Similar to PYQ Asked in JEE Advanced 2024

To form a complete monolayer of butyric acid on 2 g of silica gel, 100 mL of 0.6 M butyric acid was used. Some of butyric acid remained unadsorbed. To neutralise the unadsorbed butyric acid. 40 mL of 1 M NaOH solution was required. If each molecule of butyric acid occupies $M \times 10^{-22}$ m^2 surface area on silica gel, then the value of M is ....

[Use given data :

Surface area of silica gel $= 3.5 \times 10^2$ m^{2}g^{-1};

Avogadro's number $(N_A) = 6.0 \times 10^{23}$ mol^{-1}]

Sol. (583) Number of moles of NaOH

$= 40 \times 1 \times 10^{-3} = 4 \times 10^{-2}$

Number of moles of butyric acid $= 100 \times 0.6 \times 10^{-3}$

$= 6 \times 10^{-2}$

$\therefore$ Number of butyric acid adsorbed on silica gel

$= (6 - 4) \times 10^{-2} = 2 \times 10^{-2}$

So, the number of molecules of butyric acid adsorbed

$= 2 \times 10^{-2}\ N_A$

$= 2 \times 10^{-2} \times 6.0 \times 10^{23}$

$= 12 \times 10^{21}$

Total surface area adsorbed by one molecule of butyric acid

$$= \frac{3.5 \times 10^2 \times 2}{12 \times 10^{21}}$$

$\approx 0.583 \times 10^{-19} = 583 \times 10^{-22}$

So, the value of M is 583.

Competency Enhancer 1.1

To form a complete monolayer of formic acid on 1g of charcoal, 200 mL of 0.4 M formic acid was used. Some of formic acid remained unadsorbed. To neutralise the unadsorbed formic acid. 60 mL of 1 M KOH solution was required. If each molecule of formic acid occupies $N \times 10^{-22}$ m^2 surface area on charcoal, then the value of N is ....

[Use given data : Surface area of charcoal $= 1.5 \times 10^2$ m^{2}g^{-1}; Avogadro's number $(N_A) = 6.0 \times 10^{23}$ mol^{-1}]

Elemental Practice 10.1

Type I MCQs with Only One Correct Option

1. Which one of the following statements is incorrect about adsorption?
   (a) It is a spontaneous process
   (b) It decreases the free energy of the system
   (c) It decreases entropy
   (d) It requires activation energy

2. In case of chemical adsorption, the enthalpy of adsorption is
   (a) greater than 400 kJ mol^{-1}
   (b) between 80-240 kJ mol^{-1}
   (c) less than 20 kJ mol^{-1}
   (d) negative but greater than 40 kJ mol^{-1}

3. For a gas solid system following the Langmuir adsorption isotherm, if the surface is half-covered by the adsorbate, what is the relationship between p and K?
   (a) $p = K$ (b) $p = 2K$ (c) $p = \frac{K}{2}$ (d) $p = \frac{1}{K}$

4. Graph between $\log\left(\frac{x}{m}\right)$ and $\log p$ is a straight line at angle 45° with intercept OA as shown. Then $\left(\frac{x}{m}\right)$ at a pressure of 0.2 atm is :

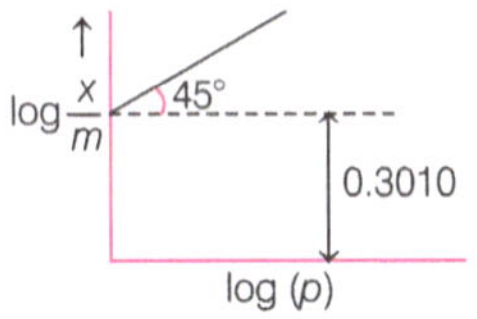

   (a) 0.2 (b) 0.4 (c) 0.6 (d) 0.8

5. In magneson test of Mg^{2+}, (magneson 4-(4-nitro phenolazo) resorcinol is a reagent to test Mg^{2+}) precipitate of $Mg(OH)_2$ attains blue colour due to
   (a) adsorption of magneson on $Mg(OH)_2$ (a solid adsorbent)
   (b) presence of OH^- ions
   (c) oxidation of the reagent
   (d) formation of metal dye complex

6. Given below are two statements.
   Assertion (A) The effectiveness of adsorbents in removing coloured impurities from solution is due to the selective adsorption of coloured molecules.
   Reason (R) Only large, non-polar molecules tend to be adsorbed onto adsorbents which leads to the removal of colour from the solution.
   In the light of the above statements, choose the correct answer from the options given below.
   (a) Both (A) and (R) are correct and (R) is the correct explanation of (A).
   (b) Both (A) and (R) are correct but (R) is not the correct explanation of (A).
   (c) (A) is correct but (R) is incorrect.
   (d) (A) is incorrect but (R) is correct.

7. Which of the following differs adsorption and absorption in terms of equilibrium behaviour?
   (a) Adsorption reaches equilibrium more slowly than absorption.
   (b) Adsorption reaches equilibrium only at very high temperatures while absorption reaches equilibrium at any temperature.
   (c) Adsorption reaches equilibrium when surface is saturated, whereas absorption involves the entire volume and may not saturate as easily.
   (d) Adsorption equilibrium depends on the volume of the substance, while absorption equilibrium does not.

8. Match List I with List II.

	List I (Freundlich Adsorption Isotherm)		List II (Equation or concept)
(A)	Condition for adsorption at intermediate pressure	(1)	$\frac{x}{m} \propto p^0$
(B)	Condition for adsorption at high pressure	(2)	$\frac{x}{m} \propto p^{\frac{1}{n}}$
(C)	Condition for adsorption at low pressure	(3)	Power of pressure lying between 0 and 1
(D)	Value of n in Freundlich isotherm	(4)	$\frac{x}{m} \propto p$

   Choose the correct answer from the options given below.
   (a) $A \rightarrow (1), B \rightarrow (2), C \rightarrow (3), D \rightarrow (4)$
   (b) $A \rightarrow (2), B \rightarrow (1), C \rightarrow (3), D \rightarrow (4)$
   (c) $A \rightarrow (2), B \rightarrow (1), C \rightarrow (4), D \rightarrow (3)$
   (d) $A \rightarrow (1), B \rightarrow (2), C \rightarrow (4), D \rightarrow (3)$

9. At 298 K, a fixed amount of charcoal adsorbs equal volumes of gases. The order of adsorption capacity (based on the volume adsorbed per gram of charcoal) for the following gases is
   (a) $NH_3 > CH_4 > CO_2 > H_2$ (b) $NH_3 > CO_2 > CH_4 > H_2$
   (c) $CO_2 > NH_3 > CH_4 > H_2$ (d) $CO_2 > NH_3 > H_2 > CH_4$

10. The graph that shows the effect of temperature on adsorption at constant pressure for physisorption process is

(a)
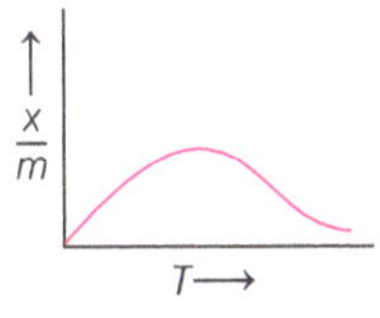

(b)
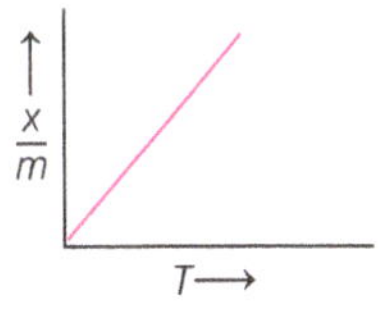

(c)
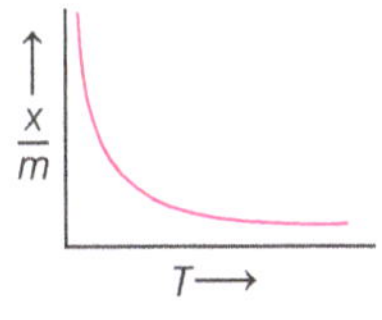

(d)
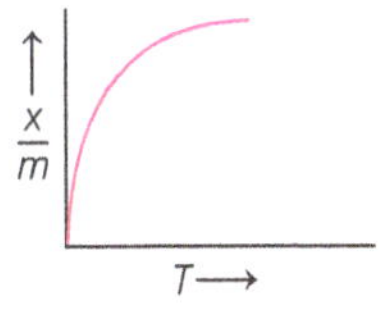

11. Given below are two statements.

Statement I At low temperatures, both physisorption and chemisorption can occur simultaneously on an adsorbent surface.

Statement II Physisorption is non-specific and reversible because the adsorption is due to weak van der waals' forces that can be easily disrupted by changing temperature or pressure.

In the light of the above statements, choose the correct answer from the options given below.

(a) Both Statement I and Statement II are true.
(b) Both Statement I and Statement II are false.
(c) Statement I is true but Statement II is false.
(d) Statement I is false but Statement II is true.

12. At a pressure of 1 atm, the amount of gas adsorbed is 0.5 mol/g. At a pressure of 4 atm, the amount of gas adsorbed is 1.5 mol/g. Then the values of *K* and *n* are

(a) 0.2, 1.16 (b) 0.3, 1.46
(c) 0.5, 1.26 (d) 0.4, 1.36

13. A sample of 20 g of charcoal is placed in a 1.5 L vessel at 25°C, where it adsorbs CO_2 gas. The pressure of the gas in the vessel falls from 800 torr to 550 torr when the charcoal is introduced. The density of charcoal is 1.5 g/cm^3. Calculate the volume of CO_2 gas adsorbed per gram of the charcoal at 550 torr and 25°C.

(a) 0.03466 L/mg (b) 0.03466 mL/mg
(c) 0.03466 mL/g (d) 0.03466 L/g

14. In the process of adsorption from the solution phase, the adsorption isotherm generally follows the Freundlich adsorption model. Consider the following statements.

A. As the concentration of adsorbate in the solution increases, the extent of adsorption initially increases but eventually, it approaches a constant value due to the saturation of the adsorption sites.
B. At low concentration of adsorbate, the adsorption process follows a linear relationship with concentration and the adsorption capacity increases proportionally with the concentration of adsorbate in solution.
C. The Freundlich adsorption isotherm is valid for adsorption at low concentrations but fails at very high concentrations.
D. In case of adsorption from the solution phase, the adsorbent material and the nature of the solvent have no effect on the adsorption capacity.
E. The adsorption of a solute from a solution is a non spontaneous when ΔG is negative.

In the light of the above statements, choose the correct answer from the options given below.

(a) Statements A, B and C are correct.
(b) Statements A, B, C and D are correct.
(c) Statements A, B, C, D and E are correct.
(d) Statements B, C and D are correct.

15. Given that the Freundlich adsorption isotherm is applicable for the adsorption of gas *A* on a solid *B*. If the amount of gas adsorbed is increased by a factor of 2, the pressure of a gas must be increased by a factor of

(a) $2^{1/n}$ (b) 2^n (c) 2^{n+1} (d) $2^{-1/n}$

16. For an adsorption process, the value of $\Delta G = -30$ kJ/mol and the enthalpy change $\Delta H = -25$ kJ/mol. Then, what will be the nature of adsorption?

(a) The process is physisorption.
(b) The process is endothermic.
(c) The process is chemisorption.
(d) Entropy decreases during adsorption.

17. A gas *X* is adsorbed on the surface of solid *Y*. The amount of gas adsorbed depends on the pressure *p* and is given by $x/m = kp^{1/n}$, where *k* and *n* are constants. If the value of *n* is 2.

Which of the following statements is correct?

(a) The adsorption is of physisorption type.
(b) $\frac{x}{m}$ vs. *p* graph is a straight line with a positive slope.
(c) The adsorption is of chemisorption type.
(d) $\log \frac{x}{m}$ vs. $\log p$ is a straight line with a slope of 0.5.

18. In a gas-solid adsorption system, the ratio of the amount adsorbed to the amount of adsorbent is highest when

(a) temperature is high.
(b) the surface area of the adsorbent is small.
(c) the surface area of the adsorbent is high.
(d) pressure is low.

Type II 》 MCQs with One or More than One Correct Option

19. Which of the following statements regarding adsorption is correct?

(a) The extent of adsorption increases with an increase in temperature for chemical adsorption in a narrow temperaure range but decreases for physical adsorption.
(b) Adsorption of gases on solids is an exothermic process and the heat of adsorption increases with increase in temperature for physical adsorption.
(c) For a given temperature, the adsorption of gases on solids follows Henry's law at low pressure.
(d) In chemisorption, the adsorbed molecules form a mono layer on the adsorbent surface and the process is highly specific to the gas and adsorbent.

20. Select the correct statements.

(a) Water vapour is absorbed by anhydrous $CaCl_2$ but adsorbed by silica gel.
(b) NH_3 is absorbed by water but adsorbed by charcoal.
(c) Sugar is decolourised by animal charcoal based on adsorption.
(d) H_2O is absorbed by conc. H_2SO_4.

21. Which of the following statements are incorrect about adsorption isotherms?

(a) The Langmuir adsorption isotherm assumes that all adsorption sites are equivalent and can hold only one molecule each.
(b) The Freundlich adsorption isotherm is applicable to adsorption on homogeneous surfaces and does not predict saturation of adsorption at high pressures.

(c) The adsorption capacity predicted by Langmuir isotherm increases indefinitely as the pressure increases.

(d) In the Langmuir adsoprtion isotherm, the adsorption process is reversible and the rate of adsorption is proportional to the concentration of adsorbate in the gas phase.

Type III 》 Numerical/Integer Type Questions

22. Carbon dioxide (CO_2) is adsorbed on activated carbon. At a temperature of 273 K, the extent of adsorption is 0.5 cm^3/g when the pressure is 0.5 atm. At a higher temperature of 300 K, the same extent of adsorption is achieved at a pressure of 10 atm. Then the molar enthalpy of adsorption of CO_2 on activated carbon is .... kJ/mol. (ln 0.5 = 0.693, ln 10 = 2.30).

23. A solid adsorbent adsorbs a gas at a specific temperature and it is found that 0.25 mg of the adsorbate covers an area of 0.10 m^2 on the surface of the solid. The molar mass of the absorbate is 0.50 kg/m. The area per molecule is .... $\times 10^{-19}$ m^2.

24. A catalyst surface has a total surface area of 500 cm^2 and the density of surface site is 2×10^{17} cm^{-2}. If 30% of the surface sites are occupied by CO_2 molecules and the catalyst is heated to 310 K, where CO_2 is completely desorbed into a pressure of 0.002 atm and a volume of 0.5 L. The number of active sites occupied by each CO_2 molecule is

25. For the adsorption of a substance A from aqueous solution by charcoal at 25°C, the Freundlich constants are $n = 3.0$ and $K = 0.50$ (for $\frac{x}{m}$ in g per g and (in gL^{-1}). What weight of A will be adsorbed by 2 g of charcoal from 1 L of a solution containing 2 g of the substance? (in terms of mg)

Elemental Practice 10.1 | Chapter 10

Connect with **Answers**

1. (d)	**2.** (b)	**3.** (d)	**4.** (b)	**5.** (a)	**6.** (c)
7. (c)	**8.** (c)	**9.** (b)	**10.** (c)	**11.** (a)	**12.** (c)
13. (d)	**14.** (a)	**15.** (b)	**16.** (a)	**17.** (d)	**18.** (c)
19. (a,c,d)	**20.** (a,b,c,d)	**21.** (b,c)	**22.** (–77.761)	**23.** (3.32)	**24.** (1)
25. (1000)					

Element 2 Catalysis

Catalyst and Catalysis

A substance that can influence the rate of a chemical reaction but which itself is not consumed and remains unchanged is known as a catalyst and the phenomenon is known as catalysis.

Berzelius (1836) introduced the term catalysis and catalyst. Ostwald (1895) redefined a catalyst as, a substance which changes the reaction rate without affecting the overall energetics of the reaction.

$$2KClO_3 \xrightarrow{MnO_2} 2KCl + 3O_2$$

$$4HCl + O_2 \xrightarrow{CuCl_2} 2H_2O + 2Cl_2$$

$$2H_2 + O_2 \xrightarrow{Pt} 2H_2O$$

The substance mentioned above the arrow indicates the foreign substance (catalyst) that does not take part in the reaction.

Types of Catalysis

The classification of catalysis on different bases are given below.

Based on the Phase

On the basis of phase of reaction mixture, there are two types of catalyst:

- Homogeneous catalysis
- Heterogeneous catalysis

A third type, enzyme catalysis, is also studied separately due to its, own characteristics.

1. Homogeneous Catalysis

When the catalyst mixes homogeneously with the reactant(s) and forms a single phase, i.e. when a catalyst is present in the same phase as the reactants the catalyst is said to be homogeneous and this kind of catalysis is called homogeneous catalysis. For example,

- Iodide ion is a **solution phase homogeneous catalyst** for the decomposition of *aq.* H_2O_2because both I^- and H_2O_2 are present in same aqueous solution phase.

$$2H_2O_2(aq) \xrightarrow{I^-(aq)} 2H_2O\,(l) + O_2(g)$$

- In the atmosphere, nitric oxide (NO) is a **gas-phase homogeneous catalyst** for the conversion of molecular oxygen to ozone.

$$\frac{3}{2}O_2(g) \xrightarrow{NO\,(g)} O_3(g)$$

JEE Spotlite

Some other homogeneous catalysis examples are given below.

Process	Products	Typical catalyst
1. Oxidation of SO_2 to SO_3 in lead-chamber process	SO_3	NO
2. Oxidation of CO (*g*) by $O_2(g)$	$CO_2(g)$	NO
3. Inversion of sucrose solution	Glucose and fructose	H^+
4. Hydrolysis of an ester	Acid and alcohol	H^+
5. Aldol condensation of acetaldehyde	Crotonic aldehyde	OH^-
6. Enolisation of ketone	Enolic form	H^+ or OH^-

2. Heterogeneous Catalysis

When, the catalyst is in a different phase from that of the reactants. The catalyst is said to be heterogeneous and this kind of catalysis is called heterogeneous catalyst. In most cases, the catalyst is solid, while the reactants are either liquids or gases.

The catalyst, usually a metal or an oxide, is present in a fine state of sub-division, or is supported on asbestos, so that it may be able to present large surface area and reaction starts from the surface of the solid catalyst. This is the reason why heterogeneous catalysis is also called **surface catalysis**. For example,

In the Fischer- Tropsch process for the manufacturing of synthetic gasoline, tiny particles of a metal, such as iron or cobalt coated on alumina (Al_2O_3) catalyse the conversion of gaseous CO and H_2 to hydrocarbons such as octane (C_8H_{18}).

$$8CO(g) + 17H_2(g) \xrightarrow{Co/Al_2O_3} C_8H_{18}(l) + 8H_2O\,(l)$$

Some of other heterogeneous catalysis examples.

	Process	Products	Typical catalysts
1.	Polymerisation of propylene	Polypropylene	Titanium (IV) chloride
2.	Methane reforming with steam	$H_2(g)$ and CO (g)	Ni supported on K_2O / Al_2O_3
3.	Methanol synthesis	$CH_3OH(g)$	ZnO / Cr_2O_3
4.	Oxidation of $SO_2(g)$	$SO_3(g)$	$V_2O_5 + K_2SO_4$ on SiO_2
5.	Cracking of hydrocarbons in the presence of hydrogen	Mixture of lower alkenes and alkanes	Zeolites
6.	Polymerisation of ethene	Polyethene	$TiCl_4$ and AlR_3 (*Ziegler method*)
7.	Formation of hydrocarbon from CO and H_2	Hydrocarbon	Fe, Co, Ru (Fischer-Tropsch process)
8.	Hydrogenation of oils	Vegetable (fat), (ghee)	Ni

Based on the Mechanism

(Action of The Catalyst)

1. Auto-Catalysis

In certain reactions, one of the products acts as catalyst. The phenomenon in which one of the products itself acts as a catalyst is known as auto-catalysis. The oxidation of oxalic acid by acidified potassium permanganate, represented by the following equation takes place rapidly after sometime.

$$2MnO_4^- + 5C_2O_4^{2-} + 16H^+ \longrightarrow 2Mn^{2+} + 10\,CO_2 + 8H_2O$$

This acceleration is due to the presence of Mn^{2+} ions which are formed in the reaction.

2. Induced Catalysis

Certain reactions influence the rate of other reaction, which does not occur under ordinary conditions, this phenomena is called induced catalysis.

e.g. Reduction of $HgCl_2$ with oxalic acid is very slow but potassium permanganate is reduced readily with oxalic acid. If oxalic acid is added to a mixture of potassium permanganate and $HgCl_2$ both are reduced simultaneously. Thus, the reduction of potassium permanganate induces the reduction of $HgCl_2$. This phenomenon is called induced catalysis.

3. Positive Catalysis

If the catalyst increases the rate of reaction, it is called positive catalyst and reaction is called positive catalysis, e.g.

- Decomposition of H_2O_2 in the presence of colloidal platinum

$$2H_2O_2(l) \xrightarrow{Pt} 2H_2O(l) + O_2(g)$$

- Hydrogenation of vegetable oil in the presence of nickel

$$\text{Vegetable oil } (l) + H_2(g) \xrightarrow{Ni(s)} \text{Ghee}(s)$$

4. Negative Catalysis

In a few cases, a catalyst instead of speeding up a reaction, may actually retard it. Such substances are called **negative catalysts** or **inhibitors**, and the phenomena is called negative catalysis.

- Addition of small amount of acetanilide or glycerine slows down the decomposition of hydrogen peroxide.
- Ethyl alcohol slows down the oxidation of sodium sulphite to sodium sulphate by atmospheric oxygen.

JEE Alert

Catalytic inhibitor retards rate of reaction by itself while catalytic poison retards the rate of reaction by reducing the activity of catalyst.

Characteristics of Catalysts

Some important characteristics of catalysts are discussed below

- They become temporarily involved in a reaction, providing an alternative reaction path of lower activation energy than that for the uncatalysed reaction.
- They catalyses both forward and backward reactions to the same extent in a reversible reaction and thus have no effect on the equilibrium constant.
- The catalyst remains unchanged in chemical composition and amount remains the same at the end of the reaction. It may undergo some physical change.
- Only a small quantity of the catalyst is generally needed.
- In certain reactions, the rate of the reaction is dependent on the concentration of the catalyst, e.g. Rate of inversion of cane sugar is dependent on the concentration of H^+ used as catalyst.
- Rate of the reaction in certain heterogeneous reaction varies with surface area of the catalyst. Hence, finely divided metals are preferred in the form of catalyst.
- The catalyst does not initiate the reaction and are specific in their action.

Activity and Selectivity of Catalyst

Catalysts possess unique property of activity and selectivity which are discussed below

1. Activity

It is the ability of catalysts to accelerate chemical reactions. The degree of acceleration can be as high as 10^{10} times in certain reactions. e.g. Reaction between H_2 and O_2 to form H_2O in the presence of platinum as catalyst takes place with explosive violence. In the absence of catalyst, H_2 and O_2 can be stored indefinitely without any reaction.

2. Selectivity

It is the ability of catalysts to direct reaction to yield particular products (excluding other). e.g. Acetylene on hydrogenation in the presence of Pt or Ni or Pd catalyst gives ethane.

$$\underset{\text{Ethyne}}{H-C\equiv C-H} + 2H_2(g) \xrightarrow{\text{Pt/Pd/Ni}} \underset{\text{Ethane}}{CH_3-CH_3}$$

Hydrogenation of acetylene in the presence of Lindlar's catalyst gives ethylene.

$$\underset{\text{Ethyne}}{H-C\equiv C-H} + H_2(g) \xrightarrow[\text{Sulphur or quinoline}]{\text{Pd-BaSO}_4} \underset{\text{Ethylene}}{CH_2{=}CH_2}$$

JEE Spotlite

Zeolite : Shape Selective Catalysts

- Zeolites are alumino-silicates of the general formulae, $M_{x/n}[(AlO_2)_x \cdot (SiO_2)_y] \cdot mH_2O$
  where, M may be simple cation like Na^+, K^+ or Ca^{2+}, n is the charge on the simple cation. m is the number of molecules of water of crystallisation.
- It has open structure which is provided by silica in which aluminium occupies $\frac{x}{(x+y)}$ fraction of tetrahedral sites.
- The negative charge of the alumino silicate framework is neutralised by the replacable cations. The void space forms more than 50% of the total volume, which is occupied by water molecules.
- ZSM-5 is a zeolite having formula $H_x[(AlO_2)_x \cdot (SiO_2)_{96-x}] \cdot 16H_2O$. It converts alcohol to gasoline (petrol) by dehydrating the alcohol and producing a mixture of wide variety of hydrocarbons.
- In its protonated form, ZSM-5 catalyses the reaction of ethene with benzene to produce ethylbenzene.

$$CH_2CH_2 + H^+ \longrightarrow CH_2CH_3^+ \xrightarrow{C_6H_6} C_6H_5CH_2CH_3 + H^+$$

Theories of Catalysis

These theories explaining the mechanism of catalysis are discussed below

1. Chemical Theory or Intermediate Compound Theory

According to this theory, the catalyst combines with the reactants to form an intermediate compound which is unstable and therefore, decomposes readily to give the product.

$$\underset{\text{First reactant}}{AB} + \underset{\text{Catalyst}}{X} \longrightarrow \underset{\text{Intermediate}}{AX} + \underset{\text{First product}}{B}$$

$$AX + \underset{\text{Second reactant}}{C} \longrightarrow \underset{\text{Second product}}{AC} + \underset{\text{Catalyst regenerated}}{X}$$

The overall reaction is $AB + C \xrightarrow[\text{Catalyst}]{X} AC + B$

e.g. The catalytic decomposition of $KClO_3$ in the presence of MnO_2 takes place in the following sequence.

$$2KClO_3 + 2MnO_2 \longrightarrow 2KMnO_4 + Cl_2 + O_2$$

$$2KMnO_4 \longrightarrow K_2MnO_4 + MnO_2 + O_2$$

$$K_2MnO_4 + Cl_2 \longrightarrow 2KCl + MnO_2 + O_2$$

Overall reaction is

$$2KClO_3 \xrightarrow[\text{Catalyst}]{MnO_2} 2KCl + 3O_2$$

This mechanism is supported by the fact that oxygen obtained in this reaction along with some Cl_2 and secondly if reaction mixture is cooled suddenly by plunging the flask into cold water, purple colour appears indicating the presence of $KMnO_4$.

Thus, this theory explains why the catalyst remains unchanged in mass and chemical composition at the end of reaction.

2. Adsorption Theory

This theory explains the mechanism of heterogeneous catalysis. It is a combination of intermediate compound formation theory and adsorption theory.

According to this theory, the surface of catalyst has active sites on which one or a more reactants get adsorbed in the form of a unimolecular layer (due to some residual forces of the catalyst). If both the reactants molecules are adsorbed on the surface, the reaction takes place readily due to more proximity of the reactants. The reactant molecule attached to the surface may hit the other reactant moving freely as a gas or liquid and the product formed is desorbed.

Basically, heterogeneous catalysis involves

(i) adsorption of reactants on the solid surface (chemisorption).

The adsorption step is thought to involve chemical bonding of reactants to the highly reactive metal atoms on the surface with accompanying breaking or at least weakening of bonds in the reactants.

(ii) diffusion of reactants along the surface.

(iii) reaction at an active site to form adsorbed product called the **activated complex.**

(iv) desorption of the product and the catalyst surface is regenerated.

The surface of the catalyst unlike the inner part of the bulk has free valencies which provide the seat for chemical forces of attraction. With increase of these valencies on the surface of a catalyst, the catalytic activity will be greatly enhanced. Thus, these free valencies are responsible for the catalytic activity.

The free valencies can be increased in the following two ways

- By fine division of the catalyst.
- By rough surface of the catalyst.

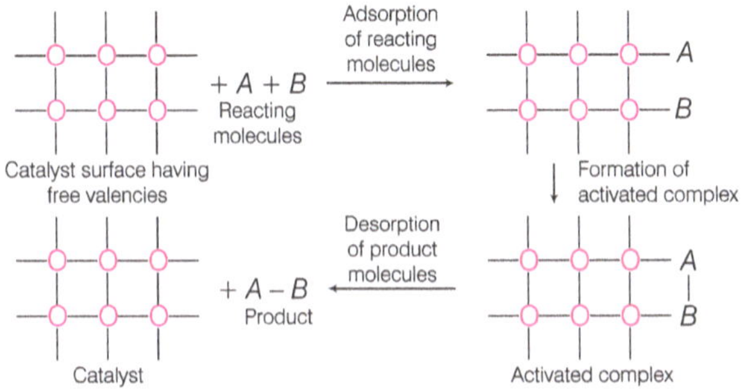

JEE Alert

- Intermediate compound theory only accounts for the homogeneous catalysis.
- Adsorption theory does not explain the action of catalytic promoters and catalytic poisons.

3. Combination of Intermediate Compound Theory and Adsorption Theory

Intermediate compound theory and adsorption theory both have combined effect to explain catalyst activity.

(i) Catalyst increases the rate of reaction by lowering the activation energy of reaction.

(ii) Catalyst provides an entirely new path for the reaction in which a newly adsorbed activated intermediate complex of lower potential energy is formed.

(iii) The active centres on the surface of catalyst play an important role in governing the amount of adsorption.

(iv) Number of free active sites can be increased by increasing surface area by increasing roughness of catalyst surface or by preparing the catalyst in colloidal form.

(v) Catalyst activity of many transition metals and their compounds is due to their ability to exhibit multiple oxidation states and to provide larger surface area for adsorption.

Enzyme Catalysis

Enzymes are complex nitrogeneous substances secreted by low forms of vegetable and animal organisms. Reactions catalysed by enzymes are called **enzyme catalysis**. Either the organisms in bulk (like yeast) or the chemicals synthesised by and extracted from them (like yeast extract) may be used for catalysing certain reactions.

The catalytic activity of enzymes is due to their capacity to lower the activation energy for a particular reaction.

Examples of Enzymes catalysis

Reaction	Catalyst
1. $\underset{\text{Sucrose}}{C_{12}H_{22}O_{11}} + H_2O \longrightarrow \underset{\text{Glucose}}{C_6H_{12}O_6} + \underset{\text{Fructose}}{C_6H_{12}O_6}$	Invertase
2. $\underset{\text{Maltose}}{C_{12}H_{12}O_{11}} + H_2O \longrightarrow \underset{\text{Glucose}}{2C_6H_{12}O_6}$	Maltase
3. $\underset{\text{Starch}}{(C_6H_{10}O_5)_n} + n\,H_2O \longrightarrow \underset{\text{Maltose}}{C_{12}H_{22}O_{11}}$	Diastase
4. $\underset{\text{Glucose}}{C_6H_{12}O_6} + \longrightarrow \underset{\text{Ethanol}}{2C_2H_5OH} + CO_2$	Zymase
5. $\underset{\text{Urea}}{NH_2CONH_2} + H_2O \longrightarrow 2NH_3 + CO_2$	Urease
6. $CO_2(aq) + H_2O(l) \rightleftharpoons H^+(aq) + HCO_3^-(aq)$	Carbonic anhydrase (in human body)
7. $N_2(\text{atmospheric}) \longrightarrow NH_3$	Nitrogenase

Characteristics of Enzyme Catalysis

(i) In the case of enzyme catalysis, the rate of the reaction is much more dependent on the amount of the catalyst (enzyme) than it is in the case of the other types of catalysis.

(ii) The enzyme reactions are sensitive to temperature; optimum temperature for maximum enzyme activity varies between 15°C to 25°C.

(iii) Enzyme reactions are far more sensitive to catalytic poisons than any other types of catalytic reaction. The enzyme poisons are biological poisons too. e.g. are HCN, H_2S, CS_2 etc.

(iv) The addition of electrolyte deactivates enzyme. It is due to coagulation of enzymes.

Mechanism of Enzyme Catalysis

Enzymes have a specific active site on their surface, which are actually the active centres on the surface of enzyme particles. When the substrate molecules of reactant bind at active site, a chemical change is initiated and an activate complex is formed which then decomposes to yield the products.

Concept Visualizer

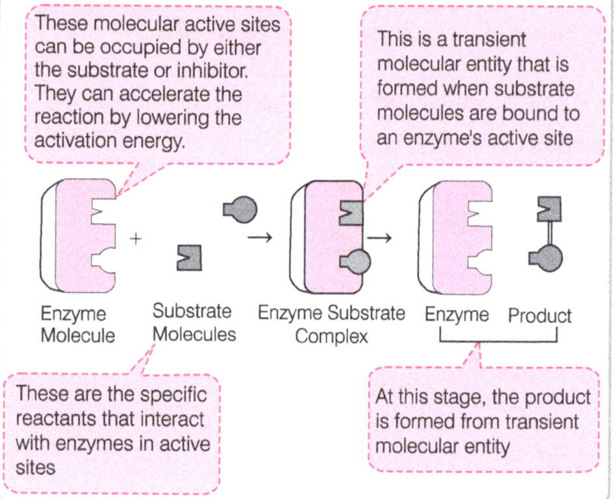

Two models of enzyme action has been proposed.

1. 'Lock-key' Fit Theory of Enzyme Action

Enzyme catalysed reactions are highly specific. A given enzyme performs a particular type of reaction on a given substrate only. The rates of catalysed reactions are often as high as 10^6 min^{-1} and the catalysis is dependent on the conditions like temperature, solvent and pH. The three-dimensional (3-D) structure of the protein molecule that acts as an enzyme is visualised to have a specific geometric cavity called active site and the substrate is accommodated in this geometric cavity much like a key fit into a lock.

2. Induced-Fit Model

This model visualises a flexible site of enzyme substrate attachment and the substrate induces a change in the enzyme shape to fit the shape of the substance. In some cases the enzyme might wrap itself around the substrate and thus, form the converted shape of lock and key.

Elemental Practice 10.2

Type I 》 MCQs with Only One Correct Option

1. Which of the following statement is correct regarding homogeneous and heterogeneous catalysis?
   (a) Heterogeneous catalysis typically exhibit a greater tolerance to poisioning compared to homogeneous catalysts.
   (b) In homogeneous catalysis, the catalysts and the reactants are in same phase, which often results in better selectivity for specific reactions.
   (c) The rate of reaction in heterogeneous catalysis is often proportional to the concentration of reactants and is less dependent on surface area.
   (d) Le Chatelier's principle can be applied directly to reactions involving heterogeneous catalysts, but it does not apply to homogeneous catalysis.

2. Which of the following statement is incorrect regarding the activity of catalysts?
   (a) The activity of catalyst is related to the number of active sites available on its surface for the adsorption of reactant molecules.
   (b) Catalysts with a larger surface area generally have a higher activity, as they provide more surface area for the adsorption of reactants.
   (c) The adsorption of reactants on the catalyst surface is an essential step in the reaction mechanism of catalytic processes.
   (d) The activity of a heterogeneous catalyst is independent of the adsorption characteristics of the reactant molecules.

3. Match the List I with List II.

	List I (Processes)		List II (Catalysts Used)
A.	Oxidation of ammonia to nitric oxide	1.	MnO_2
B.	Decompostion of hydrogen peroxide	2.	Ruthenium
C.	Fischer-Tropsch synthesis	3.	Nickel
D.	Methanation	4.	Platinum

Choose the correct answer from the options given below.
(a) $A \rightarrow 4$, $B \rightarrow 1$, $C \rightarrow 3$, $D \rightarrow 2$
(b) $A \rightarrow 1$, $B \rightarrow 4$, $C \rightarrow 3$, $D \rightarrow 2$
(c) $A \rightarrow 4$, $B \rightarrow 1$, $C \rightarrow 2$, $D \rightarrow 3$
(d) $A \rightarrow 1$, $B \rightarrow 4$, $C \rightarrow 2$, $D \rightarrow 3$

4. Which of the following is wrong in case of enzyme catalysis?
   (a) Enzymes increases the rate of reactions by lowering the activation energy.
   (b) Enzyme catalysis always results in the formation of a covalent bond between the enzyme and the substrate.
   (c) Enzymes provide an active site where the substrate binds and undergoes the reaction.
   (d) Enzyme activity can be influenced by factors such as temperature, pH and substrate concentration.

5. For the reaction $R \rightarrow P$, the following information is provided :
   (i) The reaction rate increases when concentration of *B* is increased.
   (ii) The presence of *A* in the reaction mixture decreases the rate of reaction.
   Which of the following statement is true based on this information?
   (a) *B* acts as an inhibitor in the reaction.
   (b) *A* acts as an inhibitor in the reaction.
   (c) *B* increases the activation energy of the reaction.
   (d) *A* enhances the formation of products in the reaction.

6. Given below are two statements.
   Statement I The adsorption capacity of a catalyst increases with the increase in temperature, as the number of available active sites increases with higher temperature.
   Statement II The adsorption theory is applicable only to reactions in which the catalyst is in a same phase as reactants.
   In the light of the above statements choose the correct answer from the options given below.
   (a) Both Statement I and Statement II are correct.
   (b) Both Statement I and Statement II are incorrect.
   (c) Statement I is correct but Statement II is incorrect.
   (d) Statement I is incorrect but Statement II is correct.

7. Which of the following acts as a negative catalyst?
   (a) Decomposition of H_2O_2 in the presence of colloidal platinum.
   (b) Ethyl alcohol in the oxidation of sodium sulphite to sodium sulphate by atmospheric oxygen.
   (c) Zeolites in the cracking of petroleum.
   (d) Decomposition of nitroglycerine.

8. *A* and *B* react in the presence of a metal catalyst as shown with free valencies, the activated complex is shown by

(a) 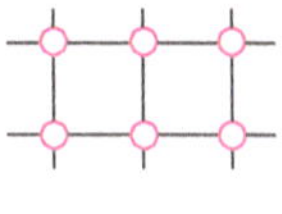

(b) 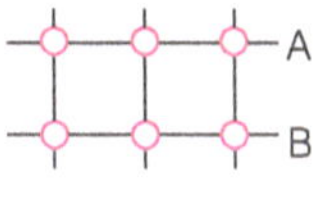

(c) 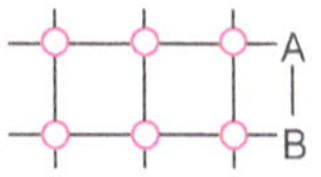

(d) 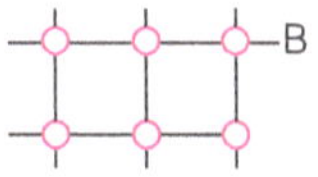

9. Select the correct statement regarding the effect of catalysts on thermodynamic factor.
   (a) A catalyst lowers the activation energy of a reaction but does not effect the rate of the reaction.
   (b) A catalyst affects the equilibrium constant of a reaction by shifting the equilibrium position to favor the products.
   (c) The addition of a catalyst decreases the overall ΔG of the reaction, making the reaction more thermodynamically favourable.
   (d) A catalyst provide alternate reaction pathway but does not change the thermodynamic properties like ΔH, ΔS or ΔG.

10. Choose the correct statement regarding the acidic nature of zeolites.
   (a) Zeolites exhibit Bronsted acidity due to presence of protonated aluminosilicate groups in their framework.
   (b) The acidity of zeolites is caused by Lewis acidic sites formed by exchangeable alkali metals cations such as Na^+ and K^+.
   (c) Zeolites with high aluminium content have lower acidity because aluminium decreases the availability of protonated sites.
   (d) The open structure is provided by silica in which aluminium occupies $\frac{x+y}{x}$ fraction of tetrahedral sites.

11. Given below are two statements.
   Assertion (A) In auto catalysis, the product of a reaction acts as a catalyst for the reaction iteself, leading to a non-linear increase in the rate of reaction as the concentration of the product increases.
   Reason (R) Auto catalysis involves the formation of a positive feedback mechanism, where the product acts as a catalyst, which accelerates the rate of reaction and this leads to the accumulation of more product, further enhancing the rate.
   In the light of the above statements, choose the correct answer from the options given below.
   (a) Both (A) and (R) are true and (R) is the correct explanation of (A).
   (b) Both (A) and (R) are true but (R) is not the correct explanation of (A).
   (c) (A) is true but (R) is false.
   (d) (A) is false but (R) is true.

12. Which of the following is not true for selectivity of a catalyst?
   (a) Regioselectivity and stereoselectivity are types of selectivity that determine. Position of reactants during a reaction or specific orientation.
   (b) Selectivity in catalysts is solely determined by the particle size of the catalyst with smaller particles always providing higher selectivity.
   (c) High selectivity in catalytic reactions implies that the catalyst promotes the formation of a single product.
   (d) A catalyst can enhance both reaction rate and selectivity of the reaction.

13. Which of the following statements about catalyst deactivation is correct?
   (a) Catalyst deactivation is always irreversible.
   (b) Coke deposition is common cause of catalyst deactivation.
   (c) Catalyst sintering occurs in heterogeneous catalysis.
   (d) Catalyst poisoning is more problematic in homogeneous catalysis.

14. In a heterogeneous catalytic reaction, which of the following can decrease the catalytic selectivity?
(a) Increasing the reaction temperature.
(b) Decreasing the partial pressure.
(c) Increasing catalyst surface area.
(d) Adding a selective promoter.

15. The rate expression for an enzyme-catalysed reaction can be written as :

rate $= K_1[E][S] - K_2[ES]$

Which of the following statements about this expression is correct?
(a) The rate is first order with respect to both the enzyme and substrate concentration.
(b) The rate is second order with respect to the substrate concentration.
(c) Enzymes are stereoselective as they recognise and bind to specific three-dimensional shapes of substrate molecules.
(d) The rate of independent of the reverse reaction rate constant, K_2.

Type II 》 MCQs with One or More than One Correct Option

16. Consider the following reversible reaction in a closed container :
$PCl_3 + Cl_2 \rightleftharpoons PCl_5$. The reaction is catalysed by a solid SiO_2. Which of the following statements are correct?
(a) The SiO_2 catalyst does not alter the equilibrium constant K_C.
(b) The catalyst increases both the forward and backward reaction rates equally.
(c) The catalyst provides an alternative reaction pathway with a lower activation energy.
(d) The presence of SiO_2 changes the equilibrium concentrations of reactants and products.

17. Select the cases of heterogeneous catalysis out of
(a) decompostion of hydrogen peroxide using potassium iodide (KI) as a catalyst in aqueous solution.
(b) haber process for ammonia synthesis using iron (Fe) as a catalyst.
(c) oxidation of sulphur dioxide (SO_2) to sulphur trioxide (SO_3) in the contact process using vanadium pentaoxide (V_2O_5) as a catalyst.
(d) hydrolysis of ester in the presence of dilute hydrochloric acid (HCl) as a catalyst.
(e) decomposition of ozone (O_3) on the surface of solid platinum (Pt).

18. Select the statements that involve catalyst poisoning.
(a) Sulphate ions (SO_4^{2-}) absorbing on the surface of Ni catalysts used for hydrogenation, reducing its activity.
(b) Lead poisoning of platinum cataysts used in catalytic converters in automobiles.
(c) Adsorption of carbon monoxide (CO) on the surface of iron catalyst in the Haber process.
(d) The addition of a ligand in a homogeneous catalytic reaction decreases the reaction rate without binding to the active catalytic site.

19. Which of the following statements are not correct regarding zeolites?
(a) The shape-selective catalysis of zeolites is based on the specific interaction between the active sites and the reactant molecules.
(b) Zeolites can be used for softening hard water by exchanging Ca^{2+} and Mg^{2+} ions with Na^+ ions.
(c) Before using zeolites as a catalyst, zeolites are not heated in vaccum.
(d) ZSM-5 is one such zeolite having formula $H_X[(AlO_2)_X \cdot (SiO_2)_{96-X}] \cdot 16H_2O$. This converts alcohol to gasoline (petrol) by dehydrating the alcohol and producing a mixture of wide variety of hydrocarbons.

20. Which of the following statements are true regarding Lock and Key Model and the Induced Fit model?
(a) The Lock and Key model assumes a pre-formed rigid active site, while induced fit model assumes a flexible active site that changes shape upon substrate binding.
(b) The Induced Fit model is better at explaining the formation of the transition state compared to the lock and key model.
(c) The Lock and Key model implies static binding, whereas the induced fit model suggests dynamic interaction between enzyme and the substrate.
(d) The Induced Fit model can explain the catalytic versatility of enzymes by allowing the active site to adjust and accomodate substrates of slightly different shapes, whereas Lock and Key model cannot.

Type III 》 Numerical/Integer Type Questions

21. The number of examples that represents the acid-catalysed reactions are :
(i) $R{-}COOH + R'{-}OH \longrightarrow R{-}COOR' + H_2O$
(ii) $R{-}COOR' + H_2O \longrightarrow R{-}COOH + R'{-}OH$
(iii) $R{-}CHO + R'{-}CHO \longrightarrow RCH(OH){-}\overset{O}{\overset{\|}{C}}{-}R'$
(iv) $R{-}CH_2OH \longrightarrow R{-}CH{=}CH_2 + H_2O$
(v) $C_6H_6 + HNO_3 \longrightarrow C_6H_5NO_2 + H_2O$

22. Select the statements about promoters in catalysis.
(a) A promoter is a substance that enhances the activity of a catalyst but is not itself active in the catalytic reaction.
(b) Promoters can increase the adsorption of the reactant on the catalysts surface , there by increasing the rate of reaction.
(c) In case of heterogeneous catalysis, promoters can alter the active site of the catalyst, making it more effective for a specific reaction.
(d) A promoter is always a substance that increases the overall reaction rate and never a substance that decreases it.

23. Number of reactions catalysed by the homogeneous catalysis are :
(i) $CH_2{=}CH_2 + CO \longrightarrow CH_3COOH$; $[Rh(CO)_2I_2]^-$
(ii) $CH_2{=}CH_2 + \frac{1}{2}O_2 \longrightarrow CH_3CHO$; $PdCl_2/CuCl_2$
(iii) $RCH{=}CH_2 + CO + H_2 \longrightarrow RCH_2CH_2CHO$; $[HCOC(CO)_4]$
(iv) $CO + H_2O \longrightarrow CO_2 + H_2$; $[Ru(H_2O)_6]^{2+}$
(v) $R{-}CH{=}CH_2 + H_2 \longrightarrow R{-}CH_2{-}CH_3$; $[RhCl(PPh_3)_3]$

24. The number of correct statements related to mechanism of catalysis are
(a) In heterogeneous catalysis, mechanism involves adsorption of reactants on the catalyst surface followed by the formation of an intermediate complex.
(b) In homogeneous catalysis, mechanism involves direct interaction between the catalyst and the reactants, followed by the reaction intermediate complex.
(c) Enzyme catalysis involves the enzyme forming a stable complex with the substrate where enzyme changes its shape to facilitate the reaction.
(d) In surface catalysis, the mechanism is based on the formation of an absorbed reaction complex.

25. The number of correct statements about the characteristics and applications of different catalyst types are
(a) Bifunctional catalysts possess both acidic and basic sites, allowing them to catalyse reactions involving both acid-base interactions and redox processes.
(b) Transition metals are exclusively used as homogeneous catalysts and cannot be employed in heterogeneous catalytic systems.
(c) Zeolites are examples of porous, solid state heterogeneous catalysts that are widely used in the petrochemical industry due to their shape selectively.
(d) Enzyme-based bio catalysts typically operate under mild conditions (low temperature, atmospheric pressure) and exhibit high substrate specificity compared to traditional chemical catalysts.

Elemental Practice 10.2 | Chapter 10

Connect with **Answers**

1. (b)	2. (d)	3. (c)	4. (b)	5. (b)	6. (b)
7. (b)	8. (c)	9. (d)	10. (a)	11. (a)	12. (b)
13. (b)	14. (a)	15. (c)	16. (a,b,c)	17. (b,c,e)	18. (a,b,c)
19. (a,c)	20. (a,b,c,d)	21. (5)	22. (3)	23. (5)	24. (3)
25. (3)					

Element 3 Particle Size and Colloidal State

Colloidal State

Thomas Graham observed that crystalline substances, such as sugar, urea, sodium chloride etc., could diffuse very readily in solution and could pass through animal and vegetable membranes, while others like glue, gelatin, gum, starch, proteins, etc., did not. He named the former **crystalloids** and the latter **colloids.**

According to Graham, the inability of the colloids towards diffusion is due to their high molecular weights (big particle size, thus low osmotic pressure).

However, the term colloid does not apply to a particular class of substances. It is a state of any substance, regardless of its nature, could be converted into a colloid by subdividing it into particles of colloidal size.

Classification of Solution

On the basis of size of particles of the dispersed phase (internal phase or discontinuous phase) and dispersion medium (external phase or continuous phase), a solution may be divided into following classes

(i) **True solution** In a true solution (e.g. sugar or salt in water), the dispersed particles are as single molecules or ions. Thus, the diameter of the dispersed particles ranges from 1Å to 10Å (0.1-1 mμ).

(ii) **Suspension** In a suspension (e.g. sand stirred into water), the dispersed particles are aggregates of millions of molecules. The diameter of these particles is of the order of 2000Å (0.2μ).

(iii) **Colloidal solutions** The colloidal solutions are intermediate between true solutions and suspensions. Thus, the diameter of dispersed particles range from 10 Å to 2000 Å (1 mμ-0.2 μ)

A colloidal system is made of two phases. The substance distributed as the colloidal particles is called the **dispersed phase, discontinuous phase** or **internal phase**.

The second phase in which the colloidal particles are scattered is called the **dispersion medium, continuous phase** or **external phase**. e.g. For a colloidal solution of copper in water, copper particles form dispersed phase and water is dispersion medium.

Distinction among True, Solutions Colloids and Suspensions

Property	True solutions	Colloids	Suspensions
Particle size	<10^{-7} cm or 10 Å or 1 mμ	10^{-7} cm to 10^{-5} cm or 10 Å to 10^3 Å or 1 mμ to 100 mμ	>10^{-5} cm or 10^3 Å or 100 mμ
Visibility	Not visible with any of the optical means	Visible with ultra microscope	Visible with naked eye
Separation			
(i) with filter paper	Not possible	Not possible	Possible
(ii) with membranes	Not possible	Possible	Possible
Diffusion	Diffuses rapidly	Diffuses very slowly	Does not diffuse
Settling	Does not settle	Does not settle but it may settle under centrifuge	Settles under gravity
Nature	Homogeneous	Heterogeneous	Heterogeneous
Appearance	Clear	Generally clear	Opaque

Classification of Colloids

Colloids are classified on several basis which are given below in table.

I. On the basis of physical states of the dispersed phase and dispersion medium.

On the above basis, colloidal solutions are of following eight types (colloidal dispersion of one gas in another is not possible).

Different Types of Colloidal Systems

Type name	Dispersed phase	Dispersion medium	Examples
Foam	Gas	Liquid	Whipped cream, shaving cream, soda- water froth
Solid foam	Gas	Solid	Cork, pumice stone, foam rubber.
Aerosol	Liquid	Gas	Fog, mist and clouds.

Type name	Dispersed phase	Dispersion medium	Examples
Emulsion	Liquid	Liquid	Milk, hair cream
Solid emulsion (Gel)	Liquid	Solid	Butter, cheese
Smoke	Solid	Gas	Dust in air
Sol	Solid	Liquid	Paint, ink, colloidal gold, protein, starch ruby glass (gold dispersed in glass), alloys, rock salt
Solid sol	Solid	Solid	Salt

The colloidal solutions in water are termed as **hydrosols** or **aquasols.**

When the dispersion medium is alcohol or benzene, the sols are termed as **alcosols** and **benzosols,** respectively.

JEE Alert

A colloidal system of gas is not possible as gases are completely miscible and always form homogeneous true solution.

II. Depending upon the nature of interaction between dispersed phase and dispersion medium. Colloidal sols are divided into two classes.

1. Lyophilic Colloids

The colloidal solutions in which dispersed particles have strong affinity for the dispersion medium, are called lyophilic colloids.

These colloids have strong interactions with the dispersion medium. This form of the colloidal solution are directly called as intrinsic colloids. They are much stable and cannot be coagulated easily. On evaporation of the dispersion medium from colloidal sol, residue obtained again passes into colloidal state, hence they are reversible colloids.

2. Lyophobic Colloids

The colloidal solutions in which dispersed phase has a weak interaction with the dispersion medium are called lyophobic colloids.

These substances; therefore, do not pass into colloidal state readily.

- They are much less stable, as they get coagulated easily on the addition of small amounts of electrolytes, by heating or by shaking.
- They are irreversible colloids, since residue left on the evaporation of the dispersion medium cannot be readily converted into sol.

Distinction between lyophilic and lyophobic sols

S.No.	Property	Lyophilic sols	Lyophobic sols
1	Surface tension	Lower than that of the dispersion medium	Same as that of the dispersion medium
2	Viscosity	Much higher than that of the medium	Same as that of the medium
3	Reversibility	Reversible	Irreversible
4	Stability	More stable	Less stable
5	Visibility	Particles cannot be detected even under ultramicroscope	Particles can be detected under ultramicroscope
6	Migration in an electric field	Particles may migrate in either direction or may not migrate in an electric field	Particles migrate either towards cathode or anode in an electric field
7	Action of electrolyte	Addition of smaller quantity of electrolyte has little effect	Coagulation takes places
8	Hydration	Extensive hydration takes places	No hydration takes place

III. On the basis of types of particles of the dispersed phase. On the above basis colloidal sols includes the following:

1. Multimolecular Colloids

On dissolution, atoms of smaller molecules of substances (having diameter less than 1 nm) aggregate together to form particles of colloidal dimensions, the particles thus formed are **multimolecular colloids.** These atoms or molecules are held together by van der Waals' forces. They show generally lyophilic character. e.g.

- Gold sol contains particles of various sizes having several atoms of gold.
- Sulphur sol consists of particles containing about a thousand of S_8 molecules.

2. Macromolecular Colloids

In macromolecular type of colloids, the particles are themselves large molecules (usually polymers) which on dissolution form size in the colloidal range. They show generally lyophobic character. e.g.

- Starch, cellulose, proteins, enzymes gelatin etc., are the examples of naturally occurring macromolecules.
- Nylon, polythene, plastics, polystyrene etc., are examples of synthetic macromolecules.

3. Associated Colloids

At high concentration when a substance dissolved in a solution its molecules aggregate spontaneously in a dispersion medium to form particles of colloidal dimensions, called as associated colloids. Such colloids occur in case of soaps or detergents, whose molecules are smaller than colloidal size but they aggregate in concentrated solution to colloid size.

The colloidal aggregates of soap or detergent molecules formed in the solvent are referred to as **micelles.**

Their molecules contain both lyophilic and lyophobic behaviour. These are the cluster or aggregated particles formed by association of colloids in solution. Micelles may contain 100 or more molecules. These are capable of forming ions. e.g. Soap (sodium stearate, $C_{17}H_{35}COONa$) is a typical example of micelles. When soap is dissolved in water, it gives Na^+ and $C_{17}H_{35}COO^-$ ions.

$$\underset{\text{(Sodium stearate)}}{C_{17}H_{35}COONa} \rightleftharpoons \underset{\text{(Stearate ion)}}{C_{17}H_{35}COO^-} + Na^+$$

The stearate ions associated to form **ionic micelles** of colloidal size. It has long hydrocarbon part of $C_{17}H_{35}$ which is **lyophobic** and COO^- part which is **lyophilic.** When the concentration of the solution is below from its CMC (10^{-3} mol L^{-1}), it behaves as **normal electrolyte.** But above this concentration, it aggregates to behave as **micelles.** The main function of a soap is to reduce oily and greasy dirt to colloidal particles (as emulsion). Soap are known as **emulsifying agent.**

Concept Visualizer

Water acts as the medium and plays a crucial role in the formation and action of soap micelles.

The head of the soap molecule is polar and interacts well with oils.

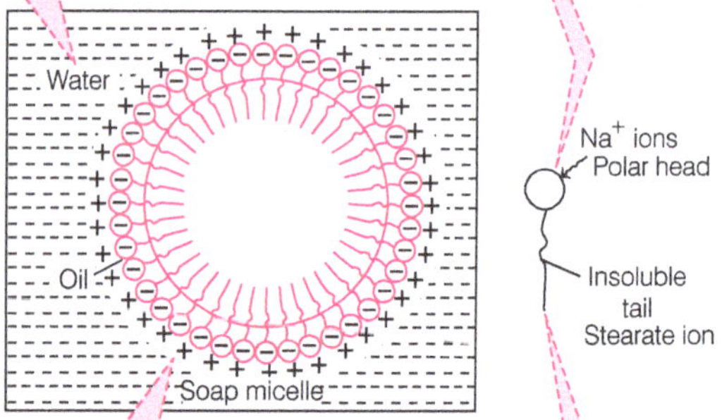

Micelle formation

It is a spherical or globular structure formed by soap molecules when they are mixed with water, particularly in the presence fo grease, oils or dirt.

The tail of the soap molecule is non-polar and repels water, but it interacts well with oils

The cleansing action of soap are

- The grease stain is absorbed into the interior of the micelle, that means which behaves like liquid hydrocarbon.
- When soap solution is added to a fabric, the tails of the soap anions, i.e. hydrophobic part are pegged into the grease stain. The polar head, i.e. hydrophilic part, protrude from the grease surface and form a charged layer around it. Thus, by mutual repulsion, the grease droplets are suspended in water. This emulsified greases stains are washed away with excess of water.

Some other examples of soap micelles are sodium palmitate ($C_{15}H_{31}COONa$), sodium lauryl sulphate [$CH_3(CH_2)_{11}SO_3O^-Na^+$], cetyl trimethyl ammonium bromide [$CH_3(CH_2)_{15}(CH_2)_3N^+Br^-$] etc.

Critical Micelle Concentration (CMC)

- It is the lowest concentration at which micelle formation appears. It increases with the total surfactant concentration. At higher concentration than CMC, they form extended parallel sheets, known as **lamellar micelles** which resemble to biological membranes.
- Increasing the hydrophobic part of the surfactant molecules favours micelle formation. Micelle formation is opposed by thermal agitation and CMC would be expected to increase with increasing temperature.
- With ionic micelles, the addition of simple electrolyte reduces the repulsion between the charged groups at the surface of the micelle by the screening action of the added ions. The CMC is lowered.

Kraft point It is the temperature above which a surfactant forms micelle.

Solved Booster 3.1

Identify the correct molecular picture showing what happens at the critical micelle concentration (CMC) of an aqueous solution of a surfactant (polar head; ~ non-polar tail; • water).

A. 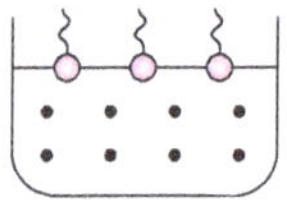

B. 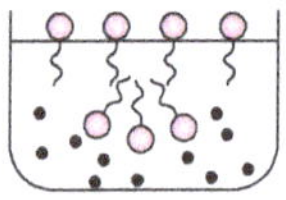

C. 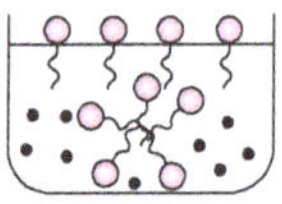

D. 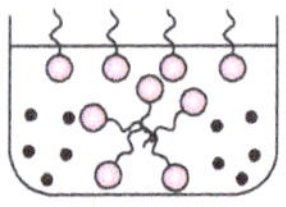

(a) *C* (b) *B*
(c) *D* (d) *A*

Solution

(c) CMC (critical micelle concentration) is the concentration of a surfactant in a bulk phase, above which aggregates of surfactant molecules, so called micelles, start to form.

A micelle is an aggregate of monomer surfactant molecules dispersed in a liquid colloid.

Hydrophilic 'Head' regions in contact with surrounding solvent, sequestering the hydrophobic 'Tail' regions in the micelle centre.

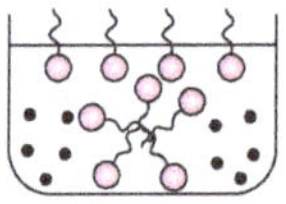

Hence, option (c) is correct.

JEE MAPPER

Example Similar to PYQ Asked in JEE Advanced 2016

The qualitative sketches I, II and III given below show the variation of surface tension with molar concentration of three different aqueous solutions of NaCl, CH_3CH_2OH and $CH_3(CH_2)_{15}\overset{+}{N}(CH_3)_3Br^-$ at room temperature.

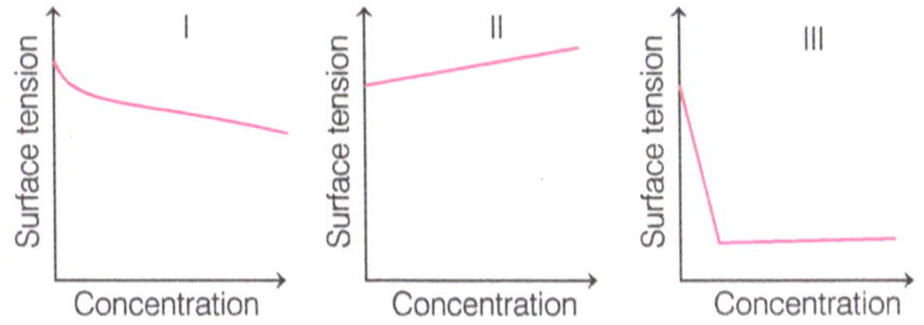

The correct assignment of the sketches is

	I	II	III
(a)	NaCl	CH_3CH_2OH	$CH_3(CH_2)_{15}\overset{\oplus}{N}(CH_3)_3Br^{\ominus}$
(b)	$CH_3(CH_2)_{15}\overset{\oplus}{N}(CH_3)_3Br^{\ominus}$	CH_3CH_2OH	NaCl
(c)	NaCl	$CH_3(CH_2)_{15}\overset{\oplus}{N}(CH_3)_3Br^{\ominus}$	CH_3CH_2OH
(d)	CH_3CH_2OH	NaCl	$CH_3(CH_2)_{15}\overset{\oplus}{N}(CH_3)_3Br^{\ominus}$

Sol. (*d*)

I. (CH_3CH_2OH) Surface tension decreases as concentration increases.

II. (NaCl) Surface tension increases with concentration for ionic salt.

III. $CH_3(CH_2)_{15}\overset{+}{N}(CH_3)_3Br^-$ it is a cationic detergent.

On increase in concentration surface tension decreases, and after CMC is attained, there is no change in surface tension.

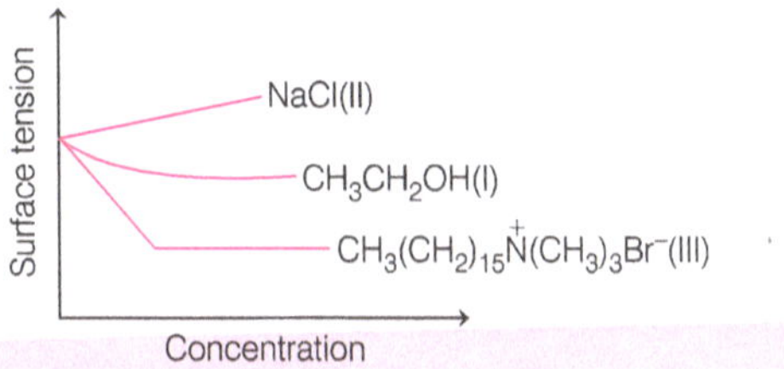

Competency Enhancer 3.1

Consider the statements given below:

Statement I Micelles are formed by surfactant molecules below the critical micelle concentration (CMC).

Statement II The conductivity of a solution having surfactant molecules decreases sharply or (CMC).

Choose the correct option

(a) Both Statement I and II are correct.

(b) Both Statements I and II are incorrect.

(c) Statement I is correct and Statement II is incorrect.

(d) Statement I is incorrect and Statement II is correct.

Preparation of Colloidal Solutions

Lyophilic colloids can be formed simply dissolving the colloidal particles in dispersion medium. e.g. colloidal solution of starch, gelatin, gum etc.

Lyophobic colloids need special method, i.e. **dispersion method** (by breaking down the bulk particles to fixer colloidal particles), or by **condensation method** (by aggregating the particles to form aggregates of colloidal size).

Dispersion Methods

In these methods, the larger particles are broken down into the smaller colloidal size. Some dispersion methods are given below.

1. Mechanical Dispersion

This method involves mechanical grinding of substance particles into the size of the colloidal particles using **colloid mill** which consists of two metal discs revolving at high speed in opposite direction. The materials to be converted into colloidal sol is fed in between the two discs in the form of a wet slurry (or suspension). The particles get broken to colloidal dimensions by the operating shearing force and then dispersed in a liquid. A stabliser is often added to stabilise the colloidal solution. e.g. Tanin is used as a stabiliser in the preparation of colloidal graphite between gum arabic in lamp black colloidal solution.

Some sols can be prepared by mechanical dispersion in a high intensity ultrasonic generators operating at a frequency of 20 kHz and above. This method is useful in cases where the substance being dispersed is of low mechanical strength such as sulphur, graphite, resins and gypsum.

JEE Alert

This method is not suitable when the dispersion medium is an organic liquid as considerable charring occurs.

2. Electrical Dispersion (Bredig's arc method)

In this method an electric arc is struck between two electrodes of a metal like platinum, gold silver or copper in water containing traces of an alkali. The metal first changes into vapour (molecular state) on account of the heat of the spark and the vapours then condense in water to give aggregate of colloidal range.

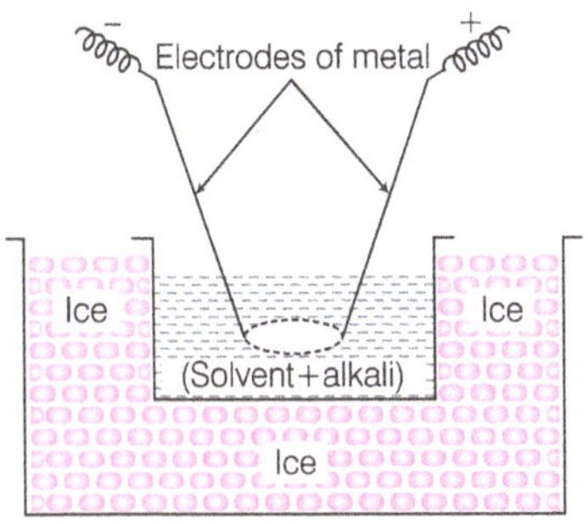

Bredig's arc method

3. Peptisation

In peptisation, some freshly precipitated ionic solids are dispersed into colloidal solution in water by the addition of small quantities of electrolytes, particularly containing a common ion.

The precipitate adsorbs the common ions and become electrically charge. These charged particles then split from the precipitate as colloidal particles.

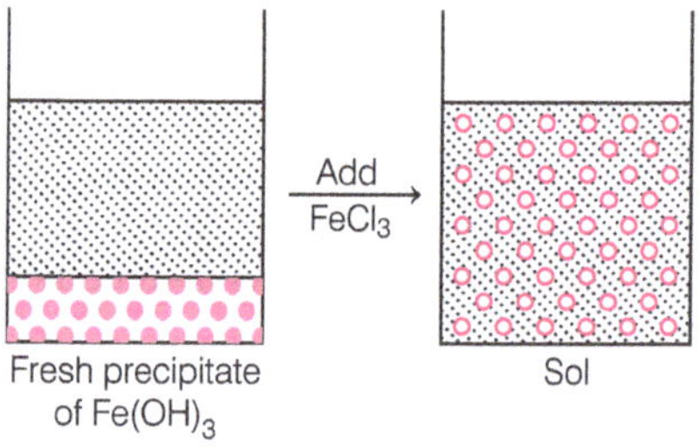

Procedure of peptisation

The dispersal of a precipitated material into colloidal solution by the action of an electrolyte in solution is termed as **peptisation** and the electrolyte is called a **peptising agent,** e.g.

- $AgCl$ can be converted into a sol by adding HCl.
- $Fe(OH)_3$ yields a sol by adding $FeCl_3$.

Condensation Methods

In condensation methods, particles of molecular dimensions are allowed to grow up to colloidal size. This may be carried by chemical and physical methods:

1. Chemical Method

In chemical methods colloidal molecules or aggregates are formed by means of chemical reactions such as decomposition, hydrolysis, oxidation or reduction. Examples of each of the reactions are given below.

(i) **Double Decomposition** As_2S_3 colloidal sol is obtained on passing H_2S gas into cold 1% As_2O_3 solution.

$$As_2O_3 + 3H_2S \longrightarrow As_2S_3 + 3H_2O$$

(ii) **Hydrolysis** On adding $FeCl_3$ to a large excess of hot distilled water, red sol of hydrated ferric oxide, commonly known as ferric hydroxide sol, is obtained.

$$FeCl_3 + 3H_2O \xrightarrow{\Delta} Fe(OH)_3 + 6HCl$$

(iii) **Reduction** A number of metals, such as silver, gold and platinum have been obtained in colloidal state by reducing aqueous solutions of their salts with reagents, such as formaldehyde, phenyl hydrazine, carbon monoxide, phosphorous acid, tannic acid, etc.

$$\underset{\text{Chloroauric acid}}{2H[AuCl_4]} + 5K_2CO_3 \longrightarrow \underset{\text{Potassium aurate}}{2KAuO_2} + 5CO_2 + 8KCl + H_2O$$

$$2KAuO_2 + \underset{\text{Formaldehyde}}{2HCHO} + K_2CO_3 \xrightarrow{\Delta} 2Au(sol) + 3HCOOK + KHCO_3$$

(iv) **Oxidation** A colloidal solution of sulphur can be obtained by bubbling oxygen through a solution of hydrogen sulphide in water.

$$2H_2S + O_2 \longrightarrow 2H_2O + 2S$$

$$2H_2S + SO_2 \longrightarrow 2H_2O + 3S$$

The presence of oxidising agents such as chromates, manganates, permanganates and nitric acid, causes the formation of colloidal sulphur in Group II of the qualitative analysis.

2. Physical Methods

In physical methods, techniques like solvent exchange by transferring solution from one solvent to other, excessive cooling or condensation of vapour, etc.

(i) **Exchange of Solvents** If a solution of sulphur in alcohol is added to water, a colloidal sol of sulphur is obtained due to lower solubility in water.

(ii) **Excessive Cooling** The colloidal sol of ice in an organic solvent (as $CHCl_3$ or ether) can be obtained by freezing a solution of water in the solvent. The molecules of water which can no longer be held in solution separately combine to form particles of colloidal size.

Purification of Colloidal Solutions

The presence of impurities, particularly the electrolytes, renders the sol unstable. These sols are purified by the following techniques.

1. Dialysis

It involves keeping the sol in a bag made of parchment or cellophane and suspending the bag in pure water. Small molecules and ions can pass through the membrane, through diffusion but the sol is retained.

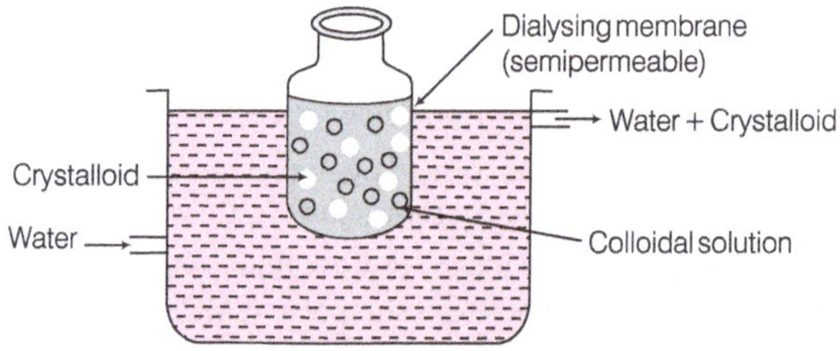

Demonstration of dialysis

When an electric field is applied during dialysis, we refer to it as electrodialysis.

In electrodialysis, the ions present in colloidal solution migrate out to the oppositely charged electrodes.

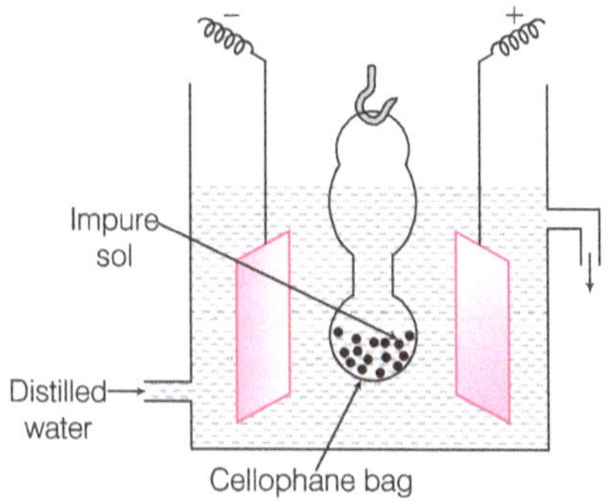

Electrodialysis

- Dialysis can be used for removing HCl from the ferric hydroxide sol.
- The process of dialysis is similar to osmosis except that both solvent molecules and small solute particles can pass through the semipermeable dialysis membrane. Only large colloidal particles such as cells and large molecules such as proteins cannot pass.
- The most important medical use of dialysis is in artificial kidney machines, where **haemodialysis** is used to cleanse the blood of patients whose kidneys have malfunctioned.

2. Ultra Centrifugation Method

In this method, colloidal sol is taken in a tube placed in an ultra centrifuge. On centrifuging, high speed, colloidal particles settle down at the bottom while impurities remain in solution (centrifugate). Sol is regenerated by mixing the settled colloidal particle with suitable dispersing medium like water containing peptised agent.

3. Ultra Filtration Method

Colloidal sols can also be purified by carrying out filtration through special type of graded filters called ultra filters this method called **ultra filtration method**. These ultra filter papers allow only the electrolytes to pass through under the influence of pressure or suction pump. Filter papers are made of particular pore size by impregnating ordinary filter paper with collodion solution to stop the flow of colloidal particles. The usual collodion solution is 4% solution of nitrocellulose in a mixture of alcohol and ether.

Properties of Colloids

General Properties

The important general properties of colloids are

(i) **Heterogeneous Nature** Colloidal sols are heterogeneous in nature. They consist of two phases : the dispersed phase and the dispersion medium.

(ii) **Colligative Properties** Due to formation of associated molecules, observed values of colligative properties like relative decrease in vapour pressure, elevation in boiling point, depression in freezing point, osmotic pressure are smaller than expected.

In arsenic sulphide sol, each particle is composed of about 1000 molecules. Thus, for a given mass of arsenic sulphide, the number of particles in the sol will be only $(1/1000)$ of the number present in true solution. Colligative properties depend on number of particles and thus these are much less for colloidal sols.

(iii) **Surface Area** Colloidal particles have larger area than the area of substance in a solid form. The adsorption tendency of colloids is due to the increased surface area.

(iv) **Surface Tension and Viscosity** In lyophobic sols, surface tension and viscosity are same as that of pure solvent. But in case of lyophilic sols the viscosity is higher and surface tension is lower as compared to pure solvent.

Mechanical Properties

The important mechanical properties of colloids are

(i) **Brownian Movement** It movement involves motion of colloidal particles in *zig-zag* paths. This type of erratic motion is due to the moving molecules of the dispersion medium constantly colliding with colloidal particles. During collision, molecules of dispersion medium impart momentum to colloidal particles. An English botanist, Robert Brown, observed this phenomenon, in 1827, with pollen grains suspended in water.

This is not observed in ordinary suspensions because the mass of each particle in this case is so large that the bombardment by molecules of the dispersion medium produces little effect on them.

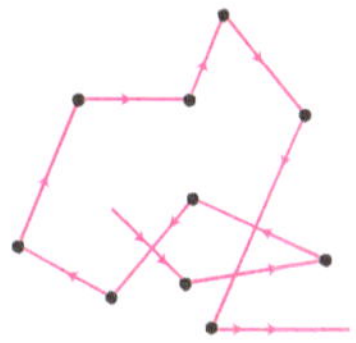

Brownian movement

- This offers a visible proof of the random kinetic motion of molecules in a liquid.
- It provides a direct demonstration of ceaseless motion of molecule as postulated by kinetic theory.
- It counters the force of gravity acting on colloidal particles and thus helps in providing stability to colloidal sol by not allowing them to settle down.

(ii) **Diffusion** Colloidal particles have a tendency to diffuse from a region of higher concentraction to that of lower concentraction.

JEE Quicker

The statement "Brownian motion of colloidal particles does not depend upon the size of particles but depends upon viscosity of the solution" is incorrect. *JEE Adv. 2017*

- Brownian motion depends upon both the size of particles and the viscosity of medium. Brownian motion is more pronounced for smaller particles as they experience greater random impact from the molecules of the surrounding medium.
The viscosity of the medium affects the motion because it determines the resistance to particle movement. Higher viscosity reduces the extent of Brownian motion.

(iii) **Sedimentation** Colloidal particles in a solution have a tendency to settle down under the effect of gravity.

Electrical Properties

In a colloidal solution the colloidal particles always carry electric charges which is same in nature, i.e. it is either positive or negative.

Some common sols with the nature of charge on their particles are given below.

- **Positive Charged Sols** Haemoglobin (blood), basic dye stuff, e.g. methylene blue sol. oxides (TiO_2 sol); Hydrated metallic oxides ($Al_2O_3 \cdot xH_2O$, $CrO_3 \cdot xH_2O$ and $Fe_2O_3 \cdot xH_2O$), etc.
- **Negative Charged Sols** Metallic sulphides, e.g. As_2S_3, Sb_2S_3, Cds sols; Acid dye stuffs, (eosin, congo red, sols); metals, (copper, silver, gold sols); sols of starch, gum, gelatin, clay, charcoal etc.

The stability of the colloidal solution is due to the presence of equal and similar charges on the colloidal particles. These similar charges create repulsive forces, due to which aggregation, condition does not takes place.

The charges on the sol particles is due to various reason *viz.*,

- due to electron capture by sol particles during electron dispersion of metals.
- due to preferential adsorption of ions from solution.
- due to formulation of electrical double layer.

The positive and negative charge on the colloidal particles is due to preferential adsorption of positive or negative ions present in the dispersion medium. The ions preferred by colloidal particles are those, which are common with their own lattice, few examples are given below.

(i) Sol formed with the help of diluted solution of silver nitrate and potassium iodide.

- **Positive Charged Sol** When KI solution is added to $AgNO_3$ solution the AgI precipitate formed absorb Ag^+ ion from the dispersion medium and form positive charged sol.

$$AgI/Ag^+$$

Positive charged

- **Negative Charged Sol** When $AgNO_3$ solution is added to KI solution to give AgI precipitate. These precipitate absorb iodide ions (I^-) from the dispersion medium and form negative charged sol.

$$AgI/I^-$$

Negative charged

(ii) Sol formed with the help of $\mathbf{FeCl_3}$ and excess of hot water/NaOH solution.

- **Positive Charged Sol** A positive charge sol of hydrated ferric oxide is formed due to adsorption of Fe^{3+} ions when $FeCl_3$ is added to excess of hot water.

$$Fe_2O_3 \cdot xH_2O/Fe^{3+}$$

Positive charged

- **Negative Charged Sol** A negative charge sol of hydrated ferric oxide is formed due to adsorption of OH^- ions when $FeCl_3$ is added to NaOH solution

$$Fe_2O_3 \cdot xH_2O/OH^-$$

Negative charged

- **Electrokinetic Potential or Zeta Potential** After selective adsorption of positive or negative ions from dispersion medium they acquired a positive or a negative charge on the surface of a colloidal particle. This layer attracts counter ions from the medium forming a second layer.

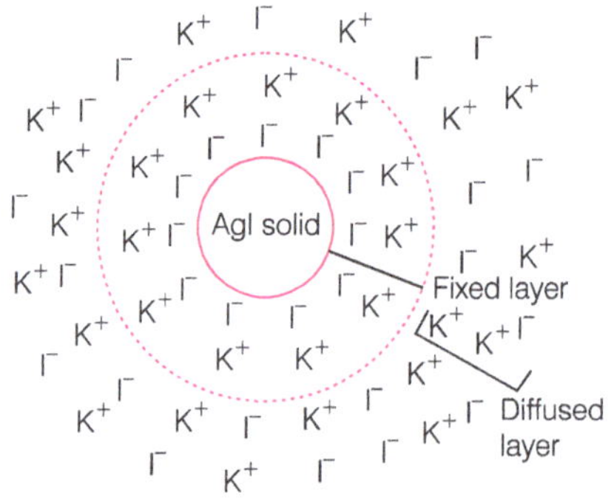

Formation of double layer

- The combination of the two layer of positive and negative charges around the sol particles is called **Helmholtz electrical double layer**.

JEE Spotlite

According to modern views, the first layer of ions is firmly held and is called fixed layer while the second layer is mobile and is called diffused layer. The opposite charges on the fixed and diffused parts of the double layer result in a potential between these layers. This potential difference between the electrical double layer is called **zeta potential** or **electrokinetic potential**, Z, given by $Z = \frac{4\pi\eta u}{D}$

where, η is called coefficient of viscosity, D is dielectric constant of the medium and u is velocity of the colloidal particles when an electric field is applied.

Electrophoresis

The phenomenon of migration of colloidal particles towards oppositely charged electrodes under the influence of applied electrical potential is called electrophoresis. It involves the movement of colloidal particles either towards the cathode or anode, under the influence of the electric field.

The electrophoretic mobility of colloidal particles is defined as the distance travelled by them in one second under a potential gradient of one volt per centimeter. Since, different colloidal materials have different mobilities, it is possible to separate them from one another from their mixtures.

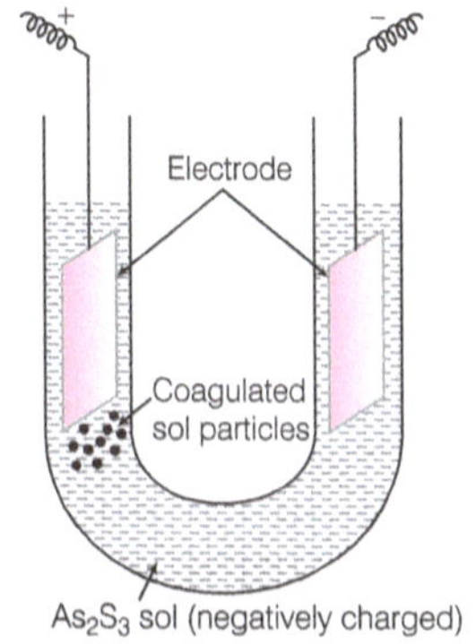

Electrophoresis

Electro-osmosis

When electrophoresis of dispersed particles in a colloidal system is prevented by suitable means, it is observed that the dispersion medium itself begins to move in an electric field.

This phenomenon is called **electro-osmosis**.

Tyndall Effect (Optical Properties)

When light passes through a sol, its path becomes visible because of scattering of light by particles. It is called Tyndall effect.

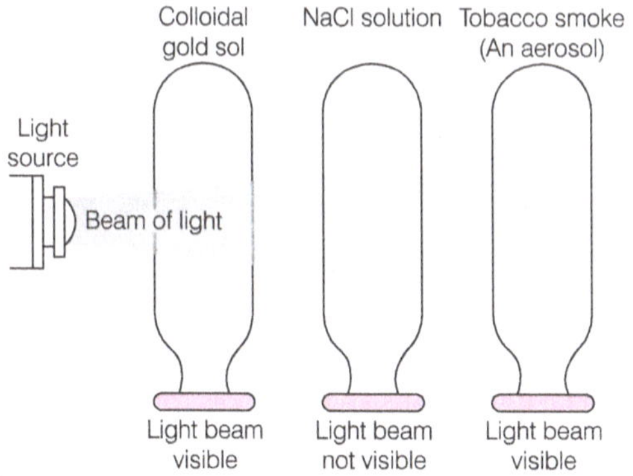

The dispersion of a beam of light by colloidal particles is called the Tyndall effect. The presence of colloidal particles is easily detected with the aid of a light beam

In a true solution, there are no particles of sufficiently large diameter to scatter light and hence, no Tyndall effect is observed.

The intensity of the scattered light depends on the difference between the refractive indices of the dispersed phase and the dispersion medium. In lyophobic colloids, the difference is appreciable and therefore, the Tyndall effect is well defined. But in lyophilic sols, the difference is very small and the Tyndall effect is very weak.

Coagulation and Hardy-Schulze Rule

Colloids are stable due to the presence of similar charges. If some how, charge is removed, the particles come nearer to each other and coagulate.

The phenomenon of change of colloidal state to suspended state is known as **coagulation** or **flocculation of colloidal solutions**.

Methods of Coagulation

1. By the Addition of Suitable Electrolyte

On the addition of electrolytes, colloids interact with ions carrying charge opposite to that present on them and cause neutralisation. This, leads to coagulation. The ion responsible for the neutralisation of charge on the particles is called coagulating ion.

Coagulation of positively charged sol takes place by the addition of negative ion of suitable electrolyte and *vice-versa*.

The coagulating power of ion is decided by Hardy-Schulze rule.

JEE Spotlite

Hardy-Schulze rule states **"the greater the valency of the coagulating ion added, the greater is its power to cause coagulation".**

Thus, to cause the coagulation of negative sol of As_2S_3 the coagulating power of different cations will be in the order.

$$Al^{3+} > Mg^{2+} > Na^+$$

Similarly, to coagulate a positive sol of $Fe(OH)_3$, the coagulating power of different anions will be in the order

$[Fe(CN)_6]^{4-} > PO_4^{3-} > SO_4^{2-} > Cl^-$

Flocculation value The minimum concentration of an electrolyte required to cause coagulation or flocculation of a sol is called its **flocculation value**. This is usually expressed in terms of **millimoles per litre**.

2. By the Mutual Action of Sols

If two oppositely charged colloidal sols are mixed, coagulation takes place.

3. By Persistent Dialysis

If the sols are subjected to prolonged dialysis, traces of electrolytes present in colloidal sols pass through the dialyser and the colloids become unstable.

4. By Mechanical Method

Violent stirring of a sol causes coagulation. Vibratory action caused by ultrasound may also cause coagulation

Solved Booster 10.2

The coagulating power of electrolytes having ions Na^+, Al^{3+} and Ba^{2+} for arsenic sulphide sol increases in the order

(a) $Al^{3+} < Ba^{2+} < Na^+$ (b) $Na^+ < Ba^{2+} < Al^{3+}$

(c) $Ba^{2+} < Na^+ < Al^{3+}$ (d) $Al^{3+} < Na^+ < Ba^{2+}$

Solution *(b)*

According to Hardy Schulze rule, greater the charge on oppositely charged ion, greater is its coagulating power. Since, arsenic sulphide is a negatively charged sol.

Thus, the order of coagulating power is $Na^+ < Ba^{2+} < Al^{3+}$.

Protective Colloidal Sols and Gold Number

Lyophilic colloidal sols are much more stable than lyophobic colloidal sols. This is due to the extensively solvation of lyophilic colloidal sols, which forms a protective layer of a liquid in which they are dispersed outside it and this prevents it from forming associated colloids.

Lyophilic colloidal sols also protect lyophobic colloidal sols from precipitation by the action of electrolytes. This is due to formation of a protective layer by lyophilic sols outside lyophobic sols. Lyophilic colloidal sols are called **protective sols**. Gelatin (lyophilic) protects gold sol (lyophobic) from coagulation on the addition of sodium chloride solution.

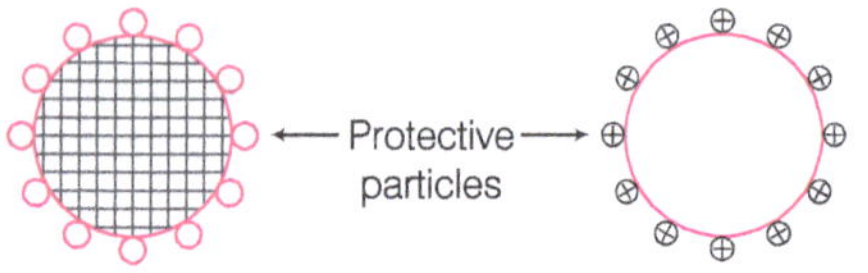

Protective powers of different colloidal sols are measured in terms of **'gold number'** (Zsigmondy). **It is defined as** the amount of protective sol in milligrams that prevents the coagulation of 10 mL of a given gold sol on adding 1 mL of 10 per cent solution of sodium chloride. **Thus, smaller the gold number of a lyophilic sol, the greater is the protective power.** Gold number of some lyophilic colloidal sols are given table.

Gold numbers

Lyophilic sols	Gold number
Gelatin	0.005-0.01
Casein	0.01
Haemoglobin	0.03
Gum arabic	0.15
Sodium oleate	0.4
Gum tragacanth	2
Potato starch	25

Therefore, reciprocal of gold number is a measure of the protective power of the colloid. Hence, out of the above list given in table 3.3, gelatin is the best protective colloid.

Applications of Colloidal Sols

(i) **Foods** Many of our foods are colloidal in nature. Milk is an emulsion of fat dispersed in water. It is stabilised by casein which itself is a lyophilic colloid and, being a protein, is a nutrient of great value.

(ii) **Medicines** A number of medicinal and pharmaceutical preparations are colloidal in nature, which are more effective and are easily assimilated. Colloidal gold and calcium are used to increase the vitality of the human system.

(iii) **Industrial Foods** So many industrial goods, e.g. detergents, varnishes, paints, gums, glues etc., are colloidal in nature.

(iv) **Tanning** Animal hides are colloidal in nature. Such hides carry positive charge and when these are soaked in a negatively charged solution of tannin, coagulation takes place. This results in the hardening of leather and process is called tanning. Chromium salts are also used in place of tannin.

(v) **Cottrell Precipitator** Smokes and dust are solid aerosols. Removal of these particles from air involves the principle of **electrophoresis**. The air from a furnace or an industrial plant carrying these particles is passed through the chamber containing metal electrodes (having charge opposite to that carried by smoke) under high voltage. The particles are discharged and deposited as precipitates on the oppositely charged electrodes.

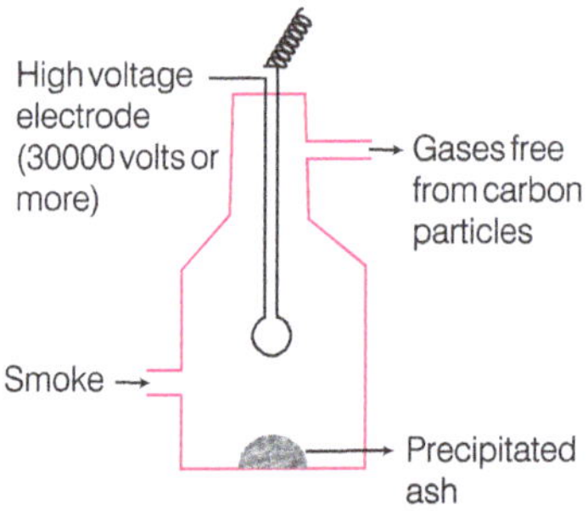

Cottrell smoke precipitator

(vi) **In sewage Disposals** Sewage water consists of particles of dirt, rubbish, mud, etc., which are of colloidal dimensions and carry electric charge. On creating an electric field in the sewage tank, coagulation takes place, again a case of **electrophoresis**.

(vii) **Purification of Water** Water carrying impurities is purified by addition of potash alum. Al^{3+} of the potash alum causes coagulation of negatively charged suspended impurities and thus waste water is made fit for drinking purposes.

(viii) **Formation of Deltas** The deltas at the river beds are formed by the precipitation of the charged clay particles, carried in suspension in the river water, by the action of salts present in sea-water.

(ix) **Artificial Rain** Cloud consist of charged particles of water dispersed in air. Rain is caused by the aggregation of these minute particles. Artificial rain can be made by throwing electrified sand from aeroplanes. Similarly, artificial smoke screens can be made by throwing titanium oxide in air.

Emulsions

If a pair of immiscible liquids such as olive oil and water are mixed and shaken vigorously, a dispersion of very fine droplets of one liquid in the other will result. Such a dispersion is termed emulsion.

One of the components in emulsion is water and the other one is an oily substance immiscible in water.

Emulsion droplets are bigger than sol particles ($\approx 10^{-6}$ m) and can be seen under an ordinary microscope or sometimes even with a magnifying glass.

Emulsions resemble lyophobic sols in some of the properties.

Types of Emulsions

Depending on the nature of the dispersed phase, the emulsions are classified as:

- Oil-in-water emulsion (*O/W*)
- Water-in-oil emulsion (*W/O*)

They have been shown in figure given below.

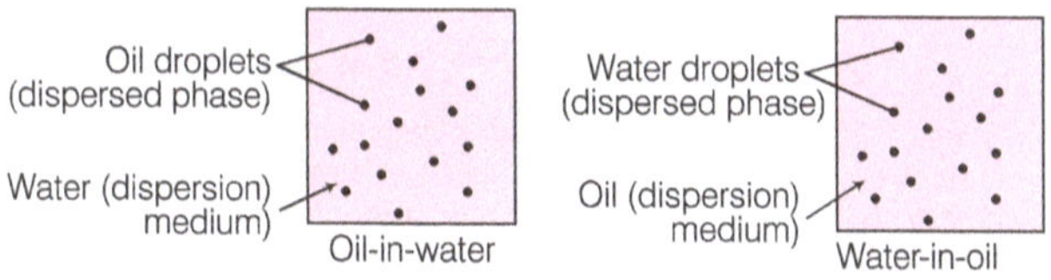

(i) **Oil-in-water Emulsions** (*O/W*) This type of emulsion is formed when oil (dispersed phase) is dispersed in water (dispersion medium).

- Milk and vanishing cream are *O/W* type emulsions. In milk liquid fat globules are dispersed in water.

(ii) **Water-in-oil Emulsions** (*W/O*) This type of emulsion is formed when water is dispersed in oil (dispersion medium).

- These are also called oily emulsion.
- Cold cream and butter are *W/O* type emulsions.

Identification of the type of Emulsions

The type of emulsions formed in a given case depends mainly on the relative proportions of the dispersed phase and the dispersion medium.The two types of emulsions may be identified by:

(i) **Dilution Test** An emulsion can be diluted with any amount of the dispersion medium, whereas the addition of dispersed phase forms a separate layer. Thus, if a given emulsion can be diluted with water, it is (*O/W*) type otherwise (*W/O*) type.

(ii) **Dye Test** An oil-soluble dye is shaken with the given emulsion to be identified. If the whole background is coloured, emulsion is (*W/O*) type. If coloured drops are seen on looking at the drop of it under microscope, the emulsion is of (*O/W*) type.

(iii) **Physical Test** Surface tension of water is greater than that of the oil hence, formation of drops in (*O/W*) emulsion is easier.

- Oily emulsions are more viscous than the aqueous emulsions.
- Electrical conductivity of aqueous emulsion is higher than that of oily emulsions and increases if any electrolyte (say KCl) is added due to its dissolution into aqueous dispersion medium.

Characteristics of Emulsion

Emulsions show all the properties of sols (or colloids) like Tyndall effect. Brownian movement, electrophoresis etc. They can be diluted with liquid forming the dispersion medium in the emulsion.

(i) Emulsions scatter light and thus exhibit Tyndall effect.

(ii) Brownian motion is also observed in emulsions, where size of the particle is near to the limit of 10^{-6}m.

(iii) Stability of an emulsion is determined by the toughness of the emulsifier film (which helps to prevent the coalescence of droplets of the dispersed phase) and by the electric charge on the emulsoid particles.

(iv) Coagulation or demulsification of an emulsion (breaking of emulsion to give constituent liquids) can be done by

- addition of a substance which would destroy the emulsifier.
- addition of an electrolyte which would destroy the charge.
- addition of a dehydrating agent or alcohol [for (W/O) emulsions only].
- heating, freezing and centrifuging.

Applications of Emulsions

(i) Cleansing action of soap is due to formation of emulsions. Soaps and detergents emulsify the grease alongwith the adhering dirt and carry them away in the wash water.

(ii) For concentrating ores, the finely powdered ore is treated with an oil. Oil forms emulsion with the ore particles. When air is bubbled into the mixture, emulsion containing the particles of the mineral are carried to the surface.

(iii) Several oily drugs are prepared in the form of emulsions to facilitate their adsorption in the body. Many of the lotions, creams and ointments are emulsions of oil-in-water or water-in-oil type.

(iv) Petroleum products get emulsified in the oil-well causing problems. However, they can be demulsified into constituent liquids by physical methods such as centrifugation, freezing, filtration, electrostatic precipitation etc.

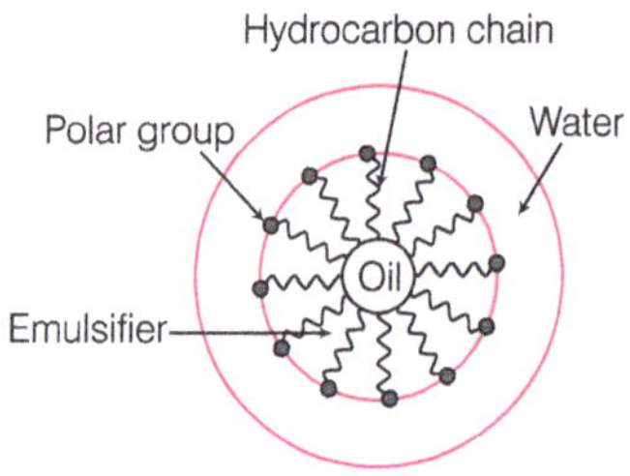

Emulsification of an oil droplet

Emulsifiers

Emulsions are generally prepared by vigorously agitating a mixture of the relevant oil and water. The emulsions obtained by simple mechanical stirring are unstable and the two components (oil and water) tend to separate out. To obtain a stable emulsion, a suitable stabilising substance, called **emulsifier is added**.

Substances which can act as emulsifiers are soaps, detergents, long-chain sulphonic acids, lyophilic colloids like gelatin, albumin, casein, etc. In milk, casein acts as the emulsifier.

Role of Emulsifier

The main function of the emulsifier is to reduce the interfacial tension between the two liquids forming an emulsion. Most emulsifiers are long-chain hydrocarbon derivatives containing a polar end group such as, sulphonic ($—SO_3^-$), carboxylic ($—CO_2^-$) etc.

The polar end group is hydrophilic and thus water-soluble and the hydrocarbon chain is hydrophobic and thus oil-soluble. When a suitable emulsifier is added to an oil-water system, the molecules of the emulsifier arrange themselves in such a way that the polar end groups dip in water and the hydrocarbon chains dip into the oil. Thus, the emulsifier forms an adsorbed film around the dispersed droplets and prevents their coagulation.

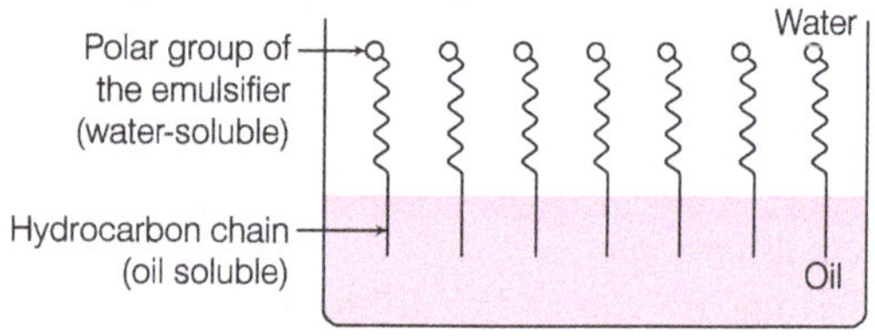

Orientation of an emulsifier at water oil interface

Gels

A gel is a colloidal system in which a liquid is dispersed in a solid. Under certain conditions, the lyophilic sols may be coagulated to give a semi-solid jelly-like mass which encloses all the liquid present in the sol. The process of gel formation is called gelation and the colloidal system formed is called gel. The common examples of gel are: gum arabic, gelatin, processed cheese, silicic acid, ferric hydroxide, etc. Gels are formed by the interlocking of the particles of solid dispersion medium in the form of a loose framework inside which liquid (dispersed phase) is contained.

When the gel is allowed to stand for a long time, it shrinks and loses the entire liquid held by it. This shrinking of gel is termed as syneresis (meaning spontaneous explusion of liquid from gel).

Gels may be classified into two types:

(i) Elastic gels

(ii) Non-elastic gels

Main point of difference between the two gels are as follows:

	Elastic gels	Non-elastic gels
(i)	Gels which possess the property of elasticity, i.e. they change to dehydratic solid mass which can again be converted into gel by addition of water followed by heating and cooling.	Gels which do not possess the property of elasticity, i.e. they change into solid mass on dehydration which becomes rigid and cannot be converted into the original form by heating with water.
(ii)	When placed in contact with water they absorb water and swell. This property is called imbibition.	They do not show the phenomenon of imbibition. (The absorption or adsorption of a liquid by a solid or a gel accompanied by swelling of the latter.)
(iii)	Examples include gelatin, agar-agar, starch, etc.	Most common example is silicic acid.

Elemental Practice 10.3

Type I MCQs with Only One Correct Option

1. Physical properties as molar conductivity, surface tension and osmotic pressure of colloidal sols shows a drastic change in their properties from a particular concentration as shown.

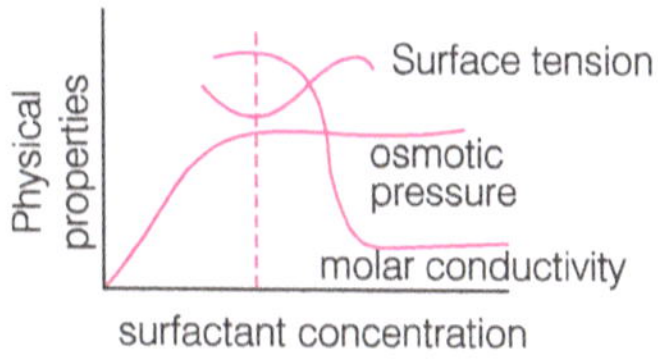

Thus, the concentration is called

(a) CMC (b) VMC
(c) TMC (d) EMC

2. Consider a colloidal solution of As_2S_3 (arsenic trisulphide). The coagulation of this sol is studied by adding different electrolytes. The flocculation values of the electrolytes are as follows,

$Al^{3+} = 10^{-3}$ M, $Ba^{2+} = 10^{-2}$ M, $Na^{+} = 10^{-1}$ M

Which of the following conclusion is correct?

(a) Na^+ will cause fastest coagulation.
(b) Ba^{2+} will cause fastest coagulation.
(c) Al^{3+} will cause fastest coagulation.
(d) Ba^{2+} and Na^+ will cause same rate of coagulation.

3. Which of the following is not a property of hydrophobic sols?

(a) They are generally less stable in the presence of electrolytes.
(b) The particles are stabilised mainly by adsorption of charged ions on their surface.
(c) They show strong Tyndall effect due to scattering of light.
(d) They are highly stable and do not get easily coagulated by electrolytes.

4. Which of the following reactions is commonly used in the preparation of colloidal sol?

(a) $AgNO_3 + NaCl \longrightarrow AgCl + NaNO_3$
(b) $2Mg + CO_2 \longrightarrow 2MgO + C$
(c) $FeCl_3 + 3H_2O \longrightarrow Fe(OH)_3 + 3HCl$
(d) $NaOH + HCl \longrightarrow NaCl + H_2O$

5. Match the List I with List II.

List I		List II	
A.	Brownian motion	1.	Coagulation of colloid particles by an electrolyte
B.	Tyndall effect	2.	Movement of particles in a colloidal solution due to random collisions with molecules.
C.	Lyophilic sol	3.	Colloids that can easily be dispersed in a solvent and form a stable sol.
D.	Flocculation value	4.	Effect of light scattering by colloidal particles in a dispersion medium.

Choose the correct answer from the options given below.

(a) A-2, B-4, C-3, D-1 (b) A-2, B-4, C-1, D-3
(c) A-4, B-2, C-3, D-1 (d) A-3, B-1, C-2, D-4

6. Given below are two statements.

Statement I In the process of dialysis, the colloidal sol is placed in a semi-permeable membrane allows the passage of small ions but prevents the passage of colloidal particles.

Statement II In ultrafiltration, a colloidal sol is passed through a membrane with pores that are small enough to retain the colloidal particles but allow the passage of solvent.

In the light of the above statements choose the correct answer from the options given below.

(a) Both Statement I and Statement II are correct.
(b) Both Statement I and Statement II are incorrect.
(c) Statement I is correct but Statement II is incorrect.
(d) Statement I is incorrect but Statement II is correct.

7. Select the correct statement regarding electro-osmosis.

(a) The movement of the liquid is always towards the cathode when an electric field is applied.
(b) Electro-osmotic flow is observed only in hydrophobic colloidal sols.
(c) The direction of electroosmotic flow depends on the charge on the particles of medium.
(d) Electro-osmosis occurs only in non-aqueous solvents.

8. Which of the following is most appropriate application of the Tyndall effect?

(a) Detection of colloidal particles in solution.
(b) Separation of colloidal particles using ultrafiltration.
(c) Purification of water using reverse osmosis.
(d) Coagulation of colloidal sols using electrolytes.

9. Given below are two statements.

Assertion (A) The addition of electrolytes, particularly those with high charge density leads to the coagulation of colloidal sols.

Reason (R) Electrolytes neutralise the charge on colloidal particles, reducing the repulsive forces between them and causing them to aggregate and settle.

In the light of the above statements, choose the correct answer from the options given below.

(a) Both (A) and (R) are true and (R) is the correct explanation of (A).
(b) Both (A) and (R) are true but (R) is not the correct explanation of (A).
(c) (A) is true but (R) is false.
(d) (A) is false but (R) is true.

10. Gold numbers of protective colloids A, B, C and D are 0.50, 0.01, 0.06, 0.005 respectively. The correct order of their protective powers is

(a) $D < A < C < B$ (b) $C < B < D < A$
(c) $A < C < B < D$ (d) $B < D < A < C$

11. Which of the following statement is correct regarding cationic and anionic surfactants?
(a) Cationic surfactants are typically used as detergents and are effective in hard water.
(b) Anionic surfactants carry a positive charge on their hydrophilic head and are commonly used in shampoos and conditioners.
(c) Cationic surfactants are used as fabric softeners due to their ability to form a thin, smooth layer on fabrics.
(d) Anionic surfactants are more effective than cationic surfactants in reducing the surface tension of water.

12. A colloidal sol of ferric hydroxide ($Fe(OH)_3$) requires 25 mL of 0.2 M NaCl to coagulate 100 mL of the sol. If the same sol requires 30 mL of 0.1 M $BaCl_2$ to coagulate 100 mL of the sol. Then the relative coagulation power of Ba^{2+} with respect to Na^+ is
(a) 2 (b) 1
(c) 3 (d) 4

13. Given below are some statements regarding the mechanical dispersion method of preparing colloidal sols.
I. Mechanical dispersion method involves breaking a bulk substance into small particles using high-speed agitation or grinding.
II. This method is suitable for preparing sols of substances like gold and silver by dispersing them in water.
III. The method produces stable colloidal sol without the need for stabilising agents.
IV. This method is generally ineffective for substances with high solubility in water like NaCl.
V. The dispersion can be further stabilised by adding a small amount of an electrolyte or by using a stabilising agent after dispersion.
In the light of the above statements, choose the correct statement from the options given below.
(a) I, II, III and IV
(b) I, III, V
(c) I, IV, V
(d) I, II, III, IV and V

14. Which of the following is an application of the electrophoresis method?
(a) Separation of colloidal particles based on their size.
(b) Separation of proteins in a mixture based on their charge and size.
(c) Formation of colloidal sols from bulk substances.
(d) Prevention of coagulation in colloidal solutions.

15. The flocculation value of $ZnCl_2$ for As_2S_3 sol is 0.68 (millimoles of electrolyte needed per litre of sol). Then millilitre of 0.24 M $ZnCl_2$ required to start the coagulation of 300 mL of sol is ....
(a) 0.55 mL (b) 0.65 mL
(c) 0.75 mL (d) 0.85 mL

16. The surfactants that will form micelles in aqueous solution at the lowest concentration is
(a) hexadecyltrimethyl ammonium chloride (HTAC)
(b) sodium dodecyl sulphate (SDS)
(c) polyethylene glycol (PEG)-based surfactants
(d) Lauryl alcohol

17. Select the statements related to the electrical double layer (EDL).
(a) Electrical double layer forms only in non-aqueous solution.
(b) The inner layer of the electrical double layer is composed of oppositely charged ions adsorbed on the surface of the particles.
(c) The thickness of the electrical layer decreases as the ionic strength of solution increases.
(d) The electrical double layer is formed only at the interface between a gas and solid phase.

18. Which of the following emulsions is correctly identified as water-in-oils (W/O), where water droplets are dispersed in oil as the continuous phase?
(a) Mayonnaise
(b) Hair oils
(c) Ice cream
(d) Milk of magnesia

Type II 》 MCQs with One or More than One Correct Option

19. For a mixture of lyophobic and lyophilic colloids in the same medium, which of the following are true?
(a) The lyophobic colloid can enhance the stability of the lyophilic colloid.
(b) The lyophilic colloid can increase the stability of the lyophobic colloid through the formation of a protective layer.
(c) Such mixtures exhibits higher viscosity than individual lyophobic colloids.
(d) The Tyndall effect becomes less pronounced in this mixture.

20. Which of the following are correct for the condensation methods of colloidal preparation?
(a) Colloidal sol of sulphur can be prepared by passing hydrogen sulphide gas into a solution of sulphur dioxide.
(b) Colloidal ferric hydroxide can be prepared by hydrolysis of ferric chloride.
(c) In double decomposition, the resulting sol always requires a stabilising agent to prevent coagulation.
(d) Reduction of silver nitrate using tannic acid can produce a colloidal sol of silver.

21. For a negatively charged colloidal solution, the order of coagulation power of the following electrolytes is observed as :
$$Al_2(SO_4)_3 > CaCl_2 > NaCl$$
Which of the following statements are correct?
(a) The colloidal sol is likely a negatively charged sol because the coagulation power is based on the valency of the cations.
(b) The order of coagulation power can be explained using the Hardy-Schulze, where the effectiveness of coagulation is directly proportional to the valency of the coagulation ion.
(c) If the coagulation solution were positively charged, the order of coagulation power would be same : $Al_2(SO_4)_3 > CaCl_2 > NaCl$
(d) Increasing the concentration of $Al_2(SO_4)_3$ will have a greater impact on the coagulation of the colloid compared to $CaCl_2$ and NaCl.

22. Select the statements which are not true for emulsions.
(a) Emulsions show both positive and negative deviations from Raoult's law based on the interaction between the dispersed phase and the dispersion medium.
(b) The addition of a surfactant with a HLB (Hydrophilic-Lipophilic balance) value less than 10 favours the formation of oil-in-water (O/W) emulsions.
(c) Emulsions are thermodynamically unstable systems but can be kinetically stabilised by using emulsifying agents.
(d) Microemulsions have smaller droplets size compared to regular emulsions and are thermodynamically stable due to their low interfacial tension.

23. Select the correct statements about macromolecular colloids.
(a) Macromolecular colloids tend to have high osmotic pressure compared to other types of colloids due to the large size of their particles.
(b) Gelatin, starch and rubber are examples of macromolecular colloids that show electrostatic stability in their colloidal form.
(c) The solubility of macromolecular colloids in a solvent depends on the temperature and polarity of the solvent.
(d) Macromolecular colloids are always thermodynamically stable and do not undergo aggregation or coagulation under any conditions.

24. Choose the statements which are correct regarding critical micelle concentration (CMC) and surfactants.
(a) The CMC of a surfactant decreases with increasing temperature for ionic surfactants.
(b) The CMC can be determined experimentally by measuring the change in the conductivity or surface tension of the surfactant solution with varying concentrations.
(c) The value of CMC is inversely related to the hydrophilic-lipophilic balance (HLB) of a surfactant, higher HLB leads to a higher CMC.
(d) The presence of electrolytes in a surfactant solution can lower the CMC as the electrolytes reduce the electrostatic repulsion between the surfactant molecules.

25. Select the correct statements.
(a) Residual force field on a surface is responsible for adsorption.
(b) Rate of adsorption is very rapid in the beginning but decreases until equilibrium is attained.
(c) Adsorption and desorption follow similar mechanism.
(d) When multilayer are formed, desorption takes place.

Type III 》 Numerical/Integer Type Questions

26. The molecular formula of a synthetic polymer *P* is represented as $(C_4H_8O_2)_m$. If the gold number of polymer *P* is 5.4 and 0.02 millimoles of *P* are required to just prevent the coagulation of 10 mL of a red gold sol upon the addition of 1 mL of 10% NaCl. The value of *m* is ....

27. A volume of 450 mL of 2% w/w KCl solution with a density of 1.1 g/mL is required to completely coagulate 150 mL of a gold sol in 1.5 hours. The coagulation value of KCl is .... m mole/litres.

28. When $FeCl_3$ and Na_2SO_4 are mixed in a 1:2 molar ratio; a negatively charged colloidal sol of C is formed. Moles of C that are coagulated by 5 moles of $BaCl_2$ is ....

29. A solution of sodium stearate $(C_{17}H_{35}COONa)$ becomes a colloidal sol at its critical micelle concentration (CMC) which is 10^{-4} M. At this concentration, the total number of micelles in 1 liter of the solution is 5×10^{20}. Then, the total number of ions present in 1 liter of the solution at CMC is ....

30. Total number of the correct statements regarding peptization is
(a) It is commonly used in the preparation of sols such as gold sol and ferric hydroxide sol.
(b) $AlCl_3$ is a stronger peptizing agent than NaCl for $Fe(OH)_3$.
(c) The addition of an electrolyte like NaOH to a colloidal solution can lead to coagulation, not peptization.
(d) Peptization is a reversible process, and the colloidal sol can be converted back to precipitate by adding excess electrolyte.

31. The number of colloids that have positively charged colloidal particles are ....
(i) ZrO_2 sol (ii) Starch
(iii) CdS sol (iv) Haemoglobin
(v) Al_2O_3

Elemental Practice 10.3 | Chapter 10

Connect with **Answers**

1. (a)	2. (c)	3. (d)	4. (c)	5. (a)	6. (a)
7. (c)	8. (a)	9. (a)	10. (c)	11. (c)	12. (b)
13. (c)	14. (b)	15. (d)	16. (a)	17. (b)	18. (b)
19. (b,c)	20. (a,b,d)	21. (a,b,d)	22. (a,b)	23. (a,c)	24. (a,b,d)
25. (a,b,d)	26. (3)	27. (880)	28. (5)	29. 1.120×10^{21}	
30. (4)	31. (3)				

Advanced Exclusive Different Strokes

Applications of Adsorption

(i) **In making moisture free atmosphere** Silica gel, alumina etc. are used to remove moisture as they adsorb water. This is why, small packets of silica gel are kept with delicate instruments.

(ii) **In removal of colouring matter** For decolorisation of sugar cane juice, it is passed over activated animal charcoal, where colouring matter gets adsorbed on the surface of charcoal.

(iii) **In production of high vacuum** High vacuum can be generated by adsorption of traces of air on charcoal.

(iv) **In purification of water** Ion-exchange resins are used to soften hard water and the process involves adsorption.

(v) **Separation of inert gases** Using coconut charcoal at different temperatures, the adsorbed inert gases gets released.

(vi) **In the extraction of metals** Froth floatation process used for the concentration of ores is based on **preferential adsorption** of ore particles.

An adsorbate having stronger adsorbing tendency adsorbs more effectively than weaker adsorbates. A strongly adsorbable substance can adsorb even by displacing the pre adsorbed weak substance.

It is known as **preferential adsorption**, *e.g.*, in gas masks finely divided charcoal contains N_2, O_2 etc. which have poor adsorbing power. These pre adsorbed gases are replaced by strongly adsorbable gases like, CH_4, Cl_2, etc.

(vii) **Adsorption indicators** Some dyes like, eosin, fluorescein etc. get adsorbed on the surface of precipitates (AgCl) and this property serves as basis for adsorption indicators.

(viii) **Industrial applications** In coalmines, gas masks use activated charcoal (or mixture of adsorbents) which adsorbs poisonous gases and thus makes the inner gas useful for breathing.

In the manufacture of

- **NH_3**, iron catalyst adsorbs N_2 and H_2 reactants.
- **H_2SO_4**, finely divided Pt adsorbs SO_2 and O_2.
- **Vanaspati** (fat), finely divided Ni adsorbs H_2.

(ix) **Chromatography** ⟶ To separate a mixture of compounds.

Thin Layer Chromatography

(Based on adsorption)

- A thin layer of an adsorbent (SiO_2 in water, slurry) is spread over a glass plate and then allowed to dry. It is referred as TLC plate.
- The solution of the mixture where components are to be separated is applied as a small spot, 2 cm above one end of the TLC plate. The procedure is repeated 4-5 times.
- The plate is then vertically placed in a closed jar containing a suitable solvent for developing the chromatogram. Ensure that the spot stays above the solvent level.
- As the solvent moves up the plate by capillary action, the components of the mixture also move up through the adsorbent layer at different rates depending on their degree of adsorption.
- Each compound ascends to a different height but less than that of the solvent.

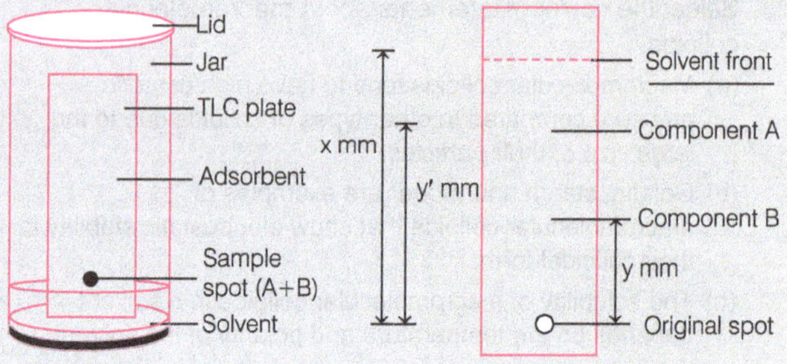

Developed chromatogram

$R_f(B) = \frac{y}{x}$ $R_F(A) = \frac{y'}{x}$

- When solvent front reaches near the top of plate, the plate is taken out of the jar.
- The solvent front is marked with a pencil and the plate is allowed to dry.
- The spots of the separated components are visible on the TLC plate if the compounds are coloured.
- Sometimes, the spots are made visible by spraying the plate with an appropriate reagent, which forms colourful products with the compounds. For example, amino acids form violet coloured products on spraying with NINHYDRIN.
- The relative rate of migration of the mixture with respect to the developing solvent used is expressed in terms of retention factor (R_F value).
- $R_f = \dfrac{\text{distance travelled by compound from origin}}{\text{distance travelled by solvent from origin}}$
- R_F value is characteristic of a compound for a given developing solvent at a given temperature and it can be used for identification of the compound.
- Component with higher R_F value will the one which is least strongly adsorbed.
- R_F value depends on the type of chromatography used, mobile phase, also on stationary phase and temperature.
- R_F value cannot be more than one.
- Chromatography is based on the principle of adsorption related to application of adsorption are frequently asked in JEE Advanced.

PRACTICE ELEMENT

Target JEE Advanced

Single Correct Choice MCQs

1. The adsorption of nitrogen gas (N_2) on a solid adsorbent follows the Langmuir adsorption isotherm at 300 K. It was found that 0.5 g of the adsorbent can adsorb a maximum of 1.2 mL of N_2 at 1 atm pressure and 300 K. The suface area of the adsorbent in m^2/g if each nitrogen molecule occupies an area of 0.162 nm^2 is

   (a) 8.49 (b) 9.49 (c) 10.46 (d) 11.49

2. Consider the following statements.

   I. The selectivity of an enzyme refers to its preference for a particular substrate.

   II. The activity of an enzyme decreases with increasing temperature beyond the optimal temperature due to denaturation.

   III. Inhibitors can bind to the enzyme's active site or allosteric site to decrease its activity.

   IV. Promoters increase the enzyme activity by binding to the enzyme's active site.

   V. The catalytic efficiency of an enzyme can be affected by the concentration of substrate and enzyme.

   In the light of the above statements, choose the correct statement from the options given below.

   (a) I, II and III (b) I, III, IV and V
   (c) I, II, III and V (d) I, II, III, IV and V

3. When gelatin is added to a silver sol, then gelatin

   (a) causes the silver nanoparticles to aggregate destabilising the sol.
   (b) adsorbs onto the surface of silver nanoparticles, preventing aggregation and stabilising the sol.
   (c) causes the silver nanoparticles to become larger in size, turning the sol into a suspension.
   (d) increases the rate of coagulation of the silver sol.

4. Given below are two statements.

   Assertion (A) In heterogeneous catalysis, the rate of reaction depends on the adsorption of reactants on the catalyst surface and the desorption of products.

   Reason (R) The rate-determining step in heterogeneous catalysis is often the desorption of the product, because once the product is desorbed, the catalyst surface becomes available for the next cycle of the reaction.

   In the light of the above statements, choose the correct answer from the options given below.

   (a) Both (A) and (R) are true and (R) is the correct explanation of (A).
   (b) Both (A) and (R) are true but (R) is not the correct explanation of (A).
   (c) (A) is true but (R) is false.
   (d) (A) is false but (R) is true.

5. Given below are two statements.

   Statement I Higher the value of T_C (critical temperature) of a gas, the more easily it will be liquified and therefore, more easily it will be adsorbed on the surface.

   Statement II The ease with which a gas can be liquified is dependent on T_C.

   In the light of the above statements, choose the correct answer from the options given below.

   (a) Both Statement I and Statement II are correct.
   (b) Both Statement I and Statement II are incorrect.
   (c) Statement I is correct but Statement II is incorrect.
   (d) Statement I is incorrect but Statement II is correct.

6. When a lyophilic colloidal solution is observed under the Tyndall effect. It is observed that

   (a) the scattering of light occurs lesser as compared to lyophobic colloidal solution.
   (b) the scattering of light occurs more as compared to lyophobic colloidal solution.
   (c) the colloidal particles aggregate and settle out of the solution.
   (d) the colour of the colloidal solution changes due to light absorption.

7. Freundlich adsorption isotherm is given by $\frac{x}{m} = kp^{\frac{1}{n}}$, where $\left(\frac{x}{m}\right)$ is the amount of adsorbate adsorbed per gram of the adsorbent at pressure (p). Which graph is correctly shown when it is plotted between $\log\left(\frac{x}{m}\right)$ and $\log p$ when $n = 1$.

   (a)
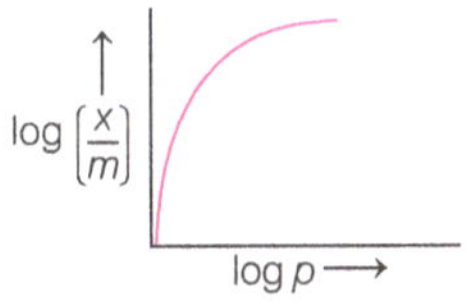

   (b)
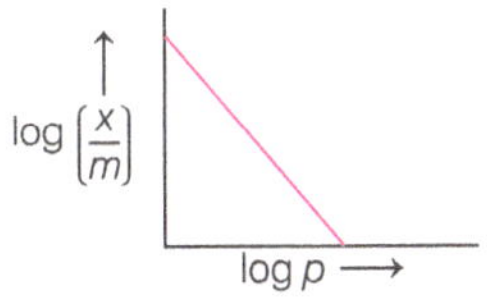

   (c)
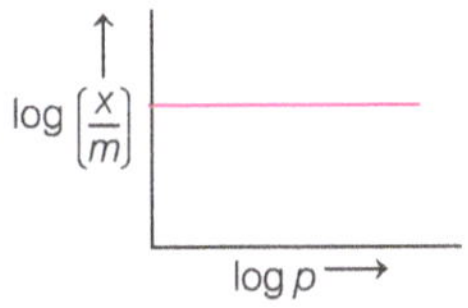

   (d)
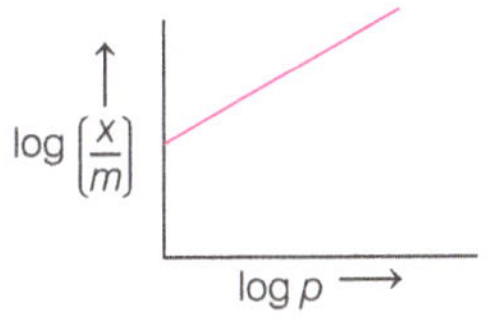

8. Which of the following statement is incorrect?
(a) Addition of sodium chloride to the gold sol causes coagulation, which can be prevented by adding a small amount of gelatin before the salt is added.
(b) During electrophoresis, the gold sol particles move towards the cathode, indicating that the gold sol particles are positively charged.
(c) In an emulsion stabilised by soap, the soap acts as an emulsifying agent by forming a protective layer around the dispersed phase.
(d) The gold number is a measure of the protective power of a lyophilic colloid, a lower gold number indicates a more effective protective colloid.

9. Arrange the following processes in increasing order of the extent of adsorption on a solid surface.
I. Physisorption of N_2 on activated charcoal at 300 K.
II. Chemisorption of H_2 on nickel at 500 K.
III. Physisorption of N_2 on activated charcoal at 273 K.
IV. Physisorption of N_2 on activated charcoal at 285 K.
(a) I < III < IV < II
(b) I < IV < III < II
(c) I < IV < II < III
(d) I < II < III < IV

10. Consider four different colloidal sols :
AgI, $Fe(OH)_3$, As_2S_3 and $Al(OH)_3$. Each sol is subjected to flocculation using different electrolyte. Given the flocculating values of different ions for these sols are as follows.
For AgI sol (negatively charged) :
Na^+ (52 mM), Ca^{2+} (0.90 mM), Al^{3+} (0.093 mM)
For $Fe(OH)_3$ sol (positively charged)
Cl^- (40 mM), SO_4^{2-} (0.60 mM), $[Fe(CN)_6]^{4-}$ (0.020 mM)
Which of the following statement is incorrect?
(a) The flocculating power of Al^{3+} is greater than that of Ca^{2+} for the AgI sol.
(b) The flocculating value of $[Fe(CN)_6]^{4-}$ is lower than that of SO_4^{2-} for the $Fe(OH)_3$ sol, indicating higher flocculating power.
(c) The effectiveness of flocculating ions follows the Hardy Schulze rule, where ions with higher valency are more effective at lower concentrations.
(d) The Na^+ ion will be more effective than Al^{3+} in flocculating AgI sol due to its lower flocculating value.

One or More than One Correct MCQs

11. Consider a lyophobic colloidal sol, such as $Fe(OH)_3$ or AgI. The stability of this colloidal sol is influenced by various factors. Which of the following statements are correct?
(a) The stability of a lyophobic sol is mainly due to charge on its colloidal particles, which results from the preferential adsorption of ions.
(b) Adding a small amount of a lyophilic sol like gelatin or starch can increase the stability of a lyophobic colloidal sol.
(c) A lyophobic collidal sol is less stable in the presence of electrolytes with high valency counter ions compared to monovalent counter ions.
(d) Potential difference between the fixed layer and the diffused layer of opposite charges around the colloidal particles increases the stability of lyophobic particle.

12. The given graph data I, II, III and IV represent general trends observed for different physisorption and chemisorption processes under mild conditions of temperature and pressure. Which of the following choice(s) about I, II, III and IV are correct?

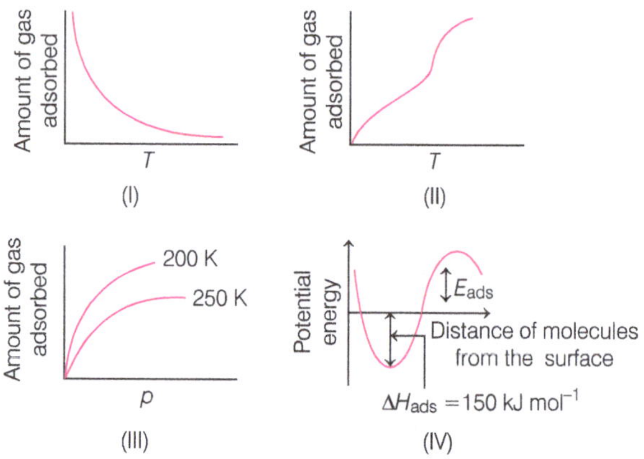

(a) I is physisorption and II is chemisorption.
(b) I is physisorption and III is chemisorption.
(c) IV is chemisorption and II is chemisorption.
(d) IV is chemisorption and III is chemisorption.

13. When a negatively charged colloidal sol of AgI is added to positively charged sol of $Al(OH)_3$ the following observations can be made. Which of the following statements are correct?
(a) The addition of AgI sol will result in the coagulation of $Al(OH)_3$ sol.
(b) The coagulation is due to the mutual repulsion between the particles of AgI and $Al(OH)_3$.
(c) The coagulation can be reversed by adding a suitable electrolyte like NaCl.
(d) The stability of $Al(OH)_3$ sol will decrease due to the electrostatic attraction between oppositely charged AgI and $Al(OH)_3$ particles.

14. Select the examples of negative catalyst.
(a) Hydrogen gas in the oxidation of oil (e.g. in the rancidification of fats)
(b) Lead (IV) oxide (PbO_2) in the decomposition of H_2O_2.
(c) Phosphoric acid in the polymerisation of ethene.
(d) Sulphur dioxide (SO_2) in the oxidation of carbon monoxide to carbon dioxide.

15. Which of the following statements regarding adsorption isotherms are correct?
(a) The Langmuir adsorption isotherm assumes a monolayer adsorption and is valid for high-pressure conditions.
(b) In the Langmuir adsorption isotherm, the adsorption is assumed to occur on a surface with heterogeneous adsorption sites.

(c) The Freundlich isotherm suggests that the amount of adsorption increases with increasing pressure but at a decreasing rate.

(d) The Langmuir isotherm assumes that there is no interaction between the adsorbed molecules and that the surface is composed of identical adsorption sites.

16. Which of the following statements regarding different enzyme-catalysed reactions are correct?

(a) The conversion of glucose to glucose-6-phosphate is catalysed by hexokinose.

(b) The conversion of pyruvate to acetyl Co-A is catalysed by pyruvate dehydrogenase.

(c) The conversion of lactate to pyruvate is catalysed by lactate dehydrogenase.

(d) The conversion of ammonia to urea in urea cycle is catalysed by urease.

17. Select the correct statements.

(a) Gels are a type of colloidal system in which the dispersed phase is a solid and the continuous phase is liquid.

(b) A colloidal solution can be differentiated from a true solution based on the Tyndall effect.

(c) Macromolecules are characterised by large molecular weight and are not typically soluble in water under standard conditions.

(d) The formation of gels from colloidal systems involves the formation of a three dimensional network, which entraps the liquid phase, resulting in a semi-solid structure.

18. Choose the correct statements.

(a) Zeolites are crystalline materials used as molecular sieves.

(b) Ultrafiltration uses a membrane to separate particles by size.

(c) Ultracentrifugation separates particles based on density.

(d) Zeolites are used in ultrafiltration to block large molecules.

19. The adsorption of iodine from its aqueous solution on activated charcoal at 25°C follows the Freundlich adsorption isotherm. If x is the mass of iodine adsorbed per unit mass of charcoal and C is the equilibrium concentration of iodine in the solution. Which of the following statement is incorrect?

(a) x increases as C increases.

(b) The process of adsorption is exothermic.

(c) At higher concentrations, the adsorption reaches a saturation point.

(d) The value of n in the Freundlich isotherm is greater than or equal to 1.

Integer/Numerical Type Questions

20. A solution of stearic acid (Molar mass = 284 g/mol) in hexane contains 2.84 g of acid per dm^3. When this solution added to a water surface, the hexane evaporates, leaving behind a monomolecular film of stearic acid. If an area covered by a monolayer is 600 cm^2 and area occupied by one molecule of stearic acid is 0.22 nm^2. Then, the required volume of stearic acid is .... mL.

21. 2 g of activated carbon is added to 200 mL of a 0.01 M methylene blue solution. After adsorption reaches equilibrium, the concentration of methylene blue reduces to 0.008 M. The surface area of the activated carbon is 500 m^2/g. Then the surface area of the activated carbon adsorbed by each molecule of methylene blue is ...... nm^2

22. A solution of cetyltrimethyl ammonium bromide CTAB, a cationic surfactant, forms micelles at its critical micelle concentration (CMC) of 0.009 M. Each micelle contains 100 CTAB molecules on average. Also, the molar volume of CTAB is 0.75 m^3/mol. The average volume of each micelle in cm^3 is .... $\times 10^{-16}$.

23. In a colloidal system, 0.02 g of a protective colloid is added to 50 mL of a gold sol. After adding 3 mL of a 10% NaCl solution, the precipitation of the gold sol is just prevented. Then the gold number of the protective colloid in (g) is

24. A 5 g sample of activated charcoal is used to adsorb acetic acid from a 0.5 M aqueous solution. After adsorption, the concentration of acetic acid in the solution is reduced to 0.2 M. The final volume of the solution is 100 mL. The value of k, if the adsorption follows the Freundlich isotherm is .... $\left(\text{where } \frac{1}{n} = 0.5\right)$

25. The adsorption of a dye from a solution on charcoal is governed by the Freundlich isotherm in which $n = 2$ and $K = 6.8$. The concentration of the dye is expressed in millimoles/cc and the amount absorbed in millimoles/gm. If 10 g of charcoal is shaken with 100 cc of 0.1 M solution of the dye, the equilibrium concentration of the dye will be ....

26. The number of correct statements related to colloids are

(a) Polyvalent ions are more effective at coagulating sols than monovalent ions.

(b) Cloud brusting in atmosphere occurs due to large amount of water present in the cloud.

(c) The viscosity of a lyophilic colloidal solution is higher than that of dispersion medium.

(d) In electrophoresis, the velocity of a colloidal particle depends on its charge, size and the viscosity of the medium.

27. A certain solid sample adsorbs 0.38 mg O_2 at pressure of 20 kPa and 300 K. Under isothermal condition 0.19 mg O_2 at a pressure of 4 kPa is adsorbed. Then, the fraction of surface covered $\theta_1 + \theta_2$ is

Assume fraction of the gas adsorbed follows equation, $\frac{kp}{1+kp}$.

28. Number of given compounds that are used as a positive catalyst in a chemical reaction are :

NO, Zeolites, $KMnO_4$, Platinum black, Alcohol, Tetraethyl lead

Matching Type Questions

29. Match the List-I with List -II

List I		List II	
A.	Positive catalyst	1.	$2Na_2SO_3 + O_2 \xrightarrow{Alcohol} 2Na_2SO_4$
B.	Negative catalyst	2.	$CO + 2H_2 \xrightarrow[K_2O]{ZnO/Cr_2O_3} CH_3OH$
C.	Poison	3.	$2KClO_3 \xrightarrow{MnO_2} 2KCl + 3O_2$
D.	Promoter	4.	$N_2 + 3H_2 \underset{H_2S}{\overset{Fe}{\rightleftharpoons}} 2NH_3$

Choose the correct answer from the options given below.
(a) A →3, B →1, C →2, D →4
(b) A →1, B →3, C →2, D →4
(c) A →3, B →1, C →4, D →2
(d) A →1, B →3, C →4, D →2

30. Match the Column-I with Column-II

Column I		Column II	
A.	Adsorption	1.	Ammonia gas passed through water to form NH_4OH
B.	Absorption	2.	Adsorption of gases on metals at high temperature
C.	Langmuir Adsorption Isotherm	3.	Acetic acid on activated charcoal
D.	Freundlich Adsorption Isotherm	4.	Removal of impurities from water using activated carbon

Choose the correct answer from the options given below.
(a) A →4, B →1, C →2, D →3
(b) A →4, B →1, C →3, D →2
(c) A →1, B →4, C →2, D →3
(d) A →1, B →4, C →3, D →2

31. Match the List-I (Colloid system) with List-II (dispersed phase and dispersion medium)

List I (Colloid system)		List II (Dispersed phase and Dispersion medium)	
A.	Ink	1.	Solid and liquid
B.	Butter	2.	Solid and gas
C.	Shaving Cream	3.	Liquid and liquid
D.	Mist	4.	Gas and liquid

Choose the correct answer from the options given below.
(a) A →1, B →2, C →3, D →4
(b) A →1, B →3, C →2, D →4
(c) A →1, B →3, C →4, D →2
(d) A →3, B →2, C →1, D →4

32. Match the Column-I (Purification Method) with Column-II (Applications)

Column I (Purification Method)		Column II (Applications)	
A.	Dialysis	1.	Used for separating colloidal particles from larger particles
B.	Ultrafiltration	2.	Used for purifying colloidal sols like protein solutions
C.	Electrophoresis	3.	Used to remove ions
D.	Coagulation	4.	Used for removing the dispersed phase from a colloidal system

Choose the correct answer from the options given below.
(a) A →3, B →1, C →2, D →4
(b) A →3, B →1, C →4, D →2
(c) A →1, B →3, C →2, D →4
(d) A →1, B →3, C →4, D →2

33. Match the Column I with the type of solution formed in Column II.

Column I		Column II	
A.	Sulphur vapours are passed through cold water	1.	Normal electrolyte solution
B.	Soap mixed with water above CMC	2.	Molecular colloidal sol
C.	Soap mixed with water below CMC	3.	Associated colloidal sol
D.	White of egg whipped with water	4.	Macromolecular colloids

Choose the correct answer from the options given below.
(a) A →2, B →3, C →4, D →1
(b) A →2, B →3, C →1, D →4
(c) A →3, B →2, C →1, D →4
(d) A →3, B →2, C →4, D →1

34. Match the List-I (Surfactants) with List-II (their types).

List I (Surfactants)		List II (Types)	
A.	Egg yolk	1.	Anionic surfactant
B.	Polyethylene glycol	2.	Cationic surfactant
C.	Sodium lauryl sulphate	3.	Emulsifying agent
D.	Hexadecyl pyridinium chloride	4.	Non-ionic surfactant

Choose the correct answer from the options given below.
(a) A →3, B →4, C →2, D →1
(b) A →4, B →3, C →2, D →1
(c) A →3, B →4, C →1, D →2
(d) A →4, B →3, C →1, D →2

Paragraph Based Questions

Paragraph 1

3 g of activated charcoal was added to 50 mL of 0.06 M acetic acid solution in a flask.

After an hour, 10 mL of residual CH_3COOH required 14 mL of 0.03 M NaOH.

35. Equilibrium concentration of CH_3COOH is ....

36. If Freundlich adsorption isotherm is followed $\frac{x}{m} = k(c)^{1/2}$ then k is .... (x is the amount of adsorbate in gram absorbed per gram of adsorbent and C is equilibrium concentration in millimoles).

Paragraph 2

In surface chemistry, adsorption is a key phenomenon where molecules or atoms adhere to the surface of a solid or a liquid. The extent of adsorption is influenced by factors such as surface area, temperature and pressure.

37. The surface area of solid adsorbent is found to be 150 m^2/g. If 0.6 grams of this adsorbent is used in an experiment, calculate the total surface area available for adsorption in nm^2.

38. For 1 g adsorbent, the amount of gas adsorbed at a particular temperature is given by Freundlich isotherm. If $k = 3$ and $n = 1.5$, pressure of gas is 2 atm. Calculate the amount of gas adsorbed on the adsorbent.

Paragraph 3

A solid with surface area independent of temperature adsorbs 2 mg of a gas when in contact with the gas at a pressure of 10 kPa and 283 K. The amount of heat absorbed is 80 J when 2 millimoles of the gas is desorbed.

39. Enthalpy of adsorption is ....

40. Equilibrium pressure for the adsorption of 2 moles of the gas at 323 K is ....

Species Selection (with 5 Species)

41. The number of following reactions that are involved in the preparation of colloidal solutions are
    (i) $As_2O_3 + 3H_2S \longrightarrow As_2S_3 + H_2O$
    (ii) $2AuCl_3 + 3SnCl_2 \longrightarrow 2Au + 3SnCl_4$
    (iii) $Br_2 + H_2S \longrightarrow 2HBr + S$
    (iv) $FeCl_3 + 3H_2O \longrightarrow Fe(OH)_3 + 3HCl$
    (v) $Fe(OH)_3 + FeCl_3 \longrightarrow [Fe(OH)_3Fe]^{3+} + 3Cl^-$
    (a) 4 (b) 3 (c) 5 (d) 2

42. Number of examples having dispersed phase gas and dispersion medium solid are
    (i) pumice stone
    (ii) styrene foam
    (iii) rubber form
    (iv) whipped creamsoap-suds
    (v) boot polish
    (a) 3 (b) 4 (c) 5 (d) 2

43. Number of gases that can be easily liquified are
    (i) H_2S (ii) CO_2
    (iii) NH_3 (iv) H_2
    (v) O_2
    (a) 4 (b) 3 (c) 5 (d) 1

Species Selection (with 7 Species)

44. The number of surfactants that are classified as anionic surfactants are
    (i) Alkylbenzene sulphonates
    (ii) Sodium dodecyl benzene sulphonates
    (iii) Sodium lauryl sulphate
    (iv) Benzalkonium chloride
    (v) Hexadecyltrimethyl ammonium chloride
    (vi) Decyl glucoside
    (vii) Polyethylene glycol
    (a) 5 (b) 6 (c) 3 (d) 7

45. The number of substances that forms true solution are
    (i) Ethanol in water
    (ii) Oxygen and water
    (iii) Water and lemon juice
    (iv) Carbon dioxide and water
    (v) Ammonium chloride in water
    (vi) Sea water
    (vii) Glucose solution
    (a) 6 (b) 7 (c) 5 (d) 4

46. Number of system that belongs to solvent loving colloidal solutions are
    (i) Starch in water (ii) Gold in water
    (iii) $Fe(OH)_3$ in water (iv) Gelatin in water
    (v) Protein in water
    (vi) As_2O_3 in water
    (vii) Metal hydroxides
    (a) 6 (b) 5 (c) 4 (d) 3

47. The number of reactions that are catalysed by an enzyme are
    (i) Inverting cane sugar
    (ii) Breaking down lactose
    (iii) Breaking down acetylcholine
    (iv) Converting glucose to ethanol
    (v) Food browning
    (vi) Conversion of proteins into peptones
    (vii) Hydrogenation of vegatable oils
    (a) 7 (b) 5 (c) 4 (d) 6

48. Number of applications that corresponds to the mechanical method of colloids are
    (i) Paints and pigments production
    (ii) Preparation of metal sols
    (iii) Pharmaceutical suspensions
    (iv) Water purification
    (v) Food industry
    (vi) Inks and dyes
    (vii) Rubber and polymer dispersions
    (a) 6 (b) 5 (c) 4 (d) 7

Check Through PYQs

Element 1 Adsorption

1. To form a complete monolayer of acetic acid on 1g of charcoal, 100 mL of 0.5 M acetic acid was used. Some of the acetic acid remained unadsorbed. To neutralise the unadsorbed acetic acid, 40 mL of 1 M NaOH solution was required. If each molecule of acetic acid occupies $P \times 10^{-23}$ m^2 surface area on charcoal, the value of P is ....

   [Use given data: Surface area of charcoal $= 1.5 \times 10^2$ m^2g^{-1}; Avogadro's number (N_A) $= 6.0 \times 10^{23} mol^{-1}$] *2024 Adv.*

2. The correct option(s) related to adsorption processes is (are) *2022 Adv.*

   (a) chemisorption results in a unimolecular layer.
   (b) the enthalpy change during physisorption is in the range of 100 to 140 $kJ\ mol^{-1}$.
   (c) chemisorption is an endothermic process.
   (d) lowering the temperature favours physisorption processes.

3. When O_2 is adsorbed on a metallic surface, electron transfer occurs from the metal to O_2. The true statement(s) regarding this adsorption is (are) *2015 Adv.*

   (a) O_2 is physisorbed.
   (b) heat is released.
   (c) occupancy of π^*2p of O_2 is increased.
   (d) bond length of O_2 is increased.

Element 3 Particle Size and Colloidal State

4. Consider the following statements related to colloids. *2023 Adv.*

   I. Lyophobic colloids are not formed by simple mixing of dispersed phase and dispersion medium.
   II. For emulsions, both the dispersed phase and the dispersion medium are liquid.
   III. Micelles are produced by dissolving a surfactant in any solvent at any temperature.
   IV. Tyndall effect can be observed from a colloidal solution with dispersed phase having the same refractive index as that of the dispersion medium.

   The option with the correct set of statements is

   (a) I and II
   (b) II and III
   (c) III and IV
   (d) II and IV

5. The correct statement(s) related to colloids is(are) *2021 Adv.*

   (a) the process of precipitating colloidal sol by an electrolyte is called peptisation.
   (b) colloidal solution freezes at higher temperature, than the true solution at the same concentration.
   (c) surfactants form micelle above critical micelle concentration (CMC). CMC depends on temperature.
   (d) micelles are macromolecular colloids.

6. The correct statement(s) about surface properties is (are) *2017 Adv.*

   (a) The critical temperatures of ethane and nitrogen are 563 K and 126 K, respectively. The adsorption of ethane will be more than that of nitrogen of same amount of activated charcoal at a given temperature.
   (b) Cloud is an emulsion type of colloid in which liquid is dispersed phase and gas is dispersion medium.
   (c) Adsorption is accompanied by decrease in enthalpy and decrease in entropy of the system.
   (d) Brownian motion of colloidal particles does not depend on the size of the particles but depends on viscosity of the solution.

HINTS & Solutions

Solutions : Competency Enhancer

1.1. ***(125)*** Number of moles of NaOH

$$= 60 \times 1 \times 10^{-3} = 6 \times 10^{-2}$$

Number of moles of formic acid $= 200 \times 0.4 \times 10^{-3}$

$$= 80 \times 10^{-3} = 8 \times 10^{-2}$$

$\therefore$ Number of formic acid adsorbed on charcoal

$$= (8-6) \times 10^{-2}$$
$$= 2 \times 10^{-2}$$

So, the number of molecules of formic acid adsorbed

$$= 2 \times 10^{-2} N_A = 2 \times 10^{-2} \times 6.0 \times 10^{23}$$
$$= 12 \times 10^{21}$$

Total surface area adsorbed by one molecule of formic acid

$$= \frac{1.5 \times 10^2 \times 1}{12 \times 10^{21}}$$
$$= 0.125 \times 10^{-19} = 125 \times 10^{-22}$$

So, the value of N is 125.

3.1. ***(d)*** Statement I is incorrect and Statement II is correct. The correct form of Statement I is

Micelles are formed by the surfactant molecules above the critical micelle concentration.

Elemental Practice 10.1

1. ***(d)*** Not all types of adsorption requires activation energy. Physisorption typically does not need activation energy because it involves weak intermolecular forces.

2. ***(b)*** Enthalpy of adsorption is high in chemical adsorption as chemical bonds are formed and range lies between 80-240 kJ mol^{-1}.

3. ***(d)*** Langmuir adsorption isotherm is given by

$$\theta = \frac{Kp}{1+Kp}$$
$$\theta = 0.5$$
$$0.5 = \frac{Kp}{1+Kp}$$
$$0.5(1+Kp) = Kp$$
$$0.5 + 0.5Kp = Kp$$
$$0.5 = 0.5Kp$$
$$1 = Kp$$
$$\Rightarrow \quad p = \frac{1}{K}$$

4. ***(b)*** By Freundlich's adsorption isotherm,

$$\log\left(\frac{x}{m}\right) = \log K + \frac{1}{n}\log p$$
$$y = C + mx$$
$$\text{Slope} = \frac{1}{n} = \tan 45° = 1$$
$$\log K = 0.3010$$
$$\therefore \quad K = 2$$
$$\therefore \quad \log\left(\frac{x}{m}\right) = \log 2 + 1\log p = \log 2p$$
$$\frac{x}{m} = 2p$$
$$\frac{x}{m} = 2 \times 0.2 = 0.4$$

5. ***(a)*** In magneson test of Mg^{2+}, precipitate of $Mg(OH)_2$ attains blue colour due to adsorption of magneson on $Mg(OH)_2$ (a solid adsorbent).

6. ***(c)*** (A) is correct but (R) is incorrect.

   Adsorption of coloured impurities depend on various factors including the polarity, size and functional group of the molecules. Both polar and non-polar impurities can be adsorbed, depending on the nature of the adsorbent.

7. ***(c)*** Adsorption occurs only on the surface and saturates once all surface sites are filled. Absorption involves the entire volume and continues until the bulk is saturated, which can take longer or may not saturate easily depending on the conditions.

8. ***(c)*** The correct match is :

   A → (2), B → (1), C → (4), D → (3)

9. ***(b)*** The adsorption capacity of gases on charcoal depends on their ease of liquefaction, which is determined by the critical temperature of the gases. Gases with higher critical temperature are more easily liquefied and are adsorbed more readily. The critical temperature of the gases are NH_3 – 405.5 K; CO_2 – 304.2; CH_4 – 190.6; H_2 – 33.2 K

   The correct order is :

$$NH_3 > CO_2 > CH_4 > H_2$$

10. ***(c)*** At low temperature, rate of adsorption is high. But as the temperature increases, rate of adsorption decreases.

11. ***(a)*** Both Statement I and Statement II are true.

12. ***(c)*** The Freundlich adsorption isotherm for a particular gas on a solid adsorbent is given by :

$$\theta = Kp^{1/n}$$
$$\theta_1 = 0.5 \text{ mol/g}, p_1 = 1 \text{ atm}$$
$$\theta_2 = 1.5 \text{ mol/g}, p_2 = 4 \text{ atm}$$

Taking the logarithm in Freundlich adsorption isotherm

$$\log\theta = \log K + \frac{1}{n}\log p$$

At $p_1 = 1\text{ atm}$ and $\theta_1 = 0.5$ mol/g

$$\log 0.5 = \log K + \frac{1}{n}\log 1$$

$$-0.3010 = \log K$$

$$\Rightarrow \quad k = 10^{-30.10} \approx 0.5$$

At $p_2 = 4\text{ atm}$, $\theta_2 = 1.5$ mol/g

$$\log 1.5 = \log 0.5 + \frac{1}{n}\log 4$$

$$\log 1.5 = -0.3010 + \frac{1}{n} \times 0.6021$$

$$0.1761 = -0.3010 + \frac{0.6021}{n}$$

$$n = \frac{0.6021}{0.4771} = 1.26$$

13. ***(d)*** Final volume of gas at 550 torr

$$V_2 = \frac{p_1V_1}{p_2}$$

$$= \frac{800 \times 1.5}{550} = 2.18\text{ L} = 2180\text{ mL}$$

Volume occupied by gas = Volume of vessel – Volume occupied by charcoal

$$= 1500\text{ mL} - \frac{20}{1.5} = 1486.67\text{ mL}$$

Difference comes in volume due to the adsorption of gas by charcoal

Volume of gas adsorbed by charcoal

$$= 2180 - 1486.67\text{ mL}$$

$$= 693.33\text{ mL}$$

Volume of gas adsorbed per gram of charcoal

$$= \frac{693.33}{20}$$

$$= 34.66\text{ mL/g} = 0.03466\text{ L/g}$$

14. ***(a)*** Statements *A*, *B* and *C* are correct whereas *D* and *E* are incorrect. The correct form of *D* and *E* is

In case of adsorption from the solution phase, the adsorbent material and the nature of solvent both effects the adsorption capacity.

The adsorption of a solute from a solution is a spontaneous when ΔG is negative.

15. ***(b)*** For Freundlich isotherm :

$$\frac{x}{m} = Kp^{\frac{1}{n}}$$

$\frac{x}{m}$ becomes $2 \times \frac{x}{m}$, then

$$2 \times Kp^{\frac{1}{n}} = K(p')^{\frac{1}{n}}$$

$$2 = \left(\frac{p'}{p}\right)^{\frac{1}{n}}$$

$$2^n = \frac{p'}{p}$$

$$p' = 2^n p$$

16. ***(a)*** The adsorption is spontaneous (as $\Delta G < 0$). Further, since the enthalpy of adsorption is in the range of 20-40 kJ mol^{-1}, which is typically of physisorption. The process is physisorption.

17. ***(d)*** The given equation is $\frac{x}{m} = Kp^{\frac{1}{2}}$

Taking logarithms on both sides

$$\log\frac{x}{m} = \log K + \frac{1}{2}\log p$$

This indicates a straight line graph with slope $\frac{1}{2}$ or 0.5.

18. ***(c)*** More surface area provides more active sites for adsorption which leads to higher adsorption capacity per unit mass of adsorbent.

19. ***(a, c, d)*** Statements (a, c, d) are correct while statement (b) is incorrect.

The correct form of (b) is

Adsorption of gases on solids is an exothermic process and the heat of adsorption decreases with an increase in temperature for physical adsorption.

20. ***(a, b, c, d)*** All the statements are correct.

21. ***(b, c)*** Statements (a, d) are correct while (b, c) are incorrect. The correct form of b and c is

The Freundlich adsorption isotherm is applicable to adsorption on heterogeneous surfaces but it does not predict saturation of adsorption at high pressures.

The adsorption capacity predicts a maximum adsorption capacity as the pressure increases. It does not predict indefinite increases in adsorption capacity.

22. ***(–77.761)*** Pressure $(p_1) = 0.5$ atm

Pressure $(p_2) = 10$ atm

Temperature $(T_1) = 273$ K

Temperature $(T_2) = 300$ K

Gas constant $(R) = 8.314$ J mol^{-1} K^{-1}

According to Clausius Clapeyron equation

$$\ln\frac{p_1}{p_2} = \frac{\Delta H_{ads}}{R}\left(\frac{1}{T_1} - \frac{1}{T_2}\right)$$

$$\ln\frac{0.5}{10} = \frac{\Delta H_{ads}}{8.314}\left(\frac{1}{273} - \frac{1}{300}\right)$$

$$\ln 0.5 = -0.693, \ln 10 = 2.30$$

$$-0.693 - 2.30 = \frac{\Delta H_{ads}}{8.314}(0.00032)$$

$$\frac{-2.993 \times 8.314}{0.00032} = \Delta H_{ads}$$

$$\Delta H_{ads} = -77761.881\text{ J/mol}$$

$$= -77.761\text{ kJ/mol}$$

23. ***(3.32)*** Mass of adsorbate = 0.25 mg

$$= 0.25 \times 10^{-6} \text{ kg}$$

Area covered = 0.10 m^2

Molar mass = 0.50 kg/mol

$$\text{Moles of adsorbate} = \frac{\text{Mass}}{\text{Molar mass}}$$

$$= \frac{0.25 \times 10^{-6} \text{ kg}}{0.50 \text{ kg / mol}}$$

$$= 5 \times 10^{-7} \text{ moles}$$

Number of molecules = Number of moles × Avogadro's number

$$= 5 \times 10^{-7} \text{ moles} \times 6.022 \times 10^{23} \text{ molecules/mol}$$

$$= 3.011 \times 10^{17} \text{ molecules}$$

$$\text{Area per molecule} = \frac{\text{Total area}}{\text{Number of molecules}}$$

$$= \frac{0.10 \text{ m}^2}{3.011 \times 10^{17}}$$

$$= 3.32 \times 10^{-19} \text{ m}^2$$

24. ***(1)*** Number of CO_2 molecules

$$= \frac{0.002 \text{ atm} \times 0.5 \text{ L} \times 6.022 \times 10^{23}}{0.082 \text{ L atm mol}^{-1} \text{K}^{-1} \times 310 \text{ K}}$$

$$= 2.36 \times 10^{19}$$

∴ Number of active sites per molecule

$$= \frac{500 \times 2 \times 10^{17} \times \frac{30}{100}}{2.36 \times 10^{19}} = 1.27$$

≃ 1 active sites per molecule

25. ***(1000)*** By Freundlich adsorption isotherm for adsorption of solution on a solid surface

$$\frac{x}{m} = K(C)^{\frac{1}{n}}$$

$$\Rightarrow \quad \frac{x}{m} = 0.50\,(C)^{\frac{1}{3}}$$

Let solute adsorbed = x g

then equilibrium concentration = $(2 - x)$ g

$$\frac{x}{m} = 0.50\,(2 - x)^{\frac{1}{3}}$$

$$x = 1(2 - x)^{\frac{1}{3}}$$

$$x^3 = (2 - x)$$

$$x^3 + x - 2 = 0$$

$$x = 1 \text{ g} = 1000 \text{ mg}$$

Elemental Practice 10.2

1. ***(b)*** In homogeneous catalysis, the catalysts and the reactants are indeed in the same phase, which results in better selectivity because the molecules can often have more freedom to interact uniformly and the catalyst can more easily modify the reaction pathway.

2. ***(d)*** Statements (a), (b), (c) are correct whereas (d) is incorrect. The correct form of (d) is

   The activity of a heterogeneous catalyst is dependent on the adsorption characteristics of the reactant molecules.

3. ***(c)*** The correct match is :

$$A \rightarrow 4,\ B \rightarrow 1,\ C \rightarrow 2,\ D \rightarrow 3$$

4. ***(b)*** Enzyme catalysis does not always results in the formation of a covalent bond between the enzyme and the substrate. In many cases, enzyme substrate interactions are non-covalent.

5. ***(b)*** A decreases the rate of the reaction which is a characteristic of inhibitor. Inhibitors slow down or prevent the reaction from occurring.

6. ***(b)*** Both Statement I and Statement II are incorrect.

   The correct form is :

   Statement I The adsorption capacity of a catalyst typically decreases with increasing temperature.

   Statement II The adsorption theory is applicable to heterogeneous catalysis only.

7. ***(b)*** Ethyl alcohol slows down the oxidation of sodium sulphite to sodium sulphate by atmospheric oxygen.

8. ***(c)*** Adsorption of reacting molecules, formation of activated complex and desorption of products are shown as

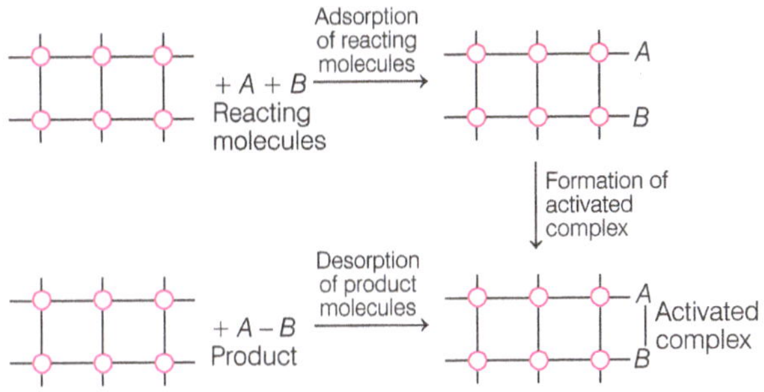

9. ***(d)*** A catalyst provides an alternative reaction pathway with a lower activation energy, which increases the rate of the reaction. It does not affect the overall thermodynamic properties.

10. ***(a)*** Zeolites exhibit Bronsted acidity because of protonated aluminosilicate groups. The presence of protons (H^+) on the framework oxygen is responsible for the Bronsted acidic sites.

11. ***(a)*** Both (A) and (R) are true and (R) is the correct explanation of (A).

12. ***(b)*** Particle size of a catalyst influences the activity due to surface area it does not solely determine selectivity. Selectivity is determined by the nature of active sites, reaction conditions.

13. ***(b)*** Coke deposition is a well known cause of catalyst deactivation, especially in heterogeneous catalysis.

14. ***(a)*** Increasing temperatures can often decrease catalyst selectivity. Higher temperatures can lead to the activation of side reactions and reduce the ability of the catalyst to selectively favour the desired reaction pathway.

15. ***(c)*** According to induced fit model, the precise fit between enzyme's active site and substrate ensures that the reaction proceeds in a way that favours the formation of one stereoisomer.

16. ***(a, b, c)*** Statements (a), (b), (c) are correct whereas (d) is incorrect. The correct form of (d) is

    The presence of a catalyst does not alter equilibrium concentrations, it only accelerates the rate of reaching equilibrium.

17. ***(b, c, e)*** Statements (b, c, e) are correct whereas (a, d) are correct.
    (a) Decompostion of hydrogen peroxide using KI in solution is homogeneous catalysis because both the catalyst and reactants are in the same phase.
    (b) The Haber process uses solid iron as a catalyst with gaseous nitrogen and hydrogen making it heterogeneous catalysis.
    (c) The contact process uses solid V_2O_5 with gaseous reactant, so it is heterogeneous catalysis.
    (d) Hydrolysis of ester in the presence of HCl is homogeneous catalysis because HCl is in the same aqueous phase as the reactants.
    (e) Decomposition of ozone on a solid surface is heterogeneous catalysis because the catalyst is in a different phase from the gaseous reactants.

18. ***(a, b, c)*** Statements (a, b, c) are correct whereas (d) is incorrect. The correct form of (d) is

    The addition of a ligand that reduces the reaction rate without binding directly to the catalytic active site is an example of non-competitive inhibition, not poisoning, as the ligand does not block the active site directly but changes the catalyst's environment.

19. ***(a, c)*** Statements (b) and (d) are correct whereas (a) and (c) are incorrect. The correct form of (a) and (c) is
    (a) The shape-selective catalysis of zeolites is based on the size and shape of the pores that allow certain molecules to enter while excluding others, but not on the direct interaction of active sites with reactants.
    (c) Before using zeolites as a catalyst, zeolites are heated in vaccum so that water of crystallisation is lost.

20. ***(a, b, c, d)*** All the statements are correct.

21. ***(5)***

$$R\text{—COOH} + R'\text{—OH} \xrightarrow{H_2SO_4} R\text{—COOR}' + H_2O$$

$$R\text{—COOR}' + H_2O \xrightarrow{H^+} R\text{—COOH} + R'\text{—OH}$$

$$R\text{—CHO} + R'\text{—CHO} \xrightarrow{H^+} RCH(OH)\text{—}\overset{O}{\overset{\|}{C}}\text{—}R'$$

$$R\text{—}CH_2OH \xrightarrow{H_2SO_4} R\text{—CH}{=}CH_2 + H_2O$$

$$C_6H_6 + HNO_3 \xrightarrow{H_2SO_4} C_6H_5NO_2 + H_2O$$

22. ***(3)*** Statements (a), (b) and (c) are correct whereas (d) is correct. The correct form of (d) is

    Not all promoters increases the reaction rate, some may alter the catalytic properties to make process more selective.

23. ***(5)*** All are the examples of homogeneous catalysed reactions.

24. ***(3)*** Statement (a), (b), (c) are correct whereas statement (d) is incorrect. The correct form of (d) is

    In surface catalysis, the mechanism is based on the formation of an adsorbed reaction complex.

25. ***(3)*** Statements (a, c, d) are correct whereas statement (b) is incorrect.

    Transition metal complexes can be used as both homogeneous and heterogeneous catalysts, depending on the system design.

Elemental Practice 10.3

1. ***(a)*** Physical properties as molar conductivity, surface tension and osmotic pressure of colloidal sol shows a drastic change in their properties from a particular concentration is known as the CMC (Critical Micelle Concentration).

2. ***(c)*** The flocculation value of an electrolyte is the minimum concentration of that electrolyte needed to coagulate the colloidal particles. The lower the flocculation value, the faster the coagulation.

   Al^{3+} has lowest flocculation value (10^{-3} M), indicating it will cause the fastest coagulation of the As_2S_3 sol.

3. ***(d)*** Hydrophobic sols are less stable compared to hydrophilic sols and can be easily coagulated by adding small amount of electrolytes.

4. ***(c)*** The reaction of $FeCl_3$ with water results in the formation of $Fe(OH)_3$ which is a classic method to prepare a colloidal sol of ferric hydroxide.

5. ***(a)*** The correct match is A-2, B-4, C-3, D-1

6. ***(a)*** Both Statement I and Statement II are correct.

7. ***(c)*** The direction of electroosmotic flow depends on the charge on the colloidal particles on the charged surface of the medium. A negative charge on the surface causes the liquid to move towards the anode and a positive charge causes movement towards the cathode.

8. ***(a)*** The Tyndall effect is primarily used to detect colloidal particles in a solution by observing the scattering of light.

9. ***(a)*** Both (A) and (R) are true and (R) is the correct explanation of (A).

10. ***(c)*** Higher the gold number, lesser will be the protective power of colloid.

11. ***(c)*** Cationic surfactants (such as quarternary ammonium compounds) are used as fabric softeners due to their positive charge, which interacts with negatively charged fibers, making them feel smoother and softer.

12. ***(b)*** Coagulation value of $Na^+ = \frac{0.2\text{ M} \times 0.025\text{ L}}{0.1\text{ L}}$

$= 0.05$ mol/L

Coagulation value of $Ba^{2+} = \frac{0.1\text{M} \times 0.030\text{ L}}{0.1\text{ L}} \times 2$

$= 0.06$ mol/L

Relative coagulation power $= \frac{\text{Coagulation value of } Ba^{2+}}{\text{Coagulation value of } Na^+}$

$= \frac{0.06}{0.05} = 1.2 \simeq 1$

13. ***(c)*** Statement I, IV and V are correct and statements II and III are incorrect. The correct form of II and III are

    II. Gold and silver are not typically prepared using mechanical dispersion method. They are usually prepared by chemical methods.

    III. The mechanical dispersion method does not always produce stable colloidal sols by itself.

14. ***(b)*** Different proteins having varying charges and sizes/allowing for effective separation when an electric field is applied.

15. ***(d)*** Flocculation value of $ZnCl_2 = 0.68$

Thus, 1000 mL of As_2S_3 sol $ZnCl_2$ required $= 0.68$ mmol

For 300 mL of As_2S_3 sol $ZnCl_2$ required $= \frac{0.68 \times 300}{1000}$

$= 0.204$ mmol

Let volume of 0.24 M $ZnCl_2 = V$ mL

then $0.24 \times V = 0.204$

$$V = \frac{0.204}{0.24} = 0.85\text{ mL}$$

16. ***(a)*** Hexadecyltrimethyl ammonium chloride (HTAC) is a cationic surfactant. Cationic surfactants typically have lower CMCs compared to anionic or non-ionic surfactants.

17. ***(b)*** The inner layer consists of ions adsorbed directly on the surface of the particle, and these ions are oppositely charged to the particle's charge.

18. ***(b)*** Hair oils are typically water-in-oil (W/O) emulsions, where water droplets are dispersed in oil. The continuous phase is oil and water droplets are embedded in it.

19. ***(b, c)*** Statements (b) and (c) are correct whereas (a) and (d) are incorrect. The correct form of (a) and (d) are

    (a) Lyophobic colloids are inherently unstable in the medium. They tend to aggregate and precipitate. They cannot enhance the stability of lyophilic colloids, which are already stable.

    (d) The Tyndall effect depends on the particle size and concentration. The protective layer actually increases particle size. This would typically make the Tyndall effect more pronounced, not less.

20. ***(a, b, d)*** Statements (a), (b) and (d) are correct whereas (c) is incorrect. The correct form of (c) is

Double decomposition can produce stable sols without additional stabilizers. The stability often comes from adsorbed ions from reactants.

21. ***(a, b, d)*** Statements (a, b, d) are correct whereas statement (c) is incorrect. The correct form of (c) is

For the positively charged sols, anions are the coagulating ions. The order would depend on SO_4^{2-} *vs* Cl^- valency. The order would be different not same.

22. ***(a, b)*** Statements (c), (d) are true about emulsions whereas (a), (b) are not true.

The correct form of (a), (b) are

    (a) Deviations from Raoult's law are observed in solutions due to non-ideal interactions, but emulsions are not simple solutions, they are colloidal dispersions. Raoult's law does not apply directly to emulsions because do not exhibit simple behaviour like molecular solutions.

    (b) The HLB value (Hydrophilic-Lipophilic Balances) of a surfactant determines its tendency to form o/w or w/o emulsions.

HLB < 10 : Tends to form w/o emulsions (more lipophilic)

HLB > 10 : Tends to form o/w emulsions (more hydrophilic)

23. ***(a, c)*** Statements (a, c) are correct whereas (b, d) are incorrect. The correct form of (b, d) is

    (b) Electrostatic stability is commonly associated with lyophobic colloids, where charge stabilisation is critical. Macromolecular colloids, however are often stabilised through steric stabilisation, where the large size and the polymeric nature of the particles prevent aggregation due to physical hinderance.

    (d) Macromolecular colloids are not always thermodynamically stable. They can undergo aggregation or coagulation under certain conditions, especially if the solvent conditions change significantly.

24. ***(a, b, d)*** Statements (a), (b), (d) are correct whereas statement (c) is incorrect. The correct form of (c) is

Higher HLB means more hydrophilic. More hydrophilic surfactants have higher CMC. So, the relation is not inverse.

25. ***(a, b, d)*** Statements (a, b, d) are correct whereas (c) is incorrect. The correct form of (c) is

Adsorption and desorption are opposite terms and follows different mechanism.

26. ***(3)*** Mass of polymer P = Moles × Molar Mass

$= 2 \times 10^{-5} \times M$

The gold number is the minimum amount of polymer (in mg) required to prevent coagulation of 10 mL of gold when 1 mL of 10% NaCl is added.

Given gold number is 5.4 mg

$$2 \times 10^{-5} \times M = 5.4 \text{ mg}$$
$$= 5.4 \times 10^{-3} \text{ g}$$
$$2 \times 10^{-5} \times M = 5.4 \times 10^{-3} \text{ g}$$
$$M = 270 \text{ g/mol}$$

Molar mass of $C_4H_8O_2 = 4 \times 12 + 1 \times 8 + 2 \times 16$
$$= 88 \text{ g/mol}$$
$$88\,m = 270$$
$$m = \frac{270}{88}$$
$$m \simeq 3$$

27. ***(880)*** Mass of KCl used $= (450 \text{ mL} \times 1.1 \text{ g/mL}) \times \frac{2}{100}$
$$= 9.9 \text{ g}$$
Moles of KCl used $= \frac{9.9 \text{ g}}{74.55 \text{ g/mol}} = 0.132$ moles

$\therefore$ Coagulation value $= \frac{0.132 \times 10^3}{\frac{150}{1000}}$
$$= 880 \text{ millimoles/litre}$$

28. ***(5)*** $FeCl_3 \rightleftharpoons Fe^{3+} + 3Cl^-$

$Na_2SO_4 \rightleftharpoons Na^+ + SO_4^{2-}$ ions

The negative charge on the colloidal particle will come from SO_4^{2-} ions and the sol formed will be negatively charged $Fe_2(SO_4)_3$.

Thus, the colloidal sol (C) is likely $Fe_2(SO_4)_3$ with a negative charge due to adsorption of SO_4^{2-} ions.

$BaCl_2 \rightleftharpoons Ba^{2+} + 2Cl^-$

Since, colloidal sol (C) is negatively charged, it will be coagulated by the Ba^{2+} ions.

According to Hardy-Schulze Rule,

Higher the charge (valency) of the coagulating ion, more efficient it will coagulate the sol.

Since, the valency of Ba^{2+} is 2, the coagulating power of $BaCl_2 = (2)^2 = 4$.

Ba^{2+} is divalent (+2). Each colloidal particle has (−2) charge. One Ba^{2+} can coagulate one colloidal particle.

$\therefore$ 5 moles of Ba^{2+} will coagulate 5 moles of C.

29. ***(1.120 × 10^21)*** $C_{17}H_{35}COONa \longrightarrow Na^+ + C_{17}H_{35}CO\overset{\oplus}{O}\overset{\oplus}{Na}$

At 10^{-4} M CMC, there are 10^{-4} moles of sodium stearate per litre. Since, each molecule dissociation into 2 ions.

Total number of ions from dissociation
$$= 2 \times 10^{-4} \times \text{Avogadro's Number}$$
$$= 2 \times 10^{-4} \times 6.022 \times 10^{23}$$
$$= 1.204 \times 10^{20} \text{ ions}$$

Since, the number of micelles in 1 liter is 5×10^{20} and each is formed from $C_{17}H_{35}COONa$ molecules.

Total number of ions from micelles
$$= 2 \times 5 \times 10^{20}$$
$$= 10 \times 10^{20} \text{ ions}$$

$\therefore$ Total ions in 1 L solution
$$= 1.204 \times 10^{20} + 1 \times 10^{21}$$
$$= 1.120 \times 10^{21} \text{ ions}$$

30. ***(4)*** All the given statements are correct.

31. ***(3)*** ZrO_2, Al_2O_3 and Haemoglobin are the positively charged colloid particles whereas starch and CdS are negatively charged colloidal particles.

Practice Element : Target JEE Advanced

1. ***(c)*** Moles of $N_2 = \frac{\text{Volume of gas adsorbed}}{\text{Molar volume at STP}}$
$$= \frac{0.0012 \text{ L}}{22.4 \text{ L/mol}}$$
$$= 5.36 \times 10^{-5} \text{ moles}$$

Number of N_2 molecules adsorbed
$$= 5.36 \times 10^{-5} \text{ moles} \times 6.022 \times 10^{23} \text{ molecules/mol}$$
$$= 3.23 \times 10^{19} \text{ molecules}$$

Total area occupied by N_2 molecules
$$= 3.23 \times 10^{19} \times 0.162 \text{ nm}^2$$
$$= 5.23 \times 10^{18} \text{ nm}^2$$
$$= 5.23 \times 10^{18} \times (10^{-9})^2 \text{ m}^2$$
$$= 5.23 \times 10^{18} \times 10^{-18} \text{ m}^2$$
$$= 5.23 \text{ m}^2$$

Surface area per gram $= \frac{5.23 \text{ m}^2}{0.5 \text{ g}}$
$$= 10.46 \text{ m}^2/\text{g}$$

2. ***(c)*** Statements I, II, III and V are correct whereas statement IV is incorrect. The correct form of IV is

Promoters do not bind to the enzyme's active site. Instead, they increase enzyme activity by interacting with other parts of the enzyme or its environment.

3. ***(b)*** Gelatin acts as a stabiliser by forming a protective layer around the silver nanoparticles, preventing aggregation and stabilising the sol.

4. ***(c)*** (A) is true but (R) is false.

Desorption is an important step in heterogeneous catalysis, it is often the adsorption of the reactants that becomes the rate-determining step, not the desorption of the product.

5. ***(a)*** Both Statement I and Statement II are correct.

6. ***(a)*** In lyophilic colloidal sol are highly solvated. The difference between refractive index between the particles and the medium is not large. So, scattering is lesser as compared to lyophobic colloidal sol.